Capacity Building for Environmental Law in the Asian and Pacific Region

Approaches and Resources

VOLUME II

Edited by

DONNA G. CRAIG
Associate Professor, Centre for Environmental Law
Macquarie University (Australia);
and
Vice Chair (Oceana) 1994-2001
IUCN Commission on Environmental Law

NICHOLAS A. ROBINSON
Professor of Law
Co-Director, Center for Environment Legal Studies
Pace University School of Law (New York);
and
IUCN Legal Advisor and Chairman
IUCN Commission on Environmental Law

KOH KHENG-LIAN
Professor, Faculty of Law
National University of Singapore;
Director, Asia-Pacific Centre for Environmental Law;
and
Vice Chair for South and East Asia
IUCN Commission on Environmental Law

Asian Development Bank

April 2003

This publication was prepared under the Asian Development Bank's (ADB's) Regional Technical Assistance No. 5658-REG: *Capacity Building for Environmental Law Training in the Asian and Pacific Region.*

ADB encourages use of the material presented herein, with appropriate credit.

This volume contains quoted materials from other sources, which are printed here as originally presented. In such cases, country names and designations may not adhere to ADB norms. Here are some of the most commonly occurring examples.

ADB Usage	*Names as Appearing in Quoted Text*
Cambodia	Kampuchea
People's Republic of China	China, PRC
Hong Kong, China	Hong Kong
Democratic People's Republic of Korea	North Korea
Republic of Korea	South Korea
Lao People's Democratic Republic	Lao PDR, Laos
Myanmar	Burma
Taipei,China	Taiwan
Viet Nam	Vietnam

However, commentaries by the editors conform to standard ADB style on country names.

In all cases, the term "country" and use of country names does not imply on the part of ADB any judgment as to the legal or other status of any territorial entity.

The analyses and assessments contained herein do not necessarily reflect the views of the editors, ADB, or its Board of Directors or the governments they represent.

ISBN No.: 971-561-504-X
Stock No.: 090503

Published by the Asian Development Bank
P.O. Box 789, 0980 Manila, Philippines

Front cover photo: © Graham Dwyer
The other pictures used for this publication are courtesy of the ADB photo library.

For more information on ADB, visit http://www.adb.org

VOLUME II: Summary of Contents

VOLUME I: Summary of Contents

Contents

Chapter 12
Sustainable Use of Freshwater Systems and Dams

Chapter 13
Sustainable Use of Forests and Fisheries

Chapter 14
Integrated Coastal Zone Management

Chapter 15
Cultural and Natural Heritage

Chapter 16
Regional Environmental Law Cooperation: ASEAN and Others

Chapter 17
Introduction to International Environmental Law

Chapter 18
Marine Environmental Law

Chapter 19
Trade and Environment

Chapter 20
Biological Diversity

Chapter 21
Protecting the Ozone Layer

CHAPTER 22
CLIMATE CHANGE

CHAPTER 23
FINANCING SUSTAINABLE DEVELOPMENT

Chapter 24
The Future

Appendixes

Foreword

In his 4 September 2000 opening statement at the Fourth Ministerial Conference on Environment and Development in Asia and the Pacific held in Kitakyushu City, Fukuoka, Japan, Asian Development Bank (ADB) President Tadao Chino emphasized ADB's long-standing commitment to "protecting the environment and improving human and social capital to enable the region to reduce poverty" and quoted from the opening provisions of the 1992 Rio Declaration on Environment and Development: "Human beings are at the center of concerns of sustainable development. They are entitled to a healthy and productive life in harmony with nature." He also declared in his opening statement that "[i]mproving the quality of governance includes supporting legal and institutional frameworks to provide accountability, participation, predictability, and transparency."

The 1992 Rio Conference agenda for environmental action in the 21st century, otherwise known as Agenda 21, provides in paragraph 8.20 that the "competent international and academic institutions could . . . cooperate to provide, especially for trainees from developing countries, postgraduate programmes and in-service training facilities in environmental and developmental law."

Much earlier, ADB had recognized the importance of environmental dimensions in the development process. Thus, in 1994, ADB welcomed a request from the IUCN-The World Conservation Union, in partnership with the Faculty of Law of the National University of Singapore and the United Nations Environment Programme (UNEP), to strengthen and expand the environmental law expertise of people and institutions of the Asia and Pacific region, and particularly universities, governments, private sector and nongovernment organizations. In December 1995, ADB provided a technical assistance grant of US$600,000 to IUCN to work with the Faculty of Law of National University of Singapore, UNEP and others, including the United Nations University and the United Nations Institute for Training and Research, to teach intensive environmental law courses in the summers of 1997 and 1998 at the National University of Singapore.

More than 30 resource persons taught in each of these two courses, on a pro bono basis. The 63 law professors participating in these courses were from 15 countries, consisting of Bangladesh, Cambodia, People's Republic of China, Fiji Islands, India, Indonesia, Lao People's Democratic Republic, Malaysia, Myanmar, Nepal, Pakistan, Philippines, Sri Lanka, Thailand, and Viet Nam. Subsequently, IUCN, acting through three editors, Professors Donna Craig, Nicholas Robinson, and Koh Kheng-Lian, produced this environmental law book to facilitate the development of environmental law in the Asian and Pacific region using local resources and novel frameworks appropriate for this region.

We believe that this publication is a pioneering work because it is the first comprehensive environmental law book based primarily on materials from the Asian and Pacific region. It is also innovative in its combination of national, sectoral and international approaches to the teaching of environmental law in the region. This book follows ADB's first publication in the area of environmental law and policy entitled *Mutilateral Development Banking: Environmental Principles and Concepts Reflecting General International Law and Public Policy* (2001) by Günther Handl.

This two-volume work adopts a broad view of sustainable development as the basis of modern environmental law with an emphasis on social justice and equity. This requires that environmental law address and incorporate social, cultural, and economic dimensions in addition to the physical environment.

Chapters 1 and 2 recognize that environmental law must be policy-oriented, contextual, problem-oriented, and multi-method[1] in order to optimize the sustainable use of resources. Environmental law is quintessentially interdisciplinary and necessarily involves closely working with experts and professionals in related and intersecting disciplines. It also highlights social and cultural issues such as the role of customary law and the rights of indigenous peoples. Chapter 3 is a framework for environmental law capacity building and the role of education and training in that process.

A wide range of training courses can draw on the book, and Chapter 3 provides examples of these:

1. Core National Environmental Law—the field, its main frameworks and examples of its legal provisions. This can be supplemented with examples of national environmental laws in the country or jurisdiction where the course is given.

Chapters 1, 2, 3, 4, 5, 7, 9, 10, 12, 13, 15, 23, 24

2. International Environmental Law —the patterns of international public law on the environment, and how these are implemented within states.

[1] Harold D. Lasswell & Myres S. McDougal, *Jurisprudence for a Free Society: Studies in Law, Science and Policy*, 1992.

Chapters 1, 2, 3, 14, 16, 17, 18, 19, 20, 21

3. Procedures and Practice of Environmental Law — the processes, institutions, and rules for implementing environmental laws.

Chapters 1, 2, 3, 6, 7, 8, 9, 10, 11, 14, 15, 23

4. Selected topics of Environmental Law—a survey of advanced issues, beyond those covered in the basic core environmental law course such as forestry, fisheries, and water resources.

Chapters 1, 12, 15, 16, 20

5. Economic aspects of implementing environmental laws—A survey of the leading economic means to attain implementation of environmental norms.

Chapters 1, 3, 6, 8, 9, 10, 20, 23

Samples of existing syllabi are also provided in the Introduction and in Chapter 3.

The first volume introduces this broad concept of environmental law and capacity building; offers a comparative overview of Asian and Pacific environmental law (Chapter 5); and an overview of major strategies, mechanisms, processes, and sectoral concerns of environmental law.

The second volume deals predominantly with international environmental law and regional cooperation, including the ASEAN legal framework in Chapter 16 and financing sustainable development in Chapter 23.

Dr. Parvez Hassan, Chair of the IUCN Commission on Environmental Law from 1990 to 1996, and Singapore's Ambassador-at-Large, Professor Tommy Koh, deserve credit for their vision and leadership of this capacity building effort. The helpful oversight of Dr. Francoise Burhenne-Guilmin, head and representative of the IUCN-Environmental Law Centre during the implementation of this technical assistance, and the contributions of the three editors and their faculties of law at Macquarie University in Australia, Pace University in New York, and the National University in Singapore deserve special praise. Without their years of concerted effort, we would not have the benefits of this book. The inputs of UNEP, United Nations University, United Nations Institute for Training and Research and more than 200 commentators, resource persons, and technical assistants were also crucial to the production of this book as well as the success of the two intensive summer "Train the Trainers" courses.

The following Preface by Dr. Hassan, the Editors' Acknowledgements, and the detailed table of contents of this book describe in more detail those who made all of these invaluable contributions. It is estimated that the value of the in-kind and in some cases financial donations of these contributors more than matched the value of ADB's initial grant of $600,000 for this technical assistance.

Special recognition must also be very gratefully given to John A. Boyd, who as Senior Counsel and later as Senior Sector Specialist (Sustainable Development), and Dr. Jyrki Wartiovaara, Environment Specialist, were involved from the beginning in the conception, implementation, and realization of this technical assistance.

ADB, IUCN, and UNEP will make hardback and CD-ROM copies of this book available throughout the world. We hope that lawyers, judges, legislators, public officials, and administrators, private sector executives and business leaders, representatives of civil society, students, and others interested in environmental law and sustainable development will find this book a useful learning tool. We also hope that it might enable them to participate effectively in the negotiation and implementation of the growing number of international environmental agreements as well as in the creation of legal and institutional frameworks through national and local laws. We are confident that the book will continue the momentum of the Training the Trainers technical assistance so that experts, consultants, and educators in environmental law development will be locally engaged in the process for the long term.

Any book of this nature dealing with such a wide range of issues and rapidly evolving norms, policies, and practices is unlikely to arrive at any universal consensus. Nor can such a text reflect the position of ADB or all or even most governments of the Asian and Pacific region on the complex range of subjects and issues encompassed by this book. Nevertheless, we believe that the scholarly work of Professors Craig, Robinson, and Koh as well as other contributors can usefully add to our environmental law educational resources. We invite comments by mail or through the Internet at adbpub@adb.org as well as inquiries about purchasing copies of this book or its CD-ROM edition. Your comments will help us to increase our ability to contribute to environmentally sound development.

We hope that this publication and the related efforts to build and deepen our regional expertise and capacity in environmental law in Asia and the Pacific will contribute significantly to the achievement of sustainable development, protection of the environment, and reduction of poverty.

December 2001

Foreword to the Second Edition

In early 2002, the Asian Development Bank (ADB) launched the pioneering work, *Capacity Building for Environmental Law in the Asian and Pacific Region: Approaches and Resources.* This two-volume work, available in hardcover and CD-ROM, was the first comprehensive publication to focus on environmental law in the region.

The book, which was launched in 2002 in several locations, has received wide approval.

ADB, the International Union for the Conservation of Nature (IUCN), and the United Nations Environment Programme (UNEP) first launched the book at the Environmental Law Institute in Washington, DC, in March 2002. Those attending that launch included representatives from the World Bank, the US Agency for International Development, nongovernment organizations, private law firms, the American Bar Association, the Association of American Law Schools, and law students.

At the Singapore launch in May 2002, Singapore's Minister for State for Health and the Environment, Dr. Balaji Sadasivan, described the book as a "trends- and standards-setter in environmental law and practices in the Asia and Pacific region," and a "new platform for information exchange on environmental law."

More than 135 people attended the book launch in Lahore, Pakistan, in June 2002, among them the deans of leading law schools, judges, lawyers, and civil society representatives. Former Chief Justice Nasim Hasan Shah of the Supreme Court of Pakistan gave the keynote address.

At the Bonn book launch, also in June 2002, an alumni of the "train the trainer" courses explained first-hand the benefits of this publication, saying the book was an "inspiration to young legal professionals in the region."

The book was launched in Japan in November 2002 at a symposium entitled "The Second Generation of Environmental Laws," organized by IUCN, the Institute for Global Environmental Strategy, and ADB. In attendance were representatives of Japanese universities, the Japanese government, NGOs, Japanese and international aid agencies, and research institutes. The Japanese Ministry of Finance representative, Yasuro Narita, a former Alternate Executive Director of ADB's Board of Directors, received a copy of the book on behalf of the Japanese government. In his address, Mr Narita noted the importance of international cooperation in capacity building in environmental law.

The book has received widespread critical acclaim. It has been deemed a fine example of cooperation between many individuals and organizations, including ADB; IUCN; the 200 environmental experts and others who contributed to the compilation of the text; the editors, Professors Donna Craig, Nicholas Robinson, and Koh Kheng Lian; UNEP; and the Asia Pacific Centre for Environmental Law (APCEL).

One reviewer, Klaus Bosselmann, Associate Professor of Law at the University of Auckland, and Director of the New Zealand Centre for Environmental Law at the University of Auckland, wrote in the New Zealand *Journal of Environmental Law*, that the book "is quite simply one of the most useful environmental law texts ever produced."

He wrote: "As such, it is a most comprehensive resource book of environmental law and an excellent teaching tool for academics in the region, and other parts of the world. What's more, working with this book saves a lot of time as it brings together articles, book extracts, unpublished papers, topic-oriented references and documents that are not readily available otherwise."

The example of *Capacity Building for Environmental Law in the Asian and Pacific Region: Approaches and Resources* has encouraged environmental law initiatives in other regions. In October 2002, Professor Robinson addressed more than 50 judges from Bahrain, Egypt, Jordan, Kuwait, Lebanon, Morocco, Oman, Qatar, Tunisia, and Yemen at the first Conference on the Role of the Judiciary in the Development of Environmental Law in the Arab Region.

In his address to that Conference, Professor Robinson spoke of the efforts of IUCN and UNEP to actively engage the judiciary from around the world. He said: "The bar and the bench are only now coming to understand how pervasive environmental laws are. They touch on practically every other field of law, as demonstrated in the chapters of Agenda 21, the action plan adopted at the 1992 Earth Summit in Rio de Janeiro."

New information in this second edition of *Capacity Building for Environmental Law in the Asian and Pacific Region: Approaches and Resources* includes the full text of the Plan of Implementation adopted at the World Summit on Sustainable Development in Johannesburg in 2002. It includes the Strategic Plan of Action on the Environment 1994-1998, formulated by ASEAN; Kota Kinabalu Resolution on the Environment, October 2000; and the ASEAN Agreement on Transboundary Haze Pollution, 2002.

As Mr. Bosselmann says in his review, "the presentation of environmental law as an evolving, dynamic, and interdisciplinary subject makes the book invaluable to all environmental law teachers."

With related efforts to build and deepen our regional expertise and capacity in environmental law in the Asia and the Pacific region, we hope this book will continue to contribute significantly to the achievement of sustainable development, protection of the environment, and the reduction of poverty.

Gerald Sumida
General Counsel
Office of the General Counsel
Asian Development Bank

Rolf Zelius
Chief Compliance Officer and Deputy Director General
Regional and Sustainable Development Department
Asian Development Bank

December 2002

Preface

When, in 1990, I was elected Chair of the IUCN Commission on Environmental Law at the General Assembly of IUCN–The World Conservation Union held at Perth, Australia, I knew that there were expectations of my special responsibilities to the developing countries. International environmental law was by then a flourishing discipline in the universities and law schools of the developed societies but had been grossly neglected on the campuses of the developing world. Lack of a trained faculty had prevented most universities in Asia, Africa, and South America from including even the teaching of environmental law in their law schools. Pakistan, for example, which then had a population of about 110 million, did not even have a single law school with environmental law courses.

Against this background, the developing countries were expected to be full global partners in the quest for sustainable development, which was anchored by the Rio Declaration on Environment and Development and Agenda 21 adopted at the Rio Earth Summit in 1992. The developing countries were expected to participate meaningfully in the evolution, adoption, and implementation of a plethora of multilateral environmental agreements. They were also expected to transform these international obligations into national laws and implement them through a dedicated cadre of environmental lawyers. At the national level, the developing countries were further expected to integrate environmental considerations into their development processes and to structure national institutions, regimes, and legislation to facilitate environmental protection and appropriate resource management. The expectations were high but the capacity of the developing countries to meet the growing environmental challenges was severely limited.

Something had to be done, and fast. As Chair of the IUCN Commission on Environmental Law, I prioritized the building of the capacity in environmental law education in developing countries as a foundation for sustainable development. One option was to start training courses in more than 100 developing countries that needed to pioneer environmental law education in their law schools, but this would have moved at a glacial speed. Instead, we moved in the direction of developing "training the trainers" courses in selected venues in the developing countries, hoping to catch the multiplier effect of this approach.

Our first project was the creation of such a center in the Asian and Pacific region. As I am from this region, I felt that it would be easier for me to arrange funding for this vision since the IUCN global financial commitments did not leave space for funding this regional project. There were many venues in the region but Singapore was chosen for several reasons. First, it is easy to reach (including the granting of visas). Second, the language of instruction in Singapore is English. Third, the National University of Singapore has an excellent law faculty. But the overwhelming factor in favor of Singapore was the dynamism and commitment of Ambassador Tommy Koh who welcomed, exuberantly, my initiative and offered local resourcing. The die was cast and we next approached the Asian Development Bank (ADB) for funding. What followed was an extensive process that involved detailed negotiations among the following: the Faculty of Law of the National University of Singapore (represented by the then Dean Chin Tet Yung, Professor Koh Kheng-Lian and the Protem Asia-Pacific Centre for Environmental Law [APCEL] Committee), IUCN (Professor Nicholas Robinson, then Deputy Chair of the Commission on Environmental law (CEL), Francoise Burhenne, then Head of the IUCN Environmental Law Centre, and I represented the Union) and ADB (Dr. Kazi F. Jalal, former Chief, Office of Environment and Social Development, Dr. Bindu N. Lohani, Dr. Jyrki Wartiovaara, and then Senior Counsel John Boyd represented ADB). The result was the welcome establishment of APCEL (web site address: http://sunsite.nus.edu.sg/apcel). The next step was for APCEL and IUCN with UNEP joining to develop two "Training the Trainers" courses for law teachers in the Asian and Pacific region. IUCN's and UNEP's participation was guided by the zealous commitment of Professor N.A. Robinson and Mr. Lal Kurukulasuriya. They together with the APCEL team and others from members of CEL, Associate Professor Donna Craig and Professor Ben Boer formed the core of planning the syllabus for the training courses. I warmly extend my personal gratitude to all these visionaries who facilitated the project.

Professor Koh Kheng-Lian has ably run APCEL as its founding Director and she and her team have brought much dedication and commitment to the success of the teaching at the IUCN/APCEL/UNEP Training the Trainers Courses on Capacity Building for Environmental Legal Education (1997 and 1998). The focus of APCEL has been the training of teachers and government officials from developing countries in the Asian and Pacific region and exposing them, for the first time, to environmental law courses. Most of these "Training the Trainers" alumni have, on return to their countries, introduced the teaching of environmental law based, generally, on the syllabus and materials developed at the two intensive "Training the Trainers" courses. The four alumni from Lahore in Pakistan have, since this year, initiated the teaching of environmental law at Pakistan's leading Punjab University Law College in Lahore.

The teaching materials used at the IUCN/APCEL/UNEP Training the Trainers Courses have been revised, updated, and edited by Donna Craig, Nicholas Robinson, and Koh Kheng-Lian for wider dissemination and use in the region. The present two volumes are a result of that effort. My felicitations and gratitude to the three editors who have done such a remarkable job in laying a blueprint for the teaching of environmental law in the various countries of the Asian and Pacific region. They have particularly relied on cases and materials from within the region that will have a special resonance in the area.

Three law schools have been particularly generous in the provision of their teachers as pro bono resource persons, among other things, and I gratefully acknowledge their enormous contributions to the success of our effort: the Faculty of Law at the National University of Singapore, the Centre for Environmental Law at Pace University in the United States, and the Centre for Environment Law, Macquarie University in Australia. To this list should be added other institutions such as the United Nations Institute of Training and Research and the United Nations University.

APCEL has been a success story in capacity building and is already being replicated in other regions. In 2000, the Arab Center of Environmental Law (ARCEL) was launched in Kuwait by the new CEL Chair, Nicholas Robinson, to carry forward the vision in the Gulf countries. It is my sincere hope that APCEL and ARCEL are further duplicated in the other developing regions so that environmental law education enters the mainstream of the curricula of universities in developing countries. This will augur well for the success of sustainable development in the present millennium.

Dr. Parvez Hassan
Co-Chair, Advisory Committee, APCEL
Chair, IUCN CEL, 1990-1996
Lahore (Pakistan)
December 2001

Editors' Acknowledgements

This publication is designed to add to the endogenous environmental law expertise (i.e., that of local people with local knowledge) in the Asian and Pacific region, particularly for universities, governments, the private sector, and NGOs. It is based on some of the material used in the two training courses (1997 and 1998) known as *IUCN/APCEL/UNEP Training the Trainers Courses on Capacity Building for Environmental Legal Education*, held in Singapore in 1997 and 1998. The aim of the training courses was to develop and enhance the capability of law schools to teach environmental law and to become centers of resource and excellence for the development of environmental law within their countries, and in the Asian and Pacific region as a whole.

The initiative for the courses came substantially from the then Chairman of the IUCN Commission for Environmental Law (CEL), Dr. Parvez Hassan (1990–1996), and Singapore's Ambassador-at-Large, Professor Tommy Koh. They remained crucial supporters throughout the project. The syllabus was drafted over four years by a planning committee chaired by Professor Nicholas A. Robinson (Deputy Chair of CEL, prior to 1996, and Chair of CEL, 1996–present), and consisted of Professor Koh Kheng-Lian, who served as a co-chair for the Committee, and the APCEL faculty members (Associate Professor Lye Lin Heng, Associate Professor Robert C. Beckman, Associate Professor Penna Laksmikanth R., Mr. Simon Tay Seong Chee, Ms. Lim Lei Theng and Mr. Alan Tan Khee Jin), Ambassador Amado Tolentino (Philippines), Mr. Lal Kurukulasuriya of UNEP and others, including IUCN–CEL members Associate Professor Donna Craig and Professor Ben Boer. Dr. Francoise Burhenne-Guilmin and Professor Koh Kheng-Lian administered the project on behalf of the Asian Development Bank and IUCN.

The preparation of this publication grew out of the extensive teaching material used in each of the two training courses and developed by the Course Planning Committee. This material was too voluminous to reproduce in full. Thus, the editors, Professor Donna Craig, Professor Koh Kheng-Lian, and Planning Committee Chair Professor Robinson began a process to distill the material into the core components essential to teach environmental law in the Asian and Pacific region. Further contributions were sought to complete the range of teaching material needed; for instance, Professor Charles Okidi provided important case law precedents from around the world. Since it was apparent that the original course materials did not readily translate into a useable book for courses on environmental law in the Asian and Pacific region, the editors used the foundation of the original course format and outline to substantially revise the content and scope of the teaching materials selected. They also updated material where needed and selected additional material to fill gaps or better illustrate points of law. A final review of all material was held at APCEL by the editors in the spring of 2001. One of the editors, Associate Professor Donna Craig, undertook the lead responsibility to prepare this book for publication, and her two companions acknowledge with appreciation the tremendous task and intellectual effort that she contributed.

Training the Trainers Courses

We would like to acknowledge the numerous resource persons and others, including institutions and individuals, for their many contributions to these two training courses. A detailed list of these contributors is given, *infra*. The courses were jointly organized by IUCN and APCEL in partnership with the United Nations Environment Programme (UNEP). UNITAR and UN University also provided resource persons and some of the course materials and books for participants.

Preparation of Capacity Building for Environmental Law in the Asian and Pacific region: Approaches and Resources

Besides the resource persons who have contributed materials and updates in the preparation of this book, the editors wish to acknowledge the substantial contributions made by the following resource persons:

- Associate Professor Robert C. Beckman (Chapters 14 and 18),
- Dr. Francoise Burhenne-Guilmin (Chapter 20), and
- Professor Ben Boer (Chapter 15).

The book was brought to completion through the research and assistance of David Browne and Rachel Carey, who transformed a basic collection of material into a coherent and near final working draft. Their contributions were invaluable and their dedication remarkable. They have been a great team.

ADB provided funding for the "Training the Trainers" project, which was extended to cover some of the cost of this publication.

Thanks also go to IUCN–CEL member Dr. Catherine Tinker, and Danielle Cavill, for their assistance in scanning and assembling the course material for the editors to work on in the early stages of this project. Christopher Campbell and Jane Steele provided research assistance, which greatly helped the authors. Our thanks also go to Maggie Liston for endless hours of typing and formatting.

Funding

This project (the "Training the Trainers Courses" and this resulting publication) would not have been possible without the generous funding of two main institutions, namely, ADB, which contributed US$600,000, and the National University of Singapore, which provided a S$250,000 in-kind contribution in terms of facilities, academic and administrative support, the IUCN Commission on Environmental Law which contributed US$50,000 in kind, the in-kind contribution of IUCN's Environmental Law Centre, and the pro bono support of a considerable number of Commission members over a number of years. In-kind contributions to the publication of the book were also made by the Centre for Environmental Legal Studies of Pace University School of Law, New York. Early phases of this project were also supported by UNEP and the UN University.

We wish to particularly thank the Centre for Environmental Law at Macquarie University, Australia, which provided the in-kind resources for most of the preparation of the final manuscript. We thank as well NUS, both the Law Faculty, including Carol Wee, Assistant Librarian, Law Faculty, National University of Singapore, and APCEL, and the University as a whole, for the many large and small—but always invaluable—contributions by NUS, above and beyond the significant funding that was provided for the courses themselves.

We also greatly acknowledge the many resource persons who served on a pro bono basis from throughout the many regions of the world. Their goodwill, knowledge, and dedication is priceless. The names of each of these individual resources experts appear, *infra*.

We thank all authors and publishers whose material has been included in this book for their intellectual contributions to the field of environmental law and express our debt for ourselves and for the many professors and students who will in the future use these materials for their public interest in supporting capacity building in the field of environmental law. This publication is a public service to fulfill the capacity building recommendations made in Chapter 8 of Agenda 21. As a noncommercial publication, it constitutes a significant voluntary contribution to making sustainable development attainable. The editors commend to all who use these materials, and the published books and articles from which the excerpts included in this work have been extracted, and recommend that those who use these materials also seek to collect for their own libraries the various publications included or referenced herein.

Last, we wish to give our deep thanks to our colleagues in ADB who have tirelessly and generously supported the training courses and this resulting book over the last five years. It is now recognized as a unique project for the region and the rest of the world and we could not have done it without their support. In particular we wish to thank these ADB officers: Bindu N. Lohani, former Manager of the Environment Division and currently Secretary of the ADB; Kazi F. Jalal, former Chief of the Environment and Social Development (OESD); Rolf Selrod Zelius, currently Chief of OESD; Gerald A. Sumida, General Counsel; E. Suzuki, Deputy General Counsel; J. Warren Evans, Manager of the Environment Division; John Boyd, Senior Sector Specialist (Sustainable Development); and Jyrki Wartiovaara, Environment Specialist. Helen Cruda, Lily Bernal, Emma Bides, Elizabeth del Mundo, Vilma Fabros, Marotte Favis, and Ma. Victoria J. Mabugat deserve credit for their part in preparing the final manuscript. Thanks also go to ADB staff consultant Graham Dwyer and Segundo dela Cruz Jr. for their work on the design and format of the book.

The ultimate acknowledgement goes to all who will use these materials to design courses in environmental law. The source materials have their greatest value when combined with the intellect of the many teachers and legal experts who make use of them. It is in each user's added value that the success of this publication will be found.

The Editors

Acknowledgements

The following publishers have requested to be acknowledged in accordance with a format suggested by them. We duly give the following acknowledgements as suggested:

1. The American Society of International Law
   - "United Nations: Convention on Environmental Impact Assessment in a Transboundary Context," 30 ILM 800-19 (1991); "World Trade Organization: United States-Import Prohibition of Certain Shrimp and Shrimp Products," 38 ILM 118 (1999); "United Nations Conference on the Human Environment: Final Document, 1972, Report of the UN Conference on the Human Environment, UNDoc A/Conf.46/14," 11 ILM 1358-66 (1972).
   - Reproduced with permission from 30 ILM 800-19 (1991); 38 ILM 118 (1999); 11 ILM 1416-69 (1972); 11 ILM 1358-66 (1972).
2. Elsevier Science
   Dr. Chua Thia Eng
   "From sectoral to integrated coastal management" (1997), 37 Ocean and Coastal Management.
   Reprinted with permission from Elsevier Science.
3. Lynne Rienner Publishers, Inc.
   The Third World in Global Environmental Politics by Miller, M. (1995).
   Reprinted with permission from Lynne Rienner Publishers, Inc.

The editors gratefully acknowledge permission granted to reproduce material by the following publishers and authors:

I. Publishers

1. Academic Press
2. American Bar Association
3. American Planning Association
4. Asian Development Bank
5. Asia-Pacific Centre for Environmental Law
6. Aspen Law and Business
7. Australian Institute of Criminology
8. Blackwell Science
9. Center for International Environmental Law (Washington, DC)
10. Centre for Strategic and International Studies (Indonesia)
11. Colorado Journal of International Environmental Law and Policy
12. Secretariat Convention on Wetlands (Ramsar)
13. Edmond Montgomery Publications
14. Federation Press Pty. Ltd.
15. Foundation Press
16. Georgetown International Law Review
17. Imperial College Press
18. Institute of Developing Economies, JETRO
19. Intergovernmental Panel on Climate Change, UNEP
20. International Bar Association
21. IUCN–The World Conservation Union
22. John Wiley & Sons
23. Journal of the American Planning Association
24. Juta Press
25. Kluwer Law International
26. Kogan Page/Earthscan
27. Law Book Company
28. Longmans Scientific & Technical Publishing
29. M. E. Sharpe (London)
30. Macquarie University Centre for Environmental Law
31. Ministry of the Environment, New Zealand
32. National Environmental Enforcement Journal University of Connecticut
33. Oceana Publications
34. Oregon Law Review, University of Oregan School of Law
35. Pace Environmental Law Review
36. Princeton University Press
37. Royal Institute of International Affairs
38. Singapore Journal of Legal Studies
39. Standard University Press
40. Taylor & Francis Inc., Routledge, Inc., Garland Publishing
41. The University of Richmond Law Review
42. The Yale Journal of International Law
43. Times Academic Press
44. UNITAR
45. United Nations Environment Programme
46. UNU Press (United National University Press)
47. Willamette Law Review
48. World Bank
49. World Commission on Dams
50. Wuhan University Press
51. Yale Journal of International Law

II. Authors

1. Ansari, H.
2. Appan, A.
3. Atkinson, N.
4. Batuwitage, L. P.
5. Beckman, R.
6. Bernstein, J. D.
7. Blastigue, T. T.
8. Boer, B.
9. Brown Weiss, E.
10. Casey-Lefkowitz, Susan
11. Chee, W. L.
12. Chen, H. K.
13. Chua, S. C.
14. Connaughton, J. L.
15. Craig, D.
16. Dan, T. D.
17. Dias, A.
18. Dobbin, J.
19. Egede, I.
20. Fredericks, I.
21. Freeland, S.
22. Hassan, P.
23. Huu, D.
24. Jeffery, M.
25. Johannes R. E.
26. Khew, E.
27. Koh, K.-L.
28. Kurukulasuriya, L.
29. Lakshman, S. M.
30. Lipman, L.
31. Madhyamankura, K.
32. Mallikamarl, S.
33. Malone-Lee, L. C.
34. McCallum, D.
35. Nomwa, Y.
36. Qnicho, R.
37. Robinson, N.
38. Ruddle, K.
39. Salm, R.
40. Swaigen, John
41. Tan, Q. H.
42. Turberfield, D.
43. Vaughan, S.
44. Verlaan, P.
44. Wang, X.

Introduction

Training the Trainers Course on Capacity Building for Environmental Legal Education in Asia and the Pacific

This book results from a very long-term capacity building project, described below, with the objective of using universities and academics (particularly legal academics) to develop environmental law in every part of the Asian and Pacific region. With the publication of this book and the truly wonderful colleagues who participated in the 1997 and 1998 courses, we have great faith that local, regional, and international capacity building for environmental law and legal education will continue the momentum from the courses in Singapore.

Background to "Training The Trainers" Course: 1997–1998

The International Commission on Environmental Law of the International Union for the Conservation of Nature and Natural Resources (IUCN) has worked since the late 1960s to develop environmental law at international and national levels. By the 1990s the Steering Committee of the Commission became convinced that there was a need to strengthen the capacity of states to implement environmental law, starting with university educational services. This began with a program to acquaint law professors with the scope of curricular opportunities and teaching techniques appropriate for environmental legal education. Out of this program, this textbook emerged.

Sometime in 1992, the idea of setting up a regional center for environmental law in Singapore for capacity building in response to the call of Agenda 21, paragraph 8.26, was mooted by Dr. Parvez Hassan (then Chairman of IUCN-CEL) and Professor Tommy Koh, Singapore's Ambassador-at-Large. Paragraph 8.26 stated that:

> "A major part of the programme should be oriented towards improving the legal-institutional capacities of countries to cope with national problems of governance and effective law-making and law-applying in the field of environment and sustainable development."

As a result, the Asia-Pacific Centre for Environmental Law (APCEL) (http://sunsite.nus.edu.sg/apcel) was established on 15 February 1996 by the Faculty of Law, National University of Singapore. This was in partnership with IUCN (The World Conservation Union–Commission on

Environmental Law) and with the collaboration of UNEP (the United Nations Environment Programme). In the leadup to the establishment of APCEL, IUCN-CEL (World Conservation Union-Commission on Environmental Law) prepared a "Concept Project" in June 1993 for the then proposed APCEL, the background and purpose of which was outlined thus:

> "This project is conceived by the IUCN Commission on Environmental Law to develop the capabilities of the Asian and Pacific region to deal with the increasingly complex legal and regulatory requirements of the post-UNCED environmental order. The implementation of the vast emerging multilateral and bilateral treaty network would require, among others, skills not only to transform these international obligations into domestic ones through drafting new laws but also to monitor and enforce these new laws. The region, unfortunately, is not equipped to handle these challenges. Even today, most of the law schools in the region do not include environmental law in their curriculum. Repeated requests to the IUCN for support in this area by developing countries has highlighted the need to develop these skills within this region."

From 1994 to 1995, a Planning Committee comprising a group of experts from ADB, IUCN, UNEP, ESCAP and members of the Faculty of Law, National University of Singapore, held some seven meetings to draft the syllabus for the training course. The syllabus focused on both the methodology of teaching environmental law at university level as well as a content suited to the needs of the Asian and Pacific region.

Hitherto, environmental law teachers have had to rely on books written by Western writers, as there was almost a complete dearth of "local" textbooks and materials in the region. The group of experts carefully drafted a syllabus encompassing topics that were of relevance to the region, with case studies culled from the region, for example, the People's Republic of China (PRC), India, Indonesia, Malaysia, Philippines, and Singapore.

Organization, Resourcing and Teaching, "Training The Trainers" Course: 1997–1998

The Asia-Pacific Centre for Environmental Law (APCEL) of the Faculty of Law of the National University of Singapore, the Commission on Environmental Law of the World Conservation Union (IUCN-CEL) and UNEP, prepared a four-week course for university law professors in Asia and the Pacific on how to introduce, prepare, and teach courses in environmental law. The main objective of this capacity-building course was to equip law graduates in the region to develop the legal aspects of sustainable development, as recommended in Chapter 8 of Agenda 21. There were two courses, the first was held from 9 June to 5 July 1997, and the second was held from 8 June to 3 July 1998. Participants for the two courses were selected from the following countries: Bangladesh, Cambodia, PRC, Fiji Islands, India, Indonesia, Laos, Malaysia, Myanmar, Nepal, Pakistan, Papua New Guinea, Philippines, Sri Lanka, Thailand and Viet Nam. The courses were funded by ADB, and supported by the National University of Singapore (NUS), and a number of other institutions including IUCN–Environmental Law Centre, United Nations Training and Research (UNITAR), Pace Centre for Environmental Law and the United Nations University (UNU).

Organizers

ADB Consultants for Course Materials

- Associate Professor Donna Craig
- Professor Koh Kheng-Lian

Planning Committee (for Course Syllabus and Schedule)

- Prof. Nicholas Robinson (IUCN) Co-chair
- Prof. Koh Kheng-Lian (APCEL) Co-chair
- Dr. Francoise Burhenne-Guilmin (IUCN)
- Prof. Ben Boer (IUCN)
- Associate Professor Donna Craig (IUCN)
- Mr. Lal Kurukulasuriya (UNEP)
- Assoc. Prof. Robert C. Beckman (APCEL)
- Assoc. Prof. Lye Lin Heng (APCEL)
- Assoc. Prof. L.R. Penna (APCEL)
- Mr. Simon S.C. Tay (APCEL)
- Ms. Lim Lei Theng (APCEL)
- Mr. Alan Tan Khee Jin (APCEL)

Management Committee

- Prof. Koh Kheng-Lian
- Prof. Nicholas Robinson
- Dr. Francoise Burhenne-Guilmin

Acknowledgement

The organizers acknowledge with thanks the following individuals and institutions for their contribution of course syllabi, materials, books, computers aids, and other assistance (designations as at 1997).

- Assoc. Prof. K Bosselmann, Law Faculty, University of Auckland, New Zealand
- Assoc. Prof. Donna Craig, Centre for Environmental Law, Macquarie University, Australia
- Prof. Michael Jefferey, Centre for Environmental Law, Macquarie University, Australia
- Prof. David Farrier, University of Wollongong, Australia
- Prof. Tommy Koh, Ambassador-at-Large & Executive Director, Asia-Europe Foundation (ASEF)
- Prof. Nicholas A. Robinson, Centre for Environmental Legal Studies, Pace University
- Dr. Donald Rothwell, Australian Centre for Environmental Law (ACEL)
- Prof. Wang Xi, Research Institute of Environmental Law, Wuhan University
- Dr. Parvez Hassan, Former Chairman, IUCN-CEL
- Ambassador Amado S. Tolentino, Philippines Ambassador to Papua New Guinea
- Mr. J. Wartiovaara, Asian Development Bank
- Mr. J. Boyd, Asian Development Bank
- Mr. Brij Kishore, Economic and Social Commission for Asia and the Pacific
- Dr. M.A. Khan, Economic and Social Commission for Asia and the Pacific
- Dr. Wimala Ponniah, United Nations Environment Programme
- Dean Richard L. Ottinger, Center for Environmental Legal Studies, Pace University
- Ms. Mary Stagliano, Center for Environmental Legal Studies, Pace University
- Mr. David McDowell, Director General, ESCAP (Economic and Social Commission for Asia and the Pacific)
- Assoc. Prof. Chin Tet Yung, Dean, Faculty of Law, National University of Singapore
- ADB (Asian Development Bank)
- ACEL (Australian Centre for Environmental Law)
- APCEL (Asia-Pacific Centre for Environmental Law)
- Center for Environmental Legal Studies, Pace University
- Faculty of Business Administration, National University of Singapore
- ESCAP (Economic and Social Commission for Asia and the Pacific)
- IUCN Secretariat
- IUCN-CEL (Commission on Environmental Law of IUNC-The World Conservation Union)
- IUCN-ELC (Environmental Law Centre of IUCN-The World Conservation Union)
- CEL (Centre for Environmental Law) Macquarie University
- UNEP (United Nations Environment Programme)
- UNU (United Nations University)

Thanks are also due to the following who served *pro bono* as guest speakers, panelists, etc.:

- Mr. Colin Campbell, Montgomery Watson, Singapore
- Mr. Chan Kean, SONY International (Singapore) Pty Ltd
- Mr. Vincent Chan, Managing Director, Galax Services Pte Ltd
- Assoc. Prof. Chia Lin Sien, Dept. of Geography, National University of Singapore
- Assoc. Prof. Chou Loke Ming, School of Biological Sciences, National University of Singapore
- Mr. Foong Chee Leong, Chief Engineer, Pollution Control Dept, Ministry of the Environment, Singapore
- Mr. Lindsay Gow, Deputy Secretary for the Environment, Ministry for the Environment, New Zealand
- Prof. Wang Xi, Institute for Environmental Law, Wuhan University, People's Republic of China
- Assoc. Prof. Avijit Gupta, Geography Department, National University of Singapore
- Dr. Ho Hua Chew, Dept of Philosophy, National University of Singapore
- Mr. Edwin T.F. Khew, Chairman, SAFECO (Singapore Association of Environmental Companies)
- Mrs. Malone-Lee Lai Choo, School of Building & Estate Management, National University of Singapore
- Dr. Clive Mason, Regional Institute of Environmental Law (RIET)
- Mr. Daniel B. Navid, Senior Special Fellow, UN Institute for Training & Research (UNITAR)
- Mr. Antonio A. Oposa, Philippines
- Dr. Peck Thiam Guan, Executive Director, Environmental Technology Centre, Singapore Productivity & Standards Board
- Mrs. Helen Tan, Director of Housekeeping, National University Hospital
- Prof. Edith Brown Weiss, Georgetown University Law Center
- And others

Faculty and Resource Persons for Training the Trainers Courses, 1997 and 1998

Dr. Abdul Haseeb Ansari, Faculty of Law, International Islamic University, Kuala Lumpur, Malaysia

Assoc. Prof. Adhityan Appan, School of Civil & Stuctural Engineering, Nanyang Technological University, Singapore

Ms. Nicola Atkinson, Singapore

Dr. Bharat Desai, Director, Centre for Environmental Law, WWF-India

Assoc. Prof. R.C. Beckman, Deputy Director, Asia-Pacific Centre for Environmental Law, Faculty of Law: National University of Singapore

Dr. Philippe Bergeron, Managing Director, Regional Institute of Environmental Technology, Singapore

Prof. Ben Boer, Director, Australian Centre for Environmental Law (ACEL), Faculty of Law: University of Sydney

Mr. John A. Boyd, Senior Sector Specialist (Sustainable Development), Asian Development Bank, Manila, Philippines

Prof. Edith Brown Weiss, Georgetown University Law Center, United States of America

Dr. Francoise Burhenne-Guilmin, Head, IUCN–Environmental Law Centre, Bonn, Germany

Mr. Colin Campbell, Senior Environmental Engineer, Montgomery Watson Asia, Singapore

Mr. Vincent Chan, Managing Director, Galaxy Services Pty. Ltd., Singapore

Dr. Chhatrapati Singh, Director, Centre for Environmental Law, World Wide Fund for Nature–WWF India (Dr. Singh passed away in 1998).

Mr. Chan Kean, Asian Environment Office, SONY International Pty Ltd. (Singapore)

Assoc. Prof.Chia Lin Sien, Department of Geography, Faculty of Arts & Social Sciences: National University of Singapore

Assoc. Prof. Chou Loke Ming, School of Biological Sciences, Faculty of Science: National University of Singapore

Mr. Mark Christensen, Partner, Anderson Lloyd Caudwell, New Zealand

Dr. Chua Thia-Eng, Regional Programme for the Prevention & Management of Marine Pollution in the East Asian Seas, UNDP–Department of Environment & Natural Resources (DENR) Compound, Manila Philippines

Assoc. Prof. Donna Craig, Director, Centre for Environmental Law, Macquarie University, Sydney, Australia

Ms. Ayesha Dias, Natural Resources Division, UN Department of Economic and Social Affairs (DESA), New York

Mr. David Freestone, The World Bank Group, Washington, DC

Mr. Foo Kim Boon, Senior State Counsel, Attorney-General's Chambers, Singapore

Mr. Lindsay Gow, Ministry for the Environment, New Zealand

Prof. Lim Hock, Director, Centre for Remote Imaging, Sensing and Processing, Faculty of Science, National University of Singapore

Prof. Douglas Johnston, Centre for Asia-Pacific Initiatives, University of Victoria, Canada

Dr. Ho Hua Chew, Dept. of Philosophy, Faculty of Arts & Social Sciences: National University of Singapore

Mr. Edwin T.F. Khew, Chairman, Singapore Association for Environmental Companies (SAFECO)

Prof. Koesnadi Hardjasoemantri, Wisma Kagama, Bulaksumur Yogyakarta, Indonesia

Prof. Koh Kheng-Lian, Director, Asia-Pacific Centre for Environmental Law, Faculty of Law: National University of Singapore

Prof. Tommy Koh, Executive Director, Asia-Europe Foundation (ASEF), Singapore

Dr. James LaFrankie, Director, Asia Program, Center for Tropical Forest Science, Nanyang Technological University, National Institute of Education, Singapore

Ms. Lam Kit Wing, Deputy Chairman, Singapore Chemical Industry Council, Chairman, Responsible Care Committee

Mr. Lal Kurukulasuriya, Chief, Regional Environmental Law Programme, UNEP/ROAP, Thailand

Ms. Lim Lei Theng, Asia-Pacific Centre for Environmental Law, Faculty of Law: National University of Singapore

Assoc. Prof. Lye Lin Heng, Asia-Pacific Centre for Environmental Law, Faculty of Law: National University of Singapore

Mr. Zafrul Alam, 2nd Assistant Director (International), Policy Division, Maritime & Port Authority of Singapore

Dr. Malone-Lee Lai Choo, School of Building & Estate Management, Faculty of Architecture & Building: National University of Singapore

Dr. Clive Mason, Director (Asia), Regional Institute of Environmental Technology, Singapore

Mr. Daniel B Navid, Senior Special Fellow, UN Institute for Training & Research, Geneva, Switzerland

Prof. Charles Odidi Okidi, Task Manager, UNEP/UNDP Joint Project, UNEP, Nairobi, Kenya

Mr. Antonio A. Oposa, Oposa Law Office, Manila, Philippines

Assoc. Prof. L.R. Penna, Asia-Pacific Centre for Environmental Law, Faculty of Law: National University of Singapore

Ms. Mere Pulea, School of Law, The University of the South Pacific, Fiji Islands

Prof. M. K. Ramesh, National Law School of India University, Bangalore, India

Assoc. Prof. Ausafur Rahinan, Department of Geography, Faculty of Arts & Social Sciences: National University of Singapore

Prof. Nicholas Robinson, Center for Environmental Legal Studies, School of Law, Pace University, New York

Mr. Mas Achmad Santosa, Executive Director, Indonesian Centre for Environmental Law, Jakarta, Indonesia

Mr. Lalchand Sheri, Legal Officer, Policy Division, Maritime & Port Authority of Singapore

Mr. Alan Tan Khee Jin, Asia-Pacific Centre for Environmental Law, Faculty of Law: National University of Singapore

Mr. Richard Tarasofsky, Barrister & Solicitor, IUCN Environmental Law Centre, Bonn, Germany

Mr. Simon Tay Seong Chee, Asia-Pacific Centre for Environmental Law, Faculty of Law: National University of Singapore

Prof. Wang Xi, Research Institute of Environmental Law, Wuhan University, People's Republic of China

List of Participants 1997 and 1998 (designations as at 1997)

Bangladesh

Dr. M. Ershadul Bari, Professor & Dean, Faculty of Law, University of Dhaka

Mr. Liaquat Ali Siddiqui, Assistant Professor, Department of Law, University of Dhaka

Ms. Bahreen Khan, Senior Staff Lawyer, BELA, House No. 9, Dhaka

People's Republic of China

Prof. Wang Xi, Research Institute of Environmental Law, Wuhan University

Mr. Ke Jian, Research Institute of Environmental Law, Wuhan University

Dr. Shi Tian Tao, Law Department, Faculty of Law, Tsinghua University

Ms. Du Qun, Lecturer, Environment & Resources Sciences School, Beijing Normal University

Ms. Gao Ling-yun (Linda), International Law Department, East China University of Politics and Law

Dr. Song Ying, International Law Institute, Beijing University

Assistant Prof. Liu Renwen, Law Institute, Chinese Academy of Social Sciences

Cambodia

Mr. Sam Chamroeun, Deputy Director, Planning & Legal Affairs, Ministry of Environment

Mr. Soeung Pahnavuth, Office of Department Criminal and Civil Affairs, Ministry of Justice

Fiji

Ms. Mere Pulea, Senior Lecturer, Department of Law, The University of the South Pacific

Mr. Isoa Tirikula Korovulavula, Coordinator, South Pacific Action Committee for, Human Ecology and Environment (SPACHEE), University of the South Pacific

Ms. Rita Morris, School of Law, University of the South Pacific, Fiji Islands

India

Dr. Chhatrapati Singh, Director, Centre for Environmental Law , World Wide Fund for Nature–WWF India

Prof. M. K. Ramesh, National Law School of India University

Prof. H. D. Pithawalla, Government Law College, Mumbai

Prof. Vijay S. Chitnis, Department of Law, University of Mumbai

Dr. Brinderpal Singh Sehgal, Dean, Faculty of Law, University of Jammu

Dr. Onkar Nath Tiwari, St Andrews College, Department of Law

Prof. A.K. Saxena, Head, Law Department, University of Allahabad

Ms. Deepa B., National Law School of India University, Centre for Environmental Education Research and Advocacy (CEERA)

Indonesia

Mr. Sukanda Husin, Environmental Law Teacher, Faculty of Law, Andalas University

Prof. Dr. Siti Sundari Rangkuti, Faculty of Law, Airlangga University

Mrs. Lie Li Tjuen, Faculty of Law, Pattimura University

Ms. Nurdjanah Anwar Saleh, Faculty of Law, Tanjungpura University

Marsudi Triatmodjo, Faculty of Law, Gadjah Mada University

Mr. Stefanus Haryanto Triyono, Bandung

Ms. Suhartati S., S.H.M. Hum, Faculty of Law, The University of Jember

Ms. Martina Oscar SH, c/o Fakultas Hukum, Universitas Indonesia

Ms. Sukma Violetta Sani, Indonesian Centre for Environmental Law (ICEL)

Lao PDR

Mr. Kongsaysy Phommasay, National Law School (Training Course), National Environment Institute for Training, Department of Environment Management (DEM)

Mr. Chanhthaly Douangvilay, Ministry of Justice

Malaysia

Ms. Izura Masdina Binti Mohamed Zakri, Faculty of Law, University of Malaya

Ms. Lizuryaty Azrina Abdullah, Institue for Environment and Development (LESTARI), University Kenangsaan Malaysia

Myanmar

Prof. Tee Tee Cho, Department of Law, Dagon University, c/o National Commission for Environmental Affairs (NCEA)

Daw Wai Wai Kyi, Department of Law, University of Distance Education

Nepal

Dr. Amber Prasad Pant, Faculty of Law, Nepal Law Campus, Tribhuvan University

Mr. Bijay Sing Sijapati, Faculty of Law, Mahendra Multiple Campus, Nepal

Mr. Nrisingh Kumar Khatri, Mahendra Ratna Multiple Campus, Ilam

Pakistan

Prof. Ahmad Ali Khan, Dean, Faculty of Law, University of Peshawar

Prof. Ashfaq A. Khan, Assistant Professor, Punjab University Law College, Lahore, Pakistan

Mr. Jawad Hassan, Advocate, High Court, Lahore; Lecturer, Punjab Unversity Law College, Lahore

Prof. Mohamed Sadiq Dar, Head of Law Department, International Islamic University

Mr. Syed Mansoor Ali Shah, Advocate High Court, Lecturer Lahore University of Management and Science and Pakistan College of Law

Mr. Anjum Jawaid Khan, Advocate High Court, Former Vice-President, Lahore High Court Bar Association

Philippines

Mr. Mikhail Lee L Maxino, Attorney and Lecturer in Law, Dumaguete City, Philippines

Ms. Maria Socorro Z Manguiat, Lecturer, Environmental Law, Ateneo de Manila University

Ms. Joan Dymphna G. Saniel, University of San Carlos, College of Law

Ms. Brenda Jay C. Angeles

Sri Lanka

Ms. Camena Guneratne, Department of Legal Studies, Open University of Sri Lanka, Nawala, Nugegoda, Sri Lanka

Mrs. Nirmala Perera, Senior Lecturer, Faculty of Law, University of Colombo

Mr. Arulanantham Sarveswaran, Faculty of Law, University of Colombo

Thailand

Dr. Sunee Mallikamarl, Faculty of Law, Chulalongkorn University, Bangkok, Thailand

Prof. Vichai Suthamtarikul, Faculty of Law, Assumption University, Bangkok, Thailand

Ms. Pannipa Buraphacheep, Faculty of Social Sciences and Humanities, Mahidol University

Mr. Tanansak Borwornnuntakul (Mike), St John's University Law School

Viet Nam

Ms. Vu Thu Hanh, Faculty of Law Economics, Hanoi University of Law

Mr. Vu Tuan Minh, Faculty of Law, Vietnam National University

Ms. Nguyen Phuc Thuy Hien, Ho Chi Minh City College of Law

Introduction

The purpose of this book is to provide appropriate resources for academics and other trainers in environmental law for use in the Asian and Pacific Region. The scope of this task is enormous as the region encompasses half of the people in the world. Therefore, the emphasis is on environmental law capacity building through education and institutional development to enable as many people as possible to address current problems and develop laws for the long-term aspiration of sustainable development. The IUCN/APCEL/UNEP Training the Trainers Course(s) on Capacity Building for Environmental Law in the Asia Pacific Region, conducted in Singapore in 1997 and 1998, were the first steps in this process. In many ways, these courses involved two-way learning due to the wonderful qualities and experience of our participants, many of whom were senior academics in the region. The next step, from Singapore, is the production of this book to provide teaching materials for the more intensive development of environmental law in the curriculum of each country in the region. Already, more country specific training courses, arising from the Singapore experience, are being delivered in India and Indonesia.

The scope of this book includes international, regional, national, and local dimensions of environmental law. Following our experiences in the Training the Trainers Course, these levels of environmental law are not treated in isolation. In many situations we focus on issues (such as natural resource management and heritage protection) or processes (such as environmental impact assessment and environmental quality systems) and deal with the many "levels" of environmental law that are involved. We take a more thematic and interdisciplinary approach than is usual in many legal texts and resource books. The reasons for this approach are articulated in Chapters 1, 2, and 3, as well as the reasons for orientation of the materials toward developing countries and the objective of sustainable development. In this context the North-South debate, the evolving relationship between environmental ethics and law, and broad principles of social justice and equity are fundamental. The more specific—and evolving—legal principles relevant to sustainable development are also articulated in Chapter 2 and evident throughout the book. Some examples of these principles are

- intergenerational and intra-generational equity;
- the right to environmental quality;
- the obligation not to cause environmental harm;
- the precautionary principle;
- the common heritage of humankind;
- the polluter and user pays principles;
- obligation to prevent pollution;
- the right of public participation and access to information; and
- environmental impact assessment of projects and proposals likely to have significant environmental impacts.

Increasingly, environmental law development, review and change draws on international environmental law and related areas, such as human rights and indigenous rights regimes, comparative study of environmental law systems and of environmental laws related to sectors (for example, forestry) or processes (for example, environmental impact assessment). In federalist systems of national government, there may be similar comparative studies and influences generated by the environmental law within nations.

Many environmentalists argue that the most effective changes toward sustainable development will be from the "bottom up." Therefore, the global Convention on Biodiversity was an important starting point but local capacity building, funding, and implementation strategies will be the real engine of global change. Therefore, the sources of inspiration, ideas, and useful comparative experiences for environmental legal change are diverse. We particularly emphasize the techniques of comparative environmental law discussed by Nicholas Robinson in Chapter 2. Throughout the book, we have used examples and studies of environmental law development and approaches drawn from the Asian and Pacific region.

In some areas, such as integrated environmental legal systems, (for example, the New Zealand Resource Management Act 1991, discussed in Chapter 6), integrated coastal zone management (discussed in Chapter 10), and in constitutional development and judicial decision making (discussed in Chapter 11), the Asian and Pacific region provides extraordinary examples of best practice in environmental law and implementation. The extract by Mahesh Chander Mehta, and the cases extracted in Chapter 11, provide powerful examples of how activist citizens and judiciaries can bring about environmental change even without the resources and funding of developed country environmental organizations and institutions.

In spite of some significant victories, such as the *Oposa* case in the Philippines, enduring issues remain throughout the region, such as the need to improve citizen participation, access to information, access to decision making, and empowerment. These issues are discussed in Chapter 10. In order to address many of the systemic problems that disadvantage citizen participation and environmental values in decisions, and the growing consensus about the objective of sustainable development, it is timely to consider how many international and national environmental regimes should be redeveloped. At the international level, the IUCN has proposed a global covenant for sustainable development, the IUCN Draft Covenant on Environment and Development, 1995, which integrates and develops principles of international law for sustainable development. The proposed Covenant is reproduced and discussed in Chapter 24. The purpose is to integrate these principles under an umbrella convention, to be negotiated in the future, rather than the many overlapping and inadequate conventions that currently exist.

Designing national systems for sustainable development is a never-ending task due to the immense environmental, cultural economic, geographic, and social diversity that often exists within nations as well as between nations. This book emphasizes the importance of designing environmental law systems that are appropriate, given this diversity, and particularly has regard to cultural and equity issues and institutional capacity. The examples drawn from Islamic jurisdictions, the needs and rights of indigenous and tribal peoples, and the small island states in the Pacific provide good illustrations of the need to consider these issues in designing environmental law systems.

With this basis, environmental law development needs to be informed by rapidly emerging trends in environmental regulation strategies market mechanisms enforcement and compliance such as those discussed in Chapter 5. Nations may choose, for good reason, to adopt customary law rather than some other form of regulation and enforcement. However, there may be situations where even the smallest of nations is drawn into an increasingly global political and economic system such as trading regimes. It is increasingly difficult for their needs to be reflected in these circumstances. There are examples where an association of nations, using clever strategy and representation, ensured that their voices were heard. This is illustrated by the Association of Small Island States which played and important role in negotiating the Framework Convention on Climate Change, 1992 (see Chapter 22).

The book proceeds to consider various other aspects of environmental legal systems, such as: national governmental approaches to institutionalizing sustainable development through national conservation strategies, policies, and laws,

- processes such as environmental impact assessment, and environmental quality systems for air, water, and waste;
- environmental management systems such as ISO 14000;
- sustainable use of fresh water systems, forests, fishing, and aquaculture; and
- integrated coastal zone management and heritage protection.

The international law dimensions of many of these areas are discussed under the topics outlined in the previous paragraph. However, environmental legal education draws heavily on regional and international environmental law. Increasingly there is a blurred line between international regimes and national regimes because of the speed of implementation of many environmental conventions, demonstrated by the Montreal Protocol on Ozone Depleting Substances, and the importance of international standard setting in the global economy, particularly in areas such as marine environmental law and the role of nonlegally binding standards such as ISO 14000. Chapter 17 provides a general introduction to international environmental law. In Chapter 16 the Association of Southeast Asian Nations region is used as an example of regional environmental law cooperation and development. The book deals with the specific areas of marine protection, trade, and environment, biodiversity, protecting the ozone layer, and climate change in the subsequent chapters.

Again, the overlap between international and national environmental law and policy is evident in the crucial discussion of financing sustainable development in Chapter 23. The particular needs and funding issues for the Asian and Pacific region are discussed in the extract by Oogai and Tanaka. The current approaches to environmental financing by additionality and the provision of incremental costs is discussed using the particular example of biodiversity conservation, the role of the Global Environment Facility and the World Bank. John Boyd continues this theme, in the regional context, through a detailed discussion on the role of the Asian Development Bank in sustainable development.

The need to develop innovative financial mechanisms is graphically illustrated in the extract by Michael Jeffery (Chapter 22) where he discusses flexibility mechanisms such as carbon trading and the clean development mechanisms under the Kyoto Protocol. The longest experience that we have with an innovative financial mechanism for sustainable development is probably the "debt swap" that was initially developed by nongovernment conservation groups to leverage conservation in biodiversity rich countries, such as Costa Rica. This mechanism is being utilized in a wide range of circumstances beyond the early nature conservation objectives. The role of more recent debt for equity swaps is reviewed by Steven Freeland in Chapter 23. These examples provide hope for improved environmental funding and outcomes in spite of the decline in the percentage of government budgets being allocated foreign aid.

The book concludes with a look forward, highlighting the challenges and opportunities that await environmental law and lawyers of the Asian and Pacific region in the 21st Century. The Draft Covenant on Environment and Development and the Earth Charter are both extracted in full, as they provide inspiration and suggested approaches to comprehensive and more integrated international law for sustainable development. Two recurrent themes that are emerging for environmental law relate to environmental issues and good governance, which is becoming the basis for funding capacity building in environmental law and related areas. The article by Parvez Hassan highlights the far-reaching potential of this emerging approach. Armed conflict and the environment is also a high priority for the future development of environmental law, as demonstrated by the conflicts and environmental damage in the Persian Gulf region. These issues are briefly covered by Lakshmikanth Penna in his extract.

International, comparative, regional, and national environmental laws are increasingly and inextricably linked to basic concerns about the right to life, the right to development as highlighted by concerns about the carrying capacity of the environment, renewable resources, and food security. This interface between environmental responsibility, sustainable development, and social justice is particularly relevant to the Asian and Pacific region where more than half of the world's population lives. This book has emphasized these aspects in seeking to promote approaches to environmental law for sustainable development in the region.

CHAPTER

12

SUSTAINABLE USE OF FRESHWATER SYSTEMS AND DAMS

CONTENTS

1

Introduction

Natural resources are either renewable, such as forests and fisheries, or nonrenewable, such as minerals and energy materials, for example oil and coal. The objectives of natural resources law are damage limitation, pollution abatement and prevention, and ecological restoration. National legal regimes on natural resources and the environment are often undeveloped or underdeveloped and ambiguous, with selective and arbitrary enforcement. Hussain discusses the important role of tenure, in the context of sustainable use of natural resources in Asia, in Chapter 13. A fundamental issue in many regimes relates to the determination of various forms of property rights in relation to the ownership and use of resources. These issues take on an infinite variety of forms in the various jurisdictions throughout the region. However, the materials in this chapter, and the chapter following, predominantly deal with regimes providing for the reasonable use and management of natural resources. It must be emphasized that these materials are not intended to deal specifically with the issues of property rights and natural resource use.

The themes in,this chapter relate to water resources in the urban context, regional and international approaches to shared water resources, and the enduring controversies associated with large dams. Chapter 13 examines the use of natural resources in forests and fisheries. These two chapters consider relevant issues from international, regional and national perspectives. The planning, management and use of natural resources often generate intense conflicts within and between nations as well as occasions for corruption. In terms of modern environmental law, these conflicts need to be addressed and we need to find new approaches to regional cooperation to deal with transboundary issues and trade issues.

Regional law on natural resources and environment has the advantages of a greater stringency of standards and variety of monitoring and enforcement mechanisms, but it has the potential disadvantage of an "unlevel" playing field that places burdens on operators. International environmental law allows universal application and can harmonize conflicting laws. However, enforcement mechanisms at the global level are weak. Types of international law relating to natural resources include: investment law, health and safety law, environmental law, development law, trade law, and human rights laws. Comparative natural resources law allows for a comparison of how core concepts in natural resources law are dealt with in national law, and an evaluation of the impact of various implementation mechanisms and enforcement practices.

In this chapter, we focus on national initiatives in Singapore and Malaysia to reduce pollution and make more efficient use of their water resources. This is described in the extract by Appan. There are also important issues pertaining to the financial aspects of natural resources, which are discussed in Chapter 22 by Salzman et al. The international legal framework, characterized by a carefully drafted modern environmental treaty, is demonstrated in the extract from the *UN Convention on the Law of Non-Navigational Uses of International Watercourses*. However, the implementation of global agreements requires regional initiatives as well as national and local ones. The extracts from the Mekong River Basin Agreement, the Singapore experience with regional negotiations and cooperation and the Ganga/Mahakali River treaties are used as examples of regional approaches to shared water resources.

On a far more detailed level, this chapter explores the very important issue of large dams. Several extracts discuss the

A fundamental issue in many regimes relates to the determination of various forms of property rights in relation to the ownership and use of resources. These issues take on an infinite variety of forms in the various jurisdictions throughout the region.

environmental and social issues associated with large dams and question their contribution to sustainable development. This culminates in the recent report by the World Commission on Dams of which a summary is extracted. These complex issues and concerns cannot be discussed in the abstract. The chapter concludes with three case studies: the Sardor Sarovar Dam, the Bakun Dam, and the Three Gorges Dam. The case studies provide important insights into the environmental issues, cultural and national priorities, legal frameworks, and the role of international financing institutions (particularly the World Bank). They present obvious cross references to issues such as Environmental Impact Assessment (Chapter 9), Citizen Participation (Chapter 10), and the rights and roles of indigenous and tribal peoples (Chapter 15). The case studies provide dramatic examples of the problems in implementing sustainable development.

A

Beckman R., "Teaching Guide for Water Resources," prepared for *IUCN/APCEL/UNEP Training the Trainers Course on Capacity Building for Environmental Legal Education*, Singapore, 1998

Objectives

- To make students understand that the protection of the quality and supply of freshwater resources is primarily a national problem which requires the application of integrated approaches to the development, management and use of water resources;
- To make students understand that water resources becomes a matter of international concern when they are shared by two or more countries, and that regional cooperation is essential to manage and protect shared water resources; and
- To make students understand the efforts in the global and regional arenas to establish principles, norms, procedures and institutions to manage and protect shared water resources, and the reasons why some states are reluctant to enter into binding treaty obligations with respect to shared water resources.

Reading List

1. *Agenda 21*: Earth's Action Plan
   Chapter 18—Protection of the quality and supply of freshwater resources
2. Programme for the Further Implementation of *Agenda 21*, Paras. 34–35 (Adopted by the General Assembly at its nineteenth special session, 23–28 June 1997, reprinted as annex to UNGA Resolution S/19-2 of 19 September 1997) available at the home page of Commission on Sustainable Development: http://www.un.org/esa/earthsummit/ [*Editors Note: This site was accessed 03/04/2001*]
3. UNEP Environmental Law Training Manual
   Chapter 6, Part B—International Law of Shared Water Resources (pp 171–182)
4. UNEP Handbook of Environmental Law
   Text of Convention and Annexes, and Status of Ratification (pp 224–251)
5. Philippe Sands, Principles of International Environmental Law
   Chapter 9—Freshwater Resources (pp 346–367)
6. IUCN Draft International Covenant on Environment and Development
   Article 19—Water and Article 34—Transboundary Natural Resources

[*Editors Note: See the Additional References for further reading and research material*]

Teaching Methodologies

This topic is ideal for a simulation or negotiation using an actual case study. By assigning students to represent different states as well as interested NGOs or local communities, the students will be able to appreciate the difficulties of negotiating regional treaties on the protection and use of shared water resources. An example of such an exercise is provided at the end of Chapter 17—Introduction to International Environmental Law.

2

Water Resources

A

Singapore

(i) Appan A., "Alleviating the Impact of Urbanization and Industrialization in Water Resources Development," paper presented at the *IUCN/APCEL/UNEP Training the Trainers Course on Capacity Building for Environmental Legal Education*, Singapore, 1997

INTRODUCTION

The primary goal in water resources development is the abstraction of a raw water by as simple and economic systems as possible. Treatment of such water will follow so that the target levels defined by the potential user of the water are met. The raw water quality obtained in any catchment is largely influenced by the activity within [the] catchment. Conventional catchment areas, which are normally located at quite a distance, have limited pollution loads, as they are uninhabited. In catchments located in urbanized areas, the raw water quality can be largely influenced by high-density population and industrial activities. The main objectives of this paper are:

- to define the quality of raw water from protected and urban catchments and to compare total treatment costs; and
- to outline the procedures adopted in the investigation and development of a major water resources projects in an urbanizing catchment and to draw some conclusions and make recommendations on water resources development in urbanized catchments.

WATER QUALITY AND TREATMENT COSTS IN DIFFERENT CATCHMENTS

Types of Water Catchment

In normal water supply schemes, catchments are located far away from the area to which water is to be supplied. Due to the distance factor and the fact that water impoundment schemes will involve large tracts of land, these catchment areas are not inhabited. Consequently, the water running off the surface is not unduly polluted. In some countries, the pollution-contributing activities are totally prohibited so as to ensure that the collected water is of a high order. Such catchments can be classified as "protected" catchments. However, as cities tend to expand and reach mega-city standards or when there is very limited land area, as in the case of Singapore, catchments are progressively encroached upon and the ensuing urban activities lead to pollution of the catchment. In such catchments, some measures are taken to limit or control the pollution-contributing factors. Such catchments are referred to as "partly-protected" catchments in some urban catchments, there could be practically no control on waste discharges and these are classified as "unprotected" catchments.

Water Quality

The quality of the rainwater that falls on a catchment runs off the surface and finds its way to a collection point like an impounding reservoir. In the process, the rainwater is subjected to various pollution loads that could emanate from the ground surface itself or could be the result of human activities associated with urbanization. It follows therefore that water collected in protected catchments will exhibit higher quality values when compared to that found in urban catchments...The levels of the parameters reflect the quality of the raw water. Such raw water has to be subjected to some form of treatment, particularly when the treated water has a specified standard. Such standards will depend on the use to which the treated water is going to be put. In most instances, water is used for drinking purposes and guidelines have been well-defined by the World Health Organisation (WHO). These guideline values are used in countries that have no specific standards...The potable water in Singapore is of a marginally higher order than that of WHO.

As cities tend to expand and reach mega-city standards or when there is very limited land area, as in the case of Singapore, catchments are progressively encroached upon and the ensuing urban activities lead to pollution of the catchment.

Cost of Treatment

The cost of treating water will largely depend on its inherent quality and the level to which it has to be treated. In the case of raw waters from sources lying in protected catchments, the treatment is quite conventional and water sludge quite minimal. However, when the source has higher levels of pollution, the quantity and variety of chemicals to be added will be greater. Besides, there could also be need for special disinfection procedures to be adopted and much larger volumes of water sludge will be encountered. Though there could be a wide variation in treatment costs, generally the transmission costs tend to remain constant.

Case Study

The Kranji-Pandan Scheme and Associated Problems

The scheme...involved the damming of an estuary in the northwestern part of Singapore forming the Kranji reservoir, the construction of dyke and collection of selectively pumped water into the Pandan reservoir and pumping of raw waters from the Jurong Lake into the Kranji catchment. The reliable yield from the whole project was estimated to be 46 mgd (210 x 10^3 m^3/d) and the total catchment area was about 120 km^2...

Methodology adopted for anti-pollution measures:

a) Liaison: The sole responsibility for implementation of the scheme lay with the Water Department of the Public Utilities Board, Singapore. To obtain relevant information on the vast catchment area meant liaising with six different government and quasi-government departments. Hence a powerful Ad hoc Committee on Anti-pollution Measures was set up where all these agencies were represented. The Committee became functional very early in the project and continued till most of the anti-pollution measures were defined.

b) Pollution Survey: Very early in the project it was apparent that there was the need to identify and enumerate all sources of pollution within the catchment. A system of grids and micro-grids was designed and the survey carried out by semi-skilled staff. To appraise the quality of the water within the Kranji catchment, sampling points were selected in all tributaries and also a number of points within the reservoirs. Water samples were collected from streams (weekly) and the reservoir (monthly).

c) Data and analysis: The voluminous data [was] obtained from the field pollution survey. The Kranji catchment had three main sources of pollution from humans, animals and industries. It has been shown that, at the time of the survey, in terms of organic and nutrient parameters the major source of pollution was from the pig-farming sector followed by human and industrial sectors.

The whole system and series of sub-systems that contributed towards the pollution loads were studied and the inputs were decomposed...The net input into the Kranji Reservoir was computed and the input-output system was modeled. A cost optimization exercise was then carried out to minimize anti-pollution costs and to pinpoint the specific areas in which action had to be taken so that water quality within the reservoir will be reduced to the levels of that in a protected catchment. Each of the sources of pollution was allocated a cost and efficiency of removal...

d) Matrix of proposals: The final costs that will be incurred for attaining pre-determined levels in the reservoir [were calculated]. The highest costs were for measures to be taken to attain Phosphorus levels, which are critical in terms of eutrophication. It was also shown that by taking the necessary measures to meet the required Phosphorus levels, all other parametric levels could be attained.

e) Monitoring of water quality: Regular monitoring of streams and reservoirs was carried out to ensure that the anti-pollution measures are effective...[T]he effect of the anti-pollution measures in the Kranji Reservoir from 1973 to 1994 [is shown by] both the nutrient parameters phosphorus and nitrogen [which] have decreased drastically and have almost attained the values prevalent in a protected catchment. Besides, the unsightly weeds and hyacinth are no more to be found in the reservoir. The reservoir has definitely attained a mesotrophic level in a tropical condition...

Legislation and Amendments to Regulations

[A]ction has to be primarily directed in the pig-farming sector, followed by the human sector with no action necessary in the industrial sector. However, stricter control was planned in all three sectors to take into current and future conditions affecting the catchment.

Banning of pig farming

A number of attempts were made to resettle farmers in non-catchment areas and to help farmers with treatment technology of their wastes. However, this treatment exercise proved to be quite expensive and was tantamount to subsidizing the pork market. Finally a decision was made that animals with hoofs should be banned from being reared in any of the water catchments (*Cattle Restricted Area Notification, 1977*).

Upgrading of Trade Effluent Regulations

In 1971, there were stipulated standards for trade effluents that were being discharged into any watercourse (*The Environmental Public Health Act, 1971*). However, this set of standards were amended (*Trade Effluent Regulations 1976*) and implemented. In this regulation, standards were set for three types of discharges viz., discharges into public sewers, discharges into a "controlled" watercourse, which lies in a water catchment area, and into discharges into any watercourse, which lies in a non-catchment area. These standards have been more stringent and are to act as a deterrent to potential dischargers. Over a period of time, practice has shifted such that all industries having trade effluents are now discharging into public sewers.

Human Wastes

At the time of the survey, hardly 50 percent of the population within the catchment had sewage treatment facilities. However, almost all human wastes are currently discharged into small sewage treatment works or into the sewerage system.

Conclusions and Recommendations

For water projects that have urbanized catchments where there is no legislation on trade effluent discharges or if the regulations are not strictly followed, a series of steps has to be taken to ensure that the sources and types of pollution are identified, the input analyzed and anti-pollution measures taken to minimize the impact of high pollution loads. The need for strong administrative support from relevant agencies is crucial for successful implementation of such projects.

Based on the findings of the pollution survey, bold steps have to be taken to promulgate new laws and to amend or upgrade existing regulations, wherever found necessary. Appropriate monitoring of the water quality, both in watercourses and reservoirs, has to be undertaken to ensure that the anti-pollution measures adopted are effective and there is an improvement in the runoff quality.

For the successful implementation of such systems where a number of agencies are involved in investigating the area, taking necessary action and amending and introducing new legislation, it is imperative that there should be the political will to fully support such undertakings.

3

Shared Water Resources— Regional and International Approaches

A

International Cooperation

(i) *UN Convention on the Law of Non-Navigational Uses of International Watercourses*, 36 ILM 700, 1997

[*The UN Convention on the Non-Navigational Uses of International Watercourses illustrates the process of international environmental law making (see Chapter 15). The treaty only recently emerged from years of drafting by the International Law Commission of the United Nations. It has been ratified by states willing to recognize the duty of states to protect and preserve the ecosystems of international watercourses, principles such as equitable and reasonable utilization, importance of exchange of data and information, the duty to cooperate, and the obligation not to cause significant harm. Like most multilateral environmental agreements (MEAs), the shared watercourses agreement includes an agreement to arbitrate disputes arising under the convention.*]

Bold steps have to be taken to promulgate new laws and to amend or upgrade existing regulations, wherever found necessary.

Part I. Introduction

Article 1—Scope of the Present Convention

1. The present Convention applies to uses of international watercourses and of their waters for purposes other than navigation and to measures of protection, preservation and management related to the uses of those watercourses and their waters.

2. The uses of international watercourses for navigation is not within the scope of the present Convention except insofar as other uses affect navigation or are affected by navigation.

Article 2—Use of Terms

For the purposes of the present Convention:

(a) "Watercourse" means a system of surface waters and groundwaters constituting by virtue of their physical relationship a unitary whole and normally flowing into a common terminus;

(b) "International watercourse" means a watercourse, parts of which are situated in different States;

(c) "Watercourse State" means a State Party to the present Convention in whose territory part of an international watercourse is situated, or a Party that is a regional economic integration organization, in the territory of one or more of whose Member States part of an international watercourse is situated;

(d) "Regional economic integration organization" means an organization constituted by sovereign States of a given region, to which its member States have transferred competence in respect of matters governed by this Convention and which has been duly authorized in accordance with its internal procedures, to sign, ratify, accept, approve or accede to it.

Article 3—Watercourse Agreements

1. In the absence of an agreement to the contrary, nothing in the present Convention shall affect the rights or obligations of a watercourse State arising from agreements in force for it on the date on which it became a party to the present Convention.
2. Notwithstanding the provisions of paragraph 1, parties to agreements referred to in paragraph 1 may, where necessary, consider harmonizing such agreements with the basic principles of the present Convention.
3. Watercourse States may enter into one or more agreements, hereinafter referred to as "watercourse agreements", which apply and adjust the provisions of the present Convention to the characteristics and uses of a particular international watercourse or part thereof.
4. Where a watercourse agreement is concluded between two or more watercourse States, it shall define the waters to which it applies. Such an agreement may be entered into with respect to an entire international watercourse or any part thereof or a particular project, program or use except insofar as the agreement adversely affects, to a significant extent, the use by one or more other watercourse States of the waters of the watercourse, without their express consent.
5. Where a watercourse State considers that adjustment and application of the provisions of the present Convention is required because of the characteristics and uses of a particular international watercourse, watercourse States shall consult with a view to negotiating in good faith for the purpose of concluding a watercourse agreement or agreements.
6. Where some but not all watercourse States to a particular international watercourse are parties to an agreement, nothing in such agreement shall affect the rights or obligations under the present Convention of watercourse States that are not parties to such an agreement.

Article 4—Parties to Watercourse Agreements

1. Every watercourse State is entitled to participate in the negotiation of and to become a party to any watercourse agreement that applies to the entire international watercourse, as well as to participate in any relevant consultations.
2. A watercourse State whose use of an international watercourse may be affected to a significant extent by the implementation of a proposed watercourse agreement that applies only to a part of the watercourse or to a particular project, program or use is entitled to participate in consultations on such an agreement and, where appropriate, in the negotiation thereof in good faith with a view to becoming a party thereto, to the extent that its use is thereby affected.

Part II. General Principles

Article 5—Equitable and Reasonable Utilization and Participation

1. Watercourse States shall in their respective territories utilize an international watercourse in an equitable and reasonable manner. In particular, an

international watercourse shall be used and developed by watercourse States with a view to attaining optimal and sustainable utilization thereof and benefits therefrom, taking into account the interests of the watercourse States concerned, consistent with adequate protection of the watercourse.

2. Watercourse States shall participate in the use, development and protection of an international watercourse in an equitable and reasonable manner. Such participation includes both the right to utilize the watercourse and the duty to cooperate in the protection and development thereof, as provided in the present Convention.

Article 6—Factors Relevant to Equitable and Reasonable Utilization

1. Utilization of an international watercourse in an equitable and reasonable manner within the meaning of article 5 requires taking into account all relevant factors and circumstances, including:
   (a) Geographic, hydrographic, hydrological, climatic, ecological and other factors of a natural character;
   (b) The social and economic needs of the watercourse States concerned;
   (c) The population dependent on the watercourse in each watercourse State;
   (d) The effects of the use or uses of the watercourses in one watercourse State on other watercourse States;
   (e) Existing and potential uses of the watercourse;
   (f) Conservation, protection, development and economy of use of the water resources of the watercourse and the costs of measures taken to that effect;
   (g) The availability of alternatives, of comparable value, to a particular planned or existing use.
2. In the application of article 5 or paragraph 1 of this article, watercourse States concerned shall, when the need arises, enter into consultations in a spirit of cooperation.
3. The weight to be given to each factor is to be determined by its importance in comparison with that of other relevant factors. In determining what is a reasonable and equitable use, all relevant factors are to be considered together and a conclusion reached on the basis of the whole.

Article 7—Obligation Not to Cause Significant Harm

1. Watercourse States shall, in utilizing an international watercourse in their territories, take all appropriate measures to prevent the causing of significant harm to other watercourse States.
2. Where significant harm nevertheless is caused to another watercourse State, the States whose use causes such harm shall, in the absence of agreement to such use, take all appropriate measures, having due regard for the provisions of articles 5 and 6, in consultation with the affected State, to eliminate or mitigate such harm and, where appropriate, to discuss the question of compensation.

Article 8—General Obligation to Cooperate

1. Watercourse States shall cooperate on the basis of sovereign equality, territorial integrity, mutual benefit and good faith in order to attain optimal utilization and adequate protection of an international watercourse.
2. In determining the manner of such cooperation, watercourse States may consider the establishment of joint mechanisms or commissions, as deemed necessary by them, to facilitate cooperation on relevant measures and procedures in the light of experience gained through cooperation in existing joint mechanisms and commissions in various regions.

Article 9—Regular Exchange of Data and Information

1. Pursuant to article 8, watercourse States shall on a regular basis exchange readily available data and information on the condition of the watercourse, in particular that of a hydrological, meteorological, hydrogeological and ecological nature and related to the water quality as well as related forecasts.
2. If a watercourse State is requested by another watercourse State to provide data or information that is not readily available, it shall employ its best efforts to comply with the request but may condition its compliance upon payment by the requesting State of the reasonable costs of collecting and, where appropriate, processing such data or information.
3. Watercourse States shall employ their best efforts to collect and, where appropriate, to process data and information in a manner which facilitates its utilization by the other watercourse States to which it is communicated.

Article 10—Relationship Between Different Kinds of Uses

1. In the absence of agreement or custom to the contrary, no use of an international watercourse enjoys inherent priority over other uses.
2. In the event of a conflict between uses of an international watercourse, it shall be resolved with reference to articles 5 to 7, with special regard being given to the requirements of vital human needs.

Part III. Planned Measures

Article 11—Information Concerning Planned Measures

Watercourse States shall exchange information and consult each other and, if necessary, negotiate on the possible effects of planned measures on the condition of an international watercourse.

Article 12—Notification Concerning Planned Measures with Possible Adverse Effects

Before a watercourse State implements or permits the implementation of planned measures which may have a significant adverse effect upon other watercourse States, it shall provide those States with timely notification thereof. Such notification shall be accompanied by available technical data and information, including the results of any environmental impact assessment, in order to enable the notified States to evaluate the possible effects of the planned measures.

Article 13—Period for Reply to Notification

Unless otherwise agreed:

(a) A watercourse State providing a notification under article 12 shall allow the notified States a period of six months within which to study and evaluate the possible effects of the planned measures and to communicate the findings to it;

(b) This period shall, at the request of a notified State for which the evaluation of the planned measures poses special difficulty, be extended for a period of six months.

Article 14—Obligations of the Notifying State During the Period for Reply

During the period referred to in article 13, the notifying State:

(a) Shall cooperate with the notified States by providing them, on request, with any additional data and information that is available and necessary for an accurate evaluation; and

(b) Shall not implement or permit the implementation of the planned measures without the consent of the notified States.

Article 15—Reply to Notification

The notified States shall communicate their findings to the notifying State as early as possible within the period applicable pursuant to article 13. If a notified State finds that implementation of the planned measures would be inconsistent with the provisions of articles 5 or 7, it shall attach to its finding a documented explanation setting forth the reasons for the finding.

Article 16—Absence of Reply to Notification

1. If, within the period applicable pursuant to article 13, the notifying State receives no communication under article 15, it may, subject to its obligations under articles 5 and 7, proceed with the implementation of the planned measures, in accordance with the notification and any other data and information provided to the notified States.
2. Any claim to compensation by a notified State which has failed to reply within the period applicable pursuant to article 13 may be offset by the costs incurred by the notifying State for action undertaken after the expiration of the time for a reply which would not have been undertaken if the notified State had objected within that period.

Article 17—Consultations and Negotiations Concerning Planned Measures

1. If a communication is made under article 15 that implementation of the planned measures would be inconsistent with the provisions of articles 5 or 7, the notifying State and the State making the communication shall enter into consultations and, if necessary, negotiations with a view to arriving at an equitable resolution of the situation.
2. The consultations and negotiations shall be conducted on the basis that each State must in good faith pay reasonable regard to the rights and legitimate interests of the other State.

3. During the course of the consultations and negotiations, the notifying State shall, if so requested by the notified State at the time it makes the communication, refrain from implementing or permitting the implementation of the planned measures for a period of six months unless otherwise agreed.

Article 18—Procedures in the Absence of Notification

1. If a watercourse State has reasonable grounds to believe that another watercourse State is planning measures that may have a significant adverse effect upon it, the former State may request the latter to apply the provisions of article 12. The request shall be accompanied by a documented explanation setting forth its grounds.
2. In the event that the State planning the measures nevertheless finds that it is not under an obligation to provide a notification under article 12, it shall so inform the other State, providing a documented explanation setting forth the reasons for such finding. If this finding does not satisfy the other State, the two States shall, at the request of that other State, promptly enter into consultations and negotiations in the manner indicated in paragraphs 1 and 2 of article 17.
3. During the course of the consultations and negotiations, the State planning the measures shall, if so requested by the other State at the time it requests the initiation of consultations and negotiations, refrain from implementing or permitting the implementation of those measures for a period of six months unless otherwise agreed.

Article 19—Urgent Implementation of Planned Measures

1. In the event that the implementation of planned measures is of the utmost urgency in order to protect public health, public safety or other equally important interests, the State planning the measures may, subject to articles 5 and 7, immediately proceed to implementation, notwithstanding the provisions of article 14 and paragraph 3 of article 17.
2. In such case, a formal declaration of the urgency of the measures shall be communicated without delay to the other watercourse States referred to in article 12 together with the relevant data and information.
3. The State planning the measures shall, at the request of any of the States referred to in paragraph 2, promptly enter into consultations and negotiations with it in the manner indicated in paragraphs 1 and 2 of article 17.

Part IV. Protection, Preservation and Management

Article 20—Protection and Preservation of Ecosystems

Watercourse States shall, individually and, where appropriate, jointly, protect and preserve the ecosystems of international watercourses.

Article 21—Prevention, Reduction and Control of Pollution

1. For the purpose of this article, "pollution of an international watercourse" means any detrimental alteration in the composition or quality of the waters of an international watercourse which results directly or indirectly from human conduct.
2. Watercourse States shall, individually and, where appropriate, jointly, prevent, reduce and control the pollution of an international watercourse that may cause significant harm to other watercourse States or to their environment, including harm to human health or safety, to the use of the waters for any beneficial purpose or to the living resources of the watercourse. Watercourse States shall take steps to harmonize their policies in this connection.
3. Watercourse States shall, at the request of any of them, consult with a view to arriving at mutually agreeable measures and methods to prevent, reduce and control pollution of an international watercourse, such as:

(a) Setting joint water quality objectives and criteria;

(b) Establishing techniques and practices to address pollution from point and non-point sources;

(c) Establishing lists of substances the introduction of which into the waters of an international watercourse is to be prohibited, limited, investigated or monitored.

Watercourse States shall, individually and, where appropriate, jointly, protect and preserve the ecosystems of international watercourses.

Article 22—Introduction of Alien or New Species

Watercourse States shall take all measures necessary to prevent the introduction of species, alien or new, into an international watercourse which may have effects detrimental to the ecosystem of the watercourse resulting in significant harm to other watercourse States.

Article 23—Protection and Preservation of the Marine Environment

Watercourse States shall, individually and, where appropriate, in cooperation with other States, take all measures with respect to an international watercourse that are necessary to protect and preserve the marine environment, including estuaries, taking into account generally accepted international rules and standards.

Article 24—Management

1. Watercourse States shall, at the request of any of them, enter into consultations concerning the management of an international watercourse, which may include the establishment of a joint management mechanism.
2. For the purposes of this article, "management" refers, in particular, to:
   (a) Planning the sustainable development of an international watercourse and providing for the implementation of any plans adopted; and
   (b) Otherwise promoting the rational and optimal utilization, protection and control of the watercourse.

Article 25—Regulation

1. Watercourse States shall cooperate, where appropriate, to respond to needs or opportunities for regulation of the flow of the waters of an international watercourse.
2. Unless otherwise agreed, watercourse States shall participate on an equitable basis in the construction and maintenance or defrayal of the costs of such regulation works as they may have agreed to undertake.
3. For the purposes of this article, "regulation" means the use of hydraulic works or any other continuing measure to alter, vary or otherwise control the flow of the waters of an international watercourse.

Article 26—Installations

1. Watercourse States shall, within their respective territories, employ their best efforts to maintain and protect installations, facilities and other works related to an international watercourse.
2. Watercourse States shall, at the request of any of them which has reasonable grounds to believe that it may suffer significant adverse effects, enter into consultations with regard to:
   (a) The safe operation and maintenance of installations, facilities or other works related to an international watercourse; and
   (b) The protection of installations, facilities or other works from willful or negligent acts or the forces of nature.

PART V. HARMFUL CONDITIONS AND EMERGENCY SITUATIONS

Article 27—Prevention and Mitigation of Harmful Conditions

Watercourse States shall, individually and, where appropriate, jointly, take all appropriate measures to prevent or mitigate conditions related to an international watercourse that may be harmful to other watercourse States, whether resulting from natural causes or human conduct, such as flood or ice conditions, waterborne diseases, siltation, erosion, salt-water intrusion, drought or desertification.

Article 28—Emergency Situations

1. For the purposes of this article, "emergency" means a situation that causes, or poses an imminent threat of causing, serious harm to watercourse States or other States and that results suddenly from natural causes, such as floods, the breaking up of ice, landslides or earthquakes, or from human conduct, such as industrial accidents.
2. A watercourse State shall, without delay and by the most expeditious means available, notify other potentially affected States and competent international organizations of any emergency originating within its territory.
3. A watercourse State within whose territory an emergency originates shall, in cooperation with potentially affected States and, where appropriate, competent international organizations, immediately take all practicable measures necessitated by the circumstances to prevent, mitigate and eliminate harmful effects of the emergency.

4. When necessary, watercourse States shall jointly develop contingency plans for responding to emergencies, in cooperation, where appropriate, with other potentially affected States and competent international organizations.

Part VI. Miscellaneous Provisions

Article 29—International Watercourses and Installations in Time of Armed Conflict

International watercourses and related installations, facilities and other works shall enjoy the protection accorded by the principles and rules of international law applicable in international and non-international armed conflict and shall not be used in violation of those principles and rules.

Article 30—Indirect Procedures

In cases where there are serious obstacles to direct contacts between watercourse States, the States concerned shall fulfil their obligations of cooperation provided for in the present Convention, including exchange of data and information, notification, communication, consultations and negotiations, through any indirect procedure accepted by them.

Article 31—Data and Information Vital to National Defence or Security

Nothing in the present Convention obliges a watercourse State to provide data or information vital to its national defence or security. Nevertheless, that State shall cooperate in good faith with the other watercourse States with a view to providing as much information as possible under the circumstances.

Article 32—Non-Discrimination

Unless the watercourse States concerned have agreed otherwise for the protection of the interests of persons, natural or juridical, who have suffered or are under a serious threat of suffering significant transboundary harm as a result of activities related to an international watercourse, a watercourse State shall not discriminate on the basis of nationality or residence or place where the injury occurred, in granting to such persons, in accordance with its legal system, access to judicial or other procedures, or a right to claim compensation or other relief in respect of significant harm caused by such activities carried on in its territory…

(ii) Koh K.L., "Institutional Cooperation Relating to Water Resources—The Singapore Experience," presented at the *Workshop on Water Security in Southeast Asian and Oceania*, Canberra, 1998

Introduction

Freshwater resources in the world are shrinking and calls have been made in *Agenda 21* that all countries adopt water policies. The water policies adopted by one country will also affect its water supplies to another country which is dependent on such supplies. In a number of countries where one country has to rely on another for its water supply, there is emerging a source of potential conflict. Singapore has never underestimated the importance of water. Indeed, she has always regarded it as a national security. Malaysia from whom Singapore obtains about half her supplies is now awakening to its importance in all spheres of activities and a call has been made in Malaysia to elevate water to the status of a security item and a strategic resource. Indonesia, one of Singapore's potential sources of supply is also realizing the importance of the issue. This recognition underlies how important institutional cooperation is if water is not to be a source of potential conflict. In 1996, Worldwatch warned: "Political leaders are vastly underestimating the influence of water scarcity on food production, natural systems and regional peace and stability. As a result, some unpleasant surprises may lie in store.

According to World Resources 1998/1999, the internal renewal water resources of 1998 per capita cubic meter of Singapore, Malaysia and Indonesia are as follows:

- Singapore—172 cubic meters per person a year
- Malaysia—21,259 cubic meters per person a year
- Indonesia—12,251 cubic meters per person a year

According to Malin Falkenmark's of the Swedish Water Institute, the stress level of renewable water is 1,000 cubic meters per person a year. We see, therefore, that Singapore is way below the stress level.

Against this backdrop, let us examine the extent of cooperation and conflict between Singapore on the one hand, and Malaysia and Indonesia on the other hand, in respect of Singapore's water supplies from these two countries.

This paper is timely as recent months have highlighted the problems Singapore may face regarding her future freshwater supplies from Malaysia, particularly as one of her two water agreements with the State of Johor, Malaysia, will expire in 13 years' time—2011.

Our analysis will demonstrate four main areas that may affect institutional cooperation or conflict, as the case may be, in regard to Singapore's future water supplies from her neighbors—Malaysia and Indonesia:

(a) Malaysia herself is facing recurring water shortage, and recently all states with surplus water supplies have agreed to channel their excess water to those states with short supply. What priority then would Singapore have in the future as against water-hungry states in Malaysia;

(b) The political relations over the last year between Singapore and Malaysia have shown that they can spill over to the water issue—current and future;

(c) Water has become a cross-cutting issue. Thus, future water issues with Malaysia and Indonesia will proceed within a framework of wider cooperation as part of a package deal rather than on a sectoral basis.

What are the prospects for future institutional cooperation?

Singapore will operate and maintain the dam but these will remain Malaysian property.

Singapore–Malaysia Water Agreements: Terms and Conditions

A word on Singapore's needs on freshwater. As a tiny island state with virtually no natural water from rivers or takes she has some 14 reservoirs which supplies about 680,000 cubic meters which is about half of her water consumption. The rest of her water needs come from Johor. Indonesia is expected to provide part of her water supplies at some future date.

The following are Singapore's two main water agreements with the State of Johor Government.

Water Agreement between the Singapore Public Utilities Board and the State of Johor Government, 1961–2011

The main terms and conditions are:

- Singapore has the right to draw water from Gunong Pulai, the Pontain and Gunong Pulai Reservoirs, as well as the Skudai and Terbrau rivers. Singapore pays RM$0.034 for every 1, 000 gallons of water piped across the causeway. In return Singapore supplies Johor with up to 12 per cent of the water delivered to Singapore or not less than four million gallons per day.
- Johor can request for more purified water up to a maximum not exceeding the yield from the Pulai catchment. Singapore also has to pay a yearly rent of S$5 per acre (0.4 ha) of land reserved for its water works.
- A review of water rates will be undertaken 25 years from the day of signing. The maximum yield from source is 138 million gallons per day.

This Agreement expires on 2011.

The Johor River Agreement, 1962–2061 as amended by the 1990 Agreement

The terms under this Agreement are similar to that in 1961, with the following additions:

- Singapore has the right to draw up to a maximum of 250 million gallons a day from the Johor River, at the rate of RM$0.3 per 1,000 gallons.
- This Agreement is valid for 99 years and will expire in 2061.
- The water rates are to be reviewed.

In November 1990 an Agreement was made in the 1962 Agreement to allow additional water to be drawn.

Memorandum of Understanding on Water and Gas, June 1988

This MOU was signed by the Prime Minister of Singapore and Malaysia relating, *inter alia*, to the supply of more water to Singapore. It is an extension of the 1961 and 1962 Water Agreements. Most of the terms and conditions in the MOU were subsequently incorporated in an Agreement between Singapore and Johor in November 1990.

Under the 1961 and 1962 Water Agreements, Singapore undertook to sell processed water back to Johor. This means that Singapore treats the raw water it obtains from Johor and sells the treated water back to Johor.

Under the 1961 Water Agreement, Singapore has the right, *inter alia,* to draw water from Skodai under the 1988 MOU. Singapore undertook to develop and to bear the entire cost to facilitate the supply of more water to Singapore. This involves the construction of a dam across Sungei Linggiu, a tributory of Johor River, and embarkments that will create a reservoir holding 70 million cubic meter storage capacity, Singapore is also to provide for the treatment of water at a site around Johor River for the treatment site to be built.

Singapore will operate and maintain the dam but these will remain Malaysian property.

The Linggui project was completed in June 1993. The cost was S$306 million. The reservoir enables over 1,100 thousand cubic meter of water a day to be drawn from the Johor River as provided for under the 1962 Johor River Water Agreement. Work was also carried out on the sludge treatment plant to treat wastewater from the water treatment plant. The estimated cost is S$32.2 million. This was completed in mid-1995 to transmit the water to Singapore. She constructed a 2,200 mm diameter and 32.5 km pipeline from Johor River Waterworks to the Straits of Johor. The work, commenced in 1992, was completed in May 1995, costing an estimated $54 million.

In order to increase the current capacity from 727,000 cubic meter per day to 1,137,000 cubic meter per day extension is being carried out by Singapore on the Johor River Waterworks. This includes the construction of intakes, water treatment and sludge dewatering facilities, clear water tanks, pumping stations, generator house, installation of electrical and mechanical plant, pipelines and other ancillary works. Estimated at S$213 million, the project is expected to be completed in 2000.

Singapore-Malaysia Water Issue: Whither?

Let us analyze the cooperation/conflict of the Singapore–Malaysia water issue in the context of the areas outlined earlier.

Malaysia's Recurrent Water Shortage and Singapore's Future Access to Malaysia's Water Supply

Some headlines of an article on the water crises in Malaysia reported in The Straits Times, 26 May 1998 bring home how critical the water situation is and can in future be in parts of Malaysia. The headlines read: "Malaysia—water woes may derail KL's recovery"; "Malaysia's water shortage is forcing plants to cut their output and may undermine investor's confidence in the country's infrastructure"; "This is the worst crises the company has faced since we began operation in 1974. I am afraid of losing my job as the frustrated Japanese bosses may decide to shut the plant" and "water shortage have caused it to slash output by 50 percent" (these statements were made by an official from the local unit of Japanese silicon manufacturer Shin-Etsu Handotai); "Water rationing hits home—domestic life now in a mess". Thus water shortage will affect the country's economy, down to the home. In May–July 1998, water shortages hit Perlis, Kedah, Kelantan, Penang, Selangor and Negri Sembilan. The Prime Minister of Malaysia, Dr. M. Mahathir, speaking at the newly established National Water Resources Council in July 1998, said that all states with surplus water have agreed to supply states with such shortage of water.

The future of the 1961 and 1962 Johor/Singapore Water Agreements will also depend on whether Malaysia will bring water under Federal jurisdiction. There have been calls from some quarters including the water-poor states and the Federation [of] Malaysian Consumer Associations (the latter recently called for an amendment of the Constitution to put water on the Federal List, under the Federal Constitution) that the Federal government should have ownership of the water rights. It was pointed out that if the Federal government takes over only the planning, control and development of water resources, but leave the question of ownership and right to sell water to the states it would reduce the Federal function to only a policy coordinating one. As has been described, this would be a 'toothless tiger' at the mercy of state governments. Currently, as Johor is benefiting financially from the Water Agreement with Singapore, it might be easier for Singapore to negotiate if it is [a] State matter and not a Federal one.

Johor is in the process of privatizing its water treatment works. As a matter of politics, it is a matter of time that Johor may not want to be dependent on Singapore for treated water, and be self-sufficient at least. When Johor reaches self-sufficiency level, it can bargain for a high rate for sale of water to Singapore.

Singapore–Malaysia Relationship and the Water Issue

Political relations between Singapore and Malaysia over the last two years have given rise to concern over many agreements between the two countries including the water agreements. Some examples may be given of one such political tension that resulted in spilling over to the water issue. The Prime Minister of Malaysia, Dr. Mahathir was upset about certain statements made by Senior Minister Lee Kuan Yew. These were contained in an affidavit made sometime in January 1997 regarding a political candidate in Singapore, Tan Liang Hong, who fled to Johor because he feared for his life. In an application for a Mareva Injunction to freeze Tang's assets, the Senior Minister queried Tang's fear with a counter statement that Johor is a place "notorious for shootings, muggings and car-jackings." This statement upset the Prime Minister of Malaysia. Although the Senior Minister subsequently made an unreserved apology, nonetheless, the youth branch of UMNO called upon the Malaysian Government to review all agreements including the two water agreements. After some weeks, the matter was not pursued and in the Singapore Parliament, it was stated that Malaysia would continue to supply water to Singapore. The Chairman of the Johor Works and Public Utilities Committee, Datuk Zainalabidin Zin, assured that there were no plans to review or amend the water supply agreements, and all the terms and conditions remained unchanged. This statement was made sometime in April 1997. Indeed, certain other incidents (though unwittingly) have aggravated the relations. Also, cooperation between the two countries in other areas such as joint projects [for] defense were subsequently suspended. The latest in a series of political tensions is the account given in the Senior Minister Lee Kuan Yew's memoirs, *The Singapore Story*, that the Singapore riots of 1969 were partly instigated by the UMNO party in Malaysia.

It is not clear what terms and conditions would cover an extension of the first Water Agreement which expires in 2011. An article appeared in The Sunday Star, a Malaysian newspaper, on the water issue between Malaysia and Singapore which contained some misconceptions on the part of Malaysia that the 1961 and 1962 Agreements were "lopsided and exploitative at a ridiculous rate" and needed to be reviewed "before we can talk about fresh agreements".

Singapore pointed out that it costs RM$2.40 to treat 1000 gallons of water and Johor buys this treated water from Singapore for only RM$0.50, which is the price stated in the two Agreements. Johor sells this water to its people at an average price of RM$3.95. Thus Singapore is subsidizing RM$1.90 for Johor. It is cheaper for Johor to buy treated water from Singapore than to treat the water herself. Such misunderstandings might stand in the way of cooperation.

The Sunday Times, 6 September 1998 reported that the current talks between the two countries on the water issue had broken down because Singapore wanted 750 million gallons of raw water. This is more than double its present ceiling under the 1961 Agreement of 350 million gallons. The 1961 Agreement cannot be amended but the current talks give an indication that there will be tough negotiations on the quantity as well as the *quality* of the water, and also its price.

Water Issue within the Framework of Wider Cooperation

On 6 November 1998, The Straits Times reported that Mr. Goh Chok Tong, and Dr. Mahathir resumed their discussions which started in April this year, on matters of common concern to Singapore and Malaysia.

Among the issues raised was Singapore's requirements for water from Malaysia. Malaysia's commitment to supply water to Singapore beyond the existing two agreements which end on 2011 and 2061 respectively was supposed to have been confirmed in April 1998. However, this matter was shelved after bilateral ties met with some problems arising from a series of issues including the location of Malaysia's Customs Immigration and Quarantine (CIQ) facilities in Singapore [and] the use of Malaysia airspace by the Republic of Singapore Air Force.

The water issue will be discussed in the context of a framework of wider cooperation including how Singapore can assist Malaysia's needs of RM$60 (S$ 26 billion) to help revive its current recession.

Water Agreements with Indonesia

Since 1990, Singapore has entered into a number of agreements with Indonesia for water supply. The source of supply in Indonesia [is] from Riau, on the Indonesian islands near Singapore. The agreement constitutes part of a larger framework for economic cooperation which is to develop in the Growth Triangle which has been described as "a new horizon of ample opportunity to improve the standard of living for the Indonesian people." This novel approach of economic cooperation whose brain-child is the Singapore Prime Minister, Mr. Goh Chok Tong, attempts to lay down "the groundwork for a long-term basis for cooperation", not only for water, but also trade, tourism, investment, infrastructural and spatial development, industry, capital and banking, and the exchange of advisers, experts and technicians. A Joint Indonesia-Singapore Committee on the development of Riau was also established.

In June 1991, pursuant to the earlier Agreement of August 1990, an Agreement was drawn up which gives Singapore the right to obtain up to 1,000 million gallons a day. Singapore is to pay one S$0.01 per cubic meter as royalty. In January 1993, Singapore signed a Memorandum of Understanding to develop water resources of the Sungei Kampar Basin in Sumatra for sale to Singapore.

Institutional Cooperation in Water Resources: From Sectoral to Framework of Cooperation

A comparison of the Malaysian Water Agreements in the 1960s with the November 1990 amendments, and also the 1990s Water Agreements with Indonesia demonstrates a change in approach. The early Agreements were sectoral in approach in that they were not tied to a wider framework of cooperation. The more recent trend is to tie water agreements to other areas of cooperation. The economic interdependence of the three countries—Johor (Malaysia), Indonesia and Singapore for potential industrial growth—makes it viable for Singapore to include the water issue as part of a larger "package deal" of the Growth Triangle Concept—with Malaysia, Singapore and Indonesia—forming the triangle for growth. The package includes not only in the case of Johor, of contributing M$320 million for the land in Sungei Linggui for the construction of a dam but also M$164 million for the cost of the dam.

In the case of Indonesia, the 'package' includes the joint partnership in construction of an industrial estate in Bintan Island, and also development of water resources for Bintan and Batam.

This institutional cooperation along the lines of a package deal gives Singapore the opportunity of jointly managing water resources in Johor and Indonesia. While this approach advance governance in water resource management among states the mechanism can also be vulnerable to the political relationship between the states. We have seen that the current political tension[s] between Singapore and Malaysia have threatened the water issue. Singapore is not taking any chances of being left in short supply after the first Water Agreement with Malaysia expires in 2011. She is currently, considering other alternatives such as the construction of desalination plants. These might replace the current water supply under the 1962 Agreement with Johor.

Prospects for Future Institutional Cooperation

The Singapore experience underlines some important issues which may also be common in other countries:

Should there be a Regional Agreement: If so what are some of the Guiding Principles for Access to and Management of Water Resources?

On the question of access perhaps the idea of "access to genetic resources" under Art 15 of the *Convention of Biological Diversity* may assist in developing a similar approach in water resources, even though water is not a 'genetic' resource. It is as important, if not more as water is the fountain of life. Without it, mankind will perish. The relevant parts of Article 15 of CBD read:

> 15(1) Recognizing the sovereign rights of states over their natural resources, the authority to determine access to genetic resources rests with the national government and is subject to national legislation.
>
> (2) Each Contracting Party shall endeavor to create conditions to facilitate access...and not to impose restrictions that run counter to the objective of this Convention…
>
> (3) Access, where granted, shall be on mutually agreed terms ...

One of the objectives of the Convention is the "fair and equitable sharing of the benefit arising from the use of genetic resources"…The CBD approach to access to genetic resources views such resources as a commodity to be traded. Similarly, should not access to water resources be equally regarded as a traceable commodity like forests, natural gas or oil? Are there any prospects for ASEAN to enter into a regional agreement on water resources? If not, what are the prospects of future bilateral/tripartite cooperation?

Singapore Resolution on Environment and Development (18 February 1992)

The call for cooperation among members of ASEAN on freshwater resources is contained in the Resolution which was made in the context of an *ASEAN Common Stand on the United Nations Conference on Environment and Development (UNCED) and Related Issues*. The ASEAN Ministers called for: "[g]reater efforts to protect freshwater resources and to ensure *access* of all people to this vital commodity."

After UNCED, the ASEAN Senior Officials on the Environment, at its Fourth Meeting held in July 1993 in Bangkok, developed an ASEAN Action Plan which was to be the ASEAN Plan of Action on the Environment 1994–1998. In mapping out New Directions, Objectives and

Strategies for this Plan some of the items in *Agenda 21* were included. Among them was Chapter 18 of *Agenda 21* entitled "Protection of the Quality and Supply of Freshwater Resources: Application of Integrated Approaches to the Development, Management and Use of Water Resources" was considered relevant for ASEAN.

It may not be too optimistic to say that a state which is blessed with an abundance of water supply should regard such a life-giving source as a "common heritage of mankind" and should be shared upon fair and equitable terms. The question of sovereignty should not be used as an obstacle in the path of quenching the thirst of other less fortunate mankind.

Also, some of the rules for sustainable management of fresh water resources in the Convention on the Non-Navigational Uses of International Watercourses adopted by the UN General Assembly in April 1997, may be useful in negotiating the terms and conditions of a water agreement (although the Convention has no direct application to the Singapore–Malaysia or–Indonesia situation). Some of these include:

- Kinds of activities to which water is to be applied affect the regulation of apportionment (e.g., irrigation, industry, domestic or other uses) must be identified.
- Obligation to cooperate and not to cause harm. An obligation to cooperate implies working together to achieve common or comparable objective.
- Where there is integrated management among states, as in the water agreements between Singapore and Malaysia, and also between Singapore and Indonesia, there should be prior notification of intended activities as well as their possible impact on the environment, whether positive or negative. Where impacts are positive, parties may plan joint activities to promote economies of scale and also that of efficient utilization of the water resources.
- The provision of prior information should include obligations as to the consequences should a party disagree—for example, some form of settlement of dispute should be included.
- The agreement should cover financial costs of projects, cost of measures for water conservation.
- Exchange of information, such as in joint research projects.

Whatever extension of the Water Agreements that might be entered into with Malaysia, Singapore is working towards eventual self-sufficiency in her water resources and is looking into alternatives such as the desalination of water, recycling of water for potable use and importing glacier water.

It may not be too optimistic to say that a state which is blessed with an abundance of water supply should regard such a life-giving source as a "common heritage of mankind" and should be shared upon fair and equitable terms. The question of sovereignty should not be used as an obstacle in the path of quenching the thirst of other less fortunate mankind.

(iii) Bharat D., "Sharing of International Water Resources; The Ganga and Mahakali River Treaties," 3(2) *Asia Pacific Journal of Environmental Law*, 1998, pp 172-177

INTRODUCTION

Rivers have been called lifelines of nations. Since time immemorial, towns and trade centers have flourished on their banks, making them important contributors to development. States have fought wars to control and harness river waters in their favor. This trend very much exists in present times as well. Customary international law has recognized the concept of an international river, which has been defined as any river flowing through the territory of two or more states. The conflict, if it may arise, between the riparian states, is resolved on the basis of mutuality, which implies that waters are to be utilized in conformity with equitable sharing.

It is this very issue of equitable apportionment, which dominated the dispute between India and Bangladesh regarding sharing of the Ganga waters as well as the Indo-Nepal dispute over the Mahakali River. In this review an effort has been made to understand the bone of contention and the subsequent solutions worked out by respective governments. It has to be understood here that foreign policies of the South Asian countries essentially center on issues relating to sharing of water resources. Constant skirmishes often disturb peaceful relations. However, it is this very issue, if tackled effectively, that can pave the way for cooperation in economic development as well as generate goodwill which may pave the way for tangible solutions to plaguing regional problems too.

India–Bangladesh

The Ganga River Treaty

Farakka has been the bane of Indo-Bangladesh relations for over three decades. The dispute arose in the 1960s when India constructed a barrage across the Ganges river in the township of Farakka, 12 kilometers upstream of the Indian border with Bangladesh. The purpose behind this construction was to ensure access of ships to the Calcutta port. Bangladesh protested stiffly that the reduction of water flow in the dry seasons would have serious implications on the fragile Bangladesh economy.

Phases of the Dispute

The dispute can be broadly categorized into five phases comprising 1951-1971, 1972-1975, 1975-1981, 1981-1995 and the 1996 phase, which led to the signing of the Ganges Water Treaty between India and Bangladesh.

The initial phases were marked by acrimony and distrust. Repeated dialogues were held between the newly independent countries, India and Pakistan. In 1971 when Bangladesh gained its political freedom, the debate was still reigning strong and repeated Secretary level meetings were conducted to reach possible solutions. Light was seen in the form of a 25-year "Treaty of Friendship, Cooperation and Peace". No agreement, however, could be reached on the Indian proposal of diverting the Brahmputra waters to Farakka through a link canal across Bangladesh. The plan was rejected by India as being unrealistic and exaggerated in character, whereas Bangladesh rejected the mammoth link canal as technically infeasible and politically unacceptable, as it would displace many and divide the country in two.

During 1975–1977, India continued with massive unilateral withdrawals at Farakka. The dispute gained international character when Bangladesh raised it at the NAM (Non-Aligned Movement) Summit conference and at the Special Committee of the United Nations General Assembly in 1976. Despite this, nothing much happened except the importance Iraq accorded to the issue, when it stated at the 1977 United Nations Water Conference (Mar Del Planta) that:

> "In the absence of an agreement between riparian countries on the sharing and development of a transboundary river, countries should endeavor not to start any major work which may have significant effect on another country."

However, the long process of negotiations culminated in the form of a five-year water sharing agreement in 1977 that agreed on the quantum of water to be released by India to Bangladesh.

Bangladesh inserted a guarantee clause in the sense that if during a particular ten day period the flow at Farakka came down to such a level that the share of Bangladesh was lower than 80 percent of the stipulated share, the release to Bangladesh during the ten day period shall not be below 80 percent of the quantum stipulated in the agreement. This Treaty proved to be the predecessor to the recent Treaty on sharing of Ganga/Ganges water at Farakka between the two countries.

The 1996 Treaty on Water Sharing

The 1996 Treaty is an endeavor "to promote and strengthen India-Bangladesh relations of friendship and good neighborliness." It highlights the need and importance to find "a solution to the long-term problem of augmenting the flows of the Ganga". It is primarily concerned with: "Making the optimum utilization of the water resources of the region in the fields of flood management, irrigation, river basin development and generation of hydropower for the mutual benefit of the people of the two countries."

There are 12 articles in the Treaty. It is to remain in force for 30 years, renewable on the basis of mutual consent. A Joint Committee consisting of equal representatives of both countries is constituted, to observe and record daily flows. The Committee has an added responsibility of submitting annual reports to the two governments. Article II, along with Annexure I, of the Treaty has dealt with water sharing arrangements as specified for the dry season. The Treaty has tried to rationally balance requirement of the Ganga waters between India and Bangladesh. Accordingly, in the lean season (1 January to 31 May), the sharing formula is based upon water availability at Farakka:

i) 70,000 cusecs or less: both India and Bangladesh get 50 percent share of water;
ii) 70,000 cusecs: Bangladesh gets 35,000 with India receiving the balance of flow;
iii) 75,000 cusecs or more: India's share is 40,000 cusecs with Bangladesh getting the balance of the flow.

Moreover, conditionality is attached in the sense that both sides receive a minimum guaranteed 35,000 cusecs of water in alternate three ten day periods during the period 1 March to 10 May.

There are 12 articles in the Treaty. It is to remain in force for 30 years, renewable on the basis of mutual consent.

The Treaty drastically affects the interests of GalGutta port, which needs 6,000 cusecs of water through Bhagirathi canal to stop the siltation of the navigable channels and to reduce the salinity of the Hoogly River. Since the Ganga flow at Farakka has greatly reduced, the Government of India has started negotiations with the Bhutanese Government on the Sankosh Hydel Project, which would add another 10,000 cusecs of water to the Farakka Barrage. The water is to be stored by a 110–meter high dam and flow through a 143 kilometers canal to the Teesta Barrage, from where the water will be carried in the Teesta Canal to Farakka.

However, the Treaty has proven a point. It is a step in a direction of good neighborly relations between India and Bangladesh. By tilting the Treaty in Bangladesh's favor, the Government of India has shown its magnanimity and an effort to work towards strengthening South Asian regional cooperation. Bangladesh occupies a strategic position on the map and an effort of this kind will only contribute in consolidating the goodwill existing between the two nations.

India–Nepal

The Mahakali River Treaty

The Mahakali Treaty, concluded between the Governments of India and Nepal, has been labelled as an historic accord as it reaffirmed the two nations' determination to promote friendship and cooperation in sharing water resources of the Mahakali River, which is a boundary river between India and Nepal.

Focus on Integrated Development

The Treaty has focused its attention on the integrated development of Mahakali River including Sarada Barrage, Tanakpur Barrage and Pancheshwar Project. It overrides and replaces the 1920 understanding "on the utilization of the waters of the Mahakali River form the Sarada Barrage and Tanakpur Barrage". Under Article II of the Treaty, the Nepalese Government has agreed to allow India the use of a piece of land of Nepalese territory to make the Tanakpur plan operational. The Treaty explicitly recognizes that India shall construct the head regulator near the left under sluice of the Tanakpur Barrage and also the waterways of the required capacity up to the Nepal-India border. Such head regulators in waterways shall be operated jointly.

The Pancheswar project is to be constructed on the Mahakali River under the joint execution of India and Nepal. There is also an agreement on joint utilization of waters "without prejudice to their respective existing consumptive uses". A Detailed Project Report is to be worked out jointly.

There is a provision for the formulation of a Mahakali River Commission, entrusted with the task of providing expert evaluation of the projects and also to coordinate and monitor plans of action arising out of the implementation of this treaty. The Mahakali Treaty water sharing arrangement is based on the principles of "equality, mutual benefit and no harm to either party". The basic objective of this Indo-Nepalese accord is to ensure optimum utilization of the water resources of the Mahakali River. Under the auspices of the Treaty it is envisaged that:

i) two power stations of equal capacity will be made on both the Nepalese and the Indian sides; these stations would be jointly operated; the energy generated would be shared; and
ii) costs of the project would be shared in proportion to the benefits.

There is also a provision in the Treaty under which India would buy a portion of Nepal's share of the energy for which the price would be mutually agreed upon. The issue of conservation is touched upon under Article I, Paragraph (2). This is to ensure the minimum flow of water to be maintained by India downstream of the Sarada Barrage in the Mahakali in order to maintain and preserve the river ecosystem. The Treaty also specifies that "each party undertakes not to use or obstruct or divert the waters of the Mahakali River adversely affecting its natural flow and level except by an agreement between the Parties". The importance of the Treaty cannot be underestimated. It saw a joint bid to work effectively to uplift the backward regions of western Nepal and Uttar Pradesh in India. It shows a sincere willingness on the part of parties to develop various infrastructure facilities, which would create vast opportunities for development in both the regions. One of the important and striking features of this Treaty is the initiation of economic cooperation between India and Nepal, through interdependence. This interdependence is an important tool in reducing monopolistic attitudes in either of the countries. A close look at the Treaty reveals that various articles are drafted in such a way that neither Nepal nor India can do anything without ensuring each other's cooperation in harnessing the water resources of this important river. A sort of symbiotic relationship is worked out under which Nepal provides the hydropower and India supplies the much needed investment in the form of financial resources and basic infrastructure. The

Mahakali Treaty did raise high expectations as it marked a successful culmination of diplomatic efforts.

Conclusion

The Ganga Treaty and the Mahakali Treaty are indicators of growing regional cooperation by India with her neighbors. In fact, it reflects a bid to move step by step from diplomatic negotiations to economic considerations: a process of sharing economic benefits amongst countries of the same region. It is this very regional cooperation which facilitates "regionally informed bilateration", thereby ensuring the requisite tapping of potential resources. South Asia demands this kind of cooperation owing to the close proximity among nations of the region and commonality of problems of development. The region also has within itself developing potential that at present lacks proper utilization but nevertheless, developments are being thought about and efforts made to resolve small skirmishes over the distribution of water. If tackled effectively, these river basins can go a long way in helping the people of these countries to get out of their cycle of poverty and herald a promising future in regional cooperation and development. Befitting her stature in world affairs, India has played a commendable role under both the treaties in going beyond narrow regional interests. On the bedrock of this vision of good neighborliness lies the future regional cooperation under the auspices of the South Asian Association for Regional Cooperation (SAARC). India has a crucial role to play in this vital process.

B

Regional Cooperation

(i) Case Study: The Mekong River Basin

(a) Lee E., "The Mekong River Basin Agreement," 1(1–2) *Asia Pacific Journal of Environmental Law*, 1996, pp 134–139

Introduction

Water is a precious resource and without it the planet would be lifeless and barren. As human populations increase, the demand for water also increases. Likewise, climate change has the potential to have a substantial impact upon the availability of water. The management and utilization of water has always been a matter of concern for individual countries, especially those which suffer from drought and lack naturally-occurring water sources such as lakes and rivers. The management of watercourses which cross state boundaries has been a further matter of concern with a range of initiatives developed to assist in the transboundary management of the water resource. The management of transboundary watercourses, especially rivers, has increasingly become subject to developments in international law. One principle which has been developed is equitable utilization. However, this has increasingly become problematic and difficult to attain as states compete for access to and utilization of water resources. This was recognized in *Agenda 21* which noted that: "The holistic management of freshwater as a finite and vulnerable resource...is of paramount importance for action in the 1990s and beyond"...

Notwithstanding the difficulty in managing transboundary watercourses a number of agreements have been reached to deal with the problem.

Background

The Mekong River is the tenth largest river in the world and the third largest river in Asia next to the Ganges/Brahmaputra and the Indus. The river stretches for 4,200 km with its headwaters in Tibetan China before meandering through Burma/Myanmar, Laos, Thailand, Cambodia and Vietnam prior to entering the South China Sea. The Mekong Basin covers an area of 795,000 km^2 with approximately 60 million occupants.

The Mekong River has distinctive wet and dry seasons due to the melting of the winter snow in the Himalayan Mountains and the monsoonal climate of the region. As a consequence, the river troughs in May and peaks in September.

The Committee for Coordination for the Comprehensive Development of the Lower Mekong Basin, or the Mekong Commission, was established in 1957 by the lower riparian states of Cambodia, Laos, South Vietnam and Thailand. Its functions were to "promote, coordinate, supervise and control the planning and investigation of water resources development projects". The Committee hoped to achieve this through developing a Basin Indicative Plan, which was a scheme that united all the development projects within the Basin constructing a comprehensive blueprint for development. The withdrawal of Cambodia from the

Committee meant that an Interim Mekong Committee was established in 1978.

Since the 1950s hydropower was seen as the key to social and economic changes. However, due to political and financial constraints these projects could not proceed. Today, this is not the case. With the region no longer in conflict, rapid economic growth is fostering development and exploitation of regional resources. It is this growth that was the catalyst for the Mekong River Basin Agreement.

The Mekong River Basin Agreement

In 1995, the Mekong River Commission was established through the *Agreement on the Cooperation for the Sustainable Development of the Mekong River Basin*. It focuses on developing "natural assets...for the economic and social well-being and living standards" of the people. The Agreement was signed on 5 April 1995 by Cambodia, Laos, Thailand and Vietnam. China and Burma/Myanmar, the uppermost basin states, are not party to the Agreement. The Agreement is divided into seven chapters addressing varying issues. These chapters are: Preamble, Definition of Terms, Objects and Principles of Cooperation, International Framework, Addressing Differences and Disputes, and Final Provisions.

Since the 1950s hydropower was seen as the key to social and economic changes. However, due to political and financial constraints these projects could not proceed.

While the focus of the Agreement is sustainable development and the utilization of Mekong Basin resources, there are few mechanisms which provide for environmental protection. The phrase "sustainable development, utilization, conservation and management of the Mekong River Basin and related resources" appears throughout the Agreement, but is adopted developmentally rather than from a conservation perspective. This is reinforced by the expressions "to optimize the multiple use and mutual benefits" and "the development of the full potential of sustainable benefits".

Article 3 provides the Mekong River Basin with environmental protection. It states that the parties agree to "protect the environment, natural resources, aquatic life and conditions, and ecological balance of the Mekong River Basin from pollution or other harmful effects resulting from any development plans and uses of water and related resources in the Basin". Other articles are consistent with customary international water law and provide for:

(a) the prevention and cessation of harmful transboundary effects of development;

(b) state responsibility for damage and liability of the state for injury to another;

(c) freedom of navigation and the right to move freely throughout the Mekong River; and

(d) notification and consultation in situations which constitute an emergency requiring an immediate response.

To ensure that development within the basin is sustainable and that other parties are not affected by certain types of development, the Agreement establishes the Mekong River Commission. The Commission is an institution whereby states have a forum to discuss development and establish a center to gather information to assist the decision-makers. To this end the Commission has three permanent bodies: the Council, the Joint Committee and the Secretariat.

The Council is the decision-making body. It consists of one member from each riparian state, at the ministerial or cabinet level who are empowered by their state to make policy decisions. The functions of the Council are to resolve disputes; to decide on policy matters necessary to implement the Agreement; and to make policy to promote, support and cooperate in activities and projects in a "constructive and mutually beneficial manner for the sustainable development, utilization, conservation management of the Mekong River Basin and related resources".

The Joint Committee implements the decisions of the Council. It comprises one member at the head-of department level, from each state. The functions of the Joint Committee are to implement the decisions of the Council; to formulate the basin development plan; to update and exchange information; to conduct appropriate studies and assessments for the protection of the environment and maintain the ecological balance of the Mekong River Basin; to assign tasks and to supervise the Secretariats; to resolve issues and differences that may arise between regular sessions of the Council; to review and approve studies and training for the personnel of the riparian member countries; and to make recommendations to the Council regarding organizational structure of the Secretariat.

The Council and the Joint Committee are empowered to resolve disputes. When this fails, the Agreement allows for negotiation through diplomatic channels or mediation through an entity or party mutually agreed upon. If this is not successful they are to proceed according to the principles of international law.

The Secretariat provides technical services and financial administration to the Council and Joint Committee. Its functions are to carry out decisions and tasks assigned by the Council and Joint Committee; to formulate annual work programs; to assist the Joint Committee in the implementation and management of projects and programs; to maintain databases of information; to prepare for sessions of the Council and Joint Committee; and to carry out all other assignments as requested.

The core to an agreement on sustainable development of a river basin lies in equitable utilization of the waters. The variable nature of the flow, plus the damming and diversionary schemes within the Mekong River makes equitable apportionment difficult. Aside from trapping water in dams (intra-basin usage), water is pumped out of the Mekong River Basin to other catchments (inter-basin usage). To ensure that all riparian states receive an equitable portion of the Mekong waters, Article 5 declares that the states will utilize the waters in a reasonable and equitable manner in their respective territories, pursuant to all relative factors and circumstances. The Joint Committee is responsible for allocating inter-basin and intra-basin water usage during the dry season and for the wet season. States must notify the Joint Committee for intra-basin usage and prior consultation for inter-basin diversion.

The Joint Committee is responsible for the development of the "Rules for Water Utilization and Inter-Basin Diversions", as stipulated in Article 26. In determining these rules the Joint Council must consider the time frame for wet and dry seasons; the location of hydrological stations; the criteria for determining surplus quantities of water during the dry seasons; improving mechanisms to monitor intra-basin usage; and the mechanisms to monitor inter-basin diversions from the mainstream.

The Agreement does not allow for any retroactive effect for projects and activities which existed prior to the date of signature. This will have a significant impact on the Mekong Basin. Prior to 5 April 1995, there were approximately 60 dam projects, including the Paki Mong Dam in Thailand and the Nam Them 2 Dam in Laos.

The Mekong River Basin Agreement provides the foundation for cooperation among the lower-basin states of the Mekong. The establishment of the Mekong River Commission will assist in the long-term development of resources. The development of its resources must be approved by the Secretariat, the Joint Committee and the Council. Additionally, the formulation of the Basin Development Plan will ensure the sustainable development, utilization, conservation and management of the Mekong River Basin Resources.

Assessment

Despite its apparent harmonious nature, the Agreement has serious shortcomings. First, not all basin states are signatories to the Agreement. China and Burma are not members. Thus, it will be impossible for the Basin Development Plan to reflect equitable utilization and the right to shared freshwater resources for all the riparian states. For example, China has recently constructed a series of dams without seeking prior approval of the downstream users. Although China and Burma only contribute proximately 20 percent of the total water volume, the distinctive monsoonal flow the Mekong means that during low-flow periods, the effect of dams and diversiony schemes is intensified.

Secondly, the Basin Development Plan does not contain enough detail. The Basin Development Plan is defined as "the general planning tool and process that the Joint Committee would use as a blueprint to identify, categorise and prioritise the projects and progams to seek assistance for and to implement the plan at the basin level". This single-strategy solution for development amongst the lower-basin states is ideal, but mechanisms such as environmental impact assessment and public participation are vital for the protection of the environment. The Joint Committee would be the appropriate body to perform these tasks and their functions are to formulate the Basin Development and to gather information on the hydrology of the Mekong River Basin...

The term "sustainable development" is an integral element of the Mekong River Basin Agreement. But is this goal achievable? Development includes among other activities, irrigation, hydropower, navigation, flood control, fisheries, timber floating recreation and tourism. This is an inherent contradiction. Hydropower cannot be developed sustainably. Development of water and related resources degrades the environment. Hydropower affects society and ecology upstream, downstream and at the dam site.

Sustainable development is also a feature of the *Agreement on the Action Plan for the Environmentally Sound Management of the Common Zambezi River System.* The Agreement provides that an objective of the Zambezi River Action Plan is to overcome the current and potential problems and implementation of environmentally sound water resources management in the whole river system. It will contribute to the incorporation by the river basin slates of environmental considerations in water resources management while increasing long-term sustainable development in the river basin.

The "long-term" approach to sustainable development in the Zambezi Agreement is to be contrasted with the approach adopted in the Mekong Basin Agreement.

It is inevitable that states within the Mekong River Basin will continue development. The single-strategy solution through the Basin Development Plan and the establishment of the Mekong Commission will assist riparian countries in the equitable utilization of its resources. However, the holistic management of the Basin and its resources will not be achieved unless all riparian states are party to the Agreement

(b) Agreement on the Cooperation for the Sustainable Development of the Mekong River Basin

The Governments of The Kingdom of Cambodia, The Lao People's Democratic Republic, The Kingdom of Thailand, and The Socialist Republic of Viet Nam, being equally desirous of continuing to cooperate in a constructive and mutually beneficial manner for sustainable development, utilization, conservation and management of the Mekong River Basin water and related resources, have resolved to conclude this Agreement setting forth the framework for cooperation acceptable to all parties hereto to accomplish these ends, and for that purpose have appointed as their respective plenipotentiaries...

Chapter II—Definitions of Terms

For the purposes of this Agreement, it shall be understood that the following meanings to the underlined terms shall apply except where otherwise inconsistent with the context:

Agreement under Article 5: A decision of the Joint Committee resulting from prior consultation and evaluation on any proposed use for inter-basin diversions during the wet season from the mainstream as well as for intra-basin use or inter-basin diversions of these waters during the dry season. The objective of this agreement is to achieve an optimum use and prevention of waste of the waters through a dynamic and practical consensus in conformity with the Rules for Water Utilization and Inter-Basin Diversions set forth in Article 26.

Acceptable minimum monthly natural flow: The acceptable minimum monthly natural flow during each month of the dry season.

Acceptable natural reverse flow: The wet season flow level in the Mekong River at Kratie that allows the reverse flow of the Tonle Sap to an agreed upon optimum level of the Great Lake.

Basin Development Plan: The general planning tool and process that the Joint Committee would use as a blueprint to identify, categorize and prioritize the projects and programs to seek assistance for and to implement the plan at the basin level.

Environment: The conditions of water and land resources, air, flora, and fauna that exists in a particular region.

Notification: Timely providing information by a riparian to the Joint Committee on its proposed use of water according to the format, content and procedures set forth in the Rules for Water Utilization and Inter-Basin Diversions under Article 26.

Prior consultation: Timely notification plus additional data and information to the Joint Committee as provided in the Rules for Water Utilization and Inter-Basin Diversion under Article 26, that would allow the other member riparians to discuss and evaluate the impact of the proposed use upon their uses of water and any other affects, which is the basis for arriving at an agreement. Prior consultation is neither a right to veto the use nor unilateral right to use water by any riparian without taking into account other riparians' rights.

Proposed use: Any proposal for a definite use of the waters of the Mekong River system by any riparian, excluding domestic and minor uses of water not having a significant impact on mainstream flows.

Chapter III—Objectives and Principles of Cooperation

The parties agree:

Article 1—Areas of Cooperation

To cooperate in all fields of sustainable development, utilization, management and conservation of the water and related resources of the Mekong River Basin including, but not limited to irrigation, hydro-power, navigation, flood control, fisheries, timber floating, recreation and tourism, in a manner to optimize the multiple-use and mutual benefits of all riparians and to minimize the harmful effects that might result from natural occurrences and man-made activities.

Article 2—Projects, Programs and Planning

To promote, support, cooperate and coordinate in the development of the full potential of sustainable benefits to all riparian States and the prevention of wasteful use of Mekong River Basin waters, with emphasis and preference on joint and/or basin-wide development projects and basin programs through the formulation of a basin development plan, that would be used to identify, categorize and prioritize the projects and programs to seek assistance for and to implement at the basin level.

Article 3—Protection of the Environment and Ecological Balance

To protect the environment, natural resources, aquatic life and conditions, and ecological balance of the Mekong River Basin from pollution or other harmful effects resulting from any development plans and uses of water and related resources in the Basin.

Article 4—Sovereign Equality and Territorial Integrity

To cooperate on the basis of sovereign equality and territorial integrity in the utilization and protection of the water resources of the Mekong River Basin.

Article 5—Reasonable and Equitable Utilization

To utilize the waters of the Mekong River system in a reasonable and equitable manner in their respective territories, pursuant to all relevant factors and circumstances, the Rules for Water Utilization and Inter-basin Diversion provided for under Article 26 and the provisions of A and B below:

a) On tributaries of the Mekong River, including Tonle Sap, intra-basin uses and inter-basin diversions shall be subject to notification to the Joint Committee.

b) On the mainstream of the Mekong River:

   1. During the wet season:
      - Intra-basin use shall be subject to notification to the Joint Committee.
      - Inter-basin diversion shall be subject to prior consultation, which aims at arriving at an agreement by the Joint Committee.
   2. During the dry season:
      - Intra-basin use shall be subject to prior consultation, which aims at arriving at an agreement by the Joint Committee.
      - Any inter-basin diversion project shall be agreed upon by the Joint Committee through a specific agreement for each project prior to any proposed diversion. However, should there be a surplus quantity of water available in excess of the proposed uses of all parties in any dry season, verified and unanimously confirmed as such by the Joint Committee, an inter-basin diversion of the surplus could be made subject to prior consultation.

Article 6—Maintenance of Flows on the Mainstream

To cooperate in the maintenance of the flows on the mainstream from diversions, storage releases, or other actions of a permanent nature; except in the cases of historically severe droughts and/or floods:

a) Of not less than the acceptable minimum monthly natural flow during each month of the dry season;

b) To enable the acceptable natural reverse flow of the Tonle Sap to take place during the wet season; and,

c) To prevent average daily peak flows greater than what naturally occur on the average during the flood season.

The Joint Committee shall adopt guidelines for the locations and levels of the flows, and monitor and take action necessary for their maintenance as provided in Article 26.

Article 7—Prevention and Cessation of Harmful Effects

To make every effort to avoid, minimize and mitigate harmful effects that might occur to the environment, especially the water quantity and quality, the aquatic (eco-system) conditions, and ecological balance of the river system, from the development and use of the Mekong River Basin water resources or discharge of wastes and return flows. Where one or more States is notified with proper and valid evidence that it is causing substantial damage to one or more riparians from the use of and/or discharge to water of the Mekong River, that State or States shall cease immediately the alleged cause of harm until such cause of harm is determined in accordance with Article 8.

Article 8—State Responsibility for Damages

Where harmful effects cause substantial damage to one or more riparians from the use of and/or discharge to waters of the Mekong River by any riparian State, the party(ies) concerned shall determine all relative factors, the cause, extent of damage and responsibility for damages caused by that State in conformity with the principles of international law relating to state responsibility, and to address and resolve all issues, differences and disputes in an amicable and timely manner by peaceful means as provided in Articles 34 and 35 of this Agreement, and in conformity with the Charter of the United Nations.

Article 9—Freedom of Navigation

On the basis of equality of right, freedom of navigation shall be accorded throughout the mainstream of the Mekong River without regard to the territorial boundaries, for transportation and communication to promote regional cooperation and to satisfactorily implement projects under this Agreement. The Mekong River shall be kept free from obstructions, measures, conduct and actions that might directly or indirectly impair navigability, interfere with this right or permanently make it more difficult. Navigational uses are not assured any priority over other uses, but will be incorporated into any mainstream project. Riparians may issue regulations for the portions of the Mekong River within their territories, particularly in sanitary, customs and immigration matters, police and general security.

Article 10—Emergency Situations

Whenever a Party becomes aware of any special water quantity or quality problems constituting an emergency that requires an immediate response, it shall notify and consult directly with the party(ies) concerned and the Joint Committee without delay in order to take appropriate remedial action.

Chapter IV—Institutional Framework

Mekong River Commission

Article 11—Status

The institutional framework for cooperation in the Mekong River Basin under this Agreement shall be called the Mekong River Commission and shall, for the purpose of the exercise of its functions, enjoy the status of an international body, including entering into agreements and obligations with the donor or international community.

Article 12—Structure of Mekong River Commission

The Commission shall consist of three permanent bodies:

- Council
- Joint Committee, and
- Secretariat

Article 13—Assumption of Assets, Obligations and Rights

The Commission shall assume all the assets, rights and obligations of the Committee for the Coordination of Investigations of the Lower Mekong Basin (Mekong Committee/ Interim Mekong Committee) and Mekong Secretariat.

Article 14—Budget of the Mekong River Commission

The budget of the Commission shall be drawn up by the Joint Committee and approved by the Council and shall consist of contributions from member countries on an equal basis unless otherwise decided by the Council, from the international community (donor countries), and from other sources.

Council

Article 15—Composition of Council

The Council shall be composed of one member from each participating riparian State at the Ministerial and Cabinet level, (no less than Vice-Minister level) who would be empowered to make policy decisions on behalf of his/her government.

Article 16—Chairmanship of Council

The Chairmanship of the Council shall be for a term of one year and rotate according to the alphabetical listing of the participating countries.

Article 17—Sessions of Council

The Council shall convene at least one regular session every year and may convene special sessions whenever it considers it necessary or upon the request of a member State. It may invite observers to its sessions as it deems appropriate.

Article 18—Functions of Council

The functions of the Council are:

a) To make policies and decisions and provide other necessary guidance concerning the promotion, support, cooperation and coordination in joint activities and projects in a constructive and mutually beneficial manner for the sustainable development, utilization, conservation and management of the Mekong River Basin waters and related resources, and protection of the environment and aquatic conditions in the Basin as provided for under this Agreement;

b) To decide any other policy-making matters and make decisions necessary to successfully implement this Agreement, including but not limited to approval of the Rules of Procedures of the Joint Committee under Article 25, Rules of Water Utilization and Inter-Basin Diversions proposed by the Joint Committee under Article 26, and the basin development plan and major component projects/ programs; to establish guidelines for financial and technical assistance of development projects and programs; and if considered necessary, to invite the donors to coordinate their support through a Donor Consultative Group; and

c) To entertain, address and resolve issues, differences and disputes referred to it by any Council member, the Joint Committee, or any member State on matters arising under this Agreement.

Article 19—Rules of Procedures

The Council shall adopt its own Rules of Procedures, and may seek technical advisory services as it deems necessary.

Article 20—Decisions of Council

Decisions of the Council shall be by unanimous vote except as otherwise provided for in its Rules of Procedures.

Joint Committee

Article 21—Composition of Joint Committee

The Joint Committee shall be composed of one member from each participating riparian State at no less than Head of Department level.

Article 22—Chairmanship of Joint Committee

The Chairmanship of the Joint Committee will rotate according to the reverse alphabetical listing of the member countries and the Chairperson shall serve a term of one year.

Article 23—Sessions of Joint Committee

The Joint Committee shall convene at least two regular sessions every year and may convene special sessions whenever it considers it necessary or upon the request of a member State. It may invite observers to its sessions as it deems appropriate.

Article 24—Functions of Joint Committee

The functions of the Joint Committee are:

a) To implement the policies and decisions of the Council and such other tasks as may be assigned by the Council.

b) To formulate a basin development plan, which would be periodically reviewed and revised as necessary; to submit to the Council for approval the basin development plan and joint development projects/ programs to be implemented in connection with it; and to confer with donors, directly or through their consultative group, to obtain the financial and technical support necessary for project/program implementation.

c) To regularly obtain, update and exchange information and data necessary to implement this Agreement.

d) To conduct appropriate studies and assessments for the protection of the environment and maintenance of the ecological balance of the Mekong River Basin.

e) To assign tasks and supervise the activities of the Secretariat as is required to implement this Agreement and the policies, decisions, projects and programs adopted thereunder, including the maintenance of databases and information necessary for the Council and Joint Committee to perform their functions, and approval of the annual work program prepared by the Secretariat.

f) To address and make every effort to resolve issues and differences that may arise between regular sessions of the Council, referred to it by any Joint Committee member or member state on matters arising under this Agreement, and when necessary to refer the matter to the Council.

g) To review and approve studies and training for the personnel of the riparian member countries involved in Mekong River Basin activities as appropriate and necessary to strengthen the capability to implement this Agreement.

h) To make recommendations to the Council for approval on the organizational structure, modifications and restructuring of the Secretariat.

The Council shall adopt its own Rules of Procedures, and may seek technical advisory services as it deems necessary.

Article 25—Rules of Procedures

The Joint Committee shall propose its own Rules of Procedures to be approved by the Council. It may form ad hoc and/or permanent sub-committees or working groups as considered necessary, and may seek technical advisory services except as may be provided for in the Council's Rules of Procedures or decisions.

Article 26—Rules for Water Utilization and Inter-Basin Diversions

The Joint Committee shall prepare and propose for approval of the Council, inter alia, Rules for Water Utilization and Inter-Basin Diversions pursuant to Articles 5 and 6, including but not limited to:

1) establishing the time frame for the wet and dry seasons;
2) establishing the location of hydrological stations, and determining and maintaining the flow level requirements at each station;
3) setting out criteria for determining surplus quantities of water during the dry season on the mainstream;
4) improving upon the mechanism to monitor intra-basin use; and,
5) setting up a mechanism to monitor inter-basin diversions from the mainstream.

Article 27—Decisions of the Joint Committee

Decisions of the Joint Committee shall be by unanimous vote except as otherwise provided for in its Rules of Procedures.

Secretariat

Article 28—Purpose of Secretariat

The Secretariat shall render technical and administrative services to the Council and Joint Committee, and be under the supervision of the Joint Committee.

Article 29—Location of Secretariat

The location and structure of the permanent office of the Secretariat shall be decided by the Council, and if necessary, a headquarters agreement shall be negotiated and entered into with the host government.

Article 30—Functions of the Secretariat

The functions and duties of the Secretariat will be to:

a) Carry out the decisions and tasks assigned by the Council and Joint Committee under the direction of and directly responsible to the Joint Committee;
b) Provide technical services and financial administration and advise as requested by the Council and Joint Committee;
c) Formulate the annual work program, and prepare all other plans, project and program documents, studies and assessments as may be required;
d) Assist the Joint Committee in the implementation and management of projects and programs as requested;
e) Maintain databases of information as directed;
f) Make preparations for sessions of the Council and Joint Committee; and
g) Carry out all other assignments as may be requested.

Article 31—Chief Executive Officer

The Secretariat shall be under the direction of a Chief Executive Officer (CEO), who shall be appointed by the Council from a short-list of qualified candidates selected by the Joint Committee. The Terms of Reference of the CEO shall be prepared by the Joint Committee and approved by the Council.

Article 32—Assistant Chief Executive Officer

There will be one Assistant to the CEO, nominated by the CEO and approved by the Chairman of the Joint Committee. Such Assistant will be of the same nationality as the Chairman of the Joint Committee and shall serve for a co-terminus one-year term.

Article 33—Riparian Staff

Riparian technical staff of the Secretariat are to be recruited on a basis of technical competence, and the number of posts shall be assigned on an equal basis among the members. Riparian technical staff shall be assigned to the Secretariat for no more than two three-year terms, except as otherwise decided by the Joint Committee.

Chapter V—Addressing Differences and Disputes

Article 34—Resolution by Mekong River Commission

Whenever any difference or dispute may arise between two or more parties to this Agreement regarding any matters covered by this Agreement and/or actions taken by the implementing organization through its various bodies, particularly as to the interpretations of the Agreement and the legal rights of the parties, the Commission shall first make every effort to resolve the issue as provided in Articles 18.C and 24.F.

Article 35—Resolution by Governments

In the event the Commission is unable to resolve the difference or dispute within a timely manner, the issue shall be referred to the Governments to take cognizance of the matter for resolution by negotiation through diplomatic channels within a timely manner, and may communicate their decision to the Council for further proceedings as may be necessary to carry out such decision. Should the Governments find it necessary or beneficial to facilitate the resolution of the matter, they may, by mutual agreement, request the assistance of mediation through an entity or party mutually agreed upon, and thereafter to proceed according to the principles of international law.

Chapter VI—Final Provisions

Article 36—Entry Into Force and Prior Agreements

This Agreement shall:

a) Enter into force among all parties, with no retroactive effect upon activities and projects previously existing, on the date of signature by the appointed plenipotentiaries.

b) Replace the Statute of the Committee for Coordination of Investigations of the Lower Mekong Basin of 1957 as amended, the Joint Declaration of Principles for Utilization of the Waters of the Lower Mekong Basin of 1975, the Declaration Concerning the Interim Committee for Coordination of Investigations of the Lower Mekong Basin of 1978, and all Rules of Procedures adopted under such agreements. This Agreement shall not replace or take precedence over any other treaties, acts or agreements entered into by and among any of the parties hereto, except that where a conflict in terms, areas of jurisdiction of subject matter or operation of any entities created under existing agreements occurs with any provisions of this Agreement, the issues shall be submitted to the respective governments to address and resolve.

Article 37—Amendments, Modification, Supersession and Termination

This Agreement may be amended, modified, superceded or terminated by the mutual agreement of all parties hereto at the time of such action.

Article 38—Scope of Agreement

This Agreement shall consist of the Preamble and all provisions thereafter and amendments thereto, the Annexes, and all other agreements entered into by the Parties under this Agreement. Parties may enter into bi- or multi-lateral special agreements or arrangements for implementation and management of any programs and projects to be undertaken within the framework of this Agreement, which agreements shall not be in conflict with this Agreement and shall not confer any rights or obligations upon the parties not signatories thereto, except as otherwise conferred under this Agreement.

Article 39—Additional Parties to Agreement

Any other riparian State, accepting the rights and obligations under this Agreement, may become a party with the consent of the parties.

Article 40—Suspension and Withdrawal

Any party to this Agreement may withdraw or suspend their participation under present Agreement by giving written notice to the Chairman of the Council of the Mekong River Commission, who shall acknowledge receipt thereof and immediately communicate it to the Council representatives of all remaining parties. Such notice of withdrawal or suspension shall take effect one year after the date of acknowledgment or receipt unless such notice is withdrawn beforehand or the parties mutually agree otherwise. Unless mutually agreed upon to the contrary by all remaining parties to this Agreement, such notice shall not be prejudicial to nor relieve the noticing party of any commitments entered into concerning programs, projects, studies or other recognized rights and interests of any riparians, or under international law.

Article 41—United Nations and International Community Involvement

The member countries to this Agreement acknowledge the important contribution in the assistance and guidance of the United Nations, donors and the international community and wish to continue the relationship under this Agreement.

Article 42—Registration of Agreement

This Agreement shall be registered and deposited, in English and French, with the Secretary General of the United Nations.

4

Large Dams

A

Darcey, T. et al. (eds), "Summary Report of the Workshop," *Large Dams Learning from the Past Looking at the Future,* IUCN, Gland, Switzerland, 1997, pp 3–5

[One of the outcomes of this workshop, held in Gland, Switzerland, in 1997, was the decision to establish the World Commission on Dams (WCD) as an independent body with "a mandate:

- *to review the development effectiveness of dams and assess alternatives for water resources and energy development, and*
- *to develop internationally-acceptable criteria and guidelines to advise future decision making in the planning, design, construction, monitoring, operation, and decommissioning of dams." See http://www.dams.org/about/history.htm, which was accessed 03/04/2001*

A synopsis of the findings of the WCD, released in November 2000, is extracted later in this chapter]

There has been mounting controversy, particularly over the last two decades, about the role of large dams in development.

...Dams have played a key role in development since at least the third millennium B.C., when the first great civilizations evolved on major rivers, such as the Nile, Tigres-Euphrates and Indus. From these early times, dams were built to supply water, control floods, irrigate agriculture and provide for navigation. More recently, since the onset of the industrial revolution in the 18th century, they have also been built to produce motive power and electricity. In the 20th century, new technologies have made possible the construction of increasingly large dams to meet various mixes of these purposes; the 221-meter-high Hoover Dam, inaugurated in the United States in 1935, ushered in a new era of big dams. In the last half of this century, construction around the world accelerated, with some 35,000 large dams being built between 1950 and the late 1980s, the largest of which, Nurek in Tajikistan, reached 300 meters high.

However, there has been mounting controversy, particularly over the last two decades, about the role of large dams in development. As development priorities changed and experience accumulated with the construction and operation of large dams around the world, various groups argued that expected economic benefits were not being produced and that major environmental, economic and social costs were not being taken into account. In the 1980s proposals for large dams began to be fundamentally questioned by locally affected interests and global coalitions of environmental and human rights groups (for example, Sardar Sarovar). In the 1990s this has resulted in a succession of calls for a moratorium on World Bank funding and reparations for those affected by construction of large dams.

World Bank Review

When he was appointed president of the World Bank in 1995, James Wolfensohn announced his intention to undertake a review of its development effectiveness. Although it had been involved in the financing of a relatively small proportion of the large dams, the World Bank Group had become a major focus of criticism because of the number of problematic projects, including some of the biggest and most controversial, in which it was involved. It was in this context that the independent Operations Evaluation Department (OED) of the World Bank began a review of large dam projects. The first phase was designed to be an internal desk study of 50 large dams assisted by the Bank and was completed by OED in September 1996. The second phase was planned to be a broader study, involving the collection of new data and participation by other stakeholders, to evaluate the development effectiveness of large dams in terms of technical, economic, social land environmental implications for future financing by the World Bank Group, as well as other sources.

Using available data for projects completed between 1960 and 1995, the dams were classified according to their economic justification and whether they satisfied the impact mitigation and management policies existing at the time of their approval, or could have been planned so as to satisfy policies that the Bank had introduced over the intervening years. OED concluded that while 90 percent of the dams reviewed met the standards applicable at the time of approvals, only about one quarter were implemented so as to comply with the World Bank's current, more demanding policies. The review also concluded that mitigation of the adverse social and environmental consequences of large dams would have been both feasible and economically justified in 74 percent of the cases. The main conclusion was OED's conditional support for the construction of large dams, provided that they strictly comply with Bank guidelines and fully incorporate the lessons of experience. The analysis, conclusions and recommendations were summarized and made public in an OED Precis (1996).

World Bank Partnership with IUCN—The World Conservation Union

One of the initiatives of the director-general of IUCN, David McDowell, upon his appointment in 1994, was to seek strategic partnerships with key international agencies so that they might work together to resolve controversial issues and meet joint interests. An agreement negotiated with the World Bank and signed in 1994 was one of the early partnerships to be established. It was under this agreement that the Bank approached IUCN in 1996 with the idea that they might jointly host a workshop to discuss the findings of the OED desk review (Phase I) and their implications for the design, methodology and process of a proposed in-depth study (Phase II) on large dams to be undertaken in 1997–1998.

B

Goodland R., "Environmental Sustainability in the Hydro Industry: Disaggregating the Debate," in Darcey, T. et al. (eds), *Large Dams Learning from the Past Looking at the Future*, IUCN, Gland, Switzerland, 1997, pp 69–73

[*Editors' Note: This article has been selectively extracted and in some cases the precise order of the original has been altered to enhance presentation.*]

Proponents of hydroelectric dams (hydros) and other renewable energy sources are losing the fight to promote them. Hydros have not yet become fully environmentally sustainable. Hydro opponents have been so successful in pointing out inadequacies that hydro development is slowing and coal is burgeoning—precisely the retrogressive course. Hydro proponents have not been totally successful in persuading opponents that hydro's benefits clearly outweigh the costs. (Box 1)

Part of the controversy is caused by confusion on the precise nature of the issues between hydro proponents and opponents, even by parties who should be well informed...

The many benefits of big dams are not the focus of this paper. However, the major benefits of big dams may not be as well known or as frequently posed as what needs to be improved. Dam proponents may want to emphasize which dams have worked well, as that case is often assumed, rather than documented. The case that many big dams have created valuable economic rates of return is clearly portrayed in the Big Dams Review. Recent major improvements in turbine efficiencies and the huge non-hydro benefits such as flood control, navigation, irrigation, water supply and river regulation to improve water use downstream must be acknowledged... [however] the record of industrial country dams is probably better than that in developing countries for compelling reasons...

Part of the controversy is that hydro can be made sustainable and renewable, but only with more effort than is customary. Hydro is on the cusp between fully renewable and clearly non-renewable.

The important point...is that the old-fashioned approach of tit-for-tat mitigation for each individual impact is inherently weak. The project-level Environmental Assessment (EA) is [thus] being complemented by the much more powerful sectoral approach. The retail project-specific environmental assessment and mitigation cannot influence project selection, [however], it is precisely during the project selection phase that most impacts can be prevented or minimized. Once the project has been selected, the weaker project-level EA should still be applied, but is severely constrained in what it can mitigate.

International best practice is converging on the notion that most impacts are better reduced in the selection process of low-impact projects or site selection, rather than mitigating impacts of previously selected projects. This Sectoral Environmental Assessment (SEA) approach is

Box 1. Examples of Controversial Dams

1. Thailand's 576-megawatt ($352 million) Nam Choan was indefinitely postponed by the Royal Thai cabinet in 1982 because the 140–square-kilometer reservoir would flood 4 percent of the 4,800–square-kilometer Thung Hai Wildlife Sanctuary. This sanctuary was (and is even more since) being actively logged and poached, both of which the project could have halted. This is just one example of the many hydro projects that are indeed dropped on environmental grounds.
2. Sweden has banned further hydro projects on half of its rivers. The new government may rescind this decision partly because of availability of Finland's nuclear energy.
3. Norway until recently derived 100 percent of its energy from hydro, which was considered good and sustainable. Norway has now postponed all new hydros because of excess capacity and opposition.
4. Slovakia is defying the EC and the EC-appointed tribunal looking into the Danube's Gabcikovo Dam. The dam is alleged to have lowered the water table in Hungary's prime agricultural area (yields dropped 30 percent) by 6 meters in the lower central pan of Hungary's Szigetkoz wetland. Most Danube fish are reported to have since declined. Work was halted for a period in mid-construction.
5. In the United States, New York State (NY Power Authority) canceled its 20-year $12.6 billion contract to buy 1,000 megawatts of Quebec's James Bay power, reportedly for environmental and social reasons, in March 1992. Demand-side management in New York played a role too. HydroQuebec indefinitely postponed Great Whale hydro in 1994.
6. India requested that the World Bank cancel the outstanding $170 million Sardar Sarovar (Narmada) loan on March 31, 1993, partly because the contractual agreement schedule was unlikely to be met on time. This was the world's most intense dam controversy for years on environmental and social impacts.
7. Nepal's 401-megawatt Arun hydro, which created a 43-hectare reservoir and caused little resettlement, twice entered Nepal's Supreme Court in 1994 because of opposition related to the 122-kilometer access road and complaints about the lack of transparency. A petition was lodged with the World Bank's Inspection Panel in 1994, and the project was dropped in 1995 largely because of financial risk, although environment was criticized by opponents.
8. China's approximately 16,000-megawatt Three Gorges, the largest in the world, had US support withdrawn in December 1993, when the US Secretary of the Interior ordered the Bureau of Reclamation to cease collaboration.. The US Export-Import Bank withdrew support in 1994. According to World Rivers Review, the export credit agencies of Switzerland, Japan and Germany (Hermes-Buergschaften Ex-Im Bank) were involved as of 1997.
9. Chile's 400-megawatt Pangue hydrodam, the first of five planned for the BioBio river (IFC's first major dam, $150 million, approved in 1992 and completed March 6, 1997), came under litigation in Chile's Supreme Court in 1993, partly because the EA failed to address downstream impacts. An independent review commissioned by IFC and led by Jay Hair, former president of IUCN-World Conservation Union, is said to be very critical of both the project process and IFC; World Bank Group President James Wolfensohn threatened on February 6, 1997, to declare default to Finance Minister Aninat. On March 11, Chile severed ties with IFC by prepaying IFC's loan and obtaining cheaper money from the Dresdner Bank, with fewer environmental conditions.

essentially integrating the tried-and-true economic least-cost analysis with environmental and social criteria…if environmental criteria are used in project selection, then only projects with the least impacts are selected…

The goal of both the sectoral and the project EA is to make hydro projects sustainable…While the project-level EA is essential and needs to be strengthened, using the SEA to select the better projects is far more powerful. In addition, the hydro industry needs to foster transparency and participation, as well as show that conservation is well in hand and that electricity pricing is adequate before new capacity is contemplated. The biggest impact of hydros, involuntary resettlement, needs the most attention. Oustees must be better off promptly after their move.

C

Scudder T., "Social Impacts of Large Dam Projects," in Darcey T., et al. (eds), *Large Dams Learning from the Past Looking at the Future,* IUCN, Gland, Switzerland, 1997, pp 41-44

Overview

Whether short-term or cumulative, adverse social impacts are a serious consequence of large dams. When combined with adverse health impacts, it is clear that large-scale water resource development projects unnecessarily have lowered the living standards of millions of local people. The emphasis in this paper is on the low-income rural majority that live in subtropical and tropical river basins. The analysis will deal mainly with resettlers, host populations and those other project affected people (OPAPS), especially downstream residents, who are neither resettlers nor hosts.

Resettlers

According to the World Bank's former senior advisor for social policy and sociology, "forced population displacement caused by dam construction is the single most serious counter-developmental social consequence of water resource development." The Bank's senior environment advisor concurs: "involuntary resettlement is arguably the most serious issue of hydro projects nowadays."

A wide range of difficulties is involved. They include the complexity of the resettlement process; the lack of opportunities for restoring and improving living standards; the problem of sustainability of what development occurs; the loss of resiliency and increased dependency following incorporation within a wider political economy; inadequate implementation of acceptable plans due to such factors as timing, financial and institutional constraints; unexpected events, including changing government priorities; lack of political will on the part of governments; host-resettler conflicts; and the lack of empowerment of relocated and host populations.

For those removed, and for the host populations among whom they are resettled, the goal of resettlement must be to become project beneficiaries. This means that the income and living standards of the large majority must improve. Analysis of the global record in regard to resettlement suggests that realizing this goal is possible but very difficult. The main resource is those relocated. The global experience is that resettlers can contribute to the stream of project benefits if appropriate opportunities and security of tenure over their natural resource base are present.

If more local people are to become beneficiaries, not only must World Bank-type guidelines for resettlers be extended to all project affected people, but the horizon of environmental and social impact assessments must be expanded to include all habitats and human populations that are likely to be affected.

The main theoretical framework dealing with dam resettlement is a four-stage model developed during the late 1970s. Briefly, the four stages are characterized by

(1) planning,
(2) efforts by the resettlers to cope and to adapt following removal,
(3) economic development and community formation, and
(4) handing over and incorporation.

Successful resettlement takes time. At the minimum it should be implemented as a two-generation process.

Following the initial planning and recruitment stage, the second stage is characterized by the struggle to adjust to the loss of homeland and to new surroundings. That stage is characterized by multidimensional stress, with physiological, psychological and sociocultural components synergistically interrelated. During the initial year following removal, income and living standards can be expected to drop. If new opportunities are available, the third stage of economic development and community formation can begin once a majority of resettlers have adjusted to their new habitat and gained a measure of household self-sufficiency. The tragedy of most resettlement to date is that a majority of resettlers never reach stage three. Rather as the resettlement process proceeds, they remain, or subsequently become, impoverished.

Stage three development must be sustainable into the next generation for the resettlement component to be considered successful. Stage four commences when the next generation of settlers takes over from the pioneers and when that generation is able to compete successfully with other citizens for jobs and other resources at national and local levels. It is also characterized by the devolution of what management and facilitation responsibilities may be held by specialized resettlement agencies, nongovernmental organizations (NGOs) and others to the community of resettlers and to the various line ministries.

Hosts

Even when political leaders among the host population agree to the movement of resettlers into their midst, sooner or later conflicts between the two can be expected. They arise because of competition among a larger population over a diminished land base, as well as over access to job opportunities, social services and political power.

It is best to anticipate the inevitability of host-resettler conflicts. The best approach for minimizing them is to include the host population in the improved social services and economic development opportunities intended for the resettlers. While such an approach will increase the financial costs of resettlement in the short run, in the long run it will enhance the possibility of multiplier effects as well as reduce the intensity of conflict. Unfortunately, such incorporation of the host population within resettlement programs is rare.

Other Project Affected People (OPAPS)

Large-scale river basin development projects speed the incorporation of all project affected people, including resettlers and hosts, within wider political economies. Theoretically that should be a plus in terms of national development. The studies that have been completed suggest, however, that such incorporation is more apt to reduce than improve the living standards of a majority. This is especially the case with OPAPS living below mainstream dams.

Aside from run-of-the-river installations, a major function of dam construction is to regularize a river's annual regime. Though few detailed studies have been completed on the impacts of such regularization, those that exist have shown them to have a devastating effect on millions of people. The topic has been best researched in West Africa in connection with mainstream dams on the Senegal River and a number of dams in Nigeria. After three years of studies, an Institute for Development Anthropology team showed that the Manantali Dam as managed by the trinational Senegal Valley Development Authority (OMVS) was adversely affecting up to 500,000 people below the dam. Below the Kainji Dam on the Niger, adverse downstream impacts include reductions in swamp rice and yam production and in the productivity of the riverine fishery. On a Niger tributary further upriver, costs of the Bakolori Dam to downstream villagers is estimated to exceed the benefits realized from the project.

As for OPAPS living in the vicinity of large-scale dams, Hydro-Quebec's James Bay Project illustrates the impoverishing impact on an entire cultural area. For example, the 1975 James Bay and Northern Quebec Agreement split the Cree into eight geographically isolated bands whose exclusive control of surface rights involved only 5 percent of their former lands. More specifically, implementation of the La Grande Phase of the project has had two quite different types of negative impacts. One is the mercury contamination of reservoir fish to the extent that mercury contamination of some Cree, for whom fish are an all-important dietary component, significantly exceeds World Health Organization standards. Causality in this instance can rather easily be ascertained. Such is not the case with the other type of impact, which includes an increased incidence of sexually transmitted diseases and social pathologies such as spousal abuse and suicide, especially among young women.

Immigrants

Immigrants, both temporary and permanent, from without a particular river basin are major beneficiaries of river basin development projects. Seeking the new opportunities created by a project, they are able to out-compete local people. Two major benefits of large dams are the reservoir fishery and irrigation. Though both involve project affected people as well as immigrants, the latter tend to dominate unless a special effort is made to select and increase the competitive abilities of local people.

Helping Project Affected People Become Beneficiaries

...In recent years, the need for local people to have greater involvement in project planning, implementation, management and evaluation has been increasingly emphasized. That emphasis is welcome and important. As with the implementation of plans that actually make project affected people beneficiaries, however, the extent to which local people have actually been involved has been disappointing. Aside from lack of political will on the part of governments to actually decentralize decision-making, there are several other issues that must be dealt with. These include differences in definition as to what local participation means, failure to link decentralization of decision-making with decentralization of financial resources for implementing those decisions, and social disorganization at the community level.

Ironically, increased emphasis on the need for local participation is occurring at a time when customary participatory institutions are weakening because of increasing incorporation of local communities within wider political economies and growing emphasis on private ownership of resources. Moreover, within communities, educated individuals are placing increasing emphasis on household and individual interests, as opposed to extended kin groups and customary institutions of cooperation.

Such circumstances must be dealt with if local participation is to play the role it should in improving the living standards of project affected people. A prerequisite will be participatory appraisal. While customary institutions may be adjusted to new conditions, new socioeconomic and political institutional forms will probably be required.

Regardless of the type of institutions utilized or developed, effective local participation must involve a much broader range of actors than just project affected people. At the national level, commitment must be reflected in the necessary legislative and judicial framework. The assistance of NGOs in institution-building would also be necessary in many cases, as would be the financial assistance of various donors. Also important would be private-sector involvement in various joint ventures as well as assistance from universities and research institutions to develop appropriate monitoring and evaluation capabilities.

D

"Executive Summary," in World Commission on Dams, *Dams and Development: A New Framework for Decision-Making*, WCD, 16 November 2000

[*Editors Note: The WCD report which contains this extract, and the extract immediately following, can be found at <http://www.dams.org/report/execsumm.htm>. This site was accessed 03/04/2001.*]

The global debate about large dams is at once overwhelmingly complex and fundamentally simple. It is complex because the issues are not confined to the design, construction and operation of dams themselves but embrace the range of social, environmental and political choices on which the human aspiration to development and improved well-being depend. Dams fundamentally alter rivers and the use of a natural resource, frequently entailing a reallocation of benefits from local riparian users to new groups of beneficiaries at a regional or national level. At the heart of the dams debate are issues of equity, governance, justice and power—issues that underlie the many intractable problems faced by humanity.

The dams debate is simple because behind the array of facts and figures, of economic statistics and engineering calculations, lie a number of basic and easily understood principles. If adhered to and routinely applied, these principles would not only go a long way towards responding to the controversy surrounding dams, but would markedly improve decision making on water and energy resources, achieving better outcomes. In identifying these principles, the World Commission on Dams (WCD) has not had to look far; they are the same principles that emerge from the global commitments to human rights, development and sustainability...

The dams debate is simple because behind the array of facts and figures, of economic statistics and engineering calculations, lie a number of basic and easily understood principles.

We believe there can no longer be any justifiable doubt about the following:

- Dams have made an important and significant contribution to human development, and the benefits derived from them have been considerable.
- In too many cases an unacceptable and often unnecessary price has been paid to secure those benefits, especially in social and environmental terms, by people displaced, by communities downstream, by taxpayers and by the natural environment.
- Lack of equity in the distribution of benefits has called into question the value of many dams in meeting water and energy development needs when compared with the alternatives.
- By bringing to the table all those whose rights are involved and who bear the risks associated with different options for water and energy resources development, the conditions for a positive resolution of competing interests and conflicts are created.
- Negotiating outcomes will greatly improve the development effectiveness of water and energy projects by eliminating unfavorable projects at an early stage, and by offering as a choice only those options that key stakeholders agree represent the best ones to meet the needs in question.

The direction we must take is clear. It is to break through the traditional boundaries of thinking and look at these issues from a different perspective. Our recommendations develop a rationale and framework that responds to this critical need and offers scope for progress that no single perspective can offer on its own. It will ensure that decision-making on water and energy development:

- reflects a comprehensive approach to integrating social, environmental and economic dimensions of development;
- creates greater levels of transparency and certainty for all involved; and
- increases levels of confidence in the ability of nations and communities to meet their future water and energy needs.

There are no shortcuts to equitable and sustainable development. The evidence of success and failure we present in this report provides the best rationale why the 'business as usual' scenario is neither a feasible nor a desirable option.

Water and Development— The Changing Context

The key decisions are not about dams as such, but about options for water and energy development. They relate directly to one of the greatest challenges facing the world in this new century—the need to rethink the management of freshwater resources. A number of global initiatives and reports have documented the dramatic impact of human-induced water withdrawals from the world's lakes, rivers and ground aquifers. Total annual freshwater withdrawals today are estimated at 3,800 cubic kilometers— twice as much as just 50 years ago.

The unfolding scenario for water use in many parts of the world is one of increasing concern about access, equity and the response to growing needs. This affects relations:

- within and between nations;
- between rural and urban populations;
- between upstream and downstream interests;
- between agricultural, industrial and domestic sectors; and
- between human needs and the requirements of a healthy environment.

The challenge is not to mobilize so as to compete successfully, but to cooperate in reconciling competing needs. It is to find ways of sharing water resources equitably and sustainably—ways that meet the needs of all people as well as those of the environment and economic development. These needs are all intertwined, and our challenge is to resolve competing interests collectively. Achieving equitable and sustainable solutions will be to the ultimate benefit of all.

The imperative to supply growing populations and economies with water in a context of depleting groundwater resources, declining water quality and increasingly severe limits to surface water extraction has brought sustainable water resources management to the top of the global development agenda. Although increasing competition for water suggests an expanding scope for conflict, it also provides an incentive for new forms of cooperation and innovation. Dire scenarios for water demand must not overshadow the fact that development paths that meet and manage the demand exist and are available for us to choose. History demonstrates that the path of cooperation has more often been followed than the path of conflict. The same must be true for our future.

During the 20th century, large dams emerged as one of the most significant and visible tools for the management of water resources. The more than 45,000 large dams around the world have played an important role in helping communities and economies harness water resources for food production, energy generation, flood control and domestic use. Current estimates suggest that some 30-40 percent of irrigated land worldwide now relies on dams and that dams generate 19 percent of world electricity.

From the 1930s to the 1970s, the construction of large dams became—in the eyes of many—synonymous with development and economic progress. Viewed as symbols of modernization and humanity's ability to harness nature, dam construction accelerated dramatically. This trend peaked in the 1970s, when on average two or three large dams were commissioned each day somewhere in the world.

While the immediate benefits were widely believed sufficient to justify the enormous investments made—total investment in large dams worldwide is estimated at more than $2 trillion—secondary and tertiary benefits were also often cited. These included food security considerations, local employment and skills development, rural electrification and the expansion of physical and social infrastructure such as roads and schools. The benefits were regarded as self-evident, while the construction and operational costs tended to be limited to economic and financial considerations that justified dams as a highly competitive option.

As experience accumulated and better information on the performance and consequences of dams became available, the full cost of large dams began to emerge as a serious public concern. Driven by information on the impacts of dams on people, river basins and ecosystems, as well as their economic performance, opposition began to grow. Debate and controversy initially focused on specific dams and their local impacts. Gradually these locally driven conflicts evolved into a global debate about the costs and benefits of dams. Global estimates of the magnitude of impacts include some 40–80 million people displaced by dams while 60 percent of the world's rivers have been affected by dams and diversions. The nature and magnitude of the impacts of dams on affected communities and on the environment have now become established as key issues in the debate...

The WCD Global Review of Large Dams

A large part of the Commission's work involved a broad and independent review of the experience with large dams. The resulting WCD Knowledge Base includes eight detailed case studies of large dams, country reviews for India and China, a briefing paper for Russia and the Newly Independent States, a Cross-Check Survey of 125 existing dams, 17 Thematic Review papers, as well as the results of public consultations and more than 900 submissions made available to the Commission. This provided the basis for the assessment of the technical, financial, economic, environmental and social performance of large dams, and the review of their alternatives. The review underlined the critical issues relating to governance and compliance that have come to be associated with large dams.

The evaluation was based on the targets set for large dams by their proponents - the criteria that provided the basis for government approval. In reviewing this experience the Commission has studied a broad spectrum of dams. Its analysis gave particular attention to understanding the reasons why, how and where dams did not achieve their intended outcome or indeed produced unanticipated outcomes that explain the issues underlying the dams debate. Presenting this analysis does not overlook the substantial benefits derived from dams but rather raises the question of why some dams achieve their goals while others fail.

Performance of Large Dams

The knowledge base indicates that shortfalls in technical, financial and economic performance have occurred and are compounded by significant social and environmental impacts, the costs of which are often disproportionately borne by poor people, indigenous peoples and other vulnerable groups. Given the large capital investment in large dams, the Commission was disturbed to find that substantive evaluations of completed projects are few in number, narrow in scope, poorly integrated across impact categories and scales, and inadequately linked to decisions on operations.

In assessing the large dams reviewed by the Commission we found that:

- Large dams display a high degree of variability in delivering predicted water and electricity services—and related social benefits—with a considerable portion falling short of physical and economic targets, while others continue generating benefits after 30 to 40 years.
- Large dams have demonstrated a marked tendency towards schedule delays and significant cost overruns.
- Large dams designed to deliver irrigation services have typically fallen short of physical targets, did not recover their costs and have been less profitable in economic terms than expected.
- Large hydropower dams tend to perform closer to, but still below, targets for power generation, generally meet their financial targets but demonstrate variable economic performance relative to targets, with a number of notable under- and over-performers.
- Large dams generally have a range of extensive impacts on rivers, watersheds and aquatic ecosystems—these impacts are more negative than positive and, in many cases, have led to irreversible loss of species and ecosystems.
- Efforts to date to counter the ecosystem impacts of large dams have met with limited success owing to the lack of attention to anticipating and avoiding impacts, the poor quality and uncertainty of predictions, the difficulty of coping with all impacts, and the only partial implementation and success of mitigation measures.
- Pervasive and systematic failure to assess the range of potential negative impacts and implement adequate mitigation, resettlement and development programs for the displaced, and the failure to account for the consequences of large dams for downstream livelihoods have led to the impoverishment and

suffering of millions, giving rise to growing opposition to dams by affected communities worldwide.

- Since the environmental and social costs of large dams have been poorly accounted for in economic terms, the true profitability of these schemes remains elusive.

Today, a wide range of options for delivering water and electricity services exists, although in particular situations the cost and feasibility of these options will vary in the face of constraints such as natural resource endowments and site location.

Perhaps of most significance is the fact that social groups bearing the social and environmental costs and risks of large dams, especially the poor, vulnerable and future generations, are often not the same groups that receive the water and electricity services, nor the social and economic benefits from these. Applying a 'balance-sheet' approach to assess the costs and benefits of large dams, where large inequities exist in the distribution of these costs and benefits, is seen as unacceptable given existing commitments to human rights and sustainable development.

Options for Water and Electricity Services

Today, a wide range of options for delivering water and electricity services exists, although in particular situations the cost and feasibility of these options will vary in the face of constraints such as natural resource endowments and site location. The Commission found that:

- Many of the non-dam options available today—including demand-side management, supply efficiency and new supply options—can improve or expand water and energy services and meet evolving development needs in all segments of society.
- There is considerable scope for improving performance of both dam projects and other options.
- Demand management, reducing consumption, recycling and supply and end-use efficiency measures all have significant potential to reduce pressure on water resources in all countries and regions of the world.
- A number of supply-side options at all scales (ranging from small, distributed generation sources or localized water collection and water-recovery systems to regional-interconnection of power grids) have emerged that—on their own or collectively—can improve or expand the delivery of water and energy services in a timely, cost-effective and publicly acceptable manner.
- Decentralized, small-scale options (micro hydro, home-scale solar electric systems, wind and biomass systems) based on local renewable sources offer an important near-term, and possibly long-term, potential particularly in rural areas far away from centralized supply networks.
- Obstacles to the adoption of these options range from market barriers to institutional, intellectual and financial barriers. A range of incentives—some hidden—that favor conventional options limit the adoption rate of alternatives.

Decision Making, Planning and Institutional Arrangements

The decision to build a dam is influenced by many variables beyond immediate technical considerations. As a development choice, the selection of large dams often served as a focal point for the interests and aspirations of politicians, centralized government agencies, international aid donors and the dam-building industry, and did not provide for a comprehensive evaluation of available alternatives. Involvement from civil society varied with the degree of debate and openness to political discourse in a country. However, the WCD Global Review documents a frequent failure to recognize affected people and empower them to participate in the process. In some cases, the opportunity for corruption provided by dams as large-scale infrastructure projects further distorted decision-making.

Once a proposed dam project passed preliminary technical and economic feasibility tests and attracted interest from financing agencies and political interests, the momentum behind the project often prevailed over other considerations. Project planning and appraisal for large dams was confined primarily to technical parameters and the narrow application of economic cost-benefit analyzes. Historically, social and environmental impacts were left outside the assessment framework and the role of impact assessments in project selection remained marginal, even into the 1990s.

Conflicts over dams have heightened in the last two decades due largely to the social and environmental impacts of dams that were either disregarded in the planning process or unanticipated. However, it also stems from the failure by dam proponents and financing agencies to fulfil commitments made, observe statutory regulations and abide by internal guidelines. Whereas far-reaching improvements in policies, legal requirements and assessment procedures have occurred in particular countries and institutions, in the 1990s it appears that business-as-usual too often prevailed. Further, past shortcomings and inequities remain unresolved, and experience with appeals, dispute resolution and recourse mechanisms has been poor.

Core Values for Decision Making

As the Global Review of dams makes clear, improving development outcomes in the future requires a substantially expanded basis for deciding on proposed water and energy development projects—a basis that reflects a full knowledge and understanding of the benefits, impacts and risks of large dam projects to all parties. It also requires introducing new voices, perspectives and criteria into decision making, as well as processes that will build consensus around the decisions reached. This will fundamentally alter the way in which decisions are made and, we are convinced, improve the development effectiveness of future decisions.

The Commission grouped the core values that informed its understanding of these issues under five principal headings:

- equity,
- efficiency,
- participatory decision making,
- sustainability, and
- accountability.

These five are more than simply issues—they are the values that run through the entire report. They provide the essential tests that must be applied to decisions relating to water and energy development. If the report advances these values significantly we will emerge at our destination—improved decision-making processes that deliver improved outcomes for all stakeholders.

The debate about dams is a debate about the very meaning, purpose and pathways for achieving development. This suggests that decision-making on water and energy management will align itself with the emerging global commitment to sustainable human development and on the equitable distribution of costs and benefits. The emergence of a globally accepted framework of norms rests on the adoption of the *Universal Declaration of Human Rights* in 1948 and related covenants and conventions thereafter. These later resolutions include the *Declaration on the Right to Development* adopted by the UN General Assembly in 1986, and the Rio Principles agreed to at the *UN Conference on Environment and Development* in 1992. The core values that inform the Commission's shared understanding are aligned with this consensus and rest on the fundamental human rights accorded to all people by virtue of their humanity.

Rights, Risks and Negotiated Outcomes

Reconciling competing needs and entitlements is the single most important factor in understanding the conflicts associated with development projects and programs—particularly large-scale interventions such as dams. The approach developed by the Commission of recognizing rights and assessing risks (particularly rights at risk) in the planning and project cycles offers a means to apply these core values to decision-making about water and energy resource management. Clarifying the rights context for a proposed project is an essential step in identifying those legitimate claims and entitlements that may be affected by the project or its alternatives. It is also a pre-condition for effective identification of legitimate stakeholder groups that are entitled to a formal role in the consultative process, and eventually in negotiating project-specific agreements relating, for example, to benefit sharing, resettlement and compensation. The assessment of risk adds an important dimension to understanding how, and to what extent, a project may impact on people's rights. In the past, many groups have not had an opportunity to participate in decisions that imply major risks for their lives and livelihoods, thus denying them a stake in the development decision-making process commensurate with their exposure to risk. Indeed, many have had risks imposed on them involuntarily. Risks must be identified and addressed explicitly. This will require the notion of risk to be extended beyond governments or developers to include both those affected by a project and the environment as a public good. Involuntary risk bearers must be engaged by risk takers in a transparent process to negotiate equitable outcomes. An approach based on the recognition of rights and assessment of risks can lay the basis for greatly improved and significantly more legitimate decision-making on water and energy resource development. It offers an effective way to determine who has a legitimate place at the negotiation table and what issues need to be included on the agenda. Only decision making processes based on the pursuit of negotiated outcomes, conducted in an open and transparent manner and inclusive of all legitimate actors involved in the issue are likely to resolve the complex issues surrounding water, dams and development.

Recommendations for a New Policy Framework

Researching and analyzing the history of water resources management, the emergence of large dams, their impacts and performance, and the resultant dams debate led the Commission to view the controversy surrounding dams within a broader normative framework. This framework, within which the dams debate clearly resides, builds upon international recognition of human rights, the right to development and the right to a healthy environment.

Within this framework the Commission has developed seven strategic priorities and related policy principles. It has translated these priorities and principles into a set of corresponding criteria and guidelines for key decision points in the planning and project cycles.

Together, they provide guidance on translating this framework into practice. They help us move from a traditional, top-down, technology-focused approach to advocate significant innovations in assessing options, managing existing dams—including processes for assessing reparations and environmental restoration, gaining public acceptance and negotiating and sharing benefits.

The seven strategic priorities each supported by a set of policy principles, provide a principled and practical way forward for decision making. Presented here as expressions of an achieved outcome, they summarize key principles and actions that the Commission proposes all actors should adopt and implement.

Gaining Public Acceptance

Public acceptance of key decisions is essential for equitable and sustainable water and energy resources development. Acceptance emerges from recognizing rights, addressing risks, and safeguarding the entitlements of all groups of affected people, particularly indigenous and tribal peoples, women and other vulnerable groups. Decision making processes and mechanisms are used that enable informed participation by all groups of people, and result in the demonstrable acceptance of key decisions. Where projects affect indigenous and tribal peoples, such processes are guided by their free, prior and informed consent.

Comprehensive Options Assessment

Alternatives to dams do often exist. To explore these alternatives, needs for water, food and energy are assessed and objectives clearly defined. The appropriate development response is identified from a range of possible options. The selection is based on a comprehensive and participatory assessment of the full range of policy, institutional and technical options. In the assessment process social and environmental aspects have the same significance as economic and financial factors. The options assessment process continues through all stages of planning, project development and operations.

Addressing Existing Dams

Opportunities exist to optimize benefits from many existing dams, address outstanding social issues and strengthen environmental mitigation and restoration measures. Dams and the context in which they operate are not seen as static over time. Benefits and impacts may be transformed by changes in water use priorities, physical and land use changes in the river basin, technological developments, and changes in public policy expressed in environment, safety, economic and technical regulations. Management and operation practices must adapt continuously to changing circumstances over the project's life and must address outstanding social issues.

Sustaining Rivers and Livelihoods

Rivers, watersheds and aquatic ecosystems are the biological engines of the planet. They are the basis for life and the livelihoods of local communities. Dams transform landscapes and create risks of irreversible impacts. Understanding, protecting and restoring ecosystems at river basin level is essential to foster equitable human development and the welfare of all species. Options assessment and decision-making around river development prioritizes the avoidance of impacts, followed by the minimization and mitigation of harm to the health and integrity of the river system. Avoiding impacts through good site selection and project design is a priority. Releasing tailor-made environmental flows can help maintain downstream ecosystems and the communities that depend on them.

Recognizing Entitlements and Sharing Benefits

Joint negotiations with adversely affected people result in mutually agreed and legally enforceable mitigation and development provisions. These recognize entitlements that improve livelihoods and quality of life, and affected people are beneficiaries of the project. Successful mitigation, resettlement and development are fundamental commitments and responsibilities of the State and the developer. They bear the onus to satisfy all affected people that moving from their current context and resources will improve their livelihoods. Accountability of responsible parties to agreed mitigation, resettlement and development provisions is ensured through legal means, such as contracts, and through accessible legal recourse at the national and international level.

Ensuring Compliance

Ensuring public trust and confidence requires that the governments, developers, regulators and operators meet all commitments made for the planning, implementation and operation of dams. Compliance with applicable regulations, criteria and guidelines, and project-specific negotiated agreements is secured at all critical stages in project planning and implementation. A set of mutually reinforcing incentives and mechanisms is required for social, environmental and technical measures. These should involve an appropriate mix of regulatory and non-regulatory measures, incorporating incentives and sanctions. Regulatory and compliance frameworks use incentives and sanctions to ensure effectiveness where flexibility is needed to accommodate changing circumstances.

Sharing Rivers for Peace, Development and Security

Storage and diversion of water on transboundary rivers has been a source of considerable tension between countries and within countries. As specific interventions for diverting water, dams require constructive cooperation. Consequently, the use and management of resources increasingly becomes the subject of agreement between States to promote mutual self-interest for regional cooperation and peaceful collaboration. This leads to a shift in focus from the narrow approach of allocating a finite resource to the sharing of rivers and their associated benefits in which States are innovative in defining the scope of issues for discussion. External financing agencies support the principles of good faith negotiations between riparian States...

From Policy to Practice— The Planning and Project Cycle

The Commission's recommendations can best be implemented by focusing on the key stages in decision making on projects that influence the final outcome and where compliance with regulatory requirements can be verified. Among the multitude of decisions to be taken, the Commission has identified five key decision points. The first two relate to water and energy planning, leading to decisions on a preferred development plan:

- Needs assessment: validating the needs for water and energy services, and
- Selecting alternatives: identifying the preferred development plan from among the full range of options.

Where a dam emerges from this process as a preferred development alternative, three further critical decision points occur:

- Project preparation: verifying that agreements are in place before tender of the construction contract,
- Project implementation: confirming compliance before commissioning, and
- Project operation: adapting to changing contexts.

Social, environmental, governance and compliance aspects have been undervalued in decision making in the past. It is here that the Commission has developed criteria and guidelines to innovate and improve on the body of knowledge on good practices and add value to guidelines already in common use. Seen in conjunction with existing decision-support instruments, the Commission's criteria and guidelines provide a new direction for appropriate and sustainable development.

Bringing about this change will require:

- planners to identify stakeholders through a process that recognizes rights and assesses risks;
- States to invest more at an earlier stage to screen out inappropriate projects and facilitate integration across sectors within the context of the river basin;
- consultants and agencies to ensure outcomes from feasibility studies are socially and environmentally acceptable;
- the promotion of open and meaningful participation at all stages of planning and implementation, leading to negotiated outcomes;
- developers to accept accountability through contractual commitments for effectively mitigating social and environmental impacts;
- improving compliance through independent review; and
- dam owners to apply lessons learned from past experiences through regular monitoring and adapting to changing needs and contexts.

The Commission offers its criteria and guidelines to help governments, developers and owners meet emerging societal expectations when faced with the complex issues associated with dam projects. Adopting this framework will allow states to take informed and appropriate decisions, thereby raising the level of public acceptance and improving development outcomes.

Beyond the Commission—An Agenda for Change

The Commission's report identifies the key elements of the debate on water and energy resources management and the role of dams in this debate. It summarizes the lessons learned from our Global Review of experience with large dams. It elaborates the development framework within which the controversies and underlying issues can be understood and addressed and proposes a decision-making process anchored in a rights-and-risks approach and based on negotiated outcomes. It offers a set of strategic priorities, principles, criteria and guidelines to address the issues around existing dams and to use in exploring new water and energy development options.

The report is not intended as a blueprint. We recommend that it be used as the starting point for discussions, debates, internal reviews and reassessments of what may be established procedures and for an assessment of how these can evolve to address a changed reality.

E

The Ecological Consequences of Dams

(i) "Ecosystems and Large Dams: Environmental Performance," in World Commission on Dams, *Dams and Development: A New Framework for Decision-Making*, 16 November 2000

Introduction

The nature of the impacts of large dams on ecosystems is generally well known and scientists, NGOs and professional groups such as the International Commission on Large Dams (ICOLD), International Hydopower Association (IHA) and the International Energy Agency (IEA) have written extensively on them. A useful indicator of the scale of human intervention in this regard is a recent estimate that dams, inter-basin transfers, and water withdrawals for irrigation have fragmented 60 percent of the world's rivers.

Ecosystem impacts can be classified according to whether they are:

- first-order impacts that involve the physical, chemical, and geomorphological consequences of blocking a river and altering the natural distribution and timing of streamflow;
- second-order impacts that involve changes in primary biological productivity of ecosystems including effects on riverine and riparian plant-life and on down-stream habitat such as wetlands; or
- third-order impacts that involve alterations to fauna (such as fish) caused by a first-order effect (such as blocking migration) or a second-order effect (such as decrease in the availability of plankton).

In addition, modifying the ecosystem changes the biochemical cycle in the natural riverine system. Reservoirs interrupt the downstream flow of organic carbon, leading to emissions of greenhouse gases such as methane and carbon dioxide that contribute to climate change. The current state of knowledge indicates that large dams have many mostly negative impacts on ecosystems. These impacts are complex, varied and often profound in nature. In many cases dams have led to the irreversible loss of species populations and ecosystems. Because the ecosystem impacts are many and complex it is hard to give a precise and detailed prediction of the changes likely to result from the construction of a dam or series of dams. Based on the geographical location of a dam and the natural river regime it is possible to give a broad indication of the type and direction of impacts with decreasing certainty, from first-to third-order impacts. To date efforts to counter the ecosystem impacts of large dams have had only limited success. This is due to limited efforts to understand the ecosystem and the scope and nature of impacts, the inadequate approach to assessing even anticipated impacts and the only partial success of minimization, mitigation and compensation measures.

This [extract] describes the nature of the impacts in general, supported by the Case Studies, the Cross-Check Survey and the Thematic Reviews on Ecosystems and on Global Change. Given that the WCD Knowledge Base describes a large number of ecosystem impacts, the focus is on summarizing these impacts by grouping them as follows:

- the impacts of reservoirs on terrestrial ecosystems and biodiversity;

- the emission of greenhouse gases associated with large dam projects and their reservoirs;
- the impacts of altered downstream flows on aquatic ecosystems and biodiversity;
- the impacts of altering the natural flood cycle on downstream floodplains;
- the impacts of dams on fisheries in the upstream, reservoir and downstream areas;
- the enhancement of ecosystems through reservoir creation and other means; and
- the cumulative impacts of a series of dams on a river system.

The extent to which efforts to reduce or eliminate these impacts were undertaken in the past is described at the end of each discussion.

The final subsection contains a further assessment of past experience with efforts to avoid, mitigate, minimize or compensate these impacts. Current efforts to restore environmental function through decommissioning are also reviewed.

Terrestrial Ecosystems and Biodiversity

The construction of a storage dam and subsequent inundation of the reservoir area effectively kills terrestrial plants and forests and displaces animals. As many species prefer valley bottoms, large-scale impoundment may eliminate unique wildlife habitats and affect populations of endangered species. Efforts to mitigate the impacts on fauna have met with little success. Construction of irrigation infrastructure may have similar impacts. Flooding a reservoir may lead to the occupation and clearing of upstream catchment areas as replacement for land lost to the reservoir. Land use change provoked in this manner not only has direct effects in terms of habitat loss, elimination of flora and fauna and, in many cases, land degradation, but also feedback effects on the reservoir through alterations in hydrologic function. The resulting loss of vegetative cover leads to increases in sedimentation, stormflow, and annual water yield; decreases in water quality; and variable changes in the seasonal timing of water yield.

Greenhouse Gas Emissions

The emission of greenhouse gases (GHG) from reservoirs due to rotting vegetation and carbon inflows from the catchment is a recently identified ecosystem impact (on climate) of storage dams. A first estimate suggests that the gross emissions from reservoirs may account for between 1percent and 28 percent of the global warming potential of GHG emissions. This challenges the conventional wisdom that hydropower produces only positive atmospheric effects, such as a reduction in emissions of carbon dioxide, nitrous oxides, sulphuric oxides and particulates when compared with power generation sources that burn fossil fuels. It also implies that all reservoirs—not only hydropower reservoirs—emit GHGs. Consequently, reservoir and catchment characteristics must be investigated to find out the likely level of GHG emissions. All large dams and natural lakes in the boreal and tropical regions that have been measured emit greenhouse gases (carbon dioxide, methane, or sometimes both)...

The construction of a storage dam and subsequent inundation of the reservoir area effectively kills terrestrial plants and forests and displaces animals.

Establishing that a reservoir emits GHGs is not enough to assess the impact of a dam on climate change. Natural habitats (undisturbed by dams) may also emit GHGs. Alternatively they may store carbon or act as a net carbon sink. For example, a floodplain tropical forest in Amazonia may emit methane from soils and, at the same time, absorb carbon dioxide in leaves. The balance of all these potentially counteracting effects would determine the profile of GHG emissions from the natural habitat without the dam. A further complication is that the land use change induced by displacement of people, resource extraction and other economic activities may also form part of the net contribution to GHG emissions associated with the construction of the dam. Calculations of the contribution of new reservoirs to climate change must therefore include an assessment of the natural pre-dam emission or sink in order to determine the net impact of the dam.

Even in this case there is no data on emissions without the dam, making a conclusion on the net effect impossible. This applies more generally to other dams that have even less information available. Current understanding of emissions suggests that shallow, warm tropical dams are more likely to be major GHG emitters than deep cold boreal dams. In the case of hydropower dams, tropical dams that have low installed capacity and large shallow reservoirs are more likely to have gross emissions that approach those of comparable thermal alternatives than those with small, deep reservoirs and high in-stalled capacity.

To date, no experience exists with minimizing, mitigating, or compensating these impacts. Pre-inundation removal of vegetation is one alternative, but the net effects of such an activity are not well understood. The outcome of global negotiations on climate change may bear on future penalties and incentives for net GHG emissions from dams.

Downstream Aquatic Ecosystems and Biodiversity

Storage dams are intended to alter the natural distribution and timing of stream-flow. They compromise the dynamic aspects of rivers that are fundamental to maintaining the character of aquatic ecosystems. Natural rivers and their habitats and species are a function of the flow, the quantity and character of the sediment in motion through the channel, and the character or composition of the materials that make up the bed and banks of the channel. The defining river discharge includes both high- and low-flow elements. These dynamics, not the average conditions of controlled dam operations, determine a stream's physical foundation, which in turn ensures ecosystem integrity.

The extent of impacts will also depend on whether water is extracted or diverted for consumption, or left instream. Introduction of non-native species, modified water quality (temperature, oxygen, nutrients), loss of system dynamics, and loss of the ability to maintain continuity of an ecosystem result in ecologically modified river systems. The establishment of a new dynamic has positive effects on some species and negative effects on others.

Impacts of changes in flow regimes

Flow regimes are the key driving variable for downstream aquatic ecosystems. Flood timing, duration and frequency are all critical for the survival of communities of plants and animals living downstream. Small flood events may act as biological triggers for fish and invertebrate migration: major events create and maintain habitats by scouring or transporting sediments. The natural variability of most river systems sustains complex biological communities that may be very different from those adapted to the stable flows and conditions of a regulated river. Finally, water temperature and chemistry are altered as a consequence of water storage and the altered timing of downstream flows. Algal growth may occur in the reservoir and in the channel immediately downstream from dams because of the nutrient loading of the reservoir releases. Self-purification processes diminish this effect downstream. Storage dams, particularly hydropower peaking plants, can significantly disrupt the whole flow regime, resulting in both high seasonal and day-to-day fluctuations that differ greatly from natural flow levels. [T]he construction of Glen Canyon dam on the Colorado River in the United States reduced daily average flows during the annual September peak from about 2,000 m^3/sec to about 700 m^3 /sec. In addition, streamflow can fluctuate daily more than 425 m^3/sec due to dam releases for electricity generation during the peak daytime demand periods. These changes in flow have dramatically altered the riverine environment, creating consistently colder temperatures due to release of water from the bottom of the reservoir. A general decline in native fish abundance in the Colorado River is attributed specifically to the cold-water release from large dams there. The population of the fish *Tandanus tandanus* in Australia's Murray River disappeared due to short-tern fluctuations in water level caused by reservoir releases in response to downstream water user requirements.

Particularly high hydropower dams cause gas to become supersaturated when water flows over the spillway. This causes fish deaths due to a condition similar to the bends that can affect divers who dive too deep for too long. The Grand Coulee Case Study reports that this is a particular problem on the Columbia River in the United States, where regulators have fixed a maximum total dissolved gas concentration to reduce impacts on migratory fish. The modified habitats resulting from large dams often create environments that are more conducive to non-native and exotic plant, fish, snail, insect, and animal species.

These resulting non-native species often out-compete the natives and end up modifying ecosystems that may become unstable, nurture disease vectors, or are no longer able to support the historical environmental and social components. Compared with a natural river, the root systems of plants in rivers below dams experience reduced effects of scour, the plants themselves suffer less stress from high discharges and the rate of channel migration is reduced, so that an area of the channel-bed available for the development of aquatic plants can be stabilized. In both Africa and Australia, the elimination of high discharges to flush systems has allowed the extensive development of the aquatic weeds Water Hyacinth *(Eichhornia crassipes*) and Water Fern *(Salvinia molest*a). The Orange River Pilot Study documents the colonisation by reeds *(Phragmites australis)* of 41,000 ha of riverbed has occurred as a result of stabilized flows on the Orange River.

Biological linkages also extend laterally away from and parallel to the river, pushing the effect of river changes onto a band of varying width. As long as the river flow is sufficient, other wildlife such as deer, antelope, and elephants will come to the water, especially in the dry/hot season, to drink. Hippos in Africa will use water of sufficient depth as a daytime refuge, emerging to forage at night. Many species of birds and bats fly in to drink. These lateral movements can extend to several kilometers from the river. Thus any wildlife species in a fairly wide strip of land on either side of the river depend upon it, and they may all be affected when the flow of the river is disrupted by the construction of a large dam. Equally, long reservoirs that extend many kilometers up river valleys present a barrier for terrestrial species inhabiting each riverbank that were previously able to cross the river.

When waters of one basin are diverted into another one, changes in volume and seasonality of flow result. New biota from the source basin may invade the recipient basin and compete with the native species. If all the water is diverted from the source basin, this will clearly have serious impacts on any unique species or genetically different stocks. In South Africa, for example, the diversion of the Orange River into the Great Fish River resulted in a six-fold increase in flow, making the Great Fish River permanent rather than intermittent. The Orange River Case Study reports that one beneficiary is the larvae of the blackfly *Simulium chutteri*, which does not tolerate desiccation. In the absence of control measures, this biting fly causes livestock losses, reduces recreational use, and irritates local farmers.

Efforts to minimize the impacts of changes in flow regime have relied on measures to restore the streamflow regime through the setting of environmental flow releases (EFR).

Impacts of trapping sediments and nutrients behind a dam

The reduction in sediment and nutrient transport in rivers downstream of dams has impacts on channel, floodplain and coastal delta morphology and causes the loss of aquatic habitat for fish and other species. Changes in river water turbidity may affect biota directly. For example, plankton production is influenced by many variables, including turbidity. If this is reduced due to impoundment, plankton development may be enhanced and may occur in new sections of a river. Reduction in sediment moving downstream from the dam leads to degradation of the river channel below the facility. This can lead to the elimination of beaches and backwaters that provided native fish habitat, and the reduction or elimination of riparian vegetation that provides nutrients and habitat for aquatic and waterfowl species, among others. Impounding rivers invariably results in increased degradation of coastal deltas due to reduction in sediment input. For example, the slow accretion of the Nile Delta was reversed with the construction of the Delta barrage in 1868. Today, other dams on the Nile, including the Aswan High Dam, have further reduced the amount of sediment reaching the delta. As a result, much of the delta coastline is eroding by up to 5–8 meters per year, but in places this exceeds 240 meters per year. The consequence of reduced sediment also extends to long stretches of coastline where the erosive effect of waves is no longer sustained by sediment inputs from rivers. It is estimated that the coastlines of Togo and Benin are being eroded at a rate of 10–15 meters a year because the Akosombo dam on the Volta River in Ghana has halted the sediment supply to the sea. Another example is the Rhone River in France, where a series of dams has reduced the quantity of sediment transported by the river to the Mediterranean from 12 million tons in the 19th century to only 4 to 5 million tons today. This has led to erosion rates of up to 5 meters per year for the beaches in the regions of the Camargue and the Languedoc, requiring a coastal defense budget running into millions of dollars. Measures for mitigating the impacts of trap-ping sediments and nutrients are limited. Where feasible, flushing sediments can be part of a program of managed flood releases.

Blocking migration of aquatic organisms

As a physical barrier the dam disrupts the movement of species leading to changes in upstream and downstream species composition and even species loss. River-dwelling species have several migratory patterns. These include anadromous fish such as salmon and catadromous fish such as eels. Adults of the former migrate up rivers to spawn and the young descend, while the reverse occurs with the latter. But many other freshwater fish move up rivers or their tributaries to spawn, while the glochidia larvae of freshwater mussels are carried by host fish. To help counteract the drift downstream of their larvae, aquatic insect adults such as mayflies and stoneflies move upstream to lay their eggs. Dams block these migrations to varying degrees. The WCD Cross-Check Survey found that impeding the passage of migratory fish species was the most significant ecosystem impact, recorded at over 60 percent of the projects for which responses on environmental issues were given. In 36 percent of these cases, the impact of the large dam on migratory fish was not anticipated during project planning. Migratory fish require different environments for the main phases of their life cycle: reproduction, production of juveniles, growth, and sexual maturation. Many anadromous fish populations such as salmon and shad have died out as a result of dams blocking their migratory routes. The sturgeon populations in the Caspian Sea now rely on stocking from hatcheries (mainly in Iran), as dams built by the former Soviet Union on rivers entering the sea halted natural spawning migrations.

Detailed studies in North America indicate that dam construction is one of the major causes for freshwater species extinction.

Detailed studies in North America indicate that dam construction is one of the major causes for freshwater species extinction. For example, a study of the threatened fish of Oklahoma suggested that the loss of free-flowing river habitat due to reservoirs had led to 55 percent of the human-induced species loss, while a further 19 percent was caused by dams acting as barriers to fish migration.

The best-documented examples of disrupted fish migrations are from the Columbia River in the United States, where many stocks of salmon have been lost. The impact of these disruptions on the productivity of the fishery are described below.

Floodplain Ecosystems

Reduction in downstream annual flooding affects the natural productivity of riparian areas, floodplains and deltas. The characteristics of riparian plant communities are controlled by the dynamic interaction of flooding and sedimentation. Many riparian species depend on shallow floodplain aquifers that are recharged during regular flood events. Dams can have significant and complex impacts on downstream riparian plant communities. High discharges can retard the encroachment of true terrestrial species, but many riparian plants have evolved with and become adapted to the natural flood regime. Typically, riparian forest tree species are dependent on river flows and a shallow aquifer, and the community and population structure of riparian forests is related to the spatial and temporal patterns of flooding at a site. For example, the eucalyptus forests of the Murray floodplain, Australia, depend on periodic flooding for seed germination, and headwater impoundment has curtailed regeneration. Conversely, artificial pulses generated by dam releases at the wrong time—in ecological terms—are recognized as a cause of forest destruction. For example, *Acacia xanthophloea* is disappearing from the Pongolo system below Pongolapoort dam, South Africa, as a result of the modified flood regime.

The control of floodwaters by large dams, which usually reduces flow during natural flood periods and increases flow during dry periods, leads to a discontinuity in the river system. This, together with the associated loss of floodplain habitats, normally has a marked negative impact on fish diversity and productivity. The connection between the river and floodplain or backwater habitats is essential in the life history of many riverine fish that have evolved to take advantage of the seasonal floods and use the inundated areas for spawning and feeding. Loss of this connection can lead to a rapid decline in productivity of the local fishery and to extinction of some species. Additionally, dewatering of stream channels immediately downstream from dams can be a serious problem.

The direct loss of annual silt and nutrient replenishment as a consequence of upstream impoundment is thought to have contributed to the gradual loss of fertility of formerly productive floodplain soils as used in agriculture and flood-recession agriculture. Dramatic reductions in bird species are also known, especially in down-stream floodplain and delta areas, where wetlands may not be replenished with water and nutrients once a dam is installed. Finally, recharge of groundwater in flood-plain areas is severely diminished once floods are eliminated.

In Africa, the changed hydrological regime of rivers has adversely affected floodplain agriculture, fisheries, pasture and forests that constituted the organizing element of community livelihood and culture. Economically important wetlands in Africa include river floodplains, freshwater lakes and coastal and estuarine environments. In the Sahel, there are major wetlands in the Delta Intérieur of the River Niger in Mali and Lake Chad (on the border between Niger, Chad, Cameroon and Nigeria). These have counterparts elsewhere in semi-arid Africa, notably the Sudd in Sudan and the

Okavan-go Delta in Botswana, and in humid areas, such as the swamps of eastern Zaire. Some of these wetlands cover extensive tracts of land. The fringing floodplain of the Senegal River covers some 5,000 km^2 in flood, and shrinks to 500 km^2 in the dry season. The fringing floodplain of the Niger covers about 6,000 km^2 in the flood season, shrinking to about half that at low water, while the Niger Inland Delta extends to 20,000 to 30,000 km^2 in the flood season, shrinking to 4,000 km^2 at low water. In the Logone-Chari system, flooding covers some 90,000 km.

Efforts to restore floodplain ecosystem functions rely on reversing the effects of the dam through a program of managed floods designed to simulate the floods that occurred prior to the dam.

Fisheries

As indicated earlier, the blockage of sediment and nutrients, the re-regulation of streamflow, and elimination of the natural flood regime can all have significant, negative effects on downstream fisheries.

Marine or estuarine fisheries are also negatively affected when dams alter or divert freshwater flows. Still, productive reservoir fisheries can follow from dam construction, although they are not always anticipated or part of project design proposals. Substantial losses in downstream fishery production as a result of dam construction are reported from around the world. Along with subsistence agriculture, fisheries constitute an important livelihood activity among large rural populations in the developing world. Many of these households depend on fisheries either as a primary or supplementary source of livelihood. For example, the partial closing of the river channel by Porto Primavera dam in Brazil blocked fish migration and diminished upstream fish catch by 80percent, affecting livelihoods. In areas of rich fish species diversity, such as the lower Mekong region in East Asia, community livelihoods and culture are woven around fisheries. The Pak Mun Case Study reports a drastic decline in upstream fish catch once the dam had effectively blocked fish migration from the Mekong River upstream into tributaries of the large Mun River watershed.

Data on the losses to downstream fishery production as a result of dam construction are reported from river basins in Africa as well. For example, 11,250 tons of fish per year from the Senegal River system were lost following dam construction. Studies on the Niger have shown that fish productivity increases linearly with the volume of river flow. Other basins in the WCD Knowledge Base reporting loss in fish production include the *yaeres* in Cameroon, the Pongo-lo flood plain in South Africa, and the Niger in West Africa below Kainji dam. Adverse impacts have been felt in the delta and estuary areas in the lower Volta region, in the Nile delta, and on the Zambezi in Mozambique.

Freshwater flows also help support marine fish production as many marine fish spawn in estuaries or deltas. A decrease in freshwater flow and in nutrients due to dam construction affects the nursery areas in a number of ways, including increasing salinity, allowing predatory marine fish to invade, and reducing the available food supply. These impacts are well illustrated by the effect of the Aswan High Dam on the coastal waters of the Mediterranean, where reduction in nutrients transported to the sea has lowered production at all trophic levels, resulting in a decline in catches of sardines and other fish. In the Zambezi delta, the impact of modified seasonal flows on local shrimp fisheries has been estimated at $10 million per year.

Dams can enhance some riverine fisheries, particularly tailwater fisheries immediately below dams that benefit from discharge of nutrients from the upstream reservoir. If discharge is from the lower layer of water in the reservoir, lowered temperatures in the receiving tailwater can curtail or eliminate warmwater river fisheries and require stocking with exotic coldwater species such as salmonids (assuming that the water is sufficiently oxygenated). Productive tailwater fisheries targeting these coldwater fish can result but generally require supplemental hatchery programs and the introduction of coldwater invertebrates to serve as food for these fish.

Productive reservoir fisheries often follow from dam construction, although they are not always anticipated or part of project design proposals. While practically all the WCD Case Study dams have reservoir fisheries, predictions of fish production were made in only three cases. In the case of Aslantas, consultants estimated a production of 580 tons, and actual figures are 86–125 tons (for 1987–1995). At Pak Mun, actual production came to only one-tenth of prediction. In both cases targets were not met as the predictions depended partly on a functional stocking program that was not fully implemented. At Kariba estimates were made for the artisanal fishery but not for the more productive open-water commercial fishery. On the other hand, an unanticipated but productive fishery has developed in Tucurui. In addition to commercial production at Tucurui, a local sport-fishing industry has developed around the sought-after Peacock Bass, *Cichla ocellaris* (known in Tucurui as *tucunaré*), Kariba has seen a similar development of a vibrant sport fishery. At Grand Coulee, the lack of a fish pass deprived salmon of over 1,000 kilometers of upstream spawning grounds, and affected First Nations tribes in the United States and Canada, while a fish hatchery largely maintained salmon numbers (but not genetic diversity) in downstream runs in the United States.

Data from before and after the construction of Tucurui illustrate the changing nature of species composition and fish production in the downstream, reservoir and upstream areas. The experimental catch data document that the number of species found in each of the three areas has declined significantly (by 30–50 species) following impoundment. The data suggest that in total 11 species are no longer found in these areas. Within the reservoir and to a lesser degree upstream, species now include more piscivorous species at the expense of the detritivores that were more common prior to construction. In production terms, the harvest upstream of the reservoir remained stable for the first 10 years or more, but now appears to be increasing. Meanwhile, the downstream fishery has shown a continued downward trend. However, the reservoir fishery has expanded tenfold in the last 20 years, with the result that the total fishery (upstream, downstream and in the reservoir) has tripled in size to 4,700 tons per year since the dam was created.

Mitigation or compensation measures have been used to reduce the impacts of changes in fisheries. Fish passages are the most prevalent measure and have been of limited applicability and usefulness. Compensation measures consist of fish hatcheries and stocking programs designed to reproduce the productivity of the fishery.

Ecosystem Enhancement

The WCD Knowledge Base provides a number of examples of the ecosystem enhancement effects of large dams. The Case Studies show, for example, that productive wetlands have been created by pumping Grand Coulee water through a previously dry area in the Columbia River Basin, and along the shores of Lake Kariba, with considerable wildlife and tourism values resulting. Some reservoirs support globally threatened reptiles (for example Hillsborough dam, Trinidad), and others have been declared Ramsar sites of international importance for birds. Indeed, one measure of the environmental value of water bodies is to consider the list of sites designated as internationally important for waterfowl under the *Ramsar Convention on Wetlands*. Of 957 sites designated by December 1998, only 10 percent included artificial wetland types, while 25 percent included natural lake types. Many of the designated artificial wetlands are dammed sites: of the almost 100 artificial wetlands designated as internationally important, 78 include water storage areas.

A study by Wetlands International for WCD showed that the wintering waterfowl assembled on natural and dammed lakes in Switzerland are broadly similar, and the same species occur most abundantly on both types of lake. The study also showed that the situation in South Africa is very different, as it lacks natural permanent water bodies and almost all permanent water bodies are reservoirs. At least 12 reservoirs support major and important concentrations of waterbirds. Large dams in South Africa have provided generally beneficial conditions for pelicans, darters and cormorants. They provide suitable moulting sites for waterfowl: for example, at least 70 percent of the global population of the South African Shelduck, *Tadorna cana*, moults at only 23 localities in South Africa, 21 of which are large reservoirs. Dam reservoirs provide dry-season or drought refuges for many water-fowl species in the semi-arid parts of the country.

But productive wetlands are most likely to be created around reservoirs where these are shallow or have shallow margins and limited reservoir drawdowns. Where sediment inflows from the catchment are heavy, small deltaic wetlands may evolve at the inflow. In general, deeper reservoirs that have steep sides or high seasonal water-level fluctuations are unlikely to support major wetland habitats. Dammed lakes support a more restricted range of species, and several common and uncommon species from natural lakes were not recorded on dammed lakes by Wetlands International.

The damming of rivers has increased the number of open water sites available to wintering waterfowl in Switzerland and provided a more suitable habitat for these birds than the generally fast-flowing stretches of river in-between. However, these sites support only relatively small numbers of birds, of mostly common and widespread species and do not appear to provide as diverse a waterfowl habitat as the natural lakes in the area. Eleven of the

2,596 British reservoirs support substantial and important wintering waterfowl populations, while 60 natural inland waters and 52 estuaries support populations of international importance.

Cumulative Impacts

Many of the major catchments in the world now contain multiple dams. Within a basin, the greater the number of dams, the greater the fragmentation of river ecosystems. An estimated 60 percent of the world's large river basins are highly or moderately fragmented by dams. The magnitude of river fragmentation can be very high. In Sweden, for example, only three major rivers longer than 150 km and six minor rivers have not been affected by dams.

Although seldom analyzed, cumulative impacts occur when several dams are built on a single river. They affect both the physical (first-order) variables, such as flow regime and water quality, and the productivity and species composition of different rivers. The problems may be magnified as more large dams are added to a river system, resulting in an increased and cumulative loss of natural resources, habitat quality, environmental sustainability and ecosystem integrity. The cumulative impacts of inter-basin water transfers can be of special concern, as this often involves the transfer of species into new watersheds. The WCD Knowledge Base documents a number of cumulative impacts that include water quantity, water quality and species impacts. Flood regimes are clearly affected as increasing the total storage volume by adding additional dams reduces the flood flows downstream. In Pakistan, the Tarbela Case Study reveals that only 1 percent of the historical dry season flow of the Indus reaches the delta; the rest is diverted for irrigation and water supply by 22 dams and barrages. Since the Kotri barrage was commissioned in the early 1960s, the average number of days with no river flow downstream in the dry season increased from zero to 85 (the average from 1962 to 1997). Similar impacts have occurred around the Aral Sea and in Australia where 80 years of river regulation, construction of additional storages, and diversion of water from the Murray Darling River have reduced the median flow reaching the sea to 21 percent of the pre-regulated flow.

Water quality parameters recover only slowly when water is released from a dam. Oxygen levels may recover within a kilometer or two, while temperature changes may still exist 100 km downstream. Where the distance between dams does not allow recovery to natural levels, the biology of many hundreds of kilometers of river may be affected by a handful of dams. Examples from the WCD Case Studies include the Orange-Vaal river in South Africa, where the impacts of 24 dams may have led to 2,300 km (63 percent) of the river having a modified temperature regime. On the Columbia River, Grand Coulee dam receives water that is already high in total dissolved gasses as a result of upstream Canadian dams. Before the levels can recover to natural values, spill at Grand Coulee increases them again, passing the problem further downstream.

Construction of a series of dams may therefore have increasing impacts on downstream ecosystems and biodiversity. Also on the Columbia River, the cumulative impact of an additional dam on salmon migrations is significant. It is estimated that 5–14 percent of the adult salmon are killed at each of the eight large dams they pass while swimming up the river.

What is not well researched is the change in the magnitude of the incremental response of ecosystem function and biodiversity as a river is increasingly fragmented. Thus it is not known if there is some threshold level at which the marginal impacts of the addition of one or more dams to a particular cascade of dams will begin to decline. It is therefore a case by case call whether the ecosystem impacts of further modifying a particular river may at some point be of less consequence than, for example, putting the first dam on a free-flowing river.

Anticipating and Responding to Ecosystem Impacts

Examination of efforts to counter the ecosystem impacts of large dams in the WCD Knowledge Base indicates that they have met with limited success owing to:

- the lack of attention paid to anticipating and avoiding impacts,
- the poor quality and uncertainty of predictions,
- the difficulty of coping with all impacts, and
- partial implementation and success of mitigation measures.

Anticipating and Predicting Ecosystem Impacts

In order for ecosystem impacts to be addressed properly, they have to be understood and predicted. The Cross-

Check Survey found that for the 87 projects that provided data on ecosystem impacts, almost 60 percent of the impacts identified were unanticipated prior to project construction, largely due to inadequate studies. While the sample size is small for some time periods, the Cross-Check also suggests that over time the trend is increasingly to anticipate impacts. This confirms the expectation that the trend towards the use of environmental impact assessments (EIA) would result in improved identification of potential impacts. Anticipating an impact is, however, not synonymous with accurately predicting the direction and magnitude of its effect on ecosystems and biodiversity. Nor does it guarantee understanding of the further impact of such changes on the livelihoods and economic welfare of affected people. While the generalized impacts of reservoir creation on terrestrial ecosystems and biodiversity are well-known, specifics, such as the net emissions of greenhouse gases from a particular dam site, cannot be predicted with any certainty at present. Further research into the factors determining net emissions may reduce this uncertainty over time.

Downstream impacts on aquatic ecosystems and biodiversity and on floodplain ecosystems represent the sum of many complex interactions and thus are inherently difficult to predict where baseline data are absent or unreliable. However, the overall direction of the impacts is generally negative. As shown for the case of floodplain effects, the impact of large dams on these ecosystems will vary. With regard to fisheries, while it appears that the effect on species composition is generally negative at all levels (upstream, reservoir and downstream), downstream losses in productivity may be accompanied by increases in reservoir fishery production. Finally, the nature of cumulative impacts as additional dams are added to a river system may be significant, but a lack of research on the topic makes predictive assessment difficult.

In sum, past anticipation and prediction of ecosystem impacts was limited, in part due to a lack of reliable baseline data, scientific uncertainty regarding the nature of the interactions, inadequate attention paid to these issues and a correspondingly limited ability to model these complex systems. While improvements in measurement, scientific understanding and modelling capability have occurred over time, most ecosystem impacts remain site-specific. Their exact nature cannot be predicted in the absence of appropriate field studies of individual river systems.

Avoidance, Minimization, Mitigation, Compensation and Ecosystem Restoration

The WCD Knowledge Base reveals that efforts to avoid or minimize impacts through choice of alternative projects or alternative designs were more successful than efforts to manage the impacts once they were built into the design of the dam. Avoidance and minimization of impacts, by their very nature, reduce ecosystem impacts on the site concerned. But where alternative sites or designs have been chosen, the net consequences for ecosystems have rarely been recorded.

Project planners and proponents have employed five principal measures to respond to ecosystem impacts:

- measures that avoid the anticipated adverse effects of a large dam through the selection of alternative projects;
- measures to minimize impacts by altering project design features once a dam is decided upon;
- mitigation measures that are incorporated into a new or existing dam design or operating regime in order to reduce ecosystem impacts to acceptable levels;
- measures that compensate for unavoidable residual effects by enhancing ecosystem attributes in watersheds above dams or at other sites; and
- measures to restore aspects of riverine ecosystems.

The primary option for avoiding ecosystem impacts from large dams has been not to build the dams in the first place. This is given a legal basis in Austria, Finland, France, Norway, Sweden, Switzerland, the United States and Zimbabwe, where legal 'set-aside' provisions to protect particular river segments or basins from regulation or development have been established.

Good site selection, such as not building large dams on the main-stem of a river system, and better dam design also played significant roles in avoiding or minimizing impacts in a number of cases in the WCD Knowledge Base. The International Energy Agency also supported such policies in its recent policy paper *Hydropower and Environment*. As reported earlier, an increasing number of countries are using environmental flow requirements to minimize downstream impacts sometimes in the form of managed floods.

Mitigation was the most widely practiced response to ecosystem impacts for the large dams in the WCD Knowledge Base. As noted earlier, mitigation has failed or worked only sporadically in the case of wildlife rescue operations and fish passes. In the Cross-Check sub-sample of 87 projects for which ecosystem impacts were recorded, mitigation was undertaken for less than one-quarter of the anticipated ecosystem impacts (10 percent of all ecosystem impacts that occurred). Of these projects, 47 also recorded the effectiveness of mitigation measures implemented. Respondents stated that about 20 percent worked effectively, 40 percent did not mitigate the impact, and 40 percent were moderately effective. The conclusion can be drawn that only a small percentage of ecosystem impacts that occurred were actually mitigated effectively, while the relative significance of these impacts remains unknown. While there are cases of good mitigation, the success is nevertheless contingent upon stringent conditions including:

- a good information base and competent professional staff available to formulate complex choices for decision-makers;
- an adequate legal framework and compliance mechanisms;
- a co-operative process with the design team and stakeholders;
- monitoring of feedback and evaluation of mitigation effectiveness; and
- adequate financial and institutional resources.

If any one of these conditions is absent, mitigation is unlikely to succeed. Mitigation, though often possible in principle, presents many uncertainties in field situations and is therefore at present not a credible option in all cases and all circumstances. In addition, the weaknesses of the EIA process for many projects reduces the possibility of positive outcomes. This supports the use of alternative strategies rather than simply one of mitigation. Compensation for lost resources may be 'in-kind' (for example construction of a fish hatchery for lost fish spawning areas) or 'out-of kind' (for example watershed protection in the upper catchment for loss of riverine or wetland habitat). Compensation may also be paid 'in-basin' (for example restoration of forest area within the river basin for forest lost to inundation) or 'out-of- basin' (for example assistance in expanding management capability at similar locations in another river basin). These are applied to offset ecosystem and biodiversity loss, as well as to replace lost productive use of natural resources (as with fish hatcheries). Concerns with the effectiveness of compensation include questions about the possibility of 'replacing' ecosystem functions and species (for example, are fish raised in a hatchery equivalent to native fish stocks?) and the consequences of such efforts, for example whether fish hatcheries actually damage native fish stocks through disease and competition.

Restoring ecosystem through decommissioning

Ecosystem restoration has been undertaken in a range of countries where evolving national legislation has required higher standards of environmental performance. In the United States and France, dams have been decommissioned to restore key environmental values, often related to migratory fish (salmon), and often as a condition of project relicensing. Ecosystem impacts of decommissioning are also complex and site-specific. One major issue in dam decommissioning is what to do with possibly polluted sediment accumulated behind the dam. The fate of this sediment when the dam is removed is frequently a major obstacle to restoration. Current large dam designs are often not sufficiently flexible to allow for changed operating regimes to meet environmental (or other) goals. Global experience shows that these long-lived structures may be called on to operate differently in the future than in the past as society's needs and values evolve and as other dams are added in the catchment area. In some cases, the dam design is completed before the environmental flow needs are determined, and cannot accommodate water releases of the required quantity and quality.

Current large dam designs are often not sufficiently flexible to allow for changed operating regimes to meet environmental (or other) goals.

Five dams on the Colorado River have now been retroactively fitted with variable level offtakes to draw off surface water, increase the temperature of the downstream river, and satisfy the needs of native fish.

Findings and Lessons

Large dams generally have extensive impacts on rivers, watersheds and aquatic ecosystems. From the WCD Knowledge Base it is clear that large dams have led to:

- the loss of forests and wildlife habitat, the loss of species populations and the degradation of upstream catchment areas due to inundation of the reservoir area;

- emissions of greenhouse gases from reservoirs due to the rotting of vegetation and carbon inflows from the basin;
- the loss of aquatic biodiversity, upstream and downstream fisheries and the services of downstream floodplains, wetlands and riverine estuarine and adjacent marine ecosystems;
- the creation of productive fringing wetland ecosystems with fish and water-fowl habitat opportunities in some reservoirs; and cumulative impacts on water quality, natural flooding, and species composition where a number of dams are sited on the same river.

The ecosystem impacts are more negative than positive and they have led, in many cases, to irreversible loss of species and ecosystems. In the Cross-Check Survey 67 percent of the ecosystem impacts recorded were negative. The social consequences of environmental impacts are examined in Chapter 4. Efforts to date to mitigate the ecosystem impacts of large dams in the WCD Knowledge base have met with limited success owing to the lack of attention given to anticipating and avoiding impacts, the poor quality and uncertainty of predictions, the difficulty of coping with all impacts and the only partial implementation and success of mitigation measures. More specifically: it is not possible to mitigate many of the impacts of reservoir creation on terrestrial ecosystems and biodiversity, and efforts to 'rescue' wildlife have met with little sustainable success; the use of fish passes to mitigate the blockage of migratory fish has had little success, as the technology has often not been tailored to specific sites and species; good mitigation results from a good information base, early co-operation between ecologists, the dam design team and affected people, and regular monitoring and feedback on the effectiveness of mitigation measures; environmental flow requirements (which include managed flood releases) are increasingly used to reduce the impacts of changed streamflow regimes on aquatic, floodplain and coastal ecosystems downstream; and avoidance or minimization of ecosystem impacts can be achieved through legislative or policy measures that set-aside particular river segments or basins, or through good site selection (such as avoiding main stem dams).

Finally, a number of countries, particularly the United States, are making efforts to restore ecosystem function and native fish populations by decommissioning large and small dams.

F

Case Study—India

(i) Sardar Sarovar Dam

The settlement of inter-state river disputes in the Indian legal system depends on the Constitution of India, Article 262, the River Boards Act of 1956, and the Inter-State Water Disputes Act of 1956. The institutions involved in the Narmada project included: the Narmada Control Authority, Environment and Rehabilitation Subgroups; Sardar Sarovar Narmada Nigam Limited (State of Gujarat); the Narmada Valley Development Authority (State of Madhya Pradesh); and instrumentalities of the State of Maharashtra. The initial resistance to the project grew and the campaign was internationalized. The World Bank played a role in the project through financing and through the commissioning of an independent review of the dam. This review was undertaken by an Independent Review Committee, which issued a report highly critical of the project. Environmental issues included the catchment area, the downstream area, the canal's command and water service area, and The National Committee on Environmental Planning and Coordination. There were also human rights issues.

(a) Fisher W.F., "Development and Resistance in the Narmada Valley," in Fisher W.F. (ed), *Toward Sustainable Development: Struggling Over India's Narmada River*, M.E. Sharpe, London, 1995, pp 1–46

Of Blood and Water

With their hands tied, symbolizing their non-violent intent, twenty-five volunteers stepped forward as their names were called and, to the beating of tribal drums, crossed the border from the Indian state of Madhya Pradesh to the state of Gujarat on January 2, 1991. Behind them stood tens of thousands of participants in the Jan Vikas Sangharsh Yatra (the People's Struggle for Development Procession), a march organized by opponents to the construction of the Sardar Sarovar Dam along the Narmada River in western

India. The Yatra, the result of months of planning, had begun in the town of Rajghat on December 25, 1990, when villagers from the submergence area of the Sardar Sarovar Dam and activists from all over India crossed under a 100–foot-long sign reading *Koi Nahin Hatega, Bandh Nahin Banega* (No one will move, the dam will not be built). The stated objective of the Yatra was to compel a comprehensive review of the Sardar Sarovar Project (SSP), an objective the organizers hoped to achieve by physically stopping work on the dam through a Gandhian-style, non-violent *satyagraha* at the dam site. But the marchers would never reach the dam site; they would never get beyond the village of Ferkuwa on the Gujar at Madhya Pradesh border.

On the other side of the border, the road was blocked by tens of thousands of Gujaratis participating in a government supported, pro-dam counterally (or Shanti Yatra) that welcomed the Sardar Sarovar Project's promise of water for drought-stricken areas, and hailed the dam and its 250–mile-long canal as "the lifeline of Gujarat." The 25 anti-dam volunteers, their hands bound with ribbon, slowly made their way toward this crowd. Inside the Gujarat border, halfway between the pro- and anti-dam groups, they were stopped by the police. They settled down on the ground, surrounded by police, where their supporters brought them food, water, and tea. The prodam rally broadcast opinions and slogans over loudspeakers while the anti-dam protesters responded with songs about their homes along the Narmada River, the sanctity of the river, and their struggle.

The ensuing standoff at Ferkuwa between the pro- and anti-dam rallies continued for a month. During the two days following the initial confrontation, additional groups of anti-dam volunteers with their hands tied crossed the border into Gujarat to join the first group. On the third day, the police rounded them up, loaded them into buses, carted them away, and released them miles from the confrontation. Undeterred, yet another group of nonviolent, anti–dam marchers entered Gujarat, this time led by Baba Amte, a renowned Gandhian social worker and activist. This group proceeded no further than the first sets of protesters had, but they were allowed to remain halfway between the pro- and anti–dam rallies. Convinced that they needed a new strategy to break the impasse, the anti–dam marchers selected seven individuals—Shatiben, Laxmiben, Khaja Bhai, Mathur Bhai, Medha Patkar, Devram Bhai, and Meghnath—who began a hunger strike in an effort to force the government's hand. The hunger strikers lay on mattresses by the side of the road, determined to fast until the government agreed to talks that would lead to a review of the Sardar Sarovar Project. For three weeks, the government remained unresponsive, the hunger strikers grew weaker, and their supporters grew angrier, until the anti-dam marchers decided to withdraw, unwilling to further endanger the lives of the fasters.

Although the Jan Vikas Sangharsh Yatra, or the "long march," as it came to be known, failed to achieve its immediate objective, it further galvanized opposition to the dam within the Narmada valley. As the Yatra withdrew from the border at the end of January 1991, the marchers, feeling that the government had been callously unresponsive to the three-week fast, declared their determination to cease attempts at dialogue with the government and to actively pursue alternative strategies. The slogan "*Hamare gaon mein hamara raj*" (Our villages, our rule) expressed their new commitment to ban government officials, especially those conducting surveys or other work related to the Sardar Sarovar Project, from the villages that would be submerged by the reservoir if the Sardar Sarovar Dam were completed. Manibeli, the first village in the state of Maharashtra that would be submerged by the rising waters of the Sardar Sarovar reservoir, became a focus of the resistance to the dam, and it remains a powerful symbol to both pro- and anti-dam forces. It was in Manibeli that many residents of the valley first swore public oaths, declaring, "we will drown, but we will not move," and symbolically sealed these vows with their own blood.

These actions—marches, rallies, counter rallies, hunger strikes, and determined oaths— typify the high drama and emotional intensity of the confrontations over the construction of the Sardar Sarovar Dam. Within India, opposition to the dam has been marked by a series of events, such Harsud rally in 1989, the Jan Vikas Sangarsh Yatra in 1990–1991, of the Manibeli *satyagraha* of 1991, the "invasion" of Manibeli in 1992, and the Narmada *satyagraha* of 1994, which have become powerful symbols of the struggle of local peoples against the imposition of centrally design managed development initiatives. These events are the most visible component of a widespread and ongoing resistance movement. These relatively local events have become national symbols with international ramifications.

Opposition to the dam has been growing since 1988 when numerous social action groups shifted from their earlier stand of seeking comprehensive resettlement package. Since then, representatives of rural communities along the Narmada and independent non-government organizations or social action groups have lobbied prime ministers of India, chief ministers of the states of Gujarat, Maharashtra, and Madhya Pradesh state and national bureaucrats, the Japanese government, the World Bank and other governments funding the Bank. These actions have relied on the formation of national alliances among organizations and movements from across India and on international linkages with non-governmental organizations and individuals in more than twenty countries. Loosely linked together as the Narmada Action Committee...these organizations and individuals ensured that news of events in India spread around the world with remarkable speed in the press, by facsimile, and through small informational meetings.

In December 1994, "Narmada" remained an open story, its outcome not yet resolved.

This innovative activity is reshaping the arena of political action both within India and internationally. In the face of public pressure the Japanese OECF withdrew its commitment to provide a loan for the project. On March 14, 1991, in response to growing criticism of the project and under pressure from the global campaign of international nongovernmental organizations against the project, the president of the World Bank commissioned an unprecedented independent review of the Sardar Sarovar Project. Charged with assessing the environmental impacts and the resettlement and rehabilitation of the population to be displaced or otherwise affected by the Sardar Sarovar Project, the review began its work in September 1991. Its final report, submitted in June 1992; was very critical of the World Bank's involvement in the project and stated:

> "[w]e think the Sardar Sarovar Projects as they stand are flawed, that resettlement and rehabilitation of all those displaced by the Projects is not possible under prevailing circumstances, and that the environmental impacts of the Projects have not been properly considered or adequately addressed. Moreover, we believe that the Bank shares responsibility with the borrower for the situation that has developed."

The report further recommended that the World Bank step back from the project pending the completion of ongoing environmental studies and a review of the project design.

Predictably, in an instance where widely disparate opinions were held with sincere conviction and clothed in powerful, emotional rhetoric, the report fanned rather than extinguished the flames of controversy. The state governments condemned the report as biased...The Narmada Control Authority, responding to the position taken by the Independent Review that the cultural uniqueness of tribal and indigenous people who would be affected by the Sardar Sarovar Project required that they receive special consideration from the World Bank and the government of India, termed "deplorable" what it saw as the attempt of the Independent Review "to create a rift between SC/STs [scheduled castes and scheduled tribes] and the rest of society." In Gujarat there were public bonfires of the report.

World Bank funding of the Sardar Sarovar Project continued for ten months after the submission of the final report of the Independent Review. While the president of the World Bank acknowledged deficiencies in the Bank's performance, particularly its failure to insist that the national and state governments consult with affected parties, develop socioeconomic data on project-affected people, and assess their implementation capacity for resettlement, the Bank management staff argued that adequate steps to improve the resettlement and rehabilitation of the oustees and to address environmental impacts could be taken simultaneously with the continuing construction of the dam. In October 1992, the executive directors of the Bank agreed to continue funding conditional upon the achievement of some benchmark improvements by March 31, 1993. On the eve of that deadline, when it was clear that the conditions could not be met, and before the benchmarks were to be reviewed, the government of India announced that it would not seek the remaining balance of the committed World Bank loan for the Sardar Sarovar Project. The central and state governments vowed to construct the dam without World Bank assistance and to adhere to or even to surpass the environmental and rehabilitation standards that had been set by the Bank.

In December 1994, "Narmada" remained an open story, its outcome not yet resolved. Despite lawsuits, nonviolent *satyagraha*, coordinated international lobbying, an unprecedented independent review of a World Bank project, and the Indian government's rejection of the World Bank funding for the project, the dam was half built. Court permission to close the sluices at the base of the dam had been granted (the gates were closed in February 1994, permanently impounding water behind the dam for the first time), the villagers of Vadgam and other threatened villagers were evicted in June 1994, backwater of the Sardar Sarovar Dam submerged Vadgam and parts of other villages in the Narmada valley twice during the 1994 monsoon. The government of Gujarat remained determined to complete the dam as planned, the government of Maharashtra remained determined to resettle the villagers from the submergence area, and the Narmada Bachao Andolan remained just as determined to oppose the completion of the dam and the resettlement of the villagers.

"Narmada" has captured the imagination of many actors on many stages: depending on the audience, the name may evoke the hopeful image of an exploitable and renewable resource, refer to a homeland in the river valley, stand for the river itself as a powerful religious symbol, or denote a historic religious pilgrimage site. In the national and international arenas, "Narmada" has also become a symbol for the struggle for local autonomy against forced displacement associated with state-directed and internationally funded development. The wide range of issues embedded in the Narmada conflict is reflected in the coalition supporting the Narmada Bachao Andolan that includes nongovernmental organizations (NGOs) working on the environment, human rights, development, religion, housing, agriculture, energy, and indigenous people's rights. The Sardar Sarovar Project has certainly made more headlines and been more widely debated in the public sphere than any World Bank–funded project. The struggle over "Narmada" provides a poignant example of how local people are caught between the threat of destruction of a way of life and the promises of development, while government agencies, nongovernmental organizations, and activists step forth to speak for them.

Contending Notions of Sustainable Development

As the report of the Independent Review commissioned by the World Bank noted in 1992:

> "To some it [Sardar Sarovar] represents economic development which will bring enormous benefits to millions; others regard it as an imposition upon the land which will impoverish—culturally and economically—hundreds of thousands of people and irrevocably alter, if not destroy, the natural environment which the Narmada River supports"...

Dam proponents and opponents seem sincere in their commitment to goals of sustainable development and social justice, but what they mean by these terms differs. Sharing the same rhetoric to describe profoundly different goals and means disguises fundamental philosophical differences and maintains confusion in the global debate about development. While widespread commitment to the term "sustainable development" might suggest a growing worldwide consensus on the need for development that is sustainable, there is no agreement about the specific goals of sustainable development or the appropriate means to achieve them...

Two specific issues are central to the debate over Sardar Sarovar and sustainable development—the environment and the interests and participation of project-affected people. Sardar Sarovar has come under scrutiny during a decade marked by the rapid evolution of worldwide ecological awareness, in the course of which standards of acceptable environmental impact have changed and continue to evolve. Simultaneously there has been growing concern about the rights of indigenous people. The rising ecological and human rights awareness and the changing standards have led to increasing criticism of large-scale development projects. Large dams everywhere have become a target of those concerned with the ecological and social effects of large infrastructural projects, particularly those in relatively remote areas inhabited by indigenous people.

In India, many individuals who acknowledged India's need for large dams and irrigation schemes are increasingly concerned about the high financial, human, social, and environmental costs associated with these projects. Others have been unequivocal in their criticism. Sunil Roy, former chairman of the Environmental Ministry Working Group on the Environmental Impact of the Tehri Dam, has noted that "this picture of dams solving food and malnutrition problems is a total illusion. Since Independence in India, 18.5 million people have been displaced—70 percent of them because of dam projects and another 500,000 are likely to be displaced every year for the next ten years. All supposedly for the benefit of the majority. With 1,500 major dams and 3,600 medium dams built over the past 40 years, there are still 350 million

Indians permanently living on the borderline of starvation."

Heightened attention has been paid to the need to establish the right balance between the promised benefits of large dams, the interests of people adversely affected by the dams, and the environment. Increased public awareness has placed a greater burden of responsibility on development planners to accurately assess and fairly compensate for the social and environmental impact of projects. This responsibility is difficult to meet when technologies have not yet sufficiently advanced to provide for the precise prediction of social and environmental impacts. For better or for worse, Sardar Sarovar has been affected by these evolving standards, and the growing concern about social environmental issues associated with the Sardar Sarovar Project fueled worldwide controversy about both the project and the World Bank's involvement with it.

The proponents of the Sardar Sarovar Dam insist that sustainable development is compatible with large-scale, ambitious, centrally controlled schemes, which are capable of mitigating the effects of natural catastrophes and meeting the increasing needs of a growing economy for food, water, and energy. The project was designed to alleviate severe drought and irrigation problems, a goal that fit well with the World Bank's goal of increasing irrigated agriculture in India. The primary concern of the project planners was sustaining agricultural growth in Gujarat by using an available and previously untapped water resource. From their perspective, the Narmada runoff is a perennially renewed resource that currently goes to waste. Dam advocates argue that domesticating this untapped resource would enable Gujarat to "sustain" its economic growth and the standard of living of its population. Project planners and supporters argue that the readily apparent and increasing needs for water in drought-prone areas, for both agricultural growth and a growing economy, justify the projected means and the costs of damming the Narmada and relocating those currently resident in the submergence area of the reservoir. Y. K Alagh acknowledges that not all large dams in the world or in India can be justified, but he argues that, unlike other dams, Sardar Sarovar uses a balanced, sustainable strategy of generating and protecting water resources and that it is an example of highly decentralized development...

Critics of the Sardar Sarovar Project, including not only some of those who will be directly displaced, but also academics, journalists, human rights activists, and environmental activists—question the portrayal of Sardar Sarovar as an example of sustainable development and see it instead as another project that will over-exploit the available resources to the detriment of the poor and the benefit of the rich. They argue that by any measure the project is unsustainable and unjust. These critics ask, "Who will benefit? Will the project alleviate drought in the most stricken areas? Are there other viable alternatives?" They note that the size and comprehensiveness of schemes like Sardar Sarovar require that these schemes be initiated, financed, and managed by the state as the guardian of the interests of the people. For these critics, sustainable development is not top-down but bottom-up. It requires that development efforts be decentralized and requires the involvement of local people at all levels of the design, appraisal, and implementation of projects. They do not seriously question the need to address the problems of the drought-prone areas and to increase irrigation, but for them sustainable development should be as concerned with justice and equity as it is with an ecologically sustainable use of resources. From the perspective advocated by these critics, large-scale, centrally controlled schemes are incompatible with sustainable development: the state's role as guarantor of national and international capital interests makes it inappropriate as the guardian of the interests of the poorest people in the society. They argue that large projects like Sardar Sarovar tend to benefit those who are able to make their interests heard at the state and national level. In their view, political pressure has encouraged the planners to expand the command area to be as large as possible and to use statistics that are more optimistic than would be justified by previous experience in irrigation projects in India...

[Some] opponents see their actions against the Sardar Sarovar Project not merely as a rejection of one specific development project nor as an opposition to development per se but as a movement for an alternative form of development. Smitu Kothari has argued that this movement

> "is neither anti-national nor anti-development. It is representative of a different vision. It is trying to articulate both nationally and internationally the need to strengthen linkages to question current strategies of industrial development...and ways in which the mechanisms of

> accountability of institutions like the World Bank can be strengthened. The [Narmada Bachao] Andolan is operating within this larger context, not as an anti-development movement but to promote [social justice and ecological sustainability], and to underline the fact that good ecology is good economics."

This tension between opposed visions of development lies at the heart of the controversy over the Sardar Sarovar Project. A detailed illustration of a major paradigm shift in process, the Narmada controversy represents a working out, through conflict and struggle, of the nature of sustainable development and social justice that concerns communities the world over.

Overview of the Sardar Sarovar Project: Dreaming of Water

At the center of the controversy is a dam that has been long in the making. Tapping the resources of the Narmada has been the dream of political leaders and development planners for decades—the idea of damming the Narmada was first suggested in 1946. indeed, proponents believe that construction should have begun long ago. Initially, the realization of this dream was complicated by the fact that the river passes through three states, which could not agree upon an equitable distribution of the river water. In 1960 and 1961, 2,000 villagers near Kevadia in Gujarat were moved from their land to allow for the construction of a dam and the canal. Prime Minister Jawaharlal Nehru laid the foundation stone for this dam in 1961. This project was delayed and, in 1965, a committee headed by Dr. A. N. Khosla was appointed by the government of India to develop a detailed plan for the development of the Narmada basin. The committee report, which recommended the construction of a dam and a canal in Gujarat and twelve major projects in Madhya Pradesh, was endorsed by the government of Gujarat but rejected by the governments of Madhya Pradesh and Maharashtra.

Subsequently, in 1969 the issue was referred to the Narmada Water Disputes Tribunal, which was established under India's *Interstate Water Disputes Act of 1956*. The Tribunal considered the issues for a decade and made its final award in 1979. This award, which provides for the diversion of 9.5 million acre-feet (MAF) of water from the reservoir into a canal and irrigation system, has guided the design of the current Sardar Sarovar Project. Financing to initiate the current project was secured in 1985, when the World Bank entered into credit and loan agreements with the governments of Gujarat, Madhya Pradesh, and Maharashtra, providing US$450 million for the construction of the dam and the canal. Construction of the dam began in earnest in 1987.

Sardar Sarovar is an ambitious and technologically complex irrigation scheme which is to draw upon the flow of the Narmada River to alleviate the water needs of large areas of the state of Gujarat. The Narmada River, 1,312 kilometers in length, the largest westward flowing river in India, rises in the state of Madhya Pradesh in central India and passes through the states of Maharashtra and Gujarat on its way to the Gulf of Khambhat. The Narmada drainage basin covers 98,796 square kilometers, with an estimated population of 22 million people. Ninety percent of the Narmada's flow occurs during three months of monsoon rains, from June through September: floods are intense and sudden, reaching their peaks in a few days. Harvesting this flow would require a large reservoir system. The river is the subject of the largest river development scheme in the world that would include, if it were to be completed, 30 major, 135 medium, and about 3,000 minor dam projects in the Narmada River valley. Sardar Sarovar is conceived as the terminal dam of the basin-wide scheme.

The Sardar Sarovar Project, alone one of the largest water resource projects ever undertaken, includes a dam, a riverbed powerhouse and transmission lines, a main canal, a canal powerhouse, and an irrigation network. Its projected impact extends over a large area, and it will potentially affect 25–40 million people. The components of the project are designed to irrigate a vast area of Gujarat as well as the districts of Barmore and Jallore in Rajasthan, and to bring drinking water to areas of central and northern Gujarat. The water is to be delivered by creating a storage reservoir on the Narmada River with a full reservoir level of 455 feet, along with an extensive canal and irrigation system. The dam is being constructed in a hilly region, and the reservoir created behind the dam will resemble a narrow lake extending from the dam over 200 kilometers upstream, submerging approximately 37,000 hectares of land in three states: Gujarat, Maharashtra, and Madbya Pradesh. While the full impact of the project remains in dispute, it is generally acknowledged that at least 100,000 people in 245 villages will be affected by the reservoir submergence. Many of these people, especially in Gujarat and Maharashtra, are considered to be "tribals" and have no formal title to their land. A larger number of farmers, perhaps as many as 140,000, will lose land to the canal and irrigation systems. In addition, thousands of people living downstream will find their lives affected by the projects. The main canal will have the largest capacity in the world, extending 450 kilometers to the Rajasthan border and crossing nineteen major rivers and 244 railroad lines or roads. With 31 branch canals, the aggregate length of the distribution system will be 75,000 kilometers, which will require approximately 80,000 hectares of land. The main canal will be 250 meters wide at the head and 100 meters wide at the border: the capacity of this canal system is such that it will be able to empty the proposed reservoir storage of 4.77 MAF in less than two months.

The complexity of the project allows for considerable dispute about how to best calculate and compare the projected costs and anticipated benefits. The project's proponents emphasize the enormous benefits it is expected to bring to millions of people at the cost of displacing comparatively few. They ask that these projected benefits—the provision of drinking water to as many as 40 million people and the irrigation of 1.8 million hectares of land in Gujarat—be weighed against the relatively small number of people who will be displaced from land that is, in their view, of marginal value. From their perspective this balance weighs heavily in favor of the project.

The opponents of the project question both the projected benefits and the costs of the project. They argue that the irrigation benefits have been vastly overestimated and that adequate drinking water may never reach the most needy drought-prone areas of Gujarat such as Kutch. Economic costs, in their evaluation, are based upon unrealistic figures and have been vastly underestimated. Even worse, from their perspective, the human and environmental costs have been grossly misunderstood and underestimated. These costs include under-estimations of the number of people to be affected by the project, misunderstandings of the extent to which people will be affected, and miscalculation of the costs of cultural disruption that will occur when tribal peoples are moved from their traditional lands. In their opinion, tallies of the numbers of people to be affected must include not only those in the submergence area but others who were not considered in the original project plans—including those displaced by construction of infrastructure at Kevadia, those affected by the canal, and those living downstream whose lives and livelihoods will be affected. Echoing their concerns with the process of development, many of the project opponents argue that the lack of early involvement of local people in the planning process has resulted in difficulties that cannot be overcome at this late stage, an analysis supported by the report of the Independent Review.

The Actors: Planners, Funders, Debunkers and Resisters

The Narmada conflict has been frequently portrayed in the press as a struggle between a powerful multinational development apparatus, on the one side, and relatively weak and defenseless local nongovernmental organizations, on the other. The reality is more complex than this and does not break down neatly into a simple pro-Sardar Sarovar versus anti-Sardar Sarovar controversy, nor can it be seen simply as conflict between local nongovernmental groups and a large state-supported development structure. Numerous institutional and individual players are involved in the controversy over the Sardar Sarovar Project who interact within and across three levels or arenas of action—local, national, and transnational. Complex linkages and conflicts occur within and between arenas, while within each arena, linkages and conflicts occur within and among national and international development institutions and nongovernmental organizations...

Three kinds or levels of criticisms have been made against Sardar Sarovar. The most basic level involves criticisms of implementation or "tactics". Recommendations about "tactics" are what were asked of the Independent Review, and it is this level of criticism proponents of the project have been willing to accept. The Independent Review team, however, felt that it was "irresponsible to put together a series of recommendations on implementation" and aimed their criticisms at another level, highlighting fundamental flaws in the project. This second level of criticism questions the general rationale or program of the project and not merely the way that program is being implemented. Even more radical criticisms that emerge from the Sardar Sarovar controversy question the fundamental assumptions of contemporary development interventions. This third kind of criticism attacks Sardar Sarovar not as one bad project that emerged from a basically positive process but as a typical project that emerged from a basically oppressive process.

Many critics of the project share a set of assumptions with the proponents of the project that stress the positive *potential* of development interventions initiated by the existing development "apparatus" (those formal national and international institutions that plan, fund, and implement development projects). Criticisms of development that emerge from within this perspective assume the positive potential of development interventions and focus on flaws in their design or execution, suggesting that development may require its implementers to muddle through, to take two steps forward and one step backward...Conflicts and debates within this perspective concern tactical decisions about how to implement the basic strategy of top-down development initiatives.

The more radical critics share a different set of assumptions about the limitations for change imposed by existing political and economic structures. Criticisms of development from this perspective argue that since interventionist development efforts emerge from existing structures of power, they necessarily serve to maintain and support those structures...

Dam Supporters, Governmental Agencies, and Alliances

Sardar Sarovar is a project designed, initiated, and managed by the national and state governments. At this level, the project involves a variety of institutions and ministries: the various interests of the central government are overseen by the Ministries of Finance (MOF), Environment and Forests (MOEF), and Water Resources (MOWR). The Narmada Control Authority (NCA), located at Indore, Madhya Pradesh, was established by the Narmada Water Disputes Tribunal to oversee and coordinate the actions of the three state governments with regard to the development of the Narmada valley. Each of the state governments of Gujarat (GOG), Madhya Pradesb (GOMP), and Maharashtra (GOM) has established a unique institutional structure for addressing issues related to the project. The heavily financed and well-staffed Sardar Sarovar Narmada Nigam, Ltd. (SSNNL, or the Nigam) administers the Sardar Sarovar Project for the government of Gujarat. The Narmada Valley Development Authority (NVDA) is the Madhya Pradesh equivalent of the SSNNL overseeing development along the entire stretch of the Narmada River that lies in the state. Maharashtra operates through its existing agencies with the assistance of the Additional Collector for resettlement and rehabilitation stationed in Dhule...

The principal international player in the Narmada controversy has been the World Bank. The Bank's involvement in a project is significant for three reasons: first, other potential lenders view World Bank financing as "a seal of approval." Second, World Bank involvement leads to a dramatic shift from a two-level domestic arena to the three-level international arena, thus opening up a state's "domestic" projects to international scrutiny, criticism, and politics. Bank involvement increases the opportunities for international nongovernmental organizations to indirectly pressure the borrower to revise environmental, human rights, or other policies related to the project. Third, World Bank involvement also subjects a project to the standards suggested by Bank policies. Policies concerning the environment and resettlement have become increasingly progressive over the past decade even though the implementation of Bank projects has not reflected these changing standards. While the Bank management staff has largely supported Sardar Sarovar, the reaction of the World Bank to the Narmada controversy has not been monolithic. The report of the Independent Review highlighted the significant differences between the Bank's policy statements and the actions of the Bank management staff. These differences between standards and performance make the Bank vulnerable to the lobbying of international nongovernmental organizations. The international campaign against the Sardar Sarovar Project brought pressure upon the executive directors of the Bank who, in turn, put pressure upon Bank President Barber Conable who, for the first time in the history of the Bank, called for a review of a Bank project by an impartial committee.

> *The principal international player in the Narmada controversy has been the World Bank.*

The Independent Review

The Independent Review was commissioned by the president of the World Bank in March 1991 as "the result of a specific controversy over the question whether India and the three state governments have complied with India's own policies, especially the 1979 award of the Narmada Water Disputes Tribunal, relating to resettlement and rehabilitation and amelioration of environmental impact, and the Bank's conditions, set out in the 1985 credit and loan agreements, touching on both subjects." As the terms of reference for the Independent Review laid out, the review was to

> "conduct an assessment of the implementation of the ongoing Sardar Sarovar Projects (SSP)...as regards (a) the resettlement and rehabilitation of the population displaced/affected by the construction of the Sardar Sarovar Project infrastructure and by the storage reservoir, and (b) the amelioration of the environmental impacts of all aspects of the projects."

This was the first review of its kind in the history of the World Bank and was seen by many as the reflection of a new interest in public accountability on the part of the Bank. The review was headed by Mr. Bradford Morse former administrator of the United Nations Development Programme, and former representative to the US Congress. The Deputy Chairman of the Review was the Honorable Thomas R. Berger, a Canadian lawyer known for his work on aboriginal, environmental, and human rights issues. The members of the review team began their work in September 1991 and for the next six months conferred with ministers and other central and state government officials, traveled throughout the Narmada valley and the command area of Gujarat, met with concerned citizens and nongovernmental organizations, and reviewed hundreds of written submissions. The final report was issued in June 1992.

As an actor on the "Narmada" stage, the Independent Review team had a brief run but its report has had a far-reaching influence. The Independent Review's report was critical of the way in which the project was repeatedly supported by the Bank staff in the face of reports that warned of potential problems. The report further criticized the Bank staff for operating as advocates of the project and for limiting the information made available through their report to others in the Bank. While some members of the Bank staff privately expressed concern about the social and environmental impacts of Sardar Sarovar and the inadequacy or absence of actions designed to mitigate them, the public statements of Bank officials were always supportive of the project.

Nongovernmental Critics and Opponents of the Project

Dozens of nongovernmental organizations, at the local, national, and international levels, have become involved in the Narmada issue both in opposition to and in defense of the Sardar Sarovar Project. The month-long standoff at Ferkuwa, described earlier in this chapter, emblematized the ongoing confrontation between pro- and anti–dam nongovernment organizations. Many Gujarati organizations, including Narmada Abhiyan, Anand Niketan Ashram, and the Narmada Foundation, have been strong supporters of the project. In Gujarat, just outside the submergence area, a few organizations like Arch-Vahini have focused their efforts on assisting those project-affected people willing to accept the offers of resettlement and rehabilitation. Organizations working within the submergence area of the project and with strong ties to the project-affected people are generally opposed to the construction of the dam and have become remarkably influential. In addition, numerous nongovernmental research institutes in India have conducted and published reports on aspects of the project and the valley, either on their own initiative or at the request of the government or the World Bank. These include the Tata Institute of Social Science (TISS), the Tribal Research Institute (TRI), Center for Social Studies (CSS), Lokayan, and Multiple Action Research Group (MARG). After the dam opposition in the submergence area began closing the villages to government officers in 1989, these groups, particularly those conducting surveys on behalf of the government, found it increasingly difficult to conduct further research.

Among NGOs, differences in perspective about the project have emerged and evolved over time—in some cases opposition has hardened and in others it has softened... Patel discuss the evolution of their activism in the Narmada valley. In the Narmada case, as with dam projects elsewhere, much of the local opposition has been fueled by a persistent failure on the part of the project planners and implementers to anticipate and handle resettlement issues promptly and adequately; but opposition to the dam is bay no means limited to the single issue of resettlement and rehabilitation. Opposition to the project has evolved through two distinct phases. In the first phase, from 1984 until 1988, a number of nongovernmental organizations within Maharashtra, Madhya Pradesh, and Gujarat worked collectively and individually to win a better resettlement and rehabilitation policy for the people to be displaced by the project. At this time, the potential "oustees" knew little about the project, their imminent displacement, or their entitlements...Anil Patel, one of the first activists to work with the potential oustees, recall[s] his early experiences:

> "We were aware ourselves of our inexperience and powerlessness...we knew nothing about the maze of land laws, the Forest Act, or the Tribunal's decisions on resettlement and rehabilitation. We didn't even know of the World Bank guidelines, and even if we knew, of what good could that be to us? The World Bank, even to us, was distant, remote and powerful mere abstraction. If we had known of these intricacies and the legal tangles, we would have been repelled by the sheer immensity of the task. Happily, we did not know this."

Even before the signing of the loan and credit agreements in 1985, local nongovernmental organizations had begun to make connections with and receive support from international nongovernmental organizations. The process of organizing the "tribals" in Maharashtra and Madhya Pradesh was begun in 1986 by two organizations that initially made demands for resettlement and rehabilitation policies similar to the demands that were being made in Gujarat.

The second phase of opposition to the project began after Gujarat offered an improved resettlement and rehabilitation policy in December 1987. At this time, the interests and strategies of these nongovernmental organizations working with the potential oustees began to diverge. Some groups, like Arch-Vahini (Action Research in Community Health and Development), a Gujarat-based, nongovernmental organization, were convinced of the need to ensure fair and just resettlement and rehabilitation of the project-affected persons, and they began to cooperate with the Gujarat government Sardar Sarovar Narmada Nigam to ensure that the new Gujarat resettlement and rehabilitation policy was fully and fairly implemented. Other nongovernmental organizations, including the Narmada Ghati Nav Nirman Samiti (the Committee for a New Life in the Narmada Valley) in Madhya Pradesh, the Narmada Dharangrast Samiti (Committee for Narmada Dam-Affected People) in Maharashtra, and the Narmada Asargrastha Samiti (the Committee for People Affected by the Narmada Dam) in Gujarat, had become convinced that a top-down decision making structure could never bring about social justice or sustainable development and vowed to oppose the construction of the dam despite the new resettlement policy. The focus of those who continued to oppose the Sardar Sarovar Project expanded from the initial objective of obtaining a better compensation package for the resettled tribals to include the issues of environmental degradation and the cost-benefit ratio: project opponents came to question not just the validity of the Sardar Sarovar Project but the centrally planned approach to development in India. These groups became part of the Narmada Bachao Andolan, a national coalition of environmental and human rights activist groups, scientists, academics, and project-affected people who espouse Gandhian nonviolent resistance techniques and stress their grassroots membership and goals. Commenting on the evolution in their thinking, one member of the Narmada Bachao Andolan explained:

> "more and more facts came to light, and the enormity of the environmental impacts became clear, as well as our realization that the very rationale of the project—the project benefits—were highly doubtful. All this led us to challenge the project itself. The struggle has now widened from resettlement to encompass the whole of sustainable development. We feel that development is planned on the whims of the wealthiest portion of the population. We want a model of development where the first priority is ensuring the minimum needs of the maximum population."

The divergence in strategies and goals is not surprising in light of the different constituencies and experiences of the various nongovernmental groups. The new Gujarat resettlement and rehabilitation policy appeared to provide the opportunities for which groups like Arch-Vahini had lobbied, though it represented a significant step forward only for those project affected people willing to resettle in the state of Gujarat. Unfortunately, the Gujarati policy was not matched by similar policies in Madhya Pradesh and Maharashtra where the Narmada Ghati Nav Nirman Samiti and the Narmada Dharangrast Samiti, respectively, had their constituencies. In order to take advantage of the new resettlement and rehabilitation package, project-affected persons from these areas had to move to Gujarat. While there is considerable disagreement about the number of villagers unwilling to make this move and about the cause and degree of resistance, it is still clear that many, if not most, project-affected people in Madhya Pradesh and Maharashtra are reluctant to move to Gujarat. While current resistance to the project is no longer based solely or even primarily on the inadequacies of the resettlement policies, it is clear that the differences among the three states' policies toward resettlement had a hand in fueling the continued resistance to the project.

The second phase of opposition to the project is characterized by a cleavage between local groups who had been united in their efforts during the first phase. Members of the Narmada Bachao Andolan and their allies argued that despite the December 1987 Gujarat resettlement and rehabilitation policy, the tribals were bound to be much worse off after they are resettled. They broadened their critique of the project and insisted that the tribals would prefer to be drowned by the rising waters of the dam than give tacit approval to this destructive scheme by agreeing to move. Arch-Vahini and others raised questions about what the tribals really prefered. Based on their own experience, members of Arch-Vahini were confident that the tribals in Gujarat, although apprehensive and suspicious about the government's true intentions, wanted to get the 1987 policy implemented. They suspected that tribals in Maharashtra and Madhya Pradesh would have made the same choice, and they were disappointed that the organizations working with the tribals in these other two states abandoned the campaign to achieve similar policies.

Manibeli had become a synecdochic representation for the whole valley.

These different assessments of the best interest of the tribals came to a clash in late March 1992, just after the Independent Review team members had left India, and as members of the Narmada Bachao Andolan and the government of Gujarat were gathering in New York for the international conference on Narmada...In a surprise morning operation, a crowd of 800 individuals—including 400 private citizens; a few former residents of Manibeli; members of their families and other supporters; members of Gujarati nongovernmental organizations; the Additional Collector of Dhule District, Maharashtra; and over 400 policemen—entered the village of Manibeli to assist the former residents who wanted to salvage building materials from their former residences. The fifty or so activists and residents of the village present when the operation began were initially cordoned off despite their protests as approximately twenty houses belonging to families who had accepted the government's offer to resettle in Gujarat were dismantled by the resettlers, their relatives, and members of Gujarati nongovernmental organizations, including Narmada Abhiyan, a strongly pro-Sardar Sarovar, Gujarati-based, nongovernmental organization, and Arch-Vahini, a nongovernmental organization facilitating the resettlement of oustees in Gujarat. The confrontation between the authorities and the antidam villagers in Manibeli continued for weeks. Tensions ran high as those residing in Manibeli continued to protest what they characterized as an invasion of Manibeli by government-supported outsiders and the press reported charges of police brutality and countercharges of violence or illegal disorder on the part of the villagers and the Andolan. Several fact–finding teams were sent to investigate negative reports about the police operation. By mid-April, the government had built a road to the village, installed a generator and flood lights, and established a camp of one hundred policemen in the village.

To understand why a small, previously ignored, relatively remote village became the center of a struggle among the government, the activists, and the press, one has to recognize the tremendous symbolic importance Manibeli had come to hold for pro- and anti–dam advocates alike. Manibeli had become a synecdochic representation [using the name of the part to represent the whole] for the whole valley; the state governments, Gujarati nongovernmental organizations assisting with resettlement, and the Narmada Bachao Andolan competed for this powerful symbol, each group claiming that it represented the true interests of the people and marshalling statistics to support its respective claim. Dam proponents argued that, in fact, a high number of Manibeli residents had either already relocated or had agreed to shift to relocation sites. Dam opponents challenged these assertions and argued that some villagers who had previously agreed to move to a resettlement site had returned to Manibeli. The long decision-making process associated with relocation and the ambivalence of many oustees who were weighing their options allowed pro- and anti–dam advocates to make conflicting claims about the number of residents who had already shifted or who had agreed to shift, on the one hand, and the number who had not shifted or had shifted but wished to return, on the other. In fact, the attempts to divide the villagers into two camps those who had shifted and those who had not—obscured the realities of the Manibeli situation. Most residents were somewhere betwixt and between, having expressed interest or made some gestures toward moving, but were not yet fully committed to resettlement. The information could be presented in various ways, depending on the point one wanted to make, by lumping together in one category people who were in various situations or states of indecision, including, for example, those who shifted before 1985 taking their house materials and belongings; those who had received land and partly shifted, leaving behind some belongings and houses; those who had received land and fully shifted, leaving their house with a relative at Manibeli; those who had received some benefits but had not shifted; and those who had received no benefits and had not shifted.

Transnational Nongovernmental Linkages and Local Opposition to Sardar Sarovar

Through its first eight years of existence, the Narmada Bachao Andolan has proven to be a formidable opponent to the government. The resilience and endurance of the organization emerges from and continues to depend upon several factors. First among these is the commitment of the villagers not to move. This commitment has been continually demonstrated and was reflected in the blood oaths marking their refusal to move. Tens of thousands of villagers throughout the submergence zone of the Sardar Sarovar Project have vowed that they will drown before they will leave their homes. The *Samarpit Dal* (Save or Drown Squads) further demonstrated this resolve by remaining in villages as the waters rose. But while local support is the heart and soul of the resistance to the dam, the moral *sine qua non* upon which all actions are based, a second, essential factor for the challenge the dam opponents have raised to the government and the World Bank is the broad-based national and international support that has been articulated through ongoing linkages and alliances.

It has been widely recognized in recent development literature that while the problems posed by environment and development policy choices are often experienced most acutely at the grassroots level, local community groups often have little voice in the policymaking process. If they are heard at all, it is in resistance to policies already decided elsewhere and implemented locally. The Narmada case is no different: Local people had no voice in the policymaking process. However, they have made their voices heard in resistance to these policies through transnational alliances that include local grassroots groups, nongovernmental advocacy groups, support organizations, and international nongovernmental organizations. The strength of these alliances comes from joining the information-sharing and political-influence skills of northern environmental and human rights advocacy organizations with the moral imperative of grassroots organizations. These alliances or social movements draw strength from their existence as "imagined communities." These movements share values and goals about development, or perhaps more precisely, they share a critical stance toward the dominant paradigm of development, a stance that characterizes both their ideology and their actions They have proven effective as reactive rather than as proactive forces affecting policy choices. That is, they have little or no opportunity for a direct role in shaping policy, but they have been able to contribute to blocking policy decisions that have been made without local community input and that threaten to have negative environmental and social effects on that community The international campaign to end Japanese and World Bank funding to the Sardar Sarovar Project welded the coalition of Indian activist groups affiliated through the Narmada Bachao Andolan with a loose coalition of international nongovernmental organizations, advocacy groups, and individuals through the Narmada Action Comrnittee...The alliance of southern and northern nongovernmental organizations against the Sardar Sarovar Project and the resulting strategies - relaying information about events in India through fax networks, letters, and regular informational meetings, and lobbying the World Bank's executive directors and its principal sources of funding, while publicly measuring the implementation of the Bank's loans against its own announced environmental and human rights policies in a way that is not done internally within the Bank—may provide a model for other southern nongovernmental organizations to emulate.

The Narmada case may be seen, as Lori Udall describes it...as a symbolic "test case" of the ability of a transnational alliance of nongovernmental organizations to pressure the World Bank either to expand its authority on social and environmental issues or to acknowledge its own lack of accountability on these issues. The effect of the pressures brought by the international alliance in the Narmada case has been to force all the proponents of the project, including the World Bank, the government of India, the state governments, and even those nongovernmental organizations supporting the dam whose funding came from international sources, into a defensive posture reacting to protests against the darn. This reversed the normal proactive and reactive stances of the government and the project opponents and forced the dam proponents to exert considerable energy and divert resources from project implementation to project justification. As the Narmada case demonstrates, this strategy can lead to a kind of paralysis in which each player is reacting to the actions and charges of the others and no player is able to take a proactive stance to break the impasse. Government and World Bank officials have been blunt about the degree to which the anti-Sardar Sarovar protests have occupied their time and effort, tied their hands, and frustrated their efforts. Where the structure of development decision-making provides no active role for nongovernmental organizations, these organizations are left with few alternative strategies. In the transnational arena, there was initially no voice competing with that of the anti-dam coalition: their presentations to the US and Japanese governments went largely unchallenged by the dam proponents. Only in 1991 did the Nigam and the Indian government begin aggressively to press their case in international forums.

While a transnational alliance of nongovernmental organizations relies on the ability of the northern nongovernmental organizations to keep information flowing and to lobby those who can place pressure on the international agencies, it draws its legitimacy from its local grassroots connections. This moral authority requires that the local nongovernmental organization be seen as the true representative of the interests of its constituency, and not fall susceptible to the almost inevitable charge that it is a tool of international interests. Because interaction with international nongovernmental organizations may expose domestic nongovernmental organizations to attack within their countries for taking domestic issues to the international arena, participation in transnational alliances is not without its costs for southern groups. Within India, for instance, the Narmada Bachao Andolan has been frequently attacked for raising a national issue at the international level. An additional liability of these alliances may be exposed when independent local groups find their own interests at odds with those of international nongovernmental advocacy groups. Allied with northern groups, they may lose control of the debate over issues. These are certainly tensions felt within India as some groups, including the Narmada Bachao Andolan, vigilantly guard their financial and intellectual independence from their northern allies.

Since the authority of transnational alliances depends upon the degree to which the Narmada Bachao Andolan can be said to represent the people of the valley, it is not surprising that this representation has been called into question by state and domestic actors in India. Strategies like *gaon bandhi*, which make it difficult for pro-Sardar Sarovar Project officials to make independent contact with the project-affected people in the submergence area, and the *lok nivada*, reinforce and protect the ties of the Andolan to the people of the valley. But these strategies also work against the Andolan, as state and Nigam officials blame the Narmada Bachao Andolan for preventing the government and other nongovernmental organizations from providing services and accurate information to the valley residents. Other local level actors, notably those working with ArchVahini, or the Additional Collector of Dhule District in Maharashtra, challenged the Narmada Bachao Andolan claims about the commitment of the villagers by citing their own successes in persuading project-affected persons to accept resettlement and rehabilitation benefits from the states of Gujarat and Maharashtra... They argue that if it were not for the strategy of *gaon bandhi*, which, they claim, prevented them from contacting project-affected people and providing them with up-to-date information concerning resettlement policies, their success in resettling villagers would have been far greater.

Issues

Two broad topics—resettlement and rehabilitation and the environment—lie at the heart of the disagreements over the Sardar Sarovar Project...The Independent Review's critique of resettlement and rehabilitation is particularly sharp, stating, "involuntary resettlement resulting from the Sardar Sarovar Projects offends recognized norms of human right—human rights that India and the Bank have been in the forefront to secure". Involuntary resettlement has been disastrous in a number of large dam projects and the risks are well-known. In the past decade it has become more widely acknowledged that not only should the costs of resettlement and rehabilitation and sacrificed future productivity be deducted from project benefits, but also that much of the opposition to dam projects has been generated by a persistent failure to address resettlement issues. But while the need for measures to mitigate the human costs of involuntary displacement are acknowledged in theory and in policies, there is still a wide disparity between the policies and the practices associated with resettlement and rehabilitation. It is easy to acknowledge the necessity for those who gain from development projects to fully compensate those who lose; it is much more difficult to determine what constitutes full, fair, and appropriate compensation. In the Narmada case, this difficulty is further beset by a practical dilemma. How does one identify and appropriately compensate project-affected people in remote areas where many of the people who will be affected by the project do not have legal property rights to their assets, and their full relationship to the land is not well understood by those who determine compensation?

This central concern of compensation pervades the discussions of Sardar Sarovar resettlement and rehabilitation: there are disagreements about what constitutes full, fair, and appropriate compensation, and further disagreements about whether all the oustees will or can be fully, fairly, and appropriately compensated under the present circumstances. With respect to appropriate compensation, some critics of past experiences argue that displacement should be treated as a development opportunity and that project affected people should not only regain their standard of living but also be treated as the first beneficiaries of the project. For project proponents, high costs attached to resettlement and rehabilitation reduce the cost-benefit ratio, making it more difficult to raise political and financial support. Even in cases where project benefits make it possible to offer attractive resettlement and rehabilitation packages, high awards are opposed by politicians and development planners who fear setting a precedent of high awards that could not be met by all future projects. The report of the Independent Review notes that World Bank policy acknowledges that oustees usually belong to marginal and disempowered communities and requires that all people affected by the project must "improve or at least regain the standard of living they were enjoying prior to their displacement". This is a minimal requirement. Given the size of the expected benefits of the Sardar Sarovar Project, it would appear to be possible, in economic terms, to fully compensate the project-affected people. However, World Bank policies are more complicated when the people to be displaced are indigenous or tribal people. As discussed below, it then becomes more difficult to determine fair and appropriate compensation.

While any number of people might be affected by the Sardar Sarovar Project in direct or indirect ways, the major concern about compensation has focused on the category of "oustee," identified in the *Development Credit Agreement* as an individual "whether landed or landless, who since at least one year prior to the date of publication of the notification under Section 4 of the *Indian Land Acquisition Act, 1894*, as amended to the date of this Agreement, has been ordinarily residing, or cultivating land, or carrying on any trade, occupation, or calling or working for gain in Gujarat, Madhya Pradesh, and Maharashtra, who would be displaced from his usual habitat due to the carrying out of the Project." Two factors affect the compensation to which a Sardar Sarovar Project "oustee" is entitled. One is the assessment of an "oustee's" right to compensation, which is complicated by the profound disparity between the way the government administers, registers, and taxes land and the way people conceive of and use resources. A second is that the resettlement and rehabilitation policies of the three states of Gujarat, Madhya Pradesh, and Maharashtra vary in the compensation they make available to the "oustees." As noted above, the states' policies are not identical: they have evolved over time, and two of the states, Madhya Pradesh and Maharashtra, have been under pressure since 1988 to change their policies to match Gujarat's policy. The three states vary in their treatment of "major" sons (sons over the age of eighteen), encroachers (those residing on and cultivating land to which they do not have legal title), and the landless. Current Gujarat policy makes no distinction between landed and landless oustees and offers full benefits to major sons. According to the award of the Narmada Water Disputes Tribunal, all people displaced by the Sardar Sarovar reservoir have the right to settle in Gujarat, if they so choose. Undoubtedly, so long as Gujarat's resettlement and rehabilitation benefits are significantly better than those offered by the other states, many displaced people are apt to take this option. Indeed, Madhya Pradesh resettlement plans anticipate that only 10 percent of the displaced people from that state will want to remain in the state. In the opinion of the Independent Review, unequal compensation violates the spirit of the Tribunal Award which provides that all oustees may remain in their home states. To do so under current policies would entail a financial sacrifice for some, while relocation to Gujarat would mean for many "a long cultural journey". While the right of choice still exists in principle, the disparity in benefits means a choice between migration to another state or a lower standard of living.

The policies of the three states also vary with respect to encroachers: Madhya Pradesh and Maharashtra treat encroachers as if they were landless with no entitlement to land. The debate about "encroachment" hinges on different notions of land use and legal versus customary land rights. Land use by tribal peoples in the valley has not been regularly recorded nor have tribal land usage patterns lent themselves to the kind of land records that states use to calculate fair and adequate compensation. As M. S. Gill concedes, land usage is difficult to determine. The government's perspective on legal land rights and the reality of land use in the submergence villages are often quite are different. A Tata Institute of Social Science (TISS) study has shown that the distinction between landed and landless in the Sardar Sarovar submergence area is artificial, and that those not holding revenue land are cultivating encroached plots of similar size and making use of the same grazing land and other resources as those on revenue land. The report of the Independent Review states that the economies of villages in the submergence region of Maharashtra "depend on a wide range of resources, including forest and river products, and extensive grazing. Much of the forest is harvested and grazed on a communal basis, while many agricultural plots are encroached. As is typical of tribal communities in the Narmada valley, the disparity between government administration of land and the people's way of owning and using resources is profound". Others argue that the use of forest products is less significant than claimed by the review and will, in any case, be more than offset by the compensation packages being offered. Dam proponents note that so-called "encroachers" who can prove they were cultivating land prior to a certain date will have to be treated as landed. Even after taking these attempts to legitimate many of the encroachers into consideration, the report of the Independent Review estimated that 60 percent of the tribals will not receive adequate land on resettlement.

Where legal ownership has little significance, resettlement policies that define land ownership more rigidly are bound to come as a rude awakening. Living in an isolated area, individuals in the Sardar Sarovar submergence area could "encroach" upon whatever land was available. With resettlement, land is no longer an unlimited resource but becomes a severely limited commodity. In the Narmada case, as elsewhere, displacement is bound to affect people differently. Those with clear title to the land are entitled to be compensated for that land, while marginal groups are finding it difficult to be recognized as groups deserving attention in the resettlement and rehabilitation process. People are also not compensated for assets more intangible than land: local markets, community resources, and social networks are undervalued. Land itself is treated as a fungible commodity without regard for social and spiritual ties people have to the land. The state is unwilling or unable to compromise its legal interpretations and is thus unable to be flexible in the compensation it offers.

As one would expect where studies reveal that the state and the people have profoundly disparate views of the land, the pattern and the significance of land use and resource exploitation in the valley remain in dispute. The report of the Independent Review advocates compensation that allows project-affected "tribals" to maintain their lifestyle. This position follows the guidelines set in 1987 by the United Nations World Commission on Environment and Development that states, "[t]he starting point for a just and humane policy for such groups is the recognition and protection of their traditional rights to land and other resources that sustain their way of life-rights they may define in terms that do not fit into standard legal systems." Others, including Vidyut Joshi, who conducted village studies in the submergence area, question this concern with conserving a way of life. Joshi asks "why should anyone oppose when tribal culture[s] change? A culture based on lower level of technology and quality of life is bound to give way to a culture with superior technology and higher quality of life. This is what we call 'development'". Beyond the conflicting goals of conserving or changing tribal culture remains the more fundamental issue of choice. Appropriate compensation cannot be determined by outsiders using some purely objective or economic criteria but instead must be determined in consultation with the project-affected people. The report of the Independent Review notes that the needs and wishes of the people at risk from the Sardar Sarovar Project have not been taken into consideration and concludes that, in keeping with World Bank objectives of involving local people, "people who live in the villages and depend on the resources of the valley should have played a central role in determining the Projects' impacts". As the report repeatedly points out, there is no substitute for the participation of the affected people, and in cases where early consultation has been forgone, there is no remedy that can be applied later. They note that "[t]he vacuum left by the Bank's own lack of appraisal was filled by measures that would not be adequate. Thereafter everyone was left with the task of making the best of a bad job."

This assessment was particularly distressing to groups like Arch-Vahini which had and continues to have a relationship with some of the project affected people and which has been working valiantly for years to assist displaced people in Gujarat. Having struggled to obtain what they felt was a just resettlement package, and having worked since 1988 to ensure that the policies are fully and fairly implemented, they anticipated that the report of the Independent Review would make recommendations that would further assist with this effort. But the evaluation of the Independent Review that the Sardar Sarovar Project was built upon a fatal flaw that could not be undone and that, despite all efforts, adequate and timely resettlement and rehabilitation was impossible, was a terrible blow to their morale and suggested that their years of effort were all for naught. Instead of advice and recommendations that would aid their task, their efforts were dismissed as part of the task of "making the best of a bad job." For these groups, this conclusion was unacceptable. In their view, the advice given by the Independent Review that the World Bank "step back" from the project was not only untenable but also morally irresponsible. People have already been affected by the project and remedies must be found to compensate for the disruption to their lives and environment. World Bank staff response to the Independent Review was qualified and took issue with many of the conclusions about resettlement and rehabilitation reached by the Independent Review. Their response began by stating, "[t]he experience with the Independent Review has been salutary and carries certain wider lessons that extend beyond the Narmada projects." The Bank management staff accepted the description of the resettlement and rehabilitation situation in each of the three Indian states and in the canal area. It also accepted the conclusions about the shortcomings in the preparation and appraisal of the project's resettlement and rehabilitation aspects. The staff disagreed, however, in one fundamental way with the assessment of the potential for resettlement and rehabilitation; the Bank management expressed the belief that if Madhya Pradesh state were to adopt a policy equivalent to that of Gujarat state, that policy could be implemented. Many individuals in India also disputed the assessment of the Independent Review that the implementation of resettlement and rehabilitation in Madbya Pradesh could not be done in time and that it would be impossible for Gujarat to resettle and rehabilitate all of the individuals displaced by the Sardar Sarovar Projects...

Environmental issues are another key area of continued controversy over the Sardar Sarovar Project. These issues include the threat of malaria, damage to river and estuarian fisheries, deforestation and soil erosion in the watersheds, and water logging and salinity in the command areas. Debates and discussions generally focus on three distinct areas affected by the project—the catchment area, the downstream area, and the canal's command and water service areas...Critics have called Sardar Sarovar "the world's biggest planned environmental disaster," while proponents argue that environmental impacts can and will be mitigated as they develop. These differences of opinion revolve around three general issues: first, the gap between World Bank and Indian government policies and the practices followed by the Sardar Sarovar Project; second, the quantity and quality of environmental studies completed so far; and third, whether studies done *pari passu* with the completion of a project can substitute for full environmental impact assessments done in anticipation of a project.

This controversy has developed despite steps taken during the past two decades, by both the World Bank and India, to ensure the accurate and timely assessment of environmental risks. The World Bank has been active in the global movement seeking to integrate environmental considerations into economic development decision making. Current Bank directives note that the purpose of an environmental assessment is to improve decision making and to ensure that the project options under consideration are environmentally sound and sustainable. These directives make clear that environmental risks should be recognized early in the project cycle and taken into account in siting, planning, and designing—and project plans should prevent, minimize, mitigate, or compensate for adverse affects. Environmental impact assessments are to be part of project preparation and are intended to avoid costly remedial measures.

India's environment-related laws, policies, and procedures, like those of the World Bank, have evolved over the past two decades. India's fourth five-year economic plan (1969–1974) stated that "planning for harmonious development...is possible only on the basis of a comprehensive appraisal of environmental issues." In 1972, the government of India created the National Committee on Environmental Planning and Coordination to advise the Department of Science and Technology on controversial environmental issues. By 1980 there was growing concern about the environment and the sixth five-year plan (1980–1984) declared, "environmental conservation is, in fact, the very basis of all development." In that year the Tiwari

Critics have called Sardar Sarovar "the world's biggest planned environmental disaster," while proponents argue that environmental impacts can and will be mitigated as they develop.

Committee was appointed by the government of India to make recommendations concerning environmental protection. November 1980 saw the creation of the Department of Environment, which became part of the Ministry of Environment and Forests in 1985. Concern about the loss of forests nationwide led to the passing of the *Forest (Conservation) Act, 1980*. By 1985, the year the credit and loan agreements for Sardar Sarovar were signed with the World Bank, India required an environmental impact assessment for all major irrigation projects, multipurpose river valley projects, and hydroelectric projects.

New environmental policies have not always found their way into practice. There is some question, for example, about whether implementation of the World Bank's environmental impact assessments achieves the Bank's stated goals. The World Bank's 1991 India Irrigation Sector Review, for instance, notes that "project implementation often still falls short of addressing the environmental concerns and objectives identified in Environmental Impact Assessments". As the report notes:

> "[the] environmental clearance process is frequently used simply as a delaying or blocking mechanism against any project with potential negative impact. Unfortunately, political pressures are frequently employed to get round this constraint with the result that projects with real environmental problems may be approved without the appropriate overview and addressment of environment issues."

The Independent Review was asked to make recommendations to improve project implementation concerned with the amelioration of the environmental impact of the project. However, the report notes that "the absence of proper impact assessments and the paucity of undisputed data have limited our ability to make project-specific recommendations of the kind that were contemplated". At the heart of its criticisms of the Sardar Sarovar Project was what the Independent Review termed the "original sin"—the failure to sufficiently appraise and provide basic data regarding the environment, resettlement, and the desires and interests of those living in the valley. This criticism of the failure to appraise and provide basic data before the credit agreements were signed pervades the report of the Independent Review. It is their opinion that master plans could not make up for this shortcoming and that the *pari passu* approach, which means that studies are done concurrently with the construction of the dam, "subverts any acceptable notion of ecological planning". They insist that "environmental impact studies, to be effective, must precede construction". Though the report of the Independent Review acknowledges the positive resettlement and rehabilitation and environmental policies of the World Bank and the environmental policies of India, the report argues that by any reasonable standard (of either the Bank or the government of India), the failure to comply with Bank legal requirements and government of India environmental clearance conditions "ought to be unacceptable". Thus the review finds it difficult to escape the conclusion that "there has been gross delinquency". In their opinion:

> "there is a fundamental difference in the meaning and practical value of *pari passu* between environmental assessment (i.e., what is to be affected, how, what can be done in project design, etc.) and environmental mitigative measures, some of which could be expected to proceed concurrently with construction."

The debates over irrigability, waterlogging, salinity, and drainage were not resolved by the Independent Review. The enormous size and complexity of the catchment and command area of the Sardar Sarovar Project pose difficult assessment problems. The World Bank staff has claimed that Sardar Sarovar Project planning represents a "break with past approaches to the planning, design, construction, and operation of irrigation projects in India". But the Independent Review dismissed the strategies designed to correct the command area difficulties as "speculative." The Bank management agreed that delays in the completion of environmental studies had occurred and that there remained a need for more effective central management or coordination regarding environmental impact studies and mitigation programs. Nevertheless, they did not feel that the environmental consequences of the delay were as potentially severe as predicted. Dissenting opinions expressed by the Bank management staff and others argued that more studies of the environment were either unnecessary or could be done simultaneously with the completion of the technical aspects of the project. The *pari passu* approach has led to a major divide among those who feel that it is a reasonable and responsible way to proceed with the necessary studies...and those who feel that this approach is fundamentally in error...

Seckler has argued that, with large projects like Sardar Sarovar, "one encounters conditions of pure uncertainty where no amount of study of past and present will enable one to know more about future consequences". Critics have argued that the *pari passu* approach treats both resettlement and rehabilitation and environmental studies as afterthoughts to the technical plans for dam and irrigation projects and sends the message that these aspects of project planning do not matter as much as the economic costs and benefits. Le Moigne, Rangeley, Mermel, and Guggenheim have noted that if World Bank policies concerning social and environmental impacts are to have any bite they need to be treated with the same concern given to the technical planning of the dam. They argue that plans based on World Bank policies on resettlement and rehabilitation should be treated as a technical part of dam planning. In other words, plans to ameliorate environmental and social impacts are of importance equal to the technical design and should be treated accordingly. These general criticisms are consistent with the Independent Review's evaluation of the Sardar Sarovar *pari passu* strategy.

THIS VOLUME AND THE CONTROVERSIES OVER THE PROJECT

...[The authors] make criticisms of all three kinds noted earlier—tactical, programmatic, and ideological. And their criticisms generally fall into one of the two basic analytical approaches toward development: they assume either the positive potential of the development process or its oppressive nature...[A] third approach,...[an] analytic approach, focuses on what actually happens in the development process above and beyond the stated intentions and goals of the development planners. The frame of study is not simply some problem that needs solving, some underdeveloped sector that needs developing, or a traditional people that need modernizing, but a process that includes the local setting and the development institutions as part of the field of study. It looks at the effect on local communities of a specific development intervention, and the professional or institutional discourse within which it originates. Change doesn't happen only within the context of the goals set by the project, but also in the broader context that includes resistance to and attempts to redirect development interventions toward alternative solutions and alternative means.

The Narmada case—examined as a struggle between the development "apparatus" and local, national, and international nongovernmental organizations also illustrates the importance of national and international civil society. This focus on civil society suggests the extent to which human beings can alter otherwise determinant structures, encourages us to consider unexpected possibilities, and leads us not to assume outright that change can be positive, nor that real change is impossible, but that changes have probably already happened—even without our awareness of it...

As a vivid illustration of a major paradigm shift in process, the Narmada controversy represents a working out, in a specific time and place, of the nature of sustainable development and social justice in an ongoing process that shapes international consciousness and affects local, national, and transnational communities.

G

Case Study—Malaysia

(i) Bakun Dam

(a) Raman M., "The 1996 Malaysian High Court Decision concerning the Bakun Hydroelectric Dam Project," 2(1) *Asia Pacific Journal of Environmental Law*, 1997, pp 93–97

A milestone in Malaysian legal history in the area of environmental law was created by the High Court in Kuala Lumpur in its 1996 decision in the Bakun Dam case [*Kajing Tubek v Ekran Bhd and Ors* [1996] 2 MLJ 388]. The decision dealt with the law on environmental impact assessments (EIAs) and has firmly entrenched the principle that, as a matter of right, the public is entitled to copies of detailed EIA reports prepared by project proponents and submitted to the Director-General of Environment for approval. They also have a right to be heard and make representations, prior to its approval by the Director General. The Court held that a denial of these rights would be contrary to legal provisions and would amount to an injustice.

The decision of the High Court in June 1996 was issued in the wake of a legal challenge mounted by three natives living in the Belaga district in Sarawak, East Malaysia, which is the site of the highly controversial Bakun Hydro-Electric Dam project (BHEP). The BHEP would inundate almost 70,000 hectares of land, displace around 10,000 native inhabitants and destroy valuable tropical rainforests. The plaintiffs claimed that the BHEP would adversely affect them and directly involve the destruction of their long houses, ancestral burial sites as well as land and forests from which they seek shelter, livelihood, food and medicine.

Background to the Case

The BHEP was approved by the Malaysian Cabinet in September 1993, and the project is being undertaken by Ekran Bhd Limited at a cost of RM13.6 billion (US$5.4 billion).

The EIA for the project had in this instance been approved by the Sarawak Natural Resources Board. This news caught the interested groups and affected natives by complete shock and led to much confusion and anguish.

On 20 April 1995, three natives who would be affected by the project if it was approved, Kajing Tubek, Saran Imu and TaLu Lujah, commenced legal proceedings against the company, the Director-General of Environment and the Government of Malaysia. On the direction of the High Court judge, Mr. Justice Datuk James Foong, the Sarawak Government and the Environment Board of Sarawak were also added as defendants.

The Plaintiffs sought a declaration that before Ekran could carry out the construction of the dam, they had to comply with the *Environmental Quality Act (1974)* (EQA 1974), and its regulations and guidelines prescribed under section 34A of the Act. Section 34A of EQA 1974 and the subsidiary legislation under it requires the submission of environmental impact assessment reports for certain prescribed activities, including the construction of dams, to the Director-General of Environment for approval prior to the commencement of any works. An omission to do so is an offence.

According to the guidelines for EIAs, prior to its approval, a project proponent must make the detailed EIA available for public viewing and comments. The public has about a month to give comments to a review panel which is set up by the Director-General and is comprised of an independent body of experts or representatives of interested organizations. The task of the review panel is to evaluate the environmental impacts, assess the cost and benefits of the project and make a recommendation to the Director-General for final approval.

Since the commissioning of the BHEP in March 1994, several Ministers, including the Minister of Environment, had given public assurances that the EIA for the project would be made available to the public for comment before approval. However, on 1 April 1995 it was reported in the Malaysian press that the first part of the EIA in relation to reservoir preparation submitted by Ekran had been approved by the Director-General of Environment. The EIA had not been made public nor were public views sought. The Director-General subsequently clarified that the EIA was not subject to Federal law under EQA 1974, but rather that the laws of the State of Sarawak applied in this instance. The EIA for the project had in this instance been approved by the Sarawak Natural Resources Board. This news caught the interested groups and affected natives by complete shock and led to much confusion and anguish.

Unlike EQA 1974 and its regulations, the Sarawak *Natural Resources and Environment (Prescribed Activities) Order 1994*, whilst requiring EIAs for certain projects, does not require the EIA to be made public for comments prior to its approval. In fact, this prompted the High Judge to call this omission a "most notorious difference".

As it subsequently turned out, the Federal Minister of Environment had in March 1995 passed an order known as the *Environmental Quality (Prescribed Activities) Environmental Impact Assessment (Amendment) Order 1995* to amend the Federal laws so that certain activities in relation to Sarawak, like the BHEP, were excluded. To compound matters further, though this order was gazetted in April 1995, it was to apply retrospectively with effect from 1 September 1994.

By these acts, the Plaintiffs claimed that they had been deprived of their accrued and vested rights to obtain a copy of the EIA, and to be heard and make representations before the EIA was approved. The Plaintiffs also sought a declaration that the 1995 Amendment Order made by the Minister was invalid.

The High Court Decision

The High Court on 19 June 1996 decided in favor of the native Plaintiffs and declared that the 1995 Amendment Order made by the Minister of Environment was invalid. It further held that that Ekran, before carrying out the construction of the dam, had to comply with the Federal law and meet the requirements of EQA 1974, and its regulations and guidelines. The Plaintiffs were also granted costs.

In what is commonly regarded as a landmark judgment, Justice Datuk James Foong made the following comments:

> "Under the guidelines prescribed by the Director-General, as provided for under the EQA itself, a valid assessment of an EIA prepared by the project proponent of the prescribed activities cannot be made without some form of public participation. This is essential, for interaction between people and their environment is fundamental to the concept of environmental impact. For this, a right is vested on the plaintiffs to obtain and be supplied with a copy of the EIA coupled with the right to make representations and be heard. While waiting to exercise their rights and being assured by the executive through their leaders—including those directly in charge that the relevant procedures of the EQA will be adhered to—the Minister suddenly strikes a mortal blow...[in gazetting amendments to the Federal EIA law to exclude certain activities in Sarawak]. Though it is claimed by the defendants that this amendment order only alters the procedure in the evaluation of the EIA on the BHEP, in substance and in fact and visible to all, it tantamounts to the removal of the entire rights of the plaintiffs to participate and give their views before the EIA is approved. This Court shall not stand idly by to witness such injustice especially when the plaintiffs have fumed to this institution to seek redress."

The High Court, in declaring invalid the 1995 Amendment Order seeking the exclude activities such as the BHEP from the purview of the Federal jurisdiction held that there is no express provision in EQA 1974 to permit the Minister to make any amendments retrospectively. "Section 34A(1) of the EQA empowers the Minister to prescribe activities including, as this court has ruled, making of amend meets thereto to cater for changes, but these changes are in anticipation of the future and not for the past," said the judge.

Further, the Court also held that the plaintiffs had acquired vested an accrued rights to be supplied with a copy of the EIA and to be heard and make representations under EQA 1974 and its subsidiary legislation. However, the repeal of section 34A of EQA 1974 and the subsidiary legislation under it, by the Amendment Order, should not affect any right acquired or accrued under the repealed law. This is provided for by section 30 of the *Interpretation Act 1948* in Malaysia.

The Attorney General of Sarawak had also questioned the usefulness of the declarations sought by the plaintiffs. He had emphasized that after the EIA was submitted to the Sarawak Board for consideration, the Board which also consisted of the Federal Director-General of Environment as one of its members, had deliberated and approved the EIA. Hence, what useful purpose would it now serve to re-submit the EIA to comply with section 34A of EQA 1974? For, after all, the Director-General will similarly approve it as he did as a member of the Sarawak Board. To this, the High Court judge remarked that:

> "it is elementary that it is not the Director-General who approved the EIA in Sarawak, but the Sarawak Board. He may be a constituent of the Sarawak Board but, it is not in his capacity as the Director-General under the EQA to approve the EIA. The Sarawak Board and the Director-General under the EQA are two separate institutions, each guided by its own set of legal procedures and the most notorious difference is the absence in the Sarawak Order of the right of the public to a copy of the EIA, and the right to be heard and make representations before the approval is granted. This difference may change the whole course of things as input through public participation as provided by the Guidelines may cause the approving authorities under the EQA to take an entirely different course of action, or impose certain conditions that may be beneficial to the project and the public as a whole....the interaction between the public and their environment is fundamental to the concept of impact. Thus, it is relevant, and indeed

> mandatory for the authorities to hear the views of the public first, before granting its approval. Even if the views of the public are rejected, of which they are entitled to do, at least the law as promulgated by the elected representatives of the people is being followed. It makes a mockery of the whole issue to say the EIA can be approved first and if the public has any constructive ideas, they can submit later. This certainly is illogical, deprived of good sense and sound reasoning...."

Response to the Decision

The natives and the public at large were elated by the decision. It was a vindication of the public's right to be heard on projects which have considerable environmental and social ramifications. Many who read the judgment which was widely publicized in the media, lauded the decision as being bold and courageous. Several of the major mainstream newspapers reproduced the decision almost in its entirety.

However, the decision did not go down well with the Malaysian government. Some 11 days after the decision, the company carrying out the project obtained an *ex parte* suspension of the High Court orders from the President of the Court of Appeal. Subsequently, on hearing lengthy arguments *inter partes*, the Court of Appeal affirmed the suspension of the High Court decision. The defendants, following the High Court decision, also filed an appeal with the Court of Appeal. The appeal was heard early in 1997 and in February the Court of Appeal quashed the High Court's 1996 ruling thereby opening the door for the BHEP to continue.

[*On Appeal to the Court of Appeal 17 February 1997, it was held that the State of Sarawak had exclusive jurisdiction over its lands, that Sarawak had its own environmental laws, and that the Federal Constitution includes 'land' under the list of State powers. Therefore, since the project related to land and rivers within Sarawak, it was the Sarawak law, and not the Environmental Quality Act, which applied. Therefore, there could be no claim based on a breach of the EQA. With regards to standing, the Court of Appeal held that the plaintiffs had threshold locus standi, but not substantive locus standi. The Court of Appeal also held that the plaintiffs were not representative in character and that they had suffered no special injury. The plaintiff's victory in the High Court was therefore overturned.*

Subsequent to this case, in September 1997, construction of the Dam was halted as the owners of the Dam terminated their contracts with the Swiss and Brazilian companies involved and President Mahathir announced an indefinite suspension. There were a number of factors at play in the decision to suspend the construction of the Dam, not the least of which was the advent of the Asian economic crisis, which descended on the region during this period.

The Bakun Dam project was revived in 1999 and in February 2001 Dr Mahathir announced that construction would re-commence. The plans were amended to remove four submarine electricity cables linking the Dam and Peninsula Malaysia (the efficiency of which had been a source of much criticism). The power generated by the Dam will now only go to the Borneo states. The total cost of the project was, therefore, reduced from RM13.5 billion to RM9 billion. Environmentalists have suggested that the omission of the cables removes any hydro-power justifications for the project. Nevertheless, construction has resumed and the Dam will proceed on its original scale.]

H

Case Study—China

(i) Three Gorges Dams

The Changjiang (Yangtze River) is the world's third largest river and China's largest. It is the lifeblood of the Yangtze River Valley which supports roughly one third of China's population, producing 40 percent of the nation's grain and 70 percent of its rice. The river flows through the mountains of southwestern China and then heads northeast, passing through a 200 kilometer reach of deep, narrow Canyon known as the Three Gorges.

Since its conception in the 1920s the proposal to dam the Three Gorges has endured a turbulent history. Efforts to push the Three Gorges Dam Project through China's decision-making process have been interrupted by war, ideological struggles, economic troubles and prolonged governmental debate.

The Yangtze River has produced some of China's worst natural flood disasters. Indeed, the driving rationale for building the Gorges Dam was originally to protect roughly

10 million people living along the river banks and flood plains from life-threatening floods.

In the 1940s, the US Bureau of Reclamation cooperated with Chinese engineers to develop preliminary plans for various dam sites. Yangtze river floods in 1954, which left 30,000 people dead and millions homeless, brought a sense of urgency to the project and subsequently, the Yangtze Valley Planning Office (now the Changjiang Water Resources Commission) was established to conduct design and feasibility studies for the Three Gorges Dam. In 1958, deliberations between Chairman Mao, government officials and soviet experts concluded that the justification for the Dam's construction could not solely be flood control. The dam was thus was redesigned to be multi-purpose to additionally provide hydropower and navigation. Hundreds of government agencies, bureaucracies and academics have since participated in detailed studies of all aspects of the project.

Construction plans for the Three Gorges Dam were delayed for decades as key issues were unable to be resolved. For instance, the proposed height of the dam has always been a highly contentious issue as it is the Dam's height which is ultimately determinative of the area to be flooded and hence the number of people who need to be relocated.

Enthusiasm for the hydropower potential of the Three Gorges Project was boosted in the late 1970s by Premier Deng Xiaopeng's modernisation plans. However, this was tempered by the growing realization and concern about the destructive environmental consequences of the previous decades of industrial development and Chairman Mao's "grain-first" policy, which promoted the conversion of all available land and forest into grain fields. Academics, intellectuals and the media began to voice concerns about the project's environmental consequences; its potentially destructive effects on agriculture; freshwater and estuarine fisheries; wildlife habitat; and water quality.

Opposition to the Three Gorges Project gained increasing national and international attention when the Chinese People's Political Consultative Committee (CPPCC) conducted a 38 day field trip in 1986 to gather opinions about the proposed dam. The Committee visited eight cities that would be affected by the dam and convened forums to hear from concerned ministries, bureaus, experts, scholars and local and national CPPCC members. Their subsequent report made a number of strong conclusions, finding that the cost of the project would exceed the official estimates threefold and would actually have detrimental effects on flood control, navigation and the safety of the Yangtze River Valley. The CPPCC's conclusions generated a heated debate within China and prompted the National People's congress to postpone a decision to build the dam for five years despite the fact that by this time the Yangtze Valley Planning Office had completed a preliminary design report and an environmental impact statement for the various dam heights under consideration.

In 1986, the Canadian International Development Agency, (CIDA) arranged with China's Ministry of Water Resources and Electric Power for CIDA to finance a feasibility study to be conducted by a Canadian consortium, comprising three private companies and two state owned utilities. In the same year, China commissioned its own final feasibility study, to be conducted by the State Planning Commission. The Canadian feasibility study recommended in 1989 that the Three Gorges Project go ahead, concluding that a 185 meter-high-dam with a reservoir level of 160 meters is technically and environmentally feasible. The Chinese feasibility study was completed shortly thereafter, recommending that the wall be 185–meters with a reservoir level of 175 meters, with building to commence in 1992.

Within China, prominent citizens, scientists, intellectuals and artists gathered to condemn the recommendations that the dam be built and released "Yangtze! Yangtze!", a collection of interviews and essays critical of the Three Gorges Project. The CPPCC denounced the Chinese feasibility study and called for a complete reappraisal of the entire project under the leadership of the National People's Congress.

The controversy surrounding the Three Gorges Project was eclipsed by the events in 1989 at Tiananmen Square. Repercussions from the Tiananmen Square massacre included condemnation by foreign governments and international financiers and led to the temporary suspension of the project. In 1990, Premier Li Peng called a meeting of experts to revive deliberations on the fate of the Project. Foreign involvement began to reappear and the pro-dam movement was given a boost following floods in June/July 1991, which took the lives of nearly 3,000 people. At this time, opposition from the academic and scientific community within China began to reappear for the first time since the Tiananmen Square massacre.

Criticism of the project continued overseas and in February 1992, prompted by concerns about economic, social and environmental consequences of the project, a case was brought to the International Water Tribunal in Amsterdam by Probe International against the government of China, the government of Canada and Canadian firms that completed the CIDA financed feasibility study. After hearing the evidence, the jury ruled that the very high ecological and socioeconomic risks of the "mega-dam" had not been adequately addressed by the defendants' feasibility studies for reasons of expediency. Nevertheless, in 1992 two thirds of the 2600 delegates to the National People's Congress voted in favor of including the Three Gorges Dam in the 1990-2000 ten year plan. Shortly thereafter CIDA announced in Canada's Parliament that it would provide no more money for the project.

(a) Wang Xi, "The Three Gorges Project and the Major Environmental Issues," paper presented at the *IUCN/APCEL/UNEP Training the Trainers Course on Capacity Building for Environmental Legal Education*, Singapore, 1998

Introduction

The Changjiang (Yangtze River) is the largest river in China and the third largest river in the world. The Changjiang Three Gorges Water Control Pivot Project ("Three Gorges Project") is a key project for harnessing and developing the Changjiang river basin of China. The heart of the project is construction of a high dam in the Three Gorges area of Changjiang. After many years study and debate, the National People's Congress finally approved the construction of the dam on 3 April 1992. It will take 17 years for the whole project to be completed. The construction of the dam was inaugurated on 14 December 1994 and the first period of the project was completed on 8 November 1997. On that day the river flow was diverted to an open diversion channel. Construction of the dam will now begin at the riverbed of the main stream. The second period of the project will be completed in 2003. By that time, the first group of electrical generators will start to produce electrical power. The project will be completed in total by 2010.

The Purpose and Necessity of the Project

The major purposes of the project are:

1. preventing and alleviating floods in the middle and lower reaches of the Changjiang;
2. providing hydroelectric power; and
3. improving the navigation conditions of the upper and middle reaches of the Changjiang.

Flood Prevention and Alleviation

The middle and lower reaches of Changjiang River include 126,000 square km of alluvial plain and lakes, which is about half the area of the United Kingdom and three times the area of Denmark. The area is densely populated with 80 million people, which is about the same as the population of Germany. The area has 6,000 square km of farmland and is a most important production base for grain, cotton and oil-bearing crops. Industry, transportation and commerce in the cities and towns of the area are well developed. Most of the important industrial and commercial cities, including the largest one in central China, the City of Wuhan, are located along the Changjiang.

The area is under serious threat of flood in flood seasons. In flood seasons, the water level of the river is higher than the level of the land along the river from a few meters to ten meters. The safety of the area is dependent upon the 3,600 km of dykes along Changjiang and 30,000 km of dykes along the tributaries of Changjiang area. The current flood resistance capability of the dykes in this area is low, as they can only resist floods of one in ten to 20 year occurrence. Changjiang is winding in its middle section, the Jinjiang section. The winding section causes difficulty for the discharge of flood waters and makes the Jinjiang section the most vulnerable section of the river.

The area has a high frequency of floods. Throughout the 20th century, very serious flood disasters have occurred on four occasions. In 1931 and 1935, flood caused 145,000 and 142,000 deaths respectively. In 1954, 18.88 million people were effected by another serious flood. There were 30,000 people dead in the pestilence caused by the flood. The only railway transportation across the country from the north (Beijing) to the south (Guangzkou) at that time was interrupted for 100 days by the flood. If a flood of once per 100 year occurrence occurred in the area, it would not only cause severe casualties and property damage in this area again, but also seriously disturb and hinder the development of China's national economy.

The flood waters of the middle and lower sections of Changjiang mostly come from the upstream area.

According to historical data, 95 percent of the incoming water for Jinjiang section and 55 to 76 percent of the incoming water for Wuhan City come from upstream of the river. The dam site is near the division between the upstream and middle stream of the river. Its favorable geographic location makes it possible to effectively intercept and control flood waters from upstream areas, which cover about one million square km.

The key to controlling the flood in the middle and lower reaches of Changjiang is to reduce or safely store the amount of the incoming floodwater which exceeds the flood discharge capability of the Jinjiang section. With the large flood control capacity of the Three Gorges Reservoir and correct operation of the Three Gorges Dam, this goal can be achieved. According to historical data and scientific calculations, the maximum excessive incoming floodwater for the Jinjiang section is 14.33 billion cubic meters in a flood of once every 100 years. The Three Gorges Reservoir has 22.15 billion cubic meters flood control capacity. It can handle the 14.33 billion cubic meters excessive floodwater. The maximum excessive incoming floodwater will reach 32.67 billion cubic meters in a flood of once per thousand year occurrence. With the 22.15 billion cubic meters of flood control capacity and the flood water storage capability of Jinjiang Flood Diversion Area and other flood diversion areas, the 32.67 billion cubic meters of excessive floodwater can be safely handled. In any case, the 22.15 billion cubic meters flood control capacity plays a crucial and irreplaceable role in the flood control of the river.

Effective flood prevention and alleviation of the Three Gorges Project can help China avoid large economic costs caused by flooding of the Changjiang. China has to invest a huge amount of money annually to prevent and combat flooding of the Changjiang. The average economic costs of flood avoided by the project will be US$12.5 million annually in normal flood years. In higher flood years, the economic costs saved by the project will be higher.

Providing Hydroelectric Power

The Three Gorges Power Plant will be the largest hydroelectric power plant in the world. The project will be very helpful for China to overcome the serious problem of electricity shortage in central and eastern China. Central and eastern China have well developed industry, agriculture and commerce. Many important cities are located in these areas, including Shanghai, Nanjing and Wuhan. The hydroelectric generators installed on the dam will generate 84.68 billion kilowatts per hour in electricity per year. The electrical power will be sent to those areas and greatly promote the further economic development of those areas. The eastern part of Sichuan Province, a poor mountain area, will also be supplied with a large amount of electrical power.

In addition, the Three Gorges Power Plant will be the backbone of a nationwide electrical power network. China has developed several regional electrical power networks, such as regional networks of northeast China, north China, west China, central China, and east China. Soon, the south China network will be established. But those regional networks have not been connected as a nation-wide network. The reason is the lack of a powerful enough and properly located electrical power plant. With its huge electrical power output and proper location, the Three Gorges Power Plant will take the role of the central power plant and work as a connection point for the regional electrical power network. With the support of the Three Gorges Power Plant, the production and distribution of electrical power in China will be much more efficient and economic than before In this sense, the Three Gorges Project is a strategic project in the development of China's electrical industry.

The Three Gorges Power Plant will be the backbone of a nationwide electrical power network.

Improving Navigation

When the Three Gorges Project is completed, navigation along the Changjiang will be improved. The Three Gorges Reservoir will make it possible for 10,000–ton class barges to reach Chongqing, the largest industrial and commercial city of southwest China. Meanwhile, the cost of waterway transportation will be reduced by approximately 35 percent. That will benefit the economic development of the southwest part of China. The navigation conditions on the river downstream of the dam will also be improved, because the dam will release more water into the downstream during the dry season.

The Dam and Reservoir

The Dam

The dam will be a concrete gravity dam 185 meters crest high. There will be 26 turbine generators each with 700,000 kilowatt capacity installed on the two sides of the dam. In the middle of the dam, there will be 23 water escaping gates. There will also be a ship lift and a ship lock on the left side of the dam.

The Reservoir

The dam will result in a reservoir 580 km long (in a flood of once per 20 year occurrence), average width 1,100 meters, and average depth 70 meters. The area of the reservoir will be 1,084 square km. The width of the reservoir will be double the original width of the river. The reservoir will be long and narrow. It will be a typical canyon shape[d] reservoir. The reservoir is seasonally adjustable. The total water storage capacity of the reservoir is about 39.3 billion cubic meters, with 22.15 billion cubic meters as flood control capacity.

The operation of the reservoir should take care of the interests of flood control, electrical power generation and navigation. The nominal water storage level of the reservoir is 175 meters. But in June, the level will be lowered to 145 meters and kept at this level for receiving floodwater until the flood season is finished in September. The lower water storage level will also be helpful for washing out the soil and sand deposited during the dry season when the water storage level is high. From late September to November, when the flood season is finished, the water level of the reservoir will be gradually raised to 175 meters and kept at that level for the full operation of the electrical generators until late December. In January, when the incoming water is less, the reservoir will start to release its stored water gradually so as to keep the electrical generators operating. This process will last until May, when the water level of the reservoir is lowered to 155 meters. The level of 155 meters is the lowest for keeping the reservoir navigable and the electrical generators operating. In May, when the new flood season begins, the water level will be further lowered to 145 meters.

The Major Issues

The Three Gorges Project has undergone a long period of study and debate. The scope, duration and depth of the study and debate for the project is seldom seen in hydroelectric construction projects around the world. The final adoption of the project by the National People's Congress represented approval for the extensive study and deliberation by thousands of scientists, scholars, and engineers. The major issues discussed and debated in the past 40 years include:

- the necessity of the project (as explained above),
- alternatives to the project,
- sediment,
- earthquake,
- the security of the dam in wartime,
- environmental impacts,
- population resettlement, and
- economic reasonableness and feasibility of the project.

The remainder of this note deals with the issues of alternatives, sediment, environmental impacts, and population resettlement.

Alternatives to the Project

The proposed alternatives to the Three Gorges Project were:

- alternative flood control methods,
- alternative electrical power supply, and
- alternative navigation and transportation improvement methods.

Alternative Flood Control Methods

Alternative flood control methods include the excavation of flood diversion canals north of Changjiang, including the alternative of excavating flood diversion canals to divert flood water from the Jinjiang section and re-filling the water into Changjiang at a point up to Wuhan City, and the alternative of excavating a large and long flood diversion canal along Changjiang and diverting the flood water from the Jinjiang section all the way to the East China Sea. The studies showed that the first alternative required difficult and extensive engineering work and involved the rearrangement of existing water resources facilities and transportation systems. It would involve huge costs and be difficult to control the diverted flood. Moreover, re-filling floodwater into Changjiang at a point up to Wuhan would increase the difficulty of flood prevention in Wuhan. The second alternative involved several provinces, which would disturb the existing irrigation systems along the river, require extensive excavation work, occupy large areas of farmland and resettle 2 million people. Therefore, both alternatives were not feasible.

Alternative two is to designate and construct more flood diversion areas. It should be remembered that using flood diversion areas is a way of sacrificing a small area for protecting a large area. However, it should only be used when there is no effective way to control the flood upstream. As mentioned above, when the Three Gorges Project is completed, the possibility and necessity of using flood diversion areas will be greatly reduced. The Jinjiang area now has a high density of population and well developed agriculture and industry. The enlargement of flood diversion areas will increase the costs of flood control. Moreover, the flexibility and reliability of using flood diversion areas cannot compare to those of the Three Gorges Dam.

Alternative three is to raise the height of the Changjiang Dykes. Studies have shown that to prevent a flood similar to the 1954 flood, the dykes of the middle and lower reaches of Changjiang need to be raised 2–3 meters. That requires a total excavation of 760 million cubic meters, occupying over 100,000 hectares of land, and resettling one million people. The total economic cost is not less than the cost of the Three Gorges Project. Moreover, the security and reliability of the dykes is uncertain, since the dykes are so long and so old.

Alternative four is to build more reservoirs on the upstream tributaries of Changjiang instead of building the Three Gorges Dam. Studies have shown that the total flood control capability of those reservoirs is 22.57 million cubic meters. It is equivalent to that of the Three Gorges Reservoir. However, there is a major storm rainfall area of 300,000 square km between the area controlled by those reservoirs and the Three Gorges Dam. The area is out of the control of the reservoirs on upstream tributaries. Therefore, those reservoirs cannot sufficiently safeguard the Jinjiang section from the huge excessive floodwaters, because there are possibilities that large amounts of rainfall cannot be caught by those upstream reservoirs.

Alternative Electrical Power Supply

According to the electrical energy development plan of the electrical networks of central and east China from 1985 to 2015, the two networks need to increase their capacity by 200 million kilowatt by 2015. The electrical expert group of the feasibility study for Three Gorges Project studied all the relevant proposals, including alternatives of developing other hydraulic power plants, developing other hydraulic power plants and coal burning power plants, and developing other coal burning power plants. The conclusion from the study was that the Three Gorges Project was economically superior than the alternatives. In addition, considering the rapid economic development and the serious shortage of electrical energy in China, all the feasible alternative hydraulic power plants will be built sooner or later, irrespective of whether the Three Gorges Power Plant is built or not.

Alternative Methods for Navigation Improvement

The navigation expert group studied two alternative proposals to the Three Gorges Project in terms of improving navigation conditions upstream of Changjiang. One alternative is a large scale waterway dredge and harnessing. The Three Gorges Project can meet the objective of 50 million tons of annual downstream transportation upstream of Changjiang by 2030. It is uncertain whether the dredge and harnessing can reach that objective. According to the study of the expert group there is a possibility that annual downstream transportation may reach 43 million tons by 2030. But that will only be achieved through very hard underwater work in the upstream of the river. To achieve that goal, the total excavation will be 38 million cubic meters, which would be seven times of the total excavation in the past 30 years. The other alternative is the combination of waterway dredge with railway transportation. This alternative requires the building of a 716 km railway.

The Three Gorges Project is better than both the alternatives in terms of navigation and transportation improvements. The Three Gorges Reservoir will allow for the passage of 10,000 tons barge fleet. But the alternatives can only allow for the navigation of a 5,000 tons barge fleet. The downstream transportation efficiency of the Three Gorges Reservoir will be 68 ton per hour per kilowatt hour, while the alternatives can only reach 49 ton per hour per kilowatt hour. The Three Gorges Reservoir can raise water level down the dam by releasing water in the low water level season. But the alternatives cannot achieve this. In addition, economically, the Three Gorges Project is better than the alternatives, because the latter requires larger investment.

Sediment

Chinese experts have studied the sediment issue of the Three Gorges Project for over 30 years. According to their study, experiments, and the experience of other reservoirs in China, the sediment problem can be solved. The Chinese experts have adopted a method called "keeping the clean water and discharging the muddy water" for the operation of the reservoir. By this method, the reservoir will lower the water level to 145 meters in the flood season. The deposited soil and sand will be washed out with the floodwater. When the dry season comes, the water level of the reservoir will be raised to 175 meters. The water in dry season contains much less soil and sand than that of flood season. So, the water stored in the dry season is cleaner than that of the flood season. When next flood season comes, the reservoir will lower the water level and wash out the deposited soil and sand again. Chinese experts have estimated that after about 100 years operation, the silting of the reservoir will be stabilized and 83.3–85.8 per cent of the flood prevention capacity and 88.9-91.5 percent of the adjustable capacity of the reservoir will be kept. Therefor, the reservoir will not be silted up completely. The method of "keeping the clean water and discharging the muddy water" has been proved to be effective by the experience of a number of reservoirs in China.

Flood prevention and control is the largest beneficial environmental impact of the Three Gorges Project.

The sediment of the Three Gorges Reservoir will have some impacts on Chongqing City, which is located at the higher end of the Three Gorges Reservoir and is the largest industrial and commercial city in southwest China. Chinese experts have found by mathematics modeling and physical model experiments that the water level in Chongqing may raise five meters in a flood of once per 100 year occurrence. The main streets and districts of the city will not be effected by the increase of the water level. Considering the reforestation in the upstream area and the construction of other reservoirs in the upstream tributaries, the actual water level will be lower than five meters. The sediment may cause some problems for the operation of Chongqing Port, but those problems can be solved by optimizing port operation and port dredge.

As to the impacts of the Three Gorges Reservoir downstream and to the mouth of the river, studies by Chinese experts have shown that the river bed of the downstream will be lower than before because the water released from the dam will be carrying less soil and sand than before and because of intensified washing against the river bed. The lowering of the river bed has both positive and negative effects. The positive effects include that it will increase the flood discharge capability of the river, improve the farmland quality by accelerating the de-saltification process of the land, and supply soil and sand for the river water so as to help keep the stability of the land and beach of the river mouth. The negative effects are the risk of collapse of the river bank and the difficulties for navigation in a few places with river sand banks. But those problems can be solved by enhancing the protection of the river bank and other engineering measures.

Environmental Impacts

The environmental impacts of the Three Gorges Project include both positive and negative impacts.

Positive Impact: Flood Prevention and Control

As mentioned above, flood prevention and control is the principal purpose of the Three Gorges Project. Flood prevention and control is the largest beneficial environmental impact of the Three Gorges Project. By effectively preventing and controlling floods in the river, the Three Gorges Project can protect the life and property of 80 million people and a large area and provide the people living in the middle and lower reaches of Changjiang with a safe natural environment. In addition to that, the benefits of flood prevention and control provided by the Three Gorges Project include avoiding ecological environmental deterioration and infestation by pests, especially the blood fluke (*schistosomiasis*) in the flood diversion areas. The Three Gorges Project can also help to prolong the life of the Tongting Lake, a large lake connected to Jinjiang section and the largest natural floodwater diversion area. When the Three Gorges Reservoir is completed, the sediment of the reservoir will cause the reduction of the sediment in Tongting Lake. That will help the construction of the harnessing facilities of the lake.

Positive Impact: Providing Clean Energy and Avoiding the Emission of Greenhouse Gases

Hydroelectric power is a renewable and clean form of energy. The rapid development of the Chinese economy demands the dramatic increase of electrical energy and to that end hydroelectric energy is a better choice than fossil energy. If the annual 84 billion kilowatt per hour output of electricity from the Three Gorges Power Plant is to be replaced by coal burning power plants, China needs to build a coal burning power plant requiring 32 million tons of standard coal annually. That means, in addition to the discharge of a large amount of hot water and coal ash, an increase of two million tons of sulfur dioxide, 10,000 tons of carbon monoxide, 370,000 tons of nitrogen oxides, 100 million tons of carbon dioxide, and a large amount of particulates and dusts.

Positive Impact: Improving Water Quality in the River

The reservoir will release more water in dry season which will increase the water level downstream and improve the living condition for fish. In addition, the increased release of water by the reservoir in dry season will help the downstream to dilute and purify more pollutants discharged into the river. The increased release of water in the dry season will reduce the strength of the salty water intrusion from the river mouth.

Positive Impact: Improving the Local Climate

The reservoir will cause a slight improvement in the local climate. It is estimated that although the annual mean temperature of the reservoir area will not change dramatically, the monthly mean temperature in winter will increase by 0.3–1.0°C. In Summer, it will decrease by 0.9–1.2°C. The improvement of the local climate will also benefit agricultural development.

Negative Impacts of the Reservoir

The reservoir will affect historical heritage property, and the natural landscape of the Three Gorges and the farmland in the reservoir area. According to many years of investigation, the reservoir area has 108 historical heritage sites. Among the 108 sites, 44 will be affected by the reservoir. Among the 44 sites, one is a national major historical heritage conservation unit, five are provincial protected units, and ten are city protected units. For those that will be submerged by water, the government plans to excavate, move to other place, or protect on site.

The change of the landscape of the Three Gorges will be limited. The major change will be the loss of water flow. Because of the reservoir, the water flow will be slowed down. The high and steep valleys will remain. For example, the most beautiful valley, Kuimen Gorge will remain 350 meters above the current water level. The water level in the gorge will increase about 40 meters when the reservoir is completed. The increased water will only cover the foot of the gorge. The steep and high canyons of the gorge will remain.

The reservoir will submerge 23,790 hectares of farmland and 5,000 hectares of orange orchard land. By inundating such a large amount of farmland, the reservoir will intensify the tension between the demand for grain and the limited land supporting capacity of the area. The available land for grain farming is limited and inadequate in the reservoir area. In addition, the cultivation of large new farmlands in mountain areas will increase the problem of soil erosion. The population resettlement expert group of the feasibility study for the Three Gorges Project, therefore suggested that 40 percent of the resettled farmers be redeployed to work in industry and the service sector. The rest of the resettled farmers will still work in the agriculture sector. But they will be encouraged to engage in forestry, fruit production, fishery and animal husbandry. The government will subside the resettled farmers with grain.

Negative Impact of Population Resettlement

Soil erosion may be intensified by destroying the vegetation and the opening up of new farmland in the resettlement area. The resettled factories and industrial facilities may cause new pollution. To prevent and control soil erosion and pollution, a number of measures have been proposed and carried out, including land use zoning, land harnessing, reforestation, a prohibition on opening up land on slopes, strictly controlling the size of the land for resettled factories and population, and requiring the resettled industries to switch to clean production.

Negative Impact on Forest Habitats and Rare Animals and Plants

The impacts on forest habitats and rare animals and plants in the reservoir area will be limited. The forest coverage rate of the reservoir area is only 15 percent. The threat to the remaining forests will be the needs of the resettled people for wood for housing and other construction projects, and for firewood. Therefore, measures need to be adopted to strengthen the protection of the existing forests. Almost all the first class state protected rare plants in the area are located in high mountains. They will not be seriously affected by the project. One of the second class state protected wild plants grows in low areas. If effective measures are taken, the wild plant and its habitat can be protected. There are 26 rare animals living in the area, including four first class state protected animals and 22 second class state protected animals. They are living in either high mountains or the areas of tributaries of the Changjiang. They will not be seriously affected by the reservoir

Negative Impacts Upon Aquatic Animals

The project will affect mainly five kinds of aquatic animals of the ever. They are white fin dolphin, white sturgeon, Yanzhi fish, Chinese sturgeon and the fish groups living in the deep water of the reservoir area. The white fin dolphin is a first class state protected species. Its number has fallen to less than 200. There are about 30 of them living in the middle reaches of the Changjiang. The increased clean water washing in the riverbed in the dry season may change some of their natural habitats. The rest of the white fin dolphin are living in the lower reaches of the Changjiang. They will not be affected.

The Chinese Government has called on other provinces and major cities to help the resettled towns with profitable projects.

Measures have been taken to protect white fin dolphin, including the use of abandoned old river courses as their reserves in the middle reach of the river.

White sturgeon is another first class state protected species. They live in the whole Changjiang basin, including large lakes connected to the ever. Scientists have found that they have breeding grounds on both sides of the Gezhouba Dam. The construction of the Three Gorges Dam will only affect the habitats of the groups of white sturgeon living in the upstream area.

Yanzhi fish is a second class state protected species. They are found in the whole Changjiang basin. The major groups of the fish are in the upstream of Changjiang. The Gezhouba Dam has blocked the migration route of the fish. An investigation in 1986 found that the fish can develop in the water down from the Gezbouba Dam. The Three Gorges Dam will not seriously change the current living conditions of the fish.

Chinese sturgeon is a large migrating fish and can be found in the upper, middle and lower reaches of the river. Gezhouba Dam blocked its migration route in the 1980s. Investigations have found that the sturgeon has developed its new breeding ground down from the Gezhouba Dam. How the operation of the Three Gorges Reservoir will affect their breeding is a question needing further study. Chinese biologists have successfully invented a way of artificially breeding the Chinese sturgeon. Investigations have found that the number of young Chinese sturgeon in the mouth of the river have increased dramatically.

The habitats of the fish groups living in the deep water of the reservoir area will be seriously affected by the reservoir. When the reservoir is completed, the water flow will be slower than before, the water will be much deeper than before, the soil and sand deposition will be different from before, and the food composition under the water will change. All these changes will affect the living conditions of deep water fishes and they will have to move to areas beyond the reservoir.

Negative Impacts Upon Water Quality of the Reservoir

When the reservoir is completed, pollution along the shores of the reservoir will be increased. At present, the waste water discharge in the reservoir area has reached 1 billion tons annually. The wastewater discharged into the upstream and the main tributaries of the upstream reaches 3 billion tons annually. When the reservoir is completed, the water flow will be much slower than before, especially in dry seasons. This will result in an increase in the concentration of pollutants in the reservoir. Experts have called for strengthening environmental management in the reservoir area. Their suggestions include construction of sewage treatment plants, controlling the total amount of the industrial waste water, enforcing the waste water discharge standards, reforestation and soil conservation, and controlling the pollution caused by ships.

Population Resettlement

Population resettlement is a key factor in the Three Gorges Project. According to a 1985 study, there are 720,000 people to be resettled in the reservoir area. Considering the growth of population in the whole period of the project, the final total population resettled will reach 1.13 million. The most difficult task will be the resettlement of a 364,000 rural population in the reservoir area.

The government has adopted a population resettlement plan and a plan for moving and reconstruction of new cities and towns. Each town and village in the reservoir area has adopted a population plan for implementing the general population resettlement plan. A special fund has been earmarked for carrying out population resettlement plans. The population experiment started in 1984. Experience showed that the new population resettlement policy is correct. The resettlement will be carried out step by step during the construction of the dam. It will last over 20 years.

The policy for population resettlement is aimed at helping the resettled to establish the capacity of long-term development, and not just to compensate them once and provide no further assistance. According to this policy, each resettled family will be compensated for their houses and other private property losses. Resettled rural families will be assigned a piece of land for agricultural purposes. Local governments will also assist resettled rural families to establish new businesses in addition to helping them to re-establish their farms on new land. Forestry, fruit production, animal husbandry, and fishery will also be encouraged by government. For resettled factories and the urban population, government will not only help in the building of new factories in new areas, but also assist in the opening or enlarging of markets for their products. The Chinese Government has called on other provinces and major cities to help the resettled towns with profitable projects.

Conclusion

The Three Gorges Project is intended to be a multi-beneficial project. The decision to proceed with the project was based on many factors and interests. The essential and decisive factors were the welfare and interests of the majority of the Chinese people, including that of the current generation and their future generations. The Report of the Feasibility Study for the Three Gorges Project (1989) concluded that "the Three Gorges Project is necessary for the four modernization of China, technologically feasible, and economically reasonable. To build (the dam) is better than not to build, to build (it) early is more beneficial than to build (it) later". The National People's Congress of China voted to proceed with the project in 1992 and the project is now undergoing construction. The merits of the project and the decision of the National People's Congress of China will only be finally determined by history.

5 Questions for Discussion

(a) Study the materials circulated on the Narmada/Sardar Sarovar Dam and discuss the following hypothetical problem.

Assume that John Doe has been appointed as the President of the World Bank with effect from 1 January 2000. He is determined to implement the commitment of World Bank to the mitigation of poverty particularly in Asia. Before assuming his new office, he studied all the major projects around the world in which World Bank was involved. He is convinced that the Narmada/Sardar Sarovar Project in India, when completed would make the Narmada River basin area drought proof, provide drinking water to over 40 million people, generate 1,500 MW of electricity, prevent flooding of large areas, and thus alleviating poverty in the region. He examined the Report of Independent Review Committee appointed in 1991 by the former World Bank President. He is also conscious of the unfavorable public image of the Narmada/Sarovar dam and the activities of the NGOs. Now that the Supreme Court of India had lifted the ban on the construction of the dam, John Doe wants to take a fresh look at the Narmada/Sarovar dam. Meanwhile, the Government of India, expressed its willingness to accept financing from World Bank for the project.

John Doe asks for you, as an expert in environmental studies, for your balanced analysis, for funding the Narmada/Sarovar Project.

(b) Does the 1997 *UN Convention on the Law of Non-Navigational Uses of International Watercourses* properly balance the interests of the upper riparian and lower riparian states as well as the interests of the international community as a whole?

(c) Does this 1997 UN Convention contain any innovative provisions with respect to the prevention of pollution and protection of the environment of the watercourse?

(d) Do the provisions in the *IUCN Draft International Covenant on Environment and Development* go further than the existing national and international practice?

6 References for Chapter 12

Crow B., *Bridges over Troubled Water? Conflict and Cooperation Over the Waters of South Asia*, Unpublished Paper, November 1996.

Abbas B.M., *The Ganga Water Dispute*, Dhaka University Press, Dhaka, 1982.

Agreement on the Cooperation for the Sustainable Development of the Mekong River Basin, 1995 34 ILM 864.

China Yangtze Three Gorges Project Dvelopment Corporation and Changjiang Water Resources Commission, *The Three Gorges Project*, China Yangtze Three Gorges Project Dvelopment Corporation and Changjiang Water Resources Commission, Beijing, 1994.

Hirsch P. and Cheong G., "Natural Resource Management in the Mekong River Basin: Perspectives for Australian Development Cooperation", *AusAID Report*, 1996. This is available at http://www.usyd.edu.au/su/geography/hirsch (accessed 25/05/01).

Kajing Tubek v Ekran Bhd and Ors [1996] 2 MLJ 388.

7 Additional References

Asian Development Bank, Handbook on Resettlement: A Guide to Good Practice, 1998.

Asian Development Bank, Resettlement Policy and Practice in Southeast Asia and the Pacific, 2000.

Asian Development Bank, Towards Effective Water Policy in the Asian and Pacific Region, Vol. 1: Overview of Issues and Recommendations, edited by Wouter Lincklaen Arriens, Jeremy Bird, Jeremy Berkoff, and Paul Mosley, 1996.

Asian Development Bank, Towards Effective Water Policy in the Asian and Pacific Region, Vol. 2: Country Papers, 1996.

Asian Development Bank, Towards Effective Water Policy in the Asian and Pacific Region, Vol. 3: Theme Papers and Comments, 1996.

Bangladesh–India: Treaty on Sharing of the Ganges Waters, 12 December 1996, reprinted in 36 *I.L.M.* 519 (1997).

Barber M. and Ryder G. (eds), *Damming the Three Gorges: What Dam Builders Don't Want You to Know—A Critique of the Three Gorges Water Control Project Feasibility Study*, 2nd ed., 1993, Probe International, Canada.

Cambodia-Laos-Thailand-Vietnam: Agreement on the Co-operation for the Sustainable Development of the Mekong River Basin, 5 April 1995, reprinted in 34 *I.L.M.* 864 (1995).

Dams and Development: A New Framework for Decision-Making, The Report of the World Commission on Dams, accessed at http://www.dams.org [*Editors' Note: This site was accessed 03/04/2001*].

Darcey T., et al (eds), *Large Dams: Learning from the Past Looking at the Future,* IUCN, Gland, Switzerland, 1997, pp 3-5.

Helsinki Rules on the Uses of the Waters of International Rivers, International Law Association, 1966, 52 *ILA* 484, 1976.

ICJ Judgement in Case Concerning the Gabcikovo-Nagymaros Project (Hungary-Slovakia), 25 September 1997, reprinted in 37 *I.L.M.* 162 (1998) available on ICJ site on world wide web: http://www.icj-cij.org, [*Editors' Note: This site was accessed on 03/04/2001. See also Chapter 12, Judicial Decisions*].

India-Nepal: Treaty Concerning the Integrated Development of the Mahakali River, 12 February 1996, reprinted in 36 *I.L.M.* 531, 1997.

IUCN Draft International Covenant on Environment and Development. Available on the worldwide web at http://www.iucn.org/themes/law/covenant.pdf [*Editors' Note: This site was accessed on 03/04/2001*].

International Rivers Network. The web site of the International rivers network has information from NGOs on river issues around the globe, including most major dam projects. The address is: http://www.irn.org/ [*Editors' Note: This site was accessed on 03/04/2001.*].

UN Convention on the Law of Non-Navigational Uses of International Watercourses, United Nations, 21 May 1997, UN Doc. A/51/869, reprinted in 36 *I.L.M.*700 (1997); available on UN web site at http://www.un.org/law/watere.htm [*Editors' Note: This site was accessed on 03/04/2001.*].

UN Convention on the Protection and Use of Transboundary Watercourses and International Lakes, 17 March 1992; reprinted in 31 *I.L.M.* 1312 (1992).

CHAPTER

13

Sustainable Use of Forests and Fisheries

Contents

1 Introduction

Central to both this and the previous chapter are the important issues of sustainable use and sustainable yield of natural resources. These concepts are particularly relevant to the discussion of fisheries below. The practical and theoretical definitions of sustainable use and sustainable yield remain deeply controversial. There is often a lack of baseline research and quantified data as well as lack of reporting and monitoring mechanisms relating to use. Important concerns, relating to traditional and indigenous sustainable use, are often not addressed by international and national laws. Hussain discusses these issues and particularly considers how they relate to tenure in Asian legal systems.

The first part of this chapter deals with the national and international issues associated with the sustainable use management and conservation of the world's forests. The need for greater action to preserve the world's forests is evident at every level—local, national regional, and international. The relevant international "soft law," *Agenda 21* (Chapter 11—Combating Deforestation) and the *Non-Legally Binding Authoritative Statement of Principles for a Global Consensus on the Management, Conservation and Sustainable Development of All Types of Forests*, is extracted for reference.

Following the *Rio Forest Principles* (1992), the Intergovernmental Panel on Forests has been considering the issue of whether there ought to be a global forest convention. The extract from Tarasofsky considers several options and dilemmas associated with this initiative. In some quarters it is argued that, in the light of the current fragmentation of the international forests regime, a new convention on forests is the best avenue through which to achieve coherence. Most commentators agree that we need more research and data about forest related problems and potential solutions. Only then will it be possible to consider the best legal and other means of implementing the solution. In particular, Tare warns that even perfect international institutions will not be enough in themselves to bring about the necessary changes. The traditional international legal system is not conducive to creating the effective public-private partnerships that are essential for dealing with current forest problems. Tarasofsky proceeds to consider all relevant global instruments and institutions and how they could develop further and create synergies to protect the world's forests.

Ansari focuses on the various international forest agreements, policies, and institutions, such as the International Tropical Timber Agreement (ITTA), and their effectiveness in the Asian and Pacific region. Ayesha Dias and Phillipa England continue to explore these issues with England focusing on the national implementation issues in Thailand. An interesting cross reference is the *Oposa v Factoran* case extracted in Chapter 11 and discussed by Quicho in Chapter 10. An issue in this landmark case was whether the citizens of the Philippines had a right to the forest resources of their country.

Section Three of the Chapter deals with international regimes, such as the Rio Principles and treaties relating to the world's oceans and fisheries, and comparative national approaches in dealing with fishing and aquaculture. The principal international treaties and "soft law" instruments are extracted. They are:

- The *Convention for the Prohibition of Fishing with Long Driftnets in the South Pacific*;
- Agenda 21 Chapter 17: Protection of the Oceans;
- General Assembly Resolution on drift nets and unauthorized fishing, 1997; and
- The Agreement arising from the *Conference on Straddling Fish Stocks in Highly Migratory Fish Stocks*.

The practical and theoretical definitions of sustainable use and sustainable yield remain deeply controversial. There is often a lack of baseline research and quantified data as well as lack of reporting and monitoring mechanisms relating to use.

The article by Menasveta explores the international regime and critically evaluates the role of fisheries management and sustainable development in the South East Asian region. The focus is on maximum sustainable yields, particularly within the exclusive economic zones under the United Nations *Convention on the Law of the Sea,* and the preconditions for an effective management system for fisheries. Importantly, she explores the role for regional cooperation in this area. Hewison takes the theme of precautionary approach to environmental management and explores it having regard to its application by the United Nations *Conference on Straddling Fish Stocks in Highly Migratory Fish Stocks.* In particular, he examines a "precautionary" approach to the maximum sustainable yields the Asian fisheries. Zou Keyuan provides a national study of the law on enforcement relating to the People's Republic of China's (PRC's) marine fisheries resources. In particular, this article notes the decline in fish stocks over the last four decades and the legal, administrative and institutional response of the PRC Government to this decline. His discussion of enforcement, in the PRC, provides some important insights into regional fisheries management.

A

Hussain S., "Tenure in the Context of Sustainable Use of Natural Resources in Asia," in Oglethorpe J. (ed), *Tenure and Sustainable Use*, IUCN, Gland Switzerland, 1999

Introduction

There are many factors that affect the sustainable use of resources. On the social front literacy, population growth, and urbanization are important factors. Among economic factors, structure of the economy, links to the international economy, and political ideology of a country are most notable. Tenure is another factor that affects sustainability of resource use, cross cutting as it does through economic and social dimensions.

Most of the literature on tenure exists as a part of two larger disciplines: it is analysed either from the standpoint of the political economy of development of newly liberated states, or, it is analyzed from a social and anthropological perspective. From a conservation point of view, very limited literature exists on tenure and resource use sustainability.

At first sight, the concept of tenure is straightforward enough. "[Tenure] is a system of rights regulating the ownership or use of land". Broadly speaking tenure can exist either formally—as a legal document originating from a central legislature—or informally as a result of orally established local property rights and community-based consensus. It is sometimes also referred to as a property right regime. Property rights regimes include two components:

1. property rights: entitlements defining rights and duties in the use of natural resources, and
2. property rules: the rules under which those rights and duties are exercised.

The aim of this paper its not to pinpoint the exact relation between different tenure arrangements and their effect on sustainability of resource use in Asia. Rather it is to bring the issue of tenure into the sustainability equation, and draw some generic lessons from Asia.

This paper is also intended to highlight the role of tenure as an important factor in conservation and sustainable use and for its consideration in international policy arenas. For the purpose of focus, I have limited the literature review to selective renewable natural resources such as forest and its products i.e., wild species of flora and fauna, pastures and protected areas.

Background To Asia

Intertwined with the broad ecological diversity of the Asian continent are a wide range of historic cultures that preach prudent use of nature for community benefit. The great cultures of Buddhism, Hinduism, and Shamanism and later Islam, as part of their general teaching, have promoted wise and prudent use of nature and its resources for a community as whole. Buddhist communities in the northern part of the sub-continent (China, Mongolia, and Southeast Asia) emphasized the upkeep of the ecosystem in balance with religious fervor and authority [state Germeraad and Enebisch].

> "In the past Mangolian nomadic society was strongly determined by principles related to behavior focused on surviving in the harsh environment, in which Shamanism and later Lamaism played a major role. These religions emphasized the importance of living in

> harmony with nature, and their written texts and customs included a series of basic nomadic land-use principles and guidelines. These were related primarily to the use of land, water, soil and vegetation and simultaneously formed a framework for adjudicating related conflicts between users of the land.

The leading principle for nomadic land use was related to what we may now describe as 'sustainable' principles."

The destruction of nature was checked through sanctions and the promotion of a compatible set of collective social behavior guidelines. For example, greed, wasteful behavior, and accumulation of wealth are condemned and emphasis is laid on equity, simplicity, and communal harmony. These social goals were the guiding principle for all social, political, and economic institutions in Asian societies.

Tenure in an Asian Perspective

The predominant tenure system in Asia was communal tenure. In this system, whole communities owned a resource and had communal rights to its use. They managed the resource through local institutions that set their own rules for resource use. Within the community, tenure was granted to individuals, a household, or a clan. In the case of land a communal tenure system may divide the whole land into small plots and grant use rights on an individual basis. This system works like a private property system in which individuals can exercise the right to exclude other individuals from their plot of land.

Tenure could also be extended to naturally growing resources on communal land, without allowing for cultivation. For example, in northern Pakistan, under the communal tenure system over forest, members of the community exercised the right to harvest herbs and grasses or collect fuelwood for subsistence. Collection of resources was not allowed for commercial purpose; resources could only be collected for subsistence use.

Individual property rights were very frequently traded or sold. For example, a member of the community who did not live in the community area and thus did not use the resources could trade his right of use to other individuals. In some cases, communal rights were granted to only those members who lived in the community. Resident status was also defined using various other criteria. For example, members living permanently outside the community could have resident status (and the rights this conferred on them) if they owned a house within the community area, or their livestock grazed on the community pasture.

Rights were defined for water and pastures. These resources were managed in the same way (i.e., by defining criteria for exclusion and inclusion). Often these rights were based on very old traditions. For example, in northern Pakistan, communities managed irrigation water through a system that dated back at least four hundred years.

Rights to use of wildlife were also very complex. For example, in Wakhan, Afghanistan, hunting was allowed but only for certain members of the community. However, if a hunter killed an animal and other non-hunting community members arrived at the scene, they had the right to claim a share of the meat. This arrangement was probably devised to ensure a degree of equity in access to the benefits from wild game.

In some cases tenure systems over some resources changed seasonally. Mostly of the privately held agriculture land, in the central Asian mountain communities, became an open access resource after the harvesting season. During this time, livestock grazed freely on anybody's land and individuals did not have the right to fence their land in order to stop communal livestock from grazing. This system reflected the adaptation made to fight shortage of livestock feed in these communities and the relative role livestock played in the economy.

The predominant tenure system in Asia was communal tenure. In this system, whole communities owned a resource and had communal rights to its use.

Management of Tenure— The Traditional Advantage

Matters relating to tenure were usually managed by a traditional village committee, made up of village elders. The main function was to resolve conflicts and disputes, and provide a fair and inexpensive judicial system that was sensitive to the prevailing climate of social, economic, and ecological values. Access to a quick and fair system of conflict resolution avoided the chances of resource degradation, as a resource that was under an unclear or conflicting tenure arrangement encouraged resource degradation.

In most of the Asian rural communities, the village-level committee formed an efficient and inexpensive management system, entailing coordination of resource use, implementation of mutually agreed upon laws, and adaptation in tenure arrangement as needed. It was inexpensive due to its low transaction costs—the costs incurred in keeping a resource under control and keeping a tenure system functional. In the case of communal tenure systems, evolved from within the communities and carrying the sensitivities and views of whole communities, compliance was voluntary, thus incurring very little transaction cost. Due to a low rate of violation and fairly secure control over communal resources, very few resources were wasted, thus making the system economically efficient.

Transformation of Asia

In the last quarter century, Asian values and institutions have been subject to transformation. This transformation has been caused by both internal and external, social, ideological, and economic forces. Among external forces, have been the rise of the global economy and global culture, each with its own distinct set of values, making them important factors in the equation. Due to technological advancement at the global scale, linking of local economies with the global economy has become inevitable. The exposure to global culture has inspired many Asian cultures to take on values that conflict with traditional Asian values. The new values promote self interest over communal interest, pursuit of material wealth, and less regard for resource sustainability. In most cases, this exposure to alien values was not voluntary, but forced upon Asian societies.

Colonization of Asia by the industrially advanced and wealthy Europe in the middle of the nineteenth century played a significant role in forcing a change and breakdown in local values and institutions. Perhaps the most drastic change was forced in the institution of property rights.

Several Land Alienation Acts and Land Ordinances were passed in colonial Asia in the name of 'public interest' and 'security'. These laws were imposed on all natural resources including farmland, wasteland, forests, fisheries, and wildlife. Under these pieces of legislation tenure of natural resources passed from local communities to the government. Any remaining property judged communal was managed under rules defined by the colonial legislation. Ownership of agricultural land was concentrated in the hands of local people loyal to the colonial powers.

The goal of colonial tenure policy was completely opposite to that of pre-colonial Asia: it was to exploit natural resources, to generate the material resources necessary to expand the empire deep into new geographical areas in order to further continue resource extraction. Such a process helped create a status quo in support of colonial rule.

Not surprisingly, imposed tenure policies never gained legitimacy amongst the majority of local people, nor could they be effectively enforced. As a result, traditional and customary tenure systems continued to exist, albeit 'illegally' and with weakened authority.

Asia Becomes Independent

After independence and the emergence of new sovereign states, no significant changes were made to the colonial system of tenure. No attempt was made to reintroduce and legalize the customary and traditional tenure systems.

The single most important reason in keeping with the status quo was that new states wished to pursue a goal of economic growth through industrialization. Such a process was based on the import of machinery and expertise from the west. The nations of Asia financed this goal principally through the continuing sale and non-sustainable exploitation of natural resources.

Until recently, conservation of resources did not fit with the economic development goal of many countries. In fact, some countries regarded conservation as counter-productive to the efforts of economic development. Therefore, State-defined tenure systems over natural resources did not take conservation measures into account. Natural resources continued to be exploited on a non-sustainable basis either to earn much needed hard currency to pay interest on huge foreign debts or to fuel import substitutions industrialization.

Current Situation

Today there are four types of common property rights regimes in Asia. These are:

- open access,
- communal property,
- private [property], and
- State property.

Open access resource is usually a public good (e.g., water bodies, parks and mountains that are accessed by all segments of public). It is essentially a system in which rights are not defined. Most open access resources, however, are State property, but without a management regime—it is a laissez faire system. Historically, most of the open access resources were under communal tenure and were later alienated from local people.

In management terms, the communal property regime is perhaps the most common property regime in Asia. In communal property, a resource is controlled by a community, who can exclude non-community members and regulate use. Most of this management is considered 'illegal' as communities do not have formal title to these resources. The resources over which communities extend their communal property rights are, in legal terms, under either a State property or an open access regime—both formally owned by the State. Communities in Asia continue to deny the State's encroachment on their resources and struggle to keep their traditional systems alive in order to protect their livelihoods. The State, on the other hand, exerts its pressure to keep control over these resources. It is this state community conflict that forms the core of tenure and resource sustainability debate in Asia. This conflict is nowhere more intense than in State-run protected areas.

Legally, State property is the most common type of property regime in Asia, all of wildlife and most of the forest and rangeland falls under the State property regime. The State owns these resources and all rights to access and use are vested exclusively in the State. Part of this State control over resources evolved in to the Protected Area Management System (PAMS). Very few natural wild resources are held under private property regimes.

Tenure and Management of Protected Areas

The protected area management system was first introduced in 1960 in Asia. The thinking behind the system was laudable enough, shadowing conventional attitudes towards conservation prevalent at the time. Governments sought, through legislation, to reduce the pressure of resource use in natural areas, principally by excluding people and removing their rights to tenure. Laws were drafted on the central assumption that human activity in sensitive areas was necessarily destructive. Unfortunately, in most cases, this assumption proved correct. However, the underlying reason for the failure of PAMS was not the resource use method of local communities, but the effects flowing from a bad law.

For the efficient management of a tenure system, transaction costs have to be lower than the benefits received from the resource. Experience demonstrates that low transaction costs are achieved through equitable management. Equity does not mean that resource users get equal shares, but it does mean that management of a tenure system is consistent with social standards for representations, distribution, openness, and conflict resolution. PAMS meets none of these criteria because it has an inherent notion of illegitimacy in the eyes of the local people, who encourage non-compliance with its management system.

Due to weak government control illegal activities such as poaching, hunting, and felling thrive. This has resulted in driving some species of wildlife to the verge of extinction. Illegal poaching and hunting are a direct result of weak State enforcement capacity and absence of communal control. Poachers from outside come in and take animals without checks. Most states in Asia have fully fledged national parks departments. These departments consume scarce government resources without actually achieving their objectives—sustaining biodiversity of the protected areas. High transaction costs of PAMS and no apparent benefits render their management inefficient [states Berkes].

> "The sustainable use of natural capital will be facilitated by those property rights regimes capable of responding to feed back from natural capital. . . A systems view of the difference between common property and open access systems. Common property systems have two way feedback between the resource, the regime, and the institution. These linkages enable institutions (rules in use) to regulate resource use. In the case of open access systems however, there are no institutions to respond to signals from the resources and no negative feedback (stabilizing feedback) or rules to regulate use. The result is that open access system tend to turn into positive feedback loops (vicious circles) whereby resource depletion leads to more intensified use, which leads to more depletion."

State of the Asian Forests

State forests in Asia are mainly managed by providing concessions, licenses, and quotas to private, non-local operators. These operators could be national or international timber companies, fishing fleets, or mining companies. It is no surprise that run at a profit seeking commercial enterprises, the motive of these concession holders is economic efficiency and productivity gains, with no regard to the sustainability of resource extraction. The situation is further exacerbated as companies prefer to have short-term concessions. The companies want only short–term rights because of their obvious lack of interest in the long-term future of the resource. Then there are problems of actually monitoring the compliance with the terms and conditions of the concessions (i.e., the rights granted for resource extraction). With poor management structure, inadequate capacity, and pervasive corruption in the State governance systems, short-term rights act as a strong incentive for illegal resource extraction.

If forest cover is taken as a proxy indicator of biodiversity richness, Asian countries have suffered significantly.

If forest cover is taken as a proxy indicator of biodiversity richness, Asian countries have suffered significantly. Loss of forest cover has a direct bearing on biodiversity. Habitat destruction is the number one cause of biodiversity loss. Both national and international logging companies have cleared a large part of the natural forest in the insular Southeast Asia (Brunei, Indonesia, Malaysia, the Philippines, Papua New Guinea) and continental Southeast Asia (Cambodia, Laos, Burma, Thailand, Vietnam).

It is estimated that at the turn of the century two-thirds of Thailand were covered under forest of remarkable ecological diversity. Now it has only 15 percent of the total land area under patchy forest cover. Indonesia is second only to Brazil in tropical forest area. It harbors a rich range of fauna and flora and has the largest mammal diversity on earth with 515 species. The country is continuously plagued by conflicts between State and local people, with the end result of forest and biodiversity degradation. In 1934, 57 percent of the Philippines was covered by forest. By 1980, this figure had fallen to 20 percent. A report from the Interpress Third World News Agency (IPS) states that according to a study carried out by the FAO on Asian tropical forests, in 1980 the rate of deforestation was estimated at two million hectares per year. In 1990, this rate had almost doubled to 3.9 million hectares per year. This is 50 percent more than the loss rate for Latin America.

The case of illegal logging and smuggling of wood in the South-east Asian region is the biggest example of how short–term, centrally administered property rights lead directly to the unsustainable use of forest in a region. The forests of Southeast Asia are not being degraded by the logging companies alone. The local communities, who continue to deny the government-imposed tenure structure, also engage in 'illegal activities'. Lack of government capacity to carefully govern the State property rights regime has rendered most of the areas as de facto open access. The result of this is devastating. The communities who once used the forest and its resources, and managed it for its long-term future, can no longer do this even among themselves. Their communal regimes and management systems have been undermined by State institutions, creating an incentive for the community and its individual members to extract as much as possible from the resources within an uncertain time frame.

All this happened not only because of the type of tenure, but as IPS puts it,

> "The Asian Development Bank said a macroeconomic and inter-sectoral approach to forestry is crucial because deforestation is linked to rural poverty, population growth, agricultural practices, the development of infrastructure and alternative livelihood options and energy policies".

The ADB also said that

> "(it) will support fuelwood production by local communities and farmers by promoting incentives such as land use reforms, security of property rights and alternative energy sources and by restricting access to previously 'free' resources".

Paradigm Shift

In most cases nationalization of resources in Asia has resulted in social dislocation and resource degradation. Governments are beginning to realize that excluding people has done more damage to resources than conserving. Nepal nationalized its forest in 1957 to combat desertification. Communal rights of locals were denied, but new tenure regimes could not be enforced. As a result, locals saw the forest as an open access resource and the rate of deforestation increased. Later, government recreated communal property rights in 1976. This introduced a new compromise approach to forest management in Asia-social forestry. Social forestry is essentially a new tenure arrangement over resources that are co-managed by the

State and community. This approach gained currency in Asia, especially in the rural mountain communities, and social forestry is now practiced in Bhutan, China, India, Nepal, Pakistan, and Central Asian States.

The experience of co-management in social forestry has so far proved to be very successful although limited in scale. Its success has prompted governments to test the co-management approach in other resources areas as well. The most important example comes from Northern Pakistan, where government has given partial ownership of wildlife to the community, who manages it on a sustainable basis.

Conclusion

Conservation, sustainability, and sustainable use are concepts for the long term. Implicit in these terms is society's continued interest and stake in the access, use, and flow of resources. Uncertainty of access to resources undermines this long-term view. Uncertainty breeds chaos, which leads to uncoordinated behaviors in human society. Coordination plays a central role in keeping social stability and ensures long-term endurance of human society. It begins with identification of collective goals, setting of roles and responsibilities among different players, and putting in place a mechanism for accountability. Coordination and accountability are governed by social institutions. The institution that facilitates accountability in the use of resources is property rights or tenure.

At the interface between natural resource exploitation and conservation are local people. Historically rights of tenure have been handed down through generations, a line of custodianship that safeguarded the local biodiversity while enabling people to sustainably exploit the natural resources around them.

Man is an entrepreneurial explorer with a gift for inventing and exploiting technology. As we have seen, the arrival of colonial powers in previously balanced agrarian societies led to a breakdown in local tenure rights and opened up natural resources to exploitation for reasons other than survival and small-scale trade. The rights and responsibilities of tenure were removed from people and centralized within government. Without properly monitored contracts, this diffusion of power created a vacuum that both commercial interests and local people filled, each 'illegally' exploiting resources within an increasingly short and desperate time frame. Pressures from the global market place, population growth, and corrupt governments all combine to make natural resources more vulnerable and rarer than ever and the need for action increasingly urgent.

For a management system to be economically efficient, control over resources should be secure. In the case of State property, the system lacks secure control over resources and makes transaction costs high, while management becomes inefficient as resources are wasted and degraded.

It will be a long haul to get centralized, bureaucratic administrations to hand back custodianship of natural resources to local people. The ownership of tenure is a powerful tool, one that governments have used to build societies.

2

Forests

A

Documents and Instruments Relating to Forests

In the absence of a global convention protecting all types of forests and governing acts relating to forest degradation, the most important international instrument negotiated so far is the international tropical timber agreement administered by the ITTO. Even though the scope of this treaty has been extended, in recent times, there is considerable dispute over its current operation and scope. Therefore, it is important to look at the sections of Agenda 21 related to forests and the "Non-Legally Binding Authoritative Statement of Principles for a Global Consensus on the Management, Conservation and Sustainable Development of All Types of Forests" (The Forests Principles) extracted below. The text of Agenda 21, Chapter 11: Deforestation, was largely agreed upon prior to the Earth Summit. During the lead up period there grew increasing debate regarding the desirability of a binding treaty on forests. The push against such a convention was lead by Developing Countries who argued that such a convention was contrary to their sovereign rights over such resources. The Forest Principles, extracted below, represents the compromise document which resulted from this North-South polarization.

Following the Earth Summit, the Commission on Sustainable Development (CSD) took over from the ECOSOC in a period of "Post-Rio" confidence building. This was designed to support and encourage emerging North-South partnerships in an attempt to facilitate the implementation of the Forest Principles and to work towards the implementation of "appropriate legal mechanisms" in the future. The outcomes of this confidence building are manifested in the intergovernmental panel on forests (IPF) and an intergovernmental forum on forests (IFF). However, despite the work of these bodies, no clear consensus emerged.

In October 2000, ECOSOC established a new permanent body, the United Nations Forum on Forests (UNFF) designed to build upon the IPF and the IFF. Participants in the organisational meeting for this new body shared the view that the UNFF would facilitate and monitor the progress of the implementation of IPF/IFF proposals.

(i) United Nations, "Chapter 11: Combating Deforestation," *Agenda 21 Programme of Action for Sustainable Development*, Rio de Janeiro, Brazil, A/CONF.151/26 (Vol. II), 13 August 1992

[*Each Chapter of Agenda 21 is separated into various program areas that focus on particular areas of concern. Within each program area, there are a number of sub-headings. The Basis for Action is the first of these. Each of the four program area headings and its Basis for Action are extracted below. The other headings deal with Objectives, Activities and Means of Implementation.*]

Sustaining the Multiple Roles and Functions of All Types of Forests, Forest Lands and Woodlands

Basis for Action

There are major weaknesses in the policies, methods and mechanisms adopted to support and develop the multiple ecological, economic, social and cultural roles of trees, forests and forest lands. Many developed countries are confronted with the effects of air pollution and fire damage on their forests. More effective measures and approaches are often required at the national level to improve and harmonize policy formulation, planning and programming; legislative measures and instruments; development patterns; participation of the general public, especially women and indigenous people; involvement of youth; roles of the private sector, local organizations, non-governmental organizations and cooperatives; development of technical and multidisciplinary skills and quality of human resources; forestry extension and public education; research capability and support; administrative structures and mechanisms, including intersectoral coordination, decentralization and responsibility and incentive systems; and dissemination of information and public relations. This is especially important to ensure a rational and holistic approach to the sustainable and environmentally sound development of forests. The need for securing the multiple roles of forests and forest lands through adequate and appropriate institutional strengthening has been repeatedly emphasized in many of the reports, decisions and recommendations of Food and Agricultural Organization, International Tropical Timber Organization, UNEP, the World Bank, IUCN and other organizations.

Enhancing the Protection, Sustainable Management and Conservation of All Forests, and the Greening of Degraded Areas, Through Forest Rehabilitation, Afforestation, Reforestation and Other Rehabilitative Means

Basis for Action

Forests worldwide have been and are being threatened by uncontrolled degradation and conversion to other types of land uses, influenced by increasing human needs; agricultural expansion; and environmentally harmful mismanagement, including, for example, lack of adequate forest-fire control and anti-poaching measures, unsustainable commercial logging, overgrazing and unregulated browsing, harmful effects of airborne pollutants, economic incentives, and other measures taken by other sectors of the economy. The impacts of loss and degradation of forests are in the form of soil erosion; loss of biological diversity, damage to wildlife habitats and degradation of watershed areas, deterioration of the quality of life and reduction of the options for development.

The present situation calls for urgent and consistent action for conserving and sustaining forest resources. The greening of suitable areas, in all its component activities, is an effective way of increasing public awareness and participation in protecting and managing forest resources. It should include the consideration of land use and tenure patterns and local needs and should spell out and clarify the specific objectives of the different types of greening activities.

Objectives

The objectives of this programme area are as follows:

...(e) To facilitate and support the effective implementation of the non-legally binding authoritative statement of principles for a global consensus on the management, conservation and sustainable development of all types of forests, adopted by the United Nations Conference on Environment and Development, and on the basis of the implementation of these principles to consider the need for and the feasibility of all kinds of appropriate internationally agreed arrangements to promote international cooperation on forest management, conservation and sustainable development of all types of forests, including afforestation, reforestation and rehabilitation...

Promoting Efficient Utilization and Assessment to Recover the Full Valuation of the Goods and Services Provided by Forests, Forest Lands and Woodlands

Basis for Action

The vast potential of forests and forest lands as a major resource for development is not yet fully realized. The improved management of forests can increase the production of goods and services and, in particular, the yield of wood and non-wood forest products, thus helping to generate additional employment and income, additional value through processing and trade of forest products, increased contribution to foreign exchange earnings, and increased return on investment. Forest resources, being renewable, can be sustainably managed in a manner that is compatible with environmental conservation. The implications of the harvesting of forest resources for the other values of the forest should be taken fully into consideration in the development of forest policies. It is also possible to increase the value of forests through non-damaging uses such as eco-tourism and the managed supply of genetic materials. Concerted action is needed in order to increase people's perception of the value of forests and of the benefits they provide. The survival of forests and their continued contribution to human welfare depends to a great extent on succeeding in this endeavor.

The greening of suitable areas, in all its component activities, is an effective way of increasing public awareness and participation in protecting and managing forest resources.

Establishing and/or Strengthening Capacities for the Planning, Assessment and Systematic Observations of Forests and Related Programs, Projects and Activities, Including Commercial Trade and Processes

Basis for Action

Assessment and systematic observations are essential components of long-term planning, for evaluating effects, quantitatively and qualitatively, and for rectifying inadequacies. This mechanism, however, is one of the often neglected aspects of forest resources, management, conservation and development. In many cases, even the basic information related to the area and type of forests, existing potential and volume of harvest is lacking. In many developing countries, there is a lack of structures and mechanisms to carry out these functions. There is an urgent need to rectify this situation for a better understanding of the role and importance of forests and to realistically plan for their effective conservation, management, regeneration, and sustainable development.

(ii) United Nations, "Non-Legally Binding Authoritative Statement of Principles for a Global Consensus on the Management, Conservation and Sustainable Development of All Types of Forests," *Report of the United Nations Conference on Environment and Development*, A/CONF.151/26 (Vol. III), Rio de Janeiro, 1992

[*This document, known commonly as the Forest Principles, was one of the documents produced at Rio. It followed a global debate on the efficacy of a global binding treaty which brought about no concrete results. There was much controversy associated with the Forest Principles particularly due to its status as a "Non-Legally Binding Authoritative Statement of Principles" as opposed to a binding instrument requiring both action and obligation. The embryonic nature of this area is noted in the section of the Preamble extracted below. This is followed by the complete text of the principles.*]

PREAMBLE

...(d) These principles reflect a first global consensus on forests. In committing themselves to the prompt implementation of these principles, countries also decide to keep them under assessment for their adequacy with regard to further international cooperation on forest issues...

PRINCIPLES/ELEMENTS

1. (a) States have, in accordance with the Charter of the United Nations and the principles of international law, the sovereign right to exploit their own resources pursuant to their own environmental policies and have the responsibility to ensure that activities within their jurisdiction or control do not cause damage to the environment of other States or of areas beyond the limits of national jurisdiction.

   (b) The agreed full incremental cost of achieving benefits associated with forest conservation and sustainable development requires increased international cooperation and should be equitably shared by the international community.

2. (a) States have the sovereign and inalienable right to utilize, manage and develop their forests in accordance with their development needs and level of socio-economic development and on the basis of national policies consistent with sustainable development and legislation, including the conversion of such areas for other uses within the overall socioeconomic development plan and based on rational land-use policies.

   (b) Forest resources and forest lands should be sustainably managed to meet the social, economic, ecological, cultural and spiritual needs of present and future generations. These needs are for forest products and services, such as wood and wood products, water, food, fodder, medicine, fuel, shelter, employment, recreation, habitats for wildlife, landscape diversity, carbon sinks and reservoirs, and for other forest products. Appropriate measures should be taken to protect forests against harmful effects of pollution, including airborne pollution, fires, pests and diseases, in order to maintain their full multiple value.

   (c) The provision of timely, reliable and accurate information on forests and forest ecosystems is essential for public understanding and informed decision making and should be ensured.

   (d) Governments should promote and provide opportunities for the participation of interested parties, including local communities and indigenous people, industries, labor, nongovernmental organizations and individuals, forest dwellers and women, in the development, implementation and planning of national forest policies.

3. (a) National policies and strategies should provide a framework for increased efforts, including the development and strengthening of institutions and programs for the management, conservation and sustainable development of forests and forest lands.
   (b) International institutional arrangements, building on those organizations and mechanisms already in existence, as appropriate, should facilitate international cooperation in the field of forests.
   (c) All aspects of environmental protection and social and economic development as they relate to forests and forest lands should be integrated and comprehensive.
4. The vital role of all types of forests in maintaining the ecological processes and balance at the local, national, regional and global levels through, inter alia, their role in protecting fragile ecosystems, watersheds and freshwater resources and as rich storehouses of biodiversity and biological resources and sources of genetic material for biotechnology products, as well as photosynthesis, should be recognized.
5. (a) National forest policies should recognize and duly support the identity, culture and the rights of indigenous people, their communities and other communities and forest dwellers. Appropriate conditions should be promoted for these groups to enable them to have an economic stake in forest use, perform economic activities, and achieve and maintain cultural identity and social organization, as well as adequate levels of livelihood and well-being, through, inter alia, those land tenure arrangements which serve as incentives for the sustainable management of forests.
   (b) The full participation of women in all aspects of the management, conservation and sustainable development of forests should be actively promoted.
6. (a) All types of forests play an important role in meeting energy requirements through the provision of a renewable source of bio-energy, particularly in developing countries, and the demands for fuelwood for household and industrial needs should be met through sustainable forest management, afforestation and reforestation. To this end, the potential contribution of plantations of both indigenous and introduced species for the provision of both fuel and industrial wood should be recognized.
   (b) National policies and programs should take into account the relationship, where it exists, between the conservation, management and sustainable development of forests and all aspects related to the production, consumption, recycling and/or final disposal of forest products.
   (c) Decisions taken on the management, conservation and sustainable development of forest resources should benefit, to the extent practicable, from a comprehensive assessment of economic and non-economic values of forest goods and services and of the environmental costs and benefits. The development and improvement of methodologies or such evaluations should be promoted.
   (d) The role of planted forests and permanent agricultural crops as sustainable and environmentally sound sources of renewable energy and industrial raw material should be recognized, enhanced and promoted. Their contribution to the maintenance of ecological processes, to offsetting pressure on primary/old-growth forest and to providing regional employment and development with the adequate involvement of local inhabitants should be recognized and enhanced.
   (e) Natural forests also constitute a source of goods and services, and their conservation, sustainable management and use should be promoted.
7. (a) Efforts should be made to promote a supportive international economic climate conducive to sustained and environmentally sound development of forests in all countries, which include, inter alia, the promotion of

sustainable patterns of production and consumption, the eradication of poverty and the promotion of food security.

(b) Specific financial resources should be provided to developing countries with significant forest areas which establish programmes for the conservation of forests including protected natural forest areas. These resources should be directed notably to economic sectors which would stimulate economic and social substitution activities.

8. (a) Efforts should be undertaken towards the greening of the world. All countries, notably developed countries, should take positive and transparent action towards reforestation, afforestation and forest conservation, as appropriate.

The efforts of developing countries to strengthen the management, conservation and sustainable development of their forest resources should be supported by the international community.

(b) Efforts to maintain and increase forest cover and forest productivity should be undertaken in ecologically, economically and socially sound ways through the rehabilitation, reforestation and re-establishment of trees and forests on unproductive, degraded and deforested lands, as well as through the management of existing forest resources.

(c) The implementation of national policies and programmes aimed at forest management, conservation and sustainable development, particularly in developing countries, should be supported by international financial and technical cooperation, including the private sector, where appropriate.

(d) Sustainable forest management and use should be carried out in accordance with national development policies and priorities and on the basis of environmentally sound national guidelines. In the formulation of such guidelines, account should be taken, as appropriate and if applicable, of relevant internationally agreed methodologies and criteria.

(e) Forest management should be integrated with management of adjacent areas so as to maintain ecological balance and sustainable productivity.

(f) National policies and/or legislation aimed at management, conservation and sustainable development of forests should include the protection of ecologically viable representative or unique examples of forests, including primary/old-growth forests, cultural, spiritual, historical, religious and other unique and valued forests of national importance.

(g) Access to biological resources, including genetic material, shall be with due regard to the sovereign rights of the countries where the forests are located and to the sharing of mutually agreed terms of technology and profits from biotechnology products that are derived from these resources.

(h) National policies should ensure that environmental impact assessments should be carried out where actions are likely to have significant adverse impacts on important forest resources, and where such actions are subject to a decision of a competent national authority.

9. (a) The efforts of developing countries to strengthen the management, conservation and sustainable development of their forest resources should be supported by the international community, taking into account the importance of redressing external indebtedness, particularly where aggravated by the net transfer of resources to developed countries, as well as the problem of achieving at least the replacement value of forests through improved market access for forest products, especially processed products. In this respect, special attention should also be given to the countries undergoing the process of transition to market economies.

(b) The problems that hinder efforts to attain the conservation and sustainable use of forest resources and that stem from the lack of alternative options available to local communities, in particular the urban poor and poor rural populations who are economically and socially dependent on forests and forest resources, should be addressed by Governments and the international community.

(c) National policy formulation with respect to all types of forests should take account of the pressures and demands imposed on forest ecosystems and resources from influencing factors outside the forest sector, and intersectoral means of dealing with these pressures and demands should be sought.

10. New and additional financial resources should be provided to developing countries to enable them to sustainably manage, conserve and develop their forest resources, including through afforestation, reforestation and combating deforestation and forest and land degradation.

11. In order to enable, in particular, developing countries to enhance their endogenous capacity and to better manage, conserve and develop their forest resources, the access to and transfer of environmentally sound technologies and corresponding know-how on favorable terms, including on concessional and preferential terms, as mutually agreed, in accordance with the relevant provisions of Agenda 21, should be promoted, facilitated and financed, as appropriate.

12. (a) Scientific research, forest inventories and assessments carried out by national institutions which take into account, where relevant, biological, physical, social and economic variables, as well as technological development and its application in the field of sustainable forest management, conservation and development, should be strengthened through effective modalities, including international cooperation. In this context, attention should also be given to research and development of sustainably harvested non-wood products.

(b) National and, where appropriate, regional and international institutional capabilities in education, training, science, technology, economics, anthropology and social aspects of forests and forest management are essential to the conservation and sustainable development of forests and should be strengthened.

(c) International exchange of information on the results of forest and forest management research and development should be enhanced and broadened, as appropriate, making full use of education and training institutions, including those in the private sector.

(d) Appropriate indigenous capacity and local knowledge regarding the conservation and sustainable development of forests should, through institutional and financial support and in collaboration with the people in the local communities concerned, be recognized, respected, recorded, developed and, as appropriate, introduced in the implementation of programs. Benefits arising from the utilization of indigenous knowledge should therefore be equitably shared with such people.

13. (a) Trade in forest products should be based on non-discriminatory and multilaterally agreed rules and procedures consistent with international trade law and practices. In this context, open and free international trade in forest products should be facilitated.

(b) Reduction or removal of tariff barriers and impediments to the provision of better market access and better prices for higher value-added forest products and their local processing should be encouraged to enable producer countries to better conserve and manage their renewable forest resources.

(c) Incorporation of environmental costs and benefits into market forces and mechanisms, in order to achieve forest conservation and sustainable development, should be encouraged both domestically and internationally.

(d) Forest conservation and sustainable development policies should be integrated with economic, trade and other relevant policies.

(e) Fiscal, trade, industrial, transportation and other policies and practices that may lead to forest degradation should be avoided. Adequate policies, aimed at management, conservation and sustainable development of forests, including, where appropriate, incentives, should be encouraged.

14. Unilateral measures, incompatible with international obligations or agreements, to restrict and/or ban international trade in timber or other forest products should be removed or avoided, in order to attain long-term sustainable forest management.

15. Pollutants, particularly air-borne pollutants, including those responsible for acidic deposition, that are harmful to the health of forest ecosystems at the local, national, regional and global levels should be controlled.

B

Tarasofsky R.G., "Assessing the International Forest Regime: Gaps, Overlaps, Uncertainties and Opportunities," in Richard Tarasofsky (ed), *Assessing the International Forest Regime,* IUCN Environmental Policy and Law Paper No. 37, IUCN, Gland Switzerland, 1999, pp 3–12

Options and Dilemmas

It is beyond dispute that [the] current international forest regime, as a whole, is not having the effect it should. It is not creating the conditions for national, sub-national and private actors to ensure the conservation, sustainable management and sustainable development of all types of forests. It does not sufficiently provide for the means for achieving this objective, for example:

- clear rules and measurable standards,
- appropriate financing and positive incentives,
- technology transfer,
- consensus on a bottom up and holistic approach,
- coordination between institutions and policies at all levels, and
- a permanent forum for dialogue and equitable resolution of conflicts.

Does this mean that the only solution is a new global convention on forests? It is argued in some quarters that the fragmentation of the international forest regime is such that a new convention on forests is the best means to establish coherence. However, this matter is rather complex.

IUCN–The World Conservation Union is neither for nor against the *per se* establishment of a new convention. Rather its primary concern is the conservation of the integrity and diversity of nature and the use of natural resources in a manner that is equitable and ecologically sustainable, and therefore is in favor of an international forest regime which most effectively supports this end, whatever the form. That said, IUCN cannot be oblivious to the risks of undertaking negotiations on a new legal instrument at this time:

- The complex negotiations will be lengthy, and consume significant financial and technical resources from all countries thereby possibly slowing much needed action on the ground. Even if a new instrument is adopted, it may not enter into force quickly, while effective implementation will take even longer.
- The divisions within the international community may lead to a weak set of norms reflecting the lowest common denominator. This risk is particularly significant given the current lack of substantive global consensus on key issues.
- A new instrument may undermine the efforts being taken under the myriad of other instruments and institutions that deal with forest issues.

It is not as if these risks cannot be overcome—they can. But their significance suggests that there is an onus on those advocating a new convention to demonstrate that such an exercise will indeed be worthwhile.

Indeed, a more constructive approach is for matters of substance to be the point of departure. Once effective solutions to forest related problems are identified, it is then possible to consider vehicles for delivering these solutions: e.g., legal instruments and international institutions. Given that we are not beginning from a legal or institutional void—far from it—a key criterion for selecting among the various options is the extent to which they support a synergistic relationship with what already exists. A second, perhaps even more significant, criterion is how conducive the options are to effective implementation on the ground, given the reality that political will to make actual change tends to be less than it ought to be. As the World Commission on Forests and Sustainable Development puts it:

> "[T]here is a crisis of credibility given the myriad [of] international legal agreements that await serious implementation, which could bring significant dividends to forests, and given that the global compact based on one earth, one world, a common future envisaged in the Earth Summit, is far from being a political reality."

Although one may intuitively concur with the World Commission's opinion, the international forest regime is complex, where both successes and failures regarding implementation have taken place. An objective analysis of which aspects of precisely which treaties and programmes are having an impact, and why or why not, would be very useful indeed. Indeed, it is hoped that this book will provide a basis for this next necessary phase of analysts.

Finally, it must be emphasized that even perfect international legal instruments and institutions will not be sufficient in themselves to bring about the necessary change. These entities are inherently flawed by the fact that they tend not to involve all the major stakeholders in a meaningful way. By focusing mainly on the governmental level, especially for the formulation of their mandates, but also for their implementation, the traditional international legal system is not conducive for creating the effective public-private partnerships that are essential for dealing with current forest problems. Indeed, it is sobering to consider that despite the lack of progress at the international policy level, some elements of the private sector have proceeded to break new ground by giving effect to norms which are still "emerging" at the governmental level.

Reviewing the Current International Forest Regime

The following draws on and builds upon some key points made by the contributors to this book. A more exhaustive treatment of each of these issues, and others, is to be found in the individual chapters.

Moving Forward from the IPF Proposals for Action

...*Prima facie,* the IPF Proposals for Action can, in principle, provide helpful guidance in the implementation of relevant treaties, since these treaties tend to contain general obligations of result rather than detailed instructions on how these results are to be achieved. However desirable this potential for synergy might appear to be, in reality there are at least three key obstacles to achieving it. The first is that the IPF Proposals themselves are not always explicit as to how they relate to existing instruments. Secondly, many of the IPF Proposals are neither specific enough nor reflect a true international consensus so as to be easily implementable. Third, several treaties are currently at early stages of implementation and key points of controversy in the IPF are also reflected in these instruments.

There is, however, enough of a basis to begin building synergies. As such, Dr. Skala-Kuhmann makes a number of recommendations aimed at national and international levels. Because many actions required for achieving the necessary synergies are country-specific, national forest programs (NFPs), or their equivalent, should be the organizing framework for implementation of the IPF Proposals and relevant treaty obligations. This will entail, as first step, coordinating NFPs with the treaty requirements to prepare national biodiversity and desertification strategies, as well as national strategies to deal with climate change. Meanwhile, at international level, governing bodies of relevant treaties and institutions should focus more clearly on how they should relate to each other, and should provide increased guidance and support for synergistic implementation. Other key actions to be done at the national level include coordinating information and reporting systems, so as to support a more coordinated approach at the international level.

Existing Instruments and Institutions

The approach taken in this book is to examine all relevant global instruments and institutions so as to identity, where possible, the following:

- The mandate of each institution and its relationship to the conservation and sustainable management of forests;
- The forest and forestry-related programmes and the human and financial resources for these programs;
- The strength and weakness of each institution with respect to matters such as the technical expertise of staff, financial resources, and political support for its mandate;
- The potential for future success and the identification of obstacles that might block progress on implementation of forest related programs or obligations.

International Legal Instruments

The [scope of] the *Convention on Biological Diversity* (CBD) is...such that it could encompass most, if not all, issues relating to the conservation and sustainable use of forests. However, the nature of the CBD, i.e., not being self-executing—and the design of its mechanisms mean that sufficient political will and commitment at both national and international levels is necessary [to] give effect to its full legal promise. The history of the Debate on forests within the CBD reveals that obstacles at various stages have prevented the harnessing of this will.

Some of these obstacles have to do with differing visions among Parties about the convention itself, while others have to do with the fact that the relationship between the CBD and the IPF/IFF has not been fully defined. This latter ambiguity has, to some extent, led to a kind of perverse "competition" between the two, where progress in one is prevented by the existence of the other. It is also the case that the fundamental disagreement about desirability of a new convention on forests has had the unfortunate result of some countries preventing the CBD from developing to its full potential, for fear that this might undermine their case.

The main output in relation to forests of the CBD process so far is the work program on forest biodiversity. But the content of this program in that it concentrates mainly on information gathering, research and coordination, rather than substantive measures, is not action oriented (at least in its first phase), again reflecting the fundamental ambiguities surrounding the role of the CBD. It remains to be seen how effective this work program will be, given that there is no explicit role laid out for secretariat, and given that the Conference of the Parties (COP) has declined so far to establish a technical panel on forest issues. Although the CBD COP will review progress made on its various thematic work programmes at its next meeting in 2000, the COP will only pay particular focus to forest biodiversity at its 6th meeting, which will take place only in 2001 or 2002, i.e., after the UN Commission on Sustainable Development (CSD) will decide, in 2000, how to follow up on the IFF. This may mean that the CBD will be restricted to a reactive role to whatever is decided by the IFF or the CSD.

David R. Downes examines the remaining global treaties that impact on forests. He begins by considering the *Ramsar Convention* and the *World Heritage Convention*, which impact on the conservation of forests. Both these are shown to be useful, and indeed could be made even more so, but it must be emphasized that even in the best case scenario they will only apply to a relatively small class of forests—mangroves in the former case and forests of outstanding natural or cultural value in the latter. *UNESCO's Biosphere Reserves,* also examined here, are similarly useful instruments, but again limited in scope.

A strong basis for defining equitable rights for indigenous peoples who are forest dwellers or otherwise connected to forests is to be found in *International Labor Organization (ILO) Convention 169*. So far, however, that instrument has not attracted universal support—in fact only a handful of countries are party to it. Another weakness is that it sits uneasily in the framework of the ILO, whose main program is substantively different. The *Draft UN Declaration on the Rights of Indigenous Peoples* may help to build support for certain key norms, but, it is not at all obvious at this stage that the final version of the Declaration will contain sufficiently powerful provisions. The CBD may ultimately prove to be the most effective venue for defining the rights of indigenous forest dwellers, e.g., through its recently created open-ended working group, although it is still too soon to tell. It must be recalled, however, that the wording of Article 8 (J), which addresses indigenous matters, heavily qualifies these rights by making them subject to national legislation.

The examination of the international trading regime suggests some mixed results for forests. On the one hand, some positive synergies may exist between trade liberalization and the conservation, sustainable management and sustainable development of forests. On the other hand, it is evident that trade liberalization can exacerbate the effects of unsustainable management practices in a variety of ways. The legal instruments and institutions only provide a partial answer. Indeed, the debate within the *World Trade Organization* (WTO) on its relationship to the environment, which is far from over, reveals considerable differences between members. Where the WTO has taken clear decisions regarding the environment, primarily in its dispute settlement body, the results have not been favorable to environmental conservation. Furthermore, concerns persist that voluntary incentives for sustainable forest management, such as certification and labeling under the Forest Stewardship Council, may be ruled inconsistent with the WTO. It must be stressed that at present the WTO itself has no specialisation in forest issues and neither do the member representatives tend to have any capacity in this regard, and therefore does not have the capacity to deal with these issues on its own. Nonetheless, by virtue of its active dispute settlement system, the WTO may soon be faced with these issues, i.e., before a normative basis for resolving these conflicts has been fully developed. A more appropriate solution would be to craft a constructive relationship between the WTO and other international environmental instruments and institutions, including those which belong to the international forest regime.

Uncertainty about consistency with the WTO rules also exists in relation to trade measures taken under multilateral environmental agreements. One such agreement, the *Convention on International Trade in Endangered Species of Wild Fauna and Flora (CITES),* is considered an effective tool at controlling trade in endangered species threatened by trade as well as providing a useful framework for managed trade in species which risk is becoming threatened by trade. Although CITES has been applied to tree and woody species, this has not happened consistently or to the Convention's full potential. Nonetheless, the positive experience with the Convention's Timber Working Group suggests that CITES may become more significant for forests in the future, once its full potential to contribute to both conservation and sustainable trade are more widely appreciated.

The *Kyoto Protocol to the Climate Change Convention,* once in force, ought to lead to more forests being conserved and sustainably used. However, this promise must be put into perspective. Firstly, the approach to forests will be based primarily on only one of many values: i.e., how well they store carbon. Secondly, instruments like the Clean Development Mechanism and "joint implementation" will not operate in all countries with forest cover. Thirdly, there are still several fundamental controversies to work out before these instruments become operational. These include the definition of terms like "reforestation", the measurement of baselines, and unexpected "leakage" from projects. It is also not at all clear what the impact on forests of tradeable emission rights will be. Similarly, overall potential of the Kyoto Protocol diminishing the adverse impact of climate change on forests is also clouded by several uncertainties.

By contrast, the challenges faced by the *Desertification Convention* do not tend to include definitional issues, but rather very practical ones. This Convention has considerable potential to assist countries affected by desertification and drought to develop a sustainable ecosystem approach to managing their forests, and other natural resources. Its holistic and grassroots-oriented approach is ambitious and will require a significant financial investment in order to be effective.

International Institutions

...Some of these institutions are members of the *Interagency Task Force on Forests* (ITFF), which was created to support the work of the IPF. Although the ITFF has been a forum for international organisations to meet, and even build partnerships around the IPF Programme Elements, it cannot yet be asserted that it is a comprehensive coordinating mechanism.

Several institutions appear to have recently been, or currently are, at critical turning points. The *UN Food and Agriculture Organisation* (FAO) is one such example. Prior to the *UN Conference on Environment and Development* (UNCED) it held an uncontested leadership role in international policy development, however, several controversies undermined its credibility in the early 1990s. Nonetheless, the FAO remains a critical actor, not least because it is the task manager in the UN System for Chapter 11 of *Agenda 21*, but also because it has reformed significantly over the past few years. In particular, the FAO's reorientation in support of National Forest Programmes is significant, given the central role advocated for such programmes by the IPF. The FAO also has considerable technical resources to provide legal assistance, information dissemination, and analysis, although these resources pale in comparison with other FAO programs. The FAO Committee on Forestry (COFO) may no longer be the central intergovernmental arena for global policy discussions on forests, but as the multilateral forum underpinning the FAO work on forests, it has the potential to send out wider policy signals. In addition, with the FAO's regional forestry commissions and its field-level work, the depth of the FAO's reach surpasses other institutions. A key challenge facing FAO, and indeed the larger international community, is in how best to define its niche and role in relation to other international instruments and institutions relating to forests. This challenge may become more acute once IFF ends.

The *International Tropical Timber Organization* (ITTO) has also reoriented itself following the entry into force in 1997 of the 1994 International Tropical Timber Agreement (ITTA). While some of ITTO's early work was pioneering from the conceptual standpoint, its potential contribution to sustainable forest management suffers from at least two factors. The first is that it is primarily a commodity trade organisation limited to only a portion of global trade and, secondly, the ITTA 1994 was the subject of particularly acrimonious negotiations. The ITTO has recently produced some useful policy guidelines and has adopted its Objective 2000—"enhancing the capacity of members to implement a strategy for achieving exports of tropical timber and timber products from sustainably managed sources by the

The Kyoto Protocol to the Climate Change Convention, once in force, ought to lead to more forests being conserved and sustainably used.

year 2000". But the Organization has been previously criticized for not being able to ensure implementation of these policy developments on the ground. Nonetheless, the creation of the Bali Partnership fund to support the Objective 2000 is a positive step, and so too are some aspects of the recently adopted Libreville Action Plan. Again, though, it remains to be seen how these will be translated into practice. ITTO has an important technical role to play, which if properly harnessed, can help steer the tropical timber trade in a more sustainable direction. At the same time, though, for the reasons mentioned above, it cannot be expected that ITTO will be the venue where global trade and environment issues relating to forests will be decided, even though the ITTO is lead agency for this topic in the IFF.

The United Nations Development Programme's (UNDP) work on forests is largely technical in nature. However, its recently established Programme on Forests can be expected to contribute to better understanding of public-private partnerships for sustainable forest management, strategies, NFPs, and innovative financial mechanisms. This latter topic will usefully contribute to UNDP's work at the IFF on financing issues, for which it is the lead agency. A key strength of UNDP's approach is that it conducts activities at both the field and international levels—with the appropriate feedback loops in place, this can be a powerful combination. UNDP also is strong in providing capacity building, through its Forest Capacity Programme. Perhaps a key challenge for UNDP, in addition to attracting sufficient financial, as well as political, support for its Programme on Forests, is to effectively reconcile its development-centered approach with the ecological values of forests not associated with direct human use and consumption.

The *United Nations Environment Programme* (UNEP) has a relatively modest programme on forests, and given its "catalytic role", mostly undertakes activities in partnership with other organizations and initiatives. Although much of the work is technical, e.g., participating in the development of regional criteria and indicators, UNEP also has an important conceptual role to play. Strengthened by the fact that UNEP usefully integrates its forest related work into its broader biodiversity program, which may allow it to create some interesting policy linkages it is also the lead organization in ITFF for examining underlying causes of deforestation. However, this topic is enormous, and whether UNEP's actual impact will be significant may largely depend upon the financial and technical resources available to it. It also remains to be seen whether UNEP's recent restructuring activities will help raise its effectiveness in relation to forests.

The *World Bank's* role in assisting developing countries in relation to conservation and management of forests is certainly significant if only by virtue of its massive spending power, although it must be noted that the allocation for forest-related work is relatively small. However, the Bank's record has been criticized from several perspectives. Firstly, there are concerns that notwithstanding its 1991 *Forest Policy*, it has not taken a sufficiently cross-sectoral approach to lessening pressures on forests (including from sectors where it also provides significant funding). A second concern is the breadth and depth of consultation procedures with interested and affected parties. Thirdly, it has failed to mainstream global environmental values, such as biodiversity, into its work. However, the Bank has recently undertaken some interesting initiatives, such as its alliance with WWF on protected areas and certification that may prove fruitful. Finally, the Bank is currently reviewing its 1991 Forest Policy, which may lead to a more effective deployment of its human, technical and financial resources.

The *Global Environment Facility* (GEF), as the financial mechanism of CBD and FCCC, is of critical importance not only in relation to the goals of those treaties, but also because it has an operational programme concerning forests. Although the amount of funding available under the GEF was considered by the recent independent evaluation to be small in relation to needs, GEF has been successful in leveraging significant amounts of co-financing.

The potential for the International Monetary Fund's structural adjustment programs to adversely affect forests is briefly noted. Although general points are made about some potentially negative impacts of such programs on forests, this was an area where further research is necessary.

Focusing on the Regional Perspective

There is one region in the world that has a legally binding instrument on forests which is in operation, namely, Central America. While... [it is possible to] identify some successes which the *Central America Forest Convention* can be credited with, it is clear that there are some unique factors in that region that help make this so. One is the overall drive and commitment to regional integration on a host of environment and development issues, which has enjoyed a high political profile. Indeed, [the] *Central American Forest Convention* is to be understood as part of a wider web of legal instruments and institutions and indeed it itself was only developed after a solid legal and institutional foundation had been laid. Secondly, the countries of the region sufficiently like minded in their evolving approach to the management of forests, which involves using incentive measures, rather than simply command and control.

Thirdly, a defining feature of the Central American process has been the heavy involvement of civil society in the decision making. The institutions created by the *Central American Forest Convention*, and other regional environmental treaties, have made meaningful engagement with relevant stakeholders a priority, with the result that working partnerships have been cultivated. In some cases, these institutions have even facilitated the creation of civil society groups with whom it can have dialogue. Given that Central America has used regional treaties to implement global norms in a regionally specific manner. It stands out as a useful model for building synergies between these norms in a constructively participatory manner. This has proven particularly important in the case of forests, which ultimately requires the buy-in of non-State actors if viable solutions are to be found. This is certainly so in Central America, but also elsewhere.

Findings

Given the lack of certainty about the true impact of the current regime, and that it is fluid and continuously evolving, it is difficult to precisely identify gaps, overlaps and opportunities. Nonetheless, some findings are possible.

Gaps

If one considers gaps as lacunae in the law or in the spectrum of institutional mandates as regards their coverage of important forest issues or problems, then several exist in the current international forest regime, although they are of different orders of scale. Of particular importance is that several key underlying causes of deforestation are not covered: e.g. agrarian land reform in relation to landless peasants, environmental aspects of mining, and activities of transnational corporations. Another, perhaps more manageable, gap is the lack of an international mechanism to control illegal trade in forest products. This would be a fairly straightforward matter to address through international law—e.g., through universal agreement on permitting and control schemes. However, this has so far not been attempted.

Overlaps

This book points out some areas where overlaps between the mandates of more than one instrument or institution exist. However, one should not over emphasize the dangers of overlaps, since they, like their mandates, tend to be at the general level. For example, the World Heritage, Ramsar and CBD all cover forest conservation, but each instrument and institution has its own specialized perspective, which can be valuable. The real challenge is to find synergy on the ground in a manner that brings out the strength of each instrument or programme. But this is a challenge that can be overcome, as suggested in the following chapter in this book. Thus, the various requirements to develop national strategies, plans and programmes should be linked where appropriate the onus being on countries themselves to determine how best these should be implemented in their particular contexts. At the international level, it should also be possible to coordinate obligations relating to technology transfer, information exchange and research.

Uncertainties

This book reveals that there are certain important aspects of the international forest regime that are uncertain. At the conceptual level, a key one is international trade, where there currently appears to be significant potential for clashes between rules and principles for trade and those for sustainable development. A second type of uncertainty arises from differences of opinion about the actual meaning of norms or how they should be implemented. One example is the amount of financing that should be provided by the North to the South. Another relates to the entitlements of indigenous peoples dependent on forests. These are fundamental matters; uncertainty about them diminishes the political credibility of the overall regime, and impacts on the ability of national forest authorities to raise the position of forests on the national agenda. However, not all uncertainties are equally problematic. For example, the uncertainty created by the lack of definitions of key concepts, such as "conservation", "sustainable management" and "sustainable development", may not be such a large problem in practice, as discussed below.

Opportunities

The current international forest regime offers considerable opportunity for enhancement in terms of substance, effectiveness of delivery, and synergy among various instruments and institutions. All the instruments and institutions surveyed here tend to be living entities that have the capacity to evolve in these directions. Indeed, virtually all of the gaps and uncertainties identified in this book can, from the legal point of view, be resolved within the existing framework. The key is marshalling sufficient political will to make this happen. As suggested below, harnessing this political will requires more than simply engaging government officials who deal with forest issues, but a more cross sectoral input with heavy buy-in from civil society.

Final Observations

This book helps demonstrate that there is still much the existing regime can offer, if it was effectively implemented. This requires more political will than that which exists to date. Indeed, those advocating a new convention must recognize that while a legal instrument helps leverage some political will to implement it, the amount is rarely sufficient on its own. The experience with the *Central American Convention* is cautionary—while it is considered to be a qualified success, it has not halted deforestation in that region.

The lack of effective implementation may also reveal the limits of government action. Although governments play a critical role in defining and enforcing rules and standards, they alone cannot achieve conservation, sustainable management and sustainable development of all forests. As globalization has gathered pace in this last decade, industry, communities, NGOs, and individuals have increased in importance relative to the public sector. This is not to say that the empowerment of non-State actors has been uniform or equitable—far from it. But what is now clear is that public/private partnerships are needed, as are incentives and clear "rules of the game" for members of civil society to take positive action in relation to forests. The role of law is to create the framework conditions for this to happen, which includes, in part, regulating these new power relations. The failure to attract sufficient political will is a failure to involve all relevant sectors of society in setting a common vision for forests; in part this is to be understood as a failure in national and international legal systems in setting the stage for this to happen.

Although governments play a critical role in defining and enforcing rules and standards, they alone cannot achieve conservation, sustainable management and sustainable development of all forests.

The existing regime is rich, but fragmented. Key gaps and uncertainties remain. A stronger and more cohesive regime is necessary, especially one which focuses and supports implementation. It is tempting to think that the only solution is a holistic convention on forests. While in ideal circumstances a convention can help achieve objective of the international forest regime, in reality risks, as outlined above, are significant.

At the same time, prospect of the international forest policy process being endlessly paralyzed over the "convention" debate, will mean that "business as usual" (i.e., continuing deforestation) will continue to operate in a vacuum. There can be little doubt that this will mean the continued devastating rate of deforestation, and therefore a tremendous failure of the international forest regime. Thus, the IFF must not be distracted by this debate, but should, as a first and urgent priority, forge substantive consensus on the actions necessary to achieve the conservation, sustainable management and sustainable development of all forests. This involves, at the very least, elaborating concepts that will bridge the gaps identified here and resolve the persisting uncertainties. It cannot be expected that the IFF alone can operationalize these concepts, but a strong and clear message from the IFF will be influential.

To succeed in facilitating this consensus-building process, the IFF will have to set priorities, so that it can focus on matters that are truly pressing. In so doing, it is not advisable for it to deal with issues that are still largely abstract. For example, while the lack of definitions of key terms create uncertainties and possibly contribute to the fragmented nature of the international forest regime, the time may not yet be ripe to undertake definitional exercises. These are concepts that need to be informed by actual experience over time, including with the application of criteria and indicators.

Finally, in dealing with Category III of its work programme (i.e., international arrangements and mechanisms to promote the management, conservation and sustainable development of all types of forests), the members of the IFF must come to closure on the debate about new legal instruments. However, this discussion should not continue to take place at the current level of abstraction and theory. Therefore, it is recommended that the IFF should:

- accelerate the systematic examination of the effectiveness of the international forest regime, focusing particularly on impacts on the ground;
- examine feasibility of existing international instruments and institutions to address the gaps and uncertainties in the current regime; and
- examine the feasibility of mechanisms, in addition to a new convention, to achieve the necessary coordination at the international level.

C

Ansari H., "International Forest Agreements and Sustainable Management of Forests: A Critical Appraisal," paper presented at the *IUCN/APCEL/UNEP Training the Trainers Course on Capacity Building for Environmental Legal Education*, Singapore, 1997

Forests, a valuable gift to man, have been the green frontiers of mankind since time immemorial—a seemingly limitless resource for human expansion, with their supply of timber, fuelwood, fodder, genetic material, herbal medicine, a rich variety of other products, including underground water and a crucial source of raw materials for human society. Many ancient civilizations would not have developed without the availability of forests and their products, and many of them delayed or disappeared after depletion of these forests. Forests thus fulfill extremely important protective, regulatory and productive functions, both for the natural environment and for the well-being and development of the society…

In the early 1980s tropical deforestation was estimated by the *Food and Agricultural Organization* (FAO) and the National Academy of Sciences to be around 75,000 km per year, which is about 1.8 percent per year. A survey made by Norman Myers in 1990 reveals that the annual amount went up to 120,800 km, an area half of the British Isles. In early 1990, FAO repeated its tropical forest survey. It revealed that during the 1980s rates of tropical deforestation had increased by 50 percent. Recently, the 1995 United Nations Report on "The States of the Environment in Asia-Pacific" notes that the Asia-Pacific accounts for the world's highest rate of deforestation with an annual increment of 2 million hectares during 1976–1981 to 3.9 million hectares for 1981–1990. At the prevailing rate, the report says, an area of about 50 million hectares is estimated to be deforested in the next 10 years…

Deforestation is occurring generally due to logging activities, legal and illegal, shifting cultivation, urbanisation, population and settlements, mining, cattle ranching, lack of enforcement of law, agriculture and plantation. In particular areas some specific reasons have been identified. In Brazil and other states of the central America and Amazonia, cattle ranching is mainly responsible for deforestations. In Southeast Asia illegal logging has been identified as one of the main reasons [for] deforestations. Likewise, in Myanmar, Thailand, Cambodia and Vietnam, shifting cultivation is [responsible] for a big area of deforestation. In some of the African countries logging is mainly carried out for reducing the burden of debts. This has been enhanced due to lack of adequate pricing of logs and wood products and export of unprocessed logs. These states get comparatively less income, because timber licenses and concessions are distributed through a political process rather than competitive bidding.

N. Myres notes that deforestation is not altogether the responsibility of tropical forest nations. Other nations contribute as well by virtue of international trading linkages. The spread of cattle ranching was the result of the demand from North America for artificially cheap beef. There has been a parallel phenomenon of developed world consumerism driving deforestation in Thailand by way of cassava connection with the European Community. Similar linkages operate with respect to the developed world demand for tropical timber, again at prices that do not reflect the full deforestation costs of timber extraction. Yet another exogenous factor lies with the demand of timber and wood products in developed world and the price is not properly revised.

Loss of forests means deprivation of the benefits mentioned above, but what is most bothering is the loss of biological diversity. This may be noted here that the tropical forests have very rich biodiversity. While covering only 6 percent of Earth's land surface, they are estimated to contain at least 70 percent and possibly even 90 percent of Earth's species. Half a square kilometer of Malaysia's forest can feature as many tree and shrub species as the whole of the United States and Canada. It is estimated that at least 15 percent of Earth's plant species [were] threatened with extinction by the year 2000 or shortly there after together with hundreds of thousands of animal species. By the year 2025 we could well lose one-quarter of all Earth's plant species in these forests, again accompanied by the elimination of large numbers of animal species. Once the biological diversity in an area is gone, reafforestation cannot bring it back.

Other things, which are bothering the world are flash flood, soil erosion, loss of underground water, loss of source of herbal medicines, unusual weather conditions and global warming. The northern countries are worried about the phenomenon of global warming and the resultant unusual weather conditions and other related consequences. Forests are sink[s] for carbon dioxide, resulting from industrialization and urbanization that has increased the number of vehicles. They absorb carbon dioxide and release oxygen...

Efforts to Safeguard Remaining Forests

In spite of the fact that in [the] 1980s states and their people, through NGOs, started making efforts to reduce forest degradation and deforestation, the result was discouraging, [and] deforestation in [the] 1990s increased. This is because of lack of enforcement of law, lack of enough forest conservation programs, lack of financial resources and lack of political will for sustainable use of forests. This attracted international efforts.

The Tropical Forests Action Plan

At the instance of the Committee on Forest Development in the Tropics in 1983 FAO launched a study that led in 1985 to develop a Tropical Forestry Task force, which was jointly acted upon by the UNDP, the World Bank and other development banks, NGOs and representatives from more than 70 tropical countries. The result was a Tropical Forestry Action Plan (TFAP), the first international document for conservation of tropical forests. The main objective of the TFAP was to coordinate the actions of developing countries, international government organizations and financing agencies to combat deforestation. It thus broadly aimed to foster sustainable logging, tree planting, watershed rehabilitation, research and education, species protection, and enhanced forestry management. One of the salient moves in the TFAP was a "new moratorium" on logging projects and the transfers of forestry division[s] moving [them] to an independent forest authority in a given state so as "to build up the institutional capacity to conserve and manage forest resources, and to establish national policy-making and planning process that will lead to sustainable development". The TFAP outlines five priority areas: first, forestry in land use; second, forest-based industrial development; third, fuel and energy; fourth, conservation of tropical forest ecosystems; and fifth, removing the institutional constraints which impede the conservation and wise utilization of tropical forest resources.

The World Resource Institute (WRI) and FAO further presented a plan for conservation and sustainable development of tropical forest areas. This plan provided a conceptual framework for the TFAP. In particular, it emphasized the importance of community involvement in the planning process and in the development of mechanisms, which would ensure local collaborations in the future long-term activities of the program. The WRI and FAO identified the following points: the participation of local populations in the planning process; the identification of local uses for forestry resources; the integration of local needs in development plans; the encouragement and support of sustainable land use practices; and the development of incentives for local populations in order to invite their participation in the development of conservation and natural resources management systems. Thus the main object of the TFAP was to encourage the tropical forest countries to develop their own action plan, based on their forest policies for sustainable use of the forests and community involvement in the planning processes for sustainable forest management, and to coordinate for their enforcement.

For some, the TFAP has been a credible process for forestry management. E. Kasimbazi finds the TFAP in broadening international participation in sustainable management of tropical forests. It may be noted that the TFAP, apart from the international institutions and NGOs, by 1990 involved over 88 countries with 85 percent of the Earth's tropical forest countries. Also, it has helped to expand regional cooperation in terms of training, exchange of information and enforcement of action plans. The TFAP has developed a sense of mutual assistance in the area of sustainable forest management. The TFAP has actively coordinated with the states in developing action plans for sustainable forest management. For enforcement of the plans, it has provided, through the World Bank and other development banks, financial assistance to develop sustainable forest management projects and enhance technical capabilities. It is helping to improve natural resources management in the member states. E. Kasimbazi notes that it has fostered training programs on forest planning. In Sierra Leone, for example, it helped to consolidate all forestry extension and training programmes and helped improve the effectiveness of the Wildlife Conservation Units. In Columbia, the TFAP facilitated unprecedented intersectoral coordination and land use planning. In Jamaica, the TFAO highlighted the need for a national land-use strategy and endorsed the need for environmental impact assessment (EIA) before any major land-use plans were commenced. In short, the achievements of the TFAP are not very significant, but, at least, it has been able to attract the minds of the planners to work for conservation and sustainable use of forests, individually and collectively.

For some others, the TFAP is not a success story, rather it has contributed to unsustainability of forests. In Papua New Guinea, the World Bank worked for commercialization of the logging activities, which became responsible for deforestation of a very large area. Funds moved to the tropical forest countries were mainly utilized for forest-based industries, forestry in land use and fuel wood/energy. Conservation received only about 10 percent of these. Therefore, the vital national and international goals of sustainable management of tropical forests were not given priority. The TFAP does not have mandatory rules. It has, therefore, not received sufficient importance by the member states. Forest as a source of finance and the idea of ownership have been priority issues. There is yet another criticism that the TFAP has not been able to mobilize enough funds for the tropical forest countries.

Myres notes that the TFAP did not live up to expectations. The largest responsibility for this must lie with FAO. Ironically FAO had refused to collaborate with the World Bank's Task Force on the grounds that there was no tropical forest problem that warranted further effort, and that FAO, as the leading U.N. agency in the field, would take care of any problem that arose. But when FAO saw the plan was to go ahead anyway, it swiftly moved to join in the exercise. The result was that FAO was appointed the chief executive agency, despite its less than satisfactory record in the tropical forestry field over a period of decades. TFAP's overriding purpose was to stem deforestation by promoting sustainable forestry through a number of cross-sectoral strategies, including in particular a programme to assist subsistence farmers outside the forests and so deter them from becoming "shifted cultivators". But FAO was inclined to view the TFAP as a means to enhance support for traditional forestry activities, despite the essential character of the plan with its major new proposals. In its execution of the plan, FAO offered scant regard for non-forestry activities, despite the plan's original intent to integrate forestry with agriculture and thereby to address root causes of deforestations. It did not even direct much attention to forestry associated issues, such as bio-diversity and climate change. Worst of all, it did next to nothing to instigate policy reform, especially concerning the factors that generate the shifted cultivator.

The *International Tropical Timber Agreement* [ITTA-83], which was negotiated and adopted by 36 producing countries and 33 consuming countries, was the world's first commodity agreement on tropical timber. At the instance of the International Union for Conservation of Nature and Natural Resources (IUCN), which recommended to include the impact of timbering in reducing natural forests, the negative environmental effects of timbering [and] the need to retain positive values for a better forest management and reforestation, ...the ITTA-83 included some elements of sustainable forest management.

The narrow meaning of sustainable development of forest means sustainable yield of timber, which simply means that forestry will be performed in such a way that the future potential cut never falls below the current actual cutting level. This narrow view was taken in Europe because there forests were shrinking very fast, states were doubtful about the future supply of timber and environmental and social services of forests were not so significant. It was only after the Stockholm Declaration that the states started emphasizing upon the relationship of forests and environment. But the phenomenon of global warming has significantly contributed to this, because forests are sink[s] for carbon dioxide, and if deforestation is not checked, the mean world temperature will rise at a faster rate. Since the North is mainly responsible for the increased ratio of carbon dioxide in the atmosphere, and since the disastrous effects of global warming will not spare the northern countries, rather they will be held responsible for these, the northern states have given priority [to] conserving the forest ecosystem and managing forests in such a way that the welfare effects of forestry activities should not decrease in future. In this context, if production of timber is to be genuinely sustainable, there should be irreversible reduction of the potential of the forests as a resource. There should be no irreversible loss of soil, soil fertility and there should be no loss of biodiversity. This includes benefits to the volume yield and wood quality, in addition to maintaining positive environmental factors. Thus, sustainable development of forests was defined by Helsinki Forest Meeting of June 16-17, 1993 as:

> "[T]he stewardship and use of forests and the forest land in a way, and at a rate, that maintains their biodiversity, productivity, regeneration capacity, vitality and their potential to fulfill, now and in the future, relevant ecological, economic and social functions, at local, national and global levels and does not cause damage to other ecosystems."

The ITTA-83, along with facilitating trade in tropical timber, contains provisions about promoting sustainable utilization and conservation of tropical forests. The preamble states:

> "[T]he parties recognize the importance of, and the need for, proper and effective conservation and development of tropical forests, with a view to ensuring their optimum utilization while maintaining the ecological balance of the regions conserved and biospheres".

Similarly, the objectives, *inter alia,* are to provide an effective framework for cooperation and consultation between producers and consumers, to encourage development of national policies aimed at the sustainable utilization and conservation of tropical forests and their genetic resources, and to maintain the ecological balance in the regions concerned.

Along with facilitating the tropical timber trade, the substantive part of the ITTA-83 provides for discouraging overharvesting and deforestation. The International Tropical Timber Council (ITTC) and the Committee on Reforestation and Forest Management were responsible for enforcement of these provisions, by sponsoring certain projects in various tropical forest countries. Through regular meetings, they assessed the problems and took steps accordingly. The NGOs tried to get the *International Tropical Timber Organization* (ITTO) to adopt codes of conduct for producers and consumers, and to get an action plan committing the Organization to sustainable management of forests. But the ITTO Council made no perceptible move toward change in the system of forest exploitation. In 1990 the Council adopted a target date of the year 2000 by which all tropical timber exports should come from sustainable-managed forests. Proposal for curbs on export of tropical timber, which would in turn check deforestation, were not acceptable to the exporting countries, because they took it as interference in their sovereignty over their forests. However, in some individual cases when the Council demanded reduction in timber extraction in particular areas, its requests were honored. For example, when in 1990, the Council issued a report for calling for a 50 percent [reduction] in Sarawak's annual timber cut, Malaysia agreed to carry it out, but without any independent means of enforcing the pledge.

Inadequacies in the Provisions

Although the ITTA-83, along with TFAP, aimed for conservation of tropical forest, deforestation has been proceeding faster than ever. This is because of the inherent weaknesses they carry. The following weaknesses of the ITTA-83 have so far been noted:

(1) The objectives contained in Article 1 para (a) to (g) were: the diversification of international trade in tropical timber, the promotion of wood utilization, the improvement of market intelligence and the increased processing of encouragement of industrial tropical timber exports. Only para (h) introduced the need for sustainable utilization and the conservation of tropical forests and their ecological balance. This proves that basically the ITTA-83 was a commodity agreement [and that] conservation of forests was incidental to it.

(2) The ITTA-83 covered only tropical timber. Thus temperate timber and boreal timber, which supply more than 75 percent of the world's industrial wood, remained out of the ambit of the agreement.

(3) So far as sustainable management of forests is concerned, the ITTA-83 provided only general guidelines; thus the specific and detailed guidelines were left for the member states to develop. This, therefore, lead to confusion and lack of uniform criteria, because each state is guided by its own conditions.

(4) There were not enough resources for projects of sustainable use and utilization of forests.
(5) The ITTA-83 could not [impact] significantly in the area of transfer of technology to tropical forest countries.
(6) The ITTA-83 did not have provisions for protection of biodiversity and the ecosystem.
(7) The ITTA-83 lacked supervisory power. Therefore, it could not do monitoring about the compliance of the sustainable related provisions. Perhaps, this power was not given to the Council and the three committees, because this would have been considered as an interference in the sovereignty of the state.
(8) The ITTA-83 did not give right[s] to the state parties to impose sanction[s] against the defaulting state.

To sum up, the ITTA-83 was not a success story for sustainable management of the tropical forests, yet it attracted the support of almost all producing countries and consuming countries. It remained active for its 10–year tenure. On its expiry, a new ITTA (hereinafter referred as ITTA-94) was negotiated by the parties to the ITTA-83.

ITTA-94

Before a series of meetings between producers and consumers in Geneva under the auspices of the UNCTAD for a new ITTA, the producing countries along with NGOs demanded that the new agreement should include matters pertaining to temperate and boreal timber. This was in the wake of the unequal trade security on tropical timber in comparison with temperate and boreal wood. This move was objected [to] by the consuming countries. They were of the opinion that widening of the scope of the ITTA will divert the concentration of the ITTO, which is now engaged in fostering trade in tropical timber along with sustainable management of the tropical forests. They promised to meet the year 2000 target and report statistics and information on their own trade. This dichotomy was echoed in the meeting held in January 1994 for adopting the ITTA. The countries, however, agreed for a compromise by which the consumer countries pledged to implement "guidelines and criteria for sustainable management of their forests comparable to those developed by the ITTO". Some countries, including Malaysia, accepted the compromise formula reluctantly, because they had no choice but to accept the decision as the [consuming] countries were adamant about excluding their products from the agreement. This was not appreciated by the NGOs, also. For example, the Worldwide Fund for Nature (WWF) expressed its disappointment at the failure of the ITTA-94 to produce a new agreement covering both tropical and temperate timbers. WWF Malaysia Director of Conservation said [that] negotiators had ducked the issue by having an agreement which allow[ed] them to wait at least another four years before reopening the issue.

The ITTA-94 retains most of the provisions of the ITTA-83. But from the point of view of sustainable management of forests the following notable additions have been made:

(1) Timber will be extracted from sustainable sources.
(2) Reforestation and forest management activities as well as rehabilitation of degraded forestland, with due regard to local communities, will be encouraged.
(3) It will encourage the members to develop national policies aimed at sustainable utilization and conservation of timber-producing forests and their genetic resources and at maintaining the ecological balances and the regions concerned.
(4) It provides for new and additional financial resources to attain the objectives of the agreement. It also establishes a new account to be known as Bali Partnership Fund to enhance the capacity of members to implement a strategy for achieving exports of tropical timber and timber products from sustainable managed sources by the year 2000.
(5) The Preamble recalls the *Rio Declaration on Environment and Development*, the *Non-Legally Binding Authoritative Statement of Principles for a Global Consensus on the Management, Conservation and Sustainable Development of all types of Forests* and the relevant chapters of *Agenda 21*, and the *Convention on Biological Diversity*.
(6) It also recognizes the need to encourage forest management activities with regard for the interests of local communities dependent on forest resources.
(7) It envisages that members, except some exceptional situations, shall use their best endeavors and cooperate to promote the attainment of its objectives and to avoid any action contrary thereto.

Some of the inadequacies of the ITTA-83 are continued in the ITTA-94. They are as follows:

The Worldwide Fund for Nature expressed its disappointment at the failure of the ITTA-94 to produce a new agreement covering both tropical and temperate timbers.

(1) In spite of the modest arguments given by the tropical timber producing countries for inclusion of the temperate and boreal forests within the jurisdiction of the ITTA-94, due to opposition of the consuming countries, who generally have temperate or boreal forests, the scope of the ITTA-94 could not be widened. The consuming countries gave arguments for this (see supra), but these arguments, we think, were given to protect their timber-related vested interests. Maybe they argued so because some of them have over-logged their forest (for example, UK), or some of them have very high deforestation rate (Canada), or they do not want any interference in their forest management from outside. Whatever might be the reason, we are of the opinion that non-inclusion of the temperate and boreal forests within the scope of the ITTA-94 is [a] negation of the commitments of the producing countries to the *Agenda 21* (see infra) and the Forest Principle of the Rio Declaration.

This issue is so important that the tropical timber countries are stressing on this issue even now. Dr. Mahathir Mohammad, the Prime Minister of Malaysia, in his speech given at the Asian Parliamentarians Conference on Environment and Sustainable Development said, "[t]heir (the developing countries of South) exports are increasingly subjected to new and arbitrary requirements and conditionalities related to certification and labelling of forest management....If the developed countries are genuinely concerned about the sustainability of the forest utilization and management, the standards and criteria imposed on tropical timber should be applied fairly and equally on all timber products, including those from temperate and boreal forests."

(2) The promises for funding towards projects of developing countries through the Special Account and the Bali Account Suffer from uncertainty, as mobilization of resources depend on voluntary contribution[s] of the donor member states.

(3) Basically, the ITTA-94 is a commodity agreement; conservation of forests is incidental to it.

(4) The Agreement includes no special procedure or program for increasing public participation. The Agreement does not involve NGOs. It is silent on indigenous rights [and] recognition, and only marginally mentions the needs of local communities. This undermines the conservation of forests because they are not accorded, economic, social and environmental values. The Agreement does not make provisions for sustainable forest management; for example, there is no provision for certification programs of timber or independent review powers to be exercised by the Council (or any other body). The Council is merely mandated to include in its annual reports information supplied by members on their progress toward the sustainable management of their timber–producing forests.

The International Tropical Timber Organization

The idea to have an organization in the line of the *International Natural Rubber Agreement* was mooted by Japan, who had the maximum of voting rights on the side of the consuming countries, but while the *International Tropical Timber Organization* (ITTO) took its final shape, because forests involves a large number of flora and fauna and it has immense environmental, economic and social services, the arena of interaction of the ITTO along with timber extraction and trading activities included conservation of forests also. Basically, the ITTA functions through the *International Tropical Timber Council* (ITTC) and the three Committees, the ITTO is the supervisory body to look after the operational mechanism of the ITTA. Its objectives include:

(1) to expand the timber industries in the producing states, so that they could export processed timber. This may be noted here that this will require less volume of timber to be exported, it will bring more money and it will generate employment in the producing countries;

(2) to regulate the international timber trade for more balanced exploitation of tropical forests and to develop means of better forestry development;

(3) to sponsor studies on tropical timber pricing, utilization and forestry management; and;

(4) to encourage sustainable use and conservation of tropical forests and their genetic resources, and maintaining ecological balance.

The ITTO appears to have set up reasonably effective methods of monitoring tropical timber production. It acts as [an] inter-governmental organization responsible for conducting research and project activities. It has succeeded in achieving almost comprehensive membership among producing and consuming countries. The ITTO provides an international forum for the countries involved in the tropical timber trade. This has contributed significantly to enhance consultation and cooperation between governments, conservationists and timber trade associations.

Temperate timbers and boreal timbers have been excluded from the scope of the Agreement, probably because the consuming countries in their formal statement have agreed to manage their forests on sustainable basis and to follow the year 2000 target of managing timber only on sustainable basis, and the ITTO can bring programmes for coordination between the tropical timber-producing countries, boreal timber-producing countries and temperate timber–producing countries. But such programs, we feel, will be successful only when the countries other than tropical timber-producing countries keep their promise.

History reveals that the ITTO has not been able to establish itself as a useful organization for conservation of forests. It has been noted by the World Bank that: "It appears true that sustainability of natural forests has to be proven". Its 1995 report "The State of the Environment in Asia-Pacific" reveals that deforestation in this region is [on] the increase.

Although the ITTO is officially committed to sustainable use and conservation of tropical forests and their genetic resources, both consuming and producing countries have interests that rule out any change in its free trade mandate. It has proven more a center of lobbying by the states by protecting their respective interests. For instance, Japan, holder of the maximum votes on the timber-consuming side, is interested in maintaining its consumption. Most EU countries are also interested in maintaining a flow of hardwoods to produce and export furnitures. The United States, which is world's largest importer of finished tropical hardwood products and, incidentally, the world's largest exporter of softwood products, which compete with tropical timber products, has been unwilling to put itself at odds with producing states, such as Malaysia and Indonesia.

The main interest of producing countries in the ITTO, meanwhile, has been to maintain demand, to earn, to take financial aids from the developed countries, to take technological advantage from developed countries, to keep trade restrictions away from the timber trade, and not to allow the developed countries to link aid with environment. Proposals for curbs on export of tropical timber products that are not sustainably managed have activated a veto condition of tropical forest countries. These proposals were said to be arbitrary and discriminatory, and also violative to the spirit of the ITTO. We are of the opinion that, in spite of the promise made by all timber-producing countries to produce timber only from sustainably managed forests and to accept eco-labelling as a measure, without a political will on the part of the countries to do so, nothing significant is going to happen in the near future.

One of the weaknesses of the ITTO is that it is reluctant to address greater non-technical issues such as the political, social and economic realities in producer countries. By strictly focusing on the concept of "sustainable forestry", the ITTO has neglected to address a multitude of influences on the continuing destruction of forest ecosystems. The ITTO's conservation objectives have failed to promote sustainable forest management. It has not developed measures for adopting an appropriate code of conduct, defining sustainable management or creating a fund to protect forest areas of high biological importance. Worse still, it neither provides data in the form of annual reports of rate of loss and areas protected nor promotes "a real price" of tropical timber which internalizes costs of reforestation and conservation. Further, the ITTO does not have sufficient powers to resolve disputes.

The ITTO has recently accepted new guidelines for certain environmental activities and biodiversity protection. But the organizations record in its area of purported expertise, sustainable logging, must raise severe questions about its capacity to implement the new proposals. We are of the opinion that the year 2000 target can be achieved successfully, if the ITTO becomes able to strike a balance between profit and conservation.

Steps Towards an International Forest Convention

The supporters of an international convention on forests generally argue that the existing instruments, the ITTO and the TFAP, have utterly failed in conservation of forests, [and that] during the period of existence of these, deforestation has been proceeding faster than ever. They [argue that this] can be solved by negotiating a *Global Forests Convention* leading to a World Forest Organization backed by a Tropical Forest Fund. They feel that a holistic approach on forest use, and forest management will serve the purpose of conserving forests with its biological diversity and ecosystems, ensuring social services and protecting economic interests of the states. According to them, only [then will] a meaningful, financial and technological cooperation emerge. It would offer a forum for continuous contributions from nongovernmental bodies, especially those that promote environmental values and grassroots interests, such as those representing indigenous people.

The idea of having a global forest convention could not get [the] support of the developing countries, especially the tropical forest countries.

The communique of the Group of Seven Summit in Houston in July 1990 declared: "We are ready to begin negotiations...a global forests convention or agreement, which is needed to curb deforestation, protect biodiversity, stimulate positive forestry actions, and address threats to the world's forests." This goal was reaffirmed at the London summit in July 1991: "We aim to achieve the following by the time of UNCED...Agreement on principles for the management, conservation and sustainable development of all types of forest, leading to a framework convention".

The tropical forest countries [did] not agree [with] a global convention, because they fear[ed] that any such convention [would] bring a great deal of restrictions, and thus it [would] be an interference in their sovereign rights over their forests. This apprehension, we feel, was due to economic interests of the states. They were also of the opinion that, in future, to meet the demands of development, they will need to clear [a] certain area of their forests. A global convention might create an impediment [to] this process. Even among developed countries, some were of the opinion that an international convention will give birth to yet another international agency....We feel that a global convention on forests can not be achieved in the near future. It will be possible only when developing countries (especially the tropical forest countries) and developed countries (especially boreal forest countries and temperate forest countries) develop confidence in each other.

The Forest Principles

In the UNCED the difference of opinion could be seen. The idea of having a global forest convention could not get [the] support of the developing countries, especially the tropical forest countries. The deadlock was never broken. Most of the developing countries, out of fear of outside intervention, did not concede to this idea. However, there was a range of views. Brazil did not want any intervention in its internal affairs; whereas, Malaysia was of the view that every country should preserve at least 30 percent of its territory under forests or provide fund[s] to do it elsewhere.

Since consensus on a global forest convention could not be reached the states hurriedly picked up a set of principles and named it as "Forest Principles". This may be noted that the Principles cover all types of forests. The principles may be divided into two parts: Preamble and Principles. The Preamble recognizes the environmental and economic and social importance of forests, and suggest[s] that they should be used in such a way that the services provided by them are not reduced over time. The principles may be summarised as follows:

(1) Forests should be sustainably managed.

(2) There should be individual and joint action for conservation and sustainable development of forests. These require [states]:
   (a) to increase the forest cover;
   (b) to intensify reforestation and other forest rehabilitation measures;
   (c) to mobilize funds for conservation and sustainable management;
   (d) to ensure free trade in timber and timber products;
   (e) to formulate guidelines for sustainable management of forests;
   (f) to enforce environmental impact assessment;
   (g) to encourage and improve training and technology transfer, research, exchange of information; and
   (h) to teach various aspects of forests to the students at primary, secondary and University levels.

(3) Efforts should be made to tell the people about the importance and utility of forests and to seek their participation in conservation and sustainable management processes.

(4) The states shall have sovereign rights on [over] their forests. They will exploit their forests without inflicting any harm to the neighbouring countries.

(5) Attempts should be made to assess the economic value of forests in each country.

The "Forest Principles" is a non-legally binding document and suffers from repetitions and contradictions. However, it includes all types of forests, and thus might help in collective and concerted efforts for conservation and sustainable management of all forests. The Intergovernmental Working Group on Global Forests, in its first meeting held at Kuala Lumpur, on April 18–21 1994, has noted that the "Forest Principles" together with chapter 11 of the *Agenda 21* constitute the first consensus on forests. The "Forest Principles", therefore, serve a useful basis for an international agenda on forests. But at the end of the meeting it was declared that the following points should be stressed in future:

(1) Effective participation in forest management decision making processes by all stakeholders [Principles, 2(d), S(b)].
(2) Full public access to essential information [Principle 2(c)].
(3) Comprehensive, cross-sectoral integration, including land use planning and management and the influence of policies external to the traditional forest sector [Principles 3(c), 8(e), 9(e), 13(d) and 13(e)].
(4) Protection of the customary rights of indigenous and other forest-dependent peoples [Principle (a)].
(5) Equitable resolution of land tenure conflicts [Principle 5(a)].
(6) Use of EIA [Principle 8(h)].
(7) Development of methodologies for the comprehensive valuation of forest goods and services [Principle 6(c)].

Agenda 21

We have noted above that Chapter 11 of the *Agenda 21* together with the "Forest Principles" are the first international consensus on all types of forests of the world. The principles contained in this chapter have been desired to fight against deforestation. It has four programme areas:

(1) Sustaining the Multiple Roles and Functions.
(2) Enhancing Conservation and Sustainable Management.
(3) Promoting Efficient Utilization and Assessment to Recover Full Valuation of the Goods and Services Provided by Forests.
(4) Establishing and/or Strengthening Capacities for Planning, Assessment of Forest and Related Programmes.

Chapter 11 of the *Agenda 21* is a comprehensive program for sustainable development, which lays greater emphasis on closer cooperation between developed and developing countries in the area of conservation and sustainable development of forests. It has specified financial implications for each programme area. We are of the opinion that if the programmes are sincerely carried forward by the states and if the developed states generously contribute toward funds established for them, the problem of sustainable development of forests can easily be solved.

Conclusions and Suggestions

Although the world community has failed to have consensus on a global forest convention and a world forest organization, joint and several attempts are being made in the area of conservation and sustainable management of forests. Although the recent reports on forests reveal that the deforestation has increased, this will be a temporary phenomenon. The tropical forest rich countries have agreed in principle that they would follow the guidelines prepared by the ITTO and by the year 2000 would manage all their forests on sustainable basis. The temperate/boreal forest-rich countries have also vowed to follow the guidelines. But we are of the opinion that the tropical forest-rich countries will be able to keep their promise only when they get enough financial support and technical help for this from the developed countries. Financial support becomes more important for those countries [which] financially depend on their forests. This may also be noted that the developing countries in the UNCED and after UNCED have decided to maintain [a] certain part of their territory as forests. They also demand the other states to maintain, at least, 30 percent of their lands as forests. We are of the opinion that, if the idea of maintaining 30 percent of the total land area of the world is scientifically sustainable, this should be observed by all countries developed and developing. If the countries can not keep this, they must pay for maintaining more than 30 percent of the land area as forests, elsewhere. We are of this opinion that this is equitable and in the line of "polluter-pays-principle." But the question of sustainable management and conservation of forests should not be linked with aid.

The efforts for sustainable management of forests are continuously being made. Some of them are: the *Global Forest Conference* held in February 1993, in Indonesia; the *Forestry Forum for Developing Countries* held in India in September 1993; the *Indo-UK Forest Initiationers*; the *Ministerial Conference on the Protection of Forests in Europe* and its follow-up (Helsinki Process), Meetings of the *Intergovernmental Working Group on Global Forests*; the

1995 session of the *U.N. Commission on Sustainable Development* (UNCSD); the follow-up to the *Seminar of Temperate and Boreal Forests* held under the auspices of the *Conference on Security and Cooperation in Europe* (Montreal Process); and the regular meetings of the ITTO. The ITTO in February 1996 entrusted a three-year project to the Asean Institute of Forest Management for developing strategies for conservation of forests and their genetic resources of commercial tree species in the Asia-Pacific. On a similar project a group of scientists under the leadership of Prof. S.M. Swaminathan is already working on 360,000 hectares of land in Guyana. This project, along with other agencies, is being funded by the ITTO. We are of the opinion that these, and in [the] future some other joint, regional and international efforts will certainly help [in] building a political will on the part of the forest-rich countries to conserve their forests and manage them on [a] sustainable basis, and on the part of the other countries, to help in these processes. This will ultimately lead to a global forest convention and a world forest organization.

D

Dias A., "Causes of Deforestation and Environmental Impacts," summary of outline presented at the *IUCN/APCEL/UNEP Training the Trainers Course on Capacity Building for Environmental Legal Education*, Singapore, 1997

...[C]auses include logging, cattle ranching, mining, development projects such as highways and dams, and colonization schemes. Deforestation leads to floods and draughts, soil erosion, atmospheric warming and climate change, and depletion of biological resources. There are two shifts in emphasis on forest issues: identifying the problems unique to tropical forests, and seeking solutions in international responses from international institutions, rather than locally. A basic issue is who should control tropical forests. International confrontations have resulted from attempts to relate trade issues to tropical timber, and from attempts to lobby for an international forest convention. The *International Tropical Timber Agreement* (ITTA) of 1985 is the only global convention addressing tropical deforestation, but it has a narrow scope, soft obligations, weak monitoring and enforcement mechanisms, limited involvement by NGOs and forest dwellers, and funding constraints. The Agreement was renegotiated in 1994 so that the objectives are now more balanced, the concept of sustainable development is included (although without a code of conduct to deal with sustainable management), and a new fund has been established to assist in the goal of sustainable managed forests. However, the funding commitments are not clear, there is no mention of indigenous rights, and temperate and boreal forests are not included. Producers vote according to the amount of timber they export; Japan, as the leading consumer of timber, has the largest number of votes.

E

England P., "Thailand and The Rio Statement on Forest Principles: National Factors and Lessons for International Forest Policy" 2(1) *Asia Pacific Journal of Environmental Law*, 1997, pp 3-25

In this article, the author argues that international initiatives to protect the environment will only succeed when they are compatible with national agendas. This is particularly so with respect to international forest policy where domestic political and commercial considerations influence states' positions in international fora. In support of this argument, the Malaysian and Thai contributions to the *United Nations Conference on Environment and Development* (UNCED) and the domestic factors which influenced the positions are examined.

This article is concerned with the national factors, legal and extra legal, which influence States' contributions to international environmental lawmaking. Given the global nature of many environmental problems it is arguable that international law should increasingly govern or at least significantly contribute to national environmental law. However, this article is based on a different premise, that is, because international law is made by nation States whose governments are concerned, first and foremost, with their own domestic political agendas, international environmental law is and will continue to be determined by accumulated national factors. International initiatives which do not meet relevant national agendas are, in practical terms, doomed from the outset. Only those international initiatives which are compatible with national agendas will prove to be long lasting and effective. Thus, international law can only be understood from the perspective of individual States legal and policy dilemmas.

The Malaysian and Thai contributions to the *United Nations Conference on Environment and Development* (UNCED), [and the] *Non-Legally Binding Authoritative Statement of Principles on the Management, Conservation and Development of All Types of Forests,* exemplify these issues. A discussion of the factors which influence their national forest policy illuminates the process of international environmental law-making and suggests new directions for international initiatives.

Background to the UNCED

In December 1989, the United Nations (UN) General Assembly passed a resolution calling for a Conference on Environment and Development in 1992 at Rio. The purpose assigned to the Conference was the formulation of strategies to integrate environment and development in every aspect of economic life.

Over the next three years, rigorous preparations were made. The fourth and final meeting of the Preparatory Committee for the Conference was held in March 1992. At this stage, negotiations on the *Convention on Biological Diversity* and the *Convention on Climate Changes* were complete and a framework document for the *Rio Declaration on Environment and Development* was in preparation. Still to be completed were the negotiations on *Agenda 21* and *Statement of Forest Principles.* It was this last item which promised to be the most intractable issue for the Conference.

In April 1992, developing countries met in Kuala Lumpur to express a common policy stance for the Group of 77 at the UNCED. The resulting *Kuala Lumpur Declaration on Environment and Development 1992* affirmed the commitment of the developing countries to addressing environment and development issues in an integrated, comprehensive and balanced manner. On the question of conservation of forests, the Declaration made three points—that forest resources are part of the national patrimony subject to sovereign rights of control; that the conclusion at Rio of a *Non-Legally Binding Authoritative Statement of Principles on the Management, Conservation and Development of All Types of Forests* would render unnecessary the negotiation of a binding international treaty and that, while developed countries should increase their national forest cover they should avoid unilateral measures such as bans and restrictions on international trade in tropical forest products.

It is significant that this meeting was convened by and took place in Malaysia at a time so close to UNCED. By April 1992, the Malaysian Prime Minister, Dr. Mahathir bin Mohamad, had made clear his concerns about the pending Conference at Rio. For him, the key issues were safeguarding national sovereignty over natural resources and securing international recognition that the primary responsibility for environmental degradation lay with the developed world. Ten earlier considered boycotting altogether the UNCED, the Kuala Lumpur meeting demonstrated that the Prime Minister had now decided to take an active role in the deliberations and to push his own agenda. Thus, Clause 3 of the *Kuala Lumpur Declaration on Environment and Development 1992* reflects his concerns:

> "We call for a new global partnership based on respect for sovereignty and the principles of equity and equality among states for the achievement of sustainable development, taking into account the main responsibility of developed countries for the deterioration of the environment and the need for sustained economic growth and development of developing countries."

At the Kuala Lumpur meeting Dr. Mahathir bin Mohamad was able to rally the support of the Group of 77 around his controversial agenda. For the Group of 77 to adopt a hard line at this stage was a sound negotiating strategy, in view of the simultaneous discussions occurring in Tokyo regarding the level of financial commitment required of the developed world for the UNCED proposals. However, the meeting of Eminent Persons in Tokyo ended without detailed agreement on the amount of funding that would be made available through this mechanism by the developed world. Thus, the dawn of the UNCED was marked by a confrontational statement from the developing world but still only weak promises from the developed countries.

Malaysian and Thai Viewpoints on Tropical Forests Expressed at the UNCED

Dr. Mahathir's staunch opposition to international involvement in tropical forest conservation, including the adoption of a legally binding treaty, continued throughout UNCED. He continued to champion the terms of the *Kuala Lumpur Declaration on Environment and Development 1992* and showed no leeway in his negotiating stance. Although only India was as vocal in its opposition to an international treaty, the developed countries failed to divide the Group of 77 and win over the support of those governments which stood to gain from the United States' last minute offer to double international forest conservation assistance.

The general environment of hostility created by the developed world's reluctance to put up significant new finance, and the United States' procrastinations on climate change and technology transfer help to explain this outcome. The fact that the United States, which was so clearly unwilling to accept any restraints on its own economic freedom, was firmly in favor of a tropical forest treaty only served to highlight the apparent hypocrisy of the developed countries and to polarise the Group of 77 in their opposition to a forest treaty. The developed countries were far from agreement among themselves on many issues. Their performance, and that of the United States in particular, provided no justification for developing countries with views less confrontational than Malaysia to break away from the fold.

In contrast to the vocal and hotly political presence of Dr. Mahathir at Rio, the Thai presence was led by Professor Dr. Her Royal Highness Princess Chulaborn Mahidol. Her statement to UNCED included general observations on the need for sectoral integration and area-specific development programs taking into account local factors. The diplomatic overtones of the Thai delegation are in marked contrast to the Malaysian Government's contribution. Nevertheless, Thailand, like other developing countries, was not lured away from the Group of 77's.

Outcomes of the UNCED for Tropical Forest Policy

The *Non-Legally Binding Authoritative Statement of Principles for a Global Consensus on the Management, Conservation and Sustainable Development of All Types of Forests (Statement of Forest Principles)* was the principal document on forests to emerge from the UNCED. The *Statement of Forest Principles* declares that it reflects a first global consensus on forests, without expressly committing States to a follow up treaty, as favored by the United States. The Statement opens with a re-affirmation of national sovereignty over natural resources and this is followed by a call for increased international cooperation for forest conservation and sustainable development. Calls for increased financial assistance to developing countries re-occur throughout the text. There are several references to the need to respect the rights of indigenous forest communities and to enhance their participation in the development, planning and implementation of national forest policies. The need for a cross-sectoral, integrated environment and development approach is acknowledged at several points. In particular, attention is drawn to the need to address the debt problem of developing countries, the need for economic and social substitution to replace unsustainable forest exploitation practices and the need for the transfer of relevant environmental technology to developing countries on preferential terms. There is also an ambitious call for the "greening of the world". The most notorious provisions however, are found in principles 13 and 14 which deal with the international timber trade and unilateral measures to prevent free trade in forest products. Principle 13 states that open and free international trade in forest products should be facilitated and the local processing of forest products should be encouraged. Principle 14 states:

> "Unilateral measures, incompatible with international obligations or agreements, to restrict and/or ban international trade in timber or other forest products should be removed or avoided, in order to attain long term sustainable forest management."

The *Statement of Forest Principles* was quickly condemned by nongovernmental organizations (NGOs) as a "Chainsaw Charter". It was criticized for the generality of its provisions, and for its condemnation of unilateral bans on the timber trade. On the other hand, the Statement did incorporate some more enlightened ideas, including references to wider economic constraints on development and the rights of indigenous communities. The Statement was clearly a compromise agreement with developing countries in the ascendancy.

Forestry issues were also an element in the *Convention on Biological Diversity* and the *Framework Convention on Climate Change*. The first of these Conventions requires each contracting party to establish a system of protected areas and to develop national strategies, plans or programs for the "conservation and sustainable use of biological diversity". The Convention once again affirms national sovereignty over all natural resources and contains stipulations requiring the transfer of technology on favorable terms, especially to countries from which relevant genetic resources are obtained.

The *Framework Convention on Climate Change* allocates the leading responsibility for combating climate change to developed countries. It does, however, commit all contracting parties to promoting the conservation and sustainable management of "sinks and reservoirs" for greenhouse gases including forests. The Convention recognizes the necessity of affording special consideration to the needs and circumstances of countries which may shoulder an abnormal burden under the Convention.

Lastly, a blue print for action to conserve and sustainably manage all types of forests was included in *Agenda 21*. The matters addressed in Chapter 11 of *Agenda 21* fall into four categories—sustaining the multiple roles and functions of all types of forests; enhancing the protection, sustainable management and conservation of all forests and the greening of degraded areas; promoting efficient utilization and assessment to recover the full value of the goods and services provided by forests; and strengthening capacities for planning, assessment and systematic observations of forests and related programmes, including commercial trade and processes. The objectives for each of these categories are stated and activities to be pursued are outlined. If implemented, the Chapter would serve to strengthen national forest institutions, address some of their research requirements and facilitate the integration of forestry issues into national decision making. However, the estimated cost of implementing all the provisions of *Agenda 21* is $125 billion per annum. As the money on offer from the developed world at Rio fell short of $10 billion, doubts about the prospects for *Agenda 21* appear to be well founded.

In summary, the UNCED adopted some progressive principles on forest conservation but at a high price. The Conference polarized views along a North-South divide, generated insufficient finance and gave credence to the view that sustainable timber exploitation is possible and desirable. Critics who regard the UNCED as a retrogressive step, at least on the forestry issue, have good grounds for their pessimism.

In the aftermath of the UNCED, little substantial progress has been made towards implementing the *Statement of Forest Principles* or reconciling the conflicts that emerged during the Rio negotiations. At the first *Ministerial Conference of the Forestry Forum for Developing Countries* (FFDC) representatives of developing countries declared their continuing support for the *Statement of Forest Principles*, while emphasizing their commitment to the principle of national sovereignty over forest resources. At the first session of the Commission for Sustainable Development's (CSD) Intergovernmental Panel on Forests (IPF) in 1995 old conflicts between developed and developing countries were only avoided by focusing, *inter alia*, on national projects and reporting programs. Similarly, the work of the Intergovernmental Working Group on Forests (IWGF), set up by Canada and Malaysia in 1994, has focused on specific, technical issues relating to forest conservation and management. In these forum, members of the G77 have resisted any proposals that could forseeably lead to a loss of national control over forests and forest products.

In the aftermath of the UNCED, little substantial progress has been made towards implementing the Statement of Forest Principles *or reconciling the conflicts that emerged during the Rio negotiations.*

It is tempting to attribute a good proportion of the blame for so little progress on forestry issues at Rio to Dr. Mahathir. Critics may argue that he used the issue to score political points at home and with the Group of 77. His views certainly helped to polarise the debate along familiar but intractable North-South lines. However, his insistence on the need for increased financial assistance to developing countries to facilitate broad based environmental and development programs and his hard line on the need for developed countries to do more to combat their own pollution were, in the light of any environmental analysis, entirely well founded. Indeed, the inclusion of broad based recommendations on environment and development within the *Statement of Forest Principles* can be viewed not only as a triumph for Dr. Mahathir and the Group of 77 who blame the developed countries for the lack of progress at Rio but as a forward step in the progressive realization of sustainable development as originally propounded in the report of the *World Commission on Environment and Development*.

National Factors Influencing the Foreign Policy of Malaysia and Thailand at the UNCED

In this section, significant political and legal factors at the national level, which help to explain the different political overtones of the Malaysian and Thai delegations to the UNCED are examined. These fundamental political and legal constraints suggest the boundaries within which international policy-making must operate, barring radical and improbable political reforms at the national level.

National Factors Influencing the Malaysian Viewpoint

Two national factors in particular appear to influence the Malaysian viewpoint. These are, first, the official commitment to sustainable timber exploitation and free trade in forest products and second, the Federal Constitution's allocation of rights over forest resources to the states in Malaysia.

Sustainable Exploitation

...Logging peaked in peninsular Malaysia in 1976 (at 411,000 hectares) and has since declined to 149,000 hectares per annum (1986). In East Malaysia (Sabah and Sarawak) logging increased during the 1980s. In 1985, log production in East Malaysia exceeded 22 million cubic meters. East Malaysia was the world's largest exporter of tropical hardwood logs at the end of the 1980s. Causes of deforestation include unsustainable logging and government–sponsored forest clearance for resettlement schemes. The high level of species diversity in Malaysia, combined with the rapid pace of deforestation and the economic significance of the timber industry indicate the intensely political, national background which informs Malaysia's foreign policy on forests...

Faced with these competing demands on its forests, the Malaysian Government has adopted the goal of sustainable timber exploitation. Thus, the Government plans to reduce its timber felling from approximately 23 million cubic meters per annum in 1990 to 15 million cubic meters.

That sustainable exploitation is the bed rock of forest policy in Malaysia is demonstrated by the response of the Sarawak State Government to anti-logging protests focused on that state. Since the 1980s national and international NGOs have exposed the rapid pace of deforestation in that state and the drastic consequences this is having on indigenous communities. In 1988, the former European Economic Community (EEC) acted to ban all imports of hardwoods from Sarawak "until it can be established that the logging does not cause unnecessary environmental damage and does not threaten the way of life of the indigenous peoples". In response to growing criticisms at home and abroad, the Government invited the *International Tropical Timber Organisation* (ITTO) to visit and report on the state of forest exploitation in Sarawak. In its report, the ITTO confirmed that forest resources were being over cut causing considerable environmental damage. The recommendations of the ITTO included increasing the number of skilled forest staff; abandoning logging on slopes greater than 60 percent; improving the protection of watershed catchment areas and reducing the rate of logging to 9.2 million cubic meters. Subsequently, the state Govemment of Sarawak agreed to reduce its log production from 12.5 million cubic meters per annum to 9.2 million in 1994 in an attempt to put exploitation on a more sustainable footing.

It is unlikely that this agreement will be strictly enforced, that the forests of Sarawak will henceforth be sustainably exploited or that indigenous forest communities will in future be any more secure in their legal rights than they were before the visit of the ITTO.

Nevertheless, the official commitment to reduce logging made by the Government of Sarawak in the aftermath of the ITTO Report is the most promising development in that state to date. The ITTO may have reaped a qualified success where policy-making both national and international, could not.

What is most surprising about developments in Sarawak is their approximate congruence in time to the Rio Conference in June 1992. While federal and state governments on the home front were making conciliatory moves towards accepting limits on forest exploitation, Dr. Mahathir staunchly objected to international intervention at Rio. The ITTO, with its trade oriented bias, was evidently seen as a relatively sympathetic, less politicized and more technocratic forum with which to cooperate. Conversely, the UNCED was a political event of notorious proportions. In these circumstances, how could such a vocal politician as Dr. Mahathir reject such an inviting opportunity to pursue the North-South debate and condemn the US for its environmental legacy?

The Malaysian commitment to promoting sustainable timber exploitation indicates constraints and opportunities for international law-making. It is clear that Malaysia will reject proposals which condemn or prohibit the continue[d] exploitation of forests. On the other hand, its approach to the ITTO suggests there is a place for discrete technical and financial assistance which may help to slow the pace of exploitation. The use of the international ban on timber imports can only be viewed as a qualified success. While the former EEC ban encouraged the Malaysian Government to resort to the ITTO, it was an important factor contributing to the condemnation of unilateral trade bans in the *Statement of Forest Principles*. Additionally, the ready tropical timber markets of the Far East meant the ban created no real financial reason for Malaysia to curb its rate of timber exploitation.

Constitutional Constraints and Federal-State Relations

The Constitution of Malaysia vests control of forests, native reserves and land tenure generally in the states. External affairs and taxation fall within the exclusive domain of the Federal Government. National parks and wildlife protection fall within the concurrent list of items subject to federal and state supervision. The Federal Government is not without jurisdictional power over state land if that land is needed for federal purposes and land proclaimed as a development area is subject to federal regulation or matters contained in the development plan for that area. In addition, Federal Parliament may make laws pertaining to subjects in the State list on the following grounds—for the purpose of implementing international treaty obligations; for the purpose of promoting uniformity in the laws of two or more states; or, if requested so to do by the Legislative Assembly of any state. Laws enacted on the basis of the last two grounds will only be operative if states subsequently adopt the legislation as their own. The *National Forestry Act 1984*, for example, has not been adopted in Sarawak.

Since the early 1970s, the Federal Government has attempted to play an active role in states' forest administration. A National Forest Policy was proposed in 1972 but only accepted by the National Land Council in 1978. The aim of the Policy is to foster a sustainable forest industry throughout the country and detailed specifications for sustained yield management are made. The inclusion of policies relating to urban expansion, indigenous rights and the protection of national parks suggest that the need for an integrated approach to forestry, environment and development issues was appreciated long before the UNCED. The fact that these wide ranging provisions, now endorsed by the UNCED proceedings, aroused opposition from within and outside the Forestry Department is indicative of the institutional obstacles which hinder the implementation of the UNCED.

The *National Forestry Act 1984* incorporated the least controversial aspects of the Policy. Its measures aim to encourage uniformity between the states while leaving primary responsibility for forest matters with the state governments. It empowers state authorities to constitute permanent forest reserves and to classify them into uniform, national categories. It provides for the establishment of State Forest Development Funds. These can be used to pay for management plans and reafforestation programs. The Federal Government can make grants to each State Forest Development Fund. Strict controls on logging and the recognition of indigenous land rights, however, found no place in the legislation. Not all states have adopted the Act and those that have, are free to amend its terms in their own state legislatures. Even after adoption, enforcement is a problem. Hurst reports that states have, in practice, only allowed federal intervention in support of rehabilitation projects.

The fate of the *National Forestry Act 1984* is indicative of the underlying problems for forestry in Malaysia. Some observers have argued that the large measure of state autonomy over forests prevents a more responsible attitude to forest management. This is because the states, which have limited sources of revenue, have been quick to grant forest concessions in order to increase state revenue. As the Federal Government would be less dependent on forests as a source of income, the centralization of control could, they argue, reduce the pressure to make quick profits from the sale of concessions. In addition, the prospects for sustainable exploitation may be enhanced as the emphasis of national development policy is on industrialization, including the export of more refined timber products. Reliable and sustained supplies of timber in the long term are essential if the necessary investment in more sophisticated types of processing is to be encouraged. Dr. Mahathir has political support in the business community and his opposition to trade embargoes in international fora is consistent with the objective of industrial development in the forest sector. He might, therefore, prove to be surprisingly sympathetic to sustainable development strategies. Recent attempts by the Forestry Department, acting under the National Forest Policy, to ban the export of unprocessed logs and to limit the annual logging rate are some evidence of an official commitment at the Federal level to sustainable production.

Centralized control of forest resources is not a sufficient strategy, by itself, however, to secure the sustainable management of forest resources. The Federal Government, which is anxious in so many respects to control the economy from the center, has majority support in all but one of the state legislatures. It deliberately turns a blind eye to excessive and destructive logging rates in return for political allegiance to the ruling coalition from the states, especially Sabah and Sarawak, and because of the financial significance of the timber industry in the national economy. Thus, legal control over forest concessions is a form of political patronage used as much by the Federal Government as by the states themselves.

It deliberately turns a blind eye to excessive and destructive logging rates in return for political allegiance to the ruling coalition from the states, especially Sabah and Sarawak, and because of the financial significance of the timber industry in the national economy.

Dr. Mahathir's close allegiance with the business community may also be counter productive. There is over capacity in the timber mills of the peninsular so the pressure to continue logging at excessive rates in East Malaysia, where resources are not yet so depleted, in order to meet industrial needs, is great. What is in fact needed is retrenchment in the milling sector as well as further investment in more sophisticated types of processing mills. A failure to match available supplies against production capacity is a recipe for further destruction of the forest estate, yet the government is likely to resist unpalatable industrial retrenchment. In summary, the Prime Minister has always made it clear that economic development in a centrally directed, plural state is the overriding concern of his Government. Although in theory, the Federal Government could intervene to legislate on forests in order to satisfy an international obligation, it is in practice most unlikely to do so because state control over forest exploitation is part of the political *quid pro quo* maintaining the stability of the federal system of government. Thus, the Federal Government is likely to continue to reject any international obligations, which may upset the sensitive federal-state balance of power.

National Factors Influencing the Thai Viewpoint

Reservation and Protection

Thailand has one of the worst records of deforestation in southeast Asia to date. Forest cover has decreased from 72 percent (36.9 million hectares) in 1938 to 29 percent (14.8 million hectares), in 1985. Some estimates put the remaining area of natural forest as low as 22 percent...

A case study of Malaysia and Thailand provides some striking contrasts in the causes of forest depletion. In Malaysia, illegal and unsustainable logging activities are known to be principal causes of deforestation. In Thailand, which has a population approximately four times that of Malaysia, the chief cause of deforestation in the postwar period has been illegal forest clearance by migrating farmers seeking land for cash crops. Nevertheless, intensive, frequently illegal, logging activities have also contributed to forest degradation in Thailand, not the least because of their role in facilitating farmers' incursions into the forest.

In the mid 1980s, efforts to stop illegal logging activities were increased but the activities of illegal loggers became only more sophisticated in response. Tensions came to a head in November 1988 when flash floods in southern Thailand killed 350 people. The Government responded by suspending logging activities in the southern region and subsequently banning logging throughout Thailand. This action won popular support and was therefore legally entrenche[d] despite the opposition of vested logging interests. The Government was able to deal with this opposition by making a controversial deal with Burma allowing the import of logs from that country to supply Thai saw mills. Illegal logging also continues. Thus, the ban has not led to more sustainably oriented policies but simply to a shift in the geographical location of logging activities.

Various attempts at reservation and protection of remaining forest land have been made. The principal forest statutes include the *Forest Act 1941*, and the *National Forest Reserve Act 1964*. The latter provides for the reservation and protection of forest reserves. Since the 1960s, the Royal Forestry Department (RFD) has pursued an active program of reservation despite the rapid pace of deforestation. In 1985, the area of forest reserves extended to 42 percent of all Thailand, despite the reduction of natural forest area to 22 percent. It is estimated that 1.2 million families, approximately 20 percent of Thai farmers, are in illegal occupation of land in forest reserves. Attempts by the RFD to compulsorily reclaim the land have led to outbreaks of violence in affected communities because many farmers simply have nowhere else to go.

An internationally sponsored project bordering the Khao Yai National Park has had some success in preventing forest encroachment and illegal hunting. Its integrated approach offers a more constructive approach than compulsory removals. The project is based on the premise that forest protection and rural development are interrelated. The project sponsors credit, education and collective business ventures in villages bordering the Park. A cooperative credit society, the Environmental Protection Society, has been formed and villagers who agree to abide by the National Park Regulations, which prohibit farming encroachments in the Park, are eligible to receive credit from the Society. In addition, there has been work created for some villagers in low key tourism developments. The project has stalled some forest encroachment and is regarded as successful. The greatest challenge, however, is to replicate the project with its demanding resource requirements, in other areas.

At first sight, the shortage of funds to replicate successful forest projects in Thailand suggests that Thailand's viewpoint at the UNCED was incongruous. Given the belated offer of the United States to increase overseas aid for forest projects in developing countries, why was the Thai Government not persuaded to break away from the hard line espoused by the Group of 77? Leaving aside the international diplomatic repercussions that such a change in position would most probably have incurred, there are convincing reasons in the domestic sphere which also help to explain the Thai position. These reasons relate to the reafforestation programs which the Thai Government was actively pursuing at the time of the UNCED.

Reafforestation

The *National Forest Policy 1985*, sets an ambitious goal of attaining 40 percent actual permanent forest cover, of which 15 percent will be completely protected and 25 percent will be classified as productive forest. The emphasis since the 1980s has been on commercial reafforestation involving, primarily, eucalyptus plantations. A facilitative legal framework and considerable fiscal incentives have been set up to support this policy objective but plantation forests have led to local riots. This is because farmers without title to land in forest reserves can, at any time, have their land requisitioned by the RFD for re-allocation to commercial enterprises and influential landowners for plantation forests. Even when compensation is payable, the rate is only one half to one third of the market price. At the time of UNCED, the army was actively engaged in implementing plans to move 1.25 million people to release their farm land for reafforestation. This was despite the protests of environmentalists, farmers and the King who opposed the eucalyptus plantations on environmental grounds.

Puntasen, Siripachai and Punyasavatsut trace the international and national commercial interests which have influenced the policy of promoting industrial plantations at the expense of local communities' well being. It is clear that these interests have constrained government policy even when environmental issues have been perceived as a vote winner. With the direct involvement of the military in reafforestation programs, the Government at the time of UNCED was under pressure from both sides of the political spectrum—the military, who have successively intervened in politics to overthrow civilian regimes and safeguard their own interests, and the pro-democracy, business community who are a valuable ally in expensive electoral campaigns.

The political situation at the time of UNCED is particularly illustrative of the power of these interest groups. In February 1991, the elected government of Chatichai Choonhaven was ousted in a military coup. The military swiftly appointed an interim government under Mr. Anand Panyarachan to lead the country into elections under a new constitution. Elections in February 1992 led to victory for a coalition government involving a top military leader, Suchinda Kraprayoon, but resentment at the continuing military role triggered public rioting in May 1992. The riots were crushed by dramatic military intervention which left 50 dead and hundreds wounded. Fresh elections were called for September 1992 and Mr. Anand was reinstalled in the interim. As a respected businessman and an appointee of the military, Mr. Anand was particularly sensitive to both the interest groups which favor plantation forestry. In reality, he was holding reins, attempting to broker a political compromise between these interests.

The reasons why Thailand was not tempted to abandon the Group of 77's hard line on forestry at Rio are now clear. Because forestry is such a sensitive issue in domestic politics, the internationalization of forestry issues, particularly the call for a binding international treaty, was naturally resisted. The past record of deforestation in Thailand did not place the Government in a strong position to advocate forest conservation. International funding, in so far as it is wanted, had already been promised to Thailand.

Understandably, the Government did not wish to expose itself to adverse publicity regarding the impact of the eucalyptus plantation program. The turbulent political events of 1992 help to further explain the Thai contribution at Rio. Mr. Anand was serving only a temporary period in office. This, combined with the difficult political situation at home, made an official trip by the political head of Government to Rio look improper. Radical changes in Thailand's international policy position on forests would also have been inappropriate.

This is not to say that the UNCED proceedings aroused very little interest in Thailand. On the contrary, in the same month that the UNCED took place, the interim government passed the *Enhancement and Conservation of the National Environmental Quality Act 1992*. This makes provision for environmental policymaking at a high level in government while recognizing the role of provincial and local level authorities in implementing environmental projects. The Act establishes an Environment Fund and encourages public participation by recognizing the right to greater freedom of information and the role of NGOs in protecting the environment. This Act demonstrates that while the Thai Government is responsive to increasing environmental awareness, it reserves the right to set its own agenda for action. Thus, while the holistic, integrated approach to environment and development has been accepted at this general level, forestry issues were not subjected to the same progressive regime.

Conclusion: Lessons for International Forest Policy

Forestry issues in Thailand, as in Malaysia, fall firmly within the domestic sphere of policy consideration. Commercial interests in both Malaysia and Thailand play a growing role in national politics. Governments in both countries are committed to economic growth including privatization of business and free international trade. Given the actual (Malaysia) and potential (Thailand) commercial significance of forests, governments in Malaysia and Thailand look set to continue their opposition to the internationalization of forest issues.

The following conclusions arise out of this analysis of forest policy in Malaysia and Thailand:

(a) Some of the ideas which were hailed as innovative developments at Rio have already been attempted, without great success, in Malaysia and Thailand. International law in this area lags far behind national developments. For example, an integrated approach to forestry and rural development, as canvassed in the *Statement of Forest Principles*, figured in the Malaysian National Forest Policy 1978, and in some projects in Thailand since the 1970s. The former suffered due to institutional rivalries, the latter due to competition with vested political interests.

(b) A high political price was paid for the inclusion of these "progressive" elements in the *Statement of Forest Principles*. The Statement solidly reaffirms that forest resources are subject to national sovereignty while Principle 14 condemns unilateral trade bans. This effectively undermines the legitimacy of the ban imposed by the former EEC on Sarawakian timber imports, a measure which prompted the Malaysian Government to call upon the ITTO for assistance in Sarawak.

(c) Linking forest conservation with the global environmental problems of climate change and loss of biodiversity is an open invitation for North-South divisiveness in international fora. Developing countries have sufficient reasons, which manifest themselves at the local level, to be concerned about deforestation. The November 1988 floods in Thailand are ample evidence of this.

(d) Despite the negative political rhetoric at the UNCED, the international community can play a constructive role in forest affairs. Discrete technical assistance facilities and well construed project assistance is needed and will be called upon by even the most reluctant States when such assistance meets their own political agendas. Malaysia's resort to the ITTO is evidence of this. This finding makes it essential that the policies of international institutions are transparent and in harmony with the more progressive elements of the UNCED *Statement of Forest Principles*.

(e) Financial assistance is not a sufficient incentive to induce developing countries to surrender absolute national control over forest resources. This is because the short-term profits from unsustainable exploitation are sufficient to make foreign aid for forest initiatives a peripheral consideration. On the contrary, it is the use of forest resources as a source of political patronage which dominates the forest agenda in both countries.

(f) National governments are responsive to powerful interest groups but they will also, at least occasionally, respond to local public opinion, particularly when it manifests itself in a sufficiently vocal or disturbing form. In Thailand, the publicity afforded to the floods in 1988 are a pertinent example of this. In Malaysia, the campaign against the logging of Sarawak's forests had domestic as well as international dimensions. At the same time as the former EEC ban, indigenous communities in Sarawak were actively organizing blockades in logging concession areas prompting legal and military interventions. In view of their actual and potential impact, local environmental groups and rural communities are interest groups worthy of much greater support from the international community.

(g) The sustainable exploitation of forest resources has not been achieved in Malaysia or Thailand. Continuing forest destruction in both countries gives environmentalists few reasons for optimism. This makes measures of last resort, including ex situ conservation of endangered species, an essential component of forest planning.

3

Fisheries

A

Documents and Instruments Relating to Fisheries

(i) *Convention for the Prohibition of Fishing with Long Driftnets in the South Pacific*, Wellington, 24 November 1989, 29 ILM 1454

[*This convention was adopted by the South Pacific Forum following a debate among the states of the Southwest Pacific. Its adoption was the inspiration for a series of United Nations initiatives some of which are extracted below. An instrument not extracted, but of some considerable relevance, is the Convention on the Conservation and Management of Highly Migratory Fish Stocks in the Western and Central Pacific Ocean, Signed in Honolulu, Hawaii, on 5 September 2000. The text of this more recent convention can be found on the Internet at http://sedac.ciesin.org/entri/texts/fish.west.cent.pac.2000.html*]

Article 1—Definitions

For the purposes of this Convention and its Protocols:

(a) the "Convention Area",
  (i) subject to sub-paragraph (ii) of this paragraph, shall be the area lying within 10 degrees North latitude and 50 degrees South latitude and 130 degrees East longitude and 120 degrees West longitude, and shall also include all waters under the fisheries jurisdiction of any Party to this Convention.
  (ii) In the case of a State or Territory which is Party to the Convention by virtue of paragraph 1(b) or 1(c) of Article 10, it shall include only waters under the fisheries jurisdiction of that Party, adjacent to the Territory referred to in paragraph 1(b) or 1(c) of Article 10;

(b) "driftnet" means a gillnet or other net or a combination of nets which is more than 2.5 kilometers in length the purpose of which is to enmesh, entrap or entangle fish by drifting on the surface of or in the water;

(c) "driftnet fishing activities" means:
  (i) catching, taking or harvesting fish with the use of a driftnet;
  (ii) attempting to catch, take or harvest fish with the use of a driftnet;
  (iii) engaging in any other activity which can reasonably be expected to result in the catching, taking or harvesting of fish with the use of a driftnet, including searching for and locating fish to be taken by that method;
  (iv) any operations at sea in support of, or in preparation for any activity described in this paragraph, including operations of placing, searching for or recovering fish aggregating devices or associated electronic equipment such as radio beacons;
  (v) aircraft use, relating to the activities described in this paragraph, except for flights in emergencies involving the health or safety of crew members or the safety of a vessel; or

(vi) transporting, transhipping and processing any driftnet catch, and cooperation in the provision of food, fuel and other supplies for vessels equipped for or engaged in driftnet fishing;

(d) the "FFA" means the South Pacific Forum Fisheries Agency; and

(e) "fishing vessel" means any vessel or boat equipped for or engaged in searching for, catching, processing or transporting fish or other marine organisms.

Article 2—Measures Regarding Nationals and Vessels

Each Party undertakes to prohibit its nationals and vessels documented under its laws from engaging in driftnet fishing activities within the Convention Area.

Article 3—Measures Against Driftnet Fishing Activities

(1) Each Party undertakes:

(a) not to assist or encourage the use of driftnets within the Convention Area; and

(b) to take measures consistent with international law to restrict driftnet fishing activities within the Convention Area, including but not limited to:

(i) prohibiting the use of driftnets within areas under its fisheries jurisdiction; and

(ii) prohibiting the transhipment of driftnet catches within areas under its jurisdiction.

(2) Each Party may also take measures consistent with international law to:

(a) prohibit the landing of driftnet catches within its territory;

(b) prohibit the processing of driftnet catches in facilities under its jurisdiction;

(c) prohibit the importation of any fish or fish product, whether processed or not, which was caught using a drift net;

(d) restrict port access and port servicing facilities for driftnet fishing vessels; and

(e) prohibit the possession of driftnets on board any fishing vessel within areas under its fisheries jurisdiction.

(3) Nothing in this Convention shall prevent a Party from taking measures against driftnet fishing activities which are stricter than those required by the Convention.

Article 4—Enforcement

(1) Each Party shall take appropriate measures to ensure the application of the provisions of this Convention.

(2) The Parties undertake to collaborate to facilitate surveillance and enforcement of measures taken by Parties pursuant to this Convention.

(3) The Parties undertake to take measures leading to the withdrawal of good standing on the Regional Register of Foreign Fishing Vessels maintained by the FFA against any vessel engaging in driftnet fishing activities.

Article 5—Consultation with Non-Parties

(1) The Parties shall seek to consult with any State which is eligible to become a Party to this Convention on any matter relating to drift net fishing activities which appear to affect adversely the conservation of marine living resources within the Convention Area or the implementation of the Convention or its Protocols.

(2) The Parties shall seek to reach agreement with any State referred to in paragraph 1 of this Article, concerning the prohibitions established pursuant to Articles 2 and 3.

Article 6—Institutional Arrangements

(1) The FFA shall be responsible for carrying out the following functions:

(a) the collection, preparation and dissemination of information on driftnet fishing activities within the Convention Area;

(b) the facilitation of scientific analyses on the effects of driftnet fishing activities within the Convention Area, including consultations with appropriate regional and international organisations; and

(c) The preparation and transmission to the Parties of an annual report on any driftnet fishing activities within the Convention Area and the measures taken to implement this Convention or its Protocols.

(2) Each Party shall expeditiously convey to the FFA:

(a) information on the measures adopted by it pursuant to the implementation of the Convention; and

(b) information on, and scientific analyses on the effects of, driftnet fishing activities relevant to the Convention Area.

(3) All Parties, including States or Territories not members of the FFA and the FFA shall cooperate to promote the effective implementation of this Article.

Article 7—Review and Consultation Among Parties

(1) Without prejudice to the conduct of consultations among Parties by other means, the FFA, at the request of three Parties, shall convene meetings of the Parties to review the implementation of this Convention and its Protocols.

(2) Parties to the Protocols shall be invited to any such meeting and to participate in a manner to be determined by the Parties to the Convention.

Article 8—Conservation and Management Measures

Parties to this Convention shall cooperate with each other and with appropriate distant water fishing nations and other entities or organisations in the development of conservation and management measures for South Pacific albacore tuna within the Convention Area.

Article 9—Protocols

This Convention may be supplemented by Protocols or associated instruments to further its objectives.

Article 10—Signature, Ratification and Accession

(1) This Convention shall be open for signature by:

- (a) any member of the FFA; and
- (b) any State in respect of any Territory situated within the Convention Area for which it is internationally responsible; or
- (c) any Territory situated within the Convention Area which has been authorised to sign the Convention and to assume rights and obligations under it by the Government of the State which is internationally responsible for it.

(2) This Convention is subject to ratification by members of the FFA and the other States and Territories referred to in paragraph 1 of this Article. The instruments of ratification shall be deposited with the Government of New Zealand which shall be the Depositary.

(3) This Convention shall remain open for accession by the members of the FFA and the other States and Territories referred to in paragraph 1 of this Article. The instruments of accession shall be deposited with the Depositary.

Article 11—Reservations

This Convention shall not be subject to reservations.

Article 12—Amendments

(1) Any Party may propose amendments to this Convention.

(2) Amendments shall be adopted by consensus among the Parties.

(3) Any amendments adopted shall be submitted by the Depositary to all Parties for ratification, approval or acceptance.

(4) An amendment shall enter into force thirty days after receipt by the Depositary of instruments of ratification, approval or acceptance from all Parties.

Article 13—Entry Into Force

(1) This Convention shall enter into force on the date of deposit of the fourth instrument of ratification or accession.

(2) For any member of the FFA or a State or Territory which ratifies or accedes to this Convention after the date of deposit of the fourth instrument of ratification or accession, the Convention shall enter into force on the date of deposit of its instrument of ratification or accession.

Article 14—Certification and Registration

(1) The original of this Convention and its Protocols shall be deposited with the Depositary, which shall transmit certified copies to all States and Territories eligible to become Party to the Convention and to all States eligible to become Party to a Protocol to the Convention.

(2) The Depositary shall register this Convention and its Protocols in accordance with Article 102 of the Charter of the United Nations.

(ii) United Nations, "Agenda 21 Chapter 17: Protection of the Oceans, All Kinds of Seas, Including Enclosed and Semi-Enclosed Seas, and Coastal Areas and the Protection, Rational Use and Development of Their Living Resources," *Programme of Action for Sustainable Development*, A/CONF.151/26 (Vol. II), Rio de Janeiro, Brazil, 1992

Program Areas

(a) Integrated management and sustainable development of coastal areas, including exclusive economic zones;

(b) Marine environmental protection;
(c) Sustainable use and conservation of marine living resources of the high seas;
(d) Sustainable use and conservation of marine living resources under national jurisdiction;
(e) Addressing critical uncertainties for the management of the marine environment and climate change;
(f) Strengthening international, including regional, cooperation and coordination; and
(g) Sustainable development of small islands.

Integrated Management and Sustainable Development of Coastal and Marine Areas, Including Exclusive Economic Zones

Basis for Action

The coastal area contains diverse and productive habitats important for human settlements, development and local subsistence. More than half the world's population lives within 60 km of the shoreline, and this could rise to three quarters by the year 2020. Many of the world's poor are crowded in coastal areas. Coastal resources are vital for many local communities and indigenous people. The exclusive economic zone (EEZ) is also an important marine area where the States manage the development and conservation of natural resources for the benefit of their people. For small island States or countries, these are the areas most available for development activities.

Despite national, subregional, regional and global efforts, current approaches to the management of marine and coastal resources have not always proved capable of achieving sustainable development, and coastal resources and the coastal environment are being rapidly degraded and eroded in many parts of the world.

Marine Environmental Protection

Basis for Action

Degradation of the marine environment can result from a wide range of sources. Land-based sources contribute 70 percent of marine pollution, while maritime transport and dumping-at-sea activities contribute 10 percent each. The contaminants that pose the greatest threat to the marine environment are, in variable order of importance and depending on differing national or regional situations, sewage, nutrients, synthetic organic compounds, sediments, litter and plastics, metals, radionuclides, oil/hydrocarbons and polycyclic aromatic hydrocarbons (PAHs). Many of the polluting substances originating from land-based sources are of particular concern to the marine environment since they exhibit at the same time toxicity, persistence and bioaccumulation in the food chain. There is currently no global scheme to address marine pollution from land-based sources.

Degradation of the marine environment can also result from a wide range of activities on land. Human settlements, land use, construction of coastal infrastructure, agriculture, forestry, urban development, tourism and industry can affect the marine environment. Coastal erosion and siltation are of particular concern.

Marine pollution is also caused by shipping and sea-based activities. Approximately 600,000 tons of oil enter the oceans each year as a result of normal shipping operations, accidents and illegal discharges. With respect to offshore oil and gas activities, currently machinery space discharges are regulated internationally and six regional conventions to control platform discharges have been under consideration. The nature and extent of environmental impacts from offshore oil exploration and production activities generally account for a very small proportion of marine pollution.

A precautionary and anticipatory rather than a reactive approach is necessary to prevent the degradation of the marine environment. This requires, inter alia, the adoption of precautionary measures, environmental impact assessments, clean production techniques, recycling, waste audits and minimization, construction and/or improvement of sewage treatment facilities, quality management criteria for the proper handling of hazardous substances, and a comprehensive approach to damaging impacts from air, land and water. Any management framework must include the improvement of coastal human settlements and the integrated management and development of coastal areas.

Sustainable Use and Conservation of Marine Living Resources of the High Seas

Basis for Action

Over the last decade, fisheries on the high seas have considerably expanded and currently represent approximately 5 percent of total world landings. The provisions of the United Nations Convention on the Law of the Sea on the marine living resources of the high seas sets forth rights and obligations of States with respect to conservation and utilization of those resources.

However, management of high seas fisheries, including the adoption, monitoring and enforcement of effective conservation measures, is inadequate in many areas and some resources are overutilized. There are problems of unregulated fishing, overcapitalization, excessive fleet size, vessel reflagging to escape controls, insufficiently selective gear, unreliable databases and lack of sufficient cooperation between States. Action by States whose nationals and vessels fish on the high seas, as well as cooperation at the bilateral, subregional, regional and global levels, is essential particularly for highly migratory species and straddling stocks. Such action and cooperation should address inadequacies in fishing practices, as well as in biological knowledge, fisheries statistics and improvement of systems for handling data. Emphasis should also be on multi-species management and other approaches that take into account the relationships among species, especially in addressing depleted species, but also in identifying the potential of underutilized or unutilized populations.

Sustainable Use and Conservation of Marine Living Resources Under National Jurisdiction

Basis for Action

Marine fisheries yield 80 million to 90 million tons of fish and shellfish per year, 95 percent of which is taken from waters under national jurisdiction. Yields have increased nearly fivefold over the past four decades. The provisions of the *United Nations Convention on the Law of the Sea* on marine living resources of the exclusive economic zone and other areas under national jurisdiction set forth rights and obligations of States with respect to conservation and utilization of those resources.

Marine living resources provide an important source of protein in many countries and their use is often of major importance to local communities and indigenous people. Such resources provide food and livelihoods to millions of people and, if sustainably utilized, offer increased potential to meet nutritional and social needs, particularly in developing countries. To realize this potential requires improved knowledge and identification of marine living resource stocks, particularly of underutilized and unutilized stocks and species, use of new technologies, better handling and processing facilities to avoid wastage, and improved quality and training of skilled personnel to manage and conserve effectively the marine living resources of the exclusive economic zone and other areas under national jurisdiction. Emphasis should also be on multi-species management and other approaches that take into account the relationships among species.

Fisheries in many areas under national jurisdiction face mounting problems, including local overfishing, unauthorized incursions by foreign fleets, ecosystem degradation, overcapitalization and excessive fleet sizes, underevaluation of catch, insufficiently selective gear, unreliable databases, and increasing competition between artisanal and large-scale fishing, and between fishing and other types of activities.

Problems extend beyond fisheries. Coral reefs and other marine and coastal habitats, such as mangroves and estuaries, are among the most highly diverse, integrated and productive of the Earth's ecosystems. They often serve important ecological functions, provide coastal protection, and are critical resources for food, energy, tourism and economic development. In many parts of the world, such marine and coastal systems are under stress or are threatened from a variety of sources, both human and natural.

Management of high seas fisheries, including the adoption, monitoring and enforcement of effective conservation measures, is inadequate in many areas and some resources are overutilized.

Strengthening International, Including Regional, Cooperation and Coordination

Basis for Action

It is recognized that the role of international cooperation is to support and supplement national efforts. Implementation of strategies and activities under the program areas relative to marine and coastal areas and seas requires effective institutional arrangements at national, subregional, regional and global levels, as appropriate. There are numerous national and international, including regional, institutions, both within and outside the United Nations system, with competence in marine issues, and there is a need to improve coordination and strengthen links among them. It is also important to ensure that an integrated and multisectoral approach to marine issues is pursued at all levels.

(iii) United Nations, "Agreement for the Implementation of the Provisions of the United Nations Convention on the Law of the Sea of 10 December 1982 Relating to the Conservation and Management of Straddling Fish Stocks and Highly Migratory Fish Stocks," *United Nations Conference on Straddling Fish Stocks and Highly Migratory Fish Stocks*, Sixth Session, UN Doc. A/CONF. 164/37 (1995); 34 ILM 1542 (1995)

Article 2—Objective

The objective of this Agreement is to ensure the long-term conservation and sustainable use of straddling fish stocks and highly migratory fish stocks through effective implementation of the relevant provisions of the Convention.

Article 3—Application

1. Unless otherwise provided, this Agreement applies to the conservation and management of straddling fish stocks and highly migratory fish stocks beyond areas under national jurisdiction, except that articles 6 and 7 apply also to the conservation and management of such stocks within areas under national jurisdiction, subject to the different legal regimes that apply within areas under national jurisdiction and in areas beyond national jurisdiction as provided for in the Convention.
2. In the exercise of its sovereign rights for the purpose of exploring and exploiting, conserving and managing straddling fish stocks and highly migratory fish stocks within areas under national jurisdiction, the coastal State shall apply mutatis mutandis the general principles enumerated in article 5.
3. States shall give due consideration to the respective capacities of developing States to apply articles 5, 6 and 7 within areas under national jurisdiction and their need for assistance as provided for in this Agreement. To this end, Part VII applies mutatis mutandis in respect of areas under national jurisdiction...

Part II—Conservation and Management of Straddling Fish Stocks and Highly Migratory Fish Stocks

Article 5—General Principles

In order to conserve and manage straddling fish stocks and highly migratory fish stocks, coastal States and States fishing on the high seas shall, in giving effect to their duty to cooperate in accordance with the Convention:

(a) adopt measures to ensure long-term sustainability of straddling fish stocks and highly migratory fish stocks and promote the objective of their optimum utilization;

(b) ensure that such measures are based on the best scientific evidence available and are designed to maintain or restore stocks at levels capable of producing maximum sustainable yield, as qualified by relevant environmental and economic factors, including the special requirements of developing States, and taking into account fishing patterns, the interdependence of stocks and any generally recommended international minimum standards, whether subregional, regional or global;

(c) apply the precautionary approach in accordance with article 6;

(d) assess the impacts of fishing, other human activities and environmental factors on target stocks and species belonging to the same ecosystem or associated with or dependent upon the target stocks;

(e) adopt, where necessary, conservation and management measures for species belonging to the same ecosystem or associated with or dependent upon the target stocks, with a view to maintaining or restoring populations of such species above levels at which their reproduction may become seriously threatened;

(f) minimize pollution, waste, discards, catch by lost or abandoned gear, catch of non-target species, both fish and non-fish species, (hereinafter referred to as non-target species) and impacts on associated or dependent species, in particular endangered species, through measures including, to the extent practicable, the development and use of selective, environmentally safe and cost-effective fishing gear and techniques;

(g) protect biodiversity in the marine environment;
(h) take measures to prevent or eliminate overfishing and excess fishing capacity and to ensure that levels of fishing effort do not exceed those commensurate with the sustainable use of fishery resources;
(i) take into account the interests of artisanal and subsistence fishers;
(j) collect and share, in a timely manner, complete and accurate data concerning fishing activities on, inter alia, vessel position, catch of target and non-target species and fishing effort, as set out in Annex I, as well as information from national and international research programmes;
(k) promote and conduct scientific research and develop appropriate technologies in support of fishery conservation and management; and
(l) implement and enforce conservation and management measures through effective monitoring, control and surveillance.

Article 6—Application of the Precautionary Approach

1. States shall apply the precautionary approach widely to conservation, management and exploitation of straddling fish stocks and highly migratory fish stocks in order to protect the living marine resources and preserve the marine environment.
2. States shall be more cautious when information is uncertain, unreliable or inadequate. The absence of adequate scientific information shall not be used as a reason for postponing or failing to take conservation and management measures.
3. In implementing the precautionary approach, States shall:
   (a) improve decision making for fishery resource conservation and management by obtaining and sharing the best scientific information available and implementing improved techniques for dealing with risk and uncertainty;
   (b) apply the guidelines set out in Annex II and determine, on the basis of the best scientific information available, stock-specific reference points and the action to be taken if they are exceeded;
   (c) take into account, inter alia, uncertainties relating to the size and productivity of the stocks, reference points, stock condition in relation to such reference points, levels and distribution of fishing mortality and the impact of fishing activities on non-target and associated or dependent species, as well as existing and predicted oceanic, environmental and socioeconomic conditions; and
   (d) develop data collection and research programmes to assess the impact of fishing on non-target and associated or dependent species and their environment, and adopt plans which are necessary to ensure the conservation of such species and to protect habitats of special concern.
4. States shall take measures to ensure that, when reference points are approached, they will not be exceeded. In the event that they are exceeded, States shall, without delay, take the action determined under paragraph 3 (b) to restore the stocks.
5. Where the status of target stocks or non-target or associated or dependent species is of concern, States shall subject such stocks and species to enhanced monitoring in order to review their status and the efficacy of conservation and management measures. They shall revise those measures regularly in the light of new information.
6. For new or exploratory fisheries, States shall adopt as soon as possible cautious conservation and management measures, including, inter alia, catch limits and effort limits. Such measures shall remain in force until there are sufficient data to allow assessment of the impact of the fisheries on the long-term sustainability of the stocks, whereupon conservation and management measures based on that assessment shall be implemented. The latter measures shall, if appropriate, allow for the gradual development of the fisheries.
7. If a natural phenomenon has a significant adverse impact on the status of straddling fish stocks or highly migratory fish stocks, States shall adopt conservation and management measures on an emergency basis to ensure that fishing activity does not exacerbate such adverse impact. States shall also adopt such measures on an emergency basis where fishing activity presents a serious threat to the sustainability of such stocks. Measures taken on an emergency basis shall be temporary and shall be based on the best scientific evidence available.

States shall make every effort to agree on compatible conservation and management measures within a reasonable period of time.

Article 7—Compatibility of Conservation and Management Measures

1. Without prejudice to the sovereign rights of coastal States for the purpose of exploring and exploiting, conserving and managing the living marine resources within areas under national jurisdiction as provided for in the Convention, and the right of all States for their nationals to engage in fishing on the high seas in accordance with the Convention:
   (a) with respect to straddling fish stocks, the relevant coastal States and the States whose nationals fish for such stocks in the adjacent high seas area shall seek, either directly or through the appropriate mechanisms for cooperation provided for in Part III, to agree upon the measures necessary for the conservation of these stocks in the adjacent high seas area;
   (b) with respect to highly migratory fish stocks, the relevant coastal States and other States whose nationals fish for such stocks in the region shall cooperate, either directly or through the appropriate mechanisms for cooperation provided for in Part III, with a view to ensuring conservation and promoting the objective of optimum utilization of such stocks throughout the region, both within and beyond the areas under national jurisdiction.
2. Conservation and management measures established for the high seas and those adopted for areas under national jurisdiction shall be compatible in order to ensure conservation and management of the straddling fish stocks and highly migratory fish stocks in their entirety. To this end, coastal States and States fishing on the high seas have a duty to cooperate for the purpose of achieving compatible measures in respect of such stocks. In determining compatible conservation and management measures, States shall:
   (a) take into account the conservation and management measures adopted and applied in accordance with article 61 of the Convention in respect of the same stocks by coastal States within areas under national jurisdiction and ensure that measures established in respect of such stocks for the high seas do not undermine the effectiveness of such measures;
   (b) take into account previously agreed measures established and applied for the high seas in accordance with the Convention in respect of the same stocks by relevant coastal States and States fishing on the high seas;
   (c) take into account previously agreed measures established and applied in accordance with the Convention in respect of the same stocks by a subregional or regional fisheries management organization or arrangement;
   (d) take into account the biological unity and other biological characteristics of the stocks and the relationships between the distribution of the stocks, the fisheries and the geographical particularities of the region concerned, including the extent to which the stocks occur and are fished in areas under national jurisdiction;
   (e) take into account the respective dependence of the coastal States and the States fishing on the high seas on the stocks concerned; and
   (f) ensure that such measures do not result in harmful impact on the living marine resources as a whole.
3. In giving effect to their duty to cooperate, States shall make every effort to agree on compatible conservation and management measures within a reasonable period of time.
4. If no agreement can be reached within a reasonable period of time, any of the States concerned may invoke the procedures for the settlement of disputes provided for in Part VIII.
5. Pending agreement on compatible conservation and management measures, the States concerned, in a spirit of understanding and cooperation, shall make every effort to enter into provisional arrangements of a practical nature. In the event that they are unable to agree on such arrangements, any of the States concerned may, for the purpose of obtaining provisional measures, submit the dispute to a court or tribunal in accordance with the procedures for the settlement of disputes provided for in Part VIII.
6. Provisional arrangements or measures entered into or prescribed pursuant to paragraph 5 shall take into account the provisions of this Part, shall have due regard to the rights and obligations of all States concerned, shall not jeopardize or hamper the reaching of final agreement on compatible conservation and

management measures and shall be without prejudice to the final outcome of any dispute settlement procedure.

7. Coastal States shall regularly inform States fishing on the high seas in the subregion or region, either directly or through appropriate subregional or regional fisheries management organizations or arrangements, or through other appropriate means, of the measures they have adopted for straddling fish stocks and highly migratory fish stocks within areas under their national jurisdiction.
8. States fishing on the high seas shall regularly inform other interested States, either directly or through appropriate subregional or regional fisheries management organizations or arrangements, or through other appropriate means, of the measures they have adopted for regulating the activities of vessels flying their flag which fish for such stocks on the high seas.

Article 9—Subregional and Regional Fisheries Management Organizations and Arrangements

1. In establishing subregional or regional fisheries management organizations or in entering into subregional or regional fisheries management arrangements for straddling fish stocks and highly migratory fish stocks, States shall agree, inter alia, on:
   (a) the stocks to which conservation and management measures apply, taking into account the biological characteristics of the stocks concerned and the nature of the fisheries involved;
   (b) the area of application, taking into account article 7, paragraph 1, and the characteristics of the subregion or region, including socioeconomic, geographical and environmental factors;
   (c) the relationship between the work of the new organization or arrangement and the role, objectives and operations of any relevant existing fisheries management organizations or arrangements; and
   (d) the mechanisms by which the organization or arrangement will obtain scientific advice and review the status of the stocks, including, where appropriate, the establishment of a scientific advisory body.
2. States cooperating in the formation of a subregional or regional fisheries management organization or arrangement shall inform other States which they are aware have a real interest in the work of the proposed organization or arrangement of such cooperation.

Article 10—Functions of Subregional and Regional Fisheries Management Organizations and Arrangements

In fulfilling their obligation to cooperate through subregional or regional fisheries management organizations or arrangements, States shall:

(a) agree on and comply with conservation and management measures to ensure the long-term sustainability of straddling fish stocks and highly migratory fish stocks;
(b) agree, as appropriate, on participatory rights such as allocations of allowable catch or levels of fishing effort;
(c) adopt and apply any generally recommended international minimum standards for the responsible conduct of fishing operations;
(d) obtain and evaluate scientific advice, review the status of the stocks and assess the impact of fishing on non-target and associated or dependent species;
(e) agree on standards for collection, reporting, verification and exchange of data on fisheries for the stocks;
(f) compile and disseminate accurate and complete statistical data, as described in Annex I, to ensure that the best scientific evidence is available, while maintaining confidentiality where appropriate;
(g) promote and conduct scientific assessments of the stocks and relevant research and disseminate the results thereof;
(h) establish appropriate cooperative mechanisms for effective monitoring, control, surveillance and enforcement;
(i) agree on means by which the fishing interests of new members of the organization or new participants in the arrangement will be accommodated;
(j) agree on decision-making procedures which facilitate the adoption of conservation and management measures in a timely and effective manner;

(k) promote the peaceful settlement of disputes in accordance with Part VIII;
(l) ensure the full cooperation of their relevant national agencies and industries in implementing the recommendations and decisions of the organization or arrangement; and
(m) give due publicity to the conservation and management measures established by the organization or arrangement.

(iv) United Nations General Assembly, "51/36. Large-scale pelagic drift net fishing; unauthorized fishing in zones of national jurisdiction; and fisheries by-catch and discards," Resolution Adopted by the General Assembly, General A/RES/51/36, 21 January 1997

The General Assembly,

Reaffirming its resolutions 46/215 of 20 December 1991, 49/116 and 49/118 of 19 December 1994 as well as other relevant resolutions,

Reaffirming also its resolution 50/25 of 5 December 1995 on large-scale pelagic drift net fishing and its impact on the living marine resources of the world's oceans and seas, unauthorized fishing in zones of national jurisdiction and its impact on the living marine resources of the world's oceans and seas, and fisheries by-catch and discards and their impact on the sustainable use of the world's living marine resources,

Conscious of the need to promote and facilitate international cooperation, especially at the regional and subregional levels, in order to ensure the sustainable development and use of the living marine resources of the world's oceans and seas, consistent with the present resolution,

Mindful that the Agreement for the Implementation of the Provisions of the *United Nations Convention on the Law of the Sea* of 10 December 1982 relating to the Conservation and Management of Straddling Fish Stocks and Highly Migratory Fish Stocks 1 provides in its general principles that States shall minimize pollution, waste, discards, catch by lost or abandoned gear, catch of non-target species, both fish and non-fish species, and impacts on associated or dependent species, in particular endangered species, through measures including, to the extent practicable, the development and use of selective, environmentally safe and cost-effective fishing gear and techniques, and further provides that States shall take measures, including the establishment of regulations, to ensure that vessels flying their flags do not conduct unauthorized fishing within areas under the national jurisdiction of other States,

Noting that the Code of Conduct for Responsible Fisheries sets out principles and global standards of behavior for responsible practices to conserve, manage and develop fisheries, including guidelines for fishing on the high seas and in areas under the national jurisdiction of other States, and on fishing gear selectivity and practices, with the aim of reducing by-catch and discards,

Expressing deep concern at the detrimental impact of unauthorized fishing in areas under national jurisdiction, where the overwhelming proportion of the global fish catch is harvested, on the sustainable development of the world's fishery resources and on the food security and economies of many States, particularly developing States,

Reaffirming once again the rights and duties of coastal States to ensure proper conservation and management measures with respect to the living resources in areas under their national jurisdiction, in accordance with international law as reflected in the *United Nations Convention on the Law of the Sea*,

Taking note of the report of the Secretary-General on large-scale pelagic drift net fishing and its impact on the living marine resources of the world's oceans and seas, unauthorized fishing in zones of national jurisdiction and its impact on the living marine resources of the world's oceans and seas, and fisheries by-catch and discards and their impact on the sustainable use of the world's living marine resources,

Acknowledging with appreciation the measures taken and the progress made by members of the international community, international organizations and regional economic integration organizations to implement and support the objectives of resolution 46/215,

Recognizing the efforts that international organizations and members of the international community have made to reduce by-catch and discards in fishing operations,

Once again expressing deep concern that there are continuing reports of activities inconsistent with the terms of resolution 46/215 and unauthorized fishing inconsistent with the terms of resolution 49/116,

1. Reaffirms the importance it attaches to compliance with its resolution 46/215, in particular to those

provisions of the resolution calling for full implementation of a global moratorium on all large-scale pelagic drift net fishing on the high seas of the world's oceans and seas, including enclosed seas and semi-enclosed seas;

2. Notes that a growing number of States and other entities as well as relevant regional and subregional fisheries management organizations and arrangements have adopted legislation, established regulations or applied other measures to ensure compliance with resolutions 46/215 and 49/116, and urges them to enforce fully such measures;
3. Urges all authorities of members of the international community that have not done so to take greater enforcement responsibility to ensure full compliance with resolution 46/215 and to impose appropriate sanctions, consistent with their obligations under international law, against acts contrary to the terms of that resolution;
4. Calls upon States to take the responsibility, consistent with their obligations under international law as reflected in the *United Nations Convention on the Law of the Sea* 2 and resolution 49/116, to take measures to ensure that no fishing vessels entitled to fly their national flags fish in areas under the national jurisdiction of other States unless duly authorized by the competent authorities of the coastal State or States concerned; such authorized fishing operations should be carried out in accordance with the conditions set out in the authorization;
5. Urges States, relevant international organizations and regional and subregional fisheries management organizations and arrangements to take action to adopt policies, apply measures, including through assistance to developing countries, collect and exchange data and develop techniques to reduce by-catches, fish discards and post-harvest losses consistent with international law and relevant international instruments, including the Code of Conduct for Responsible Fisheries;
6. Reiterates its call on development assistance organizations to make it a high priority to support, including through financial and/or technical assistance, efforts of developing coastal States, in particular the least developed countries and the small island developing States, to improve the monitoring and control of fishing activities and the enforcement of fishing regulations, including through financial and technical support for regional and subregional meetings for this purpose;
7. Requests the Secretary-General to bring the present resolution to the attention of all members of the international community, relevant intergovernmental organizations, the organizations and bodies of the United Nations system, regional and subregional fisheries management organizations, and relevant nongovernmental organizations, and invites them to provide the Secretary-General with information relevant to the implementation of the present resolution;
8. Also requests the Secretary-General to ensure that reporting on all major fisheries-related activities and instruments is effectively coordinated and duplication of activities and reporting minimized and that relevant scientific and technical studies are disseminated to the international community, and invites the relevant specialized agencies, including the Food and Agriculture Organization of the United Nations, as well as regional and subregional fisheries organizations and arrangements, to cooperate with the Secretary-General to that end;
9. Further requests the Secretary-General to submit to the General Assembly at its fifty-second session and biennially thereafter a report on further developments relating to the implementation of resolutions 46/215, 49/116 and 49/118, taking into account the information provided by States, relevant specialized agencies, in particular the Food and Agriculture Organization of the United Nations, and other appropriate organs, organizations and programs of the United Nations system, regional and subregional organizations and arrangements and other relevant intergovernmental and nongovernmental organizations;
10. Decides to include in the provisional agenda of its fifty-second session, under an item entitled "Oceans and law of the sea", a sub-item entitled "Large-scale pelagic drift-net fishing; unauthorized fishing in zones of national jurisdiction; and fisheries by-catch and discards".

77th plenary meeting
9 December 1996

B

Menasveta D., "Fisheries Management in the Exclusive Economic Zones of Southeast Asia Before and After Rio and Prospects for Regional Cooperation" in Koh K.L., Beckman R. and Chia L.S. (eds), *Sustainable Development of Coastal and Ocean Areas in Southeast Asia: Post-Rio Perspective* Singapore, 1995, pp 98–134

Introduction

Fisheries management is an essential tool for the sound, sustained development of fisheries. It is thus an integral part of the development process. Fisheries management has been based on the concept of sustainability and has been the central issue of interest to the global fisheries community for many decades. The sustainability concept was strengthened by the *International Conference on Over-fishing*; the *International Conference on the Conservation of Living Resources of the Sea*; the *FAO Technical Conference on Fishery Management and Development*; and the *FAO World Conference on Fishery Management and Development*. The wisdom that emanated from these conferences is included in the definition of sustainable development adopted by the FAO Council in 1988. The definition states: "such sustainable development in the fishery sector conserves the resources, is environmentally non-degrading, technically appropriate, economically viable and socially acceptable".

The *United Nations Conference on Environment and Development* (UNCED), a sequel to the *UN Conference on Human Environment* and to the work of the *World Conference on Environment and Development ("Brundtland" Report)* was convened in Rio de Janeiro, Brazil in June 1992. Its goal was to promote the integration of development and environment objectives, i.e., sustainable development. The above-mentioned definition of sustainable development is embodied in its *Rio Declaration on Environment and Development*. Issues related to the conservation and sustainable use of the oceans and their resources were among the elements extensively discussed at the Conference. Issues which could not be resolved when UNCED ended included those relating to the high seas, in particular, straddling fish stocks and highly migratory fish stocks. These issues are being considered at an intergovernmental conference convened by the United Nations.

UNCED culminated in the *Rio Declaration on Environment and Development*; in a program of action called "*Agenda 21*"; and two conventions, one on biodiversity and the other on climate change, now opened for signature. UNCED's outcome confirms the validity of the *Strategy for Fisheries Management and Development* and the five Programmes of Action adopted by the 1984 FAO World Fisheries Conference, but with additional emphasis on integrated coastal zone management, environmental protection and responsible fishing.

Agenda 21 has a number of chapters. Those that have direct implications on fisheries are Chapter 15 on the Conservation of Biological Diversity; Chapter 17 on the Protection of the Oceans, All Kinds of Seas, Including Enclosed and Semi-enclosed Seas, and Coastal Areas and the Protection, Rational Use and Development of Their Living Resources; and Chapter 18 on the Protection of the Quality and Supply of Freshwater Resources: Application of Integrated Approaches to the Development, Management and Use of Water Resources.

Chapter 17 of *Agenda 21* contains seven program areas concerning marine living resources and environment:

a) Integrated management and sustainable development of coastal areas, including exclusive economic zones;
b) Marine environmental protection;
c) Sustainable use and conservation of marine living resources of the high seas;
d) Sustainable use and conservation of marine living resources under national jurisdiction;
e) Addressing critical uncertainties for the management of the marine environment and climate change;
f) Strengthening international, including regional, cooperation and coordination; and
g) Sustainable development of small islands.

This paper, as its title indicates, focuses attention on the above item (d), noting that separate papers will be prepared for the present Conference on items (a) and (b).

It reviews the evolution of fisheries in the Southeast Asian region in the period prior to UNCED (1960 to 1991); highlights fisheries management issues which remain to be resolved; describes existing frameworks for international and regional cooperation and coordination in the region, as well as mechanisms for solving some of the major regional issues, with a view to accelerating the sustainability of fisheries of the Southeast Asian countries.

Southeast Asian Region

Southeast Asia, in the context of this study, covers the South China Sea and the countries and political/legal entities bordering that sea; namely, Brunei Darussalam, Cambodia, Hong Kong, Indonesia, Malaysia, People's Republic of China, the Philippines, the Republic of China (Taiwan), Singapore, Thailand and Vietnam. Laos is the only country in the Southeast Asian region which is land-locked. The South China Sea does not include any high seas area.

The extent and physical characteristics of the South China Sea have been described in detail in a number of studies and reports. In this paper, only a brief description of that sea will therefore be given.

The South China Sea is a semi-enclosed sea. It has extensive continental shelf areas and a deep basin. With the East China Sea to the north, it contains approximately 20 percent of the shallow water areas of the world. The main shelf areas are the Mainland Shelf in the north and northeast and the Sunda Shelf including the Gulf of Thailand, in the south and southwest. The total area of the South China Sea is about 3.5 million km^2, of which 1.5 million km^2 are contained in the South China Sea basin and 2 million km^2 are in the shelf areas, which are less than 500 meters in depth. The South China Sea basin has an average depth of about 4,000 m and a maximum depth of about 5,000 m located off Palawan. Within this basin lie the submerged banks (Macclesfield Banks or Chungsha) and island groups; viz., the Paracels (Hsisha), and the Dangerous Ground, including the Spratly Islands group (Nansha Islands).

Contiguous waters to the South China Sea proper are the Malacca Straits; the Java, Flores, Banda, Ceram, Molluca, Celebes and Sulu seas and the Philippine seas. Including these, the total area of Southeast Asian waters is about 8.9 million km^2, which represents about 2.5 percent of the world's ocean surface. Most of the sea areas mentioned are under the jurisdiction of the archipelagic States, viz., Indonesia and the Philippines.

The South China Sea is influenced by the tropical monsoon regime, and the climate is dominated by two monsoons annually, i.e., the southwest monsoon (May to October) and the northeast monsoon (November to April). The monsoons induce changes in the circulation pattern of surface water and also induce spotted upwellings, creating vertical mixing over many areas of the shelves. These monsoons therefore influence the biology and bionomics of the living resources therein. Nutrient enrichment is brought about by the vertical mixing of the water layers in the shelf areas, and by discharges from large rivers such as the Chao Phya in Thailand and the Mekong in Vietnam, and from many other rivers and streams in the region. This has led to the high biodiversity and production of fish, crustaceans and molluscs in the shelf areas, predominantly short-lived tropical species, estimated at more than 2,500 species. Hence, the South China Sea is one of the most productive areas in the world in terms of living resources.

A wide diversity of ethnic, cultural, political, religious and language backgrounds exists among the countries and the peoples of Southeast Asia. Diversity also exists with respect to the size of each country and its population, GNP, the status of the fishing industry, etc. Despite these differences, there are a number of similarities; these include the generally low level of income, a high birth rate in several countries in the region and the importance of fisheries in the economic and social development of the countries in the region.

Other similarities include the same range of marine fauna and flora (the Indo-Malay region), the currently intense exploitation of the fishery resources in many fishing grounds of the exclusive economic zones of the countries concerned, and high per capita consumption of fish among the populations. Furthermore, all countries in the region need to improve information and statistical data on the resources exploited and to exercise effective fisheries management and environmental protection to ensure the sustainable use of the fishery resources.

It is felt that the countries in the region tend to form a natural management unit with respect to fisheries, and most of the countries recognize the advantages of concerted action and attitudes.

It is felt that the countries in the region tend to form a natural management unit with respect to fisheries, and most of the countries recognize the advantages of concerted action and attitudes. The concept of a natural management unit has been used by FAO when the UNDP/FAO *South China Sea Fisheries Development and Coordinating Programme* (SCSP) was implemented from 1973–1984. The concept is still valid and has been used by the Indo-Pacific Fishery Commission (IPFC) in its attempt to revitalize its activities in the technical and policy fields; in particular, those of its subsidiary bodies such as the *Committee for the Development and Management of Fisheries in the South China Sea* (CDMSCS), as recommended by the FAO Committee on Fisheries (COFI) at its Eighteenth Session.

Southeast Asian Fisheries, 1960–1991

Although fish has been important in the diet of Southeast Asian people since time immemorial, the contribution of the Southeast Asian fisheries to world fish production prior to 1960 was relatively insignificant, with the regional total catch estimated at less than two million tons or less than ten percent of the total world catch. This perhaps was due to the lack or incompleteness of statistical records on fish production in many countries of the region before 1960. At that time, fish, predominantly small-sized pelagic species such as mackerels, sardines and anchovies, were captured in inshore and coastal waters by a large number of small-scale fishermen, employing traditional types of fishing gear, mainly stationary, such as stake traps, lift nets, set bag nets, beach seines, and hooks and lines. The fishing boats employed were mostly small and non-motorized. Marine fish were consumed mostly by the populations inhabiting the coastal areas.

Inland capture fisheries prior to the sixties was important as a source of food for rural populations. Aquaculture was concentrated on a few freshwater fish species employing traditional techniques and was practiced by farmers to augment fish supplies from natural waters. Of the above regional total, it was estimated that inland fisheries and aquaculture contributed about 20–25 percent in the fifties.

Since the early sixties, there has been a remarkable increase in the fish production of Southeast Asian countries, particularly from the marine fisheries sub-sector. Thailand is notable, beginning with the introduction of trawl net fishing in the Gulf of Thailand and adjacent waters. The rising regional trend of fish production continued in the eighties and early nineties with an increasing contribution from aquaculture to augment the landings. The estimated annual fish production of the South China Sea countries rose from some 2 million tons in 1950 to 8.9 million tons in 1970, and to 25 million tons in 1991. The production in 1991 was about 26 percent of the world production. Excluding China, the total production of the South China Sea countries in 1991 was about 12 million tons or 12.6 percent of the total world catch.

Marine Fisheries

Marine fisheries of the region has been traditionally characterized by the use of multi-gear by a vast majority of traditional small-scale fishermen (estimated at more than four million) to exploit a wide variety of tropical and sub-tropical marine organisms. Since the sixties, commercial fisheries has developed rapidly and, on many occasions, has had conflicts with the traditional fisheries, competing for the fishery resources in inshore and coastal waters. The commercial fisheries employ bigger and more efficient types of fishing gear, including trawl nets, purse seines and drift nets as well as fishing and navigation aids to ensure successful fishing operations. A few decades ago, tropical waters such as the South China Sea were generally believed to have low productivity. However, the rapid development of marine fisheries in these waters has confirmed that the Sea is highly productive. The major producing countries were China, Indonesia, Philippines and Thailand. The production in 1991 accounted for about one-fifth of the world marine fishery production, valued at more than US$8,000 million. Excluding China, the value of the catch was estimated at US$6,800 million.

The rapid expansion of marine fisheries in the region since the sixties has been due to a number of factors:

(1) the importation of modern technologies and techniques for fishing, such as monofilament nylon gill nets of various sizes, used widely by the small-scale fisheries sector in coastal and inshore waters, and trawl net fishing used by the industrial and commercial fisheries sector;
(2) the improvement in the design of fishing boats and their motorization;
(3) technical assistance rendered by economically developed countries and international organizations;
(4) capital investment and/or financial assistance from industrialized countries for building required infrastructures such as processing facilities, cold storages and ice plants;
(5) the discovery of new fishing grounds in offshore waters in the South China Sea and contiguous waters as well as the Indian Ocean; and

(6) the general policy of the Southeast Asian governments in the sixties and early seventies to promote offshore or deep sea fisheries.

The increased exploitation has also been fueled by the increasing demand of developed countries for higher quality and higher valued species such as shrimps and prawns. This has prompted fisheries companies and traders in some developed countries to invest or enter into joint venture agreements with key producers in the major fish producing countries in Southeast Asia. Another factor that influenced the expansion of marine fish production was the increase in demand due to the expanding urban populations in the region, with higher purchasing power. Also, as a result of improved transportation and infrastructure in many countries, marine fishery products which were once consumed mainly by the populations inhabiting coastal areas have become national consumer goods and have been transformed from domestic to international commodities.

Although trawl fisheries constitutes only a small part of the overall fishing industry in the region, which is predominantly small-scale, it is this modern fisheries sub-sector which has caused, more than any sub-sector, the rapid expansion of marine fisheries in the region during the period mentioned. The introduction of trawl net fishing to Thai fisheries in the early sixties led to the spectacular increase of that country's fish production. The total annual landing rose from some 200,000 tons in 1960 to 1,400,000 tons in 1970. By 1980 more than 85 percent of the Thai marine fish catch was by trawl fisheries. The success of the Thai trawl fisheries led to the subsequent expansion of the trawl fisheries in Malaysia and Indonesia in the late sixties. The pace of marine fisheries development in the Philippines has likewise been significant, especially with the use of gill nets by artisanal fishermen in municipal fisheries, and purse seine and "basnig" nets for catching pelagic fish and tuna by commercial fisheries in the coastal waters.

The rapid and uncontrolled expansion of trawl fisheries has had a negative impact on the fishery resources exploited. The Philippines experienced biological overfishing in Manila Bay in the sixties and seventies. The past three decades have seen biological overfishing phenomena in the Gulf of Thailand, which has forced larger Thai trawlers to fish further in the South China Sea, in the Indian Ocean and other distant waters. There have been conflicts between trawl fishermen and traditional fishermen along the coasts of Thailand. Malaysia and Indonesia have experienced the same problems. These developments led to the revision of fisheries legislation in Malaysia, including the zoning of fishing operations, and a ban on trawling activities in the Java Sea and part of Malacca Strait by Indonesia in the early eighties.

The intense trawl fishing on the Sunda Shelf, particularly in the Gulf of Thailand, has resulted in smaller sizes of demersal fish being caught and in changes in species composition of the catch whereby long-lived and higher valued species are replaced by short-lived and lower-valued species. The available fisheries statistics indicate that more than 65 percent of the trawl catch in the Gulf of Thailand now consists mainly of trash fish and contributes only 16 percent of the total landed value. The production of trash fish in the region has remained relatively constant since 1978, i.e., about one million tons annually. There is still demand for trash fish, especially by animal feed and aquaculture industries.

The trawl ban in western Indonesia by the Government of Indonesia has reportedly resulted in the landing of more demersal fish of suitable size for human consumption, and satisfactory returns to small-scale fishermen. The production is currently back to the level prior to the trawl ban.

Attempts in the past have been made, despite limited information and statistical data, to ascertain the sustainable yields of the fish stocks in the South China Sea and its contiguous waters. The recent estimate of the potential yield of the Southeast Asian waters was made by Chikuni. For comparison, the author adds the estimated catches in 1990 of the various groups of fish, crustaceans and molluscs. The catch of demersal fish in 1990 surpassed the estimated potential yield. A further increase of about 200,000 tons might be obtained from coastal pelagic fish and there is room for increased exploitation of cephalopods in the region.

It is believed that most demersal fish stocks in the region have been fully exploited or overexploited, with the exception of those in the central Sunda Shelf, the northern Arafura Sea and the central Java Sea; the worst situation exists in the inner part of the Gulf of Thailand and in the Strait of Malacca. A recent Seminar on the Rehabilitation of the Thai Seas conducted by the Fisheries Department of Thailand in 1993 concluded that demersal resources in the Gulf have been overfished for the past two decades; the reduction of the number of trawlers was strongly recommended as a fisheries management measure. Prawn and shrimp stocks in the coastal waters of the region which are exploited mainly by trawl nets have generally been fully exploited or overfished in many areas. In the Gulf of Thailand, the decline in the total catch of penaeid and smaller shrimps has recently been observed. There may be some oceanic shrimp resources for future use; however, the lack of an economical means of catching them and the small size of the schools may be impediments to increased exploitation.

The rapid development of marine fisheries in Southeast Asia during the past three decades has had both a positive and negative impact and has brought the countries concerned closer to the full utilization of marine fisheries resources in their individual exclusive economic zones.

With the decline of predator species due to intense trawling, the popular lions of cephalopods, mainly squids and cuttlefish, have increased substantially, now supporting both small-scale and commercial fisheries in the region. The landing of cephalopods in the region rose from 60,000 tons in 1970 to 250,000 tons in 1990. Cephalopods are the only resource from which a substantial catch can be made in many parts of the region. Intensive fishing on cephalopods has, however, been observed in the Gulf of Thailand, and it is believed that the resources have been fully exploited.

The decline in the abundance of demersal fishery resources has stimulated the fishing industry in the region to increase the exploitation of pelagic fish stocks, using purse seines or purse seines with luring lights. A number of fishing grounds for small and medium-sized pelagic fish such as scads were discovered in the middle of the Gulf of Thailand. This contributed to the increased production of pelagic fish in the seventies and eighties. In the late eighties, about three million tons of these small and medium-sized pelagic fish were caught annually.

The coastal pelagic resources in many areas of the region may also have been fully exploited. In Thai waters, most of these resources have been over exploited, except Indian mackerel *(Rastrelliger kanagurta)* which could sustain an increase in fishing effort by about 20 percent over the 1991–1992 level.

Oceanic pelagic fish such as skipjack and yellowfin tuna are fished mainly by Indonesia and the Philippines. The estimated total landing of tuna and tuna-like fishes in the region was about 400,000 tons in the late eighties. It is believed that the oceanic tuna stocks exploited by the Southeast Asian fisheries are part of the entire stocks widely distributed in the Pacific Ocean beyond the eastern border of the region. A moderate expansion of the fisheries in the region for skipjack and yellowfin tuna can be made as the exploitation of the Pacific Ocean stocks of skipjack still remains at a moderate level and the state of exploitation of the yellowfin tuna stocks is unclear.

It can therefore be concluded that the rapid development of marine fisheries in Southeast Asia during the past three decades has had both a positive and negative impact and has brought the countries concerned closer to the full utilization of marine fisheries resources in their individual exclusive economic zones. It is felt that within this decade distant water fishing countries will have increasing difficulties in gaining access to fish in the exclusive economic zones of the coastal countries in the region because of the steady decline in the abundance of fishery resources therein. Conditions of access rights will have to be subject to review by the coastal countries concerned.

Inland Fisheries

While the trend of the annual world production from inland fisheries during 1970–1990 was on the decline (9 million tons in 1970 to 8 million tons in 1980 and 7 million tons in 1990), the production from inland fisheries of the South China Sea rose during the same period. The total value of the inland fish production in 1990 was more than US$500 million. China, Indonesia and the Philippines are the major producing countries in the region. The production in Thailand and Vietnam has stagnated around 100,000–140,000 tons during the past two decades.

Since the end of the Second World War, reservoir fisheries has gained an increasingly important role in the production of inland fish because of the number of dams constructed for hydroelectric, irrigation and other purposes. In China and Thailand, artificial propagation for stocking fish fry and juveniles in natural and reservoir waters for culture-based fisheries in these waters has been practiced. The development of dams has reportedly had a negative impact on the productivity of the floodplains and water areas below, as the amount of water released downstream is regulated for use in agriculture or other purposes, thus reducing the flooded areas which are commonly used by fish to spawn and feed. Furthermore, the dams interfere with the upstream migration of fish, thus reducing the amount of riverine fish in the upstream area of the dam. The author has no access to any quantitative analysis of the productivity gained from reservoir fisheries as compared to the loss of productivity of the floodplain fisheries. While the current increasing trends of inland fish production in some countries in the region are noted, it is felt that, in the long term, the production from inland capture fisheries in the Southeast Asian region, especially in the Mekong Basin will not increase substantially from the present levels but may decline (Interim Committee for Coordination of Investigations of the Lower Mekong Basin, 1992). There are a number of factors limiting the future expansion of inland fisheries. These include population expansion; decline in the abundance of resources due to increased fishing pressure; degradation of water quality and fish habitats due to water pollution and deforestation; increasing conflicts in land and water use; and ineffective management of the resources and the fisheries, based on insufficient and unreliable data.

Future attention to inland fisheries development in the region should thus be focused on effective fisheries management in both natural waters and reservoirs with a view to at least maintaining the present level of production and preventing further environmental degradation. This should be based on improved data on fisheries statistics, improved information on the ecosystems, and on more knowledge of the impact on fisheries of environmental changes caused by development activities and vice versa.

Aquaculture

Aquaculture has been practiced in Southeast Asia for generations, employing traditional systems which are usually site-specific (the systems are integrated with surrounding activities). The rapid development of aquaculture has taken place only during the past few decades, due to better knowledge of the species cultivated, improved methodologies and techniques in fish breeding and nutrition, and increasing demand for food fish from the rapidly expanding populations in Southeast Asia as well as an increasing demand from economically developed countries for higher-valued species such as shrimps and prawns, sea bass, and grouper. Aquaculture production of the Southeast Asian countries rose rapidly from about 3 million tons in 1972 to 9 million tons in 1990, representing a threefold increase. The production in 1990 accounted for 60 percent of the world's aquaculture production, valued at more than US$10,000 million. It comprised 52 percent from freshwater culture; 11 percent from brackishwater culture; and 37 percent from mariculture. China had the highest aquaculture production in 1990 (7 million tons). If China is excluded, the total aquaculture production of the countries in the region in 1990 was about 2 million tons or 13 percent of the world aquaculture production, valued at US$3,000 million.

In recent years attention has been focused on developing an intensive shrimp culture with a view to exporting the products. The total shrimp production from aquaculture, including China and Taiwan, was about 500,000 tons (excluding China and Taiwan, 300,000 tons). The culture of marine fish is not yet as intensive as that of crustaceans.

Intensive shrimp culture which has been promoted in many countries in the region may have a negative impact on coastal capture fisheries and the environment. It has been reported that, in Thailand and Vietnam, mangrove deforestation for expanded shrimp culture activities has resulted in the loss of habitats for breeding and spawning of a number of commercially important species of fish, crustaceans and mollusks and could have a long-term negative impact on coastal fisheries. With the conversion of one third (100,000 ha) of the mangrove forests along the Mekong tidal flats into shrimp ponds, it is observed that the fish catch in the coastal waters of the delta region have decreased sharply with the annual catch of the Mekong fish species now down to 100,000 tons.

The deforestation of mangrove forests also has an impact on the shrimp culture itself as the latter's success, if the traditional method of culture is used, depends on the amount of post larvae in the wild for stocking in ponds. For the intensive culture system, the number of spawners caught in coastal waters, which are used for breeding in hatcheries may decrease because the wild shrimp populations also use mangrove swamps as their feeding ground.

Other negative effects of the destruction of mangrove forests to make way for fish ponds in coastal areas include water pollution, due to release of pond effluents; sedimentation due to release of solid material from ponds; the interruption of water flow regimes; the introduction of disease-causing organisms; the loss of the natural shrimp and fish stocks due to increased pollutants and product contamination due to indiscriminate use of chemicals. In recent years, an epidemic was prevalent among intensive cultured fish and shrimp in a number of Southeast Asian countries; this might have been due to mismanagement in fish culture, e.g., high stocking density, overfeeding, etc. Chemicals and antibiotics have also been used in fish and shrimp culture recently to prevent and control bacterial and viral diseases; the implications of this on human health are not clear.

Aquaculture has also been promoted by some governments in the region for the production of fish for stocking in natural waters and reservoirs (culture-based fisheries), as the rapidly expanding rural populations in a number of Southeast Asian countries has resulted in the reduction of the catch of subsistence inland capture fishing. It felt that the development and transfer of appropriate methodology and techniques for aquaculture based on traditional methods should also be made available to subsistence fish farmers in rural areas to enhance their fish farming.

There exists a potential for aquaculture expansion in the next two decades. It is estimated that at least 6 million ha are still available for aquacultural expansion in the region. However, there are a number of issues which remain to be resolved: control of diseases and epidemics; development of suitable fish feed and nutrition; and prevention of environmental degradation caused either by development activities or aquaculture. In order to ensure the sustainable development of aquaculture, it is felt that the countries should continue to refine aquaculture techniques, to promote environmentally friendly aquaculture practices, and to gain a better understanding of the ecosystems in which they would like to introduce aquaculture, bearing in mind their relationship to various socioeconomic settings. For the development of culture based fisheries, a quantitative assessment should be made of the cost/benefit of the stocking exercise and of the performance in natural waters or reservoirs, Special attention should also be given to low-input aquaculture systems to produce cheap food fish for expanding rural populations and the urban poor.

Post-Harvest Development

The past two decades saw the improvement of facilities and infrastructure for fish handling, product development, distribution and marketing in several Southeast Asian countries. Imported post-harvest technology has resulted in better handling of catch on board and improved product quality, thus increasing the value of the catch. However, in some countries such as Cambodia and Vietnam, there is still a need to improve facilities and infrastructure for fish processing, distribution and marketing.

There is a high catch utilization rate among the Southeast Asian rural populations especially for freshwater fish and marine fish caught in inshore and coastal areas. The fish are mostly consumed fresh. Traditionally processed products available in markets are sun-dried, salted and dried, steamed/boiled and fermented. High-valued and high-quality fish and shrimps from both inland and marine sources are usually frozen, filleted or canned, with an increasing amount of them destined for export. During the past two decades modern factories have been established in Thailand for producing canned and frozen fish and fishery products such as shrimp and tuna; the raw material of the latter is imported for processing. Rapid development in post-harvest technology during the past two decades has made Thailand one of world's top exporters of canned and frozen tuna.

Trawl net fishing in the Gulf of Thailand has produced a large amount of "by-catches" comprising low-valued small fish (the so-called trash fish), crustaceans and mollusks (many are juveniles of commercially important species). This has promoted Malaysia and Thailand to set up more than 150 fish reduction plants. In Thailand, about one million tons of trash fish (about 40 percent of the 1990 catch) were reduced to fish meal for use locally and for export. Fish meal is used not only for animal feed but also in aquaculture.

Despite the remarkable development in the utilization of fish and fishery products in the region during the past two decades, there is still room for the improvement of post-harvest practices in Southeast Asia; these include increased efforts to reduce post-harvest losses, improved quality of products for local consumption and quality assurance for export products as well as the development of products from low-valued species such as small pelagic and trash fish for direct human food. The Indo-Pacific Fishery Commission at its Twenty-fourth Session in November 1993, endorsed the view of its Executive Committee that collaborative research networks on fish technology between its member countries should be encouraged with a view to promoting continued research on quality control and inspection as well as full utilization of low-value species.

Export and Trade

Fisheries plays an important role in the economic and social development of Southeast Asia; besides its contributions to the food supply and employment opportunities, it has also contributed to foreign exchange earnings. The total export value of fishery commodities of the Southeast Asian countries (excluding China) in 1990 was estimated at US$6,580 million with a trade balance of

US$3,484 million. This represents a fivefold increase over the export value estimated for 1983. Major exporters are Indonesia, Taiwan and Thailand with the export value accounting for 70 percent of the total export value of the region in 1990. Outside the region, fish and fishery products are exported to major markets such as Japan, the United States, some European countries and the middle East.

Within the region, Hong Kong, Taiwan, Thailand and Singapore are the major importers. Hong Kong, Singapore and Taiwan import fish and fishery products mainly for consumption while Thailand imports raw materials, in particular, tuna, for processing and re-export.

Prospects for export and trade appear to be bright. However, in the long term, it is felt that many countries may become net importers because of the limited fishery resources in the South China Sea and the steady increase of the region's population. Hence, long-term planning to ensure full utilization of the fishery resources through proper management is essential.

Government Policies and Strategies for Fisheries Development and Management

A number of countries in Southeast Asia, such as Indonesia, Malaysia, the Philippines and Thailand have, since the sixties, implemented their respective national, economic and social development plans, with fisheries being an integral part. The survey conducted by FAO in 1975 on the objectives for the fisheries sector within the national development plans indicated that the most common objectives were:

(i) to increase the food supply for domestic consumption, thus ensuring food security; and
(ii) to export fish and fishery products for foreign exchange earnings.

Other objectives indicated in the development plans for the fisheries sector vary from one country to another. These include employment opportunities, rural development, income distribution, etc., and reflect the governments' concern with the social aspects of the national development plans. It is noted that such objectives may conflict, particularly when the exploitation of many fishery resources may have almost reached full utilization.

To achieve the fisheries development objectives as envisaged, the governments concerned have adopted policies and strategies for fisheries development and management which seem to follow a relatively similar pattern.

In the sixties, with the assumption that there was a great abundance of fish in the South China Sea and its contiguous waters, the development of offshore or deep-sea fisheries strategy was generally adopted. This has resulted in several countries in the development and expansion of commercial fishing fleets, construction of fishing harbors and on-shore facilities such as cold storages and ice plants; in several cases, with financial and technical support from developed countries or loans from multilateral financing institutions. The strategy has also resulted in the implementation of a number of country and regional projects aimed at improving the capability of local personnel for such deep sea fishing activities. Fishermen's training centers were established in several countries. At the regional level, the Southeast Asian Fisheries Development Center (SEAFDEC) was established in 1967 at the recommendation of the Ministerial Conference for the Economic Development of Southeast Asia. The main objectives of the Center in the earlier years included training in deep sea fisheries for personnel from its member countries.

With the decline in the productivity of the marine fishery resources, especially the demersal resources and the rising conflicts between commercial (mainly trawlers) and traditional fishermen in the region in the seventies, more attention was given in that period to alleviating such conflicts. The plight, and potential contribution to the food supply, of traditional and small-scale fishermen, who had hitherto not been in the mainstream of economic and social development, were recognized. The national policies and strategies since the seventies have, therefore, been to assist small-scale fishermen to increase their productivity, thus improving their standard of living. It is now recognized that small-scale fisheries should be an integral part of rural development.

The policies and strategies since the late seventies have been focused on aquaculture development, not only to augment food supplies for local consumption, but also to produce high-value fish products for export. The strategies to develop aquaculture, especially brackishwater aquaculture, are also used to alleviate fishing pressure on marine fish stocks in the inshore and coastal waters.

In the eighties, accelerated aquaculture development, with special reference to shrimp culture to boost revenues from export products, seemed to be the common strategy for fisheries development in the region. Increased attention has also been paid to the reduction of post-harvest losses, to quality assurance of exported fish and fishery products, and to the integration of fisheries in the overall coastal area management.

Fisheries Management Prior to and After UNCED

Fisheries Management Prior to UNCED

The 1984 FAO World Fisheries Conference stated in its Resolution No. 2 that "management is an essential basis for the sound, sustained development of fisheries" and that "management requirements should be fully integrated into fishery development plans".

The important role of fisheries management has generally been recognized by governments in the region. Wahyono stated that the Government of Indonesia had taken into account the need for rational management and sustainable development of fishery resources in its development policy and strategy since the launching in 1968 of the First Five-Year Development Plan (PELITA). In Thailand, the conservation of fishery resources and rehabilitation of their habitats have appeared as management policies since the Fourth National Economic and Social Development Plan (1977–1981). The Philippine Government, based on the recommendations of the National Conference on Fisheries Policy and Planning in 1987, has recently formulated and implemented the Fisheries Sector Programme (1990–1994) with emphasis on fisheries management. The Malaysian Government adopted in 1981 a comprehensive fisheries licensing policy in order to solve problems arising from the conflicts between traditional fishermen and trawlers in inshore waters.

It is observed that in the early sixties, fisheries management was not explicitly indicated in the governments' policies and plans; management measures are, however, stipulated in the fisheries laws and regulations of several countries. Fisheries management was on a sectoral basis aimed at resolving such issues in capture fisheries as protection of fish spawning and breeding areas and the alleviation of conflicts among resource users in the sector.

Marine fisheries management schemes varied from country to country and from fishery to fishery. As marine fishery resources are treated as common property resources, the measures adopted are aimed at effort controls: the limitation of fishing units (licensing of fishing boats and gear, limitation of entry into a fishery); the restriction of the average catching power of fishing units (prohibition of certain types of gear and vessels); and limitation of the amount of time spent on fishing (closed area, closed season). Other techniques such as fishermen quotas, economic controls and territorial use rights in fisheries were not common practices.

No clear management policies or strategies with respect to aquaculture development were indicated. Environmental and other impacts external to the sector were not taken into account in formulating the management options. Only recently have several countries in the region endeavored to adopt an integrated approach to the management of capture fisheries, especially in the coastal areas and aquaculture.

Ideally, fisheries management measures should have a sound scientific basis, supported by reliable information and statistical data on the stocks and the industry that exploits them. Many of the measures formulated and implemented in many countries in the region are still based on limited information and data on the resources exploited, and on the logic and experience of fisheries administrators and policy makers themselves. The involvement of the private sector, e.g., the fishing industry, is rather minimal. It is felt that these measures are better than nothing at all, but certainly there is room for improvement.

A common problem experienced by almost all countries in the region is the lack of effective enforcement of the adopted management measures. This is due to budgetary and personnel limitations; administrative wrangling among concerned agencies; a lack of understanding of the fisheries management measures by the industry, and the non-involvement of fishermen in the planning and implementation of such measures.

EEZ Fisheries Management After UNCED

It is generally agreed that the recommendations arising out of UNCED under relevant chapters of *Agenda 21* will help coastal States to effectively exercise their rights and responsibilities in order to achieve the goal of fisheries sustainability, in compliance with the relevant provisions of the 1982 UNCLOS, which will come into force in November 1994.

The complexity of the issues involved will, however, have far reaching implications on Southeast Asian countries, especially in adjusting and implementing their development policies and strategies for the rational use and conservation of natural resources. To implement relevant UNCED recommendations, fisheries management actions after UNCED will have to be based on a holistic understanding of all factors, not only biological and economic aspects, but also environmental and sociological ones.

The *Indo-Pacific Fishery Commission's Committee for the Development and Management of Fisheries in the South China Sea* (IPFC/CDMSCS) at its Seventh Session (Hong Kong, 1991) reviewed the state of marine fishery resources and trends in fisheries development of the region in recent years. It identified the following issues as having implications on fisheries management, which remained to be resolved:

(a) inadequate resource assessment, insufficient information in statistics and fisheries;
(b) over-exploitation of traditional marine fishery resources;
(c) protection of the environment (reduction or elimination of destructive fishing methods and the destruction of fish habitats);
(d) improving fish trade and value-added strategies;
(e) conflicts among resource users (e.g., conflicts between trawlers and small-scale operators);
(f) aquaculture development; and
(g) post-harvest losses and inadequate facilities.

The Indo-Pacific Fishery Commission at its Twenty-fourth Session (Bangkok, 1993) endorsed the views of CDMSCS and agreed that solutions to these issues should be accelerated through mutual cooperation among the countries in the region and that external assistance would continue to be required from FAO and other multilateral agencies.

The abovementioned issues fall within the scope of the UNCED recommendations as contained in Chapter 17 of *Agenda 21*, especially the program areas concerned with the sustainable use and conservation of marine living resources under national jurisdiction and of the high seas.

Articles 61-64 of the 1982 UNCLOS provide broad guidelines for the management of a stock within an exclusive economic zone. Under Article 63, shared and straddling stocks are treated together. Technically, the reference points for fisheries conservation and management of shared stocks do not differ from those for straddling or highly migratory stocks.

The author's comments on the above regional issues are given below.

Fisheries Statistical Data and Information

The lack of reliable statistical data and information for fisheries development and management planning has been voiced since the early sixties in many fisheries fora at the subregional, regional and international levels. At its Twentieth Session (Rome, 1993), the FAO Committee on Fisheries expressed concern "at the need to improve the collection of data and the provision of statistical information which, in spite of the emphasis given to training, had not appeared to have reached acceptable levels".

In Southeast Asia, although progress has been made in improving the collection, collation and analysis of fisheries statistics and information during the past few decades, the scope, quality and format of statistical data and information produced, and their timely dissemination, need further improvement. Reference should be made to the dearth of socio-economic data, e.g., cost and earning in fisheries, which are vital in the consideration of fisheries management options.

In Southeast Asia, although progress has been made in improving the collection, collation and analysis of fisheries statistics and information during the past few decades, the scope, quality and format of statistical data and information produced, and their timely dissemination, need further improvement.

To assist the countries in resolving the above problem, FAO in cooperation with SEAFDEC organized in Bangkok in January 1994 a Regional Workshop on Fishery Information and Statistics in Asia. The Workshop identified issues and constraints impeding progress in the improvement of fisheries information and statistics in South and Southeast Asia and recommended actions for consideration by the participating governments and international organizations/agencies concerned. SEAFDEC and FAO/ RAPA were recommended by the Workshop to jointly coordinate future efforts in this respect.

Knowledge of the Fishery Resources and Fisheries Research

Knowledge of the Southeast Asian marine fishery resources also needs to be strengthened, especially those on the central Sunda Shelf and in the South China Sea basin.

At least 40 commercially important fish stocks are thought to be shared by two or more countries in the South China Sea and the Malacca Strait (FAO, 1986; Hongskul, 1980). Knowledge of their migratory patterns such as transboundary movement is fragmentary. Moreover, there is conflict in species identification, e.g., in the scad and sardine groups, and a lack of information on the biology and bionomics of many of these fish stocks. More efforts will have to be made collectively by the countries in the region to effect rational management of these resources.

Progress has been slow in the development of suitable stock assessment techniques applicable to tropical multigear-multispecies fisheries. At present, the assessment of fish stocks in the region is based on only a few mathematical models. These models were developed primarily for a single-species fisheries in temperate waters. The application of these models implies that the assumptions of each model have to be fulfilled, which would be rather difficult in the case of mutigear-multispecies fisheries. More work is needed to develop suitable methodologies for assessing the state of the fish stocks in the region.

Recent efforts have been made in the region to develop better fisheries management-oriented research. Training workshops on fish stock assessment and fishery research planning have been held occasionally in the region with the help of organizations such as FAO (e.g., FAO/DANIDA project GCP/INT/392/DEN) and ICLARM. Recently Indonesia, Malaysia, Philippines and Thailand in cooperation with FAO have experimented with the application of big-economic analysis of fisheries to assist in the formulation of effective management options. At the Twenty-fourth Session of IPFC (Bangkok, 1993), it was agreed that the highest priority should be given to the strengthening of the national capacity to conduct applied research necessary for management and development, with special attention to research on users of the resources.

Marine Fisheries Management

The regulation of marine fisheries in exclusive economic zones through effort controls have been discussed in the past at various international and regional meetings concerned with fisheries, e.g., IPFC and its subsidiary bodies (SCORRAD and CDMSCS). The four general techniques discussed, viz., license limits, fishermen quotas, economic controls and territorial use rights in fisheries, are now familiar to fisheries administrators in the region. However, the pros and cons of each of these methods need to be examined further to ensure the most desirable results because global experience in effort controls is limited and there is still incomplete understanding of all of the consequences that may occur from such management measures.

Many fish stocks in the region move freely through man-made boundaries, e.g., the Indo-Pacific mackerel and Spanish mackerel stocks on the east coast of the Gulf of Thailand migrate through the exclusive economic zones of Cambodia, Thailand and Vietnam, and in the Malacca Strait the fish migrate between the EEZs of Indonesia, Malaysia and Thailand. Management action taken by one country without the cooperation of the others would be futile, resulting in the subsequent depletion of the resources. There is thus a need to strengthen regional cooperation and develop a suitable mechanism for the management of transboundary or straddling fish stocks. Such a mechanism should help the countries in improving data and information for the conservation and management of these fishery stocks, in harmonizing national and regional management measures of the same stocks, and in the monitoring, control and surveillance of the fisheries.

Environmental Management Consideration

Environmental management became a new emphasis in fisheries management for both capture fisheries and aquaculture after UNCED. The problems of environmental management in the South China Sea fall into three overlapping categories: (i) the conservation and preservation of marine biodiversity; (ii) the prevention and control of marine pollution; and (iii) integrated coastal area management.

Many countries in the region are reluctant to make significant inputs into environmental management because of the complexity of the issues. At the country level, besides lacking sufficient funds and expertise, especially in environmental impact assessment, planning and legislation, there seems to be no effective central mechanism in many countries for timely decision making, as environmental issues are relevant to several agencies in a government. Also, cooperation between the public and private sectors in the field of environmental protection has not yet been effective. Furthermore, there are no adequate baseline studies on environmental impact on capture fisheries/aquaculture and vice versa, e.g., a quantitative assessment of the impact of intensive aquaculture in mangrove forests on coastal fisheries.

As marine pollution and integrated coastal area management are the subjects of separate studies at this conference, comments will only be made on the conservation and preservation of marine biodiversity.

After UNCED, actions required for the conservation and preservation of marine biodiversity should include:

(a) further improvement of fisheries information, data and statistics and promotion of their exchange; this should include the updating of the inventory of marine living resources in the region;
(b) monitoring of the state of the stocks in the South China Sea and its adjacent waters;
(c) promotion of the rational use of fishery resources through responsible fishing and elimination of destructive fishing gear and methods such as dynamite, poison and environmentally unfriendly gear;
(d) development of collaborative resources and management-oriented research, aimed at the sustainable development of fishery resources;
(e) development of management strategies with full participation of fishermen;
(f) improvement of fisheries, laws and regulations and the monitoring, control, and surveillance of fisheries;
(g) strengthening one of the existing regional fishery bodies to serve as the main mechanism for management of shared, straddling and highly migratory fish stocks, and for improvement of coordination among fishery bodies;
(h) collaboration with competent bodies in the formulation and implementation of a code of practice for the introduction and transfer of marine and freshwater organisms in order to reduce the environmental and health risks of such transfers.

Aquaculture Development

Many problems remain to be resolved as indicated in Section III. There is potential for further development, especially in semi-intensive and extensive pond culture and culture of short food chain species, to augment protein supplies for rural populations. In coastal waters, mussel culture has great potential. When new species and new methods are used in aquaculture, efforts should be made to appraise their impact on existing aquaculture practices and other land and water use activities and on the ecosystems. The development of legislation aimed at sustainable development of aquaculture should be among the priority actions of the countries in the region.

Post-harvest Technology Development

Fishery management relating to this issue after UNCED should ensure that the resources are used properly in accordance with the principle of full utilization. Continued efforts should be made to convert low-value fish and trash fish for products which the poorer populations can afford. A network for research in fish technology to ensure the full utilization of low-value resources as direct human food, and on quality control and inspection, should be reactivated. The Sixty-fifth Session of the IPFC Executive Committee noted that some programmes similar to the above were being planned by the Asia-Pacific Economic Cooperation (APEC) Fisheries Working Group and the Pacific Economic Cooperation Conference (PECC) and recommended that cooperation should be sought to avoid duplication of effort.

International Trade of Fish and Fishery Products

While progress has been made to ensure the better quality of fish and fishery products exported, continued efforts have to be made by the industry regarding product safety and quality assurance in the light of the EEC sanitary legislation for fishery products and the changes in mandatory fish inspection in the US market. It should be noted that Codes of Practice and standards for processing and handling of fishery products are being developed by the Codex Alimentarius Commission. A unified action by the countries in the region with a view to alleviating trade barriers on fish and fishery products should be adopted.

Conflicts Among Resource Users

This has already been mentioned in Section III. It is expected that the governments will pay increasing attention to this issue in the context of integrated coastal area management. A Symposium on Socioeconomic Issues in Coastal Fisheries Management, held in conjunction with the Twenty-fourth Session of IPFC (Bangkok, 1993), made a number of valuable recommendations in the light of the decline and overexploitation of marine resources of the region. These include, *inter alia,* limitation of access to heavily exploited fish stocks; promotion of economic diversification and enterprise development in rural coastal fishing communities in order to reduce fishing pressure on coastal resources; strengthening of community-based management systems; and encouraging fishermen's organizations to co-manage the resources. Other recommendations of the Symposium included education and training; promotion of the application of indigenous methods of fisheries and resource management; environmental protection; and improvement of communication between scientists, administrators, the fishing industry and fishermen's communities.

Human resource development is a long-term process requiring education and training at various levels.

Marine Ecosystems

In addition to the above-mentioned issues, UNCED also recommends in Chapter 17 that States should "identify marine ecosystems...through, *inter alia,* designation of protected areas". A number of countries in the region have had protected areas and marine parks in their development plans or are implementing the above recommendations under their respective laws and regulations.

At its Seventh Session (Bangkok, 1993), the IPFC *Standing Committee on Resources Research and Development* (SCORRAD) discussed the concept of Large Marine Ecosystems and in application to marine monitoring and assessment. It noted that a paper entitled "Assessment and Monitoring of Large Marine Ecosystems" published by IOC lists the South China Sea, Sulu-Celebes Seas and Indonesian Seas among LMEs of the world. SCORRAD was of the view that external funding should be acquired to support fisheries management experiments in the South China Sea and Java Sea, which could benefit other tropical countries.

The South China Sea basin also deserves special consideration as a unique marine ecosystem. A number of coastal countries of the South China Sea have made conflicting claims to the Spratley Islands group and its surrounding waters with the main objective of reaping anticipated economic benefits from both living and non-living resources. Some peaceful solutions, including joint area development, especially in marine fishery exploitation and development, have been proposed. It is hoped that the disputing parties will consider, as a primary step for such cooperation, the feasibility of undertaking marine fishery research in the South China Sea basin in order to gain a better understanding of the state of the fish stocks and level of exploitation in these waters. There are a number of reasons for this proposed cooperative action:

(a) There is at present no accurate information on the state of the fish stocks and fisheries in these waters;

(b) Marine fishery research or investigation is a very expensive endeavor; cooperative research/ investigation would be more economical;

(c) Such cooperation would be in line with the relevant provisions of UNCLOS and the recommendations of UNCED with respect to international cooperation in marine scientific research.

(d) There are a number of intergovernmental/regional organizations in the region such as FAO/IPFC, SEAFDEC, ASEAN and NGOs such as ICLARM that are prepared to assist participating countries in undertaking this cooperative research or investigation. The majority of the claimants are members of at least two of these organizations.

Human Resource Development and Capacity Building

These two issues are of great importance to the Southeast Asian countries in their continued effort to conserve and manage living resources in their exclusive economic zones to ensure fisheries sustainability. Human resource development is a long-term process requiring education and training at various levels; people in and outside the fisheries sector should be made aware of the importance of the proper use of the living resources and environmental protection, and of the implications of various management measures. UNCED recommends that marine living resources and environment should be important topics in educational curricula at all levels.

Capacity building for the fisheries sector is also a long-term process and poses a challenge to government agencies and the private sector, including fishermen's communities. In the course of building indigenous capacities, the countries will have to appraise manpower and institutional requirements. Efforts will have to focus on those areas in which new approaches are needed: human resources, policy and planning, evaluation and monitoring tools, and information gathering. These are being addressed by UNDP in collaboration with other UN specialized agencies.

Prospect for Regional Cooperation

At its Seventh Session (Hong Kong, 1991), the IPFC/ CDMSCS noted that although a decade has lapsed since the adoption of UNCLOS in 1982, the Southeast Asian countries have not yet achieved the long-term objective of self-reliance in developing and managing their own fisheries and resources as envisaged in the Convention. The countries have expressed a continuing need to strengthen their capabilities in fishery research, development and management and reaffirmed the important role of regional and international cooperation in this respect.

The above Committee also noted that during the past three decades there had been a proliferation of organizations and programs involved with fisheries and maritime affairs in the region. While expressing concern over the limited development assistance funds available to these organizations, it felt that the scarce funds should be used more efficiently to obtain maximum benefits for the region.

A Study Group was set up by the Committee to "review the mandate, programs and mode of operations of international bodies that have fishery and fishery-related projects and/or concerns in the countries of the South China Sea region" and "to determine the feasibility of establishing an intergovernmental technical secretariat for CDMSCS in order to ensure that its decisions and recommendations will be properly executed". The recommendation of CDMSCS was endorsed by the IPFC Executive Committee at its Sixty-fifth Session.

The report of the Study Group was discussed at the Eighth Session of CDMSCS and at the Twenty-fourth Session of IPFC (Bangkok, 1993). It was noted that there are more than 20 intergovernmental organizations, both within and outside the framework of the United Nations, and nongovernmental organizations, currently engaged in promoting cooperation and collaboration between the Southeast Asian countries is the field of fisheries research, development and management. In addition there are numerous programs and projects at both regional and country levels assisted by multilateral financing institutions and donor countries.

The Study Group analyzed the mandate, functions and current activities of these organizations and ranked the first 12 organizations that are actively engaged and/or are promoting regional collaboration in various aspects of fisheries development and management in the following order FAO, IPFC, ASEAN, SEAFDEC, UNDP, ADB, Bay of Bengal Programme (BOBP), INFOFISH, ICLARM, AADCP, IOFC and NACA.

Among the 12 organizations mentioned, FAO, IPFC, ASEAN and SEAFDEC have the broadest scope for cooperation in fisheries development and management. IPFC at its Twenty-fourth Session (Bangkok, 1993) approved the change of its name to "Asia-Pacific Fishery Commission" and changes in its structure and functions. The Secretariat is now seeking approval of the remaining memberships. With its new structure IPFC will have two committees, one dealing with inland fisheries and aquaculture, and the other with marine fisheries (the former CDMSCS). The Committee on Marine Fisheries, concerned primarily with fisheries policy and planning and management aspects, will be assisted by working parties/working groups, e.g., in the analysis of major fish stocks in the South China Sea region and in the review of fisheries management options.

ASEAN's Coordinating Group in Fisheries has recently been disbanded. All fisheries matters are to be reviewed periodically by the meetings of the ASEAN Senior Officers of the Ministries of Agriculture and Forestry. ASEAN is seeking external support to hold in 1994 an *ASEAN Conference on the Development and Management of Fisheries* in the Region for the year 2,000. This would hopefully facilitate the organization's future policy concerning fisheries, especially fisheries management.

Although the main function of SEAFDEC is fisheries training, the organization has recently adjusted its strategy to give more emphasis to fisheries and resource management by establishing the Marine Fishery Resources Development and Management Department in Kuala Trengganu, Malaysia.

Countries in the region presently cooperate in various aspects of aquaculture development through FAO, IPFC, NACA and AADCP and in fish processing, distribution, marketing and trade through FAO, IPFC, and INFOFISH.

ICLARM has recently joined the Consultative Group on International Agricultural Research (CGIAR). With the latter's mandate, ICLARM plans to implement a program for strategic research on living aquatic resources management, with special emphasis on inland, coastal and coral reef resources systems. It is expected that this strategic research will help reinforce the applied fisheries management oriented research to be conducted by the countries and the concerned organizations in the region.

Asia-Pacific Economic Cooperation (APEC) whose membership includes all countries in the South China Sea region except Cambodia, Laos and Vietnam, was established in 1989 and its Fisheries Working Group, established in 1991. APEC receives high-level political support from its Member Governments. Its fisheries program as outlined by its Fisheries Working Group appears to duplicate the work of IPFC, especially CDMSCS and ASEAN.

Another organization is the Pacific Economic Cooperation Council (PECC) Fisheries Task Force, including the Western Pacific Fisheries Consultative Committee (WPFCC). This is a nongovernmental organization established in 1980, and its task force for fisheries development and management was established in 1983. Its membership includes all Southeast Asian countries with the exception of Cambodia and Vietnam. PECC/WPFCC is expected to work closely with APEC to promote fisheries cooperation in the Western Pacific. The main interest of WPFCC is to promote collaboration between the ASEAN countries and Pacific Island Nations (PINs) in fisheries training, research and management, with special reference to tuna research.

All of the abovementioned organizations have, however, only an advisory function. There is no fisheries management body in the region empowered with a regulatory function like the Inter-American Tropical Tuna Commission (I-ATTC).

The most recent attempt to provide a suitable mechanism for concerted action at the regional level for fisheries management was proposed by the CDMSCS Study Group mentioned earlier. It was proposed that one of the existing regional fishery bodies in the region such as SEAFDEC should be strengthened to serve as a technical secretariat for the three organizations in the region, viz, IPFC/CDMSCS, ASEAN and SEAFDEC, with special attention to the coordination of cooperative studies and provision of management advice to the countries in the region. However, CDMSCS at its Eighth Session did not support this proposal but agreed that informal consultations among the Secretariats of SEAFDEC, ASEAN and FAO should be carried out to find ways and means of enhancing technical cooperation in fisheries in the region. The Committee also agreed to down-sizing its activities to marine fisheries management, excluding inland fisheries, aquaculture and post-harvest matters from its mandate. It requested the Secretariat to review the procedures for establishing an autonomous budget for the Committee.

The above review indicates that there is already a regional framework for cooperation in the region in various aspects of fisheries management and development. However, the activities of the various organizations need to be coordinated with a view to effecting wise use of limited development assistance funds and avoiding the duplication of effort.

Summary and Conclusion

The rapid development of marine fisheries in Southeast Asia has had both a positive and negative impact on the countries in the region. The positive impact is the significant contribution of the fisheries to the economies of the countries; the negative impact includes the depletion of the fishery resources exploited, low economic returns to fishermen conflicts between different groups of fishermen, and environmental degradation.

There is thus a need for effective fisheries management in order to ensure the sustainability of fisheries of the region. After UNCED, fisheries management will have to cover a broad spectrum of actions, including the conservation of fishery resources through responsible fishing; prevention of environmental degradation; integrated coastal area management; environmentally friendly aquaculture practices; improvement of fish and fishery products, marketing and trade; upgrading the livelihood of small-scale fishing communities and support of their participation in management decisions and implementation; education and training; fisheries policy and planning; and improvement of fisheries legislation.

A framework for fisheries cooperation is already in existence. The main task is to coordinate the activities of these organizations/agencies to ensure the wise use of limited development assistance funds and the prevention of the duplication of effort. Formal consultations among the concerned organizations in the region should be held on a regular basis; the recommendation of the Indo-Pacific Fishery Commission to have a consultation among the Secretariats of FAO/IPFC, ASEAN and SEAFDEC to find ways and means of enhancing technical cooperation in the conservation and management of fishery resources in the South China Sea is a step in the right direction.

As the exploitation of the region's marine fishery resources approaches full utilization, there must be serious cooperation in fishery research and investigation, particularly in the South China Sea basin, and in the effective management of shared and straddling fish stocks. The countries should endeavor to develop a regional cooperative mechanism, preferably by upgrading one of the existing regional fishery bodies, to monitor the state of the shared or transboundary stocks and to implement fisheries management. Doing so would constitute compliance with the relevant provisions of UNCLOS and UNCED. It would be a challenge to the region to have a collective effort in the conservation and management of marine fishery resources. If there is only a promise to cooperate with no action, the forecast will be that there will be no sustainability of fisheries in the region.

C

Hewison G., "The Precautionary Approach to Fisheries Management: An Environmental Perspective," *International Journal of Marine and Coastal Law*, Vol.11, 1996, pp 301–332

Introduction

Application of a "precautionary approach" to international environmental management is only a recent phenomenon, but follows a worldwide trend of integrating preventative approaches to management of the environment and living resources. Moreover, as these types of mechanisms become progressively utilized in environmental management generally, they are now also being considered for application to international and national fisheries management.

Indeed, introduction of the precautionary approach into international fisheries discussions follows a development on the part of the environmental movement from a focus on the capture of non-target species, such as marine mammals, turtles and seabirds in fishing operations, to a more holistic appreciation of the overall environmental, ecological and social impact of modern fishing. For instance, a decade ago Greenpeace International's concerns about fishing activities were almost exclusively that of the capture of whales and other cetaceans. Today, however, most of the environmental movement, including Greenpeace, is concerned with over-exploitation of fish stocks, threats from fishing to the survival of marine wildlife, by-catch of non-target fish species, over capacity in the world fishing fleets, migration of fishing fleets from North to South, fish and food security, and mismanagement, particularly of high seas fisheries.

While originally adopted by the Federal Republic of Germany in the early 1980s, within a decade the principle of precaution has now been adopted in a wide range of international legal instruments, and has been the subject of considerable legal scrutiny. Most recently, precaution was adopted as Principle 15 of the *Rio Declaration on the Environment and Development*, which provides that: "Where there are threats of serious or irreversible damage, lack of full scientific certainty shall not be used as a reason for postponing cost-effective measures to prevent environmental degradation". Although it now appears that there is international consensus on the need for precautionary approaches to environmental management, there remains considerable debate concerning the practical bounds of a "precautionary approach", in particular with regard to its application to fishing...

This paper seeks to briefly explore the nature of the precautionary approach to environmental management and clarify some of its bounds from an environmental perspective, particularly regarding its application by the *United Nations Conference on Straddling Fish Stocks and Highly Migratory Fish Stocks* to high seas fisheries.

The paper has two main parts. The first discusses the status of the precautionary approach in international law, and includes an examination of some of the more significant references made to the approach in international legal instruments and its role in international fisheries management. The question of whether the approach has become founded in customary international law and its relationship to other norms of international law as well as some of the existing definitions of the approach are also examined.

The second part of the paper provides an environmental perspective on the precautionary approach to fisheries management and, in particular its application to high seas fisheries. This includes an analysis of the combined views of several environmental nongovernmental organizations and individual environmental campaigners. Several concepts raised by environmentalists are examined in detail including the predicament of having insufficient data, the demand for science-based management procedures, the setting of stock levels and anticipatory reference point safeguards against ecological degradation, and participation in decision making.

The Precautionary Approach in International Law

A precautionary approach to environmental management has been adopted in an increasingly wide range of international legal settings. Subsequent to the Federal Republic of Germany's introduction of the concept of precaution in the early 1980s *("das Vorsorgeprinzip"),* it has found broad application in the field of marine pollution, protection of the ozone layer, reduction of greenhouse gases and the conservation of nature. Of note is the adoption of the precautionary approach by the OECD Ministers of the Environment, in their Declaration of 31 December 1991; by the Governing Council of the United Nations Environmental Programmer in its Fifteenth Session of 1990; by the African states in the *Bamako Convention on the Ban of the Import Into Africa and the Control of Transboundary Movement and Management of Hazardous Wastes Within Africa*; by the *Montreal Protocol on Substances that Deplete the Ozone Layer*; by the United Nations General Assembly, in Resolution 44/225 concerning high seas drift net fishing; and by the *United Nations Conference on Environment and Development*, including its adoption as Principle 15 of the Rio Declarations.

As noted above, while the precautionary approach may have traditionally been applied only to marine pollution, it is now being adopted in other areas (such as ozone depletion and climate change) and potentially has application wherever human activity creates impacts on the environment.

The Precautionary Principle and the U.N. Resolutions on Drift Net Fishing

The United Nations General Assembly has addressed the issue of [large] scale pelagic high seas drift net fishing on several occasions including resolution 44/225 of 1989, resolution 45/197 of 1990, resolution 46/215 of 1991, resolution 47/443 of 1992 and resolution 48/445 of 1993.

At its forty-fourth session in 1989, the General Assembly considered issue of high seas drift net fishing for the first time. Following considerable [formal] and informal debate among opposing parties within the UNGA Second Committee on 22 December 1989, the Assembly adopted by consensus resolution 44/225 large-scale pelagic drift net fishing and its impact on the living marine resources of the world's oceans and seas.

In operative paragraph 4 of this resolution, the Assembly recommend[ed] that all members of the international community agree to implement a moratorium on drift net fishing on the high seas by 30 June 1992, with the understand[ing] that it would not be imposed in a region, or could be lifted, if effective conservation and management measures were taken. In addition, the resolution recommend[ed] an immediate reduction in drift net fishing activities in the South Pacific region dating from July 1991 and prohibited further expansion of drift-net fishing on high seas of the North Pacific and all other high seas outside the Pacific Ocean.

At its forty-sixth session, in resolution 461215 of 20 December 1991, the General Assembly noted that grounds for concern about the impacts of high seas drift net fishing in resolutions 44/225 and 45/197 had been confirmed and that evidence had not demonstrated that those impacts could be fully prevented. The General Assembly, agreeing that the moratorium was required, set a revised timetable by which it would be implemented. This included a reduction in effort, beginning on 1 January 1992, so as to achieve, by 30 June 1992, a 50 percent reduction in effort, with full implementation of the global moratorium on high seas driftnet fishing by 31 December 1992.

This was the first significant occasion in which the precautionary principle was applied to the management of a high seas fishery. Resolution 44/225 first recognized the uncertainty of information regarding high seas drift net fishing and then recommended imposition of a moratorium based on concerns that the existing information indicated over-exploitation of the target stock and an unacceptable by-catch of non-target species. The resolution reversed the normal burden of proof so that it fell on those using drift nets, requiring them to show that effective conservation and management measures could be taken to prevent any unacceptable impacts and to ensure conservation. The conservation and management measures proposed in the resolution were to be based upon statistically sound analysis jointly made by those countries having an interest in the fishery.

Considerable controversy has arisen with regard to the General Assembly's resolutions on high seas drift net fishing and, in particular, the Assembly's application of the precautionary approach. As a precedent for application of the precautionary approach to high seas fishing, the resolutions on drift nets unfortunately steered initial debate of the issue in a radical direction. Fishers became concerned that if these principles were applied to all high seas fisheries, and by association fisheries within EEZs, that fishing would be severely curtailed. Prof. Burke points out: "If this position were an acceptable interpretation of general principles of the law of the sea, few lawful high seas fisheries would be conducted without extremely costly and complex prior international investigations". In addition, environmental campaigners did not initially seem to have a clear understanding of the difference between applying a precautionary approach to all fisheries management and applying a more extreme version of these measures as in the special case of drift net fishing.

Perhaps if they had made clear earlier that application of a moratorium was to be taken in extraordinary circumstances, introduction of the precautionary [approach] as a [general] tool of fisheries management may have proved more acceptable [to] fishers.

The Precautionary Principle and International Fisheries

Application of the precautionary approach to international fisheries management has become a matter of serious debate within international fisheries circles. Following an endorsement at UNCED and at the United Nations General Assembly the management of high seas fisheries has recently come under concentrated scrutiny. The FAO held a Technical Consultation on High Seas Fisheries which initiated discussions that in part examined the role of precaution in seas fisheries management. At this initial meeting, Japan, South Korea, Norway and the Russian Federation "expressed grave reservations over the use of precaution...as a tool of fisheries management", while Sweden questioned view, noting that "the precautionary [principle] had been adopted by the *United Nations Conference on the Environment and Development* in the Rio Declaration". The FAO itself argued that the practical application of precaution "raises...socio-economic concerns and technical difficulties, particularly in complex...ecosystems. In the absence of agreement on acceptable levels of uncertainty, impacts, on which the principle does not provide any guidance, it would be little practical value and unlikely to gain general acceptance." The *Fisheries Act* of Japan also argued against the use of the principle on the grounds that application of precaution would obstruct sound development of international fisheries and would inequitably shift the burden of proof entirely to high seas fishing nations. This was felt to be particularly inequitable where high seas stocks were exploited within exclusive economic zones by coastal states and on the high seas by distant water fishing nations.

In the draft Report from the Technical Consultation, prepared by FAO, adopted on 15 September 1992, it was indicated that a precautionary approach should not be applied to fishing because it was an activity fundamentally differ[ent] from other more damaging practices such as toxic waste dumping, for which approach[es] had been originally adopted. If a precautionary approach was to be applied to fishing, noted the FAO, then measures taken in the application of it should not be unnecessarily restrictive, nor discriminatory, nor in all cases require a moratorium, and should be able to be revised or revoked when new information became available. In addition, the relevant precautionary measures should be contained in the FAO Code of Conduct on Responsible Fishing. Greenpeace International recommended that the Report be rejected because it did not reflect evolving state practice.

Application of the precautionary approach to international fisheries management has become a matter of serious debate within international fisheries circles.

In July 1993, the *United Nations Conference on Straddling Fish Stocks and Highly Migratory Fish Stocks* met for its first substantive session in New York to address the issues raised at UNCED regarding high seas fisheries management. This meeting faced a similar debate to the previous Technical Consultation concerning the role, if any, of a precautionary approach in the management of fisheries. The European Union (EU), in particular, argued that precautionary approaches were limited to ocean pollution. Opponents of the adoption of the approach implied that its use in fisheries management meant an absolute ban on fishing, contrary to the doctrine of sustainable development. Other nations, along with environmental nongovernmental organizations, countered by indicating that absolute bans were exceptional and that precautionary approaches to fisheries management already existed and merely required further elaboration. After considerable discussion, a consensus emerged indicating general support for adoption of some form of precautionary measures. The draft agreement adopted by this meeting included an explicit reference to precaution, which required members of the international community to "apply appropriate precautionary measures...[w]here there are threats of serious or irreversible damage to straddling stocks or highly migratory fish stocks, the lack of full scientific certainty shall not be used as a reason to postpone such measures." In addition, Annex II of the draft agreement provided more detailed precautionary mechanisms that were to be adopted. The Conference also requested that the FAO respond to growing concerns about the application of a precautionary approach by preparing a report for consideration at the next meeting of the parties in March 1994.

At that meeting, the FAO produced an information paper entitled, "The Precautionary Approach to Fisheries with Reference to Straddling Fish Stocks and Highly Migratory Fish Stocks". This document was one of the first to seriously consider the limits of the precautionary approach with regard to fishing and [was] considered by a working group of representatives at the conference. Environment nongovernmental organizations were generally opposed to the views express[ed] about precaution by the FAO, although more acceptable language finally appear[ed] in the Chairman's draft agreement.

The delegates to the Straddling Fish Stocks Conference met again in August 1994 for another substantive session and here again there was some debate over the application of the precautionary approach. By the conclusion of the meeting almost all parties present had accepted application of the precautionary approach to high seas fisheries management and felt comfortable that the boundaries of the approach had been relatively well drawn. Article 6 and Annex 2 of the present Draft Agreement contain provisions concerning the precautionary approach to high seas fisheries management, although these provisions have to be read within the context of the entire Agreement. The future of these provisions appears relative secure, although questions about whether the Agreement will be advanced as [a] legally binding document or will be kept as declaratory may mean further work on the bounds of the precautionary approach.

Definitions of the Precautionary Principle

Unfortunately, there are a number of slightly different definitions of the precautionary principle or precautionary approach existing in relevant scholar[ly] literatures and in official documents. Furthermore, a number of slightly different terms have been adopted, including: "precautionary principle", "precautionary approach", "precautionary action", "precautionary measures", "precautionary management", "precautionary policy" and "principle of precautionary action". Hey argues that "[a]lthough it has been suggested that [these] different terms imply substantial differences in content...this is not the case and ...if substantial difference[s] were intended, the delineation has not been pursued systematically".

Nevertheless, as noted above, the *United Nations Conference on Straddling Fish Stocks and Highly Migratory Fish Stocks* began with some debate over whether the conference should adopt the "precautionary principle" or "precautionary approach". The debate centred on whether adopting a precautionary "principle" had greater legal significance and a more restrictive connotation than adoption of a precautionary "approach", which seemed to have lesser legal significance and be more flexible. The FAO in their report to the 1994 UN Fisheries Conference made a sharp distinction between the concept of a precautionary "principle" and "approach". The FAO viewed the precautionary principle as a far more rigid concept than the precautionary approach, and more susceptible to "radical application", as in the case of the moratorium on all high seas drift net fishing. In addition, use of a precautionary approach, argued the FAO, includes a requirement to balance economic factors (or cost effectiveness) against environmental outcomes in making decisions. As noted above, while environmentalists initially advocated use of the precautionary principle, they have, at least with regard to fisheries, shifted position to accommodate use of the term "approach". The definition finally adopted by the conference uses the term "precautionary approach":

> "The precautionary approach [to management of fisheries] shall include all appropriate techniques and be aimed at setting stock specific minimum standards for conservation and management taking into account the best scientific information available. States shall be more cautious when information is poor. The absence of adequate scientific information shall not be used as a reason for postponing or failing to take conservation and management measures."

This definition is further supported by an elaboration of the means for applying the approach, contained in both Article 6 and Annex II of the Agreement.

Precaution as Customary International Law

Article 38 of the Statute of the International Court of Justice defines customary international law as "evidence of a general practice accepted as law." Customary international law arises when a practice among nations is extensive and virtually uniform, and is accompanied by a conviction that it is obligatory under international law. If the concept of precaution were characterized as customary international law, then all states would be legally bound to observe it.

Adoption of precaution by the *United Nations Conference on Straddling Fish Stocks and Highly Migratory Fish Stocks* appears to have been accepted, in part, because of its inclusion in many other international instruments and, most importantly, the *Rio Declaration on the Environment and Development*. Although delegates to the *United Nations Conference on Straddling Fish Stocks and Highly Migratory Fish Stocks* may not have accepted a legally binding obligation to apply precautionary measures, there was certainly early consensus that these measures should be applied in practice.

Relationship between Precaution and other Norms of International Law

Apart from questions concerning the status of the principle as customary international law, several legal commentators have also questioned the relationship between this emerging norm of international law and other elements of international law. While a precautionary approach has been adopted in an increasing number of international legal instruments, others, particularly older instruments, either do not incorporate this approach, or apply principles contrary to the concept of precaution. Of particular interest here is the relationship between the precautionary approaches to management of the environment and the high seas fisheries provisions of the *United Nations Convention on the Law of the Sea*. The FAO has argued that as "[Article 119 of the *LOS Convention*, which concerns the conservation measures to be applied to high seas fishing] permits the goal of maximum sustainable yield to be qualified by, *inter alia* environmental factors, [this] could support the incorporation of an environmental principle such as the precautionary principle into to the application of conservation measures...". In addition, the use in the *LOS Convention* of the requirement to use the "best scientific evidence" in international fisheries management may also provide room for application of precautions approaches. Environmental nongovernmental organizations have argued that precaution is fundamental to, and supported by, the concepts of conservation [and] sound fisheries management enunciated in Articles 61, 63(2), 64 and 117, 118 and 119 of the *LOS Convention*. It is worth noting that at present the Agreement states that it is "for the implementation of the provisions of the [*LOS Convention*] relating to the conservation and management of straddling stocks and highly migratory fish stocks." Overall, it appears that the language used in the *LOS Convention* is flexible enough to accept use of the concept of precaution in applying [existing] *LOS Convention* fishery management tools.

An Environmental Approach to the Application of the Precautionary Principle to Fisheries Management

The present status of many fishery resources around the world indicate clearly that management practices need to be improved or altered to achieve long term sustainable management of these resources and, in particular, high seas fishery resources including straddling fish stocks and highly migratory fish stocks. Environmental nongovernmental organizations have objected strongly to current fishery management structures that have led to over-exploitation, excess fleet capacity overcapitalization, the use of destructive fishing technology, the migration of fleets from North to South, fish becoming an issue of global food security, denial of the rights of fishers, poor enforcement and compliance, degradation of the marine environment and loss of marine biodiversity. While many environmental campaigners accept the utility of fishing, they are concerned that poor management undermining the long-term productiveness of these resources.

One of the management tools environmental nongovernmental organization[s] have been advocating to improve fisheries management is more widespread [use] of the precautionary approach. Initially, environmental campaigners simply appropriated the concept of the precautionary approach from its previous utilization in managing marine pollution. It was in this field that environmentalists first advocate[d] the concept and it seemed useful to push for its adoption in other areas of environmental management. At first only very general statements were made about adoption of the concept, with much of the environmental literature calling for managers to err on the side of caution. However, very quickly some environmental campaigners recognized that these types of statements were insufficient. These campaigners became concerned that unless a more detailed understanding of precaution was undertaken, particularly with regard to its application to high sea fisheries, then the environmental movement risked having the term mis- or re-interpreted by the traditional fishing community.

The role of undertaking a study of the precautionary approach, and determining how environmental nongovernmental organizations would apply it to fisheries management, fell primarily on Justin Cooke of IUCN and Michael Earle of Greenpeace. Much of their work was undertaken during 1993, several years after environmental nongovernmental organizations advocated adoption of the precautionary approach in fisheries management. In undertaking this determination a shift in emphasis also occurred. While the Rio Declaration and many other definitions of the precautionary approach qualify its application to only those circumstances where there are threats of serious or irreversible damage, Cooke and Earle suggest that the precautionary approach be applied at all times in fisheries management.

Where information about a fishery is sparse, environmental campaigners have argued strongly that the permitted levels of catch should be set conservatively.

Consequently, Cooke and Earle's characterization of the precautionary approach to fisheries management begins with the premise that it will be applied in all circumstances. Central to their system is recognition of uncertainty regarding all aspects of fishery science and information and the reversal of the burden of proof under these circumstances. Recognizing this uncertainty requires [a] management strategy that is very conservative in its setting of management objectives (such as catch limits) and able to observe these objectives. The system must also be able to take adequate account of the impact of fishing on the marine environment and be open to participation by non-users in decision making.

Insufficiency of Data

An inherent problem in the management of fishery resources (although it is also a recognized problem in the management of many other natural resources as well) is the high degree of uncertainty in the scientific, technical, economic and political information upon which managers and fishers base their decisions. For instance, the FAO noted that "[a] major problem is that the properties of fishery resources—their 'fluid' nature, the poor quality of fishery data, the limitation of scientific models and research funds, the inherent difficulty of research in the high seas and the fluctuations of economic parameters—tend to limit scientific understanding of the fisheries ecosystems."

Where information about a fishery is sparse, environmental campaigners have argued strongly that the permitted levels of catch should be set conservatively. As information about a fishery increases, however, management may then make more confident decisions about raising the levels of catch. Cooke and Earle [argue] that "[t]his mechanism attaches a positive effective value to fisheries data and [opens] the way to data collection programs financed by resource users or through [a] levy on catches or vessels." The corresponding relationship between catch, risk and information is such that for modest levels of catch relatively little information is needed to avoid risk to the stock, but that the required amount of information increases as catch levels are raised and risk escalates.

The information requirement suggested by Cooke and Earle is that there be a minimum estimate of stock biomass. They claim that "[f]ishing a stock [of] which there is not even a reliable estimate of abundance is contrary to any definition of precaution." In the case of fisheries where current exploitation rates are low, Cooke and Earle suggest that a cap on annual catches should be set at 1 percent of the minimum biomass estimate as an interim arrangement until a fully-fledged management procedure is put in place. They further suggest that prior to deploying new fishing gear on a commercial scale or in a new area, experimental trials of the gear, including observation of disturbance to habitat and by-catch, should be undertaken and the data arising from the trials evaluated independently.

Apart from questions relating to the intrinsic value of these approaches forwarded by Cooke and Earle, there are also questions of whether these approach[es] are consistent with provisions of the *LOS Convention*. The requirement in Article 119 of the Convention is that when establishing "conservation measures for the living resources of the high seas, States shall: (a) take measures which are designs on the best scientific evidence available to the States concerned, to maintain restore populations of harvested species at levels which can produce the max[imum] sustainable yield." It appears that the approach formulated by Cooke and Earle where fishing effort is constrained by the evidence available, is consistent with this Article. Article 119 requires states to take conservation measures which are designed to maintain stocks at levels which can produce

[Maximum Sustainable Yield] MSY. The requirement is not that the measures must produce MSY, but that they can. The use of the word "levels" also implies that the levels of allowable catch may alter over time seemingly as more scientific evidence becomes available indicating the level which will produce MSY.

Article 119 also suggests a direct relationship between the conservation measures imposed and the best scientific evidence available. Conservation measure must be based on the best scientific evidence available. This indicates that where evidence is poor, conservation measures should be designed to reflect that lack of information, but as more evidence becomes available, consecration can be altered to reflect the greater understanding of the fishery. It seems to make little sense to design liberal conservation measures when scientific evidence is poor or lacking. Most environmental nongovernmental organizations have not taken the position that where there is no scientific evidence there should be absolutely no fishing, but that in these circumstances states should proceed very carefully, and test the gear being used and its impact on the fishery appropriately. This approach also seems consistent with the *LOS Convention*.

The obligation to conserve the living resources of the high seas, found not only in Articles 116–119 of the *LOS Convention*, but also now in a number of other international agreements and declarations, seemingly obliges states to take measures that respect the level of knowledge about the fishery in question. The UNGA resolutions on drift net fishing also accept a direct relationship between scientific evidence (in this case statistically sound analysis) and the imposition of conservation measures, although in the case of drift nets the requirement was that until it could be demonstrated that there were no unacceptable impacts, the conservation measure imposed was a moratorium. Nevertheless, the resolutions provided for lifting of the moratorium where scientific evidence did not demonstrate any unacceptable impact and the international community could be satisfied that the conservation measures imposed would conserve fish stocks and other related marine species in question.

While perhaps not going as far as Cooke and Earle, the FAO has at least accepted that cautious management recognizes that the higher the uncertainty and/or risk, the greater the need for caution. The *Draft Agreement on Straddling Fish Stocks and Highly Migratory Fish Stocks* also accepts this when data is poor and adopts precaution to the extent that "absence of adequate scientific information shall not be used as a reason for postponing or failing to take conservation and management measures." There is also the question of when precautionary approaches should be adopted by fisheries management. The Draft Agreement seems to imply that precautionary approaches need only be adopted when a fishery is either new or is under stress, although the text is not entirely clear on this point. By contrast, Cooke and Earle advocate that precautionary approaches are to be applied at all times, but perhaps more rigorously where there is little information about a fishery or it is under stress.

With regard to new or exploratory fisheries, the Draft Agreement require[s] that "conservation measures including, *inter alia,* catch and effort limits shall [be] established as soon as possible and shall remain in force until there [are] data to allow assessment of the impact of the fishery on the long-term sustainability of the stocks."

The FAO has also accepted the role of experimental fisheries. While in [not] going as far as "no data–no fish" and failing to suggest appropriate catch and effort limits in new or exploratory fisheries, the Draft Agreement at least recognizes the need to proceed carefully during the first phases of fishing. Cooke and Earle also suggest that data from new or exploratory fisheries be independently verified. This seems useful and expands upon the existing requirement[s] for states to share the best scientific information available. A suggestion of the United States that fishers participating in new and exploratory fisheries be required to fish according to a data collection plan also seems worthwhile.

Scientifically-Based Management Procedure

In addition to setting an appropriately conservative target level for fish [stocks] in the high seas where information is sparse and uncertainty great, environment[al] nongovernmental organizations have also required that management systems [be] established that ensure that the objectives set for sustainable catches from the fish[eries] will be achieved. The basis of precautionary fisheries management, according to Cooke and Earle, is that all stocks be subject to a scientifically-based and tested management system. Clearly defined and unambiguous objectives are required, which make it possible not only to know if the objectives are being met, but also what must be done to revise them if they are not being achieved. The system should determine in advance which compliance measures are to be implemented for a particular fishery, so as to meet the declared objectives of management.

Cooke and Earle describe these measures in the form of a feedback loop, where data are initially collected and analyzed from both the fishery and independent surveys, assessment is made of the status of the fish stocks and management measures, such as total allowable catch limits, are established. However, it is not enough to simply design such a system and assume it will work under all conditions. It has been argued by Cooke and Earle that the system must be evaluated through the use of simulation studies under a wide range of possible scenarios, including fluctuations in ecological conditions, fish recruitment and interactions among species. Usually several management procedures for a fishery will be evaluated, and the one giving the best all-round performance selected. The process of evaluation itself will also indicate ways in which a candidate management procedure can be improved. Account should also be taken of the extent to which the proposed management measures are enforceable, and the results of non-compliance with the measures.

Cooke and Earle point to the Revised Management Procedure adopted by the International Whale Commission as an example of a set of rules for determining the allowable catch of whales that has been shown to provide reasonable levels of catches while ensuring a low risk of depletion.

The system proposed by Cooke and Earle is similar to many fishery management systems that already exist. As Garcia notes, most modern fishery management systems determine the theoretical production of the stock, calculate the corresponding level of fishing effort, recommend ways in which this can be achieved, and assess the effects of fishing. However, the significant difference is that in traditional systems the burden of proof rests with the management system. Here, scientists have to demonstrate that harm is being done to the stocks before conservation measures can be imposed on the fishing industry.

One criticism of Cooke and Earle's description of a scientifically-based management procedure is that it is not detailed enough. While a management procedure that is testable and tested with regard to its management objectives is an essential requirement for all fisheries management, environmental campaigners need to go further in their description of what specific management procedures should be adopted. While the *LOS Convention* does not provide any guidance on the types of management procedures that might be adopted by a high seas fishery, there is at least a clear obligation to establish them. The FAO has provided a list of precautionary management tools, as well as their Code of Conduct on Responsible Fishing, that are intended to be adopted in high seas fisheries. A number of other management requirements have also been adopted in the *Draft Agreement on Straddling Fish Stocks and Highly Migratory Fish Stocks.*

Cooke and Earle also do not develop ideas to tackle two of the central difficulties in managing fisheries. They provide little advice on how the problem of decision making by consensus can be overcome or the issue of resource allocation. As Garcia notes, "[i]n international management, the best principles are useless if the decision-making process leading to their practical implementation is flawed and inefficient." Management will remain deficient unless some basic issues are overcome. Owing to the principle that states are not expected to accept limitations on their sovereignty without their consent, for instance, management must contend with states failing to accept legal obligations, or opting out of obligations, exercising veto over the acceptance of others, or failing to achieve consensus for any proposition other than at the lowest common denominator. Cooke and Earle also need to address management failure resulting from the common property nature of fisheries, especially those on the high seas, and the general lack of will to control fishing effort where there is an absence of explicit allocation of the resource. Without addressing these two fundamental issues, Cooke and Earle's system of scientific management may suffer the same fate as any other management system applied to high seas fisheries resources.

Stock Levels

Environmental nongovernmental organizations have been critical of the continued use of "maximum sustainable yield" and "optimum yield" as management reference points, particularly in high seas fisheries where there is usually much uncertainty about the actual state of the stocks. Greenpeace cites many dangers in attempting to take a yield close to the maximum, including the requirement for complete knowledge of the stock and its dynamics, as well as accurate and detailed data on levels of catch; dependence of the fishery the strength of a few recent year classes, which can result in wide variation of yields from year to year; and possible ecological damage caused through by-catches or habitat disturbance following the high fishing effort required to catch the yield. They also note that excessive fishing effort implies lower catch-per-unit-effort rates resulting in higher costs (in both monetary and energy terms). In addition, MSY reference points often take very little account of the actions of the fishers themselves, including levels of high-grading and misrepresentation of actual catch.

To replace MSY or other existing reference points, Cooke and Earle argue that fishing should be undertaken in such a way that the overall ecosystem remains close to its unexploited state. Stock levels, they suggest, should not be fished substantially below their range of natural variation in abundance. Instead, their average biomass should remain at a level that is high in proportion to the average biomass that would exist if fishing had not taken place. Where stocks have already been depressed substantially below their natural range, they should be allowed to recover. A precautionary approach should also prevent stocks from being depleted in the first place, rather than having to drastically reduce fishing effort once the decline becomes evident, which will often be politically difficult, especially where fishing operators have invested heavily in expectation of constant catch levels. "An essential feature of a precautionary approach to fisheries is that management action not be delayed until definite scientific evidence of the need for management action is at hand...". Cooke and Earle have suggested that while the appropriate level may vary somewhat from species to species, depending upon the biological characteristics of a certain stock, as a general rule, the objective of management should be to aim at maintaining average stock levels in the order of 80 percent of the average biomass prior to fishing. They contend that there are many advantages to fishers from exploiting the ecosystem under these conditions: habitat would be less disturbed; species more abundant and the interactions among species less prone to severe changes, resulting in more long-term certainty for fishers. If fish stocks were at greater levels of abundance, catch rates would be higher and less effort and capacity would be required, leading to higher levels of profitability. For many species the size of individual fish would be larger, with easier processing [and] higher prices.

Despite the objections of some environmental campaigners and some states, the Draft Agreement has retained the concept of maximum sustainable yield as the primary reference point for any fishery. It appears that the main reasons for retaining MSY is its use throughout the *LOS Convention*, both in relation to fishing on the high seas and within EEZs and the fact that fisheries managers generally understand the concept of MSY. In addition to MSY, however, the Draft Agreement also contains a range of other objectives for determining catch limits, as well as the by-catch of any associated species, and the impact of fishing on the marine ecosystem generally. It also establishes in Annex II a set of guidelines for the application of precautionary reference points to high seas fishing.

Ecological Safeguards

The impact of fishing activity is not limited just to catches of the target species. Most fishing gear also catches other species that are not desired by the fisher, and are often thrown away. Some gears also damage marine habitat, such as the capture or destruction of various benthic species by bottom trawlers and continued ghost fishing by lost traps and gillnets.

While environmental campaigners argue that if overall fishing effort is kept at moderate levels, that in itself will tend to limit any adverse effects on the environment. They also contend that precautionary management requires further specific action. In particular, damage to marine habitat and catches of non-target species should be minimized and any damaged habitat allowed to recover. "Where ...data indicate that some gear results in excessive catches of non-target species, or undersized individuals of target species, gear types shall be phased out rapidly, unless modifications have been developed for reducing the by-catch to minimal levels." Where there are alternatives, fishing methods that minimize damage or disturbance to habitat should replace those which cause greater harm. Environmentalists have also suggested that before a new fishing method is deployed on a commercial scale, experimental fishing be conducted to determine its impact on the marine environment. The FAO has accepted the promotion of the use of selective fishing gear and practices that minimize waste of target catch and by-catch of non-target species, but qualified their use as long as social and economic factors are taken into account.

Environmentalists also suggest that where any fishing method involves substantial disturbance to habitat, certain representative sub-areas be closed to fishing so as to conserve part of the habitat in its undisturbed state. The concept of marine reserves has been employed in order to maintain at least part of the habitat in an undisturbed state. Cooke and Earle argue that "[i]f the entire fishing ground has already been subject to major disturbance, closed areas covering at least 50 percent of the fishing ground [should] be established to permit recovery of part of the habitat." Precedence should also be given to the conservation, protection or restoration of populations of associated, dependent and ecologically related species and ecosystems over the objective of maximizing target catches.

The concerns of environmentalists relating to the by-catch of non-target species and the marine environment generally have, to some extent, been recognized in the Draft Agreement and the work of the FAO. In Article 6 of the Draft Agreement, the impact of fishing activities on non-target and ecologically related species, associated ecosystems, as well as oceanic and environmental conditions must be considered. The FAO, noting the difficulties in assessing impacts on ecosystems from fisheries activities, argues that some of the aims found in the management charter of the Commission for the Conservation of Antarctic Marine Living Resources (CCAMLR) include aspects that could be applied more generally to fisheries management. These include minimizing conversion of critical ecosystems to "lower" conditions, compensating habitat conversion with restoration, maintaining ecological relationships, maintaining populations at greatest net annual increment, restoring depleted populations and minimizing risk of irreversible change in the marine ecosystem.

Participation and Open Decision-Making

Environmental non-governmental organizations consider current fisheries difficulties to be, at least partly, a result of non-transparent decision making, policies and management bodies, which have excluded nongovernmental organization (NGOs) and interested citizens from participation. In order to contribute to solving the present challenges, environmental campaigners argue that mechanisms must be established that ensure transparency, effective NGO and citizen participation and public accountability in fisheries decision-making processes. In addition, some environmental NGOs have called for involvement in binding dispute resolution and third party settlement regarding fisheries activities.

The FAO has also accepted the need for a more formal role for nongovernmental organizations in fisheries management. Nevertheless, the Draft Agreement makes no mention of any role for NGOs, either in applying the precautionary approach or in fisheries management more generally.

Conclusions

The present status of many fisheries clearly indicates that management practices need to be improved. Environmental nongovernmental organizations have objected to existing fishery management structures and are now beginning to advocate the application of new structures, as well as new principles.

One of the management tools advocated to improve fisheries management is more widespread application of the precautionary approach. Of particular [note] has been the work of Cooke and Earle. They have taken the concept of precaution beyond its existing boundaries and widened its scope in their application of it to fisheries management. For instance, the Rio Declaration qualifies application of the precautionary approach to only those circumstances where there are threats of serious or irreversible damage. Cooke and Earle have argued that the uncertainty inherent in fisheries management justifies use of the precautionary approach at all times. Their depiction of the precautionary approach to fisheries management begins with a clear view that it will be applied in all circumstances. Central to this view is recognition of uncertainty in all aspects of fisheries science and information and the placing of the burden of proof on fishers. They also argue that in a situation of almost complete uncertainty, any management strategy must be very conservative in its setting of management objectives (such as catch limits) and be able to observe these objectives. Catch limits must also take into account the impact of fishing on non-target as well as target species and the marine environment generally. It must also be open to participation by non-users, such as environmental NGOs.

The system developed is not, however, without imperfection. In the first instance, while Cooke and Earle have advocated adoption of precaution at all times in fisheries management, they do not make the basis of this claim clear. While there appear to be useful arguments that due to the uncertainty inherent in high seas fisheries management, and the increasingly more powerful (and potentially more destructive) fishing gear applied to fishing the high seas establish a situation where there tend[s] always to be threats of serious or irreversible damage, Cooke and Earle do not make it clear that this is the basis for their argument. Second, in developing their management system, they have tended to overlook some of the more serious reasons for fisheries mismanagement on the high seas. It seems essential that environmental campaigners consider how they might overcome issues of allocation, participation in management by all states and ineffective decision making. Cooke and Earle forward some useful suggestions in relation to the setting of conservative stock levels, particularly in new and exploratory fisheries. Again, perhaps there is some need for further detailed examination of how their catch limits would affect the long-term sustainability of certain stocks or fisheries. In particular, they need to consider the effects of applying their system to multispecies fisheries, such as those in the tropics or those targeting shrimp. Much of the work of environmentalists regarding concerns over the impact of fishing on associated species, non-target species and the marine ecosystem generally have been taken into account and applied in the Draft Agreement. However, advocacy of ideas, such as marine reserves and phasing out of destructive fishing technology need to be promoted more forcefully by environmental campaigners. Finally, public participation in decision making also seems to require more promotion, particularly in regard to introducing this principle into the Agreement.

Environmental scrutiny of fisheries management is a logical extension of decades of concern for interactions between fishing and marine wildlife, and the campaign for a ban to all whaling. Environmental NGOs are supported strongly by the public for their work in these areas and this also contributes to their continued vigilance. Focus on application of the precautionary principle by environmental campaigners is also unlikely to shift. It forms a fundamental basis for a number of important environmental concerns outside of fishing, including ozone depletion, climate change and the dumping of toxic wastes into the marine environment. Its application to high seas fisheries management is a natural extension of the use of the precaution[ary priciple], although, as noted above, there are some concerns about exactly how the concept should be applied.

D

Zou K., "Towards Sustainable Management of China's Marine Fishery Resources: Law and Enforcement," 2(3-4) *Asia-Pacific Journal of Environmental Law*, 1997, pp 293–318

Introduction

...The 1982 *United Nations Convention on the Law of the Sea* (UNCLOS), by establishing the 200-mile Exclusive Economic Zone (EEZ), has put an additional 35 percent of ocean areas under national jurisdiction. Meanwhile, it also obligates coastal States to ensure that the living resources in their EEZs are not endangered by overexploitation. Thus, not only do coastal States have the legal power to apply sound principles of resource management within this area, but they also have an obligation to do so. China, as a coastal State, has an obligation to introduce effective conservation and management principles and measures to manage the marine living resources in the sea areas within its jurisdiction in accordance with UNCLOS. This article reviews and assesses the situation of law and enforcement in regard to the management of marine fisheries in China to see whether and to what extent the management measures have been implemented and the management goals realized, and what China should do to develop and improve its legal framework in the future.

Advocacy of ideas, such as marine reserves and phasing out of destructive fishing technology need to be promoted more forcefully by environmental campaigners.

The Natural Setting

...China's sea areas from north to south (3°N to 41°N) extend through three climate zones: tropical, sub-tropical and temperate. They have a varied physical, geographical environment and are rich in natural resources. They are also under the strong effect of a monsoon-like climate, which promotes the use of the coastal area. The southern coastal waters have high surface temperatures all year round, with an annual temperature range variation of only 2°C, whereas in the northern part of the Bohai Sea and the Yellow Sea, the sea water annual temperature range is as much as 28°C, and the area freezes for a short winter period.

The hydrology of these seas is strongly affected by both the Pacific Ocean and the large rivers flowing out from the mainland. A considerable volume of fresh water empties into the shallow western area of the Bohai Sea and the other three seas, generating long shore currents of low salinity. Meanwhile, the strong Kuroshio or Japanese Current, which is of high temperature and salinity, influences the eastern part of the neighbouring seas as it flows primarily east of Taiwan. The current system contributes to the formation of several good offshore fishing grounds, especially near estuarine areas, where the ocean current, of high temperature and salinity, is mixed with the fresh waters of such large rivers as the Yangtze River and the Pearl River. Hence, marine biological and chemical resources are plentiful in China's sea areas, with economical fish species more than 1,500...Thus the extensive seas adjacent to the Chinese continent have some of the highest marine productivity rates in the world.

After the foundation of the People's Republic of China in 1949, and with deepening investigations of marine resources and the growth of fishing technologies, the fishing grounds have been expanded and the catch has significantly increased. There are more than 40 fishing grounds offshore and about ten outer sea fishing grounds, with a total area of 2.8 million square kilometers. The main grounds are the Bohai and Yellow Sea Fishing Ground, Lusi, Dasha, Zhoushan, Mindong, Minnan, South China Sea Offshore, Dongsha, Yushan, Wentai, and Beibuwan (the Gulf of Tonkin) Fishing Ground. Among them, the largest four fishing grounds are the Bohai and Yellow Sea, the Zhoushan, the South China Sea, and the Beibuwan. The four major traditional marine aquatic products are Greater Yellow Croacker, Lesser Yellow Croacker, hairtail and cuttlefish. In addition, prawn and jellyfish are also important fishing targets.

Mainly due to over-fishing, China's traditional fishing targets have declined to different degrees. For instance, the annual yield of the Greater Yellow Croacker was 220,000 tons in 1934, 197,000 tons in 1974, but only 26,000 tons in 1985. The annual yield of the Lesser Yellow Croacker has also decreased, from 270,000 tons in 1934, to 163,000 tons in 1957, and more recently to 31,000 tons in 1985. Other marine species have also declined through over-exploitation, such as Pacific herring, cod, and hairtail. In pursuance of more catches, fishing gear has been developed for high and steady productive capacity, and trawl-nets and set-nets are widely used, resulting in serious destruction of demersal marine living resources. Meanwhile, marine pollution, 80 percent of which is land-based, has had a harmful influence on marine resources. In polluted sea areas, marine species have been depleted, the fishing grounds moved outwards, and fishing seasons have failed. In order to prevent overexploitation, to seek rational utilization of marine living resources, conservation and management is urgently required, in which law and enforcement should play a major role as a safeguarding measure.

A Legal Framework

As early as the 1950s, there were two different opinions regarding the development of fishery policy in China. One policy relied upon State-run enterprises, careful regulation, and developing distant seas and catches with priority to fishery development. The other placed emphasis on collective enterprises, deregulation, development of islands and offshore fisheries, giving priority to aquaculture. Although the latter prevailed, it could not be implemented partly due to the lack of necessary law and enforcement. In 1979, China put forward a new policy on the basis of summarizing the past lessons and experiences of the aquatic industry. According to this policy, the aquatic industry has three focal points:

- to protect effectively and rationally utilize resources,
- to speed up marine aquaculture, and
- to enhance the quality of aquatic products.

Accordingly, several laws and regulations were enacted, such as:

- the *Regulations on the Production of Aquatic Product Resources* in 1979,
- the *Standards of Fishery Water Quality* in 1979,
- the *Fisheries Law* in 1986, and
- the *Regulations on the Implementation of the Fisheries Law* in 1987.

Thus, the conservation and management of marine fishery resources were put under legal control.

Principles and Institutions

The Fisheries Law and the relevant regulations are formulated for the purpose of enhancing the protection, increasing the development, and reasonable utilization of fishery resources, developing artificial cultivation, protecting fishery workers' lawful rights and interests, and boosting fishery production. All productive activities of fisheries, such as aquaculture and catching or harvesting of aquatic animals and plants in the island waters, tidal flats and the territorial sea of China, or in other sea areas under the jurisdiction of China must be conducted in accordance with the law and regulations concerned. The state encourages research in fishery science and advanced technology in order to raise the level of China's fishery science and technology. Governments at various levels, accordingly, give moral encouragement or material awards to units and individuals who make outstanding contributions to the increase and production of fishery resources, to development of fishery production, or to research in fishery science and technology. They include fishery production in their economic development plans and take measures to enhance the overall planning and comprehensive utilisation of water areas.

The Department of Fishery Administration under the State Council is in charge of the administration of fisheries throughout the country. Departments of Fishery Administration under governments at or above county level are in charge of fisheries in their respective areas. These departments are authorized to set up fishery superintendency agencies in important fishing areas and fishing ports.

State superintendency of fisheries operates under the principle of unified leadership and decentralized administration. With the exception of those sea areas and fishing grounds with specially designated fishery resources that the State Council has put under the direct administration of its fishery department, marine fishery is under the superintendency of Departments of Fishery Administration of coastal provinces, autonomous regions and centrally administered municipalities. Fisheries in sea areas under Chinese jurisdiction but which lie outside "the line of the State Council-designated areas where bottom trawl by motor-driven fishing vessels is banned", are under the superintendency of the Department of Fishery Administration under the State Council and its subordinate marine fishery superintendency agencies. Fisheries in the sea areas inside the above-mentioned "line" are subject to the superintendency of the Department of Fishery Administration under governments at the provincial level, with the exception of those areas specially designated by the state.

The fishery administration and fishing port superintendency agencies exercise superintendency over fisheries and fishing ports on behalf of the state. The Department of Fishery Administration under the State Council exercises administrative and superior authority over external relations pertaining to fisheries and fishing ports. It may set up fishery superintendency agencies in three areas of the Yellow Bohai Seas, the East China Sea, and the South China Sea. When necessary, it may also establish fishery administration and fishing port superintendency agencies in marine fishing ports, frontier waters and big rivers that run through several provinces.

Production in fishing grounds and seasons is subject to catch quotas of fishery resources and the principle that such operations are conducive to the production, increase, and rational utilization of fishery resources and that priority is given to adjacent regions while due considerations are given to other regions. The Department of Fishery Administration under the State Council or the units entrusted by it arrange the fishing operations in major fishing grounds, seasons and across the demarcation lines of different marine superintendencies. The major fishing seasons and grounds include the winter hairtail season in the Zhoushan Fishing Ground, the Greater Yellow Croacker season in the Zhejiang Province fishing ground, and in the fishing ground of east and central Fujian Province, the Greater Yellow Croacker, the Lesser Yellow Croacker, and Pomfret seasons in the Lusi Fishing Ground, and the autumn prawn season in the Bohai Fishing Ground. The common important and migratory fishery resources are subject to the superintendency of the Departments of Fishery Administration under local governments. Fishery inspectors, who are appointed by fishery superintendency agencies, are authorised to examine the certificates and licenses of all fisheries and fishing vessels, and to inspect fishing vessels, fish gear, catches, and fishing methods.

Fishing Operations

Fishing has a long history in China, with Chinese fishermen being recorded as having used bamboo fish hedges and barriers to catch fish as early as 770 BC. Under the existing legal framework, the state should encourage and support the development of offshore and deep-sea fisheries and provide for the rational arrangement of fishing capacity for inland and inshore fisheries. The classification of inshore and offshore fishing grounds is as follows:

- the Bohai Sea and the Yellow Sea are inshore fishing grounds;

- the sea areas inside the lines connecting to the base points of 33°N and 125°E, 29°N and 125°E, 28°N and 124.5°E, and 27°N and 123°E, are inshore fishing grounds of the East China Sea and the sea areas outside those lines are offshore fishing grounds of the East China Sea;
- the sea areas inside the bathometric lines of the 80 meter bathometric line east of 112°E, and the 100 meter bathometric line west of 112°E are inshore fishing grounds of the South China Sea and the sea areas outside these lines are offshore fishing grounds of the South China Sea.

Fishing licenses must be obtained for fishing operations. For a general permit, any unit or individual who wants to engage in offshore or deep-sea fishing must submit an application which is examined by the Department of Fishery Administration at the provincial level, and finally approved by the Department of Fishery Administration under the State Council. Fishing vessels engaged in offshore fishery must operate within the approved sea areas and fishing seasons, and are not allowed to fish in inshore waters. Licenses for using large trawls and purse seines in inshore fishing are approved and granted by the Department of Fishery Administration under the State Council. Fishing licenses for other fishing operations in inshore waters are approved and granted by the provincial Departments of Fishery Administration in accordance with the State-stipulated standards of fishing vessels, gear, and nets.

The fundamental purpose of the licensing system is to reasonably arrange fishing operations, to avoid overexploitation and to ensure the sustainable use of the fishery resources.

Fishing in prohibited fishing areas and closed seasons, using banned fishing gear and methods, or catching the species of fishery resources under special protection for scientific research and other special purposes must be approved through a special permit by the Department of Fishery Administration at or above the provincial level. The fundamental purpose of the licensing system is to reasonably arrange fishing operations, to avoid overexploitation and to ensure the sustainable use of the fishery resources.

Fishing licenses may not be sold, leased or transferred by other illegal means, and they may not be altered. Units and individuals engaged in inland water and inshore fisheries must conduct their operations in accordance with their licenses concerning the types of operation, location, time limits and quantity of fishing gear, and they must also abide by the relevant regulations on protection of fishery resources. All fishing vessels that are built, rebuilt, purchased or imported must be examined and inspected by fishing vessel inspection agencies before they are launched for operation. No fishing licenses shall be granted to those who:

- employ fishing gear or methods that cause damage to fishery resources and are banned by formal decrees;
- build, rebuild, buy or import fishing vessels without obtaining permission in accordance with State regulations; and
- fail to obtain fishing vessels books, navigation signatory books, officer's certificates, ship household registers, and fisherman's certificates.

As to foreigners and foreign fishing vessels, they should obtain permission from the relevant department under the State Council before entering China's jurisdictional waters to carry on fishing operations or investigations, and must abide by the *Fisheries Law* and other related laws and regulations of China. If those persons and vessels belong to countries that have signed relevant accords or agreements with China, their activities should be conducted in accordance with those accords or agreements. No Sino-foreign joint fishery ventures should engage in inshore fishing in waters under Chinese jurisdiction without the permission of relevant departments in charge under the State Council.

Conservation of Fishery Resources

A number of marine species are now protected, including hairtail, Greater Yellow Croacker, Lesser Yellow Croacker, sardine, Pacific herring, Chinese herring, cod, butterfish, grouper, mackerel, prawn, and shrimp. Catch limits are partly based on the sexual maturity of the fish. For any target species, it is necessary to prescribe the catch standards (including weight and length), and the allowable proportion below the catch standards. A sufficient amount of spawning parent species should be preserved so as to enable a stable increase of such resources. The catching of fry of aquatic species of important economic value is prohibited. Catching such fry or spawning aquatic species under protection for artificial breeding or for other special purposes must be approved by the Departments of Fishery Administration at or above the provincial level, and it must be conducted in designated areas at specific times and strictly in accordance with the quotas assigned.

Any units or individuals who directly channel or use water in key producing areas of the fry of fish, shrimp, crab, and shellfish must take protective measures such as avoiding dense schooling periods and areas of such fry or erecting net screens. When building sluices and dams on the migration routes of fish, shrimp and crab which will have serious effects on fishery resources, the construction units must build fish passages or adopt other remedial measures. Without approval from the governments at or above county level, it is not allowed to reclaim land from water areas that are used as major seedling producing centers or aquatic breeding grounds. To conduct underwater explosions, exploration and construction that may have serious effects on fishery resources, the construction units should consult in advance with the departments concerned and take measures to prevent or minimize the damage to fishery resources.

In accordance with the *Marine Environmental Protection Law* and the *Water Pollution Prevention Law*, governments at all levels should take measures to protect and improve the ecosystem of fishery waters, prevent pollution and investigate the responsibility for any unit or individual that pollutes fishery waters. The Departments of Fishery Administration monitor the pollution of fishery waters with a monitoring network of fishery environmental protection incorporated within the national environmental monitoring network. The breaking up or scuttling of ships is prohibited in key fishery waters, while in other fishery waters compensation must be paid if there is a loss in fishery resources. In addition, there have been a series of laws and regulations relating to marine environmental protection which also have implications for the protection of the marine fishery ecosystem.

Enforcement

Enforcement is a necessary and integral part of the realization of the purposes and objectives of law. According to China's existing fisheries law, there are a number of legal measures to enforce the law. Each of these are discussed below.

Legal Measures

Conservation Fees

According to the *Fisheries Law*, Departments of Fishery Administration under the governments at or above the county level should determine overall plans and take measures to increase fishery resources in the fishery waters under their respective jurisdiction. These departments may collect fees from the units and individuals who obtain profits from the use of such waters, and devote the money thus collected to the increase and protection of fishery resources. China began to collect "resource fees" from the fishing sectors benefiting directly from resource enhancement and protection programs in 1989.

Prohibited Fishing Activities

Use of explosives and poisons in fishing is prohibited. It is not permitted to fish in prohibited fishing areas and during closed seasons, to fish with gear and methods banned by the fishery authority, or to use fishing nets with mesh smaller than the minimum prescribed size. Departments of Fishery Administration have the right to designate the species of fishery resources under special protection and establish standards for catching these species. For spawning, feeding, over wintering grounds, and migration passages of important species of fish, shrimp, crab, shellfish, algae and other aquatic animals and plants, these departments designate prohibited fishing areas and closed seasons, banned or restricted fishing gear and methods and minimum mesh-sizes, and should work out other measures to protect fishery resources. Building artificial fishing reefs must be approved by the Departments of Fishery Administration concerned, and shall avoid main navigation channels and important anchorages. The Departments of Fishery Administration prescribe the limits to the number of net stakes and operational grounds, and designate closed seasons. Bottom-set marine fishing should not be carried out beyond "the line of sea areas where bottom trawling by motor-driven fishing vessels is banned".

Legal Liability

Anyone who uses explosives or poisons in fishing, fishes in violation of the regulations or in prohibited fishing areas and/or during closed seasons, uses prohibited fishing gear and methods, or catches rare aquatic animals under state protection without permission shall have their catch and unlawful income confiscated and be fined, in addition, the fishing gear may be confiscated and license revoked. In serious cases, criminal liability is instituted in accordance with Article 129 of the *Chinese Criminal Law*.

Anyone who poaches or seizes the aquatic products of other fishermen, or damages aquaculture water bodies and facilities may be ordered to pay compensation for any damages and shall be concurrently fined. Anyone who fishes without a fishing license, or in violation of the type of operation, location, limit, and amount of fishing gear stipulated in a license, or trades in, leases or transfers fishing licenses by other illegal means, shall have any unlawful income confiscated, their fishing license revoked, and may be concurrently fined.

Any foreigner and foreign fishing vessel which enters waters under Chinese jurisdiction without permission to carry out fishing production or survey fishery resources will be ordered to leave or be expelled by the Departments of Fishery Administration or their subordinate fishery superintendency agencies. In addition, these departments or agencies may also impose a fine and confiscate the catch and fishing gear of a foreign violator.

Enforcement Mechanism

In order to implement the relevant laws and regulations, a necessary enforcement mechanism should be established to carry out the authorized functions, such as surveillance, including patrol of ships and aircraft and radar monitoring to see whether there may be any violations of the law. Powers of inspection, including the inspection of ships and platforms also need to be provided for. Finally, punishment, which may be imposed upon those who have violated the relevant laws and regulations may be imposed by the administration or judicial organs, including compensation and civil liability.

In China's marine legal system, a competent authority is usually provided (sometimes more than one) to enforce relevant laws or regulations. For example, in the *Marine Environmental Protection Law*, the environmental protection department under the State Council is in charge of marine environmental protection in the whole country while other governmental departments assume specific responsibilities to implement the law. In the case of the State Oceanic Administration, it has power to organize the investigation, monitoring, and surveillance of the marine environment and to conduct scientific research as well as to be in charge of environmental protection against marine pollution damage caused by offshore oil exploration and exploitation and by the dumping of wastes into the sea. In the case of the Harbour Superintendency Administration, it is responsible for overseeing, investigating, and dealing with the discharge of pollutants from vessels, and for the Fishery Administration and Port Superintendency Agencies, to control pollution from fishing vessels and other sources in fishing ports.

It is important to enforce fishery laws and regulations, to manage fishing vessels and fishing ports, and to protect marine fishery resources. As the existing enforcement mechanisms relating to marine affairs in China is fragmented and the power is distributed among the relevant governmental departments, the authority to enforce fisheries laws belongs to the Ministry of Agriculture, which has subordinated Fishery Administration and Fishing Port Superintendency Agencies. The Bureau of Fisheries Management and Fishing Port Superintendency was first established in 1978 and four years later was affiliated to the Ministry of Agriculture. Under this Bureau, there are four direct fishing superintendency divisions in the Yellow Sea, the Bohai Sea, the East China Sea, and the South China Sea. In addition, there are 11 superintendency agencies at the provincial level. At the fishing ports there are about 300 administrative agencies. The main tasks of these organs are:

- to be responsible for maintaining the fishery interests in China's sea areas and the high seas and to oversee the implementation of the fishery agreements concluded with foreign parties;
- to manage the coastal fishing industry, including issuing fishing licenses, inspection of certificates of fishing vessels, gear and methods, and dealing with illegal fishing activities, and to protect fishery resources;
- to manage the technical inspection of fishing vessels and main vessel products;
- to supervise the management of security and order of fishing ports, fishing use areas in the non-fishing ports and fishing waters, and to investigate and deal with fishing vessel incidents; and
- to protect the fishing environment and precious aquatic fauna and flora.

A network of fisheries monitoring stations was established in China in August 1985. These stations monitor, inspect, and investigate environmental pollution accidents.

Problems in Enforcement

There are two major problems in law enforcement. One is the actual fact that the marine fishery stocks are continuing to be depleted, and the other is that there is a lack of effective means to enforce the relevant laws and regulations.

Continuing Depletion of Fish Stocks

According to a Food and Agricultural Organization (FAO) fishery expert, the optimal yield for China's waters is approximately 3.7 million tonnes. However, since the beginning of the 1980s, marine fishery resources in China have obviously been declining, for which there were two main reasons: over-exploitation of the resources, and deterioration of the marine environment. Take the East China Sea Fishing Ground as an example. The East China Sea Fishing Ground is the largest in China, but among the four traditional main economic species in the East China Sea, the Greater Yellow Croacker, and the Lesser Yellow Croacker no longer exist, cuttlefish fishing is no longer sustainable, and the hairtail has greatly decreased with its 1990 catch only about 50 percent of the historical record. During the hairtail season in the winter of 1989 and spring of 1990, the total production by more than 20,000 fishing vessels were 95,000 metric tons, a 13.1 percent decrease from the lowest production in 1989. In May 1989, when the State Council approved to set up protected zones for spawning hairtail and protected seasons for the peak period of spawning, the infant hairtail increased two times more than in 1989, but at the beginning of July 1990 a number of fishing vessels, disregarding the State law and regulations, sailed to the East China Sea to harvest infant hairtail, and severely destroyed the resource basis of the winter hairtail season. The Greater Yellow Croacker was once abundant in the East China Sea, but in 1989, its production decreased to 2,000 metric tons, one percent of the highest annual production. The Lesser Yellow Croacker had a similar destiny. Since the 1960s there has been no Lesser Yellow Croacker seasons in the Lusi Fishing Ground in Jiangsu Province. In 1980, it was closed for eight years, but there was no notable resource restoration, and in 1987 the government had to continue the closed season for another five years.

Another reason for the destruction of marine living resources is the deterioration of the marine environment. With the development of industry and agriculture in coastal regions, a large amount of toxic substances flow into the sea, and the water quality has had a severe impact upon inshore fishery resources. According to monitoring data, oil and heavy metals in coastal waters adjacent to Jiangsu, Zhejiang provinces and Shanghai Municipality have exceeded fishery water quality standards. In the waters of the famous Zhoushan Fishing Ground, inorganic nitrogen is 9.25 times beyond the standards, inorganic phosphorus 1.42 times, and inorganic copper 1.25 times. The pollutants in water have resulted in the death of plankton while a number of fish species have shifted their migratory routes, and fishing grounds have moved outwards. More than 6.4 billion tons of wastewater are discharged into the sea annually, containing chemical oxygen demand (COD), oil, copper, arsenic, zinc, aluminium, chromium— cadmium and mercury. These pollutants have destroyed the spawning, nursery, feeding and overwintering grounds of the main economic species.

Ineffectiveness of Enforcement

Although the *Fisheries Law* and other regulations provide for conservation and protection of marine living resources, violations are still very common. For example, while fishing with explosives is prohibited by law, during the spring and summer seasons in 1989, there were about 100 incidents of explosion fishing in the East China Sea. There are several reasons for the ineffectiveness of enforcement. First, fishermen are indifferent to the legal systems. They may believe that if they did not fish, the fish would belong to others. In the eyes of violators, penalties can be recovered through additional fish catch. During the first three years after the Fisheries Law came into effect, in the Zhoushan Fishing Ground alone about 3,000 cases of violation occurred annually. Second, another important issue in the enforcement of the fishery law and regulations is the weakness of the fishery administration, irregular enforcement, insufficient personnel in the fishery administration, poor equipment, and lack of financial means. For example, Zhoushan city has half of the fishing forces in Zhejiang Province, but only has 26 fishing inspectors and 12 fishery administrative vessels, to administer 9,000 square kilometers with more than 10,000 motor-driven fishing vessels as well as vessels from other provinces. That is to say, on average each inspector is responsible for more than 400 fishing vessels and each administrative vessel has to supervise and administer about 1,000 fishing vessels. According to Yu, the problem of enforcement does not rest with a lack of policy, law or regulation, but rather with a shortage of enforcement personnel and implementation mechanisms. Apart from inadequacies in operational funds, the limited number of qualified personnel and facilities for enforcement, a governmental agency's attitude towards enforcement tends to be dominated by its sectoral interests when its permitted projects run into conflict with use permitted by other sectors. There is no general permitting mechanism for coastal and marine projects which oversees or coordinates the sectoral permitting procedures in China.

At the international level, conflicting uses occur between or among States adjacent to the East China Sea, the Yellow Sea and the South China Sea. In these three sea areas, there are many fishing grounds for fishermen from both China and from other countries, thus resulting in a congested fishery. In the early 1950s many Japanese fishing vessels conducted fishing just near the Chinese coast. In 1955 and 1963, China and Japan signed nongovernmental fishing agreements which set up three military zones and a protected zone in the Yellow Sea and the East China Sea to prevent the resources from being destroyed by trawl-net boats. In 1975, the two Governments signed a formal fishing agreement which designated three prohibited fishing zones and two recovery zones from 1 September to 30 November annually and drew a prohibited line between 38°N and 29°N for the operation of 600 horsepower fishing boats between 100-150 nautical miles from the coast in the Yellow and East China Sea. Japanese vessels conduct fishing activities every year offshore China, and in recent years South Korean fishermen have joined in the same operations. They fish just near the outer limit of the prohibited fishing line set by China, and this behavior is an incentive for Chinese fishermen to be involved in an international grapple for fish despite the prohibited line or seasons. There are also fishing problems in the South China Sea.

New Approaches and Measures

China's fishery laws have been implemented now for more than a decade. During that period, many new changes have occurred. First, the United Nations Conference on Environment and Development and its various instruments became operative. Second, UNCLOS entered into force in 1994 and an agreement was adopted in 1995 to implement its provisions on fisheries on the high seas. Third, China ratified UNCLOS in 1996 and at the same time declared an EEZ. Fourth, China also adopted *China Agenda 21* and *China Ocean Agenda 21* respectively in 1994 and in 1996 as national documents to implement the global *Agenda 21*.

That period also witnessed the emergence of quite a number of new concepts applicable to the management of marine fisheries, such as sustainable development, the precautionary principle, responsible fishing, and the ecosystem approach. These concepts need to be considered in China's law and enforcement in order to achieve a better management of marine fisheries.

Introduction of New Concepts

In order to realize the goal of sustainable use of marine living resources, a number of new legal concepts should be introduced into China's management strategy as well as its relevant legal framework. Chapter 17 of *Agenda 21* reiterates some of the principles embodied in UNCLOS on the management of marine living resources by calling for coastal States to maintain or restore populations of marine species at levels that can produce maximum sustainable yield as qualified by relevant environmental and economic factors, taking into consideration relationships among species. Thus, the first concept which should be applicable is the precautionary principle.

The Precautionary Principle

...This principle is now embodied in a number of international fishery agreements. An example is the 1995 *Agreement for the Implementation of the Provisions of the United Nations Convention on the Law of the Sea Relating to the Conservation and Management of Straddling Fish Stocks and Highly Migratory Fish Stocks*. Article 6 calls for the contracting States to apply the precautionary approach, particularly with caution when information is uncertain, unreliable or inadequate. In implementing the precautionary approach, States shall:

(a) improve decision making for fishery resource conservation and management by obtaining and sharing the best scientific information available and implementing improved techniques for dealing with risk and uncertainty;

(b) apply the guidelines set out in Annex II and determine, on the basis of the best scientific information available, stock-specific reference points, and the action to be taken if they are exceeded;

(c) take into account, *inter alia*, uncertainties relating to the size and productivity of the stocks, reference points, stock condition in relation to such reference points, levels and distribution of fishing mortality, and the impact of fishing activities on non-target and associated or dependent species, as well as existing and predicted oceanic, environmental and socioeconomic conditions; and

(d) develop data collection and research programs to assess the impact of fishing on non-target and associated or dependent species and their environment, and adopt plans which are necessary to ensure the conservation of such species and to protect habitats of special concern.

These provisions, though applicable to the conservation of fisheries on the high seas, are also applicable to the conservation and management of fishery resources within national jurisdiction...

Ecosystem Approach

The ecosystem approach was first provided for in the 1980 *Convention on the Conservation of Antarctic Marine Living Resources* (CCAMLR). According to Article II of CCAMLR, a decrease in the size of any harvested population to levels below those which ensure its stable recruitment should be prevented. For this purpose, its size should not be allowed to fall below a level close to that which ensures the greatest net annual increment. The ecological relationships between harvested, dependent, and related populations of marine living resources should be maintained and the depleted populations should be restored to a sustainable level. It is necessary to prevent changes or minimize the risk of changes in the marine ecosystem which are not potentially reversible over two or three decades, taking into account the state of available knowledge of the direct and indirect impact of harvesting, the effect of the introduction of alien species, the effects of associated activities on the marine ecosystem and of the effects of environmental changes, with the aim of making possible the sustained conservation of marine living resources. Thus the CCAMLR ecosystem approach contains three basic elements or conservation principles: maximum net recruitment; maintenance of ecological relationships; and the avoidance of non-reversible reductions of any species in the Southern Ocean. It is in contrast to other conventions on fisheries such as those administered by the International Whaling Commission or the North Atlantic Fisheries Commission where the aim is sustainable yield of the target species and the welfare of the industry dependent upon it....

Thus, the ecosystem principle which has been governing the management and conservation of Antarctic marine living resources as well as the protection of the marine environment can be used in the management of marine resources in other sea areas of the world. As Belsky advocates:

> "The international community has accepted an obligation to protect the marine environment so as to protect its use for future generations, and to manage living and non-living resources so as to reduce or eliminate overexploitation. The only scientific means to accomplish this goal is through a total ecosystem approach."

China began to pay attention to the ecosystem approach in the late 1980s and adopted the ecosystem approach in *China Ocean Agenda 21,* which has attached to it a project proposal on the sustainability and protection of the Yellow Sea large marine ecosystem for the purpose of restoring the degrading Yellow Sea ecosystem, promoting sustainable development of natural resources, and mitigating and preventing environmental threats. However, realization of the above purposes needs a guarantee from law and enforcement.

Integrated Management

The "Integrated approach" to ocean management was formally articulated in *Agenda 21* which underscores the importance of integration in the ocean management process. Chapter 17 prescribes that States establish or strengthen mechanisms for integrated ocean management at both national and local levels charged with, *inter alia,* preparing plans; conducting environmental impact assessments; adopting guidelines for coastal management; adopting management measures to improve coastal settlements, conservation of critical habitats, integrating sectoral programmes, and maintaining biodiversity; and developing capacity in integrated coastal and ocean management. There have been many efforts since UNCED to further operationalize the concept of integrated coastal management and to assist nations in implementing the practices. In the past, increased multiple conflict uses and pollution problems demonstrated the failure of single sector–oriented management. China reflected therefore the integrated approach in its *Ocean Agenda 21* as an important way of ensuring sustained, rapid, and healthy development. Accordingly, integrated management relies on administrative, legal, economic, scientific, technological, and educational means to organize, guide, coordinate and supervise marine development activities with the aim of ensuring rational use of various resources in the sea areas, promoting a coordinated and orderly development of various industries, and increasing the economic, social, and ecological benefits of the entire sea area. The above

The ecosystem approach was first provided for in the 1980 Convention on the Conservation of Antarctic Marine Living Resources.

approach is closely related to the ecosystem approach since integrated coastal and ocean management covers ecosystems including the EEZ on the seaward side and the watershed on the landward side.

Improving the Existing Legal System and Enforcement Mechanisms

In 1996, China ratified UNCLOS and thus, has an obligation to bring its relevant domestic laws, including those governing fisheries, into line with the Convention. In order to improve the existing marine legal system, China has to harmonize its domestic law with UNCLOS and to enact new laws to fill the gap in its legal system. The *China Ocean Agenda 21* has recognized that:

China's marine legal system is not yet perfect, much remains to be done to make it complete. The laws and regulations already formulated and implemented are mostly special-purpose industrial ones while the basic marine law and the integrated management law are non-existent, and the existing ones are not yet complete and systematic, some of which are just the extensions of land ones into the sea, lacking consideration of the inherent nature of the sea; some of the industrial laws proceed largely from their own departments without giving consideration to other industries, especially the interests of the ocean as a whole.

Thus, the Chinese marine legal system needs improvements as well as new legislation to make it complete. It is summarized in one Chinese source that there are about 20 legal regimes to be established in accordance with UNCLOS, among which 18 should be realized through the domestic legislation process. In the Chinese marine legal system, there will be up to 11 new laws to be enacted domestically, which are related to navigational rights in China's territorial sea, EEZ, the continental shelf, management of EEZ living resources, enforcement and judicial process for the management of living resources, and regional marine environmental protection. According to *China Ocean Agenda 21,* the following laws and regulations should be promulgated for the Chinese marine legal system:

- Law on the EEZ and the Continental Shelf;
- Law on Management of Marine Development;
- Law on Management of Fee-Based Use of Sea Areas; Law on Coastal Zone Management;
- Regulations Concerning Marine Natural Reserves and Specially Protected Areas; and
- Regulations on Coastal Engineering.

Many of these laws will be directly related to the management of marine living resources. The *Fisheries Law* was promulgated in 1986, but now, after a decade, some of its provisions are obviously outdated and should be revised and replaced by taking into account the concepts and approaches addressed above. Finally, the provisions on marine living resources in UNCLOS should also be implemented in China in the form of law and enforcement. If there is any inconsistency in the existing marine fishery legal system, it should be eradicated in order to harmonise with the Convention.

As to enforcement, there have been some recent positive developments. In 1995, China began to close the summer season in the Yellow and East China Sea. The order was strictly carried out and after this measure, the catch of hairtail in 1996 reached 740,000 metric tons, a 14.2 percent increase on the previous year. For this reason, China is ready to turn the above measure into a permanent one and is considering extending the closed period from two to three months. China has also encouraged fishermen to develop mariculture to partly lift the pressure upon the fishing operations. China ranks first in the world in mariculture with a total culture area of over 400,000 hectares, a total output of 2.78 million tons and a workforce of over 3 million people. Despite such improvement, further measures are still required. First, it is necessary to establish a comprehensive administration center or department to coordinate various marine uses at the national level. Sectoral management of marine uses has caused many conflicts, however currently there is no national coordinated central mechanism. Thus, a comprehensive administration is very important in China, especially for law enforcement. In order to resolve conflicts over shared resources and environmental degradation, interprovincial coordination between or among the coastal provinces is also required. Secondly, it is necessary to enhance the legal conscience of fishermen to let them realize the importance of observing laws and regulations. Thirdly, it is necessary to strengthen and enhance training of administrative personnel so as to enhance the capacity building process.

Strengthening International Cooperation

International cooperation is critical in fisheries management, particularly in semi-enclosed seas, a number of which adjoin China's maritime areas. UNCLOS requires coastal States bordering semi-enclosed seas to engage in close cooperation between and/or among themselves. In particular, Article 123 provides that: "States bordering an enclosed or semi-enclosed sea should cooperate with each other in the exercise of their rights and in the performance of their duties under this Convention." To this end they shall endeavour, directly or through an appropriate regional organization to coordinate the management, conservation, exploration, and exploitation of the living resources of the sea, the implementation of their rights and duties with respect to protection and preservation of the marine environment, and their scientific research policies.

With regard to fisheries, UNCLOS [Article 63(1)] further requires that:

> "Where the same stock or stocks of associated species occur within the exclusive economic zone of two or more coastal States, these States shall seek, either directly or through appropriate subregional or regional organizations, to agree upon the measures necessary to coordinate and ensure the conservation and development of such stocks."

Since all the coastal States adjacent to China's seas are now parties to UNCLOS (except North Korea) and have the right to establish their respective EEZs, the delimitation of these EEZs are under way. Cooperation regarding fishery management will thus become more important than in the past.

In China's interest, UNCLOS grants a number of rights including the right of fisheries in EEZ, but on the other hand, China will lose a number of traditional fishing grounds after its neighbors have established their own EEZs. Other countries bordering China's seas will also face a similar situation. As a result, unauthorized fishing activities may occur in other EEZs. On 9 November 1994, the Chinese Ministry of Agriculture issued an order to require Chinese fishing vessels operating in waters beyond China's national jurisdiction to comply with international law and practices. Unauthorized fishing in the EEZ of any country will be punished according to Chinese law. However, such unilateral measures may be not enough and there should be regional cooperation to develop a common approach to such activities. Furthermore, the unilateral management by each country itself of marine living resources shared by many countries has resulted in some contradictions and conflicts, leading to resource destruction and the inadequate conservation of the ecosystems. For example, when China conducted a summer closed season in the East China Sea, fishing vessels from Japan and South Korea were still operating there, thus diminishing the efforts made by the Chinese side. Management of transboundary fishery stocks after the boundary delimitation of EEZs between China and other countries therefore depends upon regional cooperation.

In terms of treaties, China has concluded bilateral fishery agreements with neighbouring countries including Korea, Japan, and Vietnam. They serve only for limited purposes and limited geographical areas. For example, the *Sino-Japanese Fishery Agreement* applies to part of the Yellow and East China Sea and actually allows Japanese fishermen to carry on fishing operations in China's de facto EEZ.

The lack of contemporary regional arrangements is one of the political features around the China seas. Apart from the above experience, there are two existing international institutions which are facilitating international cooperation of fisheries in the China seas. They are the newly reconstructed Asia-Pacific Fishery Commission, a regional body established under the FAO, and the Fisheries Working Group of Asia Pacific Economic Cooperation forum (APEC). It is also worth recalling that in 1990, the former Soviet Union put forward a draft convention on the conservation of anadromous fishery resources in the North Pacific to 33°N, and intended to invite the States concerned including China to negotiate a legal regime. However, when a formal convention was finally negotiated in 1992, China was excluded as an original signatory. Since China is a State of origin for anadromous species in the North Pacific, it is reasonable to wonder whether the Convention could be effectively implemented without China's involvement. Finally, environmental security and sustainable development of marine natural resources are also two major factors which will influence this area in the future. In short, necessary regional cooperation of ocean management among the countries concerned should therefore be initiated and formulated to negotiate a regional agreement on conservation and management of marine living resources, and to establish a fishery commission so as to take effective measures.

Conclusion

Since 1990, China has become the world's largest fish producer contributing to one fifth of global production.

Although there are still many fishery resources in the seas adjacent to China, major economic fish species have declined and should be urgently conserved and protected. For marine living resources, conservation and management has become even more important. A legal regime is essential, especially one providing for effective law enforcement. From a legal perspective, future strategies should be directed to:

- strengthen the legislation and enforcement by innovative concepts and approaches; establish a central comprehensive and coordinated administration; introduce measures of responsible fishing and precautionary fishery management; strengthen other related and associated marine environmental protection laws and their enforcement; and
- initiate active international cooperation with neighbouring countries.

It is predicted that with the establishment of respective EEZs in the China seas, the task of sound management will be heavier for China.

It is predicted that with the establishment of respective EEZs in the China seas, the task of sound management will be heavier for China. Without reasonable law and effective enforcement, it will not be not possible for China to realize the resource management goals set out in *China Ocean Agenda 21.*

4

Questions for Discussion

(a) Discuss the inter-relationship between the various global regimes and institutions in international forests and fisheries policy. Is it realistic to expect these various actors to cooperate in implementing *Agenda 21*, given that they each hold different mandates and each serve and protect separate interests?

(b) Critically evaluate the International Tropical Timber Agreement. What role (if any) would it play in proposed global forestry regimes?

(c) "Despite the apparent wealth of international forestry regimes, the primary focus on international actors is upon the short-term economic value of forests. Conservation is incidental." Discuss.

(d) Discuss the importance of economic development in relation to forests with reference to the issues surrounding the North–South divide.

(e) Can international forest policy transcend the real politics of individual nation states? Discuss the role of sovereignty in the protection (or otherwise) of forests.

(f) There is a gulf between well intentioned formal protection, at the international regional and national level, and poor environmental outcomes. How might this be breached?

(g) Outline the key national and international schemes relating to Forest Certification and Eco-labelling. What role could these initiative have in sustainable forest management?

(h) How can international forest law and policy support community based forest management by indigenous and tribal peoples and local communities?

(i) The soft law "Forest Principles" replaced the intended global convention on Forests at UNCED. Should we proceed toward a global forest Convention or develop existing regimes, such as the *Convention on Biological Diversity*, and concentrate on regional forest regimes. What are the arguments for and against a global forests convention? Critically evaluate the role of the Intergovernmental Panel on Forests in this context.

(j) Compare the major points, both of congruence and divergence, between forestry and fishery regulatory regimes. What does this comparison reveal about international environmental law?

(k) "Abstract notions such as the precautionary principle can play no useful role in the management of fisheries. Instead, management decisions—such as maximum sustainable yield—should be left to those best in a position to adjudge the requirements of sustainable fishing." Discuss.

(l) Discuss the UNCLOS provisions relating to marine living resources. Why UNCLOS been insufficient as a global regime for the sustainable management of fisheries. Give an example of another regional initiative that has been more effective. How can we create greater synergies and reduce overlaps between legal, political and management processes related to fisheries?

(m) What "mechanisms" or "controls" seem to be most effective as measures to prevent over fishing? Give examples.

(n) What lessons may be learned from the Chinese experience in fisheries management? Can these lessons be applied to circumstances in other fisheries?

5

References for Chapter 13

Asian Development Bank. 1994. ADB News Release No. 20/95.

Belsky M.H., "Developing an Ecosystem Management Regime for Large Marine Ecosystems," in Sherman K. and Alexander L.M. (eds), *Biomass Yields and Geography of Large Marine Ecosystems*, Westview Press, Boulder, 1989.

Cooke J., and Earle M., "Towards a Precautionary Approach to Fisheries Management," 2 *Review of European Community and International Environmental Law*, 1993, 252.

Food and Agriculture Organization, United Nations, 1984, *Report of the FAO Conference on Fisheries Management and Development, Rome, 27 June–6 July 1984*, FAO, Rome, 1984.

Food and Agriculture Organisation, United Nations, *Follow-up to the United Nations Conference on Environment and Development (UNCED)*, Twenty Fourth Session of the Indo-Pacific Fishery Commission, Bangkok, Thailand, 1993, document IPFC/93/4.

Germeraad and Enebisch, 1994, *A View on Landscape Planning in Mongolia*. Unpublished Research Paper.

Gulland J.A., *The Fish Resources of the Ocean*, West Byfleet, Surey, 1971.

Kuala Lumpur Declaration on Environment and Development, April 1992, GA Doc-A/47/203.

SEADEC, *Fishery Statistical Bulletin for the South China Sea Area 1990*, Southeast Asian Fisheries Development Centre, Bangkok, Thailand, 1993.

Selected Papers Presented at the SEAPOL International Workshop on Challenges to Fishery Policy and Diplomacy in South-East Asia, December 1992, Rayong, Thailand, South East Asian Programme in Ocean Law, Policy and Management, Bangkok, 1992.

Stanley D.H., *et al.*, "Marine Fishery Resource Management in PR China" (1992) 16 *Marine Policy*, 197.

State Oceanic Administration (SOA), *China Ocean Agenda 21*, Ocean Press, Beijing, 1996.

World Commission on Forests and Sustainable Development, *Our Forests... Our Future*, Summary of Draft Report Prepared for the IFF, 1998.

6

Additional References

Tarasofsky R. (ed), *Assessing the International Forest Regime*, IUCN Environmental Policy and Law Paper No. 37, IUCN, Gland Switzerland, 1999.

CIEL, *Current Issues in Timber Eco-Labelling and Trade Policy: The WTO Agreement on Technical Barriers to Trade*, CIEL, London, 1997.

Global Forestry Policy: Project Linkages. http://www.iisd.ca/linkages/forestry/forest.html *[Editors' Note: This site was accessed on 03/04/2001.]*

Homepage of Rainforest Alliance, a group of NGOs working on rainforest conservation. http://www.rainforest-alliance.org/ *[Editors' Note: This site was accessed on 03/04/2001.]*

Links page for the goodwood site with links to other certification organizations. http://www.goodwood.org/goodwood/goodwood-list/goodwood-list.html#Cert.ag *[Editors' Note: This site was accessed on 03/04/2001.]*

Search under Intergovernmental Forum on Forests and Intergovernmental Panel on Forests in the UN site: http://www.un.org/esa/sustdev/csd.htm *[Editors' Note: This site was accessed on 03/04/2001.]*

Ganguli, Barin N., *Breakthroughs in Forestry Development: Experience of the Asian Development Bank*, 1995.

Hunter D., Salzman J., Zaelke D., et al., *International Environmental Law and Policy*, New York, Foundation Press, 1998, pp 695-731 "Marine Living Resources" and 1,107-1,146 in "International Protection of Forests."

KohK.L., Beckman R., and Chia L.S. (eds), *Sustainable Development of Coastal and Ocean Areas in Southeast Asia: Post-Rio Perspective*, Singapore, 1995.

Convention for the Prohibition of Fishing with Long Drift Nets in the South Pacific.

Conference on Straddling Fish and Highly Migratory Fish Stocks.

Convention on Biological Diversity in Marine and Coastal Habitats.

United Nations Convention on the Law of the Sea.

Marine Pollution Convention 1973.

Van Dyke J., et al. (eds) *Freedom for the Seas in the 21st Century: Ocean Governance and Environmental Harmony*, 1993.

"Straddling and Migratory Stocks Agreement in the Pacific", 11 *International Journal of Marine and Coastal Law* 406, 1996.

United Nations Forum on Forests web-site, <http://www.un.org/esa/sustdev/forests.htm> or <http://www.un.org/esa/sustdev/unff_2001.htm> [*Editors' Note: These sites were accessed 02/08/01.*]

CHAPTER

14

Integrated Coastal Zone Management

Contents

1 Introduction

For most of the Asian and Pacific region, coastal states' concerns reflect the habitats and ecosystems found in coastal regions and the dependence of their economies on income from coastal tourism, fishing, oil and shipping. The coastal zone is where human activities affect both the terrestrial and the marine environment. Integrated coastal zone management (ICZM) is a resource management tool and planning process based on the concept of sustainable development that is designed to strike a balance between competing interests and uses. The concept of ICZM and how it works is discussed in the extracts from UNEP and Chua Thia-Eng. The role of training and cross-sectoral planning and decision making is emphasized in these extracts and is discussed further by Bateman in his discussion of the relationship between *Agenda 21* and ICZM. In particular, he focuses on the need for synergies between a range of initiatives, including training, data collection, regional coordination, and improved communication, in order to bring about improvements in sustainable development and capacity building.

Since the 1992 UN *Conference on Environment and Development* (UNCED) in Rio de Janeiro, there has been a consistent call by the global community for the use of ICZM as a tool to manage the resources and environment in coastal and marine areas. Although terms other than ICZM are used in many of these documents, the calls are in essence for what is generally referred to as "ICZM". For example:

1. One of the main goals sought in Chapter 17 of *Agenda 21* is the integrated management and sustainable development of coastal areas.
2. The comprehensive Programme of Action adopted at the 1994 *United Nations Global Conference on the Sustainable Development of Small Island Developing States* calls for the formulation of new policies and programs in the context of integrated coastal area management in three areas: (1) climate change and sea-level rise, (2) coastal and marine resources, and (3) tourism resources.
3. ICZM has also been recommended as a tool for implementing the 1992 *Convention on Biological Diversity* (CBD) in marine and coastal areas. In 1995, the Conference of Parties to the CBD adopted a program of action known as the *Jakarta Mandate on the Protection of Biological Diversity in Marine and Coastal Areas*. The *Jakarta Mandate* encourages Parties to establish and/or strengthen institutional, administrative, and legislative arrangements for the development of integrated management of marine and coastal ecosystems and the integration of such arrangements within national development plans
4. Last, one of the most important recommendations in the 1995 *Global Programme of Action on Prevention of Pollution of the Marine Environment from Land-Based Activities* is for the development of comprehensive, continuing, and adaptive programs of action within the framework of *integrated coastal area management.*

In response to the various calls for ICZM in the global arena, integrated coastal management projects have been undertaken in many countries in the Asian and Pacific region.

Some of the international organizations seeking to apply ICZM as a result of these calls have given the following definitions.

The United Nations Environment Programme (UNEP), in its *Guidelines for Integrated Management of Coastal and Marine Areas* prepared in response to Chapter 17 of *Agenda 21*, states that:

Integrated coastal zone management is a resource management tool and planning process based on the concept of sustainable development that is designed to strike a balance between competing interests and uses.

> "Integrated coastal and marine areas management (ICAM) is defined as an adaptive process of resource management for sustainable development in coastal areas."

The World Bank, in consultation with UNEP, Food and Agriculture Organization of the United Nations (FAO), and IUCN-The World Conservation Union, prepared *Guidelines for Integrated Coastal Zone Management*, in response to UNCED, which state:

> "ICZM is a process of governance and consists of the legal and institutional framework necessary to ensure that development and management plans for coastal zones are integrated with environmental (including social) goals and are made with the participation of those affected."

Two specific aspects of ICZM are considered in more detail. These relate to the control of land-based marine pollution and the role of traditional resource use and traditional ecological knowledge. The inter-relationship between the terrestrial and the marine environment, a feature of ICZM, is further discussed by VanderZwaag. The importance of traditional resource use is discussed by Johannes and Ruddle. This latter extract continues the focus in this book upon the importance of local indigenous and tribal knowledge and custom in environmental law. The extract, therefore, should be read along with those in Chapter 1, dealing with cultural issues, and the Hussain article in Chapter 13, which examines this in the context of forestry.

To complement these extracts, the chapter also examines two case studies, the Batangas Bay project in the Philippines and the Xiamen project in the People's Republic of China. These demonstration sites were established under the GEF/IMO/UNDP Programme for Prevention and Management of Marine Pollution in the East Asian Seas, which is generally regarded as having developed some of the most successful ICZM projects in the Asian and Pacific region.

These readings are followed by a note on The Role of Law and Lawyers in ICZM. The ideas in this note are derived from an article by Robert Beckman and Brady Coleman in the *International Journal of Marine and Coastal Law.*

Law teachers interested in examining the role of law and lawyers in the ICZM process in more detail should consult that article, as well as the other materials in the Additional References at the end of this chapter.

Instructors teaching this topic may want to consider teaching it fairly late in the course, after the students have been exposed to the principles of international environmental law that relate to the marine and coastal environment, including the law of the sea, Chapter 17, and the protection of biological diversity, Chapter 20. In particular, issues relating to the Conservation of Wetlands are covered in Chapter 20; however, they are also closely linked to the material in this chapter.

2

ICZM—What it is, How it Works, Managing Growth

A

Network for Environmental Training at Tertiary-Level in Asia and the Pacific (NETTLAP), United Nations Environment Programme Regional Office for Asia and the Pacific (UNEP-ROAP), *Coastal Zone Management Training Issues*, NETTLAP/UNEP-ROAP, 2001

[*This document can be found on the Internet at <http://www.roap.unep.org/nettlap/Organization/CZMIssues.html>. This site was accessed on 29/06/01.*]

The coastal environment features prominently in Asia and the Pacific. In most countries, a high percentage of the population is located within coastal settlements, many of which are major cities. Expanding population and rapid coastal development are placing increasing pressures on coastal resources, resulting in habitat destruction, marine pollution and diminished resources.

The loss or degradation of coastal ecosystems, such as mangroves, coral reefs and seagrasses, represents more than just a simple loss of habitat. The full ecological benefits and contributions of the habitat are also eliminated, leading to a decline of other living resources dependent or associated with the habitat. According to the Food and Agriculture Organization of the United Nations, some 90 percent of the world's marine fish catch (based on weight) reproduces in coastal habitats. Over-exploitation, together with habitat destruction, have dwindled coastal living resources to irrecoverable levels in many areas.

Pollution of waters around coastal cities and settlements is contributed by various sources, including those located inland and upstream. Nutrient overload from sewage discharge, agricultural runoff, erosion and other land-based sources, has been identified by a UNEP Group of Experts on the Scientific Aspects of Marine Environment as the most widespread and serious cause of coastal pollution, worldwide. Toxic chemical pollutants are another cause for concern. Algal blooms disrupt marine life, toxic red tides threaten human life, while pathogenic bacteria and viruses create human health problems. Only a few cities in the region treat sewage before discharging it into rivers or coastal waters.

The need to manage the coastal zone has long been recognized, but it is only recently that effective measures have been examined and evaluated. Implementation of coastal zone management plans has yet to occur on a widespread basis. To ensure success, a coastal zone management plan has to be an integrated one, taking into account the needs and effects of all the different sectors. The formulation of such a plan takes time as it involves lengthy discussion between the various sectors on their needs, and mutual agreement on a spatial zonation scheme, a relevant legislative framework, and an effective institutional framework. While the reasons for creating a new organizational structure to implement the integrated management plan are generally readily apparent, the reluctance to do so is not uncommon.

The need to manage the coastal zone has long been recognized, but it is only recently that effective measures have been examined and evaluated.

The coastal zone involves both land and sea, and management is effective only through a structure which has jurisdiction over land and sea areas. Many examples show why integrated coastal zone management cannot be effective under existing management frameworks set up initially to develop and manage assets in which they have a specific and narrow interest. A common example of the consequence of piece-meal resource management is the constant clash of interest between forestry and fisheries authorities with respect to mangroves. One wants to maintain the ecosystem while the other wants to convert it to shrimp or fish ponds. Conflicts arise also in situations in which one authority controls the land and another controls the sea. Development on land without the proper controls to prevent erosion and the siltation of the sea would hamper the other authority's attempt to manage marine living resources.

Integrated coastal zone management plans (on a national or local scale) have been drawn up for a significant number of countries in the region. On a local scale, plan implementation appears to present less problems as fewer levels of authority are involved. Going down the scale, community-based management has been shown to be effective, but most of these programs are largely sectoral, e.g., management of reef resources. However, they do demonstrate that management is essential in preventing irreversible depletion of resources. Moving to the other end of the scale, problems are compounded by conflicts between local and federal government policies, further highlighting the necessity of an integrated approach.

Sustainable development has been accepted as a goal that allows for development and reduce environmental destruction. With development, loss of environmental assets cannot be totally avoided, but it can be effectively minimized with appropriate planning and management. Integrated coastal zone management is one of the best ways to achieve ecologically sustainable development.

Integrated coastal zone management is also a relatively recent concept. It involves an integrated, multi-disciplinary approach and requires appropriately trained personnel. Some universities in both developed and developing countries have started offering degree courses in coastal zone management and organized short-term training courses, often through twinning arrangements with institutions of higher learning in other regions. Hopefully it is therefore only a matter of time before the region acquires sufficient numbers of trained personnel in coastal zone management.

B

United Nations Environment Programme, *Asia-Pacific Environment Outlook*, UNEP, Environment Assessment Programme for Asia and the Pacific, 2000

[*This document can be found on the Internet and was accessed on 29/06/01. The address is <http://www.eapap.unep.org/apeo/toc.html>.*]

Emerging Issues: Marine and Coastal Environments

The Asia-Pacific marine environment comprises three major sea regions, namely the South Asian, the East Asian and the Pacific Islands region. The South Asian seas region includes Bangladesh, India, the Maldives, Pakistan and Sri Lanka, as well as the bordering country Myanmar. The East Asian seas region covers six ASEAN countries, i.e. Brunei Darussalam, Indonesia, Malaysia, the Philippines, Singapore, and Thailand, as well as other bordering countries, i.e., Viet Nam, Cambodia and the People's Republic of China. The Pacific Island sea region, which is characterized by coral reefs and lagoons, seagrass beds and mangroves, is partially surrounded by Asian, Indian and Australian land masses.

A large majority of the population in the region resides along the coasts and one quarter of the world's 75 largest cities are situated near, or on, the region's coastlines. Growth rates of coastal populations are generally higher than the national average as a result of migration to coastal urban areas and industrial centres. Most of these large cities and industrial areas are located in highly productive, low lying estuarine areas.

The marine resources of the region are economically important to most countries. Forty seven percent of world fisheries production occurs in this region, of which marine and freshwater fisheries account for 76 percent and 24 percent respectively. This region is also the centre of global mariculture (87 percent of total world production), which has major consequences for coastal habitats and coastal water quality. For insular and archipelagic states, marine resources are the key source of external earnings for development, and marine-based tourism is playing an increasingly important role in the economy of such countries. Most countries in the region rely almost exclusively on fisheries products for dietary protein...It is evident from the trends that in almost all of the subregions the marine fish catch is steadily increasing. A major cause for concern throughout the region is over-fishing and the use of destructive fishing techniques, particularly in the highly diverse coral reef systems. Most fish stocks throughout the region are currently being fully harvested, while some are being exploited at unsustainable levels.

Coastal and marine water pollution in this region is mainly due to direct discharges from rivers, surface run-off and drainage from port areas, domestic and industrial effluent discharges through outfalls and various contaminants from ships. Rivers in this region are generally heavily contaminated with municipal sewage, industrial effluent and sediments. Asian rivers account for nearly 50 percent of the total sediment load (13.5 billion tons per year) transported by the world's rivers. Unfortunately, most of the coastal cities in this region discharge their domestic and industrial wastes directly into the sea without any treatment.

As much as 70 percent of the waste effluent discharged into the Pacific Ocean has no prior treatment. Over 40 percent of marine pollution in the region is derived from land-based activities (via riverine discharge) and maritime transport contributes a further 12 percent. The Government of Korea estimates that over 80 percent of pollutants in the Yellow Sea and South Sea of the Korean peninsula come from inland activities (domestic and industrial) via the four largest Korean rivers.

The major sources of heavy metal contamination are industrial effluents and the dumping of land-based solid waste into the sea. In India, for example, exceptionally high concentrations of lead (820 micrograms per litre) and cadmium (336 micrograms per litre) have been observed in Thane creeks on the Bombay Coast and the mercury concentration was 778 micrograms per litre. Sediment along the creeks and off-shore stations was also reported to contain significant concentrations of lead. In Pakistan, heavy metal contamination has been detected in water and sediment from the coastal area within the mouth of the Indus River. Moreover, there is increasing evidence that these toxic substances are getting into the food chain.

Marine pollution also arises from sea-based activities, including marine transportation and offshore mineral exploration and production activities. Accidental oil spills are frequently reported in this region. In the Straits of Malacca alone, 490 shipping accidents were reported between 1988 and 1992, resulting in a considerable amount of oil spillage at sea. Beach tar is also considered a severe problem along the west coast of India, with total deposits of up to 1,000 tonnes a year. In the port of Chittagong in Bangladesh, it is estimated that about 6,000 tonnes of crude oil are spilled a year and crude oil residue and wastewater effluent from land-based refineries amount to about 50,000 tonnes per year. Approximately 5 million tonnes of oil enter the Arabian Sea each year and the Bay of Bengal receives some 400,000 tonnes from similar sources. Oil pollution from shipping and offshore oil rigs is also a concern in the East Asian seas. The highest hydrocarbon concentrations occur in the South China Sea off the southern part of Viet Nam and the Straits of Malacca, both of which are major shipping areas.

The increased use of agro-chemicals in this region also contributed to marine pollution. Fertilizer consumption in Asia and the Pacific rose 74 percent, from 33.3 million tons to 57.8 million tons, over the period 1982–1992. The use of pesticides to enhance agricultural productivity appears to be increasing, especially in the developing countries in the region. For example, in South Asia, India alone uses 55,000 metric tons of pesticides a year (herbicides, insecticides and fungicides), of which 25 percent are thought to end up in the sea. An estimated 1,800 tons of pesticides enter the Bay of Bengal each year. The increased use of pesticides in some areas has resulted in contamination of shell and finfish.

There is a substantial loss of coastal habitats in Southeast Asia as mangroves are used for the construction of shrimp ponds and for paddy rice cultivation. These activities affect, indirectly, commercial demersal fisheries that rely on the mangroves as nursery areas. Thailand and the Philippines are typical examples, where some 208,218 hectares and 200,000 hectares (during 1961–1993), respectively, were cleared. Identical problems resulting from shrimp culture have occurred in Bangladesh, India and Sri Lanka. One example of this destructive sequence of events is the Chakaria Sundarbans in eastern Bangladesh, which have been almost completely cleared for aquaculture.

Coastal construction, particularly for tourist facilities and inland mining, and poor land-use practices have resulted in increased sediment loads in coastal waters in countries such as Fiji, Malaysia, Indonesia and Thailand. The increased sediment has adverse impacts on sensitive coral reef systems, but in Thailand there has been a significant improvement in the condition of the reefs as a result of the efforts of nongovernmental organizations (NGOs) and local people.

Tourism, tourism encroachment and recreational activities can themselves be a threat to marine and coastal environments. The construction activities which accompany most tourism developments, such as hotels, beach clubs and marinas, have a range of direct and indirect impacts on coral reefs through infilling, dredging and the resuspension of contaminated silts. Furthermore, pressure from large numbers of visitors can lead to continuing impacts, such as physical damage to reefs from trampling, boat abrasion and the removal of coral ecosystem for "souvenirs"; discharge of untreated or partially treated sewage; operational leaks and discharges of hydrocarbons; and waste dumping.

The occurrences of "red tides" caused by blooms of particular plankton species have become an environmental problem of major concern in the coastal areas of the region. In addition to depleting oxygen levels such that mass deaths of aquatic organisms occur, the red tides also cause paralytic shellfish poisoning (PSP) with serious risks to the health of people consuming affected shellfish. An outbreak of red tides in the Philippines in 1990 caused economic losses for the fish and shellfish industries. The frequency of red tides in Tolo Harbour, Hong Kong ranged from two in 1977 to nine in 1994. The People's Republic of China is also experiencing increasing occurrences of red tides in its coastal waters, with a total of 19 incidents in 1993.

Coastal erosion, resulting from increased land subsidence from groundwater extraction, sediment starvation as a consequence of inland dam and irrigation barrage construction, and off-shore mining of sand are notable problems in some localities in the region. The high volume of maritime traffic and increasing numbers of international tourist arrivals pose additional threats to the marine and coastal environments of the region.

Although the consequences of marine environmental pollution are becoming increasingly evident, the level of pollution in most coastal waters is still manageable.

Although the consequences of marine environmental pollution are becoming increasingly evident, the level of pollution in most coastal waters is still manageable. The countries of Asia and the Pacific have joined various international and regional agreements to resolve the problem. Over the past five years, the situation in the coastal zone has improved in a few localities in the region. This has been helped along by extensive use of remote sensing in the region as part of a pilot project to obtain data on suspended sediments in the water column, topography, bathymetry, sea state, water colour, chlorophyll-a, sea-surface temperature, fisheries, oil slicks, and submerged and emergent vegetation, including mangroves and seagrass

Policy Responses and Directions: Marine and Coastal Environments

National Initiatives

The Environmental Impact Management Agency (BAPEDAL) in Indonesia, a non-departmental Government Agency, has developed a marine and coastal pollution control program to overcome negative impacts on the coastal and marine environment. The program includes pollution control in sea ports, tourist beaches, and in tanker service zones in the Malaya Strait, Macassar Strait and Lombok Strait.

In India, the National Environmental Engineering Research Institute (NEERI) is engaged in research to develop biotechnological methods to clean up oil spills and protect marine resources.

Regional Initiatives

The Coastal and Marine Environment Management Information System (COMEMIS) is a collaborative project among three member countries (Cambodia, China, and Viet Nam), ADB, and UNEP/EAP-AP. It aims to develop, improve and increase the capacities of all the countries in the South China Sea Region to engage in multi-sectoral analysis and to apply geographic information systems (GIS) to environmental impact assessment and management.

The ASEAN Strategic Plan of Action on the Environment, Strategy 6 promotes the protection and management of coastal zones and marine resources. The main actions under this strategy are the improvement of regional marine and coastal environmental coordination and the development of a framework for the integrated management of regional coastal zones. The South Asian Cooperative Environment Program (SACEP) Strategy and Programme also includes regional cooperation in conservation of corals, mangroves, deltas and coastal areas, and regional cooperation in the regional sea program, as one of the 15 priority subject areas.

Other examples of regional cooperation for coastal and marine environment protection and management include action plans under the Regional Seas Programmes initiated by UNEP. These include South Asian Seas (SAS) Region Action Plan, the East Asian Seas (EAS) Region Action Plan, and the North West Pacific Action Plan (NOWPAP). The ASEAN Senior Officials on Environment (ASOEN) Working Group on Association of Southeast Asian Nations (ASEAN) Seas and Environment, the ASEAN Council of Petroleum's Plan for the Control and Mitigation of Marine Pollution and the South Pacific Regional Environment Programme (SPREP) are also effective regional cooperation programs.

Some of the bilateral and multilateral projects that have contributed to the management and protection of the marine environment are the ASEAN/United States Agency for International Development (USAID) Coastal Resources Management Project, the ASEAN/Australian International Development Assistance Bureau (AIDAB) Projects on "Red Tides and Tidal Phenomena" and the present project on "Living Coastal Resources Management", the ASEAN/

Canada Project on assessment of marine pollution by heavy metals, and the Global Environment Facility (GEF) Project on the prevention and management of marine pollution which covers nine countries (Brunei Darussalam; China, People's Republic of; Indonesia; Korea DPR; Malaysia; Philippines; Singapore, Thailand and Viet Nam).

C

Chua T.E., "Essential Elements of Integrated Coastal Zone Management," 21 *Ocean and Coastal Management* 1993, pp 81–108

Introduction

The coastal zone comprises a narrow strip of coastal lowlands and a vast area of coastal waters. While the coastal zone represents approximately 10 percent of the earth's surface, its coastal lowlands are inhabited by more than 50 percent of the world population. The coastal zone has become the major site for extensive and diverse economic activities. Many of the coasts developing countries depend heavily on the scarce coastal resources for their economic growth.

Rapid urbanization and economic development in many countries of the world spawn a host of complex resource-use conflicts and environmental degradation problems in the coastal zone. The issues have become more serious in many coastal developing nations beset with hunger, unemployment, poverty and rapid population growth.

Such adverse impacts, however, are not clearly discernible in coastal nations with a small and sparsely distributed population, abundant natural resources and a rural economy. This situation will gradually change as increasing population and market forces are expected to exert a heavier influence on resource exploitation and use patterns.

Conventional sectoral management is not effective in addressing the complex management issues of the coastal zone. These issues are often cross-sectoral in nature wherein the activity of one sector adversely affects the development of others. The coastal management issues have become a major threat to economic sustainability and environmental quality; intensifying use conflicts, creating social unrest and destabilizing the national economy. The need for an alternative but effective management system is obvious. A growing number of policy makers and resource managers in both developed and developing nations are pressing for a blueprint for sustainable coastal development.

An integrated management approach to coastal resource utilization has been attempted in the United States (US) since the early 1970s with varying degrees of success. Since then, a number of coastal nations have attempted or practised various forms of coastal management. Since the last decade, integrated coastal zone management (ICZM) has been widely considered as a viable alternative to conventional sectoral management. Thus, national and international efforts have been directed towards promoting public awareness and ICZM programs in the Caribbean, Europe, Latin America, South and East Asia, and Southeast Asian nations.

Recognizing the socioeconomic importance of the coastal zone, the recently concluded United Nations Commission on Environment and Development (UNCED) has prominently placed integrated management of the coastal and marine areas in the now famous *Agenda 21*. Many donor agencies and banking institutions have responded by investing enormous funds in coastal management projects. More coastal nations are now focusing greater attention than before on the planning, development and management of their coastal zone.

Despite the above efforts, the problem in the application of ICZM lies in the lack of an appropriate typology and adequate guidelines for adoption in different climatic, political, cultural and socioeconomic environments.

Since 1986, the Association of Southeast Asian Nations (ASEAN) had initiated a regional project to address the issues of natural resource depletion and coastal environmental degradation under the sponsorship of United States Agency for International Development (USAID).

The project (1986–1992) successfully adopted a multi-pronged approach towards the adoption of integrated management in the region by:

- creating a strong national and regional political alliance among policymakers and the public to enhance awareness of the severity of environmental degradation caused by unsustainable development in the coastal zone;

- involving the concerned planning and line agencies in the preparation of the ICZM program;
- undertaking institutional capacity building through training and workshop to establish a core group of nationals in the region with the necessary capability to execute ICZM programs;
- incorporating the ICZM program into the planning requirements of coordinating and line agencies and ensuring national budgetary allocation for program implementation.

The 7-year project focused on increasing public awareness of the coastal and marine environment, promoted the concept of sustainable development and adopted a holistic, integrative approach in addressing coastal development problems. The purpose of the project was to develop the necessary experience and methodologies to effectively manage environmental problems associated with coastal developments. Valuable lessons have been learned in planning and implementing ICZM programs in the ASEAN region which consists of nations with diverse political, cultural and socioeconomic conditions but with close similarity in biogeographical features. The ASEAN experience in ICZM presents useful insights for future development and implementation of ICZM programs not only in the region but also in other parts of the world.

The purpose of this paper is to discuss the essential elements and application of ICZM based largely on the experiences and conclusions drawn from the ASEAN ICZM program.

Integrated Management

Characteristics of the Coastal Zone

An in-depth understanding of the functions of the coastal resource systems and their characteristics is fundamental to a better appreciation and application of ICZM. The coastal zone is the interface between the land and the sea but concern and interest are concentrated on that area in which human activities are interlinked with both the land and the marine environments. This area has the following characteristics:

- Presence of habitats and ecosystems (e.g., estuaries, coral reefs, seagrass beds, mangrove swamps, lagoons, bays, gulfs), which provide goods (e.g., fish, oil, gas, minerals) and services (e.g., natural defense against storms and tidal waves, recreation, transportation) to the coastal communities. These natural productive and defence systems are maintained in ecological equilibrium through the interaction of a set of physical, chemical and biological processes of the coastal systems.
- Competition of various stakeholders for land and sea uses, often resulting in severe conflicts and destruction to the functional integrity of the resource systems. Stakeholders are groups in the communities having a special interest or involvement in the use of the resources as common property.
- Backbone of most national economies of coastal states as a substantial proportion of the gross national product depends on the outputs from coastal activities such as the oil and shipping industries, coastal tourism and some primary industries.
- Usually has a high concentration of human settlements and is a preferred site for urbanization.

Management Goals

ICZM is a resource management system which employs an integrative, holistic approach and an interactive planning process in addressing the complex management issues in the coastal area. It could serve as the blueprint for attaining the goals and objectives of sustainable development by:

- maintaining the functional integrity of the coastal resource systems,
- reducing resource-use conflicts,
- maintaining the health of the environment, and
- facilitating the progress of multisectoral development.

Integration and Coordination

The coastal management system is built on the essential elements of integration and coordination throughout the entire program. The operational component of the ICZM program is a series of specific policies and management actions with enormous and broad implications on the livelihood and economic activities of the concerned stakeholders. These policies and management actions need to be adequately coordinated to measure effectiveness of the management system.

Integration

Integration is an essential aspect of the management system which ensures not only internal consistency between policies and actions, projects and programs but also linkages between the process of planning and implementation. Integration provides a broader and cohesive perspective of the entire ICZM program to focus efforts on attaining sustainable development goals. Three broad categories of integration have been identified: system, function and policy.

System integration takes into consideration the spatial and temporal dimensions of the coastal resource systems in terms of physical (including seasonal) changes of the environment, resource-use patterns and the socioeconomic setting. This form of integration ensures that the relevant management issues arising from the physical, social and economic linkages are adequately addressed. A coastal environment profile may provide sufficient information for integrating the various elements of the resource systems of the management area of concern...Examples could be obtained from the various coastal environment profiles and ICZM plans of the five other ASEAN members.

Functional integration relates to the linkages among various management actions such that programs and projects are internally consistent with goals and objectives. Functional integration is also promoted among concerned line agencies to avoid duplication but facilitate complementarity. The establishment of a coastal zonation scheme which allocates natural resources for specific uses is one effective form of functional integration. It determines the types and levels of activities permissible in line with the goals and objectives of the ICZM program; limits the types of projects and programs that could be implemented; and refines the responsibilities of concerned line agencies. Thus, for example, in Malaysia the Trade and Industry Department plays a major role in the development and management of industries within the industrial zone while the Fisheries Department wields more authority in the management of the areas allocated for aquaculture development and fishing...Projects and programs are developed to address specific or a combination of management issues and therefore must be functionally and structurally integrated...

Policy integration is very essential to ensure internal consistency of the ICZM program in terms of national and local government policies and management actions; to maintain coordination; and to ensure complementarity and rationalism between programs and projects as well as among concerned public agencies. The final aim is to integrate ICZM programs into national or local economic development plans. Therefore, coastal policy and management strategies must respond to the challenges of change in the coastal zone and be consistent with national economic development goals. Some of the projects may conflict with existing polices of either the national or local government. A case in point is the land-use conflict in Segara Anakan involving the rights in the use of accreted land caused by the rapid sedimentation rate. The conflict is caused by different interpretations of the *Local Government Act* by the Bupati (local government) and the Perhutani (State Forestry Department). Another example of a policy conflict between a local government and a government agency can be seen in the issuance of fishing licenses for commercial trawlers to operate in Lingayen Gulf. While the local government policy is to lessen commercial trawlers in the gulf in order to reduce fishing efforts, issuance of trawling licenses is the jurisdiction of the Department of Agriculture which permits trawlers to operate anywhere outside 15 km from the coast. Cases of policy conflicts are many and it is essential that under the ICZM program, these conflicts are carefully studied and resolved.

Coordination

One of the key features of ICZM, the coordination mechanism, brings about a better understanding and cooperation among various stakeholders in addressing a wide range of coastal development and management issues. Appropriate institutional coordination must occur at the central and local level during the program planning and implementation stages. The ASEAN ICZM experience shows that such coordination strengthens policy and management integration of the ICZM program. It also facilitates smooth implementation of program activities. Integration can be achieved through an effective coordinating mechanism at both the program planning and implementing levels.

The coordination mechanism as applied in the ASEAN ICZM initiatives in fact contributes to vertical coordination between agencies of the central and the local government to ensure policy complementarity and internal consistency, technical assistance and budget allocation. Equally important is coordination at the horizontal level among various implementing agencies in executing management actions of the program. However, interagency conflicts at various levels of the government often pose serious constraints to interagency coordination. Thus it is necessary to involve strong political will and commitment right at the beginning of any ICZM programs.

An interagency coordinating body is usually preferred to implement an ICZM program. Most projects of the program will be implemented by the respective local line agencies as part of their normal functions. The coordinating body, on the other hand, oversees the implementation of the projects; monitors and evaluates progress and impacts; and undertakes cross-agency activities, particularly implementation of zonation schemes, community mobilization, legislative proceedings, public hearings, etc.

Most countries do not have a special department or ministry for coastal zone development and management. Thus, the interagency body has to be a new establishment with the appropriate legislative authority. It can be in the form of an interagency council (e.g., in Brunei, Darussalam), an authority (e.g., proposed for Lingayen Gulf, Philippines), a task force (e.g., in Segara Anakan, Indonesia) or a committee (e.g., in South Johore, Malaysia) as long as the functions are clearly outlined. In some cases, the existing administrative structure oversees the ICZM programs. For example, the Sri Lanka Coastal Area Management Plan is coordinated through the Coastal Conservation Department of the Ministry of Fisheries. In Thailand, coastal zone management programs are organized through the Ministry of Science, Technology and the Environment, while the People's Republic of China has the State Oceanic Administration...

This Brunei model has least disruption to the existing institutional structure but provides a close institutional linkage for the coordination of policies and management actions undertaken by various agencies belonging to different ministries. The establishment of the Environmental Council is an initial step in the government's commitment. Already interagency coordination has helped to preserve the valuable mangrove wetlands in the country and the avoidance of sewage outfall into the Serasa Bay which has been designated for mariculture development.

ICZM: The Coastal Management System

Ideally, an ICZM program should operate within a closely integrated, coherent management framework within a defined geographical limit. The coastal zone is viewed in its entirety as a special geographical area wherein its productive and natural defense functions are intimately linked with the physical and socioeconomic conditions far beyond its physical boundary. Hence, any policy and management action designed to address coastal development conflicts must be founded on a solid understanding of the productive capacity of the natural systems, the assimilative capacity of the environment, the political, sociocultural and economic conditions, present and future demands as well as social costs involved.

Government policies, strategies and actions for coastal management are formulated and implemented systematically through a series of planning and implementation processes; collectively forming the coastal management system. This system is made up of three mutually supporting dimensions, viz. processes, issues and actions.

The three dimensions are closely intertwined and should be considered in their entirety. To ignore one may lead to the collapse of the whole management system or render it ineffective. ICZM should not be mistaken as a development program although its ultimate objective is to allow multisectoral development with the least intended setbacks. It provides a planning and management framework which permits the rational utilization of natural resources and their sustainable development.

For a better understanding of the concept and operation of ICZM, Scura *et al.* describe the coastal management system as a cube consisting of three basic dimensions—processes, issues and actions. The management processes identify and analyze management issues and develop the necessary policy and management options. The management processes consist of three essential sequential components: planning, implementation, and monitoring and evaluation (M&E). The planning component constitutes the basic layer of the cube. The management issues relate to conflicts arising from resource allocation, exploitation and utilization as well as other adverse effects of sectoral development. Management issues could be categorized primarily into those related to resource use, environmental quality and institutional concerns. Management actions form the third dimension. All three dimensions are of equal importance and mutually dependent. Unlike sectoral management which is represented by one sector of the cube (e.g., overfishing), the spillover effects of one form of development will be addressed under the present form of integrated management system.

The management system is analogous to a Rubick's cube. It is in a perfect form when each segment of all the three dimensions are closely coordinated and orderly in place such that coastal management issues are adequately addressed, economic development could be sustained without compromising the coastal or the marine environment. This ideal situation is seldom if not ever achievable as it is never easy to get the same color on each side of the Rubick's cube. It is therefore logical to assume that sustainable development is not easily attainable, but there is a way to get there. A perfect ICZM system is indeed the blueprint for sustainable development of the coastal zone. In the real world, coastal planning and management is a continuous process improving with time and experience.

Essential Elements of the Management Processes

Integrated Planning

Integrated planning is an essential component of the coastal management system because of the complexity and magnitude of management issues. ICZM planning consists of the following fundamental steps: inception, research/ analysis, program formulation, adoption, execution/ implementation and monitoring and evaluation (M&E). While the level and detail in planning may vary according to the conditions of the site and experience and knowledge of the planning team, the fundamental steps are essentially the same.

A review of the past planning process for ICZM programs in the Southeast Asian region provides a number of lessons discussed below.

Composition of Planning Team

A multidisciplinary team should be established at the initial phase of program development to provide the framework for the management program, establish the planning process and identify the key participating agencies. It is important to avoid concentrating the jurisdiction of resources on a single agency. The ASEAN/ US Coastal Resources Management Project experienced considerable initial difficulties in maintaining a broad approach for the coastal issues, particularly in countries where a single line agency had been appointed. This approach will have far-reaching effects on the outputs. For example, the ICZM programs for Lingayen Gulf and Segara Anakan put more emphasis on fisheries since the key coordinating and implementing agency is the Fisheries Department. Scura *et al.* suggest that the planning team should be made up of a core staff of six members comprising a coastal management expert, a regional planner, a resource economist, an ecologist, a sociologist and an environmental engineer. Specialists could be invited to join the planning team depending on the resources and their use patterns. Some of the pertinent disciplines include fisheries, aquaculture, coastal erosion, pollution, marine park management and environmental legislation.

Planning Process

The planning process adopted at the ASEAN ICZM ranged from two to five years. The unduly long process is partly due to the time-consuming technical research and other information gathering activities. This resulted in a loss of interest and momentum among policymakers and the communities in the initial phase of program development. Even the enthusiasm of the national coordinating and implementing agencies waned considerably. Therefore, it is absolutely necessary to reduce the planning process to one and not more than two years. In fact, the lessons learned from past ICZM efforts in the US and ASEAN showed that existing secondary information is sufficient to prepare a strategic management plan and specific research needs could be integrated into the plan and be undertaken as part of the management program.

It is absolutely necessary to reduce the planning process to one and not more than two years.

A fast-track management planning process has been developed that modifies the techniques used for rapid rural appraisal. Known as Rapid Appraisal of Coastal Environments (RACE), its techniques and procedures complement but not replace the conventional planning process. The RACE framework includes secondary data analysis in relation to the planning or research objectives identified. It also espouses a participatory approach for the three RACE types.

- Exploratory RACE explores key problems and opportunities in the coastal zone as a way to plan research and development projects.
- Topical RACE investigates specific issues identified under the exploratory phase.
- Monitoring RACE assesses and predicts the impacts (success or otherwise) of a proposed management or development intervention.

By integrating RACE into the conventional planning stage, the process of generating the necessary outputs is shortened and a rapid monitoring procedure to track the project's performance is made possible.

Relevant Research

Information gathering is an important component of the planning process. Unfortunately, a large amount of the data gathered may not be relevant to the planning requirements. On the other hand, essential data for estimating the assimilative capacity of the management area as well as for resource valuation and legislation are usually left out. This is partly because they are difficult to gather but basically due to the lack of a multidisciplinary team to undertake adequate program planning. Leaving the scientists to tackle the initial stage of data gathering and program formulation and planning thereafter is a major mistake. The types of data needed for planning and program formulation should be clearly spelled out in the initial phase. Research should only be conducted to provide specific answers to the technical and management questions identified during the RACE process as well as in the implementation of the strategic plans.

Program Revision and Refinement

The projects and programs formulated during the planning process must undergo a series of consultations and evaluations before they can be implemented. Sometimes technical recommendations are substantially revised to accommodate special political or sociocultural considerations. A successful ICZM program does not necessarily have the best technical content but is one that receives public approval and meets the needs of a large number of stakeholders. Adequate consultation should be undertaken with the concerned resource management agencies of national and local governments, the coastal communities and other involved stakeholders.

Implementation

Implementation of projects and programs is a critical stage of ICZM. In the past, many ICZM initiatives (e.g., Philippines, Tonga) were not able to proceed beyond the planning phase. There are many reasons for this. ICZM programs developed outside the government planning or concerned line agencies have the tendency of being ignored by these organizations and often end up shelved, irrespective of the comprehensiveness of the programs. On the other hand, if the planning and line agencies were involved right at the initial stage of ICZM program development, there is a greater likelihood of the program being integrated totally or partly into the respective development plans of the relevant agencies.

Establishing a new agency to implement the program usually takes time. The ICZM initiatives in the six ASEAN members give credence to the above situation. The ICZM program for Lingayen Gulf had the National Economic Development Authority (NEDA) as the lead agency that prepared the plan with inputs from other line agencies and experts from research organizations and universities. The program sailed through the Regional Development Council and received budget allocation for its implementation. On the other hand, the strategic management plan for Singapore, essentially prepared by a university professor with inputs from government line agencies and experts, was received as a major reference document; only some of its recommendations (e.g., the southern island management plan) were considered by the national planning agency.

Funds and human resources are the most important ingredients needed for program implementation. Government funds could be used only if the policymakers are convinced of the program's potential economic and social benefits. The success of project implementation primarily depends on the project design and capability of the implementing agencies. The coordinating body should ensure sufficient technical backstopping for program implementation.

Not all projects and programs of ICZM developed must be implemented at any one time. In fact, they are best implemented in stages over the proposed timeframe. In the ICZM program of Segara Anakan (Indonesia), the local government formed the interagency Task Force first and then implemented the aquaculture project before other activities were undertaken. In Brunei Darussalam, the various activities identified in the ICZM program were being taken up by concerned line agencies and implemented with their own annual financial allocations.

Monitoring and Evaluation

This important component of the management processes should be incorporated into the ICZM program at the planning and implementation stage. Monitoring of progress and evaluation of impacts should be undertaken annually by the respective implementing and coordinating agencies. The purposes are to see how the projects and programs are doing; determine what could be done for better performance; find out opportunities that could be explored and developed; and assess the impacts and lessons learned. The ultimate objective of this exercise is to ensure timely intervention to assist projects and programs in meeting set objectives. M&E provides opportunities for refinement or for increase or decrease in financial and logistic support.

External reviews of the progress and impacts of the program should be encouraged in the middle of program implementation and at the termination of the program phase.

Standard M&E protocol is available and could be adopted, such as the use of a logical framework. M&E measures the changes that have occurred in relation to the set objectives within the timeframe given and also assesses the impacts of outputs against the values of inputs. M&E also identifies the strengths and weaknesses of program implementation with respect to efficiency and effectiveness.

Essential Elements of the Management Issues

A wide range of management issues and problems is related to coastal development. Some of the issues are caused directly by sectoral activities, others may be indirectly related to the spillover effects of sectoral development. The management issues could be grouped under the following broad categories: resource utilization, environmental quality, institutional concerns and natural hazards. Management issues associated with resource utilization and environmental quality vary with the types of resources available and their use patterns. These categories also include archaeological/cultural or historical resources that require specific legal protection. Institutional concerns are related to institutional capacity to enforce legislation and implement programs. Finally, there are coastal management issues caused by natural hazards such as typhoons, storms and tidal waves. Moreover, the potential direct or indirect impacts of sea temperature and sea level rise may pose a series of new management problems that require careful consideration under the ICZM program.

Some management issues are very obvious and can be easily identified by site inspection, while many others may require appropriate survey instruments or field research. In most cases, coastal zone management issues could be identified through appropriate consultative meetings with the local communities, local government officials and members of the nongovernment organizations working in the field. For example, the vast experience and knowledge of the fisherfolk would easily provide the needed information on biodiversity, endangered species, overfishing, destructive fishing methods, law enforcement as well as the changes in the environmental quality or weather conditions.

Not all issues and problems can be resolved at once; many may require a longer time frame. The ICZM system helps to characterize and prioritize management issues that should be addressed to enable the development of a long-term management strategy.

Essential Elements of the Management Actions

While the first two dimensions of the management system provide the instrument and contents for planning, analysis and program formulation, the third and most important dimension is the application of actions/measures geared towards realizing the desired changes. Such changes are expected in relation to maintaining the functional integrity or productive capacity of the resource systems, improving environmental quality; and changing human behavior towards the desirable ICZM goals.

Institutional and Organizational Arrangements

Institutional and organizational arrangements are imperative in carrying out the projects and programs. Since ICZM is a government program, it must have the necessary legitimacy in implementation. An ICZM program developed outside the government framework will often encounter great difficulties. Even under the concept of co-management or community management, the government must first devolve management authority to the concerned communities or local authorities. The government is still required to provide the necessary supervision, technical assistance and in most cases, financial support.

The enactment of coastal laws is an important step towards providing the necessary legal framework. For example, the USA enacted the *Coastal Zone Management Act* of 1972 primarily to protect natural resources, reduce coastal development conflicts and improve seafronts. Under this federal legislation, a large number of coastal states developed their coastal zone management programs. As another example, the French enacted in 1986 the *National Law on Planning, Protection and Development of the Coastal Space* which provides the necessary measures to regulate coastal development and protect the environment.

Policy considerations are among the top of the list of management actions for an ICZM program. Government policies and legislation need to be formulated or clarified with respect to the promotion of sustainable development in inland, coastal and marine areas, and the protection of territorial use rights, biodiversity, coastal habitats and environmental quality. Management actions are also required to address organizational deficiency, particularly with respect to law enforcement and clarification of duties and responsibilities. In short, the most common management actions under this category include the following:

(a) clarifying and defining legal rights and obligations,
(b) determining organizational jurisdiction and responsibilities,
(c) strengthening enforcement capability, and
(d) undertaking monitoring and evaluation.

Government policies and legislation need to be formulated or clarified with respect to the promotion of sustainable development in inland, coastal and marine areas, and the protection of territorial use rights, biodiversity, coastal habitats and environmental quality.

Command and Control

A large number of management measures fall under this category. Both incentives and regulatory measures are necessary for effecting human behavioral changes in line with ICZM goals. Incentives such as tax exemption or reduction, government subsidy and technical assistance or disincentives such as heavy or new taxes, license fees, closed season, limiting access to specific resources are some of the measures to promote environmental protection or discourage pollutive or destructive practices.

The most common management actions pertaining to command and control to mitigate adverse environmental effects could be grouped under the following types:

(a) imposing new regulatory measures;
(b) strengthening existing regulatory measures;
(c) establishing and implementing standards, e.g., water quality, emission/discharge; and
(d) providing incentives.

Direct Public Investment

This category of management actions involves a direct investment by government to bring about public awareness or provide basic infrastructure, conduct research, build capabilities or offer opportunities which will lead to the solution of issues and problems related to coastal development. For example, considerable investment in research is necessary for a better understanding of the factors that maintain the functional integrity of the resource systems; the assimilative capacity of the marine environment; the social costs of a poorly managed environment, the technologies for waste management, etc.

The most common management actions under this category are as follows:

(a) research and development;
(b) training and education;
(c) public awareness and information dissemination;
(d) public infrastructure, e.g., roads, embankments, waste collection and disposal systems/facilities; and
(e) technical assistance.

Discussion

The application of ICZM requires a full understanding of the management system so that the various essential elements are effectively used to accurately diagnose the causes and effects of the identified management problems and to prescribe the appropriate solutions. Like physicians, the coastal planners must be skillful in applying the appropriate management tools and methods in designing the ICZM program. As ICZM is relatively new in most parts of the world, resource managers will need to acquire the necessary skills and experience before the system can be effectively adopted.

The ASEAN experience demonstrates that it is possible to bring various government line agencies to work together and genuine political and public support exists for the application of the management system.

Although it is ideal to develop a national ICZM program such as that of Brunei Darussalam, it is more realistic to develop a site-specific ICZM program manageable by the local authorities. With experience and a firmer grasp of its concept, a systematic application of ICZM could gradually cover the rest of the entire coastal zone. A national coastal policy could be established first with the provision to incorporate integrated planning and management into the development plans of national and local governments.

The ICZM program provides a strong legal and institutional framework within which control of pollution, protection of biodiversity and management of sectoral development could be effectively undertaken. The ineptness of many sectoral (e.g., fisheries, coral reefs and mangroves) or special area (marine parks/reserves) management programs outside the ICZM framework springs from the inability to resolve legislative, interagency and other cross-sectoral conflicts.

The positive results of integrated management cannot be discerned immediately as it takes time for the desired changes to occur. These require a shift in perception and stronger support on the part of the policymakers and sectors affected by the implementation of the ICZM programs.

Although ICZM provides a general management framework, this can vary in emphasis in response to the major issues of the management area. For example, the management plans for Lingayen Gulf and Segara Anakan focus on fisheries while those of the Upper South, Thailand and South Johore, Malaysia lean more towards general area management. The Brunei management plan is comprehensive while the coastal zone management plan for Sri Lanka, the coral reef management program for Phuket, Thailand and the coastal resource management of the Salt Pond region of Rhode Island in the USA emphasize resource conservation. The management plan for Turkey, on the other hand, centers on land management, particularly with respect to tourism development. Regardless of the emphasis, the basic elements contributing to the development of a viable coastal management system remain the same."

D

Caribbean Environment Programme, United Nations Environment Programme, "Development and Implementation of ICAM Programmes," in *Guidelines for Integrated Planning and Management of Coastal and Marine Areas in the Wider Caribbean Region*, UNEP, 2001

[*The following material has been selectively extracted, a necessity brought on by detail of the original. The Guidelines document is available on the Internet at <http://www.cep.unep.org/pubs/techreports/guidelines/index.html#contents>. This site was accessed on 29/6/2001. The extract begins with a point form summary. This is designed to give the reader an indication of the scope of the ICZM development and implementation process. Following this, selections of the program phases are extracted to provide an indication of their substance.*]

Phase 1: Program Initiation

- First Steps: Preliminary Tasks
- Public Support
- Goals
- Strategic Planning
- Data Generation, Assessment, Interpretation and Management
- Concept Paper
- Program Instruments and Deliverables
- Considerations

Phase 2: Resource Characterization and Problem Definition

- Overview
- Technical and Scientific Characterization
- Targeted Information Needs
- Management Characterization

Phase 3: Program Planning

- Elements of the Plan: Concept Formulation
- The Plan Formulation Team
- Selecting An Agenda
- Planning Phase for Information Needs
- Geographic Information System Needs
- Interagency Coordinating Mechanisms
- Critical Elements For An ICAM Plan
- Operational Considerations For Planning

Phase 4: Plan Implementation

- Implementation of the Management Plan
- Administrative Elements of ICAM Implementation
- Intersectorial Strategies for ICAM Implementation
- Monitoring and Enforcement

This section outlines a model process for developing and implementing an ICAM program. It is a prototype approach which may be difficult for many countries to fully emulate. Nevertheless, this section could serve as preliminary guidelines for countries in the Wider Caribbean Region seeking to improve existing coastal area management programs. It is not intended to meet the requirements of all, nor is it suggested that each step must be followed exactly as presented.

A four-phase process is suggested for the development and implementation of ICAM programmes; each phase is presented in detail in the four subsections which follow.

- Phase 1: Opening or program initiation phase during which the program focus is set, issues reviewed, goals and objectives established, and preliminary planning put in motion.
- Phase 2: A program analysis phase during which a number of parallel investigations are carried out which determine what problems will be addressed and what actions are needed under the ICAM program.
- Phase 3: A program design phase during which a coastal management plan and related planning tools are assembled.
- Phase 4: The final phase during which the coastal management plan is implemented, with ongoing provisions for program evaluation and modification.

Program Initiation: Phase 1

There is a general agreement among coastal area program specialists that there is no unique best scenario for the start-up and implementation of a new coastal area management programme, integrated or otherwise. In several case studies done antecedent to World Coast 1993, the International Conference on Coastal Zone Management held in the Netherlands, it was evident that a wide variety of successful programme initiatives exist but that they differ widely...

This is, of course, a favorable finding as it suggests there is a reasonably broad set of tactical options, tools and approaches that the would-be coastal program planner can choose from, selecting those that appear best suited to local conditions and circumstances. However, this also suggests the need for a pre-project review of what has worked elsewhere and under what specific conditions comparable to those prevailing locally.

This section outlines some of the pre-start up optional activities that have proven effective as first-stage, constituency-building and energizing procedures for the development of ICAM programs.

Resource Characterization and Problem Definition: Phase 2

Overview

An ICAM action programme consists of objectives and activities aimed at reducing or preventing certain stresses in the coastal zone, usually forms of resource misuse, pollution, or habitat destruction that threaten the ecological, economic or aesthetic health of the coastal ecosystem. The key question is how to pinpoint the problem. Phase 2 of ICAM— Resource Characterization and Problem Definition—provides for information gathering to determine which problems will be addressed under ICAM and what actions are needed. Two parallel investigations provide the necessary information:

1. a technical and scientific characterization, and
2. a management characterization.

This second program design phase of ICAM shifts focus from recruiting leadership and identifying expert counsel, institutional support, and information to developing the planning framework and carrying out a multi-stage design and planning project for ICAM. For example, Phase 1 sought institutional support from local and national organizations connected with marine and coastal activities for help in identifying issues and in preparing and reviewing draft work plans. This work is assumed to continue only until the program planning component is completed and officially approved and the implementation phase is ready to go operational.

In this second phase, the emphasis is on a diagnostic assessment of the state of health of both:

1. the prospective "clients" (coastal ecosystems, habitats, wildlife and other "systems"); and
2. the perspective helping institutions (government and nongovernment) which might become part of the national ICAM program team(s).

Additionally, Phase 1, by way of contrast, had no advance structure and therefore had—as presented and as would be the case in real life—an opportunistic quality about it. It is an architectural process, shaping a framework, and only becomes product focused as it reaches its concluding tasks.

This Phase 2, however, will be more product focused from the outset, with serious concerns for quality control, reporting standards, defensible science, reliable conclusions, technical accuracy, and the administrative detail of good documentation, meticulous record keeping, source tracking and up-to-date contact lists for use in ICAM public education and information dissemination...

Program Planning: Phase 3

Elements of the Plan: Concept Formulation

Basic elements to be added to the concept paper, the preparatory environmental inventory and institutional assessment work done under Phase 1 and Phase 2 (which generated a ranked agenda of coastal issues and problems awaiting attention or action) are the following:

- a monitoring and evaluation system;
- an information/documentation system;
- an applied research program or strategy;
- a public participation and educational plan and program; and
- a unit of government formally committed to lead responsibility for administering the program and for updating the core plan as needed (i.e., in charge of feedback flows from the evaluation and monitoring plan-based activities).

The countries already with coastal programmes also have documentation on the above which can have instructive value for those designing new programs. Planners of new initiatives are counselled to aggressively seek examples of this documentation if only to get a clear picture of development alternatives before making commitments to a specific track or strategy.

For guidance in evaluating such existing "model" plans from elsewhere and in shaping a locally adapted conceptual framework for a new plan in a new location, it is useful to turn to existing published guidelines on the subject, such as World Bank, 1993; Awosika, et al., 1993; Clark, 1992; Sorensen, et al., 1984; and Cicin-Sain, 1993 [*see References for Chapter 14, below*].

Since geography and unique regional geomorphological and other coastal features are significant determinant variables in any Caribbean coastal planning effort, it is recommended that a complete regime of coastal management planning documents be obtained by any planning team leader from at least one Caribbean country or territory with an existing or developing coastal zone or coastal area management program. These include Barbados, Belize, British Virgin Islands, Colombia, Cuba, Dominican Republic, Mexico, Puerto Rico, U.S. Virgin Islands, and Venezuela…

Plan Implementation: Phase 4

Implementation of the Management Plan

The final phase of developing an ICAM program is [implementation]. On one track, the focus is on putting into operation the salient components of the basic plan and its component and supplementary sub-plans. These include, among other components and its component and supplemenatary sub-plans, zoning categories (if any), proposed "special areas", a monitoring plan and an evaluation plan. These combined with previous and now continuing public participation, public education, training and information management plans, all developed in previous phases…

Before action can be taken on the basic management plan, however, formal adoption by government is required for the following:

- Adoption of the ICAM Plan and its policies, goals, new management measures and initial projects.
- Establishment of the interagency coordinating mechanism.
- Enactment, sometimes by legislation, of coastal zone management boundaries and zoning scheme.
- Approval of staffing and organizational changes that may be required.
- Approval of the funding allocation for the ICAM program.

From the very outset, the interface of the ICAM program with other regulatory and resource management activities, and with other governmental management units at the national and local level, will raise the issue of consistency. Improperly handled, it will generate controversy and place the new ICAM program at risk of premature and hasty amendments to its program plan. A procedure for addressing questions of inconsistency that arise during the implementation phase, especially at the local level, needs to be established.

There could be a quasi-formal testing period, given the time usually necessary to obtain the required executive and legislative approvals. Some parts of the ICAM programme may start to function earlier than others. Major legislative initiatives are not always required. In some countries, a decree or administrative rule is sufficient.

There is a longer-term consistency issue arising out of the permitting and leasing conditions established, and the fee schedules and standards put in place. This will require close tracking to ensure both fairness (and a public perception of fairness) that will best be achieved when such matters are eminently transparent and components like permit conditions and fee schedules are freely made available to the public and circulated widely…

Training

Training should be provided for at several levels. This includes:

- policy makers in the political directorate, government ministers and community leaders, to be educated to appreciate the purpose and importance of ICAM;
- senior management in ICAM-related agencies responsible for critical or secondary ICAM tasks, to establish the need for interagency communication and coordination;
- within the agency responsible for ICAM, to understand the functions of management and the importance of information exchange and communication;
- technical support staff, in skills for data collection and analysis, and to improve interactions with resource users in the field;
- marine police, park/reserve rangers, and other law enforcement officers, in the special requirements for interpretation and application of the regulations and standards for ICAM.

Raising the level of awareness of the general public and user groups through education is critical to the success of ICAM. There can be no appreciation of, or compliance with, an ICAM program if citizens do not know it exists, or if they are unaware of its structure, potential benefits and infringements. User groups within the area are likely to vary widely, so that specially tailored approaches are needed to avoid feelings of alienation and irrelevance. Target audiences who should be sensitized to ICAM during implementation include:

- specific user groups such as fishermen, diving and tour operators, beach vendors, researchers;
- developers, architects, engineers, and planners in both the private and public sectors;
- residents of specific geographical units impacted by the coastal zone;
- educators in the school system;
- special groups, such as community action groups, NGOs, women in
- development groups, media reporters, and cultural and/or linguistic minorities...

Evaluation

A statutory requirement for the performance of the ICAM program on some recurring schedule should be written into the enabling legislation. Changes in factors external to the project, such as revisions to economic, land use, physical planning or other policies at the national or regional level of government can influence the achievement of plan objectives. There should be provision for reevaluation if these policy changes occur. Similarly, it is essential that ICAM program managers use all available channels to maintain their own inputs to revisions of higher-level government policy.

Monitoring and Enforcement

Monitoring may be defined as the "watchdog" of the ICAM process, aiming to establish the necessary flow of information on decisions, actions and investments as these relate to the implementation of ICAM. Evaluation utilizes the information generated by continuous monitoring and analyses of the effectiveness with which ICAM decisions have been carried out, the efficiency of the investments undertaken, the equity in the distribution of benefits among the various social groups of the community, and the impacts of ICAM actions on the environment.

Monitoring can take several forms:

- *Ambient Conditions.* Ongoing routine observations of environmental and socioeconomic parameters (sometimes called "status and trends") allow the changing conditions of the managed area to be updated.
- *Compliance or surveillance monitoring.* This establishes the extent of human activities in the managed area, and the infringements of regulations or standards that may occur.
- *Structure monitoring.* Where investments have been made in structural measures for coastal defense or shoreline stabilization, ongoing performance monitoring should be undertaken, even if the feasibility of the structures has been studied previously.
- *Program monitoring.* A reporting and evaluation system must be established to ensure that the objectives are being achieved within the implementation schedule.

Enforcement is a sensitive area that can have major negative effects on implementation if it is not conducted in a manner that assists the maintenance of rapport between program managers and user groups. Several levels of enforcement are possible and perhaps should start with education and outreach before punitive or legal actions are taken. The integration of ICAM enforcement activities with other enforcement undertakings in the country—for example, those undertaken by wildlife and park rangers or port authorities—will require special attention and careful planning.

3

Agenda 21 and ICZM

A

Bateman S., "Technical Cooperation For Sustainable Development: Capacity Building," in Kusuma-Atmadja A., Mensah T.A., Oxman B.H. (eds), *Sustainable Development and Preservation of the Oceans: The Challenges of UNCLOS and Agenda 21*, Proceedings of The Law of the Sea Twenty-Ninth Annual Conference, Bali, Indonesia, 1995

Introduction

The broad agenda for the sustainable development of the coastal and ocean environments of the world, including their living resources, is contained in Chapter 17 of *Agenda 21* agreed at the United Nations Conference on Environment and Development (UNCED) in Rio de Janeiro in 1992. This builds on the regime for managing the oceans and seas of the world established by the 1982 UN *Convention on the Law of the Sea* (UNCLOS). *Agenda 21* Chapter 17 provides a long list of what countries ought to do in the following program areas:

- integrated management and sustainable development of coastal areas, including exclusive economic zones;
- marine environmental protection;
- sustainable use and conservation of marine living resources of the high seas;
- sustainable use and conservation of marine living resources under national jurisdiction;
- addressing critical uncertainties for the management of the marine environment and climate change;
- strengthening international, including regional, cooperation and coordination; and
- sustainable development of small islands.

The actions required by Chapter 17 are complex, innovative, and well beyond the capabilities of most countries. Developing countries in particular face considerable difficulties in developing their capacity to fulfil their obligations under Chapter 17 and to follow sustainable development paths. The guidance to assist developing countries in capacity building is provided by Chapter 37 of *Agenda 21*. This chapter contains the following description of the process of capacity building:

> "Specifically, capacity building encompasses the country's human, scientific, technological, organisational, institutional and resource capabilities. A fundamental goal of capacity-building is to enhance the ability to evaluate and address the crucial questions related to policy choices and modes of implementation among development options, based on an understanding of environmental potentials and limits and of needs as perceived by the people of the country concerned."

Capacity building in developing countries requires cooperation between these countries and relevant United Nations organizations, regional associations and with developed countries, as well as among the developing countries themselves. The aim of this process is to enhance the capacities of developing countries in the areas of data and information, scientific and technological means, and human resource development. In summary, capacity is usually regarded as including at least three elements: human resources, institutions, and enabling environment.

Chapter 37 of *Agenda 21* goes on to note that:

> "Technical cooperation, including that related to technology transfer and know-how, encompasses the whole range of activities to develop or strengthen individual and group capacities and capabilities."

Capacity building in developing countries requires cooperation between these countries and relevant United Nations organizations, regional associations and with developed countries, as well as among the developing countries themselves.

Technical cooperation is the most important element of capacity building. It involves moving beyond the exhortative language of documents such as *Agenda 21* to the identification and implementation of practical measures which will assist developing countries with integrated management and sustainable development. The benefits of technical cooperation accrue not only to the developing countries, which are the recipients of the assistance, but also to the entire international community as a result of the overall better management of the world's oceans and seas at all levels—global, regional, and national. The solution to many of the transnational and common problems of marine environmental management often lies in the transfer of capacity to states which lack it.

This paper explores the problems with building the capacity of developing countries to exercise their rights and fulfil their responsibilities under UNCLOS and UNCED. The paper considers factors which inhibit policy development and progress towards the more sustainable use of coastal and ocean environments and their resources. It suggests ways in which technical cooperation with developing countries may be improved to assist them in meeting the objectives of UNCLOS and UNCED.

Scope

The scope of marine affairs and oceans and coastal management included within the vision of Chapter 17 of *Agenda 21* is very large. Almost every central Government department in a coastal or island state has some policy responsibility related to the sea, and important regulatory responsibilities are invariably shared between a range of government agencies. Furthermore, all levels of government (i.e., central, provincial, and local) are involved to some extent in marine affairs. The consequent problems of jurisdictional boundaries between the different levels of government are particularly acute in countries such as Australia, with a Federal system of government and extensive powers resting or remaining with the constituent states or provinces that comprise the federation. Cooperation and coordination between the levels of government is then of obvious importance.

To assist in our analysis of technical cooperation and capacity building, it is useful to break up the scope of marine affairs and ocean management into three categories of sectoral interest. Firstly, we can talk about policy outputs or objectives. These embrace both the policy goals and the activities either carried out at sea or associated with the sea, and include:

- Integrated management and sustainable development of coastal and marine areas, including the conservation and protection of the marine environment and the prevention of marine pollution;
- Marine transport and communications, including the development of ports, marine safety, the prevention of ship-sourced pollution, and the security of sea lines of communication (SLCs);
- The exploitation and sustainable development of living and non-living marine resources;
- Other marine industries (e.g., shipbuilding, marine biotechnology, ship design, aquaculture, marine tourism, etc.); and
- Maritime security and defense, including surveillance and patrol of marine areas under national jurisdiction and the enforcement of national maritime laws.

Secondly, there are the inputs which enable these activities to be carried out and for which separate policies need to be developed. Inputs to the process include:

- human resource development (training and education);
- marine science and technology;
- coastal and offshore engineering;
- data and information needs; and
- the legal framework, including national legislation, bilateral or multilateral arrangements with neighboring countries, and international treaties.

In many ways, these inputs, along with financial resources and appropriate institutions, constitute what is meant by "capacity" for the integrated management of coastal and marine areas. They represent the skills and arrangements which a country should have in place before it can properly exercise its rights, undertake sustainable development; and discharge its responsibilities in coastal and offshore areas.

Lastly, there are the different categories of coastal and ocean space for which policies are required. These are:

- the coastal zone
- the marine areas under full national sovereignty (i.e., internal waters, territorial sea, and archipelagic waters);
- the areas where the coastal State has sovereign rights over marine resources either living or non-living (i.e., the exclusive economic zone (EEZ) and the Continental Shelf); and
- the high seas and the deep seabed.

Alternatively, we can think separately about the coastal zone and oceanic areas. The coastal zone embraces the interface between the land and the sea and various geographical definitions are possible with, in some cases, the coastal zone extending seawards to include the EEZ. However, the two significant factors about the coastal zone are at, firstly, what happens in that zone, such as waste disposal and coastal urban development, has a profound effect on the health of the nearby oceans, and secondly, the greatest political, legal, and administrative difficulties are encountered with management of the coastal zone. This is because of both the complexity of the issues involved as well as the number of agencies with responsibilities in the coastal zone.

The brief categorization of the scope of oceans management and policy highlights the reality that any holistic or integrated approach to the topic has to be an inter-disciplinary one with historians, lawyers, economists, and political scientists working with engineers, biologists, chemists, and physicists on common ocean problems. Also, there has to be close involvement of industry in this process of dialogue to ensure that environmentally sustainable marine-based industries are developed. The capacity-building process should comprehend the multifaceted nature of the issues involved.

An integrated approach to sustainable development requires that there be integration in several different dimensions—between inputs, outputs, and the zones of jurisdiction, as well as within each of these categories. Thus we are looking at a great number of matrices to show the extent of the possible relationships and impacts and to highlight the main conflicts which can arise. Rather than sub-optimizing with policy-making for each sector (input, output, or zonal), integration requires that we think much more than we have in the past about how our actions in one policy area affect other policy areas and other nations.

In summary integration has several dimensions. These comprise:

- integration among the various sectors of maritime activity and industry (i.e., the 'outputs' identified above);
- integration among the different disciplines involved in marine and coastal management (i.e., the "inputs" listed above);
- integration between the land and the water sides of the coastal zones and between the various maritime zones;
- integration among levels of government (i.e., national, provincial or state, and local); and
- integration between nations.

Outputs

Integrated Coastal and Marine Zone Management

The vulnerability of the coastal zone and adjacent marine areas to poor planning and over-development has attracted considerable attention. A more integrated approach to policy formulation and management is perceived as the main way of overcoming the problems which have arisen in the past.

Section (A) of *Agenda 21* Chapter 17 requires that coastal states commit themselves to "integrated management and sustainable development of coastal areas and the marine environment under national jurisdiction." This section goes on to call for integrated policy and decision-making processes and institutions:

Each coastal state should consider establishing, or where necessary strengthening, appropriate coordinating mechanisms (such as a high level policy planning body) for integrated management and sustainable development of coastal and marine areas and their resources, at both the local and national levels. Such mechanisms should include consultation, as appropriate, with the academic and private sectors, nongovernmental organizations, local communities, resource user groups, and indigenous people.

The concept of integrated coastal and marine zone management to achieve sustainable development is a relatively recent development. It has developed in response to the jurisdictional revolution in the law of the sea reflected in UNCLOS, the expansion of economic activities at sea, increasing concern over conflicts of interest between the various uses of coastal and sea areas (i.e., navigation, fishing, mining, dumping, tourism, recreational, etc.), the possible implications for environmental quality with unconstrained development, and the idea of ecologically sustainable development (ESD) that treats all natural environments as interacting systems.

Coordination, cooperation, and consultation are fundamental themes of integrated coastal and marine zone management. UNCLOS stresses the importance of coordinated policies by recognizing "that the problems and opportunities of ocean space are closely interrelated and need to be considered as a whole." Several articles of UNCLOS go on to point out a requirement for regional cooperation (Article 276, for example, calls for the establishment of regional marine scientific and technological research centers, and Article 277 describes the functions of such centers). Chapter 17 of *Agenda 21* stresses the importance of consultation and coordination and calls for support for "centers of excellence" in integrated coastal and marine management.

Section (B) of *Agenda 21* Chapter 17 addresses the problems of marine pollution both land-based and sea-based. The section notes that, although land-based sources contribute 70 percent of marine pollution, "[t]here is currently no global scheme to address marine pollution from land-based sources," and that:

> "Research facilities should be strengthened or, where appropriate, developed in developing countries for systematic observation of marine pollution, environmental impact assessment and development of control recommendations and should be managed and staffed by local experts."

A particular difficulty of coastal and marine zone management relates to the uncertainty of the data that is available as an input to the process. Section (E) of Chapter 17 of *Agenda 21* notes the vulnerability of the marine environment to climate and atmospheric changes and that the rational use and development of coastal and marine areas require better information on the present state of these systems and the ability to predict future conditions.

Maritime Transport

The regulation of the maritime transport (both shipping and ports) is attracting increasing attention as an element of overall marine policy and sustainable development. Incidents such as the grounding of the *Exxon Valdez* in Alaska, the foundering of the Greek *Aegean Sea* off the Northwest coast of Spain, the breaking up of the Liberian *Braer* off the Shetland Islands, and the burning of the Danish-owned *Maersk Navigator* near the northern entrance to the Malacca Strait have attracted considerable public attention and highlighted the risks to the marine environment posed by the carriage of dangerous or hazardous cargoes at sea.

While high profile marine accidents attract considerable publicity, they need to be kept in perspective as a source of marine pollution. They account for only about 30 to 40 percent of ship-generated oil pollution of the oceans with intentional activities (e.g., bilge-pumping and tank-cleaning) accounting for the remainder. In turn, and as was noted in *Agenda 21* Chapter 17, ship operations are responsible for only about 30 percent of marine pollution with the remainder due to land-based sources, natural seepage, and offshore production.

There is a paradox that ships such as the *Exxon Valdez, Braer* and *Maersk Navigator* may not have been judged unsafe by International Maritime Organization (IMO) standards. Nevertheless, the catastrophes that befell them have drawn attention to the problems of unsafe ships at sea and have led to tighter international controls over shipping, as well as providing an incentive for regional cooperation to achieve the objective of "safer ships and cleaner seas."

Developments in the regime of Port State Control (PSC) have been an important element in international efforts to manage the problem of sub-standard ships. It involves the inspection by the officers of a national maritime authority of foreign vessels visiting the country's ports to ensure compliance with the international maritime safety and marine pollution conventions. It is based on the rule of international law, according to which a state exercises full jurisdictional powers within its internal waters and has the right to deny access to such waters. It supplements the primary responsibility of the Flag State for ensuring the compliance of ships flying its flag with the relevant international conventions.

While responsibility for safety standards onboard ship primarily rests with the Flag State and standards should be maintained by shipowners, classification societies, and insurers, casualty rates have indicated that these "checks and balances"are not working. Hence PSC emerged as the "last safety net" to eradicate substandard ships. Port States control the condition of visiting ships to ensure conformity with recognized international standards prescribed by the IMO. A regional approach, rather than an individual country or global approach, has been favored as the most effective and manageable means of achieving the necessary coordination between participating countries.

An *Asia-Pacific Memorandum of Understanding* (MOU) on PSC was opened for signature on 2 December 1993 and has now been signed by seventeen countries (Australia, Canada, China, Fiji, Indonesia, Japan, Republic of Korea, Malaysia, New Zealand, Papua New Guinea, Philippines, Russian Federation, Singapore, Thailand, Vanuatu, and Vietnam with Hong Kong as an Associate Member). This MOU is based on the Paris MOU on PSC adopted in 1982 as an international agreement between the maritime authorities of 15 European countries aimed at the establishment of a harmonized system of PSC and an effective data exchange system on PSC inspections. Similarly the Asia-Pacific MOU provides for regional cooperation on ship inspections with a regional database and agreement on target inspection rates for foreign ships visiting the ports of participating countries. With an effective system of PSC now covering East Asian waters, unsafe or sub-standard ships will find it very difficult to trade in the region.

PSC is proving to be an effective system but it depends on both regional cooperation and the capacity of participating countries to monitor the condition of ships. Developing countries may suspect that the system favors the developed world and it is perhaps significant that no system of PSC has yet been introduced in the Indian Ocean region...

Legal Frameworks

The last 20 years have witnessed the formulation and implementation of a comprehensive international law of the sea regime enshrined in the 1982 UNCLOS. Indeed, without this regime serious consequences were afoot, with so many conflicting interpretations of the extent of the territorial sea, jurisdiction over offshore resources and navigational freedoms. With an international framework in place it is important now to look for the supporting national legal frameworks.

Issues associated with the national legal framework for coastal development are particularly complex. Problems include how to define the coastal zone, the jurisdictional boundaries between different levels of government, the development of national regulatory measures, particularly through the institutionalizing of environmental impact statements, and the availability of data.

Limitations are apparent with existing legal regimes for the management of offshore resources, including with the provisions of UNCLOS. With regard to the powers and obligations of the coastal state in managing resources, UNCLOS has been seen as a political document which addresses the fragile relationship between coastal states and distant water fishing states, and it may be debated whether UNCLOS provided any framework for resource management.

Tensions exist between sovereign rights and exploitation on the one hand and conservation on the other. There is nothing in UNCLOS about how to manage resources of the continental shelf, although the resources of the EEZ are covered to some extent. These are shared concerns of coastal states, when less than 400 miles apart generally or less than 700 miles apart where there are overlapping continental shelves. Agreed legal regimes over offshore areas are fundamental to the resolution of disputes. UNCLOS lacks an integrated approach itself, but at the national level, "Coastal Zone or EEZ Management Acts" may be preferable to Fisheries, Petroleum Acts, etc., and may help to overcome constitutional problems.

Much more work is necessary in this field, including possible model legislation implementing UNCLOS and the environmental principles contained in Chapter 17 of *Agenda 21*. Integrated coastal zone management is a process which requires developed legal and institutional frameworks, but few countries have these established yet.

Despite these criticism of UNCLOS, the treaty has to be judged in its historical context. Terms such as "sustainable development," "the precautionary principle," and "integrated coastal zone management" were not in common use when UNCLOS was negotiated. The weakest environmental provisions in UNCLOS are those related to pollution from land-based sources, even though about 70 percent of marine pollution is from these sources. Whereas states have claimed rights under UNCLOS in domestic legislation, they have been much slower to legislate for their obligations. A structure for this is provided by part XII of the Convention, which places an affirmative obligation on states to take action to preserve and protect the marine environment. As countries give effect to the provisions of UNCLOS, national marine law should be reviewed in a more holistic, integrated sense which recognizes both rights and obligations.

As countries give effect to the provisions of UNCLOS, national marine law should be reviewed in a more holistic, integrated sense which recognizes both rights and obligations.

Developing countries face problems with determining whether to ratify particular conventions. There are numerous areas of deficiency with regard to the state of ratification of conventions dealing with the marine environment, maritime safety, and pollution from ships. Conventions such as the *London Dumping Convention* 1972, MARPOL 73/78, and the *Convention on Oil Pollution Preparedness, Response and Cooperation* 1990 (OPRC) are not extensively ratified by developing countries.

States face a significant task in reviewing their position with regard to the various IMO conventions to determine whether it is in their interest to become parties to them. Furthermore, a number of countries, although having ratified these conventions, have not given domestic effect to them. These problems lead to the idea of "laggard" nations, which are those which either avoid obligations by not ratifying international treaties or accept commitments but then do not lead up to them. Lack of capacity to assess the implications of international treaties is a major reason for countries slipping into the laggard category.

There appears to be a need for greater attention to these conventions, enhanced legal education, and better domestic legislation. To some extent this is the crux of the problem with maritime and coastal zone planning and management. The intellectual capacity to redress these problems has not necessarily been established yet in many developing countries, and there is scope for cooperation to assist in building the required skills and expertise. [Nollkaemper suggests that] the main objective of the Technical Cooperation Programme adopted by IMO in 1992 is:

> "to enhance the capability of developing countries to engage in safe and pollution-free maritime transport operations and, in particular, to assist developing countries to adopt IMO global rules and standards."

Transnational issues pose further problems. There are ambiguities in the international legal system with key treaties not coinciding with regard to their areas of application, a plethora of overlapping regimes, and considerable difficulties evident in translating global environmental treaties down to the local and operational level. Given the proliferation of maritime regimes in recent years, the time may have come for a more systematic appraisal of overlap, whether it arises from common geographical areas, substantive provisions of conventions or protocols, or the domestic implications of international provisions.

Human Resource Development

Human resource development is an essential element of capacity building and a priority for technical cooperation. In this regard, the importance of multi-disciplinary training and education for coastal and marine managers is well recognized. As Kenchington has noted in the context of integrated coastal zone management, although his observation applies equally to maritime zone management more generally:

> "The priorities lie in interdisciplinary or transdisciplinary training which will bridge the gulf of understanding between communities, governments, business, economists and scientists to produce true integration in management."

The UNEP Network for Environmental Training at Tertiary Level in Asia and the Pacific (NETTLAP) was established in 1992 with coastal management as one of the three initial priorities. It recognizes the massive training task required to develop the capacity of regional countries and the importance of networks of professional support to assist the trainers and institutions of the region to develop and deliver a wide range of courses and programs. Diverse experiences and views on curriculum objectives, guidelines, and content need to be disseminated among those involved in education and training activities related to integrated coastal zone and marine management in developing countries.

NETTLAP has strongly supported a move away from discipline based education and training in coastal zone management towards structured education, particularly at the tertiary level, with inputs from many disciplines and an adjustment of present operational and administrative procedures. The training programs required include those at the degree level, as well as short-term, intensive training courses. The inputs to these courses should come from oceanography, geography, environmental science, economics, social studies, law and public policy with considerable emphasis on case studies and project work.

A 1993 survey of present tertiary-level curricula, both degree and short-term programs, in coastal zone management in Asia and the Pacific showed that all degree programs are at present offered by universities in developed countries while programs in the developing countries remain on the drawing-board. Short–term programs tend also to be offered by institutions from the developed countries, although they may be hosted in a developing country. Clearly an objective of technical cooperation should be to move these courses into the developing countries as soon as possible. This would maximize the benefits for capacity building and properly reflect the environmental diversity and peculiarities of different regions.

The United Nations has identified three major and complimentary fields of management and associated training related to coastal and marine areas: coastal zone management, ocean management, and sectoral management with intersections between each of these areas, as well as between all three. A variety of UN organizations (e.g., FAO, UNEP, UNCTAD, UNIDO, ESCAP, etc.), international institutions (e.g., World Bank, ICLARM, IOC, WMO, World Maritime University) and nongovernmental organizations offer programs in one or more of these areas or where they intersect.

Nongovernmental organizations (NGOs) are important in the process of human resource development in developing countries, both as donors and recipients of training and education. The International Oceans Institute is particularly active in this field with its professional training programs for international participants, Regional Leadership Seminars on Marine/Ocean Affairs, and the *Pacem in Maribus* conferences.

Zones

Relating policy development and capacity to different zones and areas reflects both the definitions of the law of the sea and the responsibilities of different areas of government. However, the obvious problem with a zonal approach is that arbitrary jurisdictional boundaries are involved which do not reflect natural processes, features, or phenomena.

Internal Waters and Territorial Sea

The responsibility for management of the water under full national sovereignty can vary from one area to another. In federal systems of government, responsibility for internal waters and the territorial sea may be delegated to state or provincial governments. This may be a full functional delegation or just for particular activities. Enforcement responsibilities can also vary. In the case of Malaysia, for example the Marine Police has primary responsibility for territorial waters while the Royal Malaysian Navy has the policing tasks in the EEZ.

The coastal zone provides the basis of all human activities in the ocean—the ports for marine transportation, fishing, and marine transportation. It also gives rise to some of the more significant tensions between economic use and environmental protection.

The degradation of mangrove and coral reef habitats are coastal zone issues of great concern to developing counties. As a highly significant natural habitat and a very valuable resource, mangroves play a vital role in preserving and protecting coastal ecosystems and as sanctuaries to many animal communities, but vast areas have been destroyed for economic use or to facilitate development. Similarly, coral reefs have great economic significance and economic value but have been heavily exploited for use as building materials or have been destroyed by pollution or fish dynamiting.

Exclusive Economic Zone

The EEZ has been an important feature of the new law of the sea regime in UNCLOS providing, as it does, a common geographical limit to the rights of a coastal State over the resources of its coastal areas. The need for an integrated, multiple-use management approach is implicit in the EEZ concept, and this has been specifically included within the gamut of integrated management of coastal and marine areas in *Agenda 21* Chapter 17.

Nevertheless, some doubts have emerged over the effectiveness of the EEZ for managing enclosed for managing enclosed and semi-enclosed seas, including on the grounds of the difficulties of deriving straightline maritime boundaries for seabed and water column jurisdiction and the transnational nature of environmental problems.

Developing countries pushed strongly for the introduction of the EEZ regime in the 1982 UNCLOS, but the regime has not necessarily produced the anticipated benefits. In many ways the regime has produced a more favorable benefit-cost ratio for the developed countries with relatively large areas of EEZ under their jurisdiction rather than that of the developing countries. (The total size of world's EEZs has been estimated at nearly 95,000 square kilometres, of which a little over 40,000 square kilometers, or about 43 percent, is under the jurisdiction of developed countries.) Also, with the dramatic increase in concern over the health of the world's oceans and seas during the last decade, the responsibility of the coastal states for stewardship of their EEZs on behalf of the international community is not to be under-estimated. The sovereign rights to marine resources gained under the EEZ regime are not without their costs in terms of obligations for preserving and protecting the marine environment and conserving species.

High Seas

All countries have an interest in the management of the high seas, which constitute the ocean areas of the world not closed off as internal waters, territorial sea, archipelagic waters, or an EEZ of a coastal state. This interest arises both in a generalized sense as members of the global community but also, in the case of coastal and island states, with a concern for the areas of high seas adjacent to waters under national jurisdiction. The 200-mile limit in the oceans is not like a land boundary, firmly determining the limits of sovereignty and interests of adjacent nations. Effective management and control of sovereign rights in an EEZ require that countries should also be concerned about what is happening in the waters immediately beyond the limits of their jurisdiction.

This problem is manifest most prominently with the management of living resources and fishing in areas outside but adjacent to the EEZs of several coastal nations. The recent dispute involving Canada and the EU nations is the well-known recent example. The problem arises in part from the inconsistent regulatory regimes established by the 1982 UNCLOS:

The Convention actually helped create the difficulty by extending sovereign rights to 200 miles but preserving freedom to fish beyond subject only to uncertain and debatable restrictions to recognize coastal state rights, duties and interests over the same stocks within the EEZ. In exercising their sovereign rights, coastal states either eliminated entirely or significantly reduced foreign access to stocks within the EEZ, leading the fishing states concerned to focus on the high seas stocks.

Problem Areas and Possible Solutions

Generally, countries have been slow to articulate an integrated approach to ocean and coastal management, the state of which is—weak and primitive—at the national level.

Major problem areas are firstly, that the state of ocean and coastal zone management at the national level in most countries remains poor, and secondly, finding solutions to the difficulties faced by developing countries in building their capacity to manage their ocean and coastal environments and to follow sustainable development paths. Generally, countries have been slow to articulate an integrated approach to ocean and coastal management, the state of which is—weak and primitive—at the national level. Both recipient and donor countries need to have their act together before technical cooperation will be entirely credible and effective.

Particular reasons for slow progress with establishing policies and institutions for oceans management and sustainable development include the low priority accorded oceans affairs in many countries, a shortage of resources, a perceived lack of equity in the process, residual conflicts and differences (both nationally and internationally) over ocean jurisdiction, and the difficulties of sustaining the capacity-building effort.

Lack of Funds

Lack of funds will always be a major problem, particularly as increasing environmental concerns are probably causing the list of tasks, which need to be done, to grow faster than the list of projects which have been completed. The funding requirements have always been high. As Chapter 37 of *Agenda 21* noted:

> "The cost of bilateral expenditures to developing countries for technical cooperation, including that related to transfer of technology and know-how, is about $15 billion or about 25 percent of total official development assistance."

The anticipated "peace dividend" allowing increased development assistance as a result of lower defense spending following the end of the Cold War has not eventuated. Extensive UN peacekeeping operations around the world have drained the funds that may have been available, and very worthwhile schemes such as the UNEP/IOMAC Indian Ocean Basin Experiment to provide an oceanwide or holistic approach to marine environmental issues in the Indian Ocean have not received funding.

Equity

In an area as complex as sustainable development, inevitably considerations of equity will arise between different sectors and between countries at different levels of development. There is a perception that the developed countries dominate the international organizations, such as the IMO, responsible for the development of international standards. This adds to the belief that the process is inequitable and weighted against developing countries. At a national level, there is a view that some sectors of industry have to carry a unfair share of the financial burden associated with preserving an protecting the marine environment, especially in applying the precautionary principle. There is a difference between environmental protection and pollution prevention, with much higher costs associate with the former.

Developing states face a particular problem with meeting international environmental standards that are beyond their capacity in terms of both available technology and resources. In this sense [according to Lotilla], maximum international standards are as much a problem as minimum international standards designed to allow scope for individual States to adopt more restrictive standards:

> "There is an interest on the part of developing States to ensure that the maximum standards remain within the reach of their technology, in as much as individual States may opt to adopt in their national legislation the maximum allowable international standard. Should that occur, anti-pollution standards which are much too stringent, though established as maximum international standards, would become the absolute national standards and may have the effect of excluding, on anti-pollution grounds, economically disadvantaged States from participating directly in the use of the marine resources of the coastal State adopting such standards."

The perception that the developed countries dominate the international organizations, such as the IMO, responsible for the development ¢f international standards adds to the belief that the process is inequitable and weighted against developing countries. As Lotilla has suggested, regional marine-related nongovernmental organizations, such as the South East Asian Programme on Ocean Policy, Law and Management (SEAPOL), potentially have an important role in formulating a regional position on marine standards.

At a domestic level, there is a real risk that the various sectors of maritime industry may well have to carry an unfair share of the financial burden associated with the precautionary principle. A recent report issued by the Australian and New Zealand Environment and Conservation Council (ANZECC) seeks to apply the precautionary Principle to the maritime industry. Shipping and port operators are prepared to observe the principle that the "polluter pays" but it is questionable how far they should be required to meet the costs of application of the precautionary principle when the supporting scientific data is not available and a large element of subjective decision is involved.

Lack of Priority

The requirement to develop relevant priorities poses two thoughts with the suggestion of a "Catch-22" relationship between them. Institutional arrangements for coastal and marine management are required in individual countries to develop national priorities. Yet these will not be established until an integrated approach to marine and oceans policy is given higher priority. And [Vallejo states] this is not the case:

> "The basic problem is the fact that currently, marine affairs are not at the top of the policy agenda, neither do they capture sustained public attention, with the exception of environmental disasters or accidents at sea."

As Biliana Cicin-Sain has pointed out in respect of integrated coastal management, the actions "are not at all self implementing" and:

> "Nations have to choose priorities among the large number of important actions that are called for regarding oceans and coasts; key concepts need to be further defined and operationalized; appropriate institutions and/or processes need to be strengthened or established; funding needs to be obtained and committed; and additional funding and technological assistance from international donors must flow to developing countries."

One explanation of the lack of priority for marine affairs lies in the fundamental tension between economic imperatives to exploit both the marine resources and the tourist potential of the coastal zone and the need to preserve and protect the marine environment. This tension is particularly acute in developing countries which may be instinctively biased towards development and exploitation rather than environmental management.

Institutions

Capacity-building involves the strengthening of the policy-making capabilities of developing countries. [Vallejo notes that] this requires particular attention to the institutional framework:

> "[T]he core of the matter resides in the need to re-adjust the existing institutional framework for integrated marine policymaking oriented to medium- and long-term goals, and closer cooperation at the regional and bilateral levels."

Networks of institutions are important to develop cooperative research needs, to facilitate exchange of expertise, and to share experience on particular issues or management strategies. An example of networking is provided by the International Coral Reef Initiative (ICRI) which has brought together countries and organizations concerned with the health of coral reef habitats to produce a framework for action to redress the serious decline of coral reefs globally. This framework includes capacity building to establish and strengthen human resource and institutional capabilities for coral reef management, research, training, and education.

Sustaining Effort

While there has been a proliferation of capacity-building projects around the world, long-term benefits are not necessarily being achieved. A perverse outcome of some projects in developing countries, involving consultants from developed countries, may well be the building of the consultant's capacity to undertake consultancies rather than capacity building in the recipient country for sustainable development.

If the capacity-building effort is to be sustained, programs are required rather than one-time projects. Technical cooperation should include an element of "after sales service" [as Crawford et al. note]:

> "It will do a country little good in the long run if assistance is provided only for planning and implementation, for the effort may well not be sustained long past the life of the project if human capacity is not present."

Building institutions as part of the overall process of capacity building is more than just establishing an organization. It must include norms and behaviours that will be sustained over time.

The "Second Track" Approach

What is variously known as "Second Track Diplomacy" or "Track Two Dialogue" involves discussion of regional issues by academics, "think tank" analysts, and officials who take part under the polite fiction that they acting "in their private capacity. This process runs parallel to and frequently influences the official channels through ministers and officials. CSCAP (Council for Security Cooperation in the Asia Pacific) is a contemporary example of institutionalized "second track" dialogue. CSCAP is designed to focus the research activities of nongovernmental agencies working on security issues in Asia and the Pacific and to provide linkage between these activities and official regional security cooperation processes.

Of relevance to this paper, CSCAP has established a working group to look specifically at maritime security cooperation in Asia and the Pacific. This group has adopted a broad view of security and is taking onboard a range of small "s" security issues, such as marine safety, resources conservation, coastal zone management, and unlawful activities at sea (e.g., drug smuggling, illegal population movements, piracy), as well as more conventional maritime security issues. These maritime activities are regarded as excellent vehicles for developing the habit of cooperation and the concept of common security in the region.

The process of "second track diplomacy" in Asia and the Pacific appears to be better developed in the more theoretically sensitive areas of foreign policy and defense than it is in other, possibly less sensitive areas at sea, such as the protection of the marine environment, marine safety, conservation of fish stocks, resource exploration and exploitation, and other transnational oceans management issues. These issues still tend to be handled by officials from specialist areas of government. A wider "second track" forum could help the capacity building process.

Synergy

The synergy between maritime activities should be reflected in policy development and capacity building. This is an essential attribute of the holistic and multi-disciplinary approach to marine affairs that recognizes the interrelationship between different activities and uses of the sea.

As has already been noted, all the inputs and outputs are to some extent inter-related. The sum of their whole may well be greater than the sum of their parts when measured in terms of the contribution to human resource development and the establishment of institutions and an enabling environment. Developments in one area facilitate those in another (for example, personnel trained in one field may transfer their skills to another). The nature of these linkages will vary from one country to another depending on the extent of maritime interests, size and importance of areas of maritime jurisdiction, etc.

Communications

Good communications at all levels and between all areas are obviously an essential element of an integrated approach to sustainable development. They facilitate the synergy between different activities and reduce the risks of a less beneficial program proceeding at the expense of a more beneficial one.

One study has suggested that the continual increase in the number of programs is making international communications, coordination, and information exchange increasingly difficult. The proliferation of plans for integrated coastal zone management in developing countries could well be counterproductive, particularly if plans are prepared at the expense of supporting the implementation of existing plans. Clearly it is better to do a few well than to have many in the pipeline.

Regionalism

As has already been noted, several articles of the LOSC stress the importance of regional cooperation in ocean management. Similarly Chapter 17 of *Agenda 21* supports a regional approach:

> "States should use existing subregional and regional mechanisms, where applicable, to

develop knowledge of the marine environment, exchange information, organize systematic observations and assessments, and make the most effective use of scientists, facilities, and equipment."

Lee Kimball has noted the special advantages of regional organizations that these offer: better scope for cross-fertilization of ideas with the "local knowledge" of regional needs and conditions; a stronger bargaining position for dealing with extra-regional ocean users and donors; and the scope for regional trans-sectoral organizations to promote integrated regional ocean management.

Marine scientific research is an area where regional cooperation is particularly important. Sharp contrasts can occur in hydrography, circulation, continental shelf width, submarine topography, coastal geomorphology, marine species, and biodiversity between closely adjacent bodies of water, and the division between differing features is quite unrelated to jurisdictional boundaries in the ocean. Unfortunately, however, the priority attached to marine scientific research, and the capacity to undertake it, will also vary very much from one country to another with the result that the will to undertake regional cooperative marine scientific research may be lacking. Various regional organizations, such as SEAPOL and IOMAC, have sought to overcome this problem and it is not surprising that cooperative marine scientific research has received emphasis at the workshops on Managing Potential Conflict in the South China Sea.

The South Pacific provides some excellent examples of effective regional organizations active in the field of coastal and marine zone management. The following paragraphs briefly describe some of the organizations which have been developed in the South Pacific and now demonstrate the advantages of countries with shared concerns getting together to address region-wide issues and problems and to build their joint capacity.

The South Pacific Forum

This was established in 1971 and has a membership of fifteen independent or self-governing countries. The Forum Secretariat manages a regional work program encompassing economic development, civil aviation, marine, energy, trade and investment, legal and political, and telecommunications sectors. The Forum Secretariat Marine Division is an excellent institutional example of capacity building. This was formed [notes Morrison] in 1986 "...to assist Forum member governments to plan, fund and implement on a coordinated regional basis, maritime development in the Pacific".

The South Pacific Regional Environment Programme (SPREP)

This is the primary environmental organization in the South Pacific region. Its membership includes French, American, and British Territories in the region, as well as the Forum countries and France, United Kingdom, and the United States. It is the South Pacific component of the UNEP Regional Seas Programme and manages an Action Plan covering the following areas of work:

- Conservation of Biological Diversity;
- Global Climate Change;
- Environmental Planning and Management;
- Coastal Management and Planning;
- Prevention and Management of Pollution;
- Planning and Response to Pollution Emergencies;
- Environmental Education and Training, Environmental Information; and
- Regional Environmental Concerns.

The South Pacific Forum Fisheries Agency (FFA)

The FFA is a specialized regional fisheries organization with many achievements that demonstrate the benefits of regional coordination. These include the development of a strong negotiating position in reaching agreements on access and management controls with extra-regional fishing countries; a collective position on surveillance and enforcement and the provision of a wide range of legal advice and services, including help with the drafting of fisheries legislation in member countries.

Clearly the South Pacific countries have decided that these interests are sufficiently similar and that the benefits of cooperation exceed any costs. The decision whether or not regional cooperation serves the needs of any individual country better than unilateral action is a decision for that particular state. The ability to make a correct decision in this regard ultimately depends on the decision making capacity of the country, and unfortunately it may be possible for developing countries to decide against cooperation due to lack of information and an overly protective approach to sovereignty.

The Association of Southeast Asian States (ASEAN) also has been active in adopting regional measures designed to ensure the sustainable development of coastal and marine areas. This has included environmental impact assessment (EIA) systems within national legal frameworks and the introduction of a variety of effective and national controls over coastal developments.

As well as at the regional level, regional cooperation must be made operational at the national and local levels. A review of the current state of regional cooperation with the sustainable development of coastal and marine areas in Southeast Asia has suggested that the management of particular problem areas was preferable to generalized regional approaches requiring the non-specific support of individual countries. "Bottom up" planning processes are important in implementing "sustainable development" and making it mean something more than just international jargon. The capability, skills, and knowledge of local community groups are important inputs to regional cooperation.

Conclusion

The ways and means of improving the current situation with technical cooperation for sustainable development and capacity-building discussed in this paper include developing a better appreciation of the synergy between different maritime activities, multi-disciplinary training and education, the development of appropriate legal frameworks, improved data collection and information management, regional coordination and better communications between all parties. Concepts from regional security forums, particularly "second track diplomacy" and "building blocks", are also relevant.

The training task to develop the capacity of regional countries is very large. Networks of professional support will assist prospective trainers and institutions to develop and deliver a wide range of courses and programs. Nongovernment organizations (NGOs) are important in the process of human resource development in some developing countries, both as donors and recipients of training and education. Multi-disciplinary training and education, [states Kenchington], requires attention:

> "Training in single disciplines is generally reasonably covered by orthodox tertiary programmes. Nevertheless this does not address the needs for integrated coastal zone management because of the need for some level of coverage of a wide range of disciplines. This raises the need for multi-disciplinary and interdisciplinary training at a number of levels."

With international legal regimes largely in place, it is important now to develop supporting national legal frameworks. More work is necessary in this field, including possible model legislation implementing UNCLOS and the environmental principles contained in Chapter 17 of *Agenda 21*. Integrated ocean and coastal zone management, including the regulation and enforcement of national maritime and marine laws, are processes which require a developed legal and institutional framework and this is not yet available in most countries.

Acceptance of the ideas of sustainable development and integrated coastal and marine zone management has a profound impact on the need for marine information and how we use that information. Data collection is a necessary prerequisite for the effective development and management of all marine and coastal zones.

Good communications and dialogue (vertical and horizontal) are essential at all levels and between sectors. The extension of "second track" diplomacy, involving officials, academics, and consultants in coastal and marine management programs is an important means of understanding the problems and developing the way ahead. Governments tend to be pre-occupied by short-term or immediate problems, and longer term research may be neglected. The research areas of universities in the fields of law, geography, geology, marine science, economics, public policy, etc., need to be more fully harnessed to the problems of capacity-building.

While the level of disputation over uses of the sea could increase, there is a risk of developing countries being marginalized in this regard. These countries lack the human, institutional, and financial resources to cope with disputes. This is evident in the level of involvement of developing countries in IMO and their current participation in relevant international conventions. This problem could be compounded with another round of international conventions forthcoming on big-diversity, climate change, migratory species, etc.

A major challenge remains in redressing the balance between developed and developing countries in meeting the requirements of sustainable development and international standards for preserving and protecting the marine environment. The problem is particularly acute in the smaller states which lack the skills and institutional frameworks to develop the policies required for integrated management of their coastal and maritime zones, including the sustainable development of resources and the regulation and enforcement of national jurisdiction. The challenge now lies in moving from the rhetoric and proliferation of "one-off" projects to programs which can be sustained for the longer term.

4

The Role of Traditional Resource Use and Traditional Ecological Knowledge

A

Johannes R.E. and Ruddle K., "Human Interactions in Tropical Coastal and Marine Areas: Lessons from Traditional Resource Use," in *Application of the Biosphere Reserve Concept to Coastal Marine Areas*, papers presented at the UNESCO/IUCN San Francisco Workshop of 14-20 August 1989, IUCN Gland Switzerland, 1993

Introduction

The *Bali Action Plan*, which came out of the 1982 World National Parks Congress, contains a recommendation to:

> "investigate and utilise the traditional wisdom of communities affected by conservation measures, including implementation of joint management arrangements between protected area authorities and societies which have traditionally managed the resources".

This marks a substantial if belated shift in the perception of traditional users of protected areas by natural resource managers. No longer regarded as intruders in their own territories, traditional users are becoming recognized as integral parts of the ecosystem.

Creating a biosphere reserve entails making tradeoffs that enable both traditional users and the world at large to benefit through sounder resource management. Here we outline what some fishermen and other traditional users of coastal marine resources in the tropics can offer marine biosphere reserve planners in this respect and, very briefly, what planners can offer in return.

Creating a biosphere reserve entails making tradeoffs that enable both traditional users and the world at large to benefit through sounder resource management.

According to the *Final Report of the Task Force on Criteria and Guidelines for the Choice and Establishment of Biosphere Reserves*:

> "the MAB program should give high priority to biotic regions in which there are no or few reserves. Particular attention should be given to tropical forests and grasslands, island ecosystems, tropical coasts and coral reefs".

Here we focus on the traditional users of (i) the reef and lagoon habitats of the islands of Oceania, and (ii) the wetlands found along many tropical coasts. Both of these ecological systems are often intimately linked with, and dramatically affected by, changes in adjacent terrestrial ecosystems, especially those of forest and grassland. No marine biosphere reserve should be designated in such areas without some control being exercised over these adjacent ecosystems. Our focus is thus on people who live in those types of biotic communities identified by biosphere reserve planners as needing particular attention, or who traditionally use, or are otherwise directly influenced by these communities.

Oceania

On the majority of islands of Oceania, people have for centuries depended on a typically narrow fringe of coastal waters for a very large portion of their animal protein. The finite nature of marine resources became apparent to these islanders long before it did to continental peoples with access to wide continental shelves and large terrestrial sources of animal protein. Consequently, different Pacific island peoples devised all the basic means of fisheries conservation in use today—size restrictions, gear restrictions, closed seasons, closed areas and, most importantly, limited entry—centuries before the need for marine fisheries conservation was even recognized in the west.

Traditional practices that function to conserve marine resources remain widespread among the traditional fishermen of Oceania, and merit serious study by marine biosphere reserve planners in the region. As we will discuss below, the traditional knowledge of island fishermen concerning marine resources can make an important contribution to marine reserve planning.

Some traditional marine resource management practices in the region have eroded or been forcibly abandoned as a consequence of the myriad pressures associated with the uneven conflict between western-style, resource-extractive development strategies and adaptive traditional resource-use strategies. In other areas, marine conservation may never have existed because it was not needed. In some lightly populated coastal areas, for example parts of Melanesia, marine resources have always existed in quantities surplus to human needs. Overexploitation is now occurring for the first time in some of these areas and there are no cultural precedents to underpin an effective local response. Reserve development in such areas may require a major education programme to help create a local conservation ethic, which can be defined as an awareness of man's ability to deplete or otherwise damage natural resources, coupled with a commitment to reduce or eliminate the problem.

Coastal Wetlands

Some of the world's highest population densities are found in the long-reclaimed former wetland areas which form the deltas and coastal plains of South and Southeast Asia. Some vast, relatively unutilized areas do remain and elsewhere ecologically similar regions, like the Orinoco Delta in South America or the Niger Delta of West Africa, rank among the world's more sparsely populated regions.

As regions containing large tracts of young alluvia, and hence tropical soils of above average fertility, many former wetlands in South and Southeast Asia have been converted into highly productive "breadbaskets". In South America, in contrast, apart from a few isolated areas of human settlement, wetlands have largely been regarded as marginal areas if not outright wastelands.

Wetlands provide diverse, renewable natural resources which support mixed traditional economies based on capture fisheries, aquaculture, agriculture, animal husbandry, the use of forest products, and hunting and gathering. Among the more specialized uses of wetlands is one that is ubiquitous throughout Southeast Asia—the millennia-old conversions to irrigated ricefields, often in association with fish culture or capture.

Despite the seasonal dominance of the aquatic environment in wetlands, terrestrial habitats are also important biosphere components in these areas. Grasslands, and mangrove and other forests support game and useful plants. Levee soils provide fertile, non-flooded cultivable areas. Many of the resource systems employed by traditional communities to exploit tropical wetlands are basically agro-aquatic systems that transform the natural communities into more specialised and managed ones. A few species of primary importance to the human community are cultured but the fundamental structure and functions of the natural ecosystems are maintained.

One of the simplest resource systems is the widespread cultivation of irrigated rice and associated ricefield fisheries. Other systems are more mimetic of the wetland environment in that they maintain a wider diversity of biotic elements, while changing selected elements within it. This is exemplified by shifting cultivation and the transition to perennial crops in wetlands, as among the Banjarese and Buginese pioneer settlers in some Indonesian coastal zones, and especially by those systems that closely integrate agriculture and aquaculture as in southern China.

Other adaptive strategies, such as cattle herding, subsistence or small-scale commercial hunting, fishing and gathering, merely crop or cull natural resources. If not overly intensive they result in little modification of wetland ecosystems.

Customary Marine Tenure

Customary marine tenure (CMT) is a practice which involves the observation of exclusive fishing rights. These rights generally apply to specific areas, and may include rights to particular species, or to use of a particular gear type. CMT has been documented for coastal and estuarine waters on all continents, but it is particularly widespread in the tropics, especially in Oceania.

The importance of this custom for marine biosphere reserve planners, or indeed any marine resource managers in such areas, is that fishermen with marine property rights are less likely to overfish than those without. This is because it is generally in the best interests of those who control access to a renewable resource to exploit it in moderation since they will reap the benefits in future years It is not assumed here that all CMT systems are or were necessarily effective in conserving marine resources any more than it is assumed that contemporary fisheries management by means of limited entry always succeeds. But it is widely accepted by fisheries scientists that fisheries conservation is all but impossible without some form of exclusive fishing rights.

A second reason marine resource managers must be aware of these customs is that CMT owners are just as attached to their rights as land owners. Thus they do not look kindly upon those who would try to include their fishing grounds in reserves simply by negotiating with their governments.

Many Oceanian societies do not conceptually divide natural resources and the space they occupy into aquatic and terrestrial components. Thus local principles of sea tenure often differ little from those that govern land tenure and the use of terrestrial resources. Among these peoples, in addition, individuals and society are often looked upon as integral parts of nature. One consequence is that the entire physical, economic and spiritual life of such communities is centred on their natural resource assemblage and the space containing it. For such people this focus is so central to their conception of themselves that alienation of their natural resources and tenured marine (and terrestrial areas) is unthinkable. The fundamental importance of this view is sometimes not appreciated by westerners.

In some regions CMT was destroyed by colonial powers who considered the practice of restricting entry to fishing grounds to be primitive. Despite this disruption (sometimes motivated by foreign businessmen wanting access to island fishing grounds) CMT remains strong in many areas today, most notably in Oceania. In some countries its legitimacy is recognized in law. In others the practice persists firmly despite lack of such recognition. Its significance began to be realised by researchers only in the late 1970s.

Much of the earlier research on CMT is characterized by a lack of appreciation of its basis within larger socioeconomic systems. In the Pacific Basin, for example, such tenure arrangements vary from the sole quasi-ownership of specific localized sites by individuals, families, clans or other small social groups, to the complex state legal system of Japan.

Local CMT needs to be well understood and documented before any efforts are made to introduce new management arrangements associated with marine reserves. Proposed new arrangements may heighten the perceived value of local resources and trigger the invention of fictional ownership, or stimulate conflicting traditional claims to resources and thus generate local conflict.

During the Third South Pacific National Parks and Reserves Conference, held in Apia, Western Samoa, in 1985, it was noted that although CMT serves as a marine conservation measure, this custom has not been used to advantage in establishing protected areas in waters under traditional ownership. Coastal biosphere reserves in Oceania would help address this opportunity.

Traditional Ecological Knowledge of Marine Resources

The knowledge possessed by local users of natural resources can play a vital role in siting and managing protected areas, especially in areas where recorded knowledge of local environments and biota is inadequate. In clear, warm tropical waters which facilitate dive fishing and underwater observation, knowledge among traditional fishermen may be remarkably sophisticated.

Traditional ecological knowledge (TEK) offers a shortcut to the acquisition of some of the basic natural history data needed to understand better the natural environments of traditional peoples. It is often superior in important respects to information gained by means of conventional resource surveys performed by imported consultants whose work is constrained by insufficient time and money. Local fishermen know, for example, the timing and location of a host of significant biological events. Certain otherwise unremarkable beaches may serve as rookeries for nesting sea turtles, or come alive with spawning land crabs during certain lunar periods and

Fishing rights in waters in the vicinity of major population centres have rarely persisted because the large numbers of migrants overwhelm the rights of the original inhabitants.

seasons. What may look like an insignificant and relatively barren islet to a reserve planner during a site inventory made in one season, may be thronged with breeding seabirds or sea snakes, in others. Researchers doing biotic inventories are also liable to overlook unfamiliar species whose value as food, medicine, and tools, for example, is known only to local people.

Tropical fishermen in some regions also know of the wide range of reef food fishes which aggregate at specific and invariable locations, at particular seasons and, often, at particular moon phases year after year, in order to spawn. The widespread existence and importance of this phenomenon was recognized by biologists almost entirely as a consequence of information obtained from fishermen in the Caribbean and tropical Pacific. Because these aggregations occur at predictable times and places, they provide biologists with an excellent opportunity to monitor stocks. In addition, because of the often exceptionally large catches, they provide a useful focus for management. (Salmon fisheries are a well developed temperate zone model for this form of stock monitoring and management). Such spawning areas do not always coincide with areas judged to be important on the basis of aesthetic qualities, species diversity or other common criteria for choosing protected areas. But they often deserve protection for the purpose of fisheries conservation. The fishermen sometimes protect these areas with traditional taboos or village-based fishing regulations.

TEK is sometimes embedded in a matrix of myth and ritual and is thus difficult to discern. Ideally, therefore, this knowledge should be recorded and evaluated by researchers who possess not only an appropriate background in biology and resource management, but also anthropological skill in interpreting information from one culture and language to another. Because TEK is dwindling around the world at an alarming rate, recording it is an urgent matter. Biosphere reserves can help with this task. Allowing TEK to vanish would amount to throwing away centuries of priceless practical environmental knowledge.

Conclusions

Where protected status is being sought for areas over which villagers traditionally exert control, they cannot be expected to cooperate with reserve planners without some consequent benefits. Local people who reveal their natural resource management strategies or TEK are relinquishing a certain amount of status or power. Naturally they may be reluctant to do so if they see no benefits from its disclosure or if they fear that competitors might learn of it and profit at their expense, or that a biosphere reserve would restrict their activities.

Planners should therefore have some incentives in mind, for example, lease payments, greater legal recognition of local village authority over local resources, better protection from outside encroachment, enhanced income from tourism, and representation in dealings with the outside world. One recognized function of terrestrial reserves is the protection of sacred sites, notably of Aboriginal peoples in Australia. Much less well known, let alone well protected, are the sacred marine sites found here, as well as in Oceania and elsewhere.

In areas where marine tenure is secure its holders may choose to reject the establishment of protected areas What can be done in such circumstances? An option rarely feasible on land which is sometimes available for coastal waters is the establishment of protected areas in untenured areas adjacent to major population centres. Fishing rights in waters in the vicinity of major population centres have rarely persisted because the large numbers of migrants overwhelm the rights of the original inhabitants. Here, protected areas may be established without fear of violating existing tenure arrangements. Enforcement of management regulations is eased by the proximity of such reserves to population centres where they are more readily subject to surveillance.

Overfishing is usually a problem near district centres. But degraded marine ecosystems typically regenerate faster than terrestrial ecosystems and once a marine area is protected, populations of fish and invertebrates may recover within a few years. The replacement rates of marine communities are comparatively fast because marine animals and plants are more mobile than terrestrial biota; they reproduce at early ages compared with dominant terrestrial species; and, with the noteworthy exception of some corals, they have relatively short life-spans.

Protected marine areas provide opportunities to help preserve valuable traditional fishing practices in developing countries. Traditional skills are being lost as fishermen substitute fibre glass launches with outboard motors for sail-powered native craft, nylon for locally-produced fibre nets and lines, and so forth. Few may wish to go back to the humbler technology, but retention by a few individuals of the skills needed to make and use such traditional technology should nevertheless be encouraged in case of eventual need. Such a need may arise through economic difficulties, perhaps following the withdrawal of foreign aid support. Tourists are often interested in such activities, and income from tourism in marine reserves can provide the incentive needed to maintain or reactivate some of this technology.

Most traditional resource use systems in tropical coastal regions involve the integrated use of a primary resource as a subsistence base, together with its nutritional and economic complements and other local raw materials. Policymakers generally foresee more specialised and "modern" uses for reclaimed tropical coastal regions. They often tend to think of utilization in terms of non-integrated agriculture, aquaculture, animal husbandry or forestry; the abstraction of water for irrigation, industrial and domestic uses; or industrial development and human settlement. Biosphere functions are sometimes not even perceived, let alone regarded as useful. In such areas biosphere reserves could provide a framework for more integrated resource management that prevents such piecemeal thinking and disconnected development.

Conflicts arise and waste occurs when resource-use strategies are not properly coordinated, potential alternative and complementary strategies are not evaluated and tradeoffs are not made. More research is needed on the ecological consequences of both traditional and more modem uses of tropical ecosystems in order to provide sound scientifically based guides for the formulation of alternative strategies.

Interaction among resource systems is an especially complex subject for which the theoretical base and the data needed to frame hypotheses are poorly developed throughout the tropics. Relationships among linked resource systems comprise a particularly important focus of regional management for sustainable coastal zone development. The majority of incompatibilities or conflicts in coastal resource use occur in such intensively used and circumscribed areas as estuaries, straits and lagoons. While problems often arise directly from local interventions, an additional and more insidious process is the destructive impact of inappropriate uses of "upstream" resources on "downstream" parts of the system.

In the more densely populated parts of Southeast Asia, for example, almost any river basin, from its watershed to the inshore coastal marine waters into which it flows, provides examples of environmental, resource and socioeconomic problems that have arisen from intervention in closely linked upstream systems. Similarly, coral reef communities are extremely vulnerable to certain human activities affecting adjacent terrestrial ecosystems. Bad land management, for example, has almost certainly degraded or destroyed more coral reef communities through smothering by eroded soil than all other forms of human activities combined. Biosphere reserves could serve to diminish these problems through the promotion of more integrated resource use patterns.

Integrating traditional and modern law will also often be necessary in the process of creating biosphere reserves. This presents unusual and challenging difficulties. A passage from the publication, *Integrated Renewable Resource Management for Insular Areas*...neatly addresses an important issue:

> "To the western-trained lawyer, such a judicial system (i.e., a blend of traditional and western law) seems to invite imprecision into a (western) system of law that values precision. The western insistence on precision, however, tends to denigrate custom, which by definition, is unrecorded, internalized and integrated with culture. If precision is valued, the written statute or case will always defeat custom. If preservation of custom is the goal, judges must reach beyond the demand for precision, and experience the cultural milieu of the custom".

In addition, the fixing of traditional custom through explicit, detailed legal definitions framed in terms of state law may weaken the adaptive flexibility of traditional systems.

Modern management programs that are patterned as much as is practicable after traditional practices are more likely to be understood and respected by traditional resource users. Public acceptance of management schemes is especially critical in the tropics because government enforcement is very expensive and thus almost always inadequate. Enforcement is often largely through informal social pressure and the authority of local village leaders, and is more likely to succeed if management measures are familiar and their purposes understood.

5

Control of Land-Based Marine Pollution

A

VanderZwaag D., *International Law and Control of Land-Based Marine Pollution/Activities: Screams, Dreams and Despair,* South East Asian Programme in Ocean Law, 2001

[*This article can be found on the Internet and was accessed 29/06/01. The URL address is <http://www.seapol.org/PAPERSpercent20REPORTS.htm>.*]

Introduction

Primal scream therapy...perhaps that should be a recommended therapeutic treatment for professors, students, managers and others who venture to face the reality of international law governing the control of land-based pollution/activities. The subject area can be dangerous to psychological health with risk of violent mood swings. Periods of extreme depression may be mixed with episodes of euphoria.

Three moods capture the present realities of international law relating to land-based marine pollution/activities control. At least three reasons exist to scream, "We can't take it anymore!" Reasons to feel extremely frustrated include:

- the lack of concrete, legally binding pollution control standards at the global level;
- minimal development of regional agreements/arrangements for addressing land-based pollution/activities; and
- the "snail's pace" development of state responsibility and liability for transboundary pollution.

However there are also reasons to be hopeful, to dream about a better environmental future. The *Global Programme of Action for the Protection of the Marine Environment from Land-Based Activities*, adopted by over 100 States on November 3, 1995, pledges national, regional and global actions to address land-based activities. Sustainable development principles, such as the precautionary approach emanating from the *Rio Declaration on Environment and Development* and *Agenda 21* among other post-*Law of the Sea Convention* documents, promise to shift decision making at the international and national levels towards greater pollution prevention and a more balanced approach to economic development. The 1982 *Law of the Sea Convention* (LOSC) promises to usher in a new era of binding dispute resolution for marine environmental disputes.

A third prevalent mood is despair. The long-range transport and transboundary movements of toxic chemicals are largely uncontrolled at the global level. With some 1,000 chemicals being added per year to the existing 100,000 chemicals, the distressing question arises of whether the world is developing management measures "far enough, fast enough."

Screams

Lack of Concrete, Legally-Binding Standards for Land-Based Marine Pollution

While the world community has developed a "Code for the Oceans" through the 1982 *Law of the Sea Convention* (LOSC), entering into force on November 16, 1994 and having 320 articles plus 9 annexes, the Convention focuses largely on zoning the oceans whereby coastal state rights are balanced against the rights of other States. For example, in the 200 nautical mile exclusive economic zone, coastal states receive the sovereign right to explore and exploit both living and non-living resources against the rest of the world. There is only a minimal obligation to share fisheries with other States if there is a surplus beyond coastal state harvesting capabilities.

Environmental standards in the *Law of the Sea Convention* are left general and aspirational. Article 192 sets out the general obligation: "States have the obligation to protect and preserve the marine environment." Article 194, while requiring States to take necessary measures to prevent, reduce and control pollution to the marine environment from all sources, leaves considerable national discretion in standard setting through the malleable language "using ... the best practicable means at their disposal and in accordance with their capabilities...." States are also given the general target of minimizing to the fullest extent possible the release to toxic, harmful or noxious substances, especially those that are persistent. Article 207, covering land-based pollution, does not set any concrete environmental standards but calls on states to "endeavor to establish global and regional rules, standards and recommended practices and procedures..."

The *Law of the Sea Convention* provides, for an ongoing Conference of the Parties, a common feature in recent international environmental treaties such as those on Climate Change and Biological Diversity, for furthering the progressive development of environmental standards. A somewhat fragmented review framework has thus emerged. The UN Commission on Sustainable Development, the key international mechanism for reviewing progress in national sustainable development commitments made at the United Nations Conference on Environment and Development (UNCED) in 1992, at its Fourth Session in 1996 decided that marine environmental protection issues would be subject to periodic review. Through Resolution 51/34 of December 9, 1996 the UN General Assembly decided to place oceans and law of the sea on the agenda of its 52nd Session. Article 319 of the *Law of the Sea Convention* grants discretion to the Secretary-General of the United Nations to convene "necessary meetings of State Parties...."

Only two maritime activities have had concrete environmental standards established. The *London Convention* 1972 has controlled ocean dumping through a "black list" of prohibited substances, a "gray list" of substances only to be disposed of with special care, and a general national permitting requirement. The *International Convention for the Prevention of Pollution from Ships* (MARPOL 73/78) sets regulatory standards for various types of vessel-source pollution through five annexes; Annex I (oil), Annex II (noxious liquid substances), Annex III (harmful substances in packaged form), Annex IV (sewage) and Annex V (garbage). The legal reality, frustrating at least to some, are major treaty "gaps" especially in the area of land-based marine pollution control. No global conventions control, in general, land-based pollution or toxic chemicals, including pesticides. Voluntary schemes have prevailed, such as the FAO Code of Conduct on the Distribution and Use of Pesticides and the London Guidelines for the Exchange of Information on Chemicals in International Trade whereby participating countries may elect to follow a prior informed consent (PIC) requirement on trade in chemicals that are banned or severely restricted.

Minimal Development of Regional Agreements/ Arrangements for Addressing Land-Based Pollution/ Activities

A second major reason for vocalizing frustration is that most of the regional and sub-regional seas of the world do not have agreements/arrangements establishing land-based pollution standards. Only four of UNEP's 13 Regional Seas Programmes—the Mediterranean, Kuwait, South-East Pacific and the Black Sea—have adopted regional protocols on controlling land-based pollution. Only a few regional sea areas outside the UNEP Program, specifically the Northeast Atlantic and the Baltic, have adopted land-based pollution standards.

"Snail's Pace"Development of State Responsibility/ Liability for Transboundary Pollution

A second source of possible screaming is the "snail's pace" at which States have developed the international law of state responsibility and liability. Only one case of transboundary pollution, the famous air pollution controversy between Canada and the United States over the Trial Smelter, has been decided on the merits by an international tribunal and that was way back in 1941. A rather "permissive" approach was adopted whereby the State complaining of transboundary pollution would have to demonstrate a serious interference and injury by clear and convincing evidence. Numerous questions were left in the wake of the case, such as the basis of liability (strict versus fault-based) and the type of damages, including whether environmental/natural resource damages may be recoverable.

The International Law Commission, while having the lofty objective of promoting the progressive development and codification of international law, has spent close to 50 years trying to codify the law of state responsibility and liability but as yet has not finalized the provisions. Although the General Assembly in 1953 requested the ILC to undertake codification of principles of international law governing state responsibility, the ILC in 1996 was still submitting the 60 draft articles to governments for comment with response requested by January 1, 1998. In 1978 the ILC established a working group to study the international liability for injurious consequences arising out of acts not prohibited by international law, but by 1996 the ILC had yet to complete first reading of 22 draft articles. The ILC reported the draft articles to the General Assembly and asked for government comments.

The *Law of the Sea Convention* simply restates a form of the "good neighborliness" principle already articulated in the Stockholm Declaration and the *Rio Declaration* on Environment and Development. Article 194(2) provides:

> "States shall take all measures necessary to ensure that activities under their jurisdiction or control are so conducted as not to cause damage by pollution to other States and their environment, and that pollution arising from incidents or activities under their jurisdiction or control does not spread beyond the areas where they exercise sovereign rights in accordance with this Convention."

Rather than detailed provisions on state responsibility and liability, LOSC merely encourages the implementation and further development of international law in the area. Article 235(3) provides:

> "With the objective of assuring prompt and adequate compensation in respect of all damage caused by pollution of the marine environment, States shall cooperate in the implementation of existing international law and the further development of international law relating to responsibility and liability for the assessment of and compensation for damage and the settlement of related disputes, as well as, where appropriate, development of criteria and procedures for payment of adequate compensation, such as compulsory insurance or compensation funds."

Dreams

At least three rays of hope stand out for better addressing land-based marine pollution/activities within the framework of international law. They are the *Global Programme of Action for the Protection of the Marine Environment from Land-based Activities*; key principles of sustainable development, such as precaution, which promise to catalyze law reforms at the international and national levels; and binding dispute resolution provisions of the *Law of the Sea Convention*.

The Global Programme of Action for the Protection of the Marine Environment from Land-Based Activities (GPA)

The GPA, while not a treaty document, nevertheless promises to energize numerous positive actions at the national, regional and global levels for addressing land-based pollution/activities. Chapter II of the GPA urges States to develop within a few years national programs of action through a six step methodology. States are asked to: identify and assess pollution and physical alteration problems; establish priorities for action; set management objectives for priority problems; identify, evaluate and select management strategies and measures; develop criteria for evaluating the effectiveness of strategies and measures; and ensure adequate program support elements, such as new legislation and innovative financial arrangements.

Chapter V suggests specific national objectives and actions for addressing nine source categories, namely, sewage, persistent organic pollutants (POPs), radioactive substances, heavy metals, oils (hydrocarbons), nutrients, sediment mobilization, litter and physical alterations/destruction of habitats. For example, for sewage, states are urged to: promote primary, secondary, and where appropriate and feasible, tertiary treatment of municipal sewage; identify productive uses of sewage such as land spreading and composting; establish research programs to develop wastewater treatment technologies; provide sufficient training for local administrators to plan, build and run adequate sewage treatment facilities; and implement public awareness campaigns on environmental sound sewage facilities. For POPs, States are urged to among other things:

- establish an environmental monitoring program;
- give priority to phasing out or banning chemicals posing unreasonable or unmanageable risks to human health and the environment;
- establish information services for industry and agriculture on safer substitutes and least environmentally hazardous handling and use of POPs; and establish or strengthen management institutions.

The GPA also promises to further catalyze regional cooperation in addressing land-based pollution/activities.

Chapter III recommends development of regional programs of action and strengthening of regional and sub-regional arrangements. Regional programs of action are to consider: harmonizing environmental standards; adopting consistent approaches to environmental monitoring and assessment; steps to protect critical habitats and endangered species; using innovative financing mechanisms; and identifying regional centers of excellence for research and training. Chapter V suggests additional regional actions for the nine source categories. For example, countries are urged to develop regional programs for exchanging information regarding environmentally sound sewage treatment. States are encouraged to adopt targets and timetables for reduction and/or elimination of POPs releases on a regional basis. Provision of regional reception and recycling facilities for oily wastes is to be considered, as well as regional arrangements for solid-waste management. Regional establishment of systems of marine and coastal protected areas is also urged.

The GPA also pushes for greater international cooperation. Chapter IV, entitled International Cooperation, calls for actions in four categories. Capacity building is urged partly through a clearing-house mechanism, that is, a referral system providing up-to-date information about practical experiences and scientific/technical expertise including cleaner production techniques, for addressing land-based activities. Mobilizing financial resources is emphasized including invitation to the Global Environment Facility (GEF) to support GPA follow-up activities, particularly those activities falling within the GEF funding priorities of protecting international waters and biodiversity. An international institutional framework for GPA implementation is suggested including a mandate for UNEP to revitalize its Regional Seas Programme, to act as a secretariat and to convene periodic intergovernmental meetings to review progress. Fourthly, States should give global priority to addressing inadequately treated waste waters and the control of persistent organic pollutants.

Chapter V suggests additional international actions for the nine source categories. For example, States are urged to provide scientific, technical and financial assistance to countries in need for installing, operating and monitoring environmentally sound sewage facilities.

While the GPA offers numerous promises, the document certainly is not the ultimate dream world for addressing land-based pollution and may be critiqued on many fronts. The document uses lots of "jargon", such as calling on States to apply best available techniques, best environmental practices and integrated coastal area management without providing explanations. In many ways the GPA restates the obvious, such as the reality that States can choose from a menu of management tools including economic instruments, regulatory measures, technical assistance and education/public awareness.

The document is laden with generalities, such as suggesting States consider the need for new legislation and appropriate enforcement mechanisms. No concrete guidance is provided on legislative innovations found in many countries, such as spelling out corporate director's liability, providing for high fines, allowing creative sentencing options for judges to impose on polluters, (e.g., community service, publication of facts of offence, costs to restore the environment) and providing for administrative penalties as an alternative to prosecution before the courts.

The greatest potential obstacle muffling the potential power for change within the GPA is the failure to adequately address financing for capacity building and technology transfer. The GPA leaves financing for the development and implementation of national and regional programs of action largely with each country's own public and private sectors. The polluter pay and user pay principles are recommended, and the GPA merely provides an illustrative list of funding sources and mechanisms as an Annex. The idea of establishing an environmental revolving fund to go towards sewage treatment in particular, was not accepted even though it was proposed in the draft GPA text developed at the Reykjavik meeting. Neither was a proposal for an explicit GEF commitment under its international waters "funding window" accepted at the Washington Conference due to strong donor positions on no new funds and no new institutions.

The idea of establishing an environmental revolving fund to go towards sewage treatment in particular, was not accepted even though it was proposed in the draft GPA text developed at the Reykjavik meeting.

The possibilities for strong, financial support to assist developing countries implement GPA responsibilities do not look good, given the larger picture of donor countries not meeting the *Agenda 21* goal of increasing official development assistance (ODA) to 0.7 percent of GNP. Average ODA for the period 1993-1995 was the lowest in 30 years and only four countries—Denmark, the Netherlands, Norway and Sweden—achieved the *Agenda 21* target in development assistance. In 1995 donor country official development assistance stood on average 0.27 percent of GNP, far from the 0.7 percent goal.

Law Reform Power of Sustainable Development Principles

Perhaps the most powerful outcome of the Rio Conference was the new emphasis on principled decision-making. In the past, international law had largely focused on interstate relations and taken an almost "hands off" approach to interfering with national sovereignty including State rights to exploit natural resources. Through the *Rio Declaration* and *Agenda 21*, UNCED articulated numerous "soft law" principles that should guide not only international but also national law and policy reforms. Those principles include integration, precaution, pollution prevention, intergenerational equity, polluter pays, public participation, community-based management, indigenous rights and women and development.

The *Global Programme of Action for the Protection of the Marine Environment* in Chapter 1 recognizes how protection of the marine environment from land-based pollution/activities must "placed squarely in the context of sustainable development". Key sustainable development principles identified as critical for controlling land-based activities include: application of preventative, precautionary and anticipatory approaches; integration of protection of the marine environment into relevant environmental, social and economic development policies; development of economic incentives and application of the polluter pays principle; and prior assessment of activities that may have significant adverse impact upon the marine environment.

Because time does not permit a detailed look at each principle, this paper briefly focuses on implementation challenges raised by two principles of particular importance, namely precaution and integration.

Precaution

One challenge facing coastal and marine managers is to obtain a settled definition of precaution, as over 12 different definitions have appeared in various international treaties and declarations. The *Rio Declaration* states the precautionary principle in Principle 15:

> "In order to protect the environment, the precautionary approach should be widely applied by States according to their capabilities. Where there are threats of serious or irreversible damage, lack of full scientific certainty shall not be used as a reason for postponing cost-effective measures to prevent environmental degradation."

The Rio version of the precautionary principle displays the need for further thinking and clarification on how to operationalize the principle. What should trigger the principle? What does serious or irreversible harm mean? What are the roles of public perceptions, the science of risk assessment, ethics and economics? How precautionary should control measures be? For example, should the principle require zero discharge for toxic substances or merely the use of best available technology?

A number of core notions have emerged to give some "flesh" to the principle. They include:

1. proaction, a willingness to take action advance the formal scientific proof;
2. cost effectiveness of action, that is, some consideration for proportionality of costs;
3. providing ecological margins of error;
4. intrinsic value of non-human entities;
5. a shift in the onus of proof to those who propose change;
6. concern with future generations; and
7. paying for ecological debts through strict/absolute liability regimes.

Various approaches to "legalizing" the precautionary principle/approach in the pollution control field have been suggested. Those approaches include:

1. requiring industries to use best available technologies;
2. adopting a reverse listing approach to toxic chemical management (where instead of allowing chemicals to be manufactured, imported and used with limited exceptions, a general prohibition would be imposed with a list of "acceptable" chemicals and substances); and
3. requiring waste minimization and pollution prevention plans as preconditions for pollution approvals and licenses.

The precautionary principle might also be applied to all proposed development activities, such as construction of fish ponds or aquaculture projects. Proponents might have to demonstrate that a project would not cause serious or irreversible harm to the environment before being allowed to proceed. Such an approach runs counter to the dominant management approach of the past requiring citizens or government regulators to prove harmful effects before control actions would be taken.

The precautionary principle/approach is also in the process of being adopted in the fisheries management field. While considerable uncertainties still exist as to the exact management implications a number of approaches are emerging. They include: requiring environmental assessments and management plans before allowing new commercial fisheries to open; imposing cautious catch limits such as not allowing fishing beyond 80 percent of the unexploited level; a move from quota controls to cautious effort controls, for example, through selective gear types, greater use of closed areas/seasons and marine protected areas. A continuing debate continues to exist over the role of science and precautionary quotas in the fisheries management field.

The precautionary principle/approach also promises to shift judicial doctrines and decision making towards greater protection of the environment. A couple of cases from the New South Wales Land and Environment Court in Australia demonstrate the potential power of the principle. In *Leatch v National Parks and Wildlife Service* [*see Chapter 11 Judicial Decisions*], a city council was proposing to build a road through a forested area known to be inhabited by a number of endangered species including the giant burrowing frog. Even though little environmental assessment had been undertaken on the potential impacts of road building on the endangered frogs, the city council was able to obtain a license from government to allow "taking" of endangered species. A concerned citizen, Ms. Leatch, challenged the licensing decision based on the precautionary principle and argued that the development proponent should bear the burden of proving serious or irreversible harm would not occur to an endangered species before a license could be granted.

Justice Stein, after noting the precautionary principle is a matter of "common sense" and has been endorsed in numerous international documents such as the *Rio Declaration*, revoked the license since inadequate scientific assessment had been carried out. In *Northcompass v. Hornsby Shire Council*, a citizens group challenged the granting of government approval for the operation of a proposed composting facility close to residential and school areas because of potential nuisance from odors. Based on the precautionary principle, the Court found the burden of proof was with the developer to show a nuisance would not be caused, and the court revoked the government's development consent.

A case presently before the Supreme Court of Ireland demonstrates how the precautionary principle might be used to challenge land-based marine pollution in particular. In *Short v. Ireland, the Attorney General and British Nuclear Fuels*, a group of residents along the East Coast of Ireland are challenging the radioactive gaseous and liquid emissions from the Sellafield nuclear reprocessing plant. Residents are seeking an injunction to stop the pollution including the discharges of radioactive substances into the Irish Sea. Arguments include the failure of British Nuclear Fuels, the operator of the nuclear reprocessing plant to live up to the precautionary principle through adequate pollution prevention actions and the failure to complete an environmental impact assessment for the project. The case has yet to be decided on the merits.

Not all cases have "warmly welcomed" the precautionary principle, and it remains to be seen how strictly judges will interpret the principle. For example, in *R. v. Secretary of State for Trade and Industry, ex parte Duddridge*, parents living in North East London, worried about leukaemia risks to their children from the laying of new high voltage underground cables emitting non-ionizing radiation, and launched a lawsuit trying to force the Secretary of State for Trade and Industry to issue regulations setting precautionary emission standards. The English courts rejected the plaintiffs' claim and found that although the precautionary principle is articulated in the *Treaty on European Union* in Article 130r, the principle had not yet been implemented in national legislation and was not, therefore, legally binding. In *Nicholls v. Director-General National Parks and Wildlife Service*, the Land and Environment Court of New South Wales, in a case almost mirroring the facts in the *Leatch case*, allowed logging of a forested area inhabited by endangered species to proceed in accord with strict license conditions. The Court noted the need to take a practical approach in applying the precautionary principle.

The fundamental shifts required by the precautionary principle in environmental management philosophy and regulatory approach are not limited to the national level. The best example of a global ocean management regime undergoing the "conversion of precaution" is the *London Convention* 1972. In 1992 the Parties changed the name of the Convention from the previous title "*The London Dumping Convention*" o the *London Convention* 1972. In late 1996, parties met to adopt an amending protocol to the Convention incorporating the precautionary approach. A shift to a "reverse listing" approach has been taken involving a general prohibition on dumping with limited listed exceptions, such as fish wastes, dredged materials and inert, inorganic geological materials, rather than the "black list" and "grey list" previously followed.

Integration

The issue area of integrated management is mired in conceptual confusion and muddied by lack of clarity and terminology.

A form of the integration principle is stated in the *Rio Declaration* in principle 4: "In order to achieve sustainable development, environmental protection shall constitute an intregal part of the development process and cannot be considered an isolation from it".

The issue area of integrated management is mired in conceptual confusion and muddied by lack of clarity and terminology. Numerous terms tend to be used interchangeably, such as integrated coastal zone management, integrated coastal area management, integrated coastal management, integrated coastal resource management, integrated island systems management and just plain integrated management. Integration is a "buzz word"in the ocean law and policy field, most often linked to the idea of integrating conflicts of uses and fragmented governmental decision making for a critical geographical area—the coastal zone. The term has gradually taken on "excess baggage" of other meanings, including the need to integrate environmental concerns with economic needs which begins to merge the term with the concept of sustainable development. To begin to get a grip on integrated management, four clarifying "handles" are useful. They are: understanding the multiple meanings of integration; sorting out the spectrum of institutional "governance arrangements" or fostering integrated coastal management; realizing integration can be promoted through various legal mechanisms; and observing that integrated management does not depend on law alone.

(i) Understanding the Multiple Meanings of Integration

The term integration has at least seven common meanings, and users should be careful of which version or combination of meanings is being referred to. Certainly the most common meaning in the oceans management context has a geographical focus, that is the integration of uses in the land/coast/sea area. Land use and watershed activities have to be managed along with coastal and sea uses. Competing demands needing to be sorted out included tourism, shipping, fisheries, port development, recreational activities, mining, offshore hydrocarbon exploration/ development, waste disposal and defense activities. Coordinating decision making among different levels of government—local, provincial and national—is often referred to as vertical integration. A third type of integration is among various sectoral departments and agencies within government, such as transportation, communications, environment, agriculture, forestry and fisheries, often referred to as horizontal integration. A fourth variety of integration referred to is interdisciplinary integration. Attempts are made to harness various disciplines, such as engineering, ecology, law, sociology, anthropology and economics to understand and address ocean management challenges. A fifth variety of integration is seeking to harmonize national laws and policies with international obligations. A sixth version, gaining in popularity after United Nations Conference on Environment and Development (UNCED) is the need to integrate environmental concerns with economic needs and is sometimes referred to as "external integration". Lastly, integrated pollution control refers to governmental attempts to streamline environmental management through a single agency and simplified permitting process, often through comprehensive environmental legislation repealing a fragmented array of legislative and regulatory provisions.

(ii) Sorting Out the Spectrum of Institutional Arrangements for Integrated Coastal Management

At least three main avenues are available to overcome fragmented sectoral agency mandates and resolve coastal conflicts. A new centralized agency or authority with coastal zone management planning and permitting powers could be established, such as the Coast Conservation Department (CCD) in Sri Lanka. A lead agency from existing government departments might be tasked and empowered to undertake coastal planning activities. This is the recent approach taken by Canada in its new *Oceans Act* where the Department of Fisheries and Oceans is mandated to develop integrated management plans and a national oceans management strategy. A coordinating council/committee might also be established. According to the Oceans chapter of *Agenda 21*, the global plan of action adopted at Rio for implementing sustainable development,

States are encouraged to involve various groups in coordination arrangements, including academics, NGOs, local community representatives, resource user groups, industry and indigenous people.

A key issue is the means of involving "major groups". For example, direct representation of various groups on an intergovernmental council/committee is possible. Creation of a broader public advisory committee, in addition to an intergovernmental council/committee, is a further option. Informal consultations might also be followed. Supplementary arrangements may also be a envisioned. For example convening of an ad hoc panel/task force or advisory committee to study coastal zone and ocean conflicts and to recommend ways to address challenges is possible. Use of a facilitator, mediator or arbitrator for resolving disputes among coastal actors or government agencies is also possible.

(iii) Realizing Integration Can Be Promoted Through Various Legal Mechanisms

Various options exist for establishing frameworks for integrated coastal area management. The most direct approaches are specific coastal zone/area management legislation, such as the 1972 US *Coastal Zone Management Act* or an *Oceans Act*, such as the one recently passed in Canada. Comprehensive environmental legislation may be a more indirect legal mechanism for facilitating integration and coastal zone management. For example, Nova Scotia's new *Environment Act* mandates preparation of a water resource management strategy (including coastal and marine waters) and allows the Minister of the Environment to send any environmental disputes, including those relating to coastal conflicts, to alternative dispute resolution. Perhaps one of the greatest post-UNCED challenges is to move from bureaucratic and ad hoc experiments in integrated coastal area management to concrete, empowering legal frameworks for coastal area management. Canada's new *Oceans Act* perhaps demonstrates a difficulty governments are having in being "true to" integrated coastal area management. The legislation grants the Minister of Fisheries and Oceans broad discretion to establish a advisory or management bodies to develop and implement integrated management plans. However, no detailed process or geographical areas are established for developing management plans, and no long-term funding program is enshrined in legislation. The "enforceability" of integrated management plans is also open to question with the federal government passing and implementing regulations as one possible option.

Perhaps one of the greatest integration challenges is to expand integration beyond the limited geographical focus of the coastal zone to address environment/economy integration at the broader national level for which other legal mechanisms have emerged. For example, Canada through amendments to its *Auditor General Act* is requiring all government departments to develop sustainable development strategies and has appointed an independent Commissioner of the Environment and Sustainable Development to review the strategies and report to Parliament. Proposed government plans, programs and policies might also be made subject to environmental impact assessment review through a clear requirement in legislation.

The need for broader integration than just a coastal fixation has been recently highlighted by the recent report by the Secretary–General to the UN Commission on Sustainable Development on the progress in implementing coastal area management in small island developing states. The report concluded:

Most of the efforts in integrated coastal area management, though technically innovative, and in various cases successful at the local level (generally associated with small geographical areas and/or a limited range of activities), have evolved in isolation from the mainstream of the national development process and have not been effectively integrated into the national development planning.

(iv) Observing That Integrated Management Does Not Depend on Law Alone

Integration in decision making relating to marine affairs need not involve formal legislation. For example, more informal techniques might be used to coordinate responsibilities among agencies, such as memorandum of understandings (MOUs) among or between departments.

Perhaps the greatest challenges lie outside law as recently recognized by the Report of the Secretary General to the Fifth Session of the Commission on Sustainable Development, scheduled for New York, April 5–25, 1997. The report noted implementation of legal obligations are lagging for three main reasons:

While legal and institutional instruments have definitely improved the basis for sustainable development of oceans and coastal areas, implementation lags behind due, inter alia, to: (a) the difficulty in making political decisions regarding resources and wealth allocation; (b) the difficulty in improving inadequate or inefficient institutions; and (c) in many cases, difficulties in meeting the related financial commitments.

Binding Dispute Resolution Provisions of LOSC

A major weak point in international law enforcement has been the lack of binding dispute resolution provisions, perhaps best demonstrated by the limited jurisdiction of the International Court of Justice, often referred to as the World Court. States can only be "dragged" before the Court with their consent. As of July 31, 1995 only 59 States had accepted the compulsory jurisdiction of the Court.

The 1995 case of *New Zealand v. France*, regarding proposed French underground nuclear tests in the South Pacific, highlights the traditional enforcement hurdle. While New Zealand was prepared to make numerous international environmental law arguments against the French testing, including the application of the precautionary principle whereby France should have to prove no marine contamination would occur from nuclear testing, the majority of the World Court decided the Court could not exert jurisdiction since France had withdrawn its acceptance of compulsory jurisdiction back in the 1970s.

The 1982 *Law of the Sea Convention* offers new hope for the rule of law through binding dispute resolution provisions. States are free to chose by means of a written declaration a preference among four binding dispute resolution options, the International Tribunal for the Law of the Sea, the International Court of Justice, a general arbitral tribunal (constituted in accord with Annex VII) and a special arbitral tribunal (established in accord with Annex VIII). In cases where a State Party has not issued a declaration or where parties to a dispute have not accepted the same procedure, binding arbitration under Annex VII will be required.

Only limited exceptions exist to binding dispute resolution for controversies over interpretation or application of the *Law of the Sea Convention*. For example, States may declare in writing that they do not accept binding dispute resolution procedures for sea boundary delimitation disputes. The discretionary powers of coastal states to determine harvesting capacity for fishers resources in the exclusive economic zone and the allocation of surpluses are also beyond binding dispute resolution.

Despair

The long-range transport of hazardous chemicals across national boundaries and into the Arctic region in particular is a growing concern. The Arctic environment acts as a "sink" for air pollutants from Europe, Asia and North America. Persistent organic pollutants (POPs), involving persistent pesticides such as dieldrin, DDT, toxaphene and chlordane, as well as industrial compounds (like PCBs) and by-products of combustion (like dioxins and furans), are prone to bioaccumulate in fatty tissue and because of their semi-volatile nature may travel long distances. Thirty-five individual organochlorines have been measured across the Arctic in polar bear fat. Up to six tons of PCBs have been estimated to fall on the Canadian Arctic annually from long-range sources.

Arctic residents, heavily dependent on traditional food sources of fish and marine mammals, may be especially at risk. The diet of fats may be high given the preference for lipid rich animal parts such as organs, skin and in the case of marine mammals, blubber. Levels of PCBs in milk of Arctic women, consuming large amounts of fish and wildlife, have been found to be two to ten times higher than in the southern population. Arctic residents have been found to have among the highest levels in the world of some POPs, such as dioxins, furans and PCBs.

Human health and environmental effects still remain uncertain and subject to ongoing studies. Dozens, even hundreds, of chemicals may be present in organisms giving rise to possibilities for complex interactions and inability to pinpoint cause-effective relations. Effect from low-level chronic exposure to POPs may be subtle rather than obvious such as impairing immune system functions, causing reproduction abnormalities and failures and contributing to development and behavior impairments. One study has indicated infection rates may be 10 to 15 times higher for children in Southern Quebec versus those in Northern Quebec.

What is the world doing? The Governing Council of UNEP at its 19th Session in early 1997 called for an intergovernmental negotiating committee to begin work by early 1998 on developing an international legally binding instrument in POPs and requested the Executive Director of UNEP to convene a diplomatic conference for adoption of a legally binding instrument to reduce/eliminate releases of POPs preferably by the year 2000. Pursuant to the 1979 *Convention on Long-Range Transboundary Air Pollution* (LRTAP), concluded under the auspices of the UN

Economic Commission for Europe, Parties at the Executive Body meeting in November 1996 requested the Working Group on Strategies to begin developing a regional protocol on POPs, and a protocol text could be ready for signature in 1998.

While such initiatives are positive, one might also despair over the conservative and slow regulatory pace. UNEP has targeted merely an initial 12 persistent organic pollutants for actions, often referred to as the "dirty dozen." The list includes PCBs, dioxins and furans, aldrin, dieldrin, DDT, endrin, chlordane, hexachlorobenzene, mirex, toxaphene and heptachlor. The ECE chose 14 chemicals to focus on initially.

Such steps might be described as "minuscule" or a form of regulatory tinkering amid chemical roulette. Authors of the recent book, *Our Stolen Future*, describe the present world situation of managing hazardous chemicals as "flying blind". Over 100,000 chemicals are known to exist with as many as 1,000 or more chemicals being added per year. More than 51 different synthetic chemicals substances, not all of them persistent in the environment, are suspected of mimicking or interfering with hormones found in wildlife and humans and interrupting nervous, endocrine and immune systems. Scientific assessment of chemical risks is hardly comprehensive with the Intergovernmental Forum on Chemical Safety, established by governments in 1994 to promote environmentally sound management of chemicals, recommending a target of evaluating 500 chemicals by the year 2000.

The Arctic scenario raises an interesting case study in the application of the precautionary approach. To what extent can the world wait for science to identify serious or irreversible harms? Shouldn't the principle be triggered more by ethics and social justice concerns?

The "voice" from the North might well be, "let's turn around the regulatory philosophy at the international level towards greater pollution prevention and reversing the burden of proof to polluters and those proposing to introduce new chemicals into the environment." For at least new chemicals, proponents should be required to demonstrate a lack of a serious threat to the environment or human health before introducing a chemical into commerce. Eventually, the reversed burden might also be applied to existing chemicals.

The negotiation of a Convention on POPs is not likely to be easy. Numerous issues remain to be addressed including the need to assist developing countries in regulatory capacity building and seeking alternatives to harmful chemicals. Some POPs, such as DDT, are employed to control insect vectors associated with transmission of a number of infectious diseases (e.g., malaria, sleeping sickness, river blindness) and, therefore, immediate cessation in use without alternatives may be difficult.

The *Global Programme of Action for the Protection of the Marine Environment* has, therefore, expressed a "move slowly" approach towards addressing POPs in light of developing country concerns. Paragraph 88(b) provides:

In developing the instrument called for above, the nature of the obligations undertaken must be developed recognizing the special circumstances of countries in need of assistance. Particular attention should be devoted to the potential need for the continued use of certain POPs and the difficulty of acquiring substitutes and of the transfer of technology for the development of those substitutes. This will require special consideration to be given to economically feasible and environmentally sound ways of ceasing to use, discharge or emit POPs selected for priority action. The reduction and/or elimination of use, emissions and discharges of POPs should, if necessary, be taken on a step-by-step basis.

Additional despair can also be raised with the potential fragmented approach to managing hazardous chemicals at the international level. UNEP and FAO have jointly convened the Intergovernmental Negotiating Committee (INC) for an *Internationally Legally-Binding Instrument for the Application of the Prior Informed Consent Procedure for Certain Hazardous Chemicals and Pesticides in International Trade*. UNEP's Governing Council at the 19th Session invited the INC to conclude negotiations in 1997 and for the Executive Director to convene, in 1997, together with the Director-General of the Food and Agriculture Organization of the UN, a diplomatic conference for adopting a legally binding instrument on the prior informed consent procedure for banned or severely restricted chemicals in trade. UNEP's Governing Council itself recognized the potential problem of fragmentation and it has invited the Executive Director, in close collaboration with the Inter-Organization Programme for the Sound Management of Chemicals, to develop a report outlining options for enhanced coherence and efficiency among international activities related to chemicals and to submit the report to the Governing Council at its twentieth session.

6

Batangas Bay, the Philippines—Case Study in ICZM

A

UNDP, "Batangas Bay Demonstration Project," *UNDP Updates: Regional Programme for the Prevention and Management of Marine Pollution in the East Asian Seas*, Vol. II, No. 2, June 1996

During the development stage of the GEF/UNDP/IMO Regional Programme for the Prevention and Management of Marine Pollution in the East Asian Seas (MPP-EAS), the need to demonstrate the viability and appropriateness of the integrated coastal management (ICM) as a framework to address pollution from land-based sources identified the Batangas Bay as one of its three demonstration sites. The Batangas Bay region, located in the southern part of Batangas Province facing the Verde Island Passage, is in the throes of industrialization, and the presence of the Programme is timely while the problems are not yet severe. The Batangas Bay Demonstration Project (BBDP) was officially launched on April 28, 1994, with the signing of the *Memorandum of Understanding* among the United Nations Development Programme, the International Maritime Organization, the Department of Environment and Natural Resources (DENR), the Provincial Government of Batangas, the Municipal Governments of San Pascual, Bauan, and Mabini, the City Government of Batangas City, and the Batangas Coastal Management Resources Foundation, Inc.

The bay region was chosen as a demonstration site to illustrate how ICM can be applied to:

(a) prevent and manage land-based pollution sources in an area moving towards heavy industrialization;

(b) encourage the active cooperation of industries with the city/municipal and provincial governments to minimize pollution risks from existing economic activities and future developments; and

(c) involve nongovernment organizations as strong partners in the protection of the coastal and marine environments.

The geographic boundaries of the Batangas Bay region covers the whole of the Batangas Bay, including the coastal municipalities of San Pascual, Bauan, Mabini, Tingloy, and Batangas City. Its inland extent covers the watersheds that include eight interior municipalities with a total area of 871.1 km^2. The BBDP began operation in late 1994, with the establishment of a project office in Batangas City, provided by the Provincial Government. Since then, a number of activities have been initiated.

One of the objectives of the Programme is to ensure the long-term sustainability of marine pollution prevention and management mechanisms in the demonstration sites. In addition to financial aspects of such mechanisms, the institutional framework in which it will be operating also needs to be strengthened. Over the past two years, the BBDP has embarked on a number of activities leading to such an endeavor, one of which was the establishment of an environmental management unit, known as the Environment and Natural Resources Office.

The Environment and Natural Resources Office

In January [1996], the provincial government of Batangas created the Environment and Natural Resources Office, headed by an Environmental and Natural Resources Officer. (Henceforth, this office shall be referred to as ENRO.) Through the BBDP, the Programme has been instrumental in the establishment of the ENRO which is provided for under the 1991 Local Government Code (LGC). Under the LGC, the local government units were mandated to participate in the management and protection of the environment and natural resources within their jurisdiction and are tasked to implement functions related to environmental management which had been devolved to them by the DENR and other national agencies. The ENRO is the environmental management arm of the provincial government; among its functions are:

- to develop and implement plans and strategies related to environment and natural resources programs and projects which the governor is empowered to implement; to establish and coordinate with local governments, other agencies, and nongovernment organizations in the implementation of ICM programs, including the implementation of waste management action plans; and

- to enforce pollution control and environmental protection laws, rules, and regulations.

The ENRO is working closely with the BBDP in the implementation of project activities. Eventually, it will take over BBDP's management. To ensure the sustainability of project activities and related efforts, it is important to strengthen the local capacity on ICM and environmental management through training and the improvement of technical facilities, especially for planning and pollution monitoring. Some of these activities are already on the pipeline for the second half of 1996. Such a move also ensures that project efforts will be integrated into the mainstream government activities.

Recently, a study was undertaken to determine the most appropriate organizational structure with responsibility and authority to undertake and implement the environmental management plans for the bay region. The study recommended the creation and establishment of a coordination mechanism such as a council rather than a centralized authority.

An ordinance (creating the Batangas Bay Council for ICM) was passed last May 1996, catalyzed by the project. The council will be responsible for guiding and supervising the formulation, adoption, governance, implementation, and policy direction of the strategic management plan of the bay region and related environmental action plans. Amendments to the ordinance to enhance some of its provisions on environmental management, legal, and institutional arrangements will be made in July 1996. This will also include the adoption of the SEMP and the integrated waste management action plan.

The Batangas Bay Management Council is composed of the Governor of Batangas; the Mayors of Batangas City and the municipalities of Bauan, Mabini, San Pascual, and Tingloy; the head of the local office of DENR-Community Environment and Natural Resources Office; the representatives of the Philippine Ports Authority, Philippine Coast Guard, the local office of the Department of Agriculture, and a nongovernment organization; the President of the BCRMF to represent the industry; and the Chairperson of the Committee on Environment of the *Sangguniang Panlalawigan*.

The ENRO is the technical secretariat of the council.

Ongoing Projects

There are 33 subprojects under the Batangas Bay Demonstration Project. The following highlights some of the ongoing project activities:

Hydrodynamics Study

Two scientists from the University of the Philippines Marine Science Institute, Dr. Cesar Villanoy and Mr. Jonathan Molina, conducted the initial phase of the Batangas Bay Oceanographic Survey on February 25–28, 1996. A total of 19 sampling stations for conductivity-temperature-depth (CTD) measurements were established throughout the bay, extending from the surface up to a maximum depth of 200 m. Processing and analysis of the CTD data are ongoing which will be used to prescribe the initial density structure of the hydrodynamic model.

In a related study, the Korea Ocean Research and Development Institute (KORDI), Republic of Korea, donated and installed a real-time wave monitoring system at the Pilipinas Shell Refinery in Tabangao, Batangas City, to measure wave heights and tide data. This low-maintenance equipment has been continuously recording environmental data which are periodically downloaded to a PC computer via a modem. This activity is being carried out in coordination with Dr. Kyung-Soo Bahk and Kwang-Soon Park of KORDI.

The study recommended the creation and establishment of a coordination mechanism such as a council rather than a centralized authority.

Geographic Information Systems (GIS) for ICM

The GIS subproject is now on its second year of operation. A large part of the activity is on data acquisition and encoding. The project is currently building up a spatial database with GIS as the core spatial tool. The geographical boundaries of the database cover the whole province of Batangas and the adjacent coastal waters up to 10 nautical miles. However, a subset of the province, covering mainly the management area, is also included. At present, several maps have already been digitized: 1985 land use, geology, bathymetry, slope, physiography, soil, rainfall, administrative boundaries (municipalities), some barangay boundaries (cadastres), and elevation. Most of the municipal zone plans are not geographically referenced; while several cadastral maps have boundary disparities. A total of 14 map sheets cover the Batangas Province at a scale of 1:50,000. The next phase of the GIS project will deal with the construction of a zonation scheme for the bay region, using current zone plans of the municipalities within the region and evaluating it from a regional perspective. Also, landuse change studies using optimization functions will be undertaken. The initial GIS training of local project staff was conducted in February 1996, but a more intensive course is scheduled in August, when a set of hardwares and the SPANS GIS will be installed at the ENRO.

Batangas Bay Integrated Waste Management Action Plan

Wastes generated from households, commercial, and industrial operations are significant problems in the Batangas Bay region, as these relate to public health risk and the marine environment of Batangas Bay. While industrial wastes are usually taken care of by the industries themselves, the lack of facilities will have an important impact on the existing land-based waste disposal systems, such as those run by the municipal governments in the bay region. The imposition of the global ban on ocean dumping of industrial wastes beginning January 1, 1996—as adopted by the Contracting Parties to the *London Convention* of 1972, of which the Philippines is a signatory—would certainly have a bearing on land-based disposal facilities, notwithstanding the issue of ship and port wastes. Thus, a comprehensive waste management program is needed to address the various waste concerns of several sectors.

An integrated waste management action plan is currently being implemented in the bay region's coastal municipalities. The plan has the following objectives:

1. to eliminate existing waste handling and disposal practices which pose immediate risks to public health or threat to the environmental quality of Batangas Bay;
2. to improve the standard of waste management and disposal in the bay region consistent with existing policies;
3. to guide the implementation of short-term actions by the various sectors in the bay region, identifying interim targets that lead to long-term waste management goals; and
4. to gain experience and build appropriate capacities in regulatory controls and economic instruments, information gathering and reporting systems, monitoring and compliance programs, and legal, technical, and scientific knowledge bases.

The general framework of the five-year action plan proposes four priority waste streams: municipal waste, industrial hazardous waste, ship and port waste, and municipal sewerage. Mr. Adrian Ross, IMO Senior Technical Officer who is implementing this subproject, conducted a series of dialogues with various stakeholders (e.g., industries and local government units) in the bay region to refine the proposal. The plan is now being implemented although formal adoption by the Batangas Bay Management Council will be made in July 1996. One of its initial activities is the implementation of the voluntary agreement on waste minimization. The first step of this activity is to quantify and characterize the waste being generated by the municipal, industrial, and maritime sectors.

In a related activity, the BBDP organized a Workshop on Pollution Management Appraisal, introducing the Industrial Environment Management Project (IEMP) and its activities on waste management and minimization, which is being implemented by the DENR's Environmental Management Bureau. The IEMP is being funded by the United States Agency for International Development. The workshop was held on May 15–17, 1996, in Batangas City, where the pollution appraisal process was presented to the industries and local government units. The appraisal process is a waste management audit system that calls for the voluntary participation of various sectors, especially the industries, to minimize the generation of both hazardous and nonhazardous wastes. The target is to reduce hazardous waste generation by 25 percent and 50 percent plantwide to include nonhazardous wastes by the year 2000. The voluntary agreement scheme has been adopted by the waste management project as one of its initial activities.

Batangas Bay Coastal Environmental Profile and the Strategic Environmental Management Plan

The coastal environmental profile of the Batangas Bay region was completed and is presently being edited for publication, along with the Strategic Environmental Management Plan (SEMP), by the third quarter of 1996. The profile covers the state of the coastal and marine environments of the bay region, including the critical analysis of the important issues related to marine pollution and resource use within the ICM framework. On the other hand, the SEMP focuses on the major issues affecting the bay region and proposes a number of strategies and actions to resolve them, including the financial implications. Consultations with relevant agencies, institutions, and groups were conducted, including a wrap-up workshop held on May 14, 1996, in Batangas City, to refine the SEMP. The plan is due for adoption by the Batangas Bay Management Council in July 1996.

4

Xiamen, PRC—Case Study

A

UNDP, "Xiamen Project Shows Significant Achievements!" *UNDP Updates: Regional Programme for the Prevention and Management of Marine Pollution in the East Asian Seas*, Vol. II, No. 1, March 1996

The operation of the Xiamen [China] project formally started in January 1994. Its objective was to mitigate marine pollution by applying the integrated coastal management approach, formulating and executing action plans to prevent and control marine pollution, and demonstrating the experience for the countries of East Asia.

Xiamen Coastal Environmental Profile and Strategic Management Plan Completed

The Integrated Task Team, composed of 12 agency managers and scientists from various institutions and universities, prepared the profile, based on secondary information related to the Xiamen coastal and marine conditions. The profile focused on the analysis of marine environmental quality and adequacies of institutional arrangements, e.g., organizational structures, functions, and activities in coastal management; existing legislation and enforcement of environmental laws and regulations; inputs and sources of marine environmental fund. It described the management issues of the Xiamen coastal resources and environment, their causes, priorities, and consequences in order to provide scientific basis for developing the strategic management plan and other demonstration activities. The team made suggestions on the management of the Xiamen coastal waters. The profile is now being prepared for publication.

Based on the profile, the team developed a strategic environmental management plan, focusing on the medium- and long-term goals of Xiamen's socioeconomic development for the years 2000 and 2010. The plan addressed the management problems identified in the profile. It emphasized the balance between economic development and environmental management, particularly in the sustainable use of coastal and marine resources. It also addressed the resource use conflicts, especially in the allocation of sea and land spaces for various economic activities, and the coordination of coastal management functions involving various government agencies. Comments and suggestions on the plan were gathered from various government departments, industrial sectors, and experts in different scientific disciplines. Finally, the Xiamen Municipal Government approved and adopted the strategic plan as a general framework for marine environmental management. Various recommendations of the plan are being implemented.

Two factors enhanced the preparation of the profile and plan. Firstly, the multiple membership of the task team broke the boundary among government departments and scientific institutions. This promoted data sharing, facilitated a smooth exchange of information, and motivated the members to accomplish their task. As a consequence, the profile and plan became scientific, instructive, and workable. Secondly, the team used workshops, discussions, etc., and these proved to be effective in disseminating the integrated management concept for coastal environmental pollution control, mitigation, and prevention.

Public Awareness and Concern on Marine Environment Increased

The Xiamen project undertook a great deal of public awareness activities in the last two years: two books were published—the *Haiyang yu Xiamen (The Sea and Xiamen)* and *We Own the Sea* (a compilation of articles written by various sectors); regular articles came out in the local press; and a contest on marine environmental awareness was conducted. These activities helped the discussion on the number of topics on marine environment at the Municipal and Provincial People's Congress and the Political Consultative Conference. As a result, the local government focused its attention and priority to the marine environmental problems.

Perceptions Changed

The Xiamen Demonstration Project has successfully promoted a change of attitude at various levels of the government and communities.

The Xiamen Demonstration Project has successfully promoted a change of attitude at various levels of the government and communities, i.e., among policymakers, agency managers, scientists, and even the common people, towards the need for integration and coordination to better resolve resource use conflicts, reduction of the impacts of marine pollution, improvement of the chances of sustainability, and increase in the efficiency of environmental management at the local level. A clear example was the transfer of the Marine Management Division from the Science and Technology Commission to the direct supervision of the Xiamen Municipal Government. This showed the change of focus from a research-related body to an authoritative resource management agency.

Xiamen Marine Management and Coordination Committee and its Office Established

The Executive Committee, an ad hoc multisectoral body under the Municipal Government, began the implementation of the Xiamen project. Recognizing, however, the serious problem the body faced in working with various offices (both government and private) and following the specific recommendations in the strategic plan, the Xiamen Municipal Government established the Marine Management and Coordination Committee and its implementing Office in November 1995. The body was given the responsibility for the planning, development, management, and coordination of the marine area. In particular, it was tasked to undertake the following:

1. prepare a functional zonation scheme,
2. protect and manage the marine environment,
3. enact local coastal and marine management regulations,
4. enforce the law jointly with relevant agencies to address coastal use conflicts, and
5. manage the activities covering the use of coastal resources.

The Office, on the other hand, was responsible for the planning, development, construction, management, and coordination of the areas beyond the high tide line.

The establishment of the Committee and its Office is a very important action of the Xiamen Municipal Government, because it enabled the accomplishment of the first goal of the project—to develop an institutional mechanism which would undertake and coordinate marine management. Through this mechanism, various marine-related activities in the Xiamen demonstration site have been coordinated and managed efficiently. Being a permanent government establishment, the Committee is also assured of a continuing budgetary allocation which, in turn, ensures its sustainability beyond the project life. In addition, it was also a clear testimony of the local government's political will to do away with the old pattern and get over the problem of weak and disorderly marine management. Finally, this ensured that the integrated coastal management approach being promoted by the Programme would continue to be an operational system for the sustainable development of the coastal and marine areas.

Marine Pollution-related Legislation Integrated

Various agencies responsible for the implementation of specific activities in environment, agriculture, transportation, tourism, harbor, etc., in Xiamen's coastal areas used to formulate their own rules and policies, without consulting each other. The creation of an institutional mechanism enabled the integration of these legislations, resulting in concrete improvements of marine management at the demonstration site.

Integrated Law Enforcement Task Force Created

In the beginning of the Xiamen project, these same agencies also went their own ways in enforcing their respective policies and laws, without coordinating with each other. With the new mechanism, an integrated task force was created, composed of law enforcers coming from the marine agencies concerned. This contributed to the efficient execution of coastal and marine laws.

Government Investments in Marine Environmental Management Increased

Motivated by the project activities and public concerns, the Xiamen Municipal Government increased its investments in the development and management of marine environment. Likewise, the Science and Technology Commission also increased its funding for marine management research.

Capacity Building Enhanced

Another significant achievement of the project was the strengthening of the Marine Management Division and its later transformation into the Xiamen Marine Management and Coordination Office. To improve the Office's operational efficiency, its facilities were upgraded.

Demonstrative Effects

The Xiamen project has successfully applied the integrated coastal management approach for the protection of the marine environment. This valuable experience has a big demonstrative value which may be extended elsewhere in China and to the other participating countries in the East Asian region."

B

Chua T.E., Huming Y., and Chen G., "From Sectoral to Integrated Coastal Management: A Case in Xiamen, China," 37 *Ocean and Coastal Management*, 1997, pp 233-251

Indicators of Change

...The implementation of the Xiamen Project has promoted positive changes in the perception and attitude of government officials and researchers resulting in organizational and institutional improvements in marine environmental management. These changes have been reported in the March [1996] issue of UPDATES and are summarized below.

Perception and Attitude

Although it is difficult to quantify socioeconomic or ecological impacts arising from the positive changes of attitude and perception at various levels of the government and communities, it is essential to document these changes. Therefore, this study will document changes among policymakers, agency managers, scientists and the common public, qualitatively.

The Project was initially perceived by many (including policy-makers and scientists) as a scientific research program because it was originally coordinated through the Science and Technology Commission instead of the Municipal Government. This perception has indeed created difficulties in the initial phase of developing a management-oriented research and the formulation of an action plan. Much time and effort spent to forge a change of perception has brought about a delay in the implementation of the initial phase.

Subsequently, this perception change of policy makers and many others has led to the establishment of MMCO, the creation of a more proactive environmental policy, a consensus to enact local ordinances to harmonize with national legislative measures, the adoption of a management-oriented and interdisciplinary research, and, the adoption of integrated planning and management.

Proactive Environmental Policy

The development policy of the municipal government has provided economic development directions and goals. This has enabled the integration of marine environmental management in the SEMP to promote a proactive environmental policy, and has allowed the reactive management of strategies to correct adverse environmental impacts. The adverse environmental conditions of the Yuandang lagoon and the high cost in its clean-up were useful lessons in promoting environmental consciousness and a stronger political commitment to prevent its occurrence. The political leadership is now more receptive to a proactive approach.

Organizational Arrangement

The establishment of MMCO marked a major organizational change in the history of the management of the marine area in Xiamen. In the past, there was no single organization or interagency consultative mechanism for resolving use-conflicts, to address adverse environmental problems, or to execute proactive environmental management programs. MMCO now has the necessary mandate and legal authority to coordinate with concerned agencies on the use and management of the marine areas.

Management Approach

The acceptance of an integrated management approach is a major change from the conventional management regime that is manifested through a series of management actions involving policy, planning, legislation, law enforcement, monitoring and research.

Research

Most researchers in Xiamen had little or no experience in undertaking interdisciplinary, management-oriented research. Although a multidisciplinary team was established, most research proposals showed little or no coordination with each other. There were even difficulties in the use of a log-framework. There were also initial resistance amongst scientists to meet the stringent management-oriented research requirements.

It took a considerable amount of time through lectures, open discussions and exercises before such management-oriented research was accepted and implemented. The change from the conventional research approach to a management-solving approach was finally realized.

In fact, according to the Science and Technology Commission, there was an increase in research fund allocation for management-oriented research as a result of the ability of the researchers to submit proposals that met management requirements.

Lessons Learned

1. Much has been learned from the implementation of the Xiamen Project. The major lessons learned to date are listed below:
2. Make ICM a government initiative/program and fully involve the local government in ICM program development and implementation;
3. Harmonize national legislation, which is an essential step toward the effective application of laws and regulations at the local level;
4. Coordination mechanisms should be established as soon as possible to undertake the formulation and execution of ICM program;
5. A sustainable financing mechanism must be established within the project-life in order to sustain ICM activities;
6. The public awareness campaign can be used as a tool to forge political commitments and cooperation of the stakeholders, in addition to raising general environmental concerns;
7. Initial efforts should be placed in the identification of local leadership and to strengthen the local capacity to implement the ICM project;
8. The ICM program should build upon the capacity of local agencies to enable them to undertake integrated management;
9. Management decisions in ICM rely heavily on scientific information. Scientific investigation should therefore address identified management issues;
10. The time taken to formulate an ICM program should not be too long. Detailed planning should be integrated into the implementation process; and
11. Consultation and consensus building among stakeholders helps to resolve interagency and use-conflicts.

Conclusion

The initiation of ICM in Xiamen has indeed created a strong impact on the management regime of sea space and marine resources in Xiamen. There is greater public of environmental concerns, a stronger political will to address environmental problems, and improved perception on the integrated management system among the resource managers and concerned scientific community.

The ICM program that is taking shape in Xiamen was manifested through the establishment of an institutional and organizational arrangement, improvement of legislative framework, development of sustainable financing mechanism, strengthening of local capacity, and the integration of law enforcement and environmental monitoring programs. More importantly, the ICM approach and objectives complement the government's economic development goals for Xiamen and certainly fall within the framework of Chapter 17 of *Agenda 21*. In fact, the ICM program is a testimony of *Agenda 21* in action, at the local level.

8

The Role of Law and Lawyers in ICZM

A

Beckman R. and Coleman B., "Integrated Coastal Management: The Role of Law and Lawyers," 14(4), *International Journal of Marine and Coastal Law*, 1999, pp 491-521

[*This note has been adapted and summarized by the original authors from the above source. The following text serves only as an outline of the issues and should not be regarded as a thorough discussion or analysis of these issues involved in ICZM.*]

The call for ICZM is evidence that in most countries the traditional approach to managing and developing the resources and environment in the coastal zone has not worked. One reason is that the traditional institutional and legal structure that governs activities in the land and marine areas in the coastal zone makes it almost impossible to adopt an integrated approach to the management and development of the resources and environment in the coastal zone.

In most countries local or provincial governments are usually given control over land (and sometimes over natural resources) and land use planning in the coastal zone is usually under the jurisdiction of the local or provincial government. National government agencies usually have representatives in the coastal region, and they share their responsibility with the state/provincial and local government for development of the land areas and resources in the coastal zone. However, the power of the state/provincial and local governments often does not extend into the sea areas off the coast. If it does, the jurisdiction of the state/provincial and local government usually varies between a few hundred meters and three nautical miles.

The national government usually has control over central economic planning. In most countries, it also has control over industrial development and major infrastructure projects. It usually has control over mineral resources, including oil and gas reserves. The national government usually has control over the sea area off the coast. The national agencies that have functions and powers in the sea areas off the coast often have no functions and powers over the adjoining land areas. Ministries and departments such as fisheries, the marine department and the coast guard usually operate exclusively in the sea areas.

In most countries, the national government is divided into various ministries and departments. Each ministry or department is traditionally responsible for a particular sector, such as agriculture, forestry, transportation, industry, fisheries, environment, etc. The various ministries and departments of many countries carry out their programs in accordance with a national development plan. In some cases, little or no attempt is made to integrate their policies and programs with those of other ministries or departments.

In most cases, there is a plethora of national, state/provincial and local institutions and laws regulating particular activities in the coastal zone. The laws and regulations issued by one department at one level of government may conflict with the laws and regulations issued by another department. Among the types of legislation that may regulate activities in the coastal zone are land use planning laws, building codes and laws, pollution laws (water, waste, industrial, chemicals, air and noise), agricultural laws, forestry laws, fishing laws, shipping and port laws, national parks and reserves laws, environmental impact assessment laws, etc.

It is becoming increasingly recognized that at the national level the traditional sectoral approach to managing the marine and coastal areas has not worked in most countries. Unresolved—but often inherent—conflict between different coastal economic activities (e.g., tourism, fishing, offshore oil and gas development, etc.) harms overall national development and creates economic inefficiencies. Just as important, coastal resources and the environment are being continually degraded and polluted. It is now recognized that the land and water in the coastal areas are part of the same ecosystem, and are very dependent on each other. It is also recognized that the best way to manage the resources and environment in the coastal zone is to adopt an integrated, holistic approach.

Unfortunately, the governments in most countries are organized along sector lines, and it is often difficult for them to adopt an integrated, holistic approach.

Although ICZM is generally considered a domestic issue, the principles and rules of international law are also relevant to ICZM. The legal regime governing uses of the coastal zone, especially the ocean areas, is to some extent governed by international treaties. Most States have become parties to global treaties that impose rights and obligations on them under international law. States may be obligated under the treaties to pass certain laws and regulations relating to activities in the coastal zone, such as pollution from vessels, pollution from dumping, protection of wetlands and preservation of marine and coastal biological diversity. National legislation implementing international legal obligations often has an impact on the management of the coastal zone at the state/provincial and local levels. Furthermore, even if a State is not a party to an applicable global treaty, it will nevertheless be expected to act in conformity with certain principles and rules of general international law relating to the marine environment. Therefore, it is important that managers, policymakers and lawyers working in ICZM understand the global legal framework relating to the coastal zone.

To date, ICZM has been seen as the realm of policymakers, managers, scientists, coastal resource economists, and others, rather than the realm of lawyers.

To date, ICZM has been seen as the realm of policymakers, managers, scientists, coastal resource economists, and others, rather than the realm of lawyers. Nevertheless, law and lawyers can, and arguably should, play a role at all stages of the ICZM process. Ideally, ICZM legal consultants should have a broad range of knowledge and experience in both international legal treaties as well in certain fundamental national law principles, so that coastal zone policies will be designed and carried out with a critical understanding of the laws and institutions needed for the long-term success of an integrated coastal management program.

At the Planning Stage, an audit should be made of institutions and laws that regulate activities and uses in the proposed coastal zone, with a particular focus on the problem areas that have been identified as requiring a more integrated approach. It is also necessary to conduct a review of whether there are any commitments and obligations under international instruments that must be taken into account in the ICZM process.

At the Formulation Stage of ICZM, lawyers are required to draft a legal definition of the coastal zone so that it meets the particular circumstances of the coastal area as well as the policy objectives of the government in establishing ICZM. They can also assist policymakers in deciding on the institutional arrangements for implementing ICZM and in drafting the legislation required to create new institutions or give new powers to existing institutions. Lawyers are also important in advising policymakers and managers about the legal principles that must be taken into account when formulating an ICZM plan.

At the Implementation Stage, lawyers can assist in developing an Integrated Coastal Master Plan and in ensuring that the plan is integrated with other national and state/provincial plans that have an impact on the coastal zone. They can also advise policymakers on the various legal mechanisms that are available to implement ICZM, including zoning and setback lines, permits and licenses, protected areas, environmental impact assessment procedures, and other regulatory and economic instruments.

In the end, the most important role that lawyers can play in the ICZM process is to help put laws and institutions in place that result in the establishment of a process of management in the coastal zone that is based upon the 'rule of law'. If a management system based upon the rule of law can be established, the ICZM process is likely to succeed, not only in the short term, but in the long term.

9

Questions for Discussion

(a) Describe the process of integrated coastal zone planning and management, known as ICZM, and how it responds to problems created existing ad hoc approaches by institutions, legal, planing and management regimes.

(b) The need for integrated coastal zone management has been clear for a long time. Discuss why ICZM has been slow to evolve in most jurisdictions including your own.

(c) ICZM is a classic example of interdisclipinary and integrated decision making. Discuss the role that applied scientific research should have in an ICZM regime. Outline the processes that appear to be an essential part of an ICZM regime.

(d) Describe and compare the ICZM process in Batangas Bay and in Xiamen demonstration projects. What role can environmental lawyers play in projects such as these?

(e) Chua Thai-Eng emphasizes the important role of conflict resolution between agencies and all other participants in ICZM and public participation. He argues that "consultation and consensus building amongst stakeholders helps to resolve interagency and use-conflicts". Discuss these issues.

(f) A key lesson from the experiences with ICZM is that it appears to promote positive changes in the perception and attitude of government officials, stakeholders and researches resulting in organizational and institutional improvement in the marine environmental management. Is this approach to integrated environmental planning and management applicable to other areas other then the coastal zone?

10

References for Chapter 14

Awosika L., Boromthanarat S., Comforth R., Hendry M., Koudstall R., Ridgley M., Sorenson S., De Vrees L., and Westmacott S., *Management Arrangements for the Development and Implementation of Coastal Zone Management Programmes*, World Coast Conference Organising Committee, International Conference on Coastal Zone Management, the Netherlands, 1-5 November 1993.

Cicin-Sain, B., "Sustainable Development and Integrated Coastal Management," *Ocean and Coastal Management*, 21, 1993, pp 11–43.

Clark J., *Integrated Management of Coastal Zones*, FAO Fisheries Technical Paper 327, Food and Agriculture Organization of the United Nations, Rome, 1992.

Crawford B.R., Cobb J.S., and Friedman A., "Building Capacity for Integrated Coastal Management in Developing Countries," 21 *Ocean and Coastal Zone Management*, 1993, pp 313.

Kenchington R., "Training Today's Coastal Managers: A Perspective for Asia and the Pacific", Contribution to *Training and Coastal Zone Management in the Asia-Pacific Region* and *Report of the First NETTLAP Resources Development Workshop for Education and Training and the Tertiary Level in Coastal Zone Management*, Cheano, Thailand, NETTLAP Publication No. 7, 1993.

Kenchington R., "Coastal Zone Management Training Programmes for Educators, Managers and the Public", Contribution to *Training and Coastal Zone Management in the Asia-Pacific Region* and *Report of the First NETTLAP Resources Development Workshop for Education and Training and the Tertiary Level in Coastal Zone Management*, Cheano, Thailand, NETTLAP Publication No. 7, 1993.

Lotilla R., "The Efficacy of the Anti-Pollution Legislation Provisions of the 1982 *Law of the Sea Convention*: A View from South East Asia," *International and Comparative Law Quarterly* 41, 140, January 1992.

Morrison J., "Coastal and Maritime Zone Planning and Management Relationships Between Australia and the South-West Pacific", *Paper presented at the Workshop on Coastal and Maritime Zone Planning and Management—Transnational and Legal Considerations*, University of Wollongong, September, 1994.

Nollkaemper A., "*Agenda 21* and Prevention of Sea-Based Marine Pollution—A Spurious Relationship," *Marine Policy*, November 1993.

Scura L.F., Chua T.E., Pido M.D., and Paw J.N., "Lessons from Integrated Coastal Zone Management: The ASEAN Experience," in Chua T.E. and Scura L.F. (eds), *Integrative Framework and Methods for Coastal Area Management*, ICLARM Conference Proceedings 37, 1992.

Sorensen J.C., McCreary S.T., and Hershman M.J., *Institutional Arrangements for Management of Coastal Resources*, Renewable Resources Information Series, Coastal Management Publication No. 1., prepared by Research Planning Institute, Inc., Columbia, SC, for US National Park Service and US Agency for International Development, 1984.

UNESCO, *Final Report of the Task Force on Criteria and Guidelines for the Choice and Establishment of Biosphere Reserves*, UNESCO, 1974.

US Congress Office of Technology Assessment, *Integrated Renewable Resource Management for Insular Areas*, US Congress Office of Technology Assessment, 1987.

Vallejo S., "Integrate Marine Policies: Goals and Constraints," in Fabbri P. (ed), *Ocean Management in Global Change*, Elsevier Applied Science, Oxford, 1993.

World Bank, *Noordwijk Guidelines for Integrated Coastal Zone Management*, World Coast Conference, Noordwijk, the Netherlands, 1-5 November 1993, the World Bank, Environment Department, Land, Water and Natural Habitats Division, Washington, DC, 1993.

11 Additional References

ADB, *Proceedings of the Workshop of Coastal and Marine Environmental Management*, Bangkok, Thailand, 1995.

Boelaert-Suominen S. and Cormac C., *Legal and Institutional Aspects of Integrated Coastal Area Management in National Legislation*, Department Law Service Legal Office, Food and Agriculture Organization of the United Nations, 1994.

Cicin-Sain, B. and Knecht R., *Integrated Coastal and Ocean Management: Concepts and Practices*, Island Press, 1998.

Clark J., *Coastal Zone Management Handbook,* Lewis Publishers, 1996.

Hotta K. and Dutton I., *Coastal Management in the Asia-Pacific Region: Issues and Approaches*, Japan International Marine Science and Technology Federation, Tokyo, 1995.

Kay R. and Alder J., *Coastal Planning and Management,* E & FN Spon, 1999.

Post J. C. and Lundin C. (eds), *Guidelines for Integrated Coastal Zone Management*, Environmentally Sustainable Development Studies and Monographs Series No. 9, the World Bank, 1996.

Sorensen J., "The International Proliferation of Integrated Coastal Zone Management Efforts," 21 *Ocean and Coastal Management,* 1993, pp 45-80.

UNEP, Guidelines for Integrated Management of Coastal and Marine Areas, UNEP Regional Seas Reports and Studies No. 161, 1995.

CHAPTER

15

CULTURAL AND NATURAL HERITAGE

CONTENTS

1 Introduction

Historic and cultural preservation is an important part of environmental law, as the history of a people and its culture can become endangered by the same forces of development that threaten living species and ecosystems. War and civil disruption; the forces of urbanization; industrialization; pollution of the air, water, and soil; and overpopulation all result in pressures that can destroy fragile architectural and archaeological heritage as well as natural heritage of significant aesthetic or scientific value. The materials chosen suggest that it is correct to say that what society chooses to preserve of the past defines who we are today, creates our collective memory, and constrains our new developments. The challenge for every state in the Asian and Pacific region is to answer such questions, mediating between competing public visions and goals.

Section 2 of this chapter extracts the *Convention Concerning the Protection of the World Cultural and Natural Heritage* (1972), known as the *World Heritage Convention*. The extract by Ben Boer, Ross Ramsay, and Donald Rothwell provides an overview of the *World Heritage Convention* and other significant conventions, such as the *Convention on the Means of Prohibiting and Preventing the Illicit Import, Export and Transfer of Cultural Property* (*UNESCO Convention)*, and discusses their significance for the Asian and Pacific region. They argue that there are a great many sites, as well as moveable property, which are worthy of protection in the region. It is a useful exercise for students to search out how many of the Asian and Pacific region nations have ratified the various heritage conventions referred to in this article.

The two further extracts by Ben Boer discuss important issues associated with the implementation of the *World Heritage Convention*, assisted by the *Operational Guidelines*. National implementation and management laws and process are critical aspects. Australia has a very large number of World Heritage Sites, national implementing legislation, and a strong citizen environmental movement. However, Boer discusses the significant disputes associated with World Heritage listings and management in Australia. He particularly focuses on the recent dispute over whether Kakadu National Park should be placed on the World Heritage in Danger List because of the effects of the Jabiluka uranium mine. Given the relative affluence and environmental abundance in Australia, this gives some insight into the kinds of conflicts that may occur in other parts of the Asian and Pacific region. Boer notes that there are relatively few World Heritage Listings in the Pacific islands, apart from Solomon Islands, but that several more sites are being proposed for listing.

Developing country issues and perspectives and presented in the extracts by Narayan Belbase (Nepal) and Teresita Blastique (Philippines). Belbase gives some insights into endangering processes and the operation of the World Heritage in Danger List. However, the Government of Nepal has taken significant steps to try and remedy some of the threats to its World Heritage, often in partnership with NGOs such as the IUCN-The World Conservation Union. Technical and financial resources and legal and administrative capacity remain constant problems. In the Philippines, there are three sites inscribed on the World Heritage List and two sites under nomination. Blastique describes the sites and the process and criteria for inscription.

Indigenous cultural heritage is an aspect of existing and emerging regimes to recognize the comprehensive rights of indigenous peoples and their aspirations for self-determination (such as the *Draft UN Declaration on the Rights of Indigenous Peoples*). This wider context of indigenous heritage is discussed in the extract by Donna

War and civil disruption; the forces of urbanization; industrialization; pollution of the air, water, and soil; and overpopulation all result in pressures that can destroy fragile architectural and archaeological heritage as well as natural heritage of significant aesthetic or scientific value.

Craig and Diane Ponce-Nova in Chapter 1. The extract in this chapter, by Boer, Ramsay, and Rothwell, suggests that indigenous cultural heritage protection is not well developed in the Asian and Pacific region, although there is an awareness, in many countries, of this need to protect indigenous material and intangible heritage, including oral traditions. They particularly focus on the issues of intangible heritage. The protection of underwater heritage in the region is also dealt with by these authors. The potential for controversy in the area of cultural heritage is further explored in the extract from Fergie who discusses the consequences for heritage arising from the Hindmarsh Island Bridge affair in South Australia.

Heritage protection provides an important opportunity to highlight environmental values and to develop protective management mechanisms in the Asian and Pacific region. It is early days and the extracts indicate that heritage protection needs to be integrated into other areas of environmental law, such as pro-active planning and pollution control, in order for its full potential to be realized.

2

International and Regional Conventions on Natural and Cultural Heritage

A

Boer B., Ramsay R., and Rothwell D.R., "Conservation of Natural and Cultural Heritage," *International Environmental Law in the Asia Pacific,* Kluwer, 1998, pp 71–86

...Cultural heritage can be divided into two types: tangible and non-tangible. Tangible cultural heritage can include whole cities and towns, as well as individual sites, and movable heritage items (artefacts, books, furniture, machinery, etc). Intangible cultural heritage can include cultural and spiritual practices, indigenous cosmology, folklore, skills, dances, and other traditions. At the international level, the area of cultural heritage conservation is a major concern of the United Nations Educational, Cultural and Scientific Organization (UNESCO). UNESCO administers the 1954 *Convention and Protocol for the Protection of Cultural Property in the Event of Armed Conflict* (*Hague Convention*), the 1970 *Convention on the Means of Prohibiting and Preventing the Illicit Import, Export and Transfer of Ownership of Cultural Property* (*UNESCO Convention*), and the 1972 *Convention for the Protection of the World Cultural and Natural Heritage* (*World Heritage Convention*). It also assists in the administration of the 1995 *Convention on Stolen or Illegally Exported Cultural Objects* (*UNIDROIT Convention*).

While there are a great many heritage areas and sites, as well as movable property, which are worthy of protection in Asia and the Pacific, relatively few countries have become signatories to these Conventions. The impact of development activities in many countries in the region has meant that there is an accelerating decline in the natural and cultural heritage of those countries. The freer movement of goods in the region has also meant an increase in the movable heritage being traded, both legally and illegally. There is no doubt that if these Conventions were adopted and implemented adequately in Asia and the Pacific, they would make a significant difference to the protection of natural and cultural heritage at a national and regional level.

In the past few years, the growth of cities in Asia has become a major concern of the UNESCO World Heritage Centre and the International Council on Monuments and Sites (ICOMOS). In 1970, the World Heritage Centre noted that Asia and the Pacific included only eight cities of more than five million inhabitants. In 1996, there are more than 30 which host this number. Being aware of the pressures of population and development, the World Heritage Centre has launched a Programme for the Safeguarding and Development of Asian World Heritage Cities for the 21st Century, the aim of which is:

> "to preserve the historic fabric of cities, testifying to the past and enshrining a 'heritage' on which to base each city's identity and future development. The idea is to manage socioeconomic and cultural development to promote the city as an entity instead of as an ever-expanding urban sprawl...The programme, founded on the principle of international cooperation as enunciated in the *World Heritage Convention,* involves municipal and provincial authorities, academics, tourism authorities, and the local populations of the Asian cities as well as those of the donor states."

A recent UNESCO report, *Our Creative Diversity,* has drawn close links between the need to develop economically and the need to retain cultural diversity; it argues that development must be seen "in terms that include cultural growth."

A recent UNESCO report, Our Creative Diversity, *has drawn close links between the need to develop economically and the need to retain cultural diversity.*

1954 Convention and Protocol for the Protection of Cultural Property in the Event of Armed Conflict (Hague Convention)

The *Hague Convention* was negotiated as a result of looting and plunder of cultural heritage during the Second Word War. It is aimed at the protection of both immovable and movable cultural heritage.

Article 1 states that "cultural property" under the Convention covers monuments of architecture, art or history, archaeological sites, groups of buildings of historical or artistic interest, works of art, manuscripts, books and other objects of artistic, historical or archaeological interest, as well as scientific collections. It also covers buildings whose main purpose is to preserve or exhibit that movable heritage, and centers containing a large amount of cultural property, as well as buildings which house movable cultural property, such as museums, libraries and archives, and centers containing monuments.

The main obligations under the Convention are for states to reduce the effects of armed conflict on cultural heritage, by taking preventive measures both in time of armed conflict and in time of peace. Protection under the Convention comprises the safeguarding of and respect for the property (Article 2). The parties undertake to safeguard cultural heritage by taking appropriate measures in peacetime against the foreseeable effects of an armed conflict (Article 3). Respect for cultural property includes obligations to refrain from using heritage property for purposes which are likely to expose it to destruction or damage during armed conflict. These obligations can only be waived in cases of military necessity (Article 4 (2)). Parties further agree to prohibit, prevent and stop any theft, pillage, misappropriation or vandalism against cultural heritage property.

A party to the Convention who is in occupation of another Party's territory also undertakes to support the national authorities of the occupied country in safeguarding and preserving its cultural property, or to take protective measures where the occupied country is unable to do so (Article 5). Parties may introduce specialist services or personnel within military forces whose purpose is to secure respect for cultural property and cooperate with civilian authorities responsible for safeguarding it during times of armed conflict (Article 7). Special protective measures may be initiated to protect items in refuges which shelter movable cultural property, and centers containing monuments and other important immovable property (Article 8). Special protection may also be accorded to transport of movable cultural property; parties undertake to refrain from any act of hostility in relation to transport under special protection (Articles 12 and 13). Cultural property may be marked with a special emblem to indicate its cultural heritage status (Articles 6, 16 and 17). Emblems can be placed, for example on particularly important buildings and monuments. The Convention applies to armed conflicts both of international character as well as of a non-international character (Article 19).

The Protocol to the *Hague Convention,* adopted at the same time as the Convention, is directed towards the prohibition of export of cultural property from occupied territory, and requires return of the property to the state from which it was removed. The Protocol requires the relevant state party to "take into its custody cultural property imported into its territory either directly or indirectly from any occupied territory. This shall either be effected automatically upon the importation the property or, failing this, at the request of the authorities of that territory" (Article I(2)). In addition, the party must return any cultural property exported in contravention of the Protocol (Article I(3)).

> "...While a country may be a member of the Convention, there is of course no guarantee that cultural property will not be lost by less direct means than the destruction of or looting of monuments. For example, in the Asia Pacific region, Cambodia has not only suffered major losses of Khmer archaeological heritage, particularly from Angkor, as a result of armed conflict, but also the loss of expertise. The fact that nearly all trained conservators in that country lost their lives as a result of armed conflict has been described as "a tragedy that has caused almost complete discontinuity in the Cambodian tradition of temple reconstruction and maintenance."

As at 15 July 1996, there are 88 states who are party to the *Hague Convention* and the Protocol; however, only eight of them are from Asia and the Pacific. [These are Australia, Cambodia, India, Indonesia, Malaysia, Myanmar and Pakistan]

UNESCO Convention

The objective of the 1970 *Convention on the Means of Prohibiting and Preventing the Illicit Import, Export and Transfer of Ownership of Cultural Property (UNESCO Convention)* is to ensure the protection of cultural property of state parties against illicit import, export and transfer of ownership of that property. The Convention recognizes in its preamble that the interchange of cultural property between countries for scientific, cultural and educational purposes increases knowledge of human civilization, enriches the cultural life of all peoples and inspires respect and appreciation among nations. It says that it is the duty of every state to protect the cultural property in its territory against theft, clandestine excavation and illicit export. It recognizes that protection of the cultural heritage can only be effective if organized both nationally and internationally by states working in close cooperation.

Cultural property is defined in Article 1 as "property which, on religious or secular grounds, is specifically designated by each state as being of importance for archaeology, prehistory, history, literature, art or science." Article 1 goes on to specify that the cultural property must also belong to one or more of a range of categories. These include: rare collections and specimens; property relating to history; products of archaeological excavations; elements of artistic or historical monuments or archaeological sites that have been dismembered; antiquities over 100 years old; objects of ethnological interest; property of artistic interest; rare manuscripts, postage and similar items; archives; articles of furniture over 100 years old; and old musical instruments.

Basic Obligations

Parties to the Convention recognize that the illicit import, export and transfer of ownership of cultural property is one of the main causes of impoverishment of the cultural heritage and that international cooperation is one of the most efficient means of protecting each country's cultural property from loss by these means. States undertake to oppose such dealings in cultural property with "the means at their disposal, and particularly by removing their causes, putting a stop to current practices, and by helping to make the necessary reparations" (Article 2).

Services for the Protection of Cultural Heritage

States undertake to set up national services for the protection of the cultural heritage, with a qualified staff sufficient in number to draft relevant laws, establish and maintain a list of important public and private cultural property; safeguard this property against export; promote establishment or development of scientific and technical institutions (museums, libraries, laboratories etc.) for ensuring the preservation and presentation of cultural property; supervise archaeological excavations; establish ethical rules for looking after the cultural heritage; promote educational measures in relation to the cultural heritage; and give appropriate publicity to disappearance of items of cultural property (Article 5).

States also undertake to provide national services for the protection of its cultural heritage with an adequate budget and where necessary, the establishment of a special fund (Article 14).

Export and Import Procedures

States further undertake to introduce procedures for the authorization of export for cultural property by way of a certificate, and to prohibit export from their territory unless accompanied by an export certificate (Article 6). In addition, states undertake to prevent museums and similar bodies within their territories from acquiring cultural property which has been exported illegally from another country, to prohibit imports stolen from museums or other bodies in other countries, and to take appropriate steps to recover and return such property (Article 7). States also agree to impose penalties and sanctions on persons who contravene the prohibitions in Articles 6 and 7. States are obliged to restrict the movement of illegally removed cultural property by education, information and vigilance, to oblige antique dealers to maintain a register of all cultural property, and to inform buyers of any export prohibitions to which the property may be subject (Article 10).

Further undertakings relate to prevention of transfers of ownership likely to promote illicit import or export, cooperation of the relevant agencies to facilitate return of property, allowing actions through courts and other bodies by the rightful owners and recognizing the right of states to declare any cultural property inalienable and therefore not able to be exported (Article 13).

International Assistance

States may call on other parties to assist in concerted international efforts to safeguard their archaeological or ethnological material (Article 9). States may also call on the technical assistance of the United Nations Educational, Scientific and Cultural Organization (UNESCO), particularly in regard to information and education, consultation and expert advice, coordination and diplomatic assistance (Article 17).

Implementation of the UNESCO Convention in Asia and the Pacific

The problem of transfer of movable cultural property in a number of Asian and Pacific countries is quite significant. This issue is perhaps best illustrated by the example of the People's Republic of China (PRC) which has for many years been the source of cultural material in spite of the 1982 *Law of the People's Republic of China on the Protection of Cultural Relics.* In more recent times, there has apparently been a vigorous antiquities trade out of the PRC through Hong Kong and Macau.

As of 15 June 1996, there were 85 states parties to the Convention, with only nine members from Asia and the Pacific. [These were Australia, Bangladesh, Cambodia, China, India, Nepal, Pakistan, Republic of Korea and Sri Lanka.]

As of 15 June 1996, there were 85 states parties to the Convention, with only nine members from Asia and the Pacific.

Link between the UNESCO Convention and the UNIDROIT Convention

The *UNESCO Convention* must now be read in the light of the *UNIDROIT Convention,* agreed in 1995...The two conventions are designed to be complementary. While the *UNESCO Convention is* directed to obligations upon states, the *UNIDROIT Convention* is directed to private actions.

World Heritage Convention

The motivation for the 1972 *Convention Concerning the Protection of the World Cultural and Natural Heritage (World Heritage Convention)* was the recognition of increasing threats of destruction to the world's cultural and natural heritage, not only by the traditional causes of decay, but also with changing social and economic conditions of many countries because of industrialization. The Convention recognizes the destruction of items of the world's heritage as affecting all nations. For this reason it sees the protection of the world's heritage as a responsibility of the international community as a whole. The cultural heritage and natural heritage as defined in Articles 1 and 2 form the World Heritage List under Article 11. The properties must be regarded as having "outstanding universal value" in terms of the criteria that the Committee has established, and which it publishes in the *Operational Guidelines.* Article 11(3) makes it clear that the inclusion of a property in the World Heritage List requires the consent of the state concerned.

[*The authors continue by quoting the text of Article 1 of the Convention. The reader is directed to section C infra which contains the Convention in its entirety.*]

Outstanding Universal Value Criteria of Cultural Properties

In relation to cultural properties, the *Operational Guidelines* specify that a monument, group of buildings or a site nominated for inclusion in the World Heritage List will be considered to be of outstanding universal value for the purposes of the Convention when the Committee finds that it meets one or more of the criteria set out below, as well as the test of authenticity. It states that each property nominated should:

"(a) i. represent a unique artistic achievement, a masterpiece of the creative genius; or

ii. have exerted great influence, over a span of time or within a cultural area of the world, on developments in architecture, monumental arts or town-planning and landscape design; or

iii. bear a unique or at least exceptional testimony to a civilization or cultural tradition which has disappeared; or

iv. be an outstanding example of a type of building or architectural ensemble or landscape which illustrates (a) significant stage(s) in human history; or

v. be an outstanding example of a traditional human settlement or land-use which is representative of a culture (or cultures), especially when it has become vulnerable under the impact of irreversible change; or

vi. be directly or tangibly associated with events or living traditions, with ideas, or with beliefs, with artistic and literary works of outstanding universal significance (the Committee considers that this criterion should justify inclusion in the List only in exceptional circumstances or in conjunction with other criteria); and

(b) i. meet the test of authenticity in design, material, workmanship or setting and in the case of cultural landscapes their distinctive character and components (the Committee stressed that reconstruction is only acceptable if it is carried out on the basis of complete and detailed documentation on the original and to no extent on conjecture); and

ii. have adequate legal and/or traditional protection and management mechanisms to ensure the conservation of the nominated cultural property or cultural landscapes. The existence of protective legislation at the national, provincial or municipal level or well-established traditional protection and/or adequate management mechanisms is therefore essential and must be stated clearly on the nomination form. Assurances of the effective implementation of these laws and/or management mechanisms are also expected. Furthermore, in order to preserve the integrity of cultural sites, particularly those open to large numbers of visitors, the state party concerned should be able to provide evidence of suitable administrative arrangements to cover the management of the property, its conservation and its accessibility to the public"...

Duties under the Convention

Article 3 provides that it is "...for each state party to this Convention to identify and delineate the different properties situated on its territory mentioned in Articles 1 and 2." In other words, state sovereignty is preserved in respect of the decision as to which properties to nominate to the World Heritage List. Articles 4 and 5 set out the duties that states take on under the Convention. Article 4 recognizes:

> "...that the duty of ensuring the identification, protection, conservation, presentation and transmission to future generations of the cultural and natural heritage referred to in Articles 1 and 2 and situated on its territory, belongs primarily to that state. It will do all it can to this end, to the utmost of its own resources and, where appropriate, with any international assistance and cooperation, in particular, financial, artistic, scientific and technical, which it may be able to obtain."

Article 5 then sets out steps to achieve protection, conservation and presentation of the cultural and natural heritage...

While these are at first sight rather onerous duties, the capacity of states to put such measures into place is recognized in Article 5 by the words "in so far as possible, and as appropriate for each country."

World Heritage in Danger List

The Committee also maintains a World Heritage in Danger List. This is a list of properties already on the World Heritage List in respect of which the Committee considers major operations necessary for their conservation, and for which assistance has been requested. Article 11(4) provides that the List may only include properties threatened by:

> "...serious and specific dangers, such as the threat of disappearance caused by accelerated deterioration, large-scale public or private projects or rapid urban or tourist development projects; destruction caused by changes in the use or ownership of the land; major alterations due to unknown causes; abandonment for any reason whatsoever; the outbreak or the threat of an armed conflict; calamities and cataclysms; serious fires, earthquakes, landslides; volcanic eruptions; changes in water level, floods and tidal waves."

The *Operational Guidelines* specify further criteria for judging when a cultural or natural property is faced with an ascertained or potential danger. When a property is placed on this List, the Committee is obliged to develop, in consultation with the state party concerned, a program of corrective measures. Funds for assistance can be allocated for these corrective measures from the World Heritage Fund. Current properties which are on the World Heritage in Danger List in Asia and the Pacific region are Angkor in Cambodia and the Manas Wildlife Sanctuary in India, both placed on the World Heritage in Danger List in 1992.

Cultural Landscapes

In 1992, the World Heritage Committee added a new category of "cultural landscapes" under the *Operational Guidelines.* The category of cultural landscapes allows for the recognition of places on the World Heritage List which present a combination of cultural and natural elements. There are three main categories:

(1) the clearly defined landscape designed and created intentionally,

(2) the organically evolved landscape, and

(3) the associative cultural landscape.

Examples of cultural landscapes include agricultural areas and natural areas significant to specific groups of people. Examples of associative cultural landscapes include Uluru-Kata Tjuta National Park in the Northern Territory of Australia and Tongariro National Park in New Zealand, which were renominated to the World Heritage List in 1994, complementing their earlier World Heritage listing for their natural values.

Specialist Advice

The Committee may receive advice from IUCN–the World Conservation Union, the International Centre for the Study of Preservation and Restoration of Cultural Property (the Rome Centre) and the International Council of Monuments and Sites (ICOMOS) (Article 13(7)).

World Heritage Fund

A "Fund for the Protection of the World Cultural and Natural Heritage of Outstanding Universal Value" (Article 15) is established under the Convention. It draws its funds from member states and from private organizations and individuals. The Fund is to be directed towards requests from the parties for international help to support the conservation of places forming part of the World Heritage and to meet the needs of places on the World Heritage in Danger List. . . .

UNIDROIT Convention

Negotiations on the *1995 UNIDROIT Convention on Stolen or Illegally Exported Cultural Objects (UNIDROIT Convention)* were completed in June 1995. It is designed to be complementary to the 1970 *UNESCO Convention.* It is aimed at the actions of private persons who are involved in transactions relating to movable cultural property, rather than the actions of states, which is the major concern of the *UNESCO Convention.* In contrast to the *UNESCO Convention,* cultural objects do not need to be "designated" by the state party before the *UNIDROIT Convention* can operate.

Accordingly cultural objects stolen from private homes, from all kinds of religious buildings, from private collections which are not registered with the state and from traditional communities, can be claimed back, even though the state has neither registered nor designated them.

The Convention concentrates on two particular matters: the conflict between a person who has been dispossessed of the cultural object by theft and who therefore has a legitimate interest in claiming its recovery, and a person who, having subsequently acquired the object in good faith, wishes to retain it. The second aspect addresses movement of cultural property across national borders contrary to the law of the state from which the property came.

Scope of the Convention

Article 1 provides that the Convention applies to claims of "an international character" for:

"(a) the restitution of stolen cultural objects; and

(b) the return of cultural objects removed from the territory of a Contracting state contrary to its law regulating the export of cultural objects for the purpose of protecting its cultural heritage."

The definition of "cultural objects" is found in Article 2. They are cultural objects which, on religious or secular grounds, are of importance for archaeology, prehistory, history, literature, art or science and belong to one of the categories listed in the Annex to the Convention. Essentially, the definition and the categories are identical to that in the *UNESCO Convention,* except that, as noted above, the items in the *UNIDROIT Convention* need not be "designated" by the state party before the Convention applies.

Obligations

The basic obligation under the Convention in relation to stolen objects is that the possessor of a cultural object which has been stolen shall return it. A claim for restitution must be brought within three years of a claimant knowing of the location of the object and the identity of its possessor (Article 3). This provision only applies to objects stolen after the Convention enters into force.

In relation to the return of illegally exported cultural objects, Article 5 allows a contracting state to request a court of another contracting state to order the return of a cultural object, within three years of the requesting state knowing of the location of the object and the identity of the possessor. Fair and reasonable compensation is payable under Article 6 to possessors who acquired the object after it was illegally exported, if the possessor neither knew or ought reasonably to have known that the article had been illegally exported (i.e., a bona fide purchaser). Alternatively, instead of compensation, the possessor may, in agreement with the requesting state, retain ownership of the object, or to transfer it to a person of its choice residing in the requesting state who "provides the necessary guarantees." Guarantees were seen to be necessary so as to ensure that the object would be adequately protected on its return, and not again be illegally exported. These provisions only apply to objects exported after the Convention enters into force.

Entry into Force

The Convention will enter into force six months after the date of deposit of the fifth instrument of ratification, acceptance, approval or accession (Article 12). As of 9 August 1997, 24 states had signed the Convention. Cambodia and China are the only states in Asia and the Pacific to have signed the Convention to date.

ASEAN Agreement on the Environment: Protection of Cultural and Natural Heritage

The 1985 *ASEAN Agreement on the Environment* contains provisions for the protection of natural and cultural heritage, in addition to its provisions in relation to the protection of the environment more generally.

[*Editors' Note: See Chapter 16–Regional Environmental Law Cooperation for a detailed discussion of the ASEAN agreement.*]

B

Boer B., "World Heritage in the Asia Pacific," 4 *Asia Pacific Journal of Environmental Law*, 1999, pp 1–4

The 1972 *Convention Concerning the Protection of the World Cultural and Natural Heritage* has been in force for over 25 years. The interpretation and implementation of the Convention is considerably assisted by *Operational Guidelines* developed by the World Heritage Committee, which are regularly updated. The Committee, created under the Convention, meets on an annual basis to consider new nominations of sites. The Committee is advised by two expert bodies. In the case of natural sites, the body is IUCN–The World Conservation Union; in relation to cultural sites from ICOMOS. For mixed nominations, both bodies are involved. The Committee also deliberates over which listed sites are appropriate to be added to the List of World Heritage in Danger. To be placed on the In Danger List, sites must be threatened by either ascertained or potential "serious and specific dangers", as judged by an expert panel of advisers from IUCN and/or ICOMOS.

The main criterion for listing of World Heritage properties is that they must be of "outstanding universal value." Parties to the Convention take on serious obligations in signing the Convention, including the establishment of legal and administrative mechanisms to ensure that World Heritage sites under their jurisdiction are identified, protected, conserved, presented and transmitted to future generations.

The inclusion of the concept "transmission to future generations" in the Convention gave early recognition to the concept of intergenerational equity, an idea which has become mainstream in the last few years, and is these days closely tied up with principles such as the precautionary principle and the principle of biological diversity and ecological integrity, which underlie the concept of sustainable development. These latter concepts are now also able to be related to the idea of World Heritage, particularly concerning the question of management prescriptions and the criteria that might be used to judge whether or not it is necessary or desirable to place a property on the World Heritage in Danger List.

There are now 582 properties on the World Heritage List worldwide, divided into 445 cultural sites, 117 natural sites and 20 mixed sites. [*Editors Note: At March 2001 the number of sites on the World Heritage List had reached 690 worldwide, of which 529 are cultural, 138 natural and 23 are mixed sites.*] Many of these sites are found in the Northern Hemisphere, and most of those are in Europe. While this is hardly surprising given the origins of the Convention, this does not mean that there are few sites of outstanding universal value in other regions. In Asia, there are 16 States which are members of the Convention and which have World Heritage listings. They are Australia, Bangladesh, Cambodia, China, India, Indonesia, Iran, Japan, Laos, Nepal, Pakistan, Philippines, the Republic of Korea, Sri Lanka, Thailand and Vietnam. In total there are some 111 World Heritage sites listed in these countries. In the Pacific, four States are members: Fiji, New Zealand, Papua New Guinea and Solomon Islands. Only the Solomon Islands has a listed World Heritage site. There are of course many other potential World Heritage sites throughout Asia and the Pacific.

A question that arises is what can be done not only to encourage more countries to become members of the Convention, especially in the Pacific, but also to ensure that those that are members are in a position to adequately protect their natural and cultural heritage. This issue is clearly bound up with the development of domestic environmental law. There is a clear need to improve regulatory regimes relating to pollution, planning and development control in general before many countries can even contemplate establishing particular legal, administrative and other measures to look after their potential World Heritage sites. One positive step that is being encouraged by the World Heritage Committee and the *Operational Guidelines* is for local communities to become more particularly involved in the nomination process, and the protection and management of sites, as has occurred with the 1998 Solomon Islands nomination of Rennell Island.

In considering the matter of improving the record of Asia and the Pacific in relation to World Heritage membership and nominations, it is disappointing to witness the task that the Australian Government has recently undertaken to try to avoid the listing of the spectacular Kakadu National Park on the List of World Heritage in Danger. Throughout the region Australia has often been looked to as holding the moral high ground on environmental questions, particularly in relation to matters of World Heritage. With the Kakadu controversy, it appears that Australia has lost more of the high ground that it began to lose with its dismal performance over the Climate Change negotiations in Kyoto in 1997. The matter of placing Kakadu on the In Danger List has arisen out of the determination of the Australian Government to allow a uranium mine, Jabiluka, to be established and operated within the general area of the park, although not within the park boundaries as such. The Jabiluka mine has been proposed to operate in addition to the Ranger mine that has been operating in the same area for some 20 years. The World Heritage Committee, at its meeting of December 1998, had before it a comprehensive report from an expert IUCN mission. The mission's report pointed to:

> "[T]he serious concerns and preoccupations expressed by some of Australia's most eminent scientists as to the unacceptably high degree of scientific uncertainties relating to the Jabiluka mine design, tailings disposal and possible impacts on catchment systems. The mission shares these concerns and therefore recommends the application of the Precautionary Principle which requires that mining operations at Jabiluka be ceased."

The report also recorded the threat of "visual encroachment" of the mining site as an ascertained danger, as well as threats to the cultural values of the property, concerning in particular the interests of the traditional Aboriginal owners of the lands. The Australian Government's response to the mission report and to the concerns of the December 1998 World Heritage Committee meeting is embodied in a comprehensive document entitled *Australia's Kakadu: Protecting World Heritage* published in April 1998. That Report was subsequently analyzed by IUCN, ICOMOS and an independent expert, and was found to be inadequate in relation to the concerns of the original IUCN mission report, and the concerns raised at the December 1998 meeting. The question of whether Kakadu should be now be placed on the In Danger List in December 1998 is a live question at the time of writing, and will be decided at an extraordinary session of the World Heritage Committee in July 1999.

Apart from the issues raised by the expert reports in relation to the threats posed to the World Heritage values of the area by the proposed mine, there is also a vital legal matter which is pertinent to the Committee's deliberations. This matter concerns the application of an international law doctrine called the intertemporal rule. The intertemporal rule, following from interpretations of the *dictum* of Judge Huber in the *Island of Palmas Arbitration*, has traditionally been understood to mean that the validity and interpretation of provisions of a treaty are determined by reference to the law as it was when the instrument was drafted. Although it would appear that certainty in the content of this rule is necessary and important, the jurisprudence of the International Court of Justice has significantly varied over the years. Human rights provisions and generic terms in treaties have come to be regarded as exceptions to this general rule. It has been suggested that the intertemporal rule now includes considering the "intention of the parties, reflected by the reference to the objects and purpose." This view does not extend to determining the validity of treaties, but only in relation to their interpretation, and this is the issue that concerns us here.

In the International Court of Justice in the 1997 *Gabcikovo-Nagymaros* case, Vice President Weeramantry's separate opinion argued that the intertemporal rule could not be applied to prevent the application of current environmental norms when interpreting the 1977 *Danube River Treaty*. Judge Weeramantry's conception of the intertemporal rule clearly included applying contemporary environmental norms and principles to interpret a treaty, even if the parties intended otherwise. He noted that "no action should be permissible which is today considered environmentally unsound, even though it is taken under an instrument of more than 20 years ago."

On the basis of this *dictum,* it can be argued that the World Heritage Committee has the right to consider the interpretation of the Convention in the light of modern scientific and legal understandings of World Heritage values. In particular it should revisit the question of whether a new uranium mine ought to be allowed on the edge of a World Heritage area, where there is significant scientific uncertainty about the effects of the mine's operations and where there is little room for doubt that the traditional Aboriginal owners are not in favor of the mine proceeding. The precautionary principle, combined with the principles of intergenerational equity, the conservation of biological diversity and ecological integrity, as elements of sustainable development, can clearly be applied in this situation.

Apart from being endorsed in a variety of modern international environmental instruments, these principles can be argued to be of great force in the Australian context, as they are found in the Australian Government's 1992 *Intergovernmental Agreement on the Environment*, and enacted through a large number of federal and state statutes. It is particularly significant to note, in the light of the IUCN's urging of the application of the precautionary principle in its recommendation, that the Australian Government's latest piece of proposed legislation, the *Environmental Protection and Biological Diversity Conservation (No 2) Bill 1998*, specifically includes the provision that the precautionary principle applies when plans are being made for managing a property that is included in the World Heritage List and is entirely within one or more Commonwealth areas.

The way in which the World Heritage Committee decides this question of placing Kakadu on the List of World Heritage in Danger, and how the matter is ultimately resolved by the Australian Government, is likely to influence the way in which the Convention is applied and interpreted in relation to development pressures in the future, not just in the Australian context, but also throughout Asia and the Pacific. A decision to let the mine go ahead, and not to place Kakadu on the In Danger List, will send a clear signal to other countries in the region, and to the world at large, that the outstanding universal values recognized by the *World Heritage Convention* are no longer more important than the allegedly outstanding universal values of the export dollar.

C

Convention Concerning the Protection of the World Cultural and Natural Heritage, 11 I.L.M. 1358, 1972 (*World Heritage Convention*)

[*This treaty can be accessed within the UNESCO web site. The address is <http://www.unesco.org/whc/nwhc/pages/doc/main.htm>. This site was accessed on 21/05/01.*]

DEFINITION OF THE CULTURAL AND NATURAL HERITAGE

Article 1

For the purposes of this Convention, the following shall be considered as "cultural heritage":

- *monuments:* architectural works, works of monumental sculpture and painting, elements or structures of an archaeological nature, inscriptions, cave dwellings and combinations of features, which are of outstanding universal value from the point of view of history, art or science;
- *groups of buildings:* groups of separate or connected buildings which, because of their architecture, their homogeneity or their place in the landscape, are of outstanding universal value from the point of view of history, art or science; and
- *sites:* works of man or the combined works of nature and man, and areas including archaeological sites which are of outstanding universal value from the historical, aesthetic, ethnological or anthropological point of view.

Article 2

For the purposes of this Convention, the following shall be considered as "natural heritage":

- natural features consisting of physical and biological formations or groups of such formations, which are of outstanding universal value from the aesthetic or scientific point of view;
- geological and physiographical formations and precisely delineated areas which constitute the habitat of threatened species of animals and plants of outstanding universal value from the point of view of science or conservation; and

On the basis of this dictum, *it can be argued that the World Heritage Committee has the right to consider the interpretation of the Convention in the light of modern scientific and legal understandings of World Heritage values.*

- natural sites or precisely delineated natural areas of outstanding universal value from the point of view of science, conservation or natural beauty.

Article 3

It is for each State Party to this Convention to identify and delineate the different properties situated on its territory mentioned in Articles 1 and 2 above.

National Protection and International Protection of the Cultural and Natural Heritage

Article 4

Each State Party to this Convention recognizes that the duty of ensuring the identification, protection, conservation, presentation and transmission to future generations of the cultural and natural heritage referred to in Articles 1 and 2 and situated on its territory, belongs primarily to that State. It will do all it can to this end, to the utmost of its own resources and, where appropriate, with any international assistance and cooperation, in particular, financial, artistic, scientific and technical, which it may be able to obtain.

Article 5

To ensure that effective and active measures are taken for the protection, conservation and presentation of the cultural and natural heritage situated on its territory, each State Party to this Convention shall endeavor, in so far as possible, and as appropriate for each country:

- to adopt a general policy which aims to give the cultural and natural heritage a function in the life of the community and to integrate the protection of that heritage into comprehensive planning programs;
- to set up within its territories, where such services do not exist, one or more services for the protection, conservation and presentation of the cultural and natural heritage with an appropriate staff and possessing the means to discharge their functions;
- to develop scientific and technical studies and research and to work out such operating methods as will make the State capable of counteracting the dangers that threaten its cultural or natural heritage;
- to take the appropriate legal, scientific, technical, administrative and financial measures necessary for the identification, protection, conservation, presentation and rehabilitation of this heritage; and
- to foster the establishment or development of national or regional centers for training in the protection, conservation and presentation of the cultural and natural heritage and to encourage scientific research in this field.

Article 6

While fully respecting the sovereignty of the States on whose territory the cultural and natural heritage mentioned in Articles 1 and 2 is situated, and without prejudice to property right provided by national legislation, the States Parties to this Convention recognize that such heritage constitutes a world heritage for whose protection it is the duty of the international community as a whole to cooperate.

The States Parties undertake, in accordance with the provisions of this Convention, to give their help in the identification, protection, conservation and presentation of the cultural and natural heritage referred to in paragraphs 2 and 4 of Article 11 if the States on whose territory it is situated so request.

Each State Party to this Convention undertakes not to take any deliberate measures which might damage directly or indirectly the cultural and natural heritage referred to in Articles 1 and 2 situated on the territory of other States Parties to this Convention.

Article 7

For the purpose of this Convention, international protection of the world cultural and natural heritage shall be understood to mean the establishment of a system of international cooperation and assistance designed to support States Parties to the Convention in their efforts to conserve and identify that heritage.

Intergovernmental Committee for the Protection of the World Cultural and Natural Heritage

Article 8

An Intergovernmental Committee for the Protection of the Cultural and Natural Heritage of Outstanding Universal Value, called "the World Heritage Committee," is hereby established within the United Nations Educational, Scientific and Cultural Organization. It shall be composed of 15 States Parties to the Convention, elected by States Parties to the Convention meeting in general assembly during the ordinary session of the General Conference of the United Nations Educational, Scientific and Cultural Organization. The number of States members of the Committee shall be increased to 21 as from the date of the ordinary session of the General Conference following the entry into force of this Convention for at least 40 States.

Election of members of the Committee shall ensure an equitable representation of the different regions and cultures of the world.

A representative of the International Centre for the Study of the Preservation and Restoration of Cultural Property (Rome Centre), a representative of the International Council of Monuments and Sites (ICOMOS) and a representative of the International Union for Conservation of Nature and Natural Resources (IUCN), to whom may be added, at the request of States Parties to the Convention meeting in general assembly during the ordinary sessions of the General Conference of the United Nations Educational, Scientific and Cultural Organization, representatives of other intergovernmental or non-governmental organizations, with similar objectives, may attend the meetings of the Committee in an advisory capacity.

Article 9

The term of office of States members of the World Heritage Committee shall extend from the end of the ordinary session of the General Conference during which they are elected until the end of its third subsequent ordinary session.

The term of office of one-third of the members designated at the time of the first election shall, however, cease at the end of the first ordinary session of the General Conference following that at which they were elected; and the term of office of a further third of the members designated at the same time shall cease at the end of the second ordinary session of the General Conference following that at which they were elected. The names of these members shall be chosen by lot by the President of the General Conference of the United Nations Educational, Scientific and Cultural Organization after the first election.

States members of the Committee shall choose as their representatives persons qualified in the field of the cultural or natural heritage.

Article 10

The World Heritage Committee shall adopt its Rules of Procedure.

The Committee may at any time invite public or private organizations or individuals to participate in its meetings for consultation on particular problems.

The Committee may create such consultative bodies as it deems necessary for the performance of its functions.

Article 11

Every State Party to this Convention shall, in so far as possible, submit to the World Heritage Committee an inventory of property forming part of the cultural and natural heritage, situated in its territory and suitable for inclusion in the list provided for in paragraph 2 of this Article. This inventory, which shall not be considered exhaustive, shall include documentation about the location of the property in question and its significance.

On the basis of the inventories submitted by States in accordance with paragraph 1, the Committee shall establish, keep up to date and publish, under the title of "World Heritage List," a list of properties forming part of the cultural heritage and natural heritage, as defined in Articles 1 and 2 of this Convention, which it considers as having outstanding universal value in terms of such criteria as it shall have established. An updated list shall be distributed at least every two years.

The inclusion of a property in the World Heritage List requires the consent of the State concerned. The inclusion of a property situated in a territory, sovereignty or jurisdiction over which is claimed by more than one State shall in no way prejudice the rights of the parties to the dispute.

The Committee shall establish, keep up to date and publish, whenever circumstances shall so require, under the title of "List of World Heritage in Danger", a list of the property appearing in the World Heritage List for the conservation of which major operations are necessary and for which assistance has been requested under this Convention. This list shall contain an estimate of the cost of such operations. The list may include only such property forming part of the cultural and natural heritage as is threatened by serious and specific dangers, such as the threat of disappearance caused by accelerated deterioration, large- scale public or private projects or rapid urban or tourist development projects; destruction caused by changes in the use or ownership of the land; major alterations due to unknown causes; abandonment for any reason whatsoever; the outbreak or the threat of an armed conflict; calamities and cataclysms; serious fires, earthquakes, landslides; volcanic eruptions; changes in water level, floods and tidal waves. The Committee may at any time, in case of urgent need, make a new entry in the List of World Heritage in Danger and publicize such entry immediately.

The Committee shall define the criteria on the basis of which a property belonging to the cultural or natural heritage may be included in either of the lists mentioned in paragraphs 2 and 4 of this article.

Before refusing a request for inclusion in one of the two lists mentioned in paragraphs 2 and 4 of this article, the Committee shall consult the State Party in whose territory the cultural or natural property in question is situated.

The Committee shall, with the agreement of the States concerned, coordinate and encourage the studies and research needed for the drawing up of the lists referred to in paragraphs 2 and 4 of this article.

The World Heritage Committee shall be assisted by a Secretariat appointed by the Director-General of the United Nations Educational, Scientific and Cultural Organization.

Article 12

The fact that a property belonging to the cultural or natural heritage has not been included in either of the two lists mentioned in paragraphs 2 and 4 of Article 11 shall in no way be construed to mean that it does not have an outstanding universal value for purposes other than those resulting from inclusion in these lists.

Article 13

The World Heritage Committee shall receive and study requests for international assistance formulated by States Parties to this Convention with respect to property forming part of the cultural or natural heritage, situated in their territories, and included or potentially suitable for inclusion in the lists mentioned referred to in paragraphs 2 and 4 of Article 11. The purpose of such requests may be to secure the protection, conservation, presentation or rehabilitation of such property.

Requests for international assistance under paragraph 1 of this article may also be concerned with identification of cultural or natural property defined in Articles 1 and 2, when preliminary investigations have shown that further inquiries would be justified.

The Committee shall decide on the action to be taken with regard to these requests, determine where appropriate, the nature and extent of its assistance, and authorize the conclusion, on its behalf, of the necessary arrangements with the government concerned.

The Committee shall determine an order of priorities for its operations. It shall in so doing bear in mind the respective importance for the world cultural and natural heritage of the property requiring protection, the need to give international assistance to the property most representative of a natural environment or of the genius and the history of the peoples of the world, the urgency of the work to be done, the resources available to the States on whose territory the threatened property is situated and in particular the extent to which they are able to safeguard such property by their own means.

The Committee shall draw up, keep up to date and publicize a list of property for which international assistance has been granted.

The Committee shall decide on the use of the resources of the Fund established under Article 15 of this Convention. It shall seek ways of increasing these resources and shall take all useful steps to this end.

The Committee shall cooperate with international and national governmental and non-governmental organizations having objectives similar to those of this Convention. For the implementation of its programs and projects, the Committee may call on such organizations, particularly the International Centre for the Study of the Preservation and Restoration of cultural Property (the Rome Centre), the International Council of Monuments and Sites (ICOMOS) and the International Union for Conservation of Nature and Natural Resources (IUCN), as well as on public and private bodies and individuals.

Decisions of the Committee shall be taken by a majority of two-thirds of its members present and voting. A majority of the members of the Committee shall constitute a quorum.

Article 14

The World Heritage Committee shall be assisted by a Secretariat appointed by the Director-General of the United Nations Educational, Scientific and Cultural Organization.

The Director-General of the United Nations Educational, Scientific and Cultural Organization, utilizing to the fullest extent possible the services of the International Centre for the Study of the Preservation and the Restoration of Cultural Property (the Rome Centre), the International Council of Monuments and Sites (ICOMOS) and the International Union for Conservation of Nature and Natural Resources (IUCN) in their respective areas of competence and capability, shall prepare the Committee's documentation and the agenda of its meetings and shall have the responsibility for the implementation of its decisions.

Fund for the Protection of the World Cultural and Natural Heritage

Article 15

A Fund for the Protection of the World Cultural and Natural Heritage of Outstanding Universal Value, called "the World Heritage Fund," is hereby established.

The Fund shall constitute a trust fund, in conformity with the provisions of the Financial Regulations of the United Nations Educational, Scientific and Cultural Organization.

The resources of the Fund shall consist of:

- compulsory and voluntary contributions made by States Parties to this Convention;
- contributions, gifts or bequests which may be made by other States, the United Nations Educational, Scientific and Cultural Organization, other organizations of the United Nations system, particularly the United Nations Development Programme or other intergovernmental organizations;
- public or private bodies or individuals;
- any interest due on the resources of the Fund;
- funds raised by collections and receipts from events organized for the benefit of the fund; and
- all other resources authorized by the Fund's regulations, as drawn up by the World Heritage Committee.

Contributions to the Fund and other forms of assistance made available to the Committee may be used only for such purposes as the Committee shall define. The Committee may accept contributions to be used only for a certain program or project, provided that the Committee shall have decided on the implementation of such program or project. No political conditions may be attached to contributions made to the Fund.

Article 16

Without prejudice to any supplementary voluntary contribution, the States Parties to this Convention undertake to pay regularly, every two years, to the World Heritage Fund, contributions, the amount of which, in the form of a uniform percentage applicable to all States, shall be determined by the General Assembly of States Parties to the Convention, meeting during the sessions of the General Conference of the United Nations Educational, Scientific and Cultural Organization. This decision of the General Assembly requires the majority of the States Parties present and voting, which have not made the declaration referred to in paragraph 2 of this Article. In no case shall the compulsory contribution of States Parties to the Convention exceed 1 percent of the contribution to the regular budget of the United Nations Educational, Scientific and Cultural Organization.

However, each State referred to in Article 31 or in Article 32 of this Convention may declare, at the time of the deposit of its instrument of ratification, acceptance or accession, that it shall not be bound by the provisions of paragraph 1 of this Article.

A State Party to the Convention which has made the declaration referred to in paragraph 2 of this Article may at any time withdraw the said declaration by notifying the Director-General of the United Nations Educational, Scientific and Cultural Organization. However, the withdrawal of the declaration shall not take effect in regard to the compulsory contribution due by the State until the date of the subsequent General Assembly of States parties to the Convention.

In order that the Committee may be able to plan its operations effectively, the contributions of States Parties to this Convention which have made the declaration referred to in paragraph 2 of this Article, shall be paid on a regular basis, at least every two years, and should not be less than the contributions which they should have paid if they had been bound by the provisions of paragraph 1 of this Article.

Any State Party to the Convention which is in arrears with the payment of its compulsory or voluntary contribution for the current year and the calendar year immediately preceding it shall not be eligible as a Member of the World Heritage Committee, although this provision shall not apply to the first election.

The terms of office of any such State which is already a member of the Committee shall terminate at the time of the elections provided for in Article 8, paragraph 1 of this Convention.

Article 17

The States Parties to this Convention shall consider or encourage the establishment of national public and private foundations or associations whose purpose is to invite donations for the protection of the cultural and natural heritage as defined in Articles 1 and 2 of this Convention.

Article 18

The States Parties to this Convention shall give their assistance to international fund-raising campaigns organized for the World Heritage Fund under the auspices of the United Nations Educational, Scientific and Cultural Organization. They shall facilitate collections made by the bodies mentioned in paragraph 3 of Article 15 for this purpose.

Conditions and Arrangements for International Assistance

Article 19

Any State Party to this Convention may request international assistance for property forming part of the cultural or natural heritage of outstanding universal value situated within its territory. It shall submit with its request such information and documentation provided for in Article 21 as it has in its possession and as will enable the Committee to come to a decision.

Article 20

Subject to the provisions of paragraph 2 of Article 13, sub-paragraph (c) of Article 22 and Article 23, international assistance provided for by this Convention may be granted only to property forming part of the cultural and natural heritage which the World Heritage Committee has decided, or may decide, to enter in one of the lists mentioned in paragraphs 2 and 4 of Article 11.

Article 21

The World Heritage Committee shall define the procedure by which requests to it for international assistance shall be considered and shall specify the content of the request, which should define the operation contemplated, the work that is necessary, the expected cost thereof, the degree of urgency and the reasons why the resources of the State requesting assistance do not allow it to meet all the expenses. Such requests must be supported by experts' reports whenever possible.

Requests based upon disasters or natural calamities should, by reasons of the urgent work which they may involve, be given immediate, priority consideration by the Committee, which should have a reserve fund at its disposal against such contingencies.

Before coming to a decision, the Committee shall carry out such studies and consultations as it deems necessary.

Article 22

Assistance granted by the World Heritage Committee may take the following forms:

- studies concerning the artistic, scientific and technical problems raised by the protection, conservation, presentation and rehabilitation of the cultural and natural heritage, as defined in paragraphs 2 and 4 of Article 11 of this Convention;
- provisions of experts, technicians and skilled labor to ensure that the approved work is correctly carried out;
- training of staff and specialists at all levels in the field of identification, protection, conservation, presentation and rehabilitation of the cultural and natural heritage;
- supply of equipment which the State concerned does not possess or is not in a position to acquire;
- low-interest or interest-free loans which might be repayable on a long-term basis;
- the granting, in exceptional cases and for special reasons, of non-repayable subsidies.

Article 23

The World Heritage Committee may also provide international assistance to national or regional centers for the training of staff and specialists at all levels in the field of identification, protection, conservation, presentation and rehabilitation of the cultural and natural heritage.

Article 24

International assistance on a large scale shall be preceded by detailed scientific, economic and technical studies. These studies shall draw upon the most advanced techniques for the protection, conservation, presentation and rehabilitation of the natural and cultural heritage and shall be consistent with the objectives of this Convention. The studies shall also seek means of making rational use of the resources available in the State concerned.

Article 25

As a general rule, only part of the cost of work necessary shall be borne by the international community. The contribution of the State benefiting from international assistance shall constitute a substantial share of the resources devoted to each program or project, unless its resources do not permit this.

Article 26

The World Heritage Committee and the recipient State shall define in the agreement they conclude the conditions in which a program or project for which international assistance under the terms of this Convention is provided, shall be carried out. It shall be the responsibility of the State receiving such international assistance to continue to protect, conserve and present the property so safeguarded, in observance of the conditions laid down by the agreement.

Educational Programs

Article 27

The States Parties to this Convention shall endeavor by all appropriate means, and in particular by educational and information programs, to strengthen appreciation and respect by their peoples of the cultural and natural heritage defined in Articles 1 and 2 of the Convention.

They shall undertake to keep the public broadly informed of the dangers threatening this heritage and of the activities carried on in pursuance of this Convention.

Article 28

States Parties to this Convention which receive international assistance under the Convention shall take appropriate measures to make known the importance of the property for which assistance has been received and the role played by such assistance.

Reports

Article 29

The States Parties to this Convention shall, in the reports which they submit to the General Conference of the United Nations Educational, Scientific and Cultural Organization on dates and in a manner to be determined by it, give information on the legislative and administrative provisions which they have adopted and other action which they have taken for the application of this Convention, together with details of the experience acquired in this field.

These reports shall be brought to the attention of the World Heritage Committee.

The Committee shall submit a report on its activities at each of the ordinary sessions of the General Conference of the United Nations Educational, Scientific and Cultural Organization...

Article 34

The following provisions shall apply to those States Parties to this Convention which have a federal or non-unitary constitutional system:

- with regard to the provisions of this Convention, the implementation of which comes under the legal jurisdiction of the federal or central legislative power, the obligations of the federal or central government shall be the same as for those States parties which are not federal States;
- with regard to the provisions of this Convention, the implementation of which comes under the legal jurisdiction of individual constituent States, countries, provinces or cantons that are not obliged by the constitutional system of the federation to take legislative measures, the federal government shall inform the competent authorities of such States, countries, provinces or cantons of the said provisions, with its recommendation for their adoption...

3

Illustrative National Heritage Management Systems and Laws

A

Australia

(i) Boer B., "World Heritage Disputes in Australia," 7 *Journal of Environmental Law & Litigation*, 1992, pp 247-279

Introduction

With its ratification in 1974, Australia became one of the first countries to adopt the *World Heritage Convention*. Since then, however, a number of Australian states have questioned whether the federal government should have the power to nominate items within state boundaries to the World Heritage List without the consent of the state concerned. The states also have resisted federal decisions concerning the management of listed areas, and have disputed federal determinations concerning the compensation they are entitled to as a result of a listing...

Political conditions include virulent "states' rights" debates over the power to control development and exploitation, and a constitutional framework *perceived* to be inadequate for resolving these debates. The strengths and weaknesses of political leaders, their factional affiliations, and their abilities to influence their Cabinets have affected the outcome of these disputes. Finally, the power of the "green" vote in Australian politics in the past decade has exerted a significant influence in most of these debates over heritage areas. This mixture has produced a unique political picture and has resulted in long, hard-fought court battles, contentious public inquiries, and elections in which state governments stand or fall on the basis of environmental issues.

The fallout from these disputes has raised Australian environmental consciousness and has stimulated the enactment of environmental protection legislation at the federal, state, and local levels. In particular, all states and territories in Australia have enacted some form of heritage legislation in the past two decades to protect items of the natural and cultural heritage.

In addition, most jurisdictions have specific provisions to protect Aboriginal heritage sites. The Aboriginal heritage is a complex mixture of what non-Aboriginal people would call natural and cultural heritage issues. These issues include questions of land rights, self-determination, skills, corroborees, and spiritual practices. In short, Aboriginal heritage preservation requires a broad understanding of Aboriginal cosmology.

Although it would seem that the states and the federal government seek to achieve similar aims in terms of environmental protection, they often have disagreed on the scope of their respective powers to implement their goals. The states have objected to federal initiatives on the ground that the federal government lacks direct constitutional power to enact environmental measures. This is hardly surprising, given that the environment was not an issue when the *Australian Constitution* was enacted in 1900. As a result, in passing a range of environmental legislation in the past 17 years, including the *World Heritage Properties Conservation Act* of 1983, the federal government has had to rely on its constitutional power to legislate in a variety of areas which have no necessary connection with environmental, heritage, or resource issues. Such powers include those relating to the regulation of trade, taxation, corporations, Aboriginal affairs, and external affairs. Since the federal government also has international obligations arising under the *World Heritage Convention*, the states have, in addition, had to wrestle with the duties the federal government has taken on in carrying out the provisions of the Convention. Over the past nine years, a number of cases have examined constitutional arguments over these matters in great detail. Many of the cases have implications that extend beyond Australian law and concern the extent of the obligations of all countries which have signed the Convention, particularly since no other signatory country has generated legal actions of the kind canvassed here. Australia is thus the only country which has built up any jurisprudence of World Heritage.

This article examines the obligations placed on signatory countries that ratified the *World Heritage Convention*. It focuses on the constitutional and political issues surrounding the implementation of the Convention in Australia, particularly through the federal *World Heritage Properties Conservation Act* of 1983. The article also considers how cases brought by the states and the Commonwealth in the Federal Court and the High Court have helped to define the Commonwealth's powers to implement the Convention. It also briefly examines the activities of the Commission of Inquiry into the Lemonthyme and Southern Forests in Tasmania. Finally, the article comments on the use of the legal system in resolving disputes and concludes that broader input into environmental decision making will likely result in more satisfactory decisions.

The World Heritage Convention

Obligations of Signatory Countries

...Each state party to the Convention is obliged to identify and delineate the World Heritage properties situated within its territory. The Convention imposes a general obligation on signatory countries to provide for its cultural and natural heritage...

[*As noted by Boer et al (1998) and as set out in the Convention, both extracted above, the duties that countries take on under the Convention are set out in Articles 4 and 5.*] The combination of obligations in [these articles] is significant. However, the "duty" mentioned in Article 4 is tempered somewhat by the words "to the utmost of its own resources," and "with any international assistance...which it may be able to obtain." Article 5 similarly qualifies its provisions: each state party "shall endeavor" to act along these lines "in so far as possible, and as appropriate for each country." One commentator, Marc Denhez, refers to these provisions as a "best efforts clause." He states that "although a 'best efforts' clause does dilute a treaty's obligations, it does not obviate them altogether," and the provisions do in fact contain legal obligations.

A consideration of the Australian cases interpreting the Convention and the *World Heritage Properties Conservation Act* of 1983 backs Denhez's view by spelling out these legal obligations to some extent. In the first of these cases, *Commonwealth of Australia v. State of Tasmania* (the *Franklin Dam* case), Justice Mason stated:

> "Article 5 itself imposes a series of obligations on parties to the Convention, one of which is the obligation dealt with in para (d) which includes the taking of legal measures. The imposition of this obligation is an element in a general framework which has as its foundation:
>
> (a) the responsibility of each State under art 3 to identify and delineate the different properties situated in its territory which answer the descriptions of "cultural heritage" in art 1 and "natural heritage" in art 2; and
>
> (b) the first sentence in art 4 which amounts to a recognition of the general or universal responsibility for the protection, preservation, etc. of the heritage and a declaration of what each State will do in the discharge of the responsibility affirmed by the first sentence...
>
> Article 5 cannot be read as a mere statement of intention. It is expressed in the form of a command requiring each party to endeavor to bring about the matters dealt with in the lettered paragraphs. Indeed, there would be little point in adding the qualifications "in so far as possible" and "as appropriate for each country" unless the article imposed an obligation. The first qualification means "in so far as is practicable" and the second takes account of the difference in legal systems. Neither of these qualifications nor the existence of an element of discretion and value judgment in para (d) is inconsistent with the existence of an obligation. There is a distinction between a discretion as to the manner of performance or nonperformance. The latter, but not the former, is inconsistent with a binding obligation to perform...And it is only natural that in framing a command to States to take measures of the kind described in para (d) in relation to their heritage the command will be expressed in terms of endeavor, subject to the qualifications mentioned."

The Convention makes clear, in Article 6 as well as by language employed in the opening paragraph of Article 5, that each party may decide for itself how it will best fulfill its obligations, as long as each carries them out in good faith. Thus, signatory governments may consider a range of factors when determining whether to nominate a property, where to set its boundaries, whether to allow any development, and how to manage it. Article 6 further requires that each party pledge not to take any deliberate measures which might damage directly or indirectly items of the cultural and natural heritages of other countries...

Signatory governments may consider a range of factors when determining whether to nominate a property, where to set its boundaries, whether to allow any development, and how to manage it.

The Federal Clause

Article 34 of the Convention confers the power to nominate areas to the World Heritage List only upon the *national* governments of signatory countries; states and provinces in federally organized countries such as Australia, Canada, the Federal Republic of Germany, and the US have no direct input into the nomination process...[*See the World Heritage Convention above for the text of Article 34.*]

In Australia, the Federal Government implements some of its obligations under the Convention through its Australian Heritage Commission, but vests primary responsibility for implementation in the federal Department of the Arts, Sport, the Environment, Tourism and Territories (DASETT). Ideally, the federal, state, and Northern Territory governments should carry out research and documentation to support the nomination on a co-operative basis. The lack of cooperation between the federal, state, and territory governments in some of the Australian listings seems to be contrary to the spirit of Article 34 and indicates a lack of political maturity in relations between the elements of the Australian federation in environmental management...

The Australian Listings

...Australia has listed eight areas to date. While all of these relate largely to natural heritage, the Kakadu, Uluru,

Willandra Lakes, and Tasmanian Wilderness listings also include important Aboriginal heritage components.

The *World Heritage Convention* also calls for tentative lists of places which may be considered for nomination at some future time. In Australia it appears that when an area or item is put on a tentative list, the *World Heritage Properties Conservation Act* of 1983 can be invoked in order to protect it. DASETT states:

> "This factor, in itself, requires the Federal Government to take its responsibility to prepare a tentative list very seriously. Australia will not merely be listing a wide range of Australian sites without first being sure that the stringent criteria [sic] of "outstanding universal value" is maintained. These considerations have precluded the submission of an Australian tentative list at this time.

DASETT has in fact drawn up a list of possible future heritage sites, but has declined to make it public because inclusion of a property on a tentative list means that the consequences for that property under the *Australian World Heritage Properties Act* seem to be exactly the same as if the property has actually been listed on the World Heritage List. "Identifying" a property under section 3A of the Act may subject the government to legal action if a property is threatened in some way. A property not so "identified" does not attract the protection of the Act.

The view of Justice Dawson, who delivered a separate opinion in *Queensland v. The Commonwealth*, is instructive here:

> "What emerges from the terms of the Convention with clarity is that it is for a State Party to identify for itself the cultural and natural heritage on its territory. It is not a matter for the World Heritage Committee. The obligation of a State Party to protect, conserve, present and transmit to future generations the cultural and natural heritage situated on its territory does not flow from any listing upon the World Heritage List. It flows from the identification by the State Party of its cultural or natural heritage, an identification which the State Party is under a duty to make. Once identified, even if there is a refusal to enter such a property on the World Heritage List, it does not cease to be part of the cultural or natural heritage and the obligations imposed by the Convention in relation to it remain in force. While the inclusion of a property in the World Heritage List may, in a practical sense, confirm the appropriateness of the identification of that property by a State Party as part of its cultural or natural heritage, it leads to no consequence under the Convention other than eligibility for international assistance."

The Australian Disputes

In addition to the controversy surrounding the creation of Kakadu National Park, there have been three major cases in the High Court of Australia relating to World Heritage. Two relate to Tasmania and one to Queensland. They are: *Commonwealth of Australia v. State of Tasmania* (the *Franklin Dam* case), *Richardson v. State of Tasmania and Gunns Kiln-Dried Timber*, and *State of Queensland v. Commonwealth of Australia*. All created a great deal of political controversy.

One indication of the importance of a constitutional dispute between the Commonwealth and one of the states occurs when other states intervene in the action, normally through their Solicitors-General. In the *Franklin Dam* case, for example, the states of New South Wales, Queensland, and Victoria intervened along with the Tasmanian Wilderness Society. States normally intervene to ensure that their interests in constitutional and other relevant questions are fully considered, even if they have no direct interest in the precise subject matter under litigation. Courts almost always give a state leave to intervene.

An important issue that arises in cases of this kind concerns the extent of "states' rights" vis-a-vis the Federal Government. This question confronted the drafters of Australia's *Constitution* in the 1890s and has resurfaced every few years in constitutional cases before the High Court. More recently, the conservative Liberal/National Party Government of Prime Minister Fraser between 1976 and 1983 saw the rise of "co-operative federalism," wherein the Federal Government withdrew from various areas which had previously been in its domain, ostensibly to reduce the central government's powers and enhance those of the states. Since 1983, resolution of World Heritage litigation before the High Court has depended partly on recognition of federal and state powers in relation to environmental matters.

Another major feature of these disputes concerns the balance of powerful development interests against a growing conservation movement which questions the wisdom of resource exploitation, particularly in ecologically sensitive areas and areas significant to Aboriginal people. Although this movement has arisen only in the past two decades or so, the increase in public awareness and a remarkable growth in the number of people joining conservation groups around the country has underscored the fact that politicians must take environmental issues seriously, if only for their political survival. Partly as a result of the 1989 Tasmanian election, the Federal Labor Government dramatically increased its efforts to capture the conservation vote.

The Franklin Dam Case

Commonwealth of Australia v. State of Tasmania involved a political and constitutional dispute arising out of a determination by the Hydro-Electric Commission of Tasmania to press ahead with a large hydro dam on the Franklin River in South West Tasmania. By the time the case reached the High Court, the proposed dam site had been inscribed on the World Heritage List as part of the nomination of the Western Tasmania Wilderness National Parks. This inscription had been preceded by a great deal of political debate, the arrest of 1,272 people involved in a land and water blockade of the Franklin River and access to it, the rise and fall of a number of state premiers and governments, and the election of the Hawke Labor government, which had as one of its election platforms the saving of the Franklin River.

After coming to power in March 1983, the Labor Government enacted the *World Heritage Properties Conservation Act* 1983. This Act is the only statute enacted in the world to ensure the domestic implementation of the World Heritage Convention. It was drafted with the specific intention of stopping the construction of the dam. The constitutional bases on which such a piece of legislation could be enacted had been canvassed both within the Labor Party and by the conservation movement. As drafted and enacted, the legislation drew on the Federal Government's corporations power, the "people of any race" power, and the external affairs power. The legislative powers of the Commonwealth Parliament are found primarily in section 51 of the Australian Constitution. The Preamble and relevant provisions of section 51 are:

> "The Parliament shall, subject to this Constitution, have power to make laws for the peace, order, and good government of the Commonwealth with respect to:
>
> - (xx) Foreign corporations, and trading or financial corporations formed within the limits of the Commonwealth;
> - (xxvi) The people of any race, for whom it is deemed necessary to make special laws;
> - (xxix) External affairs."

It is well to note that in Australian constitutional interpretation, there is no requirement that Commonwealth legislation be exclusively about one of the granted heads of power. Indeed, there is no requirement that in terms of its intent or practical effect, the legislation be primarily, predominantly or even substantially concerned with the granted head of power...In other words, the fact that there is no specific Commonwealth power over the environment, or over mining or natural resources, in no way prevents the Commonwealth from legislating with respect to those matters, provided the law is also, in a formal sense, a law "with respect to" one of the granted heads of power.

Although there was no obvious link between these three heads of power and the protective provisions of the *World Heritage Properties Act* 1983, these provisions were based primarily on these Constitutional powers.

Three sections of the Act specifically alluded to the external affairs, corporations, and "people of any race" powers. As anticipated, the Tasmanian government immediately challenged the Act in the High Court. In a 4-3 judgment, the Court upheld the Act, ruling that the Federal Government could use both the external affairs power and the corporations power under the Australian Constitution almost without limitation. The external affairs power, the Court held, would enable the Federal Government to resolve environmental disputes so as to meet Australia's international obligations. The corporations power, furthermore, allowed the Federal Government to regulate as a separate matter the activities of trading and financial corporations. A majority of the High Court specifically held that the Hydro-Electric Commission was a trading corporation, because of its sale of electricity. The Commonwealth Parliament, through the corporations power, was able to control the activities of the Commission with respect to construction of the dam, by virtue of section 10(4) of the Act.

The Franklin Dam decision also rested in part on a precedent set in *Koowarta v. Bjelke-Petersen*, which had held that the Federal Government had the power to enact laws against racial discrimination because Australia had signed the *International Racial Discrimination Convention*. In *Koowarta*, the Court had to decide whether the Federal Government's external affairs power under Section 51 of the *Australian Constitution* allowed it to enact legislation to implement the provisions of treaties at a domestic level regardless of the treaty's subject matter (the "wide" view), or whether it could enact legislation to implement only those treaties whose subject matter could be described as "international in character" (the "narrow" view).

The nomination of Kakadu National Park in the Northern Territory to the World Heritage List has been the subject of controversy for some years.

The minority judges in *Koowarta* expressed the "narrow" view of the power, stating: "A law which carries into effect the provisions of an international agreement will only have the character of a law with respect to external affairs if the provisions [of the legislation] to which it gave effect answer that description." The minority opinion held that those laws which operate only internally and which involve no relationship with persons, things, or countries outside Australia did not implicate the Federal Government's external affairs power.

Because the majority judges took different approaches in their opinions, it is difficult to state precisely what the decision stood for. One commentor's view was that "in a negative sense, *Koowarta* was authority for the proposition that there is no requirement, in ascertaining whether a treaty is 'international in character,' that the treatment of the subject matter must involve a physical or transactional relationship between Australia and other countries." Justice Stephen held that it would be sufficient if the matter was of "international concern" for the subject matter of the treaty to be regarded as "international in character."

In the *Franklin Dam* Case, the High Court ultimately upheld this "wide" view. In effect, this meant that the *World Heritage Properties Conservation Act* implementing the *World Heritage Convention* was sufficient to make that legislation valid under the external affairs power. The implications of this view raise questions concerning the political nature of constitutional interpretation. Under the "wide" view of the application of the external affairs power, it is possible for the Federal Government to enact a broad range of legislation which would override the legislative powers of the states pursuant to the "inconsistency" clause in the Constitution. The temptation to do so, however, is constrained by political limitations imposed by the strongly held views of "states'—righters." This type of limitation has been referred to as an expression of the "political" constitution, as distinct from the formal or "legal" constitution, or, put another way, the "real" as opposed to the "imagined" constitution.

The Nomination of Kakadu National Park

The nomination of Kakadu National Park in the Northern Territory to the World Heritage List has been the subject of controversy for some years. The Federal Government established the 17,000 square kilometer park in 1978. It has great ecological value and scenic beauty and includes a number of examples of Aboriginal rock art and Aboriginal cultural sites of world significance. It contains some of the earliest recorded rock art and ceremonial and spiritual places.

The first stage of Kakadu was listed under the *World Heritage Convention* in 1981 and the second stage in 1987. Stage three is presently undergoing nomination procedures. The Aboriginal people own the park pursuant to the *Aboriginal Land Rights (Northern Territory) Act* with an arrangement for a lease-back to the Federal Government.

The controversy erupted, among other reasons, because the area has valuable mineral potential. Within the boundaries of the park, but excised from it, sits the Ranger Uranium Mine, which has operated for some years. Because of the mine within its boundaries, conservationists have characterized the park as having "a hole in its heart." It was this mine, and the environmental inquiry which paved the way for its approval, that prompted the creation of the park. Other mining interests, eager for a slice of the action, launched a number of cases in the Federal and High Courts to block nomination of the various stages of Kakadu National Park. These efforts have met with a consistent lack of success.

Controversy still rages, however, about stage three. This stage comprises the southern end of the park, which shows high potential for mineral exploitation. In 1985, the Federal Government announced a five-year exploration period in an area it called the "conservation zone" (in reality, the "exploration zone"). The Government has yet to declare the commencement of that five-year period. At that point, the zone comprised some 2,252 square kilometers of the park. The estimated total worth of minerals in this zone was originally estimated to be between seven and fifteen billion Australian dollars. The park includes at least 1,275 types of plants, 280 types of birds (a third of the total Australian bird species), more than 100 different types of reptiles, more than 62 mammal species, 77 fish species, and an estimated 10,000 species of insects.

Conservation and mining interests have focused in the past few years on a one square kilometer area around Coronation Hill, a former uranium mine. This area may contain more than one million ounces of gold and is rich in platinum and palladium. Aboriginal owners of the site call it "sickness country" because they believe that a legendary figure, Bula, lived on it, and that Bula would bring retribution and death if the land were disturbed.

In late 1989, because of pressure by conservation interests, and directly contrary to the wishes of the Northern Territory government and mining interests, the Federal Government withdrew 98 percent of the conservation zone from mining development. Although the decision was popular, it left open to mining the 2 percent of the area known as "Coronation Hill," which contains both a high percentage of the zone's minerals and the most environmentally sensitive species. Although the federal Resource Assessment Commission was given a reference for an inquiry to resolve the issue, the decision on the mining of Coronation Hill was delayed until the Commission had conducted a single, coherent assessment of the economic, social, environmental, and cultural considerations relating to land uses. The whole of the newly reduced inquiry period happily coincided with the March 1990 federal election, in which the Federal Government used its environmental record, and especially the conservation of Kakadu, as an election issue.

When the Commission finally reported in early 1991, it indicated that the environmental aspects of the mining proposal, though significant, were not as important as the issues concerning Aboriginal cultural matters, in particular the social impact on the traditional Aboriginal owners, the Jawoyn. The Federal Government decided that mining would not be permitted in the Conservation Zone, and that the whole area would be added to the Kakadu National Forest. In effect, this means that it will be included in the already listed World Heritage Area...

Lawyers in World Heritage and Other Environmental Disputes

The World Heritage disputes in Australia in the past few years have featured large contingents of lawyers in various court actions, as chairs for most of the public inquiries, and as representatives of the major participants. The involvement of lawyers almost inevitably prolongs the decision-making process. Protracted proceedings, in turn, often make full participation by ordinary citizens difficult because of the time and expense involved. The use of legal aid funds in Australian public interest environmental legal actions is not widespread, and members of conservation groups are normally not able to fund their own actions. Development interests and governments, on the other hand, have the capacity to inject large sums of money into this type of litigation. It is perhaps time that governments realized that resolving these issues with the broadest possible participation is clearly in the public interest. Certain jurisdictions have begun to accept intervenor funding as a way to assist public interest participants.

Notwithstanding financial and time problems, most environmental and heritage disputes in Australia are resolved judicially, particularly when conflicts arise between federal and state governments. Courts and quasi-judicial tribunals, in contrast to inquiry processes, usually have the advantage of settled procedures to test evidence and to make final decisions. Inquiries generally have the power only to make recommendations to government...

Future Disputes in Australia

The federal system of government, as it is practiced in Australia, will no doubt continue to generate environmental disputes between the Federal Government and the states and territories...

In future years, disputants will probably use a broader range of mechanisms to resolve environmental conflicts. These include increasingly sophisticated negotiation and mediation techniques, and environmental "round tables" at the government and intergovernment level. Specially constituted tribunals and courts dealing with environmental, as opposed to general, issues have some hope of coping with the complex problems often involved in environmental disputes. The men and women who constitute the specialist bodies can build up a range of expertise not possible in generalist bodies.

It does appear likely that public interest litigation, because of a broader range of inputs, has a greater guarantee of generating decisions which not only reflect the broad public interest, but also have some hope of attaining ecologically sound decisions. In Australia, decisions made by courts and Commissions of Inquiry on World Heritage matters could be said to be overly legalistic. This is hardly surprising, given the parameters within which courts and inquiries operate. However, once judicial decisions or inquiry recommendations are handed down, the remaining questions which involve conflicting values are often resolved politically–-and haphazardly. The introduction of more uniform legislation in environmental matters by the states or the enactment at the federal level of more broadly applicable environmental and heritage legislation may bring more coherence and consistency into the process of environmental decision making. Although this would be most conveniently done on the basis of a constitutional amendment giving the Federal Government power over national environmental matters, it seems to be clear that as a result of the World Heritage cases in the High Court, the Federal Government can enforce environmental regulations under the Constitution's external affairs and corporations powers.

B

Nepal

(i) Belbase N., "Country Reports: Nepal" *Asia Pacific Journal of Environmental Law*, 1996, pp 93–104

Introduction

Nepal is confronted with a series of conflicts due to poverty, increasing population and environmental degradation. Kathmandu, the capital city, is growing at a rate in excess of 7 percent per annum largely as a result of movement of people from rural areas. Out-migration from rural areas is creating many social changes. The relationship between people and natural resources is also changing as a result of these social changes.

Environmental pollution is a serious problem throughout urban Nepal. The situation is acute in Kathmandu, where the discharge of raw sewage and industrial effluent into the Bagmati river has severally degraded the rivers, particularly in the dry season. Emissions from vehicles, brick kilns and a large cement factory have caused the air quality to be significantly worse than WHO standards. The quality of drinking water in Kathmandu is very poor due to bacterial contamination. Because of the low level of industrialization, pollution from industrial sources is low compared to municipal sewer and solid waste.

Community forestry programmes have improved the quality of forests in Middle Hills. In many areas, forests are increasing and the density is improving. Policy and legislation have drastically changed to bring them into line with the reality of rural conditions. However, the condition of the forests in the high mountains (above 2,000 meters) and on the Terai (the southern flat area) is deteriorating steadily above the zone of permanent cultivation. There are very few community forestry programmes in the Terai and virtually no programmes in high-elevation forests.

Nepal is well known for its natural and cultural heritage. The cultural heritage of Nepal has a long history dating back to approximately the first century BC. The art and architecture of Nepal, expressed in terms of stone and bronze images, wood carvings, scroll paintings, wall paintings, temples, monasteries and mosques speaks of the rich national heritage. Nepal is rich in natural heritage as well. The main efforts by governments in natural-heritage conservation have involved an extensive network of national parks and protected areas developed over the past two decades, covering more than 15,000 square kilometres, about 14 percent of Nepal's total land area. The protected-area network includes eight national parks, four wildlife reserves, two conservation areas and one hunting reserve. Sagarmatha and Royal Chitwan National Parks have been included on the World Heritage List due to their outstanding natural values, and the Koshi Tappu Wildlife Reserve has been included in the List of Wetlands of International Importance under the 1971 *Convention on Wetlands of International Importance Especially as Waterfowl Habitat.*

However, these resources are facing pressure and encroachment. The pressures of population growth, uncontrolled development, poverty, tourism, inadequate legislation and social breakdown have all contributed to a perilous situation. Conflicts have developed between local residents and authorities in areas surrounding some of the designated protected areas and national parks. In order to improve the relationship between the local communities and park management, and ensure effective protection of

World Heritage Sites, the buffer-zone concept is being introduced. It is intended that 30–50 percent of the revenue generated by the parks be spent on community development in the buffer-zone areas. Areas adjacent to cultural and historical monuments and religious shrines are being damaged by encroachment, poor maintenance and unsanitary conditions. Excessive congestion along the most popular trekking and mountaineering routes is leading to an accumulation of solid waste and localized deforestation.

The Nepal country office of the IUCN (the World Conservation Union) has critically reviewed cultural-conservation programs and agencies in Nepal. To support government initiatives, IUCN has developed a register of national heritage sites and a database encompassing 1,500 heritage sites of national importance. However, the register has not been made public yet because of the Government's ineffective security arrangements. This work supplements the *Master Plan for the Conservation of Cultural Heritage in the Kathmandu Valley*, which was prepared by UNDP and UNESCO in 1977…

Legislative and Policy Measures for Implementing the World Heritage Convention in Nepal

Nepal became a party to the *World Heritage Convention* in June 1978. Nepal's seven cultural-heritage sites and two natural-heritage sites are inscribed on the World Heritage List. Although Nepal has taken various legislative and policy measures for the conservation of national heritage, Nepal's obligations in fulfilling the requirements of protecting cultural heritage sites listed on the World Heritage List has to date been unsatisfactory. The UNESCO/International Council of Monuments and Sites (ICOMOS) Review Mission of 14-30 November 1993 highlighted the threats to cultural heritage in Nepal. It recommended that several World Heritage Sites of the Kathmandu Valley be placed on the List of World Heritage in Danger. The sites are only to be returned to the World Heritage List within a period of one to three years, after 16 specific matters of concern are met. This is not a recent phenomenon. In 1989, on the tenth anniversary of the nomination of the Kathmandu Valley to the World Heritage List, Professor W. Brown Morton III inspected all seven sites to evaluate the degree to which their inclusion on the World Heritage List had contributed to their preservation. He found uncontrolled new development everywhere, including development within the boundaries of the World Heritage Sites. The American Folklife Center's paper shows a disturbing picture of the World Heritage Sites:

> "Worst of all, [Professor Morton] discovered that the Department had somehow managed to lose the original maps he had developed with them in 1979 to establish the boundaries for the World Heritage nomination, and, in the interim, the government had adopted new, and in every case, smaller boundaries for the sites. In short, it became quite clear that inclusion on the World Heritage List as Cultural Heritage of 'Outstanding Universal Value' had little or no effect on the preservation of the sites themselves, in spite of six of the seven sites having been officially designated as protected monuments zone by the Government in 1987."

Some of the conditions set by the 1993 Joint UNESCO/ICOMOS Review Mission included:

- delimiting the boundaries of the heritage sites; publishing them in the Government Gazette;
- preparing an inventory of public and religious monuments; mapping heritage sites;
- preparation of master plans for renovation or preservation;
- controlling expansion of the city within heritage sites;
- stopping demolition of structures in monument zones;
- implementation of the *Ancient Monuments Preservation Act*; and
- restricting vehicular traffic.

The most important and the first condition put forth by the UNESCO/ICOMOS Review Mission was "that the next [fifth] amendment to the *Ancient Monuments Preservation Act* should be consistent with the *Convention Concerning the Protection of the World Cultural and Natural Heritage* and its guidelines." To date, initial steps taken by Nepal to meet these concerns include the restriction of vehicular traffic in and around ancient palace squares of the Kathmandu Valley and a ban on demolishing structures belonging to monument areas.

With respect to the conservation of natural heritage, Nepal has been relatively successful in fulfilling its obligations primarily through the implementation of the *National Parks and Wildlife Conservation Act* 1972. The IUCN in Nepal has been monitoring the status of the Royal Chitwan National Park and Sagarmatha National Park for the past two years and is satisfied with the level of protection being afforded these sites.

Policy Measures

National Conservation Strategy

Nepal was one of the first countries to prepare a National Conservation Strategy (NCS) in 1987. Preparation of the NCS involved inputs from a substantial cross-section of concerned Nepalese. More than 100 meetings were held in villages and towns across Nepal to solicit views on resource-conservation problems. These inputs and others were distilled and shaped into the NCS, which provides a long-term perspective on natural-resource management in Nepal.

The NCS recognizes the exceptional wealth of Nepal's cultural heritage and its importance at the local, national and international levels. It indicates that theft, damage and, in some cases, destruction of idols, monuments, temples and other physical assets of Nepal's cultural heritage and encroachment on heritage sites, religious forests and sacred grounds has occurred and continue to occur at an increasing rate. In response to these concerns the *NCS Conservation Action Agenda* recommended, inter alia, that:

(a) the Department of Archaeology undertakes responsibility for the protection of national heritage;

(b) public awareness of the value of heritage and the public's participation in the maintenance and protection of such property be improved; and

(c) urban and regional land-use planning and city planning be undertaken on a scale that will protect and enhance heritage sites and monuments, buildings of cultural value and religious and sacred grounds.

In relation to natural heritage, the *NCS Conservation Action Agenda* for national parks and protected areas identifies gaps in the present network of protected areas. In particular there is a shortage of sites necessary for the preservation of biological diversity, sites of unique scientific and research value and sites having significant cultural, archaeological or historical value. One of the recommendations to enable the better selection of protected areas is for the current broad classification of geographic divisions to be refined, taking into account other factors like flora and fauna. Furthermore, where a park or protected area is proposed, the preparation of management plans in consultation with the local communities is recommended. A 1994 assessment of Nepal's conservation of protected areas assessed the present network of parks and protected areas as incomplete, with not all physiographic zones fully represented, despite the NCS recommendations six years before. Physiographic zones poorly represented include tropical mixed evergreen forests, temperate broadleaf forests and particularly the middle mountain region with only 1 per cent of protected area.

Nepal Environmental Policy and Action Plan

The *Nepal Environmental Policy and Action Plan* (*NEPAP*) was prepared in 1993 in response to the World Bank's instruction to the government to prepare an Environment Action Plan in order to qualify for IDA credit. The *NEPAP* identifies that one of the most serious threats to heritage sites in urban areas is uncoordinated development that results in unsuitable buildings being erected close to temples, shrines and other important monuments. *NEPAP* maintains:

> "The solution of preserving Nepal's cultural heritage lies in developing local institutions to support heritage sites that local people value, and encouraging international institutions to support sites whose importance extends beyond national concerns, and for which local resources may not be sufficient for adequate preservation."

Nepal is faced with various constraints in maintaining its heritage including a lack of information, legislative measures and institutional arrangements. Therefore, *NEPAP's* recommendations include the preparation of a detailed strategy document for cultural-heritage preservation; developing Heritage Conservation Action Plans; assessing the effectiveness of the Guthi Sansthan in providing resources for preserving cultural sites and the investigation of possible alternative institutional arrangements; and developing a priority listing of heritage sites in need of preservation and/or restoration.

C
Philippines

(i) Blastique T.T., "Case Study: *World Heritage Convention* for Biodiversity Conservation in the Philippines," paper presented at the 2nd *ECPA Forum on Protected Areas in Asia-Pacific,* 5–12 December 1998, Pakse, Lao PDR

Introduction

On November 16, 1972, the General Conference of UNESCO adopted the International Treaty called the *Convention Concerning the Protection of the World Cultural and Natural Heritage*...[T]he Philippine Government did not ratify it until September 19, 1985. The long delay can be attributed to the fact that during the 1970s, the conservation movement in the Philippines did not have much strength as the development approach adopted by the country was anchored more on the exploitation of its natural resources...

Inscriptions/Nominations to the World Heritage List

...At present, the Philippines has three sites inscribed in the World Heritage List, and two sites under nomination. The inscribed sites include one natural heritage––the Tubbataha Reefs National Marine Park (TRNMP), while the two cultural heritage sites include the Baroque Churches and the Rice Terraces of the Cordilleras. The two sites under nomination include the St. Paul Subterranean National Park as a possible World Natural Heritage Site, and the Historic Town of Vigan as a possible World Cultural Heritage Site....

Baroque Churches

Description

...[F]our churches were inscribed into the World Cultural Heritage List as outstanding examples of the Philippines' interpretation of the Baroque style.

The Church of the Immaculate Conception of San Agustin is box-like and rather plain. Two-bell towers were added to the squat facade in 1854, but the northern cracked in the 1880 earthquake and had to be demolished. The interior of the church is more important than the exterior. The existing wall painting dates from the 19th century, but research has shown that they overlie the original tempera murals. Of special interest is the series of cryptocollateral chapels lining both sides of the nave. The wall separating them act as buttresses, similar to the Wandpfeiler of German Baroque churches. The stone vault, dome, and arched vestibule are all unique in the Philippines. A monastery complex was formerly linked to the church by a series of cloisters, arcades, country yards, and gardens, but all except one building were destroyed in 1945.

Unlike other town churches in the Philippines, which conform with the Spanish tradition of siting them on the central plaza, the Church of Nuestra Seòora de la Asuncion in Santa Maria with its convent are on a hill completely surrounded by a sturdy defensive wall. Also unusual is the siting of the convent parallel to the facade of the church and that of the separate bell tower (characteristics of Philippine-Hispanic architecture) at the midpoint of the nave wall. This arrangement was dictated by the topography of the hill on which it is situated.

Built in brick, the Church of Nuestra Seòora de la Asuncion follows the standard Philippine layout, with a monumental facade masking a straight roofline covering a long rectangular building. It is alleged to have been built on a solid raft as a precaution against earthquake damage. The walls are devoid of ornament but have delicately carved side entrances and strong buttresses, also designed to resist earthquakes. The curved pediment motif is repeated in the church, school, and cemetery.

The Church of Santo Tomas de Villanueva stands on the highest point of Miag ao, with its towers serving as lookouts against Moslem raids. These and the squat appearance of the Church underline its role as a fortress, and as the finest surviving example of "fortress Baroque". The sumptuous facade epitomizes the Filipino transfiguration of western decorative elements, with the figure of St. Christopher on the pediment dressed in native clothes, carrying the Christ Child on his back, and holding on to a coconut palm for support. Massive tapering bell towers of unequal heights flank the entire riotously decorated facade.

The Church of San Agustin at Paoay is considered to be the most outstanding example in the Philippines of "earthquake Baroque," first defined by Pal Kelman in

The long delay can be attributed to the fact that during the 1970s, the conservation movement in the Philippines did not have much strength as the development approach adopted by the country was anchored more on the exploitation of its natural resources.

relation to Latin America. Fourteen buttresses are ranged along the lines of a giant volute supporting a smaller one and surmount by pyramidal finials. A pair of buttresses at the midpoint of each nave wall serve as stairways for access to the roof. The lower part of the apse and most of the walls are constructed of coral stone blocks, the upper levels being finished in brick; but this order is reversed on the facade. The massive coral stone bell tower, which was added half a century after the church was completed, stands at some distance from the church, again as a protection against damage during earthquakes.

Process and Criteria for Inscription

The National Commission on Culture and Arts was created in 1991 to coordinate the work of a committee that facilitated the preparation of the nomination dossier of the Baroque Churches. The dossier for these sites were submitted [in]...November 1992, while the actual inscription into the World Heritage List took place during its 17th committee Session held at Columbia in December 1993.

The inscription of the Baroque Churches into the World Heritage List was based on Criteria (ii) and (iv). This group of churches features a style of building and design that was adapted to the physical conditions in the Philippines, and had an important influence on later church architecture in the region (Criterion (ii)). The Baroque Churches of the Philippines represent the fusion of European church design and construction with local materials and decorative motifs to form a new church-building tradition.

Rice Terraces of the Philippine Cordilleras

Description

The Rice Terraces of the Cordilleras are obviously an unmistakable example of a landscape resulting from the combined works of nature and man, illustrating the evolution of human society and settlement over time, under the influence and physical constraints presented by their natural environment and successive social, economic and cultural forces.

The Rice terraces are an expression of the Ifugao's mastery of the watershed ecology and terrace engineering. It is also a complex farming system consisting not only of the terrace ponds but also the swidden farms and the *muyongs* (advocate private forest). All of these components of the terrace system must be taken together if the terraces are to be considered and maintained.

The inscription of the Rice Terraces of the Philippine Cordilleras into the World Heritage List was based on the criteria (iii), (iv) and (v). The Rice Terraces of the Philippine Cordilleras are outstanding examples of living cultural landscapes. They illustrate the traditional techniques and remarkable harmony between humankind and the natural environment.

Process and Criteria for Inscription

The nomination process of the Rice Terraces began in 1992. A series of consultations with local communities and government agencies was organized through the initiative of the Philippine World Heritage Committee and the Cordillera Administrative Region Office of the Department of Tourism. The consultations led to the first interagency meeting held [in]...March 1993. Due to the press releases regarding the consultation process and the clamor for an institution that will oversee the conservation of the site, the President of the Philippine Government created the Ifugao Rice Terraces Commission in 1994. During that same year the Rice Terraces of the Cordilleras were nominated to the World Heritage List. Subsequently, in December 1995, the Rice Terraces were inscribed during the 19th Session of the World Heritage Committee in Berlin, Germany.

Historic Town of Vigan, Ilocos Sur

Description

This historic town...has an area of around 2,740 hectares. It is located in the province of Ilocos Sur, situated close to the northeast tip of the Luzon Island. The approximate area of the Historic Core Zone is 12.75 hectares; while that of the Buffer Zone of Vigan is 12.75 hectares.

Vigan belongs to the 18th and 19th century network of Asian trading cities whose lifestyle and architecture blend Asian and western culture such as Malacca, Penang, Pekalongan, Goa, Macau, Singapore and Hoi-An. In contrast to these cities, however, Vigan shows a distinctly Filipino approach in adapting to the current of architectural concepts [prevalent] throughout Asia in that era.

Process and Criteria for Inscription

In February 1975, the National Museum, in cooperation with the Ministry of Tourism and the provincial government of Vigan, organized a seminar in Vigan for the homeowners of the ancestral houses, local officials, local ecclesiastical representatives, teachers and civic leaders. This paved the way for the management of this cultural heritage by various groups and to its nomination in August 1987 to the World Heritage List. This nomination was referred back, however, because no inventory had been conducted of the houses. Renomination of the Vigan Houses to the World Heritage was submitted in 1991 together with an inventory of Vigan homes. In 1995, or after four years, a conservation plan for the Historic Center was prepared including a survey and analysis of maps of the sites. In 1996, the inventory of 120 Vigan Ancestral Homes was completed, while in 1997, a mission to assist the Save Vigan Homes Association Inc. (SVAHAI) was undertaken. With more initiatives in place, the nomination dossier for the Historic Town of Vigan to the World Heritage List was resubmitted in April 1998.

Vigan is unique among Philippine towns and cities because it is the country's most extensive and only surviving historic town that dates from the 18th century Spanish colonial era. It is an urban center of remarkable visual and architectural unity. Its inscription into the World Heritage List can be attributed to its satisfaction of criteria (ii) to (v) for world heritage sites. Criterion (ii) requires proposed sites to exhibit an important interchange of human values, over a span of time or within a cultural area of the world, on developments in architecture or technology, monumental arts or town planning and landscape design. Vigan, part of the 18th and 19th century network of Asian trading cities, demonstrates a unique architecture that effortlessly fuses Ilocano, Filipino, Chinese and Spanish influences. It also demonstrates, in a tropical Asian setting rather than in the New World, the typical Spanish colonial urban layout as specified by the Ley de las Indias, thus linking Vigan to another network of colonial cities in Latin America.

Criterion (iii) requires sites to bear a unique or at least exceptional testimony to a cultural tradition or to a civilization which is living or which has disappeared. Vigan is testimony to the Filipino cultural traditions and lifestyle of the 18th, 19th and 20th centuries. Its domestic architecture allows business to be conducted on the ground floor and for the family to reside above [and] reflects deep kinship with its Asian neighbours, where entrepreneurs preferred to live and work out of their houses. The lifestyle gave rise to streets lined with shop-houses, similar to the rows of narrow streets. The urban ensemble of Vigan is a group of buildings that, because of its architecture, its homogeneity, its place in and relationship to the landscape, is truly of outstanding universal value from the point of view of history and art.

Criterion (iv) requires that sites bear an outstanding example of a type of building or architectural or technological ensemble of landscape that illustrates a significant change in human history. The architecture of Vigan is truly reflective of its roots. It is built from the wood, tone shells and (*kapis*), and terracotta garnered from its surrounding. The houses are in the traditional bahay na bato (house of stone) style where the ground floor is covered with stone walls and the upper level is constructed entirely out of wood. A variant to the style exists in Vigan where both stories of some houses are built entirely of stone or brick.

Criterion (v) requires that sites [are] to serve as an outstanding example of a traditional human settlement or land use that is representative of a culture (or cultures) especially when it has become vulnerable under the impact of irreversible change. Vigan is well known in the Philippines as the last urban area that has maintained its architecture and urban planning that was established during the Spanish colonial era. Modernization and progress are pressuring the transformation of many structures in the Historic Core Zone as well as the buffer zone. However, Vigan is determined to maintain its authenticity...

Legal and Institutional Framework for the Management of World Heritage Sites in the Philippines

The nomination and inscription of selected sites in the country as part of the World Heritage List led to the creation of site-specific institutions tasked with ensuring the protection and management of the sites...

Baroque Churches of the Philippines

The central agency responsible for overall maintenance of the churches is the National Commission on Culture and Arts created in 1991. It has the role of coordinating the work of a committee for each property with representatives from the following national agencies and organizations: ICMOS Philippines; Department of Tourism; Department of

Education, Culture and Sports; National Museum; Historical Institute; and the concerned provincial and local authorities.

Only the Manila Church is the subject of a management plan, drawn up by the Municipal Administration of Intramuros. It was designated as a Special Historic Zone by the municipality, which makes the services of its conservation architects available for work...

Indigenous cultural heritage is a very significant question in Asia and the Pacific, particularly in those countries, or parts of countries where traditional communities continue to exist on a subsistence basis.

Historic Town of Vigan

The Philippine Government as evidenced by the existing national and municipal legislation to protect the site is committed to the preservation of the Historic Town of Vigan. Programs of the Department of Tourism, National Museum, National Historical Institute, and the National Commission for Culture and Arts focus on the preservation of various aspects of the unique cultural heritage of Vigan.

The National Commission for Culture and the Arts is concentrating on a series of awareness programs and skills training workshops to increase the level of awareness to conservation and to improve the level of skills and technical proficiency for the conservation of Vigan. The National government has set up the Vigan Heritage Commission with the mandate to coordinate the conservation programs for Vigan...

Rice Terraces of the Philippine Cordilleras

The Ifugao Rice Terraces Commission established in 1994 ensures the preservation of the terraces and has identified the following areas as its priorities:

A. Natural Hazard Management Program
   - Assessment and monitoring of geologic activities in the active faults existing within the site;
   - Delineation of hazard zones; definition of building; and
   - Prevention of landslides through slope stabilization (reforestation, engineering interventions).

B. Agricultural Management Program
   - Increase productivity;
   - Agricultural zoning to determine which terraces are to be planted to rice and which can be planted to higher value crops.

C. Watershed Management Program
   - Stabilization of watershed ecology;
   - Re-establishment of awareness of importance of maintaining good forest cover;
   - Advocate private forest (muyong) as sustainable forest management scheme; and
   - Improvement of water supply.

D. Transport Development Program
   - Improvement of road network.

E. Tourism Development
   - development of a tourism program sensitive to the site and its culture, and
   - involvement of the population in tourism activities and programs.

4

Indigenous Cultural Heritage

A

Boer B., Ramsay R., and Rothwell D.R., "Conservation of Natural and Cultural Heritage," *International Environmental Law in the Asia Pacific,* Kluwer, 1998, pp 87-91

[*Indigenous cultural heritage is an aspect of the existing and emerging regimes to recognize the comprehensive rights of indigenous peoples and their aspirations for self-determination. The reader should refer to Chapter 1 for a discussion of this wider context of indigenous cultural heritage.*]

Indigenous Cultural Heritage

Indigenous Cultural Heritage in Asia and the Pacific

Indigenous cultural heritage is a very significant question in Asia and the Pacific, particularly in those countries, or parts of countries where traditional communities continue to exist on a subsistence basis. The dispersal of indigenous peoples as distinct groups has been an ongoing process in Asia and the Pacific region, particularly in those countries where there has been pressure, often external, to exploit natural resources such as minerals or forests (including in Australia and New Zealand). The culture, language and traditional knowledge of those groups is often lost before it is adequately documented.

The legal protection of indigenous cultural heritage is not well developed in most Asia and the Pacific countries, with the international instruments and declarations cited above not having any substantial effect domestically. On one level, the need to set up formal systems of protection is an indicator of how the traditional cultural systems are breaking down. On another level, it is an indicator of the increasing awareness on the part of non-indigenous people of the value of indigenous knowledge and culture, both intrinsically and in terms of its instrumental value for environmental management. In some countries, the encroachment of and impact on indigenous lands, particularly through logging and mining, has been culturally destructive and politically controversial, with accusations of breaches of human rights being leveled at national governments.

The category of "associative cultural landscapes" under the *World Heritage Convention* and its *Operational Guidelines* is seen as particularly relevant to this region, "where the link between the physical and spiritual aspects of landscape is so important. This is especially so given the nature of cultural practices of indigenous peoples and of long-standing migration patterns through Asia to Australia and across the Pacific ocean."

In the Pacific region, there is an awareness in many countries of the need to protect indigenous material and intangible heritage, including oral traditions. [Elisabeth Harding] gives a flavor of Southwest Pacific island heritage matters, and illustrates the problem of defining it, and therefore using mechanisms to protect it:

> "The cultural heritage of Pohnpei represents both the foundation upon which rests modern Pohnpeian society, and the identity of the Pohnpeian people. Pohnpeian cultural identity is reflected in the Pohnpeian language and its unique oral traditions. Although oral traditions are frequently associated with natural features of the landscape, such as natural depressions, large coral boulders, or lengthy stretches of land, traditions also respect an intangible heritage. Intangibles like community practices, information or ideas are often exchanged and celebrated through oral traditions."

Some southwest Pacific island states have enacted legislation to address cultural heritage, though not specifically in order to implement international conventions. Nevertheless, some of the present legislation could be used to that effect.

In Australia and New Zealand, various pieces of legislation are directly or indirectly used to maintain indigenous cultural heritage. In New Zealand these include the *Resource Management Act 1991* and the *Treaty of Waitangi Tribunal Act 1975*. In Australia at national level, the *Aboriginal Land Rights (Northern Territory) Act 1976*, the *Aboriginal and Torres Strait Islander Heritage Protection Act 1984* and the *Native Title Act 1993* contribute to the maintenance of Aboriginal and Torres Strait Islander heritage, by recognition of connection with traditional country through statutory land claims and common law native title as well as by the protection of sites and objects of significance for Aboriginal and Torres Strait Islander peoples through various mechanisms.

Intangible Heritage

The protection of intangible heritage is highly problematic, as noted by the Secretary-General of UNESCO, Federico Mayor:

> "Since...intangible culture consists of a whole corpus of languages, knowledge, songs, dances and rites that are transmitted by tradition and have only in very rare cases been transcribed, recorded or described, it can only be handed down from generation to generation by the people who have preserved its memory. This was imaginatively encapsulated by the distinguished sage Amadou Hampate Ba of Mali who, speaking before UNESCO's Executive Board, uttered the still celebrated phrase: 'In Africa, when an old man dies, a library goes up in flames.' Indeed, a very rich heritage of languages, songs and proverbs is in danger of disappearing if care is not taken to collect them while there is still time, so that they can be passed on to future generations."

There are obvious difficulties in attempting to protect intangible heritage through international conventions or domestic legislation. However, the conservation of buildings and other structures, as well as culturally important objects, can themselves contribute substantially to the maintenance of intangible cultural heritage, as can "cultural landscapes." The sub-category of the associative cultural landscape developed in the *Operational Guidelines* under the *World Heritage Convention* is helpful in this regard:

> "The inclusion of such landscapes on the World Heritage List is justifiable by virtue of the powerful religious, artistic or cultural associations of the natural element rather than material cultural evidence, which may be insignificant or even absent."

The question of maintenance of intangible cultural heritage is particularly important in relation to indigenous heritage, in relation to matters of language, skills, lifestyles and ways of living in general.

B

Fergie D., "Federal Heritage Protection Where to Now? Cautionary Tales from South Australia," in Finlayson J. and Jackson-Nakano A. (eds), *Heritage and Native Title: Anthropological and Legal Perspectives*, Native Title Research Unit, Australian Institute of Aboriginal and Torres Strait Islander Studies, Canberra, 1996, pp 40-52

Introduction

In 1995, the Federal Minister for Aboriginal and Torres Strait Islander Affairs faced adverse findings from the Federal Court in respect of separate decisions to protect Aboriginal heritage in the Hindmarsh Island Bridge (South Australia) and Broome Crocodile Farm (Western Australia) cases. In addition, the South Australian Government's Hindmarsh Island Bridge Royal Commission's finding that "women's business" had been "fabricated" made the Federal Government's administration of Aboriginal heritage protection a prominent issue on the national political agenda in the run-up to the 1996 Federal election.

The credibility problem faced by the Commonwealth in respect of heritage protection is a far broader issue than Aboriginal heritage. The Federal Government's administration of the *World Heritage Properties Conservation Act* 1983 (hereafter the World Heritage Act) has been no less a prominent and contentious issue on the Australian political agenda. The application of each of these Acts by Federal Governments shares some important characteristics and problems. Recent South Australian cases provide cautionary tales to be considered when addressing the shortcomings of Federal heritage protection processes in Australia.

In this paper I suggest that an evaluation of Federal practice would profit from a comparative analysis of the broadest context of heritage recognition and protection in Australia. As a contribution to such an analysis, I present some preliminary thoughts on two cases from South Australia with which I have some familiarity--the Lake Eyre Basin World Heritage proposal and the Hindmarsh Island Bridge case.

Heritage Protection: A Demarcation Dispute?

Heritage protection in Australia is a complicated matter. In part, this is a consequence of the division of powers between the Commonwealth and the States under the Australian constitution. Each of the States and Territories has in place their own legislation and administrative structures to protect and recognize heritage items and values within their boundaries. In addition, the Federal Government has legislation which relates to the recognition and/or protection of heritage within the nation as a whole.

It is the Commonwealth power in the Constitution over Aboriginal and external affairs which gives it power over the States in respect of two areas of heritage recognition and protection. These Federal powers are expressed in and administered through the *Aboriginal and Torres Strait Islander Heritage Protection Act* 1984 (hereafter the *Federal Aboriginal Heritage Act*) on the one hand and the *World Heritage Act* on the other. The Commonwealth also takes responsibility for the listing of items of national heritage as part of the national estate and entails Commonwealth agencies in their protection under the *Australian Heritage Commission Act* 1975.

In respect of the Commonwealth's powers and responsibilities for Aboriginal affairs, its responsibility for the protection of Aboriginal heritage has been exercised most notably through the *Federal Aboriginal Heritage Act*. This Act is regarded as a safety net Act [as explained by the Aboriginal and Torres Strait Islander Commission]:

> "[It] exists essentially to ensure that areas of significance to Aboriginal and Torres Strait Islander people are not under threat of injury or desecration as a result of deficiencies in State or Territory legislation for the protection of such sites and objects, or from a failure by State or Territory administration to apply the protections available to them."

The safety net may thus be brought to bear where areas and objects "of significance to Aboriginal people according to Aboriginal tradition" are not protected by State or Territory legislation. This is possible in particular because of the different orientation to heritage significance between the relevant State/Territory Acts and the Commonwealth. As Ritchie has noted:

> "In many jurisdictions the only laws protecting Aboriginal cultural heritage derive from a period in which Aboriginal culture was conceived of in the past tense and the emphasis was on preserving 'relics'."

The *Federal Aboriginal Heritage Act*, on the other hand, is concerned with the protection of areas and objects of significance to Aboriginal peoples under Aboriginal tradition. In practice, the Federal Act has protected the heritage of 'living tradition'.

The Commonwealth legislation can be invoked when the protective provisions of State and Territory legislation apply to different things from those protected under the Federal Act. The *Federal Aboriginal Heritage Act* may also be brought to bear when, for political or other reasons, a State or Territory declines to use its own statutory powers to protect Aboriginal heritage. This was indeed the circumstance of Federal intervention in the Hindmarsh Island Bridge case.

The other prominent context in which the Commonwealth has taken on heritage protection is in terms of its commitment to the World Heritage Convention, given power through the *World Heritage Act*. The World Heritage listing process in Australia is well-known as the subject of controversy and political conflict. The legislation was put in place in response to a conflict between the Federal Government and the State Government of Tasmania over the Franklin Dam.

Setting the Scene: The Lake Eyre Basin World Heritage Proposal

On the eve of the 1993 Federal election, the Prime Minister, Paul Keating, as part of his party's environment platform, announced:

> "Australia now has ten magnificent World Heritage properties. The International Union for the Conservation of Nature has praised the Federal Labor Government for 'having done more to implement the *World Heritage Convention* than any other single country.' While we are proud of this achievement, we believe that the job is not yet complete...
>
> Today I am pleased to announce that the South Australian Government has agreed to work with the Commonwealth to assess the environmental values of the magnificent and unique Lake Eyre region for World Heritage listing. Once the necessary survey is complete, I am confident that a World Heritage nomination will proceed this year. If eventually accepted by the World Heritage Committee, this will represent a major step onward for the conservation of our fragile arid regions."

The State Labor Government was more subdued about the prospects of the initiative in its answering press release. While noting that his Government welcomed the announcement, the Labor Premier's statement focused on support for the environmental study of the region...

That was in March 1993. The State Government's coolness was underpinned among other things by a strong opposition to the idea within its own ranks. The Minister of Mines, for example, is understood to have strongly opposed the proposal in Cabinet. The position of his department was no doubt deeply affected by the importance of the Roxby Downs uranium mine. Olympic Dam, as it is known, lies just beyond the border of the Basin and is absolutely dependent on water from the Great Artesian Basin just beneath it. There had been an ongoing campaign about the effect which extracting water might have on mound springs and the Great Artesian Basin since the Roxby anti-uranium blockages in the early '80s. Indeed, this seems to be an important facet of the South Australian Conservation Council's original initiation of the Lake Eyre Basin World Heritage proposal in 1985. The mining lobby was also concerned about the threat to other mineral and gas resources in the area (which boasts the Moomba gas fields).

The local pastoral industry was also a significant contributor to the State's export earnings and a significant supplier of domestic markets. Their energetic campaign against the proposal, facilitated by the recent installation of telephones in the area, was a significant cultural development in its own right. Their opposition focused on the Commonwealth's failure to manage successfully similar areas on the World Heritage List. First among their examples was the Willandra Lakes area where, 14 years after listing, no management plan for the area had been set in place. Pastoralists also drew attention to the financial implications for local landholders. They noted the drop in property values in the wake of nomination and the fact that land use can be substantially varied under the provisions of the Federal Act without any obligation on the Government to compensate those who suffer loss as a consequence. This group of stakeholders also drew attention to the absence of assessment and decision-making protocols and, indeed, any necessary obligations for consultation with local stakeholders. A constant theme of the protest was what was to be gained by Federal intervention when it was argued the State Government already had in place land management measures which could effectively protect heritage values in an area of clear economic importance to the State.

Although it was pastoralists and mining interests which led opposition to the initiative, especially with the formation of a coalition of opponents as the Lake Eyre Catchment Protection Group, local Aboriginal politics was also drawn into the matter. A split in the local Aboriginal community expressed itself as a break between the Arabanna Peoples Committee and the Dieri Mitha. The emergence and consolidation of this split in the local Aboriginal community was clear throughout my fieldwork in the area from 1988 to 1990. It has been entrenched since then and is a factor of more recent native title applications. In respect of the World Heritage proposal, each of these groups has aligned itself in a variety of ways with opposing lobby groups and interests. The Dieri Mitha group, for example, is reported to have signed an agreement on consultation and heritage protection matters (among other things) with Western Mining Corporation. The Marree Arabanna Peoples Committee, formed in the context of the Roxby protests, has had long-term and largely informal links with green groups.

Despite the complex web of interests in the Lake Eyre Basin and its fringe areas and the development of increasingly sophisticated opposition, the State Labor Government was committed to legislating what it saw as progressive values in the area. It saw itself as having taken important legislative steps to ensure sensitive environmental management of the region. At the end of the 1980s, and after a long period of contestation and negotiation, the Bannon Labor Government had reformed a variety of State legislation affecting the area. The *Pastoral Act*, for example, was replaced by the *Pastoral Land Management and Conservation Act 1989.* Other legislative initiatives aimed at the management of the region included the *Soil Conservation and Landcare Act 1989* and the *Wilderness Protection Act 1991.*

The cautious commitment of South Australia's Labor Government to the Lake Eyre Basin World Heritage investigation of the grounds for nomination was to be a solitary one. Within months of the Prime Minister's announcement of the Commonwealth's hopes for the Basin, it had become clear that the proposal at this stage would focus on the South Australian part of the Basin. Conservation hopes that the listing might include portions of the Basin in Queensland and the Northern Territory were deferred.

Meanwhile, local opposition, particularly by the Lake Eyre Catchment Protection Group, became focused and well-organized. In May 1993, for instance, hundreds travelled to one of their public meetings held in Birdsville. Speakers included the chief executive of the Queensland Mining Council and the secretary of the Willandra Lakes Protection Group. Though invited to attend and in the region at the time, the Federal Minister, Ros Kelly, declined to attend. Members of the Protection Group subsequently travelled to Canberra to lobby the minister and other members of parliament personally. They sought public support in a variety of ways and were vocal in the demand that their interests be properly considered in any assessment of the proposal.

By mid-December 1994, the South Australian Labor Government had fallen, in the wake of public conviction about massive financial mismanagement. A landslide victory went to the Liberal team of Dean Brown. The Lake Eyre Basin World Heritage proposal was now poised at a brink of State and Federal cross-party politics. Unlike their predecessors, the Liberal Government in South Australia was clear that it did not favor the Lake Eyre Basin World Heritage proposal going forward. Nevertheless, under Federal Minister Ros Kelly, the Commonwealth appeared determined to push the initiative forward despite the non-acquiescence of the new State Government.

Minister Kelly is widely considered to have been the target of a successful Federal Liberal campaign in the controversy which has come to be known as the "sports rorts" affair. In its wake, she resigned from the Parliament and John Faulkner took her place as Federal Minister for the Environment. Under his stewardship a process known as the Lake Eyre Basin "reference group" was instigated. It gave local stakeholders and conservationists a voice in the ministerial consideration of the matter. The creation of the reference group was a political decision with important consequences for the credibility of the assessment process.

For arguably quite separate political reasons, the Federal Labor Government's determination to nominate the Lake Eyre Basin for World Heritage listing gradually became less audible in the run-up to the 1996 election campaign.

The Lake Eyre Basin World Heritage proposal can be read, in large part, as an exemplary case of how not to go about making a proposal for listing and carrying out an evaluation of heritage significance. It seems clear that when the Prime Minister included it in his party's 1993 election platform, insufficient groundwork had been undertaken with the State Government or those who would be directly affected by the initiative. The way it was announced, and its subsequent handling by Minister Kelly, served to fuel conflict, suspicion and anxiety at the local level and to galvanize an effective campaign of opposition by some stakeholders. Minister Faulkner's establishment of a consultative reference group showed more political acumen by making provision for the incorporation of local voices and disparate views in the assessment and decision-making process. One is left to wonder how the matter might have proceeded had he been its overseer from the beginning and had there been established protocols for community consultation and the assessment process.

Perhaps the most important point to make out of the Lake Eyre Basin case is the need for State and Federal initiatives to dovetail in the effective management of the heritage of areas in ways which include, rather than exclude and alienate, those who are at their front line. This issue is highlighted in a Uniting Church Submission to an Inquiry into World Heritage Area made to Government in May 1995. It suggested that, because the *World Heritage Act* was enacted to preserve the Franklin River (an uninhabited "wilderness" area in Tasmania) and because:

> "...the Franklin River was not a complex multiple-use land situation where people were already in residence and earning an income in the area, the legislation appears to have left out the requirements for adequate compensation for dislocation of people, a process for the assessment of a particular area, the production of a management plan, the ongoing management of the area and, for when there are disputes, an appeal system."

A number of these shortcomings are shared with the operation of the *Federal Aboriginal Heritage Act.*

Minister Kelly is widely considered to have been the target of a successful Federal Liberal campaign in the controversy which has come to be known as the "sports rorts" affair.

Setting the Scene: Hindmarsh Island Bridge

A legacy of a Bannon State Labor Government decision also came to a head in the early days of Dean Brown's State Liberal Government. In November 1988, a South Australian development company, Binalong, had applied to extend their marina on Hindmarsh Island. A year later, a draft environmental impact statement had been submitted which included a proposal for the building of a bridge between the town of Goolwa and Hindmarsh Island. The initial proposal had entailed the developers meeting the costs of the building of the bridge in the first instance, with the State Government then contributing towards the costs on the basis of its savings on the existing ferry service. Following serious financial difficulties which came to a head a year later, the company's financiers only agreed to continue financing the project when, in March 1991 (a month after he announced the collapse of the State Bank), Labor Premier John Bannon agreed to a complete reversal of the original funding arrangement for the bridge.

The incoming Liberal minister for transport was to describe the deal in the following terms [during parliamentary debate] in early 1994:

> "The new scheme required the Government to construct the bridge and provide the total funding up front. The scheme also required Binalong to meet in full its obligations to Westpac and also Beneficial Finance Corporation before making any contribution towards the cost of the bridge. This reflected the deteriorating position of the Binalong company and the concerns of its financiers that the company would be unable to meet its obligations.
>
> Notwithstanding this concern, and against the advice of Treasury, the former Government allowed taxpayers' funds to be invested in a bridge at a higher level of risk than the exposure of the financiers of the development of Hindmarsh Island."

Despite the clear public recognition of the perilous state of South Australian financial affairs and particularly the size of the State Government's financial liabilities, in March 1993 the Labor Government, under Bannon's successor, Lynn Arnold, entrenched the State's legal obligation by signing a binding deed between the Minister for Transport and Development, the Goolwa and Port Elliott Local Government Council and Binalong, the marina developers. Despite the clear opposition of the Liberal contenders to the new financial arrangements for the building of the proposed Hindmarsh Island Bridge in the lead up to the State election in December 1993, and notice from Aboriginal peoples that they believed that the developers' obligations to consult with them had not been met, the Liberals were caught in an unusual bind once they came to office. It seemed they were still legally obliged to build the bridge. They appointed a former Royal Commissioner and retired judge to inquire into the matter. The new State Government was reluctantly led to the conclusion that the contract was watertight and that the State, already in serious financial difficulties, would become liable for substantial damages if the Government decided not to proceed with the bridge. Holding costs on construction alone amounted to an estimated $6,000 a day.

In May 1994, the State Government used a provision of its *Aboriginal Heritage Act* 1988 to get it out of its bind. The Minister for Aboriginal Affairs, charged under the Act with the protection of Aboriginal heritage, stated in Parliament: 'I have concluded that I need to authorise damage to the [Aboriginal] sites to allow construction of the bridge to go ahead.' He then informed the House that he had issued an authorization to the Department of Road Transport to do as much damage to Aboriginal sites as was necessary for the building of a bridge to Hindmarsh Island.

On 11 May 1994, nine days after the State Minister had authorized damage to Aboriginal sites, and following requests from Ngarrindjeri people, the Federal Minister issued an emergency declaration banning further disturbance over the immediate bridge area. On 2 May 1994, Professor Cheryl Saunders was appointed the Minister's reporter on the matter under the Act. She invited written submissions to be made to her between 28 May and 11 June 1994. Saunders received in excess of 400 written submissions, an unprecedented number at the time. Even before the final date for receiving written submissions, it was necessary for the Federal Minister to make the second and final 30-day stay of development permitted under Section 9 of the *Federal Aboriginal Heritage Act*. In the week beginning 19 June 1994, Saunders travelled to South Australia to receive verbal submissions on the application, including submissions from Aboriginal women on their claims of relevant secret traditions. I was engaged by their legal representatives, the Aboriginal Legal Rights Movement (ALRM), to facilitate meetings between Ngarrindjeri women and Professor Saunders in that week. It was anticipated at that stage that this 'safety net' role would entail two or three days work. However, on 26 June 1994 the ALRM asked me to prepare a report on the women's tradition which would be forwarded to Saunders as a Supplementary Submission by 1 July 1994. Saunders reported to the Federal Minister on 7 July 1994. On 10 July 1994, following receipt of Saunders' report, Federal (Labor) Minister Tickner banned for 25 years the building of a bridge to Hindmarsh Island.

The Premier of South Australia expressed outrage at this intervention in State affairs by the Commonwealth. Privately produced pamphlets drew attention to the Federal Minister's Hindmarsh Island decision and suggested that the Federal *Aboriginal Heritage Act* amounted to a "Super Mabo". The pamphlets suggested that every Australian's backyard was at risk under the Act.

Compensation was a clear issue with the developers, against whom liquidation proceedings had been halted while the Federal process was carried out, making it clear that they would vigorously pursue a compensation claim through the courts.

The political stakes in this matter ran high. Mrs Wendy Chapman, one of the developers, was Lord Mayor of Adelaide in the early years of John Bannon's Labor premiership. Oean Brown, leader of the opposition and then Liberal Premier, was the local member in the State legislature. The local member in the Federal Parliament was Ian McLachlan, whose political aspirations suffered a serious setback when he resigned his position on the Liberal opposition's front bench in the wake of an indiscretion relating to this matter. Also suffering embarrassment in what has become known as the "McLachlan affair" was another South Australian opposition front bencher, opposition spokesperson on Aboriginal Affairs, Chris Gallus.

McLachlan had sought unsuccessfully to have Federal Minister Tickner's ban overturned on the floor of Parliament in 1994. In late May and early June 1995, allegations were made that the cultural matters which were part of the process under the Federal Act were fabricated. On 8 June 1995, the State Premier announced that he would establish a Royal Commission to investigate these allegations. It was established on 16 July and reported to the Government on 19 December 1995 in the lead up to the announcement of a Federal election. Contesting the claims of the significance in Aboriginal tradition presented to me and Saunders were 13 Ngarrindjeri women and a small number of experts. The Royal Commission, aware that it must tread carefully in the light of both the Australian Constitution and the *Racial Discrimination Act 1975*, proceeded to inquire into the matter with an awesome and powerful display of ethnocentrism. The document which was central to the Commission's terms of reference did not come before the Commission. Nor did the inquiry require that its contents be disclosed. Proponents of those claims, with one parting exception, boycotted the Royal Commission. Nevertheless, the State Government's Royal Commission found unequivocally that "women's lousiness" had been fabricated in order to stop the building of the Hindmarsh Island Bridge.

Within weeks of the conclusion of the Hindmarsh Island Bridge Royal Commission, the Matthews Inquiry—a second inquiry, commissioned by the Federal Labor Government under the Federal *Aboriginal Heritage Act*, into Ngarrindjeri claims that the building of a bridge to Hindmarsh Island would damage or desecrate their tradition—commenced its work. Unless it is held up or stopped in the courts, the Matthews Inquiry is expected to report to the new Federal (Liberal) Minister for Aboriginal and Torres Strait Islander Affairs in June 1996.

Complex political and cultural forces intersected across the three tiers of Australian Government to create the many competing facets of the Hindmarsh Island Bridge case. The matter is still unfolding.

What is already clear in the Hindmarsh Island Bridge case is that a State Liberal Government has successfully used a Royal Commission to undermine Federal Labor intervention into its earlier administration of heritage protection at the State level. In this process, limitations in assessment processes under the Federal *Aboriginal Heritage Act* have been highlighted. This case has brought the general absence of assessment and decision-making protocols, and the limitations of those which are part of the existing Act, into sharp relief.

There are few guidelines for the process of assessment leading to a ministerial decision on heritage status and protection. Indeed, the time constraints of this Act arguably put the assessment process at risk of serious critique, particularly if there is an active debate on the matter among relevant experts or when relevant Aboriginal peoples are in dispute. This is a feature of the more recent history of the Hindmarsh Island Bridge.

In addition, the "safety net" aspect of the Act, intended to locate the Federal *Aboriginal Heritage Act* delicately in respect of State provisions, has particular entailments for the credibility of assessment processes. If the Federal Minister intervenes in response to an emergency under Section 9 of the Federal *Aboriginal Heritage Act*, then the report to the Minister, and quite possibly the longer-term ministerial decision-making process, must be concluded in no more than 60 days from the Emergency Declaration.

In the 60-day period following an Emergency Declaration under the Act, a reporter to the Minister must be appointed, advertise for public submissions, receive and consider them and report to the Minister in time for the Minister in turn to properly consider the matter (and the submissions), consult Cabinet and make a decision in respect of a longer period of protection. Clearly this is not a long period for inquiries and evaluations to be undertaken and advice to be presented.

On the other hand, if the Minister instigates a report under Section 10 of the Act without making an *Emergency Declaration* under Section 9, then the 60-day outside limit does not apply and inquiries can take place and advice be furnished to the Minister over a longer and more realistic period. This is the context in which, as I write, the Matthews Inquiry has so far been operating. The decision to proceed to the making of a Section 10 report, then, is a finely tuned one for it must be established that there is a prima facie case, both in respect of the Aboriginal significance of the area or object and the failure of State or Territory legislation to protect it. The time constraints of the Federal *Aboriginal Heritage Act* are one of the Act's weak points. They present a minister with the problem of potentially acting prematurely and invoking State wrath, and balancing the possibility that waiting too long would necessitate making an Emergency Declaration under Section 9 of the Act. If that occurs, then the process is constrained to take place within the 60-day limit. In this case the process is vulnerable to the kind of attack launched on it in the Hindmarsh Island case by opposing interests.

Two broad consequences of the Hindmarsh Island Bridge case are already clear: the public credibility of heritage protection is undermined at every level of government in Australia; and Aboriginal peoples have had their selves, identity and heritage assaulted in political processes which surrounded a request for the protection of their cultural heritage.

The Hindmarsh Island Bridge case showed up the real limitations of the 60-day limit following an emergency ban. In the Hindmarsh Island Bridge case, an *Emergency Declaration* was made before the appointment of the reporter to the Minister. Work on building the bridge was expected to proceed as soon as the *Emergency Declarations* lapsed. This meant that the Minister's assessment and consideration process had to be concluded within the 60-day limit. The 60-day problem was compounded by further shortcomings, delays and failures in the process.

Nearly a fortnight was lost in the first 30-day *Emergency Declaration* during the period before Professor Saunders was appointed as reporter on 23 May 1994. No expert (anthropological) assistance was appointed to assist her, or the Aboriginal Legal Rights Movement, at that time. I was not appointed as facilitator until 17 June 1994, after almost another month or so had passed and the process had moved a week into the final 30 days of an emergency ban permitted under Section 9 of the Act. I was asked by ALRM to prepare a report at the eleventh hour on 26 June, only two weeks before the Minister was required to determine the matter and about 10 days before Saunders reported to him.

In the final analysis, particularly in view of the power of the confluence of political forces which intersected in this case, I am not sure whether those extra days necessarily would have made a substantial difference to the way in which this case has unravelled. The delay in appointing Saunders as reporter might have been addressed by having a standing list of appropriate persons to act as reporter to the Minister and having established mechanisms for appointing them efficiently.

However, even if the appointment of reporter and, as importantly, expert assistance had been more efficient, the political outcome might not have been substantially different. I suggest this because, whichever way you look at it, 60 days is a short period of time unless large teams are at work in the documentation and assessment of the matter. I am also conscious of the fact that the popular perception of these processes as political and ideological makes them especially vulnerable to attack when there is the kind of confluence of political interest and circumstance which was clear in the Hindmarsh Island Bridge case.

The proceedings of the *Hindmarsh Island Bridge Royal Commission* also offer salutary lessons. The Royal Commission underlined the vulnerability of Federal assessment and decision-making processes to political attack. It also demonstrated the need for inquirers and counsel to be experienced in cultural matters and conversant with salient dimensions of anthropological knowledge and debate. The Hindmarsh Island Bridge Royal Commission demonstrated what the consequences of a potent combination of a quasi-judicial inquiry operating outside rules of evidence accepted in most courts and an aggressive adversarial process can be. Its excesses are to be avoided.

Two broad consequences of the Hindmarsh Island Bridge case are already clear: the public credibility of heritage protection is undermined at every level of government in Australia; and Aboriginal peoples have had their selves, identity and heritage assaulted in political processes which surrounded a request for the protection of their cultural heritage.

Reflections

These two cases point up the need for experts like anthropologists, who will be entailed in processes which are part of the administration of legislation, to engage actively in its formulation and amendment. It is, after all, not only ministers whose careers and reputations are put on the line in these processes and, when heritage protection processes fail, some Australians lose a great deal more than others in the process.

The relatively recent enactment of the Federal *Aboriginal Heritage Act* and the *World Heritage Act* (in 1984 and 1983 respectively) changed a taken for granted status quo in the relationship between the exercise of State and Federal powers. There is no question that both Acts are perceived by many members of the public as tools through which Federal Governments exert their political will on State Governments, particularly State Governments of an opposing political party. In effect, the exercise of decision making under these Acts is often seen as an unwarranted and coercive intervention. Processes under both these Acts feed into States' rights arguments. There is a case to be made that Federal responsibilities for heritage protection are clearer in law than they are in public perception. Interestingly, in two separate State Royal Commissions during 1995, the Liberal Governments of South Australia and Western Australia demonstrated that they have pioneered an effective quasi-judicial weapon for turning this balance of powers on its political head.

The particular limitations of these Acts also feed into public perceptions about public accountability, failures and limitations in assessment processes, an absence of justice in respect of people affected by ministerial decisions, and demonstrable failure to properly manage "protected" areas. These are the political realities within which experts like anthropologists work in the assessment of claims of heritage significance under these Acts.

The exercise of ministerial political discretion under these Acts also presently renders unreliable the heritage protection these Acts appear to offer. As ministerial decision-making processes are vulnerable to political attack, so too are they open to political forces which might mean that, despite the merits of a case in its own terms, the Minister might decline for political reasons to make a declaration for protection. Some more reliability is needed in the process. Heritage protection is, after all, a government responsibility established in Australian law.

The *Hindmarsh Island Bridge Royal Commission* pointed up more than ever that, if Federal Governments are to take their responsibilities for heritage protection seriously, there is a need to remove them from their present relationship to cross-party conflict between the different levels of government. State and Federal heritage protection laws need to be reconsidered in concert. Commonality of purpose (namely heritage recognition, protection and management) rather than conflict of political interest needs to be nurtured between the different levels of government.

In addition there is a good case for distancing assessment and decision-making processes in respect of Federal heritage protection from their direct relationship to the political process and separating the process of assessing heritage significance from decisions about protecting and managing it.

One model for achieving this broader separation is the creation of a Federal Heritage Protection Tribunal which could, with appropriate protocols and protections, assess heritage significance on the one hand and make recommendations to government for protection management and compensation on the other. The appointment of part-time members of the tribunal could ensure that a range of appropriate Aboriginal peoples and experts were available to act on any application. A National Heritage Assessment Tribunal could conceivably assess, and make recommendations on, all heritage protection matters under Commonwealth jurisdiction. The composition of the tribunal panel assessing a claim could be varied, according to the particulars of the case. There might also be a case for the national tribunal to assess claims under both State and Federal legislation, especially when they are contentious.

In the end, however, what is needed is broader public acceptance that protection of significant heritage is in all our interests and that the Commonwealth does, in fact, have bona fide responsibilities for heritage protection and management.

It is important that the Commonwealth seeks to make its heritage assessment and decision-making processes full, transparent and accountable. Removing them from ministerial discretion in the context of retributive political agendas would go a long way towards this aim. Working with States to formulate reliable and complementary heritage legislation across the nation should be a priority of government.

5

Underwater Heritage

A

Boer B., Ramsay R., and Rothwell D.R., "Conservation of Natural and Cultural Heritage," *International Environmental Law in the Asia Pacific,* Kluwer, 1998, pp 91–93

Draft Convention on the Underwater Cultural Heritage

The draft *Convention on the Protection of the Underwater Cultural Heritage* was completed in Buenos Aires in 1994. It recognizes that there are growing threats to the underwater cultural heritage, including construction activity, advances in technology which allow for easier identification of as well as access to wrecks, the exploitation of marine resources and the commercialization of efforts to recover underwater cultural heritage. The subject of underwater cultural heritage is of great significance in some countries in Asia and the Pacific. For example in the southwest Pacific, the Chuuk Lagoon in the State of Chuuk in the Federated States of Micronesia, and the island of Guadalcanal in the Solomon Islands are host to many shipwrecks and aircraft wrecks as a result of military action in World War II. The Australian coastline is also littered with wrecks, dating from the earliest days of exploration.

The underwater cultural heritage is defined to mean (Article 1):

> "All underwater traces of human existence including:
>
> a. sites, structures, buildings, artifacts and human remains, together with their archaeological and natural contexts; and
>
> b. wrecks such as a vessel, aircraft, other vehicle or any part thereof, its cargo or other contents, together with its archaeological and natural context."

Article 2 states that the Convention is intended to cover underwater cultural heritage which has been lost or abandoned and is submerged underwater for at least 100 years. However, the Article also allows any party to protect underwater cultural heritage, which has been submerged for less than 100 years. However, it does not apply to any warship, military aircraft, naval auxiliary, or other vessels or aircraft owned or operated by a state and used for the time being only on government non-commercial service, or their contents. Thus in the case of the Solomon Islands and the Federated States of Micronesia, the World War II military wrecks would not appear to be covered under the terms of the proposed Convention as presently drafted.

The general principle of the draft Convention, as stated in Article 3, is that "All state parties shall take all reasonable measures to preserve underwater cultural heritage for the benefit of humankind". This General Principle is said to encapsulate Article 149 of the 1982 *United Nations Convention on the Law of the Sea,* and is "cast as a general duty rather than one applying only in a specific maritime area." The "reasonable measures" clearly would include the specific mechanisms in the Convention. These are found in Articles 5 to 14, pertaining to the declaration of Cultural Heritage Zones, the obligation to transmit copies of the *Charter for the Protection and Management of the Underwater Cultural Heritage* to all relevant authorities within their jurisdiction, national provisions on prohibition of use of territory in support of activities which violate the *Charter,* prohibition of activities by nationals and ships affecting the underwater cultural heritage, establishment of a permit system for excavation and retrieval in accordance with the *Charter,* seizure of underwater cultural heritage which has been excavated or retrieved outside the provisions of the *Charter,* provision for penal sanctions, notification of seizure to relevant states, record-keeping and display of heritage seized, collaboration and information-sharing and a duty to undertake education of the public as to the value of underwater cultural heritage. Apart from these measures, the mode of implementation is likely to vary considerably, depending in particular on the cost and physical difficulties of preservation of specific items.

Conclusion

While a number of countries in the region have enacted legislation for the protection of natural and cultural heritage, this legislation has been largely ineffective to protect the rich cultural and natural heritage of those countries. The adequate protection of cultural and natural heritage in Asia and the Pacific through international conventions and domestically thus remains at a low level for most countries. It may well be desirable to use regional bodies such as the South Asian Association for Regional Cooperation (SAARC), South Asia Cooperative Environment Programme (SACEP), ASEAN and SPREP as vehicles for the regional and national implementation of the various conventions discussed in this chapter.

6

Questions for Discussion

(a) Discuss the definitions of natural and cultural heritage. Can they be clearly distinguished? To what extent do they cover living cultures and oral traditions?

(b) Outline the process to be followed for World Heritage Listing and for the placing of a property on the World Heritage in Danger List. What role is there for nongovernmental organizations (NGOs)? Is there any measure that can be taken by NGOs, or others such as state and provincial governments, if the national government will not take action to list or protect World Heritage Sites?

(c) List the World Heritage Sites in Asia and the Pacific. Take one national jurisdiction (e.g., Australia or Philippines) and outline what national, legal and administrative measures have been taken to implement the *World Heritage Convention*. What particular problems of implementation are faced by developing nations?

(d) Discuss the adequacy of the *Operational Guidelines* under the *World Heritage Convention*. How might they be improved?

(e) The Jawoyn Aboriginal owners of the proposed Jabiluka mining site also have indigenous rights that they seek to exercise, and protect, in the adjacent World Heritage Area of Kakadu National Park. Indigenous people do not define territory, and their associated cultural concerns, in the same way as other experts and governments. They do not have such precise "boundaries". To what extent should indigenous "definitions" determine cultural heritage?

7

References for Chapter 15

Aboriginal and Torres Strait Islander Commission, *Heritage and Development: The Operation of the Aboriginal and Torres Strait Islander Heritage Protection Act 1984*, ATSIC Issues Paper No. 1, May 1992.

The American Folk Life Centre, *Cultural Conservation: Reconfiguring the Cultural Mission*, on file Australian Centre for Environmental Law, Sydney, Australia.

Australia v. State of Tasmania (Franklin Dam Case) 46 A.L.R. 625, 1983.

Belbase N. et.al., *Nepal Environment Policy and Action Plan*, Environment Protection Council, HMG/N, Kathmandu, 1993.

Brown Morton W., *The Kathmandu Valley of Nepal: Cultural Conservation in Siege*, 1989.

Department of the Arts, Sport, the Environment, Tourism and Territories, *Australia and the World Heritage Convention* 8, 1988.

Environment Australia, *Response by the Government of Australia to the UNESCO World Heritage Committee regarding Kakadu National Park*, April 1999, accessible at http://www.environment.gov.au/bg/kakadu/kakadu/jabiluka/summary.html [*Editors' Note: This site was accessed on 29/05/01*].

Harding E., *Federated States of Micronesia Review of Environmental Law*, SPREP/Autralian Centre for Environmental Law, Sydney, 1993.

His Majesty's Government of Nepal (HMG/N) and IUCN, *Building on Success: The National Conservation Strategy for Nepal*, IUCN Kathmandu, 1988.

Koowarta v. Bjelke-Petersen 39 A.L.R. 417 (1982).

Mayor F., *Memory of the Future*, UNESCO, Paris, 1995.

Queensland v The Commonwealth of Australia, 86 A.L.R. 519, 1989.

Ritchie D., *Abstract of Australian Heritage Protection Law: An Overview*, paper presented at the MS/AIATSIS Workshop on Heritage Issues, Canberra, 14-15 February 1996.

Rochelle V., "The World Heritage Treaty: A Means to Federally Regulate Private Property for the Preservation of Cultural and Natural Heritage," 23 *Arizona Law Review* 1033, 1981.

State of Queensland v. Commonwealth of Australia, 86 A.L.R. 519 (1989).

Stevens I.E., *Report of the Hindmarsh Is/and Bridge Royal Commission,* State Print, Adelaide, 1995.

UNESCO/ICOMOS Review Mission, *Kathmandu Valley World Heritage Site*, UNESCO/ICOMOS, Kathmandu, 1993.

UNESCO, *Our Creative Diversity*, Report of the World Commission on Culture and Development, 2nd Revised Edition, 1996.

Uniting Church in Australia, Submission to the Inquiry into World Heritage Areas, March 1995.

World Heritage Centre, *Cities of Asia: Heritage for the Future*, Programme for the Safeguarding and Development of Asian World Heritage Cities for the 21st Century, World Heritage Centre, 1996.

World Heritage Committee, *The Operational Guidelines for the Implementation of the World Heritage Convention*, World Heritage Centre, 1994 and 1996.

World Heritage Committee Bureau, *Report of the Rapporteur on the Twenty-Second Extraordinary Session of the World Heritage Committee*, WHC-98/CONF.203/5, Kyoto, November 1998. This document can be accessed at http://www.unesco.org/whc/archive/repbur98b.htm [*Editors' Note: This site was accessed on 29/05/01*].

The Netherlands v United States of America (Island of Palmas Arbitration), 2 Reports of International Arbitral Awards, 829.

8 Additional References

Boer B. (ed.), *Environmental Law in the South Pacific*, IUCN, Gland, Switzerland, 1996.

Boer, B., "Protection of Moveable Cultural Heritage Property Act 1986," 4 *EPLJ*, 1987, pp 63-66 and pp 161-163.

Boer B., Ramsay R., and Rothwell D., *International Environmental Law in the Asia Pacific,* Kluwer, 1998.

Case Concerning the Gabcikovo-Nagymoros Project (Hungary v Slokavakia), 1998, 37 *ILM* 162.

Consultation of Specialists on Ways and Means of Safeguarding the Heritage of the Pacific Region, International Council of Museums, on behalf of UNESCO and in association with South Pacific Commission, Tahiti, 1980.

Craig D. and Ponce-Nova D., "Indigenous Peoples' Rights and Environmental Law" in *UNEP's New Way Forward: Environmental Law and Sustainable Development*, Sun Lin and Lal Kurukulasuriya (eds), 1995, pp 119-120.

Islands of Palmas Arbitration (*The Netherlands v United States of America*), 2 Reports of International Awards 829.

O'Keefe P. and Prott L., *Law and the Cultural Heritage*, Vol. 3, Chapter 14, 1989 pp 491-492, 730, 741.

Posey D., *Traditional Resources Rights; International Instruments for Protection and Compensation for Indigenous Peoples and Local Communities*, IUCN, Gland, Switzerland, 1996.

Report of the World Heritage Committee Bureau (WHC-98/CONF.203/5, 29 November 1998) www.unesco.org/whc/archive/repbur98b.htm [*Editors' Note: This site was accessed on 03/04/2001*].

World Heritage List at www.unesco.org/whc/heritage.htm, [*Editors' Note: This site was accessed on 03/04/2001.*] and World Heritage List in Danger at www.unesco.org/whc/danglist.htm [*Editors' Note: This site was accessed on 03/04/2001.*]

CHAPTER

16

Regional Environmental Law Cooperation: ASEAN and Others

Contents

1 Introduction

The various subregional organizations in Asian and Pacific region, namely, the South Pacific, the ASEAN region, and South Asia, have initiated a number of environmental instruments and programs only in the last two decades. Their responses to environmental issues and problems in their subregions and to international treaties have resulted in a number of hard and soft law instruments and program activities.

In some instances, significant progress has been made in environmental management at the subregional as well as national levels. The roles of the various subregional organizations in developing environmental policies and in integrating environment and development are considered in this chapter.

The ASEAN subegion is used as a case study of the various roles it has played and can play in sustainable development and its linkages to international organizations. The extent to which ASEAN can bring about the harmonization of environmental law within the region is also considered.

A Teaching Guide

(i) ASEAN: Cooperation in the Field of Environment

- Understand the roles of ASEAN in the development of environmental law and policy through regional cooperation.
- Be aware of how international environmental law can trickle down from the global to the regional, and from the regional to the national levels, as well as percolate up.
- Be familiar with the organizational structure of ASEAN in the context of the environment.
- Understand the various modes and levels of cooperation among ASEAN states and also among/ between ASEAN and non-ASEAN member states.
- Trace the process of integration/coordination in the field of environment.
- Appreciate the strengths and weaknesses in networking within a regional grouping.

(ii) Synopsis of a Lecture on ASEAN

Introduction

- Establishment of ASEAN (1967)
- International Environmental Developments in the 1970s
- ASEAN's Cooperation and Integration Patterns in the Field of Environment

ASEAN Organizational Structures in Environmental Management

- ASEAN Institutional Framework in Environmental Management and Cooperation
- ASEAN Organizational Structure in Environmental Cooperation on Haze
- ASEAN Regional Centre for Biodiversity Conversation (ARCBC)

ASEAN Modes and Levels of Cooperation and Integration

A. *Role of ASEAN as a Subregional Organization in the Field of Environment*

- National, Regional and International Levels
- Scope

In some instances, significant progress has been made in environmental management at the subregional as well as national levels.

B. Formulation of ASEAN Policy Guidelines on Environment and Sustainable Development

- *Manila Declaration on the ASEAN Environment*, 1981
- *Jakarta Resolution on Sustainable Development*, 1987
- *Singapore Resolution on Environment and Development*, 1992

ASEAN's Priorities in the Field of Environment

- ASEAN Environment Programmes I, II and III (1978–1992)
- ASEAN Strategic Plan of Action on the Environment (1994–1998)
- Hanoi Plan of Action (1999–2004)
- ASEAN Cooperation Plan on Transboundary Pollution (1995)
- Regional Haze Action Plan (RHAP) (1997)

Some Specific Issues

- *Agreement on the Conservation of Nature and Natural Resources*, 1985
  - Should Singapore, Brunei and Malaysia ratify the Agreement?
  - Are there any constraints to ratification and implementation?
  - ASEAN Regional Centre for Biodiversity Conservation, 1998
- The Indonesian Fires

(III) Teaching Methodologies (Sample)

The subject will be taught by way of lectures, discussions and simulation of an ASEAN Ministerial Meeting on the Environment involving the forest fires in Indonesia.

A. Lecture: General information on ASEAN and the development of environmental law/policy (1 hour)

B. Students to draft a memorandum stating why the *ASEAN Agreement on the Conservation of Nature and Natural Resources, 1985* should/should not be ratified by Singapore, Brunei and Malaysia? Comments by other students (1.5 hours)

C. Student Participation: Simulation of an ASEAN Ministerial Meeting on the Environment (1.5 hours)
- Discussion of the *Cooperation Plan on Transboundary Pollution 1995*, and other action plans on the Indonesian haze.
- Students to represent Singapore, Malaysia and Indonesia on Transboundary Atmospheric Pollution relating to the haze caused by forest fires in Kalimantan, Indonesia
- Raise issues for drafting a Cooperation Plan on Atmospheric Pollution, e.g.:
- Origin and cause of local/regional haze,
- Whether haze can be prevented,
- Nature and type of regional cooperation,
- Use of environmentally sound technologies—any problems,
- Developing national and regional emergency response plans,
- Short-term fire-prevention strategies,
- Early warning system,
- Information sharing,
- Prohibitions, Regulations,
- Monitoring (remote sensing),
- Common air quality index,
- Role of ASEAN Specialized Meteorological Centre,
- Role of ASEAN Institute of Forest Management,
- Adequacy of national, subregional and international law,
- Others, for examples, UNEP, WWF, governments, etc.

Students are required to do research for the above "meeting".

2

Asia-Pacific Subregional Organizations Relevant to the Environment

Some of the main regional organizations/programs for environmental management in Asia and the Pacific are: South Pacific Commission, South Pacific Forum, South Pacific Forum Fisheries Agency, South Pacific Regional Environmental Programme, (SPREP), Association of South East Asian Nations (ASEAN), South Asia Cooperative Environment Programme (SACEP), Asian Development Bank (ADB), UNEP Regional Programme, Economic and Social Commission for Asia and the Pacific (ESCAP), and others.

The main roles of these various organizations are briefly considered in the extract following:

A

Boer B., Ramsay R., and Rothwell D.R., Chapter 2, "International Organizations and International Environmental Law," in *International Environmental Law in the Asia Pacific,* Kluwer Law International, 1998, pp 39–46

Regional Organizations in the Pacific Region

There are four major international organizations which provide the forums for economic and environmental decision making in the southwest Pacific region.

South Pacific Commission

The South Pacific Commission, established in 1947, is based in Noumea, New Caledonia and has a Charter to provide a range of services to its constituent countries. These include the giving of technical advice, training programs and information in social, health, economic and cultural fields. The Commission was the sponsor of the South Pacific Regional Environment Programme.

South Pacific Forum

The South Pacific Forum consists of all of the independent and freely associated countries of the Pacific region. The Forum, established in 1971, is essentially an annual meeting of Heads of State of the member countries. It is made up of the Prime Ministers and Presidents of the 15 independent and self-governing island states of the South Pacific. It also includes the Prime Ministers of New Zealand and Australia. Although an informally constituted political forum, its resolutions are said to be taken by its member countries as virtual directives. The Forum seeks to encourage and promote regional cooperation in trade and economic development of Pacific island countries and also focuses on various major environmental issues.

> *The Forum seeks to encourage and promote regional cooperation in trade and economic development of Pacific island countries and also focuses on various major environmental issues.*

South Pacific Forum Fisheries Agency

The South Pacific Forum Fisheries Agency, based in Honiara, Solomon Islands, was established in 1979 as an independent body under the auspices of the South Pacific Forum. Its mandate is to promote and regulate the development of fisheries within the exclusive economic zones of the South Pacific region, focusing on harmonizing and facilitating the implementation of fishing policies and encouraging cooperation between South Pacific countries. The Forum Fisheries Agency is supported by the *1979 South Pacific Forum Fisheries Convention*, the preamble of which states in part:

> "that the common interest of the South Pacific States is in the conservation and optimum utilisation of the living marine resources of the South Pacific region and in particular the highly migratory species."

The existence of the *Forum Fisheries Convention* underlines the vital economic importance of the marine fisheries in the South Pacific region. As stated by Tsamenyi:

> "The Forum Fisheries Agency has grown into an effective organization with significant

> resources and international clout to control access to the Exclusive Economic Zones of the South Pacific. The South Pacific countries have developed effective harmonized policies in relation to conservation, surveillance and enforcement of the fisheries jurisdiction, and the setting of common minimum terms and conditions in agreements with nations outside the region in relation to fishing activities."

South Pacific Regional Environment Programme

[*Editor's Note: These regions are discussed by Boer in the extract immediately following this.*]

Regional Organizations in Asia

Association of South East Asian Nations (ASEAN)

The Association of South East Asian Nations was established in 1967 by the ASEAN Declaration....

[*For a more detailed account of ASEAN, see Section 4, below.*]

Economic and Social Commission for Asia and the Pacific

The Economic and Social Commission for Asia and the Pacific (ESCAP) was established by the United Nations General Assembly in 1947 (originally named the Economic Commission for Asia and the Far East). Its formal aim is to carry out the commitment of the Economic and Social Council of the United Nations to promote economic development. In recent years, ESCAP has adopted the policy principle of "environmentally sound and sustainable development".

The ESCAP region [notes Kibria]:

> "extends from Mongolia in the north to New Zealand in the south and Cook Islands in the east to the Islamic Republic of Iran in the west. A large part of the region is marine, embracing the world's largest ocean, the Pacific (165 million sq km), the third largest ocean, the Indian (73 million sq km) and a range of important seas."

Presently there are 49 members of ESCAP, and ten associate members.

South Asia C-operative Environment Programme

The South Asia Cooperative Environment Programme (SACEP) is an intergovernmental institution headquartered in Colombo, Sri Lanka. Its members are Afghanistan, Bangladesh, Bhutan, India, Iran, Maldives, Nepal, Pakistan and Sri Lanka. Its work programme includes the development of environmental impact assessment, environmental quality standards, development of technology for renewable and non-renewable energy resources, environmental legislation, conservation of mountain ecosystems and watersheds, social forestry, marine conservation, environmental education and information and training in wildlife management. It has also coordinated the preparation of a Regional Seas Programme for South Asian Seas, in collaboration with UNEP. Its environmental law program includes the publication of reports on environmental legislation; workshops for senior policymakers and assistance in the drafting of legislation.

Asian Development Bank

The Asian Development Bank (ADB) was established in 1966. It is a development finance institution based in Manila. It is owned by 40 countries in Asia and the Pacific and 16 countries outside the region. It promotes economic and social development in its developing member countries. Its main functions are:

(a) to make loans and equity investments for economic and social advancement;
(b) to provide technical assistance for the preparation and execution of development projects and advisory services;
(c) to promote investment of public and private capital for development purposes;
(d) to respond to requests for assistance in co-ordinating development policies and plans of its developing member countries.

The Bank is also required under its Charter to give special attention to the needs of smaller and less developed countries, and to give priority to regional, subregional and national projects and programmes which contribute to the harmonious economic growth of the region as a whole.

In the recent past, the ADB has been criticized for funding development projects which have had adverse environmental and social effects, particularly in relation to indigenous peoples. As a result in part of lobbying from conservation organizations, ADB's environmental policies have been revised. The policy now includes a provision that all projects assisted by the Bank which have potentially adverse impacts on the environment must have an EIA conducted in relation to them. There is provision for public and NGO comment on the EIA, and environmental safeguards must be built into the project before funding can be approved. It is now the case that development projects need to be focused, and are being focused, toward environmentally sustainable development for the rural poor of Asia. This is important because the vast majority of the population in Asia is agrarian-based. Historically, development projects have disenfranchised the poor by displacing them from their lands and by changing their traditional ways of living.

The ADB has paralleled the development of environmental policies of the World Bank (see above) over the past few years. It has set up a Board Inspection Committee, which supervises inspections and provides expertise on the Bank's policies and procedures. Applications for inspection can only be filed by communities, organizations and groups residing in the borrower country where the project the subject of a Bank loan is located. [According to Hunter and McRae] applicants for inspections:

> "must present reasonable evidence that their rights or interests have been adversely affected by an action or omission of the Bank as a result of the Bank's failure to follow operational policies and procedures in connection with a proposed or ongoing Bank project."

It would appear that the ADB has come to the realization that, as the major financial institution in the region, it too has an integral role to play in the achievement of sustainable development.

UNEP Regional Seas Programme

UNEP began its Regional Seas Programme in 1974. It now covers 13 regions and involves over 140 states. The premise of the Programme is that countries of each of the world's ocean regions share a common interest in safeguarding the marine environment and have a mutual need for sustainable development of marine resources. Coastal waters, estuaries and enclosed and semi-enclosed seas suffer the earliest and most severe degradation from effects of urbanization, industrialization, agriculture, transportation and other human activities.

Concurrently, they contain ecosystems which are among the highest in biological productivity, with some 90 percent of the total marine catch coming from these areas. The regional approach allows particular priorities, needs and capabilities to be taken into account when action plans are being formulated to address environmental problems of the oceans as a whole. The Programme is meant to represent a "comprehensive, progressive assault upon degradation of the marine environment". It is designed to "link assessment of the marine environment and the causes of its deterioration with activities for the management and development of the marine and coastal environment".

Action plans are being formulated for each of the regional seas. These are supported by regional conventions and protocols to give them legal expression. The conventions are directed to the prevention, reduction and control of marine pollution, and have also served as frameworks for monitoring and combating marine pollution, and allowing for concerted action for emergency responses.

The South Pacific Regional Environment Programme constitutes one of the regional seas programs. Other regional seas programs operating in the Asia Pacific are the East Asia Seas Action Plan, the South Asian Seas Action Plan and the Northwest Pacific Action Plan. Each of these Action Plans are in the form of a convention or agreement.

Conclusion

It seems to be clear that as international environmental law develops further within the region, there will be a greater dependence on the role of global and regional organizations in implementation of the legal regimes and environmental policy. In addition, on experience so far, the intergovernmental environmental organizations in Asia and the Pacific contribute substantially to the development of collaboration between countries in relation to environmental matters. In subsequent chapters, these collaborative developments, particularly as evidenced by new environmental agreements within the regions, will be explored.

3

Pacific Regional Environmental Law Cooperation

A

Boer B., Ramsay R., and Rothwell D., "Southwest Pacific," *International Environmental Law in the Asia Pacific*, Kluwer Law International, 1998, pp 243–283

Membership of the Convention is open to members of the South Pacific Forum and such other states and territories as approved by the Forum.

South Pacific Forum Fisheries Agency Convention and Related Instruments

The 1979 *South Pacific Forum Fisheries Agency Convention* (*FFA Convention*) establishes the South Pacific Forum Fisheries Agency (FFA). The Agency, based in Honiara, Solomon Islands, is directed to ensuring that the South Pacific Island states can take full advantage of the exploitation of the resources of their EEZs. The Convention and the existence of the Agency underline the vital economic importance of the marine fisheries in the South Pacific region. It is also a manifestation of the need for countries in the region to cooperate closely in ensuring that their fisheries are exploited in a way that is both sustainable and equitable for them. The preamble to the *FFA Convention* states in part:

> "...that the common interest of the South Pacific states is in the conservation and optimum utilization of the living marine resources of the South Pacific region and in particular the highly migratory species."

Membership of the Convention is open to members of the South Pacific Forum and such other states and territories as approved by the Forum (Article II). The Convention recognizes that coastal states have sovereign rights, for the purpose of exploiting, conserving and managing the living marine resources, including highly migratory species, within the EEZ (Article III). The Committee established by the Convention is charged with the promotion of intra-regional coordination and cooperation in relation to harmonization of policies for fisheries management, cooperation with distant water fishing nations, cooperation in surveillance and enforcement, onshore processing, marketing and in respect of access to the 200 miles zones of other Parties (Article V). The Parties are also obliged to provide information to the Agency in relation to catch statistics within its EEZ, relevant laws, regulations and international agreements, biological and statistical data and action with respect to decisions taken by the Committee (Article IX). The Agency itself is seen as 'strictly facilitatory'. There have however been a number of subregional and bilateral fishing access agreements concluded with distant water fishing nations. Some 30 bilateral agreements have been drawn up with the assistance of the Forum Fisheries Agency between countries in the region with countries outside the region. The countries from outside the region include Japan, Russia, South Korea, Taiwan, and, Thailand. In addition, FFA members have had agreements collectively with the United States of America and Japan for some years, and are negotiating an agreement with the European Union.

In order to achieve harmonization of fisheries management in the South Pacific, the *FFA Convention* contemplates that further international arrangements will be made (Articles III, V(2)(a)). The 1982 *Nauru Agreement Concerning Cooperation in the Management of Fisheries of Common Interest* is one of these arrangements. Parties to the agreement are the Federated States of Micronesia, the Republic of Kiribati, the Marshall Islands, the Republic of Nauru, the Republic of Palau, Papua New Guinea and Solomon Islands. The parties "seek, without any derogation of their sovereign rights, to co-ordinate and harmonize the management of fisheries with regard to common stocks within the Fisheries Zones, for the benefit of their peoples (Article 1)". The Agreement states that a coordinated approach to the fishing of common stocks will involve the establishment of principles for the granting of priority to applications by fishing vessels by parties to the Agreement to fish within the Fisheries Zones, over other foreign fishing vessels. In addition, the Agreement seeks to establish, among other things, uniform terms and conditions for the grant of licences for foreign fishing vessels, standardization of logbooks, timely reporting of information about the activities of foreign fishing vessels and standardized identification of foreign fishing vessels.

The actual enforcement of access agreements in the Southwest Pacific has proved to be problematic because of the huge distances involved, combined with the lack of infrastructure regulating the use and abuse of the fisheries of the EEZs. The *1992 Niue Treaty on Cooperation in Fisheries Surveillance and Law Enforcement in the South Pacific Region* is an instrument negotiated pursuant to Article V of the *FFA Convention*, with respect to intra-regional coordination and cooperation in fisheries surveillance and law enforcement. The preamble notes 'the vast areas of ocean covered by the exclusive economic zones and the fishing zones of coastal states in the South Pacific Region and the vital economic significance of such zones' to the economic development of those states. The preamble goes on to indicate the aim of the agreement, which is to enhance the ability of these states to effectively enforce their fisheries laws and deter breaches of these laws. The Treaty is open to any member of the FFA, as well as any Territory of a member of the FFA which has been authorised to sign the Treaty (Article XIII). This Treaty goes further than the Nauru Agreement, by covering not only harmonization of terms and conditions for access, exchange of information etc, but extending to cooperation in surveillance and enforcement, and in particular, cooperation in prosecutions and enforcement of penalties (see Articles VI, VII and VIII).

At a national level, many Southwest Pacific countries have enacted marine or fisheries legislation to provide for the establishment of their EEZs, and to protect and manage their marine resources. The main difficulties in terms of enforcement and surveillance for individual countries are lack of patrol boats, aircraft, staff and finance. However, through the regional and subregional arrangements coordinated by the FFA, these problems of surveillance and enforcement are beginning to be addressed. It might also be noted here that at least in respect to fisheries, the Southwest Pacific is in the process of building a comprehensive legal regime for the management of its natural resources. While fisheries are perhaps the most obvious natural resources to take primacy for the building of a comprehensive regime, it is also a tribute to the cooperative spirit which permeates Pacific island environmental management and which has contributed to the emergence of it.

South Pacific Nuclear Free Zone Treaty

The 1985 *South Pacific Nuclear Free Zone Treaty* (*Treaty of Rarotonga*) is an attempt to make the South Pacific a nuclear-free zone. The main thrust of the Treaty is to try to ensure that the nuclear powers do not continue nuclear testing in the South Pacific. By the Treaty, Parties undertake not to manufacture, possess or have control over any nuclear explosive device anywhere inside or outside the South Pacific Nuclear Free Zone, and agree to abide by safeguards in the provision of nuclear material and equipment. They also undertake to prevent the stationing of any nuclear explosive device on their territory and agree not to dump radioactive wastes and material at sea in the South Pacific Nuclear Free Zone. Each Party also undertakes to prevent in its territory the testing of any nuclear explosive device or to assist any other State in doing so. The Treaty provides for prevention of dumping of radioactive wastes or other radioactive matter within the South Pacific Nuclear Free Zone (Article 3). The Treaty applies to the whole of the area covered by the South Pacific countries, including Australia and New Zealand.

Convention on the Conservation of Nature in the South Pacific (Apia Convention)

The *Convention on the Conservation of Nature in the South Pacific* (*Apia Convention*) was completed in 1976, but did not come into force until 1990. It is presently of limited effect, due to its lack of comprehensiveness and the low number of ratifications. The Convention is primarily concerned with the creation of protected areas and the continued existence of national parks, which are defined to include flora and fauna and areas of natural and cultural heritage significance (Article 2). It urges restrictions on their exploitation for commercial profit 'except after the fullest examination'. Under Article 3(3), the hunting, killing, capture or collection of specimens of flora or fauna in national parks is prohibited 'except when carried out by or under the direction or control of the appropriate authorities or for duly authorized scientific investigations'.

The importance of traditional practices is recognized in Article 6, which allows customary use of areas and species in accordance with traditional cultural practices. Under Article 7(ii) the parties shall 'wherever practicable' conduct research relating to the conservation of nature.

Article 7(v) provides they are also obliged to 'examine the possibility of developing programmes of education and public awareness relating to conservation of nature'. Unfortunately, the Convention lacks enforcement provisions or Articles relating to management plans, community participation or consultation with affected interests in relation to the establishment of protected areas.

Some South Pacific countries have established national parks, reserves and protected areas. Nevertheless, a more vigorous promotion of the need for national parks and protected areas is urgently needed in a number of countries. For example, in the Solomon Islands, a country of high endemicity of flora and fauna, but where logging is a major industry, only one national park has been declared under the relevant legislation. Unfortunately the park, close to Honiara on Guadalcanal, has fallen into disuse and has been encroached upon. Many other areas of spectacular beauty in the Solomon Islands, as well as elsewhere in the Pacific, have no protected area status of any form.

1986 Convention for the Protection of the Natural Resources and Environment of the South Pacific (SPREP Convention)

The SPREP *Convention* was adopted in 1986, together with protocols on cooperation in Combating Pollution Emergencies and Dumping. It came into force in 1990 at the same time as the *Apia Convention*. The Preamble to the Convention recognizes:

> "the threat to the marine and coastal environment, its ecological equilibrium, resources and legitimate uses posed by pollution and by the insufficient integration of an environmental dimension into the development process."

In the Preamble the parties also recognize the need for cooperation among themselves and with competent international, regional and subregional organizations in order to ensure the co-ordinated and comprehensive development of the natural resources of the region. The Convention seeks to ensure that resource development shall be in harmony with the maintenance of the unique environmental quality of the region and the evolving principles of 'sustained resource management'.

The Convention is meant to be a broadly-based instrument for the protection of the natural resources and the environment of the South Pacific, as reflected in its name. However, the scope of the Convention is in fact rather narrow. Article 1 provides that, except as otherwise provided by way of a Protocol, the Convention Area shall not include internal waters or archipelagic waters of the Parties. Article 2 defines the Convention Area as the 200 nautical mile zones off the Pacific island countries (as listed in the Article), those areas of high seas which are enclosed from all sides by those 200 nautical mile zones, and areas of the Pacific Ocean which have been included in the Convention Area under Article 3. Article 2 thus does not refer to terrestrial areas as such. However, there is an apparent internal contradiction in the application of the convention, where it talks in the Preamble about the need to ensure a coordinated and comprehensive development of the natural resources of the region, and recognizing the desirability for the wider acceptance and national implementation of international agreements already in existence concerning the marine and coastal environment. Further, Article 14 is aimed at taking measures to protect and preserve rare or fragile ecosystems and depleted, threatened or endangered flora and fauna and their habitat, and for all state parties to take 'all appropriate measures' to protect and preserve rare or fragile ecosystems and depleted, threatened or endangered flora and fauna as well as their habitat 'in the Convention area'. It states that they 'shall, as appropriate, establish protected areas, such as parks and reserves, and prohibit or regulate any activity likely to have adverse effects on the species, ecosystems or biological processes that such areas are designed to protect'. Article 14 does not restrict parks and reserves to marine parks and reserves, but leaves the matter open. It is therefore assumed that the drafters of the Convention contemplated that the Convention Area could at some stage be expanded pursuant to Article 3 to cover specific terrestrial areas, as well as archipelagic and territorial waters presently excluded under Article 1(b). Article 3 provides that any Party may add areas under its jurisdiction within the Pacific Ocean (as defined) to the Convention Area.

The general provisions of the Convention encourage the parties to conclude bilateral or multilateral agreements, including regional or subregional agreements, for the protection, development and management of the marine and coastal environment (Article 4). Article 4(6) directly reflects Principle 21 of the *Stockholm Declaration*:

> "Nothing in this Convention shall affect the sovereign right of states to exploit, develop and manage their own natural resources pursuant to their own policies, taking into account their duty to protect and preserve the environment. Each Party shall ensure that activities within its jurisdiction or control do not cause damage to the environment of other states or of areas beyond the limits of its national jurisdiction."

Given the interconnected nature of the marine environment, Article 4(6) would seem to place a substantial onus on Pacific island states to ensure that the marine areas under their control are not polluted or overexploited.

The two Protocols to the *SPREP Convention* are directed to the combating of pollution emergencies and the prevention of pollution by dumping. The Protocols are in effect an integral part of the Convention, by virtue of Article 27(1) which spells out the relationship between the Convention and its Protocols:

> "No state may become a Party to this Convention unless it becomes at the same time a Party to one or more Protocols. No State may become a Party to a Protocol unless it is, or becomes at the same time, a Party to this Convention."

The Convention and Protocols concentrate primarily on pollution prevention, reduction and control. They cover pollution from vessels, from land-based sources, from sea-bed activities, from airborne sources, from disposal of wastes, the storage of toxic and hazardous substances and the testing of nuclear devices. They also cover mining and coastal erosion (see Articles 6 to 13). These provisions are consistent with the environment protection requirements in Part XII of *UNCLOS*.

However, the obligations under the Convention go beyond the Parties taking 'all appropriate measures' in relation to pollution prevention, reduction and control, and extend to environmental conservation of specially protected areas, particular ecosystems and fauna and flora, which gives force to the assertion that the Convention can apply to terrestrial areas.

There is little in the way of direct prohibition of activities, except in the case of the storage of radioactive wastes or other radioactive matter in the Convention Area (see Article 11). The *SPREP Convention* is intended to be carried out in part through the SPREP Action Plan:

> "The Action Plan provides a framework for a South Pacific regional approach to environmental issues addressing the unique needs and of the countries and peoples in the region."

The implementation of the Convention is envisaged to include the enactment of national legislation. Article 5(5) provides that Parties shall 'endeavor to establish laws and regulations for the effective discharge of the obligations prescribed in this Convention'. The process of implementation has been assisted to an extent in a number of countries through the *National Environmental Management Strategies* developed for a number of the countries in the region, as well as by a SPREP initiative begun in 1994 to facilitate the exchange of information on the implementation of environmental conventions in the region, including standardized reports for the *Apia* and *SPREP Conventions*. Carew-Reid has suggested that these two Conventions and associated Protocols, the Action Plan and the *Nature Conservation Action Strategy* should be meshed into one regional structure. Through the 1993 *Agreement*, SPREP has started to move in this direction. The *National Environmental Management Strategies* mentioned above are one indication of these aspirations.

1989 *Convention for the Prohibition of Fishing with Long Drift Nets in the South Pacific*

This Convention provides that Parties undertake to prohibit nationals and vessels documented under its laws from engaging in drift net fishing activities within the Convention Area (Article 2). The Convention obliges each State Party to prohibit the import of fish products caught using a drift net and to restrict port access to drift net fishing vessels. Initially, this Convention faced significant enforcement problems because of the difficulty of surveillance in such a large region. However, because of international pressure placed on the major users of drift nets, primarily through the United Nations, together with the use of air surveillance provided by Australia and New

Zealand, the practice appears to have been successfully prohibited.

United Nations Framework Convention on Climate Change

...Because a number of Southwest Pacific island countries, or parts of them, are constituted by atolls, and many others have low-lying areas of coast, the potential impact of sea-level rise caused by global warming may be much more drastic than for other countries in the Asia Pacific region. The Convention states that each country should enact effective environment legislation and that the environmental standards, management objectives and priorities should reflect the environmental and developmental context to which they apply.

The Convention places obligations on developed countries to take the lead in combating climate change and its adverse effects. It places obligations on all countries to take precautionary measures to anticipate, prevent or minimize the causes of climate change and to mitigate its adverse effects. It recognizes that developed and developing countries have different responsibilities (according to the state of industrialization and development of pollution control technology) and that economic development is perceived to be essential for adopting measures to address climate change, in the context of the promotion of sustainable development. In the Pacific island countries, there is generally no capacity to directly address the causes of climate change, and equally, to address its effects, apart from the building of seawalls for low-lying atolls and coastal areas, or, more realistically shifting whole communities to higher ground within their own countries where possible, or to other countries.

The Convention calls on each of the developed countries to commit themselves specifically to a range of programs. The Convention states that in the implementation of its various commitments, full consideration should be given to what actions are necessary to meet the specific needs and concerns of developing countries arising from the adverse effects of climate change, as well as the impact of response measures. It identifies specific types of countries in terms of these needs, concerns and measures. Among those countries are small island countries, countries with low-lying coastal areas, countries prone to natural disasters and countries with fragile ecosystems, including mountainous ecosystems (Articles 2(5)(6) and (7)). All of these types are found in the Southwest Pacific region.

The dilemma which the Pacific island countries find themselves in is neatly encapsulated in the plea from [Paeuiu] the Prime Minister of Tuvalu, an atoll country:

> "Now it is up to the decision makers of the world, particularly those of the leading industrialized nations, to respond with decisiveness and conviction. We know from all the scientific evidence collected to date that the fragile and delicate atmosphere balance on which life and our existence depend has been upset. The threat to the atmosphere comes predominantly from the breath of industrialized civilization. We in the island nations cannot afford to wait for more studies and research. We would like to have firm and pragmatic solutions to curb the negative impact of climatic changes on our lives. We live on these small and fragile islands and we know that the problems are *now* and not tomorrow. The time to act is now or never."

The Federated States of Micronesia (FSM) has gone so far as to pass a resolution in relation to global warming expressing serious concern over the threat to the FSM posed by its effects. The Congress states that continued unrestricted release of carbon dioxide, methane, nitrous oxide and other greenhouse gases into the Earth's atmosphere will accelerate the process of global warming and climate change, with possible catastrophic consequences to the FSM. By this legislative declaration, FSM joins many other low-lying and high island nations in the developing Pacific in the attempt to influence and educate the world community regarding the specific dangers to island states of unregulated harmful atmospheric emissions.

Resolution 7-24 gives warning that the FSM citizens stand to be among the first on Earth to become victims of sea-level rise, intensified storms, saltwater invasion and destruction of marine life as a consequence of industrial and agricultural activities in other nations. It urges the President, the Department of Human Resources and the Department of External Affairs to work with the newly-formed 'Alliance of Small Island States' to encourage broader expression of island views during the United Nations-sponsored negotiations toward the global *Framework Convention on Climate Change*.

Convention on Biological Diversity

...The implementation of this Convention requires, at a minimum, that all Parties review all legislation and administrative policies which affect the use and conservation of all components of the natural environment. A number of countries in the Pacific have begun this process, either specifically or more generally, with a view to putting in place adequate mechanisms, both administrative and legal, to meet the obligations under the Convention. To date in most countries, the legislation in relation to the conservation of biological diversity has been rather narrowly focused. SPREP has established a major South Pacific Biodiversity Conservation Programme (linked with an Integrated Conservation and Development Programme), financed by the Global Environment Facility. The program is intended to promote sustainable development through the management of conservation areas in both terrestrial and marine environments. It emphasizes involvement by local communities and NGOs in collaboration with government agencies.

Waigani Convention

In 1992, Papua New Guinea proposed to the 23rd South Pacific Forum that a regional convention be drafted to ban the import of and control the movement and management of hazardous wastes in the South Pacific region. The Convention was completed in draft form by the end of 1994, and was presented to the 25th South Pacific Forum in that year. The *Convention to Ban the Importation into Forum Island Countries of Hazardous and Radioactive Wastes and to Control the Transboundary Movement and Management of Hazardous Wastes within the South Pacific Region* (*Waigani Convention*) was adopted by the heads of government at the South Pacific Forum meeting in Port Moresby in August 1995. The Convention is drafted to be consistent with the 1989 *Convention on the Control of Transboundary Movements of Hazardous and their Disposal* (*Basel Convention*). It is intended to act as an agreement under Article11 of that Convention. Article 11 provides for bilateral, multilateral and regional agreements or arrangements to be made, which are 'not less environmentally sound' than those provided for by the *Basel Convention*, 'in particular taking into account the interests of developing countries'. Under its General Obligations, the Convention obliges Parties to formulate national definitions of wastes considered or defined as hazardous under its national legislation (Article 3). Each Pacific Island Developing Country Party is obliged to take appropriate legal, administrative and other measures to ban the import of such materials from outside the Convention Area. Other Parties (Australia and New Zealand, under Annex IV) must also take such measures to ban the export of all hazardous and radioactive wastes to all South Pacific Forum countries (Article 4). Parties are also obliged to provide a 'competent authority' for implementation of notification procedures and a 'focal point' for transmission and receipt of information (Articles 5, 6 and 7). Further Articles provide for a duty to re-import wastes which have been authorized for transboundary movement, but where the movement cannot be completed according to the contract or under Convention procedures (Article 8), procedures for dealing with illegal traffic (Article 9), cooperation among Parties and international cooperation (Article 10), and for further bilateral, regional or multilateral agreements or arrangements (Article 11).

The *Waigani Convention* includes two concepts which are not found in the *Basel Convention*: use of the 'precautionary principle', and 'cleaner production.' The definition of the precautionary principle in the Convention, found in Article 1, is virtually identical to that found in Principle 15 of the *Rio Declaration*. However, the principle is not otherwise referred to in the Convention except in Article 13(3), where it is stated that the first meeting of the Conference of the Parties 'shall consider the adoption of additional measures in accordance with the precautionary principle relating to the implementation of the Convention. It is possible therefore that the Conference of the Parties may wish to conclude a Protocol on additional measures that might be taken in accordance with the precautionary principle.

In a similar vein, the Convention includes the recently developed concept of 'cleaner production', found in Article 10, which is concerned with cooperation among Parties and with international cooperation. Article 10(4) states that, taking into account the needs of developing countries, Parties shall encourage, among other things, 'the adoption of new technologies which are environmentally sound, including cleaner production technologies'. SPREP is designated as the body to carry out the Secretariat functions under the Convention. Legislative action to implement the Convention will now be required in the Pacific Island countries.

The Waigani Convention includes two concepts which are not found in the Basel Convention: use of the 'precautionary principle', and 'cleaner production.'

Barbados Declaration

The *Global Conference on Sustainable Development of Small Island States*, agreed to at UNCED in 1992, was held in Barbados in 1994. A United Nations General Assembly resolution of late 1992 called on the Conference to elaborate strategies and measures to enhance the sustainable development of small island developing states, and urged increased national and international efforts to promote sustainable and environmentally sound development worldwide.

The resolution also called for the adoption of plans and programs to support sustainable development in small island states and for the utilization of their marine and coastal resources. This included meeting essential human needs, maintaining biodiversity and improving the quality of life of island people. A review of current socioeconomic development trends of island states, examining their particular vulnerabilities and defining specific actions and policies on environment and development planning was also called for. The Conference was further called on to enhance the capacity of states through development of expertise and access to environmentally sound technology. Southwest Pacific countries were involved in the conference through SPREP.

The Conference adopted a *Programme of Action for the Sustainable Development of Small Island States*, which set out provisions on all major concerns relating to small island developing states, including assistance for the enhancement of national institutions and administrative capacity.

Further, a regional mechanism for consultation on implementation was established by the 25th South Pacific Forum in October 1994, consisting of support units in the Pacific Operations Centre of the United Nations Economic and Social Commission for Asia and the Pacific as well as in SPREP.

Implementing International Environmental Conventions in the South Pacific

As with many developing countries, there are political, economic, geographic and cultural factors which operate to inhibit the consistent implementation of the conventions and agreements operating in the Pacific in relation to environmental matters. In the past, the lack of participation by South Pacific countries in some of these conventions arises partly from the lack of involvement by many of these countries in their drafting. Without a feeling of 'ownership' of the process of producing the instruments, there is less commitment to becoming a party or implementing their provisions. Further, because of a lack of resources and appropriately trained personnel to draft and administer national legislation, the opportunity to implement international agreements at the national level is limited. These problems were addressed to an extent in relation to the *Convention on Biological Diversity,* the *Framework Convention on Climate Change* and *Agenda 21*, particularly because SPREP was able to coordinate the representation of these countries in the UNCED negotiations. However there continues to be a need to build the institutional capacity required for proper implementation. The *Capacity 21* project initiated by UNDP through SPREP in 1994 is intended to help Pacific island countries to strengthen both governmental and nongovernmental capacity for sustainable development. It encourages the participation of the general public, especially women, and NGOs in development planning and incorporates customary systems of land and marine tenure and management practices into future policies. The programme is designed to build on the National Environment Management Strategies generated in the early 1990s. One of its anticipated results is the reform of legislation to support land and sea management.

Future of Environmental Law in the Pacific

As a result of the stimulation provided by UNCED and the Global Conference on the Sustainable Development of Small Island States, and because of the major initiatives taken by SPREP and its supporters, through various programs, a gradual strengthening in regional arrangements is occurring in relation to the management of marine and coastal environments in the Pacific region. There is also a growing awareness of the need for the implementation of international agreements at a domestic level. The targeted funds being made available through the Global Environment Facility and the UNEP's *Capacity 21* program, and the work being carried out by the Food and Agricultural Organization as well as through overseas development assistance bodies, means that it is more likely that national institutions will be strengthened, which will in turn assist in the drafting and implementation of modern environmental and natural resources legislation.

4

ASEAN Cooperation in the Field of Environment

A

Establishment of ASEAN

ASEAN was established by the *ASEAN Declaration* (*Bangkok Declaration*) on 8 August 1967. Its five founder members are Indonesia, Malaysia, the Philippines, Singapore and Thailand. Brunei joined in 1985, Vietnam 1995, Laos and Myanmar 1997 and Cambodia 1999.

The *Bangkok Declaration of 1967* stated, as one of its aims, the acceleration of economic growth and promotion of matters of common interest in, *inter alia*, economic fields. Although no mention was made of cooperation in environment, world events in the area of the environment culminating with the *Stockholm Declaration 1972* which called for regional cooperation in environment, led to ASEAN's Subregional Environment Programme beginning in 1978.

A word must be said about the ASEAN way of doing things. The cooperation at the subregional level is done through consensus. There is no ASEAN Parliament to issue laws/regulations/directives to its member countries and no enforcement agencies. Would this state of affairs change in light of the Indonesian haze?

The various environmental instruments emanating from ASEAN, e.g., the Meeting of the ASEAN Heads of Government, the ASEAN Ministerial Meeting on the Environment (AMME), ASEAN Senior Officials on the Environment (ASOEN) and its subsidiary Working Groups will strengthen national policies and development of local environmental instruments. The various ASEAN negotiated instruments on the environment will also facilitate the harmonization of laws among ASEAN countries, such as air pollution and water quality. In the absence of enforcement at the ASEAN sub-regional level, the role of each of its member states in implementation and enforcement becomes critical. Thus, at the present moment the role of ASEAN is essentially the guiding force. Each member state must play its part in implementing the various ASEAN instruments.

B

ASEAN Organizational Framework in Environmental Management and Cooperation

Institutions provide the mechanisms for cooperation and coordination. The following are some of the important ASEAN institutions that have contributed to the development of various environmental instruments ranging from biodiversity, marine pollution to urban and industrial environmental management (see Organization Chart, *infra*).

ASEAN Heads of Government

Comprising Presidents or Prime Ministers of the member countries, they meet once in three years. Environmental matters may feature in the agenda of such meetings. One of the landmark meetings was held in Bangkok in 1984 which led to the *Bangkok Declaration on the ASEAN Environment*, 29 November 1984 (see *infra*). Another notable meeting was the Singapore Summit in 1992 where the Heads of Government met in Singapore just before the United Nations Environment and Development meeting in Rio de Janeiro, 1992. At this meeting it was agreed that regional cooperation be enhanced. In promoting regional cooperation towards sustainable development some policy guidelines were laid down pertaining to pollution, biodiversity, climate change, forests, etc.

ASEAN Ministerial Meeting on the Environment (AMME)

The AMME occurs once every three years in order to ensure that decisions of the Heads of Government are implemented and also to promote ASEAN cooperation. Apart from formal meetings, AMME may have informal meetings, e.g., to discuss the "Indonesian Haze". One of the meetings in which a Resolution was passed included the harmonization of environmental quality standards for ambient air and river quality to be attained by the year 2010—this was the meeting held on 24 April 1994 in Bandar Seri Begawan.

ASEAN Senior Officials on the Environment (ASOEN)

The predecessor of ASOEN is the ASEAN Expert Group on the Environment (AEGE) established in 1977 and replaced by ASOEN in 1989. It meets annually to consider the reports of its various ASEAN Working Groups. There were originally six Working Groups, namely, ASEAN Seas and Marine Environment, Environmental Economics, Nature Conservation, Environmental Management, Transboundary Pollution and Environmental Information, Public Awareness and Education. In addition, there is a special institution set up in 1995 to operationalize and implement the measures recommended in the ASEAN Cooperation Plan on Transboundary Pollution relating to atmospheric pollution.

There is a special institution set up in 1995 to operationalize and implement the measures recommended in the ASEAN Cooperation Plan on Transboundary Pollution relating to atmospheric pollution.

In 1998 the six Working Groups were restructured and streamlined into three Working Groups, namely, Working Group on Nature Conservation and Biodiversity, Working Group on Coastal and Marine Environment and Working Group on Multilateral Environmental Agreements. The rationale for restructure of the Working Groups is to make them more efficacious in responding to emerging issues.

ASEAN's responsibilities and functions include the following:

- Recommend policy guidelines and provide the catalytic impetus towards the implementation of the principles of sustainable development to ASEAN Governments and relevant ASEAN committees;
- Monitor the state of ASEAN's natural resources and the quality of the ASEAN environment;
- Promote ASEAN cooperation on regional environmental matters, focusing on land-based pollution, urban and rural pollution and others;
- Promote cooperation with other government agencies, the private/business sectors, professional associations, NGOs and other organizations.

The ASOEN Subsidiary Bodies

As mentioned above the current Working Groups are:

- Working Group on Nature Conservation and Biodiversity
- Working Group on Marine and Coastal Environment
- Working Group on Multilateral Environment Agreements

The ASEAN Secretariat

The Secretariat is based in Jakarta and the Environment Unit of the Functional Cooperation Bureau deals with both administrative and substantive matters pertaining to environmental cooperation.

National Focal Points

Each ASEAN member country has a focal point. Generally a ministry which deals with environmental matters would link up with the ASEAN institutional arrangements, particularly ASOEN and its subsidiary bodies. There are also national biodiversity reference units in most member state for the ASEAN Regional Centre for Biodiversity (ARCBC, *infra).* There is a separate organizational structure for ASEAN environmental cooperation on haze (see diagram, *infra*), and also one for biodiversity conservation (see diagram, *infra*).

C

ASEAN Regional Centre for Biodiversity Conservation (ARCBC)

[*Readers interested in this initiative can contact the Centre via E-mail: arcbc@laguna.net.*]

The ASEAN Regional Centre for Biodiversity Conservation (ARCBC) serves as the main focal point for networking and institutional linkage among ASEAN member countries (AMCs) and between ASEAN and European Union (EU) partner organizations to enhance the capacity of ASEAN in promoting biodiversity conservation.

EU provides the means for networking, applied research, training and technical assistance while ASEAN provides office space and facilities and support personnel. The Department of Environment and Natural Resources (DENR) is the Project's Executing Agency.

ARCBC will intensify biodiversity conservation through improved cooperation in a comprehensive regional context, by assisting in setting up a network of institutional links

ASEAN Institutional Framework in Environmental Management and Cooperation

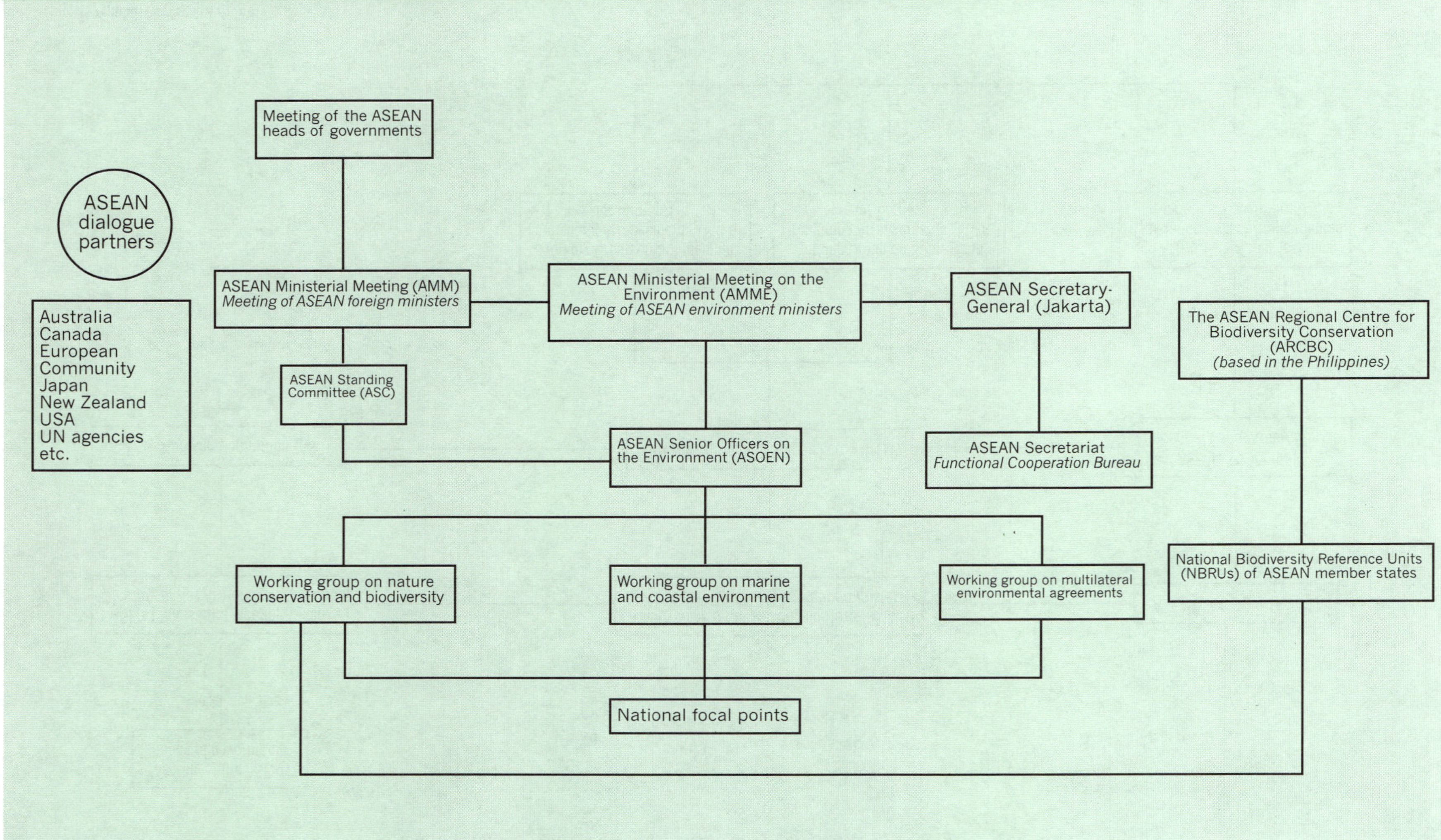

Source: Koh Kheng-Lian, 1 January 2000.

Organizational Structure of ASEAN Environmental Cooperation on Haze

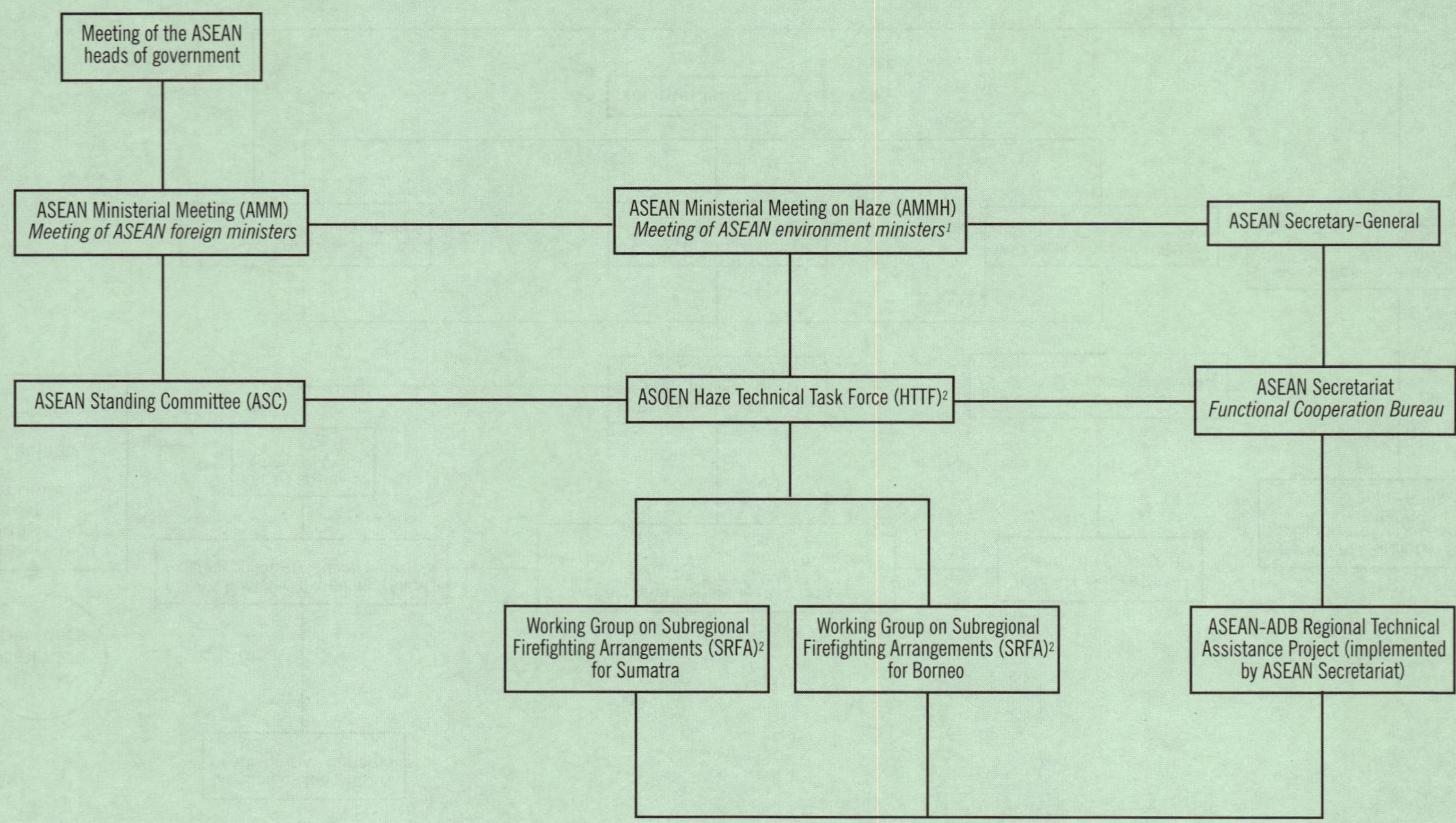

[1]AMMH meets regularly every 1-2 months.
[2]HTTF and SRFAs meet regularly every month.
Source: ASEAN Secretariat.

among ASEAN countries and between ASEAN and EU partner organizations.

The objectives of ARCBC are to

- Establish an intra-ASEAN and ASEAN/EU network of institutional links;
- Foster collaborative partnership between ASEAN and European institutions in the field of training, research and information management;
- Assess and strengthen human resources capability;
- Assess and improve the flow of information;
- Analyze, document and disseminate information on regional biodiversity conservation;
- Establish and maintain an appropriate database and information referral system;
- Assist institutions and stakeholders in policy analysis;
- Formulate proposals to coordinate regional initiatives on biodiversity conservation;
- Intensify awareness and participation of institutions and other stakeholders on regional biodiversity issues; and
- Assist in improving curricula on biodiversity conservation.

The Project components of ARCBC are

- Networking and Institution Building

  This component establishes a regional network via the National Biodiversity Reference Units (NBRUs) to link scientific knowledge and promote information exchange and synergies on biodiversity. It will likewise develop and implement an exchange program for professors and researchers among ASEAN institutions and invite European leading experts (Biodiversity Visiting Chairs) to facilitate the transfer of knowledge and experience. It will design and implement thematic workshops and policy fora on biodiversity conservation.
- Training and Extension

  This component will conduct Training Needs Assessment (TNA) of institutions and human resources in order to design training packages and methods for individuals and stakeholders involved in biodiversity conservation. Assessment and improvement of biodiversity curricula in academic and training institutions will be part of this component.
- Research and Development

  This component will set up guidelines to define research priorities, organize conference to finalize the regional research agenda, identify research institutions, and provide funds for applied biodiversity research activities.
- Database and Information Management Systems

  This component will create and maintain electronic repositories for ASEAN and link to other international databases. It will also establish guidelines for information handling services and publish newsletters and documentation on biodiversity consrvation.

There are NBRUs from the following ASEAN countries:

- Brunei Darussalam
- Indonesia
- Malaysia
- Philippines
- Singapore
- Thailand
- Viet Nam

D

ASEAN Policy Guidelines on the Environment

The following are some of the ASEAN environmental instruments which deal with policy guidelines. (All numbering is as per original document to facilitate further examination by the reader.)

(i) *Manila Declaration on the ASEAN Environment*, 1981

The Parties:

1. Do hereby declare their agreement to strengthen regional cooperation and collaboration in the field of environment by adopting the following objective policy guidelines:

   (a) Objective:

   To ensure the protection of the ASEAN environment and the sustainability of its natural resources so that it can sustain continued development with the aim of eradicating poverty and attaining the highest possible quality of life for the people of the ASEAN countries.

(b) Policy Guidelines:

(1) Foster a common awareness among the people of the ASEAN countries of the biological, physical and social environment and its vital significance for sustained development to proceed apace;

(2) Ensure, as far as practicable, that environmental considerations are taken into account in development efforts, both on-going and future;

(3) Encourage the enactment and enforcement of environmental protection measures in the ASEAN countries;

(4) Foster the development of environmental education programmes;...

(ii) *Jakarta Consensus on ASEAN Tropical Forestry of The Third Meeting of The ASEAN Economic Ministers on Agriculture and Forestry*, 1981

ASEAN Common Forestry Policy

Recognizing the importance of a common policy in developing the forestry sector in ASEAN Countries as a strong basis for the long term and effective sound development of that sector to improve the lives of the rural communities, maintain and create renewable resources for industrial development and sustain environmental amenity and ecological stability, the Ministers agree to adopt a common Forestry Policy pertaining to the:

(a) Conservation, Reforestation and Management of Forest Resources:

1. establishment/consolidation of adequate, permanent forest estates for protection, production, conservation/recreation and other purposes;
2. management of the forest resources based on the principles of sustained yield and appropriate/optimal land use;
3. reforestation and forest development consistent with the objectives of forest management and the concept of sustained yield.

(b) Utilization of Forest Resources: Production, Processing and Marketing

1. utilization of the forest resources based on technically, environmentally and socioeconomically sound land and resource-use strategies, plans and programmes;
2. rationalization of forest industries development based on maximum possible utilization of materials removed from the forest and highest possible value-added processing;
3. marketing of wood products based on concerted action and standardization of nomenclature, grading rules and specification;
4. application of appropriate technology based on optimal inputs of manpower, knowledge, capital and other relevant productive resources;
5. development of greater domestic processing of timber through the scaling down of log exportation and generating the production of more value-added products for exports.

Research and Development

Promotion of research and development in all relevant areas of forest resources conservation, management and development as well as in timber production and marketing.

Education and Training

Development of adequate and appropriate manpower at all levels of forest management, research and operations.

[*Editors Note: For further examination of issues relating to forests management see Chapter 13 Sustainable Use of Forests and Fisheries.*]

(iii) *Bangkok Declaration on the ASEAN Environment*, 1984

Objective

To implement the ASEAN Development Strategy through an integrated approach entailing advance or forward planning in the environmentally related activities with a view to incorporating environmental dimension in development planning right at the base level in order to achieve sustained development and long-term conservation of environmental assets and at the same time improving the quality of life for all.

Policy Guidelines

To achieve the objective noted above, the following policy guidelines shall be adopted for application throughout the ASEAN region:

(1) With respect to environmental management:

i. Foster the development of macroeconomic-cum-environmental development plans which can be accommodated by the environmental carrying capacity of the region.

ii. Continue and strengthen the use of Environmental Impact Assessment (EIA) process and extended Cost-Benefit Analysis for minimizing the adverse effects and for ensuring proper consideration of environmental values in all projects and programmes under government that are likely to produce significant environmental impact and its gradual extension to the private sector including industry.

iii. Develop a system of procedures for conducting EIAs and for their review which can be practically utilized within the ASEAN region.

iv. Continue and increase efforts for establishing environmental units in the planning divisions of major project implementing agencies to ensure that environmental consciousness permeates government departments and that development policy and planning in all sectors reflect systematic consideration of the environment.

v. Establish techniques for quantifying the impact of development projects on environment both favorable and unfavorable.

vi. Evolve criteria for augmentation of renewable resources and economical use of non-renewable resources.

vii. Prepare an optimal land use pattern and zoning plan.

(2) With respect to nature conservation:

Develop new and practicable approaches for preserving forests wildlife, and other ecological systems in the face of continuing population pressure.

(3) With respect to marine environment:

Develop practicable methods for the management of pollution discharges so that economic development of coastal resources may proceed in coexistence with preservation of the quality of coastal beaches and resorts and the marine environment.

(4) With respect to industry:

i. Adopt practicable methods of ensuring reasonable control of waste discharges from the earliest stages of project formulation.

ii. Wherever practicable adopt low waste and non-waste technology and more effective reuse and recycling of waste in production.

iii. Develop a Toxic and Hazardous Waste Control Programme and stimulate efforts by government agencies and industry to develop suitable systems for control.

(5) With respect to urban environment:

Increase efforts to provide waterborne sewerage systems with central sewage treatment facilities at least for the major towns.

(6) With respect to environmental education and training:

i. Continue efforts to enhance public awareness in respect of the importance of environmental protection and support governmental actions in these regards.

ii. Provide environmental training of personnel involved in decision making on projects, programmes, policies and plans with emphasis on cause and effect relationship that exists between an individual's environment and his health.

iii. Introduce stronger general environmental theme into school and university syllabi.

iv. Provide technical training for staff engaged directly in the work of environmental protection agencies and in environmental programmes of other agencies.

(7) With respect to environmental information systems:

i. Develop a comprehensive environmental system to facilitate decision-making.

ii. Initiate or strengthen efforts for establishment of suitable national data bank/storage and retrieval system.

iii. Intensify efforts for establishing monitoring programmes for continuing surveillance of sensitive environmental resources.

iv. Promote increased use of remote sensing as a means of establishing environmental databases.

(8) With respect to wider involvement in environmental management:
Encourage and promote cooperation between Government, Non-Governmental Organizations, Universities, Business Communities within ASEAN in the field of environmental management.

(9) With respect environmental legislation:
Develop appropriate legislation to support the proper management and development of the environment.

(10) With respect to international cooperation on environmental management in the ASEAN countries:
Establish cooperation with developed and other developing countries and international agencies for transfer of technology and share experiences in the management of the environment.

(iv) *Singapore Resolution on Environment and Development*, 1992

Enhancing Regional Cooperation

To promote regional cooperation towards sustainable development, we agree that ASEAN member countries shall:

Policies

- introduce policy measures and promote institutional development that will encourage the integration of environment factors in all developmental processes;
- work closely on the inter-related issues of environment and development;
- cooperate in setting basic environmental quality standards and regulations at national level, work towards harmonized environmental quality standards in the region, and adopt long term quantitative goals relating to ambient air quality and river water quality;
- harmonize policy directions and step up operational and technical cooperation on environmental matters such as transboundary air and water pollution, natural disasters, forest fires, oil spills, and the transboundary movements and disposal of toxic chemicals and hazardous wastes, and undertake joint actions to address the anti-tropical timber campaign.

E

Some Areas of ASEAN Environmental Cooperation

(i) *Agreement on the Conservation of Nature and Natural Resources*, 1985

[*This is the only environment treaty of ASEAN. Of the six ASEAN member states that signed the Agreement, the following have ratified it, namely, Indonesia (10 July 1986), Philippines (4 September 1986), and Thailand (19 May 1986). Brunei Darussalam, Malaysia, and Singapore have not ratified the Agreement. The Agreement has not entered into force; it shall enter into force on the thirtieth day after the deposit of the sixth Instrument of Ratification (Article 33).*]

Chapter I: Conservation and Development

Article 1: Fundamental Principle

(1) The Contracting Parties, within the framework of their respective national laws, undertake to adopt singly, or where necessary and appropriate through concerted action, the measures necessary to maintain essential ecological process and life support systems, to preserve genetic diversity, and to ensure the sustainable utilization of harvested natural resources under their jurisdiction in accordance with scientific principles and with a view to attaining the goal of sustainable development.

(2) To this end they shall develop national conservation strategies, and shall coordinate such strategies within the framework of a conservation strategy for the Region.

Article 2: Development Planning

(1) The Contracting Parties shall take all necessary measures, within the framework of their respective national laws, to ensure that conservation and management of natural resources are treated as an

integral part of development planning at all stages and at ail levels.

(2) To that effect they shall, in the formulation of all development plans, give as full consideration to ecological factors as to economic and social ones.

(3) The Contracting Parties shall where necessary, take appropriate action with a view to conserving and managing natural resources of significant importance for two or several Contracting Parties.

Chapter II: Conservation of Species and Ecosystems

Article 3: Species—Genetic Diversity

(1) The Contracting Parties shall, wherever possible, maintain genetic diversity by taking action aimed at ensuring the survival and promoting the conservation of all species under their jurisdiction and control.

(2) To that end, they shall adopt appropriate measures to conserve and plant species whether terrestrial, marine and freshwater, and more specifically

- (a) conserve natural, terrestrial, freshwater and coastal or marine habitats;
- (b) ensure sustainable use of harvested species;
- (c) protect endangered species;
- (d) conserve endemic species; and
- (e) take all measures in their power to prevent the extinction of any species or subspecies.

(3) In order to fulfil the aim of the preceding paragraphs of this Article the Contracting Parties shall in particular endeavor to

- (a) create and maintain protected areas;
- (b) regulate the taking of species and prohibit unselective taking methods;
- (c) regulate and, where necessary, prohibit the introduction of exotic species; and
- (d) promote and establish gene bank, and other documented collections of animal and plant genetic resources.

Article 4: Species—Sustainable Use

The Contracting Parties shall pay special attention to harvested species, and, to that effect, shall endeavor to

(1) Develop, adopt and implement management plans for those species, based on scientific, studies and aiming at

- (a) preventing decrease in the size of any harvested population to levels below those which ensure its stable recruitment and the stable recruitment of those species which are dependent upon, or related to them;
- (b) maintaining the ecological relationship between harvested, dependent and related populations of living resources of the ecosystem considered;
- (c) restoring depleted populations to at least the level referred to in subparagraph (a) of this paragraph; and
- (d) preventing changes or minimizing risk of changes in the ecosystem considered which are not reversible over a reasonable period of time.

(2) Take the appropriate and necessary legislative and administrative measures on harvesting activities in the light of their national interests whereby

- (a) such activities must conform to the management plans referred to above;
- (b) the conduct of such activities is controlled by a permit system;
- (c) all indiscriminate means of taking and the use of all means capable of causing local extinction of, or serious disturbance to, populations of a species of related species are prohibited,
- (d) such activities are prohibited or strictly regulated at certain periods, seasons or places of importance in the life cycle of the species;
- (e) such activities may be regulated more strictly, temporarily or locally in order to assist restoration of population level, or counterbalance any threat caused by special circumstances;
- (f) special measures, such as restocking, are provided for whenever the conservation status of species so warrants; and
- (g) trade and possession of specimen or products of specimens are regulated whenever such regulations meaningfully contribute to the implementation harvesting regulations.

Article 5: Species—Endangered and Endemic

(1) Appendix 1 to this Agreement shall list endangered species recognized by the Contracting Parties as of prime importance to the Region and deserving special attention. The Appendix shall be adopted by a meeting of the Contracting Parties;

Accordingly, Contracting Parties shall, wherever possible,

(a) prohibit the taking of these species, except for exceptional circumstances by special allowance from the designated authorities of the Contracting Parties;

(b) regulate the trade in and possession of specimens and products of those species accordingly;

(c) especially protect habitat of those species by ensuring that sufficient portions are included in protected areas, and

(d) take all other necessary measures to improve their conservation status, and restore their populations to the highest possible level.

(2) Each Contracting Party shall, wherever possible, apply the above measures to species endangered at national level.

(3) The Contracting Parties recognize their special responsibility in respect of species that are endemic to areas under their jurisdiction and shall undertake accordingly to take, wherever possible, all the necessary measures to maintain the population of such species at the highest possible level.

Article 6: Vegetation Cover and Forest Resources

(1) The Contracting Parties shall, in view of the role of vegetation and forest cover in the functioning of natural ecosystems, take all necessary measures to ensure the conservation of the vegetation cover and in particular of the forest cover on lands under their jurisdiction.

(2) They shall, in particular, endeavor to

(a) control clearance of vegetation; endeavor to prevent bush and forest fires; prevent overgrazing by, inter alia, limiting grazing activities to period and intensities that will not prevent regeneration of the vegetation;

(b) regulate mining exploration operations with a view to minimizing disturbance of vegetation and to requiring the rehabilitation of vegetation after such operations;

(c) set aside areas as forest reserves, inter alia, with a view to conserve the natural forest generic resources;

(d) in reforestation and afforestation planning avoid as far as possible mono-culture causing ecological imbalance;

(e) designate areas whose primary function shall be the maintenance of soil quality in the catchment considered and the regulation of the quantity and quality of the water delivered from it;

(f) ensure to the maximum extent possible the conservation of their natural forests, particularly mangroves with a view, inter alia, to maintaining maximum forest species diversity; and

(g) develop their forest management plans on the basis of ecological principles with a view to maintaining potential for optimum sustained yield and avoiding depletion of the resource capital.

Article 7: Soil

(1) The Contracting Parties shall, in view of the role of soil in the functioning of natural ecosystems, take measures, wherever possible towards soil conservation, improvement and rehabilitation, they shall, in particular, endeavor to take steps to prevent soil erosion and other forms of degradation, and promote measures which safeguard the processes of organic decomposition and thereby its continuing fertility.

(2) To that effect, they shall, in particular, endeavor to

(a) establish land use policies aimed at avoiding losses of vegetation cover, substantial soil losses, and damages to the structure of the soil;

(b) take all necessary measures to control erosion, especially as it may affect coastal or freshwater ecosystem leading to siltation, of downstream areas such as lakes or vulnerable ecosystems such as coral reefs, or damage critical habitats in particular that of endangered or endemic species; and

(c) take appropriate measures to rehabilitate eroded or degraded soils including rehabilitation of soil affected by mineral exploitation.

Article 8: Water

(1) The Contracting Parties shall, in view of the role of water in the functioning of natural ecosystems, take all appropriate measures towards the conservation of their underground and surface water resources.

(2) They shall to that effect, in particular, endeavor to
  - (a) undertake and promote the necessary hydrological research especially with a view to ascertaining the characteristics of each watershed;
  - (b) regulate and control water utilization with a view to achieving sufficient and continuous supply of water for, inter alia, the maintenance of natural life supporting systems and aquatic fauna and flora; and
  - (c) when planning and carrying out water resource development projects take fully into account possible effects of such projects on natural processes or on other renewable natural resources and prevent or minimize such effects.

Article 9: Air

The Contracting Parties shall, in view of the role of air in the functioning of natural ecosystems, endeavor to take all appropriate measures towards air quality management compatible with sustainable development.

Chapter III: Conservation of Ecological Processes

Article 10: Environmental Degradation

The Contracting Parties, with a view to maintaining the proper functioning of ecological processes, undertake, wherever possible, to prevent, reduce and control degradation of the natural environment and, to this end, shall endeavor to undertake, in addition to specific measures referred to in the following article:

- (a) to promote environmentally sound agricultural practices by, inter alia, controlling the application of pesticides, fertilizers and other chemical products for agricultural use, and by ensuring that agricultural development schemes, in particular for wetland drainage or forest clearance, pay due regard to the need to protect critical habitats as well as endangered and economically important species;
- (b) to promote pollution control and the development of environmentally sound industrial processes and products;
- (c) to promote adequate economic or fiscal incentives for the purposes of subparagraphs (a) and (b) above;
- (d) as far as possible to consider the originator of the activity which may lead to environmental degradation responsible for its prevention reduction and control as well as, wherever possible, for rehabilitation and remedial measures required;
- (e) to take into consideration, when authorizing activities likely to affect the natural environment, the foreseeable interactions between the new activities proposed and those already taking place in the same area, and the result of such interactions on the air, waters and soils of the area; and
- (f) to pay particular attention to the regulation of activities which may have adverse effects on processes which are ecologically essential or on areas which are particularly important or sensitive from an ecological point of view, such as the breeding and feeding grounds of harvested species.

Article 11: Pollution

The Contracting Parties, recognizing the adverse effect that polluting discharges or emissions may have on natural processes and the functioning of natural ecosystems as well as on each of the individual ecosystem components, especially animal and plants species, shall endeavor to prevent, reduce and control such discharges, emissions or applications in particular by

- (a) submitting activities likely to cause pollution of the air, sea, freshwater, or the marine environment, to control which shall take into consideration both the cumulative effects of the pollutants concerned and the self-purificating aptitude of the recipient natural environment;
- (b) making such controls conditional on, inter alia, appropriate treatment of polluting emissions; and
- (c) establishing national environment quality monitoring programmes, particular attention being paid to the effects of pollution on natural ecosystems, and cooperation in such programmes for the Region as a whole.

Chapter IV: Environmental Planning Measures

Article 12: Land-Use Planning

(1) The Contracting Parties shall, wherever possible in the implementation of their development planning, give particular attention to the national allocation

of land usage. They shall endeavor to take the necessary measures to ensure the integration of natural resource conservation into the land use planning process and shall, in the preparation and implementation of specific land use plans at ail levels, give as full consideration as possible to ecological factors as to economic and social ones. In order to achieve optimum sustainable land use, they undertake to base their land use plans as far as possible on the ecological capacity of the land.

(2) The Contracting Parties shall in carrying out the provisions of paragraph (1) above, particularly consider the importance of retaining the naturally high productivity of areas such as coastal zones and wetlands.

(3) They shall, where appropriate, coordinate their land use planning with a view to conserving natural resources of significant importance for two or several Contracting Parties.

Article 13: Protected Areas

(1) The Contracting Parties shall as appropriate establish, in areas under their jurisdiction, terrestrial, freshwater, coastal or marine protected areas for the purpose of safeguarding

(a) the ecological and biological processes essential to the functioning of the ecosystems of the Region;

(b) representative samples of all types of ecosystems of the Region;

(c) satisfactory population levels for the largest possible number of species of fauna and flora belonging to those ecosystems; and

(d) areas of particular importance because of their scientific, educational, aesthetic, or cultural interests; and taking into account their importance in particular as:

i. the natural habitat of species of fauna and flora; particularly rare or endangered or endemic species;

ii. zones necessary for the maintenance of exploitable stocks of economically important species;

iii. pools of genetic material and said refuge for species, especially endangered ones;

iv. sites of ecological, aesthetic or cultural interest;

v. reference sources for scientific research; and

vi. areas for environmental education.

They shall, in particular, take all measures possible in their power to preserve those areas which are of an exceptional character and are peculiar to their country or the Region as well as those which constitute the critical habitats of endangered or rare species, of species that are endemic to a small area and of species that migrate between countries of Contracting Parties.

(2) Protected areas established pursuant to this Agreement shall be regulated and managed in such a way as to further the objectives for the purpose of which they have been created. Contracting Parties shall, wherever possible, prohibit within such protected areas activities which are inconsistent with such objectives.

(3) Protected areas shall include

(a) National Parks

i. This expression denotes natural areas that are sufficiently large to allow for ecological self-regulation of one or several ecosystems, and which have not been substantially altered by human occupation or exploitation.

ii. National Parks shall be placed under public control, their boundaries shall not be altered nor shall any portion of any National Park be alienated except by the highest competent authority.

iii. National Parks shall be dedicated to conservation and to scientific, educational and recreational uses and the common welfare of the people.

(b) Reserves

i. This expression denotes areas set aside for the purpose of preserving a specific ecosystem, the critical habitat of certain species of fauna or flora, a water catchment area or for any other specific purpose relating to the conservation of natural resources or objects or areas of scientific, aesthetic, cultural, educational or recreational interest.

ii. After reserves have been established their boundaries shall not be altered nor shall any portion of such reserves be alienated except by the authority establishing them or by higher authority.

iii. Reserves shall be dedicated to the purposes for which they have been created and, in the light of the national interests of the Contracting Parties any activity inconsistent with such purposes shall be prohibited.

(4) Contracting Parties shall, in respect of any protected area established pursuant to this Agreement

(a) prepare a management plan and manage the area on the basis of this plan; and

(b) establish, wherever appropriate, terrestrial or aquatic buffer zones that shall be located around protected areas and which, in the case of marine areas, may include coastal land areas or watersheds of rivers flowing into the protected area; in such buffer zones all activities that may have harmful consequences on the ecosystems that such areas purport to protect shall be prohibited or regulated and activities which are consistent with the purpose of the protected area shall be promoted.

(5) Contracting Parties shall, in respect of any protected area established pursuant to this Agreement, endeavor to

(a) prohibit the introduction of exotic animal or plant species;

(b) prohibit the use or release of toxic substances or pollutants which could cause disturbance or damage to protected ecosystems or to the species they contain; and

(c) to the maximum extent possible, prohibit or control any activity exercised outside protected areas when such activity is likely to cause disturbance or damage to the ecosystems or species that such protected areas purport to protect.

(6) Contracting Parties shall cooperate in the development of principles, objectives criteria and guidelines for the selection establishment and management of protected areas in the Region, with a view to establishing a co-ordinated network of protected areas throughout the Region giving particular attention to those of regional importance. An Appendix containing such principles, objectives, criteria and guidelines shall be drawn up in the light of the best scientific evidence, as adapted to the conservation requirements of the Region and shall be adopted by a meeting of Contracting Parties.

(7) In addition to the establishment of the protected area referred to in paragraph 3 of this Article, Contracting Parties shall promote, through the adoption of appropriate measures, the conservation of natural areas by private owners, community or local authorities.

Article 14: Impact Assessment

(1) The Contracting Parties undertake that proposals for any activity which may significantly affect the natural environment shall as far as possible be subjected to an assessment of their consequences before they are adopted, and they shall take into consideration the results of this assessment in their decision-making process.

(2) In those cases where any such activities are undertaken, the Contracting Parties shall plan and carry them out so as to overcome or minimize any assessed adverse effects and shall monitor such effects with a view to taking remedial action as appropriate.

Chapter V: National Supporting Measures

Article 15: Scientific Research

The Contracting Parties shall individually or in cooperation with other Contracting Parties or appropriate international organizations, promote and, whenever possible, support scientific and technical programmes of relevance to the conservation and management of natural resources, including monitoring, research, the exchange of technical information and the evaluation of results.

Article 16: Education, Information and Participation of the Public Training

(1) The Contracting Parties shall endeavor to promote adequate coverage of conservation and management of natural resources in education programmes at all levels.

(2) They shall circulate as widely as possible information on the significance of conservation measures and

their relationship with sustainable development objectives, and shall, as far as possible, organize participation of the public in the planning and implementation of conservation measures.

(3) Contracting Parties shall endeavor to, individually or in cooperation with other Contracting Parties or appropriate international organizations, develop the programmes and facilities necessary to train adequate and sufficient scientific and technical personnel to fulfil the aims of this Agreement.

Article 17: Administrative Machinery

(1) The Contracting Parties shall identify or maintain the administrative machinery necessary to implement the provisions of this Agreement, and, where several governmental institutions are involved, create the necessary coordinating mechanism for the authorities dealing with designated aspects of the environment.

(2) They shall endeavor to allocate sufficient funds to the task necessary for the implementation of this Agreement, as well as sufficient qualified personnel with adequate enforcement powers.

Chapter VI: International Cooperation

Article 18: Cooperative Activities

(1) The Contracting Parties shall cooperate together and with the competent international organizations, with a view to coordinating their activities in the field of conservation of nature and management of natural resources and assisting each other in fulfilling their obligations under this Agreement.

(2) To that effect, they shall endeavor

(a) to collaborate in monitoring activities;

(b) to the greatest extent possible, coordinate their research activities;

(c) to use comparable or standardized research techniques and procedures with a view to obtaining comparable data;

(d) to exchange appropriate scientific and technical data, information and experience, on a regular basis; and

(e) whenever appropriate, to consult and assist each other with regard to measures for the implementation of this Agreement.

(3) In applying the principles of cooperation and coordination set forth above, the Contracting Parties shall forward to the Secretariat

(a) Information of assistance in the monitoring of the biological status of the natural living resources of the Region;

(b) Information, including reports and publications of a scientific, administrative or legal nature and, in particular information on

(i) measures taken by the Parties in pursuance of the provision, as of this Agreement;

(ii) the status of species included in Appendix 1; and

(iii) any other matter to which the Conference of the Parties may give special priority.

Article 19: Shared Resources

(1) Contracting Parties that share natural resources shall cooperate concerning their conservation and harmonious utilization, taking into account the sovereignty, rights, and interests of the Contracting Parties concerned in accordance with generally accepted principles of international law.

(2) To that end, they shall, in particular

(a) cooperate with a view to controlling, preventing reducing or eliminating adverse environmental effects which may result in one Contracting Party from the utilization of such resources in another Party;

(b) endeavor to conclude bilateral or multilateral agreements in order to secure specific regulations of their conduct in respect of the resources concerned;

(c) as far as possible, make environmental assessment prior to engaging in activities with respect to shared natural resources which may create a risk of significantly affecting the environment of another sharing Contracting Party or other sharing Contracting Parties;

(d) notify in advance the other sharing Contracting Party or the other sharing Contracting Parties of pertinent details of plans to initiate, or make a change in, the conservation or utilization of the resource which can reasonably be expected to affect significantly the environment in the territory of the other Contracting Party or Contracting Parties;

(e) upon request of the other sharing Contracting Party or sharing Contracting Parties, enter into consultation concerning the abovementioned plans;

(f) inform the other sharing Contracting Party or other sharing Contracting Parties of emergency situations or sudden grave natural events which may have repercussions on their environment; and

(g) whenever appropriate, engage in joint scientific studies and assessments, with a view to facilitating cooperation with regard to environmental problems related to a shared resource, on the basis of agreed data.

(3) Contracting Parties shall especially cooperate together and, where appropriate, shall endeavor to cooperate with other Contracting Parties, with a view to

(a) the conservation and management of

(i) border or contiguous protected areas,

(ii) shared habitats of species listed in Appendix 1, and

(iii) shared habitats of any other species of common concern;

(b) the conservation, management and, where applicable regulation of the harvesting of species which constitute shared resources

(i) by virtue of their migratory character, or

(ii) because they inhabit shared habitats.

Article 20: Shared Resources

(1) Contracting Parties have in accordance with generally accepted principles of international law the responsibility of ensuring that activities under their jurisdiction or control do not cause damage to the environment or the natural resources under the jurisdiction of other Contracting Parties or of areas beyond the limits of national jurisdiction.

(2) In order to fulfil this responsibility, Contracting Parties shall avoid to the maximum extent possible and reduce to the minimum extent possible adverse environmental effects of activities under their jurisdiction or control, including effects on natural resources, beyond the limits of their national jurisdiction.

(3) To that effect, they shall endeavor

(a) to make environmental impact assessment before engaging in any activity that may create a risk of significantly affecting the environment or the natural resources of another Contracting Party or the environment or natural resources beyond national jurisdiction;

(b) to notify in advance the other Contracting Party or Contracting Parties concerned of pertinent details of plans to initiate, or make a change in, activities which can reasonably be expected to have significant effects beyond the limits of national jurisdiction;

(c) to enter into consultation concerning the abovementioned plans upon request of the Contracting Party or Contracting Parties in question; and

(d) to inform the Contracting Party or Contracting Parties in question of emergency situations or sudden grave natural events which may have repercussion beyond national jurisdiction.

(4) Contracting Parties shall, in particular, endeavor to refrain from actions which might directly or indirectly adversely affect wildlife habitats situated beyond the limits of national jurisdiction, especially habitats of species listed in Appendix 1 or habitats included in protected areas.

Chapter VII: International Supporting Measures

Article 21: Meeting of the Contracting Parties

(1) Ordinary meetings of the Contracting Parties shall be held at least once in three years, in as far as possible in conjunction with appropriate meetings of ASEAN, and extraordinary meetings shall be held at any other time upon the request of one Contracting Party provided that such request is supported by at least one other Party.

(2) It shall be the function of the meetings of the Contracting Parties, in particular:

(a) to keep under review the implementation of this Agreement and the need for other measures, in particular the Appendices;

(b) to adopt, review and amend as required any Appendix to this Agreement;

(c) to consider reports submitted by the Contracting Parties in accordance with Article 28 or any other information which may be submitted by a Party, directly or through the Secretariat;

(d) to make recommendations regarding the adoption of any Protocol or any amendment to this Agreement;

(e) to establish working groups or any other subsidiary body as required to consider any matter related to this Agreement; and .

(f) to consider and undertake any additional action including the adoption of financial rules, that may be required for the achievement of the purposes of this Agreement.

Article 22: Secretariat

On the coming into force of this Agreement the Contracting Parties shall designate the Secretariat for carrying out the following functions:

(a) to convene and prepare the meetings of Contracting Parties;

(b) to convene diplomatic conferences for the purpose of adopting Protocols;

(c) to transmit to the Contracting Parties notifications, reports and other information received in accordance with this Agreement;

(d) to consider inquiries by, and information from, the Contracting Parties, and to consult with them on questions relating to this Agreement;

(e) to perform such other functions as may be assigned to it by the Contracting Parties; and

(f) to ensure the necessary coordination with other competent international bodies and in particular to enter into the such administrative arrangements as may be required for the effective discharge of the secretariat functions.

Article 23: National Focal Points

In order to facilitate communications with other Parties and the Secretariat, the Contracting Parties shall designate an appropriate national agency or institution responsible for co-ordinating matters arising from consultations and channelling communications between Contracting Parties or with the Secretariat.

Article 24: Adoption of Protocols

(1) The Contracting Parties shall cooperate in the formulation and adoption of Protocols to this Agreement, prescribing agreed measures procedures and standards for the implementation of this Agreement.

(2) The Contracting Parties, at a diplomatic conference, may adopt Protocols to the Agreement.

(3) The Protocols of this Agreement shall be subject to acceptance and shall enter into force on the thirtieth day after the deposit with the Depository of the Instruments of Acceptance of all the Contracting Parties.

Article 25: Amendment of the Agreement

(1) Any Contracting Parties to this Agreement may propose amendments to the Agreement. Amendments shall be adopted by a consensus of the Contracting Parties.

(2) Amendments to this Agreement shall be adopted by a consensus of the Contracting Parties.

(3) Acceptance of amendments shall be notified to the Depository in writing and shall enter into force on the thirtieth day following the receipt by the Depository of notification of the acceptance by all the Contracting Parties.

(4) After the entry into force of an amendment to this Agreement any new Contracting Party to this Agreement shall become a Contracting Party to this Agreement as amended.

Article 26: Appendices and Amendments to Appendices

(1) Appendices to this Agreement shall form an integral part of the Agreement;

(2) Amendments to an Appendix:

(a) Any Contracting Party may propose amendments to an appendix at a meeting of the Contracting Parties;

(b) Such amendments shall be adopted by a consensus of the Contracting Parties; and

(c) The Depository shall without delay communicate the amendment so adopted to all Contracting Parties.

The adoption and entry into force of a new Appendix to this Agreement shall be subject to the same procedure as for the adoption and entry into force of an amendment to an Appendix as provided for in paragraph (2) of this Article provided that, the new Appendix shall not enter into force until such time as the amendment to the Agreement enters into force.

Article 27: Rules of Procedure

The Contracting Parties shall adopt rules of procedure for their meetings.

Article 28: Reports

The Contracting Parties shall transcript to the Secretariat reports on the measures adopted in implementation of this Agreement in such form and at such intervals as the meetings of Contracting Parties may determine.

Article 29: Relationships with Other Agreements

The provisions of this Agreement shall in no way affect the rights and obligations of any Contracting Party with regard to any existing treaty, convention or agreement.

Article 30: Settlement of Disputes

Any dispute between the Contracting Parties arising out of the interpretation of implementation of this Agreement shall be settled amicably by consultation or negotiation.

Article 31: Ratification

This Agreement shall be subject to ratification by the Contracting Parties. The Instruments of Ratification shall be deposited with the Secretary-General of the ASEAN Secretariat, who shall assume the functions of Depository.

Article 32: Accession

(1) After the entry into force of the Agreement any Member State may accede to this Agreement subject to prior approval by the Contracting Parties to this Agreement.

Instrument of accession shall be deposited with the Depository.

Article 33: Entry into Force

(1) This Agreement shall enter into force on the thirtieth day after the deposit of the sixth Instrument of Ratification.

(2) Thereafter, this Agreement shall enter into force with respect to any Contracting Party on the thirtieth day following the date of deposit of the instrument of accession by that Contracting Party.

Article 34: Responsibility of the Depository

The Depository shall inform the Governments which have signed this Agreement:

(a) of the deposit of instruments of ratification, acceptance or accession;

(b) of the date on which the Agreement will come into force.

Article 35: Deposit and Registration

(1) The present Agreement shall be deposited with the Depository who shall transmit certified true copies thereof to the Governments of all Contracting Parties which have signed the present Agreement or acceded to it.

(2) As soon as the present Agreement enters into force, the text shall be transmitted by the Depository to the Secretary-General of the United Nations for registration and publication, in accordance with Article 102 of the Charter of the United Nations.

(ii) *Memorandum of Understanding on ASEAN Sea Turtle Conservation and Protection*, 1997

[*This Memorandum can be found on the Internet at <http://www.arbec.com.my/>. This site was accessed 22/06/01*]

Preamble

The Government of Negara Brunei Darussalam, the Government of the Republic of Indonesia, the Government of Lao People's Democratic Republic, the Government of Malaysia, the Government of the Union of Myanmar, the Government of the Republic of the Philippines, the Government of the Republic of Singapore, the Government of the Kingdom of Thailand, and the Government of the Socialist Republic of Vietnam (hereinafter referred to as the "Parties" and individually as the "Party").

Recognizing the significance of the sea turtle populations and their habitats in ASEAN waters;

Recognizing also that sea turtles are migratory species and the waters of ASEAN countries form a contiguous area of waters without any interval;

Realizing that effective conservation efforts cannot be independently realized at a national level and that multilateral efforts are necessary to ensure the long-term survival of sea turtles in the ASEAN region;

Desiring to jointly manage, protect and conserve all species of sea turtle and their habitats in the ASEAN region through a unified approach in the formulation and attainment of the management, conservation and protection strategies;

Have agreed as follows:

Article I: Definitions

For the purposes of this Memorandum of Understanding (hereinafter referred to as "MOU"):

1. "Sea turtle" means any of the species as follows: Leatherback Turtle (Dermochelys coriacea) Green Turtle (Chelonia mydas) Hawksbill Turtle (Eretmochelys imbricata) Olive/Pacific Ridley (Lepidochelys olivacea) Loggerhead (Caretta caretta) Flatback Turtle (Natator depressa).
2. "Sea turtle habitats" mean all those aquatic and terrestrial environments where sea turtles live at any state of their life cycles.
3. "Parties" means ASEAN countries which have consented to be bound by this MOU and in which this MOU is in force.

Article II: Objectives

The objectives of the Memorandum of Understanding on ASEAN Sea Turtle Conservation and Protection are to promote the protection, conservation, replenishing and recovery of sea turtles and of the habitats based on the best available scientific evidence, taking into account the environmental, socioeconomic and cultural characteristics of the Parties.

Article III: Areas of Application

The areas of application of this MOU shall include the land territories and the maritime areas over which the Parties exercise sovereignty, sovereign rights or jurisdiction in accordance with international law as reflected in the United Nations *Convention on the Law of the Sea*, concluded at the Montego Bay, Jamaica on 10th December 1982 and came into force on 16th November 1994.

Article IV: Proposed Mechanism

1. This MOU shall recognize that all matters or issues concerning sea turtles conservation and protection shall be subjected to the existing national laws and regulations of each Party.
2. When necessary, Parties to this MOU would consider harmonizing their existing national laws and regulations, and enact new laws on sea turtle conservation and protection to suit with current situations.

Article V: Coordinator and Technical Expert Working Group

1. A Coordinator shall be designated to coordinate and implement the proposed mechanism in Article IV when this MOU enters into force and report directly to the ASEAN Fisheries Working Group.
2. Considering its long-term experiences and strong efforts on sea turtle conservation, Malaysia shall be designated as the Coordinator under this MOU.
3. Each Party shall designate expert(s) to form the Technical Expert Working Group to prepare an ASEAN program and work plan on sea turtle conservation and protection, for the endorsement of the ASEAN Fisheries Working Group and the approval of the Senior Officials Meeting of the ASEAN Ministers on Agriculture and Forestry (SOM-AMAF).
4. ASEAN member countries, recognizing the Southeast Asian Fisheries Development Center (SEAFDEC) as the competent technical regional organization on marine issues in the ASEAN region, shall seek close cooperation and collaboration with SEAFDEC in undertaking its sea turtle conservation and protection program.

Article VI: Coordination and Linkages

1. Each Party shall designate an appropriate agency to coordinate with the Co-ordinator as specified in Article V.
2. The coordinations and linkages among the Parties under this MOU shall be done on a networking basis.
3. The Coordinator shall be responsible in organizing meeting of the Expert Technical Working Group as soon as this MOU enters into force.

Article VII: Final Provisions

1. This MOU shall enter into force on the date of signature.
2. This MOU shall be deposited with the Secretary General of ASEAN.

3. Accession to this MOU shall take effect from the date on which the instrument of accession is deposited with the Secretary General of ASEAN.
4. Any Contracting Party may propose an amendment to the provision of this MOU. Such amendment shall only come into force after it has been accepted by all the other Contracting Parties.
5. A Contracting Party may at any time give formal notice of its intention to withdraw from this MOU and such withdrawal shall take affect one year from the date of the submission to the notification to the Secretary General of ASEAN.

IN WITNESS WHEREOF, the undersigned being duly authorized by their respective governments, have signed this MOU.

Done at Bangkok on this Twelfth day of September in the year One Thousand Nine Hundred and Ninety Seven in English language.

(iii) *Hanoi Plan of Action, 1999-2004*

The second ASEAN Informal Summit, held at Kuala Lumpur on 15 December 1997, adopted the ASEAN Vision 2020 which sets out a broad vision for ASEAN in the year 2020. The Hanoi Plan of Action (HPA) has a six-year time frame covering the period from 1999 to 2004. The progress of its implementation shall be reviewed every three years to coincide with the ASEAN Summit Meeting.

Protect the Environment and Promote Sustainable Development

The following are the relevant aspects of the HPA on the environment:

- Fully implement the ASEAN Cooperation Plan on Transboundary Pollution with particular emphasis on the Regional Haze Action Plan by the year 2001.
- Strengthen the ASEAN Specialized Meteorological Centre with emphasis on the ability to monitor forest and land fires and provide early warning on transboundary haze by the year 2001.
- Establish the ASEAN Regional Research and Training Centre for Land and Forest Fire Management by the year 2004.
- Strengthen the ASEAN Regional Centre for Biodiversity Conservation by establishing networks of relevant institutions and implement collaborative training and research activities by the year 2001.
- Promote regional coordination for the protection of the ASEAN Heritage Parks and Reserves.
- Develop a framework and improve regional coordination for the integrated protection and management of coastal zones by the year 2001.
- Strengthen institutional and legal capacities to implement *Agenda 21* and other International environmental agreements by the year 2001.
- Harmonize the environmental databases of Member Countries by the year 2001.
- Implement an ASEAN regional water conservation programme by the year 2001.
- Establish a regional centre or network for the promotion of environmentally sound technologies by the year 2004.
- Formulate and adopt an ASEAN Protocol on access to genetic resources by the year 2004.
- Develop a *Regional Action Plan* for the Protection of the Marine Environment from Land-based and Sea-based Activities by the year 2004.
- Implement the Framework to Achieve Long-Term Environmental Goals for Ambient Air and River Water Qualities for ASEAN Countries.
- Enhance regional efforts in addressing climatic change.
- Enhance public information and education in awareness of and participation in environmental and sustainable development issues.

F

Koh K.L., "Ecosystem Management Approach to Biodiversity Conservation: The Role of ASEAN," *The First ASEAN Environmental Forum*, 20-24 September 1999, Hanoi, Viet Nam

Introduction

The ASEAN region is very rich in biodiversity with a variety of ecosystems ranging from forests (tropical, subtropical and alpine forests), mangroves, corals, tidal marshes, estuaries, delta and lagoonal river mouths. These ecosystems yield an abundant variety of products such as timber, food and medicine, not to mention fauna and flora, much of which are of educational, research, recreational, tourism and other values. Thus, biodiversity conservation in the context of socioeconomic development and sustainable development of a country is vital and should be of concern to policymakers, environmental ministries and agencies, industrialists, scientists, stakeholders, local communities, NGOs and the public. The benefits from biodiversity are tremendous but at the same time, environmental damage that exploitation or over-exploitation can bring about could result in loss of biodiversity. During the last two decades, ASEAN countries have embarked on a massive economic development aimed at raising the standards of living of its peoples. Consequently, the impacts of these activities have affected the region's biodiversity.

The benefits from biodiversity are tremendous but at the same time, environmental damage that exploitation or over-exploitation can bring about could result in loss of biodiversity.

Until recently, little was done from an ecosystem management approach to biodiversity conservation. Little wonder as the concept of ecosystem management was little known. The concept is complex and is still a developing one, as we shall see. Be that as it may, in 1978, 11 years after its establishment, ASEAN began to play a role in the management and conservation of biodiversity when "nature conservation and terrestrial ecosystems" was included as one of the six priority projects in the ASEAN subregional programs (ASEP I). It was then realized that that the capacities for assessment, study and systematic observation and evaluation of biodiversity need to be reinforced at national, regional and international levels.

This paper explores the emerging concept of ecosystem management approach to biodiversity conservation and examines the role of ASEAN.

Establishment of ASEAN (1967)

ASEAN, the Association of South East Asian Nations, was established by the ASEAN Declaration (*Bangkok Declaration*) in Bangkok, on 8 August 1967. The five founder members are Indonesia, Malaysia, Philippines, Singapore and Thailand subsequently joined by Brunei (1984), Viet Nam (1995), Lao PDR (1997), Myanmar (1997) and Cambodia (1999)...

What is Ecosystem Management?

"Ecosystem" means different things to different people. Let us take the definition in the *Convention on Biodiversity* (CBD):

> "Dynamic complex of plant, animal and microorganism communities and their non-living environment interacting as a functional unit."

The structure of an ecosystem is the interaction of the living (plants and animals) and the non-living (e.g., air and water) components forming a functional unit. Thus an ecosystem approach must take into consideration not only the species but the air, water, soil sunlight and much else besides.

The term "environmental management" has been used in many contexts but it is still an emerging concept. It has, for example, been defined in Article 3 of the *Indonesian Environmental Act, 1997* as:

> "Environmental management which is performed with a principle of national responsibility, a principle of sustainability, and a principle of exploitation, in a framework of the holistic development of the Indonesian human and the development of an Indonesian community in its entirety which is faithful and devoted to God the Almighty."

At the recent UNITAR/KIWC Training Workshop on Integrated Conservation and Development Planning: Role of Multilateral Agreements Concerning Biodiversity, held from 27 August to 3 September 1999, some elements were recommended for developing a set of Guidelines on Ecosystem Management Approach to Biodiversity Conservation. These elements are not exhaustive, and suggestions are welcome...

As we can note from Appendix 2, the elements are wide ranging and include an interaction of socio-economic, scientific, ecological and even religious elements; land use planning; air and water laws; policy considerations; governance; cooperation; training and research, to mention a few. Those who would like to add further elements for the development of the UNITAR Guidelines, can email to Daniel Navid@unitar.org

In considering what is an ecosystem management approach, it might be well to note what is not an ecosystem approach. In a word, the traditional approach, which is focused on only discrete areas that are to be managed on a sectoral basis, is not an ecosystem-based approach.

Role of ASEAN in Developing an Ecosystem Management Approach

The role of ASEAN in developing an ecosystem management approach must begin with a recognition that the ASEAN region is to be considered as one ecosystem. What does this mean, considering the vast area encompassed by the five founder members and subsequently, by the other five members? This concept can be said to have its genesis in the *Manila Declaration on the ASEAN Environment* dated 30 April 1981, when the Declaration considered the need to safeguard the "ASEAN Environment" and the "the natural resources". In 1994, during the Indonesian haze at the Informal ASEAN Ministerial Meeting on the Environment in Kuching, the Ministers reiterated that the entire region is one ecosystem. Indeed, at the Third ASEAN Experts Meeting on the Environment in the 1980s, the following criteria for consideration of a project for the ASEAN Environment Programme were set out:

(1) It is participated by at least three countries. (Hence, in the Indonesian haze, the transboundary pollution need not affect all ASEAN countries to come within the ASEAN concept of one ecosystem. Again, for example, in the case of transmigratory species, like marine turtles, the ASEAN Conservation Programme of Marine Turtles affects five of the ten ASEAN countries, namely, Indonesia, Malaysia, Philippines, Thailand and Viet Nam.);
(2) It is endorsed by all ASEAN members;
(3) It benefits the ASEAN region;
(4) It strengthens national capabilities;
(5) It develops ASEAN cooperation.

Indeed, in 1978 when the ASEAN Subregional Environment Programme (ASEP I) was launched, it recognized that ASEAN is to be considered as "one ecosystem"—the Nature Conservation and Terrestrial Ecosystem Programme (one of the six programs under ASEP I). The Programme itself speaks of "Ecosystem". ASEAN has continued to play an important role in developing an ecosystem management approach in biodiversity conservation. Its role is in the following main areas set forth below:

Setting Policy Guidelines on Biodiversity Conservation

Policy guidelines are important as they set out the vision and objectives for future actions. Policies may also form the basis of subsequent laws and regulations. At a meeting of the ASEAN Ministers of the then six ASEAN member states (Brunei, Indonesia, Malaysia, Philippines, Singapore and Thailand) held in Bangkok on 29 November 1984 the Governments represented there made a declaration, known as the *Bangkok Declaration on the ASEAN Environment.*

The objective of the Declaration was to "implement the ASEAN Development Strategy through an integrated approach entailing advance or forward planning in the environmentally related activities with a view to incorporating environmental dimension in development planning right at the base level in order to achieve sustained development and long-term conservation of environmental assets and at the same time improving the quality of life"...The Declaration then sets out Policy Guidelines to achieve the objective. These Guidelines include the conservation of nature and the marine environment as follows:

> **"(i) Nature Conservation**
>
> Develop new and practicable approaches for preserving forests wildlife, and other ecological systems in the face of continuing pressure. It is significant to note that this Policy Guideline recognizes the ecosystem approach to nature conservation. In an earlier soft law instrument, namely, the *Jakarta Consensus on Tropical Forestry* which emanated from the Third Meeting of the ASEAN Economic Ministers on Agriculture and Forestry, held in Jakarta, 12–14 August 1981, an ASEAN Common Forestry Policy was adopted.
>
> The Meeting recognized the importance of a common policy in developing the forestry as a basis for long term and effective sound development to improve the lives of the rural communities and maintain renewable

> resources for industrial development and sustain environmental amenity and ecological stability. It was recommended that the Common Forestry Policy should cover a number of areas including conservation, reforestation and management of forest resources. In this sector the Policy called for the establishment of adequate "permanent forest estates for protection, production, conservation, recreation and other purposes; management of forest resources based on the principles of sustained yield and appropriate optimal land use; and reforestation and forest development to obtain sustainable yielded."
>
> **(ii) Marine Environment**
>
> To develop practicable methods for the management of pollution discharges so that economic development of coastal resources may proceed in coexistence with preservation of the quality of coastal beaches and resorts and the marine environment.
>
> To develop policy guidelines which are also relevant to biodiversity conservation pertaining to education and training and environmental information systems. In biodiversity conservation, data regarding the status of flora and fauna are crucial to determining the type of measures to be taken. The Policy Guidelines call for the establishment of suitable national bank/ storage and retrieval system. It also calls for the use of remote sensing as a means of establishing environmental data."

The Policy Guidelines above have been translated into various ASEAN hard and soft law instruments and have influenced some of the policies relating to these areas at the national levels.

Developing Hard Law Instruments on Biodiversity: An Ecosystem System-Based Approach

Agreement on the Conservation of Nature and Natural Resources, 1985

The *ASEAN Agreement for the Conservation of Nature and Natural Resources* (ASEAN Agreement) was signed by the then six ASEAN member states in 1985 and has been ratified by Indonesia (10 July 1986), Philippines (4 September 1986) and Thailand (19 May 1986), but Brunei Darussalam, Malaysia and Singapore have yet to ratify it.

This Agreement was drafted with the technical assistance of the IUCN Environmental Law Centre and its Commission on Environmental Policy, Law and Administration. It has been regarded as one of the most progressive and forward instruments on the conservation of nature and natural resources. The approach adopted in the Agreement is an ecosystem-based approach. The main object of the Agreement is the conservation of wild flora, fauna and renewable resources (e.g., soil, vegetation, fisheries) through the protection of ecosystems, habitats and endangered species, and by ensuring sustainable use of harvested ones.

Thus the Preamble recognizes the "interdependence of living resources, between them and with other natural resources, within ecosystems of which they are part..." and calls upon parties to develop *national conservation strategies* and to coordinate such strategies within the framework of a *conservation strategy in the region.*

Viewed in the context of the development of international environmental law generally, the Agreement has been viewed by many as "remarkable" and "progressive", even today—14 years after it was signed. In the *Foreword to Legislation for Implementation of the ASEAN Agreement on the Conservation of Nature and Natural Resources: Country Reports (1994)*, it was stated:

> "It's [i.e., the Agreement] provisions reflect the most advanced state of the art of conservation and natural resource management at that time. Consequently, it contains a number of concepts which were unfamiliar in international agreements and which will call for a high degree of care in their transformation into national legislation."

The subject matter of the Agreement demonstrates a holistic/integrated approach, which was ahead of its time. The wide scope of the Agreement testifies to the ecosystem-based approach.

Chapter II: Conservation of Species and Ecosystems: This chapter deals with genetic diversity, sustainable use and, endangered and endemic species; vegetation and forest resources; the role of soil, water and air in the functioning of the natural ecosystems.

Chapter III: Conservation of Ecological Processes: This chapter deals with environmental degradation and pollution.

Chapter IV: Environmental Planning Measures: This chapter deals with land use planning, protected areas; impact assessment.

Chapter V: Environmental Planning Measures: This chapter deals with land use planning, protected areas; impact assessment.

Chapter VI: International Cooperation: This chapter covers matters like shared resources, and transfrontier environmental effects.

Chapter VII: International Supporting Measures: This chapter deals with organizational matters as meeting of contracting parties and the work of the Secretariat; and setting up of national agencies for coordination.

Chapter VIII: Final clauses include adoption of protocols, amendment, settlement of disputes, ratification, accession, and entry into force. The concept of "sustainable development" was introduced in this 1985 Agreement, even before the *Brundtland Report* was published in 1987, where the concept was stated as "development that meets the needs of the present without compromising the ability of future generations to meet their own needs." The WCED had started deliberations in 1984—it can be said that the 1985 Agreement had a preview of the WCED Report in 1987 when it noted in its Preamble that the interrelationship between conservation and socioeconomic development implies both that conservation is necessary to ensure sustainability of development, and that socioeconomic development is necessary for the achievement of conservation on a lasting basis.

Another aspect of the Agreement requires careful and innovative implementation measures in national legislation. Thus Article 2 calls for an integrated approach to development planning by taking into account the conservation and management of natural resources. Article 4 directs parties to develop management plans for maintaining the ecological relationship between harvested, dependent and related populations of living resources of the ecosystems in order to prevent the diminution of those species. For this purpose, a number of administrative measures are recommended such as a permit system.

The concept of "protected areas" contained in Article 13 is considered very innovative and sophisticated. It deals with the terrestrial, freshwater, coastal or marine ecosystems of the region and lays down the criteria for the protection of national parks and reserves. The main thrust of this Article is to safeguard the ecological and biological processes essential to the functioning of the ecosystems of the region including areas of particular importance from the scientific, educational, aesthetic or cultural viewpoints. The guidelines suggest an integrated ecosystem approach and involve the preparation of a management plan and the establishment of buffer zones. The Article also calls for the prohibition of exotic species and toxic substances and pollutants, the cooperation in the development of principles; objectives for the management of protected areas in the region.

As earlier noted, the Agreement is holistic as it deals, inter alia, not only with the substantive issues of conservation but also with the processes that conserve the functioning of the natural ecosystems, such as vegetation cover and forest resources, soil, water and air. For example, in the case of forests, it addresses the prevention of forest fires and also development plans of reforestation and afforestation. It also covers the implementation process such as land use planning, environmental impact assessment, pollution control, monitoring of environmental quality, education, information and training, international cooperation and supporting measures.

The Agreement is far-sighted as it not only incorporates some of the principles in the *Stockholm Declaration 1972*, the Commission on Sustainable Development (*Brundtland Report*) 1978, but also many of the concerns, policies, and institutional mechanisms discussed at UNCED (see supra), which are holistic. The Rio Conference of 1992, which introduced *Agenda 21*, also provided some environmental guidelines for the international community as well as regional, sub-regional and national organizations and these should give further impetus and urgency to conservation strategies and management both to ASEAN as a whole, as well as to its member states.

At the 7th and 8th meetings of ASOEN, held on 9-11 September 1996 and 8-11 September 1997, respectively, a call was made to assess the relevance of the ASEAN Agreement "in present context" i.e., in light of several international instruments relating to biodiversity, for example, the *Convention on Biodiversity* (CBD) and *Ramsar* (conservation and wise use of wetlands of international importance). In a paper I presented at the IUCN Workshop on Environmental Treaties, held from 25 to 26 November 1997 in Hanoi, I argued that the ASEAN Agreement has an important role to play at the subregional as well as national levels in that it reinforces and supplements these international instruments.

(Draft) ASEAN Framework Agreement on Access to Genetic Resources, 1999

At the Meeting of the ASEAN Senior Officials on the Environment held in the Philippines in September 1997, it was decided "to develop a common protocol among ASEAN member countries pertinent to the issue of access to genetic resources and intellectual rights." Pursuant to this decision, the Technical Experts of the ASEAN Working Group on Nature Conservation and Biodiversity (AWGNCB) together with some NGOs held a Workshop in the Philippines from 3 to 6 December 1998 and drafted a Framework Agreement on Access to Genetic Resources. This Framework is a major effort on the part of ASEAN countries which have common ecosystems and genetic resources to harmonize their laws on the question of access, sustainable use and conservation.

It would also lead to environmental auditing of all the resources in the ASEAN region, so important in an ecosystem-management approach. Countries with the same genetic resources could draft similar laws and contracts relating to their utilization and this will prevent "forum shopping" by users, which may lead to undesirable competitiveness. As this is only a Framework Agreement, it allows for flexibility in the determination of access.

Among the issues dealt with in the Agreement are prior informed consent and participation of key stakeholders (Art 7), fair and equitable sharing of benefits (Art 8) and environmental and social impact and biosafety concerns (Art 10).

Developing Soft Law Instruments on Biodiversity Conservation

Soft law instruments (declarations, resolutions, consensus, programs, plan of actions, etc.), though not binding often form the basis of subsequent laws. In any case, soft laws can be as effective as hard laws if implemented. Some of the important ASEAN soft law instruments on the environment deal with biodiversity conservation and are back-to-back with the *1985 ASEAN Agreement*, as they reinforce and supplement it.

Let us consider a few of them.

ASEAN Declaration on Heritage Parks and Reserves, 1984

This Declaration facilitates the management of some conservation areas in order "to maintain ecological processes and life support systems, preserve genetic diversity, ensure sustainable utilisation, educational, research, recreational and tourism values." Eleven national heritage sites and reserves in five ASEAN countries were declared under this Declaration. In some of these sites and reserves, national legislation has been passed to protect and manage them. Article 13 of the ASEAN Agreement lays down the criteria for *in situ* conservation and calls for a system of protected areas.

Jakarta Consensus on ASEAN Tropical Forestry, 1981, and Singapore Resolution on Environment and Development, 1992

One of the relevant ASEAN soft law instruments which include the conservation of fauna and flora as well as the protection of ecosystems is the *Jakarta Consensus on ASEAN Tropical Forestry, 1981*, earlier mentioned. This Consensus also calls for closer cooperation among ASEAN countries in the fields of environment and wildlife protection. Another instrument is the *Singapore Resolution on Environment and Development.* This Resolution was made at the Singapore meeting of the heads of the then ASEAN countries to develop a Common Stand at the UNCED held in Rio de Janeiro in 1992. Among the various common stands were issues pertaining to the protection and conservation of biodiversity and of the ecosystems of oceans and seas.

Developing Environmental Programs and Plans of Action

Since 1987, ten years after its establishment, ASEAN had its first Sub-Regional Environment Programme, known as ASEP I (1978–1982). There were six priority programs, one of which was Nature Conservation and Terrestrial Ecosystems. The Programme continued with ASEP II (1983–1987) and ASEP III (1988–1992) and was subsequently replaced by the ASEAN Strategic Plan of Action (ASPEN) 1994–1998 (see below). ASEPs I, II and III dealt with biodiversity conservation including:

- Implementation of a regional program on nature conservation with emphasis on the conservation of wild flora and fauna of the region; the harmonization of the list of endangered species of ASEAN countries; and the training of park and reserve wardens,

- Development of regional programs on the management of wetland ecosystems; management of wildlife species of economic importance; and the protection of migratory species that cross ASEAN borders,
- Development and implementation of a regional program for the development, protection, and rational exploitation of forest resources of the ASEAN region; and the establishment of adequate and proper monitoring; management and information system for the control of soil erosion and the practice of shifting cultivation.

ASEAN Strategic Plan of Action, 1994–1998 (ASPEN)

ASPEN was drafted to take into account, inter alia, the recommendations of *Agenda 21* at UNCED and to introduce policy measures to encourage the integration of environmental factors at national and regional levels,

Strategy 5 of ASPEN established a regional framework on biological diversity conservation and sustainable utilization of its components. The following are the actions to be carried out:

Promote the Development of a Framework for the Protection and Conservation of Heritage and Endangered Species

ASEAN has long recognized the importance of nature and biodiversity, and thus heritage areas. Despite these management and monitoring efforts, the threat of these identified areas persists owing to continued habitat destruction, overharvesting, pollution and threats posed by the introduction of exotic species (both plants and animals) which either replaces or competes with the endemic species. The absence of a regional framework for the protection and conservation of heritage areas and endangered species has designated areas that are to be preserved as national parks, nature reserves and only exacerbates the situation as management efforts are left to individual member countries. There is a need to develop a framework for the protection of these areas and species so as to ensure that conservation approaches are rationalized.

Strengthen Capacities for R&D to Enhance Biodiversity Conservation in the Region

In support of the areas designated for biological diversity conservation are efforts to improve the knowledge and understanding of species found in these areas. The current stage of knowledge on the status and distribution of many animal and plant species is still poor and inadequate. As a result, effective conservation measures cannot be implemented. ASPEN should invest in this field and seek assistance from the international community both in public and private sectors. Strong support to systematic and taxonomic research which ranges from undertaking surveys and inventories to monitoring wildlife movement and control should be pursued by the region....

Strategy 6 noted that:

> "Southeast Asian seas are natural habitats for numerous species of fish and invertebrates. They provide the supply of marine products and source of livelihood for many of the region's fishermen. All ASEAN countries have extensive fishing industries. Yet, many of the major nearshore fishing areas in the region are over-fished and polluted from land based sources and oil spills. The Straits of Malacca, for example, is one of the major shipping lanes for crude oil transport and is vulnerable to oil spills. There has been a notable increase in the occurrence of red tides which is attributed to domestic sources of pollution. This incidence poses not only a health hazard but also affects export earnings. Similarly, many mangroves are disappearing to make room for brackish water prawn farming, housing and industrial development. Coral reefs are also being degraded and require rehabilitation. Accordingly, there is an urgent need for a more coordinated, proactive and collective action to protect ASEAN's coastal zones and marine resources."

The actions to be carried out under this strategy are:

ASEAN has long recognized the importance of nature and biodiversity, and thus heritage areas.

Improvement of Regional Marine and Coastal Environmental Coordination

Cooperation among the ASEAN countries in the field of marine sciences and marine environments have been carried out through three distinct regional bodies, namely, the Coordinating Body on the Seas of East Asia (COBSEA), the ASOEN Working Group on ASEAN Seas and Marine Environment (WGASME) and the COST Sub-committee on Marine Science (SCMS). While the WGASME and the SCMS are official ASEAN bodies, the latter being under the purview of the ASEAN Committee on Science and Technology (COST), COBSEA comes under the purview of the United Nations Environment Programme (UNEP). There is a need to streamline these cooperative mechanisms, as they create unnecessary overlaps and contusion and fritter away scarce technical and financial resources.

Development of a Framework for the Integrated Management of Regional Coastal Zones

It is recognized that while several programs have been developed on a bilateral and regional basis to protect and manage coastal zones in the region, these developments are not tied to any framework that could integrate its approaches on a regional basis. The impacts, therefore, of these programs have been localized and its regional benefits have not been fully appreciated or felt. In order to enhance the effects of these activities, ASEAN could initiate the development of a framework for the integrated management of regional coastal zones. This framework could serve as a guide in the development of the respective coastal zone management interventions by member countries.

Apart from ASPEN, it should be mentioned that other ASEAN programs such as those in ASEAN Cooperation Plan on Transboundary Pollution, 1995 have an indirect as well as direct impact on biodiversity conservation.

Hanoi Plan of Action, 1999–2004

The Hanoi Plan of Action is to protect the environment and promote sustainable development. The following are the recommendations:

- Fully implement the *ASEAN Cooperation Plan on Transboundary Pollution* with particular emphasis on the *Regional Haze Action Plan* by the year 2001 which have a direct or indirect impact on biodiversity conservation. Strengthen the ASEAN Specialised Meteorological Centre with emphasis on the ability to monitor forest and land fires and provide early warning on transboundary haze by the year 2001.
- Establish the ASEAN Regional Research and Training Centre for Land and Forest Fire Management by the year 2004.
- Strengthen the ASEAN Regional Centre for Biodiversity Conservation by establishing networks of relevant institutions and implement collaborative training and research activities by the year 2001.
- Promote regional coordination for the protection of the ASEAN Heritage Parks and Reserves.
- Develop a framework and improve regional coordination for the integrated protection and management of coastal zones by the year 2001.
- Formulate and adopt an ASEAN Protocol on access to genetic resources by the year 2004.
- Develop a *Regional Action Plan* for the Protection of the Marine Environment from Land-based and Sea-based Activities by the year 2004.
- Enhance public information and education in awareness of and participation in environmental and sustainable development issues.

Other actions under the Plan relating to biodiversity are as follows:

- Strengthen institutional and legal capacities to implement *Agenda 21* and other international environmental agreements by the year 2001.
- Harmonize the environmental databases of Member Countries by the year 2001.
- Implement an ASEAN regional water conservation program by the year 2001.
- Establish a regional center or network for the promotion of environmentally sound technologies by the year 2004.
- Implement the *Framework to Achieve Long-Term Environmental Goals for Ambient Air and River Water Qualities for ASEAN Countries.*
- Enhance regional efforts in addressing climatic change.

Some Current Projects of ASEAN Working Group on Nature Conservation/Biodiversity

Some of the current ASEAN projects on biodiversity conservation which would involve an ecosystem management approach are Transborder Parks and other Protected Areas for Conservation within the Greater

ASEAN Region. The components of this project include a Management Plan for ASEAN Heritage Parks and Reserves (see ante, on *ASEAN Declaration on Heritage Parks and Reserves 1984*, where a number of parks and reserves were listed). Such management would include cooperation among the countries concerned and training and assistance. Another project is the ASEAN Turtle Conservation Programme. The ASEAN region is considered a critical habitat for six species of marine turtles. Various species of turtles are found mainly in Berau and Irian Jaya in Indonesia, Philippines, Sabah Turtle Islands (Malaysia) and Viet Nam.

Threats to these species of turtles have been due to over-exploitation and habitat degradation with the result that there has been a rapid decline over the last 50 years. Sea turtles are migratory and, hence, conservation in the ASEAN region requires concerted effort among the ASEAN countries. In 1991, at the 2nd AWGNC Meeting, the Philippines proposed a symposium on marine turtles, and this materialized when the 1st ASEAN Symposium-Workshop on Marine Turtles Conservation was held in Manila in December 1993, the output of which was the ASEAN Marine Turtle Conservation Programme with the following components which are again ecosystem-based, for example:

- Institution Building—which calls for the creation of ASEAN Marine Turtle Specialist Network to collaborate the implementation of the regional program and to formulate and recommend policies and programs to the AWGNC;
- Information System Development which involves the establishment of regional database and information network for marine turtles;
- Management-Oriented Research and Monitoring to enhance and collaborate research and monitoring activities particularly on population status and distribution, turtle harvest management and other augmentative researches relevant to the conservation and protection for all stages of the life of marine turtles;
- Education and Conservation Awareness to coordinate training and education not only for then personnel involved in marine turtle conservation and management but also for the local communities affected by the program;
- Resource Management to work out for the declaration of globally and regionally significant habitats for marine turtles as ASEAN Heritage/Conservation Areas. The identified significant marine turtle areas/habitats in the ASEAN Region include the:
  - Turtle Island of Philippines and Sabah, Sipadan, Malaysia; and the Berau Islands of Indonesia for green turtles;
  - Pantai Utara Kepala Burung Irian Jaya of Indonesia for leatherbacks and green turtles; and
- International Linkages to encourage member countries to accede to international conventions such as the CITES and the IUCN-SSC Marine Turtle Specialist Group, among others.

This Program was endorsed by ASOEN at its 4th AWGNC Meeting in 1994. Subsequently, an ASEAN Marine Turtle Specialist Network was included. This was submitted to the ACU for appraisal and the Appraisal Report considered this Network and the Conservation Programme as consistent with the ASEAN Plan of Action on the Environment (ASPEN) 1994–1998, under Strategic 5.1 "Promote the development of a framework for the protection and conservation of heritage areas and endangered species."

Other current projects of the ASEAN Group on Nature Conservation/Biodiversity such as the ASEAN/Australia Wetlands Waterbirds Project, the ASBAN/Australia Marine National Parks Staff Exchange project are all part of the ecosystem approach to biodiversity conservation.

Conclusion

Since 1978 ASEAN has developed legal instruments, programs and plans of action concerning biodiversity conservation from an ecosystem-based approach, with the 1985 *ASEAN Agreement on the Conservation of Nature and Natural Resources* as the epitome. However, all these are in most parts only "frameworks" (of necessity), and must be further developed in order to implement them. Some have been developed or are in the process of being further developed at the regional and national levels. The Indonesian fires (which have been detrimental to the biodiversity in Indonesia, among other types of damage) have brought to the fore the need for, inter alia, sound conservation policies, sustainable development and utilization, forward planning, effective laws at the subregional and national levels, EIAs at the regional and national levels, participation from local communities, institutional restructuring and strengthening, training and research, regional and international cooperation.

All these elements have already been incorporated in the various instruments, programs and plans of action but, as mentioned, the details have to be worked out. As a regional institution, ASEAN is well placed to develop an effective regional network to coordinate with the national units in the ASEAN member countries as well with the international community to protect the ecosystem in the whole of the ASEAN region and beyond, if necessary. The establishment of the ARCBC, with its links to the ASEAN countries and the European Community, is a great step forward. More networks should be established with regional institutions concerned with biodiversity.

More networks should be established with regional institutions concerned with biodiversity.

Together with the ASEAN Secretariat and the AWGNCB, more can be achieved, However, these ASEAN institutions and the national units on biodiversity need to be strengthened in terms of "jurisdiction" (e.g., at the national level there are some countries which experience conflicting jurisdictions), governance, personnel, training and research. From the viewpoint of management, it is also desirable for representatives of various countries attending meetings (e.g., AWGNCB) to continue to be represented at subsequent meetings (as far as possible) so that they will be able to follow through the discussion of a particular topic to its conclusion.. This will make for more effective participation as the representatives will be able to follow through the whole discussion.

Over the last few years, the 10 ASEAN countries have ratified and are still in the process of ratifying many international instruments concerning biodiversity such as the CBD, Ramsar, Bonn and the *World Heritage Convention*. ASEAN should play a bigger role to see what common issues can be addressed at the regional level and it could also influence the process of biodiversity conservation at the national level. It could, for example, facilitate the synergies relating to these conventions at the intra-ASEAN as well as at the national levels. ASEAN has taken a more pro-active stand as witnessed by the establishment of ARCBC in 1998 and the current work of the AWGCNB. What is needed is a stronger political will and closer cooperation to "develop national conservation strategies, and co-ordinate such strategies within the framework of a conservation strategy for the region"(Article 1).

[*Information regarding the IUCN Regional Biodiversity Programme, Asia can be found on the Internet at http:// www.rbp-iucn.lk. This site was accessed 22/06/01.*]

G

ASEAN Cooperation Plan on Transboundary Pollution, 1995

[*The ASEAN Plan of Cooperation on Transboundary Pollution represents a significant milestone in ASEAN environmental cooperation and reflects the common resolve of ASEAN member countries to join hands in addressing an important problem facing in the region. This Plan addresses the following three programme areas: transboundary atmospheric pollution, transboundary movement of hazardous waste, and transboundary shipborne pollution.*]

Programme Area 1: Transboundary Atmospheric Pollution

Objectives

This Programme Area has the following objectives:

(1) to assess the origin and cause(s), nature and extent of local and regional haze incidents;

(2) to prevent and control the sources of haze at both national and regional levels by applying environmentally sound technologies and by strengthening both national and regional capabilities in the assessment, mitigation and management of haze; and

(3) to develop and implement national and regional emergency response plans.

Strategies

The best short-term strategy to address transboundary atmospheric pollution issue to prevent anthropogenically induced forest fires, especially in land clearing activities in timber and agricultural estates and transmigration projects. The following measures should be undertaken:

(1) timely detection and prevention of forest fires through early warning systems, the deployment of ground forces and preparedness of local communities;

(2) prohibit burning and prevention of biomass generated largely by development projects during dry periods, particularly in the region affected by dry weather;
(3) during haze episode, to minimize any generation of pollution from local sources, to activate communication network for the sharing of information, and to activate relevant joint activities; and
(4) promote investments in alternative uses of biomass.

As a long term strategy, zero-burning practices and technologies which would result in pollution reduction should be promoted in all economic sectors through attractive financing by lending agencies. The longer term measures also comprise awareness building efforts to eliminate the use of fire in land clearing activities, as well as introducing improvement of land clearing activities through economically sound and environmentally friendly methods in agriculture. Areas susceptible to spontaneous outbreaks of fire, such as coalbeds and peat fields, should be developed to enable investments in appropriate activities.

Activities

The following activities shall be undertaken:
(1) establish National Focal Points in each country with inter alia the following functions:
 (a) make an inventory of existing resources, and
 (b) establish types of information to be shared/ disseminated.
(2) expand the role of the ASEAN Specialized Meteorological Centre (ASMC) to develop an atmospheric transport model in order to predict the tracts and spread of smoke haze;
(3) establish procedures for reporting/alerting of fires by the Forestry and other relevant agencies;
(4) develop a common air quality index and harmonize air quality sampling techniques;
(5) develop a regional fire danger rating system;
(6) share knowledge and technology in the prevention and mitigation of forest fire and other emission sources;
(7) establish a mechanism for cooperation in combating forest fires and other emission sources and their points of activation;
(8) expand the role of ASEAN Institution of Forest Management (AIFM) to strengthen national capacity through training in forest fire management; and
(9) enhance national and regional capabilities to deal with forest fires and other emission sources.

Institutional Arrangements

National Focal Points

The National Focal Points for this component of the Action Plan appear in Annex A.

Regional Institutions and Arrangements

In addressing the issue of transboundary pollution, the involvement of several existing ASEAN institutions and arrangements have been identified as follows:
(a) The ASEAN Specialised Meteorological Centre (ASMC)
 ASMC being the regional facility for developing specialized weather forecasting capability for the region, should serve as a focal point for coordinating the detection and monitoring of transboundary atmospheric pollution in cooperation with the national meteorological services of the ASEAN member countries.
(b) ASEAN Institute of Forest Management (AIFM)
 AIFM's expanded role should focus on upgrading of skills and capabilities in the field of forest fire management, namely:
 • establish linkages with developed countries and multilateral organizations regarding the use of fire danger rating system, GIS and remote sensing technologies in forest fire monitoring and mapping of fire-prone areas;
 • develop and implement a regional forest fire danger rating system;
 • develop and implement a regional strategy for responding to forest fire emergencies; and
 • coordinate development of training standards where applicable.
(c) ASEAN Working Group on Forestry, ASEAN-EC Joint Consultative Committee (JCC) Sub-Committee on Forest, and Brunei-Indonesia-Malaysia-Philippines (BIMP). The East ASEAN Growth Areas (EAGA) Sub-Committee on Forest ASOEN should explore ways to work closely with the above bodies to enhance cooperation to combat forest fire.

Programme Area 2: Transboundary Movement of Hazardous Wastes

Objective

The objective of this program is to prevent and control illegal transboundary movement of hazardous wastes.

Strategy

To control the transboundary movement of hazardous wastes, all ASEAN member countries should accede to the *Basel Convention* as soon as possible.

Activities

In subscribing to the provisions of the *Basel Convention* the following activities shall be undertaken:

(1) identification of focal points in each ASEAN country;

(2) exchange of information on list of hazardous wastes and control procedures on the movement of such wastes as adopted by each country;

(3) training programs and capacity building on the management of hazardous wastes; and

(4) development of national legislation to control the management of hazardous waste within the country as well as for its movement from abroad.

Institutional Arrangement

The National Focal Points for this programme area appear in Annex B.

Programme Area 3: Transboundary Shipborne Pollution

Objective

The National Focal Points for this Programme Area appear in Annex C.

Resources and Extra-Regional Support

Cooperative links shall be established with multinational agencies and third countries to strengthen national and regional capabilities in addressing the transboundary pollution problem. With regard to Programme Area 1, the following needs have been identified for resourcing:

(1) Resources for Assessment

  (a) modelling technique which can accurately simulate and predict long-range transportation of haze over the ASEAN region and evaluate the impact of transboundary haze on local air quality;

  (b) remote-sensing data acquisition for early detection of forest fire through satellite and aircraft; and

  (c) development and use of fire danger rating system, GIS and vegetation fuel modelling for mapping of fire-prone areas.

(2) Resources for Management

  (a) capacity building in the prevention and mitigation of forest fire and other emission sources through development of standardized training program.

  (b) project demonstration relating to up-to-date technology in biomass utilization such as composting and generation of electricity which can bring returns to investment; and

  (c) investment in biomass utilization.

Indonesia Fires Internet Sites:

[*These sites were all accessed on the 22/06/01.*]
http://www.haze-online.or.id/
http://www.asean.or.id/news/ar_haze.htm
http://www3.itu.int/MISSIONS/Myanmar/jps00001.htm
http://www.reliefweb.int/w/rwb.nsf
http://icsea.org/sea-span/SCIPOL2/STUDY323.htm
http://www.env.gov.sg/info/press/pr99/rel-84-99.html
http://www.fs.fed.us/global/globe/asia/indonesia/links/regionalfire.htm
http://eapei.home.att.net/2001cp.htm
http://www.unep.org/unep/per/for_fire/sitrep.pdf
http://www.middlebury.edu/SouthChinaSea/why.html

(i) Tay S.S.C., "The South-East Asian Fires and Sustainable Development: What Should be Done About the Haze?," *Indonesian Quarterly*, xxvi (2), pp 99–117

Introduction

Environmental law and policy struggles with the simple fact that ecology does not respect national borders. The natural world of wind, water and animals moves according to their own patterns and cycles. The world of politics and law, in contrast, is built upon borders and rests on the

Westphalian structure of states, each being sovereign within its borders and over its foreign agreements.

Consequently, environmental concerns that cross boundaries between nations or regions, or that span the globe, require systems of cooperation among sovereign nations. Conversely, environmental concerns that lie within the borders of a single State are often seen as a function of domestic jurisdiction, which is reserved to the representatives of that State. To make law and policy respond effectively to environmental concerns therefore requires thinking through different levels or *loci* for action: international, regional, national and local communities. This needs then to be paired to a search for the right policies and instruments, especially as between coercive measures or "sticks" and cooperative action and incentives, or "carrots". The ability of environmental law to work at different levels and by varied policies and instruments is severely tested by the fires and smoke haze experienced by Southeast Asian countries.

The fires in 1997 and 1998 have been described by the *United Nations Environment Programme* (UNEP) chief, Dr. Klaus Topfer, as one of the world's worst environmental disasters. There are clear and considerable impacts in the region on human health, the environment, natural resources and economic activity.

From the fires of 1997, estimates are that between 800,000 and 4.5 million hectares of forests and bush in the Indonesian islands of Sumatra and Kalimantan were burnt. For the 1998 fires, as at end April, official Indonesian estimates were that 395,000 hectares of forest and ground cover were destroyed. The economic damage for 1998 in log and timber damage alone, without environmental and health costs, were set at US$912 million. The fires and haze have had considerate economic impacts. An early estimate for the 1997 fires is that Indonesia, Malaysian and Singapore have in total lost some US$1.4 billion in increased health care, and foregone receipts in tourism.

Clearly, the fires are (or should be) of immediate concern to Indonesia, where the vast majority of the fires have originated, and which suffers the vast majority of ecological, economic and other damages. Indonesia's immediate neighbors Singapore and Malaysia, need be concerned too.

Our perspective on the nature of the problem shapes our response. Despite the grave effects on the local environment, human health, economic activity, resources and global environmental concerns, our perspectives are betrayed by the terms we use to describe the problem.

The tendency in the region is to talk about the "haze", rather than pollution. The use of the term, "haze", understates the risk to human health. The perception of "haze" also contrasts to a focus on the fires that cause it. The term "haze" suggests that, if winds change direction, there is no problem for West Malaysia or Singapore. This may help explain the inaction among the ASEAN governments after initial attempts following the 1991 and 1994 incidents of haze in the region. Changing our perception to focus on the cause—the fires—might help sustain action in the medium to longer term, even when the cities and countryside of the region are not smogged in. Focusing on the fires would help preventive and precautionary thinking and planning.

The fires have implications for regional and inter-regional politics too. The ability of ASEAN to react to the fires, or their inability to do so, will test the working relations between the member states and affect the grouping's credibility in the eyes of others. But, beyond this, our perceptions should be challenged in viewing this as a regional or subregional problem, entangling only ASEAN or the subgroup of Brunei, Indonesia, Malaysia and Singapore. It is important to note the wider implications of the Southeast Asian fires. There are also considerable impacts on global environmental concerns with biodiversity and climate change, issues which confront the international community. As such, the fires and smoke haze are directly related to global environmental issues and are reason for the legitimate concern among nations far beyond the region. As such, the ability and commitment of the international community and of international institutions will also be tested.

In looking at the use of fire, we must bear in mind the clear satellite evidence in 1997 that most fires were started on large land-holdings and plantations. These are run by large conglomerates, many with international and regional investors. The main source of the fires, as the Indonesian government itself stated, is not small-scale indigenous farmers. These large businesses have continued to use fires for land clearing not because of tradition but because it is a cheaper alternative to other, less pollutive methods. This is despite Indonesian laws that prohibit the use of fire.

In discussing the fires and haze, some perspectives have emphasized the El Niño climatic effect. Such a perspective can easily lead to fatalism: that we should do nothing but wait for the weather to change. It must be noted however that there have been fires and haze occurrences in years when there was no El Niño and, conversely, there have been previous El Niño phenomenon which did not coincide with the fires.

Others have taken the perspective that the current political and economic uncertainties faced by Indonesia exacerbate the problems. This perspective is useful in emphasizing the realism of the current situation. It should not however be turned into a blanket excuse for inaction. It must be recognized that the fires and severe haze also occurred in 1994 and in the early 1980s, years when Indonesia was stable and flourishing. Present economic-political uncertainties may lessen our ability to respond effectively to the problem, but are not their root.

Given the focus on fires, it may seem that fire-fighting is the key response. Some emphasize the use of high-tech fire-fighting, moreover, with fire-bombing from airplanes or helicopters. Clearly, when fire has broken out, fire-fighting is needed, especially timely and quick fire-fighting, backed with well trained and equipped fire-fighting units on the ground. But fire-fighting should not be our only response. Rather, the fires need to be addressed in the medium to longer term, to prevent the recurrence that the past years have witnessed, in both El Niòo cycles and at other times. Taking a medium to longer term perspective emphasizes prevention, rather than emergency response. What we should do then goes beyond the immediate task of fire-fighting to look at education and other methods to prevent, limit or control the use of fire in clearing land. Management and strategy are needed. In contrast, fire-fighting will always be just that: fire-fighting.

The following table summarizes the keywords for our perspective to take action on the Southeast Asian fires, in contrast to misperceptions that foster inertia, misdirected attempts or palliative efforts:

Once we take the perspective for action, the first and primary cause of the fires also becomes clear. It is the failure of the Indonesian system to enforce its own laws and regulations, and to manage its resources so as to pursue sustainable development. The attempts by Indonesia to deal with the fires, or the lack of such attempts, must first be examined before we look to regional and other responses.

Beyond this, the article will also consider the rights and duties of those outside Indonesia to act in the absence of effective action by Indonesia. What exactly non-Indonesians can and should do is open to question. Much depends on how we answer three primary questions:

(1) What are the causes of the problem?
(2) What are the answers and remedies?
(3) How do we conceive the appropriate role of nations and agencies outside Indonesia?

There are, as such, a matrix of different policy responses that arise from these three primary questions. For instance, we may believe that the cause is Indonesia's lack of capacity in addressing the issue, or we may diagnose cronyism and corruption. If we think capacity is the root problem, we may prescribe giving financial and technical assistance, and providing equipment. This has been captured in the principle of international environmental law of recognizing common and differentiated responsibilities. Neighboring states may contribute and cooperate for a solution by drawing from their own resources.

On the other hand, even if we see capacity and financial assistance as keys to a solution, we may still feel that it is not our duty to contribute substantially to finance and other forms of help. States in the region may call for extra-regional resources, given their own inadequacies or because of the implications for the global environment.

TABLE 1: MISPERCEPTIONS AND PERSPECTIVES FOR ACTION

Misperception for Inertia	Perspective for Action
• Haze	• Fires, pollution
• Local effects only	• Local, regional and global effects
• El Niño fluke	• Recurrent
• Traditional small-scale farmers	• Primary from large businesses
• Problem caused by poverty and problems	• Response weakened by poverty and problems in Indonesia
• Indonesia	• Fire-fighting prevention, control, integrated forest management and fire-fighting
• Lack of development	• Unsustainable development

On the other hand, if we see cronyism and corruption as the problems, we might not grant monetary assistance, feeling that funds will be misspent. Instead, we may believe that sanctions and other "sticks" are the keys to getting Indonesia to bear its legal responsibility and address the problem. This is consonant with the international law principle of State responsibility, enshrined in Principle 21 of the *Stockholm Declaration on the Human Environment*

Still, even if we believe that State responsibility must be imposed on the guilty parties, if we are neighboring states, we may still, for bilateral relations, wish to have someone else—international bodies such as the International Monetary Fund (IMF) or a superpower like the US—take those measures and incur their resentment.

Given the many different possibilities, this article will focus first on Indonesia, where most of the fires have started. Then, it will consider the rights and duties of ASEAN at the regional level and of the international community and institutions. Finally, it will sketch possible actions at the level of citizens—by NGOs, companies and individual consumers. The article briefly reviews efforts to date: what we have done. It also considers suggestions on what more should be done.

While there are many suggestions, the article tries to recognize the context of ASEAN and emphasize what may be politically acceptable to Indonesia and other parties. It does not however accept the ASEAN way as a given, but tries to seek ways to evolve the modes of cooperation to seek a solution. Of the many suggestions surveyed, the emphasis of this article is to link economics and environment towards sustainable development. Such a linkage is controversial in an ASEAN context. The argument is, however, that there is no other means to bring sufficient priority and attention to the issue in Indonesia. Additionally, the article will seek to center the link between economics and the environment not on sanctions, but in more positive ways.

What Indonesia Has and Has Not Done to Date

Given the largely manmade beginnings of the fires, and their primary location within one nation—Indonesia—national legislation and policy making might be expected to be sufficient to prevent and control the environmental problem, yet national responses have been ineffective. As noted, this is due in part to the fact that Indonesia currently faces not only the environmental disaster of the fires, but also the economic downturn and uncertainty in its once booming economy. With its economic problems, there are doubts that Indonesia presently has the financial wherewithal to stop the problem, even if the political will exists. It is clear, and understandable, that Indonesia is giving priority to its economic crisis, the resultant political tensions and an increasing famine in some areas, resulting from both crop failure and the sharp depreciation of their currency.

While not a priority, some environmental efforts have been made. The use of fire to clear land has been illegal under Indonesian law since 1993. Penalties for the use of fire to clear land were increased in 1997 to a maximum of 15 years jail and a maximum fine of 250 million rupiahs. New laws also allow the government to seize the assets and close down the activities of companies found guilty. The critical failure in Indonesia is not that laws are missing, but that laws have not been effectively enforced.

With its economic problems, there are doubts that Indonesia presently has the financial wherewithal to stop the problem, even if the political will exists.

The names of some 180 major companies thought to be involved were released in 1997. None, however, have been successfully prosecuted to date and only five have recently begun to face prosecution by Indonesian governmental agencies.

The lack of effective enforcement is systemic. The Indonesian Ministry for the Environment does not have direct jurisdiction over the agricultural and forestry lands involved. Nor can it command provincial authorities to enforce the laws.

Many observers blame the failure of enforcement and the misallocation of natural resources on institutional weakness, corruption and cronyism; much like the economic problems. Reform of the legal and administrative system is the advice.

There are additional and differing analyses. Some commentators emphasize the lack of capacity in Indonesia. They argue that even assuming that there is political will to address the environmental issues, there is a lack of capacity in fire-fighting and other relevant institutions, especially at the provincial level. Their response would be to increase assistance to Indonesia, in terms of funding, equipment and technical assistance, both for fire-fighting.

Others believe that problems stem from misguided development policies and inappropriate land use, often with short or uncertain land tenure. These cause:

- a higher rate of conversion of land from forest to plantation (with the use of fire);

- irrational allocation of lands for conversion, by which virgin forest is converted and not degraded forest or *alang-alang* (wild grass) lands; and
- the lack of any incentive of companies to adopt sustainable practices in forestry, such as re-planting.

Different suggestions arise from the identification of these problems. Some would urge us to stop the conversion of virgin forest land to plantation land, and to conserve those lands for nature. Some conservationists urge this perspective. Many from developing countries would however view this as another disguised constraint on economic development, in contradiction of the right to permanent sovereignty over natural resources, the right to development and the principles of sustainable development.

Other forestry experts do not emphasize conservation per se, but that a priority be established for land conversion. By such priority, degraded forest and *alang-alang* fields in Kalimantan would first be converted to plantation land, rather than virgin forest and peat swamps. Such a recommendation would seem to allow the development of plantations while avoiding the greater harm to rainforests, striking a better balance for sustainable development. This has been the thrust of several programs in Indonesia by agencies such as the *International Tropical Timber Organization* and the German GTZ agency. It remains to be seen if the Indonesian government will consider and commit to such reforms.

What, in sum, Indonesia has failed to do is:

(1) to ensure compliance with its own existing laws,

(2) develop sufficient capacity to deal with the fires, and

(3) shape and change land use and other policies for sustainable development.

The following steps would assist Indonesia in addressing the underlying causes of the fires:

(1) Agencies must be activated to enforce their own laws and regulations. These agencies must necessarily go beyond the Ministry of Environment, to involve and coordinate between agencies with appropriate jurisdiction and reach, such as the Ministries of Agriculture and Forestry, the BAPEDAL agency and provincial authorities.

(2) Enforcement of the laws must be equal and even, extending to companies involved in cronyism and corruption, as well as those with foreign investments.

(3) As regards land use, the tenure of land concessions and ambiguous property rights in Indonesia may also have to be considered.

(4) Without preventing sustainable development by Indonesia, the rational use of land should be encouraged. In particular, oil palm and other plantations might be developed not in virgin rainforest, but rather in degraded forests or *alang-alang* fields. This would require initial efforts and inputs but conserve the ecological and other values of the rainforests.

The first and best remedy to the fires clearly lies within Indonesia itself. There are, however, reasons to look beyond Indonesia's efforts at the national level. International and regional organizations and communities can assist and support Indonesia's efforts. This may be a necessity to supply Indonesia's lack of capacity. There may also be a need for international and regional efforts to supplement or override the national efforts, if we take the reason for Indonesia's failure to date to be systemic cronyism and corruption.

The Role of Those Outside

What should we do, from outside Indonesia? Much depends on our view of the appropriate role of ASEAN, the international community and the private sector.

Some in Indonesia and ASEAN believe that nothing should be done by those outside the nation, as this would constitute a breach of the norm of non-intervention. This is a key tenet of the ASEAN way. In this view, the fires are the internal affair of Indonesia, over which no State or ASEAN itself can legitimately take action.

Such a conception of the ASEAN way is misconceived. First and foremost, the haze is not a purely internal matter for Indonesia. There are clear and severe external, transboundary effects and damage. This transboundary character removes it from the realm of exclusive jurisdiction. The effect of the fires on global issues of biodiversity and climate change have similar effect.

A second and connected reason is international law holds that a State is responsible for transboundary harm that results from activities on its territory, carried out by the State or within its control. This, arguably, stems from the general international law of State responsibility and the landmark *Trail Smelter Arbitration*, and is enshrined as Principle 21 of the 1972 *Stockholm Convention on the Human Environment*.

Based on this principle, Indonesia should be held responsible to the affected countries for the consequences of its failure to enforce its own laws and to control the fires. There have also been suggestions that ancillary or procedural duties arise. Such duties require States to generally prevent, mitigate, repair for harm and notify others of risks. These principles of State responsibility and liability for transboundary harm clearly limit the norm of non-intervention.

There are difficulties in applying Principle 21 and the *Trail Smelter* case. Establishing legal responsibility would be difficult given the lack of a threshold for transboundary pollution in terms of the haze, established by either custom or treaty. In the ASEAN context, it is very unlikely that any State is likely to try to impose State responsibility on Indonesia, in a strict, legal meaning and hold it liable to harm. Although intra-ASEAN disputes have recently been referred to the International Court of Justice for peaceful settlement, a litigious attitude over the fires might be seen to be antithetical to the ASEAN way. It may also be unrealistic, given the limits of Indonesian capacity to respond.

To date, the Indonesian government has accepted moral but not legal responsibility, with then President Suharto offering a public apology at an ASEAN environment ministers meeting in 1997. The Governments of Singapore and Malaysia, the two most affected neighbors, have not to date publicly complained to Indonesia, claimed any legal right against Indonesia or pursued any legal approaches to seek compensation. But recognizing the norm of State responsibility is a strong basis to suggest that Indonesia has a duty to consult and cooperate with affected States, and take good faith measures within its capacity to further agreed actions.

The principle of agreement is a third factor that must be noted. Where Indonesia consents to action plans, offers of assistance and other cooperative measures, there is no interference in Indonesia's domestic affairs.

ASEAN Responses

ASEAN has not been inactive on the issue of the fires specifically, or on the environment, more generally. Its record has, however, been mixed. ASEAN countries have often come under criticism from environmentalists and NGOs. This is especially in respect of tropical deforestation and the lack of conservation efforts. To date many countries in the region have been impacted by industrialization on one hand, and the continuing problems of poverty and the lack of infrastructure on the other hand.

As a grouping, ASEAN took its first step forward on the environment in 1978. Its first Ministerial level declaration on cooperation on environmental issues followed in 1981. It has however been better known as taking a pro-developing country stand at the 1992 Earth Summit. ASEAN countries also rallied to lobby successfully against Austrian eco-labels on tropical timber. Most recently, ASEAN countries have been central to the challenge in the World Trade Organization against US laws against shrimp imports, where production methods do not safeguard against the killing of sea turtles.

More positively, ASEAN members have undertaken some steps towards improving environmental cooperation among themselves, and with other states. These have taken the form of environmental programs, evolving through three phases to an ASEAN Strategic Plan of Action (1994–1998). The strategies cover a broad range of environmental concerns and adopt many of the approaches recommended in *Agenda 21*.

The effectiveness of such measures however suffer from weakness in monitoring, assisting and ensuring State compliance. This is in view of the "ASEAN way" and its preference for non-interference in the domestic affairs of member states; for non-binding plans, instead of treaties; and for central institutions with relatively little initiative and resources. As such, the ASEAN environmental undertakings may be characterized as plans for cooperation between national institutions, rather than the creation or strengthening of any regional institutions as a central hub for policy making or implementation. These same characteristics of the ASEAN way find expression in the specific agreements on the fires and resulting haze.

ASEAN environment ministers agreed to a Cooperation Plan on Transboundary Pollution in June 1995. The Cooperation Plan set out the broad policies and strategies to deal with atmospheric and other forms of transhoundary pollution. This followed the haze in 1994. The Cooperation Plan outlined efforts to be made at both national and regional levels to deal with the haze. At the national level, each country undertook to establish focal points and enhance national capabilities to deal with forest fires. Countries also agreed to share knowledge and technology on the prevention and mitigation of forest fires, and establish a mechanism for cooperation in combating forest fires.

A common air quality index and a regional fire danger rating system was to be developed for the region. ASEAN institutions like the Specialized Meteorological Centre were asked to develop ways of predicting the tracts and spread of smoke haze.

The Cooperation Plan also envisaged seeking support from countries outside the region, from countries with knowledge in fire management systems, like New Zealand and the US, as well as institutions such as the International Tropical Timber Organization, based in Japan.

The Cooperation Plan is not as formal as comparable treaties in other regions, like Europe, which deal with long distance transboundary harm. Its principles and approach, however, might seem workable and indeed commendable. First and foremost, perhaps, the Cooperation Plan recognized that the region was a single eco-system. Additionally, it emphasized the need to build on both national and regional efforts so that one complements the other, and incorporated principles of prevention and of mutual assistance and cooperation. It also recognized that while all states have a common interest in reducing or avoiding a recurrence of the haze, they have different abilities and responsibilities in working towards a solution. In this respect, the Cooperation Plan gives expression to the principle of common and differentiated responsibility, recognized in the Rio Declaration, at a regional level.

Following the 1997 fires, the ASEAN environment ministers agreed in December 1997 to a further Regional Haze Action Plan to provide further commitments and detail.

But the failure of the Cooperation Plan has been in its implementation. Very few steps envisaged were actually taken. The outbreak of fires in 1997 showed up the lack of follow up to the Cooperation Plan in almost all areas. Singapore's assistance to Indonesia by providing satellite imaging of fires and "hot spots" was the exception that proves the rule. Instead of working within an agreed system of cooperation, countries were left to bilateral arrangements and emergency discussions especially between Indonesia and Malaysia, and Indonesia and Singapore. The international assistance that was given in 1997, mainly for fire-fighting, was largely piecemeal and uncoordinated.

Following the 1997 fires, the ASEAN environment ministers agreed in December 1997 to a further Regional Haze Action Plan to provide further commitments and detail. Again, the objectives of the Action Plan are commendable: to prevent land and forest fires; to establish operational mechanisms to monitor fires; and to strengthen regional fire-fighting capabilities. The Action Plan reiterates the need for regional monitoring and to identify sources of technical assistance within and outside ASEAN, from other countries and from international organizations such as the Asian Development Bank and UNEP. The primary emphasis of the Action Plan continues to be on national plans and capabilities. However, the Action Plan agreed to establish a procedure by which fire-fighting resources could be pooled for regional fire-fighting operations.

Upon review in April 1998, the Action Plan agreed to establish two sub-regional Firefighting Arrangements for Kalimantan and for the Sumatra/Riau provinces in Indonesia. Indonesia also announced that it would lay down the framework for an ASEAN Research and Training Centre for Land and Forest Fire Management in Central Kalimantan. Further details and arrangements under the Action Plan may be expected between ASEAN member states.

Clearly, the Action Plan is a welcome attempt to kick-start the stalled work of the earlier and more general Cooperation Plan. Doubt however remains on the ability of ASEAN as an organization to supply the omissions of the Indonesian national system. This is primarily because of the ASEAN norm for non-intervention in the domestic affairs of member states and the dominant role that Indonesia plays in the grouping. The relative weakness of central institutions in ASEAN is another major factor.

In the face of these obstacles, ASEAN has to date been unable to supplement failures by Indonesia to address the Southeast Asian fires. There have instead been recent attempts by ASEAN to internationalize the issue. Can international institutions and principles suffice?

The International Community and Institutions

In March 1998, the Asian Development Bank committed itself to provide regional technical assistance in management policy and enforcement, monitoring mechanisms and enhancing firefighting capabilities. ASEAN also agreed that UNEP should play the lead role in coordinating international assistance to combat and control the regional fires.

This takes a step forward towards finding solutions to the fires at the international level. This seems to be the only possibility left, given the failures at the national and regional levels. But while there may be no other alternative, it still remains to be seen if international institutions and principles of international law are strong enough to deal effectively with the fires and the issues that arise.

Institutionally, the key international organization that has responded to the fires is UNEP. Understandably, UNEP is giving priority to fire-fighting, taking a key role in the UN Disaster Assessment and Coordination Team that assessed the impact of the Kalimantan fires and convening an international meeting of donors. In response to the fires, international assistance has come from a large number of countries and agencies. Some of the assistance has been in terms of fire-fighting equipment. Australia and the US have also provided assistance in terms of water-bombing.

Such assistance has had some palliative effect but clearly did not engender a stable situation to prevent the recurrence of fires in 1998. Fire-fighting by means of water-bombing, in particular, would seem a spectacular but expensive waste of money and scarce water in drought-stricken areas, unless supported by sufficient efforts on the ground.

The present challenge of international assistance is therefore to go beyond fire-fighting to find and implement strategies of prevention and control at the national level. It remains to be seen whether the international community and relevant international organizations can do this effectively.

In the international community, as with ASEAN, no State has sought to hold Indonesia responsible for the fires and haze, and their global consequences. Instead, the approach of ASEAN's plans, as already noted, and now of international donors, has been to emphasize cooperation with Indonesia. This may fit the realities of the Southeast Asian fires. But it makes for unfavorable principles to govern the international community.

At best, the arrangements of the international community and of ASEAN may be said to reinforce an idea akin to the principle of common and differentiated responsibilities; that if all have an interest in putting a stop to the fires of Southeast Asia, then the regional and international communities must render assistance to Indonesia. Arguably, Indonesia has a reciprocal duty to cooperate and make good faith efforts to take steps agreed with other states.

Given the current attention to fire-fighting and to improving indigenous fire-fighting capability in Indonesia and among its neighbors, it may be understandable that principles of international environmental law may be de-emphasized. But what has been done may not be sufficient to meet the problem of the fires. What else can and should be done?

What More Should be Done?

In moving ahead, assistance will have to go beyond fire-fighting to deal with the causes of the fires and to set up systems of prevention and control. One approach would be to increase the capacity of the relevant Indonesian agencies. A second approach is to strengthen the systems of international cooperation, especially in ASEAN. The third, and perhaps key approach, is to ensure that the issue receives sufficient priority, and stimulate the internal reform of Indonesia's system to achieve that end.

The first approach, of increasing capacity, largely looks to the provision of incentives or "carrots" for Indonesia. The second approach is largely functional, seeking to improve the regimes of cooperation. The third, of increasing the priority that Indonesia gives to the issues, can include a variety of measures of enforcement or "sticks". They may therefore be controversial.

ASEAN

At the regional level, ASEAN may have to reconsider and adapt the "ASEAN way" if it is to be relevant and effective in situations of transboundary harm. Non-interference cannot be maintained as an icon in the face of ecological disaster that knows no border. A regional treaty setting thresholds for transboundary harm and creating sufficiently strong institutions to monitor and assist their compliance would be a step towards guarding themselves against future fires.

Suggestions for improvements in ASEAN can be discussed in two clusters:

(i) more specifically, on options in treaty-making for transboundary pollution; and

(ii) more generally, on reconciling ASEAN norms and strengthening institutions.

Treaty-Making for Transboundary Pollution

As noted earlier, the ASEAN Plans may be characterized as cooperative approaches rather than attempts to create liability regimes or set specific environmental limits. Since these latter types of treaties have had more success in dealing with transboundary pollution, steps might be taken to evolve the ASEAN Plans towards one or the other type of treaty. Liability regimes are relatively few and far between. In the ASEAN context, it seems unlikely to be politically acceptable. If, however, that would be the intention, a number of proposals might be made to make it more acceptable.

The first is that more types of transboundary pollution should be covered, and not just the atmospheric pollution and, even more specifically, the haze. Focusing on the haze alone would give Indonesia very few reasons to agree or, even if they agreed, to comply with any such regime. The approach to any liability regime should be to place equal emphasis on seaborne pollution, especially in the Straits of Malacca, and the shipment of hazardous waste. Given that Singapore and, to a lesser extent, Malaysia have been criticized for these forms of transboundary pollution, because of their heavier involvement with trade and shipping, this might create a greater balance of interests for Indonesia and a more reciprocal system between the states.

The second suggestion is that any system of liability should be devolved from the State level to the level of private actors. This would allow citizens of the States to invoke proceedings in the courts of another State. The target could be, instead of the government of that State, any private corporation involved. This would follow, in part, the example of the *1974 Nordic Convention on the Protection of the Environment*. This would lessen the possibility of political embarrassment and intergovernmental confrontation, which are antithetical to the ASEAN way.

Another direction would be to evolve the ASEAN Plans towards setting specific targets for atmospheric pollution fires and haze. This might well be difficult, given different environmental priorities, stage of industrial development and administrative and technical capacity between countries. There are even different measurement systems in ASEAN for airborne pollutants. Harmonizing limits, such as seen in the European Community experience, in such a situation might not be achievable.

If a common system cannot be achieved, an alternative would be to hold States to set their own national laws and limits and then to hold them to it, through an intergovernmental panel. This approach is seen in a number of agreements on transboundary pollution. It is less difficult than reaching common limits, agreed by all. It also avoids the imposition by any one country of its own unilateral standards. Instead, like the Golden Rule, each country is held to do to others what it would do domestically for itself.

In the immediate to medium terms some may believe that ASEAN Plans must remain, essentially, agreements for cooperative, national behavior. Even as such, they may still be strengthened. One measure is to have regular and more open review of national plans and implementation. The ASEAN Action Plan as implemented in early 1998 improves on the 1994 Cooperation Plan by having a regular review by Ministers and, more regularly, by officials. Holding such reviews is the most common mechanism for encouraging State compliance.

There are however differences between different modes of review. For example, who participates in the reviews? On one hand, review could be internalized and limited to officials, as it is in the ASEAN Action Plan. At the end of the range of possibilities, there might be a more open review, with the involvement of recognized NGOs with expertise and interest. At an interim position, review might be open to relevant inter-governmental organizations, such as the secretariats for the UN *Convention on Biological Diversity* and the *Framework Convention on Climate Change*; both global issues which are connected to the Southeast Asian fires and haze.

Alternatively, the ASEAN Secretariat itself might serve a role in commenting on reviews, from a more impartial point of view. Such a role for the ASEAN Secretariat would, however, require that the organization be strengthened in knowledge and capacity, and have the legitimized role of providing such review.

Reconciling Norms and Strengthening Institutions

It must be recognized that the ASEAN norm against non-interference does not preclude lawful actions as regards transboundary pollution. By its very nature, transboundary pollution is not a purely domestic affair. Steps in this direction have already been taken by ASEAN through recognizing the issue and promising cooperative actions. The further step that needs to be taken is for the pooling and mobilization of joint resources, such as fire-fighting units. This again has been promised by ASEAN and bilateral agreements. It appears however that there continues to be considerable implementation problems and obstacles on the ground, arising from political sensitivities. There is no immediate solution.

In the medium to longer term, however, confidence building measures might be suggested to assist. Joint exercises between fire-fighting units and other involved agencies in ASEAN member states would assist. First, if

Indonesian sensitivities remain, perhaps these exercises might be conducted initially on East Malaysian or Bruneian territory, or even further afield, in ASEAN member states like the Philippines Thailand. The latter countries are not so primarily affected by the present fires but have comparable experiences in forestry and the control of forest fires. The participation or even leadership of neutral agencies, such as UNEP and ASEAN, might also assist in defusing sensitivities.

Secondly, there must be a mutual recognition of the human, economic and other costs of the fires and haze. This follows from the precept that the seriousness of the harm increases the prospect of finding cooperation and, conversely, the relative insignificance of the problem lowers those prospects.

At present, many of the cost estimates have come from NGOs and think tanks. ASEAN governments will need to take these estimates into their official consideration or to generate figures of their account. This may assist the Indonesian political system in recognizing the real costs to their own people and economic system. It would also be a basis for affected states to make the economic commitment to fund the necessary steps for the prevention and control of future fires. This has not been done to date.

Perhaps for this reason, despite NGO estimates of losses running into hundreds of millions, neither Malaysia nor Singapore have been forthcoming on the suggestion for a multilateral revolving fund or, to some degree, to assist in UNEP's request for US$10 million for interim fire-fighting measures.

It is common sense that cooperation will only succeed if, for all parties, the benefits are greater than the costs. Part of the response to this reality must then be to fully recognize the benefits to be gained.

Thirdly, ASEAN's general capacity for environmental policy making will need to be strengthened. As noted, ASEAN's institutional capacity has been limited because the ASEAN way doubts the effectiveness of supranational institutions. Within ASEAN too, environment has not been emphasized. This may have to be addressed in dealing with transboundary pollution, as much as national capacities. ASEAN should have sufficient resources and knowledgeable personnel to add value to national efforts to deal with the transboundary pollution. This might assist and help smooth matters if and when bilateral discussions become ruffled. The use of good offices of the ASEAN Secretary-General might also be strengthened.

Fourthly, the possibility of linking environmental and economic concerns within ASEAN should be considered. It is clear that initiatives such as the SIJORI Growth Triangle, between Singapore, southern Malaysian states, and the Riau Islands and Sumatra provinces of Indonesia, thicken economic interdependence, as do ASEAN-wide programs, such as the ASEAN Free Trade Agreement and ASEAN Investment Agreement. It is also discernible that environmental standards have an economic impact on traders and, especially, investors. Higher standards might exact higher costs for businesses and, therefore, to attract investment, countries may lower, or be loathe to increase environmental protections. There is, therefore, economic sense to connect ASEAN's economic agenda to its environmental concerns. Conversely, linking the environment to economics would help prioritize the former. On the whole, such connections would help ASEAN countries take steps towards sustainable development, reconciling environment and economics. A first step in this direction would be to call for a sustainable development forum at which both economic and environment ministers for each country would attend.

International Community

At the international level, environmental policy making must continue to strengthen both institutions and principles.

As regards institutions, the role of UNEP in responding to the fires in 1998 has not been fully played out. With so many bilateral donors and the efforts of other UN-related or other agencies involved, UNEP may face considerable difficulties in effectively coordinating the efforts. What happens in Southeast Asia, in this sense, may have wider implications on UNEP's perceived effectiveness as a catalyst and coordinator for international community efforts, especially under a new executive director. ASEAN and other countries should make an effort to strengthen and support UNEP.

In terms of principles, this article has already pointed out how the practices of ASEAN in reacting to the fires differ from Principle 21 of the Stockholm Declaration, which holds out State responsibility and liability. Even if States do not set out to hold Indonesia liable, their practice should make it clear that Indonesia has obligations to cooperate and take necessary actions to abate the fires, and to accept and properly utilize assistance.

The fires also put pressure on the *Framework Convention on Climate Change* and the *Convention on Biological Diversity* and the emerging principles of international cooperation embodied therein. These conventions can and should find ways to bring in developing countries in ways that do not impose impediments to growth, while helping environmental protection. The Secretariats of these Conventions should join with UNEP to consider such medium to longer term measures. For instance, the *Clean Development Mechanism* and the concept of *Joint Implementation in the Climate Change Convention* can be of use in efforts to deal with the fires.

Beyond UNEP and environmental institutions, another suggestion would be for economic institutions such as the World Bank and IMF to link economic assistance to environmental improvements. By this, we would not necessarily call for conditionality nor to justify sanctions, as seen in the recent case in which the IMF withheld assistance to Cambodia because of illegal and uncontrolled timber trade. Rather, it is suggested that the international institutions and international community as a whole embrace the principle of additionality. The principle, embodied in the Rio Declaration and a number of other documents that emerged from the *UN Conference on Environment and Development*, emphasizes that new and additional funding and assistance should be given for environmental causes. By such means, the international community might help assuage Indonesia that economic-environmental links are not eco-imperialism but legitimate efforts to further sustainable development.

Private Sector

Given the scale of the fires and their global consequences, it may seem that the private sector and individuals can do little. It is likely that some efforts, such as fire-fighting and any water-bombing, are best left to governments and intergovernmental agencies. There are, however, other efforts that the private sector may usefully be involved with.

Consideration needs to be given to fostering and enforcing compliance within the relevant industries in Indonesia. This can be assisted by both internal economic measures and externally driven incentives, such as voluntary eco-labels. Such eco-labels would help consumers discriminate in favor of those companies and products that do not use fires in clearing land, thereby lessening consumer demand for those that do.

Similar economic incentives from the private sector can be pursued by what has been called, "ethical" funds; investment funds that pursue both profit and a good environmental record in the companies in which they invest. Private bank lending and insurance coverage too might make a difference. It would be of sound economic sense for both banks and insurers to take steps to ensure that their clients have no environmental liabilities, such as the use of fire. Such investments and business practices might also be acceptable to Indonesia if they help tap into new and additional funds and economic opportunities that will help their economy recover more quickly.

Conclusion

In asking the question, "what should we do," we raise questions about the nature of the problem as well as the ability and legitimate place of countries, institutions and private sector individuals to deliver acceptable solutions. If "we" are not Indonesians, international law's central concept of sovereignty dictates that we operate as outsiders, from a distance, like advice or interference from a back-seat driver.

What can such outsiders do? What tone and tactics should they take? The measures that environmental efforts turn to are often associated with political pressure by lobby groups and NGOs and sanctions, often unilaterally employed. ASEAN has expended considerable energies protesting such measures, often with success. If "sticks" are predominantly used, this is likely to be unacceptable to Indonesia and to ASEAN members, even perhaps those affected by the haze. An over-emphasis on sanctions or other "sticks" can also be argued to run against the emerging trend of environmental law principles in fostering cooperation, and the approach of recognizing common and differentiated responsibilities to assist developing countries meet environmental goals.

Instead of sticks, as such, there can be an emphasis on "carrots". In the present climate of economic concern, tying additional economic assistance and private funds to environmental problems caused by the fires would help give priority to those problems. Increasing institutional ability and capacity—at the national level, in ASEAN, and among the relevant international institutions—is another approach that has been canvassed. Both economic assistance and efforts to enhance institutional capacity should be met not only by Indonesia and states causing the fires, but also by neighboring states and, because of the global consequences, by the international community as a whole.

What we should do is to embrace the idea of common but differentiated responsibilities, wherein states make efforts to achieve a common goal according to their different abilities. What we should do is to emphasize the principles of cooperation that are strong in international environmental law and in ASEAN. In so doing, we may take steps that seem to some to go beyond the ASEAN way as presently conceived as well as to extend the reach of international environmental law and institutions into the nation-State of Indonesia, gently and persuasively, but also persistently and firmly.

Appendix I

Chairman's Statement, Singapore Environment Council, *"International Policy Dialogue on the Southeast Asian Fires"*

On 4 and 5 June 1998, the Singapore Environment Council held its first International Policy Dialogue on the Southeast Asian Fires. The Dialogue was organized with support from the Singapore Institute of Intemational Affairs and the Foundation for International Environmental Law and Development (FIELD-UK) and sponsorship from Shangri-La Hotel, Far East Organization and the Hanns Siedel Foundation.

The Dialogue brought together some 40 representatives of international, regional and local nongovernment organizations (NGOs), think tanks and academic institutions, and the private sector, as well as international and governmental institutions. These included:

NGOs: the Nature Conservancy (USA-Indonesia), the Nature Society of Singapore, NGOs for Integrated Protection Areas (the Philippines), Singapore Environment Council, Worldwide Fund for Nature (WWF-Indonesia and WWF-Regional), and World Resources Institute (Regional).

Think Tanks and Academic Institutions: Asia-Pacific Centre for Environmental Law (APCEL-Singapore), Centre for Remote Imaging, Sensing and Processing (CRISP-NUS), Centre for International Forestry Research (Indonesia), Center for Tropical Forest Science, Environment and Economy Programme for South East Asia (EEPSEA-Canada), Foundation for International Environmental Law and Development (FIELD-UK), Institute of Southeast Asian Studies (ISEAS), Institute of Policy Studies (IPS-Singapore), Institute of Strategic and Intemational Studies (ISIS-Malaysia), the Max Planck Institute (Germany), and Singapore Institute of International Affairs.

Private Sector: Bombardier Aerospace, Golden Hope Plantations (Malaysia), Singapore International Chamber of Commerce, and Shell-Brunei.

International and Governmental Organizations: Asian Development Bank (ADB), ASEAN Secretariat, BAPEDAL (Indonesia), *United Nations Environment Programme* (UNEP), US State Department, US-Asia Environment Programme and World Conservation Union (IUCN).

The Dialogue called attention to the fires in Southeast Asia, and especially Indonesia, as a matter of regional and global significance. It called on Indonesia and other countries with fires to take appropriate actions to mitigate the present fires and prevent future fires. It called for coordinated action among the regional countries, ASEAN, the international community, international organizations, and NGOs.

The Dialogue called attention to the fires in Southeast Asia, and especially Indonesia, as a matter of regional and global significance.

The Dialogue noted that NGOs can contribute to solutions to the fires and called for greater coordination between NGOs working in Indonesia, the region and at the international level. It also called for regular dialogue to be established between NGOs and ASEAN officials.

Members of the Dialogue noted, with great concern, that the fires in Indonesia:

- were recurrent in nature, mostly of manmade origins, although worsened by El Niño climate conditions;
- related to the use and clearance of forest and other land, mainly by big business, engaged in logging and palm oil;
- could have been foreseen, given climatic forecasts and patterns of forest use;
- burnt up to 4.5 million hectares in 1997 alone, according to satellite monitoring by CRISP;
- caused harm to human life and health, and damage to the environment, nature, and to economic activity, estimated to be worth more than US$4.4 billion by a study by EEPSEA and the WWF;
- caused damage to Indonesia's neighboring states, especially Brunei, Malaysia and Singapore, by reason of transboundary air pollution or "haze";
- caused damage to the global commons, by the release of greenhouse gases, estimated to exceed the total greenhouse gas emissions of Western Europe in a single year, and by the loss of biodiversity, especially

in mega-diversity areas of Indonesia and East Malaysia; and

- caused enormous harm and damage to the people, environment and economy of Indonesia.

Members of the Dialogue noted:

- ASEAN has promulgated the 1995 Cooperation Plan on Transboundary Pollution and 1997 Action Plan on the Haze, with regular reviews in 1998, promising closer cooperation and joint actions for monitoring, fire-fighting and prevention, establishing subregional fire-fighting areas in Kalimantan and Sumatra and considering shared resources for fire-fighting and prevention;
- Despite the economic difficulties facing many ASEAN members, ASEAN has shown commitment to regularly review the compliance with and possible improvements to the Action Plan;

And called for ASEAN and its member states to:

- recognize that the norm against intervention in the internal affairs of a State should not prevent effective response to transboundary pollution insofar as the damage is suffered by another State or the global commons;
- recognize the human, environmental and economic costs of the fires; help mobilize funds to prevent and control fires; further focus plans for the subregional fire-fighting areas by prioritising specific sites for strengthened fire-fighting and prevention, based on factors such as greater biodiversity, ecological value and the potential to release harmful gases if affected by fire; strengthen their existing Plans by fully recognizing international principles and laws, including those relating to state responsibility for transboundary pollution, biodiversity and climate change, and to ensure compliance; make satellite monitoring and other information relating to the fires available as widely as possible, especially to NGOs and local communities; institutionalize review of actions taken on the fires by all concerned government officials and, further, to invite expert and concerned international organizations, scientists and academics and NGOs for dialogue and review; balance economic cooperation with environmental concerns for sustainable development in regional plans such as the ASEAN Free Trade Agreement and ASEAN Investment Area and subregional economic cooperation, especially the SIJORI Growth Triangle, linking Singapore and parts of Indonesia and Malaysia; and
- strengthen the capacity of the ASEAN Secretariat, especially in matters concerning the environment and sustainable development.

Noted:

- The important role of international law, especially Principle 2 of the Rio Declaration, and that Indonesian authorities had accepted moral responsibility for the effects of the fires and haze;
- Indonesia has ratified the international conventions on Climate Change and on Biological Diversity:
- Indonesian authorities have sought to address the issue by passing laws to prohibit the use of fire, and increasing fines and penalties for offenders, naming some 180 suspected companies; and
- The Indonesian Government, experiencing a time of economic hardship, humanitarian emergencies in some regions, and political change, has promised reform, especially to eradicate nepotism, corruption and cronyism;

And called for Indonesia to:

- recognize a duty and obligation to cooperate with other countries and the international community in dealing with the fires;
- seek sustainable development, balancing economic growth with environmental concerns;
- enforce its current laws against the use of fire against corporate offenders, effectively, efficiently and equally, without favor or prejudice to any Indonesian or foreign business or investors;
- coordinate their response both internally, between different agencies and ministries, and externally with countries, institutions and NGOs that offered technical and other assistance;
- update its land use plans and to reform its land use policy so as to ensure sustainable use, so as to prioritize any land conversion to better protect forest land, rationally use marginal and degraded land, and exercise extreme caution in any conversion of deep peat swamps; and
- grant secure and sufficient tenure to users, empowering and recognizing the interests of local communities.

Noted:

- More than 18 different donors from the international community rendered assistance to Indonesia in 1997;

- The LTN Environment Programme has been welcomed by ASEAN to coordinate international efforts for fire-fighting and prevention;
- The Asian Development Bank has undertaken to provide technical assistance for ASEAN; and
- The International Monetary Fund, World Bank and Asian Development Bank are working with the Indonesian Government to deal with the economic crisis in that country by making necessary reforms.

Fund called for International Organizations and Bilateral Donors

- to support efforts by the UN Environment Programme and Asian Development Bank to coordinate assistance;
- not to over-emphasize fire-fighting, especially by high-technology methods;
- instead, to develop medium and longer-term responses to the fires and their causes, including education, systems of control, reforestation and agreed principles for the sustainable management of forests;
- to provide new and additional aid and assistance to Indonesia in response to the fires and for the environmental and humanitarian concerns arising;
- to work with the respective convention secretariats to develop appropriate policies and mechanisms to link the prevention of fires in southeast Asia to the *Climate Change Convention*, and the *Biological Diversity Convention*; and
- for the IMF and other assistance programmes and packages not to raise the risk of fires by inappropriate policies and to further sustainable development, especially by addressing inappropriate subsidies and other policies affecting the rational and sustainable use of land.

Noted:

- The efforts of NGOs in Indonesia and the concern of NGOs in the region and internationally; and
- The welcome extended by ASEAN Ministers for the Environment in 1998 for contributions by NGOs.

And called upon NGOs to:

- coordinate among NGOs in Indonesia, and at the regional and international levels, for mutual assistance and support; and to avoid wasteful duplication;
- establish regular dialogue with ASEAN officials;
- mobilize public concern on the fires;
- work with national authorities and local communities, as appropriate, for early detection and small-scale fire suppression, to increase their concern and capacity to deal with fires and their underlying causes;
- work with intergovernmental organizations, where appropriate, to provide information, assist in monitoring, undertake programs and advise on policies; and
- advocate and implement the increased use of credible environmental certification for timber and forest products, and for oil palm, to highlight companies which are good examples of best practice and expose the logging and plantation companies which are guilty of using fire to clear land.

Noted:

- Businesses and private sector companies are both involved with and affected by the fires and resulting "haze" pollution.

And called upon Businesses and Private Sector Companies to:

- faithfully comply with Indonesian national laws against the use of fire;
- transfer appropriate technology to enable zero burn land clearing for palm oil and other plantations, and increasing efficiency in logging and timber processing;
- review their business practices to lessen environmental damage that results from their economic activity, to establish and uphold best practices in their industry and expose the misdeeds of pollutive producers; and
- seek appropriate certification for their products to ensure sustainable management of resources under their stewardship.

(ii) Robinson N.A., "Forest Fires as a Common International Concern: Precedents for the Progressive Development of International Environmental Law," 18 *Pace Environmental Law Review*, 2000

Transnational air pollution from forest fires, for the first time, became a tragic reality on a worldwide basis during 1997 and 1998. Occasioning lost of human life and property, these same fires also caused enormous loss of biodiversity since they raged in the rich tropical forests around the equator and in rich Siberian boreal forests on three different continents. The acute air pollution in Southeast Asia alone impaired the health and property of millions of people. In addition to the immediate damage caused by forest fires, the releases of carbon dioxide, which has a warming effect as greenhouse gas, and of aerosols, which reflect sunlight and thus have a cooling effect, have a complicated effect on Earth's climate. Many of these fires started as the result of human activities, and most burned without the benefit of any fire control measures.

The scope of these fires was unprecedented. In May 1998, state environmental protection officials in Texas declared the air unfit to breathe from the coast of the Gulf of Mexico for over 100 miles inland and the entire state went on an air pollution alert. Hazy skies were reported as far north as Colorado and South Dakota. The smoke caused health problems and cut visibility. The fires were burning in Mexico, which was experiencing its worst drought in 70 years. The number of forest fires reached 11,000 from an average of 7,000. Over 1,500 square miles burned.

The transnational air pollution caused health problems and measurably damaged the economy in Brunei, in Singapore, and in Malaysia.

Meanwhile, during the same year, forest fires in Central America consumed 2,150 square miles of forests, primarily in Guatemala, Honduras and Nicaragua. The Mexican fires affected this region also. Smoke from the fires caused dense haze across the region, closing all four international airports in Honduras.

During the same period, forest fires in Africa burned around Mt. Kilimanjaro in Tanzania, as well as in Kenya, Rwanda, Congo and Senegal, all exacerbated by the drought accompanying El Nièo weather patterns in Africa. In South America, fires in Brazil consumed some 20,000 square miles, or an area half the size of New York State; the journal *Nature* called the Brazilian patterns of unmanaged logging that led to new surface fires and a cycle of forest impoverishment that contributed to further fires, a kind of "cryptic deforestation." In Siberia, 15,000 forest fires in 1997 and over 19,000 in 1999 burned with little effective means of extinguishing them. Some fire fighting forces and equipment reached the peat forest fires in Belarus and European Russia, but substantial burning was not controlled.

Perhaps the most extensive and acute forest fire phenomena were found in South East Asia. The fires of 1997 in Kalimantan and Sumatra, Indonesia, and in parts of Malaysia and Papua New Guinea, produced plumes of smoke that blanketed Singapore and Malaysia and reached the Philippines and Thailand. To imagine the breadth of the disaster, it is as if forest fire smoke covered an area as extensive as either the United States, or both East and West Europe. Singapore, which has strong domestic air pollution control systems and clear air, was enveloped with air unfit to breathe. The transnational air pollution caused health problems and measurably damaged the economy in Brunei, in Singapore, and in Malaysia.

The occurrence of these forest fires in the same temporal span has been attributed to the climate phenomenon of the El Niño/Southern Oscillation, which brings drought conditions to the areas where these fires took place. The dry weather also heightens the likelihood of fires, and the lack of rain exacerbates the dispersion of the air pollution from the fires. El Niño is a shift in Pacific Ocean temperatures and atmospheric conditions that alter wind patterns. This phenomenon was first identified nearly a century ago by Peruvian fishermen, who gave it the name of the Christ child since the peak of the phenomenon appears around the December celebration of Christ's birth. It is now thought that these events appear cyclically, and have been going on for a much longer period of time. Contemporary advances in scientific detection, monitoring and modeling have made it possible to study the El Niño/Southern Oscillation effects. After the drought and El Niño, the wind patterns shift and the La Niña phenomenon brings excessive rainfall, often to the same regions that endured the drought. If forest fires have denuded the hills, this deluge of rain can cause severe erosion and flooding since tree cover no longer exists to soak up the rain and the roots no longer hold the soil against the water run-off.

While the dry conditions of El Niño may have prepared the dry and hot conditions that fanned the flames, the weather was not the cause of the forest fires. The fires ignited and grew out of control because of a variety of causes, which were overwhelmingly induced by human behavior. In each region, however, some variables remained the same. Some fires were caused by lightning but many were set to clear tropical forest cover for agricultural purposes. Except in Russia, the human populations are increasing in the regions where the fires take place. Many people live in and near the forests, as population growth has brought human habitats closer to forest lands. In every case there was no long-standing system of local fire prevention, no training to curb fires, and virtually no organized fire fighting capacity. In each case, the fires were not fully extinguished by man but by the rains of nature.

In most places there was no alternative but to get out of the way of the fire and wait for the rains, which were slow to come because of the dry weather conditions. Finally, all of these fires took place in some of the most biologically diverse and rich areas of the Earth; the loss of forest habitat adversely affects endemic and migratory species.

Traditionally, the law and governmental policy have regarded forest fires, like fires in cities, quintessentially as local matters to be addressed by domestic policy and municipal legal frameworks. For decades, if a nation chose to allow its forest fires to burn until rainfall extinguished them, as was largely the case in the Soviet Union, such a governmental response was not considered an appropriate question for international law. Even at the United Nations Conference on the Human Environment (UNCED), the 1992 "Earth Summit," there was an assumed consensus among the sovereign states that a nation's forests were its own business. UNCED declined to advance proposals for a treaty on forests and their management, and adopted "non-binding forest principles" as a modest foundation for future discussions. These Forest Principles recognize the responsibility of States to ensure that activities within their jurisdictions do not damage the environment of other states or areas beyond the limits of national jurisdiction, but at the same time considered that each State has a "sovereign right to utilize, manage and develop their forests," and that this should be done in an ecologically sustainable way. Never do the Principles address the phenomena of forest fires, although they extol the many and varied values of the forest for human society. Since fires ravish these values, the failure to reference forest fires is remarkable; so intent were the delegates in preserving their national rights to control their forests that they neglected the potential roles for international cooperation in preventing and containing forest fires.

The failure to reference forest fires at UNCED also is found in the principal outcome of the Earth Summit, its action plan, *Agenda 21*. The *Agenda 21* chapter on "Combating Deforestation," pays scant attention to forest fires by merely including references to the "lack of adequate forest-fire control" and the anti-poaching of timber in a long list of threats to forests worldwide. There is no mention of international or regional cooperation to address the need to build capacity to combat forest fires. In the chapters of *Agenda 21* on combating desertification, managing montane regions, or on conserving biological diversity, there is no mention of how forest fires leave the land denuded and subject to erosion, thereby inducing desertification, eroding mountains and causing flooding, and destroying biologically diverse habitats. It is as if the nations at the Earth Summit chose to assume that each nation could look after its own forest fires and that the issue should not be inscribed on the priority list for the world.

The worldwide forest fire events of 1997 and 1998 have changed this situation, even if Earth's nations remain slow to acknowledge the fact. What was once deemed exclusively to be a problem of domestic, municipal law, is now squarely a common concern of nations and a proper focus for international public law. This is so because of the transboundary pollution caused by the smoke of fires, and the destruction of habitat for migratory species, but is also so because of the destruction of biodiversity in contravention of undertakings in the *Convention on Biological Diversity* to integrate the conservation and sustainable use of biodiversity into each nation's plans, programs and policies. Insofar as the burning of Earth's forests contributes to climate change, a "common concern" of humankind, the fires do not protect the climate system "for the benefit of present or future generations of humankind." The devastating effects of forest fires in 1997–1998 are likely to be revised during the next El Niño phenomena, and before that eventuality is the time for the international community to take action.

This article will examine:

(a) how traditional principles of state responsibility under international public law address the issue of transboundary pollution from forest fires;

(b) what the application of basic rules of international cooperation under the United Nations Charter meant for the fires of Mexico and Indonesia; and

(c) since both the rules of state responsibility and of the obligation to cooperate are woefully short of producing sustainable human systems to prevent and cope with forest fires, how the principles of environmental law should be marshalled to guide governmental systems to manage forest fires consistently at the local, national or international levels. Unless the governmental and commercial and public interest nongovernmental interests that care about the health and biodiversity of the world's forests give forest fire protection a much higher priority than they do at present, their efforts to pass on the forest resources of Earth to the next generations will fall woefully short.

Forest fires today have become more than an "Act of God" or a dramatic and tragic isolated event within a state. Such fires now endanger the public health and safety across national borders, and affect the climate as a commons. In addition, forest fires impoverish the world's genetic resources, diminishing a global resource that is also of common concern to mankind. Since humans began to use wood for their needs, some 80 percent of the forests that originally covered the various continents have been cleared and converted to fragmented, degraded or nonforest uses. The remaining forest lands with biological value are found in the Amazon Basin, Central Africa, Southeast Asia, as well as the boreal forests of Canada, Russia and the US. Of these regions, only Canada and the US, and portions of Western Europe, have developed the capacity to use prescribed burning in forests as a management technique and are able to detect and control forest fires. Even in these states, however, the task is not easy. Vast fires in the Florida Everglades required evacuations in 1998, and horrific fires in New Mexico in 1996 burned vast areas of parks and national forests, as well as human settlements.

Without a more effective and comprehensive global effort to prevent and cope with forest fires, the remaining wild forests' resources of the world are at risk. Quite apart from the present loss of commercial timber and species habitat, and the present problems of flooding and erosion in the aftermath of fires, the loss of these wooded lands will reduce the capacity of regions to absorb carbon dioxide through photosynthesis, thereby making the challenge of managing emissions of greenhouse gases all the more problematic. Forests sequester carbon in their woody tissue as a result of photosynthesis, release oxygen into the atmosphere and are often termed the "lungs" of the Earth. The recurring forest fire events put much more at stake than just the apparently transient and dramatic event of the fire itself. How does, or should, environmental law attend to this situation?

Traditional International Law and State Responsibility

Under the United Nations Charter and principles of international law, states have the "responsibility to ensure that activities within their jurisdiction or control do not cause damage to the environment of other states or of areas beyond the limits of national jurisdiction." This settled principle of international law, Principle 21, makes it clear that if a state allows air pollution from its forest fires to damage another state, then it is responsible for compensating the other state for that damage. This Principle has been cited in the case of treaties dealing with abatement of industrial acid rain and indeed was codified from the early air pollution arbitral decision in *The Trail Smelter Arbitration* (*United States and Canada*). The Principle was reiterated in the Declaration of Rio de Janeiro on Environment and Development adopted at the UN Earth Summit in 1992.

Whether one considers the air pollution from the fires to have damaged a nation's people and resources under the *Corfu Channel case* or considers the damage to have harmed a common and shared resources in the "air shed" under the analogous situation in the *Lake Lanoux Arbitration* it is evident that the state which is the source of the pollution would be liable for the damage caused.

Yet, would claims of injury and demands for compensation, arbitration or litigation before the International Court of Justice have any beneficial effect in such a circumstance? Forest fires erupt rapidly and are unplanned events. The El Niño weather conditions for a fire threat can be forecast, as can the ground conditions, including the presence of forest litter from logging operations or the patterns of using fires for land clearing, but except in an extreme situation there appears to be scant possibility of the threat of forest fires being a basis for a claim in international public law between nations. One such extreme situation may exists in the failure of a State to put an end to the pattern of commercial interests using fires, unlawfully under national law, to clear forest to plant palm oil plantations in Indonesia and parts of Malaysia. When there is a fire, there is precious little time for prior notice and consultation with states located down-wind about an impending transboundary impact. After the event, the quantification of the widespread damage often is difficult at best; a State will doubtless ask whether it has the expertise or resources to make the investigation needed in order to determine if it is worth the effort of calculating the quantification of widespread injury. Even if a State could calculate the claims of natural resource damage and costs of restoration and quantum of injury to a State's nationals, how would the damaged State in turn deal with the demand demands of injured parties or compensate its own nationals? What State, States, or intergovernmental organization, can press a claim for damage to the commons, if that could be established?

Finally, even if secured would a damage award achieve deterrence or encourage better care to prevent the forest fires? After the fires, there is vast damage to repair and scarce resources to prevent future fires. Moreover, even if one were to view the statistical likelihood that there will be more forest fires, and thus further predictable damage in the future, is this not a risk that the State enduring the fires is taking, and a risk that the State suffering the air pollution is aware of and perhaps even acquiescing in by its inaction? States are reluctant to press claims that might appear to be interfering in the internal affairs of another State, and in failing to press colorable claims before or after fires, the injured States diminish the likelihood that any international law remedies will be employed.

In light of these considerations, it is difficult to see how the concepts of liability and state responsibility in international law may be useful doctrines to either deter future forest fires or as means to insist on measures to prevent the fires. It is evident that traditional international public law has little to offer to solve the problems of transnational forest fire air pollution.

One analogous situation is the air pollution caused by Iraq's burning of the oil wells and reserves in Kuwait during the Persian Gulf War. Iraq deliberately bombed the largest Kuwaiti oil field, two refineries, an offshore loading terminal, tank and tankers, and other oil related facilities in its war with Kuwait, inflicting substantial environmental damage in Kuwait and in the region. Although the armed conflict ceased on 1 March 1991, the fires continued to burn for weeks, emitting a plume 22,000 feet into the atmosphere and causing blackened snow in the Himalayan Mountains of Pakistan and Nepal. The health impacts on people and the continuing damage to ecosystems has been assessed as part of the post-war claims settlements. Once the claims are determined, the methodology and quantification of air pollution damage claims may provide a precedent that could be used for acute injury from forest fire incidents. Whatever the use of the evidentiary measures to quantify damage to natural resources from the fires in the Gulf War, the precedent is not of much further value with respect to forest fires. The remedies ordered by the Security Council under the United Nations Charter arising out of the Gulf War, however, are not likely to be ordered by either some United Nations body or the International Court of Justice. Would a national claim that the threat of fires constitutes a threat to its national security and peace, and present such a claim to the Security Council? The fear of forest fires, and the scope of their damage, is not yet likely to be deemed to reach the threshold of national security.

While there are other examples of transboundary pollution damage akin to that of the forest fires, there are few useful precedents. There have been no effective claims or remedies from the transboundary radioactive pollution that resulted from the fires at the Chernobyl nuclear power reactor in the USSR on 26 April 1986. People continue to suffer a slow death in Belarus from this incident in the Ukraine. Given the failure of international public law to address the aftermath of Chernobyl itself, it is hard to envision states organizing to address the equally troublesome aftermath of the forest fires. Ministries of Foreign Affairs in States where injuries are documents have chosen not to raise troublesome claims with their neighboring States, and the members of the public are either denied legal recourse or are too passive to demand action from their foreign affairs ministries. Unlike the air pollution from Kuwaiti fires resulting from armed conflict, where the UN Security Council had a clear responsibility, the civilian forest fires or the civilian nuclear reactor fires have not produced concerted state recourse to the traditional rules of international law.

The leading legal commentator on the Indonesian fires has also concluded that traditional rules of State Responsibility are poorly equipped to resolve the forest fire threats. Prof. Alan Khee-Jin Tan examined Indonesia's responsibility under international law for its transboundary pollution of Malaysia and Singapore in 1997 and 1998. He applied the terms of the UN International Law Commission's Draft Articles on State Responsibility which reflect in their codified form the customary international law, to the events in Indonesia leading up to the air pollution in the Malay Peninsula. Prof. Tan demonstrates how the Indonesian authorities knew that fires were being set unlawfully and failed to prevent the acts which caused the fires which resulted in the transboundary pollution and damage. He notes that Indonesia did cooperate with other States to try to extinguish the fires after they were out of control, but finds that:

> "what constitutes the basis of Indonesia's responsibility is its failure to control effectively the timber and plantation companies operating within its territory. It is with respect to this failure that Indonesia has not exercised due diligence in preventing transboundary harm to other States and to other areas beyond

> its national jurisdiction, thereby attracting State responsibility for its conduct."

Notwithstanding his view that a case for holding Indonesia responsible exists, Prof. Tan concludes that "it does not appear that political realities will provide for that natural consequence of responsibility to unfold," and he sadly notes in a postscript that "it appears that a repeat of the forest fire and haze episode—perhaps with even greater degrees of severity—cannot be ruled out this year, or at any time in the near future."

If a solution to the forest fire situation is to be found, it appears not to be in the realm of State Responsibility. Rather, what is needed is a most substantial recourse to the international law of cooperation.

The Obligation of Cooperation Under International Law

The Charter of the United Nations is premised on the principle of cooperation. Through the Charter, states founded the United Nations "to achieve international cooperation in solving international problems of an economic, social, cultural or humanitarian character..." In the words of Professor Wolfgang Friedmann, international law is strengthened by:

> "the gradual emergence of an international law of cooperation, implemented by an increasing number of international organizations, pursuing the common interests of mankind in the fields of economic and social development, health, communications, and other matters of human welfare."

Given the interdependence of the natural systems of the biosphere, it is normal that states seek to cooperate on common matters of environmental protection. The Rio Declaration on Environment and Development of 1992 expressly provides that:

> "States shall cooperate in a spirit of global partnership to conserve, protect, and restore the health and integrity of the Earth's ecosystem. In view of the differentiated contributions to global environmental degradation, States have common but differentiated responsibilities."

Cooperation on matters of environmental protection is widely accepted as a basic obligation of international law. The duty to cooperate is the foundation of the State obligations under the *Convention on Biological Diversity* (Article 5, "Cooperation"). The question that should be asked, however, is what minimum level of cooperation, beyond merely not frustrating cooperation "by sitting on the sidelines," is sufficient for a State to meet its duty to cooperate. It is evident that whether or not a State has satisfied its duty to cooperate should depend on a good faith effort to act effectively, given the common, but differentiated, responsibilities various states may have depending on their circumstances.

The test to determine whether this obligation to cooperate in international law has been satisfied should be whether the response was proportional to the demand, in light of the resources of the States involved. If States effectively cooperated to abate the problem, then the level of such action may be deemed adequate to satisfy the duty to cooperate under International Law. If the problem continued or worsened, despite the cooperation, then patently, the duty to cooperate was not satisfied. This proportionality test, put in context by the "common but differentiated responsibilities" prescription of the UN *Framework Convention on Climate Change*, provides a measuring system by which to test the performance of States in observing their duty to cooperate. A proportionality test makes the duty to cooperate more concrete, and facilitates an objective analysis of State conduct. The test would apply to any duty to cooperation, and would taken on specific meaning in the context of the factual setting in which the duty to cooperate arises whether it is forest fire prevention and control, or control of diseases, or any other subject. A proportionality test permits the analysis of state conduct, with respect to the obligation to cooperate, in the same way that state responsibility does with respect to the obligations of Principle 21 discussed above.

In the context of the forest fires during the El Niño years, as soon as the transnational threat became apparent, all States should inaugurate substantial efforts at international cooperation. The United States of America, not directly affected by pollution from Southeast Asia or Russia or South America, has nonetheless placed is satellite remote sensing systems are the use of all nations; international cooperation through the National Atmospheric and Oceanic Administration (NASA), which provides real time monitoring of forest fire phenomena, available over the Internet. The Member States of the Association of South East Asian Nations (ASEAN) developed an ASEAN Cooperation Plan on Transboundary Pollution in Kuala Lumpur in June of 1995, however it is doubtful that this Plan has stimulated the level of cooperation needed to avert the next period of fires, any more than it did in 1997–1998. In the other regions of Asia, Russia, Africa, or South America, there is not even a comparable plan to begin defining the context for cooperation.

Present international measures at regional cooperation to combat forest fires, therefore, barely begin to address—much less adequately meet—the minimal threshold required for observing the duty of cooperation when those measures are judged a proportional assessment of the actual responses made to the dangers and the likely injuries. As this article seeks to illustrate, the worldwide danger of forest fires requires States to take more substantial, immediate and focused measures *before* as well as during and after a forest fire.

While this article examines the fires in Indonesia and Mexico, most other States also presently fall far short of being able to demonstrate that they meet their duty of international cooperation to ensure that future fires will be averted or contained. In 1997–1998, while belated, sincere and apparently well-intended measures were taken to cooperate in the abatement of the fires, the responses could not satisfy the proportionality test posited above. Nonetheless, at the same time it is clear that States did acknowledge their duty of cooperation under international law, thereby motivating many humanitarian actions to help fight the fires.

If State conduct is proportionally defined relative to the threat of further forest fires, it is likely that that objective test would motivate many more concrete steps to address forest fire prevention and control than would the theoretical recourse to rules of State Responsibility. This proposition can be examined in the disposition of largely bilateral assistance for the fires in Mexico and in the context of the largely multilateral assistance for the fires in Indonesia. In light of what was not done in these two nations, it will then be possible to prescribe some of the minimal elements of cooperation needed for coping with forest fires.

The Mexican Forest Fire Catastrophe

Once the magnitude of the Mexican fires became apparent, the US undertook to offer assistance. Brian Atwood, head of the United States Agency for International Development, made clear that the US' interest in the problem extended nationally, and not just as a regional US interest to protect the affected regions of Texas. In Atwood's words:

> "This disaster in Mexico has to be the most serious of its kind we have seen anywhere in the world, including the fires in Indonesia. American people wonder why we should care about the fires here in Mexico. It's not just the smoke and haze that's affecting the United States as far north as Wisconsin and as far east as Georgia, but it's the potential loss of biodiversity."

Atwood's concerns were justified, although there is only doubtful value in trying to compare the magnitude of the seriousness of the Mexican fires to those in Indonesia. They were both calamitous. In Mexico, the fires in the Chimalapas Biological Reserve, for instance, endangered 1,500 of the world's most endangered species of plants and 90 percent of the migratory birds that fly between the US, Canada and South America and use the Reserve. Similar claims can be made for the effects on biodiversity in Indonesia.

The fires in Mexico roared through 11 of the 32 Mexican states and caused extensive damage to a quarter of the forest in the Desierto de Los Leones National Park at the edge of Mexico City, cloaking the capital in soot for over a week.

The fires in Mexico roared through 11 of the 32 Mexican states and caused extensive damage to a quarter of the forest in the Desierto de Los Leones National Park at the edge of Mexico City, cloaking the capital in soot for over a week. The Mexican Secretariat of the Environment (SEMARNAP) reported that 80 percent of the fires were burning in areas inhabited by people, with grave risk to life and health. In Chiapas, the smoke and fog were so thick that headlights were needed at midday. In response, Mexico mobilized resources to fight the fires and to avert their recurrence. Thirty thousand military personnel and 6,000 civilians were reportedly deployed to fight the fires. The volunteers had little training, or for that matter, time for it. It was reported, as of April, that six helicopters and two light aircraft were tracking the fires, but only one Canadian aircraft equipped to water bomb the fires was in use. The fire patterns could not be tracked because the smoke's thickness prevented the planes from flying at an adequate range. Only in May did the US Government provide a King Air plane equipped with infrared sensors to find fires beneath the cloud forest canopy of the tropical forest. The US sent 45 fire-fighting experts to assist from 16 May to 6 July 1998. Some $8 million was allocated to assist Mexico. Over 50 fire fighters and members of special brigades died in Mexico fighting the fires. In the central state of Michigan, 100 villagers tried to save part of the forest areas used as the wintering habitat for the migratory Monarch Butterfly, by bringing buckets of water two hours from their village. Given the lack of resources to fight such widespread fires and the magnitude of the fires, these response efforts were simply insufficient to bring the crisis under control. Despite these efforts, many fires burned until extinguished by the rains in late June, while others kept burning into July.

The causes of the Mexican fires were varied, yet 90 percent were attributed to human negligence and only 10 percent to natural causes. These causes include actions by farmers to clear land for expanded agricultural uses and others by narcotic traders to raise poppies or marijuana. Many fires were started by the careless disposal of cigarettes by drivers of cars and trucks, others by recreationalists or vacationers. A small percentage were created by natural causes. In response, Mexico is reported to have proposed an educational program to persuade farmers not to use fire to burn off trees in preparation for planting or grazing. At the time, some voices proposed that setting of intentional fires should be classified as an environmental crime. Even if criminal laws apply, evidence of arson is most difficult to obtain. However, as of mid-May, only 109 investigations of the some 10,000 fires had been undertaken. Even if the leads for investigations are promising, the fires destroy all evidence of negligent or criminal activity; arson is nearly impossible to establish absent eyewitnesses.

It is interesting to note that the North American Commission on Environmental Cooperation (CEC), organized under the Environment Side Agreement for the North American Free Trade Agreement (NAFTA), would have the legal authority to fashion a cooperation between Canada, the US and Mexico and the US to address forest fire management. Unlike the Association of South East Asian Nations (ASEAN), which at once began consultation regarding how to cooperate to prevent and cope with fires in Asia, the CEC has yet to respond seriously to this tragic economic and ecological and human disaster in its territory. There is already effective cooperation between provinces in Canada and states in the US, and ironically this may be a reason that the CEC has not addressed a NAFTA-wide approach to cooperation, adding Mexico and its states. While some might argue that the CEC is, perhaps, too new an institution to take on such a task, the reasonably effective compacts and treaties for the deployment of fire fighters from various provinces and states in and Canada and the US; the model already exists among two of the three partner nations. The CEC would do well to facilitate the operational cooperation with Mexico to replicate such systems between that nation and the other two. This potential for cooperation remains to be realized.

These accounts of the responses to the Mexican and Central American forest fires indicate that there was an immediate humanitarian response to cooperate with Mexico on the part of the US. However, the rapid expansion of the fires, exacerbated by the very dry El Niño weather patterns, rendered the national and international responses inadequate to the problem. Whether the rules of international cooperation are being effectively embraced must be measured by whether the response is proportional effectively to meet the need for that cooperation. In the case of Mexico, the national Mexican response was not adequate to the emergency and the international response on the part of the US, as a neighboring state, was also clearly insufficient. The US did not mobilize the resources it could have, and nor did Canada.

The Indonesian and SE Asia Forest Conflagration

Mexico's crisis coincided with that of Indonesia, and the media coverage of these two regions eclipsed reports of similar crises in Russia, Central African States and Brazil. The Southeast Asian international response was as problematic as that in North America. In Asia, a much more deliberative plan for cooperation had emerged, launching a more extensive framework for cooperation; these steps, however, did not have much more of an effect than ultimately was seen in the North American context. Like the bilateral help to Mexico, this system of cooperation provided too little, too late, to be effective in helping to prevent or to cope with the fires. The international cooperation was not proportional to the task.

Indonesia confronted the worst drought in 50 years, extending over more than one year. For the first 89 days of 1998, not a drop of rain fell in East Kalimantan. In June the fires began, and efforts to protect the people and to save the remaining 20,000 orangutans proved difficult. Wildlife conservation teams rescued some 200 orangutans, many were badly burned. Villages have captured many abandoned baby orangutans, hoping to sell them to get cash to live on. As Willie Smits of the Warariset Forestry Station described it [and quoted by Nash], "In East Kalimantan, the situation is desperate—for both people and orangutans. There is now a conflict for survival." This vignette captures the crisis. People have died because of the lack of food and protection and biodiversity has been lost in Indonesia. Ill-equipped citizens rose to fight the fires and protect the rare habitats around them, such as the Kota Kinabatangan forests. Indonesia is estimated to have lost $4.5 billion in fire related damage, including loss of timber, agriculture, biodiversity, health impacts, loss of tourism, loss of industrial output, and other related losses. This sum is more than double all the foreign assistance received by Indonesia annually the year before, and is about 2.5 percent of Indonesia's gross national product. Had a foreigner caused the damage, the claim in this amount would be more than the combined legal liabilities assessed by the Exxon Valdez and Bhopal tragedies.

In light of the losses of forests in Indonesia (estimated at 4.5 million hectares in 1997 alone), and given that many more millions of people were injured throughout Southeast Asia than had been injured in Mexico, it is evident that the head of the United States Agency for International Development was preoccupied with the crisis at hand and was speaking out of ignorance when he characterized the horrific losses in Mexico as worse than those in Indonesia. As the Assistant Executive Director of the UNEP [Jorge Illueca] stated:

> "The forest fires of Indonesia have been categorized as an environmental emergency of exceptional proportions. UNEP endorses that conclusion, aware as it is of the status of Indonesia as one of the twelve 'maga-biodiversity' countries of the world, rich in species, many unique to that nation and deserving of international protection. Indonesia possesses 11 percent of the world's known flowering plans, 12 percent of the world's mammals, 15 percent of all amphibians and reptiles, and some 37 percent of the world's fish."

States cooperated internationally to assist Indonesia with the fires as they worsened. As noted above, the United States National Atmospheric and Oceanic Administration (NOAA) monitored the Indonesia crisis by satellite because the area where fires were widespread was too vast for monitoring by airplane and the satellite systems were in place to monitor the fires (See NASA Earth Observatory, at <http://earthobservatory.nasa.gov/cgi-bin/printall/Library/GlobalFire/fire.html>. The US and ADB allocated $6 million to assist Indonesia and neighboring states to cope with the environmental disasters of the fires. Other States also made similarly modest bilateral contributions of humanitarian assistance.

Both the forest fires in Mexico and in Indonesia were unprecedented and enormous, but if one measures the environmental and economic impact that Indonesia had on its neighbors, it is evident that the Indonesian crisis eclipses the great loss in Mexico. Malaysia and Singapore each provided air pollution alert information on the Internet, so that individuals could take action to protect their health by assessing the pollution index directly. The air pollution, or "haze," caused damage to Singapore that has been estimated at $74.1 million and the damage to Malaysia may exceed $310 million. The lost tourism income from the air pollution is readily quantified. In addition, the impacts of the Indonesian fires that were located on the island of Borneo, on the adjacent nation of Brunei Darussalam, and on the adjacent Malaysian states of Sabah and Sarawak, were acute in health impacts and lost of natural resources.

Brunei Darussalam does not have the problem with palm oil or timber plantations that Indonesia or parts of Malaysia experience. Fires spread into Brunei from over the Indonesian and Malaysian border. This disrupted life in Brunei substantially. The experience of the Shell Oil refinery in Brunei illustrates this. The Brunei Shell Petroleum Company is responsible for some 4,000 persons, including dependents. The air pollution was so acute in Brunei during the period of the fires that it exceeded maximum health limits (100 PSI) repeatedly; indoor air was often measured at 200 PSI. Workers regularly had to volunteer to fight fires in order to prevent their spread. Shell had to invest $3 million just in disbursements to fight fires, secure the health of its workers, and keep its refinery open in conditions of near zero visibility; this figure does not include the lost revenues when production was shut down.

The causes of the fires in Indonesia were partially natural but mostly human. One of the major causes was the burning of land to plant new, lucrative palm oil plantations. Although the use of fire to clear land had been made illegal in 1993 in Indonesia, the government undertook no enforcement of this law, and indeed, with corruption, the practice continued unabated. Professor and Ambassador Tommy Koh of Singapore has advocated that it is time to name the corrupt companies and individuals who cause these problems.

> "It's not El Niño that set the fires. A United Nations report said that 80 percent of the fires were set by logging companies and palm oil plantations. If we want to prevent a recurrence of the haze, the only thing to do is to stop these bad guys...the only way to prevent the haze was to publish names of culprits who start fires and turn public opinion against them."

The pattern of international cooperation to control forest fires in Indonesia and the other areas of Southeast Asia has been developing for some years.

A German forest expert [quoted by Nathan], Ludwig Schindler, noted that most of the fires began on commercial plantations and on concession lands; he urged that the companies should be obliged to put fire fighting teams and equipment in place on their concession lands. In addition, large paper and pulp mills in Indonesia, just west of Singapore and Malaysia, induce behavior that allows forest first to develop, since they demand salvage timber and are supplied by new incursions into forest lands. Fires have also spread along degraded lands. Unlike Mexico, the use of "slash and burn" agricultural clearing by small farmers was not the major cause of the fires in Indonesia.

The pattern of international cooperation to control forest fires in Indonesia and the other areas of Southeast Asia has been developing for some years. Because of past cooperation, a system had developed to cooperate to track the fires in Indonesia. However, the magnitude of the 1997 and 1998 fires was greater than expected and the systems of cooperation to supply assistance to fight the fires was not up to the magnitude of the task. Fire and air pollution smoke incidents had taken place in Indonesia before the 1997–1998 crisis in 1982–1983, 1987, 1991, and 1994. As a result, a conference was called by Indonesia in Bandung in 1992, following the 1991 fires. The 1982–1983 fires had caused some $8-9 billion worth of damage, and those a decade later were more severe.

The Bandung Conference recommended a number of measures of international cooperation to prepare Indonesia and other states to be able to cope with the forest fire problem. The purpose was the development of an international program to initiate a "Long-Term, Integrated Forest Fire Management Programme" for Indonesia. The Programme was to involve national agencies involved in forest fire control and international experts and donors. Beginning in 1995, Indonesia's Environmental Impact Management Agency (BAPEDAL) established a "National Coordination Team on Land and Forest Fire Management." Projects were launched by the Canadian, German, Japanese, and US bilateral aid agencies, and by the European Union and the UN Food and Agriculture Organization. A workshop in 1997 developed "National Guidelines on the Protection of Forests Against Fires," and in 1998 the Bogor Agricultural University established the Research Center for Forest Fire and Land Studies.

The Bandung strategy did engage the system of international cooperation. It stimulated the development of a forest fire management program in the Association of South East Asian Nations (ASEAN). The ASEAN member states conducted workshops and meetings between 1992 and 1996 on "Transboundary Haze Pollution." This led to one bilateral agreement and on 12 December 1997 Malaysia and Indonesia entered into a Bilateral Memorandum of Understanding to jointly tackle the "haze problem" (meaning the transboundary air pollution) and to manage any other disasters. It also led to multilateral undertakings. For instance, in 1998, based on the 1997 ASEAN Regional Haze Action Plan described below, the ADB provided financial support through a regional technical assistance (RETA) to assist ASEAN to strengthen cooperation among the ASEAN states affected by the fires and the air pollution from the smoke.

At a meeting in June of 1995, the ASEAN Environment Ministers agreed on the ASEAN Cooperation Plan on Transboundary Pollution, which forms the basis for the ASEAN Regional Haze Action Plan. Parenthetically, it can be noted that the gentleness of phrase by which the transboundary air pollution is referred to as "haze," describing its national manifestation in the polluted states, is a diplomatic way to avoid having to confront the states that cause the problem with the issues of state responsibility that are evident here. Cooperation is encouraged if the issues of liability are set aside. As one of the region's leading legal commentators, Professor Simon S.C. Tay, has observed, ASEAN policy and practice build consensus and cooperation by recognizing "the norm of non-interference in another state's affairs," by adopting "non-binding plans, instead of treaties and legalistic rules," and by relying "on national institutions and actions, rather than a stronger central bureaucracy."

The Secretary General of ASEAN, Dato' Ajit Singh, has described the ASEAN Cooperation Plan on Transboundary Pollution as consisting of three program areas:

- Transboundary Atmospheric Pollution;
- Transboundary Ship-borne Pollution; and
- Transboundary Movement of Hazardous Wastes.

In each program area, the objectives, strategies, activities and institutional arrangements are further elaborated. The Plan of Cooperation also contains a section on resources and extra-regional support which describes the various sources of technical expertise and financial assistance that are available or can be mobilised to support ASEAN's efforts in implementing the Plan. The Plan further includes a section on implementation and evaluation which outlines the steps required to implement the Plan and evaluate the progress made.

The Plan provides for a short-term strategy to "prevent anthropogenically induced forest fires, especially in land clearing activities in timber and agricultural estates and transmigration projects," by prohibiting the "burning of biomass generated largely by development projects during dry periods," and by early detection of fires and enhancing communications to share information and deploy relevant activities. Long-term goals include finding alternative uses of biomass and employing zero burning practices.

The air pollution of 1997 stimulated measures toward implementation of the 1995 Cooperation Plan through the actions set forth in The Regional Haze Action Plan. The 1997 fires produced very acute regional air pollution from July to October of 1997 in Brunei, Indonesia, Malaysia and Singapore and to a lesser extent in the Philippines and Thailand. The public was demanding action because of the unprecedented health problems affecting, literally, millions of people in these states. The Regional Haze Action Plan has three primary objectives: "(a) to prevent land and forest fires through better management policies and enforcement; (b) to establish operational mechanisms to monitor land and forest fires; and (c) to strengthen regional land and forest fighting capability and other mitigation measures." The activities identified as priorities to attain these ends are all technical, e.g., preparing inventories, enhancing remote sensing of fire phenomena, developing a common air quality index, better communications and cooperation. The institutional arrangements involve greater roles for the ASEAN Specialised Meterological Centre (ASMC) and the ASEAN Institute of Forest Management (AIMF). ASEAN "should explore ways to work closely" with the following list of bodies in order "to enhance cooperation to combat forest fire": the ASEAN Working Group on Forestry; ASEAN-EC Joint Consultative Committee (JCC) Sub-Committee on Forest; Brunei-Indonesia-Malaysia-Philippines (BIMP), and the East ASEAN Growth Areas (EAGA) Sub-Committee on Forest.

It is evident from the details of the Plan that it is a rudimentary set of recommendations, rather far removed from actually building the capacity in any single nation to more effectively combat the forest fires. This may be partially ascribed to inexperience, especially with fires on such a vast scale. However, it is also the result of the weakness of the ASEAN Environment Ministries, vis à vis the economic development ministries, and the fact that many of the fires are associated with powerful plantation and timber developers who either do not wish to have government scrutinize their activities or have corruptly prevented government from enforcing the applicable laws supervising their endeavors. Nonetheless, the full agreement on the strategies established a firm foundation on which to build more substantive work, which may promise more immediate benefit for fire fighting and prevention.

The Regional Haze Action Plan, underwritten by the Asian Development Bank's RETA, takes the Cooperation Plan to a stronger level of endeavor. This Action Plan expressly calls for:

(a) an adoption of legislation to ban open burning;
(b) strict enforcement of laws;
(c) more effective systems of air quality monitoring of all sources of air pollution;
(d) guidelines to discourage activities which can lead to land and forest fires; and
(e) operating procedures for the early mobilization of resources to prevent the spread of fires.

It spells out the roles for regional monitoring through ASMC. It includes a detailed plan for strengthening national and regional fire fighting capability; inventories of existing capacity; compiling lists of needed equipment; acquisition of such equipment; establishing operating procedures to deploy fire-fighting resources in each country; regional fire-fighting operations; and for establishing a mechanism to update the Regional Haze planning. A Regional Haze Task

Force is to meet monthly to review the progress on implementing the Plan. In May of 1998, ASEAN convened an inception workshop on strengthening ASEAN capacity to mitigate transboundary haze, and the cooperation continues at a technical level to advance aspects of the Action Plan.

One striking aspect of the ASEAN Action Plan is that it is essentially a call for consistent and parallel measures at the national level. Only the ASMC role in providing regional services that none of the states can secure on their own, is truly operational, and it only detects the problem and its scope. In the area of fire prevention and response, virtually nothing is outlined for international cooperation. The Action Plan does provide that national fire fighting measures will be strengthened by establishing an operating procedure for the deployment of fire-fighting resources in each country for regional fire-fighting operations." However, the financial crisis in the region and the political and socio-economic transformations in Indonesia have meant that there has been neither the rapid development of national forest fighting teams or a management system for the regional deployment of forest fighting resources. All the Asian Development Bank funds are for studies and analysis, and do not supply the needed cooperative action itself.

As far as it goes, the ASEAN Action Plan is sound. The ASEAN States have set a goal in the Hanoi Plan of Action for the years 1999–2004, to "fully implement the ASEAN Cooperation Plan on Transboundary Pollution with particular emphasis on the Regional Haze Action Plan by the year 2001." ASEAN has established a "Haze Technical Task Force" (HTTF) initially under the aegis of the ASEAN Senior Officials on The Environment (ASOEN), and now reporting directly to the ASEAN Ministerial Meeting on Haze (AMMH) which meets every other month. The HTTF meets monthly, facilitated by the ASEAN Secretariat's Functional Cooperation Bureau. The HTTF reports both to the ASEAN Standing Committee, which in turn reports to the ASEAN Meeting of Foreign Ministers, and to the ASEAN Ministerial Meeting on Haze, comprised of the Region's Environment Ministers. In principle, this framework should produce cooperation to implement the Regional Haze Action Plan. Under the HTTF there are two Working Groups on Sub Regional Fire Fighting Arrangements (SRFA), one each for Sumatra and Borneo. ADB provides a RETA for the Regional Haze Action Plan, to be implemented by the ASEAN Secretariat.

Despite the care and coordination invested in the design and operation of this framework for cooperation, and notwithstanding the goodwill involved, the process is not able to leverage fully what is needed to prevent and combat forest fires. The magnitude of the forest fire problem is far greater than the current levels devoted to implementing the Plan. First, for forest fires to have the priority needed in each State, the Prime Ministers need to be involved. The environment ministers are relatively weak and under-funded agencies. If the ASEAN Defence Ministries were to assign battalions for training in combating forest fires, and if specialized military units were allocated to fire prevention and fighting, then there would be a cadre of fire fighters sufficient to address the regions needs. Second, the financial resources are not sufficient to maintain comprehensive forest fire surveillance and prevention measures, and the prioritization of tasks leaves potential forest fire areas at risk. Third, the environmental law systems for compliance and enforcement are weakly structured, without the needed public education and public participation measures. Finally, despite the continuing assistance of NASA, the approach remains regional, and if the regional systems are insufficient during the next El Niño episode, there remains no effective standby plan for marshaling the needed international assistance to the region. Local officials cannot make much use of the best information from remote sensing if they lack the capacity to fight a fire on the ground. The UN humanitarian relief and environmental systems are not yet capable of organizing the level of international mutual aid needed to again meet the sort of crisis that the world faced in 1997–1998.

Taking the fires of the last El Niño as a benchmark, the level of regional or international cooperation is not yet proportional to meet the threat of forest fires. This further dimension of cooperation that needs to be realized in the future. In terms of the 1997–1998 fires, the allocation of material, technical assistance, and finance from the international community was wholly inadequate to combat the raging fires. Good intentions to cooperate, tied to modest cooperation, cannot objectively be deemed to be effective cooperation. The undertakings are disproportionate to the threat posed by the fires. So far the States attempting to cooperate together have failed to marshal the activity to satisfy their duty to cooperate. It is likely that the fires will again devastate the region, and that the phenomenon of transboundary air pollution will be repeated, with the attendant loss of human life, biodiversity, and natural resources.

What threshhold of cooperation could be sufficient to be proportional to the threat? There are precedents from other regional responses that are minimally sufficient. These exist at the subnational level, and have been largely ignored by the UN or other international intergovernmental bodies that deliberate about the world's forest fire phenomena. If the international legal obligation to cooperate is to carry more promise than the law of State Responsibility, States need to examine what does already work internationally to combat forest fires, and use that context as the measure to define whether their own undertakings are proportionate.

Tentative Early International Deliberations on Forest Fires

One measure that forest fires have become a common concern of States internationally are the wide range of intergovernmental consultations that now address fires. Beyond the bilateral cooperation and discussions between Mexico and the US, or the regional multilateral negotiations with ASEAN, the UN system has taken up the issue. The UN FAO had long worked on fires as a matter of technical assistance in forest management. The UN Division of Humanitarian Affairs in New York has assisted in organizing relief for states engulfed in vast forest fires, along with other "natural" disasters. But the magnitude of the 1997–1998 worldwide fire phenomenon raises the legitimate question of whether the UN should facilitate more effective international cooperation to cope with fires.

In order to build consensus that international cooperative measures were needed, the UN convened numerous meetings and consultations of experts. These meetings, in and of themselves, did not produce immediate action. It can take some years before the political consensus emerges to support a new UN cooperative venture and for new financial support to be donated by states to allow the cooperation to advance. In the interim, of course, the problem of the forest fires continues to get worse and little is done to actually work on resolving the problem. At best, the UN's meetings build toward the day action will be agreed upon; at worst, the meetings educate a range of officials and give the appearance of activity which is too often disconnected from remedial measures.

The acute publicity given to the fires in 1997 and 1998 prompted the UNEP to convene a meeting of experts on "Coordination of UN Response to Indonesian Fires" on 20–21 April 1998 in Geneva, Switzerland. That meeting was followed by a World Meteorological Organization Workshop (WMO) on "Regional Transboundary Smoke and Haze in South-East Asia" in Singapore on 2–5 June 1998 and the WMO approved a "Programme To Address ASEAN Regional Tranbsboundary Smoke (PARTS)." WHO convened a workshop in Lima, Peru, on 3–7 August 1998 on "Guidelines for Forest Fire Emergencies." In late 1998, WMO and the UN International Decade for Natural Disaster Relief convened an inter-agency review and retrospective of the 1997/1998 El Niño events.

UNEP's Executive Director, Dr. Klaus Topfer, announced that UNEP would take on a central coordinating role for building capacity to cope with forest fires. UNEP, for instance, has undertaken to assist "the development and improvement of the fire early warning component of the action plan within the UNEP/GEF project on Emergency Response to Combat Forest Fires in South-East Asia." The Global Environment Faculty (GEF) allocated to UNEP a grant of $850,000 for work in Indonesia, Malaysia, Philippines, Singapore, and Thailand in order to set up the basic consultation procedures for the deployment of emergency fire fighting help as between the governments, the international agencies, and non-governmental organizations. The product will be public education about fire prevention and ultimately "a strategy to combat the fires, and make recommendations to donors." (Id). The UNEP efforts are intended to complement the WMO/NOAA Programme To Address ASEAN Regional Transboundary Smoke ("PARTS"), which will result in an aerial fire surveillance regime for Sumatra under a Sub-Regional Fire Fighting Arrangement. UNEP has indicated that it is ready also to work with the UNDP on regional protocols and agreements in Asia, although no negotiations for such appear to have been initiated.

The commendable willingness of UNEP's Executive Director to serve a coordinating role in coping with forest fires is not yet matched by the willingness of the nations to support that role. There is rarely coordination among the national positions among the different international organs. A nation like the US can take a leadership role in one arena through certain agencies, such as through NOAA's contribution of remote sensing and fire monitoring assistance in Southeast Asia, and yet take a small role through another agency, such as the United States Agency for International Development's weak presence in the Asian forest fire area and its higher public profile but disproportionately weak involvement in the assistance to Mexico. These agency positions are no more coordinated than is that of the US State Department delegation to the UNEP Governing Council meetings in Nairobi with respect to whether or not to support a UNEP coordination role, or whether forest fires should be discussed in the context of debates on biodiversity in the Second Committee of the United Nations General Assembly or the Commission on Sustainable Development. Other nations have a similarly segmented decision-making process. States have neither signalled a consensus to support UNEP's lead on the forest fire issues nor proffered the needed technical and financial support.

Moreover, among other international agencies there is not yet much response to UNEP's leadership. Other agencies have proposed a different model of cooperation. For instance, a UN Team of Specialists on Forest Fires from FAO and UN Economic Commission for Europe (UNECE) prepared a multi-agency program proposal to link UNEP, FAO, UNESCO, WMO, the International Tropical Timber Organization (ITTO), and the IDNDR in a coordinate effort at cooperation. The initiative was endorsed by a UN FAO/UN ECE/ ILO Conference on "Forest, Fire and Global Change," held at Shushenskoe in the Russian Federation in 1996. The FAO and UNECE Team of Specialists on Forest Fires had earlier submitted the proposal as "A Possible Role of the UN System in Fire Research and Wildfire Disaster Management" as an Annex of the Yokohama Strategy for a Safer World, at the World Conference on Natural Disaster Reduction (Yokahama, May 1994), and it was considered at the International Conference on "Wildland Fire '97" in Vancouver, British Columbia, Canada.

Thus, in the aftermath of the 1997–1998 forest fire catastrophes around the world, it is evident that many international intergovernmental organizations have *begun* to address the problem of how to cooperate to prevent or cope with the fires. At the same time, this international cooperation is fragmented among many agencies, and has such a low level of financial support that it cannot be expected to make a significant contribution to solving the forest fire problem. Moreover, much international assistance seems focused primarily on the problem of Southeast Asia, while the need is for a response to build capacity in every region since the forest fire phenomena are worldwide. Central Africa and South and Central America and Siberia require a measure of international cooperation as well.

Despite these international deliberations, it is fair to assess that the response of States through their UN multilateral system to the duty to cooperate is no more effective today with respect to forest fires and transboundary air pollution than is their response at the bilateral or regional levels. Action may not be galvanized until the next tragic wave of forest fires. It may be that the world community must await an even greater loss of human life and biodiversity in the next El Niño/Southern Oscillation phenomena before States will find the political conviction to act with effectiveness that is proportionate to the challenge.

One reason that international deliberations are still at an inconclusive stage is that the expertise in preventing and fighting forest fires exists only with parts of western Europe, the provinces of Canada, the states of the US and a few federal agencies responsible for the stewardship of public lands. Even this capacity is stretched thinly, and because it functions outside the ambit of foreign affairs, its experience tends to be neglected by the diplomats tending to the international negotiations. It is to the practical experience of these governmental units that the effective precedents may be found for coping with forest fires.

Roles for Environmental Law in Sustaining Development and Preventing Fires

If neither the public international law principles of State Responsibility, nor the present understanding of the level of conduct needed to observe the obligation of cooperation, provide an effective working legal framework to motivate States to respond to forest fires accompanying El Niño, then what role can law serve? One answer is provided by the still emerging field of environmental law. Because forest fires are intimately a part of land stewardship, it is appropriate to examine the contributions of environmental law as the field of law whose doctrine and process most closely address all aspects of the forest fire phenomena.

Environmental laws provide a legal system that works across political borders, whether within a nation or transnationally. The field of environmental law provides a set of rules and principles designed to bring human conduct into accord with the scientifically understood operations of Earth's natural systems. To be sure, it can be (and too often still is) evaluated solely in traditional legal terms, as either municipal law or international law, but upon a deeper reflection, it is apparent that environmental law integrates both the domestic and the regional or global levels. It is this integrative role of environmental law that makes it a most useful system for the challenge of preventing forest fires. Environmental law builds systems and relationships across the sectors of government agencies and the territories of different jurisdictions, and the levels of authority from the local government to the UN.

Environmental law in Indonesia or Mexico or any other state is not an isolated sector of municipal law. It is a network of related legal regimes serving a common worldwide public policy objective. Environmental legislation within nations becomes the means to conserve the world's biological diversity, to stabilize Earth's climate under the UN *Framework Convention on Climate Change*, and to maintain natural resource use and develop in sustainable ways. Internationally, States have common but differentiated responsibilities as they cooperate to contain vast releases of carbon dioxide (whether from forest fires or other sources), into the atmosphere as well as maintaining forests as sinks which sequester carbon dioxide through photosynthesis, and to share data obtained from the scientific studies of El Niño/Southern Oscillation phenomena, including the use of remote sensing satellite technology from orbital space, is necessarily an effort engaging the scientists of all nations. At regional and local scales, preventing or containing forest fires is essential to safeguarding public health whether domestically or across national borders from air pollution. These shared and common global purposes are advanced by each nation's forest fire management systems, and retarded by the lack of such systems. The substance and procedures of environmental law, adapted to the conditions and cultures of the states which embrace them, provide the relevant legal framework for forest fire prevention.

Forest fires will not be prevented unless sustainable land use systems are established in each nation. These regimes cannot be imposed by a treaty system, but rather must be built from the cultures and environments of each nations or area. In the parlance of "common but differentiated responsibilities," each geographic region with forest habitat has the common responsibility to prevent forest fires, and each can and must implement this responsibility in different ways, according to the differentiated conditions prevailing in their area.

In the case of Indonesia, the nation had enacted environmental legislation and requited the teaching of environmental law in State Law Schools since the mid 1970s. Lapses in enforcement and weak administrative implementation, complicated by extensive corruption, undermined the effectiveness of these measures. Without a sound environmental law system, development patterns were not sustainable, contributing to the conditions that exacerbated forest fires. IUCN experts summed up the problems thus:

> "Since 1982, large-scale forest exploitation and conversion activities in Sumatra and Kalimantan have led to a rapid increase in fire hazard. Inappropriate logging and land-clearing methods, carried out by agro-industrial companies and transmigration projects, have left a patchwork of degraded forest cover that burns easily. Land acquisition by large companies without sufficient consideration for the rights of local people has led to land disputes, which are often solved or avenged through fire.
>
> The impact of these practices has been aggravated by inadequate infrastructure, unclear policies, weak legislation, and unenforced and ineffectual regulations. Finally, the Asian Economic Crisis caused a resource crunch that made things worse; funding, facilities, trained personnel, and incentives for community participation were withheld; fire prevention and protection measures were kept to a minimum. Under these conditions, the prevention and containment of fires was impossible."

Lapses in enforcement and weak administrative implementation, complicated by extensive corruption, undermined the effectiveness of these measures.

Without an adequate municipal environmental law regime, no amount of international cooperation will prevent forest fires. For this reason, *Agenda 21* in Chapter 8 recommended that all States enhance their national legislation and administration of laws governing environment and development. Cooperation toward this end is essential if the societal conditions that cause or exacerbate forest fires are to be ameliorated. This can be illustrated by the history of forest fires and economic development in the State of New York.

From this description of New York State's legal regime for the stewardship of the forests of the state, the role of environmental law is evident. Fire fighting is not relegated to a special sector of government, and then starved for the funds and personnel to make it effective. Nor is fire fighting asked to compensate for the failures of land stewardship or negligent timbering. Rather, fire fighting is an essential part of a system of forest stewardship.

Mutual Aid Agreements—A Defining Threshold for Cooperation to Combat Forest Fires

New York State regularly deploys its forest rangers and forest fighting equipment to other States and Provinces with which it has negotiated mutual aid agreements. These are essentially like treaties, since the States retain the sovereignty over their lands and forests, and have the right to enter into agreements with each other. In an interesting precedent, Canadian Provinces have also entered into these agreements. This formal process for preventing and cooperation for combating forest fires can provide a useful precedent for fashioning regional mutual aid pacts, as in the ASEAN region, or internationally through the UNEP...

Following forest fires in Maine in 1947 that burned over 250,000 acres, the states decided to enter into an interstate Compact in 1947 to promote effective protection and control of forest fires in the north-eastern states of the US and adjacent portions of Canada. New York State joined together with the States of Connecticut, Maine, Massachusetts, New Hampshire, Rhode Island and Vermont. Congress approved the Compact in 1949. Quebec joined the Compact, and in 1970 New Brunswick did likewise; in 1997 Nova Scotia joined. Canadian Provincial participation in the Compact was approved by Congress in 1952.

The Member States and Provinces of the Northeast Compact pay membership fees based on their share of the protected area of 66,047,101 acres of forest in the region. The Commission's mandate is to provide the means for its member states and provinces to cope with fires that might be beyond the capabilities of a single member through information, technology and resource sharing (mutual aid) activities. The Rules of the Commission provide that it is a fact-finding, coordinating and deliberative body with power to make recommendations to the member states. Each Member State or Province can send three Commissioners, one from the fire fighting service, one from its Governor and one from its legislature. This ensures that the Commission recommendations can be heard by each branch of government responsible for equipping and financing forest fire protection. Over the years a technical committee of State Foresters was set up to co-ordinate training, and formulate procedures for all technical issues of fire control. Under the overall supervision of an Executive Committee, working teams have been set up for

(a) training
(b) prevention
(c) equipment
(d) aviation
(e) fire weather.

An Executive Director manages the affairs of the Commission.

The Northeastern Compact functions well because each member state and province has established its own professional forest fire fighting agencies, with trained personnel and equipment. Each member can call on the others for mutual aid in case of a fire that its own team of fire fighters cannot contain. The Compact helps advise its members on what they need to do to maintain adequate accreditation of member services and scheduling of periodic reviews of the services, for preparation of the findings of review teams and the presentation of recommendations for program improvements to the full Commission.

When a state of province calls on the other members of the Compact for mutual aid, the fire fighting teams of equipment requested are deployed, After the fire is contained, the members requesting the aid pay the member that contributed the assistance for the costs of services. The compact works well.

Similar arrangements exist among the federal agencies that manage the public lands of the US, primarily in the west. The US Department of the Interior and Department of Agriculture prepared an Action Plan for Federal Wildland Fire Management in 1996. The plan calls for establishing "Geographic Coordinating Groups" to work with all local state and tribal partners in forest fire management. The Plan aims to develop interagency preparedness for wildfire management, including developing training tools and programs, common management procedures and objectives, implementation strategies, and fire prevention activities.

An Interagency Management Review Team is to establish fire management qualifications and qualification standards. In 1997, the US Forest Service announced a goal of resolving the problems of the large, catastrophic forest fires on the 39 million acres of forest at high risk of fires by the year 2015. The plans call for employing programs to monitor forest health and developing a comprehensive strategy for reducing accumulated vegetation that fuels fires.

The examples of the Northeastern Compact, and the federal agency wildfire strategies, provide concrete examples of practical measures that States are taking to combat forest fires. The procedures, techniques, training and financial systems have all been developed. While that would always need to be adapted to the different ecological, social and economic conditions of each nation, the broad outlines are evident. Fire fighting is an applied activity, not merely a planning process. The sooner teams of actual fire fighting services start to work together, with the full support of their governments, the sooner forest fires can be brought under control. International cooperation needs to begin from that premise. The successful models of inter-state cooperation exist. They should be adapted and emulated. If States wish to get results, they should insist that further international diplomatic deliberations over forest fires focus on putting in place the practical fire fighting service units, and bringing these services into cooperative alliances. This has worked over the years in New York and in the northeast of North America.

Environmental Law Goals in Developing Nations

The illustrative case of New York is useful in the context of states such as Indonesia and Mexico. While New York built its systems of law and forest management gradually, the pressures for development on natural resources in the developing nations, and in the economies in transition, require that these States move rather more rapidly to establish their environmental laws and forest fire protection systems.

Environmental law is clearly understood as a relevant body of law by each nation. Both have made the teaching of environmental law a requirement for their law degrees. Both supported *Agenda 21*, which in Chapter 8 calls for the strengthening of legal systems as essential for sustainable development. The public in both nations is increasingly frustrated with the poor administration of the basically sound environmental legislation, and there is growing impatience because of the evidence of corruption in the administration of the laws generally in both states. The stewardship and remedial aspects that characterize the observance of environmental law in New York are not yet realized in these states. Nonetheless, the gradual strengthening of environmental law will bring the benefits of sustainable development.

It is important to note that New York developed its forest fighting and environmental law capabilities largely by itself, as a developing economy and society. In this respect, also, the illustration is germane to the needs of developing states. As Professor Tommy Koh has observed, "Developing countries must avoid the mistake that cooperation at the international level can substitute for the needed sacrifices and hard work at the national level." New York was rich in natural resources but at the time was squandering its forest wealth, and no foreign aid came to help New York with its problems. There was no international cooperation at the time, and aid from the federal government would not come into existence until the institution of the Income Tax and the expansion of federal government roles during process of rebuilding the economy after the Great Depression in the 1930s.

In light of the weak response of the international community to the forest fire problems during 1997–1998, it is safe to say that developing states can only rely upon themselves to establish systems that will prevent or control forest fires in the future. Current levels of bilateral and multilateral assistance are inadequate to carry the burden of subsidizing the capacity building for national or subnational forest fighting. The ADB RETA or the UNEP proposals for forest fire monitoring both pay scant attention to the reality that the forest fires must be prevented locally and contained and extinguished locally.

Developing nations can take measures to control their forest fires in relatively short order. They can do so in cooperation with neighboring states. International organizations can provide the funds for the basic training and equipment needed to get forest fire services in place. But just as the fires destroy the resources base of each nation, so it must essentially be the decision of each nation to invest its own financial and human resources in systems to combat fires. Since it takes a disciplined force to fight fires, and airplanes are needed it would make sense for States initially to direct that their armed forces assume the responsibility for combating forest fires.

Fire prevention succeeds when self-help is employed. If international assistance and cooperation are to advance the cause of sustainable development, it must catalyze local measures for self-sufficiency. When nations, like Indonesia and Mexico, already have make a commitment to such self-sufficiency by enacting stewardship norms through their national environmental laws, international development efforts would benefit from recognizing and strengthening those national efforts. This can be done on two fronts. The first is to strengthen the systems that characterize environmental law in each nation, and not to shy from such a task simply because certain economic interests seek to continued or vested their exploitation of natural resources. The second is to provide the basic training for community leaders to organize local fire protection programs.

Community organization to fight fires is the first step in self-sufficiency.

Community organization to fight fires is the first step in self-sufficiency. Examples of organizing in this way can be found in developing nations. For instance, the first volunteer fire-fighting corps in Chile was organized in 1850 in Valparaiso. The model took hold there much as it did in New York State. There are now some 35,000 volunteers in 1,100 fire companies in Chile. Even in rural areas there are usually one and two volunteer fire companies. These are organized under 276 fire departments, or corps, and they raise funds locally for a barracks, a fire truck, communications equipment, and fire fighting tools. The corps are essentially private nongovernmental corporations. In 1970, the Junta Nacional de Cuerpos de Bomberos de Chile was founded to provide national integration of the system. There is a National Fire Fighters Academy (Academia Nacional de Bomberos) which coordinates the training for all the volunteers, and the national budget allocates some $11 million to the network.

Building this community volunteer network to fight fires is fundamental to successful forest fire management. It is used in other sectors, some also related to El Niño phenomena. For instance, in India, Dr. M.S. Swaminathan instituted an integrated monsoon management strategy to micromanage the planting of crops based on actual rainfall during the problematic El Niòo period. As he describes it,

> "First, establish in every district a Crop Weather Watch Group consisting of climatologists, farm scientists, representatives of farmers and women's organizations, members of the mass media and officials of government and financial institutions. The tasks to be addressed by the group include monitoring monsoon progression, developing contingency plans and alternative cropping strategies to suit different weather probabilities, building seed reserves of alternative crops and intensifying efforts in the area of water harvesting and minor irrigation"

To extend this approach, he advocates training "in each village panchayat at least one male and one female member in the science and art of monsoon management." The unpredictability of the effect of El Niño on the important monsoon rains for agriculture requires this community level involvement in cropping. The same approach can be seen in the initial organization of fire districts and towns in New York, or the volunteer fire corps in Chile.

What is missing from the reports of the follow-up to the Mexican forest fires, or the ASEAN Regional Haze Action Plan, and the ADB's RETA to assist after the Indonesian fires, is a commitment to assign high priority to this sort of community based organizing. There is also a lack of interest in creating economic instruments to generate the funds within each nation to secure the needed equipment and underwrite the ongoing training. Beyond establishing user fees, especially for the larger scale commercial agriculture and silvaculture enterprises, to pay for building fire-fighting capacity, little to no attention has been paid to develop more sophisticated economic instruments such as fire insurance system. Not only would insurance help compensate for unavoidable fire losses and prepare local communities to fight the next wave of fires, but by employing graduated levels of insurance premium fees, the system could reward those low risk insureds who employ strong fire prevention systems while assessing higher fees to high risk enterprises. This system would, thereby, provide economic incentives for sound fire prevention practices. The inattention to insurance in the aftermath of the 1997–1998 fires is a mistake. It is more than a little ironic that the World Bank and others are examining new emission trading systems for emitting and sequestering carbon dioxide under prospective greenhouse gas management schemes for the UN *Framework Convention on Climate Change*, and virtually no one is developing the needed fire insurance programs to help ensure that sustainable local economies will be there to manage and safeguard forests.

Similarly, there are proven forestry techniques to avert fires, and zero burn techniques for palm oil plantations and other agricultural activity. Golden Hope Plantations Berhad in Malaysia has been recognized by UNEP as its Global 500 Roll of Honor at the 1992 Rio de Janeiro Earth Summit for shredding old palm fronts and vegetation and replanting the new palms amidst the decomposing old, rather than burning the biomass. This technique should be taught and mandated throughout Indonesia and Malaysia and elsewhere as a sound and sustainable agricultural practice that obviates the need for burning and thus forest fires.

New equipment, such as the Bombardier aerospace turboprop amphibian airplanes which can load with surface water while in flight ("water scooping") and make repeated passes delivering water to remote fire areas, can be added to a nation's defence forces. There is no rational explanation for a nation having a large air force "to defend" against a foreign force, and have no equipment to help fight off the common foe of fire. Canada, France, Greece, Italy and Spain, along with heavily populated areas such as Los Angeles County in California, employ these planes effectively. Thailand has acquired two such aircraft. Developing nations cannot afford to squander funds on military aircraft which may or may not ever be needed against "theoretically possible" enemies when their nations need these fire fighting aircraft to fight recurring and predictable fires. The shift in military budgets for this purpose is within the capacity of each developing nation to achieve. In Indonesia, most areas are within a short distance of water. In Mexico, while water may be more remote, the fires are often in places inaccessible to fire fighting equipment and fire suppression by aircraft may be essential.

One thoughtful commentator on the problem of transboundary air pollution from forest fires is Professor Simon S.C. Tay, of the law faculty of the National University of Singapore, and a Member of Parliament in Singapore. Professor Tay has noted that nations have not worked effectively at the regional or bilateral level to collaborate to end the fires, for instance, as in not creating a regional fund to pay for measure to tackle the "haze" problem. At an Asia–Pacific Regional Workshop on Transboundary Pollution in Singapore in May 1998, he advocated six measures in the private sector that would induce more government action:

(a) a full account of the costs and losses from the pollution would "be a basis for affected states to make the economic commitment to fund the necessary steps for the prevention and control of future fires";
(b) a regional treaty to set environmental limits and establish a basis for holding states responsible;
(c) establishing access to the courts for private citizens to seek compensation for their losses;
(d) having a more open and routine review of regional plans (such as in ASEAN), including a range of experts and NGOs;
(e) conducting joint training of fire fighting units in the region, to build confidence in transboundary cooperation as well as the enhanced skills in fire fighting; and
(f) connecting regional economic incentives to better fire prevention, as in regional trade relations.

Professor Tay has effectively argued that inactivity in Southeast Asia results from the perspective that governments, media and the public take to the problem. If the air pollution is seen as merely haze, a local concern, an unusual El Niòo event, caused by many small fire incidents with no one at fault, and solvable just by organizing fire fighting, then there will be no response to the 1997–1998 fires. If, on the other hand, fires are seen as recurring dangers, the air pollution as a threat to health, that fires can be prevented more effectively than fought, and that commercial enterprises can be held accountable for their behavior, then a government can be motivated to act.

Of course, inertia tends to move governments toward the first characterization. News about the fires in the media and regular reporting of the health impacts and costs of the transboundary air pollution, can build political pressure toward collaboration to develop more effective fire prevention and containment. The strategies recommended by Professor Tay depend on full and transparent sharing of knowledge about the fires and their causes, and this in turn on ensuring access to information, as well as public participation in decision making, and ultimately access to justice. These principles lie at the heart of environmental law procedures, and have recently be reaffirmed in the United Nations Economic Commission for Europe's *Convention on Freedom of Information, Public Participation and Access to Justice* signed in Aarhus, Denmark, in June

1998 [*This convention is extracted in Chapter 10—Citizen Participation*]. The pre-conditions in civil society, for Professor Tay's recommendations to take root, will depend on other regions, beyond Europe, developing similar agreements.

Conclusions

It is evident that much more is at stake in the response to the forest fires of 1997 and 1998 than the cause of fire fighting. The strengthening of civil society, to become responsible for the stewardship of fire and forests, is a fundamental premise for sustainable development. Careful use of natural resources will not advance amidst corruption and avoidance of environmental management systems. Nations with inefficient or corrupt governments will neglect good forest management and experience an escalation of forest fire damage and loss.

Yet it is not simply the developing states that must reorder their thinking if the forest fires are to be contained. There is a myopia in developed lands as well. Most environmental organizations devote substantial resources to establishing preserves to safeguard Earth's biodiversity, and yet spend virtually nothing on building the community level systems for forest conservation and forest fire prevention. The environmental advocates and actors need to add the challenge of forest fire prevention and management to their priorities. They need to help support the training of local forest rangers and facilitate the development volunteer fire prevention and fighting programs. Because the citizens and parliaments of developed states tend to assume that the fire phenomena is under control in their nations, they seem oblivious to the fact that it is out of control in most other regions.

The fires of 1997 and 1998 may have elevated forest fires to the global agenda of concerns for journalists, but foreign ministries and national governments appear not to have embraced that agenda. For many leaders in government and nongovernmental sectors alike, the economic problems flowing from the economic depression in the markets of Southeast Asia and the weak economy in Mexico, and the stressed economies of Brazil or the states in Africa, have eclipsed the worry about forest fires. The rains return and the urgency to prepare for the next wave of fires is clouded over.

Fire fighting in the biologically rich areas of the Earth requires an environmental priority at least as sustained and important as that served by the International Committee of the Red Cross and the Red Cross and Red Crescent Societies. Humanitarian concerns never leave the agenda, and the team of volunteers who mobilize in the wake of natural disaster or armed conflict are always in training and preparation. If the United Nations system is not prepared to mobilize the systems for the sustainable use and defense of forests, then organizations, such as the International Union for the Conservation of Nature and Natural Resources (IUCN), should be encouraged to add this work to their agenda and commit to it for the long term.

The work of IUCN, through its World Commission on Protected Areas or its Species Survival Commission, will be gravely threatened by a repeat of the forest fires of 1997–1998. For instance, in the Primorski Krai, a maritime region in the Far East of the Russian Federation, there were 120 large-scale forest fires out of 546 fires in 1998, which burned 43,820 hectares of forestland. These were the worst forest fires in the region since 1921 and burned some 4,000 hectares in the Sikhote-Alinski and Lazovski Zapovedniki, which are the habitat for the endangered Siberian Tiger. NGOs contributed a mere $18,500 for fighting the fires, and rainfall in July 1998 finally extinguished the fires. Such setbacks to biodiversity protection can be seen in every region where forest fire damage escalates. The states that are members of IUCN and support its work would benefit from examining how this intergovernmental organization, founded in 1948, with its forest and wildlife ministry members and NGO members, can address the new global threats of forest fires. IUCN may be able to catalyze the international cooperation which is presently so disproportionate to the need.

Put positively, it is the local authority that must be the first defense against fire. In the parlance of the European Union, considerations of subsidiarity support this conclusion. At the same time, regionally there must be a shared effort towards training and transferring forest fire prevention knowledge and technology. At the interregional or international level, there must be sharing of remote sensing data for the detection of forest fires and gathering and disseminating formation on climatic and weather conditions. Environmental law can shape the links between sustaining managing forests in ways to prevent fires and coordinating the fire detection and fighting. It is a continuum, from the local to the global, transcending the traditional lines of governmental authority and between international and municipal law.

What animates the progressive development of international law today? Principles of state responsibility and international cooperation provide scant help in coping with forest fires around the world because of the way they treat, in a static way, the status relations among states. The law must evolve to be relevant to social problems or it becomes a dead letter. Environmental law emerges as a legal system that is evolving as the needs of nations, people and nature dictate and with the scientific advances in better understanding nature. The Earth's people cannot add more concentrations of larger numbers of people to fragile forest areas and fail to also improve their management of the forest ecology.

Forest fires are a clear and present danger, not merely to territory within a nation, but globally and transnationally. It is unlikely that a worldwide approach to fires will become a priority, at least until the next wave of El Niño induced forest fire tragedies. Until that time, the role of environmental law must be to support procedures that provide remediation to those afflicted by fires and catalyze reforms to avert such afflictions were possible. This transformative mission is the hallmark of environmental law.

5

Other International Organizations Operating in Asia and the Pacific

There are many international, intergovernmental, quasigovernmental, nongovernmental, private stakeholder organizations which assist in the implementation of environmental law and policy. Some of these organizations also provide funds for environmental projects in the region. They also contribute to the collaboration among countries in the region in relation to environmental matters. These organizations include the UN and its agencies (e.g., UNEP–ROAP in Bangkok), ESCAP, UNDP (e.g., its offices in Viet Nam, People's Republic of China and Thailand), UNESCO (e.g., UNESCO Man and Biosphere with its regional secretariat in Jakarta), IUCN (e.g., Pakistan Regional Directorate and country offices in Bangkok, Lao PDR, Viet Nam, etc.), World Bank, Commission on Sustainable Development (with representation from Asian states), ADB, WTO, APEC, WWF, ICS, ICC, etc. The roles of these organizations are set forth in the following extract.

A

Boer B., Ramsay R., and Rothwell D., "International Organizations and International Environmental Law," in *International Environmental Law in The Asia Pacific*, Kluwer Law International, 1998, pp 39-46

World Trade Organization

The World Trade Organization (WTO) (formerly the General Agreement on Tariffs and Trade or GATT) is the primary instrument for the regulation of multilateral trade. Its fundamental tenet is trade liberalization, with its central policy being non-discrimination. It aims to remove barriers to trade between nations by demanding that countries do not discriminate between domestic products and imports, between domestic products and exports, or between imports from different countries except in accordance with agreed exceptions.

The WTO can be seen as potentially problematic for environmental protection. It allows environmental policies which are consistent with international standards and allows for the domestic protection of the environment by the regulation of production or consumption of products if this is done consistency over domestic and imported products. However, the WTO may disallow environmental policies which discriminate against trading with one or more countries.

The Asia Pacific Economic Cooperation Forum

The Asia Pacific Economic Cooperation Forum (APEC) was established in Canberra in 1989, in the light of a realization that a framework for regional cooperation had become necessary. APEC comprises 18 countries, which account for some 40 percent of the world population. Thirteen of the present members are from Asia and the Pacific. APEC has taken a number of resolutions in recent years committing members to environment protection and sustainable development, including an "APEC Environmental Vision Statement".

[*The following paragraph discusses the "APEC Environmental Vision Statement." It is taken, out of its original order, from the current reference—Ben Boer, ibid, p 194*]

In the statement, the ministers reiterated the commitment of APEC to sustainable development, recognizing that environmental protection and economic growth are inseparably linked. The statement supported the integration of "environmental considerations into relevant policy development and economic decisions throughout the region." The ministers recognized the potential for regional approaches to address global environmental problems, and called on APEC to take the lead in addressing them and developing solutions consistent with the *1992 Rio Declaration on Environment and Development.*

[*The extract below returns to Boer, Ch. 2 pp 36-42*]

Nongovernmental Organizations

Non-governmental organizations (NGOs) can play an important role in the development of environmental policy at national, regional and international levels. NGOs are generally established with a view to promoting a particular interest in the public arena. NGOs concerned with environmental issues include not only those established primarily for this purpose, such as World Wide Fund for Nature (WWF), Greenpeace and Friends of the Earth, but also those established for other purposes such as industry associations which may be affected by environmental regulation or which wish to influence environmental issues. These include the International Chamber of Shipping (ICS), the International Chamber of Commerce (ICC) and the Business Council for Sustainable Development. One manifestation of the growing influence of NGOs in the environmental debate was the conduct of the Global Forum, which took place at the same time as UNCED in Rio de Janeiro in 1992. The Global Forum was attended by thousands of people from around the world, many as representatives of nongovernment conservation organizations. *Agenda 21* recognizes the importance of NGOs as well as other groups:

> The continued active and effective participation of non-governmental organizations, the scientific community and the private sector as well as local groups and communities are important in the implementation of *Agenda 21*.

Conservation organizations in recent years have often played a part in the development of treaties and in Conferences of the Parties, as well as acting as watchdogs in treaty implementation. They have also influenced negotiations on environmental protection in agreements such as the World Trade Organization and play a role in the accountability of the multilateral development banks, such as the World Bank and the Asian Development Bank, in relation to loans made for development projects. The main NGOs active in the Asia Pacific region are briefly described below.

IUCN–The World Conservation Union

The IUCN, also known as the World Conservation Union, was formed in 1948 as an organization comprising states and public law authorities as well as a diverse range of non-government organizations. It is based in Gland, Switzerland. The IUCN presently comprises 74 states, 105 government agency members, and over 700 non-governmental organizations, with representation of 133 countries in this membership. It convenes a General Assembly (as of 1996 the General Assembly has been known as the World Conservation Congress) every three years, at which members negotiate and pass resolutions to present to governments and to relevant intergovernmental organizations.

The IUCN has six Commissions: Environmental Law; Ecosystem Management; World Commission on Protected Areas (formerly the Commission on National Parks and Protected Areas); Species Survival; Education and Communication; and Environmental Strategy and Planning. These Commissions are responsible for overseeing the work of the IUCN. They represent a global network of over 6,000 scientists and other professionals working in the environmental field. The work programs of the Commissions are approved by IUCN members at the World Conservation Congress.

Although resolutions of the World Conservation Congress are not binding on members in any legally enforceable sense, the organization has nevertheless played a significant and influential role in the development of international environmental policy and law. For example, the *1980 Wind Conservation Strategy* was largely the work of the IUCN. In 1991 the IUCN released the successor to the *World Conservation Strategy*, entitled Caring for the Earth. The IUCN was also the instigator of the *1982 World Charter for Nature* and the *1992 Biodiversity Convention.* Its commission on Environmental Law presented its proposed International Covenant on Environment and Development to a 1995 conference at the United Nations.

The IUCN is also an information source and research coordinator for environmental issues globally. It publishes the IUCN Red List of Threatened Animals, which contains comprehensive lists of endangered species, and Species Action Plans, which assess international conservation priorities for groups of species. In addition, it provides information on national parks and protected areas, nature reserves, World Heritage sites and biosphere reserves. Over the past decade it has assisted the development of National Conservation Strategies in partnership with member governments and nongovernment organizations. A number of these have been generated in Asia and the Pacific.

Greenpeace

Greenpeace is an independent international conservation organization, with a worldwide membership of over 5 million in some 158 countries. It has offices in 43 countries, and has its international headquarters in Amsterdam. In Asia and the Pacific, Japan, Fiji Islands, Australia and New Zealand have national offices.

Worldwide Fund for Nature

The Worldwide Fund for Nature (WWF), formerly known as the World Wildlife Fund, has its headquarters in Gland, Switzerland. It has some 4.7 million supporters, and a global network of 27 national organizations. It has action-oriented conservation programs and support services in 96 countries, including a number in Asia and the Pacific. It works closely with the IUCN in many initiatives, for example the *1980 World Conservation Strategy* and its successor, Caring for the Earth. Its mission is stated to be:

> "To conserve nature and ecological processes by:
>
> preserving genetic, species and ecosystem diversity, ensuring that the use of renewable natural resources is sustainable now and in the longer term, for the benefit of all life on Earth; and
>
> promoting actions to reduce to a minimum pollution and wasteful exploitation and consumption of resources and energy."

WWF's ultimate goal is to stop, and eventually reverse, the accelerating degradation of our planet's natural environment, and to help build a future on which humans live in harmony with nature.

The Nature Conservancy

The Nature Conservancy (TNC) is a United States-based private conservation organization which commenced operation in 1951. Its mode of operation is to raise funds for the purchase of (generally) large areas of land. To date, it has protected 9.5 million acres of land within the United States and has assisted with the protection of 42 million acres outside the United States. It has a membership of over 800,000, with corporate associates numbering some 1,385. It operates in a wide range of countries, and owns and manages over 1,600 preserves. In Asia and the Pacific, it has programs focused on Indonesia, Japan and various southwest Pacific countries. An example of its work includes a collaborative project in the Arnavon Islands (part of Solomon Islands), which has protected the habitat of the Hawksbill turtle...

B

South Asian Association for Regional Cooperation (SAARC)

Introduction

The South Asian Association for Regional Cooperation (SAARC) comprises the seven countries of South Asia, i.e., Bangladesh, Bhutan, India, Maldives, Nepal, Pakistan and Sri Lanka. SAARC is a manifestation of the determination of the peoples of South Asia to work together towards finding solutions to their common problems in a spirit of friendship, trust and understanding and to create an order based on mutual respect, equity and shared benefits. The primary objective of the Association is the acceleration of the process of economic and social development in member states, through collective action in agreed areas of cooperation.

SAARC is a manifestation of the determination of the peoples of South Asia to work together towards finding solutions to their common problems in a spirit of friendship, trust and understanding and to create an order based on mutual respect, equity and shared benefits.

Evolution

The idea of regional cooperation in South Asia was first mooted in November 1980. After consultations, the Foreign Secretaries of the seven countries met for the first time in Colombo in April 1981. This was followed up, a few months later, by a meeting of the Committee of the Whole, which identified five broad areas for regional cooperation. The Foreign Ministers, at their first meeting in New Delhi in

August 1983, adopted the *Declaration on South Asian Regional Cooperation* (SARC) and formally launched the Integrated Programme of Action (IPA) in the five agreed areas of cooperation, namely, Agriculture, Rural Development, Telecommunications, Meteorology, and Health and Population Activities. Later, Transport, Postal Services, Scientific and Technological Cooperation, Sports, Arts and Culture were added to the IPA.

The Heads of State or Government at their First SAARC Summit held in Dhaka on 7–8 December 1985 adopted the Charter formally establishing the South Asian Association for Regional Cooperation (SAARC).

The objectives, principles and general provisions as mentioned in the SAARC Charter are as follows:

Objectives

- To promote the welfare of the peoples of South Asia and to improve their quality of life ;
- To accelerate economic growth, social progress and cultural development in the region and to provide all individuals the opportunity to live in dignity and to realize their full potential;
- To promote and strengthen collective self- reliance among the countries of South Asia;
- To contribute to mutual trust, understanding and appreciation of one another's problems;
- To promote active collaboration and mutual assistance in the economic, social, cultural, technical and scientific fields;
- To strengthen cooperation with other developing countries;
- To strengthen cooperation among themselves in international forums on matters of common interests; and
- To cooperate with international and regional organizations with similar aims and purposes.

Principles

- Cooperation within the framework of the Association is based on respect for the principles of sovereign equality, territorial integrity, political independence, non-interference in the internal affairs of other States and mutual benefit.
- Such cooperation is to complement and not to substitute bilateral or multilateral cooperation.
- Such cooperation should be consistent with bilateral and multilateral obligations of Member States.

General Provisions

- Decisions at all levels in SAARC are taken on the basis of unanimity.
- Bilateral and contentious issues are excluded from the deliberations of the Association.

Institutional Set-up

Summit

The highest authority of the Association rests with the Heads of State or Government, who meet annually at Summit level. To date, 10 Meetings of the Heads of State or Government have been held in Dhaka (1985), Bangalore (1986), Kathmandu (1987), Islamabad (1988), Malé (1990), Colombo (1991), Dhaka (1993) New Delhi (1995), Malé (1997), and Colombo (1998), respectively. The Eleventh and Twelfth SAARC Summits will be held in Nepal (1999) and Pakistan (2000), respectively.

The Heads of State or Government during the Ninth SAARC Summit agreed that a process of informal political consultations would prove useful in promoting peace, stability and amity and accelerated socioeconomic cooperation in the region.

Council of Ministers

Comprising the Foreign Ministers of Member States, the Council is responsible for formulating policies; reviewing progress; deciding on new areas of cooperation; establishing additional mechanisms as deemed necessary; and deciding on other matters of general interest to the Association. The Council meets twice a year and may also meet in extraordinary session by agreement of Member States. It has held 20 regular sessions till December 1998. The Twenty-first Session of the Council will be held in Colombo in March 1999.

A Commemorative Session of the Council, to mark the First Decade of SAARC, was also held at New Delhi on 18 December 1995, during the Sixteenth Session of the Council of Ministers.

Standing Committee

The Standing Committee comprising the Foreign Secretaries of Member States is entrusted with the task of overall monitoring and coordination of programs and the modalities of financing; determining intersectoral priorities; mobilizing regional and external resources; and identifying new areas of cooperation. It may meet as often as deemed necessary but in practice normally meets twice a year and submits its reports to the Council of Ministers. The Committee has held 25 regular sessions and two special sessions till December 1998. The Twenty-sixth session of the Committee will be held in Colombo in March 1999.

The Standing Committee may also set up Action Committees comprising of Member States concerned with implementation of projects as per Article VII of the Charter.

The Standing Committee is assisted by a Programming Committee, an ad hoc body, comprising senior officials, to scrutinize the Secretariat Budget, finalize the Calendar of Activities and take up any other matter assigned to it by the Standing Committee. The Programming Committee has also been entrusted to consider the Reports of the Technical Committees and the SAARC Regional Centers and submit its comments to the Standing Committee. The Programming Committee has held 20 sessions till December 1998.

Technical Committees

Comprising representatives from the Member States, the Technical Committees formulate programmes and prepare projects in their respective fields which make up the Integrated Programme of Action under SAARC. They are responsible for monitoring the implementation of such activities and submit their reports to the Standing Committee through the Programming Committee. There are currently eleven Technical Committees, the Chairmanship of which rotates among Member Countries in alphabetical order every two years.

C

South Asia Cooperation on Environment Programme (SACEP)

(i) Kaniaru D., "Introduction," in *Compendium of Summaries of Judicial Decisions in Environment Related Cases*, SACEP, UNEP, NORAD, 1997, pp XIV

SACEP has, since it was set up as a South Asian intergovernmental organization to provide a regional focus on environmental issues of special significance to the countries in this region, carried out several programs to assist in the strengthening of the national and regional capabilities in the area of environment and development. Among these are the Development of a Curriculum for Regional Training for the Management of Protected Areas and Coral Island Ecosystems in South Asia, the Assessment of Biodiversity in the South Asian Countries and the Training in the area of Environmental Management. SACEP, with assistance from UNEP and the Asian Development Bank, has also set up the SACEP Environmental Natural Resources Information Centre (SENRIC). In recognition of the major role that SACEP has played in promoting regional cooperation in environmental matters, it was recently made the Secretariat for UNEP's Regional Seas Programme for South Asia. SACEP would also be implementing the South Asian segment of the Global Programme of Action on Land Based Sources of Marine Pollution.

6

Questions for Discussion

(a) What are the roles of regional/subregional organizations in the development of environmental law?

(b) Evaluate the levels of cooperation in your region. Are there obstacles to cooperation, and, if so, can these be overcome?

(c) The *ASEAN Agreement on the Conservation of Nature and Natural Resources, 1985* has not been ratified by three of the six signatory member states. Should the Agreement be ratified by them? What is the interrelationship between this Agreement and other global biodiversity conventions such as the *Convention on Biological Diversity*, 1992? Do these various conventions render the ASEAN Agreement otiose?

(d) What are the relevant policies and instruments that can respond to the Indonesian fires at international, regional and national levels?

(e) In what ways can ASEAN play a role in the Indonesian forest fires?

(f) "Traditional rules of state responsibility are ill-equipped to resolve forest fire problems." Discuss.

(g) Draft a Treaty/Protocol for a Cooperation Plan on Atmospheric Pollution in the ASEAN Region. Give an "Explanation" for the Treaty or Protocol of the provisions in your Draft.

7

References for Chapter 16

Atwood, "Species could be lost in Mexico Forest Fires," *Chicago Tribune*, 6 June 1998, p 1.

Corfu Channel case, 1949 I.C.J. 4.

Federal Wildland Fire Management Policy and Program Review—Implementation Action Plan, available at http://www.fs.fed.us/land/wdiap.htm [This site was accessed 24/04/2001].

Friedmann W., "The Role of International Law in the Conduct of International Affairs," 20 *Int'l J.* 1965, p 158.

Hunter D. and McRae A., *The Asian Development Back,* 1994, 5 YEIL.

Illueca J., *Address to the Singapore Environment Council Policy Dialogue on Southeast Asian Forest Fires*, 4-5 June 1998.

Kibria S.A.M.S., "Foreword," in *State of the Environment in Asia and the Pacific 1990*, 1992.

Koh T., *The Straits Times*, 5 June 1998, p 53.

Koh T., "The Quest for World Order; Perspectives of a Pragmatic Idealist," *Institutional Policy Studies*, p 62.

Lake Lanoux Arbitration, 12 UN R.I.A.A. 281, 1957.

Nash J.M., "Floods and Fires? They're just the Beginning of El Niño's Impact," *Time*, 1 June 1998, p 26.

Nathan D., "Repeat of Fires a 'Death Penalty'; The Kalimantan fires which may flare up during the July dry season will be 10 times more devastating than the 1982-83 episode, says fire expert," *The Straits Times*, 28 May 1998.

Nolan L., *Artic Legal Regime for Environmental Protection*, West Coast Environmental Law Research Foundation, forthcoming.

Paeuiu B., "Address to the Second World Climate Conference," Geneva, 6 November 1990, as quoted in Blakely R., "Global Warming: A Pacific Perspective," 2 *Transnational Law and Contemporary Problems*, 1992, p 202

Rio Declaration on Environment and Development, UN Doc AS/Copnf.151/26, reprinted at 31 ILM 874, 1992.

Swaminathan M.S., "Pokhran, El Niño and the Monsoon," *The Hindu*, 28 May 1998, p 12.

Tan A.K.J., "Forest Fires of Indonesia: State Responsibility and International Liability," 48 *Int'l & Comparative L. Q.* 826 (1999).

Tay S.S.C., "Inertia Over Haze Problem—Need to Work Out Full Costs of Haze," *Straits Times*, 28 May 1998, p 33.

The Trail Smelter Arbitration (*United States and Canada*), 3 UN Rep. International Arb. Awards 1911, 1938 (1941); reprinted at 35 *Am J. Intl. L.* 684, 1941.

Tsamenyi B.M., "Regional Cooperation in International Law in the South Pacific Region," 7 *Queensland University of Technology Law Journal*, 1991.

8

Additional References

ADB Reform of Environmental and Land Legislation in the People's Republic of China, ADB, 2000.

ASEAN Agreement on Transboundary Haze Pollution. See http://www.fire.uni-freiburg.de/se_asia/projects/ASEAN-Agreement.pdf, Appendix V in this Volume II at page 1045.

ASEAN Strategic Plan of Action on the Environment 1994–1998, Appendix III in this Volume II at page 1041.

ASEAN Vision 2000-2020, ASEAN Secretariat. (http://www4.gov.sg/asean/mirror/aseansec/).

IGES, *IGES Policy Recommendations on Forest Conservation in the Asia-Pacific*, 2001.

IGES, *Regional/Subregional Environmental Cooperation in Asia*, 2001.

Jakarta Declaration on Environment and Development, 18 September 1997 (http://www. aseansec.org/).

Kato K. and Takahashi W., Regional/Subregional Environmental Cooperation in Asia, IGES, 2001.

Koh K.L., *Selected ASEAN Documents on the Environment*, APCEL Document Series, Issue No.1, July 1996.

Koh K.L., "ASEAN Agreement on the Conservation of Nature and Natural Resources, 1985: A Question of Ratification and Implementation," paper presented at *Environmental Treaties—The Asia-Pacific Dimension: International Conference*, Darwin, Australia, 21-22 July 1995 (unpublished).

Koh K.L., ASEAN Air Plan: Up in Smoke in International Environmental Protection: A 50th Anniversary Status Report, *The Environmental Forum: The Policy Journal of the Environmental Law Institute*, Vol. 15, No. 1, January/February 1998, pp 50-51.

Koh Kheng Lian & N.A. Robinson, "Regional Environmental Governance: Examining the Association of Southeast

Asian Nations (ASEAN)", in *Global Environmenal Governance: Options & Opportunities* (Daniel C Esty & Maria H Ivanova eds.), pp. 101-120 [Yale Center for Environmental Law & Policy: 2002, http://www.yale.edu/envirocenter].

Kota Kinabalu Resolution on the Environment, 7 October 2000 (http://www.aseansec.org/), Appendix IV in this Volume II at page 1043.

Lye L.H., "The ASEAN Agreement on the Conservation of Nature and Natural Resources—Its Implementation in the Regulation of Wildlife Trade in the Region," paper presented at *Environmental Treaties—The Asia Pacific Dimension An International Conference*, Darwin, Australia, 21-22 July 1995 (unpublished).

Memon P.A., Designing Institutional Arrangements for Environmental Policy: Implications for ASEAN Countries of Recent New Zealand Reforms, *ASEAN Journal of Environmental Management*, Vol. 3, No. 2, November 1995, pp 147–157.

Qadri S.T., *Fire, Smoke, and Haze: The ASEAN Response Strategy*, Asian Development Bank, 2001.

Sakumoto N., The ASEAN Agreement on the Conservation of Nature and Natural Resources and the ASEAN Strategic Plan of Action, Chapter 14 in *Environmental Law and Policy in Asia: Issues of Enforcement* (Yoshiro Nomura & Naoyuki Sakumoto (eds), 1997.

Tan A.K.J., Integrating International Conventions on Nature Conservation in the Domestic Legal Framework, in *Conventions on Nature Conservation*, National Environmental Agency, Ministry of Science, Technology, and Environment, Hanoi, Viet Nam, 1998.

Tan A.K.J., Land/Forest Fires: Indonesian Environmental Legislation and its Implementation, in *South East Asian Land/Forest Fires: Science and Policy*, Douglas Johnston and Lim Hock (eds), World Scientific and Singapore University Press, 1998.

Tan A.K.J., Forest Fires of Indonesia: State Responsibility and International Liability, in *International and Comparative Law Quarterly*, October 1999, pp 826–855.

Tay S.S.C., "Modes of Regional Agreement," *Transboundary Pollution Germany-Singapore Environmental Technology Agencies Workshop*, Singapore, 27–28 May, 1998 (unpublished).

Tay S.S.C., What Should Be Done About the Haze? in *Indonesian Quarterly*, xxvi, 2, 1998, pp 99–117.

Tay S.S.C., South East Asia Forest Fires: Haze Over ASEAN 7 No. 2, *Review of European Community and International Environmental Law* (United Kingdom), August 1998, pp 198–204.

Tay S.S.C., What Should We Do About the Haze? South East Asia and Sustainable Development (editorial section), 3, No.3 *Asia Pacific Journal of Environmental Law*, (Australia), 1998.

Tay S.S.C., South East Asian Fires and Haze: Law Responsibility and Cooperation, 1998, Lawasia.

Tay S.S.C., "Transboundary Pollution in ASEAN: Cooperative Approaches," in *Environmental Law and Policy*, Edith Brown Weis, McCaffrey, McGraw, Szasz and Lutz eds, Asian Law and Business, New York, 1998, pp 601–603.

Tay S.S.C., "South East Asian Fires and Sustainable Development" (Abstract), presented at *Singapore Environment Council International Policy Dialogue on the South East Asian Fires*, 4-5 June 1998, Singapore.

Tay S.S.C., "South East Asian Fires: Implications for ASEAN and International Environmental Law," presented *at NUS Workshop on South East Asian Land and Forest Fires: Science and Policy*, 15-16 May 1998, Singapore (unpublished).

Tookey D.L., "The ASEAN Cooperation Plan on Transboundary Pollution: A Step Towards Pollution Control," *Environmental Liability*, Vol. 4, Issue 2, pp 36-40.

Tolentino A.S., *The Role of the ASEAN in Developing Environmental Law at the National and Regional Levels* (unpublished).

CHAPTER

17

INTRODUCTION TO INTERNATIONAL ENVIRONMENTAL LAW

CONTENTS

1

Introduction

International environmental law, a new field blossoming only in recent decades, is an integrated paradigm of environmental and international law, not only comparative law. It is a field that melds natural environment and science with law and the transboundary aspects of international politics and institutions. This approach recognizes environmental law as multidisciplinary and based on a natural science format and philosophical premises that include consideration of both the effect of humans and our population and consumption patterns, and the role of humans in the global ecosystem. The field is trans-species, recognizing human, plant, animal, and other forms of life such as bacteria and microbes, all interrelated in ecosystems and the biosphere.

The development of modern international environmental law began with the United Nations conferences in 1972 and continued in 1992, building up an extensive body of treaties and "soft law" documents that establish the tone of international cooperation and the search for modalities and aspirational principles, even if these principles are not yet crystallized into binding international law. Many times, the debates and drafting challenges turn on moral and philosophical as well as economic and social concerns and cultural values from different parts of the world. The process of formulating "soft law" documents is equally important, emphasizing the degree of public participation through nongovernment organizations, major groups, communities, and business/industry in addition to governments and institutional representatives.

The role of international environmental lawyers is thus based on substantive legal knowledge of several different fields of expertise, environmental and international, as well as specialized applications of tax law and policy, financing, trade, intellectual property, and land use planning. These lawyers also must understand scientific principles and methodologies and the use of scientific data in determining policy and law. International environmental lawyers deal extensively with policymakers inside legislative and ministerial bodies as well as with international diplomats and nongovernment organizations. The complexity and the challenge of the field are attracting some of the most creative and thoughtful lawyers, and professionals from other disciplines, who want to find ways of saving the quality of life for this and other generations, for other species, and to achieve sustainable development. Studying the legal and non-legal aspects of issues in the field of international environmental law presents unique rewards and challenges for students, professors, professionals, and policy-makers from every region of the world and from both the public and private sectors.

The international concern for the environment is clear in common areas such as coastal areas and shared water resources (dealt with in Chapter 14 and Chapter 12), the high seas (Chapter 18), outer space, and Antarctica. Through the United Nations, rules have been developed to apply more generally to the human environment and to sustainable development, relating to transborder and marine pollution (see the material on the *Basel Convention* in Chapter 7), preservation of biological diversity (Chapter 20), weather modification, population growth, and depletion of the ozone layer (Chapter 21). In fact, one of the new treaties of the 1990s, the *Convention on Desertification*, creates a significant number of legal obligations for parties and emphasizes the role of local communities in sustainable development.

The articles reproduced below provide an introduction to the field of international environmental law and its history. The material from Beckman and UNEP provide a very useful introduction to international law generally and lead on to an overview of environmental treaties, generally known as Multilateral Environmental Agreements (MEAs) or Conventions. If students do not have any experience in international law they may require supplementary reading in a basic international law text relating to the concepts

Many times, the debates and drafting challenges turn on moral and philosophical as well as economic and social concerns and cultural values from different parts of the world.

and principles raised in this introductory material. A more detailed introduction—*New Directions in International Environmental Law*—is provided by Brown Weiss in Chapter 1. This foundation material is essentially an introduction to international law and the rapidly evolving field on international environmental law.

International environmental law challenged many of the existing approaches to treaty making, enforcement, and the subject matter of international law. The extract from Stone raises provocative ethical and legal issues about who is responsible for protecting the global commons and what legal mechanisms can be used for this purpose. He includes a proposal for a global commons trust fund. His second article *Treaties as Antidotes* raises some of the problems associated with the use of treaties as the basis of a common action by nations. He expresses doubt that the slow growing body of general principles of international law (those rules that prevail in the absence of any special treaty) should be relied upon to provide significant protection of the biosphere. This points to the advantage of bilateral and multilateral treaties negotiated for this purpose. However, he goes on to critically evaluate why there are not more worldwide environmental treaties and why truly effective treaties are difficult to negotiate in this area.

The early development of the principles of international environmental law is highlighted by Principle 21 and Principle 22 of the *Stockholm Declaration*, extracted below. Further examples of these principles are extracted in Chapter 2 where the progression over 20 years from the *Stockholm Declaration* to the *Rio Declaration* is outlined. An example of the practical application of these basic principles, relating to responsibility for transboundary pollution, is the *Trail Smelter Arbitration* between the United States and Canada decided 60 years ago. It is clear that environmental law had to move beyond this sort of ad hoc evolution of general principles and arbitrations. However, the extracted arbitrations in Chapter 19 demonstrate that there is still an attachment to such mechanisms especially where economic concerns are at play.

The evolution of modern environmental law is described in the extract from Handl. He discusses the role of "soft law", framework conventions, and implementing protocols, uniform environmental standards and asymmetrical rights and obligations, and the interplay of local, national, regional, and global environmental standard setting. His general discussion of implementation and enforcement of international environmental law is followed by a more detailed discussion of new legal principles relating to nation states and entitlement to use environmental resources. The emerging precautionary principle and the wider notion of sustainable development are used as the basis for analyzing legal responsibility for significant transboundary risk and intergenerational responsibility.

Throughout the UN conferences, in 1972 and 1992, and in the negotiation of the modern MEAs, the issues of North–South conflict have always been ever present. These issues have many dimensions that are often related to concerns over the erosion of sovereignty, negotiating power, allocation of responsibility for global environmental problems, resources for implementation of sustainable development mechanisms, additional funding to facilitate compliance, technology transfer, and concern over trade and competitiveness issues. These issues in turn are inextricably linked to another crucial issue: the concept of development and the relationships between developing and developed economies.

The dilemma for developing countries (and indeed for the international community as a whole) is how to develop sustainably with access only to the cheapest, which in most cases also means most environmentally damaging, technologies. In Chapter 8, Doherty deals with the increasingly important issue of technology transfer in the context of environmental management. In the same chapter, Ottinger discusses the role of technology transfer in the promotion of energy efficiency. These articles clearly relate to issues of international environmental law and should be studied accordingly. Additional funding, through specific funds set up under treaties such as the *Framework Convention on Climate Change*, 1992, through the Global Environmental Facility, the Asian Development Bank, or foreign aid, may take many forms. This is discussed in Chapter 23 with a particular emphasis on "additionality," whereby the difference in cost between the polluting and the environmentally appropriate alternative developments are funded.

The politics of the North–South divide are a recurring theme of international environmental law. These debates can be quite intense during environmental negotiations. See, for example, the discussion in Chapter 13 of the politics surrounding a global response to the issue of forest depletion. In the current chapter, the extracts from Handl and Ambassador Koh detail the nature of these conflicts. Koh presents a positive argument that environmental negotiations provide unique opportunities for cooperation in North-South relations. An example of this cooperation could be the initiatives for North-South partnerships for the sustainable management of forests such as the Canada-Costa Rica initiative.

The reality in most environmental regimes is that additional funding and technology transfer is provided for, although often inadequately. The most significant concession to North-South concerns seems to have been the concept of differential responsibilities whereby the North and South are allocated different "targets" and/or timing concessions for the meeting of targets or other obligations. Even this concession is being challenged by new concepts of differential responsibility being argued for by nations, such as Australia, in the context of the Kyoto Protocol and the position of the United States Senate which appears to insist that South commit to targets around the same time as the North. Presumably there would still be differentiation in targets within and between these blocks. Chapter 22 discusses the issues surrounding climate change and the attendant political and legal problems surrounding the implementation of this MEA.

The Boer extract provides a more expansive interpretation of sustainable development and how it is incorporated in MEAs and strategies for implementation at the global and regional level. Finally, this chapter concludes with a problem exercise, provided by Beckman, to demonstrate the problem method of teaching involving a dispute over transboundary water pollution.

A

Teaching Guide

(i) Beckman B., "The Law of Treaties and the System of Multilateral Environmental Agreements and other Instruments," prepared for *IUCN/APCEL/UNEP Training the Trainers Course on Capacity Building for Environmental Legal Education*, Singapore, 1997

The following guide is a point form outline of essential principles, processes, terms, instruments and trends in international law.

Law of Treaties—Important Terms

Definition

- An international agreement,
- concluded between States in written form, and
- governed by international law.

Common designations

- Agreement
- Convention
- Treaty
- Protocol
- Covenant
- Pact
- Exchange of Notes

Classification of treaties

- Bilateral
- Regional
- Global or Multilateral

Treaty Making Process for UN Conventions Prepared By International Law Commission (ILC)

1. [A] Series of reports and draft articles [are] prepared by [a] Rapporteur from among the members of the ILC.
2. Over several years and sessions of the ILC, draft articles are approved and adopted by the ILC and sent to General Assembly.
3. Draft Articles are accompanied by an official commentary for each article.
4. [The] General Assembly refers [the] Draft Articles to 6th Committee (Legal Committee)
5. [The] 6th Committee refers [the Draft Articles] to [the] General Assembly
6. [The] General Assembly passes [a] resolution convening UN Diplomatic Conference to which all members are invited.
7. [The] treaty is debated at the Conference, adopted by a resolution and opened for signature.
   - vote to adopt the treaty and signature does not mean that the state is bound by the treaty
   - signature generally signifies agreement in principle

Treaty Making Process for Major Global Environmental Agreements

1. Identify forum or institution to serve as the legislative forum

- Negotiate under auspices of UNEP (e.g., 1992 *Biodiversity Convention*)
- Negotiate under auspices of General Assembly (e.g., 1985 *Climate Change Convention*)

2. Establish the negotiating process
   - Informal ad hoc working group of experts (e.g., established by UNEP Governing Council for *Ozone Convention*)
   - Formal institutional structure (e.g., GA Resolution established Intergovernmental Negotiating Committee for *Climate Change Convention*)
3. Convene international diplomatic conference to adopt the text and then open the treaty for signature

Procedure for Becoming a Party to a Treaty

1. Depositary—a UN official which has the responsibility of keeping the official records with respect to the treaty
2. Consent to be bound: a State expresses its consent to be bound by the treaty by depositing one of the following official documents with the depositary
   - Instrument of Ratification—if it is a signatory
   - Instrument of Accession (if it is not a signatory)
   - Instrument of Acceptance or Approval—modern terms used by some States in lieu of Instrument of Ratification
3. Entry into force—global treaties contain a provision stating exactly when they will enter into force with respect to states which have expressed their consent to be bound (e.g., 30 days after deposit of the 35th instrument of ratification or accession)
4. Party—a state which is legally bound by the treaty because it has deposited and instrument of ratification or accession and the treaty has entered into force

General Principles of the Law of Treaties

1. *Pacta Sunt Servanda*—treaties are binding on the parties and must be performed by them in good faith (Art 26)
2. A treaty binds only parties, not third states.
3. Grounds for termination or suspension
   - Material Breach
   - Fundamental Change of Circumstances
   - Impossibility of Performance
4. Grounds not accepted for termination or suspension
   - Break in diplomatic relations
   - Cannot perform obligation due to domestic law
5. Breach of international obligation under treaty gives rise to state responsibility
6. Dispute Settlement
   - Treaties can provide that any dispute between parties on the interpretation or application of the provisions of the Convention may be unilaterally referred by either party to the dispute to adjudication, arbitration, or conciliation

Vienna Convention on the Law of Treaties

Adopted: Vienna 23 May 1969
Depositary: UN Secretary-General
Entry into force: 27 January 1980
Text: 1155 UNTS 331 (UN Treaty Series)
8 ILM 679 (1969) (Int'l Legal Materials)
Parties: 81 as of 16 June 1997 (from UN web site)

Negotiating History

Conference Records

UN Conference on the Law of Treaties, *Official Records*, First and Second Sessions, 1968 and 1969, UN Doc. A/Conf. 39/11 and Add. 1

Rules on the Interpretation of Treaties

Article 31—General Rule of Interpretation

A treaty shall be interpreted in good faith in accordance with the ordinary meaning to be given to the terms of the treaty in their context and in light of their object and purpose.

Article 32—Supplementary Means of Interpretation

Recourse may be had to supplementary means of interpretation, including the preparatory work of the treaty and the circumstances of its conclusion, in order to confirm the meaning resulting in the application of Article 31, or to determine the meaning when the interpretation according to Article 31:

(a) leaves the meaning ambiguous or obscure; or
(b) leads to a result which is manifestly absurd or unreasonable.

ILC Draft Articles and Commentary

Yearbook of the International Law Commission, Volume II, Part Two, pages 177-274

Secondary Materials

Sinclair, *The Vienna Convention on the Law of Treaties* (2nd ed. 1984)
Rosenne, *The Law of Treaties: A Guide to the Legislative History of the Vienna Convention (1970)*

Soft Law Instruments

1. Action Plans or Programmes of Action
   - 1995 *Washington Programme of Action on the Preventior of Pollution of the Marine Environment form Land-Based Activities*
   - *Agenda 21*, UN Conference on Environment and Development (UNCED, 1992)
   - *ASEAN Programme of Action on the Environment* 1996
2. Declarations of Conferences
   - 1972 *Declaration of the UN Conference on the Human Environment* (*Stockholm Declaration*)
   - 1992 *Agenda 21* of the UN Conference on the Environment and Development (UNCED)
3. Guidelines
   - 1985 *Montreal Guidelines for the Protection of the Marine Environment from Land-Based Sources*
4. Memorandums of Understanding (MOUs)

Major Global Environmental Instruments (excluding marine environment)

1971 *Ramsar Convention on Wetlands of International Importance* (*Ramsar Convention*)

1972 *Convention Concerning the Protection of the World Cultural and Natural Heritage* (*World Heritage Convention*)

1972 *Declaration of the United Nations Conference on the Human Environment*

1973 *Convention on International Trade in Endangered Species of Wild Flora and Fauna* (CITES)

1979 *Convention on the Conservation of Migratory Species of Wild Animals* (*Bonn Convention*)

1985 *Convention for the Protection of the Ozone Layer* and 1987 *Montreal Protocol* (*Ozone Convention* and *Montreal Protocol*)

1989 *Basel Convention on the Control of Transboundary Movements of Hazardous Wastes and their Disposal* (*Basel Convention*)

1992 *Rio Declaration on the Environment and Development*

1992 *Agenda 21* (UNCED, 1992)

1992 *Convention on Biological Diversity* (*Biodiversity Convention*)

1992 *United Nations Framework Convention on Climate Change* (*Climate Change*)

Methods of Encouraging Compliance with Treaties

Obligations

1. Traditional Treaties
   - No provisions to ensure compliance
   - Only mechanism is dispute settlement mechanism if dispute arises between two parties
2. Modern Global Environmental Agreements
   - Secretariat
   - Conference of the Parties
   - Reporting requirements
   - Phasing-in of obligations
   - Technical and financial assistance to developing countries

Trends in Law-Making Treaties

1. Secretariats and Conferences of the Parties playing important role in encouraging compliance
2. Common but differentiated responsibilities for developed and developing countries
3. Many treaties now provide a general framework, and details are left to Annexes and Appendices. Appendices and annexes can be updated through meetings of the Conferences of the Parties or by decisions or resolutions of the Conference of the Parties. Another example of procedures for updating treaties is the "tacit amendment" procedure utilized in most IMO Conventions.
4. Traditional distinction between treaties and soft-law instruments is becoming less clear and less important
   - Some recent instruments [are] framed as treaties but drafted in soft-law language—no precise legal obligations, only vague and general commitments
   - Can be argued that distinction is increasingly of little practical importance, as states seldom invoke dispute settlement mechanism for treaties

- If states willingly follow the commitments and guidelines laid down in soft-law instruments, it can have the same practical effect as if the commitments were set out in a treaty as legal obligations
- Soft-law instruments are still used in areas where there is a lack of consensus in the international community
- Soft-law instruments are very effective when states are willing to make a good faith commitment to change their conduct, but are unwilling to undertake a precise obligation which is binding under international law

(ii) UNEP, "Introduction to International Law Relating to the Environment," *Environmental Law Training Manual*, UNEP, 1997

What is International Law?

International law, otherwise known as the law of nations, is the system of law which governs relations among States. At one time. States were the only bodies enjoying international legal personality, i.e., having right and duties under international law, but today, international organizations, companies and individuals are also seen as having an international personality in certain situations. However international law may still be considered as primarily concerned with States.

Sources of International Law

Regarding the sources of international law, reference is often made to Article 38 (1) of the Statute of the International Court of Justice which provides:

> "The Court, whose function is to decide in accordance with international law such disputes as are submitted to it, shall apply:
>
> (a) international conventions, whether general or particular, establishing rules expressly recognized by the contesting States;
>
> (b) international custom, as evidence of a general practice accepted as law;
>
> (c) the general principles of law recognized by civilized nations;
>
> (d) [...] judicial decisions and the teachings of the most highly qualified publicists of the various nations, as subsidiary means for the determination of rules of law."

This provision is usually accepted as constituting a list of sources of international law. However, some writers have criticized it on the ground that it does not list all sources. Soft law, such as declarations, guidelines, codes of ethics, are also often referred to as an authoritative source of international law.

The various sources listed in the Statute of the International Court of Justice are examined below.

International Custom

International customary law is primarily to be found in the actual practice of States, which usually derive either from their reciprocal understanding on the way to interact in specific areas, or from a broad and long recognition and acceptance of rules already elaborated in international legal instruments.

Initial evidence of these practices can be gathered in published material, i.e., newspapers, reports of international meetings, or States' official documents, reflecting actions of States or Statements made by government officials. Evidence of international customary rules can also be gathered in judgments and advisory opinions of the International Court of Justice, as well as arbitral and other international tribunals.

To be established as customary rules, States' practices must answer two main criteria:

Constant and Uniform Usage

A single precedent is not enough to establish a customary rule. There must be a degree of repetition over a period of time. Furthermore, the practice should not be tainted by major inconsistencies. that is a large number of practices which go against the "rule" in question. Minor inconsistencies do not prevent the creation of a customary rule.

Opinio Iuris Sive Necessitatis

The practice should be seen by States as governed by international law. As such the exchange of greetings between the crew of two warships passing, although a long established custom, is not recognized as falling under international law.

In recent years, there has been a tendency to codify customary law into international legal instruments. Such codifications present obvious advantages: the rules become more precise and more accessible; new States are more willing to accept rules which they themselves have helped to codify. In view of the divergence between the practices of different States, to be successful, codification of customary law should proceed slowly in order to allow time for adjustments in State' practices towards their harmonization. Acceleration produces the risk of failure, as happened at the codification conference of The Hague in 1930, and at the first and second *United Nations Conferences on the Law of the Sea* in 1958 and 1960 in their attempt to reach an agreement on the width of the territorial sea.

General Principles of Law

The line of demarcation between customary law and general principles of law is often not very clear, since customary law, understood in a broad sense, may be considered as including all that is unwritten in international law. Nevertheless, unlike customary law which consists of specific rules formulated for practical purposes, general principles of law are rather general propositions underlying the various rules of law. As such, they provide guidance in the interpretation and application of international law.

General principles of law mainly derive from principles recognized in municipal law of all or nearly all States. Among these general principles, it is worth mentioning the principle of good faith which applies in several areas of international law

Pacta Sunt Servanda

[The PCIJ has noted that] "contracting parties are always assumed to be acting honestly and in good faith". [Similarly, it is noted by Moore that] "treaties of every kind, when made by the competent authority, are as obligatory upon nations as private contracts are binding upon individuals [...] and to be kept with the most scrupulous good faith." As such a party may not unilaterally "free itself from the engagements of a treaty, or modify the stipulations thereof, except by the consent of the contracting parties, through a friendly understanding."

Abuse of Rights—Sic Utere Tuo Ut Alienum Non Laedas

States must exercise their rights in a manner compatible with their various obligations arising either from treaties or from the general law. The application of the theory of Abuse of Rights can be illustrated in the famous *Trail Smelter Case,* the *Corfu Channel Case* and the *Lake Lanoux Case* (see [this extract] below the section "Judicial Decisions").

In international environmental law, the theory of Abuse of Rights has been further developed in Principle 21 of the Declaration of United Nations Conference on the Human Environment, Stockholm, 1972, and in Principle of the *Agenda 21* on Environment and Development, Rio de Janeiro, 1992, which States:

> "States have, in accordance with the Charter of the United Nations and the principles of international law, the sovereign right to exploit their own resources pursuant to their own environmental and developmental policies, and the responsibility to ensure that activities within their jurisdiction or control do not cause damage to the environment of other States or of areas beyond the limits of national jurisdiction."

Duty to Notify

Although a State is ordinarily free to pursue and alter its own policy, domestic and foreign, it may be obliged in certain circumstances to notify other States of a proposed change in its policy when such change pertains to those States. In international environmental law, this duty has been further developed in several instruments, including the *Agenda 21*...which states in its Principles 18 and 19 that:

> "States shall immediately notify other States of any natural disasters or other emergencies that are likely to produce sudden harmful effects on the environment of those States [...].'

> "States shall provide prior and timely notification and relevant information to potentially affected States on activities that may have a significant adverse transboundary environmental effect and shall consult with those States at an early state and in good faith."

Allegans Contraria Non Est Audiendus: called 'Estoppel'

This principle obliges States to be consistent with previous commitments/statements and to avoid by unilateral acts, changes in their relation with other States which may have prejudicial effects to those States.

Further to the general principles of international law, some of which have been further developed in international environmental law, new principles specific to international environmental law have also been established. They include:

- Principle of preventing damage to the environment,
- Principle that reparations should be made for environmental damage,
- Principle that the survival of endangered species should be assured.

Furthermore, in order to answer to new environmental challenges in the context of sustainable development, new concepts have been developed and are currently emerging in international environmental law:

- Concept of sustainable development,
- Concept of intergenerational equity,
- Concept of common concern of mankind,
- Concept of global partnerships,
- Concept of common but differentiated responsibilities,
- Concept of valuation of biodiversity,
- Concept of environment security.

Some of these emerging concepts have been given full consideration in recently developed regimes. such as the concept of common but differentiated responsibility which has been incorporated in the United Nations *Framework Convention on Climate Change*. This provided the basis for global partnership.

Judicial Decisions

Judicial decisions recognized in international law are those adopted by the International Court of Justice (ICJ), as well as by arbitral and other international tribunals.

Once the competence of the ICJ to decide on a case is recognized by the parties to a dispute, decisions adopted by the ICJ have no binding force except between the parties to the dispute and in respect of the particular case. Although the ICJ is not obliged to conclude on a new case in accordance with previous decisions, it usually takes into account previous decisions which are relevant to the case in question.

Although jurisprudence is referred in the Statute of the ICJ as a subsidiary source for determining applicable rules of law, judgments and advisory opinions of the ICJ and other tribunals are important since they are often considered as the affirmation or the revelation of international customary rules.

Among the decisions adopted by international judicial bodies, the arbitral judgment of 11 March 1941 in the *Trail Smelter* case should be given particular attention since it is considered as having laid the foundations for international environmental law, at least regarding transfrontier pollution. In its conclusion, the Arbitral Tribunal stated that:

> "No State has the right to use or permit the use of its territory in such manner as to cause injury by fumes in or to the territory of another or the properties or persons therein [...]-

This rule has been confirmed by a more general principle enunciated in the *Corfu Channel Case*, where the International Court of Justice concluded that "[n]o State may utilize its territory contrary to the rights of other States", and favourably referred to in the *Lake Lanoux* Arbitration between France and Spain, where the tribunal stated:

> "It could have been argued that the works would bring about a definite pollution of the waters of the Canal or that the returned waters would have a chemical composition or a temperature or some other characteristic which could injure Spanish interest."

Teachings of the Most Highly Qualified Publicists of the Various Nations

As with judicial decisions learned writings can be evidence of customary law. They can also play a role in developing new rules of laws.

Learned writings of scientific and professional associations and of eminent lawyers are significant sources of international environmental law. For example, the *Helsinki Rules* on waters of international rivers which has been developed by the International Law Association, are considered as highly authoritative. The theory of intergenerational equity, as expounded by Brown-Weiss, is currently considered as emerging concept of international environmental law.

International Conventions

International conventions are an increasing important source of international law, and, in particular of international environmental law. At the outset of this century, only a few international regimes to protect some natural resources had been established through international conventions. Today, hundreds of international conventions exist in the field of the environment. The UNEP 1993 Register of Treaties and Others Agreements in the Field of the Environment lists 170 multilateral environmental conventions.

The Vienna Convention on the Law of Treaties

Because of the importance of treaties as a source of international law, and the need for certainty in treaty practice and interpretation, customary rules on the law of treaties have been developed for a long time. This law has been codified in the 1969 *Vienna Convention on the Law of Treaties* (VCLT). The VCLT deals with a great range of matters affecting treaties. It is important to have an understanding of its provisions and of general treaty law in order to appreciate some of the legal and practical issues which impact on treaties. As an important threshold issue, it should be noted that the VCLT deals with treaties between States (Art. 1). This is a reflection of the fact that treaties are international instruments, traditionally entered into only by States, and not between States and individuals. Recently, there has been recognition of the fact that treaties are now being entered into between States and international organizations and a separate Convention now exists on that subject.

Definition of a Treaty

The VCLT describes a treaty as being "an international agreement concluded between States in written form and governed by international law, whether embodied in a single instrument or in two or more related instruments and whatever its particular designation." (Art. 2(l)). It is therefore important to note that a treaty must be in written form and that an oral agreement does not constitute a treaty in international law.

Title

An international agreement or instrument is normally called a treaty or a convention, while terms such as Protocol, Agreement, Accord, Act, Statute, Covenant, or Charter may also be used. It is important to distinguish these legal instruments from other documents which are not governed by international law.

Whether an international instrument or document is to be governed by international law depends on the intention of the parties. This can sometimes be ascertained by the language used in the instrument, its title (such as whether it is a Declaration or Statement of Principles) or by Statements made by the State parties during its negotiation or subsequently.

Although the type of an international agreement is not formally determined by the name given to it, there are some customs commonly followed, for example:

- Peace agreements are usually called treaties:
- Agreements constituting important organizations are often called charters, convents or statutes; and
- Agreements amending or complementing an already existing agreement, are usually called protocols.

Types of Treaties

Treaties can be either bilateral, that is between two contracting States, or multilateral, between more than two States. Multilateral treaties dealing with the environment can also have either global application or only apply within a certain region. The area of intended application of the treaty will have an important impact upon the number of States, and which States become parties to the treaty. For example, the 1972 *Convention on the Prevention of Marine Pollution by Dumping of Wastes* is a treaty of global application and has 69 contracting parties. By contrast, the 1972 *Oslo Convention for the* Prevention *of Marine Pollution by Dumping from Ships and Aircraft* is a regional convention which applies in the North Atlantic and Arctic Ocean and has only 13 contracting parties.

The area of intended application of the treaty will have an important impact upon the number of States, and which States become parties to the treaty.

Whether the treaty is bilateral or multilateral may also determine the way in which it is negotiated. Bilateral treaties are often negotiated at a Ministerial or government-to-government level. Multilateral treaties are often negotiated at diplomatic conferences, either convened by an international organization such as the UN or one of its agencies, or at the invitation of a particular State. Because of the large number of States which may be invited to participate at a multilateral diplomatic conference, and the complexity of the issues under discussion, the time required to negotiate a multilateral treaty can vary considerably. For example, the 1982 UN *Convention on the Law of the Sea* was negotiated at the Third UN Conference on the Law of the Sea, which held 11 sessions between 1973 and 1982. This lengthy period of negotiation reflected the complexity of the Convention and also the number of States which participated at the Conference. In contrast, the 1972 *Convention on the Prevention of Marine Pollution by Dumping of Wastes and Other Matters* was negotiated at a single meeting held in London in November and December 1979.

Entry Into Force

The procedures for adoption and entry into force of a treaty can be complex and vary depending on its type. A bilateral treaty will be agreed upon by mutual consent of the parties. Once the text has been finalized, it will be signed by both States. Depending on the terms of the treaty and the internal constitutional arrangements of the parties, it may also be necessary to deposit acts of ratification prior to the treaty eventually entering into force. This will only occur after both parties have signed and ratified it. A multilateral treaty can also be adopted by the consent of all States which participated in its drawing up, though a two-thirds vote may sometimes also be sufficient (VCLT, Art.9).

In nearly all cases, multilateral treaties will be open for a period of signature following their conclusion. It is common at this stage for most of the States which participated in the negotiation of the treaty to sign it. While it is possible under the terms of the treaty for it to enter into force upon the receipt of a certain number of signatures (VCLT, Art. 12), this is not common practice. Rather, most treaties will require the deposit of instruments of ratification from a certain number of States prior to the formal entry into force of the treaty (VCLT, Art.14).

Ratification is a process whereby the relevant authority in a State notifies the convention depositary of that State's formal acceptance of the terms of the convention. In some States ratification is an act of the executive government or the head of State. In some instances, States have created certain procedures which must be followed prior to ratification. For example, in the United States of America, the Senate must approve ratification.

The number of signatures or ratifications required to bring a treaty into force will be determined by the actual terms of the treaty (VCLT Art.24). For example, the 1987 *United Nations Convention on the Law of the Sea* required 60 ratifications before it could enter into force. The *Basel Convention on Transboundary Movements of Hazardous Wastes and their Disposal* required 20 ratifications. It is unusual, however, for a requirement to exist that all States which participated in the negotiation of the treaty or which have signed the treaty must ratify prior to entry into force.

In the interim period between negotiation, signature, and ratification, a treaty does not have any legal force. However, the VCLT does provide that States are not to engage in "acts which would defeat the object and purpose of a treaty" during this interim period until such time as they have made clear that they do not intend to become a party or that it has become clear that the treaty will not enter into force (VCLT, Art. 18). The States who have conclusively accepted a treaty which has entered into force, by way of ratification or some other act, are often referred to as 'contracting parties'.

Even though a treaty has entered into force it remains possible for States which participated in its negotiation and previously signed the treaty to still become a contracting party by depositing an instrument of ratification. States which were not part of this process may also become a contracting party under the specific terms of the treaty. In these cases, acts of acceptance, approval, accession or adhesion will be sufficient (VCLT, Art.16). Once a treaty has entered into force it becomes binding upon the contracting parties to perform the treaty in good faith: a doctrine known as *pacta sunt servanda* (VCLT, Art.26).

Domestic Legal Effect of a Treaty

Because treaties are international instruments between States, they create legal obligations between States and not individuals. Whether a treaty has domestic effect is a separate issue which will often depend on the domestic legal system of the contracting party.

The constitutional arrangements which exist in each State may be important in determining the legal effect of a treaty. For example, in the United States of America, treaties have domestic legal effect once they have been ratified by the President. In some other States, treaties only have legal effect once they have been formally implemented by some act of the legislature, parliament, executive government, or the President. Yet another issue arises in federal States. Under the terms of the constitution of a federal State, the central government may not have the power to make laws dealing with a treaty. This power may reside with the regional or provincial governments or may only be exercised with the agreement of those governments.

While the domestic status of a treaty does not affect a contracting State's international obligations under the treaty, it does have an important impact on the domestic law of the State. If the treaty has not been formally given effect to, or has no status in the domestic legal system, then it has no domestic legal effect. This is most important in treaties dealing with the protection of the environment, especially those which anticipate some change in domestic regulation of certain activities. An example would be greenhouse emissions into the atmosphere by industry.

A treaty may have domestic legal effect in a number of ways. It may impact on the domestic legal system as a result of:

- domestic legislation or law;
- proclamation by the Head of State (President or equivalent);
- the State having simply ratified the treaty; or
- the courts recognizing the effect of the treaty.

In each one of these instances, the potential exists for the treaty to regulate certain activities of citizens, including corporations, of the contracting State.

Reservations and Declarations

An important feature of treaty law is the ability of contracting parties to make either reservations or declarations upon their formal acceptance of the treaty. This procedure is always governed by the strict terms of the treaty and in some treaties it is not possible to make a reservation (VCLT, Art.l9). A reservation is a unilateral Statement made upon signature or ratification of a treaty which purports to exclude or to modify the legal effect of certain provisions of the treaty in their application to that State (VCLT. Art.2(1)(d)). The content of a reservation may be wide-ranging, unless it is incompatible with the object and purpose of the treaty (VCLT, Art.19).

Certain rules exist dealing with the making of reservations governed by both treaty law and the terms of the treaty itself (VCLT, Art.20). The most important effect of a reservation, however, is its impact on the legal relations between the contracting parties and its modification of the terms of the treaty. If there is no objection to the reservation, then its effect is to modify the legal relations between contracting parties to the extent of the reservation (VCLT, Art.21 & 29).

It is possible for States which do not agree to the reservation to make an objection to it. Providing an objecting State does not oppose the entry into force of the treaty between itself and the State making the reservation, the provision to which the reservation relates does not apply as between the two parties (VCLT, Art.21(3)). Unless otherwise provided by the treaty, a reservation or objection can be withdrawn at any time (VCLT, Art. 22).

Principle of Good Faith

Apart from the principle of *pacta sunt servanda* (see above), a fundamental rule of treaty law is that a treaty is to be interpreted in good faith and in accordance with the ordinary meaning to be given to the terms of the treaty in their context and in the light of its object and purpose (VCLT, Art.31(1)).

Interpretation

The interpretation of a treaty can sometimes be made simpler by the definition of various terms which are found throughout the treaty. This is most important in environmental treaties where technical or scientific terms may be relied upon. In addition to the preamble and annexes to a treaty, it is also possible to refer to other documents. Documents or agreements made at the time of the conclusion of the treaty can be helpful, such as the Final Act of a negotiating conference, and other documents made by the parties and accepted as an instrument related to the treaty (VCLT, Art.31.(2)).

Subsequent agreements or practice between the parties regarding interpretation of the treaty, and relevant rules of international law applicable in the relations between the parties can also be taken into account (VCLT, Art.31 (3)). If there remains some uncertainties resulting in an ambiguous or obscure meaning or an interpretation which is manifestly absurd or unreasonable, it is also possible to take into account as a subsidiary means or interpretation the preparatory work of the treaty and the circumstances of its conclusion (VCLT. Art. 32). In many instances, multilateral treaties are concluded in two or more languages. Unless otherwise provided in the treaty, each text is equally authoritative (VCLT, Art.33).

Amendment and Revision

Many multilateral treaties contain provisions for their own amendment. These procedures can range from meetings of all the contracting parties, to meetings convened by the governing international organization or the treaty secretariat. A variety of procedures can also be relied upon in order to amend treaties. In some instances, a formal procedure resulting in the negotiation of an instrument such as a Protocol may occur which will only become legally binding once all contracting parties have adopted the Protocol. In other instances, the operational scope of treaties can be expanded by the adoption of Annexes dealing with specific topics. In some cases, it is considered acceptable if not all contacting parties to the treaty adopt the Annex.

Less formal procedures exist for the amendment of some treaties, and this has the advantage of ensuring that detailed standards included within a treaty can be adjusted as needed. These procedures operate most effectively when there is a treaty secretariat or international organization responsible for coordinating these amendments.

Under the terms of the VCLT, formal procedures do exist for the amendment of a treaty (VCLT. Artt.39-41). However, because many treaties include their own amending rules, these procedures are rarely used. Bilateral treaties are often amended by way of agreement between the parties, which can in some instances result in a completely new treaty. Because bilateral treaties only have two contracting parties, it is easier to amend their terms than in the case of multilateral treaties which must accommodate the desires of a large number of parties.

Role of Depositary

In all multilateral treaties, it is normal practice for either a contracting party or an international organization to act as a depositary for the treaty. This will actually be provided for under the terms of the treaty. The depositary will note signatures of the treaty and also receive instruments of ratification, acceptance, or accession acknowledging formal adherence to the treaty. The Depositary will be required to maintain lists of the status of all contracting parties and signatories to the treaty and of any amendments made to the treaty.

It is normally the depositary's role to also ensure that the treaty has been registered with the Secretariat of the United Nations (Charter of the United Nations. Art. 102). If there is no secretariat to the treaty, then the depositary may also have the responsibility of convening meetings to review the treaty and discuss possible amendment. However, such meetings would normally only be called under procedures provided for under the treaty or with the agreement of a majority of contracting parties.

Role of Other bodies

Depending on the complexity and scope of the treaty, there may be several bodies established under a convention to ensure the achievement of its objectives. These bodies usually aim at following-up the implementation of the convention by the Parties, assisting the Parties in that regard, and further developing or amending the convention when necessary. To this end, the following bodies may be established:

Plenary, Non-Standing Body

A plenary, non-standing body, i.e., the Conference of the Parties, is usually the highest body of a convention. It consists of representatives of all Parties to the convention, and convenes on a regular basis to adopt decisions necessary for the achievement of the objectives of the convention.

Non-Plenary, Standing Body

In order to implement decisions adopted by the plenary, a non-standing body, a non-plenary, standing body, i.e., Standing Committee, or Commission may be established. It consists of a limited number of members elected by the plenary, non-standing body, and meets as often as necessary.

Advisory body

Advisory bodies may be set up to provide technical or scientific advice to the abovementioned bodies or to the Secretariat.

Secretariat

A secretariat may also be established. It will take on many of the roles of the depositary but also be involved in the day-to-day administration of the treaty regime. This may include receiving reports from the contracting parties dealing with implementation of the treaty and reported infringements. It would also include the role of convening and administering any annual or other meetings of review among the contracting parties, or other conferences called to discuss specific issues under the terms of the treaty or related issues. If a secretariat is created to administer a treaty, the contracting parties will need to finance the operation of the secretariat. It will often be the case that the secretariat will have a director and other permanent staff plus a headquarters located within the territory of one of the contracting parties.

2

Defending the Global Commons

A

Stone C., "Defending the Global Commons," in Sands P. (ed), *Greening International Law*, Earthscan, London, 1994, pp 34–49

Introduction

Across the world, the environment is in peril. Forests are being stripped, stressed, and burned. Natural habitats are vanishing. Deserts are advancing. Croplands suffer from water-logging in some regions, overgrazing and salinization in others. The atmosphere and ozone shield are under assault. The oceans are being loaded with pollutants and swept of marine life. We are sullying the polar regions, perturbing the climate, and eradicating species.

All these alarms, and more, have been widely sounded. There is no reason to belabor them: what we need now are answers. I have two to put forward: a system of Global Guardianships, and a Global Commons Trust Fund. They alone will not solve our complex environmental predicaments, but together they would constitute a major stride forward, a foundation for an appreciable "greening" of international law.

To understand these proposals, a good start is to mark the distinction in outlook between the scientist, on the one hand, and the international lawyer and Statesperson, on the other. Scientists—such as geophysicists, geochemists and the like—have the luxury of contemplating the planet from the grand panorama of astronauts. From such a removed state, national boundaries fade and the mind can be struck by the marvellous wholeness of the Earth and the interconnection of globe-spanning phenomena that sustain its tenants: one great swirling envelope of atmospheric gases, the great body of ocean, and the broad globe-spanning belts of weather and vegetation.

International lawyers and Statespersons operate from a more cramped and mundane vista. Ours is an inherited world in which all that grand unity has been disrupted into political territories. We all know that most of these penciled borders have little to do with the great natural processes that the scientist is drawn to; that they are often the legacies of chance, intrigue, vanity, avarice, and military battles that could have gone either way. But for all their caprice and impermanence, the boundaries that mark the diplomats' world, hardened as they commonly are, by pronounced cultural, religious, and socioeconomic differences, are no less to be reckoned with than carbon.

Broadly speaking, the diplomats' maps (the foundation for received international law) divide the world into two sorts of regions: those which fall under Territorial Sovereignty, and those that lie outside the political reach of any nation State—the global commons.

In this view of things, the territorial sovereignty each nation enjoys is co-extensive with its geographic boundaries, extends upwards through its air traffic space, and, in the case of the many nations with coastal borders, extends across an Exclusive Economic Zone (EEZ) running 200 nautical miles seaward.

The global commons refers to those portions of the planet and its surrounding space which lie above and beyond the recognized territorial claims of any nation. That includes the atmosphere, outer space, and the high seas, together with the potentially valuable seabeds and subsurfaces that have yet to be "enclosed" by any coastal State as part of its territorial extension. On some accounts, much the same commons status does, or should, apply to the resource-rich Antarctic, which comprises 10 percent of the planet's land mass, and whose ownership is currently in limbo.

The global commons refers to those portions of the planet and its surrounding space which lie above and beyond the recognized territorial claims of any nation.

Viewed within the constraints of traditional international law, this two-fold division into national territories and commons areas has crucial significance for all efforts to defend the environment. Within its sovereign territory, a nation can, by and large, do whatever it wants. Each nation, and it exclusively, has the right to pull up its forests, bulldoze habitats, wipe out species, fish, farm, and mine—and not have to answer to any "outside" authority for any repercussions on its own environment.

If the "outside" world wishes to influence a country's internal behavior—to constrain deforestation, for example—its recourse is limited. International organizations can try to persuade a developing country's leaders of the long-term benefits of a scale and pace of development which is environmentally kind. Funding sources, preeminently the World Bank, can withhold support from massive projects that are environmentally disruptive. Wildlife groups have been known simply to pay a country to set aside an exotic habitat as a wildlife reserve, often arranging so-called "debt-for-Nature swaps". However, as long as a nation is chewing up only its own insides, it is not, in the eyes of international law, doing anything it can be sued over. It is true there are *declarations* that all the environment, including internal environments, are to be valued; but they are consistently undermined by conflicting declarations that a nation's use of its own resources is a matter of sovereign prerogative. The counterbalance could be resolved in a "green" direction that is, conceivably, grave damage to internal environments could someday come to be considered a sort of "ecocide", and, likened to human rights violations, made a violation of international law. Unfortunately, such a development does not appear imminent. In the meantime, "outside" influence is constrained to such tactics as bargaining, loan conditions, and perhaps trade pressures. As we know all too well, desertification and deforestation continue, and thus far, neither these tactics nor any others have been able to arrest the degradation of internal environments.

As frustrating as one finds it to have an effect on the "internal" scenarios, the situation in the commons areas is, in many regards, even worse. All the nations of the world are faced with deterioration of their internal environments, with the result that resources required for cleaning up the commons have to compete with resources required to clear up internal environments. This is a competition in which the domestic demands have a clear advantage. When a country's interior deteriorates—as urban areas become smoggy, or fish die in lakes—there is at least a political constituency of directly aggrieved voters to focus pressure on whichever government (State, federal or local) to provide relief. In contrast, when we turn to the commons, the areas lack, by definition, their own citizens to complain, and those who do in fact have complaints cannot locate a competent authority to complain to.

However, the plight of the commons reflects more than a jurisdictional vacuum. Important economic and bargaining considerations reinforce the inclination to give the commons short shrift. When a nation turns its attention inward, it can select the most pressing problem on its own political agenda, be it water quality or soil treatment. Since a nation has full control over its domestic programs, it can arrange to fund only those projects for which it receives at least a dollar benefit for each dollar it spends. However, suppose we were to ask the same nation to invest a million dollars in mending the commons—to restrict carbon emissions, for example, and thereby reduce the risks of climate change. In expenditures to clean up the commons, the nation stands to capture some fraction of the benefits (the seduced risks of climate change). But most of the benefit will be diffused among all 180 or so members of the world community, some of whom will fail to shoulder their proportionate share of the burden.

One can put the point in familiar public finance terms: the maintenance of the commons is a public good, and efforts to provide for the public good are notoriously dogged by the manoeuvers of those who wish to "free ride" on those who contribute. Of course, domestic governments face the same problem when they undertake any public finance project: parks, police and so on. The problem is that combatting strategic behavior and securing cooperation in the international arena is considerably more difficult than overcoming the analogous obstacles in domestic contexts. In domestic democratic societies subject to majority rule, dissenters—potential "free riders"—can be simply forced to pay their share by law. In the international community, however, a corollary of sovereignty is that no nation can be forced into any agreement in which it does not assent: in essence, unanimity, not majority, is the collective choice rule. As a consequence, every country is wary of getting drawn into a fragile multilateral agreement in which it may find itself under pressure to pay out a larger share of the costs than its benefits warrant. (This is one basis for the United States' reluctance to put teeth into a climate change convention). Each nation may incline to mend its own local disorders even when it would make more sense overall (if cooperation could be ensured), for all the nations of the world to turn their joint attention to more ominous problems they have in common.

This "no man's land" feature of the commons has important implications for the design of institutional remedies. The fact that the degraded area lies outside anyone's exclusive jurisdiction presents impediments to monitoring deterioration, and presents even more serious obstacles to securing legal and diplomatic relief.

Invasion of Territories

Speaking realistically, international law does not enter the picture until something a nation does—releasing a radioactive cloud, for example—sweeps across its boundaries and damages a neighboring country. In those circumstances it is generally agreed, at least it is universally verbalized, that the injured neighbor has grounds for diplomatic and legal remedies. In the 1940s, the US successfully sued Canada over sulphur fumes from a Canadian lead smelter that were wafting across the boundary into the State of Washington. The US once even acquiesced to a Mexican diplomatic demand that it eliminate offensive transboundary odors that were blowing south from a US stockyard. Such results in transboundary contexts are rare; but relief is at least a theoretical option that potential polluters have to consider in the design of factories etc.

When, however, fumes blow across a frontier not into a neighboring nation, but up into the commons region of higher atmosphere, or out across the sea, however many soft declarations may denounce it, resort to law becomes appreciably more problematic. In a typical nation-to-nation transboundary conflict, such as the US–Canada case referred to, one can assume there are officials of the injured state on hand at the site of the harm to inspect the damage and determine where it is coming from. In that dispute, the fumes could be characterized as an "invasion" (however modest) of US sovereignty, the sort of thing international law has customarily sought to mend.

By contrast, when the open sea or the atmosphere is degraded, who is on hand to keep watch? Are significant loadings of heavy metals working their way into the deep seas and seabed? If so, are the levels dangerous and are they insinuating their way into the food cycle? Who is responsible for cleaning them up? To answer these questions, even to gather the relevant facts in a scientifically and internationally credible way, goes beyond any single nation's ordinary motivation and competence; it practically necessitates a multi-national coordinated effort.

Even then, if the appropriate institution *could* be established, and the monitors *could* identify substantial and worrisome changes in the environment and pin down their source, there would remain judicial obstacles of legal interest and standing. If someone should come onto your yard, and steal your pet turtle from your pond, you would have a suit because it would be a trespass and injury to your property. But if some nation's fleet of fishing vessels, sweeping the high seas with nets, obliterates scores of rare sea turtles or dolphins, customary international law—that is, international law as it stands absent some specially-tailored treaty—is unlikely to grant a remedy to any nation that objects. Who can prove that the destroyed creatures would have been captured by the objecting nation? On the high seas, because the turtles do not belong to anyone, it is unclear that anyone has the legal interest which the law requires to complain. Besides, what is the market value (the law would want to know) of turtles and dolphins? Where was the legal damage?

Who is Responsible?

One should understand that the liberty of each State to impair the commons is not a principle that is condoned. There are, in fact, any number of lofty declarations of international conferences and commentators which solemnly (although usually with saving double-speak qualifications) renounce abuse of the commons areas. There are even scraps of legal doctrine from which a suit to protect the commons areas might be constructed. Some government could argue that a country responsible for a massive injury to the commons had committed a wrong *erga omnes* (crime against the community of nations), a notion historically invoked to legitimate the power of any nation to punish piracies on the high seas. But the fact is, aside perhaps from the special case where the complaining nation was able to show that the offender violated an express agreement (such as a treaty), no claim arising out of commons despoliation has yet to be pressed, and the prospects of such a suit would have to be regarded at present as rather doubtful.

Thus, whatever lip service environmental diplomats will pay the commons areas at great *Earth Summits*, nations still find it expedient to let vast proportions of their pollutants simply blow away into the global atmosphere or run off untreated into the open sea...

Some of the stuff that has been dumped is even worse. Sitting on the seabed right now are hundreds of thousands of tons of World War II munitions, including unfired chemical weapons, to which we have more recently added untold canisters of nuclear waste that were deposited in the sea for 'safe storage', which are already showing signs of fatigue." An ex-Soviet official recently admitted that for nearly 30 years the Soviet military had been jettisoning its nuclear wastes (including thousands of canisters, 12 old reactors and one damaged submarine) into the Arctic Sea in the most heedless way imaginable. The important thing now is, no one is responsible for cleaning up the whole mess.

This does not mean that the commons are utterly undefended. While no nation can be compelled to protect the commons, various protective conventions and declarations have garnered the cooperation of enough countries to monitor the rate of deterioration. The 1985 *Vienna Convention on Substances that Deplete the Ozone Layer* is achieving a dramatic reduction in the release of ozone-depleting agents. The 1991 UN General Assembly Resolution against Drift netting is, technically, no more than that, a legally nonbinding 'resolution'. Yet, the announced willingness of the major drift netting nations, Japan, Taiwan and Korea, to respect it is a promising development of some significance. Also there is a whole patchwork of other conventions in other areas, each with its own aspirations and attainments. These include the ban on weapons testing in space, the *International Whaling Convention* (IWC), the Antarctic treaty system, and the *London Convention on the Prevention of Marine Pollution by Dumping of Wastes*.

If one looks behind the various lofty declarations and examines the prevailing practices...one finds that, aside from a few areas provided for by special treaty, much of the commons is only partially and feebly protected.

The present picture can best be summarized as this: If one looks behind the various lofty declarations and examines the prevailing practices...one finds that, aside from a few areas provided for by special treaty, much of the commons is only partially and feebly protected. In essence, since the commons are available for purposes of wealth exploitation—anyone can sweep it for fish or scoop up deep seabed minerals without answering to the world community: questions about the pollution of the commons are going unanswered. What is to be done?

Voice for the Environment: Global Commons Guardians

One approach is to negotiate more and stronger multinational treaties specially tailored to protect designated portions of the commons, along the lines of the Ozone Agreements, and the more recent, still nebulous, *Framework Convention on Climate Change* that emerged from the *Earth Summit* at Rio. Those efforts deserve further support.

Yet, there is another approach, in some ways bolder, and in some ways integral and supplementary to the treaty efforts. As we saw, one of the reasons for overexploitation of the commons is the lack of a plaintiff clearly qualified to demonstrate both standing and injury. Hence, the first proposal; to establish a system of guardians who would be legal representatives for the natural environment. The idea is similar to the concept of legal guardians (sometimes 'conservators') in familiar legal systems. Presented with possible invasions of the interests of certain persons who are unable to speak for themselves, such as unrepresented infants, the insane, and the senile, courts are empowered to appoint a legal guardian to speak for them. So too, guardians can be designated to be the legal voice for the otherwise voiceless environment: the whales, the dolphins, important habitats, and so on.

The guardians could either be drawn from existing international agencies that have the appropriate focus, such as the United Nations Environment Programme (UNEP) and the World Meteorological Organization (WMO), or from the many nongovernmental organizations (NGOs) such as Greenpeace or The Worldwide Fund for Nature (WWF). Certainly the guardians would not be given plenary and unreviewable powers to halt any activity they disapproved of. Rather, the guardian would be built into the institutional process to ensure that environmental values were being identified and accounted for. Take the oceans, for example. To ensure that oceanic ecosystems were being adequately accounted for, an Ocean Guardian might be designated, perhaps the Joint Group of Experts on the Scientific Aspects of Marine Pollution (GESAMP) with supplementary legal staffing.

As guardian, its first chore would be to monitor. It would review ocean conditions not just to gather facts 'scientifically', but with a specific eye towards assuring compliance with conventions already in place. One weakness of the 1972 *London Dumping Convention* (LDC) and many fishing agreements is that compliance depends almost entirely on 'self-monitoring,' without any independent effort to survey the activities of signatories. The guardian could provide that monitoring. By doing so, it would improve the willingness of every State to comply, since each country will no longer feel hesitant that if they observe the rules, they will be the only nice, law-abiding 'sucker'. Everyone would benefit from the mutual assurances.

Second, the guardian would exercise legislative functions, not as a legislative body, but as part of the complex web of global policy-making institutions. In exercising the monitoring: function it would undoubtedly come across problems uncovered by existing agreements, which would prompt it to recommend and stimulate formation of new multinational agreements. The guardian could appear before international agencies and even the domestic legislatures and administrative agencies of nations considering ocean-impacting actions to counsel moderation and to suggest alternatives on behalf of its 'client'.

Third, it could be authorized to appear as a special intervenor-council for the unrepresented environmental 'victim' in a variety of bilateral and multilateral disputes. For example, whenever there is a proposal to dam an international river, one or more of the nations along the river may initiate international negotiations to assure the fair division of the water flow, electric and irrigation benefits, etc. However, we have learned, often too late and to our chagrin, that such dam projects inevitably affect the environment, including life in the oceans to which they feed. The ocean guardian would appear as a 'third party' before the appropriate body to assure, not necessarily that the viability of the ocean environment was the conclusive issue, but at least that it was raised in the most effective manner possible.

The final function simply takes the intervenor concept one step further. International treaties should endow the guardian with standing to initiate legal and diplomatic action on the ocean ecosystem's behalf in appropriate situations; to sue at least in those cases where, if the ocean were a sovereign State, the law would afford it some prospect of relief. The law could be arranged so that, even if a violating nation refused to appear, the guardian could secure a declaratory judgement that the conduct in question was indeed unlawful. Such a judicial pronouncement is far less steely than an injunction, but is not the sort of thing members of the world community would simply brush off either.

The notion of legal standing for nature is hardly farfetched. Indeed, many guardianship functions are currently recognized in US environmental laws on a more modest scale. For example, under the *Superfund Legislation*, the National Oceanic and Atmospheric Administration (NOAA) is designated trustee for fish, marine mammals, and their supporting ecosystems within the US fisheries zone. NOAA has authority to institute suits to recover restoration costs against any patty that injures its 'ward'. A major lawsuit is presently proceeding in a federal court in Southern California, in which NOAA attorneys are suing local chemical companies allegedly responsible for seepage of PCBs and other chemicals into the coastal water ecosystem. There is no reason such a system could not be replicated internationally.

A Case for Seals

A recent case in Germany even invoked the guardianship concept in a case with global commons implications. In 1988, approximately 15,000 dead seals mysteriously washed up on the beaches of tile North and Baltic Seas. Widespread alarms were sounded, amid considerable concern that the massive deaths were a portent of an impending ecological disaster. This most flagrant insult to the North Sea's chemistry was widely considered to be titanium and other heavy metals that were being produced by incineration and dumping on the high seas by permit of the West German Government.

Conceivably, any of the States bordering the sea might have tried to challenge Germany's actions. However, recall that, so long as the harm was being done on, or affecting life only in the high seas, the authority of any nation to sue was (and is) doubtful. For Poland, say, to trace through a legally compensable injury would have been nearly hopeless. From the point of view of national fishing interests, the reduction, or even elimination, of the seals might even have been regarded as an economic benefit. (The harbor seals involved, unlike fur seals, are themselves commercially valueless but compete with fishermen for commercial fish stocks.) Moreover, all the sea-bordering nations were contributing to the pollution, and thus, had any of them objected, their case might have been met by Germany with an 'unclean hands' defence: 'you can't complain, because you're as guilty as we are'.

Who then, was to speak for the seals, and, in so doing, represent all the elements of the ecological web whose hazardous fortunes were intertwined? In comparable situations in the US, courts have shown willingness to interpret the *Administrative Procedure Act* and other laws as giving a public interest group standing to challenge the government's actions. German law, however, is much more stringent about allowing 'citizen's suits'.

The solution was for a group of German environmental lawyer, (with the encouragement and advice of the author) to institute an action in which the North Sea Seals were named the lawsuits principal plaintiffs, with the lawyers appearing essentially as guardians, speaking for them. What better plaintiffs? No one could accuse the seals, surely, of unclean hands (or fins). The injury to them, furthermore, did not appear as problematical as it was one step less removed from the harm that the other littoral nations might have raised.

The administrative law court rejected the seals' standing on the grounds that seals were not 'persons' and no specific legislation had authorized standing on their behalf. There were two lessons. First, the very filing of the case and attendant news media coverage was considerable and favorable. When the time came for the government to renew the ocean dumping permit, the authorities who initially gave their permission were forced, by a kindled public opinion, to revoke it. Germany has committed to limit or phase out disposal of heavy metals in the North Sea. The seals lost the battle in court, but emerged hardier in the war.

On the other hand, the technical defeat underscored the advantage of institutionalizing any system for commons guardians in advance. When local (lander) statutes so provide, even German courts will allow specially designated environmental groups to challenge forest-threatening actions.

In the international context, formal recognition of commons guardians could be achieved through reforms within existing legal frameworks—for example, appropriate amendments of the charters of the United Nations and of the International Court of Justice.

The institutionalization of guardians would have the virtue of designating one responsible voice for each part of the environment. There is at least one drawback that grows out of that virtue, however. The more power a guardian were to have, and the more exclusively its voice were made to be the voice that counted, the greater the political pressures to compromise its scientific and legal integrity.

Furthermore, while a system of commons guardians would be a step forward, it would be no panacea for biosphere degradation. Those commons areas that were placed under guardianships, such as living ocean resources, would be elevated to a legal and diplomatic standing on a par with sovereign states. But unfortunately, under present law the powers even of sovereign States are limited which it comes to protecting themselves from transfrontier pollution. Hence, the success of a guardianship regime would depend not only upon legitimation and institutionalization of the guardians as legal representative, but upon significant changes in the substantive law which the guardian would be empowered to invoke—for example, conventions proscribing levels of pollution hazardous to sea life. The oceans not only need their own independent voice, they need the world community to adopt more diligently protective standards.

Financing the Repair: The Global Commons Trust Fund

Supporting a system of guardianships—indeed, any counterattack on global degradation—will cost money. Where will it come from? I have already observed the understandable inclination of political leaders to give priority to their hard-pressed domestic agendas before they address the commons areas. If any nation unilaterally and voluntarily lays out a hundred million dollars to clean up the ocean floor or atmosphere, it just relieves the pressure on other nations to pay up, if they can bank on getting a 'free ride' on the benefits of others' expenditures. Meager or non-cooperation becomes a dominant strategy.

Of course, as noted above, problems of 'free riding' confront any domestic society when it plans the provision of any public goods, such as the payment for police and fire protection, and the maintenance of public parks. But the difference, once more, is that domestic democratic societies have the power to tax. When the majority decides on a programme for the general welfare, it can compel a raising of the needed funds. The world community enjoys no comparable power to levy a 'world tax' for world public welfare.

While 'One World' idealists have proposed such a tax, it is not presently a viable alternative.

There already exists one financial mechanism to tackle the job without appeal to taxes, the Global Environment Facility (GEF). The GEF is a pilot programme originally conceived to support energy conservation, preserve ecological diversity, arrest depletion of the ozone shield, and protect the marine environment. It has been able to garner $1.3 billion in voluntary financial commitments from the industrialized countries for the years 1991, 1992 and 1993. As a financial mechanism, however, purely voluntary contributions are not a dependable basis on which to build a stable infrastructure. In fact, the pilot phase of GEF is soon to expire and its future level on funding is highly uncertain.

Exacerbating the GEF's problems has been a continuous conflict over how the fund is to be governed. The developed countries, as donors want a proportionately stronger voice. They, therefore, favor governance somewhat along the lines of the World Bank, which allots each nation voting power in proportion to its contributions. In 1997, the World Bank formula gave the US 19.47 percent of the voting power; Egypt had just 0.52 percent. Such a weighted voting plan may be explained on pragmatic grounds: it induces the wealthy to keep giving. But the unevenness rankles the Third World as being clearly undemocratic, and unresponsive to a pattern of historical wrongs that make wealth transfers now a matter of compensation and obligation, not of largesse. Hence, Third World countries resist transporting the same standards into the environmental field; even more specifically, they fear any such formula will slant funding towards projects favored by the developed countries, such as ozone depletion, and away from the more immediate concerns of the Third World, notably desertification and treating water. All parties have agreed in principle to come up with 'some other formula'. However, friction over the issue, and the continued inability of anyone to produce a mutually acceptable alternative, is one more impediment to the GEF's long-range viability.

Implementing a Global Commons Trust Fund

These considerations suggest the advantages of a fund that is not wholly dependent on voluntary contributions. More specifically, a financial mechanism that sought levies from legal obligations would both make the flow of funds relatively dependable from year to year, and, by removing the present element of 'largess', perhaps eliminate the governance element that arises out of donor-donee frictions. That is what the proposed Global Commons Trust Fund (GCTF) aims to achieve. The idea is that in order to finance the repair of global commons, we look to levies on uses of the commons areas themselves. Let us expand on how this might be accomplished. As I have already observed, under present practice all the commons areas can be used and abused with relative impunity—free of charge. If we were to rectify this practice, and charge even a fraction of the fair worth for the various uses to which nation-States put the global commons, we would advance two goals at once. The charges would dampen the intensity of abuse, and at the same time underwrite the costs of providing public order such as marine resources management and the repair of environmental damages. Because the resources raised would not be founded on 'largesse' but on what could be presented as legitimate obligations, the supply of funds would be relatively more stable from year to year.

The revenue, while difficult to estimate, is potentially enormous. Consider some rough projections.

The Oceans

The world harvests 185 billion pounds of marine fish annually. A tax of a mere one-tenth of one percent of the commercial value would raise approximately $200 million for the proposed fund. The same token rate on oil and gas produced in the EEZs would add perhaps $80 million more. As for the use of the oceans as a dump site, the official figures, almost certainly underreported, amount to 212 million metric tons of sewage sludge, industrial wastes, and dredged materials yearly. A tax of only a dime a ton would raise an additional $20 million. A charge on ocean transport such as tanker traffic, that imperil waters and beaches, would swell the fund further.

The Atmosphere

By burning fossil fuels and living forests, humankind thrusts 22 billion metric tons of carbon dioxide (CO_2) into the atmosphere annually. A CO_2 tax of only ten cents a ton would raise $2.2 billion each year, 30 times the current budget of the United Nations Environmental Programme (UNEP). Taxing other greenhouse gases (GHGs) such as nitrous oxides at a comparably modest (dime-a-ton) rate, indexed to their 'blocking' equivalent to CO_2 would bring the total to $3.3 billion. The same ten cents a ton tax could be levied on other (non-GHG) transfrontier pollutants; a sulphur dioxide levy, for example, would produce $16 million more.

Space

Tapping the wealth of the planets may still be far off, but the rights to 'park' satellites in the choice slots is a potential source of enormous wealth right now. Most valued are points along the 'geostationary orbit', the volume of space 22,300 miles directly above the earth's equator in which a satellite can remain in, a relatively fixed point relative to the surface below. The number of available points is restricted by minimal distances required between satellites to avoid interference. Rights to spots above the Earth's equatorial belt are also valued because they are exposed to exceptionally long hours of sunlight, and are therefore ideally situated for production of energy from solar radiation, as a support for special operations such as high-tech gravity-free manufacturing, and, perhaps, ultimately for commercial redirecting to Earth. These positions, and ancillary frequencies in space, 'the most resource of the telecommunication ages'—worth to users an estimated $1 trillion globally over the next decade—are now parcelled out free of charge in a system that can only be labelled absurd. The tiny island nation of Tonga, after being awarded 3–6 orbital positions gratis, subsequently put them up for auction, recently striking a deal with a satellite company for $2 million a year rental. It is reportedly seeking more such deals. Why should the rights to any of these slots and spectrum positions, a limited resource that is the legacy and province of all humankind, and worth trillions of dollars to users, be doled out like free lottery tickets, while those who would mend the planet are severely limited by a lack of resources? As auction of slots and frequencies would yield several hundred million dollars annually.

Biodiversity

I am little more ambivalent about including biodiversity as part of the Common Heritage of Humankind in the sense of making it a tax base for the fund. While tuna are (often) in the high seas, beyond any nation's exclusive jurisdiction, many biological riches lie within the territories of nations. Of course, when we talk of biotechnical potential, we are not talking about seizing physical matter from forests, trees, and so on, as mush as copying and exploiting genetic information. It presumably makes small difference to the biologically rich nations such as Columbia and Brazil, who would regard global demands to share the fortune of their biological wealth about the same way the Saudis would react to arguments that the world should co-own its oil. The proposal may simply intrude too far into their sovereign space and prerogatives, which is why the Rio negotiators rejected labelling biodiversity part of the Common Heritage in favor of the limper 'common concern'....

Areas in Need of the Global Commons Trust Fund

That brings us to the functions of the GCTF: what would the raised revenue be used for? To begin with, the GCTF would pay the costs of the Guardianship system, previously described. Any number of potentially critical treaties, including the 1972 *London Dumping Convention*, the 1973 *Convention on International Trade in Endangered Species*, the 1987 *Basel Convention on the Movement of Transboundary Wastes*, and the 1992 UN *Resolution on Drift netting*, are simply under-policed; the GCTF would make policing viable. The monies would support improved scientific monitoring and modelling of the common areas, and underwrite the transfer of environment-friendly technology to developing nations. They could also promote institutional readiness to respond to various sorts of crises with the global equivalent of 'fire fighters'. To illustrate, no single nation anticipates incidents in its own waters enough to warrant keeping on alert a full-time staff trained and equipped to contain oil spills. But a force with global responsibilities, financed out of the fund, might well be cost-effective. It has been estimated that $150 million a year would underwrite an effective worldwide system to ensure early detection of major new viral diseases, for instance, so that the next AIDs–type epidemic does not catch us off guard.

Notwithstanding the mutual and widespread value of such measures, not every country would readily submit: one can anticipate resistance among the already struggling developing nations, in particular. Yet they do not face the highest levies, and the fund, therefore, does not depend on them. For the developed countries, the 4 billion–5 billion dollars or so is a lot more realistic than many of the figures that have been bandied around in the wake of Rio.

Some countries will object to any tax activities within their territories or, in the case of the coastal States, within their self-proclaimed EEZs. However, the charges are not for what nations do within their sovereign territories; they are levied largely for the effects of their activities on the 'outside' world. Moreover, many non-coastal, landlocked nations—along with many scholars—continue to regard as semi-legitimate, at best, the coastal States' proclaimed EEZs of 200 miles and more from their coasts. Allowing the coastal States to supply exclusive management across these zones makes a certain amount of sense; some management of ocean resources is better than none. But allowing the coastal States to snatch all the wealth without any accounting to the rest of the world, just because it happens to be closer to them, is indefensible. That is why I would incline to tax activities such as fishing and oil production undertaken anywhere beyond the traditional territorial boundaries of three or 12 miles from the coastline, and not merely in the smaller region beyond their EEZs.

Many people will object to the pollution charge component of the proposal calling it immoral to permit pollution-for-pay. The answer is that some pollution is inevitable, and it is more of an outrage that the polluters get away with it, as they presently do, free of charge.

Indeed, if there is a real objection to the proposed GCTF, it is that the initial rates I have suggested are probably too paltry. Many would say that, viewed as a strategy for reducing environmental damage, the levels advanced for discussion—ten cents a ton for carbon usage—are unlikely to confront the polluting nations with the full costs of the damage they are causing, and therefore will fall short of inducing the 'right' amount of conservation and pollution control. Viewed from the reverse side, as a strategy for maximizing revenues for the environmental infrastructure, the proposed rates will often fall short of extracting the full value of what users would pay if they were required to bid for restricted rights at an internationally conducted auction.

It is true that, superficially, similar proposals have been advanced in the past, without making much political headway. But the GCTF can be distinguished from the other similar sounding plans—distinguished in ways that may make the GCTF both more effective and more 'saleable' politically.

First, the GCTF can be differentiated from a host of plans, such as that put forward by the late Rajiv Gandhi of India, to tax each developed nation a fraction of its Gross National Product and to distribute the funds to less-developed countries. While Gandhi called his proposal a Planet Protection Fund, the transparent intent was to redistribute wealth from rich countries to poor. The aim may be noble, but it ought not to be confused with the GCTF, which would link levies not to each nation's wealth per se, but to its use of the commons, and would restrict application of the revenue raised to the maintenance and repair of the commons.

Second, most proposals have been limited to a single source or activity. Recently the focus has been on carbon use. Years ago, during the Law of the Sea, negotiations were advanced, unsuccessfully, to tax users of ocean space. Although the ocean tax proposals failed the public atmosphere, in terms of environmental consciousness, is more sympathetic today than 20 years ago. The proposed ocean taxes, moreover, were designed to pay off third world countries, rather than being earmarked to repair the ocean environment. By contrast, both with the carbon and ocean tax, the idea of the GCTF is comprehensive: to bring all economic uses of the commons under an overall plan, from uses of the ocean to uses of the atmosphere and of space.

Conclusion

It is true that the GCTF, by focusing on the global commons, would have unaffected many pressing problems that occur wholly within sovereign boundaries. The answer is that these 'internal' problems, bad as they are, are better attended to by existing institutions. In fact, the International Development Agency (a subsidiary of the World Bank) has had no trouble collecting a $3 billion 'earth increment' to provide virtually free grants to help poor nations protect their internal ecological systems. To some extent, the relative disadvantage of the commons is a question of out of sight, out of mind; and partly, while dolphins may have friends in Greenpeace, they don't vote or form potentially irksome alliances. For both reasons the commons is, once more, a low priority.

The guardianship proposal would help fill the void. It would establish a 'police' mechanism for the global commons are as, an international public service for an international public good. The GCTF is the mechanism to pay for it. The Global Commons Trust Fund is not merely a roundabout scheme to take wealth from the rich nations and redistribute it to the poor. It simply seeks, from users of the global commons, a reasonable fee for their use of the commons so as to apply it back to the commons, for its maintenance and repair. What could be more reasonable? Or, given the afflictions of our planet, more crucial?

The GCTF can be distinguished from the other similar sounding plans—distinguished in ways that may make the GCTF both more effective and more 'saleable' politically.

3

Overview of International Environmental Law

A

Role of Treaties in International Environmental Law

(i) Stone C., "Treaties as Antidotes," in Stone C., *The Gnat is Older than Man: Global Environmental and Human Agenda*, Princeton University Press, 1993, pp 96–121

The Virtues of a Treaty-Based Approach

I have expressed doubts that the slow-growing body of general principles of international law (those rules that prevail in the absence of any special treaty) should be relied upon to provide significant protection for the biosphere. Part of the explanation lies in the list of hurdles a litigating nation faces: getting the defendant to submit to jurisdiction; resolving complicated questions about causality; meeting standards of state responsibility; obtaining satisfaction on a judgment, should one eventually be forthcoming; and so on.

All of these defects in the general rules point to the advantage of bilateral and multilateral treaties that are hammered out and specially tailored to anticipate specific disputes in advance. In conference, the negotiators can translate the nebulous contours of the customary law (which often amount to little more than "don't use your territory in such a way as to injure others") into a more specific, reckonable and realistic set of obligations. Although treaties bind only the signatories, which is a distinct limitation, the other side of that coin is that the signatories have control over whom they are going to deal with, and who will be counted.

There are several virtues to such agreements. First, while customary international law moves slowly, treaty negotiations provide focal opportunities both to clarify the controlling law and to establish the empowered to call them to act governing procedures. For example, treaties can flexibly specify which sorts of disputes will lead to diplomatic response, and which will be fumed over to arbitrators or to courts for binding third-party disposition. The International Court of justice can be given compulsory jurisdiction if the signatories so desire.

There is a medley of other alternatives. Under a 1974 environmental accord, the Nordic states (Denmark, Finland, Norway, and Sweden) agree that each of them, in permitting a potentially harmful activity, has to account for the interests of the other states that may be affected. And then, to solidify the obligation, the convention empowers any citizen of a contracting state (and not merely an official) who is or may be affected by an emanating nuisance to institute proceedings before the appropriate forum of the offending state. In other words, if a Swede is aggrieved by actions taking place in Denmark, and for some reason of diplomacy, the Swedish public representatives will not press a claim on the citizen's behalf, the individual Swede can take her cause into Denmark herself—and the Danish courts and agencies have to give her standing.

Under treaties, the distinctive problems of assuring protection for the commons areas can be provided for and, to some extent, overcome. Moreover, treaties characteristically adopt a preventive approach, reducing or eliminating risks before they have ripened into legally provable injuries. The ozone agreements display this preventive emphasis. Whatever compliance measures are finally agreed to, if any (the issue of sanctions has been deferred to subsequent negotiations), the duties are spelled out in terms of *usage,* not *harm.* This means that a complaining nation need not demonstrate actual injury, much less prove a causal link between that injury and the violator's CFC emissions. A nation is in violation of the agreement once it has exceeded its allowable level of use, period.

In addition, if a nation has reservations about putting itself under externally imposed hard and fast "laws," treaties can provide for international agencies that can promulgate non-compulsory standards to which many nations will voluntarily subscribe. The Food and Agricultural Organization (FAO), International Labor Organization (ILO), World Health Organization (WHO), and International Maritime Organization (IMO) among them have much authority that coordinates and encourages without being "compulsory" in a sense familiar to domestic legal systems.'

The Impediments to Treaty Formation

The question to turn to now is this: Considering the worldwide concern over the environment, and the relative advantages of treaties, why are there not more worldwide agreements? What are the impediments that led to such disappointments at Rio?

There are several reasons why environmental treaties—truly effective treaties—are hard to negotiate. Some of the difficulties stem from problems that hinder the formation of any sort of international accords in any subject area. Others are specific to particular areas of current environmental concern. Let us look at these two sorts of problems in turn.

Some General Problems in Treaty Formation

Constructing Coalitions

The first general impediment to treaty formation arises from the freedom nations retain not to be bound. Within an ordinary democratic society, a decision by the majority binds all members, including dissenters. But under international law, states are bound only by the rules to which they have expressly consented, with a few exceptions for the most basic precepts of the world community. For example, the obligation of nations to honor their commitments and the immunity of diplomats from prosecution by the host state are considered so basic that each state, on achieving statehood, can be presumed to consent to be bound by them. But rules of this sort are largely irrelevant for the contemporary environmental situation, since no one pretends that the principles of modern conventions on weapons testing or sulfur dioxide are part of a long-established body of law that has become universally applicable.

These far-ranging prerogatives of sovereignty exacerbate the "freerider" problem, a strategic obstacle inherent in any effort to arrange for the supply of a public good (public safety, protection from disease, parks, and so on). The benefits of such goods being indivisible (I get as much police or ozone-shield protection as anyone else, whether I chip in and pay for it or you do), it is a principle challenge of all governments to arrange for their supply. Especially as societies are large and diversified (and what society is larger or more diversified than the world's?), each benefiter is tempted to withhold its share of support in the hope that the other benefiters will make up the deficit. Majority rule and taxes provide a way of overcoming the problem—where they prevail. But in the world community, not majority rule but a sort of unanimity rule (no one goes along unless they choose to) prevails. There is, indeed, no "legislative" body, and in all events no system of taxation, as such, exists. Hence, cooperation for the overall public good is all the more difficult to achieve.

As with any public good, these global ones confront regulators with two major issues. What is the right level of supply (which can be viewed as the optimal level of fishing, emissions, monitoring, etc.)? And, how is the cost of achieving that right supply to be apportioned among the benefiters? Any answer, particularly one hardened into effective regulation, will require widespread international cooperation. But it is the achievement of that cooperation which free-riding and other strategic behavior frustrates. In so large and diverse a community, each member is tempted to conceal preferences (understate its true interest in a proposal) and withhold a fair share of support, in the hope that the other benefiters will shoulder the burden and make up the deficit.

These aspects of the world community—150 sovereign states and growing, all politically equal—are a general impediment to a cooperation. But efforts to secure cooperation are hardly futile. In some established forums, such as the UN General Assembly and within certain international agencies, majority rule or variations upon it are built into the practice.

Moreover, in many contexts, a convention does not need universal support in order to be effective. Although 117 states have now signed the 1963 *Treaty Banning Nuclear Weapons Tests in the Atmosphere, in Outer Space and Under Water*, considerable effectiveness was virtually secured with the agreement between only two powers, the United States and the Soviet Union. Coal burning, a principal source of greenhouse-creating CO_2, presents a similar opportunity. In view of the fact that nearly 60 percent of the world's coal is consumed by only three nations—China, United States, and former Soviet Union (in that order) — an agreement among those states on coal alone would have a noticeable impact on the global atmosphere. And, as we have seen, many problems, such as pollution of the Mediterranean, can best be established on the regional, not global level. Thus, the first point is, not every nation has to sign an international convention for it to make a substantial difference.

The Question of Compliance

A second general problem is how to get nations that assent to a treaty to comply with their commitments. As noted above, there is no sure way to compel a nation to appear before a national or international tribunal to answer charges against it. And even when nations do appear to answer charges, the sanctions that international law makes available tend to be far less intimidating than those available to the ordinary nation internally. Save, perhaps, for the case of war crimes, the international community does not itself mete out direct punishments to individuals (such as imprisonment) or impose punitive damages or fines on the nation. There is not even what would pass, in a domestic court, for an injunction. Even damage awards against states, while available, are infrequent, slow to extract, and generally, by US standards, leanly calculated when awarded. What is there then to make nations comply?

Compliance with international law, in the absence of any international sheriff with badge and pistol, is a large subject on which a great deal has been written. (The eminent English philosopher John Austin declared that, lacking these elements, international law should not be honored as law.) But, as with sovereignty and the unanimity rule, the limitations ought not to be overstated.

Granted, the compliance problem is serious. Any nation that refrains from joining a ban on trade in ivory or rhinoceros horns stands to reap the benefit of the higher prices that the reduced supply will invite. Nations that refuse to participate in a convention restricting fishing have that many more fish to catch. The prospect of these "rewards" for non-cooperators undermines efforts to form an effective coalition.

But the foundations of the world order are not as flimsy as they are often depicted. Even the commonplace that there is no international criminal liability must be understood with qualification. There may be no international criminal court, but international agreements can oblige the parties to use their own judicial systems to punish violators. For example, the 1954 international *Convention for the Prevention of Pollution of the Seas by Oil* obliges the offender's state to provide penalties "adequate in severity to discourage any such unlawful discharge and [which] shall not be less than the penalties which may be imposed under the law of that territory in respect of the same infringements within [its] territorial sea." Then, too, while international law traditionally depended upon nation states to press enforcement, compliance, especially in the US, is increasingly achieved through suits by nongovernmental organizations and private parties.

Moreover, sheriff or no sheriff, there is no reason why those nations that do sign an international convention have to sit idly by and let the nonsigners "free-ride" on their efforts. The international community has its own special carrots, such as technology transfers and economic assistance. And, that failing, the world community has its own sticks. In September 1992, in the wake of outrage over aggression and atrocities in the former Yugoslavia, the UN expelled the Serbian-dominated Yugoslav federation. In response to apartheid, South Africa has been suspended, draconian measures range from censure by the United Nations or other formal body, to making a cheater ineligible to receive loans from multinational development banks. There is even the potential "sanction of non-participation," that is, the exclusion of delinquent states from participating in international scientific and technical organizations and programmes

In addition, the non-cooperator's products can be subjected to special tariffs contrived to offset its unfair advantage. At least one bill introduced in the Senate would put the US in a position to impose countervailing duties on just such a basis. But the concerted boycott involving a larger community of nations is the more common rejoinder Countries that sign the *Convention on International Trade in Endangered Species* (CITES) agree to prohibit trade in endangered species and their products with nonsignatory nations, thereby restricting (unfortunately, not eliminating) markets. The same sort of non-trade provision exists under the *Montreal Ozone Protocol*. The agreement to reduce CFC production would be undermined if signatories were allowed to sell production technology to non-signing nations. But the Protocol closes this loophole by prohibiting the signatories from engaging in such trade.

The informal constraints of good neighborliness have a definite influence too. Although nations are under no compulsion to go along with the majority, they generally wish to be considered responsible members of the world community. Indeed, on one theory of hegemonic power, the leading nations may be particularly sensitive to do the right thing, even if it entails, as it often will, bearing a disproportionate share of the financial costs in exchange for the glory of world leadership.

The desire to be a good—or leading—world citizen is not only a motivation to sign international accords, it may even induce some non-signing nations to meet a convention's standards even though they have not formally bound themselves to do so. Both the United States and the United Kingdom have declined to become formal parties to the 1985 *Helsinki Sulfur Protocol*, under which states commit to achieve 30 percent reductions in transboundary fluxes. Yet both countries, mindful of world opinion, are careful to stress that they have met the requirements with substantially reduced sulfur dioxide (SO_2) emissions in the 1975–1984 period, the United States by 33 percent and the United Kingdom by over 40 percent. Community pressures have operated in the same way in the area of atmospheric nuclear weapons testing. Neither France nor China has signed the 1963 test ban treaty but both have displayed some sensitivity to its demands.

Of course, even in the face of these legal levers and "social" pressures, nations may be willing to suffer a little tarnish in image when the benefits of lawbreaking, in terms of some national self-interest, are viewed as worth it. (Just as ordinary people sometimes calculate an advantage, on balance, in breaking a lease or contract.) But the dominant

The desire to be a good—or leading—world citizen is not only a motivation to sign international accords, it may even induce some non-signing nations to meet a convention's standards even though they have not formally bound themselves to do so.

fact remains: even in the absence of many familiar formal sanctions, most nations are inclined to advance global interests and to honor their undertakings, if only because there are reciprocal advantages of being considered a reliable citizen of the world community.

Yet undeniably, these two general problems—getting nations to enter into conventions, and then getting the signers to comply—have two important consequences on the shape and mood of international law.

The first is that treaty targets tend to be set at relatively undemanding levels: making ambitions "realistic" is the easiest way to muster consensus and assure compliance. The 30 percent reduction in SO_2 agreed to at Helsinki represented not the level that would check acidification (some environmentalists believed that would have required a 90 percent reduction) but simply a figure that the governments involved could live with. Indeed, SO_2 emissions had been decreasing, even without a treaty, at about the same pace the treaty confirmed. Second, as we have seen, the sanctions for failure to comply, if any, tend to be more vague and more mild than their domestic counterparts.

Special Obstacles Confronting Environmental Agreements

If we go beyond the general problems that beset the making of all international conventions and focus on the obstacles to the negotiation of contemporary environmental treaties, we form a better idea of why the UNCED *Earth Summit* at Rio fell so short of its advance billing. The fact is, the major global environmental problems that drew the world leaders to Rio—loss of biodiversity, thinning of the ozone layer, thickening of the greenhouse blanket, the pressures on living marine resources—each contain the germ of potentially divisive conflicts. There are reasons why nations may decline to enter global agreements on them in the most earnest good faith—i.e., even putting aside displays of strategic behavior that one has to anticipate in any multiparty negotiation.

Judgment About Impacts

In many negotiations over the environment, there can be, as we saw in Rio, perfectly good-faith disagreement as to whether some alleged phenomenon—actually taking place on a serious scale—for example, whether we are actually witnessing a statistically significant increase in world temperature, or a decline in total marine resources. The uncertainty is amplified when future effects are projected:

When, if ever, will the level of atmospheric CO_2 double, and what consequences would such a doubling have, for, say, soil moisture and sea level? When so many scientists are in disagreement, it is hard to expect diplomats to put their fullest weight behind ameliorative programs that compete for resources with other legitimate, and in most ways more immediate, demands, such as the elimination of AIDS, poverty, drugs, and so on.

Judgment About Causes

Even if the global community is in general agreement that a certain perceived effect (a thinning of the ozone shield) is truly occurring, rather than apparent or illusory, negotiation may be hampered by disputes over cause.

For example, periodically the oceans are marked by "blooms"—sudden swellings in oceanic algae populations. These episodes have lethal effects on marine life (and occasionally, indirectly, on people who consume them), either through depriving other marine life of adequate oxygen or, in the case of "red tides," poisoning them through associated toxins. There is considerable concern that the algae blooms are fostered by man-made pollution, including run-off from fertilized agricultural land, sewage discharge, and possibly acid rain, all of which can inject surges of nutrients that swell the algae population. On the other hand, "red tides" (as they are often called) have been reported periodically through human history. Exodus 7:21 records an episode as one of the plagues visited on the Egyptians—long before our tampering with the environment had reached significant levels.

Moreover, even if human activities, as seems likely, are exacerbating the algae blooms, there is considerable room for uncertainty as to what chemical agents and which nations' activities are causally responsible. Nation A may point the finger at nitrogen emanating from Nation B's agriculture; Nation B blames phosphorous and trace metals from Nation A's industrial waste—and there may well be a grain of truth to each position.

Similarly, while human activity may be affecting climate in significant ways, the principal determinants of global climate remain natural forces, as we saw—most notably solar radiation, the tilt of the earth's axis with respect to the ecliptic, and the eccentricity of the earth's orbit. These relations continually shift over long cycles, signalling ice ages and their retreats. There are enormous and wide-ranging climatic effects of such other natural processes as solar activity, volcanic debris, and the El Niòo, as well. All these "background" processes complicate efforts to determine the extent to which any perceived changes in the environment can be pinned on human activity—and therefore be subject to mitigation by changes in human conduct, through law.

Negotiating Linkages

Even where the contribution of human activity has been segregated out, negotiation will often face considerable controversy over questions of linkage. No one doubts that the blanket of greenhouse gases is thickening. But the blanket consists of a number of gases. Carbon dioxide, largely a by-product of fossil fuel burning, is the most abundant and has therefore attracted the most attention. But methane, substantially connected to agriculture, has been increasing more rapidly, at least until quite recently. While the expected residence in the atmosphere of each carbon dioxide molecule may be ten or 15 times that of a methane molecule, each methane molecule is perhaps 50 times more effective a "blanketer" of outbound energy, molecule per molecule, than CO_2.

This background complicates climate negotiations considerably. The US negotiators, and perhaps other major fossil fuel burners (China, Russia, and Germany), have understandable reservations about diminishing their fossil fuel use unless these reductions are linked to sacrifices by those who affect the greenhouse blanket in other ways. The others would include India, the primary producer of methane, and Brazil, whose massive forest burnings not only result in major CO_2 emissions, but obliterate one of the planet's major "sinks" for drawing excess CO_2 out of the atmosphere. These demands for linkage do not appear to be unreasonable, considering, for example, the suspicion that at the present margin, a reduction in methane could be achieved more cheaply.

The various greenhouse gases (GHGs) can be related to a common blocking power index on the basis of their expected atmospheric residences, absorptive power, and various yet uncertain climatic feedbacks. Several methodologies for doing so are under consideration. But to give a flavor of the feelings that the negotiators will have to face if they insist on pressing linkage, before the Rio conference an Indian policy center decried as "greenhouse imperialism" a study by the World Resources Institute that dared nothing more than to compare the emissions of the less developed countries (largely methane) with the emissions of the industrialized world (largely CO_2). That, the center complained, was to compare "survival emissions" with "luxury emissions" and would be "criminal" if used as a basis for international action.

Negotiating Baselines

The solution to many problems requires agreement on some baseline upon which negotiated restrictions will operate. To sort out the alternatives is to enter a diplomatic and moral quagmire. Take GHGs, once more. Should a reduction formula be proportioned to historic levels of emission, laissez-faire levels (that is, projected levels absent agreement), Gross Domestic Product (GDP), territory, population, a threat point (that is, what each nation *could* emit if it, say, exploited its coal reserves at full pace without scrubbing), or someone's calculations of need, that is, "survival" versus "luxury" emissions?

Temporal baselines are every bit as knotty. Every negotiation that looks to an agreed-upon rollback of emissions has to agree on how far back to go to find the benchmark year. Ordering cutbacks from levels current at the time of negotiations may convey a perverse message: it suggests to any nation considering voluntary reductions that it may be required to make even deeper, more expensive cuts (from its new, self-imposed baseline) later. Frictions are rife. One of the draft agreements in the nitrogen oxide (NOx) negotiations called for nations to freeze emissions to the 1987 levels by 1994. But the United States balked, pointing out that it had already cut NOx emissions substantially under its Clean Air legislation, and raking the position—ultimately successful—that each nation should be allowed to pick a base year, presumably the year in which its output was at its peak. Great Britain raised a comparable objection in refusing to join the sulfur protocol.

Costs

To get nations to cooperate, there has to be some consensus that the benefits of the undertaking merit the costs. There are several reasons why the costs may not seem "worth it" to key negotiators, with consequent pressure on the consensus.

Most obviously, a nation may object to some proposal on the grounds that it is being asked to bear a disproportionate sacrifice. At Rio, the United States, as the heaviest producer of CO_2, put up the largest resistance to CO_2 constraints. On some estimates, to restrict carbon dioxide emissions over the next century to 1990 levels (one of the Rio proposals) would have cost the United States in the range of $800 billion to $3.6 trillion. That is the principal reason why the United States, while assenting to the vaguely aspirational *Framework Convention on Climate Change* (which the Senate approved by voice vote in October 1992), used its influence to squeeze out any firm reduction targets. On the other hand, the United States was second to none in the fight against tropical deforestation; the leading deforesters, such as Brazil, the Philippines, and Malaysia, foiled in their bid to plug the United States' carbon, succeeded in derailing the antilogging measures.

The Uneveness of Impacts

Even among the hazards we refer to as "global"—say, ozone depletion and climate change—the damages are projected to fall unevenly across regions. As a result, some nations will place a higher value on collaborative action than the others.

The world witnessed some such regional divisiveness at the London ozone negotiations. The thinning of the ozone shield poses its gravest threat to light-skinned populations living at high latitudes; that is because the thinning is most pronounced toward the poles and its principal direct human health hazard is skin cancer of a sort to which fair-skinned people are most susceptible.

This is not to imply that dark-skinned midlatitude populations, among which sun-induced skin cancer is rare, positively want an ozone thinning. But the phasing out of CFCS poses trade-offs in terms of development, and it was not surprising that at the London negotiations it was the Scandinavian countries, Germany and Canada in the Northern Hemisphere, and New Zealand and Australia in the Southern, that appeared to take the lead in pressing for the most rapid phase out of ozone-depleting agents.

When we turn to climate change, the situation is even more complex. After all, everyone agrees that ozone thinning is bad; people simply differ on the sacrifice warranted to achieve any particular level of constraint. By contrast, some nations may actually believe (or can credibly claim) that the odds favor their benefiting from greenhouse warming. This can be expected to hinder negotiations even more severely.

To illustrate, recall that if the earth heats up, precipitation worldwide is expected to increase. A warmer, moister, more carbon dioxide-rich atmosphere, together with longer (frost-free) growing seasons, is generally viewed as favorable to the growth of biomass overall (with some variable impacts on plants depending on species and local conditions).

Consider what the position of former Soviet republics is likely to be. According to a study by the United Nations Environmental Programme (UNEP), the effect of a 1.5° C increase in temperature in the Central European area of the former Soviet Union would be "a 30 percent increase in wheat yield. Additionally, the area suitable for wheat cultivation would increase by 26 percent, providing an overall increase in wheat production of 64 percent."

The old Soviet region stood second among nations in contributions to global CO_2 additions—and therefore might expect to bear one of the highest burdens in any reduction agreement. Can we expect nations so situated, with all their other worries, to pay more for heat and energy today in order to have less to eat tomorrow?

Indeed, on the basis of present knowledge, can we really dismiss the possibility that carbon consumption, moderately masked by available technology, could not meet Kaldor-Hicks criteria for efficiency? In ordinary parlance, that means while some will win and some will lose from continued GHG emissions, it is an open question whether the gains from enhanced agriculture will not dominate the losses from floods, etc., both across space and across generations The very fact that it is an open question hinders—and indeed, ought to hinder-the garnering of a worldwide consensus that radically stringent carbon-constraining policies are an ideal— even before we get to the difficulties of implementation.

Discrepancies in Value

Across the world, one hears strong support for the environment. But the real question in negotiation is how sturdily environmental values, such as respect for species and lifeless tundra, will be maintained when they come in conflict with the value of human lives and qualities of living. The values that are put in play vary enormously among individuals within our own nation, and the range varies all the more as we move across cultures. Some cultures regard the earth and life upon it as relatively insignificant in comparison with eternal paradise; others regard all of Nature (of which *homo sapiens* are just another ingredient) as sacred; still others are relatively homocentric. Some nations value whales in the ocean; others, on their plates.

Such valuative differences are compounded when long-term effects are accounted for. Many of today's controversial actions, such as the storage of nuclear wastes and the elimination of wilderness areas, involve a shifting of risks onto the unborn. This raises a series of terribly complex problems, on which different nations are apt to differ. There are, of course, the straightforward empirical uncertainties. We cannot be sure what the remote effects of our actions will be, particularly in light of the technology that will be available to our distant progeny. Will they really care that the oceans are whaleless? They may be far better off than we, looking back on our lives (as we regard those of the late Middle Ages) as short, nasty, brutish, and deprived. And even if we do conclude that some of our present actions will affect our descendants in adverse ways, how do we mediate between their interests and ours? We may be leaving them hazardous waste sites; but we are also bestowing on them Shakespeare and Beethoven and VCRs. ("What," some ask, "have future generations done for us?") These raise knotty inquiries for philosophers, on which little consensus can be expected worldwide.

Finally, there are different valuative postures that arise not so much from differences of cultural and philosophical attitudes as from sheer differences in wealth. Those under the pressures of poverty (and international debt repayments) are destined to bring a sense of urgency to the present and to discount the future correspondingly. Of the populous nations, Egypt and Bangladesh probably have the most reason to worry about sea-level rise in the next century. But they also face terribly pressing economic problems right now. If each were given a "budget" and told that they could apply it either to reduce the risks to future generations or relieve the present suffering, who can really doubt which they would choose?

Strategic Options

Suppose that nations can agree on all of the above: that some effect is taking place; that some identified agent is the cause; that the consequences are bad; that the benefits of eliminating the risks warrant a joint global effort, even if the costs rise to such and such an amount; and so on. Negotiations can still break down over strategy—on how best to tackle the problem.

Some international accords prohibit certain conduct outright-for example, those that forbid trade in endangered species, or nuclear weapons testing in the atmosphere, or war crimes. But note that prohibition is feasible in those instances because the forbidden activity is almost universally condemned. There is no redemptive value in mistreating POWs. By contrast, much of the global degradation results from activities that, while hazarding the environment, have associated benefits. Transporting oil by tanker and burning fossil fuels are representative. The underlying activities cannot be eliminated outright without significant sacrifice in global welfare. In these "grey" areas, the question is not to ban, but how to regulate the activity so that competing legitimate interests are maximized. In this area, negotiators have to weigh the merits of economically more sensitive control techniques, including user charges, marketable pollution rights, and so forth.

The technique favored—for example, whether to ban ocean dumping or allow it subject to permits, or to empower the injured to sue—will of course reflect competing national priorities regarding economic growth. But the fashioning of relief can also be impeded by unsettled factual questions. Consider ocean dumping. While the loudest voices call for a halt to the practice, there are respectable voices, including the National Research Council of the National Academy of Sciences and the National Advisory Committee on Oceans and Atmosphere, who reason that deep-ocean dumpsites, carefully monitored, may be the best resting ground for some of our worst waste. The issues are highly complex, but their point, essentially, is that while fail-safe containment or destruction would be ideal, it is presently unachievable; deposited on land, the waste is ordinarily more of a hazard to human populations; and that, given the law of gravity, much of our waste is now reaching the deep ocean anyway, meandering through river and wetlands, doing more damage on its way than if we just deposited it in the deep oceans at the start.

Strategic debates are shaping up in regard to biodiversity as well. Mathematicians have questioned present emphasis on preserving the most endangered species: they maintain that biological diversity should be measured by the evolutionary distance between available species, and what conservationists should aim to optimise is a function of that distance. A prominent economist has reminded us that efforts to save the most highly endangered species are apt to be the most costly and futile; when the costs and benefits are considered, rational policy should include making presently un-endangered species safer. And a zoologist has queried whether the single-minded focus on rain forests may not be misdirected: worldwide, dry areas are more threatened and are more important custodians of "higher taxonomic categories"—notably mammals, which store, species for species, more genetic information than the lower life with which the wetter jungles teems.

Strategic agreement can be plagued, too, by the existence of diverse cultural and national "tastes" toward various specific strategies. We would have to defer to the cultural anthropologists to opine the depth and breadth of their influence. My impression is that the United States displays a relatively high preference for clear rules spelled out in advance, is accustomed to settle differences through litigation, but is prepared to experiment with economic instruments such as pollution rights. Other countries are more accustomed to living with cloudier guidelines (which means more administrative discretion), inclined to mediation over litigation—and regard economic instruments as the cryptic handiwork of the capitalist devil.

The North-South Conflicts

As we saw at Rio, the most fractious dissensions arise from North-South conflicts. the nations of the earth enter into global negotiations with a profoundly unequal distribution of wealth. As a result, two sets of issues are in play—each of which would be intimidating even if presented singly. First, there are the public-goods questions: how to define and provide for the "right" rate of GHG emissions or ocean fishing or habitat preservation. In that discussion, the negotiations assume the character of a cooperative, potentially positive sum game. What is sought is an agreement that improves upon non-agreement, with the benefits and burdens of mutual cooperation so distributed that no nation emerges worse off than when negotiations began.

Note that on this first view of the process, the negotiators are regarded as accepting the prevailing wealth and rules as a given—the "no agreement point" that serves as a baseline from which advances are sought. Any questioning of the starting point is severed for a focused discussion in the context of agencies specifically charged with development and redistribution, including the development banks and various UN agencies.

For many of the LDCs, however, the starting point is the question. For them, the remote vulnerability to an environmental collapse, while worrisome, is in general secondary to the immediate threats of stagnation and poverty. The LDCs are thus not inclined to delink the issues. Rather, negotiations over climate or anything else are seen as an opportunity to reduce the underlying disparities in wealth and power." Some nations, the rich, should emerge worse off, having transferred some of their affluence to the poor.

It is this tension between rich and poor that marked the exchanges at Rio. Those focusing on the environment (largely, from the environmental nongovernment organizations [NGOs] and some First World representatives wanted to maximize environmental protection—as much protection as available money could buy. The poor nations showed that they want, foremost, to pull themselves up from poverty. It is that conflict between the environment focusers and development focusers that gives rise to talk about "sustainable development," a term meant to suggest that conservation and development can go hand in glove. And, indeed, the environmental literature is full of case studies in massive and mindless developmental projects that managed to set back the local economy at the same time they were destroying the environment. There undoubtedly exist *some* projects where developmental and environmental goals are fully congruent, and these should be identified and vigorously pursued. But more often there are tensions that cannot be obscured by diplomatic rhetoric. Environmental quality, economic development, and, for that matter, distributional justice are all potentially in conflict. In particular, the more a nation develops, some poverty-linked environmental problems, such as desertification, may be mitigated. But a larger number associated with carbon and chemicals—and these are the pollutants with the largest transfrontier effects—is positively linked. We may be able to lessen the correlation through technology transfer, for example, but we are not about to eliminate it.

Nor, however, can those tensions be ejected from North-South negotiations by dividing some talks into "the environment," to be attended to by environmental

Strategic agreement can be plagued, too, by the existence of diverse cultural and national "tastes" toward various specific strategies.

agencies such as UNEP, and others into "development," to be relegated to the jurisdiction of the International Monetary Fund (IMF), World Bank, and traditional developmental agencies. While the values of environment and development often conflict, they are also inseparable. Restrictions in the name of the environment, whether on fossil fuels or methane or anything else, are destined to affect rates of development and relative distribution of wealth.

The fact is, too, that the bargaining power of the Third World collapsed with the end of the Cold War. The developed nations are turning attention inward, and giving the old Eastern bloc an inside track on much of what is leftover. The LDCs do not have many cards to play. Developmental assistance is provided on the developed world's terms. In environmental negotiations, by contrast, the developed countries are more anxious about the global environment than the LDCs whose cooperation they are courting. This gives the LDCs something to bargain over. And it is quite understandable they might want the bargaining to be opened up beyond the international public goods (the ideally thick greenhouse blanket, ozone shield, and level of biodiversity, whatever they may be), and to encompass some raw reallocation of wealth. If the poor get more assistance from the rich, they can make the funds available for local environmental challenges such as desertification and dirty water, as well as, of course, food, health care, and infrastructure. As in the Law of the Sea context, in which the same North-South clash arose, adding cards to the deck raises the risk that the environment will get lost in the shuffle. And it is easy to show that in any negotiation in which majority rule prevails, a coalition of poor voters, provided with ample freedom to define the issues, probably *will* go beyond an "efficient" solution to the public-goods problem and wind up redistributing a little wealth in their favor.

On the other hand, the insistence on linkage must appear to the LDCs no less legitimate than the United States' occasional gestures linking human rights to trade. Adding pure redistribution to the agenda adds another unit of currency for bargaining, and hence another dimension along which advances in aggregate welfare may be sought-not a bad dimension, given plausible assumptions about the declining marginal utility of wealth. That is, if we admit the legitimacy of interpersonal comparisons of utility, it seems credible that a transfer of $1 billion from the United States to Bangladesh would bring about a net increase in welfare, their population gaining more in utility than ours loses.

In sum, even if an environmental convention provides an imperfect framework for resolving inequalities in global wealth, some degree of North–South economic conflicts cannot be avoided. The *UNCED Earth Summit* was convened, after all, in the name of environment and development. But the broadened focus at Rio proved to be—and will continue to be—an obstacle to achieving outcomes that are ideal environmentally, at least as environmentalists understand that term. From the environmental perspective, and probably from that of development, resuming development policies and strategies as much as possible to the IMF, World Bank, and traditional assistance agencies would tidy both of the working areas considerably.

Under What Circumstances are International Negotiations Likely to Succeed?

It is not my intention to add to the post mortems on the 1992 meeting in Rio. With thousands of government officials, NGO representatives, observers, activists, media, and movie stars gathered together in one tent for two weeks to repair every problem under the sun, it is small wonder that the *Earth Summit* disappointed the expectations that no one should have held for it. It is rather a surprise that agreement on anything survived collapse under the weight of so ample an agenda and glamorous a multitude. I have made clear enough my views why climate change may have been a poor—perhaps the worst possible—choice for a focal point.

The disappointments of Rio should not obscure the fact that, even in the face of all these potential conflicts, declarations are proclaimed and treaties do get signed. Thus, in closing this discussion of treaty formation, a better use of history—and horse sense—is to speculate why progress has been made in some areas and not in others. Specifically, if we are not to tackle every problem at once, what characteristics make an area of negotiation a propitious target for successful international negotiations?

Let me suggest (in some instances, review) a few features that appear to favor success of multilateral agreement not necessarily if displayed singly, but certainly where they appear in combination. The first is that the agreement doesn't (yet) matter. Several early conventions regarding outer space, the moon, and celestial bodies were hammered out successfully because negotiations began when their effects were still distant in space and time. This suggests the advisability of getting an early start—anticipating rather than reacting—before potential vetoing constituencies have an opportunity to form.

A related point is that the easier it is to conclude a treaty, the fewer the number of nations whose cooperation is required to make it effective. This was true of the 1963 *Treaty Banning Testing of Nuclear Weapons in the Atmosphere*, and also the CFC cutbacks under the *Montreal Ozone Protocol*: in both cases, many nations ultimately signed, but success was sealed with the assent of a relatively small core.

It appears, too, that treaties come easiest when the activities to be regulated are on the global commons. Regulation of pollution on the high seas has been achieved far ahead of controlling pollution *of* the high seas from land-based sources. Partly, this results from the world community's readiness to recognize the legitimacy of international restrictions on activities that affect, particularly those that take place on, the shared space of the global commons. But the failure to stem land-based pollution also reflects another, more obvious factor: agreements are more likely when the costs of restrictions are low. That, as we saw, was a major distinction between controlling ozone-depleting agents and controlling GHGs.

There is a suggestion, too, that coalitions may be strengthened if it is feasible at least to monitor (and if possible, to enforce) compliance. Critical to the banning of nuclear weapons testing was the conviction that violations could be monitored. There was considerably more resistance to the banning of underground testing until is was shown that seismic equipment for measuring earthquakes could detect underground explosions as well. The ban then became effective just because violations could be detected, even though there were no "real" liabilities for violators. Monitoring difficulties are another factor why the Economic Council of Europe (ECE) had a hard time producing a transboundary NOx agreement as a sequel to its SO_2 accord. The bulk of SO_2 is produced by a relatively small number of major coal-burning sources, such as utilities. NOx derives from so many point sources—automobiles are a major contributor—that NOx was not as easy to clamp down on.

It helps, too, when the consensus as to need for action is strong and the technical experts are in agreement. Scientists and other technical experts do not make treaties; but consensus among experts certainly helps move negotiations along. This boost results not so much from any influence experts exert on the political process directly. It is more that the political path is straighter when the experts report, for example, that technical fixes are not foreseeable. To illustrate, the concern in the United States over sea level rise, and hence the willingness to negotiate a CO_2 agreement, would be stronger if there were no technical undercurrent that future engineers and construction technology will be able to defend such areas as New York City without insurmountable difficulty.

It may seem obvious, but it bears reminding, that the proposed restrictions have to be practically achievable. The CFC reduction levels reached at Montreal and London were made possible only when the prospect of CFC substitutes, principally HCFCs that at least at the time were believed to be generally acceptable, lifted the resistance of US manufacturers. The schedule for phasing out haloes, used in fire extinguishers, is less ambitious, not because haloes are less threatening to the ozone layer pound for pound, but because there is yet to be developed a comparable substitute—and fires are a continuing worldwide concern more lethal right now than ultraviolet radiation.

Conclusion

Where are we left by all this—the virtues of treaties, the various impediments to treaty formation, the circumstances that may be, hopefully, favorable for their growth? In some circumstances, as we shall see in the succeeding chapters, the obstacles are significant enough that they invite alternative approaches—specifically, unilateral action, and various styles of more modestly scaled bilateral and small numbers undertakings.

But the notion of more ambitious multilateral conventions will and should go forward. In that evolution, the impediments are best viewed not as absolute barriers to agreement, but as factors that shape the structure and timing and mode of international action.

For example, where conflict takes the form of disagreement over effects or causes, there can be a first-stage agreement to cooperate on modelling and data gathering. While nations can and do act separately in scientific matters, joint sponsorship of the efforts is likely to make the results more credible internationally and probably more accurate as well. While the facts are being gathered, treaty negotiations, even the execution of softly textured conventions such as "declarations of principle," can proceed. But until the scientific uncertainties are resolved, progress toward stringent and widely acceptable restrictions is apt to be limited—and often rightly so.

On the other hand, in cases where the reservations arise from fears that "the other fellow's" cheating cannot be monitored, the answer is concerted efforts to improve the monitoring. In light of the difficulty of tracking causal links, such as whose chemical agents are showing up where, it is encouraging to consider recent advances in the ability of scientists to trace some particles and gases to their place of origin. In describing pollution of the Arctic, *National Geographic* reports that 'the Arctic pollutants showed a signature unknown to Western scientists. One investigator found arsenic, selenium, antimony, and indium, in a combination that pinned most of the pollution to a mineral-rich smelting region in the Soviet Union's Ural Mountains. Other investigators found dry-cleaning freons and degreasing solvents used commonly by the Russians but rarely by Western nations. Similar advances in data gathering and processing could facilitate global agreements appreciably, and should be fostered as a matter of deliberate policy.

Where the conflicts arise over evaluation and choice of strategy, the marginal value of gathering additional facts or improving detection is minimal.

Where the conflicts arise over evaluation and choice of strategy, the marginal value of gathering additional facts or improving detection is minimal. The arguments there are not over what is, but what ought to be. What is required, at the least, is a continuing frank dialogue on international values and community.

Nonetheless, no one should doubt that even without "hard" sanctions backing them up, treaties, and even vague, aspirational declarations of principle, have significant effects on patterns of behavior in the international community. Indeed, no one should doubt the salutary effects in the mere process of bringing diplomats together to discuss global problems. One well-informed commentator, Charles Pearson, has observed of the 1972 United Nations-sponsored meeting at Stockholm that produced the Declaration on the Environment:

> "It is difficult to assess the actual results of Stockholm. In part this is because the process of conference preparation and participation can be viewed as an objective that was more important than the Declaration... itself... Preparations for the conference... force[d] governments into awareness of international environmental issues."

Twenty years from the *Earth Summit* in Rio—and 20 years is not long in geologic or diplomatic time—the same may be said. Awareness of, and even the appreciation of, deepening conflicts has increased. This is less likely to mean that efforts to reach consensus will cease, as that the focus of efforts will shift. Important issues on which agreement is possible will be delinked, compartmentalized, and shunted to more favorable forums. There, details can be worked out in a more productive (and sometimes less public) negotiating environment. In many areas significant advances are less likely to be achieved by agreement on governing rules (even in the limp form of aspirational targets), as on the creation of an infrastructure of agencies, informed as much by scientists as by diplomats, that can oversee and guide, step by step, the development of particular regimes.

B

Examples of Early Principles of International Environmental Law

The *Stockholm Declaration* was adopted by the *United Nations Conference on the Human Environment* held at Stockholm in 1972. It was adopted by acclamation by the 113 participating states. It contains 26 principles which provide the basis of an international policy for the protection and improvement of the environment, of which Principles 21 and 22 directly concern international law. Due to their significance, these particular principles are also extracted in Chapter 2.

The potential significance of the *Stockholm Declaration* in the environmental field has been compared with that which the *Universal Declaration on Human Rights* has come to have in respect of human rights. Principle 21 states, as a matter of current international law, the right of a state to exploit its own natural resources and its duty not to cause harm to others or to places outside of its territory in the course of their exploitation. The *Trail Smelter* case, extracted following, gives some idea of the content of this duty. Principle 22 imposes an obligation *(quaere* a legal one) to cooperate to develop the duty further. Areas "beyond the limits of national jurisdiction" include the high seas and Antarctica.

(i) "Stockholm Declaration on the Human Environment," *Report of the UN Conference on the Human Environment*, UN Doc. A/CONF. 48/14; I.L.M. 1416, 1972

Principle 21

States have, in accordance with the Charter of the United Nations and the principles of international law, the sovereign right to exploit their own resources pursuant to their own environmental policies, and the responsibility to ensure that activities within their jurisdiction or control do not cause damage to the environment of other States or of areas beyond the limits of national jurisdiction.

Principle 22

States shall cooperate to develop further the international law regarding liability and compensation for the victims of pollution and other environmental damage caused by activities within the jurisdiction or control of such States to areas beyond their jurisdiction.

(ii) *The Trail Smelter Arbitration US v. Canada* (1938 and 1941), Arbitral Tribunal: Hostie, Chairman; Warren, US member; Greenshields, Canadian member; 3 R.I.A.A. 2905

A Canadian company began smelting lead and zinc at the beginning of the century at Trail, on the Columbia River about 10 miles from the border between the two countries on the Canadian side. In the 1920s, the company stepped up production and by 1930 over 300 tons of sulphur, containing considerable quantities of sulphur dioxide, were being emitted daily. Some of the fumes were being carried down the Columbia River Valley and across into the United States where they were allegedly causing considerable damage to land and other interests in the state of Washington. After negotiations between the two countries, Canada agreed that the case should be referred to the International Joint Commission. This is a body established by the two countries by the Boundary Waters Treaty of 1909 with jurisdiction over problems concerning their common water boundaries. It is a notable early example of one kind of standing administrative body that can be of use in controlling international air or water pollution. The Commission reported in 1931 that damage had indeed occurred and assessed it at 5,350,000. Canada which had not disputed the question of liability, agreed to pay this amount. But the smelter at Trail continued to operate and the question whether damage had been caused after 1931 for which compensation should be paid was raised and referred, this time, to arbitration. The United States claimed about $2 million compensation. In 1938, the Tribunal allowed the claim in part, awarding $578,000 compensation in respect of damage caused between 1930 and 1937. The Tribunal was also asked [this] question—"whether the Trail Smelter should be required to refrain from causing damage in the State of Washington in the future and, if so, to what extent?" It is this question that is considered in the following extract.

1941 Report of the Tribunal

The first problem which arises is whether the question should be answered on the basis of the law followed in the United States or on the basis of international law. The Tribunal, however, finds that this problem need not be solved here, as the law followed in the United States, in dealing with the quasi-sovereign rights of the States of the Union, in the matter of air pollution, while more definite, is in conformity with the general rules of international law.

Particularly in reaching its conclusions as regards this question as well as the next, the Tribunal has given consideration to the desire of the high contracting parties "to reach a solution just to all parties concerned."

As Professor Eagleton puts it: "A State owes at all times a duty to protect other States against injurious acts by individuals from within its jurisdiction." A great number of such general pronouncements by leading authorities concerning the duty of a State to respect other States and their territory have been presented to the Tribunal.... But the real difficulty often arises rather when it comes to determine what, *pro subjecta materie, is* deemed to constitute an injurious act.

A case concerning, as the present one does, territorial relations, decided by the Federal Court of Switzerland between the Cantons of Soleure and Argovia, may serve to illustrate the relativity of the rule. Soleure brought a suit against her sister State to enjoin use of a shooting establishment which endangered her territory. The court, in granting the injunction, said: "This right (sovereignty) excludes...not only the usurpation and exercise of sovereign rights (of another State)...but also an actual encroachment which might prejudice the natural use of the territory and the free movement of its inhabitants." As a result of the decision, Argovia made plans for the improvement of the existing installations. These, however, were considered as insufficient protection by Soleure. The Canton of Argovia then moved the Federal Court to decree that the shooting be again permitted after completion of the projected improvements. This motion was granted. "The demand of the Government of Soleure," said the court, "that all endangerment be absolutely abolished apparently goes too far." The court found that all risk whatever had not been eliminated, as the region was flat and absolutely safe shooting ranges were only found in mountain valleys; that there was a federal duty for the communes to provide facilities for military target practice and that "no more precautions may be demanded for shooting ranges near the boundaries of two Cantons than are required for shooting ranges in the interior of a Canton."

No case of air pollution dealt with by an international tribunal has been brought to the attention of the Tribunal nor does the Tribunal know of any such case. The nearest analogy is that of water pollution. But, here also, no decision of an international tribunal has been cited or has been found.

There are, however, as regards both air pollution and water pollution, certain decisions of the Supreme Court of the United States which may legitimately be taken as a guide in this field of international law, for it is reasonable to follow by analogy, in international cases, precedents established by that court in dealing with controversies between States of the Union or with other controversies concerning the quasi-sovereign rights of such States, where no contrary rule prevails in international law and no reason for rejecting such precedents can be adduced from the limitations of sovereignty inherent in the Constitution of the United States....

The Tribunal, therefore, finds that the above decisions, taken as a whole, constitute an adequate basis for its conclusions, namely, that, under the principles of international law, as well as of the law of the United States, no State has the right to use or permit the use of its territory in such a manner as to cause injury by fumes in or to the territory of another or the properties or persons therein, when the case is of serious consequence and the injury is established by clear and convincing evidence

The decisions of the Supreme Court of the United States which are the basis of these conclusions are decisions in equity and a solution inspired by them, together with the regime hereinafter prescribed, will, in the opinion of the Tribunal, be "just to all parties concerned," as long, at least, as the present conditions in the Columbia River Valley continue to prevail.

Considering the circumstances of the case, the Tribunal holds that the Dominion of Canada is responsible in international law for the conduct of the Trail Smelter. Apart from the undertakings in the Convention, it is, therefore, the duty of the Government of the Dominion of Canada to see to it that this conduct should be in conformity with the obligation of the Dominion under international law as herein determined.

The Tribunal, therefore, answers Question No. 2 as follows: (2) So long as the present conditions in the Columbia River Valley prevail, the Trail Smelter shall be required to refrain from causing any damage through fumes in the State of Washington; the damage herein referred to and its extent being such as would be recoverable under the decisions of the courts of the United States in suits between private individuals. The indemnity for such damage should be fixed in such manner as the Governments, acting under Article XI of the Convention, should agree upon.

C

Trends in International Environmental Law

(i) Handl G., "Environmental Security and Global Change: The Challenge to International Law," in Lang W. *et al.* (eds), *Environmental Protection and International Law*, Graham and Trotman, 1991, pp 60–83

Introduction

In 1972, Maurice Strong noted

> "The essential theme of modern age is interdependence, the interdependence of all the elements which sustain life on the planet,

> of man with those elements, of the natural system with man's needs and aspirations, and most of all man with man."

Today, almost twenty years later, on the eve of the 1992 United Nations Conference on Environment and Development, global environmental interdependence has become painfully obvious, its manifestations distinctly threatening, its ramifications all-engrossing Some commentators conclude that global environmental degradation has reached a "pre-crisis stage". Others, quite persuasively, maintain that we are in the middle of a process of unavoidable global environmental change that threatens possibly catastrophic economic, social, and political consequences. Whatever the perspective on the present state of affairs, there is broad agreement that environmental resource management has become a matter of paramount importance, an issue involving national security, and thus, by definition, international, indeed global security.

If, therefore, the present state of the global environment poses a serious challenge to both national and international decision makers and to the international public order system itself, it offers also an opportunity for, indeed holds out the promise of, unprecedented international cooperation. The end of the cold war signals the possibility of broad and intensifying East-West accommodation and, in its wake, of global cooperation. In general, we see, as Professor Falk has pointed out, a "dramatic shift from the perception of international relations as a zero-sum game to a positive sum game"... The notion of "spaceship earth", long accepted as a metaphor for the existence of a global community in an ecological sense, may finally inspire international political and legal action. Successful responsive action however, will depend on whether and how decision makers act upon the special characteristics of today's environmental crisis and its specific implications for the international legal system.

The scientific, economic, and social context in which the global environmental crisis unfolds, is subject to change at increasing speed. Indeed, certain features of the factual setting change at exponentially increasing speed. The result has been an enormous strain on the capability of the international legal system, and, particularly, of the international legislative process, to keep up with the rate of change, to reorder regulatory priorities, and, most importantly, to adjust procedurally and institutionally to increasing demand for quick legislative action.

A second characteristic ingredient of the crisis is the fact that environmental issues that rise to the level of international concern have progressively advanced from purely local transboundary, to regional/continental and, lately, global dimensions. This has meant that the international regulatory focus had to expand accordingly, ultimately necessitating the building of environmental global regimes. The geographically expanding scope, in turn, has rendered international standard-setting a much more delicate task, an exercise in balancing the objectives of minimum state participation, discouragement of free riders, and avoidance of unreasonably low levels of environmental protection.

Finally, the present global environmental situation acquires crisis proportions because of the intensity or severity of its present or potential manifestations. There is a risk of serious irreversible or cumulative effects, of an environmental system overload producing cascading effects throughout ecological subsystems. Thus, international environmental law must come to reflect a much greater emphasis on precautionary policies and a systematic rather than segmented approach to environmental resource management.

The question thus arises whether the international legal system can meet these challenges, whether it will be able to ensure to this and future generations a modicum of environmental security in the face of rapid global change. The following review thus will attempt to sketch an answer by identifying critical policy themes and by evaluating evolving international community responses to specific issues that are likely to bear on success or failure of the international legal system.

International Protection of the Environment: The Evolving Process

Legal Instruments and Lawmaking Techniques

Framework Conventions and Implementing Protocols

If international protection of environmental resources requires an increasingly high degree of adaptability or responsiveness of the legal system to rapid and frequent change," a traditional, ad hoc, treaty-based approach to international environmental standard-setting, is evidently ill-suited to meet the task. The disadvantages of the classic treaty approach are obvious: the drafting, adoption, and putting into effect of treaties as well as revisions or amendments involve elaborate and time-consuming exercises in diplomacy. In the aggregate, transaction costs of this approach become unacceptably high because, as legislative international intervention will be repeatedly required to respond to an evolving international environmental problem, this approach offers simply too many opportunities to states for "opportunistic" behavior.

The need to facilitate international environmental decision making of a less cumbersome and time-consuming nature without sacrificing at the same time on the objective of broad state adherence to adequate environmental standards, has prompted a restructuring of multilateral legislative processes: diplomatic "*ad hocracy*", is being abandoned for institutionalized, periodic, and informal review of international regulatory regimes with simplified amendment procedures.

While there are other indications of this development in international environmental standard-setting (note, for example, the simplified amendment procedures of Article 313 of UNCLOS) it is only in the context of more recent environmental framework conventions and implementing protocols that the trend has become conspicuous. For example, the *Montreal Protocol on Substances that Deplete the Ozone Layer* expressly provides for the periodic review and assessment of control measures taken and their adjustment or supplementation whenever deemed necessary." Similarly, the 1989 *Basel Convention on the Transboundary Movement of Hazardous Wastes* (although, strictly speaking, not a framework convention) authorizes the regularly scheduled meetings of the Conference of the Parties to take legislative initiatives to ensure the effectiveness and continuous improvement of the regime. Significantly, as regards adoption of technical annexes under either regime, parties must "opt out" so as to avoid being bound by the new standards." Simplification of the formal standard-setting procedure is, moreover, accompanied by an acceleration of meetings of the parties, thus by increased opportunities for legislative initiatives. In the case of some of the regimes concerned, this may well offer the prospect of a virtually continuous legislative enterprise."

The resulting intrinsic flexibility or adaptability of the legislative process comes, as some might be apt to object, with a substantial price tag. The framework-cum-implementing protocols approach necessarily entails a significant degree of indeterminacy of the normative landscape thus being created: States tend to settle first broad policy outlines through the device of framework conventions and leave nettlesome details to be worked out in future protocols. This institutionalizes international lawmaking within the individual environmental context as defined by the framework convention. By necessity, this approach thus also signals a certain open-endedness of the legislative enterprise.

More significantly still, states may leave the definition of key legal parameters regarding the scope and very nature of conventional obligations to which they contract to be settled at a later date. Consider, for example, the *Basel Convention*: The finalization of at least two such concepts, namely that of "environmentally sound management of wastes" and of "liability", have been left for decision by the parties until after the Convention formally enters into force.

International legislation under this guise is no longer a single well-defined product carried by expectations of stability for a foreseeable future. It is rather a fragile, temporary legal signpost in an institutionalized process in which legal positions are subject to constant review and susceptible to frequent and speedy alteration. Those who might be troubled by this fact might do well to heed Professor Sax's admonition on the function of domestic environmental law which applies with equal, indeed greater force to international legal mechanisms for protecting environmental resources globally:

> "[W]e must put aside the dominating idea that the legal system is to be designed to instinitionalize stability and security. Probably nothing is more urgently required than institutions for controlled instability."

Some aspects of this development may be undesirable. For example, the institutional dynamics of multilateral regimes (with regard to both the setting and implementation of standards), may be such as to decouple decision making within the regime from traditional national processes of control and supervision. In this sense, the new type of environmental regime may signal an emerging "democratic deficit". Other implications of such regimes might be merely inconvenient. However, on balance, there can be little doubt that the evolving international legislative process represents progress towards better international legal management of increasingly demanding global environmental problems.

"Soft Law"

It is against the background of the special regulatory exigencies of international environmental problems, that so-called "soft-law", plays an important role in the evolution of international environmental law. "Soft law" denotes international prescriptions that are deemed to lack the requisite characteristics of international legal norms proper, but which, notwithstanding this fact, are capable of producing certain effects. "Soft law", of course, travels in tandem with "hard law", its counterpart on the other side of the threshold of international normativity.

There are international lawyers who harbour serious reservations about usage of the term, defining it as a "pathological phenomenon", of international law, as introducing a graduated scale of normativity; as a practice that lends itself to legal pretension. The concept, so the argument goes, tends to blur the line between law and nonlaw, be that because merely aspirational norms are accorded "legal" status, albeit of a secondary nature; be that because the effect of the usage of the term may be to undermine the status of an established legal norm.

On the other hand, "soft law" can be a valuable instrument for enhancing or supplementing international law proper. In fact, frequently "soft law" will capture emerging notions of international public order and thus help extend the realm of legitimate international concern to matters of previously exclusive national jurisdiction. This is especially true of the use of soft law with regard to the protection of the environment. In this sense, soft law is the thin end of the normative wedge of international environmental law, perhaps the "Trojan Horse of environmentalists".

There is, of course, abundant and well-known evidence of the effectiveness of soft law declarations as catalysts in the evolution of international environmental law proper. The so-called *Helsinki Rules on the Uses of Waters of International Rivers*, the 1972 *Stockholm Declaration on the Human Environment*, or the 1982 General Assembly Resolution entitled *World Charter for Nature*, to name only a few, all have proved to be agents in the "legalization of international environmental protection."

In the final analysis, though, soft law concepts pose both a challenge for and an obligation on international lawyers. First, the declining reliability of formal criteria as guideposts to what actually constitutes international law...requires an adequate theory about international law, namely as a process of communication, and thus sensitivity to those signals indicating international normativity and those that do not. Second, international environmental lawyers must heed the normative dividing line and avoid misrepresenting aspirational norms for "hard law" and thereby rendering a disservice to the very cause they purport to serve, namely the strengthening of the legal protection of the environment globally.

Uniform Environmental Standards and Asymmetrical Rights and Obligations

In his recent study on international environmental standard-setting, Peter Sand endorses asymmetrical standards or differential obligations as a way to induce broad state acceptance of a regulatory regime, yet beat the "lowest common denominator problem". The usefulness, indeed indispensability of selective incentives, is, of course, a reflection of the fact that expected benefits and costs of any regime will vary from state to state. Thus, incentives such as delayed compliance schedules or economic/ financial assistance may be necessary to offset the absence of reciprocal state interest in the proposed regime. As an axiom of international cooperation, such measures have long been part and parcel of international standard-setting efforts. By the same token, the intrinsic merit of differentiating standards that account for variations in state parties' contributions to the problem to be regulated, is equally self-evident.

From a legal policy perspective, any asymmetry in rights and obligations is a sensitive matter.

Nevertheless, from a legal policy perspective, any asymmetry in rights and obligations is a sensitive matter. Sometimes the nature, possibly also the scope, of asymmetrical standards may raise a fundamental question about the appropriateness of such multilateral regime-building devices. Indeed, in the absence of special justifications, such as causation-related allowances in the case of environmental regimes addressing a transnational pollution problem, any international regulatory system that discriminates among states with regard to its core obligations, is bound to be problematical in the long run.

Consider, for example, the *Nuclear Non-Proliferation Treaty* to which Sand refers as an example of a successful incentive-based regulatory approach. To many observers the NPT may illustrate also the dangers inherent in any asymmetrical standard-setting: the persistence of the temporarily sanctioned legal discrimination along the lines of nuclear "haves" and "have-nots" has exacerbated diplomatic controversies over implementation of the treaty and repeatedly threatened to unravel the whole regime."

As regards international environmental legislation, asymmetrical normative standards that bear on the essence of the regulatory regime, unlike incentives, are generally undesirable. First, they invariably entail higher administrative costs given the greater complexity of the system; second, inevitable distortions in international trade are likely to be more difficult to reverse than would be the case if brought about by, for example, financial incentives to induce disadvantaged states to comply fully with internationally uniform, but stringent standards; third, such standards might be counterproductive in terms of long-term environmental benefits, especially where less developed countries are involved. A dilution of the normative demands on developing countries is likely to impede progress by those countries towards an adequate level of local environmental protection, the acquisition of technological know-how and managerial ability on which "sustainable development" locally will depend. Thus, developing country status cannot justify in and by itself an automatic lowering of international standards.

To oppose such differentiation in environmental standards does not imply rejection of a state's ability to control the risk of untoward environmental impacts—quite apart from its contribution to the problem—as the ultimate basis of international responsibility for safeguarding internationally sensitive environmental resources. As a matter of fact, retaining uniformity with regard to core obligations while taking into account states' socioeconomic conditions, are entirely compatible objectives for multilateral regulatory regimes.

Take, for example, the *Basel Convention on the Transboundary Movement of Hazardous Waste*. It establishes very broad international obligations for the protection of would-be importing countries. Yet, there is little evidence that the regime reflects the abandonment of the rules of classic state responsibility or the ascendancy of social welfare concept in international relations, as some might be tempted to argue. Rather, rights and obligations within the essentially bilateral context of exporting and importing states are fairly well balanced. They are in line with the traditional international principle to allocate responsibility to the state party best able to act towards minimization of the costs of untoward waste transfers. In particular, the Convention does not proceed from the unwarranted assumption that the responsibility of the state of import is automatically diminished whenever the latter falls into the developing country category.

In the end, rejection of a purely wealth-sensitive or development status-oriented international standard-setting philosophy, quite obviously brings into sharper focus the issue of equity in North-South relations and the need for alternative mechanisms to redress the problem of underdevelopment as it bears on international environmental regime building.

The Formal Legal Structure of Regulatory Regimes

To be effective, international environmental regimes must not only attract the support of all relevant states, but also reach effectively the activities of major transnational non-state actors, especially transnational corporations (TNCs) and multilateral lending institutions. Given the immense influence of activities of some of these non-state actors on national policies and operational decisions affecting internationally sensitive environmental resources, as well as these actors' often quasi-autonomous conduct in the transnational arena, the question arises of how best formally to structure environmental regulations.

One possibility might be legally to treat these entities as formally independent of states in recognition of their frequent de facto independence in the transnational arena. Another would be to couch international regulations in terms of private legal obligations directly incumbent on the principal actors, instead of in language that focuses on states' international responsibility as the underlying cardinal principle. Indeed, the definition of the relationship between private legal obligations and explicit norms of state responsibility has become a significant issue in recent efforts at international standard-setting related to environmental protection.

Some transboundary regulatory regimes of a highly technical nature, most notably those relating to liability for transboundary damage, already evince a so-called "private law approach". While the legal instruments by which these regimes are established represent formal international agreements among states proper, their objective is the regulation of rights and obligations not among states themselves, but among private individuals. Similarly, the *OECD Guidelines for Multinational Enterprises* as well as the proposed *UN Code of Conduct on Transnational Corporations* directly address responsibilities of TNCs.

Finally, there is the phenomenon of limited direct international regulation of environmentally sensitive private conduct as in the *Convention on the Regulation of Antarctic Mineral Resource Activities* (CRAMRA), or the draft regulations drawn up by the UN Preparatory Commission for the International Sea-Bed Authority and for the International Tribunal for the Law of the Sea.

However, neither existing "private law" liability regimes, nor other, presently proposed, international regulations that might directly address private conduct more broadly, should obscure the fact that the ability to invoke state responsibility principles remains a necessary alternative to asserting nonstate actors' responsibility. Thus, to single out TNCs, it is unlikely that, any time soon, their international legal status would be upgraded to the point where they could be both direct claimant and respondent under international law without any mediation by states. Nor is it likely that international control, for example under United Nations auspices, would replace present "home" state control, and that thereby United Nations responsibility would replace "home" state responsibility."

In short, the principle of state responsibility proper is likely to remain an essential legal underpinning of any transboundary regulatory regime. States are the repository of ultimate power to enforce transnational community standards. Accordingly, in the interest of strengthening international environmental regulations, the principle of state responsibility should be made explicit especially where it already extends implicitly to controlling activities of nationals, including multinational corporations. At the same time, it will be necessary to continue to strengthen the direct transnational accountability of key actors, such as TNCs. This will not, however, diminish state responsibility for the conduct of corporate nationals abroad. Rather, greater specificity of TNC obligations will strengthen the hand of host states in dealing with TNCs while introducing a more demanding standard against which to assess "home" state compliance with its international obligation to control corporate nationals.

The Interplay of Local, Regional, and Global Environmental Standard-Setting

Heightened awareness of international environmental interdependence and rising threats to globally shared resources, such as the atmosphere, have had a dramatic impact on the locus of standard-setting bearing on internationally sensitive environmental resources. Two basic trends are discernible. First, international law making on environmental matters is rapidly becoming more centralized, thus reducing the room for standard-setting at the individual state level. Evidence of this shift can be found in many regulatory contexts, including, for example, marine pollution. Unlike the early 1970s, when Canada could unilaterally set offshore pollution prevention standards which, though primarily intended to protect national environmental interests, cut broadly across international interests, today, in an analogous situation, national discretion would be severely limited: UNCLOS and special international marine pollution legislation establish clear international procedures for authoritative standard-setting that preempt unilateralism. At the same time, global regimes are susceptible to the de facto veto power of strategic individual countries. Consider, for example, the recent United States *Oil Pollution Liability and Compensation Act* which allows federal states to set higher than internationally agreed upon limits on liability. Most observers agree that this legislation will seriously undermine, if not kill, the 1984 Protocols amending the 1969 *Oil Pollution Liability Convention*, and the 1971 *Fund Convention*.

Second, international standard-setting tends to occur—not surprisingly—at a level consistent with what, in a different context, is often referred to as the principle of "subsidiarity" of legislation. Frequently, the appropriate level for international environmental legislative action will be the regional one. Regionalization, as Sand points out, offers an opportunity for custom-built regimes and more stringent environmental standards as limited membership is likely to imply a higher common denominator. Recognition of the merits of this approach can be seen in the fact that many global regimes leave room for supplementary regulation at regional or bilateral levels. For example, the *Basel Convention* specifically accommodates bilateral, multilateral, or regional agreements or arrangements regarding the transboundary movement of hazardous wastes, provided "environmentally sound management" at least equivalent to that required under the Convention will be assured. By contrast, the 1986 *Convention on Early Notification of Nuclear Accidents* and *Convention on Assistance* represent bare-bones framework conventions which in effect render bilateral or regional implementing regimes a necessity.

Regional standard-setting, of course is not only a process of intrinsically regional importance. The dynamics of the "small group-high common denominator" function may result in stringent or innovative environmental standards at regional level. Such standards are often precedent-setting for the larger community of states. Indeed, it would be difficult to overlook the major contribution of regional organizations to the evolution of general international environmental law. Mention need only be made of various OECD initiatives, such as Council recommendations or decisions related to the "polluter-pays-principle", equal right of access, or "risk communication". Yet, there are intrinsic limits to the ability of regional organizations to offer precedent-setting environmental legal solutions for global problems. Often, global issues render globally arrived-at solutions simply inevitable.

There are intrinsic limits to the ability of regional organizations to offer precedent-setting environmental legal solutions for global problems.

There is yet another problematical and critically important aspect to the phenomenon of environmental standard—setting at venous levels of territorial organization. The problem is that of legal precedence among conflicting standards, and, specifically, of the interrelationship between local standards that vary from those of the larger communities involved. By and large, treatment of the issue on an international/global level mirrors that at regional, e.g., within the European Community or, at national, levels within federal systems of government. Uniformity, even at the cost of the lowest common denominator, tends to be given preference to acceptance of stricter local or national standards whenever the latter are deemed to restrain national or international trade and to amount to a level of environmental protection that is "disproportionate" to the effect on trade.

It is true that neither GATT's general rules, nor the Tokyo Round's *Subsidy Code*, or *Agreement on Technical Barriers to Trade*, prohibit states from adopting standards that affect the international trade in goods for the bona fide purpose of protecting the local environment. On the other hand, a state's unilateral environmental standard-setting that nullifies or impairs another state's pre-existing trade concession might open the former to claims for compensation even if the standards themselves are found not to violate GATT. For the moment, this provision of GATT remains a dead letter. That might change. In any event, the present Uruguay Round of negotiations on further liberalization of world trade, especially the push for a reduction or elimination of agricultural subsidies, has rekindled justified concerns that multilateral progress in facilitating international trade, may come at the price of eliminating individual states' freedom to set stricter than international minimum standards and thereby endanger local natural resource conservation. Conversely, GATT negotiations could result in a strengthening of the hand of those governments that might seek to impose countervailing duties on imports from countries with liberal or non-existent environmental protection standards, on the grounds that the export of such goods is indirectly subsidizcd.

Conceivably, Peter Sand's conclusion that "it is the trade regime that determines, if not the bottom line, at least the margin of tolerable asymmetries in the EEC's environmental regime" might well come to characterize also global environmental standards. Yet, if, ultimately, economic aspirations must be compatible with the principle of 'sustainable development', very careful attention will have to be paid to the finalization and subsequent application of emerging new GATT, regional, or bilateral trading rules so as to avoid setting up an international regulatory system in which the trade tail wags the environmental dog.

Implementation and Enforcement of International Environmental Law

A first observation concerns the dearth of arrangements for compulsory third-party decision making in environmental disputes. The well-known general resistance of states to submit to third-party decision making may pose a particularly severe threat to the effectiveness of international environmental regimes. International disputes involving environmental problems are as likely to arise over underlying issues of science and technology as over conflicting views on applicable legal principles and detailed norms. Thus, the absence of "in advance agreed to" impartial fact-finding, or, generally speaking, of authoritative third-party decision making can be a significant impediment to full realization of the respective regime s environmental protection objectives.

There are, however, some offsetting factors that must be mentioned here. First, in the decision-making environment characteristic of some of the regimes described above, a prime example of which is the ozone protection layer regime, in which formal legal criteria might be disregarded for the sake of pragmatic advancement of the regulatory agenda, the absence of compulsory formal dispute settlement procedures may actually be an advantage...However, any international tribunal or court, might be overtaxed when asked to adjudge the merits of a legal dispute. Measured against formal international legal criteria, some of the decisions that have evolved within these environmental regimes might be found not to meet the test of "legality".

Second, some of these regulatory regimes feature special internal implementation mechanisms based on reporting requirements and review procedures some what akin to supervisory procedures in the field of human rights. For example within the framework of the ECE *Convention on Long-Range Transboundary Air Pollution*, the Protocols on sulphur and nitrogen oxide emissions establish national reporting requirements vis-a-vis the Executive Body for the Convention and provide for the independent calculation of pollutant budgets, transboundary fluxes, and deposition by EMEP, the Cooperative Programme for the Monitoring and Evaluation of the Long-Range Transmission of Air Pollutants in Europe. It is against this database that national responses are being reviewed at annual meetings of the Executive Board and individual states' compliance with obligations under the Protocols is being evaluated. Leaving aside the formal dispute settlement mechanisms of the respective Protocols, this process of verifying compliance is an essential element in the regimes' enforcement mechanisms.

Institutionalized periodic peer review of states' performance is a basic feature also of the *Montreal Protocol*. Article 8 specifically calls upon the parties to consider procedures and institutional mechanisms for determining non-compliance with the Protocol. The 1990 London amendments to the *Montreal Protocol* now establish an "Implementation Committee" which reviews allegations of non-compliance and acts as an initial arbiter in disputes over the implementation of obligations under the Protocol. This approach thus internalizes, at least to some extent, dispute settlement that might otherwise be entrusted to third parties.

A second observation concerns the increasingly important role of nongovernmental organizations (NGOs), in the application and enforcement of international environmental standards. Of course, environmental NGOs, like those working in the field of human rights, have a long history of active participation in international legal decision making. Most notable among these involvements is the gathering and dissemination of environmental information, policy advocacy, and the appraisal of failure or success of policies in the light of avowed public policy objectives.

Against the background of an explosive growth of interest and grass-root political activism regarding international environmental issues, NGO involvement in international decision making related to enforcement of and compliance with international environmental standards, is likely to continue to intensify and expand. Consider, for example, the emerging international regime on the transboundary movement of hazardous waste Experience shows that, at the national level, controlling movement of hazardous wastes is notoriously difficult, notwithstanding relatively strict reporting requirement and elaborate monitoring and policing efforts. On the international level, these difficulties are bound to be significantly greater. Thus, although the *Basel Convention* establishes a formal procedure for the verification of compliance and leaves room for the establishment of subsidiary bodies to assist in this task, the Convention's effectiveness may ultimately turn on various informal monitoring and verification processes involving non-state actors. In the past, NGOs have been key players in the tracking of hazardous waste exports, and in alerting both would-be importing countries and the international public of illegal or unsound waste disposal plans and operations. Clearly, NGO input in the international system of supervision thus can be expected to be an indispensable factor in rendering the *Basel Convention* an effective regime.

Private enforcement of environmental legal standards through "citizen suits" is an essential component in the effectiveness of domestic law. An analogous enhancement of the status of NGOs on the transnational environmental plane therefore might be highly desirable. NGOs, it has recently been suggested, could "actually be appointed to perform inspections or serve even as expert mediators or arbitrators of disputes".

While a few environmental NGOs have formal consultative stands with international organizations and some more may have observer status on specific international bodies entrusted with environmental matters, NGOs continue to suffer from limited access to environmental decision-making bodies in the transnational arena. As a minimum, existing relationships between international organizations and NGOs, therefore, ought to be expanded and formalized so as to allow for a more effective NGO input in the international environmental decision making process which would most likely benefit the quality of the decision outcome.

Directly related is a third observation that regards empowerment at local level. By now it is almost a truism that, as the conclusions of the *Siena Forum* note "environmental protection begins at the local level." Protection of internationally sensitive natural resources, including the global commons, depends on support at local level. This "think globally, act locally" maxim, however, can only be realized if citizens have access to pertinent environmental information as well as to relevant environmental decision-making forums.

Traditionally, international legal efforts had focused on ensuring access by individuals, potentially or actually affected by injurious transboundary activities, to foreign decision-making forums on a basis of equality with nationals of the foreign State concerned. More recently, the international regulatory focus has begun to expand beyond the limited transboundary context to environmental empowerment of citizens in general. For example, a 1989 OECD Council Decision commits member countries to ensure local hazard communication: the public must be provided with and have access to pertinent information about local industrial hazards. The Decision also obliges Member States to ensure the affected public of an opportunity to participate in decisions concerning hazardous installations and the development of community emergency preparedness plans. The *European Council Directive on Freedom of Access to Information on the Environment* goes a significant step beyond the OECD Decision by establishing a general obligation for Member States to make environmental information held by public authorities available to any person. Finally, the *World Charter of Nature* endorses a general or broadly conceived right of individuals to be involved in decisions bearing on the environment. Article 23 stipulates that "[a]ll persons...shall have the opportunity to participate, individually or with others, in the formulation of decisions of direct concern to their environment...". Although the Article does not amount to an unqualified endorsement of local environmental empowerment, it signals recognition in principle of the fundamental importance of extending participatory democracy to local and national environmental decision-making processes to ensure success at protecting the global ecological system as a whole.

The Changing Nature and Scope of States' Entitlement to the Use of Environmental Resources

The Precautionary Principle

State Autonomy and Significant Transboundary Risk

The self-evident truth that an ounce of prevention is better than a pound of cure, has for sometime now been reflected in the international law related to the environment, even though unto this day the notion has persisted that customary international law does not yet include such an obligation. The evolution of a duty of prevention can be traced from its conceptual origin in the venerable Trail Smelter decision, all the way to the International Law Commission's focus on prevention in its work on the liability topic. Evidence of state practice supportive of the existence, in principle. of a customary international legal duty to prevent transboundary harm, includes such relatively early multilateral environmental treaties as the *Baltic Sea Convention*, the 1974 Paris *Convention for the Protection of Marine Pollution from Land-Based Resources* and the 1982 *United Nations Law of the Sea Convention,* quite apart from more recent multilateral environmental regimes.

The obligation concerned is one of due diligence and requires a state to abstain from conduct that carries a significant risk of harm. It is an obligation that has several procedural companion-elements, namely the duty of prior information and of consultation. By now, both these obligations have become part of customary international law. A third procedural obligation, namely to analyze the risk of transboundary environmental impact, is, logically speaking, a necessary appendix of the obligations of prior information and consultation. However, the life of the law has seldom been logic, but experience. International acknowledgement of the intimate relationship among these procedural obligations—all of them reared towards prevention of significant transboundary environmental harm—and concomitant acceptance that transboundary environmental assessment, as much as prior information and consultation, would be required under international law, has not been clearly reflected in the practice of states. However, in light of recent state practice, including finalization of an ECE draft *Convention on Environmental Impact Assessment in Transboundary Context,* which is to be adopted in early 1991, as well as recent national legislative developments, it will be increasingly difficult to maintain that states are not (yet) obliged under customary international law to assess potential transboundary effects.

An essential aspect of precautionary environmental policy, then, is the taking of remedial action even in the absence of provable environmental harm, simply upon evidence of a significant risk thereof. This is, of course, the approach that inspires the international ozone layer regime. On the other hand, in the context of, for example, the North American acid rain problem, while Canada proposed that the United States take specific remedial action as required under international law, the US government invoked "scientific uncertainty regarding 'traceability' and thus 'redressability' of pollutant emissions" as a reason for non-compliance.

Today, it should be axiomatic that the greater the risk of harm threatened, the lower the evidentiary burden concerning source-specific causal linkage and injurious transboundary environmental impact. Obviously, only such a conceptual starting point is appropriate in addressing the global warming issue or in attempting to ensure biological security. It is not surprising, therefore, that the Ministerial Declaration adopted at the *Bergen Conference on Sustainable Development*, focuses attention on this crucial aspect of precautionary action: "Environmental measures must anticipate, prevent and attack the causes of environmental degradation." It goes on to emphasize that "[w]here there are threats of serious or irreversible damage, lack of full scientific certainty should not be used as a reason for postponing measures to prevent environmental degradation." By the same token, the parties to the *Third International Conference of the North Sea*, in committing themselves to apply the "precautionary principle", pledged "to take preventive action...even when there is no scientific evidence to prove a causal link between emissions and effects."

"Precautionary Action" as a General International Canon of Environmental Conduct?

These and other recent references to precautionary action have encouraged advocacy of a "precautionary principle" as a basic restraint on environmentally sensitive action generally. Indeed, state practice, resolutions of international organizations, and other pertinent indicia point to the emergence of community expectations that, at least as a matter of basic international policy, activism potentially affecting the environment be subject to restraint. Three general notions underlie these emerging expectations. First, although precautionary action is advocated as an international standard of conduct, its application is not limited to transboundary risks of harm, but instead reaches environmentally sensitive activities generally, i.e., irrespective of a direct transnational impact potential. Second, restraint is advocated not just in face of present and clear danger to environmental resources but as a corollary of our inherently limited knowledge of the ecological implications of human activities through time and space. Third, "precautionary action" implies a broad, systemic approach to global environment management. The "react and correct model" of international environmental legislation must, as the conclusions of the *Siena Forum* emphasize, [must] be complemented by a "forecast and prevent approach".

Notwithstanding the relative clarity of these notions, at present the precautionary principle is not a term of art. The principle's exact political and, *a fortiori* legal implications remain "elusive". One reason for this is the fact that postulations of precautionary action evince also a strong undercurrent of preservationist concerns. It must remain open to doubt, therefore, whether, ambiguous as it is, as a broadly defined concept, the "precautionary principle" can evolve into an effective international canon of environmental conflict. On the other hand, there is no denying that international environmental law already addresses some of the concerns epitomized in the principle of precautionary action, such as the call for restraint on state autonomy in creating significant risks of transboundary environmental harm, or for conserving biological diversity of the planet. By the same token, a limited number of general maxims of environmental action such as adoption of "best available pollution control technology", "controlling pollution at the source", or the setting of reasonable margins of safety in environmental policy making which are basic ingredients of precautionary environmental action, appear to be well on their way to becoming part of the customary international law of the environment.

Sustainable Development/Intergenerational Equity

Sustainable development might be defined as "development that meets the needs of the present without compromising the ability of future generations to meet their own needs. This concept of living off nature's "income", rather than squandering its "capital", is a key tenet of the report of the World Commission on Environment and Development, and has since been supported by a number of decisions of the United Nations or other international organizations, agencies within the UN system, and various conferences of states. It is thus fast becoming the basic criterion against which international or transnational environmental initiatives and, increasingly so, ostensibly merely "local" environmental activities are being evaluated politically.

Its potential normative reach is narrower than that of "precautionary action". "Sustainable development" envinces a strictly utilitarian view of environmental protection: it imposes restraints on developmental activities only in so far as these would undermine the environmental basis for further development in the long run. Indeed, "sustainable development" is non-preservationist; it reflects a commitment to promote development, albeit of a special qualitative nature. This perspective, in contrast to the no-growth strands that are part of the complex policy fabric of the precautionary principle, makes "sustainable development" internationally a broadly attractive concept. Not surprisingly, it has thus turned out to be a notion around which legally significant expectations regarding environmental conduct have begun to crystallize. Indeed, before long the concept might turn into mandatory standard of international legal evaluation, a peremptory norm of international law.

The reasons for such a possible ascendancy are intuitively persuasive "Sustainable development" is a *conditio sine qua non* for human life on this planet in the long run. It stands to reason, therefore, that other legal arrangements would have to measure up to the principle. "Sustainability" thus would safeguard not simply individual state interests but act as a restraint in "the higher interest of the whole international community" in preserving the ecological basis for human civilization.

To ascribe *jus cogens* character to the objective of "sustainable development", however, tends to highlight the special problems any peremptory norm raises in the co-hierarchical and decentralized decision-making process of the international legal system. Without authoritative third-party decision making, conflicting claims about the concept's specific normative implications will abound and disputes over application will be exceedingly difficult to resolve. This will be all the more so because "needs" will vary from country to country, and the consistency of state conduct with "sustainable development" will thus depend on context."

For the moment, in any event, the concept per se poses a more preliminary, i.e., fundamentally definitional, problem. Thus, while the prospect of "sustainable development" eventually gaining *jus cogens* status cannot be ruled out, it is difficult to see how the concept could be readily operationalized. To begin with, the concept suffers from internal tension: "Sustainable development" as an international policy or legal concept, clearly implies some measure of international accountability, yet, as generally endorsed, it is also accompanied by an express disclaimer of any intended encroachment upon state sovereignty. The initial challenge, therefore, will be to reach a clear international understanding on pathways to sustainable development and [a clear] agreement on the specific markers that lead to that goal.

Notwithstanding increasingly frequent affirmations of "sustainable development" as a cardinal principle of international environmental decision making, we are still at a very early stage of this task. Recent calls for "sustainable development practices" as, for example, in the Bergen Ministerial Declaration, by the Council of Europe's Parliamentary Assembly, or the Interparliamentary Conference on the Global Environment, are couched in fairly abstract and general terms. On the other hand, the list of criteria developed within the UN Centre on Transnational Corporations, as well as, for example, the 1989 OECD *Council Recommendation Concerning an Environmental Checklist for Development Assistance*, or the World Bank's *Environmental Assessment Operational Directive*, provide more specific guidance to decision makers at corporate management, national governmental, or international organizational levels.

Irrespective of the concept's international normative weakness at the moment, it is evident that "sustainable development" is shaping environmental policy debates in a fundamental way. More significantly, it has begun to act as a de facto constraint on environmental decision makers both internationally as well as domestically.

The conceptual or philosophical underpinning of this emerging obligation to reorient natural resource use towards sustainability, is the notion of intergenerational equity. The idea that present generations accept restraints on their use of natural resources for the benefit of future generations has attracted overwhelming international support ever since the Maltese proposal of a "common heritage of mankind" to the United Nations General Assembly in 1967. States have expressly re-endorsed the principle of intergenerational responsibility ever since it was first formally adopted by a conference of states in the 1972 *Stockholm Declaration*.

Today, few could thus deny that the concept of intergenerational responsibility is a fundamental tenet of international public policy. Rather, if there is a debate about the concept per se, it will be, first, over whether the obligations of restraint emanating from the concept are of an international legal, rather than of a merely moral nature; and, second, whether they arise vis-a-vis future generations for which the present generation holds the planet in trust or, whether they are obligations of conduct on behalf of future generations that members of the present generation owe each other directly.

As indicated above, the twin notion of "sustainable development" appears close to becoming an international legal standard for the evaluation of state conduct bearing on the environment. It appears also to be the one that would be more readily acceptable from an ideological viewpoint. As regards the second issue, the normative basis of obligations for intergenerational responsibilities, it is evident that the protection or insulation of norms guaranteeing sustainable development or fairness to future generations against unwarranted changes or tampering by members of the present generation ought to be a matter of concern. But, as to the quality of protection provided, it is not self-evident which conceptual basis would he more effective. In any event, and whatever the underlying philosophical justification for sustainability obligations, Lothar Gundling reminds us that "without equity within the present generation, we will not be able to achieve equity among generations".

D

North-South and Sovereignty Issues

(i) Handl G., "Environmental Security and Global Change: The Challenge to International Law," in Lang W., *et al.* (eds), *Environmental Protection and International Law*, Graham and Trotman, 1991, pp 83–87

The North-South Issue

Against the backdrop of the existing North-South divide, one of the most contentious issues in international standard-setting for globally sensitive environmental resources is the question of incentives to poor countries. Protection of such resources typically will require widespread, if not universal, international cooperation, thus rendering Third World participation essential to securing the environmental objectives of the regimes concerned. Traditionally, Third World aid demands and, conversely, grants and concessions by developed countries, had been viewed in terms of a moral obligation of donor countries to redress past wrongs of colonialism or to respond to calls for international solidarity. Now, with international concern over the conservation of internationally sensitive natural resources on a sharp rise, developing countries have begun to insist publicly that conservation measures—they are being asked to undertake locally—be paid for by developed nations. Thus, development assistance in general, and selective treaty incentives to developing countries in particular, have become the focus of an entitlement reinterpretation. A peak in this development thus far has been the debate accompanying the diplomatic drive to increase state participation in the ozone layer protection regime. Another high point will probably be reached when negotiations begin in earnest on an international convention on climate change.

There is no denying that, more often than not, incentives to encourage developing country participation in global environmental regimes are justified as a matter of fundamental international equity. International regulations, for example, for the protection of the ozone layer or of climate stability, tend to become necessary because past uses and abuses of the environment have created an environmental crisis situation. While the benefits of such regulations, in terms of mitigation or avoidance of harm, might be spread among developing and developed nations alike, the costs of compliance would weigh more heavily on developing countries. More importantly, while developed nations would be asked to pay up belatedly for globally experienced or threatened environmental costs associated with their economic and social development, developing nations whose contribution to the problem might be minor are asked to share the burden of controls without having derived comparable compensating socioeconomic benefits. Finally, international regulations deemed necessary to protect critical global resources, may preempt developing nations from exercising what might have been their "natural" development options.

There is no denying that, more often than not, incentives to encourage developing country participation in global environmental regimes are justified as a matter of fundamental international equity.

It can be hardly surprising, therefore, that in such a situation, developing countries should insist on compensatory and/or technical incentives in exchange for support of international regulatory restrictions. Indeed, if a Third World country incurs opportunity costs by foregoing a natural development option to preserve environmental resource that are of global interest of special interest to other states, it should be recognized as entitled to compensation. The fact that restraint would also be in the long-term interest of the developing country itself should not detract from compensation as a matter of right. For such claims for compensation merely amount to a vindication of the principle of equitable utilization, a principle long recognized as a basic legal tenet that underlies the use of internationally shared natural resources.

The moral, political, and, ultimately, legal persuasiveness of claims by developing countries to financial or technical assistance in protecting resources of global significance, are foreshadowed in the declarations adopted at the UN Environmental Conferences in Stockholm in 1972 and in Nairobi in 1982. Since then, the basic international consensus on support measures for developing countries' environmental efforts has matured into a strong conviction about international burden-sharing with regard to the preservation of internationally sensitive environmental resources. Thus, innovative financial assistance arrangements, such as debt-for-conservation swaps, international debt forgiveness strategies, and the proposal for a Global Environmental Facility, as well as numerous formal and informal declarations by conferences of states, etc., all testify to growing recognition of the legitimacy of developing countries' claims.

At an international regulatory level, the change in the entitlement perspective can be seen in specific concessions granted to developing countries. Thus Article 5 of the *Montreal Protocol* invites parties to undertake to facilitate access by developing countries to alternative technology as well as to provide them with financial assistance for the use of alternative technology and for substitute products. At the Second Meeting of the Parties to the Protocol, finally, agreement was reached on an international financial mechanism in fulfilment of the mandate of Article 5.

Environmental interdependence, as reduced in the need to enlist the cooperation of key developing countries in order to ensure the success of international regimes for the protection of globally sensitive natural resources, thus, may be a turning-point in North–South relations. Unlike the postulation of a "new economic order" in the 1970s, presently proposed strategies to counter the threat to global environmental security may lead to the empowerment of developing countries. By forcing developed countries squarely to face the effects of underdevelopment on global environmental protection objectives, developing countries might succeed in shedding their traditionally marginal roles as international actors. In any event, the new dialogue and evolving patterns of North-South cooperation can only work to the benefit of the community of states as a whole.

Redefining Sovereignty

Any student of transnational environmental issues will readily acknowledge that the nature and scope of state sovereignty or autonomy is undergoing dramatic change. Across-the-board, decision-making powers on matters that hitherto had been exclusively in the national domain are increasingly shared with other states or have completely devolved upon the international community at large.

This process is at work also with regard to "local" natural resources management. Its focal point is an increasingly restrictive interpretation of the classic international entitlement rule which-absent special circumstances-limits states' autonomy only in the sense of enjoining domestic environmental practices from causing transboundary harm or posing a significant risk thereof.

Restrictions on state autonomy are hinted at in concepts such as "inter-generational equity", "sustainable development", or "common concern of mankind." Notwithstanding frequent disclaimers, all of these notions have been invoked authoritatively to intimate limits on nation-states' freedom of action for the sake of protecting the larger community interest at stake. Together they provide a conceptual platform from which the international community advances its claim to review or participate in certain national decision-making processes related to internationally sensitive environmental resources, irrespective of their location or the presence of direct or immediate transnational environmentally harmful effects.

Whether a certain matter is or is not solely within the domestic jurisdiction of a state is, as the Permanent Court of Justice noted [in 1923], "an essentially relative question; it depends upon the development of international relations". By this standard, the protection of globally sensitive natural resources is a matter of legitimate international concern. However, it is equally clear that general acquiescence in expressions of international concern over local environmental management is one thing; states' acceptance of specific international normative standards and rules that might impose severe limits on natural resource policies locally, is quite another. Frequent allegations of foreign interference with national environmental decision making or the reiteration of a "sovereign right to administer freely [national] natural resources" are reminders of the extreme sensitivity of the "internationalization process". Still, as vehement as some of these objections may be, in the final analysis, they represent rearguard action by defenders of an anachronistic view of national sovereignty.

It is well to remember that state sovereignty is a functional concept. Territorial sovereignty, Max Huber noted in the *Island of Palmas* case, "serves to divide between nations the space upon which human activities are employed, in order to assure them at all points the minimum of protection of which international law is the guardian". Today the rights that emanate from the concept of sovereignty, are not, as Philipp Allott reminds us, unfettered freedoms but powers shared between the holder of the power and the community of states. In other words sovereignty signals no longer a simple *status negativus*, a legal basis for exclusion, but has become the legal basis for inclusion, or of a commitment to cooperate for the good of the international community at large: *souverainete oblige.*

(ii) Koh T., "North–South Relations: Conflict and Cooperation," in *The Quest for World Order: Perspectives of a Pragmatic Idealist,* The Institute of Policy Studies, Times Academic Press, 1997, pp 58–63

Beyond the North–South Divide

Until about ten years ago, international relations was dominated by the East–West confrontation. Over the past decade, a different confrontation has emerged. The relationship between the developing countries and the developed countries had become increasingly acrimonious. The dialogue between the North, representing the developed countries and the South, representing the developing countries is often confrontational. The purpose of my talk tonight is to try to explain the political and economic significance of the negotiations between these two groups of countries.

The Developing Countries

There are about 110 developing countries. They vary considerably in size, in wealth and in the levels of their economic development. A handful of developing countries, i.e., some of the oil-exporting countries, are extremely rich. The three countries with the highest GNP per capita income in the world are Kuwait, Qatar, and the United Arab Emirates. There is another group of countries which have made considerable strides in their economic development. These include Brazil, Argentina, Mexico, South Korea, Taiwan, Malaysia, the Philippines, Thailand, and Singapore. The great majority of the developing countries are, however, extremely poor. There are 19 countries whose GNP per capita income is between US$500 and US$875. There are 30 countries whose per capita income is between US$875 and US$1,425. The great majority of the people in the majority of the developing countries live in dire poverty. They have barely enough food to eat. They rarely have enough potable water. Health conditions are extremely inadequate. When work is available, the pay is usually low and the conditions are often deplorable. Malnutrition, illiteracy, disease, a high birth rate, employment, underdevelopment and low income are their constant companions.

Human Solidarity

Do the richer people in your society and mine have a duty to help those who are poorer? The answer, undoubtedly, is "Yes". What is the moral basis of this duty? The moral basis of this duty is human solidarity. In the same way, I would argue, that because of human solidarity, the richer moral [have a] duty to help the poorer nations. I cannot, therefore, accept the argument of the Soviet Union and her East European allies that because they did not exploit the developing countries in the past, they therefore do not have a duty to help them.

Apart from the human solidarity, there are other sound economic reasons for helping the developing countries. In the last few years, the world economy has been in a slump due to rampant inflation and to the slowdown in or stagnation of the economies of the West. If the developed countries can inject more dynamism into the economies of the developing countries, this will increase their purchasing power which will have a tonic effect on the economies in the West and on the world economy. Secondly, some of the causes of the present economic crisis stem from structural deficiencies. In order to cure these structural deficiencies in the world economic system, it is necessary for the developed and the developing countries to work together. This is the rationale for the proposed global economic negotiations.

I would now like to say a few words about the agenda of the global economic negotiations currently under discussion at the UN. The agenda will consist of five major areas. These are raw materials, trade, development, energy, money, and finance.

Global Economic Negotiations at the UN

Raw Materials

In the area of raw materials, the North–South negotiations have led to some concrete achievements in the last few years. At the Fourth UN Conference on Trade and Development, held in Nairobi in 1976, the developing countries proposed an Integrated Programme for Commodities. The purpose of an integrated program was to strengthen the markets, as well as to stabilize the prices, of 26 commodities of interest to the developing countries. The way in which this would be done would be to maintain buffer stocks of the 16 commodities. By selling the buffer stocks when prices are going up and buying them when prices are going down, it is hoped that the fluctuation of commodity prices will stabilize. A Common Fund of about US$6 billion was proposed as the centerpiece of the Integrated Programme for Commodities. The idea was that the Common Fund would lend money to enable the managers of the 16 commodity buffer stocks to buy when the prices of the commodities are falling. The loans from the Common Fund would be offset by income derived from the sale of buffer stocks.

The areas of energy, on the one hand, and money and finance, on the other, are closely interrelated.

After more than four years of intensive negotiations, the articles of agreement on the Common Fund were adopted in June 1980. The negotiations on the Common Fund were closely linked to the negotiation of a series of individual commodity agreements or arrangements. So far, commodity agreements have been concluded on tin, coffee, cocoa, sugar and rubber. Preparatory meetings have been held on copper, cotton, tea, jute, hard fibres, vegetable oils, bananas, meat and tropical timber.

The dialogue between the developed and developing countries in the area of raw materials includes the question of the participation of developing countries in the trade, transportation, marketing and distribution of their commodities and raw materials. It also includes the question of local processing and storage of commodities and raw materials produced by developing countries.

Trade

Turning from raw materials to trade, the questions for negotiation include access for the exports of developing countries to markets in the developed countries and the twin problems of protectionism and structural adjustment.

Development

In the area of development, several specific questions are involved. First, there is the question of what positive adjustment policies and incentives the developed countries can adopt to facilitate the industrialization of the developing countries. What we mean by "positive adjustment policies and incentives" is that the developed countries would adopt policies to phase out their obsolete and uncompetitive industries; that they would help the affected industries to diversify to or to specialize in areas in which the developed countries maintain a comparative economic advantage over the developing countries, as well as to adopt programs to retrain the workers and to cushion the adverse social consequences resulting from the restructuring of their industries. The second question is what measure can be adopted to support the transfer of technology to developing from developed countries, including the adaptation and application of such technology. The third question concerns measures to enhance and improve the transfer of resources from developed to developing countries for the purpose of promoting economic development.

Energy, Money, and Finance

The areas of energy, on the one hand, and money and finance, on the other, are closely interrelated. The industrialized countries wish to have assurances of regular and adequate supplies of energy at predictable prices. The developed countries also wish to minimize disruptive movements in financial markets. The oil-exporting countries wish to safeguard the real value of their exports and their financial reserves. They also wish to avoid an excessively rapid depletion of their non-renewable resources.

Thirdly, the oil-exporting countries wish to have technological support for their economic development from the developed countries, particularly in sectors of their economy which are based upon hydrocarbons. Finally, all countries, whether oil-exporting or oil-importing, whether developed or developing, have an interest in ensuring that the financial balances generated in the energy sector help to stabilize and not disrupt the international financial and monetary system.

Conclusion

I shall conclude my remarks on the North–South dialogue by asserting the following propositions. First, human solidarity requires that the richer nations should help poorer nations just as in our individual nations, the rich are required to help the poor through progressive income tax and other social measure. Secondly, I cannot accept the thesis of the Soviet Union that it has no moral duty to help the developing countries because it did not exploit them in the past. Since the duty to help is based upon human solidarity, I would like to see the communist countries of Eastern Europe participate more actively in the process of re-ordering international economic relations. Thirdly, by helping the developing countries, the developed countries are indirectly helping themselves because if the developing countries have greater purchasing power, this would be used to purchase technology, food, and brain services from the developed countries.

Fourthly, if the developing countries succeed in growing at a more rapid pace, this will have a positive effect on the expansion of the world economy which will benefit all countries, including the developed countries. Fifthly, the present world economic crisis is due, in part, to structural deficiencies in the world economic system. To cure these structural deficiencies, it is necessary for developed and developing countries work together. This is the logic behind the proposal of the developing countries for global economic negotiations. These negotiations should adopt an integrated approach as opposed to a sectoral approach. The negotiation should look at the measures which are necessary in the short, medium and long terms. The negotiations should focus on specific issues and problems in five broad areas: raw materials, trade, development, energy, money, and finance. The negotiations should avoid polemics and rhetorics, and should focus on finding solutions to problem which are economically sound and morally equitable.

Finally, I think I should say a word about the duty of the developing countries in the context of the New International Economic Order. I believe that the primary responsibility for their economic development rests upon the developing countries themselves. No amount of external assistance can transform a developing country into a developed country if it is not prepared to help itself. What do I mean by a developing country helping itself? By this, I mean several things. A developing country should inculcate [in the] population the values and social attitudes which will promote economic development. For example, the government should inculcate in its people the values of hard work and thrift. The government should have the political courage to ensure that the growth of its population does not exceed the growth of its economy. It must channel its resources into productive rather than consumptive ends, and practise fiscal responsibility and live within its means. The government must ensure that the fruits of economic development are equitably distributed to all sections of the population. Politicians and civil servants should be free of corruption. If a developing country follows this recipe, it will have a good chance of succeeding in its economic development.

The goal of building a New International Economic Order can only be achieved through action at the international and at the national level. Developing countries must avoid the mistake of thinking that cooperation at the international level can substitute for the needed sacrifices and hard work at the national level. It cannot be done. Our dream of a more prosperous and more equitable world can only be realized if all of us are prepared to work hard at home and to develop the habit of consultation and cooperation at the international level. The growing inter-dependence of our economies make global economic cooperation an imperative of our time.

4

Institutionalizing Sustainability

A

Boer B., "Institutionalizing Ecologically Sustainable Development: The Roles of National, State, and Local Governments in Translating Grand Strategy into Action," 31 *Willamette Law Review*, 1995, pp 312–333

The Problem of Unsustainability

Some modern analysts argue that the earth has reached its human capacity limit. In some countries, unsustainability is more obvious because of higher levels of pollution, mortality rates, and resource depletion. Consequently, unsustainability can remain "hidden" longer in wealthier countries. In its guide to sustainable development strategies, the IUCN [in its *Strategies Handbook*] has pointed some of the main problems associated with unsustainability:

(1) Rising human numbers and consumption of resources: Since the industrial revolution, human numbers have grown eightfold. Water withdrawals have grown from 100 to 3,600 cubic kilometers a year. The 5.3 billion people now on Earth use 40 percent of its most elemental resource: the energy from the sun made available by green plants on land.

(2) Poverty: More than a billion people live in poverty. One person in five cannot get enough food to support an active working life. One quarter of the world's people are without safe drinking water. Every year, millions of children die from malnutrition and preventable disease.

(3) Resource depletion: In less than 200 years, the planet has lost six million square kilometers of forest. An estimated 60,000-70,000 square kilometers of agricultural land is made unproductive by erosion each year. The sediment load from soil erosion has risen threefold in major river basins and by eight times in smaller, more intensively used ones.

(4) Pollution: Human inputs of nutrients into coastal waters already equal natural sources. Human-caused emissions of many heavy metals now range from double those from natural sources (for example, arsenic and mercury) to five and even 18 times higher than natural rates (cadmium and lead respectively).

(5) Global climate change: The climate regime to which people and other forms of life have long been adapted is threatened by human impact on the atmosphere. Since the mid-18th century, human activities have more than doubled the methane in the atmosphere, increased the concentration of carbon dioxide by 27 percent, and significantly damaged the stratospheric ozone layer.

(6) Debt: The combined cumulative debt of lower-income countries is more than $1 trillion, and interest payments alone have reached $60 billion per year. As a result, since 1984 there has been a net transfer of capital from lower-income to upper-income countries. Nonetheless, many upper-income countries also run substantial deficits.

Interpretations of Sustainable Development

The international instruments agreed to at the Rio Conference incorporate the concept of sustainable development. The concept is rapidly evolving as an environmental mandate for the world. A number of countries have incorporated sustainable development strategies into their environmental legislation. Various private and intergovernmental organizations are beginning to embrace the concept, as well. It is therefore vital that policymakers understand the concept and its application.

Over the past few years, sustainable development has been interpreted in a variety of ways. *Our Common Future* defines sustainable development as "development that meets the needs of the present without compromising the ability of future generations to meet their own needs." This definition can be criticized because it invites narrow interpretations such as "sustainable economic development," without explicitly requiring concern for or focus on the continued viability of ecosystems. *Caring for the Earth* states:

> "The term has been criticized as ambiguous and open to a wide range of interpretations, many of which are contradictory. The confusion has been caused because 'sustainable development', 'sustainable growth' and 'sustainable use' have been used interchangeably, as if their meanings were the same. They are not. 'Sustainable growth' is a contradiction in terms: nothing physical can grow indefinitely. 'Sustainable use' is applicable only to renewable resources: it means using them at rates within their capacity for renewal."

"Sustainable development" is used in this Strategy to mean improving the quality of human life while living within the carrying capacity of supporting ecosystems. A "sustainable economy" is the product of sustainable development. It maintains its natural resource base. It can continue to develop by adapting, and through improvements in knowledge, organization, technical efficiency, and wisdom. However, the definition used in *Caring for the Earth* may also be seen as problematic, as it is arguably anthropocentric and utilitarian in orientation. It casts the environment into a supporting role, viewing it simply as an instrument or resource for the exploitation of humans, with lesser regard for the needs of the natural environment. The Australian government makes the focus of its concern more explicit, by using the term ecologically sustainable development, defining it as "development that improves the total quality of life, both now and in the future, in a way that maintains the ecological processes on which life depends.

In its handbook on the implementation of sustainable strategies, the IUCN states:

> "Sustainable development means improving and maintaining the well-being of people and ecosystems. This goal is far from being achieved. It entails integrating economic, social and environmental objectives, and making choices among them where integration is not possible. People need to improve their relationships with each other and with the ecosystems that support them, by changing and strengthening their values, knowledge, technologies and institutions.
>
> Major obstacles include lack of agreement on what should be done, resistance by interest groups who feel threatened by change, and uncertainty about the costs and benefits of alternatives. Overcoming these obstacles requires continuing public discussion, negotiation and mediation among interest groups, and development of a political consensus."

Sustainable development involves the integration of environmental and developmental aspirations at all levels of decision making. Additionally, sustainable development involves the concepts of intragenerational and intergenerational equity, application of the precautionary principle, the conservation of biological diversity and integrity, and the internalization of environmental costs. These concepts are now briefly examined.

Intergenerational Equity

Intergenerational equity embodies the notion that the present generation holds the earth's resources in trust for future generations. In her book, *In Fairness to Future Generations*, Edith Brown Weiss states:

> "At any given time, each generation is both a custodian or trustee of the planet for future generations and a beneficiary of its fruits. This imposes obligations upon us to care for the planet and gives us certain rights to use it....The proposed theory of intergenerational equity postulates that all countries have an intergenerational obligation to future generations as a class, regardless of nationality. This is necessary because the condition of the planet will have a profound impact on the welfare of our descendants. There is increasing recognition that while we may be able to maximize the welfare of a few immediate successors, we will be able to do so only at the expense of our more remote descendants, who will inherit a despoiled natural and cultural environment. Our planet is finite, and we are becoming increasingly interdependent in using it. Our rapid technological growth ensures that this interdependence will increase. Thus our concern for our own country must, as we extend our concerns into longer time horizons and broader geographic scales, focus on protecting the planetary quality of our natural and cultural environment. This means that, even to protect our own future nationals, we must cooperate in the conservation of natural and cultural resources for all future generations."

The Australian Intergovernmental Agreement on the Environment of 1992 recognizes the concept of intergenerational equity by declaring that "the present generation should ensure that health, diversity and productivity of the environment is maintained or enhanced for the benefit of future generations."

Intergenerational equity raises many questions: How far into the future should we look? What assumptions should we make about the needs of future generations? Further, are we talking only of human generations to which the principle applies?

Intragenerational Equity

Intragenerational equity refers to the idea that people, and arguably other life forms, within a single generation have equal rights to benefit both from the exploitation of resources and from the enjoyment of a clean and healthy environment. Intragenerational equity can be understood in both a national and an international sense. At a national level, it implies equal access to common natural resources, clean air in local airsheds, and clean water in national watercourses and the territorial sea. It also raises the question of government restrictions on the use of private property. At an international level, intragenerational equity implies equitable allocation of international air, water, and marine resources. Biodiversity poses a major conceptual problem here due to collective ownership of resources existing beyond the jurisdiction of any particular country. Although biodiversity questions appear at first sight to be national, the idea of international ownership, or more controversially, the idea that biodiversity of the earth cannot be owned, is a matter that needs to be addressed.

A recent analysis refers to intragenerational equity as "equity between the earth's inhabitants at any one time." The concept means that all people are entitled to basic needs, which may be taken to include a healthy environment, adequate food and shelter, and cultural and spiritual fulfillment. To achieve this, a transfer of wealth and technology from higher to lower income countries may be necessary in many cases. It also implies that wealthier nations in particular must reduce their consumption of material goods, water, and air. The concept of intragenerational equity is obviously fraught with political, economic, social, and practical difficulties.

It should be immediately obvious that if governments are to take intragenerational equity seriously, they must instigate far-reaching changes to the way societies are organized, business operates, and people live.

The Precautionary Principle

The *Rio Declaration* defines the precautionary principle as follows: "Where there are threats of serious or irreversible damage, lack of full scientific certainty shall not be used as a reason for postponing cost-effective measures to prevent environmental degradation." In effect, this means spending intellectual effort, imposing environmental regulation, and allocating financial resources to avoid environmental degradation, even though decision makers are not one-hundred percent certain of the seriousness of the environmental effects of a proposed activity or program. More generally, where there is doubt about the possible consequences of action, a decision should err on the side of caution.

Conservation of Biological Diversity

The conservation of biological diversity is a key element of sustainable development. As stated in the draft National Strategy for the Conservation of Australia's Biological Diversity:

> "Biological diversity is the variety of all life forms—the different plants, animals and microorganisms, the genes they contain and the ecosystems of which they form a part.
>
> Biological resources provide all our food and many medicines and industrial products.
>
> Biological diversity underpins human well-being through the provision of ecological services such as those that are essential for the maintenance of soil fertility and clean, fresh water and air. It also provides recreational opportunities and acts as a source of inspiration and cultural identity."

It is broadly agreed that plant and animal species are being lost through human-caused extinction at a rate which is much higher than the natural, or "background," rate.

The 1992 *Convention on the Conservation of Biological Diversity* addresses in detail the question of biodiversity conservation. The Convention urges the use of in situ conservation where possible (i.e., conserving species in their natural habitat). Ex situ conservation (i.e., conserving species in environments other than their natural habitat, such as botanical gardens or zoos) is seen as less desirable than in situ conservation.

Special measures for the planning and control of development are critical in order to achieve conservation of biological diversity. The use of environmental impact assessment is especially important. A recent Australian case dealing with the continuing disputes over logging practices illustrates these principles. A legal action was brought in 1991 against the National Parks and Wildlife Service, alleging that in its consideration of the granting of a logging license, the Service did not sufficiently take into account the effect of the proposed logging on fauna in the area [*Editors Note: See Leatch v National Parks and*

Wildlife Service (1993) in Chapter 11 Judicial Decisions]. As a result of the case, the relevant legislation was amended to specifically require a fauna impact statement in any development application or approval process where endangered species are likely to be present.

The Internalisation of Environmental Costs

The internalization of environmental costs involves "the creation of economic environments so that social and private views of economic efficiency coincide. It is concerned with structures, reporting mechanisms and tools to achieve this end." In essence, the principle requires that all burdens placed on the environment by a particular activity be taken into account in the decision making process. It also means that previously unquantified costs (e.g., loss of "free" or "public" goods such as clean air or clean water) should be quantified as far as possible, and included in economic calculations about the financial viability of a particular proposed or ongoing activity. In other words, "those who use the public good are forced to pay costs equivalent to the value of their use on others and the opportunities that their actions take from others."

The standard ways in which these costs can be internalized are: regulations prohibiting or controlling actions that cause environmental costs or externalities; pollution charges for quantified amounts of pollution released; the use of leases, licenses, and permits to restrict the permitted range and nature of economic activity; and the use of institutional mechanisms and education to change community attitudes, values, and behavior. None of these strategies seems to be sufficient on its own; however, a combination of them can promote long-term changes to individual and corporate behavior.

Institutionalizing Sustainability at Global, Regional, and National Levels

Integration of Environment and Development in Agenda 21

Chapter 8 of *Agenda 21*, one of the more important sections of the document in terms of legal implementation of sustainable development, addresses the practicalities of integrating environment and development in decision making. It recognizes that governments must make fundamental changes to their processes to put environment and development at the center of economic and political decision making. It urges countries to:

- integrate environment and development at the policy, planning, and management levels;
- adopt a national strategy for sustainable development;
- provide an effective legal and regulatory framework;
- make effective use of economic instruments and market and other incentives;
- establish systems for integrated environmental and economic accounting.

The Development and Minimum Content of Sustainability Law

"Sustainability law" refers to legislation drafted to incorporate the principles of sustainable development. The term is preferable to "sustainable development law" used in *Agenda 21* because the term does not imply that development should necessarily take place, but nevertheless includes that possibility.

Documents such as *Our Common Future* and *Caring for the Earth* make it clear that integration of environmental safeguards and economic decision making, embodied in the concept of sustainable development, is the key to sustainability of resource use and the achievement of environmental conservation. The achievement of sustainability is a complex task, involving a broad range of governmental, community, and industry initiatives. These initiatives must be implemented globally, regionally, nationally, locally, and individually.

The achievement of sustainability is a complex task, involving a broad range of governmental, community, and industry initiatives.

To achieve long-term economic and environmental viability, however, comprehensive institutional and legal changes must be made. As noted in the previous section, *Agenda 21* recognizes that these include the introduction of integrated mechanisms for the generation and implementation of economic and environmental policy, and the enactment of legislation to ensure that policies can be carried out within a consistent and enforceable legal framework. *Agenda 21* recognizes the need for sustainability law to be generated globally. The next few years will see an increasing effort by many countries to enact adequate environmental laws to fulfil the obligations of *Agenda 21* and the various other instruments agreed upon at UNCED.

Caring for the Earth spells out the minimum content of "sustainability law":

The national legal system should provide for:

- the application of the precautionary principle and the use of best available technology, when standards for pollution prevention are set;

- use of economic incentives and disincentives, based on appropriate taxes, charges and other instruments;
- the requirement that all proposed new developments and new policies should be subject to environmental impact assessment;
- the requirement that industries and government departments and agencies be subject to periodic environmental audit;
- effective monitoring, permitting detection of infringements, and adjustment of regulations where necessary; and
- granting public access to EIA assessments, environmental audit data and monitoring results, and to information about the production, use and disposal of hazardous substances.

According to *Caring for the Earth*, penalties must be severe enough to deter noncompliance, and liability systems should recognize economic, ecological, and "intangible" costs, including restoration of damaged ecosystems. The system also should include strict liability for accidents involving hazardous substances, and should include provisions for insurance or other financial indemnification.

Importantly, citizen access to the courts is vital to enforcement of sustainability laws. Nevertheless, government agencies ultimately are responsible for implementing and enforcing environmental law and should be held accountable for their actions. Moreover, corporate directors and officers should be held accountable for the effect of their organizations' activities on the environment. The broad changes required by the adoption of sustainability law clearly must be introduced in legislation and administrative policy within a coherent philosophical and practical framework.

The Role of the Global Environment Facility

Implementation of sustainable development programs requires both adequate administrative machinery and sufficient financial support. *Our Common Future* calls for "new approaches as well as new sources of revenue for financing international action in support of sustainable development." This was also recognized in *Agenda 21* and the other UNCED instruments.

The Global Environment Facility (GEF), originally a three-year pilot program established by the United Nations in 1991, provides grants to developing countries for projects, technical assistance and research, and also allows access to environmentally benign technologies. To qualify for GEF funding, projects must address global, rather than merely local, environmental issues. The GEF focuses on four major environmental problems: global warming, pollution of international waters, destruction of biodiversity, and destruction of the stratospheric ozone layer.

The United Nations Environment Programme, the United Nations Development Programme, and the World Bank jointly oversee the GEF. In 1993, the GEF was restructured into a permanent program, with a governing board composed of a balanced and equitable representation of developing and developed countries. With its proposed $2 billion budget, the GEF can serve as a funding mechanism for the implementation of some of the more recent global environmental conventions.

The Commission on Sustainable Development

The Commission on Sustainable Development was formally established by the Economic and Social Council of the United Nations in February 1993. Representatives from 53 countries comprise the Commission, which strives to maintain an equitable geographic distribution by including thirteen representatives from African states, eleven from Asian states, ten from Latin-American and Caribbean states, six from East European states, and thirteen from Western European and other states. The functions of the Commission are as follows:

(1) to monitor progress in the implementation of *Agenda 21* and activities related to the integration of environmental and developmental goals through the United Nations system. This it will do through analysis and evaluation of reports from all relevant United Nations bodies;

(2) to consider information by governments, particularly in relation to activities to implement *Agenda 21*, concentrating on problems associated with this implementation, for example financial resources and technology transfer;

(3) to review progress in the implementation of commitments contained in *Agenda 21*, including those related to finance and technology transfer;

(4) to review and monitor the United Nations target of 0.7 percent of Gross National Product of developed countries for official development assistance;

(5) to review the adequacy of funding for the objectives of *Agenda 21*;
(6) to receive and analyze input from nongovernment organizations, including the scientific and private sector, in the context of the implementation of *Agenda 21*;
(7) to enhance the dialogue within the United Nations with nongovernment organizations and the independent sector as well as bodies outside the United Nations;
(8) to consider progress in the implementation of environmental Conventions;
(9) to provide recommendations to the United Nations General Assembly through the Economic and Social Council on the implementation of *Agenda 21*;
(10) to consider the results of the review by the Secretary-General of the United Nations of all recommendations of the UNCED Conference for capacity-building programs, information networks, task-forces and other mechanisms to support the integration of environment and development at regional and subregional levels.

The Commission charted a course for future actions in its first annual meeting, held in June 1993. In discussing the degree of involvement of various participants, the Commission also decided to review five "cross-cultural clusters" of *Agenda 21*, as follows:

(1) Critical elements of sustainability: this includes international economic policies, combating poverty, changing consumption patterns, demographic dynamics, and sustainability.
(2) Financial resources and mechanisms.
(3) Education, science, transfer of environmentally sound technologies, cooperation, and capacity building: this involves the consideration in particular of the areas in *Agenda 21* of biotechnology, technology, science, education, and capacity-building.
(4) Decision–making structures: this involves the integration of environment and development in decision making, including the role of environmental law, international institutional arrangements, international legal instruments and mechanisms, and information for decision making.
(5) Roles of major groups: this includes concentration on nongovernment organizations and private sector organizations.

The Commission formulated a five-year plan that emphasized:

- 1994: Health, human settlements and fresh water, toxic chemical,s and hazardous waste;
- 1995: Land, desertification, forests and biodiversity;
- 1996: Atmosphere, oceans, and all seas;
- 1997: An overall review and appraisal of *Agenda 21* and its implementation."

The IUCN, based in Gland, Switzerland, is arguably the most important global environmental organization. Its membership comprises governments, government agencies, and environmental nongovernment organizations. The IUCN has played a significant and influential role in the development of international environmental policy and law.

Since the publication of the World Conservation Strategy in 1980, the IUCN has sponsored a wide range of workshops and programs to develop national strategies for sustainability. In a 1993 Latin American workshop on strategies, the first steps in preparing a strategy were seen to include:

(1) diagnosis of a country's environmental status through an intersectoral analysis including biophysical, socioeconomic, institutional, and legal factors (this is often done through a State of the Environment report or similar document);
(2) establishment of strategy objectives;
(3) training of government staff and key participants in multisectoral strategy development and community-based problem solving and participation.

The IUCN maintains that the purpose of national sustainable development strategies and other multisectoral strategies is to mobilize and focus a society's efforts to achieve sustainable development. It states that:

> "National strategies for sustainability are participatory and cyclical processes of planning and action to achieve economic, ecological, and social objectives in a balanced and integrated manner. NSDSs aim to achieve all three objectives; other strategies for sustainability emphasize one or two of them. The process, in most cases, encompasses the definition of policies and action plans, their implementation, monitoring, and regular review."

In essence, a sustainability strategy must be internalized into all development planning and resource allocation processes by government, the private sector, and nongovernmental organizations throughout the functioning of society.

Integration of Sustainability Strategy into Government Processes

As a "participatory and cyclical process of national planning," a sustainability strategy should be developed by a broad range of parties, including government officials from relevant departments, private sector interests, and representatives of relevant nongovernment organizations. The sustainability strategy process should therefore be integrated within the broader processes of government, particularly developmental and planning mechanisms. There should also be a clear vision of what the benefits of such strategies are and a realistic view of the cost of implementing each aspect of the strategy.

In addition to its integrative aspects, it is important that the strategy include a capacity-building process, including environmental education for the community as well as specific technical training for those who are involved in both the generation and implementation of the strategy. Because governments may change, it is important for the strategy to be developed and accepted by representatives of both government and nongovernment political parties. Responsibility should also be spread over a range of relevant government departments, in order to minimize the possibility of adverse administrative or political changes.

In essence, a sustainability strategy must be internalized into all development planning and resource allocation processes by government, the private sector, and nongovernmental organizations throughout the functioning of society. This can be done effectively only if public participation processes are adequate.

The IUCN's Project and Regional Offices, as well as the IUCN Secretariat and the IUCN Commission on Environmental Strategy and Planning, have been instrumental in instigating and assisting the development of these strategies. Currently, more than sixty national strategies, and dozens of provincial and local strategies, exist in various stages of preparation and implementation. The IUCN is developing a comprehensive database on these strategies, and has produced two volumes of regional reviews of sustainability strategies analyzing each country's progress. The first volume includes countries in South and East Asia; namely Bangladesh, Malaysia, Nepal, Pakistan, Sri Lanka, and the Philippines. The second volume includes overviews of strategies in Africa, including Ethiopia, Guinea-Conakry, Nigeria, Serengeti, Tanzania, Uganda, Zambia, Zimbabwe, and Arid and Semi-Arid Lands of Kenya. Further volumes are anticipated as more progress is made.

The Importance of Public Participation in Strategies for Sustainability

Both *Agenda 21* and the *Rio Declaration* recognize the vital importance of public participation to the achievement of environmental goals...

The nature of this participation is not one of simple "consultation" but a genuine exchange of information and a role in decision making. Participation is a form of partnership implying a long-term commitment. The IUCN places great importance on broad participation in strategies. It states:

> "Sustainable development involves trade-offs between economic, social and ecological objectives. Such trade-offs cannot be determined by "scientific' means alone, no matter how multi-disciplinary. They are value judgments, and therefore "people-centered' approaches to sustainable development strategies are needed. Participation of stakeholder groups is critical for decision making, and for all tasks of the strategy cycle, taking different forms for each task. The result will be a more realistic strategy, with a broader base of knowledge, understanding and commitment from the groups involved, and with better links to promising local initiatives.
>
> The challenge of participation is considerable: "horizontal' participation across sectors and geographic regions has to be complemented by "vertical' participation from national to local levels. Although existing structures and methods for participation are usually weak, it is best to begin by using them. Introducing new elements—participatory inquiry, communications /information and education campaigns, round tables and special committees—is relatively easy and can have great impact. NGOs and local governments can help bring this about. It is a mistake to think that participation is entirely a non-government affair: ultimately,

governments need to find appropriate roles as facilitators in participation, and hence to continually increase the effectiveness of strategies."

The Role of Regional Intergovernmental Groups in Institutionalizing Sustainability

A feature of the UNCED process is the refocusing of work programs of major intergovernmental groups to assist implementation at regional and national levels. In the Asian and Pacific regions, two bodies are important: the United Nations Economic and Social Commission for Asia and the Pacific (ESCAP), which is based in Bangkok, Thailand, and the South Pacific Regional Environment Programme (SPREP), based in Apia, Western Samoa. [*These organizations are also discussed in Chapter 16—Regional Environmental Law Cooperation.*]

5 Example of Problem Method of Teaching International Environmental Law

A

Beckman R., *Introduction to Problem Method of Teaching*, Asia Pacific Centre for Environmental Law (APCEL), National University of Singapore, 1998

This session is intended to introduce the problem method of teaching international environmental law. In the problem method of instruction, students are required to do a substantial amount of preparation prior to the session, and to actively participate in the class discussion. The focus of discussion in the class is on a hypothetical problem. The students are provided with readings which introduce the principles, rules and precedents governing the area of law. In preparation for class, the students are required to apply the principles, rules, and precedents to a hypothetical problem.

When this method of instruction is employed, students are usually asked to "role-play". The instructions can vary. The problem can be framed as a hypothetical case (or moot) before an international tribunal, in which students are required to present legal arguments on behalf of one of the parties in the case. The problem can also be framed as a mediation or negotiation, with several stakeholders or parties.

The problems can also be framed to require students to conduct further research on the problem, and to prepare a written opinion advising one of the parties.

Problem: The Dispute Concerning the Use and Pollution of the White River

1. Alpha and Beta are neighboring countries sharing a common land border. Alpha is a rich developed country which is highly industrialized. Beta is less developed, but possesses a wealth of natural resources. The citizens of Alpha are very environmentally conscious.
2. The White River originates in the mountains of Beta, and flows through both Beta and Alpha on its way to the ocean. Alpha is the lower riparian state. In 1992, Beta granted a license to a local company to build a huge petrochemicals factory on the banks of the White River, 8 kilometer north of the Alpha border. No environmental impact assessment was done prior to construction the factory, as none are required under Beta law. The Government of Alpha was not consulted or notified about the construction of the petrochemical plant. The factory began operation in January 1995.
3. On April 4, 1991, an accident occurred at the factory due to faulty design, causing large amount of toxic chemicals to flow into the White River. On the same day, scientists from Alpha detected a massive increase in the quantities of toxic chemicals in the river at a monitoring station just south of the border with Beta. In addition, citizens in Alpha began to report that large amounts of fish and river life began dying on the same day. On April 8, the Government of Alpha closed fishing and recreational activities on the White River. Unfortunately, the incident occurred at the height of the tourist and fishing season in Alpha.

4. The government of Beta never informed the government of Alpha about the accident. Alpha found out about the accident only through its own intelligence operations, which were set in motion after the scientific monitoring station in Alpha reported a massive increase in toxic chemicals in the river. Intelligence reports in Alpha indicate that the Beta government did conduct an investigation on the same day of the accident, but there were no reports in newspapers in Beta, and there was no announcement of any kind by the Beta Government. After repeated official requests to the Government of Beta for information about the toxic spill, the Beta Government informed the Alpha Ambassador after 5 days (on April 9) that there had been a minor accident at the plant and that it had been investigated, and the investigation had revealed that the accident had caused no serious or long-term damage to the environment. He further stated that he could provide no more information because the investigation was an internal government matter.
5. Scientists in Alpha reported that the massive increase in toxic chemicals from the factory began to decrease after 6 days, and that the level of toxic chemicals returned to normal after 10 days. Normal recreational activities on the river in Alpha were resumed after 14 days, but the Alpha government has not allowed fishing activities to continue until its scientists complete a study to determine whether there are any long-term effects on the living resources of the river, including the shell fish. Alpha has been having difficulty completing this study, as its scientists have reported that they still do not know exactly what chemicals were spilled into the river, and that it is therefore extremely difficult to determine the long-term effects on the ecosystem of the river. The petrochemical factory in Beta has been closed since the incident, but is apparently making plans to resume operations.
6. In 1993, before the factory was built, the Minister of Environment of Beta had reassured the environmental groups in Beta to the following effect: "We will take all necessary precautions to ensure that the operations of the petrochemical factory shall not pollute the environment, especially the White River. We undertake to compensate anyone who can show any damage to their interests arising from the activities of the factory."
7. Both Alpha and Beta have signed the Stockholm and *Rio Declarations*. They are both parties to the Statute of the International Court of Justice. They are not parties to any other relevant treaty.

Directions

1. Assume the following. Alpha and Beta have agreed to submit the dispute to a Special Tribunal at the NUS Faculty of Law, and has asked the tribunal to decide the case according to the rules and principles of general international law. The *compromis* asks the tribunal to decide the following two legal questions:
   - Whether Beta is internationally responsible and liable to Alpha for the damage caused to the environment of Alpha and to its citizens as a result of the accident at the petrochemical plant in Beta, and if so, what remedies are appropriate;
   - Whether Beta's decision to license the construction and operation of the petrochemical factory without requiring an EIA and without consulting the Government of Alpha, and its failure to immediately notify and consult Alpha after the accident, were in violation of its international legal obligations to Alpha, and if so, what remedies are appropriate;
2. Students/participants should divide themselves into 4 teams—Alpha 1, Alpha 2, Beta 1 and Beta 2. Alpha 1 will prepare a written outline of legal arguments on behalf of Alpha on the first issue, Alpha 2 will prepare a written outline of legal arguments on behalf of Alpha on the second issue. Beta 1 will prepare a written outline of legal arguments on behalf of Beta on the first issue, and Beta 2 will prepare a written outline of legal arguments on behalf of Beta on the second issue. Each team should appoint one member of its team to serve as its advocate. The advocate will have 10 minutes in class to outline the key arguments on his issue to the tribunal, which shall be comprised of resource persons.

6

Policy Questions for Discussion

(a) What is "soft law" and what do you think of its effectiveness?

(b) Can trade restrictions enforce environmental agreements? See also Chapter 15. Is this usage consistent with international trade law and the GATT? Compare the *Montreal Protocol* with CITES in regard to treatment of imports or exports from states not party to the agreement.

(c) Consider the process by which customary international law may be codified in treaties through evidence of state practice and the binding nature of legal obligations on states. Where does "soft law" fit into this traditional lawmaking process on the international level? Has the practice changed in regard to multilateral environmental agreements?

(d) Should international environmental law treaties prohibit all reservations? Is it preferable to have more states parties to weaker treaties, by allowing reservations which may affect obligations under the treaty? Or is it preferable to have a strong treaty at the cost of fewer states parties or the absence of a major state whose interests or practice is important to the subject matter of the treaty?

(e) Is "sustainable development" a general principle of international law or customary international law? Is equity? Or the precautionary principle?

(f) Has Principle 21 of the *Stockholm Declaration* on the Human Environment crystallized into a principle of customary international law binding on states?

7

References for Chapter 17

Allot P., "Power Sharing in the Law of the Sea," 77 *AJIL* 1, 1983.

Austin J. *The Province of Jurisprudence Determined*, Noonday, New York, 1954.

Australian Government, *National Strategy for the Conservation of Australia's Biological Diversity*, Australian Government Printing Service, 1994.

"Bergen Ministerial Declaration on Sustainable Development in the ECE Region," in *Yearbook of International Law*, pp 753, 1990.

Brown-Weiss E., *In Fairness to Future Generations*, Dobbs Ferry, New York, 1989.

Carew-Reid J., *et.al.*, *Strategies for National Sustainable Development: A Handbook for Their Planning and Implementation*, 17 IUCN, IIED, Earthscan, 1994.

Convention on the Law of Treaties between States and International Organizations or Between International Organizations, 1986, 25 ILM 543.

Convention on the Law of Treaties, Vienna, 22 May 1969, in force 27 January 1980, 1155 UNTS 331.

Falk, "The Capacity of International Law to Respond to the Environmental Challenge," *Proceedings, Canadian Council on International Law*, 1989, p 35.

Gundling L., "The Status in International Law of the Principle of Precautionary Action", in 5 *IJECL* 23, 1990.

Huber M., *Island of Palmas Case*, (Netherlands US), 2 UNRIAA 839.

PCIJ: *Tunis—Moroco Nationality Decrees*, *PCIJ* Ser.B, No.4, 24, 1923.

PCIJ: *Lighthouse Case* (1934), France/Greece, Separate Opinion by Seferiądes, in: Series A/B, *Judgements, Orders and Advisory Opinions of the Permanent Court of International Justice*, 1931-1940, fasciles No. 62.

Pearson C.S., *International Marine Environmental Policy*, Baltimore, John Hopkins University Press, 1975.

Sand P., *Lessons Learned in Global Governance*, 1990.

Sax, "A General Survey of the Problem", in *Science for Better Environment, Proceedings of the International Congress on the Human Environment*, 1976, pp 753.

"Conclusions of the Siena Forum on International Law of the Environment," in *Yearbook of International Law*, 1990, p 704.

World Resources Institute, *World Resources 1990–1991*, New York Basic Books, 1992.

8

Additional References

Books

Asian Development Bank, *Asian Development Outlook 2001: Asia's Globalization Challenge*, Oxford University Press, 2001.

Asian Development Bank and IUCN-The World Conservation Union, *Biodiversity Conservation in the Asia Pacific Region: constraints and Opportunities*, Asian Development Bank, Manila, 1995.

Asian Development Bank, *Technology Transfer and Development: Implications for Development Asia*, Asian Development Bank, Manila, 1995.

Birnie P.W., and Boyle A.E., *International Law and the Environment,* Oxford UniversityPress, 1992.

Blakely R., "Global Warming: A Pacific Perspective," 2 *Transnational Law and Contemporary Problems*, 202, 1992.

Brown-Weiss E., McCaffrey, McGraw, Szasz, and Lutz, *International Environmental Law and Policy,* Aspen Law & Business, 1998.

Brown Weiss E. and Jacobson H., *Engaging Countries: Strengthening Compliance with International Accords,* MIT Press, Cambridge, Massachusetts, 1998.

Gillespie A., "The Malaysian Agenda and Influence on the International Tropical Deforestation Debate," 1 *Asia Pacific Journal of Environmental Law,* 1996, p. 25.

Guruswamy, Palmer, and Weston, *International Environmental Law,* West, 1994.

Henkin, Schachter, Pugh, and Smits, *International Law,* 3rd ed. West, 1995, Chapter 16, pp. 1,375-1,393.

Hunter, Salzman, and Zaelke, *International Environmental Law and Policy,* Foundation Press, 1998 (New Edition Forthcoming).

IUCN, *Draft International Covenant on Environment and Development,* 1997.

IUCN, *Caring for the Earth: A Strategy for Sustainable Living,* 1991, ICUN, UNEP, WWF.

IUCN, *Caring for the Earth: A Strategy for Survival,* 1995, IUCN, UNEP, WWF .

IUCN Law Commission, *Environmental Law in the South Pacific*, IUCN Law Commission, Gland, Switzerland, 1996.

Kiss and Shelton, *International Environmental Law,* Transnational, 1991.

Koh K., Bechman R., and Chia L., *Sustainable Development of Coastal and Ocean Areas in South East Asia: Post-Rio Perspectives,* National University of Singapore, Singapore, 1995.

Lang W. (ed), *Sustainable Development and International Law*, International Environmental Law and Policy Series, Graham and Trotman, 1995.

Litfin K, *The Greening of Sovereignty in World Politics,* MIT Press, Cambridge, Massachusetts, 1998.

Nanda V.P., *International Environmental Law & Policy*, Transnational, 1995.

Sands P. (ed), *Greening International Law*, London, Earthscan Publications Ltd, 1993.

Sands P., *Principles of International Environmental Law*, Manchester Univ. Press, 1995.

Sun Lin and Kurukulasuriya L. (eds), *UNEP's New Way Forward: Environmental Law and Sustainable Development,* UNEP, 1995.

Victor D., et al., *The Implementation and Effectiveness of International Environmental Commitments: Theory and Practice,* MIT Press, Cambridge, Massachusetts, 1998.

Wolf A., *Quotas in Environmental Agreements*, Earthscan, London, 1997.

Journals

Asia Pacific Journal of Environmental Law

Environmental Policy and Law

Environmental and Planning Law Journal

Review of European Community and International Environmental Law

Yale Journal of International Law

CHAPTER

18

Marine Environmental Law

Contents

1

Introduction

The oceans and their resources have long been taken for granted and have consequently suffered the effects of mismanagement at the national, regional, and global levels. Many of the world's marine living resources are severely depleted, and in some areas of the world, commercial fishing has had to be suspended. Marine and coastal biological diversity forms the foundation of natural ecosystems that produce and maintain fisheries and other biological resources on which humanity depends and the richest marine biodiversity in the world is found in Southeast Asia. However, coastal ecosystems in many countries in the Asian and Pacific region are seriously threatened by human activities, and in many places the damage to mangroves and other wetlands of enormous ecological value is beyond repair.

The impacts of land-based marine pollution continue to worsen, constituting the most alarming single threat to the marine environment. Global conventions regulating ship-generated pollution and ocean dumping have been adopted through the work of the International Maritime Organization (IMO), but these sophisticated and technical regulatory mechanisms create their own difficulties for many developing countries, not least those in the region. Meanwhile, efforts continue to establish an international regulatory regime to govern land-based activities that cause serious pollution of the marine environment. Questions also arise as to how to implement the 1992 *Convention on Biological Diversity* in marine and coastal areas, and how to safeguard particularly sensitive sea areas from pollution by vessels and land-based activities.

These issues are addressed in an evolving area of environmental law that we refer to as Marine Environmental Law. Marine Environmental Law is a relatively new field of public international law. It reflects the inroads made by a modern branch of international law—environmental law—into a more traditional branch of international law—the law of the sea.

The profound importance of Marine Environmental Laws in the Pacific Region is self-evident. The dependence of island nations upon effective marine regimes is illustrated in the overview of environmental laws in Tonga and Vanuatu included in Chapter 5. The entire ocean surrounding the countries of Southeast Asia have at times been described as a semi-enclosed sea. More accurately, this area consists of several bodies that could be individually described in this way, such as the semi-enclosed waters of the Gulf of Thailand. UNEP has facilitated the development of the *East Asia Seas Action Plan* under the UNEP regional seas program which was adopted in 1981. As an area of environmental law, marine environmental protection needs to be given a very high priority due to its importance throughout the Asian and Pacific region. Increasingly, marine law is being incorporated into integrated coastal zone management regimes and the present chapter should be read with Chapter 14 of this book which deals with ICZM. In particular, the piece in Chapter 14 from VanderSwaag focuses on the issue of land-based pollution and the 1995 GPA and should be considered along with this chapter. The high level of use, threats to, and pollution of marine areas in this region create considerable environmental problems, but there also exists a strong commonality of interests and concerns which could become a focal point for regional cooperation.

In this chapter we focus on marine pollution and the efforts of the international community to prevent, reduce, and control pollution of the marine environment. We first examine the significance of the 1982 United Nations *Convention on the Law of the Sea* (1982 UNCLOS) and in particular we extract selected Articles from Parts V, VII and XII.

The impacts of land-based marine pollution continue to worsen, constituting the most alarming single threat to the marine environment.

Following this we provide a selection of brief extracts which deal with the concepts of Regional Seas and Marine Protected Areas. Our focus in this chapter is on global instruments and on their implementation in national law. However, many issues of marine environmental law cannot be adequately addressed unless a regional or subregional approach is adopted. Asia lags behind other regions in developing effective regional regimes for dealing with issues of marine environmental law, such as the UNEP regional seas programs. An overview of these UNEP programs and a brief commentary are included in this chapter. Students interested in doing further research in marine environmental law may find it useful to examine the regional regimes that have been developed in Europe and the Caribbean to deal with issues of marine environmental law. The extract from the Caribbean Environment Programme in Chapter 14 provides a useful point of departure for such research. Although obviously focused on ICZM, the original source provides a wealth of information across a range of marine issues.

Sections 5, 6, and 7 of the chapter examine the major global legal instruments relating to marine pollution. This includes an examination of the issues relating to the national implementation of one of the major global instruments relating to marine pollution, the 1973/78 *Convention on the Prevention of Pollution from Ships*, known as *MARPOL73/78*.

We will not be examining other areas of marine environmental law such as the conservation and sustainable development of marine living resources, the conservation of marine and coastal biological diversity, and the exploitation of off-shore hydrocarbon resources. However, other chapters in this book provide students with a framework for analyzing issues relating to the conservation of biological diversity (Chapter 20), and the sustainable use and development of renewable and non-renewable resources (Chapters 8, 12, 13, and 14). The framework in those chapters can be used to analyze issues of marine environmental law relating to fisheries resources, the conservation and protection marine mammals, and the conservation of biological diversity in marine and coastal areas.

This chapter will provide students with an overview of the law of the sea and the efforts of the international community to develop global and regional regimes to govern the uses of the oceans. We focus on marine pollution and, to a lesser extent, marine protected areas. We aim to highlight the importance of planning and management to protect ecologically important marine areas and to emphasize the role of international and regional regimes in the solution of these problems.

A

Beckman R., *Syllabus for Marine Environmental Law and Policy*, 2000–2001, National University of Singapore, 2000–2001

[*An extensive list of references, including many from this syllabus, is included at the conclusion of this chapter. Note that this course description extends beyond the material in this chapter and requires supplementation with material on domestic law for the protection of marine and coastal ecosystems and biodiversity, as well as material from other chapters in this book, referred to above.*]

Course description and objectives

Marine environmental law is a relatively new field of public international law. It reflects the inroads made by a modern branch of international law—environmental law—into a more traditional branch of international law—the law of the sea. It also reflects inroads made by global instruments into areas traditionally governed solely by national law. In this course, we will examine the efforts of the global community to protect and preserve the coastal and marine environment and to prevent, reduce and control pollution of the marine environment.

Throughout the course, we will be focussing on the legal regime established in: (a) the 1982 UN *Convention on the Law of the Sea*, which establishes a legal framework for the oceans; (b) Conventions adopted by the UN organization charged with dealing with ship-based marine pollution and ocean dumping, the International Maritime Organization (IMO); and (3) Conventions and "soft-law instruments" adopted through the international organizations responsible for protecting and preserving the marine environment and marine and coastal habitats. We will also be examining the role of the institutions, both governmental and nongovernmental, that are involved in making policy and establishing legal regimes. We will also be examining the extent to which the emerging law and policy reflects a balance of the interests of the various stakeholders. including states' economic groups, scientists, local communities and nongovernmental organizations.

The objective of the course is to study the process by which marine environmental law is being developed, as the international community recognizes that new institutions, new commitments, new management tools and new levels of cooperation are required if oceans resources and environment are going to be managed in a wise and rational manner in the 21st century.

Tentative List of Seminar Topics

Topics will focus on the pollution of the marine environment, and the steps by the international community to prevent, reduce and control pollution of the marine environment from pollution from various sources. A recurring theme will be the action required at the regional and local levels to implement the policies, standards and procedures established at the global level.

The next theme will be the conservation and management of the living resources of the oceans. We will examine two issues. First, the efforts of the international community to regulate, manage and conserve whales. Second, the issues relating to the conservation and management of coastal fisheries, that is, fisheries over which coastal states have sovereign rights and jurisdiction under the new law of the sea. We will not be studying the attempts of the international community to conserve and manage high seas fisheries, straddling fish stocks and highly migratory fish stocks, as this topic is covered in the course on Ocean Law and Policy.

The final theme in the course will be to examine the various measures being recommended to preserve and conserve marine and coastal biodiversity and marine and coastal ecosystems. Finally, we will look at the pros and cons of regional cooperation to protect and preserve the marine environment.

Topic 1: Global Institutions and the Marine Environment

Class Plan

1. Students will be expected to have done the readings in advance and to come to class prepared to discuss the roles played by the various UN organizations and NGOs in the marine environment.
2. Students should also be prepared to discuss the information in the readings about pollution of the marine environment and fisheries.

Topic 2: Major Global Instruments

Class Plan

The following questions will serve as the focus of discussion in class.

1. Check on the current status of 1982 UNCLOS. How many states are Parties? Which ASEAN countries are not Parties?
2. What are the major provisions in the 1982 UN *Convention on the Law of the Sea* (1982 UNCLOS) which provide a legal framework for the protection, preservation and conservation of the marine environment?
3. What are the major differences between 1982 UNCLOS and the two soft-law instruments—Chapter 17 of *Agenda 21* and the Stockholm Action Plan? What is the relationship between them?
4. Which principles in the Stockhohn and Rio Declarations that are likely to have an impact on the development of international rules relating to the marine environment?
5. According to the Earth Summit +5, what is necessary for further implementation of Chapter 17 on protection of the oceans?

Topic 3: Pollution from Ships

Class Discussion

1. What are the effects of oil and plastics on the marine environment?
2. How many states are Parties to MARPOL 73/78 and the Annex on Garbage? How many ASEAN countries are Parties? (Note: use IMO web page at www.imo.org)
3. The main IMO Convention on the prevention of pollution from ships is MARPOL 73/78. How does the legal regime established by MARPOL attempts to prevent pollution from ships. In particular, what is the relevance of the following?
   - Standards of construction and equipment
   - Reception facilities
   - Oil record book
   - Certificates
   - Inspections of certificates

- Inspections of vessels
- Tacit acceptance procedure for amendments to annexes

4. What is the link between MARPOL and UNCLOS? What are the rights and obligations of coastal states, flag states and port states to enforce MARPOL rules? How do the rights of coastal states differ in the territorial sea, exclusive economic zone and in international straits?
5. What is Port State Control and how does it work? Is it authorized under 1982 UNCLOS? Can Singapore prosecute the captain of a ship who illegally discharged oil in the Territorial Sea or EEZ of Malaysia?
6. What is the environmental problem posed by ballast water, and how is it being dealt with?

Topic 4: Liability and Compensation for Oil Pollution

Class Discussion

1. Explain the system of liability and compensation under the CLC 69. When does the Convention apply? Who is liable? To what extent? What limits? What types of damage? To whom? Are there any exceptions? When considering whether to become a party, what are pros and cons for coastal states?
2. Explain the system of liability and compensation under Fund 71? When does it apply? Who is liable? When does it come in? What exceptions? What limits the amount or type of damage? Who contributes to the Fund? Who manages the Fund? What are the roles of the IOPC Fund and ITOPF in the case of major oil pollution incidents?
3. Outline the major changes to the CLC and Fund regimes as a result of the 1992 Protocols? (Limits, exceptions, types of damage, etc.)
4. Check the current status of the conventions to find out the number of Parties and the status within ASEAN countries. Which ASEAN countries are not Parties to any of the CLC or Fund Conventions? If you were advising them, which would you advise them to become parties to, and why?
5. Assume that major oil spill occurs in the Straits of Singapore following a collision involving a fully-laden VLCC. Extensive damage is caused to all three littoral states, Singapore, Malaysia and Indonesia. The damage by oil includes damage to fish farms, coral reefs and mangroves. What are the limits on the amount of compensation that could be recovered by the three states under the CLC and Fund Convention regimes. To what extent would the States be able to recover for environmental damage to reefs and mangroves?

Topic 5: Pollution from Dumping

Class Plan

1. Can it be argued that States parties to UNCLOS are under a legal obligation to regulate ocean dumping by their ships and in their maritime zones?
2. Check on the status of the 1972 Convention and the 1996 Protocol generally and in ASEAN.
3. Be prepared to discuss the development of the legal regime governing ocean dumping from 1972 to 1996. Focus in particular on the major differences between the 1972 Convention and the 1996 Protocol.
4. What is your view of the role of scientists and NGOs in the development of the London Convention? Does it reflect a conflict between science and ethics in the making of ocean policy? Has the London Secretariat been hijacked by Greenpeace?

Topic 6: Pollution from Land-Based Activities

Discussion Questions

1. Compare the UNCLOS provisions on land-based activities to those on pollution from vessels and from dumping. To what extent do they make inroads into the sovereignty of coastal states? What actions were called for in Chapter 17 of *Agenda 21* to deal with pollution from land-based activities?
2. What are the purposes and objectives of the GPA? Who is to implement it? What are problems in implementing it?
3. Examine the LBS Protocol for the Wider Caribbean? What are its objectives and major features? To what extent do the states legally bind themselves to take action? What mechanisms are there to promote cooperation, coordination and compliance?

2

The Significance of 1982 UNCLOS

A

United Nations Convention on the Law of the Sea (Montego Bay), 21 ILM, 1261, 1982

Part I: Introduction

Article 1—Use of Terms and Scope

1. For the purposes of this Convention:
   (4) "pollution of the marine environment" means the introduction by man, directly or indirectly, of substances or energy into the marine environment, including estuaries, which results or is likely to result in such deleterious effects as harm to living resources and marine life, hazards to human health, hindrance to marine activities, including fishing and other legitimate uses of the sea, impairment of quality for use of sea water and reduction of amenities;
   (5) (a) "dumping" means:
         (i) any deliberate disposal of wastes or other matter from vessels, aircraft, platforms or other man-made structures at sea;
         (ii) any deliberate disposal of vessels, aircraft, platforms or other man-made structures at sea;
       (b) "dumping" does not include:
         (i) the disposal of wastes or other matter incidental to, or derived from the normal operations of vessels, aircraft, platforms or other man-made structures at sea and their equipment, other than wastes or other matter transported by or to vessels, aircraft, platforms or other man-made structures at sea, operating for the purpose of disposal of such matter or derived from the treatment of such wastes or other matter on such vessels, aircraft, platforms or structures;
         (ii) placement of matter for a purpose other than the mere disposal thereof, provided that such placement is not contrary to the aims of this Convention.

Part XII : Protection and Preservation of the Marine Environment

Section 1—General provisions

Article 192—General Obligation

States have the obligation to protect and preserve the marine environment.

Article 193—Sovereign Right of States to Exploit their Natural Resources

States have the sovereign right to exploit their natural resources pursuant to their environmental policies and in accordance with their duty to protect and preserve the marine environment.

Article 194—Measures to Prevent, Reduce and Control Pollution of the Marine Environment

1. States shall take, individually or jointly as appropriate, all measures consistent with this Convention that are necessary to prevent, reduce and control pollution of the marine environment from any source, using for this purpose the best practicable means at their disposal and in accordance with their capabilities, and they shall endeavor to harmonize their policies in this connection.
2. States shall take all measures necessary to ensure that activities under their jurisdiction or control are so conducted as not to cause damage by pollution to other States and their environment, and that pollution arising from incidents or activities under their jurisdiction or control does not spread beyond the areas where they exercise sovereign rights in accordance with this Convention.
3. The measures taken pursuant to this Part shall deal with all sources of pollution of the marine environment. These measures shall include, inter alia, those designed to minimize to the fullest possible extent:
   (a) the release of toxic, harmful or noxious substances, especially those which are persistent, from land-

based sources, from or through the atmosphere or by dumping;

(b) pollution from vessels, in particular measures for preventing accidents and dealing with emergencies, ensuring the safety of operations at sea, preventing intentional and unintentional discharges, and regulating the design, construction, equipment, operation and manning of vessels;

(c) pollution from installations and devices used in exploration or exploitation of the natural resources of the sea-bed and subsoil, in particular measures for preventing accidents and dealing with emergencies, ensuring the safety of operations at sea, and regulating the design, construction, equipment, operation and manning of such installations or devices;

(d) pollution from other installations and devices operating in the marine environment, in particular, measures for preventing accidents and dealing with emergencies, ensuring the safety of operations at sea, and regulating the design, construction, equipment, operation and manning of such installations or devices.

4. In taking measures to prevent, reduce or control pollution of the marine environment, States shall refrain from unjustifiable interference with activities carried out by other States in the exercise of their rights and in pursuance of their duties in conformity with this Convention.
5. The measures taken in accordance with this Part shall include those necessary to protect and preserve rare or fragile ecosystems as well as the habitat of depleted, threatened or endangered species and other forms of marine life.

Article 195—Duty Not to Transfer Damage or Hazards or Transform One Type of Pollution into Another

In taking measures to prevent, reduce and control pollution of the marine environment, States shall act so as not to transfer, directly or indirectly, damage or hazards from one area to another or transform one type of pollution into another.

Article 196—Use of Technologies or Introduction of Alien or New Species

1. States shall take all measures necessary to prevent, reduce and control pollution of the marine environment resulting from the use of technologies under their jurisdiction or control, or the intentional or accidental introduction of species, alien or new, to a particular part of the marine environment, which may cause significant and harmful changes thereto.
2. This article does not affect the application of this Convention regarding the prevention, reduction and control of pollution of the marine environment.

Section 2—Global and Regional Cooperation

Article 197—Cooperation on a Global or Regional Basis

States shall cooperate on a global basis and, as appropriate, on a regional basis, directly or through competent international organizations, in formulating and elaborating international rules, standards and recommended practices and procedures consistent with this Convention, for the protection and preservation of the marine environment, taking into account characteristic regional features.

Article 200

Studies, research programs and exchange of information and data States shall cooperate, directly or through competent international organizations, for the purpose of promoting studies, undertaking programs of scientific research and encouraging the exchange of information and data acquired about pollution of the marine environment. They shall endeavor to participate actively in regional and global programs to acquire knowledge for the assessment of the nature and extent of pollution, exposure to it, and its pathways, risks and remedies.

Article 201—Scientific Criteria for Regulations

In the light of the information and data acquired pursuant to article 200, States shall cooperate, directly or through competent international organizations, in establishing appropriate scientific criteria for the formulation and elaboration of rules, standards and recommended practices and procedures for the prevention, reduction and control of pollution of the marine environment.

Section 3—Technical Assistance

Article 202—Scientific and Technical Assistance to Developing States

States shall, directly or through competent international organizations:

(a) promote programs of scientific, educational, technical and other assistance to developing States for the protection and preservation of the marine environment and the prevention, reduction and control of marine pollution. Such assistance shall include, inter alia:
   (i) training of their scientific and technical personnel;
   (ii) facilitating their participation in relevant international programs;
   (iii) supplying them with necessary equipment and facilities;
   (iv) enhancing their capacity to manufacture such equipment;
   (v) advice on and developing facilities for research, monitoring, educational and other programs;

(b) provide appropriate assistance, especially to developing States, for the minimization of the effects of major incidents which may cause serious pollution of the marine environment;

(c) provide appropriate assistance, especially to developing States, concerning the preparation of environmental assessments.

Article 203—Preferential Treatment for Developing States

Developing States shall, for the purposes of prevention, reduction and control of pollution of the marine environment or minimization of its effects, be granted preference by international organizations in:

(a) the allocation of appropriate funds and technical assistance, and

(b) the utilization of their specialized services.

Section 4—Monitoring and Environmental Assessment

Article 204—Monitoring of the Risks or Effects of Pollution

1. States shall, consistent with the rights of other States, endeavor, as far as practicable, directly or through the competent international organizations, to observe, measure, evaluate and analyze, by recognized scientific methods, the risks or effects of pollution of the marine environment.
2. In particular, States shall keep under surveillance the effects of any activities which they permit or in which they engage in order to determine whether these activities are likely to pollute the marine environment.

Article 205—Publication of Reports

States shall publish reports of the results obtained pursuant to article 204 or provide such reports at appropriate intervals to the competent international organizations, which should make them available to all States.

Article 206—Assessment of Potential Effects of Activities

When States have reasonable grounds for believing that planned activities under their jurisdiction or control may cause substantial pollution of, or significant and harmful changes to the marine environment, they shall, as far as practicable, assess the potential effects of such activities on the marine environment and shall communicate reports of the results of such assessments in the manner provided in article 205.

Section 5—International Rules and National Legislation to Prevent, Reduce and Control Pollution of the Marine Environment

Article 207—Pollution from Land-Based Sources

1. States shall adopt laws and regulations to prevent, reduce and control pollution of the marine environment from land-based sources, including rivers, estuaries, pipelines and outfall structures, taking into account internationally agreed rules, standards and recommended practices and procedures.
2. States shall take other measures as may be necessary to prevent, reduce and control such pollution.
3. States shall endeavor to harmonize their policies in this connection at the appropriate regional level.
4. States, acting especially through competent international organizations or diplomatic conference, shall endeavor to establish global and regional rules, standards and recommended practices and procedures to prevent, reduce and control pollution of the marine environment from land-based sources, taking into account characteristic regional features, the economic capacity of developing States and their need for economic development. Such rules, standards and recommended practices and procedures shall be reexamined from time to time as necessary.

When States have reasonable grounds for believing that planned activities...may cause substantial pollution of, or significant and harmful changes to the marine environment, they shall, as far as practicable, assess the potential effects of such activities on the marine environment.

5. Laws, regulations, measures, rules, standards and recommended practices and procedures referred to in paragraphs 1, 2 and 4 shall include those designed to minimize, to the fullest extent possible, the release of toxic, harmful or noxious substances, especially those which are persistent, into the marine environment.

Article 208—Pollution from Sea-Bed Activities Subject To National Jurisdiction

1. Coastal States shall adopt laws and regulations to prevent, reduce and control pollution of the marine environment arising from or in connection with sea-bed activities subject to their jurisdiction and from artificial islands, installations and structures under their jurisdiction, pursuant to articles 60 and 80.
2. States shall take other measures as may be necessary to prevent, reduce and control such pollution.
3. Such laws, regulations and measures shall be no less effective than international rules, standards and recommended practices and procedures.
4. States shall endeavor to harmonize their policies in this connection at the appropriate regional level.
5. States, acting especially through competent international organizations or diplomatic conference, shall establish global and regional rules, standards and recommended practices and procedures to prevent, reduce and control pollution of the marine environment referred to in paragraph l. Such rules, standards and recommended practices and procedures shall be reexamined from time to time as necessary.

Article 209—Pollution from Activities in the Area

1. International rules, regulations and procedures shall be established in accordance with Part XI to prevent, reduce and control pollution of the marine environment from activities in the Area. Such rules, regulations and procedures shall be reexamined from time to time as necessary.
2. Subject to the relevant provisions of this section, States shall adopt laws and regulations to prevent, reduce and control pollution of the marine environment from activities in the Area undertaken by vessels, installations, structures and other devices flying their flag or of their registry or operating under their authority, as the case may be. The requirements of such laws and regulations shall be no less effective than the international rules, regulations and procedures referred to in paragraph 1.

Article 210—Pollution by Dumping

1. States shall adopt laws and regulations to prevent, reduce and control pollution of the marine environment by dumping.
2. States shall take other measures as may be necessary to prevent, reduce and control such pollution.
3. Such laws, regulations and measures shall ensure that dumping is not carried out without the permission of the competent authorities of States.
4. States, acting especially through competent international organizations or diplomatic conference, shall endeavor to establish global and regional rules, standards and recommended practices and procedures to prevent, reduce and control such pollution. Such rules, standards and recommended practices and procedures shall be reexamined from time to time as necessary.
5. Dumping within the territorial sea and the exclusive economic zone or onto the continental shelf shall not be carried out without the express prior approval of the coastal State, which has the right to permit, regulate and control such dumping after due consideration of the matter with other States which by reason of their geographical situation may be adversely affected thereby.
6. National laws, regulations and measures shall be no less effective in preventing, reducing and controlling such pollution than the global rules and standards.

Article 211—Pollution from Vessels

1. States, acting through the competent international organization or general diplomatic conference, shall establish international rules and standards to prevent, reduce and control pollution of the marine environment from vessels and promote the adoption, in the same manner, wherever appropriate, of routing systems designed to minimize the threat of accidents which might cause pollution of the marine environment, including the coastline, and pollution damage to the related interests of coastal States. Such rules and standards shall, in the same manner, be reexamined from time to time as necessary.
2. States shall adopt laws and regulations for the prevention, reduction and control of pollution of the

marine environment from vessels flying their flag or of their registry. Such laws and regulations shall at least have the same effect as that of generally accepted international rules and standards established through the competent international organization or general diplomatic conference.

3. States which establish particular requirements for the prevention, reduction and control of pollution of the marine environment as a condition for the entry of foreign vessels into their ports or internal waters or for a call at their off-shore terminals shall give due publicity to such requirements and shall communicate them to the competent international organization. Whenever such requirements are established in identical form by two or more coastal States in an endeavor to harmonize policy, the communication shall indicate which States are participating in such cooperative arrangements. Every State shall require the master of a vessel flying its flag or of its registry, when navigating within the territorial sea of a State participating in such cooperative arrangements, to furnish, upon the request of that State, information as to whether it is proceeding to a State of the same region participating in such co-operative arrangements and, if so, to indicate whether it complies with the port entry requirements of that State. This article is without prejudice to the continued exercise by a vessel of its right of innocent passage or to the application of article 25, paragraph 2.

B

Beckman R., *The Significance of Universal Acceptance of 1982 UNCLOS*, Asia-Pacific Centre for Environmental Law (APCEL), National University of Singapore, December 2000

Background

The 1982 United Nations *Convention on the Law of the Sea* (1982 Convention) is one of the most significant achievements of the international community since the founding of the United Nations. The 1982 Convention was the culmination of eight years of negotiations at the Third UN Conference on the Law of the Sea. More than 150 countries, representing all regions of the world, all political systems, and all degrees of socioeconomic development, participated in these negotiations. Never before had the international community taken on so monumental a challenge in international negotiation and international lawmaking.

The 1982 Convention aimed to establish a 'constitution for the oceans', that is, a comprehensive regime dealing with all matters relating to the law of the sea which would remain viable into the next century. Its text comprises 320 articles and nine annexes which were intended to establish principles and rules governing all uses of ocean space.

The 1982 Convention entered into force on 16 November 1994, one year after the sixtieth State deposited an instrument of ratification or accession with the United Nations. Most of the 60 states that ratified the Convention prior to 1994 were developing countries from the African regional group or the Latin American/Caribbean regional group. Only one developed state from Western Europe, Iceland, was among the first 60. Indonesia and the Philippines were the only countries from this region among the first 60.

Deep seabed provisions and the 1994 Interpretation Agreement

The major reason why more developed countries did not ratify the 1982 Convention is that the United States and many of its Western allies were unhappy with the provisions in Part XI relating to deep sea-bed mining. Because of this, the United States refused to sign the Convention in 1982, and most of the developed countries refused to ratify it. This dispute between the First and Third world countries over Part XI threatened to prevent the Convention from ever becoming universally accepted.

However, in the early 1990s steps were taken in the United Nations to address the concerns of the developed countries on the deep seabed provisions so that the 1982 Convention could become universally acceptable. A series of informal consultations were convened by the UN Secretary-General and chaired by Ambassador Satya Nandan of Fiji. The consultations were with a group of states representing all regions and interest groups, including the United States, Germany and the United Kingdom. The result of the four years of informal

Since 1994 most of the states in this region have also become parties to the 1982 Convention as amended by the 1994 Interpretation Agreement.

consultations was an agreement that significantly amended the deep seabed provisions to take into account the concerns of the United States. On 28 July 1994 the General Assembly adopted a resolution by a vote of 121-0-7 that contained an *Agreement Relating to the Implementation of Part XI* of the 1982 Convention.

The terms of the 1994 *Implementation Agreement* were ingeniously drafted to encourage states to become parties to the 1994 Interpretation Agreement (and to the 1982 Convention) as soon as possible. The *Interpretation Agreement* also contained a unique procedure to allow for its provisional application and for provisional membership of the Authority (the body charged with responsibility for administering Part XI on the deep seabed). Under the terms of the Agreement all states which voted for its adoption in the General Assembly applied it provisionally from 16 November 1994.

The adoption of 1994 *Implementation Agreement* in July 1994 paved the way for near universal acceptance of the Convention. As of 1st September 1998 a total of 127 States are parties to the Convention. Most of the OECD countries have become parties to the Convention. Notable exceptions are the United States and Canada.

Since 1994 most of the states in this region have also become parties to the 1982 Convention as amended by the 1994 Interpretation Agreement. All of the states in Southeast Asia are now parties except Cambodia and Thailand. All of the states in Northeast Asia are now parties except the Democratic People's Republic of North Korea, and all of the States in South Asia are parties except Bangladesh and the Maldives.

Major provisions of the Convention

Certain portions of the 1982 Convention, such as those relating to the high seas, were a codification of existing rules of international law. Other provisions, however, were new. They were often the result of long and arduous negotiations among the various groups of states. For example, the major coastal states were often most interested in extending their rights and jurisdiction over a larger area of ocean space, whereas the major maritime and naval powers were most interested in preserving traditional freedoms of navigation and overflight. Many provisions of the 1982 Convention reflect delicate compromises designed to protect the competing interests of various groups of states.

Expanded Rights of Coastal and Archipelagic States

The 1982 Convention resolved the existing controversies relating to the breadth of the territorial sea, the right of coastal states to claim an exclusive fishing zone or exclusive economic zone, and the right of mid-ocean archipelagic states to claim archipelagic waters. Under the 1982 Convention, coastal states can claim a 12 nautical mile Territorial Sea. They can also claim a 200 nautical mile Exclusive Economic Zone, where they have sovereign rights over the living and non-living resources in the water as well as on and under the seabed and subsoil on their continental shelf. The 1982 Convention also recognized that mid-ocean Archipelagic States such as Indonesia and the Philippines could draw straight baselines connecting the outermost points of their outermost islands, and claim the waters within the baselines as their archipelagic waters.

The result of these provisions is that coastal states now have jurisdiction and control over 95 percent of the living resources (fisheries) of the oceans and almost all of the off-shore hydrocarbon resources (oil and gas). Less than 5 percent of the fisheries resources are now in the high seas, beyond the jurisdiction of the coastal states.

Rights of Passage Made More Secure

At the same time as the 1982 Convention extends the rights and jurisdiction of the coastal states, it also protects the interests of other states by preserving their right to passage on routes used for international navigation, even when such routes are through International Straits, Exclusive Economic Zones and Archipelagic States. All states have freedom of navigation and overflight on the High Seas (beyond 200 miles from coast) and in the Exclusive Economic Zone (from 12 to 200 miles from coast) of other states. The ships of all states have the right of innocent passage through the Territorial Sea (within 12 miles of coast) of other states. In addition, special passage regimes ensure the right of navigation and overflight on routes used for international navigation through International Straits such as the Straits of Malacca and Singapore, and on major international routes through Archipelagic States such as Indonesia and the Philippines.

Protection of the Marine Environment

Another major achievement of the Convention is that it is the first global convention that contains comprehensive provisions placing obligations on all states to take measures to prevent, reduce and control pollution of the marine environment. It also contains provisions designed to enhance the world community's interest in the conservation and optimum utilization of living resources of the oceans. States parties to the Convention must adopt laws and regulations to prevent, reduce and control pollution of the marine environment from all sources, including vessels, ocean dumping, offshore installations and land-based activities. The provisions to prevent pollution from ships are the most detailed, and are closely linked to the conventions adopted under the auspices of the International Maritime Organization. The provisions relating to pollution of the marine environment from land-based activities, which account for as much as 80 percent of marine pollution, are the most vague and general.

Mandatory Settlement of Disputes

The 1982 Convention is also significant in that it contains the most sophisticated system ever devised for the mandatory settlement of disputes arising from the interpretation or application of its provisions.

Common Heritage of Mankind

Finally, the Convention provides that the resources of the deep seabed are the common heritage of mankind. Part XI contained detailed provisions that attempted to establish principles, institutions and arrangements for a fair and workable system governing their exploitation. Part XI has subsequently been amended by the 1994 Interpretation Agreement, but the principle of common heritage remains unchanged.

Matters not dealt with adequately in the Convention

Though comprehensive, the 1982 Convention does not contain provisions that will resolve all of the important issues relating to the oceans. For example, the Convention has no provisions on the resolution of competing claims to sovereignty over disputed islands or territory such as those to the Spratly Islands in the South China Sea. Also, although the Convention contains a comprehensive system for the mandatory settlement of disputes, existing territorial disputes between states are not subject to the mandatory system of dispute settlement.

Subsequent developments

The provisions of the 1982 Convention governing the exploitation of fisheries resources on the high seas, as well as straddling stocks and highly migratory species, proved to be inadequate. As a consequence, a UN conference was convened to supplement the 1982 Convention's provisions relating to these issues. An Interpretation Agreement to establish new rules to govern straddling fish stocks and highly migratory fish stocks was adopted in 1995. This agreement, commonly referred to as the 1995 *Straddling Stocks Agreement*, will enter into force after it is ratified by 30 states. To date, only 19 states have ratified it. The future of the 1995 *Straddling Stocks Agreement* will remain in doubt until it is accepted by the major distant water fishing states. To date, Russia is the only distant water fishing state to have ratified it. Unless the 1995 *Straddling Stocks Agreement* is accepted by other major distant water fishing states such as Korea, Japan, Spain and Poland, the rules governing high seas fisheries will remain a subject of controversy and possible conflict.

The provisions of the 1982 Convention on the preservation and protection of the marine environment represented a very significant step in the development of the law of the sea. However, they only provide a general framework and general principles. Detailed obligations and actions plans must be worked out for specific sources of pollution. The most significant gap is pollution from land-based activities. This issue is so sensitive that it is not possible to get states to agree to specific international rules and standards to prevent pollution of the marine environment from land-based activities. As a result the international community is working to develop non-binding guidelines in "soft-law" instruments such as action plans. A significant step forward was made in 1995 by the adoption of the *Washington Programme of Action on the Prevention of Pollution of the Marine Environment from Land-Based Activities.*

The 1992 UN Conference on Environment and Development (1992 UNCED) also considered the state of the oceans and the marine environment. The Action Plan adopted at 1992 UNCED, which is called *Agenda 21*, contains a chapter on Protection of the Oceans. Chapter 17 of *Agenda 21* affirms that the international rules governing the uses of the oceans are those set out in the 1982 Convention. However, Chapter 17 clearly states that the regime set out in the 1982 Convention is not adequate to protect and preserve the ocean environment. Chapter 17 calls for the adoption of an integrated holistic approach to the protection and preservation of the marine environment, including the biological diversity of the marine environment. Chapter 17 also calls for the adoption of new approaches such as integrated coastal zone management, and the adoption of modern principles of international environmental law, such as the precautionary approach and the "polluter-pays-principle."

Significance of near universal acceptance of the 1982 Convention

The near universal acceptance of the 1982 Convention is significant for four reasons.

First, the 1982 Convention provides a sound legal framework that can be used as the basis for further adapting and developing the international law of the sea and for addressing issues which were not dealt with adequately in the 1982 Convention.

Second, there is now a clear set of legal rules governing the uses of the marine areas in the region, and setting out the rights, jurisdiction and obligations of states, there are less likely to be misunderstandings or conflicts arising because of differing views as to what rules are applicable.

Third, if disputes do arise between states that are parties to the Convention as to the interpretation or application of the rules in the Convention, the states concerned will have the option of invoking the compulsory system of dispute settlement under the Convention. With a wider choice of means for resolving disputes by peaceful means, states are less likely to resort to other means to resolve their disputes.

Fourth, the 1982 Convention establishes a framework for cooperation at the regional and subregional level with respect to uses of the oceans. In many areas, such as the protection of the marine environment, the 1982 Convention merely provides the basic structure and framework. It envisages that states will cooperate at the regional and subregional level to fully address certain types of issues. An example in this region is the Straits of Malacca and Singapore. The problems of safety of navigation and protection of the marine environment cannot be resolved without the cooperative efforts of the three bordering states. Now that all three states are parties to the 1982 Convention, they have accepted that the basic rules governing the Straits of Malacca and Singapore are those set out in the Convention on straits used for international navigation. Therefore, it should be easier for them to explore ways and means to cooperate to improve the safety of navigation and to protect the marine environment, within the framework of the 1982 Convention.

C

IUCN, *The Law of the Sea: Priorities and Responsibilities in Implementing the Convention*, IUCN, Gland, Switzerland, 1995

[*The following material is comprised of excerpts selected from throughout an extensive IUCN publication.*]

Executive Summary

"The United Nations *Convention on the Law of the Sea* was the most ambitious attempt ever to provide an internationally agreed regime for the management of the oceans. The resulting Convention represents a major step towards an integrated management regime for the oceans. Indeed, the most significant initial action that nations can take in the interest of the oceans' threatened life support system is to ratify the *Law of the Sea Convention*." [Our Common Future World Commission on Environment and Development (1987)]

"International law, as reflected in the provisions of the UN *Convention on the Law of the Sea*, referred to in this chapter of *Agenda 21*, sets forth rights and obligations of States and provides the international basis upon which to pursue the protection and sustainable development of the marine and coastal environment and its resources. This requires new approaches to marine and coastal area management and development, at the national, subregional, regional and global levels, approaches that are integrated in content, and are precautionary and anticipatory in ambit...." [*Agenda 21*, Chapter 17]

The UN *Convention on the Law of the Sea* was adopted and opened for signature in 1982. On November 16, 1994, it entered into force for 68 countries. Many others have initiated ratification processes.

The Convention establishes a comprehensive framework for use of the ocean and its resources. Its 320 articles, supplemented by nine detailed annexes, specify the rights all nations may exercise in the world oceans and their responsibility to do so with due regard for the rights and interests of other nations. The preservation and protection of the marine environment and the conservation of marine living resources are fundamental obligations.

The reasons for the long delay between adoption and entry into force are explained in Section I. What is important is that this comprehensive ocean law regime become binding on all States, now that the obstacles to its universal ratification have been removed...

The Opportunities

The LOS Convention governs activities undertaken both in the oceans and on land that impact marine and coastal ecosystems. Its framework of objectives, obligations, and principles is linked to an increasing number of more detailed international agreements for marine environmental protection and the conservation and management of marine species. Taken together, they present a dynamic vehicle for expanding and upgrading each nation's responsibilities. The references in the LOS Convention that protect rare or fragile ecosystems and the habitat of threatened or endangered species provide a hook for ensuring that activities governed by the Convention respect area and species designations pursuant to other terrestrial and marine agreements. The Convention's dispute settlement system permits its framework obligations to be interpreted and applied drawing on this wide range of evolving, more specific legal regimes.

This legal foundation establishes the basis for management actions that integrate marine environmental protection with marine living resources conservation. Convention building blocks include unqualified obligations to prevent, reduce, and control marine pollution, the definition of pollution (which includes harm to marine life), and references to the effects of pollution on habitat or through the introduction of new or alien species. Specifically for marine living resources, they include the requirement that conservation and management measures take into account environmental factors, the interdependence of stocks, and effects on associated or dependent species, which would include marine mammals and seabirds. That such measures may address fishing gear and practices permits further regulation to avoid incidental catch and marine debris.

The Convention's support for management based on natural systems and the geographic scales that reflect them is found in requirements for cooperation regarding marine living resources throughout the range of the stock or species. It is found also in obligations to protect rare or fragile ecosystems. Where all species of coral reef, seagrasses, and mangrove have been listed for protection under a Caribbean regional agreement, for example, this establishes a legal basis for system-wide protection. In addition, the LOS Convention facilitates the protection of clearly defined, vulnerable marine areas within national jurisdiction; concerted international management of ship-based activities affecting larger sea areas, such as the Baltic Sea or the Antarctic Treaty area; internationally-coordinated research and management in enclosed and semi-enclosed seas; and the harmonization of national laws at the regional level, specifically for land-based and offshore seabed sources of marine pollution.

The Convention's provisions on land-based sources of marine pollution are particularly important. For if the cumulative effects of contaminants, nutrients, and sediments manifested in coastal/marine areas are to be addressed, this will require assessment, planning, and management processes that encompass the full range of coastal and/or watershed activities. The legal term "land-based sources of marine pollution" expresses the basis for "integrated coastal area planning and management" and "integrated watershed planning and management". As agreements on land-based sources of marine pollution are elaborated, this will fundamentally affect the application of these management concepts. Several governments have recently indicated their support for utilizing land-based pollution obligations as a means to promote agreements on pollution in shared rivers. This can advance sustainable use of freshwaters, coastal zones, and marine areas. The LOS Convention's monitoring and assessment requirements, and the duty to communicate the results internationally, will support and update these planning and management processes.

Mounting solid wastes and their various pathways to the sea increasingly compel a new look at wastes reduction, management, and disposal strategies, encompassing both marine and terrestrial activities. This includes wastes generated on land that may be dumped at sea, particularly in nearshore waters; wastes carried out to sea by rivers, tides, and currents; wastes deposited in coastal landfills or marshes from which pollutants are leached into the marine environment; and wastes received in port from ships. The interaction between waste disposal at sea and on land is compounded by linkages between offshore operations and coastal facilities. As human activities increase, national and regional strategies must be capable of anticipating and responding to these complex and interactive effects. The LOS Convention furthers an integrated approach to pollution/wastes management strategies at national and regional levels by its requirement that states do not transform one type of pollution into another nor transfer damage or hazards from one area to another.

Without the forcing factor of international legal obligations, it is unlikely that many of these objectives would be tackled, let alone realized, except in the face of major disasters. The LOS Convention's unqualified obligations become the impetus for national implementing measures where other international agreements are less imperative. And they may exact more specific international agreements, for example, in the case of pollution from land-based sources, including that borne to the sea by shared rivers. Special opportunities exist for international agreements to reinforce each other in relation to coral reefs and other vulnerable coastal and marine areas, and in relation to marine and coastal species that are protected by broader international agreements. Collaborative ventures for coral reef research, assessment, and management could be developed under the *Framework Convention on Climate Change* (FCCC), the *Biodiversity Convention*, the *Law of the Sea Convention*, and related oceans agreements, making use of the LOS Convention's binding obligations. For areas and species protected under other agreements, the oceans agreements may support the application of additional protective measures. A thorough evaluation of the respective values afforded protection under these and other agreements, and of the measures countries may apply to achieve them, may reveal constructive synergies and gaps...

Section One: The 1982 United Nations *Convention on the Law of the Sea*

This section summarizes the origins of the LOS Convention and highlights major advances in the rules of international law as they affect marine environmental protection and the conservation of marine species. Section A notes how the 1994 Agreement to modify the Convention's seabed mining regime came about. Section B outlines the zones of coastal state jurisdiction progressively developed and codified in the Convention. Section C indicates what's new about the Convention ocean law regime, and Section D elaborates on the political, economic, and environmental trends that influenced Convention negotiations.

The Third UN Conference on the Law of the Sea (UNCLOS III)

The UN General Assembly decided in 1970 by consensus to convene an international conference for the purpose of concluding a comprehensive agreement on ocean law. Its purpose was to update and expand the four *Geneva Conventions*, concluded at the first UN Conference on the Law of the Sea in 1958. Preparatory discussions from 1968 to 1973 laid the groundwork for the conference, which lasted for ten years. The agenda included navigation and overflight, fishing and conservation of marine living resources, marine mammals, the development of minerals in offshore and deep seabed areas, marine environmental protection, marine scientific research, maritime boundaries, the laying of submarine cables and pipelines, artificial islands and seabed installations, piracy, illicit drug trafficking, and dispute settlement.

For the many countries that achieved independence after 1960, the LOS Conference was a novel experience in international negotiation. It was the first time that over 150 nations took part in drafting an international agreement, and the most comprehensive agenda ever contemplated by a treaty-making conference. The process served as a diplomatic academy for many of the international environmental negotiations that have followed. On April 30, 1982 the Convention was adopted, and it was opened for signature from December 10, 1982 to December 9, 1984. It received 159 signatures during that period, all subject to ratification.

The 1994 Agreement on Deep Seabed Mining

The delay from adoption to entry into force of the LOS Convention is attributable to one issue: its provisions governing development and management of seabed mineral resources beyond national jurisdiction. Criticisms of this portion of the Convention were advanced most prominently by the United States in the early 1980s, although many of the US concerns came to be shared by other industrialized nations. By the end of the decade, rapidly changing political and economic circumstances worldwide presented an opportunity to modify the deep seabed mining provisions and thus achieve universal support for the Convention. UN Secretary-General Perez de Cuellar and his successor Boutros-Ghali convened a series of informal consultations from 1990 to 1994. These took on a more urgent pace when Guyana deposited the both instrument of ratification in November 1993, triggering entry into force one year later. The consultations culminated on July 28, 1994, with the adoption by the 48th UN General Assembly of the *Agreement Relating to the Implementation of Part XI of the UN Convention on the Law of the Sea of 10 December 1982.*

The new Agreement clarifies and replaces many of the Convention's original deep seabed mining provisions. It is to be interpreted and applied as a single instrument with the Convention, and it prevails in the event of any inconsistency. To avoid a period before entry into force of the Agreement during which different regimes for deep seabed mining would apply—one to countries that ratified the Convention before November 16, 1994 but have not yet ratified the Agreement, and one to countries that ratify the Convention together with the new Agreement—the Agreement will be provisionally applied once the Convention enters into force on November 16, 1994. The Agreement remains open for signature for one year from July 29, 1994. By the end of 1994, it had been signed by 70 countries, including virtually all of the western industrialized nations and such developing nations as Argentina, Brazil, China, India, Indonesia, and Kenya. Among the industrialized nations, already Australia and Germany had ratified the Convention together with the Agreement. The Agreement will enter into force once 40 nations have consented to be bound by it. That number must include seven of the states defined as "pioneer investors" in seabed mining, of which at least five must be developed states.

Ocean Zones

The LOS Convention sets forth the rights and obligations of all States in the following offshore zones:

- internal waters,
- a territorial sea of up to 12 nautical miles (n.m.),
- a contiguous zone of up to 24 n.m.,
- an exclusive economic zone (EEZ) of up to 200 n.m., and
- the continental shelf, which may extend beyond 200 n.m. but not beyond 350, depending on the configuration of the seabed.

The Convention grants coastal states substantial control over activities in these zones, but the degree of control they exercise over use by other states varies with the zone and the activity in question. Most fundamentally, the Convention balances the rights and obligations of coastal states to use and protect offshore zones with worldwide freedoms of navigation and telecommunications essential for international security and commerce. As the zones move further offshore, coastal state authority over foreign activities diminishes. A fundamental distinction exists between the sovereignty of the coastal state out to the 12-mile limit of the territorial sea, and the less absolute authorities the coastal state may exercise in the other offshore zones.

Beyond the limits of national jurisdiction, all states have the same rights and obligations on the high seas (the water column), and a unique regime is established for the international seabed and its mineral resources. Further refinements of states' rights and obligations obtain in international straits and archipelagos... States bordering enclosed or semi-enclosed seas are specifically directed to cooperate as they exercise their rights and perform their duties under the Convention.

Beyond the limits of national jurisdiction, all states have the same rights and obligations on the high seas (the water column), and a unique regime is established for the international seabed and its mineral resources.

The establishment of different ocean zones has been criticized for drawing artificial boundaries that truncate marine ecosystems, ignore the movements of marine species, and turn a blind eye to the winds and currents transporting pollutants. On the other hand, it would be impossible to encompass within a single geographic unit or a single management authority all the complex and interactive factors that affect marine environments and species...

What's New About the Convention Ocean Law Regime?

Several significant shifts from the earlier international ocean law regime occurred as a result of the Third UN Conference on the Law of the Sea. Most importantly, the Convention recognizes:

- that the expansion of coastal states' rights to develop and manage offshore resources must be linked to duties to conserve living resources and protect the marine environment;

- that advancing scientific knowledge and the pace of political, economic, and technological change require radical new approaches to the progressive development and implementation of a rule of law for the oceans; and
- that cooperation to strengthen all nations' scientific, technical, and management capabilities is essential if the Convention is to be meaningfully implemented.

While much of the LOS Convention has been considered binding as customary international law during the last decade, its entry into force reaffirms and stabilizes customary law developments, adds important refinements, and puts in place the most elaborated arrangements for compulsory and binding dispute settlement of any international environmental agreement to date.

Coastal State Resource Rights

The coastal state enjoys sovereign rights over resources within the 200-mile EEZ. With respect to living resources, high seas fishing freedoms no longer exist in the EEZ and coastal state rights have expanded. For the first time, these rights are qualified by conservation obligations, and, in an attempt to retain benefits for the wider international community, by the obligation to share any surplus resources (resources that are not harvested by the coastal state) with other countries. The coastal state's exclusive control over continental shelf resources is reaffirmed and explicitly extended to the edge of the continental margin. It is obliged to share revenues with the international community from any mineral resources exploited beyond 200 n.m. That is, for nations lucky enough to have very wide continental shelves, the extension of their exclusive resource rights entails some contribution to international well-being…

Other Coastal State Economic Rights

Within the EEZ, the coastal state has sovereign rights not only over resources but also over other activities for the economic exploitation and exploration of the zone, such as the production of energy from water, currents, or winds. Within the EEZ and on the continental shelf, the coastal state has jurisdiction over the establishment and use of artificial islands and most installations and structures. In short, the Convention grants rights to control all activities carried out for economic development purposes to the coastal state, including activities carried out by other states that may prejudice these rights.

Coastal State Environmental Rights and Duties

The Convention recognizes that environmental protection must go hand in hand with control over development activities if the viability of those activities is to be sustained. Coastal state rights are subject to explicit obligations to protect and preserve the marine environment. Within the EEZ, the coastal state has jurisdiction for this purpose and acquires a greater degree of authority to set and enforce rules for foreign vessels in order to protect its marine resources and coastlines, balanced with obligations to respect international navigation rights. Port states (countries in whose ports vessels are voluntarily located) are granted additional rights to enforce international rules and standards applicable to foreign ships even if the violation has taken place outside a port state's EEZ.

Environmental/Conservation Obligations and Principles

The Convention establishes for all states the unqualified obligation to protect and preserve the entire marine environment. Its comprehensive framework addresses many aspects of this obligation, mandating in many cases, that more detailed, supplementary agreements be reached through appropriate international fore. Also articulated are a number of principles to guide the formulation of additional international rules and standards. As these more detailed rules and standards are elaborated and updated, they are incorporated by reference to the LOS Convention. The Convention, as elaborated, forms the basis for national law and policy.

The obligations and principles in the Convention have set the pace for international environmental law. They have shaped ecosystem-based marine living resources agreements and evolving concepts of marine protected areas. They support a preventive approach to marine pollution and require caution in the use of technologies and the introduction of new or alien species. Principle 21 of the *Stockholm Declaration*—a state's responsibility to ensure that activities within its jurisdiction or control do not cause damage to the environment of other states or to areas beyond national jurisdiction—is codified in the *Law of the Sea Convention* with respect to marine pollution, without qualification. It is strengthened by obligations to assess the potential adverse effects of planned activities, monitor the results, and communicate the findings internationally. An integrated approach to wastes management and pollution control is promoted by the duty not to transform one type of pollution into another nor transfer damage or hazards from one area to another. The entry into force of the Convention will more firmly ground these and other forward-looking principles as the basis for the progressive development of international ocean law.

Compliance, Enforcement, and Dispute Settlement

The LOS Convention contains new rules on compliance and enforcement, particularly with respect to pollution by vessels, high seas fishing, and any future deep seabed mining. In addition, it establishes an unprecedented system for the settlement of oceans disputes. If more voluntary procedures fail, most disputes may be submitted by any disputant to binding international arbitration or adjudication. All environmental disputes and many fisheries disputes are subject to these procedures. The entry into force of the Convention will bring this system into effect for its parties and establish a new International Tribunal on the Law of the Sea. The system provides an important point of reference to ensure that framework Convention provisions, as supplemented by related agreements, are consistently interpreted and applied.

Marine Scientific Research

The coastal state gains jurisdiction over marine scientific research carried out in its EEZ. While the 1958 *Continental Shelf Convention* already required the consent of the coastal state for foreign research on the shelf, the 1982 Convention adds a requirement for coastal state consent to foreign research in the EEZ (effectively, the water column). The balance between coastal state control and foreign access, however, is more subtle. Although coastal state concerns over possible commercial or military "research espionage" shifted the balance toward coastal state control, there are numerous stipulations in the Convention that facilitate access for all states to carry out "basic" or "fundamental" research—as opposed to research of direct significance for the exploration and exploitation of natural resources (Articles 246, 252). They also facilitate research programs undertaken under the auspices of an international organization (Article 247). Moreover, the thrust of the relevant articles is to respond to coastal State interest in taking part in research ventures and in sharing and interpreting the results, and to ensure that research results are made internationally available (Articles 244, 249).

A New Global Bargain

In order to conclude a comprehensive package deal, the participants in UNCLOS III struck several global bargains. On the one hand, these represent trade-offs among the specific interests and concerns of the nations taking part in the Conference. On the other, they introduce major new dimensions in international lawmaking, including universal participation in multilateral negotiations and recognition of the need for international cooperation to assist developing nations implement treaty provisions.

The Trade-Offs

Among the 'deals' incorporated into the Convention, the major maritime nations conceded extended coastal state jurisdiction in exchange for guaranteed rights of international navigation, overflight, and telecommunications, in particular through international straits and archipelagos. To ensure this balance, some concessions were made to developing nations in structuring the regime for the international deep seabed. In addition, coastal states endowed with bountiful offshore zones agreed to share a portion of these resources with the international community. The major industrialized nations with multinational resource interests and the nations with distant-water fishing capabilities effectively conceded to coastal states the right to exact a price for granting foreigners access to EEZ resources. For marine research programs, the price of access to coastal state zones was explicit: the right to participate in research ventures and learn from the results. In making use of national rights, all nations agreed to preserve and protect the marine environment and to conserve marine living resources.

The regime for the international deep seabed—beyond the EEZ and the continental shelf—establishes the seabed and its resources as the "common heritage of mankind". For the first time, the international community fashioned a system for collective management of common property resources not subject to national sovereignty or appropriation. This "common heritage" concept has been usefully distinguished from the term "common concern"—employed in the *Framework Convention on Climate Change* and the *Convention on Biological Diversity*. The latter conventions apply primarily to activities taking place in areas subject to national sovereignty, whose cumulative results add up to a "common concern". The collective management of deep seabed resources required new international machinery to ensure international recognition of rights and avoid conflicts; to promote the orderly development of the resources; to guarantee human safety and environmental protection; and to ensure that mankind as a whole benefited. The deal struck in the 1982 Convention, as modified by the 1994 Agreement, offers the developing nations equitable participation in resource management decisions, and financial and technical benefits once deep seabed mining becomes commercially feasible.

New Dimensions in International Lawmaking: Participation in Decision Making and International Technical and Financial Support

The resolutions adopted annually by the UN General Assembly on the law of the sea have consistently emphasized the needs of states arising from the new legal regime, including the need for technical and financial assistance.

The international politics of the time, brought about by changing political and economic circumstances, produced explicit recognition of the importance of universal participation in the elaboration of the law. It reaffirmed that the law should ensure more substantial international cooperation in the use and development of the oceans, so that the entire world community would benefit. This goes well beyond the regime developed for the international deep seabed. It permeates every aspect of ocean use. In the Convention preamble, states parties:

> "Recogniz[e] the desirability of establishing ... a legal order for the seas and oceans which will ... promote the peaceful uses of the seas and oceans, the equitable and efficient utilization of their resources, the conservation of their living resources, and the study, protection and preservation of the marine environment, ... and
>
> Bear in mind that the achievement of these goals will contribute to the realization of a just and equitable international economic order which takes into account the interests and needs of mankind as a whole and, in particular, the special interests and needs of developing countries, ... "

Part XII of the Convention, "Protection and Preservation of the Marine Environment", requires states, directly or through competent international organizations, to promote scientific, educational, technical and other assistance to developing states for environmental purposes, and requires that international organizations grant developing states preference in allocating resources and special services for these purposes (Articles 202, 203). Parts XIII and XIV of the Convention address cooperation in "Marine Scientific Research" and the "Development and Transfer of Marine Technology". They are supplemented by Annex VI (Resolution on Development of National Marine Science, Technology and Ocean Service Infrastructures, Final Act of the Third UN Conference on the Law of the Sea), which foreshadows more recent developments in international environmental agreements and *Agenda 21*. The resolution recognized that unless urgent measures were taken, rapid advances in marine science and technology would widen the gap between developed and industrialized nations, endangering the very foundations of the new regime. It supported national and international action to strengthen national capabilities, and called for states to determine priorities in national development plans for strengthening their marine science, technology, and ocean services.

Anticipating current efforts to improve and increase technical and financial assistance for national implementation, the resolution urged international support for national programs and more co-ordinated efforts on the part of the UN system. It recommended that the World Bank, the regional banks, the UN Development Programme, and other multilateral funding agencies augment and coordinate their operations to this end. The resolutions adopted annually by the UN General Assembly on the law of the sea have consistently emphasized the needs of states arising from the new legal regime, including the need for technical and financial assistance.

UNCLOS III: The Context

Several factors influenced the 1970 decision of the UN General Assembly to convene a comprehensive global conference on the law of the sea. From a national security perspective, the major powers feared that a growing number of excessive claims by coastal states would undermine traditional freedoms of navigation and overflight. The conferees who drafted the 1958 Conventions had been unable to agree on the limits of coastal state territorial sovereignty or coastal state exclusive jurisdiction over fisheries. The second law of the sea conference in 1960 also failed to resolve these questions. A compromise proposal on a six-mile territorial sea and a further six-mile zone of exclusive fisheries jurisdiction did not quite win sufficient support. While there was a general international understanding, based on long-standing custom, that coastal states were entitled to a three-mile territorial sea and more limited rights in the nine miles beyond, this was beginning to erode.

The distinction between the territorial sea, subject to national sovereignty, and natural resource rights (fishery zone, EEZ) is an important one. Territorial sovereignty is an inclusive concept of coastal state authority; within the territorial sea the coastal state wields discretionary control over all activities, subject only to the limited international right of "innocent passage" for ships navigating on the surface. (Unless otherwise agreed, submarines must navigate on the surface and airplanes need permission to fly over.) Resource rights are restricted to exploring, exploiting, and managing resources. Beyond the territorial sea, international high seas rights of navigation and overflight may not be curtailed, nor the laying of submarine cables and pipelines.

During the late 1960s, more and more nations extended their claims offshore, both in limits and in scope. These proliferating claims threatened fundamental security interests in freedom of navigation and overflight; they raised the spectre of multiple conflicts over resources and other ocean uses; and they created a patchwork of unilaterally-declared zones subject to different and changing rules, further undermining a stable and predictable climate for international commerce and ocean use.

Clearly, wider territorial seas would restrict submarine navigation and overflight, and hamper surface transit. The extension from three to twelve miles subjected approximately 100 international straits less than 24 n.m. wide to the more restrictive "innocent passage" rule. Many of these straits represent the sole point of entry (Straits of Hormuz and Bab el Mandeb to the Persian Gulf) or a major short-cut, reducing the time and cost of alternative routes (Strait of Malacca, adjacent to Indonesia, Malaysia, and Singapore, which is the main sea route between the Indian and Pacific Oceans; or the Strait of Gibraltar, which provides access to the Mediterranean and, through the Suez Canal, to the Indian Ocean). As a result, the LOS Conference defined the right of "transit passage" through international straits to preserve important traditional navigation rights through and over such straits.

Claims to 200-mile territorial seas caused particular concern, for in addition to potentially restricting high seas freedoms, they would reduce areas subject to conservation obligations for living resources and were likely to curtail high seas fishing rights and the possibility of scientific research undertaken by foreign vessels. There were also fears that claims to protect the marine environment would be used as a back-door approach to restricting foreign navigation, whether in the Canadian or (then) Soviet Arctic or in the Strait of Malacca.

Many of the newly independent nations in the 1960s did not endorse the 1958 *Geneva Conventions*. They believed that the limits on coastal state resource rights favored the major maritime and industrialized nations with their distant water fishing and deep-water technological capabilities. A few coastal states objected to alleged foreign surveillance activities just beyond the three-mile territorial sea, manifested by North Korea's seizure of the US Pueblo in 1968. Others were wary of foreign research vessels, whose findings seemed to give the advantage to foreign firms in locating fish and offshore minerals or negotiating resource development contracts. Vocal constituencies in some of the industrialized nations sought expanded coastal state jurisdiction over fisheries.

The growing importance of offshore oil and gas in future world energy scenarios had a major influence on both developed and developing nations. Their aim was to reaffirm exclusive rights over these resources and thus improve the potential for national energy self-sufficiency and/or resource revenues. (Oil and gas resources form in the sediments deposited from the continental land mass, throughout the continental margin. The abyssal plain of the deep seabed lies beyond these sediments.) While exclusive coastal State rights to continental shelf resources were recognized in the 1958 Convention, the outer limit of these rights was elastic, contingent on technological developments; that is, "where the depths of the superjacent waters admits of the exploitation of the natural resources". Even though further legal judgments defined the shelf as the natural prolongation of the continental land mass, there was still no agreement about how to determine the outer boundary.

When the mineral resource potential of the deep seabed began to be discussed (and exaggerated) in the late 1960s, there was virtually unanimous opposition to permitting a free-for-all of national claims. From the perspective of the major maritime states, this could impede traditional high seas activities—notably, submarine navigation and detection. From the perspective of the developing nations, the technologically-advanced states would have a clear advantage. A 1967 speech by Ambassador Arvid Pardo of Malta led to a UN resolution calling for the seabed beyond national jurisdiction to be reserved exclusively for peaceful purposes and for its resources to be used for the benefit of all mankind, taking into account the special interests and needs of the developing nations. As international machinery was designed to administer exploration and exploitation rights and to give concrete expression to the idea that mankind as a whole should benefit from deep seabed minerals development, the debate centered on the allocation of control between international and national authorities and the system of international decision-making.

Broader international developments also affected the law of the sea negotiations. Growing disparities in wealth made the debate over economic development increasingly contentious between the industrialized and developing nations. In addition to asserting permanent national sovereignty over natural resources, developing nations favored price and production controls and international trade preferences as a means of increasing returns to raw materials producers. Many sought strong international directives that would facilitate access to scientific and technical information and rapidly developing new technologies. Stringent investment codes and high taxes for multinational corporations were perceived as a means of ensuring substantial benefits to host countries, and the establishment of state-controlled enterprises a way to avoid and control direct foreign investment.

From the perspective of environmental protection, the LOS Conference was captive to the most visible and widely-reported incidents of marine pollution at the time. These included the 1967 Torrey Canyon oil spill off Land's End, England, and Thor Heyerdahl's accounts of tarballs in the mid-Atlantic near major shipping routes. Offshore oil development had also produced disastrous blow-outs like the 1969 Santa Barbara Channel oil spill off California. It was not until 1982 that the first comprehensive assessment of The Health of the Oceans emerged, followed by a second in 1990. These reports began to call attention to the chronic land-based sources of marine pollution and the problems of coastal and habitat degradation, which were far more significant than pollution from vessels. The LOS Convention elaborates a more detailed regime for vessel-source pollution, carefully balancing coastal and maritime interests, and maintains that balance for other sea-based activities that could impede navigation freedoms. For land-based activities, it establishes a solid foundation of obligations and principles to be elaborated through supplementary agreements.

The issue of land-based activities was affected by the same tension that had surfaced at the 1972 Stockholm Conference. The developing nation view of economic development as the means to cure their major environmental problems contrasted with the developed nation view of economic development as the source of their environmental problems. During the LOS Conference, there was a substantial debate over the "double standard"; that is, whether to specify that developing nations could adopt lower standards for protection of the marine environment than the industrialized nations to avoid impeding their development. By demonstrating that mounting marine pollution off the larger coastal cities of the South was every bit as serious as in the North, the conferees forged agreement on common commitments. The trade-offs were both explicit and implicit. Without assistance, there were limits to what the developing nations could accomplish in dealing with land-based activities. They would employ means "at their disposal" and ``'in accordance with their capabilities." It was up to the industrialized nations to live up to their commitments to provide assistance.

From the perspective of conserving marine living resources, the political momentum behind wider zones of coastal state control over fisheries was reinforced by concern to avert the "tragedy of the commons", defined by Garrett Hardin in 1968. Coastal fishing communities in both industrialized and developing nations sought coastal state authority out to 200 miles in order to get rid of foreign competition over the 90 percent of world fisheries found in these zones. Many also saw the EEZ as a way to vest conservation responsibilities in coastal states. For some of the developing nations, the EEZ offered, in addition, a basis for contractual arrangements with foreign fishing interests that would increase benefits to the coastal State, whether in terms of revenue, equipment, or technical assistance. Ironically, the failure to stem the decline in world fisheries is primarily the result of coastal state failures to exercise their expanded authorities and duties in environmentally-sound ways.

The ten-year LOS Conference negotiations took place in a climate of growing international insecurity over navigation and overflight rights, coastal state desires to expand control over offshore resources, expectations of substantial international benefits from deep seabed mineral resources, and heightened North–South tension. The Convention's provisions on resources conservation and marine environmental protection (other than vessel-source pollution) were least affected by these trends. In retrospect, they benefited from that 'neglect'. Were nations to negotiate these issues today in a series of limited-purpose agreements, or modelled on more recent global environmental agreements, it is unlikely that the same sweeping, fundamental obligations could be achieved.

Section Seven: Capacity Building

The Marine Environment

Previous sections outline the general obligations of all states to protect and preserve the marine environment, without qualification. They note the implicit and explicit trade-offs and balances inherent in the LOS Convention, where it was recognized that if international obligations were to be met, international assistance would be necessary: for sea-based activities, international rules and standards constitute minimum standards; whereas for land-based (and airborne) sources of marine pollution, assistance would be necessary to upgrade the means available to developing nations. Specific obligations to assist developing countries are found in relation to environmental assessment, environmental monitoring, and emergency response. Obligations to promote the capacity of states requesting assistance in marine research and technological capabilities in relation to protection and preservation of the marine environment are also specified below.

Regarding technical assistance to protect and preserve the marine environment, the Convention specifies that developing states shall be granted preference by international organizations in the allocation of appropriate funds and technical assistance and in utilizing their specialized services. [Article 202] elaborates on the responsibilities to be undertaken by states, directly or through competent international organizations, as follows:

"(a) promote programs of scientific, educational, technical and other assistance to developing states for the protection and preservation of the marine environment and the prevention, reduction and control of marine pollution. Such assistance shall include, inter alia,

(i) training of their scientific and technical personnel;

(ii) facilitating their participation in relevant international programs;

(iii) supplying them with necessary equipment and facilities;

(iv) enhancing their capacity to manufacture such equipment;

(v) advice on and developing facilities for research, monitoring, educational and other programs;

(b) provide appropriate assistance, especially to developing states, for the minimization of the effects of major incidents which may cause serious pollution of the marine environment;

(c) provide appropriate assistance, especially to developing states, concerning the preparation of environmental assessments."

In relation to deep seabed mining, states are obliged to promote international cooperation and programs for scientific and technical training, technical assistance, and research in marine science and technology and marine environmental protection (1994 Agreement, Annex, Section 5, Article l.c.).

More generally, states are to cooperate and exchange results, directly and through competent international organizations, in rule-making, emergency response, and research and studies related to marine pollution and its remedies; marine pollution monitoring; and establishing scientific criteria as a basis for rule-making (Articles 197-201, 204.1). Regarding the results of marine scientific research, every state is obliged to provide other states with a reasonable opportunity to obtain information necessary to prevent and control damage to human health and safety and to the marine environment (Article 242).

Marine Living Resources

In the context of the conserving marine living resources, both within the EEZ and on the high seas, the regular exchange of scientific information and catch and effort statistics is required through competent international organizations (Articles 61.5, 119.2). The Convention is also explicit regarding terms and conditions that coastal states may establish for access by other states' nationals to fish in the EEZ. These include the conduct of fisheries research programs, requirements for personnel training, transfer of technology, and enhancing research skills related to fisheries (Article 62.4).

Marine Research and the Transfer of Technology

To promote collaboration in scientific research, states and international organizations must make available information on proposed major research programs and the resulting knowledge. They must cooperate to promote the flow of scientific data and information and the transfer of knowledge, especially to developing states, and to strengthen marine research capabilities in developing states (Article 244). With respect to coastal state rights regarding research by foreign states or international organizations in its EEZ and continental shelf, it may participate in research projects and receive data, results, samples, and assistance in interpreting them (Article 249).

Collaboration to promote the development of marine science and technology and its transfer on fair and reasonable terms and conditions is to be undertaken directly by states and through competent international organizations. This includes the acquisition, evaluation, and dissemination of information, data, and knowledge on marine technologies as well as the development of appropriate marine technologies (Articles 266, 268, 269). States are also to promote the development of marine scientific and technological capacity of states which may need and request technical assistance for resource activities, marine scientific research, and the protection and preservation of the marine environment (Article 266). Anticipating later international agreements and *Agenda 21*, states are encouraged to foster economic and legal conditions favorable for the transfer of marine technology, and for the benefit of all parties concerned, with due regard for the rights and duties of holders, suppliers, and recipients of marine technology (Articles 266.c, 267, 269). Acting directly or through international organizations, they are to promote the development of the necessary technological infrastructure and human resources to facilitate marine technology transfer (Articles 268, 269).

The Convention calls for states, acting directly or through international organizations, to promote and support the establishment of national and regional centers for marine scientific and technological research, particularly in developing coastal states. The functions of regional facilities include study programs related to the protection and preservation of the marine environment and the acquisition, processing, and dissemination of information on marine research and technologies, as well as systematic information systems on technology acquisition and marketing (Articles 275-277).

Funding and Coordination

Other articles encourage bilateral, regional, and multilateral cooperative programs to facilitate appropriate international funding for ocean research and development. They urge that the efforts of competent international organizations be coordinated in the field of marine technology transfer (Articles 27-274). Moreover, the competent international organizations dealing with marine science and marine technology are themselves obliged to "take all appropriate measures to ensure, either directly or in close cooperation among themselves, the effective discharge of their functions and responsibilities" (Article 278).

Institutional and Legal Developments

A review of the many international programs that provide support for capacity building related to use and protection of marine and coastal areas and marine living resources would be voluminous. These have developed to support the implementation of specific legal agreements—for example, IMO's Integrated Technical Cooperation Programme, trust funds established pursuant to the UNEP regional seas programs, or FAO support for fisheries agreements—and to enhance capabilities more generally with respect to marine research and marine management, with significant programs in FAO and IOC. Virtually all of the marine agreements contain language promoting international cooperation, directly and through competent international organizations. Numerous international agencies are involved, as well as bilateral donors.

More concerted support for implementation of the regional marine programs has begun to develop in the Mediterranean and Black Seas. The Environmental Program for the Mediterranean, launched in 1988, and the Mediterranean Environmental Technical Assistance Program, have been supported by the World Bank, UNDP, European Investment Bank, and Commission of the European Communities. The Black Sea program is supported by UNDP and the Global Environment Facility (GEF). The former built upon the UNEP regional seas program but was not directly linked to it; the latter subsumes the regional agreement initiated by UNEP. The GEF has also supported efforts furthering the implementation of the *Baltic Sea Convention*.

The GEF—a tripartite arrangement among UNEP, UNDP, and the World Bank—focuses on marine and freshwater initiatives through its "international waters" component. In addition to the two regional agreements noted above, it has funded projects that contribute to the implementation of MARPOL 73/78 in the Wider Caribbean and in China. Its role regarding the other regional marine agreements remains to be defined. Two recent documents, the *Programme of Action of the SIDS Conference* and the *Draft Implementation Agreement from the UN Fisheries Conference*, explicitly name the GEF, in addition to other traditional funders, as potential sources of assistance for developing states.

In the final act of UNCLOS III, the call for national development plans to strengthen capabilities in marine science, technology, and ocean services, and better co-ordination among international agencies in support of these initiatives, warrants renewed attention. As with every other aspect of the environmental development web, the marine/coastal sector cannot be dealt with in isolation. It should be merged with sustainable development assessment, planning, and management at local, national, and regional levels. From a sectoral standpoint, national (and regional) plans for biodiversity and species conservation, freshwater management, forests management, and airborne pollution control need to take into account, explicitly, causes and effects related to the marine/coastal sector. From these specialized plans, a coordinated national strategy needs to be forged, which can focus external assistance on national concerns and priorities. IUCN experts are in a position to shape and influence national assessment and planning at all levels of governance, and to help formulate criteria for determining priorities. They can bring to bear expertise in marine and coastal issues, wetlands, biodiversity and other areas and deal constructively with interactions and synergies.

International cooperation to strengthen research, assessment, and monitoring capabilities as a basis for improved management is essential. The transfer of management skills within and among regions is vital. The IUCN network of experts already contributes to such capacity building and is ideally suited to promote information exchange among regions.

IUCN has urged governments to develop global networks to enhance management capacity and training to maximize sharing between nations and regions regarding experience, research, and technical information on integrated management of coastal, shallow sea, and marine environments and resources (Resolution 19.46).

In relation to the transfer of technology and other management skills and practices, the LOS Convention's call for states to foster economic and legal conditions favorable to transfer end that benefit all those involved, resonate in light of *Agenda 21* and other emphases on the constructive role that may be played by the private sector.

Specifically, pursuant to the LOS and *Biodiversity Conventions*, the guidelines for granting access to foreign researchers in the EEZ, developed pursuant to the LOS Convention, should be drawn upon as cooperative arrangements are developed for research and shared benefits relating to genetic resources in marine areas under national jurisdiction.

3

Regional Seas Treaties and Programmes

A

UNEP Water Branch, *Regional Seas Programme: General Strategy*, UNEP, 2001

International cooperation to strengthen research, assessment, and monitoring capabilities as a basis for improved management is essential.

[*This extract is accessible on the Internet and was accessed on 12/07/01. The address is <http://www.unep.org/unep/program/natres/water/regseas/regseas.htm>.*]

The Regional Seas Programme was initiated in 1974 as a global program implemented through regional components. *Agenda 21*, the UN General Assembly of the Governing Council of UNEP endorsed the Regional approach. The Programme at present includes thirteen regions involving more than 140 coastal States and Territories.

The Regional Seas Programme is an action-oriented program and focuses not only on the mitigation or elimination of the consequences but also on the causes of environmental degradation. It has a comprehensive, integrated, result oriented approach to combating environmental problems through the rational management of marine and coastal areas.

General Strategy

The Regional Seas Programme was initiated by UNEP in 1974 as a global program implemented through regional components. Since then the Governing Council of UNEP has repeatedly endorsed a regional approach to the control of marine pollution and the management of marine and coastal resources and has requested the development of regional actions plans.

The Regional Seas Programme at present includes 13 regions and has over 140 coastal States and Territories participating in it. It is conceived as an action-oriented program having concern not only for the consequences but also for the causes of environmental degradation and encompassing a comprehensive approach to combating environmental problems through the management of marine and coastal areas. Each regional action plan is formulated according to the needs of the region as perceived by the Governments concerned. It is designed to link assessment of the quality of the marine environment and the causes of its deterioration with activities for the management and development of the marine and coastal environment. The action plans promote the parallel development of regional legal agreements and of action-oriented program activities.

The program is under the overall co-ordination of the Water Branch of UNEP but its success critically depends on the work of specialized organization and centers dealing with specific regions covered by the program or with specific subjects common to most or all of the regions.

The substantive aspect of any regional program is outlined in an "Action Plan" which is formally adopted by an intergovernmental meeting of Governments of a particular region before the program enters as an operational phase. In the preparatory phase leading to the adoption of the action plan, Governments are consulted through a series of meetings and missions about the scope and substance of an action plan suitable for their region. In addition, with the cooperation of appropriate global and regional organizations, reviews on the specific environmental problems of the region and in corresponding priorities to be assigned to the various activities outlined in the action plan.

All action plans are structured in a similar way, although the specific activities for any region are dependent upon the needs and priorities of that region. An action plan usually includes the following components:

(i) Environmental Assessment. This concerns assessing and evaluating the causes of environmental problems as well as their magnitude and impact on the region. Emphasis is given to such activities as: baseline studies, research and monitoring of the sources levels and effects of marine pollutants, ecosystem studies, studies of coastal and marine activities and social and economic factors that may influence, or may be influenced by, environmental degradation, and the survey of national environmental legislation.

(ii) Environmental Management. Each regional program includes a wide range of activities in the field of environmental management. Examples of such activities are:

- cooperative regional projects on training in environmental impact assessment,
- management of coastal lagoons, estuaries and mangrove ecosystems,
- control of industrial, agricultural and domestic wastes,
- formulation of contingency plans for dealing with pollution emergencies.

(iii) Environmental legislation. An umbrella regional convention, elaborated by specific technical protocols, most often provides the legal framework for cooperative regional and national actions. The legal commitment of Governments clearly expresses their political will to manage individually and jointly their common environmental problems.

(iv) Institutional Arrangements. When adopting an action plan, Governments agree upon an organization to act as the permanent or interim secretariat of the action plan. Governments also are expected to decide upon the periodicity of intergovernmental meetings which are to be responsible for reviewing the progress of the agreed workplan and for approving new activities and the necessary budgetary support.

(v) Financial arrangements. UNEP, together with selected United Nations and other organizations, provide "seed money" or catalytic financing in the early stages of regional programs. However, as a program develops, it is expected that the Governments of the region will progressively assume the full financial responsibility. Government financing is usually channeled through special regional trust funds to which governments make annual contributions. These funds are administered by the organization responsible for the secretariat functions of the action plan. In addition,

Governments contribute by supporting their national institutions participating in the program or by financing specific project activities.

It is essential to bear in mind that all components of a regional program are independent. Assessment activities identify the problems that need priority attention in the region. Legal agreements are negotiated to strengthen cooperation among States in managing the identified problems. They also provide an important tool for national policy makers to implement national control activities. Management activities, aimed at controlling existing environmental problems and preventing the development of new ones, are one of the means by which States fulfill their treaty obligations.

The key to the success of any regional seas action plan is the political agreement of the Governments concerned and the execution of the program primarily by national and other appropriate institutions from the region in close cooperation with the relevant components of the United Nations system, regional organizations and other appropriate organizations. The successful implementation of any regional seas action plan also depends to a considerable degree on sound preparations which take into account the specific socioeconomic and political situation in a given region, the priorities in environmental protection as defined by the Governments of the region, the recognized capabilities and needs of the national institutions which are participating in the action plan, and the results of past and ongoing activities.

Consultations with the Governments concerned, the United Nations system and other appropriate organizations are essential for the preparatory phase of a regional program. As a result of such consultations, the general strategy of developing a regional program should be clarified, priority program elements should be proposed, and the timing of, and responsibility for, substantive actions during the preparatory phase should be determined.

The procedures and activities followed in developing an action plan are instrumental in determining the Governments' and experts' long-term commitment to the implementation of the plan's activities and whether or not the action plan corresponds to the real priorities and needs of the region. Without a strong governmental commitment and a realistic program, efforts to promote regional environmental cooperation will be short-lived. Consequently, the process leading to the adoption of an action plan is crucial.

B

Verlaan P., "Lecture on the International Legal Context for the Management of the Marine Environment," in UNEP/UNITAR/ UNCHS(Habitat) Training Program, *Environmental Law and Policy*, Nairobi, 1995

Introduction

It is important to note at the outset that the management of ocean space and the rule of law on the oceans have been addressed by the international community of nations with increasing sophistication and complexity for hundreds of years. Now, in 1995, marine environmental lawyers have to deal with, inter alia:

- the UN *Convention on the Law of the Sea* (UNCLOS) of 1982
- nine Regional Seas Conventions, 24 Protocols and twelve Action Plans,
- nine related maritime pollution conventions concluded under the auspices of the International Maritime Organization
- the Conventions dealing with the North Atlantic and the Baltic (Bonn, Oslo, Paris & Helsinki)
- various multilateral fisheries agreements the Antarctic Treaty System
- the International Whaling Convention the Wellington Convention on Drift Net Fisheries

In this presentation, I would like to focus on a very few, but very important action points for your consideration.

The 1982 United Nations *Convention on the Law of the Sea*

The importance to your work in both the marine AND the terrestrial environment of the entry into force of the 1982 United Nations *Convention on the Law of the Sea* (UNCLOS) last November cannot be overemphasized. This is the overarching global convention within which all matters relating to the marine environment must be cast. UNCLOS is a global constitutional Convention. It establishes, inter

UNCLOS also recognizes the need for international and regional cooperation in achieving the requirement that States MUST protect and preserve the marine environment.

alia, a comprehensive and obligatory public international law framework for the management of the marine environment, in application of one of its founding principles, namely that "the problems of ocean: space are closely interrelated and need to be considered as a whole." (Preamble.) Consequently, UNCLOS also recognizes the need for international and regional cooperation in achieving the requirement that States MUST protect and preserve the marine environment.

Consequences of the Entry into Force of UNCLOS

The entry into force of UNCLOS has, inter alia, the following consequences for States-Parties:

- They MUST adopt and enforce measures for the protection of the marine environment;
- They MUST adopt these measures even though it may mean promulgating legislation relating to what are normally considered purely terrestrial concerns. UNCLOS applies to pollution of the marine environment from ANY source. For example, consider Article 207: "States shall (emphasis added) adopt laws and regulations to prevent, reduce and control pollution of the marine environment from land-based sources, including rivers...." and Article 212: "States shall (emphasis added) adopt laws and regulations to prevent, reduce and control pollution of the marine environment from or through the atmosphere, applicable to air space under their sovereignty...."
- They *must* apply *and enforce*, as a minimum, internationally or regionally agreed rules, regulations, recommended practices and procedures, even if these rules, etc., are promulgated under a global or regional agreement to which they are not a party.
- They MUST cooperate, globally and regionally, in the formulation of these rules, etc.
- They MUST submit to compulsory and binding dispute settlement procedures, with a very few exceptions not relevant here.

National Legal and Policy Implications

The national legal and policy implications of the preceding include [the following].

States which are parties to UNCLOS but not parties to, for example, their regional seas conventions and action plans, are OBLIGED to apply the provisions of those regional conventions and action plans. However, as non-parties to the latter, they have no right to be consulted on the application of those conventions or to receive whatever financial assistance may be available under those regional conventions or action plans for their implementation. On the other hand, they are obliged to cooperate with the regional convention's States—Parties in the promulgation of new rules, etc., but again without any right to a vote or to financial assistance for such cooperation.

The same is true for States which are parties to UNCLOS but not parties to other global multilateral marine environmental agreements. Here I wish to draw your particular attention to the agreements promulgated and administered under the auspices of the International Maritime Organization (IMO).

The same will be true for States who are parties to UNCLOS but who are not intending to become parties to the proposed *Global Convention on High Seas Fisheries and Straddling Stocks* and the proposed *Global Programme of Action for the Protection of the Marine Environment from Land-Based Activities* (these titles may change when these instruments are finally adopted, which is presently expected to be by the end of 1995).

The same is true for States who are parties to UNCLOS but not parties to any international or regional fisheries agreements. For details on these, please consult with the Fisheries Department of the UN Food and Agricultural Organization (FAO).

The same is true for States who are parties to UNCLOS but not to the *International Whaling Convention* or the *Marine Mammal Action Plan*. For details on these, please consult with the Programme Officer responsible for marine mammals at UNEP-OCA/PAC. In the same context, please note that States-Parties to UNCLOS are under a more stringent set of obligations to protect their marine biodiversity than are States-Parties to the *Biodiversity Convention*.

Note: The foregoing is not intended to be an exhaustive list of international legal instruments relating to the marine environment.

For those States who have signed but not ratified UNCLOS please note that not ratifying does not significant) assist in postponing the obligations of UNCLOS, a signing an international treaty obliges States at the very least not to act inconsistently with that treaty.

For those very few States who have not signed UNCLOS at all, unless they make it very clear that they do not agree with this Convention, they will be confronted with the possibility that certain parts of the Convention may still be applied to them in cases of dispute.

UNCLOS embodies a set of rights and benefits that are carefully balanced against the concomitant undertaking of duties and obligations by States-Parties. The former cannot be asserted without also complying with the latter. Please note that it is probably not possible, even for clear non-parties, to claim a right or benefit under UNCLOS while denying the concomitant and balancing obligation or duty.

The duties and obligations under UNCLOS are extensive and complex; they are not contingent or qualified. The rights and benefits cannot be exercised unless due regard is paid to the rights of other States and the concomitant duties and obligations are implemented. As stated in Article 235 with regard to the marine environment, States-Parties "shall be liable in accordance with international law." Furthermore, in that same Article, States "shall ensure that recourse is available in accordance with their legal systems for prompt and adequate compensation or other relief in respect of damage caused by pollution of the marine environment by natural or juridical persons under their jurisdiction." Thus, an unqualified requirement for implementation and enforcement is immediately effective when a State becomes a party to UNCLOS, and UNCLOS provides no grounds for relief from these obligations on grounds, for example, of lack of staff, skills, finances, other resources, assistance from other countries or other sources should a State-Party be obliged to defend itself against allegations of non-compliance with its obligation to protect and preserve the marine environment.

In conclusion on this point, the national legal and policy consequences of the coming into force of UNCLOS for the countries represented here may be bluntly summarized as requiring the development, passage, implementation and enforcement of the appropriate national legislation.

The Regional Seas Programme

Compliance with the environmental obligations of UNCLOS is not a trivial task, and its accomplishment will be made considerably more difficult if it is attempted in isolation. Fortunately, countries need not do so alone unless they specifically so choose. In addition to the excellent services provided by, inter alia, UNEP's Environmental Law Unit and the United Nations Office of Ocean Affairs and the Law of the Sea in New York, every country has available to it, if it chooses, the services of a tailor-made, regionally designed, managed, financed, and agreed—at plenipotentiary level—legal instrument and implementing program for the protection and preservation of the marine environment which it shares with its neighboring countries. These services are provided by UNEP's Regional Seas Programme, one of the premier mechanisms for the implementation of UNCLOS, and which was designed to be so from its inception. Joining a Regional Sea Programme also makes available the full panoply of skills and twenty years of experience in facilitating the protection and preservation of the marine environment offered by UNEP.

The scope of and tasks undertaken by a Regional Sea Programme is limited only by the desires of its constituent governments. Any Regional Sea Programme can choose to focus on designing, implementing and enforcing legislation to protect and preserve the marine environment, and it is considerably more cost-effective and efficient, not to mention required by UNCLOS, to do so as a region than individually. At the annual Intergovernmental Meetings under which all Regional Seas Programmes operate, the governments can decide whether and how much money from the Trust Funds to allocate to marine environmental legislation purposes for the region. Furthermore, as the Regional Seas Programmes also function under the legislative authority granted by UNEP's Governing Council, and are granted catalytic funding by UNEP accordingly, the Council may request the Director of UNEP to allocate additional for these purposes from UNEP's Environment Executive Resources Fund. This will require close coordination between the government officials responsible for the representation of their respective countries within the Regional Sea Programme and those responsible for representing their countries to the Governing Council. Facilitating this coordination, and ensuring that the responsible national finance and budgetary officials are also involved, is one of the most important functions that a governmental legal adviser on environment could perform for his or her country in endeavoring to achieve the design of appropriate environmental legislation.

Even if one is not a party to UNCLOS, it is essential that countries wishing to benefit from the advantages of the presence of a Regional Sea Programme in their vicinity, formally join those Programmes, become full members of the relevant Conventions, Protocols and Action Plans and participate fully in the work of the Programme. Of course participation is not free of charge: nothing is free in this world. So also with the Regional Sea Programmes; financial obligations are incurred by participation in the Programme. A Regional Sea Programme is only set up at the specific request of governments, with legislative authority of UNEP's Governing Council and on the explicit assumption that governments find the Programme sufficiently useful to eventually assume full financial responsibility for its operation. These financial obligations can be very modest, they are not externally imposed, but are negotiated by the countries among themselves, and they are a direct measure of the amount of work the governments wish to undertake in the marine environment. Here also considerable economies of scale may be achieved, where the whole is greater than the sum of its parts but which guarantee the sustainability of the Programme for the mutual benefit of all the participants.

Adhesion to the appropriate legal instruments will facilitate the attraction of outside assistance, should this be necessary, if this is undertaken as a region rather than by countries individually. For certain forms of assistance, such as from the Global Environment Facility, for example, formal membership of the relevant regional or international conventions is now a condition precedent for any country to be able to receive financial assistance under the International Waters tranche of that funding mechanism

Follow-up Action

As the legal advisers on the environment to your governments, it is therefore recommended that you consider in the first instance completing the accession to, or ratification of, as appropriate, the relevant marine environmental conventions referred to above, and joining the relevant action plans, insofar as your governments have not already done so.

Please be aware that lack of money is not usually the primary obstacle to achieving the goal of protecting the environment. Nor is it the lack of appropriate legal skills. Far more important is the absence of coordination and the lack of communication between sectors and ministries. As has already been indicated above, if you could include in your role as legal adviser that of an inter-sectoral and inter-ministerial facilitator on matters relating to the environment, so that such measures as those adopted by your governments are not mutually contradictory, you will have achieved far more for the benefit of the environment—marine or terrestrial—than any amount of even the most carefully crafted legislation could, because the latter cannot function in an uncoordinated national context.

Finally, it is necessary to turn the attention of the Regional Seas Programmes more towards management and control of the marine environment. To that end it is imperative that domestic implementing legislation be coordinated at the regional level, because countries should not want to distort intra-regional competitive conditions, and they should wish to facilitate enforcement of that legislation, which is far more easily and cheaply achieved jointly than severally.

4

Marine Protected Areas

A

Salm R. and Dobbin J., "Planning, Management, and Administrative Processes for Marine Protected Areas," in *Application of the Biosphere Reserve Concept to Coastal Marine Areas*, Papers presented at the UNESCO/IUCN San Fransico Workshop of 14–20 August 1989, IUCN, Gland, Switzerland, 1993

Introduction

There are many different approaches to marine-protected area planning, management, and administration. The choice of approach should be influenced by the prevailing resources as well as environmental, social, political, and economic parameters. The climate of the area and the species living within it must also be considered. These parameters help to identify the boundary of the "target marine protected area" and its interactions with:

- linked environments and component species (the ecological component);
- the pressures on these by human needs and activities (the socioeconomic component); and
- the political, administrative, and institutional influences and constraints (the political component).

An understanding of the interaction among these three components will ultimately lead to the appropriate management strategy. The process for determining the final management and administrative strategy is called the planning process. In other words, planning is the deliberate action between knowledge (scientific and objective understanding of an environmental problem) and implementation (putting solutions to the problem into effect).

In developing administrative and management approaches to marine protected areas the following definition [from Koontz and O'Donnell] is helpful for planning:

> "Planning is deciding in advance what to do, how to do it, and who is to do it. Planning bridges the gap from where we are to where we want to go. It makes it possible for things to occur which would not otherwise happen. Although the exact future can seldom be predicted and factors beyond our control may interfere with the best laid plans, without planning, events are left to chance. Planning is an intellectual process, the conscious determination of courses of action, the basing of decisions on purpose, facts, and considered estimates."

It would be wrong to assume that a universal blueprint or design can be applied to every marine protected area. Because each site has different characteristics, dynamics, resources, uses, issues, and management objectives, there can be no one definitive model. For example, compare the planning for a small offshore island (having important turtle or seabird nesting sites, no inhabitants, no special management issues, no conflicting uses) with a vast mainland estuarine complex (having settlements, expanding fisheries, recreation, agriculture, and port development potential). The two sites would necessarily have vastly different types and levels of management and administrative systems.

However, it is possible to follow the planning and design process which has been applied over many years to real projects by landscape architects, architects, and regional environmental planners. Their experience has resulted in a planning process that provides basic elements which can be adapted as needed to individual cases. This planning process includes the flow of relevant information through problem identification, data collection, data analysis, and data synthesis as the major phases. The emphasis is on the "process"—or the path one follows to achieve results. That path should include interdisciplinary teamwork, cross-sectoral planning, and participation by the end users and/or the manager throughout the planning process.

The small offshore island mentioned above could be afforded strict protection without conflict with any existing uses, and may not require a management presence. In cases of a low level of conflict, there could be the need for minimal surveillance or perhaps seasonal presence of rangers. A strict nature reserve of this sort would require minimal administrative support—possibly restricted to a cooperative agreement with the Coast Guard or Navy for periodic surveillance and enforcement.

This type of protected area takes us all the way back to Ray's original "critical marine habitats" (CMH) concept. Ray's CMH approach requires identification and strict protection of areas of intense biological diversity or sensitivity. What is missing—how to fit the CMH concept into the larger environmental, socioeconomic, and administrative context—is something that can be achieved through coastal and ocean planning.

Advance planning (prospective planning) is the key to resolving current issues and setting up the process to deal with future issues. It is more effective than reactive planning which responds to one issue at a time. Therefore, even the smallest and most strictly controlled areas cannot be protected in isolation.

In the vast mainland wetland area example. we might also use the CMH concept to identify "hot spots" on which to focus intensive management action. However, these sites cannot stand alone. and we would need to fit them into a cohesive framework. The definition of this framework, and the fitting of the critical marine habitats into it, requires an appropriate level of environmental planning. There is the need for thorough identification of the issues, review of development options, and careful assessment of their social and environmental consequences. Generally, the resulting planning process will need to:

- resolve urgent and important management issues;
- provide for appropriate levels of protection and management of CMHs and other sites of vital importance in context with the region; and
- anticipate the emergence of future management issues during the course of the development process and provide a framework to resolve them.

This type of planning will result in very different management and administration processes for the two examples. The process of determining management actions, however, is the same for both areas.

In the remainder of this paper, we will address the following related management questions. Are small CMHs likely to survive as discrete units? How can the above three management needs be tied together in the planning process? Is there a single prototype management and administrative system? If so, what is it?

Survival of Small "Cookie Cutter" Marine Protected Areas

The natural linkages among coastal, marine, and inland realms preclude the effective management of coastal and marine areas as independent entities. This is the principle obstacle to long-term survival of "cookie-cutter" reserves—small discrete sites cut out of large heavily developed areas. Of course there are exceptions. A remote rocky islet with a seasonal seabird colony may well survive management as a discrete unit. Generally, there is value in protecting small areas that are essential for safeguarding such vital habitats, but their management should be integrated with that of the surrounding region.

Integrated Planning

One solution is to include the planning of marine protected areas as part of general coastal land use planning, for example, through coastal zone management (CZM). Establishment of marine protected areas in the broader context of CZM planning has been recommended as an effective technique for the management of upstream and other interactive activities and processes, and this has yet to be fully exploited. The goals of CZM are to build policies into overall land use planning to meet the needs mentioned above.

Appropriately conceived and developed CZM plans can achieve a vast multiple use reserve for the entire coastal zone of a nation. Within the coastal zone all valuable resource areas (CMH) can be managed to avoid damaging activities and pollution through development policies controlled by specific legislation, or contained by zoning plans. The entire coastal zone of the country essentially functions as a large conservation area in which all significant ecosystems receive protection without the deployment of permanent field managers. Thus, only the minimal core areas need specific management attention. Management activities are free to focus on protection of CMHs or core areas, reducing conflict between user groups, and enabling the restoration of damaged areas. There are many parallels between planning for CZM and planning for biosphere reserves.

As for marine biosphere reserves, one could consider a nation's entire exclusive economic zone (EEZ) as a management unit within which special areas may be identified as marine biosphere reserves. It is possible to use the existing regional institutional framework for the EEZ, such as legislation and regulations for fishing, pollution control, and fisheries management, to designate and manage biosphere reserves.

Land use policies can also be used to achieve *de facto* protection for a range of sensitive and scenic environments (including beaches, dunes, wetlands, estuaries, coastal cliffs and mountains, and headlands). This generally under exploited means of protecting critical habitats and scenic areas enables broad environmental protection without the need to define, legislate, and manage numerous small and scattered "cookie-cutter" reserves.

There are three action components of the CZM planning process as designed for the Sultanate of Oman which illustrate the integrated planning approach:

1. Establishment of planning policies which would provide a broad-brush approach to guide development in the coastal zone, and avert the emergence of new management issues. If built into the central planning system, an advantage of these planning policies is that they can achieve protection of a vast number of small, sensitive or productive coastal habitats, such as dunes and wetlands without requiring formal site protection or a management presence. For example, a setback

policy for development along the coast can keep coastal structures off unstable dune ridges and beaches; and wetlands policy can restrict encroachment of tidal lands, and prevent landfill, dumping, and destruction of vegetation.

2. Establishment of protected areas to enable intensive management of specific sites of particular value including:
   - Nature reserves, which are designed primarily for the conservation management of wildlife and other natural resources;
   - Scenic reserves, which are designed primarily to safeguard aesthetic resources through the control and monitoring of development activities; and
   - Recreation areas, which are designed to protect prime recreation areas for the public through varying levels of control over adjacent lands, and which provide different types of utilities and services.
3. Definition of issue-specific actions which recommend specific remedial actions for particular management issues in the coastal zone and assign these to a responsible agency for implementation. In this way, all concerned authorities are brought into the field of environmental management and conservation, and the burden of comprehensive CZM is spread among them.

Three Models for Planning, Management, and Administration of Marine Protected Areas

Consider the three approaches used for marine protected area management in Indonesia, Oman, and Australia's Great Barrier Reef, each of which is affected differently by their respective environmental, social, economic, administrative, and political characteristics.

Indonesia

In Indonesia, the Directorate General of Forest Protection and Nature Conservation (PHPA) has the mandate for all conservation activities, including the establishment and management of marine protected areas. Here, the marine protected areas are first gazetted to achieve rapid legal protection for a vast array of areas. Conservation management plans are then prepared for priority sites and, once funds are obtained, management is implemented. The marine protected area system includes a variety of representative environments, CMHs, and resource types, and aims to protect these and endangered species from damage or elimination.

Active site management is necessary to control localized, small-scale, but destructive activities. Once conservation management plans are prepared and funds are obtained, a reserve manager is appointed whose task it is to interpret and implement the plan.

Actual formulation of the conservation management plans was guided as much as possible by scientific principles, including island biogeography theory, which influenced the location, size, shape, and distribution of zones; by social parameters which also influenced the design of zones, but which mainly influenced the types and levels of use and development of the different zones; and by economic parameters which influenced the extent of management activity. This approach requires that marine protected areas be large enough to enable direct control by reserve personnel of all activities and developments which may affect the included ecosystems.

Active site management is necessary to control localized, small-scale, but destructive activities.

This approach is appropriate to the Indonesian situation where there is heavy dependence on the marine environment by resident communities; a bewildering variety of candidate marine protected areas with vastly differing resource values spread over a huge area; and where it is funding, not manpower, which primarily limits marine protected area management activities. Manpower is readily available, and with a certain amount of training and supervision, can be directed towards management of marine protected areas.

Sultanate of Oman

In contrast, manpower is the primary limiting factor to marine protected area management and administration in the Sultanate of Oman. Here, the CZM model was developed primarily as a means to reduce dependence on a large force of administrative and field personnel, and to reduce the size and number of conservation areas.

Experience in the Sultanate has shown the CZM approach to have distinct advantages. First, it draws marine protected area management into an integrated land-sea-use planning process, effectively establishing the entire coastal zone as a vast multiple use reserve, similar in concept to a biosphere reserve. It should be noted here that the coastal zone planning process bears little resemblance to coastal zone planning in the United States. In the Oman project, a great deal of emphasis was placed on resources on the "wet" side of the coastline with field survey central to data collection and analysis. Second, there was complete integration and inclusion of all the relevant agencies who manage resources and activities in the coastal zone, as well as emphasis on spatial planning techniques and overlay mapping in order to locate resource concentrations, conflicts, and compatibilities. Third, the Sultanate of Oman coastal zone management plans are based on a shared responsibility for administration and management of the coastal zone among concerned agencies. These factors reduce the requirement for huge conservation areas and a large management force. Management of defined marine protected areas remains the responsibility of the Ministry of Environment which also coordinates all CZM activities.

Australia (GBRMPA)

There are similarities between the CZM model of Oman and that of the Great Barrier Reef Marine Park Authority (GBRMPA), but they differ in certain important aspects. CZM ideally should tie terrestrial and marine elements into a single planning framework, thereby guiding inland development in such a way that reduces risk to downstream marine areas. The GBRMPA model is more of marine zone management planning, being bounded by the sideline.

Prospective planning for the definition of conservation and activity zones is used both in Indonesia and Oman. This form of management planning entails evaluation of marine environments on the basis of their intrinsic values, and where necessary may require the control or exclusion of existing activities which conflict with resource conservation in the most valuable sites. In other words, zonation reflects intrinsic resource values. The GBRMPA model is more retrospective in the sense that existing uses play a significant role in the definition of zones. Zonation reflects current patterns of use, which is not necessarily what uses should be.

The Great Barrier Reef is an exceptional case with a number of characteristics which have enabled GBRMPA to be more accommodating of existing uses in overall design of the marine park. These include the sentiment of the reef as an object of national pride and the considerable public will to preserve it; the low resident population and vast areas with no history of resident communities dependent on its resources; relatively low levels of resource/use conflicts; and the great number of alternative undamaged sites for location of different resource uses, developments, and conservation areas.

By way of contrast, Indonesia has a disparate system of coral reefs, most of which are exploited by resident communities which subsist to a large extent on the reef resources. All parts of it are exploited by itinerant collectors of mother-of-pearl shell and turtles who use extremely destructive collection methods.

Focusing Management on Marine Protected Areas

These three case studies show that there can be quite different approaches to planning, management, and administration of marine protected areas dictated by the prevailing conditions. There is a common pattern for defining goals, deploying staff, isolating priority actions, and implementing management programs. The primary goals of marine protected area planning are generally to prohibit the pursuit of any damaging activities, to control fisheries, recreation, and shore or inland developments as necessary, and to restore degraded areas.

To be effective, marine protected areas require staffing. A low-level staff presence is relatively easy to achieve and its mere presence can often make a considerable contribution to control of the most damaging activities. But management activities require further effort. The first action should be the identification and resolution of management issues: management should be issue-driven. By focusing on immediate problems, management is directed to resolving the most urgent issues, in addition to everyday problems (fuel orders, maintenance, personnel problems, surveillance, public contact, enforcement). In the process of everyday implementation of management, a host of additional issues, particularly those related to inadequacies in the administrative system, will become apparent. These can be dealt with on an *ad hoc* basis, if the system allows it, or they can be addressed in a comprehensive long-term management plan. The advantage of this approach is that it allows management efforts to start on a small but focused scale, and to evolve toward the more comprehensive ideal as funds, personnel, and other essential institutional requirements become available.

Conclusion

Every nation has its particular marine environments, resources, and administrative opportunities and constraints, and these special conditions dictate the development of appropriate marine protected area management planning. A model that is applicable in one country would probably not be appropriate elsewhere—but the overall planning process does have universal elements.

A widely applied approach is the nature reserves model, where, in the more traditional view, marine protected areas evolve as independent units to be lobbied for and decreed before incorporation into land-use plans. This approach is used in Indonesia and suits the country's immediate needs. However, a more effective means to achieve marine protected area administration and management is through advanced CZM, as in the model for the Sultanate of Oman.

One goal of coastal zone management is to establish protected areas as an integral component of regional land-use policy and planning. Thus, it circumvents the more traditional view of marine protected areas as independent areas. Instead, the CZM plan uses traditional land-use planning methods and techniques as the vehicle, with policies and site plans as tools to facilitate the protection and management of numerous tracts of sensitive or valuable coastal and marine environments, leaving marine protected area management to focus on activities in the critical marine habitats or core areas.

5

The High Seas

A

de Fontaubert A.C., "Legal and Political Considerations," in WWF/IUCN (eds), *The Status of Natural Resources on the High-Seas*, WWF/IUCN, Gland, Switzerland, 2001

Introduction: The Rationale for High-Seas Marine Protected Areas

WWF and others have demonstrated that marine biodiversity found in the high-seas is abundant, valuable and increasingly threatened. Currently, 90 percent of fish harvested is caught within the exclusive economic zone (EEZ) of coastal States, however, this restricted focus has generally been a result of poor understanding of the wealth of resources available on the high-seas, combined with the natural human tendency to exploit resources closer to home before going furtherafield. But once coastal resources become severely impacted, we can expect exploitation efforts to be directed toward other resources, further offshore and thus more difficult to reach, but where in some measure, freedom of fishing still prevails. This move into the high-seas is already becoming apparent.

Unfortunately, the historical collateral to freedom of fishing has been, and still is, the Tragedy of the Commons, where users engage in a race to harvest resources before others can get to them, often with detrimental effect. In addition to fishing, some other activities impact on high-seas marine biodiversity and emanate from fishing activities, dumping, mining, or even scientific research. Many deep-sea resources are being destroyed even before we have fully explored and assessed their potential value.

Some of the most valuable resources under threat in the high-seas include:

- hydrothermal vents;
- seamounts;
- deep-sea trenches;
- deep-water, reef-forming corals;
- submarine canyons;
- seabirds;
- cetaceans; and
- high-seas fish stocks.

In addition, high-seas biodiversity is at threat from the potential exploitation of the following:

- polymetallic nodules,
- cold seeps and pockmarks, and
- gas hydrates.

To-date, the track record of the fishing industry in managing marine living resources is dismal.

According to the UN Food and Agriculture Organization, 69 percent of the fish stocks worldwide are fully exploited, depleted, or slowly recovering. Fish stocks are becoming depleted, some species disappear before we can even identify them, marine pollution is on the rise, and changing global climate poses significant risks. There seems to be no limit to the extent of human impact on our oceans environment. In most cases, we discover these impacts after the fact.

Along the coast, more often than not, we are able to monitor this impact, and can even put a value (post hoc of course) on the resources we have squandered, though that is not always so in some developing countries.

For most resources of the high-seas, however, this is simply not the case. It is often said that we know more about the surface of the moon than we do about the bottom of our oceans. Certainly, more funds have been devoted to various space programs than to the exploration of our oceans and sea-floors. As a result, we know very little about the resources of the deep. Scientists and the general public have long believed that no life could be sustained on the abyssal plains, only to discover later on that a wealth of species live there. An example that has recently come to light is that of hydrothermal vents, which are veritable oases, teaming with life, rich in biodiversity and often host to endemic species. We have yet to examine or understand fully the extent to which our uses so far (from trawling to dumping of waste) have impacted such biodiversity, and the situation is about to get worse.

"Pulse fishing" is a common fisheries practice, where fishing fleets move into previously un-fished area, over-harvest the resource to the point where it is no longer commercially viable, and then move on to a new, unexploited area. As ludicrous as it may sound, pulse fishing is still practised by some distant water fishing fleets, but the problem is about to become much more complicated.

Pulse fishing is still practised by some distant water fishing fleets, but the problem is about to become much more complicated.

As explained in further detail below, international law now recognizes that a major portion (perhaps most) of known, exploitable marine living resources are now under the exclusive sovereign jurisdiction of coastal States. A significant part of the marine area that used to be considered "the high-seas" is now regulated by the regime of 200-mile exclusive economic zones (or EEZs), as embodied in the 1982 UN Convention on the Law of the Sea (or UNCLOS).

As a result, the same distant water fishing fleets that used to engage in pulse fishing off the coasts of coastal (often developing) States have been displaced beyond these zones of national jurisdiction onto the high-seas. Consequently, we are facing a potential worst-case scenario, where first, we know very little about the resources (and thus are hard pressed to manage them sustainably) and, second, the resources are not under the jurisdiction of any single State, but rather are placed under the so-called regime of the high-seas, where their sustainability is dependent on collective restraint being exercised by all users. As serious as the fisheries crisis is, the problem is actually much broader, after decades of using the high-seas, abyssal plains, and deep-sea trenches as a repository for the world's unwanted wastes, nuclear and otherwise, under the erroneous assumption that no life could be sustained in such environments and that the waste dumped would be contained in these areas. These same unwise fishing activities not only impact the target fish stocks, but also seriously threaten seabirds, sea turtles, marine mammals and deep-water corals, to name a few. Inappropriate exploitation of the high-seas has already begun, and is unlikely to diminish soon.

Policy makers and resource managers have at their disposal an arsenal of measures to address these threats and to manage resources sustainably, at least in theory. Unfortunately, most of the time these tools are either mis-applied or ineffective. Marine protected areas, though far from being a panacea, are emerging as a flexible, targeted alternative to traditional management measures. As highlighted by Salm and Clark, all MPAs are not created with the same purpose in mind, though they generally aim to regulate the use of a resource that is deemed worthy (and in need) of protection. MPAs are not necessarily marine and coastal areas where all uses are restricted. Rather, MPAs provide a framework in which uses can be regulated and organized. For instance, MPAs are sometimes necessary to organize different, mutually exclusive uses in a limited area. In addition, different uses, and levels of use can be organized within a single MPA. For instance, the Great Barrier Reef Marine Park, which is the largest MPA in the world, is divided in different zones, where different uses are allowed but regulated, including tourism, fishing and other extractive uses of marine resources. Irrespective of the level of use that is allowed or restricted, the main advantage of MPAs is that they allow to manage an ecosystem rather than a single species, a series of stocks or a mineral resource.

Inter alia, measures taken in MPAs can fulfil the following objectives:

- to help protect vulnerable habitats and threatened species,
- to increase fisheries productivity (including through the export of biomass),
- to protect breeding populations, and
- to reduce the adverse impacts of human activities.

In addition, MPAs can embody an emerging new principle of international law—the precautionary principle. The principle is worded differently by various international legal instruments but can be interpreted in two ways:

- that the absence of definite scientific information should not be an excuse for inaction in curtailing harmful activities, and
- that the putative new user of a resource should be able to show that the uses intended will not have a detrimental effect on the said resource.

Either interpretation of the principle applies to our current situation on the high-seas, where scientific understanding is inadequate and where many States are:

- either interested in exploiting the resources but are unable to show that theirs will be a sustainable use, or
- unwilling to curtail other activities that might have an impact on marine biodiversity.

Within national territorial waters, as well as EEZs, MPAs still represent a relatively recent approach to marine resource management. This initial experience, however, has given us a substantive understanding of how MPAs can and should be established, what we can expect them to accomplish and how to combine them with other, traditional measures. Inherently, MPAs incorporate the precautionary principle, because they provide for the protection of the resource through the restriction (though not necessarily the prohibition) of uses. It is important to note that MPAs usually represent a balance between conservation of the resource (expected benefit of the MPA) and the regulation of the uses of the same resource or others that will have a detrimental impact (the clearest and most immediate cost of the MPA). Along with the benefit of conservation comes a price, which can be very high and tends to be immediate for the displaced or regulated user.

To date, our experience with MPAs has generally been limited to coastal areas and to action taken by a single State or, in exceptional cases, by a handful of adjacent, coastal States. With a few exceptions, which will be examined in more detail later in this paper, MPAs have not been established on the high-seas. One of the main reasons for this state of affairs is that beyond national jurisdiction, no single authority can designate the MPA, adopt the management measures that it requires and see to it that these measures are enforced.

Currently, however, a number of States, along with WWF and IUCN, have expressed a strong interest in exploring the possibilities of MPAs on the high-seas. This effort is a reflection of the dire situation that prevails on the high-seas (and is expected to worsen) and recognizes the failure of traditional management measures.

This paper will first determine whether or not high-seas MPAs are permissible in international law. Secondly, it will assess how to make the best use of international law and to modify and build on the existing regime to enhance the recognition of MPAs on the high-seas. Finally, it will highlight some of the political obstacles that are likely to arise in the process, along with some recommendations on how to overcome those obstacles. The status of natural resources on the high-seas Legal and political considerations

The Current International Legal Regime of the High-Seas

The current international legal regime can best be described as a mosaic of different instruments (treaties, programs of action, etc), including global and regional instruments, whether "legally-binding" documents or "soft law". From this disparate ensemble, a legal regime emerges that regulates who can and should do what, and where. The existing international legal regime that regulates use of the high-seas strongly encourages cooperation among States, does not prohibit the establishment of MPAs, and is furthermore susceptible to evolution and could endorse HSMPAs more explicitly.

The Framework: The UN Convention on the Law of the Sea

The United Nations Convention on the Law of the Sea (UNCLOS) has been dubbed a constitution for the oceans, because it effectively delineates most of the rights and obligations of all States. Most importantly, it divides the oceans in different zones of jurisdiction, where different States have different rights.

- The territorial sea extends from the baseline up to 12 nautical miles. Within that zone, the coastal State exercises exclusive sovereignty and jurisdiction, almost as it would in its land territory.
- The contiguous zone extends from 12 to 24 nautical miles. There the coastal State may take measures to prevent and punish infringement of national laws as they relate to customs, fiscal, immigration and sanitary matters, as long as these infringements took place within its territory or territorial sea.

- From 12 to 200 nautical miles, the coastal State can declare an exclusive economic zone (EEZ), where it exercises sovereign rights over living and non-living marine resources and jurisdiction over marine scientific research and the protection and preservation of the marine environment.
- From 200 nautical miles outwards, the so-called regime of the high-seas applies, where all States have the right to engage in fishing, subject to treaty obligations and the rights of other States. (In practice, most fishing on the high-seas is now regulated, to some extent, by regional fisheries management organizations). A separate regime will apply to the exploitation of mineral resources on the deep seabed.

UNCLOS represents a very carefully crafted balance between the interests of all States. It was negotiated over a 15-year period, following two earlier attempts to reach agreement. As a result, UNCLOS is the bedrock of international law as it relates to ocean uses. One should note that though the Convention was adopted in 1982, it only came into force in 1994, after its regime of deep seabed mining was amended by the so-called 1994 Mining Agreement. In addition, the regime of UNCLOS was further supplemented in 1995 with the adoption of the UN *Agreement on Straddling Fish Stocks and Highly Migratory Fish Stocks*. The adoption of both the mining agreement and the fish stocks agreement reflect the evolving views of the negotiating Parties. In the former case, the original text was substantially modified to reflect changing economic and political circumstances. The fish stocks agreement, on the other hand, elaborates and supplements the original text, but it has not yet entered into force. In any event, both agreements are a clear reflection that UNCLOS is a living treaty, subject to modifications or elaboration, as reflected by the will of its Parties.

As the Convention stands, the most important and relevant provisions of UNCLOS for our purposes, are divided as follows:

- The provisions that regulate fishing on the high-seas (Articles 116-120), and
- The provisions that regulate the protection of the marine environment (notably, Articles 192 and 194).

The Fisheries Regime

The Law of the Sea devotes a whole section to the conservation and management of the living resources of the high-seas. Under Articles 116 and 117, the States' freedom to fish on the high-seas is limited both by the right of other States to do so and by their duty to cooperate "as may be necessary for the conservation of the living resources of the high-seas." The right to fish is therefore a limited one, and definitely does not stretch to a right to overfish on the high-seas. With the right to fish comes a responsibility to respect the rights of other States and to ensure that the stocks do not become depleted.

To that end, Articles 117 and 118 provide details as to how States should cooperate and the kind of measures they should take to ensure conservation of the resources. Inter alia, UNCLOS provides that States shall cooperate to establish subregional or regional fisheries management organizations (or RFMOs), as appropriate, and take measures "which are designed, on the best scientific evidence available…, to maintain or restore populations of harvested species at levels which can produce the maximum sustainable yield." In other words, States have a clear mandate to conserve and cooperate, but the manner in which they achieve that goal is left for them to decide. The reference to the best scientific evidence available is a clear indication that the measures called for will depend on knowledge of the state of the stocks, and must therefore take into account past uses.

One could argue that in cases where the stocks have been severely impacted, strong measures, such as the designation of an MPA (e.g., no take area, closed area) would be completely justified under UNCLOS, as long as this measure is adopted as a result of the cooperation among the States involved. In fact, certain regional fisheries management organizations (RFMOs) have already adopted such measures on the high-seas. Whilst UNCLOS does not refer specifically refer to MPAs on the high-seas, it does not prohibit them either, rather the States have carte blanche to adopt any measures they have negotiated and deemed necessary for the conservation of the stocks. In addition, Article 119 of UNCLOS calls on States to take measures on the high-seas that take into account the interdependence of stocks and associated species, which can be achieved through the protection of a whole area rather than a mere target stock.

The Environment Regime

Part XII of UNCLOS is devoted entirely to the protection and preservation of the marine environment. Article 192 provides a very clear indication that "States have the obligation to protect and preserve the marine environment." Article 193 also provides that States have the right to exploit their natural resources pursuant to their environmental policies and in accordance with their duty to protect and preserve the marine environment. The duty to protect and preserve is further developed in Article 194, which provides that:

- States shall act individually, or jointly as appropriate to take all measures necessary, using the best practicable means at their disposal (including the adoption of MPAs, which are not prohibited here);
- States shall take measures to ensure that activities under their jurisdiction or control are so conducted as not to cause damage by pollution "beyond the areas where they exercise sovereign rights." In other words, the State is responsible for the activities of vessels flying its flag, even when those are on the high-seas and no longer in its EEZ;
- States shall take measures to deal with all sources of pollution of the marine environment;
- States also have a duty to take measures to protect and preserve "rare or fragile ecosystems as well as the habitat of depleted, threatened or endangered species and other forms of marine life."

Underlying all these measures that States must take is the obligation to cooperate with other States since, "States shall refrain from unjustifiable interference with activities carried out by other States in the exercise of their rights and in pursuance of their duties in conformity with this Convention."

By combining the fisheries regime and the protection of the marine environment component, States are therefore in a position to take strong conservation measures on the high-seas, as long as they cooperate with other States, show that the measures they want to take would enhance the conservation of resources and that they are based on the best scientific evidence available. Under these circumstances nothing in the Law of the Sea Convention precludes the adoption of some form of marine protected areas on the high-seas.

Soft Law vs. Hard Law

As has been noted above, UNCLOS provides the framework within which the whole legal regime rests, but the treaty was adopted close to 20 years ago and international law has evolved since, sometimes in dramatic fashion. New principles have emerged that were not expressly incorporated into the Law of the Sea Convention, including the precautionary principle and the ecosystem approach. Often, this evolution of new legal concepts has been tied to scientific discoveries or experimentation in new management approaches. The emergence of marine protected areas as a management tool has followed that pattern and MPAs are now incorporated into a number of recently negotiated instruments, both in hard law form and as soft law.

Hard law is usually understood as legally-binding, i.e., the rights and obligations of States as incorporated in treaties and conventions. Once a State becomes party to a treaty or convention, it is bound by the measures of that instrument. Other Parties may be able to bring disputes to be solved under binding dispute settlement mechanisms, such as the International Tribunal for the Law of the Sea (ITLOS) in Hamburg. The Law of the Sea Convention, the Convention on Biological Diversity and the International Convention for the Regulation of Whaling are all constitutive of hard law. Soft law, in contrast, is usually adopted when a new principle emerges, where States recognize the value of that principle, but are not yet willing to be bound by it. Agenda 21, the program of action adopted at the outcome of the UN Conference on Environment (the "Earth Summit" held in Rio in 1992) is a perfect example of soft law, where measures to be taken are suggested but not required. Likewise, the Rio Declaration of Principles contains a series of principles that were adopted and recognized but were not given the force of treaty law. Yet often once States recognize a new legal principle under soft law, that principle is ultimately codified into treaty law.

In the case of marine protected areas, their role in international law has developed informally. The initial stage of their development occurred as a result of national initiatives. As governments became fully aware of the usefulness of MPAs, other area-based mechanisms for protection of species and habitats have found their way into international law, providing a basis for broadening the use of MPAs into EEZs and international waters. Although fully recognized as measures that can be taken in the EEZ, the use of MPAs on the high-seas has yet to be incorporated formally into international instruments. It is important to note that the creation and use of protected areas is in no way prohibited on the high-seas. States recognizing that MPAs are a necessary mechanism for achieving critical international objectives in the realm of biodiversity conservation are within their rights, and arguably under an obligation to start adopting them as one element of their duty to "take all measures necessary to protect and preserve the marine environment" (UNCLOS, Article 193).

To that end, States can also use the following legal instruments.

The Convention on Biological Diversity and its Jakarta Mandate

The Convention on Biological Diversity (CBD) was opened for signature at the UN Conference on Environment and Development (UNCED, or the Earth Summit), which was held in Rio de Janeiro in June 1992. The objectives of the CBD are the conservation of biodiversity, the sustainable use of biodiversity's components and the equitable sharing of benefits derived from genetic resources. State Parties are called upon, inter alia, to take measures to ensure the conservation and sustainable use of biodiversity, to monitor biodiversity in their territories, to identify and take measures for the control of destructive activities, and to integrate consideration of biodiversity into national decision making.

Biodiversity conservation can be achieved though a combination of both in situ and ex situ conservation. The former is most important and the Convention provides that the Parties, "shall, as far as possible and as appropriate, establish a system of protected areas or areas where special measures need to be taken to conserve biological diversity." The CBD does not refer specifically to marine or terrestrial ecosystems in its discussion of in situ conservation, but during the 1995 Conference of the Parties, the so-called Jakarta Mandate was issued, which outlined a program of action for implementing the Convention with respect to marine and coastal biodiversity. Decisions pursuant to the Jakarta Mandate identify five areas in which the State Parties can take practical steps to apply the Convention to marine habitats. They include:

- implementing integrated coastal area management; ensuring the sustainable use of coastal and marine living resources;
- implementing environmentally sustainable mariculture practices;
- preventing the introduction of alien species; and establishing marine and coastal protected areas.

MPAs are therefore one of the five pillars of the Jakarta Mandate.

With regards to implementation of the Convention on the high-seas, Article 4 clearly states that the scope of the Convention extends:

- in areas within the limits of national jurisdiction in the case of components of biological diversity, and
- within national jurisdiction or beyond the limits of national jurisdiction for processes and activities carried out by a member State, regardless of where their effects occur (i.e., including on the high-seas).

Furthermore, Article 5 calls on States to cooperate with other contracting Parties, as far as possible and as appropriate, in respect of areas beyond national jurisdiction. Article 8 also calls on States to, "establish a system of protected areas or areas where special measures need to be taken to conserve biological diversity."

Under the CBD, Parties are responsible for actions of their nationals that may impact biodiversity on the high-seas, are invited to establish protected areas to conserve biological diversity and are required to cooperate for the conservation and sustainable use of biodiversity on the high-seas. Combined, these requirements present a strong mandate for the establishment of MPAs on the high-seas, constrained only by the need to negotiate with other Parties in areas beyond national jurisdiction.

The UN Fish Stocks Agreement

The UN Agreement of Straddling and Highly Migratory Fish Stocks was adopted in 1995 and aimed to fill some of the gaps that had been left in the framework of UNCLOS. The UN Conference on Straddling and Highly Migratory Fish Stocks was specifically called for in Chapter 17 of Agenda 21. After more than three years of negotiations, the Agreement was adopted and embodies a compromise reached between the interests of coastal States and those of distant water fishing nations. This instrument acknowledges the biological reality that while some stocks straddle EEZs and the high-seas, they nevertheless need to be managed throughout their range (according to the so-called biological unity of the stocks). Efforts to elaborate measures for the conservation of these stocks were unsuccessful during the UNCLOS negotiations, due to the conflict of interest between coastal and distant water fishing States.

The 1995 Agreement takes things further by requiring that Parties settle their differences by adopting compatible measures, but the Agreement does not indicate which measures shall prevail in case of conflict.

The precautionary approach is also given considerable emphasis in the Agreement and the whole of Article 6 is devoted to it. This Article is particularly interesting because it aims to articulate what, in concrete terms, can be undertaken to apply that approach. The adoption of this article represents a major shift in fisheries management, as it reverses the burden of proof between conservation and exploitation objectives. Throughout the history of fishing, remedial measures had been taken following the collapse or severe depletion of stocks and thus were, in essence, reactive. Likewise, conservation measures were only agreed to after managers had shown that a) the stocks were being unduly impacted, and b) the management measures would likely remedy this situation. The precautionary approach, as prescribed under Article 6, requires that the conservation and management measures be based on the best scientific evidence available, that States be more cautious when information is uncertain, unreliable or inadequate and that the absence of adequate scientific information not be used for postponing or failing to take conservation and management measures. Inasmuch as the designation of high-seas MPAs may give effect to the application of the precautionary approach, such designation by the relevant regional fisheries management organizations would be both appropriate and called for.

The Fish Stocks Agreement has not yet entered into force but it is already being implemented by the Parties that have ratified it. Those Parties could conceivably enter into a scheme where they could designate an MPA in an area of the high-seas, under the auspices of the relevant RFMO. Once an MPA is adopted by an RFMO, all Parties to the Fish Stocks Agreement would be bound by this measure since under the Agreement other States should respect the conservation measures taken by the competent RFMOs.

The International Convention for the Regulation of Whaling, 1946

The ICRW was adopted in 1946 to provide for "the proper conservation of whale stocks" and to ensure "the orderly development of the whaling industry." In its more than 50 years of existence, the Convention has evolved dramatically from an instrument that was meant to regulate whaling, to one that currently prohibits it. This evolution reflected the changing political objectives of the majority of its Parties, which have now taken consistent measures to ban most whaling and to restrict it to very few exceptions, notably scientific and traditional whaling. Most noteworthy here is the fact that the Convention provides for the adoption of regulations designed to open and close waters, including the designation of sanctuaries in which no whaling is allowed. These sanctuaries can be declared in all waters in which whaling takes place, and therefore are clearly applicable in areas of the high-seas, beyond national jurisdiction. In this regard, the Convention provides for a very specific type of MPA, where the conservation measure aims to restrict just one use: whaling. Nevertheless, it provides an interesting precedent and is particularly noteworthy in that it was adopted in 1946, long before MPAs became a common tool for management and conservation of marine resources.

The Convention provides for the adoption of regulations designed to open and close waters, including the designation of sanctuaries in which no whaling is allowed.

Agenda 21

Agenda 21 may well be the most important soft-law instrument that recognizes the possibility of enacting MPAs on the high-seas. In the course of the UN Conference on Environment and Development (UNCED) all participating States negotiated and adopted Agenda 21, a blueprint, the status of natural resources on the high-seas, legal and political considerations for sustainable development. Agenda 21 is divided into 40 chapters and one of them, Chapter 17, deals with "Protection of the Oceans, all kinds of seas, including enclosed and semi-enclosed seas, and coastal areas and the protection, rational use and development of their living resources." One of the main sections of Chapter 17 deals with integrated management and sustainable development of coastal and marine areas and calls on coastal States to undertake "measures to maintain biological diversity and productivity of marine species under national jurisdiction,...including...establishment and management of protected areas."

Agenda 21 also calls for cooperation in areas of the high-seas, beyond national jurisdiction. Paragraph 17.46 calls for States to conserve marine living resources of the high-seas, including through the protection and restoration of endangered marine species and the preservation of habitats and other ecologically sensitive areas.

Agenda 21 is widely recognized as a useful guide for States aiming to achieve sustainable development. Its level of detail also ensures that States can refer to it for practical recommendations of concrete steps to take to that end. In that context, MPAs are clearly marked as a necessary tool for the protection of coastal marine environment and nothing precludes their adoption on the high-seas, as long as this approach is negotiated among all States involved.

Particularly Sensitive Sea Areas Designated under the IMO Regime

The International Maritime Organization is the UN forum in which shipping issues are discussed and relevant international regulations adopted. Within the IMO a new concept has emerged, that of particularly sensitive sea areas (PSSAs). PSSAs are defined as "areas which need special protection through action by IMO because of their significance for recognized ecological, socioeconomic or scientific reasons, and which may be vulnerable to damage by maritime activities." Through these measures, the international shipping community reconizes its responsibility to limit the adverse environmental impacts of shipping. A member State or group of States of the IMO may submit an area for designation as a PS SA. This application is reviewed by the Marine Environment Protection Committee (MEPC), the IMO's arm of the organization that reviews measures designed to limit the impacts of shipping on the marine environment. Guidelines were recently adopted that list ecological, social, cultural and economic or scientific and cultural criteria that must be met for an area to be designated as PSSA. Once a PSSA is designated, special protective measures can be adopted, which must be respected by the vessels flying the flag of all IMO members. Such measures may include traffic separation schemes, pilotage, vessel traffic services and no discharge areas and are designed to avoid the risk of collision, grounding and other adverse impacts resulting from shipping. The measures are then legally-binding and constitutive of hard law.

PSSAs are thus another clear manifestation of the international community's willingness to restrict some uses (in this case shipping) to protect areas that warrant special protection.

Global vs. Regional Approaches

All the instruments reviewed so far, both legally binding and soft-law in nature, are global in scope. In addition, a series of regional approaches have evolved, illustrating the realization by member States of the importance of adopting regional approaches to the protection of the marine environment and sustainable use of marine living resources.

UNEP's Regional Seas Programmes

Under the auspices of the UN Environment Programme (UNEP), multilateral regional seas conventions have been adopted in eight regions. Each regional seas program is organized around a framework treaty, under which specific protocols can be adopted to deal with a number of specific issues. Protocols dealing specifically with marine protected areas have been adopted in four regions: the Mediterranean, the South Pacific, East Africa and in the Wider Caribbean. In some of these Conventions, the scope of application includes areas of the high-seas.

The Protocol on Specially Protected Areas and Wildlife (SPAW) to the Cartagena Convention provides a good example of the importance of regional approaches to MPAs. The 1990 SPAW Protocol is the second protocol to the 1983 Cartagena Convention, which is the major legal instrument of the Caribbean Environment Programme, set-up under UNEP's Regional Seas Programme. Within the structure of the Regional Seas Programmes, the States of the Wider Caribbean collaborated on a substantive aspect through the adoption of an action plan, which was formally adopted by an intergovernmental meeting and then adopted an umbrella regional convention.

The SPAW Protocol refers specifically to the establishment of protected areas and includes a series of protection measures that can be adopted by the Parties to meet the objectives of the Protocol, but the implementation is to be carried out by the States as they see fit. There is, however, a major aspect of the SPAW Protocol, which indicates that the regional marine protected area regime it sets up could amount to more than the sum of its national parts. Marine protected areas serve a wide variety of functions and the Protocol recognizes the various objectives that can be pursued. The goal pursued through the designation of an MPA will actually often dictate its shape, size and the means of implementation. If, for instance, a Party intends to protect an endemic and particularly threatened species and the goal is the protection of a single vulnerable habitat type, the design and management of the protected area can be relatively simple. If, however, the goal of the MPA is to protect a wide range of habitats or resources, the protected area established will be more complex. In the case of protected areas where the goal is the protection of the ecosystem and its processes, the underlying ecology in the region dictates the outer boundaries of the area to be protected. In the case of the Wider Caribbean, and given the objectives of the Protocol, marine protected areas planners need to work towards conserving ecosystem integrity and thus to design networks of marine protected areas.

Three approaches can be adopted in designating networks of protected areas:

- preserving ocean or coastal "wilderness" areas,
- resolving conflicts among users, or
- restoring degraded or overexploited areas.

In the case of the Wider Caribbean, choosing one approach over another depends on the state of the resources one aims to protect (and thus whether the approach is proactive, interactive or reactive). There is mounting evidence from physical oceanography in the Caribbean that in order to protect coral reefs in some areas, seed sources of recruits need to be identified and protected in other areas, sometimes hundred of miles removed. This in turn points to the importance of adopting a multilateral approach, which is likely to work more efficiently than the sum total of unilateral efforts that ignore the system dynamics. The SPAW Protocol provides the framework within which a regional network would allow for the protection at the ecosystem level.

Similar models were followed for the Nairobi, Noumea and Barcelona Conventions and all four cases are part of a growing regional approach to MPAs. In all cases, the scope of application of the Conventions is specified in the original forming treaty and it should be noted that they often apply both in areas of national jurisdiction and beyond, when the activities of member States are concerned. As a result, State Parties can agree to restrict their own activities on the high-seas.

An even more interesting case in that regard is that of the Noumea Convention because in the South Pacific some areas of the high-seas are enclosed by the EEZs which have been proclaimed by the coastal States in the region. In that case, any State wishing to use resources of the high-seas must first transit through the EEZ of a coastal State, which makes it easier to monitor their activities.

Overall, therefore, the geographical scope of the regional agreements tends to be more limited than the global treaties but conversely, States appear to be more willing to restrict some of their activities if they trust their neighbors in the region to do the same. On paper at least, the potential for networks of MPAs, including some on the high-seas appears greater at the regional than at the global level.

International Precedents

In addition to hard law and soft law as they have been described above, another important source of law is known as customary international law, where law is "made" through the practice of States who may not in theory be legally bound, yet agree to act in a coordinated fashion, over a substantive period of time, and with the intent of binding themselves. For instance, the Law of the Sea Convention was adopted in 1982 and did not enter into force until 1994. In the interim, most States had demonstrated by their activities (the so-called State practice) that they recognized most sections of the Convention as binding, even if they had neither signed nor ratified the Convention. The concept of EEZ for instance is now widely acknowledged as being part of customary international law.

In that respect, several examples have emerged that appear to show the willingness of States to see wide areas of the high-seas set aside in order to restrict at least some limited uses. Two such examples occurred within the work of the International Whaling Commission, the other within the UN General Assembly. Under the IWC regime, two sanctuaries were designated on the high-seas, first in the Indian Ocean and then within the Southern Ocean. Through the designation of these sanctuaries, the IWC endorsed the idea that a single use (whaling) can be restricted, and in this case completely banned, in an area of the high-seas. A more remarkable phenomenon occurred when the UN General Assembly adopted a ban on the use of drift-nets on the high-seas, because UN General Assembly Resolutions are not legally binding.

It is very important to note, however, that at least in the case of the IWC sanctuaries some States have expressed their refusal to be bound by the measures. Such a refusal is perfectly legal since the Whaling Convention allows States to object and opt out of measures adopted by the Commission. Any State can also refuse to be bound by an emerging legal principle. But the reverse is also true, in that a community of nations is entitled to bind itself under international law, even if it is well aware that its intention is not shared by other States. Legally, therefore, a group of States is allowed to designate an MPA on the high-seas, where it can agree to limit uses for those States willing to be bound. The only limit to such a possibility is that any such measure can only be applied to States willing to be bound.

Making the Most of the Existing Legal Regime and Fostering Change

As the previous section has shown, the current legal regime should not be viewed as an obstacle to the designation of high-seas MPAs. Although many parts of the legal framework are unclear on the relevant points, it is clear that a lot can be achieved by making full use of its parts. Nevertheless, it is important to identify the areas of the regime that might hamper the establishment of high-seas MPAs since these are clearly a tool that may become more useful as pressure on the resources increases. By identifying what flaws may exist in the regime, States with an interest in high-seas conservation stand a chance to address them, by encouraging change and adaptation in the regime.

Marine protected areas are sometimes described as an insurance scheme, a mechanism through which we protect what we know to be of significant value, even if clear impacts cannot yet be identified.

Paving the Way for New Law: Leading by Example in Customary International Law

Marine protected areas are sometimes described as an insurance scheme, a mechanism through which we protect what we know to be of significant value, even if clear impacts cannot yet be identified. In that respect, MPAs can be a true embodiment of the precautionary principle, where we protect a resource either because we are not sure what impacts it is submitted to (as is often the case in the marine realm), or because we are not sure what use would be sustainable. In doubt, the reasoning goes, protect the resource until you know that the use you are planning will be sustainable over time. This approach to MPA management, however, is much more theoretical than practical, and few States have the foresight or resources to protect marine resources in such a way.

This may also be due to the fact that precaution is a very new legal principle, whose implementation is still somewhat random and often inadequate. There is, however, comfort to be drawn from the fact that the new generation of post-UNCED international instruments have, more often than not, incorporated this principle. This outcome is the result of the political will of some States who, when they negotiate international instruments insist on its incorporation. International environmental law rarely emerges spontaneously. MPAs are a balance between conservation objectives and restriction of uses, a State willing to designate, and abide by a high-seas MPA commits to restricting its use on the high-seas where, in theory at least, it could avoid to do so. In this case the benefit of the MPA (conservation of the resource) is greater than the cost (further restriction of uses that might have been permissible) for the State involved.

Because of the inherent nature of international law, no State is bound on the high-seas unless it is willing to do so. The UN General Assembly Resolution was effective only because States agreed to abstain from using drift nets on the high-seas. Likewise, the IWC Southern Ocean sanctuary measure is not applicable to those members who indicated that they did not want to be bound. As a result, States cannot expect others to follow measures that they themselves are not willing to abide to. Furthermore, the only hope for an evolution in the regime, and for a fuller incorporation of the precautionary and ecosystem approaches on the high-seas, will be through the action of some States willing to restrict their own uses on the high-seas, in the hope that others will follow suit. Some States have already indicated that they would be willing to try and adopt such a strategy and, insofar as their objective is the conservation of high-seas resources, their efforts should be encouraged and supported. Naturally, no one State can hope to end overfishing on the high-seas singlehandedly. Like-minded States are likely to cooperate as they restrict their uses but the impact of their effort will be limited unless the main users in the area cooperate. On an equity level, such cooperation also makes sense as few States have an interest in conserving the resources if they know that others will take advantage of their restraint to fish even more, thus undermining any conservation measure. As far as fisheries are concerned, most States fishing on the high-seas now have a blank slate with the adoption of the Fish Stocks Agreement. The Agreement clearly refers to the duty of States to cooperate, and to set up regional fisheries management organizations where they do not exist and to strengthen existing ones. Within that context, States can demonstrate their commitment to conservation by closing some areas to fishing, for instance around previously un-fished seamounts. If one RFMO is successful in taking such an approach, others are likely to follow suit.

At each level, whether regionally or globally, States have an opportunity to cooperate and develop international law to recognize the unique role that can be played by high-seas MPAs. Another option is to actually modify the existing legal regime through new negotiations.

The UNCLOS Precedents

A number of legal experts have argued that UNCLOS is such a carefully crafted instrument that it cannot and should not be amended lest the balance that it strikes be imperiled. This view however, is somewhat static and does not take into account the evolution that has taken place since the adoption of the Convention close to twenty years ago. At the very least, one needs to acknowledge that the balance embodied in UNCLOS is actually shifting and that we now know much more than we did then. If UNCLOS were to be negotiated today, it would most certainly look different and more recent concerns that have emerged in the last twenty years would be more specifically outlined and incorporated. In fact, precedent has shown us that when it was inadequate the UNCLOS regime was either amended (in the 1994 Agreement on deep-sea mining) or built upon (in the 1995 Fish Stocks Agreement and in the various Regional Seas Conventions).

The negotiations on straddling and highly migratory fish stocks are a perfect example of an issue that was first tackled during the Law of the Sea negotiations, was then taken up in the course of the Earth Summit and where, after both these efforts failed, the issue was taken up again in the course of a conference called for in Agenda 21. The first two failures were no indication that the issue was not urgent, but rather that most States had not yet reached the point where they were willing to relinquish enough sovereignty over fishing on the high-seas to give birth to a new regime.

The question at this point, then, is to know if enough States are concerned enough about high-seas biodiversity to amend, or build upon the UNCLOS regime to give greater importance to high-seas protection. Even if this is not yet the case, those States with an interest to do so can nevertheless start modifying customary international law through their own State practice.

Political Obstacles and How to Overcome Them

The Lowest Common Denominator

The designation of MPAs on the high-seas is an eminently political exercise. Establishing any sort of jurisdiction over a high-seas area that is sure to raise the concern of States that have traditionally made the most of the Freedom of the high-seas. The problem here lies in the absence of a centralized, overarching jurisdictional authority that could take action and impose measures on States on the high-seas. As a result, any single State or group of States that refuses an evolution in international law can single-handedly undermine the efforts of the international community as a whole. It is therefore in the common interest to try and focus on approaches that will meet with consensus, or at least quasi-consensus. Several practical steps can be taken to that end.

First, and because they tend to provoke such negative reaction, the adoption of high-seas MPAs should really be restricted to cases where no other traditional measures could achieve the same goal. Again, the UN Resolution on drift nets is a good example of a measure, in that case gear restriction, that was targeted to the problem at hand.

Second, it might be wise to focus initially on resources that are under direct and actual threat, rather than on those that may (or may not) come under threat in a number of years. With an increased sense of urgency comes the realization that action must be taken fast.

Third, one should always keep in mind the costs and benefits of MPAs on the high-seas. One of the inherent flaws of MPAs tends to be that the winners and losers are not clearly identified, that the costs tend to overshadow the benefits and that the winners do not always compensate the losers. A perfect illustration of that point would be an MPA established merely to keep an area pristine for future generations, where the current users are ignored and/or fail to be compensated. In such a case, costs could be limited, for instance, by restricting the size of the MPA to that which is strictly necessary or by allowing all other uses that will not adversely impact the resource protected. Another (environmentally undesirable) alternative would be to wait for the pressure on a resource to increase, until the benefit of protecting it overtakes the costs incurred as a result of the protection.

Fourth, sufficiently strict measures can be taken on the high-seas without incorporating them stricto sensu into an MPA. This change in label may appear as a cosmetic measure, but adverse political reaction can sometimes be averted through such modification.

Fifth, if and when a high-seas MPA is established, its management should be carefully monitored and the restrictions on the uses adapted to reflect the status of the resources. In other words, on the high-seas it may not be possible to be as generous with conservation measures (perceived by some as use restrictions) as one might be in the coastal area or in waters under national jurisdiction.

Sixth, any effort to set up an MPA on the high-seas will depend on a careful assessment of the international political climate. This climate in turn can be somewhat influenced by the collection and timely dissemination of relevant scientific information. Some States may be insufficiently informed as to the state of resources on the high-seas and better information may very well sway their opinion as to the necessity of designating MPAs.

Finally, at some point, action may be required even if a State or group of States is still reluctant to see the existing regime in any way amended or strengthened. First, the number of States participating can hope to have a significant impact (albeit one less important than if consensus had been reached). Second, one can hope that once a sub-regime is established among cooperating States, others more recalcitrant will be brought into the fold through a number of diplomatic measures.

The "Seamount Experiment"

While they wait for the international legal regime to evolve, States should seriously consider an experiment by establishing high-seas MPAs over a seamount where fishing has not yet begun. One of the benefits of such an experiment would be to show other States, who may have another interest in high-seas resources, that a voluntary MPA scheme can work beyond national jurisdiction. In such an endeavor, however, it will be very important to ensure that it can and does work. Where a successful effort will carry a very high value as a demonstration of the value of this mechanism, an unsuccessful one may unjustly doom all future uses of the concept.

Focusing on a seamount also makes sense because history has shown that fisheries in these areas are infallibly unsustainable and recent evidence shows that given the chance fishing fleets will move into un-fished areas where they feel return on their investment will likely be high.

From a legal standpoint, States wishing to participate in a seamount experiment can also avail themselves of the Fish Stocks Agreement and establish an RFMO with a declared objective to adopt a precautionary approach, through the designation of an MPA.

An additional benefit of setting up an MPA over an un-fished seamount is that only future uses would be restricted and no current users would be displaced (and no losers would need to be compensated). Access to other users, such as shipping traffic, could remain unrestricted. In short, a seamount may be the one area where an experimental MPA would be most likely to succeed because of the reality of the threat on the resources, the political will of some States who have expressed an interest in the issue and the existence of a usable legal sub-regime to draw from (the Fish Stocks Agreement and possible RFMOs). Paradoxically, however, the designation of an MPA could also be a signal to distant water fleets that valuable resources are found around that seamount and encourage them to start fishing in the area, if they are flying the flag of a State that is not Party to the Fish Stocks Agreement.

Conclusion

As all the scientific evidence points out, urgent action is required to conserve marine living resources of the high-seas. Whether or not such action takes the form of high-seas MPA, action is required now. This action should take place both immediately and over the longer term.

6

Major Global Instruments Relating to Marine Pollution

A

Beckman R., *An Outline of the Major Global Instruments Relating to Pollution of the Marine Environment*, Asia-Pacific Centre for Environmental Law (APCEL), National University of Singapore, December 2000

Introduction: Definition and Sources

This paper is intended to provide an overview of the major global instruments governing pollution of the marine environment. It contains a brief description of the scope of the major instruments, presented in a historical context. It is not intended to provide a detailed analysis of any of the conventions or of the many outstanding issues with respect to marine pollution. Also, it does not deal with global instruments governing the conservation and sustainable use of the living resources of the oceans.

In Article 1 of the 1982 UN *Convention on the Law of the Sea*, "pollution of the marine environment" has been defined to mean:

> "the introduction by man, directly or indirectly, of substances or energy into the marine environment, including estuaries, which results or is likely to result in such deleterious effects as harm to living resources and marine life, hazards to human health, hindrance to marine activities, including fishing and other legitimate uses of the sea, impairment of quality for use of sea water and reduction of amenities."

When most laymen think of marine pollution, they think of major oil spills, and television scenes of oil–soaked birds and beaches come immediately to their minds. However, oil pollution from ships, although the most dramatic and visible source of marine pollution, is not the only serious marine pollutant. In fact, it accounts for a relatively small amount of the marine pollution. According to the 1990 GESAMP Report on *The State of the Marine Environment*, marine pollution is derived mainly from land-based sources and the atmosphere. In that report, it was estimated that the relative contribution of all potential pollutants from various human activities entering the sea is as follows:

Offshore Production	1 percent
Maritime Transportation	12 percent
Dumping	10 percent
Run-off and land-based discharges	44 percent
Atmosphere	33 percent

The position prior to World War II

Under the rules of customary international law governing the oceans, the principle of *freedom of use* was the prevailing norm. The resources of the oceans were regarded as inexhaustible. The oceans were also viewed as ideal dumping grounds which were so vast that they were not capable of being polluted through the activities of man.

The potential for ships to pollute the marine environment was recognized as early as the 1920s, and a conference was convened in Washington in 1926 to draw up a draft convention on pollution from ships. However, it was only after World War II that the international community began to realize that international action may be required to regulate pollution of the marine environment.

Oil Pollution Convention, 1954

The 1954 International *Convention on the Prevention of Pollution of the Sea by Oil* was the first international convention to attempt to prevent pollution of the sea by oil from tankers. It prohibited the discharge of oil or oil mixture by tankers within prohibited zones. It originally applied to all sea-going ships over 500 tons or more, but was amended in 1962 to cover tankers of 150 tons or over.

Amendments were made to the 1954 *Oil Pollution Convention* in 1969. It was amended to provide for more stringent requirements for operational discharges which were consistent with the "load-on-top system" of operating which had been adopted by oil tankers. In 1971 the Convention was amended to impose new standards on the construction of oil tankers.

This convention has been superseded by the 1973/78 *MARPOL Convention*, which will be discussed later in this paper.

Geneva Convention on the High Seas, 1958

The 1958 *Geneva Convention on the High Seas* contained only two provisions relating to marine pollution. Article 24 recognized the potential harmful effects of oil pollution from ships and from off-shore oil exploration and exploitation. It placed an obligation on all states to draw up regulations to prevent pollution of the seas by the discharge of oil from ships or pipelines or resulting from the exploitation and exploration of the seabed and its subsoil, taking account of existing treaties on the subject. It thus had an indirect reference to the 1954 Convention, but only obliged states to take it into account.

Article 25 of the 1958 Convention continued two provisions relating to pollution of the marine environment. First, it required states to take measures to prevent pollution of the seas by the dumping of radioactive waste. Second, it provided that states had a general obligation with respect to 'activities with radioactive materials or other harmful agents'. States were obliged to cooperate with the 'competent international organizations' in taking measures in the prevention of the pollution of the seas from such activities.

IMO International Maritime Dangerous Goods Code

This code was introduced by a resolution of the IMO Assembly in 1965. It classifies dangerous goods and sets out detailed requirements as to marking, labeling, packaging and documentation. It has been updated on a regular basis in response to developments in the shipping and chemical industries. It is widely observed and the IMO has recommended that states adopt it as the basis for national legislation. It supplements several IMO conventions, and is essential for their effective implementation. The IMDG Code is regularly amended. Amendments made in 1994 were so extensive that the entire 2500 page Code has been reprinted.

Intervention, Civil Liability and Fund Conventions

The *Torrey Canyon* disaster in 1967, in which a Liberian tanker carrying over 119,00 tons of crude oil, caused considerable pollution damage along the coasts of France and the United Kingdom. This prompted two international conventions in 1969 to deal with the problem of oil spills from maritime casualties—the *Intervention Convention* and the *Civil Liability Convention.* These two conventions were supplemented by the 1971 *Fund Convention.*

Intervention Convention, 1969

The *Convention Relating to the Intervention on the High Seas in Cases of Oil Pollution Casualties* was adopted in Brussels on 29 November 1969. It entered into force on 6 May 1975.

This treaty gives coastal states special powers to take self-help measures beyond the limits of their territorial sea following a maritime casualty involving oil pollution from ships which may reasonably be expected to result in major harmful consequences. Coastal states may take such measures as may be necessary to prevent, mitigate or eliminate grave and imminent danger to their coastline or related interests from pollution or threat of pollution of the sea by oil.

A Protocol adopted in 1973 extends the Convention to substances other than oil. The 1973 Protocol entered into force on 30 March 1983.

Civil Liability Convention, 1969

The 1969 *International Convention on Civil Liability for Oil Pollution Damage* was also adopted in Brussels in 1969. It entered into force on 19 June 1975.

The 1969 *Civil Liability Convention* creates a scheme of liability for oil pollution damage caused by oil tankers. The Convention provides that the shipowner is strictly liable for oil pollution damage, without any need to prove negligence or fault, except in certain circumstances, such as war and insurrection. They allow persons who suffer damage from oil pollution to have recourse directly against the owner of the vessel, without involving states. Under the 1969, Convention the owner's liability is limited according to a formula related to the tonnage of the ship and the overall total, unless the incident occurred as a result of his actual fault.

The 1969 Convention was amended by a Protocol in 1976, which entered into force on 8 April 1981.

Fund Convention, 1971

The 1971 *Convention on the Establishment of an International Fund for Compensation for Oil Pollution Damage* (1971 *Fund Convention*) was adopted in Brussels in 1971. It entered into force on 16 October 1978.

The purpose of the 1971 *Fund Convention* is to establish a fund to provide additional compensation so that within the limits of the Fund's total liability, the victims are fully and adequately compensated. The fund is established from a levy on oil importers, who are mainly the oil companies whose cargoes the vessels are likely to be carrying. The 1969 *Fund Convention* provides that the owner who is liable under the 1969 *Civil Liability Convention* is entitled to have recourse to the fund in order to relieve a portion of his liability, even where the total amount of his liability does not exceed the limits established by the 1969 Convention.

The 1969 *Fund Convention* also provides compensation even where no liability for damage arises under the *Civil Liability Convention*, or where the shipowner is financially incapable of meeting his obligations under the *Civil Liability Convention.* The *Fund Convention* thus provides a form of security for claimants who have suffered pollution damage. However, the Fund established by the Convention is not available in certain exceptional circumstances, including where the claimant cannot prove that the damage resulted from an incident involving one or more ships.

Stockholm Conference on the Human Environment, 1972

The recognition of the need for international cooperation to prevent pollution of the marine environment was given further impetus by the 1972 Stockholm Conference on the Human Environment. The Stockholm Conference called upon all states to accept and implement existing legal instruments on the control of marine pollution. It also supported proposals for new conventions on dumping and pollution from ships.

London Convention, 1972

The proposals at the Stockholm Conference led to the adoption in the following year of the 1972 *Convention on the Prevention of Marine Pollution by the Dumping of Wastes and other Matter* (*London Convention*). Draft articles which had been prepared for the 1972 Stockholm Conference were adopted at an intergovernmental conference convened in London in which more than 90 states took part. The Convention entered into force on 30 August 1975.

The purpose of the *London Convention* is to regulate the dumping of wastes at sea. It regulates the deliberate disposal at sea of certain substances, including oily wastes, dredgings and land-generated wastes. It does not govern oil pollution caused by operational discharges from the normal operation of ships. Nor does it govern pollution caused by maritime casualties.

Under the *London Convention* contracting parties pledge themselves to take all practicable steps to prevent the pollution of the sea by the dumping of waste and other matter that is liable to create hazards to human health, to harm living resources and marine life, to damage amenities or to interfere with other legitimate uses of the sea. Contracting Parties are obliged to take effective measures to prevent marine pollution caused by dumping and to harmonize their policies in this regard.

Two provisions are of special interest to less developed countries. First, the obligation to take individual measures is 'according to their scientific, technical and economic capabilities'. Second, parties are obliged to promote support for other parties who require training of personnel, supply of equipment, and facilities for research and monitoring and disposal and treatment of waste.

The *London Convention* contains a 'black list' of Annex I substances that may not be dumped at sea, a 'grey list' of Annex II substances that may be dumped subject to a special permit. Annex III contains criteria for determining whether other substances may be dumped at sea, pursuant to a general permit.

The International Maritime Organization (IMO) is the competent organization which is responsible for secretariat duties under the Convention. Contracting Parties have obligations to make notifications on various matters to the IMO. The IMO convenes consultative meetings of the parties to review the implementation of the Convention, adopt amendments, promote regional cooperation, etc. Periodic reviews and amendments of thc Convention are made through the regular Consultative Meetings. The Convention was amended in 1978. Under a tacit amendment procedure, amendments to the annexes take effect for all parties within a certain time, unless they object within 100 days. Under this procedure, the annexes have been amended several times.

Beginning in 1991, the Contracting Parties to the *London Convention* began to adopt what might be described as a 'precautionary approach' to ocean dumping. Under this approach, "appropriate preventive measures are taken where there is reason to believe that substances or energy introduced in the marine environment are likely to cause harm even where there is no conclusive evidence to prove a causal relation between outputs and their effects.' The effect of the new amendments to the annexes has led to a complete ban on the dumping of radioactive waste, to a phaseout of the dumping of industrial waste and to a ban on the incineration of waste at sea.

> *The purpose of the* London Convention *is to regulate the dumping of wastes at sea. It regulates the deliberate disposal at sea of certain substances, including oily wastes, dredgings and land-generated wastes.*

The *London Convention* is supplemented by regional agreements in many parts of the world. For the most part, the regional agreements do not elaborate substantially on the 1972 Convention. In some respects, however, the regional agreements set the trend for proposed amendments to the *London Convention*. For example, the 1992 Baltic and Northeast Atlantic agreements expressly cover dumping in internal waters, which is not governed by the *London Convention*.

MARPOL Convention, 1973/1978

The Stockholm Conference was an impetus for the adoption of the 1973 Convention for the Prevention of Pollution from Ships (1973 *MARPOL Convention*) in the following year. The 1973 *MARPOL Convention* replaced the 1954 Convention. The 1954 Convention had not been particularly successful. Not all flag states were parties to it, and the enforcement record of flag states which were parties was weak. The Stockholm Conference had called on states to accept and implement the available international instruments and to ensure compliance by vessels flying their flag.

This convention is known as the 1973/1978 *MARPOL Convention.* The initial 1973 text was adopted by the IMO in 1973. Before it received a sufficient number of ratifications to enter into force, it was substantially amended by a protocol in 1978 to facilitate its entry into force. The Convention, as amended by the 1978 Protocol, entered into force on 2 October 1983.

The object of the Convention is to prevent the pollution of the marine environment by the operational discharge of oil and other harmful substances and to minimize the accidental discharge of such substances. States parties are obliged to apply the provisions of the convention to ships flying their flag and to ships within their jurisdiction.

The Convention has had a major impact on the construction of tankers, and in practice, all tankers built after 1975 have been built to meet MARPOL requirements. In practice, the vast majority of ships today conform to MARPOL standards.

Amendments adopted in 1992 and which entered into force in 1995 impose new standards to improve the safety of tankers. All new tankers ordered after July 1993 of 5,000 gwt and above must be fitted with double bottoms and double hulls. In addition, the construction requirements for tankers of 25 years of age or above (those built prior to 1970) were amended to require the mandatory fitting of double hulls or an equivalent design. In addition, the 1992 amendments provided for an enhanced system of inspection for oil tankers aged five years and above. The effect of these amendments is likely to be that aging tankers which were constructed prior to the *MARPOL Convention* will be either upgraded to modern standards or scrapped.

Implementation of the Convention is based in part upon the right of inspection by port states. Parties are obliged to cooperate in the detection of violations and the enforcement of the provisions of the convention. Ships in the port or offshore terminals of any party to the convention are required to hold certificates issued pursuant to the Convention, and are subject to inspection by the port state to verify the certificate. If any ship in port does not carry a valid certificate, or if there are clear grounds for believing that the condition of the ship or its equipment does not correspond substantially with the particulars of its certificate, a more detailed inspection is required. In such case, the Party carrying out the inspection is obliged to take such steps as will ensure that the ship shall not sail until it can proceed to sea without presenting an unreasonable threat of harm to the environment.

The *MARPOL Convention* relies mainly on technical measures to limit oil discharges, including standards for the construction of new oil tankers. Discharges of small quantities of oil are permitted, but only when the vessels are enroute and more than 50 miles from land. The Convention allows that certain areas can be designated as 'special areas' where all discharges are prohibited.

The Convention is not confined to oil pollution. It also regulates other types of pollution caused by the operation of ships, including the bulk carriage of noxious liquids and garbage. The Convention contains five annexes which contain regulations governing different types of pollutants. The annexes are:

- Annex I: Oil Discharges
- Annex II: Noxious Liquid Substance Discharges
- Annex III: Harmful Substances in Packaged Form and Containers
- Annex IV: Sewage Discharges
- Annex V: Garbage Discharges

All of the annexes are in force except Annex IV on Sewage Discharges. All parties are bound by Annexes I and II.

States parties to the *MARPOL Convention* are obligated to supply reception facilities. However, the record of port States in supplying such facilities has been not been good in some parts of the world because of financial constraints. Another problem for implementation by port States is the cost of administering a system of inspection and enforcement, including the training of the necessary personnel.

It has also been observed that there has been lack of effective implementation of the Convention by many flag states. Among the reasons cited for this are a lack of trained and experienced personnel to carry out the inspections, especially the need to train and retain qualified and experienced surveyors.

It is generally believed that the participation costs for developing countries will be reduced if there is cooperation on a regional basis in implementing the Convention. Under Article 17 of the Convention, States parties are obligated to promote, in consultation with the IMO and with assistance and cooperation from UNEP, support for Parties requesting assistance for the training of scientific and technical personnel and the supply of necessary equipment and facilities for reception and monitoring. Another benefit of regional cooperation is the standardization of rules and procedures.

The International Maritime Organization (IMO) serves as secretariat for the convention. It receives reports, acts as depository, and considers amendments to the Convention and its annexes. Article 16 of the Convention provides for amendments to the Convention, its appendices, annexes, and protocols either by a Conference of the Parties or through the IMO. In practice, Appendices, Annexes and Protocols have been amended by the IMO through the Marine Environment Protection Committee (MEPC). The MEPC is responsible for coordinating work with other IMO conventions and with relevant UNEP conventions (such as the 1989 *Basel Convention*).

IMO Conventions on Maritime Safety

Other IMO conventions and instruments, although technically dealing with maritime safety, are also relevant to prevention of pollution of the marine environment. The most important of these are:

(a) 1974 *Convention on Safety of Life at Sea* (SOLAS);
(b) 1972 *International Regulations for Preventing Collisions at Sea* (COLREGS); and
(c) 1978 *Standards of Training, Certification, and Watchkeeping*.

United Nations Convention on the Law of the Sea, 1982

In 1973, the Third UN Conference on the Law of the Sea was convened. The deliberations lasted for nine years, and resulted in the 1982 *Convention on the Law of the Sea*. The 1982 Convention was intended to provide a global constitution for the oceans. It entered into force on 16 November 1994.

The 1982 Convention is of critical importance because it is increasingly regarded as a constitutional document which sets out the basic legal framework for the oceans. It is a major law-making treaty which has significance for all states, whether or not they are parties to it. As a law-making or constitutional document it can be regarded as the "best evidence" of the existing rules of general international law governing the oceans. All of the global conventions covering specific areas, such as the IMO and UNEP conventions, are generally read subject to the 1982 Convention. Subsequent documents of fundamental importance, such as Chapter 17 of *Agenda 21*, are also read so as to be consistent with the 1982 Convention.

The 1982 Convention is the strongest comprehensive global environmental treaty in existence. It established for the first time a comprehensive legal framework for the protection and preservation of the marine environment. It is significant because it represents the first attempt to set out in a global convention a general framework and structure for a legal regime which establishes the obligations, responsibilities and powers of states in matters of marine environmental protection. Part XII of the 1982 Convention (articles 192 to 237) sets out state's obligations with respect to the marine environment generally and also their obligations with respect to the major sources of marine pollution. I shall now highlight some of the most important provisions in the 1982 Convention.

General Provisions

Prior to the 1982 Convention states had the right to pass legislation to protect and preserve the environment, but no clear duty to do so. The 1982 Convention represents a major change because in Article 192 it places an affirmative obligation on states to take action to preserve and protect the marine environment. Article 193 recognizes that although states have a sovereign right to exploit their natural resources, they must do so pursuant to their environmental policies and in accordance with their duty to protect and preserve the marine environment. To this extent, the provision recognizes that the sovereign right of states to exploit their natural resources is subject to its obligations to protect and preserve the marine environment.

Article 194 provides that states shall take all measures consistent with the Convention to prevent, reduce, and control pollution of the marine environment from any source. It recognizes that because of different levels of development and expertise, all states may not be able to take the same measures. It provides that states must use the best practicable means at their disposal and in accordance with their capabilities. Nevertheless, states are obliged to take all measures necessary to ensure that activities under their jurisdiction or control are so conducted as not to cause damage by pollution to other states and their environment. States are also obliged to take measures to ensure that pollution arising from incidents or activities under their jurisdiction or control does not spread beyond the areas where they exercise sovereign rights in accordance with the 1982 Convention. Article 194 also provides that the measures taken in accordance with this Part shall include those necessary to protect and preserve rare or fragile ecosystems as well as the habitat of depleted, threatened or endangered species, and other forms of marine life.

Global and Regional Cooperation

Section 2 of Part 12 is also significant because it specifically provides that states have an obligation to cooperate on a global basis, or as appropriate, on a regional basis. Article 197 provides that States shall cooperate directly or through competent international organizations, in formulating and elaborating international rules, standards and recommended practices and procedures for the protection and preservation of the marine environment. Such cooperation must take into account regional features. Article 200 provides that states shall cooperate for the purpose of promoting studies, undertaking programs of scientific research, and encouraging the exchange of information and data acquired about pollution of the marine environment. Article 200 also provides that states shall endeavor to participate actively in regional and global programs to acquire knowledge for the assessment of the nature and extent of pollution, exposure to it, and its pathways, risks, and remedies.

Article 200 provides that states shall cooperate for the purpose of promoting studies, undertaking programs of scientific research, and encouraging the exchange of information and data acquired about pollution of the marine environment.

Monitoring and Environmental Assessment

The most significant provision of the 1982 Convention relating to environmental impact assessments is Article 206. It provides that when states have reasonable grounds for believing that planned activities under their jurisdiction or control may cause substantial pollution of or significant and harmful changes to the environment, they shall, as far as practicable, assess the potential effects of such activities on the marine environment.

Pollution from the Various Sources

The 1982 Convention represents an important advance over the prior law because it addresses all of the sources of marine pollution. It contains detailed provisions on vessel-source pollution, and also places a specific obligation on states to pass laws to regulate ocean dumping. Specific obligations are also set out for other sources of pollution, such as pollution from sea-bed activities, pollution from the atmosphere and pollution from land-based activities.

Links to IMO Conventions

The provisions of the Convention concerning pollution from ships and from dumping contain some important principles and rules. The provisions are significant because they incorporate by implication the provisions of other major environmental conventions such as the 1972 *London Convention* and the 1973/78 *MARPOL Convention.* In certain cases, the international rules and standards established in the IMO conventions are established as a "minimum." States are obliged in certain cases to apply rules and standards no less onerous than "generally accepted international rules and standards." In other cases, the international rules and standards act as a "maximum." For example, in certain cases coastal states are permitted (but not obliged) to pass laws and regulations, and if they do, they must be laws and regulations "conforming to and giving effect to generally accepted rules and standards".

In other words, the 1982 Convention uses the IMO conventions to define the detailed content of the obligations on states to protect the marine environment from pollution from ships and from dumping. Although there is some disagreement on the precise legal effect of these provisions, their effect seems to be that states which become parties to the 1982 Convention will be under an obligation to adopt the rules and standards set out in many of the major IMO conventions, even if they are not parties to the IMO conventions. This is an important step forward in the development of international law relating to the protection of the marine environment as it ties certain states to the international standards in the IMO conventions even though they may not have accepted those conventions.

Also, it should be noted that there is nothing in the 1982 Convention which is inconsistent with the provisions of the 1969 Intervention Convention relating to the right of coastal states to take measures to avoid pollution arising from maritime casualties. Neither is there anything in the 1982 Convention which is inconsistent with the liability regimes established in the *Civil Liability* and *Fund Conventions*.

Pollution from Ships

The provisions on pollution from ships are among the most detailed in the Convention. They attempt to strike a balance between the interests of coastal states and maritime interests.

With respect to flag states, the generally accepted international rules and standards are the minimum. Article 211(2) obliges flag states to adopt laws and regulations which at least have the same effect as the international rules. (This provision should be read together with Article 94, which addresses in part the problem of flags of convenience. Article 94 sets out new, stricter duties on flag states with respect to vessels flying their flag, including duties regarding the safety of navigation which are set out in IMO conventions.)

With respect to coastal states, the rules in Article 211 are complex and complicated. With respect to vessels entering their ports or internal waters, the Convention makes it clear that coastal states have the power to establish their own requirements relating to pollution from ships as a condition of entry of foreign ships into their ports or internal waters. This power, if used as the basis for a cooperative agreement among port states within a region, provides the legal basis for regional port state control. It enables port states to impose international rules and standards such as those set out in the *MARPOL Convention* on all vessels entering the ports in the region.

With respect to vessels passing through their territorial sea, coastal states have the power under Article 211(4) to establish requirements relating to pollution from foreign vessels. (see also Art. 19(2)(b) and Art. 21). The powers of the coastal states are more limited with respect to pollution from foreign ships in their exclusive economic zone. Under Article 211(5), coastal state regulations governing pollution from ships in their Exclusive Economic Zone must conform to and give effect to generally accepted international rules and standards. However, article 211 of the Convention gives coastal states the power, in consultation with the competent international organization (IMO), to designate special areas where it can apply stricter rules and standards.

The provisions on enforcement recognize that the flag states are still the most important, but they also give increased powers to coastal states and port states. The 1982 Convention contains one important development concerning pollution from ships. Article 220 of the 1982 Convention gives increased powers to port states to take action against a vessel in respect of any discharge from that vessel, even if the discharge was in one of the maritime zones of another state. For example, if a vessel is voluntarily in port in State A, and is believed to have committed a discharge violation which has occurred in, caused or threatened damage to the internal waters, territorial sea or exclusive economic zone of State B, State A is required, as far as practicable, to comply with a request from State B for investigation of the discharge violation. Therefore, if the 1982 Convention becomes universally acceptable, major port states are likely to play an increasingly important role in the enforcement of laws and regulations concerning pollution from ships.

Pollution from Dumping

Dumping is defined in Article 1 of the 1982 Convention. Article 210 obligates states to adopt laws and regulations, and take such other measures as may be necessary, to prevent, reduce and control pollution of the marine environment by dumping. It further provides that such laws, regulations and measures shall be no less effective that the global rules and standards. It is generally accepted that the global rules and standards referred to in Article 210 are those set out in the London Convention.

The 1982 Convention specifically covers one issue which is not clearly set out in the *London Convention*. It provides that no dumping can be carried out within the territorial sea and the exclusive economic zone or onto the continental shelf without the express prior approval of the coastal state. It also makes it clear that coastal states have the power to regulate or prohibit dumping in such areas.

Article 216 provides that the laws and regulations and dumping shall be enforced by the coastal state with respect to dumping within its territorial sea or its Exclusive Economic Zone or onto its continental shelf, and by the flag state with respect to vessels flying its flag. It does not provide for enforcement by port states.

Pollution from Land-Based Sources

It is generally recognized that the weakest environmental provisions in the 1982 Convention relate to pollution from land-based sources, even though it is estimated that as much as 70 percent of marine pollution is from land-based sources. The obligation on states with respect to land-based sources of pollution is set out in Article 207. It is only to take into account internationally agreed rules, standards and recommended practices and procedures. Furthermore, the obligation on states to endeavor to establish global and regional standards with respect to land-based sources of marine pollution expressly provides that the economic capacity of developing states and their need for economic development must be taken into account.

The weaker provisions with respect to land-based sources of marine pollution reflect the lack of consensus in the international community on the establishment of agreed rules and standards in this area, as well as the debate between developed and developing states on the proper balance between development and the environment. It should also be noted that at the time of the 1982 Convention there was no global instrument governing land-based sources of marine pollution.

Implementation of Marine Pollution Provisions

Most coastal states who benefited from the new entitlements under the 1982 Convention, such as the sovereign right over the resources in the Exclusive Economic Zone, have been very quick to enact laws and regulations claiming sovereign rights over the resources within their Exclusive Economic Zone. The same states have been much slower, however, in adopting the laws and regulations which they are required to take under Chapter XII of the 1982 Convention.

For example, those states which have ratified the 1982 Convention have a legal obligation to enact laws and regulations to prevent, reduce and control pollution of the marine environment by dumping, and such laws and regulations must be at least as effective as those of the *London Convention*. However, many states which have ratified the 1982 Convention still have no laws and regulations preventing ocean dumping by ships flying their flags.

UNEP Guidelines and Conventions

In the 1980s, the following international instruments of relevance to the marine environment were promulgated by UNEP:

(1) 1982 *Guidelines Concerning the Environment Related to Offshore Mining and Drilling Within the Limits of National Jurisdiction*; and
(2) 1985 *Montreal Guidelines for the Protection of the Marine Environment from Land-based Sources*; and
(3) 1989 UNEP *Guidelines and Standards for the Removal of Offshore Installations and Structures on the Continental Shelf and in the EEZ.*

In addition, an important UNEP convention adopted in 1989, the *Basel Convention* on the Control of the Transboundary Movement of Hazardous Wastes and their Disposal, represented the first global attempt to regulate the transboundary movement of hazardous waste.

Montreal Guidelines on Land-based Marine Pollution, 1985

No global treaty exists for the control of land-based sources of marine pollution. Regional agreements exist in several areas, but not in this region.

In 1985 UNEP adopted a non-binding instrument known as the *Montreal Guidelines for the Protection of the Marine Environment Against Pollution from Land-based Sources.* These guidelines offer a checklist for national legislation, as well as for the development of global, regional or subregional agreements. The guidelines call for the negotiation of internationally agreed rules and standards. The annexes give guidance on control strategies and the classification of substances.

Basel Convention, 1989

This UNEP Convention is entitled the *Convention on the Control of the Transboundary Movements of Hazardous Wastes and their Disposal* [*Editors Note: See also Chapter 7*]. It is a global convention designed to minimize and control international trade in hazardous waste. The Convention entered into force on 5 May 1992.

It governs the transboundary movement of hazardous substances produced on land which are disposed of, or intended for disposal, excluding radioactive waste. Hazardous wastes are listed in Annexes to the Convention. It regulates the export of hazardous waste to another state or the passage of such waste through another state. Its regulatory regime is based upon the principle of prior-informed consent.

The *Basel Convention* is not directly on marine pollution. However, it is related to other marine pollution conventions in the sense that it forms an integral part of a regime governing the movement of hazardous waste. The 1972 *London Convention* controls the dumping of such wastes in the oceans, the 1973/1978 *MARPOL Convention* regulates the manner of storing and packing such substances during transit on the oceans, and the *Basel Convention* regulates their transboundary movement to other states, including the transit of such substances through other states.

Ships carrying hazardous substances are regulated by the 1973/1978 *MARPOL Convention* and by the IMO

International Maritime Dangerous Goods Code. The *Basel Convention* further provides that packaging, labeling, and transporting of such substances should conform to 'generally accepted rules and standards' and take account of 'internationally recognized practices', whether or not they are obligatory. Thus, like the 1982 *Convention on the Law of the Sea*, it contains an indirect reference to standards established in other conventions.

It has been recognized that there is a need to study whether all of the provisions of the *Basel Convention*, the 1972/1978 *MARPOL Convention* and the 1972 *London Convention* are compatible. There is also a need for states to understand that the three conventions complement one another and that there may be gaps or lacunae in their laws if they do not ratify and implement all three conventions. Therefore, there is a need for states to ensure that the domestic legislation implementing the three conventions are consistent with one another.

Convention on Oil Preparedness, Response and Cooperation, 1990

In 1990, following the *Exxon Valdez* disaster off the coast of Alaska, the IMO adopted a global instrument entitled the *Convention on Oil Pollution Preparedness, Response and Cooperation* which sets out general obligations for cooperation and assistance to deal with major oil pollution incidents. Its purpose is to help Governments combat major oil pollution incidents. It entered into force on 13 May 1995, one year after being accepted by 15 states.

The Convention is intended to encourage the establishment of oil pollution emergency plans on ships and offshore installations, and at ports and oil handling facilities. It also is intended to encourage the establishment of national and regional contingency plans, and a framework for international cooperation.

Amendments to the 1973/1978 *MARPOL Convention* were adopted in 1991 in response to this Convention. The amendments, which came into force in 1995, require oil tankers of 150 gross tons and above to carry a shipboard oil pollution emergency plan adopted in accordance with IMO guidelines.

UNCED—Chapter 17 of *Agenda 21*

The major development in the 1990s with respect to marine pollution came out of the 1992 UN Conference on the Environment and Development (UNCED, or Earth Summit) in the form of an action plan rather than a global convention. Chapter 17 of *Agenda 21* contains recommendations and guidelines relating to the pollution of the marine environment from the various sources.

Chapter 17 of *Agenda 21* is not a binding legal instrument. It is an action plan designed to give guidance to states on how to develop strategies and plans to protect and preserve the marine environment at the global, regional, and national levels. It recognizes that the 1982 UN *Convention on the Law of the Sea* sets out the basic framework with respect to the rights and responsibilities of states with respect to the marine environment and marine pollution. It calls upon states to ratify and effectively implement the existing treaties governing all sources of marine pollution. Its major contribution is that it emphasizes the need for an integrated approach to marine and coastal areas. It also recognizes the need for greater cooperation at the regional and subregional levels.

Protocols to the *Civil Liability* and *Fund Conventions*, 1992

In 1984 amendments to the 1969 *Civil Liability Convention* and 1971 *Fund Convention* were adopted. The major purpose of the amendments was to increase the amount of compensation payable to victims of oil pollution incidents under the two conventions. The approximate limit to shipowners under the *Civil Liability Convention* was US$22 million; further compensation under the *Fund Convention* could bring the maximum total amount to approximately US$93 million. These amounts were clearly not adequate in the case of major oil incidents.

The 1984 Protocols never entered into force, largely because the United States refused to accept them because it felt the maximum limits proposed were too low. Also, the requirements for entry into force of the 1984 amendments were too onerous. The 1984 Protocols were replaced and superseded by the 1992 Protocols. The less onerous requirements for entry into force of the 1992 Protocols have been met, and they will have entered into force on 30 May 1996.

The 1992 Protocols have the same substantive provisions as those adopted in 1984. They amend the conventions in order to widen their scope of application and provide higher limits of compensation. In order to widen the pool of potential contributors to the Fund, they lower the threshold of annual oil imports at which a liability to contribute arises. They substantially increase the liability of the shipowner, from a limit of $22 million to a limit of $92 million. The total amount of compensation payable by the Fund under the 1992 Protocol is increased from $92 million to $208 million.

Other changes are also introduced in the 1992 Protocols. First, shipowners will bear the full costs up to the limit of their total liability under the *Civil Liability Convention.* The fund's resources will only be available for losses above the shipowner's limit. Second, the 1992 Protocol attempts to clear up ambiguities with respect to compensation for damage to the environment. Under the 1992 Protocol, compensation for environmental damage is limited to 'the costs of reasonable measures of reinstatement actually undertaken or to be undertaken'. The new definition also allows recovery for loss of profit arising out of impairment of the environment.

Global Programme of Action on Land-based Activities, 1995

The major weakness of the efforts of the international community has been the failure to deal effectively with marine pollution caused by land-based activities, which accounts for nearly 70 percent of all marine pollution. In 1995 an attempt was made to deal with this complex problem. An intergovernmental conference to adopt a *Global Programme for the Protection of the Marine Environment from Land-based Activities* was held in Washington, D.C. from 23 October to 3 November 1995. The Conference, which was organized by UNEP in response to recommendations made at the UNCED Conference in Rio de Janeiro in 1992, unanimously adopted a detailed Programme of Action aimed at preventing the further degradation of the marine environment from land-based activities. The Programme of Action not only identifies the problems and ecosystems under threat, but also recommends specific practical actions at international, regional and national levels to address it.

HNS Convention, 1996

The *International Convention on Liability and Compensation for Damage in Connection with the Carriage of Hazardous and Noxious Substances by Sea* (HNS) was prepared by the legal committee of the IMO and adopted at a diplomatic conference in May 1996. The *HNS Convention* establishes a system for compensation and liability covering in principle all kinds of hazardous and noxious substances.

The *HNS Convention* introduces strict liability for the shipowner, with higher upper limits than are available under existing general limitation regimes. It also introduces a system of compulsory insurance and insurance certificates. The shipowner's liability is supplemented by an HNS Fund, which is financed by cargo interests. Contributions to the HNS Fund will be levied on persons within the territory of contracting Parties who receive a certain minimum quantity of HNS cargo during a calendar year.

The *HNS Convention* goes further in its scope than the oil pollution compensation regime in that it covers not only pollution damage but also the risks of fire and explosion. The draft convention defines its scope of application by reference to existing lists of hazardous substances in other instruments, such as the lists in Annex II to the 1973/78 *MARPOL Convention* and in the *International Maritime Dangerous Goods Code* (IMDG).

Protocol to *London Convention*, 1996

A Protocol to the *Convention on the Prevention of Marine Pollution by the Dumping of Wastes and Other Matter*, 1972, was adopted at a conference held at IMO headquarters in London in November 1996. The Protocol will enter into force 30 days after ratification by 26 countries, 15 of whom must be Contracting Parties to the 1972 treaty.

The Protocol represents a major change of approach to the question of how to regulate the use of the sea as a depository for waste materials. One is to introduce the "precautionary approach." This requires that "appropriate preventative measures are taken when there is reason to believe that wastes or other matter introduced into the marine environment are likely to cause harm even when there is no conclusive evidence to prove a causal relation between inputs and their effects."

The Protocol also provides that "the polluter should, in principle, bear the cost of pollution" and it emphasizes that Contracting Parties should ensure that the Protocol should not simply result in pollution being transferred from one part of the environment to another.

The 1972 Convention permits dumping to be carried out provided certain conditions are met. The severity of these conditions varies according to the danger to the environment presented by the materials themselves and there is a "black list" containing materials which may not be dumped at all. The Protocol is much more restrictive. It states (in Article 4) that Contracting Parties "shall prohibit the dumping of any wastes or other matter with the exception of those listed in Annex 1." These materials include:

1. Dredged material
2. Sewage sludge
3. Fish waste, or material resulting from industrial fish processing operations
4. Vessels and platforms or other man-made structures at sea
5. Inert, inorganic geological material
6. Organic material of natural origin
7. Bulky items primarily comprising iron, steel, concrete and similar unharmful materials for which the concern is physical impact and limited to those circumstances, where such wastes are generated at locations, such as small islands with isolated communities, having no practicable access to disposal options other than dumping.

The only exceptions to this are contained in Article 8 which permits dumping to be carried out "in cases of force majeure caused by stress of weather, or in any case which constitutes a danger to human life or a real threat to vessels..."

Incineration of wastes at sea was permitted under the 1972 Convention, but this practice has since been ended and it is specifically prohibited by Article 5 of the Protocol. Incineration at sea of industrial waste and sewage sludge had already been prohibited under amendments to the *London Convention* adopted in 1993.

In recent years concern has been expressed at the practice of exporting wastes which cannot be dumped at sea under the 1972 Convention to non-Contracting Parties. Article 6 of the Protocol states that "Contracting Parties shall not allow the export of wastes or other matter to other countries for dumping or incineration at sea." Article 9 requires Contracting Parties to designate an appropriate authority or authorities to issue permits in accordance with the Protocol.

The Protocol recognizes the importance of implementation and Article 11 details compliance procedures under which, no later than two years after the entry into force of the Protocol, the Meeting of Contracting Parties "shall establish those procedures and mechanisms necessary to assess and promote compliance..."

A key provision is the so-called transitional period (Article 26) which allows new Contracting Parties to phase in compliance with the convention over a period of five years. This provision is supported by extended technical assistance provisions.

The Protocol contains three annexes. Annex 1 is described above and the other two deal with assessment of wastes and arbitral procedures. Amendments to the annexes are adopted through a tacit acceptance procedure under which they will enter into force not later than 100 days after being adopted. The amendments will bind all Contracting Parties except those which have explicitly expressed their non-acceptance.

Conclusion

In this paper, I have attempted to provide an overview of the major international and regional instruments relating to marine pollution in this region. Many of the conventions are highly technical in nature, and it is doubtful whether anyone can claim to be knowledgeable about the details of all of them. It is important, however, that government policy-makers have a broad overview of the various instruments that exist before they undertake a detailed examination of any one instrument. I hope that this paper has been of some assistance in providing this overview.

Many of the conventions are highly technical in nature, and it is doubtful whether anyone can claim to be knowledgeable about the details of all of them.

As this paper demonstrates, there is no lack of global conventions and other instruments to control marine pollution. The international community is not in dire need of new conventions. What is needed is effective implementation at the regional level of the existing conventions and instruments. The number of ratifications of the major global conventions by states in Southeast Asia and South Asia is sorely inadequate. Also, there are no regional conventions to supplement the major global conventions and adapt them to meet the particular needs and circumstances of the regions.

In my view, environmental lawyers and government officials in Southeast Asia and South Asia should undertake a responsibility to study these conventions with a view to addressing the following issues:

1. Would it be in the best interests of the marine environment if the states in this region were to ratify and effectively implement these conventions?
2. What are the major impediments to states in the region ratifying the conventions, and how can this impediments be overcome?

3. What are the major impediments to the effective implementation of each of the conventions by the states in the region?
4. Can enhanced cooperation among legal experts from the states in the region help overcome some of these impediments?
5. Would greater cooperation and coordination among the states in the region in the implementation of the conventions, including the harmonization of domestic laws and regulations, and the harmonization of standards, practices and procedures, enhance the effective implementation of the conventions at the regional level?
6. Would it be in the best interests of the states in the region if they adopted regional conventions or instruments which complement and supplement some of the global conventions and which take into consideration the particular characteristics, needs and interests of the region?

7

National Implementation of Global Conventions on Marine Pollution—Problems in Implementing MARPOL 73/78

A

Problems of implementation

(i) Beckman R., *National Implementation of Global Conventions on Marine Pollution—Problems in Implementing MARPOL 73/78* Asia-Pacific Centre for Environmental Law (APCEL), National University of Singapore, December 2000

Although *MARPOL* 73/78 has been widely accepted, one of its major problems is that many states have been unable or unwilling to implement its provisions effectively. The provision of adequate reception facilities is one problem. Effective enforcement is another. It has also been observed that there has been lack of effective implementation of the Convention by many flag states. Among the reasons cited for this are a lack of trained and experienced personnel to carry out the inspections, especially the need to train and retain qualified and experienced surveyors.

Port State Control

Because of the failure of many flag states to effectively implement the Convention, there has been a gradual movement to rely more on port states to implement the Convention. *MARPOL* 73/78 was amended in 1995 to enhance the system of port state control. Previously, the system of port state control in IMO conventions was limited to the port state making inspections to ensure that the ship had the necessary certificates and that the physical condition of the ship and its equipment were in order. The 1995 amendments extend port state control by making it possible for ships to be inspected in the ports of other parties to the Convention to ensure that crews are able to carry out essential shipboard procedures relating to marine pollution prevention.

Assistance to Developing Countries

Under Article 17 of the Convention, states parties are obligated to promote, in consultation with the IMO and with assistance and cooperation from UNEP, support for Parties requesting assistance for the training of scientific and technical personnel and the supply of necessary equipment and facilities for reception and monitoring.

It is generally believed that the participation costs for developing countries will be reduced if there is cooperation on a regional basis in implementing the Convention. Another benefit of regional cooperation is the standardization of rules and procedures.

In recent years the IMO has increased its programs to provide technical assistance to developing countries that require assistance in preparing to implement the Convention, especially if it is done on a regional basis. For example, in 1996 APCEL hosted a three-day regional

Workshop on the Ratification and Implementation of *MARPOL* 73/78. The Workshop was held at the Faculty of Law, National University of Singapore from 30 October to 1 November 1996. It was cosponsored by the International Maritime Organization (IMO), the Asia-Pacific Centre for Environmental Law (APCEL) and the Maritime and Port Authority of Singapore (MPA). Government officials from Cambodia, Indonesia, Philippines and Viet Nam attended the workshop, which focused on problems of effectively implementing the Convention.

Developing a System for the Effective Implementation of MARPOL 73/78

Obtain and Study the Convention

Before considering ratifying or taking steps to more effectively implement MARPOL 73/78, the legal and marine specialists in the country must carefully study and analyze the provisions of the Convention and its five Annexes, the Unified Interpretation of the provisions of the Annexes, the Appendices to the Annexes, the Appendices to the Unified Interpretation, as well as the relevant IMO resolutions, guidelines and circulars. The relevant documents must be obtained from the IMO Secretariat in London. The starting point is the 1991 *Consolidated Edition of MARPOL 73/78.* Subsequent amendments to this volume have been issued as an insert or published separately by the IMO.

MARPOL—How to Do it

The starting point for any state which desires to understand the practical implications of ratifying and implementing MARPOL 73/78 is the 1993 IMO publication entitled *MARPOL—How to do it (Manual).* This 128 page Manual provides useful practical information to governments, particularly those of developing countries, on the technical, economic and legal implications of ratifying and implementing *MARPOL* 73/78. Its objective is to provide practical information, in an easily understandable form, on the technical, economic, and legal implications encountered by governments and the shipping industry when ratifying and implementing *MARPOL* 73/78. The Manual contains practical information on the following:

- the obligations which a state undertakes when ratifying the convention
- the means of meeting the obligations of the convention
- the basic marine administration necessary
- the legal requirements
- the requirements of each annex
- possible delegation of certain duties by an administration to other organizations
- the cost of the necessary ships' equipment and shore reception facilities

As this Manual makes clear, a country must possess certain minimum requirements before it can effectively ratify a complex legal instrument like *MARPOL* 73/78. Most important, it must have in place a basic marine administration, with the trained manpower necessary to fulfill its obligations under the convention, including qualified marine surveyors and inspectors, administrative staff and legal staff. Smaller states often delegate some of their responsibility, such as the survey of ships, to classification societies. The Manual has detailed provisions on how states can undertake such delegation of duties.

Implementing Legislation

Parties agree to make laws and regulations to give effect to the Convention in its national legal system, as well as to give effect to any Annexes to which they are parties. Most states are parties to IMO conventions on maritime safety such as 1974 *SOLAS*, 1966 *Load Lines* and 1972 *COLREG*. The legal officers should first examine how these conventions have been implemented into the national law. It may be possible to integrate the *MARPOL* implementing legislation into existing maritime legislation, such as a Merchant Shipping Act. However, most states appear to have found it more convenient to enact new legislation for the specific purpose of implementing *MARPOL* 73/78. An example is the *Prevention of Pollution of the Sea Act* of Singapore.

When considering implementing legislation, it is important to remember that *MARPOL* 73/78 is constantly being amended and updated through the tacit acceptance procedure which applies to amendments and through IMO resolutions and recommendations. Therefore, it is highly desirable to establish a system of implementation which enables the subsequent amendments to the Annexes and Appendices to be incorporated into the domestic *MARPOL* legislation without having to have an amending act passed by the legislature. Most states find it convenient to have their legislature pass a broad enabling act to implement the main Convention, and to delegate to a Minister or some other government body the power to implement the detailed annexes and appendices through regulations or subsidiary legislation.

Issue and Acceptance of Certificates

Maritime administration must provide that ships under their flag are surveyed and inspected and issued certificates in compliance with *MARPOL* 73/78. Parties are required to accept certificates issued by other parties. Port states are permitted to inspect ships to verify that they have a valid certificate. If a ship does not carry a valid certificate, or the port state has doubts about the condition of the ship or equipment, the port state can prevent the ship from sailing until it is satisfied that the ship presents no harm to the marine environment. Parties are to apply these same requirements to the ships of states which are not party to *MARPOL* 73/78.

Detection of Violations and Enforcement

Parties are required to cooperate in monitoring compliance with the Convention and in detecting violations. Where necessary, a coastal or port states are obligated to inspect a ship in order to verify whether it has made a prohibited discharge and, where such a discharge is proved, to take appropriate measures. In response to a request from another party, a port state is obligated to inspect a ship in order to verify whether it has committed a violation in the waters of the requesting state.

One of the obligations which states have found most difficult to meet is the obligation to ensure the provision of reception facilities adequate to meet the needs of ships using their ports or terminals.

Reports on Incidents Involving Harmful Substances

Parties are obligated under Protocol I to make reports of any actual or probable discharge into the sea of a harmful substance or effluents containing such substance.

Violations and Sanctions

Parties are required to prohibit violations and to provide sanctions under their law and take procedures against offenders. In particular, states must:

- apply the *MARPOL* requirements to their flag ships wherever they may be;
- take proceedings against their own flag ships if sufficient information and evidence is provided by another Party, and inform that Party and IMO of the actions taken;
- take proceeding against other ships which commit a violation within their jurisdiction or inform the flag administration and provide information and evidence of the violation; and
- make penalties adequate in severity to discourage violations.

Undue Delay of Ships

Flag states and port states undertake to avoid unnecessary delay to a ship in carrying out their obligations to issue certificates, undertake inspections, detect violations and take proceedings against offenders.

Communication of Information to IMO

Parties undertake to provide IMO with various documents and reports relating to their marine administration and their implementation of the Convention.

Provision of Reception Facilities

One of the obligations which states have found most difficult to meet is the obligation to ensure the provision of reception facilities adequate to meet the needs of ships using their ports or terminals. Such reception facilities are required for oil under Annex I, for noxious liquid substances under Annex II, for sewage under Annex IV, and for garbage under Annex V. The IMO has a publication entitled *Guidelines on the Provision of Adequate Reception Facilities in Ports*. They provide in some detail the method of assessing the capacity of reception facilities in ports or terminals to meet the needs of ships visiting them. The Manual advises that ports and terminals should be aware of the needs of ships and arrange the provision of the necessary reception facilities before implementing each Annex.

An important point to note is that obligation in the Convention is for the government to ensure the provision of reception facilities. This does not mean that the government is legally obligated to fund and provide the reception facility. In practice, many governments require port authorities or terminal operators in their countries to provide the reception facilities. This is often the most realistic and practical approach, especially for developing countries. The regulations in the Manual reflect this approach.

8

Case Study on Implementation of MARPOL—Singapore

A

Singapore's Implementation of MARPOL

(i) Beckman R., *National Implementation of Global Conventions on Marine Pollution—Problems in Implementing MARPOL73/78*, Asia-Pacific Centre for Environmental Law (APCEL), National University of Singapore, December 2000

Singapore is strategically located at the crossroads of major shipping routes linking Europe and the Middle East with East Asia. In 1997 Singapore was the busiest port in the world. More than 130,000 vessels called at its ports, including more that 16,000 oil tankers. In addition, up to a thousand laden very large crude carriers (VLCCs) transit the Singapore Strait annually. Singapore is also a major oil refining center, and the port and shipping sector is a vital part of its economy.

Singapore places great importance on preventing marine pollution from ships, and it has adopted a comprehensive approach to improve the safety of navigation through the Singapore Strait and to prevent pollution from vessels navigating the Strait.

The ratification and implementation of the major global conventions relating to marine pollution has been an integral part of Singapore's comprehensive approach to protect the marine environment.

Singapore became a contracting party to *MARPOL* 73/78 in 1990. The Singapore authorities had studied the Convention for several years prior to becoming a party to it. They had extensive consultations with all of the stakeholders that would be affected by the implementation of *MARPOL* 73/78, including shipping companies and oil companies. The authorities also made arrangements with the stakeholders for the provision of adequate reception facilities for oil waste and chemicals. On 30 August 1990, the Singapore Parliament passed the Prevention of Pollution of the Sea Act (PPSA) in order to implement *MARPOL* 73/78.

MARPOL 73/78 entered into force for Singapore on 1 November 1991. The Prevention of Pollution of the Sea Act (Cap.243, 1991 Ed.) implementing the *MARPOL* 73/78 was brought into force on the same day that the convention came into force for Singapore, 1 February 1991. The maritime authorities in Singapore were prepared to implement the new legislation immediately.

The PPSA is modeled on the implementing legislation of Australia and the United Kingdom and it fulfills the obligations established in *MARPOL* 73/78. The PPSA prescribes measures to prevent operational pollution and minimize pollution from ships anywhere in the world as well as other ships while using Singapore waters.

There are six parts to the PPSA. Part I deals with preliminary matters such as the title and definitions. Part II deals with prevention of pollution from land and apparatus used for transferring oil to or from a ship. Part III prohibits the discharge of any oil or oily mixture from Singapore ships into any part of the sea (including Singapore waters) and from foreign ships into Singapore waters. Part IV deals with preventive measures against pollution of the sea. Part V deals with cleaning up costs and their recovery. Part VI contains wide enforcement powers. The PPSA also empowers the Minister of Communications to make regulations pursuant to the Act. The PPSA gives the Singapore authorities wide powers of enforcement, including the power to detain ships. In addition, it provides for heavy penalties for the illegal discharge of oil, including fines of up to $500,000 and imprisonment of up to two years.

The Minister of Communications has issued various regulations to give effect to some of the Annexes of *MARPOL* 73/78. These include the following:

- *The Prevention of Pollution by Oil Regulations* 1991
- *The Control of Pollution by Noxious Liquid Substances in Bulk Regulations* 1991
- *The Reporting of Incidents Regulations* 1991
- *The Reception Facilities for Pollutants Regulations* 1991
- *The Detergents and Equipment for Pollution Reduction Regulations* 1991

Singapore became a Party to Annex III of *MARPOL 73/78* in 1994 and ships have been required to comply with Annex III relating to harmful substances in packaged form in 1994. Annex III was implemented by means of regulations issued by the Minister.

B

Singapore's Implementation of the Civil Liability and Fund Conventions for Oil Pollution Damage

(i) Beckman R., *National Implementation of Global Conventions on Marine Pollution—Problems in Implementing MARPOL73/78*, Asia-Pacific Centre for Environmental Law (APCEL), National University of Singapore, December 2000

In 1981, Singapore became a party to the international *Convention on Civil Liability for Oil Pollution Damage* 1969 (CLC 69). The Singapore legislation implementing CLC 69 was the *Merchant Shipping (Oil Pollution) Act* (MSOPA), [CAP 180, 1985 Revised Edition]. The MSOPA made the provisions in CLC 69 part of Singapore law. This enabled the persons in Singapore who suffered damage from pollution caused by an oil spill from a tanker to make claims against the owners or their insurers, as provided in CLC 69.

CLC 69 provides that when oil is discharged or escapes from a ship into the territorial waters of a state party to the Convention, the shipowner is liable for any pollution damage as a result of such discharge, the cost of any remedial measures taken and any damage caused as a result of such remedial measures being taken. The shipowner is required under the Convention to take out liability insurance. The shipowner is allowed to limit his liability to an amount linked to the tonnage of the ship.

Singapore never became a party to the 1971 *International Convention on the Establishment of an International Fund for Compensation for Oil Pollution Damage* (Fund 71). Fund 71 established in international compensation fund to compensate victims of oil pollution when the damage exceeds the amount for which the owner is strictly liable under CLC 69. The compensation fund was established by governments under Fund 71, but was financed by the importers of oil by sea, which in most cases is oil companies.

On 18 September 1997 Singapore deposited an instrument of accession with the IMO to become a party to the 1992 Protocol to the *Civil Liability Convention* (CLC 92). On 31 December 1997 Singapore deposited an instrument of accession with the IMO to become a party to the 1992 Protocol to the *Fund Convention* (Fund 92). Under the provisions of the Conventions they would enter into force for Singapore 12 months later. The 1992 Protocols substantially raise the level of compensation that victims can claim as a result of an oil pollution incident.

To implement CLC 92 and Fund 92 under Singapore law, a new act was passed on 31 July 1998. It is entitled the *Merchant Shipping (Civil Liability and Compensation for Oil Pollution) Act* 1998 [No. 33 of 1998]. Parts I, II and IV of the Act came into force on 18 September 1998, the same day that CLC 92 entered into force for Singapore. Part III of the Act governing the fund came into force on 31 December 1998, the same day that Fund 1992 entered into force for Singapore.

During 1997 and 1998 the Singapore authorities consulted the various members of the shipping and oil communities to advise them on what new regulations would be required to implement the 1992 Protocols. The authorities also took other measures to ensure that they were ready to implement the new law and their convention obligations when they entered into force.

The Singapore government has a procedure in place to ensure that it has the implementing laws and regulations in place on the same date that its international obligations under the international conventions enter into force. Not only is the legislation in place, but the administrative authorities are prepared, and the stakeholders whose activities will be regulated under the new legislation have been fully briefed on what is required under the new legislation.

Unfortunately, very few if any other countries in Southeast Asia are as diligent as Singapore in ensuring that they are ready to fulfill their international obligations under the Conventions from the date they enter into force. In some cases, states have been parties to conventions for many years and have yet to make any serious effort to implement their obligations under the Conventions.

C

Song San Case Study on the Enforcement of Marine Pollution Laws in Singapore

(i) Beckman R., *National Implementation of Global Conventions on Marine Pollution—Problems in Implementing MARPOL73/78*, Asia-Pacific Centre for Environmental Law (APCEL), National University of Singapore, December 2000

The Singapore government fully understands that passing legislation to implement their obligations under the international conventions is not adequate. They take many steps to ensure that persons whose conduct will be regulated have been informed of the requirements of the law, and have been provided with adequate notice to bring their conduct into compliance. The authorities also try to educate the persons whose conduct is being regulated on the need to pass the laws in order to protect the marine environment.

However, the Singapore authorities also take the position that an important method of ensuring compliance with the legislation is to strictly enforce them, especially in situations where the laws are flouted. They are willing to make an example out of persons who flout the law so that it will serve as a deterrent to others.

This policy of strict enforcement is illustrated in the *Song San Case*. Following a serious pollution incident in August 1996 which polluted Singapore's harbor and a beach resort, the authorities conducted a clean-up operation and an investigation of the source of the oil pollution. After several days they were reasonably certain that they that a ship anchored off-shore had caused the pollution. However, the master and crew of the ship and its Singaporean owner denied any wrongdoing. A full investigation was then launched by the maritime authorities using all means available, including satellite photographs and computer-generated models of oil spill incidents, to trace the source of the oil.

After several weeks, the authorities had gathered a sufficient amount of evidence and they were certain that the suspected vessel was the source of the oil. Criminal charges were brought in the Singapore court against the owner, the master and the chief officer on a series of charges relating to the oil spill and the attempted cover-up. They were charged not only for illegally discharging oil under the PPSA. They also faced over one hundred additional charges related to the tanker's failure to record oil operations in her oil record books as required by the *MARPOL Convention*, failing to cooperate with the investigating authorities, making false and misleading statements to the investigating authorities, etc.

In the end, all three persons pleaded guilty in the Magistrates Court. What is most significant is that the Singapore court took the matter just as seriously as the maritime authorities and prosecutors who had investigated the case and brought the charges. The judge imposed the heaviest sentence in the Singapore's maritime history. The owners were fined S$400,000 (approximately US$250,000) for discharging oil into the sea, plus S$50,000 on the failure to maintain oil record books. The Master was fined S$400,000 and sentenced to 13 months and two weeks' imprisonment on the charges of discharging oil into the sea, failing to maintain oil record books, and giving false or misleading statements. The Chief Officer was sentenced to six weeks' imprisonment for giving false or misleading statements.

This is the first time that a Singapore court had imposed imprisonment for marine pollution and the non-maintenance of oil record books as prescribed by the MARPOL 73/78 Convention to prevent pollution of the sea by oil.

The Magistrate hearing the case noted that Singapore is the busiest port in the world, and is strategically placed, making it very vulnerable to pollution. The Magistrate found it shocking that the offenses were committed in flagrant disregard of any concern for the marine environment, despite the fact that marine and leisure activities, which require waters free from pollution, are increasing.

9

Questions for Discussion

(a) What are some of the problems faced by governments in monitoring and enforcing marine pollution laws? To what extent can the policies and practices of the Singapore government on the implementation of maritime conventions be difficult to replicate in many developing countries?

(b) What steps can be taken at the national, regional and global levels to establish an effective system of enforcement of marine pollution laws?

(c) Is there a possible role for nongovernment organizations (NGOs) in ensuring that government authorities are effectively implementing the major global conventions relating to marine pollution?

(d) *Agenda 21* makes it clear that to address the problems of the marine environment in the next century, states must adopt an integrated holistic multi-disciplinary ecosystem approach to the marine environment, and they must greatly increase their cooperation at the regional and global levels. Are such actions compatible with the framework for the oceans that is set out in the 1982 *Convention on the Law of the Sea*, which emphasizes the sovereignty and sovereign rights of coastal states in various maritime zones?

10

References for Chapter 18

Agreement for the Implementation of the Provisions of the United Nations Convention on the Law of the Sea relating to the Conservation and Management of Straddling Fish Stocks and Highly Migratory Fish Stocks, 10 December, 1982.

de Fontaubert A.C., "Institutional and Legal Framework of Marine Protected Areas," in Salm R. and Clark J., *Marine and Coastal Protected Areas: A Guide for Planners and Managers*, 3rd edition, IUCN, Gland, 2000.

de Fontaubert A.C., Downes D.R., and Agardy T.S., *Biodiversity in the Seas: Implementing the Convention on Biological Diversity in Marine and Coastal Habitats*, IUCN.

de Fontaubert A.C., *The Convention for the Prevention of Fishing with Long Drift Nets in the South Pacific*, Oxford University Press Encyclopaedia of Global Change, in Press, 2001.

de Fontaubert A.C., with Agardy T.S., "Critical Analysis of the Protocol on Specially Protected Areas and Wildlife to the Cartagena Convention: The Dilemma of Regional Cooperation," *University of Miami Inter-American Law Review*, 30:85-98, 1998.

Expert Workshop on Managing Risks to Biodiversity and the Environment on the High-Seas, including Tools such as Marine Protected Areas—Scientific Requirements and Legal Aspects, 27 February–4 March 2001, Vilm, Germany, 2001.

Freestone D., "Protection of Marine Species and Ecosystems in the Wider Caribbean—The Protocol on Specially Protected Areas and Wildlife," *Marine Pollution Bulletin*, Vol.22, No. 12, 1992, pp. 579–581, Gland, 1998.

Kimball L.A., "The United Nations Convention on the Law of the Sea: A Framework for Marine Conservation," in IUCN, *The Law of the Sea: Priorities and Responsibilities in Implementing the Convention*, IUCN, Gland, 1995.

Kimball L.A., *How to Use International Law and Organizations to Achieve Sustainable Use of Marine Resources: Fishing Sustainably, Controlling Marine Pollution and Preserving Marine Habitat and Ecological Services*, IUCN, Gland, in press, 2001.

Kimball L. "The United Nations Convention on the Law of the Sea: A Framework for Marine Conservation," in IUCN, *The Law of the Sea: Priorities and Responsibilities in Implementing the Convention*, IUCN, Gland, 1995.

Koontz H. and O'Donnell C., *Principles of Management: An analysis of managerial functions*, 5th ed. McGraw Hill, New York, 1972.

Ray G.C., "Critical Marine Habitats," in *Proceedings of an International Conference on Marine Parks and Reserves*, IUCN Publication No. 37, Gland, Switzerland, 1976.

Roberts C.M., "Connectivity and Management of Caribbean Coral Reefs," *Science Magazine*, Vol. 278, No. 5342, 21 November 1997, pp. 1,454-1,457.

Salm R. and Clark J., Marine and Coastal Protected Areas: A Guide for Planners and Managers, 3rd edition, IUCN, Gland, 2000.

11

Additional References

Robinson N., "Chapter 17. Protection of the Oceans," in Robinson N., *Agenda 21: Earth's Action Plan*, pp 357-411.

Bautista Payoyo, P. (ed) *Ocean Governance: Sustainable Development of the Seas*, United Nations University Press, 1994.

Boer B., Ramsay R., and Rothwell D.R. (eds), *International Environmental Law in the Asia Pacific,* London, Kluwer Law International, 1998.

Berman M., "Protection of the Marine Environment from Land-Based Activities," in *UNEP's New Way Forward: Environmental Law and Sustainable Development*, Sun Lin and Kurukulasuriya L. (eds), 1995, p. 237.

de Fontaubert A.C., Downes D.R., Agardy T.S., *Biodiversity in the Seas: Implementing the Convention on Biological Diversity in Marine and Coastal Habitats*, IUCN, CIEL, 1996.

Birnie P.W. and Boyle A.E. (eds), *Basic Documents on International Law and the Environment*; Oxford: Clarendon Press, 1995.

Birnie P.W. and Boyle A.E., *International Law and the Environment*, Oxford: Clarendon Press; New York: Oxford University Press, 1992.

Boyle A.E. and Freestone D.A.C. (eds), *International Law and Sustainable Development: Past Achievements and Future Challenges*, New York: Oxford University Press, 1999.

Churchhill and Lowe, *The Law of the Sea*, Manchester Univ. Press, Rev. Ed. 1988.

Cicin-Sain B. and Knecht R., *Integrated Coastal and Ocean Management: Concepts and Practices*, Island Press, 1998.

Crawford J., and Rothwell D.R. (eds), *The Law of the Sea in the Asian Pacific Region: Developments and Prospects*, Dordrecht; Boston, M. Nijhoff , 1995.

Dupuy and Vignes (eds), *A Handbook on the New Law of the Sea*, Vols. I & II, Martinus Nijhoff, 1991.

Eteuati K., *The Law of the Sea and the South Pacific*, UNEP, 1991.

Independent World Commission on the Oceans, *The Ocean, Our Future*, Cambridge University Press, 1998.

Kelleher G. (ed), *Guidelines for Marine Prtected Areas*, World Commission on Protected Areas, IUCN, Gland, Switzerland, 1999.

Sands P., Tarasofsky R., and Weiss M. (eds), *Documents in International Environmental Law*; Manchester University Press, 1994.

Nordquist M.H. (ed), *United Nations Convention on the Law of the Sea, 1982: A Commentary*, 5 volumes, Kluwer Academic Publishers, 1985.

Sands P., *Principles of International Environmental Law 1 Frameworks, Standards, and Implementation*, Manchester University Press, 1994.

Sands P. (ed), *Greening International Law*, New York: New Press, 1994.

Salin R.V., Saiirila E., and Clarke J.R. (eds), *Marine and Coastal Protected Areas: A Guide for Planning and Management*, 3rd Edition, IUCN, 2000.

Society of International Law (Singapore), *Research Guide, Ocean Law and Policy*, http://www.sils.org. For a list of links to documents and web sites relating to ocean law and policy. [*Editor's Note: This site was accessed on 03/04/ 2001.*]

Zou K., *Curbing Marine Environmental Degradation: China's New Legislation*, EAI Working Paper No. 66, 2001.

Internet References

[The following web sites were all accessed on 18/07/01.]

"Marine Environment," from web site of the Division for Ocean Affairs and the Law of the Sea (DOALOS), at http://www.un.org/Depts/los/losmel.htm

"An Introduction to the IMO," from web site of International Maritime Organization (IMO), at http ://www.imo.org/

"Regional Seas"' from the web site of the UNEP Regional Seas Programme, at http://www.unep.ch/seas/rshome.html

"Our Mission," from the web site of the Fisheries Department of the FAO at http://www.fao.org/fi/struct/mission/english.asp

"Origin of GESAMP," from the GESAMP web page at http://gesamp.imo.org/intr.htm

"GESAMP Statement of 1998 Concerning Marine Pollution Problems from GESAMP Home Page at http://gesamp.imo.org/ocean.htm

"About WRI" downloaded from the web site of the World Resources Institute at http://www.wri.org/wri.html

Center for Marine Conservation, at http://www.cmc-ocean.org/

"Endangered Seas Campaign" and "Creating a Sea Change for Fisheries," from the web site of the World Wide Fund for Nature (WWF) at http://www.panda.org/endangeredseas/

"Global Overfishing," from the web site of Greenpeace International at http://www.greenpeace.org/~oceans/

1982 UNCLOS (United Nations *Convention on the Law of the Sea)*, 1982. gopher://gopher.un.org

1972 Stockholm, United Nations Conference on the Human Environment, 1972 *Stockholm Declaration* on the Human Environment. http://www.unep.org/Documents/Default.asp?DocumentID=97&ArticleID =1503

1992 Earth Summit, UN Conference on Environment and Development, Rio de Janeiro, 1992 (1992 UNCED): Rio Declaration. http://www.igc.org/habitat/agenda21/rio-dec.html

Chapter 17 of *Agenda 21* on Protection of the Oceans http://www.igc.org/habitat/agenda21/ch-17.html

Earth Summit + 5, Special Session of the General Assembly to Review and Appraise the Implementation of *Agenda 21*, New York, 23-27 June 1997, http://www.un.org/esa/earthsummit/

Status of MARPOL 73/78: http://www.imo.org/

"Oil Pollution", from Smithsonian's Ocean Planet. http://seawifs.gsfc.nasa.gov/OCEAN_PLANET/HTML/peril_oil_pollution.html

"Plastic in Our Oceans". http://www.umassd.edu/Public/People/Kamaral/thesis/plasticsarticle.html

"Marine Debris" from Centre for Marine Conservation at http://www.cmc-ocean.org/mdio/MDIO.php3

Global Ballast Water Management Programme, http://globallast.imo.org/

Tokyo MOU on Port State Control http://www.iijnet.or.jp/tokyomou

"An Overview of Land Based Sources of Marine Pollution" http://www.cep.unep.org/issues/lbsp.html

Washington Declaration on Protection of the Marine Environment from Land-Based Activities, 1995. http://www.gpa.unep.org/documents/gpa/wadeclaration/default.htm

"About the GPA" by GPA Clearing House. http://www.gpa.unep.org/about/default.htm

London Convention Summary of GPA. http://www.londonconvention.org/GPA.htm

UNEP's Progress Report on Implementation of the Global Programme of Action, Second London Workshop on Oceans, 10-12 December 1998. http://www.gpa.unep.org/documents/status/unepprogressdec98/default.htm

Protocol Concerning Pollution from Land-Based Sources and Activities in the Wider Caribbean Region. http://www.cep.unep.org/pubs/legislation/lbsmpnut.html

"Report of The Secretary-General on the Protection of the Marine Environment" (document A/44/461 of 18 September 1989), UN Division of Ocean Affair and LOS. http://www.un.org/Depts/los/a44_461.htm#iii

CHAPTER

19

Trade and Environment

Contents

1 Introduction

The links between the environment and trade are now generally recognized, at least to some extent, although the conclusions to be drawn from this linkage are subject to ongoing debate. Environmentalists want to block further pollution and destruction of ecosystems and species, which they see as an inevitable byproduct of industries moving to countries with no or lax environmental regulation. On the other hand, free traders see a trade advantage in countries with inadequate environmental regulation over countries which do not regulate corporate or governmental conduct to protect the environment. Thus there has been an effort to extend international environmental law and national laws implementing treaties and agreements to address international trade. This debate is discussed in the extracts from Brack and Tay and Esty.

There can be no conclusions in this field as the debates have far to run before the issues in contention are resolved. Issues of competitiveness, which are never far from the center of economic discourse, are discussed in the extracts Section 4 of this chapter. The issues here are related to numerous other chapters of this book. In particular, see the North-South debate discussed in Chapter 17, the *Basel Convention* material in Chapter 7, Ozone and Climate Change issues discussed in Chapters 21 and 22, and Financing Sustainable Development discussed in Chapter 23. It is apparent, even from this very broad list of cross references, that economic considerations are permeating further and further into the environmental debate.

The breadth of issues under the umbrella terms "Trade and Environment" require a variety of differing approaches. One such approach, begun by the international community almost 30 years ago, is the specific regime aimed at regulating the global trade in endangered species. In Section 3, we extract both the convention and four separate discussion pieces that detail the operation of this regime both generally and through specific examples.

A contrasting approach is the attempt to utilize, for environmental ends, the *General Agreement on Tariffs and Trade* (GATT), which is implemented by an international organization; the World Trade Organization (WTO). The materials selected here introduce GATT and WTO as well as provide examples of their dispute resolution panels, which have issued decisions in a number of contested trade cases with environmental implications. Included in these materials are extracts of these panel decisions—*Tuna-Dolphin I*—followed by a discussion of this decision with reference to a later case—*Tuna-Dolphin II*. The second case study is the *Shrimp Turtle* WTO decision from 1999. These materials illustrate the extent to which trade can impact on the environment, and the difficulty of drawing lines between trade and environment, or deciding the debate over whether trade is good for the environment. They explore situations where governments have regulated (or attempted to regulate) international trade in particular products, claiming the restraint on trade was necessary to achieve national goals of environmental protection and health. The reasoning of the dispute resolution panels, and the way factual and legal issues were addressed, are interesting to the environmental lawyer.

Much of the focus of this book has been on the philosophical foundations for environmental law. The contrast between these foundations and those which ground economic reasoning are quite stark. The philosophical and policy disputes are far from resolved, however, even after these GATT/WTO decisions (concerning the scope and applicability of Article XX exceptions to the general GATT policy of prohibiting any restraints on international trade). At issue is still the legitimacy of the effort of one state to use trade incentives and sanctions to force environmental reform in other states.

Environmentalists want to block further pollution and destruction of ecosystems and species, which they see as an inevitable byproduct of industries moving to countries with no or lax environmental regulation.

A
Teaching Guide

(i) Vaughan S., "Lecture Outline on Trade and Environment: An Introduction," in UNEP/UNITAR/UNCHS (Habitat) Training Program, *Environmental Law and Policy*, Nairobi, 1995

Sustainable Development Objectives: Integrate Economics and Environmental Policy. Reference Points:

(a) 1972 Stockholm Conference: (Need for higher environmental protection, but not at the cost to developing countries because of development priorities—Principle 23).

(b) OECD "Polluter Pays Principle" and "User Pays Principle"—the cost of using natural resources, and the cost of clean-up pollution, should be borne by user and polluter, and not passed to society.

(c) 1987 Brundtland Commission Report—*Our Common Future* recognizes need to integrate ecology into development and economics.

(d) UNCED—clarified cross-sectoral implications of sustainable development, including links between international trade and trade liberalization, and environmental protection. UNCED calls for trade and environment to be "mutually supportive".

Trade and Environment cannot be separated from development priorities.

General agreement on important points between economists and environmentalists, including:

(a) Trade is needed to improve the efficient allocation of resources, including many environmental resources.

(b) Trade is needed to improve development conditions, since trade is an important engine of economic development: example, export intensity of newly industrialized countries.

(c) Trade can help improve per capita incomes, which in turn strengthens public demand and the ability to afford higher environmental conditions.

Post-UNCED debate: Trade and Environment emerge as the most visible and debated areas, in integrating economic and environmental policies.

Why? [The] main reason is that international trade represents one of the most important engines of economic growth in the last fifty years. Annual growth in international trade has been around 4 percent per year since the early 1960s, it is much faster than the annual development growth. As markets become more global, national economies increase dependence on international market for economic growth.

Today, the world economy is closely interlinked and interdependent. International trade in goods and services generates $3 trillion per year to the global economy. One implication is that the national policies of one country—especially with a larger market—has direct economic impacts on an exporting country. This includes environmental policies.

Growth in environmental standards, regulations and international laws:

(a) Since 1972, environmental policies at national and international levels have become more stringent and more comprehensive. Economic implications of environmental policies are now in the vicinity of 2 percent of national GDP in OECD countries and rising in transitional and developing economies.

(b) At the international level, some 180 international and environmental agreements are now in place. Some agreements use trade measures as means to help achieve environmental objectives.

(c) As important environmental policies rely heavily on how goods are produced, environmental impact assessments address the production process by which products are made. This includes new developments in "life cycle assessments".

To summarize, trade and environment are the two most important developments in international law. International trade is covered under the World Trade Organization (WTO), and its predecessor, the General Agreement on Tariffs and Trade (GATT). By contrast, environmental policies are covered under hundreds of different national laws, and a growing number of regional and international laws.

The challenge in the post-UNCED era is to ensure that these two bodies of legal and economic importance work together, to strengthen sustainable development. This compatibility is not altogether clear.

The main issue in understanding links between trade and environment can be addressed by two main questions:

[Firstly], What are the trade and economic effects of environmental policies?

(a) Can environmental policies—which address primarily the way in which products are produced—conflict with GATT-WTO rules, which primarily address the characteristics of the product itself.

(b) Numerous examples of possible clashes between products and production process methods—"Tuna-Dolphin" dispute. Other examples: higher process standards; "eco-labelling standards".

(c) Green taxes and charges, which also look at life cycle, and may hurt un-taxed imports.

(d) Underlying Fears—especially from developing countries—that the "greening of the GATT—represents no more than intentional protectionism. This fear is especially acute in less developed countries and transitional economies, where the production process and other environmental standards are generally lower than in OECD countries. Examples of this are textiles and tropical timbers.

(e) These and other issues are being addressed in the WTO Committee on Trade and Environment, and its predecessor, the GATT. Discussions are also underway in UNCTAD, OECD and CSD.

Second Question—What are the environmental impacts of free trade?

(a) Work in this area is not as advanced. There is considerable difficulty in assessing economy-wide effects of macro-economic policies, including the environmental implications of trade liberalization, structural adjustment and price stabilization, and other policies.

B

Craig D., *Introduction to Trade and Environment*, Centre for Environmental Law, Macquarie University, August, 2000

General Agreement on Tariffs and Trade

Trade is an engine of economic growth. The example of the newly industrialized economies of Asia demonstrates export-led industrialization and globalization, based on improvements in technology and transport. Trends in international trade include further liberalization, expansion into newer areas, e.g. services, investment and intellectual property, and the development of the World Trade Organization (WTO).

The core principles of the *General Agreement on Tariffs and Trade* (GATT), the agreement which is implemented and interpreted by the WTO since the organization itself was created in 1993, are the principles of non-discrimination and of no quantitative restrictions.

A general exception is found in Article XX, which permits states to act to protect human, plant, and animal life Art. XX(b) or for conservation of natural resources Art. XX(g). However, any measures undertaken under Art. XX must be those "least restrictive" of trade and only where necessary, as narrowly construed.

Disputes under GATT may be brought by states, which are parties to GATT, before dispute resolution panels of the WTO. Decisions of these panels are binding on states parties to GATT. The tendency is for a state to rely on the dispute settlement system to handle difficult political disputes, with a trend toward a rules based system.

The tendency is for a state to rely on the dispute settlement system to handle difficult political disputes, with a trend toward a rules based system.

GATT could pose one of the main challenges to the continued protection of the environment including the World's forests. The reason for this is that the international conventions that protect the environment by way of constraints on trade (such as CITES, *Basel Convention on the Control of Transboundary Movement and Management of Hazardous Wastes* 1989 and the *Montreal Protocol*) have the potential to be challenged as contrary to free trade, despite the preamble of WTO which declares that it seeks the "optimal use of the world's resources in accordance with the objectives of sustainable development seeking to protect and preserve the environment". At the present time, it appears that global measures "constraining" trade are less likely to be considered to breach the GATT than national measures. Regional Trading blocks, such as NAFTA and the EC, may be able to impose greater measures and protect the environment within their trading block. However, the issue of competitiveness, in a global economy, remains a serious concern.

Article 20 of the GATT permits exceptions to the wide limitations and prohibitions under Gatt. It provides that:

> "Subject to the requirements that such measures are not applied in a manner which would constitute a means of arbitrary or unjustifiable discrimination between countries where the same conditions prevail,

> or a disguised restriction on international trade, nothing in this Agreement shall be construed to prevent the adoption or enforcement by any contracting party of measures ...b) necessary to protect human, animal, or plant life or health ...g) relating to the conservation of exhaustible natural resources if such measures are made more effective in conjunction with domestic production or consumption."

World Trade Organization

The WTO Committee on Trade and Environment, inactive for 20 years, has been resurrected and certain suggestions have been put forward on the need to open up the closed process by which all GATT decisions are currently taken. The suggestions include the following:

- The need to incorporate Principle 10 of the *Rio Declaration* relating to public participation and access to information into the practices of the WTO under the GATT.
- That the GATT/WTO dispute settlement system should allow for amicus interventions by NGOs or international institutions (e.g., UN agencies) having a demonstrated interest in the claim. Amicus interventions, by WWF, were allowed by the panel in the recent shrimp/turtle appeal.
- The need for GATT/WTO panels considering trade disputes to contain better representation by experts in environmental law and policy.
- The need for environmental impact assessment (EIA) of the GATT trade process and there should be EIA guidelines for GATT policies and agreements.
- The need for a trade system that incorporates the full cost of environmental impacts. That is, the GATT system should incorporate the "polluter pays" principle and the precautionary principle.

The Uruguay Round *Trade Related Investment Measures* (TRIMS) seeks to facilitate investment across international frontiers to increase the economic growth of all partners and the *Trade Related Aspect of International Property Rights* (TRIPS), which acts as a guarantee for the national and international protection of patents, copyrights, etc. need to be looked at in terms of their relationship with the CBD, access to genetic resources and SFM. Other GATT issues relating to transportation issues need to be looked at in terms of their effect on atmospheric loadings. Product standard issues in relation to technical regulations, packaging, labelling and recycling and the issue of exports of domestically prohibited goods also need to be further explored.

Some commentators, such as Cameron, believe that the WTO does not have the expertise, institutional capacity and agenda to tackle many trade and environment issues. Proposals for change have included a new Intergovernmental Panel on Trade and the Environment to provide the WTO Environmental Committee with expert information and advice and that the CSD should expand its role in this area.

Regional Trade Agreements

It is significant that regional trade agreements such as the *European Community Treaty* and the *North American Free Trade Agreement* (NAFTA) have been far more effective in getting accepted measures which more strongly support the environmental aspects of trade. In particular, the *NAFTA Environmental Supplemental Agreement* (Article 104) provides that in the event of any inconsistency between NAFTA and the specific environmental agreements, which are listed, the environmental obligations shall prevail to the extent of the inconsistency. NAFTA provides for a Commission for Environmental Cooperation which includes a public advisory committee. Each party is required to enforce its environmental laws effectively and citizens seeking environmental enforcement and compensation for environmental damage have the right to go to court. The *Supplemental Agreement* also provides for public participation through the publication of policy enforcement procedures and non-compliance and for public comment prior to the adoption of legislation.

Proposed Multilateral Agreement on Investment

Another major development in trade is a proposal known as the multilateral agreement on investment (MAI). The purpose of the MAI is to facilitate "free trade" in foreign investments. This will have enormous implications internationally. For example, will national environmental standards be construed as a trade barrier to foreign investment and will affirmative action and negotiated agreements which benefit indigenous peoples be construed as special treatment vis-à-vis foreign investors?

2

The Trade and Environment Debate

A

Brack D., "Introduction: The Trade and Environment Debate," in *Trade and Environment: Conflict or Compatibility*, Royal Institute of International Affairs, London, 1998, pp 1–25

Introduction

The gradual evolution of global trade and environmental regimes continues to raise the possibility of conflict. The international community is in theory committed *both* to trade liberalization, through the Uruguay Round extension of the *General Agreement on Tariffs and Trade* (GATT) and the creation of the World Trade Organization (WTO), *and* to environmentally sustainable development, through the agreements signed at the UN Conference on Environment and Development, the 'Earth Summit' of 1992.

In principle, the pursuit of both objectives should be entirely compatible. According to the theory of comparative advantage, trade allows countries to specialize in the production of goods and services in which they are relatively most efficient. In other words, trade enables countries to maximize output from a given input of resources—which is a movement in the direction of environmental sustainability. Furthermore, trade liberalization can help to remove distortionary subsidies and pricing policies, improving the efficiency of resource allocation, and can encourage the spread of environmentally friendly technology. The higher rate of growth of income resulting from trade also helps to generate the resources needed for investment in environmental protection—although this is not an automatic link, and appropriate policies need to be pursued simultaneously.

Given modern systems of economic activity, however, trade can also harm the environment. To the extent that environmental externalities are not incorporated in economic prices and decision making, trade can act to magnify unsustainable patterns of economic activity, exacerbating problems of pollution and resource depletion. Where externalities are being incorporated (through environmental taxation, for example, or regulation), the process is invariably proceeding at different speeds in different countries. Yet trade rules are set internationally, and the multilateral trading system (the complex of agreements centered around the GATT and administered by the WTO) may fail to allow for such differences in national efforts at achieving environmental sustainability, even when policies are aimed at controlling transboundary or global environmental problems. In addition, a country with strict environmental regulations may fear that its economy will be undermined by competition from other countries with more lax environmental standards (and hence potentially lower production costs).

A country with strict environmental regulations may fear that its economy will be undermined by competition from other countries with more lax environmental standards.

Trade and environmental policies are therefore inextricably interlinked. Conflict between trade liberalization and environmental protection has already erupted in a number of instances as regulations drawn up in pursuit of the objective of environmental sustainability have been challenged as erecting barriers to trade, notably in several cases brought before disputes panels of the GATT and WTO. The very first dispute under the WTO (which went through both a panel and the Appellate Body) was on a trade-environment case. The WTO itself, on its creation on I January 1995, established a Committee on Trade and Environment (CTE), taking forward the work carried out in the former GATT Working Group on Environmental Measures and International Trade (formally created in 1971 but inactive until 1991). Its aim is 'to identify the relationship between trade measures and environmental measures, in order to promote sustainable development', and 'to make appropriate recommendations on whether any modifications of the provisions of the multilateral trading system are required. The Committee reported to the first WTO Ministerial Meeting in Singapore in December 1996, and had its mandate renewed; aspects of its discussions and conclusions are highlighted below.

Many other international organizations, including the OECD, the UN Environment Programme (UNEP), the UN Conference on Trade and Development (UNCTAD) and a large number of academic institutes and NGOs, have also published work in the area. Two new organizations were established during 1996: the International Panel on Trade,

Environment and Sustainable Development, established by the World Wide Fund for Nature and sponsored by a number of European governments; and the Geneva-based International Centre for Trade and Sustainable Development, supported by the International Union for the Conservation of Nature.

This paper aims to provide an outline of the major issues involved in the trade and environment debate.

Use of Trade Measures for Environmental Purposes

The central aim of the GATT is to liberalize trade between contracting parties. Article I ('most favored nation' treatment) requires that any trade advantage granted by any contracting party to any product either for import or export must also be applied to any 'like product' originating in or bound for any other contracting party. Article III ('national treatment') similarly requires imported and domestic 'like products' to be treated identically with respect to internal taxes and regulations. WTO members, in other words, are not permitted to discriminate between other WTO members' traded products, or between domestic and international production.

The GATT does, however, permit certain unilateral trade restrictions in the pursuit of environmental protection under particular circumstances. Article XX ('General Exceptions') states that:

> "Subject to the requirement that such measures are not applied in a manner which would constitute a means of arbitrary or unjustifiable discrimination between countries where the same conditions prevail, or a disguised restriction on international trade, nothing in this Agreement shall be construed to prevent the adoption or enforcement by any contracting party of measures:
>
> ...
>
> (b) necessary to protect human, animal or plant life or health;
>
> ...
>
> (g) relating to the conservation of exhaustible natural resources if such measures are made effective in conjunction with restrictions on domestic production or consumption."

Countries can, therefore, ban or restrict the import of products that will harm their own environments, as long as the standards applied are non-discriminatory between countries and between domestic and foreign production. Environmental grounds have indeed become more widely cited as an objective and rationale for applying trade-restrictive regulations including, most notably, measures aimed at controlling air pollution and hazardous chemicals. Any agreement permitting a restriction in trade, however, runs the risk of capture by protectionist interests using environmental justification as a disguise. To that end, the CTE spent some time discussing transparency requirements for such measures. The Uruguay Round agreement incorporated many improvements in the requirements for notification of measures under the *Agreements on Technical Barriers to Trade* (TBT), *Sanitary and Phytosanitary Measures, and Subsidies and Countervailing Measures.* While considering that no further modifications to WTO rules were necessary, the CTE concluded that the establishment of a central database of trade-related environmental measures would be helpful. Relatively little analysis has in fact been carried out on the impact of such measures, but at least one study has concluded that they are relatively inexpensive, tend to be short-term and are often well worth the cost in terms of environmental benefits.

Product Requirements

Generally speaking, environmental regulations apply either to products or to processes. Product requirements, as well as outright bans, include regulations and/or voluntary agreements governing labelling, packaging, recycling and recycled content. Increasingly, such requirements are based on life-cycle assessments of the product's environmental impact during production, consumption and disposal. Although these can be valuable instruments of environmental policy, the application of such requirements to imported products can pose significant difficulties. Information, particularly in life-cycle assessment cases, may be wholly or partially lacking. Characteristics chosen for labelling may reflect domestic environmental priorities, and criteria used in different national schemes may vary widely. Schemes that focus only on particular products (e.g., tropical timber) may create artificial advantages for products that are not subject to similar requirements (e.g., temperate timber or substitutes such as plastics or metals) but whose consumption and production nevertheless have environmental impact. Packaging regulations that require recovery and reuse (e.g., returnable bottles) clearly create problems for non-domestic producers. Foreign governments and industries are highly unlikely to be involved in designing and implementing such schemes. Not only do these problems combine to create barriers to trade (particularly for developing countries), but they may also lead to resource misallocation and potentially inappropriate environmental policies.

The TBT Agreement aims to ensure that regulations such as these do not create unnecessary obstacles to international trade; environmental protection is singled out as a legitimate objective of technical requirements and standards. The Agreement requires, *inter alia,* that all such measures should be as transparent as possible and based on international standards where feasible. The CTE, which spent most of its time under this item discussing voluntary ecolabelling schemes, stressed the importance of sticking to the Agreement's provisions and ensuring fair access to foreign producers. It is unclear, however, whether recycling and waste management requirements, and labelling schemes incorporating information about production processes, are covered by the Agreement, and the CTE resolved to consider these issues further. The OECD has proposed a series of steps to minimize disruption to trade, including transparency; transitional adaptation periods; sensitivity to non-domestic conditions and particularly to the special needs of developing countries and economies in transition; greater harmonization of life-cycle methodologies; and a requirement for genuine environmental justification for all such measures.

A specific issue related to the trade in products is the export of domestically prohibited goods. Goods that are restricted in domestic markets, on the grounds that they present a danger to human, animal or plant life or health, or to the environment, may often be legally exported. This may cause a problem for the importing country, where information is lacking on whether and why the product is banned: exporters may make false declarations, customs authorities (particularly in developing countries) may lack adequate product testing facilities, and undeveloped or ineffective consumer protection legislation may, for example, enable products to be marketed beyond their expiry dates. Trade in hazardous waste is covered by the *Basel Convention*, and the negotiation of further multilateral environmental agreements (MEAs) may prove the best way to make progress on this issue. A legal requirement for 'prior informed consent' for export is increasingly common within the European Union (for example for the export of restricted chemicals) and this may also provide a way forward. As with many other trade-environment topics, transparency of measures, and the provision of technical assistance to developing countries, are key issues.

Process and Production Methods

Environmental regulations based on process and production methods (PPMs), as opposed to product standards, cause more complex interactions with trade. Although the GATT's 'like product' provisions were not drawn up with environmental issues in mind, a GATT dispute panel applied them in the case of the well-known US-Mexico tuna-dolphin dispute in 1991. It ruled that the trade restriction in question (the US import ban on Mexican tuna caught with dolphin-unfriendly nets) was in breach of the GATT because it discriminated against a product on the basis of the way in which it was produced, not on the basis of its own characteristics; i.e., it discriminated against a 'like product'.

The meaning of 'like product' has become one of the most difficult issues in the trade-environment arena. In 1994 another GATT panel, ruling on an EU-US dispute over car imports, slightly relaxed the definition, considering that vehicles of different fuel efficiency standards could be considered not to be like products. However, it placed strict boundaries on this conclusion, arguing that Article III of the GATT referred only to a 'product as a product, from its introduction into the market to its final consumption'. Factors relating to the manufacture of the product before its introduction into the market were, therefore, still irrelevant. Another panel in 1996 found that chemically identical imported and domestic gasoline were like products regardless of the environmental standards of the producers.

Even if one does not adopt the panels' viewpoints, PPM-based environmental trade measures can be difficult to justify. Different parts of the world vary widely in their ability to assimilate pollution, depending on factors such as climate, population density, existing levels of pollution and risk preferences. Environmental regulations suited to industrialized nations, with high population densities and environments that have been subject to pollution for the past 200 years, may be wholly inappropriate for newly industrializing countries with much lower population densities and inherited pollution levels—and yet trade measures based on PPMs could in effect seek to impose the higher standards regardless. Carried to its logical extreme, enforcing similarity of PPMs could deny the very basis of comparative advantage, which rests on the proposition that countries possess different cost structures for the production of various goods. It is hardly surprising that many developing countries view the motives of those wishing to introduce this issue to the debate as protectionist. Another argument rests on practicalities. By their very nature, PPMs cannot generally be determined by inspection of the products. Importers wishing to apply PPM-based controls must therefore enjoy the cooperation of the exporting country or country of origin in certifying how the goods are produced.

Carried to its logical extreme, enforcing similarity of PPMs could deny the very basis of comparative advantage, which rests on the proposition that countries possess different cost structures for the production of various goods.

PPM-based measures are, however, becoming increasingly important in strategies for environmental sustainability. Particularly where the use of energy is involved (as it is in virtually every manufacturing and processing activity), the pollution caused stems from the PPM and not the product. Life-cycle approaches have similarly focused attention on the way in which products are manufactured, grown and harvested, as well on product characteristics themselves. In terms of trade measures, an important distinction can be drawn between PPMs that cause pollution that is restricted to the country of production, and those that cause pollution that is transboundary or global. In the latter case, differentiating, as the panels' interpretation of the GATT effectively does, between pollution associated with the consumption of a product and that associated with its production is more difficult to justify, and would rule out any trade measure aimed at protecting a country's environment, or any aspect of the global commons, from damage caused by transboundary pollution originating from production.

Inclusion of PPM-based trade measures in MEAs may provide a solution, and in fact the *Montreal Protocol* (on ozone-depleting substances) includes provision for such measures, though they have not so far been deployed. The OECD has accepted that in some cases PPM-based trade restrictions may have a place in MEAs. Recognizing the difficulties involved in determining the PPMs used from physical inspection of the product, it has called for the development of verification and certification systems and for the mutual recognition of such systems.

The negotiation of international treaties is frequently, however, a difficult and slow process. A number of participants in the debates have therefore called for the GATT to be amended to set out objective criteria under which trade measures directed against PPMs could be taken (including requirements such as non-discriminatory and transparent measures and evidence of significant transboundary environmental problems), subject to challenge under normal GATT rules. This issue does not feature explicitly on the agenda of the CTE, but underlies many other areas of concern, and is likely to feature increasingly in trade disputes. Recent debates over actual or potential trade restrictions against fur caught in leghold traps, genetically engineered maize and shrimps fished by methods that kill sea turtles all focus attention on processes, not products.

Economic Instruments

Economic instruments—taxes and charges, traceable permits, deposit refund systems and subsidies—are playing an increasingly important role in environmental policy as complements to regulatory instruments and voluntary agreements. In principle, they aim to ensure that environmental externalities are incorporated in decision-making, and in general they are more efficient and more transparent than simple regulatory measures.

The WTO agreements already cover to a certain extent the impact of economic instruments on trade. Subsidies are dealt with in the *Agreement on Subsidies and Countervailing Measures*, which permits government assistance to promote the adaptation of existing facilities to new environmental requirements, as long as this is limited to 20 percent of the cost.

WTO members are permitted to adjust tax rates at the border—i.e., to impose taxes on imports and rebate taxes on exports so that domestic producers and exporters are not undercut by foreign producers—inasmuch as these are applied to traded products. Following the discussion on PPMs above, it would appear that taxes and charges related to processes and production methods cannot be so adjusted, though the GATT is not completely clear on this and a Working Party on Border Tax Adjustments in 1970 failed to draw any conclusion on so-called *taxes occultes* (consumption taxes on materials and services used in the production and transport of other goods). The 1987 GATT dispute panel on the US Superfund regulations ruled that import taxes applied to certain chemicals and to derivatives of them were permissible, that the same case can be made for energy consumed in the production process, and that border tax adjustments for carbon or energy taxes should therefore be permissible. In fact, the *Subsidies Agreement* explicitly provides for special treatment for rebating indirect taxes on energy, fuels and oils used in the production process for *exports.*

There are, however, very severe problems involved with the practicalities of border tax adjustments, including the valuation of the appropriate level of tax, the likely wide diversity in national tax rates (given, as noted above, that environmental costs vary not only with products and processes but also with location) and the difficulty of verifying PPM-based damage from an inspection of products. The CTE undertook only a preliminary examination of some of the issues in this complex and controversial topic, and called for further work.

Multilateral Environmental Agreements

As Principle 12 of the *Rio Declaration* states, international agreement is clearly preferable to unilateral action in tackling transboundary or global environmental problems. More than 180 MEAs already exist, of which about 20 incorporate trade measures. These include three of the most important: the *Basel Convention* on hazardous waste, the *Convention on International Trade in Endangered Species* (CITES) and the *Montreal Protocol on Ozone-Depleting Substances.* In the absence of any comprehensive framework of global environmental law, the negotiation of further MEAs—such as the *Kyoto Protocol* to the *Framework Convention of Climate Change*—will form an increasingly prominent part of the international agenda.

On the face of it, however, there would appear to be some conflict between current GATT rules and MEAs that contain trade provisions. The *Montreal Protocol,* for instance, permits parties to ban imports of chlorofluorocarbons and other controlled substances from non-parties, which breaches the 'most favored ration' end 'national treatment' clauses of GATT. It is widely accepted, however, that the inclusion of this measure in the *Montreal Protocol* has contributed significantly to its success in attracting signatories, and future MEAs may similarly benefit from the inclusion of trade restrictions.

This topic became one of the most important items of debate on the CTE, with members putting forward proposals designed variously to define under what conditions trade measures taken pursuant to an MEA could be considered to be 'necessary' under the terms of the GATT's Article XX, or to establish a degree of WTO oversight on the negotiation and operation of trade provisions in future MEAs. No consensus was reached about the need for modifications to trade rules. The CTE noted, however, that:

> "Trade measures based on specifically agreed upon provisions can also be needed in certain cases to achieve the environmental objectives of an MEA, particularly where trade is related directly to the source of an environmental problem. They have played an important role in some MEAs in the past, and they may be needed to play a similarly important role in certain cases in the future."

The Committee also recognized that a range of provisions in the WTO can already accommodate the use of trade measures in MEAs; these include the provisions of Article XX, and also of Article XXV, which permits the waiver of other GATT provisions, though on case-by-case and time-limited bases. NGOs have tended to argue for amendment to the GATT to create a presumption of compatibility with MEAs. It is worth noting, however, that no complaint has yet arisen within the GATT or WTO with respect to trade measures taken in pursuit of an MEA, and this may well continue to be the case; in instances such as the *Montreal Protocol,* where the trade provisions were designed to encourage countries to accede, this has been so successful that there are virtually no non-parties left against whom trade measures could be taken in any case.

Environmental Policy, Market Access and the Removal of Trade Distortions

In what is probably the only area of broad consensus, it is generally agreed that the ending of economically distortionary practices such as subsidies for agriculture or energy would benefit both trade (improving allocative efficiency) and the environment (removing support for environmentally unsustainable activities). Similarly, ending the practice of tariff escalation, by which developing countries face higher tariffs against exports of manufactured and processed goods than for raw materials and primary products (common particularly in the timber and wood products sector), would encourage economic diversification and help end environmentally damaging systems of resource extraction. The GATT Uruguay Round made progress on this issue in the areas of agriculture and textiles, where the system of quotas on developing-country exports known as the Multi-Fibre Arrangement is due to be phased out over a ten-year period. CTE discussions on this item focused in particular on the needs of countries that are currently marginal participants in world trade, and on small and medium-sized enterprises.

International Competitiveness

The impact of environmental regulation on economic competitiveness is much debated. Firms in countries with high environmental standards and costs of compliance may fear that they will be undercut by competition from companies based in countries with less strict regulation and lower costs. In theory, this may lead to entire industries departing for countries with lower standards, the so-called 'pollution havens'. Solutions that have been advocated in order to avoid a general lowering of environmental standards include the equalization of costs through countervailing duties. The purpose of these measures (sometimes referred to 'ecodumping' duties or 'ecoduties') is to level the playing field by ensuring that products imported from countries with lower environmental standards are subject to duties or tariffs to offset the implicit subsidy they enjoy from lower environmental costs.

In practice, however, there does not appear to be much evidence for industrial migration. For most industries, costs attributable to environmental regulations rarely exceed about 1.5 percent of the total. Countries with initially low environmental standards are not immune to pressures to raise them. Indeed, it can be argued that, in a dynamic business environment, higher environmental standards may in practice act as a spur to innovation and competitive success. Trade may be a key factor in the ratcheting-up of standards, as manufacturers seek to expand markets for the products they are required to produce for countries with the higher standards. Nevertheless, it has been argued that concerns over competitiveness may become more relevant as the costs of environmental compliance rise, particularly for sectors such as energy-intensive manufacturing and processing.

Unsurprisingly, this topic does not feature in the work program of the CTE. Although it could be argued that a failure to incorporate environmental costs is equivalent to an implicit subsidy, and should be countervailable under GATT's Article VI if the subsidized imports cause material damage to domestic production, the Subsidies Agreement carefully defines a subsidy as "a financial contribution by a government or any public body"—i.e., not an implicit subsidy arising from lower environmental standards. Even ignoring this, the concept of ecoduties raises many practical problems, including the appropriateness of the standards being defended, the danger of capture by protectionist interests, the possible removal of competitive pressures on domestic industry and the ever-present fear of retaliation.

The practical problems of border tax adjustment have been considered above. Nevertheless, some participants in the debate' have argued that it may be necessary to contemplate countervailing duties to defuse industrial opposition to higher environmental standards and to prevent concerns that loss of competitiveness may become a significant drag on environmental legislation. The OECD, while affirming its opposition to countervailing duties, considered that further research on the extent of the problem would be helpful.

Dispute Settlement

The World Trade Organization's *Disputes Settlement Understanding* established a unified system which applies to all WTO agreements. It operates to stricter time limits and is more transparent than the GATT system it replaced, and the findings of disputes panels are adopted automatically by WTO members unless they decide by consensus otherwise: the reverse of the pre-Uruguay Round position. The Understanding also enables panels to request written advisory reports from expert groups, and CTE members have underlined the importance of following this procedure in areas of trade-environment interaction—while recognizing that it is not within the mandate of panels to question the merits of national or international environmental objectives. In general, it is believed that the new system is a considerable improvement on the old, and panel findings have certainly been published much more speedily than before. CTE discussions largely concentrated on the interaction between WTO and MEA disputes settlement mechanisms but, as with the wider question, failed to reach any conclusion.

Conclusion

The trade-environment debate is not going to go away. On the contrary, the combination of the growth in trade anticipated from the implementation of the Uruguay Round agreements and the accumulating evidence of global environmental degradation, together with the pressure for international action that will result, seems likely to lead to more, and more serious, conflicts. Set against this background, the findings of the first report of the World Trade Organization's Committee on Trade and Environment—which were little more than that more work was needed—were a disappointment to many.

It may be, however, that the CTE will never be able to conclude very much by itself. The GATT/WTO regime tends to progress through negotiating 'rounds' (such as the Uruguay Round, the most recent) covering a very broad sweep of topics; trade-offs are then possible which ensure that every participant benefits directly from at least some of the elements of the final package. It may be that progress on the trade-environment issue will have to wait until the next WTO round, for which there are already calls.

More fundamentally, it may be that the WTO by itself, even in the context of a new trade round, will not be able to resolve the trade-environment conflict. One of the problems inherent in this issue is that debates are conducted within, but rarely between, two separate communities, each encompassing governments, international organizations, NGOs and businesses: those motivated by trade liberalization and those motivated by environmental protection. These two groups of people possess different assumptions, values and modes of operating, and tend to lack a full understanding and appreciation of each other's position.

Where the two sides can be brought together—as they can, for instance, within the European Union, where the European Court of Justice is enabled to strike a balance in disputes between the two Treaty of Rome objectives of trade and environment—then the pursuit of their two objectives can be brought into harmony. Further research and analysis, joint discussion and open debate are the prerequisites for progress in resolving the conflicts inherent in the pursuit of trade liberalization and environmental protection.

B

Tay S.S.C. and Esty D., "Trade and Environment; Context and Controversy," in Tay S.S.C. and Esty D. (eds), *Asian Dragons and Green Trade*, Times Academic Press, 1996, pp 1–17

Trade and the environment is an issue that has come into prominence in the 1990s. This follows years of parallel development of the two fields as largely separate areas of international law and policy. Their intersection can be traced to two major trends.

First, the completion of the Uruguay Round of the *General Agreement on Tariffs and Trade* (GATT) and the establishment of the World Trade Organization (WTO) has revitalized interest in trade liberalization. This development promises to establish a regime of market access trade rules that will further liberalize global trade, and bind together the economies of nations. Many have come to believe that trade liberalization is important in enhancing world economic welfare. And, as freer trade takes hold and there is progress in reducing tariffs, new worries about "non-tariff barriers", including environmental regulation, have emerged.

Second, the international community now recognizes that protecting the environment is important. Building on from the 1992 Earth Summit in Rio, nations around the world now adhere to sustainable development as the guiding principle for economic growth. At the international level, this objective requires cooperation among nations in addressing global environmental harms. To tackle concerns such as global warming, the depletion of the ozone layer and deforestation, common rules are needed so that the protective efforts of one country are not undermined by others. As economists remind us, there can be no "free riders". The international community has committed itself to an emergent and interlocking regime of multilateral environmental agreements (MEAs), regional treaties and national laws.

These two currents of international policy converge in the issue of trade and the environment. Environmentalists believe that increased and uncontrolled trade will hasten environmental degradation. Those who promote freer trade fear that environmental rules may be used as a disguised tool for protectionism and impede economic growth. Issues arise that are important to all who believe that trade liberalization can and should be reconciled with environmental protection and lead to "green trade".

It is against this backdrop that the WTO has come to consider the relationship between trade and the environment. There has also been consideration of environmental issues in regional trade contexts: the European Union (EU), the *North American Free Trade Agreement* (NAFTA), the Asia Pacific Economic Cooperation (APEC) area and the Association of Southeast Asian Nations (ASEAN). In each area, where economic integration is proceeding, the environment has also come into consideration.

There is a complementary movement in environmental matters. Environmental agreements at the international level have turned to trade measures as a means to achieve their goals. As environmentalists come to terms with the concept of sustainable development, there has been an increased emphasis on finding the right economic tools and policies to maximize benefits with the greatest efficiency. This is particularly the case as we look beyond the environmental problems such as the conservation of species to those that are primarily associated with poverty and the least developed countries—the lack of potable water and sanitation, adequate housing, diminishing agricultural lands and the depletion of natural resources to meet basic needs, such as deforestation arising from the use of wood for fuel.

What can be expected? How will the WTO and other regional regimes balance the scales between the different concerns of trade and the environment? How will environmental rules affect the economic dynamism of many Asian nations? What are the likely effects on countries, companies and consumers?

It was to enquire further into these and other questions that the Asia Conference on Trade and the Environment was convened in Singapore in June 1996. That conference provided one of the first occasions to focus on the Asian dimension of trade and the environment...

This book seeks to reconcile the two perspectives of trade and the environment and to identify ways to achieve trade liberalization and environmental protection, and to make for "green" trade. It attempts to supply three needs in the discussion of trade and the environment.

First, it seeks to highlight the importance of trade to Asia, and the importance of the region's growing trade and economic dynamism to the world economy. Much of the earlier discussion of trade and environment issues centered on European and North American experiences. In comparison, Asia's concerns have been largely neglected. This book endeavors to bring the Asian dragons into the center of the trade-environment debate. Second, it aims to identify environmental pressures that Asia has experienced in tandem with accelerated economic growth. The region has considerable environmental riches as well as its share of environmental problems. Third, this book strives to take in different perspectives on the issues of trade and the environment. Perspectives can differ in respect of a number of axes: between developed and developing countries; between environmentalists and those who are pro-trade; and between different sectors of government, business, nongovernmental organizations and academia. These perspectives are in conflict about what should be done. Indeed, they differ essentially on the definition of the problems at hand and how they see the connections and priorities between trade and the environment....[T]his chapter gives some background to these issues...

Different Perspectives and Theories

The WTO's mission is to increase and further liberalize trade. In the Uruguay Round of multilateral trade negotiations, initiatives were taken in new areas, such as trade in services, trade-related intellectual property and investment measures. The WTO has also tried to define and limit the circumstances in which a nation may object to imports as not meeting national standards. The WTO is keen to follow through on the gains of the Uruguay Round and to maintain momentum towards freer trade. Regional economic groupings like NAFTA, APEC and ASEAN (with its ASEAN Free Trade Area—AFTA), also seek to facilitate trade and business across borders. Trade is seen by many, especially in Asia, as an engine for economic growth.

The effect of trade liberalization on the environment is more controversial. Some environmentalists see "limits to growth". They believe trade will have a detrimental impact on the environment, because it encourages greater production and economic development while constraining national regulations that might encourage environmental protection and clean-up. These environmentalists wish to put trade into a subservient role. Other environmentalists support "sustainable development" and argue that freer trade can benefit the environment in two ways. First, countries will be able to specialize and he more efficient in production, thereby reducing waste and environmental damage. Secondly, they believe that trade will help countries achieve economic progress which will, in turn, give them additional resources to invest in environmental protection. While concerned for the environment, they do not reject trade. Such views are confirmed by the *Rio Declaration*, made at the 1992 Earth Summit. Article 12 called for trade and the environment to be, "mutually supportive in favor of sustainable development".

The search for sustainable development has led environmentalists to look at economic tools to reconcile growth and efficiency with increased environmental protection. Some do not call for all countries, both richer and poorer, to set the same environmental standards. Instead, they feel this should be governed by a corrected market that would fully and accurately price environmental resources. It is this market-based idea of cost-effectiveness that determines the efficient allocation of resources between environmental and other concerns. Market based environmentalism would only justify higher environmental standards when the marginal benefits of that protection would be equal to the marginal costs. The technology to deal with the increasing pollution may not, for example, be cost-effective, or there may be other pressing socioeconomic demands with priority over environmental issues.

How can these economic tools be made to work for the environment? Can trade measures and access to larger and richer markets in the United States and Europe be used to provide both the incentives and punishments to increase environmental standards in developing countries?... Theories and concepts that undergird the economic analysis of environmental issues include economic externalities and market failure and the "polluter pays principle". Pearson considers the ability of economics to sufficiently and accurately "price" the environment to promote both protection and efficient use. In this, the relationship between classical trade theory—that promotes free trade and open markets—and environmental standards is considered.

The polluter pays principle is another mechanism for dealing with the economic advantage (or disadvantage) that may arise from environmental concerns. Economists suggest that the environment will be better protected if policies aim to "get prices right" by reducing subsidies on environmentally harmful products and activities. The polluter pays principle requires that consumers of these goods and services pay prices that reflect full costs, including environmental factors.

Pearson surveys some of the empirical studies that seek to prove, or disprove, these theories, as well as the general relation of trade and open markets to environmental protection. He considers that empirical studies have largely been inconclusive, and suggests that four conclusions be drawn. First, there is no sharp or certain difference between environmental protection that results from external rules and demands by foreign markets, and that which responds to domestic regulations. Second, environmental protection measures may place the small and medium-sized enterprises in especially difficult positions, without access to facilities, technology and know-how, and capital to adapt to new environmental rules. Third, the growing number of eco-labelling schemes will impair market access. Fourth, developing countries have largely been able and willing to respond to export quality requirements.

The search for sustainable development has led environmentalists to look at economic tools to reconcile growth and efficiency with increased environmental protection.

It is true that some countries have lower environmental standards than others. This may result from a lack of adequate and updated legislation or from weaknesses in monitoring and administration. In some cases, it may be that the country has a different capacity to absorb and tolerate pollution. In other cases, environmental priorities are different. In the United States, for example, rare wildlife like the Bald Eagle and excessive radon levels in households are among the highest environmental concerns of average people. In contrast, for poorer countries, key environmental issues may be basic needs such as the lack of clean water and proper sanitation.

Environmental regulation may effect the comparative advantage of different countries in the production and trade of goods. There is very often a cost associated with environmental protection. Those countries with higher standards may then be imposing a higher cost on their producers, resulting in more expensive and potentially less competitive goods. Conversely, countries with lower standards may act as "pollution havens" to attract foreign investment.

How valid is it to see lower environmental standards as an "unfair" advantage that can enhance economic competitiveness? Do developing countries in fact lower standards to attract investors?...In the face of "unfair" competition, some environmentalists may fear that even countries which want to protect the environment will lose their prerogative to set higher domestic standards. Instead, environmental standards will tend to the lowest common denominator. Environmentalists are concerned that uncontrolled trade and economic competition between nations will lead to a race to the bottom.

Esty points out that, although fears of industry migration to pollution havens have not been proven by empirical studies, there is considerable anecdotal evidence to support concerns about pressure on lower environmental standards. He suggests that the result is not a race to the bottom, but rather a "regulatory chill" in the environmental policy process, obstructing movement towards better standards. Different policy approaches to deal with different levels of environmental standards between different countries are also examined.

Esty identifies various responses to competitiveness concerns: *laissez-faire* approaches; the use of trade restrictions; different techniques of harmonization; the mutual recognition of standards between countries; and requiring countries to enforce their own domestic standards. Harmonization policies need not mandate uniform standards but can be further refined. Balance, Esty suggests, is essential for good trade and environmental policy.

Another difference in perspectives on trade-environment issues lies between developed and developing countries. This does not exactly correspond to the pro-trade and environmental perspectives already mentioned. There are many in developed countries who are staunchly pro-trade, and there are also environmentalists in developing countries.

However, at the risk of over-generalization, it can be said that most developing countries are now pro-trade. This is especially true in Asia, where the newly industrialized economies have set the example of export-oriented growth for other, larger economies such as China, Vietnam and India. One of the worries for developing countries is that environmental standards may serve as disguised barriers to trade. Green issues may then be used as an excuse for developed countries to reduce competition and blunt their comparative advantage. Even those who believe in protecting the environment may fear that protectionists march behind a green flag.

Developing countries are concerned with competitiveness; in particular, competitiveness between companies. Larger companies may find it relatively easy to adjust to new standards. But, in comparison, the small and medium sized companies that predominate in many sectors in poorer countries may lack the capital, technology and know-how to successfully adapt to and meet the costs of environmental protection... Vossenaar and Jha draw on country studies by UNCTAD and other international institutions to examine the effects of trade on environmental policies in developing countries.

They differentiate between effects that result from domestic policies, external market requirements and multilateral agreements, and consider that the results differ according to a variety of factors that may be specific to a firm or sector. Development and macro-economic policies at the national level can also influence the outcome. Developing countries are not, as such, wholly or equally vulnerable to higher environment standards. National policies at these different levels and in different sectors can be of use. Vossenaar and Jha suggest some policy responses for developing countries to maximize the environmental improvements while minimizing negative effects on the economy.

Controversies and Experiences

The different perspectives on trade and the environment—between free-traders and environmentalists, developed and developing countries—have led to controversies and conflict between nations.

Perhaps the best known trade-environment controversy was the 1991 tuna-dolphin case involving the American ban on Mexican tuna imports. American laws sought to stop the incidental slaughter of dolphins in commercial tuna fishing by banning tuna caught using methods that killed dolphins. Mexico challenged the ban and a GATT dispute settlement panel ruled that the extraterritorial effect of the trade restrictions were contrary to GATT rules in 1991. More recently, the United States has again been asked by the WTO to change some anti-pollution laws that were deemed to discriminate against gasoline imports from Brazil and Venezuela.

Outside of the WTO, there has also been controversy over environmental measures in other regional trade groupings. When Mexico joined Canada and the United States in NAFTA in 1993, green groups and others argued that Mexico would act as a pollution haven, pulling jobs and investment away with the promise of lower environmental requirements, and obstructing American and Canadian initiatives to raise environmental standards. This led to a side agreement on environment to supplement the main trade treaty...

Although their standards were not harmonized, the environmental measures in NAFTA go much further than anything in the WTO or Asia to date on at least three important points. First, NAFTA countries have agreed it would be inappropriate for any country to lower its environmental standards to attract investment. Second, a persistent failure to observe environmental laws by one country in NAFTA can lead to another member taking economic measures against it. Third, specific multilateral environmental agreements [MEAs] are exempted from NAFTA trade rules. Alanis-Ortega, an environmentalist, suggests that this has assisted those in Mexico who wish to ensure the better enforcement of environment standards set by the country itself.

The EU is a regional grouping of nations with relatively similar levels of economic development. Despite this, there have also been trade-environment disputes. One example of this followed Denmark's renewables recycling. The rules limited the type and the shape of beer and soft drink containers. Companies in other EU countries were disadvantaged in relation to domestic producers and complained. Part of the Danish rules were challenged by the EU as being too restrictive of trade and "unnecessary" for environmental protection.

Damien Geradin...reminds us that it is not simply a question of what standards are set, but who sets them. He notes that, in contrast with NAFTA, harmonization of environmental requirements has been the cornerstone of the EU response to trade and environment concerns. The integration seen in the EU may be an unsuitable model for the WTO or a more diverse grouping such as APEC. But there may also be lessons to extract from the experience. Among these is Geradin's reminder that even within the relative economic homogeneity of the KU, differences still exist. He points out various ways in which the EU has sought to deal with these differences while seeking harmonization of standards and rules.

The experience of Asian countries differs from those found in the European Union and NAFTA. Like many developing countries, Asian countries favor continuing to liberalize trade to stimulate economic growth. They argue that trade and economic growth will bring the resources to deal with environmental problems effectively. Cutting off trade would, as such, be counter-productive if they are impoverished. As such, there have been relatively few steps to harmonize environmental standards among Asian nations in APEC or the ASEAN. Nor has any one Asian country sought to set environmental standards to influence or compel others to follow.

The Asian experience in trade-environment issues to date has largely been a defensive response against attempts by developed countries to impose environmental standards. They have responded to initiatives derived from unilateral measures, such as the American tuna-dolphin laws, multilateral agreements like the *Montreal Protocol* protecting the ozone layer, as well as consumer-based initiatives, such as eco-labels and the setting of environmental management standards under the ISO 14000 series.

While the tuna-dolphin case has been resolved, other unilateral measures have arisen. A current and still unresolved controversy concerns American laws that prohibit the import of shrimps, where the harvesting methods used result in the killing of sea turtles, an endangered species. This conflict affects a number of Asian and ASEAN countries.

Even when environmental measures are taken on a multilateral basis, some have felt that the burdens have been unequally placed on Asian countries. There are, however, some models for North-South collaboration. The *Montreal Protocol*, for example, gives developing countries a longer period to phase out their production of chlorofluorocarbons (CFCs) and other ozone depleting substances. It also promises multilateral funding to assist developing countries in acquiring CEC substitutes and encourages technology transfer to minimize industrial dislocation.

Eco-labels have also recently come into focus. Rather than banning a product, the eco-label seeks to steer consumers to favor environmentally friendly products. ASEAN countries have been troubled by eco-labels that affected tropical hardwood products. The scheme was started by some European countries as they felt that such products contributed to the destruction of rainforests. ASEAN countries protested that the schemes had no basis because no similar eco-label scheme was imposed on temperate forest products, which can also contribute to environmental damage.

Countries in Asia, like other developing countries, have also had to consider the effect of ISO 14000 standards on their competitive position. Set by the International Standards Organization (ISO), these new management guidelines promote environmental activities such as audits and life-cycle analysis. Like eco-labels, these are not compulsory laws. They can, however, influence buyers of products as a mark of quality, like the preceding ISO 9000 series…

Intal acknowledges that economic growth and industrialization has placed environmental stress on Asian countries. He examines the parallel concern that higher environmental standards may erode competitiveness. Intal regards competitiveness as a multi-dimensional concept and suggests that the best way forward—for both environmental protection and economic growth—is to increase efficiency. He considers the ways that ASEAN countries can successfully respond and adapt to standards set by eco-labelling schemes, ISO 14000 and multilateral environmental agreements (MEAs). Keeping their economies open and furthering trade liberalization can be one key to ensuring ASEAN countries can respond robustly to changing environmental rules.

A very wide range of proposals has been generated on how to deal with possible conflict between environment and trade in the WTO.

Pangestu and Roesad share the experience and perspectives of Indonesia. The country has received increasing foreign investment in industrial sectors in which pollution is potentially severe. Some foreign companies in these sectors have applied their home country standards above and beyond the requirements of Indonesian legislation, but others have not. They find that the theories of competitiveness disadvantage and of pollution havens are not easy to substantiate in practice. The widescale adoption of the polluter pays principle, the deregulation of the economy and institutional integration are, however, recommended by Pangestu and Roesad.

In the controversies settled to date, environmental regulations have largely been abandoned or amended because of economic and free trade considerations. Throughout the 1980s and into this decade, GATT decisions have almost always favored trade concerns over the environment. In a number of cases, national governments have had to change their laws or face penalties for failing to meet trade obligations. These outcomes have reassured those in favor of trade. But they have not dissipated environmental concern. They have instead renewed the call for change.

Even those who are cautious about environmental trade measures may wish to heed that call, for environmental concerns cannot be held at bay. The environmental regimes are proceeding independently. From the trade perspective, there is concern that MEAs will increasingly employ trade measures and that such measures may be inconsistent with WTO rules. If so, there will be difficulty in resolving which of these two separate and equal international obligations should take precedence. Moreover, if attempts to reconcile trade and the environment at the multilateral level are thwarted, this may lead to nations turning to unilateral actions out of frustration.

Both these scenarios—of conflict between two multilateral obligations, and of increasingly diverse and divergent unilateral measures—would undermine the consistency and certainty that is needed both for international trade and for the protection of the environment. For these reasons, considerable attention in the trade-environment debate has focused on the WTO.

Issues and Institutional Change in the WTO

A very wide range of proposals has been generated on how to deal with possible conflict between environment and trade in the WTO. The WTO has played a primary role in promoting free trade among the majority of nations. The GATT has provided the international community with a rule-based regime for making decisions and resolving disputes.

The GATT was initiated after World War II to liberalize trade. The International Trade Organization (ITO) was meant to be the institution to promote the GATT but was abandoned before it began. It was only some 40 years later, after the GATT had achieved substantial reductions in trade barriers, that the WTO was created in the Uruguay Round of GATT negotiations to serve as its umbrella administration. The WTO is directed by a "ministerial conference" of all member nations that meets at least once every two years. In December 1996, the first post-Uruguay Round Ministerial Conference will be held in Singapore. The primary goal of this conference is to continue to promote freer trade among countries, and to follow up on the Uruguay Round agenda that has expanded trade to new issues and sectors. The WTO works on the premise that countries enjoy comparative advantages in different aspects and attributes, so increased trade will be more efficient and provide mutual benefit for all. The core principles of the GATT are:

- Most favored nation: to treat all foreign goods alike;
- National treatment: not to discrimination between domestic and foreign goods in internal taxation and regulation.

General exceptions for GATT obligations are found in Article XX. The environment and MEAs are not explicitly listed. However, environmental concerns can potentially be addressed if the actions taken are, "necessary to protect human, animal or plant life or health" in Article XX (b). Actions that may relate to, "the conservation of non-renewable natural resources" may be protected under the exception of Article XX (g). These exceptions under Article XX are, however, limited quite narrowly to:

- What is "necessary" or least restrictive of trade;
- Protection of the domestic environment of the country enacting the regulations, and not that of another country or of the global commons;
- Products, not the production and process methods (PPMs) that may cause environmental harm.

In the Uruguay Round, the GATT refined provisions relating to product standards, such as technical barriers to trade (TBT) and sanitary and phytosanitary measures (SPS). The new areas of the GATT potentially admit environmental exceptions as well.

When environmental measures are taken by one country, they are subject to challenge by affected parties. The dispute is referred to a GATT dispute panel, which has a quasi-judicial function to decide whether trade rules have been infringed.

The development of the GATT and the birth of the WTO has, however, largely been isolated from the growth in environmental law and policy. Recognition of the environment as an important international concern can be marked by the 1972 Stockholm Declaration on the Human Environment. This was reinforced by the *Rio Declaration* exactly 20 years later at the 1992 Earth Summit. In between these two events, environmental concerns grew in at least two major ways. First, the concept of the environment, at first associated primarily with conservation, widened to encompass broader economic and other developmental factors, as captured in the term, "sustainable development". Second, international laws and policies concerning the environment have grown rapidly, with a range of new MEAs, especially in response to global environmental harms. The isolation between the trade regime on the one hand and the environmental regime on the other, has only come to be addressed relatively recently with the activation of the WTO Committee of Trade and the Environment (CTE).

The Marrakesh meeting of the Uruguay Road gave the CTE the task of examining ten specific items concerning trade and the environment. The items on the CTE agenda are:

1. the relationship between the provisions of the multilateral trading system and trade measures for environmental purposes, including those pursuant to MEAs;
2. the relationship between environmental policies relevant to trade and environmental measures with significant trade effects and the provision of the multilateral trading system;
3. the relationship between the provisions of the multilateral trading system and
   (a) charges and taxes for environmental purposes; and
   (b) requirements for environmental purposes relating to products, including standards and technical regulations, packaging, labelling and recycling;
4. the provisions of the multilateral trading system with respect to the transparency of trade measures used for environmental purposes and environmental measures and requirements which have significant trade effects;
5. the relationship between the dispute settlement mechanisms in the multilateral trading system and those found in MEAs;
6. the effect of environmental measures on market access, especially in relation to developing countries, in particular to the least developed among them, and environmental benefits of removing trade restrictions and distortions;
7. the issue of exports of domestically prohibited goods;
8. environment-related provisions in the Agreement on Trade Related Aspects of Intellectual Property Rights;
9. the work program envisaged in the 1994 Uruguay Round Decision on Trade in Services and the Environment; and
10. appropriate arrangements for relations with nongovernmental organizations referred to in Article V of the WTO and transparency of documents.

Of these items, discussion has focused mainly on four issues: the relationship of MEAs to trade rules the relationship between WTO and MEA dispute settlement mechanisms; eco-labelling; and the impact of trade liberalization on environmental standards.

Some have been disappointed by the slow pace of progress in the CTE. [I]t becomes clear that the CTE has met marked difficulties in proceeding with trade-environment discussions, resulting from the different perspectives and interests of developed and developing countries. Some environmental advocates have, on that basis, questioned whether the CTE should continue its work. Reiterer, to the contrary, argues that the CTE should become a permanent organ of the WTO.

Different proposals have been considered to clarify the consistency of MEAs with trade rules. There are three major MEAs which use trade measures to meet environmental aims: [The] 1973 *Convention on International Trade in Endangered Species of Wild Fauna and Flora* (CITES); [the] 1987 *Montreal Protocol on Substances that Deplete the Ozone Layer* (Ozone treaty); and the 1989 *Basel Convention on the Control of Transboundary Movements of Hazardous Wastes and their Disposal* (*Basel Convention*).

The compatibility of MEAs with GATT obligations on free trade is uncertain. The three major MEAs mentioned have not been challenged in the WTO to date. But controversy remains over future MEAs that may be agreed. Such future MEAs are likely to increase their reliance on trade measures as one of the few sanctions available to meet environmental goals. Proposals for reform are divided between incorporating specifically named MEAs into the GATT or trying to set criteria for inclusion of present and future MEAs. This creates the need to coordinate and reconcile them with trade rules. Reiterer considers different techniques of doing so: by amendment, interpretation or waiver of relevant WTO rules; and by issuing guidelines for MEA negotiators on the limits of acceptable trade measures....

The insights of business are important on trade and environment issues. While governments may set the rules, it is business and the private sector who produce and trade. [Robert] Heine is concerned that MEAs will affect businesses negatively. This is because it is not simply the nature of the products but the production and process methods (PPMs) that are often in question, as they are in eco-labelling schemes. PPMs potentially require businesses to reveal proprietary know-how and technology to bureaucracies. There is danger, as such, that they may be revealed to others. As only specified and fixed methods would be acceptable, moreover, PPMs may also stifle innovation and new, more environmentally effective and efficient methods.

Unilateral environmental measures, such as those used by the United States in the tuna-dolphin and the recent gasoline law cases, which Murase considers, have been widely criticized. Article 12 of the *Rio Declaration*, issued at the 1992 Earth Summit, suggests that such unilateral measures should be avoided. If trade rules are similarly interpreted to prohibit unilateral measures, this would create at least one area of consistency between the two regimes.

But while Murase does not support unilateral measures, he argues that they may not be unsupportable. Unilateral measures by nations, short of the use of force, are allowed under general principles of international law. They would, as such, be illegal in trade matters only if the WTO system is considered to be a self-contained system. This, Murase tries to show, is not necessarily the case.

He gives special attention to WTO dispute settlement system. Dispute settlement in the GATT has achieved a credible reputation as regards trade issues. The new WTO is armed with perhaps the most comprehensive and potentially effective dispute settlement mechanism in international law. It allows for enforcement with economic bite. Murase suggests that the system will not help settle trade-environment disputes unless it is given sufficient jurisdiction and the ability to provide suitable remedies.

Suggestions for reform of the WTO dispute settlement system are also the focus...[of] Winfried Lang. There have been proposals to increase the transparency in the WTO dispute settlement system and allow environmentalists to participate in decision making. The level and purpose of that participation is however in question. Some suggest that environmentalists should only provide information that might assist trade experts in making decisions. Others have gone so far as to suggest the creation of an entirely new international institution, to bridge gaps between the trade and environmental regimes.

Lang examines the different perspectives of those who are in favor of bringing environmental considerations into the WTO, and those who are sceptical of such suggestions. He presents seven options to involve environmental expertise and institutions in the WTO dispute settlement system when there are trade-environment disputes. The more conservative options would he to include one or more environmental experts as members of dispute settlement panels. This draws on existing WTO procedures to include independent expertise from outside the trade community. Far more extensive suggestions would be for institutional changes to allow appeal from the WTO to the international Court of Justice or even *ad hoc* arbitration that equally represent both trade and environmental interests.

Lang...look[s] at the possibility of minimizing or avoiding conflict over trade and environment. This would depend on better coordination between the trade regime and the environment regime, as both fields of international law and policy grow. To bridge the two regimes, Lang calls for greater transparency and dialogue, by having consultations before environmental measures with trade effects are undertaken.

Steve Charnovitz...considers increasing the part that independent environmental experts can play, as well as interaction between the WTO and other international governmental organizations, such as the United Nations Environmental Programme. But beyond this, Charnovitz focuses on exploring how environmental nongovernmental organizations (NGOs) might be involved.

The relationship between NGOs and the WTO has been the source of considerable tension. NGOs have been among the strongest critics of the WTO. On its part, unlike the United Nations and other organizations, the WTO has not developed a structure to recognize NGOs and allow them to participate in its deliberations or even attend many of its discussions. This is in sharp contrast to the environmental regime, in which NGO participation is an accepted principle. The WTO has been seen as one of the most closed and secretive international organizations. This closed culture, Charnovitz points out, runs counter to the WTO mandate to open up, both under its present rules and from the original conception of the International Trade Organization, the WTO's stillborn predecessor. Surveying possible objections to the increased participation of NGOs, Charnovitz argues that this would not slow down negotiations of new trade agreements and rules. It would instead assist in making such agreements more representative of the world's demands and interests.

A Context for Future Dialogue

Proposals on issues in trade and the environment are numerous and detailed At their core, there are important and fundamental questions. How will environmental standards be set? Who decides if those standards are being met? What trade measures should be allowed? What assistance is committed to help those who want to comply? How do we coordinate and reconcile our different commitments to trade and to the environments?

Given its scope and complexity, the trade-environment debate seems here to stay. Indeed, as laws and policies in both the fields of trade and environment expand and go forward with the separate agendas, the potential for conflict will increase. Much of Elvis will continue to focus on the WTO. But trade and environment issues will also arise in other regional economic groupings, such as APEC, ASEAN and Asia's reinvigorated ties with Europe in the wake of the Asia-Europe meeting. What should be the context for continuing work and dialogue on the issues of trade and the environment?

...David Runnalls considers what the richer countries of the North must do to engage the global South. He looks back to the 1992 Earth Summit and argues that the opportunity for co operative, win-win solutions was foregone. Instead, discussion has proceeded on separate agendas for development, on one side, and the environment, on the other. The result has been conflict, rather than cooperation for sustainable development.

Among developed countries, there has been a sense of both frustration and exhaustion in environmental efforts. Donor fatigue has also led to the failure of the developed countries to make the substantial transfers of assets that were promised in the Earth Summit. This fails to meet the principle of common but differentiated responsibilities agreed at the Earth Summit, whereby developed countries would bear' greater responsibilities for meeting environmental concerns. Runnalls believes the developed countries have largely failed to provide leadership in meeting environmental challenges.

Runnalls calls for this Rio bargain to be renewed. He examines a number of areas where developing countries have had reason to suspect protectionism disguised by environmental concerns. Ways to protect against increased protectionism are proposed. Transparency can ameliorate the effects of ecolabelling and ISO 14000 schemes on small and medium-sized enterprises. Greater certainty and less suspicion can come from avoiding unilateral measures and reforming MEAs. The willingness of developing countries to cooperate can be enhanced by amending the WTO rules on intellectual property to grant them access to technology on easier terms, and increasing their capacity to understand and deal with trade environment conflicts. By such means, Runnalls believes that the developed and developing countries can engage and cooperate with each other.

...Simon Tay looks at future cooperation on the trade environment issues from Asia's point of view. Especially for the developing countries in the region, environmental concerns cannot be pursued at the cost of stopping economic growth. But two different scenarios of growth can be sketched: the first of starkly unequal and unsustainable growth, and the second of development that takes human and environmental factors into account.

Like Runnalls, Tay is concerned that the Rio bargain on the environment has unravelled. He looks at reasons for Asia to act, despite this failing, to protect its own environment. These reasons relate to overcrowded megacities, overtaxed agricultural land and water resources. Tay urges attention to an environmental agenda that is more immediately related to the problems of Asia than other issues such as conservation and global warming.

Tay also considers that the bargain on trade issues, established in the Uruguay Round, might also be in doubt. The crux of the trade bargain is mutual benefit from mutually freer trade. Many countries in the region have therefore opened their own market to foreign imports and investment in expectation that their exports would grow. If environmental measures arise that reduce the access for Asian goods to the markets of the developed countries, this may unravel the trade bargain.

Tay therefore suggests a new context for dialogue. Consensus and cooperation must be emphasized in the relationship between trade and the environment as both require nations to work together. Preference and assistance for developing countries is also justified by principles found in both environmental and trade regimes. Given the rise of regional initiatives in Asia, Tay suggests that these groupings might find ways of going ahead with trade issues in ways that the more rigid and rule-bound WTO cannot.

Conclusion

The need for growth continues. Despite economic dynamism and the emergence of Asian dragons, the developing countries in Asia and elsewhere still face the pressures of poverty. The challenge for the trade regime is to demonstrate that more open markets will help governments and societies fulfil those needs. The importance of environmental protection is also felt by both developed and developing countries, not only within their respective borders but also, increasingly, on the global level. The challenge of the environmental regime is to address these common concerns, while ensuring an equitable distribution of the costs and responsibilities.

In their evolution to date, trade and environmental regimes have largely gone their own way. Where they have come together, the context has been beset by controversy, conflict and suspicion. This has to change. All regions benefit from free trade. Equally, all countries have a responsibility to cooperate to protect the environment. In that context conflict between trade and environmental needs, between free-traders and environmentalists, and between developed and developing countries, is not inevitable. Trade and the environment can be made mutually supportive. This has been recognized by the trade regime in the Preamble to the 1994 GATT Agreement and the environmental regime in the *Rio Declaration*...This emphasis does not mean that what is good for trade will automatically be good for the environment, or vice versa. Rather, it is a call for concerted action to make the two regimes more mutually reinforcing.

3

Trade and Multilateral Environmental Agreements: Convention on International Trade in Endangered Species of Wild Fauna and Flora (1973)

A

Introduction to CITES

(i) Cyrille de Klemm and Clare Shine, *International Environmental Law: Biological Diversity*, Programme of Training for the Application of Environmental Law, UNITAR, UNEP, IUCN, 1998, pp. 63–72

Background

Whilst man has always exploited or overexploited certain species, it is only in recent decades that international trade in natural products has become large-scale. Demand has grown sharply, essentially in developed countries, for luxury products (from furs and reptile-skins to mother-of-pearl), pets (from raptors to tropical fish), ornamental plants (cacti, orchids), animals for bio-medical research and collector's items such as shells and butterflies. Other factors influencing trade are the need to provide specimens for zoos; the use of wild plants for the extraction of genetic material to make the pharmaceutical products; the use of certain animal species, such as whales, to obtain industrial products; and the importance of certain animal and plant derivatives (including bear gall bladder and rhino horn) for traditional medicine, particularly in Asia.

Trade in wild animals, plants and their products now represents an annual turnover of several thousand million dollars. However, overexploitation for trade purposes aggravates the threats already posed by habitat destruction. If uncontrolled, such trade could not only impoverish global biodiversity and the natural heritage of the countries concerned, but also deprive producer countries of substantial economic resources. In many such countries, the competent authorities do not have the means necessary to enforce relevant laws, especially to prevent illicit exports of wild animals and plants.

Measures for international control of trade in natural products, with importing States verifying the legality of exports to their territories, were included in conservation conventions for Africa and the Americas as early as 1933. However, these instruments could not adequately address the problem of international trade as they are regional, not global, and have no institutional mechanisms to secure the enforcement of their provisions. The initiative for a global convention equipped with measures to ensure compliance was taken by IUCN in 1963. Ten years later, the Convention on International Trade in Endangered Species of Wild Fauna and Flora (CITES) was signed in Washington on 3 March 1973. It came into force on 1 July 1975.

Objectives and Scope of the Convention

CITES plays a critical role in biodiversity conservation as the sectoral instrument dealing with the last link in the chain of causes of species extinction. Its dual objectives, relating to conservation as well as trade, are:

- to strengthen international protection of endangered species by banning international trade therein; and
- to ensure that commercially exploited species which are not currently threatened do not become endangered, thus ensuring the maintenance of sustainable trade and economic benefits for exporting countries.

CITES controls apply to specimens of animal and plant species listed in three Appendices.

Specimen is defined as meaning:

> "any animal or plant, whether alive or dead, belonging to a species listed in a CITES Appendix, as well as the readily recognizable parts of derivatives of such species" (Article I(b)).

Identification of such parts and derivatives is essential to the successful implementation of CITES, but interpretation of "readily recognizable" can vary widely between Parties, especially for less well-known products. The Conference of the Parties (COP) has therefore adopted several resolutions clarifying the term and establishing standardized names for parts and derivatives. There is now a presumption that where a label, mark or other circumstance indicates that a specimen is a part or derivative of a CITES species, this shall be taken as correct even if made by mistake or fraudulently (as in "turtle soup" with no turtle content...).

The inclusion of species in Appendices I and II is subject to decision of the COP, with amendments being subject to a simplified procedure (Article XV). Detailed criteria for including species in these Appendices were first adopted on 1976 and replaced by the COP in 1994. Known as the Everglades Criteria, these reaffirm that biological and trade criteria should remain the basis for listing species in the Appendices, contain numerical guidelines for what constitutes a threat of extinction and specifically incorporate the precautionary principle. This means that considering any proposal to amend Appendix I or II, Parties must apply the precautionary principle so that scientific uncertainty should not be used as a reason for failing to act in the best interest of the conservation of the species.

Trade in wild animals, plants and their products now represents an annual turnover of several thousand million dollars.

Main Obligations of the Parties

National institutional mechanisms are essential to the operation of CITES controls. Each party must designate one or more Management Authorities responsible for granting CITES permits in accordance with the rules laid down for species listed in each Appendix (see below). It must also establish one or more Scientific Authorities whose function is to advise the Management Authorities. The names and addresses of the Management Authorities must be communicated to the Depositary of the Convention which is located in Switzerland.

Parties are specifically required under CITES to take appropriate measures to enforce its provisions and to prohibit trade in breach of its rules: this includes penalizing illegal trade in or possession of CITES specimens and providing for their confiscation or return to the State of export (Article VIII). These provisions are not "self-executing" (not directly applicable in the territory of the Parties). Each Party must therefore take the necessary legislative and administrative measures to equip itself with a firm legal basis for prohibiting or regulating certain kinds of trade and imposing penalties for violations of those controls.

Trade Controls

Appendix I Species (Articles II.1 and III)

Appendix I lists species threatened with extinction which are or may be affected by international trade: it includes over 500 species, mostly mammals and birds, the majority of which are very rare. Trade in such specimens is made subject to particularly strict regulation, based on a double control system operated by the States of export and import.

An export permit may only be granted if an import permit has already been issued by the State of import, the State of export's Scientific Authority has advised that the export will not be detrimental to the survival of that species, and the specimen has not been obtained in breach of that State's laws.

An import permit may only be granted if an export permit/re-export certificate has already been issued by the State of export, the State of import's Scientific Authority has advised that the import will be for purposes which are not detrimental to the survival of the species, and that State's Management Authority is satisfied that the specimen is not to be used for "primarily commercial purposes". The last two rules also apply to introductions from the sea (for example, where an animal has been captured in the high seas outside the limits of national jurisdiction: no export permit can be presented as there is of course no State of export).

A re-export certificate (for the export of specimens previously imported into a given country) may only be granted by the State of re-export's Management Authority if it is satisfied that the specimen was imported into that State in accordance with the provisions of the Convention.

Appendix II Species (Articles II.2 and I)

Appendix II includes species which, although not necessarily threatened with extinction at present, may become so unless trade therein is strictly regulated to prevent exploitation incompatible with their survival. It has a much higher number of species than Appendix I since it includes whole zoological groups (from all monkeys and parrots to all cacti and orchids: the last-named family alone comprises between 20,000 and 30,000 species). Species which are very similar to the abovementioned species may also be listed, to avoid the risk of confusion and ineffective implementation of controls.

An export permit may only be granted if the State of export's Scientific Authority has advised that such export will not be detrimental to the survival of that species and its Management Authority is satisfied that the specimen has not been obtained illegally.

Imports require the prior presentation of an export permit/re-export certificate. Any introduction from the sea requires the prior grant of a certificate from the State of introduction's Management Authority, and its Scientific Authority must advise that such introduction will not be detrimental to the survival of the species concerned.

A re-export certificate may only be granted if the State of re-export's Management Authority is satisfied that the specimen was imported in accordance with the provisions of the Convention.

Appendix II listing makes it possible to monitor levels of trade and to take action if this begins to threaten populations of the species concerned. Each Scientific Authority is required to monitor export permits granted and actual exports of Appendix II specimens (Article IV.3): if it determines that exports should be limited to maintain one of these species at a level consistent with its role in the ecosystems in which it occurs (and well above the level at which it might become eligible for inclusion in Appendix I), it must advise the appropriate Management Authority of measures to be taken to limit the grant of export permits for such specimens.

Appendix III (Articles II.3 and V)

Unlike Appendices I and II, Appendix III only contains species which have been individually listed by Parties (around fifteen have so far done so). A species should only be included in Appendix III if a Party needs the cooperation of other Parties in the control of trade (Article II.3), as where a State has legislation regulating the export of species not listed in Appendices I and II and needs international support to enforce its laws. Where domestic legislation is adequate to protect the species concerned, however, it should not be so listed. Guidelines for the inclusion of species have been provided by the COP: these provide that a Party on whose territory such a species is present must have appropriate legal measures to prevent or restrict its exploitation and must declare to the CITES Secretariat that it wishes to include this species in Appendix III.

An export permit may only be granted by the State which included the species in Appendix III if the specimen concerned was legally obtained within that State. Imports are subject to the prior presentation of a certificate of origin. Where the specimen is imported from a State which included the species in Appendix III, its import is subject to the presentation of an export permit from that State.

Trade with States not Party to the Convention

CITES trade controls apply to all transactions of specimens, whether conducted between Parties or between Parties and non-Parties. Since non-Parties cannot be made to issue identical documents to those required under the Convention, Article X provides that "comparable documentation" issued by the competent authorities in non-Party States of import or export may be accepted, provided that it substantially conforms to CITES requirements for permits and certificates. Detailed guidance to Parties on the implementation of this provision has now been provided by Resolution Conf. 9.5 (Fort Lauderdale, 1994).

Transportation of Live Animals

The transport conditions of live animals are frequently appalling and mortality very high. Articles III-V therefore subject the issue of CITES permits/certificates to conditions for the transport of live animals and the necessary reception facilities in the countries of import. The COP has adopted several resolutions on this subject. Guidelines for Transport and Preparation for Shipment of Live Wild Animals and Plants have been prepared whilst, in respect of air transport, Parties are urged to comply with the International Air Transport Associations *IATA Live Animals Regulations* which are amended annually.

Exceptions to CITES Trade Controls

Transit

CITES trade controls do not cover the transit or transshipment of specimens through or in the territory of a Party while the specimens remain in Customs control (Article VII.1) Since this has facilitated fraudulent trade, the COP has adopted several resolutions in order to improve the control of shipments in transit. Essentially, specimens should only qualify for this exemption whilst they are moving through the State of transit under Customs control. All shipments that fall outside this narrow definition, such as shipments to no named consignee or to a consignee in the very country where they are nominally in transit, should be considered as imports subject to the normal CITES trade controls. Parties are also encouraged to apply the export requirements applicable to CITES specimens to specimens in transit and to adopt legislation allowing them to seize and confiscate specimens in transit without valid export documentation.

Breeding in Captivity and Artificial Propagation

There are two situations where specimens of Appendix I species are treated as if they were listed in Appendix II: animals bred in captivity for commercial purposes and plant species artificially propagated for commercial purposes (Article VII.4). If the State of Export's Management Authority is satisfied that a specimen has originated in this way, it issues a certificate to this effect which takes the place of an export permit. However, since this exception related to Appendix I species threatened with extinction, the COP has had to adopt several resolutions to prevent specimens being taken from the wild and then traded under such certificates, whether issued in good or bad faith.

With regard to animals, the COP has defined breeding in captivity as closed-circuit operations requiring, once established, only occasional addition of wild specimens to prevent deleterious inbreeding. Specimens benefiting from the exception must be offspring of parents which were themselves in captivity when mating took place. Comprehensive procedures for qualifying, registering and monitoring commercial captive-breeding operations for Appendix I species have been established pursuant to Resolution Conf. 8.15.

Greater problems of detection and control can arise for plants than for animals, because specimens taken from the wild are often mixed with artificially propagated ones in plant consignments. Since artificial propagation of certain plants could form an economic alternative to traditional agriculture in countries of origin and increase conservation interest in the areas of natural distribution, the COP has taken steps to reduce the administrative burden for plant traders whilst maintaining protection for wild plants and helping exporters to comply with the requirements of the Convention. These include the establishment of Guidelines for the Registration of Nurseries exporting artificially propagated specimens of Appendix I species and the compilation of a Register of Commercial Nurseries.

Ranching

Ranching operations use specimens taken from the wild, generally as eggs or juveniles. These do not benefit from the captive-bred exemption under the Convention, which means that ranched specimens of Appendix I species cannot be traded for primarily commercial purposes.

To prevent fraudulent trade, a uniform marking system has been developed for ranched specimens and inspection and reporting procedures have been developed for ranching operations.

This rule proved unjust (preventing controlled exploitation for the benefit of the producer State even where a species was still abundant) and often contrary to the conservation interests of some species (removing any economic incentive to maintain wild populations, particularly species widely considered as harmful such as crocodiles). Ranching can in fact bring substantial benefits to the States concerned and also requires populations to be maintained in their wild state so that eggs or juveniles may be taken. Consistent with modern approaches to species management, ranching allows States to derive economic benefit from rationally exploiting their wild fauna without endangering the survival of the species in question.

The COP has therefore developed a system allowing the populations of some species to be downgraded from Appendix I to Appendix II, in line with detailed criteria. To prevent fraudulent trade, a uniform marking system has been developed for ranched specimens and inspection and reporting procedures have been developed for ranching operations. Guidelines for evaluating ranching proposals for particular species have also been adopted.

The COP has adopted resolutions establishing quota systems to permit limited trade in certain species. Specific quotas have been adopted in respect of hunting trophies from certain species (leopard, cheetah, markhor). Special criteria have been adopted for the transfer of taxa from Appendix I to Appendix II where the countries of origin agree to introduce a quota system.

Other Exceptions

Article VII also provides for the following exceptions, which cannot be examined in detail here:

- Specimens acquired before the Convention's provisions became applicable to them.
- Personal or household effects (specific resolutions have been adopted with regard to the Control of tourist souvenir specimens).
- Specimens which are loaned, donated or exchanged between scientists or scientific institutions, including herbarium specimens.
- Specimens which form part of a zoo, a circus, a menagerie or a travelling exhibition, provided that these are either pre-Convention specimens, animals bred in captivity or artificially propagated plants.

Institutional Mechanisms

The Convention provides for the establishment of a Conference of the Parties. This meets about every two years to consider and adopt amendments to Appendices I and II, review the implementation of CITES and make recommendations for improving the effectiveness of the Convention. Nongovernmental organizations may attend the sessions as observers.

The CITES Secretariat is provided by the Executive Director of the United Nations Environment Programme (UNEP) and is based in Geneva. Its powers and duties, set out in Article XII, are quite extensive. It studies the reports of Parties and may request extra information where necessary to ensure implementation of CITES and it can make recommendations for the implementation of the aims and provisions of the Convention. Where it determines that an Appendix I or II species is being adversely affected by trade or that the provisions of the Convention are not being effectively implemented, it must communicate such information to the authorized Management Authority of the Parties concerned. The Secretariat thus plays a crucial role in the implementation of CITES: it centralizes information on offenses, informs the Parties of the specific measures that each of them can take, gives its opinion on the advisability of measures and so on.

As originally drafted, CITES did not provide for the funding of the Secretariat and the Conference. The Convention was therefore amended at an extraordinary meeting of the Conference of the Parties (Bonn, 1979). The amendment, which authorized the COP to adopt the necessary financial measures, only entered into force in 1987, but the majority of Parties paid voluntary contributions pending that date. At each of its meetings, the COP now adopts a budget.

The COP has established a Standing Committee, composed of the representatives of nine Parties, which is responsible, during the periods between meetings, for supervising budgetary expenditure, for guiding the Secretariat in discharging its duties and for carrying out such interim activities on behalf of the Conference as may be necessary. The COP has also set up four other committees: an Animals Committee, a Plants Committee, an Identification Manual Committee and a Nomenclature Committee, which is concerned with the standardization by nomenclatural references of the taxonomy used in the appendices to the Convention.

B

Convention on International Trade in Endangered Species of Wild Fauna and Flora (Washington), 993 UNTS 243; 12 ILM 1085, 1973

[*This treaty is available on the Internet at the following address and was accessed on 22/06/01 <http://www.cities.org>.*]

Article 1—Definitions

For the purpose of the present Convention, unless the context otherwise requires:

(a) "Species" means any species, sub-species, or geographically separate population thereof;

(b) "Specimen" means:

i. an animal or plant, whether alive or dead;

ii. in the case of an animal: for species included in Appendices I and II, any readily recognizable part or derivative thereof; and for species included in Appendix III, any readily recognizable part or derivative thereof specified in Appendix III in relation to the species; and

iii. in the case of a plant: for species included in Appendix I, any readily recognizable part or derivative thereof; and for species included in Appendices II and III, any readily recognizable part or derivative thereof specified in Appendices II and III in relation to the species;

(c) "Trade" means export, re-export, import and introduction from the sea;

(d) "Re-export" means export of any specimen that has previously been imported;

(e) "Introduction from the sea" means transportation into a State of specimens of any species which were taken in the marine environment not under the jurisdiction of any State;

(f) "Scientific Authority" means a national scientific authority designated in accordance with Article IX;

(g) "Management Authority" means a national management authority designated in accordance with Article IX;

(h) "Party" means a State for which the present Convention has entered into force.

Article 2—Fundamental Principles

1. Appendix I shall include all species threatened with extinction which are or may be affected by trade. Trade in specimens of these species must be subject to particularly strict regulation in order not to endanger further their survival and must only be authorized in exceptional circumstances.
2. Appendix II shall include:
   (a) all species which although not necessarily now threatened with extinction may become so unless trade in specimens of such species is subject to strict regulation in order to avoid utilization incompatible with their survival; and
   (b) other species which must be subject to regulation in order that trade in specimens of certain species referred to in subparagraph (a) of this paragraph may be brought under effective control.
3. Appendix III shall include all species which any Party identifies as being subject to regulation within its jurisdiction for the purposes of preventing or restricting exploitation, and as needing the cooperation of other parties in the control of trade.
4. The Parties shall not allow trade in specimens of species included in Appendices I, II and III except in accordance with the provisions of the present Convention.

Article 3—Regulation of Trade in Specimens of Species Included in Appendix I

1. All trade in specimens of species included in Appendix I shall be in accordance with the provisions of this Article.
2. The export of any specimen of a species included in Appendix I shall require the prior grant and presentation of an export permit. An export permit shall only be granted when the following conditions have been met:
   (a) a Scientific Authority of the State of export has advised that such export will not be detrimental to the survival of that species;
   (b) a Management Authority of the State of export is satisfied that the specimen was not obtained in contravention of the laws of that State for the protection of fauna and flora;
   (c) a Management Authority of the State of export is satisfied that any living specimen will be so prepared and shipped as to minimize the risk of injury, damage to health or cruel treatment; and
   (d) a Management Authority of the State of export is satisfied that an import permit has been granted for the specimen.
3. The import of any specimen of a species included in Appendix I shall require the prior grant and presentation of an import permit and either an export permit or a re-export certificate. An import permit shall only be granted when the following conditions have been met:
   (a) a Scientific Authority of the State of import has advised that the import will be for purposes which are not detrimental to the survival of the species involved;
   (b) a Scientific Authority of the State of import is satisfied that the proposed recipient of a living specimen is suitably equipped to house and care for it; and
   (c) a Management Authority of the State of import is satisfied that the specimen is not to be used for primarily commercial purposes.
4. The re-export of any specimen of a species included in Appendix I shall require the prior grant and presentation of a re-export certificate. A re-export certificate shall only be granted when the following conditions have been met:
   (a) a Management Authority of the State of re-export is satisfied that the specimen was imported into that State in accordance with the provisions of the present Convention;
   (b) a Management Authority of the State of re-export is satisfied that any living specimen will be so prepared and shipped as to minimize the risk of injury, damage to health or cruel treatment; and
   (c) a Management Authority of the State of re-export is satisfied that an import permit has been granted for any living specimen.
5. The introduction from the sea of any specimen of a species included in Appendix I shall require the prior grant of a certificate from a Management Authority of the State of introduction. A certificate shall only be granted when the following conditions have been met:
   (a) a Scientific Authority of the State of introduction advises that the introduction will not be detrimental to the survival of the species involved;
   (b) a Management Authority of the State of introduction is satisfied that the proposed recipient of a living specimen is suitably equipped to house and care for it; and
   (c) a Management Authority of the State of introduction is satisfied that the specimen is not to be used for primarily commercial purposes.

Article 4—Regulation of Trade in Specimens of Species Included in Appendix II

1. All trade in specimens of species included in Appendix II shall be in accordance with the provisions of this Article.
2. The export of any specimen of a species included in Appendix II shall require the prior grant and presentation of an export permit. An export permit shall only be granted when the following conditions have been met:
   (a) a Scientific Authority of the State of export has advised that such export will not be detrimental to the survival of that species;
   (b) a Management Authority of the State of export is satisfied that the specimen was not obtained in contravention of the laws of that State for the protection of fauna and flora; and
   (c) a Management Authority of the State of export is satisfied that any living specimen will be so

prepared and shipped as to minimize the risk of injury, damage to health or cruel treatment.

3. A Scientific Authority in each Party shall monitor both the export permits granted by that State for specimens of species included in Appendix II and the actual exports of such specimens. Whenever a Scientific Authority determines that the export of specimens of any such species should be limited in order to maintain that species throughout its range at a level consistent with its role in the ecosystems in which it occurs and well above the level at which that species might become eligible for inclusion in Appendix I, the Scientific Authority shall advise the appropriate Management Authority of suitable measures to be taken to limit the grant of export permits for specimens of that species.
4. The import of any specimen of a species included in Appendix II shall require the prior presentation of either an export permit or a re-export certificate.
5. The re-export of any specimen of a species included in Appendix II shall require the prior grant and presentation of a re-export certificate. A re-export certificate shall only be granted when the following conditions have been met:
   (a) a Management Authority of the State of re-export is satisfied that the specimen was imported into that State in accordance with the provisions of the present Convention; and
   (b) a Management Authority of the State of re-export is satisfied that any living specimen will be so prepared and shipped as to minimize the risk of injury, damage to health or cruel treatment.
6. The introduction from the sea of any specimen of a species included in Appendix II shall require the prior grant of a certificate from a Management Authority of the State of introduction. A certificate shall only be granted when the following conditions have been met:
   (a) a Scientific Authority of the State of introduction advises that the introduction will not be detrimental to the survival of the species involved; and
   (b) a Management Authority of the State of introduction is satisfied that any living specimen will be so handled as to minimize the risk of injury, damage to health or cruel treatment.
7. Certificates referred to in paragraph 6 of this Article may be granted on the advice of a Scientific Authority, in consultation with other national scientific authorities or, when appropriate, international scientific authorities, in respect of periods not exceeding one year for total numbers of specimens to be introduced in such periods.

Article V—Regulation of Trade in Specimens of Species Included in Appendix III

1. All trade in specimens of species included in Appendix III shall be in accordance with the provisions of this Article.
2. The export of any specimen of a species included in Appendix III from any State which has included that species in Appendix III shall require the prior grant and presentation of an export permit. An export permit shall only be granted when the following conditions have been met:
   (a) a Management Authority of the State of export is satisfied that the specimen was not obtained in contravention of the laws of that State for the protection of fauna and flora; and
   (b) a Management Authority of the State of export is satisfied that any living specimen will be so prepared and shipped as to minimize the risk of injury, damage to health or cruel treatment.
3. The import of any specimen of a species included in Appendix III shall require, except in circumstances to which paragraph 4 of this Article applies, the prior presentation of a certificate of origin and, where the import is from a State which has included that species in Appendix III, an export permit.
4. In the case of re-export, a certificate granted by the Management Authority of the State of re-export that the specimen was processed in that State or is being re-exported shall be accepted by the State of import as evidence that the provisions of the present Convention have been complied with in respect of the specimen concerned.

Article VI—Permits and Certificates

1. Permits and certificates granted under the provisions of Articles III,IV and V shall be in accordance with the provisions of this Article.
2. An export permit shall contain the information specified in the model set forth in Appendix IV, and may

only be used for export within a period of six months from the date on which it was granted.

3. Each permit or certificate shall contain the title of the present Convention, the name and any identifying stamp of the Management Authority granting it and a control number assigned by the Management Authority.
4. Any copies of a permit or certificates issued by a Management Authority shall be clearly marked as copies only and no such copy may be used in place of the original, except to the extent endorsed thereon.
5. A separate permit or certificate shall be required for each consignment of specimens.
6. A Management Authority of the State of import of any specimen shall cancel and retain the export permit or re-export certificate and any corresponding import permit presented in respect of the import of that specimen.
7. Where appropriate and feasible a Management Authority may affix a mark upon any specimen to assist in identifying the specimen. For these purposes "mark" means any indelible imprint, lead seal or other suitable means of identifying a specimen, designed in such a way as to render its imitation by unauthorized persons as difficult as possible.

Article VII—Exemptions and Other Special Provisions Relating to Trade

1. The provisions of Articles III, IV and V shall not apply to the transit or transshipment of specimens through or in the territory of a Party while the specimens remain in Customs control.
2. Where a Management Authority of the State of export or re-export is satisfied that a specimen was acquired before the provisions of the present Convention applied to that specimen, the provisions of Articles III, IV and V shall not apply to that specimen where the Management Authority issues a certificate to that effect.
3. The provisions of Articles III, IV and V shall not apply to specimens that are personal or household effects. This exemption shall not apply where:
   (a) in the case of specimens of a species included in Appendix I, they were acquired by the owner outside his State of usual residence, and are being imported into that State; or
   (b) in the case of specimens of species included in Appendix II:
      i. they were acquired by the owner outside his State of usual residence and in a State where removal from the wild occurred;
      ii. they are being imported into the owner's State of usual residence; and
      iii. the State where removal from the wild occurred requires the prior grant of export permits before any export of such specimens;

   unless a Management Authority is satisfied that the specimens were acquired before the provisions of the present Convention applied to such specimens.
4. Specimens of an animal species included in Appendix I bred in captivity for commercial purposes, or of a plant species included in Appendix I artificially propagated for commercial purposes, shall be deemed to be specimens of species included in Appendix II.
5. Where a Management Authority of the State of export is satisfied that any specimen of an animal species was bred in captivity or any specimen of a plant species was artificially propagated, or is a part of such an animal or plant or was derived therefrom, a certificate by that Management Authority to that effect shall be accepted in lieu of any of the permits or certificates required under the provisions of Articles III, IV or V.
6. The provisions of Articles III, IV and V shall not apply to the non-commercial loan, donation or exchange between scientists or scientific institutions registered by a Management Authority of their State, of herbarium specimens, other preserved, dried or embedded museum specimens, and live plant material which carry a label Issued or approved by a Management Authority.
7. A Management Authority of any State may waive the requirements of Articles III, IV and V and allow the movement without permits or certificates of specimens which form part of a travelling zoo, circus, menagerie, plant exhibition or other travelling exhibition provided that:
   (a) the exporter or importer registers full details of such specimens with that Management Authority;
   (b) the specimens are in either of the categories specified in paragraphs 2 and 5 of this Article; and
   (c) the Management Authority is satisfied that any living specimen will be so transported and cared for as to minimize the risk of injury, damage to health or cruel treatment.

Article VIII—Measures to be Taken by the Parties

1. The Parties shall take appropriate measures to enforce the provisions of the present Convention and to prohibit trade in specimens in violation thereof. These shall include measures:
   (a) to penalize trade in, or possession of, such specimens, or both; and
   (b) to provide for the confiscation or return to the State of export of such specimens.
2. In addition to the measures taken under paragraph 1 of this Article a Party may, when it deems it necessary, provide for any method of internal reimbursement for expenses incurred as a result of the confiscation of a specimen traded in violation of the measures taken in the application of the provisions of the present Convention.
3. As far as possible, the Parties shall ensure that specimens shall pass through any formalities required for trade with a minimum of delay. To facilitate such passage, a Party may designate ports of exit and ports of entry at which specimens must be presented for clearance. The Parties shall ensure further that all living specimens, during any period of transit, holding or shipment, are properly cared for so as to minimize the risk of injury, damage to health or cruel treatment.
4. Where a living specimen is confiscated as a result of measures referred to in paragraph 1 of this Article:
   (a) the specimen shall be entrusted to a Management Authority of the State of confiscation;
   (b) the Management Authority shall, after consultation with the State of export, return the specimen to that State at the expense of that State, or to a rescue center or such other place as the Management Authority deems appropriate and consistent with the purposes of the present Convention; and
   (c) the Management Authority may obtain the advice of a Scientific Authority, or may, wherever it considers it desirable, consult the Secretariat in order to facilitate the decision under sub-paragraph (b) of this paragraph, including the choice of a rescue center or other place.
5. A rescue center as referred to in paragraph 4 of this Article means an institution designated by a Management Authority to look after the welfare of living specimens, particularly those that have been confiscated.
6. Each Party shall maintain records of trade in specimens of species included in Appendices I, II and III which shall cover:
   (a) the names and addresses of exporters and importers; and
   (b) the number and type of permits and certificates granted; the States with which such trade occurred; the numbers or quantities and types of specimens, names of species as included in Appendices I, II and III and, where applicable, the size and sex of the specimens in question.
7. Each Party shall prepare periodic reports on its implementation of the present Convention and shall transmit to the Secretariat:
   (a) an annual report containing a summary of the information specified in sub-paragraph (b) of paragraph 6 of this Article; and
   (b) a biennial report on legislative, regulatory and administrative measures taken to enforce the provisions of the present Convention.
8. The information referred to in paragraph 7 of this Article shall be available to the public where this is not inconsistent with the law of the Party concerned.

As far as possible, the Parties shall ensure that specimens shall pass through any formalities required for trade with a minimum of delay.

Article IX—Management and Scientific Authorities

1. Each Party shall designate for the purposes of the present Convention:
   (a) one or more Management Authorities competent to grant permits or certificates on behalf of that Party, and
   (b) one or more Scientific Authorities.
2. A State depositing an instrument of ratification, acceptance, approval or accession shall at that time inform the Depositary Government of the name and address of the Management Authority authorized to communicate with other Parties and with the Secretariat.
3. Any changes in the designations or authorizations under the provisions of this Article shall be communicated by the Party concerned to the Secretariat for transmission to all other Parties.
4. Any Management Authority referred to in paragraph 2 of this Article shall if so requested by the Secretariat or

the Management Authority of another Party, communicate to it impression of stamps, seals or other devices used to authenticate permits or certificates.

Article X—Trade with States Not Party to the Convention

Where export or re-export is to, or import is from, a State not a Party to the present Convention, comparable documentation issued by the competent authorities in that State which substantially conforms with the requirements of the present Convention for permits and certificates may be accepted in lieu thereof by any Party.

Article XII—The Secretariat

1. Upon entry into force of the present Convention, a Secretariat shall be provided by the Executive Director of the United Nations Environment Programme. To the extent and in the manner he considers appropriate, he may be assisted by suitable intergovernmental or nongovernmental international or national agencies and bodies technically qualified in protection, conservation and management of wild fauna and flora.
2. The functions of the Secretariat shall be:
   (a) to arrange for and service meetings of the Parties;
   (b) to perform the functions entrusted to it under the provisions of Articles XV and XVI of the present Convention;
   (c) to undertake scientific and technical studies in accordance with programs authorized by the Conference of the Parties as will contribute to the implementation of the present Convention, including studies concerning standards for appropriate preparation and shipment of living specimens and the means of identifying specimens;
   (d) to study the reports of Parties and to request from Parties such further information with respect thereto as it deems necessary to ensure implementation of the present Convention;
   (e) to invite the attention of the Parties to any matter pertaining to the aims of the present Convention;
   (f) to publish periodically and distribute to the Parties current editions of Appendices I, II and III together with any information which will facilitate identification of specimens of species included in those Appendices.
   (g) to prepare annual reports to the Parties on its work and on the implementation of the present Convention and such other reports as meetings of the Parties may request;
   (h) to make recommendations for the implementation of the aims and provisions of the present Convention, including the exchange of information of a scientific or technical nature;
   (i) to perform any other function as may be entrusted to it by the Parties.

Article XIII—International Measures

1. When the Secretariat in the light of information received is satisfied that any species included in Appendices I or II is being affected adversely by trade in specimens of that species or that the provisions of the present Convention are not being effectively implemented, it shall communicate such information to the authorized Management Authority of the Party or Parties concerned.
2. When any Party receives a communication as indicated in paragraph 1 of this Article, it shall, as soon as possible, inform the Secretariat of any relevant facts insofar as its laws permit and, where appropriate, propose remedial action. Where the Party considers that an inquiry is desirable, such inquiry may be carried out by one or more persons expressly authorized by the Party.
3. The information provided by the Party or resulting from any inquiry as specified in paragraph 2 of this Article shall be reviewed by the next Conference of the Parties which may make whatever recommendations it deems appropriate.

Article XIV—Effect on Domestic Legislation and International Conventions

1. The provisions of the present Convention shall in no way affect the right of Parties to adopt:
   (a) stricter domestic measures regarding the conditions for trade, taking, possession or transport of specimens of species included in Appendices I, II and III, or the complete prohibition thereof; or
   (b) domestic measures restricting or prohibiting trade, taking possession, or transport of species not included in Appendices I, II or III.

2. The provisions of the present Convention shall in no way affect the provisions of any domestic measures or the obligations of Parties deriving from any treaty, convention, or international agreement relating to other aspects of trade, taking, possession, or transport of specimens which is in force or subsequently may enter into force for any Party including any measure pertaining to the Customs, public health, veterinary or plant quarantine fields.
3. The provisions of the present Convention shall in no way affect the provisions of, or the obligations deriving from, any treaty, convention or international agreement concluded or which may be concluded between States creating a union or regional trade agreement establishing or maintaining a common external customs control and removing customs controls between the parties thereto insofar as they relate to trade among the States members of that union or agreement.
4. A State Party to the present Convention, which is also a Party to any other treaty, convention or international agreement which is in force at the time of the coming into force of the present Convention and under the provisions of which protection is afforded to marine species included in Appendix II, shall be relieved of the obligations imposed on it under the provisions of the present Convention with respect to trade in specimens of species included in Appendix II that are taken by ships registered in that State and in accordance with the provisions of such other treaty, convention or international agreement.
5. Notwithstanding the provisions of Articles III, IV and V, any export of a specimen taken in accordance with paragraph 4 of this Article shall only require a certificate from a Management Authority of the State of introduction to the effect that the specimen was taken in accordance with the provisions of the other treaty, convention or international agreement in question.
6. Nothing in the present Convention shall prejudice the codification and development of the law of the sea by the United Nations Conference on the Law of the Sea convened pursuant to Resolution 2750 C (XXV) of the General Assembly of the United Nations nor the present or future claims and legal views of any State concerning the law of the sea and the nature and extent of coastal and flag State jurisdiction.

C

Implementation and Enforcement

(i) Kobayashi M., "The Enforcement of CITES," in Nomura Y. and Sakumoto N. (eds), *Environmental Law and Policy in Asia: Issues of Enforcement*, Institute of Developing Economies, Japan, 1997

Introduction

There are a number of factors pushing wildlife species toward extinction. The main ones are:

1. destruction of habitat,
2. introduction of exotic species into natural ecosystems, and
3. overexploitation of species.

A study by the World Conservation Union showed that among the fauna extinct since 1600, 39 percent were due to introduction of exotic species, 36 percent to habitat destruction, and 23 percent to overexploitation. Narrowing the focus to wildlife extinction caused by overexploitation, another study indicated that this was the primary cause of extinction for 23 percent of the mammals, 32 percent of the reptiles, 11 percent of the birds, and 4 percent of the fish that had gone extinct. What is more, over-exploitation continues to threaten wildlife, especially mammals and reptiles.

The exploitation of wildlife is carried out on a broad scale to supply both domestic and international markets. Exploitation for international trade is lesser than that for domestic trade, and so in comparison with habitat destruction and the introduction of exotic species, it cannot be considered a main factor driving wildlife species to extinction. But international trade is indeed a threat to a number of wildlife species. Certain species are overexploited and driven to extinction in order to satisfy demand from other countries and in response to economic motives. Innumerable species have been led to extinction through overexploitation for the foreign consumers who seek things like furs and ivory. Demand for wildlife and their products is also linked to the rise in income levels, so that in addition to Western countries and Japan, which have heretofore been major importers, imports in the economically growing Asian region are also increasing.

This creates ever-increasing pressure for more exploitation. This paper will therefore conduct an overview of the *Convention on International Trade in Endangered Species of Wild Fauna and Flora* (CITES), whose purpose is controlling international trade in endangered wildlife species, and examine the problems in its implementation, especially its domestic enforcement.

Background

It was at the seventh General Assembly of the International Union for Conservation of Nature and Natural Resources (IUCN) in 1960 that the danger to wildlife species posed by international trade was first discussed. The following IUCN General Assembly in 1963 passed a resolution calling for an international convention to regulate the export, transit, and import of rare or threatened wildlife species, or their skins and other forms of trophies, and this marked the beginning of drafting a convention to control such international trade. The 1972 United Nations Conference on the Human Environment held in Stockholm also took up this matter and recommended that "a plenipotentiary conference be convened as soon as possible, under appropriate governmental or intergovernmental auspices, to prepare and adopt a convention on export, import, and transit of certain species of wild animals and plants". In response to this, a meeting of plenipotentiaries from 88 countries was held in Washington, D.C. in 1973. Here CITES was proposed, and the attending representatives adopted this convention to control international trade in wild animal and plants so that the continued existence of these species would not be threatened by commercial trade.

Owing to the awareness that unrestricted commercial trading presents a major threat to wildlife species, the convention's direct purpose is to control international trade in endangered wildlife species and their products.

Overview of CITES

CITES took effect in 1975 with its ratification by the tenth country, and as of June 1996 there were 131 parties to the convention. Owing to the awareness that unrestricted commercial trading presents a major threat to wildlife species, the convention's direct purpose is to control international trade in endangered wildlife species and their products.

Controls on International Trade

Species subject to CITES controls are classified into Appendices I through 111 depending on the degree of protection, which differs according to species...

Appendix I includes species threatened with extinction which are or may be affected by international trade. It lists about 700 species including gorillas, tigers, elephants, rhinoceroses, sea turtles, and giant salamanders. Controls on trade in these specimens are especially strict so as to prevent it from further endangering their survival, and international trade is generally prohibited (Art. 11 Para. 1). Trade is permitted in exceptional cases such as for academic research, but this requires the prior issuance of an import permit and either an export permit or a re-export certificate. Permits are granted only when the scientific authority is satisfied that the specimen will not be used for commercial purposes (Art. 111).

Appendix II includes species that are not necessarily threatened with extinction now but may be threatened if trade is not strictly regulated, and other species that must be regulated for effective enforcement of the convention. It lists over 34,000 species including primates, cetaceans, members of the cat family, Falconiformes, cacti, and orchids (Art. 11 Para. 2).. Commercial trade in specimens of these species is permitted but to prevent unrestricted trade, it requires an export permit or re-export certificate (Art. IV).

Appendix III includes wildlife species which any party identifies as being subject to domestic regulations for the purpose of protecting its wildlife resources and thus needs the cooperation of other parties (Art. II Para. 3). Trade controls are roughly the same as those on Appendix 11 species. A certificate of origin and an export permit are required.

Of important note here, "specimen" means not only living individuals, but also dead individuals, parts, and derivatives (Art. I). "Part" means ivory, horns, tortoise shells, feathers, furs, skins, and the like, while "derivative" means their products, such as handbags shoes, and clothing accessories. Parts and derivatives make up the greater proportion of trade in wildlife species, so it is important to control them.

CITES also provides for exceptions to these controls. For example, the provisions of Articles III-V do not apply to specimens that are "personal or household effects" (Art. VII Para. 3). And when a specimen has been "bred in captivity" or is "artificially propagated," the usual permits are not required (Art. VII Para. 5). Further, although parties may not make general reservations, they can make specific reservations on species listed in Appendices I–III when they become parties or when an appendix is amended (Arts. XV, XVI, and XXIII).

Domestic Measures

In addition to classifying wildlife species to be protected and defining international rules to control trade according to each appendix, CITES sets forth a number of measures that parties are to enact domestically. For instance, CITES requires states to enforce the convention and take appropriate measures to prevent trade in specimens that violate it (Art. VIII Para. I). These measures must include the following two. First, to penalise the trade in or possession of specimens in violation; second, to provide for the confiscation of such specimens or their return to the exporting state. And when necessary, parties must provide for the reimbursement of expenses incurred by confiscation (Art. VIII Para.2).

Parties must also keep records of trade in the specimens of species listed in Appendices I–III (Art. VIII Para. 6), and must, in addition to other information pertaining to CITES implementation, incorporate this information into periodic reports and transmit them to the secretariat (Art. VIII Para. 7). Parties must also designate management authorities and scientific authorities who are responsible for enforcement of the treaties within their countries (Art. IX).

Enforcement Problems

It is thought that CITES is very strictly enforced, and is highly regarded as one of the most successful international treaties for wildlife protection. It also has some problems, however, which are well illustrated by the violations reported at conferences of the parties. This means that international trade does not conform to the Convention, and that the parties are not taking effective measures. For example, the scope of wildlife species to which CITES applies is specified as an individual or any readily recognisable part or derivative of a species listed in Appendices I–III (Art. I), but it is possible for parties to interpret this definition in a way that suits the purposes of their own countries. And even if specimens are Appendix I species, which would be subject to especially strict control, there are special provisions for exemptions, thus making it possible to export items recognized under those provisions as "personal or household effects" (Art. VII Para. 3). The most serious matter is that parties can make reservations to listed species when becoming parties to CITES or when an appendix is amended, which allows them to legally continue trading in those species (Art. XXIII). The fact that a large quantity of listed species is continuously being legally traded is a problem in of itself, but in addition to that, criticism is being levelled on reservations, which are being used as a smoke screen which results in abetting illegal trading.

Another problem is that while CITES regulates international trading, it has no direct effect on the parties' domestic wildlife protection, and for that reason the convention's controls do not directly show up in domestic controls. Let's say, for instance, that when amending the appendices at a conference of the parties, a certain species is moved from Appendix II to Appendix I. Although international commercial trading in that species is now forbidden this has no effect on domestic laws, so domestic commercial trading will still be allowed. Furthermore, even if strict controls are enacted on imports, parties would have to have domestic laws to control trading within their countries; if not, once a specimen is illegally brought into a country there would be no way to exercise control over it. Because, CITES is not a self executing treaty, each party must discharge its responsibilities pursuant to the convention by providing ways to implement it domestically. Although such domestic measures by the parties are indispensable for the convention's success, a considerable number of parties currently lack even the domestic legislation to enforce CITES, a fundamental obligation.

Even when parties have domestic laws for CITES enforcement, the laws themselves are in many cases inappropriate. Only a few parties have specific and comprehensive laws for carrying out CITES, and most of them depend on legislation such as general wildlife protection laws, or on customs laws and foreign trade laws. And when such domestic laws are those passed before parties joined CITES, they often lack provisions needed to sufficiently address the convention's purpose. Even when parties have wildlife protection laws, those laws' scope of application is in some instances too narrow. Examples of such problems are: (1) fish, plants, and invertebrates are excluded from controlled species, (2) Appendix III species are not included, and (3) laws are limited to parties' endemic species. Such laws cannot therefore completely protect CITES-listed species and some domestic laws have other problems because they lack provisions for penalties and confiscation. Foreign trade laws classify CITES-listed species as mere prohibited or restricted items that require special permits for import and export, which makes it possible their implementation will not conform to the purpose of CITES, which is to protect wildlife.

Domestic Implementation Requirements

Presently the parties' legislation of domestic laws for CITES implementation is the key to the domestic enforcement which CITES calls for. This is because just ratifying the convention is not enough to assure effective enforcement unless there are also suitable domestic laws. CITES calls for the passage of domestic laws, and the conferences of the parties have repeatedly pointed out the importance of this.

Domestic Legislation

The rules of international law hold that states are bound by the treaties they become party to, but under the legal institutions of most countries, international conventions do not automatically become legally binding on their citizens. Normally, domestic implementation of conventions requires new legislation for that purpose.

Domestic legislation for CITES is especially required for Article II Paragraph 4 and in Article VIII Paragraph 1. In the case of the former, parties are required to permit no trading whatsoever in listed species except when done in accordance with the provisions of CITES. Parties are thus required to take measures prohibiting trade in listed species as long as there are no conditions for such trade provided for by CITES.

Article VIII Paragraph I more clearly obligates parties to pass domestic legislation. Parties must pass domestic laws that implement the convention and prevent trade in violation, and those laws must at the least prohibit all trade that violates CITES. "Trade" here is a broader concept than mere buying and selling, and includes all international transfers of specimens.

Article VIII Paragraph I further sets forth two conditions that must be included in domestic legislation. First, domestic laws must have provisions to penalize individuals who trade in or possess specimens in violation of CITES. Second, domestic laws must provide for the confiscation of specimens, including cases when they are resumed to the state of export. These requirements can be considered the core of CITES. The absence of penalties would make it impossible to enforce laws effectively, but many legal systems can only establish penalties by parliamentary legislation or documents with the same level of force. CITES recognizes this fact and imposes a clear obligation upon parties. In consideration of the great variety of legal systems among parties, these obligations are stated in the most general terms, thereby allowing the parties to legislate in a way that accommodates their own legal systems.

After parties have established domestic laws that include the aforesaid items, only then is a connection forged between international and domestic trade in endangered wildlife species; only then are individual citizens of the parties bound by CITES; and only then is the convention effectively enforced in accordance with its provisions.

Trends in Conferences of the Parties

Conferences of the Parties showed an early awareness of the importance of implementing CITES domestically, and have documented their intentions in the form of resolutions. Although these resolutions are not legally binding, they express Conference of the Parties decisions for heightening the effectiveness of CITES enforcement. Among them are the following recommendations, which were resolved in connection with domestic legislation.

Resolution Conf. 3.9 recommends abiding strictly by all provisions of the convention and carefully regulating trade. It also recommends that parties should immediately take appropriate measures pursuant to Article VIII Paragraph 1, to penalize the offender and take other proper actions in the event that CITES provisions are violated.

Resolution Conf. 6.3 asks parties to enhance import controls and rigorously check documentation. This request was made in consideration of the facts that parties are obligated to observe the convention, including the enactment of measures to confiscate illegally imported specimens pursuant to Article VIII Paragraph I (b), and that it is essential for all parties to implement and abide by established restrictions in order for CITES to work effectively.

Resolution Conf. 8.4 directs the secretariat to, among other things, and within the scope of funding available to it and in accordance with the basic awareness that a considerable number of parties had not taken proper measures to enforce the provisions of the convention:

1. to identify those Parties whose domestic measures do not provide them with the authority to:
   (i) designate at least one Management Authority and one Scientific Authority,

- (ii) prohibit trade in specimens in violation of the Convention,
- (iii) penalize such trade, or
- (iv) confiscate specimens illegally traded or possessed.

2. to seek from each Party so identified information indicating the procedures, action and time frames that are needed in order to establish the measures necessary to properly enforce the provisions of the Convention; and
3. to report its findings, recommendations or progress to the Standing Committee and at the ninth meeting of the Conference of the Parties. As this shows, all parties that have not appropriately adopted measures for implementing CITES domestically are prodded by resolutions to enforce the convention.

At the ninth meeting of the Conference of the Parties in 1994 the secretariat delivered a report (Doe. 9.24) on "National Laws for Implementation of CITES". This report consisted of an analysis by TRAFFIC and the IUCN Environmental Law Centre (ELC) of the domestic laws of 81 parties with much trade in CITES-listed species. This analysis showed that only 15 parties had domestic laws that generally satisfied the requirements of CITES, and that 27 parties' domestic laws hardly satisfy CITES requirements at all.

The Conference of the Parties passed a resolution asking parties without adequate domestic laws to take all measures for passing domestic legislation, improve their domestic laws to address the problems pointed out by the analysis, and report the results to the secretariat; all these actions were to be taken by the 10th meeting of the Conference of the Parties. This resolution took a stand on this problem that was more rigorous than before. For instance, it clearly stated that countries whose domestic laws had, according to the analysis, failed to generally satisfy the demands of CITES would either have to take positive action no later than the following Conference of the Parties, or sanctions would be enacted, including limitations on trade in CITES-listed species with those countries. In connection with this, the conference also passed a resolution on enforcement (Resolution Conf. 9.8).

Implementing Resolutions

As recommended in resolutions, it is essential that all parties to CITES pass domestic laws that accommodate the convention in order to effectively protect wildlife, which is the purpose of CITES. Many parties have produced domestic legislation within the framework of CITES, but the convention itself states clearly that its provisions in no way restrict parties from adopting even stricter domestic measures (Art. XIV Para. I). There are at least three conceivable ways to create the domestic laws needed for domestic CITES implementation:

1. Include a clause in existing wildlife protection laws, which would prohibit the import, export, and possession of, as well as domestic trade, in all wildlife species or in all CITES-listed species unless there is a permit;
2. Include in CITES ratification laws or all related laws, such as wildlife protection laws, a basic clause that prohibits all actions in violation of CITES for all CITES-listed species; or
3. Pass individual laws aimed exclusively at controlling international trade in wildlife species.

Conclusion

There is indeed criticism of CITES' underlying ideas because the convention concerns itself only with wildlife species that are endangered by international trade, while it is not concerned at all with alleviating other factors driving wildlife toward extinction, or with the protection of species not traded internationally," but CITES has in fact performed a major role ,in wildlife protection. Right now, the most important task for making the convention do its job fully within its framework is the passage by the parties of the domestic laws needed to make their own government agencies and individual citizens implement the treaty's provisions.

The underlying idea of CITES is that the use of wildlife species jeopardizes their survival, but recently the contention that wildlife should be protected instead by encouraging its use is gaining currency. A few developing countries in particular claim that wildlife species, which are also resources, are unjustly controlled, and advocate their use. So, the eighth meeting of the Conference of the Parties in 1992 adopted a resolution (Resolution Conf. 8.3) stating that the body "recognizes that commercial trade may be beneficial to the conservation of species and ecosystems and/or to the development of local people when carried out at levels that are not detrimental to the survival of the species in question." While the overall worldwide trend is toward sustainable development and use, there is also a tendency to give precedence to economic development and short shrift to preventive principles, so this cannot be accepted without criticism. It is important to continue maintaining the spirit of CITES, which is the idea of preventing excessive use that would cause the extinction of wildlife species. To achieve that purpose, it is hoped even more that all parties will pass the needed domestic laws, and cooperate internationally, especially among developed and developing countries.

(ii) De Klemm, C. *Guidelines for Legislation to Implement CITES*, IUCN Gland, Switzerland and Cambridge, UK, 1993, pp 5–9

THE NEED FOR CITES IMPLEMENTATION LEGISLATION

Sixteen years after the entry into force of the Convention, only a small number of Contracting Parties have so far enacted specific and relatively comprehensive legislation to implement it. These include Australia, Austria, Belgium, Denmark, France, Germany, Malta, the Netherlands, New Zealand, Switzerland, the United Kingdom (including Hong Kong), the United States and Zimbabwe. A few others, such as Canada, have legislation under development. In addition, a certain number of other Parties including Argentina, Colombia, Italy, Japan, Liberia, Nigeria, Papua New Guinea, Portugal (including Macau), Singapore, Thailand, all four South African provinces and Sweden, as well as the European Community, have adopted legislation covering at least certain aspects of the implementation of CITES. Another Party, Tunisia, merely provides in its legislation that the import or export of specimens of CITES-listed species is to be governed by the provisions of the Convention. Likewise, but in a slightly different manner, the law of the People's Republic of China provides that import or export permits must be obtained for specimens of CITES-listed species and that in the case of differences between national wildlife legislation and CITES the latter should always prevail.

A large majority of the Parties, however, have so far enacted no specific legislation to implement the Convention. They have, therefore, to rely on their general wildlife legislation and in certain cases on their Customs or foreign trade legislation to control trade in CITES specimens.

These laws are, however, generally ill-adapted to the specific purpose of implementing CITES especially, as is often the case, when they have been adopted before the entry into force of the Convention in the country concerned.

Most wildlife laws are limited in their scope and only cover certain categories of species, products or operations, as they are mainly or exclusively concerned with the protection of native fauna.

There are, however, considerable differences between these laws. Some only provide for export controls (and less frequently also import controls) on indigenous protected or game species. They cannot, therefore, be used to control trade in all other CITES species. In addition, in some cases controls only apply to trade in live specimens.

In a few other countries, export and import controls generally apply to both indigenous and exotic species but only to certain groups of organisms, usually vertebrates. Invertebrates and plants are generally excluded, as are sometimes also fish. In these cases there are no legal means available to control trade in those species. Examples are the laws of Botswana, the Gambia and Zambia, which are restricted to vertebrates except fish, and the law of Tanzania, which is restricted to vertebrates. An exception is the law of Cameroon, which requires permits for the import or export of all wild animals or plants whether alive or dead.

A few countries, for example India, mostly rely on their foreign trade legislation for the implementation of CITES. CITES specimens are characterised under these laws as prohibited or restricted goods, the import or export of which require special licences. These laws are, however, generally ill-adapted to the specific purposes of CITES.

The reasons why such a large majority of CITES Parties have so far failed to enact implementation legislation, or have enacted legislation which is limited to certain aspects of the Convention, are unclear. It has sometimes been argued that such legislation was unnecessary since, once ratified, the Convention automatically became a part of the national legislation of the Party concerned and was, therefore, directly binding upon private citizens.

This may well be true, at least in some legal systems, from a purely theoretical point of view. But to implement the Convention in practice, implementation legislation is essential for the reasons outlined below.

CITES as a Non-Self-Executing Treaty

International lawyers distinguish between self-executing and non-self-executing provisions in a treaty. Self-executing provisions are those which are directly applicable by a Party without a need for any additional national legal instrument. Non-self-executing provisions, on the contrary, cannot be implemented until specific legislation has been adopted for that purpose. These include, in particular, provisions which create specific obligations for private persons, as such obligations cannot be enforced in the courts and penalties cannot be applied for non-compliance unless expressly provided for by domestic legislation.

The main non-self-executing provisions of CITES appear in Articles II.4 and VIII.1. Article II.4 requires that Parties do not allow trade in specimens of species included in the Convention Appendices except in accordance with the provisions of the Convention. As a result, Parties are under the obligation to take measures prohibiting trade in CITES specimens whenever the conditions laid down by the Convention have not been complied with.

This general rule is supplemented by Article VIII. I, which requires that Parties take appropriate measures to enforce the provisions of the Convention and to prohibit trade in specimens in violation thereof. Therefore, Parties have to take the specific measures required to implement the Convention and make its provisions binding not only upon public agencies but upon private persons as well.

The scope of Article VIII.1 is quite broad and allows, therefore, for a certain degree of discretion by Parties on the type of measures they must take to enforce the Convention. There are, however, two categories of measures which must be taken under that Article: firstly, measures to penalize trade in specimens in violation of the Convention, or the possession of specimens so traded, or both (Article VIII. 1 (a)); and secondly, measures to confiscate such specimens or return them to the State of export (Article VIII.l(b)).

These obligations must be considered as the very keystone of the Convention since without effective penalties it is obvious that enforcement will be impossible. As, however, in most if not all legal systems, criminal penalties may only be imposed by an Act of Parliament or an equivalent instrument, the Convention provides a clear obligation for Parties to enact appropriate legislation. The failure to do so constitutes a violation of the Convention.

Thus, the mere ratification of CITES without the adoption of appropriate implementation legislation can never be sufficient to ensure an effective enforcement of the Convention, if only because penalties for violations of the provisions of CITES can only be imposed by national legislation.

Self-Executing Provisions Require Further Elaboration

The self-executing provisions of the Convention only provide a broad framework, which must be supplemented by national legislation. There are many matters of detail which must be settled at national level and for which enabling legislation is in many cases requited. Legislation is usually also required to set out clearly which authorities are in charge of implementing and enforcing the Convention and to specify their respective powers. In particular, the implications of the Convention on the operations of the various government agencies concerned, such as the department in charge of wildlife, the Customs, the police, etc., should be clearly stated in order to avoid overlaps, inconsistencies or gaps in implementation and enforcement. It is also necessary that the various categories of enforcement agents be clearly designated.

Legislation is usually also required to set out clearly which authorities are in charge of implementing and enforcing the Convention and to specify their respective powers.

The need for national legislation to implement at least some of the self-executing provisions of the Convention is, therefore, clear. This was recognized by the Conference of the Parties, which by Resolution Conf. 6.6 urged Parties whose domestic legislation did not fully carry out requirements of Articles III, IV and V of the Convention to take measures necessary to conform their legislation to them and by Resolution Conf. 8.4 urged all Parties that have not adopted the appropriate measures to fully implement the Convention to do so.

Other Reasons for Implementation Legislation

(a) The adoption of implementation legislation adapted to the specific requirements of the national legal system and institutions is also important as a way of informing all the parties concerned, i.e. government agencies, the courts, traders and the public in general, of the changes in the trade rules which have occurred as a result of the ratification of the Convention and of the penalties that are incurred if the new rules are violated. Likewise, the courts are generally much more at ease with the enforcement of national legislation than with treaties, the implications of which may not always be entirely clear, especially if there are inconsistencies between the text of a treaty and national legislation.

(b) Implementation legislation may also be necessary to clarify what are the effects of CITES on other domestic legislation relating to trade in wild species and to eliminate potential inconsistencies or contradictions between the two.

(c) Article XIV.1 of the Convention provides that Parties have the right to adopt stricter domestic measures regarding the conditions for trade, taking, possession or transport of species listed on the Convention appendices. The adoption of national legislation is of course necessary for that purpose.

(d) CITES has to adapt itself to changes in circumstances, many of which could not have been foreseen by the original drafters of the treaty. As a result, the Conference of the Parties has adopted a large number of resolutions, either to provide a commonly agreed interpretation of certain terms or provisions of the Convention, or to recommend that the Parties take certain action. In addition, the Secretariat, by the means of notifications to the Parties, frequently invites Parties to take certain specific measures, particularly to assist other Parties in their conservation efforts or to advise Parties not to accept documents or shipments originating from certain countries It is clear, however, that without adequate legislation empowering the appropriate authorities to take those recommended measures, Conference resolutions and notifications to Parties, which in themselves are not binding, cannot be implemented. They have to be incorporated into legislation if they are to be enforced. To take an example, Resolution Conf. 6.4 urges all Parties to prohibit imports of wildlife illegally exported from neighboring countries. This implies that Parties are able either to institute a system of import permits, which they may refuse at their discretion if they have grounds to believe that they are faced with an illegal export, or to refuse to accept apparently valid export permits accompanying specimens, the export of which is prohibited by the law of the State of export. Clearly, none of these measures can be taken without legislation empowering the competent authorities of the State of import to do so. Indeed, if these measures were taken by simple administrative decision without a firm basis in the law, there would be a serious risk that aggrieved traders would apply to the courts to have them made void. There are some examples of court decisions of that kind.

(iii) Chen H.K., "Effective CITES Implementation," in *Workshop Proceedings on International Conventions and Treaties*, 1999

In order to be able to effectively implement CITES, it is important to understand the basic obligation of membership of the Convention. The four main obligations are:

- To only allow import, export and re-export of listed specimens when carried out in accordance with the Convention;
- To take appropriate measures to enforce the provisions of the Convention, to prohibit trade in specimens in violation of the Convention's provisions (including measures to penalise offenders and confiscate illegal specimens);
- To designate one or more Management Authorities (see Annex I for list of functions) responsible for granting permits of certificates and maintaining trade records and to designate one or more Scientific Authorities (see Annex 2 for list of functions) to provide technical advice to the Management Authority; [and]
- To contribute annually to the CITES Trust Fund which finances the operation of the Convention's Secretariat and the meetings of the Conference of the Parties (contributions are based on a UN scale).

Vietnam has been a party to CITES since the middle of 1994. It has already fulfilled the latter two obligations, and it remains to be seen how effective Vietnam is in meeting the obligations outlined in the first two of the above.

This presentation will not be looking at the weaknesses and ineffectiveness that may exist in the present structure and mechanisms of implementing CITES in the country. All countries to a greater or lesser degree have their own problems in meeting their CITES obligations.

We propose to highlight the many affective mechanisms and structures that other countries, albeit only a small number of countries, have put in place to try and overcome or reduce the problems encountered.

...[T]his presentation will cover the narrower but highly critical procedures that ensure that the system is as effective as possible and to highlight the broader aspects of themes that relate to CITES, which is the other side of the coin in meeting the objective of CITES to conserve species in the wild.

The narrower focused elements of making CITES work is as follows:

Administrative Systems

The Management Authority has two basic roles firstly, it is responsible for granting permits and certificates under the teens of the Convention, and secondly, it is responsible for communicating with the Secretariat and other Parties regarding all CITES matters in order to do that, it is imperative that the Management Authority has an information System for the issuance of CITES certificates and monitoring of import/re–export activities of CITES-listed species. USA is considered to have a relatively effective system, and the other system that is considered as highly effective is that used in Italy.

The system in Italy consists of the following elements:

(i) a "central core"—the Coordination Center—responsible for the organization and operation of the CITES Management Authority, and also for monitoring the overall trade situation in Italy. The Centre supervises the activity and the management of information resources;

(ii) in some "peripheral branches", operational units to identify the identity of specimens and to check authenticity of their documents at Customs and the Ministry of Foreign trade, and for automatic issue of authorisation and support to the control of documents through data updating and querying. The ministry issues import licences for non–European Union countries.

The system provides for:

- systematic identification of the issued certificates;
- checks on the accuracy of the input data;
- during data acquisition, the system also automatically displays any directives and observations issued by the Coordination Center concerning the species and the country from which the specimen originates, or the country of destination;
- an immediate exchange between the Operational units of the CITES Management Authority;
- information on the licences and certificates is issued to a single centralised database;
- Constantly updated information which can be analysed on the basis of a defined criteria; which allows for faster document verification as well as identification of possible fraud;
- Automatic function for checking the remaining amount of each import transaction (quota); and
- Checks for whether, for import of raw materials, no corresponding re-export certificates were issued for an excessively large amount of finished products with respect to production capacity.

As part of the information system, a number of databases have also been created under the system:

- non-EU import licences issued by the Ministry of Foreign Trade;
- non-EU import certificates;
- re-export certificates to EU and non-EU countries issued by the CITES Management Authority;
- births in captivity and holding of protected species;
- protected species;
- lists of firms working in the import/re-export field (supplemented by the Tax Authorities database);
- the association between species and areas of origin;
- species protection status corresponding to country of origin; and
- reporting and directives (thousands of Items to support the issuance of certificates with information received from national and international organisations)

If you review the system above against the role and function of a Management Authority (MA) of any country, you will notice that the system fulfils much of the requirements of an MA.

It should also be remembered that in most countries, a system of licensing is also in force to allow the MA to recoup part of the administrative cost of operating an MA. Therefore it is imperative that the government institute a schedule of fees that allow the MA to maximise the capture of the full cost of the import/export inspection program. For example, USA has a fee system that has recently been amended to do just that.

The fee structure includes:

- import/export license,
- import/export license fee (paid once a year),
- inspection fee (paid for each shipment),
- overtime fee (paid for inspections outside of normal working hours (including Sundays),
- federal holidays, and
- non–licensees fee.

The latter is to differentiate between those traders that are licensed by the government to import and export wildlife and its products and those that do so irregularly.

An important point to note is that the inspection and the administrative support should have a direct correlation between the value of wildlife shipments and the operation costs incurred by the MA in inspections of wildlife that cannot be made.

An integral part of the administrative system is the development and publicising of the standard permit to be used in Vietnam. There are a number of requirements that need to be fulfilled in developing the permit, including clarity, space for writing, local language (and in addition, at least in [the] United Nations languages of English French and Spanish), proper and relevant codes to use and statement about IATA live animal transport regulation. The checking of permits require[s] experience but the fundamentals of what to check in certifying the authenticity of the permits can be taught. All permits should have a security stamp which is only obtained from the CITES Secretariat and the serial numbers are unique to each country.

An integral part of the administrative system is the development and publicising of the standard permit to be used in Vietnam.

Your will notice that, once the administrative system is in place, the Management Authority will be able to meet the demand of annual reporting to [the] CITES Secretariat in a quality report, that is produce[d quickly] and includes all the useful data in monitoring global trade and identifying possible infractions of the Convention. The obligatory reporting includes producing the biennial report on legislation, regulatory and administrative measures taken to enforce CITES. The system would also be able to track the infraction cases that are handled by each Party and report it in a timely manner to CITES Secretariat.

Legislative Development/Enhancement

This theme includes the review and development of existing legislation with improved and effective results, either through modification of current legislation or implementation of new legislation.

In this respect, the leading role in developing Improved wildlife legislation to govern wildlife trade has been the European Union. Considerable effort has been spent in developing and refining comprehensive new draft legislation which has taken 10 years to reflect. The *Council Regulation (EC) No. 338/97 on the Protection of Species of Wild Fauna and Flora by Regulating Trade Therein* became effective on 1 June 1997.

While there is no obligation on Parties to have legislation that is stronger than those required under CITES, it is very useful for a country to have improved legislation that builds upon those required by CITES, and the EU legislation include painstaking lessons learnt over 10 years, such as clearly prescribes procedures, specific definitions, assigns responsibilities, and outlines stringent measures and restrictions.

Among the improvements of the new EU legislation include:

- clarification of procedures to be followed by personnel involved in its application;
- application of stricter and stronger controls at the EU's external borders, with all designated ports to be provided with sufficient and adequately trained staff;
- requirements for a set of penalties for specific infractions;
- live, listed specimens arriving in Community ports of entry without valid documentation must be seized and may be confiscated, including from shipments in transit;
- improved flexibility to respond to changes in conservation status of species, by adding to, or removing from, the list of species governed by the Regulations;
- non–CITES species that meet specific criteria have been added;
- a requirement for import documentation to be checked at the first port of entry;
- To control internal trade in species to include "purchase, offer to purchase, acquisition for commercial purposes and use for commercial gain";
- prohibition of possession of certain specimens; and
- must inform citizens and enforcement agencies of the government of the new legislation.

Many of the points above have an impact or relates to the other themes in this paper. However, having it stated in writing as part of a legislation ensures that the framework is the same for all government agencies and enforcement agencies.

Anti–Smuggling Initiatives

In order to be able to take the initiatives to reduce illegal trade in wildlife, enforcement officers need to be aware of the various types of infraction and fraud that occur with the permit system of CITES. A chief source of information is the CITES Secretariat Alleged infractions Report which are compiled biennially and which describes numerous representative cases of invalid documentation and where inadequate controls have resulted in infractions of the CITES regulations. Among the infractions are:

- Instances of outright smuggling (absence of documentation);
- issuance of export permits for Appendix I species before an import permit is obtained;
- issuance of permits for Appendix I species for commercial purposes;
- lack of presentation of import documentation for Appendix II species issuance of export permits for species with zero quotas; acceptance of permits its issued by unauthorized authorities; issuance of re-export certificates without checking specimens; acceptance of imports without checking specimens;
- acceptance of imports without ensuring the validity of export permits: issuance of re-export certificates for illegally obtained Specimens; acceptance of permits with incomplete information;
- retroactive issuance of permits;
- fraudulent use of permits; inadequate transit controls issuance of pre-Convention certificates without date of acquisition, country of origin; and.
- fraudulent use of the terms 'artificially–propagated' and 'captive-bred' or other CITES Article II exemptions.

There are various methods and systems that can be employed to undertake anti-smuggling fraud activity which is to reduce smuggling in CITES specimens through detection, dissuasion and prevention.

Two examples that appear to have been effective is the formation of a Species Protection Department (SPD) with the Zambian Anti-Corruption Commission (ACC) and the UK Customs and Excise CITES Enforcement Team (HMCE).

You will notice that the SPD and HMCE are both independent of the Management Authorities of those countries even though they work closely together. The key to successful investigation and prosecution of illegal wildlife traffickers is the timely access of intelligence information gathered during the course of past and ongoing operations.

The SPD depends heavily on a computerised system which is used in tracking of CITES permit data and also to generate reports on trade in CITES-listed species. The database has been a useful tool in providing a solid base of information which can be analysed and target trade and traders.

The HMCE is a Team or eight personnel that is responsible for all aspects of CITES control and intelligence exchange. The Team establishes close links with the Police, Wildlife agencies, and NGOs. The Team is involved in proactive intelligence analysis to identify trade trends, problem areas, illegal traders, couriers and smuggling routes. Targeting of shipments is also a priority and frequently results in seizures. The Team is also involved in developing public awareness programs, including public speaking, media interviews, and provision of information and advice. Each Team member is an expert on a different taxonomic or trade types. The most powerful tool that is used by the Team is the computerised identification database called "green parrot". The database includes such information as:

- visual keys for identification,
- color images of CITES and non-CITES species,
- an analytical system that the identification characteristics [are] entered [into] to provide the species of best fit,
- CITES-listing information,
- source country information, and
- notes.

The system is developed so far to cover nearly all parrots, the majority of raptors, many reptiles and amphibians a large selection of butterflies, corals, traditional Chinese medicines and derivatives. The resulting database is still growing and will be made available online to all HMCE CITES officers nationally and may be offered to Customs in other countries.

Identification/Marking/Forensics

These activities are, to some extent, innovative processes which may not be appropriate for use in Vietnam at the moment, particularly forensics, partly due to a lack of resources, training, and funds. However, the identification and marking applications are important to deter fraud.

Taiwan has developed forensic techniques to determine the origin of bear gallbladder, bile and medicinal products to differentiate between species as the bear populations in various parts of the world are placed in different Appendices I and II.

Coral identification is another problem as CITES differentiate[s] between living, fossil and hard corals. CITES has placed all scleractinia and other hard corals belonging to the Anthipatharia, Milleporidae, Stylasteridae,

Coenathecalia and Tubiporitiae in Appendix II, in order to aid identification and avoid instances where shipments could be confiscated if not accompanied by a necessary or incorrect permit. [T]he Netherlands has developed a system to conclusively differentiate between living rock and marine organisms such as corals.

Markings is another issue that is very important to prevent fraud. Therefore it is essential that the MA is up-to-date on the various making used for different species. Tags for crocodile skins, ring bands for live birds, microchip for fish and some mammals, tatoos for mammals, clippings of body parts such as the ears, fins, in reptiles and fish, etc. CITES Secretariat has a full list of approved marking methods and can help to source for secure techniques that can be used.

The broader level of implementation of CITES includes [the following].

Training Initiatives

Training includes development and application of programmes to train those who implement and enforce CITES, as well those that are part of the process, such as those involved in transport systems.

In many cases identification of species is an issue, especially for those front-line officials such as Customs. This is where training initiatives to develop and provide research materials for identification guides is crucial to successful monitoring and enforcement. Thailand has developed an illustrated manual in Thai language which focuses on *Paphiopedilum* and *Vanda* species of orchids. The manual form the basis of any training for enforcement officers in Thailand on orchid trade control. This manual was developed with the help of the UK CITES Scientific Authority, the Royal Botanical Gardens, Kew.

There is also a great need for developing and implementing a programme for training that targets different audiences. The training programme should include basic workshop on CITES implementation especially for MA, Sa, anti other relevant authorities, enforcement workshops specifically for MA and Customs and Police, as well as other investigative agencies that may be engage[d] in wildlife trade enforcement. A number of countries have carried out basic CITES training workshops, often with the help of the CITES Secretariat. Vietnam is further along in this training as [it has] carried out regional training courses as well.

However, it is important to note that the most effective briefing materials are those in local languages. While materials produced overseas are a good source of reference, not many will be able to understand anti interpret the materials effectively.

Partnerships and Cooperation

In the preamble to the next of the Convention, it states that the best protector of wildlife in a country is the people of the country herself, and it goes on to state that international cooperation is critical for effective Implementation of this role. International and national links and joining together of groups such as governmental, nongovernmental and/or commercial to look at problems, share information, investigate issues and implement changes will enhance the efficiency and effectiveness of a country in conserving its natural resources.

There a number of different partners that could be formed for different and overlapping reasons—coordinating body that also produces materials for use, enforcement, legislative changes, etc. Some of the more effective partnerships include [the following].

UK Partnership for Action Against Wildlife Crime (PAW)

This is a creation of a permanent national committee, the PAW, composed of the CITES Management Authority, the Home Office, the UK Police Forces, H.M. Customs and Excise nongovernmental organizations involved in wildlife law enforcement and other official bodies with some relevance to this subject area. This Committee meet bi-annually and is closely involved in the review, coordination and collaboration o CITES related issues.

PAW formed a series or working group to take forward particular issues and providing a sounding board for development of initiatives The working groups include subject areas such as data management; legislation and policy; DNA and forensic analysis; media; and the Police Wildlife Liaison Officer Conference. The Committee produced the *Guide for Wildlife Law Enforcement in UK*, setting out all information pertinent to every aspect of the law, policy, practical advice, contracts, resources, and many other issues. A kit for sampling blood and materials for DNA analysis from live birds and derivatives was developed with instructions for use by enforcement officers.

PAW has created a forum and mechanism that allows a comprehensive, structured and coordinated approach to improving wildlife law and enforcement in the UK. The results have included useful products for law enforcement personnel, or changes in legislation as well as targeted enforcement activities resulting in significant prosecutions.

Wildlife Taskforce in Los Angeles, USA

This Task Force is a multi-agency effort to interdict illegal wildlife imports and exports. The members are officers and inspectors from US Customs. US Fish and Wildlife Service, Food and Drug Administration, and the US Department of Agriculture.

The Task Force meet regularly to discuss the successes and failures of past efforts and how to improve future interdiction plans, which primarily involve concerted law enforcement initiatives targeted at routes where illegal wildlife trade is most likely. The areas of action include international mail division, where every parcel from specified target countries is opened and inspected, international cargo presented to US Customs as informal (non-commercial or low value) entries, passenger flights from target countries so that each passenger's luggage can be opened and examined.

The Task Force is successful because it brings a number of agencies together to work for a common goal. When working together, each agency is attuned to the priorities of its partners. Further, the interest generated in these efforts continues beyond the individual projects, develop contacts and improves communication dissemination among agencies, and makes each agency more effective in its wildlife trade interdiction efforts.

National Coordination Committee of India

The NCC consists of representatives of 10 different enforcement agencies and an NGO, TRAFFIC India. The objective of the NCC is to promote effective interdepartmental coordination for the control of illegal trade in wildlife and wildlife products in the country. The NCC meets bi-annually. In function, it is similar to PAW in UK.

Covenant in the Netherlands

The Dutch Covenant was created in response to a recommendation of a report on wildlife crime in the Netherlands in 1994. This is an inter-ministerial body, comprising of representatives of the Ministry of Justice, Ministry of Internal Affairs (Police), AID-Ministry of Agriculture and Customs, and meets with NGOs to discuss wildlife crime and enforcement. The Covenant is simply a mechanism to facilitate cooperation, mutual understanding, sharing of intelligence information and concerted targeting of problem areas in wildlife trade and CITES.

Commercial Sector Action

By its very nature, wildlife trade involves a number of different levels of entrepreneurs, traders, commercial companies, in particular transport companies, among others. Success in getting them involved in the practice of sustainable harvest and utilization of wildlife has been limited to a large degree as it depends on the moral obligations which are tenuous at best, and good will of many individuals directly involved in wildlife trade. These are the actions that do not involve punishment and penalties and rewards for doing good.

However, Cathay Pacific Airlines has developed an environmental policy to improve all aspects of resource use, pollution reduction, environmentally sound purchasing, and now transport codes for wildlife. In 1996, it was recognized that the airline had a role in the international transport of live wildlife and derivatives, both at the freight level and at the passenger level. The management decided to implement a system of staff and passenger awareness about wildlife trade and the legal requirement of CITES

The Airline made a complete review of all procedures and practical methods of raising awareness and reducing unwitting complicity in the illegal trade in CITES specimens. The process is ongoing and it is hopeful of success. Staff training and awareness materials are being developed and will be incorporated into training schemes at all levels. Monitoring and checking of freight with a purview of looking for wildlife and derivatives is being established. Educational materials for passengers are being developed to inform them of the issues of transporting CITES specimens The procedures will also include liaison and cooperation with local enforcement agencies

Public Awareness and Education

Public awareness anti-education is the single most important action that may have an impact far beyond the enforcement and monitoring measures that can be undertaken in the near term. However, it is also the one action where the results are not immediate and do not affect all individuals equally. The groups of people that such activities would target include the public, governments, official bodies and traders of particular elements which may improve effectiveness of the implementation or enforcement of CITES.

New legislation once adopted has to be made known to the general public and enforcement officers. Campaigns that attempts to ensure smooth transition to the new regulation, increase awareness of the problems of illegal trade and provision of information on the effects of unsustainable trade can overcome such impediment to proper enforcement. The EU has a *CITES Information Campaign* and Hong Kong has the *Protect Endangered Species Campaign*. The Hong Kong campaign differs in that it uses a three-prong approach to increasing public awareness about trading in endangered species

(i) The first element focused upon traditional Chinese medicines and aimed to encourage the public to refrain from purchasing tiger and rhinoceros parts and medicines which claimed to contain them;

(ii) The second element requested that the public inform the authorities of any illegal activities relating to trading in endangered species in general, in addition, to traditional Chinese medicines.

Both the above were supported by a leaflet which outlines the regulations which refer to the import and export of wildlife and lists the species which are covered by these regulations. The information leaflet for the campaign was produced in Chinese and English and was distributed to traders, relevant authorities and schools.

(iii) The third element of the approach was awareness for new recruits involved in the control of trade, including Customs and Excise officers and airport workers.

Publicity was also crucial towards getting the attention of the public on the issues at hand. Major prosecutions were highlighted in the press, including the very large fines and jail sentences. Hong Kong took an important step forward in acknowledging the problems of wildlife conservation by taking a tough stance on those who contravene the law, including very large sums of money in fines and lengthy jail sentences. The judges and judiciary have also been made aware of the seriousness of the crime of illegal wildlife trade and mete out punishment accordingly.

Scientific Authority

Continued commercial trade in Appendix II–listed specimens require scientific evidence to demonstrate that the trade is sustainable and CITES requires that the Scientific Authority in each Party to monitor exports of specimens of Appendix II species, in order to limit trade to sustainable levels. The full list [of] functions of a Scientific Authority is found in Annex 2.

There are a number of reasons why Scientific Authorities may not be functioning well. The Infractions report identified several reasons:

- a Scientific Authority exists but only on paper,
- the Scientific Authority is technically incompetent or has competence limited to certain fields only,
- the Scientific Authority is not consulted,
- there is insufficient funds for the proper functioning of Scientific Authority, and
- a lack of commitment by the government to implement the Convention.

This is not a reflection on Vietnam and, in fact, Vietnam has been very progressive in assigning competent Scientific Authorities. The only constraint of ours is the lack of funds to carry out the work. [*The following two annexes are from the original Workshop Proceedings.*]

Annex I—The Role and Functions of a Management Authority

The Management Authority has two basic roles. Firstly, it is responsible for granting permits and certificates under the teens of the Convention, and secondly, it is responsible for communicating with the Secretariat and other Parties regarding all CITES matters.

Procedures for Granting Permits and Certificates

Granting of Import Permits

In the case of a species listed in Appendix I, import shall require the prior grant and presentation of an import permit, which shall only be granted when the following conditions have been met:

(a) The Scientific Authority has advised that the import will be for purposes which are not detrimental to the survival of the species involved;

(b) The Scientific Authority of the Management Authority is satisfied that the proposed recipient of a living specimen is suitably equipped to house and care for it.

(c) The management Authority is satisfied that the specimen is not to be used for primarily commercial purposes.

Granting of Export Permits

An export permit is required for any species listed in Appendix I or II and for Appendix II species if listed by a country.

An export permit shall only be granted when the following conditions have been met:

- The Scientific Authority has advised that such export will not be detrimental to the survival of that species;
- The Management Authority is satisfied that the specimen was not obtained in contravention of the laws of Vietnam for the protection of fauna and flora;
- The Management Authority is satisfied that any living specimen will be so prepared as to minimise the risk of injury damage to health or cruel treatment;
- in the case of a species listed under Appendix I, the management Authority is satisfied that an import permit has been granted for the specimen.

Granting of Re-Export Certificates

The re-export of any CITES-listed specimen shall require the prior grant of a re-export certificate. For species listed in Appendices I or II a re-export certificate shall only be granted when the following conditions are met.

(a) the management Authority is satisfied that the specimen was imported in accordance with the provisions of the Convention;

(b) the Management Authority is satisfied that any living specimen will be so prepared as to minimize the risk of injury, damage to health or cruel treatment; and

(c) in the case of a living specimen of a species listed under Annex I, the Management Authority is satisfied that an import permit has been granted.

Exception

Exceptions to these provisions may be granted in accordance with the provision of CITES at the discretion of the Management Authority for: Specimens which were acquired before the Convention came into force; personal or household effects: animals bred in captivity; or artificially propagated plants.

The Management Authority is responsible for assessing whether such exceptions are justifiable on a case-by-case basis and issuing per-Convention certificates and certificates of captive breeding/ artificially propagation as appropriate.

Communication, Reporting, and Other Responsibilities

Communication with the Secretariat and other Parties

The Management Authority has the primary responsibility for communicating with the CITES Secretariat and other Parties. For example, such communications may involve verification of permits and certificates; providing information on the status of species in trade, and on the basis upon which scientific decisions have been made; and participation in regional meetings and training seminars.

The re-export of any CITES-listed specimen shall require the prior grant of a re-export certificate.

Participation in Meetings of the Convention of the Parties

The Management Authority will normally be responsible for preparing for the biennial meeting of the Conference of the Parties; and preparing advice for the government delegation on species listing and administrative proposals.

Production of Periodic Reports

The Management Authority is responsible for compiling an annual CITES trade report containing a luminary of all permits and certificates granted during the year, and for producing biennial reports on legislative, regulatory, anti administrative measures taken to enforce the provision of CITES.

Registration

The Management Authority is responsible for a number of registration duties under the Convention, including registration of captive-breeding operations, nurseries anti scientific institutions.

Development and Implementation of National Provisions to Implement the Convention

The Management Authority must ensure that all provisions of the Convention are respected anti implemented and that decisions of the Conference of the Parties are entered into force.

Education and Information Functions

Although not a specific requirement of the Convention the Management Authority should provide information as required to the general public and traders to ensure knowledge and encourage compliance with the provisions of the convention.

Annex 2—The Role of a Scientific Authority

The Scientific Authority has an essential role to play as, under Article III and IV of CITES, its advice is required before Management Authorities can issue of refuse a permit. Under CITES, a Scientific Authority has five tasks:

1. To advise the Management Authority on whether or not a proposed export of an Appendix I or II specimen will be detrimental to the survival of the species involved.
2. In the case of a proposed import of an Appendix I specimen to advise the Management Authority on whether or not the purposes of that import are detrimental to the survival of the species involved.
3. In the case of a proposed import of a live Appendix I specimen, to state whether or not its is satisfied that the proposed recipient of the specimen is suitably equipped to house and care for it.
4. To monitor the export permits granted for Appendix II specimens as well as the actual exports of such specimens, and to advise the Management Authority of suitable measures to the taken to limit the grant of export permits where it has determined that this is necessary to maintain that species throughout its range at a level consistent with its role in the ecosystems, and well able the level at which that species might become eligible for inclusion in Appendix I.
5. To advise the Management Authority on the choice of a rescue center or other place for the disposal of confiscated specimens.

The Scientific Authority has extremely important functions, which [are] considered absolutely essential for the implementation of CITES.

(a) Monitoring. To be able to determine whether a proposed export will be detrimental to the survival of a species, or whether exports of a particular species must be limited to maintain it at a level consistent with its role in the ecosystems, and well above the level at which it would be eligible for Appendix I listing, the Scientific Authority must have at its disposal the best of all relevant scientific research or field work. If the information does not exist, the Scientific Authority should be able to cause the undertaking of the necessary research or work.

(b) Provision of advice. The second function of the Scientific Authority is to provide advice to the Management Authority on several matters. This advice does not bind the Management Authority except in one particular important case: as the CITES Convention clearly states, When the Scientific Authority has advised that a proposed export will be detrimental to the survival of a species, the Management Authority is bound by that advice under CITES.

D

National Implementation of CITES in Singapore

(i) Lye L.H., "The Implementation of the Convention on International Trade in Endangered Species in Singapore," 2:1 *Journal of International Wildlife Law & Policy*, 1999, pp 46–62

Twenty-six years ago, on 3 March 1973, the *Convention on International Trade in Endangered Species of Wild Flora and Fauna* (commonly referred to as "CITES") was opened for signature. It came into force on 1 July 1975, 90 days after the deposit of the tenth instrument of ratification. As of 13 March 1999, there are 146 parties to the Convention, including Singapore, which acceded to the Convention on 30 November 1986.

Sited at the crossroads of Southeast Asia, one of richest areas of biological diversity in the world, with well-developed transportation and communication networks, it is not surprising that Singapore has been accused of facilitating trade in wildlife. Indeed, a large volume of wildlife trade passes through Singapore's doors, on transit to other regions. However, it should be noted that CITES does not regulate transshipments. Additionally, much of this trade comprises non-CITES species. Is this, therefore, a fair accusation?

This paper examines the implementation of CITES in Singapore. It first examines the provisions of the implementing legislation, the *Endangered Species (Import and Export) Act* (hereinafter referred to as "ESA"); it then examines implementation from practical perspectives, as gleaned from interviews with the Primary Production Department, which is the designated Managing and Scientific Authority in Singapore. Several case studies are highlighted. The paper then discusses the inadequacies in the laws, including enforcement problems, and concludes with recommendations for improvement.

Accession to CITES

Member States that accede to the Convention are given 90 days to implement its provisions. Singapore started its implementation on 9 February 1987, 77 days after its accession. From that date, all commercial imports and exports of wild flora and fauna and their derivatives, had to be approved by the Primary Production Department (PPD), the designated authority for implementation of CITES. The Primary Production Department is both the Management and the Scientific Authority in charge of enforcing CITES. It has a special CITES Unit, manned by six staff members. Traders were made aware of these changes through seminars organized by the Trade Development Board and the PPD. The *Endangered Species (Import and Export) Act*, was passed to implement CITES, to take effect beginning 17 March 1989. The Act requires a permit from the PPD for the import, export, re-export or introduction from the sea of all endangered species. It provides powers of search, entry, and seizure to facilitate investigation and enforcement. It was amended in 1992 to provide for stricter control on domestic trade in endangered species.

Ten years have passed since the enactment of the ESA. Initially, Singapore had entered reservations on one species of alligator (*caiman crocodilus crocodilus)*, and two species of crocodiles *(crocodilus porosus* and *crocodilus novaeguineae novaegzcineae*). These reservations were necessary to allow local traders to adjust to the system, and have since been withdrawn, (on 31 August 1990 for the crocodiles, and on 15 February 1992 for the Caiman alligator), as traders became familiar with the system. Since then, Singapore has not placed any reservations under CITES.

The Endangered Species (Import and Export) Act—An Overview

Protected Species

The *Endangered Species (Import and Export) Act* (ESA) is comprised of 22 sections and 3 schedules, which list animals, animal parts and their derivatives, and plants, respectively.

The term "animal" is defined as any animal, whether dead or alive, including the egg, young or immature form. "Plant" is defined as a live or dead plant and any readily recognizable part or derivative of a plant. The Act prohibits international as well as domestic trade in "scheduled species," which encompasses scheduled animal parts and animals, or a scheduled plant.

The ESA makes no reference to the three CITES appendices. The ESA's First Schedule lists all animals in CITES Appendices I and II. The Second Schedule lists their parts and derivatives. It begins with a wide provision for the derivatives of all scheduled animals listed in the First Schedule, covering "substantially complete parts of dead specimens (either in natural form, stuffed, chilled, preserved, dried or otherwise treated meat)." The derivatives of particular animals are then listed, e.g., elephants—"Tusk, and any part of any such tusk, whether simply prepared or worked"; sea turtles—"The shell and scales, if unworked or simply prepared, the waste of the shell and scales. The flippers and limbs. The cartilage and eggs. The whole or any part of any raw hide or skin, whether or not split, and the leather." The Third Schedule lists protected plants contained in CITES Appendices I and II.

Species listed in CITES Appendix III do not appear in ESA's Schedules because the PPD takes the view that Appendix III is not subject to sufficient scrutiny. As it stands, it is being abused by some countries that do not properly enforce CITES themselves, but simply list all their species, so that others are obliged to control them. The PPD, however, selectively controls the importation of Appendix III species, via the licensing provisions of the *Animals and Birds Act*. This Act requires a certificate of origin for all live animals and birds imported into Singapore.

The three Schedules are updated promptly after each Conference of the Parties (COP). In 1997, a complete set of Schedules was published, incorporating changes from the last COP. This facilitates easy reference.

Where a corporation commits an offense with the consent or connivance of any director, manager, secretary or other officer, the officer as well as the body corporate will be guilty of an offense and liable to prosecution.

Permits

The import, export, re-export or introduction from the sea of any scheduled species requires a permit from the Director of PPD. The Director may issue a permit, licence, certificate or written permission, either conditionally or unconditionally, or refuse to do so (s.5). A permit may be cancelled at any time if any condition of the permit has been contravened or the permit is later discovered to have been issued as a result of a misleading statement or a misrepresentation of a material fact (s.6). Failure to return a cancelled permit is an offense (fine S$2,000).

Although the three Schedules do not indicate whether the animals or plants listed are Appendix I or 11 species, in practice, permits are granted or refused according to the provisions contained in the Convention. Thus, a permit for a specimen falling within Appendix I would be granted only in accordance with the terms of CITES Article 111.

Offenses Under ESA

There are three main offenses under the ESA.

- First, the Act prohibits the import, export, re-export or introduction from the sea of "any scheduled species" without a permit from the Director of Primary Production (s.4(1)).
- Second, it is an offense for anyone to "have in his possession, under his control, sell, offer or expose for sale or display to the public, any scheduled species which has been imported or introduced from the sea without a permit." (s.4(2)).

The penalty in both cases is a fine of up to S$5,000 or imprisonment up to one year, or both. In the case of a second or subsequent conviction, the fine is doubled to S$10,000, with a maximum of a year's imprisonment or both fine and imprisonment.

- Third, it is an offense to "sell, offer or expose for sale, or display to the public such scheduled species as the Minister may, by notification in the Gazette, specify." (s.4A(1)). The penalty is a fine of up to S$2,000, or imprisonment of up to three months, or both. (s. 4A(2)).

The third offense was added in 1992 to address domestic sales of endangered species. To date, two species have been gazetted: rhinoceros horns, derivatives and products—prohibited as of 20 November 1992; and tiger parts and products (including medicines containing tiger parts, such as tiger bone wine, plasters, pills, etc.)—prohibited as of 4 November 1994. Breaches of these laws fall within s. 4A, and entail a fine of up to S$2,000 or a jail term of up to three months, or both.

Abetment

It is an offense to abet the commission of any offense under the Act. (s.7). However, the penalty for abetment is set forth in the ESA. It would thus appear to fall within s. 12, which applies to all offenses for which a specific penalty has not been specified. The penalty is a fine of up to S$2,000 or imprisonment up to 6 months, or both. It should be noted that under s. 109, Penal Code, the penalty for abetment where no penalty is specified, is similar to that for the main offense. In order to serve as sufficient deterrence, the punishment for abetment of an offense should be the same as that for the offense itself, as in s.109 of the Penal Code.

Corporations

Where a corporation commits an offense with the consent or connivance of any director, manager, secretary or other officer, the officer as well as the body corporate will be guilty of an offense and liable to prosecution (s. 12).

Enforcement

Officers authorized under the Act have extensive powers, including the authority, without warrant, to enter and search any place or premises, to stop and board any conveyance which they reasonably suspect to contain any scheduled species, and authority to seize, detain or remove any species and all other relevant items. These powers extend to the breaking of any door, window, lock, fastener, compartment, box, container or any other interference. Officers may also search any person found in such premises or conveyance, and may arrest without warrant, any person who has committed or whom they reasonably suspect to have committed an offense under the Act or its rules. (s.9).

It is an offense to obstruct any authorized officer in the execution of his duty, or to fail, without reasonable excuse, to furnish information or render all necessary assistance as may bc required or directed by an authorized officer. (s.10)

It is also an offense to make any false statement, declaration, representation or information, or produce a license that one knows or has reason to believe is false or has been tampered with. (s. 11).

These offenses carry a fine of up to S$2,000 and/or imprisonment up to 6 months.(s.12).

If the Director suspects that any scheduled species has been imported, he may require the person with custody to furnish such information as he may require. (s.15)

The Director and his officers are empowered to investigate any matter under the Act, and may require the production of any books; documents, paper or information. Failure to comply is an offense (s. 16).

Exemption

The Director may exempt any person, scheduled species or group, or description or persons or species from all or any of the provisions of the Act (s. 18).

Compounding of Offenses

Offenses may be compounded for a sum not exceeding S$1,000, but the species and any other thing seized shall be forfeited.

The PPD has developed a system for the compounding of offenses, where the less serious cases are let off with a composition that usually ranges from S$200 to S$500. Much depends on whether the accused is a trader, the nature of the species (whether Appendix I or II), whether it is a first offense, etc. Statistics are not available, but many offenses are compounded, and only the more severe cases are prosecuted.

Forfeiture

Where a person has been convicted under s. 4 or s. 4A, forfeiture of the scheduled species is effected immediately without the need for a further order. Where the person charged with an offense under s. 4 or s. 4A is acquitted or given a discharge, the court may order that the species be returned to him or be forfeited (s. 13).

Forfeiture can also be effected where the importer or exporter cannot be ascertained or is outside national jurisdiction. However, the Director of PPD must first give the person from whom the species was seized seven days notice of his intention to forfeit. No notice is required if the species are live animals.

The Director has full discretion to dispose of species that have been forfeited. All incurred expenses are recoverable from the owner, importer, exporter or re-exporter, as a debt in any court of competent jurisdiction.

In practice, live specimens are sent to the Singapore Zoological Gardens, the Jurong Birdpark, or, in the case of specimens from the sea, to the Underwater World at Sentosa Island. Non-live specimens are given to the National University of Singapore's Raffles Collection. Products and derivatives from scheduled species are either destroyed or kept by the PPD.

Marking of Species

The ESA provides that the PPD may require the marking of certain species (s.14) e.g. birds must be ringed and reptile skins tagged; arowanas are marked by a special chip inserted in their bodies.

Implementation and Enforcement

The CITES Unit at PPD

The six staff members in the CITES Unit of PPD are kept very busy, attending to the following matters:

- Documentation—the issuance of permits, keeping of records of species traded;
- Enforcement—attending to complaints, conducting raids; checking of stocks of traders;
- Inspections—at the airports, Woodlands checkpoint (for incoming road and rail traffic from Malaysia);
- Correspondence—with the CITES Secretariat and other Managing Authorities;
- Strategic planning—charting the future directions of CITES and its enforcement in the years ahead.

It is clear that the Unit is understaffed and more personnel are needed. Due to staff constraints, inspections of bird shops and other establishments are not as frequent as they should be. There are not sufficient labor resources to conduct public awareness education, and stock-takings are very difficult as there is no time to count every item. The number of staff has not been increased since the Unit commenced its work in 1987. The Unit should comprise at least ten members.

The Customs Authorities

The role of the Customs Authority is to detect illegal shipments of endangered species and their derivatives. The CITES Unit conducts classes for Customs officers, to acquaint them with the workings of CITES and to train them to identify those species (95 percent) that are commonly traded. These classes used to be held once a month, but are now conducted at least twice yearly. Where Customs officers are unsure of the species, they may be detained and PPD can be called upon for assistance in identification.

Trade in Endangered Species

In 1995, 12,873 CITES permits were issued for the import and export of wildlife and related products. These include reptile skins, reptilian leather manufactured products, live birds, zoo animals, arowanas and CITES plants such as orchids and American wild ginseng.

In 1996, some 10,996 CITES permits were issued for the import and export of reptile skins, reptilian leather manufactured products, live birds, zoo animals, arowanas and CITES plants, worth some S$80 million.

In 1997, a total of 7,914 CITES permits were issued for the import and export of zoo animals, birds, reptile skins, reptilian leather manufactured products, dragon fish and CITES plants, such as orchids, agarwood and American wild ginseng. The majority of imports of CITES-listed species into Singapore in 1997 were specimens of live birds and reptile skins. Other imports included live mammals, stony corals, butterflies, Agarwood and American ginseng. Major re-exports of CITES species included live birds, reptile skins and manufactured reptile products.

Attendance at Conferences of the Parties (COPs)

Singapore attends all Conferences of the Parties. Amendments to the lists of species in Appendices I and II are implemented promptly by a revision of the laws.

Pre-CITES Species

The ESA does not provide for pre-Convention species. According to the PPD, upon Singapore's accession to CITES, letters were sent to all traders, informing them about CITES, and requiring them to declare their existing stocks. PPD would check these stocks to ensure they are accurately declared. There are no obligations on non-traders or householders.

Captive Breeding

Singapore has registered four Saltwater (Crocodylus porosus) and three Dragon fish (Sderopages formosus) captive breeding operations with the CITES Secretariat.

Infringements of the Law

Infringements come to the PPD's attention at the Customs checkpoints, through the alertness of Customs officers, or through public information e.g. tip-offs, complaints.

Each case is investigated, but sometimes, the investigations are not sufficiently expeditious. There are allegations that birdshops and aquariums in Singapore often contain live CITES species, even Appendix I species (e.g., arowana); that shop owners know the law well, and are very defensive when asked about these species. They immediately claim the species are not for sale and are only for "display." There is also considerable domestic trade in endangered species. These shops also contain species that are strictly protected in their home countries and are not allowed to be traded, the inference being that these must therefore be illegally obtained.

The writer does not have complete statistics of cases of infringements of the law as many of these are compounded, and do not appear in the PPD's Annual Reports. However, seizures are reported in the annual yearbooks published by the Ministry of Information and the Arts, along with the number of CITES permits granted, and cases that are prosecuted.

In 1995, the PPD confiscated a total of 16,209 turtle eggs, 31 birds and 20 boxes of Chinese pills containing powdered rhinoceros horn.

In 1996, there were seven cases of enforcement actions for illegal import, export or possession or endangered species. In all, 1,750 live pythons, macaws, cockaroos and tortoises were confiscated. Offenders paid between S$200 and S$2,000 in fines.

In 1997, there were nine cases of enforcement action, mainly for possession of illegally imported endangered species, which resulted in fines of up to S$5,000 and confiscation of all seized specimens.

In 1998, the number of enforcement cases rose to 41 (up from nine in 1997). The Head of PPD's Regulatory Branch, Dr. Leong Hon Keong, has attributed this rise to a better informed public, which is more forthcoming in reporting cases of illegal trade or possession of animals. Although illegal trade is not widespread, and the PPD no longer sees cases of "crude smuggling," Dr. Leong believed a few groups of traders were bringing the animals in for collectors. The traders would either offer the animals to their contacts or advertise them over the Internet, using their pager numbers and false names.

There is also an increasing number of cases of thefts of animals and birds. The most notable was the theft in January 1999 of two tamarins and two marmosets from the Singapore Zoo. The loss generated great publicity and the animals were found a few days later, abandoned in a cage. Petshop owners claim they have been approached by men who offer them wild animals or birds at very low prices. A spokesman for the Zoo said many of the animals that the authorities seize and hand over to the zoo come from illegal traders or from people who had bought them from illegal traders. A police spokesman, however, said it was still too early to say if syndicates were involved in animal thefts. . . .

Selected Cases

There are no cases reported in the Law Reports, as the decisions emanate from the lower courts and do not warrant written judgments. There have been no appeals from these decisions. The writer is thus compelled to rely on reports contained in the newspapers, as well as interviews with the PPD.

The following cases have been reported in the newspapers:

(a) Turtle eggs—a businessman attempted to smuggle over 16,000 eggs of the endangered Green Turtle. PPD officers were on a routine patrol of the Jurong Fishing Port when they spotted the man leaving the port in a green van. When he made a sudden detour back to the Fish Merchant's Complex, the officers became suspicious. They found 20 cartons in the van, each containing about 800 marine turtle eggs. The eggs were believed to be worth about S$6,400 if sold to restaurants for consumption. The perpetrator pleaded guilty, but was only fined S$2,000!

(b) Birds—a bird trader who claimed to import only non-CITES bird species from China was found to have 30 Fischer's Lovebirds that require CITES permits. The trader was only fined S$200 for importing the birds without proper documentation. The birds were confiscated.

(c) Birds—a company was caught attempting to re-export 36 birds without proper permits, of which 26 were endangered species. The birds were estimated to be worth some S$38,000. The company and its manager were each fined $5,000, the maximum under s. 4, ESA, for first offenders.

(d) Star tortoises—in 1997, some 500 star tortoises were seized by the PPD from a small supermarket. The owner was fined S$5,000.

(e) Pythons—An aquarium was fined S$2,000 for having nine young pythons on display in the shop.

(f) Assorted—Another aquarium owner was fined S$1,000 for having a variety of CITES listed species such as arowanas, iguanas and spiders imported without PPD permits.

Inadequacies

Low Fines

It is clear from an examination of these cases that the fines imposed by the courts are too low to serve as a sufficient deterrent of illegal trafficking in wildlife Under the ESA, the maximum fine is only S$5,000 for conducting international trade without a permit. The fine is even lower (S$2,000) in the case of domestic trade. Additionally, the fines are imposed on a per consignment species, not a per specimen species. It should be noted that while CITES requires a separate permit or certificate for each consignment of specimens (Art. VI(5)), its main provisions (Articles III, IV and V) apply to "any specimen of a species." Courts also do not treat these offenses with sufficient gravity.

The problem is compounded by the practice of bringing most cases before the Magistrates' courts, where fines are limited to only S$2,000. Prosecutors from the PPD are not legally trained and prefer the less formal, more expeditious trial process of the magistrates courts, obviating imposition of the maximum penalty (S$5000) provided for under the ESA.

It is submitted that the law should be amended to raise the fines substantially. PPD agrees that it should be raised to at least S$50,000. Additionally, where the offense relates to a large consignment, the law should empower the imposition of the fine on a per specimen basis. Offenses under Singapore's national law for the protection of wild animals and birds impose a fine of up to S$1,000 per animal or bird (s. 4 *Wild Animals and Birds Act*). Thus, in one case, a Malaysian who attempted to smuggle some 775 birds (non-CITES species) and 50 rabbits in 24 boxes across the Causeway into Singapore, in his car, was fined S$50 per bird. His total fines amounted to S$41,750 and he was also sentenced to 6 months imprisonment. As he could not raise the money, he had to serve another nine months in prison.

Jail Sentences

Jail sentences are seldom imposed on the offenders. It is submitted that as the fines are grossly inadequate, and thus may be simply viewed as a cost of doing business, offenders should be imprisoned, even if it is a first offense. Singapore's pollution laws prohibit illegal dumping, or contamination of the water supply by discharge of any toxic substance, both of which carry, in addition to a fine, a mandatory jail sentence of one to twelve months imprisonment for repeat offenders. The principle should be extended to illegal trade in wildlife.

Onus of Proof

The law should make it easier to prove guilt, by reversing the onus of proof. As it stands, to obtain a conviction under s.4(2), the prosecutor must prove that the animal being offered for sale was imported without a permit. There should be a presumption that mere possession of a scheduled animal or its derivative, is an offense, unless a permit is produced, the onus falling on the accused to prove otherwise.

Enforcement

The law should provide for stronger powers of enforcement, which should include the power to examine persons, take down written statements which are admissible in court, the power to demand the names and addresses of persons involved, and power to require the attendance of witnesses in court.

Regulations

Legal experts have recommended that detailed rules on the implementation of the Convention should be embodied in regulations, and the Ace itself should be limited to laying down general rules, prohibitions, the designation of enforcement agents, penalties and the granting of powers necessary for the government to make further regulations that are necessary for implementation.

However, unlike the more comprehensive laws of some countries such as the USA, Canada, Australia or Hong Kong, Singapore's ESA does not lay down any detailed rules, except relating to the payment of fees for permits. The ESA and its rules are not sufficiently comprehensive. Many areas have not been specifically covered either under the ESA or its regulations (e.g., the status of pre-Convention species; the types of permits required, the form they should take, their period of validity; issues relating to captive breeding). It is also unclear if any resolutions passed at conferences of the parties have been adopted. They do not appear in any legislation or regulations (apart from amendments to the Schedules). While some decisions may have been adopted as part of the PPD's administrative practice, this is not apparent to members of the public.

Licensing of Endangered Species

The *Wild Animals and Birds Act* prohibits the killing, taking or keeping of any wild animal or bird. It provides for the licensing of certain species of wild animals, (including animals that are endangered species under CITES), but there are no provisions for the licensing of birds. Under strict construction of the Act, it is illegal to keep any wild bird. However, this prohibition is not observed, as keeping birds is a popular hobby in Singapore. There have been many calls for the licensing of certain wild birds, particularly endangered species protected under CITES, and non-CITES species that are protected under the laws of their countries of origin, particularly species from the region. It is hoped that these calls will soon be answered.

For birds and animals that are protected under CITES, it should follow that license provisions for these endangered species should be contained in the *Endangered Species (Import and Export) Act*, instead of under the *Wild Animals and Birds Act*.

Trans-shipments

As Singapore is often the transit point for trade in wildlife, it is important that specimens in transit be subject to the provisions of the Convention. However Article VII of CITES states that it does not apply to the "transit or trans-shipment of specimens through or in the territory of a Party while the specimens remain in Customs control." Resolution Conf. 7.4 recommended that parties "inspect transit shipments, check the presence of valid export documentation as required under the Convention or satisfactory proof of its existence" and "adopt legislation allowing them to seize and confiscate transit shipments without such documentation or proof thereof." Resolution 8.8 went further, recommending that documentation comparable to that which is required between Parties be required for transit shipments passing through the territories of parties, even if the shipment is in transit between two non-party states.

A few countries have adopted laws that apply CITES controls to transits and trans-shipments. For example, Germany and Switzerland allow transit only upon presentation of valid export permits issued by the country of export. A few countries have even extended protection to specimens brought in which do not fall within Customs control, such as cases where goods are transported in a carrier that only makes a stop in the country, with the goods remaining on board or arrive in one conveyance and are then loaded and transferred to another conveyance—e.g., Hong Kong requires the presentation of valid export documentation even if the specimens remain at all times in the vessel or aircraft in which they were brought in; the USA construes the term "import" very broadly, including specimens that are on a plane that makes an unscheduled landing at a US airport.

In Singapore, scheduled species in transit in Singapore do not fall within the meaning of the terms "import" or "export" as defined in s. 2(2) ESA and are thus not subject to the requirement of a permit. Section 2(2) states that a scheduled species shall be deemed to be in transit if it is brought into Singapore solely for the purpose of taking it out of Singapore and:

(a) remain at all times in or on the conveyance in or on which it is brought into Singapore;

(b) is removed from the conveyance in or on which it was brought into Singapore and either returned to the same conveyance or transferred directly to another conveyance before being despatched to a place outside Singapore; and is kept under the control of the Director or an authorized officer while being so removed, returned or transferred; or

(c) is removed from the conveyance in or on which it was brought into Singapore and kept under the control of the Director or an authorized officer for a period not exceeding 14 days or such longer period as the Director may permit pending despatch to a place outside Singapore.

In practice, Singapore does control the trans-shipments of live animals and birds via the Animals and Birds Act, which requires a trans-shipment licence if the specimens are alive. This necessitates an import as well as an export permit. Thus, CITES is enforced indirectly. Regulations prescribed by the International Air Travel Association must also be complied with, otherwise no trans-shipment license will be granted. PPD claims that cases are checked if they are transferred to another carrier or if they leave the airplane and proceed over land, to Malaysia. However, it is not possible to check those cases that remain on the same plane.

The present practice of inspecting trans-shipments that contain live specimens should continue, but efforts should be made to extend inspections to all trans-shipments of wild flora and fauna, live or otherwise. The writer acknowledges that this may not be possible in all cases, given the large volume of trade that passes through Singapore each day. Nonetheless, it is essential that efforts should be made to fully implement the Convention, including resolutions adopted by the Conferences of the Parties. Additionally, these powers of inspection should be provided under the ESA and not under the Wild Animals and Birds Act. The latter legislation serves an altogether different purpose, focusing on the importation of domestic animals or animals imported into Singapore as food. As such, its extension to wild animals and birds may be challenged.

Separate Agency

A separate agency should be established to administer CITES. The Primary Production Department's priorities are the ensuring of safe and wholesome food, animal and plant health issues, and regulation of agro-technology. With the growing importance of CITES in the years to come, it is only fitting that Singapore should devote more resources and facilitate better and more comprehensive monitoring and implementation of wildlife trade law. The agency should have more staff and resources, to enable it to undertake more comprehensive prevention and enforcement measures as well as public education. Given the present constraints, it is difficult for preventive measures to be undertaken. Thus, the Unit is compelled to engage in reactive enforcement.

The police should also be called upon to provide assistance, and a special unit should be set up to investigate the smuggling of wildlife.

With the growing importance of CITES in the years to come, it is only fitting that Singapore should devote more resources and facilitate better and more comprehensive monitoring and implementation of wildlife trade law.

Conclusion

Singapore has carried out its obligations under the Convention faithfully; but it does not go beyond what CITES prescribes. Its enforcement officers are free of corruption, cases of alleged infringements are always investigated, records are dutifully and carefully kept and submitted to the Secretariat, offenders are prosecuted and punished. However, there are inadequacies, in the law as well as in its implementation, which is primarily attributable to a shortage of staff and resources. It is hoped they will soon be addressed, and that Singapore can be viewed (as it rightly should be) as a full partner in the worldwide effort to eradicate illegal trade in wildlife.

Looking beyond trade in endangered species, to the broader issues of the conservation of biological diversity and habitat protection, many species in the region are protected by national laws, but not under CITES. These species should be listed under Appendix III. Ideally, countries in the region should enlist the help of Singapore to ensure that such trade is controlled. This can be realised if there is a common conservation strategy in the region. This is precisely one of the aims of the ASEAN Agreement on the Conservation of Nature and Natural Resources, signed in 1985 by the then six ASEAN states, namely Brunei, Indonesia, Malaysia, Philippines, Singapore and Thailand.

Drafted with the assistance of the World Conservation Union (IUCN), the Agreement was considered to be the most progressive instrument of its time, viewing the region as one eco-system, and requiring parties to "develop national conservation strategies" and "coordinate these strategies within the framework of a conservation strategy for the region."

Under the terms of the Agreement, it can only come into force if ratified by all signatory countries. To date, only Indonesia, Philippines and Thailand have ratified the Agreement. It is thus, most regrettably, still not in force, as Brunei, Malaysia and Singapore have yet to ratify. At a recent Conference of the Judiciary in ASEAN, enticed "The Role of the Judiciary in Sustainable Development," held in Manila from 4-7 March 1999, a Resolution was passed requesting the ASEAN Secretariat to:

(a) approach those States that have not yet ratified the ASEAN Agreement, to do so; and

(b) to propose to those States that became members of ASEAN after 1985, to accede to the ASEAN Agreement once it enters into force.

It is hoped that Singapore, Malaysia and Brunei will ratify this Agreement and bring it into force very soon. Thereafter, we hope to see a new era in ASEAN cooperation on matters relating to nature and the conservation of natural resources. This should translate into better laws and administrative measures not only for the enforcement of CITES in the region, but for better regional protection of all flora and fauna, even they fall outside the ambit of CITES.

4

Competitiveness Theory

A

Esty D., "Environment Regulation and Competitiveness: Theory and Practice," in Tay and Esty (eds), *Asian Dragons and Green Trade,* Times Academic Press, 1996, pp 33–47

One of the most challenging issues in the effort to promote environmental protection alongside trade liberalization derives from the fear that more open markets will put countries with high environmental standards at a competitive disadvantage in a globalized world economy. This chapter explores the various types of competitiveness concerns that arise in the "trade and environment" context and the responses that policy makers might consider to competitiveness pressures. First we explore three different categories of competitiveness issues. Next, we will look at the tools that can be used in response to these concerns. Finally, we shall offer some concluding observations and policy recommendations.

A Theoretical Perspective

Traditionally, when people speak about "competitiveness" concerns, they have in mind the possibility that companies will be unable to sell their goods and services profitably in the marketplace at prices that are attractive to buyers. In the trade and environment context, this fear stems from the possibility that producers in high-standard countries will bear heavier costs for compliance with environmental regulations than their counterparts in low-standard countries, making it harder for them to sell at low prices or to earn comparable profits. As a result, they will suffer lost sales and market share in competition with these other producers.

That differences exist in the rigour of environmental standards from country to country is not in doubt. What is at issue is the effect of these differences and whether the competitiveness concerns created require a policy response.

Industry Migration

The economics literature has two, somewhat opposite, perspectives on this competitiveness issue. First, under the theory of "comparative advantage", economists observe that variations in environmental standards reflecting differences in local circumstances like climate, weather, population density, wealth, or stage of development, existing pollution levels and risk preferences are not a bad thing. From this viewpoint, countries with low environmental standards are simply using their comparative advantage. The fact that some industries (presumably relatively pollution-intensive ones) move to the jurisdictions offering low standards is neither surprising nor troubling. It is simply the work of the market in action. The differences in environmental standards, like other differences in circumstances, allow for specialization in production and make gains from trade possible.

Even if high-standard countries "lose" industries as a result of this dynamic, the traditional economic perspective sees no competitiveness problem. Rather, this is an appropriate reallocation of resources and production that enhances welfare. Although jobs will be lost in those industries that migrate, they will be replaced by other jobs in other sectors, which presumably the society values more highly. The goods in question will still be available as imports and perhaps at lower cost because they are made under less stringent environmental circumstances abroad. The consumers in the high-standard country benefit not only from access to lower-price goods but also from the healthier environment that follows shutting down high-pollution factories. Ironically, while economists argue that comparative advantage and differences in regulatory rigour should lead to the migration of "dirty" industries from high-standard to low-standard countries, they also tend to observe that there is little evidence of any such movement towards "pollution havens". A number of studies have looked for evidence that companies suffer competitive disadvantage from environmental regulations resulting in shifts in the location of production. None of these studies, however, showed any significant degree of industry migration or competitive pressure on industry. The authors of these studies have therefore concluded that, in general, environmental compliance costs are too small a factor. For most companies, it does not make much of a difference in their competitive position in general and their production location decisions in particular.

Distortions of Competition

Of course, shifting production to a new location often entails writing off existing capital investments, spending money on new facilities and other significant expenditures. Thus, companies migrate to new locations only under extreme circumstances. As such, to equate competitiveness effects to the relocation of industries is unlikely to produce much evidence of competitiveness effects. It is much more common that companies simply suffer a profit squeeze, loss of market share, or other subtle competitiveness pressures as a result of environmental costs that are disproportionate to their competitors.

In fact, one of the problems with all of the empirical studies cited above is their narrow focus on "pollution control expenditures". The impact of environmental regulation on industry competitiveness is much more likely to be seen in other variables, such as the degree to which energy prices reflect full environmental costs. Industry sensitivity to energy costs is hard to measure but there is substantial anecdotal evidence that it is a major factor in competitiveness. The European Union (EU), for example, has not moved forward with its plans for new energy taxes because the proposal for a carbon/energy tax to combat greenhouse gas emissions is expressly linked to a willingness by the EU's major trade partners (Japan and the United States) to do the same. Similarly, the Clinton Administration's efforts in the United States to impose a new energy tax in 1993 collapsed under the weight of protests from energy-intensive industries who complained that their competitiveness in the International markets to be harmed.

Thus, to test rigorously the hypothesis that higher environmental standards will create competitive disadvantages, one must look at a broad array of environmental burdens including energy tax levels, time delays due to regulatory roadblocks, and resources devoted to environmental management systems as well as spending on pollution controls. It is important, furthermore, to note that while economists see no evidence of competitiveness effects from stringent environmental regulation, politicians and business people are absolutely convinced of such impacts. Part of the reason for this diametrically opposite perspective is that businesses (and the politicians who advance their interests) are focused on sectoral effects while economists usually worry only about economy-wide competitiveness impacts.

Economists observe that while certain industries might be competitively disadvantaged by high environmental standards, by definition a country cannot lose comparative advantage in everything. Resources that are freed up by the closing of high-pollution steel mill will be re-deployed in new productive activities that yield greater net benefits to society But politicians, unlike economists, focus on the transition costs and redistributive effects of such changes. Notably, they respond to the distress of steelworkers who are laid off and whose new employment may pay much less than their former mill jobs. These redistributive effects and the concentration of the losses from economic evolution unleash a familiar "public choice" dynamic. Politically, the visible loss of jobs overrides the less visible gains from re-deploying productive assets. As a result, many competitiveness effects never appear as measurable economic harms. Instead, as explained below, they play out as downward pressure on environmental standards where, again, the losses are harder to see.

The "Race to the Bottom"

The spectre of competitive disadvantage appears to have its most pronounced impact on the environmental policy process. Faced with the prospect of reduced sales, lost jobs and diminished investment from high environmental standards, government officials act strategically and choose not to raise environmental standards, or even to relax enforcement of the standards currently in existence. This competitiveness-driven impact on environmental standards is known as the "race to the bottom". Note that the race is not really "to" the bottom but rather "toward" the bottom. In fact, governments rarely lower standards. The actual effect is thus one of "political drag" or "regulatory chill", making it difficult for governments to move toward better environmental policies.

Faced with the prospect of reduced sales, lost jobs and diminished investment from high environmental standards, government officials act strategically and choose not to raise environmental standards, or even to relax enforcement of the standards currently in existence.

This policy "stickiness" would not be a problem if, in general, governments had relatively good environmental programs in place. But this is not the case. Across the board and across the world, there exists a need to sharpen environmental regulatory programs by moving away from "command and control" standards to the use of "market mechanisms" that internalize environmental externalities in a more systematic and refined way. But the shift to more "transparent" economic incentive-based regulatory approaches is very difficult for governments to do unilaterally.

Being the first jurisdiction to impose appropriate environmental taxes, for example, exposes your own industries to costs and pressures which their competitors do not face. Thus, even if the policy will yield better long term results by internalizing pollution spillovers that currently go unattended to, the risk of transitional burdens on industry looms large. Moreover, such policies would shift from paying the price for pollution through public health and ecological harms that are spread diffusely across society (and perhaps even spilled, in part, onto other jurisdictions) to a regime of highly visible price signals. This presents substantial political challenges, as those who have been externalizing their pollution are forced to pay for the harm they cause. Having to overcome the claims of competitive disadvantage which—no matter that they are advanced by special, sector specific interests, appear in the relatively concrete and visible form of reduced profits, factory closures and job losses—makes the shift to more optimal environment regulation nearly impossible.

Interestingly, there has recently been considerable debate in the academic literature over whether the race to the bottom is a legitimate concern. In particular, Professor Richard Revesz has suggested that race to the bottom arguments in the environmental arena have been made "with essentially no theoretical foundation". Revesz argues that, far from causing a race to the bottom, jurisdictions with differing environmental standards actually enhance social welfare. He sees the pressure put on governments to reduce the environmental compliance costs imposed on their industries as likely to be valuable as a mechanism for streamlining government regulation and unlikely to yield standards that are suboptimal. His claim that "regulatory competition" will be efficiency-inducing builds on the work of a number of economic and legal scholars including Tiebout, Fischel, and Oates and Schwab. These theorists have demonstrated that, under carefully defined circumstances, interjurisdictional competition can enhance social welfare. Unfortunately, a number of the assumptions that must be made to achieve the proffered positive results do not appear likely to exist in the environmental domain.

In particular, Oates and Schwab have demonstrated that a race to the bottom will not arise from regulatory competition unless governments tax capital (which they all do). Oates and Schwab also note that if public choice distortions exist, meaning that environmental policies do not faithfully and accurately represent the public's will, suboptimal results will arise. Of course, the environmental policy realm represents the classic arena where public choice distortions are rampant. Furthermore, it is widely recognized that if transboundary externalities exist (i.e., the public good in question is not purely local), then regulatory competition will not necessarily improve social welfare.

Special interests contort standard-setting in the environmental domain. The public, moreover, is often not in a very strong position to judge whether it is getting the right level of environmental protection. Indeed, given the prevalence of time lags in the appearance of public health and ecological harms, threshold effects and confusion arising out of the technical complexity of environmental problems, it seems unlikely that the "market" for location rights would operate efficiently enough for regulatory competition to enhance welfare.

Product or Production and Process Method Standards

In discussing the competitiveness issues that relate to environmental regulation, it is important to distinguish between "product" and "production and process method" (PPM) standards. PPMs governing how companies make the goods they sell and, in particular, mandating certain efforts to prevent or control pollution in the production process are generally what people worry about in the competitiveness context. Product standards specifying required attributes of what companies make, such as emissions standards for cars or pesticide residue limits on food-are much less likely to have negative consequences. The *General Agreement on Tariffs and Trade* (GATT) has long recognized that governments may specify public health and ecological standards for products to be sold in their market, so long as they apply equally to domestic and foreign producers. Countries that mandate strict product standards do not disadvantage their own industries. Nor do they create any pressure for the adoption of suboptimal environmental policies. On the contrary, David Vogel argues that high standards for products in one jurisdiction may induce other jurisdictions to follow suit. For example, once the Japanese automakers had to meet the tough pollution control standards of the United States, it made a great deal of sense to apply similar standards in the Japanese market.

Product standards can, nevertheless, become barriers to trade. The requirements that a country imposes on products to be sold within its jurisdiction can be structured in ways that advantage domestic producers. If so, foreign companies will have cause for complaint. Indeed, it is the essence of the international trading system and the rules of the GATT that countries do not "discriminate" against imported products from other countries. Thus, while concerns about product-based environmental regulations being used as unfair barriers to trade arise in the trade and environment context, the issue is not fundamentally one of competitiveness.

Policy Tools to Respond to Environmental Competitiveness Concerns

Government officials have a variety of policy choices to consider in response to competitiveness concerns that arise from differential levels of environmental protection. In this section, these alternatives are described and evaluated.

The Laissez-Faire Approach

One response to the pressures created by differing degrees of environmental rigour across jurisdictions is to do nothing. In fact, many economists argue that, in general, no policy intervention is required and that the differences in standards are, as noted, simply differences in circumstances and preferences which play out in the marketplace. More dramatically, advocates of regulatory competition suggest that any attempt to mitigate or eliminate the differences in standards will reduce social welfare by eliminating a dimension of comparative advantage and thereby reducing the benefits of specialized production and trade.

If, however, the varying environmental standards do not reflect underlying differences in circumstances or the variations trigger strategic behavior in policy making and a race toward the bottom, then a laissez-faire approach to the competitiveness question is likely to yield poor results. In addition, if transboundary environmental harms exist, decentralized (country-by-country) regulation cannot be counted upon to produce optimal results. Harms (or benefits) that fall beyond the regulating authority's borders tend not to be counted, skewing the regulatory cost-benefit calculus. Thus, whenever pollution externalities are present, some form of over-arching governmental intervention will be required to avoid market failure and allocative inefficiency. At the very least, a regime that allows for the clarification and vindication of the property rights of those who suffer pollution spillovers must be established. Other regulatory regimes might be preferable depending on the significance or transaction costs in the circumstances.

Trade Restrictions

A second response to differences in environmental standards across jurisdictions would be for the governments of high-standard nations to seek to eliminate the cost differentials their companies face through trade measures. If, for example, cement produced in the United States costs 30 percent more to make because of pollution controls than the comparable product coming from Mexico (where environmental requirements are less stringent), adherents to the "level playing field" school would argue for a 30 percent "eco-duty" to be imposed on Mexican cement imports into the United States. A number of politicians and environmental groups have argued for the imposition of such eco-duties. The rationale for imposing such charges on imported goods is that any cost differential arising from lower environmental standards is unfair and amounts to a subsidy. In fact, the notion of an eco-duty arises from the well established trade concept of imposing "countervailing" duties whenever a government finds that other governments are providing their industries with subsidies that distort the prices at which a product enters the market-place.

Free traders object vehemently to the use of eco-duties, arguing that such policy instruments, far from equalizing the terms of trade, actually distort bad" relationships by eliminating the comparative advantages that lie with countries whose circumstances dictate that they follow less stringent environmental standards. This logic is sound if the lower standards derive from legitimate differences in circumstances between low-standard and high-standard countries. Thus, for example, sparsely-populated Sweden might legitimately have less strict air pollution standards for pulp mills than densely populated Germany. In this case, the Swedish comparative advantage in papermaking would derive from the fact that any emissions from pulp mill; would affect far fewer people than would comparable emissions from a plant in Germany. Under these circumstances, it could be considered unfair to the Swedish paper producer to subject it to eco-duties for its products entering Germany. Similarly, consider the position of a Mexican paper producer selling his product in the United States. Such a producer has lower costs than his American counterpart because Mexico is at a less advanced stage of development and therefore imposes less strict environmental standards. The Mexican producer's cost advantage in the United States market should be seen as a legitimate element of Mexico's comparative advantage, not unfair "eco-dumping".

If, however, low environmental standards reflect the fact that a government does not take seriously the pollution control interests of its citizenry, then the cost advantage obtained in the global marketplace should be deemed an "unfair" advantage and subject to eco-duties. A Chinese paper producer, for instance, whose capacity to keep costs down derives from the fact that Chinese environmental standards do not reflect the will of the people should not be seen to have a legitimate comparative advantage.

Harmonization

Within federal government structures, perhaps the most common response to fears about competitiveness is to mandate some form of centralized standards. For example, the United States adopted a wide range of federal environmental laws in the 1970s to respond, in part, to fears that state-by-state environmental regulation was not adequately dealing with pollution problems and that state-versus-state competition for industry was making movement toward better environmental programs difficult. Similarly, the EU has undertaken a program of developing EU-wide "environmental directives" to ensure that all members meet certain minimal environmental standards.

It is important to note that adoption of federal standards need not mean uniform standards. In fact, "harmonization" is probably a bad rubric for centrally coordinated environmental policies in so far as the term connotes a single uniform standard. Indeed, there are a great number of ways that harmonization can be undertaken, as discussed below.

Total Harmonization

Total harmonization implies uniform standards across all jurisdictions. This means that each regulating authority would implement exactly the same environmental requirements. Neither higher nor lower standards would be permitted. There are several advantages to total harmonization. First, there can be no confusion about what the rules are. Because everyone must adhere to the same standard, any deviation in performance can be easily recognized. In addition, there are likely to be some benefits to those charged with enforcing the rules in so far as they can achieve economies of scale in their regulatory activities by piggybacking on the work of others who are enforcing exactly the same requirements. In addition, there may be some administrative gains from "network effects" that arise where adherence to a common standard allows for efficiency in developing pollution control technologies, training programs, legal systems, or any other aspect of an environmental regime that would otherwise consume resources in each jurisdiction individually. Total harmonization also eliminates any possibility of competitiveness concerns or a race to the bottom across competing jurisdictions.

These advantages, however, come at what may be a high price specifically, a single standard across all jurisdictions allows for no tailoring of the requirements imposed to local needs, circumstances, or preferences. To the extent that the world is heterogeneous, single standards have a tendency to reduce welfare. Under conditions of relative homogeneity, the advantages of uniform standards might outweigh the losses that arise from ignoring diversity in conditions and values.

Minimum Standards

'Minimum standards' implies the adoption of a regulatory floor below which no jurisdiction can go. Minimum standards ensure that all governments require at least a baseline level of environmental protection from their industries. Under a program of minimum standards, jurisdictions remain free to impose higher standards if they so desire.

Minimum standards reduce environmental cost differentials across jurisdictions and therefore constrain the possibility of a race to the bottom. Indeed, game theory suggests that properly structured minimum standards may diminish strategic behavior and thereby narrow the risk that inter-jurisdictional competition will yield suboptimal environmental results. A regime of minimum standards thus allows for some tailoring of standards to meet local conditions but there is no unlimited variation in environmental requirements. Such an approach offers the promise of providing some of tile benefits of uniform standards, such as opportunities for scale economies in the administration of environmental regulations, without surrendering all of the welfare gains from having standards that match local requirements.

Maximum Standards

Maximum standards, which impose a ceiling on the stringency of environmental regulations, protect industries from the costs of facing differential standards in the various markets in which they operate. In general, maximum product standards are especially helpful in promoting freer trade, as diminished variations in product requirements facilitate the entry of companies into new markets and may reduce regulatory administration costs as well. Maximum process or PPM standards do much less to facilitate trade flows. Maximum standards also do very little to address the environmental concerns that might arise out of a competitiveness dynamic. Specifically, if countries are free to pursue standards as low as they want, there is no brake on a race to the bottom. Maximum PPM standards thus make little sense as a policy prescription in response to competitiveness concerns.

Multi-Tier Harmonization

There is another way to obtain some of the benefits of standards tailored be local conditions without losing all of the advantages of uniform requirements. This is by establishing a multi-tier regulatory regime with different standards for different groups of countries. To the extent that the most important variable determining the optimal level of environmental protection is a country's wealth and level of economic development, a system of standards that are unified for those at a comparable level of development might prove: quite valuable. One could imagine, for example, a set of environmental, standards developed for the industrialized countries (e.g., members of OECD) that would reflect quite a high degree of environmental protection. A second, set of standards, with more modest requirements, might then be developed for industrializing countries whose needs for environmental protection are great but whose capacity to afford high-level standards is limited. Finally, a baseline set of standards could be defined for countries whose economic position is so modest as to make anything more than a very limited set of environmental goals unaffordable and whose capacity to develop their own regulatory regime might be constrained.

Such a multi-tier system would provide for economies of scale and network effects among the countries within each regulatory tier. At the same time, the existence of multiple tiers would ensure that standards would be at least roughly in line with the individualized needs of countries. Such a program would also provide for the opportunity to have countries "graduate" into higher degrees of environmental protection as their economic development warrants.

Convergence

Another approach to the issue of harmonization would be to establish a system that had both minimum and maximum standards. Countries would then be free to set their standards anywhere within the established band. This would eliminate the wide variations in environmental standards that pose a risk of a race to the bottom. This "convergence" of requirements would also provide for some administrative efficiency while still permitting considerable tailoring of environmental programs to local conditions.

Van den Bergh, Faure, and LeFevere have proposed such a regulatory regime for the EU. They suggest creating an "environmental margin", within which standards may fluctuate. This would offer the best balance between the benefits of standards that are purely tailored to local conditions and the advantages of uniform controls. Specifically, Van den Bergh and his co-authors argue for broad environmental quality standards and goals to be set at the EU wide level. But each member state would determine for itself how to achieve the EU-wide target. In effect, the goals are harmonized but the implementation of specific environmental programs and the identification of precise emission standards would be decentralized.

Differentiated Harmonization

Another approach to the competitiveness dilemma is a regulatory program that sets standards centrally but not uniformly Under such a regime, central authorities would identify environmental targets but would provide for different degrees of stringency (in "time" or "level" of accomplishment) depending on the sub-jurisdiction in question. The United States uses this sort of differentiated approach in its *Clean Air Act*. Metropolitan areas are ranked based on the severity of their air pollution problems extreme, severe, serious and moderate. The more severe an area's "non-attainment" problem, the more time the jurisdiction is given to come into compliance with the national clean air goals. Under this structure, Los Angeles, for instance, has 17 extra years to meet the established national ambient air quality standards. In the international domain, the *Montreal Protocol* has more stringent requirements for developed countries than for developing countries which are permitted an extra ten years to phase out their production of ozone-depleting CECs.

Differential standards are more efficient than total harmonization, and yet the common goals ensure that wide variations in the rigour of environmental protection efforts do not persist over time. Again, this mechanism serves to balance the benefits of diverse standards set at the local level with the benefits of reduced competitiveness stresses obtained by more centralized standards.

Limited Harmonization

Another approach to harmonization is to mandate uniform requirements but only for a small number of essential environmental goals. Under such a system, uniformity across the spectrum of environmental issues would not be undertaken. Instead, common standards would be established for only the most important areas of environmental regulation. Such an approach would allow; local control over less important dimensions of the environmental policy domain but would ensure that the most critical issues are dealt with in a more systematic fashion.

Process Harmonization

The issue of divergent regulatory standards can also be approached by mandating conformity with certain established environmental processes, but not insisting that all jurisdictions adopt identical substantive standards. By guaranteeing that at least a rudimentary regulatory structure is in place, such a regime might help to reduce the number of cases where divergent standards arise from public choice failures rather than variations in local needs and conditions. In doing so, a harmonized process approach to environmental regulation would go some distance towards blunting the risk of a race to the' bottom in the environmental regulatory domain. The disadvantage of this approach is that there may be little convergence in the substantive requirements that are imposed from jurisdiction to jurisdiction on industry. As a result, wide variations in environmental compliance costs may persist and competitiveness effects may endure.

The EU's Environmental Management and Auditing System (EMAS) offers a model of process harmonization. The EMAS requirements impose basic management standards on participating companies, but do not establish any strict set of standards that must be followed. Similarly, the International Standards Organization (ISO) is developing a set of environmental management requirements (ISO 14000) which may well become a recognized baseline for environmental performance in many industries. In both of these cases, participation in the regime is voluntary.

One of the interesting questions that has already arisen in the context of process standards is who designs them. One alternative is for the standards to be designed by governments. Another approach is for the standards to emerge out of private sector negotiations. Similarly, the question of who enforces such standards is open to several alternatives. Governments might require that companies operating within their jurisdictions adhere to basic process requirements or subject companies which agree to such a program to less stringent regulation. Alternatively, companies might insist that their suppliers meet certain standards as a condition for doing business with them, using market pressures as the primary enforcement tool.

Pre-Standard Harmonization

Many of the benefits of harmonized standards can be achieved if jurisdictions coordinate their regulatory systems so that they use common testing protocols, scientific methodologies and risk assessment procedures. This type of harmonization offers the promise of substantial cost benefits for companies operating in multiple jurisdictions. For example, a pesticide maker that has met the testing requirements for selling its product in the Japanese market would then be able to bring the data used to meet the Japanese regulatory standard to the United States and have a regulatory judgement made by the United States Environment Protection Agency on the basis of the data from Japan. With adequate quality controls, such an interjurisdictional system of mutual recognition ensures that the company does not need to go through additional years of testing and proving their product. This reduces the cost and time for regulatory reviews. To the extent that one of the stumbling blocks to good environmental protection is the dearth of good scientific and analytical work on which to base regulations, ensuring that the technical efforts of one country are made available to those in other countries is an important advantage.

While achieving economies of scale in testing, such an approach offers the additional benefit or allowing individual jurisdictions to tailor their substantive standards to their own diverse needs. Thus, for example, if the pesticide in question were to be used on rice, the Japanese (who consume a great deal more rice than American citizens) might demand a substantive standard that was considerably stricter than the rice pesticide residue levels that would be permitted in the United States.

Public Information Harmonization

A final type of harmonization relates to the information that the public is provided about the environmental qualities of the products that they might purchase. If countries develop standardized approaches to delivering information to consumers, the public will benefit from being able to understand the environmental consequences of the purchasing choices they make. If a common "eco-label" is developed for products across the world, companies would not have to go through separate analyses and label development processes for each market they wish to enter. In addition, consumers would become well-versed with a specific set of environmental criteria and be better able to make environmental judgements about what kinds of products they want to buy. Such an approach to the harmonization issue does little to deal with varying substantive standards and risk of competitive pressures arising from the regulatory requirements of high-standard countries. Nevertheless, such a regime would bring market pressure to bear in favor of products offering environmental advantages that consumers find worth paying for.

If a common "eco-label" is developed for products across the world, companies would not have to go through separate analyses and label development processes for each market they wish to enter.

Mutual Recognition

Rather than agreeing to accept each other's regulatory data, countries might agree to accept into their market any product that meets the environmental requirements of another country. Although there is much talk of such a "mutual recognition" approach in Europe, the EU's environment policy does not really work on this basis. Indeed, for governments to agree to a mutual recognition scheme, they must be confident that the jurisdictions from which they are accepting products will carry out adequate environmental programmes so as to ensure that the goods being exported meet acceptable standards.

Mandatory Enforcement of Domestic Standards

A final mechanism for addressing competitiveness tensions is a rule which requires each jurisdiction to strictly enforce its own environmental standards. Such an approach allows jurisdictions to determine their own appropriate levels of environmental protection, ensuring the advantages of local tailoring of standards. At the same time, the mutual commitment to enforcement' approach provides at least a modest mechanism to blunt the risk of a race to the bottom. This structure is likely to be especially useful if the countries that are in a trading relationship have relatively similar standards but the sufficiency of enforcement has been in doubt in one or more jurisdictions.

The NAFTA adopts such an approach to the question of differential environmental standards between the United States, Mexico and Canada. American and Canadian producers (and environmentalists) feared that their products would suffer competitively in a marketplace where low-cost Mexican goods might achieve a price differential because of less stringent Mexican environmental standards. These concerns were addressed by a provision in the treaty that requires each country to strictly enforce its own environmental standards. If one country perceives that a persistent pattern of non-enforcement has arisen in another, it can complain to the trade authorities that implement the NAFTA and seek a determination that the party {ailing to uphold its environmental standards is derogating from its NAFTA obligations.

Conclusion and Policy Recommendations

Designing an international environmental regime which permits national regulations tailored to local conditions and prevents competitiveness driven strategic behaviour, or other negative effects, presents a significant policy challenge. Complete decentralization risks unleashing a race to the bottom with suboptimal standards being adopted in some, if not all, jurisdictions. Even if industries are not moving with great frequency to pollution havens, there exists a risk that competitiveness pressures arising from more open world markets will adversely affect the environmental policy making dynamic in some countries.

A wide variety of policy tools can be adopted to respond to environmental competitiveness pressures. Depending on the nature and circumstances of the problem at hand, some form of coordinated standard setting might well be appropriate. Strict harmonization would rarely be the optimal choice, but there are a great many other approaches to environmental policy convergence that offer some of the benefits of a centralized regulatory regime. These would simultaneously permit jurisdictions to maintain their comparative advantages and tailor their standards to their own needs, at least to some degree. Striking this optimal balance must be the policy-makers goal.

B

Asian Perspectives on Competitiveness Theory

(i) Vossenaar R. and Jha V., "Competitiveness: An Asian Perspective," in Tay and Esty (eds), *Asian Dragons and Green Trade,* Times Academic Press, 1996, pp 49–68

Asian developing countries are an important center of economic growth and development, fuelled largely by international trade. Dynamic export growth has contributed significantly to poverty alleviation in these countries. Economic growth has also helped to alleviate environmental problems associated with poverty and low levels of development. Alongside economic growth, however, other environmental problems have emerged. Since Asian developing countries will continue to rely heavily on exports as a major source of economic development, integrating trade, environment and developmental policies in the framework of national sustainable development objectives, is among the important challenges for countries in this region.

In developing effective strategies to achieve such integration, the relationship between environmental protection and international competitiveness is of crucial importance. First, Asian countries themselves are implementing domestic environmental measures to address environmental problems which emerge with rapid economic growth. An important aspect of any environmental policy measure, particularly in the short term, is its impact on production costs, product prices and international competitiveness. Asian developing countries thus have to find cost effective ways to move towards environmentally sound development while maintaining dynamic export growth.

Second, environmental requirements are emerging in developed countries in sectors of export interest to Asian developing countries, such as textiles, leather, furniture, footwear and other consumer goods. New trading opportunities may also arise for environmental goods and services. Asian developing countries must ensure that their industries remain competitive in the light of environmental requirements emerging from external markets. In this context it is important to note that small and medium-sized enterprises (SMEs), which tend to have more difficulties in complying with environmental requirements, account for a relatively large share of production and exports in a number of Asian developing countries.

Third, addressing global environmental problems through multilateral environmental agreements (MEAs), while yielding global environmental benefits, may have broad economic consequences. For example, in the case of the *Montreal Protocol on Substances that Deplete the Ozone Layer*, Asian developing countries have to address competitiveness effects of measures required to meet their own targets under the Agreement, as well as effects of market-driven phase-out, such as dwindling supplies of ozone-depleting substances or the shrinking international market for products using ozone depleting substance technology. The phase-out of ozone-depleting substances may require relatively large adjustments in many Asian developing countries, given their high growth rates, in particular in sectors which traditionally use ozone-depleting substances, such as refrigeration, airconditioning and electronics.

This chapter first briefly reviews how the competitiveness debate is evolving in developed countries, in particular with regard to North-South trade. It draws from studies on trade and environment linkages in selected Asian countries to identify a number of factors which may influence the competitiveness effects of environmental policies, standards and regulations on Asian developing countries. It also discusses policies and measures to address such effects, at the national and regional levels in particular.

The Competitiveness Debate in Developed Countries

The linkages between environmental policy and international competitiveness are complex. Firms and sectors gain or lose international competitiveness on account of many factors, among which environmental requirements are only one element, if a factor at all. While it is difficult to isolate environmental requirements from other elements, studies on developed countries indicate that environmental policies may have both positive and negative competitiveness effects. Impacts vary from sector to sector, and from plant to plant. In general, however, effects of existing policies have been small to the point of relatively little policy concern.

The relationship between environmental policy and competitiveness is perhaps one of the issues on which the trade and environment debate has most evolved. Originally, competitiveness concerns were seen primarily as a potential source of conflict between environmental and trade policies.

Industry was concerned that environmental policy standards and regulations would undermine their ability to compete internationally. Fear was expressed that stringent environmental regulations could result in trade and investment losses to countries where standards are less stringent or where enforcement is difficult The environmental community saw competitiveness concerns as an obstacle to the implementation of more stringent environmental standards, particularly in the context of the ongoing process of globalization and liberalization of the world economy. It was also feared that competitive deregulation would exacerbate negative environmental effects of trade liberalization. Demands for "levelling the competitive playing field" could, in particular, target dynamic export-oriented developing countries in Asia.

Analyses and debate in recent years have contributed to alleviating some of these fears, thus reducing or eliminating sources of potential conflict. For example, it has not been possible to find evidence to substantiate fears that trade liberalization negotiated under the Uruguay Round would lead to competitive deregulation and a race to the bottom in environmental standards; or that polluting industries would relocate to countries with lower environmental stringency.

Studies carried out in Asian developing countries also contributed to correcting the wrong perception that differences in environmental standards across countries would result in "unfair" competitiveness advantages for companies in developing countries or other countries where costs of compliance with environmental standards are relatively low. It is now widely believed that "eco-dumping" is not an issue. For example, studies have pointed out that there is no rational ground for developing countries to base development strategies on artificially low environmental standards. Also, several studies have shown the important role that international trade can play in the dissemination of environmental standards worldwide, thus contributing to a greater convergence of such standards across countries. Indeed, companies in developing countries that sell in external markets where environmental requirements are stringent tend to make relatively larger investments in environmental management than companies that operate predominantly in the domestic market. Thus, companies tend to raise rather than lower environmental standards when they enter international markets.

The question now arises in developed countries whether competitiveness effects of environmental policies is a policy issue at all.

An encouraging development is that governments have taken a strong view against the use of trade-restrictive measures to address differences in costs arising from differences in environmental standards across countries. At the United Nations Conference on Trade and Development (UNCTAD) and the Commission on Sustainable Development, developing countries have joined Organization for Economic Co-operation and Development (OECD) governments in firmly rejecting "demands sometimes made to introduce so-called 'green countervailing duties', or other protectionist or WTO inconsistent trade measures, to compensate for negative competitiveness effects, whether real or perceived, of environmental policies".

The question now arises in developed countries whether competitiveness effects of environmental policies is a policy issue at all. First, the implications for international competitiveness of environmental policies are no different in principle from those of other policies which also differ across nations, including social or welfare policies.

Second, as mentioned above, empirical studies in developed countries show that existing environmental standards on average have had only small effects on production costs. A dynamic approach to analyzing the linkages between environmental policies and competitiveness tends to emphasize the fact that properly designed environmental standards may induce innovation, resulting in cost savings which may at least partially offset the costs of compliance. According to the "Porter hypothesis", well-designed environmental policies can even improve competitiveness at the company levels Also, companies may be able to pass on costs to consumers or may even gain price premiums in "green" niche markets.

Third, to the extent that environmental policies aim at correcting existing market and policy failures, resulting changes in competitiveness at the company or sector level and consequently in production patterns can be seen as desirable and welfare-enhancing. Thus, according to some, the important issue is not competitiveness, but the concept of national welfare.

Fourth, it is contended that since successful companies have a broad-based capacity to respond to market changes, including environmental regulatory processes, competitiveness effects do not necessarily require policy action. In any case, government and industry can work together to shape environmental policies in a manner that removes strong negative impacts on competitiveness.

The above would indicate that competitiveness effects of environmental policies currently do not appear to be a major policy issue in developed countries. A debate may again emerge if compliance costs with environmental policies, in particular those addressing global environmental problems, become more significant. For example, increased efforts to avert the problem of global warming may have strong trade and competitiveness effects.

The Experience of Asian Developing Countries

For developing countries, the major concern in relation to the competitiveness effects of environmental policies, is how these policies impinge on their development process. As mentioned above, one of the major challenges for Asian countries in the field of trade and environment is to find complementarily between export-led growth and environmentally sound development, in accordance with national sustainable development Objectives. International competitiveness is of key importance in this context.

So far, systematic empirical studies on environment-related competitiveness effects have focused on assessing the impacts of domestic environmental measures on domestic industries in developed countries. One of the first attempts to analyze trade and environment linkages in developing countries is being undertaken in the context of the UNCTAD/UNDP and UNCTAD/UNEP country case studies. Other studies on developing countries have been undertaken or are under way elsewhere. In the Asian region, both the secretariats of the Association of Southeast Asian Nations (ASEAN) and the Economic and Social Commission for Asia and the Pacific (ESCAP) are undertaking country case studies on trade and environment linkages and preliminary results of these studies are now becoming available.

In order to examine the relationship between environmental policy, competitiveness and development, three kind of linkages can be distinguished for analytical purposes:

(1) domestic environmental policies and competitiveness,

(2) trade and competitiveness effects of external environmental requirements, and

(3) competitiveness effects of MEAs.

Domestic Environmental Policies

In Asian developing countries there has been considerable progress in alleviating environmental problems which are primarily related to poverty or to a low level of economic development. In several countries, such as Malaysia, investment in infrastructure, carried out as part of national development policies, has alleviated a number of environmental problems. For example, household water supply and sanitation facilities have improved significantly. With economic growth, however, some environmental problems tend to intensify. For example, agricultural activities and agro-based industries may contribute to water pollution. Air pollution has become a matter of concern, especially in large urban areas. More recently, rapid industrialization is generating large volumes of solid waste in several Asian countries. Asian countries have enacted important domestic regulations to address emerging environmental problems and to improve the management of natural resources.

Perhaps the most fundamental economic consequence of any environmental management or control measure is the immediate impact on the cost of production, product prices and international competitiveness. Any such impact will initially be felt within specific sectors. The effects of environmental policies on trade and export competitiveness depends to a large extent on the ability to pass the costs of pollution control on to product prices.

Case studies show that in highly competitive markets, such as palm oil, it is difficult to incorporate even small increases in production costs into export prices. In other sectors, such as consumer electronics, however, it is more likely that the costs of pollution control can be incorporated into export prices.

In this context, it is worth noting, as the World Commission on Environment and Development has done, that developing countries have often been less successful than developed countries in ensuring that export prices reflect environmental costs and resource values. There is thus a need to strengthen capacity in developing countries to become more competitive in international markets while at the same time developing production and export capacities in a sustainable manner.

Linkages between domestic environmental policy and competitiveness are analyzed in a number of studies undertaken in Asian countries. A macro-economic study on the Philippines indicates that, by and large, pollution abatement could be achieved without substantially increasing costs in most industries. In some sectors, however, international competitiveness could be affected significantly. In the case of forest and wood-based industries, which are already non-competitive, pollution abatement would further decrease competitiveness. Thus, according to the study, imports of wood were desirable to reduce resource pressure and encourage domestic wood processing. According to the study, internalizing environmental costs could also affect international competitiveness in the textile sector.

These results must be qualified, however. The study on the Philippines itself, as well as other studies, indicate that SMEs are more likely to have difficulties in complying with the regulations. This may be mainly because economies of scale are significant in environmental investments. In addition, unlike large firms for which internally generated sources of financing tend to be available, SMEs may find it difficult to gain access to capital for environmental investments due to low or negative private returns. Hence, according to the study, there is a need to grant more leeway to smaller companies in the course of enforcing regulations on domestic industry as a whole.

An analysis of Malaysia's experience indicates that strategies aimed at poverty eradication and economic development can be fully compatible with efforts to improve the quality of life through environmental management. A study by the Malaysian Institute for Strategic International Studies shows that, in the case of Malaysia, improved environmental protection and increased pollution control are being achieved simultaneously with high rates of export led economic growth. The study attributes this to several factors, such as the emphasis on technology development and the close cooperation between government and industry. This has enabled the Department of Environment to enact cost-effective environmental regulations, for example, by allowing variation in domestic environmental standards in different areas and at different times.

Environmental Requirements from External Markets

Export-oriented firms in developing countries may also need to adjust to environmental requirements emerging from external markets in order to sell in these markets. While in many cases the effects of environmental policies on trade may be similar to or exacerbate those arising from constantly changing conditions in the marketplace such as changes in technology, consumer preferences, price and availability of raw materials, it can be argued that in many aspects environmental requirements are different from other factors, such as product quality or fashion. For example, environmental requirements, especially those related to production and process methods (PPMs), may be based on value judgements, and pressure groups may be especially vocal on issues of environmental protection, even outside their own countries. Examples can be found with regard to tropical timber. In addition, importers often require their foreign suppliers to comply with certain PPM-related requirements.

Fears are sometimes expressed that gains arising from trade liberalization in certain sectors could be eroded if compliance with environmental requirements were to lead to cost increases or discrimination against their exports. Developing countries are in particular concerned that environmental requirements may be used for protectionist purposes.

An analysis of trade flows shows that there are some grounds for such concerns in the case of Asian developing countries. Environmental policies and consumer concerns in developed countries are to a large extent sector specific, affecting such sectors as fishery and forestry products, leather and footwear, textiles and clothing, and certain consumer products. A number of product requirements, such as bans on the use of specific chemicals, packaging regulations and eco-labelling, apply to these sectors. A preliminary analysis indicates that, on average, about one-third of the value of total exports and about half of the value of manufactured exports of developing countries originate in sectors where environmental requirements would be emerging. This may be particularly relevant for Asian developing countries, since over 60 percent of their manufacturing exports, in value terms, originates in such Sectors. For example, textiles and electronics account for a high share of Asian exports to developed countries.

Also, the comparative advantage of developing countries has largely been their ability to sell standardized mass-produced products at low prices, which also explains their concern about environmental standards and requirements. Product differentiation is low in the case of homogenous products, and producers generally find it difficult to recover increased costs owing to environmental improvements through price premiums. In addition, since the home demand for "environmentally friendly" products may be insignificant, the domestic market generally does not allow companies to recover incremental costs.

Furthermore, a number of studies have pointed out that adapting to environmental standards may be especially difficult for SMEs in specific sectors, for example, the leather and footwear industries as well as the textile and garment sectors. This is largely because, for small and spatially dispersed producers, common effluent treatment is not a realistic option and therefore environmental standards can result in higher costs. Even in cases where common effluent treatment is technically feasible, its costs may be prohibitive. Finally, the variable cost component of complying with environmental standards is high. For example, in the leather tanning sector in India, the costs of chemicals required to meet international standards were approximately three times higher than the costs of conventional chemicals.

Where external environmental requirements are different from domestic requirements, transaction costs may arise if companies have to manufacture different products for the domestic and external markets. If exports are significant, governments may introduce domestic regulations which are similar to external regulations. Win-win situations may exist where environmental policies can induce both improved environmental management and increased export competitiveness. A study on India recommends that governments should take proactive stands, in particular where domestic environmental concerns coincide with those in major export markets. The Indian government has already intervened in the case of benzidine content in dyes and pesticide usage in tea and other agricultural products.

A different situation arises if compliance with external environmental requirements, while entailing significant costs, is of limited environmental benefit to the country of production. Here, incurring such costs may be a good investment from a commercial point of view—that is, to maintain export markets—but may yield inferior results from an environmental point of view compared to other investments. For example, a study on the Philippines suggests that a dollar invested in industrial pollution abatement is expected to contribute less to environmental improvement than a dollar invested in basis infrastructure, such as sewerage and drainage systems. A study on India also points out that, at times, there may be trade-offs between addressing domestic environmental concerns and investments in specific environments improvements in response to requirements emerging from external markets

There has been some debate on whether environmental requirement emerging from developed country markets are already affecting developing country exports A few remarks should be made here. First, relatively stringent environmental requirements are emerging only in specific markets and in specific sectors. Even within these sectors, competitiveness effects tend to vary in accordance with many factors. Therefore, one should not expect that environmental requirements have generalized effects on market access and export competitiveness. Such requirements, however, may have more significant effects in specific sectors. For example, environmental requirements are becoming increasingly important for Indian textile exports.

Environmental requirements should not be expected to have generalized effects on market access or export competitiveness. A number of Asian developing countries, however, have experienced specific cases which have received a considerable amount of attention, and which could be considered as high profile cases in the trade and environment debate. These include a German ban on leather and leather products containing pentachlorophenol, affecting India in particular; an Austrian eco-label for tropical timber affecting Indonesia, Malaysia and other Asian countries, and boycotts directed against tropical timber originating in Malaysia, Thailand and other countries.

Competitiveness Effects of MEAs

Consideration must also be given to the competitiveness and development effects of policy harmonization in the context of MEAs. The costs of standard Implementation may differ widely among parties to an MEA based on variables such as the specificity of the standard, the availability and adequacy of substitutes, the degree of patent protection of specified technologies, existing environmental standards prior to the implementation of the international standard, administrative costs and other factors. Standard implementation in the framework of MEAs shows that the same environmental standards may not eve similar competitiveness effects across all countries and situations. Unlike domestic environmental policies, which have focused on the competitiveness effects of differing standards across countries, analysis of implementation pursuant to MEAs can provide a better understanding of the effects of factors such as the levels of national development.

An example of this is the implementation of the *Montreal Protocol* to phase out ozone-depleting substances. Studies on India and the Republic of Korea indicate that the trade and competitiveness effects of ozone-depleting substance phase-out may be large. A study on Malaysia, however, suggests a phase-out of ozone-depleting substances has had relatively little effect trade and competitiveness. This can be attributed to a number of factors:

(1) The strong cooperation between the Government and industry has helped identify cost-effective approaches for the phase-out of ozone-depleting substances, based on the incorporation of sector-specific elements into a national strategy;
(2) The use of a combination of approaches in setting industry phase-out targets, including regulations, voluntary measures, investment incentives and capacity-building;
(3) Technological development;
(4) The structure of industries using ozone-depleting substances, in particular the predominance of affiliates of transnational corporations; and
(5) International finance provided by the Multilateral Fund under the *Montreal Protocol.*

The Multilateral Fund of the *Montreal Protocol* provides a financial mechanism to assist developing countries in meeting their obligations and in acquiring new technologies. Technically, the Multilateral Fund should meet the full incremental costs of phase-out by developing countries, but these costs are hard to define and beneficiary countries have had to bear at least some of the cost. Another question is whether the Fund is sufficient to meet the needs of Asian developing countries. It is to be noted that there is no fixed size of the Multilateral Fund, and Article 10 would imply that funds will be made available to cover the agreed incremental costs of Article 5 developing countries. Financial commitments under the Multilateral Fund are considered by some studies to be inadequate.

With regard to the promotion of access to and transfer of technology, the *Montreal Protocol*, in Article 10A, contains provisions to encourage the transfer of substitutes and related technologies to developing countries under fair and most favorable terms. Although it is difficult to determine the magnitude of technological transfer to developing countries, the majority of companies which have actually received new technology were either foreign joint venture partners or subsidiaries of transnational corporations. A number of Asian developing countries feel that the relationship between the WTO *Agreement on Trade-Related Aspects of Intellectual Property Rights* (TRIPs) and the transfer of environmentally friendly technology is an important issue, requiring further examination. This issue is being raised, for example, in the context of the transfer of ozone-friendly technology under fair and most favorable terms.

Asian countries could examine ways and means to facilitate the implementation of the *Montreal Protocol*, for example, through incentives that encourage trade in environmentally friendly substitutes, voluntary mechanisms on foreign direct investment (FDI), technology transfer and market-based instruments. With regard to FDI, for example, according to a recent UNEP report, many Japanese, North American and European automobile, chemical, consumer product, electronics and petroleum companies pledged to help the Government of Vietnam to protect the ozone layer by investing only in modern, environmentally friendly technology in their Vietnam projects.

Another example is Thailand, which is encouraging subsidiaries of multinational companies operating in Thailand to phase out ozone-depleting substances technology at the same rate as in their home countries or elsewhere. Subsidiaries of transnational corporations and joint ventures are major users of ozone depleting substances in Thailand. A recent study indicates that transnational corporations and joint ventures account for up to 97 percent of the consumption of solvents (which constitute 40 percent of Thailand's consumption of CFCs). A large part of a recent increase in the use of ozone depleting substances in Thailand was reportedly attributed to a rapid expansion of Japanese, European and United States companies operating wholly-owned subsidiaries or joint ventures with Thai companies, lending some support to the proposition that certain production based on ozone depleting substances technology may have relocated to Thailand. The measures adopted by the Thai government would be aimed at halting such development.

Factors Determining Competitiveness Effects of Environmental Policies, Standards and Regulations

In developing countries, particularly the least developed among them, several factors may adversely affect competitiveness, such as lack of information, access to inputs and technology, finance and infrastructure. Other areas of concern to developing countries include the sectoral composition of their exports and their typically undiversified export baskets; the important role of SMEs in exports; the emergence of new environmental requirements in sectors of export interest to developing countries; the low domestic demand for environmentally friendly products; and the homogenous nature of exports and the price-taker position of developing countries that make any cost increases critical.

For analytical purposes, factors that may have an important bearing on the effects of environmental policies on competitiveness could perhaps be classified as follows:

(1) company or sector specific factors,
(2) development policies,
(3) macro-economic policies, and
(4) regional and international cooperation. These issues are set out in more detail below.

Company or Sector Specific Factors

Among the many company or sector-specific factors influencing competitiveness effects are the following: destination of exports; cost structures; basis for export competitiveness; company size; availability of raw materials, specialized inputs, technology and information; and relationship with foreign companies.

Destination of Exports

Environmental requirements vary largely across different markets. Studies show that Asian exports may face stringent environmental requirements for food products in all developed country markets, including Japan and the United States. More stringent environmental requirements for manufactured products, such as textiles, leather and furniture tend to emerge in particular in European markets, such as Germany and the Netherlands. Any competitiveness effects thus depend on the destination of exports. Apart from compliance cost, there may be transaction costs if environmental requirements differ between different export markets.

Cost Structures

The competitiveness effects of increased environmental compliance costs will depend on the share of corresponding cost categories in total production costs. This may affect low value-added products. For example, packaging requirements may have more significant effects on certain fruit and vegetables than on high value-added products. In the case of commodities, a large proportion of total costs is accounted for by the cost of raw materials. Thus environmental policies affecting raw material costs may have significant competitiveness effects.

A case in point is textiles. A number of environmental requirements refer to dyes and chemicals. A study on India estimates that, on average, raw materials, of which dyes are a significant proportion, represent around 60 percent of the cost of production. Thus, switching to more expensive environmentally friendly dyes may have a significant bearing on production costs. In this context, it is to be noted that while benzidine dyes cost only US$3 per kilo, non-benzidine dyes were priced at US$8-10 per kilo. Some of this cost difference can be passed on to the export prices.

Basis for Export Competitiveness

Complying with environmental regulations frequently results in increased production costs, at least in the short term. This may make the product less competitive in segments of the international market where competition is based largely on the ability to sell at low prices, particularly if the prices of competing products are not increased similarly. It is to be noted that in many Asian developing countries, international competitiveness is based largely on price.

If export competitiveness is based on price, environmental policies that lead to cost increases are more likely to have an adverse impact on competitiveness. For homogenous products, product differentiation on the basis of environmental quality with a view to obtaining price premiums may be more difficult.

Company Size

Perhaps the most important conclusion from studies undertaken so far is that in general it is more difficult for small companies to comply with environmental regulations and standards, both domestic and external, than it is for large companies. The constraints faced by SMEs in meeting environmental standards and regulations can be divided into two categories:

(1) those which are endemic to the nature of their operation, and

(2) those which can be specifically linked to environmental requirements.

The first category includes factors such as poorer access to information, raw materials, capital and technology. The second category includes constraints such as the fact that the economic use of environmentally sound technologies may require a minimum scale of operation, often beyond that of small companies. Environmental policies may thus need to address the concerns of small companies specially.

Availability of Raw Materials, Specialized Inputs, Technology and Information

The availability of raw materials, inputs, technology and information is of key importance for the production of "environmentally friendly" products. For example, complying with environmental requirements in the textile and footwear sectors poses special conditions on dyes and leather. Required input materials may often be several times more expensive than conventional materials. While large firms may be in a position to use their economic power to obtain special inputs at prices which are more in line with those of conventional materials, SMEs normally face difficulties in obtaining the required inputs at competitive prices. Thus, maintaining international competitiveness may require attention to be given to the relationship between manufacturers/exporters of final products and producers of intermediate products. Government policies towards the intermediate product sectors may also have to be addressed.

The availability of raw materials, inputs, technology and information is of key importance for the production of "environmentally friendly" products.

Relationship with Foreign Companies

Companies that have links with foreign companies often find it easier to comply with environmental requirements. The strong presence of subsidiaries of transnational corporations in many Asian developing countries should contribute to high environmental management standards in these countries. Governments should ensure, including through regional cooperation, that subsidiaries of transnational corporations and joint ventures use the most environmentally sound technologies.

Development Policies

In many Asian countries, development and industrial policies have played an important role in achieving high rates of growth in production and exports, as well as a larger degree of export diversification, for example by promoting technological development and competitiveness. In a number of countries, such as Malaysia and the Republic of Korea, the government plays a relatively large role in setting development objectives and defining strategies for their achievement, even though market forces play an essential role in ensuring allocative efficiency within the framework of industrial development plans. Government policies to support private sector-led growth, for example, through support for research and development, facilitate the ability of firms to respond to environmental challenges. The traditional close cooperation and coordination between government and the private sector in many Asian countries, including Japan, may be one reason why the relationship between environmental policy and international competitiveness may be considered more as an issue of policy concern in these countries, as compared to Europe or the United States, where this relationship may be considered more as a sectoral or company-level issue, than a policy issue.

Infrastructural Development

Improvements in environmental infrastructure play an important role in reducing the cost of compliance, particularly for small companies. Improved infrastructure can reduce the cost of compliance with effluent standards. For example, the electronics industry generates a considerable amount of waste. The Malaysian government has decided to build an Integrated Scheduled Waste Treatment and Disposal Facility, which is managed by a consortium of companies. It started receiving waste for storage in July 1996 and is expected to be fully operational by June 1998.

Testing and Certification

Certification of environmentally friendly products may be costly, in particular when producers in developing countries depend on testing and certification bodies in the developed countries. The establishment of standardization bodies—or expansion of existing bodies—in Asian developing countries is of key importance. Countries such as Malaysia are encouraging the development of certification bodies, including for ISO 14000.

Capacity for Innovation

Whether firms can find innovative and cost-saving responses to environmental requirements determines whether compliance costs can be offset or even competitiveness improvements gained. To promote innovation, governments can either provide broad enabling conditions for innovation, or take a more active part in fostering innovation.

The Institute for Strategic International Studies study on Malaysia stresses that the central role of technology within Malaysia's development strategy is vital for environmentally sustainable economic growth. The acquisition of efficient technologies through foreign direct investment and through domestic research and development by both industry and the government is providing necessary technological know-how. Technological progress has been strongly encouraged by the government's development policy.

Cooperation Between Government and Industry

Cooperation of industry with the authorities in the standard-setting process can ensure the design of feasible standards and facilitate their implementation. Cooperation between government and the private sector has been mentioned as one of the factors explaining Malaysia's success in finding cost-effective solutions for environmental problems. For example, strong cooperation between the government and industry has helped to identify cost-effective approaches for the phase-out of ozone-depleting substances, based on the incorporation of sector-specific elements into a national strategy.

Technical Cooperation

Technical cooperation between developed and developing countries can play an important role in assisting companies in developing countries to adjust to environmental requirements. For example, technical assistance provided by Germany has helped Indian leather exporters to eliminate the use of PCP in leather tanning.

Dissemination of information

Developing country exporters often lack timely and precise information about emerging environmental standards and regulations in their export markets. In addition, increased awareness of new environmental standards and regulations and consumer preferences for "green" products is of crucial importance. This includes the ability to recognize trends in consumer preferences and to adjust to them through changes in product design and marketing policies.'

Capacity-building efforts could focus on the identification of sources of information on product standards and regulations in external markets, as well as the establishment of information systems for exporters. Experience indicates that larger companies tend to cooperate with each other, for example, in the exchange of information on existing and emerging environmental requirements in external markets. SMEs tend to have more difficulties in obtaining information and in adjusting to environmental requirements in external markets. Capacity-building efforts may help promote a process whereby the know-how and experience acquired by larger companies is transmitted to smaller companies.

Macro-Economic Policies

To a large extent, integrating trade and environment policies while maintaining international competitiveness requires sustained economic growth and sound macro-economic and environmental policies. An important challenge for Asian developing countries is to build on the synergies between broad economic reform and improved environmental management. A recent study proposes that sustainable development strategies in developing countries will increasingly have to rely on domestic sources of financing, which have to be generated through policies in many areas. The strong commitment of Asian developing countries to sustained economic growth and openness through the promotion of trade and investment, together with improved environmental management, are key elements of their sustainable development strategies.

Sustained economic growth

The competitiveness effects of environmental policies in the case of developing countries are to a large extent determined by the ability of the country to trade and to grow; stagnant economies being less able to implement environmental standards. Such economic growth should be seen to imply not more of the same kind of goods, but cleaner products produced with cleaner processes. Furthermore, growth allows negative effects in some sectors to be compensated elsewhere.

Openness of the economy

The more open and dynamic the economy, the greater is the exposure of companies to environmental requirements. However, openness also tends to provide better conditions to adapt to environmental requirements because o f easier availability of information, inputs and technologies. Economic openness may also induce industrial restructuring, and the need to reduce production costs may adversely affect environmentally obsolete industries while resulting in environmental improvements in other industries.

Conclusion

The debate on environmental policies and competitiveness seems inconclusive at the present time. The dominant view in the developed countries appears to be that, at their existing levels, environmental policies are unlikely to have significant adverse effects on trade and competitiveness, and that their effects can even be positive. Currently, competitiveness effects of environmental policies would not be of great policy concern. Future impacts, however, may be different if the level of environmental protection is significantly raised.

The developing countries, for their part, are concerned about the implications for international competitiveness and development of environmental policies, including measures required to meet the targets of MEAs. They continue to be particularly concerned that environmental policies, particularly when they are based on requirements related to PPMs, may affect market access or be used for protectionist purposes.

There are many factors determining the competitiveness effects of domestic and external environmental policies, standards and regulations. An examination of these factors, in particular structure of exports and firm size, indicates that, in principle, Asian developing countries may be relatively more vulnerable to external environmental requirements than other developing regions. However, the competitiveness effects of environmental policies can be mitigated by appropriate policies and measures at the national and international levels. Asian developing countries should strive to ensure that existing market access conditions are not eroded by emerging environmental policies, standards and regulations and that they take advantage of new trading opportunities in environmental goods and services.

Many countries in Asia have been successful in achieving high export growth rates while moving towards improved environmental management. With regard to policies and measures at the national level, the following can be highlighted:

- Successful policies aimed at enterprise development and the promotion of competitiveness;
- Government policies aimed at promoting technology development, infrastructure, and cooperation with the private sector in finding cost-effective solutions for environmental problems; and
- Asia's sustained economic growth and economic openness.

Many countries in Asia have been successful in achieving high export growth rates while moving towards improved environmental management.

Certain policies and measures could be developed at the regional level, for example, in the areas of technological development, product harmonization, the establishment or further development of testing and certification bodies, the promotion of environmentally friendly raw materials, such as dyes, and coordination of approaches to FDI with a view to ensuring access to and transfer of environmentally sound technologies.

Multilateral deliberations and negotiations, in particular in the WTO, have important impacts on the international economic and legal context in which developing countries and countries with economies in transition can frame their domestic policies for sustainable development. Developing countries must utilize these deliberations to ensure that environmental measures do not unnecessarily erode some of the market access opportunities expected from trade liberalization. They could do that by supporting a process aimed at building consensus on principles and propositions and designing positive measures. Principles for consensus are needed on the interface of trade, environment and development. These include adequate transparency, the consideration of potentially less trade restrictive measures to achieve the environmental objective, attention for special conditions and development needs of developing countries, exploring concepts such as mutual recognition and equivalencies, as well as common but differentiated responsibility for addressing global environmental problems. The positive measures developing countries should look to include improved market access, improved access to finance, transition mechanisms, access to and transfer of technology, capacity building and special provisions for SMEs. These would assist developing countries in achieving sustainable development objectives, including the multilaterally agreed targets of MEAs.

(ii) Ewing K.P. and Tarasofsky R.G., *The Trade & Environment Agenda: Survey of Major Issues and Proposals—From Marrakesh to Singapore*, IUCN, Gland, Switzerland and Cambridge, UK, 1997, pp 23–26

Environmental Measures with Trade Effects

[The following materials will examine "the relationship between environmental policies relevant to trade and environmental measures with significant trade effects and the provisions of the multilateral trading system."]

Summary of Issues

Discussions in the CTE under this heading have largely been exploratory so far, to identify environmental measures indirectly affecting trade and, similarly, to identity the effects of trade on environmental protection policies. Several issues have received some scrutiny so far, including "pollution havens" and "green countervailing duties", "take-back" and recycled content obligations, as well as more general questions of how trade and environmental policies interact.

Pollution Havens

Although not environmental measures themselves, pollution havens arise when States intentionally maintain lower environmental standards or enforcement policies to attract investment. More generally, discussions about pollution havens concern the possibility that countries may suffer competitively if they adopt stricter environmental policies. A widely cited OECD study in 1991 suggests that pollution havens may not be a common phenomenon, although the OECD has recognized that its research has not covered all sectors. According to the study, environmental costs make up only a small proportion of most industries' costs. There is little evidence of significant movement by industries from States with stricter environmental standards and enforcement to States with less strict standards or enforcement, although some movement may be occurring in some industries, such as textiles and leather tanning, more heavily affected by environmental controls. Several other academic studies have reached similar conclusions. Some commentators have pointed out, however, that these studies have focused largely on the costs of abating industrial pollution, without taking into account other environment-related costs such as for complying with workplace health and safety or industrial zoning requirements. Nor do they appear to account for the costs of strict protection for the natural resources used in production but not passed along as components of consumer prices, because the product is a commodity. The studies are also based on historical averages, which fail to reflect the great costs in certain sectors and do not take adequate account of the likely rise in environmental costs as the less costly technical measures are exhausted. Thus one analyst has noted that industrial migration may become more significant if *e.g.* fossil fuel consumption is restricted to control greenhouse gas emissions. The OECD and others are continuing to conduct further research into the consequences of environmental regulation on the relative competitiveness of States.

Green Countervailing Duties

One possible response to pollution havens is to impose "green countervailing duties" on imports from pollution havens. Such duties would be additional import duties on products found to be produced under lax environmental requirements. The theory is that such duties can force producers to internalize the true environmental costs of production. At the very least it is argued such duties can minimize the commercial disadvantage that domestic industries suffer when competing with imports from manufacturers subject to less strict environmental controls. In this view they make stricter domestic environmental controls an economic and political possibility. Many have argued however, that determining what the appropriate level of environmental protection should be and translating that level into the costs that should be borne by the imports is an extremely difficult task involving many subjective judgments and hence rife with the potential for protectionist abuse. Some have also contended that the entire theory of attempting to equalize the costs of environmental regulation would undermine the very basis for international trade—i.e., comparative advantage.

Take Back and Recycled Content Obligations

Certain new environmental measures have also been the subject of discussion among them take-back and recycled content obligations. Take-back-obligations generally require manufacturers to provide a mechanism by which consumers of their products may return to the manufacturer certain materials associated with their products. Such obligations have been applied to a wide range of materials such as waste oil, packaging or CFCs. Their purposes also vary. For instance, obligations to take back CFCs in consumer products and to provide technical services for handling them are intended to ensure that CFCs are not released into the environment but are re-used or disposed of properly. Take-back obligations for waste oil achieve similar ends. More generally, by forcing byproducts back into the hands of manufacturers, take-back obligations shift to manufacturers some of the costs of handling and disposing of the byproducts, providing a disincentive to incorporating them in the end product to begin with.

The added costs of take-back programs can disproportionately burden imports. As was argued before the European Court of Justice in the *Danish Bottles Case* (see below The *Danish Bottles Case*), higher transportation costs generally make it more costly for importers to reclaim returned materials than for domestic producers to do so. The materials subject to the obligation, such as drink containers, may also need to be strengthened to withstand the increased use and shipping, further increasing transportation and materials costs. To arrange for taking back returned materials, foreign suppliers may even be required to establish a larger, more permanent presence in the market imposing the take-back obligation than would otherwise be warranted by their market share. In addition, environmental conditions and technical expertise in the producing State may differ from those justifying the take-back obligation in the State imposing them. All of these greater burdens on importers result in higher costs for them and can effectively pose a barrier to smaller producers, particularly in developing countries.

Recycled content obligations can pose problems for foreign suppliers similar to those posed by take-back obligations. Examples include the obligation to include a minimum amount of recycled paper in newsprint or a minimum amount of recycled plastic or glass in beverage containers. Like take-back obligations, recycled content obligations are generally intended to ensure that less of the material at issue is produced. Foreign suppliers, however, may be unable to secure adequate quantities of the recycled materials in their home State, forcing them to incur the added costs of importing them.

If the only source of such recycled materials is the State imposing the obligation, the obligation may also constitute a violation of the GATT Article III:5 obligation not to maintain quantitative regulations requiring that a specified proportion of a product be supplied from domestic sources. Manufacturers may also be forced to make costly changes to manufacturing processes to handle the recycled materials. These costs can pose a barrier to producers with smaller market shares, such as smaller producers or producers supplying several markets not all of which impose similar recycled content requirements.

Other Issues

In addition to considering environmental measures with trade effects. Discussions have begun to address more general questions about the effect of trade rules on environmental protection policies and *vice versa.* Questions being asked in the CTE include:

- Should trade rules, such as the principle of non-discrimination. be modified in light of environmental principles, such as the Producer Pays Principle or the Precautionary Approach? Conversely, should trade rules insist upon different principles, such as "sound science" in addition to or instead of environmental principles?
- Should the WTO establish common understandings on how such concepts as "necessity", "effectiveness", "least trade-restrictiveness" and "proportionality" apply to environmental policies?
- Do trade rules permit a sufficiently wide range of policy options to address environmental concerns? For instance, do they permit cost internalization and environmental instruments based on PPMs?
- Do trade rules contribute to non-sustainable production and consumption patterns? Should the Subsidies Agreement, for instance, be modified to address environmentally detrimental energy or agricultural subsidies?

The Danish Bottles Case

In the 1988 *Danish Bottles Case,* the European Court of Justice considered a challenge to Danish regulations that required both domestic and foreign suppliers of beer and soft drinks to use returnable and recyclable containers in shapes approved by the Danish National Agency for the Protection of the Environment. The regulations effectively required the use of glass containers. Importers complained that the regulations disproportionately burdened them because glass containers weighed more and. hence. cost more to transport, than other materials; higher transportation costs meant that compliance with the take-back obligation cost importers more; and being forced to use approved shapes hindered importers' ability to use distinctive bottle designs in competing with domestic suppliers. Denmark modified the law to exempt suppliers of less than 3,000 hectoliters per year from the shape-authorization requirements. Unsatisfied, the European Commission sued Denmark before the European Court of Justice for a declaration that the regulations constituted a measure having an effect equivalent to that of a quantitative restriction, in violation of Article 30 of the Treaty of Rome establishing the European Economic Community.

The Judge Advocate General, an official associated with the Court to provide it with an unbiased legal analysis and recommendation, agreed that Denmark's objective to preserve its environment by reducing the amount of waste to be disposed of in the country could justify the regulations in principle. In practice, however, both the take-back and the shape-authorization requirements were disproportionate to the burdens they caused on trade and should be declared a violation.

The European Court of Justice agreed only partially. It found that protection of the environment could be an adequate justification not only in principle, but also in fact for the mandatory take-back obligations. Of special significance was the Court's ruling that environmental protection was a mandatory objective of the Community, even in the absence of express language to this effect in the Treaty of Rome at the time. Accordingly, the Court concluded that the mandatory take-back obligations were a necessary element of the system and hence necessary to achieve the environmental aims being pursued The Court agreed with the Advocate General, however, that the added burden of requiring approval of container shapes was disproportionate to any environmental harms that might he caused by allowing an unlimited number of containers to be used, since these would still be required to be returnable and recyclable. The Court concluded that the take-back obligation did not violate the Treaty of Rome, but the ban on sales without official authorization of the container did violate the Treaty.

The *Danish Bottles Case* stands as a recognition that environmental objectives may justify burdening trade, but the trade restrictions must be proportionate to the environmental aims.

Summary of Proposals

Concrete proposals for addressing the issues discussed under this heading within the international trade regime have not yet been made. Instead, further study of the possible environmental measures is underway. Some general proposals have also been made, including the following:

To minimize trade effects of strong domestic environmental legislation, Switzerland has suggested increasing technical assistance to developing countries, increasing the role of the ISO, and considering how WTO provisions regarding special and differential treatment of developing countries might be used.

The United States has suggested that the WTO endorse *ex post* environmental reviews of trade agreements by member governments. The WTO Secretariat could collect and publish both the results and the methodologies of such reviews.

India has expressed interest in elaborating on the application to environmental policy of the trade concepts of MFN, national treatment, transparency, necessity, effectiveness, least trade-restrictiveness, and proportionality, as well as the environmental principle of common but differentiated responsibility and the trade concept of special and differentiated treatment of developing countries. It also suggested that the WTO CTE monitor TREMs, particularly unilateral measures with extra-territorial application.

Summary of CTE Recommendations

The CTE's report on Item 2 of its agenda included the following:

- "Further examination and analysis of [trade-related environmental policies and measures not covered elsewhere in the work program] will be required, including analysis of their effects on trade."
- "There has also been some discussion of the use by governments at the national level of environmental reviews of trade agreements, and of the relationship and compatibility of general trade and environmental policy making principles.... Further work will be required on this Item in the CTE."

Charges & Taxes and Packaging, Labelling, and Other Product Standards

[The following material will examine] "the relationship between the provisions of the multilateral trading system and: (a) charges and taxes for environmental purposes [and] (b) requirements for environmental purposes relating to products, including standards and technical regulations, packaging, labelling and recycling."

Summary of Issues

Charges and Taxes

Most analysts agree that internalizing the environmental costs attributable to a product would be the most efficient method for minimizing the environmental consequences of trade in that product. Cost internalization is the foundation for the Polluter Pays Principle (PPP), adopted by the OECD in 1972 and since incorporated, at least normatively, in several environmental treaties. This Principle declares that the costs of pollution prevention, control and reduction measures are to be borne by the polluter; essentially the "external" costs of environmental harm should not be subsidized by the state, society or future generations. Principle 16 of the *Rio Declaration* builds on the PPP to call for national authorities to promote the internationalization of environmental costs. One method for doing so would be to impose charges or taxes on products reflecting the environmental costs associated with the product. States may, for instance, comply with their obligations under the *Climate Change Convention* by adopting a "carbon tax" on products reflecting the products' energy inputs and hence the ancillary creation of carbon dioxide by combustion.

In principle, the GATT does not prevent members from imposing any cost internalizing taxes domestically. The national treatment obligations of GATT Article III:2 forbid only the imposition of charges or taxes on imported products in excess of those imposed on like domestic products or in a manner that would afford protect to the domestic products. GATT thus allows States to impose taxes on domestic products, even if they are not also imposed on imports. It also allows States that impose a tax on a domestic product to impose an equivalent tax on the same imported product, known as a border tax adjustment, so taxes paid on domestically produced goods, if they are to be exported. Thus in *United States—Taxes on Petroleum and Certain Imported Substances*, a GATT dispute resolution panel concluded that the United States' imposition under its Superfund law of a tax on imported petroleum higher than that on domestic petroleum violated GATT Article III, even though no adverse effect on the volume of imported petroleum had been shown; but it upheld a different tax on certain imported hazardous substances equivalent to a tax imposed by the United States on domestic sales of chemicals used to produce the substances. In reaching the latter conclusion, the panel also made clear that a border tax adjustment would not violate the GATT even if the environmental purpose of the domestic tax would not be furthered directly by imposing the equivalent tax on importers.

In practice, however, the limitations of GATT's permission for border tax adjustments may prevent States from adopting a wide range of measures to achieve cost internalization. It is generally politically infeasible to impose cost-internalizing taxes or charges on domestic industries if a State is not able to "level the playing field" against foreign competitors by providing equivalent border tax adjustments. For instance, the European Commission proposed to introduce taxes on carbon and energy use to meet the European Community's obligations under the *Climate Change Convention*, but only on condition that other OECD countries do so as well and after excluding energy-intensive industries on competitiveness grounds. Yet GATT Article II:2(a), which provides rules covering border tax adjustments, has been interpreted to apply only to direct taxes, such as sales taxes, specific excise duties or value-added taxes. Consequently, it is argued, governments may not adjust for differences in "indirect" taxes such as social security taxes, or for "taxes occultes" such as taxes on capital equipment, transportation or energy inputs, much less for costs incurred to meet regulatory burdens.

Border adjustments for charges or taxes on, for instance, environmentally inappropriate capital improvements, environmentally damaging PPMs or such "inputs" as energy and transportation, may thus violate the GATT. Some analysts have argued that language in Annex II of the Uruguay Round Agreement on Subsidies and Countervailing Measures suggests that at least some such border adjustments may now be allowable. That annex allows rebates of "prior-stage cumulative indirect taxes levied on inputs that are consumed in the production of [an] exported product" and defines "inputs consumed in the production process" to include "energy, fuels and oil used in the production process and consumed catalysts". It has been pointed out, however, that the negotiating history of that Agreement suggests that this language was not intended to legalize border adjustments for energy taxes. More generally, some analysts have expressed concern that a wholesale shift from indirect taxes, such as social security and other payroll taxes, that are currently not eligible for border tax adjustments to an energy tax eligible for border tax adjustment would unravel the trading system. In their view, variation in payroll and other social taxes constitutes part of what gives States comparative advantages over other States. Shifting these forms of taxation to other forms eligible for equalizing border tax adjustments would eliminate these comparative advantages and with them some of the reasons for international trade.

Packaging

There are generally two types of packaging requirements: (1) content and other requirements that must be met for packaging to be allowed to be used and (2) process-related requirements concerning return, reuse, recycling, or disposal of packing materials. These give rise to separate trade-related concerns.

Regulations requiring minimum content of recycled material may reflect the relative importance and availability of such materials in the importing State, but not in the exporting State. As discussed above under Item 2 regarding recycled content obligations generally, exporting States may have difficulty securing sufficient recycled materials to include in the product, particularly if their own State does not require similar recycling. If the only source for acceptable recycled materials is the State imposing the recycling requirement, the requirement may violate GATT Article III:5, which bars regulations requiring minimum domestic content.

Mandatory return programs, also known as take-back requirements or extended producer responsibility programs, could be costlier for foreign companies than for their domestic competitors, particularly for foreign companies with small market shares. As revealed in discussions under Item 2, the added costs of take-back programs can burden imports more than domestic products. Foreign suppliers may also be required to establish a larger, more permanent presence in the market imposing the obligation than would otherwise be warranted by their market share, effectively posing a barrier to smaller producers. Without such a presence, importers will be required to pay the generally higher costs of transporting the returned materials back to the source State, where, in addition, environmental conditions and technical expertise may differ from those justifying the take-back obligation in the State imposing them.

As a general matter, foreign suppliers may need more packaging to transport their products over the greater distances to their export markets than do domestic suppliers. Cost-increasing requirements concerning packaging materials may, consequently, affect foreign suppliers more than they do domestic suppliers.

Eco-Labelling

The term "eco-labelling" generally refers to programs under which certain products are awarded the right to affix a label attesting to the consumer that the product meets some standard of "environmental friendliness".

Eco-labelling programs may serve a wide variety of purposes, but they generally are intended to improve the sales and image of the labelled product by identifying products which are preferable, from the environmental standpoint, to similar products. Proponents thus consider eco-labelling programs an alternative to the traditional governmental regulation of industry, by harnessing market forces to shift production and consumption toward less environmentally harmful products and manufacturing processes. Others question their effectiveness, however, arguing that eco-labels rarely give consumers the whole picture, may be based on criteria that become outdated as technology advances, may apply a single set of standards to varying environmental conditions, and may fail to compare products that consumers consider substitutes, thus misdirecting consumer demand.

Eco-labelling programmes have taken a wide variety of forms. Almost all are voluntary, although they may become so important as to become a *de facto* prerequisite to participation in the market. So-called "third-party" programmes are established by private organizations (e.g., Green Seal (USA)) or by or with the help of governments (e.g., Germany's Blue Angel. India's Ecomark). Other "second-party" programmes, are established by industry groups (e.g., the Chemical Manufacturer's Association's Responsible Care Program). Under "first-party" programmes individual manufacturers make claims about their own products. Some programmes focus on one or a few attributes of the products concerned, but most attempt to consider all significant environmental aspects of a product "from cradle to grave"—so-called life-cycle analysis (LCA) covering use of raw materials, production, distribution, consumption and disposal, re-use or recycling. Often these impacts may be found in the processes or production methods (PPMs) used to create the product.

The rapid spread of eco-labelling programs, particularly third-party programs based on the still-young science of life-cycle analysis, has given rise to concerns about possible effects on trade, especially for products from developing countries. Several potential trade-distorting effects have been identified:

- Eco-labelling programs may tail to take the characteristics of foreign producers' environments into account. For instance, the foreign producer's environment may be more capable of accepting a given quantity of pollution than the environment of the State establishing the labelling program. Imports may thus be denied the benefits of an eco-label even though their impact on the producer's environment is perfectly acceptable.
- Eco-labelling programs developed nationally or regionally may be based on assumptions about how products are made that do not reflect how imports are actually produced. Imports may thus be denied the use of eco-labels on the basis of criteria inappropriate to their production processes.
- The category of product defined as the object of the eco-labelling program may favor domestic producers by failing to include similar or competing products from foreign producers, thus placing imports at a

The term "eco-labelling" generally refers to programs under which certain products are awarded the right to affix a label attesting to the consumer that the product meets some standard of "environmental friendliness".

disadvantage. On the other hand, some business interests have expressed concern that over-inclusive definitions used for general labels of "overall friendliness" may tail to be specific enough about environmental impacts to distinguish appropriately between competing products.

- Conformance with labelling criteria, the certification process and even the eco-labels themselves may be costlier for foreign producers, particularly in developing or least developed countries.
- Foreign producers may have no notice or access to the various stages of the development of eco-labels nor the technical expertise to participate in the standard-setting stages even if they do have notice and access.
- Foreign producers may be more reluctant than domestic producers to reveal business confidences as required for certification, particularly if they have only a small share of the market in the State establishing the eco-labelling program.

Some of these concerns might be ameliorated by implementation of the new TBT Agreement. This Agreement provides disciplines for both mandatory "technical regulations" and voluntary "standards" set by governments and nongovernmental bodies. There is still controversy, however, over the applicability of the TBT Agreement to all eco-labelling programs. Most agree that the TBT Agreement applies to eco-labelling programs to the extent that they address characteristics of the products, as well as PPMs reflected in the end products themselves. What is not unanimously agreed is whether the TBT Agreement covers or should cover aspects of eco-labelling programs addressing non-product related PPMs, because the Agreement's definition of the terms "technical regulation" and "standard" may be interpreted either to exclude or specifically to include non-product related PPMs.

Doubts have also been expressed about the emphasis in both the TBT Agreement and the S&PS Agreement on international standards. The International Organization for Standardization (ISO) is in the process of developing common terms, definitions, symbols, testing and verification methodologies and advertising techniques to harmonize at least these aspects of eco-labelling programs. Yet lack of funding and technical expertise have made it difficult for developing countries to participate in setting some of the standards. Some observers also question whether the WTO should play any role regarding voluntary, third-party programmes.

Eco-labelling issues are being addressed in several fore, including the WTO CTE and the WTO Committee on Technical Barriers to Trade, ISO, UNEP, UNCTAD, OECD, EU, and a conference of over a dozen national eco-labelling programs known as the Global Eco-Labelling Network.

The TBT Agreement

The Agreement on Technical Barriers to Trade (TBT Agreement) concluded in the Uruguay Round provides disciplines regarding the setting and enforcement of technical standards to reduce associated burdens on international trade. Specifically, the TBT Agreement applies to any "document" that sets mandatory standards (referred to as "technical regulations") or voluntary standards (referred to simply as "standards") for products. Separate Agreements cover technical standards relating to government procurement and to sanitary and phytosanitary measures. Unlike its predecessor, the TBT Agreement covers not only standards for characteristics of products themselves, but also standards for "related processes and production methods". It is not yet clear precisely what standards based on PPMs are covered and what not, but many believe that the Agreement is intended to cover only PPMs that are reflected in the product itself. Thus, for instance, laws requiring the incorporation of recycled materials in a final product may be covered, but laws banning the importation of hardwood products derived from unsustainably managed tropical forests may not.

The TBT Agreement attempts to foster the harmonization of technical regulations and standards by favoring the use of international standards. Whenever a member has adopted or expects to adopt technical regulations for a product, it is required to participate, within the limits of its resources, in efforts to set international standards for that product (Article 2.6). If "relevant international standards" exist, then WTO members must use them as the basis for their technical regulations, unless the international standards would be "ineffective or inappropriate means for the fulfilment of the legitimate objectives pursued" in establishing the standards (Article 2.4). Protection of human health or safety, animal plant life or health or the environment constitutes an objective explicitly recognized as legitimate (see Article 2.2). If members do impose a technical regulation for a legitimate objective and based on available international standards, then the technical regulation is "rebuttably presumed not to create an unnecessary obstacle to international trade" (Article 2.5). Similar requirements apply to any procedures to assess conformity with either technical regulations or standards (see Articles 5.4-5.6).

If international standards are not followed, the TBT Agreement imposes both procedural and substantive requirements. When proposing technical regulations or conformity assessment procedures not based on international standards, members must provide prior notice and opportunity to comment "at an early appropriate stage, when amendments can still be introduced and comments taken into account" (see Articles 2.9 & 5.6). Members must also publish final technical regulations and any conformity assessment procedures promptly (see Articles 2.1 1 & 5.1) and must establish "enquiry points" to which other Members and interested parties may turn for information (see Article 10). Substantively, technical regulations and conformity assessment procedures must obey the existing GATT obligations regarding national and most favored nation treatment (see Articles 2.1 & 5.1). In addition, the TBT Agreement imposes a new rule known as the "least trade restrictive" test: Technical regulations "shall not be more trade-restrictive than necessary to fulfil a legitimate objective, taking account of the risks non-fulfilment would create" (Article 2.2). Conformity assessment procedures must meet a similar test (see Article 5.1.2) and, whenever possible, governments must accept the results of equivalent procedures in other members, even if different (see Article 6).

The disciplines of the TBT Agreement apply directly to central governments. They also form the basis for an annexed Code of Good Practice to which nongovernmental bodies establishing standards may adhere. Central governments are required to take reasonable measures to ensure that other governmental entities and nongovernmental standardizing bodies abide by similar rules.

The S&PS Agreement

The *Agreement on the Application of Sanitary and Phytosanitary Measures* (S&PS Agreement) provides disciplines for Members imposing sanitary and phytosanitary (S&PS) measures that might affect international trade. In broad terms, sanitary and phytosanitary measures are those taken to protect human, animal or plant life or health from risks arising from the entry for spread of pests and diseases, or from contaminants in foods, beverages or feedstuffs (see Annex A.1). They include a wide variety of requirements including those regarding characteristics of products and processes or production methods (PPMs) related to the end product (see id.). The S&PS Agreement is similar to the TBT Agreement in certain respects (see Box 10: The TBT Agreement), but generally imposes stricter requirements, in part because it does not contain the usual GATT, MFN or national treatment disciplines.

Like the TBT Agreement, the S&PS Agreement favors international standards. It requires WTO members to base S&PS measures "on international standards, guidelines or recommendations where they exist, except as otherwise provided in this Agreement" (Article 3.1). Measures conforming to such international standards are "presumed to be consistent with the relevant provisions of this Agreement and of GATT 1994" (Article 3.2). Unlike the TBT Agreement, which leaves open the source of international standards to be followed. Annex A to the S&PS Agreement specifies the Codex Alimentarius Commission as the international source relating to food, the International Office of Epizootic, relating to animals, and the *International Plant Protection Convention* relating to plants.

Pursuant to Article 3.3 members may introduce S&PS measures more stringent than international standards "if there is a scientific justification, or as a consequence of the level of sanitary or phytosanitary protection a Member determines to be appropriate" pursuant to procedures to assess risks (Article 3.3). In assessing risks, WTO members must take several specified factors into account, including "available scientific evidence" (Article 5.2) and certain economic factors (Article 5.3). In setting the appropriate level of safety, they must take into account the "objective of minimizing negative trade effects" (Article 5.4) and must "avoid arbitrary or unjustified distinctions in the levels [they consider] to be appropriate in different situations, if such distinctions result in discrimination or a disguised restriction on international trade" (Article 5.5).

Substantively, S&PS measures must be (1) "applied only to the extent necessary to protect human, animal or plant life or health", (2) "based on scientific principles", (3) "not maintained without sufficient scientific evidence" and (4) "not more trade-restrictive than required to achieve their appropriate level of sanitary or phytosanitary protection, taking into account technical and economic feasibility" (Articles 2.2, 5.6). A footnote clarifies that the fourth requirement is met "unless there is another measure, reasonably available taking into account technical and economic feasibility, that achieves the appropriate level of sanitary and phytosanitary protection and is significantly less restrictive of trade" (Article 5.6 n.3). If relevant scientific evidence is "insufficient", members may take provisional measures based on whatever scientific evidence is available, but must seek further information and review the measures within a reasonable period of time (Article 5.7). They must also accept the S&PS measures of other members as equivalent, even if different, so long as the exporting member "objectively demonstrates" to the importing member that its measures achieve the importing member's appropriate level of S&PS protection (Article 4.1).

The International Organization for Standardization was founded in Geneva in 1946 to foster international commerce by establishing harmonized standards.

Annex B to the S&PS Agreement establishes transparency requirements pursuant to which WTO members must provide interested parties "notice at an early stage" of proposed S&PS measures, as well as an opportunity to comment on them. WTO members must promptly publish final S&PS measures and establish an "enquiry point" to supply relevant documents and answer reasonable inquiries from interested WTO members.

Committee on Sanitary and Phytosanitary Measures acts as a forum for consultations on S&PS issues, as well as to foster the international harmonization of S&PS standards (Article 12). Provision is made for technical assistance and special treatment for developing countries (Articles 9-10), including delays in implementation of 5 years for least developed countries and 2 years for other developing countries (Article 14).

Like the TBT Agreement, the S&PS Agreement applies directly only to measures of central governments, but obliges central governments to take "such reasonable measures" to ensure that non-governmental and regional bodies follow the same disciplines (Article 13).

The International Organization for Standardization

The International Organization for Standardization (ISO) was founded in Geneva in 1946 to foster international commerce by establishing harmonized standards. Comprised of over 100 national standard-setting bodies, ISO has established thousands of technical and safety standards. Although voluntary, ISO standards often become *de facto* requirements for conducting business, as treaties or domestic legislation incorporate them, governments and major private purchasers adopt them, and consumers, lenders, insurers or competitors insist upon them. Two events have propelled ISO the into midst of the trade and environment discussions: The Uruguay Round agreements require WTO members to use available international standards, such as those developed by ISO, as the basis for their own technical regulations and ISO has decided to develop standards explicitly addressing environmental issues collectively known as ISO 14000.

Modelled on the successful ISO 9000 series of standards for quality control, ISO 14000 will be comprised of a core standard establishing criteria for environmental management systems (EMS), and five guidance documents regarding environmental auditing, environmental performance evaluation (EPE), eco-labelling, life cycle assessment (LCA), and environmental aspects in product standards. An accelerated schedule has produced final drafts for EMS (ISO 14001) and environmental auditing ISO 14010), and work is continuing for the other standards.

The heart of the series, ISO 14001, is intended to improve the environmental performance of an organization by specifying the elements of an effective EMS. It does not specify substantive standards like limits on pollution or energy consumption. Instead, ISO 14001 requires organizations to define and adopt an environmental policy, plan how to satisfy the policy's objectives, implement the plan, continually monitor compliance with the plan, correct problems that are discovered, and have upper management regularly review and revise the EMS. Companies may either self-certify that they satisfy ISO 14001 or seek official registration after undergoing an independent audit. Successful registration allows the company to use an ISO 14001 certificate in marketing and advertising.

The other standards elaborate on the requirements of ISO 14001. The two most important will probably be those for LCA and eco-labelling. The LCA standard is intended to harmonize methodologies for assessing the environmental impact of a product across its entire life-cycle. Because of scientific uncertainty and disagreements on how to accommodate different cultural and environmental conditions, consensus is only slowly emerging about how to inventory the environmental impacts of a product and is not yet in sight on other aspects of LCA. These disagreements have also slowed work on eco-labelling, which is based on LCA. ISO's aim for eco-labelling is not to establish an eco-label, but again to harmonize methodologies, terms, and principles for others doing so. Three types of labels are being considered: Type I labelling programs, under which third parties certify that products meet criteria for overall environmental impact, have generated the most controversy. In addition to the uncertainties surrounding LCA, difficult questions include how to define product categories, how to address technological change, and how to prevent regional or national biases in their specification and enforcement. ISO's efforts to define terms for Type II labelling programs, under which companies make claims about environmental attributes of their own products, and Type III labels, which inform consumers quantitatively about a product's environmental impacts, have been less controversial.

ISO 14000 raises both environmental and trade-related concerns. Despite their incorporation into the TBT and S&PS Agreements, these standards may become non-tariff barriers to trade: For instance, companies in the many countries without entities accredited to certify ISO 14000 compliance may be forced to incur the greater costs of hiring foreign certifiers; even certification by local accredited entities may be prohibitively expensive for smaller companies. ISO 14001 has also been criticized for failing to require publication of environmental information or to impose substantive environmental standards. More generally, ISO is dominated by large multinational companies and industry-related government standard-setting bodies from developed countries, particularly Europe; small businesses, consumer and environmental advocates, and companies from developing countries often cannot afford to participate or have inadequate technical expertise. As a result, standards may fail to give due regard to environmental impacts, such as loss of biodiversity or desertification important to less industrialized countries or otherwise fail to reflect products or environmental realities of under-represented countries. Although many of these concerns have been brought to the attention of ISO. Little has been done to alleviate them, giving rise to calls for ISO to be restructured.

Summary of Proposals

Charges and Taxes

As regards border tax adjustments, several analysts have proposed that countervailing duties or other charges on imported products be allowed to reduce the pressure of concerns about competitiveness on the adoption of more stringent environmental policies. One observer has suggested that such charges or export rebates be allowed when imports have been given a competitive advantage by domestic environmental legislation, so long as:

- the domestic environmental legislation seeks to address global or physical transboundary environmental problems by more stringent policy than in the past;
- the charge or rebate is strictly limited in time, for instance to three years after introduction of the environmental legislation;
- the amount of the charge or rebate is based on independently audited estimates by the industry concerned of the cost to them and consequent rise in product prices of the environmental legislation, above a minimum threshold, for instance, of 5percent;
- the estimates would be independently reviewed one year after the introduction of the legislation, and the charges or rebates immediately revoked if the estimates prove high;
- the charge or rebate would be announced in advance and open to challenge; and
- the proceeds would be placed in a fund to help developing countries improve environmental performance.

Packaging

No proposals have been made on this topic in the CTE.

Eco-Labelling

In the CTE, Canada proposed a draft decision which includes the following elements:

- mandatory eco-labelling measures, voluntary eco-labelling measures, and eco-labelling compliance procedures, both governmental and nongovernmental, are within the scope of the TBT Agreement and its Code of Good Practice;
- since eco-labelling programs are established by standardizing bodies, for purposes of the TBT

Agreement, such bodies should accept the TBT Code of Good Practice;

- the CTE and the Committee on Technical Barriers to Trade should jointly analyze the impact of developing international standards based on life-cycle approaches; and
- the draft decision would not prejudge whether eco-labels based on non-product-related PPMs are within the scope of the TBT.

The United States too proposed a draft decision which focuses on enhancing transparency in the design and implementation of eco-labelling programs, but which is not intended to be construed as altering the relationship of such programmes to WTO rules.

Other proposals made in the CTE and elsewhere, overlapping to some extent the Canadian proposal, include the following:

- an interpretation clarifying the applicability of the TBT Agreement to government-sponsored and private schemes, both mandatory and voluntary, as well as to voluntary programs based on non-product related PPMs (European Union);
- further study of the relationship between eco-labelling and the TBT Agreement, eco-packaging and technical assistance (Egypt);
- a Code of Good Practice for voluntary eco-labelling schemes similar to the TBT Agreement's Code of Good Practice (Norway, European Union);
- the possibility of appeal of adverse decisions by eco-labelling programs regard application to particular products;
- guidelines to cover non-product related PPM aspects of life cycle analysis underlying eco-labelling schemes;
- mutual recognition of environmental criteria, certification agencies, evaluation and auditing procedures, to be developed in international fora such as UNCTAD and UNEP and taking into account differing ecological conditions.

In addition, the United States has proposed that the WTO Committee on Trade and Environment develop a common understanding with the WTO Committee on Technical Barriers to Trade on when in the process of developing and implementing eco-labelling programs the transparency obligations of the TBT Agreement require an opportunity for comment from interested parties. The United States believes that comment should be allowed at a stage early enough to be taken into account in selecting criteria, setting standards, and developing procedures for assessing conformity to the resulting standards.

Statements from the business community have also recommended the following disciplines for eco-labelling programs:

- criteria should be based on sound science and internationally agreed testing;
- criteria should be accurate, verifiable, relevant and non-deceptive;
- criteria should not be based on PPMs;
- programs should be voluntary, open to all producers, and non-discriminatory;
- programs should be developed and implemented in transparent proceedings open to participation by all interested parties; and
- programs should promote technological and environmental innovation.

Summary of CTE Recommendations

The report of the CTE about its work under Item 3 of its agenda included the following conclusions and recommendations:

Charges and Taxes

- "Scope exists under WTO provisions for Member governments to apply environmental charges and taxes.... Further work on this Item is needed."

Packaging

The CTE reported no separate conclusions or recommendations regarding packaging.

Eco-Labelling

- "Well-designed eco-labelling schemes/programmes can be effective instruments of environmental policy to encourage the development of an environmentally-conscious consumer public."
- "The CTE felt that an important starting point for WTO Members to address some of the trade concerns raised over eco-labelling schemes/programmes is by discussing how to ensure adequate transparency in their preparation, adoption and application, including affording opportunities for participation in their preparation by interested parties from other countries. The transparency provisions contained in

the TBT Agreement, including the Code of Good Practice for standardizing bodies contained in Annex 3 of the Agreement provide a reference point to the further work of the CTE in enhancing transparency of eco-labelling schemes/programs."

- "Without prejudice to the view of WTO Members concerning the coverage and application of the TBT Agreement to certain aspects of ... voluntary eco-labelling schemes/programs and criteria. i.e., those aspects concerning non-product-related PPMs, and therefore to the obligations of Members under this Agreement regarding those aspects, the CTE stresses the importance of WTO Members following the provisions of the TBT Agreement and its Code of Good Practice, including those on transparency."

The CTE will conduct further work on all issues under this Item ....

5

Case Studies

A

Tuna-Dolphin Dispute

(i) *General Agreement on Tariffs and Trade: Dispute Settlement Panel Report on United States Restrictions on Imports of Tuna*, 30 I.L.M. 1594, 1991

[The following is an extract from the decision of the GATT panel in a case known as Tuna Dolphin I. A later case, known as Tuna-Dolphin II, is discussed in the extract immediately following. These cases provide examples of the reasoning used in international trade disputes that have attendant environmental issues. The extract below is reproduced from the text provided by the General Agreement on Tariffs and Trade (GATT). The Panel Report was not adopted by either the United States or Mexico as it was feared this would endanger the negotiation process for the North American Free Trade Agreement. On 29 November 1991, the Report was de-restricted at the joint request of Mexico and the United States. There were no objections.]

Introduction

After consultations with the US concerning its restrictions on imports of tuna, Mexico requested a GATT Panel to consider their complaint...

Finding

Introduction

[5.1.] The Panel noted that the issues before it arose essentially from the following facts: the *Marine Mammal Protection Act* (MMPA) regulates, *inter alia*, the harvesting of tuna by United States fishermen and others who are operating within the jurisdiction of the United States. The MMPA requires that such fishermen use certain fishing techniques to reduce the taking of dolphin incidental to the harvesting of fish. The United States authorities have licensed fishing of yellowfin tuna by United States vessels in the ETP on the condition that the domestic fleet not exceed an incidental taking of 20,500 dolphins per year in the ETP.

[5.2.] The MMPA also requires that the United States Government ban the importation of commercial fish or products from fish caught with commercial fishing technology which results in the incidental killing or incidental serious injury of ocean mammals in excess of United States standards. Under United States customs law, fish caught by a vessel registered in a country is deemed to originate in that country. As a condition of access to the United States market for the yellowfin tuna or yellowfin tuna products caught by its fleet, each country of registry of vessels fishing yellowfin tuna in the ETP must prove to the satisfaction of the United States authorities that its overall regulatory regime regarding the taking of marine mammals is comparable to that of the United States. To meet this requirement, the country in question must prove that the average rate of incidental taking of marine mammals by its tuna fleet operating in the ETP is not in excess of 1.25 times the average incidental taking rate of United States vessels operating in the ETP during the same period. The exact methods of calculating and comparing these average incidental taking rates have been specified by regulation.

[5.3.] The MMPA also provides that ninety days after imports of yellowfin tuna and yellowfin tuna products from a country have been prohibited as above, importation of such tuna and tuna products from any "intermediary nation" shall also be prohibited, unless the intermediary nation proves that it too has acted to ban imports of such tuna and tuna products from the country subject to the direct import embargo.

[5.4.] Six months after either the direct embargo or the "intermediary nations" embargo goes into effect, the United States authorities are required to take action which triggers Section 8 of the *Fishermen's Protective Act* (the Pelly Amendment). This provision enables the President in his discretion to prohibit imports of all fish or wildlife products from the country in question, "for such duration as the President determines appropriate and to the extent that such prohibition is sanctioned by the *General Agreement on Tariffs and Trade*".

[5.5.] Under the MMPA, the United States currently prohibits importation into its customs territory of yellowfin tuna and yellowfin tuna products from Mexico which were caught with purse-seine nets in the ETP. A predecessor embargo was imposed on such tuna and tuna products on 28 August 1990; the embargo in its present form has been in place since 26 March 1991. Since 24 May 1991 the United States has also implemented the "intermediary nations" embargo provisions of the MMPA by prohibiting the importation of yellowfin tuna or yellowfin tuna products from any other country if the tuna was harvested with purse-seine nets in the ETP by vessels of Mexico. If either of these prohibitions is in effect six months after its inception, then as of that date the President will have the discretionary authority under the Pelly Amendment to prohibit imports of all fish products of Mexico or of any "intermediary nation" for such duration as he determines appropriate and to the extent that such action is "sanctioned by the General Agreement".

[5.6.] The *Dolphin Protection Consumer Information Act* (DPCIA) provides that when a tuna product exported from or offered for sale in the United States bears the optional label "Dolphin Safe" or any similar label indicating it was fished in a manner not harmful to dolphins, this tuna product may not contain tuna harvested on the high seas by a vessel engaged in driftnet fishing, or harvested in the ETP by a vessel using a purse-seine net unless it is accompanied by documentary evidence showing that the purse-seine net was not intentionally deployed to encircle dolphins. The use of the label "Dolphin Safe" is not a requirement but is voluntary. The labelling provisions of the DPCIA took effect on 28 May 1991.

[5.7.] The Panel decided to examine successively:

(a) the prohibition of imports of certain yellowfin tuna and certain yellowfin tuna products from Mexico imposed by the United States and the provisions of the MMPA on which it is based;

(b) the prohibition of imports of certain yellowfin tuna and certain yellowfin tuna products from "intermediary nations" imposed by the United States and the provisions of the MMPA on which it is based;

(c) the possible extension of each of these import prohibitions to all fish products from Mexico and the "intermediary nations", under the MMPA and Section 8 of the Fishermen's Protective Act (the Pelly Amendment); and

(d) the application to tuna and tuna products from Mexico of the labelling provisions of the DPCIA, as well as these provisions as such.

In accordance with the established practice, the Panel further decided that it would examine each of the above issues first in the light of the provisions of the General Agreement which Mexico claims to have been violated by the United States and then, if it were to find an inconsistency with any of the provisions invoked by Mexico, in the light of the exceptions in the General Agreement raised by the United States.

Prohibition of Imports of Certain Yellowfin Tuna and Certain Yellowfin Tuna Products from Mexico Categorization as Internal Regulations (Article III) or *Quantitative Restrictions (Article Xi)*

[5.8.] The Panel noted that Mexico had argued that the measures prohibiting imports of certain yellowfin tuna and yellowfin tuna products from Mexico imposed by the United States were quantitative restrictions on importation under Article XI, while the United States had argued that these measures were internal regulations enforced at the time or point of importation under Article III:4 and the Note Ad Article III, namely that the prohibition of imports of tuna and tuna products from Mexico constituted an enforcement of the regulations of the MMPA relating to the harvesting of domestic tuna.

[5.9.] The Panel examined the distinction between quantitative restrictions on importation and internal measures applied at the time or point of importation, and noted the following. While restrictions on importation are prohibited by Article XI:1, contracting parties are permitted by Article III:4 and the Note Ad Article III to impose an internal regulation on products imported from other contracting parties provided that it: does not discriminate between products of other countries in violation of the most-favored-nation principle of Article I:1, is not applied so as to afford protection to domestic production, in violation of the national treatment principle of Article III:1; and accords to imported products treatment no less favorable than that accorded to like products of national origin, consistent with Article III:4. The relevant text of Article III:4 provides:

> "The products of the territory of any contracting party imported into the territory of any other contracting party shall be accorded treatment no less favorable than that accorded to like products of national origin in respect of all laws, regulations and requirements affecting their internal sale, offering for sale, purchase, transportation, distribution or use".

The Note Ad Article III provides that:

> "Any internal tax or other internal charge, or any law, regulation or requirement of the kind referred to in [Article III:1] which applies to an imported product and the like domestic product and is collected or enforced in the case of the imported product at the time or point of importation, is nevertheless to be regarded as an internal tax or other internal charge, or a law, regulation or requirement of the kind referred to in [Article III:1], and is accordingly subject to the provisions of Article III".

[5.10.] The Panel noted that the United States had claimed that the direct import embargo on certain yellowfin tuna and certain yellowfin tuna products of Mexico constituted an enforcement at the time or point of importation of the requirements of the MMPA that yellowfin tuna in the ETP be harvested with fishing techniques designed to reduce the incidental taking of dolphins. The MMPA did not regulate tuna products as such, and in particular did not regulate the sale of tuna or tuna products. Nor did it prescribe fishing techniques that could have an effect on tuna as a product. This raised in the Panel's view the question of whether the tuna harvesting regulations could be regarded as a measure that "applies to" imported and domestic tuna within the meaning of the Note Ad Article III and consequently as a measure which the United States could enforce consistently with that Note in the case of imported tuna at the time or point of importation. The Panel examined this question in detail and found the following.

The MMPA did not regulate tuna products as such, and in particular did not regulate the sale of tuna or tuna products.

[5.11.] The text of Article III:1 refers to the application to imported or domestic products of "laws, regulations and requirements affecting the internal sale ... of products" and "internal quantitative regulations requiring the mixture, processing or use of products"; it sets forth the principle that such regulations on products not be applied so as to afford protection to domestic production. Article III:4 refers solely to laws, regulations and requirements affecting the internal sale, etc. of products. This suggests that Article III covers only measures affecting products as such. Furthermore, the text of the Note Ad Article III refers to a measure "which applies to an imported product and the like domestic product and is collected or enforced in the case of the imported product at the time or point of importation". This suggests that this Note covers only measures applied to imported products that are of the same nature as those applied to the domestic products, such as a prohibition on importation of a product which enforces at the border an internal sales prohibition applied to both imported and like domestic products.

[5.12.] A previous panel had found that Article III:2, first sentence, "obliges contracting parties to establish certain competitive conditions for imported products in relation to domestic products". Another panel had found that the words "treatment no less favorable" in Article III:4 call for effective equality of opportunities for imported products in respect of the application of laws, regulations or requirements affecting the sale, offering for sale, purchase, transportation, distribution or use of products, and that this standard has to be understood as applicable to each individual case of imported products. It was apparent to the Panel that the comparison implied was necessarily one between the measures applied to imported products and the measures applied to like domestic products.

[5.13.] The Panel considered that, as Article III applied the national treatment principle to both regulations and internal taxes, the provisions of Article III:4 applicable to regulations should be interpreted taking into account interpretations by the contracting parties of the provisions of Article III:2 applicable to taxes. The Panel noted in this context that the Working Party Report on Border Tax Adjustments, adopted by the contracting parties in 1970, had concluded that:

> "there was convergence of views to the effect that taxes directly levied on products were eligible for tax adjustment ... Furthermore, the Working Party concluded that there was convergence of views to the effect that certain taxes that were not directly levied on products were not eligible for adjustment, [such as] social security charges whether on employers or employees and payroll taxes".

Thus, under the national treatment principle of Article III, contracting parties may apply border tax adjustments with regard to those taxes that are borne by products, but not for domestic taxes not directly levied on products (such as corporate income taxes). Consequently, the Note Ad Article III covers only internal taxes that are borne by products. The Panel considered that it would be inconsistent to limit the application of this Note to taxes that are borne by products while permitting its application to regulations not applied to the product as such.

[5.14.] The Panel concluded from the above considerations that the Note Ad Article III covers only those measures that are applied to the product as such. The Panel noted that the MMPA regulates the domestic harvesting of yellowfin tuna to reduce the incidental taking of dolphin, but that these regulations could not be regarded as being applied to tuna products as such because they would not directly regulate the sale of tuna and could not possibly affect tuna as a product. Therefore, the Panel found that the import prohibition on certain yellowfin tuna and certain yellowfin tuna products of Mexico and the provisions of the MMPA under which it is imposed did not constitute internal regulations covered by the Note Ad Article III.

[5.15.] The Panel further concluded that, even if the provisions of the MMPA enforcing the tuna harvesting regulations (in particular those providing for the seizure of cargo as a penalty for violation of the Act) were regarded as regulating the sale of tuna as a product, the United States import prohibition would not meet the requirements of Article III. As pointed out in paragraph 5.12 above, Article III:4 calls for a comparison of the treatment of imported tuna as a product with that of domestic tuna as a product. Regulations governing the taking of dolphins incidental to the taking of tuna could not possibly affect tuna as a product. Article III:4 therefore obliges the United States to accord treatment to Mexican tuna no less favorable than that accorded to United States tuna, whether or not the incidental taking of dolphins by Mexican vessels corresponds to that of United States vessels...

Articles XI and XIII

[5.17.] The Panel noted that the United States had, as mandated by the MMPA, announced and implemented a prohibition on imports of yellowfin tuna and yellowfin tuna products caught by vessels of Mexico with purse-seine nets in the ETP. The Panel further noted that under United States customs law, fish caught by a vessel registered in a country was deemed to originate in that country, and that this prohibition therefore applied to imports of products of Mexico.

[5.18.] The Panel noted that under the General Agreement, quantitative restrictions on imports are forbidden by Article XI:1, the relevant part of which reads:

> "No prohibitions or restrictions ... whether made effective through quotas, import or export licenses or other measures, shall be instituted or maintained by any contracting party on the importation of any product of the territory of any other contracting party ..."

The Panel therefore found that the direct import prohibition on certain yellowfin tuna and certain yellowfin tuna products from Mexico and the provisions of the MMPA under which it is imposed were inconsistent with Article XI:1. The United States did not present to the Panel any arguments to support a different legal conclusion regarding Article XI.

[5.19.] The Panel noted that Mexico had also argued that the prohibition imposed on imports from Mexico was inconsistent with Article XIII. In view of the finding that this measure is inconsistent with Article XI:1 the Panel found that it was not necessary to make a finding on the question of whether it was also inconsistent with Article XIII.

Section 8 of the *Fishermen's Protective Act* (Pelly Amendment)

[5.20.] The Panel recalled that Mexico had also argued that the possible extension of import prohibitions to all fish products of Mexico under Section 101(a)(2)(D) of the MMPA and Section 8 of the *Fishermen's Protective Act* (the Pelly Amendment) was inconsistent with Article XI. The Panel noted that the Pelly Amendment authorized such an embargo, but gave the United States authorities discretion to refrain from taking any trade measures at all. Such an embargo was not now in effect, and might not be imposed by the United States authorities. In the Panel's view, therefore, the question presented to it was whether a statutory provision that authorizes but does not require a measure inconsistent with the General Agreement constituted in itself a measure in conflict with the General Agreement.

[5.21.] The Panel recalled that it had been recognized by the contracting parties in previous cases that legislation mandatorily requiring the executive authority of a contracting party to act inconsistently with the General Agreement may be found to be inconsistent with that contracting party's obligations under the General Agreement, whether or not an occasion for its actual application has yet arisen, but on the other hand, legislation merely giving those executive authorities the power to act inconsistently with the General Agreement is not, in itself, inconsistent with the General Agreement. Accordingly, the Panel found that, because the Pelly Amendment did not require trade measures to be taken, this provision as such was not inconsistent with the General Agreement.

Article XX

[5.22.] The Panel noted that the United States had argued that its direct embargo under the MMPA could be justified under Article XX(b) or Article XX(g), and that Mexico had argued that a contracting party could not simultaneously argue that a measure is compatible with the general rules of the General Agreement and invoke Article XX for that measure. The Panel recalled that previous panels had established that Article XX is a limited and conditional exception from obligations under other provisions of the General Agreement, and not a positive rule establishing obligations in itself. Therefore, the practice of panels has been to interpret Article XX narrowly, to place the burden on the party invoking Article XX to justify its invocation, and not to examine Article XX exceptions unless invoked. Nevertheless, the Panel considered that a party to a dispute could argue in the alternative that Article XX might apply, without this argument constituting *ipso facto* an admission that the measures in question would otherwise be inconsistent with the General Agreement. Indeed, the efficient operation of the dispute settlement process required that such arguments in the alternative be possible.

[5.23.] The Panel proceeded to examine whether Article XX(b) or Article XX(g) could justify the MMPA provisions on imports of certain yellowfin tuna and yellowfin tuna products, and the import ban imposed under these provisions. The Panel noted that Article XX provides that:

> "Subject to the requirement that such measures are not applied in a manner which would constitute a means of arbitrary or unjustifiable discrimination between countries where the same conditions prevail, or a disguised restriction on international trade, nothing in this Agreement shall be construed to prevent the adoption or enforcement by any contracting party of measures...
>
> (b) necessary to protect human, animal or plant life or health;
>
> (g) relating to the conservation of exhaustible natural resources if such measures are made effective in conjunction with restrictions on domestic production or consumption;"

The United States considered the prohibition of imports of certain yellowfin tuna and certain yellowfin tuna products from Mexico, and the provisions of the MMPA on which this prohibition is based, to be justified by Article XX(b).

Article XX(b)

[5.24.] The Panel noted that the United States considered the prohibition of imports of certain yellowfin tuna and certain yellowfin tuna products from Mexico, and the provisions of the MMPA on which this prohibition is based, to be justified by Article XX(b) because they served solely the purpose of protecting dolphin life and health and were "necessary" within the meaning of that provision because, in respect of the protection of dolphin life and health outside its jurisdiction, there was no alternative measure reasonably available to the United States to achieve this objective. Mexico considered that Article XX(b) was not applicable to a measure imposed to protect the life or health of animals outside the jurisdiction of the contracting party taking it and that the import prohibition imposed by the United States was not necessary because alternative means consistent with the General Agreement were available to it to protect dolphin lives or health, namely international cooperation between the countries concerned.

[5.25.] The Panel noted that the basic question raised by these arguments, namely whether Article XX(b) covers measures necessary to protect human, animal or plant life or health outside the jurisdiction of the contracting party taking the measure, is not clearly answered by the text of that provision. It refers to life and health protection generally without expressly limiting that protection to the jurisdiction of the contracting party concerned. The Panel therefore decided to analyze this issue in the light of the drafting history of Article XX(b), the purpose of this provision, and the consequences that the interpretations proposed by the parties would have for the operation of the General Agreement as a whole.

[5.26.] The Panel noted that the proposal for Article XX(b) dated from the Draft Charter of the International Trade Organization (ITO) proposed by the United States, which stated in Article 32, "Nothing in Chapter IV [on commercial policy] of this Charter shall be construed to prevent the adoption or enforcement by any Member of measures: (b) necessary to protect human, animal or plant life or health". In the New York Draft of the ITO Charter, the preamble had been revised to read as it does at present, and exception (b) read: "For the purpose of protecting human, animal or plant life or health, if corresponding domestic safeguards under similar conditions exist in the importing country". This added proviso reflected concerns regarding the abuse of sanitary regulations by importing countries. Later, Commission A of the Second Session of the Preparatory Committee in Geneva agreed to drop this proviso as unnecessary. Thus, the record indicates that the concerns of the drafters of Article XX(b) focused on the use of sanitary measures to safeguard life or health of humans, animals or plants within the jurisdiction of the importing country.

[5.27.] The Panel further noted that Article XX(b) allows each contracting party to set its human, animal or plant life or health standards. The conditions set out in Article XX(b) which limit resort to this exception, namely that the measure taken must be "necessary" and not "constitute a means of arbitrary or unjustifiable discrimination or a disguised restriction on international trade", refer to the trade measure requiring justification under Article XX(b), not however to the life or health standard chosen by the contracting party. The Panel recalled the finding of a previous panel that this paragraph of Article XX was intended to allow contracting parties to impose trade restrictive measures inconsistent with the General Agreement to pursue overriding public policy goals to the extent that such inconsistencies were unavoidable. The Panel considered that if the broad interpretation of Article XX(b) suggested by the United States were accepted, each contracting party could unilaterally determine the life or health protection policies from which other contracting parties could not deviate without jeopardizing their rights under the General Agreement. The General Agreement would then no longer constitute a multilateral framework for trade among all contracting parties but would provide legal security only in respect of trade between a limited number of contracting parties with identical internal regulations.

[5.28.] The Panel considered that the United States' measures, even if Article XX(b) were interpreted to permit extrajurisdictional protection of life and health, would not meet the requirement of necessity set out in that provision. The United States had not demonstrated to the Panel—as required of the party invoking an Article XX exception—that it had exhausted all options reasonably available to it to pursue its dolphin protection objectives through measures consistent with the General Agreement, in particular through the negotiation of international cooperative arrangements, which would seem to be desirable in view of the fact that dolphins roam the waters of many states and the high seas. Moreover, even assuming that an import prohibition were the only resort reasonably available to the United States, the particular measure chosen by the United States could in the Panel's view not be considered to be necessary within the meaning of Article XX(b). The United States linked the maximum incidental dolphin taking rate which Mexico had to meet during a particular period in order to be able to export tuna to the United States to the taking rate actually recorded for United States fishermen during the same period. Consequently, the Mexican authorities could not know whether, at a given point of time, their policies conformed to the United States' dolphin protection standards. The Panel considered that a limitation on trade based on such unpredictable conditions could not be regarded as necessary to protect the health or life of dolphins.

[5.29.] On the basis of the above considerations, the Panel found that the United States' direct import prohibition imposed on certain yellowfin tuna and certain yellowfin tuna products of Mexico and the provisions of the MMPA under which it is imposed could not be justified under the exception in Article XX(b).

Article XX(g)

[5.30.] The Panel proceeded to examine whether the prohibition on imports of certain yellowfin tuna and certain yellowfin tuna products from Mexico and the MMPA provisions under which it was imposed could be justified under the exception in Article XX(g). The Panel noted that the United States, in invoking Article XX(g) with respect to its direct import prohibition under the MMPA, had argued that the measures taken under the MMPA are measures primarily aimed at the conservation of dolphin, and that the import restrictions on certain tuna and tuna products under the MMPA are "primarily aimed at rendering effective restrictions on domestic production or consumption" of dolphin. The Panel also noted that Mexico had argued that the United States measures were not justified under the exception in Article XX(g) because, inter alia, this provision could not be applied extra-jurisdictionally.

[5.31.] The Panel noted that Article XX(g) required that the measures relating to the conservation of exhaustible natural resources be taken "in conjunction with restrictions on domestic production or consumption". A previous panel had found that a measure could only be considered to have been taken "in conjunction with" production restrictions "if it was primarily aimed at rendering effective these restrictions". A country can effectively control the production or consumption of an exhaustible natural resource only to the extent that the production or consumption is under its jurisdiction. This suggests that Article XX(g) was intended to permit contracting parties to take trade measures primarily aimed at rendering effective restrictions on production or consumption within their jurisdiction.

[5.32.] The Panel further noted that Article XX(g) allows each contracting party to adopt its own conservation policies. The conditions set out in Article XX(g) which limit resort to this exception, namely that the measures taken must be related to the conservation of exhaustible natural resources, and that they not "constitute a means of arbitrary or unjustifiable discrimination ... or a disguised restriction on international trade" refer to the trade measure requiring justification under Article XX(g), not however to the conservation policies adopted by the contracting party. The Panel considered that if the extrajurisdictional interpretation of Article XX(g) suggested by the United States were accepted, each contracting party could unilaterally determine the conservation policies from which other contracting parties could not deviate without jeopardizing their rights under the General Agreement. The considerations that led the Panel to reject an extrajurisdictional application of Article XX(b) therefore apply also to Article XX(g).

[5.33.] The Panel did not consider that the United States measures, even if Article XX(g) could be applied extrajurisdictionally, would meet the conditions set out in that provision. A previous panel found that a measure could be considered as "relating to the conservation of exhaustible natural resources" within the meaning of Article XX(g) only if it was primarily aimed at such conservation. The Panel recalled that the United States linked the maximum incidental dolphin-taking rate which Mexico had to meet during a particular period in order to be able to export tuna to the United States to the taking rate actually recorded for United States fishermen during the same period. Consequently, the Mexican authorities could not know whether, at a given point of time, their conservation policies conformed to the United States conservation standards. The Panel considered that a limitation on trade based on such unpredictable conditions could not be regarded as being primarily aimed at the conservation of dolphins.

[5.34.] On the basis of the above considerations, the Panel found that the United States direct import prohibition on certain yellowfin tuna and certain yellowfin tuna products of Mexico directly imported from Mexico, and the provisions of the MMPA under which it is imposed, could not be justified under Article XX(g).

Secondary Embargo on Imports of Certain Yellowfin Tuna and Certain Yellowfin Tuna Products from "Intermediary Nations" *Under The MMPA*

Articles III and XI

[5.35.] The Panel noted that Mexico had claimed that the "intermediary nations" embargo was inconsistent with Articles XI and XIII. The United States considered that these measures fell instead under Article III and the Note Ad Article III as they provided for enforcement of requirements for yellowfin tuna harvested in the ETP using purse-seine nets. The Panel found that since the United States domestic regulations on tuna harvesting were not applied to tuna as a product, the "intermediary nations" embargo did not fall within the scope of the Note Ad Article III, and was therefore a quantitative restriction subject to Article XI.

[5.36.] The Panel further noted that the MMPA required that the United States authorities implement a prohibition on imports of yellowfin tuna and yellowfin tuna products from "intermediary nations", and that the United States was refusing entry to yellowfin tuna unless the importer declared that no yellowfin tuna or yellowfin tuna product in the shipment were harvested with purse-seine nets in the ETP by vessels of Mexico. The Panel therefore found that these measures and the provisions of the MMPA mandating such an embargo were import restrictions or prohibitions inconsistent with Article XI:1. The United States did not present to the Panel any arguments to support a different legal conclusion regarding Article XI.

[5.37.] The Panel recalled its finding on the Pelly Amendment in paragraph 5.21 above, namely that this provision as such was not inconsistent with the obligations of the United States under the General Agreement because the Pelly Amendment does not require trade measures to be taken. The Panel considered that this finding was equally valid in the case of the "intermediary nations" embargo.

Article XX(b) and XX(g)

[5.38.] The Panel noted that the United States had argued that the intermediary nations embargo was justified as a measure under Article XX(b) and XX(g) to protect and conserve dolphin, and that the intermediary country measures were necessary to protect animal life or health and related to the conservation of exhaustible natural resources. The Panel recalled its findings with regard to the consistency of the direct embargo with Articles XX(b) and XX(g) in paragraphs 5.29 and 5.34 above, and found that the considerations that led the Panel to reject the United States invocation of these provisions in that instance applied to the "intermediary nations" embargo as well.

Article XX(d)

[5.39.] The Panel then proceeded to examine the consistency of the "intermediary nations" embargo with Article XX(d), which the United States had invoked. The relevant part of Article XX(d) reads as follows:

> "Subject to the requirement that such measures are not applied in a manner which would constitute a means of arbitrary or unjustifiable discrimination between countries where the same conditions prevail, or a disguised restriction on international trade, nothing in this Agreement shall be construed to prevent the adoption or enforcement by any contracting party of measures
>
> . . .
>
> (d) necessary to secure compliance with laws or regulations which are not inconsistent with the provisions of this Agreement"

[5.40.] The Panel noted that Article XX(d) requires that the "laws or regulations" with which compliance is being secured be themselves "not inconsistent" with the General Agreement. The Panel noted that the United States had argued that the "intermediary nations" embargo was necessary to support the direct embargo because countries whose exports were subject to such an embargo should not be able to nullify the embargo's effect by exporting to the United States indirectly through third countries. The Panel found that, given its finding that the direct embargo was inconsistent with the General Agreement, the "intermediary nations" embargo and the provisions of the MMPA under which it is imposed could not be justified under Article XX(d) as a measure to secure compliance with "laws or regulations not inconsistent with the provisions of this Agreement".

Dolphin Protection Consumer Information Act (DPCIA)

[5.41.] The Panel noted that Mexico considered the labelling provisions of the DPCIA to be marking requirements falling under Article IX:1, which reads:

> "Each contracting party shall accord to the products of the territories of other contracting parties treatment with regard to marking requirements no less favorable than the treatment accorded to like products of any third country".

The United States considered that the labelling provisions were subject not to Article IX but to the most-favored-nation and national-treatment provisions of Articles I:1 and III:4. The Panel noted that the title of Article IX is "Marks of Origin" and its text refers to marking of origin of imported products. The Panel further noted that Article IX does not contain a national-treatment but only a most-favored-nation requirement, which indicates that this provision was intended to regulate marking of origin of imported products but not marking of products generally. The Panel therefore found that the labelling provisions of the DPCIA did not fall under Article IX:1.

[5.42.] The Panel proceeded to examine the subsidiary argument by Mexico that the labelling provisions of the DPCIA were inconsistent with Article I:1 because they discriminated against Mexico as a country fishing in the ETP. The Panel noted that the labelling provisions of the DPCIA do not restrict the sale of tuna products; tuna products can be sold freely both with and without the "Dolphin Safe" label. Nor do these provisions establish requirements that have to be met in order to obtain an advantage from the government. Any advantage which might possibly result from access to this label depends on the free choice by consumers to give preference to tuna carrying the "Dolphin Safe" label. The labelling provisions therefore did not make the right to sell tuna or tuna products, nor the access to a government-conferred advantage affecting the sale of tuna or tuna products, conditional upon the use of tuna harvesting methods. The only issue before the Panel was therefore whether the provisions of the DPCIA governing the right of access to the label met the requirements of Article I:1.

[5.43.] The Panel noted that the DPCIA is based *inter alia* on a finding that dolphins are frequently killed in the course of tuna-fishing operations in the ETP through the use of purse-seine nets intentionally deployed to encircle dolphins. The DPCIA therefore accords the right to use the label "Dolphin Safe" for tuna harvested in the ETP only if such tuna is accompanied by documentary evidence showing that it was not harvested with purse-seine nets intentionally deployed to encircle dolphins. The Panel examined whether this requirement applied to tuna from the ETP was consistent with Article I:1. According to the information presented to the Panel, the harvesting of tuna by intentionally encircling dolphins with purse-seine nets was practised only in the ETP because of the particular nature of the association between dolphins and tuna observed only in that area. By imposing the requirement to provide evidence that this fishing technique had not been used in respect of tuna caught in the ETP the United States therefore did not discriminate against countries fishing in this area. The Panel noted that, under United States customs law, the country of origin of fish was determined by the country of registry of the vessel that had caught the fish; the geographical area where the fish was caught was irrelevant for the determination of origin. The labelling regulations governing tuna caught in the ETP thus applied to all countries whose vessels fished in this geographical area and thus did not distinguish between products originating in Mexico and products originating in other countries.

[5.44.] The Panel found for these reasons that the tuna products labelling provisions of the DPCIA relating to tuna caught in the ETP were not inconsistent with the obligations of the United States under Article I:1 of the General Agreement.

Concluding Remarks

[6.1.] The Panel wished to underline that its task was limited to the examination of this matter "in the light of the relevant GATT provisions", and therefore did not call for a finding on the appropriateness of the United States' and Mexico's conservation policies as such.

[6.2.] The Panel wished to note the fact, made evident during its consideration of this case, that the provisions of the General Agreement impose few constraints on a contracting party's implementation of domestic environmental policies. The Panel recalled its findings in paragraphs 5.10 to 5.16 above that under these provisions, a contracting party is free to tax or regulate imported products and like domestic products as long as its taxes or regulations do not discriminate against imported products or afford protection to domestic producers, and a contracting party is also free to tax or regulate domestic production for environmental purposes. As a corollary to these rights, a contracting party may not restrict imports of a product merely because it originates in a country with environmental policies different from its own.

[6.3.] The Panel further recalled its finding that the import restrictions examined in this dispute, imposed to respond to differences in environmental regulation of producers, could not be justified under the exceptions in Articles XX(b) or XX(g). These exceptions did not specify criteria limiting the range of life or health protection policies, or resource conservation policies, for the sake of which they could be invoked. It seemed evident to the Panel that, if the contracting parties were to permit import restrictions in response to differences in environmental policies under the General Agreement, they would need to impose limits on the range of policy differences justifying such responses and to develop criteria so as to prevent abuse. If the contracting parties were to decide to permit trade measures of this type in particular circumstances it would therefore be preferable for them to do so not by interpreting Article XX, but by amending or supplementing the provisions of the General Agreement or waiving obligations thereunder. Such an approach would enable the contracting parties to impose such limits and develop such criteria.

[6.4.] These considerations led the Panel to the view that the adoption of its report would affect neither the rights of individual contracting parties to pursue their internal environmental policies and to cooperate with one another in harmonizing such policies, nor the right of the contracting parties acting jointly to address international environmental problems which can only be resolved through measures in conflict with the present rules of the General Agreement.

Conclusions

[7.1.] (a) The prohibition of imports of certain yellowfin tuna and certain yellowfin tuna products of Mexico and the provisions of the Marine Mammal Protection Act under which it is imposed are contrary to Article XI:1 and are not justified by Article XX(b) or Article XX(g).

(b) The import prohibitions imposed by the United States with regard to certain yellowfin tuna and certain yellowfin tuna products of "intermediary nations" and the provisions of the *Marine Mammal Protection Act* under which they are imposed are contrary to Article XI:1 and are not justified by Article XX(b), XX(d) or XX(g).

(c) The Panel recommends that the contracting parties request the United States to bring the above measures into conformity with its obligations under the General Agreement.

[7.2.] The provisions of Section 8 of the *Fishermen's Protective Act* (the Pelly Amendment) as such are not inconsistent with the obligations of the United States under the General Agreement.

[7.3.] The tuna products labelling provisions of the Dolphin Protection Consumer Information Act relating to tuna caught in the Eastern Tropical Pacific Ocean are not inconsistent with the obligations of the United States under Article I:1 of the General Agreement."

A contracting party may not restrict imports of a product merely because it originates in a country with environmental policies different from its own.

(ii) Donald Goldberg, "GATT Tuna-Dolphin II: Environmental Protection Continues to Clash with Free Trade," *CIEL Brief*, June 1994, No. 2

Introduction

In June 1992, the European Economic Community (EEC) requested the Contracting Parties to the *General Agreement on Tariffs and Trade* to establish a dispute resolution panel to review US restrictions on the import of tuna and tuna products under the federal *Marine Mammal Protection Act* (MMPA). On may 20, 1994 the panel issued its report, concluding that the US embargo violated the GATT prohibition on quantitative restrictions and does not fall under any of the exceptions to the GATT's general obligations.

The MMPA prohibits the taking of any marine mammal in connection with the harvesting of fish and bars import into the United States of tuna and tuna products from countries that do not meet the Act's requirements. It also bars imports of tuna and tuna products from "intermediary" nations—nations that both import and export tuna products—unless they certify that they have not imported any tuna or tuna products subject to the US ban within the past six months.

This was not the first GATT challenge to the MMPA. In 1991, Mexico successfully challenged the Act in what is now know as the *Tuna-Dolphin I case*. That panel decision has no direct legal effect, however, since neither Mexico nor the US asked the GATT Council to adopt the decision, primarily because delicate negotiations over the *North American Free Trade Agreement* were taking place at the time. Nevertheless, *Tuna-Dolphin I* was viewed as a guide for action that future panels are likely to take in adjudicating GATT disputes.

The central message of *Tuna-Dolphin I* was that trade measures to protect global environmental resources face high, and perhaps insurmountable, barriers. That message appears to be little changed by the decision in *Tuna-Dolphin II*, the case settled in May [1994]. There are, however, significant differences between the analytical paths taken in the two decisions. These differences will play a role in determining whether any trade measures for protecting global environmental resources may pass muster with GATT and, if so, how they should be designed.

This article describes MMPA trade restrictions and the panel findings in the cases. It then assesses the cases and discusses implications for future disputes over environmentally motivated trade measures.

US MMPA Trade Restrictions

...In addition to placing restrictions on fishing operations under US jurisdiction, the MMPA bans the import of tuna harvested by a method that results in killing or injury of marine mammals in excess of US standards. Countries seeking to export tuna harvested in the ETP to the United States must show that they have adopted a regulatory program comparable to the US program and that their incidental taking rate is not greater than 1.25 times the US rate. Alternatively, they may enter into a formal agreement with the United States, under which they must ban the practice of deploying purse seine nets on marine mammals, require observers on all vessels using purse seine nets in the ETP, and reduce dolphin mortality from their fishing operations by a statistically significant margin....

Tuna-Dolphin I

Mexico challenged the MMPA in 1991. In considering Mexico's challenge a GATT panel (Panel 1) found that the United States had violated the proscription in Article XI of the GATT against adopting quantitative restrictions on imports. The United States argued that the restrictions were internal regulations enforced at the point of entry as permitted by Article III:4. The panel rejected the argument on grounds that Article III restrictions could only be applied to 'products' as such, and could not be based on the 'process' by which the product was produced. Since regulating dolphin mortality incidental to fishing operations does not affect the final product, the panel found Article III:4 did not apply. The panel then found that the US embargo of Mexican tuna was a quantitative restriction prohibited by Article XI.

The United States next argued that even if its restrictions were prohibited by other provisions of GATT, they were permitted as exceptions to the general obligations by Article XX(b), (d), and (g). Article XX provides that:

> "Subject to the requirement that such measures are not applied in a manner which would constitute a means of arbitrary or unjustifiable discrimination between countries where the same conditions prevail, or a disguised restriction on international trade, nothing in this Agreement shall be construed to prevent the adoption of enforcement by any contracting party of any measure: ...
>
> (b) necessary to protect human animal or plant life or health ...
> (d) necessary to secure compliance with laws or regulations which are not inconsistent with the provisions of this Agreement ...
> (g) relating to the conservation of exhaustible natural resources if such measures are made effective in conjunction with restrictions on domestic production or consumption."

The panel found, based on what many consider to be a flawed analysis, that Article XX(b) was not intended to be applied "extrajurisdictionally"(the panel did not say whether it is the damaging activity—tuna fishing—or the protected resource—migratory tuna—that must be located within the jurisdiction of the party taking measures). The panel also found even if extrajurisdictional application were permitted, the measures in question were not "necessary" within the meaning of Article XX(b). To be necessary, the panel said, the contracting party invoking Article XX(b) must show that no GATT consistent measures were reasonably available. The panel found that the United States had not exhausted all reasonable GATT—consistent options, in particular negotiation of an international cooperative arrangement to protect dolphins (ignoring the 20-year effort by the United States to negotiate an agreement through the Inter-American Tropical Tuna Commission to protect dolphins in the ETP).

Furthermore, the panel found that the US measures were to unpredictable to be considered necessary to protect dolphins. Because the permitted rate of Mexican incidental taking of dolphins was linked to the actual rate of the US fleet during the same period, Mexican authorities could not know in advance whether they were in compliance with the MMPA. The panel also held the Article XX(g), like Article XX(b), could not be applied extrajurisdictionally. The panel interpreted the requirement that measures under XX(g) be taken "in conjunction with restrictions on domestic production or consumption" to mean that they must be "primarily aimed at rendering effective" those restrictions. The panel reasoned that a country can only control natural resource or consumption of a natural resource if that production or consumption is under its jurisdiction. Therefore, the drafters must not have intended Article XX(g) to be applied extrajurisdictionally. This argument ignores the possibility that countries with large markets might effectively protect a species by banning consumption within their borders.

Applying the same reasoning, the panel decided the "intermediary" nation embargo could not be justified under Article XX(b) or (g). It also found that, since the MMPA is inconsistent with GATT, Article XX(d) could not apply.

Tuna-Dolphin II

The panel in *Tuna-Dolphin II* (Panel 2) reached the same conclusion as Panel 1 concerning Article III: 4. It held that the article only applies to measures relating to products as such, and therefore the MMPA trade restrictions must be considered quantitative restrictions prohibited by Article XI. Like Panel 1, it also held that the exceptions contained in Article XX do no apply. However, Panel 2's reasoning was markedly different from the reasoning of Panel 1, and on some points even contradictory.

To interpret Article XX(g), the panel set out a three part analysis:

1. Article XX(g) must be invoked to further policies to conserve exhaustible natural resources;
2. The measure in question must be "related to" the conservation of exhaustible natural resources and made effective "in conjunction" with restrictions on domestic production or consumption; and
3. The measure may not be applied in a manner that would constitute a means of arbitrary or unjustifiable discrimination between countries where the same conditions prevail, or a disguised restriction on international trade.

In addressing the first element of this test, the panel quickly rejected the EEC's contention that dolphins are not an exhaustible natural resource. The panel noted that it is not relevant whether, at any given time, the stocks of dolphins are actually depleted. Rather the issue was whether the resource could in fact be depleted, and dolphins [being a resource] could [be depleted].

Next the panel turned to whether Article XX(g) could apply to a resource outside the territory of the United States. The panel rejected the US argument that other international agreements, specifically environmental agreements, could be used as evidence of subsequent agreement and practice, or as a supplementary means on interpreting GATT. Nevertheless, it found nothing to support the conclusion that Article XX(g) only applies to protect resources located within the territory of the country invoking it. The panel observed that Article XX(g) does not spell out and limitation on the location of the living things to be protected; that other panels had applied Article XX(g) without distinguishing between resources located within and outside the territory of the contracting parties; that measures could be taken under other paragraphs of Article XX concerning things located and actions taken outside the jurisdiction of the party taking the measure; and that under general principles of international law states are not barred from regulating outside their territory the conduct of their nations, of

The panel asserted that, by themselves, the embargoes "could not possibly" further the US conservation objectives; the US objectives could be achieved only if the primary exporting country changed its policies and practices.

vessels having their nationality, or of any persons on those vessels.

In part two of its analysis, the panel noted that a previous panel had concluded that the terms "relating to" and "in conjunction with" in Article XX(g) meant "primarily aimed at". The panel pointed out that, under both the primary and intermediate nation embargoes, imports of tuna could be barred regardless of whether harvesting of the particular tuna involved had resulted in any incidental taking of dolphins. The panel asserted that, by themselves, the embargoes "could not possibly" further the US conservation objectives; the US objectives could be achieved only if the primary exporting country changed its policies and practices. This assertion ignores the possibility that by denying countries that refuse to change their policies access to the vast US market, fewer tuna may be harvested and, as a result, fewer dolphins taken. The panel then considered whether measures taken to force other countries to change their policies and practices could be "primarily aimed at" the conservation of exhaustible natural resources rendering effective domestic restrictions on their production or consumption. It noted that the text of Article XX(g) does not provide a clear answer.

At this point the panel seems to have abandoned the logic of its step-by-step analysis. It claimed that if Article XX were interpreted to permit measures taken to force other countries to change their policies, the "balance of rights and obligations" among contracting parties would be seriously impaired. Here, as one commentator has pointed out concerning a similar statement by Panel 1, the panel assumes what it tries to prove. Both the rules and the exceptions have to be considered together to ascertain, in any particular dispute, the rights and obligations of the parties concerned. Indeed, the plain language of the Article XX preamble ("...nothing in this Agreement shall be construed to prevent the adoption or enforcement by any contracting party of measures...") suggests that there are no rights or obligations conveyed by GATT that cannot be overridden by a measure that meets all the requirements of Article XX. Of course, the measures must accord with the Article XX preamble ("... such measures [may not be] applied in a manner which would constitute a means of arbitrary or unjustifiable discrimination between countries where the same conditions prevail, or a disguised restriction on international trade..."). But in this dispute there was no suggestion that the US measures were protectionist or otherwise failed to comport with the preamble.

The panel concluded that measures taken to force other countries to change their policies, and that would be effective only if such changes occurred, could not possibly by "primarily aimed" within the meaning of Article XX(g). Having found that the MMPA fails second part of its test, the panel did not examine the MMP in light of the third part.

The panel used a similar three-part test to interpret Article XX(b):

(1) Article XX(b) must be invoked to further policies to protect human, animal, or plant life or health;

(2) The measure in question must be "necessary" to protect human, animal, or plant life or health; and

(3) The measure may not be applied in a manner which would constitute a means of arbitrary or unjustifiable discrimination between countries where the same conditions prevail, or a disguised restriction on international trade.

The panel found that Article XX(b) was not limited to the territory of the contracting party invoking it. Since the EEC had conceded that the embargo was intended to protect the life or health of dolphins, the panel held that the US embargo falls within the rage of policies promoted by Article XX(b).

The panel disagreed with the US contention that "necessary" means "needed". Instead, the panel found that necessary means that no alternative exists. The panel agreed with a previous panel that "in cases where a measure consistent with other GATT provisions is not reasonable available, a contracting party is bound to use, among measures reasonable available to it, that which entails the least degree of inconsistency with other GATT provisions."

The panel did not identify any other less GATT-inconsistent measure reasonably available to the United States to accomplish its legitimate objectives. Instead, it found that any measure taken to force other countries to change their policies, and that would be effective only if such changes occurred, could not be considered "necessary" within the meaning of Article XX(b). Having found that the MMPA fails the second part of its test, the panel did not examine the Act in light of the third part.

The panel also found that, since the MMPA is inconsistent with GATT, Article XX(d) could not apply.

Comparisons and Analysis of the Two Cases

At first glance, Panel 2 seems to have overruled a highly criticized element of the first panel's decision: the limitation of Articles XX(b) and (g) to the jurisdiction of the contracting party invoking them. But by putting the Article XX exceptions off limits for the purpose of changing another country's policies and practices, Panel 2 may have taken back with one hand what it gave with the other. Most environmentally oriented trade restrictions, whether adopted unilaterally or multilaterally, are aimed at encouraging a change in policies and behavior. Moreover, since Panel 2 did not distinguish between unilateral and multilateral measures, as did Panel 1, the decision could have serious implications for multilateral environmental agreements such as the *Montreal Protocol*, the *Convention on International Trade in Endangered Species* (CITIES) and the *Basel Convention*.

There may, however, be a somewhat less ominous reading of the case. Given the language of the decision, it is possible that measures targeted to change behavior—without requiring countries to change their policies—would pass GATT scrutiny.

B

Shrimp–Turtle Dispute

(i) *World Trade Organization: United States —Import Prohibition Of Certain Shrimp And Shrimp Products,* 38 I.L.M. 118; 1999

[*This Document was reproduced, edited and reformatted from the text appearing at the World Trade Organization web site visited on 12/22/98. The WTO report, which is the subject of the analysis in the extract below, can now be found at <http://www.wto.org/english/tratop_e/dispu_e/distab_e.htm>. This site, which produces the report without the introductory note, written by Nancy L. Perkins, was accessed on 03/04/2001. Of the report itself, only a very brief exert is included here.*]

Introductory Note

In a decision issued on 12 October 1998, the Appellate Body of the World Trade Organization (WTO) upheld the judgment of a WTO dispute settlement panel that the United States' ban on imports of shrimp harvested without turtle-excluder devices (TEDs) (which protect sea turtles during shrimp harvesting) violates WTO rules. The Appellate Body agreed with the panel that, contrary to the arguments of the United States, the import ban was not justified as a natural resource conservation measure under Article XX(g) of the *General Agreement on Tariffs and Trade* of 1994 (GATT 1994) (part of the WTO Agreement), which provides an exception from general WTO rules for trade-restrictive measures "relating to the conservation of exhaustible natural resources." Although the Appellate Body found that the US law prescribing the import ban was within the scope of measures covered by Article XX(g), because the ban was applied by the United States in an arbitrary and discriminatory manner, it nevertheless was not permissible.

The Appellate Body ruling represents an important step forward in elucidating the parameters and proper application of GATT Article XX. In particular, the decision clarifies the relationship of Article XX's introductory clause, or "chapeau," to the exceptions from general WTO rules that are subsequently enumerated in Article XX, including Article XX(g). Under the "chapeau", none of those enumerated exceptions may serve to justify a restriction on trade if that restriction is "applied in a manner which would constitute a means of arbitrary or unjustifiable discrimination between countries where the same conditions prevail, or a disguised restriction on international trade."

Both the panel and the Appellate Body in the shrimp/turtle case found that the challenged US import ban could not be squared with the conditions of the Article XX chapeau. However, they reached this finding by different routes, and the Appellate Body soundly rejected the approach taken by the panel. The panel had reasoned that since none of the exceptions enumerated in Article XX could apply unless the chapeau conditions were met, it made sense to analyze the chapeau's application to the import ban before considering the terms of the specific Article XX exceptions. The Appellate Body found this was a serious doctrinal error that led the panel to an overly broad ruling regarding the types of measures excluded from coverage under Article XX. Through its preferred method of analysis—considering the chapeau conditions only after analyzing the application of the specific exceptions in Article XX—the Appellate Body determined that the U.S. import ban was among the types of measures covered by Article XX(g), but nevertheless was not justified because of the particular method in which it was applied. The Appellate Body's findings under Article XX(g) convey several notable messages—some implicit—about the types of trade restrictions, properly applied, that WTO Members may use to achieve environmental protection.

First, the Appellate Body implicitly indicated that the WTO does not categorically disallow the use of trade restrictions that are based not on the characteristics of the product(s) to which they apply, but rather on the processes or production methodologies (PPM) from which the product(s) are derived. The Appellate Body's silence regarding the fact that the US import ban was a PPM-based measure (since it applied depending on how shrimp is harvested, rather than based on any characteristic of shrimp itself), signals a tolerance for PPM-based trade restrictions that is of considerable importance to the international trade community. The use of PPM-based measures has generated a contentious debate in the WTO, particularly between developed and less-developed WTO Members. Many less-developed nations, including at least one of the claimants in the shrimp/turtle case (Thailand), have argued that authorizing PPM-based trade barriers would open the door to highly coercive measures by powerful trading nations, effectively forcing less powerful nations to adopt particular production policies (including, for example, specific labor policies). The Appellate Body, in finding that the US shrimp import ban was within the scope of measures covered by Article XX(g), signaled a level of tolerance for PPM-based restrictions that is plainly unwelcome by these WTO Members.

A second message sent by the Appellate Body is that the WTO does not categorically proscribe trade-restrictive measures imposed by one nation to protect the environment outside that nation's territory. The Appellate Body carefully limited its suggestions in this regard to the facts of the shrimp/turtle case, specifically stating that "we do not pass upon the question of whether there is an implied jurisdictional limitation in Article XX(g), and if so, the nature or extent of that limitation." However, noting that the United States did not purport to exercise any special jurisdiction over sea turtles swimming freely in their natural habitat—the oceans—the Appellate Body found that, since at least some of the waters where sea turtles occur are within US jurisdiction, "there is a sufficient nexus between the migratory and endangered marine populations involved and the United States for purposes of Article XX(g)." This finding indicates that a WTO Member may rely on Article XX(g) to justify a trade-restrictive measure aimed at protecting environmental resources in the "global commons" so long as there is at least some jurisdictional relationship between those resources and that WTO Member. Since at least two GATT panels that addressed the issue expressed serious doubt about the possibility of such justification, the Appellate Body's opinion on this point may give notable comfort to advocates of trade restrictions aimed at global environmental protection.

Third, the Appellate Body confirmed the panel's finding that it is generally not acceptable for one WTO Member to restrict trade based on the failure of other Members to conform their natural resource conservation (or presumably other) policies to the unilateral dictates of that WTO Member. The Appellate Body observed that, as a condition for avoiding the US shrimp import ban, the United States "requires other WTO Members to adopt a regulatory program that is not merely comparable, but rather essentially the same, as that applied to the United States shrimp trawl vessels." This, the Appellate Body found, establishes an unacceptably "rigid and unbending standard" for achieving the goal of protecting sea turtles. Both by failing adequately to examine other nations' individual circumstances and policies regarding sea turtle protection before applying the shrimp import ban, and by failing to pursue bilateral or multilateral negotiations on appropriate protection methods, the United States unjustifiably imposed its own standards on other nations in an arbitrary and discriminatory manner inconsistent with the requirements of the Article XX chapeau. "The unilateral character of the application" of the import ban, the Appellate Body emphasized, "heightens the disruptive and discriminatory influence of the import prohibition and underscores its unjustifiability."

The reactions of the United States, other WTO Members, and interested nongovernmental organizations to the Appellate Body ruling are illustrative of the high degree of sensitivity surrounding the trade-and-environment issue. The US reaction was among the most positive, despite obvious disappointment with the ultimate judgment. In announcing the US intention to abide by the judgment, the US Trade Representative to the WTO stated:

"We are pleased that the Appellate Body found no inconsistency between the US legislation at issue [as opposed to the application of that legislation] and our obligations under the WTO. We are also pleased that the Appellate Body made a number of important and positive findings that help clarify the critical relationship between WTO rules and measures taken to protect the environment." Ironically, Thailand, one of the prevailing claimants in the case, was less laudatory in its reaction. While applauding the final judgment, Thailand sharply criticized the Appellate Body for showing "deference to underlying political concerns" about the WTO's sensitivity to environmental protection, admonishing that "public relevant concerns should not be used to invalidate negotiated treaty obligations." Further, Thailand expressed serious concern about the Appellate Body's apparent tolerance for PPM-based trade restrictions, predicting that the Appellate Body opinion;

> "will result in an explosive growth in the number of environmental (and perhaps labor) measures applied to PPMs and justified pursuant to Article XX,...[which] is likely to have profound systemic implications for the future application of the WTO rules and disciplines."

Simultaneously, some nongovernmental organizations reacted with dismay to the Appellate Body ruling, alleging WTO bias against environmental protection. The World Wildlife Fund, for example, asserted that the decision "reveals the profound bias of the WTO against environmental policies, and in favor of 'free trade' at any cost." According to the World Wildlife Fund:

> "The Appellate Body ruling ... perpetuates a contorted interpretation of ... Article XX of the WTO Agreement [which] plainly states that governments are free to limit trade in non-protectionist ways when doing so is necessary to protect the environment."

These contrasting reactions, and the strong sentiments they reflect, indicate that the WTO's approach to environmentally based trade restrictions will continue to be hotly contested. In the context of dispute settlement, the debate will likely engage nongovernmental organizations in a more directly active role in the future, since the Appellate Body, as part of its opinion in the shrimp/turtle case, held that WTO dispute settlement panels are free to consider unsolicited information received from non-WTO Members. Rejecting the contrary opinion of the panel below, the Appellate Body found that the WTO dispute settlement rules grant a panel "the discretionary authority either to accept and consider or to reject information and advice submitted to it, whether requested by a panel or not." This determination is obviously a welcome one for those nongovernmental organizations that have sought to influence WTO decision making and trade policy. It may, perhaps, serve to dilute the criticism by many of these organizations that the WTO dispute settlement process is unduly insulated and myopic in focus.

On that basis and in its substantive guidance regarding the scope and application of GATT Article XX, the Appellate Body decision in the shrimp/turtle case represents a significant advancement in WTO jurisprudence...

[WTO] Findings and Conclusions

[187] For the reasons set out in this Report, the Appellate Body:

(a) reverses the Panel's finding that accepting non-requested information from nongovernmental sources is incompatible with the provisions of the DSU;

(b) reverses the Panel's finding that the United States measure at issue is not within the scope of measures permitted under the chapeau of Article XX of the GATT 1994, and

(c) concludes that the United States measure, while qualifying for provisional justification under Article XX(g), fails to meet the requirements of the chapeau of Article XX, and, therefore, is not justified under Article XX of the GATT 1994.

[188] The Appellate Body recommends that the DSB request the United States to bring its measure found in the Panel Report to be inconsistent with Article XI of the GATT 1994, and found in this Report to be not justified under Article XX of the GATT 1994, into conformity with the obligations of the United States under that Agreement.

6

Improving Trade and Environment Regimes

A

Asian Perspectives and Future Trends

(i) Simon Tay, "The Way Ahead in Asia," in Tay and Esty (eds), *Asian Dragons and Green Trade,* Times Academic Press, 1996, pp 189–201

The connections between trade and the environment are complex and multi-faceted. There is not one subject but many. The core of issues discussed in the World Trade Organization (WTO) relates to the consistency of multilateral environmental agreements and eco-labels with trade rules. But other issues are also voiced in the debate, often by developing countries and nongovernmental organizations. In this wider context, there is concern with the connection of the WTO regime of trade-related intellectual property rights to environmental resources, biodiversity and indigenous knowledge. There are also matters that involve other institutions beyond the WTO. These include the question of how to institute a system of international supervision over the export of domestically prohibited goods (DPGs), which are banned in their country of origin but still sent to poorer countries without prior warning; and the recognition of environmental considerations by the International Standards Organization (ISO) in awarding its ISO 14000 series certification for products.

Asia too is a complex entity. The region is large and diverse, with large and small countries, with differing cultural and historical heritages. Economically, there are developed countries such as Japan; the four "little dragons" or newly industrialized economies of Hong Kong, Singapore, South Korea and Taiwan; the near-NIEs like Malaysia, Thailand and Indonesia; industrializing countries and the least developed. The region has some economies that have traditionally been open to international trade and foreign investment, as well as others like China, Vietnam and India that have been opening up only recently to the world economy.

To discuss trade and the environment in Asia comprehensively is then to multiply the wide range of issues by the varying attitudes, comparative advantages and developmental stages of the different Asian countries. This is clearly beyond the reach of the present chapter. What can be done is, first, to characterize the trade and environment debate in Asia at the present and, second, to offer some suggestion on ways ahead for the region. These suggestions describe a context for dialogue.

The Present Scene

Asia's rise has become a common and easy prediction. Its economies are growing at the highest rates of any region in the world. Its share of world trade has been increasing at almost twice the world average, catching up with Europe and North America. A handful of Asian countries like China and the member-states of the Association of South East Asian Nations (ASEAN) absorb the lion's share of the foreign direct investment made in developing countries. Intra-regional investment and trade between different Asian countries is also increasing...

The truth is that Asia's rise is not a proven fact. Growth lines in many of the graphs and charts drawn towards the future are straight line extrapolations, drawn optimistically towards the horizon of the year 2000 or 2020. The prediction rides, as such, on the assumption that things will be more or less as they have been, except more and better. These assumptions stand to be proved or disproved. Asia's rise to equality and greater prominence is not inevitable but contingent... Human, social and environmental challenges stand before the region. Indeed, in many instances, today's successes may in fact increase the tension and difficulty in meeting tomorrow's needs and aspirations. Asian economies, like too many cars on city streets, may become stuck on the highway to success.

Regional leaders seem to understand this. Thus, while they are justifiably proud of what has been done to date, most feel they are not ready to take on the laurels of fully-developed status. The race towards that status in development is a marathon that they have not completed. They therefore remain cautious about measures that may undermine their competitiveness in that race. That is a concern that is voiced in many different fore, on many different initiatives. It is the concern that underlines, and perhaps undermines, the discussion of trade and the environment in Asia.

Asian countries care about trade. It is seen as the region's engine of growth. The NIEs have provided a model for others, based on export-oriented industrialization. Larger countries like China, Vietnam and, to a lesser degree, India, have followed suit to emphasize trade. Initiatives for further trade liberalization have been seen in both the Asia-Pacific Economic Cooperation (APEC) area and the ASEAN Free Trade Area (AFTA).

Do Asians care about the environment? At the national level, many Asian countries have committed themselves to ambitious plans and legislation, much of it built on the international soft law guidelines such as *Agenda 21* or tied to the accession to international environmental treaties. At the regional and subregional level too, in ASEAN and APEC, Asia has shown progress on the environment.

APEC is first and foremost an economic institution. In 1994, however, after the *Rio Summit* and *Agenda 21*, APEC held its first Environmental Ministers meetings. This meeting issued the APEC *Environmental Vision Statement* as well as a *Framework of Principles for Integrating Economy and the Environment in APEC*. It also notable that the 1994 APEC *Foreign Investment Guidelines* provides, among other things, that environmental standards should not be lowered to attract foreign investment.

ASEAN, established in 1967, aimed initially to ensure political stability and security in the region. Its scope has since widened to include economic and environmental matters. In 1977, the first ASEAN environmental program was initiated. The grouping has undertaken one major environment treaty, the 1985 Agreement on the Conservation of Nature and Natural Resources. There have also been numerous ministerial declarations on the environment, most notably in the run-up to the 1992 Earth Summit. Beyond this, environmental cooperation between the ASEAN countries on both national and regional issues has proceeded more pragmatically, through action plans and coordinating meetings between senior officials.

Environmental and economic concerns came together in the AFTA, in 1992. When work on AFTA continued after the Earth Summit, ASEAN recognized the need to consider the intersection of trade and environmental issues. Three specific strategies were proposed to that end:

(1) studies on the development of policies that would support sustainable development;

(2) mechanisms and economic incentives to encourage both government and the private sector to adopt appropriate environmental standards; and

(3) information links and networks between government and the private sector on technology, expertise and facilities for environmental management.

Some may feel that it is encouraging that these institutions have placed the environment on their agenda. Others, however, may wish that these institutions would go further and faster in dealing with environmental problems. Impatient with Asian results, developed countries have on occasion sought to use trade restrictions to push for faster and stronger action.

Consequently, the experiences of ASEAN countries with trade and environmental issues have been largely negative and defensive responses to initiatives by developed countries. They have been on the receiving end of eco-labels against tropical hardwood products, and unilateral measures under American conservation laws. They have been hit with sanctions for failing to control imports of tiger bones and rhino parts and, even more recently, for failing to comply with US-made laws against shrimping that leads to the killing of sea turtles.

The experiences of ASEAN countries with trade and environmental issues have been largely negative and defensive responses to initiatives by developed countries.

Between its own efforts and externally imposed measures, do Asia and ASEAN care for the environment? What is clear is that much depends on what we mean by environmental problems. It makes a difference whether the problem is climate change, or the pollution of a local source of drinking water. It makes a difference if the environmental damage is blown or washed away to another country, externalized, or has immediate effects to those living there. And it makes a difference whether environmental issues are local, national, transboundary or global.

Global environmental problems and some conservation issues dear to the heart of green groups in developed countries are harder to fix in the priorities of Asia. But many in the region understand or are beginning to understand that they face a future in which populations, especially in cities, will grow rapidly, and tax resources of water, land, food and energy. This latter set of environmental problems can be understood and made a priority for both sound economic and environmental reasons. This division of environmental issues has been characterized as distinguishing between the environmental problems of affluence and those of poverty.

APEC, in particular, seems to have taken on this environmental agenda of environmental problems associated with poverty. The APEC Ministers Meeting on Sustainable Development was held in the Philippines in July 1996. Environmental cooperation schemes have been discussed in three different areas, including sustainable cities and urban management; clean production and technology; and the sustainability of the marine environmental. The APEC emphasis shows key differences from the vision of the 1992 Earth Summit. As regards the challenges identified at Rio, there has been a notable lack of official development assistance from the developed countries to meet the costs of environmental problems. The concern is that the developed world has reneged on their part of this compact, that the bargained package of the Earth Summit has been unravelled.

There is danger that the same thing seems to happening to the bargain on trade rules that was made in the Uruguay Round of GATT negotiations. The promise of trade in classical trade theory is that it is good for all countries, a win-win situation. So it made sense that the goods of developing countries would find a place in the markets of developed countries, and vice versa. Accordingly, for the promise of trade-led growth, the formerly closed or protected markets in Asia and elsewhere have begun to open to imports. Whole new regimes in the Uruguay Round like Trade-Related Investment Measures, Trade-Related Intellectual Property and new sectors of the economy—like telecommunications and other services and the phased cessation of special multi-fiber and agriculture agreements, were part of that bargain. Some Third World thinkers already believe developing countries have paid too high a price for that bargain. They seek to re-open some of the past discussions, and to question the entire basis of international trade.

There are others in Asia—and they are the majority for now at least—who want to uphold the bargain and the promise of free trade. But their belief can be shaken if seems that this trade bargain—in parallel with the environmental bargain—is in danger of unravelling. This makes the prospect of environmental conditions on trade unsettling. Similarly, there is caution in most of Asia over the initiatives in labor standards, corruption, and so many other conditions that have come up for consideration in the trade agenda. More generally, talk of "containment" of Asia, and some Asian countries, or even of disinterest and disengagement from the region, does not reassure.

A Context for Dialogue and Progress

Against this context, what can be done to further dialogue and progress on this issue in the region? Certain principles in the discussion of trade and the environment may be briefly suggested, as follows:

A Need for Consensus and Cooperation

First, consensus and cooperation must be emphasized. Both international trade and environmental problems require nations to work together...Dialogue is essential.

Asians may suspect disguised protectionism by developed countries. But silence will not make green issues go away. In this dialogue, the three major trading regions of Europe, North America and Asia must have equal voices. Trade-environment issues must be negotiated with an emphasis on multilateralism. Different sectors must be involved: governments and NGOs, think-tanks and business. Research must be furthered. We should begin to provide facts and figures where theory and rhetoric have gone ahead in this debate. The recent work led by UNCTAD, ESCAP and ASEAN should only be the start...

Observing the Environmental Bargain

A second starting point is that environmental concerns must be acknowledged by Asia. Growth in the region cannot mean hubris in the face of environmental degradation. Asia must take the initiative in facing the uncertain future of limited agricultural land and water, and overcrowded urban centers. Asia must seek ways of avoiding or shortcutting the inverted U pattern of pollution. The period in which pollution and environmental costs rise in Asia must be shortened. The good day when those production patterns become more environmentally friendly must be hastened.

The region must also play its part in helping with global problems. This would reassure environmentalists in developed countries and elsewhere that Asia is not neglecting its due environmental responsibilities. But as that reassurance is given, technical assistance, technology transfer and funding from developed countries are also needed for effective action. The environmental bargain reached at the Earth Summit must be observed. Trade measures are a poor substitute for assistance. They are, as economists have observed, sub optimal because the damage is often done not by trade per se, but by production and consumption. They still have a role to prevent free riders and to give incentives for participation in environmental accords, as seen in the *Montreal Protocol*, but they are not sufficient in themselves. "Carrots" and incentives are needed for Asia to improve its environmental record, more than "sticks" and sanctions.

Observing the Trade Bargain

A third suggestion is that there should be recognition that, while all countries stand to benefit, free trade has a special importance to Asia. All countries should observe the trade bargain of the Uruguay Round. Asia needs assurance in this regard. Developed countries cannot put forward new items on a piecemeal basis, especially on subjects on which there is little or no international consensus in definition. Environmental issues that lack multilateral endorsement and international understanding cannot be realistically advanced by the developed countries in the WTO.

On their part, developing countries in Asia and elsewhere will wish to raise issues such as DPGs, the export of waste and the connection of the TRIPs regime to issues such as biodiversity. Avenues should be open to these discussions, either within the WTO or, as a first step, in the context of seeking a multilateral treaty that crystallizes international consensus on these issues.

Preference and Assistance for Developing Countries

My fourth suggestion picks up a point that is shared in both the trade rules and the principles of international environmental law. This is that developing countries—and the majority of Asian countries come into this category-should receive preference. Trade rules have long recognized this, although the sentiment seems somewhat watered down at present. Environmental law has developed the principle of "common but differentiated responsibilities" as stated in the *Rio Declaration*.

But while recognized in principle, preference and assistance to developing countries is increasingly difficult to operationalize. The Secretary-General of the Earth Summit, Maurice Strong, envisaged that US$125 billion in official development assistance per year was needed to operationalize *Agenda 21* and to give due priority to the environment. Instead of meeting this challenge, there has been a vast scaling back of the financial commitments in the developed countries.

While governments should do more, we should not ignore the role of the private sector. We must accept that being green can be good for business and that business can be good for green goals. Although this is not always so, the right policies and incentives can encourage synergy. In the gap left by developed country governments, we may let private sector initiatives assist the environmental cause. This would not be for altruism. Rather, the private sector would be best equipped to identify which schemes will work and which won't. Companies might pay their own way, going ahead only if it helped their bottom line. Or there could be more financial incentives for private sector activity with such aims, rather than the bulk of funding going to government projects.

The WTO

My fifth point addresses the role of the WTO. I think we may face a choice. We can take up the call by some to open a new round of global trade negotiations, despite exhaustion. This could take in the environment, and all the issues I have mentioned, and even aspirations for new sectors of services to be opened and an investment treaty to be agreed.

Alternatively, we can consolidate the present, fixed agenda, and avoid hastily taking on new initiatives for a time, perhaps until the benefits of the Uruguay Round are more clearly evident to all. In suggesting this approach for consolidation, I recognize that time is of the essence for environmental concerns. I do not mean to excuse inaction. But I think it is also essential that we appreciate the precaution of taking deliberate steps, even at the cost of a slower pace, rather than doing the wrong thing quickly.

I add that, in consolidating the existing agenda, environmental concerns must lay claim to a priority over new issues like labor and corruption. This is by virtue of the work of the WTO CTE. It would also reflect the surrounding and continuing context of controversy as well as some possible middle ground on topics such as MEAs and eco-labelling. If we can assert the priority of trade and the environment issues over the new items, modest but real progress can be made.

This might be criticized by some as a lack of ambition. It can conversely be criticized by others who believe that little or nothing will be done by the WTO. Be that as it may, I think those of us who want to see trade and the environment move forward have to be careful of championing other conditions to trade. I want to link this aim of modest and real progress in the WTO with my next point.

A Role for Regional Initiatives

My sixth point concerns regional initiatives. In parallel with the WTO's progress on the global level, regional initiatives for closer economic ties involving Asia have also come in the APEC area, in the follow-up to the Asia-Europe Meeting (AEM) and within ASEAN. The idea of "open regionalism" seeks to ensure that these inter-regional and subregional initiatives will be consistent with the global GATT and the WTO.

What does this mean for environmental issues in these different fora? As briefly considered in this chapter, the environment has been on the agenda for ASEAN and it has begun to be discussed in APEC. It cannot be faraway for Asia's reinvigorated ties with Europe in the ASEM.

Some have expressed scepticism about these regional initiatives as being mere "talk shops" because there is a general lack of rules that "bite", compared to the primarily rule-based and legalistic GATT and the WTO. This view applies equally in the environmental sphere, as to other areas of regional cooperation. The Asians in these groupings have said that such criticism misunderstands the "Asian" way. They seek to build these regional initiatives around consensus and consent, rather than rules and compulsion.

Asia should recognize that the region need not always lean on Europe or North America.

My suggestion is that this approach should also guide regional initiatives as they take up environmental issues in their relation to trade and to investment. In this respect, their lack of hard rules and potential decision making powers—compared to the WTO—may assist, rather than hinder. Discussion in these fora may go forward more freely and at a faster pace, where penalties are less threatening than at the WTO.

The dialogue process of these regional initiatives also seem better able to involve more sectors, and to take in environmental issues and the related concerns of assistance, technology transfer and funding in ways that GATT is unable to do. The flexibility and relatively new identity of APEC and ASEM may be a strength. If this is taken up, the regional initiatives will play a role that is relevant to the trade-environment issue in the WTO context; a role that the WTO itself is unable or unwilling to undertake.

There are two further ways in which Asia, as a region, may proceed with trade-environment issues. First, Asia should recognize that the region need not always lean on Europe or North America. The region has developed countries, such Japan and South Korea, and more advanced developing countries, as well as newly emergent economies such as Laos and Cambodia. Just as intra-Asian investment has increased, intra-Asian assistance on the environment may be of increasing importance. Second, the special subregional arrangements seen in growth triangles, like the one between Singapore-Southern Malaysia Indonesia or in the Mekong Delta, hold promise. These arrangements share common resources such as air and water. As trade and investment flow between the parts of the growth triangle, there may be increasing need to deal with the question of environmental standards that may differ from one part and another. As the experiences of these special regimes in growth areas accumulate, they may then be generalized for the region…

B

Governance Issues

(i) Steve Charnovitz, "Improving Environmental and Trade Governance," *International Environmental Affairs*, Vol. 7. No. 1, Winter 1995, pp 59–76

The trade and environment debate—as it has flowered during the 1990s—is a significant event in the evolution of international governance. Although much attention has been devoted to the ways in which trade policies may interfere with environmental goals and the ways in which environmental policies may interfere with trade goals, it is important not to lose sight of the fundamental complementarities between the trade and environment regimes. Open trade and investment should normally be good for environmental protection. Pollution control and biodiversity protection should normally be good for transnational business.

There are many ways in which the two regimes can proceed independently. There is no need to transform the *General Agreement on Tariffs and Trade* (GATT) or the World Trade Organization (WTO) into an environmental agreement. There is no need to subordinate one regime to the other. Nevertheless, it is important that the trade and environment regimes attain greater harmony. As *Agenda 21* cogently stated: "Environment and trade policies should be mutually supportive." Given the large number of issues on which the two regimes share a mutual interest, it would be useful to seek coordination—and some interpenetration—between trade and environment treaties and organizations.

In this chapter, I shall focus on the WTO, rather than environmental conventions. I shall consider three institutional issues: first, building on the Uruguay Round of trade negotiations; second, the link between the WTO and intergovernmental organizations; and third, and in more detail, links between the WTO and nongovernmental organizations.

Building on the Uruguay Round

The Uruguay Round was a monumental achievement in lowering tariffs and establishing new disciplines on non-tariff barriers and subsidies. It is vital that the Singapore Ministerial keep this momentum going. To that end, several initiatives should be considered.

First, the Ministers could make a commitment to achieve worldwide free trade by a certain year... Free trade should also be good for the global environment if appropriate environmental policies are in place at the national and international levels.

Second, the Ministers could establish a schedule for the phase-out of the reduced obligations on developing countries to lower their trade barriers. Reducing lingering protectionism will be good not only for the economies of developing countries but also for their domestic environments.

Third, renewed attention could be given to the problem of subsidies in international trade. Some environmentalists have put forward a win-win scenario wherein the WTO Committee on Subsidies and Countervailing Measures develops a work program aimed at reducing environmentally harmful subsidies. Reducing such subsides—for example in agriculture and energy sectors—is called "win-win" because it would be good both for the economies and the environments of countries that still retain such subsidies. This is one area where environmentalists and free traders could join forces to pursue sustainable development.

Fourth, the Ministers should begin a process of making the WTO more compatible with international public law. In that regard, the trade regime could follow in the path of international environmental law. As Professor Murase has noted in his recent lecture to the Hague Academy, some environmental treaties create general obligations that go beyond the reciprocal contractual obligations in traditional treaties. One area in which the WTO might do this involves the treatment of non-members, particularly, those who are trying to join the WTO. Right now, WTO members are free to ignore WTO norms, such as non-discrimination, in their dealings with China. Another way of improving the WTO would be to incorporate principles of openness and free trade as general obligations.

Fifth, the Trade Policy Review Mechanism could be expanded to include trade-related environmental issues. This is already happening to some extent, for example, in the recent report on Sri Lanka. But it would be useful to codify this development by amending the understanding achieved during the Uruguay Round.

Sixth, the upcoming Ministerial meeting is expected to address the so called new issues of international trade policy. Several of these new issues have significant environmental implications. One in particular is investment. In the past couple of years, the Organization for Economic Co-operation and Development (OECD) has been developing a new code for international investment. Some countries would like to see this code brought to the WTO for further work. So far, the OECD effort has focused only on commercial concerns about investment. It has yet to consider the environmental dimension. These issues need to be brought into the debate at the earliest available opportunity.

The WTO and Intergovernmental Organizations

The second topic I want to discuss is the relationship of the WTO to international organizations that pursue environmental objectives. The WTO treaty provides that, "The General Council shall make appropriate arrangements for effective cooperation with other intergovernmental organizations that have responsibilities related to those of the WTO". Since the Preamble to the WTO Agreement notes the objective of "sustainable development", it seems clear that other intergovernmental organizations, including the United Nations Environment Programme (UNEP), the United Nations Conference on Trade and Development (UNCTAD) and the Commission on Sustainable Development, are within the purview of this mandate.

In the first one and a half years of the WTO, the General Council has not taken steps to achieve effective cooperation with agencies working on environmental matters. This omission is particularly noticeable in light of the good working relationships that have developed between UNCTAD and UNEP on trade and environment issues. While it is true that representatives from UNEP are allowed to attend and observe meetings of the WTO Committee on Trade and Environment, they are not allowed to speak at these meetings. It is hard to accept that this constitutes "effective cooperation".

Ambassador Winfried Lang has proposed one modality for achieving cooperation, namely, joint sessions of the WTO with UNCTAD, UNEP and Bretton Woods Institutions. Such sessions, according to Lang, would allow for a periodic dialogue facilitating the exchange of views. They would not be negotiations, but would serve a purpose of exploring cross-cutting issues. For example, one might imagine a joint meeting of the UNEP Governing Council and the WTO General Council.

The WTO should also develop effective cooperation with the World Conservation Union (IUCN). Although the IUCN is not an inter-governmental organization, it has government members, and thus qualifies under the WTO mandate. Despite the fact that the GATT and the IUCN both came into being in 1948, and are in close locational proximity, they have had surprisingly little contact with each other.

Effective cooperation between the WTO and environmental organizations will be helpful to both regimes. The trade regime has developed an effective dispute settlement mechanism that the environmental regime can learn from. The environmental regime has developed techniques for negotiating complex agreements quickly that the trade regime can learn from. Both regimes could work together in assessing the trade impact of environmental policies and the environmental impact of trade policies.

WTO and Nongovernmental Organizations

The third topic I want to discuss is the relationship of the WTO to nongovernmental organizations—or NGOs—that pursue environmental objectives. The WTO treaty provides that, "The General Council may make appropriate arrangements for consultation and cooperation with nongovernmental organizations concerned with matters related to those of the WTO."

In the first one and a half years of the WTO, the General Council has not taken steps to consult and cooperate with NGOs, despite the apparent willingness of international NGOs to engage in such relationships. Although some WTO Secretariat officials and national ambassadors have met occasionally with NGOs, this is not a substitute for formal consultation and cooperation.

It is unclear why the WTO has moved so slowly to implement this mandate. One reason may be that the WTO lacks robust decision making rules. Decisions are taken by consensus and therefore persistent objectors can block progressive action. In my own informal discussions with ambassadors to the WTO, I have got the impression that many of them view the WTO as a sealed, self-contained set of relationships that have little to do with public international law or international civil society. From that parochial perspective, the fact that most other international organizations have ongoing relationships with NGOs says nothing about whether the WTO could institute the same kinds of constructive relationships.

NGOs should be given opportunities to participate in the work of the WTO. Such opportunities need not be unbounded; they can be structured carefully to maximize the benefits of NGO participation and to minimize any ensuing costs. But it is important that the WTO abandon the insularity and secrecy that characterized its predecessor, the GATT. Eliminating the most resilient and restrictive barriers to trade will require popular approval. Thus, it is vital for the public to understand the aims of the WTO and to develop trust in that organization.

The issue of public participation in the GATT did not originate in the "trade and environment" debate. In fact, a primary American objective in the previous Tokyo Round was the adoption of international fair labor standards and of public petition and confrontation procedures in the GATT. That objective was never achieved. Fifteen years later, when the issue of public participation arose again, some environmental NGOs cleverly borrowed the term "transparency", a word which at that time in GATT circles referred to the trade laws and practices of each country. The NGOs reasoned that if transparency was an appropriate norm at the national level, it was also appropriate at the international level. In calling for more transparency, the NGOs challenged the GATT to live up to its own principles by increasing the flow of information to and from the public.

These efforts towards transparency, initiated by NGOs, stimulated governmental pressure within the GATT and resulted in several advances toward openness. For instance, the GATT, and now the WTO, release Secretariat-drafted studies sooner; the Secretariat staff holds informal consultations with NGOs; the new WTO dispute settlement rules permit governments to publicly disclose statements of the positions they are taking in a pending dispute; and the WTO recently joined the World Wide Web.

Yet in many other ways, the WTO remains as distant from the public as the GATT was. Dispute settlement panels continue to hold closed sessions; the WTO will not release basic biographical information about panelists that would be useful in assessing qualifications or potential conflicts of interest; panel reports are not released to the public until after a report is adopted; NGOs may not observe regular meetings of the WTO General Council and, indeed, minutes of these meetings remain secret for two years; and finally all WTO committees, including the Committee on Trade and Environment, convene in closed sessions that NGO representatives may not attend.

The criticism of the GATT/WTO by NGOs is broad-based. Environmental NGOs have been at the forefront of the criticism, but have been joined by NGOs from labour, development, consumer, public interest and farm groups. Their arguments can be summarized by stating that the World Trade Organization must look at the interests of the entire world. This globalized perspective cannot be achieved effectively with input only from those governmental trade officials who routinely attend WTO meetings.

NGOs are on solid legal ground in seeking greater transparency and participation in the WTO. Drawing on the expertise of NGOs is a hallmark of other intergovernmental organizations and institutions. For example, *Agenda 21*, a program of action implemented by the United Nations Conference on Environment and Development (UNCED), states that:

> "[A]ll intergovernmental organizations and forums should, in consultation with nongovernmental organizations, take measures to...enhance existing or, where they do not exist, establish, mechanisms and procedures within each agency to draw on the expertise and views of nongovernmental organizations in policy and program design, implementation and evaluation; [and]...[p]rovide access for nongovernmental organizations to accurate and timely data and information to promote the effectiveness of their programmer and activities ..."

In fact, most other international organizations have done far more than the WTO to involve NGOs in their work. For example, the OECD has active advisory groups drawn from business and trade unions. The International Labor Organization (ILO) includes workers and employers as delegates to that organization. Especially in recent years, NGOs have become important players in many international conferences and organizations.

Indeed, the World Bank is searching for a new kind of employee it calls an "NGO Specialist". Of course it should be noted that NGOs remain largely shut out of the International Monetary Fund, as well as international military, nuclear and law enforcement organizations.

NGOs are playing increasingly important roles in direct negotiations with governments. For example, in September 1995, several environmental groups undertook discussions with the Government of Mexico to explore the possibility of a new convention to protect dolphins during tuna fishing. This compromise led to a declaration by 12 nations, calling for a binding international agreement to be signed by 1996. In January 1996, the Worldwide Fund for Nature reached an agreement with the Government of Finland and a major forestry company in Finland to permit a recommencement of logging operations in Russia's Karelian forest.

It is sometimes suggested that NGO involvement in the GATT/WTO would contradict the principles upon which the global organization was established. This argument, however, ignores the early attempts by the postwar multilateral trading system to involve NGOs. The original plan of the Bretton Woods system provided for an International Trade Organization (ITO) to be flanked by the World Bank and the International Monetary Fund (IMF). The United Nations initiated negotiations for ITO in 1946 and concluded in 1948 with the Charter for the International Trade Organization. Article 87(2) of the ITO Charter provided that "[t]he Organization may make suitable arrangements for consultation and cooperation with nongovernmental organizations concerned with matters within the scope of this Charter".

For various political reasons, the ITO never came into existence. Instead, the GATT—which was originally intended to be superseded by the ITO—replaced the ITO as a *de facto* treaty and organization. It is instructive, however, to look at how the Interim Commission for the ITO intended to implement ITO Article 87(2). In May 1949, the Interim Commission Secretariat—which later become the GATT Secretariat prepared a report for the first ITO

Conference which, among other topics, proposed procedures for NGO involvement in the ITO. This proposal suggested that:

(1) appropriate NGOs be listed as consultative organizations;
(2) these listed organizations be invited to ITO Conference sessions;
(3) NGO representatives be able to make statements on items at the discretion of the chairpersons; and
(4) these organizations receive ITO documents as necessary for effective consultation. Member governments extensively discussed these procedures and would likely have adopted them if the ITO came into existence.

The fact that the negotiators of the ITO treaty provided for NGO participation, combined with evidence that the Interim ITO was prepared to implement this provision, together demonstrate that NGO participation is consistent with the design and aspirations of the multilateral trading system. That the GATT behaved in a more introverted way does not detract from the intention of the founders of the trading system.

The WTO Agreement provides that "[t]he General Council may make appropriate arrangements for consultation and cooperation with non-governmental organizations concerned with matters related to those of the WTO". So far, the WTO General Council has not begun to implement this provision. There is a wide range of opinion on what is "appropriate" for NGOs to see, hear and do. Nevertheless, the straightforward nature of this provision, and its similarity to the original provision in the ITO, make it difficult for WTO members to argue convincingly that the WTO is different from other international organizations in its ability to institutionalize NGO participation.

There are two major issues relating to NGO participation in the WTO. The first is NGO participation in the policy work of the WTO as carried out in various committees, such as the Committee on Technical Barriers to Trade. The second is NGO participation in the WTO dispute resolution process as plaintiffs, *amici curiae,* witnesses, or observers. These general issues are separable. The WTO could involve NGOs in the policy committees but not in dispute resolution on the grounds that public disclosure would harden positions, chill negotiations and hinder settlements. Likewise, the WTO could open up dispute resolution but not the policy committees on the grounds that fact collection and adjudication should be insulated from interest group pressure.

Participation in WTO Policy Making

Some may be concerned that member countries would be unwilling to entrust negotiations involving sovereignty to any entity other than themselves. Assuming this is true, there remain a number of useful NGO activities which fall short of this. For example, NGOs can facilitate negotiations in several ways by providing expert information, serving as a sounding board for possible compromises, injecting new ideas into a substantive debate, securing public support necessary for parliamentary approval, and serving as monitors to enforce governmental commitments.

Another concern about NGO involvement is that it would slow down WTO policy-making, which would be an undesirable effect. On the other hand, NGO participation in the GATT Uruguay Round, which took over seven years to negotiate, might have expedited the negotiating process. The NGOs might have catalyzed trade negotiators and encouraged them to look beyond mercantilist interests. Certainly, the involvement of NGOs in the environment regime has not caused undue delay in negotiating environmental agreements. In fact, during the seven years of Uruguay Round negotiations, no less than seven global environmental agreements were reached.

One reason why the Uruguay Round took so long to complete was because little occurred during extended periods of time as governments either stewed at each other or awaited national elections in individual countries. With NGOs at the table, the governments might have been prodded toward more diligent negotiations. NGO involvement also might have stimulated the trade negotiators to obtain more significant results than those that were achieved.

The presence of NGOs may seem to undermine the apparent authority of governments, and thus their ability to negotiate trade policies. While it is true that NGOs could have that effect, NGOs also could stimulate the opposite reaction. A government backed by NGOs might actually find its credibility strengthened in negotiations as other countries perceive an enhanced ability to follow through on its commitments. One need not posit a failure in democracy to support greater NGO participation in international organizations. On the contrary, NGO participation should be viewed as an exemplification of the democratic vision.

The case for policy making participation of national NGOs in international organizations is not premised on the incompetence of national governments to balance domestic interests. Instead, the contention is that international organizations will perform more effectively if they have the input of interest groups. The same argument justifies NGO involvement in domestic rule-making. Why should NGOs be involved in the creation of national law, but not international law?

The case for the policy making involvement of international NGOs in international organizations is a different matter. While one can argue that the views of national NGOs are represented by national governments, the same argument cannot be made for international NGOs, such as the Worldwide Fund for Nature, the International Confederation of Free Trade Unions, or the International Chamber of Commerce. International NGOs have no national government to represent them; they only have international organizations.

Critics may suggest that any scheme would not equitably allow for direct participation by all of the citizens of the world. This view is correct. Nobody, however, calls for such direct participation, but rather NGOs advocate an organized process of NGO involvement. Borrowing from the procedures of the United Nations Economic and Social Council, the OECD, the ILO, and the 1949 ITO Secretariat proposals, the WTO General Council could easily formulate a workable set of arrangements for NGO participation.

Some groups would have greater resources for participation than others, but the issue of disparate resources is a pervasive problem in any organization. In fact, disparate resource allocation is currently a problem for *governmental* representation at the WTO. After all, the United States Trade Representative has more staff in the WTO headquarters city of Geneva than does the Geneva delegation of the trade ministry of the Congo.

The most serious concern is that trade scholars believe that the GATT's "low public profile" was "one of the largest contributors to trade liberalization over the past fifty years". Even if the GATT's low public profile largely contributed to trade liberalization in the past—and it is possible that the GATT's low public profile was the main reason why trade liberalization proceeded so slowly over the past 50 years—it seems unlikely to remain so in the future as trade assumes a larger role in American political discourse.

A recent American public opinion poll found strong support among American citizens for protectionism. Over 68 percent of the public would support the imposition of "tariffs on products from countries that have a trade imbalance with the United States". In recent years, there has been a resurgence in protectionist literature and in 1995, with the advent of a Republic-controlled Congress, trade liberalization proposals stalled. By winter 1996, trade became a key issue in the Republic Presidential campaign.

Given the heightened public attention to trade, it is unlikely that the WTO will be able to maintain the anonymity of the GATT. Nor should it. The WTO should actively engage in educating the public about the dangers of protectionist trade policies, just as the World Health Organization educates the public about communicable disease.

The notion that the international trade regime should be a buffer between the makers of trade policy and the public is an elitist view that should not find refuge in liberal governance. The founders of the international trade regime were well aware of the need to obtain popular support in removing domestic trade barriers. Indeed, the American reciprocal trade agreements program, begun in 1934, contains institutional procedures for broad public participation. Individuals and NGOs will need to become more deeply involved in the legislative process by which the world trade community creates rules and standards. The trading regime must be more inclusive in order to integrate both trade and non-trade values.

Critics may suggest that any scheme would not equitably allow for direct participation by all of the citizens of the world.

If the WTO is going to expand its work into new areas such as investment, competition policy, environment, labor standards and corrupt practices, it will need a broader base of participation than just national trade ministers. However, even if the WTO were to focus only on narrow issues of trade liberalization, the case to include NGOs would still be strong' primarily because eradicating protectionism is an enormous task which requires the full involvement of all stakeholders.

Participation in WTO Dispute Resolution

For better or worse, no government or major NGO argues that NGOs ought to have "standing" as a plaintiff to invoke WTO dispute resolution. Instead, the contemporary debate addresses whether an NGO ought to be able to submit an *amicus* brief or testify before a dispute panel in a public hearing. NGOs also seek access to government briefs. At this point, NGOs are not pursuing the right to make oral arguments before a panel, nor the right to cross-examine the plaintiff or defendant governments.

If history is a guide, whether NGOs should have standing as WTO plaintiffs is an interesting legal question that surely will arise in the next century and has been resolved in other contexts. For example, as delegates to the ILO, employers and worker NGOs do have standing to lodge complaints about a government's conformity with its responsibilities under a ratified ILO convention. Furthermore, environmental NGOs have standing in American courts to challenge federal actions as "interested" humans, but not generally as representatives of nature. In the European Union, individuals who are challenging laws in national courts may seek to refer the case to the European Court of Justice under Article 177 for a determination as to whether a national law is violative of provisions of the Treaty of Rome ensuring the free flow of goods. The *North American Free Trade Agreement* (NAFTA) contains a provision giving a private investor the right to invoke arbitration when it believes that a NAFTA member government has violated NAFTA's rules on investment. This provision was invoked for the first time in March 1996 by a Mexican drug company who complained about Canadian regulations of generic drugs.

One certainly can imagine a system whereby NGOs or individuals would be able to invoke the WTO dispute process. For example, the European Union has entered into an agreement with several developing countries to limit imports of bananas. A consumer group in Europe should be able to file a complaint that this agreement violates GATT Article XI, which requires the general elimination of quantitative restrictions, especially if no government is willing to do so.

For the foreseeable future, however, the WTO seems unlikely to grant that sort of standing. A logical interim step would be to give the WTO Secretariat the right to lodge complaints, in the same way that the European Commission has the right to bring a matter before the European Court of Justice. In one area, the WTO does require standing for private parties in national tribunals. The Agreement on Trade-Related Aspects of Intellectual Property Rights provides that:

> "[A] member shall ... adopt procedures to enable a right holder, who has valid grounds for suspecting that the importation of counterfeit trademark or pirated copyright goods may take place, to lodge an application in writing with competent authorities, administrative or judicial, for the suspension by the customs authorities of the release into free circulation of such goods."

> Environmental and public interest NGOs are seeking an opportunity to participate in WTO dispute resolution because the WTO has become an important forum for international environmental adjudication. As Ernst-Ulrich Petersmann pointed out, "[t]he GATT dispute settlement system has been used more frequently for the settlement of 'environmental disputes' between states than any other international dispute settlement mechanism".

There are two main justifications for NGO participation in dispute resolution. First, NGO participation will increase the information available to the panel, thereby leading to better informed—and hopefully better quality—panel decisions. Second, a closed dispute resolution process will undermine popular support. The general public of a country that loses a WTO dispute will be more apt to cooperate with the required legislative change if the WTO dispute resolution process seems fair.

An impetus behind NGOs' desire to participate in WTO dispute resolution is that the GATT panels have not performed well in adjudicating environmental disputes, particularly in the tuna-dolphin controversy. The tuna panel decisions were neither thorough nor entirely logical. The low quality of these environmental decisions—as compared to typically high quality GATT decisions in the more common commercial disputes—suggests a need to improve the information provided to a WTO panel. Although it does not provide a mandate for NGO *amicus* briefs, the Uruguay Round Agreement does take steps to improve the adjudication process. Most importantly, the Uruguay Round established an appellate review process that will provide a mechanism for correcting erroneous panel decisions.

Those critical of direct access by NGOs to WTO panels usually argue that NGOs should filter comments through their sovereign governments. There are, however, several problems with this argument. First, as noted above, international NGOs do not fit the traditional citizen-government model Second, NGOs from countries who are not members of the WTO are not represented by governments with WTO participatory rights. Thus, environmental NGOs in large nations like China or Russia might have valuable information for a WTO panel, but are prevented from supplying such input. Third, a government may not want to present a point urged by one of "its" NGOs. There could be a benign reason for this: the point could be incorrect. But, there might also be a less benign reason: a government might not want to repeat an NGO point if doing so could undermine the government in another WTO case or in domestic litigation. For example, while the United States Trade Representative defended the American tuna import ban against the European Commission, the United States Trade Representative pressed the Commission to repeal a pending ban on the import of furs caught in countries permitting leg-hold traps. Perhaps the United States Trade Representative withheld arguments in the tuna-dolphin case for fear that the Commission would turn those arguments against the United States in a fur trapping case or in another subsequent panel. Such latent conflicts of interest would provide a compelling reason to allow NGOs to present their best points directly.

Additionally, there is the possibility that defendant governments-particularly the United States with its separation of powers might prefer to lose a WTO case if the executive branch dislikes the law being contested. Similarly, one group within a government, such as the trade officials who speak before WTO panels, might mount a weak defense. In such scenarios of conflicting governmental interest, assumptions that governments can be depended on to synthesize and balance values are not warranted.

Even some supposedly pro-participation governments are sometimes reluctant to listen to NGOs. For example, in March 1994, the Clinton Administration, with great fanfare, created a trade and environment NGO advisory committee. Two years later, however, the administration had not yet held the first meeting of this advisory committee.

We should not be overly concerned about the spectacle of a domestic constituency opposing the position of the government that is supposed to represent that constituency. Surely, we are used to that by now. Domestic opposition to a governmental position is quite common in domestic public law litigation and is increasingly common in transnational public law litigation. One such spectacle occurred in 1981 when the United States Senate restaurant workers lodged an ILO complaint stating that the Senate management refused to negotiate with them. The ILO performed a fair investigation without irreconcilable dissonance.

Thus far, I have focused on possible inadequacies in the representations made by governments to WTO panels, yet there is even a more fundamental reason to move to allow NGOs a role: defects within the WTO itself.

Fundamentally, the WTO Agreement fails to recognize the global environment. It is a treaty about trade across economic borders. If there were no ocean, no atmosphere, no Antarctica, no cross-border pollution and no biodiversity, not a single word in the WTO would need to be rewritten. The WTO is replete with constructive rules on the topic of economic interdependence, but it is vacuous on the topic of ecological interdependence.

The absence of attention to ecological interdependence necessitates fundamental reform of the WTO. In the meantime, to fill this gap it would be useful to permit NGOs to make written presentations to WTO panels. Each panel might also hold one day of public hearings where NGOs could testify. An appropriate time for such NGO input would be after the panel completes a draft on the factual background of the dispute and summarizes the positions of the parties. The WTO should release these interim factual and positional drafts to the public before the hearing so that those testifying can comment on them. It will be impossible to hear from thousands of NGOs. As with any legislative hearing, the chairperson can determine who will be allowed to speak. Alternatively, NGOs could act collectively to select their spokespersons.

If direct participation by NGOs produces too much incoherence, the WTO might try a more organized approach. For example, the WTO could ask an intergovernmental environmental organization, such as the United Nations Environment Programme or the World Conservation Union, to name an "Environmental Advocate" to speak in WTO environmental disputes. The Environmental Advocate would work with NGOs and scientists to produce a report discussing the significance of the environmental treaty or law challenged in the WTO dispute resolution procedure.

Another model that could assure a just representation of environmental interests before WTO panels existed within the Permanent Court of International Justice. This court provided for a special chamber for labor issues only in which the judges appoint "technical assessors" who would be chosen with a view to ensuring a just representation of the competing interests.

Conclusion

The establishment of the WTO should improve international trade governance. The WTO has the authority to consider new trade rules, to review national trade laws, and to adjudicate disputes. The Charter of the ITO, written between 1946–1948, recognized the need for involving NGOs. Although that organization never came into existence, the birth of its nephew, the WTO, provides an opportunity to correct the GATT practice of excluding NGOs.

If it is appropriate for NGOs to provide input to national governments about trade issues, then it is also appropriate for NGOs to provide input to international organizations about trade issues.

NGOs play constructive roles in numerous international organizations. It seems clear that these roles will increase in the years ahead. If it is appropriate for NGOs to provide input to national governments about trade issues, then it is also appropriate for NGOs to provide input to international organizations about trade issues.

Simply put, there are no good reasons for the WTO to refuse to provide systematic participation rights for NGOs. One hopes that WTO members will feel this reality while the WTO still enjoys the goodwill afforded to new International institutions. As United States Secretary of State, Cordell Hull [said] in 1944, "[n]o institution will endure unless there is behind it considered and complete public support".

7

Questions for Discussion

(a) What impact does international trade have on the environment? How should or do economic institutions such as the World Trade Organization deal with environmental concerns?

(b) Should economic institutions such as the World Trade Organization coordinate their policies with environmental institutions? If so, how? What role should nongovernmental organizations play with the WTO?

(c) Should any one country be allowed to use unilateral national measures to protect the environment beyond its territory? Or should action be confined only to situations where there is an international consensus? Should national and international levels of environmental policy and law be coordinated? If so, how?

(d) Are concerns with "race to the bottom" and "pollution havens" valid? Do different countries have a legitimate right to set their own environmental standards? Do different countries need to coordinate national and international laws and policies in economic activity and for environmental standards? Why?

(e) What are the concerns with developing countries over the linkage between trade and the environment? How can these concerns be best met?

8

References for Chapter 19

Barcelo J.J. III, "Product Standards to Protect the Local Environment—The GATT and the Uruguay Round Sanitary and Phytosanitary Agreement," 27 *Cornell Int'l L.J.*, 1994, pp 755–776.

Bousquet P. and Berlin K., "Environmental Trade: The Question of Standards," 12 *Envtl. L.*, March 1993, pp 1–5.

Charnovitz S., "The Regulation of Environmental Standards by International Trade Agreements," 16 *Int'l Env. Rep.* (BNA), 25 August 1992, pp 631-635.

Charnovitz S., "The World Trade Organization and Environmental Supervision," *Int'l Env. Rep.* (BNA), 26 January 1994, pp 89-93.

Chaytor B. and Cameron J., *Taxes for Environmental Purposes: The Scope for Border Tax Adjustment under WTO Rules,* A WWF International Discussion Paper. Gland, Switzerland: World Wide Fund for Nature, October 1996.

Dawkins K., *Ecolabelling: Consumers' Right-to-Know or Restrictive Business Practice*, Draft, Minneapolis, MN, US: Institute for Agriculture and Trade Policy, 1995.

Demaret P. and Stewardson R., "Border Tax Adjustments under GATT and EC Law and General Implications for Environmental Taxes," 28 *J. World Trade,* August 1994.

Esty D.C., *Greening the GATT: Trade, the Environment and the Future,* Washington, DC, Institute for International Economics, 1994.

Esty D.C., "Environmental Regulation and Competitiveness," paper presented at the *Asia Conference on Trade and Environment*, Singapore, 27–28 June 1996.

GATT Secretariat,"Agenda Item 3: Packaging and Labelling Requirements," GATT Doc. TRE/ W/12, paper prepared for *GATT Group on Environmental Measures and International Trade*, June 1993.

International Council of Chemical Associations [ICCA], "Position Statement on Product Requirements," 11 April 1995.

Jha J., *et al.*, "Eco-labelling and International Trade: Preliminary Information from 7 Systems," paper prepared for *United Nations Conference on Trade and Development* [UNCTAD] International Trade Division, Trade and Environment Section, New York: UNCTAD, 1993.

Lee J. "Process and Product: Making the Link Between Trade and the Environment: 6 *Int'l Envtl. Aff*, September 1994, pp 200–348.

Levinson A., "Environmental Regulations and Industry Location: International and Domestic Evidence," in I Jaydish N. Bhagwati & Roberl E. Hudec (eds). *Fair Trade and Harmonization: Prerequisites for Free Trade?* Cambridge. Massachusetts & London, England, MIT Press, 1996.

Mathews C.A., "The ISO 14001 Environmental Management System Standard: An Innovative Approach to Environmental Protection." 2 *Envtl. Law.*, 1996, p 817.

Organization for Economic Cooperation and Development [OECD] "Environmental Costs and Industrial Competitiveness," OECD Doc. DSTI/IND(91)46, 2 October 1991.

OECD, *The Environmental Effects of Trade,* Paris, OECD, 1994.

OECD Secretariat,"Report on Trade and Environment to the OECD Council at Ministerial Level," OECD Doc. OCDE/ GD(95)63, 1995.

Pearson C., "Trade and Environment: Theory, Empirical Studies and Their Limitations," paper presented at the *Asia Conference on Trade and Environment*, Singapore, 27-28 June, 1996.

Prudencio R., *Guarding the Green Choice: Environmental Labelling and the Rights of Green Consumers*, A National Wildlife Federation [NWF] Trade and Environment Report, Washington, DC:NWF, 1996

Reiterer M., "GATT, the WTO and the Environment: The Agenda of the CTE, in particular MEAs, Eco-Labelling and Trade Liberalization," paper presented at the *Asia Conference on Trade and Environment*, Singapore 27 28 June 1996.

Repetto R., *et al.*, *Green Fees: How a Tax Shift Can Work for the Environment and the Economy,* A World Resources Institute [WRI] Report. Washington, DC: WRI, November 1992.

Roht-Arriaza, N., "Shifting the Point of Regulation: The International Organization for Standardization and Global Lawmaking on Trade and the Environment," 22 *Ecology L.Q.*, 1995, p 479.

Salzman J., "Trade Law Issues of Eco-Labelling and Extended Producer Responsibility TakeBack Programs," working draft of a discussion paper for the Global Environment & Trade Study, presented at the *Asia Conference on Trade and Environment*, Singapore 27-28 June 1996.

Snape W.J. III and Lelkovitz N. B., "Searching for GATT's Environmental *Miranda:* Are 'Process Standards' Getting Due Process?", 27 *Cornell lnt'1 L. J.*, 1994, 777.

Stevens C.,"Trade and Environment: The PPMs Debate," in Winfried Lang, *Sustainable Development and International Law*, London: Graham & Trotman/Martinus Nijhoff, 1995.

Stonehouse R., *et al., Environmental Data, Risk Assessment and Environmental Standards*, UNEP Environment and Trade Series No. [4'], New York: UNEP, 1994.

Terra Choice Environmental Services Inc., Eco-labelling: A Possible Framework for Cooperation," background paper prepared for Government of Canada to facilitate discussions in WTO CTE and Committee on Technical Barriers to Trade, 25 March 1996.

UN Conference on Trade and Development [UNCTAD] Secretariat, "International Cooperation on Eco-Labelling and Eco-Certification Programmes and Market Opportunities for Environmentally Friendly Products," UN Doc. TD/B/WG.6/2, paper prepared for the *Trade and Development Board Ad Hoc Working Group on Trade, Environment and Development*, 6 October 1994.

UNCTAD Secretariat,"Trade, Environment and Development Aspects of Establishing and Operating Eco-Labelling Programmes," UN Doc. TD/B/WG.6/5, paper prepared for the Trade and Development Board *Ad Hoc* Working Group on Trade. Environment and Development, 28 March 1995.

US Council for International Business [USCIB], *Statement on Trade Barriers Which Arise From Government-sponsored Eco-labelling Programs*, 21 March 1995.

World Trade Organization [WTO] Secretariat, "GATT/WTO Activities on Trade and Environment 1994-95," *Trade and Environment Bulletin* No. 2., WTO Doc. PRESS/TE002, 8, May 1995.

WTO Secretariat, "WTO Trade and Environment Committee Agrees on Work Programme in Preparation for The Singapore Ministerial Meeting and Continues Examination of Trade Measures in Multilateral Environmental Agreements and Eco-labelling," *Trade and Environment Bulletin* No.6., WTO Doc. Press/ TE006, 8 December 1995.

WTO Secretariat, "WTO Trade and Environment Committee Discusses Proposals on Trade Measures in Multilateral Environmental Agreements and on Eco-labelling," *Trade and Environment Bulletin* No. 6., WTO Doc. Press/TE006, 29 April 1996.

World Wide Fund for Nature [WWF], *The Uruguay Round's Technical Barriers to Trade Agreement*, Gland. Switzerland: World Wide Fund for Nature, 1993

9 Additional References

Agenda 21, Ch. 34—"Transfer of Technology."

Barsh R.L., "Is the Expropriation of Indigenous Peoples' Land GATT-able?," *Review of European Community and International Environmental Law*, v.10 (1), 2001, pp 13–26.

Brack D., 'Balancing Trade and the Environment,' *International Affairs*, 71:3 July 1995.

Cameron J., Demaret P., and Geradin D. (eds), *Trade and Environment: The Search for Balance*, London, Cameron May 1994.

Charnovitz S., "Improving Environmental and Trade Governance," 7 *International Environmental Affairs* 1995, pp 59–76.

Charnovitz S., 'GATT and the Environment: Examining the Issues' *International Environmental Affairs*, 4:3, Summer 1992.

Esty D., *Greening the GATT: Trade, Environment and the Future*, Washington, DC: Institute for International Economics, 1994.

Floum J.R., "Defending Dolphins and Sea Turtles: On the Front Lines in an 'Us-Them' Dialectic," 10 *Georgetown International Environmental Law Journal* (1998), pp 943–955.

The Global Environment and Trade Study web site <http://www.gets.org> contains links to other trade and environment resources, as well as much useful material of its own [*Editors' Note: This site was accessed on 03/04/2001*]. (GETS is a collaborative enterprise involving the Foundation for International Environmental Law and Development, Yale University Center for Environmental Law and Policy and the US Institute of Agriculture and Trade Policy.)

Hardcastle R., "Environmental Trade Measure Under Seige: The WTO *US Shrimp* Case," *Asia Pacific Journal of Environmental Law*, Vol. 3, Issue 2, 1998, pp 157–171.

House of Commons Environment Committee, *World Trade and the Environment*, London: HMSO, HC 149, June 1996.

International Centre for Trade and Sustainable Development web site (http://www.ictsd.org) contains much useful trade and environment material, including in particular the *BRIDGES Weekly Trade News Digest* and *BRIDGES Monthly Trade Review*. [*Editors' Note: This site was accessed on 03/04/2001.*]

International Trade Law Reports, (reprinting WTO panel findings together with a commentary, as they occur), Cameron May.

Hughes L., "Limiting the Jurisdiction of Dispute Settlement Panels: The WTO Appellate Body Beef Hormone Decision," 10 *Georgetown International Environmental Law Journal*, 1998, pp 915–942.

Jha V., Hewison G., and Underhill M., *Trade, Environment and Sustainable Development: A South Asian Perspective*, St Martins Press, New York, 1997.

Kingsbury B., "The Tuna-Dolphin Controversy, The World Trade Organization, and the Liberal Project to Reconceptualize International Law," 5 *Yearbook of International Environmental Law*, 1994, p 1.

Repetto R., *Trade and 5ustainable Development*, Geneva, UNEP, 1994. (This is the first of the UNEP 'Environment and Trade' series of booklets.)

Shenk M. D., "Standards for Reformulated and Conventional Gasoline," 90 *American Journal of International Law* October, 1996, pp 669–674.

Tay S.S.C. and Esty D. (eds.), *Asian Dragons and Green Trade*, Times Academic Press, 1996.

United Nations Conference on Trade and Development [UNCTAD] Secretariat, "Newly Emerging

Environmental Policies with a Possible Trade Impact: A Preliminary Discussion," UN Doc. TD/B/ WG.6/ 9, paper prepared for *Trade and Development Board's Ad Hoc Working Group on Trade, Environment and Development*, Third Session. Geneva 6 November 1995, item 3 of the provisional agenda, 28 August 1995.

Vossenaar R. and Jha V., "Environmental Policy and International Competitiveness: An Asian Development Perspective", paper presented al the *Asia Conference on Trade and Environment*, Singapore, June 1996.

Walker S., *The TRIPS Agreement, Sustainable Development and the Public Interest*, IUCN Law and Policy Paper No.41, IUCN, Gland, Switzerland, 2001.

Won A., "Note: Environmental Subsidies Under the GATT and the Polluter Pays Principle: A Case Study of the Republic of Korea," 5 *Geo. Int'l Envtl. L. Rev.*, 1993, pp 761–782.

WTO web site: http://www.wto.org [*Editors' Note: This site was accessed on 03/04/2001.*]

World Trade Organization [WTO] Secretariat, "Relationships between Environmental Policies and WTO Services and Intellectual Property Agreements Examined", *Trade and Environment Bulletin* No. 4, WTO Doc. PRESS/TE004, 14 August 1995.

WTO Secretariat, "WTO Trade and Environment Committee Takes Up The Issues of Market Access and Domestically Prohibited Goods," *Trade and Environment Bulletin* No.5., WTO Doc. PRESS/ TE005, 10 October 1995.

WTO Secretariat, "WTO Trade and Environment Committee Discusses Proposals on Transparency, Multilateral Environmental Agreements. Market Access and Domestically Prohibited Goods and Adopts Work Programme to Singapore," *Trade and Environment Bulletin* No. 10., WTO Doc. PRESS/ TE010, 1 July 1996.

CHAPTER

20

BIOLOGICAL DIVERSITY

CONTENTS

1

Introduction

Biological diversity is the variety (or variability) of life on Earth. This variation occurs at several levels—those of genes, species, and ecosystems. Species diversity refers to the variety of species within a region; genetic diversity refers to the variation of genes within species. The complexes of species, interacting together and with the physical environment they inhabit, create the diversity of ecosystems found around the planet. Genes, species, and ecosystems are all components of biological diversity.

These components, which constitute the totality of biological resources of the Earth, or of a given region, are of fundamental importance to humans from the ecological and economic as well as aesthetic points of view: the biological diversity of the planet maintains the cycles of the elements that are essential for the future of all forms of life, including human life; it provides the basic material for food, clothing, medicines, housing and major industries; it also has intangible—cultural and aesthetic—values.

Regulatory mechanisms for the conservation of biological resources and the uninterrupted provision of the services they render to humans are not new: rules concerning the taking of animals and the collection of plants are as old as the human communities using them; those rules, however, evolved in parallel to the knowledge and understanding of the complexity of relationships and processes which exist within nature.

Thus, nationally, the evolution has been toward creating regulatory mechanisms that approach their specific aims (e.g., the use of a particular population of p lants or animals) in the context of ecological unit management.

The rationale for internationally agreed regulatory mechanisms has also evolved, originally only based on the need to cooperate bilaterally, regionally or globally whenever unilateral measures are not sufficient to achieve the conservation of specific populations or ecosystems either because:

- the species or ecosystems concerned are outside any area under national jurisdiction: or
- they are distributed across national boundaries (shared resources); or
- they are threatened by factors that originate in other states (transboundary threats).

It is based on this rationale that a number of early treaties on terrestrial and aquatic resources uses have been concluded; only exceptionally did this rationale justify action at global level, for regulating such activities as fishing on the high seas or international trade in endangered species, which is discussed in Chapter 19.

It is only relatively late that the need for concerted global action has been recognized, first in two specific instances: for one ecosystem, particularly as a habitat, type—wetlands (*Ramsar Convention*), and for sites with exceptional global values (*World Heritage Convention*, discussed in Chapter 15).

These two texts marked an essential step in the evolution of international biodiversity law, as they recognized a common interest of the international community as a whole in the unilateral, but concerted, conservation of specific components of biological diversity, dispersed throughout the world.

The way was paved for the recognition that biological diversity as a whole is a common concern of humanity, and that in spite of—or, more logically, because of—the sovereign rights of states over its constituent components, they have a duty to cooperate in achieving the conservation of biological diversity, as well as an individual responsibility to conserve and use sustainably the biodiversity components on which they exercise such rights. This was done with the adoption of the 1992 *Convention on Biological Diversity*.

The complexes of species, interacting together and with the physical environment they inhabit, create the diversity of ecosystems found around the planet. Genes, species, and ecosystems are all components of biological diversity.

The material in this chapter:

- introduces the concept of biological diversity, its nature and values;
- provides information on the *Convention on Biological Diversity* (CBD), addressing its constituent elements (conservation, sustainable use, sharing of benefits) and giving an illustration of an Asian (Viet Nam) strategy to implement the Convention;
- gives an overview of earlier international instruments of relevance to biological diversity with particular on the *Ramsar Convention* (CITES, another important convention, is dealt with in Chapter 19);
- considers the consequences of the co-existence of the CBD with other biodiversity-relevant international accords; and
- considers elements of national legislation needed to implement the CBD and, generally, international treaty law in the field of biodiversity.

A
Teaching Guide

At the conclusion of this chapter, students should:

- understand the values of biological diversity and the importance of its conservation and sustainable use for sustainable development;
- be aware of the relationships between international treaties in the field of biological diversity, at the global as well as regional levels;
- be familiar with the breadth of subjects covered by the CBD (conservation, sustainable use, access and benefit-sharing, biosafety) and with the main elements/techniques of implementation in national legislation; and
- appreciate the relationships between this field of international law and the relevant rules of the international trade regime.

Synopsis of a Lecture on Biodiversity Law

A. Introduction
- what is Biological Diversity
- what are its values
- how is it threatened

B. The evolution of treaty law in the field of biodiversity
- the early treaties
- from Stockholm to Rio: 20 years of treaty making:
  - global conventions
  - regional conventions
  - species specific accords
- the UN *Convention on Biological Diversity*
  - conservation, sustainable use and benefit sharing
  - indigenous and local communities and their knowledge
  - resources for food and agriculture
  - biotechnology and biosafety

C. The relationships
- between treaties dealing with biological diversity at the global level
- between global and regional treaties, e.g., the ASEAN Agreement on Conservation of Nature and Natural Resources
- between obligations deriving from biodiversity treaties and those deriving from WTO-related agreements

D. Implementation through National Legislation
- the need for coordinating mechanisms between the various sectoral laws and institutions involved
- the need to support sectoral legislation with cross sectoral links: national biological diversity strategy and planning cycle
- tools: command-and-control techniques; incentives measures; EIAs; risk assessment and management

Teaching Methodologies

The subject will be taught by way of lectures, discussions and simulation of governmental meetings on specific subjects.

A. Lecture: General information about biological diversity and the development of law and policy in this field.

B. Students to draft a memorandum stating why the revised FAO Undertaking on Genetic Resources should become a Protocol under the CBD. Comments by other students.

C. Student participation: Simulation of a parliamentary hearing in a country of the region considering the elements needed for the drafting of a legislation dealing with access to genetic resources and benefit sharing mechanisms related thereto.

- Students to represent the concerned regulatory agency, the indigenous communities, and the private sector, including environmental NGOs
- Discuss issues which need to be considered in order for the future legislation to achieve the third objective of the CBD:
  - Scope of application
  - Institutions needed to oversee access to genetic resources
  - Granting access:
- application
- notification of the public
- discussion of mutually agreed terms
- approval – denial
- appeal
  - Monitoring of implementation—short and long term

Students are required to do research for the above 'hearing'.

D. Questions for further discussion and research
- conservation and sustainable use objectives: legal mechanisms to empower local community management of biological resources
- processes and activities affecting biological diversity: legal techniques to provide incentives in achieving their control
- synergy starts at home: legal and institutional means to induce implementation of biodiversity-related international instruments in an integrated manner

2

Biological Diversity: Nature and Values, Losses and their Causes

Biological Diversity, or biodiversity, is a relatively new term, which has the merit of providing an overarching concept for a number of fields which have been of interest and concern to scientists and policy-makers for decades. In order to teach and study what is now referred to as biodiversity law, it is important to understand the concept. Even more important is to understand the role of biological diversity components in supporting human livelihoods and aspirations—and thus its relationship to development. Finally, action to conserve it, including legal strategies, demands an understanding of the causes which have generated a steady erosion of the diversity of genes, species and ecosystem.

A

WRI/IUCN/UNEP, *Global Biodiversity Strategy: Guidelines to Save, Study and Use Earth's Biotic Wealth Sustainably and Equitably*, WRI/IUCN/UNEP, 1992, pp 1–5, 7–18

The Nature and Value of Biodiversity

Earth's plants, animals, and microorganism—interacting with one another and with the physical environment in ecosystems—form the foundation of sustainable development. Biotic resources from this wealth of life support human livelihoods and aspirations and make it possible to adapt to changing needs and environments. The steady erosion of the diversity of genes, species, and ecosystems taking place today will undermine progress toward a sustainable society. Indeed, the continuing loss of biodiversity is a telling measure of the imbalance between human needs and wants and nature's capacity.

The human race had 850 million members when it entered the industrial age, sharing Earth with life forms nearly as diverse as the planet has ever possessed. Today, with population nearly six times as large and resource consumption proportionately far greater, both the limits of nature and the price of overstepping them are becoming clear. A turning point is upon us. We can continue to simplify the environment to meet immediate needs, at the cost of long-term benefits, or we can conserve life's precious diversity and use it sustainably We can deliver to the next generation (and the next) a world rich in possibilities or one impoverished of life; but social and economic development will succeed only if we do the first.

The Value of Biodiversity's Components

From both wild and domesticated components of biodiversity humanity derives all of its food and many medicines and industrial products. Economic benefits from wild species alone make up an estimated 4.5 percent of the Gross Domestic Product of the United States—worth $87 billion annually in the late 1970s. Fisheries, largely based on wild species, contributed about 100 million tons of food worldwide in 1989. Indeed, wild species are dietary mainstays in much of the world. In Ghana, three out of four people look to wildlife for most of their protein. Timber, ornamental plants, oils, gums, and many fibers also come from the wild.

The current economic value of domesticated species is even greater. Agriculture accounts for 32 percent of GDP in low-income developing countries and 12 percent in middle-income countries. Trade in agricultural products amounted to $3 trillion in 1989.

The components of biodiversity are also important to human health. Once, nearly all medicines came from plants and animals, and even today they remain vital. Traditional medicine forms the basis of primary health care for about 80 percent of people in developing countries, more than 3 billion people in all. More than 5,100 species are used in Chinese traditional medicine alone, and people in northwestern Amazonia have tapped some 2,000 species. Traditional medicine is now encouraged by the World Health Organization, and in many countries—including industrialized countries—its use is expanding rapidly. Nearly 2,500 plant species in the Soviet Union have been used for medicinal purposes and the demand for drug plant material has tripled in the last decade.

As for modern pharmaceuticals, one-fourth of all prescriptions dispensed in the United States contain active ingredients extracted from plants, and over 3,000 antibiotics—including penicillin and tetracycline—are derived from microorganisms. Cyclosporin, developed from a soil fungus, revolutionized heart and kidney transplant surgery by suppressing the immune reaction. Aspirin and many other drugs that are now synthesized were first discovered in the wild. Compounds extracted from plants, microbes, and animals were involved in developing all of the 20 best-selling drugs in the United States, drugs whose combined sales approached $6 billion in 1988.

Biotic resources also serve recreation and tourism. Fully 84 percent of all Canadians fish, photograph wildlife, or base other recreational activities on nature—a national passion and pastime worth $800 million annually. Worldwide, nature tourism generates as much as $12 billion in revenues each year. In Namibia, the national constitution itself includes a call to protect the "beauty and character" of the environment. And for many, simply knowing that a particular species or ecosystem exists is inspiring or comforting.

The Value of Diversity

The sheer *variety* of life has enormous value. The variety of distinctive species, ecosystems, and habitats influence the productivity and services provided by ecosystems. As the variety of species in an ecosystem changes—legacy of extinction or species introduction—the ecosystem's ability to absorb pollution, maintain soil fertility and micro-climates, cleanse water, and provide other invaluable services changes too. When the elephant—a voracious vegetarian—disappeared from large areas of its traditional range in Africa, the ecosystem was altered as grasslands reverted to woodlands and woodland wildlife returned. When the sea otter was all but exterminated from the Aleutian Islands by fur traders, sea urchin populations swelled and overwhelmed kelp production.

The value of variety is particularly apparent in agriculture. For generations, people have raised a wide range of crops and livestock to stabilize and enhance productivity. The wisdom of these techniques—including their contributions to watershed protection, soil fertility maintenance, and receptivity to integrated pest-management strategies—is being reaffirmed today as farmers around the world turn to alternative low-input production systems.

The genetic diversity found within individual crops is also of tremendous value. Genetic diversity provides an edge in the constant evolutionary battle between crops and livestock and the pests and diseases that prey on them. In age-old systems, several genetically distinct varieties of crops are planted together as a hedge against crop failure. The Ifugao of the Philippine island of Luzon can name more than 200 varieties of sweet potato, and Andean farmers cultivate thousands of varieties of potatoes.

Breeders and farmers also draw on the genetic diversity of crops and livestock to increase yields and to respond to changing environmental conditions. The opportunities provided by genetic engineering—which allows the transfer of genes among species—will further increase the opportunities genetic diversity provides for enhancing agricultural productivity. A wild tomato, found only in the Galápagos Islands, can grow in seawater and possesses jointless fruitstalks—a trait that has been bred into domesticated tomatoes to make them easy to harvest mechanically. A wild relative of rice collected in India provided a "resistance gene" that now protects high-yielding rice varieties in South and Southeast Asia from their nemesis, the brown plant-hopper. Plant breeding is to thank for fully half of the gains in agricultural yields in the United States from 1930 to 1980: an estimated $1 billion annually has been added to the value of US agricultural output by the widened genetic base.

Genetic diversity provides an edge in the constant evolutionary battle between crops and livestock and the pests and diseases that prey on them.

Over time, the greatest value of the variety of life may be found in the opportunities it provides humanity for adapting to local and global change. The unknown potential of genes, species, and ecosystems represents a never-ending biological frontier of inestimable but certainly high value. Genetic diversity will enable breeders to tailor crops to new climatic conditions. Earth's biota—a biochemical laboratory unmatched for size and innovation—hold the still-secret cures for emerging diseases. A diverse array of genes, species, and ecosystems is a resource that can be tapped as human needs and demands change.

Because biodiversity is so closely intertwined with human needs, its conservation should rightfully be considered an element of national security. It has become increasingly apparent that national security means much more than military might. Ecological dimensions of national security cannot be ignored when countries fight over access to water or when environmental refugees strain national budgets and public infrastructure. A secure nation means not only a strong nation, but also one with a healthy and educated populace, and a healthy and productive environment as well. National security will be strongest in countries that care for their biodiversity and the services it provides.

For many, these technical definitions and economic calculations may be eclipsed by still more basic reasons for conservation. Attitudes toward biodiversity and the respect that people show for other species are strongly influenced by moral, cultural, and religious values. The reason is not surprising.

Biodiversity is closely linked to cultural diversity—human cultures are shaped in part by the living environment that they in turn influence—and this linkage has profoundly helped determine cultural values. Most of the world's religions teach respect for the diversity of life and concern for its conservation. Indeed, the variety of life is the backdrop against which culture itself languishes or flourishes.

Even so, some reduction in biodiversity has been an inevitable consequence of human development, as species-rich forests and wetlands have been converted to relatively species-poor farmlands and plantations. Such conversions are themselves an aspect of the use and management of biodiversity, and there can be no doubt that they are beneficial. But many ecosystems have been converted to impoverished systems that are less productive—economically as well as biologically. Such misuse not only disrupts ecosystem function, it also imposes a cost. In the United States, the destruction of estuarine ecosystems between 1954 and 1978 cost over $200 million annually in revenues lost from commercial and sport fisheries alone. Expensive engineering was needed to defend against storms as substitutes for the natural defenses provided by coastal wetlands.

The many values of biodiversity and its importance for development suggest why biodiversity conservation differs from traditional nature conservation. Biodiversity conservation entails a shift from a defensive posture—protecting nature from the impacts of development—to an offensive effort seeking to meet peoples' needs from biological resources while ensuring the long-term sustainability of Earth's biotic wealth. It thus involves not only the protection of wild species but also the safeguarding of the genetic diversity of cultivated and domesticated species and their wild relatives. This goal speaks to modified and intensively managed ecosystems as well as natural ones, and it is pursued in the human interest and for human benefit. In sum, biodiversity conservation seeks to maintain the human life support system provided by nature, and the living resources essential for development.

Losses of Biodiversity and Their Causes

Biological diversity is being eroded as fast today as at any time since the dinosaurs died out some 65 million years ago. The crucible of extinction is believed to be in tropical forests. Around 10 million species live on earth, according to the best estimates, and tropical forests house between 50 and 90 percent of this total. About 17 million hectares of tropical forests—an area four times the size of Switzerland—are now being cleared annually, and scientists estimate that at these rates roughly 5 to 10 percent of tropical forest species may face extinction within the next 30 years. This estimate may prove conservative, however. Rates of tropical forest loss are accelerating, and some particularly species-rich forests are likely to be largely destroyed in our lifetime. Some scientists believe that about 60,000 of the world's 240,000 plant species, and perhaps even higher proportions of vertebrate and insect species, could lose their lease on life over the next three decades unless deforestation is slowed immediately.

Tropical forests are by no means the only sites with endangered biodiversity. Worldwide, nearly as much temperate rain forest—once covering an area nearly the size of Malaysia—has also been lost. Although the total extent of forest in the northern temperate and boreal regions has not changed much in recent years, in many areas the species-rich, old-growth forests have been steadily replaced by second-growth forests and plantations. Evidence of accelerating clearance of temperate forests is also appearing: between 1977 and 1987, 1.6 million hectares of forest was lost in the United States alone.

In several spots in Europe, fungal species diversity has dropped by 50 percent or more over the past 60 years. In such "Mediterranean" climes as California, South Africa, central Chile, and Southwest Australia, at least 10 percent of all plant and animal species are imperilled. The largest number of recent extinctions have been on oceanic islands: some 60 percent of plant species endemic to the Galapagos Islands are endangered, as are 42 percent of the Azores' endemic species and 75 percent of the endemic plant species of the Canary Islands.

The biodiversity of marine and freshwater systems faces serious loss and degradation. Perhaps hardest hit of all are freshwater ecosystems, battling long-term pollution and the introduction of many alien species. Marine ecosystems too are suffering from the loss of unique populations of many species and are undergoing major ecological changes.

The number of documented species extinctions over the past century is small compared to those predicted for the coming decades. This difference is due, in part, to the acceleration of rates of habitat loss over recent decades but also to the difficulty of documenting extinctions. The vast majority of species has not yet even been described, and many may disappear before they are even known to science. Moreover, species are generally not declared to be extinct until years after they have last been seen—so figures for documented extinctions are highly conservative. Finally, some species whose populations are reduced by habitat loss below the level necessary for long-term survival may hang on for several decades without hope of recovery as their population dwindles—these are the "living dead."

Still, evidence of extinction, especially of distinct populations of species, is only too plentiful. In 1990, the otter died out in the Netherlands, and in 1991 Britain declared the mouse-eared bat extinct. In the eastern Pacific, elevated sea temperatures in the 1980s caused the extinction of a hydrocoral. In the past decade, at least 34 species or unique populations of plants and vertebrates have become extinct in the United States while awaiting federal protection. Worldwide, over 700 extinctions of vertebrates, invertebrates, and vascular plants have been recorded since 1600. How many species went extinct elsewhere, unnoticed?

Habitat loss not only precipitates species extinctions, it also represents a loss of biodiversity in its own right. In many countries, relatively little natural vegetation remains untouched by human hands. In Bangladesh, only 6 percent of the original vegetation remains. Forests around the Mediterranean Sea probably once covered 10 times their current area, and in the Netherlands and Britain, less than 4 percent of lowland raised bogs remain undamaged.

The dramatic losses of species and ecosystems obscure equally large and important threats to *genetic* diversity. Worldwide, some 492 genetically distinct populations of tree species (including some full species) are endangered. In the northwestern United States, 159 genetically distinct populations of ocean-migrating fish are at high or moderate risk of extinction, if they have not already slipped into oblivion.

Loss of genetic diversity could imperil agriculture. How much the genetic base has already eroded is hard to say, but since the 1950s, the spread of modern "Green Revolution" varieties of corn, wheat, rice, and other crops has rapidly squeezed out native landraces. Modern varieties were adopted on 40 percent of Asia's rice farms within 15 years of their release, and in Indonesia and Philippines, and some other countries, more than 80 percent of all farmers now plant the new varieties. In Indonesia, 1,500 local rice varieties have become extinct in the last 15 years. A recent survey of sites in Kenya with wild coffee relatives found that the coffee plants in two of the sites had disappeared, three sites were highly threatened, and six were possibly threatened. Only two were secure.

The impact of such losses of genetic diversity often registers swiftly. In 1991, the genetic similarity of Brazil's orange trees opened the way for the worst outbreak of citrus canker recorded in the country. In 1970, US farmers lost $1 billion to a disease that swept through uniformly susceptible corn varieties. Similarly, the Irish potato famine in 1846, the loss of a large portion of the Soviet wheat crop in 1972, and the citrus canker outbreak in Florida in 1984 all stemmed from reductions in genetic diversity. In such countries as Bangladesh, where some 62 percent of rice varieties come from a single maternal plant, Indonesia (74 percent), and Sri Lanka (75 percent), such outbreaks could occur at any time.

Gene banks have slowed the loss of genetic diversity, but the high costs of periodically regenerating the seeds and the risk of mechanical failures make seedbanks less than fail-safe. In 1980, experts estimated that even in developed countries between one-half and two-thirds of the seeds collected in past decades had been lost. In 1991, representatives of 13 national germplasm banks in Latin America reported that between 5 and 100 percent of the maize seed collected between 1940 and 1980 is no longer viable.

The loss of genetic, species, and ecosystem diversity both stems from and invites the loss of cultural diversity. Diverse cultures have bred and sustained numerous varieties of crops, livestock, and habitats. By the same token, the loss of certain crops, the replacement of traditional crops with export crops, the extinction of species embedded in religion, mythology, or folklore, and the degradation or conversion of homelands are cultural as well as biological losses. Since 1900, experts say, about one Indian tribe has disappeared from Brazil each year. Almost one half of the world's 6,000 languages may die out in the next 100 years. Of the 3,000 languages expected to survive for a century, nearly half will probably not last much longer.

Causes and Mechanisms of Biodiversity Impoverishment

The current losses of biodiversity have both direct and indirect causes. The direct mechanisms include habitat loss and fragmentation, invasion by introduced species, the overexploitation of living resources, pollution, global climate change, and industrial agriculture and forestry. But these are not the root of the problem. Biotic impoverishment is an almost inevitable consequence of the ways in which the human species has used and misused the environment in the course of its rise to dominance.

As people awaken to the damage unsustainable development is increasingly inflicting on the web of life and the human prospect, the search for solutions must turn inward.

As people awaken to the damage unsustainable development is increasingly inflicting on the web of life and the human prospect, the search for solutions must turn inward. The roots of the biodiversity crisis are not "out there" in the forest or on the savannah, but embedded in the way we live. They lie in burgeoning human numbers, the way in which the human species has progressively broadened its ecological niche and appropriated ever more of the earth's biological productivity, the excessive and unsustainable consumption of natural resources, a continuing reduction in the number of traded products from agriculture and fisheries, economic systems that fail to set a proper value on the environment, inappropriate social structures, and weaknesses in legal and institutional systems. Just as biodiversity is an essential resource for sustainable development, finding sustainable ways to live is essential if biological diversity is to be conserved.

Six Fundamental Causes of Biodiversity Loss

The Unsustainably High Rate of Human Population Growth and Natural Resource Consumption

In most countries with high fertility rates, about half the population is under the age of 16. The resulting demographic momentum—that is, high birth rates in coming years due to the large number of people who will be reaching their reproductive years—means that global population will continue to grow for at least the next half century and probably longer, barring catastrophe. Another billion people are likely to be added to the world population for each of the next three decades. The rates and magnitude of this growth and the eventual size at which the global population stabilizes—critical considerations for biodiversity—depend on social and economic measures, especially on the rate of economic development in the developing countries.

As numbers have increased and new technologies have developed, humanity has appropriated an ever-increasing share of the earth's resources. People consume, divert, or destroy an estimated 39 percent of the terrestrial productivity of photosynthetic plants, algae, and bacteria, the fundamental source of the energy available for virtually all living systems. This trend is unsustainable. The world's biotic systems simply cannot accommodate an evergrowing claim on primary productivity to meet further growth in human population and consumption. The inherent limits of the natural resource base will impose a corresponding limit on the number of people who rely on it. Of course, an ecosystem's (or, for that matter, a planet's) "ecological carrying capacity" can be increased by technology (as the history of agriculture demonstrates), but ultimate constraints on consumption are nevertheless real.

Critical environmental resources are now under stress. Emissions of pollutants, including greenhouse gases, are already overtaxing the tolerance of ecosystems and the dispersal capacity of the atmosphere. Ozone layer depletion, acid rain, and air pollution are all taking a toll on biodiversity today and may threaten it even more severely in the future, particularly if climate change accelerates. Excessive consumption of minerals and other non-renewable resources and a gross overuse and waste of energy, especially by the industrialized nations, aggravates these problems. The developed countries bear the principal responsibility for these impacts, and they need to move swiftly toward a more sustainable way of life. New patterns of development are essential if projected population growth is to be accommodated without straining the planet's carrying capacity.

The Steadily Narrowing Spectrum of Traded Products from Agriculture, Forestry, and Fisheries

For millennia, the world was a patchwork of relatively autonomous regions. Knowledge, subsistence strategies, and social structures evolved in each region more or less independently, and people's demands on the environment rarely exceeded nature's capacity. In forest areas, traditional agriculture did not appreciably erode diversity where population densities remained low, market pressure was slack, and the combination of shifting cultivation, hunting, fishing, and the gathering of forest products that formed the backbone of most traditional subsistence strategies was well-balanced. No one group could undermine biodiversity overall, and some even enhanced it. But the global exchange economy that has emerged over the past century, based on principles of comparative advantage and specialization, has increased both uniformity and interdependence.

In agriculture, producers now specialize in the relatively few crops that provide an edge in the world economy. As the number of crop species declines, local nitrogen-fixing bacteria, mycorrhizae, predators, pollinators, seed dispersers, and other species that coevolved over centuries with traditional agricultural systems die out. The use of fertilizers, pesticides, and high-yielding varieties to maximize production and profits over the short-term exacerbates this loss. In forest areas, the rapid and total conversion of forests (often to monocultural cash crops) is widespread. When the price of coffee or palm oil drops, the plantation cannot quickly revert to the biologically diverse forest that preceded it, even if left alone. Similarly, large global markets have fostered the development of what might be called blanket fishing. Monofilament drift nets, for instance, catch enormous quantities of target species—and enormous numbers of "incidental" marine mammals, birds, and so-called nontarget fish.

Economic Systems and Policies that Fail to Value the Environment and its Resources

Many conversions of natural systems—such as forests or wetlands to farmlands and rangelands—are economically and biologically inefficient. They happen partly because of the urgent need for land to cultivate, regardless of how sustainable cultivation is, and partly because natural habitats are commonly undervalued economically.

There are several reasons for the misvaluation of biological resources. First, many biological resources are consumed directly and never enter markets. Among forest products, sawn timber, pulpwood, rattan, and gums are likely to be marketed while much of the food, fuelwood, and medicinal plants harvested by local people and the clean water supplied by the forest to the rivers will not. Accordingly, the economic values of logging and other potentially exhaustive uses are overestimated while sustainable uses (and aesthetic and spiritual benefits) are underestimated, creating incentives to impoverish the forest.

Second, biodiversity's benefits are in large part "public goods" that no single owner can claim. Wetland protection, for example, benefits the public tangibly and quantifiably, but the benefits are so diffuse that no market incentives for wetland conservation ever develop. This undervaluation then justifies government policies—such as tax incentives—that further encourage wetland conversion to use with greater "market" value.

Third, property rights are more likely to be granted to those who clear and settle forests and other lands covered with natural vegetation than to forest dwellers living by the sustainable harvest of natural products. Formal property rights are also often easier to obtain by people living in cities and working in the formal sector of the economy—which itself favors the extraction and marketing of products such as timber over the sustainable harvest of products with limited market value. Any uncertainty over property rights weakens incentives for stewardship and encourages overexploitation. Few farmers will plant woodlots that they might not own five years later. People who do not benefit from a tourist industry, but need food, are more likely to kill than to protect wild animals. People who have no stake in a resource are the least likely to care for it and the most likely to alter it if doing so establishes ownership.

Correctly valued, biologically diverse natural systems are major economic assets. But because such systems are commonly undervalued, biodiversity conservation is seen as a cost rather than an investment. Correcting this error is essential to conserving global and national biodiversity.

Inequity in the Ownership, Management and Flow of Benefits from Both the Use and Conservation of Biological Resources

In most countries, ownership and control of land and biotic resources, and all the benefits they confer, are distributed in ways that work against biodiversity conservation and sustainable living. The rapid depletion of species and the destruction of habitats are the norm in many countries where a minority of the population owns or controls most of the land. Quick profits from excessive logging or overfishing flow to the few, while the local communities dependent on the continued production of the resources pay the price.

A second problem arises from the concentration of resource control and responsibility for environmental policy decisions primarily in the hands of urban men. In many societies women manage the environment and possess far greater knowledge of biodiversity's value to farming and health.

A third issue is the way international trade, debt and technology transfer policies and practices foster inequities that resemble—and often reinforce—those found within nations. By 1988, developing countries were transferring $32.5 billion net to industrialized countries, excluding other implicit resource transfers not involving direct financial flows. (At the beginning of the decade, $42.6 billion had been flowing to developing countries.) To conserve biodiversity, industrialized countries must reverse this flow. If the developing countries continue to be shut out of markets, deprived of access to technology, and burdened with debt, they will have neither the means nor the incentive to conserve their resources for the future.

Deficiencies in Knowledge and its Application

Scientists still do not have adequate knowledge of natural ecosystems and their innumerable components. This ignorance is compounded by the destruction of cultures that possess a traditional understanding of nature. Even where knowledge exists, it does not flow efficiently to decision-makers, who have in consequence often failed to develop policies that reflect the scientific, economic, social and ethical values of biodiversity. Information also fails to flow properly between central decision-makers and the local communities who depend directly on biological resources, and who may have their livelihood jeopardized by inappropriate development projects and other actions. A final difficulty stems from public reluctance to accept policies that reduce excessive resource consumption, no matter how logical or necessary such policies may be.

Legal and Institutional Systems that Promote Unsustainable Exploitation

Ecological and economic realities clearly call for a cross-sectoral approach to biodiversity conservation and management. Yet, many national and international institutions operate along rigidly sectoral lines, and many environmental institutions are small and short of resources. Cross-sectoral coordinating machinery is being introduced, both at international level and within countries, but it has yet to prove its effectiveness.

A second problem is the overcentralization of government and corporate planning, which hinders local implementation, discourages local participation, and closes the process to citizen's groups and nongovermental organizations.

A third problem is the weakness of most agencies and organizations charged with nature conservation. Few have the personnel or financial resources needed even to support minimal programs. Their efforts are commonly fragmented and overlapping; what conservation planning they do is neither comprehensive nor strategic, and they do not integrate *in situ* and *ex situ* conservation tools and technologies.

Adding to these difficulties, many countries lack an adequate system of environmental laws and other instruments to ensure the protection of the environment and the sustainable use of its resources. In many developing countries, customary laws that conserved biological resources well have been replaced by less effective legal systems; national policy-making and planning processes are ineffective, the use of economic instruments to promote environmental protection is insufficient, and basic scientific knowledge is inadequate.

Largely because of these legal and institutional constraints, biodiversity conservation has typically been piecemeal and concentrated on traditional wildlife protection techniques—a protected area here, a regime for managing an endangered or threatened species there. Even multiplied many times, such efforts seldom fulfill species' habitat requirements, particularly those of migratory animals, since land-use practices outside protected areas can alter water supplies, introduce pollutants, and change microclimates. And such efforts do nothing to ensure that policies for sustainable resource use are integrated, which is at the heart of biodiversity conservation.

Regionwide management approaches are needed to address the habitat needs of whole biotic communities and to integrate conservation with regional development. In most situations, managing entire regions as national parks, forest reserves, or marine reserves is inappropriate. But lack of the integrated expertise and authority needed to manage a mix of developed and wild ecosystems impedes sound regional management. Regions big enough for effective development and resource management incorporating biodiversity conservation typically come under various local, state, or provincial government jurisdictions, and some involve two or more nations—an administrative nightmare.

3

Preconvention on Biological Diversity: International Instruments and Initiatives

International cooperation to conserve certain species and certain natural areas dates back to the beginning of this century, with treaties concluded on certain migratory species (in particular birds), and regional instruments for Africa (1933) and the Western Hemisphere (1940), some of which are now obsolete.

Under the impetus of the Man and Biosphere Conference (UNESCO, 1968), and the Stockholm Conference on the Human Environment, the value of species and ecosystems—and generally the natural environment—became increasingly recognized. The need for cooperation and concerted unilateral action was formally recognized in soft law instruments, starting with the *Stockholm Declaration* (see Principles 2 and 4), and followed by the *World Charter for Nature* (1982) and the *Rio Declaration* (1992). The negotiation of binding international instruments on specific issues accompanied this process. Four major global conventions were adopted in the period 1972-1992. They are:

- The *Convention on Wetlands of International Importance*, Ramsar, 1971
- The *Convention for the Protection of the World Cultural and Natural Heritage*, Paris, 1972
- The *Convention on International Trade in Endangered Species*, Washington, 1973
- The *Convention on the Conservation of Migratory Species of Wild Animals*, Bonn, 1979

Chapter 15 is dedicated to the *World Heritage Convention*. Chapter 19 contains an examination of CITES. Therefore, the reader is directed to those chapters for the relevant material. The *Ramsar Convention* is discussed in this chapter and the introduction to the convention within the following extract is designed to lead straight into that discussion. Finally, the following extract is the only material in this book which explicitly covers the *Bonn Convention*. It is, by necessity, an introductory piece and the reader is directed to the additional references for further study in this area.

Until the *Biodiversity Convention* was adopted, all broadly-based biodiversity-related instruments were regional. Two are relevant to Asia:

The first is the *Agreement on the Conservation of Nature and Natural Resources*, Kuala Lumpur, 1985 (ASEAN Agreement), which is dealt with extensively in Chapter 16.

The other is the *Convention on the Conservation of Nature in the South Pacific* (Apia, 1976). The Convention provides for the creation of protected areas and the protection of species, lists of which are to be drawn up by each Contracting Party. Secretariat functions are provided by the South Pacific Regional Environmental Programme (SPREP), but the Convention does not provide for meetings of its Contracting Parties.

Regional Seas Conventions, adopted in the framework of the UNEP Regional Seas Programme, are also relevant here. The UNEP Regional Seas Programme is briefly discussed in Chapter 18.

Finally, Conventions have been concluded which deal with the conservation and management of particular species: terrestrial species, in particular birds, freshwater species, and marine mammals are the subject of early treaties (e.g., the *Whaling Convention*), as well as agreements under the *Migratory Species Convention*. A brief overview of these treaties, as well as of the relationship between fisheries law and marine biodiversity conservation law, including UNCLOS, can be found in the UNITAR/UNEP/ IUCN source which is extracted below.

A

The Convention on the Conservation of Migratory Species of Wild Animals

(i) de Klemm C. and Shine C., "International Environmental Law: Biological Diversity," Course 6, Programme of Training for the Application of Environmental Law, UNITAR/UNEP/IUCN, 1998, pp 63–72, 78–96

Convention on the Conservation of Migratory Species of Wild Animals (Bonn, 23 June 1979)

Background

In the course of this century, there has been gradual acceptance by the international community that migratory species should be considered as shared resources for which Range States should exercise joint responsibility. A series of bilateral and multilateral treaties have been concluded for certain species (see below), but their coverage was restricted to a few regions of the world and they often excluded part of the migration routes concerned.

These factors made it necessary to conclude a global convention enabling States to address the conservation problems of all migratory species worldwide and to coordinate an effective response to threats ranging from habitat destruction, excessive hunting along migration routes and degradation of feeding sites. Recommendation 32 of the 1972 *Stockholm Conference Action Plan* therefore called on governments to take into consideration *"the need to enact international conventions and treaties to protect species inhabiting international waters or those which migrate from one country to another"*. In 1974, the Federal Republic of Germany took the initiative by preparing a preliminary draft treaty which was submitted to all States. The definitive text of the Convention was adopted in Bonn on 23 June 1979 and it entered into force on 1 November 1983.

Objectives and Scope of the Convention

The Convention is intended to provide a framework within which Parties take appropriate action, individually or in cooperation, to conserve migratory species and their habitats by:

- adopting strict protection measures for endangered migratory species (Appendix I);
- concluding multilateral Agreements for the conservation and management of migratory species that have an unfavorable conservation status or would benefit significantly from international cooperation (Appendix II); and
- undertaking joint research activities.

The Convention applies to all migratory species, defined in Article I.1 as:

> "the entire population or any geographically separate part of the population of any species or lower taxon of wild animals, a significant proportion of whose members cyclically and predictably cross one or more national jurisdictional boundaries".

This definition covers marine species which migrate between adjacent Exclusive Economic Zones or between areas under coastal State jurisdiction and the high seas: on the other hand, it excludes the few species which live only in the high seas as these do not cross jurisdictional boundaries.

The Conference of the Parties (COP) plays an essential role in establishing and amending (by simplified procedure) the two Appendices. Where a species is endangered and likely to benefit from international cooperation for its conservation, it may be listed in both Appendices (Article IV.2).

Main Obligations of the Parties

Obligations under the Convention attach to the Range States of a particular migratory species. These include not only the States (and, where appropriate, regional economic integration organizations) that exercise jurisdiction over any part of the range of that migratory species but also States whose flag vessels are engaged outside national jurisdictional limits (e.g., on the high seas) in taking that migratory species.

Conservation Measures for Species Listed in Appendix I (Article III)

Parties must prohibit any "taking" of such species, defined to include hunting, fishing, capturing, harassing and deliberate killing. Limited exceptions are possible in specific cases (e.g., for scientific purposes or to satisfy the needs of traditional subsistence hunting), but these must be specific as to what they cover, be limited in space and time and not operate to the disadvantage of the species concerned.

Parties must also "endeavor" to conserve and, where feasible, restore the important habitats of these species; to prevent, remove, compensate for or minimize the adverse effects of activities or obstacles that seriously impede or prevent migration; and to prevent, reduce or control factors that endanger or are likely to endanger these species. This includes strictly controlling the introduction of exotic species and controlling, limiting or eliminating species which have already been introduced.

Agreements for the Conservation of Appendix II Species (Article IV)

The only requirement in respect of Appendix II species is a non-binding provision for Parties to "endeavor" to conclude international agreements. Since CMS entered into force, three categories of regional instruments have been developed for this purpose. These are collectively known as Agreements.

Agreements (Article IV.3)

Agreements are intended to benefit migratory species listed in Appendix II, especially those with an unfavorable conservation status, over their whole range. Their object must be to restore the migratory species concerned to a "favorable conservation status" (as defined at Article I.1.c). They are open to accession by all Range States of the species concerned, including those that are not Parties to CMS. They take the form of treaties as they provide for the creation of institutions and contain financial provisions: they must therefore be ratified.

The substantive content of Agreements is shaped by Guidelines in Article V. These comprehensively list the types of measure which should be taken to ensure the conservation and management of the species concerned, including: periodic reviews of the conservation status of the species concerned; coordinated conservation and management plans; research into the ecology and population dynamics of these species; conservation and, where required and feasible, restoration of important habitats; control of exotic species; maintenance of a network of suitable habitats appropriately disposed in relation to migration routes, elimination of activities and obstacles which hinder or impede migration; prevention, reduction or control of the release of polluting substances into the habitats of the species concerned, measures based on ecological principles to manage the taking of the species, etc.

Agreements in the Form of Treaties (Article IV.4)

These Agreements are not restricted to Appendix II species. They may be concluded for any population or any geographically separate part of the population of any species or lower taxon of wild animals, members of which "periodically" cross one or more national jurisdictional boundaries. This makes them particularly suitable for species or populations which cannot be listed in Appendix II because they do not fulfil the listing criteria in Article IV.1 or the slightly different definition of "migratory" in Article I.1.a. Agreements should preferably be restricted to species or populations which are not listed in Appendix II to avoid overlap with Agreements.

Agreements do not have to cover the whole range of the species concerned, nor need they be open to all Range States. Although CMS does not lay down any substantive rules for their content, the Article V Guidelines have been applied to some existing Agreements and should preferably be applied to future Agreements in the interests of harmonization.

Memoranda of Understanding (Article IV.4)

Administrative agreements, such as Memoranda of Understanding (MOU), may also be concluded under Article IV.4. The two MOU concluded to date are intended to initiate and coordinate short-term administrative and scientific measures to be taken by Range States in collaboration with specialized international NGOs. Although desirable, it is not mandatory for MOU to cover the whole range of the migratory species concerned or to be open to accession by all Range States.

MOU are not legally binding in the same way as Agreements in the form of treaties. Nevertheless, they constitute official undertakings signed by authorized government representatives, usually from the wildlife departments of the States concerned, which should be implemented fully. They usually enter into force for a fixed period on the date of signature and list specific conservation undertakings from each State in an annexed Action Plan. They provide a relatively simple way to establish a limited framework for regional cooperation for the conservation of certain migratory species, possibly as an interim step to the conclusion of a binding Agreement.

A weakness of non-binding agreements is that States cannot be required to make financial contributions. However, there is nothing to prevent MOU from stating that Parties should use their best endeavors to this end or to stop a State from providing technical and financial assistance to signatory States on a purely voluntary basis.

MOU are not legally binding in the same way as Agreements in the form of treaties. Nevertheless, they constitute official undertakings signed by authorized government representatives, usually from the wildlife departments of the States concerned, which should be implemented fully.

Institutional Mechanisms

Article VII provides for the establishment of a Conference of the Parties as the decision-making organ of the Convention, entrusted with keeping its implementation under review, making any amendments to Appendices and adopting the necessary financial provisions. The Conference meets approximately every three years.

The Convention establishes a Secretariat. Provided by UNEP, this has its offices in Bonn, Germany (it is co-located with the Secretariat of the UN *Framework Convention on Climate Change*). A Standing Committee, consisting of representatives from five geographic regions, the Depositary (Germany) and the hosts of the last and next meetings of the Conference, has been established to provide policy and administrative guidance between regular meetings of the COP.

In accordance with Article VIII, the COP established a Scientific Council at its first meeting. This is a consultative body which advises on scientific matters. The Council is composed of experts nominated by the Parties and the Conference may choose to nominate additional experts. The COP also determines the functions of the Council.

B

RAMSAR

The Convention on Wetlands of International Importance especially as Waterfowl Habitat (Ramsar, 2 February 1971)

Background

The ecological and economic importance of wetlands was poorly understood for many years. Commonly understood to include marshes, mangroves, lagoons and all shallow stretches of water generally unsuitable for agriculture, wetlands were either seen as wastelands without any utilitarian purpose for society or as actively damaging to public health (as sources of diseases such as malaria).

Many countries directly supported the drainage of wetlands by means of legislation providing for tax benefits and subsidies or even by compulsory regulations: large-scale drainage projects were often undertaken directly by the State.

Scientists have now established, however, that wetland ecosystems have multiple functions in maintaining natural balances and that upsetting these balances may have serious environmental, social and economic costs.

Despite the growth in understanding of these ecological functions and economic values, the development of comprehensive conservation and planning measures for wetlands has been a slow process. In many countries, destruction continues unabated: wetlands remain one of the most threatened ecosystem types on Earth.

Scientists and conservation organizations, worried by what they consider to be a genuine catastrophe, have long attempted to check this trend. In 1962, a joint project known as MAR (the first letters of the word "marsh" in several languages) was launched by several international NGOs to protect wetlands of international importance for migratory birds in Europe and North Africa. The possibility of concluding an international convention on wetland conservation was first discussed that same year: nearly nine years later, negotiations came to fruition with the signature of a global wetlands treaty on 2 February 1971 in Ramsar, a small Iranian town on the Caspian Sea.

The *Ramsar Convention*, which entered into force in 1975, had a number of lacunae in its procedural clauses which hampered its early development. It has consequently been amended twice since its entry into force. The first amendment, adopted in Paris on 3 December 1982, consisted of a protocol to insert into the Convention provisions to establish an amendment procedure (omitted by the original negotiators) and to make the French version of the text an authentic version. The other languages of the United Nations were also designated to be "official" languages for the *Ramsar Convention*. The *Paris Protocol* entered into force in 1986. The second amendment was made at an extraordinary meeting of the Parties in Regina (Canada) in 1987 and which entered into force in 1994. It formally established the Conference of the Parties (COP) as an institution of the Convention by means of an amendment to Article 6, which empowered the COP to review and promote the implementation of the Convention.

Objectives of the Convention

The main purpose of the *Ramsar Convention* is "to stem the progressive encroachment on and loss of wetlands now and in the future". In line with developments in international environmental policy and law as expressed at UNCED, the Convention's mission has been expanded to cover "the conservation and wise use of wetlands by national action and international cooperation as a means to achieving sustainable development throughout the world".

Wetlands are defined very broadly to include:

> "areas of marsh, fen, peatland or water, whether natural or artificial, permanent or temporary, with water that is static or

> flowing, fresh, brackish or salt, including areas of marine water the depth of which at low tide does not exceed six meters." (Article 1.1).

The Convention therefore applies to all natural and manmade wetlands, from rivers and lakes of any size to seashores, from peatbogs to artificial reservoirs and aquaculture ponds.

To achieve this objective, the Convention contains a very general obligation to promote as far as possible the wise use of wetlands and a more specific obligation to conserve wetlands included in a List of Wetlands of International Importance. Parties must also establish nature reserves to protect wetlands, whether or not included in the List and cooperate with other countries for the conservation of shared wetlands, water systems and wetland fauna and flora. These obligations are described in more detail below, together with relevant decisions on their implementation which have been adopted by the COP.

Main Obligations of the Parties

Wise Use of Wetlands

Contracting Parties are required to

> "formulate and implement their planning so as to promote ... as far as possible the wise use of wetlands in their territory" (Article 3.1).

This obligation requires States to review, and if necessary, modify their policies and programs so as to provide for the sustainable use of all wetlands within their territories to remove any incentives to wetland destruction and to encourage positive legal and institutional frameworks for wise use.

Listing and Conservation of Ramsar Sites

To become a Party, a State must designate at least one of its wetlands for inclusion in the List of Wetlands of International Importance: the boundaries of the wetland must be delimited on a map and may incorporate riparian and coastal zones adjacent to the wetlands, and islands or bodies of marine water deeper than six meters at low tide within the wetlands, especially where these have importance as waterfowl habitat (Art. 2.1). The Party concerned must maintain the ecological character of listed wetlands and inform the Secretariat of any changes in such condition at the earliest possible time. A Party may delete a Ramsar wetland from the List, but should compensate the loss by listing another wetland (this has never yet happened). A State which deletes all the wetlands that it has included on the List will cease to be a Contracting Party.

International Cooperation

Parties sharing the same wetlands or water systems are required to consult with each other about implementing their obligations under the Convention and to seek to coordinate policies and regulation for the conservation of wetlands and their fauna and flora (Article 5).

International cooperation between neighboring States is of critical importance to the successful implementation of the Convention. Conservation and wise use of a wetland often depends on this, especially where the feed-waters of Ramsar sites come from a neighboring country (at least 300 major river basins and many large lakes cross the national boundaries of two or more countries).

If the quantity or quality of those waters is impaired, the State on whose territory the wetland is located may be unable to prevent the destruction of that site unless its neighbor agrees to prevent or alleviate the damage.

Article 5 thus provides a clear legal basis for the development of appropriate forms of international cooperation, *inter alia* on the basis of existing regional river agreements. The COP and the Ramsar Strategic Plan have given active support to the listing of transboundary Ramsar sites, an important—if geographically limited—way of strengthening the management of shared wetlands. There are already several examples of bilateral cooperation in respect of listed Ramsar sites. The Netherlands, for instance, is cooperating with Mauritania in order to protect the Banc d'Arguin, one of the most important wetlands in the world for waterfowl, fish habitat and an endangered mammal, the monk seal. The Wadden Sea is a trilateral Ramsar site for whose management the riparian states (Denmark, Germany, and The Netherlands) have established a special coordination secretariat.

Institutional and Financial Mechanisms

The Conference of the Parties is responsible for reviewing the implementation of the Convention as amended. It must meet at least every three years and has powers to take decisions, including on financial matters. The Convention

The ambitious aim of the Convention is "to stem the progressive encroachment on and loss of wetlands now and in the future" and to support wetland conservation "by combining far-sighted national policies with coordinated international action".

now has its own budget approved by the Parties and financed by their mandatory contributions: the scale of contributions is based on the United Nations practice.

The Secretariat of the Convention, known as the Ramsar Bureau, was initially provided by IUCN but has, since 1987, been an autonomous body whose operation is completely financed by the Parties. The Bureau is still located at the headquarters of IUCN in Gland, Switzerland.

A nine-member Standing Committee was established in 1987 to carry out any necessary activities between meetings of the COP, supervise the activities of the Bureau and provide it with guidance on implementing the Convention and preparing meetings of the COP.

A permanent Scientific and Technical Review Panel was created by the COP in 1993. The panel is composed of seven experts and provides advice to the Conference of the Standing Committee and the Bureau.

In 1990, the COP established a Wetlands Conservation Fund, now called the Ramsar Small Grants Fund for Wetland Conservation and Wise Use. This provides developing country Parties with financial support for wetland conservation activities. The Fund is financed by a small amount from the Convention budget (70,000 Swiss francs per year in the current budget) and by voluntary contributions which amounted to around 300,000 Swiss francs in 1997.

(i) de Klemm C. and Shine C., "The Emergence of Legal Responses at International Level," in *Wetlands, Water and the Law: Using Law to Advance Wetland Conservation and Wise Use*, IUCN, Gland, Switzerland, pp 27–42

...In the legal arena, a series of global or regional instruments and programmes have been developed to promote conservation and management of particular species, ecosystems and resources and to address specific categories of environmental threats. This chapter provides an overview of the development of international principles and obligations related to wetlands before considering issues related to national implementation.

Ramsar Convention on Wetlands (1971)

The *Convention on Wetlands of International Importance especially as Waterfowl Habitat* was adopted in Ramsar (Iran) on 2 February 1971. It was the first globally applicable environmental convention and, nearly three decades on, is still the only treaty to address the specific requirements of one type of ecosystem.

Background

...The *Ramsar Convention* entered into force on 21 December 1975. Since that date, it has been amended on two occasions to remedy omissions in its procedural clauses that hampered its early development. An extraordinary meeting of the Parties (Paris, 3 December 1982) adopted a protocol to insert an amendment procedure into the Convention provisions and to make the French version of the text an authentic version. The Paris Protocol entered into force in October 1986. It provided the legal basis for convening a further extraordinary meeting (Regina, 1987) at which the administrative arrangements established under Article 6 of the Convention were amended. These amendments provide for the formal establishment of the Conference of the Parties as an institution of the Convention.

Objectives, Obligations and Mechanisms

Although the Convention's title emphasizes one aspect of wetlands (as waterfowl habitat), its Preamble shows clearly that negotiators were concerned with the full range of wetland benefits. The Preamble recognizes the "fundamental ecological functions of wetlands as regulators of water regimes and as habitats supporting a characteristic flora and fauna, especially waterfowl". The ambitious aim of the Convention is "to stem the progressive encroachment on and loss of wetlands now and in the future" "and to support wetland conservation "by combining far-sighted national policies with coordinated international action".

Contracting Parties are bound by three main groups of obligations which, consistently with Ramsar's very broad definition of wetlands, apply equally to inland and coastal wetlands and water systems:

- Site-specific measures: To designate one or more suitable wetlands of international importance for inclusion in the List of Wetlands of International Importance (Art. 2), to promote the conservation of listed wetlands (Art. 3.1) and to establish nature reserves on wetlands and provide adequately for their wardening (Art. 4.1);
- Non-site-specific (generally applicable) measures: To formulate and implement their planning so as to

promote, as far as possible, the "wise use" of wetlands in their territory (Art. 3.1);

- International cooperation: To consult with other Parties about implementing obligations arising under the Convention in respect of transboundary wetlands, shared watercourses and coordinated conservation of wetland flora and fauna (Art. 5).

Article 4 generally requires Parties to encourage wetland research, to endeavor to increase waterfowl populations on wetlands and to promote the training of personnel.

This combination of localized, general and international measures is of particular interest. Whereas area-based conservation mechanisms were already well established in international and national law, the open-ended concepts of wise use and multifaceted transboundary cooperation were more pioneering. The *Ramsar Convention* was concluded right at the start of the twenty-year period that saw the emergence and crystallization of fundamental principles and concepts framing international environmental law, including the now familiar concepts of "sustainable use" and "sustainable development". It did not define "wise use" or establish requirements for its implementation nor did it require Parties to ensure that activities carried out on their territory or in areas under their jurisdiction do not cause damage to the environment in other States. In contrast to modern environmental instruments, which set out comprehensive definitions, principles and measures, Ramsar's substantive obligations are very general in character and lack legal precision.

Possibly for this reason, Ramsar was for a long time exclusively associated with the conservation of important wetlands and implementation by many Contracting Parties tended to be concentrated on a few flagship sites. However, as described above, wetlands are exceptionally vulnerable to changes in the quantity or quality of their water supply generated by activities at considerable distances. While site-specific mechanisms are of great importance and can act as a catalyst for wetland conservation on a wider scale, they are rarely designed to safeguard individual wetlands against harmful impacts of external activities. Site-specific mechanisms should thus be seen as a component, albeit an essential one, of generally applicable policies and practical measures for wetland conservation and wise use.

International cooperation on wetland-related issues is another key component of wise use. A shared water system or transboundary wetland cannot be rationally managed as a functional ecological unit without cooperation between neighboring States. If a wetland's feed-waters come from a neighboring country where their quality or quantity is adversely affected, the country on whose territory the wetland is located will be unable to prevent the destruction of its wetland unless its neighbor agrees to stop or alleviate the damage. Article 5 provides a clear legal basis for bilateral or multilateral cooperation to promote compatible approaches to management of shared water resources consistently with the wise use obligation. It also supports rationalized approaches to species conservation across political boundaries. Waterfowl and some other migratory species are biologically dependent on the maintenance of wetland habitats along their migration routes. As they migrate, they come successively under the sovereignty or jurisdiction of each State situated along these routes. If just one State fails to take adequate conservation measures or destroys an important migration staging post, the conservation and management efforts of the other States involved may be seriously undermined. It follows that migratory species cannot be rationally managed by one country in isolation.

The interpretation and implementation of Ramsar's obligations is supported by the following institutions established under the Convention:

- The Conference of the Parties (COP) meets at least every three years. It has broad powers to review and take decisions relating to the Convention's implementation, including on financial matters. It approves the Convention's budget, which is financed by mandatory contributions from Contracting Parties, according to a scale of contributions based on the United Nations scale. Six meetings have been held to date: Cagliari, Italy (1980); Groningen, the Netherlands (1984); Regina, Canada (1987); Montreux, Switzerland (1990); Kushiro, Japan (1993); and Brisbane, Australia (1996). The Seventh Meeting of the COP will be held in Costa Rica in May 1999.
- Between meetings of the COP, the Convention's activities are governed by a nine-member Standing Committee (established in 1987) which includes representatives from each of the seven regions of the world and carries out such interim activities as may be necessary.
- The day-to-day work of implementation and the preparation of meetings of the COP are carried out

by a small secretariat known as the Ramsar Bureau. The Bureau was initially provided by IUCN–The World Conservation Union but became an autonomous body in 1987 with its operations completely financed by the Parties. The Bureau is still co-located with the IUCN headquarters in Gland, Switzerland.

- A permanent Scientific and Technical Review Panel (established in 1993) is composed of seven experts appointed by the COP who act in their individual capacity rather than as national representatives. The Panel provides advice to the Conference, the Standing Committee and the Bureau and meets at least once a year. It now works closely with the Subsidiary Body on Scientific, Technical and Technological Advice (SBSTTA) established under the 1992 *Convention on Biological Diversity* and with scientific bodies advising other environmental conventions.

The Convention itself does not establish a financial mechanism to assist Parties to implement its obligations. Moves to remedy this weakness were taken as early as 1980, when the COP recommended that Parties should give financial and technical assistance to developing countries for the purposes of wetland conservation. However, it was not until 1990 that the COP established the Wetland Conservation Fund to support activities that improve the management of listed sites or promote the wise use of wetlands. The Ramsar Small Grants Fund for Wetland Conservation and Wise Use (as it was renamed in 1996) is financed by a small amount from the Convention budget and by voluntary contributions. Any developing country seeking to accede to the Convention may apply for a grant to support activities necessary for the identification, delineation and mapping of a site to be included in the Ramsar List. All countries on the List of Aid Recipients established by the Development Assistance Committee of the OECD are eligible to receive assistance from the Fund.

Evolution of the Convention and Current Status

The *Ramsar Convention* now enjoys considerable success, measured in terms of the increasing number of Parties and the growth in the number and surface area of the wetlands included in the List. By April 1999, there were 114 Contracting Parties and 965 Ramnsar sites worldwide, covering 70,471,806 hectares (this compares favorably to 1991, when there were only 538 listed sites covering about 33 million hectares). The largest Ramsar site is currently the Okavango Delta in Botswana, which covers around 6.8 million hectares.

Despite this progress, there are still many States that have not yet ratified the Convention and many existing Parties have only designated one or very few wetlands. Many wetlands of international importance thus remain unprotected, while around 84 percent of sites which have been listed are thought to be under some form of threat. More far-reachingly, no Party has yet applied the *Ramsar Convention* to the fullest extent and it would be misleading to claim that any Party has managed to achieve wise use of all its wetlands.

The Ramsar institutions have worked hard with Contracting Parties to develop a range of: strategic tools to promote more comprehensive implementation of all key provisions of the Convention. This incremental approach has made it possible to respond over time to developments in environmental science, international law and institutional processes. The range of such tools, discussed in detail in the appropriate sections of this book, is briefly summarized here.

The Convention's original emphasis on wetlands as waterfowl habitat has been systematically broadened by the COP. A more holistic approach to wetland classification has been developed which takes account of other species (including fish) and the ecological functions of wetlands within water systems, as well as the role of wetland restoration in improved water management. Several decisions have focused on the central role of local communities, indigenous peoples, wetland users and other stakeholders in wise use and the importance of participative approaches to wetland management planning (the theme chosen for the Seventh Meeting of the COP in 1999 is *Wetlands and People—The Vital Link).* The scope of international cooperation under Article 5 has also been broadly interpreted to include development assistance affecting wetlands.

The concept of wise (sustainable) use has been promoted as the unifying theme for Ramsar's future development and the COP has adopted a series of detailed guidelines to assist Parties towards more effective implementation. Special emphasis is now placed on the development and implementation of national wetland policies, or the incorporation of wetland conservation requirements into National Environmental Action Plans or equivalent policy instruments, as a mechanism for delivering wise use. A sizeable minority of Parties have now initiated or completed wetland policy-making and planning processes.

The *Ramsar Convention's Strategic Plan* 1997–2002, adopted by the COP in 1996, provides a clear conceptual framework and ordered structure for the next phase of implementation. Its Mission Statement for the Convention—"the conservation and wise use of wetlands by nation action and international cooperation as a means to achieving sustainable development throughout the world"—is intended to anchor Ramsar firmly within the body of more modern environmental instruments founded on the concept of sustainable development.

The Strategic Plan lays down a series of general and operational objectives that are supported by specific actions to translate the treaty's broad goals into practice. Responsibility for carrying out each suite of actions is assigned to the Parties, Ramsar institutions or partner (nongovermental) organizations, as appropriate. The eight General Objectives are as follows:

- To progress towards universal membership of the Convention (at least 120 Contracting Parties by 2002).
- To achieve the wise use of wetlands by implementing and further developing the Ramsar Wise Use Guidelines.
- To raise awareness of wetland values and functions throughout the world and at all levels.
- To reinforce the capacity of institutions in each Contracting Party to achieve conservation and wise use of wetlands.
- To ensure the conservation of all sites included in the List of Wetlands of International Importance (Ramsar List).
- To designate for the Ramsar List those wetlands which meet the Convention's criteria, especially wetland types still under-represented in the List and transfrontier wetlands.
- To mobilize international cooperation and financial assistance for wetland conservation and wise use in collaboration with other conventions and agencies, both governmental and nongovermental.
- To provide the Convention with the required institutional mechanisms and resources.

It is clear from this list that Ramsar's goals continue to be ambitious, nearly 30 years after its conclusion. While the Convention has undoubtedly served as a catalyst for international recognition of wetlands as reservoirs of biological diversity and economically valuable components of inland and coastal water systems, much remains to be done. The achievement of wise use is acknowledged to be highly complex, requiring new combinations of policies, mechanisms and actors at all levels of implementation to address issues of political and public sensitivity.

The following sections consider the extent to which more recent environmental treaties and institutional processes provide a legal basis for national action for wetland conservation and wise use.

Development of Other International Instruments Relevant to Wetlands

The principles that underpin the *Ramsar Convention* received broad political consensus in 1972, when the United Nations World Conference on the Human Environment (Stockholm) adopted the non-binding *Declaration of Principles for the Preservation and Enhancement of the Human Environment.* For the first time in a text adopted by almost all States of the world, an inclusive approach to ecosystems and biological resources was recognized as fundamentally important for mankind. The Declaration affirmed that the natural resources of the earth, including air, water, land, flora and fauna and especially representative samples of natural ecosystems, "must be safeguarded for the benefit of present and future generations through careful planning or management, as appropriate"; that the capacity of the earth to produce vital renewable resources must be maintained and, wherever practicable, restored or improved; and that in view of man's special responsibility to wisely manage the heritage of wildlife and its habitat, nature conservation "must receive importance in planning for economic development".

Since Stockholm, the conceptual basis for international environmental policy has been extended by many other non-binding instruments that have contributed to the reinforcement of existing legal principles and the recognition of emerging international customary law rules.

The *World Charter for Nature*, adopted and solemnly proclaimed by the UN General Assembly on 28 October 1982, declared that essential ecological processes must not be impaired and the genetic viability of the earth not be compromised. "Ecosystems and organisms, as well as the land, marine and atmospheric resources that are utilized by man, shall be managed to achieve and maintain optimum sustainable productivity, but without endangering the integrity of those other ecosystems or species with which they coexist". Nature conservation should he integrated into the planning and implementation of social and economic development activities, taking into consideration the long-term capacity of natural systems to ensure the subsistence and settlement of human populations.

The 1992 *Rio Declaration on Environment and Development* adopted a much more anthropocentric approach to these issues. It proclaims that individuals and communities are at the center of concerns for sustainable development and affirms the need equitably to meet developmental and environmental needs of present and future generations. States must cooperate in a spirit of global partnership to conserve, protect and restore the health and integrity of the Earth's ecosystem, with developed countries bearing particular responsibility for sustainable development in view of the pressures their societies place on the global environment and of the technologies and financial resources they command. The Declaration affirms *inter alia* the importance of public access to environmental information and participation in decision making processes, the need to enact effective environmental legislation and the need for States to recognize and support the vital role of indigenous people and other local communities in environmental management and development.

The binding environmental instruments adopted since the Stockholm Conference can be loosely grouped into 'generations' which may be considered as mutually reinforcing.

Treaties adopted during the 1970s were essentially concerned with the regulation of environmental sectors: oceans, inland waters, air, soil and wildlife. The three global conservation treaties concluded during this period dealt with very different issues: area-based protection of cultural and natural heritage of global significance, which can include wetlands; the control of international trade in endangered animal and plant species, which potentially provides a mechanism for regulating commercial exploitation in wetland-dependent species such as corals, crocodiles and fish; and legal mechanisms to conserve migratory species and their habitats, which have since been implemented at regional level for different groups of wetland-dependent species.

In the 1980s, international law-making focussed more systematically on potential sources of environmental harm, addressing the impacts of human activities and products across all sectors. "Transsectoral" or "transversal" regulatory frameworks were developed during this period *inter alia* for toxic or dangerous products and wastes, radioactivity, nuclear wastes and hazardous activities. However, regulatory regimes established during this period tend not to be inclusive: in other words, processes, activities, habitats and species do not benefit from management or conservation measures unless specifically covered by applicable legal frameworks.

A notable exception is the 1985 *Agreement on the Conservation of Nature and Natural Resources*, concluded between the six states of the Association of South-East Asian Nations. The ASEAN Agreement is probably the most complete conservation instrument in existence. It aims to achieve comprehensive environmental protection through the implementation of specific measures on air. water, soil, plant cover, forests, fauna, flora and ecological processes. The Agreement specifically addresses the need to prevent, reduce and control environmental degradation and reduce pollution and establishes requirements for land planning and land use, impact studies and transboundary cooperation. Regrettably, this Agreement has still not entered into force moreover, it is of limited geographical scope, given the size and population of the Asian continent.

The most recent phase of legal development has been characterized by the adoption of comprehensive global mechanisms to address planet-wide problems such as the depletion of the ozone layer, global warming, desertification and loss of biological diversity. These modern instruments generally take the form of framework conventions that lay down general principles and obligations and also provide for the adoption of detailed protocols or annexes were considered necessary in the light of new scientific evidence and technical and technological developments.

At regional or subregional level, a large number of environmental agreements have been concluded between States or under the auspices of regional economic integration organizations such as the European Union. Regional processes make it possible to tailor the implementation of environmental objectives to the particular characteristics and capacities of a given region and to build on commonalities between a relatively small group of countries. In the context of wetlands, verifiable obligations related to conservation of migratory species and habitat types have been established *inter alia* under two important Directives adopted by the European Community. From a global perspective, however, regional treaty coverage remains patchy. Some parts of the world, notably much of Asia, have no convention at all while others, including America and Africa are covered by older treaties which do not provide for institutional mechanisms to review and facilitate national implementation.

Legal regimes for the protection of inland waters have long been regional in character, dominated by treaties between countries sharing a river or a lake. Early water agreements concerned navigation, broadening slowly over time to address non-navigational economic uses related to transboundary water resources such as irrigation, pollution or dam building. The scope of such agreements has been extended significantly over the last decade, as international legal frameworks have sought to reflect the link between water resource development, drainage basin management and conservation of aquatic ecosystems, including wetlands. Modern treaties based on this type of integrated approach include the 1992 *Convention on the Pollution and Use of Transboundary Watercourses and International Lakes* and the 1997 *Convention on the Law of Non-Navigational Uses of International Watercourses.* The latter contains a series of globally applicable obligations for the protection, preservation and management of the ecosystems of international watercourses.

Legal regimes are also beginning to take better account of the interrelationship between terrestrial and maritime activities and the quality of the marine and coastal environment. A series of shipping disasters (notably involving the Torrey Canyon and Amoco Cadiz tankers) led to the development of a treaty regime for the prevention of pollution from ships. The 1982 United Nations *Convention on the Law of the Sea* (UNCLOS) requires States *inter alia* to preserve and protect the marine environment; to prevent, reduce and control pollution from land-based sources, including rivers, estuaries, pipelines and outfall structures; and to protect "rare or fragile ecosystems as well as the habitat of depleted, threatened or endangered species and other forms of marine life". A legal framework for regional marine and coastal conservation has been developed under the Regional Seas Programme, established in 1974 by the United Nations Environment Programme. Action Plans have been prepared for 13 regional seas, with more than 80 coastal States and territories participating.

Finally, two other processes damaging to wetlands—sea level rise and desertification—are addressed more or less directly by two recent treaties of global application.

The 1992 United Nations *Framework Convention on Climate Change* establishes commitments to stabilize greenhouse gas concentrations in the atmosphere at a safe level, over the long term, and to limit emissions of greenhouse gases by developed countries in accordance with nonbinding targets and timetables. Implementation programs in different countries have *inter alia* included measures to promote energy efficiency and to develop renewable non-carbon emitting energy sources. The promotion of renewables could in the long term be beneficial for certain wetlands, such as mangrove forests, which are often deforested in areas where local communities have no alternative fuel sources. Scientific research suggests that wetlands, especially peatbogs, may play a positive role in combating climate change by functioning as natural carbon sinks. If such functions are confirmed, this could provide a powerful incentive for large-scale expansion of wetland creation, restoration and protection programs. Cooperative research and planning between the *Ramsar Convention* and the treaty secretariats dealing with climate change and biological diversity is currently under consideration.

Five of the 35 wetland types included in the Ramsar Classification System for Wetland Types are frequently found in inland arid zones and are recorded in over a third of Ramsar sites.

The 1994 *Convention on Desertification* is directly relevant to wetlands in arid zones. Five of the 35 wetland types included in the Ramsar Classification System for Wetland Types are frequently found in inland arid zones and are recorded in over a third of Ramsar sites. These sites are severely threatened by processes that reduce water supply as well as overgrazing, erosion and pollution through agricultural runoff.

The *Desertification Convention* applies to arid, semi-arid and dry sub-humid countries of the world and promotes integrated action at all levels to achieve sustainable development in affected areas. It promotes sustainable water resource management, *inter alia* through the development of integrated strategies for the rehabilitation, conservation and sustainable management of land and water resources and the promotion of cooperation among affected country Parties for environmental protection and the conservation of land and water resources. Parties undertake to strengthen existing legislation or enact new laws and establish long-term policies and action programs. The Convention covers the identification and management of damaging processes, the development of sustainable irrigation programs and the development of integrated approaches to physical, biological and socioeconomic problems. In an innovative example of a global treaty combining general principles and obligations with region-specific guidelines and measures, the *Desertification Convention* establishes four regional implementation annexes for Africa, Asia, Latin America and the Caribbean, and the Northern Mediterranean. A Memorandum of Cooperation was signed on 5 December 1998 between its Secretariat and the *Ramsar Convention* Bureau.

Action on the Ground: the Challenge of National Implementation

As this chapter has shown, wetlands have not been neglected by international law: indeed there is now a relatively extensive treaty framework relating directly or indirectly to conservation and sustainable use of wetlands and wetland biodiversity. This is of course no more than a beginning. Conventions and international institutions provide political solidarity and technical and financial assistance which are essential for creating a favorable climate for action on wetlands. In the long term, however, if countries do not act within and across their boundaries to implement their obligations to safeguard wetland functions and values, treaty institutions can do little more than apply moral and political pressure.

A common characteristic of conservation treaties is that their provisions are deliberately very broad in order to accommodate diversity of national conditions, legal systems and institutional and technical capacity. In addition, their provisions are frequently tempered by 'best endeavors' formulae along the lines of "as far as possible and as appropriate", which leave their Parties considerable latitude in how to implement their international undertakings: such aspirational formulae are often a necessary precondition to reaching agreement among treaty negotiators. The combined result of these two factors is that most conservation treaties lack commonly-understood standards and norms and many key provisions are too imprecise to be capable of legal verification.

In recent years, the decision-making bodies established under certain treaties have taken a more proactive stance towards improving standards of implementation and strengthening national reporting requirements. Ramsar's Conference of the Parties has issued prolific policy and technical guidance to flesh out the treaty's general provisions and has established support mechanisms ranging from the site management guidance procedure to regional coordinators who ensure regular contact with and between Parties in each biogeographic region. The emphasis on practical 'tools' for implementing the Convention represents a welcome innovation in the realm of international conservation law.

In choosing to become party to a treaty, a state commits itself to take the necessary measures appropriate to its legal and institutional system to implement its treaty obligations in domestic law. The actions necessary for this purpose vary according to the nature of the treaty, the level of precision of its obligations and the constitutional requirements or legal traditions of individual States. Certain States deem treaty obligations to be 'self-executing' or 'self-implementing': in other words, once the treaty has been duly ratified, its obligations must be applied in domestic law and may be enforced by domestic courts or agencies without the need for legislation, executive decree or other implementing measure. Many other States adopt the approach that specific legislative action must be taken to incorporate or transpose treaty obligations into domestic law.

Because of their very general character, it is extremely difficult to consider conservation treaty obligations as self-executing: moreover, they do not lend themselves to simple transposition into national law. For example, the commitment to promote wise use is likely to remain largely rhetorical or operationally ineffective unless each country translates this broad concept into detailed and coordinated legislative and policy instruments adapted to its traditions and conditions. Such instruments need to be backed by clear lines of institutional responsibility at national and/or subnational level, with adequate powers being conferred on those institutions to ensure proper monitoring and enforcement of applicable legislation. This is far from being the case in most countries.

[L]egal measures to support wetland conservation and wise use need to be comprehensive and multi-sectoral. There has been dramatic progress in extending the scope and techniques of environmental protection legislation in recent years, but many of these legal and institutional changes have still to be digested and translated into workable systems on the ground. Moreover, environmental issues still tend to be addressed within a sectoral framework which prevents wetland issues from being mainstreamed' (integrated) into sectors whose activities may adversely affect wetlands (including agriculture, forestry and fisheries; energy generation, mining and industrial development; terrestrial and maritime transport links and facilities, including ports and marinas; and residential, tourism and leisure development). Policy coordination and consistency in implementing international commitments can be particularly complex in countries with decentralized or federated structures.

The interface between national implementation and transboundary cooperation also needs to be strengthened and seen in a broader context. As indicated above, international cooperation between Parties (and where appropriate regional economic integration organizations) is required under both the *Ramsar Convention* and the CBD. Such obligations are not restricted to transboundary management issues but extend to international assistance for wetland-related programs and projects. States should also support improved coordination between treaty institutions competent in areas related to wetlands and water resource management, in order to avoid duplication or inconsistency between parallel or overlapping processes.

The central question for this book is how countries can adapt or develop legal tools and institutional frameworks to circumscribe actions and policies that contribute to wetland loss or degradation and to promote a broadly-haled culture of public support for and participation in sustainable land and water use.

(ii) D'Cruz R., "Implementation of the Ramsar Strategic Plan 1997–2002 in the South East Asia Region," *Workshop on International Conventions and Treaties Proceedings*

Introduction

The 6th Meeting of the Conference of the Contracting, Parties, held in Brisbane in March 1996, adopted the *Ramsar Strategic Plan* 1997–2002. Execution of the Plan is largely in the hands of the Contracting Parties who, in full recognition of the sovereignty of the state, have agreed to work together towards implementing obligations accepted under the Convention.

Through this Plan, the Convention's long-standing technical work in wetlands is strengthened, and a new catalytic role vis-a-vis the development assistance community is established. The Convention's technical and policy work becomes more closely related to the broader concerns of the *Convention on Biological Diversity*, and its traditional involvement with waterfowl is related more clearly to the *Convention on Migratory Species*. The long-standing link between it *Ramsar Convention* and its international partner organizations, IUCN–The World Conservation Union. Wetlands International, the World Wide Fund for Nature (WWF) and Birdlife International are maintained and enhanced, and new partnerships in the area of wise use of wetlands sought.

Mission Statement

> "The Convention's mission is the conservation and wise use [which is considered as synonymous with sustainable use] of wetlands by national action and international cooperation as a means to achieving sustainable development throughout the world."

General Objectives

Within the overall mission the General Objectives of this Strategic Plan are:

1. To progress towards universal membership of the Convention.
2. To achieve the wise use of wetlands by implementing and further developing the Ramsar Wise Use Guidelines.
3. To raise awareness of wetland values and functions throughout the world and at all levels.
4. To reinforce the capacity of institutions in each Contracting Party to achieve conservation and wise use of wetlands.
5. To ensure the conservation of all sites included in the List of Wetlands of International Importance (Ramsar List).
6. To designate for the Ramsar List those wetlands which meet the Convention's criteria, especially wetland types still underrepresented in the List and transfrontier wetlands.
7. To mobilize international cooperation and financial assistance for wetland conservation and wise use in collaboration with other conventions and agencies, both governmental and nongovermental.
8. To provide the Convention with the required institutional mechanisms and resources.

General Objective 1: To Progress Towards Universal Membership of the Convention

Rationale

In order for the Convention to achieve its mission, as many states as possible should be Contracting Parties. Membership has grown steadily to encompass all regions of the world, with 93 Contracting Parties at the time of the Brisbane meeting and 103 today. Nevertheless, some parts of the world (notably the Caribbean, the Near East, Southern Africa, and the South Pacific) are less well represented and states in these regions will be encouraged to join as will the remaining states in better represented regions. A special effort will be made to encourage Small Island Development States to join, in recognition of their special needs and significant wetlands, including coral reefs, sea-grass beds and mangroves. On the basis of growth in recent years, the objective of at least 120 Contracting Parties by 2002 appears attainable.

In order for the Convention to achieve its mission, as many states as possible should be Contracting Parties.

Current Status in SEA

Four Contracting Parties:

- Viet Nam (20.01.89);
- Indonesia (08.08.92);
- Philippines (08.11.94); and
- Malaysia (10.03.95).

Several non-member states have expressed their intention to accede to the Convention:

- Cambodia,
- Lao PDR,
- Myanmar, and
- Thailand.

Further Efforts

To pursue membership in the SEA region through

(a) the efforts of existing Parties, the Standing Committee and the Convention Bureau, and

(b) providing information on the benefits of membership.

General Objective 2: To Achieve the Wise Use of Wetlands by Implementing and Further Developing the Ramsar Wise Use Guidelines

Rationale

Under article 3.1 of the Convention, Contracting Parties agree to "formulate and implement their planning so as to promote as far as possible the wise use of wetlands in their territory". Through this concept of "wise use" the Convention has always emphasized that human usage on a sustainable basis is entirely compatible with Ramsar listing and wetland conservation in general. The Conference of the Contracting Parties has determined that the concept of wise use applies to broad planning affecting wetlands, and has therefore adopted Guidelines for the implementation of the wise use concept (Recommendation 4.10) and additional guidance for the implementation of the wise use concept (Resolution 5.6).

In the coming triennia, the greatest emphasis in Ramsar implementation will be placed on wetlands in the context of land-use planning, water resource management and other decisions affecting wetlands. Where Contracting Parties are developing national wetland policies (or other policies encompassing conservation and wise use of wetlands), such policies should be in conformity with other national environmental planning measures. Legislative changes may also he necessary. The present section of the Strategic Plan accordingly addresses the interaction between wise use and legislation, institutions, policy development, planning, and general decision-making.

Current Status in SEA

- Development of National Wetland Policies: Cambodia (draft), Indonesia, Malaysia (draft), Philippines, Thailand (draft), and Viet Nam.
- Development and implementation of Environmental Impact Assessment (EIA) procedure and legislation for development projects, including in wetlands.
- Development of a *Directory of Coastal Wetland Restoration and Rehabilitation Projects* in SEA.
- Increasing involvement of local communities in the management of wetlands through broad stakeholder membership in wetland management committees.
- Increasing involvement of the private sector in the conservation and wise use of wetlands.

Further Efforts

- Promote greater efforts to develop national wetland policies and associated legislative mechanisms.
- Promote the development, wide dissemination and application of documents and methodologies for the economic valuation of wetland benefits and functions.

- Encourage the systematic application of EIA procedures in wetland sites so as to mitigate any adverse effects of proposed development, resource exploitation, or changes in land/water use.
- Promote the active and informed participation of local communities in sustainably managing wetland areas and resources by providing for their involvement in management committees.

General Objective 3: To Raise Awareness of Wetland Values and Functions Throughout the World and at All Levels

Rationale

Public support is essential to generate political and legislative action, to obtain financial resources, and to ensure the successful implementation of wetland legislation and management, In turn, public support can, only be achieved through information about, and understanding of, the issues, including the benefits that individuals and societies can derive from wetlands.

Current Status in SEA

- World Wetlands Day (2 February) has been celebrated in the SEA region since 1996. In that year, national level celebrations were marked by: a 3-day celebration at the Olango Island Ramsar site (Philippines), a family-oriented 2-day event at a local shopping center including wetland exhibits and contests for children, and TV broadcasts by the Ministers of Forestry and Environment and a children's art competition (Indonesia).
- Production of new, and translation of existing information material on the benefits and values of wetlands in local languages: translation of *Wetland Benefits* into Vietnamese, Khmer, Malay, Indonesian and Thai.
- Establishment of educational centers at wetland sites in Indonesia, Malaysia, Philippines, and Thailand.
- Inclusion of modules related to wetlands in the curricula at all levels of education and the production of wetland teachers' kits (Indonesia).
- Development and maintenance of the Ramsar Worldwide Website and the Ramsar Forum to provide information on current activities and initiatives within member states and promote discussion and exchange of information on wetland issues.

Further Efforts

Support and assist in implementing, in cooperation with partner organizations and other institutions, and international program of education and public awareness on wetlands, their functions and values, to encourage transfer of information, knowledge and skills between wetland education centers and educators.

Develop and encourage national programs of education and public awareness on wetlands, targeted at a wide range of people, including key decision-makers, people living in and around wetlands, other wetland users and the public at large.

Explore and develop partnerships with the media and seek private sector support for education and public awareness initiatives.

Promote the establishment of educational centers at wetland sites and forge linkages with educational centers in other countries of the region.

While several universities have begun to incorporate wetland subjects in their curricula, the link has traditionally been made in the fields of biology, ecology and environmental science, other fields, such as engineering and urban planning have been slow to adopt wetland, including catchment wide, management as an integral component of environmentally-sound development.

General Objective 4: To Reinforce the Capacity of Institutions in Each Contracting Party to Achieve Conservation and Wise Use of Wetlands

Rationale

The Wise Use Guideline: emphasize that conservation and wise use of wetlands require appropriately structured institutions in each Contracting Party. There is a need in all regions and at all levels, in particular in developing countries, to strengthen the capacity of the institutions responsible for achieving the Convention's mission and objectives.

In order to strengthen existing institutions, an extensive program of training is required. A strategic approach to identifying the precise training needs and target audiences will take account of the differences between regions, countries and sites. Furthermore, existing training opportunities need to be developed and supported, and new initiatives developed in regions and subjects where such opportunities are lacking. A high level of international cooperation, including the transfer of environmentally sound technology and the exchange of information, will be a significant feature of this approach.

Current Status in SEA

A regionwide training needs analysis workshop was organized in 1994, with the participation of all 10 SEA countries; however, progress on implementation of the recommendations arising from the discussions has been slow.

Several international partner organizations are active in organising general and specialised training courses for key target groups: Cambodia; Indonesia; Lao PDR; Malaysia; Philippines; and Viet Nam (e.g., Training Programme for Wetland Managers in collaboration with Kakadu National Park (Australia)).

Further Efforts

- Review, and implement recommendations arising from the 1994 training needs analysis and develop new training initiatives and programs in areas where the need is greatest.
- Review existing capacity in national institutions responsible for the conservation and wise use of wetlands, and implement appropriate measure to overcome limitations where they exist
- Develop new training activities and modules for application of the Wise Use Guidelines, with a focus on integrated catchment/river basin and coastal zone planning and management, integrated site management planning, wetland restoration and rehabilitation, and education and public awareness techniques.
- Provide increased opportunities for manager training through personnel exchanges on the job, and developing wetland manager training facilities and courses at Ramsar sites.
- Exchanging information, technical assistance and advice, and expertise on the conservation and wise use of wetlands with other countries of the region e.g., through the development of regional training opportunities.

General Objective 5: To Ensure the Conservation of all Sites Included in the List of Wetlands of International Importance (Ramsar List)

Rationale

Designation of a wetland for the Ramsar List is only the starting point, since Contracting Parties accept an undertaking to conserve listed sites. The Conference of the Parties has placed increasing emphasis on maintaining the ecological character of Ramsar sites, as a key to their conservation. This does not preclude human usage but aims to avoid fundamental adverse changes to wetland functions, values or attributes. The aim is at least to maintain the ecological character recorded at the time of designation, and, in many cases, additional measures will be required to restore functions, values or attributes lost prior to designation.

Working Definitions of "ecological character" and "change in ecological character" and Guidelines for describing and maintaining the of ecological character of listed sites were adopted at the 6th COP in Brisbane, 1996. The Conference of the Parties has adopted mechanisms to assist the Contracting Parties; the Montreux Record (Recommendation 4.8, Resolution 5.4, and Resolution VI.1) identifies Ramsar sites in need of priority action; the Management Guidance Procedure (Recommendation 4.7 and Resolution VI.14) enables the Bureau to provide Parties with expert advice. Resolution 5.7 calls for all Ramsar siters to have a management plan and its annexes includes guidelines on management planning for Ramsar Sites and other wetlands; one management option is to decide that no specific action is required.

Current Status in SEA

- Management plans have been, or are currently being developed for Ramsar sites in Indonesia, Malaysia and the Philippines.
- Zoning measures have been taken at Ramsar sites in Indonesia, Malaysia and the Philippines.
- Ramsar Information Sheets have been prepared for all Ramsar sites in Malaysia, Indonesia, Philippines and Viet Nam.
- None of the Ramsar sites in SEA have been listed on the Montreux Record.

Further Efforts

- Conduct review to identify changes in the ecological character of Ramsar sites, with input from local communities NGOs, and other stakeholders.
- Take remedial action, where necessary, to mitigate changes in ecological character (e.g., by listing on the Montreux Record) and promote rehabilitation efforts.
- Develop, and implement management plans for all Ramsar sites, consistent with the Convention's Guideline on Management planning and emphasizing the involvement of local communities and other stakeholders.
- Ensure that, by the 8th COP (2002), management plans and other mechanisms are in place for at least half of all Ramsar sites in each Contracting Party.
- Obtain regularly updated information on Ramsar sites, and forward these to the Bureau.
- Promote the establishment and implementation of zoning measures related to larger Ramsar sites, wetland reserves and other wetland.
- Support the establishment of national wetland databases, compatible with the Ramsar Database, and develop a common protocol to facilitate exchange and interaction.

General Objective 6: To Designate for the Ramsar List Those Wetlands Which Meet the Convention's Criteria, Especially Wetland Types Still Underrepresented in the List and Transfrontier Wetlands

Rationale

The inclusion of wetlands in the Ramsar List has proved to be an effective means of conserving wetland, especially in cases where they have not been formally designated as protected areas. The number of sites on the List has grown at a steady pace over the years as new Contracting Parties have joined the Convention and as existing Parties have designated additional sites. As of 27 March 1996, the List includes over 800 sites, covering over 500,000 square kilometers. While this is a welcome development, over 500 of these sites are in only 24 Contracting Parties which are developed countries, and more than 80 sites are located in 15 Contracting Parties that are countries with economics in transition. Much greater effort is required to promote the listing of sites by developing countries. The listing of underrepresented wetland types and transfrontier sites also requires priority attention.

Criteria for identifying wetlands of international importance have been adopted by the Conference of the Parties (Recommendation 4.2) while the 6th Conference of the Parties (1996) adopted criteria on wetlands important for fish (resolution VI.2). The Ramsar criteria have served in developing regional or national scientific inventories of wetlands (Recommendation 4.6) and thus in identifying candidate Ramsar sites.

Current Status

- Malaysia, Philippines, and Viet Nam have listed only one site to the Ramsar List of Wetlands of International Importance.
- A regionwide inventory of wetlands was prepared in 1989, but the information is relatively out-of-date given the rapid pace of development in the region.
- National inventories of wetlands have been prepared in Indonesia (1989, now on database), Malaysia (1987), Philippines (1990) and Viet Nam.
- The existing Ramsar sites in SEA comprise inland freshwater, coastal/mangrove, and peatland systems. There are no coral reef sites listed in the entire Asian region.
- No transfrontier sites have been listed in the Asian region.

Further Efforts

- Increase the number of designated Ramsar sites priority should be given to wetland types currently underrepresented on the Ramsar List (and in particular, coral reefs, mangroves, sea-grass beds and peatlands) and sites currently enjoying no special conservation status at national level.
- Update, and where necessary, expand, national inventories of wetlands according to the Ramsar criteria.
- Develop priority listing of wetland sites of international and national importance.
- Consider designating transfrontier wetland areas as Ramsar sites, as a step towards fostering regional cooperation.

General Objective 7: To Promote International Cooperation and Mobilize Financial Assistance for Wetland Conservation and Wise Use in Collaboration with other Conventions and Agencies, both Governmental and Nongovermental

Rationale

Under Article 5 of the Convention, Contracting Parties accept an obligation to consult one another over implementation of the Convention, particularly in the case of wetlands extending over the territories of more than one Party and of water systems shared by Contracting Parties. This Article also refers to coordination of policies on wetlands and their flora and fauna. The Parties have further interpreted Article 5 to cover development assistance affection wetlands (Recommendation 4.13).

The Convention will intensify its international cooperation activities, *inter alia* those related to transfrontier wetlands, will develop further the coordination of activities with other global and regional conventions on natural resources use, and will promote coordination at national level in implementaion of such conventions. In order to achieve the preceding General Objectives, the Convention will develop its catalytic role in ensuring that funds are available, especially to developing countries and to countries whose economies are in transition, for implementation of these states' Ramsar obligations.

Current Status in SEA

- While there has been considerable action at national level in the implementation of the Convention, regional cooperative efforts, involving member states and nonmember states is lacking.
- Several regional agencies and groups (e.g., ASEAN) have working groups on nature conservation and environment. So far, wetlands have not been considered as a distinct ecosystem type in the deliberations of the groups.
- Development assistance agencies provide financial support for a variety of projects which have the potential to adversely affect wetland benefits and functions.
- Networks such as the Global Water Partnership, International Coral Reef Initiative (ICRI) and Waterwatch Asia are active in the region, and provide the framework for enhanced regional cooperation in wetland-related initiatives.
- Some member states have designated sites to the Shorebird Reserve Network (Brisbane Initiative).

Further Efforts

- Existing member states should use the opportunity of their participation in regional groupings to promote and encourage membership to the Convention.
- Identify transfrontier wetlands of international importance (including those within shared catchment/river basins) and encourage preparation and implementation of joint plans for such sites using a catchment approach.
- Encourage twinning of transfrontier wetland sites and other wetlands with similar characteristics.
- Strengthen cooperation and synergy with the *Convention on Biological Diversity*, in particular as regards inclusion of wetland concerns in national biodiversity strategies, and planning and execution of projects affecting wetlands.
- Enhance contribution to international cooperation on shared wetland species, notably through cooperative arrangements with the Convention on Migratory Species, flyway agreements, networks and other mechanisms dealing with migratory species.
- Participate in, and provide active support for, the efforts of regional and global networks (e.g., ICRI, Global Water Partnership and Waterwatch Asia).
- Allocate funds for conservation and wise use of wetlands in national budgets.
- Include projects for conservation and wise use of wetlands in development plans funded by development assistance agencies.

General Objective 8: To Provide the Convention with the Required Institutional Mechanisms and Resources

Rationale

The operation of the Conference of the Parties and of Ramsar subsidiary bodies and mechanisms Standing

Committee, Scientific and Technical Review Panel, Bureau, Small Grants Fund, Montreux Record and Management Guidance Procedure will be kept under review to ensure that they function as effectively as possible. Resources will be sought to guarantee the efficient operation of these mechanisms. Furthermore, new mechanisms may be required at international and at national level to promote more effective implementation of the Convention. The present General Objective provides the institutional structures and resources required to achieve the previous General Objectives.

Current Status in SEA

Malaysia is the current Regional Representative for Asia on the Standing Committee.

The upcoming Ramsar Regional meeting in Malaysia (February 1998) will provide the opportunity for members states to review progress in implementation of the Strategic Plan, and participate in the development of a Regional Action Plan for Asia.

Indonesia, Malaysia and Thailand have established multisectoral National Wetland/ Ramsar Committees to coordinate and oversee the implementation of the Convention in their respective countries. The establishment of similar committees is reported to be underway in the Philippines and Viet Nam).

Most Administrative Authorities in member states have active working relationships with one or more of the Ramsar partner organizations.

Further Efforts

- Participate actively in regional and subregional meetings, and in the preparation and implementation of regional action plans for effective implementation of the Convention.
- Support and encourage the efforts of National Wetland/Ramsar Committees; where they do not currently exist, enhance efforts to establish such committees.
- Strengthen cooperative planning mechanisms with Ramsar partner organizations, at national and regional levels.
- Give priority of funding for training programs, education and public awareness work, development of the Ramsar database, and the Convention's Communications Strategy.

(iii) Hassan P., *Legal Framework for Wise Use of Wetlands: A Regional Perspective*, Keynote address at the Asian Wetlands Symposium 2001, Penang, Malaysia, Ramsar Center, Japan, Universiti Sains Malaysia, Wetlands International-Asia and Pacific, and the Ministry of Science, Technology and the Environment, Government of Malaysia, 2001

On its 30th anniversary this year, the *Ramsar Convention on the Conservation of Wetlands*, 1971 can look to its several successes in first pioneering and, over the years, consolidating and strengthening the recognition, at national, regional and international levels, of the "fundamental ecological functions of wetlands as regulators of water regimes and as habitats supporting a characteristic flora and fauna, especially waterfowl" and that "wetlands constitute a resource of great economic, cultural, scientific, and recreational value, the loss of which would be irreparable" (Preamble). It held out the wisdom that the Contracting Parties shall "formulate and implement their planning so as to promote the conservation of the wetlands ... and as far as possible the wise use of wetlands in their territory" (Article 3).

As a Pakistani, I want to start with the announcement that, in May this year, Pakistan designated eight new wetlands to be included in the list of Wetlands of International Importance. The total area covered by these new additions is 222,246 hectares. There are now sixteen (16) Ramsar sites in Pakistan. The new sites include (1) an extensive mangrove forest extending along Gawater Bay on the Arabian Sea to the Iranian border, and contiguous with Iran's Govater Bay and Hur-e-Bahu Ramsar site; (2) an uninhabited island off the coast, as well as other sandy beach coastal sites, which are important for the endangered Olive Ridley and Green turtles; and (3) a 170-km stretch of the Indus River that is vital for the survival of the once-common Indus dolphin. IUCN-Pakistan and WWF-Pakistan have both been very active, not only in biodiversity studies and management planning for these areas, but also in technical preparations for these Ramsar designations.

Despite this good news, the problem of reduction in wetlands and deterioration in their quality continues. According to an estimate the world has lost half of its

Indonesia, Malaysia and Thailand have established multisectoral National Wetland/ Ramsar Committees to coordinate and oversee the implementation of the Convention in their respective countries.

wetlands during the course of the previous century. Mounting populations have put great pressure on wetlands in the developing countries. There is, undeniably, need for an urgent review of the causes of this global trend and for us in Asia and the Pacific, to particularly identify remedial measures in this region. My professional and geographical background enables me to submit a regional perspective on the legal framework for wise use of wetlands.

At the pace-setting Asian Wetlands Symposium held in Kushiro, Japan in October 1992 I had, in a keynote address, *From Lyon to Otsu: Laws on Conservation and Wise Use of Wetlands*, submitted ten (10) guidelines and goals for a legal regime for the wise use of wetlands:

(1) strengthening the law as an essential tool in wetland conservation, including wise use, by systematically considering this aspect in policy reviews, as well as case studies, and thus providing information on positive and negative aspects of a particular legal system.

(2) systematically reviewing national legislation to determine those provisions which induce or enable wetland destruction, and work towards their abolition.

(3) legislation should provide for a variety of protected area types, ranging from national parks, strict nature reserves, and generally highly protective instruments, to multiple use areas and softer regimes.

(4) the panoply of national conservation legal instruments should include "biotopetype protection measures," and to include wetlands as one of the ecosystem types covered.

(5) legislative provisions should cover activities and processes affecting a particular wetland, even when they take place outside its boundaries.

(6) in a federation, instituting a legal system satisfactory from the conservation point of view in all the component parts of the State, including adequate coordination between the provinces/ regions, and between these and the federal government.

(7) regulatory regimes should include elements which facilitate their implementation through public participation in decision-making, and provide for enforcement mechanisms, including, but not limited to, sanctions.

(8) legislation should where appropriate, allow for site-specific mechanisms, including provisions for autonomy in site-governance and ability to regulate and control human activity.

(9) fostering coordination and cooperation between the existing conventions in the field of biological diversity conservation such as Ramsar, and the then newly adopted *Convention on Biological Diversity*.

(10) increasing expertise building and improving services in the field of wetland conservation related law through pooling information and knowledge.

The role of constitutional provisions on environmental protection and sustainable development and of the judiciary in facilitating sustainable natural resource management has also been particularly acknowledged by me. It is a measure of the slowness with which things have moved in respect of attempts to provide a legal regime for the conservation of wetlands in Asia that much of what I stated in Kushiro, eight years ago, continues to remain fully valid. In fact, there is a more compelling urgency that the suggestions be heeded.

Of course, this is not to say that there has been no progress since Kushiro. The several Ramsar Conferences of the Parties (COP), particularly since 1987, at Regina (1987), Montreux (1990), and Kushiro (1993), have developed definitions and guidelines for the interpretation of "wise use" mentioned in the *Ramsar Convention*. The 1996 COP (Brisbane) adopted the *Ramsar Strategic Plan*, 1997–2002 and the 1999 COP (San Jose) adopted the *Guidelines for Developing and Implementing National Wetland Policies*, and the *Guidelines for Reviewing Laws and Institutions to Promote the Conservation and Wise Use of Wetlands*; these duly impact on the "wise use" concept. These developments have duly accounted for the subsequent work on sustainable development including by the 1992 World Conference on Environment and Development, and the 1992 *Convention on Biological Diversity*. In fact, the 1993 *Kushiro Additional Guidance* acknowledges that:

> "this guidance must be applied in the light of other national and international obligations for nature conservation, including the conservation of biodiversity, climate change and pollution control measures, as adopted by the UN Conference on Environment and Development and in other international fora".

It is increasingly acknowledged that the wise use of wetlands can be effectively promoted through legislation: the 1990 *Guidelines for the Implementation of the Wise Use Concept* prioritized five categories for national action:

(1) improvement of institutional and government organizational arrangements;
(2) review of existing and future legislation and other national policies affecting wetlands;
(3) development of awareness and knowledge of wetland functions and values;
(4) inventory and economic valuation of wetlands for setting site management priorities; and
(5) establishment of actions on a site-specific basis such as legal protection mechanisms and habitat restoration (emphasis added).

The 1993 *Kushiro Additional Guidance* recommends several components for general wise use legislation and for site-specific legal protection. But while we recognize that this Guidance will impact significantly on the future planning of legal regimes for wetlands, it would be well to acknowledge the six basic conclusions that led to their development:

(1) Social and economic factors are the main reason for wetland loss and therefore need to be of central concern in wise use programs;
(2) Special attention should be given to local populations, the primary beneficiaries of improved management of wetland sites, and to the values that indigenous people can bring to all aspects of wise use;
(3) Wise use programs should seek to involve all public and private institutions in addition to the wetland conservation agency where such institutions have expertise relevant to the effective long-term management;
(4) Site-specific projects many often demonstrate the need for more general institutional requirements for the wise use of wetlands;
(5) Wise use should take account of surrounding coastal zones of catchments where wetlands form an integral part thereof;
(6) Activities affecting wetlands should be governed by the precautionary principle where knowledge of ecological constraints of a wetland system is not available.

The challenge before the Asian Wetlands Symposium 2001 now being held in Penang, Malaysia, is to move the 1993 *Additional Guidance* and the 1999 *Guidelines for Reviewing Laws* and the actions thereunder forward. How can we do this? Should we recommend a model legislation for the conservation of wetlands? If so, should such a legislation be part of a general national law on environmental protection and sustainable development or should there be a model legislation for site-specific wetlands. When the United Nations Economic and Social Commission for Asia and Pacific (ESCAP) pioneered in grasping the importance of environmental protection legislation in the region, I was requested to overview these developments in the region and to present recommendations for a future course of action by the countries in the Asia Pacific region. Following an extended travel to most of the countries in the region, I submitted the *Status of Environmental Protection Legislation in the Asia and Pacific Region* in 1978. It was a major conclusion of this Report that the diversity of political and legal history, the different stages of economic development and the different legal systems in the region, did not permit a "model legislation" approach. Each country had different resources and different capacity and it was recommended that it would be best to identify essential elements that would go into legislation for environmental protection. Almost a quarter century later, I reiterate the sound basis of this conclusion and recommend that, instead of developing model wetland legislation for our region, we should seek to identify basic elements that should be included in any legal regime for the conservation of wetlands. These guidelines can provide an appropriate checklist for draftsmen of such laws in national jurisdictions. This paper builds on this essential conclusion.

The *Ramsar Convention* itself provides a beginning in the search of such elements by providing for the "wise use" of wetlands. The work of the Ramsar Conference of the Parties (COP) and the practices recommended by the Ramsar Bureau and adopted by the COP, are all important navigational compasses. Several elements can be drawn particularly from the 1993 *Kushiro Additional Guidance*. These, however, need to be supplemented with the help of developments in the field of sustainable development since 1971 when the *Ramsar Convention* was finalized. The *Stockholm Declaration on the Human Environment*, 1972, the *World Charter of Nature*, 1982, the UNCED process anchored by the *Rio Declaration on Environment and Development*, 1992, and *Agenda 21*, and reinforced by a proliferation of Multilateral Environment Agreements (MEAs) have all contributed to a growing acceptance of certain principles of international environmental law. These principles, which can be the basis for the development of national and regional legal regimes for wetlands, include:

(1) respect for all life forms,
(2) global environment is a common concern of humanity,
(3) inter-generational equity,
(4) preventive principle,
(5) precautionary principle,
(6) right to development, and
(7) eradication of poverty.

To these could be added state sovereignty, international cooperation, information and assistance in environmental emergencies, consultations in relation to transboundary events, access to information, public participation, and good environmental governance.

The 1992 Convention on Biological Diversity *has, particularly, influenced the development of the wise use concept used in the* Ramsar Convention.

The 1992 *Convention on Biological Diversity* has, particularly, influenced the development of the wise use concept used in the *Ramsar Convention.* In fact, the first interpretation of "wise use" came in the 1987 COP as the "sustainable use of wetlands for the benefit of mankind in a way that is compatible with maintaining the natural properties of the ecosystem". But it was the 1996 COP that, in considering the relationship between the Ramsar concept of wise use and the provisions of the *Convention on Biological Diversity*, declared that the Ramsar concept had developed substantially to be "considered ... synonymous with "sustainable use". The result of these and subsequent developments is that, today, the wise use concept means more than conservation of listed sites, reserve creation and international cooperation. It has come to include the broader concerns related to sustainable development, biodiversity conservation and water resource management.

Article 20 of the IUCN *Draft International Covenant on Environment and Development* dealing with "Natural Systems" also recognizes the importance of wetlands and the need to maintain their ecological integrity:

"1. Parties shall take appropriate measures to conserve and, where necessary and possible, restore natural systems which support life on Earth in all its diversity, including biological diversity, and to maintain and restore the ecological functions of these systems as an essential basis for sustainable development, including *inter alia*,...
(b) fresh water wetlands and floodplains as recharge areas for groundwaters, floodwater buffers, filters and oxidizing areas for contaminants....
2. Parties shall, within their jurisdiction, manage natural systems as single ecological units..."

In drafting these provisions, we took the view that the optimal management of a natural system, that is its conservation, maintenance and restoration, is accomplished when it is treated as a single ecological unit. This consideration should be at the core of any legal regime for the wise use of wetlands.

There are many different categories of users that compete for wetlands and water resources. Competition could include over access or title to wetlands and their products. Rising populations put pressure for uses such as housing, agriculture, and industry which may conflict with existing uses by local populations. National wetland polices are recommended for resolving these complex issues in line with the wise use concept. Many governments have announced national wetland policies and these provide an impressive mosaic of commitments to wise use and sustainable development. Equally impressive is the wetland policy of the European Union which is based on four principles:

(1) no further loss of wetlands
(2) no further wetland degradation
(3) wise use of wetlands
(4) wetland improvement and restoration

The 1993 *Additional Guidance* recommends that the wise use of wetlands should consider the following difficulties:

(1) a lack of institutional mechanisms designed to encourage the involvement of both public and private sectors of the society, at regional or local level as well as at national level;
(2) insufficient coordination among public agencies;
(3) policies that discourage conservation and wise use objectives;
(4) inadequate policy research programs; and
(5) lack of cooperative arrangements with neighboring countries for joint management of shared wetlands or wetland species.

There are many different ways in which countries may attempt to overcome these obstacles. A few examples are given in the Guidance:

(1) At international level, countries may wish to establish cross-boundary water commissions or other coordinating boards to avoid action in one country adversely affecting wetlands in another country and to guarantee that water quality and quantity are maintained in such a way as to preserve the functional values of wetlands. In addition, countries that are range states for migratory species dependent on wetlands may wish to establish coordinated conservation programmes for those species and set common guidelines on development aid in the field of conservation and wise use of wetlands.

(2) At national level, countries might create inter-ministerial boards or commissions, national wetland committees or other bodies to oversee coordination and cooperation for wetland management. These bodies should include a wide representation (based on a catchment approach) from the authorities with responsibility for wetlands and might include government agencies dealing with environment, nature conservation, agriculture, forestry, aquaculture, hunting, fishing, shipping, tourism, mining, industry, health, development assistance, and other relevant subjects; they should also include interested governmental and nongovernmental conservation organizations.

(3) At local level, countries might establish procedures to guarantee that local populations are involved in the decision-making process related to wetland use and to provide local populations with sufficient knowledge of planned activities to assure their meaningful participation in this decision making process.

National or regional wetland policies provide an appropriate basis for the next phase of wise use: the development of national legislation or legal regimes for the wise use of wetlands. Governments can use several instruments to promote policy such as legislative tools. The Guidance identifies five different mechanisms to implement wise use in practice:

(1) Periodical review of existing legislation to ensure that it is generally compatible with the wise use obligation, and make adjustments if necessary; this applies to particular legislation regarding mandatory wetland destruction or to that which encourages such destruction through tax benefits and subsidies.

(2) General wise use legislation for wetlands should consider the following:

(a) inclusion of wetlands in the zones of land-use plans which enjoy the highest degree of protection;

(b) institution of a permit system for activities affecting wetlands. This should include a threshold under which a permit would not be required, as well as a general exemption for activities which, because of their nature, are deemed to be compatible with any performance obligation;

(c) execution of an environmental impact assessment in order to determine if a proposed project is compatible with the general requirements of wise use and the maintenance of the ecological character of the wetlands concerned. Special rules relating to the contents of an environmental impact assessment will be needed in order to ensure that no important factor specifically related to wetlands is overlooked. The cumulative effects of separate projects should also be taken into consideration. Environmental impact assessments should also be prepared not only for activities and projects in the wetlands concerned but also for activities outside these areas when they may have significant effect on wetlands. Environmental impact assessments should also cover the long-term effects of proposed activities, projects, plans and programmes as well as interactions between all components of the water system at the catchment level.

(d) monitoring of the effects of authorized actions and carrying out unbiased environmental audits of these actions when they have been completed;

(e) institution of a system of management agreements between relevant government agencies, landowners and landusers to provide for positive management measures by the latter when this is required for the maintenance of the ecosystem;

(f) provision of financial incentives including taxes and subsidies to encourage activities which are compatible with the maintenance of wetlands, and which promote and contribute to their conservation. Financial tax incentives should not permit activities which have detrimental effects upon wetlands;

(g) obligation to refrain from introducing invasive alien species, and to take preventive measures to minimize the risk of accidental introductions;

(h) obligation to make all appropriate efforts to eradicate introduced and translocated species which may cause significant ecological disturbances in water systems and, in addition, provide for the possibility of claiming civil damages from those responsible for unlawful introductions; and

(i) right of appeal by private organizations against governmental agency decisions which might violate obligations laid down by law.

(3) Legislation for the conservation and wise use of specific wetland sites (e.g., Ramsar sites, ecologically sensitive areas, areas with a high degree of biodiversity, sites containing endemic species, wetland nature reserves) will generally apply to large wetland areas where human activities compatible with the conservation of the ecosystem should be maintained, encouraged and developed for the benefit of local populations. This legislation will be in addition to those provisions laid down in the previous paragraph in respect of wetlands in general. It should consider the following points:

(a) definition of a special legal status for large wetland areas allowing for the control of any potentially damaging activity, including agriculture, forestry, tourism, fishing, hunting, aquaculture;

(b) division of those wetlands into different zones with particular regulations applying to each type of zone; these regulations would be defined to ensure that the carrying capacity of the area concerned is not exceeded in respect of each activity authorized;

(c) encouragement of traditional and other ecological and sustainable activities in these areas through incentives and advice;

(d) establishment of a management system in each area which should have legal support and of a management body to oversee the implementation and to ensure that regulations are observed;

(e) association of populations living in or close to the area with its management, through appropriate representation; scientific institutions and conservation NGOs should also be associated with management, at least in an advisory capacity;

(f) application of special environmental impact assessment rules to these areas in view of their particular environmental sensitivity; and

(g) submission of activities which may have adverse effects on the area, to environmental impact assessment or to other forms of evaluation. Such activities should only be authorized when the evaluation has shown that no significant damage to the area will occur.

(4) Review of division of jurisdiction among government agencies is important to the success of regulatory wetland regime. This issue, which concerns both territorial and functional matters, often constitutes a considerable obstacle to integrated management of wetlands since it needs to be based on a catchment-wide approach. A review of legal and administrative constraints which prevent management at the correct scale (e.g., catchment-wide management) should be undertaken with a view to developing appropriate solutions to jurisdictional problems. Particular attention should be paid to the need to manage coastal wetlands as single units, irrespective of the usual division of jurisdiction between land and sea.

(5) It is important to develop cooperative arrangements for water systems shared between two or more countries to achieve wise use.

The 1999 *Guidelines for Reviewing Laws and Institutions to Promote the Conservation and Wise Use of Wetlands* is the most recent law-specific attempt by Ramsar to progress the wise use concept. It identifies the need for a legal and institutional review, the elements for the preparation and carrying out of such a review. The review process is intended to help the Parties to take stock of how existing laws and institutions contribute to or work against wetland conservation and wise use. A particularly helpful part of these Guidelines, paragraphs 32–35, is in respect of issues to be developed in adaptation to national circumstances:

"In relation to non-site specific measures:

(a) Is the legal definition of wetlands or the scope of wetland-related legal and institutional measures sufficiently broad to apply to all categories of wetland covered by the *Ramsar Convention*?

(b) Is it possible under land-use planning legislation (national, provincial or local) to confer protective status on wetlands and to limit urban, industrial and recreational development which might adversely affect wetland functions, values and benefits, including in a transboundary context?

(c) Do principles, standards and techniques applicable to socio-economic activities, including environmental impact assessment rules, support the maintenance of wetland functions, values and benefits and incorporate a precautionary approach?

(d) Is there a legal basis to encourage positive conservation measures and stewardship by wetland owners, users and nongovernmental organizations (e.g., contracts, conservation easements or tax provisions)?

(e) Where development involves wetland loss or degradation, is there a legal requirement to make monetary or other compensation, consistent with the polluter pays principle?

(f) Are civil or administrative law remedies available to interested parties where wetlands are unlawfully destroyed or damaged?

(g) Where wetland loss or degradation constitutes a criminal offense, are enforcement procedures adequate and are penalties set at a meaningful level?

Site-specific considerations could include:

(a) Is the legal status conferred on Ramsar sites and wetland nature reserves sufficient to ensure their conservation and wise use?

(b) Is it possible legally and institutionally to designate and manage coastal protected wetlands, even though they may include terrestrial and marine areas?

(c) Where wetlands are designated as protected areas, does legislation authorise continued access and use by indigenous and local communities where this is consistent with the conservation and wise use of the particular site?

(d) Is legislation supportive of customary laws, practices, tenure systems and institutions of indigenous and local communities, which promote sustainable use of wetland resources?

(e) Do wetland users, including indigenous and local communities and other stakeholders, have the right to information, representation and participation in site management?

(f) Does legislation support the preparation and implementation of wetland management plans?

(g) Is there a legal requirement for wetland management bodies to be consulted about potentially damaging external activities?

Considerations related to jurisdictional and institutional coordination could include:

(a) Do procedures exist for horizontal (cross-sectoral) coordination between wetland administrative authorities and relevant sectoral departments and agencies?

(b) Do procedures exist for vertical coordination on conservation and wise use issues between different tiers of government, particularly in countries with federal or decentralized systems?

(c) What, if any, steps have been taken to promote consistency between sectoral plans, policies and programs and obligations related to wise (sustainable) use?

(d) What legal and institutional measures have been taken to coordinate and integrate management of inland water systems (river basins, catchments, watersheds) and coastal areas?

(e) Have legal and institutional measures been taken to involve stakeholders in wetland policy-making and wise use planning?

(f) Do national or sub-national administrative authorities have adequate powers and human, technical and financial resources to implement wetland conservation and wise use programs?

Possible transboundary and international cooperation considerations include:

(a) Is there a legal and institutional basis for coordinated management of shared wetlands, international watercourses or wetland flora and fauna with one or more neighbouring countries? If so, could institutional coordination and joint management programs be made more effective or extended in the future?

(b) Have steps been taken under other international environmental agreements to develop bilateral or multilateral cooperation? If so, could these be used as a basis for strengthening coordinated international action on wetland and water resource issues?

(c) Are procedures in place to ensure that foreign and domestic investment and development cooperation/aid programmes do not support activities which could damage wetlands and are fully compatible with the wise use obligation?"

It is possible to conclude that, as has been shown, the concept of wise use, vague or general as it may have been in 1971 when it was included in the *Ramsar Convention*, has by now developed a precise content aided by the corpus of interpretation and practices of the Ramsar COP, including particularly by the 1990 *Guidelines for the Implementation of the Wise Use Concept*, the 1993 *Kushiro Additional Guidance*, the 1999 *Guidelines for Reviewing Laws and Institutions to Promote the Conservation and Wise Use of Wetlands*, the multilateral environmental agreements and the general principles of international environmental law. All these are relevant and should guide the development of legal regimes in Asia and the Pacific. But the following need to be reiterated for their special importance to our region:

(1) provisions in the Constitution on environmental protection and sustainable development highlight a national priority and will facilitate the specific objective of wise use of wetlands. Experience particularly in India, Pakistan, Philippines and Sri Lanka has demonstrated that the judiciary has used even general (human rights) provisions to advance conservation and sustainable natural resource management. Additionally, provisions in the Constitution clarify, in a federation, the respective competences of the Federal and Provincial Governments in natural resource management thereby facilitating cooperation between the Federal and Provincial Governments.

(2) the diversity of the region does not allow a "model" wetland legislation.

(3) the local populations in the wetlands should be involved in any legal regime of the wetlands; such participation will enhance the enforcement of the legal regime.

(4) good environmental governance, particularly in countries with large poor populations, would require poverty eradication as an integral part of its wetland policies.

(5) public interest litigation should be strengthened by improving standing to sue concepts; this will facilitate NGOs and civil society to seek judicial interventions to promote the wise use of wetlands.

(6) access to information legislation will improve transparency and accountability in respect of Governmental actions or failure to act further to wetland policies or legal regimes.

The above are highlighted in recognition of the most serious problem in the region: enforcement and implementation. The region has, in many cases, been found to have forward-looking policies and laws on sustainable development and natural resource management but these are largely unimplemented.

The importance of effective implementation of national laws and obligations under MEAs such as the *Ramsar Convention* can hardly be exaggerated. The conditioning factors that impede implementation in the Asia and Pacific region include (1) increasing poverty, (2) growing populations, (3) lack of financial and technical resources, (4) lack of capacity, and (5) low levels of education and awareness. The Asian and Pacific region will have to make a concerted attempt in these areas to move forward to wisely use its wetlands. Facilitation of this would be one of the major challenges before the upcoming World Summit on Sustainable Development at Johannesburg, South Africa, next year.

C

UNESCO Biosphere Reserves

Although not specifically deriving from a treaty, the Biosphere Reserve Concept plays an important role in the conservation of biodiversity. The material here is intended to demonstrate the different courses a government might take in its overall strategy for biodiversity. The Biosphere Reserve Concept should, therefore, be viewed as a supplement to the Instruments discussed above, namely RAMSAR and the *Migratory Species Convention*, and, of course, the *Convention on Biological Diversity*.

(i) Conservation International-UNESCO, *Biospheres Reserve Partnerships*, CI-UNESCO, 2001

[*The text of the following extract can be found on the Internet. The address is <http://www.conservation.org/science/cptc/capbuild/unesco/>. This site was accessed on 12/07/01.*]

The Biosphere Reserve Concept

In 1968, the UNESCO Conference on the Conservation and Rational Use of the Biosphere gave rise to the Man and the Biosphere (MAB) Programme within UNESCO. The biosphere reserve concept was key to achieving MAB's objective of striking a balance between conserving biodiversity, encouraging economic and social development, and preserving cultural values

Biosphere reserves are areas of terrestrial and coastal/marine ecosystems where, through appropriate zoning patterns and management mechanisms, the conservation of ecosystems and their biodiversity is ensured. Each biosphere reserve has three basic functions:

- a conservation function: *to contribute to the conservation of landscapes, ecosystems, species and genetic variation;*
- a development function: *to foster economic and human development which is socially and ecologically sustainable; and*
- a logistic function: *to provide support for research, monitoring, education and information exchange related to local, national and global issues of conservation and development.*

For management purposes, each reserve is divided into three zones:

- core zone: *strictly protected areas with very little human influence, which are used to monitor natural changes in representative ecosystems and serve as conservation areas for biodiversity;*
- buffer zone: *areas surrounding the core zone where only low impact activities are allowed, such as research, environmental education, and recreation; and*
- transition zone: *the outer zone where sustainable use of resources by local communities is encouraged and these impacts can be compared to zones of greater protection.*

While traditional parks often attempt to form small protected areas in a world increasingly dominated by severe human impacts, biosphere reserves are designed to bring people and nature together to demonstrate how to both use and preserve nature.

The Global Picture

A primary goal of UNESCO-MAB is the exchange of scientific knowledge and management experience. There are currently more than 335 biosphere reserves in 85 countries, forming a global network of scientists and natural resource managers working to maintain the long-term survival of fragile ecosystems. Because of its unique structure, this biosphere reserve network has the ability to serve as a medium for the worldwide exchange of ideas and information on conserving biodiversity and monitoring ecological changes in the environment.

A major international conference held in Seville, Spain in 1995 refined and strengthened the strategy for this global cooperative effort. By recognizing the value of partnerships among local communities, government institutions, nongovermental organizations and private enterprises—such as that between UNESCO, CI, Intel, and NEC—the network is capitalizing on the shared strengths and needs among each of its participants.

Biosphere reserves are areas of terrestrial and coastal/marine ecosystems where, through appropriate zoning patterns and management mechanisms, the conservation of ecosystems and their biodiversity is ensured.

Biosphere Reserves

Biosphere reserves are areas designated by their national governments to provide examples of sustainable development, through integrating conservation, research, and the use of natural resources to meet human needs. Often these reserves are based on national parks, but the biosphere reserve concept emphasizes that they should also work with surrounding communities, since nearby activities will effect the parks and vice-versa.

Currently the international biosphere reserve network includes over 350 reserves in more than 80 countries. In 1995 representatives from around the world met and finalized the "Seville Strategy for Biosphere Reserves," which emphasizes the need to develop mechanisms for exchanging experiences and standardized data between reserves.

To help strengthen this international biosphere reserve network and the management of individual reserves, CI and UNESCO have selected 25 reserves from Latin America, Asia, and Africa to receive a special grant of computer, an Internet connection, and training in specialized applications.

Project Background

Biosphere reserves are designed to answer one of the most challenging questions that the world is facing as we move towards the 21st century: How can we conserve the diversity of plants, animals and microorganisms which make up our living "biosphere" and maintain healthy natural systems while, at the same time, meet the material needs and aspirations of an increasing number of people? In contrast to traditional parks, biosphere reserves contain strictly protected areas surrounded by buffer and transition zones where a range of human activities is permitted. By recognizing the important role of people in the long-term survival of parks and protected areas, biosphere reserves ensure that local communities have incentives for using natural resources sustainably.

> "The Biosphere Reserve Network should facilitate exchange of information on the experience acquired in a vast range of biogeographic, bioclimatic, economic, social, and cultural development patterns." [Frederico Mayor Director General of UNESCO]

Despite these important goals, many biosphere reserves have faced critical shortages in technology and human capacity. High technology is becoming accessible and commonplace in the industrial countries. However, those in the developing world confront a wide gap between the technological needs that growing populations, intensified resource use, and dwindling frontier lands have made on their societies, and the technical skills that exist within their countries today.

To address these issues, Conservation International and the United Nations Educational, Scientific and Cultural Organization's Man and the Biosphere Program (UNESCO/MAB) have joined together to develop an institutional strengthening program for biosphere reserves that combines intensive, hands-on training in scientific analysis with long-term technical support through an international user network. By linking the institutions that manage even the most remote and inaccessible biosphere reserves into the global information network, we can help prove their planning and decision-making capacities, while encouraging greater national and international attention to their needs.

As Coordinator of the International Network of Biosphere Reserves, UNESCO will be responsible for arranging agreements between the participating Biosphere Reserves and Conservation International, and assisting CI with networking and communications exchange. As part of its broad institutional strengthening program, CI will direct the training workshops and technical support activities. Intel Corporation and NEC Corporation are providing the financing for equipment procurement, training and technical support, and the implementation of the communications network.

4

The Convention on Biological Diversity

A

Overview

The *Convention on Biological Diversity*, negotiated and adopted in the wake of the Rio Summit on environment and development, is an attempt to provide an overarching framework for the biodiversity concept. All-encompassing, it deals with all levels of biodiversity (genes, species and ecosystems); with wild and domesticated species; with conservation *in situ* and *ex situ*; and with biodiversity components within and outside national jurisdictions. It addresses area-based, species-based, and process-oriented regulatory techniques to keep the threats to biodiversity under control, while also mandating cross-sectoral legal mechanisms to achieve its aims: biodiversity planning, EIA, incentives, and benefit-sharing. An overview of the Convention is provided below.

(i) Glowka L., Burhenne-Guilmin F., and Synge H., in collaboration with McNeely J. and Guendling L., *A Guide to the Convention on Biological Diversity*, IUCN, 1994, pp 1–7

Introduction

On 22 May 1992, in Nairobi, the nations of the world adopted a global *Convention on Biological Diversity*. Later, on 5 June 1992, at the UN Conference on Environment and Development in Rio de Janeiro, a record number of over 150 States signed it. Approximately 18 months later, on 29 December 1993, the Convention entered into force.

The treaty is a landmark in the environment and development field, as it takes for the first time a comprehensive rather than a sectoral approach to conservation of the Earth's biodiversity and sustainable use of biological resources. It recognizes the vital point made in the *World Conservation Strategy (1980), Caring for the Earth* (1991), the *Global Biodiversity Strategy* (1992) and many other international documents that both biodiversity and biological resources should be conserved for reasons of ethics, economic benefit and indeed human survival. It implicitly accepts the telling point that the environmental impact which future generations may most regret about our time is the loss of biodiversity, in part because most of it—for example loss of species—cannot be reversed.

The Convention, however, goes beyond the conservation of biodiversity *per se* and the sustainable use of biological resources, to encompass such issues as access to genetic resources, sharing of benefits from the use of genetic material and access to technology, including biotechnology.

The fact that biological diversity is unevenly distributed around the globe is also recognized in the Convention. The North, biologically poorer, has depleted its biodiversity reserves over time, but such reserves are still found in the biologically South. If biodiversity is to be conserved, this imposes a heavier burden on the South, at a time when the use of biological resources is of paramount importance for developing countries in achieving development. The Convention recognizes that this burden, in turn, can only be alleviated by additional contributions (not only financial) from the industrialized North and through increased partnership between both developed and developing countries.

The Character of the Convention

The *Convention on Biological Diversity* is a framework agreement in two senses. In the first sense, it leaves it up to individual Parties to determine how most of its provisions are to be implemented. This is because its provisions are mostly expressed as overall goals and policies, rather than as hard and precise obligations as in, for example, the *Convention on International Trade in Endangered Species of Wild Fauna and Flora* (CITES). Nor does it tend to set targets, as does, for example, the recent European Council Directive On the Protection of Natural and Semi-natural Habitats and of Wild Fauna and Flora, which lists hundreds of species that should be brought back to "satisfactory levels". Instead, the emphasis in the *Convention on Biological Diversity* is to place the main decision making at the national level: unlike other treaties related to the conservation of biological diversity, there are no lists, no annexes of accepted sites or of species to be protected.

With regard to the provisions on conservation and sustainable use, the focus on action at the national level is emphasized by two crucial articles—article 1 which sets out the Convention's objectives, including the conservation of biological diversity and the sustainable use of its components, and article 6 which requires each Party to develop national strategies, plans or programs for conservation of biodiversity and sustainable use of biological resources. It will often be the case that the Parties will have to go beyond the substantive provisions in the later articles to achieve the overall objectives in article 1.

The later articles set out the policies to be followed. Article 8 sets out the major policies for effective *in-situ* conservation of biological diversity, giving Parties a set of goals against which to match their own laws and policies. Article 9 does the same for *ex-situ* conservation, article 10 for sustainable use of biological resources and article 14 for environmental impact assessment. These goals are buttressed by less detailed commitments on research and training (article 12) and on education and awareness (article 13).

The articles on access to genetic resources (article 15) and access to and transfer of technology (article 16), complex and imprecise as they are, also leave much to each Contracting Party to decide regarding their implementation. The financial articles (article 20, 21 and 39) were, to an extent, purposely left vague for the Conference of the Parties to later clarify; this part of the Convention's text simply reflects the level of agreement that could be achieved in time for the deadline of signature at UNCED in Rio de Janeiro on June 5, 1992.

That the Convention is a framework agreement is evident in the second sense because emphasis is placed on the possibility for the Conference of the Parties to further negotiate annexes and protocols.

Origin and History

In 1987, the UNEP Governing Council recognized the need to increase and streamline international efforts to protect biological diversity.

Well before the intergovernmental negotiations began under the aegis of the United Nations Environment Programme (UNEP), international experts had been promoting the idea of a global convention on biological diversity and working to develop elements for such an instrument.

Following recommendations from its General Assemblies, in particular in 1984 and 1987, IUCN-The World Conservation Union—had been exploring the possibilities for a treaty on the subject and from 1984 to 1989 had prepared successive drafts of articles for inclusion in a treaty. The IUCN draft articles, which were prepared by IUCN's Commission on Environmental Law and the IUCN Environmental Law Centre with help from numerous experts, notably the Joint IUCN/WWF Plant Advisory Group, concentrated on the global action needed to conserve biodiversity at the genetic, species and ecosystem levels, and focused on *in-situ* conservation within and outside protected areas. It also included the provision of a funding mechanism to alleviate the inequality of the conservation burden between the North and the South, already reflecting at the time the view that a convention without new and additional funding would not be worth pursuing.

In 1987, the UNEP Governing Council recognized the need to increase and streamline international efforts to protect biological diversity. It therefore established an *ad hoc* working group to investigate "the desirability and possible form of an umbrella convention to rationalize current activities in this field, and to address other areas which might fall under such a conventions" (UNEP Governing Council Res. 14/26 (1987)).

The first meeting of the group in late 1988 concluded that the existing conventions addressed specific questions of biodiversity conservation but, because of their piecemeal nature, did not adequately meet the needs of conserving biodiversity worldwide. At the global level, the existing conventions covered only internationally important natural sites (the *World Heritage Convention*), the specific threat of trade in endangered species (CITES), a specific ecosystem type (the *Ramsar* or *Wetlands Convention*) and a group of species (the *Migratory Species Convention*). In addition, there were various regional conventions on the conservation of nature and natural resources, some more comprehensive than others. Even taken together, these international accords could not ensure global conservation of biodiversity and so the group concluded that one or more additional legally binding mechanisms were needed at global level.

It soon became clear that the concept of developing an umbrella convention which would absorb or consolidate the existing conventions was legally and technically impossible. By early 1990, the *ad hoc* working group had reached a consensus that a new global treaty on biodiversity conservation was urgently needed—in the form of a framework treaty, building upon existing conventions.

In discussions on the scope of the Convention, it rapidly became apparent that many States were not prepared to consider only the conservation aspects in the strict sense. Some States also were not prepared to limit the discussion to wild resources. The scope for the Convention was gradually broadened to include all aspects and facets of biodiversity namely: *in-situ* and *ex-situ* conservation of wild and domesticated species, sustainable use of biological resources, access to genetic resources and to relevant technology, including biotechnology, access to benefits derived from such technology, safety of activities related to modified living organisms and provision of new and additional financial support.

With the draft articles developed by IUCN, and the later ones developed by FAO before them for consideration, as well as a number of studies commissioned by UNEP, the working group prepared a large number of elements for possible inclusion in a global treaty on biological diversity. The UNEP Secretariat, assisted by a small group of legal experts, then prepared a first draft of the convention based on all the "elements" that had been produced so far.

The formal negotiating process started in February 1991, when the group was renamed the Intergovernmental Negotiating Committee for a *Convention on Biological Diversity* (INC).

The main issues were divided between two working groups for discussion article by article. Working Group I dealt with general issues, such as the fundamental principles, general obligations, measures for *in-situ* and *ex-situ* conservation and the relationship with other legal instruments. Working Group II dealt with issues of access to genetic resources and relevant technologies, technology transfer, technical assistance, financial mechanisms and international cooperation. Progress was slow and negotiation difficult, especially during the final negotiating sessions. As time passed, the self-imposed deadline for signature of the Convention—the UNCED Conference in June 1992—was approaching with alarming speed.

The negotiations were often close to breaking down. Even on 22 May, the final day of the final negotiating session in Nairobi, it was not clear until the last moment whether the Convention would be adopted. Had the UNCED deadline not been present, it is unlikely that a convention would have been adopted on that date. Yet in spite of this fact, and in spite of the tensions in the negotiation, the number of signatures to the Convention in Rio on 5 June was unprecedented. The entry into force of the Convention, only 18 months after it was adopted was equally stunning.

The Issues Covered by the Convention

The Convention can be hailed as a landmark from several points of view. It is the first time that biodiversity, as such, is comprehensively addressed, and the first time that genetic diversity is specifically covered in a binding global treaty. It is also the first time that the conservation of biodiversity is recognized as the common concern of humankind.

By including issues of access and use of genetic resources, as well as technology transfer and biosafety, the Convention demonstrates a will to address all aspects of biodiversity. By creating a mechanism to provide funds to developing countries to help them implement the Convention, the need for new and additional resources to flow from North to South is also addressed.

The major issues of the Convention are discussed below in summary form and elaborated in detail in the commentary on the individual articles.

National Sovereignty and the Common Concern of Humankind

The proposition that biodiversity should be considered as the "common heritage" of humankind was rejected at an early stage, since most components of biological diversity are situated in areas under national jurisdiction. Instead, a firm emphasis was placed on sovereign rights over biological resources, while recognizing that the conservation of biological diversity is a "common concern" of humankind. "Common concern" implies a common responsibility to the issue based on its paramount importance to the international community as a whole.

The sovereign rights of States over their natural resources are referred to in the preamble and twice in the main text. Article 3 reproduces *verbatim* Principle 21 of the *Stockholm Declaration*, recognizing that States have the sovereign right to exploit their own resources pursuant to their own environmental policies. Article 15, on access to genetic resources, again recalls the sovereign rights of States over their natural resources as a basis for the authority to determine access to genetic resources.

However, this emphasis on national sovereignty is balanced by duties deriving both from sovereignty itself and from the fact that the conservation of biodiversity is a common concern to the entire international community. Indeed, it is significant that the preamble affirms first that the conservation of biological diversity is a common concern of humankind and only thereafter reaffirms that States have sovereign rights over their own biological resources.

Emphasis is also placed on the responsibilities of States towards biological resources within their jurisdiction. The preamble makes clear that States are responsible for conserving their biodiversity and for using the biological resources constituting this biodiversity in a sustainable manner. This is also emphasized by the acceptance of detailed responsibilities and obligations on these matters, as for instance in article 6 (General Measures for Conservation and Sustainable Use), article 8 *(In-situ* Conservation) and article 10 (Sustainable Use of Components of Biological Diversity).

Conservation and Sustainable Use

The Convention contains a series of far-reaching obligations related to the conservation of biological diversity and the sustainable use of its components.

On the strategic planning side, as already mentioned, the Convention creates obligations to develop national strategies and plans, to integrate the conservation and sustainable use of biological diversity into relevant sectoral or cross-sectoral plans, programs and policies, as well as into national decision-making (articles 6 and 10).

To base their activities on good science, each Party undertakes to identify important components of biodiversity and to identify priorities which may need special conservation measures, or which may offer the greatest potential for sustainable use. Processes and categories of activities which may have significant adverse effects on conservation and use are also to be identified and monitored (article 7).

Emphasis is given to *in-situ* conservation with obligations which constitute a comprehensive agenda, and call for measures ranging from the establishment of a system of protected areas to the rehabilitation of degraded ecosystems and recovery of threatened species, the protection of natural habitats and the maintenance of viable populations of species in natural surroundings (article 8).

Ex-situ conservation measures are also called for, principally to complement the *in-situ* measures (article 9).

Obligations on the sustainable use of biological resources are interwoven into a number of articles, and are also the specific subject of article 10. Parties undertake to regulate or manage biological resources for conservation and sustainable use and to encourage the development of methods for sustainable use.

The role of indigenous and local communities in conserving biodiversity is recognized in the preamble, the importance of maintaining their knowledge and practices relevant to the conservation of biodiversity and the sustainable use of its components is also recognized, as is the need to encourage equitable sharing of benefits derived from the use of their knowledge and innovations (article 8(j)) and article 10(c)).

Finally, measures for research and training (article 12) and for public education and awareness (article 13) are required. So too is the use of techniques, such as impact assessment (article 14(l)(a) and (b)) and contingency measures for emergency situations, in support of national decision-making (article 14(l)(c)-(e)).

Four points can be made about these obligations. First, the Convention consistently makes a distinction between conservation and sustainable use. There was much debate in the negotiations about this. Many advocated that conservation should be used as a broad term which includes the concept of sustainable use, as in the *World Conservation Strategy.* In the end, sustainable use was included as a separate term and defined in article 2, to emphasize the overwhelming importance that countries, especially developing countries, attach to the use of their biological resources. By contrast, conservation is purposely not defined and is used in the Convention sometimes in a broad and sometimes in a restricted sense.

On the whole, in spite of its haziness regarding the term conservation, the Convention does justice to modern conservation thinking. Not only does it consistently recognize that sustainable use of living resources and the ecosystems of which they are a part is a prerequisite for biodiversity conservation, it also acknowledges the need for certain components to be given special care and treatment. Thus, the provisions on conservation and sustainable use reflect the full spectrum of measures needed to achieve the overall goal of the Convention.

Second, the obligations often concern individual biological resources rather than diversity *per se.* Although the conservation of the Earth's biodiversity is the fundamental goal of the treaty, this can only be achieved by implementing different sets of obligations on its different elements—ecosystems, species and genetic resources and generally on the biological resources that may be seen as the source of biodiversity. Thus, one can argue that the Convention, because it addresses the use of biological resources, has a wider aim than some would like to acknowledge or than the title connotes.

Through its attention to the components of biodiversity, the Convention addresses the causes rather than the symptoms of the loss of biodiversity, while at the same time becoming a major instrument in the context of sustainable development. This comprehensive approach, beyond biodiversity *per se,* makes the Convention important to all States, not only those particularly rich in biodiversity: all of the Earth's biological resources, as components of biodiversity, fall under its terms.

Third, the obligations of the Convention, dealing with conservation and sustainable use, are far-reaching when taken in their pure form, without qualifiers. This is why most of the articles have been prefaced by phrases limiting their application. The purpose of most qualifiers is to make the level of implementation commensurate to the capacities of each Party to meet the obligation at hand. At times, explicit distinctions are made between what is expected from developed and developing country Parties, as in, for example, article 20 on financial resources.

These qualifiers have met with considerable criticism. However, the need to differentiate between the capabilities of developed and developing country Parties has long been recognized. Such qualifiers, which are usually disliked for the elasticity they introduce in a legally binding text, are almost inherent in global conservation conventions with broad goals. The necessity to attune the obligations in Conventions to what is possible, practicable, necessary or appropriate was first illustrated in the 1982 United Nations *Convention on the Law of the Sea*, the first of this type. From both a substantive and a drafting point of view, the alternative to using such qualifiers would, in any case, be to weaken the obligation itself. After all, much more important than the qualifier is the will and the means to carry out the requirements of implementation.

The fourth point is the focus on national action, which has already been touched upon. Efforts geared at establishing international mechanisms to set priorities met with considerable resistance and were perceived by the Group of 77 developing countries as attempts of the developed countries to influence or even dictate action on biological resources under their jurisdiction. Tools such as global lists were rejected as they were seen as instruments to short-circuit national priorities and to impose globally determined ones both on conservation generally and on the protection of specific sites and species in particular. The global lists controversy was the focal point of this sensitivity and the debate ultimately resulted in the word "global" being removed from all parts of the text.

The emphasis on national action and priority-setting is desirable from several points of view. First, it is at the national and subnational levels that biodiversity can effectively be conserved and biological resources efficiently managed. Second, States are more likely to adhere to priorities developed at the national level, rather than to ones established with mainly global concerns in mind. Third, the conservation of biodiversity and the sustainable use of biological resources is so complex and so multifaceted an issue that the exact tasks can only be determined and carried out at the national, or indeed local, level. Of all environmental problems, it is probably the least amenable to top-down solutions.

However, what may be lacking as a result, is the consistency of approach and the harmonization of goals that coordination and common priority setting at the international level can bring. If each Party sets its conservation priorities based on potentially differing criteria, the need for global consistency, which generated the Convention in the first place, might not be fulfilled. The fact that a measure of priority-setting can be achieved through the financial mechanism is only a palliative. The positive role of the Conference of the Parties to guide and promote harmonized approaches may become a crucial one.

The Access Issues

Access-related issues were some of the thorniest in the negotiation of the Convention. In order to be willing to discuss and eventually take on the conservation obligations, developing countries made certain demands of their own. Not only did they press for the Convention to become more directly use-oriented, but many made their participation in the negotiations conditional on the inclusion in the Convention of obligations and measures on three types of access: access to genetic resources, which they wished to have recognized as subject to national authority; access to relevant technology, stressing that it includes biotechnology; and access for the providing States to benefits ultimately gained from the use of genetic material in the development of biotechnology.

Until the negotiation of the Convention, the principle of free access to genetic resources had prevailed, and is recognized in the *FAO Undertaking on Plant Genetic Resources* of 1983, which, however, in the context of a mounting controversy over genetic resources control, has remained a non-binding instrument. Since the early 1980s, several countries restricted access to the genetic resources under their jurisdiction, and the calls of developing nations for national controls over genetic resources have become increasingly louder. During the negotiation of the *Convention on Biological Diversity*, this point of view prevailed. As a result, article 15 recognizes that the authority to determine access to genetic resources rests with the national governments and is subject to national legislation.

This evolution is based on the view that there is no legal reason to exempt genetic resources from the principle of national sovereignty over natural resources. But it is also grounded in practical reasoning: control over access to genetic resources gives the providing Party the opportunity to negotiate the mutually agreed terms for fair and equitable sharing of benefits required by article 15(7).

That these issues are intertwined is not new and their concurrent discussion has only intensified during the past decade: increased progress in biotechnology has provoked greater attention to the value of genetic resources, while the protection developed in industrialized nations through intellectual property rights over the resulting products exacerbated the debate, and expanded it well beyond the narrow scope of new plant varieties to which it had previously been limited.

Today, the trend is for industrialized nations to extend intellectual property protection, including patents, to a wide spectrum of living organisms. These property systems reward human ingenuity, but ignore nature's handiwork—the value of the raw material that is manipulated. They also fail to take into consideration the informal contribution of indigenous peoples and farmers to the maintenance and development of genetic diversity through years of cultivation and husbandry.

In the negotiations, the goal of the Group of 77 was to ensure that the value and contribution of the raw material itself be properly recognized. One possible route for the Convention would have been to require contributions from the users of the genetic material to an international fund for biodiversity conservation and sustainable use, independent of the origin of the material. Instead, following the national orientation of the Convention, articles 15, 16 and 19 require that access to results and benefits be given on a bilateral level, so that those Parties providing the genetic material obtain a fair and equitable share of the benefits when and if these are realized. The arrangement is to be decided in each individual situation according to mutually agreed terms.

But, to effectively implement the letter, let alone the spirit, of these provisions will not be easy, and in practice there will be many difficulties at the implementation stage. The obligations under articles 15(7), 16(3) and 19(2) leave considerable discretion with the Party. In addition, the identification of material from which the benefit derives is not a simple matter, especially as it may be a decade or more before the benefit is realized and as the genetic material used may have been gathered from several sources.

Even more difficult was to find an acceptable compromise regarding the broader issue of access to and transfer of technologies. The resulting text reflects the importance developed countries place on intellectual property rights, but nevertheless creates a basic obligation to undertake to provide, or facilitate access to and transfer of, technology, including biotechnology.

Finally, the provisions on technology transfer and on access to benefits of biotechnology are limited by the definition of genetic resources in article 15(3).

Funding

It was never questioned in the negotiations that a flow of resources from the North to the South was needed to achieve the various goals of the Convention. Several innovative methods to achieve this had been discussed during the early stages, including an international fund based on fees levied on the use of biological, and especially genetic, sources in the North. Others, such as the creation of an international corporation, in which Parties could invest through buying shares, were considered during the negotiation process.

In the end, the negotiators chose to create a more classical financial mechanism to be fed by contributions of the developed country Parties for the exclusive use of the developing country Parties. The funds which, according to article 20 on financial resources, are to be new and additional, will be applied to enable developing country parties to meet the agreed full incremental costs to them of the measures needed to implement the Convention's obligations. The agreement on what exactly these costs are is to be made bilaterally between each developing country Party and the institution chosen to handle the financial mechanism.

The notion of incremental cost in this Convention poses problems. The situation with biodiversity is different from that of ozone depletion, where the concept of incremental cost has been used with some success. But in the context of the *Convention on Biological Diversity*, incremental costs are much more difficult to determine. However, as mentioned earlier, under article 20(2) the incremental costs to be met have to be agreed upon, which makes the financial obligations considerably more realistic.

The Conference of the Parties determines the amount of financial resources needed periodically and the contributions have to take into account the need for predictability, adequacy and timely flow of funds in order to meet the Convention's obligations. This provision, which caused great fears of an open financial commitment among the developed countries, was hotly debated and, at the very last moment, nearly caused the Convention not to be adopted. A joint interpretive statement at the time of adopting the Convention text on the part of 19 developed countries provided their interpretation of the adopted language for the record.

The financial mechanism, set out in article 21, provides financial resources to developing countries on a grant or concessional basis, under the authority of the Conference of the Parties to which it is directly accountable. The Global Environment Facility (GEF) was named in article 39 of the Convention as the institutional structure operating the financial mechanism on an interim basis and conditional on restructuring. There was an enormous reluctance among the developing countries to accept this solution, as they felt that the GEF did not operate in a transparent and democratic manner as required under article 21 (1).

Implementation

As already noted, the main thrust of implementation is at the national level. Each Party has much to do, considering the spectrum of actions Parties have to undertake and the wide range of policies they have to review. How they can do this is not the main subject of this volume, which is essentially an explanation of the convention article by article. Nonetheless, whenever it was felt necessary or beneficial to the understanding and implications of the articles analyzed, the commentary does present general ideas on how a Party could approach the implementation of a particular obligation.

The success of national action, seen from a global perspective, will depend on the will of both the developed and developing country parties to meet their obligations. Therefore, at this stage in the process, both, in essence, hold the success of each other in their hands. The level of implementation and enforcement will be the ultimate test of whether the compromise achieved during the Convention negotiation was a true success or an illusion.

At the international level, the machinery provided for in the Convention to steer and assist its implementation has to be set in motion. The Conference of the Parties, its Subsidiary Body on Scientific Technical and Technological Advice and the Secretariat all have key roles to play.

The financial mechanism must also be set in motion and, thus, steps must be taken to either adequately restructure the Global Environment Facility or to decide upon another institutional structure to perform the task of managing it. A pressing issue is to prepare the detailed criteria and guidelines for eligibility for access to and use of the financial resources which article 21(2) requires the Conference of the Parties to determine.

Many other crucial tasks lie ahead, such as considering the need for further negotiation of certain issues through the preparation of protocols. Article 19(3) requires consideration to be given to a protocol on the safe transfer, handling and use of any living modified organism resulting from biotechnology that may have an adverse effect on the conservation and sustainable use of biological diversity. Other protocols may become needed as implementation efforts proceed.

In order to prepare the operational phase of the implementation process, interim mechanisms and measures were called for by Resolution 2 of the Conference for the Adoption of the Convention. An Intergovernmental Committee for the *Convention on Biological Diversity* (ICCBD) was established to operate until the first meeting of the conference of the Parties at the end of 1994.

The first meeting of the ICCBD, in Geneva in October 1993, was preceded by the meetings of four experts panels convened by the UNEP Executive Director for advice in preparing the work of the ICCBD. UNEP also created an interim secretariat. The ICCBD is scheduled to meet at least one more time in 1994 in anticipation of the first meeting of the Conference of the Parties.

In both the interim and operational phase, it is important to draw from available expertise, as well as to build on existing activities. A number of international governmental and nongovermental organizations have worked on biodiversity issues for decades and it is essential to harness their knowledge and expertise in support of the implementation process. UNEP, FAO, UNESCO, and IUCN have much to contribute, as have the World Resources Institute (WRI) and other international organizations with a sectoral focus. Initiatives such as the *Global Biodiversity Strategy* will enable Parties to make implementation decisions with the best background information to hand. Of equal importance is to link these implementation efforts to existing programs, including those which are emerging from the implementation of *Agenda 21*, such as the UNDP-sponsored Capacity 21. These initiatives should not simply exist parallel to the implementation of the convention, but should play an integral part in the process and vice versa.

The success of national action, seen from a global perspective, will depend on the will of both the developed and developing country parties to meet their obligations.

In the same vein, the relationship between the *Convention on Biological Diversity* and other conventions in the field should be reconsidered and links established to enable effective cooperation and coordination. The original reason for promoting a convention on biological diversity—to fill in the gaps of the existing fragmentary regime while building upon the existing conventions—should not be lost from sight at this stage. There are a considerable number of global and regional instruments directly relevant to biodiversity and both their achievements and potential must be taken into account and integrated to the maximum extent possible in the process of implementation. The problems inherent in trying to effectively link existing treaties in a particular field are difficult. Imaginative steps are required if the overall goal of the convention, which is to lead to a truly comprehensive and integrated regime, is to be realized.

Finally, at both the national and international level, nongovermental organizations have an important role to play in the convention's implementation. This was specifically recognized in preambular paragraph 14 which stresses "the importance of ... the nongovermental sector for the conservation of biological diversity and the sustainable use of its components."

The growth of NGO interest for the Convention, in both developed and developing countries, bodes well for the convention's implementation, and it is to be hoped that Parties will take full advantage of the knowledge, skills and commitment of NGOs in their country, as well as regionally and globally, to help them implement the Convention.

B

Conservation and Sustainable Use

The first two objectives of the Convention are the conservation of biological diversity, and the sustainable use of its components. Considerable focus is placed on *in-situ* conservation, defined as 'the conservation of ecosystems and natural habitats and the maintenance and recovery of viable populations of species in their natural surroundings and, in the case of domesticated or cultivated species, in the surroundings where they have developed their distinct properties' The implication of these fundamental tenets of the Convention is illustrated below.

(i) de Klemm C., Tolentino A. Jr., Burhenne-Guilmin F., Tarasofsky R., Glowka L., and Craig D., *Conserving Biological Diversity: The Legal and Institutional Issues, Biodiversity Conservation in the Asia and Pacific Region—Constraints and Opportunities*, Asian Development Bank and The World Conservation Union, 1995, pp 408–429

Conservation of Biological Diversity and Sustainable Use of its Components

Introduction

The Preamble to the Convention sets out the reasons for conserving biological diversity and the type of measures that should be taken to this end, both for ecocentric and anthropocentric purposes. It stresses that biological diversity has not only an intrinsic value, but also an ecological, genetic, social, economic, scientific, educational, cultural, recreational and aesthetic value of benefit to present and future generations; biological diversity is necessary for the continuation of evolution and for the maintenance of the life-sustaining systems of the biosphere. The conservation of biological diversity is therefore declared in the Convention to be a "common concern of humankind", and the responsibility of States to conserve their biological diversity and use their biological resources sustainably is affirmed.

As noted above, the first objective of the Convention is the conservation of biological diversity and the sustainable use of its components. These two concepts appear in tandem because they are different points on the same spectrum, and in practice there is no division between the two; differences are of emphasis rather than nature. This is reflected in the definitions of "*in situ* conservation" and "sustainable use" in respect of species, and by the overlapping substantive requirements listed under each concept. Of particular significance is the requirement that Parties create the conditions necessary for the compatibility "between present uses and the conservation of biological diversity and the sustainable use of its components".

The Convention outlines in detail several requirements for *in situ* conservation of biological diversity and the sustainable use of its components. To achieve the former, Parties must, where appropriate, establish a system of protected areas and guidelines for their management, rehabilitate and restore degraded ecosystems, promote the recovery of threatened species, regulate the introduction of alien species, and promote the protection of ecosystems, habitats, and species in their natural surroundings. For the latter, Parties are required, as appropriate, to integrate conservation and sustainable use into their national decision-making, adopt measures relating to use which avoids or minimizes adverse effects on biological diversity, support local populations develop and implement remedial plans, and encourage cooperation between the private and public sectors.

The overwhelming threats to biological diversity are from human-induced processes and activities, such as over-exploitation, the many forms of habitat destruction, pollution, introduction of alien species, etc. Effective protection of biological diversity requires regulation and management of these process and activities. The traditional regulatory means have been to create protected areas where all processes and activities are prohibited or severely restricted, or to enact legislation aiming to control the taking of or trade in species. By addressing processes and activities *per se*, wherever they occur, the Convention represents an important innovation.

Before turning to the substance, one more point requires addressing. As important, perhaps, as the subject of regulation in this context is the attitude towards risk management. It is evident that preventive measures are required to attack the causes of loss of biological diversity at source. The difficulty is that information and knowledge regarding biological diversity is not always sufficient, which makes it urgent that scientific, technical and institutional capacities be developed to enhance the understanding upon which to plan and implement appropriate measures. Accordingly, the Preamble to the Convention states that lack of full scientific certainty should not be used as a reason for postponing conservation measures wherever there is a threat of significant reduction or loss of biological diversity. In so doing, the Convention acknowledges the importance of the "precautionary approach" in relation to the conservation of biological diversity and the sustainable use of its components.

Site-Specific Conservation Measures: Protected Areas

The Convention recognizes that a fundamental requirement for the conservation of biological diversity is the *in situ* conservation of ecosystems and natural habitats and the maintenance or restoration of viable populations of species in their natural surroundings. Site-specific conservation measures, usually in the form of protected areas, are an essential tool for this purpose.

The first protected area in the world was Yellowstone National Park, established in the United States in 1872. Since then, almost all countries in the world have enacted protected area legislation with the objective of ensuring the integrity...of such areas, both terrestrial and marine. Initially, protected areas were created to preserve spectacular scenery or particular wildlife concentrations while conservation of biological diversity was rarely a primary objective.

The protected area concept has evolved considerably in recent decades, generating the need for much more flexible legal instruments. In particular, these instruments permit adapting the regulatory scheme to the conservation goal being pursued in each case. Thus, modern protected areas legislation seeks to allow for a variety of types and mechanisms, ranging from the traditional strict prohibition of human activities to the selective regulation of those which otherwise would defeat the conservation purpose of the protected areas. A combination of those variously stringent regimes is of course permissible. For example, this is the philosophy behind the *biosphere reserve* concept developed as part of the Man and Biosphere Programme administered by UNESCO, which contemplates different categories of zones within a larger area. As such, protected areas legislation has become an effective planning tool which should be seen as permitting a continuum of controls.

"Protected area" is defined in Article 2 of the Convention as "a geographically defined area which is designated or regulated and managed to achieve specific conservation objectives". This definition reflects the evolution outlined above. Indeed, the Convention definition of protected area allows for a broad range of possible schemes.

Categories

The names given to the different categories of protected areas in national legislation vary considerably as between States, making comparisons between them difficult. Over the years, IUCN's Commission on National Parks and Protected Areas has developed a system of protected areas management categories; the focus is on the management goal, rather than on the name of the ascertained category. The recently-revised has six management categories, as indicated in Box 2.

Within a protected area, there can be areas belonging to different categories. For example, a national park (Category II) may include a scientific reserve or wilderness area (Category I), while a Category V or VI area can include Category I, II, III or IV areas and so on.

Category V areas have been created in countries with few natural areas left but which still have outstanding landscapes, often with considerable biological diversity remaining. This type of area is mostly found in Europe, the Republic of Korea, and Japan.

Category VI is appropriate in instances where there are still large natural areas but where national parks or other more protective categories are not suitable because of the presence of local populations, but where the sustainability of traditional forms of exploitation must be ensured.

The objectives for which protected areas are to be established should be clearly stated in national legislation.

Thus, Categories V and VI, while not protected areas in the traditional sense of the term, are areas where special measures are being taken to conserve biological diversity as provided for by Article 8(a) of the Convention. Conventional protected area legislation is generally limited to the first four IUCN categories. This has tended to produce a system encompassing very limited choice and based mostly on prohibitions. In order to provide for the flexibility referred to above, legislation dealing with protected areas should ideally provide for the possibility of establishing protected areas in any of the above categories. This can be achieved in two ways: (i) the legislation may provide for regulatory regimes applying to as many categories or types of protected areas as is considered appropriate in the State concerned; or, alternatively, (ii) a more selective approach as to types may be chosen, with the legislation also providing for the possibility of creating conservation areas with the specific regime to be determined by a specific legal instrument establishing each area.

Other weaknesses in most existing protected areas legislation are: (i) there is generally no requirement for a management plan to be prepared or implemented; (ii) the protected area administration has insufficient powers, especially with regard to the conclusion of contracts with local communities or landowners; and (iii) provision is inadequate for local communities concerned to participate in the preparation of a management plan or in the actual management of the protected area, nor is it possible for local communities and interests to be represented on the managing body. These observations should be kept in mind when protected areas legislation is reviewed.

Objectives

The objectives for which protected areas are to be established should be clearly stated in national legislation. It is imperative that one of these objectives be the conservation of biological diversity.

Concerning the protected areas themselves, the legislation must have the *permanence* of protected areas as a primary objective so as to guarantee, to the maximum extent possible, their long-term existence. A method used in the legislation of several countries (e.g., Australia) consists of providing for de-establishment procedures which are stricter than those for establishment. By way of example, if protected areas can be established by Government decree, as is usually the case, de-establishment should require the adoption of an Act of Parliament following a public enquiry.

Integrity should be the second major objective of protected areas legislation. This depends on the regime of the site, i.e., the restrictions imposed on activities within and outside the protected area, which is a rather complex matter since the applicable rules depend on local conditions.

Land tenure is a critical factor in preserving the integrity of a protected area since the possibilities to establish it and to regulate activities inside it will vary according to whether the land is publicly or privately owned. In many countries, natural areas such as forests, mangroves and marine areas are in public ownership. For protected areas in Government ownership, it is essential that:

- encroachment by third parties (e.g., in the form of new human settlements) should be avoided. In certain countries, those who cultivate virgin land become owners of that land in their own right. This can threaten the integrity of a protected area and the legislation should clearly exclude this type of acquisition in a protected area;
- all Government agencies should comply with the building and development restrictions imposed within the protected area. Ideally all protected areas on public land should, by law, come under the exclusive jurisdiction of the conservation agency. No other agency should have power to carry out or authorize any activity in protected areas. If this is not possible, which may well be the case particularly in Category V and VI protected areas, the conservation agency should have, if not a right of veto, at least the right to be consulted on any proposed activity.

With regard to privately owned areas important for biological diversity, the legislative means should be created to:

- facilitate public acquisition of land by right of preemption, tax incentives and, if necessary, compulsory purchase;
- impose restrictions upon landowners by regulatory measures, although this may require compensation;
- impose restrictions by means of contracts which are binding on successors in title (i.e., run with the land); and
- provide financial or other incentives for voluntary conservation, backed by regulatory measures to prevent encroachment by third parties.

There will also be cases where land is in indigenous and community ownership. Here the solution may be to conclude agreements with the community which provide incentives for conservation and sustainable use, which are backed by regulatory measures to prevent damage being caused by Government agencies, third parties and members of the local communities themselves. However, this may not always be the most appropriate solution. For example the Aboriginal Peoples Act (1954) of Malaysia states that no land within an aboriginal area can be declared a wildlife reserve or sanctuary in order to protect the well-being of aboriginal people in Peninsular Malaysia who are settled or live near park areas. On the other hand, Category V or VI under the IUCN system may protect such aboriginal rights rather than undermine them.

The preservation of the integrity of protected areas against damage caused by external sources is by no means easy. One solution is the establishment of buffer zones, namely defined 'belts' of land surrounding the protected area proper, which are still regulated in the interests of conservation but in which a wider range of human activities is permitted. Such zones must have a certain capacity to absorb the environmental impact of activities conducted outside the protected area and thus to cushion the ecosystem concerned from the full brunt of the potential damage.

Provisions of this type are, moreover, needed to comply with Article 8(e) of the Convention which requires Contracting Parties to "promote environmentally sound and sustainable development in areas adjacent to protected areas with a view to furthering protection of those areas". This provision is not limited to buffer zones although the latter are, of course, a means to the same end.

Buffer zones alone may not, however, be sufficient to afford adequate protection to the inner area itself. The legislation should therefore provide for powers to regulate activities carried on further away from the protected area whenever these threaten the latter's integrity. Since environmental impact assessments (EIA)...may be necessary to identify such activities, the legislation should require that activities liable to damage protected areas be subject to EIA.

Management of Protected Areas

No protected area can be effectively conserved without a management body. Such a body is particularly necessary in Category V or VI areas where good relations with the local population and communities are essential for the system to work properly. National legislation should therefore establish a management body for each protected area with a mandatory requirement to draw up management plans. In certain countries, such as Bhutan, these are legal documents approved by Government order. There is also often a requirement of periodic reviews.

Management requirements obviously vary from one protected area to another and, within each protected area, from one zone to another. Zoning is often necessary to allow different rules to apply to each kind of zone. This is especially so for Category V and VI areas, where there may be inhabited zones and zones in which activities not contrary to the conservation objectives of the area are authorized.

Management bodies should have powers prescribed by legislation to purchase land, to conclude contracts with landowners, to provide advice and incentives for conservation and to enforce the applicable legislation. Local communities and populations should, as far as possible, be represented on the relevant management body, as provided for in Papua New Guinea's Conservation Areas Act, and Fauna (Protection and Control) Act, and in the Philippines' National Integrated Protected Areas System (NIPAS) Law. This latter case also creates express entitlements for NGOs, including the right to participate in the planning and management of protected areas and to be represented on the management board. Alternatively, procedures could be established for these groups to be consulted in certain cases, especially where decisions liable to affect them are contemplated.

The legislation should also allow for the participation of local communities in the development of the management plans and wherever possible, provide incentives for them to care for the protected area, such as the supply of community services, concessions for services in the protected area, or a share of the income derived from the protected area itself.

It is to be noted that several States within the Asia-Pacific region have adopted innovative legislation combining many of the above suggestions. For example, in Nepal, the National Parks and Wildlife Conservation Act (1973 as amended) classifies areas into national park areas or wildlife reserves. The distinction lies in the fact that while both provide for the conservation of fauna and their habitats, national parks emphasize protection of landscapes. By a 1989 amendment, the concept of a conservation area was incorporated into the Act which is to be managed in accordance with an integrated plan for the conservation of the natural environment and the sustainable use of natural resources. Flexibility in resource management is provided for through public participation and the fact that the possibility is created for the area to be managed by an NGO.

Enforcement Issues

While the provision of incentives to induce a certain behaviour is highly desirable, as indicated above, assurance of the prescribed level of protection requires effective means to enforce the supporting regulatory measures. Two broad cases need to be considered:

(1) Enforcement against government agencies is particularly difficult. Some form of procedure—judicial or administrative—should be established by legislation to allow the management body or the conservation agency to stop unauthorized activities carried out by other government agencies.

(2) Enforcement powers against private persons should be the responsibility of the protected area authority or management body, in collaboration with the local communities concerned. With regard to penalties, imprisonment for violations of conservation legislation is provided for in some pieces of legislation where serious levels of poaching, habitat destruction or pollution occur, although this is sometimes difficult for public opinion to accept. It is often more appropriate to impose fines, especially if those fines are to be paid into the budget of the individual protected area concerned. An alternative penalty is to require work on specific management tasks in the protected area. Where serious damage is caused by a solvent person, such as a big corporation conducting illegal logging, national legislation should make it possible for civil damages to be claimed as compensation.

Systems

The Convention requires a system of protected areas to be established. This entails having a national body with the legislative mandate to assess the situation on the ground and create an appropriate system. Wherever possible, protected areas should be connected by wildlife corridors so as to avoid becoming isolated islands surrounded by developed areas, which risk losing an important proportion of their biological diversity. All this requires coordinated planning, since both protected areas and corridors must be considered in the context of the overall physical planning process.

The relationship between physical planning rules and those established within a protected area are especially important for Category V and VI areas. National legislation should provide a link between the rules applicable in the protected area and its various zones and the local physical planning rules. The latter should always be subordinate to the protected area's rules; in other words, any land use plan made under physical planning legislation should comply with the management plan for that area.

A systematic approach to establishing protected areas gives rise to an important issue regarding areas identified as important for biological diversity, but which have not yet been designated as protected areas. Where such areas are on Government land, it is essential that during that interim period, the land not be sold to private persons or put to other use. Safeguards must therefore be introduced into national legislation for this purpose. Where such areas are on private land, safeguards may also be imposed by means of land use restrictions, at least on a temporary basis. Under India's *Wildlife (Protection) Act* (1972), for example, a national park may be established only out of completely unencumbered areas or where all rights have been vested in the government. Once constituted, its boundaries can only be altered by resolution of the state legislature. Sanctuaries, on the other hand, may be set up in private lands. Cattle grazing and fishing are completely banned in national parks but may be regulated, controlled or prohibited in sanctuaries.

In this context, it is worth recalling the requirement under Article 6(b) of the Convention for Contracting Parties to integrate conservation and sustainable use of biological diversity into relevant sectoral or cross-sectoral plans, programs and policies.

Species-Based Measures

The Convention lays down three main obligations applicable to the conservation and sustainable use of species. Parties are required to: (i) promote both the maintenance of viable populations of species in natural surroundings, and the recovery of threatened species *inter alia* by the implementation of plans or other management strategies; (ii) develop or maintain legislation for the protection of threatened species and populations; and (iii) to sustainably use harvested species.

Most countries, if not all, have legislation on species. The vast majority of these are hunting, fishing and forestry laws. Legislation specifically designed to conserve species, except for endangered species, is generally lacking. This often has the following consequences:

- the species to which these laws apply are limited to those which traditionally are considered to be 'quarry' species, namely most mammals and birds, a few reptiles, fish and aquatic invertebrates of commercial importance, and forest trees. All other species, consequently, are ignored;
- the different groups of species are governed by different laws and managed by different agencies, which means that there are no uniform rules for the regulation and management of terrestrial, fresh water and marine species; and
- only a limited range of harmful activities is prohibited or regulated, such as taking possession and trade in species. Intentional trade, the control of which has become of increasing importance since the conclusion of CITES, may in fact be dealt with under completely separate legislation, i.e., that which deals with foreign trade. All other threats to species, including habitat destruction, are almost universally ignored.

Harvestable Species

Sustainable use of species has been the subject of national and international regulation. On the international level, States in the region have, for instance, entered into agreements relating to the exploitation of shared fisheries.

Although, as mentioned above, most countries in the world already have legislation regulating hunting and fishing, this is rarely applicable to the taking or collection of species other than game or fish. Plants, in turn, have traditionally been regulated only under forestry legislation, which is frequently limited in scope to the collection of forest products in public forests. Regulation of the exploitation of commercially important wild plants is still relatively undeveloped.

It is important, however, for the scope of national legislation on harvestable species to be sufficiently wide to be applicable to all animal and plant species. National legislation should empower the appropriate authorities to apply specific taking prohibitions or restrictions to any species. It should ensure that it is possible to vary these prohibitions or restrictions from one species to another, or from one class of user to another. Thus, national legislation should lay down the general rule that no commercial exploitation of any species is permitted without an appropriate permit, which may be issued subject to conditions. A logical consequence of taking restrictions is a prohibition on possession of and trade in specimens which have been illegally collected or otherwise obtained. Particular attention should be paid to controlling imports and exports, especially of those species listed in the Appendices to CITES. National legislation should, consequently, give the appropriate authority all powers necessary to control the import or export of any species of animals and plants.

National legislation should require management plans to be developed for all harvested species, based on factors such as optimum sustainable yield, the conservation of essential habitats, and the regulation and management of activities and processes liable to affect the species adversely. Regulations and management plans dealing with harvestable species, in articular harvestable animal species, should deal *inter alia* with the following subjects:

- the duration of open and closed seasons. This should be adapted to the individual requirements of each species, with particular protection afforded during the breeding season. Countries along the migration route of a migratory species should coordinate their regulations so as to protect the species adequately throughout its journey;
- the establishment of designated areas which are closed, temporarily or permanently, to hunting, fishing and collection;
- limitation, when required, on the number of hunters, fishermen or collectors, particularly by restricting the number of licenses that may be issued in a given season;
- restrictions on the type of animals or plants that may be taken. Such limitations include restrictions on the sex and age of the animals and on the number of specimens of a species that may be taken by each hunter in a specified period. Bag limits of this kind may be enforced by registration or tagging requirements;

- the prohibition of non-selective and mass methods of destruction, such as dynamite, poison, and certain types of nets and rakes to collect fungi; and
- regulation of all other methods of collection or destruction.

With regard to plant species, specific measures are needed, in particular to control the collection activities. These could include daily collection limits or other forms of control such as the 'small bunch' rule (the quantity that may be held in the hand), prohibitions on picking the aerial parts or damaging the subterranean parts of specimens of listed plant species, and, on private land, a prohibition on picking or damaging wild plants without the written permission of the landowner.

Special rules should apply to subsistence hunters, fishermen and collectors of biological resources such as plants, preferably by incorporating exemptions for their subsistence activities into the legislation. This is especially important where local populations and indigenous peoples have traditionally been and continue to be dependent on subsistence activities for a significant proportion of their diet and daily needs. Legislation in such countries has frequently taken these customary rights into account through a range of exemptions from the applicable regulations. The populations concerned may, for example, be exempted from the requirement to obtain a hunting license, except perhaps in respect of protected species, or may be permitted to hunt protected species but only with traditional methods.

This battery of measures will not suffice, however, unless the habitats of harvestable species are protected at the same time. As mentioned earlier in this paper, many species are in danger of disappearing not through over-exploitation but rather through habitat destruction or other threats. It may therefore be necessary for management plans to address not only the level of authorized taking but also other factors, including the conservation of critical habitats such as spawning and nursery areas for fish.

Species with Unfavorable Conservation Status

It is clear that species with unfavorable conservation status require priority attention and that the factors that contribute to their threatened status should be brought under control. Accordingly, the scope of the legislation concerned is an important consideration. Some countries, still relatively few but gradually increasing in number, have enacted legislation allowing for the protection of any species, including invertebrates and plants. The usual method is for legislation to list species subject to special measures.

Ideally, it should be possible under the legislation to list specific species communities when the community as a whole is endangered. In these cases, it is the community as such which should be protected and not the individual species of which it is composed.

As a growing number of species come under threat and information about the conservation status of species generally improves, the trend is towards the compilation of longer and longer lists of species, often identifiable only by a few specialists. This has caused the adoption of the "negative listing" approach in several pieces of legislation (discussed below).

As with hunting and fishing legislation, protected species conservation legislation is usually limited to taking and trade, although here the emphasis is on prohibitions, rather than regulation. For many of these species, however, taking is either not a threat or not the main threat, and such prohibitions therefore do little to preserve the species in question.

National legislation should therefore also provide for positive measures to be taken for the species in question to recover. This can be achieved by requiring the development of recovery plans or similar instruments for selected species. These would identify all existing and potential threats to these species and provide for measures inducing their recovery, including specific habitat protection measures as well as *ex situ* conservation and reintroduction where appropriate and feasible. There are only a few examples of laws so far that make provision for recovery plans. For example, under the *Law for Protection of Cultural Properties*, enacted by Japan, certain endangered species can be designated as special Natural Monuments. The Act requires the protection of the habitats of designated species and the prohibition of activities which may affect their living conditions. Although recovery plans are not a mandatory requirement under this law, activities necessary for the recovery of designated species do, in practice, have priority and special subsidies may be provided for this purpose.

Recovery of species is a costly process, especially where it requires *ex situ* measures such as captive breeding or artificial propagation in the case of plants, followed by reintroductions to the wild. Such programs require special facilities and trained staff. As the number of species in need of recovery plans increases everywhere, it will become more and more difficult to achieve the recovery of anything other than a few well-known flagship species unless adequate financing is made available.

In consequence, it will be necessary to establish priorities for recovery, e.g., on the basis of the indicative list in Annex I of the Convention. This would include wild relatives of domestic or cultivated species or species of medicinal, agricultural or other economic value. Priority should additionally be given to species which, although not belonging to the categories listed in Annex I, play a particularly important ecological role, such as pollinators or seed dispersers.

Preventive Measures

Since recovery is costly, prevention of population reduction should be actively encouraged. It follows that species protection measures should not be confined to those species which are already endangered. One approach is to adopt a strategy known as negative listing, whereby only if a species is listed is it exempted from the general prohibition against taking. In addition to its preventive character, the negative listing method makes regulation and enforcement much easier, as there is no need to be able to identify poorly known species.

This approach, however, does not tackle the problem of habitat destruction or the control of potentially damaging processes and activities. It is clearly impossible to take specific measures to protect the habitats of all species. This can only be done through protected areas and other forms of area-based conservation. Certain species, although not yet necessarily endangered, are nevertheless known to be particularly vulnerable to habitat alteration. Special measures should therefore be provided by the legislation to safeguard their habitats.

Processes and Activities

Processes and Activities Generally Affecting Biological Diversity

Outside protected areas, biological diversity is mainly threatened by human activities and processes. Some of these lead to the destruction or alteration of habitats and may thus have direct or indirect effects on species. Polluting processes and the use of toxic substances are just two types of human activity which have a negative impact on species and ecosystems, and thus on biological diversity generally. Others include the use of biocides, public works, the clearing of native vegetation, afforestation, forestry practices, intensive agriculture, over-grazing, open air recreation, the use of off-road vehicles or the dynamiting of coral reefs. Article 7(c) of the Convention leaves it to the individual Parties to identify the processes and categories of activities which have or are likely to have significant adverse impacts on the conservation and sustainable use of biological diversity and also to monitor their effects through sampling and other techniques. The Convention does, however, list two processes which may have major harmful effects on biological diversity, which should be regulated by all Parties: the use and release of living modified organisms resulting from biotechnology, and the introduction of alien species which threaten ecosystems, habitats or species.

In addition to its preventive character, the negative listing method makes regulation and enforcement much easier, as there is no need to be able to identify poorly known species.

Article 8(1) provides that where such a significant effect has been determined pursuant to Article 7, Contracting Parties must regulate or manage the relevant process or category of activities. The novel approach outlined in the Convention is rarely found in existing national legislation. The *Flora and Fauna Guarantee Act* of 1988 of the Australian State of Victoria is the first example of legislation providing for the listing and management of potentially threatening processes and the preparation of specific management plans. This Act was followed by the *Australian Federal Endangered Species Protection Act* of 1992. Under the 1988 Act in Victoria, a process is eligible for listing if, in the absence of appropriate management, it poses or has the potential to pose a significant threat to the survival or evolutionary development of a range of flora and fauna. Among the processes already listed under this Act are the alteration of the natural flow regimes of rivers and streams, the loss of hollow-bearing trees in native forests, the introduction of live exotic fish species and the use of lead shot in cartridges for the hunting of waterfowl.

The management of a potentially threatening process means either its outright prohibition, if absolutely necessary, or the restriction of certain activities which may result in significant harm to biological diversity. Restrictions may obviously vary according to areas, periods of the year or other circumstances. Stricter rules should in principle apply where a process or activity threatens a protected area, even where that activity is exercised beyond the buffer zone.

In many cases, the control of potentially damaging processes or activities does not come within the jurisdiction of conservation authorities. National legislation should, therefore, confer the necessary powers on conservation authorities to enable them to initiate and participate in the preparation of management plans for such processes.

Regarding the introduction of alien species, it is important to distinguish between voluntary and accidental introductions. Voluntary introductions should be subject to a strict permit system, where permits are only issued where there is a reasonable certainty that no significant harm to biological diversity will result from the proposed introduction. National legislation should apply not only to introductions into the country but also to introductions from one part of the same country to another. This means, for example, that the introduction of an aquatic species into a river basin where it is not naturally present would be prohibited, even if that species exists in other river basins in the same country. Introductions should also be completely prohibited in protected areas.

Accidental introductions are more difficult to control. In practice, only species imported deliberately can be regulated. The method employed by certain countries is to control imports of live animals and plants and to prohibit the entry of those considered to be potentially harmful. In addition, the keeping, transport and sale of exotic organisms should also be made subject to a permit.

Finally, national legislation should require that every effort be made to eradicate harmful or potentially harmful species which have already been introduced, whether deliberate or accidental.

Activities Affecting Certain Ecosystem Types

When activities affect certain natural or semi-natural ecosystems, it is imperative to regulate them with a view to ensuring that the use made of the ecosystem is sustainable. Again here, the legal means used to achieve this result will vary according to whether the land is publicly or privately owned.

On publicly-owned land, exploitation is carried on either directly by the Government department concerned or, more frequently, through a system of concessions. It is imperative that the legislation underlying the granting of concessions stipulate rules for sustainable use of the resource concerned; for example, it may determine a maximum number of cattle permitted to graze on range lands. In respect of mangroves, the concession must be able to specify the annual amount of wood which may be cut together with the permitted methods of cutting and charcoal making. In natural forests, it must be possible to lay down conditions in relation to logging practices, together with obligations to leave patches of forest intact to serve as reseeding stocks. Permits to collect minor forest products could also be made subject to conditions as to species, quantities allowed, time, area and collection methods. In any event, unsustainable practices, such as the clear-cutting of natural forests or the removal of coral for use as construction material, should be generally prohibited.

The restriction of activities on private lands can be particularly complex, depending on the legal system concerned. For example, some systems may contain strong constitutional protection of private property, which require the State to compensate individual owners for the imposition of restrictions on activities on their land. The thresholds which trigger compensation also varies from State to State.

As matters stand, however, natural and semi-natural areas in which the exploitation of biological resources is possible are often under public ownership. This means that the most important task is not to allow, or at least to strictly control, the sale or lease of such areas to private persons or corporations.

The attention given by the Convention to customary use of biological resources in accordance with traditional customary practices compatible with the concepts of conservation and sustainable use should be reflected in the legislation adopted to control activities affecting natural and semi-natural ecosystems.

As in the foregoing cases, regulation of processes and activities must be supported by an effective enforcement regime which will deter offenders. Where large-scale collection or destruction for commercial purposes or profit is undertaken without a permit or in violation of permit or concession conditions, this should be punishable by economic sanctions, such as confiscation of the equipment used (logging equipment, fishing boats, etc.). In cases of concessions, damage arising from a breach of the terms should be punishable by the withdrawal of the concession, together with an obligation to restore, where possible, the degraded land. These penalties should be imposed without prejudice to the payment of civil damages. Exploitation without the necessary concession or permit should again be punished by appropriate penalties, including obligations to make restoration and to pay civil damages.

(ii) de Klemm C., "The Regulation and Management of Destructive Processes: A New Type of Instrument for the Conservation of Biological Diversity," 27 *Environmental Policy and Law* 4, 1997, pp 350–354

[*Many of the measures required by the Convention to achieve conservation and sustainable use of biodiversity components are not new: area-based legal techniques (physical planning, including protected area planning) and species-based controls (taking and habitat protection) are well-known features of the law of species and ecosystem conservation and sustainable use. The Convention, however, innovates in introducing the concept of regulation of processes and categories of activities having a significant adverse effect on biodiversity. The significance of this innovative approach is explained in this extract.*]

Article 7(a) of the *Convention on Biological Diversity* lays down an obligation for Parties to identify processes and categories of activities which have or are likely to have significant adverse impacts on the conservation and sustainable use of biological diversity, and to monitor their effects through sampling and other techniques. Article 8(1) of that treaty further requires Parties, where a significant adverse effect has been determined pursuant to article 7, to regulate or manage the relevant processes and categories of activities.

For a long time the conservation of species and ecosystems has been mainly, and still generally is, achieved through species specific measures, mostly the prohibition or limitation of taking, and the establishment of protected areas. The emerging threatening process concept calls for a new category of conservation instrument which, if adequately combined with the other two, should in broadening the scope of available conservation measures make it possible to increase considerably the effectiveness of conservation action.

What are Processes?

It has been clear for a long time that if species and ecosystems were to be preserved, conservation measures should address the whole range of the threats that may affect them. Red Data Books generally list these threats, when they are known. However, the concept of threat has never, it would seem, been scientifically defined and there is often much confusion between the causes of the threats, such as agriculture, forestry, tourism or pollution and the actual processes which are directly responsible for the depletion or extinction of species. Thus, the intensification of agriculture which is, in certain countries, the prime cause of the destruction of natural habitats and of many wild species, is not a process in itself but the cause of many activities which in turn generate a large number of destructive processes.

A threatening process may be defined as a phenomenon affecting unfavorably the conservation status of a component of biological diversity, either directly because it kills living organisms or indirectly because it affects a biological process which is essential to their continued existence. In either case, the result is an increase in the mortality of the organisms concerned or a decrease in their birth rate, and their possible extinction if the process is allowed to go on unabated.

Processes should not be confused with the activities which generate them. Different activities may trigger the same process, and the same activity different processes. Thus, the lowering of the water table may be caused by draining, an excessive extraction of water, or the prevention of the periodic floods of a river. On the other hand, an activity such as the use of fertilizers is lethal to certain wild plants which can only live on nutrient poor soils, such as orchids, and may also cause the eutrophication of water bodies and a resulting loss of biodiversity in fragile aquatic habitats.

Examples of processes which may affect species directly are, of course, over-exploitation, but also the incidental taking of non-target species by fishing boats, the accidental killing of birds by electric overhead lines, or the often heavy mortality of wild animals caused by motor vehicles.

Processes which affect species and ecosystems indirectly through the alteration of the conditions necessary for their continued existence are legion. Only some examples can be given here.

Predation by, or competition with, intentionally or accidentally introduced alien organisms has been responsible for many extinctions, particularly on oceanic islands.

The systematic elimination of dead or hollow trees, and of dead wood in forests, threatens a large number of animal species which use the trees as breeding sites or shelters, or feed on decaying wood. Examples are woodpeckers, certain bats and rodents, long-horned beetles, and a host of other insects. Many plants, fungi and bacteria are also closely associated to dead or dying wood. In the long term, the very process of the decomposition of vegetable matter may be affected, as the organisms which contribute to the process are gradually vanishing.

Another example is that of fire. Fire, whether accidental or used deliberately, is a process which is often very destructive of biological diversity. It may also constitute an essential component of certain ecosystems where it is indispensable to the germination of certain plants. The suppression of fire in such cases can therefore be a very damaging process resulting in the extinction of highly specialized plant species and their associated fauna.

Fire, whether accidental or used deliberately, is a process which is often very destructive of biological diversity.

The last of the large blue butterflies *Maculinea arion* disappeared from a nature reserve in Britain because the threatening process could not be identified in time. The caterpillar of this species develops in the nests of a particular species of ant which requires a short grass habitat. The establishment of a nature reserve resulted in the discontinuation of grazing and the disappearance of the ants and therefore of the butterfly. The massive death of rabbits caused by the deliberate introduction of myxomatosis in the 1950s in Europe also resulted in undergrazing of natural grasslands and the depletion of that species of butterfly and of related species. There can therefore be cascades of processes each one triggering another with resulting threats to new species.

Processes may threaten entire ecosystems. Coral reefs may be destroyed by pollution in run-off waters or by siltation resulting from the deforestation of mountain slopes far upstream. The invasion of semi-natural habitats, such as heathlands, and non-climatic grasslands or peatlands, by woody vegetation is a natural process. It will, however, in many cases be very destructive of certain man-made ecosystems which have now become rare and must be preserved for their particular fauna and flora. The threatening process here is constituted by the abandonment of traditional farming practices, such as extensive grazing, which maintained the habitat at a particular stage of the natural succession.

Processes can be local, regional or global. Two major global processes are the depletion of the ozone layer and global warming. The management of these processes requires global action since the activities which are causing them are worldwide. The conventions on the ozone layer and climate change were concluded in recognition of this need.

At national level, the only country which has so far instituted a legal regime specific to processes is Australia. Victoria was the first of the Australian states to provide for the management of threatening processes in its *Fauna and Flora Guarantee Act* of 1988. Potentially threatening processes are defined by this law as processes which have the capacity to threaten the survival, abundance or evolutionary development of any taxon or community of fauna or flora (sec.3). Listed processes requiring management include, *inter alia*, the alteration of the natural flow or of the natural temperature of rivers and streams, the increase in sediment inputs into water courses due to human activities; the introduction of live fish into waters outside their natural range; the loss of hollow-bearing trees in native forests; the removal of wood debris from streams; soil erosion and vegetation damage in alpine regions caused by cattle grazing; predation of indigenous wildlife by feral cats and introduced foxes; and the prevention of passage of aquatic organisms as a result of the presence of instream structures.

The federal *Endangered Species Protection Act*, 1992 of Australia, which is applicable only on land under federal jurisdiction or owned by the federal government, followed a few years later. It defines a threatening process (sec.4) as a process that threatens, or may threaten, the survival, abundance or evolutionary development of a native species or ecological community. Key threatening processes are those which adversely affect two or more native species or two or more ecological communities listed as endangered or vulnerable, or could cause native species or communities to become endangered (sec.25).

In New South Wales, according to the *Threatened Species Conservation Act* of 1995, a threatening process is a process that threatens, or may have the capability to threaten, the survival or evolutionary development of species, populations or ecological communities (sec.4). A key threatening process is a process which adversely affects two or more threatened species, populations or ecological communities, or could cause species, populations or ecological communities that are not threatened to become threatened. Key threatening processes are to be listed by regulations.

Processes can be regulated or managed in relation to particular species or particular areas, or generally wherever they occur.

Species Specific Processes

For a long time species protection legislation was limited to the control of one single process: overexploitation through deliberate taking. Many countries have still not gone beyond that stage. A few, however, have instituted special measures for the protection and recovery of endangered species. Examples are certain Australian states, Spain, and the United States which all provide for the preparation of recovery plans for those species. To be effective these plans must identify the processes which are threatening the species concerned and provide for the necessary measures to eliminate them or reduce their impact to an acceptable level. In the United States and a few Australian states, the law also requires the designation of critical habitats for endangered species.

The preservation of a critical habitat requires the maintenance in the area designated as such of all the ecological conditions which are necessary to the species and therefore the identification, monitoring and elimination of the processes which are impairing, or are likely to impair, these conditions. In some cases the administrative decision designating a critical habitat lists at the same time the constituent elements of that habitat which must be maintained for the survival of the species concerned. For instance, for an endangered fish, the Maryland darter *Etheostoma sellare*, these constituent elements are the quality and permanence of stream flow in shallow areas and the presence of unsilted rocky crevices for shelter and production of aquatic insects and snails for food. For the Oregon silverspot butterfly, *Speyeria zerene hippolyta*, listed biological elements essential to the continued existence of this insect within its critical habitat include the foodplant of its caterpillar, grasses in which the larvae find shelter, the plants from which the adults obtain nectar and the spruce woods in which they shelter. The alteration of these elements therefore constitutes processes which are damageable to the species, and any activity resulting in any of these processes is, as a consequence, unlawful.

In the United Kingdom, the *Conservation (Natural Habitats) Regulations*, 1994, made to implement the European Union *Habitats Directive* of 1992, prohibits the destruction or damaging of the breeding sites or resting places of certain animal species. "Guidelines for Developers" published by English Nature, the conservation agency for England, list damaging processes for certain of those species. For the great crested newt, *Triturus cristatus*, for instance, the processes concerned include any substantial lowering of the water level of ponds where the species live, the introduction of fish into such ponds, the deepening or infilling of these ponds, the clearing of land around them and chemical pollution.

Processes affecting species may also now be regulated and managed pursuant to recent Australian legislation. The Fauna and Flora Guarantee Act of the state of Victoria provides for the making of management plans (sec.21) and the conclusion of management agreements between the conservation department and other public authorities (sec.25) in respect of processes potentially threatening particular species. At federal level, the *Endangered Species Protection Act* provides for threat abatement plans laying down the research and management actions necessary to reduce key threatening processes to an acceptable level in order to maximize the chances of the long-term survival in nature of the native species and ecological communities affected by these processes (sec.34). Plans are approved by the Minister in charge of conservation (sec.41). Federal agencies must not take any action that contravenes a threat abatement plan (sec.99). These plans may only be made for key threatening processes that occur in areas under federal jurisdiction. However, if a process also occurs outside these areas, the federal government must seek the cooperation of the states in which it occurs with the view to the preparation and implementation of a joint threat abatement plan (sec.33).

The law of New South Wales (sec.74) requires the preparation of a threat abatement plan for each key threatening process. The plan must identify the actions needed to abate, ameliorate or eliminate the effects of the process, and the persons responsible for the implementation of the measures included in the plan. Plans are approved by the Minister. Public authorities must take any appropriate action available to them to implement the measures included in a threat abatement plan for which they are responsible and must not make decisions that are inconsistent with the provisions of any such plan.

Site Specific Processes

The traditional method to control processes which may affect a particular site consists in the establishment of a protected area, and to prohibit, within that area, all or most activities which may generate damaging processes. Important as it may have been, and still is, for the preservation of sites of great importance for conservation, the protected area technique has some weaknesses. It does not, in particular, make it possible to control processes affecting the area where these are caused by activities exercised outside its boundaries. Moreover, outright prohibitions of all human activities may not always be necessary to preserve the scientific value of a site. Finally, the number of protected areas that can be established is necessarily limited because of the constraints they involve. Other means have therefore to be found to introduce more flexibility in site specific conservation instruments.

The *Nature Conservation Act*, 1992 of Queensland includes among threatening processes those which are capable of threatening the survival of protected areas. This makes it possible to control damaging activities originating from outside these areas through conservation orders and management agreements.

In the United Kingdom, the designation of an area as a Site of Special Scientific Interest (SSSI) must be followed by a notification to the owner of the land concerned of a list of potentially damaging operations which he or she cannot undertake without prior notification to English Nature. This agency will then seek to negotiate a management agreement. These "operations" are in fact largely a list of processes which must be avoided if the scientific interest of the land is to be preserved. This technique makes it possible to control only those processes the avoidance of which is essential for the maintenance of the qualities of the site. All activities which do not lead to damaging processes may then continue.

Process Specific Management

Processes which affect large numbers of species or particular habitat types or classes of areas need to be regulated and managed as such, irrespective of the places where their effects occur.

To take the example of dead and dying trees, species specific conservation of these very specialized habitats, through individual recovery plans and the designation of critical habitats, can clearly only be taken in the particular sites where the last specimens of extremely endangered species are known to survive. Site specific protection, through the establishment of protected areas together with prohibitions to remove dead trees, fallen timber and firewood in such areas, will catch a larger number of species. This will, however, not be enough as these species will survive only in isolated patches and gene movements will soon become impossible if dead trees are removed everywhere else. There is therefore clearly a need to manage the process in such a way that a minimum number of dead or dying trees be preserved in forests, and in the general countryside in hedges, gardens, small woods or even as isolated trees. Management measures could include mandatory rules to be observed by forest departments and tree owners, guidelines and adequate incentives. The compulsory felling of dying trees to prevent accidents should no longer be required by law, at least in certain cases. Rules relating to the civil liability of landowners for injuries for damage caused by falling trees would also need to be reviewed.

Process management will therefore generally require a combination of measures so that all activities contributing to the process concerned can be controlled in such a way that its harmful effects are eliminated or minimized. Instruments used for this purpose may include regulations, contracts, incentives, and disincentives such as the payment of compensatory damages.

Conclusion

The identification, monitoring, regulation and management of processes that may significantly harm biological diversity, as now required by the *Biodiversity Convention*, constitutes a new component of conservation science to the development of which scientists and lawyers should both be closely associated. Law is in this respect of particular importance because no management of processes is possible without adequate legal instruments.

A first step would seem to be the identification, for priority management, of the processes which have significant effects on large numbers of species or on particular habitat types or ecosystems. However, scientists do not specialize in processes but in groups of species. There are many species specialist groups within the Species Survival Commission of IUCN. However, for many taxonomic groups of animals and plants specialists are few and threats to the existence of these organisms poorly known. For many species therefore the causes for their decline and the processes and activities involved are still unclear. Process specialist groups do not exist. As a result, there are no lists of species that are threatened by particular processes.

A second step could be the drawing up, for each priority process, of a process management plan. Such plans should determine the avoidance or mitigation measures that appear to be the most effective and acceptable and provide for the development of management guidelines. In many cases research will be needed into the methods which are the best able to mitigate processes and the result of this research will have to be broadly disseminated. An example is the handbook for civil engineers which was published in 1996 by the *Ecole polytechnique de Lausanne*. This publication provides guidance on the methods which can be used to prevent interference between wildlife and traffic along highways, railways and waterways.

Finally, appropriate legal instruments will have to be developed and tested. Particular attention may have to be given to forms of environmental impact assessments applicable to certain new activities or to the use of certain equipment or products, because of the threatening processes they generate. To give an example, had the manufacture of large drift nets been subject to an EIA at the design stage, and conservation authorities forewarned of the considerable damage to many marine species that the use of these nets would cause, it might have been possible to prevent their introduction on the market, possibly through the conclusion of a treaty, and the incidental take of large numbers of non-target animals could then have been avoided.

Treaties may also be necessary to manage certain global or regional processes. The conventions on the ozone layer, climate change, desertification and marine or long range air pollution are examples of treaties specifically designed for that purpose. Processes specific to biological diversity could also be made the subject of particular treaties, global or regional, in some cases perhaps as protocols to the biodiversity convention. One possible case could be the regulation of the introduction of alien species into the natural environment, now prohibited or regulated by many treaties but which requires much more detailed provisions and control instruments if is to be effective. Accidental introductions of alien marine organisms through the ballast waters of ships could and probably will in the not too distant future be the subject of a global treaty under the auspices of the International Maritime Organization. For processes that have international consequences it could be possible to imagine an international permitting system, and international EIAs.

Another possible field for international action could be the making of guidelines for the management of particular processes with a view to harmonizing national measures.

The impetus for the management of processes causing significant damage to biological diversity should as much as possible come from scientific bodies or from the relevant international trade or professional associations or organizations. As an example, the International Council for the Exploration of the Sea, an international advisory governmental organization established by treaty in 1902, has adopted guidelines on the introduction of alien species into the marine environment. International trade or professional associations could be approached with a view to developing their awareness of the importance of a particular problem in their field of competence and enlisting their assistance in carrying out research work and in seeking mutually satisfactory solutions. Codes of conduct or guidelines, issued by these organizations, for the purpose of minimizing or mitigating the effects of threatening processes, may be easier to accept by their national members than regulatory measures.

As an example, the electrocution of large birds, in particular birds of prey, on high voltage power lines is a worldwide process. The impetus for necessary research work to develop suitable mitigation methods should therefore come from the specialized international organization, in the case in point the International Conference on Large High Voltage Electric Systems, of which all large electricity companies are members. Other bodies the assistance of which could be sought to promote awareness among their members and to develop acceptable process management tools could be, for instance, the International Chamber of Commerce, the International Federation of Agricultural Producers and the World Forestry Congress.

C

Access to Genetic Resources and Benefit-Sharing

The third objective of the Convention is the fair and equitable sharing of benefits derived from the use of genetic resources, defined as 'genetic material of actual or potential value', itself defined as 'any material of plant, animal, microbial or other origin, containing functional units of heredity'. A new requirement altogether, these benefit sharing provisions became a major aim for developing countries in the negotiation of the Convention, and a condition *sine qua non* of their participation. Why this requirement became a pivotal element of the Convention and what is its architecture is well documented elsewhere, and only summarized by way of introduction here.

(i) de Klemm C., Tolentino A. Jr., Burhenne-Guilmin F., Tarasofsky R., Glowka L. and Craig D., *Conserving Biological Diversity: The Legal and Institutional Issues, Biodiversity Conservation in the Asia and Pacific Region—Constraints and Opportunities*, Asian Development Bank and IUCN-The World Conservation Union, 1995, pp 434–437

Access to Genetic Resources and the Sharing of Benefits Derived from Their Use

Access to Genetic Resources

As mentioned above, one of the three primary objectives of the *Convention on Biological Diversity* is the fair and equitable sharing of benefits derived from the use of genetic resources, as defined in Article 2. Prior to the Convention, genetic resource users were typically not required to share benefits derived from their subsequent use in agriculture, medicine or industry with the States providing the genetic resources (usually developing countries and within them traditional communities), because genetic resources, in particular wild and locally domesticated plant varieties, had no recognized legal status and were *de facto* usable by anyone for any purpose. In addition to being perceived by developing countries as inequitable, this situation also eliminated a potential incentive for conserving biological diversity and sustainably using its components.

To ameliorate the inequity and provide an incentive for conservation and sustainable use, the *Convention on Biological Diversity* attempts to create a new relationship between providers and users of genetic resources. The basic idea is to create a *quid pro quo* between the Parties of the Convention which provide genetic resources and potential users: access to genetic resources in exchange for sharing of benefits derived from their use.

Article 15 provides the foundation for this *quid pro quo*. It outlines each Party's rights and obligations regarding access to genetic resources and their subsequent use and is based on three fundamental concepts: (i) sovereignty over genetic resources, (ii) access subject to mutually agreed terms, and (iii) access subject to prior informed consent.

Article 15(1) clearly establishes a government's authority to control access to genetic resources under its jurisdiction, while Article 15(2) requires Parties to facilitate access to genetic resources to other Contracting Parties for environmentally sound uses and not to impose restrictions which run counter to the Convention's objectives.

By the terms of Article 15(4), access to genetic resources is conditioned on reaching mutually agreed terms between the Party providing genetic resources and a potential user. "Mutually agreed terms" implies a negotiation between the Party granting access to genetic resources and the entity which wants to use genetic resources. This could be an individual (such as a plant collector), a company (such as biotechnology firm), an institution (such as a public or private research organization) or another State. A successful negotiation (i.e., reaching mutually agreed terms) could result in an access agreement. Access agreements will likely become the primary means to (i) authorize access to genetic resources, and (ii) establish the return of benefits from their subsequent use.

According to Article 15(5), access to genetic resources is also subject to the prior informed consent (PIC) of the Party providing the genetic resources. This means that *prior* to a potential user gaining access to genetic resources under State jurisdiction, it must obtain the government's *consent* based on *information* the potential user provides on how the genetic resources will be subsequently used. In effect, reaching mutually agreed terms would be part of the PIC process.

The PIC process has two important ramifications for a Party providing genetic resources. First, PIC can *only* be ensured through national legislation unless, of course, potential users voluntarily submit to gaining consent. Second, the State providing genetic resources has the discretion to determine what genetic resources the PIC procedure will be extended to and which users (for example, commercial or non-commercial users) will have to submit to that procedure.

Sharing of Benefits

Benefit-sharing is one of the advantages which can accrue from controlling access to genetic resources. The Convention lists some examples of benefits which may be shared, including participation in scientific research, the fair and equitable sharing of research and development results and commercial and other benefits derived from genetic resource use, access to and transfer of technology making use of genetic resources, participation in biotechnological research activities based on genetic resources, and priority access to results and benefits arising from biotechnological use of genetic resources provided. However, none of the Convention's benefit-sharing provisions actually require benefit-sharing, reflecting the fact that most benefits contemplated for sharing are in the hands of the private sector (including not only business and industry, but communities and individuals as well). Indeed, *all* Parties are required to take legislative, administrative or policy measures which "aim" for benefit-sharing, whether they are developed or developing countries.

Benefit-sharing is always to be on mutually agreed terms, which implies case by case, bilateral negotiation. The end result should be an arrangement which is fair and equitable. What is fair and equitable will change with the circumstances. In most instances it will not be possible to determine at the time of the access agreement negotiation either the type of genetic resources involved (since they have yet to be collected) or the types of subsequent use contemplated (since end-products have yet to be determined and/or a final user, whether commercial or non-commercial, may not yet be evident).

Even with this uncertainty, however, effective benefit-sharing can be provided for. For example, technology transfer can be sought without knowing how genetic resources will be used. This could take the form of research participation and sharing research results or hard technology transfer. Advance payment or per sample fees can also be established, as can minimum royalties as percentage of net sales.

Future unforeseen end-products, applications or other contingencies could be provided for in access agreements. Reporting requirements could be incorporated into such an access agreement to track subsequent use. Third-party transfers could be controlled in the same manner, perhaps by being subject to PIC.

The Convention's access provisions, and its more detailed provisions on benefit-sharing, are primarily directed to the Parties providing genetic resources (i.e., the government) and potential users, whether governmental or private. What is easily overlooked is that access agreements and the sharing of benefits may also take place between "private" providers of genetic resources (for purposes of this discussion, this term includes all providers other than the State, for example, communities and individuals) and potential users. Depending on the legal system of the country in which they are located, these providers of genetic resources may be entitled to claim a fair and equitable share of benefits derived from genetic resources and some of the same principles outlined in Article 15—such as PIC and reaching mutually agreed terms—could be applied to facilitate this. In this regard, indigenous and local communities are specifically mentioned in the Convention.

Benefit-sharing is one of the advantages which can accrue from controlling access to genetic resources.

Article 8(j) requires, Parties to "encourage the equitable sharing of benefits" derived from using the knowledge, innovations and practices of indigenous and local communities embodying traditional lifestyles. This obligation is expressly subject to the provisions of national legislation. In many countries, these communities are the grass roots stewards of genetic diversity, developing over countless generations thousands of new plant varieties, animal breeds and strains of microorganisms through informal means. These human-created genetic resources, and a rich library of accompanying knowledge, have been especially valuable to modern breeders and pharmaceutical companies in developed countries, but few benefits have gone back to the traditional communities who were the initial innovators.

Even though its language is perhaps not as strong as many would have liked, especially with the proviso regarding national legislation, Article 8(j) signals an important acknowledgement that indigenous and local innovations and knowledge are valuable, especially to "modern" society, and that as "holders" of this information traditional communities need to consent to its wider application and are entitled to equitably share in the benefits others derive from its use. The challenge will be for Parties to develop appropriate policies and legislation to ensure consent and encourage benefit-sharing, while minimizing the tendency to simply see the knowledge and innovations of indigenous and local communities as just another resource to be exploited.

(ii) Ten Kate K. and Laird S., *The Commercial Use of Biodiversity—Access to Genetic Resources and Benefit Sharing*, Earthscan Publication, 1999, pp 17–32

[*The implementation of Article 15 of the Convention and related provisions poses numerous legal and practical problems, both for Parties providers of genetic resources and those which are users of those resources. Central to these are interpretations of the provisions on scope, as well as on mutually agreed terms, and prior informed consent. These questions are examined in this extract.*]

The Scope and Requirements of National and Regional Law on Access to Genetic Resources and Benefit-Sharing

Scope

Perhaps the first question to ask concerning national laws on access and benefit-sharing is what they cover. The scope of the resources whose access is to be regulated is outlined briefly in the CBD, but since countries have national sovereignty over their natural and other resources, individual states may choose to regulate access to a broader or narrower range of resources than those encompassed by the term 'genetic resources', as defined in the CBD. This section will describe the basic provisions of the CBD regarding scope, and also provide a few examples of the scope chosen by states through the definitions used in their national and regional regulations. The issues covered in this section are genetic resources; human genetic materials; derivatives of genetic resources; traditional knowledge concerning genetic resources; *ex situ* collections of genetic resources; and marine genetic resources.

Genetic Resources

The obligations under the CBD on access and benefit-sharing refer to 'genetic resources', defined in Article 2 as 'genetic material of actual or potential value'. Genetic material is defined as 'any material of plant, animal, microbial, or other origin containing functional units of heredity'. There has, as yet, been no cause (such as an international dispute) for courts to interpret this term. Glowka *et al.* [*extracted above*] consider that 'functional units of heredity' would include whole organisms, parts of organisms or biochemical extracts from tissue samples that contain deoxyribonucleic acid (DNA) or, in some cases, ribonucleic acid (RNA).

Although the language of the CBD does not say so in so many words, it is now widely accepted that the scope of Article 15 is confined to the use of genetic resources for their genetic purposes. If this is the case, then it is only necessary to obtain prior informed consent, reach mutually agreed terms and share benefits where the use is made of the material's genetic attributes, for example, exploring the biological activity of compounds extracted from the material or using plants in a breeding program.

Under this interpretation, it would not be necessary to share benefits in return for access for 'non-genetic' uses of genetic resources, such as access to trees for timber (rather than for chemical analysis) or access to a forest for ecotourism. Most national access legislation has not resolved this ambiguity, a problem which is caught up in broader questions concerning the lack of clarity of the exact activities and resources which are regulated (see especially 'derivatives', below).

Although the language of the CBD does not distinguish between human and other categories of genetic resources, the Conference of the Parties, at its second meeting in 1996, 'reaffirmed that human genetic resources were not included within the framework of the Convention (Decision II/11)'. Most national access law and draft laws to date have also specifically excluded human genetic resources from the definition of genetic resources within the scope of their laws. Access to samples of human genetic material for research and indeed for commercialization are thus largely unregulated (although subject to common law and some statutory provisions in some countries). Since this category of research is common and raises profound ethical issues, many governments will presumably wish to consider developing law or policy on this kind of access outside the ambit of the CBD.

Derivatives

The CBD itself makes no mention of 'derivatives', although the very act of regulating access to genetic resources provides a trigger for negotiations on mutually agreed terms that could (and often do) involve a share of the benefits arising from derivatives of genetic resources, such as sales of semi-synthesized or totally synthesized compounds based on structures discovered from studying genetic resources, or sales of hybrid plants that result from access to two parents.

Recognizing that, in sectors such as pharmaceuticals and crop protection, only a few commercial products actually contain unmodified genetic resources, and that the large majority contain products derived from, patterned on or incorporating manipulated compounds and genes found in nature, many access agreements (including many agreed before the CBD) contain benefit-sharing obligations attached to sales or other use of derivatives of the genetic resources themselves. [P]artnerships can involve benefits such as joint research between the provider of genetic resources and the user on derivatives (see, for example, NCI/Calanolide). Agreements for the supply of genetic resources often involve commitments to pay royalties not only for the commercial use of the genetic resources supplied, but for any derivatives. These terms are agreed at the time when the recipient is granted access to genetic resources themselves.

A number of national laws include definitions of 'derivative', 'by-product', and 'synthesized product'. In many cases, the substantive provisions make no further reference to these definitions, so it is unclear which activities with respect to them are regulated, and to what effect. Specifically, it is unclear whether the laws require prior informed consent from the state (and possibly other stakeholders) prior to access to derivatives, or only regulate access to genetic resources themselves, but encourage the sharing of benefits arising from the commercial (and other) use of derivatives of genetic resources. For example, *Biodiversity Law* 7788 of Costa Rica defines genetic elements, biochemical elements and associated knowledge, but Article 63, the substantive provision concerning the regulation of access, simply refers to 'the requirements for access', without clarifying access to what. Similarly, the Executive Order and Implementing Regulations in the Philippines regulate the prospecting of biological and genetic resources. 'Derivatives' are defined, but not mentioned in the substantive provisions concerning access, except for an allusion to the role of the Department of Health in evaluating proposals for research and development 'including the utilization of extracts, products and by-products and derivatives for commercial and academic purposes'. 'By-products' are defined but not mentioned at all in the substantive provisions. By contrast, *Decision 391 of the Andean Pact* is clear that its objective is to regulate access to genetic resources and their derivatives (Article 2).

Regulators wishing to design laws that will capture a share of the benefits arising from sales of derived products such as pharmaceuticals are faced with a problem. On the one hand, if access to genetic resources alone is regulated, there is the danger that people will make derivatives within the country concerned and export them without ensuring a sharing of benefits, whether by selling traditional medicines or plant cultivars in the market place, or by preparing refined extracts of natural product specimens in a pharmaceutical company, and shipping the resulting samples to a subsidiary company elsewhere. On the other hand, if regulators attempt to control access to derivatives, a broad definition is needed to capture the full range of products that may be developed. However, derivatives of genetic resources are ubiquitous in daily life, so it is questionable how governments could effectively regulate access to them.

One way around this problem for legislators, depending on the law governing rights over genetic and biological resources in each country, may be to regulate access only to genetic resources, but to require benefit-sharing for the use of derivatives. Current models of access laws will probably have this effect, but more by accident than by clear design.

Traditional Knowledge

Article 8(j) of the CBD provides that each Contracting Party shall:

> "Subject to its national legislation, respect, preserve and maintain knowledge, innovations and practices of indigenous and local communities embodying traditional lifestyles relevant for the conservation and sustainable use of biological diversity and promote their wider application with the approval and involvement of the holders of such knowledge, innovations and practices and encourage the equitable sharing of the benefits arising from the utilization of such knowledge, innovations and practices."

There is a growing body of literature on this provision. An *Intersessional Workshop on Traditional Knowledge and Biological Diversity*, held under the auspices of the CBD in Madrid in November 1997, focused on Article 8(j) (UNEP/CBD/TBK/113), and a meeting of the Ad Hoc Working Group on Article 8(j) is planned for January 2000.

Several national laws on access to genetic resources define terms such as 'knowledge', 'traditional knowledge', 'intangible component' and various categories of peoples such as 'local communities' and 'indigenous cultural communities'. As with other questions of scope, such as derivatives and *ex situ* collections, the exact circumstances in which the 'prior approval' of local and indigenous communities is needed—and for what—vary from country to country and are sometimes unclear. Some access laws require prior informed consent from local and indigenous people for access to genetic resources on their lands but do not address access to their traditional knowledge concerning those resources, while others explicitly require prior approval from local and indigenous peoples for access to their traditional knowledge, but not to genetic resources or their land.

Ex Situ Collections

At the national level, the majority of countries do not have explicit laws on access and benefit-sharing that apply to ex situ *collections.*

The effect of Article 15(3) of the CBD is to exclude from the remit of its provisions on access and benefit-sharing those genetic resources acquired before the entry into force of the Convention. *Ex situ* collections of genetic resources acquired before the Convention thus fall outside these provisions. Notwithstanding, it is open to governments to consider introducing access requirements and benefit-sharing for these resources, although there are important legal considerations related to the retrospective nature of any such obligations, as well as the fact that the resources may be privately owned.

At the international level, access to pre-CBD *ex situ* collections of plant genetic resources for food and agriculture forms an important part of the negotiations under the auspices of the FAO Commission on Genetic Resources for Food and Agriculture to revise the *International Undertaking on Plant Genetic Resources for Food and Agriculture* (Chapter 5). It was also one of the most controversial issues discussed during the fourth meeting of the Conference of the Parties (COP), which requested the Executive Secretary of the Convention to invite information from Parties and relevant organizations in respect of those *ex situ* collections which were acquired prior to the entry into force of the CBD and (in order to avoid duplication of the work under the auspices of the FAO) which are not addressed by the Commission on Genetic Resources for Food and Agriculture (Decision IV/8).

At the national level, the majority of countries do not have explicit laws on access and benefit-sharing that apply to *ex situ* collections, particularly to those acquired prior to the entry into force of the Convention. However, it is important to remember that many governments have used collecting permits for decades, or even for hundreds of years, so it is likely that a large proportion of the materials in pre-CBD *ex situ* collections were acquired under this form of agreement. Prior to granting access to its accessions, an *ex situ* collection must thus establish whether it is contractually bound by the terms of specific collecting permits to treat certain accessions in certain ways.

The effect on pre-CBD collections of the laws in those countries that have introduced them is often ambiguous. For example, Section 3 of the *Philippine Implementing Regulations* does not explicitly state whether, or which, *ex situ* collections established prior to the Convention are in the 'public domain', and are thus covered by the Regulations. The *Andean Pact Common System on Access to Genetic Resources* governs those genetic resources of which the Member State is the country of origin, defined as the country which possesses those genetic resources in *in situ* conditions (much as in the CBD itself), but also genetic resources that, having been established in *in situ* conditions, are encountered in *ex situ* conditions. Since no date is mentioned, the effect of the Decision is arguably to regulate access to *ex situ* collections of national genetic resources, whether collected prior to or after the entry into force of the CBD. Furthermore, the first Transitory Provision states that:

> "All those who, on the date on which this decision enters into force, are in illegal possession, for purposes of access, of genetic resources for which the Member States are countries of origin, their derivatives or related intangible components, must negotiate such access with the Competent National Authority, subject to the terms of this decision. The Competent National Authorities shall establish deadlines for such negotiation, not to exceed twenty-four months from the entrance into force of this decision.
>
> In the event of non-compliance with this requirement, the Member States may disqualify such persons and the bodies which they represent or on whose behalf they are acting from applying for further access

> to genetic resources or their derivatives in the subregion, without prejudice to application of the corresponding penalties once the period referred to in the previous paragraph has elapsed."

As well as being clearly retrospective in effect, this clause could be interpreted as being extra-territorial (i.e., applying to pre-CBD collections of Andean material held outside the jurisdiction of the five member states). The basis for such scope is questionable in international law and may well not have been the intention of the countries, which could use other articles in the Decision to resolve the question in the future, particularly since two major international collections—Centro Internacional de Agricultura (CIAT) in Colombia and Centro Internacional de la Papa (CIP) in Peru—and several national genebanks and botanic gardens are held within their territory. Nonetheless, the provision demonstrates that treatment of its existing *ex situ* collections is likely to affect an organization's chances of securing access to genetic resources in the future.

Geographical Scope

As well as the nature of the genetic resources covered by legislation, another important aspect of defining the scope of access regulations is the location of the genetic resources concerned. As the CBD reaffirms, all countries have sovereign rights over genetic resources within their jurisdiction, and the vast majority require phytosanitary permits for import and export of genetic resources and may well control other activities such as trade in endangered species. However, the approach of different countries to regulating the collection of samples from *in situ* conditions varies. The following examples are simply generalizations to illustrate some major differences in approach. It is necessary to study the law of each individual country in order to understand where access to genetic resources is regulated.

Private Land

In some countries (for example, many in Latin America), genetic resources are the 'national patrimony' of the state, so that access to genetic resources is regulated by the state on private as well as public land. In such countries, if one wishes to access plants or microorganisms in someone's private backyard, one will need not only the landowner's permission, but also prior informed consent from the state. In contrast, in Organization for Economic Cooperation and Development (OECD) countries, the state generally does not regulate access to genetic resources on private land (but there are notable exceptions, for example certain activities involving access to particular species are regulated by domestic laws on wildlife, conservation, hunting, fishing and shooting that apply to private land). In many countries, if one wishes to obtain a plant from private land for research, the permission of the landowner to enter the land and remove the specimen is probably sufficient. No prior informed consent from the government is needed. While ownership of genes is a grey area, ownership of the specimen itself, and authority to dispose of it, probably rests solely with the landowner in these circumstances.

Public Land

Regulation of access to genetic resources on public land also varies from country to country. The scope of some countries' access regulations is sometimes defined by reference to particular categories of public land, such as protected areas. In the USA, for example, the Department of the Interior regulates access to genetic resources within the Federal National Parks through the enabling act for the National Park Service (the *National Parks Organic Act* of 1916), and the regulations under the US *Code of Federal Regulations* (36 CFR 1). A number of other departments of the US government regulate access to other Federal lands (ELI, 1996). In Madagascar (where changes in the regulation of access are currently being considered), permission from one body—the Association Nationale pour la Gestion des Aires Protegees (ANGAP)—is needed for access to protected areas, and permission from another (the Direction Generale de la Ministere des Eaux et Forets) for access to other public lands.

Marine Areas

Since several research institutes and companies are known to focus on marine genetic resources, it is perhaps surprising that access laws are often ambiguous in their application to the marine environment. National jurisdiction over marine living resources extends to inland waters, territorial waters and exclusive economic zones. National access law has not, to date, clarified whether countries will distinguish between their territorial waters and the exclusive economic zone, where the jurisdictional powers of the coastal state are understood to be less expansive. Some countries specifically include coastal and inland waters in the geographical scope of their access legislation; the laws in others are ambiguous; and in yet others it is quite clear that access to marine organisms is not covered, since the scope of the law clearly applies only to specific terrestrial areas, such as national parks. As with other issues discussed above, this is a matter that must be checked against the specific law of the country concerned. Countries considering regulating access may wish to consider that, to date, access procedures have been designed with terrestrial prospecting in mind, and may need adaptation for a marine environment.

Although few can afford to work there, researchers and companies are extremely interested in the marine environment outside national jurisdiction in the high seas, since unusual organisms and extremophiles can be found on the deep sea bed and in thermal vents. By virtue of the *United Nations Convention on the Law of the Sea* (UNCLOS), the seabed, ocean floor and subsoil thereof beyond the limits of national jurisdiction, 'the Area', are designated as 'the common heritage of mankind' (UNCLOS articles 133a and 136). An International Seabed Authority exists to ensure the fair and equitable utilization of the Area's mineral resources.

Mutually Agreed Terms

According to the CBD, access to genetic resources, where granted, shall be on mutually agreed terms. Typical terms include:

- legal acquisition,
- permitted use of genetic resources,
- restrictions on supply,
- benefit-sharing, and
- other terms.

Since mutually agreed terms for access to genetic resources involve, by definition, two or more parties, at least one party will be supplying the genetic resources and another acquiring them. The terms under which a recipient acquires the genetic resources are likely to affect its freedom to supply the same resources, or their derivatives, to a third party. Thus an important consideration for an 'intermediary' institution, be it a genebank, university department, botanic garden or company, is to ensure that any commitments it makes in agreements in which it acquires genetic resources, are honored in agreements under which it supplies them. [W]hen resources are initially collected, prior informed consent from government is likely to be required, and this may be granted to the collector subject to certain mutually agreed terms (Material Transfer Agreement 1 (MTA1)). Before supplying the resources (or their progeny or derivatives) to a third party, this collector will need to check the terms under which they were acquired. If there are restrictions, such as ensuring that the resources are not commercialized without the consent of the government, or passing benefit-sharing obligations on to any subsequent recipient, the collector will need to ensure that the materials are only supplied to any future recipient under an agreement (MTA2). The terms of MTA2, mutually agreed with the recipient (in this case, a company), will need to be consistent with those of MTA1. For its part, the company receiving materials from the collector may also wish the collector to guarantee in MTA2 that it obtained the resources lawfully and can pass title to them to the company.

Legal Acquisition

If the organization acquiring genetic resources is collecting them itself from *in situ* conditions or other situations covered by access legislation, it will need to obtain prior informed consent from the appropriate government authorities, and from others whose consent is needed, such as private landowners, protected area management boards, and local and indigenous communities. Some access laws introduce fairly heavy penalties for breach of these requirements, such as fines and imprisonment. For example, the proposed *Biological Diversity Act* in India would regulate access to biological resources for research or commercial utilization, collecting or bioprospecting, and even proposes to prohibit the transfer of research results. It states that any contravention of the provisions of the Act will be punishable with imprisonment for a term which may extend up to five years, or a fine which may extend up to Rs 10 lakhs (approximately US$25,000), or both.

If, however, the organization is not collecting genetic resources itself, but rather acquiring them (or their derivatives) from another organization, such as a botanic garden or research institute in the source country or elsewhere, this activity may well not be covered by access legislation itself (although that depends on the law in the country concerned). While a recipient is not, *prima facie*, bound by access law if it simply receives genetic resources from a supplier, engaging in such activity without ensuring that the supplier has title to the materials exposes the recipient to a number of legal and other risks. The fundamental danger for a recipient in these circumstances is that the genetic resources may not be the supplier's to provide. If the supplier (whether a public or private institution from the country of origin or from elsewhere in the world) does not lawfully own the resources itself, or have the authority to dispose of them to a third party, the recipient's right to commercialize the resources or any derivative from them is thrown into question. Depending on the circumstances and degree of knowledge of the recipient at the time it acquired the materials, it could also itself be guilty of an offense.

There are a number of possible bases for legal actions on the part of the rightful owners or right-holders (who might be a state with sovereign rights, private citizens, or a community) against a recipient of genetic resources. The possibilities depend on the legal provisions in the country of origin, in the country where the collector/supplier was based and in the country where the ultimate recipient company is based. There are two main scenarios. In the first, the supplier has collected or acquired the material legally, under a permit or some other material transfer agreement, but has then supplied the material to the recipient in breach of the express or implied terms of that agreement—the 'breach of contract' scenario. In the second, the supplier has not collected or acquired the material legally, but nonetheless goes on to supply the material to the recipient—the 'illegal acquisition' scenario. The implications of each of these scenarios will be discussed briefly in turn.

The 'Breach of Contract' Scenario

A typical example of this scenario would be the case where an academic collector obtains a 'scientific' collecting permit (and various export and phytosanitary permits) to collect and take home certain samples, but then supplies these to a company for commercial purposes. Let us imagine that the company derives a highly successful commercial product from its work on the samples. The collector would, arguably, be in breach of the terms of the permit even if the permit contained no explicit prohibition of commercialization. The courts might decide that it is an implied term of such a contract that a 'scientific' permit granted to a 'scientific' institute, ostensibly for non-commercial purposes, prohibits the use of the materials for commercial purposes. Collectors frequently complete detailed forms explaining the purposes of collection and the use to which they intend to put the material. If there was no mention in the application of commercialization, the permitting authorities might argue that they granted the permit in reliance upon the applicant's assurance that the materials would be used only as described in the application. In a clearer case, the permit may explicitly prohibit the commercialization of the samples or their derivatives, or their supply to third parties for commercialization or any other purposes.

In this scenario, the permitting authorities could sue the collector for breach of contract. This might not avail them much, if the collector was penniless and had already parted with the materials to the company. The authorities could not sue the recipient company for damages or a 'share in the benefits' since they were not parties to the same agreement. The authorities might conceivably have some ground for action against the recipient company if they could prove that the company was well aware that it was receiving the materials on terms that breached the agreement between the authorities and the collector. In practical terms, this would be extremely difficult to show. In order to avoid the risk of any such action, however, companies are increasingly likely to require their suppliers not only to guarantee that they have good title to the materials, which they are entitled to pass to the company, but also to indemnify the company against any possible actions by aggrieved source country authorities or others.

Faced with these circumstances, a company might claim damages against the collector for supplying it with materials in circumstances in which it was not entitled to do so, but the ability of the collecting institution to pay damages would depend on its standing. For this reason, companies may choose to receive materials only from well-established, reputable organizations that will examine their contractual obligations with care, and, in the worst case, would have the assets or insurance to make good any orders for damages.

However, an institution is likely to be reluctant to give any form of indemnity to a company and may well refuse to do so. The company may therefore need to verify for itself that the supply of materials was permissible.

If a challenge arose, it is questionable whether or not the company could continue with the commercialization. This would depend on the law of the country in which the company is established. That law might well permit the source country or entity to prevent this commercialization on grounds akin to intellectual property rights enforcement, namely that no license was granted to the company to use the materials for that purpose. The extent to which such preventative action would be possible is likely to depend upon the nature of the laws introduced in response to the CBD in 'user' countries, since the chances would be much higher if legal provisions in user countries complemented and reinforced those introduced laws by 'provider' countries.

The answer may also depend on the law of the source country. In all contractual (and indeed other) scenarios, the rules on conflict of laws in the countries involved would need to be considered. To give an illustration, consider a material transfer agreement between a Peruvian institution and a British company which leads to a dispute. If the material transfer agreement between the parties contained a provision such that it was governed by the laws of Peru, an English court would apply Peruvian law to any contractual dispute, subject to public policy considerations. The third transitory Provision of *Andean Pact Decision 391* states that 'The Member States may take any legal action that they deem appropriate to reclaim genetic resources, derivatives and related intangible components for which they are countries of origin and to obtain any indemnities and compensation that may be due.' It is possible that an English court could grant a remedy under that law even if the same remedy was not available under English law. However, the court would not be likely to do so if the remedy were punitory or otherwise contrary to English law.

A further practical issue that a company will need to consider is that it may have operations in many countries, including the source country. In these circumstances, it could be susceptible to the laws of, and legal action in, the source country. A company will thus need to exercise caution in its receipt of materials, in order to ensure that no possible claims arise in the countries where it operates.

The 'Illegal Acquisition' Scenario

In this scenario, the collector may not have obtained any consent to take the materials, or may not have obtained the consent of all those from whom it was required by the relevant laws. However, the collector provides some of the material to a company, and a commercial product results. As mentioned above, access legislation frequently provides for sanctions against the collector in these circumstances. In the absence of access legislation, the source country may be able to prosecute the collector for theft, obtaining by deception, fraud, or any other associated crime. Furthermore, this scenario differs from the first in that the possibility of civil and possibly even criminal actions against the recipient company itself is higher, although remedies for dealing in stolen property, whether knowingly or unknowingly, vary from country to country, and questions of jurisdiction arise where the goods concerned are involved in international trade. The risk is, however, that the company may not obtain clear title to the materials, and may face claims for their restitution by the source country authorities. Furthermore, the source country may be able to obtain an injunction preventing the company from commercializing the resulting products without its permission, which would provide the setting for benefit-sharing negotiations.

These considerations about the actions of private individuals and organizations raise a broader question concerning the obligations of the countries where the commercialization takes place. So far, *de facto*, the burden of regulating access has fallen on the countries providing genetic resources. Since all Contracting Parties are equally bound by the provisions of the Convention, it can be argued that governments are obliged to take legal, administrative or policy measures to ensure that companies and other users of genetic resources have acquired them in accordance with the Convention, and that the benefits arising from access to genetic resources are shared fairly and equitably. Several possible approaches to such measures have been mooted, including preventing genetic resources from entering countries without proof of prior informed consent; requirements to disclose the country of origin and demonstrate prior informed consent in patent applications; and national legislation which would require companies to obtain genetic resources in accordance with the Convention, and to facilitate the enforcement of claims against collectors or commercializing entities.

Thus, in some circumstances, a source country could bring an action based either in criminal or civil law against not only the collector, but the recipient of genetic resources that commercializes them. Where the collector did not literally 'steal' the materials concerned, and where the company is the passive, innocent recipient of derivatives of genetic resources in a country other than the country of origin of the resources, the chances of success and successful enforcement of such claims under present laws are questionable. However, the acquisition of samples by a company in either of the two scenarios described above throws sufficient doubt over its title to the genetic resources, their derivatives and the profits arising from their sale as to provide good legal arguments for avoiding the situation. Furthermore, there are good business arguments for doing so, namely to maintain the company's reputation with its customers and other stakeholders, and to protect the company's ability to acquire raw materials from countries around the world in the future.

The best way to avoid the risk of legal actions, loss of reputation and the risk of losing channels for the supply of raw materials in the future is to ensure that genetic resources are acquired under material acquisition agreements containing terms that clarify the rights and responsibilities of the supplier from whom the company acquires the genetic resources, and the recipient company.

Collectors and companies might feel that the collecting permits issued by many countries resolve these questions, since they appear to be proof of government agreement for access to genetic resources. There are two main points to be made about collecting permits: first, they are legal agreements between the permitting authority and the individual or organization granted access, and may set detailed terms for access. Second, they may, however, not grant sufficient authority for applicants to use the materials obtained for commercial purposes. Each of these points will be discussed in turn.

Many permits are granted in reliance upon quite detailed information provided in application forms and project proposals submitted to the permitting authority. There are strong legal arguments to suggest that the granting of the permits thus concludes contracts, whose implied terms might incorporate restrictions on the use of the materials to those described in the applications. Permitting authorities might also be able to sue for misrepresentation if an applicant subsequently used samples in a manner other than described in the application which resulted in the permit being granted.

However, collecting permits suffer from two major shortcomings as far as avoiding the legal doubts described in this section are concerned. First, they are often quite vague on the conditions under which materials acquired may be used. Frequently, they simply list the material, the collector's name, and the location where the resources were collected. A stamp shows that permission has been granted. Sometimes the permits are headed 'scientific collecting permit', or 'research permit', but often they are silent on whether the permit allows the recipient to conduct research for commercial purposes, whether the materials can be used for other specific purposes (for example, public display, DNA analysis or biochemical screening, even for ostensibly non-commercial purposes), or whether the material can be passed to third parties for these or other purposes. Second, collecting permits may be just that: permits to enter a protected area to collect. Separate permits from other departments of government may be needed to export or otherwise use the samples. For these reasons, organizations such as university departments and botanic gardens that collect genetic resources, and companies that obtain samples from them, may prefer a material acquisition agreement, rather than simple evidence of a collecting permit.

The basic terms that a company (or other organization acquiring genetic resources) might therefore wish to see reflected in a material acquisition agreement are:

- *The material was legally acquired*: confirmation that the material was collected in accordance with the law of the host country;
- *The government has authorized access*: confirmation that the supplier of that material is authorized under the laws of the host country to grant access to and to provide the material to the recipient (i.e., confirmation of prior informed consent); and
- *Terms for use of the material*: a clear statement of the terms and conditions attaching to the use of the material or, if there are none, a clear statement that this is the case.

There are two main barriers to obtaining such agreements: identifying the competent national authority, and identifying local level stakeholders whose consent is also needed.

The fundamental difficulty faced by companies and the intermediary organizations that collect and supply genetic resources is that it is often practically impossible to determine precisely who is the 'gatekeeper' authorized to grant access, and exactly what are the requirements one must follow. This makes it difficult for suppliers to give absolute guarantees that materials were legally acquired or that the correct government body has authorized access for

Many permits are granted in reliance upon quite detailed information provided in application forms and project proposals submitted to the permitting authority.

the purposes for which the recipient company wishes to use the resources.

In many countries, different government bodies are authorized to deal with different aspects of regulating access. For example, in China the Ministry of Forests is responsible for access to plants in forests and protected areas, and the Ministry of Agriculture for access to plants elsewhere. Access to insects and microorganisms is regulated by the Chinese Academy of Sciences. Further permissions may also be needed from Ministries (such as the Ministry of Public Health, in the case of medicinal plants) where work involves organizations under their jurisdiction. Until national access legislation has been introduced, it is difficult to tell which single government body is authorized to grant access, whether a number of different bodies are empowered to grant access and any one will do; whether different bodies grant access in different circumstances for different uses; or whether permission may be needed concurrently from more than one body. The challenge of finding clear answers to these questions is compounded by the fact that many representatives of the governments concerned do not themselves know the answer to the questions and also by the 'diplomatic' difficulty of raising the need for central government approval with other institutions (such as research institutes, genebanks, botanic gardens, herbaria and universities) which have, *de facto*, granted access to genetic resources for many years.

Permitted Use of Genetic Resources

One useful purpose that can be served by MTAs is to clarify the use which the recipient is entitled to make of the materials received. If the recipient is a company, it is likely that the materials will be used for research and development which may (but more likely will not) lead to successful commercialization. In that case, the agreement should state explicitly that the recipient is entitled to commercialize the material transferred, or its derivatives. While a court could, in the event of a dispute, decide upon what activities constitute 'commercialization', it is preferable to avoid any doubts by including a definition of 'commercialization' or 'commercial use' in the agreement. Many such definitions bear some similarity to the following one:

> "Commercialization shall include, but not be limited to, the following activities; sale, filing a patent application, obtaining or transferring intellectual property rights or other tangible or intangible rights by sale or license or in any other manner, commencement of product development, conducting market research, and seeking pre-market approval."

Definitions such as this serve not only to prescribe the activities which the recipient may conduct on the material acquired, but also to set various 'milestones' in the use of material by the recipient. Thus other clauses in the agreement can refer to the events listed in the definition of commercialization, which can be used as the 'trigger' for notification of the supplier, for the transfer of benefits such as milestone payments, or for further negotiations, either with the supplier, or with source country governments.

Where the main purpose of the transfer of material does not foresee commercialization, the provider may wish explicitly to prohibit commercialization of the material by the recipient, using a definition such as the one above. Alternatively, the parties may agree a list of other activities which the recipient may or may not undertake on the materials. For example, a government granting a permit to a botanic garden could stipulate that the botanic garden may only use the materials for the creation of herbarium specimens and not for public display; or for public display but not for screening or DNA extraction, etc.

Restrictions on Supply

Recipients of material need to ensure that they are clear about their rights to supply the material to third parties, or otherwise dispose of it. If the recipient is an intermediary institution such as a small company, genebank or a university department, it should establish whether it is entitled to supply the materials, or products derived from them, to third parties such as companies or other genebanks. Even a company that is likely to manufacture a final product from the materials may license out access to its libraries of extracts and compounds, or may merge with or be acquired by another company, so terms on the supply of materials to third parties may also be relevant.

Benefit-Sharing

A range of monetary and non-monetary benefits can be shared by the provider and recipient of the material transferred at several times that can be mutually agreed when the agreement is signed; for example, at the time the materials are first transferred; at various stages during the research and development process (see 'triggers' under the definition of commercialization, above); and once a product is successfully commercialized.

As well as stipulating the stage at which benefits are to be shared, the nature of the benefits and the basis for calculating them can also be set out in an MTA.

Aspects of benefit-sharing that are listed in national access legislation for incorporation nto material transfer agreements, and that are common in MTAs for the commercial use of biodiversity, include:

Monetary Benefits

- up-front fees, either for access to genetic resources, or to cover the costs of any preparation of samples, research conducted on them, and handling and shipping costs;
- milestone payments when various stages in discovery and development are reached (either independent payments, or set-off against any royalties that may be incurred in the future); and
- royalties. It is important to clarify the basis of royalty payments, for example whether they are calculated on gross or net sales.

Non-Monetary Benefits

- participation of source-country scientists (who may be third parties) in research;
- transfer of equipment, software and know-how;
- exchange of staff and training;
- in-kind support for conservation;
- acknowledgement of provider in research publications, patents and other forms of IPR;
- sharing of research results, including notification of discoveries and ensuring that copies of publications concerning research on the genetic resources provided are sent to the source country;
- voucher specimens to be left in national institutions; and
- terms for the licensing of technologies developed from research on the genetic resources transferred.

Other Terms

In addition to terms on legal acquisition, authorized uses of materials, transfer to third parties and benefit-sharing, it is common to include a number of other clauses in material transfer agreements, which may deal with the following:

- definitions;
- duty to minimize the environmental impact of collecting activities;
- duty to maintain samples in good condition;
- ownership of materials;
- representations and warranties concerning the quality, identity of the materials transferred and any liabilities arising from their use;
- indemnity against potential liability, such as that arising from civil or criminal actions connected to access and benefit-sharing brought by source countries and other providers or recipients of genetic resources;
- length of agreement;
- notice;
- the fact that the obligations in certain clauses (e.g., benefit-sharing) survive the termination of the agreement;
- independent enforceability of individual clauses in the agreement;
- events limiting liability of either party (such as Act of God, war, fire, flood, explosion, civil commotion, industrial disputes, impossibility of obtaining gas or electricity or materials), and requirement to notify the other party in the case of any such event;
- arbitration;
- assignment or transfer of rights; and
- choice of law.

Prior Informed Consent

Article 15 (5) of the CBD provides that access to genetic resources shall be subject to the prior informed consent of the Contracting Party providing such resources, unless otherwise determined by that Party. As required by Article 15(2), Parties must endeavor to facilitate access, thereby ensuring the continued exchange of genetic resources. National measures must therefore strike a balance controlling access so as to arrive at mutually agreed terms for access and to ensure benefit-sharing, and the need to ensure that access procedures and requirements do not block access.

Prior informed consent is not defined in the Convention, but several commentators have identified the key elements as being:

- '*prior*'—before access takes place;
- '*informed*'—based on truthful information about the use that will be made of the genetic resources that is adequate for the authority to understand the implications; and
- '*consent*'—the explicit consent of the government (and possibly other stakeholders, according to national law) of the country providing genetic resources.

In those cases where countries have introduced explicit access legislation after the CBD, they require consent from the state and also from certain other individuals, communities and organizations.

Whose Consent is Required?

Prior Informed Consent from the State

Although there is some debate as to the meaning of the phrase 'unless otherwise determined' in Article 15(5), the CBD is fairly unambiguous that informed consent is to be sought from national governments prior to access. In practice, identifying the appropriate organ or organs of government from whom consent must be sought is often extremely difficult. Most countries have not yet taken legal, policy or administrative steps to clarify access to genetic resources in the light of the CBD. In these circumstances, access to genetic resources is generally governed by a patchwork of different laws concerning access to protected areas, collection of specimens in various other geographical locations, scientific research, export, the *Convention on International Trade in Endangered Species of Wild Fauna and Flora* (CITES), phytosanitary provisions, biosafety, the laws of private property, and the rights of local and indigenous communities. These laws often overlap, but also often reveal important 'gaps'—such as no regulation of access to microorganisms or to marine resources. Access is often administered by an equally varied group of organizations, including several different ministries (typically, the ministries of environment, forests, agriculture, health, science, and commerce), local or regional government, para-statal organizations, institutions and individuals.

Most countries have not yet taken legal, policy or administrative steps to clarify access to genetic resources in the light of the CBD.

Governments can play a variety of roles in access and benefit-sharing arrangements established pursuant to access legislation, and these roles are reflected in the function designated for the state in terms of oversight, negotiation, approval and monitoring of access agreements. At one extreme, a government might be party to each commercial agreement. At the other extreme, a government might establish laws that guide the development of access and benefit-sharing arrangements but then remain distant from all negotiations and transactions, leaving private institutions to enter into their own agreements, consistent with the law. A range of roles for government bodies is spelled out in access regulations, and these often include assessment of the merit of each proposed access and benefit-sharing arrangement, and subsequent approval (or rejection) of the terms of access and benefit-sharing contracts. Several countries have established or are considering cross-sectoral, representative bodies to perform such tasks. These may be interministerial or inter-agency committees, which include the representation and participation of indigenous and local communities, the private sector, the research community, nongovermental organizations, and other stakeholders. In several countries, such a committee is supported by one or more technical advisory committees.

Local-Level Prior Informed Consent

Several access measures establish the requirement for the approval of local and indigenous communities prior to access either to genetic or biological resources within their territory, or to their knowledge, innovations and practices. For example, the Philippines law requires the prior informed consent of indigenous cultural communities, in accordance with customary laws, for the prospecting of biological and genetic resources within their ancestral lands and domains (PEO, Section 2). It does not, however, refer to access to their knowledge, innovations and practices.

While there is no clear provision requiring the prior informed consent of local and indigenous communities, Article 7 of Decision 391 states that the five member states of the Andean Commission 'recognize and value the rights and decision-making capacity of indigenous, Afro-American and local communities with regard to their traditional practices, knowledge and innovations connected with genetic resources and their derivatives'. The Decision states that an applicant wishing to access genetic resources or derivatives with an 'intangible component' must identify the supplier of the intangible component (Article 26(b)) and negotiate an annexe to the access contract providing for the sharing of benefits with them (Article 35). Furthermore, the Eighth

Complementary provision refers to the future development of a special system or harmonization standard 'to provide greater protection of the knowledge, innovations and traditional practices of indigenous, Afro-American and local communities'. The language itself is a little unclear, but it is plain that the intent of the legislation is to ensure that the approval of local and indigenous communities should be sought prior to access to their knowledge. Their prior informed consent may also be needed (as landholders) for access to biological resources on the land, whereas access to genetic resources in the Andean Pact is a question for the member states alone.

According to the law in each country, the consent of other individuals and organizations may also be required. For example, Section 2 of the *Philippines Implementing Regulations* includes in its definition of prior informed consent both local communities and private land owners:

> "Prior informed consent refers to the consent obtained by the applicant from the Local Community, Indigenous Cultural Communities or Indigenous Peoples (IP), Protected Area Management Board (PAMB) or Private Land Owner concerned, after disclosing fully the intent and scope of the bioprospecting activity, in a language and process understandable to the community, and before any bioprospecting activity is undertaken."

As well as its provisions that refer to annex agreements with any indigenous, African American and local communities that provide knowledge, or the 'intangible component' associated with genetic resources, Decision 391 also refers to accessory contracts between the applicant for access and the owner, holder or administrator of the biological resource containing the genetic resource, or of the property on which the biological resource containing the genetic resource is found (Article 41). In this way, access laws effectively grant rights to prior informed consent of individuals and organizations with property rights over biological resources and the land where they are found, land-owners and other private citizens, thus granting a level of prior informed consent to private land-owners as well.

The challenge for the collector is to identify, at the local level, exactly whose consent is required. While it may be possible to identify local landowners, it is often quite a challenge for scientists from foreign countries who are neither anthropological experts nor conversant in local languages or customs to identify from which local and indigenous communities consent is needed, and who can negotiate on their behalf. The necessity to obtain consent from local and indigenous communities raises a number of important questions, such as: how many distinct communities are involved? Does the legal system of the country concerned grant rights to individuals, or collective rights to communities? Does the community have legal standing to enter into agreements? Who is authorized to negotiate on behalf of the community? What happens if a certain proportion of members of a community agree to negotiated terms, but the rest do not? What happens if certain communities break away from umbrella groups that represented them and with whom access agreements were negotiated? Collectors are likely to need help from local experts, for example, from the government, that will require evidence of agreement with these communities prior to approving an access application, or from local NGOs.

The PIC Procedure

Procedures which an applicant for access must follow vary from country to country, but in access regulations such as those in the Philippines and the Andean countries, they generally involve:

- submission by the applicant to the competent national authority of a proposal (see below);
- (in some procedures) public notification through publication of elements of the proposal in national and local newspapers. The Philippines Implementing Regulations, for example, call for public notification, through various media, of any collection activities, as well as local community and relevant sector consultation and notification;
- negotiation of contracts between the applicant and the competent national authority and also, if appropriate, between the applicant and other parties such as private landowners, indigenous groups providing traditional knowledge or *ex situ* collections providing access to specimens (see below);
- approval by government of the contracts and the proposal, and procedures for appeal if access is refused; and
- implementation, for example periodic reporting by the applicant on the use it is making of the resources accessed.

Typical of the requirements for the information to be contained in an access application so that any consent granted by the state can be 'informed' are those set out in the Philippines Executive Order and Implementing Regulations. This asks applicants to provide a letter of intent and an application form setting out the kind, number and quantity of specimens sought, the purpose and places of collection, and the foreign and local-counterpart researchers (Annexe B). Applicants must also attach a research proposal setting out the objectives and date of the project, the nature of the bioresources involved, methodology, the manner of collecting, the anticipated intermediate and final destination of the bioresources, how they are to be used, a description of funding and budget, foreseen impact on biological diversity, details of immediate and long-term anticipated compensation, and a list of in-country entities likely to receive compensation (Annex A). Other accompanying documents must include a letter of acceptance from Filipino counterparts, a letter of endorsement from the head of the institution with which the applicant is affiliated, an institutional profile of the applicant, and any others that the concerned government agency may require (Article 6.1).

The kind of terms that may be mutually agreed in access agreements are described in Section 2.2 above. This section will summarize briefly the different kinds of access agreements envisaged in various models of access legislation.

The *Philippines Executive Order* distinguishes between Academic and Commercial Research Agreements. The former are to be used by duly recognized Philippine universities and academic institutions, domestic governmental entities and intergovernmental entities where the genetic resources are intended for academic and scientific purposes. In contrast, Commercial Research Agreements are to be used by private persons, corporations and foreign international entities when the genetic resources are intended directly or indirectly for commercial uses.

The Procedure to Obtain a Commercial Research Agreement in the Philippines

- Step1: The applicant submits the following requirements:
  (a) letter of intent, and
  (b) three copies of the Research Proposal to the IACBGR through the Technical Secretariat; Filing fee of P25.
- Step 2: The Technical Secretariat conducts an initial screening of the application to determine whether the research is within the coverage of EO No 247;
- Step 3: If the proposed research is within the coverage of the EO:
  (a) the Technical Secretariat provides the applicant with a checklist of additional requirements to be submitted which include, among others, the following;
    - Duly accomplished application form;
    - Company/Institution/Organization /Agency Profile;
    - Environmental Impact Assessment (EIA); as determined by the Technical Secretariat; and
    - Processing fees in the following amounts:
    - Philippine national—P1,000 per application
    - Foreign national—P2,000 per application;
  (b) the applicant submits a copy of the summary of the research proposal, duly certified by the Technical Secretariat, to the recognized head of the indigenous peoples, municipal or city mayor of the IGU, PAMB, or private land-owner concerned for the required PIC Certificate (2.2.3, p. 28).
- Step 4: If the research proposal is not within the coverage of EO No 247, the Technical Secretariat issues a Certificate of Exemption and refers the proposal to the government agency that has jurisdiction over the project.
- Step 5: The applicant submits the PIC Certificate signed by the recognized head of the IP, municipal or city mayor of the LGU, PAMB, or private land-owner concerned, together with proofs of public notification and sectoral consultation.
- Step 6: The Technical Secretariat conducts an initial review and evaluation of the application and documents.
- Step 7: The Technical Secretariat submits the result of its evaluation, including the draft Commercial Research Agreement, to the IACBGR within 30 days from receipt of all requirements.
- Step 8: The IACBGR conducts a final evaluation of the application.
- Step 9: The IACBGR submits its recommendation to the Agency concerned.
- Step 10: The Secretary of the Agency concerned considers the approval or disapproval of the Research Agreement.

- Step 11: Upon approval of the application, the applicant pays the bio-prospecting fee as determined by the IACBGR.
- Step 12: The Agency concerned transmits the signed Research Agreement to the Technical Secretariat who shall furnish a copy to the applicant, IP, local community, PAMB, or private land-owner concerned.

(iii) La Vina A.G.M., "Intellectual Property Rights and Indigenous Knowledge of Biodiversity in Asia," 2(3–4) *Asia Pacific Journal of Environmental Law*, 1997, pp. 227–252

[*A particularly difficult issue within those raised by the provisions of the Convention on access to genetic resources and benefit sharing therefrom is the situation of resources provided by indigenous and traditional communities and the knowledge related thereto. Article 8 (j) of the Convention requires Parties to respect, preserve, and maintain the knowledge, innovations, and practices of indigenous communities; to promote their wider application with the approval and involvement of their holders; and to encourage equitable sharing of benefit from their use. The articulation of these requirements with those related to access to genetic resources, benefit-sharing, and intellectual property rights (IPRs) are considered in the document reproduced below.*]

Introduction

Biodiversity and indigenous peoples have an intimate link in most of Asia. It is no accident that along with the massive loss of biodiversity, indigenous cultures with their largely undocumented knowledge base are being wiped out. Because indigenous peoples live close to the earth and their individual and collective lives revolve around nature, much of this indigenous knowledge relates to biodiversity, habitats, ecological relationships and patterns.

The loss of "vast archives of knowledge and expertise" is "leaving humanity in danger of losing its past and perhaps jeopardising its future as well". The knowledge base of indigenous peoples is "humanity's lifeline" to a time when human beings accepted nature's authority and learned through trial, error and observation. But as the world's indigenous peoples are increasingly threatened by the destruction of the forests many of them call home, their irreplaceable knowledge is threatened as well.

The specter of cultural extinction hangs over hundreds of thousands of indigenous peoples who live in the forests of Asia. The tragedy is that the people most threatened by biodiversity loss are the very people who possess knowledge about living in harmony with nature that their countrymen competing for space in the forests need to learn. By ignoring the rights of indigenous and other long-term forest dwellers and insisting that forest resources are state-owned, national governments have provided economic and political elites with easy legal access to forest resources and short-term profits have been made by the favored few. But the costs in terms of forest degradation have been staggeringly high. Moreover, all those people who live entirely in and off the rainforests, are, due to the enormous amount of practical knowledge they have gained, the only ones who have mastered the art of exploiting the rainforests on a sustainable basis. Knowledge passed on through tens of generations about food plants, medicinal species, edible insects and their larvae, and the collection of wild honey among others have value almost beyond imagination.

The disappearance of the tribes and their cultures implies one cost that even the most narrowly pecuniary of economic planners should appreciate: the loss of knowledge of how to use the diverse forest species. The medicinal and other properties of the thousands of species present in the forest are prohibitively expensive to assess if done from random samples of vegetation. Much more efficient is a program of ascertaining the uses of species as known to tribal peoples. Little of the knowledge of how to use forest species has been recorded. Recording and using the knowledge that is now the near exclusive domain of indigenous tribes should be done with all due haste because of the unique value of such knowledge and because it supports a strong argument for maintaining intact significant tracts on the forests on which these groups depend for their survival.

There are fears, however, that passing this knowledge on to the dominant society would represent a "last theft" from the tribes. Hence, the tribes' lands and their right to exist must be guaranteed, independent of any economic value that the dominant society may see in preserving their cultures. Once all useful knowledge has been gathered from the tribes, they cannot be destroyed with impunity. In the end therefore, their right to exist is not a question of economic value but one of human rights.

This dilemma is particularly crucial as played out in Asia where most of the world's indigenous peoples live. Almost

70 percent of the estimated 250 million indigenous peoples in the world live in Asia. This same region is also one of the richest in terms of biodiversity, with species richness among terrestrial orders generally in the 40–60 percent range of global diversity. The Asia Pacific region, [states MacKinnon], includes:

> "three of the eight natural realms of the planet including the very extensive Malesian rainforests stretching from Myanmar to New Guinea, the world's richest subtropical and temperate forest systems in China and Indonesia, extensive monsoon and semi-desert habitats in India, Indochina and China and the world's most extensive high altitude deserts on the Tibetan plateau."

The marine biodiversity of the region is just as impressive. The marine areas of the region extend to two oceans—the Indian and the Pacific—which account for more than half the marine organisms of the world.

The major threats to this biodiversity are the "loss of habitat of living species and unsustainable levels of utilization of renewable resources." According to Mackinnon:

> "These threats can be further categorized as logging, fuel collection, over-hunting, land conversion, climate change, desertification, pollution, spread of exotic species, etc. In the most industrialized parts of the region, pollution and acid rain are seriously threatening natural habitats. Wildlife trade is also a growing problem which is very difficult to control."

Indigenous Knowledge in Asia

The range and breadth of indigenous knowledge in Asia is well-recorded and documented. Its utility has also been recognized. Indigenous knowledge in Asia includes information about natural resource management and utilization systems particularly on agriculture and the use of forest resources, traditional medicine and pharmaceuticals, and crafts and artistic designs.

In southeast Asia, traditional healers have been documented as using about 6,500 plants. Fourteen Asian indigenous communities possess what has been called "an enormous reservoir of cultural information that can provide useful guidance as to which pieces of the natural world are worth a closer look". The implications of this information are described by Kloppenburg:

> "Tapping this reservoir of knowledge has already proven effective. Three quarters of the plants that provide active ingredients for prescription drugs originally came to the attention of researchers because of their uses in traditional medicine. Accordingly, the NCI (National Cancer Institute of the United States) collection strategy involves close attention to indigenous medical practice and especially to the expertise of traditional healers and curanderos. Similarly, the USDA's (US Department of Agriculture) crop germplasm acquisition policy now gives priority to obtaining samples for which the ethnic source of the cultivar is described."

Indigenous knowledge of medicinal plants has been described as priceless information. According to [Elisabetsky]:

> "As with genetic diversity, once lost, it cannot be recovered. Without it, we must use random screening, which is like searching for a needle in a haystack. Past experience is the best argument here: 74 percent of chemical compounds used as drugs today have the same or related use in Western medicine as they do in traditional medical systems. It has been estimated that ethnobotanical information might have increased the yield of active plants by 50 to 100 percent in the National Cancer Institute (NCI) research program in the search for anticancer and anti-AIDS drugs."

The Misappropriation of Indigenous Knowledge

The threat to indigenous knowledge comes from three sources. First, the loss of their territorial base—through the destruction of rainforests or through their displacement by government projects or the commercial utilization of natural resources—makes it impossible for many indigenous communities to sustain their knowledge as well. Second, indigenous knowledge is also threatened by the introduction of so-called "modern" practices of, among others, agriculture and medicine. These new practices frequently replace traditional practices which ironically are often more sustainable or effective than the former. Third, indigenous knowledge is increasingly endangered by misappropriation of this knowledge by outside researchers. The tragedy is that it is the North or the developing countries, which often benefit from this misappropriation or intellectual piracy.

The example of misappropriation that has often been cited is that of the neem tree. The neem tree, which is native to Asia, has been used by local people for centuries for manifold uses: as a pesticide, a medicine, an antiseptic, a contraceptive, as building material, fuel wood and for agriculture. Recently however, over a dozen patents have been granted in developed countries on the medicinal and insecticidal properties of this tree. According to Genetic Resources Action International (GRAIN):

> "While Asians consider the neem to be part of a collective heritage, companies in the North are now patenting it. Monopoly rights have been assigned for the use of neem bark against cancer, stable and storable forms of the insecticidal component, neembased toothpaste, etc. All of these uses derive from centuries of indigenous knowledge and local innovation, as well as Asian people's efforts to nurture and conserve the valuable tree. Patenting of the neem in the North has struck many as a classic case of intellectual piracy, where scientists have added nothing fundamental to the understanding and use of the indigenous neem and yet are granted an intellectual and commercial monopoly over it."

Another example is the use of the rosy periwinkle. Irving S. Johnson [quoted by Axt], former vice-president of research at Eli Lilly and Co. states that:

> "two different groups were investigating the plant because of folklore suggesting the use of a tea of the leaves for diabetes. These reports were from the Philippine Islands and Jamaica. The plant, however, grows wild or is cultivated in most temperate and semitropical parts of the world. At the time it could be harvested because of its rampant growth in India and Madagascar, and it was grown commercially in Texas."

Johnson argues that the traditional knowledge as well as the genetic resources leading to the discovery of the vinca alkaloids and their use in the treatment of cancer came from many sources, not just Madagascar. He points out that if one argues that Madagascar's contribution should be compensated, then all the other countries involved should also be paid. Besides, according to Johnson, the traditional use was a remedy for diabetes while the pharmaceutical company ultimately developed a cancer treatment.

The National Cancer Institute of the United States, for example, is actively undertaking plant collection in different parts of the world, including Asia. It can be presumed that many of these collection efforts are premised on existing research which may include documentation of indigenous knowledge.

The National Cancer Institute of the United States, for example, is actively undertaking plant collection in different parts of the world, including Asia.

Customary Norms on Indigenous Knowledge

The accepted view on how indigenous peoples perceive indigenous knowledge is that such knowledge cannot be owned and that it is to be freely shared. Indeed, this cultural refusal to claim ownership, is a major obstacle that bars the use of intellectual property laws by indigenous communities seeking to protect their rights to their traditional knowledge. As Rural Advancement Foundation International (RAFI) observes:

> "There are approximately 15,000 culturally distinct ethnic communities in the world today and, while the diversity to be found among these cultures is both marvellous and extraordinary, most indigenous peoples share a sense of communal responsibility for their land and its living resources. It is rare to find a deeply-rooted culture that permits a patent like monopoly over the products and processes of life. It is largely because of this communal tradition that many indigenous peoples look upon intellectual property—especially related to life forms as a kind of blasphemy."

However, this view of "communal ownership" should be qualified. While indigenous peoples generally do not claim to "own", in a western sense, their knowledge, this refusal does not mean that there are no rights attached to such knowledge.

There is enough anthropological data to support the conclusion that such rights exist, that, in fact, much of the information and knowledge considered indigenous and traditional are not really freely shared with just any person within or outside particular communities. Instead, indigenous knowledge is classified into different categories according to the nature, characteristics, utility and even form of the particular information. The rights of the members of the community, as well as those outside of the community, to share particular knowledge is dependent on these categories. Thus, the knowledge of the medicine man or shaman as well as that of religious and political leaders are usually restricted to those called or chosen to this position. On the other hand, information concerning seed varieties and agricultural practices are more freely shared.

The error in concluding that there are no rights over indigenous knowledge because they are communally held is similar to the mistake of those who assert that indigenous peoples "communally own" their lands. The fact is that "communal ownership" does not exclude private rights (the community can exclude others outside) as well as individual rights (some forms of property are exclusively utilised by members of the community who may exclude even other members).

In the same way that "communal ownership" of lands has been misunderstood, the perception that indigenous communities do not recognize private and individual rights over knowledge and information is based on a lack of documented data over such rights. Indeed, in the course of the study of which this article is one product, the author interviewed many anthropologists who unanimously said that the issue of rights over knowledge has rarely been looked at by anthropologists and that this probably explains why very little documentation exists, and in their own experience, they can cite many examples of community as well as individual rights over knowledge and information, which in fact frequently includes the right to exclude others within and outside the community.

Traditional Healers: Monopoly of Information

Ritual and magic are essential elements in traditional healing practices of many indigenous communities. Their presence is probably the nearest thing to intellectual property rights (IPR). Through ritual, the traditional healer controls the use of knowledge "by connecting the use of a particular treatment with rituals and magic" which he or she alone can perform. Thus, another member of the community would believe that a treatment would not be effective unless accompanied by the healer's ritual.

In the Philippines, for example, the Babaylans of the Manobos clearly restrict information and knowledge on healing rituals to themselves. Violating this exclusionary norm subjects the infringer to social ostracism as well as a threat that the *Diwatas* (spirits) will punish him or her. Many traditional healers in southern Africa feel the same way [states Cunningham]: "that this knowledge should certainly not be available to the public; even within their own societies, much of this knowledge is kept private through ritual and taboo".

To become a healer or priest is a calling that not all persons within the indigenous community are called to or are qualified to be. Among the Lisu in Thailand, for example, to become a *mo muang* (priest), a man must pass a selection test conducted in front of the village spirit shrine. Candidates are usually married men with children and have other family responsibilities. Before they become candidates they must already have a good knowledge of ritual. The position cannot be inherited and for as long as a *mo muang is* a resident in the village where he was "chosen" he cannot give up the post. His duties only end when he leaves the community.

Indigenous Knowledge and Intellectual Property Rights

What is incompatible about the concept of IPR with indigenous knowledge is not so much that the latter is freely shared but the very fact that "ownership" is claimed over it by human beings. It is this cultural refusal to claim ownership over knowledge—as well as many natural resources—that makes resort to IPR rules, as a means of protecting rights to indigenous knowledge, objectionable to many Asian indigenous peoples.

On the other hand, even in cases where information and knowledge are usually shared, many indigenous peoples, in Asia and elsewhere, rightly look with suspicion at efforts by outsiders to document such knowledge and information. Their historical experience—of their lands and minerals being taken away from them—justifies this scepticism. As McGowan and Udeinya observe:

> "The resources of indigenous peoples have long been a target of state governments and commercial enterprises. Gold, timber, crops, land, oil, minerals, water, fisheries and art have all been sought or taken from native

> peoples. Now indigenous knowledge of complex healing systems combining plant medicines, local ecology and spiritual care is yet another resource being taken and used by others. For many indigenous peoples, it looks like more of the same. Many indigenous peoples and healers refuse to share their cultural knowledge with outsiders, viewing this use of their cultural knowledge as yet another resource appropriation without permission, payment, recognition or proper respect."

This scepticism is reflected, for example, in knowledge about agriculture particularly folk seed varieties. Like their brothers and sisters all over the world most Asian indigenous peoples as well as farmers have traditionally shared seed freely with each other and with their neighbors. However the increasing privet control and manipulation of seeds by private companies for commercial gain is beginning to change this. The result is that many Asian indigenous communities are now reluctant to share their folk varieties freely. While this may be a sad development, it is also necessary. Indeed, the starting point for protecting indigenous knowledge is simply to refuse to share information with outsiders.

Indigenous peoples throughout the world are beginning to see that the protection of indigenous knowledge is intimately linked with the concept of IPR In the *Mataatua Declaration on Cultural and Intellectual Property Rights of Indigenous Peoples* [extracted by Greaves], the indigenous peoples present declared that:

> "cultural and intellectual property are central to the right of determination and that, although the knowledge of indigenous peoples is of benefit to all humanity, the first beneficiaries of indigenous knowledge must be the direct indigenous descendants of such knowledge."

The Declaration recognizes that:

> "Indigenous Peoples are capable of managing their traditional knowledge themselves, but are willing to offer it to all humanity provided their fundamental rights to define and control this knowledge are protected by the international community."

In sum, as a Maori leader articulated it, the most fundamental intellectual property right of indigenous peoples is the "right to define what their intellectual property is: the right to determine the extent and the meaning of the body of knowledge which shapes, and is in turn shaped, by their cultural heritage".

Asian Intellectual Property Rights Regimes

The IPR regimes that currently dominate in Asia all originate from the western model of intellectual property rights. The only significant difference between the IPR systems of the North and the regimes which operate in Asia is the treatment of national interest. Asian IPR systems sometimes exclude or restrict the recognition of intellectual property rights where fundamental national interests are involved.

The particular laws that are relevant to the question of indigenous knowledge and the challenges posed by biotechnology are the laws on patents, copyrights, trade secrets and trade marks. The emphasis of many of these laws has always been on individual interest and national interest and not the interest of specific communities in a state. Unfortunately, in many cases in Asia, national interests—often linked to the interests of elite economic classes—is not equivalent to the interests of communities. Indeed, historically, national interests have often collided with the interests of local communities, particularly indigenous peoples.

Asian IPR systems are individualistic because they are designed to recognize and reward individual inventors. Like western IPR systems, a major objective of Asian IPR laws is to ensure that the rights of inventors and those who support them are protected. Asian IPR regimes are also characterized by an emphasis on national and state interests. This characteristic of statism is found in many IPR laws of Asian countries and is founded on the belief that IPR systems must serve the interests of the nation state.

Like many developing countries, most Asian countries maintain generally less extensive systems of intellectual property protection. They insist on the right to design IPR systems to specific national circumstances. This differential treatment has created friction under international trade laws. China, for example, experienced trade sanctions from the United States for refusing to bow down to demands for stricter enforcement of IPR norms. This is also one reason, among others, why the developed countries insisted on the TRIPS agreement under GATT.

In general, developing countries, including most Asian countries, have seen IPRs as a barrier to development, restricting the ability of industry to innovate and imitate This perception is reflected in compulsory licensing provisions that are found in many Asian IPR systems. "Compulsory licensing" laws usually require that inventors make their invention available to all those prepared to pay. In some cases, compulsory licenses may be awarded by patent tribunals if the inventor fails to make the invention adequately available to society. Under this system, the right of the patent holder to charge royalties for the use of the invention which presumably, allows inventors to seek a fair return on the research investment, is respected.

Many patent systems in Asia are rooted in the colonial histories of the states in the region.

Patent Systems in Asia

Asian patent systems share the same basic definition of a patent as their western and northern counterparts. A patent is considered a form of industrial property right which is designed to legally protect the invention which must generally be new, and commercially useful. The granting of a patent results in the patentee having a monopoly right over the invention. With such a right, the holder of the patent can exclude others from making, using or selling the invention for a period of about ten to twenty years.

Many patent systems in Asia are rooted in the colonial histories of the states in the region. Hong Kong, India, Malaysia, Singapore and Sri Lanka, borrowed from the British legal tradition. Japan, at least outwardly, looked to Germany, and the Philippines was influenced by US law. Notwithstanding the diverse colonial backgrounds of the patent systems of many Asian states, these systems have much in common. By and large, most Asian patent systems have as common elements:

- restrictive rules on what may be patentable;
- the fact that priority is determined by the first inventor to file;
- the requirement that the patent application must be disclosed to the public;
- the opportunity given to the interested public to oppose the application;
- the requirement of public disclosure for commercial gain prior to filing results in a prohibition on its patenting;
- the fact that someone who invents and patents an improvement is generally entitled (for a fee) to work the pioneer or senior patent;
- provisions allowing compulsory licensing in specified cases; a cumbersome registration procedure; and
- an undeveloped enforcement mechanism.

For an invention to be patentable, most Asian patent laws require the same elements as in western IPR systems: the invention must be useful and novel (not publicly known or used by others), and must satisfy the standard of inventiveness or "nonobviousness". The subject of a patent may include any useful process, machine, or composition of matter. In this context, mere discoveries are not patentable.

A review of existing Asian IPR regimes reveals the following conclusions:

- On the basis of the texts of the legal provisions alone, life forms are not patentable in Asia except in Thailand which explicitly allows for the patenting of biotechnological inventions.
- The works which are patentable remain principally industrial in nature.

The widening of the scope of patent protection in the North have implications for developing countries, including those in Asia. First, even if most Asian countries continue to exclude genetically engineered life forms from the scope of patent protection, this restriction may be meaningless in the international and global context. Indeed, an exclusionary rule may work against the interests of those Asian countries which are investing heavily on biotechnology as a future industry. Second, the internationalization of IPR standards mandated by TRIPS may pressure Asian states to recognize patents from the developed countries even when these patents cover subject matter not patentable in their respective IPR systems. While countries like India have so far resisted pressure to amend its patent laws to recognize life-forms, there is no guarantee that this refusal is sustainable. Third, the present texts of Asian patent laws are not—as the experience of the United States and Europe has shown—absolute barriers to the widening of the scope of patent protection. At present, Japan, South Korea and Thailand have already widened the scope of patent protection to include most biotechnological products. There is no legal barrier to do the same in Thailand. It remains to be seen how the other countries in the region will respond to this challenge. What is certain is that in the near future, if it is not happening now, patent applications for genetically modified life forms will be filed.

A survey of the filing and registration procedures required by Asian patent systems reveals a very complex and cumbersome process. Patent application goes through the process of filing, acceptance, opposition, grant and maintenance. In most cases, publication in an official gazette or in a newspaper is essential. Other extensive preliminary requirements must be followed.

Enforcing the rights to a patent when violated is even more difficult. In most cases, weaving through the patent system of an Asian country involves engaging in both administrative and judicial litigation. Enforcement measures could range from defending an existing patent in the patent office to civil and criminal law suits involving infringement.

In sum, the filing and registration of a patent as well as enforcing rights when they are granted will require substantial financial, administrative and legal resources on the part of the patent applicant or holder.

Copyright Laws in Asia

Copyrights were traditionally designed to protect works of art and literature. Copyrights as a form of intellectual property are unlike patents in that they do not protect ideas but rather their expression. Copyrights can cover artistic and literary work, computer programs, and commercial designs. Copyright law may also indirectly protect rights relating to biodiversity, including rights of indigenous peoples to their traditional knowledge.

The common elements in Asian copyright systems are:

- the originality of the idea expressed as a condition of granting the copyright;
- protection from unauthorized use, reproduction, distribution, sale, and adaptation; and
- a period of time in which the author's rights are protected, usually the life of the author plus 50 years.

Copyright infringement results in liability for the violator who may be ordered to stop the acts of infringement, to pay damages and to deliver, for confiscation and destruction the infringing texts, materials or devices. Criminal remedies may also be resorted to. However, all these remedies, as in enforcing patent rights, are dependent on the availability of substantial financial and legal resources.

Trade Secrets and Trademark Laws in Asia

Trade secrets serve as an alternative to patent protection. Trade secrets can be availed of to protect valuable knowledge which does not meet the requirements for patentability. A trade secret can continue perpetually so long as the formula, information, or device remains secret. In plant breeding, for example, the lines used to produce a hybrid may be defended as secrets indefinitely. The owner of a trade secret may license, disclose, or assign the right to use the trade secret, subject to an agreement to hold the information in confidence.

In the Asian context however, the law on trade secrets is largely undeveloped. Like many developing countries, trade secrets are not encouraged in Asia where monopoly of knowledge and information is perceived principally as an obstacle to national development.

Trademarks are labels attached to traceable goods bearing the name (or some brand name) of their owners. They are resorted to for the purpose of identifying the source of the goods in question. Trademarks, when registered, are protected for a number of years (from ten to 20 years in Asia) with an option for renewal.

Trademark law can be useful in cases where eco-labelling is appropriate. Trademarks can protect the competitive advantage of the company providing the green product, and the revenues can be returned to the source of the product through licensing and other contractual arrangements. Indeed, a product that is perceived to have been derived in a sustainable way can enjoy a competitive advantage among consumers around the world simply because it is perceived as "green". One example where the approach has worked is in Brazil where indigenous peoples raised funds by sustainably producing nuts and materials for cosmetic products.

In sum, a trademark attesting to the authenticity of indigenous peoples' work would be useful if the trademark were widely known among consumers.

Using IPR Laws to Protect Indigenous Knowledge: Limitations and Possibilities

The foregoing survey of Asian intellectual property rights laws clearly shows that using IPR laws to protect the rights of indigenous peoples to their traditional knowledge will at best be very limited. Indeed, Asian IPR regimes were clearly not conceived to recognize the intellectual contribution of indigenous peoples.

There are three classes of problems that must be confronted in using Asian patent laws to protect the rights of indigenous peoples. First, there is frequently a cultural obstacle to the claiming of ownership over knowledge of genetic and biological resources. Second, the forms and expression of indigenous knowledge are incompatible with the requirements of patentability. And, third, applying for rights under these laws as well as protecting and enforcing rights once granted are frequently impracticable for indigenous peoples.

Ownership by Indigenous Peoples over Life-forms

Most indigenous peoples in Asia reject the proposition that knowledge of life-forms, whether natural or altered, can be owned. They share this belief with others who oppose such claims on ethical, political or economic grounds. The rejection of claims of ownership over knowledge of living matter flows logically from the refusal of many indigenous peoples to claim, at least in the western sense, ownership over natural, genetic and biological resources themselves. As such, even more unacceptable is the concept of ownership over living products and life processes including the regeneration of life.

Unless changes in the cultural worldview of indigenous peoples with respect to what can and what cannot be owned take place, it would be very difficult for indigenous communities to even make the first step in all IPR mechanisms—the filing of a claim of ownership. To some extent, this change is happening in the area of land claims where many indigenous communities are now pressing claims ownership as against the state as well as against private persons.

Whether or not indigenous knowledge fulfils the criteria of patentability becomes the next obstacle to recognition of IPR over indigenous knowledge. Of view is that since patents and copyrights are available only for new knowledge these mechanisms cannot be used to protect traditional knowledge which has existed for a long time.

From a legal point of view however, this is not an insurmountable obstacle indigenous knowledge fulfils the criteria of patentability in most cases. Besides, the conflict between international trends in IPR and the rights of indigenous people emerged precisely because there is still a substantial amount of knowledge and information which remains within the limited confines of indigenous communities—and not shared by others.

A related problem is that patents and copyrights are conferred on individual or corporations rather than community ownership. Indeed, the traditional concept of IPR is that they grant private rights to individuals to the exclusion of others within a society. Indeed, under IPR laws, the concept of community invention is not recognized. What is usually required is that an inventor is an individual or group of named individuals.

This bias in favor of individual ownership is also not an insurmountable obstacle to patenting indigenous knowledge. Fundamentally, patents and other IPR laws grant private rights and not necessarily individual rights. As in the case of land, there is nothing in IPR laws which prohibits communities from claiming ownership over ideas.

Communities however must resort to conventional legal means to acquit juridical personality. And assuming that they find an acceptable mode (such as incorporation), they would still have to contend with the issue of how to keep the IPR rights already granted to them. This is especially difficult if the knowledge patented is shared by different communities.

These questions emphasise the practical difficulties of resorting to prevailing IPR laws as modes of protecting rights to indigenous knowledge.

The Practical Difficulties of Using Patents

The more difficult obstacles to using patent laws to protect rights to indigenous knowledge are the practical problems associated with the procedures of filing and registering the patent claim, and when granted, protecting the rights conferred. The process of filing and registration as well as enforcement is complex, cumbersome and expensive.

In sum, engaging in the patent system will demand unreasonably high technical, financial, administrative and legal resources on the part of indigenous peoples. Clearly, by themselves, most indigenous peoples do not have these resources. The only way that they may successfully use the patent system is if they link up and collaborate with individuals or groups with these resources. Indeed, even if they have the necessary resources, it is probably not advisable from a cost-benefit point of view to use these resources for IPR protection.

These difficulties and obstacles also apply to other IPR laws such as copyrights, trade secrets and trade marks. In particular, the cultural barrier of refusal or reluctance to claim ownership over knowledge of living things remains a formidable obstacle.

Theoretically, communities could document their indigenous knowledge in some tangible medium and obtain a copyright under most Asian laws. Ethnobotanists may also write and publish articles or books on traditional knowledge and voluntarily share the copyright with the indigenous people.

In copyright law, as in the case of patents, the same problem of the individual's versus the community's claim of ownership is present. The "author" of traditional knowledge is rarely an individual but a community. Moreover, the period of protection, if indigenous knowledge is truly to be protected, should continue as long as the community survives. This kind of "perpetual" protection would be incompatible with the copyright system. Moreover, the copyright would only protect the specific expression, not the knowledge being expressed. Under copyright laws, others could still use the knowledge they discover or learn from books, articles, and films.

The law on trade secrets may also be resorted to by indigenous peoples. Among others, a traditional healer's knowledge of the medicinal use of a plant or of a method passed down over generations might be protected as a trade secret. However, the utility of trade secrets is limited because of the difficulty in establishing, protecting, and enforcing them. Theoretically, indigenous knowledge could be considered as a trade secret if others within and outside the community are excluded. But once this knowledge is shared or when it is documented and published, by an anthropologist for example, trade secret rights are extinguished.

Finally, utilizing the law on trademarks is also not a promising mode of protection. First, it does not meet the needs of communities to protect works that have already been widely copied. Second, the law on trademarks does not protect indigenous knowledge related to biological products or processes but protects only non-living works.

Resorting to the IPR laws which currently prevail in Asia is not, on the whole, a promising strategy for indigenous peoples to take. While small windows of opportunity are available in using IPR laws, applying the conventional IPR approaches to indigenous knowledge is likely to do more harm than good.

On the theoretical plane however, there is nothing inherent in IPR laws which prevents its use by indigenous peoples. Working with other sectors, such as public agencies, academic institutions, or nongovermental organizations, indigenous peoples might succeed in using IPR mechanisms to protect indigenous knowledge. However, to successfully weave through the IPR system, indigenous peoples might be compelled to make fundamental changes in their worldview. Moreover, the costs of engaging in the system would probably outweigh the potential economic benefits. In this sense, the decision to pursue IPR could distract attention and energy from more useful initiatives.

Asian Indigenous Peoples and the IPR Challenge: Response Strategies

The IPR challenge to the indigenous peoples of Asia and elsewhere is not a challenge for indigenous peoples to assert ownership over knowledge or living things. Rather it is how, under the shadow of the widening and strengthening of IPR on the international as well as national level, indigenous peoples can best nurture and protect indigenous knowledge.

At its core, the response to the IPR challenge must consist of efforts to affirm responsibility and control over traditional knowledge and to things produced through its application. The ultimate objective of these efforts is "to preserve meaning and due honour for elements of cultural knowledge and to insure that these traditional universes, and their peoples, maintain their vitality". Other objectives are "to manage the degree and process by which parts of that cultural knowledge are shared with outsiders and, in some instances, to be justly compensated for it.

Towards this end, the response framework to the IPR challenge should be one that allows indigenous peoples "to ensure the intellectual integrity of their ongoing innovations rather than to obtain intellectual property". According to RAFI: "Ultimately, a combination of initiatives, that could collectively be termed the 'intellectual integrity framework' may prove most appropriate."

RAFI proposes a spectrum of initiatives to realize this, including:

- Intellectual Protection—the rights of indigenous peoples to their traditional knowledge should be protected through different mechanisms within and outside the IPR system. Indigenous peoples should not be compelled to endorse or support IPR systems in order to have their intellectual integrity protected.
- Intellectual Recognition—the utility of indigenous knowledge should be recognized. Indigenous peoples must work with other sectors to ensure that credit,

and compensation where appropriate, is given to indigenous communities for their contribution to the conservation and development of biodiversity.

- Intellectual Development—indigenous peoples must be supported so that they can extend their existing systems of information-exchange and cooperation. Linkages between indigenous peoples and with other sectors—such as farmers, scientists and anthropologists—are essential to attain this objective.
- Intellectual Exchange—indigenous peoples should actively participate in the social decision process that characterizes the IPR debate. They should discuss the issue among themselves and with others, at the community, national, regional and international level.

Territorial Integrity and Intellectual Integrity

Despite differences in historical and political contexts, most indigenous peoples in Asia and elsewhere share similar problems resulting largely from colonization. To benefit from local resources and to establish effective political power, the colonizers and subsequently the nation states which replaced them "took the land away from the natives".

A common colonial history has left indigenous groups with four basic needs: "namely the need for (a) cultural protection; (b) recognition of land claims; (c) recognition of individual, economic and social (welfare) rights; and (d) political autonomy."

All these needs and the rights corresponding to them are however intimately interrelated. Demands for cultural protection, which includes the preservation of traditional subsistence patterns as well as the protection of indigenous religions and languages, cannot be separated from the recognition of indigenous land rights. Without a secure territorial base, cultural rights become meaningless.

The primary struggle then of Asian indigenous peoples continues to be their struggle for territorial integrity. Indeed, the IPR challenge must always be seen in this context for it to be meaningful for them. Initiatives to deal with this challenge must support the primary struggle. The fore provided by the IPR debate should therefore be seen as additional and new opportunities for insisting on territorial recognition.

All IPR related initiatives must be premised on the recognition of the integrity of the territory of indigenous peoples. Without a comprehensive and effective recognition of the right of indigenous peoples to control access and utilization of their ancestral lands and domains, all efforts to realize the intellectual integrity framework is irrelevant and bound to fail. Moreover, if not linked to the struggle to gain territorial integrity, all initiatives to respond to the IPR challenge would ultimately be diversionary.

Territorial integrity includes the following elements:

- the delineation of ancestral lands and domains;
- the recognition that indigenous peoples communally hold and control (not necessarily "own") these lands as against the state and other private persons;
- the acknowledgment that within indigenous territory, the customary law of the indigenous community must generally be followed; and
- in cases, where history justifies it, the recognition of political autonomy.

The ultimate success of an intellectual integrity framework, as a response to the IPR challenge, is dependent on the degree of success that Asian indigenous peoples attain in realizing the elements of territorial integrity. At the same time, the IPR challenge provides new venues and fore for their realization.

A look at specific national and international response strategies reveals how the IPR challenge presents new opportunities for indigenous peoples to assert their claim for territorial integrity. These are discussed below.

National Response Strategies

Response strategies to the IPR challenge, at the national level, may include:

- the enactment and enforcement of regulations to govern bio-prospecting and access to genetic resources;
- using existing IPR laws, limited as they are; and
- legislating new IPR norms and mechanisms such as inventor's certificates, a law protecting folklore, and recognizing community intellectual property rights.

Access Regulations and Bio-prospecting

One immediate response of Asian indigenous peoples to the IPR challenge is to lobby and work for the immediate formulation, enactment and enforcement of regulations governing access to the genetic resources within their territory. It is politically possible to attain this because it is also in the interests of most Asian states that these resources are protected from both destruction as well as piracy that may result from bio-prospecting.

At present, bio-prospecting—defined as the research, collection and utilization of biological and genetic resources for purposes of applying the knowledge derived therefrom to scientific and/or commercial purposes—is happening throughout Asia. This prospecting is done by both foreign and local collectors.

Philippine Bio-prospecting Regulation

A major problem in Asia is that there are no statutes which explicitly regulate bio-prospecting—effectively giving collectors free access to genetic resources. In the Philippines, Executive Order 247 was issued to regulate this activity. It contains provisions on prior informed consent of indigenous and other local communities which may have value for other countries. The regulation is far from perfect. Indeed, some have criticized it for even allowing bio-prospecting at all. Unfortunately, the reality is that this activity is happening and that it is being done by Filipinos themselves—usually for and on behalf of a foreign company. A major goal therefore of the regulation is to ensure that all information about bio-prospecting becomes available to the public, that before the activity is undertaken indigenous and local communities have given their prior informed consent, and that both the country and communities benefit from its result. Above all, what Executive Order 247 does is to make the activity of bio-prospecting transparent so that interested parties may make decisions and act on them with the proper information.

The order requires collectors to enter into a contract with an interagency governmental body which includes representation from nongovermental organizations and indigenous people's organizations. However, as part of the process of giving consent, indigenous communities can compel the collector to enter into a Materials Transfer Agreement—containing provisions on compensation, capacity building, and technology transfer—with them.

Corporate Practice

It should be noted that there are companies which specialize in using indigenous knowledge to facilitate prospecting. Shaman Pharmaceuticals, for example, explicitly states that it is committed to developing new therapeutic agents by working with indigenous and local people of tropical forests and in the process contributing to the conservation of biocultural diversity. Shaman is also on record as directly acknowledging ethically and financially the intellectual property rights of indigenous people with whom it works. Their strategy is to immediately compensate indigenous peoples for their contribution.

Whether Shaman will live up to its commitments is a question that remains to be seen. Whether the advantages of entering into an agreement with a company such as Shaman outweigh the dangers is a question every indigenous community must confront. The point however is that the national legal system must provide for minimum rules in which these contractual arrangements can be made. Access and bio-prospecting regulations are ways which this can be provided for.

There are companies which specialize in using indigenous knowledge to facilitate prospecting.

Rules on access to genetic resources and bio-prospecting are not the only answer to the IPR challenge. However, they have immediate utility. They can, if properly formulated and enforced, slow down the process of genetic and intellectual piracy. And they can give indigenous peoples some breathing space to acquire the needed capacity to make the right decisions.

The Case of Human Genetic Material

Collecting genetic materials from indigenous peoples, as is being done under the Human Genome Project, is a different question altogether and should be excluded from rules regulating access to genetic resources. Collecting and patenting human cell lines have both ethical and political underpinnings and cannot be considered as a simple act of bio-prospecting. Indigenous peoples must lobby and work hard for an absolute prohibition on such activity at least until they can make a more informed stand about the activity.

Using IPR Laws

It was pointed out earlier that using Asian IPR laws to protect the rights of indigenous peoples to their traditional knowledge is at best limited. Existing IPR laws are not only incompatible with the cultural worldview of most indigenous peoples, but engaging in them also requires legal, financial and administrative resources which most indigenous peoples do not have. Moreover, if they do have such resources, it is far better to spend them on the primary struggle of attaining recognition of territorial integrity.

The only way that existing IPR laws can be used by Asian indigenous peoples is if they work together with public or private institutions, such as government agencies and nongovermental agencies, to acquire and defend patents, copyrights, trade secrets or trade marks. In any case, even in this instance, indigenous communities who choose to engage in the IPR system must be willing to conform to the market and commercial premises of the system. This could include setting aside fundamental cultural and ethical biases.

One way however of using existing IPR laws is to lobby Asian governments not to recognize patents over life-forms. There is a cogent argument why national governments of the region should delay recognizing such patents. Indeed, as the Crucible Group points out:

> "No country should be coerced into adopting an IP system for living materials. There are valid ethical and practical reasons why each country should be allowed to reach its own position and either adopt an existing mechanism for protection, create a new mechanism better suited to national interests, or encourage innovation by other means altogether."

Indigenous peoples should also monitor developments in the national and international arenas, making sure that no patents, copyrights or trade marks are granted for knowledge which is based on indigenous innovation.

Another strategy for dealing with the IPR challenge is to lobby and work for new laws on intellectual property rights, laws which provide for norms and mechanisms more compatible with the nature and characteristics of indigenous knowledge. Examples of such laws includes the recognition of Inventors' Certificates, the UNESCO Model Law on Folklore and a law recognizing community intellectual property rights.

Inventors' Certificates is an IPR option which, unlike other IPR laws, is not based on an exclusive monopoly. They discard financial compensation altogether in favor of non-monetary awards and nonexclusive licensing arrangements. According to RAFI:

> "Governments can establish Inventors' Certificates through uncomplicated national legislation; they need only notify WIPO and GATT that this legislation exists. Forms of recognition or compensation can be determined either through legislation or through regulation which can vary by category or by case. Governments can adjust the terms of compensation to promote local innovations in domestic or export markets or to attract a foreign invention where access to that invention is deemed to be in the national interest."

Inventors' Certificates would permit governments the flexibility to:

- vary the methods of recognition;
- permit or exclude monetary compensation; grant exclusive or non-exclusive licenses;
- ensure that the patented technology is applied or manufactured nationally;
- establish other transfers of technology conditions beneficial to the importing country;
- vary the period of protection; and
- attach any other contractual provisions deemed beneficial.

Another option is to work and lobby for the enactment in Asian states of the Model Law on Folklore, adopted in 1985 by both UNESCO and the World Intellectual Property Organization (WIPO). According to RAFI: "This model law affords indigenous communities three unique elements that are especially appropriate to the protection of biological products and processes." First, "communities" (rather than specific individuals) can be the legally registered innovators; they can either act on their own behalf or be represented by the State. Second, community innovations are not necessarily fixed or finalized, but can be ongoing or evolutionary and still be protected by intellectual property law. Third, communities retain exclusive monopoly control over their folklore innovations as long as the community continues to innovate.

The Model Law however has been interpreted to exclude scientific inventions. Based on the experience of the application of conventional patent laws, this is not an insurmountable objection. RAFI points out that existing IPR laws:

> "Expressly exclude protection for plants, animals, pharmaceuticals, and chemicals, but many national patent offices have interpreted the law to permit the patenting of such innovations on the assumption that if legislators had known "then" what they know "now", they would not have made these exclusions."

A similar argument could apply to the case of indigenous knowledge.

Still another new initiative that could be pursued is a law recognizing an alternative rights regime for indigenous knowledge. In such a case, the claim of indigenous communities would differ from standard IPR claims which are characterized by individualism and commercialization. It is based on the premise that indigenous communities create collective rights thus the whole community will be deemed the rightful owner of such creativity or innovation. Nijar points out that this alternative rights regime rejects "the notion of a one shot concept of innovation which typifies industrial innovations". It recognizes that:

> "The creation of indigenous communities is often accretional, informal, and over time. The knowledge is continuous as it modifies, adapts and builds upon the existing knowledge. This would pave the way for the recognition of cumulative innovations and knowledge. This will also mean that the innovation cannot be dealt with without regard to the past, present and future owners' and beneficiaries of the knowledge."

A Word of Caution on New Laws

While the three alternative legal approaches discussed above hold promise for the protection of rights to indigenous knowledge, indigenous peoples must seriously weigh the consequences of supporting the adoption of any or all of them. Progressive as they appear, these alternative approaches are still, at its core, IPR mechanisms. As such, they all require registration procedures as well as elaborate administrative arrangements. Moreover, even if rights to indigenous knowledge were granted under these alternative approaches, enforcing and defending these rights would still require substantial resources from communities. The option of course is to rely on the state for protection and enforcement. Given however the political economy of most Asian states, and the extent of the marginalization of indigenous peoples within these states, it is probably not realistic to rely on such an option.

An additional factor to be considered is the fact that, as the Crucible Group observes, IPR policy and practice is in such a state of flux that: "not only the rules of the game but the game itself may be changing as science and society grapple with the marketing of new bio-materials." Given this state of IPR, governments as well as indigenous peoples should not enact policies or legislation that cannot be changed rapidly if new circumstances demand it. Indeed:

> "If governments are unable or unwilling to rescind or revise legislation, they would be ill advised to lock into new legislation now. If institutes or people's organizations find it difficult to review and revise policy, they should be equally cautious."

International Response Strategies

The national strategies must be accompanied by a coherent international plan of action. A regional response to the IPR challenge would be an essential step to formulate and implement such a plan. RAFI has proposed different initiatives that may be valuable for Asian indigenous peoples to support. Some of these initiatives are relevant only in the international arena. Others may also be applicable at the national level. Another important avenue for protecting rights to indigenous knowledge at the international level is by resorting to the emerging international law of the human rights of indigenous peoples. Indeed, this may prove to be a more effective legal mechanism for protecting indigenous cultural knowledge than the international law of intellectual property rights. By linking the IPR issue to the primary struggle of indigenous peoples for recognition of territorial integrity as well as political autonomy, a more coherent, relevant and effective response to the IPR challenge will be possible.

Conclusion: The Urgent Tasks

Responding to the IPR challenge demands three urgent tasks from the indigenous peoples of Asia:

- unity within communities,
- unity among peoples, and
- unity with other sectors.

A significant consequence of the IPR challenge is that it could be divisive of indigenous communities and peoples. Because access to indigenous knowledge could translate into commercial gain for outsiders, indigenous communities or persons within such communities will be tempted to enter into contractual arrangements with bio-prospectors or gene collectors. So long as there is prior informed consent and so long as the social decision process of the community, in particular its customary law, is followed, there should be no objection to decisions to enter into these arrangements. The problem arises when consent is not informed, when it is given only by a few or not at all or when it is given outside community processes. To deal with the IPR challenge, an indigenous community must be united.

The IPR challenge could also result in divisions among peoples. Indigenous peoples in one country and within a region could be pitted against each other and end up competing with each other over contractual arrangements. Real disputes over who has prior rights over knowledge, once freely shared, could erupt. Again, indigenous peoples, in countries, in Asia and elsewhere, must be united if they are to effectively deal with the IPR challenge. Finally, the IPR challenge demands that indigenous peoples examine closely the need to collaborate with other sectors of their respective societies as well as the international community.

Indigenous peoples must also be willing to work with lawyers, anthropologists and other social scientists.

The IPR challenge cuts across sectors. In many ways, the predicament and problems it brings to indigenous peoples is similar to what confronts most farmers of the South. There are, in a real sense, "in the same boat". Indeed, in the IPR issue, an alliance with farmers is justified and essential.

Local scientists from developing countries are confronted with analogous, if not similar, dilemmas as indigenous peoples. The need to conserve genetic resources while local capacity is being built and developed is a common concern shared by both scientists and communities. An alliance between both sectors is therefore desirable for an effective response to the IPR challenge.

Indigenous peoples must also be willing to work with lawyers, anthropologists and other social scientists. The nature of the IPR challenge is that it can only be understood and responded to in a multidisciplinary context.

Working with nongovermental organizations, ranging from environmental organizations to groups specializing in genetic resources and intellectual property, will also be useful. Resort to such organizations would particularly be important for monitoring the dizzying pace of change in IPR policy and practice.

Finally, the State. Most nation states of Asia generally emerged as successors of colonial masters. As such, historically, the Asian states and the indigenous peoples within them were usually at odds with each other. It was often seen to be in the national interest, such as national elites, to disregard the rights of indigenous peoples. Depriving indigenous peoples of their territory was seen as necessary so as to expand state power and control. In the IPR issue, however, national interests and the interests of indigenous peoples may coincide. For it is in the national interest, in an economic and political sense, of many Asian states to restrict the scope of patentability and other IPR protection. It is in the national interest for the state to ensure the conservation of genetic resources as well as the protection of indigenous knowledge. Perhaps, finally, in a common response to the IPR challenge, indigenous peoples and Asian states can be allies. In sum, the IPR challenge is not merely a threat to indigenous peoples. It should likewise be seen as an opportunity to use another approach to securing territorial integrity.

(iv) The Crucible II Group, Seeding Solutions Volume 1. *Policy Options for Genetic Resources: People, Plants and Patents Revisited*, the International Development Research Centre, the International Plant Genetic Resources Institute and the Dag Hammarskjöld Foundation, pp 53–59, 63–69

[Two other particularly problematic issues relate to agricultural genetic resources, a subject traditionally dealt with by FAO, and the Consultative Group on International Agricultural Research (CGIAR), created in 1971. Toward the end of the negotiations of the CBD, it became apparent that the rules developed under the Convention regarding access and benefit sharing, based on the concept of bilateral agreements between a provider and a user of genetic resources, were not readily applicable to the special case of genetic resources used for food and agriculture. The negotiators, therefore, adopted a resolution (Resolution 3 of the Nairobi Final Act), requesting the FAO to resolve the outstanding issues of Farmers' Rights and of the status of ex-situ collections collected prior to the entry into force of the CBD. As underlined by the Crucible II Group, and explained in this extract:

> *'The CBD's decision to cede the issue of Farmers' Rights and ex situ collections to FAO underscores some of the complexities and peculiarities of dealing with agricultural genetic resources in a bilateral framework. In contrast to those genetic resources that are rare and geographically localized, such as wild*

plant species of pharmaceutical interest, the market value of agricultural biodiversity is not easily established, and it is especially difficult to determine its origin because of the widespread diffusion and adaptation of crop genetic resources worldwide. A bilateral access and benefit-sharing framework for agricultural biodiversity is, in most cases, extremely complex, if not impossible. Negotiations under way on the revised International Undertaking (see below) are considering a broader, multilateral approach to access and benefit-sharing for some major crops which seeks to avoid the problem of linking benefits or compensation to specific transactions for specific genetic resources, and tying those benefits to a single country of origin.']

The Revision of the International Undertaking

In the late 1970s, developing countries and CSOs first raised political concerns over control, ownership and access to plant genetic resources for food and agriculture (PGRFA) at the FAO. At that time, PGRFA were considered by virtually all governments to be the 'common heritage of mankind'. Developing countries at FAO began to argue, however, that common heritage implied the existence of common responsibilities to safeguard genetic resources. They also began to question the contradictory nature of free access to plant genetic resources of the developing world in the face of proprietary rights for new plant varieties developed by institutional plant breeders. They asked: Why are proprietary seeds, originating in the developing world, bringing royalties to institutional plant breeders in the industrialized world without corresponding compensation for the original donors/innovators of the genetic material? Who is responsible for conserving plant genetic resources? Who controls access to genetic material, and what mechanisms are needed to ensure reciprocal benefits between the industrialized world and the developing world?

It was with this political background that governments created the *International Undertaking* in 1983. Now, in the light of the Rio Earth Summit and the CBD, governments are working to update the IU to address new issues—or the same old issues dressed for the nineties.

In the years following its adoption, many governments came to recognize that the IU is incomplete and contains ambiguities requiring clarification. Over the past decade, in fact, three interpretative resolutions were adopted to clarify concepts and terms in the IU. One of the main objectives of the current revision of the *International Undertaking* is to harmonize its provisions with the CBD's principles of national sovereignty over PGRFA, access, prior informed consent and sharing of benefits. The CBD negotiators specifically requested that FAO's Global System resolve two outstanding issues of particular relevance to agricultural biodiversity—the question of Farmers' Rights and the status of *ex situ* collection in existence prior to the CBD. Negotiations to revise the IU were initiated in this context in the mid-1990s, although it has not yet been decided, in its final form, whether the IU will be (1) under the FAO constitution, (2) on its own as a stand-alone treaty, or (3) under the auspices of the CBD as a protocol.

Renegotiation of the International Undertaking was on the agenda of the April 1999 session of the Commission on PGRFA. A single negotiating text was accepted as the basis for negotiation. There is a basic agreement to develop a multilateral system of access to PGRFA. Under such a system, access to PGRFA and the resulting benefits would be open to all parties who are participants in the multilateral system on access and benefit sharing. Three outstanding issues dominate the current IU negotiations: scope and access, benefit sharing and Farmers' Rights.

Scope and Access

The scope of what plant genetic resources the IU will cover, and the question of how access will be regulated, are key issues in the negotiations. It is generally agreed that the scope of the revised IU would cover all plant genetic resources for food and agriculture, but that governments may wish to determine a multi-tiered system of access ranging from 'free access' to certain species under a multilateral system, to a 'not free' or restricted access system subject to bilateral exchange agreements (which could be monitored or maintained with the assistance of a multilateral facility). There is a growing willingness to accept a relatively free flow of germplasm among signatory states for some food crops already widely dispersed and utilized by plant breeders. However, plant species less widely available and/or having high commercial value (i.e., coffee, high-value spices or medicinal plants) would be restricted and their access controlled, subject to bilateral negotiations. Initially, a limited range of crops would be available for multilateral exchange, but the lists would be maintained as an annex to the IU, and could be dynamic over time. However, some countries pointed out during the April 1999 negotiations that ongoing revision of the lists is problematic.

Many issues are not finalized. Will the revised IU apply to materials collected both before and after the CBD entered into force, or just those acquired prior to the CBD? Will CGIAR collections have a separate status? Will non-parties to the IU be denied or restricted in their access to materials (including those of the CGIAR)?

Generally speaking, many developing countries approach 'scope and access' defensively. There is concern that they are being asked to donate their germplasm freely while some industrialized countries allow for claims to temporary exclusive monopoly on the same material through intellectual property regimes. A number of independent studies have suggested that—while collectively invaluable—it is next to impossible to determine the commercial worth of single germplasm accessions. In fact, the monitoring costs of tracking gene flows could exceed the actual financial returns to countries of origin.

The status of germplasm protected under intellectual property is controversial. For many developing countries, it is particularly important that this germplasm should be fully part of the 'free' multilateral exchange system. This is material with defined commercial value and is a vital part of the contribution from the North, necessary to balance the South's richer store of unexploited potential. IP owners, however, contend that IP-protected material is already freely available, to the extent appropriate—which (they say) is for use in breeding development, rather than in direct commercial exploitation of unmodified material. Material protected by plant variety rights can be freely used in further breeding. The research exemption for patented material is generally more restrictive. In the United States it appears that the research exemption is so narrow that researchers are not allowed to use propagating material that includes patented material within it, even if the patented material is bred out of (i.e., not included in) the researcher's final product. The law in the UK on this point appears to be somewhat more lenient; there it seems that the researcher can use the material to create something new, as long as the patented portion is not in the final product. In jurisdictions that have practically useful research exemptions, the only material that researchers could not use would be that which is protected by trade secret law.

CSOs offer another range of views on the issue of access to PGRFA. Some believe that farming communities should either develop their own intellectual property regimes for farmers' varieties—or adopt non-IP, *sui generis* mechanisms to defend their rights. Others regard any non-traditional constraints to germplasm exchange (be they IP or non-IP, *sui generis*) as self-defeating since such approaches, they argue, would undermine community plant breeding.

Benefit-Sharing

How will countries that are donors of germplasm to the multilateral system share in the benefits derived from those materials? What is the benefit-sharing mechanism? Should it be voluntary or mandatory? Some governments argue that developing (and other) nations are adequately compensated for their germplasm merely by having access (free or royalty-tied) to the information and breeding material created by open, international exchange. Others consider this a 'trickle-down' approach that does not adequately recognize the contribution of farming communities and national governments. Efforts to proportion the contribution and benefits from germplasm exchange and plant breeding have left all sides uncertain and frustrated, especially in light of the fact that there are few funds available, even in industrialized countries, to support this goal. National budgets for PGRFA are facing severe constraints and cutbacks, in both industrialized and developing countries.

Some parties suggest that benefit sharing might best be achieved through the full implementation (including new and additional financing) of the Leipzig Global Plan of Action (GPA). Various scenarios have been devised under which industrialized countries would make financial contributions to the GPA through membership fees to the multilateral exchange 'club', while developing countries (as well as industrialized countries) would make their germplasm available to club members. In effect, the membership 'fee' for developing-country members would be germplasm rather than money. Again, conditions for scope and access might vary and one or more species categories could be entertained. All members of the multilateral system would be able to access the germplasm and the funds on the basis of approved programs and projects in line with the rolling GPA. Not surprisingly, there are many nuances to this scenario and many concerns about prohibiting IP claims on germplasm in the multilateral system.

There is increasing recognition that the future role of the CGIAR's international centers, and its mandate to conduct agricultural research in service to the world's poor, is one possible concrete mechanism for sharing the benefits of PGRFA. In light of the growing importance of the CGIAR centres, there is concern among governments and CSOs that aspects of ownership, trusteeship, governance and the rules regarding access and exchange of CG germplasm be strengthened and clarified.

At the First Inter-sessional Meeting of the Chairperson's Contact Group of the Commission on Genetic Resources for Food and Agriculture, held in Rome, 20-24 September 1999, negotiations focused on benefit-sharing within the multilateral system. All nongovermental observers were excluded from participation, with the exception of IPGRI, representing the CGIAR. There was general agreement that some global benefits could arise from the use of PGRFA under a multilateral system, through the exchange of information, access to and transfer of technology, capacity-building and the sharing of benefits on commercialization. Many outstanding issues are still under negotiation, including financial matters. For example: while access to technologies, improved varieties and germplasm will be provided and facilitated, will it be subject to applicable property rights and access laws? Are there special circumstances under which access to and utilization of information and technology protected by IP agreements and confidentiality can be made freely available? How can parties give practical expression to the fair and equitable sharing of commercial benefits? How will parties establish and/or strengthen programs on capacity-building, and who will determine priorities? What role will the Global Plan of Action play? Negotiations on these issues will continue at the next meeting of the Chairman's Contact Group in early 2000.

The Issue of Farmers' Rights

The principle of Farmers' Rights, endorsed by the FAO in 1989, recognizes that farmers and rural communities have contributed greatly to the creation, conservation, exchange and knowledge of genetic resources, and that they should be recognized and rewarded for their past and ongoing contributions.

Many governments and CSOs have embraced the principle of Farmers' Rights, not only as a counterpoint to Plant Breeders' Rights (as it was initially proposed), but also as recognition of the innovative role that farmers and rural communities play in the conservation and further development of genetic resources and their right to benefit from it. In 1991, the Keystone Dialogue (held by a multi-stakeholder group that brought together representatives from government, CSOs, scientists and the private sector) attempted to elaborate the meaning of Farmers' Rights by suggesting that it includes the right to germplasm, information, financial resources, technologies, and systems of research and marketing. The Keystone Group suggested that a concrete way of recognizing Farmers' Rights would be to create a fund to support genetic conservation and utilization programs. It was also agreed in Keystone that farming communities had the right to save and exchange seed. (Although an international fund was created in the 1980s by the FAO Commission as a channel for countries, governments, CSOs, private industry and individuals to support conservation and sustainable use of plant genetic resources, it was voluntary and existed primarily on paper.)

Perhaps because Farmers' Rights was conceived as a political term, it has been especially difficult to define it in legal terms. It has been debated continuously over the past decade, and is a key aspect of the ongoing renegotiation of the International Undertaking.

Support for the 'principle' of Farmers' Rights is a mile wide and (some would argue) an inch deep. As the IU negotiations proceed at FAO it remains unclear whether or not Farmers' Rights will ever be implemented—or whether their implementation will be solely at the national level and not at the international level. CSOs and some governments have posed additional elements for Farmers' Rights that may go beyond its original definition. Critics insist that the range of claims being made under the Farmers' Rights umbrella far exceed the mission of either the FAO Commission on Genetic Resources for Food and Agriculture (CGRFA) or the CBD and must either be reduced or dropped altogether. Others wish to limit the debate on Farmers' Rights within CGRFA to the right to save seed and to have access to genetic resources while leaving wider land and culture issues to the UN High Commissioner for Human Rights. Still others see Farmers' Rights as a vague statement of principle and appreciation but nothing more and insist that the realization of Farmers' Rights can only occur at the national level.

In the context of PGRFA, implementation of the Leipzig GPA (see next section) would be one way to implement Farmers' Rights effectively. Some have suggested that the implementation of Farmers' Rights through the Leipzig GPA could mean that farming communities might have special access to resources and special recognition in the governance structure for the multilateral exchange system or 'club'. Following the World Food Summit, others have suggested that some elements of Farmers' Rights might be included in the current review of 'the Right to Food' being jointly undertaken by the UN Human Rights Commission (UNHRC) and FAO. A study on the Right to Food submitted to the Human Rights Commission urges that Farmers' Rights should be addressed by the human rights community and promoted as part of the right to food. A third element has evolved along the lines of the right of farming communities to 'say no'—to opt out of germplasm exchange or enhancement systems they regard as counterproductive.

At the April 1999 Commission meeting, the debate on Farmers' Rights focused on the right of farmers to save seed from their harvest. Ten years before, when the FAO Commission recognized that Plant Breeders' Rights were not incompatible with the IU's objectives, the prevailing model of PBR (the 1978 UPOV Act) was widely presumed to permit farmers to re-use proprietary seeds. Since then, however, there has been a general tendency in government and industry to constrain or curtail the unlicensed replanting of proprietary material through national intellectual property legislation or through new scientific developments such as genetic seed sterilization (genetic use restriction technology or 'terminator' technology). Although the situation is hotly disputed, UPOV's 1991 Convention has also been widely interpreted as a move to prevent farmer plant-back. The UPOV 1991 Act contains an option for a farmers' exemption under which UPOV member states may exempt farm-saved seed from the breeders' right 'within reasonable limits and subject to safeguarding the legitimate interests' of the breeder. While the 1978 UPOV Act allowed implicitly for farmers to exchange limited amounts 'over the fence' the 1991 UPOV Act allows for farmers to use for propagating purposes on their own holdings only those seeds that they have obtained from their own holdings. This casts doubt on the possibility of exchanging seeds for planting on one's own holding. However, UPOV provides that subsistence farmers (and others) may use protected seed 'for purposes that are private and non-commercial'. These issues became central to the debate at FAO.

The Unique Role of the CGIAR in Facilitating Access and Exchange

The Consultative Group on International Agricultural Research, established in 1971, is an informal association of public and private donors that supports a network of 16 international agricultural research centres (IARCs), each of which has its own governing body. The CGIAR's mission is to use science and technology, in partnership with other organizations, to increase food security, alleviate poverty and protect the environment. With a budget of approximately US$340 million per annum, the CGIAR oversees the largest agricultural research effort in the developing world. The CGIAR Secretariat is housed in the World Bank (Washington, D.C.) and the group's major donors include the World Bank, Japan, the USA and the European Union.

Through its 16 international institutes, the CGIAR manages approximately 600,000 seed samples which amount to approximately 40 percent of the world's unique germplasm in storage worldwide. Because IARC gene banks contain 'inventoried' germplasm, their collections are considered among the most valuable genetic materials, both because they are more readily identifiable and accessible to institutional breeders than farmers' varieties or wild crop relatives and because of the large amount of information available on the individual samples. The vast majority of crop germplasm held in the IARCs was collected from farming communities in the developing world. But to whom that treasure ultimately belongs, and to whom a genebank is accountable, has been the subject of controversy and debate.

The Issue of Internationally-Held *Ex Situ* Collections (and the 1994 FAO/CGIAR Trust Agreements)

As an interim step in addressing the status of *ex situ* collections, the CGIAR and FAO signed agreements in October 1994 that place most of the gene bank material from CGIAR centres under the auspices of FAO, to be held 'in trust' for the world community. Under the 1994 Trust Agreement, all designated germplasm is to remain in the public domain, ensuring as far as possible a continuing unrestricted flow of germplasm to all researchers. The FAO Commission on Genetic Resources for Food and Agriculture is responsible for setting policy for a network of *ex situ* collections, which includes the centers' in-trust collections.

CGIAR centres routinely distribute germplasm to plant breeders through material transfer agreements (MTAs). The Trust Agreement also requires CGIAR to prohibit recipients of designated germplasm from applying for IPRs on the germplasm or related information. (Recipients who have not signed MTAs—for example those who obtained material prior to 1994—are not legally bound by these restrictions.) The Trust Agreement does not prohibit CGIAR patenting or claiming any other IPRs with regard to material isolated from designated material, such as cells, genes, etc. The CGIAR guidelines, which have never been formally adopted but only 'accepted', require the authorization of the center where a recipient wishes to apply for IPRs with regard to such isolated materials. However, these guidelines do not form part of the FAO/CGIAR Trust Agreement. Furthermore, the MTAs allow breeders to use designated material for breeding purposes and to apply for Plant Breeders' Rights with respect to their new varieties.

In late 1997 and 1998, documented examples came to light wherein recipients of CGIAR designated germplasm applied for intellectual property or otherwise asserted proprietorship over germplasm. While neither governments nor breeders are obliged to adhere to the FAO-CGIAR Trust Agreements, these acts were in contradiction to those agreements as endorsed by the governments of the institutes involved. Of course, insofar as governments or breeders are parties to the contractual provisions enshrined in a material transfer agreement they are obligated to respect those terms. These examples raised serious questions about FAO's and CGIAR's capacities to implement the accords and whether or not the trust arrangement served a useful purpose. Special concern was raised with respect to material transfer agreements used by CGIAR centers when exchanging trust germplasm.

In response to the situation, the Chair of CGIAR called for a moratorium on the granting of IP rights on all designated plant germplasm. In October 1998, FAO and CGIAR adopted a new procedure confirming what each party would do if trust germplasm becomes the subject of proprietary claims.

According to some CSOs, abuses are widespread. In September 1998 the Canadian-based Rural Advancement Foundation International (RAFI) and the Heritage Seed Curators Australia (HSCA) released a report documenting 147 examples of plant intellectual property claims (PBRs and patents), which they considered dubious. According to the HSCA/RAFI report, in more than one-third of the cases cited the plant varieties were collected in foreign countries and submitted for PBR without any evidence of breeding. According to RAFI and HSCA at least 16 of the suspect claims—granted and/or pending—are believed to involve germplasm under the FAO Trust Agreement. The report charges that systematic abuses are taking place showing that plant patents are predatory on breeding work undertaken by farmers and indigenous people around the world.

Breeders' associations and UPOV, while admitting that rights may sometimes be granted when not justified, deny that this is a general problem. They do not accept that any abuse has been proved. Registration procedures may not call for proof of breeding work—in any case, absence of evidence is not evidence of absence. Even if all the alleged 147 abuses were conclusively proved, argues the International Association of Plant Breeders for the Protection of Plant Varieties (ASSINSEL), these represent a mere 0.45 percent of all Plant Breeder's Rights granted over the past five years, and only 0.15 percent of the samples distributed by the CG centers. ASSINSEL points out that most of the alleged violations involve public breeders, who are often not completely aware of the complex system of IP and MTAs. It would not be cost-effective, argues ASSINSEL, to spend a great deal of money to monitor so few violations. In response, RAFI and HSCA note that their study focused primarily on 118 Australian claims which amount to 6 percent of all applications made to the Australian PBR office since the legislation was adopted in that country. The PBR violations, asserts RAFI, were those that were clearly visible based on available documentation—a more in-depth and well-funded study would likely uncover many more violations. ASSINSEL, however, believes that such a study would show that many of the original allegations were unfounded.

Breeders' associations and UPOV, while admitting that rights may sometimes be granted when not justified, deny that this is a general problem.

Ultimately, six Australian PBR claims were abandoned or withdrawn in 1998 after alleged abuses were brought to light. In addition, the Australian PBR Office in Canberra has published revised standards for assessing PBR applications that are designed to improve protocols and correct potential abuses. Nevertheless, in May of 1999, RAFI uncovered yet another instance, also in Australia, where a government institute was apparently claiming rights for a CGIAR-bred wheat variety. Prompt action by the center involved put an end to the claim.

What is designated germplasm under the FAO/CGIAR Trust Agreement? The Trust Agreement states that CGIAR centres shall not claim legal ownership over designated germplasm or related information. According to guidelines elaborated by the International Potato Centre (CIP), 'related information' refers to passport and characterization data, and when available in the databases of the respective genebanks, evaluation data and information on indigenous knowledge. Cells, organelles, genes, etc., from designated germplasm are not specifically mentioned in the agreement. The general rule of law is that recipients of materials do not require the permission of the provider to patent further innovations derived from such materials. The CGIAR Guiding Principles adopted in October 1996 require centers to impose obligations on recipients that they protect such derived inventions only with the agreement of the supplying center. However, the Guiding Principles do not form part of the FAO/IARC Trust Agreements, and may therefore be changed or even disregarded. In any case, they depend on the centers requiring and enforcing special agreements with recipients.

According to CIP guidelines, authorization for a recipient of designated germplasm to seek IPRs on a new variety can only be given by a center if the new product (through an intellectual contribution) is significantly different from the originally transferred material (i.e., a product whose main characteristics and aptness are other than those of the initial material provided).

Some breeders also are anxious for greater clarity in their dealings with germplasm provided by centers. They can accept wholeheartedly the obligation not to protect for their own benefit materials and information received from the centers. However, it is not clear to commercial breeders why they should be forbidden by CGIAR to apply for IPRs on materials that are significantly different. Guidelines such as CIP's are appropriate given the mandate of the centers to ensure that designated germplasm does not become encumbered by IP rights. Commercial breeders say that they will respect those restrictions. However, if they are unable to seek protection on any material derived from germplasm from gene banks, they will end up not using such germplasm. These policies, they claim, could therefore jeopardize use and further development of designated germplasm. In the absence of IP protection, the investment will not be undertaken by industry because it could not be recovered—and valuable existing materials will be neglected. Potential benefits, they claim, are withheld from farmers and consumers for fear that breeders should make profits.

The FAO/CGIAR Trust Agreement specifically refers to germplasm and related information. The latter includes, where applicable, information on indigenous knowledge which should be protected according to Article 8(j) of the CBD. However, the MTA used by the CGIAR centers to transfer designated germplasm does not specifically refer to this obligation. The FAO/CGIAR Trust Agreement does not cover cells, organelles, genes, etc., from designated germplasm, although this is covered in the centers' IP guidelines and thus it is left up to the individual center to enforce—without reference to the intergovernmental authority of the FAO.

Recent events demonstrate that it is difficult for the CGIAR centers to monitor recipients of designated germplasm. In addition, CGIAR centers lack mechanisms to counter violations of MTAs. Technically, gene markers on designated germplasm could be used to track utilization by third parties. Centers could, through FAO, alert governments in countries where violation has taken place. However, governments will not necessarily see it as their role to enforce the MTAs, which have only the status of private agreements. These problems deserve further consideration. Some would say it is not clear why it is vital for the centers to devote expensive resources to monitoring infringement of contractual IP rights arising from MTAs, yet inappropriate for them to take out other kinds of IP rights.

It remains unclear whether or not the parties to the Trust Agreement can construct an effective monitoring system that not only links information on trust germplasm to CGIAR use and exchange of that germplasm but also connects to national and international databases for PBR and patents.

Governments need to address the unresolved issue of *all* pre-CBD collections. The Nairobi Final Act, 1992, referred to the need to address all pre-CBD *ex situ* collections, meaning both domestic, national and international collections. Although the issue of rights over germplasm actually involves all pre-CDB *ex situ* collections held by any public or private institution in any foreign location, most of the international debate focuses on the CGIAR's gene bank material. Not only does the CGIAR have a vast and generally well-cared-for collection but it is the largest source of germplasm held by any 'international' body.

Some parties believe that any CGIAR material whose collection location is documented should be surrendered by IARCs to the country. The country may or may not wish to have the collection repatriated or duplicated. Among those who share this view are some who regard the FAO-CGIAR Trust Agreement as a political ploy engineered by the CGIAR even as the CBD was coming into force in order to avoid surrendering the germplasm to its rightful owners.

Some others insist that the actual history of the Trust Agreement makes it obvious that the CGIAR collectively and centres individually were forced by public pressure to accept the connection to FAO which they dearly wished to avoid. Indeed, it was the row that took place at the last meeting of states before the first COP (held in Nairobi in June of 1994) that literally railroaded the IARCs into accepting FAO authority over their collections. At that time, some governments in the CBD accused the World Bank of attempting to take over the IARC gene banks in order to bargain with the WTO for a special status for the CGIAR. The debate forced the CGIAR, they claim, to agree publicly to the Trust Agreement and to make the System rush to sign the agreement that October before the first COP session in Nassau in November.

Still others consider both of these scenarios to be too dramatic. The CGIAR's mission to increase food production, eradicate poverty and protect the environment in developing countries depends on the fullest possible exchange and use of plant genetic resources for food and agriculture (PGRFA). Furthermore, agrobiodiversity is a critical component of environmental conservation. The growing politicization and legal ambiguity posed a threat to the exchange and use of PGRFA and spurred the CGIAR to look for a means to ensure that the collections be used for the benefit of the world community. Placing the collections under the auspices of a United Nations body—the FAO—and in trust for the world community was seen as the best mechanism available (pending finalization of the revision of the IU) to ensure the collections be deployed for the benefit of the world community. They believe the concept of repatriating gene banks is not a feasible option. It is technically complex because the germplasm held in genebanks may have developed its distinguishing characteristics somewhere other than the collection location. It is no simple matter to return germplasm to its 'rightful owner'.

D

Biosafety

Article 19.3 of the CBD obliges the Parties to consider the need for a biosafety protocol, and provided some guidance for the Parties' consideration of this issue, which started soon after the CBD entered into force. A Protocol on Biosafety was concluded in Montreal in January 2000. An overview of its provisions and of the process which led to its adoption is given below.

(i) Burhenne-Guilmin F., "The Biosafety Protocol is Adopted in Montreal," *Environmental Policy and Law*, 2000

The *Cartagena Protocol on Biosafety* was adopted on 29 January, in Montreal, by representatives of some 130 nations. The adoption is a memorable event, concluding seven years of efforts. This is the first Protocol under the *Convention on Biological Diversity*.

The breakthrough came at dawn, when hope of a successful conclusion had almost been given up. It took the whole night to arrive at the last compromise formula of this difficult negotiation—dealing with the treatment of "commodities" in the text.

The subject of biosafety was already on the agenda of the negotiators of the Convention, an instrument which aims to provide a comprehensive and holistic approach to all issues of relevance to biological diversity. The matter raised such controversy that it was not possible to deal with its substance in time for the adoption of the Convention before the Rio Summit, where it had to be open for signature. Instead, negotiators agreed to postpone consideration of binding rules regarding biosafety, and adopted Article 19.3 which obliged Parties to the Convention to consider at a later date the need for, and requirements of, a protocol "setting out appropriate procedures, including, in particular, advance informed agreement, in the field of the safe transfer, handling and use of any living modified organism resulting from biotechnology that may have adverse effect on the conservation and sustainable use of biological diversity".

The mandate was not lost sight of, and a Panel was set up by the Executive Director of UNEP in 1993. The first Conference of the Parties to the Convention (COP-1) met in Nassau, the Bahamas, from 28 November to 9 December, 1994) then proceeded to establish an Open-ended *Ad Hoc* Working Group of Experts on Biosafety. The second COP (Jakarta, Indonesia, in November 1995) discussed the consequences of the results of the experts' work, in particular the fact that a large majority of the participating delegations favored the development of a Protocol: it decided to embark on a negotiation process to develop a protocol on biosafety "focusing on transboundary movements of any living modified organism (LMO) resulting from modern biotechnology", established an Open-ended *Ad Hoc* Working Group on Biosafety (BSWG), and provided it with detailed terms of references (Decision II/5).

While progress on conceptual common concerns was achieved in Vienna, it was clear that the real confrontation would take place once specific language hit the table.

After four meetings of the Group, which took place between July 1996 and February 1998, it had become clear that the goal set by the COP of completing BSWG before the end of 1998 was unrealistic. The deadline was extended until early 1999, and an Extraordinary COP convened for February 1999 in Cartagena, Colombia in order to adopt the Protocol. At the end of 1998, a set of 40 articles had been prepared, but 13 of these remained "entirely square-bracketed", indicating lack of agreement on their content. The scope of the Protocol, for example, whether products of LMOs would be covered, remained controversial, as did a series of other points, including liability provisions, and those related to the precautionary approach. Altogether, the staggering number of over 600 square brackets adorned the text!

The sixth and last meeting of the BSWG met in Cartagena immediately preceding the Extraordinary session of the COP. In spite of the efforts by delegations, as well as the Chairman of the BSWG Veit Koester (Denmark), and the President of the ExCop Juan Mayr (Colombia), the negotiations failed, and the ExCOP session was suspended. A decision gave the Bureau of COP 4, together with ExCOP Chair Mayr, the mandate to convene a resumed session if and when possible.

The shock caused by this was profound, and the nature, more than the number, of the unresolved issues was so deeply divisive that discouragement prevailed at first. Progress at Cartagena, had, however, not been negligible. Many articles had been approved provisionally; negotiating groups with specific positions had emerged. Most importantly, the very reason for which negotiations were started—to define rules for the transboundary movement of LMOs intended for introduction into the environment—had found acceptable solutions. There were four unresolved "core issues": first, the scope of the Protocol (beyond LMOs intended for introduction into the environment); second, the treatment of "commodities", a term used to describe LMOs intended for use as food, feed or for processing (LMO/FFPs); third, the precautionary approach or principle; and fourth, the relationship between the protocol and existing trade-related agreements.

Armed with these sizeable accomplishments, and a communicative energy and optimism, Chairman Mayr embarked on a series of informal consultations, first with the spokespersons of the negotiating groups which had formed in Cartagena (Montreal, July 1999); based on the expression of political will to conclude the negotiations. Mayr proceeded to convene a fully-fledged informal meeting in Vienna (September 1999), organized to allow for the exchange of views within and between groups. During the final two days, spokespersons for each group sat at a round table to address the remaining four core issues in terms of concepts rather than attempting to draft precise language. The format of the meeting became the "Vienna setting", which was used again during the third and final informal consultations, which took place in Montreal immediately before the meeting of the resumed Extraordinary COP and also during the ExCOP.

While progress on conceptual common concerns was achieved in Vienna, it was clear that the real confrontation would take place once specific language hit the table. This is what the Montreal consultations set out to produce over the four days available to the Groups. A "non-paper" from Chairman Mayr, suggesting textual elements based on the results of the Vienna consultations, facilitated the process. Each of the Groups (Miami Group, Like-minded Group, EU, Central and Eastern European Group, and Compromise Group) responded to the Chair draft, and agreed to his proposal to proceed with the discussion of clusters of issues: scope, commodities, relationships with other agreements, and precautionary approach.

Scope and commodities were tackled first, and encouraging progress was made in group negotiations behind closed doors, with periodic reports to shorter and shorter informal plenary sessions. Only shortly before the beginning of the ExCOP were the third and fourth clusters open for discussion—a consequence of their intense political nature.

On the eve of the ExCOP opening, the fate of the Protocol was still very uncertain—significant progress had been made but no final agreement reached, on two core issues; uncertainties still surrounded the "relationship" cluster, as well the treatment of the precautionary approach.

As a result, the formal negotiations during the ExCOP continued in virtually the same format as the informal ones, the only difference being that by mid-term the political climate became unbearable: over 30 ministers responsible for biosafety were in Montreal, and while there was no time to hear any formal statement they might have wished to make, the pressure of their presence and the active role they took in the behind-the-scenes talks became an important and politically decisive factor: a compromise on the remaining issues had to be found; a second Cartagena was not an option. Nevertheless, this nearly happened: while the rumors of a positive outcome on the question of relationships with WTO-related agreements and the precautionary approach led to optimistic prognosis about the end result, the final plenary session convened for 28 January in the late afternoon to adopt the Protocol was postponed from hour to hour. Just before midnight, it was clear that a final confrontation was taking place. Not about the relationship between the protocol and trade-related agreements, or scope...but still on the precautionary approach and also the requirement to identify commodities as containing or not containing LMOs.

The question of "segregation", "identification" and "documentation" accompanying commodities containing LMOs was a heated issue right from the start. It caught up with the negotiators as the last bastion defended by the Miami Group to agree on the otherwise acceptable negotiation package. The Miami Group had consistently argued that it was virtually impossible to ensure segregation and labelling, while the EU considered it a prerequisite to consumers' right to know. In the end, a compromise was agreed between the two groups, that commodities should be labelled as "may contain LMOs", a formula which leaves open the option to provide more information on whether the commodity contains LMOs or not. The compromise was apparently agreed upon by the other groups, including the Like-Minded Group, which hastily convened on the floor of the main room at 4:00 a.m. to 'take it or break it', and agreed to consent. The Plenary was reconvened at 4:40 a.m., and adopted the Protocol at 4:50 a.m. by consensus. It was a breathtaking moment—and a near escape!

The Protocol was immediately hailed as a success, auguring well for the environment and sustainable development in the new millennium. It has been hailed as a success since then, from all quarters, including the environmental community, industry and negotiators themselves.

Is this enthusiasm justified? The question must be answered to a large extent in the positive, while some aspects provide justifiable cause for anxiety. The scope of the Protocol is broad, a goal consistently pursued by the Like-Minded Group; it applies to the transboundary movement, transit, handling and use of all LMOs that may have adverse effects on the conservation and sustainable use of biological diversity. Two exceptions are mentioned in separate articles (pharmaceuticals for humans which are dealt with in other international agreements; and LMOs for transit and contained use). They are both limited in extent: in the case of pharmaceuticals, Parties remain free to subject import to risk assessment if they so wish, and in the case of transit and contained use, it is not the protocol in its entirety which does not apply, only the Advance Informed Agreement (AIA) procedure.

The most difficult question on scope had been whether LMOs intended for direct use as food, feed or for processing (LMO/FFPs) should be covered or not. These include commodities such as tomatoes and corn. Some, in particular the members of the Miami Group, argued that they should be excluded, as they pose no threat to biological diversity. Many others, in particular the Like-Minded Group, argued that once these products were in circulation, it would be impossible to ensure that they were not introduced into the environment, accidentally or not. At the end of Cartagena, the principle of the inclusion of LMO/FFPs within the scope of the Protocol was established. The question then became to what extent they would be submitted to the same rules as those LMOs intended for introduction into the environment. Here, of course, large industrial interests were at stake.

The question is linked to the cornerstone of the Protocol, namely the application of the Advance Informed Agreement (AIA). The AIA procedure provides for the Party of export to notify the Party of import before the first import of an LMO for which the procedure is mandatory. The importing party has 90 days to indicate whether the import may proceed with or without written consent. If written consent is required, the party of import has 270 days from the date of receipt of the notification to indicate whether the import is approved with or without conditions, or refused, or the decision delayed for a specific period of time, or whether additional information is requested, in accordance with the Party of import national legislation or the protocol itself (in particular risk assessment according to Annex II). The lack of a decision within the 270 day period does not imply consent. In addition, lack of scientific certainty does not prevent the Party of import from taking a decision.

The AIA clearly applies to the transboundary movement of LMOs for intentional introduction into the environment of the Party of import. However, it can be derived from various articles in the Protocol that it does not apply to pharmaceuticals for humans, LMOs in transit or intended for contained use, or LMOs which have been identified by a decision of the meeting of Parties to the Protocol as not likely to have adverse effects on biological diversity, taking into account risks to human health. It also does not apply to the transboundary movement of LMOs/FFPs for which a significantly less demanding procedure is provided.

It has been pointed out that, as a result, the AIA applies only to a limited number of LMOs, such as seeds, which are exported with a view to being grown in the country of import. Transboundary movements of LMO/FFPs—for instance, fruit and vegetables for direct consumption, or seeds for feed—are subject to another set of provisions. Parties making final decisions regarding the domestic use of a LMO/FFP shall inform the other Parties through the Biosafety Clearing House Mechanism within 15 days. Importing Parties may take a decision according to their national legislation, which has to be consistent with the objective of the Protocol. Developing countries or countries in transition which do not have such regulatory framework may apply the procedure provided by the Protocol itself, i.e., require a risk assessment, followed by a decision within a timeframe not exceeding 270 days. Again here, failure to take a decision does not imply consent to import, and lack of scientific certainty does not prevent that Party from taking the decision it deems appropriate.

While this system remains based on the decision of the country of import, it does not require notification by the exporter, and thus is less burdensome for them. In order to function, however, it requires the identification of the LMO/FFPs through accompanying documentation. The system would otherwise be unenforceable.

The question of segregation between commodities containing LMOs and those which do not, as well as the documentation which should accompany them for transboundary movements, was a critical point from the start of the negotiations, and a major concern for the Miami Group. It was the last point to be agreed upon on 29 January, with a formula which postpones "detailed requirements" until a decision is taken on this subject by the meeting of the Parties to the Protocol, within a timeframe of two years. Until then, LMO/FFPs will have to be identified, at the minimum, as "may contain" LMOs, and as not intended for introduction into the environment.

Central to the philosophy of the Protocol is the precautionary approach; yet whether and how this should be reflected in the Protocol's text remained contentious until the very last round of negotiations, when referring to it in the Preamble as a "guiding policy principle" was acceptable to all. Mentioning it in the article on "Objective" passed the acceptability test with some difficulty, but most resistance was met by the proposed inclusion of precaution language as an accepted tool of decision-making for importing Parties of LMOs for introduction into the environment and, *a fortiori*, for LMO/FFPs. The supporters of this "operationalization" of the precautionary approach (which included, prominently, the EU) prevailed: lack of scientific certainty shall not prevent importing Parties to take decisions, as appropriate, in both cases. This is a real breakthrough for all those who believe that precaution, distinct from prevention, has an important role to play at all levels of decision-making.

Last but not least, the relationship of the new Protocol with the WTO-related agreements was a very divisive subject. At the end of Cartagena, an article of the draft clearly declared the supremacy of trade rules over the Protocol, an objective of the Miami Group. In Vienna, the concept that both regimes should be mutually supportive and are of equal rank made its way to the negotiation table. In Montreal, the article was deleted, and replaced by a cluster of three clauses in the preamble, as follows:

> "Recognizing that trade and environment agreements should be mutually supportive with a view to achieving sustainable development,
>
> "Emphasizing that this Protocol shall not be interpreted as implying a change in the rights and obligations of a Party under any existing international agreements,
>
> "Understanding that the above recital is not intended to subordinate this Protocol to other international agreements".

The second clause, with an unusual "shall" in a preambular clause, is inspired by a similar clause in the preamble of the *Rotterdam Convention on Prior Informed Consent* (PIC), and thus is based on a precedent.

A typical compromise package, these statements, at first sight contradictory, probably embody the best achievable balance between the two regimes. Much will no doubt be said and written about these clauses in future. The final test would ultimately only take place should a dispute concerning the implementation of the Protocol be brought before a WTO dispute panel, for breach of WTO rules. This is a situation which naturally cannot be excluded, but which many consider extreme and undesirable—at least politically.

It would be more constructive and promising to put the emphasis on the first clause. Indeed, it may well be argued that the Protocol does not conflict with WTO-related rules but, rather, that it establishes international standards in a specific instance, or gives added specificity to trade rules. Such a course of thought and action would also reconcile States with themselves: after all, the States which have negotiated the Biosafety Protocol are the same as those who are Parties to the trade-related agreements!

If this were to happen, the Protocol could not only be hailed as a significant achievement in international environmental law, as well as another important step in the achievement of sustainable development, but it could also be hailed as an element in the progressive development of trade law.

5

Relationship Between the CBD and Other Biodiversity-Related International Instruments

The evolution of international treaty law relating to biological diversity in the past thirty years has been remarkable, culminating with the adoption of the *Convention on Biological Diversity* in 1992.

While the CBD vision and mandate is all-encompassing, sectoral and regional instruments dealing with genetic, species and ecosystem diversity remain essential to the achievement of its ultimate goal: the conservation of the planet's biological diversity. This is true for instruments which pre-date the 1992 Convention, and for those which no doubt will be concluded for specific regions, as well as for particular species, genetic resources, ecosystems, or processes affecting biological diversity in the future.

Viewed from this perspective, the *Convention on Biological Diversity* has not only a normative character of its own; it also has a role to play in orchestrating the concert of biodiversity-related international instruments, while these instruments have a role to play in the implementation of the CBD mandate.

The 'synergetic' implementation of this cluster of international instruments has become an important element of the international agenda. Many views have been offered on the role of the CBD in this regard. One of them is given below.

A

Wold C., "The Futility, Utility and Future of the *Biodiversity Convention*," *Colorado Journal of International Environmental Law and Policy*, Vol. 9, No. 1, 1998, pp 30–37

Limiting and Consolidating the Agenda

Based on the comprehensive survey, the Parties must prioritize and limit their obligations. That said, the Parties will not easily prioritize, consolidate, and limit their tasks. Significant problems relating to institutional "turf" as well as the logistics of bringing together States and secretariats make the task of effectively linking and delinking different conventions extremely difficult. In addition, the Parties must actually make these decisions. The history of the *Biodiversity Convention* suggests that this decision-making process will be slow and contentious. Also, a decision as to whether a particular issue is best addressed by a regional agreement, a habitat-specific agreement, or the *Biodiversity Convention* may not be obvious.

The *Biodiversity Convention* contemplates regional and other cooperative approaches to implementation of the Convention's obligations. Although the *Biodiversity*

Convention delegates responsibility for implementation largely to States, it specifically requires cooperation with other Parties and international organizations "in respect of areas beyond national jurisdiction and on other matters of mutual interest". It also stresses "the importance of, and the need to promote, international, regional and global cooperation among States and intergovernmental organizations and the nongovermental sector for the conservation of biological diversity and the sustainable use of its components."

The proliferation of biodiversity-related conventions also suggests that states in general believe international cooperation is essential to meaningful and successful conservation and sustainable use. Yet, these efforts may be wasted through unnecessary duplication and inconsistent application of conservation and sustainable use concepts if states do not sensibly delegate responsibility for these issues. The parties to these various conventions and especially the *Biodiversity Convention* Parties—must determine how, not if, to delegate this responsibility effectively and efficiently.

Implementation Through "Regional" Conventions

Regionalization may be one way to develop a manageable agenda. The term "regionalization" has two meanings here. First, the Parties can use existing regional conventions to implement obligations that could be addressed within the *Biodiversity Convention*. For example, the Parties could implement the habitat and species conservation and sustainable use obligations through regional agreements such as the Association of South East Asian Nations Agreement (the ASEAN Agreement) or the *African Convention on the Conservation of Nature and Natural Resources* (the *African Convention*). Second, regionalization means implementing obligations within the *Biodiversity Convention* on a regional basis. In this second use, "regional" means geographic as well as ecological and economic proximity. For example, if the Parties continue to develop rules relating to sustainable mariculture, the major consumers such as the United States should be included in any agreement or protocol with producers from Southeast Asia.

A regional approach recognizes that conservation and sustainable use of biological diversity cannot mean the same things across differing ecological conditions. For example, the Parties might be able to create general principles for sustainability that apply to the steppes of Mongolia and the tropical forests of Brazil. But, the uses of those ecosystems and their very different nature preclude specific sustainability criteria that apply equally to both. A regional approach might also effectively implement each Party's differing responsibilities, especially when the economic conditions of a regional group of Parties are similar.

Specific regional biodiversity-related conventions, such as the ASEAN Agreement, the *African Convention*, or the *Western Hemisphere Convention*, might implement *Biodiversity Convention* obligations more quickly and effectively than the *Biodiversity Convention*, because they have smaller geographic scope and fewer parties. For example, the *Biodiversity Convention* Parties must, as far as possible and as appropriate, establish protected areas, maintain viable populations of species, and promote the protection of ecosystems. Because the ranges of populations and ecosystems may include two or more political territories, national implementation alone is likely to be insufficient. To more effectively conserve such species or ecosystems, parties should cooperate with all relevant parties to implement this obligation. For a species or habitat type unique to two or three states or a particular region, the *Biodiversity Convention* probably is not the proper forum to develop policy, because educating, and accommodating the opinions of, 169 Parties about that unique species or habitat would delay any decision. If the species or habitat is unique to Southeast Asia, the ASEAN Agreement perhaps is best. Like the *Biodiversity Convention*, the ASEAN Agreement also has provisions to maintain maximum genetic diversity, create protected areas, and protect ecological processes. Other *Biodiversity Convention* obligations might also be resolved more effectively through regional agreements, such as the protection of threatened species.

In determining whether a regional convention can adequately implement *Biodiversity Convention* obligations, the Parties must assess the regional convention's institutional structure. In this regard, the ASEAN Agreement and the *Berne Convention* have superior institutional structures compared to those of the *African Convention* and the *Western Hemisphere Convention*. The ASEAN Agreement has a well-developed institutional structure with a Secretariat to handle the day-to-day operations of the Agreement and COPs to make decisions.

The *Berne Convention* creates a Standing Committee, which takes on the duties of both a secretariat and a conference of the parties. The *African Convention* and the *Western Hemisphere Convention* have neither, although the Organization of African Unity and the Organization of American States, respectively, could fill the role of secretariat until the parties develop better institutional structures.

If the members of the *African Convention* and the *Western Hemisphere Convention* fail to create permanent institutional structures, their members could meet as working groups of the *Biodiversity Convention*. The working group members would make clear that they are making decisions consistent with both the *Biodiversity Convention* and the relevant regional agreement. The use of a *Biodiversity Convention* working group could cause some difficulties relating to participation and voting, because the parties to the conventions do not perfectly overlap. Thus, the United States as a non-party to the *Biodiversity Convention* could participate in the working group but could not vote. Similarly, Belize, Canada, and others are Parties to the *Biodiversity Convention* but not the *Western Hemisphere Convention*. The *African Convention*, the *Berne Convention*, and the *ASEAN Convention* exhibit similar asymmetry. Presumably, the relevant states could develop a decision-making process that includes everyone and allows all to vote.

Implementation Through Habitat and Species Conventions

The great number of species—or habitat-specific conventions could cause confusion as to the most appropriate forum for resolving issues. Although a regional convention may provide a better forum addressing some issues, species—or habitat-specific conventions may be better able to address other issues. Knowing which to choose, especially when the issue is regional in nature, will be difficult. As with regional agreements, the comprehensive survey of biodiversity-related agreements should describe the best way to resolve these issues.

Problems relating to sea turtles in Southeast Asia exemplify the trouble in choosing the best agreement, as well as the potential for synergy. Both the *Convention on the Conservation of Migratory Species of Wild Animals* (CMS), relating specifically to migratory species such as sea turtles, and the *ASEAN Agreement*, a Southeast Asian conservation agreement, provide smaller fora for addressing sea turtle conservation and sustainable use. The Parties to the CMS already are pursuing regional agreements to protect sea turtles. However, one of the primary threats to sea turtles is shrimp trawling in coastal waters, an issue that the *Biodiversity Convention* Parties could address as part of the *Jakarta Mandate*.

In this particular case, the CMS might be the best fora, because its efforts are known and specific to the species at issue. As a result, the *Biodiversity Convention* Parties (and ASEAN Agreement members) should delete any discussion of sea turtles and shrimp trawling from its agenda. The Parties could accomplish this task through a Decision of the Parties. To ensure coordination, the *Biodiversity Convention* secretariat could notify the CMS secretariat of the Decision or enter into a memorandum of cooperation on this specific issue or a series of issues that the *Biodiversity Convention* Parries agree are better addressed by the CMS. As part of the arrangement, the CMS Parties could respond by incorporating the *Jakarta Mandate* into any sea turtle plan.

One of the primary threats to sea turtles is shrimp trawling in coastal waters, an issue that the Biodiversity Convention Parties could address as part of the Jakarta Mandate.

Consolidation of Substantive Obligations

The *Biodiversity Convention* Parties should also consolidate several biodiversity-related substantive and procedural issues. The resolution of overlapping jurisdiction will not be easy, especially for issues not capable of a regional approach or where two or more conventions have already developed policies relating to a particular aspect of biodiversity. The case of IPRs and access to and use of genetic resources illustrates this problem. Four international institutions have some jurisdiction over IPRs: The World Intellectual Property Organization, The World Trade Organization through the Agreement of Trade-Related Aspects of Intellectual Property Rights, the FAO, and the *Biodiversity Convention*. Each of these institutions has invested time and energy into different aspects of IPRs and genetic resources. To avoid duplication of efforts, the *Biodiversity Convention* Parties should consolidate or create a well-defined niche regarding IPRs and genetic resources.

Because the institutional barriers to consolidation of these issues is likely to be high due to the institutional involvement of all, the Parties might justify finding a unique niche in the area of access and benefit sharing. Focusing on these issues also plays to the strengths of the *Biodiversity Convention*. The *Biodiversity Convention* already changes international law relating to access to genetic resources and the sharing of financial and technological benefits that derive from that access. With this contentious issue resolved, the Parties should focus on developing more specific provisions for access to genetic resources and the sharing of benefits.

Similar consolidation of jurisdiction could occur in other areas, such as persistent organic pollutants. With consolidation completed and implementation of other obligations through regional, species-specific, or habitat-specific conventions determined, the Parties may approach a sensible substantive agenda with a few difficult substantive issues to address. These include, and may be limited to, access to genetic resources and fair and equitable sharing of benefits derived from that access, introduction of alien species, biosafety, and marine and coastal biodiversity.

Consolidation of Procedural Issues

The Parties should also consolidate the more procedural issues of conventions, such as reporting, identification, and monitoring obligations. In the alternative, the Parties could use the reporting, identification, and monitoring requirements of other conventions to implement similar obligations under the *Biodiversity Convention*. In addition, the Parties should create uniform reporting criteria and formats to ensure that the data submitted to each convention is comparable. By using existing reporting mechanisms and devising uniform reporting rules, the Parties will better implement their duties to identify and monitor components of biological diversity for its conservation and sustainable use and avoid redundancies with the reporting requirements of other conventions.

Such uniformity should improve decision making for both the *Biodiversity Convention* and other conventions. For example, Parties to CITES are required to submit trade data concerning imports and exports of Appendix I and II species. These data might identify a species that is traded heavily and in need of additional monitoring. Additional monitoring might include closer scrutiny of requests for import and export permits. The *Ramsar Convention* requires Parties to develop criteria to identify wetlands of international importance and to identify potential wetlands for protection, which could provide the basis for identifying and monitoring habitats and ecosystems for conservation and use. At least for international commercial trade and wetlands, the mechanisms for implementing the reporting and identification provisions of the *Biodiversity Convention* already exist, and the Parties should use them.

Financing

The Parties should ensure that funds from the Global Environment Facility (GEF), the *Biodiversity Convention*'s interim financing mechanism, can be used to implement other biodiversity-related conventions, such as CITES. Developed-country Parties to the *Biodiversity Convention* provide funding through the GEF for developing-country Parties to meet the "agreed full incremental costs" of implementing the *Biodiversity Convention*. In contrast, CITES has no financing mechanism, and very few of its Parties implement it adequately. The lack of resources to ensure that trade is not detrimental to a species—a finding that the exporting country must make prior to the export of a CITES-listed species—is perhaps the biggest concern. Yet, implementation of the "no detriment finding" is essential for protecting species from overutilization due to trade. It also is essential for meeting the obligations of the *Biodiversity Convention* relating to threatened species and for sustainable use of biological diversity. The GEF could fund "no detriment findings" of CITES in those countries that lack the funding to do so.

More generally, in funding projects concerning sustainable use, the Parties should disburse funding only to make existing uses sustainable, including support for the development of national plans and research into the legal, management, and scientific elements required to ensure that a use is sustainable. Because most uses of biodiversity are unsustainable, funding should not be used to support new uses of biological diversity.

In addition, the Parties should build on the work of other conventions. For example, they could rely on the various appendices of other conventions to prioritize funding. The Parties to Ramsar list wetlands of international importance, which could receive priority funding. Or, species listed in Appendix I of CITES—those threatened with extinction and which may be affected by trade could receive priority funding. Apparently, funding dollars migrate toward the management of species in Appendix II because these species can be commercially traded. Ironically, the more endangered Appendix I species receive far fewer dollars for management because they cannot be commercially traded.

6

Asian Strategies for Conserving Biological Diversity

A

Huu D., Minister of Science Technology and Environment, *Viet Nam National Action Plan on Biological Diversity*, the Government Socialist Republic of Viet Nam, Hanoi, 1995

Viet Nam has been endowed by nature with an abundance and diversity of ecosystems, species and genetic resources which are generally regarded as biological diversity. Investigations have shown that Viet Nam is the home of 12,000 plant species of which 7,000 species have been identified, 275 species of mammals, 800 species of birds, 180 species of reptiles, 80 species of amphibians, 2,470 species of fish, 5,500 species of insects. Viet Nam's biodiversity is relatively unique as 10 percent of the world's mammal, bird and fish species can be found in Viet Nam while over 40 percent of the local plant species are endemic and believed to be found nowhere else but in Viet Nam. In addition, many livestock species have been domesticated and selected in this country since thousands of years now [sic].

In terms of economic value, all agricultural, forestry or marine products, which come from the biodiversity resources are estimated to bring about US$2 billion to the country's revenue every year. In many places, especially in the mountainous regions, the food and foodstuff sources, medicine plants and essential source of income rely largely on the biodiversity exploitation.

However, the national rapid population growth, the decreased forest areas, the overexploitation of the big-marine resources, [and] the over-introduction of new varieties in agricultural production, have led to the reduction or loss of the ecosystems, resulting in the fact that 28 percent of mammals, 10 percent of birds, 21 percent of reptiles and amphibians are currently listed as endangered species. Once a species is lost, it will never be recovered and this also constitutes a loss of genetic resource. The speed of biodiversity degradation is more rapid in our country than that in other countries of the region.

Recognizing the great economic, scientific, cultural and social value that biodiversity can contribute to the present and future development of mankind and being aware of the full responsibility for biodiversity conservation, Viet Nam has joined many countries in the world to sign the *Convention on Biological Diversity* which entered into force in the middle of 1993.

In the 60s, Viet Nam made the official initial steps to conserve its nature. In 1972, the promulgation of the Ordinance on Forest Protection led to the recruitment of 10,000 full-time public forestry-inspectors to work at all levels throughout the country. Since the 80s, the general endeavors to protect the environment including the biodiversity protection have been more intensive and systematic.

In 1985, the *Viet Nam's National Conservation Strategy* was formulated. This strategy, the first of this kind being developed in a developing country, was highly welcomed by the world community.

In 1991, the Government approved the *National Plan on Environment and Sustainable Development* the period 1991–2000. This plan served as a basis, leading to the drafting and later on the adoption of the *Law on Environmental Protection* in 1994, as well as to the establishment of the Ministry of Science, Technology and Environment and Departments of Science, Technology and Environment in all provinces.

At the national level, it is an imperative to formulate and promulgate a *National Action Plan on Biological Diversity*.

Review of the Biological Diversity Protection Situation in Viet Nam

The Economic Utilization of Species

The economic utilization of species can be seen first of all in the wood exploitation of between 1,3–1,7 million cubic meters per year while other forestry products such as rattan, canes, bamboo and fuel are also exploited for economic purposes. About 100,000 tons of bamboo were logged for the paper industry. Of the total national demand of energy, 75 percent is supplied by fuelwood. It is estimated that between 22 to 23 million tons of fuelwood are exploited annually from the natural forests. Besides, 2,300 flora species and a number of wildlife fauna species are exploited to provide medicines, food for human being and livestock, raw materials for industries and handicrafts. A[n] increasing amount of products are being traded with the neighboring countries.

Every year, fishing products estimated at 1 million tons per year, have provided one half of the total amount of the national fauna protein. Between 60 percent to 70 percent are fish exploited from the sea resource. About 20,000 to 30,000 tons of fish, soft-shell turtles, frogs are provided by the freshwater resource, while cultured fish also yields about 200 tons a year.

The fields can be cultivated for some consecutive years then abandoned for a few years as a fallow period to wait for forest restoration before being subject again to the slash-and-burn cultivation.

Threats to the Biodiversity

With the gradual reduction of the ecosystems resulting in the gradual loss of habitats, many species are facing the danger of extinction. In Viet Nam's Red Book, scientists have listed over 300 fauna and 350 flora species as endangered species facing the danger of extinction. This situation is generally caused by:

Overexploitation

The exploitation of wood and other forestry products still poses a big threat even though there is now a strong limit on the forest areas which are legally exploitable. The large-scale exploitation of energy is hard to control and poses the biggest threat to the biodiversity in many countries. The forest quality and capacity have been more and more reduced in the areas close to human residence. In many areas, forests have been divided, becoming smaller in size and separate from one another. Consequently, they can no longer support and create the environment for the abundance of species like before.

Over-fishing is also a fact of life that occurs throughout the country. Moreover, the fishing methods are not applied according to approved standards. Destructive methods have even been in practice such as using traps, heck set-up, small-meshed nets, dynamite and toxic substances in some areas.

Coral exploitation is the highest concern in the Central Coastal Area from Da Nang to Thuan Hai Provinces. The exploitation of dead coral in the tidal areas to generate raw materials for cement production using dynamite (in Khanh Hoa, Ninh Thuan) seriously damages the living environment of many marine organisms and reduces the capacity of erosion prevention in the coastal areas.

Shifting Cultivation and the Encroachment of Arable Land

A number of ethnic minorities have practised shifting cultivation for generations. According to their practice, the fields can be cultivated for some consecutive years then abandoned for a few years as a fallow period to wait for forest restoration before being subject again to the slash-and-burn cultivation. This practice used to clear only a small size of forests while it could help enrich the species by providing habitats for new ones. Due to the population growth, this practice is no longer stable and the sequence of land use is gradually shortened with the consequences of gradual deforestation. The immigration, forest clearing for arable land or aquaculture, also contributes to the gradual area reduction of the forest ecosystems.

Shifting cultivation is also a reason for forest fire. Of the remaining 9 million hectares of forests, 56 percent is fire prone in the dry season. The forest areas being burned each year are between 20,000 to 30,000 hectares, even 100,000 hectares in certain year. Deforestation resulted in a major reduction in biodiversity.

Water Pollution

Oil pollution is regarded as the worst disaster for the marine environment. As a result of oil exploitation and sea transport the proportion of oil mixed with the coastal water has often exceeded the permissible level of between 0.4 to 1.0 mg/1 many times. Quang Ninh province also suffers a serious problem of sedimentation on the coastal areas due to coal and clay exploitation. Millions of tons of sand and mud, due to the dredging activities at the seaports (Hai Phong dredges 3–5 tons per year), often cause the estuary and coastal sedimentation which, contain oil and toxic substances, creating negative impacts on the coastal ecosystems and marine organisms.

The Degradation of the Coastal Areas

The construction of coastal aquaculture ponds, land reclamation from the sea to create fields for salt production or for agricultural cultivation, human settlement along the coastal areas often contributes to the reduction of the tidal zones, the increase in the salinity, changes in the sedimentation process, causing destruction to or serious degradation of the tidal swamps. The large-scale exploitation of sand and stones for construction and of other mineral resources causes land erosion in the coastal areas of the Southern Central Region and the reduction of water resources, affecting the lower layer of the marine ecosystems.

The Transition to the Market Economy

Changes towards the market economy mechanism have had strong impact on the farmers. The farmers are now under pressure to apply many new varieties and species in order to have the produce yields that meet the current market demands. This poses a great danger to the traditional varieties and plant species which have long been suitable to grow in the local climate and soils. They have the valuable phenotypes but may be ignored by their failure, in a short-term perspective, to meet the present market demands.

The present situation regarding the exploitation and utilization of species makes the biodiversity protection task more urgent than ever before.

Objectives of the Viet Nam National Action Plan on Biological Diversity

The long-term objective of the Plan is to protect the rich and unique biodiversity resources within the sustainable development framework of Viet Nam;

The immediate objectives of the plan are to:

- Protect the country's endemic ecosystems, the vulnerable ecosystems which are now facing the danger of reduction or destruction caused by human economic activities.
- Protect those biodiversity components which are now subject to be overexploited or ignored.
- Promote and identify the utilization values of all biodiversity components on the basis of development of natural resources in order to serve the country's economic targets.

Main Contents of the Action Plan

Biodiversity protection is a long-term task which needs to be carried out by different 5-year programs. A number of the following urgent actions should be included in Specific Plans:

Policies and Legal Issues

The Law on Environmental Protection passed by the National Assembly provides the general guidance for the environmental protection. However, many more bylaw regulations and supporting documents should be prepared in order to strengthen the enforcement of the law and other legal documents.

Law enforcement is one of the pressing issues to which more attention should be paid. This requires the strengthening of technical and management capacity for the concerned institutions, staff training is also needed for these institutions. A number of laws and regulations should be reformed while the introduction of economic instruments based on the market mechanism as well as punitive actions need to be studied and implemented.

The bylaw regulations should deal with such issues as the exploitation and sustainable use of natural resources, the control of the trading in the rare species as well as the unique bio-materials of Viet Nam, pollution prevention and control. These issues should be included also in the regulations on environmental impact assessments.

The effective protection of biodiversity requires a clarification, readjustment or strengthening of the functions, and duties entrusted to the State management organizations concerned as well as of the regulations on those activities carried out by economic establishments that have impacts on the environment. Therefore, priority should be given to the sectoral review of the functions and duties of the organizations which manage the protected areas.

Establishment and Management of Protected Areas

Immediately establish and well manage the protected areas with high biodiversity values. Planning and enlargement of forest and forest land in 87 specialized forests which have been identified. Primary priority should be given to those protected areas of high biodiversity values such as: Pu Mat (Nghe An Province); Vu Quang (Ha Tinh Province), Hoang Lien Son (Lao Cai Province), Ba Be (Cao Bang Province), Cat Ba (Hai Phong), Cuc Phuong (Ninh Binh Province), Ke Go Lake (Ha Tinh Province), Bach Ma (Thua Thien Hue Province), Nam Ca (sac Lac Province), Chu Giang Sinh (sac Lac Province), Bi Dup (Lam Dong Province), and Cat Tien (Dong Nai Province).

Strengthen and develop the buffer zones surrounding the protected areas, discourage intensive farming on sloping land, gradually stop the shifting cultivation, stabilize the life of the people and raise their awareness so that they will voluntarily join the protection force.

Develop the planning and creation of a number of important wetland areas in Ca Mau, or close to the Red River Delta, tine bird colonies and the Tam Giang Lagoon, etc. These areas are located outside the specialized forests but close to human residence where the people have great demands to exploit theses areas for many different purposes, such as aquaculture, coastal forests and waterway transportation, etc. It is therefore necessary to pay special attention right from the outset to the biodiversity protection of these wetlands and to the prevention of contamination sources, especially from the water and to the control of the water overdrainage.

Build a number of protected areas for sea and inland waterbodies. As the sea areas with high biodiversity are usually the ones that can provide high economic values, priority should be given to the protection of those sea areas that have highest biodiversity values.

Build gene banks of flora, microorganisms and domesticated animals. Supply genetic materials for hybridizing and selecting varieties to serve economic purposes as well as to ensure the genetic sources in nature. To enhance capacity of zoos which can serve as places for sight-seeing, training and raising the general awareness on the environment. These places are also useful for scientific research, conservation of wildlife which are endangered; and when conditions permit, these species should be released back to the protected areas.

Organize integrated management of the coastal areas within the framework of sustainable development. Many activities in the coastal areas should be carried out in an integrated manner, such as: developing protected forests, mangrove forest exploitation, growing aquaculture, land reclamation for farming, human settlement and coastal industry development, etc.

Enhance measures to protect agricultural biodiversity; bring into full play the various form of "farming conservation"; encourage farmers to participate in the common protection efforts; special attention should be given to the conservation of popular traditional varieties which have long been adapted to the local geography and climate.

Awareness Building

Utilize such mass media instruments as radio, television, newspapers, posters, etc. to raise the public awareness on biodiversity, encourage people to protect the general benefits of biodiversity.

Provide necessary information through short symposiums, study tours to biodiversity protection institutions within and outside the country to help management officers or policy-makers to have better understanding and knowledge concerning the biodiversity importance.

Carry out propaganda and dissemination of knowledge and methods necessary for the rational use of endemic natural resources for the ethnic communities so that they can both exploit and protect theses resources. Encouragement and technical support should be rendered to people so that they can protect the traditional plant and animals for medicines and transform gradually from their natural exploitation methods to scientific ones by raising their awareness of sustainable use of the natural resource values.

Prepare biodiversity education curriculum for the school system which could be incorporated within the biological programs or the environmental education in general.

Capacity Building and Staff Training

Give priority to the training for officers who are involved in the biodiversity management at all levels and technical staff who are directly involved in enforcement. In addition, training should also be given to the members of mass organizations, associations and farming households who participate in the protection of biodiversity.

Set up a national biodiversity database and a biodiversity databank beneficial to the management and research activities promote the international information exchange concerning these issues.

Establish a system to monitor the changes in biodiversity resources in order to timely provide necessary information to the state management organizations.

Scientific Research

Attention should be given to the following guidelines for scientific and technological research:

Carry out research on technologies which can be appropriately used in the rational exploitation and sustainable utilization of biodiversity resources. Give priority to the scientific research on the exploitation technology and the use of biodiversity components in agriculture and pharmacy.

Carry out research on the criteria and standards to evaluate the changes in biodiversity resources, using these criteria and standards as the basis for the evaluation of these resources values.

Study issues relating to bio-safety, ensuring the safe reception and transfer of biotechnology.

Carry out research on and growing of precious and rare sea organisms and forest animals that have high economic values but are subject to overexploitation and facing the consequent danger of extinction.

Study biodiversity issues occurring in neighboring countries which have natural conditions similar to ours, recognizing that Viet Nam and these countries have various common demands in the protection of their mutual benefits as well as exchange of technology.

Socioeconomic Issues

The crucial issue of the *National Action Plan on Biodiversity* is to bring about the sustainable development of the country, to examine and anticipate the interaction between the Plan and the country 's socioeconomic conditions in order to have appropriate adjustments. The plan must create conditions for, and ensure the support of, the people who live nearby the natural resources for their increased benefits. Therefore, priority should be given to projects which assist the people with the building of the buffer zones, the application of advanced technological achievements, upgrading of infrastructure, improvement of the social welfare, so as to ensure the balanced income for the people, thus preventing them from further encroachment into the protected areas.

The socioeconomic programs managed by the line ministries or branches and implemented in the areas adjacent to the protected areas should be implemented in conformity with the plan on biodiversity protection. The exploitation of natural resources must be carried out sustainability.

A number of new economic developments close to protected areas or areas which have sensitive eco-systems will be are subject to pay a fee for the environmental protection.

International Cooperation

The fact that Viet Nam has ratified the *Convention on Biodiversity* creates a good basis for a broadened international cooperation in this area. It is necessary to appeal international organizations, foreign governments and individuals, to provide practical technical training and financial assistance for the step-by-step implementation of this plan.

With regard to the neighboring countries, for the mutual interests of each country, it is necessary to strengthen cooperation in the scientific research, exchange of information and technology and to work together for the protection and development of their biodiversity values.

Activities Needed to be Carried Out in the Period 1996–2000

In the five-year plan from 1996-2000, based on the State resources, efforts should be focused on the priority targets in order to carry out the following actions:

Policies and legal issues: complete a system of bylaw regulations in order to create a legal framework for the implementation of the *Law on Environmental Protection and of the Conventions relating to Biological Diversity*:

Formulate regulations on the conservation, utilization, exploitation and exchange of. genetic resources, varieties and breeds with a view to:

- Manage rare and precious specious natural resources of the country which have immediate and long-term practical economic values.
- Protect the national sovereignty and act in conformity with those international conventions which Viet Nam has ratified concerning these natural resources.

Coordinate all the existing laws and regulations on the management, exploitation and utilization, of biological resources for whatever purposes with a view to:

- Identify the loopholes and shortcomings of those documents previously promulgated by different ministries or branches.
- Reform and rectify these documents in order to make them compatible with the new changes in the national economic management mechanism and, at the same time, to ensure the sustainable exploitation and utilization of the biological resources with a sustainable development approach.

Make public those less sustainable ecosystems in the "sensitive" terrestrial and aquatic environmental areas and promulgate corresponding protection regulations in order to prevent the degradation or destruction of these ecosystems as the result of adverse environmental impacts created by industrial development.

Establishment and Management of Protected Areas

Locate and enlarge the forest protected and land areas in order to:

- Increase the size and acreage of each specialized forests of the total 87 forests already approved by the Government.
- Legalize all land use documents concerning these areas.

Consolidate and establish the protected areas with high biodiversity values which have been identified.

Priority for investment should be first given to these areas because of their national and international high biodiversity values. Along with the consolidation and establishment of strictly protected areas, synchronized plan should be worked out to develop the buffer zones so as to stabilize the living conditions of the local inhabitants.

Carry out the selection, planning and establishment of a number of important wetlands in the identified areas.

Special protection and priority should be given to these areas as these areas are rich in biodiversity but very sensitive to the environmental pollution and usually associated with many economic activities.

Carry out the selection, planning and establishment of a number of important marine reserves in the areas of Ha Long Bay, the coastline from Khanh Hoa to Binh Thuan Province, and in the Con Dao and Phu Quoc islands.

These areas are very rich in biodiversity, inhabited by many marine species and directly interlinked with the protection of the water resources and important fish grounds of the country.

Consolidate and establish genetic conservation centers for raising plants and animals, and micro-biological organism aimed at protecting the precious and rare genetic resources with high economic values and supplying genetic materials for breeding.

Strengthen and upgrade the capacity for the zoos in Ha Noi and Ho Chi Minh City in order to better use them as facilities to educate people's consciousness of environmental protection in general and biodiversity conservation in particular. In addition, these zoos can also be used as research centers to raise the rare and precious animals which are facing the danger of natural extinction and to release them back to their habitats when conditions arise.

General Awareness Building

Keep the public constantly informed of the values of biodiversity in order to enhance the population's awareness of these values so that they will have better sense of responsibility to protect the biodiversity resources.

Provide necessary information on biodiversity to officials at all levels particularly officials at the local levels in order help them with better understanding the biodiversity values; at the same time these officials should be assisted with information to make necessary decisions concerning the protection of these natural resources.

Capacity Building and Staff Training

Organize short-term training courses, seminars within and outside the country to strengthen the capacity and professional expertise for the management and technical staff at all levels and branches who are involved in the biodiversity-related work.

Establish a national network of database on biodiversity with a view to have a unified system of database and information on biodiversity throughout the country, creating favorable conditions for the general capacity building.

Scientific Research

Conduct research and studies on technologies for the sustainable exploitation and utilization of biodiversity components, priority will be given to those technologies that could be used profitably in agriculture, medicines and pharmacy aimed at better utilizing the values of biodiversity components and thus making practical contributions to the achievement of the national socioeconomic targets.

Study the criteria and standards to assess the changes of biodiversity components in protection, supervision and assessment of the trends in biodiversity

Study the issues relating to the safety of the biodiversity values in the receipt and transfer of technologies especially biotechnology.

Conclusions

The National Action Plan on Biological Diversity is worked out to serve the long-term benefits of the country. It also demonstrates to the world community our responsibility towards the conservation of the common heritage of mankind. All organizations, branches concerned are obliged to implement this Action Plan.

B

Salim E., "Preface-Keynote Address," *The Report of the Indonesian Country Study on Biological Diversity*, UNEP, 1993

With somewhere between 15 percent and 25 percent of the world's total number of species, Indonesia is of critical importance to global biodiversity conservation efforts. This species richness is associated with the integrity of natural environments that support much of Indonesia's total economic activity. This economic contribution is not wholly quantified at present, but is know to be worth several to many billions of US dollars annually.

In this context, the realisation that Indonesia's biodiversity resources and environmental integrity are steadily being degraded is of concern both to the Government of Indonesia and to its international partners in development. With a mandate to coordinate internal governmental and nongovermental activities in this area, KLH occupies a critical position in these efforts. To help KLH meet the challenge of this responsibility, a bilateral agreement has been initiated between the governments of Indonesia and of the Kingdom of Norway, and this *Country Study on Biological Diversity* is one of the first fruits of this agreement...

Because of the economic significance of biodiversity to the Indonesian people, we feel that an adequate and well-coordinated national program to manage this resource is vitally important. This new concept of "biodiversity management" actually includes many activities that people have been doing to stay alive for thousands of years, such as hunting, gathering, fishing, forestry and agriculture.

The new term also implies, however, that these activities should be done safely, meaning that the resources being managed must not be destroyed, and that later generations of people should have the opportunity to benefit from their continued and sustainable use, But how is this to be achieved in a country as large and diverse as Indonesia, where so many different sectors of society make use of biodiversity management program.

Just as important, however, is the evolution of a strategic concept for this program, which is now emerging from the last several years of study, planning and legislation in Indonesia. This process started with the *National Strategy for the Management of Biodiversity* of 1989, and continued with Act No. 5 *Concerning the Conservation of Living Resources and the Ecosystems* of 1990, *Tropical Forestry Action Programme* of 1991, the *Biodiversity Action Plan* of 1991, and with this *Country Study on Biological Diversity* itself. The process has been further enriched by international experience, for example by this ministry's recent work with the National Biodiversity Institute (INBio) of Costa Rica, and with reference to the new *Global Biodiversity Strategy* by UNEP and others.

Although much remains to be done, the outlines of a national program are now clear. It will be a complex task, and biodiversity management is inherently difficult because it requires groups and individuals to make sacrifices by not exploiting resources for immediate gain. Nevertheless, biodiversity conservation must be achieved if Indonesia's future prosperity is to be secured. This flows from the analysis that the world's economy in the 21st Century will be dominated by a "Fourth Wave" of biotechnology-based activity (the first three "waves" being based on agriculture, industry and information technology). Since genetic diversity will be the raw material of this phenomenon, those biodiverse countries which manage to retain a large number of species will be at a competitive advantage in these circumstances.

Although much remains to be done, the outlines of a national program are now clear.

To ensure that Indonesia obtains such a competitive advantage, we will seek to base our national biodiversity management program (NBMP) on the following strategic principles, many *of* which are justified by the content of the *Country Study* report which follows.

(a) A comprehensive NBMP must involve *'saving'* biodiversity, as well as *'studying'* it and *'using'* it sustainably. Each of these three basic themes rely on *'rationalization'* (clear reason to act), *'motivation'* (a willingness to act) and *'capacity'* (an ability to act) These principles must be applied with equal efficiency at the *'central'*, *'provincial'* and *'local'* levels of society.

(b) The most important task in 'saving' biodiversity is securing an adequate system of protected areas, and this will involve the following steps:

  (i) *Investigation* of the nationwide terrestrial, coastal and marine protected area system, to determine and correct adequacy of coverage, boundaries, status, threats and needs for protective management.

(ii) *Consolidation* where appropriate of protected areas into larger conservation areas (e.g., by combining national parks with nearby nature reserves, protection forests, etc.), which may be zoned for different kinds of use.

(iii) *Integration* of these larger conservation areas into regional management units ('bioregions', otherwise called ICDPs, IPASs, biosphere reserves, protected landscapes and seascapes, etc., by various agencies), which will include surrounding production forests, agricultural lands and other ecosystems under more-or-less intensive use by people.

(iv) *Decentralization* of management authority to the conservation areas and bioregions themselves, in order to create opportunities for their management to be locally appropriate, to involve and be supported by local populations, and ultimately to create financially self sufficient conservation entities.

(c) The NBMP would therefore encourage the protected area system review, while facilitating the cross-sectoral linkages which are implied by the need to address development issues *outside* the conservation areas. This will mean providing national-level encouragement and guidance for provincial-level liaison between PHPA and the BAPPEDAs to secure cooperation of all tine agencies and other groups which are involved at the local level.

(d) The concepts of *study and sustainable use* should be linked in the NBMP. This means that it should specifically encourage scientific activity which addresses the needs of identified 'biodiversity user groups', which include:

(i) agencies concerned with scientific research, education and tourism;

(ii) agencies concerned with conservation planning and monitoring;

(iii) agencies concerned with the environmental impact of development activities (BAPEDAL and all line agencies); and

(iv) agencies concerned with the commercialization of Indonesia's biodiversity assets.

(e) One implication of a biodiversity 'study and use' approach is the need for a *National Biodiversity Inventory* (NBI). If biodiversity is to be used it must be inventoried, in much the same way that a warehouse or supermarket needs to know the nature, value and location of its stock if it is to operate profitably. The MBI should thus aim to describe and name, as well as to determine location, ecological and behavioral characteristics and actual or potential uses of each species in Indonesia.

(f) The NBI will be a major undertaking, and should be preceded by independent feasibility studies to determine how best to collect and manage data in the light of anticipated users of that data: The NBI will relate directly to a *National Biodiversity Database* (NBD), and the design of this should be examined during the same feasibility studies. The NBD will need a major graphical and mapping capability, and so should interface well with the national digitized mapping system at Bakosurtanal. The whole NBD should be designed from the same point of view as the NBI: i.e., what kind of data will the users need, how will they need it to be managed and presented, and how much will they be prepared to pay for it?

(g) Much of the information in an NBD will be most useful to Indonesia if it is provided free to the education, science, tourism, conservation and development planning communities. Commercial environmental impact assessments (AMDALs), however, would be a potential market which the NBD could in principle service.

(h) Other revenue-generating options come from the commercial potential of Indonesia's biodiversity, for example in developing new pharmaceutical or agrochemical products. These assets should not be exploited commercially without a share in the revenues being captured by Indonesia. This is important to the NBMP because commercialization of these assets can contribute at various levels and in various ways to developing the rationale, the motivation and the capacity to save them.

(i) To commercialize biodiversity data requires a different approach to that involved in simply making it available to non-commercial users, mainly because of the need to maintain data security and hence exclusivity. Since commercialization is impossible without this, the NBD would need to be designed from the start to allow data with commercial potential to be kept secure.

(j) Maintaining data security while negotiating and fulfilling contracts with the private-sector to develop new products and markets, are specialized tasks for which a new agency, the 'biodiversity marketing board' (BMB), will be needed. This could be modelled on the Costa Rican INBio, and should have a mandate to manage the 'secure' section of the NBD in order to generate net revenues to be used for biodiversity protection in Indonesia.

(k) Such revenues would come from two main sources, to be provided for in contracts between the BMB and its partners in research, development and marketing of products:
   (i) up-front payments in exchange for access to particular 'packages' of information and specimens for analysis; and
   (ii) royalty payments on sales of any product or the exercise of any patent derived from such information or specimens.

(l) The use of the net revenues of the BMB for 'biodiversity protection' implies their allocation to appropriate vehicles for the management of these revenues. These might take the form of:
   (i) *Endowment Funds* (EFs) for each conservation area, to relieve PHPA of some routine management and protection costs. A maximum of 50 percent of net BMB revenues could be divided equally on a per-hectare basis among the Endowment Funds of all Indonesia's conservation areas.
   (ii) *Sustainable Development Foundations* (SDFs) for each bioregional management unit, to be used for the benefit of the people living there by helping with education, health care, agricultural improvements, etc. A minimum of 50 percent of net BMB revenues could be allocated to the EFs and SDFs of particular conservation areas to 'reward' the use of endemic species or local ethnobiological information, and in response to particular threats to the integrity of each resource.

(m) An important final point is that technology would now allow Indonesia's biodiversity assets to be exported very easily, and this leakage can be either deliberate or as a consequence of innocent research. All relevant research should therefore be prohibited except where a contract has been signed which assigns royalty rights to Indonesia from any commercial exploitation of materials or information taken from Indonesia. The BMB would be the logical beneficiary of such a contract.

(n) Various other components will also be needed, so in summary the whole NBMP should eventually comprise:
   (i) stabilizing and securing the protected area system to achieve *in-situ* conservation (through investigation, consolidation, integration and decentralization);
   (ii) arranging for site-specific sustainable financing (through Endowment Funds and Sustainable Development Foundations);
   (iii) biodiversity data management (through the proposed National Biodiversity Inventory, Database and Marketing Board);
   (iv) complementary measures for environmental education, ecotourism development, management of the wildlife trade, and appropriate bilateral and multilateral cooperation with other countries; and
   (v) complementary *ex-situ* conservation measures (through germplasm collections, botanical gardens, etc.

Coordination of all these measures into a functional whole is the strategic vision which this Ministry is seeking to apply. In support of this, we are currently seeking on the one hand, to conduct a number of detailed feasibility studies to answer some of the many outstanding questions, and on the other to strengthen the operational mandate and capabilities of the Biodiversity Working Group in general and of this Ministry in particular.

We therefore look forward to continue working with all other agencies and governments which are willing to share in the development of a truly integrated, coordinated, and efficient program of biodiversity management in Indonesia.

Jakarta, Indonesia
7th May 1992

7

References for Chapter 20

Regional Biodiversity Forum web site

Axt J., *et al.*, *Biodiversity, Indigenous Rights, and Intellectual Property Rights: A Report by the Congressional Research Service to Congress*, Congress of the United States, Washington DC, 1993.

Burhenne-Guilmin F., "The Biosafety Protocol is Adopted in Montreal," in *Environmental Policy and Law*, Vol. 30, No. 2, 2000.

Crucible Group, *People Plants and Patents*, International Development Research Centre, Ottowa, 1994.

Cunningham A.B., "Indigenous Knowledge and Biodiversity" (Summer), *Cultural Survival Quarterly* 4, 1991.

Dutfield G., *Intellectual Property Rights, Trade and Biodiversity.* IUCN, Earthscan, Earthscan Publications Ltd, 2000

Genetic Resources Action International (GRAIN), *Intellectual Property Rights for Whom?* GRAIN Biobriefing No.4, Part 2, June 1994 .

Global Biodiversity Strategy: Guidelines to Save, Study and Use Earth's Biotic Wealth Sustainably and Equitably, WRI/IUCN/UNEP, 1992.

Glowka L., in collaboration with Shine C., Santos O.R., Farooque M., and Gündling L., *A Guide to Undertaking Biodiversity Legal and Institutional Profiles*, IUCN, Gland, Switzerland, Cambridge, UK and Bonn, Germany, 1998.

Glowka L., *A Guide to Designing Legal Frameworks to Determine Access to Genetic Resources*, IUCN, Gland, Switzerland, Cambridge and Bonn, 1998.

Glowka L., *A Guide to the Complementarities Between the Convention on Migratory Species and the Convention on Biological Diversity*, UNEP/CBD/COP/5/ INF/28, 2000.

Greaves T. (ed), *Intellectual Property Rights for Indigenous Peoples: A Sourcebook*, Society for Applied Anthropology, Oklahoma City, 1994.

Hails A.J. (ed), *Wetlands, Biodiversity and the Ramsar Convention: The Role of the Convention on Wetlands in the Conservation and Wise Use of Biodiversity,* Ramsar Convention Bureau, Gland, Switzerland, 1996.

Handbook of Incentives Measures for Biodiversity—Design and Implementation, OECD, 1999.

Kloppenburg J. Jr., "No Hunting! Biodiversity, Indigenous Rights, and Scientific Poaching, (Summer), *Cultural Survival Quarterly* 15, 1991.

Lenton R., *Synergies in National Implementation: The Rio Agreements.* UNDP Sustainable Energy and Environment Division, New York, 1997.

MacKinnon J., *Analytical Status Report of Biodiversity Conservation in the Asia Pacific Region*, paper prepared for the Regional Conference on Biodiversity Conservation Sponsored by the Asian Development Bank, June 1994.

McGowan J. and Udeinya I., "Collecting Traditional Medicines in Nigeria: A Proposal for IPR Compensation," in Greaves T. (ed), *Intellectual Property Rights for Indigenous Peoples: A Sourcebook*, Society for Applied Anthropology, Oklahoma City, 1994.

Nijar G.S., *A Conceptual Framework and Essential Elements of A Rights Regime for the Protection of Indigenous Rights and Biodiversity, Biodiversity Convention* Briefings, Third World Network, 1994.

Posey D.A. (ed), *Cultural and Spiritual Values of Biodiversity*, UNEP, 1999.

Rural Advancement Foundation International, *Conserving Indigenous Knowledge: Integrating Two Systems of Innovation*, United Nations Development Programme, New York, 1994.

Shine C. and de Klemm C., *Wetlands, Water and the Law: Using Law to Advance Wetland Conservation and Wise Use*, Gland, Switzerland, Cambridge, UK, and Bonn, Germany, 1999.

Shine C., Williams N., and Gündling L., *A Guide to Designing Legal and Institutional Frameworks on Alien Invasive Species,* IUCN, Gland, Switzerland, Cambridge, UK, and Bonn, Germany, 2000.

Walker S., *The TRIPS Agreement, Sustainable Development and the Public Interest: Discussion Paper*, IUCN, Gland, Switzerland, Cambridge, UK and Bonn, Germany and CIEL, Geneva, Switzerland, 2001.

Wijnstekers W., *The Evolution of CITES: A Reference to the Convention on International Trade in Endangered Species of Wild Fauna and Flora*, CITES Secretariat, Châtelaine-Geneva, Switzerland, 1995.

8

Additional References

Anneveldt E.and Pasman M., *Biodiversity in EIA Guidelines: A Study on the Extent to which Biodiversity is Currently Being Addressed in EIA Guidelines of the South Asiain Countries*, IUCN Asia, Kathmandu, Nepal, 2001.

Asian Development Bank, *Mobilizing Broader Support for Asia's Biodiversity, How Civil Society Can Contribute to Protected Area Management*, 1999.

Barber C.V. and Schweithelm J., *Trial by Fire: Forest Fires and Forestry Policy in Indonesia's Era of Crisis and Reform*, World Resources Institute in collaboration with WWF-Indonesia and Telapak Indonesia Foundation, 2000.

BIOLOG: The Newsletter of the Asia Regional Biodiversity Programme, IUCN, Gland Switzerland, 1999–present.

CBD Secretariat, *Assessment and Management of Alien Species that Threaten Ecosystems, Habitats and Species*, CBD Technical Series #1, Earthscan Publications 2001.

CBD Secretariat, *Handbook of the Convention on Biological Diversity* (Draft), Earthscan Publications, 2000.

Dhar B., Chaturvedi S. and Anuradha R.V., *Regime of Intellectual Property Protection for Biodiversity: A Developing Country Perspective*, Research and Information System for the Non-Aligned and Other Developing Countries (RIS), IUCN, 2001.

de Klemm C. and Shine C., *Biological Diversity Conservation and the Law: Legal Mechanisms for Conserving Species and Ecosystems*, IUCN The World Conservation Union, 1993.

de Klemm C., "The Regulation and Management of Destructive Processes: A New Type of Instrument for the Conservation of Biological Diversity," *27 Environmental Policy and Law 4*, 1997.

Downes D.R., *Integrating Implementation of the Convention on Biological Diversity and the Rules of the World Trade Organization*, IUCN, Gland Switzerland, 1999.

Dutfield G., *Intellectual Property Rights, Trade and Biodiversity*, Earthscan Publications, 2000.

French H., *Vanishing Borders: Protecting the Planet in the Age of Globalization*, Worldwatch Institute, 2000.

Girsberger M., *Biodiversity and the Concept of Farmers' Rights in International Law: Factual Background and Legal Analysis*, European Academic Publishers, Bern, Switzerland, 1999.

Giesen W. and King K., *Incremental Costs of Wetland Conservation: Case Studies in Asia and the Pacific*, Global Environment Facility and Wetlands International, 1997.

Glowka L. and Balakrishna P. (eds), *Access to Genetic Resources and Benefit-Sharing*, IUCN-Regional Biodiversity Program, Asia, 2001.

Glowka L., *A Guide to Designing legal Frameworks to Determine Access to Genetic Resources*, IUCN, Gland Switzerland, 1998.

Hardstaff P., *The Biosafety Protocol: An Analysis*, Royal Society for the Protection of Birds, March 2000.

International Affairs: Special Biodiversity Issue: Vol.76, No.2, April 2000.

Konz P. (ed), *Trade, Environment and Sustainable Development: Views from Sub-Saharan Africa And Latin America*, ICTSD and UNU-IAS, 2000.

Monagle C. and Gonzales A., *Biodiversity and Intellectual Property Rights: Reviewing Intellectual Property Rights in Light of the Objectives of the CBD*, CIEL/WWF International, Gland, Switzerland, March 2001.

OECD, *Handbook of Incentive Measures for Biodiversity: Design and Implementation by the OECD*, OECD Publications, 1999.

O'Riordan T., Cameron J. and Jordan A. (eds), *Reinterpreting the Precautionary Principle*, Cameron May Ltd London, 2000.

Oviedo G. and Larsen P.B. and Maffi L., *Indigenous and Traditional Peoples of the World and Ecoregion Conservation* (Terralingua), WWF International, November 2000.

Posey D., *Cultural and Spiritual Values of Biodiversity*, Intermediate Technology Publications, 1999.

Ramsar Convention Bureau, *The Convention Work Plan 2000–2002*, Ramsar Convention Bureau, Gland Switzerland, 2000.

Seynour F. and Dubash N., *The Right Conditions: The World Bank, Structural Adjustment and Forest Policy Reform*, World Resources Institute, 2000.

Shine C., Williams N., and Gundling L., *A Guide to Designing Legal and Institutional Frameworks on Alien Invasive Species*, IUCN-ELC Environmental Policy and Law Paper #40, IUCN Publications, 2000.

Smith S. and Martin A., *Achieving Sustainability of Biodiversity Conservation: Report of a GEF Thematic Review*, GEF, July 2000.

Svarstad H. and Dhillion S., *Responding to Bioprospecting from Biodiversity in the South to Medicines in the North*, Olaf Norlis Bokhandel, 2000.

Tacconi L., *Biodiversity and Ecological Economics: Participation, Values and Resource Management*, Earthscan, 2001.

Voumard J., *Access to Biological Resources in Commonwealth Areas Commonwealth Public Inquiry*, Environment Australia, 2000.

Walker S., *The TRIPS Agreement, Sustainable Development and the Public Interest*, IUCN Law and Policy Paper No. 41, IUCN, Gland, Switzerland, 2001.

Wood A., Stedman-Edwards P., and Mang J., *The Root Causes of Biodiversity Loss*, Earthscan Publications, July 2000.

CHAPTER

21

PROTECTING THE OZONE LAYER

CONTENTS

1 Introduction

The ozone layer has two functions: it protects the earth against harmful exposure to ultraviolet radiation from the sun; and it controls the temperature structure of the stratosphere. It also acts as a greenhouse gas at a lower altitude and can affect plant growth.

Since the 1960s, there has been an increased thinning of the ozone layer that has developed into a hole over the last five years, both over the Arctic and the Antarctic. The depletion of the ozone layer has been caused by the emission of certain inert gases including chloroflourocarbons (CFCs) and halons. On reaching the ozone layer they are exposed to ultraviolet rays and break down, releasing chlorine and bromine. The potential for increased harm to human health, plant and marine life is becoming more evident. CFCs are used as refrigerants, air conditioner coolants, and in aerosol spray cans.

The protection of the ozone layer has been the object of a series of legal conventions and protocols, starting with the 1985 *Vienna Convention for the Protection of the Ozone Layer* (the *Vienna Convention*), the 1987 *Montreal Protocol on Substances That Deplete the Ozone Layer* (the *Montreal Protocol*), and the many Amendments and Adjustments to the *Montreal Protocol*. There have been many amendments to the Protocol approximately every two years since 1987. This regime is often used by environmental law teachers as a detailed study of modern environmental treaty making, implementation, compliance, and enforcement.

The 1990 Amendments to the *Montreal Protocol* entered into force 10 August 1992, 33 of the 91 parties having ratified the 1990 Amendments by 31 October 1992. This is an indication of the speed with which international environmental law can change when a regime is in place and there is a significant degree of scientific certainty about the global problems.

The parties to the *Montreal Protocol* in 1987 agreed to reduce the production and consumption of five fully halogenated CFCs by 50 percent until the end of the century. They also agreed to freeze production and consumption of three halons, including bromine and similar compounds.

The original *Montreal Protocol* set forth legal obligations to achieve specific limitations and reductions on the level of production and consumption of certain controlled ozone depleting substances (ODSs). It gave a 10–year grace period to developing countries on a per capita emissions basis under certain limits (the so-called Article 5.1 countries). The 1990 Amendments established a financial and technical assistance mechanism that included the need to look at the position of developing countries in relation to their developmental needs, the provision of additional finances, access to relevant technologies, and the transfer of alternative technologies. The 1990 Amendments to the *Montreal Protocol* also altered certain definitional aspects of the Convention and new rules were established to deal with the transfer of calculated levels of production between parties.

The 1992 Amendments introduced changes to the timetable for phasing out certain substances under Articles 2A–2E of the amended Protocol, listed three new controlled substances and some further trade restrictions, adopted new reporting requirements and an indicative list of measures to be taken against parties who are not in compliance with the Protocol and its amendments. The 1992 Amendments also established the Multilateral Fund to provide additional financing for developing countries on a permanent basis.

Changes discussed at the Copenhagen Conference of Parties to the Protocol (1994 Amendments to the Protocol) included the automatic application of new control measures to developing countries and a scheme to enable meetings of the Parties without further amendments to the Protocol.

Key issues relating to the *Montreal Protocol* and Amendments involve building a successful monitoring and

Since the 1960s there has been an increased thinning of the ozone layer over Antarctica that has developed into a hole over the last five years, both over the Arctic and the Antarctic.

compliance regime for the Protocol and how to combat the illegal trade on ODSs. Following the phaseout of the CFCs and halons, many nations rely on "essential use" exemptions for replacement substances and other ODSs. This is a constant challenge. Funding developing nations through the (inadequate) Multilateral Fund remains a serious issue. These matters are covered in more detail in Chapter 23 particularly in relation to the Global Environment Facility (GEF). In addition, Chapter 19, Trade and Environment, contains materials that supplement the material below.

In this chapter, the extracts from Miller and Barrat Brown highlight the history, process, and content of the regime created by the *Vienna Convention* and the *Montreal Protocol*. Miller emphasizes the role and interests of developing countries, nation states, nongovernment organizations, and the multinational corporate producers in the regime creation and transformation as the Protocol has been amended with great regularity. He builds a picture of deeply political negotiations with many economic and technical factors being influential along with very significant changes in public perception caused by the dissemination of new scientific knowledge about the ozone hole. The Barrat Brown article provides a more detailed legal analysis of the Montreal Protocol. Although this article is dated 1991, and there have been changes to the Protocol since then, this article is important to the understanding of many areas of international environmental law involving treaty making and implementation. It sets out the background and history of the *Montreal Protocol* and its amendments. This is a very good analysis of environmental standard setting and compliance issues in international law and is essential reading.

The main focus, of Barrat Brown, is on monitoring and compliance regimes and she draws analogies with other areas where these are better developed, such as human rights regimes, nuclear non-proliferation regimes and the International Labour Organization. These comparisons provide a rich source of ideas and analysis for the future development of the Montreal Protocol and other multilateral environmental agreements (MEAs).

The Montreal Protocol broke important ground in the use of targets and trade sanctions in international environmental law and in the evolution of very rapid amendment processes. Many commentators see it as one of the most effective MEAs to date. However, problems persist particularly in relation to funding, monitoring, and compliance. The extract from Solow highlights the extent and problem of the illegal trade in CFCs as one of the ongoing concerns that are yet to be resolved in this complex area.

Ozone depletion is a matter of global concern. All states must participate in the regimes established to combat the problem effectively. At present, few Asian states manufacture ODSs. However, all states in Asia and the Pacific have a role to play in using substitutes and in controlling trade in illicit material.

A

Teaching Guide

(i) Craig D., *Climate Modification and Stratospheric Ozone as an Example of a Modern Multilateral Environmental Agreement*, Macquarie University, 2001

This session is intended to give an overview of one of the first important MEAs that provided for rigorous targets to be met by national governments to address the global problem of protecting the ozone layer. Prior to this, most MEAs and related international laws provided "soft" approaches to compliance with considerable discretion given to nation states and their sovereign rights in the implementation of their international obligations. There is ongoing controversy over the adequacy of the targets eventually set in the Montreal Protocol (as Amended) and the adequacy of monitoring and compliance. However, it is a sophisticated regime which has responded speedily (in international terms) to the unfolding science on public concern relating to ozone depletion. It is a fascinating study of how the regime creation has been inextricably linked to developing understanding of the underlying science. It is an appropriate example of the operation of the precautionary principle in international treaty making. There was considerable evidence supporting the phenomenon of ozone depletion from human causes, but the extent of the problem was not certain in 1985 (the *Vienna Convention for the Protection of the Ozone Layer*) and in 1987 (the *Montreal Protocol*). However, the science, and public education, proceeded rapidly and amendments to the Montreal Protocol occurred with great regularity. The process is explained with insight by Rich Benedick in his book *Ozone Diplomacy 2*.

The negotiation of the Convention and Protocol were landmarks in the evolution of treaty making to address global environmental problems. However, most contemporary concern about this regime focuses on issues such as monitoring, compliance, additional funding and technology transfer. This session will provide a broad overview of the regime and then focus on these latter issues.

At the conclusion of the session students should:

- Understand the nature of the environmental problems and causes associated with the depletion of the ozone layer;
- Critically understand the role of science, the precautionary principle, the role of nongovernment organizations and public opinion in creating a consensus and momentum for a global MEA;
- Understand the interests and conflicts associated with North-South issues;
- Evaluate the role of industry and corporations, such as Du Pont and ICI,
- Understand the legal and market mechanisms provided for in the Convention and Protocol as control measures to prevent or alleviate ozone depletion
- Critically evaluate the adequacy of the legal and market mechanisms provided for in the Convention and Protocol, and their implementation by parties, having regard to the current understanding of the causes and magnitude of ozone depletion.
- Consider the monitoring and compliance regime, particularly concern over the illegal trade in ODSs, and provide examples of how they might be improved.

The following is a summary of most of the major developments in the regime creation relating to ozone depletion which should be of assistance to teachers and students in organising the material in this chapter.

Background

The following is a brief outline of the important steps along the road to a global regime:

- 1977: US, Canada, Finland, Norway and Sweden urged UNEP to consider international regulation of ozone
- 1978: US banned principal CFCs
- 1980: EC placed limit on production of CFCs and cut use of aerosols by 30 percent
- 1977–1986: UNEP Co-ordinating Committee on Ozone Layer met 8 times during this period
- 1982–1985: UNEP Ad Hoc Working Group of Legal and Technical Experts to elaborate a framework convention
- 1985: Framework Vienna Convention
- 1985: Dramatic evidence of Antarctic Ozone hole and more data confirming role of CFCs
- 1987: Montreal Protocol negotiated
- 1988: Vienna Convention enters into force
- 1989: Montreal Protocol enters into force
- 1987–1990: Further scientific evidence that more action required on ozone depletion
- 1990: London amendments to Montreal Protocol (more substances added, phaseout accelerated, multilateral fund established)
- 1991: Fund commenced
- 1992: London amendments come into force
- 1992: Copenhagen amendments accelerating phaseout
- 1995: Vienna amendments on further adjustments to phase out
- 1997: Montreal Amendment
- 1999: Beijing Amendment

International Legal Instruments and Policies

Overview of Key Instruments

- Vienna Convention for the Protection of the Ozone Layer, 1985
  Key Features: "appropriate" means to be taken by parties according to the means at their disposal and capabilities on the basis of relevant scientific and technical considerations including systematic observations, research exchange, adoption of "appropriate" legislative or administrative measures to reduce or prevent activities harming the ozone layer and cooperate in formulating measures, procedures and standards to implement the Convention
- Montreal Protocol, 1987 (as amended)
  - Annexes of controlled substances
  - CFCs phased out by January 1 1996
  - Halons, carbon tetrachloride, methychloroform also phased out by January 1996
  - Longer term phase-out for HCFCs and methyl-bronide
  - Control mechanism—calculation of consumption and production of controlled substances

- A regional economic "bloc" (e.g., European Community) may jointly fulfil their obligations
- Developing states given a 10-year grace period (Art 5(1))
- After introduction of a financial mechanism (fund) in 1992, developing state compliance linked to implementation of financial resources and technology transfer
- Trade measure—import of controlled substances from non-parties banned from 1 January 1993
- Control and Trade Bans being gradually introduced on products containing controlled substances or produced using controlled substances
- Dispute resolution and implementation—Concerns re: "joint" targets, Art 5(1), whether phase out has been quick or effective enough, weak compliance measures

National Implementation

It is useful for teachers to provide a relevant example of national implementation of the Convention and Protocol. If there is no implementing legislation in your nation state it may be appropriate to choose a comparable jurisdiction in the region, such as Singapore.

It may also be useful to consider what policy, economic and technological steps are being implemented along with the legal regime.

Topics for Further Research and Study

(i) The ongoing concern about the illegal trade in ODSs and particularly the evidence being produced by some nongovernment organizations that it is far more widespread than previously believed.

(ii) The adequacy of additional funding and technology transfer under the Montreal Protocol Fund, the GEF and other national and regional sources.

(iii) The effectiveness role played by trade measures in the protocol and the consistency of these measures with international trade law such as the GATT or regional trade regimes.

(iv) The adequacy of targets provided given concerns over the level of compliance and the "bubble" provided for regional economic blocks such as the EC.

(v) The interface between the regime relating to ozone depletion and the evolving regime relating to climate change under the Framework Convention on Climate Change and the Kyoto Protocol 1997.

2

Nature of the Environmental Problem and Legal Regime

A

Miller M., "The Ozone Layer Protection Regime," *The Third World in Global Environmental Politics*, Lynne Reinner Boulder Publications, 1995

[*Air pollution, global warming, and ozone depletion are transforming the earth's climate and atmosphere. These changes are among the most far-reaching environmental problems people face today. Nation-states have attempted to address these issue areas at the national and international levels. Of the three areas, ozone depletion is the one in which there has been the most significant progress in regime building. UNEP established a committee to examine the ozone depletion problem in 1978, and the process culminated in a framework convention in 1985. Two years later, this convention was strengthened by the Montreal Protocol, which was amended in 1990; the amendment entered into force in August 1992.*]

The Ozone Depletion Issue

Ozone limits the amount of harmful solar ultraviolet radiation that reaches the earth. Without it, life on earth would be impossible. Under normal conditions, chemical reactions triggered by sunlight continuously destroy and replenish ozone. But with the introduction of chemicals that contain chlorine and bromine, the balance has been upset; the earth's ozone shield is being depleted by chemicals such as chlorofluorocarbons (CFCs), which contain chlorine, and halons, which contain bromine. These chemicals can survive intact in the atmosphere for more than a century and each chlorine and bromine atom can destroy tens of thousands of ozone molecules.

The stratospheric ozone layer first became a matter of international concern in 1970, when there was a fear that the supersonic transportation system could damage it significantly. This concern resurfaced in 1974, when two scientists argued that the chlorine in CFCs could destroy the ozone molecules and deplete the ozone layer.

The use of CFCs has become widespread because of their versatility. In the short time since the discovery of this class of chemicals in 1931, they have become a key part of the industrialization process. They have been used in aerosol spray cans, artificial cooling, seat cushions, computer chips, and foam insulation, and, in the 1970s, they began to be used as solvents in the electronics industry. CFCs have been particularly attractive because they have been found to be nontoxic, noncarcinogenic, and inert. The United States and the European Union are the two major producers of these chemicals. In 1986, these two areas accounted for more than 70 percent of world production and more than 50 percent of the world's consumption of CFCs.

In addition to allowing more ultraviolet radiation into the earth's atmosphere, CFCs and halons also prevent infrared radiation from leaving it; thus, they are also factors in global warming. Because of the time lag between the release of the gases and the impact on the ozone layer, even if the production of all ozone-depleting chemicals were to stop now, the gases already rising to the stratosphere and those contained in millions of appliances would continue to erode the ozone layer for many years.

In addition to allowing more ultraviolet radiation into the earth's atmosphere, CFCs and halons also prevent infrared radiation from leaving it; thus, they are also factors in global warming.

Stratospheric ozone depletion is occurring everywhere except over the tropics, although it is most extensive at high latitudes in both hemispheres. Some of the most significant depletion has been observed over the Antarctic region. But ultraviolet radiation will have negative impacts on people all over the world; these effects include increased incidence of melanoma and nonmelanoma skin cancer, eye disorders, and suppression of the immune system. Because ultraviolet radiation is damaging to some plants and ecosystems, ozone depletion will also reduce the long-term productivity of agriculture and fisheries, thereby exacerbating the problem of hunger in areas where food shortages already exist.

Evolution of the Ozone Layer Protection Regime

In the early 1970s, when scientists began to explore the theory that chlorofluorocarbons might be damaging the ozone layer, their findings were initially greeted with some skepticism. But the issue began to elicit such concern that by the late 1970s and early 1980s, some industrialized countries took steps to limit the use and production of CFCs. In 1978 the United States banned the principal CFCs for most uses; in 1980 European Community countries placed a limit on production of CFCs and cut their use in aerosol products by 30 percent. Sweden, Norway, and Canada also placed limits on CFC use.

This concern at the national and regional levels was also reflected at the global level. UNEP expressed serious concern about ozone depletion in 1975. At that time, it funded a study by the World Meteorological Society to explore the hypothesis that ozone depletion was caused by CFCs. But the definition of the issue did not begin until 1977, when the United States, Canada, Finland, Norway, and Sweden urged UNEP to consider international regulation of ozone. A UNEP conference during that year developed a *World Plan of Action on the Ozone Layer*, but ozone depletion was not yet seen as an urgent problem. In order to ascertain the extent of the ozone depletion problem, the governing council of UNEP established the Coordinating Committee on the Ozone Layer, composed of government and industry representatives involved in research on ozone depletion. It met eight times between 1977 and 1986.

Because there was little consensus on the seriousness of the problem, the fact-finding and consensus-building process was prolonged. In May 1981 the governing council of UNEP decided to start work on a global convention for the protection of the ozone layer. The council set up the Ad Hoc Working Group of Legal and Technical Experts for the Elaboration of a *Global Framework Convention for the Protection of the Ozone Layer*. Its task was to prepare a draft convention; in so doing, it met seven times between 1982 and 1985.

At the beginning of the negotiation process, the issue was not yet clearly defined, and nations brought disparate viewpoints to the negotiations. Some were in favor of a complete ban; others were reluctant to dispense with useful, inexpensive chemicals, especially when they were not convinced of their danger by the scientific evidence against CFCs.

The negotiating parties met eight times over a period of three years, but they failed to achieve consensus on the ozone issue. Consequently, they had to be satisfied with a framework convention, which was primarily an agreement to cooperate on monitoring, researching, and exchanging data. The *1985 Vienna Convention for the Protection of the Ozone Layer* imposed no specific obligations to reduce the production of ozone-depleting compounds and did not even identify the compounds that were ozone depleting. The parties did agree to resume negotiations on a binding protocol on ozone protection, which provided an opportunity for regime strengthening. UNEP Executive Director Mostafa Tolba's projection was that a protocol stipulating control measures would be adopted in April 1987.

By the time negotiations for the *Montreal Protocol* began in December 1986, there were more data confirming that CFCs were damaging the ozone layer. In 1985 the Antarctic hole had made dramatic headlines, as scientists discussed the thinning of the ozone layer over Antarctica. In addition, increases in the use of CFCs meant the scenarios on which projections were based had to be revised. These new data informed an Environmental Protection Agency (EPA)-UNEP atmospheric ozone study that became the scientific basis for the ensuing negotiations.

Although nations were still divided about the validity of the scientific evidence against CFCs, the recent evidence was more persuasive. By 1987 most nations realized some controls were necessary; the major disputes were over the extent and the timing of those controls. Lead states advocated a freeze, followed by a gradual 95 percent reduction in the production of CFCs and other ozone-depleting substances over a period of 10 to 14 years. However, other states were in favor of a production cap rather than a freeze or a reduction.

As a result of the new scientific evidence and the pressure from lead states, the parties successfully negotiated the *Montreal Protocol on Substances That Deplete the Ozone Layer*. Industrialized countries pledged that by 1999 they would cut CFC production by 50 percent of the 1986 level. During the first decade of the agreement, developing countries were permitted to increase their CFC use up to 0.66 pound per capita annually. This exception was made because these countries had been major contributors to ozone layer damage; the derogation gave them the opportunity to receive some of the industrial and social benefits of CFCs and halons. In addition, developing nations were entitled to receive technical assistance to make the transition to technologies that were not ozone depleting.

The agreement would result in a net reduction of CFCs of 35 to 40 percent, far less than the 85 percent reduction some analysts regarded as necessary to stabilize the level of ozone depletion. The parties agreed to control five CFCs (numbers 11, 12, 113, 114, and 115) and three bromine compounds (halons 1211, 1301, and 2402). As stated earlier, by 1999, production and consumption of CFCs would be cut back to 50 percent of their 1986 levels; production and consumption of halons would be frozen within three years, except for uses in which no satisfactory substitutes were available.

The *Montreal Protocol* allowed the continued production of ozone-depleting substances, such as methyl chloroform and carbon tetrachloride, and it did not prohibit the use of CFC and halon alternatives that could deplete the ozone layer. It had no provisions for monitoring production and consumption of ozone-depleting chemicals; furthermore, there were no provisions for a fund to defray the costs of CFC substitutes in the developing countries.

In September 1987, 24 nations and the European Economic Community signed the *Montreal Protocol on Substances That Deplete the Ozone Layer*. Within months of the accord, new scientific evidence indicated that more ozone damage had already occurred than the negotiators had assumed would happen in the next 100 years. New measurements by the National Aeronautics and Space Administration indicated that even with the agreement, ozone loss could result in 5 to 20 percent more ultraviolet radiation reaching populated areas within the 40 years following the accord. Exposure resulting from a 10 percent ozone loss would affect the planet's food chain, both on land and in the ocean. Human health would also suffer, as more people would have skin cancer, cataracts, and depressed immune systems.

Consequently, even before the *Montreal Protocol* came into force on schedule on January 1, 1989, a major working group had begun the process of strengthening the protocol's control measures. In March 1989 a ministerial conference in London examined developing nations' involvement in the protocol. This was followed by the Helsinki Meeting of the Parties to the *Montreal Protocol* in May 1989, which took place in an atmosphere of urgency. Many of the parties wanted to accelerate the schedule for the reduction of the production and consumption of CFCs and halons. Although time did not permit a formal amendment of the *Montreal Protocol* at Helsinki, the delegates adopted a declaration that called for phasing out the production and consumption of the five CFCs listed in the protocol by the year 2000. The agreement also addressed the phaseout of halons and reduced dependence on other ozone-depleting substances. In addition, the parties agreed to help developing countries acquire information, research, and training and to assist them in their attempts to devise ways of financing technology transfers and retooling.

In June 1990 there was a second meeting in London to amend the protocol. The attendees addressed an extensive agenda of amendments, which widened the scope of the protocol considerably. The amendments addressed timetables for phasing out ozone-depleting chemicals not included in the original protocol. The five CFCs and three halons already covered by the *Montreal Protocol* were to be completely phased out by the year 2000. In addition, the 93 nations would phase out 10 other fully halogenated CFCs and carbon tetrachloride by the year 2000 and methyl chloroform by 2005. A review of the phaseout schedule for the original five CFCs and methyl chloroform was planned for 1992.

An associated resolution addressed the phaseout of 33 partially halogenated CFCs by no later than the year 2040 and perhaps even by 2020. The parties also resolved not to authorize the production or use of 46 other halons. In addition, in order to ensure the Third World's participation, the amendment provided them with financial incentives, including technical cooperation and a fund that would help them make the switch to alternate technology. Developed countries would contribute to the fund. This amendment entered into force in August 1992.

A few months later, spurred by new scientific information, the regime was further strengthened. It was clear that even if the control measures of the amended *Montreal Protocol* were implemented by all nations, there would still be a significant increase in stratospheric chlorine that would not peak until around the turn of the century. Significant ozone losses were expected throughout the 1990s, and there was the possibility of widespread losses in the Arctic region. With new information coming in on ozone losses, 87 countries met in Copenhagen in November 1992 and agreed to accelerate the phaseout schedule to January 1, 1996.

...[1]3 years elapsed between the definition of the ozone depletion issue in 1977 and the agreement on a binding protocol in 1990. Much of that time was spent reducing scientific uncertainties and building consensus. Because of the strategy of incrementalism, it took five years to negotiate a framework convention, a protocol, and an amendment that contained explicit information on the financing mechanism for the transfer of ozone technology. If it were not for the momentum inspired by the convincing new scientific evidence that surfaced after the *Montreal Protocol*, the ozone layer protection regime would have been a relatively weak response to the problem.

Actors and Interests

Both state and nonstate actors played major roles in the regime-building process. To a large extent, their roles were determined by their position in the global economic system, but policy choices were also conditioned by the nature of the environmental problem and by unfolding scientific information. Ecological interdependence also modified the resistance of the industrialized countries to financial assistance being given to the developing countries. This section focuses on the interest of four sets of actors: the Third World, the industrialized states, corporations involved in the production of CFCs, and environmental lobby groups.

As the regime evolved and as more scientific information became available, significant differences in short- and medium-term interests made the negotiation process difficult.

The Nation-States

All of the nation-state actors embraced the same long-term goal—to protect the ozone layer. But as the regime evolved and as more scientific information became available, significant differences in short- and medium-term interests made the negotiation process difficult.

The Third World

Developing countries were slow to identify a separate set of interests on this issue. In the early stages of the process, they did not emerge as a distinct interest group; in fact, most showed no significant interest in the issue until 1987. In the beginning, ozone depletion was primarily the concern of the nations that were the major users and producers of CFCs and other major ozone-depleting chemicals. Consequently, Third World countries input at the *Vienna Convention* was limited. However, as the regime evolved, these countries realized they had significant interests at stake; therefore, when a freeze was suggested, they expressed their concerns.

CFCs are important ingredients in the industrialization process, but their fastest growing use in the developing world is for cooling. China and India, with about 40 percent of the world's population, consume only about 5 percent of all CFCs. As they continue to industrialize and as the use of refrigerators and air conditioners becomes more widespread, their need for CFCs or chemicals with similar properties will increase. The Chinese government estimated that the 1991 production of ozone-depleting substances was approximately 48,000 metric tons. This was projected to increase to 117,000 metric tons by the year 2000 if no measures were taken to control the demand.

Developing countries key interests, then, were in retaining access to CFCs or in getting assistance in acquiring substitutes. They wanted free or low-cost access to the technologies or, failing that, financial assistance to help them acquire those substitute technologies. India and China argued that it was unfair for the industrialized countries to expect the Third World to incur the costs of switching to CFC substitutes in order to solve a problem they had little part in creating. This perspective was widely held by the Third World group, with Argentina, Brazil, Egypt, Kenya, Mexico, and Venezuela prominent in representing the group's position. Some of the Third World nations pressing hardest for help in making the technological switch were countries whose industrial sectors had already begun to explore alternatives, including Brazil, China, Egypt, and Mexico. Mexico has adopted alternate propellants for use in aerosol sprays, Brazil's researchers have developed a more efficient refrigerator compressor, and China has been working on substitute refrigerants.

The Third World position also received some support from UNEP Executive Director Mostafa Tolba. Although Tolba wanted the conference delegates to agree on a strong treaty, he also supported the establishment of a fund to help the Third World countries find and buy substitute chemicals. Tolba is an Egyptian, and he saw himself as a representative not only of UNEP but also of the interests of developing countries. Because of concerns that Third World interests be represented, under Tolba UNEP financial assistance allowed delegates from about 10 developing countries to attend the ozone negotiations in February 1987.

Industrialized Nation-States

At the beginning of the negotiating process, there were divergent interests within the industrialized countries' group, interests that were put forward by two major groups: the Toronto Group and the European Community (EC). The Toronto Group was composed of the United States, Canada, Sweden, Norway, Finland, and later New Zealand, Australia, and Switzerland. The EC group included its member nations, loosely allied at various stages with Chile, Japan, and the Soviet Union. These two groups had different objectives: The Toronto Group wanted to move more quickly on the ozone matter, and so it was in favor of controlling consumption; the EC group preferred to use production controls. As the major producer and consumer state, the United States might have been expected to side with the EC group; however, it had been forced by domestic pressure to control some CFC uses, and it wanted to reduce the competitive advantage of other nations in this area. The EC included four major CFC producing states: the United Kingdom, France, the Federal Republic of Germany, and Italy. Because of these countries' production capacities, they had an economic interest in continuing production.

By the time of the London meeting on the *Montreal Protocol*, the differences between the Toronto Group and the EC had diminished significantly. Although there was some disagreement about the phaseout schedule, both groups agreed that ozone-depleting substances should be completely phased out. In addition, the Toronto Group and the EC initially found common ground in their resistance to the developing countries' requests for financial assistance.

Nongovernmental Organizations

As the ozone protection regime evolved, the role of interest groups in the process increased. According to the rules of procedure, nongovernmental organizations with expertise in fields related to the protection of the upper atmosphere could participate as observers at the meetings. The chair would ask for their perspectives after the participating nations had presented their positions.

The two major NGO groups represented were environmental interest groups and industrial groups. Their representatives made brief statements at the negotiating sessions, focusing their efforts on briefing the press and lobbying ministers and legislators in individual countries. Their tactics differed. The industry group focused on lobbying the relevant government ministers, whereas the environmental groups focused more on press briefings. Although the lobbies operated in a low-key fashion during the negotiation sessions, the presence of these NGOs did put pressure on the negotiators, either because of the press scrutiny gained by the environmentalists or because of industrial lobbies' access to governments.

Corporate Interests

The small group of CFC producers had a marked interest in the evolution of the ozone protection regime. At the time of the negotiations, 17 ozone-producing companies were operating in 16 countries. The leader was the US-based DuPont, which produced CFCs for the major markets of North America, Europe, and Japan. The company produced more than 25 percent of the global output of CFCs and controlled 50 percent of the US market.

The CFC manufacturers saw regulation of the chemicals as inimical to their interests; consequently, DuPont, and the other US manufacturers, and European manufacturers, such as Imperial Chemical Industries, tried to block the process of regime evolution. As part of this effort, the US manufacturers formed a lobbying organization, the Alliance for a Responsible CFC Policy. In the initial stages of the evolution of the ozone regime, industry representatives denied there was any scientific basis for linking ozone depletion to CFCs, and scientific dissension in the early stages of the negotiations helped to support their position. The industry group also did not want the US to implement a unilateral freeze, since this move would make its members less competitive in the world market. The industry position was weakened, however, in September 1986, when DuPont issued a statement favoring a protocol to limit CFC emissions. DuPont's change of position can be seen more as a function of the global economy than one of the unfolding scientific knowledge. The company envisioned a globally competitive position in the market for CFC substitutes, and this perspective motivated the change in its stand on the issue. Because DuPont had been engaged in the search for CFC substitutes, it was better suited to make a fast switch to a CFC-restricted market than were its competitors; consequently, international restrictions on CFCs gave the company an initial advantage.

Environmental NGOs

The general objective of these groups was to persuade decision-makers to implement policies that would halt and reverse the ozone depletion process. They also supported the establishment of a fund to assist developing countries with technology conversion, which they felt was a necessary incentive for an effective regime.

Environmental groups involved in the evolution of the ozone protection regime included Friends of the Earth (FOE), Greenpeace, the Environmental Defence Fund, and the Natural Resources Defence Council (NRDC). The NRDC got involved in the regime process in 1986 when it made the first proposal for a complete phaseout of CFCs and halons over a period of 10 years. But the bulk of the NGOs' input occurred following the signing of the *Montreal Protocol* in 1987. Three weeks after the signing, the affiliates of FOE International made ozone layer protection their top priority in a campaign that targeted both industry and consumers. These nongovernmental organizations used national lobbying, international lobbying, and consumer boycotts as tools.

Although the environmental NGOs did not have direct input into the negotiation process, through their continued pressure they did affect the process of regime evolution and were also instrumental in their support of a technology transfer fund for developing countries. A statement to that effect, representing the viewpoints of 93 NGOs worldwide, was presented at the First Meeting of the Parties to the *Montreal Protocol* in Helsinki in May 1989.

The Third World in the Regime's Evolution

The Third World countries were slow to assume active roles in the development of the ozone layer protection regime; consequently, they did not try to affect the definition of the problem. But their interest and efforts increased as the negotiation process evolved.

Defining the Problem

At the beginning of the problem definition process, there was scientific uncertainty about the gravity of the ozone depletion problem. The definition process reduced this uncertainty by accomplishing three major tasks: It confirmed that ozone depletion was occurring; it confirmed the connection between the use of CFCs and halons and the damage to the ozone layer; and it estimated the extent and rate of depletion.

The ecological epistemic community, which played a major role in defining the problem, was a transnational one. It was made up of atmospheric scientists and policymakers, including officials of UNEP, the US Environmental Protection Agency, and the US State Department's Bureau of Oceans and International Environmental and Scientific Affairs (OES). The epistemic community used a variety of channels to affect the decision-making process. In the process of drafting documents and reports, gathering data, organizing scientific panels, and lobbying delegates, it was able to substantially define the issue and modify the agenda for the negotiations. Significant components of the epistemic community participated in UNEP's Coordinating Committee on the Ozone Layer, in which they were able to share information.

The incorporation of the epistemic community into the UNEP process enhanced the community's ability to define the ozone depletion problem. The expertise of the community was accepted; consequently, it was able to suggest the policy implications of the scientific developments. The group's perspectives gained wide credibility within the political community. Because of this, the policymakers were willing to move ahead with the negotiations, even in the face of some scientific uncertainty.

Corporations involved in the production of ozone-depleting chemicals were initially opposed to the epistemic community's definition of the problem, and they tried to modify that definition. By questioning the evolving body of knowledge about ozone depletion, the corporations were able to slow the process of problem definition, but they could not substantially modify that definition.

As a group, developing countries had little to do with the definition of the ozone depletion problem. Developing country interests were not substantially represented within the epistemic community. Although the ecological epistemic community was transnational, its major components were based in the industrialized world. Much of the research was done and supported by Americans, but atmospheric scientists in Belgium, Britain, France, Japan, and Norway were also at work on the problem. Consequently, epistemic communities based in the industrialized countries defined the problem and set the scientific context for the negotiations.

Bargaining

The bargaining process over the ozone protection regime actually began before the issue was clearly defined. In the beginning, the Third World countries played a minor role in the negotiations, primarily because they did not have clearly defined interests. Nations with economic interests, however, as well as industries involved in CFC production, did have a clear understanding of the interests at stake.

Nations brought dissimilar viewpoints to the negotiations. Some favored a global ban on CFCs 11 and 12 in aerosols (except for essential purposes) and a limit on CFC emissions in nonaerosol uses. The United States, which accounted for 30 percent of worldwide production, was prepared to be the lead state. However, other nations were reluctant to undertake such sweeping actions until they felt the scientific evidence against CFCs was compelling. The latter group would have been satisfied with a framework convention.

The European Community accounted for 45 percent of world CFC output, and by the mid-1980s it was exporting a third of its production to developing states. Because of the major producer states' interests in continuing production, the EC member states constituted a veto coalition. Since these states' participation was necessary for a strong ozone protection regime, their cooperation was important. The large developing states, such as India, China, Indonesia, Brazil, and Mexico, also appear to have had some potential as a veto coalition. Their bargaining leverage was based not on their consumption of CFCs but on their potential as producers and consumers of CFCs. These countries were already producing on a small scale; although they were providing less than 5 percent of the world's CFC production, their production was increasing by 7 to 10 percent each year. However, in the negotiations on the *Vienna Convention*, these states did not take advantage of their veto power. At this stage, no Third World country played an active role.

The Toronto Group took the lead, pushing for simultaneous negotiation of a framework convention and associated protocols that would obligate states to reduce CFC use. However, the veto coalition would not support the negotiation of regulatory protocols, taking the position that the state of scientific knowledge was insufficient to support such a protocol. The lead states remained on the offensive, proposing a worldwide ban on nonessential uses of CFCs in spray cans in 1983. But the veto coalition offered a counterproposal: Total CFC production would be capped at a level that would allow EC producers to increase production by 30 percent beyond the anticipated 1985 level.

Over a three-year period there were eight negotiating sessions, but the groups failed to achieve consensus on the ozone issue. In 1985, after three years of negotiation, the United States began to define ozone depletion as an urgent issue, but still the veto coalition would not yield. As a result, the parties had to be satisfied with the *Vienna Convention*, which was a framework convention.

The *Montreal Protocol* began the process of strengthening the ozone layer protection regime. Because of new findings, most nations accepted the idea of some controls. However, the extent and the timing of the controls were contentious issues. Lead states argued for a freeze, followed by a gradual reduction in the production of ozone-depleting substances over a period of 10 to 14 years, whereas the veto coalition wanted a production cap. The Toronto Group still pressed for a cut, but as a compromise its members suggested a 50 percent cut. As late as April 1987 the EC insisted it would agree to a reduction of no more than 20 percent, but at the Montreal Conference later that year, the EC representative agreed to a 50 percent reduction.

The EC veto coalition was beginning to disintegrate. Some of its members (the Federal Republic of Germany, Denmark, Belgium, and the Netherlands) now felt it was necessary to implement stronger regulation. In addition, the United States was exerting continued diplomatic pressure on the Community. The EC realized that, by remaining inflexible, it risked being blamed for the failure of the negotiations. With the change in the EC position, the parties were able to successfully negotiate the *Montreal Protocol on Substances That Deplete the Ozone Layer*. By 1999 industrialized countries were to cut CFC production by 50 percent of the 1986 level.

Developing countries successfully pressed for some concessions; they obtained a derogation that would allow them to increase their CFC use for the first decade of the agreement. They were also to receive technical assistance as well as information and advice on CFC recycling and conservation. The fear was that without some concessions Third World countries would set up their own CFC production plants.

But these concessions did not address all of the developing countries' major concerns regarding the evolving regime. Of particular concern was the fact that there were no provisions for a fund to help them make the switch to CFC substitutes. The fund was not established because the United States, Japan, and the EC countries opposed it. Because there were no provisions for financial assistance, three major developing countries—China,

India, and Brazil—refused to sign the protocol. These were important holdouts, because they had the potential to become major producers and consumers of CFCs. They refused to participate in the regime until the industrialized countries agreed to provide financial and technological assistance. UNEP's Tolba supported them in their calls for the establishment of the fund.

Scientific revelations about ozone depletion continued to unfold, and they spurred the regime strengthening process. The *Montreal Protocol* came into force on January 1, 1989, and the negotiations on its amendment began promptly. At a meeting to amend the protocol in Helsinki in May 1989, the veto coalition began to shift its position dramatically. The EC members were among 80 nations voting for a complete CFC phaseout by the year 2000.

At the London meeting in June 1990, a new coalition of 13 industrialized states pushed for a 1997 deadline for the final elimination of CFCs. However, the four leading CFC-producing states—the United States, the United Kingdom, France, and Italy—joined by the Soviet Union offered an alternate phaseout date of the year 2000. The push by some industrialized states for a 1997 deadline caused the United States to change from a lead to a veto role.

When the London Conference began, the industrialized countries were still opposed to the establishment of a fund to assist the developing countries in their transition from CFC technologies. The United States was strongly opposed to the inclusion of this provision, not only because it meant funds would have to be provided by developed countries, but also because of the precedent that would be established. The implications could be significant for subsequent agreements, such as the *Climate Change Convention*. But the environmental NGOs and some nation-states saw the establishment of a fund as crucial to winning developing countries' cooperation. Continued unrestricted CFC use or production by Third World nations would make any agreement on a reduction or a phaseout meaningless. These countries have the power to invalidate any negotiated regime.

The switch from negotiating control measures to discussing financial mechanisms resulted in a realignment of the major actors. Initially, developing nations had not been significantly involved in the negotiation of this regime, but they identified a funding mechanism as crucial for their transition to substitute technologies that would not be ozone-depleting. Very few of these countries had been involved in the development of the *Vienna Convention*, but as the regime evolved, they became increasingly immersed in it and began to realize its implications for their own industrial development. In spite of their reluctance over, and resistance to, the establishment of a fund, the developed nations realized that the developing nations' cooperation was essential to the long-term success of the *Montreal Protocol*. After intensive bargaining and a last-minute policy reversal by the United States, participants agreed to provide developing countries with financial incentives and technical cooperation; in return, developing countries would subscribe to the amendments by becoming parties to the protocol.

Developing countries were concerned that developed countries would try to pass off current assistance as a part of this new fund, and they were largely successful in preventing such a move. Some bilateral cooperation could be included as part of a nation's contribution, but this was not to exceed 20 percent of the total. Only developed countries would be levied for contributions to the fund, but payments by developing countries, nongovernmental organizations, and international organizations were also encouraged.

From this new multilateral fund, grants and concessional disbursements would be made to developing countries, provided the parties agree to the specific expenditures. Fund policies would be the responsibility of the Annual Meeting of the Parties, and its operation and administration would be handled by an executive committee working with agencies such as the World Bank. The agreement on financing arrangements paved the way for the support of major Third World countries such as China and India.

During the course of the negotiations, some of the participants and all of the interested NGOs tried to increase their leverage through use of the media. As regime negotiations progressed, it became easier to gain increased media coverage since there was increasing public interest in the issue of protecting the world's atmosphere. By the time the *Montreal Protocol* negotiations began, media attention was significant.

Developing countries were usually at a disadvantage with respect to the size and makeup of their delegations. A developing country was likely to be represented by a single generalist, whereas the industrialized countries were more likely to have a team of specialists. Countries that had a strong economic interest in the process were usually represented by large delegations. But most delegations fell between these two extremes. They had, on average, two to four members, usually representing scientific, industrial, economic, legal, and political disciplines. The delegations that had specialists had an advantage since these people usually had special knowledge of, or experience regarding, the ozone issue.

Regime Transformation

The initial controls provided in the *Montreal Protocol* have been substantially strengthened as a result of two major changes. One is the acceleration of the CFC phaseout schedule in the new agreements made in London and in Copenhagen. The other major change involves the establishment of the fund for developing countries. Because these countries' cooperation is so important to the effectiveness of the regime, as a part of the transformation process they were able to obtain agreement on the technology transfer fund. But they were only able to do so because the community of nations was convinced by the growing fund of information about the damage to the ozone layer. Because of the nature of the atmosphere, all of the world's nations are vulnerable to any ozone layer damage done by other actors; therefore, without the cooperation of Third World countries, the regulatory regime would be ineffective.

The potential for further regime transformation still exists. With the developing countries now on board, the regime can be further strengthened by speeding up the timetable for phaseout. Transformation can also take the form of regime weakening, and the developing countries or any other large country or group of countries can render the regime ineffective by forcing the countries to delay the final phaseout date.

Conclusion

The pattern of accession to the agreements indicates the changing salience of the ozone layer protection regime for developing countries. The Third World's low level of interest in the early phase of regime evolution is indicated by the fact that during the year the *Vienna Convention* was open for signature, only 7 of the 28 signatories were Third World countries, and these did not include the most populous countries, which were potentially large users and producers of CFCs. The Third World signatories were Argentina, Burkina Faso, Chile, Egypt, Mexico, Morocco, and Peru. In contrast, all of the members of the Group of Seven, except for Japan, were signatories. The industrialized countries had a clear understanding of how this issue would affect their economic interests...shows, the Third World states were also slow to ratify the convention. By the time the *Vienna Convention* entered into force three and a half years after its adoption, only eight Third World states had ratified it, and this group did not include China, India, and Indonesia—the Third World states with the largest populations. These early ratifiers are equally divided between low and middle-income states, but with the exception of Mexico and Venezuela, they are primarily exporters of services and non-fuel primary products.

By the time of the *Montreal Protocol*, there was increased Third World interest, but the protocol was still unsatisfactory to that group's major actors. Consequently, at the time of its entry into force, only 6 of the 30 state parties were from the Third World. Once again, the parties were a mix of low and middle-income states. With the exception of Uganda and Nigeria, they were primarily exporters of services and diversified exporters.

By the time of the Montreal Protocol, *there was increased Third World interest, but the protocol was still unsatisfactory to that group's major actors.*

With the *London Amendment*, we see a change of pattern among the Third World states. Ten of the 30 states that ratified the agreement before its entry into force were from that group of states. Because of the concessions made regarding the establishment of the fund, China, India, and Indonesia—the world's most populous countries—were among the early ratifiers. Most of the early ratifiers were low-income countries, and half were primarily diversified exporters.

...[T]he early ratifiers of the ozone protection agreements are drawn from a small group of 18 Third World states, less than 14 percent of that group. All are low- and middle-income states. High-income states are not represented; nor did they play high-profile roles in the negotiations. The largest major export categories represented are diversified exporters and non-fuel primary exporters. China is the only country that is primarily an exporter of manufactures.

Finally, this group represents some of the Third World states for which the ozone issue is clearly salient, because of either circumstances or choice. For China and India, it is particularly relevant because of their large populations and growing industrial sectors. These two states, along with Egypt, Kenya, Mexico, and Venezuela, also chose to assertively represent the Third World position in the negotiations. Additionally, the early ratifiers included states—such as China, Egypt, and Mexico—for which the issue had acquired salience because of their investment in alternate technologies.

Since the ozone issue had not acquired high salience for the Third World countries in the early stages of regime evolution, they were not involved in the definition of the ozone depletion problem; nor did they have leading roles in the evolution of the regime. They had very little input in the early negotiating sessions; however, as they began to become aware of the interests at stake, they gradually directed their energy toward modifying the regime.

Because of the unique characteristics of the atmosphere, developing countries were able to modify the evolution of the ozone protection regime. Ozone depletion involves the atmosphere, which is a common property resource. It is impossible to exclude users, and a situation of open access exists. This property and access arrangement had significant implications for negotiations and implementation. A proper perception of the common-property nature of the resource heightened the sense of interdependence and had implications for the nature of the bargaining. Developing countries have the ability to sabotage efforts to reverse the damage to the ozone layer; thus, the decisions could not be based simply on the international distribution of power. Consequently, parties and interests that wanted a successful ozone layer protection regime had to take the Third World's demands and interests into account.

The globalized nature of the biosphere also has significant implications for implementation. Given the nature of the ozone issue, regime implementation is dependent on the cooperation of all nation-states. It is crucial that the parties carry through with the fund provisions and with other commitments; otherwise, some developing countries may be unable to switch to technology that is not ozone-depleting.

The ozone layer protection regime has evolved gradually. In its early stages, the progress of the Toronto Group and its supporters was slowed by nations that perceived that their economic interests were threatened. Reluctance to set up a fund for the Third World also slowed the regime's progress. However, the dynamic nature of the *Vienna Convention* allowed the participants to react quickly to advances in scientific knowledge. The end result has been an environmental regime that is generally regarded as effective and viable. The perception of viability springs from the fact that the regime has responded to a technological problem with a technological solution. Because the ozone issue is primarily technological, it can be effectively addressed through the cooperation of the state and industrial sectors. Unlike other environmental problems, it does not require significant socioeconomic change.

3

The Vienna Convention and the Montreal Protocol

A

Vienna Convention for the Protection of the Ozone Layer (1985)

(i) Hunter D., Salzman J., and Zaelke D., "Principles and Concepts in International Environmental Law," Chapter in *International Environmental Law and Policy*, New York, Foundation Press, 1998, pp 554–555

The *Vienna Convention for the Protection of the Ozone Layer* was signed by 20 countries [in 1985]. Rather than controls on CFC consumption or production, the Convention called for countries to take "appropriate measures" to protect the ozone layer and established an international mechanism for research, monitoring and exchange of information. With very little known about the scale of CFC production in Soviet bloc and developing countries, it was hoped that this data would form the basis for establishing a global production baseline. No chemicals were identified as ozone-depleting substances. Instead, in a non-threatening description, the annex listed chemicals "thought to have the potential to modify the chemical and physical properties of the ozone layer". At the end of the meeting, despite objections by the EC, a non-binding resolution was passed addressing controls. The Vienna Convention's failure to establish controls on production or consumption seemed to ensure that the future of CFCs still seemed bright.

B

The Montreal Protocol

(i) Summary of Protocol Provisions

(a) Hunter D., Salzman J., and Zaelke D., "Principles and Concepts in International Environmental Law," Chapter in *International Environmental Law and Policy*, New York, Foundation Press, 1998, pp 319–326

The Montreal Protocol on Substances That Deplete the Ozone Layer

The negotiations in Montreal could not have shown a greater contrast to the small affair two years earlier in Vienna. With over 60 countries participating (more than half from developing countries), many industrial and environmental groups, and wide media coverage, the world's attention focused on CFCs. The workshops and lobbying since Vienna paid off, for the Protocol was passed by consensus. *See* 26 I.L.M. 1550 (1987).

Coverage

In the Vienna Convention, no chemicals had been identified or regulated as ODSs. The Protocol, however, not only froze production and consumption levels of CFCs upon ratification (CFCs 11, 12, 113, 114, 115) and of halons three years later (Halons 1211, 1301, 2402), but also set in place a reduction schedule for CFCs. By 1998, a 50 percent reduction in CFC consumption was to be achieved. Because monitoring consumption of ODSs was thought infeasible, a surrogate formula was adopted defining a country's consumption of CFCs or halons as:

Consumption = production + imports - exports

Thus a major CFC producer could satisfy the reduction requirements by decreasing its domestic use but still continuing to export. An importing country would measure its consumption simply by adding domestic production and imports together.

In order to give countries flexibility in their reduction schedules, the Protocol developed a "basket" strategy. Each chemical's ozone-depleting potential (ODP) was compared to CFC 11 (arbitrarily given a value of 1). Since CFC 113 is less destructive of the ozone layer than CFC 11, its ODP is 0.8. Using the basket strategy, a country would achieve the same reduction in consumption levels either by using 8 tons less of CFC 11 or 10 tons less of CFC 113 (8 tons x ODP of 1 = 10 tons x ODP of 0.8). This arithmetic was important because CFC 113 was widely used as a solvent in the electronics industry. Countries like Japan, which had opposed CFC 113's inclusion in the Protocol, could now choose to reduce a greater percentage of other CFCs while conserving CFC 113's use.

The reduction schedules and basket strategy not only avoided chemical-by-chemical negotiations but provided clear signals for industrial development by removing uncertainty. CFC producers like DuPont and ICI could now justify heavy R&D spending in CFC alternatives. CFC users like IBM and Toshiba could justify investments for in-process recycling and recovery systems to reduce the need for additional, and certainly more expensive, CFC stocks. For businesses in ratifying countries, long-term investments in CFC production or CFC consumption technologies suddenly seemed less attractive.

Trade Measures

If the Protocol's only teeth were scheduled phaseouts of controlled substances, countries would have a strong incentive not to sign in order to gain the newly-freed market share for themselves. To avoid this free rider behavior and as an incentive for countries to join, the Protocol provided tough trade measures.

Regarding imports, parties to the Protocol are prohibited from importing from non-parties either controlled substances or certain products containing controlled substances. These products include domestic, commercial and vehicle airconditioners, refrigerators, and portable fire extinguishers. When the parties deem it feasible, the Protocol requires a ban on the import of products produced with controlled substances (this ban has not yet been implemented). The country of origin can avoid these onerous restrictions only if it demonstrates full compliance with the Protocol's reduction schedules.

Regarding exports, parties must similarly ban the export of controlled substances to non-parties unless the country of destination can demonstrate full compliance with the Protocol's reduction schedules. Exports to non-parties that are in compliance are not counted as exports

Parties were required to assess and review controls at least every four years. This would ensure that the Protocol's international controls reflected scientists' improved understanding of the mechanisms and causes of ozone depletion.

in the country's consumption calculation, so they must be offset by an equal reduction in production or imports.

As an example, if Country P is a party and Country N is a non-party and not in compliance with the protocol, there can be no trade in controlled substances between the countries, and Country P cannot import products containing controlled substances from Country N. If Country N remains a non-Party but complies with the Protocol, Country P can export controlled substances to Country N but cannot subtract this amount from imports or production in calculating national consumption. Subject to the reduction schedules, parties may freely trade controlled substances amongst themselves.

Technical and Financial Assistance

Article 5 of the Protocol addressed aid to developing countries. While developing countries' per capita consumption of CFCs was much lower than in the developed world, their domestic requirements were steadily growing. Since the manufacture of CFCs is a low-cost, low-tech operation, no practical barriers prevented cottage CFC industries from sprouting around the globe. Thus in part to accept the responsibility for having created most of the ozone-depleting substances and in part to encourage broad international participation, developed countries supported a ten-year period following ratification for developing countries to increase their consumption to 0.3 Kg per capita in order to meet basic domestic needs. Following this period, developing countries would have ten years more to reduce their consumption by 50 percent. While this allowed growth may have seemed counter- productive, even if all the developing countries increased their use of ODS to 0.3 Kg per capita the total consumption would still only have been 25–30 percent of the 1986 US and EC consumption.

Moreover, negotiators thought it unlikely parties would reach their per capita limit because they believed CFC-based technologies would be largely dead within a decade. Rather, the growth limit provided a means to ease the transition away from ozone-depleting substances. When it came to providing developing countries specific financial and technical assistance for alternative substances and new technologies, however, the Protocol provided only vague promises of facilitating access.

Ratification and Amendments

With clear restrictions negotiated, the problem remained of when the controls would enter into force. If parties were bound by the trade and reduction provisions as soon as they ratified, there would be a perverse incentive for countries to hold out and gain short-term competitive benefits by intransigence. To avoid this behavior, the Protocol entered into force only when at least 11 countries representing two-thirds of global production had ratified. This was yet other innovation in international law.

The most important innovation of the Protocol, however, was its flexibility. Parties were required to assess and review controls at least every four years. This would ensure that the Protocol's international controls reflected scientists' improved understanding of the mechanisms and causes of ozone depletion.

(ii) Schedule of Phaseouts of Ozone-Depleting Substances

(a) Hunter D., Salzman J., and Zaelke D., "The Law of Air and Atmosphere," in *International Environmental Law and Policy*, New York, Foundation Press, 1998, p 574

(iii) *The Montreal Protocol on Substances That Deplete the Ozone Layer*, 26 ILM, 1550, 1987

as adjusted and amended by the
Second Meeting of the Parties
(London, 27–29 June 1990)

and by the Fourth Meeting of the Parties
(Copenhagen, 23–25 November 1992)

and further adjusted by the
Seventh Meeting of the Parties
(Vienna, 5–7 December 1995)

and further adjusted and amended by the
Ninth Meeting of the Parties
(Montreal, 15–17 September 1997)

Article 1: Definitions

For the purposes of this Protocol:

1. "Convention" means the *Vienna Convention for the Protection of the Ozone Layer*, adopted on 22 March 1985.

Summary of Montreal Protocol Measures

Ozone-Depleting Substances	Baseline Year	Montreal 1987	London 1990	Copenhagen 1992	Vienna 1995
CFC 11,12, 113, 114, 115	1996 levels	1996 freeze 1993—20% 1998—50%	1995—50% 1997—85% 2000 ban	1994—75% 1996 ban	
10 other CFCs	1989 levels	not covered	1993—20% 1997—85% 2000 ban	1994—75% 1996 ban	
Halons 1211, 1301, 2402	1986 levels	1992 freeze	1995—80% 2000 ban	1994 ban	
Other Halons		not covered	Nonbinding resolution discouraging use; mandatory reports		
Carbon Tetrachloride	1989 levels	not covered	1995—85% 2000 ban	1995—85% 1996 ban	
Methyl Choroform	1989 levels	not covered	1993 freeze 1995—30% 2000—70% 2005 ban	1994—50% 1996 ban	
HCFCs	1989 levels	not covered	Nonbinding resolution discouraging use; mandatory reports; call for ban no later than 2040	1996 freeze 2015—90% 2030 ban	
Methyl Bromide	1995-1998 levels	not covered	not covered	1995 freeze Resolution for future reductions	2020 ban
Financial Support	total phase-out by 2020c	Facilitated bilateral and multilateral aid to LDCs	International fund controlled by parties; administered by World Bank; 3-year budget from $160 to $240 million	Established Multilateral Fund in Montreal; 3-year budget $340-500 million dollars	2010 ban Except for critical agricultural uses
Technology Transfer	phased out end of 1995	Parties will "facilitate access" of LDCs to technology	Parties will "take every practicable step" to transfer technology to developing countries fairly and most favorably		

2. "Parties" means, unless the text otherwise indicates, Parties to this Protocol.
3. "Secretariat" means the Secretariat of the Convention.
4. "Controlled substance" means a substance in Annex A, Annex B, Annex C or Annex E to this Protocol, whether existing alone or in a mixture. It includes the isomers of any such substance, except as specified in the relevant Annex, but excludes any controlled substance or mixture which is in a manufactured product other than a container used for the transportation or storage of that substance.
5. "Production" means the amount of controlled substances produced, minus the amount destroyed by technologies to be approved by the Parties and minus the amount entirely used as feedstock in the manufacture of other chemicals. The amount recycled and reused is not to be considered as "production".
6. "Consumption" means production plus imports minus exports of controlled substances.
7. "Calculated levels" of production, imports, exports and consumption means levels determined in accordance with Article 3.
8. "Industrial rationalization" means the transfer of all or a portion of the calculated level of production of one Party to another, for the purpose of achieving economic efficiencies or responding to anticipated shortfalls in supply as a result of plant closures.

Article 2: Control Measures

5. Any Party may, for one or more control periods, transfer to another Party any portion of its calculated level of production set out in Articles 2A to 2E, and Article 2H, provided that the total combined calculated levels of production of the Parties concerned for any group of controlled substances do not exceed the production limits set out in those Articles for that group. Such transfer of production shall be notified to the Secretariat by each of the Parties concerned, stating the terms of such transfer and the period for which it is to apply.

5.*bis* Any Party not operating under paragraph 1 of Article 5 may, for one or more control periods, transfer to another such Party any portion of its calculated level of consumption set out in Article 2F, provided that the calculated level of consumption of controlled substances in Group I of Annex A of the Party transferring the portion of its calculated level of consumption did not exceed 0.25 kilograms per capita in 1989 and that the total combined calculated levels of consumption of the Parties concerned do not exceed the consumption limits set out in Article 2F. Such transfer of consumption shall be notified to the Secretariat by each of the Parties concerned, stating the terms of such transfer and the period for which it is to apply.

6. Any Party not operating under Article 5, that has facilities for the production of Annex A or Annex B controlled substances under construction, or contracted for, prior to 16 September 1987, and provided for in national legislation prior to 1 January 1987, may add the production from such facilities to its 1986 production of such substances for the purposes of determining its calculated level of production for 1986, provided that such facilities are completed by 31 December 1990 and that such production does not raise that Party's annual calculated level of consumption of the controlled substances above 0.5 kilograms per capita.
7. Any transfer of production pursuant to paragraph 5 or any addition of production pursuant to paragraph 6 shall be notified to the Secretariat, no later than the time of the transfer or addition.
8.
   (a) Any Parties which are Member States of a regional economic integration organization as defined in Article 1 (6) of the Convention may agree that they shall jointly fulfil their obligations respecting consumption under this Article and Articles 2A to 2H provided that their total combined calculated level of consumption does not exceed the levels required by this Article and Articles 2A to 2H.

   (b) The Parties to any such agreement shall inform the Secretariat of the terms of the agreement before the date of the reduction in consumption with which the agreement is concerned.

   (c) Such agreement will become operative only if all Member States of the regional economic integration organization and the organization concerned are Parties to the Protocol and have notified the Secretariat of their manner of implementation.

9.
(a) Based on the assessments made pursuant to Article 6, the Parties may decide whether:
(i) Adjustments to the ozone-depleting potentials specified in Annex A, Annex B, Annex C and/or Annex E should be made and, if so, what the adjustments should be; and
(ii) Further adjustments and reductions of production or consumption of the controlled substances should be undertaken and, if so, what the scope, amount and timing of any such adjustments and reductions should be;
(b) Proposals for such adjustments shall be communicated to the Parties by the Secretariat at least six months before the meeting of the Parties at which they are proposed for adoption;
(c) In taking such decisions, the Parties shall make every effort to reach agreement by consensus. If all efforts at consensus have been exhausted, and no agreement reached, such decisions shall, as a last resort, be adopted by a two-thirds majority vote of the Parties present and voting representing a majority of the Parties operating under Paragraph 1 of Article 5 present and voting and a majority of the Parties not so operating present and voting;
(d) The decisions, which shall be binding on all Parties, shall forthwith be communicated to the Parties by the Depositary. Unless otherwise provided in the decisions, they shall enter into force on the expiry of six months from the date of the circulation of the communication by the Depositary.

10. Based on the assessments made pursuant to Article 6 of this Protocol and in accordance with the procedure set out in Article 9 of the Convention, the Parties may decide:
(a) whether any substances, and if so which, should be added to or removed from any annex to this Protocol, and
(b) the mechanism, scope and timing of the control measures that should apply to those substances;

11. Notwithstanding the provisions contained in this Article and Articles 2A to 2H Parties may take more stringent measures than those required by this Article and Articles 2A to 2H.

Introduction to the Adjustments

[The Second, Fourth, Seventh and Ninth Meetings of the Parties to the Montreal Protocol on Substances That Deplete the Ozone Layer decided, on the basis of assessments made pursuant to Article 6 of the Protocol, to adopt adjustments and reductions of production and consumption of the controlled substances in Annexes A, B, C and E to the Protocol... The adjustments to "targets" and phaseouts are summarised in Chart form above.]

Article 3: Calculation of Control Levels

For the purposes of Articles 2, 2A to 2H and 5, each Party shall, for each group of substances in Annex A, Annex B, Annex C or Annex E determine its calculated levels of:
(a) Production by:
(i) multiplying its annual production of each controlled substance by the ozone-depleting potential specified in respect of it in Annex A, Annex B, Annex C or Annex E;
(ii) adding together, for each such Group, the resulting figures;
(b) Imports and exports, respectively, by following, mutatis mutandis, the procedure set out in subparagraph (a); and
(c) Consumption by adding together its calculated levels of production and imports and subtracting its calculated level of exports as determined in accordance with subparagraphs (a) and (b). However, beginning on 1 January 1993, any export of controlled substances to non-Parties shall not be subtracted in calculating the consumption level of the exporting Party.

Article 4: Control of Trade with Non-Parties

1. As of 1 January 1990, each party shall ban the import of the controlled substances in Annex A from any State not party to this Protocol.

1*bis*. Within one year of the date of the entry into force of this paragraph, each Party shall ban the import of the controlled substances in Annex B from any State not party to this Protocol.

1*ter.* Within one year of the date of entry into force of this paragraph, each Party shall ban the import of any controlled substances in Group II of Annex C from any State not party to this Protocol.

1*qua.* Within one year of the date of entry into force of this paragraph, each Party shall ban the import of the controlled substance in Annex E from any State not party to this Protocol.

2. As of 1 January 1993, each Party shall ban the export of any controlled substances in Annex A to any State not party to this Protocol.

2*bis.* Commencing one year after the date of entry into force of this paragraph, each Party shall ban the export of any controlled substances in Annex B to any State not party to this Protocol.

2*ter.* Commencing one year after the date of entry into force of this paragraph, each Party shall ban the export of any controlled substances in Group II of Annex C to any State not party to this Protocol.

2*qua.* Commencing one year of the date of entry into force of this paragraph, each Party shall ban the export of the controlled substance in Annex E to any State not party to this Protocol.

3. By 1 January 1992, the Parties shall, following the procedures in Article 10 of the Convention, elaborate in an annex a list of products containing controlled substances in Annex A. Parties that have not objected to the annex in accordance with those procedures shall ban, within one year of the annex having become effective, the import of those products from any State not party to this Protocol.

3*bis.* Within three years of the date of the entry into force of this paragraph, the Parties shall, following the procedures in Article 10 of the Convention, elaborate in an annex a list of products containing controlled substances in Annex B. Parties that have not objected to the annex in accordance with those procedures shall ban, within one year of the annex having become effective, the import of those products from any State not party to this Protocol.

3*ter.* Within three years of the date of entry into force of this paragraph, the Parties shall, following the procedures in Article 10 of the Convention, elaborate in an annex a list of products containing controlled substances in Group II of Annex C. Parties that have not objected to the annex in accordance with those procedures shall ban, within one year of the annex having become effective, the import of those products from any State not party to this Protocol.

4. By 1 January 1994, the Parties shall determine the feasibility of banning or restricting, from States not party to this Protocol, the import of products produced with, but not containing, controlled substances in Annex A. If determined feasible, the Parties shall, following the procedures in Article 10 of the Convention, elaborate in an annex a list of such products. Parties that have not objected to the annex in accordance with those procedures shall ban, within one year of the annex having become effective, the import of those products from any State not party to this Protocol.

4*bis.* Within five years of the date of the entry into force of this paragraph, the Parties shall determine the feasibility of banning or restricting, from States not party to this Protocol, the import of products produced with, but not containing, controlled substances in Annex B. If determined feasible, the Parties shall, following the procedures in Article 10 of the Convention, elaborate in an annex a list of such products. Parties that have not objected to the annex in accordance with those procedures shall ban or restrict, within one year of the annex having become effective, the import of those products from any State not party to this Protocol.

4*ter.* Within five years of the date of entry into force of this paragraph, the Parties shall determine the feasibility of banning or restricting, from States not party to this Protocol, the import of products produced with, but not containing, controlled substances in Group II of Annex C. If determined feasible, the Parties shall, following the procedures in Article 10 of the Convention, elaborate in an annex a list of such products. Parties that have not objected to the annex in accordance with those procedures shall ban or restrict, within one year of the annex having become effective, the import of those products from any State not party to this Protocol.

5. Each Party undertakes to the fullest practicable extent to discourage the export to any State not party to this Protocol of technology for producing and for utilizing controlled substances in Annexes A and B, Group II of Annex C and Annex E.

6. Each Party shall refrain from providing new subsidies, aid, credits, guarantees or insurance programmes for the export to States not party to this Protocol of products, equipment, plants or technology that would facilitate the production of controlled substances in Annexes A and B, Group II of Annex C and Annex E.
7. Paragraphs 5 and 6 shall not apply to products, equipment, plants or technology that improve the containment, recovery, recycling or destruction of controlled substances, promote the development of alternative substances, or otherwise contribute to the reduction of emissions of controlled substances in Annexes A and B, Group II of Annex C and Annex E.
8. Notwithstanding the provisions of this Article, imports and exports referred to in paragraphs 1 to 4*ter* of this Article may be permitted from, or to, any State not party to this Protocol, if that State is determined, by a meeting of the Parties, to be in full compliance with Article 2, Articles 2A to 2E, Articles 2G and 2H and this Article, and have submitted data to that effect as specified in Article 7.
9. For the purposes of this Article, the term "State not party to this Protocol" shall include, with respect to a particular controlled substance, a State or regional economic integration organization that has not agreed to be bound by the control measures in effect for that substance.
10. By 1 January 1996, the Parties shall consider whether to amend this Protocol in order to extend the measures in this Article to trade in controlled substances in Group I of Annex C and in Annex E with States not party to the Protocol.

Article 4A: Control of trade with Parties

1. Where, after the phase-out date applicable to it for a controlled substance, a Party is unable, despite having taken all practicable steps to comply with its obligation under the Protocol, to cease production of that substance for domestic consumption, other than for uses agreed by the Parties to be essential, it shall ban the export of used, recycled and reclaimed quantities of that substance, other than for the purpose of destruction.
2. Paragraph 1 of this Article shall apply without prejudice to the operation of Article 11 of the Convention and the non-compliance procedure developed under Article 8 of the Protocol.

Article 4B: Licensing

1. Each Party shall, by 1 January 2000 or within three months of the date of entry into force of this Article for it, whichever is the later, establish and implement a system for licensing the import and export of new, used, recycled and reclaimed controlled substances in Annexes A, B, C and E.
2. Notwithstanding paragraph 1 of this Article, any Party operating under paragraph 1 of Article 5 which decides it is not in a position to establish and implement a system for licensing the import and export of controlled substances in Annexes C and E, may delay taking those actions until 1 January 2005 and 1 January 2002, respectively.
3. Each Party shall, within three months of the date of introducing its licensing system, report to the Secretariat on the establishment and operation of that system.
4. The Secretariat shall periodically prepare and circulate to all Parties a list of the Parties that have reported to it on their licensing systems and shall forward this information to the Implementation Committee for consideration and appropriate recommendations to the Parties.

Article 5: Special Situation of Developing Countries

1. Any Party that is a developing country and whose annual calculated level of consumption of the controlled substances in Annex A is less than 0.3 kilograms per capita on the date of the entry into force of the Protocol for it, or any time thereafter until 1 January 1999, shall, in order to meet its basic domestic needs, be entitled to delay for ten years its compliance with the control measures set out in Articles 2A to 2E, provided that any further amendments to the adjustments or Amendment adopted at the Second Meeting of the Parties in London, 29 June 1990, shall apply to the Parties operating under this paragraph after the review provided for in paragraph 8 of this Article has taken place and shall be based on the conclusions of that review.

1*bis*. The Parties shall, taking into account the review referred to in paragraph 8 of this Article, the assessments made pursuant to Article 6 and any other relevant information, decide by 1 January 1996, through the procedure set forth in paragraph 9 of Article 2:

(a) With respect to paragraphs 1 to 6 of Article 2F, what base year, initial levels, control schedules and phase-out date for consumption of the controlled substances in Group I of Annex C will apply to Parties operating under paragraph 1 of this Article;

(b) With respect to Article 2G, what phase-out date for production and consumption of the controlled substances in Group II of Annex C will apply to Parties operating under paragraph 1 of this Article; and

(c) With respect to Article 2H, what base year, initial levels and control schedules for consumption and production of the controlled substance in Annex E will apply to Parties operating under paragraph 1 of this Article.

2. However, any Party operating under paragraph 1 of this Article shall exceed neither an annual calculated level of consumption of the controlled substances in Annex A of 0.3 kilograms per capita nor an annual calculated level of consumption of controlled substances of Annex B of 0.2 kilograms per capita...

5. Developing the capacity to fulfil the obligations of the Parties operating under paragraph 1 of this Article to comply with the control measures set out in Articles 2A to 2E, and any control measures in Articles 2F to 2H that are decided pursuant to paragraph 1bis of this Article, and their implementation by those same Parties will depend upon the effective implementation of the financial cooperation as provided by Article 10 and the transfer of technology as provided by Article 10A.

6. Any Party operating under paragraph 1 of this Article may, at any time, notify the Secretariat in writing that, having taken all practicable steps it is unable to implement any or all of the obligations laid down in Articles 2A to 2E, or any or all obligations in Articles 2F to 2H that are decided pursuant to paragraph 1bis of this Article, due to the inadequate implementation of Articles 10 and 10A. The Secretariat shall forthwith transmit a copy of the notification to the Parties, which shall consider the matter at their next Meeting, giving due recognition to paragraph 5 of this Article and shall decide upon appropriate action to be taken.

7. During the period between notification and the Meeting of the Parties at which the appropriate action referred to in paragraph 6 above is to be decided, or for a further period if the Meeting of the Parties so decides, the non-compliance procedures referred to in Article 8 shall not be invoked against the notifying Party.

8. A Meeting of the Parties shall review, not later than 1995, the situation of the Parties operating under paragraph 1 of this Article, including the effective implementation of financial cooperation and transfer of technology to them, and adopt such revisions that may be deemed necessary regarding the schedule of control measures applicable to those Parties.

Article 6: Assessment and Review of Control Measures

Beginning in 1990, and at least every four years thereafter, the Parties shall assess the control measures provided for in Article 2 and Articles 2A to 2H on the basis of available scientific, environmental, technical and economic information. At least one year before each assessment, the Parties shall convene appropriate panels of experts qualified in the fields mentioned and determine the composition and terms of reference of any such panels. Within one year of being convened, the panels will report their conclusions, through the Secretariat, to the Parties.

Article 7: Reporting of Data

1. Each Party shall provide to the Secretariat, within three months of becoming a Party, statistical data on its production, imports and exports of each of the controlled substances in Annex A for the year 1986, or the best possible estimates of such data where actual data are not available.
2. Each Party shall provide to the Secretariat statistical data on its production, imports and exports of each of the controlled substances...
3. Each Party shall provide to the Secretariat statistical data on its annual production (as defined in

paragraph 5 of Article 1) of each of the controlled substances listed in Annexes A, B, C and E and, separately, for each substance...

3*bis*. Each Party shall provide to the Secretariat separate statistical data of its annual imports and exports of each of the controlled substances listed in Group II of Annex A and Group I of Annex C that have been recycled.

4. For Parties operating under the provisions of paragraph 8 (a) of Article 2, the requirements in paragraphs 1, 2, 3 and 3*bis* of this Article in respect of statistical data on imports and exports shall be satisfied if the regional economic integration organization concerned provides data on imports and exports between the organization and States that are not members of that organization.

Article 8: Non-Compliance

The Parties, at their first meeting, shall consider and approve procedures and institutional mechanisms for determining non-compliance with the provisions of this Protocol and for treatment of Parties found to be in non-compliance.

Article 9: Research, Development, Public Awareness and Exchange of Information

1. The Parties shall cooperate, consistent with their national laws, regulations and practices and taking into account in particular the needs of developing countries, in promoting, directly or through competent international bodies, research, development and exchange of information on:
   (a) best technologies for improving the containment, recovery, recycling, or destruction of controlled substances or otherwise reducing their emissions;
   (b) possible alternatives to controlled substances, to products containing such substances, and to products manufactured with them; and
   (c) costs and benefits of relevant control strategies.
2. The Parties, individually, jointly or through competent international bodies, shall cooperate in promoting public awareness of the environmental effects of the emissions of controlled substances and other substances that deplete the ozone layer.
3. Within two years of the entry into force of this Protocol and every two years thereafter, each Party shall submit to the Secretariat a summary of the activities it has conducted pursuant to this Article.

Article 10: Financial Mechanism

1. The Parties shall establish a mechanism for the purposes of providing financial and technical cooperation, including the transfer of technologies, to Parties operating under paragraph 1 of Article 5 of this Protocol to enable their compliance with the control measures set out in Articles 2A to 2E, and any control measures in Articles 2F to 2H that are decided pursuant to paragraph 1*bis* of Article 5 of the Protocol. The mechanism, contributions to which shall be additional to other financial transfers to Parties operating under that paragraph, shall meet all agreed incremental costs of such Parties in order to enable their compliance with the control measures of the Protocol. An indicative list of the categories of incremental costs shall be decided by the meeting of the Parties.
2. The mechanism established under paragraph 1 shall include a Multilateral Fund. It may also include other means of multilateral, regional and bilateral co-operation.
3. The Multilateral Fund shall:
   (a) Meet, on a grant or concessional basis as appropriate, and according to criteria to be decided upon by the Parties, the agreed incremental costs;
   (b) Finance clearing-house functions to:
      (i) Assist Parties operating under paragraph 1 of Article 5, through country specific studies and other technical cooperation, to identify their needs for cooperation;
      (ii) Facilitate technical cooperation to meet these identified needs;
      (iii) Distribute, as provided for in Article 9, information and relevant materials, and hold workshops, training sessions, and other related activities, for the benefit of Parties that are developing countries; and
      (iv) Facilitate and monitor other multilateral, regional and bilateral cooperation available to Parties that are developing countries;

(c) Finance the secretarial services of the Multilateral Fund and related support costs.

4. The Multilateral Fund shall operate under the authority of the Parties who shall decide on its overall policies.
5. The Parties shall establish an Executive Committee to develop and monitor the implementation of specific operational policies, guidelines and administrative arrangements, including the disbursement of resources, for the purpose of achieving the objectives of the Multilateral Fund. The Executive Committee shall discharge its tasks and responsibilities, specified in its terms of reference as agreed by the Parties, with the cooperation and assistance of the International Bank for Reconstruction and Development (World Bank), the United Nations Environment Programme, the United Nations Development Programme or other appropriate agencies depending on their respective areas of expertise. The members of the Executive Committee, which shall be selected on the basis of a balanced representation of the Parties operating under paragraph 1 of Article 5 and of the Parties not so operating, shall be endorsed by the Parties.
6. The Multilateral Fund shall be financed by contributions from Parties not operating under paragraph 1 of Article 5 in convertible currency or, in certain circumstances, in kind and/or in national currency, on the basis of the United Nations scale of assessments. Contributions by other Parties shall be encouraged. Bilateral and, in particular cases agreed by a decision of the Parties, regional cooperation may, up to a percentage and consistent with any criteria to be specified by decision of the Parties, be considered as a contribution to the Multilateral Fund, provided that such cooperation, as a minimum:
   (a) Strictly relates to compliance with the provisions of this Protocol,
   (b) Provides additional resources, and
   (c) Meets agreed incremental costs.
7. The Parties shall decide upon the programme budget of the Multilateral Fund for each fiscal period and upon the percentage of contributions of the individual Parties thereto.
8. Resources under the Multilateral Fund shall be disbursed with the concurrence of the beneficiary Party.
9. Decisions by the Parties under this Article shall be taken by consensus whenever possible. If all efforts at consensus have been exhausted and no agreement reached, decisions shall be adopted by a two-thirds majority vote of the Parties present and voting, representing a majority of the Parties operating under paragraph 1 of Article 5 present and voting and a majority of the Parties not so operating present and voting.
10. The financial mechanism set out in this Article is without prejudice to any future arrangements that may be developed with respect to other environmental issues.

Article 10A: Transfer of Technology

Each Party shall take every practicable step, consistent with the programmes supported by the financial mechanism, to ensure:

(a) that the best available, environmentally safe substitutes and related technologies are expeditiously transferred to Parties operating under paragraph 1 of Article 5; and

(b) that the transfers referred to in subparagraph (a) occur under fair and most favorable conditions.

(iv) Compatibility with the GATT

(a) Hunter D., Salzman J., and Zaelke D., "The Law of Air and Atmosphere," in *International Environmental Law and Policy*, New York, Foundation Press, 1998, p 596

Compatibility with GATT

Before they would agree to the restrictions, the EC insisted on obtaining an opinion on their compatibility with the GATT from a trade expert in the GATT secretariat, apparently expecting the expert to advise against such measures. On their face, the restrictions on trade with non-parties are quantitative restrictions, prohibited by article XI of the GATT. They also appear to conflict with the most favoured nation (MFN) principle of Article I, because they discriminate between like products of parties and non-parties.

The GATT expert concluded, however, that trade measures were justifiable under the GATT article XX exceptions, which permit restrictive trade measures "necessary to protect human, animals or plant life or health" and "relating to conservation or exhaustion of exhaustible natural resources…The legal expert stressed, however, that he was giving an opinion and that the formal decision as to whether the trade restrictions satisfied article XX's exceptions must come from the GATT contracting parties.

4

Building a Monitoring and Compliance Regime Under the Montreal Protocol

A

Barratt Brown E., "Building a Monitoring and Compliance Regime under the Montreal Protocol," 1991, *Yale Journal of International Law*, pp 519-570

Introduction

> "[A]lmost all nations observe almost all principles of international law and almost all of their obligations almost all of the time." [Henkin]

There is more than a kernel of truth in this quip about the problem of state compliance with international obligations. Without strong monitoring and compliance mechanisms, states are tempted to embrace international solutions and then not follow through with their obligations. Despite such shortcomings, multilateral agreements on issues as diverse as environment, peace, trade, and international debt have given rise to international regimes. Nowhere is this clearer than in the environmental context where recent events, such as the Soviet nuclear disaster at Chernobyl and the burning of Kuwaiti oil fields, remind us that pollution recognizes no borders.

This article focuses on a quintessentially global environmental issue, the depletion of the ozone layer, and on the *Montreal Protocol on Substances That Deplete the Ozone Layer* (Montreal Protocol), an agreement adopted in 1987 and significantly strengthened in 1990 under the auspices of the United Nations Environment Programme (UNEP). Sixty-three countries have ratified the agreement, representing over 99percent of the production and 90 percent of the consumption of ozone-depleting chemicals. As the first global agreement adopted to protect the earth's atmosphere, the *Montreal Protocol* is perhaps the greatest achievement of the UNEP regime. The Protocol not only addresses a serious global environmental crisis, it sets the stage for collective action on global warming. In February 1991, 130 countries began meeting to negotiate a treaty on global warming, a process to which the *Montreal Protocol* undoubtedly will contribute.

> *As the first global agreement adopted to protect the earth's atmosphere, the* Montreal Protocol *is perhaps the greatest achievement of the UNEP regime.*

Yet depletion of the ozone layer continues and the work of putting the *Montreal Protocol* into effect has just begun. Many of the real challenges lie ahead, including adoption of an effective non-compliance provision that will encourage countries to abide by their commitments. The parties to the Protocol are expected to meet in 1992 to discuss proposals for a non-compliance provision. This article suggests ways to build a successful monitoring and compliance regime drawing on effective features of other regimes.

The *Montreal Protocol*, its Amendments, and National Legislation

…The drafters of the *Montreal Protocol* negotiated with an unwavering commitment to include as many countries as possible in the agreement. In making ozone protection a major global initiative, they hoped to encourage a large-scale switch from ozone-depleting chemicals to substitutes by setting reduction goals and foreclosing as many markets as possible for ozone-depleting chemicals. To maximize the number of parties joining at the outset, the drafters chose a "top down" approach, one that mandates goals and deadlines but allows states the flexibility to choose their own means of phasing out restricted chemicals. A "top down" approach encourages participation by states that might otherwise find the requirements too Draconian or a threat to their sovereignty. This approach allows states to develop their own policies and regulations for meeting their obligations to reduce ozone consumption. Trade benefits and exceptions negotiated by concerned parties also encourage states to join.

The strides made at the national level in the United States, which were brought about by environmental organizations and concerned citizens, are equally impressive. In 1989, over 100 bills in 24 states were introduced calling for CFC restrictions. Also in 1989, the EPA agreed to issue regulations under the authority of the *Clean Air Act* in a settlement with the Natural Resources Defense Council (NRDC). A year later, Congress passed a reauthorized *Clean Air Act*—proposed and supported by a coalition of environmental, health, and labor organizations—containing stringent provisions for the "control of CFCs and other ozone-depleting chemicals." Congress made it clear in the amendments to the Clean Air Act that it intended the EPA to go further than the Montreal Protocol to protect the ozone layer. The amendments not only put the United States reduction obligations on a faster track, but also addressed issues the Montreal Protocol ignored, such as recycling ozone-depleting chemicals and certifying safe substitutes.

The Merits of the Protocol Approach and the Role of NGOs

...The *Montreal Protocol*'s "top down" approach is attractive for a number of reasons. Merely by becoming parties to the Protocol, states share a common definition of the problem and a plan to address it. To meet their obligations under the Protocol, they must agree to specific goals, time schedules, and promulgation of national programs. The larger the number of parties to the agreement, the faster markets for ozone-depleting chemicals will decline and manufacturers will move to substitutes. Additionally, the Multilateral Fund and the trade provisions create strong incentives for states to join and, because of trade sanctions, to encourage their trading partners to join as well. The UNEP Secretariat centralizes monitoring, data collection, and administration of the agreement for the parties.

The *Montreal Protocol* has three major weaknesses, however, all of which must be corrected by adopting more aggressive monitoring and compliance provisions. First, the structure of the agreement made it imperative that a large number of states become members. The drafters made concessions to states that could significantly alter the success of the agreement by slowing the pace of CFC reduction to accomplish that goal. Second, the agreement is necessarily quite flexible, since it leaves to individual countries the responsibility for adopting their own programs for eliminating targeted chemicals. This flexibility, however, will make the monitoring and verifying of compliance more difficult. Finally, the agreement's compliance scheme is inherently weak. The reason for this is that the main mechanism for encouraging compliance is the monitoring of country-supplied data by the Implementation Committee and the UNEP Secretariat. Both of these organizations are too small to be effective in this role.

Many States Must Comply to Realize the Protocol's Goals

In focusing on consumption, the *Montreal Protocol* requires participation by a larger group of states than would be necessary under a production formula. The drafters of the agreement made a number of exceptions to the Protocol's requirements to entice parties to sign. The most significant provides a grace period to developing countries (the Article V exception). Another important exception permits the "trading" of obligations between parties (the EC exception), while a third exception is equivalent to a grandfather clause for states with plans for CFC-producing facilities that predate the signing of the Protocol (the USSR exception).

The exception for developing countries allows any country consuming less than 0.3 kilograms of CFCs per capita to delay complying with the control requirements for up to ten years to meet "basic domestic needs." To illustrate the ramifications of this exception, an increase from the current worldwide average use of 0.2 kilograms of CFCs per capita to the 0.3 kilograms per capita allowed in developing countries would increase the worldwide production and use of CFCs by 50 percent by 1999. Even a long-term use of only 10 percent of the 1986 levels of CFCs would only delay eliminating the ozone hole until the end of the twenty-second century. This exception, however, will probably not lead to increased levels of CFC use due to the developing countries' desire to share in the Multilateral Fund, a benefit available only to those reducing their CFC use on schedule. Nonetheless, the success of the Fund is critical, for the agreement explicitly protects parties from non-compliance penalties if they are operating under Article V and are unable to meet their requirements because of inadequate implementation of the Multilateral Fund. The London Amendments also provide for a 1995 review of the strides made in financial cooperation and the transfer of technology to developing countries, and create an opportunity to revise control requirements based on this review.

The exception requested by the EC allows parties to trade obligations with other parties for the purposes of industrial rationalization within regional economic integration organizations, as long as the total production by the organization's members does not exceed the sum of the members' production limits. While the EC Council of Ministers has announced that Europe will not use the production "bubble" this policy could change. Because only three of the twelve EC countries reported separate production figures, it is difficult to determine whether the EC is complying with its stated policy.

The exception for the USSR allows parties in calculating their baseline production levels to add production from facilities under construction or contracted for prior to September 1987, as long as the facilities were included in national legislation before January 1987, thus prior to the adoption of the *Montreal Protocol*. This provision was granted during negotiations over the selection of 1986 as the baseline year from which to calculate reductions, and should only affect the Soviet requirements.

Perhaps the most serious exception in the agreement is the treatment of hydrochlorofluorocarbons, (HCFCs) as transitional substances not subject to a reduction schedule. HCFCs are attractive alternatives to CFCs because they can be substituted quickly and relatively inexpensively for CFCs. While they have only 2 percent to 14 percent of the ozone-depletion potential of CFCs, extensive use of HCFCs could delay the recovery of the ozone layer into the twenty-second century. The treatment of HCFCs became one of the most problematic issues during the negotiations over the London Amendments. Encouraging a rapid move away from CFCs by promoting investment in substitutes that are also serious ozone depleters is a poor solution. The compromise, surely to be revisited at the next meeting of the parties, requires reporting on the production, import, and export of HCFCs. It includes a nonbinding resolution declaring that HCFCs should be used only where more environmentally sound alternatives are not available and should be phased out by 2020 to 2040. The compromise also requires the Amendments to be reviewed regularly for additional measures.

Because of these exceptions, some environmentalists and policymakers; have estimated that the *Montreal Protocol* might result in only a 35 percent to 40 percent reduction in CFC consumption by the turn of the century. Others have argued that a dramatic shift in the global marketplace from CFCs to substitutes will reduce CFC consumption beyond the original 50 percent goal of the Protocol. Obviously, the ratification of the London Amendments will bring about a far larger reduction and will promote the development of substitutes. But that will mean hard work and commitment to carrying out the technology transfer and financial cooperation provisions of the Protocol and its Amendments.

The Structure of the Protocol Makes Monitoring Difficult

The *Montreal Protocol* requires that individual states design their own reduction programs. Instead of mandating a blanket ban on the use of CFCs in aerosols—a step that would be easy to monitor—the Protocol allows every state to reduce CFCs and the other restricted chemicals in whatever way it chooses provided it can show that it is meeting its reduction requirements. This structure provides great flexibility, but it takes more time to accomplish, fragments decision-making, and frustrates monitoring efforts.

Once programs are adopted, the agreement relies on the parties' good faith efforts to comply. With the exception of countries receiving money from the Multilateral Fund, there are no explicit penalties for non-compliance. The parties have the power to act on an *ad hoc* basis in response to reports from the Implementation Committee, but it is unclear whether this provision will be utilized. The fact that there will be many different state plans also increases the likelihood that changing the direction of these programs will be more difficult. To make the agreement responsive to new information about depletion of the ozone layer, the *Montreal Protocol* provides for an amendment process timed to coincide with its regular scientific, technical, and economic assessments. For example, the agreement permits parties, through the UNEP Secretariat, to call on the Protocol signatories to require sharper reductions in CFCs. These provisions were crucial in bringing the parties together to approve the London Amendments.

The Shortcomings of the UNEP Monitoring Mechanism

The placement of monitoring duties in the UNEP Secretariat may give a false sense of security. The monitoring carried out by the Secretariat consists primarily of the review of data submitted by the parties. However, with a small, impermanent, and under-funded staff, the Secretariat cannot compel parties to turn over data and will not be able to verify the data that it receives. If the Secretariat relies on data submitted by the parties, and this data is incomplete or inaccurate, then measuring the success of the *Montreal Protocol* and assessing the need for additional measures will be extremely difficult.

One of the greatest challenges will be collecting data and monitoring the activities of such a large number of parties.

One of the greatest challenges will be collecting data and monitoring the activities of such a large number of parties. The trade provisions and Multilateral Fund obviously encourage membership, but weak data collection and compliance monitoring may make it difficult to determine if parties are in fact fulfilling their obligations. Already, there is evidence that following party compliance through the reporting requirements may be difficult. Of 55 states required to submit data to the UNEP Secretariat in May of 1990, only 21 countries, including the United States, the USSR, and Japan, submitted complete data. Only three of the EC countries submitted complete data and four, including Britain, have yet to submit any data. In May 1990, in response to the poor reporting record of the parties, UNEP's Mustafa Tolba sent a letter to all the states suggesting that parties failing to submit data should be considered in non-compliance.

The EC and developing countries resisted the efforts of the United States and the Scandinavian countries to adopt a tougher measure and extend trade sanctions to non-complying parties. As a compromise measure, the parties created the Implementation Committee. The Committee serves as an important forum for reviewing the data and monitoring information collected by the UNEP Secretariat. The Secretariat, in preparing its regular reports for the parties, may submit information and observations made during its review of data to the Committee for its consideration. Additionally, parties may submit complaints to the Secretariat, which must allow the parties whose compliance is in question an opportunity to respond. The Secretariat then transmits the complaint, response, along with any additional information, to the Committee.

Unfortunately, the provision for the Implementation Committee contains several weaknesses. The Committee has no powers of investigation or enforcement. Its members are not objective experts, but state representatives who may politicize the Committee's mission. For example, they may be more hesitant to put forth tough recommendations for fear that their own countries' programs will be made the subject of the next review. If the Committee does issue a critical report, it is unclear what, if anything, the parties will do in response. Finally, information submitted to the Committee is to be kept confidential, weakening the incentives for the Committee to aggressively pursue violations.

Strengthening Monitoring and Compliance Regimes: Theory and Examples

While the "top down" approach selected by the drafters is appropriate given the desirability of having many countries ratify the *Montreal Protocol*, it leaves too much responsibility in the hands of individual states, has exceptions built in that could slow the essential progress of the agreement for many years, does not have adequate mechanisms for punishing states for non-compliance, and relies too heavily on a UNEP Secretariat ill-equipped to carry out implementation by itself. Although there are probably many fruitful approaches to take in addressing these problems, the burgeoning field of regime theory provides a particularly useful approach by placing these problems in a more theoretical context.

Regime Theory

Regime theorists attempt to explain the behavior of actors in a particular regime. These theorists look at factors such as reciprocity, reputation, repetitive dealings, and—ultimately—power to explain why and how states deal with one another. Regime theory suggests that the process of monitoring and information gathering creates "regime" expectations by providing the feedback necessary for members to appraise performance. Such feedback can help hold members to their obligations and make injunctions meaningful. One regime theorist, Robert Keohane, argues that injunctions, which prescribe certain actions and proscribe others, are the essence of a regime. Effective regimes, according to Keohane, require only a few strong players that recognize they will benefit from collective action. These players will set the rules of the game, or the injunctions, to ensure that if they play, others will play as well.

Other regime theorists, in particular those who study game theory, believe that reputation and reciprocity between parties are the essential building blocks of regime expectations. Parties confer benefits of membership only on those states that abide by what one theorist, Robert Axelrod, describes as meta-norms. States that do not abide by these norms can be denied the benefits of membership. Regime theorists describe this as the "shadow of the future" in which states, aware that their present actions may alter the future receptivity of other states to their membership, choose to comply with regime norms.

Most regime theorists assume that negotiations begin when the states come together and then occur only among states. International negotiations are in fact multi-dimensional and are heavily influenced by domestic politics, as the *Montreal Protocol* negotiations demonstrated. The players that influenced the international position of the United States, for example, included NGOs, private industry, Congress, state and municipal legislatures, and—in no small way—the agencies of the federal government itself. The United States carefully considered its position in regard to the domestic regulatory climate. In addition, the same NGO, the NRDC, that brought litigation in the United States under domestic law, organized international NGOs to express their opinions in one position paper for all the delegations to the Protocol convention.

One regime theorist who does look at states as multi-dimensional entities is Roger Putnam. He criticizes the excessive focus of other theorists on supranational institutions in the evolution of international agreements. Putnam suggests that domestic politics and third parties strongly influence regimes, and that interest groups, public opinion, and national and local politics play a central role in influencing foreign policy.

In Putnam's model, political leaders engage in negotiating that allows regime participants to minimize adverse foreign developments while satisfying domestic demand. He describes the negotiating process as having two stages. First, negotiators bargain in and among themselves and then they bargain with constituents about the shape and ultimate ratification of the negotiated agreement. Putnam's two-stage model is important because it recognizes the influence that domestic political forces, such as "third party watchdogs," have on international cooperation. Negotiators must also consider whether they have satisfied all the elements necessary to secure ratification. In his model, domestic politics broadly deemed— not simply the role of Congress in the United States, for example, but lobbying by pressure groups and the influence of public opinion—play a role in determining the content of the agreement negotiated abroad. Ultimately, Putnam argues, politicians will try to shape international agreements in ways that favour approval by domestic constituents while maintaining diplomatic credibility.

Putnam's model recognizes two elements that are powerful in shaping contemporary events but too often get short shrift in the regime theory literature: the power of domestic politics and public opinion. A fairly sophisticated version of the Putnam model is operating today in the context of the *Montreal Protocol*. The chief United States negotiator asserts that the major difference between the positions taken by the United States and the EC can be explained by the difference in public perception of the threat to the ozone layer. Even before the ban on the use of CFCs in aerosols in 1978, the use of spray cans in the United States dropped by two-thirds due to an active media and environmental community that immediately spread the word about the dangers of CFCs. As a result, the United States government took action quickly under domestic law and assumed a leadership role in the international negotiations. On the other hand, European states, which for a long time had neither a press nor constituents demanding environmental attention, were consistently opposed to taking action. In fact, the major European CFC-producing industries, ICI and Atochem, dominated the national politics that shaped the European position. Thus, the two parties had vastly different domestic political situations that accounted for their positions.

According to regime theorists, once parties have adopted an agreement, monitoring by members of the regime and sanctions against non-members or violators then become crucial to deterring potential free-riders. As noted earlier, however, the *Montreal Protocol's* current mechanisms for monitoring and compelling compliance are extremely weak. Putnam's insight into the role of domestic politics and private organizations in influencing state behavior suggests a possible solution to the problem of creating a strong monitoring and compliance regime for the Protocol. Because advocacy by NGOs and private industry played a critical role in the adoption of the Protocol, incorporating NGOs into the international compliance regime would be an effective way of compelling states to abide by their obligations. Such a role would allow NGOs to bring systematic domestic political pressure to bear on non-complying states. The ozone-protection regime is well set to accommodate such structural additions. The parties have agreed to the concept of implementation and compliance procedures, have grown accustomed to working closely with NGOs and industry, and have already centralized the existing monitoring and compliance mechanisms.

Expanding the monitoring and compliance mechanisms of the *Montreal Protocol* on the international level is critically important, and recent work in regime theory suggests that reliance on NGOs for monitoring and enforcement may be an effective solution. Such a regime need not be developed completely from scratch for there already exist three regimes that address problems similar in crucial respects to those addressed by the Protocol. These are the human rights regime, the International Labour Organisation (ILO), and the International Atomic Energy Agency (IAEA). In particular, these regimes are valuable objects of study because they provide examples of monitoring and compliance mechanisms that rely significantly on NGOs and private individuals. In spite of the fact that NGOs are acknowledged as crucial to bringing about desired policy goals under both international and domestic laws, neither international agreements nor international implementing bodies, such as UNEP, explicitly acknowledge and accommodate NGOs in their compliance mechanisms. While the international environmental regime has yet to incorporate NGOs formally into the implementation mechanisms of international agreements, the regime is beginning to struggle with that question.

The comparison of individual and NGO participatory rights in the human rights and ILO regimes with United States procedural rights is inescapable. Perhaps that is why these regimes are attractive models. As more and more regulation occurs abroad in the form of international agreements, the more citizens from countries such as the United States stand to lose in opportunities to shape regulations through notice and comment, receive a response from the agency formulating the regulations, and—most importantly—to challenge regulations and non-compliance through judicial review. This scenario is more than hypothetical. The *Montreal Protocol* internationalized the process of developing United States regulations on ozone-depleting chemicals. Unlike the 1978 EPA regulations banning CFCs in aerosols, there was little opportunity for the United States public to shape the 1988 regulations through notice and comment. Implementation and enforcement now pose a similar challenge as there is nothing comparable to citizen enforcement power at the international level.

The first and primary regime to be considered is the human rights regime. This regime provides perhaps the most salient example of how actively NGOs can be involved in the enforcement mechanisms of international regimes. The regime also has impressive procedures for addressing violations of regime norms through extensive use of commissions and courts for the review of complaints. While the human rights regime is in many ways quite different from the *Montreal Protocol*, the comparison is useful because it provides a constructive view of how international mechanisms can be put to work to correct undesirable state behavior.

The Human Rights Regime

In 1948, the United Nations adopted the *Universal Declaration on Human Rights* (Universal Declaration). NGO efforts to enforce the *Universal Declaration*, and the 30 human rights declarations, conventions, and resolutions that followed, are as important as the document itself. Amnesty International is well-known for its work to bring human rights practices to the attention of the global community, but there are literally thousands of groups and individuals who have used the monitoring and enforcement mechanisms of the regime's commissions and courts to define acceptable human rights practices. They also conduct fact-finding missions, publish reports, issue annual reports on the state of human rights around the world, and work closely with international organizations to strengthen these institutions.

Monitoring Under the United Nations Regime

The *Universal Declaration* grew out of the United Nations Charter's mandate and set a standard of achievement for all nations. As Judge Buergenthal of the Inter-American Court observes, countries that voted for the Declaration believing there was little risk of legal obligation were to be surprised by the force of its ideas. Of the two major United Nations human rights covenants that followed the

Declaration, the *Covenant on Civil and Political Rights* has the more extensive monitoring and enforcement mechanism. This Covenant requires member countries, comprising about half of the United Nations membership, to submit reports on measures adopted to comply with the Covenant. These reports are sent to a Human Rights Committee, established by the Covenant and made up of independent experts, which reviews the reports and summons each state submitting a report before the Committee for a hearing. Although the Committee takes a narrow view of its powers to evaluate or comment on the reports, it has worked closely with NGOs to determine its line of questioning, and individual members of the Committee often use information obtained from NGOs to formulate penetrating questions.

The *Optional Protocol*, adopted at the same time as the Covenants, permits individuals to submit petitions regarding violations directly to the Human Rights Committee. When a petition is submitted, the Committee must make a substantive compliance determination, but the decision is neither binding nor appealable. There are no oral hearings and many of the petitions receive only a cursory review. The Committee's jurisdiction is limited. It can consider petitions against only the approximately 45 countries that are parties to the Protocol, and it cannot consider anonymous petitions, if domestic remedies have not been exhausted, or if the matter is under consideration in another international forum. The Committee's authority to reprimand a state is limited to forwarding its views to the state concerned and to the petitioning individual. Given the risks to the petitioner and the limited potential for redress, it is not surprising that the Human Rights Committee has considered on average only twenty to 25 petitions a year. Despite its limitations, about half of the petitions received were considered admissible and, in the majority of those cases, the Committee found a breach of the Covenant.

The Commission on Human Rights, established under the United Nations Economic and Social Council (ECOSOC) and strengthened by a 1970 ECOSOC resolution, has the greatest potential for monitoring human rights violations. Prior to 1970, the thousands of petitions received every year alleging violations were simply filed without review by the Commission. The resolution expanded the Commission's authority to receive complaints, directing the Commission to investigate complaints from NGOs or individuals that appear to reveal a "consistent pattern of gross and reliably attested human rights violations" in any state. The resolution also authorized the Commission to appoint a committee to conduct fact-finding within the state being investigated. While no such fact-finding has been undertaken, regime norms are promoted simply by raising the specter of investigations.

Although the resolution cleared away a number of the drawbacks in the authority of the Commission on Human Rights, serious problems remain. The Commission's members are state representatives, not independent experts, and, as a result, their work has been politicized. The Commission members also appear to be remarkably isolated from their world. Working Groups established by the Commission must examine petitions in private and only occasionally refer summaries of petitions to the Commission. This screening procedure has inhibited the Commission from adopting a more activist role in uncovering human rights abuses. In 1978, the chairman of the Commission began announcing the identity of countries that were the subject of consideration, but the proceedings have remained secret. As a result, individuals increasingly look to the Covenant's Human Rights Committee and the regional regimes in Europe and Latin America as more responsive venues for redress of individual grievances.

Monitoring Under the European and Inter-American Regimes

In 1948, shortly after the *Universal Declaration* was adopted, Europe fashioned a sister convention, the *European Convention for the Protection of Human Rights and Fundamental Freedoms* (European Convention). At the same time, the Organization of American States (OAS) adopted its *American Declaration of the Rights and Duties of Man*, which was followed in 1969 by the *American Convention on Human Rights* (American Convention). Most recently, the Organization of African Unity has embraced a regional human rights regime modelled on the European and Inter-American regimes.

The *European Convention* is enforced by means of state and individual applications made to the European Commission on Human Rights in Strasbourg. The Commission's members are independent experts, usually lawyers, from each member state. The primary work of the Commission is to screen the applications for admissibility.

The Commission's decisions are published, as are its opinions regarding breaches of the Convention. Decisions to deny applications are appealable to the European Court on Human Rights. The fact that few states have submitted applications parallels the experience of the United Nations Human Rights Committee and Human Rights Commission. The vast majority of the applications to the Commission are from individuals. While only eleven interstate applications have been submitted, individual petitioners have submitted over 12,000 claims.

Individuals, NGOs, or groups of individual petitioners can submit applications against states that have accepted the right of individual petition. The European Commission on Human Rights then conducts fact-finding and, if necessary, visits to the state charged with violations. If the Commission is unable to secure an acceptable compromise between the parties, it forwards a report to the Ministers of the Council of Europe to consider the case for appeal to the European Court of Human Rights. Again, the defendant state must either have accepted the jurisdiction of the Court or have agreed to it in the particular case. The decisions of the Court are considered final, and are binding under an article of the *European Convention* that instructs member states to abide by the decisions of the Court.

The application process appears to be moderately effective. The European Commission on Human Rights deems the vast majority of the petitions inadmissible—out of the 12,000 petitions that have been submitted, only 500 (or 4 percent) have been admitted. However, petitioners have direct access to the Commission, as complaints need not be espoused by the petitioner's state. Additionally, the cases that are decided by the Commission or by the European Court of Human Rights often influence state practice with regard to similarly situated individuals. Similar to the *Optional Protocol* of the *U.N. Convention on Civil and Political Rights*, the European regime allows states to submit voluntarily to petitions by individuals. All twenty-one member states of the *European Convention* have agreed to this procedure, which makes it theoretically available to over 300 million people.

After the European regime, the Inter-American regime is the most developed regional human rights regime. In 1960, the OAS established the Inter-American Commission on Human Rights (Inter-American Commission) to enforce the *American Declaration of the Rights and Duties of Man* (American Declaration). In 1969, the OAS elaborated upon the *American Declaration* and strengthened the role of the Commission by creating the Inter-American Court of Human Rights (Inter-American Court). The admissibility requirements of the Commission are similar to the European example.

Because all members of the *American Convention* are subject to individual petitions, its legal powers are potentially greater than the European regime, although the American regime is less well-developed. It also works more closely with NGOs. For example, the Inter-American Commission has advisory jurisdiction over complaints of human rights abuses by any state that is a member of the OAS, and is empowered to carry out investigations in order to compile a court record. The Inter-American Court can order compliance with its decisions, including restitution and compensation, and has begun to exercise these powers. Unfortunately, like the European Court of Human Rights, the jurisdiction of the Inter-American Court is optional, and states can choose to accept its jurisdiction for a limited period, either on condition of reciprocity or on an *ad hoc* basis.

Implications for the Montreal Protocol

The integration of a broad range of NGOs within the structure of the human rights regime is unparalleled in other international regimes. By focusing international norms on domestic practice, NGOs and the monitoring and compliance mechanisms of the regime have formed a powerful partnership to remedy poor human rights practices. The investigatory work of the NGOs, including the review of reports submitted by countries, and the right of NGOs and individuals to petition courts and commissions, contribute significantly to the effectiveness of the human rights regime.

The European and Inter-American human rights regimes combine the authority of the highly regarded experts, who sit on their commissions and courts, with the commitment of NGOs and those individuals who have been subjected to the human rights abuses at issue. The courts of these regimes make legally binding decisions and, in the case of the Inter-American Court, the decisions are often based on aggressive fact-finding. Their procedures are among the strongest international legal mechanisms for accomplishing compliance with regime norms.

The *Montreal Protocol* regime is similar to the human rights regime in a number of ways. It has an active NGO and citizen network throughout member states that is ready and able to participate in the *Montreal Protocol's* implementation. The Protocol also relies on state practice to fulfil its goals, thus making state monitoring and compliance the key to its success. Finally, the parties to the Protocol have contemplated an investigatory function within the *Montreal Protocol* in adopting an interim Implementation Committee. Taking the strengths of the human rights regime—its incorporation of NGOs, its impartial and highly regarded commissions and courts, and its reporting, investigations, and other feedback mechanisms for publicizing state practice—and incorporating them into the *Montreal Protocol* regime would be a monumental step in strengthening not only the Protocol regime, but also the emerging environmental regime to which it belongs.

The International Labour Organisation regime is similar to the human rights regime in many ways. It has monitoring and compliance mechanisms that closely review country compliance and incorporate public participation. It also, in cooperation with NGOs, has conducted fact-finding missions when a country's compliance is at issue. The regime builds on the human rights regimes in a very significant way. It has for its long history incorporated NGOs into its very system of governance. By having those whose interests are directly affected sit on the committees and formulate the policy of the organization, the International Labour Organisation escapes many of the pitfalls of the United Nations Human Rights Commission and Human Rights Committee, and greatly enhances the likelihood of successful implementation of its labor standards into domestic policy of member states.

The International Labour Organisation

In 1919, the Treaty of Versailles established the International Labour Organisation (ILO) as part of the League of Nations. As its first Director-General proclaimed, the ILO was to get countries to "speak ... the same language" on labor rights. The ILO became a specialized agency of the United Nations and it has made enormous contributions to workers' rights through its international standard setting, implementation procedures, and technical assistance.

ILO mechanisms for collecting information, issuing reports and using publicity as a means of encouraging state compliance, are the strongest in the United Nations system. But the ILO is unique in another essential way. Its tripartite system of governance, in which representatives of the government, employers, and workers sit together in plenary sessions, has long recognized the value of incorporating nongovernmental interests in creating an international norm for workers' rights. Each delegation consists of two governmental representatives and one representative each for employers and workers. The nongovernmental representatives, as they are called, have voting power equal to that of the government representatives, sit on the committees and commissions that review compliance, and have full access to the information generated by member countries.

The Mutual Supervision Mechanism

The ILO is well-known for its system of standard setting and mutual supervision, in which labor standards are regularly and systematically monitored. Through its legislative body, the International Labor Conference, the ILO has adopted approximately 300 conventions and recommendations, which have become an international code of standards for workers rights. Members are required to submit regular reports on the status of these standards within their countries. In a practice that is highly unusual in international governance, the nongovernmental delegates are invited to comment on any assertions of compliance with which they disagree.

The ILO is well-known for its system of standard setting and mutual supervision, in which labor standards are regularly and systematically monitored.

As the number of standards grew, greater and greater numbers of reports were submitted. In order to continue to monitor implementation effectively, the International Labor Conference created two supervisory bodies, the Committee of Experts on the Application of Conventions and Recommendations, comprised of independent specialists in labor law, and a tripartite Conference Committee on the Application of Conventions and Recommendations. The Committee of Experts conducts a preliminary review and notes any problems with compliance by making direct requests or observations. In the case of direct requests, the Committee works with a government, perhaps asking it to submit more information or to take certain measures. These requests are sent to the nongovernmental representatives, but are not otherwise published. If there is no follow up by the government, the Committee will make observations that, in addition to being sent to the government, are published in its annual report. This method of review has been enormously successful.

Based on the Committee of Experts' report, the Conference Committee on Application of Conventions and Recommendations chooses the most egregious or persistent cases of non-compliance and calls governments before it in hearings open to the public to explain the reasons for their non-compliance. The Conference Committee then issues a report and a special list of countries failing to live up to their obligations. An extension of the special list procedure is the special paragraph procedure, which puts countries on notice that they may find themselves on the special list unless they take corrective action. The Conference Committee's lists and reports are usually adopted unanimously by the Conference and are public documents.

Even those who are sceptical about the impartiality of the ILO give high marks to what easily could have become a highly politicized process of review. The process of review ingeniously combines the authority of experts with the pressure of public opinion. As a result, governments anxious about being discussed in the Conference Committee's reports usually live up to their pledges. Thus, the process has been dubbed the "conscience of the ILO".

The Investigatory and Complaint Process

There are four basic procedures for bringing complaints within the ILO regime: representations, complaints, special procedures for freedom of association violations, and special surveys on discrimination in employment. Representations are brought by workers' or employers' organizations in cases of state non-compliance with ratified conventions, and involve minimal investigation and enforcement. The ILO Governing Body can refer a representation case for more formal investigation if it decides it should be handled as a complaint or refer it for supervision to the Experts Committee.

Complaints are similar to representations, but may be brought by a state that is a member of the convention at issue, a delegate of the ILO Conference (including the NGO delegates), or the ILO Governing Body itself. A Commission of Inquiry, comprised of three independent persons, may be established to consider complaints on an *ad hoc* basis. These commissions operate quasi-judicially and can conduct evidentiary hearings and site visits to gather information. A state may appeal to the International Court of Justice if it does not accept the Commission's recommendation. The appeal procedure has never been invoked, which reflects the high degree of resolution that is achieved through less formal procedures. As testimony to the success of the mutual supervision mechanisms as a means of ensuring party compliance, only ten representations have been investigated and only four cases considered by the Commissions.

In 1950, the ILO initiated a system to expedite review of cases involving violations of its conventions on freedom of association. Quick action was needed to respond to cases of sudden violations, such as jailing trade union activists or suppressing workers' strikes. In response, the ILO Governing Body created special procedures for accepting and acting upon complaints. The Committee on Freedom of Association receives complaints directly from workers' and employers' organizations. It may refer exceptional cases to the Fact-Finding and Conciliation Commission. Both organizations can conduct on-site investigations. The ILO has made impressive use of the Committee on Freedom of Association. Between 1950 and 1980, more than 1,000 cases were considered concerning a broad variety of free association claims.

Implications for the Montreal Protocol

The ILO is unique in its formal incorporation of nongovernmental representatives in its governance. Its legislative Conference and Governing Body are made up of workers' and employers' organizations as well as governments, and its various committees draw membership from this tripartite group. Nongovernmental representatives can review compliance reports, bring complaints, sit on committees, and order investigations as committee members. Often NGO delegates work closely with their own states through these international mechanisms. Additionally, even NGOs who do not have representative status can bring complaints through the representation process and the Committee on Freedom of Association.

The ILO's system of mutual supervision and complaint procedures makes full use of information and its investigating power to encourage states to comply with their obligations. The process of review or mutual supervision—requiring reports to be submitted first to a committee made up of experts and then to a more political committee— allows feedback that helps compel states to comply with ILO standards. States are "punished" by being listed or having a representation against them published if they fail to comply. If this process does not achieve compliance, NGOs, the ILO Governing Body, or any member state may bring actions. The mere availability of recourse to complaint mechanisms has undoubtedly strengthened the authority of the mutual supervision process.

The integration of NGOs in the ILO regime is a far cry from their nascent, and somewhat hesitant, integration under the *Montreal Protocol*. Giving NGOs a role in implementing the Protocol would be an enormously positive step in reinforcing the restrictions in the Protocol. A governing body for the agreement—similar to the ILO—could draw from environmental and industrial representatives as well as government officials, and committees could be established patterned on the mutual supervision and complaint procedures of the ILO. The process of review and listing would put a premium on compliance regime for those parties most concerned about their standing among other parties.

The final regime to be considered is the nuclear non-proliferation regime, a regime that makes monitoring and physical inspections of nuclear material and technology its central focus. Unlike the first two regimes considered, this regime conducts routine physical inspections to verify compliance with its norms.

The Nuclear Non-Proliferation Regime and the IAEA

For a quarter of a century, the International Atomic Energy Agency (IAEA) has been the heart of the nuclear non-proliferation regime. In response to President Eisenhower's "Atoms for Peace" proposal, the IAEA was created in 1957 as an autonomous organ of the United Nations. While the IAEA has played a significant role in promoting the commercial use of nuclear power, its principle function today is to verify, through safeguard procedures and on-site inspections, that nuclear facilities and radioactive materials are used for peaceful purposes and not diverted to weapons production.

The inspection mechanism is the critical component of the safeguard procedures. Between 1968 and 1982, the IAEA's staff of inspectors conducted 9,600 inspections, two-thirds of which were conducted in the last four years of this period. In 1984, over 875 installations were under IAEA safeguards, comprising 97 percent of the nuclear plants in states without nuclear weapons.

As nuclear testing by the superpowers escalated and nuclear material began to proliferate, global concern over military use grew. By the late 1960s, the non-nuclear countries were ready to trade their theoretical right to develop nuclear weapons for the tangible benefits of a system of safeguards and nuclear security. The Latin American Nuclear Free Zone Treaty and the Nuclear Non-Proliferation Treaty (NPT) were formed in response to this new attitude. The treaties imposed lead obligations on all member states to submit to IAEA safeguard procedures, thereby closing a critical loophole in the IAEA statute.

The IAEA and its Safeguard Procedures

On-site inspections are central to the safeguard procedures. The IAEA statute allows the IAEA "access at all times to all places and data" as necessary to determine compliance and to assure that the agency's health and safety standards are met. Additional authority was granted by the NPT, which requires "that the diversion of significant quantities of nuclear material from peaceful activities be promptly detected". The broad reach of the language of the statute and treaty has been narrowed by the IAEA's safeguard guidelines, which instruct the agency to keep inspections to the minimum necessary and to avoid hampering the economic and technological development of the state. Additionally, the guidelines put inspection under considerable control by the state. Member states are given at least twenty-four hour notice, and have the right to approve inspectors and to accompany them during their inspections.

In order to implement the safeguards, the agency must negotiate an agreement with the nation where it wishes to verify compliance on a facility-by-facility basis. Nonetheless, between 1961 and 1983, the agency entered into ISO safeguard agreements with 92 states. One of the main features of the agreements is its record-keeping procedure. Most of the information collected is kept confidential. Thus, there is very little access to specific information, making it difficult to evaluate the effectiveness of the safeguard procedures.

Implications for the Montreal Protocol

In regard to the *Montreal Protocol*, the most relevant feature of the IAEA is its system of inspections. In addition to the committee and commission mechanisms of the human rights and ILO regimes, a verification committee could be created under the Protocol to conduct routine inspections and to verify reductions in the production and use of restricted chemicals. This committee could also perform the investigations for compliance committees or commissions. There are several other features of the IAEA that are attractive candidates for inclusion in a *Montreal Protocol* authority. First, the IAEA's dual purpose of monitoring and providing technical assistance could serve as a role model for softening resistance to perceived incursions into state sovereignty. Thus, a verification committee under the Protocol might not only conduct inspections, but also may provide on-site technical assistance during the transition to substitute chemicals and processes. Second, the IAEA has for years served as a clearinghouse for nuclear information and technology. A verification committee under the Protocol could provide information on substitutes and aid in the technical administration of the Multilateral Fund.

Building a Monitoring and Compliance Regime Under the *Montreal Protocol*

The parties to the *Montreal Protocol* are poised to debate a non-compliance mechanism for the agreement in June 1991. While the non-compliance provisions are not scheduled for adoption until the 1992 meeting, the parties are expected to discuss progress made during the meeting of the open-ended Ad Hoc Working Group of Legal Experts. The interim Implementation Committee is a positive recognition that compliance mechanisms, similar to those of the human rights and ILO regimes, might be attractive in the context of the Protocol.

The regimes described above suggest that there is more the parties can and must do to put an effective monitoring and compliance regime in place. First, NGOs must be involved in the compliance regime chosen. The power of the environmentalists and industry in the ozone layer debate attests to the role of private actors in determining global norms. After all, it is the behavior of individuals, NGOs and industry that international law ultimately seeks to regulate, and their participation in the enforcement of the *Montreal Protocol* can play an important legitimizing role. Additionally, NGOs are purveyors of information generated within states, and can provide indispensable political and scientific information to inform international implementation efforts. Second, open and routine mechanisms to review compliance can generate "peer pressure" among states interested in maintaining their standing abroad. However, the reporting and review mechanisms of the current *Montreal Protocol* regime, as illustrated by the poor reporting record of states professing strong support for the agreement, are not creating the peer pressure that the ILO system of mutual supervision generates. Finally, verification of data and reports on party compliance can improve the accuracy of reporting by states. As the ILO recommendations and observations system illustrates, many problems with state compliance can be resolved positively in the early phases of non-compliance. Additionally, as the Inter-American Court and the ILO Committee on Freedom of Association demonstrate, investigations can be critical in resolving later complaints of non-compliance. Thus, these three factors—NGO integration, verification of compliance, and open and routine monitoring—must form the core of any proposal to put in place an effective compliance regime for the *Montreal Protocol*. A model for this compliance regime is discussed below.

Incorporating NGOs into the Compliance Regime

The *Montreal Protocol* fails to create a positive role for NGOs. By keeping them on the outside, the regime not only loses an opportunity to make use of their strengths but also risks making their participation adversarial. For example, under the agreement, NGOs and industrial representatives must notify the UNEP Secretariat of their interest in attending meetings of the parties. They will be invited only if two-thirds of the parties assent to their participation as observers. This provision alone betrays an attitude toward NGOs that is vastly different than that found in the human rights and ILO regimes.

The Montreal Protocol fails to create a positive role for NGOs. By keeping them on the outside, the regime not only loses an opportunity to make use of their strengths but also risks making their participation adversarial.

The parties should affirm a role for NGOs in the governance and implementation of the *Montreal Protocol*. Thus, NGOs should be incorporated in any governing body or committee that might set policy for the agreement. Additionally, they should be members of committees monitoring compliance. Finally, they should be empowered to bring complaints against states failing to live up to their obligations.

In a manner similar to the ILO nominating process, which requires countries to nominate those nongovernmental delegates most representative of their respective constituents, NGOs might be nominated according to their past or potential contributions to domestic and international progress toward the elimination of ozone-depleting chemicals. NGO and industrial interests should have the right to appeal directly to the UNEP Secretariat to participate on the governing and implementing bodies of the agreement if they are not selected by their home country or if their country is not a member of the *Montreal Protocol*. The governing body of the Protocol should scrutinize party nominations that are not representative of the public or their constituents or are selected primarily for other reasons (e.g., those who would rarely take a position different from that of their governments).

The Governing Body and Annual General Meetings of the Parties

The parties should adopt a governing body, comprised of developed and developing countries, NGOs, and industrial representatives—no single category of which should have veto power—to formulate policy for the meeting of the parties. This should in no way pre-empt parties from recommending amendments under the current procedures. The governing body should have a staff that aids in the implementation of the agreement and in coordinating any Working Groups and meetings of the parties.

Under the *Montreal Protocol*, the parties are to meet on a regular basis. Since the Protocol was adopted in 1987, the parties have met on an annual basis, and every meeting has been of enormous importance, even if just to build a groundswell of support for strengthening amendments. To create the expectation that the parties will put a high priority on reviewing the compliance of the parties as well as the adequacy of the agreement, the annual meetings should continue to serve as a forum to consider the progress of the agreement, the adoption of amendments, and reports from committees.

Creation of a Monitoring and Compliance Mechanism

The human rights, ILO, and IAEA regimes make extensive use of monitoring and compliance mechanisms to encourage countries to abide by their norms. The *Montreal Protocol* is well-structured for similar monitoring and compliance mechanisms. The annual reporting requirements, the trade provisions, and Multilateral Fund all provide opportunities for review by committees set up under the agreement. The parties could make the Implementation Committee a permanent body and enhance its powers or create a number of new committees that would report to the governing body and the meetings of the parties.

If the parties chose to create several committees, the first committee could conduct fact-finding investigations similar in procedure to those conducted under the ILO Commissions on Inquiry and the Committees on fact-finding and Conciliation and Freedom of Association. Modelled on the IAEA, this verification committee could consist of trained technical experts who would carry out routine investigations and verification in member countries. The committee's mandate could include verification of compliance and investigation of general problems of compliance and specific instances of non-compliance. In its investigations of non-compliance, the committee might work closely with those providing technical assistance through the Multilateral Fund. Ultimately, the committee could be responsible for dispensing a strategic reserve of CFCs and other restricted chemicals for essential uses in a manner similar to the IAEA repository of nuclear materials. Because trade between member states is one of the incentives for states to join or comply with the agreement, there should be a penalty for trading restricted products with non-parties, a prospect that becomes increasingly complicated as the list of chemicals and products expands. The committee could inspect cargo shipments to verify that trade between parties and non-party states was free of restricted raw chemicals, products, and technologies.

A second committee could receive the reports that are required by the *Montreal Protocol* and its amendments. With sixty countries now members of the agreement, there is ample technical information to evaluate the effectiveness of national control programs. This compliance review committee might be modelled on the ILO Committee of Experts on the Application of Conventions and Recommendations, which makes recommendations to states and issues observations in reviewing compliance of states with ILO labor standards in its annual report on cases of non-compliance.

In a manner similar to the ILO review mechanism, the compliance review committee's report could either be transmitted to the Implementation Committee, if it is made permanent, or to the governing body. The Implementation Committee should evaluate the most egregious cases of non-compliance for action, perhaps promulgating a list of countries similar to the ILO procedure for special listing. Again following the ILO model, the nongovernmental representatives would have a role in this review; they should be included in the evaluation of party reports and be given a forum to register any disagreement with those reports.

A third committee should be structured to hear non-compliance complaints, as now provided under the *Montreal Protocol's* interim non-compliance provision. The committee also should receive complaints from NGOs and concerned citizens, who may know more about the compliance activities within their states than other party states. The non-compliance committee would have the authority to direct the verification committee to conduct on-site investigations. The threshold for screening complaints should be kept low until the usefulness of the procedure in encouraging compliance can be ascertained.

The recommendations of the committee could be appealed to a special court, modelled on the European and Inter-American Courts for human rights cases. In order to encourage early resolution, parties failing to abide by the decisions of the non-compliance committee should have their trade benefits or funding under the Multilateral Fund revoked. In general, the trade penalties for non-parties should apply to non-complying parties.

Placement of Experts on Compliance Committees

One of the critical features of the human rights and ILO monitoring and compliance committees is the impartiality and expertise their members bring to the review and recommendations functions. When state representatives serve as members of such committees, as in the case of ECOSOC Human Rights Commission, they pursue violations far less aggressively and tend to politicize the Committee's work. It is important that the initial review of country reports be conducted by committees of experts whose recommendations command objective authority. As one long-time official of the ILO observed, the impartiality of the experts is critical in creating the confidence that international supervision will be effective.

Full Disclosure

All three Committees recommended above, and the Implementation Committee, if it becomes permanent, should adopt full disclosure as the rule rather than the exception. Secrecy in the IAEA regime has made evaluating the effectiveness of its safeguard procedures difficult. In the human rights regime, secrecy has lessened the pressure and therefore the incentives to pursue violations. In the ILO regime, on the other hand, the compliance committees not only work with an ethic of full disclosure, they also actively use disclosure, or what they term publicity, as a tool to encourage parties to comply.

Access to data is essential if nongovernmental representatives are to evaluate meaningfully the compliance of parties. NGOs are decentralized, which means they can monitor state programs on a daily basis more effectively than UNEP or the Implementation Committee. They would also play an important publication role by alerting the public, other parties, and the media to developments under the *Montreal Protocol*. Through the media, NGOs also can keep the latest scientific findings in the news, which creates another incentive for states to act and to improve compliance with the agreement.

One of the key elements in any policy of open disclosure is dissemination of the regular reports of the parties. The 1990 London Amendments require reports from the Implementation Committee and the Multilateral Fund's Executive Committee, but are not very specific about the scope and content of these reports. Requiring an annual report from all committees set up under the *Montreal Protocol* might elevate the importance of such reports as sources of information for monitoring and compliance purposes. Annual reports should include discussions of the activities of the committees and of member and non-member states, and should recommend necessary actions. All reports should be made available to the public.

Conclusion

An effective international regime will create the opportunity and incentives for states to act together. Creating a strong connection between domestic practices and international obligations is central to making the *Montreal Protocol* regime work. As another official of the ILO observed, the proper criterion for assessing the value of particular international organizations or regimes is how successfully they involve the domestic decision-making processes of states rather than how independent of states they have become. After all, as the debate surrounding the adoption of the Protocol illustrates, national commitment is the source of the political will underlying most strong regimes. For this reason, an international supervisory mechanism that integrates nongovernmental actors can create an essential system of accountability between international regimes and state practice.

The regime should encourage states to work together. There are many positive benefits of the *Montreal Protocol* regime. For example, states can share technology and financing to put less harmful substitutes in place, they can create trade benefits to reward those states that are complying, and they can move quickly to respond to changes in the scientific assessment of the causes and rate of ozone depletion. However, the regime must not become a hiding place for states that would like to appear environmentally-minded, but have no intention of living up to their obligations. The human rights, ILO, and IAEA regimes provide persuasive examples of ways to ensure that the Protocol establishes its goals through state compliance.

International environmental norms must catch up with the realities of the global environment. Ecological disasters and growing economic interdependence—epitomized by the recent Persian Gulf War—reminds us how small this earth really is. Yet the *Montreal Protocol*, held out as the greatest accomplishment of the international environmental regime, is light years behind the human rights, labour and nuclear nonproliferation regimes in its structural capacity to implement its obligations. Unless nations work together, by opening up international institutions to the public and putting in place mechanisms to create the necessary dynamic between international obligation and state practice, we risk losing nothing less than the chance to save life as we know it on this planet.

B

Yoshida O., "Soft Enforcement of Treaties: The Montreal Protocol's Noncompliance Procedure and the Functions of Internal International Institutions," 10 *Colorado Journal of International Environmental Law and Policy*, Winter, 1999, pp 95–141

A Preliminary Examination

"Soft" enforcement of environmental treaties consists of international supervision of treaty-based regulatory measures by internal international institutions. Unlike judicial tribunals such as the International Court of Justice, which are essentially confrontational and bilateral, mechanisms for dispute avoidance or settlement within environmental regimes are multilateral in character. Instead of international adjudication based on existing procedures of international law, environmental regimes increasingly focus on international supervision or control—such as environmental reporting and monitoring, fact-finding and research, data or information collection, and inspection—for compliance with treaty regime rules. International environmental regimes rely mainly on intergovernmental compliance monitoring through the collection of statistics (indicating the extent of government or private activity in a given issue—area of international environmental relations), notification of adoption of relevant domestic legislation, and detailed regulations and specific national programs. Yet because it is a kind of early warning system for noncompliance problems, self-reporting or its data analysis is only the first step toward successful international supervision.

With this background in mind, drafters of the Montreal Protocol's dispute settlement regime were concerned with the crucial question of ensuring greater compliance with the ozone layer treaty requirements that deal with the application of complex environment-related obligations. Those obligations include reducing emissions of ozone-depleting substances (ODSs) (Articles 2 and 3 and Annexes), controlling international trade in ODSs (Article 4), and national or regional reporting requirements (Articles 7 and 9). As a result of their pioneering endeavors, the Montreal Protocol added a flexible arrangement for environmental dispute avoidance and settlement—a "noncompliance procedure" (NCP) regime.

The NCP of the 1994 Oslo Sulfur Protocol closely follows the Montreal NCP model. In addition, the Conference of the Parties to the 1997 Kyoto Protocol to the United Nations (UN) Climate Change Convention decided to approve, at its first session, "appropriate and effective procedures and mechanisms to determine and to address cases of noncompliance.... including the development of an indicative list of consequences, taking into account the cause, type, degree and frequency of non-compliance" (Article 18).

Under the present international cooperation regime for protecting the ozone layer, the only legal remedy is collective treaty compliance. Monetary compensation by sovereign states consuming ODSs or by transnational corporations producing ODSs is not available. Under the Montreal NCP regime, either a member state or the United Nations Environment Programme (UNEP) Ozone Secretariat can initiate procedural mechanisms to ensure implementation of the international ozone treaties without any question of its own legal interests being involved. Therefore international NCP regime initiators do not have to exhaust any domestic legal remedies as a precondition. In this respect, the Montreal NCP is an unprecedented procedural mechanism designed to effectively enforce international obligations erga omnes, in this case the global protection of the stratospheric Ozone layer. The ozone layer regime needed a self-contained dispute avoidance and settlement system to implement international obligations erga omnes.

Although it is difficult to make generalizations about the Montreal NCP regime on the basis of its brief period of operation, the NCP regime—in which internal treaty institutions exercise regulatory and supervisory functions—can be regarded as an internalized treaty dispute avoidance and settlement mechanism based on a "collective reaction" or "multilateralism" rather than confrontational bilateralism common to formal dispute settlement mechanisms. Multilateralism is concerned with traditional collective measures such as informal persuasion and the "mobilization of shame" applied by global institutions. Compared with traditional judicial settlements that usually require time-consuming processes, the NCP regime seems to be more flexible, simple, and rapid. In light of the step-by-step negotiation processes of the NCP regime, which seek feasible and amicable solutions, the international mechanism shows a scrupulous respect for the sovereignty of ozone regime member states.

Apart from its multilateralism, flexibility, simplicity, and rapidity, the Montreal NCP regime has gradually established a close link with international financial mechanisms such as the Montreal Protocol's Multilateral Fund (MLF) and the Global Environment Facility (GEF). These mechanisms strengthen the so-called "soft" enforcement of international environmental regime rules by providing financial incentives for compliance and financial consequences for noncompliance.

This article outlines the Montreal NCP regime and discusses how it applies to current treaty violations. Section II provides a brief summary of the Montreal NCP regime negotiation process. Section III attempts to clarify the meaning of the legal term "noncompliance" within the international legal ozone regime. Section IV deals with the operational mechanics of the Montreal NCP regime, pointing out the important functions played by the specialized NCP regime institutions. Section V discusses the unique relationship between the Montreal NCP regime and the "precautionary principle," an evolving principle of international environmental law. Section VI, devoted to the Montreal NCP regime in practice, analyzes the effectiveness of specific treaty requirements such as technical reporting, ODS control measures, and international trade controls. Consideration is given to the Russian Federation's noncompliance with those ozone treaty obligations and shows the difficulties that arise under a soft enforcement regime. The conclusion identifies the Montreal NCP as a new approach to treaty enforcement, one that is well-suited to international environmental concerns.

The Negotiation of the Montreal NCP Regime

While the 1987 version of the Montreal Protocol introduced specific ODS control measures to prevent steady ozone depletion, negotiators of the international ozone regime could not complete the NCP in time for its adoption. As a result, Article 8 of the protocol provides that "The Parties, at their first meeting, shall consider and approve procedures and institutional mechanisms for determining noncompliance with the provisions of this Protocol and for treatment of Parties found to be in noncompliance."

Nevertheless, it took several years of gradual preparations to establish the existing Montreal NCP regime. The 1989 Helsinki meeting established an Ad Hoc Working Group of Legal Experts, which was to evaluate three different proposals for a noncompliance procedure submitted by the United States, the Netherlands, and Australia. Some states, the United States and Nordic countries, in particular, strongly supported a more stringent, punitive approach rather than the working group's recommendation of an encouragement-based approach.

The first meeting of the Ad Hoc Working Group was held in Geneva in 1989. The US proposal suggested a conciliation procedure based on noncompliance under the 1985 Vienna Ozone Convention, which could ultimately lead to recommendations and/or further punitive measures as approved by a Meeting of the Parties. Under an Australian proposal, the Secretariat was to be given stronger powers as the "guardian of the Protocol," which included regular reporting as to both compliance and noncompliance. After an extensive discussion about the NCP regime, it was agreed that:

(i) it was important to avoid drawing up an unnecessarily complex and duplicative system;
(ii) the procedure should not be confrontational;
(iii) action under the noncompliance procedure could be commenced by either one or a number of Parties or the Parties collectively registering concern with the Secretariat;
(iv) the procedure proposed should not alter or weaken in any way Article 11 of the Vienna Convention on the Protection of the Ozone Layer;
(v) confidentiality must be respected and specific reference to this should be made in the procedures proposed;
(vi) the Secretariat's role should be that of a servicing, administrative body rather than a judicial one;
(vii) the Secretariat should compile the necessary data and other information;
(viii) early indications of possible noncompliance might be resolved through administrative action by the Secretariat and through diplomatic contacts between Parties;
(ix) decisions on noncompliance should be recommendations, rather than mandatory directives.

The working group also agreed that there should be an international supervisory body called the Implementation Committee. Since many delegations demanded that the Implementation Committee not have a judicial function, the Ad Hoc Working Group agreed that any decisions concerning noncompliance would be made by the regime's supreme entity, the Meeting of the Parties. The working group also approved a Draft Noncompliance Procedure, which specified basic functions of the UNEP Ozone Secretariat, the Implementation Committee, and the Meeting of the Parties. The 1990 London Ozone Meeting adopted this draft NCP on an interim basis and established its institutional mechanism, the standing Implementation Committee.

In the Second Meeting of the Working Group, held in 1991, the European Community (EC) offered the most sweeping proposal. Under the EC's proposal, the functions of internal international institutions, including the UNEP Ozone Secretariat and the Implementation Committee, were essentially similar in many respects to the existing Montreal NCP regime. In addition, the EC proposal included in its draft text Indicative Lists of Steps to Bring about Full Compliance with the Protocol which dealt with three types of noncompliance: reporting requirements, ODS control measures, and trade restrictions. Apart from draft proposals submitted, many experts in this meeting argued that dispute settlement procedures under the Vienna Convention and the Montreal Protocol's NCP were "two distinct and separate procedures which could well exist in parallel."

The final draft of the Montreal NCP, as improved by the Third Meeting of the Ad Hoc Working Group, was adopted at the 1992 Copenhagen Ozone Meeting of the Parties as annexes to the Montreal Protocol (Decision IV/5). The decision is legally binding because of the enabling provisions of Articles 8 and 11(3.d). In order to strengthen the NCP, the 1997 Montreal Ozone Meeting of the Parties established a fourteen-member Ad Hoc Working Group of Legal and Technical Experts on the NCP.

The use of the legal terminology "noncompliance" in the Montreal Protocol seems to be particularly appropriate for its global regulatory rules on ODS controls.

The Meaning of "Noncompliance" in the Ozone Protocol Regime

In general, "compliance" means a "desired state of conformity with the law, a regulation, or a demand." Its working definition is dynamic rather than static. Unlike the term "enforcement," "compliance" implies that regime member states are induced to comply rather than coerced to do so. In this sense, the use of the legal terminology "noncompliance" in the Montreal Protocol seems to be particularly appropriate for its global regulatory rules on ODS controls. An instance of noncompliance could be defined as the breach of obligations owed under public international law, or an internationally wrongful act. However, possible noncompliance with the international ozone treaty provisions is not necessarily a matter of state liability requiring compensation for environmental damage.

"Noncompliance" is not defined in the legal text of the Montreal Protocol nor the Vienna Convention. One reason is that the 1992 Copenhagen Ozone Meeting was not ready to adopt an Indicative List of Possible Situations of Non-compliance with the Protocol as prepared by the Ad Hoc Working Group of Legal Experts. In the absence of such a helpful list of potential noncompliance scenarios, the risk of noncompliance is likely to increase. As Professor Michael Bothe said, "The risk of non-compliance increases if a norm is not well defined and legal loopholes remain. Compliance is furthered by the possibility of obtaining a clear determination of the content of a norm in relation to a given case."

"Noncompliance" may imply multilateral environmental disputes relating to "compatibility with the objectives of an international regime," since violation of ozone treaty obligations would affect the international community as a whole rather than a particular sovereign state or individuals under any one state jurisdiction. In this sense, potential ozone disputes differ radically from environmental conflicts concerning transboundary air pollution or natural resource conservation.

Taking account of the draft Indicative List, noncompliance regarding the following four ozone treaty obligations would first be determined by the Montreal NCP regime:

(i) noncompliance with treaty provisions relating to ODS control measures (Articles 2, 2A-2H);
(ii) noncompliance with treaty provisions relating to restrictions on trade with nonparties (Article 4);
(iii) noncompliance with time schedules for reporting data (Article 7); and
(iv) noncompliance with reporting of a summary of national ozone activities (Article 9).

Arguably, nonpayment of contributions to the financial mechanism, the MLF, could also be regarded as noncompliance with the international ozone treaties. While most donor countries consider the obligation to contribute to the MLF as legally binding, the United States interprets it as requiring merely "voluntary compliance." The legal text of the MLF is silent on this contentious matter, and the Implementation Committee has never decided the issue. Consequently, the legal status of these monetary contributions has been left intentionally ambiguous. There is no evidence that the Executive Committee has ever formally brought noncompliance problems concerning MLF operations to the NCP regime's meetings of the Implementation Committee. In addition, MLF-related decisions by the Executive Committee and the Meeting of the Parties have been monitored almost entirely by the Executive Committee and the MLF Secretariat. As David C. Victor has noted, the link between the MLF and the NCP remains "surprisingly weak."

The above analysis indicates that the definition of "noncompliance" will depend on the practical decisions of both the Meeting of the Parties and the contracting parties themselves. In this respect, Professor Martti Koskenniemi rightly observes:

> "a dispute about whether some particular type of non-compliance is a wrongful act is another dispute about interpretation or application of the treaty [i.e., "treaty disputes"] and capable of being resolved only within the procedures under Article 11 of the Vienna Ozone Convention."

Ultimately, "the question of wrongfulness is one of general international law, and not a question that can be solved, or indeed even approached, from within the special regime of the Vienna Ozone Convention and the Protocol at all." Koskenniemi therefore argues that the Meeting of the Parties, acting as a strictly judicial organ, may suspend the rights of an allegedly defaulting party only if there exists noncompliance in the sense of a wrongful act by that state party.

With regard to the relationship between Article 11 of the Vienna Convention and the Montreal NCP regime, the protocol provides that "the provisions of Article 11 of the Vienna Convention shall apply with respect to any protocol except as provided in the protocol concerned" (Article 11(6)). This means that the operation of the Montreal NCP is not necessarily stipulated as a condition precedent to the settlement mechanisms enumerated in the Vienna Convention. Moreover, since a hierarchy does not exist under the Montreal NCP for settling disputes, no ozone regime member could or would eliminate the possibility of invoking binding procedures under the Vienna Convention. For instance, an allegedly defaulting party that believes that it has not committed a wrongful act entailing state responsibility can invoke, as a means of avoiding collective suspension of rights or countermeasures, the traditional settlement mechanisms under the convention. At this stage, the Montreal NCP may not be seen as a "self-contained" regime.

The Montreal NCP provides only that:

(i) the special procedural regime (i.e., the NCP) shall apply "without prejudice to the operation of the settlement of disputes procedure laid down in Article 11 of the Vienna [Ozone] Convention;"
(ii) the Meeting of the Parties may issue an interim call and/or recommendations, pending completion of these proceedings;

(iii) the contracting parties that decide to use a dispute settlement mechanism described in Article 11 of the Vienna Ozone Convention must inform the Meeting of the Parties through the Ozone Secretariat;

These three points do not radically change the abovementioned relationship between Article 11 settlement mechanisms and the Montreal NCP regime.

The 1991 Nairobi Meeting of the Parties decided that these two processes for dealing with parties' noncompliance were distinct and separate procedures (Decision III/2). Furthermore, at the 1992 Copenhagen Meeting of the Parties, it was declared that "the responsibility for legal interpretation of the Protocol rests ultimately with the parties themselves."

Perhaps one acceptable solution for this situation is for the internally specialized treaty bodies, as legal advisers to the regime practitioners, to take account of the existing principles and rules of international law as a whole in deciding what constitutes noncompliance or breach of treaty before deciding which measures should then be taken. This solution makes sense even if members of these bodies are unwilling to provide clarity and, in the interest of flexibility, would prefer it to remain a gray area of the international legal ozone regime.

It is likely that the international institutional supervision of compliance through the Montreal NCP will be too weak to resolve certain ozone disputes. Hence, should the new NCP regime fail to settle ozone disputes, an allegedly defaulting party could still be taken to the formal dispute settlement procedure under Article 11 of the Vienna Convention, a procedure that includes binding third-party settlement. This assessment of NCP weakness is not necessarily confirmed in practice.

The Mechanics of the Montreal NCP Operation

The Basic Structure of the Montreal NCP Regime

The NCP Regime Actors

The main actors of the Montreal NCP regime, apart from the state parties, are the three specialized internal international institutions:

(1) the Meeting of the Parties,

(2) the Implementation Committee, and

(3) the UNEP Ozone Secretariat. All three are "functional" and "sectional" institutions in the field of international Ozone layer protection.

The NCP regime can be triggered—independent of causality or full scientific certainty—by

(1) one party against another party,

(2) the party which itself is or will be in noncompliance, and

(3) the UNEP Ozone Secretariat.

International financial mechanisms that support the NCP regime include the Executive Committee of the MLF, the Multilateral Fund Secretariat, the World Bank, the UNEP, the United Nations Development Programme (UNDP), and the United Nations Industrial Development Organization (UNIDO). Unlike nongovernmental organizations (NGOs) in the field of international human rights law, environmental NGOs under the Montreal NCP regime only have a minor role in releasing informal information about anticipated noncompliance.

The Principle of Good Faith

In light of its reliance on voluntary political cooperation in ensuring implementation of various technical obligations, it is noteworthy that the fundamental basis of the NCP regime is the principle of good faith (bona fides), a natural law concept of international law regarded as an implicit provision of all treaty regimes. The legal principle has formed the psychological foundation of the international ozone regime, and noncompliance in "bad faith" (e.g., illegal trade in CFCs) would likely lead to the regime's collapse. For the regime to work, states must act in good faith.

In a self-reporting system, a state party in noncompliance should have dedicated its best bona fide efforts to the fulfillment of its treaty obligations. Developed countries already have the capacity to comply fully with technical treaty obligations, and expect that developing states with their economies in transition (CEITs) will also try to comply with stringent ozone treaty obligations, precise legal regulations, and other related principles of international environmental law.

Despite the difficulties in enforcing multilateral environmental treaty rules, international reputations have political significance. As Professor Louis Henkin observed, "states recognize that stability, law and order, reliability (and a warranted reputation for reliability) are in their national interest, and therefore that they have a more-

or-less enlightened self-interest in compliance." Under the NCP, if a noncomplying party fails to respond within a fixed period or if the matter cannot be settled by diplomatic means, the UNEP Ozone Secretariat includes that information in its report of the Meeting of the Parties. The Secretariat also informs the Standing Implementation Committee. It is possible that this "sociological sanction" might have some effect.

The Functions of Internal International Institutions in the Montreal NCP Regime

The UNEP Ozone Secretariat: NCP Regime Initiators and Functions of the Ozone Secretariat

The UNEP Ozone Secretariat can request that any party provide necessary information in connection with its possible noncompliance.

The 1985 Vienna Ozone Convention established the UNEP Ozone Secretariat on an interim basis. At present, the UNEP Ozone Secretariat serves on a permanent basis. It acts at an early stage to monitor state compliance with detailed scientific and technical ozone regulations to identify potential violations.

While members of the Implementation Committee do not necessarily have technical or scientific expertise, or any special legal competence, they nonetheless deal with political and diplomatic matters as well as with all matters pertaining to technical and scientific noncompliance issues. In this respect, the importance of the UNEP Ozone Secretariat's role as a source of highly experienced technical and scientific expertise cannot be overemphasized.

The Montreal NCP regime will be invoked by the UNEP Ozone Secretariat in three circumstances. In the first case, the UNEP Ozone Secretariat:

(1) receives a report presented by any contracting parties that have reservations as to another party's implementation of its treaty obligations under the protocol,
(2) sends that submission to the party whose implementation is at issue, and
(3) transmits the submission provided by the parties to the Implementation Committee.

The submission must be supported by "corroborating information" that might include informal information offered by nonstate international actors, including environmental NGOs.

In the second case, the UNEP Ozone Secretariat obtains a written explanation given by the party with regard to the particular circumstances of the causes of noncompliance and transmits the submission to the Implementation Committee. This "self-reporting system" was included in the Montreal NCP regime on the basis of a proposal made by the former Soviet Union, several of whose successor states were the first parties to initiate the NCP dispute settlement regime.

The UNEP Ozone Secretariat can also invoke the NCP regime by itself, when it becomes aware of possible noncompliance during the course of preparing its reports. The UNEP Ozone Secretariat can request that any party provide necessary information in connection with its possible noncompliance. This is the first case in which the secretariat of a Multilateral Environment Agreement (MEA) has been empowered to invoke a formal dispute avoidance/settlement procedure in international law. In contrast, the UNEP Ozone Secretariat, under the 1989 Basel Convention, is only empowered to inform the parties of the alleged violations.

This third scenario shows how it would be possible for information derived from environmental NGOs to reach the Montreal NCP regime without any governmental support. Although government officials tend to see NGOs as "long-haired radicals" with no understanding of the complexities of the issues, NGOs' detailed information as to illegal trade in CFCs seems particularly reliable and helpful. NGOs—including industrial NGOs—have demonstrated a commitment to working toward implementation of the Montreal Protocol. It therefore may be good idea to increase NGO input into the existing NCP process. Until now, however, the UNEP Ozone Secretariat has been rather reluctant to invoke the NCP in this way.

The Implementation Committee

Some commentators view the creation of the Implementation Committee as a real breakthrough in international environmental law. The legitimate first stop in any formal discussion, the Implementation Committee, has examined and decided most of the resolvable noncompliance issues. However, more vexing questions, such as noncompliance of CEITs, may ultimately have to be referred to a Meeting of the Parties.

At present, the Implementation Committee consists of ten representatives from state parties elected to two-year terms by the Meeting of the Parties. Like many other intergovernmental conciliation committees, the composition of the Implementation Committee is based on the principle of equitable geographical distribution designed to ensure a political equilibrium in which common interests of the international community are represented. Hence, the Implementation Committee is not an independent third party but merely a mixture of ten states. The result of this composition may be that the Implementation Committee will tend to exercise its broad discretion with regard to noncompliance cases in pursuit of political goals. Professor Sir Geoffrey Palmer observes in this respect that the committee could "ignore certain rules of international law whose application might not be considered desirable and it may draw upon the body of normative expectations developed within the [Ozone] regime regardless of the formal legal status of any particular rule."

Under the Montreal NCP regime, the Implementation Committee assumes four prominent roles "with a view to securing an amicable solution of the matter on the basis of respect for the provisions of the Protocol." First, the Implementation Committee receives and considers:

(i) a report from a Party/Parties in another Party's implementation of its treaty obligations under the Montreal Protocol;
(ii) the submission provided by a Party that considers itself unable to comply fully with its obligations;
(iii) other relevant submissions, replies, and information concerned;
(iv) any information or observations with regard to compliance or production, import, and export of controlled substances received and forwarded by the UNEP Secretariat.

When analyzing these reports or submissions, the Implementation Committee must ascertain particular underlying reasons for noncompliance in order to make appropriate recommendations. In light of national data reporting from the parties, the Implementation Committee also amicably arranges the classification or reclassification of "developing countries" entitled to receive funding from the MLF. When necessary, the Implementation Committee may request further information through the UNEP Ozone Secretariat.

The Implementation Committee, therefore, is in a position to consider confidential information as to treaty performance as contained in data reports provided by the parties. Its own reports, however, must not include such delicate matters. Accordingly, members of the Implementation Committee and any party involved in its NCP processes must protect the confidentiality of information. Due partly to the fear that discussions of such confidential data might be publicly disclosed, environmental NGOs are presently totally excluded from Implementation Committee meetings.

Second, the Implementation Committee submits a report, including any recommendations on individual noncompliance cases, to the Meeting of the Parties. The Implementation Committee may also make recommendations where it considers them appropriate, although the parties concerned cannot participate in the decision-making process. In making such recommendations, the Implementation Committee, as a subsidiary body of the Meeting of the Parties, must conform to the Rules of Procedure adopted by the 1989 Ozone Meeting. While these recommendations are not legally binding on ozone regime members, they may carry some "political weight," and in many cases they are widely followed.

Third, the Implementation Committee undertakes information gathering within the national territory of a party with the consent of the party. This is the so-called "on-the-spot investigation," or a limited kind of verification.

Fourth, since financial and technical assistance are, in practice, closely related to a party's capability to comply with obligations, the Implementation Committee exchanges information with the Executive Committee of the MLF concerning this assistance.

The Ozone Meeting of the Parties to the Montreal Ozone Protocol

a. The Functions of the Meeting of the Parties in the NCP Regime

The Meeting of the Parties is the final decision-maker under the Montreal NCP regime. As the highest institution of the regulatory regime, the Meeting of the Parties retains direct control over ozone disputes raised among member states. This decision-making arrangement reveals the parties' desire to protect their various national interests in international environmental organizations rather than turning over such power to representative subgroups.

After receiving reports from the Implementation Committee, the Meeting of the Parties will consider "the circumstances of the matter, decide upon and call for steps to bring about full compliance with the Protocol, including measures to assist the parties' compliance with the Protocol, and to further the Protocol's objectives." The Indicative List of Measures lists actions that might be taken by the Meeting of the Parties in response to noncompliance with the treaty obligations:

(i) Appropriate assistance, including assistance for the collection and reporting of data, technical assistance, technology transfer and financial assistance, information transfer and training.
(ii) Issuing cautions.
(iii) Suspension, in accordance with the applicable rules of international law concerning the suspension of the operation of a treaty, of specific rights and privileges under the protocol, whether or not to time limits, including those concerned with industrial rationalization, production, consumption, trade, transfer of technology, financial mechanism, and institutional arrangements. The Meeting of the Parties may also make interim recommendations. Moreover, it can "request the Implementation Committee to make recommendations to assist the Meeting's consideration of matters of treaty noncompliance." The decisions and recommendations made by the Meeting of the Parties concerning implementation must relate to the objectives of the international cooperative ozone regime.

b. The Legal Nature of Meeting of the Parties Decisions

By September 1997, the Meeting of the Parties to the Montreal Ozone Protocol had adopted more than 200 decisions in accordance with the Rules of Procedure. Many of them are related directly or indirectly to noncompliance issues concerning international regulation of ODSs, international trade controls of ODSs, and technical data reporting. These decisions usually stipulate that regime members shall take further measures necessary to achieve the purposes of the cooperative and regulatory regime, but they often merely reiterate obligations already laid down in the articles of the international ozone treaties.

One of the primary roles of the Meeting of the Parties is to continually adapt international law for stratospheric Ozone layer protection. As the main source of regime negotiation and decision-making, the body enjoys considerable legislative autonomy. As a result of political compromise within the international environmental regime, however, its decisions are often vague and open to a variety of interpretations. In addition, the legal status of its decisions remains unsettled, and it is not clear that noncompliance with its decisions can be regarded as noncompliance with the Montreal Protocol.

During the negotiations of the Montreal NCP regime, many governmental representatives suggested that decisions of the Meeting of the Parties were distinct from articles of the Montreal Ozone Protocol's text. Some states were of the opinion that not all decisions were binding on state parties; other representatives stated that such decisions were always legally binding if they related to matters of substance. As discussed earlier, the 1992 Copenhagen Meeting did not adopt the Indicative List of Possible Situations of Non-compliance. Possible instances of noncompliance have not been formally discussed in the Meeting of the Parties, nor in meetings of the Conference of the Parties to the Vienna Convention.

The implied powers of the Meeting of the Parties are strictly limited to their so-called objectives and functions, and thus differ from state entities that have established fully independent legal personalities in international law. Generally speaking, the implied powers of the Meeting of the Parties are not well-defined by customary or general public international law, but instead are based primarily on the Montreal Protocol as a law-creating treaty. While the regular Meeting of the Parties has some supranational aspects, it is not a "super-state" organization. As Professors Patricia Birnie and Alan Boyle shrewdly point out: "the supervisory body, whether a meeting of the parties or a Commission, is in substance no more than a diplomatic conference of states, and the existence... of a separate legal personality does not alter the reality that the membership of these institutions is in no sense independent of the states they represent."

In this light, one may argue that any additional action required for achieving the purposes of the Montreal Ozone Protocol should be defined in terms of its limited functional capacity or implied powers in general international law.

One should note that internal international law and Meeting of the Parties' procedural rules are subject to customary international law governing the principles of state sovereignty and equality of states. In theory, the individual decisions adopted through the internal legal rules of the Meeting of the Parties are, in a formal sense, of secondary importance to the international regulatory ozone regime unless declared with an expressed intention to bind the parties. Thus ozone regime members may dispute the validity of a decision adopted by the Meeting of the Parties on the grounds that it violates the Rules of Procedure.

In light of these considerations, a decision cannot impose on regime member states a legal obligation to adopt measures that may conflict with the ozone treaty regime's objectives and purposes. However, certain specific decisions adopted through formal procedures provided in advance of international ozone treaties (e.g., adjustments or amendments) are legally binding on regime member states. In this context, they are properly regarded as "hard" international law.

However, it is a mistake to think that nonbinding legal instruments have no legal effects. Many decisions arguably show current evidence of consensus among regime actors and have formed certain legal norms, which are capable of creating customary international law applicable to the international legal system of the developing regulatory ozone regime. At the same time, many decisions provide essential indicators for a proper understanding of the developing cooperative ozone regime.

The "Precautionary Principle" as the Basic Philosophy of the Montreal NCP Regime: Soft Enforcement of International Environmental Law

Before examining the Montreal NCP regime in practice, an understanding of the philosophical foundation of this new dispute avoidance and settlement procedure in the sphere of international environmental protection law is necessary to place the regime in context.

The Precautionary Environmental Principle and Stratospheric Ozone Depletion

The distinctive characteristics of the Montreal NCP regime must be viewed against the background of the Montreal Ozone Protocol's technical obligations, which require both international cooperation in facilitating developing countries' capacity to comply with their obligations and acknowledgment of an evolving principle of international environmental law—the precautionary principle.

The precautionary principle involves taking certain preventive measures to protect the environment even before a causal link has been established by absolutely clear scientific evidence. The precautionary principle can be seen as a gradual development or an effective modification of the 1972 Stockholm Declaration's Principle 21, which is currently perceived to be a binding legal obligation. Given the time lag between knowledge and law, the precautionary principle should be a critical component of the ozone treaties.

Certain issues of law enforcement arise whenever states fail to comply with their legally binding obligations under MEAs or customary international law. Most reprisals or countermeasures, including the suspension of certain rights or privileges, are presented as direct responses to violations of these obligations. In early 1990, Professor Martti Koskenniemi argued that, "from the perspective of state responsibility, the Montreal NCP appears as a mechanism for collective countermeasures (or reprisals) in case of non-performance (Breach of Treaty or Noncompliance)." His statement is true, albeit within certain limitations.

More accurately, resorting to the NCP regime in itself reflects both the limitations of existing principles of customary environmental protection rules and the growing roles of international supervisory institutions. Since customary international law cannot react quickly enough to deal with environmental problems, the existence of an international institution that can establish new customary international environmental law norms on the fly may be the only effective way to deal with international environmental problems. In this author's view, Professor Koskenniemi's speculative legal argument, founded on traditional international rules on law enforcement, obscures the fact that the Montreal NCP, a "self-contained" international ozone regime, is based on the precautionary approach to environmental destruction. The NCP's redeeming characteristic is its adaptability to changing circumstances. The regime's emphasis on flexibility renders its limitations in complicated international relations less troublesome. The Montreal NCP is not the product of ignorance of general international law principles.

"Soft Enforcement" of Treaties

In examining the nature and contents of the Montreal NCP regime, it is important to note that many developing countries were reluctant to join in the international regulatory regime due mainly to restrictions on international trade in ODSs (i.e., control of trade with nonparties). This was in spite of the fact that many were not sure how to comply with the substantial technical treaty obligations, including reporting procedures, ODS control measures, and trade controls. With a few exceptions, states usually decide to participate in international treaty regimes only when they think they will comply with the legal obligations. Considerable collective countermeasures, primarily economic, which would make it possible to ensure not only treaty compliance but the necessary universal participation, were therefore employed beforehand in Article 4 of the regulatory Ozone regime.

Another important aspect of the Ozone regime is that—despite the objection of state parties—adjustments of the Montreal Ozone Protocol's ODS control measures are binding on all the parties on the basis of the revolutionary "simplified majority decision-making." This departure from the traditional principle of unanimity might become a potential cause of ozone disputes. Some dissenting minority states, aware of their inability to comply, might vehemently oppose time-targeted adjustments adopted by such a simplified procedure.

To ensure strict consistency in the international obligations of all parties to the international legal ozone regime, no reservation is allowed under the 1985 Vienna Ozone Convention or the Montreal Ozone Protocol. Nevertheless, in reality, most developed states have come to recognize that developing countries and CEITs do not necessarily have the capacity to comply fully with the technical treaty obligations, including the national reporting requirement.

In practice, the Implementation Committee has been overloaded with routine administrative work such as locating missing baseline or annual data, correcting incomplete data reports from the parties, and classifying and reclassifying "developing countries." Noncompliance with national or regional reporting requirements has stemmed from a lack of capacity among member states. In most cases, noncomplying states within the regulatory ozone regime are either "developing countries" under the Montreal Ozone Protocol or CEITs such as the Russian Federation.

In such situations, unless noncompliance results from malice or greed and is therefore considered to be intentional or systematic, the Meeting of the Parties will not resort to severe international sanctions against the party in question. Patrick Szell, former chairman of the Montreal NCP negotiations, voiced this need for differentiation:

> "A regime should be based on the recognition that noncompliance was frequently the consequence, not of malice or greed, but rather of technical, administrative or economic difficulties."

Given the aforementioned problems, one can understand why the Montreal NCP regime, in dealing with possible noncompliance, encourages a party that is willing but unable to fulfill its treaty obligations by giving appropriate financial or technical assistance. Hence, the countermeasures seen in paragraph C of the NCP regime's Indicative List would likely be counterproductive. The central aim of the Montreal NCP regime is not to take controversial countermeasures that would occasionally give rise to questions of state responsibility, but rather to seek amicable solutions to anticipated noncompliance. An extreme example of this approach to noncompliance is the NCP regime of the 1994 Oslo Sulfur Protocol to the 1979 Long-Range Transboundary Air Pollution Treaty, which does not even provide for sanctions.

The Montreal NCP regime is therefore designed to carefully apply the precautionary principle to an urgent global environmental problem—stratospheric ozone layer depletion. Under the present regulatory ozone regime, the evolving precautionary principle mandates that developed nations must provide global financial support for developing countries to assist them in fulfilling their technical treaty obligations.

One should not overlook the fact that, even if the real guarantee of treaty compliance is the system of collective sanctions, such sanctions are not intended to be directly punitive or repressive. Instead, the sanctions are intended to be coercive in the sense that they would apply sufficiently strong pressure on defaulting member states. International institutions such as United Nations specialized organs and the International Monetary Fund (IMF) usually do not invoke the power to suspend a state's rights or privileges; instead, they employ other less punitive means of securing state compliance.

Despite this, it does not necessarily follow that various principles of customary international law and state responsibility have nothing to do with the settlement of potential ozone treaty disputes. Indeed, collective response measures should be commensurate with the importance of the provision itself, as well as with the nature and degree of the compelling reasons behind noncompliance. The question of whether the NCP regime is a kind of conciliation mechanism, a quasijudicial mechanism, or merely an institutionalized negotiation process would depend in part on the nature of the issues the institution must handle.

While the NCP's flexibility has contributed to effective implementation of international Ozone treaties, one should not ignore the ultimate disadvantage of its considerable "softness." Indeed, as Professor Francesco Francioni said in a recent critique:

"This question [whether soft enforcement procedures are exclusive of countermeasures] will arise whenever the soft implementation procedure has failed to satisfy a contracting party, for instance, objects to an amicable compromise; ... or when a state reiterates the breach or becomes a systematic defaulting state. In these circumstances it would make little sense to exclude the operation of ordinary countermeasures under customary international law or under the Vienna Convention on the Law of Treaties. Soft law and soft remedies cannot be understood in such a way as to displace and curtail the operation of hard law."

The Montreal NCP Regime in Practice

Ensuring Compliance with International Ozone Treaties

The Reporting Requirements

International legal regimes are of no use if their legal rules are not put into operation in the sphere of domestic legal regimes. Most international environmental agreements impose periodic reporting requirements, which are often labeled "procedural compliance." Reports can be divided into two broad categories: reports on the overall implementation of a treaty, and reports on compliance with specific treaty obligations. In addition, the national and regional reporting systems of international environmental law have great importance in judging the effectiveness of control measures, and for adjusting existing international regulations established by internal treaty institutions of environmental regimes.

The Montreal Protocol requires contracting parties to provide the UNEP Ozone Secretariat with baseline and annual data on their production, imports, and exports of each group of controlled substances, or the best possible estimates of such data if actual data is not available. Although the international regulatory ozone regime decided that nonparties and noncomplying states were denied access to foreign markets for CFCs and ODSs, the Montreal Protocol does not currently impose any obligation to report to the UNEP Ozone Secretariat on the implementation of Article 4, which concerns the control of trade with nonparties. This is due partly to the fact that drafters could not ensure the compatibility of the terms of Article 4 with the General Agreement on Tariffs and Trade (GATT).

Since its first meeting in 1991, the Implementation Committee has dealt with continuing problems of nonreporting, insufficient reporting, and late reports from parties to the Montreal Protocol as well as nonparties. Noncompliance with data reporting has been a problem more frequently with developing countries than with developed countries. The Implementation Committee, in its Third Meeting, found that the principal reasons for reporting problems were "the turnover of personnel in the Customs service, their lack of training and experience, and the lack of qualified specialists to train them." Subsequently, the UNEP Ozone Secretariat stressed the importance of country studies and programs being carried out by the MLF's implementing organs—the UNDP, UNEP, UNIDO, and the World Bank.

International legal regimes are of no use if their legal rules are not put into operation in the sphere of domestic legal regimes.

In 1993 the Implementation Committee invited to its Seventh Meeting ten parties that had consistently failed to provide reporting data. At that meeting, the representative of Costa Rica stated that incomplete data was due mainly to delays in receiving funds from the UNDP—that is, a lack of prompt financial assistance. Italy's representative suggested that its failure was the result of purely domestic bureaucratic matters and that forthcoming legislation would resolve the problems of nonreporting. In considering the EC's significant production and consumption impacts, the Implementation Committee expressed particular concern with nonreporting by some EC members (Belgium, Greece, Italy, and Portugal) and with missing 1991 consumption data from the Commission of the EC.

The Implementation Committee also recommended that Mauritania be reclassified as a party not operating under Article 5 until it reported required data, thereby denying that government funds from the MLF. In a broader action, the Meeting of the Parties adopted Decision VI/5, which held that an Article 5 developing country will lose its status "if it does not report base-year data as required by the Protocol within one year of the approval of its country program and its institutional strengthening by the Executive Committee." In addition, the GEF made funding of ozone-related projects in CEIT party states conditional on compliance with the Montreal Protocol and its 1990 London Amendment. As with Article 4 trade restrictions, loss of MLF funding can be regarded as an enforcement "stick."

It appears that the relationship between MLF funding and compliance with the protocol's requirements is gradually strengthening. In its Twelfth Meeting the Implementation

Committee noted that reports from many parties on required information were more than two years overdue and that "it should be made clear to the Meeting of the Parties that the trend of late reporting should end, particularly in respect to those countries in which institutional strengthening projects have been carried out under the Multilateral Fund."

The Control Measures Applied to ODSs

State compliance with substantive regime control measures of ODSs under Articles 2, 2A to 2H, and the corresponding measures in Article 5, has formed the basis of the international regulatory regime for protecting the stratospheric ozone layer.

According to recent data received by the UNEP Ozone Secretariat, most non-Article 5 parties appear to comply with the detailed control measures. Most of these developed state parties have introduced national regulations that could substantially achieve the various objectives of the international cooperative ozone regime. While it is possible for the Ozone Secretariat and the Implementation Committee to dispute the scientific validity of data provided by those state parties, neither of them has taken such an action to date.

Due to the ten-year grace period, developing countries operating under Article 5 only have to phase out CFCs by 2010 and halons by 2015 in accordance with the 1990 London Adjustments. Consequently, their compliance with these international control measures remains to be seen. Given this, it is perhaps more accurate to say that both the UNEP Ozone Secretariat and other implementing agencies are, at present, trying to achieve extensive improvement in nonreporting and inadequate reporting from these developing state parties.

Some commentators believe that the Article 5 grace period has created a serious danger of weakening the precautionary principle. First, rapid increase in CFC consumption in Article 5 nations could eventually undermine earlier phaseout efforts by non-Article 5 countries. Undeniably, the ten-year grace period will retard the possible recovery of the stratospheric Ozone layer. Second, the grace period has encouraged an illegal international trade in controlled CFCs. Article 5 countries, China and India in particular, continue to produce large amounts of CFCs and illegally export them to non-Article 5 countries.

There are several examples of the Implementation Committee's efforts to resolve implementation problems. In the Tenth Meeting of the Committee, the UNEP Ozone Secretariat informed the committee that Lebanon, which was conferred the status of a developing country operating under Article 5, had exceeded the per capita consumption ceiling. Additionally, Lithuania once tried to obtain a delay of five years for the implementation of control measures, as provided in the self-executing London/Copenhagen Adjustments, even though the Implementation Committee stated that Lithuania's data reports were inadequate and that the government would not be eligible to receive assistance from financial institutions until it ratified the 1990 London Amendment. In the Eighteenth Meeting of the Committee, Lithuania submitted detailed implementation information, a timetable for ratification of the London Amendment, and its country program prepared with the UNDP and the UNEP. The committee thus recommended that international assistance, particularly from the GEF, should be considered for Lithuania.

The newly emerging illegal trade in CFCs and ODSs weakens and threatens the effectiveness of the regulatory Ozone regime as a whole. At the 1995 Seventh Meeting of the Parties to the Protocol, many representatives reported "regrettable evidence" of illegal trade in controlled substances. The Vienna Ozone Meeting, and its subsequent meetings, adopted decisions regarding illegal imports and exports of those substances. Nevertheless, the Ozone Operations Resource Group (OORG), established by the World Bank, reports that there have been startling increases in illegal CFC-12 imports into the United States. Fortunately, these eventually resulted in numerous arrests and indictments. Duncan Brack, of the Royal Institute of International Affairs in London, claims that Russia is the main source of CFCs and ODSs and that European countries and Australia are now major destinations. Until now, the United States has been the only country to take any decisive action to stop such illegal trade in ODSs, and many European countries have been relatively slow to act. It was agreed in the 1997 Montreal Ozone Meeting, however, that parties shall institute a licensing system to help national governments track international trade in ODSs and discourage unlicensed black-market trade.

A Case Study: Noncompliance by the Russian Federation and Reactions of NCP Regime Institutions

Since the early 1990s the issues concerning CEITs' noncompliance have been formally discussed in the standing Implementation Committee and in the Meeting of the Parties. Yet it was not until 1995 that the Montreal NCP regime was invoked to handle the voluntary submission of anticipated noncompliance by several CEITs, including the Russian Federation, Belarus, Bulgaria, Poland, and the Ukraine. This section concentrates on Russia's noncompliance case, rather than on CEITs' treaty noncompliance as a whole.

The Russian Federation and CEITs

There are currently 27 states with economies in a transitional state. It is worth noting that the CEITs are contributing immensely to stratospheric ozone depletion. Their estimated 1994 consumption of ODSs was approximately equal to a quarter of the world consumption in that year. The Russian Federation is one of the world's largest producers and consumers of ODSs. Russian consumption of controlled substances exceeds 60 percent of the CEIT total, and Russia is the only producer of these substances in its region. The Russian Federation is the major exporter of controlled substances to some twenty CEITs and, possibly, to other non-CEIT countries. In light of its considerable political and economic influence in the international community, the Russian Federation's noncompliance will likely undermine the stability of the regulatory ozone regime.

The former Soviet Union adopted the 1987 version of the Montreal Protocol on November 10, 1988. The Russian Federation—which formally became an independent sovereign state on August 24, 1991—has since assumed the former Soviet Union's obligations under international ozone treaties.

Russia's Noncompliance Case

In the open-ended Eleventh Ad Hoc Working Group held in May 1995, the Russian Federation submitted a joint statement on behalf of itself, Belarus, Bulgaria, Poland, and the Ukraine. In the statement, Russia argued that it did not appear possible to completely phase out ODS production and consumption by January 1996 due mainly to the difficult economic situations that faced the CEITs.

To be fair, the Russian Federation did not initially intend to invoke the mechanics of the new Montreal NCP regime. Instead, its original intention was to seek a special five-year grace period directly from the Meeting of the Parties. That request was then sent to the standing Implementation Committee. The Russian Federation first informed both the Meeting of the Parties and the Implementation Committee of anticipated treaty noncompliance. Nevertheless, the Implementation Committee regarded the Russian Federation's statement as a submission under paragraph (4) of the NCP under the Montreal Protocol regime. The Russian Federation did not attempt to deny this plausible interpretation. As a result, the standing Implementation Committee was presented with its first opportunity to address noncompliance matters under the Montreal NCP regime.

In its Tenth Meeting the Implementation Committee noted that there were no treaty provisions that would allow any Party a schedule for ODSs different from that of the Montreal Protocol regime. It further suggested that anticipated noncompliance by the Russian Federation should be addressed by a decision of the Meeting of the Parties, rather than by amending the Montreal Ozone Protocol. The committee required the Russian Federation to provide further information, including data on production and consumption of controlled ODSs, and its compliance plan, for use in developing a committee recommendation.

The Implementation Committee could not reach an agreement with the Russian Federation, particularly regarding monitoring issues and international trade. Its recommendations, then, were brought to the 1995 Meeting of the Parties without complete agreement by Russia.

After much discussion, and over the objections of the Russian Federation, the 1995 Vienna Ozone Meeting adopted Decision VII/18 with regard to anticipated noncompliance by the Russian Federation. Decision VII/18 required not only data reporting—namely, more detailed information as to its firm commitments to the Montreal Protocol—but also reporting on planned actions to prevent re-exports from the Commonwealth of Independent States (CIS) to any party to the Montreal Protocol regime. It can be said that the Meeting of the Parties consolidated, to some extent, the contents of the previous Decision VII/16 made by the Implementation Committee.

The representative of the Russian Federation, who considered such actions "discriminatory measures and sanctions against a party," strongly disputed the paragraph addressing future trade restrictions and thus regretted that Russia "had not been able to accept the draft decision in its entirety." This example of the NCP in action nicely illustrates that a conflicting opinion defended by only one party may eventually have to reconcile with stated regime objectives. This case pointedly illustrates the collective side of the Montreal NCP regime.

Despite the trade restrictions, Decision VII/18 allows the Russian Federation to export controlled substances to CEIT parties operating under Article 2 of the protocol, including Belarus and the Ukraine. The decision recommends, as an incentive, international assistance to help Russia comply with its international ozone treaty obligations. In reality, such funds would be indispensable if Russian industries are required to virtually halt ODS production and convert existing capacity to less ozone-depleting HCFC or HCF production. A potential problem is that the Russian Federation, which prefers to use national production processes, is not willing to rely on transnational corporations' proprietary processes or licenses. This may limit Russia's ability to convert its industries to more modern processes.

It appears obvious that the Russian Federation wants to ensure continuity of ODS supplies to developing countries to meet their "basic domestic needs" as permitted under the protocol.

Notwithstanding its high levels of ODS consumption, the Russian Federation is by no means a "developing country" operating under Article 5 of the protocol. As a result, the country is not entitled to receive funds from the MLF. Consequently, the only international institution that is available to contribute the necessary funds after Russian noncompliance will be the GEF, an entity that has no official legal status in the international ozone regime.

It appears obvious that the Russian Federation wants to ensure continuity of ODS supplies to developing countries to meet their "basic domestic needs" as permitted under the protocol. This is one of the main reasons that Russia would not choose to withdraw from the regulatory regime. Meanwhile the Group of 77 and China, which are fearful of the consequences of Russian illegal ODS trade in their markets, tried in vain to add clear language to Decision VII/18 that would ban export and re-export of controlled substances to Article 5 parties. The final outcome of this case, therefore, is not completely clear.

Since issuing Decision VII/18, the Implementation Committee has emphasized its requirements for further information and has reiterated that the Russian Federation should monitor and report on the implementation of trade restrictions. In recent reports of its meetings, the Implementation Committee has noted that the process of ODS phaseout in Russia is impeded primarily by the Russian Federation's desire to continue illegal exports and that the country is the only party still producing ODSs in violation of the Ozone Protocol's phaseout schedule.

At the Seventeenth Meeting of the Implementation Committee, the Russian Federation reiterated its commitment to meeting its international ozone treaty obligations. Russia also stated that a new phaseout program would be implemented in cooperation with the international community and multilateral financing agencies. In this meeting the committee decided that the Russian Federation had continued to produce ODSs during 1996 contrary to provisions of the Montreal Protocol and Decision VII/18, and that Russia was still in noncompliance with the Protocol for 1996. Moreover, the Implementation Committee found that the Russian Federation had engaged in an illegal trade in ODSs with many developed and developing countries under the Montreal Protocol regime. It was thus noted that "there was a danger of a loss of credibility for the whole Montreal Protocol process if it was seen that Parties not operating under Article 5, which should have completed phase-out, were still importing and exporting controlled substances."

After the Eighteenth Meeting of the Implementation Committee, Russia's persistent noncompliance was further discussed in the 1997 Montreal Ozone Meeting of the Parties, and Decision IX/31 was adopted at this meeting based on the recommendations made by the Implementation Committee. Decision IX/31 noted that international financial assistance—the GEF in particular—should continue in order to furnish funds for projects designed to phase out ODS production and consumption in the Russian Federation.

Conclusions

The Montreal NCP regime is essential to the operation of a rule-oriented ozone legal system in the comparatively weak realm of legal obligations concerning global environmental protection. The regime has turned out to be a great step forward in strengthening the collective state compliance, or "horizontal enforcement," of international environmental law principles such as the precautionary principle. More importantly, the regime guarantees a reliable procedure of identifying, at an early stage, possible noncompliance with treaty obligations, and provides a mechanism for avoiding and settling multilateral ozone disputes.

Yet the Montreal NCP is not meant to supplant or replace traditional legal settlement procedures under the Vienna Convention. In this respect, Professor Gunther Handl accurately points out that, "where basic constituent principles and "hard' legal parameters are concerned, disputes should be amended both technically and politically to formal third-party decision-making in accordance with international law narrowly defined."

A weakness of the Montreal NCP is that decisions as to what kind of recommendations should be made and which measures must be taken are left largely to the broad discretion of the Implementation Committee and the Meeting of the Parties. It is questionable whether such political institutions consisting of governmental representatives can always act impartially. More importantly, it still is unclear whether such bodies can responsibly act as a sincere trusteeship of the global commons—the stratospheric ozone layer. Unlike international judicial institutions or human rights committees, NCP regime operators are not independent and do not necessarily have professional prestige. In addition, we should not overlook the confidential aspects of the Montreal NCP regime's decision-making process, which are often crucial in understanding the hidden meaning of the internal regime institutions' decisions.

In 1995 the Montreal NCP regime started its active operation by handling the first formal submission of treaty non-compliance. The Meeting of the Parties' adoption of Decision VII/18 by consensus against the will of the Russian Federation demonstrates that the NCP's method of "friendly" confrontation could enhance effective operation of the existing Montreal NCP regime. An ongoing lesson from Russia's noncompliance case is that, on suitable occasions, environmental regime institutions must exert appropriate international pressure on member states that persistently violate their treaty obligations by not only offering "carrots" but also by applying an appropriate "stick." If, in this first test of the Montreal NCP regime, the 1995 Meeting of the Parties had merely followed the Implementation Committee's rather soft recommendations, considerable doubts would have arisen among the ozone regime members as to the effectiveness of this new dispute avoidance and settlement procedure against treaty noncompliance.

The Montreal NCP regime also will undergo self-review under Decision IX/35 of the 1997 Montreal Meeting of the Parties. The Ad Hoc Working Group of Legal and Technical Experts on the NCP is to consider any proposals by Parties for strengthening the NCP, including how repeated instances of significant noncompliance could trigger adoption of measures under the Indicative List of Measures with a view toward ensuring prompt compliance with the protocol, and any proposals for improving the Implementation Committee's effectiveness—including proposals to improve data reporting and the general conduct of its work. Currently the working group is considering various government proposals.

The experience of the Montreal NCP model will likely be helpful in designing future NCP environmental regimes under various international environmental treaties, including those protecting global atmosphere, biological diversity, and global forests. While the Montreal NCP regime has turned out to be a good prototype for dealing with ozone depletion, each respective environmental treaty should adopt a more suitable form of the NCP regime, depending on the nature and contents of its established legal obligations and types of potential environmental disputes. Future treaties would do well to keep in mind the philosophy of the Montreal NCP regime—collective "soft" enforcement.

5

Current Issues and Concerns

A

Illegal Trade in Ozone-Depleting Substances

(i) Solow S.P., "The Big Chill: How Federal Agencies Are Working Together to Stop CFC Smuggling," *National Enforcement Journal,* Vol. 12, No. 5, 1997, pp 9–14

Introduction

Following a ban on the importation of certain chlorofluorocarbons (CFCs) used in car air conditioners, a black market in illegally imported CFCs has developed in the United States. A nationwide federal offensive against the smugglers has resulted in the seizure of hundreds of thousands of pounds of smuggled CFCs and significant jail terms and criminal fines for smugglers. The success of the National CFC Enforcement Initiative, begun in November 1995, is the result of a tremendous level of cooperation among EPA's Criminal Investigation Division (CID), US Customs, the FBI, the IRS, US Attorneys' offices, and the Environmental Crimes Section (ECS) of the Department of Justice.

The proactive nature of the CFC Enforcement Initiative also represents the future of environmental crime enforcement at the local, state, and federal levels. As explained in greater detail below, the CFC Initiative's success was based on several key elements:

- Quick response to a few early cases that indicated a broader pattern of criminality,
- Prompt sharing of data among various federal agencies,
- Regular and complete communication among all agencies involved in the initiative.

These factors enabled the initiative to quickly build upon the information and lessons learned from the first few major cases, which were brought in the southern district of Florida. The result is a successful nationwide initiative that continues to yield results.

CFC Smuggling and the Black Market

CFCs are chemicals used as refrigerants, solvents, and propellants. Unfortunately, these chemicals eventually work their way into the stratosphere and become dangerously efficient destroyers of the ozone layer which protects the Earth from ultraviolet-B (UV-B) radiation. Excess UV-B radiation can cause skin cancer, cataracts, and suppression of the immune system in humans and other animals and disturb global ecosystems. One CFC molecule can destroy 100,000 molecules of ozone. Because of the widely recognized risks posed by CFCs, the United States joined with over 160 other countries to phase out the use of certain CFCs under the *Montreal Protocol* of 1987. The protocol separates developed from developing countries, setting the phaseout goals for CFC uses based upon a country's status.

The United States' obligations under the *Montreal Protocol* were implemented through amendments to the *Clean Air Act* of 1990. Under this plan, CFCs were to be phased out using two methods: First, an EPA-administered system of "consumption allowances" that would limit the amount of CFCs that could be imported or used each year to a declining number of pounds and, second, an increasing excise tax per pound of CFCs imported that ultimately has exceeded $6 per pound. The phaseout culminated in a ban, which went into effect on January 1, 1996, on the importation for use of the CFCs most destructive to the ozone layer, known as Class I CFCs. Developing countries have until 2010 to phase out Class I CFCs.

There has been an ongoing attempt to circumvent the United States' ban on Class I CFCs by smuggling CFCs such as dichlorodifluoromethane or R-12, a refrigerant commonly known by its former trade name Freon, into the country and selling them on the black market. The suspected major sources for the production of the black market CFCs are Russia, China, Mexico, and India. In this year alone, thousands of tons of illegal CFCs will likely be transported into the United States and will enter the black market. With approximately eighty million cars in this country still on the road that use R-12 in their air conditioning systems, there is high demand for these illegal CFCs. It is still perfectly legal to use existing stockpiles of R-12 to service cars that use the older refrigerant, but suppliers of smuggled CFCs stand to earn huge profits by selling their black market goods at near-market prices while avoiding both the excise tax and the floor tax on existing stockpiles. For example, a standard thirty-pound cylinder of R-12, imported legitimately before the end of 1995, can cost as much as $500, of which almost $180 represents the excise tax. Smugglers who have evaded the tax and who sell the same cylinder at near market prices stand to make a tremendous profit while consumers and, probably, most service stations will pay the same price for stockpiled or smuggled CFCs. Most importantly, black marketeers undermine the international effort to reduce the use of the most ozone-destructive CFCs. They are making a quick dollar at a cost to our global environment.

This illicit trade violates the *Clean Air Act* (42 U.S.C. § 7401) and triggers liability under other federal statutes. CFC smugglers have been convicted of violations of customs laws (18 U.S.C. § 545), tax laws (26 U.S.C. § 7201), and money laundering laws (18 U.S.C. § 1956) as well as under mail fraud and wire fraud (18 U.S.C. § 1341) and false statements (18 U.S.C. § 1001) statutes.

How It Began

In October 1993, a US Customs Inspector, who worked at Port Everglades, Florida, took her car in for servicing. When she received the bill, she noticed that the cost of recharging her car air conditioner had risen considerably. She spoke to her mechanic about the sudden increase. He, in turn, explained how the price of CFCs was rising because certain CFCs were being phased out. He explained EPA's requirement of consumption allowances for imports and the excise taxes triggered by the first use or sale of imported CFCs. He proved to be an excellent teacher.

About two weeks later, the Customs inspector was checking a series of shipments from Great Britain when she noticed that there were two containers entering the United States that contained about 1,800 30-pound cylinders of R-12. Recalling her mechanic's explanation for the higher repair bill, she checked with EPA to confirm that the shipment was being made with the necessary consumption allowances. When she learned that it was not, she seized the containers and notified Special Agent George White, a US Customs criminal investigator, who in turn brought in Special Agent Kevin Guarino of EPA CID. The inspector's quick thinking led to a criminal case that culminated in jail sentences and fines for the smuggling conspirators. This was the beginning of operation Cool Breeze in Miami which would involve additional agents from Customs and EPA CID along with the IRS, the Tax Division of the Department of Justice, and the US Attorney's Office in Miami.

One case led to another in this first prosecution. The CID agents and the federal prosecutor, Assistant United States Attorney (AUSA) Tom Watts-Fitzgerald, recognized that Florida was not the only port of entry being used by the smugglers. They quickly informed other Customs and EPA agents and the Environmental Crimes Section (ECS) at the Department of Justice of their growing pool of information concerning CFC smuggling and the variety of methods by which the CFCs were illegally entering the United States. These included:

Failure to Use EPA Allowances

Some smugglers reported their importation of CFCs to US Customs and then moved them into the market before their lack of consumption allowance could be determined.

Fraudulent Transhipments

CFCs can be shipped into the United States marked as destined for transport to another country. Under Customs laws, these items are not considered to have "entered" the United States. Smugglers would secretly remove the CFCs from shipping containers, replacing them with other items for transport out of the country, while the CFCs would slip into the black market. Some of the Cool Breeze defendants used this scheme, bribing the operator of a customs-licensed facility to assist in preparing paperwork to show that the containers were being shipped to Mexico.

Claiming that "Virgin" CFCs were Recycled

To encourage recycling of CFCs and to suppress demand for "virgin" product, EPA regulations have exempted recycled or recaptured CFCs from the consumption allowance system that was in effect until January 1, 1996, and from the complete ban on imports of "virgin" CFCs since January 1, 1996. EPA requires importers of recycled or reclaimed CFCs to file a petition with the EPA administrator before the shipment leaves the port of export. Some smugglers falsely represented to EPA that their material was recycled when it was, in fact, "virgin."

Mislabelling CFCs

Smugglers can attempt to import CFCs by mislabelling their shipments as a different product.

A National CFC Enforcement Initiative

In the early fall of 1995, representatives from EPA, Customs, and the ECS began to identify the location of suspected illegal CFC imports. Working closely with EPA's Stratospheric Ozone Protection Program (SOPP) and US Customs Trade Information Development Exchange (TIDE), the ECS identified 12 federal districts with the greatest number of suspicious imports. Lois J. Schiffer, the Assistant Attorney General of the Environment and Natural Resources Division, invited the United States' Attorneys' offices in the twelve districts as well as Customs, EPA, IRS, and FBI representatives to take part in the formation meeting of the National CFC Enforcement Initiative. The meeting was held in November 1995 in Washington, D.C.

At the meeting, the initiative brought together as instructors the experts in the field including the attorney who had written the relevant tax regulations, the program manager of the EPA Ozone Protection Program, the Customs experts who handle the import databases, AUSA Watts-Fitzgerald, and the agents who had already worked on the cases in Florida.

A Workgroup was then established to coordinate cases and to meet regularly to discuss case development and strategies. Particularly because it is a nationwide black market, the Workgroup has enabled participating districts to share information in a timely manner. This has led to stronger cases because districts have been able to spin off cases to other districts, share leads, avoid charging conflicts, and use cooperating witnesses and evidence in several districts. This coordination effort has met with repeated success. For example, on January 9, 1997, the Attorney General, the Administrator of EPA, and the Commissioner of Customs announced charges against smugglers from coast-to-coast. Some fifteen individuals and three companies were charged with smuggling by federal prosecutors in Los Angeles, San Diego, Houston, Miami, Savannah, Philadelphia, and Portland, Maine.

A growing number of prosecutors and investigators at the local, state, and federal levels have significant experience and expertise in the investigation and prosecution of environmental crimes.

These efforts have led to over two and one-half million pounds of black market CFCs being seized with a street value of over $18 million.

Conclusion

Environmental crime investigation and prosecution has developed rapidly over the past fifteen years. The early history of environmental crime enforcement, with some exceptions, was primarily reactive: responding to tips from informants or the public, news of spills or other incidents, and referrals from regulators. Now a growing number of prosecutors and investigators at the local, state, and federal levels have significant experience and expertise in the investigation and prosecution of environmental crimes. With over 70 joint task forces operating around the country, these experienced criminal investigators will increasingly begin to take the initiative in fighting environmental crime—looking beyond individual cases for patterns of criminality. The pattern may show up in certain industries; they may span a county or the country. By improving the communication and cooperation efforts through task forces, joint training exercises, and even through the growing number of readers of this journal, we can turn knowledge about environmental crime occurring in one place into action elsewhere.

The investigators and prosecutor in the CFC smuggling cases in Miami quickly circulated evidence that a nationwide smuggling problem existed. With the help of the initiative, agencies and prosecutors around the country were able to respond to this information, put together a coordinated enforcement effort, and produce substantial results in a remarkably short time period. This kind of rapid and aggressive response is only possible when we quickly share information and experience. Moreover, such an approach allows us to make the best possible use of our available resources and maximize the deterrent impact of criminal enforcement. Ten years from now initiatives like the CFC Enforcement Initiative may well be the norm for local, state, and federal law enforcement. For environmental criminals, that is very bad news indeed.

6

Questions for Discussion

(a) "The negotiations for the *Vienna Convention on Ozone Depleting Substances, 1985* provide a dramatic example for the importance of the precautionary principle, whereby a global framework convention was agreed prior to full scientific certainty about the problem". Discuss.

(b) Discuss the role that scientific information, public perception of risk and activist nongovernment organizations played in the negotiations for the *Montreal Protocol* and its subsequent amendments.

(c) Describe the control mechanisms, particularly the restrictions in consumption, implemented in the *Montreal Protocol*. What is the scope of the substances regulated e.g., chemicals, products and processes? Can you suggest any other regulatory approaches that could have been taken in such a global regime?

(d) The developing nations took a relatively low profile in the early stages of the development of the *Vienna Convention*. What role did they subsequently take in the development of the *Montreal Protocol*? Is there a clear unified developing nation position that emerged or are there differentiated positions between the rapidly expanding economies such as India and China and nations with very little industrialization? To what extent are there differentiated responsibilities in the *Montreal Protocol*?

(e) Hunter et al. state that "If the Protocol's only teeth were phase outs of controlled substances, countries would have incentives not to sign in order to gain the newly freed market share between themselves. To avoid this free rider behaviour and as an incentive for countries to join, the Protocol provided tough trade measures." Discuss the nature and effect of these trade measures relating to nonprotocol parties or trade that is not in compliance with the protocol.

(f) The trade measures under the *Montreal Protocol* could be considered a trade restriction under the *General Agreement on Trade and Tariffs*. Discuss the arguments for and against the operation of *Montreal Protocol* type trade provisions in global environmental regimes.

(g) The *Vienna Convention* and the *Montreal Protocol* provide a classic illustration of rapid responses to scientific developments and public opinion and an extraordinarily rapid amendment process (by international law standards). The regime now has an extraordinarily large number of nations that have ratified the treaty and the first few amendments to the protocol. In spite of these achievements, discuss the extent to which the regime is likely to reduce ozone depletion over the next forty years. In your discussion you should address issues such as the illegal trade in ozone-depleting substances, monitoring and compliance issues and the adequacy of the multilateral fund to assist developing nations.

7

References for Chapter 21

Benedick R., *Ozone Diplomacy: New Directions in Safeguarding the Planet*, Cambridge, Massachusetts Harvard University Press, 1991.

Bothe M., "Compliance Control Beyond Diplomacy: The Role of Nongovernmental Actors," 27 *Environmental Policy and Law*, 293, 1997.

Environment Australia, *The operation of the Ozone Protection Act 1989*, Environment Australia, 2001, see <http://www.ea.gov.au/about/ann_report/99-00/ozone.html> [*Editors' Note; This site was accessed on 27/07/01*].

Francioni F., International "'Soft Law': A Contemporary Assessment," in Lowe V. and Fitzmaurice M. (eds.), *Fifty Years of the International Court of Justice: Essays in Honour of Sir Robert Jennings*, 1996.

Henkin Louis, *How Nations Behave*, 2nd edition, Columbia University Press, 1979.

Koskenniemi M., "Breach of Treaty or Non-Compliance?" 3 *Yearbook of International Environmental Law* 123, 1992.

Szell P., "Compliance Regimes for Multilateral Environmental Agreements," 27 *Envtl. Pol'y & L.* 304-07, 1997.

Szell P., "The Development of Multilateral Mechanisms for Monitoring Compliance," in Winfried Land (ed.), *Sustainable Development and International Law*, 1995 .

Victor D.G., *The Early Operation and Effectiveness of the Montreal Protocol's Non-Compliance Procedure* 17, 24, 1996.

8

Additional References

Caron D., "Protection of the Stratospheric Ozone Layer and the Structure of International Environmental Lawmaking", *14 Hastings Intl. & Comp. Law Review 755*, 1991.

French H.F., "Learning from the Ozone Experience," in Brown LR., *State of the World*, W.W. Norton & Company, 2001.

Makhijani A. and Gurney K., *Mending the Ozone Hole: Science, Technology, and Policy* MIT Press, 1995.

Hunter D., Salzman, J. and Zaelke, D., *International Environmental Law and Policy*, Foundation Press, New York 1998.

Makhijani A. and Gurney K., *Mending the Ozone Hole*, MIT Press, 1995.

Miller M., *The Third World in Global Environmental Politics*, Lynne Reinner Publishers, Boulche, USA.

Home page of the UNEP Ozone Secretariat: [*Last accessed on 28/3/01*]. www.unep.org/ozone/index.shtml

CIESIN List of references: [*Last accessed on 28/3/01.*]www.ciesin.org/TG/OZ/oz-bib.html

UNEPIE OzonAction Programme under the Multilateral Fund: [*Last accessed on 28/3/01*]. www.unepie.org/ozat/aboutus/oaicdvs.html

UNEP, *Environmental Effects of Ozone Depletion: 1994 Assessment*, UNEP, 1994.

CHAPTER

22

Climate Change

Contents

1

Introduction

Scientific evidence is showing that increases in atmospheric concentrations of certain greenhouse gases caused by human activity, such as carbon dioxide, CFCs, nitrous oxide, and ozone, are leading to an increased greenhouse effect and global climate change. While changes in the global temperature are not new, what is new is the short time frame within which these temperature changes created by industrial emissions have taken place over the last 50 years. The Clayton extract details many of the scientific issues related to the phenomenon of global warming and associated with the prediction of impacts from it.

The most significant factor in global climate change appears to be the emissions from the combustion of fossil fuels, deforestation, and other agricultural and land uses, followed closely by the emissions of CFCs, methane, and nitrous oxide.

The predictions of a rise in temperature of 0.3 percent per decade by the Intergovernmental Panel on Climate Change (IPCC), constituted by the world's most renowned climate experts, in 1990 under a "business-as-usual" scenario, gave a predicted level of global mean temperature reaching 2 degrees above the mean in the next 30 years and about 4 degrees by the year 2100. This report was revisited in 1992 and the same temperature increases were predicted. The 1996 IPPC Assessment Report predicted a doubling of preindustrial levels of CO_2 (over the next 50 years) if action was not taken immediately to reduce emissions. The draft report of the IPCC, released in 2001, outlines the increase in CO_2 from 280 ppm (pre-industrial) to 365 (1998), at a rate (calculated between 1990 and 1999) of 1.5 ppm/yr (averaged between 0.9 ppm/yr and 2.8 ppm/yr), with an atmospheric lifetime of 5–200 years. The 1996 report concluded that this projected increase in the level of CO_2 would constitute a dangerous interference with the world's climate system.

A "business-as-usual" scenario assumes that we continue with our massive fossil fuel reliance and only introduce minor energy efficiency programs and continue deforestation at the present rate. Such a change in temperature will lead to increases in rainfall, diminution of ice cover over Antarctica, and a global mean sea level rise of 20 cm by 2030 and 65 cm by the end of the next century. This would cause a major threat to low estuarine and delta systems, such as in Bangladesh and many small island states. Cultures could be wiped out, either through increases in cyclone and storm damage destroying the very land mass, for example on coral atolls, or by making the water table sufficiently brackish to be unusable on these atolls.

The 1990 session of the United Nations General Assembly established a single intergovernmental negotiating process for the preparation of the *Framework Convention on Climate Change* (FCCC) which led to the signing of the Convention at UNCED in June 1992 by 155 States and the European Union. The FCCC only contained weakly worded "commitments" by States. The setting of reduction targets for greenhouse gases (GHGs) (including CO_2) was left to the Kyoto Protocol (amending the FCCC) which was signed by 59 States in December 1997. The extracts from Jeffery and Baird provide an overview of the legal regime created by the FCCC and the Kyoto Protocol in 1997. They go on to elaborate the potential application of the market mechanisms, known as flexibility mechanisms, which are incorporated in the Kyoto Protocol. The clean development mechanism is emphasized as this is the only market mechanism that is likely to involve developing countries in the Asian and Pacific region in the near future. The exact form of the market mechanisms remains unclear after the collapse of the sixth Conference of the Parties (COP6) in The Hague in November 2000. COP negotiations were ongoing in 2001.

The most significant factor in global climate change appears to be the emissions from the combustion of fossil fuels, deforestation and other agricultural and land uses, followed closely by the emissions of CFCs, methane, and nitrous oxide.

Framework Convention on Climate Change 1992

The Convention reflects a compromise between all the States and acts as a framework from which future protocols can be developed. The Convention establishes:

(a) broad commitments to stabilize greenhouse gas concentrations in the atmosphere at a safe level over the long term and to limit emissions of greenhouse gases by developed countries. There was no specific commitment to targets at this point, commitment did not occur until the Kyoto Protocol in 1997;

(b) a financial mechanism and commitment by certain developed country parties to provide financial resources for meeting certain incremental costs and adaption measures;

(c) two subsidiary bodies to the Conference of the Parties;

(d) guiding principles (in article 3) including precautionary measures and policies; and

(e) innovative implementation and dispute settlement techniques.

As regards the negotiating process of the Convention, the economic implications of the Convention played a key role in defining the bargaining positions of each country, rather than the traditional divide between North and South OECD countries and non-OECD countries.

Country Parties are listed in different annexes to the Convention according to their economic background and needs in relation to "sources" and "sinks". A "source" is defined as "any process or activity which releases a greenhouse gas, an aerosol, or a precursor of a greenhouse gas into the atmosphere". A "sink" is defined as "any process, activity, or mechanism that removes a greenhouse gas, an aerosol, or a precursor of a greenhouse gas from the atmosphere". The Convention also differentiates between groups of country Parties in relation to finance issues. There is a distinction between developed country Parties and developing country Parties.

The ultimate objective of the Convention is to achieve stabilization of greenhouse gases in the atmosphere at a level that will prevent dangerous anthropogenic interference with the climate system.

The commitments under article 4(1) include:

- the development of national inventories of anthropogenic emissions by sources and removals by sinks of all greenhouse gases not controlled by the Montreal Protocol;
- the formulation and implementation of national and, where appropriate, regional programs containing measures to mitigate climate change by addressing emissions and removals of gases by facilitation of adequate adaption to climate change;
- all Parties to promote and cooperate in the diffusion of technologies, practices, and processes that control, reduce, or prevent anthropogenic emissions of greenhouse gases;
- all Parties to cooperate in preparing for climate change;
- the taking of climate change considerations into account in all social, economic, and environmental policies as far as possible;
- all Parties to promote and cooperate in research; and
- all Parties to promote full and open exchange of information.

Article 4 establishes broad reporting requirements for information and communications and contains specific provision for making financial resources available to developing countries and for technology transfer.

The Convention established a Secretariat (now located in Bonn, Germany), a Conference of the Parties, two subsidiary bodies, and a financial mechanism. A subsidiary body for scientific and technological advice is established to provide advice to the Parties. The Global Environment Facility operates the financial mechanism.

The *Kyoto Protocol*

The first Conference of Parties of the FCCC in 1995 set in train negotiations to establish a protocol (subsidiary treaty) that would:

- strengthen the commitments of developed countries for the post-2000 period; and
- advance the implementation by all countries of their commitments under the FCCC.

These negotiations were successfully concluded at the third Conference of Parties in December 1997, where agreement was reached on the text of the Kyoto Protocol. Australia signed the Protocol on 29 April 1998.

As a result of the Kyoto Protocol, developed countries, as a whole, will strive to reduce their greenhouse gas emissions from 1990 levels by a least 5 percent by 2008–

2012. In recognition of the fact that developed countries have different economic circumstances and differing capacities and costs in making emissions reductions, each developed country has a specific, differentiated target period to no more than 8 percent above 1990 levels. Australia is a very "fossil fuel dependent" State but it is unlikely that future COPs will continue to offer Australia "special treatment" (+8 percent on 1990 GHG levels) compared to North American, EC and Japanese reduction targets (of at least 5 percent below 1990 levels by 2008–2012).

It is an interesting feature of the Kyoto Protocol that they are adopting a differentiation approach within the developed country blocks as seen by the above discussion. The issue of whether or when developing countries should commit to targets remains deeply controversial.

The targets under the Kyoto Protocol encompass all the major greenhouse gases and the range of sources and significant sinks. The Protocol therefore allows Australia to include emissions from land clearing in the calculation of its target. The target set for each country becomes legally binding when the Protocol has entered into force and that country has itself ratified the Protocol.

The role of market mechanisms in the Protocol are fundamentally important and are covered in the extracts from Jeffery and Baird. There is also considerable discussion of carbon trading and market mechanisms in Chapter 6.

Nations of the world not only have differing resources and capacities to cope with the effects of climate change, they will often experience differential impacts. For example, the extract from Ambassador Slade demonstrates that a small impact could be devastating for the small island states in areas such as the Pacific Ocean because of their vulnerability to sea level rise. This raises issues similar to the ones discussed in the context of social justice regarding how global regimes should deal with the unequal distribution of environmental costs and benefits.

There are many positive strategies that are emerging to deal with climate change impacts, many are "win/win" options as they address long-standing pollution problems in many jurisdictions. A key area for positive change is more efficient energy-use and the promotion of alternative forms of energy. These issues are canvassed in the extract from the *World Energy Assessment* and the extracts from Bradbrook and Otttinger in Chapter 8.

The FCCC and Kyoto Protocol are some of the most complex MEAs negotiated thus far. The Negotiation Exercise, included in this chapter, provides an opportunity for students to appreciate the complex issues associated with the Kyoto Protocol.

A

Nature of Global Environmental Problems and Differential Responsibilities

(i) Clayton, K. "The Threat of Global Warming," in O'Riordan T. (ed), *Environmental Science for Environmental Management*, Longman, Manchester, 1995, pp 110–130

[*Note: This article was written prior to the formulation of the Kyoto Protocol.*]

In an interesting analysis of how the science of acid rain, ozone depletion, and global warming evolved, Kowoloh reached the following conclusions:

- The discoveries evolved over a number of years, in the case of acid rain almost a century, climate warming over three quarters of a century, and ozone depletion over a decade.
- The breakthroughs come almost by accident, but always from a pool of data based on historical trends and supported by boring but vital monitoring and recording.
- Scientists learned through networks of communication and experimentation. None of these great global problems was diagnosed by a single individual, though in the history of discovery, one or two names stand out. In every case it was multidisciplinary workshops and communities of scientists that fully unravelled the mystery.
- Most, if not all, of the science was only partially funded by governments. A substantial part was privately paid for, and some even was done at the scientists' personal expense. Mega-buck science tends to follow rather than precede great discoveries.

It is an interesting feature of the Kyoto Protocol that they are adopting a differentiation approach within the developed country blocks.

On this basis it is a fair bet that the global worries of the next generation have already been discovered. What is missing is the painstaking collection of evidence, the formation of unusual collectives of scientists, the steady incorporation of the nine stakeholder groups that should dominate the global debate from now on, and the reformed role of the media. The media have to act more as lubricators and synthesizers, providing a basis for reaching agreement over common positions, not scaremongers or the peddlers of micro-.stories of transient human interest. Curiously, it is because environmental matters are diffusing into shapeless topic areas that environmental journalists are losing out to their agricultural, business, or even religious brethren. One of the great paradoxes of environmentalism is its search for integration with daily existence, yet its desire for a sharp focus so as to maintain its momentum.

The climate debate is important in that, along with ozone loss, it is the embodiment of global environmental change. A molecule of greenhouse gas emitted anywhere becomes everyone's business. CO_2, CH_4 and CFCs remain as atmospheric warming agents for 60 years, 10 years, and 100 years respectively. So each additional molecule is not just everybody's concern: it is the headache for four generations to come. The fascinating aspect of this globalization of atmospheric warming is that to find a solution, any nation or economic activity need not stop at its own borders. There is every incentive for an emitter to find either a sink elsewhere in the world, or to finance a reduction of future greenhouse gas output from another country if it is to become more efficient at the point of production These are so-called offset (i.e., buying out someone else's greenhouse gases) or joint implementation (i.e., investing in greenhouse sinks).

Both of these approaches are enshrined in the *UN Framework Convention on Climate Change*. In principle, they should become among the most novel and exciting aspects of interdisciplinary environmental science. Any offset or joint implementation scheme requires a knowledge of the radiative forcing role of each gas, of the sequestration rates of various organic systems, of the possible costs of additional amounts of the gas, discounted over four generations, and of the politics and legal aspects of actually ensuring the outcome is beneficial to all parties concerned and the world as a whole.

Such a marvellously interdisciplinary opportunity will not be easy to fulfill. Take, for example, the furor over the measurement of the radiative forcing or global warming potential (GWP) of various gases. This matter was looked at by the Intergovernmental Panel on Climate Change (IPCC) in both its 1990 and 1992 reports, but has been subject to a lot of further analysis by Allan Hammond and his associates at the World Resources Institute in Washington, DC. They tried to produce an index of greenhouse-forcing contributions based on the warming potential of current emissions. This in turn was related to residence time in the atmosphere.

So far, so good. The real trouble arises with estimates of actual emissions. National inventories of CO_2 have been developed but are still guesswork for many countries, notably where deforestation and soil disturbance rates are not known. For methane, the calculation is even more awkward, for rice paddies can emit anywhere from 25 million to 170 million tons per year, and cattle 35 kg to 50 kg per year per animal depending on what they eat and how much work they do. In a similar vein, the forcing potential of halogenated substances is very varied depending on composition.

The third difficulty is the ethical question of historical emissions versus current emissions. The Hammond index does not take into account the legacy of emissions over the past 200 years, nor does it try to anticipate the future warming potential of the current crop of emissions. This means that Indonesia and Brazil come high up the index because of deforestation and rice production (Indonesia), most of which is relatively recent, while the contributions of Western Europe and Japan, which includes demand for food and forest products that have increased CO_2 and CO_4 releases over many years, only include current emissions. Furthermore, the index does not take into account the scope for removal by sinks such as biomass, and biogeochemical cycling generally. Part of this process lies in national resources, but an unaccountable element lies in the international commons. This poses extremely awkward questions for those looking for traceable permits or negotiating positions for greenhouse gas removal and burden-sharing, not just because sequestration rates are still not known, but also because of the very great political sensitivities over rights to continue to develop, using the global commons as a free access sink.

On another tack, recent studies suggest that sulphate aerosols, caused by emissions of SO_2 in the troposphere, help to cool the lower atmosphere by reflecting solar radiation before being absorbed and re-emitted by the

Earth in the longer and atmospheric-capturing wavelengths. This could depress future warming by about 0.2–0.4°C over the next hundred years, significant enough for some to talk of future "cold pools" of differential atmospheric warming. What this does is of course to credit science with thoughtful analytical modelling in the search for greater accuracy of prediction. But for the politician, faced with a possible clamour over carbon taxation or burden-sharing higher emission removal rates to let poorer nations develop non-sustainably for longer, such calculations are unsettling and liable to encourage nitpicking diplomacy and procrastination.

One can see very quickly how science can be ambushed for ideological and political purposes. There will never be a satisfactory and independent greenhouse index. But that does not mean that the effort should not be made to construct one. The fact that the world now has a climate change convention that provides a framework for greenhouse gas inventories and removal tactics means at the very least that thoughtful science has an accommodating institutional framework in which to be of service.

Future Global Warming: How Likely Is It?

Global warming is what most scientists currently think will happen as the effect of the additions humans have made to the natural mixture of "greenhouse gases" in the atmosphere. The greenhouse gases are those that allow the short-wave radiation from the sun to penetrate the atmosphere, but absorb the lower wavelength energy which is re-radiated from the Earth's surface. The process is not really that which occurs in a greenhouse, but the term remains an effective one in public communication. We are unlikely to be able to demonstrate the reality of this warming for another one or two decades, but the predictions of an "enhanced greenhouse effect" are taken seriously and are the starting point for efforts to bring about international action even before proof is established. If we do not act to reduce emissions promptly, we leave a much more serious problem for the next generation, and were there no action at all, the eventual amount of warming might be enough to threaten not simply our lifestyle, but perhaps even the survival of people in some areas.

As I write in 1993, that is still a statement with which the majority of scientists interested in this topic would agree. But it is not so certain that every scientist supports these views, while the implications for how we ought to behave (especially when it comes to burning fossil fuel and perhaps also burning rainforests) are so considerable that many governments are reluctant to concede that anything drastic should be done. Indeed, we have a contrast with the response to the "ozone hole" in the stratosphere, where scientific proof of change convinced governments enough to bring about an international agreement to reduce the threat, known as the Montreal Protocol. Because both the amount, and especially the timing, of global warming are still uncertain, and the economic effects and the social changes required to limit CO2 emissions are much greater than those involved in limiting CFCs and halons, it is easier for our opinion leaders to suggest that we may be able to adjust to global warming and indeed that it may be a cheaper and less disruptive option than reducing fuel use.

One particular feature of the debate about the reality of future global warming is the role played by the Intergovernmental Panel on Climate Change (IPCC). This distinguished panel of international scientists has worked hard over the past few years to produce a series of carefully researched and clearly presented reports on the mechanisms of climate change and the likely rate of future warming. In particular, many of the inconsistencies in the different computer models used to forecast the effects of increased CO_2 levels have been reduced through the international cooperation achieved by the IPCC, so presenting a more convincing case that warming is probable. On the other hand, as we learn more about the very complicated feedbacks within the Earth/atmosphere system, scientists are finding that the rate (though not as yet the long-term amount) of change is likely to be considerably slower than the early reports suggested. This has the dual effect of reducing the apparent certainty surrounding the scientific predictions and also apparently allowing a longer delay before action must be taken. This is not strictly true: slower warming also means slower response to palliative measures, but that's not an easy message to get across.

Greenhouse Gases and the 'Greenhouse Effect'

The Earth is in long-term heat balance, receiving radiation from the sun and losing the same amount of heat to space. If there were no "greenhouse effect" from the atmosphere, the average temperature of the Earth's surface would be -18°C, but the current average global temperature is close to +15°C, a difference of 33°C. This difference is caused by the presence of our atmosphere and is called the "greenhouse effect". The atmosphere is mainly composed of nitrogen and oxygen, but it is the small traces of some other gases, notably carbon dioxide and water vapor, that are responsible for the insulating effect of the atmosphere.

The flow of carbon dioxide to and from the atmosphere is controlled by a complex series of largely biological processes on Earth and can be represented as a carbon budget.

The flow of carbon dioxide to and from the atmosphere is controlled by a complex series of largely biological processes on Earth and can be represented as a carbon budget. The main flows of carbon are exchanges between the atmosphere and the biosphere, that is to say the plants and animals that live on land and in the sea. Plants consume carbon dioxide in photosynthesis as a source of carbon to grow, emitting oxygen. Animals consume oxygen to live and grow, emitting carbon dioxide (CO_2). Other natural sources of carbon dioxide include gases from erupting volcanoes and natural fires, as well as the decay of plant and animal material. Long-term sinks of carbon dioxide include the fixing of carbon as calcium carbonate in the shells of marine animals which accumulate on the ocean floor as limestones and chalks and the accumulation of plant and animal materials to form peat, coal and oil. In addition, ocean water itself is an absorber of carbon dioxide and it is gradually dispersed throughout the ocean as surface water sinks and moves to great depths as deep ocean currents.

The natural balance of the carbon cycle has changed greatly over the Earth's history, perhaps especially during the ice ages of the last few hundred thousand years. We can study these natural changes by measuring the carbon dioxide in air bubbles trapped in ice deep in the polar ice sheets. This shows that if we plot past atmospheric carbon dioxide levels against past temperature there is a close correlation. We might be tempted to argue that these changes in CO_2 in the atmosphere were causing the changes in ice volume, but we believe that the effect of changing global temperature on the biological activity on Earth and on the rate at which ocean waters took up or gave out carbon dioxide (which is linked with the sinking of cold, saline water and the up-welling of deep water to the surface elsewhere) was at least of equal importance. This is supported by the fact that another greenhouse gas, methane, also varies with the same pattern, suggesting that all three curves are being driven by an external factor, in this case, the pattern of warming and cooling triggered by the Earth's orbital variations (the Milankovitch effect) and amplified by changes in the biogeochemical cycling of these gases.

Ice cores from the 18th century show carbon dioxide levels of about 280 ppm. The level today (1991) is about 25 percent higher than this (350 ppm) and measurements made on Mauna Loa, the extinct volcano of one of the Hawaiian Islands, since 1950 show a persistent upward trend. Hawaii is a good location for such measurements as there are few local sources of CO_2 and the relatively high altitude allows air typical of much of the northern hemisphere to be sampled. Inspection of the Hawaii curve shows a constant seasonal fluctuation, up every northern hemisphere autumn/winter, down every spring/summer. This reflects the importance of the land area of the world in the carbon balance, most of the world's land is in the northern hemisphere and the vegetation is more vigorous in spring and summer (so fixing carbon by photosynthesis) and an additional contribution is made by human societies (at least in Europe) burning more carbon in winter to keep warm; again, most of this activity is north of the equator. When the seasonal fluctuation is averaged out, the rise is persistent year by year with the only obvious hesitation in 1974. This was the result of the high price of oil following the Organization of Petroleum Exporting Countries (OPEC) action of 1973: For a time we used over 6 percent less of such costly oil, and this lower use of fossil carbon was at once reflected in the level of CO_2 in the atmosphere There could hardly be a more dramatic indication of the role of fossil fuel in contributing carbon dioxide to our atmosphere; indeed this is the kind of evidence on which science thrives. Proof is never absolute, but good measurements applied with sound theory (i.e., a secure understanding of the processes involved in the flows and transformations of carbon) can give us the ability to predict future changes. It is on this basis that public policy can be made with confidence, though inevitably not all environmental science can give such clear and well-found forecasts of future environmental change.

Thus a significant contributor to the increased level of carbon dioxide in our atmosphere is the burning of fossil fuel. Carbon time-warped in oil and coal millions of years ago is being returned to the atmosphere at a rapid rate as we use fossil energy to power our factories, heat our homes and drive our cars. Thus it is the annual transference of some 5 billion tonnes of CO_2 each year from this store sequestered by life on Earth hundreds of millions of years ago, which is now stressing the biosphere to the extent that it cannot quickly adapt. Year by year we transfer more additional carbon into the atmosphere than natural processes can remove, so the proportion of carbon dioxide rises. We also contribute to the present imbalance by clearing vegetation, especially that great sink for carbon dioxide, the tropical rainforest. Disturbance and clearance of forest and the underlying soil releases carbon through burning or natural decay (oxidation), and the reduced area of natural forest reduces the amount of tree growth and thus the uptake of CO_2 from the atmosphere by the natural vegetation. The IPCC estimate that 10-15 percent of the increase in atmospheric CO_2 is caused by forest clearance, and that almost all the rest is due to the use of fossil fuel.

So far we have concentrated on carbon dioxide as the most important of the world's greenhouse gases. However, although naturally it contributes almost 80 percent of the effect, other gases are also effective in trapping heat in the lower atmosphere and some of these have been increasing as a result of human activity. Most obvious are the CFCs, chlorofluorocarbon compounds, manufactured to provide stable gases for many purposes including refrigeration coolants, insulation foams, fire-fighting gases, and the cleaning of electronic components, as well as the better known use as propellants in aerosols. As recently as 1986, aerosol propellants accounted for about 25 percent of CFC use, but this has been almost entirely eliminated as substitutes have been introduced. However, their use as solvents and in insulating foam will take time to achieve, though the *Montreal Protocol* has set out a time timetable for their elimination. These gases have become notorious through their damaging effect on the stratospheric ozone layer, but they are also very powerful greenhouse gases. Indeed, molecule for molecule they can be around 16,000 times as effective as carbon dioxide, so it is fortunate they remain relatively rare in the atmosphere. Nevertheless, they account for almost 20 percent of the greenhouse effect.

Other gases with similar properties include methane and nitrous oxides. Methane is produced by many natural process and increased animal populations on the world's farms are one source, but it also comes from the decay of vegetation, from the release of gas as frozen arctic soils thaw, and from leaks in gas pipelines. Nitrous oxides are produced by a wide variety of biological sources in soils and water. Thus many of these gases too are being produced in increasing quantities as the human population of the world increases and makes ever-greater use of farm animals, motorcars, and natural gas.

Predicting the Impact of Enhanced Levels of 'Greenhouse Gases'

In order to try to predict the effect of increased levels of these "greenhouse gases" on the world's temperature balance, that future point when all the gases contribute the equivalent of double the effect of the pre-industrial revolution value of 280 ppm is often chosen. This is usually expressed as doubling of CO_2, though in fact by that time the CO_2 level will be about 410 ppm, and it is the additional effect of CFCs, methane, etc, which bring the "CO_2 equivalent" concentration to 560 ppm. When will this occur?

The prediction of future increases requires assumptions about the continuing rate of economic growth in the world, which in turn drives the use of fossil fuel. Less critical for the calculation are estimates of the future rate of forest clearance. There are problems about our incomplete understanding of the global carbon balance. The IPCC used a budget which does not actually balance. For some time it has been suggested that our estimates of the amount taken up by the oceans was at fault, but this now seems less probable as improved measurements of air-sea exchange and other oceanographic observations increase our understanding of the processes at work. Another possibility is the increased uptake of CO_2 by vegetation as its vigor increases with higher CO_2 levels. It has been suggested that this may be an important part of the full explanation for the missing carbon. However, the IPCC set these unresolved problems aside and adopted a future growth rate which assumes that recent increases in the atmospheric concentration of carbon dioxide will continue (known as "business-as-usual" scenario, often shortened to BAU). On this basis, doubling of CO_2 equivalent will occur at about 2030; consequently, this date appears in many analyzes of future change.

The prediction of the global warming to be expected by that date is not a simple matter. Were there no complications, the increased CO_2 would bring about a reduction in the energy loss to space to 236 W/m^2 and this would require a 1.2°C increase in surface temperature to bring it back up to the balancing figure of 240 W/m^2. However, there are many complications, including the atmospheric global circulation and changes in cloud cover (water vapor is a greenhouse gas, but this is closely balanced by the clouds which it forms which reflect heat from their upper surfaces) and in the albedo (reflectivity) of the Earth's surface as warming reduces the area of snow and ice.

To bring these factors into the reckoning, it is necessary to use the huge computer models known as global circulation models based on the same principles as the numerical models used to forecast the weather. These can be run for long periods on powerful computers to simulate the effects of changed CO_2 levels. Different models give different predictions of temperature rise, so some effort has gone into securing convergence and an internationally agreed estimate of future warming. The publications of the IPCC predict a figure of 1°C above the present value by 2025 and by then an increase of 0.3°C each decade, a rate well in excess of anything experienced throughout the natural changes of the last 10,000 years. This would bring total warming since the beginning of the industrial revolution to about 4°C by the end of the next century. If the figure (a global average) seems small, it is worth noting that the minimum during the last Ice Age was about 5-6°C cooler than today, and that the warming which has occurred over the last 100 years is a rise of no more than 0.5°C in the global average temperature.

One check on the assumptions made and the techniques used to model future change is to look at the known changes over the last 150 years and to see whether these are "forecast" by the model when run from a pre-industrial revolution state. When this is done, we discover that the predicted rise in temperature is rather higher than that observed, though the match is well within the range of natural variability and thus not inconsistent with the model. Broadly the model predicts a little more than 1°C warming and the observed amount to date is about 0.5°C. It is known that the southern hemisphere has warmed more than the northern and it would be encouraging if we could fully understand this. There is more ocean in the southern hemisphere and the land in the northern hemisphere carries the bulk of the world's industrial activity. It has been suggested that the increase in temperature in the northern hemisphere has been reduced by pollution, the SO_2 produced when coal and oil are burnt offsetting to some extent the effect of the CO_2. The SO_2 produces sulphate aerosols (small particles in the atmosphere) which have a direct effect on the radiation balance but also an indirect effect through their modification of the albedo of clouds. This makes the forecasting of the effect of increased SO_2 burden complex, but it is thought that this may be the cause of the lag in warming observed when the northern hemisphere is compared with the southern, and perhaps also that this century observed warming below that predicted from the increase in CO_2 and other greenhouse gases. It also has the implication that current attempts (as a consequence in part of the acid rain problem) to reduce SO_2 emissions (without reducing fossil fuel use) could bring a phase of more rapid warming as we catch up with the model.

Recently, within a set of studies discussing the risks and implications of climatic change, Wigley and others have discussed the problem of detecting climate change. They note that despite the absence of any evidence that warming is occurring, already many policymakers are moving towards global action. This is the result of the general air of confidence in the public statements of the climatic modellers (though the scientific literature is full of caveats), and the chance (for it seems unlikely to be much more than that) that the instrumental record shows irregular but real warming through the past hundred years. So they conclude the detection may well follow decisions to act, but that it could still be helpful in suggesting how to act. The key issue is the climate sensitivity, for this will determine both the amount of future change and the effect of various mitigating actions. After discussing many aspects of prediction and detection, they conclude the one essential is to improve the present observations network, moving away from a pattern designed to help in weather forecasting to observations of more value to the long-term study of climate. These will include not only the maintenance of long-term data sets, but also the collection of data that define other external forcing factors such as solar output and sulphate aerosol concentrations.

The Impacts of Future Warming

Sea-level rise

The IPCC has indicated one likely result of global warming, an increase in the rate of sea-level rise. This is not the result of melting of the major ice sheets in Greenland and Antarctica), but of the melting of smaller glaciers in mountains such as the Alps and the Himalayas, and, of equal importance, the thermal expansion of the warming oceans. These two effects will cause the sea level to rise by about 5 mm/yr in future compared with a rate little more than 1 mm/yr today. The predicted contribution from the melting of the large (and thus slow to respond) Greenland ice sheet is only about 12 percent of the total estimated rise and this is offset by the forecast that at first the Antarctic ice-sheet will actually remove water from the oceans in roughly the same proportion. The reason for this prediction is that at present the Antarctic continent is a cold desert with very low snowfall. As the world warms, so the Southern Ocean will warm, allowing increased evaporation from the ocean and hence greater precipitation in high latitudes. This will increase snowfall on the Antarctic ice-sheet, especially around the margins, but with time even far into the interior. This snow will not melt but will compact to form ice. Only when the slow movement of the ice-sheet has transported it down to the ice margin will it be returned to the ocean. Undoubtedly, this will take several hundred years, perhaps more. There has also been much discussion about the possibility that the West Antarctic portion of this great ice-sheet might be invaded by the rising sea and melt relatively quickly. This is indeed possible, but again on a timescale of many hundreds of years; it cannot contribute to sea-level rise over the next few generations. Despite scientific confidence about these lags in the huge Antarctic system, there remain individuals who persist in presenting a real long-term risk as a potential threat over the next two or three generations. They emphasize the risk of a large sea-level rise, and neglect the timescale of the lags involved, in order to add to the demand for the precautionary removal of greenhouse gases.

The cumulative predicted sea-level rise of about 30 cm by 2050 is not large, but it will make the problems of erosion and tidal flooding experienced along coastlines all over the world more difficult.

Water Balance

Although changes in sea level have received much publicity, problems of water availability (in the ground and at the tap) are likely to be more serious and perhaps more expensive to solve. Here we move from the relative certainty of predictions about future temperature and sea level to great uncertainty. We can be sure that on average, the future world will be wetter than today, probably by between 3 and 15 percent. This is because warmer seas will mean greater evaporation and as moisture cannot be stored in the atmosphere for long, more evaporation will mean more rain. However, our general computer models (OCMs) are unable to agree on the distribution of the extra rain in time or space. If areas with too little rain get less than is needed to offset the higher evaporation and plant transpiration (evapo-transpiration) which will be the result of warming, then summer droughts will be more severe. On the basis of current estimates the most likely outcome will be increased aridity in the deserts and desert margins, drier summers in the temperate latitudes, but a general tendency towards a more thundery and erosive rainfall. It is not surprising that the major global conference to establish an international convention to combat desertification was held in 1994. This is when the environmental sciences can come into their own. Hulme and Kelly suggest that about 20 percent of the increase of the Sahel is due to factors other than the change in annual rainfall possibly a combination of overgrazing and the loss of vegetation (and thus change of albedo) due to drying and warming. In short, it is possible that desertification has a feedback effect and reduces regional rainfall, so exacerbating the effects of drought. As yet the models are too primitive to prove this, and much more work has to be done to accumulate further data on rainfall, evapo-transpiration, vegetation change, and temperature. Hence the urgent need to improve the scientific capacity of the Third World. As it is, nearly 20 countries in Africa have no irrigation schemes of any size, so future climatic stress will cause many problems and much hardship. This could obviously spell long-term disaster for such drought-prone areas as the African Sahel and perhaps lead to migrations into wetter areas with the threat of increased tension and perhaps local armed conflict. This threat of instability in the Third World may prove to be the strongest pressure on the developed world to adjust its use of fossil fuel, though the arms trade which is already worth over $500 billion annually to the rich world, will doubtless get bigger as a result. Such a conclusion may sound cynical, but intelligence services the world over are interested in GCM predictions, as are the finance ministries.

But many developed countries have demands on water supply that are close to the normal available local rainfall surplus and that already have difficulty meeting needs at time of drought. New York City reservoirs have been very low at times over the last three decades; much of England suffered serious drought in 1975–1976 and again in 1990 and 1991. In most areas, abstracted water is stored above ground in reservoirs and more frequent drought will increase the pressure to build more large reservoirs, expensive to build, and often resisted by those who lose land. In other areas, aquifers below ground form natural stores, as in England where much of East Anglia, Lincolnshire, and the Thames valley depends on water in the chalk aquifer, which is normally recharged for a few months each winter. Dry winters and the increasing water demand of hot and dry summers have led to hose-pipe bans in the early 1990s and the threat of worse to come if winter rainfall (and snowfall) should fail again. In the western USA, water allocation is based on the principle of prior appropriation, namely first-come, first-allocated. Generally this has benefited the agricultural industry at the expense of urban and industrial supplies, as well as the wildlife of rivers and lakes now over-abstracted to meet legal requirements. In the USA, there is already a growing battle over the proper price to charge for water to reflect these crucial amenity and wildlife losses. Wholesale allocation of water rights and major shifts in prices will be required before too long. This will no doubt involve lengthy and expensive legal battles.

In a warmer world, summers will not only be hotter, but longer, shortening the period available for winter recharge. Thus even if rainfall does increase by 15 percent as some models predict, and even if it increases in winter at least as much as in summer, there may be too brief a period for sufficient recharge to meet the increased summer demand. Those living in drought-prone areas will then wish that plans to import water from wetter areas with surplus yield had been implemented more rapidly. Others will demand the kind of reallocative water pricing forthcoming in the USA, coupled with the metering of domestic supplies and social valuation of the minimum flows of freshwater in streams and the conservation of groundwater to maintain discharges at natural springs. It is hardly surprising that there is such an interest in the ecological economics of water charging throughout the world, though it cannot produce surplus water for redistribution where this is unavailable from the climatic water balance. Some areas that currently just make do are going to find themselves short, whatever the cost of water to the consumer.

Natural Areas and Land Use

The uncertainty that surrounds regional forecasts of future precipitation and especially future seasonal patterns of precipitation and temperature makes it difficult to forecast the effects of global warming on natural vegetation and fauna. Many nature reserves have been established to preserve plants and animals near the limit of their range, so in future they may either fall well within the natural range, or so far outside it that species that the reserve was designed to conserve will die out. It seems that the bluebell, surely that most English of spring woodland flowers, may well disappear and no doubt many other less showy species near their southern limit will go too. They will be replaced by the immigration of new plants or the increasing dominance of others already here. Bird migration patterns will change and some of our common winter visitors will stay further north than now.

However, our worst problems are trying to forecast the future of agriculture in a warmer world. This matters a great deal, since any major effects on the principal grain-producing regions of the world will have serious implications for world food supply. This would be difficult enough were nothing else changing, but the main effects on agriculture will not be the changing global environment, but the existing forces of economic policies and the rate of success of the plant breeders. The spread of maize into the UK has been the result of plant breeding, not of climatic change. The northern limit of the sunflower in France is similarly moving towards the English Channel as new varieties are developed. According to Parry every 1°C increase in mean annual temperature will shift the current agricultural belts 300 km northward in Europe and 175 km northward in the USA even without the efforts of the plant breeders to improve crops still further.

Considerable effort will be put into the improvement of regional forecasts of climatic change. To the extent that we are committed to considerable future warming regardless of how quickly we act to try to stabilize current concentrations of atmospheric greenhouse gases, we need to discover where the most serious impacts will be. In this way threats to local food supply may be offset by understanding where higher productivity will be possible. The improvement of these predictions depends on developing "nested" regional climatic models within the global models, as well as improvement of the GCMs themselves. In particular, the representation of the oceans needs improvement as does the coupling of the ocean model to the atmosphere. Other important refinements are the better representation of clouds and the feedbacks they cause. Even the chemistry of the atmosphere is being built into the more advanced models. To achieve all this will take at least ten years. That is too long to risk doing nothing in the meantime, hence the interest in the "no regrets" strategies.

What Might We Do to Reduce Future Global Warming?

We have already seen that the discovery of the depletion of stratospheric ozone over Antarctica led in 1987 to the international agreement known as the Montreal Protocol. Although driven by the threat to the protective stratospheric ozone layer (which protects the Earth's surface from harmful ultraviolet radiation from the sun), the Protocol will have the effect of reducing the contribution the halocarbons make to the enhanced greenhouse effect. To some extent this will be offset by substitutes which are less chemically active in the stratosphere, but still possess greenhouse properties in the troposphere.

The immediate outcome of the UN Environment and Development Conference held in Brazil in 1992 was disappointing for those who hoped for early action to reduce our use of fossil fuels. In scientific terms, it is essential to understand the huge reductions that would be necessary to bring about an end to increased climatic forcing. At present, most countries regard such reductions as unattainable, and likely to disrupt the world economy even more than global warming, so a compromise is likely to be sought. Currently, the Canadian government is one of the most ambitious with a proposal to seek a reduction in carbon dioxide output to 20 percent below its 1990 level by the year 2000. The EC aims at getting back to 1990 levels by 2000, though compliance will be difficult to establish since current measurements of CO_2 emissions are estimates and collected by several different methods. It could take up to ten years for the developing world to create the monitoring capacity for carbon dioxide which is needed if future output is to be managed in the light of international targets. Verifiable data collection is thus one of the most Important contributions of the environmental sciences in the coming years across the whole spectrum of global change issues.

We need to understand that even were emissions higher than those of 1750 (i.e., the pre-industrial revolution level) to be eliminated tomorrow, there is a considerable "commitment" to warming in the higher levels of greenhouse gases already in the atmosphere. The world is not in equilibrium with the higher levels of today; it is warming and that warming will continue for sometime until equilibrium is reached. Similarly, where the lag between forcing and change is longer, as is the case with sea level, then the commitment will continue for longer and be larger in amount. If international efforts were to succeed immediately sea level will continue to rise for at least another hundred years, passing 18 cm higher than today before the end of the next century. In other words, even early action on increasing atmospheric CO_2 levels will still leave the next three or four generations coping with changes brought about by the 20th century consumption of fossil fuels. Yet to take effective action and incur the social and economic costs involved in change is difficult when we are still discussing an uncertain future change; "Let's wait and see" is a popular call. Yet others would argue to play for safety and do something now rather than later the precautionary policy described as "no regrets".

Recently one comparison of the choice between early precautionary action ("no regrets") and "wait and see" (and adjust if needed) has shown how important the economic models used are in suggesting the outcomes. Here is an interesting analogy of the issue tackled by the IPCC the initial variation in the prediction of complex models all based on the same physical principles and the same mathematical rules. They found that draconian measures would retard economic development, but that there were ways in which the open dissemination of information about future change could improve areas such as energy efficiency and forest preservation for the benefit of the world's economy, as well as mitigating future rates of climatic change. A carbon tax seemed to be an important part of such policies. But they also found that whether the world acts now or waits to see, global warming will have both "winners" and "losers" in other words the costs of inaction will be as unevenly spread as the costs of action. In particular the divergencies between policies and possible threats between the North and South emphasize the difficulties in getting early agreement on a truly global basis about what, if anything, should be done. Even the attribution of "blame" for the present, less

If international efforts were to succeed immediately sea level will continue to rise for at least another hundred years, passing 18 cm higher than today before the end of the next century.

stable, state of our global environment provokes wide disagreement and the if acts about greenhouse gas emissions can be presented and analyzed in many different ways.

All this goes to show the central theme of this text, namely, that the environmental sciences exist in a world of power, prejudice, wishful thinking, and unjustified alarm. Above the level of the individual scientist, there is no independent evaluation of the evidence and no truly objective collection of facts. Data are framed by the models, the computer power, the collection methods, and the agency mandates of those who present the information for public choice. This is not to say that there is no place for rigorous science: very much the opposite. Without the networks of self-critical scientists in panels such as the IPCC there would be no credible consensus on which to base international action. The environmental sciences remain imperfect, and there is still much research to be done before complex global systems are adequately understood, but even our current knowledge is vital in world affairs.

Can the Prediction be Improved?

If the "precautionary principle", is adopted we can wait patiently for the science of global change to become more precise, confident that we have begun to adopt appropriate measures which over a long period of time will reduce the rate of change and could eventually stabilize the global heat balance. Unfortunately, there is room to argue that the precautionary principle is premature, given the uncertainties in current forecasts of change and the evidence that the present tendency is for more careful analyzes to reduce forecasts of the rate of future warming. There are even signs that scientists, convinced of the inevitability of future change and the need to act, are willing to slow down the process of enquiry and withhold revision of estimates of future warming for fear of losing the world's interest in the urgency and reality of the problem.

Clearly such a politically motivated science cannot be allowed to develop. The success of the IPCC has been its achievement of virtual unanimity through the improvement of the quality of the science. What is likely to happen is that at the global level better understanding of the role of the oceans, of the various atmospheric feedbacks (such as changes in cloud cover) and the increasing evidence for a "CO_2 fertilization" feedback, estimates of the rate of warming will continue to decline. However, at the same time, powerful CGMs are being developed that allow more detailed and thus more realistic analyzes of changes at a regional level. We may expect these to provide improved regional forecasts of temperature and precipitation change, and from these future water balance forecasts can be developed. It is very likely that despite the overall increase of rainfall implied by a warmer world, seasonal changes, coupled with higher evapo-transpiration from warmer and longer seasons, will cause adverse changes in some areas. These will quickly impact on the strategic thinking of the governments concerned, and in the case of the less adaptable economies of the developing world, on those developed nations which fear instability and its knock-on effects.

Thus we may expect that it will be increasingly easy for developed nations to argue that for them adaptation is an effective strategy, except where regional forecasts imply changes in water balance which may be harder to accommodate than changes in temperature. At the same time, the increased reliability of regional forecasts for developing countries (where temperature changes are expected to be less than at higher latitudes) may well imply changes in water balance which threaten the existing precarious balance between population and food supply. The resolution of these issues is going to take far longer than the early reactions to the first IPCC forecasts suggested. The issue of global climatic change and the appropriate measures to counteract it will not go away, but it will not be limited to the simple doom or dismiss scenarios of the last few years. It will become increasingly complex and increasingly more intertwined with other global and regional issues, including population growth, and the many issues surrounding the concept of sustainability.

(ii) IPCC Working Group I, "Summary for Policy Makers," WG I *Climate Change 2001: The Scientific Basis*, Report of Working Group I of Intergovernmental Panel on Climate Change, IPCC, January 2001

The Third Assessment Report of Working Group I of the Intergovernmental Panel on Climate Change (IPCC) builds upon past assessments and incorporates new results from the past five years of research on climate change. Many hundreds of scientists from many countries participated in its preparation and review.

This Summary for Policymakers (SPM), which was approved by IPCC member governments in Shanghai in January 2001, describes the current state of understanding of the climate system and provides estimates of its projected future evolution and their uncertainties. Further details can be found in the underlying report, and the appended Source Information provides cross-references to the report's chapters.

An Increasing Body of Observations Gives a Collective Picture of a Warming World and Other Changes in the Climate System

Since the release of the Second Assessment Report (SAR), additional data from new studies of current and palaeoclimates, improved analysis of data sets, more rigorous evaluation of their quality, and comparisons among data from different

The Global Average Surface Temperature has Increased over the 20th Century by About 0.6°C

The global average surface temperature (the average of near surface air temperature over land, and sea surface temperature) has increased since 1861. Over the 20th century the increase has been 0.6-0.2°C 5,6. This value is about 0.15°C larger than that estimated by the SAR for the period up to 1994, owing to the relatively high temperatures of the additional years (1995–2000) and improved methods of processing the data. These numbers take into account various adjustments, including urban heat island effects. The record shows a great deal of variability; for example, most of the warming occurred during the 20th century, during two periods, 1910 to 1945 and 1976 to 2000. Globally, it is very likely that the 1990s was the warmest decade and 1998 the warmest year in the instrumental record, since 1861.

New analyzes of proxy data for the Northern Hemisphere indicate that the increase in temperature in the 20th century is likely to have been the largest of any century during the past 1,000 years. It is also likely that, in the Northern Hemisphere, the 1990s was the warmest decade and 1998 the warmest year. Because less data are available, less is known about annual averages prior to 1,000 years before present and for conditions prevailing in most of the Southern Hemisphere prior to 1861.

On average, between 1950 and 1993, night-time daily minimum air temperatures over land increased by about 0.2°C per decade. This is about twice the rate of increase in daytime daily maximum air temperatures (0.1°C per decade). This has lengthened the freeze-free season in many mid- and high latitude regions. The increase in sea surface temperature over this period is about half that of the mean land surface air temperature.

Temperatures have Risen During the Past Four Decades in the Lowest 8 Kilometers of the Atmosphere

Since the late 1950s (the period of adequate observations from weather balloons), the overall global temperature increases in the lowest 8 kilometers of the atmosphere and in surface temperature have been similar at 0.1°C per decade. Since the start of the satellite record in 1979, both satellite and weather balloon measurements show that the global average temperature of the lowest 8 kilometers of the atmosphere has changed by 0.05-0.10°C per decade, but the global average surface temperature has increased significantly by 0.15-0.05°C per decade. The difference in the warming rates is statistically significant. This difference occurs primarily over the tropical and sub-tropical regions.

The lowest 8 kilometers of the atmosphere and the surface are influenced differently by factors such as stratospheric ozone depletion, atmospheric aerosols, and the El Niño phenomenon. Hence, it is physically plausible to expect that over a short time period (e.g., 20 years) there may be differences in temperature trends. In addition, spatial sampling techniques can also explain some of the differences in trends, but these differences are not fully resolved.

Snow Cover and Ice Extent have Decreased

Satellite data show that there are very likely to have been decreases of about 10 percent in the extent of snow cover since the late 1960s, and ground-based observations show that there is very likely to have been a reduction of about two weeks in the annual duration of lake and river ice cover in the mid- and high latitudes of the Northern Hemisphere, over the 20th century. There has been a widespread retreat of mountain glaciers in non-polar regions during the 20th century. Northern Hemisphere spring and summer sea-ice extent has decreased by about 10 to 15 percent since the 1950s. It is likely that there has been about a 40 percent decline in Arctic sea-ice thickness during late summer to early autumn in recent decades and a considerably slower decline in winter sea-ice thickness.

Global Average Sea Level has Risen and Ocean Heat Content has Increased

Tide gauge data show that global average sea level rose between 0.1 and 0.2 meters during the 20th century. Global ocean heat content has increased since the late 1950s, the period for which adequate observations of sub-surface ocean temperatures have been available.

In some regions, such as parts of Asia and Africa, the frequency and intensity of droughts have been observed to increase in recent decades.

Changes have also Occurred in other Important Aspects of Climate

It is very likely that precipitation has increased by 0.5 to 1 percent per decade in the 20th century over most mid- and high latitudes of the Northern Hemisphere continents, and it is likely that rainfall has increased by 0.2 to 0.3 percent per decade over the tropical (10°N to 10°S) land areas. Increases in the tropics are not evident over the past few decades. It is also likely that rainfall has decreased over much of the Northern Hemisphere sub-tropical (10°N to 30°N) land areas during the 20th century by about 0.3 percent per decade. In contrast to the Northern Hemisphere, no comparable systematic changes have been detected in broad latitudinal averages over the Southern Hemisphere. There are insufficient data to establish trends in precipitation over the oceans.

In the mid- and high latitudes of the Northern Hemisphere over the latter half of the 20th century, it is likely that there has been a 2 to 4 percent increase in the frequency of heavy precipitation events. Increases in heavy precipitation events can arise from a number of causes, e.g., changes in atmospheric moisture, thunderstorm activity and large-scale storm activity.

It is likely that there has been a 2 percent increase in cloud cover over mid- to high latitude land areas during the 20th century. In most areas, the trends relate well to the observed decrease in daily temperature range.

Since 1950, it is very likely that there has been a reduction in the frequency of extreme low temperatures, with a smaller increase in the frequency of extreme high temperatures.

Warm episodes of the El Niño-Southern Oscillation (ENSO) phenomenon (which consistently affects regional variations of precipitation and temperature over much of the tropics, sub-tropics and some mid-latitude areas) have been more frequent, persistent and intense since the mid-1970s, compared with the previous 100 years.

Over the 20th century (1900 to 1995), there were relatively small increases in global land areas experiencing severe drought or severe wetness. In many regions, these changes are dominated by inter-decadal and multi-decadal climate variability, such as the shift in ENSO towards more warm events.

In some regions, such as parts of Asia and Africa, the frequency and intensity of droughts have been observed to increase in recent decades.

Some Important Aspects of Climate Appear not to have Changed

A few areas of the globe have not warmed in recent decades, mainly over some parts of the Southern Hemisphere oceans and parts of Antarctica.

No significant trends of Antarctic sea-ice extent are apparent since 1978, the period of reliable satellite measurements. Changes globally in tropical and extra-tropical storm intensity and frequency are dominated by inter-decadal to multi-decadal variations, with no significant trends evident over the 20th century. Conflicting analyzes make it difficult to draw definitive conclusions about changes in storm activity, especially in the extra-tropics.

No systematic changes in the frequency of tornadoes, thunder days, or hail events are evident in the limited areas analyzed.

Emissions of Greenhouse Gases and Aerosols Due to Human Activities Continue to Alter the Atmosphere in Ways that are Expected to Affect the Climate

Changes in climate occur as a result of both internal variability within the climate system and external factors (both natural and anthropogenic). The influence of external factors on climate can be broadly compared using the concept of radiative forcing. A positive radiative forcing, such as that produced by increasing concentrations of greenhouse gases, tends to warm the surface. A negative radiative forcing, which can arise from an increase in some types of aerosols (microscopic airborne particles) tends to cool the surface. Natural factors, such as changes in solar output or explosive volcanic activity, can also cause radiative forcing. Characterization of these climate forcing agents and their changes over time is required to understand past climate changes in the context of natural variations and to project what climate changes could lie ahead.

Concentrations of Atmospheric Greenhouse Gases and their Radiative Forcing have Continued to Increase as a Result of Human Activities

The atmospheric concentration of carbon dioxide (CO_2) has increased by 31 percent since 1750. The present CO_2 concentration has not been exceeded during the past 420,000 years and likely not during the past 20 million years. The current rate of increase is unprecedented during at least the past 20,000 years.

About three-quarters of the anthropogenic emissions of CO_2 to the atmosphere during the past 20 years is due to fossil fuel burning. The rest is predominantly due to land-use change, especially deforestation. Currently, the ocean and the land are together taking up about half of the anthropogenic CO_2 emissions. On land, the uptake of anthropogenic CO_2 very likely exceeded the release of CO_2 by deforestation during the 1990s. The rate of increase of atmospheric CO_2 concentration has been about 1.5 ppm 9 (0.4 percent) per year over the past two decades. During the 1990s, the year-to-year increase varied from 0.9 ppm (0.2 percent) to 2.8 ppm (0.8 percent). A large part of this variability is due to the effect of climate variability (e.g., El Niño events) on CO_2 uptake and release by land and oceans. The atmospheric concentration of methane (CH_4) has increased by 1060 ppb 9 (151 percent) since 1750 and continues to increase. The present CH_4 concentration has not been exceeded during the past 420,000 years. The annual growth in CH_4 concentration slowed and became more variable in the 1990s, compared with the 1980s. Slightly more than half of current CH_4 emissions are anthropogenic (e.g., use of fossil fuels, cattle, rice agriculture and landfills). In addition, carbon monoxide (CO) emissions have recently been identified as a cause of increasing CH_4 concentration.

The atmospheric concentration of nitrous oxide (N_2O) has increased by 46 ppb (17 percent) since 1750 and continues to increase. The present N_2O concentration has not been exceeded during at least the past thousand years. About a third of current N_2O emissions are anthropogenic (e.g., agricultural soils, cattle feed lots and chemical industry). Since 1995, the atmospheric concentrations of many of those halocarbon gases that are both ozone-depleting and greenhouse gases (e.g., $CFCl_3$ and CF_2Cl_2), are either increasing more slowly or decreasing, both in response to reduced emissions under the regulations of the Montreal Protocol and its Amendments. Their substitute compounds (e.g., CHF_2Cl and CF_3CH_2F) and some other synthetic compounds (e.g., perfluorocarbons (PFCs) and sulphur hexafluoride (SF_6) are also greenhouse gases, and their concentrations are currently increasing.

The radiative forcing due to increases of the well-mixed greenhouse gases from 1750 to 2000 is estimated to be 2.43 Wm^{-2}: 1.46 Wm^{-2} from CO_2 ; 0.48 Wm^{-2} from CH_4; 0.34 Wm^{-2} from the halocarbons; and 0.15 Wm^{-2} from N_2O. The observed depletion of the stratospheric ozone (O_3) layer from 1979 to 2000 is estimated to have caused a negative radiative forcing (–0.15 Wm^{-2}). Assuming full compliance with current halocarbon regulations, the positive forcing of the halocarbons will be reduced as will the magnitude of the negative forcing from stratospheric ozone depletion as the ozone layer recovers over the 21st century.

The total amount of O_3 in the troposphere is estimated to have increased by 36 percent since 1750, due primarily to anthropogenic emissions of several O_3 -forming gases. This corresponds to a positive radiative forcing of 0.35 Wm^{-2}. O_3 forcing varies considerably by region and responds much more quickly to changes in emissions than the long-lived greenhouse gases, such as CO_2 .

Anthropogenic Aerosols are Short-Lived and Mostly Produce Negative Radiative Forcing

The major sources of anthropogenic aerosols are fossil fuel and biomass burning. These sources are also linked to degradation of air quality and acid deposition. Since the SAR, significant progress has been achieved in better characterising the direct radiative roles of different types of aerosols. Direct radiative forcing is estimated to be –0.4 Wm^{-2} for sulphate, 0.2 Wm^{-2} for biomass burning aerosols, 0.1 Wm^{-2} for fossil fuel organic carbon and 0.2 Wm^{-2} for fossil fuel black carbon aerosols. There is much less confidence in the ability to quantify the total aerosol direct effect, and its evolution over time, than that for the gases listed above. Aerosols also vary considerably by region and respond quickly to changes in emissions. In addition to their direct radiative forcing, aerosols have an indirect radiative forcing through their effects on clouds. There is now more evidence for this indirect effect, which is negative, although of very uncertain magnitude.

Natural Factors have made Small Contributions to Radiative Forcing over the Past Century

The radiative forcing due to changes in solar irradiance for the period since 1750 is estimated to be about 0.3 Wm^{-2}, most of which occurred during the first half of the 20th century. Since the late 1970s, satellite instruments have observed small oscillations due to the 11-year solar cycle. Mechanisms for the amplification of solar effects on climate have been proposed, but currently lack a rigorous theoretical or observational basis.

Stratospheric aerosols from explosive volcanic eruptions lead to negative forcing, which lasts a few years. Several major eruptions occurred in the periods 1880 to 1920 and 1960 to 1991.

The combined change in radiative forcing of the two major natural factors (solar variation and volcanic aerosols) is estimated to be negative for the past two, and possibly the past four, decades.

Confidence in the Ability of Models to Project Future Climate has Increased

Complex physically-based climate models are required to provide detailed estimates of feedbacks and of regional features. Such models cannot yet simulate all aspects of climate (e.g., they still cannot account fully for the observed trend in the surface-troposphere temperature difference since 1979) and there are particular uncertainties associated with clouds and their interaction with radiation and aerosols. Nevertheless, confidence in the ability of these models to provide useful projections of future climate has improved due to their demonstrated performance on a range of space and time-scales.

Understanding of climate processes and their incorporation in climate models have improved, including water vapor, sea-ice dynamics, and ocean heat transport. Some recent models produce satisfactory simulations of current climate without the need for non-physical adjustments of heat and water fluxes at the ocean-atmosphere interface used in earlier models. Simulations that include estimates of natural and anthropogenic forcing reproduce the observed large-scale changes in surface temperature over the 20th century. However, contributions from some additional processes and forcings may not have been included in the models. Nevertheless, the large-scale consistency between models and observations can be used to provide an independent check on projected warming rates over the next few decades under a given emissions scenario. Some aspects of model simulations of ENSO, monsoons and the North Atlantic Oscillation, as well as selected periods of past climate, have improved.

There is New and Stronger Evidence that Most of the Warming Observed Over the Last 50 Years is Attributable to Human Activities

The SAR concluded: "The balance of evidence suggests a discernible human influence on global climate". That report also noted that the anthropogenic signal was still emerging from the background of natural climate variability. Since the SAR, progress has been made in reducing uncertainty, particularly with respect to distinguishing and quantifying the magnitude of responses to different external influences. Although many of the sources of uncertainty identified in the SAR still remain to some degree, new evidence and improved understanding support an updated conclusion.

There is a longer and more closely scrutinized temperature record and new model estimates of variability. The warming over the past 100 years is very unlikely to be due to internal variability alone, as estimated by current models.

Reconstructions of climate data for the past 1,000 years also indicate that this warming was unusual and is unlikely to be entirely natural in origin. There are new estimates of the climate response to natural and anthropogenic forcing, and new detection techniques have been applied. Detection and attribution studies consistently find evidence for an anthropogenic signal in the climate record of the last 35 to 50 years.

Simulations of the response to natural forcings alone (i.e., the response to variability in solar irradiance and volcanic eruptions) do not explain the warming in the second half of the 20th century. However, they indicate that natural forcings may have contributed to the observed warming in the first half of the 20th century. The warming over the last 50 years due to anthropogenic greenhouse gases can be identified despite uncertainties in forcing due to anthropogenic sulphate aerosol and natural factors (volcanoes and solar irradiance). The anthropogenic sulphate aerosol forcing, while uncertain, is negative over this period and therefore cannot explain the warming. Changes in natural forcing during most of this period are also estimated to be negative and are unlikely to explain the warming.

Detection and attribution studies comparing model simulated changes with the observed record can now take into account uncertainty in the magnitude of modelled response to external forcing, in particular that due to uncertainty in climate sensitivity. Most of these studies find that, over the last 50 years, the estimated rate and magnitude of warming due to increasing concentrations of greenhouse gases alone are comparable with, or larger than, the observed warming. Furthermore, most model estimates that take into account both greenhouse gases and sulphate aerosols are consistent with observations over this period.

The best agreement between model simulations and observations over the last 140 years has been found when all the above anthropogenic and natural forcing factors are combined. These results show that the forcings included are sufficient to explain the observed changes, but do not exclude the possibility that other forcings may also have contributed. In the light of new evidence and taking into account the remaining uncertainties, most of the observed warming over the last 50 years is likely to have been due to the increase in greenhouse gas concentrations.

Furthermore, it is very likely that the 20th century warming has contributed significantly to the observed sea level rise, through thermal expansion of sea water and widespread loss of land ice. Within present uncertainties, observations and models are both consistent with a lack of significant acceleration of sea level rise during the 20th century.

Human Influences will Continue to Change Atmospheric Composition Throughout the 21st Century

Models have been used to make projections of atmospheric concentrations of greenhouse gases and aerosols, and hence of future climate, based upon emissions scenarios from the IPCC Special Report on Emission Scenarios (SRES). These scenarios were developed to update the IS92 series, which were used in the SAR and are shown for comparison here in some cases.

Greenhouse Gases

Emissions of CO_2 due to fossil fuel burning are virtually certain to be the dominant influence on the trends in atmospheric CO_2 concentration during the 21st century.

As the CO_2 concentration of the atmosphere increases, ocean and land will take up a decreasing fraction of anthropogenic CO_2 emissions. The net effect of land and ocean climate feedbacks as indicated by models is to further increase projected atmospheric CO_2 concentrations, by reducing both the ocean and land uptake of CO_2.

By 2100, carbon cycle models project atmospheric CO_2 concentrations of 540 to 970 ppm for the illustrative SRES scenarios (90 to 250 percent above the concentration of 280 ppm in the year 1750). These projections include the land and ocean climate feedbacks. Uncertainties, especially about the magnitude of the climate feedback from the terrestrial biosphere, cause a variation of about 10 to 30 percent around each scenario. The total range is 490 to 1260 ppm (75 to 350 percent above the 1750 concentration).

Changing land use could influence atmospheric CO_2 concentration. Hypothetically, if all of the carbon released by historical land-use changes could be restored to the terrestrial biosphere over the course of the century (e.g., by reforestation), CO_2 concentration would be reduced by 40 to 70 ppm.

Model calculations of the concentrations of the non-CO_2 greenhouse gases by 2100 vary considerably across the SRES illustrative scenarios, with CH_4 changing by –190 to 1,970 ppb (present concentration 1,760 ppb), N_2O changing by 38 to 144 ppb (present concentration 316 ppb), total tropospheric O_3 changing by 12 to 62 percent, and a wide range of changes in concentrations of HFCs, PFCs and SF_6 , all relative to the year 2000. In some scenarios, total tropospheric O_3 would become as important a radiative forcing agent as CH_4 and, over much of the Northern Hemisphere, would threaten the attainment of current air quality targets.

Reductions in greenhouse gas emissions and the gases that control their concentration would be necessary to stabilize radiative forcing. For example, for the most important anthropogenic greenhouse gas, carbon cycle models indicate that stabilization of atmospheric CO_2 concentrations at 450, 650, or 1,000 ppm would require global anthropogenic CO_2 emissions to drop below 1990 levels, within a few decades, about a century, or about two centuries, respectively, and continue to decrease steadily thereafter. Eventually CO_2 emissions would need to decline to a very small fraction of current emissions.

Aerosols

The SRES scenarios include the possibility of either increases or decreases in anthropogenic aerosols (e.g., sulphate aerosols), biomass aerosols, black and organic carbon aerosols) depending on the extent of fossil fuel use and policies to abate polluting emissions. In addition, natural aerosols (e.g., sea salt, dust, and emissions leading to the production of sulphate and carbon aerosols) are projected to increase as a result of changes in climate.

Radiative Forcing Over the 21st Century

For the SRES illustrative scenarios, relative to the year 2000, the global mean radiative forcing due to greenhouse gases continues to increase through the 21st century, with the fraction due to CO_2 projected to increase from slightly more than half to about three quarters. The change in the direct plus indirect aerosol radiative forcing is projected to be smaller in magnitude than that of CO_2.

Global Average Temperature and Sea Level are Projected to Rise Under all IPCC SRES Scenarios

In order to make projections of future climate, models incorporate past, as well as future emissions of greenhouse gases and aerosols. Hence, they include estimates of warming to date and the commitment to future warming from past emissions.

Temperature

The globally averaged surface temperature is projected to increase by 1.4 to 5.8°C over the period 1990 to 2100. These results are for the full range of 35 SRES scenarios, based on a number of climate models 10,11. Temperature increases are projected to be greater than those in the SAR, which were about 1.0 to 3.5°C based on the six IS92 scenarios. The higher projected temperatures and the wider range are due primarily to the lower projected sulphur dioxide emissions in the SRES scenarios relative to the IS92 scenarios. The projected rate of warming is much larger than the observed changes during the 20th century and is very likely to be without precedent during at least the last 10,000 years, based on palaeoclimate data.

By 2100, the range in the surface temperature response across the group of climate models run with a given scenario is comparable to the range obtained from a single model run with the different SRES scenarios. On timescales of a few decades, the current observed rate of warming can be used to constrain the projected response to a given emissions scenario despite uncertainty in climate sensitivity. This approach suggests that anthropogenic warming is likely to lie in the range of 0.1 to 0.2°C per decade over the next few decades under the IS92a scenario...

Based on recent global model simulations, it is very likely that nearly all land areas will warm more rapidly than the global average, particularly those at northern high latitudes in the cold season. Most notable of these is the warming in the northern regions of North America, and northern and central Asia, which exceeds global mean warming in each model by more than 40 percent. In contrast, the warming is less than the global mean change in South and Southeast Asia in summer and in southern South America in winter.

Recent trends for surface temperature to become more El Niño-like in the tropical Pacific, with the eastern tropical Pacific warming more than the western tropical Pacific, with a corresponding eastward shift of precipitation, are projected to continue in many models.

Precipitation

Based on global model simulations and for a wide range of scenarios, global average water vapor concentration and precipitation are projected to increase during the 21st century. By the second half of the 21st century, it is likely that precipitation will have increased over northern mid to high latitudes and Antarctica in winter. At low latitudes there are both regional increases and decreases over land areas. Larger year-to-year variations in precipitation are very likely over most areas where an increase in mean precipitation is projected.

Extreme Events

[There is] an assessment of confidence in observed changes in extremes of weather and climate during the latter half of the 20th century and in projected changes during the 21st century. This assessment relies on observational and modelling studies, as well as the physical plausibility of future projections across all commonly-used scenarios and is based on expert judgement.

For some other extreme phenomena, many of which may have important impacts on the environment and society, there is currently insufficient information to assess recent trends, and climate models currently lack the spatial detail required to make confident projections. For example, very small-scale phenomena, such as thunderstorms, tornadoes, hail and lightning, are not simulated in climate models.

El Niño

Confidence in projections of changes in future frequency, amplitude, and spatial pattern of El Niño events in the tropical Pacific is tempered by some shortcomings in how well El Niño is simulated in complex models. Current projections show little change or a small increase in amplitude for El Niño events over the next 100 years. Even with little or no change in El Niño amplitude, global warming is likely to lead to greater extremes of drying and heavy rainfall and increase the risk of droughts and floods that occur with El Niño events in many different regions.

Monsoons

It is likely that warming associated with increasing greenhouse gas concentrations will cause an increase of Asian summer monsoon precipitation variability. Changes in monsoon mean duration and strength depend on the details of the emission scenario. The confidence in such projections is also limited by how well the climate models simulate the detailed seasonal evolution of the monsoons.

Thermohaline Circulation

Most models show weakening of the ocean thermohaline circulation which leads to a reduction of the heat transport into high latitudes of the Northern Hemisphere. However, even in models where the thermohaline circulation weakens, there is still a warming over Europe due to increased greenhouse gases. The current projections using climate models do not exhibit a complete shut-down of the thermohaline circulation by 2100. Beyond 2100, the thermohaline circulation could completely, and possibly irreversibly, shut-down in either hemisphere if the change in radiative forcing is large enough and applied long enough.

Snow and Ice

Northern Hemisphere snow cover and sea-ice extent are projected to decrease further. Glaciers and ice caps are projected to continue their widespread retreat during the 21st century. The Antarctic ice sheet is likely to gain mass because of greater precipitation, while the Greenland ice sheet is likely to lose mass because the increase in runoff will exceed the precipitation increase. Concerns have been expressed about the stability of the West Antarctic ice sheet because it is grounded below sea level. However, loss of grounded ice leading to substantial sea level rise from this source is now widely agreed to be very unlikely during the 21st century, although its dynamics are still inadequately understood, especially for projections on longer time-scales.

Sea Level

Global mean sea level is projected to rise by 0.09 to 0.88 meters between 1990 and 2100, for the full range of SRES scenarios. This is due primarily to thermal expansion and loss of mass from glaciers and ice caps. The range of sea level rise presented in the SAR was 0.13 to 0.94 meters based on the IS92 scenarios. Despite the higher temperature change projections in this assessment, the sea level projections are slightly lower, primarily due to the use of improved models, which give a smaller contribution from glaciers and ice sheets.

It is likely that warming associated with increasing greenhouse gas concentrations will cause an increase of Asian summer monsoon precipitation variability.

Anthropogenic Climate Change Will Persist for Many Centuries

Emissions of long-lived greenhouse gases (i.e., CO_2 ,N_2O, PFCs, SF_6) have a lasting effect on atmospheric composition, radiative forcing and climate. For example, several centuries after CO_2 emissions occur, about a quarter of the increase in CO_2 concentration caused by these emissions is still present in the atmosphere. After greenhouse gas concentrations have stabilized, global average surface temperatures would rise at a rate of only a few tenths of a degree per century rather than several degrees per century as projected for the 21st century without stabilization. The lower the level at which concentrations are stabilized, the smaller the total temperature change.

Global mean surface temperature increases and rising sea level from thermal expansion of the ocean are projected to continue for hundreds of years after stabilization of greenhouse gas concentrations (even at present levels), owing to the long timescales on which the deep ocean adjusts to climate change.

Ice sheets will continue to react to climate warming and contribute to sea level rise for thousands of years after climate has been stabilized. Climate models indicate that the local warming over Greenland is likely to be one to three times the global average. Ice sheet models project that a local warming of larger than 3°C, if sustained for millennia, would lead to virtually a complete melting of the Greenland ice sheet with a resulting sea level rise of about 7 meters. A local warming of 5.5°C, if sustained for 1000 years, would be likely to result in a contribution from Greenland of about 3 meters to sea level rise. Current ice dynamic models suggest that the West Antarctic ice sheet could contribute up to 3 meters to sea level rise over the next 1000 years, but such results are strongly dependent on model assumptions regarding climate change scenarios, ice dynamics and other factors.

Further Action is Required to Address Remaining Gaps in Information and Understanding

Further research is required to improve the ability to detect, attribute and understand climate change, to reduce uncertainties and to project future climate changes. In particular, there is a need for additional systematic and sustained observations, modelling and process studies. A serious concern is the decline of observational networks. The following are high priority areas for action.

Systematic observations and reconstructions:

- Reverse the decline of observational networks in many parts of the world.
- Sustain and expand the observational foundation for climate studies by providing accurate, long-term, consistent data including implementation of a strategy for integrated global observations.
- Enhance the development of reconstructions of past climate periods.
- Improve the observations of the spatial distribution of greenhouse gases and aerosols.

Modelling and process studies:

- Improve understanding of the mechanisms and factors leading to changes in radiative forcing.
- Understand and characterise the important unresolved processes and feedbacks, both physical and bio- geo-chemical, in the climate system.
- Improve methods to quantify uncertainties of climate projections and scenarios, including long-term ensemble simulations using complex models.
- Improve the integrated hierarchy of global and regional climate models with a focus on the simulation of climate variability, regional climate changes and extreme events.
- Link more effectively models of the physical climate and the biogeochemical system, and in turn improve coupling with descriptions of human activities.

Cutting across these foci are crucial needs associated with strengthening international cooperation and coordination in order to better utilize scientific, computational and observational resources. This should also promote the free exchange of data among scientists. A special need is to increase the observational and research capacities in many regions, particularly in developing countries. Finally, as is the goal of this assessment, there is a continuing imperative to communicate research advances in terms that are relevant to decision making.

B

The Association of Small Island States: Vulnerability, Risk, and Differential Responsibility

The position of Small Island States, their vulnerability and their response to Climate Change is described by Jurgen Lefevere in the following terms:

> "While the impact of climate change will be felt everywhere, the IPCC has reconfirmed that small islands will be hit first and hardest through increases in sea level and extreme weather events. Not only are small islands most vulnerable, but they also have limited capacity to adapt to the worsening impact of climate change.
>
> The Alliance of Small Island States (AOSIS) the group of 43 small islands that joined forces in the climate change negotiations, thus reacted strongly to US opposition to the Kyoto Protocol. In the statement of March 2001, they said that they were 'profoundly concerned and disappointed' by US announcement, warning that the US position will not only 'severely jeopardize' the climate change negotiations in Bonn in July, but indeed 'the international momentum to deal with global climate change'.

As the gap between scientific evidence on climate change and international action to tackle this problem widens, it becomes increasingly essential that vulnerable countries are able to adapt to the adverse impact of climate change."

(i) Slade T.N., Permanent Representative of Samoa to the United Nations and Chairman of the Alliance of Small Island States (AOSIS), "Small Island States: Special Characteristics for Development," Keynote Address, *Seminar on Small Island Developing States: Their Vulnerability, Their Program of Action for Sustainable Development, Their Opportunities for Post-Lomé*, Brussels, 1–2 September, 1998

There is wide acknowledgement by the international community of the characteristics which are special to small island developing states (SIDS) and which largely condition their situation and prospects for sustainable development. These characteristics—small islands, often geographically remote, environmentally fragile and economically vulnerable—give to these states uniqueness and qualities which set them apart from other developing countries.

Principle 6 of the *Rio Declaration* promised that "developing countries most environmentally vulnerable" shall be given special priority. All SIDS would fall within this category. Chapter 17 of *Agenda 21* addressed the special problems of SIDS, noting the combination of factors giving rise to vulnerability: small size, isolation from markets, ecological fragility, geographic dispersion and limited resources. The international conventions on climate change and biodiversity, both signed in the context of the Rio process, contain specific acknowledgements of the special conditions and vulnerability of small island states. In Barbados at the 1994 global conference dedicated to SIDS, the international community recognized their special characteristics and needs, and adopted a specific *Programme of Action* to address these needs. The UN *Agenda for Development* adopted by the General Assembly in July 1997 reinforced both the acknowledgement of special circumstances of SIDS and the need for international support to help island communities with their development efforts. The ACP Heads of State and Government in their *Liberville Declaration* expressly recognized these same special circumstances and needs.

Vulnerability Index

In December 1997 the Ad Hoc Expert Group on Vulnerability Indices convened by the UN Department of Economic and Social Affairs (DESA) concluded, amongst other things, that as a group SIDS are more vulnerable than other groups of developing countries. It had been generally acknowledged, at least in the Commonwealth, that by comparison to larger countries, small states are more susceptible to environmental and economic risks, and their Governments open to territorial and political security threats. The conclusions of the outstanding Commonwealth report, *A Future for Small States: Overcoming Vulnerability*, which took an in-depth look at the vulnerability issues and the economic implications for small states in the context of globalization underscores this fact. At the recent ECOSOC session in July 1998 it seemed to have been accepted that vulnerability was a determining factor in the designation of least developed countries, although work for the improvements in criteria and methodology for such designation must continue.

Barbados Programme of Action

The *Barbados Programme of Action for the Sustainable Development of Small Island States* (BPOA) is bound to the principles and ideals of *Agenda 21*; it is a product of the Rio process. It is a blue print for sustainable development defining actions and policies in 14 agreed priority areas. What sometimes escapes attention is the fact that it is an agreed program fashioned at a global conference by the international community as a whole, including the SIDS and other developing countries as well and, for our present purposes, the European Union.

There is recognition that although afflicted by the same economic difficulties and imperatives confronting developing countries generally, SIDS also have their own "peculiar vulnerabilities and characteristics" so that the difficulties they face in the pursuit of sustainable development are particularly severe and complex. The BPOA identifies the range of these characteristics.

Many disadvantages derive from small size, magnified by the fact that many island states are not only small but

All islanders have intense attachment to their environment. Small size means that there is a close and natural interrelationship between the environment and development.

are themselves made up of a number of small islands. Disadvantages include a narrow range of resources, which forces undue specialization; excessive dependence on international trade inviting vulnerability to global developments; relatively high population density; overuse of resources resulting in early depletion; relatively limited sources of freshwater; costly public administration and infrastructure, especially in transportation and communication; and limited institutional capacities and domestic markets, which are too small to provide significant scale economies, while their limited export volumes, sometimes from remote locations, lead to high freight costs and reduced competitiveness.

All islanders have intense attachment to their environment. Small size means that there is a close and natural interrelationship between the environment and development. This is fully reflected in the BPOA where there is significant emphasis on the environmental aspects of development—perhaps more so than the *Lome Convention*. There is, in fact, some recognition by the European Commission in its Green Paper of 1996 that the Community "still lacks a clear strategy and sense of purpose to make [environmental management] operationally viable". It is a matter of observation here that, unlike other development-related international conferences that are referred to in the Green Paper, there appears to be no direct reference therein to the BPOA. Such reference in the Green Paper and perhaps the successor ACP convention no doubt serve to draw attention to the specific circumstances and vulnerabilities of SIDS. Let me say though that the Green Paper does draw special attention to the fact that ACP states are particularly exposed to the potential dangers linked to climate change, especially the increasing frequency of violent storms.

Climate Change

It is no accident that the first chapter of the BPOA deals with climate change, and neither that it leads off with the clear and, as far as I know, undisputed statement that SIDS are particularly vulnerable to global climate change, climate variability and sea-level rise. Indeed, the assessment of the Intergovernmental Panel on Climate Change (IPCC) is that SIDS are the least able to adapt to the impact of climate change. Sea-level rise is profoundly the most dangerous threat, for it touches the very life force of island communities. Serious saline intrusion into freshwater supplies, caused by rising seas, are already occurring in several small island states, in the Caribbean, Indian Ocean and the Pacific. And recent studies by the IPCC show that there are measurably significant increases in temperature and sea-level rise in the Caribbean and Pacific regions. It is why the SIDS, since 1990, through the Alliance of Small Island States (AOSIS) have made a determined and concerted effort to be heard in the global negotiations on this issue. Their concerns carry a high degree of authenticity and moral force.

The low-lying island states and atolls in particular are especially vulnerable to climate change and associated sea-level rise because in many cases (as in The Bahamas, Kiribati, Maldives and Marshall Islands), much of the land is only 3–4 meters above the present mean sea level. The higher islands, too, are vulnerable, particularly in coastal zones, where settlements, economic infrastructure and vital services tend to be concentrated. All island systems are extremely vulnerable to any changes in the frequency or intensity of extreme events whether droughts, floods, hurricanes or storm surges. Indeed, vulnerability to these and other natural hazards, including some that may not be influenced by climate change (like tsunamis and volcano eruptions) contributes to the cumulative vulnerability of SIDS.

Moreover, the cost of protection would be highly disproportionate to the ability of SIDS (questions of equity and historical responsibility quite apart). Studies in the Pacific, for instance, show that land loss from a one meter sea-level rise would destroy over 8 percent of the total land area of the Marshall Islands and over 12 percent of the territory of Kiribati. For the Caribbean small states, the IPCC estimates the cost for new construction alone to protect shorelines against future sea-level rise to be in the order of US$11 billion, an amount that would be well beyond the combined economies of the countries in that region.

Biodiversity

Let me also say that the biodiversity of islands, especially in the marine area, could be severely affected by climate change. Small islands tend to have high degrees of endemism and levels of biodiversity, but relatively small numbers of the various species impose high risks of extinction and create a need for protection. The costs of species protection, in light of a small island's international responsibilities in the matter, would again be highly disproportionate compared to its means. As I say, all these add to the cumulative vulnerability of SIDS.

Review of the Barbados Programme of Action

The particular challenge for SIDS in the immediate months ahead, is to be fully engaged in the preparations for next year's UN General Assembly special session to review the implementation of the BPOA, from the donors' roundtable meeting in February 1999, and throughout the processes of the Commission on Sustainable Development. In respect of the donors' roundtable, it is clear that SIDS will require assistance from regional and international institutions for the preparation of project proposals...In respect of the BPOA, it is vital that SIDS take the opportunity not only to demonstrate the practical problems and constraints in implementation but also, and perhaps more critically, to showcase the successes.

Regional mechanisms for interaction and cooperation among SIDS were developed partly to alleviate the problems of distance and geographic isolation. The mechanisms existing today testify to their viability and efficiency as vehicles for the achievement of sustainable development objectives. Regionalism is an essential basis for action under the BPOA. The political and economic regional arrangements in the Caribbean and the Pacific are of particular vitality; the experience of the Pacific, especially in the functioning and specialization of institutions, being quite extensive and productive. All are clear examples of effective regional action and of what SIDS can successfully do for themselves.

This is not to suggest that all is well with the BPOA. Indeed not. The overall trends with respect to sustainable development, as acknowledged by the world's political leadership at the 5-year review of *Agenda 21* last year, are worse today than they were in 1992. Of the BPOA itself, one of the main drawbacks would be the lack of assured financial support as well as the shortage of skilled human resources. The report of the UN Secretary-General to the Commission on Sustainable Development earlier in April this year in connection with the review of several chapters of the BPOA confirmed not only the shortfalls in foreign financial assistance to SIDS, but also the significant gaps in the implementation of the BPOA, especially in the strengthening of Government and regional institutions and in training opportunities and the improvement of capacity in SIDS. Capacity building is of the highest priority. At the end of the day, a country's most precious possessions are its human and natural resources.

Development Needs

There is no doubt that climate change remains a critical area for SIDS. The AOSIS countries are serious in their efforts to clarify and to develop agreed compliance rules and procedures to ensure the effectiveness and strengthening of the new mechanisms established under the Kyoto Protocol. AOSIS is paying particular attention to the Clean Development Mechanism. The question of adaptation is of critical importance to all SIDS, as an issue in the climate change negotiations as it is in the context of sustainable development projects. The problem of fossil-fuel dependence among SIDS and the need for new and renewable energy sources and techniques is fundamental both to the global climate mitigation effort and to the ultimate economic well-being of SIDS. There are many aspects of these matters that fall within the ambit of the BPOA.

There are several other priority areas, among them waste management and the increasingly urgent need for freshwater and freshwater conservation in almost all SIDS. Fast and secure modern communication systems is a requirement of the day for all countries, and no less than SIDS. AOSIS, in conjunction with UNDP is putting considerable effort in the development of SIDS/Net currently being operated by and out of the UNDP headquarters in New York. International support in all such areas would be vital.

Self-Help

It is true, indeed, that SIDS in many significant respects differ from other developing countries and are naturally and extremely vulnerable; and that consequently SIDS face additional constraints in their development efforts. Yet, in a world intent on globalization, a world of competing priorities with hunger and poverty still appallingly real among developing countries, and given that there is retreat from the sustainable development commitments and ideals agreed at Rio in 1992, it is important for SIDS to accept that the assertion of vulnerability alone is not sufficient. Much more needs to be done to build understanding and to encourage from the international community a response to the needs of SIDS, a response that is both informed and qualitatively constructive; and from the SIDS themselves, a particular focus on specific priorities and on what the SIDS can and must do.

In this respect it is important to appreciate that the primary responsibility for the success of the BPOA lies with the SIDS, first and foremost. The implementation of strategies for sustainable development must and should be undertaken by SIDS, with of course the essential support of the international community. It would be a challenge well worth the effort. For the ultimate prize, surely, is self-reliance with the assurance of strengthened local capacities, both vital ingredients for lasting sustainability.

(ii) Alliance of Small Island States, "AOSIS Submission to the CSD 9," Annex 1 to *Report of The 3rd Alliance of Small Island States (AOSIS) Workshop on Climate Change, Energy and Preparations for the 9th Session of the Commission on Sustainable Development*, AOSIS, 2001

Introduction

Small Island Developing States (SIDS) continue to share a common aspiration for economic development and improved living standards while at the same time remain strongly committed to conserving the natural and cultural heritage upon which their future depends. Participants at the workshop recognized that while there are some differences of situations among them, there are a vast amount of similarities.

The context of the discussion was the need to focus international attention on the unique and special constraints and concerns of SIDS. SIDS are vulnerable to economic as well as environmental shocks. In addition to the problems faced by most developing countries such as lack of financial resources, SIDS face a unique combination of challenges in making the transition to sustainable development. Among the many constraints are fragile natural environments, little resilience to natural disasters, growing populations, isolation from markets, a narrow resource base, difficulties arising from economies of scale, and high cost for energy, infrastructure, transportation, communication and access to other services.

In recognition of the special situation of the SIDS, the United Nations convened the first Global Conference for the Sustainable Development of SIDS in Bridgetown, Barbados in 1994, that adopted the Barbados Program of Action (BPOA), a non-binding, comprehensive blue print for action for the sustainable development of SIDS. The BPOA translates *Agenda 21* into specific policies, actions, and measures to be taken at national, regional, and international levels to enable SIDS to achieve sustainable development. At the Barbados Conference participating Governments also adopted the Barbados Declaration, a political document, meant to promote and uphold the BPOA.

To mark the fifth anniversary of the adoption of the BPOA, the United Nations convened its twenty-second Special Session of the General Assembly (UNGASS) in September 1999, to review and appraise the implementation of the BPOA. The Special Session also undertook an analysis of the BPOA with regard to achievements and setbacks, and identified a number of future possibilities for SIDS in their endeavor to achieve sustainable development. The analysis highlighted the impact on SIDS of trade liberalization and globalization, the erosion or loss of preferential treatment in economic relations or both, and the special vulnerabilities of SIDS. It was against this background that the participants considered the vulnerabilities and the sustainable development priorities for SIDS, building on these internationally agreed commitments.

One of the most serious environmental threats to SIDS is the continued increase in greenhouse gas emissions, which threaten their very existence. Most SIDS are highly vulnerable to increased sea level rise—the entire territories of ten SIDS are barely one meter above sea level. All SIDS have highly vulnerable coastal zones where the majority of the population live and work.

AOSIS members are the "frontline" states in every sense. They now suffer and expect to suffer in the most direct way the full range of climate impacts—increased cyclones, droughts, hurricanes, typhoons and coral bleaching among them. All are increasing in their frequency, intensity and impacts. It is impossible to cope adequately with these shocks. And it is not just these direct extreme climatic events that confront and will affect SIDS. There are serious economic effects—such as disruptions to food security, to the tourism, fisheries and agriculture sectors, to water supplies, which will be affected by salt-water intrusion, and the diversion of economic resources to reconstruction. The significant challenges facing SIDS have been identified as part of necessary climate change adaptation policies, which will need to consider the following:

- Loss of revenue across productive sectors.
- Loss of agricultural production.
- Shifting of fishing grounds, fish catch and overall impact on total stocks.
- Bleaching and death of coral reefs.
- Damage to infrastructure and accelerated coastal erosion.
- Availability and quality of freshwater resources, contaminated by saltwater intrusion, reduced by drought and changing weather patterns.
- Increased diversification of the economy to improve resilience, in an already difficult international context for SIDS.
- Social and cultural disruption, displacement of populations and adverse effects on traditional systems and human health.

While SIDS are thus recognized as the most vulnerable to climate change, they have made the smallest contribution to its causes. It has been estimated that SIDS are responsible for producing approximately one quarter of the per capita CO_2 emissions attributable to the average person worldwide. This is miniscule by international comparison. For example the Pacific Island Countries account for some 0.03 percent of the global emissions of CO_2 from fuel combustion despite having only 0.12 percent of the world's population. This can be compared to the OECD countries, which, with only 20 percent of the world's population, are responsible for over 50 percent of the total global emissions from fuel combustion.

In addition to the climate change stress, further stress on the island system is occurring as countries develop. Their reliance on fossil fuels has increased, in particular for producing electricity, and transportation seems to be the fastest growing consumer of petroleum, including sea and aviation transport. It is therefore important to acknowledge that in providing access to energy sources, in particular electricity, there is significant opportunity to utilize renewable energy sources. Although renewable energy technologies such as solar, hydropower, biomass and to a lesser extent wind have already been utilized in a number of SIDS to improve, communication, health, education and some small cottage industry, there remain significant opportunities and potential to further develop these and other renewable energy resources. At the same time it is quite apparent that there are also major opportunities for improving energy efficiency in SIDS, and that this should be considered in parallel to renewable energy development.

There are a number of significant constraints and barriers to the exploitation and integration of these renewable energy technologies into the urban and rural sectors. The SIDS are for the most part heavily dependent on fossil fuel based systems of energy generation. These are frequently environmentally and economically unsustainable and not accessible to many remote communities, raising serious social equity concerns. This dependency makes them vulnerable to increased costs and uncertain supplies which slows the sustainable development of SIDS, particularly in rural areas and remote islands.

It is imperative that the SIDS are provided financial and technical resources to assist in development of their strategies and priorities for the exploitation and use of new and alternative forms of energy. International, regional and bilateral cooperation are important to ensure the promotion of energy conservation, improvement of energy efficiency, adoption of renewable energy technologies, and the development and dissemination of innovative energy-related technologies.

In recent years the need for and importance of the energy sector in the SIDS regions has increased significantly. The essential role of energy sources for economic and social development and the increasing need to reduce negative environmental impacts is paramount. Furthermore, the need for sustainable patterns of production, distribution and utilization of energy are of critical importance to the above-mentioned objectives, and are among the issues facing the challenge of energy for sustainable development.

In terms of energy imports, the Pacific Islands energy imports account for 15-25 percent of their total imports and over 40 percent of the gross domestic commodity exports. A Pacific Regional Energy Assessment (PREA) (1992) report showed the tremendous impact of petroleum imports on the economy. The ratio of petroleum imports to total export earnings is very large for most Pacific Island Countries, between 40–80 percent, and alarmingly so for some countries where the figures are as high as 500 percent. This constitutes a dangerous dependency situation, for in case of major market fluctuations due to global shortages, rising prices, conflicts or other causes, the consequences for SIDS would be dramatic.

Energy consumption is often regarded as an important indicator of economic development of a nation. It is feared that excess commercialization and inequities between the urban and rural communities will result if inappropriate mechanisms are used in the development of energy resources in SIDS. SIDS must therefore be assisted in finding more appropriate energy futures. For this reason, SIDS are advocating the development of an energy agenda for SIDS to assist them with sustainable development. A conceptual framework of such an energy agenda is currently being developed.

Key Issues

Accessibility of Energy

Situation and Challenges

Accessibility of energy varies widely within and between the SIDS regions. It is estimated that in the Pacific Island Countries approximately 70 percent of the people do not have access to modern energy services, with many of these people living on remote islands or in isolated rural areas. This is a greatly different picture to the global situation where approximately 30 percent are without access to modern energy services. Meeting the basic energy requirements and sustainable socioeconomic development needs of people with subsistence incomes remains a top priority. In other regions, there is less of a problem of access, but rather of affordability. Accessibility to energy should be considered together with the reliability of supply and the affordability of prices. Accessibility is also closely linked to the issue of energy security. Storage capacity should also be improved to minimize disruption in countries where it is a frequent occurrence. For SIDS that means one must first consider petroleum, and then look at storage, transport and quality. Some small communities are not well served, and it is recognized that energy efficiency could assist in lowering prices and hence accessibility in these rural areas and remote islands. At the international level regional measures of cooperation is desirable. One example is the *San Jose Accord*, which could be considered in other regions where such measures are feasible. As far as possible such arrangements should be pursued. Recognizing that the whole issue of accessibility would be improved by greater use of renewable energy, participants stressed the need to look at capacity building, management and financing.

Strategies and Recommendations

In considering energy accessibility at the regional and national levels the following main strategies and recommendations have been identified:

- Provision of reliable energy markets that can generate a profitable income for producers, while protecting the consumers.
- Introduction of sustainable energy supplies in rural areas and remote islands to increase the standard of living of rural dwellers and in generating economic activities.
- Establishing greater reliability of the energy supply at an affordable cost.
- Utilizing renewable natural resources, such as solar, wind, biomass, hydro including mini-hydro, geothermal, ocean (wave, tidal and ocean thermal energy conversion), and hydrogen from renewable sources to meet energy demands where economically and financially feasible so as to reduce the high dependence on imported petroleum products used for electricity generation.
- Adopting national policies, strategies and action plans that ensure the basic energy requirements of low-income rural and urban dwellers are met with modern energy services at an affordable cost.
- Seeking increased official development assistance and other grant and concessional financing from international and regional funding cooperation in the development of national sustainable energy service strategies.

[*The submission continues on to discuss, in some detail, a range of energy issues relevant to developing countries and Small Island nations. To avoid duplication, this material has been excluded and the reader is directed to the two extracts in Chapter 8 (Bradbrook and Ottinger) which discuss Energy Efficiency.*]

2

Overview of the Global Regulatory Framework

A

Jeffery M. and Baird W., "Using Market-Based Incentives to Curtail Greenhouse Gas Emissions: Factors to Consider in the Design of the Clean Development Mechanism, Joint Implementation and Emissions Trading," *Asia Pacific Journal of Environmental Law*, 2001, pp 10–19

THE UNFCCC AND THE *KYOTO PROTOCOL*

In this paper the authors are assuming that the reader is familiar with the basic terms of the UNFCCC and the *Kyoto Protocol* and accordingly it is proposed to focus upon only the specific provisions of the *Kyoto Protocol* relating to the 'flexibility mechanisms'.

UNFCCC

The UNFCCC is a framework convention having as its ultimate objective the 'stabilization of greenhouse gas concentrations in the atmosphere at a level that would prevent dangerous anthropogenic interference with the climate system'. Following the recommendation of the Intergovernmental Panel on Climate Change (IPCC) and the Second World Climate Conference, the UN General Assembly established the Intergovernmental Negotiating Committee for a Framework Climate Convention (INC). Its mandate was to attempt to arrive at an international convention along the lines of the *Vienna Convention for the Protection of the Ozone Layer*, 1985. The General Assembly directed the INC to produce an agreement for signing at the Rio Earth Summit to be held in June 1992.

The US and the European Community (EC) approach to the negotiations differed significantly in the key area of whether or not the convention should contain specific targets and timetables for reduction. The US was vehemently opposed to the inclusion of specific reduction targets and moreover insisted on including CFCs within the range of greenhouse gases, notwithstanding that CFCs were already scheduled to be phased out completely.

As a result of these differences and a last minute frantic rush to meet the Rio Summit deadline, the framework convention that was ultimately adopted was a significantly watered down version from what had been originally developed in draft form. It provided for subsequent development of the climate change regime through protocols or amendments and established the administrative framework to deal with policy making, implementation and monitoring.

GUIDING PRINCIPLES

The guiding principles for the Parties to follow in implementing the UNFCCC are laid out in Article 3 and reproduced in the footnote below.

COMMITMENTS

It must be pointed out that Parties to the UNFCCC did not enter into *specific* and *quantifiable* commitments for the reduction of greenhouse gases but undertook a series of general commitments in accordance with their categorization. For the purposes of the Convention, the Parties are divided into three specific categories:

1. All Parties;
2. Annex I Parties—Industrialized countries (including those countries from the former Soviet Bloc undergoing the process of transition to a market economy); and
3. Annex II Parties—Industrialized countries (except those countries undergoing the process of transition to a market economy).

All Parties made *general* commitments regarding greenhouse gases not controlled by the *Montreal Protocol* which are summarized as follows, to:

- develop national inventories of anthropogenic emissions and removals of greenhouse gases;
- formulate and implement national and regional programs containing measures to mitigate climate

The US was vehemently opposed to the inclusion of specific reduction targets and moreover insisted on including CFCs within the range of greenhouse gases, notwithstanding that CFCs were already scheduled to be phased out completely.

change by addressing anthropogenic emissions and removals of greenhouse gases;

- promote development, application and diffusion of technologies that control, reduce or prevent emissions in all relevant sectors;
- promote sustainable management and the conservation and enhancement, as appropriate, of sinks and reservoirs of greenhouse gases;
- cooperate in preparing for adaptation to the impacts of climate change, particularly in Africa;
- take climate change considerations into account, to the extent feasible, in their relevant social, economic and environmental policies and actions;
- promote and cooperate in research related to the climate system with a view to eliminate remaining uncertainties regarding climate change;
- promote and cooperate in the full, open and prompt exchange of information related to the climate system and climate change;
- promote and cooperate in education, training and public awareness related to climate change;
- communicate to the Conference of the Parties information related to implementation.

The commitments made by the developed country Parties and other Parties included in Annex I were designed to demonstrate that developed countries were taking the lead in modifying longer-term trends in anthropogenic emissions consistent with the objective of the Convention.

In particular each of these Parties committed to adopting national policies and to taking corresponding measures on the mitigation of climate change, by limiting their anthropogenic emissions of greenhouse gases and protecting and enhancing their greenhouse gas sinks and reservoirs. It was recognized that the return, by the end of the decade in which the UNFCCC was signed, to earlier levels of anthropogenic greenhouse gases not controlled by the *Montreal Protocol* would contribute to modifying the longer-term trend. Annex I Parties specifically committed themselves to the *aim* of returning individually or jointly to their 1990 levels of anthropogenic emissions of carbon dioxide and other greenhouse gases not controlled by the Montreal Protocol. As noted above, however, that this fell far short of a legally binding commitment to in fact reduce these emissions to 1990 levels.

It was then delegated to the Conference of the Parties to review and take appropriate action on the adequacy of these commitments in the light of the best available scientific information and assessment on climate change and its impacts, as well as relevant technical, social and economic information.

The developed country Parties and other developed Parties included in Annex II agreed to provide new and additional financial resources to meet the agreed full costs incurred by developing country Parties in complying with their obligations under Article 12 paragraph 1.

In addition they agreed to take all practical steps to promote, facilitate and finance, as appropriate, the transfer of, or access to, environmentally sound technologies and know-how to other Parties, particularly developing country Parties, to enable them to implement the provisions of the Convention.

Funding

A mechanism for the provision of financial resources on a grant or concessional basis, including provisions for the transfer of technology, is set up under Article 11 of the UNFCCC. It functions under the guidance of, and is accountable to, the Conference of the Parties. Its operation under this Article was entrusted to the Global Environment Facility (GEF) a partnership of the World Bank and the United Nations system with funding provided through one of three implementing agencies, the World Bank, the United Nations Development Programme (UNDP), and the United Nations Environment Programme (UNEP). The GEF is governed by a Council of 32 countries meeting twice a year and is physically located in the World Bank building in Washington, D.C.

Dispute Resolution

In the event of a dispute between any two or more Parties concerning the interpretation or application of the Convention, the primary obligation of the Parties concerned is to seek a settlement of the dispute through negotiation or any other peaceful means of their own choice. Article 14 of the UNFCCC also provides that a Party may declare in a written instrument that, in respect of any dispute, it recognizes as compulsory *ipso facto* and without special agreement in relation to any Party accepting the same obligation, to submit the dispute to the International Court of Justice and/or to arbitration. In the case of a Party that is a regional economic integration organization, arbitration only is provided for.

If the Parties have not chosen to take the dispute to either the ICJ or arbitration and the dispute remains after 12 months following notification by one Party to another, a Party to the dispute has the further option of submitting the dispute to conciliation. In this instance a conciliation commission shall be created composed of an equal number of members of each Party concerned and a chairman chosen jointly by the members appointed by each Party. The commission shall render a recommendatory award, which the Parties shall consider in good faith.

It should be noted that the provisions under the UNFCCC relating to dispute resolution shall apply to any related legal instrument which the COP shall adopt unless the instrument provides otherwise.

The Kyoto Protocol

Background

The evolutionary road from the UNFCCC to the *Kyoto Protocol* proved difficult. Ongoing political reticence, particularly on the part of the USA, to come to terms with defined limits and timetables coupled with a continuing vociferous debate within the scientific community that climate change was actually occurring, threatened to bring further meaningful negotiations to a standstill.

In March/April 1995 the first Conference of the Parties (COP 1) convened in Berlin to review the commitments of Annex 1 Parties as required by Article 4 (2)(d) of the UNFCCC. It was here that the Parties agreed to begin a process to enable it to take appropriate action for the period beyond 2000, including the strengthening of the commitments of Annex 1 Parties in Article 4(2)(a) and (b) through the adoption of a Protocol or other legal instrument.

Also in 1995 the IPCC in its Second Assessment Report concluded:

> 'Global mean surface temperature has increased by between about 0.3 and 0.6 degrees Centigrade since the late 19th century, a change that is unlikely to be entirely natural in origin. The balance of evidence from changes in global mean surface air temperature and from changes in geographical, seasonal, and vertical patterns of atmospheric temperature, suggests a discernible human influence on global climate. There are uncertainties in key factors, including the magnitude and patterns of long-term natural variability. Global sea level has risen by between 10 and 25 cm over the past 100 years and much of the rise may be related to the increase in global mean temperature.'

This apparent consensus by the scientific community, coupled with a significant increase in the levels of global greenhouse gas emissions since the Rio Summit in 1992, galvanized some of the major players (including the United States) into taking significant steps towards breaking the impasse that had developed over limits and timetables for achieving GHG reductions.

Finally, the United States with barely six months to go before Kyoto, announced that it was now prepared to support defined targets and timetables for GHG emissions and in a speech in October 1997, President Clinton outlined the US policy.

This breakthrough opened the way for meaningful negotiations at Kyoto, which led ultimately to the adoption of the *Kyoto Protocol*.

Under the terms of the Protocol those Annex 1 Parties who made specific, quantifiable emission limitation and reduction commitments (QELRCs) were listed together with their QELRCs in Annex B. Only Parties listed in Annex B are entitled to participate in emissions trading under Article 17 of the Protocol as a way of fulfilling their commitments.

Many of the details relative to various Articles were left to be resolved by the Conference of the Parties to the UNFCCC and to Meetings of the Parties after ratification of the Protocol.

It had been hoped that much of the details to be determined by the Conference of the Parties with respect to, inter alia, the flexibility mechanisms, would have been settled at COP6 held in the Hague in November 2000. This was not to be the case as the COP6 ended without agreement and the outstanding issues deferred to a resumption of COP6 tentatively scheduled for June 2001 in Bonn, Germany.

In February 2001 the IPCC Working Group II released its Third Assessment Report. with the major findings of that assessment summarized in its '*Summary for Policymakers—Climate Change 2001: Impacts, Adaptation, and Vulnerability.*'

This summary refers...to conclusions reached by Working Group 1 that the globally averaged surface temperatures have increased by 0.6 plus/minus 0.2°C over the 20th century, and that, for the range of scenarios developed in the *IPCC Special Report on Emission Scenarios* (SRES), the globally averaged surface air temperature is projected by models to warm 1.4 to 5.8°C by 2100 relative to 1990, and globally averaged sea level is projected by models to rise 0.9 to 0.88 meters by 2100.

The globally averaged surface air temperature is projected by models to warm 1.4 to 5.8°C by 2100 relative to 1990, and globally averaged sea level is projected by models to rise 0.9 to 0.88 meters by 2100.

In addition the Report sets out...the projected *Regional Adaptive Capacity, Vulnerability, and Key Concerns* findings of the Working Group with respect to climate change for eight regions which include Africa, Asia, Australia and New Zealand Europe, Latin America, North America, Polar, and Small Island States.

In several of the regions such as the Small Island States, Latin America, Africa, and the developing countries of Asia, the adaptive capacity of human systems is rated low and vulnerability generally high. The same is true of natural systems in Polar Regions. The adaptive capacity for human systems in developed regions such as Europe and North America is generally high with vulnerability low (with vulnerability increasing for indigenous people and those dependent on climate-sensitive resources).

It is this alarming prediction, based on credible scientific data, that has infused a new sense of urgency into the continuing debate on what, if anything, can be done in the time available to address the resulting socioeconomic impacts affecting all regions of the world, in the event of a rise in surface temperatures and sea levels of this magnitude.

The Kyoto Protocol—Relevant Articles

The *Kyoto Protocol*, as an instrument based on a Framework Convention, contains specific substantive obligations that implement the general objectives of the UNFCCC. Before the Protocol comes into force and has any legal effect it must be ratified in accordance with the provisions set out in Article 25. As with any treaty, a Party must consent to be bound by the treaty. In the case of the *Kyoto Protocol*, this consent must be demonstrated by the deposit of evidence of ratification, acceptance, approval or accession with the Secretary-General of the United Nations. In most instances a Party State must approve the treaty through its own domestic political process before ratification and the treaty having a legally binding effect on such Party. The treaty or convention will normally provide when, and under what circumstances, it will come into force.

The flexibility mechanisms are contained in Articles 6, *Joint Implementation* (JI)), Article 12, *the Clean Development Mechanism* (CDM), and Article 17, *Emissions Trading* (ET). These Articles must be read in the context of Article 3, which contains the emission limitation and reduction commitments of the Parties, among other matters.

Article 3—Parties' Commitments

Article 3 sets out binding commitments of Annex 1 Parties, (i.e., those Parties listed in Annex 1 to the UNFCCC), to collectively limit and reduce greenhouse gas emissions over 1990 levels. On a global basis, Annex 1 Parties committed themselves to reducing emissions by at least 5 percent below 1990 levels in the first commitment period 2008 to 2012. The assigned amounts for Annex 1 Parties are calculated in accordance with quantified, differentiated, emission limitation and reduction commitments.

Provision is made for inclusion of emissions by sources and removals by sinks which result from direct human-induced land-use change and forestry activities. These are limited to afforestation, reforestation and deforestation since 1990. The inclusion of additional human-induced activities related to changes in greenhouse gas emissions by sources and removals by sinks in the agricultural soils and the land-use change and forestry categories, are left for later consideration.

Amid a good deal of controversy, Australia proposed the inclusion of emissions from land clearing in the determination of the baseline from which to calculate Annex 1 Parties assigned amounts. This resulted in Clause 3.7 which provides that those Parties for whom land-use change and forestry constitute a net source of emissions in 1990 shall include those in their 1990 emission base year. It has been argued that this clause effectively benefits Australia only.

Annex 1 Parties were required by the year 2005 to have made demonstrable progress in achieving their commitments under the Protocol.

Inclusion of Market- Based Mechanisms

During the Kyoto negotiations broad support for the inclusion of flexible ways in which Annex 1 Parties could meet their commitments (with the exception of the EU countries) was evident. It was argued that developed countries must be presented with cost effective ways of meeting their reduction targets and that, provided there was an overall reduction of greenhouse gases on a global bases, the methods utilized by the Annex 1 Parties was largely irrelevant.

The outcome of the debate was the inclusion of the three flexibility mechanisms, each formulated to accomplish specific objectives. However, it was evident at COP6 that disagreement with the rationale for their inclusion remains strong and was a major factor in the collapse of the COP6 negotiations. The three flexibility mechanisms cover joint arrangements between Annex 1 Parties, arrangements between Annex 1 Parties and non-Annex 1 Parties, and trading in emission credits.

Article 6—Joint Implementation (JI)

Under Article 6 Annex 1 Parties may transfer or acquire from each other emission reduction units (ERUs) resulting from projects aimed at reducing emissions or enhancing sequestration by sinks for the purpose of meeting their commitments. Participation in joint implementation is confined to Annex 1 parties only.

Article 6 incorporates the principal of additionality, that is, any reductions in emissions or enhancement of removals by sinks must be *in addition* to what would otherwise occur.

The settling of the mechanisms for the implementation and operation of each of the flexibility mechanisms remains to be determined and is by no means certain.

Article 12—The Clean Development Mechanism (CDM)

Under Article 12 project activities resulting in certified emission reductions (CERs) in non-Annex 1 Parties may be used by Annex 1 Parties to contribute to meeting part of their emission limitation and reduction commitments. The extent to which this may occur is still to be determined, it being left to the Conference of the Parties meeting after the ratification of the Protocol to do so COP(MoP).

The purpose of the CDM is to assist non-Annex 1 Parties in achieving sustainable development and in contributing to the ultimate objective of the UNFCCC and to assist Annex 1 Parties in achieving their commitments.

Certification of the emission reductions resulting from each project activity is required. Certification is to be on the basis of voluntary participation in the project, real, measurable and long-term benefits mitigating climate change. The principle of additionality applies.

Provision is made for assistance in arranging funding of certified project activities as necessary. A share of the proceeds from such activities is to be used to assist developing countries that are particularly vulnerable to the adverse effects of climate change.

Both the public and private sectors are expected to become involved in the CDM.

An executive board is to be established to supervise the CDM and provide guidance to both private and public entities, who wish to participate. The board is subject to the authority and guidance of the COP (MoP).

CERs obtained from the year 2000 up to the beginning of the first commitment period may be used in that period.

Article 17—Emissions Trading

So-called 'emissions trading' is provided for in Article 17. Annex B Parties, (that is, those Parties listed in Annex B to the Protocol as committing themselves to emission limitation or reductions quantified therein), may participate in emissions trading in order to meet their commitments. Such trading must be *supplemental* to domestic actions to meet their commitments.

Provision for the Use of 'Bubbles' to Meet Commitments

Provision is made in the Protocol for Annex 1 Parties to meet their commitments jointly through agreements with each other. This 'bubble' approach is presently being pursued by the EU. At Kyoto the EU, on behalf of its member states, agreed to reduce its combined greenhouse gas emissions by 8 percent of 1990 levels by 2008–2012. Through an internal burden sharing agreement each member state was then required to meet a specific reduction target which varies from 72 percent (Luxembourg) to 127 percent (Portugal) of 1990 GHG emissions.

The group of countries comprising the 'Umbrella group' is a loose coalition of like- minded countries, who are Parties to the UNFCCC and signatories to the *Kyoto Protocol.* This group is also exploring the use of Article 4.

3

The Kyoto Protocol

A

Kyoto Protocol to the *United Nations Framework Convention On Climate Change*, 39 ILM, 22, 1998

ARTICLE 1

For the purposes of this Protocol, the definitions contained in Article 1 of the Convention shall apply. In addition:

1. "Conference of the Parties" means the Conference of the Parties to the Convention.
2. "Convention" means the United Nations *Framework Convention on Climate Change*, adopted in New York on 9 May 1992.
3. "Intergovernmental Panel on Climate Change" means the Intergovernmental Panel on Climate Change established in 1988 jointly by the World Meteorological Organization and the United Nations Environment Programme.
4. "Montreal Protocol" means the *Montreal Protocol on Substances that Deplete the Ozone Layer*, adopted in Montreal on 16 September 1987 and as subsequently adjusted and amended.
5. "Parties present and voting" means Parties present and casting an affirmative or negative vote.
6. "Party" means, unless the context otherwise indicates, a Party to this Protocol.
7. "Party included in Annex I" means a Party included in Annex I to the Convention, as may be amended, or a Party which has made a notification under Article 4, paragraph 2(g), of the Convention.

ARTICLE 2

1. Each Party included in Annex I, in achieving its quantified emission limitation and reduction commitments under Article 3, in order to promote sustainable development, shall:
   (a) Implement and/or further elaborate policies and measures in accordance with its national circumstances, such as:
      (i) Enhancement of energy efficiency in relevant sectors of the national economy;
      (ii) Protection and enhancement of sinks and reservoirs of greenhouse gases not controlled by the Montreal Protocol, taking into account its commitments under relevant international environmental agreements; promotion of sustainable forest management practices, afforestation and reforestation;
      (iii) Promotion of sustainable forms of agriculture in light of climate change considerations;
      (iv) Research on, and promotion, development and increased use of, new and renewable forms of energy, carbon dioxide sequestration technologies and advanced and innovative environmentally sound technologies;
      (v) Progressive reduction or phasing out of market imperfections, fiscal incentives, tax and duty exemptions and subsidies in all greenhouse gas emitting sectors that run counter to the objective of the Convention and application of market instruments;
      (vi) Encouragement of appropriate reforms in relevant sectors aimed at promoting policies and measures which limit or reduce emissions of greenhouse gases not controlled by the *Montreal Protocol*;
      (vii) Measures to limit and/or reduce emissions of greenhouse gases not controlled by the *Montreal Protocol* in the transport sector;
      (viii) Limitation and/or reduction of methane emissions through recovery and use in waste management, as well as in the production, transport and distribution of energy;
   (b) Cooperate with other such Parties to enhance the individual and combined effectiveness of their policies and measures adopted under this Article, pursuant to Article 4, paragraph 2(e)(i),

of the Convention. To this end, these Parties shall take steps to share their experience and exchange information on such policies and measures, including developing ways of improving their comparability, transparency and effectiveness. The Conference of the Parties serving as the meeting of the Parties to this Protocol shall, at its first session or as soon as practicable thereafter, consider ways to facilitate such cooperation, taking into account all relevant information.

2. The Parties included in Annex I shall pursue limitation or reduction of emissions of greenhouse gases not controlled by the *Montreal Protocol* from aviation and marine bunker fuels, working through the International Civil Aviation Organization and the International Maritime Organization, respectively.
3. The Parties included in Annex I shall strive to implement policies and measures under this Article in such a way as to minimize adverse effects, including the adverse effects of climate change, effects on international trade, and social, environmental and economic impacts on other Parties, especially developing country Parties and in particular those identified in Article 4, paragraphs 8 and 9, of the Convention, taking into account Article 3 of the Convention. The Conference of the Parties serving as the meeting of the Parties to this Protocol may take further action, as appropriate, to promote the implementation of the provisions of this paragraph.
4. The Conference of the Parties serving as the meeting of the Parties to this Protocol, if it decides that it would be beneficial to coordinate any of the policies and measures in paragraph 1(a) above, taking into account different national circumstances and potential effects, shall consider ways and means to elaborate the coordination of such policies and measures.

Article 3

1. The Parties included in Annex I shall, individually or jointly, ensure that their aggregate anthropogenic carbon dioxide equivalent emissions of the greenhouse gases listed in Annex A do not exceed their assigned amounts, calculated pursuant to their quantified emission limitation and reduction commitments inscribed in Annex B and in accordance with the provisions of this Article, with a view to reducing their overall emissions of such gases by at least 5 percent below 1990 levels in the commitment period 2008 to 2012.
2. Each Party included in Annex I shall, by 2005, have made demonstrable progress in achieving its commitments under this Protocol.
3. The net changes in greenhouse gas emissions by sources and removals by sinks resulting from direct human-induced land-use change and forestry activities, limited to afforestation, reforestation and deforestation since 1990, measured as verifiable changes in carbon stocks in each commitment period, shall be used to meet the commitments under this Article of each Party included in Annex I. The greenhouse gas emissions by sources and removals by sinks associated with those activities shall be reported in a transparent and verifiable manner and reviewed in accordance with Articles 7 and 8.
4. Prior to the first session of the Conference of the Parties serving as the meeting of the Parties to this Protocol, each Party included in Annex I shall provide, for consideration by the Subsidiary Body for Scientific and Technological Advice, data to establish its level of carbon stocks in 1990 and to enable an estimate to be made of its changes in carbon stocks in subsequent years. The Conference of the Parties serving as the meeting of the Parties to this Protocol shall, at its first session or as soon as practicable thereafter, decide upon modalities, rules and guidelines as to how, and which, additional human-induced activities related to changes in greenhouse gas emissions by sources and removals by sinks in the agricultural soils and the land-use change and forestry categories shall be added to, or subtracted from, the assigned amounts for Parties included in Annex I, taking into account uncertainties, transparency in reporting, verifiability, the methodological work of the Intergovernmental Panel on Climate Change, the advice provided by the Subsidiary Body for Scientific and Technological Advice in accordance with Article 5 and the decisions of the Conference of the Parties. Such a decision shall apply in the second and subsequent commitment periods. A

Party may choose to apply such a decision on these additional human-induced activities for its first commitment period, provided that these activities have taken place since 1990.

5. The Parties included in Annex I undergoing the process of transition to a market economy whose base year or period was established pursuant to decision 9/CP.2 of the Conference of the Parties at its second session shall use that base year or period for the implementation of their commitments under this Article. Any other Party included in Annex I undergoing the process of transition to a market economy which has not yet submitted its first national communication under Article 12 of the Convention may also notify the Conference of the Parties serving as the meeting of the Parties to this Protocol that it intends to use an historical base year or period other than 1990 for the implementation of its commitments under this Article. The Conference of the Parties serving as the meeting of the Parties to this Protocol shall decide on the acceptance of such notification.
6. Taking into account Article 4, paragraph 6, of the Convention, in the implementation of their commitments under this Protocol other than those under this Article, a certain degree of flexibility shall be allowed by the Conference of the Parties serving as the meeting of the Parties to this Protocol to the Parties included in Annex I undergoing the process of transition to a market economy.
7. In the first quantified emission limitation and reduction commitment period, from 2008 to 2012, the assigned amount for each Party included in Annex I shall be equal to the percentage inscribed for it in Annex B of its aggregate anthropogenic carbon dioxide equivalent emissions of the greenhouse gases listed in Annex A in 1990, or the base year or period determined in accordance with paragraph 5 above, multiplied by five. Those Parties included in Annex I for whom land-use change and forestry constituted a net source of greenhouse gas emissions in 1990 shall include in their 1990 emissions base year or period the aggregate anthropogenic carbon dioxide equivalent emissions by sources minus removals by sinks in 1990 from land-use change for the purposes of calculating their assigned amount.
8. Any Party included in Annex I may use 1995 as its base year for hydrofluorocarbons, perfluorocarbons and sulphur hexafluoride, for the purposes of the calculation referred to in paragraph 7 above.
9. Commitments for subsequent periods for Parties included in Annex I shall be established in amendments to Annex B to this Protocol, which shall be adopted in accordance with the provisions of Article 21, paragraph 7. The Conference of the Parties serving as the meeting of the Parties to this Protocol shall initiate the consideration of such commitments at least seven years before the end of the first commitment period referred to in paragraph 1 above.
10. Any emission reduction units, or any part of an assigned amount, which a Party acquires from another Party in accordance with the provisions of Article 6 or of Article 17 shall be added to the assigned amount for the acquiring Party.
11. Any emission reduction units, or any part of an assigned amount, which a Party transfers to another Party in accordance with the provisions of Article 6 or of Article 17 shall be subtracted from the assigned amount for the transferring Party.
12. Any certified emission reductions which a Party acquires from another Party in accordance with the provisions of Article 12 shall be added to the assigned amount for the acquiring Party.
13. If the emissions of a Party included in Annex I in a commitment period are less than its assigned amount under this Article, this difference shall, on request of that Party, be added to the assigned amount for that Party for subsequent commitment periods.
14. Each Party included in Annex I shall strive to implement the commitments mentioned in paragraph 1 above in such a way as to minimize adverse social, environmental and economic impacts on developing country Parties, particularly those identified in Article 4, paragraphs 8 and 9, of the Convention. In line with relevant decisions of the Conference of the Parties on the implementation of those paragraphs, the Conference of the Parties serving as the meeting of the Parties to this Protocol shall, at its first session, consider what actions are necessary to minimize the adverse effects of climate change and/or the impacts of response measures

on Parties referred to in those paragraphs. Among the issues to be considered shall be the establishment of funding, insurance and transfer of technology.

Article 4

1. Any Parties included in Annex I that have reached an agreement to fulfil their commitments under Article 3 jointly, shall be deemed to have met those commitments provided that their total combined aggregate anthropogenic carbon dioxide equivalent emissions of the greenhouse gases listed in Annex A do not exceed their assigned amounts calculated pursuant to their quantified emission limitation and reduction commitments inscribed in Annex B and in accordance with the provisions of Article 3. The respective emission level allocated to each of the Parties to the agreement shall be set out in that agreement.
2. The Parties to any such agreement shall notify the secretariat of the terms of the agreement on the date of deposit of their instruments of ratification, acceptance or approval of this Protocol, or accession thereto. The secretariat shall in turn inform the Parties and signatories to the Convention of the terms of the agreement.
3. Any such agreement shall remain in operation for the duration of the commitment period specified in Article 3, paragraph 7.
4. If Parties acting jointly do so in the framework of, and together with, a regional economic integration organization, any alteration in the composition of the organization after adoption of this Protocol shall not affect existing commitments under this Protocol. Any alteration in the composition of the organization shall only apply for the purposes of those commitments under Article 3 that are adopted subsequent to that alteration.
5. In the event of failure by the Parties to such an agreement to achieve their total combined level of emission reductions, each Party to that agreement shall be responsible for its own level of emissions set out in the agreement.
6. If Parties acting jointly do so in the framework of, and together with, a regional economic integration organization which is itself a Party to this Protocol, each member State of that regional economic integration organization individually, and together with the regional economic integration organization acting in accordance with Article 24, shall, in the event of failure to achieve the total combined level of emission reductions, be responsible for its level of emissions as notified in accordance with this Article.

Article 5

1. Each Party included in Annex I shall have in place, no later than one year prior to the start of the first commitment period, a national system for the estimation of anthropogenic emissions by sources and removals by sinks of all greenhouse gases not controlled by the Montreal Protocol. Guidelines for such national systems, which shall incorporate the methodologies specified in paragraph 2 below, shall be decided upon by the Conference of the Parties serving as the meeting of the Parties to this Protocol at its first session.
2. Methodologies for estimating anthropogenic emissions by sources and removals by sinks of all greenhouse gases not controlled by the *Montreal Protocol* shall be those accepted by the Intergovernmental Panel on Climate Change and agreed upon by the Conference of the Parties at its third session. Where such methodologies are not used, appropriate adjustments shall be applied according to methodologies agreed upon by the Conference of the Parties serving as the meeting of the Parties to this Protocol at its first session. Based on the work of, *inter alia*, the Intergovernmental Panel on Climate Change and advice provided by the Subsidiary Body for Scientific and Technological Advice, the Conference of the Parties serving as the meeting of the Parties to this Protocol shall regularly review and, as appropriate, revise such methodologies and adjustments, taking fully into account any relevant decisions by the Conference of the Parties. Any revision to methodologies or adjustments shall be used only for the purposes of ascertaining compliance with commitments under Article 3 in respect of any commitment period adopted subsequent to that revision.

3. The global warming potentials used to calculate the carbon dioxide equivalence of anthropogenic emissions by sources and removals by sinks of greenhouse gases listed in Annex A shall be those accepted by the Intergovernmental Panel on Climate Change and agreed upon by the Conference of the Parties at its third session. Based on the work of, *inter alia*, the Intergovernmental Panel on Climate Change and advice provided by the Subsidiary Body for Scientific and Technological Advice, the Conference of the Parties serving as the meeting of the Parties to this Protocol shall regularly review and, as appropriate, revise the global warming potential of each such greenhouse gas, taking fully into account any relevant decisions by the Conference of the Parties. Any revision to a global warming potential shall apply only to commitments under Article 3 in respect of any commitment period adopted subsequent to that revision.

Article 6

1. For the purpose of meeting its commitments under Article 3, any Party included in Annex I may transfer to, or acquire from, any other such Party emission reduction units resulting from projects aimed at reducing anthropogenic emissions by sources or enhancing anthropogenic removals by sinks of greenhouse gases in any sector of the economy, provided that:
   (a) Any such project has the approval of the Parties involved;
   (b) Any such project provides a reduction in emissions by sources, or an enhancement of removals by sinks, that is additional to any that would otherwise occur;
   (c) It does not acquire any emission reduction units if it is not in compliance with its obligations under Articles 5 and 7; and
   (d) The acquisition of emission reduction units shall be supplemental to domestic actions for the purposes of meeting commitments under Article 3.
2. The Conference of the Parties serving as the meeting of the Parties to this Protocol may, at its first session or as soon as practicable thereafter, further elaborate guidelines for the implementation of this Article, including for verification and reporting.
3. A Party included in Annex I may authorize legal entities to participate, under its responsibility, in actions leading to the generation, transfer or acquisition under this Article of emission reduction units.
4. If a question of implementation by a Party included in Annex I of the requirements referred to in this Article is identified in accordance with the relevant provisions of Article 8, transfers and acquisitions of emission reduction units may continue to be made after the question has been identified, provided that any such units may not be used by a Party to meet its commitments under Article 3 until any issue of compliance is resolved.

Article 7

1. Each Party included in Annex I shall incorporate in its annual inventory of anthropogenic emissions by sources and removals by sinks of greenhouse gases not controlled by the Montreal Protocol, submitted in accordance with the relevant decisions of the Conference of the Parties, the necessary supplementary information for the purposes of ensuring compliance with Article 3, to be determined in accordance with paragraph 4 below.
2. Each Party included in Annex I shall incorporate in its national communication, submitted under Article 12 of the Convention, the supplementary information necessary to demonstrate compliance with its commitments under this Protocol, to be determined in accordance with paragraph 4 below.
3. Each Party included in Annex I shall submit the information required under paragraph 1 above annually, beginning with the first inventory due under the Convention for the first year of the commitment period after this Protocol has entered into force for that Party. Each such Party shall submit the information required under paragraph 2 above as part of the first national communication due under the Convention after this Protocol has entered into force for it and after the adoption of guidelines as provided for in paragraph 4 below. The frequency of subsequent submission of information required under this Article shall be determined by the

Conference of the Parties serving as the meeting of the Parties to this Protocol, taking into account any timetable for the submission of national communications decided upon by the Conference of the Parties.

4. The Conference of the Parties serving as the meeting of the Parties to this Protocol shall adopt at its first session, and review periodically thereafter, guidelines for the preparation of the information required under this Article, taking into account guidelines for the preparation of national communications by Parties included in Annex I adopted by the Conference of the Parties. The Conference of the Parties serving as the meeting of the Parties to this Protocol shall also, prior to the first commitment period, decide upon modalities for the accounting of assigned amounts.

Article 8

1. The information submitted under Article 7 by each Party included in Annex I shall be reviewed by expert review teams pursuant to the relevant decisions of the Conference of the Parties and in accordance with guidelines adopted for this purpose by the Conference of the Parties serving as the meeting of the Parties to this Protocol under paragraph 4 below. The information submitted under Article 7, paragraph 1, by each Party included in Annex I shall be reviewed as part of the annual compilation and accounting of emissions inventories and assigned amounts. Additionally, the information submitted under Article 7, paragraph 2, by each Party included in Annex I shall be reviewed as part of the review of communications.
2. Expert review teams shall be coordinated by the secretariat and shall be composed of experts selected from those nominated by Parties to the Convention and, as appropriate, by intergovernmental organizations, in accordance with guidance provided for this purpose by the Conference of the Parties.
3. The review process shall provide a thorough and comprehensive technical assessment of all aspects of the implementation by a Party of this Protocol. The expert review teams shall prepare a report to the Conference of the Parties serving as the meeting of the Parties to this Protocol, assessing the implementation of the commitments of the Party and identifying any potential problems in, and factors influencing, the fulfilment of commitments. Such reports shall be circulated by the secretariat to all Parties to the Convention. The secretariat shall list those questions of implementation indicated in such reports for further consideration by the Conference of the Parties serving as the meeting of the Parties to this Protocol.
4. The Conference of the Parties serving as the meeting of the Parties to this Protocol shall adopt at its first session, and review periodically thereafter, guidelines for the review of implementation of this Protocol by expert review teams taking into account the relevant decisions of the Conference of the Parties.
5. The Conference of the Parties serving as the meeting of the Parties to this Protocol shall, with the assistance of the Subsidiary Body for Implementation and, as appropriate, the Subsidiary Body for Scientific and Technological Advice, consider:
   (a) The information submitted by Parties under Article 7 and the reports of the expert reviews thereon conducted under this Article; and
   (b) Those questions of implementation listed by the secretariat under paragraph 3 above, as well as any questions raised by Parties.
6. Pursuant to its consideration of the information referred to in paragraph 5 above, the Conference of the Parties serving as the meeting of the Parties to this Protocol shall take decisions on any matter required for the implementation of this Protocol.

Article 9

1. The Conference of the Parties serving as the meeting of the Parties to this Protocol shall periodically review this Protocol in the light of the best available scientific information and assessments on climate change and its impacts, as well as relevant technical, social and economic information. Such reviews shall be coordinated with pertinent reviews under the Convention, in particular those required by Article 4, paragraph 2(d), and Article 7, paragraph 2(a), of the Convention. Based on these reviews, the Conference of the Parties serving as the meeting of

the Parties to this Protocol shall take appropriate action.

2. The first review shall take place at the second session of the Conference of the Parties serving as the meeting of the Parties to this Protocol. Further reviews shall take place at regular intervals and in a timely manner.

Article 10

All Parties, taking into account their common but differentiated responsibilities and their specific national and regional development priorities, objectives and circumstances, without introducing any new commitments for Parties not included in Annex I, but reaffirming existing commitments under Article 4, paragraph 1, of the Convention, and continuing to advance the implementation of these commitments in order to achieve sustainable development, taking into account Article 4, paragraphs 3, 5 and 7, of the Convention, shall:

(a) Formulate, where relevant and to the extent possible, cost-effective national and, where appropriate, regional programs to improve the quality of local emission factors, activity data and/or models which reflect the socio-economic conditions of each Party for the preparation and periodic updating of national inventories of anthropogenic emissions by sources and removals by sinks of all greenhouse gases not controlled by the Montreal Protocol, using comparable methodologies to be agreed upon by the Conference of the Parties, and consistent with the guidelines for the preparation of national communications adopted by the Conference of the Parties;

(b) Formulate, implement, publish and regularly update national and, where appropriate, regional programs containing measures to mitigate climate change and measures to facilitate adequate adaptation to climate change:

(i) Such programs would, *inter alia*, concern the energy, transport and industry sectors as well as agriculture, forestry and waste management. Furthermore, adaptation technologies and methods for improving spatial planning would improve adaptation to climate change; and

(ii) Parties included in Annex I shall submit information on action under this Protocol, including national programs, in accordance with Article 7; and other Parties shall seek to include in their national communications, as appropriate, information on programs which contain measures that the Party believes contribute to addressing climate change and its adverse impacts, including the abatement of increases in greenhouse gas emissions, and enhancement of and removals by sinks, capacity building and adaptation measures;

(c) Cooperate in the promotion of effective modalities for the development, application and diffusion of, and take all practicable steps to promote, facilitate and finance, as appropriate, the transfer of, or access to, environmentally sound technologies, know-how, practices and processes pertinent to climate change, in particular to developing countries, including the formulation of policies and programs for the effective transfer of environmentally sound technologies that are publicly owned or in the public domain and the creation of an enabling environment for the private sector, to promote and enhance the transfer of, and access to, environmentally sound technologies;

(d) Cooperate in scientific and technical research and promote the maintenance and the development of systematic observation systems and development of data archives to reduce uncertainties related to the climate system, the adverse impacts of climate change and the economic and social consequences of various response strategies, and promote the development and strengthening of endogenous capacities and capabilities to participate in international and intergovernmental efforts, programs and networks on research and systematic observation, taking into account Article 5 of the Convention;

(e) Cooperate in and promote at the international level, and, where appropriate, using existing bodies, the development and implementation of education and training programs, including the strengthening of national capacity building, in particular human and institutional capacities and the exchange or secondment of personnel to train experts in this field, in particular for developing countries, and facilitate at the national level public awareness of, and public access to information on, climate change. Suitable modalities should be developed to implement these activities through the relevant bodies of the Convention, taking into account Article 6 of the Convention;

(f) Include in their national communications information on programs and activities undertaken pursuant to this Article in accordance with relevant decisions of the Conference of the Parties; and

(g) Give full consideration, in implementing the commitments under this Article, to Article 4, paragraph 8, of the Convention.

Article 11

1. In the implementation of Article 10, Parties shall take into account the provisions of Article 4, paragraphs 4, 5, 7, 8 and 9, of the Convention.
2. In the context of the implementation of Article 4, paragraph 1, of the Convention, in accordance with the provisions of Article 4, paragraph 3, and Article 11 of the Convention, and through the entity or entities entrusted with the operation of the financial mechanism of the Convention, the developed country Parties and other developed Parties included in Annex II to the Convention shall:
   (a) Provide new and additional financial resources to meet the agreed full costs incurred by developing country Parties in advancing the implementation of existing commitments under Article 4, paragraph 1(a), of the Convention that are covered in Article 10, subparagraph (a); and
   (b) Also provide such financial resources, including for the transfer of technology, needed by the developing country Parties to meet the agreed full incremental costs of advancing the implementation of existing commitments under Article 4, paragraph 1, of the Convention that are covered by Article 10 and that are agreed between a developing country Party and the international entity or entities referred to in Article 11 of the Convention, in accordance with that Article.

   The implementation of these existing commitments shall take into account the need for adequacy and predictability in the flow of funds and the importance of appropriate burden sharing among developed country Parties. The guidance to the entity or entities entrusted with the operation of the financial mechanism of the Convention in relevant decisions of the Conference of the Parties, including those agreed before the adoption of this Protocol, shall apply *mutatis mutandis* to the provisions of this paragraph.
3. The developed country Parties and other developed Parties in Annex II to the Convention may also provide, and developing country Parties avail themselves of, financial resources for the implementation of Article 10, through bilateral, regional and other multilateral channels.

Article 12

1. A clean development mechanism is hereby defined.
2. The purpose of the clean development mechanism shall be to assist Parties not included in Annex I in achieving sustainable development and in contributing to the ultimate objective of the Convention, and to assist Parties included in Annex I in achieving compliance with their quantified emission limitation and reduction commitments under Article 3.
3. Under the clean development mechanism:
   (a) Parties not included in Annex I will benefit from project activities resulting in certified emission reductions; and
   (b) Parties included in Annex I may use the certified emission reductions accruing from such project activities to contribute to compliance with part of their quantified emission limitation and reduction commitments under Article 3, as determined by the Conference of the Parties serving as the meeting of the Parties to this Protocol.
4. The clean development mechanism shall be subject to the authority and guidance of the Conference of the Parties serving as the meeting of the Parties to this Protocol and be supervised by an executive board of the clean development mechanism.

5. Emission reductions resulting from each project activity shall be certified by operational entities to be designated by the Conference of the Parties serving as the meeting of the Parties to this Protocol, on the basis of:
   (a) Voluntary participation approved by each Party involved;
   (b) Real, measurable, and long-term benefits related to the mitigation of climate change; and
   (c) Reductions in emissions that are additional to any that would occur in the absence of the certified project activity.
6. The clean development mechanism shall assist in arranging funding of certified project activities as necessary.
7. The Conference of the Parties serving as the meeting of the Parties to this Protocol shall, at its first session, elaborate modalities and procedures with the objective of ensuring transparency, efficiency and accountability through independent auditing and verification of project activities.
8. The Conference of the Parties serving as the meeting of the Parties to this Protocol shall ensure that a share of the proceeds from certified project activities is used to cover administrative expenses as well as to assist developing country Parties that are particularly vulnerable to the adverse effects of climate change to meet the costs of adaptation.
9. Participation under the clean development mechanism, including in activities mentioned in paragraph 3(a) above and in the acquisition of certified emission reductions, may involve private and/or public entities, and is to be subject to whatever guidance may be provided by the executive board of the clean development mechanism.
10. Certified emission reductions obtained during the period from the year 2000 up to the beginning of the first commitment period can be used to assist in achieving compliance in the first commitment period.

Article 13

1. The Conference of the Parties, the supreme body of the Convention, shall serve as the meeting of the Parties to this Protocol.
2. Parties to the Convention that are not Parties to this Protocol may participate as observers in the proceedings of any session of the Conference of the Parties serving as the meeting of the Parties to this Protocol. When the Conference of the Parties serves as the meeting of the Parties to this Protocol, decisions under this Protocol shall be taken only by those that are Parties to this Protocol.
3. When the Conference of the Parties serves as the meeting of the Parties to this Protocol, any member of the Bureau of the Conference of the Parties representing a Party to the Convention but, at that time, not a Party to this Protocol, shall be replaced by an additional member to be elected by and from amongst the Parties to this Protocol.
4. The Conference of the Parties serving as the meeting of the Parties to this Protocol shall keep under regular review the implementation of this Protocol and shall make, within its mandate, the decisions necessary to promote its effective implementation. It shall perform the functions assigned to it by this Protocol and shall:
   (a) Assess, on the basis of all information made available to it in accordance with the provisions of this Protocol, the implementation of this Protocol by the Parties, the overall effects of the measures taken pursuant to this Protocol, in particular environmental, economic and social effects as well as their cumulative impacts and the extent to which progress towards the objective of the Convention is being achieved;
   (b) Periodically examine the obligations of the Parties under this Protocol, giving due consideration to any reviews required by Article 4, paragraph 2(d), and Article 7, paragraph 2, of the Convention, in the light of the objective of the Convention, the experience gained in its implementation and the evolution of scientific and technological knowledge, and in this respect consider and adopt regular reports on the implementation of this Protocol;
   (c) Promote and facilitate the exchange of information on measures adopted by the Parties to address climate change and its effects, taking into account the differing circumstances, responsibilities and capabilities of the Parties and their respective commitments under this Protocol;

(d) Facilitate, at the request of two or more Parties, the coordination of measures adopted by them to address climate change and its effects, taking into account the differing circumstances, responsibilities and capabilities of the Parties and their respective commitments under this Protocol;
(e) Promote and guide, in accordance with the objective of the Convention and the provisions of this Protocol, and taking fully into account the relevant decisions by the Conference of the Parties, the development and periodic refinement of comparable methodologies for the effective implementation of this Protocol, to be agreed on by the Conference of the Parties serving as the meeting of the Parties to this Protocol;
(f) Make recommendations on any matters necessary for the implementation of this Protocol;
(g) Seek to mobilize additional financial resources in accordance with Article 11, paragraph 2;
(h) Establish such subsidiary bodies as are deemed necessary for the implementation of this Protocol;
(i) Seek and utilize, where appropriate, the services and cooperation of, and information provided by, competent international organizations and intergovernmental and nongovernmental bodies; and
(j) Exercise such other functions as may be required for the implementation of this Protocol, and consider any assignment resulting from a decision by the Conference of the Parties.

5. The rules of procedure of the Conference of the Parties and financial procedures applied under the Convention shall be applied *mutatis mutandis* under this Protocol, except as may be otherwise decided by consensus by the Conference of the Parties serving as the meeting of the Parties to this Protocol.
6. The first session of the Conference of the Parties serving as the meeting of the Parties to this Protocol shall be convened by the secretariat in conjunction with the first session of the Conference of the Parties that is scheduled after the date of the entry into force of this Protocol. Subsequent ordinary sessions of the Conference of the Parties serving as the meeting of the Parties to this Protocol shall be held every year and in conjunction with ordinary sessions of the Conference of the Parties, unless otherwise decided by the Conference of the Parties serving as the meeting of the Parties to this Protocol.
7. Extraordinary sessions of the Conference of the Parties serving as the meeting of the Parties to this Protocol shall be held at such other times as may be deemed necessary by the Conference of the Parties serving as the meeting of the Parties to this Protocol, or at the written request of any Party, provided that, within six months of the request being communicated to the Parties by the secretariat, it is supported by at least one third of the Parties.
8. The United Nations, its specialized agencies and the International Atomic Energy Agency, as well as any State member thereof or observers thereto not party to the Convention, may be represented at sessions of the Conference of the Parties serving as the meeting of the Parties to this Protocol as observers. Any body or agency, whether national or international, governmental or nongovernmental, which is qualified in matters covered by this Protocol and which has informed the secretariat of its wish to be represented at a session of the Conference of the Parties serving as the meeting of the Parties to this Protocol as an observer, may be so admitted unless at least one third of the Parties present object. The admission and participation of observers shall be subject to the rules of procedure, as referred to in paragraph 5 above.

Article 14

1. The secretariat established by Article 8 of the Convention shall serve as the secretariat of this Protocol.
2. Article 8, paragraph 2, of the Convention on the functions of the secretariat, and Article 8, paragraph 3, of the Convention on arrangements made for the functioning of the secretariat, shall apply *mutatis mutandis* to this Protocol. The secretariat shall, in addition, exercise the functions assigned to it under this Protocol.

Article 15

1. The Subsidiary Body for Scientific and Technological Advice and the Subsidiary Body for Implementation established by Articles 9 and 10 of the Convention shall serve as, respectively, the Subsidiary Body for Scientific and Technological Advice and the Subsidiary Body for Implementation of this Protocol. The provisions relating to the functioning of these two bodies under the Convention shall apply *mutatis mutandis* to this Protocol. Sessions of the meetings of the Subsidiary Body for Scientific and Technological Advice and the Subsidiary Body for Implementation of this Protocol shall be held in conjunction with the meetings of, respectively, the Subsidiary Body for Scientific and Technological Advice and the Subsidiary Body for Implementation of the Convention.
2. Parties to the Convention that are not Parties to this Protocol may participate as observers in the proceedings of any session of the subsidiary bodies. When the subsidiary bodies serve as the subsidiary bodies of this Protocol, decisions under this Protocol shall be taken only by those that are Parties to this Protocol.
3. When the subsidiary bodies established by Articles 9 and 10 of the Convention exercise their functions with regard to matters concerning this Protocol, any member of the Bureaux of those subsidiary bodies representing a Party to the Convention but, at that time, not a party to this Protocol, shall be replaced by an additional member to be elected by and from amongst the Parties to this Protocol.

Article 16

The Conference of the Parties serving as the meeting of the Parties to this Protocol shall, as soon as practicable, consider the application to this Protocol of, and modify as appropriate, the multilateral consultative process referred to in Article 13 of the Convention, in the light of any relevant decisions that may be taken by the Conference of the Parties. Any multilateral consultative process that may be applied to this Protocol shall operate without prejudice to the procedures and mechanisms established in accordance with Article 18.

Article 17

The Conference of the Parties shall define the relevant principles, modalities, rules and guidelines, in particular for verification, reporting and accountability for emissions trading. The Parties included in Annex B may participate in emissions trading for the purposes of fulfilling their commitments under Article 3. Any such trading shall be supplemental to domestic actions for the purpose of meeting quantified emission limitation and reduction commitments under that Article.

Article 18

The Conference of the Parties serving as the meeting of the Parties to this Protocol shall, at its first session, approve appropriate and effective procedures and mechanisms to determine and to address cases of non-compliance with the provisions of this Protocol, including through the development of an indicative list of consequences, taking into account the cause, type, degree and frequency of non-compliance. Any procedures and mechanisms under this Article entailing binding consequences shall be adopted by means of an amendment to this Protocol.

Article 19

The provisions of Article 14 of the Convention on settlement of disputes shall apply *mutatis mutandis* to this Protocol.

Article 20

1. Any Party may propose amendments to this Protocol.
2. Amendments to this Protocol shall be adopted at an ordinary session of the Conference of the Parties serving as the meeting of the Parties to this Protocol. The text of any proposed amendment to this Protocol shall be communicated to the Parties by the secretariat at least six months before the meeting at which it is proposed for adoption. The secretariat shall also communicate the text of any proposed amendments to the Parties and signatories to the Convention and, for information, to the Depositary.
3. The Parties shall make every effort to reach agreement on any proposed amendment to this Protocol by consensus. If all efforts at consensus have been exhausted, and no agreement reached, the amendment shall as a last resort be adopted by a three-fourths majority vote of the Parties present and voting at the meeting. The adopted amendment

shall be communicated by the secretariat to the Depositary, who shall circulate it to all Parties for their acceptance.

4. Instruments of acceptance in respect of an amendment shall be deposited with the Depositary. An amendment adopted in accordance with paragraph 3 above shall enter into force for those Parties having accepted it on the ninetieth day after the date of receipt by the Depositary of an instrument of acceptance by at least three fourths of the Parties to this Protocol.
5. The amendment shall enter into force for any other Party on the ninetieth day after the date on which that Party deposits with the Depositary its instrument of acceptance of the said amendment.

Article 21

1. Annexes to this Protocol shall form an integral part thereof and, unless otherwise expressly provided, a reference to this Protocol constitutes at the same time a reference to any annexes thereto. Any annexes adopted after the entry into force of this Protocol shall be restricted to lists, forms and any other material of a descriptive nature that is of a scientific, technical, procedural or administrative character.
2. Any Party may make proposals for an annex to this Protocol and may propose amendments to annexes to this Protocol.
3. Annexes to this Protocol and amendments to annexes to this Protocol shall be adopted at an ordinary session of the Conference of the Parties serving as the meeting of the Parties to this Protocol. The text of any proposed annex or amendment to an annex shall be communicated to the Parties by the secretariat at least six months before the meeting at which it is proposed for adoption. The secretariat shall also communicate the text of any proposed annex or amendment to an annex to the Parties and signatories to the Convention and, for information, to the Depositary.
4. The Parties shall make every effort to reach agreement on any proposed annex or amendment to an annex by consensus. If all efforts at consensus have been exhausted, and no agreement reached, the annex or amendment to an annex shall as a last resort be adopted by a three-fourths majority vote of the Parties present and voting at the meeting. The adopted annex or amendment to an annex shall be communicated by the secretariat to the Depositary, who shall circulate it to all Parties for their acceptance.
5. An annex, or amendment to an annex other than Annex A or B, that has been adopted in accordance with paragraphs 3 and 4 above shall enter into force for all Parties to this Protocol six months after the date of the communication by the Depositary to such Parties of the adoption of the annex or adoption of the amendment to the annex, except for those Parties that have notified the Depositary, in writing, within that period of their non-acceptance of the annex or amendment to the annex. The annex or amendment to an annex shall enter into force for Parties which withdraw their notification of non-acceptance on the ninetieth day after the date on which withdrawal of such notification has been received by the Depositary.
6. If the adoption of an annex or an amendment to an annex involves an amendment to this Protocol, that annex or amendment to an annex shall not enter into force until such time as the amendment to this Protocol enters into force.
7. Amendments to Annexes A and B to this Protocol shall be adopted and enter into force in accordance with the procedure set out in Article 20, provided that any amendment to Annex B shall be adopted only with the written consent of the Party concerned.

Article 22

1. Each Party shall have one vote, except as provided for in paragraph 2 below.
2. Regional economic integration organizations, in matters within their competence, shall exercise their right to vote with a number of votes equal to the number of their member States that are Parties to this Protocol. Such an organization shall not exercise its right to vote if any of its member States exercises its right, and vice versa.

Article 23

The Secretary-General of the United Nations shall be the Depositary of this Protocol.

4

Flexibility of Mechanisms Under the *Kyoto Protocol*

A

Jeffery M. and Baird W., "Using Market-Based Incentives to Curtail Greenhouse Gas Emissions: Factors to Consider in the Design of the Clean Air Development Mechanism, Joint Implementation and Emissions Trading," *Asia Pacific Journal of Environmental Law*, 2001, pp 19–28

Identification of the Major Issues with respect to the Three Flexibility Mechanisms Under the Protocol

Article 12—Clean Development Mechanism

In analysing the principal causes for the collapse of the COP6 negotiations it appears that, by necessity, accommodation will have to be reached by the principal antagonists on the fundamental uses of the flexibility mechanisms. It is unlikely that the key provisions of the *Kyoto Protocol* will be rewritten in their entirety or open for future negotiation. The concept of carbon sinks forms an integral part of Article 3 of the Protocol. The debate since the Protocol has been signed has been over to what extent can carbon offsets be utilized by Annex 1 Parties in meeting their commitments. In the context of the CDM this debate centres on the use of sinks in CDM projects and the relationship between sinks in the CDM and sinks under Articles 3.3 and 3.4 of the Protocol. These issues are considered in detail later in this paper.

Emissions trading was also a last minute compromise at Kyoto, without which agreement may not have been reached. It is unlikely to be dispensed with as a flexibility mechanism as a result of future negotiations. The debate on emissions trading has centered on the *extent* to which carbon credits may be utilized to offset domestic reductions by Annex 1 Parties, rather than elimination of their use entirely. In the context of the CDM and Article 17 (emissions trading), the debate includes the trading, as well, of CERs in any global trading system that comes into existence.

The CDM provides the only basis within the confines of the Protocol for the inclusion of non-Annex 1 Parties to participate in the global reduction of greenhouse gases strategy at this point in time. Given the historical fact that non-Annex 1 Parties bear little responsibility for global warming resulting from human-induced emission of greenhouse gases, there is a persuasive argument for treating these countries differently when considering reduction targets. An argument presented by non-Annex 1 Parties is that, their development ought not be inhibited by compelling them to adhere to limitations or reductions on emission of greenhouse gases, and thereby placing them at a disadvantage not incurred by developed countries during their industrialization.

Parties to the Kyoto negotiations sought to address, on the one hand, the issue of bringing in the developing countries into what was perceived to be a global initiative, while on the other, providing the necessary economic stimulus for the developed countries to invest in and facilitate sustainable development through, inter alia, the transfer of technology in accordance with the objectives outlined in the Brundtland Report. At the same time Annex 1 Parties faced with the possibility of enormous economic cost to reduce domestic emissions needed a way of meeting their reduction targets without such cost. The option to do so was provided, in part, by way of the CDM.

This appeared to meet the objective of promoting, rather than inhibiting, development within undeveloped countries in a manner that would not contribute to global warming and, ideally, contribute to a reduction in the emission of greenhouse gases. In time the non-Annex 1 Parties were expected to enter into emission limitation and reduction commitments in a similar manner to those agreed to by Annex-1 Parties.

At COP6 the role of the CDM vis-à-vis the Parties' technology transfer commitments under the UNFCCC, were the subject of serious debate. The US, Australia, Canada, Japan and New Zealand at COP6 continued to acknowledge the potential of the CDM to facilitate and finance the transfer of environmentally-sound technologies, to enable parties to meet the provisions of the UNFCCC. Brazil with China and Thailand strongly objected to a US proposal that made reference to technology transfer and the CDM, opposing any attempts to link technology transfer under the UNFCCC to the Protocol

A number of further contentious issues relating to CDM came to the fore and fundamental differences on these issues were partly responsible for the failure of the negotiations. Some of the issues of major concern are discussed below.

Project Eligibility and Certification (Article 12.5)

This issue concerns the determination of the eligibility of projects for inclusion in the CDM and whether there should be an attempt to formulate a list of such projects or rely on some other basis for inclusion.

The EU and Hungry argued for a positive list. Japan, Australia, the US, Canada and Saudi Arabia expressed a preference for no positive list. G77/China argued that the host developing countries ought to be the sole decider on projects. The Africa group expressed concern with a proposal that submission of 'national communication' be a pre-condition for CDM participation. The U.S. expressed flexibility on the potential for small projects on condition that there was no positive list and that sinks were included. Honduras, Saudi Arabia and Hungry argued against the inclusion of nuclear power in the CDM and Australia said it was for the individual developing countries to decide. Additional issues relating to fast-tracking small projects, using nuclear facilities for generating CERs, giving expedited consideration to energy efficient improvements and renewable energy projects, and equitable distribution of CDM projects, were discussed.

Diverse views were expressed on the eligibility of Land Use, Land-Use Change, and Forest projects (LULUCF projects). Although the Parties failed to reach a compromise on these issues by the conclusion of COP6, the majority of the Parties appeared to favour no list for project eligibility.

Additionality (Article 12.5(c))

Article 12.5(c) of the Protocol requires that activities resulting in certified emission reductions must be '*additional*' to any that would occur in the absence of the certified project activity. This additionality requirement under the CDM has triggered concern on the part of those who are opposed to the inclusion of sinks, as it may be difficult to determine whether land clearing or other forms of deforestation may have occurred in the absence of the CDM activity. It is worth noting, however, that the principle of additionality (with specific reference to 'an enhancement of removals by sinks' that is additional to any that would otherwise occur) must also be applied to the generation of ERUs from JI projects under Article 6.

Supplementarity

The issue of supplementarity, i.e. the degree to which the flexibility mechanism may be used as a substitute to domestic action to reduce emissions in the context of the debate surrounding the CDM, emerged as one of the more contentious issues. The extent of this is to be determined by COP (MoP).

France, on behalf of the EU, stressed that domestic actions should be the main means for fulfilling developed country commitments.

France, on behalf of the EU, stressed that domestic actions should be the main means for fulfilling developed country commitments. Switzerland, on behalf of the Environmental Integrity Group (a coalition of countries including Switzerland, Mexico and the Republic of Korea) said the CDM should be based on an incremental approach, JI should follow a two-track approach, and emissions trading should be linked to the nature and scope of the enforcement branch of the compliance regime. Indonesia favored requiring 70 percent of the reductions to be as a result of domestic action, which could be reduced under certain conditions. Hungary and the Africa Group, opposed by the Russian Federation and Australia, advocated implementation of a quantitative limitation on the flexibility mechanisms while Japan and the US argued against renegotiating the Protocol.

The Inclusion of 'Sinks' in the CDM

This issue has been the subject of much debate both before and during the COP6 negotiations. Several developed countries have long argued for the inclusion of sink activities within the CDM, although there is no reference to sinks in Article 12.

Those countries that have argued for the inclusion of sink activity in all three flexibility mechanisms, which include Australia and the US, do so on the basis that, in part, the mechanisms be used to their *full* potential including the delivery of maximum economic and environmental benefits and participation by a wide range of countries.

Major concerns regarding the inclusion of sinks revolve around issues of permanence, carbon leakage, socio-economic impacts to the host country, impacts in the form of delays on the development of renewable forms of energy, monitoring and verification, and the potential impact on the impetus to reduce emissions at source in the Annex 1 Parties.

Many of these issues were considered at some length in the IPCC Special Report on Land Use, Land-Use Change and Forestry and options for dealing with them were examined. Some experience has been gained through pilot projects conducted under '*activities implemented jointly*' provisions of the UNFCCC. This Report noted that some pilot projects, which are designed to avoid emissions by deforestation and forest degradation, have, in some cases, produced marked environmental and socioeconomic co-benefits. These include biodiversity conservation, protection of watershed and water resources, improved forest management, local capacity building and employment and local enterprise.

As a way of mitigating potential negative socio-economic impacts various suggestions have been made regarding the eligibility of projects to be part of the CDM. These include the formulation of a positive list, a proposal that does not appear to have found favour amongst a majority of Parties at COP6, and the provision of a 'screening test' to be applied to most projects. The screening test approach has been suggested by the IPPC in their special report. Such a test would appear to envisage the application of various EIA standards and guidelines to carbon offset projects limiting the accrediting of activities under the CDM to those that pass the screening test.

The debate has, in part, focussed on sinks in the land-use change and forestry area drawing in this regard on discussion and work done in regard to Article 3 and the confinement of sinks in Article 3.3 to those resulting from 'direct human-induced land-use change and forestry activities, limited to afforestation, reforestation and deforestation since 1990. The debate on Article 3.4 as to 'which additional human-induced activities related to changes in greenhouse gas emissions by sources and removals by sinks in the agricultural soils and the land-use change and forestry categories' ought to be added to or subtracted from Annex 1 Parties' assigned amounts, also has a bearing on the debate as to the inclusion and scope of sinks in the flexibility mechanisms.

Under the *Kyoto Protocol*, as mentioned above, sink activities are not explicitly referred to under Article 12 (the CDM provision) and hence the restrictions in the Protocol on the scope of inclusion of sinks domestically in the meeting of Annex 1 Parties' commitments, do not appear to *automatically* apply to the inclusion of sinks in the CDM.

Perhaps the greatest division occurs between those who argue that the inclusion of sinks in the flexibility mechanisms is essential for the full and proper functioning of the Protocol and is indeed necessary to ensure the very ratification of the Protocol, and those who argue that such inclusion of sinks in the flexibility mechanisms (and the inclusion of additional sink activities under Article 3.4) is 'against the spirit of the *Kyoto Protocol* and creates 'loopholes' in national commitments. In this regard the Senate Environment, Communications, Information Technology and the Arts Reference Committee of the Australian Parliament expressed concern at continued perceptions of Australians attempting to maximize potential loopholes in these aspects of the *Kyoto Protocol*. While the Committee was unclear that this was the case, they were of the view that the strength of these perceptions could not be overlooked.

Funding for CDM Projects

Several non-Annex 1 Parties have expressed concern over the relationship between funding for the CDM and projects under it, and the financial mechanism of the UNFCCC. NGOs and various environmental research bodies have also raised concerns over this relationship. Concerns exist that Annex 1 Parties will have little incentive to fund the GEF or other development assistance institutions when they are able to gain CERs by financing the CDM.

Under Protocol Article 12.8, COP (MoP) must ensure that a share of the proceeds from certified project activities is used to cover administrative expenses as well as to assist developing country Parties that are particularly vulnerable to the adverse effects of climate change to meet the costs of adaptation.

At COP6, G77/China, the Africa Group, and Samoa, wanted the establishment of an adaptation fund based on a levy applied to all three flexibility mechanisms. This was opposed by the US, Canada, Japan, the Russian Federation, Hungry and Australia. Japan (opposed by China and Indonesia) supported using the UN Overseas Development Agency (ODA) funding for CDM funding.

Compliance

The issue concerning the nature of the 'compliance system' contemplated under Article 14 of the Protocol and to be determined by the COP (MoP) was the subject of heated debate at COP6 and was one of the 'crunch' issues. The positions taken by various Parties, was divergent to say the least. Poland on behalf of the Central Group Eleven wanted the treatment of non-compliance to be based on the nature of the commitment, not based on the Parties, while the Russian Federation called for flexibility for countries with economies in transition. South Africa joined the G-77/China in supporting a strong compliance system with mandatory consequences. China went on to stress that since non-compliance affects everyone, not only the trading partners of Annex 1 Parties, this must be reflected in the composition of the Compliance Committee.

The EU countries took a strong position in favor of legally-binding consequences for non-compliance arguing that this was justified both by concerns over the environmental integrity of the Protocol as well as by the necessity to provide the private sector with the confidence needed for the use of the mechanisms.

The US, while acknowledging the possibility of legally-binding consequences, argued that they need not be punitive and supported a deduction from the following commitment period with a 1.3 percent penalty rate as well as a restriction on the transfer of units also applicable to joint fulfilment Parties under Article 4.

Australia and the Russian Federation argued for a non-binding regime indicating concern about their own compliance capabilities.

Article 17—Emissions Trading

As indicated above, emissions trading has been utilized by several jurisdictions as a method of inducing regulatory compliance in a more cost efficient manner. The basic concept underlying emissions trading schemes is to provide an economic incentive to further an environmental goal at a lower cost than would otherwise be incurred through some other abatement measure. In the context of the current greenhouse gas emissions debate, acquiring carbon credits could, in some circumstances, provide regulated industry with the ability to stay in compliance with their domestic emission permits rather than to undertake other more costly abatement measures such as reducing production or installing more expensive pollution control equipment. Conversely industries with low abatement costs may generate excess credits, which may be traded at a profit.

This ability to profit from excess credits has the potential to stimulate the development of innovative technology to further lower compliance costs and also to increase profit. Ideally, the end result is the achievement of the environmental goal as determined by the particular jurisdiction and embodied in its domestic legislation and regulations. In the context of the UNFCCC, the environmental goal has been determined by the international community.

Under Article 17, Annex B Parties may participate in emissions trading to meet their reduction commitments under the Protocol. Annex 1 Parties have agreed to ensure that individually or jointly their emission of greenhouse gases will not exceed their assigned amounts. This is with a view to reducing their overall emissions of such gases by at least 5 percent below 1990 levels in the first commitment period.

In order to consider emissions trading in a practical context, it is necessary to establish a standardized or 'fungible' unit of trade which, under a global emissions trading scheme, will be referred to as an 'Assigned Amount Unit (AAU)'. The further issue of whether the AAUs derived from JI under Article 6, (resulting in the generation of ERUs, or from the CDM under Article 12, (resulting in the generation of CERs), may be traded pursuant to the emissions trading scheme contemplated under Article 17, will be dealt with later in this paper. It is of particular relevance to note, however, that AAUs, when acquired or transferred by one Party to another, *from whatever source*, may be added to or deducted from the relevant Party's assigned amount.

It would be up to the Annex B Party as to whether and how trading is devolved to legal entities over which the Party has jurisdiction. This would require that the design of any domestic trading scheme used by a Party to assist it in meeting its international commitments was implemented in a manner that was compatible with the terms of the Protocol. It is clear, therefore, that major issues must be confronted also at the domestic level. Some of these issues are considered below.

The Creation of Markets for Emission Credits

The Protocol itself has little to say on the creation and development of markets for the trading in emissions credits, other than to leave the defining of the '*relevant principles, modalities, rules and guidelines, in particular for verification, reporting and accountability for emissions trading*', to the Conference of the Parties to the UNFCCC.

Markets for emissions credits may evolve through a number of stages. They include:

- direct bilateral swaps between a buyer and seller,
- over-the-counter trading (OTC) whereby sellers provide details of what they are offering and buyers react by judging the inherent risks involved, which, in part, determines price,
- the product being traded, becoming standardized and fungible with the other elements of a public trading system being put in place, including independent verification, accounting and documentation standards, electronic depositories, etc.
- continuous trading, with market bid and offer price moving with supply and demand.

As with any emissions trading scheme it is necessary to ensure that the appropriate infrastructure is in place.

The Commodity Being Traded

Most of the interest and development of carbon trading to this point in time has revolved around carbon sequestration credits involving carbon sinks. In the development that has taken place to date, the commodity to be traded, derived from 'Kyoto consistent' forests (that is, forests planted after 1 January 1990, managed by human activity and resulting in a land-use change limited to afforestation, reafforestation and deforestation), is being defined as the perpetual storage of one ton of carbon dioxide (CO_2) equivalent emissions. Units of sequestered carbon credits (or 'Assigned Amount Units,' AAUs) would be identified and embodied in a certificate and traded over the exchange like any other commodity.

Eventually, as standardization and fungibility concerns are addressed, these AAUs are expected to be fully integrated with the other flexibility mechanisms set out in the Protocol.

Additional 'Human Induced Activities'—Article 3.4

Considerable debate is now occurring with respect to what additional human induced activities related to changes in greenhouse gas emissions by sources and removals by sinks in the agricultural soils category, and additional to afforestation, reforestation and deforestation in the land-use change and forestry category, are to be included in the determination of Annex 1 Parties' assigned amounts. These issues, to be decided by COP (MoP), are of fundamental importance to countries such as Australia, Canada, and the US who are relying to a large extent on the use of sinks in these categories to enable them to meet their commitments.

This debate impacts on the development of emissions trading under Article 17 in that, the source of the commodities traded may be increased and with it, the access at source to those commodities, will differ. The ramifications for creation and distribution of wealth are considerable.

Essential Elements of an Emissions Trading Scheme

As with any emissions trading scheme it is necessary to ensure that the appropriate infrastructure is in place. It is beyond the scope of this paper to give a comprehensive treatment of all the issues that must be dealt with when designing and implementing a global emissions trading scheme. The focus of this section will therefore be confined to a discussion of those elements that are likely to induce an Annex B Party to participate fully in such a scheme. These include an agreed upon method of defining, measuring, monitoring, reporting and verifying emissions by sources and absorption (sequestration) by sinks, of greenhouse gases. At this stage the focus is on the reduction of carbon dioxide although the other greenhouse gases defined in Annex A of the Protocol could similarly be the subject of emissions trading under Article 17.

An emissions trading scheme necessarily involves domestic consideration of a range of issues as well as consideration of elements applicable to an international regime. First and foremost on the domestic front are issues surrounding the licenses or permits to be issued by a government to meet its international commitments under the Protocol. These include, inter alia:

- permit allocation, for example:
  - grandfathering: allocation on a historical basis;
  - auctioning: government selling to the highest bidder;
  - granting: differentiation in allocation allowing for different companies circumstances i.e. a companies growth potential, export orientation, past emission abatement record etc.;
  - fixed price sale.
- permit acquittal;
- permit design;
- structure of the market in which it is traded, including:
  - cap and trade;
  - baseline and credit.
- the legal nature of the units being traded, (whether it is to be a license, a form of real property, a form of

personal property, a choice in action or profit à prendre).

It has been observed that the integration of national trading systems with international trading requirements and conventions under the Protocol is a key requirement in designing domestic systems, including dealing with permits. Emission credits generated through the CDM and JI need to be recognized and able to be readily substituted for nationally traded permits (or units) and ultimately AAUs, under the *Kyoto Protocol*.

Article 6—Joint Implementation

In the event that an international emissions trading system is established and becomes operative under Article 17, there is strong likelihood that JI activity under Article 6 will decrease for a number of reasons. The primary one is directly related to cost as it is anticipated that the transaction costs of engaging in JI activities will be significantly higher than that associated with both emissions trading and credits generated from CDM projects. Because JI activities are confined to Annex B countries where marginal abatement costs will be higher, those Parties opting to invest in project-based activities may choose to do so under the CDM rather than JI. A further incentive to invest in CDM projects is the fact that emission credits (CERs) generated from CDM projects may be used from the year 2000 up to the beginning of the first commitment period to assist Annex 1 Parties in meeting their commitments. In contrast, ERUs generated from JI projects may be acquired or transferred only *after the emissions reductions have actually occurred* and the other requirements set out in Article 6 have been met and there are no provisions for use of JI credits before the year 2008. Nevertheless, JI is available to be used by both governments and private sector entities and will, in certain cases, provide an additional, useful option.

It appears that the EU countries will utilize the provisions of Article 4 (as a EU 'bubble') rather than Article 6, which permits Annex 1 Parties to fulfil their commitments under Article 3 jointly.

The US, Australia, Canada, Japan and New Zealand submitted a proposal for a draft decision at COP6 acknowledging the potential of the CDM and JI to promote, facilitate and finance the transfer of environmentally-sound technologies to enable Parties to meet the provisions of the UNFCCC, although Brazil, China and Thailand objected strongly to any linkage of technology transfer under the UNFCCC to the Protocol.

5

Energy Issues and Climate Change

A

UNDP/UN DESA/WEC, *World Energy Assessment: Energy and the Challenge of Sustainability—An Overview*, UNDP, 2001

One way of looking at human development is in terms of the choices and opportunities available to individuals. Energy can dramatically widen these choices. Simply harnessing oxen, for example, multiplied the power available to a human being by a factor of 10. The invention of the vertical waterwheel increased productivity by another factor of 6; the steam engine increased it by yet another order of magnitude. The use of motor vehicles greatly reduced journey times and expanded human ability to transport goods to markets.

Today the ready availability of plentiful, affordable energy allows many people to enjoy unprecedented comfort, mobility, and productivity. In industrialized countries people use more than 100 times as much energy, on a per capita basis, as humans did before they learned to exploit the energy potential of fire.

Although energy fuels economic growth, and is therefore a key concern for all countries, access to and use of energy vary widely among them, as well as between the rich and poor within each country. In fact, 2 billion people—one-third of the world's population—rely almost completely on traditional energy sources and so are not able to take advantage of the opportunities made possible by modern forms of energy. Moreover, most current energy generation and use are accompanied by environmental impacts at local, regional, and global levels that threaten human well being now and well into the future.

In *Agenda 21*, the United Nations and its member states have strongly endorsed the goal of sustainable development, which implies meeting the needs of the present without compromising the ability of future generations to meet their needs. The importance of energy as a tool for meeting this goal was acknowledged at every major United Nations conference in the 1990s, starting with the Rio Earth Summit (UN Conference on Environment and Development) in 1992. But current energy systems, as analyzed in this report and summarized here, are not addressing the basic needs of all people, and the continuation of business-as-usual practices may compromise the prospects of future generations.

Energy produced and used in ways that support human development over the long term, in all its social, economic, and environmental dimensions, is what is meant in this report by the term *sustainable energy.* In other words, this term does not refer simply to a continuing supply of energy, but to the production and use of energy resources in ways that promote-or at least are compatible with- long-term human well-being and ecological balance.

Many current energy practices do not fit this definition. As noted in *Agenda 21*, "Much of the world's energy...is currently produced and consumed in ways that could not be sustained if technology were to remain constant and if overall quantities were to increase substantially". Energy's link to global warming through greenhouse gas emissions (most of which are produced by fossil fuel consumption) was addressed by the *United Nations Framework Convention on Climate Change*, adopted in 1992. And in 1997 a United Nations General Assembly Special Session identified energy and transport issues as being central to achieving a sustainable future and set key objectives in these areas.

The energy industry also recognizes the need to address energy issues within a broad context. For example, the conclusions and recommendations of the 17th Congress of the World Energy Council discuss the need to provide commercial energy to those without it, and to address energy-linked environmental impacts at all levels.

Although there seem to be no physical limits to the world's energy supply for at least the next 50 years, today's energy system is unsustainable because of equity issues as well as environmental, economic, and geopolitical concerns that have implications far into the future. Aspects of the unsustainability of the current system include:

- Modern fuels and electricity are not universally accessible, an inequity that has moral, political, and practical dimensions in a world that is becoming increasingly interconnected.
- The current energy system is not sufficiently reliable or affordable to support widespread economic growth. The productivity of one-third of the world's people is compromised by lack of access to commercial energy, and perhaps another third suffer economic hardship and insecurity due to unreliable energy supplies.
- Negative local, regional, and global environmental impacts of energy production and use threaten the health and well being of current and future generations.

More specific—and more quantifiable—elements of sustainability are identified below in the section on energy scenarios. Before looking into the future, however, some basic features of energy and its relationship to economic development are described, and the linkages between energy and major global challenges are analyzed.

....The rate of global commercial energy consumption is thousands of times smaller than the energy flows from the sun to the earth. Primary energy consumption is reliant on fossil fuels (oil, natural gas, and coal), which represent nearly 80 percent of the total fuel mix. Nuclear power contributes slightly more than 6 percent, and hydropower and new renewables each contribute about 2 percent.

Worldwide, traditional (often non-commercial) energy accounts for about 10 percent of the total fuel mix. But the distribution is uneven: non-commercial energy accounts for perhaps 2 percent of energy consumption in industrialized countries, but an average of 30 percent in developing ones. In some low-income developing countries, traditional biomass accounts for 90 percent or more of total energy consumption.

If the global growth rate of about 2 percent a year of primary energy use continues, it will mean a doubling of energy consumption by 2035 relative to 1998, and a tripling by 2055. In the past 30 years developing countries' commercial energy use has increased at a rate three and a half times that of OECD countries, the result of life-style changes made possible by rising personal incomes, coupled with higher population growth rates and a shift from traditional to commercial energy. On a per capita basis, however, the increase in total primary energy use has not resulted in any notable way in more equitable access to energy services between industrialized and developing countries. Clearly, more energy will be needed to fuel global economic growth and to deliver opportunities to the billions of people in developing countries who do not have access to adequate energy services.

However, the amount of additional energy required to provide the energy services needed in the future will depend on the efficiencies with which the energy is produced, delivered, and used. Energy efficiency improvements could help reduce financial investments in new energy supply systems, as they have over the past 200 years. The degree of interdependence between economic activity and energy use is neither static nor uniform across regions. Energy intensity (the ratio of energy demand to GDP) often depends on a country's stage of development. In OECD countries, which enjoy abundant energy services, growth in energy demand is less tightly linked to economic productivity than it was in the past.

The trend towards a reduction in energy intensity as economic development proceeds can be discerned over a long historical period...A detailed, long-term analysis of energy intensity for a number of countries reveals a common pattern of energy use driven by the following factors:

- The shift from non-commercial to commercial forms of energy, industrialization, and motorization initially increase the commercial energy-GDP ratio. (In the 1990s this ratio increased in transition in economies, mainly because of slower economic growth.)
- As industrialization proceeds and incomes rise, saturation effects, as well as an expansion of the service sector (which is less energy intensive), decrease the ratio of commercial energy to GDP after it reaches a peak. This maximum energy intensity has been passed by many countries, but not by low-income developing countries.
- As a result of worldwide technology transfer and diffusion, energy efficiency improvements can be the main limiting factor in the growth of energy demand arising from increasing populations and growing production and incomes.
- The more efficient use of materials in better-quality, well-designed, miniaturized products, the recycling of energy-intensive materials, and the saturation of bulk markets for basic materials in industrialized countries contribute to additional decreases in energy intensity.
- In developing countries, technological leapfrogging to the use of highly efficient appliances, machinery, processes, vehicles, and transportation systems offers considerable potential for energy efficiency improvements.

These drivers are leading to a common pattern of energy use per unit of GDP in industrialized and developing countries.

Energy prices influence consumer choices and behavior and can affect economic development and growth. High energy prices can lead to increasing import bills, with adverse consequences for business, employment, and social welfare. High energy prices can also stimulate exploration and development of additional resources, create a pull for innovation, and provide incentives for efficiency improvements.

Although some impacts of energy prices are fairly steady, others are more transient. For example, different absolute price levels have had little effect on economic development in OECD European countries or Japan relative to the much lower energy prices in the United States and some developing countries. What affected economic growth in all energy-importing countries were the price hikes of the 1970s. It appears that economies are more sensitive to price changes than to prices per se.

Capital investment is a prerequisite for energy development. Energy system development and structural change are the results of investment in plants, equipment, and energy system infrastructure. Difficulties in attracting capital for energy investment may impede economic development, especially in the least developed countries. Scarce public funds, especially in developing countries, are needed for many projects—ranging from rural development, education, and health care to energy supplies. Because energy supply, more than any other alternative, is often seen as more readily capable of generating early revenues, energy investments are increasingly viewed as a private sector affair. Yet private funds are not flowing into many developing countries for a variety of reasons, especially risks to investors.

Foreign direct investment approached $400 billion in 1997—up from $50 billion in 1984—and represents an increasing share of international investment flows. Foreign direct investment is generally commercially motivated, and investors not only expect to recover the initial capital but also count on competitive returns. These outcomes cannot be guaranteed in developing countries with potentially fragile governments or without free markets. In fact, very little foreign direct investment reaches the least developed countries.

Unlike foreign direct investment, official development assistance has remained flat relative to gross world product.

In 1997 it totalled $56 billion, or 0.25 percent of the GDP of OECD countries—which have agreed in principle to a target of 0.7 percent of GDP. Against this backdrop, financing is inadequate for energy projects in developing countries. Until the economic risks to foreign investors can be managed (for example, through clear and stable rules for energy and financial markets, steady revenue generation through bill collection, and profit transfers), most developing countries may have to continue to finance their energy development from domestic savings.

Although energy investment as a share of total investment varies greatly among countries and at different stages of economic development, on balance, 1.0-1.5 percent of GDP is invested in the energy sector. This ratio is expected to remain relatively stable. Based on these rules of thumb, current energy supply sector investment totals $290-430 billion a year. But this does not include investment in end-use energy efficiency.

Energy and Social Issues

Energy use is closely linked to a range of social issues, including poverty alleviation, population growth, urbanization, and a lack of opportunities for women. Although these issues affect energy demand, the relationship is two-way: the quality and quantity of energy services, and how they are achieved, have an effect on social issues as well.

Poverty is the overriding social consideration for developing countries. Some 1.3 billion people in the developing world live on less than $1 a day. Income measurement alone, however, does not fully capture the misery and the absence of choice that poverty represents. The energy consumption patterns of poor people—especially their reliance on traditional fuels in rural areas—tend to keep them impoverished.

Worldwide, 2 billion people are without access to electricity and an equal number continue to use traditional solid fuels for cooking. As shown in the next section, cooking with poorly vented stoves has significant health impacts. In addition, hundreds of millions of people—mainly women and children—spend several hours a day in the drudgery of gathering firewood and carrying water, often from considerable distances, for household needs. Because of these demands on their time and energy, women and children often miss out on opportunities for education and other productive activities.

Lack of electricity usually means inadequate illumination and few labor-saving appliances, as well as limited telecommunications and possibilities for commercial enterprise. Greater access to electricity and modern fuels and stoves for cooking can enable people to enjoy both short-term and self-reinforcing, long-term advances in their quality of life...

Limited income may force households to use traditional fuels and inefficient technologies...For low-income households, firewood is the dominant fuel. At higher incomes, wood is replaced by commercial fuels and electricity, which offer much greater convenience, energy efficiency, and cleanliness. Because convenient, affordable energy can contribute to a household's productivity and income-generating potential, its availability can become a lever for breaking out of a cycle of poverty.

Although population growth tends to increase energy demand, it is less widely understood that the availability of adequate energy services can lower birth rates. Adequate energy services can shift the relative benefits and costs of fertility towards a lower number of desired births in a family. An acceleration of the demographic transition to low mortality and low fertility (as has occurred in industrialized countries) depends on crucial developmental tasks, including improving the local environment, educating women, and ameliorating the extreme poverty that may make child labor a necessity. All these tasks have links to the availability of low-cost energy services.

The growing concentration of people in urban centres is another key demographic issue linked to energy. Although the general trend towards urbanization has many components and may be inevitable, providing more options to rural residents through energy interventions could potentially slow migration and reduce pressure on rapidly growing cities. Although the negative externalities associated with energy use in urban areas can be severe, various strategies can mitigate their effects and promote energy conservation. Taking energy into consideration in land-use planning, and in designing physical infrastructure, construction standards, and transportation systems, can reduce some of the growth in energy demand that accompanies rapid urbanization.

Transportation systems may be especially important in this regard, given the rapid growth in the number of motor vehicles worldwide. Since about 1970 the global fleet has been increasing by 16 million vehicles a year, and more than

1 billion cars will likely be on the road by 2020. Most of these cars will be driven in the cities of the developing world, where they will create more congestion, aggravate urban pollution, and undermine human health—even with optimistic projections about efficiency improvements and alternative fuels.

In developing countries, addressing the energy needs of the poor, who represent a large majority, will require major structural changes. On the other hand, in industrialized countries adequate access to affordable energy is problematic only for a minority, and thus more amenable to social policy solutions. Throughout the world, however, poor households pay a larger fraction of their incomes for energy than do the rich, and so are vulnerable to rapid increases in the price of energy. Increases in the pace of oil in the winter of 1999/2000, for example, posed a hardship for many people, even in some industrialized countries.

Eradicating poverty is a long-term goal of development. But long before that goal is achieved, convenient and affordable energy services could dramatically improve living standards and offer more opportunities to people. Today's inequity is unsustainable. Satisfying the energy needs of the poor with modern technologies has the potential to improve standards of living and health, and to create new jobs and business opportunities. Allowing one-third of the world's population to continue to endure the constraints associated with traditional energy is unacceptable from a humanitarian and moral standpoint. Making commercial energy more widely available makes sense from a political perspective as well. The wave of democratization sweeping the world is putting political power in the hands of the economically disenfranchised. Societies with grave inequalities and disparities tend to be unstable, and large populations below the poverty line are fertile ground for social upheavals.

Energy, the Environment, and Health

The environmental impacts of energy use are not new. For centuries, wood burning has contributed to the deforestation of many areas. Even in the early stages of industrialization, local air, water, and land pollution reached high levels. What is relatively new is an acknowledgement of energy linkages to regional and global environmental problems and of their implications. Although energy's potential for enhancing human well-being is unquestionable, conventional energy' production and consumption are closely linked to environmental degradation. This degradation threatens human health and quality of life, and affects ecological balance and biological diversity.

...Just in the course of the past 100 years, during which the world's population more than tripled, human environmental insults grew from local perturbations to global disruptions. The human disruptions of the 20th century—driven by more than 20-fold growth in the use of fossil fuels, and augmented by a tripling in the use of traditional energy forms such as biomass—have amounted to no less than the emergence of civilization as a global ecological and geochemical force. In other words, the accelerating impact of human life is altering the world the global level.

At every level (local, regional, global), the environmental consequences of current patterns of energy generation and use make up a significant fraction of human impacts on the environment. At the household level, solid fuel use for cooking and heat has significant health impacts. Poor air quality—at the household, local, and regional levels—is associated with increased sickness and premature death. About 2 million premature deaths a year—disproportionately of women and children—are estimated to occur from exposure to indoor air pollution caused by burning solid fuels in poorly ventilated spaces. Particulate matter (which is both emitted directly and formed in the air as the result of the emissions of gaseous precursors in the form of oxides of sulphur and nitrogen) and hydrocarbons are growing concerns worldwide. They are especially troublesome in many parts of the developing world, where dirtier fuels predominate with little emissions abatement. No safe threshold level for exposure to small particulate matter has been established.

At every level (local, regional, global), the environmental consequences of current patterns of energy generation and use make up a significant fraction of human impacts on the environment.

Fossil fuel combustion is problematic on several levels (although natural gas produces significantly fewer harmful emissions than do oil or coal). The main pollutants emitted in the combustion of fossil fuels are sulphur and nitrogen oxides, carbon monoxide, and suspended particulate matter. Ozone is formed in the troposphere from interactions among hydrocarbons, nitrogen oxides, and sunlight. Energy-related emissions from fossil fuel combustion, including in the transport sector, are major contributors to urban air pollution. Precursors of acid deposition from fuel combustion can be precipitated thousands of kilometers from their point of origin-often crossing national boundaries. The resulting acidification is causing significant damage to natural systems, crops, and human-made structures; and can, over time, alter the composition and function of entire ecosystems. In many regions acidification has diminished the productivity of forests, fisheries, and farmlands. Large hydropower projects often raise environmental issues related to flooding, whereas in the case of nuclear power, issues such as waste disposal raise concern.

Fossil fuel combustion produces more carbon dioxide (CO_2) than any other human activity. This is the biggest source of the anthropogenic greenhouse gas emissions that are changing the composition of the atmosphere and could alter the global climate system, including the amount and pattern of rainfall. Achieving a stable atmospheric CO_2 concentration at any level would require that CO_2 emissions eventually be cut by more than half from current levels. Stabilising CO_2 at close to the present concentration would require reducing emissions to half of current levels within the next few decades. Instead, CO_2 emissions continue to increase. Current CO_2 emission trends, if not controlled, will lead to more than a doubling of atmospheric concentrations before 2070, relative to pre-industrial levels. Changes have been observed in climate patterns that correspond to scientific projections based on increasing concentrations of greenhouse gases. The balance of evidence, according to the Intergovernmental Panel on Climate Change, suggests that there is already a discernible human influence on global climate.

Because, by definition, sustainable energy systems must support both human and ecosystem health over the long term, goals on tolerable emissions should look well into the future. They should also take into account the public's tendency to demand more health and environmental protection as prosperity increases.

Although the scope of environmental problems related to energy may seem overwhelming, numerous 'win-win' strategies could simultaneously benefit the environment (at several levels), the economy, and human well-being. For example, the replacement of solid fuels for cooking with gaseous or liquid fuels could have significant environmental benefits at the local, community, regional, and global scales, with attendant benefits for health and productivity.

Energy Security

Energy security means the availability of energy at all times in various forms, in sufficient quantities, and at affordable prices. These conditions must prevail over the long term if energy is to contribute to sustainable development.

Attention to energy security is critical because of the uneven distribution both of the fossil fuel resources on which most countries currently rely and of capacity to develop other resources. The energy supply could become more vulnerable over the near term due to the growing global reliance on imported oil. For example, the oil dependence (net imports as a share of total demand) of OECD countries is expected to grow from 56 percent in 1996 to 72 percent in 2010.

In addition, although energy security has been adequate for the past 20 years, and has in fact improved, the potential for conflict, sabotage, disruption of trade, and reduction in strategic reserves cannot be dismissed. These potential threats point to the necessity of strengthening global as well as regional and national energy security. Options to enhance energy security include:

- Avoiding excessive dependence on imports by increasing end-use efficiency and encouraging greater reliance on local resources (particularly those whose development will have other positive externalities such as job creation, capacity building, and pollution reduction), provided these do not involve disproportionate costs or waste scarce resources.
- Diversifying supply (including both suppliers and energy forms).
- Fostering greater political stability through international cooperation and long-term agreements among energy-importing countries and between importing and exporting countries. Examples might include wider adoption and more effective implementation of the *Energy Charter Treaty*, as well as increased sharing of infrastructure for transporting natural gas.
- Encouraging technology transfers (for example, through joint ventures and public-private partnerships) to developing countries so they can develop local resources and improve energy efficiencies.
- Increasing national and regional strategic reserves of crude oil and oil products through increased investment and advanced exploration technologies.

Although markets play a prominent role in securing energy supply in OECD countries, their role is modest in some developing countries and absent in others. Where markets do not flourish, the security of supply and services depends almost solely on government action and multinational companies, which may not serve the best interests of consumers. In such situations, energy security can be enhanced by encouraging the development of frameworks that allow markets to contribute to the allocation of energy resources.

Because of small fuel requirements, nuclear power contributes to the diversity of supply and to supply security. But public concerns about economic necessity, reactor safety, and radioactive waste transport and disposal—as well as weapons proliferation—have curbed nuclear energy development in many countries. A nuclear accident anywhere in the world or a proliferation incident linked to nuclear power could further reduce support for nuclear power programs, with long-term loss in the diversity of the energy supply mix. But if generally accepted responses could be found to the above concerns, nuclear energy could contribute significantly to secure electricity generation in many parts of the world.

Individuals and commercial enterprises are also vulnerable to disruptions of energy supply. Although the trend towards the liberalization of energy markets generally has enhanced energy security by offering more options, supplies, and competition, it has also raised concerns that those who are impoverished will be left out of the process, resulting in continued energy insecurity for some individuals.

Energy Resources

Careful analysis of the long-term availability of energy resources, starting with conventional and unconventional oil and gas, indicates that these resources could last another 50–100 years—and possibly much longer—with known exploration and extraction technologies and anticipated technical progress in upstream operations. Coal resources and nuclear materials are so abundant that they could, respectively, last for centuries or millennia. Moreover, although fossil fuel prices may rise slowly over time, the large, cost-driven increases in energy prices projected in the 1970s and 1980s will not take place in the foreseeable future.

As evidenced by rising oil prices in the winter of 1999/2000, however, prices are subject to volatility. This may occur, for example, if cartels set prices independent of production costs. Some fluctuations in prices can also be expected, especially during the transition to a large-scale use of unconventional oil and gas resources, because the timing of investments in upstream production capacities may not correspond with demand. Other cost-pushing factors could arise from the environmentally more challenging extraction of unconventional oil resources.

Renewable resources are more evenly distributed than fossil and nuclear resources, and energy flows from renewable resources are more than three orders of magnitude higher than current global energy use. But the economic potential of renewables is affected by many constraints, including competing land uses, the amount and timing of solar irradiation, environmental concerns, and wind patterns.

Although there are no real limitations on future energy availability from a resource point of view, the existence of resources is of little relevance without consideration of how these can contribute to the supply of (downstream) energy services. Rather, the key concerns are: Can technologies to extract, harvest, and convert these vast energy stocks and flows be developed in time? Will these processes have adverse implications? Will the energy services eventually generated from these resources be affordable? Historical evidence suggests that these concerns may be at least partly offset by technological progress, but that such progress needs to be encouraged-by regulations to improve market performance, temporary subsidies, tax incentives, or other mechanisms—if it is to occur in a timely fashion.

Energy End-Use Efficiency

The quadrupling of oil prices in the 1970s, the growing awareness of energy-related pollution, and the possibility of climate change have all contributed to a re-evaluation of energy use. The result has been an improvement in the efficiency with which energy is used in industry and power generation as well as in lighting, household appliances, transportation, and heating and cooling of buildings. This more efficient use of energy is a major factor contributing to the improvements in energy intensity that have occurred historically in almost all OECD countries, and more recently in many transition economies, as well as in some in fast-growing developing countries such as Brazil and China.

Today the global energy efficiency of converting primary energy to useful energy is about one-third. In other words, two-thirds of primary energy is dissipated in the conversion processes, mostly as low-temperature heat. Further significant losses occur when the useful energy delivers the energy service. Numerous and varied economic opportunities exist for energy efficiency improvements, particularly in this final conversion step from useful energy to energy services. Taking advantage of these opportunities, which have received relatively little attention, has the largest potential for cost-effective efficiency improvements. It would mean less costly energy services and lower energy-related pollution and emissions.

Over the long term, additional and dramatic gains in efficiency are possible at all stages of energy conversion, particularly from useful energy to energy services.

Over the next 20 years the amount of primary energy required for a given level of energy services could be cost-effectively reduced by 25-35 percent in industrialised countries (the higher figure being achievable by more effective policies). These reductions are mostly in the conversion step of useful energy to energy services in the residential, industrial, transportation, public, and commercial sectors. Reductions of more than 40 percent are cost-effectively achievable in transition economies. And in most developing countries—which tend to have high economic growth and old capital and vehicle stocks—the cost-effective improvement potentials range from 30 percent to more than 45 percent, relative to energy efficiencies achieved with existing capital stock.

The improvements of about 2 percent a year implied by the above figures could be enhanced by structural changes in industrialized and transition economies, by shifts to less energy-intensive industrial production, and by saturation effects in the residential and transportation sectors. These combined effects, made up by efficiency improvements and structural changes, could lead to decreases in energy intensity of 2.5 percent a year. How much of this potential will be realised depends on the effectiveness of policy frameworks and measures, changes in attitudes and behaviour, and the level of entrepreneurial activity in energy conservation.

The next few decades will likely see new processes, motor systems, materials, vehicles, and buildings designed to reduce useful energy demand. Because the demand for cars is expected to grow rapidly in the developing world, gaining greater efficiencies in this area will be very important. In addition, rapidly industrializing countries could greatly profit from the introduction of radically new and more efficient technologies in their energy-intensive basic materials processing. Because these countries are still building their physical infrastructure, they have a growing demand for basic materials. This opens a window of opportunity to innovate and improve efficiencies of production, particularly in countries undergoing market reform. The opportunities are larger at the point of new investment, relative to retrofitting.

Over the long term, additional and dramatic gains in efficiency are possible at all stages of energy conversion, particularly from useful energy to energy services. Analysis shows that current technologies are not close to reaching theoretical limits, and that improvements of an order of magnitude for the whole energy system may eventually be achieved.

For a number of reasons the technical and economic potentials of energy efficiency, as well as its positive impact on sustainable development, have traditionally been under-realized. Achieving higher end-use efficiency involves a great variety of technical options and players. Because it is a decentralized, dispersed activity, it is a difficult issue for which to organize support. And because it has little visibility, energy efficiency is not generally a popular cause for politicians, the media, or individuals looking for recognition and acknowledgement. In addition, significant barriers—primarily market imperfections that could be overcome by targeted policy instruments—prevent the realisation of greater end-use efficiencies. These barriers include:

- Lack of adequate information, technical knowledge, and training. Uncertainties about the performance of investments in new and energy-efficient technologies.
- Lack of adequate capital or financing possibilities.
- High initial and perceived costs of more efficient technologies.
- High transaction costs (for searching and assessing information and for training).
- Lack of incentives for careful maintenance.
- The differential benefits to the user relative to the investor (for example, when energy bills are paid by the renter rather than the property owner).
- External costs of energy use, not included in energy prices.
- Patterns and habits of consumers, operators, and decision makers, which may be influenced by many factors, including ideas of social presage and professional norms.

Realizing cost-effective energy efficiency potentials will be beneficial not only for individual energy consumers, but also for the economy as a whole. For example, saved energy costs can be used to produce energy-saving domestic goods and services. And as cost-effective energy improvements are realized, additional profitable opportunities for improvement will continue to open up as a result of research and development, learning curves, and economies of scale. That means that continual cost-effective energy efficiency improvements can be expected.

Energy efficiency policies that use direct or indirect price mechanisms (such as the removal of subsidies and the incorporation of externalities) are effective in lowering consumption trends in price-sensitive sectors and applications. But even without changing the overall price environment, energy efficiency policies should be pursued to address market failures. For example, efficiency standards, appliance and product labelling, voluntary agreements, and professional training or contracting can increase GDP growth by improving environmental and economic performance, using a given quantity of energy. Legal standards; well-informed consumers, planners, and decision makers; motivated operators; and an adequate payments system for energy are central to the successful implementation of energy efficiency improvements.

Renewable Energy Technologies

Renewable energy sources (including biomass, solar, wind, geothermal, and hydropower) that use indigenous resources have the potential to provide energy services with zero or almost zero emissions of both air pollutants and greenhouse gases. Currently, renewable energy sources supply 14 percent of the total world energy demand. The supply is dominated by traditional biomass used for cooking and heating, especially in rural areas of developing countries. Large-scale hydropower supplies 20 percent of global electricity. Its scope for expansion is limited in the industrialized world, where it has nearly reached its economic capacity. In the developing world, considerable potential sail exists, but large hydropower projects may face financial, environmental, and social constraints.

Altogether, new renewable energy sources contributed 2 percent of the world's energy consumption in 1998, including 7 exajoules from modern biomass and 2 exajoules for all other renewables (geothermal, wind, solar, and marine energy, and small-scale hydropower). Solar photovoltaics and grid-connected wind installed capacities are growing at a rate of 30 percent a year. Even so, it will likely be decades before these new renewables add up to a major fraction of total energy consumption, because they currently represent such a small percentage.

Substantial price reductions in the past few decades have made some renewables competitive with fossil fuels in certain applications in growing markets. Modern, distributed forms of biomass seem particularly promising for their potential to provide rural areas with clean forms of energy based on the use of biomass resources that have traditionally been used in inefficient, polluting ways. Biomass can be economically produced with minimal or even positive environmental impacts through perennial crops. Wind power in coastal and other windy regions is promising as well.

Unlike hydropower and conventional thermal power sources, wind and solar thermal or electric sources are intermittent. Nevertheless, they can be important energy sources in rural areas where grid extension is expensive. They can also contribute to grid-connected electricity supplies in appropriate hybrid configurations. Intermittent renewables can reliably provide 10-30 percent of total electricity supplies if operated in conjunction with hydropower- or fuel-based power generation. Emerging storage possibilities and new strategies for operating grids offer promise that the role of intermittent technologies could be considerably larger.

Significant barriers, which could be overcome by appropriate frameworks and policies, stand in the way of the accelerated development of renewable technologies. These barriers include economic risks, regulatory obstacles, limited availability of products, information and technology gaps, and lack of investment. The greatest challenge is financial, even though costs have come down significantly over the past several decades...

Many renewable technologies, because they are small in scale and modular, are good candidates for continued cost-cutting as a result of field experience. The cost reductions of manufactured goods, which are typically rapid at first and then taper off as the industry matures, are called experience curves. These curves resulted in industry-wide cost declines of about 20 percent for each cumulative doubling of production for solar photovoltaics, wind generators, and gas turbines—due to learning effects, marginal technological improvements, and economies of scale. Similar declines are expected for other small-scale renewables.

A rapid expansion of renewable-based energy systems will require actions to stimulate the market in this direction. This expansion can be achieved by finding ways to drive down the relative cost of renewables in their early stages of development and commercialization, while still taking advantage of the economic efficiencies of the marketplace. Pricing based on the full costs of conventional energy sources (including phasing out subsidies and internalizing externalities) will make renewables more competitive. Because internalizing external costs may be controversial for some time, 'green' pricing of electricity and heat (which lets consumers pay more for environmentally benign energy supplies if they choose) may be an immediate option in industrialized countries.

Advanced Energy Technologies

Fossil energy

Sustainability goals indicate the importance of evolving fossil energy technologies towards the long-term goal of near-zero air pollutant and greenhouse gas emissions without complicated end-of-pipe control technologies. Near-term technologies and strategies should support this long-term goal.

The technological revolution under way in power generation, where advanced systems are replacing steam turbine technologies, does support this long-term goal. Natural-gas-fired combined cycles offering low costs, high efficiency, and low environmental impacts are being chosen wherever natural gas is readily available—in some countries even displacing large new hydropower projects. Cogeneration is more cost-effective and can play a much larger role in the energy economy—if based on gas turbines and combined cycles rather than on steam turbines.

Reciprocating engines and emerging microturbine and fuel cell technologies are also strong candidates for cogeneration at smaller scales, including commercial and apartment buildings. Coal gasification by partial oxidation with oxygen to produce syngas (mainly carbon monoxide and hydrogen) makes it possible to provide electricity through integrated gasifier combined cycle (IGCC) plants with air pollutant emissions nearly as low as for natural gas combined cycles. Today power from IGCC cogeneration plants is often competitive with power from coal steam-electric plants in either cogeneration or power-only configurations.

Although synthetic liquid fuels made in single-product facilities are not competitive, superclean syngas-derived synthetic fuels (such as synthetic middle distillates and dimethyl ether) produced in polygeneration facilities that make several products simultaneously may soon be. Syngas can be produced from natural gas by steam reforming or other means or from coal by gasification using oxygen, as noted. Expanding markets for clean synthetic fuels are likely to result from toughening air pollution regulations. Synthetic fuels produced through polygeneration will be based on natural gas if it is readily available. Synthetic middle distillates so produced are likely to be competitive where low-cost natural gas is available (as at remote developing country sites); the technology might facilitate exploitation of relatively small remote natural gas fields.

In natural-gas-poor, coal-rich regions, polygeneration based on coal gasification is promising. Such systems might include production of extra syngas for distribution by pipelines to small-scale cogeneration systems in factories and buildings—making possible clean and efficient use of coal at small as well as large scales. Rapidly growing polygeneration activity is already under way in several countries based on the gasification of low-quality petroleum feedstocks—activity that is helping to pave the way for coal-based systems.

Barriers to widespread deployment of advanced cogeneration and polygeneration systems are mainly institutional. Most systems will produce far more electricity than can be consumed on-site, so achieving favorable economics depends on being able to sell co-product electricity at competitive prices into electric grids. Utility policies have often made doing so difficult, but under the competitive market conditions towards which electric systems are evolving in many regions, cogeneration and polygeneration systems will often fare well.

The near-term pursuit of a syngas-based strategy could pave the way for widespread use of hydrogen (H_2) as an energy carrier, because for decades the cheapest way to make H_2 will be from fossil-fuel-derived syngas. The successful development of fuel cells would facilitate the introduction of H_2 for energy. Fuel cells are getting intense attention, especially for transportation, because they offer high efficiency and near-zero air pollutant emissions. Automakers are racing to develop fuel cell cars, with market entry targeted for 2004–2010. The fuel cell car will compete for the role of 'car of the future' with the hybrid internal combustion engine/battery powered car already being introduced into the market.

Syngas-based power and H_2 production strategies also facilitate separation and storage of CO_2 from fossil energy systems, making it possible to obtain useful energy with near-zero emissions of greenhouse gases without large increases in energy costs. Recent research suggests that the global capacity for secure disposal of CO_2 in geological reservoirs might be adequate to dispose of CO_2 from fossil fuel use for hundreds of years, although more research is needed to be sure about this.

Other advanced technologies (ultrasupercritical steam plants, pressurized fluidized-bed combustion, coal IGCC based on partial oxidation in air for power generation, direct coal liquefaction for synthetic fuels production) offer benefits relative to conventional technologies. But unlike syngas-based technologies, such options in the near term would not offer clear paths to the long-term goal of near-zero emissions without significant increases in costs for energy services.

Nuclear Energy

Worldwide, nuclear energy accounts for 6 percent of energy and 16 percent of electricity. Although nuclear energy dominates electricity generation in some countries, its initial promise has not been widely realized. Most analysts project that nuclear energy's contribution to global energy will not grow—and might decline during the initial decades of the 21st century. Nuclear power is more costly than originally projected, competition from alternative technologies is increasing, and there has been a loss of public confidence because of concerns related to safety, radioactive waste management, and potential nuclear weapons proliferation.

But because nuclear power can provide energy without emitting conventional air pollutants and greenhouse gases, it is worth exploring if advanced technologies could offer simultaneously lower costs, boost public confidence in the safety of nuclear reactors, assure that peaceful nuclear programs are not used for military purposes, and demonstrate effective nuclear waste management practices. Unlike Chernobyl-type reactors, the light water reactors (LWRs) that dominate nuclear power globally have a good safety record—although this record has been achieved at considerable cost to minimize the risk of accidents.

The potential linkage between peaceful and military uses of nuclear energy was recognized at the dawn of the nuclear age. Efforts to create a non-proliferation regime through the Nuclear Non-Proliferation Treaty and a series of regional treaties, controls on commerce in nuclear materials and goods and services that might be used to further military ambitions, and safeguards applied to nuclear materials in peaceful nuclear applications have been largely successful in separating peaceful and military uses. If there is to be an energy future in which nuclear power eventually contributes much more than at present, stronger institutional measures will be needed to maintain this separation. These measures should be complemented by technological advances aimed at limiting opportunities to acquire nuclear weapons under the guise of peaceful nuclear energy applications and to steal weapons-usable nuclear materials.

Reactor development activity for the near term has involved both evolutionary LWRs and new concepts. Reactor vendors now offer several evolutionary LWRs with improved safety features and standardized designs, for which there can be a high degree of confidence that performance and cost targets will be met. Another evolutionary activity involves modifying LWRs to make them more proliferation resistant through a denatured uranium or thorium fuel cycle. One concept being revisited, the pebble bed modular reactor, offers the potential for a high degree of inherent safety without the need for complicated, capital-intensive safety controls. A pebble bed modular reactor could also be operated on a proliferation resistant denatured uranium- or thorium fuel cycle.

Access to low-cost uranium supplies could constrain nuclear power development based on LWRs. The plutonium breeder reactor, which requires reprocessing spent fuel to recover plutonium for recycling in fresh fuel, was once thought to be a viable option for addressing this challenge. But electricity costs for breeders would probably be higher than for LWRs, at least until late in the 21st century, and preventing proliferation is much more challenging with reprocessing and plutonium recycling than with LWRs operated on once-through fuel cycles.

Other long-term options for addressing the nuclear resource constraint are alternative breeder concepts—including particle-accelerator-driven reactors, uranium from seawater, and thermonuclear fusion. The prospective costs, safety, and proliferation resistance features of such alternative breeder concepts are uncertain, and the concepts would take decades to develop. Recent research suggests it might be feasible, at relatively low cost, to extract uranium from seawater, where its concentration is low but total quantities are vast. If the technology could be deployed at globally significant scales, it might be feasible to avoid making major commitments to nuclear fuel reprocessing and plutonium recycling. Fusion could provide an almost inexhaustible energy supply, but it will probably not be commercially available before 2050.

Radioactive waste by-products of nuclear energy must be isolated so that they can never return to the human environment in concentrations that could cause significant harm. Although the safety of long-term waste disposal has not been proven, the technical community is confident that this objective can be realized—largely because of the small volumes of wastes involved. But in most countries there is no social consensus on the goals and standards for radioactive waste disposal and on strategies (both interim and long-term) for implementing them. The issues involved are only partly technical. The current social stalemate on waste disposal not only clouds prospects for nuclear expansion, it also has made spent fuel reprocessing a de facto interim nuclear waste management strategy in some countries. This has happened even though fuel reprocessing does not offer economic gains and does not solve the waste disposal problem—it merely buys time and is creating large inventories of plutonium that must be disposed of with low proliferation risk.

Energy Scenarios

Energy scenarios provide a framework for exploring future energy perspectives, including various combinations of technology options and their implications. Many scenarios in the literature illustrate the degree to which energy system developments will affect the global issues analyzed in part 1. Some describe energy futures that are compatible with sustainable development goals. Key developments in sustainable scenarios include increases in energy efficiencies and the adoption of advanced energy supply technologies. Sustainable development scenarios are characterized by low environmental impacts (local, regional, and global) and equitable allocation of resources and wealth...

Rural Energy in Developing Countries

Between 1970 and 1990 about 800 million additional people were reached by rural electrification programs. Some 500 million saw their lives improve substantially through the use of better methods for cooking and other rural energy tasks, particularly in China. Despite these enormous efforts to improve energy services to rural populations in the past 20-30 years, the unserved population has remained about the same in absolute numbers—2 billion people.

Although the unavailability of adequate energy services in rural areas is probably the most serious energy problem confronting humanity in the near future, rural energy remains low on the list of priorities of most government and corporate planners. And the increased demands of the more influential (and rapidly growing) urban population will make it more difficult to keep rural development on the agenda.

An effective strategy to address the energy needs of rural populations is to promote the climbing of the 'energy ladder'. This implies moving from simple biomass fuels (dung, crop residues, firewood) to the most convenient, efficient form of energy appropriate to the task at hand—usually liquid or gaseous fuels for cooking and heating and electricity for most other uses. Such climbing involves not only a shift to modern fuels but is often also complemented by the synergistic use of modern, more efficient end-use devices such as cooking stoves.

Climbing the energy ladder does not necessarily mean that all the rungs used in the past should be reclimbed. In the case of cooking, for example, users do not have to go from fuelwood to kerosene to liquefied petroleum gas (LPG) or electricity. What users should do—whenever possible—is leapfrog directly from fuel-wood to the most efficient end-use technologies and the least polluting energy forms (including new renewables) available. Because of the emergence of new technologies, it is also possible to introduce new rungs on the energy ladder, and gain even greater efficiencies and environmental acceptability.

The energy-related sustainable development goals for rural areas are to:

- Satisfy basic human needs by providing all households with minimally adequate amounts of electricity for uses such as lighting and fans, in addition to cleaner cooking fuels. Specifically, all households should move away from unprocessed solid fuels (biomass and coal) for cooking and heating to modern energy forms, which may potentially be derived from renewable sources (biomass and solar) or fossil fuels.
- Provide electricity that is sufficiently affordable to support industrial activity in rural areas, which can provide employment and help curb urban migration.

In many cases the rural poor are willing and able to pay for energy services if appropriate financing options are offered to help them meet high first costs. The economics of providing basic electricity to rural households should be evaluated according to the costs of supplying comparable energy services through less efficient carriers. In most cases home solar photovoltaic systems can provide energy services at a lower cost than the kerosene and batteries they replace and can be an economically viable source of rural household power, even at relatively low levels of service provision.

The availability of affordable and adequate energy services in rural areas could lead to significant improvements in living conditions and to the fulfilment of basic human needs over a relatively short time frame. The amount of energy needed to provide such services in rural areas is relatively small. Modern ways of using biomass more efficiently could go a long way towards achieving this objective. Experience has shown that to find the most viable and appropriate solutions to rural energy, the active participation of the people who will use it is a must.

The challenge is to find ways to make modern energy carriers affordable to satisfy the basic needs of all rural residents—which may, at least initially, require subsidies. The key is to introduce market efficiencies if possible to use the smallest subsidy needed to achieve social objectives. If a subsidy is required, it might be provided as an integral part of a new social contract, whereby energy providers serve rural energy needs while simultaneously, highly competitive conditions are created in the energy sector (a key element of energy reforms). One way to finance the subsidies that might be needed would be to complement the creation of competitive markets with the establishment of a public benefits fund generated by nonbypassable wire and pipe charges on electricity and on gas providers. Such funds have been adopted or are under consideration in several countries as a means of protecting public benefits under competitive market conditions. Other options include carefully designed economic incentives, perhaps using tax regimes.

Specifically, some of these revenues could be used to subsidize the very poorest households until they are able to work themselves out of poverty. This strategy could be made entirely consistent with a shift to greater reliance on market forces to efficiently allocate resources. If, for example, a rural energy concession was the preferred approach for bringing adequate energy services at a set price to a particular rural area, and if the concession was awarded competitively, market forces would be brought into play to find the least costly mix of energy technologies with the least amount of subsidy to satisfy the concessionaire's obligation to provide affordable energy services to all.

In many cases the rural poor are willing and able to pay for energy services if appropriate financing options are offered to help them meet high first costs.

Energy and Economic Prosperity

The demand of industrialized and transition economies for energy services is likely to grow, although increasing efficiency in conversion and end uses may result in a levelling off or even a reduction in the demand for primary energy. In developing countries, however, primary energy demand is expected to grow at about 2.5 percent a year as industrialization and motorization proceed and living standards improve.

Meeting these projected demands will be essential if developing countries are to achieve economic prosperity. It will require considerable investment—on the order of 2.0-2.5 percent of the GDP of developing countries over the next 20 years. This is close to historical norms and, with good financial and economic policies should be affordable. In the past, energy investments in developing countries rested heavily—and unnecessarily—on government subsidies, and too little on the financial resources that would be generated by real cost-based pricing, regulatory policies, and efficient management.

In general, there is no reason the energy sector should not be financially self-sufficient in the following sense: appropriate pricing and regulatory policies would raise revenues to cover operating costs and generate returns on investment sufficient to attract large-scale private finance and investment. Indeed, one of the primary aims of market liberalization and the new forms of regulation introduced in many countries in the 1990s was precisely this: to reduce the need for government subvention and to attract private capital and investment to the energy sector. The other aims were to encourage innovation, cost-effectiveness, and managerial efficiency.

But temporary government subsidies may be needed to help people who are excluded from the market by extreme poverty. Just as poor areas in today's industrialised countries benefited in the past from non-market energy policies, such options should be still available, when justified, in developing countries. Moreover, the poor may need to be shielded from economic hardships caused by trends over which they have no control. In some developing countries, for instance, the oil price increases of the 1970s and early 1980s contributed to large increases in external debt-up to 50 percent in some cases. The effects of that debt-impoverishment of the country and widespread unemployment-were particularly hard on the poor, even though their main source of fuel was and continues to be firewood rather than oil. The debt burden from the 1970s persists in many developing countries.

Although there seem to be no physical limitations on total energy resources, potentially severe problems are likely if appropriate economic, technological, and environmental policies are not developed in a timely manner. Rational energy pricing is part of what is needed, but so is a willingness to prompt markets to find technological solutions to problems before they begin exacting high societal and environmental costs. Finding ways to curb energy-related greenhouse gas emissions and to address other environmental problems, while sail expanding energy services, will require enlightened research, development, and demonstration policies. Much therefore will depend on the energy and environmental policies that are introduced, and on their relationship to the forces of globalisation and liberalisation.

Thanks to technological advances and better information on impacts, developing countries are in a position to address local and regional environmental problems early in the 21st century, and at an earlier stage of development than industrialized countries did. By addressing these negative externalities of energy generation and use early on, developing countries would find their overall economic well-being and the prospects of their people improved, not diminished. The issue of global climate change, however, may prove more difficult to reconcile with high levels of economic growth.

Overall, however, the analysis in this report suggests that there are no fundamental technological, economic, or resource limits constraining the world from enjoying the benefits of both high levels of energy services and a better environment. This is not to suggest that these benefits are to be expected—only that they are achievable. As the scenarios discussed above demonstrate, sustainable futures depend on ambitious policy measures and support for technological innovation.

In analyzing appropriate policies, it is important to keep in mind key features of the political and economic environment in which new energy systems will evolve:

- The broad structure of macroeconomic and development policies—particularly those for education and broad-based growth. Below a certain level of per capita income, subsistence needs other than energy dominate household budgets and priorities. Income growth among groups without access is the most important determinant of whether they will be willing to pay for energy services (and thus provide the demand required for markets to work effectively). This, in turn, depends on policies beyond the control of energy industries.
- The widespread liberalization of energy markets and the restructuring of the energy sector. These changes are driven by inefficient monopolies, government budget constraints, and expanding technological opportunities—especially in electric power generation. Liberalization and restructuring can lower costs and generate the finance required for the expansion and extension of supplies (as long as it is profitable to do so). But in restructured energy markets, cross-subsidies will not be available to increase access in areas that are not attractive to investors, unless restructuring is accompanied by policy measures that specifically address such concerns.
- Globalization and the transformations of the information age. Related to the liberalisation of markets is globalization—the worldwide expansion of major companies and their acquisition of, or partnership with, local companies. Procurement of materials and services from distant and foreign sources has become common. New technologies are also diffusing at rates faster than ever before, spurred by worldwide access to the Internet and other information technologies. This expansion can expedite the awareness of sustainable energy options and the deployment of new technologies.

Energy Policies for Sustainable Development

The scenarios exercise showed that, although energy can contribute to sustainable development, its performance in this respect will depend on a range of factors. These include attitudes and behavior, information and technologies, the availability of finance and supporting institutions, and, in particular, policies and policy frameworks that encourage change in the desired direction. The current path of energy development, and the rate of change, are not compatible with key elements of sustainable development. The divergence of alternative futures that becomes apparent in the scenarios after about 20 years reflects the long-term nature of energy systems. It also indicates that if governments, corporations, and international institutions do not introduce appropriate policies and measures now, critical windows of opportunity are likely to close. It will then become even more difficult to change course.

The most critical issues that sustainable energy strategies and the policies derived from them need to address are how to widen access to reliable and affordable modern energy supplies, and how to ease the negative health and environmental impacts of energy use.

Given proper frameworks, pricing signals, and regulatory regimes, markets can efficiently deliver on the economic objectives of sustainable development. But markets alone cannot be expected to meet the needs of the most vulnerable groups and to protect the environment. Where markets fail to protect these and other important public benefits, targeted government policies and consistent regulatory approaches will be needed. The problem is that government interventions are usually less efficient than market approaches. Government intervention may have unintended consequences at odds with its original aims. For that reason, there is a need to try different approaches and learn from the experiences of other countries.

Policies and policy frameworks in support of sustainable development should focus on widening access, encouraging energy efficiency, accelerating new renewable energy diffusion, and expanding the use of advanced clean fossil fuel technologies, while keeping open the nuclear option. These policy areas, as well as related decisions on private-public transportation and city planning, have the greatest relevance to the environmental and safety problems associated with conventional fuels.

The broad strategies for encouraging sustainable energy systems are straightforward. But achieving them will require wide acknowledgement of the challenges we face and stronger commitment to specific policies. The strategies are largely aimed at harnessing market efficiencies to the goal of sustainable development and using additional measures to speed up innovation, overcome obstacles and market imperfections, and protect important public benefits. Among the basic strategies, six stand out.

Making Markets Work Better

Driven by the forces of competition, markets do a better job than administered systems in allocating resources. But the marketplace fails to adequately account for the social and environmental costs of energy provision and use. Policies that reduce market distortions— that level the playing field—would give sustainable energy (renewable sources, energy efficiency measures, new technologies with near-zero emissions) a considerably better market position relative to current uses and practices.

Market distortions can be reduced by phasing out permanent subsidies to conventional energy (estimated at $250 billion–$300 billion a year in the mid-1990s) and by including social and environmental costs in prices. Several countries have experimented with energy and environment taxes as a way to address the latter. In many cases incentives will be needed to induce or accelerate changes. One such option is a targeted, time-limited (through a 'sunset clause') subsidy. Where energy markets cannot function effectively because of absolute poverty, additional resources, including official development assistance, are required.

Another aspect of making markets work better is finding ways to overcome obstacles to energy end-use efficiency measures. Even in the absence of subsidies, market barriers, such as lack of technological knowledge, different interests of investors and users, and high transaction costs of individual investors, keep energy efficiency measures from reaching their cost-effective potential. Options to overcome these barriers include voluntary or mandatory standards (effectively applied) for appliances, vehicles, and buildings, labelling schemes to better inform consumers, procurement policies to achieve higher standards and economies of scale, technical training in new energy efficiency technologies and their maintenance, and credit mechanisms to help consumers meet higher first costs.

Currently applied technologies are not adequate and profitable enough to deliver the energy services that will be needed in the 21st century and simultaneously protect human health and environmental stability.

Complementing Energy Sector Restructuring with Regulations that Encourage Sustainable Energy

The ongoing, worldwide restructuring of the energy industry—largely driven by the increasing globalisation of the economy—will lead to more economically efficient energy markets. This restructuring presents a window of opportunity for ensuring that the energy-related public benefits needed for sustainable development are adequately addressed in emerging policies for energy market reform. The process could be enhanced if governments set goals that define the performance characteristics of qualifying sustainable energy technologies (for example, by specifying air pollution emission limits or minimum standards on plants, machinery, and vehicles).

These goals for suppliers can be complemented by mechanisms that favour sustainable energy technologies in energy market choices. Other regulatory approaches supportive of sustainable energy include mandating that a certain percentage of energy comes from renewable sources, requiring that energy grids be open to independent power producers, and ensuring that rural populations are served. Such regulations are based on the recognition that energy market restructuring in itself may not help achieve sustainable development.

Mobilizing Additional Investments in Sustainable Energy

Energy markets in many countries are rapidly becoming more competitive. For that reason, successful sustainable energy policies, whether involving financing, incentives, taxes, or regulations, must engage the private sector and catalyze private investment on a large scale. But for political or institutional reasons, many of the transition and developing economies that most need investment have problems attracting private enterprise and gaining access to financial markets. Reliable commercial legislation and jurisdiction, as well as incentives, may be needed to encourage private companies to invest in sustainable energy—or to defray the risks associated with such investments.

Official development assistance may also need to play a greater role in the least developed countries, especially in those where the conditions that attract private sector investment are lacking. Political stability, application of the rule of law, avoidance of arbitrary intervention, and the existence of institutions that facilitate savings and investment are generally important for promoting investment. Supportive financial and credit arrangements (including micro-credit arrangements like those now in existence) will be needed to introduce commercial energy to people excluded from markets, especially in rural areas.

Encouraging Technological Innovation

Currently applied technologies are not adequate and profitable enough to deliver the energy services that will be needed in the 21st century and simultaneously protect human health and environmental stability. Adequate support for a portfolio of promising advanced and new technologies is one way to help ensure that options will be available as the need for them becomes more acute. Energy innovations face barriers all along the energy innovation chain (from research and development, to demonstration projects, to cost buy-down, to widespread diffusion). Some of these barriers reflect market imperfections, some inadequacies in the public sector, and some different views about needs, corporate priorities, relevant time horizons, and reasonable costs.

The public support needed to overcome such barriers will vary from one technology to the next, depending on its maturity and market potential. Obstacles to technology diffusion, for example, may need to be given higher priority than barriers to innovation. Direct government support is more likely to be needed for radically new technologies than for incremental advances, where the private sector usually functions relatively effectively. Options to support technological innovation, while sail using competition to keep down costs, include tax incentives, collaborative research and development ventures, government or cooperative procurement policies, 'green' labelling schemes, and market transformation initiatives.

Supporting Technological Leadership and Capacity Building in Developing Countries

Because most of the projected growth in energy demand will occur in the developing world, innovation and leadership in energy technologies could be highly profitable for developing countries in economic, and human terms. Developing economies need to further develop their resources—human, natural, and technological—so they can create energy systems appropriate to their own circumstances. But they also need assistance with technology transfer, financing, and capacity building.

The declining share of official development assistance relative to required investment capital suggests that much of this investment will need to be led by the private sector or private-public partnerships. International industrial collaboration offers one means by which the private sector could gain markets while fostering the private research institutes, and regional institutes that provide training in technological management offer additional possibilities for furthering technology sharing and capacity building.

Encouraging Greater Cooperation at the International Level

The ongoing process of globalization means that ideas, finances, and energy flow from one country to another. Productive ways of moving forward might include combining national efforts, for example, in the procurement of renewable energy technologies. Other options include international harmonisation of environmental taxes and emissions trading (particularly among industrialized countries), as well as energy efficiency standards for mass-produced products and imports of used machinery and vehicles. The need for concerted action on energy is clear from *Agenda 21*, which emerged from the 1992 Earth Summit.

The challenge of sustainable energy includes crucial enabling roles for governments, international organizations, multilateral financial institutions, and civil society, including nongovernmental organizations and individual consumers. Partnerships will be required, based on more integrated, cooperative approaches and drawing on a range of practical experience. A common denominator across all sectors and regions is setting the right framework conditions and making public institutions work effectively and efficiently with the rest of society and other economic actors to reach beneficial, shared objectives.

Clearly, energy can serve as a powerful tool for sustainable development. Redirecting its power to work towards that overarching goal, however, will require major changes of policy within an enabling overall framework. Poverty, inequity, inefficiency, unreliable service, immediate environmental priorities, a lack of information and basic skills, and an absence of needed institutions and resources require changes to be made. Unless these changes occur within the next few decades, many of the opportunities now available will be lost, the possibilities for future generations diminished, and the goal of sustainable development unrealised.

6

Case Study Problem

A

Craig D., *Negotiation for Amendments to the Kyoto Protocol (1998) Under the Framework Convention on Climate Change*, Centre for Environmental Law, Macquarie University, 2000

1. Six Nation States/NGOs will be participating. Each country should be represented by at least two people. Choose a role and notify, (in writing), the Chairperson.
2. The role play involves proposing amendments to the 1997 *Kyoto Protocol*. The general object of the proposed amendments should be:
   (a) to impose binding commitments on developing countries to limit their emissions of carbon dioxide.
   (b) To obtain commitments by developed countries to provide developing countries with assistance to meet those limits.
3. At the beginning of the role play, each country will make a 1-2 minute opening statement. The statement must outline your proposed amendments to the *Kyoto Protocol* 1997; or (lack of them), and the reasons for your position.
4. The countries have no duty to reach an agreement. They do however, have an obligation to negotiate in good faith with the object of seeing whether agreement is possible.

Summary—Climate Change *Kyoto Protocol*, (1997)

Base: 1990 Emissions

Target Dates: 2008–2012. (Not as per *Framework Convention on Climate Change*)

Specific Targets set in 1997

- US 7 percent reduction
- Iceland 10 percent reduction
- EC 8 percent reduction
- Australia + 8 percent
- Overall Global 5 percent reduction
- Market mechanisms such as emission trading and the clean development mechanism proposed

ROLE PLAY—*KYOTO PROTOCOL* NEGOTIATIONS IN THE YEAR 2002

The following roles are assigned to re-negotiate the 1997 *Kyoto Protocol*

1. Japan—Government
   Wants significant target but less than 12 percent. They believe that they have products (e.g., less polluting cars) and industrial technology that will easily allow them to meet a target of 10 percent reduction. They will have and economic/trade advantage if targets are set at 10 percent or slightly above.
2. USA—Government
   Wants targets but the President believes that Congress will not ratify anything greater than 8-10 percent. Does not want Japan to get competitive advantage re: GHG reduction and technology, therefore they are keen on achieving reasonably high (binding) target.
3. EC wants 10 percent target because "bubble" (target is calculated by averaging EC emissions) gives it more flexibility and trade advantage. They can trade off "deficit" GHG's from Eastern Europe against Western Europe GHG's.
4. "South" Nations
   - China wants no targets for the poor nations of the world.
   - India will agree to targets of less than 5 percent only if there is a guarantee of adequate funding and technology transfer at no cost for the "South".
   - Brazil will agree to targets 10 years later then "North" nations.
5. Green NGOs and the Organization of Small Island States (including the rapidly sinking Pacific Islands) want 20 percent reduction and they meant it! They have retained expert negotiators from the Foundation for International Environmental Law (FIELD) to present their case.
6. Fossil Fuel Corporate NGOs want a target of +15 percent and voluntary measures, because they know that they work. They believe that the existing *Montreal Protocol* targets are an impractical and costly mistake.
7. The target date remains 2008–2012 (as per the 1998 Protocol) on the advice of scientists from the Intergovernmental Panel on Climate Change.

ISSUES

1. Scientific/Technical Role of Precautionary Principle
2. Differential Responsibilities of Nation States
3. Differential Economic Impacts of Nation States
4. Regulatory Mechanisms
   - Role of targets/dates
   - Role of technology transfer
   - Joint implementation
   - Carbon Trading
   - CDM: Clean Development Mechanism
   - Interim measures
5. Monitoring, Reporting and Compliance
6. Establishment of a fund to assist developing nations with compliance.

7 Questions for Discussion

(a) The issue of climate change, the extent to which it is occurring and the role of human induced greenhouse gases, raises complex scientific and policy issues. Discuss the role of the intergovernmental panel on climate change in the development of the regime created by the FCCC and the *Kyoto Protocol*. Go on to the IPCC web site and discuss the latest projections about global warming and climate change that they have made. What is the likely impact, on the world's environment, of these projections?

(b) What gases are regulated by the *Kyoto Protocol*? What problems do you anticipate, with national implementation measures relating to each of the gases the are regulated by the regime? Would it have been more appropriate, or effective, to have immediately tried to get international agreement to regulate only CO_2 emissions as soon as possible after the FCCC was agreed in 1992? What are the arguments for the more comprehensive approach adopted in the *Kyoto Protocol*?

(c) What main mitigation and adaption strategies are available to reduce the impact of climate change? Discuss particularly the potential role of energy efficient technologies and reducing demand.

(d) Discuss the differentiated responsibilities of developed and developing countries in the FCCC and the *Kyoto Protocol*. Discuss how the concept of differentiated responsibilities has evolved, particularly under the *Kyoto Protocol*. Do you believe that "fossil fuel dependent nations", such as Australia should have been given differentiated treatment under the *Kyoto Protocol*?

(e) What overall reduction in greenhouse gas emissions, from the 1990 baseline, are likely to be achieved if all parties to the *Kyoto Protocol* make *bona fide* attempts to meet their target? Discuss the adequacy of the proposed reduction having regard to the projections about climate change that are being made by the IPCC?

(f) Arguably, there can be no global regime without ratification and implementation by the European Community, United States and Japan. Discuss the role that these parties have taken in the *Kyoto Protocol* negotiations and the likelihood of their ratification.

(g) One of the significant developments, under the climate change regime, is the rapidly emerging role of flexible market mechanisms—carbon trading, joint implementation and the clean development mechanism. Discuss the role that these mechanisms could play in the regime. To what extent are they likely to contribute to the overall goals of the regime and to sustainable development? What role do forests play in these regimes and discuss the environmental issues that are associated with this?

8

References for Chapter 22

Hammond A., Rudenburg, and Moonmaw W., "The Greenhouse Index," *Environment*, 33 (1), 1991.

Hulme M. and Kelly P.M., "Exploring the Links Between Desertification and Climate Change," *Environment*, 35 (6), 1993, pp 4–46.

Kowoloh M.E., "Common Threads: Research Lessons from Acid Rain, Ozone Depletion and Global Warming," *Environment*, 35 (6), 1993.

Lefevere Jurgen, "Small Islands at the Frontline," *FIELD in Brief*, No. 9 Summer, 2001.

Wigely TM.L. and Raper S.C.B., "Implications for Climate and Sea Level of Revised IPCC Emissions Scenarios," *Nature*, 357, 1992, pp 293–300.

Wigely TM.L., Pearman G.I., and Kelly P.M., "Indices and Indicators of Climate Change: Issues of Detection, Validation and Climate Sensitivity," in Mintzer I.M. (ed), *Confronting Climatic Change: Risks Implications and Responses*, Cambridge University Press, 1992.

9

Additional References

Asiedu-Akrofi D., "Debt for Nature Swaps: Extending the Frontiers of Innovative Financing in Support of the Global Environment," 25, *The International Lawyer* 557, (Fall), 1991.*Energy End Use: An Environmentally Sound Development Pathway*, Asian Development Bank, 1993.

European Union, *Green Paper on Greenhouse Gas Emissions Trading Within the European Union* available at COM(2000)87. http://europa.eu.int/comm/environment/docum/0087_en.htm

Cameron J., Robertson D.J., and Curnow P., "Legal and Regulatory Strategies for GHG Reduction—A Global Survey," Natural Resources & Environment, ABA Section of Environment, *Energy and Resources* Vol. 15, No. 3, Winter 2001.

Goldberg D., *et al.*, *Carbon Conservation, Climate Change, Forests and the Clean Development Mechanism*, Washington, DC, Centre for Environmental Law, CEDARENA, 1998.

Ghosh P., *Implementaion of the Kyoto Protocol: Opportunities and Pitfalls for Developing Countries*, Asian Development Bank, 2000.

Grubb M., Vrolijk C., and Brack D., *The Kyoto Protocol: A Guide and Assessment*, Earthscan, 2001.

Hunter, D., Salzman, J., and Zaelke, D., *International Environmental Law and Policy*, University Casebook Series, Foundation Press, New York, 1998.

International Institute for Sustainable Development (IISD), "The Summary of the Sixth Conference of the Parties to the Framework Convention on Climate Change," The Earth Negotiations Bulletin, Vol. 12, No. 163, 27 November 2000, http://www.iisd.ca/download/asc/enb12116e.txt [*Editors' note: last accessed on 23/01/2001.*]

Jackson T., Begg K., and Parkinson S., *Flexibility in Climate Policy: Making the Kyoto Mechanisms Work*, Earthscan, 2001.

Kyoto Protocol to the United Nations Framework Convention on Climate Change, http://www.unfcc.de/fccc/docs/protintr.html [*Editors Note: This site was accessed on 26/02/2001.*]

United Nations Framework Convention of Climate Change, http://www.unfccc.int/resource/conv/conv.html [*Editors Note: This site was accessed on 03/04/2001.*]

CHAPTER

23

FINANCING SUSTAINABLE DEVELOPMENT

CONTENTS

1 Introduction

Sustainable development is clearly the most cost-effective policy option in the long run. In the short run, it is necessary to be creative in designing options for financing sustainable development to counter the immediacy of the bottom line visible to managers and financiers and corporations or banks. The materials in this chapter suggest some ways in which alternatives for financing have been utilized to preserve the environment and achieve sustainable development.

Economic incentives can include trading in pollution permits or mitigation allowances. In addition, the use of taxes, fees, and dedicated trust funds can be used to shape development and business decisions by treating some projects more favorably than others to accomplish the policy goal. Legal systems for national bonding and infrastructure investment are important tools that must not be overlooked on the national level as a means of financing sustainable development. International and regional development assistance is available through the World Bank, Asian Development Bank, and funds under some of the multilateral environmental treaties, such as the *Biodiversity Convention*, administered through the Global Environment Facility (GEF). A recent General Assembly resolution relevant to the implementation of *Agenda 21* is included.

Governments are also beginning to impose conditions on private investment for provision of infrastructure at the stage of negotiations for foreign direct investment. Current development assistance programs are in evolution. Building large project infrastructure (dams for electricity, etc.) has not induced rapid economic development, and has left substantial foreign debt to be repaid, often has produced secondary adverse environmental impacts, and has not been insulated by sound financial accounting systems so that it has fed corruption in government. Politicians in developed states are reluctant to ask taxpayers to increase overseas assistance, and increasingly limit their aid by "conditionality" or insist on requests being generated out of the embassy in the country where the aid will be spent. Multilateral development bank (MDB) donors are reassessing their assistance and investment systems. MDBs and bilateral aid are encouraging private capital investment as a preferred means for underwriting development assistance. Projects of economic development today are often a combination of public and private funds. Some key environmental issues, associated with the trend toward privatization, are discussed in the Richardson extract.

Finally, the international legal system is beginning to address liability rules, strict liability, and provision of insurance for situations where environmental degradation results from development activities. National legislation also can establish such rules as a means of protecting scarce natural resources, and the health and cleanliness of the environment.

The extracts in this chapter commence by examining the wider economic issues that form the context for environmental evaluation and funding. Oogai and Tanaka discuss the limits of traditional approaches to economics particularly in the area of valuation and environmental accounting. Basically, they argue that the provision of funding, by the private sector or MDBs, proceeds from a fundamentally flawed basis because of the failure by most nations to develop environmental economics as a tool for environmental management and investment. The second extract deals with the unequal way that environmental costs and benefits are borne, the administrative difficulties of implementing environmental policies in the Asian and Pacific region and the problems of transboundary pollution. They argue that these are the three main political and institutional obstacles to funding for environmental management. In demonstrating how different groups bear different costs and

The international legal system is beginning to address liability rules, strict liability, and provision of insurance for situations where environmental degradation results from development activities.

benefits, they look at the deeper cause of environmental destruction, such as the cycle of poverty, poor national systems of environmental law and management, insufficient environmental safeguards contained in bilateral and multilateral aid projects and destruction generated by the North-South trade structure.

Oogai and Tanaka go on to explore regional environmental problems, such as acid rain, in more detail and to propose investment and funding strategies to deal with these. They emphasize the need for a common environmental strategy for the region that will preserve the fragile ecosystems and the establishment of an organization to accelerate capacity building on a regional level, such as an Asian Regional Environment Facility. This latter issue is discussed in Chapter 16 using the issue of the Southeast Asian fires as a focus. The article therein from Robinson discusses some financial issues regarding transboundary cooperative fire fighting. Also, the intricacies of the North-South debate are covered in more detail in Chapter 17.

The issue of funding mechanisms is explored further in the context of national environmental funds that have been established in many countries and sources of additionality and the payment of incremental costs through funds under a global convention such as the *Convention on Biological Diversity*. The concepts of additionality and incremental costs are now fundamental in the financing of sustainable development and they reexplored in more detail in the extract from Jordan and Werksman. The Global Environment Facility has now been pledged more than $2.75 billion to protect the environmental and promote sustainable development. Its governing structure is significantly different from the World Bank with much stronger representation from developing countries. It levers its funding to a much greater extent by using approaches such as funding incremental costs—for example funding the difference between the cost of a polluting source of power generation and an energy efficient one.

Their focal areas for funding are biodiversity, climate change, international waters, ozone depletion and land degradation. The other significant feature of GEF funding is that it can be given to nongovernment organizations (i.e., not only governments). It has a different funding procedure to the World Bank and often GEF project grants are smaller and facilitate more local level involvement that World Bank funding. When considering funding approaches for biodiversity conservation, the operations of the multilateral fund under the Convention, the GEF, and World Bank need to be considered.

The World Bank has been rapidly evolving country studies, involving significant environmental studies, environmental impact assessment procedures for projects, and more general policies relating to funding a much wider range of projects and capacity building activities such as the development of national environmental laws and institutions. The extract by Di Leva looks at the role of the World Bank in developing international environmental law, the interaction between the World Bank and the GEF and other environmentally related policies and procedures of the World Bank. This extract gives a detailed discussion of this controversial area and institution.

Of course, in the Asian and Pacific region, the operations and policies of the Asian Development Bank are central to financing sustainable development. The extract from Boyd provides a firsthand examination of ADB and its role in the Asian and Pacific region including the targeting of loans toward particular projects, the development of projects for capacity building, the use of consultants to bring expertise to the region that otherwise may be able unaffordable and the production of ADB publications, such as this book.

Students should also be aware of other multilateral institutions such as the International Monetary Fund and the World Trade Organization which have far less developed environmental policies and programs. The issue of "green conditionality" on bilateral and multilateral aid remains very important in terms of a coordinated approach to sustainable development and the sovereignty of nation states.

An example of the potential for innovative approaches to Third World debt is through the use of the financial mechanisms known as debt swaps.

The mechanisms are described in the extract from Freeland along with a wide range of examples of debt swaps.

2

Protecting and Valuing Environmental Services

A

Salzman J., Thompson B.H. Jr., and Daily G.C., "Protecting Ecosystem Services: Science, Economics, and Law," 20 *Stanford Environmental Law Journal* 309, 2001

Introduction

By most measures, modern American environmental law has been a great success. With few exceptions our air is cleaner, our water purer, than in 1970. Despite these achievements, however, the last decade has witnessed repeated calls for a significant shift in regulatory emphasis. The top managers and scientific advisors in the United States Environmental Protection Agency (EPA) have consistently declared that maintenance of productive natural systems demands more attention and should, in fact, become one of the agency's highest priorities. In recommending that reduced ecological risk become a primary focus of EPA, its scientists and managers have revealed the single greatest failing of modern environmental law and its greatest challenge today—the inadequate protection of ecosystems and the services they provide.

Largely taken for granted, healthy ecosystems provide a variety of critical services. Created by the interactions of living organisms with their environment, these "ecosystem services" provide both the conditions and processes that sustain human life—purifying air and water, detoxifying and decomposing waste, renewing soil fertility, regulating climate, mitigating droughts and floods, controlling pests, and pollinating plants. Although awareness of ecosystem services dates back to Plato, ecologists, economists, and lawyers have only recently begun systematically examining the extent and implications of these services' valuable contributions to social welfare. Not surprisingly, recent research has demonstrated the extremely high costs to replace many of these services if they were to fail, on the order of many billions of dollars in the United States for water purification alone. Such estimates are inherently uncertain, but the extraordinary costs required to substitute for many important services by artificial means are beyond dispute.

Our unthinking reliance on ecosystem services is due in part, no doubt, to society's dissociation between the milk carton and medicines in our home, on the one hand, and the services of nutrient cycling and biodiversity, on the other, that made these possible. Thus it is perhaps not surprising that many children, when asked where milk comes from, reply without hesitation, "from the grocery store." Given their significance, one might expect that ecosystem services would be prized by markets and explicitly protected by the law. With few exceptions, however, neither has been the case.

It is perhaps not surprising that many children, when asked where milk comes from, reply without hesitation, "from the grocery store."

Despite their obvious importance to our well being, ecosystem services have largely been ignored in environmental law and policy. Provision of services is only rarely considered in cost-benefit analyses, preparation of environmental impact statements, wetlands mitigation banking, Superfund remediations, and oil spill clean-ups. Nor have significant markets arisen that capitalize on the commercial value of these services. We have no shortage of markets for ecosystem goods (such as clean water and apples), but the services underpinning these goods (such as water purification and pollination) are free. The services themselves have no market value for the simple reason that no markets exist in which they can be exchanged. As a result, there are no direct price mechanisms to signal the scarcity or degradation of these public goods until they fail. Partly as a result, ecosystems are degraded.

An explicit ecosystem services perspective provides two obvious benefits. The first is political. Understanding the role of ecosystem services powerfully justifies why habitat preservation and biodiversity conservation are vital, though often overlooked, policy objectives. While a wetland surely provides existence and option values to some people, the benefits provided by the wetland's nutrient retention and flood protection services are both universal and undeniable. Tastes may differ over beauty, but they are in firm accord over the high costs of polluted water and flooded homes.

The second benefit is instrumental. Efforts to capture the value of ecosystem services may spur institutional designs and market mechanisms that effectively promote environmental protection at the local, regional, national, and international levels. To realize this potential, however, we must first create market mechanisms and institutions that can capture and maximize service values. If given the opportunity, natural systems can, in many cases, quite literally "pay their way." The key challenge is how to make this happen.

The study of ecosystem services and their implications for environmental protection is a nascent field and we still have much to learn. There has been a great deal of enthusiasm surrounding an ecosystem services approach, and in many cases this may be thoroughly warranted. Yet such an approach offers potential pitfalls, as well. Recognition of the value provided by specific ecosystem services may offer persuasive reasons to strengthen existing protections and resist further encroachments, or it may not. In some cases, perhaps many, a focus on services will not justify conservation of biodiversity or certain natural habitats. In other cases, the services will not be amenable to market or legal-based solutions and will be largely irrelevant to environmental protection efforts. Thus, while a focus on ecosystem services provides great latent potential to promote environmental protection, its practical implications remain largely unexamined.

There are several important questions that need to be answered. Can we develop robust methodologies for the valuation of services? Absent these, how can we compare the costs of degrading an ecosystem and its service provision with the benefits of the offending activity? If ecosystem services have real but uncaptured value, what are the necessary conditions for market creation to exchange valuable services? And, critically, is the science good enough to tell us how to manage ecosystems for reliable service provision?

This issue of the *Stanford Environmental Law Journal* explores our current state of knowledge, presenting the results of interdisciplinary research conducted over the past three years on the legal, scientific, and economic aspects of ecosystem services...In probing the implications of an ecosystem services approach, Parts II and III of this article explore the ecosystem services of water purification and flood control, describing efforts to capture their value and the resulting challenges. Part IV describes a range of initiatives around the globe to value and protect nature's services. Part V considers the steps necessary to integrate the emerging science and economics of ecosystem services valuation within a legal framework of rules and incentives. The challenges of valuing and protecting ecosystem services are surely significant, but the potential is there to transform the explicit management of services from enticing anecdote to widespread practice.

The Service of Water Purification

Of all ecosystem services, water purification might provide the greatest chance for galvanizing market or regulatory action aimed at protecting ecologically important lands. The value of safe drinking water is undeniable and universally recognized. Internationally, water contamination is one of the greatest causes of human disease, illness, and death. Domestically, drinking water quality is high relative to that found in much of the world, but close to a million Americans still become sick each year as a result of drinking contaminated water, and hundreds die. Surveys, not surprisingly, repeatedly show that safe drinking water is among the most important environmental issues to the American public. If any ecosystem service is likely to capture the public's attention, water purification is it.

The linkage between watershed protection and drinking water quality is also clear. When land in the vicinity of a waterway is developed, the uses to which the land is put frequently add contaminants to the waterway. Nonpoint pollution, in the form of runoff from agriculture, livestock operations, construction sites, parking lots, roads, and other uses, as well as the leaching of waste from septic tanks, is today the major threat to the nation's waterways. Undeveloped land, moreover, helps reduce contamination. Both wetlands and soils filter out nutrients and other contamination from runoff before the runoff reaches the main course of a waterway. Vegetation slows down runoff, permitting solid pollutants to settle out, and stabilizes soil, thus reducing contamination from siltation. Land preservation thus performs double duty in protecting water quality: it eliminates a major source of contamination, while also protecting the waterway from those nonpoint sources of contamination that do exist.

Recognizing the value to water quality of natural watersheds, a number of water suppliers for years have tried to protect watersheds from development. Although the typical water supplier owns only about two percent of the land in its watersheds of supply, water suppliers in some regions of the country own a much larger percentage, sometimes including a majority of the remaining open space. The interesting question is whether government can use the value of natural water quality services to encourage water suppliers to take additional steps today to preserve ecologically valuable watershed lands.

New York City has inspired hope by embarking on a $250 million program to acquire and preserve up to 350,000 acres of land in the Catskills watershed, one of three major basins from which the city obtains its water supply. A combination of federal regulation and cost realities drove New York City to this program. Under the federal Safe Drinking Water Act, municipal and other water suppliers must filter their water supplies unless they can demonstrate that they have taken other steps, including watershed protection measures, that protect their customers from harmful water contamination. Presented with a choice between building a filtration plant and preserving the watershed, New York City easily concluded that the latter was more cost effective. New York City estimated that a filtration plant would cost between $6 billion and $8 billion to build and another $300 million annually to operate. By contrast, watershed protection efforts, which would include not only the acquisition of critical watershed lands but also a variety of other programs designed to reduce contamination sources in the watershed, would cost only about $1.5 billion.

New York City's Catskills efforts raise a number of issues. First, are New York City's efforts anomalous, or are they an example of a growing interest in preserving watershed lands for water quality purposes? In the late 1990s, EPA estimated that more than 140 cities were considering watershed conservation as a means of ensuring high drinking water quality. The Appendix to this article provides approximately a dozen important examples of this phenomenon. Few of these efforts, however, come close to New York City's preservation actions in scale or importance. And water suppliers in a few areas of the country actually are divesting themselves of watershed lands.

Several factors helped make New York City's decision to preserve watershed lands for water quality purposes relatively easy. First, New York City is the dominant beneficiary of Catskills preservation efforts. New York both draws sizable quantities of water from the Catskills and dwarfs all other cities drawing drinking water from the watershed. As a result, New York City gets virtually the entire benefit in improved water quality of its preservation efforts. A smaller city that draws on only a small portion of the supply from a watershed would face a tougher choice because only a fraction of the water-quality benefits from land preservation would go to it. In deciding whether to acquire land on its own, a smaller city might decide that the benefits were not worth it, and efforts to forge a coalition with other water suppliers drawing water from the same watershed might fail as a result of free-rider problems. Second, in deciding to protect the Catskills watershed rather than build a filtration plant, New York City benefited from century-old regulatory authority over the watershed. New York City is protecting the watershed partly through land acquisition and preservation and partly through local land-use incentive programs, but also through regulation of local uses. Whether New York City would have found it worthwhile to protect the watershed through economic means even if it had not enjoyed the regulatory power is an unaddressed question. Third, most of the land that New York City has slated for preservation is in areas that are still not highly populated and, thus the land is not astronomically expensive. Significant differences in land prices could change the cost-benefit equation for deciding whether to acquire and preserve the watershed land. Finally, the federal government put the city to a choice: protect the watershed or build an extremely expensive filtration plant. It is questionable whether New York City would have chosen to protect water quality by protecting the watershed absent that federal pressure.

The last point raises a second important issue: how can governmental policy help promote water-quality motivated investments in watershed preservation? The government can start by forcing water suppliers to take water quality seriously through regulatory schemes such as the Safe Drinking Water Act. Although consumers might prize safe drinking water, they also savor low water rates and might not be willing to support a rate increase needed to purchase land that would promise water quality services. The government also must not favor technological over natural solutions. New York City chose to protect the Catskills watershed because EPA gave it a choice between a filtration facility and watershed efforts. If EPA had required New York City to build the filtration facility, the city might not have concluded that any additional water-quality benefits from protecting the watershed were worth the cost. Governments similarly must ensure that any funding aid provided to water suppliers can be spent on either technological or natural efforts to promote water quality. Although EPA has extended its revolving loan program for water quality investments to land acquisition, EPA prohibits a state from spending more than ten percent of its loan moneys on the acquisition of fee simples or conservation easements.

Non-environmental regulations sometimes may also influence water suppliers' decision whether to acquire and preserve watershed lands. Consider, for example, the rate setting system used by public utility commissions to determine how much private water companies can charge for their services. In most cases, water rates are set to permit companies a specified rate of return on the total capital invested in their business. Land is typically included in the rate base, but at original cost. Where a water supplier purchased watershed lands in the distant past, the land might be worth far more today than its value in the rate base—encouraging the water supplier to find a way to sell the land and capitalize on the land's increased value. This phenomenon might partly explain why a number of Connecticut water companies have sold off watershed lands in the last decade. Indeed, the Connecticut Department of Public Utility Control, whose mission includes reducing the water rates that consumers pay, sometimes has encouraged the water companies to sell such lands and then use part of the proceeds to lower their water rates.

The water quality motives that drive water suppliers to acquire and preserve watershed lands might conflict in some situations with other public goals.

The simplest means that the government can use to promote water quality through land preservation, of course, would be to mandate that all water suppliers adopt a watershed preservation program demonstrated to ensure an adequate level of water quality. The choice between such an imperative regulation and the current choice given to water suppliers to either preserve the watershed or filter their water comes down to efficiency. In many settings, land preservation will not be the most economical means of ensuring adequate water quality.

A third issue is whether we currently have the scientific knowledge needed to determine which lands to preserve in order to maximize the value to water quality. As mentioned earlier, we know far more about water quality services than most other ecosystem services, but the science is still fairly rough and ready. New York City has chosen which land to preserve based on geography and the "travel time" that it would take runoff from the land to reach the city's water supply.

A final issue is the degree of "ecosystem synergy" obtained when water suppliers acquire and preserve watershed land for water quality purposes. Do the preservation efforts just ensure higher water quality, or do they also provide other valuable ecosystem services? It would be nice, for example, if the same land that water suppliers chose to preserve was also high in biodiversity or was habitat for endangered species. We do not have enough information at the moment, however, to know whether this is the case. Worse, the water quality motives that drive water suppliers to acquire and preserve watershed lands might conflict in some situations with other public goals. Given their water quality goals, for example, many water suppliers do not permit public access to or use of watershed lands owned by the suppliers. Where this is the case, public recreational interests conflict with the water quality goals. Emphasis on one ecosystem service undermines the provision of another.

On the whole, however, investments by water suppliers in watershed preservation provides one of the most exciting and significant examples of how those who benefit from ecosystem services are recognizing the services' value and taking steps to protect the services.

The Service of Flood Control

Flood control also would seem to be a strong motivation for watershed protection. Like drinking water quality, flood protection is of tremendous importance. Floods cause over $4 billion in damages in an average year and lead to dozens of deaths. Scientists have a strong understanding of the relationship between watershed preservation and reductions in flood damages. Heavy vegetation can slow the runoff of precipitation into waterways, permitting some of the runoff to seep into groundwater aquifers and reducing peak flows. Wetlands similarly serve as natural sponges, soaking up water during times of peak runoff and then releasing the water slowly over time. A 1993 study by the Illinois State Water Survey, for example, estimated that every 1 percent increase in wetlands along a stream corridor in the state decreased peak stream flows by an average of 3.7 percent. Naturally contoured lands also spread out runoff temporally, more so than do highly developed regions with channelized riverbeds. Finally, undeveloped riparian land can help provide safety valves in case of floods: peak flows can be released onto the undeveloped land, reducing the risk of flood damage to developed areas downstream.

Not surprisingly, therefore, some governmental agencies have invested in watershed preservation for flood control purposes...In one of the best known examples, voters in California's Napa County approved an initiative to spend $160 million to acquire 500 acres of flood plain, in the expectation that the acquisition will significantly reduce flood damage. Local governments near Boston have also decided that acquiring 8,000 acres of wetlands, capable of holding approximately 50,000 acre-feet of water, was a more effective approach to flood control than the construction of a $100 million system of dams and levees. But flood control has driven far fewer watershed preservation programs than drinking water quality.

In trying to evaluate the role that ecosystem services can play in ecological preservation, the important question is why flood control has proven a less significant force in watershed protection efforts. Why have numerous steps been taken to preserve watersheds for water purification and few for flood control? Here, one currently can offer only educated guesses. As noted earlier, flood control is economically extremely valuable, and traditional engineering approaches to flood control are very expensive. Although detailed studies are lacking, the economics of "natural" solutions to flood control would seem to favor such methods over engineering approaches. Water suppliers have recognized for decades the value to water quality of a protected watershed, but flood control agencies historically have relied on technological solutions to flood risks. Part of the reason for this difference might be our historical failure to understand the importance of natural terrains and features to flood potential and mitigation. The willingness and eagerness of the United States Army Corps of Engineers to become involved in flood control, along with federal funding for flood control construction, also has inevitably biased thinking toward engineering rather than natural solutions. Whatever the reason for the traditional bias toward engineering, habits die hard. Flood control experts have spent far more time studying and perfecting engineering solutions than natural solutions, and government officials trying to protect populations from flood loss are more likely to turn to the tried and true. The dominant role of the federal government in flood control also contrasts with water purification, a traditionally local activity. In the tradition of local experimentation (letting a thousand flowers bloom) one would expect a far greater range in approaches to water purification than to flood control. Controlling floods through watershed preservation also might be more difficult than providing water quality through watershed protection. In many cases, water supplies are captured, stored, and diverted from the upper reaches of a watershed where development is light and land prices relatively low; flood control, by contrast, may require land preservation up and down the reaches of a waterway, including land in prime development locations.

Governments can help overcome the traditional bias toward engineering solutions by providing both expertise and funding for natural solutions. The Army Corps of Engineers in recent years, for example, has begun to work with local communities on natural flood control measures (in part sensing that this is the growth field of the future). Efforts to rectify the bias toward engineering solutions, however, have been much slower in coming to flood control than to water purification.

Ecosystem services furnish not only a new approach to flood control but a new way of thinking about floods because scientists increasingly are recognizing that floods themselves can provide some valuable services. Floods, for example, can bring new and rich topsoil to riparian land. The potential value of floods suggests that governments should be thinking more in terms of flood management than flood control. Permitting floods to occur in some areas might both minimize flood damage elsewhere while adding a natural service value to the flooded area.

Research and restoration work currently being conducted on the Cosumnes River in California demonstrates not only the benefits of watershed preservation for flood control, but also the potential opportunity to capitalize on multiple ecosystem services through land preservation. Scientists believe that a restored Cosumnes River watershed can help reduce flood risks by storing runoff and reducing flow velocity. But scientists also believe that watershed restoration and preservation can provide additional water supplies by promoting groundwater recharge and supporting base flows; improve water quality; increase neighboring soil quality by regulating sediment flux, serving as a sink for fine sediment and nutrients, and providing a source for increased soil moisture; improve air quality by trapping airborne particulates, moderating air temperature, and sequestering carbon in floodplain forests and wetlands; and serve as valuable habitat for both fish and regional wildlife.

Initiatives Abroad

Efforts to protect ecosystem services are occurring well beyond the United States. Indeed, the most innovative mechanisms for capturing service values and rewarding economically those who protect the underlying ecosystem assets have been developed abroad. In both developed and developing countries, these initiatives have involved a range of groups—government agencies, NGOs, and private enterprises—from local to national levels. They provide an important and growing set of experiments for exploring new institutional terrain, evaluating what works and what doesn't, and improving implementation in different social and economic circumstances.

In some of these initiatives, the potential values of services have influenced public land management decisions. In Madagascar, for example, a recent government decision to establish the 2,300km^2 Masoala National Park was based not only on a national policy to promote biodiversity conservation, but also on the anticipated capture of local ecosystem service benefits including sustainable forestry, production of non-timber forest products, and ecotourism. In the Ha Tinh Province of Vietnam, changes in community-level institutions have produced significant incentives for ecosystem service-based conservation. One village, Ky Thuong, has voluntarily established a reserve for the protection of biodiversity and supply of local ecosystem services, and others are attempting to follow suit. Similar efforts are underway in India; although at an earlier stage of development, they are yielding promising changes in farming practices to preserve important ecosystem goods, such as valuable plant species.

In several southern African nations, by contrast, private cattle ranchers are cooperating to develop eco-tourism with no government encouragement (indeed, in the face of major disincentives such as government subsidies for cattle). They are removing livestock, pooling their land and eliminating internal fences, and re-establishing native wildlife for safari purposes. The amount of land under conservation is growing substantially as a consequence, and has more than doubled in some large regions.

The largest experiments in protecting services are now underway in Costa Rica and Australia, where national initiatives already operate on relatively large areas and are being designed for further scaling up. Expansion will be possible with additional funding of the programs, which is anticipated with growing government and private sector investment in carbon sequestration, and in more sustainable development generally, and with greater monitoring and accountability project results. Expansion is also likely to result from the great effort presently going into innovative policies to align economic incentives with environmental conservation. Costa Rica has been a leader on these fronts, recognizing the value of its ecosystem assets before they were badly degraded and attracting national and international investment in them. In fact, most of Costa Rica's major ecosystem investments are preventive, aimed at preserving threatened ecosystems that are still supplying services.

Costa Rica's efforts have focused on services provided by forests. Through the 1940s, most of the country was covered with forest and rates of deforestation were low. By the 1960s through the early 1990s, however, Costa Rica had one of the highest deforestation rates in the world (ca. 4.25 percent/yr). Today, the country retains 44 percent of its original forest cover, and is still undergoing deforestation, although at a somewhat lower rate. The current government has established a goal of protecting remaining primary forest, encouraging regrowth of secondary forest, and promoting tree plantations on degraded soils to meet demands for timber and paper.

The 1997 amendments to Costa Rica's 1996 *Forestry Law* provide the legal and regulatory basis to compensate landowners for "environmental services" from their lands. The services include

(i) watershed protection,
(ii) carbon sequestration and storage,
(iii) protection of biodiversity resources, and
(iv) protection of key "life zones".

By encouraging watershed protection, the government hopes to ensure the purification and supply of drinking water to urban centers, production of hydroelectric power (the main source of power for the country and a major export to neighboring countries), and flood control. By rewarding carbon-related services, Costa Rica hopes to be well-poised to capture benefits from the anticipated global market in carbon storage. By protecting biodiversity and key life zones, the country will be able to capitalize on pharmaceutical development and ecotourism.

The program has been funded primarily by a national sales tax on fossil fuel consumption, a contract with a private hydropower producer in Costa Rica (Energia Global), joint carbon sequestration implementation projects (with the United States, Norway, and the Netherlands), contracts with pharmaceutical companies for biodiversity prospecting, and from tourism admission fees to protected areas. Landowners engaged in forest protection or restoration receive approximately US$50 per hectare per annum. In regions important for ecosystem service provision, the major alternative land use is cattle ranching. This subsidy exceeds the rents for active pasture (typically \$20 to \$30 per hectare per annum) and may exceed the profits from cattle ranching (\$8 to \$125 per hectare per annum). Initially there was some concern that few landowners would volunteer to participate. Within a short time, however, the program was vastly oversubscribed, and new sources of funds are being sought to expand it.

Like Costa Rica, Australia is undertaking a systematic national assessment of its ecosystem assets and seeking ways of capturing their value. Its principal asset of concern is also forest cover, but for very different reasons than in Costa Rica. Australia's actions have been primarily restorative, reacting to extreme forms of ecosystem degradation and service impairment with severe socioeconomic consequences.

Australia has been undergoing a long period of deforestation—starting with European settlement and continuing today. Over time, the steady removal of native tree cover has allowed naturally occurring salts in the soil to rise to the surface and poison large areas of agricultural and grazing land. Deeply rooted, native trees act as pumps, transferring vast amounts of water from the soil to the atmosphere, thereby keeping the water table (and its salts) below the rooting zone of plants. With removal of native trees and other deeply rooted vegetation, this hydrological pumping service has diminished greatly: crops and pasture grasses do not transpire water to the atmosphere at nearly the same rate as the vegetation they replaced. As a result, the water table has crept invisibly upward, bringing with it the naturally occurring salts. Once the saline water table reaches the rooting zone of vegetation, it causes severe socioeconomic impacts.

Scientists fear that appreciation of the service provided by native tree cover has come too late in much of the wheat belt of Western Australia. Reversing the process of salinization is costly and slow. In the Murray-Darling River Basin (spanning Queensland, New South Wales, Victoria, and South Australia), however, there is more hope and there are major efforts to restore hydrological services and to reap many other ecosystem benefits at the same time. Even here, there is no guarantee of success. Within the New South Wales region of the Basin, 15 percent of the irrigated land is already degraded by salinity and 70-80 percent is under threat.

Linked national and state programs, many of which are just now being implemented, pay landowners for protecting or reestablishing native vegetation on critical recharge and riparian lands, for establishing tree plantations on such areas, and for introducing more suitable cropping systems (perennial or salt-tolerant pastures or intercropping of high-and low-water-using crops to minimize "leakage"). So far, funds have come from government and from private industry. State Forests of New South Wales, for instance, has a contract with Tokyo Electric Power to establish forest for carbon sequestration and storage. The forest will be planted strategically to secure salinity control benefits, as well.

Salinity targets for 2010 have been set for "end-of-valley" and "within-valley" locations in each catchment. A flexible mix of market-based mechanisms, strategic government investment, promotion of new business opportunities, and regulation is being used to achieve these targets. Through adaptive management, a wide array of pilot projects has been implemented, with ongoing assessments of their success. For instance, the Hunter Salinity Trading Scheme, established in 1995, allows trading between power stations and mines of their rights to discharge saline water into the Hunter River. The scheme has permitted economic development without increasing river salinity and may be implemented elsewhere. Further support of market-based approaches will come in the form of an Environmental Sustainability Index, to be introduced by the Australian Stock Exchange, to support individuals and fund managers in directing funds toward environmentally and socially responsible investments. Momentum is also building behind the idea of creating and trading "biodiversity credits" along with salinity and carbon credits.

Next Steps

In assessing the promise of an ecosystem services approach—an explicit focus on protecting and restoring services—the bottom line is whether this approach leads to beneficial changes in the behavior or priorities of the government and private sector. The increasing number of initiatives to value and protect ecosystem services, both within the United States and abroad, suggests that in many instances it will. There is increasing evidence that the beginnings of a broad shift are underway within environmental law and policy both in the United States and abroad—from protection of ecosystems to protection of ecosystem services.

How can we spur this transition and realize the full potential of an ecosystem services approach? Part of the challenge is educational. Most people realize neither the critical role ecosystem services play in their lives nor the threats to service provision. Part is scientific. We need to understand better the linkage between ecosystem function and provision of services so we can appropriately weigh the ecosystem management options. Part is legal, since we have little experience with institutional design and regulatory instruments to protect services. And part is economic. We need to better value services and identify the institutional barriers to their commodification.

As in environmental policy generally, there is no one-size-fits-all solution for ecosystem service protection. We suggest, however, that there are four basic issues that must be seriously examined to determine which services hold the potential for greater legal or market protection, and the form such protection should take.

The first issue is identification of the service—delineating its range, status, and salience. What is the service's scale of delivery? Local services, such as pollination, raise very different issues than regional services such as flood control or global services such as climate stabilization. Is provision of the service stable, declining, or increasing? If the service provision does raise cause for concern, what are the threats to the service? And, of critical importance to developing appropriate policy responses, is the importance of this service generally recognized by its recipients? This is generally less of an issue with water purification, for example, since we all pay for water, than for "free" goods that rely on services such as pollination or soil fertility.

The second issue is valuation of the service—assessing its economic benefits. Even if the service is under threat, we have limited resources and a wide range of pressing needs. Those services that are most valuable (to people) will receive priority. To value the service, one must ask whether it is a public or private good, and whether the service is scarce or redundant. Is it a joint service? If so, the valuation methodology should consider the various streams of benefits (e.g., in determining a wetland's value, calculate benefits of water purification and flood control and nursery habitat, etc.). Even if the service is valuable, it may still be less costly to provide the service through built structures. Thus, one must ask, are there more efficient substitutes?

The third issue concerns market development—examining the obstacles to capturing the service's benefits. Assuming the service is under threat and sufficiently valuable to warrant resources for protection, we must still identify the most efficient policy tool (or combination of tools) to do so. If relying on economic instruments, the threshold question is whether current market mechanisms signal changes in provision of the service. Are there market signals of service degradation? If not, what are the barriers to commodification of the service? Perhaps the problem is one of split incentives or free riders. Do the costs and benefits accrue to the same actor? Perhaps the problem stems, at least in part, from transaction costs. Does protection require collective action?

The last issue is regulatory development—crafting appropriate policy tools to protect the service. Market instruments rarely, if ever, operate outside regulatory proscriptions. What are the potential uses of taxes, subsidies, and fees? What are the barriers to their use? Is it feasible to create and allocate property rights? What about creating new institutional authorities, such as ecosystem service districts?

Each service will provide different answers to many of these questions, and the answers will vary depending on location, as well. In the pages that follow, volume 20, issue 2, of the Stanford Environmental Law Journal presents current research grappling with these questions, providing an intellectual base to ground the shift from theory to practical implementation. Our hope is that reading these articles will spur further interest in ecosystem service protection and shape research agendas that develop this exciting and promising approach to environmental law and policy.

3

Limits of Traditional Economic and Accounting Approaches and Environmental Funding

The extracts below analyze the serious obstacles that may be encountered when trying to obtain funds for environmental management. It seeks to answer the question, If the environment is so highly valued, why are funds so scarce? It also identifies possible ways to overcome these funding obstacles, including an examination of the potential for some type of regional funding mechanism.

Conventional approaches to policymaking using traditional economic tools have created obstacles for funding environmental projects. These traditional tools—national income accounting, cost benefit analysis and discounting—have until recently ignored or sidelined environmental issues. This review examines potential reforms to these tools, incorporating environmental and resource concerns in national income accounting, including environmental issues in the cost-benefit and cost-effectiveness criteria used in the project cycle and examining how the role of uncertainty and intergenerational equity influence the choice of the discount rate.

A

Obstacles to Environmental Financing

(i) Oogai O. and Tanaka A., "Sources of Funds for Environmental Management," in Owens G.M. (ed), *Financing Environmentally Sound Development*, Asian Development Bank, 1994, pp 101–109

Obstacles to Environmental Financing

Obstacles Due to Economic Analysis

One of the basic tasks for policymakers and investors is the creation of a rational system for decision making to be used to rank different investment choices by uniform criteria and then determine priorities. Given that investments cost money and that both government and private investors are constrained by limited budgets, one of the most common frameworks for rational decision making is economic analysis. This framework can be applied in various ways, by ensuring that investments are made with the highest rate of return, by determining that the benefits of a policy must outweigh the costs, by choosing the investment with the highest discounted net present value, or by choosing the policy that contributes most to national income.

Until recently, this economic framework did not reflect environmental concerns. As the major framework used by governments, the private sector and international organizations to determine where investments should be made, the exclusion of environmental concerns created a major obstacle to funding. Environmental investments were viewed as a poor investment because the framework assumes that the benefits of an investment can be measured with low levels of risk and uncertainty, that these benefits can be quantified in monetary terms and that they can be discounted with present gains valued more highly. Since none of these assumptions hold for environmental investments, the use of this framework creates a built-in bias against environmental funding.

This exclusion of the environment was primarily a reflection of the situation in modern academic economics that ignored environmental issues. The neoclassical economy, consisting of consumption and production, was seen in isolation from the natural world, which was viewed as infinite. Thus conventional neoclassical economics is all about the efficient allocation of resources, with no concern about the ultimate scale of economic processes. Interestingly, early economists such as Ricardo, Malthus, and Mill were very aware of the importance of natural resources.

The neoclassical economy, consisting of consumption and production, was seen in isolation from the natural world, which was viewed as infinite.

The neoclassical approach was first challenged in the 1970s when fears about the limits of natural resources were raised. Then, in the 1980s, fears about increasing transboundary and global problems, such as acid rain, global warming and ozone depletion, and the threat to overexploited but potentially renewable natural resources such as fragile ecosystems—tropical forests or wetlands, certain species, seas and rivers, and fertile soils—were raised.

It is now clear that production and consumption are both part of a finite natural system that provides natural resources for the productive process and also receives wastes discharged into the air, water and land. Thus, far from being infinite, the environment or natural capital must be conserved from the damaging scale effects of increased population and increased economic growth. This means that economic processes must be integrated with environmental issues.

As these intellectual developments have changed the way we view the economy, so we must now alter the analytical tools used by policymakers. Until this is done, sustainable development cannot be embarked upon, as environmental management will remain a secondary goal. The extent of the reform remains a matter of debate; some argue the environment should be quantified in monetary terms and then included in the conventional framework. Others argue that aspects of the economic framework will have to change.

The Problem of Valuation

If policy is decided after certain benefits are quantified in monetary terms, then the problem of valuation becomes central. Environmental concerns must be factored in using monetary values to reflect the benefits of environmental investments and the costs of environmental damage. This will avoid funding obstacles both at a micro project level and at the macro level of economic planning based on national income accounts.

Determining the value to be placed on environmental goods and services is complex and multifaceted. For example, the value of a single forest will be determined by a wide range of factors: its size, composition, location, how people use it and how it relates to economic activity. Beyond that, the ecosystem comprising the forest is itself of value only if it remains intact. In many respects, environmental values can only be understood as actions/equations.

Some commonly used methods to measure the value of the environment include:

- the examination of the cost of preventing environmental degradation and of restoring a degraded environment to its original state (the clean-up cost approach);
- the net land rent method—evaluating the gap between prevailing market prices for natural resources and the cost of logging or mining them;
- the use cost method—estimating the retained surpluses allocated to reinvestment or depreciation when the natural environment or natural resources are used;
- the contingent cost method—using direct questions to study how much people are willing to pay for conservation; and the travel cost method—evaluating the increase in travel costs that result from environmental deterioration.

Differences in measurement techniques often produce major variations in estimated environmental values. This, in turn, breeds lack of trust among the public. It will be necessary to improve and redefine these methods in the future.

National Income Accounting and the Role of Environmental Management

Until recently, conventional measures to estimate national income accounts, which form a vital guide for both public and private investors, have excluded environmental concerns. This is now being tackled by examining ways in which pollution and degradation of the environment and the depletion of natural resources can be reflected in national income accounting. One of the various ways suggested is to supplement existing national economic accounting with satellite accounts. This approach has been developed largely in France and Canada.

The United Nations Statistical Commission is considering recommendations to revise the international standards for systems of national accounting (SNA). Environmental accounts are to be included and the new accounting framework will be known as the system for integrated environmental and economic activity (IEEA). It will use SNA satellite accounts to handle the depletion of natural resources and the degradation of the environment. Resource extraction will be subtracted from net national product as depletion of capital and environmental cleanup costs will be counted as intermediate expenditures.

Although many theoretical and practical problems remain with these reforms, the introduction of environmental concerns into national income accounting will mean that regional aggregates can be used as a basis for discussing regionally based solutions in Asia and other areas. Obviously, for developing countries to use these new systems, technology transfers and support will be needed for data and information gathering. Thus, there is a need for simple, easy to use, and inexpensive information systems as well.

Environmentally Sound Project Cycle

When making investment decisions it is common to use cost benefit analyses to evaluate profitability. While it is not always easy to convert environmental impacts into economic values, serious attempts are being made to bring environmental concerns into all stages of the project cycle.

The World Bank, Asian Development Bank, Japan Overseas Economic Cooperation Fund, and Export-Import

Bank of Japan have all adopted this approach. The World Bank guidelines stipulate that the likelihood of major environmental impacts must be considered at each stage in a project:

- In the preparatory stages, the World Bank supports the environmental assessment carried out by the recipient country and drafts measures to alleviate major environmental problems. If judged necessary from an environmental standpoint, it will also specify additional studies.
- During the screening stage, the World Bank judges the success of the environmental assessment process and whether or not suitable measures are being taken in relation to the degree of environmental impact.
- When the loan is being negotiated, the World Bank will, if necessary, discuss environmental concerns with the recipient country and include environmental guidelines in the loan agreement.
- As the project proceeds, the World Bank works with the recipient to review the implementation on a regular basis, keeping records of any agreements for revisions or additional environmental measures.
- During post project monitoring, the World Bank records the environmental measures used in the project, their suitability and cost, and any problems encountered in their implementation. This information is used in future projects and also helps to determine which projects will be subject to environmental auditing.

While these are important policy improvements, practical problems remain. These include lack of understanding on the part of decision makers, a shortage of funding for environmental assessments and lack of capacity to carry them out.

Coping with Risks and Uncertainties

There are uncertainties involved in environmental investments, but one cannot wait to act until studies and research have cleared up all the uncertainties. Obstacles to environmental funding are created if investors prefer to minimize risks. Others oppose the precautionary principle, believing that it serves as an obstacle to low-cost adaptive measures and may be prohibitively expensive. However, the risks of inaction are, in fact, much greater than the cost of precautionary investments.

Discounting at the Micro Level and Interest Rates at the Macro Level

The role of interest rates and discounting is central to the conventional economic policy framework. They ensure that present gains are valued more highly than future gains. A review of individual projects shows that the World Bank and ADB usually calculate internal rates of return using a discount rate of 10 to 12 percent. The role of such high discount rates in terms of environmental management is ambiguous as discount rates affect not only individual projects on a micro level, but also all investment projects on a macro level.

The higher the discount rate, the more future gains and costs are discounted. Thus a project that may cost $1 billion to clean up in 50 years time would only be measured at a present cost of $87 million if it is discounted at a 5 percent discount rate over 50 years. Similarly, using a high discount rate, an afforestation project with trees that take 50 years to mature would be considered a less profitable investment than another project with more immediate returns. These two examples illustrate why it is often argued that high discount rates create funding obstacles for environmentally beneficial projects, while encouraging investments with high future environmental costs. Lowering the discount rate is not however a solution. All investments, not just investments with favorable environmental impacts, are affected by the discount rate. A lower rate might favor investments that do not benefit the environment at all, such as those that increase the demand for natural resources or increase the level of pollution.

This has led some to call for differential discount rates for environmental projects, while leaving other investments at the higher standard rate. Certain environmental investments could be eligible for soft loans. The real problem here is to define environmental investments since the current trend is for conventional investments to integrate environmental concerns. In addition, the encouragement of environmental investments with lower net returns may lead to a loss of income that could be used for environmental purposes.

Intergenerational Equity

The debate over discount rate is part of a much larger concern with intergenerational equity. Unlike the conventional economic framework, which aims to maximize economic welfare for the current generation, sustainable development stresses the need to take future generations into account. Indeed the Brundtland Commission makes the case for intergenerational balance. This is reflected in their definition of sustainable development the idea that development should meet the needs of people today without harming the ability of future generations to also meet their needs. Until these concepts are elevated into the principles that guide economic decisions, they remain mere ideas, and thus will not accelerate the promotion of intergenerational equity.

The idea of leaving to future generations the resources they need may be realistic in industrialized countries if populations are not growing.

But there is little agreement on exactly what intergenerational equity actually means. One attempt to solve these dilemmas is the *principle of guaranteeing options,* which says that resources should be available equally to all generations—that they should be guaranteed fair access. The problem is that this still leaves unclear what resources must be guaranteed. The tendency is to transfer natural resources into manufactured capital investment. This may or may not be seen as fair access. Because of technical change, each generation's need for natural resource inputs is dynamic rather than static. These complications lead to three distinct ways of addressing fairness in the conservation of natural resources:

- natural resources should be rigorously conserved, natural resource needs change in the course of development;
- new technologies will lead to the development of alternative resources; and
- a decline in natural resources is not in itself a particular problem as long as the revenue is reinvested in manufactured capital stock.

Consideration of intergenerational equity must also take the following issues into account:

> "In many developing countries, the concept of intergenerational equity is meaningless. It is irrational to tell the farmers of today to starve to death so that enough natural resources are left for tomorrow."

The idea of leaving to future generations the resources they need may be realistic in industrialized countries if populations are not growing. But it is not realistic to tell the people of Kenya, where the population will triple by 2025, to leave their natural resources exactly as they are now. Nor it is possible to do so on a global scale, since today's population of 5.5 billion is expected to reach 10 billion by 2050.

B

Political and Institutional Obstacles to Environmental Financing

(i) Oogai O. and Tanaka A., "Sources of Funds for Environmental Management," in Owens G.M. (ed), *Financing Environmentally Sound Development,* Asian Development Bank, 1994, pp 109–115

Political and Institutional Obstacles

The unequal way environmental costs and benefits are borne, the administrative difficulties of implementing environmental policy and the problems of transboundary pollution are three major political and institutional obstacles to funding.

Too often environmental externalities are seen as purely an efficiency issue, without an examination of the more potent political fact that these externalities are borne by different groups in society. Since the poor suffer most from environmental damage and the rich tend to gain, this provides a serious policy obstacle to financing.

To demonstrate how different groups bear different costs and benefits, environmental problems in developing countries can be classified according to their causes, effects and scope.

Environmental destruction stemming from the endless cycle of poverty

Poverty causes environmental destruction that in turn causes poverty, the two feeding off each other in an endless cycle. This is also fueled by rapid population growth, which is again both a cause and a result of poverty. The most obvious example of this is in the area of agriculture where poor farmers are occasionally forced to destroy their own environments to survive. Lack of adequate farmland forces some farmers to cultivate easily eroded hillsides. Others see their land becoming semi-arid as the soil quality deteriorates. Some may in fact be using marginal land such as former tropical rain forests that is clearly unsuited to cultivation, and where yields quickly diminish after only a few years of cultivation. Poor subsistence farmers are therefore destroyers of the environment, as well as the victims of that destruction. The underlying causes of this poverty may be political, due to the distorted land ownership systems so common in developing countries and development plans that give scant attention to the environment or to local inhabitants. The endless cycle of poverty is driven not only by natural disasters and population increases, but also by political inequalities.

Environmental destruction stemming from domestic development

Economic growth without sufficient environmental safeguards results in a damaged environment. In Thailand, the poor who live in densely populated squatters' camps lack access to safe drinking water and adequate sewage and bear the brunt of floods, landslides, industrial accidents, and the air pollution caused by industrial waste and traffic. While the rich and the powerful can take measures to protect themselves from such outcomes, the poor are defenseless in the face of environmental pressures. This trend becomes more pronounced if the gap between rich and poor widens or where income growth is stagnant.

Environmental destruction stemming from development aid

Insufficient environmental safeguards taken during bilateral and multilateral aid projects can be a direct or indirect cause of environmental destruction. When Asian countries implement energy projects that involve building dams or large agricultural development projects, these may require the wholesale displacement of the residents from the area. Large dams themselves can destroy the environment, but if there is also insufficient attention to resettlement this will create a group of refugees who cause further environmental destruction. The classic example of this sequence has been the Sardar Sarovar Dam in India. This is the largest dam in the giant Narmada irrigation project, which includes proposals for 30 large dams, 135 medium dams and over 3,000 smaller dams. Four principal benefits motivate the developers: it would irrigate 1.8 million hectares of chronically water-starved land, allowing for cultivation throughout the year; it would help to provide drinking water for approximately 30 million people by 2021; it could help to provide electricity throughout the construction of a power plant; and there would be jobs for 700,000 workers during construction and for 600,000 after construction. Yet, this huge dam was not without its costs. It would submerge 170,000 hectares of forest and 13,000 hectares of wasteland, and would require the relocation of 67,000 residents (about 100,000 by the time it was completed). An independent inquiry commissioned by the World Bank found that the environmental safeguards for the Sardar Sarovar Dam were insufficient and this led to the cancellation of the loan. Many other large aid projects have not had such intensive reexamination despite similar concerns being expressed.

Environment destruction generated by the North–South trade structure

Some damage flows from the economic relationships and trade structures between the developed and developing nations. Primary products exported by developing countries trade cheaply with prices not reflecting environmental costs. The Philippines, which now bans logging in almost all of its remaining forests, saw forest areas decline from 70 percent of total land at the end of World War II to less than 20 percent today. The Philippine government and business cut down the forests because the demand for timber by industrialized countries earned them hard currency/foreign exchange. A large percentage of Philippine timber exports went to Japan where it was used to build buildings and for furniture during the postwar period of reconstruction and growth.

Environmental destruction stemming from activities in international waters

This type of environmental destruction includes over fishing of the oceans and oil pollution of major sea lanes. With oceans open to international access, control of individual actions is impossible. Hence the temptation to abuse such common resources and, in the case of over fishing, deplete them until they no longer have the ability to regenerate. Pollution in the Strait of Malacca, a major sea lane with an average of 300 ships passing through each day, is the result of the oil spills from cleaning of tanks and repeated tanker accidents. Although full sovereignty does not extend to the high seas, the situation has nevertheless forced countries of the region to contemplate regulations and to demand that user countries pay their share. In this case, the direct beneficiaries of marine pollution are the companies that own the ships passing through the Strait of Malacca (because they do not foot the environmental costs). The direct victims are the fishermen and other people who live on the coast of the Strait of Malacca. It is possible that the destruction of aquatic life has a more wide-ranging impact as well and, thus, the number of victims increases.

Environmental destruction stemming from transboundary spillovers

Acid rain, pollution of international rivers that run through several countries and pollution of other regional water bodies are examples of environmental destruction that occur in one country and then spill over and damage neighboring countries. In Europe, acid rain occurred as a result of an idea prevalent in the sixties and seventies that the solution to pollution is dilution. This encouraged power plants and factories to build their smokestacks high so as not to pollute the surrounding environment with their emissions. But the higher the smokestack, the more likely its sulfur dioxide and nitrous oxide emissions were to be picked up by seasonal winds and carried over long distances. The beneficiaries in these cases are the people who run the power plants and factories and are able to save on pollution reduction costs. The victims are the people in many different countries who bear the brunt of the emissions. The indirect beneficiaries are the consumers of electric power, since they have access to electricity at lower costs as spending on pollution reduction is avoided.

Environmental destruction stemming from global environmental problems

Activities that damage the global environment affect everyone, including those who were originally responsible. Examples include ozone layer depletion caused by chlorofluorocarbons (CFCs) and global warming from carbon dioxide emissions, as well as the loss of tropical rain forests and wetlands. Fossil fuels burned in power plants, factories and homes are part of the problem, but because natural causes also exist, it is difficult to allocate responsibility. The initial victims of global warming are likely to be the people living in coastal lowlands (such as, the deltaic regions of Bangladesh) and farmers and ranchers whose livelihoods are influenced by even minor climatic changes. As in the case of transboundary spillovers, it is society's weakest who are unable to invest in measures to lessen the impact. However, in the long run, preventing global-scale environmental destruction produces benefits for everyone.

Winners and losers from environmental destruction

In developing countries, there is a trend in the cause-and-effect relationship at work in environmental problems. We will call this the short-term environmental nexus in environmental destruction. In this nexus:

- The immediate victims of deteriorating environmental conditions are the poor and the socially weak.
- The initial beneficiaries of sound environmental measures are also the poor and the socially weak.
- The socially strong such as the rich and powerful have the ability to avoid harm from deteriorating environmental conditions.
- Among these powerful entrenched interests are some who benefit from the destruction of the environment.

Awareness of this nexus is essential when looking for solutions to today's environmental problems. Policy decisions do not always reflect the wishes of society's weakest and are often used by a portion of society's strongest to pursue their own interests...

Initially, the benefits of environmental degradation to the strong outweigh any damages. But these benefits gradually diminish until finally, the strong are damaged as well. Note, however, that society's weakest are on the losing end from the very beginning, and as the environment deteriorates, they simply lose more and more. The left side of the break-even point represents the short-term environmental nexus; the right side, the long-term environmental nexus. As can be inferred from the figure, as long as the rich gain from environmental damage, they are unlikely to be interested in reducing this damage. The short-term environmental nexus thus represents a very common political impasse. There will be some among the strong who will actually impede efforts at conservation, since they have at that point, a negative incentive to protect the environment. For example, entrenched fishing interests will oppose conservation policies to set up no-fishing periods or to abandon drift nets loggers will oppose steps to replenish timber reserves; and factory owners will oppose tighter effluent standards.

Measures for Eliminating the Obstacles

The problems of environmental policy can be divided into problems of formulating efficient sets of regulations, of monitoring compliance with these regulations and then enforcing these regulations by punishing transgressors. In addition to policing, environmental agencies must implement positive environmental improvements such as soil conservation programs and training for energy efficiency. They also have a role in conducting environmental impact assessments: The less effective this policy process is, the more environmental damage there will be. Thus greater environmental funding will be required. If government institutions and personnel are untrained and inefficient, then they will make poor use of any funding. Eventually given major demands for funding but poor effectiveness in the use or administration of the funds, donors will no longer consider these investments worthwhile. Thus instead of facilitating the process, another major obstacle to funding will have been developed.

While international experts can provide short-term guidance, it is much more cost-effective in the long run if local administrators and researchers can become self-sufficient by improving their own local capacities. Through this process, policy administrators can lower the cost of environmental policy and make it more effective. Improving local capacities will encourage environmental monitoring by the public. This ensures that environmental information becomes publicly available.

- Promote active involvement of local people to ensure that the best policy priorities are chosen. Setting priorities for environmental management differs according to a country's characteristics degree of urbanization, average income level, and so on.
- Reduce skill shortages. Skill shortages involve problems of absolute shortages and the uneven distribution of skill among specialized fields. Shortages also occur when a country has talented people, but these people shun employment in public organizations due to poor compensation.
- Allow the decentralization of environmental policy. It is usually better in terms of both cost and effectiveness to solve environmental problems on-site. Therefore it is most effective for governments to transfer responsibility for daily management to local agencies and set them to work on the problems. To accomplish this, governments must expand personnel training to local government employees.
- Ensure the local population is supportive of environmental regulation. This can reduce monitoring and implementation costs enormously. If local governments and citizens do not accept policy, it will be difficult to assure its effectiveness. The backing of local citizens is also needed for cooperation in implementing environment-related projects, or in changing the attitudes of local businesses towards the environment.

C

Asia-Pacific Regional Environmental Problems and Funding Issues

(i) Oogai O. and Tanaka A., "Sources of Funds for Environmental Management," in Owens G.M. (ed), *Financing Environmentally Sound Development*, Asian Development Bank, 1994, pp 115–129

Regional Environmental Problems

Regional problems require intercountry agreements—national policy frameworks are inadequate. The usual problems of environmental policy (setting standards, monitoring compliance and punishing transgressors) become even more intractable. Each country must provide credible institutions and sanctions to ensure that there is no incentive to cheat or to not adhere to the agreement.

Acid Rain in Asia and the Pacific

Transboundary Acid Rain in Asia

Acid rain may become a critical problem in the region. Already there is considerable damage from acid rain in the People's Republic of China (PRC) as a result of rapid industrialization. Burning coal is one of the main causes. From 1970 to 1988, energy consumption in that country increased almost threefold—coal-fired generation accounts for 76 percent of the total. It is anticipated that this high dependence on coal will remain unchanged, at least until the end of the century. At the same time, the PRC's energy use efficiency is much lower than that of the highly industrialized countries. The PRC uses 1.7 times as much energy per $100 million GNP as the former Soviet Union, 2.1 times that of the United States, and 5.6 times that of Japan. And while Japan and the United States have coal utilization coefficients of 57 and 51 percent, respectively, that of the PRC is about 30 percent. However, some of these low efficiencies will begin to improve as energy prices are deregulated.

It has been suggested that in recent years, the PRC's air pollution has crossed the Sea of Japan and has caused transboundary acid rain to fall on the main Japanese islands. It is also claimed that acid rain from the PRC is beginning to cause the death of cedar and fir trees in Japan's Kanto region, as well as pine trees in the Chugoku region. But there are many countries in addition to the PRC that may be contributing sources of acid rain, including Russia; Republic of Korea; Taipei,China; and Japan itself. There are also effects of sulfur dioxide from natural sources such as volcanoes. This makes it difficult to identify Asia's sources of transboundary acid rain with great accuracy. At the same time, however, in view of the PRC's industrialization during recent years, as well as its future economic growth potential, it is only a matter of time before the PRC's atmospheric pollutants become the dominant cause of acid rain in other countries.

The costs required for countermeasures after environmental damage has been done are far greater than initial investments. This applies even more to environmental problems affecting vast areas that straddle national borders. Examples of such countermeasures are improving energy efficiency; coal washing to reduce noncombustible inorganic matter; changing coal to a low-emission fuel (for example, gasify it and use it as coal gas); and installing electrostatic precipitators.

Although the PRC is now receiving international aid for electrostatic precipitators and desulfurization units in its coal-fired generating plants, this affects only newly built plants. Nothing is being done for old plants. Furthermore, only installation costs, not operational costs are being financed by foreign aid. Thus, one often hears that even though such pollution control hardware has been installed, plants are operating without turning on the equipment because the costs are too high.

It is calculated that even if 0.5 percent of the PRC's GNP is invested in environmental protection, the environment will continue to be degraded. If 1 per cent is invested, the situation will remain unchanged; and if 1.5 percent is invested, the environment will begin to improve. Although the PRC's direct investment in pollution abatement reached Yuan 7.23 billion in 1989, this is still less than 0.5 percent of the country's GNP. Therefore, because the PRC not only lacks the technology but also at present does not invest enough in pollution control, it is expected that its role as— a source of pollution will steadily increase.

Funding Obstacles

Experience with acid rain elsewhere in the world has led to the identification of four closely interrelated obstacles when dealing with transboundary or regional problems.

First, the costs and benefits of remedial activities differ from country to country. This is always a factor in regional environmental problems and clearly reveals some conflict with the *polluter pays principle.* If environmental actions are advantageous to all countries there will be few political obstacles. If, however, there is a difference in the costs and benefits of such actions between the countries concerned, many problems can arise.

Second, there is, in general, little public awareness concerning the environment. There are wealth disparities among countries. Japan is the only fully developed nation in the Asian region. This is very dissimilar to the situation in Europe or North America. In developing countries, generally there is low level of education and little incentive for citizens, government or business to undertake environmental protection. There is also a division of opinion between countries that give priority to industrial development over policies for pollution abatement and countries that want to combine both objectives.

Third, there is no accumulation of basic studies and research about the environment in the region. Asia has not had as long a history of acid rain and its effects as has Europe. Because it has industrialized rapidly, many of Asia's pollution problems have appeared only recently and most of the basic studies and research about the environment have therefore just begun. To determine the costs and benefits of pollution abatement it is necessary first to identify the sources. In the absence of an incentive for international cooperation, this will be difficult. While it is essential to build monitoring systems for transboundary pollution (covering many countries), moves in this direction have only recently been made in the region. The genesis of new forms of cooperation can however be found in joint Sino-Japanese research; this involves mainly academic bodies and the Sea of Japan Interchange Sphere International *(Kannihon-kai-niigata-kaigi).*

Finally, there is no single political structure that can formulate and execute appropriate policies. It is difficult to unify public Opinion for environmental conservation across a group of nations. It is however much easier to obtain consensus if there is an international political entity. The European Community (EC) took the initiative in promoting cooperative action against acid rain among EC countries. There is no such organization to take the political initiative on regional environmental action in Asia.

Investing in the Environment

Environmental investment can be grouped under three classifications.

Type one would include environmental investments that can also be justified on economic grounds, known as *win-win* or *no regrets* policies (such as installing electricity meters that calculate energy prices progressively on the basis of the volume consumed). According to analyses carried out by the World Bank, the following types of government policy contribute to environmental conservation and the improvement of economic efficiency without burdening government finances:

- elimination of subsidies for energy investment, pesticides, fertilizers and water for irrigation;
- elimination of subsidies for logging and livestock farming;
- clarification of farmers' land rights; and
- levying taxes aimed to curb congestion on urban roads.

Other investments that are both efficient in the long-term and environmentally advantageous include: investments to reduce population pressure, thus reducing demands on governmental investment budgets as well as reducing environmental pressures; and investments that are considered capacity building, that is, they reduce the costs and improve the effectiveness of implementing environmental policy that will have both economic and environmental advantages.

Type two would include investments aimed directly at protection of the environment and that may or may not be justified by conventional economic analysis, for example, afforestation projects or soil conservation investments.

The determination of which types of investments most urgently require funding must involve an investigation of the relationship between the costs of environmental protection and expected benefits to the environment. However, the quantification of environmental benefits can be difficult, and a considerable period of time is often required for the environment to reap the benefits. Even when there may be quantifiable benefits, it is sometimes hard to tell when they will appear or it may be impossible to specify what degree of benefit has been achieved. Considering these from the viewpoint of the relative necessity of providing funds, we make the following suggestions:

- When the effect on the environment only becomes apparent after a considerably long time-span, the cost-benefit analysis must be carried out on a similarly long-term basis.
- When the benefit to the environment is unclear or irreversible, this usually means that the cost of repair will be much higher than the cost of prevention. To this end, we must emphasize preventive measures against environmental destruction.
- As for environmental investment in developing countries, lenders should prepare special environmental soft loans with interest rates differing from the standard discount rate.
- In the case of investment directly aimed at conservation, there are often nongovernmental benefits as well. This factor makes environmental investment an even higher priority, and we should value it all the more.

Type three environmental investments would include conventional investments that may have some environmental components, such as construction of a chemical plant incorporating low emission technology.

Almost all development investment has an impact on the environment. Thus, improvement must be sought for methods of environmental assessment and of assessing project feasibility to avoid implementing projects that cause environmental damage. Both conceptual and practical problems remain over the integration of environmental concerns in conventional development investments. By conducting preliminary surveys, project participants must work diligently to alleviate the environmental impact beginning with the design stage, doing their best to ensure the success of the project and viewing the project design from as broad an angle as possible.

Almost all development investment has an impact on the environment.

When an environmental impact is unavoidable, provisions must be made for some kind of compensatory countermeasure. Projects that will dislocate communities or harm weaker groups within society must be avoided. Despite this, projects involving systematic migration have been progressing.

While a few environmental investments remain that cannot be justified on conventional economic criteria, most will involve an integration of economic and environmental concerns (type 2 investments). Thus, environmental investments must be combined with efficiency (type 1 investments), and conventional economic investment must come to embody environmental technology (type 3 investments).

Financial Requirements and Sources of Funds

Financial Requirements for Environmental Management

A serious funding gap exists between official development funds invested in developing countries and environmental expenditures needed by the year 2000.

Official Development Funds Invested in DMCs

...[F]igures have been compiled based on 1990 OECD data showing how much public money in the form of bilateral and multilateral official development aid (ODA) and other official flows was being invested in the developing member countries (DMCs) of the ADB...[T]he grand total of ODA and other official flows comes to $26.3 billion with $12.1 billion of this in the form of grants. The category, "other official flows" refers to investment other than development loans and grants, often with some return expected.

How much of this money goes to environmental causes is a very interesting question. But international standards for deciding exactly what falls within the purview of environmental investment, and what does not, have not yet been established. Consequently, the data are not yet in a form where compilation of such figures would be possible. It is very important for environmental investment to be prepared according to international standards, thus allowing for the compilation of international statistics. This is one reason why a regional environment fund is being proposed. On this occasion, to present the magnitude of the total environmental investment of ODA, we have used estimates based on Japanese ODA figures.

Japanese development aid directed to environmental management is estimated at approximately 12.4 percent of total ODA, that is, $1.4 billion (Yen165.4 billion at the conversion rate of 115 to the dollar). In this case, environmental management means improvement of the living environment, forest conservation, pollution reduction, prevention of disasters and conservation of the natural environment. To date, there is little investment directly aimed at environmental management. Instead it is usually integrated into conventional development. If we apply the rate of Japanese ODA to total official development funds, around $3.3 billion may have been used for environmental purposes in 1990.

Environmental Expenditures Needed in the Year 2000

...[I]t was estimated, according to the accelerated progress scenario, that the DMCs would need $70.2 billion to cover the costs of environmental protection in the year 2000. The amount necessary for Group A countries (the lowest income group of DMCs) amounts to $46.8 billion, 66 percent of the total.

Looking at...project sector[s], only $800 million was being invested in water supply and sanitation in the DMCs in 1989. It is believed that $13.1 billion will be needed in the year 2000. Of this, $10.7 billion or 82 percent of the total will have to be handled in the form of grants for Group A underdeveloped countries. However, this will put a major strain on soft loan sources, even though Japan and other countries already place priority on such basic human needs. Underdeveloped countries should develop programs based on more cost-effective criteria by designing projects so that those who benefit most bear the heaviest part of the cost. DMCs should also clearly plan to rely less on soft loans as their economic strength grows.

Conservation costs related to generating electrical power are expected to reach $19.4 billion by the year 2000. This accounts for approximately 5.4 percent of total investment. Group A countries will need $13.7 billion or 71 percent of the total. In 1989, $4.6 billion was invested on energy supply in the DMCs. It is not clear how much of this constitutes environmental expenditure, but it is still obvious that the demand for funds in this area will be significant by 2000. Underdeveloped countries will therefore have to move quickly to find other official flows besides ODA and private loans. Japan has exerted much energy into aid related to energy supply, mostly in the form of grants. But, since energy plants are expected to eventually be profitable, the recent trend has been towards official non-ODA flows and private loans.

Environmental costs related to transportation are expected to reach $8.8 billion by 2000. This includes the cost of installing catalytic converters and engines in vehicles that run on unleaded gas. This is paid for through official non-ODA flows and private loans. However, in order to ensure investment, it is essential that appropriate laws and other mechanisms be set up.

Environmental costs related to industrial wastes are expected to reach $9 billion by 2000. This includes state-run enterprises as well. Investment comes mainly from private loans. For this kind of investment to proceed smoothly, work must be done to set up a legal framework as well as environmental assessment and inspection systems. Regarding the environmental costs to small and medium size enterprises, many have acknowledged the effectiveness of the aforementioned soft loans. For small and medium-size enterprises in developing countries, strategic soft loans such as two-step loans (which were developed by the Japanese government) should be made available.

As for environmental costs in the agriculture sector, it is expected that $2.5 billion will be needed by 2000 for the prevention of soil erosion. In addition, $3.7 billion will be needed for forest conservation, giving a total of $6.2 billion for both projects. The cost of reclaiming eroded soil is extremely high, whereas prevention is relatively inexpensive. And since the benefits of prevention are so great, it is believed that the chances of such investment taking place are excellent. The cost of forest conservation is high, but this figure covers investment aimed at sustainable development, including technical assistance. Thus, we should look into the possible necessity of soft loans.

Investment in population control and the education of women are basic environmentally oriented measures related to the vicious cycle of poverty and environmental destruction. These areas are generally recognized as an extremely high priority area for investment. By 2000, population control costs will amount to $5 billion and the cost of educating women is expected to reach $2.5 billion, 88 percent of this going to Group A countries. For these purposes, grants and soft loans should be arranged.

Plans to deal with acid rain are expected to require $700 million by 2000, but this figure is based on a mere 20 percent reduction in sulfur dioxide. The funding sources for this are discussed in later sections on the concept of a Regional Environment Facility. The cost of preventing global warming is expected to reach $5.4 billion, and the cost of preserving biodiversity will run to $100 million by the year 2000. Funding for these issues is being dealt with by the Global Environment Facility (GEF). In addition, a mechanism for financing sustainable development in fragile ecosystems such as tropical forests, wetlands and coral ecosystems in the region will be proposed.

Growing Pressures on the Environment

Predicted to be the region with the world's highest economic growth over the next ten years, the Asian and Pacific region needs sustainable development in the literal sense of the term. Along with [the increasing pressures on the environment], are new trends, including:

- the appearance of new opportunities for economic growth, principally the southern PRC economic bloc;
- increasingly active foreign trade within the Asian and Pacific region, that is, greater interdependence within the region;
- the manifestation of new interregional environmental problems, such as global warming and acid rain; and
- the rise in the sea level resulting from: global warming will present island states with a critical problem—the loss of land area.

It is anticipated that, owing to increases in population and high economic growth, the Asian region will experience far greater pressure from environmental damage than other regions. According to UN population estimates for the 37 Asian nations, the 3.1 billion population of 1990 will reach 3.4 billion by 1995, and 4.9 billion (158 percent of 1990) by 2025.

In Asia, a large number of local economic blocs are being formed. For example, there is the so-called growth triangle comprising Singapore, Riau, including the islands of Batam and Bintan, and Malaysia's Johore; the northern triangle linking the island of Phuket, Malaysia's Penang, and Indonesia's Medan, and the baht economic bloc comprising Thailand and three Southeast Asian states. In addition, there is the southern PRC economic bloc, the Yellow Sea economic bloc, and the Sea of Japan economic bloc. The intraregional trade dependency ratio of the region comprising Japan, the members of the Association of Southeast Asian Nations (ASEAN), and the PRC, already exceeds 40 percent, and a regionally unified industrial structure is in its formative stages. The current size of the Asian region's GNP totals $4.1 trillion, with the breakdown being $505 billion for the Asian newly industrialized economies (Republic of Korea; Taipei,China; Hong Kong and Singapore), $268 billion for ASEAN (Indonesia, Brunei, Malaysia, Philippines, and Thailand), $364 billion for the PRC, and $3 trillion for Japan.

Should Asia's environmental strategy remain unchanged, environmental damage will surely proceed and can be anticipated, in time, to lead to a stage where productivity falls and economic growth declines.

If the North American Free Trade Agreement (NAFTA) and EC countries continue without change in their current rather low 2 to 2.5 percent growth, and the Asian countries maintain their high rate of growth, the Asian countries will approach the economic scale of NAFTA in the year 2000, and if the EC continues with the same members as currently, then it is possible that in 2010 the size of the Asian market will outstrip that of NAFTA and the EC.

However, should Asia's environmental strategy remain unchanged, environmental damage will surely proceed and can be anticipated, in time, to lead to a stage where productivity falls and economic growth declines. The Asian region is now coming to a juncture—deemed a major one in human history as well—where Asia has the opportunity to lead other developing regions in overcoming the pressures for environmental damage induced by population increases and high economic growth, and thereby make the transition to the path of sustainable development.

The total ODA that the DMCs received for 1990 amounted to $26.3 billion. If ODA stays at its 1990 levels, as estimated earlier, $3.3 billion will be available for environmental investments in each year. Assuming that two thirds of environmental expenditures needed by the year 2000 are raised within the developing countries themselves, it follows that $23.4 billion will have to come from external sources.

We assume that the developing member countries will receive $3.3 billion in official development funding in 2000. At the Earth Summit in 1992, Japan committed to increase its environmental aid from 900 billion to 1 trillion over the following five-year period. Still, given an exchange rate of 115 yen to the dollar, this amounts to only $1.6 billion to $1.8 billion per year. A massive influx of additional capital will be necessary to bridge this gap in the future.

Four Key Environmental Needs

Despite the existing funding gap between the estimated costs and the existing sources, there remain environmental needs in the Asian and Pacific region. These needs will have to be financed by new sources as the old ones are already significantly depleted. The importance of identifying priority areas is obvious. Key funding areas include: planning and facilitating a common environmental strategy for the Asian and Pacific region; setting up an organization to preserve fragile ecosystems in the Asian and Pacific region; establishing an organization to accelerate capacity institution building; arid setting up a preliminary organization to cope with transboundary environmental problems.

Planning and Facilitating a Common Environmental Strategy for Asian and Pacific Region

This report has set out the requirements for environmental policy in the light of various funding obstacles. But it is also necessary to examine these in terms of global, regional, subregional and national environmental policy. Historically, national governments have worked in isolation on their respective environmental policies. With the emergence of global environmental problems, international institutions have led the way in promoting the development of global environmental policies. The European Community is about the only example of regional governments coming together to give consideration to regional environmental problems as well as other political issues.

Environmental policies considered by regional commissions and regional development banks are primarily those that enrich the individual environmental policies of the involved countries and those that constitute proposals and requests aimed at global environmental policy. The environmental policies of entire multinational regions/subregions have received very little attention.

Yet, regional interdependence continues to grow with the advancing specialization of tasks in regional industrial structures and the increasing mutual dependence in trade relationships. This indicates that there is an increasing need to plan and implement regional environmental policy, which will enable countries to divide up tasks and to carry out a unified environmental policy, either as economic blocs or as entire regions. This trend will no doubt intensify in the future. It is from this perspective that we have examined financing requirements and organizations for the planning and implementation of an environmental policy for Asian and the Pacific.

Economic development in the Asian and Pacific region is proceeding through evolving relationships among a number of economic blocs, a process that is likely to increase in the future. Thus, it is vital that in addition to the enhancement of individual countries' environmental strategies, that environmental strategy be planned and implemented at the level of economic blocs. The strategy should not be one for the region as a whole but rather one to be used as a common guideline for the region. In other words, it is important to identify concepts of sustainable development to be established in the diverse Asian and Pacific region. Some examples of this regional strategic planning are techniques and systems for environmental impact assessments and environmental screenings that are common to all the countries of a group linking a countries' environmental policies, including their environmental standards; multinational environmental strategies pertaining to development-related investment for regional infrastructure; locating and facilitating practical, enlightened projects and policies on the regional level; and more efficient environmental investment involving the whole region.

Tasks related to such environmental strategies are performed by the OECD, the World Bank, UNDP, UNEP, ESCAP, ADB and others. Under this arrangement, however, recommendations and requests made of individual countries or the idea of a global strategy hold sway, while any tendency to move in the direction of integration as a regional strategy is not necessarily very strong. Integration of development and environment on the one hand, and of economics and environment on the other, is the wave of the future. This trend of development and economic progress on the regional level will continue as structural links are strengthened. Thus, the regional integration of environmental strategy will be increasingly important.

This demonstrates the necessity of clearly defining the task, at the regional level, of integration of the environmental strategies that have been, and will be, proposed by various institutions. In addition, regional environmental strategies must be aggressively planned and implemented. Institutions that can best play this role include the Economic and Social Commission for Asia and the Pacific (ESCAP), Asian Development Bank (ADB), and the Asia-Pacific Economic Cooperation Conference (APEC).

The funds needed to perform these tasks are the costs of policy exploration and project development. The costs of policy and project implementation cannot always be predicted. Thus for the time being, consideration must be given to sources of funding for research, for the creation of venues for policy exploration and for decision making on instituting policy and project implementation. Covering the costs of actual policy and project implementation will have to be decided—along with how to procure the funding—at the stage when decisions are made. Since funds covering the former should not be too large, they would probably be obtainable by somewhat expanding the funding to the institutions (ESCAP, ADB) that perform these tasks. [*The remaining of the four key needs have been omitted as they do not deal specifically with the financial aspects of sustainable development and the environment.*]

4

National Environmental Funds

A

Robinson N., *Illustrative Governmental Funds Dedicated to Sustaining Environmental Service*, unpublished paper, 2001

Restoration and maintenance of environmental quality requires a sustained effort over a number of years. To ensure that such measures can be continued without interruption, it is often essential to establish special funds, set aside and dedicated to be spent on the identified environmental purpose. The money in such funds is derived from specific sources, and are collected and deposited directly into the funds rather than being subject to annual budgetary appropriation by legislative or executive branches of government. Annual disbursements of any such fund may be budgeted annually, and may not be diverted to other purposes than the specific designation for each fund.

These funds take on several characteristics:

1. Bonded projects, whose funds are derived from borrowing money from financial markets through floating bonds, with the repayment of the bonds, and interest, derived from users fees or other dedicated revenue sources.
2. Revolving funds, whose funds are derived from an initial dedication or contribution of money obtained from taxes (or donations, or other sources) and then loaded to local authorities for specified environmental purposes, and then repaid by the local authorities either from their own annual budgets or from users fees or other dedicated revenue sources.

3. Dedicated tax revenue funds, whose funds are raised annually by specified taxes on a designated natural resource extractions of sales of commodities, often related to the environmental problems that the funds are designed to address.
4. Endowed funds, whose funds are set side and only the interest from investing the funds is available annually for the specific purposes designated by the endowment, the funds being contributed by one or more donors, or from designated contributions of tax or other revenues.
5. Dedicated charitable contribution funds, whose funds are derived from annual contributions by individuals or associations, with disbursements to the specified environmental purposes made annually of the funds received annually.
6. Compensation funds, whose funds come from a payment by a company or individual who has damaged the environment and been sued in a civil action or cited in a criminal action, and who makes a payment to such a fund in lieu of the civil penalties and fines (which if collected would otherwise be paid into the general treasury and not be used necessarily for environmental remediation).
7. Funds for specific services, whose funds are paid by an applicant for a permit or license to cover the cost of environmental review or protection services being provided by the government in order to process the permit application.

Each of these types of funds can be illustrated by well established examples. Since these funds are established by a State, or sometimes by a State in cooperation with a nongovernmental organization or another governmental body, the financing examples are generic models that can be applied in any governmental setting where the political will exists to set up the funds. The following examples are drawn from experience in the State of New York and the USA.

(1) Bonds—NYS *Environmental Quality Bond Act* (see NYS *Environmental Conservation Law*)
(2) User fees—See the State revolving funds for the maintenance and upgrading of publicly owned sewage treatment works.
(3) Dedicated tax revenue funds—See the "Superfund" set up under CERCLA in the USA, and the state mini-superfunds, with taxes on petroleum and chemical feed stocks (hazardous contamination sources).
(4) Endowed funds—See Park funds, etc.
(5) Contribution funds—See US Fish and Wildlife Conservation Funds; Duck Stamp funds; etc.
(6) Compensation funds—Wetlands restoration, parks dedications, etc. paid for pay payments in lieu of fines, often paid to NGOs or specific government agencies (e.g., Puerto Rico payment, etc.)
(7) Funds for specific purposes—EIA fees to pay for scientific studies and reviews; operator permits for TSD Facilities to pay for State inspectors at hazardous waste sites

5

Financing Through Additionality and the Provision of Incremental Costs

A

Jordan A. and Werksman J., "Financing Global Environmental Protection," in Cameron J., Werksman J. and Roderick P. (eds), *Improving Compliance with International Environmental Law,* London, Earthscan, 1996, pp 247–256

UNCED and the Debate on Finance

One of the most contentious issues raised at the June 1992 United Nations Conference on Environment and Development (UNCED) was whether, and to what extent, the developed countries would meet the additional cost of measures undertaken by the developing countries to protect the global climate system and preserve biodiversity. It was generally recognized that sufficient financial incentives would need to be built into the agreements then under negotiation to encourage greater developing country support, but little discussion took place as to how these incentives would actually function in practice. After protracted negotiations, a compromise of sorts was reached.

Developing countries pledged to implement certain measures to address global environmental problems in return for new and additional finance provided by the industrialized states. The total amount of 'additionality' was not specified. However, the additional money was earmarked for the *incremental costs* incurred by developing country Parties in implementing the terms of any agreements they entered into.

Over the last five years, the terms 'additionality' and 'incrementality' have appeared with increasing regularity in international negotiations and agreements. Broad conceptual agreement on additional financing contributed to the successful re-negotiation of the *Montreal Protocol* in 1990 and to the adoption of the Conventions on *Climate Change* and *Biodiversity*. The successful use of financial bargains between North and South in these issue areas appears to have had an important precedent. An expectation has developed that financial transfer packages or other 'selective inducements' will be needed to accelerate and strengthen the process of negotiating international environmental regimes in other areas of global concern such as desertification and deforestation.

In practice, however, the two concepts have proved elusive and little agreement exists over how much money should be transferred and how it should be used. This is partly because additionality and incrementality touch the heart of deeper political debates over which countries should shoulder the responsibility for human-induced global environmental change, and on how the costs of responding to such change should be apportioned between countries. Historical grievances and the temptation to link finance to other disputed issues in international politics, serve only to complicate the debate even further. However, some measure of agreement must be sought or the implementation of agreements signed at Rio may be jeopardized.

This chapter reviews the emergence of the terms 'new and additional' and 'incremental cost' in international environmental politics. It focuses on the theoretical and practical difficulties that have arisen during initial stages of implementing the *Climate Change Convention* and in the operation of the Convention's financing institution, the Global Environment Facility (GEF).

Additionality and Incrementality

Additionality describes the origins of the financial resources needed to solve global environmental problems, while incrementality determines the total *size* of those resources needed to address a particular area of concern (e.g., biodiversity, marine pollution). The concepts, thus, interlock: the greater the incremental costs, the more additional resources will be required; the more additionality that is provided, the greater the 'total' incremental cost that can be met.

The concepts have tended to take on different meanings in different contexts. The first context is that of *regime formation* (i.e., international negotiations), where bargains are struck between countries to produce international law and policy. Finance can help to lubricate the process of international diplomacy. The second context is the more drawn out process of *operational decision making* (i.e., the implementation of international accords), where implementation programs are drawn up, individual projects are identified and ranked, and finance begins to flow. The rapid entry into force of both the Rio Conventions has forced differences of opinion, which were subsumed during the process of negotiation, to the surface.

'New and Additional' Financial Resources

At the core of the concept of additionality is a general understanding that resources should be provided by the industrialized world over and above existing flows of international finance for measures taken by developing countries to address global environmental challenges. Additionality can be viewed as the price which the South demands for its participation in international attempts to solve global environmental problems, and a small contribution to offset the North's general ecological debt. The word 'new' is generally understood to describe either the sources of funding or the financial mechanisms used to provide them. The term 'additional' suggests that the assistance supplements rather than diminishes existing flows of finance.

The Additionality Debate

The principle of additionality could now be said to form one of the central planks of the Group of 77 (G-77) developing countries' negotiating strategy in international discussions on environment and development. On a very general level, the industrialized states have been sympathetic to the South's plea for extra financial assistance but they have carefully avoided making specific commitments. Some donor states have sought to put promises into action, and have pledged their support for the new and additional funding mechanisms of the *Montreal Protocol* Multilateral Fund (MPMF) and the recently restructured Global Environment Facility (GEF). Neither fund, however, has sought to define, or even clarify, the additionality of its contributions.

The Rationale for Additionality

The concept of additionality has an intellectual coherence and is politically attractive to both North and South. The developing countries' calls for additionality are symptomatic of a number of underlying concerns, some essentially practical others with a moral and ethical dimension. First, developing countries claim that their attempts to industrialize should not be hindered by the costs of measures designed to ameliorate problems not of their making. Additionality would provide them with the inducement to leapfrog the polluting and wasteful stages of industrialization. Second, capital constraints and an overwhelming need to address domestic concerns such as poverty and food security do not allow for tackling environmental problems with the same vigor as the industrialized world. During the 1980s, flows of finance from the North (aid, private flows and export credits) declined sharply (largely as a result of reductions in private flows) and even reversed as the debt problem reached its peak in the mid to late 1980s. Calls for additionality are thus one attempt to address much deeper inequalities and economic imbalances in the world economy. During international negotiations for the Conventions and the GEF, the developing countries insisted that contributions be additional and disbursements concessional (i.e., in the form of grants or very low interest loans). They were particularly concerned that contributions to the GEF would not diminish the funds available for development assistance.

The notion of providing an extra quantum of finance specifically for the global environment holds a certain appeal for the North as well. First, allocating a certain amount of money for sustainable development or the global environment makes for good and publicly visible 'gesture politics'. Second, separating out a distinct portion of money for global warming or ozone depletion raises the hope that it will be used more 'efficiently' (in the sense that it specifically funds global environmental projects rather than development related activities), while also helping to parry criticism that existing flows of aid fail to reflect global environmental concerns.

Additionality Baselines

Additionality is a relative term, which predicates the need for some form of benchmark or baseline, above which an 'additional' increment can be discerned. The most common interpretation of additionality sets this baseline at the level of existing development assistance. Total net resource flows to the South in 1991 amounted to US$131bn (at 1990 prices) 12 of which US$73bn (56 percent) was in the form of Official Development Assistance (ODA). Although global aid volume has grown markedly in gross terms in the last 20 years, as a percentage of OECD GNP it has hardly changed and remains lodged at around 0.33 percent. Additionality, so measured, would thus constitute any increase in ODA over and above 0.33 percent.

Developing countries have pressed for a higher, aspirational baseline of 0.7 percent of GNP, which has been the UN's official target for ODA since 1970. At present only five developed countries could be said to be meeting or exceeding this target. Not surprisingly, individual OECD donors support definitions of additionality that place their practices in the best light. Sweden, a country which nets its contributions to the GEF and the MPMF from a general multilateral aid budget (thereby failing on a narrow construction of an additionality test applied specifically to Sweden itself) that is around 0.92 percent of its domestic GNP, would clearly have a strong incentive to push for the acceptance of a 0.7 percent baseline and indeed has made representations to that effect.

The US government, in the context of ozone protection, describes additionality as 'the allocation of *more* funds specifically to ozone protection, but not necessarily the allocation of funds in addition to overall resource flows' (emphasis added). On this interpretation, any extra money which is diverted to environmental protection is judged to be additional regardless of its origins. In the context of GEF's pilot phase the US announced that it was not prepared to contribute 'additional' funds to the GEF's core fund. Instead, the US negotiated a co-financing agreement with the GEF, contributions to which are re-directed from the regular US Agency for International Development (USAID) budget.

Finally, some countries have argued that additionality should be measured over and above the level of *total* net resource flows, including resources in the form of private flows of money. The US Government has implied that increased flows of North-South private investment might also be considered as releasing further additionality, even when levels of publicly financed ODA remain constant. If net financial transfers are taken as the unit of account (i.e., total flows minus interest and dividends on loans) the bench mark in 1990 would have been just US$34bn. The concept of additionality could then be stretched to include such things as debt forgiveness or 'debt-for-nature' swaps. The adequacy of money allotted to the GEF and MPMF could be judged to be either very large or relatively small, depending on the baseline adopted.

Additionality Post-Rio

The texts of the *Climate Change* and *Biodiversity Conventions* do not clarify the meaning of additionality, and merely use the umbrella term 'new and additional finance'. If 'existing flows' is to be the baseline, then what is 'additional' can only be calculated on the basis of what a donor would have done had they not entered into an international agreement or pledged to support an international fund. The absence of a definition opens up an enormous opportunity for conflicting interpretations and expectations.

An accurate calculation or indeed enforcement of additionality will be difficult to achieve not least because it would transform a general commitment to a specific obligation. But, as the demand for regular flows of development assistance continues to increase and finance becomes more closely linked with the future prospects for global environmental governance, greater scrutiny may need to be applied to the measurement and enforcement of additionality. Arguably, this may help to engender trust between Parties and may improve the quality of the overall cooperative effort.

Incremental Cost Financing

The term 'incremental cost' is important because it quantifies the size of the payment to developing countries will receive from developed countries as compensation for acceding to, and implementing the terms of, international environmental agreements. Just as with the term 'additionality', recipient Parties clearly have an incentive to try and maximize the size and scope of the total side payment; providers, the converse.

Incrementality can be traced to the text of the revised (1990) *Montreal Protocol*. During the negotiations, countries of the South expressed concern that measures to address ozone depletion, a problem they repeatedly stressed was not of their making, would 'add new burdens to their economies and adversely affect their standard of living'. What were termed 'incremental burdens' by negotiators were eventually incorporated into the text of the revised Protocol as 'incremental costs'.

In the *Montreal Protocol* the sources and technical solutions for ozone depletion are relatively easy to identify. Defining and implementing the term 'incremental cost' has proved comparatively straightforward and Parties have agreed on a broad list (an 'indicative list') of costs judged to be eligible for 'incremental' cost financing. In terms of climate change, a problem more complex and uncertain to predict and alleviate, the task will be far more challenging.

> *In the* Montreal Protocol *the sources and technical solutions for ozone depletion are relatively easy to identify.*

Much of the controversy surrounding the concept of incrementality has arisen because of expectations attached to the concept when it was expressed as a broad principle. Thus far, the work of developing a specific definition for incrementality in the *Climate Change Convention* has been carried forward by two separate but related institutions: the Convention's Conference of Parties, and the GEF, which is to serve as the interim 'operating entity' of the Convention's financial mechanism. The future of the incremental financing issue will probably be determined by the continuing interplay between these two institutions.

Incremental Costs and the Climate Convention

All Parties to the Convention, developed and developing countries alike, have committed themselves to undertake a wide range of measures to address the threat of climate change. These 'general commitments' are designed to develop, collect and disseminate information on climate change and possible responses, to implement programs containing measures to reduce net emissions of greenhouse gases and to facilitate adequate adaptation to climate change. Developed country Parties further commit themselves to provide *new and additional resources* to meet the *agreed full incremental costs* of developing country Parties. The term 'agreed full incremental cost' was, in itself, a compromise. Throughout negotiations, developed countries had advocated the use of the single qualification 'agreed', whereas developing countries preferred the term 'full'. As a last minute compromise, the two qualifiers, 'full' and 'agreed', were combined to produce the seemingly contradictory term 'agreed full incremental costs'.

Incremental Costs and the GEF

During the GEF's pilot phase (which began almost a year before the Convention was signed at Rio), donor country Participants defined incremental cost as that segment of an eligible project's total cost which directly benefits the global environment, but which would not normally be in the interest of a host nation to finance itself. Only those projects which generated global benefits, but which required extra concessional financing to be viable to the host nation (i.e., national costs exceeded national benefits), were judged to be eligible for GEF support in the pilot phase. 'Domestically beneficial' projects were to be excluded.

In the context of the GEF, then, incremental cost is the difference between the national costs and national benefits of a project designed to generate global environmental benefits. So, for example, the GEF could meet the incremental cost of re-designing a proposed coal-fired power station project to utilize a local supply of natural gas, thereby realizing the global benefit of reduced CO_2 emissions. In this example, the GEF would pay for the incremental cost of the conversion; the 'baseline' cost of the coal-fired station would have been financed by the host nation (either from its own resources or from international lending or the private sector).

Since Rio, discussions on developing an operational definition for incremental costs in the climate change context has been proceeding within the INC and the GEF on parallel tracks. The INC, a large and loosely structured intergovernmental body with limited administrative and research capacity but a wide-ranging agenda, has thus far failed to resolve the issue beyond renewing its requests to its Secretariat for further clarification of the issues. As this vacuum developed, the GEF administration launched its own multimillion dollar research Programme for Measuring Incremental Costs for the Environment (PRINCE).

Certain commentators expressed surprise over PRINCE's approach to measuring incrementality because it appeared both to erode significantly the level of financial resources that would be available under the Convention and prejudge the outcome of discussions which are scheduled to begin at the first meeting of the Convention's Conference of the Parties (COP) in 1995. The Convention provides specifically that the COP (and not the GEF) will 'decide on ... policies, program priorities and eligibility criteria' for the financial mechanism.

It is easy to imagine that the bulk of the measures to be undertaken by developing countries under the Convention will have national as well as global benefits. Because of this, GEF conceded early on that 'only a limited number of projects are likely to be...eligible for full funding from GEF'. The GEF suggests that the rest of the increment, to cover that portion of the costs seen to have 'national' benefits, should come from 'other sources of domestic and foreign funding sources'. In a later statement the GEF claimed that: 'in typical cases, the incremental cost will be a relatively small proportion of the total cost of the re-designed or alternate activity.'

'Gross' and 'Net' Incremental Costs

As policy makers begin to struggle with the implications of these early attempts to apply incremental cost principles, two competing interpretations can be said to have emerged: *gross* and *net* incremental costs. Gross incremental costs can be defined as the difference between the total costs of implementing a proposed project and that course of action which the developing country would have pursued had it not undertaken commitments under the Convention. Supporters of this interpretation rely on a direct reading of the text of the Convention and tend to lay stress upon the word *full* in 'agreed full incremental cost'. Net incremental costs, on the other hand, can be viewed as the additional cost of complying with the Convention *minus* the value of any domestic benefits thereby generated. Generally, this has been the approach taken by the GEF, and justified on the grounds that it is more 'cost-effective' then funding the full cost of projects (i.e., by funding only those aspects of a project that specifically yield global environmental benefits, more funds will be available to fund the globally beneficial aspects of further projects). The significant difference between the two approaches is that on the gross cost interpretation, developing countries are left better off than they would have been without Convention funding, whereas on the net cost interpretation developing countries are left no better off (except for their share of the global environmental benefit) than had the Convention not been adopted.

The G-77 coalition and China have signalled that they expect the costs of *all* the commitments mentioned in the *Climate Change Convention* to be met including those measures with primarily domestic benefits such as adaptation, research and training. They have expressed concern that some developed countries are attempting to reduce the scale of transfers by disallowing projects which are domestically beneficial from being eligible for funding (i.e., the net cost approach).

If the net approach is followed, developing countries may be asked to look outside the GEF for funding. To implement the Convention, developing countries may be forced to fend for themselves in financial channels ungoverned by the principles of the Convention. This may, in turn, lead to an unsystematic and uneven distribution of resources. No system would be in place to ensure funding from other sources is new and additional, and at the same time on the concessional terms agreed to under the Convention. Ironically, the net approach, if adopted, would render those countries least capable of fulfilling their obligations (and thus most likely to benefit nationally from enhanced capacity) which are least eligible for extra funding. Least developed countries would be saddled with an inequitable share of the global burden of climate change (for which they have relatively less responsibility) under a Convention in which developed country Parties have committed themselves to 'take full account of the specific needs and special situations of the least developed countries in their actions with regard to finding and transfer of technology'.

Negotiated Incremental Costs

On closer analysis, the line dividing the two interpretations is more blurred than the simple 'net' end 'gross' typology suggests. There are, for example, measures which could be taken to reduce global warming at a negligible incremental cost (correcting subsidies for example) or even a negative incremental cost (e.g., energy efficiency measures). Meanwhile, it is likely that for certain types of projects (e.g., game parks to protect biodiversity and institutional strengthening) the incremental cost might approach 100 percent (i.e., because nothing would have been done in the absence of the respective Convention). Indeed, the GEF suggests that 'there are cases when the incremental cost will be equal to the full cost of the activity'.

In practice, a balance between the gross and net interpretations will probably emerge out of a process of *negotiation,* a view now reflected in statements from the GEF. Negotiations could proceed on two levels: at a sectoral level to determine the eligibility of certain classes of activity through the preparation of indicative lists; and at the project level to determine the scale of assistance to individual interventions. What remains to be agreed on are a set of guidelines to structure and inform these negotiations. These should be agreed by the COPs and may draw upon the research emerging from the PRINCE program.

Incrementality Baselines

As with additionality, incremental costs can only be defined against some kind of hypothetical baseline which measures what a host nation would have done in the absence of an international agreement. Incremental cost baselines are as difficult to establish as additionality baselines, not least because if a proposed project is financed then the baseline situation will never occur. The baseline is intrinsically hypothetical, since it can be premised upon a number of very different scenarios and may adopt many different forms, and hence is open to manipulation. King suggests that the baseline could be based on a number of factors, including economic efficiency, equity, and existing trends. In the case of the power station example (above), the costs and benefits of a hypothetical coal-fired power station project over the next 10 to 20 years would need to be calculated. This would not be easy. The interim Secretariat to the *Climate Convention* notes that rules of 'economic, environmental, technical, and financial *reasonableness'* may need to be applied, but these have yet to be formulated and agreed upon.

Conclusions

As implementation of the Rio Conventions proceeds, the importance of measuring, verifying and perhaps enforcing additionality and incrementality will increase. Yet, both are relatively elastic terms and the potential for conflict and confusion remains high. For example, the foregoing underscores the importance of having proper baselines, calculated according to what a donor or recipient would have done had they not entered into the respective global environmental agreement. Clearly, there are enormous difficulties in estimating and, more importantly, verifying this 'counterfactual'. Further, both donors and recipient Parties have an incentive, and the latitude allowed them by the vagueness of international agreements, to push the rules of assessment in their favor, leaving plenty of room for discord and conflict in the future.

A vital need has arisen for some form of mutually acceptable calculus or set of criteria for measuring both terms. As the process of implementation begins to roll forward, the policy debate may now turn to fundamental questions about the types of institutions and decision making structures appropriate to developing and applying these criteria. Issues such as additionality and incrementality involve sophisticated social, economic, moral, scientific and political judgements. Policy makers must decide if such complex issues can be handled by rambling debates in large intergovernmental bodies such as the Conventions' COPs or the UN's Commission on Sustainable Development. The alternative is that responsibility and a degree of decision making power be delegated to more powerful organizations such as the World Bank which have a great deal of experience in international finance, or programs such as PRINCE. However, the involvement of these and other similar institutions will probably raise hackles within the green lobby and in the Third World.

The foregoing discussion challenges the simple idea that the Rio Summit resolved the issue of how to finance the transition to sustainable development. One suspects that there are very profound discrepancies in the manner that North and South perceive the need for, likely role and scope of additional financial transfers. The developed states tend towards a *minimal* interpretation; transfers being a price (to be minimized wherever possible) to be paid for enlisting the support of the South in tackling common problems. Meanwhile the developing states seek perpetually to advance a *maximal* interpretation of additionality and incrementality, arguing that 'new' environmentally related transfers are a rightful and legitimate means to address the inequities inherent in the operation of the world economy. These represent very different standpoints and do not appear to be easily reconcilable. In the short term, the task of balancing these has been delegated to the COPs and the GEF. The pathways through which these two bodies evolve in the coming years will come to represent a fascinating test case of how well international institutions can adapt to the challenge of sustainable development.

One suspects that there are very profound discrepancies in the manner that North and South perceive the need for, likely role and scope of additional financial transfer.

6

Funding for Biodiversity Conservation

A

Financing the *Convention on Biological Diversity*

(i) *Convention on Biological Diversity*, 31 ILM 818, 1992

Article 20: Financial Resources

1. Each Contracting Party undertakes to provide, in accordance with its capabilities, financial support and incentives in respect of those national activities which are intended to achieve the objectives of this Convention, in accordance with its national plans, priorities and programs.
2. The developed country Parties shall provide new and additional financial resources to enable developing country Parties to meet the agreed full incremental costs to them of implementing measures which fulfill the obligations of this Convention and to benefit from its provisions and which costs are agreed between a developing country Party and the institutional structure referred to in Article 21, in accordance with policy, strategy, program priorities and eligibility criteria and an indicative list of incremental costs established by the Conference of the Parties. Other Parties, including countries undergoing the process of transition to a market economy, may voluntarily assume the obligations of the developed country Parties. For the purpose of this Article, the Conference of the Parties, shall at its first meeting establish a list of developed country Parties and other Parties which voluntarily assume the obligations of the developed country Parties. The Conference of the Parties shall periodically review and if necessary amend the list. Contributions from other countries and sources on a voluntary basis would also be encouraged. The implementation of these commitments shall take into account the need for adequacy, predictability and timely flow of funds and the importance of burden-sharing among the contributing Parties included in the list.
3. The developed country Parties may also provide, and developing country Parties avail themselves of, financial resources related to the implementation of this Convention through bilateral, regional and other multilateral channels.
4. The extent to which developing country Parties will effectively implement their commitments under this Convention will depend on the effective implementation by developed country Parties of their commitments under this Convention related to financial resources and transfer of technology and will take fully into account the fact that economic and social development and eradication of poverty are

the first and overriding priorities of the developing country Parties.

5. The Parties shall take full account of the specific needs and special situation of least developed countries in their actions with regard to funding and transfer of technology.
6. The Contracting Parties shall also take into consideration the special conditions resulting from the dependence on, distribution and location of, biological diversity within developing country Parties, in particular small island States.
7. Consideration shall also be given to the special situation of developing countries, including those that are most environmentally vulnerable, such as those with arid and semi-arid zones, coastal and mountainous areas.

Article 21: Financial Mechanism

1. There shall be a mechanism for the provision of financial resources to developing country Parties for purposes of this Convention on a grant or concessional basis the essential elements of which are described in this Article. The mechanism shall function under the authority and guidance of, and be accountable to, the Conference of the Parties for purposes of this Convention. The operations of the mechanism shall be carried out by such institutional structure as may be decided upon by the Conference of the Parties at its first meeting. For purposes of this Convention, the Conference of the Parties shall determine the policy, strategy, program priorities and eligibility criteria relating to the access to and utilization of such resources. The contributions shall be such as to take into account the need for predictability, adequacy and timely flow of funds referred to in Article 20 in accordance with the amount of resources needed to be decided periodically by the Conference of the Parties and the importance of burden-sharing among the contributing Parties included in the list referred to in Article 20, paragraph 2. Voluntary contributions may also be made by the developed country Parties and by other countries and sources. The mechanism shall operate within a democratic and transparent system of governance.
2. Pursuant to the objectives of this Convention, the Conference of the Parties shall at its first meeting determine the policy, strategy and program priorities, as well as detailed criteria and guidelines for eligibility for access to and utilization of the financial resources including monitoring and evaluation on a regular basis of such utilization. The Conference of the Parties shall decide on the arrangements to give effect to paragraph 1 above after consultation with the institutional structure entrusted with the operation of the financial mechanism.
3. The Conference of the Parties shall review the effectiveness of the mechanism established under this Article, including the criteria and guidelines referred to in paragraph 2 above, not less than two years after the entry into force of this Convention and thereafter on a regular basis. Based on such review, it shall take appropriate action to improve the effectiveness of the mechanism if necessary.
4. The Contracting Parties shall consider strengthening existing financial institutions to provide financial resources for the conservation and sustainable use of biological diversity.

Article 39: Financial Interim Arrangements

Provided that it has been fully restructured in accordance with the requirements of Article 21, the Global Environment Facility of the United Nations Development Programme, the United Nations Environment Programme and the International Bank for Reconstruction and Development shall be the institutional structure referred to in Article 21 on an interim basis, for the period between the entry into force of this Convention and the first meeting of the Conference of the Parties or until the Conference of the Parties decides which institutional structure will be designated in accordance with Article 21.

(ii) IUCN, "The Funding Debate and the Compromise Reflected in Articles 20, 21 and 39," in *A Guide to the Convention on Biological Diversity*, IUCN, 1994, p 101

In the multilateral environmental agreements, provisions were made for funding mechanisms to help finance activities to implement the conventions in developing countries if the conventions were going to be effective. Consensus on how to organize the funding mechanism was not easily reached, however. For example, the debates over the *Convention on Biological Diversity* on the question of financing "divided along North-South lines over questions of whether and how to establish an independent biodiversity fund, what costs would be covered, and who would administer the financial resources—the Conference of the Parties, an existing institutional structure, or a new one.

Developing countries envisioned an independent fund administered under the authority of the Conference of the Parties and funded by developed countries. The goal of the developing countries was to give control over the Convention's financial resources to the Conference of the Parties, a body in which they would likely have a majority. Developed countries never denied the need to make funds available to developing countries to implement the Convention. However, they wanted the Global Environment Facility (GEF), a new financial initiative established in 1990, and jointly operated by the World Bank, the United Nations Development Programme and the United Nations Environment Programme, to become the financial mechanism under the Convention.

The text [of the treaty] represents a compromise negotiated in the final negotiating session's final hours. Article 20 and 21 both contain language that was deliberately left vague for the Conference of the Parties to later clarify. But, overall, the conference of the Parties was given control over the financial mechanism established and the designation of the institutional structure which will operate the mechanism.

Resolution 1 of the Nairobi Final Act invited the GEF to operate, on an interim basis, the financial mechanism during the period between the Convention's opening for signature and its entry into force. Article 39 designates the GEF as the interim institutional structure entrusted to operate the financial mechanism, between the convention's entry into force and the first meeting of the Conference of the Parties, or until the conference of the Parties decides otherwise, provided it is fully restructure to fulfil the requirement found in Article 21 that the financial mechanism operate in a democratic and transparent manner.

B

Incremental Costs

(i) IUCN, "Incremental Costs," in *A Guide to the Convention on Biological Diversity*, 1994, pp 103–104

Incremental cost is a theoretical concept comprising one aspect of cost/benefit analysis. Cost/benefit analysis is an attempt to quantify and compare the costs and benefits of particular actions. The process of determining costs and benefits can, in theory, help decision makers make more objective funding determinations by allowing the costs and benefits of different options to be compared. In addition to incremental cost, other aspects of cost/benefit analysis include calculating an action's total cost, incremental benefits and total benefits. Costs are measured in monetary terms. Benefits can be measured monetarily as well. In addition, benefits can also be measured in terms of "effectiveness," for example, the amount of biological diversity conserved. . . .

The simplicity of the preceding examples [of gross and net incremental cost] masks the complexity of the incremental cost concept in real world applications."' The incremental cost (and, as it turns out, incremental benefit) is highly determinant on establishing an appropriate baseline. A baseline action's cost is used as a reference point against which the cost of a proposed action can be subtracted to determine an incremental cost. A baseline cost could represent present day conditions for a particular situation. Baseline costs for actions involving mutually exclusive options (such as whether to build a dam or transfer a particular hard technology) are relatively explicit and straightforward to determine. The most simple baseline is no action, keeping in mind that inaction's costs could be quite great. . . .

In summary, incremental cost is a highly theoretical concept. While the technical problems are worked out, funding decisions may need to rely simply on which costs are "agreed" between a developing country and the institutional structure set up to administer the financial mechanism [under the *Convention on Biological Diversity* or the *Montreal Protocol* on substances that Deplete the Ozone Layer]."

7

The Role of the Asian Development Bank

A

Boyd J., *Financing and Capacity Building for Environmental Law in Asia: The Role of the Asian Development Bank*, unpublished paper, 2001

Introductory Summary

On 1 February 1980 the President of the Asian Development Bank signed in New York the *Declaration of Environmental Policies and Procedures Relating to Economic Development*, committing in part ADB to "support[ing] the principles and recommendations for action of the United Nations Conference" on the Human Environment held in Stockholm in 1972. This New York Declaration, signed by representatives of nine other development banks and United Nations organizations and programs, dealt with a wide range of environmental concerns, including policies, programs, projects, technical assistance, research, training, and publications. Since then, ADB has engaged in a wide range of activities fully within the terms of the New York Declaration. Today, these ADB activities are pursued within a Long-Term Strategic Framework and are responsive to ADB's Donor Member Countries Report for Seventh Replenishment of the Asian Development Fund (ADF VIII), which emphasizes the importance of ADB's new environmental policy.

To provide guidance to ADB officers and others, ADB has a Loan Classification System defining loans designed to protect the environment and promote "Good Governance". Under its Good Governance policy, which emphasizes predictability, transparency, accountability, and participation, ADB has developed a Law and Policy program and a yearly publication. The result is an ADB loan program which promotes new environmental legislation and regulations, requires improved environmental conditions such as the prohibition of the sale of leaded gasoline, strengthens environmental institutions, and provides training. ADB's technical assistance grant program, which depends in part on cofinancing from ADB's member countries, also features training concerning the environment which has lead to significant legislation, regulations and publications. ADB has also used its own funds to engage scholars to undertake research concerning environmental principles and concepts reflecting general international law and public policy for multilateral development banking.

This article reviews the New York Declaration, and related ADB policies, as well as the classification system, loan and technical assistance program, training and research activities to explain how ADB finances capacity building for environmental law in Asia, including total ADB lending for environmental projects surpassing $8 billion. The article concludes with a look forward, suggesting that multilateral development banks have an international legal obligation to take sustainable development concerns into account. The article ends urging everyone in the international community to increase cooperation many times over to achieve the important objectives of the Declaration of the 1972 Stockholm Conference for the Protection and Improvement of the Environment.

The New York Declaration and Recent Policies Pertaining to the Environment

On 1 February 1980 the President of the Asian Development Bank, Mr. Taroichi Yoshida, joined with representatives of nine other banks and international entities in signing in New York *the Declaration of Environmental Policies and Procedures Relating to Economic Development*. This Declaration stated that the signatories "*Will*, to the best of their abilities, endeavor to" undertake nine tasks relating to:

1. "systematic examination of all development activities, including policies, programs and projects under consideration for financing to ensure that appropriate measures are proposed for compliance with" their "support for the principles and recommendations for the United Nations Conference on the Human Environment (Stockholm, 1972)";
2. "integration of appropriate environmental measures in the design and implementation of economic development activities";

3. "technical assistance, including training, on environmental matters to developing countries";
4. "support [for] project proposals that are specifically designed to protect ... the human environment";
5. "cooperate in research and studies leading to ...project appraisal, implementation and evaluation methodologies, including ... environmental protection measures";
6. "training ... of operational staff in the environmental dimension of economic development"; and
7. "publish and disseminate documentation ... providing guidance on the environmental dimension of economic development activities."

In the more than two decades since the New York Declaration, ADB has been undertaking each of these tasks and much more.

Strategic Framework

The most recent expression of ADB's policy of protecting the environment is found in its *Long-Term Strategic Framework of the Asian Development Bank (2001-2015)*, endorsed by ADB's Board of Directors in 2001. This Long-Term Strategic Framework contains a Strategic Agenda with three "Core Strategic Areas of Intervention" consisting of "Sustainable Economic Growth", "Inclusive Social Development", and "Governance for Effective Policies and Institutions", plus three "Cross-cutting Strategic Themes":

(i) Promoting the Role of the Private Sector in Development,
(ii) Supporting Regional Cooperation and Integration for Development, and
(iii) Addressing Environmental Sustainability.

Paragraph 60 of this Long-Term Strategic Framework summarizes in part ADB's strategy for Addressing Environmental Sustainability among its Developing Member Countries (DMCs):

> "ADB's programs must be designed to promote environmentally strong development without compromise. In addition to advocating the integration of environmental policies and objectives into national development policies and objectives, ADB must ensure, in conjunction with DMCs, that environmental policies adopt an integrated resource management approach.... ADB will advocate a greater reliance on economic instruments and incentives to address environmental issues, combined with regulatory controls. The advocated environmental policy will address specific market failures, such as open access resources, and government policies that exacerbate environmental problems, such as subsidizing the extraction of scarce resources.

In a similar vein, ADB's previous strategic framework, the *Medium-Term Strategic Framework (1995-1998)*, which guided ADB operations until the recent endorsement of the Long-Term Strategic Framework, contained "five strategic development objectives:

(i) promoting economic growth,
(ii) reducing poverty,
(iii) supporting human development (including population planning),
(iv) improving the status of women, and
(v) protecting the environment."

Asian Development Fund VIII Donors' Report

The November 2000 Asian Development Fund (ADF VIII) Donors' Report entitled *Fighting Poverty in Asia* contains a chapter concerning the "Strategy for Implementing ADF VIII." This chapter consists of more than a dozen subheadings including a "Governance Action Plan", "Gender and Development", "Improving Project Quality and Portfolio Management", and "Strengthening ADB's Institutional Capacity". Concerning the environment, the Donors' Report indicated, in part, the following:

> "Donors concluded that the implementation of ADB's poverty reduction strategy, along with a new environment policy and revised guidelines for environmental assessment, as well as a performance-based allocation system including environmental criteria, provides an opportunity for improving mainstreaming of environment in all ADB operations. In this context, Donors recommended that ADB integrate environmental concerns and expertise at each stage of the Poverty Reduction Strategy country-level process leading to the Partnership Agreement between ADB and the DMC. Similarly, Donors recommended that ADB continue with the integration of environmental expertise in the country programming cycle to ensure that the CSP [Country Strategy and Program] fully

incorporates environmental concerns—both to avoid programs and projects entering the pipeline which are unacceptable from an environmental perspective, and to strengthen environmental assistance across sectors. Donors recommended that the environment policy and revisions to the environmental assessment guidelines be finalized in a timely manner so that they may apply during the ADF VIII period."

Loan Classification System

ADB's Loan Classification System, updated in a 27 November 2000 Staff Instruction, has seven thematic priorities:

- economic growth,
- human development,
- gender and development,
- good governance,
- environmental protection,
- private sector development, and
- regional cooperation.

The Staff Instruction states that concerning public sector loans "from 2001 onwards, not less than 40 percent ... of lending volume should be directed to poverty, including core poverty interventions" and that "[a]ll public sector interventions—whether poverty interventions or otherwise—will also support important thematic priorities of ADB", which should result in "a balanced public sector lending mix". This Staff Instruction "recognize[s] that interventions in each category could also promote one or more of the other thematic priorities", permits "[a]s a rule, however, only one category for purposes of this classification" but also permits "[i]n exceptional cases, where more than one thematic priority is strongly present in the project/program design, two categories for classification purposes."

To be classified as protecting the environment, a loan must have an objective "to promote sound management of natural resources" through one or more of the following:

- protection or improvement or the local, regional and/ or global environment;
- conservation of or increasing the net stock of natural resources (excluding minerals);
- strengthening of environmental policies and institutions, and promotion of environmental education; and of
- one or more components for sound management of natural resources and/or the environment account for at least 20 percent of total loan cost.

This environmental protection category "excludes the mitigation of incremental adverse effects since this is mandatory for all ADB-financed loans."

To be classified within the "Good Governance" category, a loan must contain one or more of the following main objectives:

- improve public expenditure management at national and/or subnational levels;
- promote accountable, efficient, and responsive public administration at national and/or subnational levels, including the reform of administrative procedures;
- strengthen or reform the legal system;
- strengthen public accountability institutions and fight corruption;
- increase government accountability and responsiveness through decentralization, local empowerment, or strengthening of civil society, and through improved information systems and transparency;
- improve corporate governance; or
- improve regulatory frameworks, particularly for public utilities, banking and capital markets.

Legal rights form an integral portion of the loan classification for "Gender and Development", which requires that a loan have an objective "to directly benefit women through improved access to income/employment opportunities or human development services, equality of rights to employment and equal wages and property ownership, fair treatment under the law, child support and maternity leave through improved social security, etc. and either:

- at least one third of the beneficiaries specifically targeted by the loan are women, or
- one or more components designed specifically to benefit women account for at least 20 percent of total loan costs.

To be classified as protecting the environment, a loan must have an objective "to promote sound management of natural resources."

Policy Initiatives Addressing Environmental Sustainability

Since 1995 ADB has developed many of policies and initiatives reflecting the growing concern for the need to focus more on social development and environmental sustainability. The policies developed from 1995 to 1998 include involuntary resettlement, forestry, energy, governance, inspection function, industrial pollution, cooperation with NGOs, indigenous peoples, fisheries, and gender and development. In 1999 ADB adopted its *Strategy for Fighting Poverty in Asia and the Pacific*. Currently ADB is preparing an Environment Policy through a wide-ranging process of consultation with diverse stakeholders, including DMC and donor governments, nongovernment organizations (NGOs), researchers, and others. The Policy will address the following needs:

- to reorient ADB's environmental program vis-a-vis ADB's *Poverty Reduction Strategy* (1999), *Long-Term Strategic Framework* (LTSF, 2000), and medium-term focus of ADF-VIII Agreements (2000);
- to shift ADB's lending operations to focus on policy reforms;
- to redesign ADB's business practices to require strengthening of environmental review and planning processes;
- to respond to increased external scrutiny of ADB programs and practices through establishment of a new environmental policy making explicit certain norms relating to outcomes of ADB operations and processes of environmental assessment such as a prohibition of adverse transboundary environmental impacts.

The principal environmental policy challenges for ADB are to assist DMCs:

- correct the policy mistakes of the past such as those arising from energy subsidies,
- ensure that environmental resources on which the poor depend for their livelihoods are conserved,
- integrate environmental objectives into the economic development process,
- bring about institutional change, to ensure accelerated flow of resources for environmental improvement.

Accordingly, ADB's medium-term action plan (2001–2005) for the environment would:

- propose strengthening environmental assessment processes and capacities in ADB,
- promote more effective integration of environmental considerations in sectoral policy dialogue with DMCs,
- support implementation of leading international environmental agreements; and
- recommend priorities for investment and technical assistance in environmental conservation for poverty reduction.

Governance and Law and Policy Reform

ADB's 1995 policy defined governance as "the manner in which power is exercised in the management of a country's social and economic resources for development." It then identified four elements of good governance:

(i) accountability,
(ii) participation,
(iii) predictability, and
(iv) transparency.

Law and policy reform is central to predictability, one of the four essential constituents of ADB's approach to governance. Legal and regulatory frameworks also ensure:

(i) participation,
(ii) transparency, and
(iii) accountability.

Predictability

Predictability refers to the existence of laws, regulations, policies, and procedures which regulate society and govern certain kinds of government action together with their fair and consistent application. ADB has promoted this principle by

- assisting DMCs to develop their legal systems;
- developing and training the professional groups needed to make legal systems work effectively;
- strengthening regulatory frameworks that govern infrastructure and public service providers (for example, energy and telecommunications), capital markets, and the natural environment; and
- supporting access to legal information and increasing legal literacy in the DMCs, and improving the quality of the judicial process by training judges and magistrates.

Transparency

Transparency concerns the disclosure of information regarding government rules, regulations, and decisions. It enables interested parties to assure themselves that official processes and procedures have been followed in a predictable way to a fair conclusion.

Creation of legal information systems that are readily accessible to citizens is an important pillar of the rule of law. Knowledge of the law is important to empower citizens and create a stable environment for economic transactions.

ADB has launched Project DIAL (*Development of the Internet for Asian Law*, an Internet subscription-based service for legislators and public officials in DMCs), and LAW-DEV, an Internet forum that provides a link for communication of ideas and information among more than 600 participants in 40 countries. Project DIAL, LAW-DEV, and *Bulletin on Law and Policy Reform* provide important sources of information about DMC law reform activities and technical assistance for law and policy reform.

Commitment

ADB's year 2000 paper on *Promoting Good Governance: ADB's Medium-Term Agenda and Action Plan* makes clear that commitment on the part of many is required to achieve improvements in governance:

> "The greater the commitment of a country's leadership to governance reform, the more likely it is that reforms will take root. Where commitment is absent, ADB's best response is to strengthen and reinforce constituencies for reform and maintain policy dialogue. Only when there is a critical mass of support for reform will ADB's financial support bear fruit. More than any other form of policy reform, governance reforms require shared commitments across the political spectrum, including the opposition and the individual parliamentarians. However, at times, lack of commitment results from a lack of awareness about the issues, rather than an unwillingness to address them. Therefore, efforts at raising awareness can have an important role in strengthening commitment."

Public Sector Loans Dealing with Environmental Law

On an annual basis environmental projects constitute more than 12 percent of total public sector lending volume or an annual equivalent of about $800 million. Many of these projects have environmental law components, some of which require enactment of environmental legislation on regulations. For example, in the year 2000, ADB approved twelve environmental loans, of which five required legislation:

(i) India's Gujarat Power Sector Development Project,
(ii) Nepal's Melamchi Water Supply Project,
(iii) Sri Lanka's Protected Area Management and Wildlife Conservation,
(iv) Water Resources Management Project, and
(v) Forest Resources Management Sector Project.

One loan required new environmental regulations: the Philippines' Pasig River Environment Management and Rehabilitation Sector Development Program. Six required environmental mitigation or management measures:

(i) India's Calcutta Environmental Improvement Program,
(ii) Indonesia's Marine and Coastal Resources Management,
(iii) the Tianjin Wastewater Treatment Project in the Peoples' Republic of China (PRC),
(iv) the PRC's Water Resources and Wind Power Development Project,
(v) Papua New Guinea's Provincial Towns Water Supply and Sanitation Project, and
(vi) Viet Nam's Tea and Fruit Development Project.

The remaining 72 loan projects and programs approved in 2000 by ADB were prepared pursuant to procedures, acceptable to ADB, which ensured that environmental impacts were minimized or mitigated.

The Philippines' Metro Manila Air Quality Improvement Sector Development Program

ADB loans for the Philippines' Metro Manila Air Quality Improvement Sector Development Program, approved in late 1998, highlight ways in which environmental law plays an important role in public sector environmental loans. These Philippine Sector Development Program loans consisted of

(i) a policy loan to the Government of the Republic of the Philippines of $200 million to implement the policy reforms under the Program;
(ii) an investment loan to the Land Bank of the Philippines of $25 million for the establishment of an air pollution control facility to assist industries, commercial establishments, and the transport sector to make investments necessary for monitoring and reduction of air emissions; and
(iii) an investment loan to the Government of $71 million to finance part of the necessary public sector investments. In addition, ADB provided a grant of $1,500,000 to develop air emission policies and enhance public awareness supporting abatement of air pollution.

Among the conditions of loan effectiveness for this Program loan were requirements:

In a relatively short period of time, the Government enacted and established ancillary regulations for the Clean Air Act *as well as terminated sales of leaded gasoline in Metro Manila.*

(i) that the Government's Department of Environment and Natural Resources (DENR) issue implementing rules and regulations for a Presidential Air Quality Commission;

(ii) that the DENR provide ADB with recommendations concerning fees and penalty charges for exceeding air emission standards by both mobile and point source polluters; and

(iii) that the Government provide adequate budgetary resources to implement the first year of the Program in all agencies.

A condition of disbursement of the investment loan to the Land Bank of the Philippines was that the Land Bank of the Philippines furnish ADB with detailed implementation guidelines.

The second tranche of this Philippine Program loan contains several conditions with environmental law significance:

(i) enactment of a *Clean Air Act* and establish ancillary regulations;

(ii) terminating sales of leaded gasoline in Metro Manila; and

(iii) strengthening the capacity of DENR's Pollution Adjudication Board and the Public Hearing Committee of the Laguna Lake Development Authority.

In a relatively short period of time, the Government enacted and established ancillary regulations for the *Clean Air Act* as well as terminated sales of leaded gasoline in Metro Manila. By mid-year 2002 little progress had been made with respect to strengthening the capacity of DENR's Pollution Adjudication Board or the Public Hearing Committee of the Laguna Lake Development Authority. However, the Government plans to take steps to strengthen these two regulatory bodies in the near future.

The $1,500,000 technical assistance grant is designed to assist the legal departments of the DENR and the Laguna Lake Development Authority to improve their procedures and effectiveness concerning enforcement of air emission standards. Also this technical assistance will improve legal procedures with DENR's Pollution Adjudication Board and the Laguna Lake Development Authority's Public Hearing Committee.

ADB has not provided loan funds to finance environmental law education for law students, lawyers or judiciary. However, one loan has been made to improve the capacity of the bar and bench. In November of 2000, ADB approved a loan equivalent to $54.9 million to Nepal for a Corporate and Financial Governance Project with a significant component to improve legal enforcement capacity and infrastructure including establishment of a National Judicial Academy, enhancement of the Law Books Management Board, establishment of a secured transactions center, and an initiative to establish a special commercial bench.

Pakistans' Legal and Judicial Reform Project

The December 2000 ADB *Country Assistance Plan for Pakistan (2001-2003)* indicates that ADB plans to make a program loan to Pakistan equivalent to $80 million for Judicial and Legal Reform. Page 43 of this *Country Assistance Plan* states that:

> "ADB-funded *TA* [technical assistance] *on Pakistan 2010* study, the IMF's *Framework for Pakistan* and ADB-funded TA 3015: *Legal and Judicial Reform Project*, have identified inefficiencies in the judicial and legal system as key governance issues that need to be addressed."

Though the proposed scope of this program loan makes no specific mention of environmental law, the issues described in this program loan scope will likely have a positive impact on Pakistan's sustainable development, including "governance and institutional problems", "court congestion" and "alternative dispute resolution", "addressing declining standards in legal education and legal profession", including and "promoting transparency and accountability through greater freedom of information".

Environmental Technical Assistance

In the years from 1995 to 2000, ADB annually approved on average 26 environmental technical assistance grants, and in each of these years, the average value of these environment oriented technical assistance grants was a little more than $25,150,000. These technical assistance grants have a wide range of objectives, though only a few have a focus on environmental law.

ADB Support for Reform of Legal System

In recent years ADB has supported a variety of technical assistance projects designed to reform legal systems:

- Supported the compilation and publication of laws in the PRC and Tajikistan.
- Developed further training of legal officers, from lawyers to judges, in Maldives, Mongolia, and Viet Nam.
- Reformed the legal framework for private sector development and the related credit, security, and insolvency in DMCs, such as Indonesia, Kyrgyz Republic, Mongolia, and Viet Nam.
- Completed diagnostic work for improving the judicial system for better enforcement of laws and greater access to justice in Pakistan.
- Supported the Government of Vanuatu to strengthen the State of Law Office, improve the quality of legislation, and improve the advice on reform measures.

People's Republic of China Provincial Legislation for Environmental Protection and Natural Resources Conservation

Examples of technical assistance on environmental legislation may be found in two technical assistance grants to the PRC financed by ADB and one by the Government of Norway, administered by ADB. These grants were made to the Environmental Protection Committee to improve the capacity of the PRC's legislative drafters. During the six years of collaboration, more than 100 PRC legislative drafters, both at national and provincial level were trained both in the PRC and abroad. The results of these three technical assistance projects included adoption at the national level of a revised *Water Pollution Prevention and Control Law* and a new *Land Administration Law*.

This *Land Administration Law* contains important and innovative mechanisms to more appropriately price farmland upon conversion, and to compensate farmers whose land is taken for development purposes. At the provincial level the results included *Implementation Measures of Sichuan Province on the 'Land Administration Law of the People's Republic of China'*, which added important details at the provincial and municipal level to the national Land Administration Law.

In 2000 ADB published *Reform of Environmental and Land Legislation in the People's Republic China*, which was prepared by the consultants from the New York University School of Law, the Foundation for International Environmental Law and Development, and the law firm of Sidley & Austin engaged to provide their services under these three technical assistance grants.

Regional Capacity Building for Environmental Law Training in Asia

An example of technical assistance in which the training of environmental professors formed the primary objective is found in an ADB grant from the Japan Special Fund for "Capacity Building for Environmental Law Training in the Asia and Pacific Region". In-kind cofinancing was provided by IUCN, the National University of Singapore and by the United National Environmental Program. In two summer sessions in 1997 and 1998 held in the School of Law of the National University of Singapore, 63 law professors from 16 countries were trained. The materials collected to conduct these two summer sessions were relied upon in the preparation of this environmental law book, entitled *Capacity Building for Environmental Law in the Asian and Pacific Region: Approaches and Resources*, the first of its kind for the Asia and the Pacific.

Maldives' Strengthening Legal Education and Judicial Training

In January 2000 ADB approved a grant to the Government of the Republic of Maldives for the purpose of Strengthening Legal Education and Judicial Training. The legal education component is designed to enhance the capacity of the Government's Institute of Shariah and Law to deliver legal education and to build indigenous capacity in the delivery of legal education. The judicial training component addresses the Government's need to provide suitable training for judges to improve the efficiency of the judiciary, and to provide a special judicial training program for new recruits who will fill more than 40 vacancies for island court judges.

PRC's Transjurisdiction Environmental Management

ADB environmental technical assistance grants approved in 2000 deal with a wide variety of issues, and provide continued assistance with previously identified issues. For example, through a cluster technical assistance of $2.1 million to deal with PRC's "Transjurisdiction Environmental Management," ADB will assist the PRC Government in operationalizing transjurisdictional provisions of the Water Pollution Prevention and Control Law.

Environmental Law Consultants

From time to time ADB engages as staff consultants environmental law experts to assist the Office of the General Counsel or the Office of Environment and Social

Development with various issues. For example, a staff consultant was engaged to prepare a review of the development of ADB environmental policies and practices with respect to environmental loan covenants. As a direct result, ADB published *Environmental Loan Covenants: Helping Ensure the Environmental Soundness of Projects Supported by the Asian Development Bank* and *Environmental Loan Covenants: Principles, Checklists and Samples*. The latter publication was prepared especially for members of ADB's staff but also as a reference for representatives of ADB borrowers and executing agencies.

In February 2000, ADB and Kluwer Law International published *Multilateral Development Banking: Environmental Principles and Concepts Reflecting General International Law and Public Policy* by Gunther Handl, who had been engaged as a staff consultant to prepare such work. This book consists of an article which first appeared in *The American Journal of International Law* entitled "The Legal Mandate of Multilateral Development Banks as Agents for Change Toward Sustainable Development" plus a second section on "Environmental Principles and Concepts". The second section of this book defines more than 60 Key Words and phrases, such as "Coastal Zone Management", "Cultural Property Protection", and "Desertification and Soil Protection". Other Key Words and phrases include "Involuntary Resettlement", "Treatment of Indigenous Populations", and "Environmental Manage-ment and Audit Schemes" (EMAS, ISO 14000 Series). As described Professor Handl's book, these definitions consist of:

- a summary of the contents, purpose and specific operational implications of the normative concept contained in the Key Word or phrase;
- a summary of its status;
- a statement of the normative bases for its classification as reflecting either a "legal requirement" or a "principle of public policy"; and
- an analysis of the practice of multilateral financial institutions, including the operational standards and guidelines of Multilateral Development Banks.

From time to time ADB staff consultants are requested to undertake assignments lasting a few months to analyze problems and make recommendations. The latest of these efforts involves the engagement of more than a dozen experts to prepare *An Environment and Social Development Action Plan for Asia*. This Action Plan, prepared by Antonio A. Oposa Jr., proposes implementation of a wide variety of measures including:

(i) creation of a region-wide network of environment and social development experts to assist in the design and implementation of ADB projects and programs,
(ii) preparation of country legislative and regulatory profiles incorporating rigorous analysis of areas to be improved concerning environmental and social development issues...
(iii) development of a computerized information system to facilitate the preparation and inclusion of appropriate environmental and social development loan covenants...
(iv) prior to commencement of development projects and programs, more extensive training in environmental and social concerns for implementors (such as construction contractors) and for stakeholders (such as those living in the project area)...
(v) for better monitoring by expert third parties of environmental and social development aspects of ADB projects and programs.

ADB Environmental and Other Publications

Aside from the publications mentioned above, ADB is laying the groundwork for further strengthening the integration of environmental policies in key development sectors by launching the *Asian Environment Outlook*. Reports in this publication, which is expected to be made available every three years, will form a basis for the formulation of environmentally-sound development policies and programs. The *Asian Environment Outlook* will present a prescriptive analysis of the kinds of interventions ADB could undertake in its policy-based and project loans, technical assistance, and policy dialogues.

There are a great many ADB publications which focus on environmental issues, including those with legal implications. For example, in 2000 ADB published *Implementation of the Kyoto Protocol: Opportunities and Pitfalls for Developing Countries*, edited by Prodipto Ghosh. This book consists of a compilation of research papers dealing with such issues as international environmental law, estimates of the supply of and demand for greenhouse gas abatements implied by the Protocol, economic analysis of key proposals concerning the Protocol, and inquiries into formulating baselines for the Clean Development

Mechanism and Joint Implementation projects. This book relies in part on a 13 volume study prepared under an ADB technical assistance project known as the Asia Least-Cost Greenhouse Gas Abatement Strategy (ALGAS) Project, which was financed with more than $10 million of grants from the GEF, ADB and the Government of Norway. The ALGAS Project resulted in a 13-volume study including 81 investment and technical assistance projects for greenhouse gas abatement in Bangladesh, the PRC, India, Indonesia, Republic of Korea, Mongolia, Myanmar, Pakistan, the Philippines, Thailand, and Viet Nam.

In 2001 ADB published *India: Mainstreaming Environment for Sustainable Development,* which includes a chapter on "Policies, Legislation, and Institutions for Environmental Management", and *Environments in Transition: Cambodia, Lao PDR, Thailand, Viet Nam.* The latter publication also contains a chapter on "Environmental Policies and Institutional Framework" for these four countries as well as a "Development Framework for Environmental Action", which contains strategies dealing with forestry, water resource management, coastal area management, land use planning, cleaner production and other topics. In 2000 ADB environmental publications included *Fire, Smoke, and Haze—The ASEAN Response Strategy, Regional Economic-cum Environmental Planning, Sustainable Development in Asia,* and *The Environment Program-Recent Achievements and a New Agenda for the Poor.*

In addition to environmental publications, ADB publishes a great many books, pamphlets and CD-ROMs on issues with a direct and indirect impact on the environment as well as publications on loans, technical assistance and programming of ADB in its DMCs. For example, the Annual Report presents a comprehensive view of ADB policies, strategies, operations and financial resources. In 2000 ADB published for each DMC a Country Assistance Plan for the years 2001 through 2003. ADB also published in May of 2001 CD-ROMs of the *Asian Development Outlook, Our Framework: Policies and Strategies of the Asian Development Bank, Business Opportunities with ADB,* and *Consulting Opportunities with ADB.*

A Look Forward

The *Agreement Establishing the Asian Development Bank,* which came into force on 22 August 1966, does not mention the word "environment". Article 1 of this Agreement states in part that the purpose of ADB:

> "shall be to foster economic growth and cooperation in the region of Asia and the Far East (hereinafter referred to as the "region") and to contribute to the acceleration of the process of economic development of the developing member countries in the region, collectively and individually."

Article 2 sets forth six functions of ADB:

> "(i) ... promote investment in the region of public and private capital for development purposes; (ii) ... utilize the resources at its disposal for financing development ...; (iii) ... meet the requests from members in the region to assist them in the coordination of their development policies and plans ...; (iv) provide technical assistance for the preparation, financing and execution of development projects and programs ...; (v) cooperate ... with the United Nations ... and with public international organizations and other international institutions, as well as national entities whether public or private, ... and to interest such institutions and entities in new opportunities for investment and assistance; and (vi) ... undertake such other activities and provide such other services as may advance its purpose."

As a staff consultant of ADB, Professor Gunther Handl argues...that "the debate on whether MDBs' constituent instruments, should be amended to permit the respective institution to espouse a more activist role in the pursuit of sustainable development objectives, is a red herring" [something that distracts attention from the real issue]. In part he bases this argument...on "the 1972 *Stockholm Declaration on the Human Environment,* which enjoins states to 'ensure that international organizations play a coordinated, efficient and dynamic role for the protection and improvement of the environment." To conclude that MDBs are subject to evolving general international law norms, he relies on "considerations relevant to 'economic development' and 'sound banking practices'" and "Multilateral Environmental Agreements (MEAs) as general normative benchmarks for MDB operations":

> "As members of the international community, MDBs are subject not only to evolving

> international public policy and general international law (custom and general principles of law), but also to the normative reach of those MEAs that have been adopted precisely to lay down principles and standards of global applicability."

To answer the question of whether MDBs have to adapt as a legal requirement operational policies to make sustainable development a reality, Professor Handl answers in the affirmative:

> "[While] MDBs have no special international mandate to vindicate human rights generally and hence are not subject to only (functionally) limited affirmative obligations regarding the enhancement of human rights [footnote omitted], international financial institutions (and development agencies) have been entrusted with a broad and universally recognized role in promoting sustainable development. That mandate entails a responsibility: MDBs must actively promote the objectives of international normative concepts, extant or emerging, that bear directly on sustainable development. Thus, the normative implications of, for example, 'women in development' suggest that the banks not only refrain from acting in defiance of, or at cross-purposes with, the environmental and social objectives the normative concept seeks to capture, but also act affirmatively towards their realization. It goes without saying, however, that such an affirmative obligation is neither absolute nor unlimited. Rather, MDBs will be only required to take reasonable steps in support of sustainable development."

In view of these arguments, particularly the status of "Multilateral Development Banks as Subjects of International Law", the status of MEAs as General Normative Benchmarks for MDB Operations, and the consequential responsibility of MDBs to promote the objectives of international normative concepts such as sustainable development, Professor Handl concludes that there is no need to amend the agreements which established MDBs to include provisions dealing with protecting the environment or promoting sustainable development:

> "MDBs in general are not only free to take sustainable development concerns into account, but have an international legal obligation to do so—not despite their constituent instruments, but rather, it has been submitted because of them."

This article submits that ADB has been supporting for more than 20 years the principles and recommendations for action adopted by the Declarations of the United Nations Conference on the Human Environment made in Stockholm in 1972 and that ADB is continuing to support reasonable steps in support of sustainable development. Consistent with Article 2 (v) of the Agreement Establishing ADB, ADB will also continue to cooperate with respect to environmental concerns with the United Nations as well as national entities whether public or private, including law schools and associations of lawyers and jurists, in new opportunities for investment and assistance to promote a sustainable development.

In closing, I wish to emphasize the growing importance in the coming years of such cooperation within the international community, particularly with international civil society, to achieve common objectives concerning the protection of the environment and the achievement of sustainable development. In the words of the then President of the International Court of Justice, Judge Bedjaoui, who wrote in the Advisory Opinion on the Legality of the Threat or Use of Nuclear Weapons, reprinted in 35 *International Legal Materials* 1345 at 1346, cited by Professor Handl:

> "It scarcely needs to be said that the fact of contemporary international society is much altered. Despite the still limited emergence of 'supra-nationalism', the progress made in terms of the institutionalization, not to say integration and 'globalization', of international society cannot be denied. Witness the proliferation of international organizations, the gradual substitution of an international law of cooperation for the traditional law of co-existence, [and] the emergence of the concept of 'international community'."

Whether we participate in the international community as an employee of an international organization with 59 member countries like ADB or as a member of an international law association or as an individual lawyer or professor or student, we will all need to continue and increase our cooperation many times over to achieve the lofty and important objectives of the Declaration of the 1972 Stockholm Conference.

8

The Role of the World Bank and Global Environment Facility

A

Outline of the Global Environment Facility

(i) Global Environment Facility, *What is the Global Environment Facility?*, GEF, 2001

[*This extract sources from the Global Environment Facility's Internet web-site. The address is <http://www.gefweb.org/>. This site was accessed on 03/04/2001.*]

What is the Global Environment Facility?

The Global Environment Facility was established to forge international cooperation and finance actions to address four critical threats to the global environment: biodiversity loss, climate change, degradation of international waters, and ozone depletion. Related work to stem the pervasive problem of land degradation is also eligible for GEF funding.

Launched in 1991 as an experimental facility, GEF was restructured after the Earth Summit in Rio de Janeiro to serve the environmental interests of people in all parts of the world. The facility that emerged after restructuring was more strategic, effective, transparent, and participatory. In 1994, 34 nations pledged $2 billion in support of GEF's mission; in 1998, 36 nations pledged $2.75 billion to protect the global environment and promote sustainable development.

The GEF can succeed in its global environmental mission only as part of a worldwide movement toward sustainable development. GEF brings together 166 member governments, leading development institutions, the scientific community, and a wide spectrum of private sector and nongovernmental organizations on behalf of a common global environmental agenda.

Focal Areas

The GEF funds projects in four focal areas: biodiversity, climate change, international waters, and ozone. Projects to address land degradation, as it relates to the four focal areas, are also eligible for funding. In addition to the general descriptions here, some specialized materials are available that focus on single focal areas. These options are highlighted below.

The GEF funds projects in four focal areas: biodiversity, climate change, international waters, and ozone.

Biodiversity

A wide spectrum of efforts to conserve and sustainably use earth's biological diversity makes up nearly half of all GEF projects. As the financial mechanism for the *Convention on Biological Diversity* (CBD), GEF receives guidance from the conference of parties (or COP) on policy, strategy, program priorities, and eligibility criteria related to the use of resources for purposes of the Convention. Projects generally deal with one or more of four critical ecosystem types and the human communities found there: (i) arid and semi-arid zones; (ii) coastal, marine, and freshwater resources; (iii) forests; and (iv) mountains.

Between 1991 and 1999, GEF allocated $991 million in grants and mobilized and additional $1.5 billion in cofinancing (from recipient countries, bilateral agencies, other development institutions, the private sector, and nongovernmental organizations) for biological diversity projects.

Climate Change

Projects addressing climate change make up the next largest group of GEF-funded projects. As the financial mechanism for the United Nations *Framework Convention on Climate Change* (UNFCCC), GEF receives guidance from the COP on policy, program priorities, and eligibility criteria related to the Convention. Climate change projects are designed to reduce the risks of global climate change while providing energy for sustainable development. GEF climate change projects are organized into four areas: (i) removing barriers to energy efficiency and energy conservation; (ii) promoting the adoption of renewable energy by removing barriers and reducing implementation costs; (iii) reducing the long-term costs of low greenhouse gas emitting energy technologies; and (iv) supporting the development of sustainable transport.

From 1991 to 1999, GEF allocated $884 million to 227 climate change projects and enabling activities, which was matched by more than $4.7 billion in cofinancing. For more information, click here.

International Waters

GEF projects to reverse the degradation of international waters are informed by—and help to realize the objectives of—a mosaic of regional and international water agreements. These projects enable countries to recognize and learn more about the water-related challenges they share, find ways to work together, and undertake important domestic changes needed to solve problems. The three categories of water projects are: (i) water bodies, (ii) integrated land and water projects, and (iii) contaminants. From 1991 to 1999, GEF allocated nearly $360 million to international waters initiatives.

Ozone Depletion

Phasing out ozone depleting substances (ODS) is a highly effective means to achieving immediate, and future, global environmental benefits. The GEF, in partnership with the *Montreal Protocol of the Vienna Convention on Ozone Layer Depleting Substances*, funds projects that enable the Russian Federation and nations in eastern Europe and central Asia to phase out their use of ozone destroying chemicals. After more than a decade of international cooperation, the concentration of some of these chemicals in the atmosphere has already started to decline. Between 1991 and 1999, the GEF allocated more than $155 million to projects to phase out ODS.

Land Degradation

GEF's interest in financing activities to prevent and control land degradation comes from the nature and extent of its link to global environmental change. Destroyed forests and degraded water resources imperil biodiversity, induce climate change, and disturb hydrologic cycles. Taking into account the objectives of the *Convention to Combat Desertification* (CCD), dozens of GEF projects cut across the four focal areas described above to address land degradation. Between 1991 and 1999, GEF has funded more than $350 million worth of projects focused primarily on deforestation and desertification.

(ii) IUCN, "The Funding Debate and the Compromise Reflected in Articles 20, 21 and 39," *A Guide to the Convention on Biological Diversity*, 1994, p 104

The Global Environment Facility was formally created in 1991 to assist countries with a per capita income of less than US$4,000 address four main global environmental problems: global warming, pollution of international waters, loss of biological diversity and the depletion of the stratospheric ozone layer. It provides additional grant and concessional funding to meet the agreed incremental costs for investment projects, technical assistance and a research to achieve agreed global environmental benefits. …

The GEF is operated jointly by the World Bank, the United Nations Development Programme (UNDP) and the United Nations Environment Programme (UNEP). The World Bank administers the GEF and is the repository for the Gobal Environment Trust Fund (GET). It also is responsible for the GEF financed investment projects. The UNDP provides technical assistance, identifies projects and runs a Small Grants Programme for NGOs. UNEP provides the secretariat for the Scientific and Technical Advisory Panel (STAP) and contributes environmental expertise to the GEF process. …The independent Scientific and Technical Advisory Panel is composed of 15–20 experts from industrialized and developing countries and assists in the development of criteria for project selection. It also reviews and comments on project proposals….

Since its inception, the GEF has been greatly criticized for its internal structure, the implementing agencies chosen and the design of the projects it funds. Action is being taken to address these issues. By conditioning the GEF's participation as the institutional structure for their respective financial mechanisms, the UN *Framework Convention on Climate Change* and the *Convention on Biological Diversity* have helped to instigate this change. An independent evaluation of the GEF released its report at the end of 1993 (UNEP, UNDP & World Bank, 1993). Intergovernmental negotiations on restructuring the GEF were held throughout 1993 and into 1994. The negotiations led to the GEF's restructuring. A new phase [was] initiated (GEF II) beginning in 1994 and extending to 1996.

In the case of the *Convention on Biological Diversity*, the GEF is the funding mechanism, both as an interim measure and continuing to the present. GEF pilot phase grants to Asia and the Pacific to implement the *Convention on*

Biological Diversity represented 25 percent of the total, or US$75.1 million for 11 projects through 1993. These projects cover different ecosystems...and include baseline studies, institutional strengthening, and community participation, but GEF funds cannot be used to buy land or finance debt for nature swaps. The pilot phase grants in the region were as follows:

World Bank:

- *Bhutan—Trust Fund for Environmental Conservation.* The first GEF trust fund. Includes institutional strengthening and preliminary stages of establishing a protected area network. $10 million GEF grant.
- *Indonesia—Biodiversity Conservation.* To develop and implement a regional project linking national park management with local communities, plus policy studies, a conservation awareness program, and support of ex-situ conservation. Linked to a Bank watershed development project. $12 million GEF grant.
- *Lao PDR—Forest Management and Conservation Project.* To begin a protected area system, including training and institution building. Linked to Bank's $10 million Forest Management and Conservation Project. $6 million GEF grant.
- *Philippines—Conservation of Priority Protected Areas.* Protecting 10 sites with decentralized management. Linked to Bank's $224 million Environment and Natural Resources Sector Adjustment Loan. $20 million GEF grant.

UNDP:

- *Indonesia and Malaysia Conservation Strategy for Southeast Asia Rhinos.* To support implementation of the rhino conservation strategy and action plan. especially through training. $2 million GEF grant.
- *Mongolia—Development and Institution of a National Biodiversity Conservation Plan.* To support development of a national plan, with emphasis on the 53,100 km2 Greater Gobi National Park. $1.5 million GEF grant.
- *Nepal Makalu—Barun Conservation Area Project.* Community-based management and park protection in an extension of Sagarmatha (Mount Everest) National Park, based on the Annapurna Conservation Area. $4 million GEF grant.
- *Papua New Guinea—National Conservation and Resource Management Programme.* Comprehensive biodiversity conservation program with involvement of landowners and community groups, and major emphasis on clan-owned forests. $5 million GEF grant.
- *South Pacific Biodiversity Conservation Proqramme.* To establish several large multiple-use conservation areas (terrestrial and marine), with extensive roles for private landowners, NGOs and local communities. $8 million GEF grant.
- *Sri Lanka—Wildlife Conservation and Protected Area Management.* Establishment of two new protected areas, and management plans for six others' training for government agency personnel and attention to people/elephant conflicts. $4 million grant.
- *Vietnam—Protected Areas and Wildlife Conservation Project* to support a training program and biodiversity action plan. $3 million GEF grant.

B

Charles E. Di Leva "International Environmental Law and Development," The Georgetown International Environmental Review, Vol. 10, Issue 2, Winter 1998, pp 501–549

The Concept of International Environmental Law

International environmental law has traditionally centered upon international and regional environmental treaties and agreements. More recently, the topic is often considered to include the policies, procedures, codes of conduct, and guidelines of multilateral financial institutions, such as the World Bank Group (Bank) and other United Nations specialized agencies. Although these "non-treaty" instruments are not binding in the traditional sense, they have considerable practical impact, especially throughout the developing world. In part this impact occurs because the financial leverage of institutions such as the World Bank enables them to impose environment-related instruments, such as "green" loan conditions, and environment-related policies as part of their financing activities. Further, the application of these instruments by multilateral financial institutions helps support traditional treaty law, because

Clearly, to some, the World Bank has fallen short as a model institution for the support of sustainable development.

many of these instruments explicitly or implicitly further the aims of international environmental agreements. Thus in a world where the efficacy of a legal instrument is based upon its capacity to generate compliance, the policies of the World Bank and similar institutions may be highly effective in promoting international environmental treaties—in some cases more effective than many traditional sources of international environmental law.

The focus on "non-binding" instruments does not mean that international treaties lack significance to multilateral financial institutions. Because governments are the owners of the institutions like the World Bank, and are bound to comply with the treaties they have ratified, multilateral financial institutions must be careful to ensure that if these treaties are implicated in their projects, the treaties are appropriately taken into account in project design and finance. In fact, in some cases, multilateral institutions are considered the prime means for implementing these treaties for the vast majority of the world's population, in the so-called "developing" countries. One example of this view is that the World Bank serves as the main implementing agency for the Global Environment Facility (GEF), which is the interim financial mechanism for the United Nations *Framework Convention on Climate Change*, and the *Convention on Biological Diversity*. The GEF was established in the World Bank as a pilot program to "assist in the protection of the global environment," and to do so in a way that is consistent with the promotion of "environmentally sound and sustainable economic development."

While this article notes that the growth of international environmental law has many positive aspects, to many this increase represents a troubling dilution of national sovereignty. To these concerned critics, the impact of project finance by international organizations and their decision making processes are often carried out without adequate citizen involvement. Further, they contend that international organizations often seek to make environmental practices or standards globally or regionally harmonized, with the result that the environmental standards used will represent the lowest common environmental denominator. Frequently criticized in this context are the "Bretton Woods Institutions" —the International Monetary Fund and the World Bank—and the World Trade Organization. Also accused are regional organizations such as the European Union and the administrative bodies of the North American Free Trade Agreement.

At the same time there have been clear global and local environmental benefits emanating from a broad view of international environmental law and the actions of these international organizations. As this paper attempts to portray, the application of World Bank-type environment-related policies has paved the way for increased prospects for procedural and substantive environmental improvements by all multilateral financial organizations. These improvements are apparent in that during the past few years alone a vastly wider range of stakeholders are now part of the decision making process for projects financed in whole or in part by multilateral financial institutions, and the goals of environmental treaties are much more often a part of project implementation. Perhaps more importantly, with the multilateral institutions in the forefront, these policies are likely to be increasingly utilized by the private sector in their activity in developing countries. Given that the private sector often works in developing countries with uncertain or weak environmental standards or lax enforcement, utilization of these international practices could result in major improvements over the current situation.

Clearly, to some, the World Bank has fallen short as a model institution for the support of sustainable development. To the Bank's credit, however, there are few institutions capable of bringing such a broad array of factors to seek to reconcile the tension between environment and development. A recent project that typifies this tension, but in which the Bank did not participate, was addressed in the recent ruling of the International Court of Justice in the dispute between Hungary and Slovakia over the construction of a dam on a shared watercourse [*See Chapter 11, Judicial Decisions*].

The two sides agreed that the principle of sustainable development was applicable to the case, but could not agree how to apply it. In a separate opinion Justice Weeramantry stressed the need for states to look beyond their narrow interests. In this context, Weeramantry noted, the proposition should stand that the law of sustainable development and application of environmental assessment are part of customary law.

Thus given the difficulties of balancing these competing interests in the judicial arena, even the Bank's most strident critics should agree that the Bank represents one of the most important mechanisms to influence the development of international environmental law, given its significant financial and technical resources and its global links to both the public and private sectors. In fact, as set forth in *Agenda 21* of the United Nations Conference on Environment and Development and in numerous references since the 1992 Rio Conference, international development institutions such as the Bank play a key role in promoting international environmental treaties and agreements, as well as the development of national environmental law. Indeed, while addressing the United Nations, World Bank President James D. Wolfensohn made it clear that the Bank would help to promote the goals of the global environmental conventions. This outcome is a welcome and natural progression for an institution "generally viewed as an environment-insensitive organization." The progression can be seen as an outcome of the Bank's growing support for international environmental law.

The World Bank is the first and largest multilateral financial institution. It is owned by the governments of 180 countries. Created in 1945, the Bank's Charter (*Articles of Agreement*) proclaimed that its purpose is, in part, "to assist in the reconstruction and development of territories of members by facilitating the investment of capital for productive purposes ... and the encouragement of the development of productive facilities and resources in less developed countries." As such, the Bank was created under, and undertakes its operations to be in compliance with, applicable public international law principles and rules.

Although the Bank's Articles do not refer to the terms "environment" or "sustainable development," the World Bank provides more human and financial resources for the environment than any other international development institution. With an active portfolio of 166 projects funded at close to US$12 billion, and a staff of approximately 300 specializing in the environment, the Bank is the largest international financier of environmental projects, which the Bank considers to be both "global" and "targeted"—meaning that the funds are aimed specifically at addressing environmental concerns of the international community' not just the sovereign recipient of funds. Newer international development institutions are also taking these strides, increasingly in conjunction with the Bank. In fact, the *Articles of Agreement* of the European Bank for Reconstruction explicitly refer to the need for environmental considerations in its financing activities.

While the World Bank's Charter did not refer to the environment, important Bank policy documents have done so for over two decades. The most comprehensive was a 1984 statement entitled "Environmental Aspects of Bank Work," which noted the Bank's findings about the impact on the environment as a result of development financing, and discussed the seriousness of these impacts. It also noted that the Bank had guidelines suggesting "acceptable ranges [of impact] to be followed in Bank operations, unless the borrowing country's standards are stricter."

The instructions for applying these guidelines set forth a series of principles, each of which finds support in international environmental legal instruments. For example, almost as a precursor to the phrase "sustainable development," the instruction indicates that Bank-financed projects "should not exceed the regenerative capacities of the environment." The operational statement also sets forth principles pertaining to indigenous peoples, involuntary resettlement, transboundary harm, and cultural heritage sites protected as "World Heritage sites or Biosphere Reserves." Serving as a key principle for the discussion here, the statement also provides that "the Bank will not finance projects that contravene any international environmental agreements to which the member country concerned is a party."

While the 1984 statement specifically referred to binding "international environmental agreements," its more general discussion of the need to consult with nongovernmental organizations (NGOs) and provide information to the public, as well as its concern for broader environmental goals, reflect concerns embodied in nonbinding instruments. To this extent the 1984 Bank statement can also be seen as supporting the many "soft law" instruments throughout the international community. A number of these instruments are also particularly relevant to the work of the Bank, including the *Rio Declaration on Environment and Development*, the statements of policy set forth in *Agenda 21*, and a series of principles and guidelines issued by other United Nations agencies and programs, such as the codes relating to pesticides from the Food and Agriculture and World Health Organizations.

This article contends that the Bank promotes international environmental law in a number of ways. The next section of this article points out that the Bank supports international environmental law through its lending strategy and selection of projects, as well as through its roles in relation to the Global Environment Facility and the *Montreal Protocol*. The last section of the article discusses the Bank's operational policies and procedures regarding the environment, and demonstrates how they support many goals of international environmental law.

The World Bank and Project Finance for International Environmental Law

The principle of "common but differentiated responsibilities" dictates that developed countries should undertake the major burden of meeting the goals set forth in international environmental treaties. It is important to note that, notwithstanding this principle, developing countries still have responsibilities under international agreements, such as the recently adopted *Kyoto Protocol*. The resources of the GEF can provide up to US$2 to US$3 billion dollars triennially in grants to developing countries to fulfill their responsibilities, as set forth in international environmental treaties. But GEF resources are scarce, and it is important for the multilateral financial institutions to assist with those efforts. For example, as administrator of the Ozone Trust Fund, the Bank supports activities in developing countries that are necessary to carry out the goals of the *Montreal Protocol*.

World Bank Support for Developing Country Obligations under International Environmental Law

In addition to projects that directly serve identified environmental treaties, during the last several years the Bank has also financed a number of projects supporting general environmental goals that focus on human capital, such as environmental institution capacity building, education, and awareness. These "environmental management" projects help develop environmental capacity and public participation at the national and local levels, and thereby provide indirect, but important, foundations for international environmental law.

Indeed, these environmental education projects portend well for international environmental law by introducing education on the subject to broad venues of the world's less advantaged. One example is the World Bank's India Environmental Management Project, designed to ensure that environmental law is taught at law schools in Bangalore and New Delhi. This project was prepared following discussions with government officials and scholars, as well as interviews with leading environmental lawyers such as M.C. Mehta, the internationally acclaimed lawyer who achieved notable rulings by the Indian Supreme Court against polluting industries. Thus while not falling expressly under the rubric of an environmental treaty, this project can help train the next generation of environmental lawyers in the world's largest democracy. A similar project is being prepared by the World Bank in Bangladesh.

Another example of promoting international environmental law through national planning occurred during the preparation of the Thailand Forestry Project. This project was designed to help develop sustainable forestry and use GEF resources to support the goals of the biodiversity treaty. Because receipt of the GEF-funded portion of the project was dependent upon ratification by Thailand of the *Convention on Biological Diversity* (CBD), the project sparked a national debate on the issue of ratification, including discussion during a Bank-sponsored workshop in Bangkok at which dozens of Thai NGOs attended and debated the topic. Eventually, the Thai government ratified the Convention. Thus in some cases the objectives of these projects do not necessarily come under the rubric of an international environmental treaty, yet they indirectly provide significant support for its goals.

In addition to natural resource projects supporting the goals of the CBD, the Bank is revising its energy lending to respond to the goals of the *Climate Convention*. The Bank's draft Energy and Environment Strategy Paper discusses the link between global and local environmental objectives. Under the strategy the Bank will assist clients in meeting their obligations under the *Climate Convention* and the *Kyoto Protocol*, while also serving the Bank's primary development objective-poverty reduction.

Consistent with the Strategy Paper, the Bank is poised to begin preparations for a Carbon Investment Fund (CIF) following the negotiations of the *Kyoto Protocol*. The CIF would invest in projects that result in carbon offsets. Funds would come from governments or private sector entities seeking to comply with emission limitations obligations. These projects could be part of the pipeline of projects already in the World Bank, International Finance Corporation (IFC), and other multilateral financial institutions. The CIF would operate with the goal of supporting carbon emission reduction projects, as authorized by the *Kyoto Protocol*. The Protocol authorizes these projects between countries listed in the Protocol Annex B. This list includes so-called "developed countries" and the countries with economies in transition. At some point in the future, perhaps by year 2000, it could include all developing countries. This possibility is envisioned under the *Kyoto Protocol* through the Protocol's proposed Clean Development Mechanism (CDM).

Linked to the combined goal of pollution and poverty reduction, the funds collected for the CIF could be disbursed through host country governments, or through the IFC; the ultimate recipients would be in the host country. The CIF could have its carbon offsets verified by the CDM or by CDM-approved third parties. By making these projects more energy efficient, and thereby reducing carbon emissions, the investors could receive carbon offset certificates, which could be used as evidence of their efforts to comply with the emission reduction limitations. To the extent that these actions could take place before *Kyoto Protocol* rules on emission reductions, crediting, and verification are in place, there is a need to discuss the possible grandfathering of these credits under the Kyoto Regime.

Any grandfathering effort could be aided by the knowledge gained by some projects already undertaken by the Bank during the "pilot phase" of activities implemented jointly (AIJ), as authorized through the *Climate Convention*. Consistent with that authority, the Bank established AIJ pilot-phase activities in Poland, Mexico, Burkina Faso, and India using GEF and other resources. In these projects financial resources from developed countries were used to reduce carbon emissions below the amount of carbon that would have been emitted as of the project's original design; that is, the "baseline" for the project. Through the World Bank the results of those AIJ projects have been reported to the Convention Secretariat and then to the Parties to the Convention. These projects, and projects under the future CIF, will provide important lessons for future broad-scale reduction activities.

As noted above the global problem of green house gases is also a local health problem, because many of the greenhouse gases emitted from fossil fuel-burning sources also contain particulate matter and sulfur dioxides linked to respiratory illness. Thus by addressing local pollution the Bank and others can also help alleviate the global problem. As a result, the Bank has notes [in its *Strategy for the Energy Sector*] that "polluters—whether large power plants, factories, households burning coal or firewood, or the owner of a stroke motorcycle—continue to pollute without paying the full social and environmental cost of doing so or of switching to cleaner fuels." A key step toward reducing these emissions is to find ways to demonstrate the global and local externalities arising from air pollution. The Bank, the Asian Development Bank, and others have helped develop an environmental assessment tool, "RAINS-ASIA," which, through satellite imagery and other tools, can depict acid rain "hot spots" to local regulators throughout Asia. In this way regulators and investors can devise alternative energy-development strategies.

The Bank also helps developing countries to reduce their consumption of ozone-depleting substances (ODSs). To do so the Bank plays a key role under the *Montreal Protocol* on Substances that Deplete the Ozone Layer, acting as one of four implementing agencies of the Multilateral Fund for the Implementation of the *Montreal Protocol* (Multilateral Fund). The Multilateral Fund was established to provide the funds necessary for developing countries to phase out the use of ODSs. The World Bank holds a portfolio, which now stands at close to US$250 million, that will go largely to private sector enterprises in developing countries to enable them to find substitutes for, or shut down their production of, chlorofluorocarbons, the principal chemicals destroying the ozone layer. This portfolio represents almost 25 percent of the consumption of ozone-depleting substances by developing countries.

Key to the legal component of work under the Multilateral Fund is to ensure that the recipients of the fund also contractually obligate themselves not to restart operations with ozone-depleting substances in the future. Such obligations are inserted in the World Bank's legal agreements with the fund recipients. The Bank and relevant environmental ministries undertake follow-up supervision and monitoring activities to ensure compliance with these obligations. For example, as proposed under an upcoming grant to Mexico, Bank staff and staff from the National Institute of Ecology (INE) will make supervisory visits to factories. As is standard with the Bank and its ozone project clients, the Bank and the INK will also review Mexico's overall progress in implementing national phase-out of ODSs.

Support for International Environmental Law in the Bank's Overall Lending Program

The World Bank [in *Environmental Matters* states that it] "proactively supports the objectives of the global environmental Conventions." Consistent with this message, World Bank President James Wolfensohn has noted the Bank is in the process of mainstreaming GEF resources with the Bank's portfolio. This mainstreaming strategy makes clear that the Bank is going to proactively support the global environmental agenda by, among other things, ensuring that Bank funds will be combined with GEF resources to support global environmental conventions. Indeed, as a recent independent study of the GEF Portfolio indicated, while the Bank has made progress mobilizing different sources of funds for global environmental projects finance' by the GEF, as well as accelerating the time required to prepare GEF projects, there is still considerable progress that should be achieved. Therefore, as the Bank has indicated and the GEF Study supports, for the Bank to be more effective, it "must 'mainstream' global environmental concerns into its regular lending and nor lending services and take on a major intellectual and policy leadership role." The GEF Study concluded that to achieve these goals the Bank must find ways to provide incentives to staff, so that they will put the same or greater emphasis on global concerns as they place on traditional Bank business.

To date, however, the Bank's "environmental portfolio is limited by virtue of the need for Bank resources to reach into the wide range of types of development projects through which the Bank supports developing countries. In the 1996 fiscal year the World Bank committed US$21.520 billion for projects in 94 countries. These project consisted of 129 International Bank for Reconstruction and Development (IBRD) loans in countries, and 127 International Development Association (IDA) "credits" in 49 countries.

At the same time the Bank committed to finance projects solely for environmental purposes, in the amount of US$1.63 billion. This brought the Bank's overall environmental portfolio to US$11 billion. These environmental projects are geared specifically to water and air pollution control, energy-efficiency related issues, environmental institution building, and on the "green" side, to natural resource management.

To help develop the effectiveness of the overall environmental project portfolio, the Bank is implementing measures to integrate global and national environmental goals into individual Country Assistance Strategies (CAS). The CAS is key to the Bank's overall lending program, as it is the national lending strategy document developed by the Bank and each of its borrowers. All projects financed by the Bank should be consistent with the CAS; which thus serves as an important national economic planning tool. Concern has been expressed that because the CAS is dominated by economic considerations, environmental needs were being ignored. That perspective has undergone change; beginning in 1995 Bank policy specified that environmental concerns should be taken into account in the development of the CAS. The procedure for implementing this policy, however, is not yet fully developed.

Overall lending in the energy sector is also changing, to coordinate with environmental needs. The recent draft Strategy Paper put forward by the Bank's Environment and Industry and Energy Departments indicates that reforming the CAS is crucial in order to assist countries in meeting their commitments under the *Climate Convention*. This commitment is especially important for those countries with economies in transition (EITs), as they are obligated by the Convention to abide by emissions limitations similar to those of Organization for Economic Co-Operation and Development (OECD) countries.

While there has been a measure of progress promoting environmental mainstreaming at the local level has occurred, the Bank [through Robert T. Watson in *Environmental Matters*] recognizes that "except for the phase-out of ozone depleting substances ... at the global level we are not achieving our objectives." This disappointing result can be traced by environmental indicators that reveal a continued increase in global atmospheric pollution, loss of natural habitat and biodiversity, marine pollution, and soil degradation. Indeed, a certain irony is apparent by the now tarnished trumpeting of the "East Asian Miracle's" economic growth. Even when Bank indicators noted that the Asian economy was booming, the availability of clean air and water continued to decline in the region. Recent economic difficulties do not bode well for this scenario.

From a legal perspective, improving environmental indicators requires that the Bank's lending strategy continue to take into account relevant international and national legal instruments, as well as Bank environment-related policy. Thus Bank staff should redouble their efforts to apply accepted international treaty principles that seek to protect the environment, and to continue to improve environmental assessment, which promotes the application of these principles. In this sense a key role Bank lawyers help to fulfill in project finance is to offer project-related advice that could be less tied to country lending goals, and more tied to other long-term objectives. These objectives include the need to build legal frameworks and institutional capacity as part of overall and project-specific lending. There is an urgent need to forge stronger links between economically successful projects and improved efforts toward legal and institutional capacity building.

Bank Support for the Global Environment Facility

The Bank also promotes the goals of international environmental law through its role as one of the implementing agencies of the GEF. Both the Climate Change and Biodiversity conventions recognized the need to establish a financial mechanism to function under the guidance of, and be accountable to, the Conference of the Parties. Thus with somewhat parallel approaches the conventions note that the GEF should serve as the international entity entrusted to operate the financial mechanism referred to is the conventions, and that the mechanism will operate, at least initially, on an interim basis.

In carrying out these functions, the convention bodies noted that the financial mechanism should include modalities to ensure that GEF funded projects to address climate change and biodiversity are in conformity with the policies, program priorities, and eligibility criteria established by the Conference of the Parties. The Bank, as the main implementing agency of the GEF, must ensure that the project it implements under the climate change and biodiversity focal areas of GEF operate in a manner consistent with the conventions. These GEF-financed actions represent direct and immediate support for the development of these treaties.

The GEF operates in four focal areas: climate change, biological diversity, international waters, and ozone-layer depletion. The GEF directs funds toward projects in each of these areas to "enhance and protect the global environment." In addition the GEF addresses land degradation issues, primarily desertification and deforestation, as they relate to the four focal areas mentioned above.

The GEF operates under an Operational Strategy that incorporates guidance from the Climate Change and Biodiversity conventions. The Strategy recognizes that "all GEF-funded activities in climate change will be in full conformity with the guidelines provided by the Conference of the Parties to the UNFCCC." Further, it notes that "all GEF-funded activities in biodiversity will be in full conformity with the guidance provided by the COP [Conference of the Parties] to the CBD."

GEF resources are available to GEF-eligible recipients (which can include governments and nongovernmental entities) as grants and as concessional (non-interest-bearing) loans. Since 1991, when the GEF was established, it has provided more than US$1.8 billion to recipient countries. To maximize the effect of these resources, the Bank and the GEF seek to leverage Bank and other donor funds with GEF-funded projects. To date close to US$5 billion has been leveraged from cofinancing of funds from other agencies, such as the World Bank, for projects in more than 110 countries.

Because GEF resources can only be used in conformity with the GEF-relevant Conventions and the underlying focal areas, GEF-financed and Bank implemented projects clearly support the development of the international environmental law regime pertaining to climate, the ozone layer, international waters, and biodiversity. As part of the Bank's goal to mainstream the consideration of global environmental issues into Bank lending, an increasing number of these projects will include funds from the Bank. To take advantage of leveraging, Bank borrowers must be willing to accept the importance of these environmental goals, since unlike GEF "stand-alone" financed projects, GEF/Bank projects require return payment to the Bank for the loans and credits provided by IBRD and IDA.

For climate, biodiversity, and the ozone layer GEF support is closely aligned to the relevant international treaties mentioned above, each of which specifically refers to its financial mechanism. The GEF provides protection for the ozone layer by funding non-ODS projects in economies in transition not covered by the Multilateral Fund for the *Montreal Protocol*. GEF support for the international waters focal area also conforms with relevant international environmental law, but the GEF Operational Strategy for international waters helps to promote numerous international conventions, treaties, and agreements. The reach of the topic is expanded by the large number of multilateral and bilateral agreements covering transboundary freshwater basins. Project selection criteria for this GEF focal area specify that projects will attain "consistency with national environmental planning documents and international legal obligations."

The GEF operates under an Operational Strategy that incorporates guidance from the Climate Change and Biodiversity conventions.

Bank and GEF Financing for Technical Assistance

Under the international waters focal area the GEF-financed Wider Caribbean Initiative on Ship-Generated Waste is a US$5.5 million technical assistance project undertaken at the request of 22 countries in the wider Caribbean region. The goal is to support the implementation of the *International Convention for the Prevention of Pollution from Ships* (MARPOL 73/78) and the Special Area designation of MARPOL Convention Annex V (plastic waste). Key to this project has been the development of model legislation under the auspices of the International Maritime Organization (IMO). The IMO has provided model laws to the countries of the Wider Caribbean and offered technical assistance to enable legislatures in the region to prepare the necessary implementing legislation, so that the countries have the option to ratify and implement the MARPOL Convention.

The Wider Caribbean Initiative is an ambitious effort using limited means to try to harmonize broad-reaching marine legislation. Despite grant funding for this project, finding the time and commitment to introduce potentially complicated legislation into already overburdened parliaments poses a challenging task. Even if the legislation is enacted, it will be difficult to find the capacity to implement enforcement action. Still, the participating countries recognize the urgency of developing the enforcement tools to protect the fragile Caribbean.

One example of an effort by the Bank to harmonize legislation involves the introduction of cost-recovery legislation into the countries of the Eastern Caribbean as part of the Organization of Eastern Caribbean States (OECS) Solid Waste Management Project. The relatively small countries of the eastern Caribbean depend to a great extent on tourism revenue from cruise lines. The World Bank Project team and the OECS established as a condition of project effectiveness that the OECS member countries develop cost-recovery legislation creating a per passenger charge on all cruise ships entering their ports. The revenue will go toward maintaining solid waste facilities capable of managing ship-generated waste, and thereby support the implementation of the OECS country MARPOL obligations. OECS countries were concerned that if they did not act jointly, the first country to impose the charge could lose tourist business if its colleagues did not follow through with charges of their own, or if they instituted lesser fees. It was a courageous act for the countries to put forward these measures in the face of possible cruise line industry reprisals; hopefully they will continue to consider cooperation to be in their best interest.

Another Bank project which seeks to enhance transboundary legal and political cooperation is the Lake Victoria Environmental Management Project. This project will supply both Bank (IDA) and GEF funds to protect the world's second largest body of fresh water. The lake is suffering from agricultural and industrial run-off, from deoxygenation due to water hyacinth and matting on the lake surface, and the disappearance of many species of fish. With support from the Bank and other international organizations a tripartite agreement was signed among the riparian countries (Kenya, Tanzania, and Uganda) pledging collaboration in the process of project preparation and implementation. Key to the project will be funding to develop the harmonization of laws and regulations among the three countries.

A series of other regional projects is also underway with Bank and GEF financing. The three riparian countries of Lake Malawi (Malawi, Mozambique, and Tanzania) have agreed to jointly undertake studies of the lake and take the steps required to enhance cooperative monitoring and regulation. More recently, the six countries of the Congo Basin rainforest have agreed to form a Regional Environmental Information Management Project that will share environmental information and build up environmental institutional capacity. The Bank (including the Bank's Environmental Law Unit) and the Food and Agriculture Organization will help implement the Congo Basin project, along with financial support from the GEF and the European Union.

The World Bank is also implementing GEF and Bank-financed regional transboundary water projects in a number of regional seas and international lakes. These include projects in the Aral Sea, the Black Sea, Lake Baikal, the Caspian Sea, Lake Ohrid, and the Red Sea.

GEF Financing for Setting up Environmental Trust Funds

Environmental trust funds have emerged as an innovative legal instrument to protect biodiversity. These funds can be structured in a variety of ways, but typically are designed to ensure a source of stable income to be used to pay for the ongoing costs of particular conservation efforts. The World

Bank has worked extensively with donors and stakeholders in designing such funds particularly in the area of biodiversity protection One of the first and most successful of these is the "Bhutan Trust Fund." The Bhutan Fund was started with financial assistance from the United Nations Development Programme (UNDP) and the World Wildlife Fund-US, and then received a US$10 million grant through the GEF, as well as additional donations in the range of US$10 million through several foreign governments. The Charter of the Trust Fund, which governs disbursement, states that its purpose is to promote social welfare through preservation of biodiversity. In addition the terms of the 1996 Charter require the government to maintain its forest cover at 60 percent of the country's area and set aside as protected areas the same percentage of the country's protected area as existed on the date of the signature of the Charter. The Fund is governed by a Board of Directors, of which five members are Bhutanese. The sixth member is a WWF representative, who will serve for five years and then be replaced by a Bhutanese citizen.

Currently, all of the Bhutan Trust Funds are invested outside Bhutan; program activities are funded by a portion of the investment income. If the interest on the investment income is insufficient to meet project requirements, the fund's capital can be invaded, but only up to a specified amount and with unanimous vote of the Board. Given the Fund's success to date, invasion of capital is not a high probability.

The Uganda Trust Fund for the Conservation of the Bwindi Impenetrable and Mghaniga Gorilla National Parks is also financed by the GEF. This fund follows an investment strategy similar to that in Bhutan and was devised so that a number of local stakeholders have key decision making roles. The fund's goal is to protect some of the only remaining native gorilla habitat in eastern Africa. In Mexico negotiations have recently concluded for the establishment of a GEF-financed trust that will enable a Mexican private foundation to manage the funds. The funds will be used to finance biodiversity conservation in a number of rural areas, for which Bank staff have worked with the government to prepare indigenous peoples development plans. These plans apply to areas within the government's network of protected areas, and were developed pursuant to the Bank's *Indigenous Peoples Policy*. Other trust funds are also underway, mostly with funds provided by the GEF. The projects include the Eastern Carpathian Trust Fund (for the countries of the Ukraine, Slovakia, and Poland—administered under Swiss law) and the Peru Trust Fund, as well as recent discussions about establishing a new biodiversity trust fund in Nepal.

While mobilizing financial resources is vital to protect the global environment, these valuable sums will be wasted if they are not expended in an environmentally and socially sound manner. Thus Bank project preparation and implementation must follow policies and procedures, which are discussed in the next section.

World Bank Environment-Related Policies and Procedures

World Bank management has issued a series of operational policies and procedures for staff. These policies instruct staff on the means by which projects are financed and the steps required to protect environmental and social interests in preparing and carrying out projects. The instructions, therefore, act as a form of internal management structure which, because of the Bank's global reach, could well be argued to also mean that the impact and control they exert on development finance transform them into a veritable "soft" international environmental law.

Adding to the rigor of these instructions, and to the contention that they serve as a form of "soft law," in 1993 the Bank established an Inspection Panel to address alleged noncompliance of Bank staff with these policies and procedures, especially pertaining to the policies discussed below. The stated purpose of the Panel includes:

> "Providing people directly and adversely affected by a Bank-financed project with an independent forum through which they can request the Bank to act in accordance with its own policies and procedures."

To date the Panel has handled numerous inquiries involving projects with environmental and social-related issues. By mid-1997 it had processed eight formal requests and acted upon five in fiscal 1997 alone. The discussion below provides a brief survey of the policies and their relation to international environmental law.

Development of Environment-Related Policies

Since its beginning, the Bank has been applying policies linked to environmental protection. In 1949 the Bank decided to avoid making loans for projects that involved disputed waters of the Indus River system, as the riparian countries had not been able to agree on an approach for use of the waters. The Bank's concern was to avoid contributing to water disputes between riparians.

Similarly, during the early 1950s the Bank was requested by the Government of Egypt to provide financing for the construction of the Aswan Dam. The Bank set conditions for its financing, including that Egypt and Sudan reach agreement on how to share the water resources and make arrangements for the compensation and relocation of people to be resettled due to flooding. When Egypt did not enter into discussions with Sudan, the Bank did not finance the dam; financing was ultimately provided by the former Soviet Union. For similar reasons in the same time period, the Bank did not fund other major water projects on the Euphrates river.

By 1992 the Bank had decided to convert its operational policies into a new format from what were termed "operational manual statements," "operational policy notes," and "operational directives."

Thus despite the absence of pertinent international watercourse treaties, by 1956 the Bank had set out procedures for Bank staff to follow in financing projects on international waterways. These procedures ensured that staff would investigate and notify Bank management if Bank projects could involve the use of an international inland waterway. A chief objective of these procedures was to ensure that riparians did not undertake projects with Bank financing to the detriment of other riparians, especially in the absence of adequate notice and opportunity for consultation. Thus Bank policy was largely consistent with today's international treaties many years before their development.

By the 1970s the Bank had begun to take the environment into consideration in a more formal way, through the hiring of its first environmental specialists. Then, in 1984, the Bank published an *Operational Manual Statement* which recognized that the Bank's environmental practices were still evolving, but that there was a body of international environmental law that the Bank would help to promote. Moreover it helped pave the way for the Bank's publication in 1989 of its cornerstone environmental policy "environmental assessment".

By 1992 the Bank had decided to convert its operational policies into a new format from what were termed "operational manual statements," "operational policy notes," and "operational directives." These documents serve as guidance to Bank staff. The Board decided that these policy formulations would be converted into "Operational Policies," "Bank Procedures," both of which would be binding upon staff, and non-binding "Good Practices" (collectively referred to as OP/BP/GP).

This conversion process is still underway, and some of the policies and procedures discussed herein may change. For the most part the conversion meant that the substance of the policies would not change when put into the new format. However, some policies may be revised, as in the case of indigenous peoples, involuntary resettlement, and, possibly, forestry. The Operational Directive for environmental assessment has not yet been converted, although this should occur in the very near future. The conversion has been closely monitored in and outside the Bank, given the critical relation between environmentally sound project finance and thorough, high quality environmental assessment...

Environment-Related Requirements Pertaining to Legal Instruments and the Development of Project Legal Documentation

The Bank requires that the environmental assessment (EA) process consider all relevant international environmental treaties or agreements relevant to project-related impacts. In practice this means that Bank staff should seek to ensure that the EA has noted and discussed relevant treaty obligations pertaining to the borrower/member and whether those obligations have an impact on the design of the proposed project. The Bank has also taken the position that it will not finance project activities that would contravene such country obligations, as identified during the EA.

This position helps to clarify that the EA report must include discussion about any relevant international environmental treaty obligations, and that they should be met by the project design. Where appropriate in the view of the Bank's Legal Department and the Borrower, these obligations can then be included in relevant legal conditions included in loan documents. This action is consistent with the requirement that the EA include the requisite legal, policy, and administrative framework within which the EA report is prepared.

Indeed, the Bank's recent review of its environmental assessment practices noted clearly that legal conditions included in loan documents need to be enhanced in relation to the EA applicable to the project. The report stated as follows:

> "The strength of environmental language in project legal documents appears to be a critical factor in how much attention the environment receives during supervision.

> The types of environmental issues focused on are also largely determined by the nature of these conditions and covenants. This is only to be expected, as compliance with legal clauses is one of the principal ways project performance is assessed. Projects with specific environmental clauses in the legal documents are also more likely to have environmental specialist participation in the supervision, thus further intensifying the focus on environmental aspects."

The report thus supports the Bank's Legal Department and Bank staff who have worked with borrowers to draft and include conditions in the legal documents spelling out the need to carry out environmental mitigation plans mandated by the EA. For example, in carrying out a solid waste management project negotiated over the last two years, a borrower was required to "carry out an environmental assessment in connection with each disposal site to be used under the Project," and to "ensure that all environmental mitigation and monitoring measures, recommended under each report furnished to the Bank in connection with an EA, ... shall have been carried out."

Clearly, the Bank is seeking to ensure that environmental conditions and covenants are set forth in a more uniform manner. The Bank has available on-line access to all environmental covenants set forth in its loan agreements. Further, while the Bank now routinely works to incorporate in the legal documents both the environmental mitigation measures and any environmental management plan arising from the EA, further clarification of this process has been proposed in the draft environmental assessment policy now under consideration, which will ensure added uniformity in the effort to ensure that environmental plans are carried out.

The draft environmental assessment policy will also clarify another long-standing policy pertaining to project development. Since the late 1980s the Bank has used its environmental guidelines during project preparation and environmental assessment. These guidelines are considered to be especially essential when projects take place in developing countries lacking modern environmental laws and regulations. The *Pollution Prevention and Abatement Handbook* (a revision of the 1988 *World Bank Environmental Guidelines*, prepared in 1988) sets forth the pollution prevention abatement measures and emission levels that "are normally acceptable to the Bank."

The Handbook was prepared based upon the standards and consultations with the Bank's borrowers, UN specialized agencies, national regulatory agencies, NGOs, and the private sector. The Bank's draft EA policy makes clear that these pollution measures should be taken into account in the environmental assessment. It is also clear that they will be taken into account in legal documentation, as referred to above. At the same time where local law is adequate or local conditions indicate that the guidelines are not suitable, the EA can recommend alternative emission levels to those in the Handbook, provided that the "EA report must provide full and detailed justification for the levels and approaches chosen for the particular project or site."...

International Waterways Projects

Projects on international waterways frequently require extensive environmental assessment, as many of them involve engineering activity, such as irrigation and hydroelectric schemes. Thus, when financed in whole or in part by the Bank, they must comply with the Bank's environmental assessment policy. Beyond this compliance, such projects need to be viewed in terms of long standing principles about riparian use of shared water bodies, especially in regard to the process by which countries notify each other of their proposed use. The Bank has sought to take these principles into account through Bank policy.

The Bank's policy on "International Waterways" defines the term to be, with one potentially significant exception, consistent with the "international watercourses," addressed by the *Convention on the Law of the Non-Navigational Uses of International Watercourses*. Unlike the Convention, the Bank's policy does not refer to groundwater. Under the Convention "watercourse" means "a system of surface waters and groundwater constituting by virtue of their physical relationship a unitary whole and normally flowing into a common terminus." Further, "international watercourse" is "a watercourse, parts of which are situated in effluent states."

Although the Bank's definition of "international waterways" does not refer to groundwater, its definition based upon a series of specifically identified types of water areas and waterbodies is potentially broader than those of the Convention. Besides the distinctions in definitional coverage, another interesting contrast between the Bank's policy and the Convention is that Bank policy is phrased to ensure that a project does not cause "appreciable harm." The Convention makes more prominent note of the concerns for "equitable utilization." In practice these distinctions are not likely to present barriers to a consistent approach to project finance, as both instruments stress the need to ensure that all parties receive early and adequate notice of potential issues. The Bank encourages early notice from the riparian party undertaking a project to other riparians users. Such notice may be required, even when the riparian party undertaking the project is not in a position to cause harm to other riparian parties, to ensure that the project "will not be appreciably harmed by the other riparians' possible water use." Thus notice may be required even if the project would not cause appreciable harm. Before presenting the loan to the Bank's Board, Bank staff must ensure that the project is either covered by an agreement between the relevant riparian states, has received a positive consent or no objection from the other riparians, or "will not cause appreciable harm to the other riparians."

By using the "appreciable harm" and "adverse effect" formulation, the Bank was not rejecting the "equitable utilization" formulation. In fact, it has been noted that the "equitable use" formulation is considered to be the "cornerstone" of the law in this field. In the Bank's view, however, the equitable use analysis could require the Bank to act more in the nature of a tribunal, adjudicating issues of equity and distribution between the parties, whereas the "appreciable harm" or "adverse effect" formulation is more of a purely scientific determination, akin to the environmental assessment/economic analysis required of Bank investments.

At the same time if riparian states wish to enter into negotiations on the equitable utilization of international waterways, the Bank has always stood ready to facilitate and assist countries or regional organizations with those issues to be negotiated.

From Waterways to Global Externalities

While the policy on international waterways represents one of the Bank's first formal policies to address transboundary issues of the hydrosphere, increasing attention is focused on the global issues pertaining to other natural resources, especially the atmosphere. Addressing the global externalities of Bank project financing is a relatively new phenomenon, but will require increasing devotion of resources, especially when undertaking environmental assessments. The Bank's first policy on this issue is set forth in a policy on economic analysis of Bank investments. This policy addresses, in part, project externalities that are domestic, cross-border, or global. Cross-border externalities could include the effects from a project that impact on more than one riparian state. Global externalities affect the global commons, and include emissions of greenhouse gases or ozone-depleting substances, pollution of international waters, or impacts on biodiversity.

The Bank's policy points out that these externalities and their impacts need to be taken into account during EAs when Bank-financed "payments related to the project are made under an international agreement," or "projects or project components are financed by the Global Environment Facility." If these two conditions do not exist, "global externalities are fully assessed (to the extent tools are available) as part of the environmental assessment process and taken into account in project design and selection."

The "tools" to carry out the global externality analysis are still evolving. Often the externality can be assessed in economic terms, by forecasting the monetary value an investor might be willing to pay to lower the environmental impact from the planned investment operation. An example could be the cost to undertake an environmentally friendly fuel switch at an industrial plant in order to lower atmospheric emissions. In some cases this "willingness to pay" is more easily determined in projects where there will be cofinancing. Cofinancing, especially linked to air emissions, is likely to arise from an investor or country who perceives a regulatory need to support an emission reduction project, and is willing to "cofinance" a project to achieve the reductions.

If the willingness to pay is not clear, how does one assess the externality? Precisely what is the environmental cost of an added ton of greenhouse gas to the atmosphere, and how should that cost be internalized in project finance? In the context of the United Nations *Framework Convention on Climate Change*, if a country has binding obligations under the Convention the cost of a less polluting gas might be more easily calculated by determining the cost of compliance with a regulation. Following that determination, the less polluting option might then be added to the cost of financing the project. If no binding obligations are imposed on the project financier, and the willingness to pay is not clear, determining the externality is a challenge.

Protection of Natural Habitats and Endangered Species

Recent discoveries about the value of wetland plant and animal species have demonstrated that certain natural habitats and species are of global value. The Bank's environmental portfolio will hopefully contribute to the environmental treaties for the preservation of natural habitats and endangered species, the success of which depends upon transfer of resources to developing countries. The *Ramsar Convention on the Protection of Internationally Important Wetlands* and the *Convention on the Conservation of Migratory Species* are among many treaties that seek to support our natural heritage. While Bank policy pertaining to natural habitats does not cite international conventions that seek to protect natural habitat, the policy is protective of the types of natural habitats whose survival is the objectives of these treaties. Bank policy states:

> "The Bank does not support projects involving the significant conversion of natural habitats, unless there are no feasible alternatives for the project.... If the environmental assessment indicates that a project would significantly convert or degrade natural habitats, the project includes mitigation measures acceptable to the Bank. [Further]...the Bank supports, and expects borrowers to apply, a precautionary approach to natural resource management to ensure opportunities for environmentally sustainable development... The Bank does not support projects that, in the Bank's opinion, involve the significant conversion or degradation of critical natural habitats."

"Critical natural habitats" are defined as follows:

> "Existing protected areas and areas officially proposed by government as protected areas (such as reserves that meet the criteria of the World Conservation Union classifications), areas initially recognized as protected by traditional local communities (such as sacred groves), and sites that maintain conditions vital for the viability of these protected areas (as determined by the environmental assessment process)."

Coverage of natural habitats that are not "critical" is less stringent, given the less sensitive nature of the habitat. In these cases The Bank does not support projects involving the significant conversion of natural habitats unless there are no feasible alternatives for the project...If the environmental assessment indicates that a project would significantly convert or degrade natural habitats, the project includes mitigation measure acceptable to the Bank.

The policy on natural habitats also contains another interesting reference to internationally known principles. It states at the outset that the Bank supports and expects borrowers to apply a precautionary approach to natural resource management, to ensure opportunities for environmentally sustainable development. However, the Bank has not yet had extensive discussion about this provision or determined how it will be implemented.

In 1984 the Bank stated that it would "not finance projects which would significantly modify natural areas designated by international conventions as World Heritage sites. Later the Bank expanded upon this principle, stating that it would seek to help countries conserve, maintain, enhance, and restore their cultural heritage. This policy enables the Bank to address cultural property and cultural resources. The Bank has also issued recent guidance on addressing cultural heritage issues during Bank project finance.

Sustainable Forestry

International treaty negotiations are still under development for a treaty on sustainable forestry. The Bank's forestry policy makes no explicit reference to potentially relevant international forestry agreements. Yet comparison of the Bank's policy with prominent international instruments indicates some consistency of approach, and represents a step toward the development of accepted international best practice in this field. Such policies may go a long way toward helping develop an international frame of reference for generally accepted forestry principles. Of course, key areas of consensus do not yet exist in the international regime, and efforts to conclude a forestry treaty last year were unsuccessful.

The Bank is considering revising its forestry policy, and at the same time, has efforts underway to help the international dialogue toward an approach to sustainable forestry. As it proceeds, the Bank needs to take into consideration any legal developments pertaining to the draft Forestry treaty, as well as current timber agreements.

The Bank states that its "lending operations in the forest sector are conditional on government commitment to undertake sustainable management and conservation-oriented forestry." This means that the Bank can require borrowers to "adopt policies and a legal and institutional framework" to support sustainable practices, while also promoting the "active participation of local people and the private sector." The Bank's policies toward local peoples includes its recognition of their rights, through the Bank's indigenous peoples policy. Thus, for example, as a requirement for going forward with an IDA credit to Laos for the Lao Forestry Project, the Bank required development, to its satisfaction, of a forestry law and underlying legislation supporting the customary rights of indigenous peoples, with the participation of affected local and indigenous peoples.

These and other provisions set forth in the. Bank's policy are consistent with certain provisions in the *Forestry Principles* adopted at the Rio Earth Summit. Both emphasize the need to promote participation of interested parties in the development, implementation, and planning of national forest policies, while also supporting moist forest." The *Rio Principles*, on the other hand, speak to the need to "aim" to protect "primary old growth." In this context the Bank is embarking upon the support of projects that focus on sustainable forestry, including in the private sector. Recently, the International Finance Corporation agreed to support a project in Papua New Guinea under which concessions will be granted to local villagers, provided their activities are carried out in a sustainable manner.

Rights of Indigenous Peoples

It has been estimated that there are over 250 million "indigenous peoples" in over 70 countries. Principle 22 of the *Rio Declaration* states:

Indigenous people and their communities and other local communities have a vital role to play in environmental management and development because of their knowledge and traditional practices. States should recognize and duly support their identity, culture and interests and enable their effective participation in the achievement of sustainable development.

International instruments supporting the rights of indigenous peoples were summarized recently by the United Nations Commission on Human Rights. In these discussions recognized the difficulty of developing a uniformly accepted definition of indigenous people. Many World Bank projects are in regions inhabited by indigenous peoples, and since 1982 the Bank has had an explicit policy to address these peoples, beginning with the "Tribal Peoples" policy. This policy was revised in 1991, and is now referred to as the "Indigenous Peoples" Policy. Further revisions are under consideration. The policy was broadened to extend the definition to a wider range of social groups that maintain social and cultural identities distinct from the majority and who, as a result, are vulnerable to social and political pressure. In addition the policy stresses the importance of ensuring that in cases when they are affected, indigenous peoples participate in and benefit from Bank-financed projects. It also spells out the requirements for Indigenous Peoples Development Plans, as a means to incorporate the needs of indigenous people as part of the project loan documentation.

Today it is difficult to define the types of people that fit into prescribed categories. For some the difference between indigenous peoples and tribal peoples relates essentially to the principle of self-determination. Some in the field contend that a people may be "tribal either by their own choice, or without their consent, whereas indigenous peoples are classified as such only if they choose to perpetuate their own distinctive identity and institutions." Further, as the UN Commission points out: "The United Nations system should be mindful of the conclusion of the managers of the World Bank that 'no single definition can capture the diversity of indigenous peoples worldwide."

Even if indigenous peoples could be clearly defined and identified, there is an inherent tension between, on the one hand, seeking to support indigenous rights by recognizing a group of people as a distinct entity and, on the other, seeking to integrate their participation in environmental management. Yet no more than ten countries have ratified relevant international legal instruments that seek to spell out indigenous peoples rights, such as the International Labor Organization's *Convention No. 169 on the Rights of Indigenous Peoples*. Thus a lack of clarity remains in regard to the legal rights of indigenous peoples. This places added responsibility upon lawyers and project staff involved in the process of preparing projects that affect indigenous peoples to ensure the fulsome research into the rights of indigenous peoples and, where such rights are not adequately defined, to enter into dialogue with relevant government and local officials to undertake the development of an appropriate legal regime. This task is difficult because it requires clarifying uncertain and/or unrecorded legal principles, finding additional project preparation funds, and forging a difficult political dialogue among actors who may have a history of conflict.

Despite these difficulties, rather than form a strict legalistic interpretation of the people covered under relevant terms, the Bank has taken a more regional and country-specific way of identifying groups that should be considered under its operational policy. Most important in this context, the Bank has sent a message that the progressing of projects in areas that could impact on indigenous people requires engaging qualified lawyers, sociologists, and anthropologists. The Bank's policy seeks to ensure that Bank projects that impact indigenous peoples have a plan to ensure that their rights and interests are taken into account, so as to maintain their cultures, while giving them the opportunity to improve their lifestyles. The World Bank Working Group on Indigenous Peoples Policy strives to improve upon these processes.

Some evidence of the success of this policy and its application were detailed in a Nicaraguan civil action [*La communidad Mayagna*], in which indigenous groups filed suit to require action on their behalf by government officials. As part of their claim, and as evidence of international norms supporting their rights to their native lands, they argued:

> "It stands out that the World Bank has established a normative policy in favor of the territorial rights of indigenous peoples. In its *Operational Directive 4.20* of 1991, the Bank establishes the objective of assuring that indigenous peoples do not suffer the adverse effects of development. As a result, the Directive sets forth legal acknowledgment of land tenure schemes agreeing to the rights of indigenous traditions, and to the informed participation of the same communities in the setting out and execution of any development project that could affect them."

While this case has not yet been decided, it suggests that the policies of multilateral development banks can form the basis of international norms, thereby contributing to the development of international environmental jurisprudence.

Involuntary Resettlement

Projects with major environmental impact may lead to displacement of people, in some cases involuntarily. Such human impact is difficult to separate from environmental concerns, and many cases result in an impact on the legal rights of those who are forced to move from their homes. Among the *Rio Principles* are articles setting forth the need for informed public participation and right to judicial review. The need for the thorough, just application of an involuntary resettlement policy that takes these principles into account is paramount. The Bank estimates that over the last decade close to 80 or 90 million people have been resettled as a result of infrastructure projects. World Bank activity in this period has accounted for a "small, but significant share" of this amount. In 1996 it was estimated that the Bank's portfolio at that time would involve the resettlement of 2 million people over an eight-year period.

The Bank's policy on involuntary resettlement, like that on indigenous peoples and environmental assessment, carries forward the theme of meaningful consultation and the right to independent/judicial review when resettlement is inevitable. This policy requires screening for potential resettlement requirements in cases of projects that involve land acquisition, or in which a Category A or B environmental assessment is required. Further, it requires that the project design seek to avoid involuntary resettlement or, if it is unavoidable, that resettlement be minimized to the extent possible. When resettlement must occur, a plan must be in place before the Bank can finance the project. This plan must be developed in consultation with the affected people, Bank staff (including social scientists), and the national government and must ensure that the people to be displaced receive benefits from their relocation. People displaced must be given the means to improve, or at least restore, their former living standards.

Principle 10 of the *Rio Declaration* states in part that "effective access to judicial and administrative proceedings, including redress and remedy, shall be provided." The Bank's policy requires that design of the resettlement plan encompass a thorough understanding of the legal framework, and in case of disputes, such as land acquisition disputes, there must be legal procedures available, including an appeals process with an applicable timeframe for such an appeal.

The Bank's policy seeks to ensure that Bank projects that impact indigenous peoples have a plan to ensure that their rights and interests are taken into account, so as to maintain their cultures, while giving them the opportunity to improve their lifestyles.

In addition the resettlement policy incorporates the Bank's protection of cultural heritage, also reflected in other policies. The policy notes that the potential for acceptance of a resettlement plan can be increased by ensuring that people retain access to cultural property, such as temples and pilgrimage centers.

Policies to Protect Against the Adverse Impact of Chemicals, Pesticides, and Hazardous Wastes

In a number of instances international organizations have developed or applied legal instruments to seek to protect the public from exposure to toxic chemicals and other harmful products. As an example of the application of these laws or policies, the Bank has developed and implemented policies pertaining to the use of pesticides, the handling of hazardous wastes and other hazardous materials, and the regulation of tobacco. The policy receiving the most attention applies to pesticides and their use in agriculture pest management.

Pesticides

The Bank's policies dealing with agricultural pest management take note of applicable international instruments and their effort to prevent hazardous application and exposure to dangerous pesticides. For example, the Bank's policy on "Pest Management" states:

> "In assisting borrowers to manage pests that affect either agriculture or public health, the Bank supports a strategy that promotes the use of biological or environmental control methods. The Bank uses various means to assess pest management in the country and support integrated pest management (IPM) and safe agricultural use."

Having stated the goal of minimizing the use of chemical pesticides, the policy then lays out certain requirements pertaining to procurement of pesticides. Noting that the procurement "of any pesticide in a Bank-financed project is contingent on an assessment of the nature and degree of associated risks," the policy goes on to note:

> "With respect to the classification of pesticides and their specific formulations, the Bank refers to the World Health Organizations recommended Classification of Pesticides by Hazard and Guidelines to Classification..."

Any pesticides financed by the Bank must be manufactured, packaged, labeled, handled, stored, disposed of, and applied according to standards acceptable to the Bank. The FAO's *Guidelines for Packaging and Storage of Pesticides* (Rome, 1985), *Guidelines on Good Labeling Practice for Pesticides* (Rome, 1985), and *Guidelines for the Disposal of Waste Pesticide and Pesticide Containers on the Farm* (Rome, 1985) are to be used as minimum standards. The policy further states that:

> "The Bank does not finance any formulated products that fall in WHO classes IA and IB, or formulations of products in Class II, if (i) the country lacks restrictions on their distribution and use; or (ii) they are likely to be used by, or be accessible to, lay personnel, farmers, or others without training, equipment, and facilities to handle, apply, and store these products properly."

Thus, in practice, Bank policy seeks to ensure that pesticides are only used when necessary. If they are used, however, it must be in accordance with accepted international best practice and appropriate technology financed by the Bank.

Hazardous Wastes

The Bank has also developed a policy to address the transboundary shipments of hazardous waste. Prior to the adoption and entry into force of the *Basel Convention on the Control of the Transboundary Movements of Hazardous Wastes and their Disposal*, World Bank President Barber Conable stated that the Bank "will not finance any projects that involves the disposal of hazardous wastes from another country, nor will it finance the shipment of such wastes for disposal in any developing countries." Following this approach, the Bank has undertaken projects to develop waste management facilities that support the *Basel Convention*'s goals for the environmentally sound management of their hazardous wastes.

When Bank staff prepare such projects they refer to definitions and requirements under the *Basel Convention*, or to practices required by the waste management industry. As an example, in an industrial pollution control project in India, legal conditions require that the Bank consider requests for subproject financing. Following receipt of a request for funding, the Bank notified the government's executing agency that it would have to clarify to the Bank the temperature at which an incinerator would be operated and the identity of the substances to be burned. The Bank's task manager informed the borrower that the Bank would not finance an incinerator that would burn halogens or mercury.

Hazardous Materials

In addition to the use of operational policies as a means to control use of environmentally dangerous chemicals through the Bank's applicable procurement policies, the Bank seeks to ensure that environmentally dangerous products are not purchased with Bank loans. Bank policy on "Procurement Arrangements for Adjustment Operations," in pertinent part, states:

Consistent with the Bank's policies that loan proceeds are used for development purposes, such items as military hardware, luxury goods, and environmentally hazardous goods are excluded by using a negative list ... Funds may be disbursed for any imports except those excluded by the negative list.

While this policy is not often referred to in the context of the environment, the relation between public sector procurement and "green" behavior is likely to grow over time. This is especially true given increased attention to product certification and eco-labelling.

Tobacco

While there are few treaty instruments addressing tobacco, the Bank's tobacco policy is included here. Similar to other health-threatening substances, tobacco is a substance likely to be regulated; it has already been the subject of an interesting trade-versus-environment dispute between the United States and Thailand, concerning restrictions by Thailand on cigarette imports. International organizations have also expressed concern about the manufacture of tobacco-related products, as reflected by the work of the World Health Organization, which, in turn, is reflected in a 1991 World Bank report and set forth in a policy on tobacco. The Bank's tobacco policy states:

> "The Bank does not lend directly for, invest in, or guarantee investments or loans for tobacco production, processing or marketing. To the extent practicable, the Bank does not lend indirectly for tobacco production activities....Unmanufactured and manufactured tobacco, tobacco processing machinery and equipment, and related services are included in the negative list of imports in Loan Agreements."

Perhaps just as the tribe in Nicaragua referred to the Bank's policy to support their actions, future disputes on this issue will take into account the World Bank's policy on tobacco as evidence of international norms...

Conclusion and Next Steps

As an economic institution, the Bank has extensive experience in measuring the economic performance of its borrowers and the financial return on its projects. Economic data remains proficient in providing quantitative data on project performance. Yet it is increasingly agreed that measurements of qualitative indicators are lacking. The opening statement of the Bank's report on "Monitoring Environmental Indicators" notes that "Most knowledgeable people working on environmentally sustainable development know that the empirical base for decision making is weak." Thus "green accounting" is still inexact, despite efforts to improve the use of environmental indicators.

Given this unfinished state of affairs, in which many economists have difficulty measuring the relative merit of environmental mitigation measures, there is a call for greater multidisciplinary planning in economic investment decisions, and greater adherence to the environmental and social policy measures that are drafted to ensure long-term social and environmental benefits.

Moreover, this state of affairs must embrace all actors, not just the multilateral development banks who no longer provide the bulk of finance in developing countries, but the private sector as well. The Bank is well equipped to serve as a mechanism for bringing these actors together. This is clearly a goal of the Bank under its current leadership.

The Bank can take on leadership in this regard through commitment to thorough portfolio assessment that mainstreams global environmental concerns, as well as environmental assessment that analyzes global and local impacts even if it means the "no-project" alternative is preferred, or that extra caution means delays in project finance. This effort is especially important because such efforts are not likely to be achieved by perennially underfunded environmental regulatory agencies.

To a great extent it seems that borrowers and project sponsors are more willing today to work within these natural and human resource limits. Perhaps the *Kyoto Protocol* signifies, finally, an understanding that there are limits to growth. Still, the unfortunate irony is that as resources become more scarce and fragile, the pressure is growing to maximize profit from these same resources as a means to help poorer countries improve their living standards. The World Bank is at the crossroads of this unsettling challenge.

9

Innovative Financial Mechanisms: Debt Swaps

A

Freeland S., *The Use of the Non-Equity Debt Exchange Mechanism for Environmental and Development Purposes*, Faculty of Law, University of New South Wales, Australia, unpublished paper, 2001, pp 1–2, 16–37

Without the support of the United States, there still remains the possibility that some other industrialized countries choose not to ratify the Kyoto Protocol.

Introduction

This paper submits that it is both desirable and feasible to look at innovative ways of adapting and applying the debt exchange mechanism to further promote the goal of sustainable development. Past experience has shown that, when structured to take account of all relevant considerations pertaining to a particular situation, the use of this technique can be adapted to properly address the twin needs of economic growth and sustainability of a country's important natural resources. Indeed the debt exchange mechanism can also be applied to deal with social, cultural and developmental problems and needs, and has the flexibility to extend its scope even further to embrace questions of global concern such as the distribution of technology designed to aid the achievement of sustainable development.

At a time when the international community is faced with the increasingly divisive debates regarding 'globalization' and the 'digital divide', as well as the ever-increasing economic disparities between developed countries and less developed countries (LDCs), the level of LDC debt has become a highly political question. Similarly, particular issues of environmental concern, such as the problem of climate change and international efforts to curb greenhouse gas emissions, have themselves become globalized and highly politicised. Increasingly, calls are made for cooperative action by all countries in relation to these concerns. A combination of political expediencies, scientific evidence and (sometimes militant) public protest means that they are now being addressed, albeit slowly, usually on the basis of the international environmental principle of 'common but differentiated responsibility'.

It is therefore propitious to consider whether and how the debt exchange mechanism, which can lead to the 'cancellation' of large amounts of LDC debt, can at the same time be utilized to address significant environmental issues. In this regard, an important opportunity may present itself under the terms of the framework proposed for the Clean Development Mechanism (CDM), which forms part of the Kyoto Protocol to the United Nations Framework Convention on Climate Change (UNFCCC). Much of the specific detail of the CDM was agreed by consensus—with the notable exception of the United States—at the Sixth Conference of the Parties to the UNFCCC (COP6) in Bonn in late July 2001. Following that conference, there is renewed optimism about the possibility that the Kyoto Protocol will come into force in 2002 to coincide with the 10 year anniversary of the United Nations Conference on Environment and Development (UNCED) which was held in Rio de Janeiro in June 1992.

However, without the support of the United States, there still remains the possibility that some other industrialized countries choose not to ratify the Kyoto Protocol, with the result that it may not receive sufficient ratifications to actually come into force. However, even in this case, it is anticipated that an alternate 'CDM-type' mechanism will be utilized in practice under some other form of international regime, perhaps based more on voluntary rather than legally binding commitments.

In either event, the use of the debt exchange mechanism to implement CDM projects (or projects under some alternate structure) could well prove to represent an effective way of encouraging increased cooperation between developed and developing countries with regard to one of the most pressing current issues of global concern—the effects of global warming. The implementation of the debt exchange mechanism also has the potential to lead to more meaningful and committed participation by developing countries in legal regimes directly under, or in some way based upon the structure and principles of the CDM and the wider provisions of the Kyoto Protocol ....

The debt exchange mechanism has been utilized to date in a number of ways. These include relatively simple Debt-for-Nature swaps and more complex government-to-government and Debt-for-Development transactions. The following sections of this paper briefly describe these different structures.

Steps Involved in a Simple Debt Exchange—the Debt-for-Nature Transaction

The initial debt exchange mechanism was the Debt-for-Nature (DFN) transaction. Whilst the original concept of this transaction rests on the simple notion of a reduction of external debt in return for increased domestic conservation efforts, the mechanism usually requires a series of complex negotiations and formal documentation. It involves a number of parties, often with differing agendas and priorities and from various legal jurisdictions. Among other necessary preconditions, there must be sufficient incentives on all sides to encourage compliance, as well as the appropriate government will to effectively implement the debt exchange transaction. The need for these requirements has not, however, unduly restricted the suitability and widespread acceptance of appropriately structured debt exchange mechanisms for conservation funding, nor for broader purposes relating to LDC social and economic development.

Of course, as the complexities of any specific transaction increase, so do the costs (both in terms of money and allocation of resources) associated with its implementation. The debt exchange mechanism must therefore be designed and implemented to suit the particular circumstances and with clear 'success measures' in mind. Flexibility is crucial, since what may be appropriate in one LDC may not be in another. The structure of a particular debt exchange mechanism should take account of a variety of factors including (but not necessarily limited to) local economic conditions and political expediencies, cultural and social mores, the needs and development of any affected indigenous groups and the environmental priorities of the LDC government and the local and international nongovernmental organizations (NGOs) involved.

A DFN transaction in its simplest form involves the acquisition of commercial LDC debt by an investor—typically an international environmental organization acting together with a local environmental organization in the relevant LDC or the government of a developed country. With certain forms of debt exchange mechanism, official sovereign debt is utilized rather than private commercial debt. The debt is presented to the central bank of the LDC for conversion into a local currency instrument, the proceeds of which are then used for pre-agreed conservation, environmental or development purposes.

Whilst each DFN transaction will be different, it will generally involve a 5-step process:

1. An international environmental organization (International Organization) approaches an LDC government and negotiates the terms of a proposed debt exchange transaction. Following agreement, the International Organization receives approval from the LDC government to establish a particular conservation, environmental or development project in that country. This would normally involve the participation of the LDC government, its central bank and a local environmental organization (Local Organization). Alternately, agreement is reached between the respective governments of the particular LDC and a developed country wishing to instigate a debt exchange transaction.
2. The International Organization (or, in the case of a government-to-government debt exchange, the developed country government) identifies and acquires an appropriate LDC debt instrument. This usually involves the purchase of the debt through the international secondary debt markets, which have developed over the past two decades as facilities to create liquidity in the trade of LDC debt. The purchase is generally paid for by money raised by or donated to that organization, although there have been some instances where debt has been directly donated by commercial lenders. Where,

more recently, developed country sovereign lenders have become involved, they may agree to cancel LDC debt or purchase it themselves in the international secondary debt market and then donate it to an LDC. As with any commercial arrangement, it is important to determine the associated costs as against the benefits to be gained from a proposed debt exchange transaction. Where the debt is to be acquired in the international secondary debt market, the transaction is premised on the fact that the participating LDC's external debt can be purchased for a price substantially below its face value. This discount to face value must be sufficiently large so as to outweigh establishment and implementation costs associated with the transaction. In practice, LDC debt can generally be purchased at anywhere from a few cents in the dollar to parity. The conversion of debt should also be implemented in such a way as to maximize the 'purchasing power' of the amounts involved, this leverage factor being crucial to the overall success of the transaction in achieving the desired conservation, environmental or development goals. It is generally regarded that this 'leveraging effect' of the actual funds employed represents a significant advantage of debt exchange transactions over direct aid for conservation projects, although some commentators argue that direct financing of conservation projects is a more economically sound approach given the large amounts of funding required.

3. The transfer of title to the debt instrument is effected. The precise nature of this transfer is dependent upon a number of variables, including tax, financial and accounting considerations. Title may either be initially transferred to the International Organization which then donates it to the Local Organization, acquired directly by the Local Organization (through funds provided to it by the International Organization) or transferred directly to the Local Organization which holds it as the creditor's agent. In circumstances involving government-to-government debt exchanges, the transaction may also take the form of debt relief in exchange for an agreed program of environmental management or the implementation of a particular project.
4. The foreign currency denominated debt is converted by the LDC's central bank into a predetermined amount of local currency—usually in the form of local currency bonds or cash, based on the financing needs of the particular project(s) and the need to minimize any inflationary impact associated with the transaction. Further scope for leverage may also arise at this point, depending upon the exchange rate used and the proportion of the face value of the debt that is to be converted into local currency (as compared to the discounted purchase price in the international secondary debt market). These issues will have been the subject of lengthy negotiations and agreement prior to the implementation of the transaction.
5. The implementation of the conservation, environmental or development program. The project may be managed by the Local Organization in accordance with the terms of the debt exchange agreement, sometimes in collaboration with the relevant government agencies. In other circumstances, the International Organization or a development agency may play a leading role. It is at this juncture that the issue of enforceability, either through formal legal means or, as has predominantly been the case in most debt exchange transactions to date, through informal relationships or political pressure, becomes important. Many of the earlier debt exchange transactions did not incorporate clear enforceability and dispute resolution procedures. On occasions, this was to prove to be a major omission. However, as the debt exchange mechanism continues to develop as a financing technique for a broader range of projects involving larger amounts of (sometime public) debt, the need for more rigid enforcement and dispute resolution mechanisms will inevitably increase.

A Survey of Selected DFN and Broader Debt Exchange Transactions

Commencing with a relatively simple—though, as it transpired, not entirely successful—DFN transaction in 1987, the debt exchange mechanism has gradually evolved and been adapted for uses extending significantly beyond the conservation of forests. The mechanism has subsequently been implemented to address various environmental, developmental and social issues in many LDCs. It is suggested that the debt exchange mechanism has demonstrated its adaptability and appropriateness in this regard, and should ideally (but not necessarily) be used in conjunction with other forms of financing for large-scale programs designed to achieve sustainable development, such as projects falling within the terms of the CDM (or a similar legal regime).

The following section of this paper briefly describes a number of selected debt exchange transactions that have taken place since 1987. This is not intended to be an exhaustive list of transactions, nor is it a detailed description of every facet of those transactions that have been selected. Rather, the choice of transactions is designed to illustrate the evolution and development of the debt exchange mechanism for an increasing variety of purposes, to the point where it might now be considered for CDM projects and other sustainable development programs.

Furthermore, a review of these selected transactions, and some of the other government and Multinational Development Bank (MDB) initiatives that are intended to encourage the use of the debt exchange mechanism, serves to highlight some important—and initially unexpected—issues that have emerged relating to the use of this financing technique.

'First-Generation' (Private Sector) Debt Exchange Transactions

The debt exchange mechanism was initially implemented in relatively modest terms and involved cooperation and agreement between private sector groups—usually environmental NGOs—and the LDC government and its central bank. These are often referred to as the 'First Generation' of debt exchange transactions, and first emerged in 1987 in the form of a DFN transaction designed to promote conservation in Bolivia.

Bolivia (1987) — 'Debt-for-Conservation'

In 1987, an international conservation group based in Washington D.C., Conservation International (CI), purchased US$650,000 of Bolivia's debt from private lenders in the international secondary debt market for approximately US$100,000—an 85 percent discount to face value. The funds for this purchase were provided via a grant from a private charitable foundation. Under the terms of the debt exchange, this debt was swapped for shares in a newly established company set up to preserve approximately 3.7 million acres of forests and grasslands surrounding the Beni Biosphere Reserve in north-eastern Bolivia. This reserve was noted for its biological richness and had been established in 1982 as a model for the preservation of flora, fauna, water resources and the lifestyle of the local indigenous people living in the area. CI agreed to provide ongoing advice and assistance to Bolivia and announced that it was official advisor to the Bolivian Government in the design and planning of protected areas. For its part, the Bolivian Government also undertook to provide the maximum possible legal protection—congressional law status—for the 334,200 acre Beni Biosphere Reserve and agreed to establish a local currency fund equivalent to US$250,000 to manage and administer the protected areas. Management was divided between the government and a local NGO, with title to the lands remaining with the government.

Despite the relatively simple nature of the debt exchange agreement and the obligations undertaken by the various parties, events subsequent to the announcement of the proposed transaction raised a number of problems that had not been anticipated during the various negotiation stages. Some of these problems stemmed from the fact that this was the first DFN transaction to be implemented, and thus it experienced 'teething problems' associated with an untried financing mechanism. Moreover, the Bolivian DFN was the first debt conversion of any type undertaken in that country—there was, for example, no established Debt-for-Equity (DFE) program in place in Bolivia at the time from which the various parties could draw some guidance.

When the proposed transaction was initially announced, various Latin American newspapers reported (incorrectly) that a foreign organization had purchased national heritage Bolivian land. This led to a significant degree of criticism of the debt exchange concept among several Latin American countries. Eventually the Local Organization involved was able to explain the true position—however the incident clearly demonstrated the need to handle with sensitivity the local and regional public information issues associated with these type of transactions.

It also became clear that the various parties to the debt exchange agreement had failed to adequately consult with the local indigenous people prior to finalizing the project, let alone include them as a full partner in the conservation planning. Barely two months prior to execution of the agreement, the government had created seven logging concession areas in the Chimane Forest. At the time of the debt exchange transaction, the Chimane Indians, who lived in the forest without any formal land tenure, were attempting to obtain title to the land. However, the terms of the transaction made this impossible. Already fearful of significant destruction of their habitat through indiscriminate logging activities, which would have disastrous effects on their livelihood, they were now presented with a western-type national park model, in which their ability to engage in traditional and life-supporting activities—such as using trees for fuel in the areas in which they lived—was further restricted. In effect, the Bolivian debt exchange agreement operated to divest the Chimane Indians of the traditional rights to their land, since those activities were considered detrimental to the forest conservation goals underlying the transaction.

The fact that this had happened without the opportunity for the local indigenous people to provide input into the project established under the debt exchange agreement represented a major failing of this transaction. This need to involve local communities is a particularly significant issue for the structure of many forms of debt exchange transaction, since the indigenous people living in a designated—and sometimes protected—area will often be the persons most directly affected by any restrictions relating to land use that are imposed by the agreement. Moreover the failure to involve indigenous people gives considerable credence to a frequently raised criticism of environmentalists—that they attach too great a significance to their own agendas to the exclusion of other more pertinent factors, and consequently structure conservation and environmental agreements to correspond with other personal interests.

In addition, the Bolivian Government did not make its agreed US$100,000 contribution to the local currency management account until 10th April 1989—almost 21 months after the signing of the debt exchange agreement. As a consequence, the proposed funding by the United States Agency for International Development (USAID), which was contingent upon this contribution by the Bolivian Government, was not forthcoming and approximately US$60,000 in interest for the benefit of the Reserve was lost.

Moreover, the Bolivian Government (initially) failed to enact appropriate legislation to provide for the agreed legal protections for the Reserve. The issue was mired by the fact that the Beni region was one of Bolivia's principal areas for cocaine processing and export.

Overall, the experience of a debt exchange transaction in Bolivia was considered mixed at best. The failure of the government and CI to properly consult with the local indigenous people was a major shortcoming of the process. Furthermore, the (largely unjustified but nevertheless real) perception that this form of debt exchange mechanism represented an attack on the sovereignty of LDCs—action sometimes referred to as 'ecological imperialism' or 'environmental neo-colonialism'—as well as the failure of the Bolivian Government to fully comply with its responsibilities, meant that the transaction could not be viewed as entirely successful. Yet, as with many subsequent transactions, the debt exchange agreement was negotiated with the Bolivian Government on the basis that it would contain no legally binding enforceability mechanisms, relying rather on a more 'subtle' forms of compliance enforcement involving extensive international NGO involvement in designing and implementing the project. Enforceability of the agreement based on legally binding commitments was 'sacrificed' by the environmentalists in an attempt to build a long-term relationship with the participating government without offending its sovereignty concerns.

The experience with this first DFN clearly showed that future debt exchange transactions would need to be carefully structured and adapted to accord with local conditions and sensitivities if they were to more effectively achieve broader goals. Clearly no two debt exchange transactions could be the same since there were a large number of specific local variables that had to be taken into account.

Nevertheless, despite the obvious problems associated with this transaction, it did demonstrate the potential for utilizing LDC debt, through a technique involving financial structuring, to advance conservation, environmental (and eventually developmental) goals, whilst at the same time reducing the LDCs external debt level (even if only to a relatively small degree). What was required was that appropriate adaptations could be made to the mechanism so as to take due account of relevant local conditions. Furthermore, the implementation of the Bolivian DFN transaction heightened international awareness of the close interrelationship between a developing country's external debt levels and the state of its environment. This also acted as a spur for additional and complementary environmental support—in Bolivia's case, following the implementation of the DFN transaction, the International

Tropical Timber Organization (ITTO) gave the Bolivian Government a US$1.26 million grant to continue its forestry work with CI.

CI still remains involved in a range of conservation programs in Bolivia, including the Beni Biological Station established as a result of the 1987 DFN transaction. It has also utilized its experience to conduct a several additional debt exchange transactions in Costa Rica, Guatemala, Madagascar and Mexico. These CI initiated debt exchanges have so far provided for a total of over US$15 million in funds to be designated for environmental projects in LDCs, at an acquisition cost to CI of approximately US$6,500,000.

The Bolivian DFN transaction represented the first step in a lengthy evolutionary process that still continues today. The next stages in this process took the form of debt exchange transactions in Ecuador and Costa Rica, which were implemented shortly afterwards. A number of the important issues emerging from the Bolivian transaction were duly noted. These subsequent transactions were structured in an attempt to address at least some of these concerns.

Ecuador (1987) — 'Debt-for-Environment'

Although only a small country, Ecuador is rich in biological diversity, with important natural habitats that include the Galápagos Islands, rain forests, highlands, coastal savannah and mangrove forests. Its burgeoning population and lack of financial resources have combined to place severe strains on its environment.

In an effort to arrest environmental degradation, the country undertook an ambitious debt exchange program, which was structured to reflect some of the lessons learnt from the Bolivian experience. In October 1987, the Ecuador Government agreed to facilitate debt exchange transactions involving up to US$10 million of its external commercial debt. Through transactions in 1988 and 1989, The World Wildlife Fund (WWF), The Nature Conservancy (TNC) and the Missouri Botanical Gardens acquired this debt for US$1.5 million in the international secondary debt market. The debt was then assigned to *Fundación Natura* (FN), a private Ecuadorian conservation group and, upon conversion by the central bank, was exchanged at full face value into local currency non-negotiable monetary stabilization bonds in favor of FN. The principal reflected by these bonds was used to provide for the establishment of FN itself and, upon maturity, as an endowment fund to support the organization's general activities. FN uses interest income generated by the bonds to undertake a diverse range of environmentally related projects related to the protection of Ecuador's national parks and reserves.

Therefore, in contrast to the structure established under the Bolivian transaction, this debt exchange provided for agreed conservation goals to be implemented solely by a local NGO rather than with debtor government participation (which had led to some of the problems associated with the Bolivian transaction). This is a model that has often been followed in subsequent debt exchange transactions. Moreover, by issuing bonds and using only the interest generated, as opposed to a larger lump sum amount, to apply to the specific conservation projects, the structure of this transaction minimized the potential for inflation.

From an environmental funding viewpoint, the transaction was a success. Like many LDCs, in the absence of debt exchange transactions such as these, Ecuador would almost certainly have found it difficult to devote significant financial resources to the environment given other needs of a higher priority. Despite the fact that the US$10 million of debt involved represented only a fraction of Ecuador's total external debt, the environmental funding provided by the interest income on the local currency bonds was very significant for the country's domestic environmental activities. Indeed, the first year's interest payments alone were estimated to double Ecuador's entire national park budget. Clearly, these debt exchange transactions provided additional funding for environmental programs. This 'additionality' factor is an important element to take into account when determining whether to initiate a debt exchange transaction. If, on the other hand, the particular project would have been undertaken in any event even without the debt exchange, perhaps through the use of LDC government funds, then resort to a debt exchange in these circumstances would merely be a subsidy for existing conservation investment.

In view of the overall success of its initial program, Ecuador subsequently embarked on a US$50 million debt exchange program designed to fund social, cultural, educational and environmental protection projects. The experience gained through the utilization of the initial small transactions has led to the broadening of the debt exchange structure to address other areas of concern in that country.

Although only a small country, Ecuador is rich in biological diversity, with important natural habitats that include the Galápagos Islands, rain forests, highlands, coastal savannah and mangrove forests.

Costa Rica (1987) — 'Debt-for-Conservation'

The debt exchange transactions in Costa Rica have also been significantly more successful than the initial Bolivian DFN swap. Like those in Ecuador, the structure of the Costa Rican debt exchange transactions reflected some of the lessons learnt from the Bolivian experience and, through careful planning and negotiation, the mechanism was eventually applied in respect of much larger amounts of external debt. This was mainly as a result of the involvement of developed countries in the process. Within three years, in excess of US$70 million face value of Costa Rica's external debt was swapped into local currency bonds (equivalent to US$36 million) through the implementation of four debt exchange transactions. These funds have been utilized for conservation and wider environmental purposes.

Costa Rica had already established a DFN program in 1986 designed to convert US$180 million in debt. It has a richly diverse and important ecology and, from time to time, has taken steps to preserve its biological diversity. Twelve percent of its area has been proclaimed as national parks and a further 14 percent has been granted a legally protected status. However, the country lacks the necessary resources, equipment and personnel to completely manage and police these areas, and outside of the park areas, has still had an unacceptably high rate of deforestation.

Pursuant to a 1987 debt exchange agreement and a supplementary 1998 agreement, US$5.4 million of external debt was purchased for US$918,000, representing a discount from face value of 83 percent. This purchase of debt in the international secondary market was funded by WWF, in addition to donations made to the Costa Rican National Parks Foundation (*Fundación de Parques Nacionales*) from a variety of other NGOs. The debt was converted at 75 percent of face value into local currency bonds with a maturity of five years and nine months and carrying an average annual interest rate of 25 percent. Interest generated was used to establish a fund for the conservation of natural resources in Costa Rica. One of the main beneficiaries of these funds was the Guanacaste National Park project and the program involved the purchase of land to which the government only received title after the park was fully completed and endowed.

As a result of the success of this first debt exchange, the Costa Rican central bank approved the conversion of a further US$5.6 million of external debt, allowing for a second transaction to be implemented in January 1989. CI, with the assistance of other donors, acquired the debt from American Express Bank for US$784,000 and, upon conversion, the central bank issued the local currency equivalent of US$1.7 million in five-year monetary stabilization bonds generating interest at an annual rate of 25 percent. Once again, the interest income, which exceeded US$3 million, was applied towards conservation and environmental projects.

Sudan (1988) — 'Debt for Development'

As the use of the debt exchange mechanism came to be more widely accepted, its flexibility was increasingly recognized. Interested parties realized that, as commendable as turning areas like the Amazon region into a wildlife reserve might be—at least in theory—merely concentrating on narrowly focused DFN transactions aimed simply at conservation would not contribute significantly towards the abatement of poverty and the provision of basic services in many LDCs. The existence of a high rate of poverty and a lack of essential infrastructure necessary for local community survival often are themselves significant causes of environmental degradation and resource depletion.

In addition it may be the case that preservation of areas such as rain forests will frequently conflict with completing local interests, including those of indigenous people living in that area, as well as other more immediate priorities of LDC governments. Indeed such conservation projects might even exacerbate local poverty, increase demands on already depleted government social programs and reduce any income that would otherwise be generated from engaging in the restricted activities.

Consequently, for the debt exchange mechanism to be utilized more effectively, it was important that it could be adapted and thus implemented as a way of facilitating social and economic progress in LDCs. The mechanism was sufficiently flexible to be applied for these other purposes, leading to a number of further variations from the initial DFN model. One of these new forms was the debt-for-development exchange (DFD), which was utilized to facilitate programs that more directly address immediate concerns of the local population. In a DFD transaction, a creditor bank or sovereign creditor sells or donates LDC debt to a development organization that already operates development programs in the participating LDC. These programs are primarily aimed at improving the standard of water, sanitation, reforestation, health education and nutrition, thus promoting societal development in the particular LDC. The recipient of the debt might be an international government funded development organization such as the United Nations Children's Fund (UNICEF), the United Nations High Commissioner for Refugees (UNHCR) or the World Food Program (WFP), or a voluntary NGO such as CARE. The organization then retires the debt in return for the participant LDC government commitment to support an agreed development program to be administered by that organization.

An early DFD transaction involved US$1 million of Nigerian debt owed to American Express Bank Ltd. This debt was donated by the bank to the International Foundation for Education and Self Help and was subsequently exchanged in Nigeria for local currency to be used for various development programs.

In December 1988 Midland Bank donated to UNICEF its entire US$800,000 portfolio of Sudanese debt. The Sudan Government had agreed with UNICEF that it would continue to service this debt in local currency, with these servicing payments to be utilized in a number of development programs in Sudan administered by UNICEF.

Following on from these early transactions, the use of DFD exchanges grew dramatically, far exceeding the amount of debt involved in narrower DFN transactions from which they had developed. In the period 1987–1994 it was estimated that between US$750 million and US$1 billion of external LDC debt was cancelled as a result of DFD transactions, much of it comprising official bilateral government-to-government sovereign debt. During this period, UNICEF alone exchanged US$193 million of debt. By way of comparison, a total of approximately US$177 million of external debt was converted in narrower DFN transactions during the same period.

Part of the attraction of the DFD mechanism is that, by definition, it does not involve the acquisition by foreign organizations of local assets. It therefore is designed to minimize LDC concerns regarding possible infringement of sovereignty associated (on occasions mistakenly) with some of the earlier DFN swaps. Moreover, if properly conceived, a DFD swap focuses on the immediate and direct development needs of the local communities, and are therefore less likely to be driven by the agenda of well-meaning but perhaps somewhat unrealistic environmentalists. This development-conservation paradigm adds to the complexities involved in structuring and implementing a successful debt exchange transaction, and the goals of the stakeholders must therefore be well understood by all parties and factored into the transaction as appropriate.

If this can be done, the potential for success and acceptance of DFD swaps provides a clear example of the continued development of the debt exchange mechanism and its ability, in appropriate circumstances, to be applied to significant amounts of debt in respect to a broad range of programs.

Ecuador (1990)— 'Debt-for-Education'

The success of earlier transactions in Ecuador encouraged further creativity in the application of the debt exchange mechanism in that country. On 10th July 1990, Harvard University and Ecuador entered into the first 'debt-for-education' exchange. Under the agreement, Harvard acquired US$5 million of Ecuador's external debt in the international secondary debt market at a cost of US$775,000, representing just under sixteen percent of face value. The debt was then exchanged with the country's central bank at fifty percent of face value into local currency bonds, which were then transferred to a local educational foundation formed for that purpose.

The foundation sold the bonds into the local market, with the proceeds used to purchase United States dollars, which were then re-invested by the foundation back in the United States. A large part of the interest generated by this investment—approximately US$150,000 annually—was used to fund scholarships and grants for local students from Ecuador to attend Harvard, with the balance to fund local costs of research and study in Ecuador by students and faculty members from Harvard. Approximately seventy students and academics benefited under this arrangement over a ten-year period.

'Second Generation' (Government-to-Government) Debt Exchange Transactions

The widely publicized success of some of the 'first generation' transactions, coupled with the introduction of a number of developed country initiatives and an increasing recognition of the interrelationship between the protection of the environment and LDC development, all contributed to the initiation of a new type of debt exchange mechanism. These transactions provided, for the first time, for the exchange of public debt. They were structured on a direct government-to-government basis and, as a result, developed country governments would now also play a central role in the process, often taking the place of private international environmental organizations. This adaptation added an further variable to the debt exchange mechanism—actions undertaken by creditor governments would be influenced by political as well as economic considerations.

It should be noted that government-to-government transactions potentially give rise to increased corruption, as well as greater sovereignty concerns.

It should be noted that government-to-government transactions potentially give rise to increased corruption, as well as greater sovereignty concerns. As a result, the final structure and implementation of these debt exchanges must reflect a convergence of interest between the respective governments and encompass adequate safeguards to enhance transparency and accountability. However, if this can be achieved, the 'success' of any specific government-to-government debt exchange has the potential to forge greater cooperative relationships between the participating countries.

The implementation of public debt exchange transactions represented an important development in the evolution of the debt exchange mechanism, opening the way for much larger amounts of debt to be utilized and made available for programs, not just of an environmental nature but directed towards wider goals. The involvement of developed country governments in the process would, over time, allow for the broadening of the debate as to the type of projects to be considered. A more sophisticated range of projects could be considered, extending the use of the debt exchange technique far beyond the relatively narrow concerns of those NGOs responsible for negotiating the DFN transactions.

Moreover, the successful completion of these larger and more 'high profile' transactions would also increase industrialized country government and administration familiarity with, and confidence in the use of a debt exchange mechanism for environmental and development purposes. Not only could this be a catalyst for other areas of international cooperation, but it would also enhance developed country government support for commercial ventures by their major corporations in the participating LDC countries. The involvement of private enterprise is of crucial importance in circumstances where the debt exchange mechanism is to be applied to legal regimes such as the CDM. This in turn would increase the need to make dealings between parties to the debt exchange more 'predictable', which would itself promote added confidence to participate in future transactions.

As a result, the evolution of these government-to-government transactions saw the inclusion of more substantive compliance and enforcement provisions in the facilitating agreement. It also significantly broadened the political dimensions of the transaction, adding a further element of pressure on LDCs to ensure that every effort was made to comply with the obligations to which they had agreed. The participating LDC would need to consider the potential for political, as well as economic damage it would suffer by failing to satisfactorily implement its agreement with another government.

These ongoing developments help to point the way to increased transparency in this form of transaction, and therefore (hopefully) encourage a trend towards other spheres of co-operation between governments in relation not only to the levels of LDC debt, but also on issues of global environmental and developmental concern. These factors would be crucial if more ambitious aims are to be pursued through the utilization of the debt exchange mechanism, such as its application to large-scale projects under the CDM (or a CDM-type regime).

These government-to-government agreements came to be known as 'Second Generation' debt exchange transactions. Two examples are briefly described below.

Costa Rica (1989)— 'Debt-for-Conservation' and 'Debt-for-Industry'

In addition to its early first generation transactions, two further debt exchanges involving Costa Rica were completed during 1989. In January 1989 the Dutch and Costa Rican Governments reached an agreement pursuant to which the former purchased US$33 million of Costa Rican debt in the international secondary debt market for US$5 million. The subsequent conversion resulted in the issue of local currency four-year non-negotiable monetary stabilization bonds, equivalent in value to US$9.9 million, paying interest biannually at the annual rate of 15 percent. This was the first government-to-government exchange without the involvement of NGOs.

Despite the close relationship that existed between the respective governments at the time of this transaction, the Netherlands insisted on some new, though still largely informal, means of enforcing the commitments given by Costa Rica, although the agreement did not go so far as to include a dispute resolution mechanism. Nevertheless, this marked an important step in the process towards including more rigorous enforcement provisions in debt exchange transactions.

Soon afterwards, the Swedish Government purchased approximately US$28 million of Costa Rican debt for US$3.5 million and donated it to the Costa Rican National Parks Foundation. Upon conversion, four-year stabilization bonds were created paying fifteen percent annual interest, the proceeds of which went into an endowment for research and environmental education as well as park management and land acquisition. The use of an endowment in this transaction meant that local currency funding was introduced into the domestic economy gradually and by way of smaller regular amounts rather than a large 'one-off' injection of cash. In this way, fears were allayed that the expenditure of the local currency through the implementation of this debt exchange may result in unwanted domestic inflation.

The success of these transactions prompted the Costa Rican Government to increase its efforts to promote development through the use of the debt exchange mechanism. The central bank established a new debt conversion program in 1989 to promote projects involving not only natural resource conservation but also small industry development and education. The government has continued to believe that debt exchanges are a viable means to pursue sustainable development, and the possibility of even wider utilization of this mechanism for such purposes in Costa Rica appears likely.

The involvement of developed countries in the 1989 Costa Rica debt exchanges laid further groundwork for subsequent broader transactions. Through the involvement of a much larger range of developed country participants, the debt exchange mechanism expanded, spawning additional variants including DFD swaps in LDCs such as Sudan. Debt exchange transactions involving Poland's debt to the Paris Club of creditor nations involved even greater levels of debt.

Poland (1991)— 'Debt-for-Democracy'

On 15th March 1991, seven major industrialized creditor nations in the Paris Club reached agreement with Poland to forgive half of the US$33 billion of debt that it owed those nations. In addition, individual Paris Club nations were permitted to channel payments of interest and principal into a Polish Ecofund, to be used to finance projects designed to reverse or halt environmental damage caused by pollution. In the previous year, the Paris Club for the first time had authorized its members to sell their debt, or engage in debt exchange programs involving local currency funding, and these were also permitted under the terms of the agreement with Poland.

One of the major reasons for the implementation of these initiatives was to provide tangible support for democratic and economic reforms that had been instituted in Poland, which had only recently seen the introduction of a non-communist government. As a result of many years of economic mismanagement, Poland was, at this time, suffering from severe economic stagnation which, coupled with its unsustainable debt burden, had pushed it to the brink of insolvency.

In addition, Poland was a highly polluted country. Largely in an effort to reduce the transboundary effects of this pollution on neighboring countries, the agreement reached with the Paris Club was also subject to the implementation of various environmental clean-up programs and anti-pollution measures in Poland.

The debt exchange mechanism was structured as a two-stage process. The initial stage involved a thirty percent debt relief, calculated at net present value, to be followed by a further twenty percent debt relief to take effect three years after the successful implementation of various measures, including a program stipulated by the International Monetary Fund (IMF). These formal measures were in addition to any individual debt relief proposals offered on a voluntary basis by individual creditor nations under terms permitted by the Paris Club 'rules'.

Prior to the announcement of the Paris Club agreement, the (West) German Government had agreed to forgive additional loans of up to US$60 million. These had been part of an initial package of agreements between the respective governments in 1971. The implementation of conservation and environmental assistance activities by Poland was one of the conditions for the provision of this debt relief.

Pursuant to the Paris Club program, a number of creditor nations, including the United States, Switzerland, France, Sweden, Norway and Italy concluded debt exchange agreements with Poland, resulting in significant funds being injected into the Polish Ecofund. Pursuant to these arrangements, it was agreed that the Ecofund would be subject to significant international scrutiny. Representatives of the creditor nations participated in the Ecofund's steering committee, which is responsible for the selection of appropriate environmental projects to be financed by the fund. Moreover, Polish officials have stressed that the establishment and financing of the Ecofund represents funding in addition to, rather than in lieu of previously planned environmental spending.

There is no doubt that the circumstances leading up to the debt exchange arrangements with Poland were unique. Western Governments had a strong interest in supporting the country's transition from socialism to capitalism and important political considerations were inevitably a crucial factor in the decision by the Paris Club nations to agree to these debt exchanges. Nevertheless, this does not detract from the benefits derived through these transactions. The implementation of this program represents a further expansion in the scope and magnitude of the debt exchange mechanism. The obligations agreed to by Poland extended far beyond the habitat conservation efforts associated with early DFN exchanges. Prior to the time that this program was implemented, debt exchanges had not been utilized to any significant degree to finance environmental clean-up activities. The utilization of the mechanism in this way was significant in that it provided substantial funding for the immediate needs of the country (and its local communities), rather than facilitate the mere 'setting aside' of areas for conservation—often regarded as a developed world concept— that typified the DFN transaction.

Moreover, the use of the debt exchange mechanism to fund emission control projects in Poland represents an interesting and potentially relevant model in the wider context of the proposed CDM, depending upon the final details as to what specific types of project will fall within that framework.

In view of the amounts involved and the issues to be addressed in Poland, the proposal incorporated significantly stricter enforcement mechanisms than in previous debt exchanges. This did not unduly restrict the scope of the program, the overall success of which further demonstrates the adaptability of the mechanism and its ability to be applied to significant amounts of debt in order to facilitate social and economic development.

Other Initiatives Aimed at Promoting Debt Exchange Transactions

Much of the impetus for the development of narrow DFN transactions, as well as broader forms of debt exchanges, has stemmed from various United States Congressional initiatives designed to support these forms of transactions. Whilst the United States Administration had, in response to the effects of the 1982 Latin American debt crisis, initially considered (erroneously) that its two government initiated programs intended to address the problems that arose—the Baker Plan and the subsequent Brady Plan—might resolve the situation satisfactorily, over time it realized that other measures were necessary. Ongoing LDC debt servicing problems forced the United States commercial banks to take independent measures to minimize their potential losses. This led to the development of the international secondary markets for LDC debt.

An important consideration lay in the fact that the United States had significant bilateral trade, investment and strategic relationships with a number of those countries struggling under severe debt burdens, particularly in Latin America. A significant reason for initiating efforts to address the economic plight of these countries was to protect existing United States interests. The high volume of trade between Latin American countries and the United States meant that the region's economic health was important to the economy of the United States. Stronger Latin American economies help United States interests by expanding the potential market for United States goods, services and investment capital. Moreover the United States has long regarded political stability in Latin American countries—which is more likely to be threatened in times of economic crisis—to be a major tenet of its foreign policy.

As a result the Administration has, over recent years, enacted legislation and endorsed various tax initiatives that have allowed for easier and more commercially acceptable participation in debt exchange transactions by United States lenders. These actions have also had the effect of further highlighting the debate regarding the relationship between debt and the environmental and developmental situation of LDCs.

In addition, there was growing sentiment among United States lawmakers that various MDBs such as the World Bank should be accountable for the environmental effects of previous lending policies. These institutions were, for a long time, not appropriately staffed to adequately assess environmental issues associated with many of the transactions with which it was involved. Recently they have moved to establish environmental units and have developed a more focused strategy designed to take into account of the goal of sustainable development. In mid

2001, the World Bank's Environmentally and Socially Sustainable Development Network also adopted a new strategy to ensure that development in LDCs did not result in pollution and degradation of natural resources.

The support of institutions such as the World Bank and the IMF for the concept of the debt exchange mechanism, in conjunction with their own debt relief programs under their Heavily Indebted Poor Countries (HIPC) initiative launched in 1996, further highlights the scope for very significant amounts of debt to be utilized in this way.

At the same time, the broader recognition of this debt-environment-development relationship has also led to increased international calls for far-reaching programs of debt relief, part of which is slowly being implemented by the major industrialized countries. The increasing demand among elements of the international community for debt relief and debt forgiveness has become an important focus in recent high profile protests that have accompanied major international meetings such as the 1999 World Trade Organization (WTO) meeting in Seattle and the 2001 Group of 8 (G8) industrialized countries' meeting in Genoa.

The Global Environmental Protection Assistance Act of 1989

In April 1988, the Bureau for Program and Policy Coordination at USAID issued Debt for Development guidelines proposing that it provide funding for approved debt exchanges to NGO intermediaries, which would then be (theoretically) responsible for arranging the terms of the conversion directly with the LDC recipient government and for managing the use of the resources acquired through the exchange. The final terms of this proposal were partly motivated by the need to avoid the appearance of overt debt forgiveness, which would have not been an acceptable policy to the United States Administration at the time.

After a positive reaction to these guidelines, Congress passed the Global Environmental Protection Assistance Act (GEPA) to enable funding and support for USAID's debt exchange activities. GEPA was the first United States law relating to debt exchange transactions. Under the heading 'Debt-for-Nature Exchanges', Chapter 7 of the Act authorizes USAID to grant funds to environmental NGOs for the purchase of secondary market debt of eligible countries, to be used in debt exchange transactions. To participate in a USAID funded debt exchange transaction, the debtor country must demonstrate an ability and commitment to oversee the long-term viability of the particular environment project(s) being considered. In order to avoid sovereignty concerns, the legislation prohibits the United States Government from accepting title or interest in any land located in a recipient country as a condition of the transaction.

In 1989, WWF acquired US$3 million of external Madagasy debt with funds provided by USAID. The debt was converted at face value into local currency for various measures intended to protect and manage natural areas, including the training and funding of 400 park rangers. This was the first debt exchange transaction funded by USAID money. Further USAID funded debt exchanges have since taken place in Madagascar—which had, by 1998, reduced its $100 million commercial debt by half through the implementation of debt exchanges—as well as the Philippines and Guatemala. By 1998, USAID had provided US$95 million to environmental NGOs for the acquisition of US$146 million of external LDC debt, which was subsequently used in debt exchange transactions.

Despite these achievements, there are inevitable problems associated with the disbursement of aid money to localized programs by large bureaucracies such as USAID. There is always the danger that the overheads inherent in these government organizations will absorb a significant proportion of the funds dedicated towards a debt exchange program. Moreover, decisions to fund (or not to fund) a particular project may be based on internal procedures not necessarily relevant to the proposal. Indeed, USAID has been criticized by both President George W. Bush and Senator Jesse Helms, and there have been recent calls for it to be abolished and replaced by a smaller and more streamlined quasi-governmental foundation. There are no plans at the moment for this proposal to be implemented, and it is not clear in any event whether and to what extent this would affect official United States policy regarding the funding of future debt exchanges.

Notwithstanding any uncertainties regarding the future of USAID funding for debt exchanges, the transactions with which it has been involved have been important, particularly by emphasizing funding and education of indigenous people in protected areas, as well as taking advantage of their particular skills and knowledge in capacities such as park rangers. The incorporation into the debt exchange mechanism of procedures for the education and training of local indigenous people is one way of promoting local community involvement, which may lead to more long-term and sustainable modes of development.

Enterprise for the Americas Initiative Act of 1990

In June 1990, following a meeting with various South American leaders at the Andean Summit, President George W.H. Bush first proposed the Enterprise for the Americas Initiative as a comprehensive plan to stimulate economic growth and reduce trade barriers in the Western Hemisphere. The proposal revolved around three 'pillars'—increased capital investment in Latin American and Caribbean countries, a proposed Free Trade Zone and debt reduction—and was intended to demonstrate to Latin American democracies that they would not be ignored in favor of Eastern Europe.

Although it was primarily designed to stimulate growth and free trade, the debt reduction aspects of the initiative were significant, with debt exchanges being formalized as an important component of United States policy for the region. The terms proposed further demonstrated the increasing acceptance and popularity of the debt exchange mechanism as applied to issues of environmental and development concern. In its final form, the Enterprise for the Americas Initiative Act (EAI) authorized the exchange of bilateral official United States debt for environmental protection programs in the relevant countries. This marked the first time that this type of United States government debt could be utilized in debt exchanges. Under the EAI, the United States agreed to reduce the loan principal of debt owed by eligible countries and allow interest to be paid (at concessionary rates) in local currency into a local environment fund, which would be used to finance appropriate programs.

The original proposal envisaged utilization of approximately US$5 billion of Latin American debt in debt exchanges (with another US$12 billion to be completely forgiven). In the end, as a result of intense political debate and negotiation in the period leading to the debt element of the program coming into law on 1st January 1991, Congress only agreed to a debt reduction of US$1.7 billion, representing the food assistance credits allowable under the Agricultural Trade Development Act (known as PL 480 debt) owed by EAI countries at the time. A 1992 amendment to the EAI expanded debt reduction by allowing the relevant debtor countries to purchase up to forty percent of Paris Club debt owed to the United States Agriculture Department at market price.

In order to qualify for EAI debt reduction, a country must meet certain eligibility criteria. These include 'significant progress' in establishing an open investment regime, which itself may require compliance with various World Bank or IMF macroeconomic requirements. Implementation of the EAI is by way of an Environmental Framework Agreement (EFA) between the United States and the relevant debtor country. The first EFA was signed between the United States and Chile on 27th June 1991—the first anniversary of the announcement of the initiative—and provided for the forgiveness of US$15.7 million of Chile's PL 480 debt in return for Chile allocating the interest payable on the remaining US$23.6 million of PL 480 debt towards the funding of local environmental projects. By 1993, Argentina, Bolivia, Colombia, El Salvador, Jamaica, Peru and Uruguay had also signed EFAs with the United States. These resulted in the conversion of US$875 million of debt into the local currency equivalent of US$154 million of environmental protection funding, at an overall cost to the United States Treasury of US$90 million.

Initiatives taken pursuant to the EAI have illustrated the interrelationship of a variety of broad international economic, development and financial policy issues with environmental concerns, and provided another method by which these could be incorporated into the debt exchange mechanism. They highlighted the need to consider all of these issues in tandem in light of the increasing concerns for global environmental and development issues. The program allowed for funding of a wide range of activities, from conservation to education, and from agriculture to sustainable development projects.

Due to changes in United States budget rules requiring costs incurred by the United States Treasury through the implementation of debt reduction schemes to be subject to prior appropriation in the United States budget, no EFAs have been signed since 1993. However, further amendments in 1998 facilitated a debt buy-back by Peru under the EAI. Under this form of debt exchange, Peru was able to repurchase in United States dollars fifty percent of its US$350 million debt to the United States at net present value (US$57 million). In return, Peru agreed to place the local currency equivalent of US$22 million (representing approximately forty percent of the purchase price) into a local environment fund.

The Tropical Forest Conservation Act of 1998

The Tropical Forest Conservation Act (TFC) was signed into law by President Clinton on 29th July 1998 and represents a further step in the evolution of the debt exchange mechanism. The TFC is intended to address problems relating to the inter-dependence between levels of external indebtedness and the continuing eradication of the world's tropical rain forests. It relieves developing countries of some of the costs associated with debt owed to the United States in exchange for a commitment on their part to allocate resources towards the preservation of their rain forests.

This legislation further reinforces the acceptance among major developed countries of the positive role that debt exchanges can play in alleviating issues of global concern. In its legislative findings relating to the TFC, Congress made specific reference to the role that tropical rain forests play in reducing greenhouse gases in the atmosphere. Even though the range of eligible conservation programs envisaged by the TFC is restricted—it applies only to activities relating to the conservation of rain forests—it is anticipated that its enactment will serve as a further spur towards more widespread use of the debt exchange mechanism in other circumstances as well. Furthermore, the use of the TFC structure might also become possible under the Kyoto Protocol, depending upon the future involvement (if any) of the United States within that agreement, as well as the specific provisions relating to 'carbon sinks' that are agreed under its regime.

Whilst the TFC is modelled on the EAI, it applies to any developing country with significant tropical rain forest resources, extending the range of countries beyond those within the terms of the EAI. This will give increased opportunities to some developing countries in Africa and Asia to participate in official debt exchange programs, giving them a greater understanding of the practical aspects of the mechanism, as well as its potential advantages and disadvantages. Depending upon their experiences in this regard, it may also serve to increase LDC, as well as developed country confidence and expertise in the debt exchange process, and thus expand further its potential for utilization in a wider range of projects, including those directed towards the achievement of sustainable development. As an example, Canada, Switzerland and Germany have entered into debt exchange arrangements with a number of debtor countries as a result of the success of earlier debt exchange experiences of those developing countries pursuant to agreements with the United States (under the GEPA and EAI).

The TFC provides directly for the protection of the rights of indigenous peoples and, like the EAI, encourages projects that include the involvement of local communities in planning and execution. It goes further than the EAI by facilitating funding specifically for the '[d]evelopment and support of the livelihoods of individuals living in or near a tropical forest in a manner consistent with protecting such tropical forests'.

In July 2001, the Bush Administration announced that it had successfully negotiated a US$14 million Debt-for-Forest swap with El Salvador under the provisions of the TFC. Under the arrangement, it was agreed that every dollar of debt relief would be exchanged for two dollars of local currency funding for tropical forest conservation. The Administration has also indicated that it was hoping to reach further TFC-mandated agreements with a number of other countries. Whilst these latest initiatives are, in part, intended to diffuse wider criticisms of the Bush Administration's policies on the environment – in particular its rejection in March 2001 of the Kyoto Protocol—they still represent positive developments in the formal application by the United States Government of the debt exchange mechanism to promote conservation and environmental goals.

In July 2001, the Bush Administration announced that it had successfully negotiated a US$14 million Debt-for-Forest swap with El Salvador under the provisions of the TFC.

The TFC provides for three types of debt exchange mechanism—debt reductions, debt buy—backs and debt swaps. This further demonstrates the scope for adaptability of the mechanism to apply to particular circumstances, and may well encourage other creative future uses of the mechanism in the areas of 'green' financing.

Industrialized Country and MDB Debt Relief Initiatives

In 1999, the leaders of the major G7 industrialized countries held their annual global summit meeting in Cologne and pledged to forgive the debts of at least 20 nations by the end of 2000. This pledge, however, remains unfulfilled largely due to the conditions imposed by the world's richest nations. However, seen in the context of an era of unprecedented prosperity among the industrialized nations and in response to intense lobbying by groups such as Jubilee 2000 and its successor organization Jubilee Plus, the issue of debt relief for the world's poorest countries had become a major political issue, particularly in Western Europe.

In addition, the World Bank and the IMF, partially in response to widespread criticism of their previous lending strategies and failure to address the problems of world poverty and increasing LDC debt, have embarked on their HIPC Initiative and have continued to review their funding policies in the context of increasing environmental and societal concerns. These actions have been developed with the support of the representatives of the major industrialized countries on the respective Boards of these institutions.

Concerns regarding levels of debt and the plight of the world's poorest countries have been exacerbated by the fact that the overall amount of direct foreign aid (DFA) to those countries, particularly from the United States, have been steadily falling during the 1990s. Indeed, it has been estimated that foreign aid to the poorest countries fell by nearly 25 percent during the latter part of the 1990s.

Moreover, according to figures produced by the United Nations, only 20 percent of foreign direct investment (FDI) in 2000, which totalled in excess of US$1.1 trillion, was directed to LDCs. Out of this portion, most was directed to twenty countries with already growing economies. In 1999, only 0.5 percent of FDI was directed towards the world's poorest countries.

In response to this situation, the United Nations instituted an advisory panel in late 2000 to examine and suggest ideas designed to help these countries. The major industrialized countries and MDBs, mindful of the lack of progress since the Cologne meeting and anxious to be seen to comply with their promises to coincide with the symbolism associated with the beginning of a new millennium, subsequently accelerated the process to announce debt relief proposals for twenty-two countries in late 2000. As part of these proposals, the United States has approved US$435 million of debt relief, which is fully financed by its 2001 budget.

Whilst it is beyond the scope of this paper to examine the overall levels of LDC debt and trends in FDI and DFA, it is important to note that many of these debt relief initiatives, like the Paris Club debt relief programs introduced in the early 1990s in Poland, are conditional upon the implementation, by the respective debtor countries, of projects designed to aid development. Indeed, the grant of debt relief by the G7 nations is contingent upon the debtor nation demonstrating that the money no longer used to repay debt is employed in 'constructive' ways, such as improving education, health care or economic development.

The imposition of conditions will delay—or in some cases even prevent—actual implementation of the debt relief programs. Yet many people, particularly in the debtor nations, believe that LDC debt crises have been produced by the western financial system. Others argue that much of the Latin American debt was incurred by illegal and illegitimate military dictatorships and that the funds provided were the subject of widespread fraud and corruption or were wasted on ineffective infrastructure projects. As a result, they argue that the debt associated with these projects should be unconditionally forgiven by creditors, since no tangible benefits were received by the majority of people in the particular LDC. Traditionally these views have contrasted with that of the United States, whose creditor banks have worried about the 'moral hazard' associated with unconditional debt forgiveness and do not want to promote any perception that international debt obligations are not legally binding. The European and Japanese approach advocates a partial debt forgiveness program contingent on rigorous selection criteria.

There are doubtless merits associated with each of these viewpoints. Indeed, it has been suggested that the implementation of unconditional large-scale debt forgiveness programs could also bring some advantages to industrialized economies in the form of increased employment and capacity in their export-oriented industries and various financial and political advantages arising from greater international harmony.

However, it seems that, at least for the foreseeable future, a significant proportion of large-scale debt relief initiatives will involve an element of 'conditionality'. As such, they represent a further extension of the debt exchange mechanism—designed to swap external (and foreign currency denominated) debt into pre-agreed local currency funded development projects. Assuming that these conditions are not unrealistic or, in practice, unattainable by debtor nations, the implementation of these programs highlights how the debt exchange mechanism can continue to play an ever increasingly significant role in the overall development of LDCs. The further involvement of increasing numbers of industrialized countries, perhaps also in conjunction with institutions such as the World Bank acting in the role as a 'broker' or a 'clearing house', adds another dimension to the potential of applying the debt exchange mechanism towards the attainment of sustainable development...

10

Privatization and Environmental Law

A

Richardson B., "Changing Regulatory Spaces: The Privatisation of New Zealand Environmental Law," in Richardson B., *Environmental Justice and Market Mechanisms*, Kluwer International, Netherlands, 1999, pp 209–214

Environmental Justice and Economic Policy

Economic deregulation and market-based mechanisms are transforming the regulatory space of environmental law in New Zealand. These institutional changes, and their impact on environmental justice, are the subject of this chapter. The 'regulatory space' is the institutions and processes by which environmental policies are developed and executed. Important features of such spaces are citizen participation procedures (e.g., submissions and public hearings), generation and exchange of information (e.g., environmental impact assessments), environmental standard-setting and dispute resolution processes. Environmental justice considerations permeate these spaces, especially in relation to procedural rights for participation, social redistribution questions concerning the benefits and costs of resource use, and the conceptualization of human relationships with nature. The privatization of environmental law signifies the way *public* decision processes are eroding under the influence of property rights doctrines, market devolution and commercial imperatives. While economic deregulation reforms may promote consumer sovereignty, it is argued that consumer accountability is not a proper substitute for political accountability in decision making. The normative-generating capacity of civil society has increasingly diminished in a post-modern world characterized by more information but less meaning. If ethical positions to frame our relationships with one another and nature are to be cultivated, they will at least require non-market institutional spaces that are capable of housing and projecting this ethical dialogue.

In New Zealand, tensions persist between economic deregulation and maintenance of a resource management system established to contain ecological damage and social protest. Since 1984, Conservative and Labour parties in New Zealand government have pursued a program of regulatory, economic and administrative reform unique in the nation's history. The reforms were engendered by a belief that the country's growing fiscal and budgetary dilemmas could be solved only by a comprehensive shift toward a market-oriented and internationally outward economy. This shift would entail a curtailment of government involvement in many areas of economic and social policy, with the result that various State assets and services were corporatized or privatized, and government authorities reduced in size and function. Somewhat incongruously, amidst this neo-conservative avalanche, a program of reform of environmental institutions that began in the late 1980s envisaged enhanced State involvement in environmental policy. This incongruity is now starting to unravel in a way that makes New Zealand a salient example of how environmental law might function in the context of economic deregulation.

Ever since the State in Western society became recognized as an agent for economic development, the generation of abundance has become the primary foundation of political legitimacy. The rise of the modern capitalist economy has concurrently spawned a more heterogeneous and potentially discordant society that finds its expression in an impersonal system of needs or consumer culture. The ability of the State successfully to manage this discordant culture is a further basis for its legitimacy. The environmental *sequelae* of economic growth, however, in turn have promoted social conflict over the distribution of the costs and benefits of this growth in a way that now threatens to trap the State between seemingly incompatible economic and environmental objectives. The potential 'injustices' of market activity that fuel this conflict include the externalities or 'spillover' effects on third parties, and the discounting of the interests of posterity that are not participants in current market transactions. Environmental effects and risks are not evenly spread and unforeseen effects may be irreversible. Government policy options to address these issues are highly constrained by the market economy because of the privileged position held by capital as the perceived wealth and revenue generator. This is particularly so in New Zealand, a small economy heavily integrated into an international framework, dominated by transnational capital, over which New Zealand governments have limited leverage.

The emergence of 'sustainable development' doctrines can be conceived as an attempt to reconcile the potential contradiction between protecting the environment whilst respecting capital's desire for autonomy in production decisions. Economic instruments such as taxes and traceable permits have been increasingly identified as an important means for giving operational effect to sustainability. Concepts such as 'polluter pays' and 'internalization of environmental costs' now permeate government policies. Economic instruments were introduced in Western societies as an 'alternative' to administrative regulation, condemned for its rigidities, inefficiencies and distortion by sectional interests. The use of economic instruments can be conceptualized as an attempt to change the State from a 'commander' to a 'steerer', or 'facilitator', in which the marketplace is structured to allow private enterprise to further public policy goals. A vital question is whether sustainability doctrines and economic tools can resolve these structural tensions in State decision making, and allow for both efficient economic development while accommodating ecological protection and environmental justice.

Economic instruments such as taxes and traceable permits have been increasingly identified as an important means for giving operational effect to sustainability.

In New Zealand, the foundational *Resource Management Act* (RMA) 1991 promotes 'sustainable management' as its guiding principle, and incorporates a range of regulatory, planning and economic tools. Through sustainability, the Act aims to achieve integrated resource management that encompasses biophysical, social and economic issues. The RMA was introduced after an extensive public consultation process that reflected a certain desire to ensure that the new regime would provide for comprehensive citizen participation in environmental planning and development control processes, that were now to be substantially decentralized to local councils. This participation would be ensured, for example, through rights to make submissions and objections in relation to proposed plans/policies and resource consent applications, participation rights in public inquiries and greater access to the courts to challenge inappropriate decisions. The exercise of governmental discretionary powers would also be constrained by the core environmental policy principles (RMA, ss. 5-8). Similar public consultation processes were embodied in other environmental laws.

The RMA decision processes do not, however, fundamentally challenge the hegemonic paradigm of economic development. Despite the different interests that sought to influence the design of the RMA during its preparation, the legislation can be understood essentially as a strategy to minimize the risk to capital from social protest or excessive environmental damage. The capitalist State's implicit hostility to citizen collective self-action and protest has inspired the enactment of legislative charters such as the RMA to *channel* environmental concerns into formalized, administrative structures wherein they can be contained and neutralized. Environmental law invites and authorizes citizens to advance their interests through participation in the prescribed planning and development controls, yet carefully regulates and blunts their expression. Participation tends to be confined to the terms of development activity, rather than the overall justification for economic development *per se.* In this sense, environmental law may serve to legitimate and reinforce capital's consumption of the environment. If environmental law is to truly challenge the dynamics of capital, it will need to penetrate the more fundamental bases of economic decision making such as international trade policy, financial lending practices, and gross domestic product accounting.

The problem for the State with public participation processes, however, is that they can be costly to administer and costly to developers incurring delayed resource use approvals. In particular, financing the costs of Maori involvement in RMA implementation has become much more onerous, and controversial. These concerns about escalating 'compliance costs' have extended to other domains including the *Fisheries Act* 1996. In an era of shrinking public budgets and economic recession, governments are searching for more efficient environmental regimes that promise both 'taking account of community interests' while respecting private property rights and economic growth imperatives. Economic instruments harnessing market-determined consumer preferences may be appealing for their ability to circumvent the problems posed by the declining efficacy of traditional liberal-democratic institutions." Thus, the Ministry for the Environment, an earlier opponent of economic instruments, has shown an unexpected new interest in these tools.

Ubiquitous references to economic instruments now appear in the Ministry's seminal 'Environment 2010 Strategy'. Although the 1995 Strategy is a general policy document of no legal standing, it is a key barometer of changing government thinking. Five out of the Strategy's ten guiding principles refer to economic concepts or tools, including 'internalization of external environmental costs' (principle 4); 'sustainable property rights' (principle 5); 'least cost policy tools' (principle 6); full cost 'pricing of infrastructure' (principle 8). Social equity and public participation are referenced relatively infrequently in the Strategy.

The growing drive to incorporate market-based and commercially oriented approaches in resource management is being achieved principally through:

- corporatization and privatization of environmentally significant assets and services;
- 'user pays' and related cost internalization mechanisms, such as in relation to electricity, water supplies and road transport;
- traceable resource use rights such as in relation to water and marine fisheries;
- business self-regulation and voluntary agreements.

Among local councils, there has been less interest in economic instruments, causing a growing friction between central and local government. Although the decentralization of decision making powers to local authorities under the RMA was initially perceived as consistent with the imperatives of economic deregulation, there was a failure among reformers to appreciate that local authorities are equally susceptible to bureaucratic pathologies that can stifle policy innovation and efficient administration. Developers have expressed concern about the apparently high costs and excessive information requirements for resource consent approvals, and the consequential impacts on economic enterprise. Escalating council regulation is viewed by some as incongruous with the RMA's presumption in section 9 that landholders may freely use their land unless there is a contrary rule in a relevant local plan (in which case a resource consent may be needed). This key section reflects the traditional Blackstonian view about the primacy of private property rights and the recent resurgence in many countries of private rights doctrines. In a consultancy report to the Ministry for the Environment [prepared by Pavletich and McShane], councils are accused of perpetuating the 'old planning paradigm':

> "...few, if any councils employ economists, and yet their planners pontificate on economic matters with total confidence. Even those councils which have sought economic advice on their Plans, or heard extensive submissions from the Ministry of Commerce have had that advice dismissed almost out of hand by their internal planning staff."

The Ministry has itself conceded, following the 1997 Annual Survey of Local Authorities, that there are deficiencies in local council performance that may need to be remedied through amendments to the RMA. The criticisms have not been confined to the RMA regime, and the New Zealand Business Roundtable (a leading corporate lobby group [in a report by Kerr]) has savaged the Department of Conservation for its 'environmental socialism'. Concerns with the RMA led the Minister for the Environment in early 1998 to commission consultant Owen McShane to prepare 'a think piece designed to debate extent to which regulatory control of land is justified under the Resource Management Act'. According to the 'McShane Report', as it is known:

> "[t]here is almost universal agreement that the direct costs of compliance are too high while the holding and opportunity costs are now so great as to be seriously hindering both economic and employment growth."

Blame is laid on councils for imposing excessive land use restrictions based on 'trendy' models of social and economic planning, or on idiosyncratic aesthetic preferences. The report's recommendations include adoption of a US-style 'takings' doctrine to oblige councils to compensate landowners unduly affected by regulation, and the introduction of competitive resource consent processing by either public or private bodies.

Although the McShane report has been derided for its shoddy methodology, ideological assumptions and unworkable suggestions, the government has since moved to draft amendments to the RMA to give effect to some of its controversial proposals. This reform process has also been influenced by the report of the Ministerial Environment's Reference Group. The proposed statutory amendments include limiting appeals to the Environment Court to points of law and allowing development applicants to choose government appointed commissioners rather than elected council representatives to hear their applications. Many community environmental groups have strenuously resisted the amendments.

Using market forces as a means of environmental policy may entail substituting our private 'consumer' preferences for our public 'citizen' preferences. Sagoff argued that the preferences we may hold in the marketplace are often quite different to those we may hold as citizens participating in the political process. Although economic analyses may assist decision makers by assigning prices to the values and beliefs that citizens articulate in political fore, it is inappropriate that such analyses should be determinative. It may be useful to use contingent valuation and travel cost studies or other surrogate market approaches to price our environmental preferences for the purpose of formulating eco-taxes and 'user pays' charges. However, incorporating these approaches into policy decisions may result in what Tribe described as the 'squeezing out "soft" but crucial information merely because it seems difficult to render commensurable with the "hard" data in the problem'. Asking how much a community is willing to pay for a specific environmental good may reflect the intensity of their preferences, but not their merits. The consumer sovereignty promised by economic tools such as 'user pays' pricing may allow for greater 'choice' (e.g., to purchase or not to purchase), but it is choice within the language and structure of the marketplace. Whilst economic instruments can help correct market failures in addressing environmental costs, they also facilitate the utilitarian tendency to crudely capitalize nature as an additional component of production and consumption.

The problem now, however, is that the relativism and nihilism of our pervasive postmodernist consumer culture may emasculate attempts to project theories of environmental justice and purposeful citizen action that require a restoration of belief in grand narratives. Postmodernism denies that law or other institutions can yield a stable and shared set of understandings to govern action since the poststructuralist analysis of language suggests that all is culturally mediated and there is no way of independently and objectively ascertaining an underlying reality. In contrast to the Modernist belief that language can 'mime' or refer to an underlying reality, Derrida argued that all we can examine are the language structures that purport to represent 'truth'. The signified can thus lapse into another signifier, creating an infinite chain of meanings with no fixed and stable destination. To forge a critical *ecological* legal narrative requires a multilateral strategy that aims to nurture market-insulated spaces that can allow for citizen dialogue and the exploration of new constitutional norms that are capable of being culturally sustained. Additionally, at a strategy level, the importation of economic theory into environmental law must be matched by taking ecological principles into commercial and financial policy making. By targeting company law, insurance law, lender liability and insolvency law, for example, environmental lawyers may achieve a much greater impact on the underlying structure of economic decision-making which controls *access to* capital, before contentious developments ever reach the RMA or other decision processes.

11

Foreign Investment and the Role of Multinational Corporations

A

Sornarajah M., "Foreign Investment and International Environmental Law," in Lin Sun and Kurukulasuriya L. (eds), *UNEP's New Way Forward: Environmental Law and Sustainable Development*, UNEP, Nairobi, pp 283–297

Foreign investment has been a chosen path towards economic development in many countries of the world. States in Asia, Eastern Europe, Latin America and Africa have now devised policies which have considerably liberalized legislation on foreign investment in the hope that the influx of foreign capital will engineer economic growth in their countries. Whether the rapid economic development which is desired through such foreign investment will accord with the concept of sustainable development articulated in international environmental law remains unclear. If a schism develops between the objectives of foreign investment and the goals of sustainable development, the ideals of international environmental law will suffer. Hence, techniques will have to be developed to ensure that the notion of sustainable development is the objective behind attracting foreign investment into developing countries.

An effort is made in this paper to indicate what has been achieved so far towards ensuring that sustainable development is achieved through foreign investment, and what remains to be done in the future to ensure that foreign investment does not deviate from the goals of sustainable development in the host States in which it operates.

The paper points out that existing controls over multinational corporations in international environmental law are predominantly of the "soft law" type and therefore much too weak to be effective. Nevertheless, a number of promising principles are emerging including the duty to disclose toxic emissions data, the requirement to carry out environmental impact studies prior to commencing activities and a growing recognition of the liability of the parent company for the environmentally damaging activities of its subsidiary.

The argument put forward is that if foreign investment is to promote, or at any rate not compromise, sustainable development in the host State, there must be further development of international environmental law towards controlling these activities. This would involve creating a duty on the home State of the multinational to impose liability on those multinationals which cause environmental harm abroad and the further development of the concept of an international crime for activities which cause serious environmental harm, thus enabling enforcement action to be taken under general principles on international law.

Existing Controls Over Multinational Corporations in International Environmental Law

Control systems in the law require sanctions for effectiveness. It is generally accepted that absence of sanctions in international law constitute the major weakness in international law. Environmental law, as the newest branch of international law, also has the least experience with enforcement mechanisms. The problem of compliance presents an acute problem to international environmental law, as many of its propositions are formulated as soft law propositions. The controls of international environmental law over multinational corporations are based largely on soft law. In the face of the perceived financial might of multinational corporations, the strength of these controls as existing prescription of international environmental law, the genesis of an idea of responsibility for environmental harm caused by multinational corporations in the course of their foreign investment operations. The future establishment of a more meaningful regime of control is dependent on the isolation and development of these rudimentary concepts. The idea of control involves norms which recognize the existence of wrongs, liability for wrongs and remedies for such wrongs. However, what one finds principally in international environmental law are prescriptions as to good environmental behavior made through instruments of soft law. When it comes to the field of foreign investment, the soft law prescriptions are more dominant because of the inherently controversial nature of the principles relating to foreign investment in international law. The problem falls at the interstices of two weak areas of international law. International investment law is weak because of disagreements between developed and developing countries as to what its principles should be and the prescriptions continue to be couched in non-binding, soft instruments like codes of conduct. One finds that the legal emphasis and effort are more on the formulation of codes of conduct and of precautionary principles preventing environmental harm than on the formulation of rules of recognition of liability. These developments may, however, be a prelude to the emergence of a regime of control and cannot be dismissed as having no relevance. These formulations in the codes of conduct and precautionary principles can be examined before looking at what the future evolution of the law should be.

Codes of Conduct

Codes of Conduct are usually made in areas where there is no agreement that the breach of a principle will result in liability. It has been difficult to find agreement among States as to what propositions should go into a binding code. A binding code of conduct was attempted by the now defunct United Nations Centre for Transnational Corporations (UNCTC) but the disagreement on it among the different groupings of States was such that the venture had to be abandoned. Business has generally preferred a voluntary approach to the issue of environmental protection and has strenuously resisted binding codes. The OECD has a non-binding code of conduct for multinational corporations. These instruments have prescriptions as to how multinational corporations should conduct themselves in relation to the environment of their host States. However, since one of them did not leave the draft stage and the other is non-binding the principles they give rise to have only ethical significance at best. The OECD Guidelines merely refer to a precautionary principle and do not involve the contemplation of any liability for non-observance. These Guidelines require multinational corporations to:

> "Assess and take into account in decision-making, foreseeable environmental and environmentally related health consequences of their activities, including siting decisions, impact on indigenous natural resources and foreseeable environmental and environmentally related health risks of products as well as from the generation, transport and disposal of waste."

Though the formulation addresses the issue of multinational corporations being the vehicles for the export of hazardous processes or technologies, they merely require these corporations to assess and take into account their capacity for harm. Such weak prescriptions in non-binding codes are admonitory at best and have little legal significance. The hope is sometimes expressed that these admonitions will come to be adopted later in more specific instruments in more strict language of obligation and that when an accumulation of such prescriptions comes about, it may be possible for decision making bodies to convert them into law.

The formulation in the UNCTC's draft Code of Conduct on Transnational Corporations had more definite prescriptions relating to the conduct of multinational corporations in host States. The code did not become effective and activity relating to it has ceased. Yet, there was little disagreement as to the provisions on the environment and their acceptance can be read as evincing international community support for the norms relating to the environment contained in the draft code. The three provisions on the environment read as follows:

> "43. Transnational corporations shall carry out their activities in accordance with it national laws, regulations, established administrative practices and policies relating to the preservation of the environment of the countries in which they operate and with due regard to relevant international standards. Transnational corporations should, in performing their activities, take steps to protect the environment and where damaged to rehabilitate it and should make efforts to be develop and apply adequate technologies for this purpose.
>
> 44. Transnational corporations shall, in respect of the products, processes and services they have introduced or propose to introduce in any country, supply to the competent authorities of that country on request or on a regular basis, as specified by these authorities, all relevant information concerning:
>
> - Characteristics of these products, processes and other activities including non experimental uses and related aspects which may harm the environment and the measures and costs necessary to avoid or at least mitigate their harmful effects;
> - Prohibitions, restrictions, warnings and other public regulatory measures imposed in other countries on grounds of protection of the environment on these products, processes and services.
>
> 45. Transnational corporations should be responsive to requests from Governments of the countries in which they operate and be prepared where appropriate to cooperate with international organizations in their efforts to develop and promote national and international standards for the protection of the environment."

The code contains the genesis of principles of liability and does not depend entirely on preventive principles. It requires the multinational corporation to repair the environmental harm it may cause to the host economy. It also requires the multinational corporation to report the laws used by other States, including the home State, to control the type of foreign investment proposed so that the same types of regulatory framework could be introduced by the host State. Also, since the multinational corporation would know the regulations in its home State and reporting of these are required, the host State would be put on guard that the multinational corporation is seeking entry in order to escape from the more stringent environmental standards in the home State. This will put the host State on guard as to the environmental hazards involved in the foreign investment. The reporting provision will ensure that all potential host States will have similar regulations so that competition in the use of laxer environmental standards as a means of attracting foreign investment could be avoided. These meaningful principles were unfortunately not in a final document which would have carried authority. Yet, these principles do have weight, as reflecting the desires of many States which participated in the draining of the code of conduct.

Formulation of Preventive Principles

It has been easier to formulate precautionary principles in the area as they do not initially create any liability. However, as the law gathers in strength, the failure to take precautions will entail liability and hence, these formulations will have significance to the development of the law. Again, initially, most of the precautions that were required were to be voluntarily undertaken by the corporations. The principles that are coming to be established may be looked at.

Duty to Disclose Toxic Emission Data

The major environmental hazards caused by multinational corporations, like the Bhopal and the Seveso disasters, have involved toxic emissions. In many countries, including some industrialized countries, there is no specific recognition of a duty on the part of a manufacturing corporation to disclose the extent of the pollution it generates. In many developing States, such legislation is nonexistent.

The standardization of practices relating to the duty of disclosure is much desired. *Agenda 21* endorses such a standardization of requirements of disclosure. Uniformity in disclosure requirements among developing countries will ensure that one is not favored over the other for purposes of investment entry on the basis of lower environmental standards. Though law making through general principles has generally been confined to principles evolved through precedent, there is no reason why a proposition which is supported uniformly in the legislation of the different States of the world should not be regarded as a general principle of law giving rise to a principle of international law as a result of such generality of acceptance. The recognition of such a duty of disclosure could give rise eventually to liability principles based on the failure to fulfil the duty.

The Requirement to Conduct Environmental Impact Studies

The law of many host States has now made it a requirement that foreign investment seeking entry into the host State should conduct a study as to how its operations will affect the host environment. Since the theory of foreign investment is that it would be beneficial to the host economy, this benefit may be illusory if the environmental costs of the operation of the foreign investor would have to be met by the host economy. The requirement of an environmental impact study would make the assessment of the benefits of the foreign investment meaningful. Under the law of the People's Republic of China, to take an example, the usual method of entry of foreign investment is through a joint venture with a local partner. However, entry is screened through administrative agencies which require the making of environmental impact studies as well as other feasibility studies to determine the extent to which the entry of the particular foreign investment would be beneficial to China. This position generally prevails in the foreign investment laws of Asia. Malaysia, the State in which the Langkawi Declaration on Environment was made by the Commonwealth Heads of States in 1989, has strong laws on environmental protection. These laws have an impact on the planning and implementation of projects by the foreign investor. The law requires that the building of any plant or structure must be preceded by an environmental impact report. The measures that should be taken to avoid any adverse impact must be indicated in the report. The report has to be approved by the Director General of the Department of Environment. The measures indicated in the report as well as any others which the Director may impose will have to be implemented. The project may be revoked or licenses connected with it may be canceled if there is no compliance with the requirements. To varying degrees, other Asian States require the conducting of environmental impact studies of the potential effects of the operations of the multinational corporation and its foreign investment projects prior to entry.

The requirement of an environmental impact study would make the assessment of the benefits of the foreign investment meaningful.

The major lending organizations of the world, like the World Bank, the Asian Development Bank, the African Development Bank, the European Bank for Reconstruction and Development and the Inter-American Development Bank, have instituted the practice of making environmental impact assessments prior to lending for projects involving foreign investments as well as other development projects. There are recommendations that commercial banks should also follow this practice. The institutional banks have commenced this practice in recognition of the fact that widespread harm has been caused by the failure to take into consideration the environmental impact of investment projects. Though the practices of these banks are different, there is uniformity in the requirement of making the prior environmental assessment as a condition of the loan. There could be provision for the monitoring of the progress of the project. Such a technique involves a meaningful sanction in that where there is a failure to comply with the requirements, the loan could be canceled. The monitoring of the project throughout its cycle by the lending institution may become the normal practice in the future.

The practice of making environmental assessments prior to permitting entry for foreign investments is now well entrenched in legal systems. There is an onus on the foreign investor to make full disclosure of the techniques and methods of his manufacturing and other processes. The making of fraudulent disclosures or the using of other techniques later will have legal consequences and can be the basis for the justifiable withdrawal of the operating permit for the foreign investment.

The Recognition of the Liability of the Parent Company

The law is now working towards the recognition of the liability of the parent company for the environmental damages caused by a subsidiary in a host State. The principles have not been clearly established as yet, but the subject of the parent company's tortious liability is evolving in many different legal systems, not only in respect to environmental harm but also in respect to harm caused by circulation of hazardous products (product liability). In the United States, the courts recognize the liability of parent companies for harm generated by subsidiaries. In the Bhopal litigation, the liability of the parent company was recognized though the Indian courts were regarded as the better fore for the litigation. In the Irrigation concerning oil spills by Amoco Cadiz off the French coast, an American court stated the principle of liability in the following terms:

> "As an integrated multinational corporation which is engaged through a system of subsidiaries in the exploration, production, refining, transportation and sale of petroleum products throughout the world, Standard is responsible for the tortious acts of its wholly owned subsidiaries and instrumentalities, AIOC and Transport."

In varying degrees, the notion of enterprise liability is coming to be recognized in most legal systems. The strengthening of this emergent trend towards parent liability for environmental harm caused in host countries is an important aspect of developing meaningful international environmental law in the direction of sustainable development.

A Prognosis of Future Trends

Generally, international law has not been concerned with liability which takes place within States on the grounds that it falls outside its province. It has generally been concerned with liability for transfrontier pollution. In circumstances of such environmental damage, there is liability in the domestic law of the place where these disasters took place but, often, this would be generally insufficient either because of the lack of sophistication of the local legal system or the subsidiary responsible for the harm did not have sufficient funds to pay damages. Suing the parent company in its home State also becomes difficult because of doctrines like *forum non conveniens* which require that the litigation should be brought before the courts in the more convenient jurisdiction where the incident took place and where the witnesses are available. In regard to the further development of international environmental law in this era, these issues require further examination.

A Duty on the Part of the Home States to Impose Liability on their Multinational Corporations which Cause Environmental Harm Abroad

The home States of foreign investors have always claimed the right of diplomatic protection of foreign investment which leaves their shores. Multinational corporations have relied on the diplomatic protection of the home State to ensure safety for their investments and intervention in times when they face disputes with host States. There is a duty implicit in this power of protection in that the exercise of the power is possible only to the extent that the foreign investor had acted in a manner consistent with his corporate duties in the host State. Where the foreign investor had acted to the detriment of the host State, the power of his home State to intervene on his behalf would diminish correspondingly. The recognition of the duty of good corporate citizenship on the part of the foreign investor has now become the basis on which protection can be given by the home State to its multinational corporations. It is in recognition of this fact that home States have sought to ensure that multinational corporations act in accordance with an international public policy in their operations. The United States, for example, seeks to ensure that its multinational corporations do not engage in corrupt practices while conducting business abroad. The use of extraterritoriality for these purposes is recognized by American courts.

The same situation exists in the case of environmental protection. The growth of an international environmental law creates an international public policy to ensure that a multinational corporation headquartered within its State does not harm the environment of the host State in which it operates through a subsidiary. This duty is obvious in the case of some activities such as the export of hazardous substances where conventions and customary principles may exist preventing such export. It is less clear in the case of other types of environmental harm. However, such a duty has been stated in international declarations which require that States recognize liability for environmental harm. It can also find support from international law which is moving towards the recognition of the fact that the global environment constitutes one whole and that environmental harm that occurs within another State's territory is a matter of international concern.

The *Rio Declaration* contains seeds of such a view of universal liability for environmental harm. Developed countries, which are the homes of multinational corporations have "acknowledged the responsibility they bear in the international pursuit of sustainable development". There is a specific duty on States to use their national laws in recognizing liability for environmental harm and enforcing such liability. Principle 13 of the *Rio Declaration* reads:

> "States shall develop national law regarding liability and compensation for the victims of pollution and other environmental damage. States shall also cooperate to develop further international law regarding liability and compensation for adverse effects of environmental damage caused by activities within their jurisdiction or control to areas beyond their control."

There is a clear requirement in the Declaration to recognize liability for environmental harm wherever it occurs. The Declaration also mandates that a State which has control over the situation should seek to prevent environmental harm. The home State exerts control over its multinational corporations for various purposes. The principle of nationality permits control over the multinational corporation through the fact that those who control the activities of the subsidiaries are nationals of the home State or are resident within it.

Jurisdictional Principles Relating to the Imposition of Liability

Though in international law the territoriality principle of jurisdiction is the most used basis of jurisdiction, it is increasingly becoming accepted that there are other bases o jurisdiction upon which domestic courts could enforce liability. The nationality jurisdiction has generally been accepted as a basis of jurisdiction and can be used to establish jurisdiction of the home State courts over their multinational corporations. The effects doctrine is an aspect of the territoriality principle of jurisdiction in that, courts have claimed that they can exercise jurisdiction over acts taking place abroad but intended to have effects within their own country. The effects doctrine has met pith some resistance from other States but with its espousal by the European Community courts, it is likely that it will receive wider acceptance. Despite the innovative uses to which it could be put, the use of the effects doctrine in the environmental area is limited, as it would be difficult to prove that environmental harm abroad was intended to have an effect within a country whose courts are willing to use the doctrine.

More promising, is the idea that another intermediate category of jurisdiction, which stands between the effects doctrine and the universality principle of jurisdiction, is developing, which caters to situations of obtaining jurisdiction over environmental harm committed within the territory of another country. This intermediate category includes terrorism, hijacking, smuggling of narcotics and possibly money laundering. In the case of these crimes, there is authority building up that a State could exercise jurisdiction, and indeed, has a duty to exercise jurisdiction, provided it finds the offender within its jurisdiction or has the link of nationality with the offender despite the fact that the crime was committed outside the jurisdiction of the State. There is sufficient authority building up to warrant the inclusion of the causing of environmental harm in this list.

Environmental Harm and International Crime

It has been pointed out that States which seek to confer diplomatic protection upon foreign investors have a duty to ensure that foreign investors conduct themselves in accordance with internationally accepted norms of conduct.

Evidence is mounting that the causing of serious environmental harm could be, in certain cases, an international crime. The imposition of criminal liability on domestic corporations under domestic law for environmental harm is now well recognized. Novel theories have been adopted for imposing such responsibility on parent corporations for environmental harm caused by subsidiaries under domestic law. The proposition is that similar principles are evolving in international law and that this process should be accelerated.

Firstly, there is sufficient articulation of the community interest in extending jurisdiction in the case of environmental harm beyond territorial limits. A conference of the European Ministers of Justice has recognized; the need for wider principles of criminal jurisdiction than those which exist at present to contend with the problem of environmental pollution. The Organization of African Unity in its *Resolution on the Dumping of Nuclear and Industrial Wastes in Africa* declared such dumping to be a crime against the African people and required multinational corporations responsible for such dumping to clean up the affected areas. The *ASEAN Agreement on the Conservation of Nature and Natural Resources* also urges the acceptance of responsibility of the originator of the activity which may lead to environmental degradation.

There is also the recognition of a legal obligation not to degrade the environment and State responsibility for environmental harm. As indicated above, Article 13 of the *Rio Declaration* recognizes the need to create principles recognizing liability for environmental harm. One of the most important developments in the area is the inclusion of environmental harm in the list of international crimes in the *Draft Code of Crimes Against the Peace and Security of Mankind* by the International Law Commission, in which international crimes are defined in Article 19(2) in the following terms:

> "An internationally wrongful act which results from the breach by a State of an international obligation so essential for the protection of the fundamental interests of the international community that its breach is recognized as a crime by that community as a whole constitutes an international crime."

After defining an international crime, the Article lists four crimes as examples of international crimes. The fourth relates to the environment, and states that:

> "It is a serious breach of an international obligation of essential importance for the safeguarding and preservation of the human environment, such as those prohibiting massive pollution of the atmosphere or of the seas."

Since the International Law Commission states that its concept of international crimes is based on rules of international law already in force and since the concept is dependent on the violation of fundamental principles of international law, it may be concluded that the International Law Commission was prepared to hold that there existed sufficient grounds for regarding the causing of serious environmental harm as involving violations of fundamental principles of international law. The *Draft Code* contemplates both the criminal responsibility of the State as well as of individuals. It furnishes additional authority for the argument that the causing of environmental harm falls within the intermediate category of jurisdiction, which should be exercised over the person who caused the harm if he is in the State's jurisdiction or has a nexus with that jurisdiction, wherever that harm had been caused.

Duty on the Courts which have Jurisdiction over the Parent Corporation

It has been pointed out that States which seek to confer diplomatic protection upon foreign investors have a duty to ensure that foreign investors conduct themselves in accordance with internationally accepted norms of conduct. Where there is a failure to abide by these norms, the right of diplomatic protection diminishes correspondingly. The internationally accepted norms include the duty of the transnational corporation to comply with the laws of the host State, including its environmental laws. This is applicable particularly in the case of States which have claimed it. Writing in the context of State responsibility for the marine environment, Smith has observed:

> "The legal authority of the state does not, however, end at its borders; each state possesses a measure of extraterritorial prescriptive legal authority, most clearly, for example, over its own nationals. A state performing with due diligence should logically be required to exercise such jurisdiction to proscribe for its nationals extraterritorial conduct which, if the state were the actor, would violate international law. Two points support this conclusion. First, the prescription itself may prevent such conflict. Thus, if a causal connection can be established, state responsibility and a consequential obligation to compensate should arise for a failure to exercise such authority. Moreover, it is only through the enforcement of such extraterritorial prescription that the state may fulfill the complementary due diligence obligation of punishment."

A similar argument is stated in a [1992] work [by the editors of the *Harvard Law Review*] as follows:

> "If the conduct of private parties is in question, principles of international jurisprudence require states to exercise "due diligence" to prevent conduct that, if performed by the state, would breach its primary international duties.... If a state exercises due care but private parties within its jurisdiction or control nonetheless inflict substantial harm upon the environment of another state, the source state must take all necessary steps to punish the offenders. Otherwise, the polluting conduct may be attributed to the state."

These contemporary developments in the field of foreign investment and international environmental law are a clear manifestation of the progressive development of this branch of international law in the direction of sustainable development.

12

Questions for Discussion

(a) Discuss the meaning of "green accounting". How does it differ from the more traditional approaches? What barriers and impediments are there to the development of "green accounting" as a basis for financing sustainable development in your jurisdiction?

(b) Critically evaluate the proposal by Okihiro Oogai and Akira Tanaka for an Asia-Pacific Environmental Facility. Include in your discussion the key features of the operation of the GEF and how you would modify them for the Asia-Pacific region.

(c) Is "green conditionality" for financing and aid to developing countries ever justified or is it another form of colonialism?

(d) Discuss the operation of the multilateral fund under the *Biodiversity Convention* and the GEF and its adequacy to assist developing countries with their obligations under the convention.

(e) Discuss the concepts of additionality and the provision of incremental costs. Are these approaches, and the amount of funding currently available for development initiatives, in developing countries adequate to break the cycle of poverty? Are there other measures that are needed as well?

(f) "The World Bank has come a long way in the last twenty years in developing environmental policies and environmental assessment approaches. This has been critical given the interface between international financing and global sustainable development initiatives. However, some commentators still argue that these changes result in new processes, but the majority of World Bank activities still support the old paradigm of environmentally exploitative major project development." Discuss.

(g) The use of debt swaps for conservation purposes provided a visionary example of how a relatively small amount of money could be leveraged for a considerable amount of conservation in poorer countries. However, the early debt swaps were mainly for small amounts, initiated by NGOs (such as Conservation International) and were mainly directed at the preservation of nature. There were many unintended side effects such as the effects on indigenous and local communities, who were not adequately consulted in the early swaps, and the political and institutional effects on endowing some nation NGOs with resources that were often absent in government conservation agencies. How can debt swaps evolve into a much more influential and large scale process facilitating sustainable use, environmental rehabilitation and sustainable development. Give some examples in your discussion.

13

References for Chapter 23

ADB, *Bulletin on Law and Policy Reform*, ADB, 1999.

ADB, *Country Assistance Plan for Pakistan (2001-2003)*, ADB, December 2000.

ADB, *Environmental Loan Covenants: Helping Ensure the Environmental Soundness of Projects Supported by the Asian Development Bank*, ADB, 2000.

ADB, *Environmental Loan Covenants: Principles, Checklists and Samples*, ADB, 2000.

Asian Development Bank, *Long-Term Strategic Framework of the Asian Development Bank (2001-2015)*, ADB, 2000.

Asian Development Fund (ADF VIII), *Fighting Poverty in Asia*, Donors' Report, November 2000.

Conable B., *Address to Oslo Conference on Sustainable Development*, 10 July 1998.

Declaration of Environmental Policies and Procedures Relating to Economic Development, Reproduced in Philippe Le Prestre, *The World Bank and the Environment Challenge*, Selinsgrove, 1989, Appendix A, pp. 208-9.

Derrida J., *Of Grammatology*, Baltimore, Johns Hopkins University Press, 1976.

ECOSOC, Commission on Human Rights, Sub-Commission on Discrimination and the Protection of Minorities, Working Group on Indigenous Populations, 14th Session, UN Doc., E/CN.4/Sub.2/AC.41996/2, 1996.

Foundation for International Environmental Law and Development, New York University School of Law, Sidley & Austin, *Reform of Environmental and Land Legislation in the People's Republic China*, ADB, 2000.

Gibson J.E. and Curtis R.K., "A Debt for Nature Blueprint", 28 *Columbia Journal of Transnational Law*, 331-412, 1990.

Handl G., *Multilateral Development Banking: Environmental Principles and Concepts Reflecting General International Law and Public Policy*, ADB and Kluwer Law International, February 2000.

Editors of the Harvard Law Review, *Trends in International Environmental Law*, 1992.

International Court of Justice, *Legality of the Threat or Use of Nuclear Weapons*, 35 ILM, 1345.

International Law Commission, *Draft Code of Crimes Against the Peace and Security of Mankind.*

Kerr R., "Market Mechanisms and Conservation", *Environmental Justice and Market Mechanisms: Key Changes to Environmental Law and Policy*, 5-7 March 1998, Auckland, University of Auckland Press, 1998.

Lewis A., "The Evolving Process of Swapping Debt for Nature", 10:2 *Colorado Journal of International Environmental Law and Policy*, 431–467, 1999.

La Communidad Mayagna (Sumo) de Awas Tingni, et. al. v Ing. Milton Cardenai, Et al., Recurson De Amparo dirigido al Honarable Sala de lo Civil di Tribunal de Aelaciones de Matagalpa, Case No. 11.557, Constitutional Action, Civil Tribunal of Matagalpa, 2 October 1995.

McShane O., *Land Use Control Under the Resource Management Act: A Think Piece*, Wellington, Ministry for the Environment, 1998.

Ministry for the Environment, *Annual Survey of Local Authorities*, Wellington, Ministry for the Environment, 1998.

Ministry for the Environment, *Environment 2010 Strategy*, Wellington, Ministry for the Environment, 1995.

Minister for the Environment's Reference Group, *Resource Management Act 1991: Report of the Minister for the Environment's Reference Group*, Wellington, Ministry for the Environment, 1998.

OECD, *Guidelines for Multinational Enterprises*, 15 ILM 967, 1995.

Pavletich H.J. and McShane O., *Taking the Heat Off the RMA*, Report for the Minister of Environment, Wellington Ministry of Environment, 1997.

RE Oil Spill by the "Amoco Cadiz" off the Coast of France on March 10, 1978 American Maritime Cases, 2123, 1984.

Sagoff M., "Economic Theory and Environmental Law," 79 *Michigan Law Review* 1991, p 1,393.

Smith B., *State Responsibility and the Maine Environment: The Rules of Decision*, 1988.

Tribe L., "Ways Not to Think About Plastic Trees," 83 *Yale Law Journal*, 1974, p 1,315.

UNCTC, *Draft Code of Conduct on Transnational Corporations.*World Bank, "Environmental Aspects of Bank Work," *Operational Manual Statement*, 1984.

World Bank, "Forestry," in *World Bank Operational Manual: Operational Policies*, 1992.

World Bank, "Procurement Arrangements for Adjustment Operations," in *World Bank Operational Manual: Operational Policies*, 1992.

World Bank, "Tobacco," in *World Bank Operational Manual: Operational Policies*, 1992.

World Bank, "Tribal People in Bank-Financed Projects," *Operational Manual Statement*, 1982.

World Bank, *An Environmental Strategy for the Energy Sector*, WB, 1998.

World Bank, *Environmental Matters*, Fall, 1997.

World Bank, *Global Operational Programs*, April, 1997.

World Bank, *Inspection Panel for the IBRD, Operating Procedures 5*, 1994.

World Bank, *Monitoring Environmental Progress*, WB, 1995.

World Bank, *Operational Strategy of the Global Environment Facility*, February 1996.

World Bank, *World Bank Operational Manual: Bank Procedures*, 1992.

World Bank, *World Bank Operational Manual: Good Practices*, 1992.

World Bank, *World Bank Operational Manual: Natural Habitats*, 1992.

World Bank, *World Bank Operational Manual: Pest Management*, 1992.

World Health Organizations, *Classification of Pesticides by Hazard and Guidelines to Classification*, WHO, Geneva, 1994–1995.

14

Additional References

Agenda 21, Chapter 33 (Financial Resources and Mechanisms)

Asian Development Bank web site: http://www.adb.org [*Editors' Note: This site was accessed on 03/04/2001.*]

Asian Development Bank, *Asian Development Outlook 2001: Asia's Globalization Challenge*, Oxford University Press, 2001.

Asian Development Bank, *Annual Report 2000*, Asian Development Bank, 2001.

Asian Development Bank, *Financing Environmentally Sound Development*, 1994.

Asian Development Bank, *Operations Manual*

- Section 20 – Environmental Considerations in Bank Operations, 7 January 1997
- Section 21 – The Role of Women in Development, 7 January 1997
- Section 22 – Benefit Monitoring and Evaluation, 7 January 1997
- Section 23 – The Bank's Cooperation with NGOs [under preparation]
- Section 40 – Formulation and Implementation of Loan Covenants, 12 December 1997
- Section 47 – Incorporation of Social Dimensions in Bank Operations, 7 January 1997
- Section 48 – Poverty Reduction [under preparation]
- Section 49 – Inspection, 31 August 1998
- Section 50 – Involuntary Resettlement, 7 January 1998
- Section 53 – Indigenous Peoples, 21 December 2000

Asian Development Bank, *Policies and Strategies*

Policies

- Gender and Development
- Governance: Sound Development Management
- Indigenous Peoples
- Involuntary Resettlement
- Inspection Function, Establishment of
- Inspection Policy: A Guide Book

Strategies

- Long-Term Strategic Framework, 2001–2015
- A Pacific Strategy for the New Millennium
- Poverty Reduction
- Promoting Good Governance: ADB's Medium-Term Agenda and Action Plan (2000)

Asian Development Bank, *Technology Transfer and Development: Implications for Developing Asia*, 1995.

Ayres R., *Turning Point: The End of the Growth Paradigm*, Earthscan, 2001.

Bharat Desai, "Global Accords and Quest for a New International Ecological Order: From Law of Indifference to Common Concern," 3 *Asia Yearbook on International Law*, 1994, p 546.

Bharat Desai, "Revitalizing International Environmental Institutions: The UN Task Force Report and Beyond," 40 (3) *Indian Journal of International Law*, 2000, p 455.

Brown Weiss E., Sureda A.R., and de Chazournes L.B. (eds), *The World Bank, International Financial Institutions, and the Development of International Law*, Studies in Transnational Legal Policy No. 31, American Society of International Law, 1999.

Emerton L., *Using Economic Incentives for Biodiversity Conservation*, IUCN Nature and Economy Programme, IUCN, 2000.

Financing Protected Areas Task Force of the World Commission on Protected Areas (WCP) of IUCN, *Financing Protected Areas*, IUCN, Gland, Switzerland, 2000.

GEF web site: http://www.gefweb.org/ [*Editors' Note: This site was accessed on 03/04/2001.*]

Gibson J.E. and Curtis R.K., "A Debt for Nature Blueprint," 28 *Columbia Journal of Transnational Law*, 331-412, 1990.

Global Environment Facility (GEF), *Early Impacts, Promising Future*, 1998 Annual Report, 1999.

Handl G. (ed), *Yearbook of International Environmental Law*, Vol. 4, 1993, Oxford: Clarendon Press, 1994.

Handl G., *Multilateral Development Banking: Environmental Principles and Concepts Reflecting General International Law and Public Policy*, ADB and Kluwer Law International, February 2000.

Illig P., "The Role of Nongovernmental Organizations in the Development of Environmental Policy at the Asian Development Bank," 1 *Buffalo Journal of International Law*, 1994, p. 47.

Lewis A., "The Evolving Process of Swapping Debt for Nature," 10:2 *Colorado Journal of International Environmental Law and Policy*, 431–467, 1999.

Pearce D. and Barbier E.B., *Blueprint for a Sustainable Economy*, Earthscan, 2001.

Sjoberg H., "Restructuring the Global Environment Facility," GEF Working Paper 13, 1999.

UNDP Office to Combat Desertification and Drought, *Debt-for-Environment Swaps for National Desertification Funds: An Introductory Guide*, UNDP, 1998.

UNEP, "GEF," Ch. 10, *UNEP Environmental Law Training Manual*, UNEP, 1997.

World Bank Inspection Panel: http://wbln0018.worldbank.org/ipn/ipnweb.nsf [*Editors' Note: This site was accessed on 03/04/2001.*]

World Bank web site: http://www.worldbank.org [*Editors' Note: This site was accessed on 03/04/2001.*]

Yearbook of International Environmental Law, Vols. 8-12, Oxford University Press, 1997-2001.

CHAPTER

24

THE FUTURE

CONTENTS

1

Introduction

"With increasing globalization and creation of new affiliations, the West Asia Region remains fragmented by conflicts that threaten the well-being of both our people and our environment. Comprehensive solutions to our regional ecological problems will arise only through comprehensive peace." [Mohammed Al Sarawi, "The Perspective from West Asia"]

"In order for IUCN to effectively re-define the essence of sustainability, special attention on gender is crucial. Without a solid understanding of the gender dynamics in a society, even well-intentioned activities can have detrimental effects on communities, exacerbating social inequalities." [Lee Quy An, "The Perspective from South and East Asia"]

These quotes highlight but two of the numerous issues which confront the global environment as we embark upon a new century. In addition to these we can also identify issues such as:

- Bio-technology, which has already seen the patenting of life forms and other ethically controversial practices;
- Environmental Refugees and population resettlement;
- The future of the Kyoto Protocol in the light of the Bonn Conference of the Parties and the recent shifts in US policy;
- The increasing emphasis upon the role of good governance in the quest for sustainable development; and
- The increasing awareness of the consequences for the environmental of armed conflict and war.

The last two points in this list, which is far from exhaustive, are discussed below, by Hassan and Penna respectively. This chapter is designed to give the reader a sense of what is to come. In Section 2 the *Earth Charter* provides a fundamental aspirational statement of future norms and ethics for sustainable development. Section 3 provides a framework for an integrated international environmental law through the *World Charter* and the *Draft Covenant*. These documents foreshadow significant steps toward the pursuit of environmental ideals. Their pursuit, both formally through eventual implementation, and informally through gradual immersion into international "soft law", is of fundamental importance, not only to the Asian and Pacific region, but to the planet as a whole.

A

McNeeley J., "Whither the National Challenges that will Confront Environmental Law in Asia and the Pacific?" in *Conservation Challenges of the 21st Century*, presented to the Royal Society of Edinburgh/ Scottish Natural Heritage Annual Lecture, Edinburgh, Scotland, 7 April 1999

[*As the 20th century has drawn to a close, it is timely for the conservation movement to reflect on changing environmental, social, economic, and political conditions and how it might adapt to these changes. This paper looks to the year 2025, drawing on the best available science to speculate on the evolution of global environmental trends and issues, evolving pressures on the environment, and obstacles and opportunities for effective conservation action. The paper*

These documents foreshadow significant steps toward the pursuit of environmental ideals. Their pursuit...is of fundamental importance, not only to the Asian and Pacific region, but to the planet as a whole.

addresses changes in population, consumption, and resources; cultural diversity; national security; climate; environmental pollution; economics; institutions; technology; information and communications; and biological diversity. Based on this assessment of trends, some suggestions will be made on how the evolving context will affect the niche of conservation organizations, what their emerging role might be, what key technical and organizational themes will require their attention, and what they can do to address these issues and best position themselves to be a productive force far into the future. The paper necessarily focuses on the assessment of future trends rather than specific advice, as the implications and responses for each organization are more properly the subject for much broader discussion within the concerned organizations. Generally speaking, conservation organizations should prepare for the future on two related but distinct dimensions. First, building greater understanding of the degree to which past human actions have set in motion irreversible and ongoing changes in the natural and physical environments, altering the range of options available to human communities; and second, building the capacity of human societies to understand, adapt, and respond to environmental change, a function of the cultural, social, economic, and political contexts within which they operate.]

Introduction

Those seeking to forecast the future can be distributed along a spectrum with "neo-Malthusian pessimists" at one end and "technological optimists" or "cornucopians" at the other. The neo-Malthusians—often biologists—tend to think it very likely that human industrial civilization will collapse under the weight of growing consumption of resources, growing human population, and increased environmental pollution, so human life will return to the sort that Thomas Hobbes characterized as "solitary, poor, nasty, brutish and short". According to this position, it is highly unlikely that any group of inventions or investments can permit us to continue living at the level of material affluence taken for granted by the industrial societies today. Modern industrial society has so harmed the natural environment, this position concludes, that ecological and economic turmoil are inevitable, resulting in the collapse of populations and civilizations, perhaps followed by a regrouping at a much lower level of resource use and civilization. The Club of Rome report, *The Limits to Growth*, for example, predicted that if current patterns of population growth and resource consumption continue, the world economic system would collapse by the mid-21st century. Many leading environmentalists, led by Paul Ehrlich, Vandana Shiva, Norman Myers and Lester Brown, fall toward the neo-Malthusian end of the spectrum, either implicitly or explicitly; even when they express guarded optimism about the future, it is difficult to avoid the feeling that they are just trying to avoid being labelled as prophets of doom.

At the other extreme, technological optimists—often economists—express conviction that technological advances will rescue us, and that an ever-improving base of material well-being will continue to provide humanity with the option of continuing its experiments in freedom, democracy, liberalism, peace, justice and understanding. While neo-Malthusians use the evidence of rapidly-growing consumption of non-renewable resources by growing numbers of people to logically conclude that such consumption cannot continue, the technological optimists point out that the empirical evidence is quite the contrary. Even though rapid population and economic growth have resulted in enormous increases in the extraction of metals, oil, coal, and other non-renewable resources for which logic dictates that supplies are fixed, the cornucopians insist that little evidence indicates that such resources are actually being depleted, as new resources are discovered faster than the old ones are depleted.

For many of these non-renewable resources, prices have been falling or holding steady over the past 20 years, implying to at least some economists that supplies are not declining. Therefore, they see no need to tamper with consumer behavior by dampening demand, believing that any shortcomings of today's high-consumption economy can be addressed on the supply side. Simon and Kahn, for example, argue that the 21st century will bring higher living standards and reduced human impacts on the environment as a result of technological advance and policy innovation.

Easterbrook, providing evidence for the optimists, has argued that the anti-pollution measures taken in the developed world over the past quarter century or so have been a stunning success and that environmental trends in the industrialized world are mostly positive. And in many ways, the quality of the environment has significantly improved over the rather dismal baseline of several decades earlier. For example, over the past decade, American manufacturers have reduced their releases of toxic chemicals by over 40 percent, and the success of the Montreal Protocols in reducing chemicals which threaten the Earth's protective ozone shield (CFCs) justifies at least some hope that humans can mobilize the political will to change, when the evidence for the necessity of doing so is sufficiently compelling and the measures proposed are economically and technologically feasible.

Pessimists might respond that most of these victories have been relatively easy ones against obvious, clear-cut threats to human welfare; and that such victories are relatively few. Further, the more difficult challenges, they might contend, still lie ahead, especially in addressing the loss of biological diversity, growing maldistribution of wealth, and the very real possibility of climate change. They worry that the easy advances in productivity have been made, hydroelectric facilities have been built in all the most appropriate places, and all the best agricultural soils are already in production.

For virtually any position along the Malthusian-cornucopian spectrum, ample supporting evidence can be mobilized by well-qualified scientists; no position has a monopoly on truth, justice, ethics, or reality. An empirical observation is that human societies are self-organizing complex systems involving institutions such as governments, property rights, laws, and markets. Societies are constantly evolving and adapting to satisfy human wants, providing a framework of rules within which individuals can engage in exchanges of goods and services which are perceived to be mutually advantageous. Market-oriented cornucopians argue that this happens more or less automatically, contending that little evidence exists to indicate that master plans, conservation strategies, or action plans—despite their popularity—have much of an influence on these adaptations. They go back to the 18th century economist Adam Smith to quote the power of the "invisible hand" of the market system. But of course even the "invisible hand" needs basic rules to make sure the system works, including ways to ensure that all costs are included in prices paid by consumers, and that the drive for private benefits does not overwhelm the broader objectives of society.

The more extreme free-market optimists might go even farther and blame such strategies for at least part of the problem; they might assert that many environmental problems appear to have been caused or exacerbated by well-meaning attempts to impose order on institutions from above, through one or another kind of plan. The environmental disasters of the centrally-planned economies in China and Eastern Europe are perhaps the most dramatic examples, but the generality is widespread; in some sub-Saharan African countries, for example, land degradation is at least partly due to well-meaning government policies which prevent individuals from owning land. The free-market optimists conclude that individuals need incentives to invest in the protection of the natural environment, and that the best incentive is the expectation that investments today will bring rewards tomorrow. In other words, people need confidence in the future in order to invest in it.

The key conservation issues faced by society are complex and multi-dimensional, with scientific, technical, political, economic, social, and ethical components. Problem solving and decision making in the conservation field is difficult because solutions are not clear-cut, they affect different groups in different ways, and the future consequences of alternative actions are uncertain, not least because people continually change their expectations and perceptions—and thus their behavior. Even so, the conservation community has no option but to act, and it should do so on the basis of the best available information, drawing on lessons from history.

Pessimists might respond that most of these victories have been relatively easy ones against obvious, clear-cut threats to human welfare; and that such victories are relatively few.

Lessons from the Past: Trends and Projections

This section will examine current trends in ten areas of critical interest to conservation, project these trends into the future, and suggest how conservation organizations might respond to these trends. These ten areas are treated separately, but it is clear that all are interconnected, and that complex synergies are to be expected, leading to many surprises in the future. And of course, projections are not predictions, but rather tools for helping to adapt to changing conditions...

Changes in Population, Consumption, and Resources

Optimistic as well as pessimistic forecasters of the world's future recognize increasing demand by expanding human populations as a source of immense stress on resources. The world population in 1998 was about 5.9 billion, nearly 80 percent occurring in the developing countries (effectively all countries excluding Europe, North America, Japan, Singapore, Australia and New Zealand). Significant increases are anticipated in total world population in the coming decades. Lutz *et al.* considered three components of population change—fertility, mortality and migration—and using various estimates of the range that these three components could realistically take, developed nine population scenarios. Although these resulted in a wide range of possible outcomes, three conclusions were consistent:

- World population will continue to grow and by 2030 will have increased by at least 50 percent, and may even have doubled in size. The "central scenario" suggests an increase of 80 percent with a population of 9.5 billion, but other studies conclude that this figure will not be reached until 2050.
- Developing countries will account for a greater share of the world population and will have increased to 86 percent by 2030. Under all scenarios Africa's share of the population will increase most rapidly (the central scenario estimates Africa's population will increase from 12 percent of world population in 1990 to 19 percent in 2030 and 26 percent in 2100; but the spread of AIDS is already depressing growth rates).
- All populations will become older. The more rapidly fertility declines, the faster populations will age. This "greying" of the population will have profound social, economic, and political implications, some of which are already becoming apparent in Japan and eastern Europe. One important implication of lower population growth rates (or even population declines) combined with increasing life spans is that the percentage of the economically-productive population will decline while the demands of pensioners will increase, along with their political influence.

If the demographers' consensus holds true, we are about halfway towards a level population of between 8 and 12 billion people, barring major catastrophes such as global warfare, massive volcanic eruptions, a cometary impact, or new virulent diseases of people or crops. What about the likelihood of some of these potential limiting factors? For example, despite all the efforts of modern medical science, humanity is still threatened by the resurgence of familiar diseases such as malaria, tuberculosis, cholera, bubonic plague, yellow fever, syphilis, and AIDS, as well as the newly-emerging viruses and bacterial infections that scientists are only just beginning to identify, including Legionnaire's disease, the rodent-borne hantaviruses, toxic shock syndrome, lassa fever, Marburg virus, and Ebola virus. And the growing urbanization of most societies has created dense population centres where poverty, poor sanitation, and over-extended health care systems combine to create ideal conditions for epidemics. At the same time, cheap and accessible air travel has helped to create a global village in which microbes can migrate from one remote region to another within just a few hours, long before their symptoms become apparent. Because the impact of disease over the past several decades has been relatively minor, many people act as though the threat of disease to civilization has essentially been brought under control. However, this appears to be a significant misreading of history, which demonstrates that disease organisms have a tremendous capacity to react to dense human populations by developing new and occasionally highly deadly strains. Many of these outbreaks of disease seem to be closely related to significant human modification of the environment. Thus at least some observers believe that disease will have an increasingly significant impact in the future, possibly influencing the direction of human civilization.

How many people can the Earth support? Determining optimum human population is no simple matter, as it depends very much on what kind of life people will expect to lead. The minimum viable population size is one that is just sufficiently large to ensure against extinction, while the maximum number that could be supported by the planet's life-support systems could be in the multiple billions, especially if people ate sufficiently low on the food chain to become much smaller in body size. Whittaker and Likens have estimated that an "agricultural world", in which most human beings are peasants, should be able to support 5 to 7 billion people, probably more if the large agricultural population were supported by industry-promoting agricultural activities. In contrast, a reasonable estimate for a sustainable industrialized world society at the present North American material standard of living would be one billion. At the somewhat more frugal European standard of living, two to three billion might be possible. Some scientists contend that the highest quality of life would come with a human population of around 1.5 billion, about the same number of people as existed at the turn of the 20th century …

It is often said that poverty is the worst polluter, but an even stronger case can be made that consumption is an even worse polluter. Kennedy concludes that the average American baby represents twice the environmental damage of a Swedish child, three times that of an Italian,

13 times that of a Brazilian, 35 times that of an Indian, and 280 times that of a Haitian because its level of consumption throughout its life will be so much greater. Thus even though the population of the developed world is relatively low and stable, its impact on resources is far greater than that of the developing world...

Rural populations have grown along with urban populations, though at slower rates. For the world as a whole, that is projected to remain the case through 2015. Between 2015 and 2025, however, the medium variant projection has the world's total rural population declining from 3.33 to 3.23 billion. The decline in rural populations may mean that wilderness in at least some parts of the world may well increase, not decrease. In the USA, for example, the largest rural counties tend to be those which also have the largest relative population losses. Conservation uses will often be the most plausible replacements on the land that the extractive industries will abandon, and declining rural populations will provide new opportunities for biodiversity conservation—provided that rural population decline is not accompanied by increasingly-mechanized extensive resource extraction and agricultural production to support the growing urban populations...

Many experts believe that water scarcity rather than shortage of land will be the main constraint on agricultural development in the coming decades. Global demand for water has historically increased at a rate of about 2.3 percent a year, doubling every 21 years, but supply can no longer keep up with this rate of growth. The Earth's water supply is being pressured by the demands of a growing human population for water for agriculture, industry, and domestic use; contamination of good-quality water through pollution originating from domestic waste, industry, and agricultural chemicals; and the increasing costs of developing new water sources, since most of the readily-tapped sources have already been developed.

Another disturbing trend has been the rising concentration of income worldwide. From 1960 to 1989, the share of world income going to the poorest 20 percent of its population declined from 2.3 percent to 1.4 percent, while the share of income going to the richest 20 percent increased from 70.2 percent to 82.7 percent. In other words, while per capita consumption is actually declining in many parts of the developing world, 83 percent of world income is concentrated in the hands of "biosphere people"—those who are able to mobilize resources from the entire world and who are relatively immune to local over-exploitation, and whose disproportionate share of disposable income allows them access to increasing quantities of consumer goods...

Arrow *et al.* conclude that the carrying capacity of our planet may well have significant limits, while recognizing that improvements in the management of resource systems, accompanied by resource-conserving structural changes in the environment, could enable economic and population growth to continue despite the finiteness of the environmental resource base (at least for some period of time). Others believe that an optimal human population level would be around two billion, roughly 40 percent of today's population; they do not prescribe how to achieve this reduction, which would surely involve tumultuous social and political change. However, even the optimists agree that the increasing scarcities of the resource base as the human population continues growing need to be effectively reflected within the economic system.

Changes in Cultural Diversity

The most pervasive changes to modern culture are being brought about by the spread of knowledge, which in turn depends on new information technologies. The global market and expanding communications technology mean that the world is in very real danger of having reality replaced by virtual reality, at least for urban-dwellers. If we live in a world where people do not need to travel to communicate, the depth of our understanding of different realities and different cultures inevitably will diminish, as video replaces experience and stimulation replaces contemplation. A global culture means a single language—undoubtedly some form of English—and a loss of the cultural diversity that enables people to adapt to their local conditions. Optimists will see this as an opportunity for increased welfare for all, accepting that the dominant desire of people is consumption of growing amounts of consumer products. Pessimists will be alarmed by such trends, contending that the dominance of the rich will only increase at the cost of local self-reliance.

In seeking to assess changes in cultural diversity, it is worth keeping in mind that cultural and biological diversity are closely related. Just over 83 percent of the world's languages (5,635 out of 6,760) are endemic to a single country. Of the 25 countries with the highest number of endemic higher vertebrate species (mammals, reptiles, birds, and amphibians), 16 are also among the top 25 in endemic languages—a concurrence of 64 percent. The factors which lead to high levels of species endemism—geographic isolation, large area, landscape diversity, complex geological history—also lead to linguistic endemism, so efforts to conserve biological and cultural diversity can be highly complementary...

This appears to be an inevitable side-effect of the world becoming a single global trading system, bringing new technologies and new approaches to exploiting resources. Products from local ecosystems are being harvested to feed the demands of distant, unpredictable markets rather than responding to local conditions of supply and demand. Often using heavy subsidies in the form of agricultural chemicals, fossil fuel, pesticides, and so forth, governments have replaced traditional systems of resource management with new systems imposed or adapted from other parts of the world. These new systems are able to yield considerable income, but the highest profits are earned when the full social and economic costs of resource depletion are not paid (in the economic term, "externalized"). For example, logging is far more profitable when the loggers do not need to compensate traditional owners for their loss of goods and services from the forest. Instead of being included in the prices paid for the timber, these environmental costs are transferred to society as a whole, to be paid either now or in the future. Further, royalties for local knowledge about plant varieties are not paid. UNDP estimates that the developing world would gain about US$5.4 billion per year if multinational food, seed, and pharmaceutical firms paid such royalties at even a modest rate.

Logging is far more profitable when the loggers do not need to compensate traditional owners for their loss of goods and services from the forest.

This analysis suggests that we should not be surprised that forests, grasslands, coral reefs, and the species they support have been grossly overexploited, forcing government officials into pitched battles with "poachers", conflicts with indigenous people, and draconian policy measures such as exclusion of people from resources upon which their lives depend. And since the cultural survival of many rural people depends directly on how they manage natural resources, the "nationalization" of resources—including through establishing protected areas—has had a profound impact on their cultures.

The urban centers which characterize modern industrial civilization have long viewed nature and culture as distinctly different, even opposing, concepts. Today's dominant symbol is money—a very distant and abstract way to characterize resources—and it is replacing natural symbols of proven worth to so-called "primitive" peoples. Maybury-Lewis pointed out that as the new century draws near, the modern world is marked by unprecedented degrees of confusion, insecurity, and yearning for change. industrial society—today characterized by high unemployment, growing budget deficits, ageing work forces, and social strife—is losing self-confidence in the face of the future. Under such conditions, the value of tribal wisdom can be better appreciated, bringing an opportunity to consider new models for living in balance with resources. A return to tribal or "primitive" lifestyles is not a realistic answer for the industrialized world or a feasible option for most of the world's 5.5 billion people, or for the projected doubling of the world population in the next century. Rather, new and sustainable systems of resource use could incorporate the traditional knowledge and wisdom of indigenous peoples to develop new and more sustainable relationships between people and resources. Perhaps stimulated in part by the Convention on Biological Diversity (which calls for governments to recognize the value of traditional knowledge), more governments are beginning to return at least some resource-management responsibilities to local people. Canada, Australia, New Zealand, India, and Colombia are prominent examples.

Changes in National Security

National security is already seen in increasingly environmental terms. Researchers have found considerable evidence that scarcities of renewable resources are already contributing to dislocations and violent conflicts in many developing countries. These conflicts may foreshadow more violence in coming decades, particularly in poor countries where shortages of water, forests, and fertile land are already producing considerable hardship. Unlike non-renewable resources, such as fossil fuels and iron ore, renewable resources are linked in highly complex systems, and the overuse of water, soil or forests can lead to many unforeseen, simultaneous environmental crises. Scarcities often produce insidious and cumulative social effects, such as large migrations and economic disruptions that in turn lead to ethnic strife, civil war, and insurgency.

For example, in Baidoa, Somalia, looters wrecked Somalia's new national seed bank as national security broke down. In a direct attack on the country's treasury of native genetic material, gangs emptied underground seed stores of sorghum, the local grain staple. These were particularly valuable, because the farmers had planted hundreds of varieties of their staple food crops, adapting these to the local conditions. Further, the raiding soldiers and other armed gangs often were recruited from among nomadic herdsmen clans, who made special targets of farmer clans, their age-old rivals. In the famine that followed the rural rampages, farm families often ate any remaining seed and then fled to nearby towns seeking food, leaving their fields uncultivated and the agricultural chain broken...

The close linkage between security and the environment is rapidly becoming a political reality pushed into even sharper profile by the rising tide of people who have sought the safety valve of emigration, often driven from their homes by environmental problems. But as the number of Central Americans, Haitians and North Africans migrating to North America and Europe in search of work has increased, so has unemployment, racial tension and social conflict in the towns in the North.

The strain on the United Nations and the incessant calls for more funds for humanitarian relief and peacekeeping is a growing concern of the wealthier nations. The United Nations is also now spending more money on peacekeeping than on development assistance, i.e., more money is being spent on treating symptoms than seeking cures to social conflict. At a time when the end of the Cold War was supposed to bring lasting economic benefits, new forms of domestic conflict threaten to consume even more resources than the previous military conflict, with far greater damage to the environment and serious challenges for conservationists.

Changes in Climate

The most complex manifestation of human-induced global change is that of the earth's climate. The debate over the effects of ozone depletion and airborne particulates (producing a cooling influence) and greenhouse gases (producing a warming influence) has produced a plethora of scientific material on the subject. A strong consensus of the world's climatologists believe that the "enhanced greenhouse effect", caused by the observed accumulation of carbon dioxide, methane, nitrous oxide, and chlorofluorocarbons in the atmosphere, is likely to raise mean world temperatures by about 2°C by 2030 and mean sea levels by around 30-50 cm on a comparable time scale.

Already, major ice shelves are breaking off Antarctica and for the first time in recorded history it is possible to sail around James Ross Island, formerly connected by ice to the mainland of Antarctica. According to a study by the British Antarctic Survey, continued increases in temperature could result in the disintegration of the larger Ronne and Ross ice shelves which are each roughly the size of Spain. Collapse of these ice shelves could result in land-based ice falling into the sea and cause a rise in the sea level of as much as 5 meters, flooding many coastal cities and causing massive population disruptions.

Although the magnitude and some specific effects (e.g., on clouds or on plankton) of the greenhouse effect remain hotly contested, the scale and complexity of potential changes has led to a desperate scramble to foresee the future. Large scale extinctions have occurred as a result of past major climatic changes. Although little scientific consensus has emerged on the biological impacts of apparent current changes, it appears highly likely that global warming and associated disturbance events, particularly when coupled with human population growth and accelerating rates of resource use, will bring further losses in biological diversity.

A growing body of research has also examined the possible effects of climate change on individual species and biotic communities. This research suggests that biological communities will change and shift in complex and unpredictable ways as the geographical distributions of species are altered individually rather than in community units. Further, because species are interrelated, any advantage falling to a given species in a closed system will affect other species in ways that are not always predictable. The rate of species invasions and extinctions is likely to accelerate further, bringing about complex changes in species compositions and interactions. Thus, rather than causing a simple northward or uphill shifting of ecosystems with all of their inhabitants intact, climate changes will serve to reorganize biological communities—totally new assemblages are a distinct possibility.

Peters and Lovejoy identified a number of mechanisms through which species and communities are likely to be affected as a result of the direct and indirect impacts of climate change. Populations located near the edge of a species' range, narrowly endemic species, and endangered species that exist only in protected areas or other extremely limited habitats are especially vulnerable to global vegetation shifts. Species that are already threatened by direct exploitation and habitat loss and degradation are likely to be particularly susceptible to new threats. Coastal communities may be inundated as sea levels rise, while altitudinal shifts brought about by increased temperatures would reduce or even eliminate the ranges of montane and alpine species, many of which are already relictual, having been isolated by past climate changes. In zones where genetically distinct populations meet, mate, and produce hybrids, climate change may favor some species but cause the extirpation of others.

Climate change will also affect people directly. Global warming could lead to the spread of infectious diseases such as cholera, malaria, and yellow fever. *Anopheles* mosquitoes which carry malaria are limited to areas with average temperatures of 16°C, but with global warming, the range of these mosquitoes could be dramatically extended northward. Further, warmer temperatures accelerate the lifecycles of disease-carrying insects, encouraging them to feed more often and therefore infecting significantly more people in warmer weather. One study in Rwanda found that a 1°C temperature rise caused malaria infections to increase by 337 percent.

Perhaps the biggest challenge is that problems of biodiversity and climate change lie in the deeply-ingrained everyday behavior of people, especially in their patterns of consumption of the fossil-fuel energy whose byproduct, carbon dioxide, is predicted to heat the atmosphere and make the global climate more unstable and disruptive. It is an open question whether even complete knowledge about the causes and future impacts of climate change would lead to significant changes in human behavior in time to avert the predicted changes. And even if people fundamentally changed their behavior today, the effects on climate would still be several decades into the future.

Changes in Environmental Pollution

Pollution is clearly a major concern for humanity, especially in industrial societies where environmental protection measures have been inadequate (such as eastern Europe and parts of China). So-called "persistent organic pollutants" (POPs) are carbon-based chemical compounds that resist the normal processes of degradation, are highly toxic, persistent and tend to evaluate and travel long distances. Pollutants stress ecosystems and may reduce or eliminate populations of sensitive species, as contamination may reverberate along food chains. For example, many remote arctic lakes contain a wide range of pesticides that may be toxic to humans, apparently resulting from a global distillation process in which chemicals are vaporized from soils as far away as the tropics and transported by wind to the far north, where they condense out and become concentrated in the body fat of animals at the top of the food chain—including fish, seals, otters, and humans. One recent study in Canada found that pesticide concentrations were highest in fish from lakes with the longest food chains—in other words, with the greatest biodiversity, at least as measured by ecosystem complexity. Many POPs have been found to interfere with the hormones of at least mammals, disrupting the endocrine system leading to reproductive problems in males and jeopardizing neurological development in children. Because of the wide dispersion of POPs, they have become a global problem requiring international cooperation to address.

Acid rain has made thousands of Scandinavian and North American lakes virtually lifeless, and, in combination with other kinds of air pollution, has damaged forests throughout Europe; developing countries such as Brazil, India, and China are also increasingly suffering from acid rain. Marine pollution, particularly from non-point sources, has defiled the Mediterranean and many estuaries and coastal seas throughout the world, leading to impacts on reproduction of some marine species. The key point here is that pollution is far more than a human health issue—it has significant impacts on conservation as well.

Environmental pollution is basically a side-effect of resource consumption, the result of converting useful resources into substances that are hazardous to human welfare. Most global-scale impacts of pollution have been quite recent, especially those dealing with biogeochemical cycles. For example, industrial emissions alone now multiply the annual natural releases of arsenic by a factor of three, of cadmium by seven, of mercury by ten, and of lead by 25.

Much of the pollution is related to energy consumption. Early humans consumed just enough energy to keep alive, like other animals. When they began to cook food, energy consumption doubled, only to triple again when they started to cultivate crops. Today we consume about 125 times more energy per capita than our early ancestors did. Although we still need to cook and keep warm, most of the energy is used to maintain a convenient lifestyle.

Industrial emissions can be reduced with present technology at reasonable cost. For example, the technology is available to significantly reduce the energy requirements of industry and other economic activity, so that carbon emissions can be reduced without necessarily implying a reduction in standards of living. Since 1973, Japan has increased its industrial output by 81 percent without increasing energy use. Mills et al. conclude that even allowing for continued economic growth, by the year 2000 global greenhouse gas emissions could be reduced by 10 percent from 1990 levels, at significant net economic benefit, through implementation of available energy efficiency improvements (needless to say, this is unlikely to happen, as few countries have shown willingness to reduce consumption of fossil fuel). The impacts of ozone pollution on crop production can also be reduced by reducing the use of fossil fuels, limiting losses of nitrogen fertilizers from soils, implementing nitrogen oxide emission controls, and developing ozone-resistant crops. Enhanced networks for monitoring air quality throughout the world to assess the extent and severity of ozone pollution on continental scales will aid in evaluating the benefits of these mitigating strategies.

Early environmental regulations focused on large problems where big benefits—especially in the field of pollution—easily exceeded costs. But now growing costs may outweigh dwindling gains, leading to a backlash on the part of politicians. Optimists will point out that environmentalists have won important victories, such as stopping the flow of raw sewage into waterways and air pollutants from industry, but pessimists will respond that it is much more difficult to control the broad run-off of fertilizers, silt and pesticides from farm fields and urban developments; and these "non-point sources" may be even more devastating to aquatic life and ultimately to human welfare.

Changes in Economics

Many cornucopians link their technological optimism to economic arguments, for in an era in which natural capital is the limiting factor to economic development, logic dictates that we maximize its supply and productivity. Further, the world's shift from command to market economies offers greater opportunities for research and investment, since market economies are generally more open to change in response to signals of ecological distress.

The world may be reaching a time of profound change in the structure of the way society functions. Historically, people often experience such restructuring as a depression, but optimists might contend that "structural adjustment" and global capital flows are making the process slightly less painful. The advanced industrial countries avoided the worst of the economic crisis of the 1980s largely by creating public and private credit, leading to severe indebtedness and ultimately to bad debts, bankruptcies, bank failures, reduced jobs, and lack of consumer confidence. But these structural changes will, the optimists contend, lead to increased prosperity by 2025, based on new technologies, industries, institutions, and geopolitical configurations. The US, optimists will contend, has been able to take advantage of the new conditions, but pessimists will warn that the full implications of the recent structural changes brought about by economic problems in Asia have yet to be felt.

Cleveland concludes that people governed by consent seem to want to do business (shop, invest, work, watch television) across borders that are as open as possible. This trend ensures a growing role for global companies, already the most dynamic actors in international economic affairs. It also seems bound to accelerate the leakage of power from central governments to international regulators and cooperation systems, to international nongovernments (not only the global companies but also well-organized associations of professionals, such as the international communities of scientists, lawyers, and economists) and to subnational authorities and enterprises where local governments increasingly take the initiative on issues that used to be preempted by central governments.

This globalization of markets is a major conservation issue because it leads to a lack—or at least a weakening—of feedback loops. For example, in the field of banking, the trend is toward fewer and larger banking conglomerates, with less and less diversity and ties to specific local situations. It is apparent that decision makers in today's world do not have an effective feedback loop with the environment, as they are surrounded by noise from the clamoring crowds of competing interests, a crucial measure would be reforms that would improve the economic signals that are received by resource users.

As the concept of national markets has been replaced by regional trading blocks, the relative importance of the private sector, including national and multi-national industry, has greatly increased. This globalization of the economy has been accompanied by at least a recognition of the interdependence of the world economy with the environment, an interdependence that is underlined by transboundary transport of toxic wastes, nature-based tourism, trade in endangered species, conflicts such as the "cod wars" in the North Atlantic, and numerous international agreements to address the "externalities".

The establishment of the World Trade Organization and the growing size and importance of multi-national corporations make it inevitable that the world will increasingly become a single marketplace, with profound implications on culture, resources, security, and human welfare. The economic centre of gravity is gradually shifting from the north to the south, as at least some economies in Asia and Latin America are showing annual growth rates faster than those in the north. China is today the world's second largest economy, with India sixth, and Brazil and Mexico in the top ten. Much of this economic growth in the south is driven by exports to the north, matched by exports of manufacturing jobs from north to south; but it depends on a globally-shared orientation toward production of more consumer goods. Herman Daly and others have pointed out the dangers inherent in such a global marketplace, which tends to promote local over-exploitation of resources because it is not able to detect the symptoms of over-exploitation until it is too late to change the trajectory of use, shifting easily to new resources when the old ones are depleted. Under current economic arrangements, the market is less sensitive to ecological changes than to most other sorts of change.

One of the most important underlying causes of environmental problems is market failure, what the pioneer economist Adam Smith might have called "the invisible backhand". Much current work indicates that economics will provide increasingly useful tools for improved conservation, addressing local market failures by capturing and internalizing to local populations the benefits from the goods and services derived from the environment. Increasing supply from available resources, mitigating ecological damage associated with human activities, and developing adaptive technologies depend in large part on the ability, and willingness, to reform economic pricing and markets. Markets and prices must not only account for the environmental costs of production and consumption, but also compensate economic factors for the environmental benefits of resource conservation. Brenton suggests that sustainable development will not emerge from "dense webs of regulation" or the old command and control approach to environmental conservation, but only when conditions create more democracy, greater economic prosperity and a market that works for, rather than against, the interests of biodiversity. However, it is increasingly clear that the process of market reform and "getting prices right" involves much more than simply freeing the market. For example, environmentally-damaging subsidies amount to over US$1.4 trillion per year. Markets are the creation of human cultures, policies and institutions and are therefore subject to the many limitations of human understanding and politics.

The key point for conservation organizations is that economics needs to become a tool for conservation, involving full-cost accounting, green taxes, economic incentives for conservation, and "internalizing environmental externalities". Ways must be found to send conservation-oriented signals to the marketplace and to stop subsidizing the destruction of nature.

Changes in Institutions

The main institutional actors in the conservation field include the private sector, with its emphasis on marketplace agility, the bottom line, and the public's expressions of preference; the public sector, with its emphasis on stable and codified process, regulating private action, protecting public goods, and reluctance to experiment; and the independent sector (including NGOs), with its tradition of innovation, critical thought and the checking of inequalities of wealth, status, power, and knowledge.

[T]he nation-state is no longer the principal definer of the marketplace, especially as the marketplace goes regional and global. Many structures and networks are being created and maintained by their ability to help people to communicate, irrespective of public authority. Many of these "nongovernments" have become effective users of modern information technologies, and in fact groups concerned with business and finance, population policy, human rights, various aspects of science, and so forth, are highly creative in using information technology and therefore are providing more and more of the policy initiative at both domestic and international levels. Thus we can expect the role of central governments to continue to change from primary determinant of the society's course to that of coordinator, regulator and monitor of the activities of local governments, the private sector, and NGOs. Power will be more broadly shared, and the role of the marketplace will become more dominant in establishing the conditions under which development can be made sustainable and resources conserved. The expansion of regional and global economic infrastructures also permits the reawakening of local identities and may stimulate an increasing interest in both cultural and biological diversity (as well as conflict, in the name of "nationalism"). The general trend is one of global integration but simultaneously greater local autonomy and responsibility. Managing this apparent paradox will be a major challenge in the coming years.

The UN system, the World Bank, and the International Monetary Fund were established in the post-war era when the nation-state was supreme, and were designed to serve the interests of central governments. Consequently, these institutions also reflect the limitations of the nation-state; the existing international institutional framework is not necessarily well designed to cope with the new realities. Being built around the perceptions and approaches of national government structures, these institutions are, in general, slow to react and position themselves to build upon the opportunities that have come with the formation of wider regional alliances, powerful multi-national corporations, and trading blocs. Similarly, they are slow to benefit from opportunities provided by the decentralization of authority to local government structures, and devolution of initiative to community groups such as people's associations and other community-based organizations. The change in the role of the nation-state which the organizations are designed to support means that their role will also change; it should be remembered that in global economic terms, the UN system already is inconsequential, expenditure being around one twentieth of one percent of global GDP or just over one percent of global military expenditure; more people work for the government of Winnipeg, Canada, for example, than for all of the United Nations. Bilateral development assistance agencies suffer, albeit to a lesser extent, from the same shortcoming since they too were designed to interact primarily with central governments in recipient countries.

The mechanics of the new global system are becoming increasingly apparent, being led by modern information technology and with a greatly expanded role for the private sector in both the financial and service industries. As the relative importance of central governments continues to decline, at least some of their roles will be augmented by other forms of association, such as multinational corporations, multinational membership organizations such as economic and defense alliances, NGOs or other forms of organization with large membership bases and considerable resources and/or political power. A possible problem with such privatization is that governments are public and can be scrutinized by the public, but the private sector is much more difficult to control and much more skilful at managing public opinion (but also consider the power of Greenpeace to embarrass powerful multinationals, such as Shell, or the public relations headaches of Monsanto, as it has sought to promote genetically-modified organisms on an unwilling European public). Another problem is that the private sector has not yet shown itself able to protect the common interest, especially in the case of public goods which are not able to be protected by private interests.

Changes in the independent sector, basically NGOs, will be especially important for conservation organizations, as they seek to continue providing linkages among the three main institutional actors; on the other hand, communities are likely to have more direct access to the decision making process, so the role of NGOs as intermediaries may decrease. In the meantime, NGO numbers have increased remarkably over the past two decades, especially in Europe, North America, West Africa, Asia and Latin America. In some countries, particularly in parts of Asia, it is even conceivable that NGOs will play an increasingly important role as extensions of government, as governments slim down their bureaucracies and pass the work through to the NGOs and corporate sector on a commercial basis. The Middle East and Africa have lagged behind in this change, although the NGO movement is now gathering momentum in at least some parts of Africa. In Europe and North America, it is possible that NGOs might decline in numbers and in strength as the public either tires of their messages or perceives the inevitable contradictions, duplications and inefficiencies. All of this will lead to a new emphasis on partnerships, alliances, and other arrangements that will enable groups to form a critical mass to achieve their objectives.

NGO numbers have increased remarkably over the past two decades, especially in Europe, North America, West Africa, Asia and Latin America.

Changes in Technology

All major development goals, including economic growth, environmental protection, improved health, better farming, and improved human welfare, depend on the ability of countries to absorb and use science and technology. Unforeseen technological breakthroughs could have profound and unpredictable effects on society—consider the impact of computers, nuclear weapons, and satellite communications. The key role of technology is one reason why "technology transfer" is such an important topic of discussion at intergovernmental negotiations (e.g., Article 18 of the Convention on Biological Diversity). However, much of the new technology is essentially beyond the reach of governments. Kennedy argues that the main creators and controllers of technology have increasingly become large multinational corporations with more global reach than global responsibility. They are the groups that create, control, and have access to new discoveries, and they are increasingly able to operate free of direct government control, responding instead to their customers and stockholders.

Rennie points out that a good technology must by definition be useful; it must be able to survive fierce buffeting by market forces, economic and social conditions, governmental policies, quirky timing, whims of fashion, and all the vagaries of human nature and custom. International disputes over who owns the mineral rights to the sea floor sapped the incentive that many nations and corporations had to invest in undersea mining technologies, leaving the resources untapped. Competing industrial standards can also hamper progress, as illustrated by the conflicts that froze work on high definition television. Many of the greatest innovations are unforeseen, if not unforeseeable; for example, a Technology-of-the-20th Century Symposium held in 1895 might have not mentioned airplanes, radio, antibiotics, nuclear energy, electronics, DNA, computers, or space exploration. Can anyone today truly foresee what the world will be like if, for example, genetic engineering matures rapidly to the full potential claimed by its adherents? If organisms can be tailored to serve any function, can anyone guess what a mid-21st century factory would look like?

Technological optimists often argue that even given recent evidence of the pace and scale of environmental change, human societies can continue to achieve quantitative, qualitative, and sustainable economic development through advances in science and technology. Technological innovation undoubtedly has the potential to dramatically stretch the limits of existing resources and systems in order to meet the needs of present and future human populations, and to alleviate many of the ecological and economic stresses caused by growing human populations and rising per capita resource consumption. Currently, computer chips are doubling their storage capacity while halving in cost every 18 months. Crop improvements and continuing improvements in irrigation and pest control are likely to enable rising productivity as well as reducing known environmental impacts; for example, research is now underway to develop drought-resistant cassava and crops suitable for production on acidic soils. Continuing increases in food supply can also be maintained through increased aquacultural production as well as diversification of seafood consumption. Timber consumption can be reduced dramatically simply by further development of technologies to reduce waste or to mass produce woodless paper.

As the rate and scale of global change have increased, so has the technological response. One of the most dramatic manifestations of a technological response to resource limitations is biotechnology, which offers the prospect of boosting crop yields with lower inputs of energy, water and pesticides. In the short term, potential advances which appear likely include modification of food crops to increase resistance to insects, viruses and fungi; improve processing quality or reduce spoilage; and improve nutritional content. Fermentation and enzyme technology are already used in the manufacture of animal growth hormones to increase milk production or induce faster growth and production of leaner meat. In the long term, biotechnology may help to offset the impacts of global change on food supply, for example by producing staple crops that are resistant to drought, heat, salinity, and other environmental stresses. New reproductive techniques for livestock, such as embryo transfer to stimulate production of multiple eggs for artificial insemination or cloning, could boost the reproductive rate of desirable species and reduce susceptibility to disease. And already a multinational corporation, CIBA Agriculture, has developed a spray which can immunize crops such as wheat, bananas, and rice against fungal infections in much the same way that people can be vaccinated against disease; applied at a dosage of 30 grams per hectare, this biotech breakthrough could prove to be very important in maintaining yields.

Biotechnology also brings its own set of problems and challenges. In the past, human activities have resulted in biodiversity loss through the introduction of exotic species, a problem that could recur on a grander scale with the introduction of transgenic species. Altered organisms may out-compete other species in the environments in which they are released, or spread their altered genes by reproducing with native species. Just as the Green Revolution was accompanied by hidden economic and environmental costs, the Biotechnology Revolution undoubtedly will bring with it environmental consequences that have not yet been anticipated. For example, some developing countries are concerned that biotechnology will enable the developed countries to reduce their imports of some agricultural commodities from the developing countries, with unpredictable effects on the environment.

An interesting question is why information technology, with its much wider and more intrusive impact on human behavior, has attracted so little criticism compared with the much less-developed biotechnology. One reason for this contrast may be that people appear to pay only lip service to the values which information technology may compromise, such as privacy or freedom from social control, but are truly worried when biotechnology appears to pose health risks and, most important, impinges on moral and religious agendas.

While the technology-led information economy is leading to greater automation, on balance it does not seem to save people much time or raise their living standards. Much of the innovation seems to be more trouble than it is worth, and does not really contribute to productivity in any measurable way. With the post-industrial economies increasingly focusing on services which include jobs that do not evolve with technology, much of the perceived "progress" is in fact illusory. Kuttner contends that the new information technology produces almost as many costs to productivity as it does benefits, and the rapid evolution of the technology means increasing amounts of time spent learning how to manipulate the new generation of equipment. Thus the information economy may be innovating at a rate that is faster than optimal—faster than people are able to learn how to use the new tools. And don't forget that nobody has matched Shakespeare for quality and output of literature, and he used a quill.

And while technology is surging ahead, many developing countries have lapsed into an under-class which cannot apply science and technology to meet the basic needs of their people or to enhance the efficiency of their domestic production and services to compete in world markets. One danger is that some of the new technologies may in fact harm the developing countries by making redundant certain economic activities. Clearly, economic change and technological development are seldom beneficial to all; a change is likely to benefit those groups or nations that are best able to take advantage of the newer methods, and will damage those who are less prepared technologically, culturally, and politically to respond to change. The danger that the world will become further split into the technology-rich and the technology-poor is one that must be of great concern to conservationists. Technology is not culture-free and carries with it unpredictable implications for humanity, and for our relation with the environment.

Changes in Information and Communications

Conservation has been a social movement, and like most social movements is led by information. But social movements must continue to evolve or they recede in importance. We should certainly celebrate our successes, such as the broad public awareness of endangered species (at least in developed countries), the hundreds of millions of visitors to protected areas, the continuing expansion of the global protected area estate, the greening of many governments (at least in their public statements), and various other conservation measures. But ironically, good news does not sell nearly as well as bad news, forcing conservationists to focus on bad news and alarming predictions. The disadvantage to this approach is that when advocates cling to their rhetorical palisades, their positions become more rigid, leading critics to become more exasperated. Exaggerations on one side can inspire absurd reactions on the other as debate becomes more shrill and politics grow more polarized, making compromise and informed decision making more difficult rather than more likely. A new form of rhetoric needs to be considered in order to fight the inevitable backlash from our successes (however modest they may have been).

The technology of communications also carries dangers, the pessimist might warn. Slouka foresees a sinister new world in which telecommunications replaces physical contact and meaningless abstractions replace a sense of community and place: a world where people are concerned only with themselves and become easily subject to manipulation by charismatic ideologues. As we all know, electronic documents are subject to change in all sorts of ways, establishing impermanence as the norm. The relationship among the mass information media and politics is emerging as a central problem, and it is becoming increasingly difficult to tell who the real power brokers are—the politicians or the media barons.

Information is being controlled by fewer and fewer multinational corporations, as indicated by the recent acquisition of ABC by Walt Disney, Westinghouse Electric's acquisition of CBS, Time-Warner's flirtation with CNN, and the expansion of Rupert Murdoch's Star TV from India to cover Asian markets from Dubai to Indonesia, giving all a greatly expanded global reach. Such acquisitions are expected to have a profound influence on shaping the television news industry. Clearly, the trend is more toward entertainment than information. The recent mergers have tended to drastically reduce the relative importance of the news departments, so an already diluted pool from which the values of journalism will be drawn has been reduced to peripheral importance in corporate decisions. "Truth" may become increasingly abstract and subject to manipulation by special interests.

Ecosystems that have been substantially transformed, managed, and utilized constitute about half the land surface of the ice-free earth, and no truly pristine areas remain.

Information undoubtedly will be one of the most valuable commodities of the future, but information technology tends to make at least some information freely available, which may diminish its value and its quality. Furthermore, information is increasing very rapidly, perhaps too rapidly to apply wisdom and reflection to the overwhelming flood of new data. This has been likened to "trying to get a drink from a fire hose," and is forcing the political system to become more sensitive to the transitory priorities of a public manipulated by the mass media (leading to what some observers consider a mal-adaptive "hyper-democracy").

On the other hand, optimists might contend that global communications can make information far more democratic. For all parts of the world, information and communications technology (ICT) can be a path to greater freedom. Information is power and ICT can empower people by organizing, storing, retrieving, sharing and disseminating information. Computer hardware, software and electronic communications help ensure informed decision making, make it easier to evaluate and compare options and scenarios, and allow speedy identification of experts, organizations and resources. During the 1980s and 1990s, ICT has helped to make possible an extraordinary increase in peer-to-peer communication, challenging traditional concepts of hierarchically-structured organizations and leading to the emergence of flattened structures that are based on "peer acceptance" rather than "mandate". Optimists hope for a twenty-first century world of information-based cooperatives rather than twentieth century "ivory towers" or fortress-like organizations holding exclusive "mandates".

The evolution of conservation organizations toward decentralized and regionalized ways of working is very much about creating environmental cooperatives based on "peer acceptance". But to function effectively, these cooperatives will require more than commitment, information, expertise, strategic planning and priority-setting. They will also need information and communications technology. ICT offers cost-effective tools for building the "infrastructure and highways" that extend connections, interaction and exchange as widely as possible. The success of people-led cooperatives will depend on making the best possible use of this technology in pursuit of carefully planned and clearly defined goals.

Changes in Biological Diversity

The changes described in [this paper] will all have impacts on biological diversity. A consensus of leading scientists has concluded that the scale of human impacts on biodiversity is increasing dramatically, threatening the very foundation of sustainable development. The rate at which humans are altering the environment, the extent of those alterations, and their consequences for the distribution and abundance of species, ecological systems, and genetic variability are unprecedented in human history, and pose substantial threats to both sustainable development and the quality of life.

Humans have already greatly modified the earth's surface. Ecosystems that have been substantially transformed, managed, and utilized constitute about half the land surface of the ice-free earth, and no truly pristine areas remain. Moreover, the rate of global land use and land cover change is accelerating. Conversion to cropland contributes to much of this land cover change; half of the area of cropland worldwide has been added during the past 90 years, with croplands in the tropics doubling in area in the last 50 years. Rates of forest loss in the tropics are currently increasing by an estimated 4 to 9 percent annually.

Although land use change outside the tropics has been relatively small in recent decades (the major periods of profound habitat alteration took place in Europe in the Neolithic and the Middle Ages and in 1500-1900 in North America), changes in characteristics other than area continue to occur, including loss of biomass and carbon storage; the loss of old-growth forest remains a major concern in many temperate countries. Habitat disturbance and other anthropogenic factors may also contribute to species invasions or successful introductions of exotic species. The addition of species may have wide-ranging effects on community composition and dynamics, and alter productivity, soil structure, nutrient cycling and water chemistry. A recent report by the US National Biological Service says that "If unchecked, human activities will continue to result in an upset balance of species interactions, alteration of ecosystems and extensive habitat loss". Even an environmental optimist such as Easterbrook recognizes that preservation of natural habitat "is likely to be the primary ecological issue of the coming century".

The Global Biodiversity Assessment concludes that the world is already committed to further species extinctions and the loss of populations and genetic resources, even if responsible actions were taken immediately. According to IUCN figures, since 1600 at least 484 animal and 654 plant species have become extinct. Based on historical records that span the past four centuries, the extinction rate for vertebrates and plants is estimated to be 50 to 100 times the expected natural rate. When fossil records that date back 2,000 years are used, the estimated rate for bird extinctions ranges from 500 to 1,000 times that expected. Finally, when projections of future extinction rates are based on habitat destruction and empirical studies of habitat-area relationships, the estimated rate exceeds that expected by substantially more than 1,000 times. For some groups of vertebrates and plants, between 10 and 40 percent of the identified species are already listed as being threatened with extinction. Although many areas of apparently natural vegetation remain, large animals on which many plant species are ecologically dependent may have been hunted out by humans. The result may well be the profound change of these areas, with the new ecosystems being much less useful to people though not necessarily less complex ecologically.

Habitat loss, modification and fragmentation are widely considered the most important cause of loss of biological diversity, with most current attempts to estimate and project the rate of species loss based on reductions in habitat area. Recent work has documented an "extinction debt" associated with habitat destruction, in which the rate of extinction increases as a function of the area of habitat that has already been destroyed. For instance, destruction of an additional one percent of habitat causes the extinction of 8 times more species if 90 percent versus 20 percent of a region has already been destroyed. Furthermore, an unanticipated effect of this habitat destruction may be the selective extinction of the best competitors—those species that are often the most efficient users of resources and major controllers of ecosystem functions. Thus, this extinction debt may have dramatic effects on the ecosystems of the future and the ability of these ecosystems to deliver vital services to human populations.

The opposite trend—bringing in new species—is also dangerous. A crucial element in the changing biological diversity of most ecosystems as a result of increasing global trade is the introduction of invasive exotic species. While such invasions often mean that any particular site has greater biological diversity now than formerly (England, for example, now has more species of deer than at any previous time in its history and New Zealand has more than twice as many plants), the overall impact of these invasive species is unknown.

Not only will land areas continue to be affected, but so too will marine and freshwater areas. Marine ecosystems are increasingly affected by logging of forests and mangroves, siltation, dredging and channelization, pollution, shoreline development, oil and gas development and other human modifications, as well as introduction of exotic species and offtake of fish and other marine species (both deliberate and incidental). And freshwater fish are the vertebrate group that has suffered the highest extinction rates, in both tropical and temperate regions.

Change constantly occurs on an infinite number of spatial scales—from tree falls to the impacts of meteors—and temporal scales—from continental drift to sunrise and sunset. Variability and instability are the traits necessary to retain the resilience of ecosystems, or their ability to adapt to disturbance through rapid shifts to alternate stable states or through evolutionary organisational change. An important implication of this view is that reductions in natural variability lead to fragility and lessen the likelihood that disturbance will bring about a transition to an alternate equilibrium. Condit *et al.* concluded that all biotic communities undergo constant flux as populations or individual species expand, contract, go extinct locally and remigrate in response to local ecological and evolutionary change and other major changes from outside the system (such as climate change).

In conclusion, depending on the circumstances, human activities may increase, maintain, or diminish the diversity of genes, species, or ecological communities in a given region and at a given time, but the general trend is an increasing loss of biodiversity at the global scale, a net gain in biodiversity at some locations as introduced species outnumber species extinctions and new communities are formed, and increasing human impacts on "natural" ecosystems. Some of these changes are irreversible, such as extinction of species. Other changes are more cyclical, but all present challenges in managing natural resources in a sustainable manner without losing the diversity which will enable the system concerned to adapt to change. The Convention on Biological Diversity, Convention on International Trade in Endangered Species of Wild Fauna and Flora (CITES), the Migratory Species Convention, the World Heritage Convention, the Ramsar Convention, and the Law of the Sea will provide international fora where the issues of biodiversity will continue to be debated. The effectiveness of these fora will depend very much on the willingness of governments to use them, and this in turn will depend especially on public perceptions of the importance of biodiversity to a changing world...

Conclusions

Human-induced change has shifted from the agricultural transformation of the surface of the earth, to industrial mobilization of materials and energy, to the current mix of agricultural, industrial and advanced industrial transformation. As this range has expanded, so has the secondary interaction among the changes and hence the complexity of the problems that they pose for biological systems. The impacts of human-induced change are no longer only local or regional, but now are global as well; but individual humans behave at the local level, calling for action to be focused here as well. All of this adds to the difficulty of assessing the human impacts on biodiversity, predicting the future, and defining the role of conservation organizations in the 21st century.

Given the many possible and feasible views of the future, a sensible course of action would be the following:

(1) Prepare for any kind of future, for example through continuing discussions, research, monitoring, and assessment;

(2) Maximize the possibility that our preferred set of possibilities is realized, while doing whatever we can to ensure against even a small probability of the most pessimistic scenarios being realized; and

(3) Continue to refine our understanding of the possible futures, both by adding to our knowledge about the events which will determine the relevant characteristics of the future, and by familiarizing ourselves with the terms of debate over why these events should lead one way or another.

Conservation organizations should prepare for the future on two related but distinct dimensions. The first involves building greater understanding of the degree to which past human actions have set in motion irreversible and ongoing change in the natural and physical environments, altering the range of options available to human communities. The second involves building the capacity of human societies to understand, adapt and respond to environmental change, a function of the cultural, social, economic and political contexts in which they operate.

2

Evolving International Norms and Ethics

A

The Earth Council, *The Earth Charter*, The Earth Charter Initiative, International Secretariat, The Earth Council, March 2000

PREAMBLE

We stand at a critical moment in Earth's history, a time when humanity must choose its future. As the world becomes increasingly interdependent and fragile, the future at once holds great peril and great promise. To move forward we must recognize that in the midst of a magnificent diversity of cultures and life forms we are one human family and one Earth community with a common destiny. We must join together to bring forth a sustainable global society founded on respect for nature, universal human rights, economic justice, and a culture of peace. Towards this end, it is imperative that we, the peoples of Earth, declare our responsibility to one another, to the greater community of life, and to future generations.

Earth, Our Home

Humanity is part of a vast evolving universe. Earth, our home, is alive with a unique community of life. The forces of nature make existence a demanding and uncertain adventure, but Earth has provided the conditions essential to life's evolution. The resilience of the community of life and the well-being of humanity depend upon preserving a healthy biosphere with all its ecological systems, a rich variety of plants and animals, fertile soils, pure waters, and clean air. The global environment with its finite resources is a common concern of all peoples. The protection of Earth's vitality, diversity, and beauty is a sacred trust.

The Global Situation

The dominant patterns of production and consumption are causing environmental devastation, the depletion of resources, and a massive extinction of species. Communities are being undermined. The benefits of development are not shared equitably and the gap between rich and poor is widening. Injustice, poverty, ignorance, and violent conflict are widespread and the cause of great suffering. An unprecedented rise in human population has overburdened ecological and social systems. The foundations of global security are threatened. These trends are perilous—but not inevitable.

The Challenges Ahead

The choice is ours: form a global partnership to care for Earth and one another or risk the destruction of ourselves and the diversity of life. Fundamental changes are needed in our values, institutions, and ways of living. We must realize that when basic needs have been met, human development is primarily about being more, not having more. We have the knowledge and technology to provide for all and to reduce our impacts on the environment. The emergence of a global civil society is creating new opportunities to build a democratic and humane world. Our environmental, economic, political, social, and spiritual challenges are interconnected, and together we can forge inclusive solutions.

We have the knowledge and technology to provide for all and to reduce our impacts on the environment.

Universal Responsibility

To realize these aspirations, we must decide to live with a sense of universal responsibility, identifying ourselves with the whole Earth community as well as our local communities. We are at once citizens of different nations and of one world in which the local and global are linked. Everyone shares responsibility for the present and future well-being of the human family and the larger living world. The spirit of human solidarity and kinship with all life is strengthened when we live with reverence for the mystery of being, gratitude for the gift of life, and humility regarding the human place in nature.

We urgently need a shared vision of basic values to provide an ethical foundation for the emerging world community. Therefore, together in hope we affirm the following interdependent principles for a sustainable way of life as a common standard by which the conduct of all individuals, organizations, businesses, governments, and transnational institutions is to be guided and assessed.

Principles

I. Respect and Care for the Community of Life

1. Respect Earth and life in all its diversity.
   1. Recognize that all beings are interdependent and every form of life has value regardless of its worth to human beings.
   2. Affirm faith in the inherent dignity of all human beings and in the intellectual, artistic, ethical, and spiritual potential of humanity.

2. Care for the community of life with understanding, compassion, and love.
   1. Accept that with the right to own, manage, and use natural resources comes the duty to prevent environmental harm and to protect the rights of people.
   2. Affirm that with increased freedom, knowledge, and power comes increased responsibility to promote the common good.

3. Build democratic societies that are just, participatory, sustainable, and peaceful.
   1. Ensure that communities at all levels guarantee human rights and fundamental freedoms and provide everyone an opportunity to realize his or her full potential.
   2. Promote social and economic justice, enabling all to achieve a secure and meaningful livelihood that is ecologically responsible.

4. Secure Earth's bounty and beauty for present and future generations.
   1. Recognize that the freedom of action of each generation is qualified by the needs of future generations.
   2. Transmit to future generations values, traditions, and institutions that support the long-term flourishing of Earth's human and ecological communities.

In order to fulfill these four broad commitments, it is necessary to:

II. Ecological Integrity

5. Protect and restore the integrity of Earth's ecological systems, with special concern for biological diversity and the natural processes that sustain life.
   1. Adopt at all levels sustainable development plans and regulations that make environmental conservation and rehabilitation integral to all development initiatives.
   2. Establish and safeguard viable nature and biosphere reserves, including wild lands and marine areas, to protect Earth's life support systems, maintain biodiversity, and preserve our natural heritage.
   3. Promote the recovery of endangered species and ecosystems.
   4. Control and eradicate non-native or genetically modified organisms harmful to native species and the environment, and prevent introduction of such harmful organisms.
   5. Manage the use of renewable resources such as water, soil, forest products, and marine life in ways that do not exceed rates of regeneration and that protect the health of ecosystems.
   6. Manage the extraction and use of non-renewable resources such as minerals and fossil fuels in ways that minimize depletion and cause no serious environmental damage.

6. Prevent harm as the best method of environmental protection and, when knowledge is limited, apply a precautionary approach.
   1. Take action to avoid the possibility of serious or irreversible environmental harm even when scientific knowledge is incomplete or inconclusive.
   2. Place the burden of proof on those who argue that a proposed activity will not cause significant harm, and make the responsible parties liable for environmental harm.
   3. Ensure that decision making addresses the cumulative, long-term, indirect, long distance, and global consequences of human activities.
   4. Prevent pollution of any part of the environment and allow no build-up of radioactive, toxic, or other hazardous substances.
   5. Avoid military activities damaging to the environment.

7. Adopt patterns of production, consumption, and reproduction that safeguard Earth's regenerative capacities, human rights, and community well-being.

1. Reduce, reuse, and recycle the materials used in production and consumption systems, and ensure that residual waste can be assimilated by ecological systems.
2. Act with restraint and efficiency when using energy, and rely increasingly on renewable energy sources such as solar and wind.
3. Promote the development, adoption, and equitable transfer of environmentally sound technologies.
4. Internalize the full environmental and social costs of goods and services in the selling price, and enable consumers to identify products that meet the highest social and environmental standards.
5. Ensure universal access to health care that fosters reproductive health and responsible reproduction.
6. Adopt lifestyles that emphasize the quality of life and material sufficiency in a finite world.

8. Advance the study of ecological sustainability and promote the open exchange and wide application of the knowledge acquired.

1. Support international scientific and technical cooperation on sustainability, with special attention to the needs of developing nations.
2. Recognize and preserve the traditional knowledge and spiritual wisdom in all cultures that contribute to environmental protection and human well-being.
3. Ensure that information of vital importance to human health and environmental protection, including genetic information, remains available in the public domain.

III. Social and Economic Justice

9. Eradicate poverty as an ethical, social, and environmental imperative.

1. Guarantee the right to potable water, clean air, food security, uncontaminated soil, shelter, and safe sanitation, allocating the national and international resources required.
2. Empower every human being with the education and resources to secure a sustainable livelihood, and provide social security and safety nets for those who are unable to support themselves.
3. Recognize the ignored, protect the vulnerable, serve those who suffer, and enable them to develop their capacities and to pursue their aspirations.

10. Ensure that economic activities and institutions at all levels promote human development in an equitable and sustainable manner.

1. Promote the equitable distribution of wealth within nations and among nations.
2. Enhance the intellectual, financial, technical, and social resources of developing nations, and relieve them of onerous international debt.
3. Ensure that all trade supports sustainable resource use, environmental protection, and progressive labor standards.
4. Require multinational corporations and international financial organizations to act transparently in the public good, and hold them accountable for the consequences of their activities.

11. Affirm gender equality and equity as prerequisites to sustainable development and ensure universal access to education, health care, and economic opportunity.

1. Secure the human rights of women and girls and end all violence against them.
2. Promote the active participation of women in all aspects of economic, political, civil, social, and cultural life as full and equal partners, decision makers, leaders, and beneficiaries.
3. Strengthen families and ensure the safety and loving nurture of all family members.

12. Uphold the right of all, without discrimination, to a natural and social environment supportive of human dignity, bodily health, and spiritual well-being, with special attention to the rights of indigenous peoples and minorities.

1. Eliminate discrimination in all its forms, such as that based on race, color, sex, sexual orientation, religion, language, and national, ethnic or social origin.
2. Affirm the right of indigenous peoples to their spirituality, knowledge, lands and resources and to their related practice of sustainable livelihoods.

3. Honor and support the young people of our communities, enabling them to fulfill their essential role in creating sustainable societies.
4. Protect and restore outstanding places of cultural and spiritual significance.

IV. Democracy, Nonviolence, and Peace

13. Strengthen democratic institutions at all levels, and provide transparency and accountability in governance, inclusive participation in decision making, and access to justice.

1. Uphold the right of everyone to receive clear and timely information on environmental matters and all development plans and activities which are likely to affect them or in which they have an interest.
2. Support local, regional and global civil society, and promote the meaningful participation of all interested individuals and organizations in decision making.
3. Protect the rights to freedom of opinion, expression, peaceful assembly, association, and dissent.
4. Institute effective and efficient access to administrative and independent judicial procedures, including remedies and redress for environmental harm and the threat of such harm.
5. Eliminate corruption in all public and private institutions.
6. Strengthen local communities, enabling them to care for their environments, and assign environmental responsibilities to the levels of government where they can be carried out most effectively.

14. Integrate into formal education and life-long learning the knowledge, values, and skills needed for a sustainable way of life.

1. Provide all, especially children and youth, with educational opportunities that empower them to contribute actively to sustainable development.
2. Promote the contribution of the arts and humanities as well as the sciences in sustainability education.
3. Enhance the role of the mass media in raising awareness of ecological and social challenges.
4. Recognize the importance of moral and spiritual education for sustainable living.

15. Treat all living beings with respect and consideration.

1. Prevent cruelty to animals kept in human societies and protect them from suffering.
2. Protect wild animals from methods of hunting, trapping, and fishing that cause extreme, prolonged, or avoidable suffering.
3. Avoid or eliminate to the full extent possible the taking or destruction of non-targeted species.

16. Promote a culture of tolerance, nonviolence, and peace.

1. Encourage and support mutual understanding, solidarity, and cooperation among all peoples and within and among nations.
2. Implement comprehensive strategies to prevent violent conflict and use collaborative problem solving to manage and resolve environmental conflicts and other disputes.
3. Demilitarize national security systems to the level of a non-provocative defense posture, and convert military resources to peaceful purposes, including ecological restoration.
4. Eliminate nuclear, biological, and toxic weapons and other weapons of mass destruction.
5. Ensure that the use of orbital and outer space supports environmental protection and peace.
6. Recognize that peace is the wholeness created by right relationships with oneself, other persons, other cultures, other life, Earth, and the larger whole of which all are a part.

The Way Forward

As never before in history, common destiny beckons us to seek a new beginning. Such renewal is the promise of these Earth Charter principles. To fulfill this promise, we must commit ourselves to adopt and promote the values and objectives of the Charter.

This requires a change of mind and heart. It requires a new sense of global interdependence and universal responsibility. We must imaginatively develop and apply the vision of a sustainable way of life locally, nationally, regionally, and globally. Our cultural diversity is a precious heritage and different cultures will find their own distinctive ways to realize the vision. We must deepen and expand the global dialogue that generated the Earth Charter, for we have much to learn from the ongoing collaborative search for truth and wisdom.

Life often involves tensions between important values. This can mean difficult choices. However, we must find ways to harmonize diversity with unity, the exercise of freedom with the common good, short-term objectives with long-term goals. Every individual, family, organization, and community has a vital role to play. The arts, sciences, religions, educational institutions, media, businesses, nongovernmental organizations, and governments are all called to offer creative leadership. The partnership of government, civil society, and business is essential for effective governance.

In order to build a sustainable global community, the nations of the world must renew their commitment to the United Nations, fulfill their obligations under existing international agreements, and support the implementation of Earth Charter principles with an international legally binding instrument on environment and development.

Let ours be a time remembered for the awakening of a new reverence for life, the firm resolve to achieve sustainability, the quickening of the struggle for justice and peace, and the joyful celebration of life.

3

Towards an Integrated Environmental Law

A

Robinson N.A., "'Colloquium: The Rio Environmental Law Treaties' IUCN's Proposed Covenant on Environment & Development," 13 *Pace Environmental Law Review* 133, 1995

Most nations today confront multiple challenges to the environmental quality which underpins and nourishes their socioeconomic development. The goal of the 1992 Rio de Janeiro United Nations Conference on Environment and Development (UNCED) was to establish an action plan, *Agenda 21*, by which these challenges could be effectively met. UNCED recommended concerted national and international measures to combat global trends in pollution and the exhaustion of natural resources. The need for such measures, including legal steps to promote environmentally sustainable development, have long been recognized. Former Secretary-General Perez de Cuellar stated that "the Charter of the United Nations governs relations between States. The *Universal Declaration of Human Rights* pertains to relations between the State and the individual. The time has come to devise a covenant regulating relations between humankind and nature."

The International Union for the Conservation of Nature and Natural Resources (IUCN) arrived at the same conclusion as Secretary-General de Cuellar. IUCN's Commission on Environmental Law designed a new treaty to serve as an umbrella agreement to govern the interactions of nations with the Earth's natural systems. The first drafts were adapted from the UN's *World Charter for Nature*, which IUCN had also helped draft into treaty format. By the time the UN had convened its Preparatory Committee for UNCED in 1990, the Commission had concluded that a legal mandate was required to integrate the protection of the environment with socioeconomic development. The IUCN *Draft International Covenant on Environment and Development* (*Draft Covenant*), the text of which is printed as an appendix to this article, restates and refines the relationship between society and nature. The *Draft Covenant* was the product of extensive study and negotiation. It was proposed as a basic framework treaty, to integrate the Rio Treaties on Biological Diversity and Climate Change and the post-Rio Treaties on Desertification and Highly Migratory and Straddling Fish Stocks, along with other global and regional treaties.

In order to build a sustainable global community, the nations of the world must renew their commitment to the United Nations, fulfill their obligations under existing international agreements, and support the implementation of Earth Charter principles.

Although future negotiations will probably result in revisions of the draft treaty, it nevertheless is a valuable model of how international environmental law should be integrated and made more effective. A prior version of the *Draft Covenant* was published as part of the official deliberations of UNCED's Third Preparatory Committee. Even a cursory comparison of this earlier version to IUCN's present draft suggests that diplomatic negotiators will probably have an equal opportunity to modify the present draft as they had with the previously published version. The present IUCN *Draft Covenant* reflects a mature, well researched and negotiated foundation on which these future negotiations can be based.

This article examines the genesis and scope of the IUCN *Draft Covenant*. It (a) describes IUCN's interest and experience in preparing the proposed *Draft Covenant*; (b) analyzes the roles the *Draft Covenant* can serve; and (c) identifies some illustrative precedents for the Articles of the *Draft Covenant*.

IUCN's Interests in the Covenant

IUCN was founded in 1948 by an international intergovernmental organization (United Nations Educational, Scientific and Cultural Organization, or UNESCO), and by a nongovernmental organization (the Swiss League For The Protection of Nature). One of its purposes was to develop new treaties to conserve nature and natural resources. While it was unusual in 1948 to create IUCN as a partnership of such seemingly diverse authorities, today the need for such collaboration is an integral part of *Agenda 21*'s recommendations. IUCN has grown to have a majority of its members in the southern hemisphere. Over 60 states, 95 ministries, and 500 nongovernmental organizations (NGOs) of all sorts (from university units, to professional societies, to citizen movements) today comprise IUCN. It is the largest worldwide partnership committed to building what UNCED calls "sustainable development." Headquartered in Switzerland, it is governed by a General Assembly which meets every three years, and is the only organization in which States and NGOs sit together and vote, bicamerally, to govern a worldwide organization.

IUCN has five expert commissions of volunteers who do much of its work: The Species Survival Commission (which, for instance, prepares and publishes the IUCN Red Data books), the Commission on Parks & Protected Areas (which among its tasks prepares the UN Secretary General's List of the World's Parks), the Commission on Environmental Law, the Ecology Commission and the Planning Commission. The Environmental Law Commission assists nations in preparing statutes and treaties and undertakes studies and publishes the results. For example, the Environmental Law Commission prepared and published the annotated paperback edition of *Agenda 21*, which was the 27th scholarly publication since 1972.

IUCN's Environmental Law Commission, with its secretariat in Bonn, Germany, began the *Draft Covenant* well before the UN General Assembly launched the UN Preparatory Committee for the Conference on Environment and Development. After the Third Preparatory Committee Meeting, when the draft appeared as an official UN document, the IUCN consulted and included the responses of the delegates to UNCED's Preparation Committee Meeting.

In addition to preparing several treaties, the IUCN assisted many states in preparing their own national legislation. For example, IUCN's Environmental Law Commission initiated and actively participated in negotiating the 1973 *Convention on International Trade In Endangered Species*. IUCN prepared the first draft of a Biological Diversity Treaty in 1986, stimulating the Food and Agricultural Organization (FAO) and the United Nations Environment Programme (UNEP) to take the need for such a treaty seriously. In addition, IUCN actively participated in negotiating the resulting Rio *Convention on Biological Diversity*. Furthermore, IUCN is expressly given a role under the terms of the UNESCO *Convention on Protection of the World's Cultural and Natural Heritage*. IUCN, therefore, has a strong tradition of establishing international environmental law, including significant service in preparing the *Draft Covenant*. It works inconspicuously and constructively with States to build the legal framework for what we today term "sustainable development."

IUCN decided to prepare this draft because International Public Law has no unifying umbrella agreement to facilitate integrating environment and development. UNCED's *Agenda 21* called for the further development of legal measures by which environment and developmental needs could be better integrated. UNCED's two Rio treaties (on Biological Diversity and Climate Change) did not provide such integration; instead, they elaborated new regimes for two critical natural resource sectors. The same is true for the two post-Rio treaties on desertification, and straddling and migratory fish stocks. IUCN's Law Commission agreed with many UNCED delegates that, although a new umbrella treaty was needed, it could not be realized as part of the already overcrowded UNCED Agenda. Thus, IUCN began as both a preparation for and a follow-up to UNCED, to prepare this *Draft Covenant*.

The first steps for drafting the covenant were taken in the 1980s. In 1983, the United Nations World Commission on Environment and Development (known as the

"Brundtland Commission" after its chair, Norway's Prime Minister Gro Harlem Brundtland), established an Experts Group on Environmental Law which recommended that the United Nations prepare a new universal convention on environmental protection and sustainable development. The World Commission itself, in 1986, recommended the preparation of both a Universal Declaration and a Convention on environmental protection and sustainable development. Then, in 1988, in response to the many "soft law" instruments which already existed, the IUCN General Assembly meeting in San Jose, Costa Rica, requested that IUCN's Commission on Environmental Law continue preparing an international convention on environmental protection and sustainable development.

A formal Working Group of IUCN's Commission on Environmental Law was established in November 1989 under the chairmanship of Dr. Wolfgang E. Burhenne, the Commission's Chair. The Group included international law specialists, governmental lawyers, judges, academics and private practitioners, all acting in their personal capacities. Many of these individuals had actively participated in the 1972 UN Stockholm Conference on the Human Environment, the IUCN Working Group on the World Charter for Nature, and in the Brundtland Commission's Experts Group on Environmental Law. The *Draft Covenant* on Environmental Conservation and Sustainable Use of Natural Resources, a document which contained 88 provisions, was the basis of discussion at this first Working Group. The many comments and suggestions made were incorporated into the next draft.

In March 1991, Dr. Parvez Hassan, Chair of the IUCN Commission on Environmental Law, convened the Working Group's second meeting and deputized Professor Nicholas A. Robinson to conduct the meeting. Many of the Brundtland Commission's Legal Experts became members of the Working Group. This meeting examined the concerns of developing countries and elaborated Articles concerning the transboundary movement of hazardous waste and the environmental degradation caused by commercial enterprises including transnational corporations. The IUCN Working Group then sought the active advice of the delegates to the UNCED Preparatory Committee. It was this version that Iceland requested be distributed in all UN official languages to the UNCED Preparatory Committee as a model study draft.

With the benefit of reactions from delegates to UNCED, the IUCN Working Group's third meeting, chaired by Dr. Hassan, occurred in the aftermath of UNCED. A thorough and concerted effort was made to incorporate the consensus of *Agenda 21* into the *Draft Covenant*. The IUCN Working Group decided to expand its membership to include experts who had significantly contributed to the UNCED process. Drafting, debate and redrafting actively continued.

Dr. Hassan convened a further Drafting Committee session in April, 1993, to continue the work of integrating the ideas of UNCED into the *Draft Covenant*. This meeting further restructured the *Draft Covenant* to include a section on "Fundamental Principles," designed to address such *Agenda 21* priorities as the right to development, eradication of poverty, demographic trends, wasteful consumption patterns, and international financing mechanisms. The meeting also proposed that the treaty be entitled the Draft Covenant on Environment and Development.

Dr. Hassan chaired the fourth meeting of a further expanded Working Group in Bonn, Germany, in September 1993. In light of the fundamental moral elements of the *Draft Covenant*, the members of the IUCN Ethics Working Group, organized by IUCN's Commission on Planning, were invited to attend. Since biological diversity was also a major concern of the Covenant Working Group, Dr. George Rabb, the Chair of the IUCN Species Survival Commission, also participated by invitation and actively contributed.

The articles of the *Draft Covenant* were still further tested and refined. Geo-political and regional issues emerged in the same manner as they had done in other international fora such as UNCED, and a deliberative approach was adopted to find a common ground in international law. The participants were sensitive both to the concerns of the developing countries and to the scientific realities of Earth's natural systems. The Working Group met the challenge to restate *Agenda 21*'s "sustainable development" policies in the form of draft legal principles and rules. The *Draft Covenant* was sent to other specialists for their critique.

The Working Group met again in December 1993, and in April 1994, to incorporate the comments made by the full Working Group and others into the text. In addition, the *Draft Covenant* was the subject of a two-day workshop at the IUCN General Assembly meeting in Buenos Aires in January 1994. In Buenos Aires, the response to the *Draft Covenant* was favorable, and constructive suggestions by religious and ethical leaders regarding general principles of international law were offered. Following the presentation of this article at the *Pace Environmental Law Review Colloquium* in September 1994, a small group of specialists on international liability met in New York City to edit, resolve drafting issues, and refine the provisions. The final draft text was presented to the United Nations Congress on Public International Law in March of 1995 at UN headquarters in New York.

The *Draft Covenant's* Roles

The Civil Law tradition highly values a codified set of principles to guide conduct. This approach is shared by socialist traditions and theocratic traditions alike.

As the history of IUCN's drafting suggests, the *Draft Covenant on Environment and Development* serves several roles. These perceived roles are the justification for the labors of lawyers and diplomats from around the world, and for legal specialists in civil law, common law, Islamic law and socialist law traditions, working together to prepare this text. There are ten basic reasons for developing this *Draft Covenant*.

First, there is no "hard law" consolidation of the many declaratory "soft law" resolutions on international environmental protection or development. Neither the UN General Assembly's *Declaration on the Right to Development*, nor its Resolution adopting the *World Charter for Nature*, are contained in treaties. The famous "Principle 21" from the UN Stockholm Conference on the Human Environment appears in only one multilateral treaty, the Rio *Biological Diversity Convention*.

It is time to reaffirm the principles and duties of these widely supported soft law statements and distill them into a clear treaty. UNCED's Declaration of Rio de Janeiro on Environment and Development need not be repeated in more soft law texts. Mere repetition of soft law principles, by itself, does not result in the realization of those principles. The particularly critical right of developing states to develop needs to be transformed into a juridical context. The energies expended in preparing repetitive resolutions should be focused into one treaty; and when ratified, those energies should be directed into regional and national measures for implementing the treaty undertakings. IUCN agreed with the basic premise that UNCED made in its *Agenda 21* Action Plan: if the deteriorating trends are to be reversed, it is urgent to stop talking about action and to start doing it.

There are two types of "soft law" recodified in the *Draft Covenant*. First are the well accepted legal principles, such as The Stockholm Conference's Principle 21. These are unexceptional and unobjectionable. Second are the very volatile and still tentatively accepted principles, such as the duty to restrain consumption of resources through avoiding waste, or the duty to promote a thoughtful demographic regime to manage population demand vis-a-vis the available resources. Indeed, Article 46 of the *Draft Covenant* goes beyond the consensus at Rio which had failed to quantify and provide additional international resources. IUCN's Commission on Environmental Law anticipated that as States debate the *Draft Covenant*, the first soft law category will be accepted as "hard law" and be the basis for the *Draft Covenant*, while the continued form of the second category of soft law remains problematic.

Second, the Civil Law tradition highly values a codified set of principles to guide conduct. This approach is shared by socialist traditions and theocratic traditions alike. IUCN published an analysis of the Islamic Principles of Environmental Protection based on the Koran, and was guided by these principles in preparing the *Draft Covenant*. In addition, other ethical and religious specialists were consulted, such as representatives of the Buddhist tradition, who contributed guidance at an IUCN Law Commission seminar on the *Draft Covenant* in Buenos Aires in January 1994. These common values of the diverse traditions are reflected in the general principles of the *Draft Covenant*. Until States can agree on a set of shared basic principles to guide their laws, there will always be some confusion and disagreement. The *Draft Covenant* seeks to promote consensus on these fundamental principles.

Third, just as agriculture, industry, fisheries management, trade and other economic ventures, as well as early conservation and natural resource use, were once deemed to be separate and independent sectors, it is clear from UNCED's *Agenda 21* that all these sectors are interrelated. Each aspect of sustainable development needs to be guided by the same basic rules. The *Draft Covenant* harmonizes and assembles these rules in one place for all to share.

Fourth, many States have not signed or ratified all the environmental treaties, and some states still have gaps in their own national legislation related to implementing such agreements. States need a framework to integrate their national legal and administrative systems, whether for internal or international use. Otherwise the result is a balkanization of environmental agencies which compete for budgets, contest "turf control" and oppose some forms of development rather than giving support to sustainable development. In response, many developmental interests attempt to circumvent environmental controls.

The *Draft Covenant* by itself cannot solve all these disputes, but it can steer the competing agencies into a common framework, and help them to recognize their interdependency. Law can serve as a guide. The *Draft Covenant*'s articles may tend to curb such disaggregating trends that appear in all regions.

Fifth, in addition to building a set of common legal goals for all States, the *Draft Covenant* fills some missing gaps. For instance, the duty to undertake Environmental Impact Assessment (EIA) (Article 37 of the *Draft Covenant*) is not stated as a treaty obligation for most activities. In addition, the *Espoo Convention* of the UN Economic Commission for Europe (ECE) applies only to transboundary impacts in the ECE region. Soil conservation (Article 18 of the *Draft Covenant*) is a well recognized environmental science, but is not addressed in any treaty. States should not ignore their duty to manage soil until they lose so much of it that they must adhere to the Rio *Desertification Treaty*. Moreover, all States are parties to the Vienna *Convention to Protect the Stratospheric Ozone*, and depend on this atmospheric ozone layer to shield against harmful ultraviolet solar radiation. Even States who are not yet ready to ratify the specific undertakings of the Vienna Convention and Montreal Protocol, should acknowledge a legal duty to protect the ozone layer.

Sixth, by establishing such a common set of rules, the *Draft Covenant* levels the playing field for international trade. It clarifies what is and what is not appropriate environmental protection. For example, non-tariff trade barriers could be discerned more clearly, and disputes over possible non-tariff trade barriers could be minimized.

Seventh, the *Draft Covenant* can be a guide for parties who seek to revise their other treaties or prepare supplementary protocols. These disparate existing agreements can be harmonized incrementally over time, and become mutually reinforcing. The EIA process in every sectoral treaty does not have to be repeated; once it is completed here, it can be incorporated by reference into other legal instruments. Any inconsistencies that might inadvertently arise in different negotiation sessions can be avoided. This also saves scarce diplomatic and legislative time and money.

Eighth, the *Draft Covenant* provides an environmental code for intergovernmental agencies, such as UNESCO, the World Bank, FAO, and others to use. The many regional and global intergovernmental bodies should avoid duplicative or inconsistent approaches to the same sustainable development issues that the States have addressed.

Ninth, and quite fundamentally, the *Draft Covenant* is a teaching tool. Law is most successful when it educates, identifies the path of enlightened self-interest, and induces persons or States to voluntarily follow that path. The *Draft Covenant*, by relying on principles of international cooperation, instead of coercion, illuminates the way.

Tenth is the most basic rationale, and the fundamental reason for nine years of preparation and now for worldwide debate: to revise and adopt the *Draft Covenant* on Environment and Development. Without considering both development and environment, most, if not all, nations cannot cope with the growing burden of water and air pollution, depleted natural resource stocks, meeting the needs of growing human populations, and solving related problems. The UN World Commission on Environment and Development (Brundtland Commission) made this clear in *Our Common Future*. UNCED did so even more emphatically at the Earth Summit Meetings in 1992 in Rio de Janeiro.

In the post-Rio period, a visible diplomatic process is needed to strengthen the implementation of *Agenda 21* at all levels. The high profile of the UN Commission on Sustainable Development must be maintained in order to rapidly integrate and advance the interests of both the environment and development. If the developed States seem to have lost this perspective following Rio, debate over the *Draft Covenant* can revive attention to the urgent global challenges of *Agenda 21*. This *Draft Covenant* obliges the world's political leaders to focus on the priorities it sets out in its Articles. Is this proposal a realistic effort? How can it not be?

There are those who say that the world does not need another treaty. There are those who want more soft law, an "Earth Charter" as Maurice Strong had urged at Rio, and subsequently through the Earth Council and the "Green Cross," two post-Rio new nongovernmental organizations. Such advocates often have not looked at the large number of treaties that do exist, or asked how best to integrate them.

Some may argue that the world needs implementation of *Agenda 21*'s prescriptions for action, not more treaties. Yet, in Chapters 38 and 39 of *Agenda 21*, UNCED expressly calls for more establishing law like the *Draft Covenant* in order to guide and accelerate sustainable development. The

Draft Covenant is, in fact, one of the measures that UNCED proposes for implementing *Agenda 21*. Law is essential for implementing global, regional, and national policy on environment and development. UNCED emphasized the need to integrate "environment and development issues at national, subregional, regional and international levels," including:

(a) elaborating the balance between environmental and developmental concerns;

(b) clarifying the relationships between the various existing treaties; and

(c) ensuring national participation in both developing and implementing these legal measures, with particular focus on developing countries.

Rather than competing with *Agenda 21*, the UNCED consensus supports the creation of the *Draft Covenant*.

Some may doubt that IUCN can find a consensus among States today in support of the *Draft Covenant*. IUCN faced the same objection in 1986 to its "new" idea of a biological diversity treaty. In fact, IUCN has wide support among States for this *Draft Covenant*, especially among the developing nations. Some states, perhaps even the United States, will oppose the *Draft Covenant* for a time. It took the United States three decades to ratify the *Convention against Genocide*. This opposition, if it emerges, is not likely to stop the *Draft Covenant* from going forward into formal negotiations, conclusion and ratifications. The objectives of the *Draft Covenant* can be widely realized without universal participation. The *Draft Covenant* may induce a positive and consistent State practice which can ripen into customary law for states that do not quickly become parties.

The *Draft Covenant on Environment and Development* offers support for sustainable development in many sectors. The *Draft Covenant* furthers the environmental protection articles (Part XII) of the UN *Law of the Sea Convention*, and "updates" these Articles by integrating such duties to new undertakings, unconceived of at the time the UN Conference on the Law of the Sea in 1982, such as how loss of the stratospheric ozone layer affects marine phytoplankton. The *Draft Covenant* also encourages emergency preparedness and the avoidance of harm rather than allowing damage to occur and afterwards paying for compensation. Specific duties and priorities set forth in the *Draft Covenant* make it more likely that sustainable development can proceed.

In short, this *Draft Covenant* does precisely what Dr. Emil Salim of Indonesia urged in his May 1990 address to The South-East Asia and Pacific Ocean Law Conference (SEAPOL) in Bali, Indonesia. Dr. Salim said:

> "We believe that pursuit of sustainable development is the only viable way to ensure that mankind will prevail now and in the future. That pursuit must be properly institutionalized, among others, through legal and legislative impacts."

The Precedents for the *Draft Covenant*

IUCN's *Draft Covenant on Environment and Development* is structured in nine key "Parts", and includes an opening article stating its objectives and several standard "Final Clauses." All of the seventy-two proposed articles serve the *Draft Covenant*'s central objective, "to achieve environmental conservation and sustainable development by establishing integrated rights and obligations." The following survey of the precedents which support the *Draft Covenant* illuminates how its objective may be realized.

Part II of the *Draft Covenant* states the "Fundamental Principles" on which its specific obligations are based. Five of these articles essentially restate well accepted general principles of international law, and four are basic precepts arrived at through consensus at UNCED. The World Charter for Nature provides a more detailed version of sustainability principles that were derived by reevaluating international law in light of contemporary environmental scientific knowledge. For instance, while "respect for all life forms" finds express treaty precedent in both the Rio Biological Diversity Treaty and the Berne Convention on European Wildlife, this principle is one found in every major religion. It is a genuine general principle of international law, so universally adopted that it questioned only now when mankind's unprecedented tampering with the Earth's hydrologic cycle, stratospheric ozone shield, or other actions cause the rapid extinction of species. These unnatural trends demand a restatement and reaffirmation of the principle in a treaty. A familiar situation is addressed when the *Draft Covenant* states that the environment "is a common concern of humanity."

The Articles on "Intergenerational Equity," Prevention, and Precaution are all related, and find support in Principle 21 of the *Stockholm Declaration*. While ensuring that no State will use its environment or resources so as to harm another State, the rule for precaution as stated in Article 3(3) of the *Rio Climate Change Convention* is evident and well acknowledged, as is the rule for prevention found in Article 194(2) of the UN *Law of the Sea Convention* or Article 3 of the Rio *Biological Diversity Treaty*. Even more basic is the duty of parents to provide for their descendants, and the human right of future generations to find that their ability to satisfy their needs has not been compromised by past generations. Paragraph 11 of the Vienna *Declaration of Human Rights*, restates this duty, as does Principle 3 of the Rio *Declaration on Environment and Development*.

The *Agenda 21* principles which articulate the right to develop, the eradication of poverty, the avoidance of wasteful consumption, and the recognition that peace, development, environmental protection and respect for human rights are interdependent, and are grounded in the right to life itself. Since these principles permeate most of *Agenda 21*, the Agenda itself is perhaps the best authority for these principles.

Part III of the *Draft Covenant* sets forth general obligations. These are divided into rather conventional duties of States, including Principle 21 of the *Stockholm Declaration* on the duty to cooperate as governed by the United Nations Charter itself. Less conventional is the Article on Persons. One of *Agenda 21*'s most important consensus elements is to prescribe cooperation and stewardship obligations for individuals. Just as international human rights place the individual as the subject of international law, so too do the general principles of law governing environment and development. The *Draft Covenant* incorporates these soft law elements from *Agenda 21* into a treaty standard by which to gauge human conduct. The other general obligations of Part III elaborate the basic objective of the *Draft Covenant* and restate the basic tenet of environmental protection that when states remediate an environmental harm or threat, they must not transform or transfer the harm into another form.

Among the most effective provisions of the *Draft Covenant* are those set forth in Part IV, "relating to natural systems and resources." These Articles integrate environmental scientific knowledge with social and economic actions. Whether it is the State's duty to respond to emergencies such as a Chernobyl-type accident or to protect the stratospheric ozone, or to stabilize anthropogenic interference with the Earth's climate system, or to maintain water quality systems, the *Draft Covenant* carefully restates already widely acknowledged duties. The *Draft Covenant*'s Articles on Soil, Natural Systems, and Biological Diversity are more innovative and progressive. Similarly, the Articles on Biological Diversity or on cultural and national heritage integrate existing treaties on those topics, and put them in the context of inter-sectoral duties. No treaty today reflects the teachings of soils science. It is anomalous for States to prescribe remediation for desertification according to the Rio Treaty on Desertification and yet posit no rule to prevent the desertification from developing.

The structure of the *Draft Covenant* is similar to that of the UN *World Charter for Nature* where principles are stated first and are followed by specific duties derived therefrom. Part V of the *Draft Covenant* sets forth obligations relating to human processes and activities. Here technology assessment, pollution prevention and abatement, waste minimization, and the integration of alien or modified organisms each reflect customary state practice and treaty law as it has developed since the 1972 UN Conference on the Human Environment.

Part VI of the *Draft Covenant* is primarily derived from UNCED. The Articles on "Demographic Policies" and on "Consumption Patterns" reflect the UNCED agreement to balance *Agenda 21*'s Chapter 5, "Changing Consumption Patterns," and Chapter 4, "Demographic Dynamics and Sustainability." This was the essential North-South consensus balance agreed to at UNCED. The 1994 Cairo Conference on Population elaborated the former in its Declaration and Action Plan. Further elaboration of the latter is found primarily in emerging state practice, such as the green packaging rules of Germany or electricity demand-side management reforms of several states in the United States.

Part VI also contains the more problematic articles covering "Eradication of Poverty," "Trade and Environment," and "Economic Activities of Foreign Origin." These proposed Articles were drafted to help diplomats use specific terms rather than the general expressions of consensus in their negotiations of issues that had already been arrived at in UNCED and were included in *Agenda 21*. Greater clarity of the core legal obligations is required to move these UNCED expressions of consensus from soft law to hard law. Drafting these articles presented, perhaps, the most difficult challenge in preparing the *Draft Covenant*. Their expression represents largely uncharted territory, although the 1994 Cairo Population Conference Programme of Action offers some guidance on state practice, as do the 1994 agreement establishing the World Trade Organization and other recent developments under

The *General Agreement on Tariffs and Trade*, as well as the *Environmental Side Agreement* for the *North American Free Trade Agreement*.

Although these progressive and newly defined articles lack established formulas for expressing their obligations, the duties to protect the environment in times of armed conflict are very clear. These duties are precisely defined by the Additional Protocol I (1977) to the Red Cross 1949 *Geneva Convention* and the UN 1976 *Environmental Modification Treaty*. The 1954 *Hague Cultural Property Convention* defines the protection of culture and nature, which are obligatory in time of armed conflict. Although the International Committee of the Red Cross and IUCN have proposed practical measures by which States can implement these obligations, few have done so. Here the *Draft Covenant*'s problems arise not from the need to draft new written texts, but from the persistent failure of States to take the required political steps to give effect to the rules that they understand and adapt.

In Part VII, the *Draft Covenant* returns to more conventional and well settled legal norms. Most of these duties are based on ample precedents and reflect substantial state practice; some are reflective of custom. The duties with respect to transboundary environmental effects, including prior notification and environmental impact assessment, are well established. Duties for the management of shared resources have a rich and accepted legal foundation.

The *Draft Covenant* again encounters difficulty when it restates the legal duties for "implementation and cooperation." These Articles, stated in Part III do not reflect the same kind of preliminary consensus encountered in Part VI. Rather, they are consensus norms that were agreed to at UNCED because they are in fact widely used and accepted within States around the world. What was new at UNCED is their inclusion in an international soft law context in addition to their status as national legislation. Not all States have enacted such laws. The *Draft Covenant* would require each State to promulgate comparable legislation for sustainable development.

Most nations already have enacted legislation which enumerates duties to prepare national action plans; to undertake regional land use plans and other physical planning; to enact and routinely employ environmental impact assessment; to establish environmental standards and routine controls for pollution control or natural resource management; to collect environmental data and information to ascertain clearly the facts about environmental conditions; and to cooperate on scientific and technical matters. Other treaties often also provide authority supporting such legislative duties.

Even if States acknowledge the need for such national environmental laws, the *Draft Covenant* in Part VIII effectively provides what each nation, individually cannot achieve. Missing from these national laws and the sectoral treaties on specific topics is a coordinating procedure. UNCED, like the Brundtland Commission before it, identified and confirmed the need to integrate and harmonize these various legal systems around the world. All States should have common national legal procedures and means by which to observe the treaty obligations of the *Draft Covenant*. Just as the World Charter for Nature set out guidance for national implementation of its principles, so UNCED in *Agenda 21* recognized the importance of not leaving it for the States to take the next step to establish and integrate their legal implementation machinery.

Although to diplomatic and national political leaders, Part VIII may appear to be an undistinguished part of the *Draft Covenant*, it is nonetheless probably the most important section because it induces the States to integrate environmental concerns with development. It is here that the *Draft Covenant*'s objectives must be achieved, or not at all.

Corollaries which arise out of this existing state legislative and administrative practice can be used to promote effectiveness. The remainder of the Articles in Part VIII, concerning the development and transfer of technology, the fair and equitable sharing of the benefits of biotechnologies, the exchange of information and knowledge and the furthering of education, training and public awareness, all state important duties which make implementation more efficient.

Similarly unless all nations allocate adequate national financial resources for observance and implementation, the individual States cannot succeed in meeting the legal obligations of attaining sustainable development. *Agenda 21* expressly emphasized the far reaching significance of this seemingly self-evident rule.

It will be more problematic for diplomats to restate the proposed Article on International Financial Resources in any future negotiations of this *Draft Covenant*. This Article is similar to Part VI because it relates to obligations concerning global issues. It appears in the "implementation and cooperation" part because it logically belongs there. It should be noted, however, that no treaty obligation now fixes the duty of nations to target 0.7 percent of their gross national product for official development assistance. Many nations do, in fact, make major voluntary financial contributions toward development. However, this sum has not kept pace with increases in population growth, global pollution, or natural resource depletion.

UNCED heatedly debated the need for more than merely incremental increases in each State's developmental aid. However, as reflected in the financial paragraphs in each Chapter of *Agenda 21*, consensus was difficult to achieve and little new financial support was forthcoming.

Nonetheless, if the UN target of 0.7 percent is not to be regarded hypocritically, serious efforts are needed to translate the fragile *Agenda 21* consensus on financial duties into a legal context. At least, diplomats can now negotiate the more precise terms of this legal and moral obligation to cooperate in establishing the conditions for "sustainable development," and can try to attain an acceptable restatement of such a duty. Of course, a range of treaty precedents for this obligation already exists, including the terms establishing the World Bank, the Global Environmental Facility and the undertakings noted in *Agenda 21*. It should be possible for a *Draft Covenant* on Environment and Development to state this legal duty with specificity. IUCN offers this first draft towards that end.

Part IX on "Responsibility and Liability" is a very useful melding of well settled, public international law obligations with reasonably clear private international and comparative law duties. State responsibility and liability are well restated. The obligations of cessation, restitution and compensation are also accepted. The problem with this part is its application. No actual or potential "wrong-doer" ever wants a clearly stated rule and some politicians will resist this restatement because they fear that their future conduct may be judged by it.

Regrettably, there is no universally agreed forum today where judgment for acts which violate international law and damage the environment can be had. The International Court of Justice and its environmental chamber, or the Permanent Court of International Arbitration could take on these tasks, but States routinely have not made the political decisions to assign them this responsibility.

It is all the more important, therefore, for this *Draft Covenant* to clearly state the agreed rules of responsibility and liability. Whenever courts must decide, or ad hoc arbitral panels are convened, or a compromise sends a matter to an international tribunal, Part IX of this *Draft Covenant* can provide parties with a neutral rule to apply.

Seen in this light, the *Draft Covenant*'s Part IX is extremely important in providing a mechanism for the peaceful settlement of disputes over environmental and natural resource claims. Articles on agreed exemptions from liability, the duty of States to provide civil remedies to victims of environmental wrongs and that such recourse be non-discriminatory, complete Part IX.

All the Articles in the *Draft Covenant* must be read together with the other treaties already in force that concern the same subjects. The purpose of Part X is to provide general rules of interpretation and application for a harmonious integration of the obligations set forth in the various treaties. The Vienna *Convention on the Law of Treaties* is the foundation for this Part. The Articles on the Parties' participation in these related treaties, about permitting the more stringent rules to apply, the application to the commons, and relations with non-parties provide rules for construing related duties in the specific context of environment and development. They provide the framework to expressly guide the harmonization of all the varied and still growing number of treaties that pertain to sustainable development.

All the Articles in the Draft Covenant *must be read together with the other treaties already in force that concern the same subjects.*

The Articles on national reporting, compliance, and dispute avoidance or settlement, offer practical steps by which unilateral disagreements concerning the application of these rules of interpretation may be clarified and peacefully resolved.

Finally, the *Draft Covenant on Environment and Development* contemplates the need for a forum where changes to the *Draft Covenant* can be considered. No single United Nations organ, except perhaps the General Assembly itself, has the full oversight of the matters set forth in the *Draft Covenant*. Thus, a provision has been made for a limited conference of parties to periodically review the work of this self-implementary *Draft Covenant*. There are ample precedents for such a review conference. While it may be more progressive to structure a new specialized international agency for sustainable development, or merge the UN Development Programme (UNDP) with the UNEP, there is as yet no consensus among States to take this step. States need time to independently harmonize their national endeavors under an umbrella agreement such as the *Draft Covenant*, before they can define the roles they wish such an agency to serve.

The final clauses of Part XI contain standard elements of international law. Twenty-one States must ratify this *Draft Covenant* before it enters into force, although a larger or lesser number of States could be selected. It has been proposed that the United Nations Secretary General be the Depositary for the *Draft Covenant*, although the European Union or any State could be assigned this responsibility.

Conclusions

IUCN has prepared its *Draft Covenant on Environment and Development* as a model text. Its reception awaits the debates in the UN Commission on Sustainable Development, in the UN Environment Programme's Governing Council, and elsewhere. States must resolve whether or not they wish to translate the soft law of *Agenda 21* on sustainable development into a hard law treaty, and if so, how.

Just as the first 50 years of multilateral cooperation through the UN largely addressed an agenda of international peace-keeping, human rights and disarmament, so the next 50 years of State cooperation will work to integrate environment and development and make progress toward attaining sustainable development. If it does nothing else, at least the terms of the *Draft Covenant* provide an inventory for this future agenda, which is essential to the well being of Earth and the life it sustains.

B

IUCN Commission on Environmental Law, *Draft Covenant on Environment and Development, 2nd Edition: Updated Text*, IUCN in cooperation with International Council of Environmental Law, 2000

Part I: Objective

Article 1—Objective

The objective of this Covenant is to achieve environmental conservation and sustainable development by establishing integrated rights and obligations.

Part II: Fundamental Principles

In their actions to achieve the objective of this Covenant and to implement its provisions, the Parties shall co-operate in a spirit of global partnership and shall be guided, *inter alia*, by the following fundamental principles:

Article 2—Respect for All Life Forms

Nature as a whole warrants respect. The integrity of the Earth's ecological systems shall be maintained and restored. Every form of life is unique and is to be safeguarded independent of its value to humanity.

Article 3—Common Concern of Humanity

The global environment is a common concern of humanity.

Article 4—Interdependent Values

Peace, development, environmental protection and respect for human rights and fundamental freedoms are interdependent.

Article 5—Intergenerational Equity

The freedom of action of each generation in regard to the environment is qualified by the needs of future generations.

Article 6—Prevention

Protection of the environment is best achieved by preventing environmental harm rather than by attempting to remedy or compensate for such harm.

Article 7—Precaution

Lack of scientific certainty is no reason to postpone action to avoid potentially serious or irreversible harm to the environment.

Article 8—Right to Development

The exercise of the right to development entails the obligation to meet the developmental and environmental needs of humanity in a sustainable and equitable manner.

Article 9—Eradication of Poverty

The eradication of poverty, which in particular necessitates a global partnership, is an indispensable requirement for sustainable development.

Article 10—Consumption Patterns and Demographic Policies

The elimination of unsustainable patterns of consumption and production and the promotion of appropriate demographic policies are necessary to enhance the quality of life for all humanity and reduce disparities in standards of living.

Part III: General Obligations

Article 11—States

1. States have, in accordance with the Charter of the United Nations and the principles of international law, the sovereign right to utilize their resources to meet their environmental and sustainable developmental needs, and the obligations:
   (a) to protect and preserve the environment within the limits of their national jurisdiction; and
   (b) to ensure that activities within their jurisdiction or control do not cause potential or actual harm to the environment of other States or of areas beyond the limits of national jurisdiction.
2. States have, in accordance with the Charter of the United Nations and principles of international law, the right to protect the environment under their jurisdiction from significant harm caused by activities outside their national jurisdiction. If such harm has occurred, they are entitled to appropriate remedies.
3. Parties shall take all appropriate measures to avoid wasteful use of natural resources and, in particular, to ensure the sustainable use of renewable resources.
4. Parties shall provide the public, including nongovernmental organizations, local communities and indigenous peoples, with appropriate opportunities to participate during decision making processes relating to the environment.
5. Parties who are members of international organizations undertake to pursue within such organizations policies that are consistent with the provisions of this Covenant.
6. Parties shall apply the principle that the costs of preventing, controlling and reducing potential or actual harm to the environment are to be borne by the originator.

Article 12—Persons

1. Parties undertake to achieve progressively the full realization of the right of everyone to an environment and a level of development adequate for their health, well-being and dignity.
2. All persons have a duty to protect and preserve the environment.
3. All persons, without being required to prove an interest, have the right to seek, receive, and disseminate information in respect to the environment, subject only to such restrictions as may be provided by law and are necessary for respect for the rights of others, for the protection of national security or for the protection of the environment.
4. All concerned persons have the right to participate effectively during decision making processes at the local, national and international levels regarding activities, measures, plans, programs and policies that may have a significant effect on the environment.
5. All persons have a right of effective access to administrative and judicial procedures, including for redress and remedies, to enforce their rights in respect to the environment, under national and international law.
6. Parties shall respect and ensure the rights and the fulfillment of the duties recognized in this Article and shall devote special attention to the satisfaction of basic human needs, in particular the provision of potable water.
7. Parties shall develop or improve mechanisms to facilitate the involvement of indigenous peoples and local communities in environmental decision-making at all levels and shall take measures to enable them to pursue sustainable traditional practices.

Article 13—Integrating Environment and Development

1. Parties shall pursue sustainable development policies aimed at the eradication of poverty, the general improvement of economic, social and cultural conditions, the conservation of biological diversity, and the maintenance of essential ecological processes and life-support systems.

2. Parties shall ensure that environmental conservation is treated as an integral part of the planning and implementation of activities at all stages and at all levels, giving full and equal consideration to environmental, economic, social and cultural factors. To this end, Parties shall:
   (a) conduct regular national reviews of environmental and developmental policies and plans;
   (b) enact effective laws and regulations which use, where appropriate, economic instruments; and
   (c) establish or strengthen institutional structures and procedures to fully integrate environmental and developmental issues in all spheres of decision making.

Parties shall take all appropriate measures to achieve the stabilization of concentrations of greenhouse gases in the atmosphere at a level that prevents dangerous anthropogenic interference with the climate system.

Article 14—Transfer or Transformation of Environmental Harm

Parties shall not transfer, directly or indirectly, harm or hazards from one area to another or transform one type of environmental harm to another.

Article 15—Emergencies

1. Each Party shall, without delay and by the most expeditious means available, notify potentially affected States and competent international organizations of any emergency originating within its jurisdiction or control, or of which it has knowledge, that it may cause harm to the environment.
2. A Party within whose jurisdiction or control an emergency originates shall immediately take all practicable measures necessitated by the circumstances, in cooperation with potentially affected States, and where appropriate, competent international organizations, to prevent, mitigate and eliminate harmful effects of the emergency.
3. Parties shall develop joint contingency plans for responding to emergencies, in cooperation, where appropriate, with other States and competent international organizations.

Part IV: Obligations Relating to Natural Systems and Resources

Article 16—Stratospheric Ozone

Parties shall take all appropriate measures to prevent the depletion of stratospheric ozone. To that end, Parties shall restrict human activities which modify or are likely to modify the stratospheric ozone layer in ways that adversely affect human health and the environment.

Article 17—Global Climate

Parties shall take all appropriate measures to achieve the stabilization of concentrations of greenhouse gases in the atmosphere at a level that prevents dangerous anthropogenic interference with the climate system. Such a level should be achieved within a time frame sufficient to allow ecosystems to adapt naturally to climate change, to ensure that food production, essential ecological processes, and biological diversity are not threatened, and to enable economic development to proceed in a sustainable manner.

Article 18—Soil

Parties shall take all appropriate measures to ensure the conservation and where necessary the regeneration of soils for all living systems by taking effective measures to prevent soil erosion, to combat desertification, to safeguard the processes of organic decomposition and to promote the continuing fertility of soils.

Article 19—Water

Parties shall take all appropriate measures to maintain and restore the quality of water, including atmospheric, marine, ground and surface fresh water, to meet basic human needs and as an essential component of aquatic systems. Parties also shall take all appropriate measures, in particular through conservation and management of water resources, to ensure the availability of a sufficient quantity of water to satisfy basic human needs and to maintain aquatic systems.

Article 20—Natural Systems

1. Parties shall take appropriate measures to conserve and, where necessary and possible, restore natural systems which support life on Earth in all its diversity, including biological diversity, and to maintain and restore the ecological functions of these systems as an essential basis for sustainable development, including *inter alia*,
   (a) forests as natural means to control erosion and floods, and for their role in the climate system;
   (b) freshwater wetlands and floodplains as recharge areas for groundwaters, floodwater

buffers, filters and oxidizing areas for contaminants;

(c) marine ecosystems, in particular coastal ecosystems including barrier islands, estuaries, mangroves, sea grass beds, coral reefs and mudflats as natural defenses against coastal erosion and essential habitats for the support of fisheries.

2. Parties shall, within their jurisdiction, manage natural systems as single ecological units. In particular they shall,

(a) manage aquatic systems as entire units covering the full extent of the catchment area, and

(b) manage coastal systems as entire units covering both aquatic and terrestrial components.

Article 21—Biological Diversity

1. Parties shall take all appropriate measures to conserve biological diversity, including species diversity, genetic diversity within species, and ecosystem diversity, especially through in situ conservation. To this end, Parties shall:

(a) integrate conservation of biological diversity into their physical planning systems,

(b) establish a system of protected areas, where appropriate with buffer zones and interconnected corridors, and

(c) prohibit the taking or destruction of endangered species, protect their habitats, and develop recovery plans for such species.

2. States shall regulate or manage biological resources with a view to ensuring their conservation, sustainable use, and where necessary and possible, restoration. To this end, Parties shall:

(a) develop and implement conservation and management plans for harvested biological resources;

(b) prevent a decrease in the size of harvested populations below the level necessary to ensure stable recruitment;

(c) safeguard and restore habitats essential to the continued existence of the species or populations concerned;

(d) preserve and restore ecological relationships between harvested and dependant or associated species or populations; and

(e) prevent or minimize incidental taking of non-target species and prohibit indiscriminate means of taking.

Article 22—Cultural and Natural Heritage

Parties shall take all appropriate measures to conserve or rehabilitate cultural and natural monuments, and areas, including Antarctica, of outstanding scientific, cultural, spiritual, or aesthetic significance and to prevent all deliberate measures and acts which might harm or threaten such monuments or areas.

Part V. Obligations Relating to Processes and Activities

Article 23—Prevention of Harm

Parties shall identify and evaluate substances, technologies, processes and categories of activities which have or are likely to have significant adverse effects on the environment. They shall systematically survey, regulate or manage them with a view to preventing any significant environmental harm.

Article 24—Pollution

Parties shall take, individually or jointly, all appropriate measures to prevent, reduce, control, and eliminate to the fullest extent possible, detrimental changes in the environment, in particular from radioactive, toxic, and other hazardous substances. For this purpose, they shall use the best practicable means at their disposal and shall endeavor to harmonize their policies.

Article 25—Waste

1. Parties shall ensure that the generation of waste is reduced to a minimum, particularly through the use of non-waste technology.
2. Waste shall be reused, recovered, and recycled to the fullest extent possible.
3. Waste which cannot be reused, recovered, or recycled, shall be disposed of in an environmentally sound manner, to the fullest extent possible in the source Party.
4. Under no circumstances shall there be any export of waste where the exporting Party has reason to believe that it will not be managed in an environmentally sound manner or to a place where waste import has been banned. If a transboundary

movement cannot be completed in compliance with these requirements, the exporting Party shall ensure that such waste is taken back if alternative environmentally sound arrangements cannot be made.

Article 26—Introduction of Alien or Modified Organisms

1. Parties shall prohibit the intentional introduction into the environment of alien or modified organisms which are likely to have adverse effects on other organisms or the environment. They shall also take the appropriate measures to prevent accidental introduction or escape of such organisms.
2. Parties shall regulate and manage the risks associated with the development, use and release of modified organisms resulting from biotechnologies which are likely to have adverse effects on other organisms or the environment.
3. Parties shall take all appropriate measures to control and, to the extent possible, eradicate introduced alien or modified organisms when such organisms have or are likely to have a significant adverse effect on other organisms or the environment.

Article 27—Eradication of Poverty

Parties, with the assistance of and in cooperation with other States and international organizations as appropriate, shall seek to take measures which will, directly or indirectly, contribute to the eradication of poverty, including measures to:

(a) enable all individuals to achieve sustainable livelihoods;
(b) promote food security and, where appropriate, food self-sufficiency in the context of sustainable agriculture;
(c) rehabilitate degraded resources, to the extent practicable, and promote sustainable use of resources for basic human needs;
(d) provide potable water and sanitation; and
(e) provide education.

Article 28—Consumption and Production Patterns

Parties shall seek to develop strategies to eliminate unsustainable patterns of consumption and production. Such strategies shall be designed, in particular, to meet the basic needs of the poor and to reduce use of non–renewable resources in the production process. To this end, Parties shall:

(a) collect and disseminate information on consumption patterns and develop or improve methodologies for analysis;
(b) ensure that all raw materials and energy are conserved and used as efficiently as possible in all products and processes;
(c) require reusing and recycling of used materials to the fullest extent possible;
(d) promote product designs that increase reuse and recycling and as far as possible eliminate waste; and
(e) facilitate the role and participation of consumer organizations in promoting more sustainable consumption patterns.
(f) ensure that sufficient product information is made available to the public in a manner that enables consumers to make informed environmental choices.

Article 29—Demographic Policies

Parties shall develop or strengthen demographic policies in order to achieve sustainable development. To this end, Parties shall:

(a) conduct studies to estimate the size of the human population their environment is capable of supporting and develop programs relating to population growth at corresponding levels;
(b) cooperate to alleviate the stress on natural support systems caused by major population flows;
(c) cooperate as requested to provide a necessary infrastructure on a priority basis for areas with rapid population growth; and
(d) provide to their populations full information on the options concerning family planning.

Article 30—Trade and Environment

1. Parties shall cooperate to establish and maintain an international economic system that equitably meets the developmental and environmental needs of present and future generations. To this end, Parties shall endeavor to ensure that:
   (a) trade does not lead to the wasteful use of natural resources nor interfere with their conservation or sustainable use;

(b) trade measures addressing transboundary or global environmental problems are based, as far as possible, on international consensus;
(c) trade measures for environmental purposes do not constitute a means of arbitrary or unjustifiable discrimination or a disguised restriction on international trade;
(d) unilateral trade measures by importing Parties in response to activities which are harmful or potentially harmful to the environment outside the jurisdiction of such Parties are avoided as far as possible or occur only after consultation with affected States and are implemented in a transparent manner; and
(e) prices of commodities and raw materials reflect the full direct and indirect social and environmental costs of their extraction, production, transport, marketing, and, where appropriate, ultimate disposal.

2. As regards biological resources, products and derivatives, Parties shall endeavor to ensure that:
   (a) trade is based on management plans for the sustainable harvesting of such resources and does not endanger any species or ecosystem; and
   (b) Parties, whose biological resources cannot be exported due to prohibitions imposed by a multilateral environmental agreement, shall receive appropriate compensation for losses suffered due to non-compliance by any other party to that agreement.

Article 31—Economic Activities of Foreign Origin

1. Parties shall require, from all economic entities and in regard to activities of foreign origin conducted within their jurisdiction, information on:
   (a) potential or actual harm to the environment resulting from their activities;
   (b) the relevant environmental legal requirements and standards applicable in the State of origin;
   (c) the techniques in use in the State of origin to comply with such requirements and standards; and
   (d) reasonably available data and information concerning the state-of-the-art techniques to prevent environmental harm.
2. The Party of origin shall, upon request of the host Party,
   (a) provide it with all relevant information on applicable environmental requirements and standards within the limits of its jurisdiction; and
   (b) enter into consultations with the host Party to enable the host Party to take appropriate measures regarding such activities.
3. The Party of origin shall ensure that, in the absence of equally strict or higher environmental standards in the host Party or express agreement by the host Party to the contrary, it shall cause its nationals to apply the relevant standards of the Party of origin.

Article 32—Military and Hostile Activities

1. Parties shall protect the environment during periods of armed conflict. In particular, Parties shall:
   (a) observe, outside areas of armed conflict, all national and international environmental rules by which they are bound in times of peace;
   (b) take care to protect the environment against avoidable harm in areas of armed conflict;
   (c) not employ or threaten to employ methods or means of warfare which are intended or may be expected to cause widespread, long-term, or severe harm to the environment and ensure that such means and methods of warfare are not developed, produced, tested, or transferred; and
   (d) not use the destruction or modification of the environment as a means of warfare or reprisal.
2. Parties shall cooperate to further develop and implement rules and measures to protect the environment during international armed conflict and establish rules and measures to protect the environment during non-international armed conflict.
3. All Parties involved in armed conflicts shall take the necessary measures to protect natural and cultural sites of special interest, in particular sites designated for protection under applicable national laws and international treaties, as well as potentially dangerous installations, from being subject to attack as a result of armed conflict, insurgency, terrorism, or sabotage. Military personnel shall be instructed as to the existence and location of such sites and installations.

4. Parties shall take measures to ensure that persons are held responsible for the deliberate and intentional use of means or methods of warfare which cause widespread, long-term, or severe harm to the environment.
5. Parties shall ensure that military personnel, aircraft, vessels and other equipment and installations are not exempted in times of peace from rules, standards, and measures for environmental protection.

Part VII: Transboundary Issues

Article 33—Transboundary Environmental Effects

Parties shall take appropriate measures to prevent transboundary environmental harm. When a proposed activity may generate such harm, Parties shall:

(a) ensure that an environmental impact assessment is undertaken, as provided in Article 37;

(b) give prior and timely notification, along with relevant information, to potentially affected States, and consult in good faith with those States at an early stage; and

(c) grant potentially affected persons in other States access to, as well as due process in, administrative and judicial proceedings, without discrimination on the basis of residence or nationality.

Article 33 bis—Prior Informed Consent

Prior to the export of domestically prohibited hazardous substances and of hazardous waste, Parties shall require the prior informed consent of importing and, where appropriate, transit States.

Article 34—Transboundary Natural Resources

Parties shall cooperate in the conservation, management and restoration of natural resources which occur in areas under the jurisdiction of more than one State, or fully or partly in areas beyond the limits of national jurisdiction. To this end,

(a) Parties sharing the same natural system shall manage that system as a single ecological unit notwithstanding national boundaries. They shall cooperate on the basis of equity and reciprocity, in particular through bilateral and multilateral agreements, in order to develop harmonized policies and strategies covering the entire system and the ecosystems it contains. With regard to aquatic systems, such agreements shall cover the entire catchment area, including the adjoining marine environment.

(b) Parties sharing the same species or population, whether migratory or not, shall treat such species or population as a single biological unit. They shall cooperate, in particular through bilateral and multilateral agreements, in order to maintain the species or population concerned in a favorable conservation status. In the case of a harvested species or population, all the Parties that are range states of that species or population shall cooperate in the development and implementation of a joint management plan to ensure the sustainable use of that resource and the equitable sharing of the benefits deriving from that use.

Part VIII: Implementation and Cooperation

Article 35—National Action Plans

Parties shall establish action plans, with targets and timetables, and update them as necessary, to meet the objective of this Covenant.

Article 36—Physical Planning

1. Parties shall establish and implement integrated physical planning systems, including provisions for infrastructure and town and country planning, with a view to integrating conservation of the environment, including biological diversity, into social and economic development.
2. In such planning, Parties shall take into account natural systems, in particular drainage basins, coastal areas and their adjacent waters, and any other areas constituting identifiable ecological units.
3. Parties shall take into account the natural characteristics and ecological constraints of areas when allocating them for agricultural, grazing, forestry, or other use.

Article 37—Environmental Impact Assessment

1. Parties shall establish or strengthen environmental impact assessment procedures to ensure that all activities which are likely to have a significant adverse effect on the environment are evaluated before approval.

2. The assessment shall include evaluation of:
   (a) cumulative, long-term, indirect, long-distance, and transboundary effects,
   (b) the possible alternative actions, including not conducting the proposed activity, and
   (c) measures to avert or minimize the potential adverse effects.
3. Parties shall designate appropriate national authorities to ensure that environmental impact assessments are effective and conducted under procedures accessible to concerned States, international organizations, persons and nongovernmental organizations. Parties shall also ensure that the authority deciding on approval takes into consideration all observations made during the environmental impact assessment process and makes its final decision public.
4. Parties shall conduct periodic reviews both to determine whether activities approved by them are carried out in compliance with the conditions set out in the approval and to evaluate the effectiveness of the prescribed mitigation measures. The results of such reviews shall be made public.
5. Parties shall take appropriate measures to ensure that before they adopt policies, programs, and plans that are likely to have a significant adverse effect on the environment, the environmental consequences of such actions are duly taken into account.

Article 38—Environmental Standards and Controls

1. Parties shall cooperate to formulate, develop, and strengthen international rules, standards and recommended practices on issues of common concern for the protection and preservation of the environment and sustainable use of natural resources, taking into account the need for flexible means of implementation based on their respective capabilities.
2. Parties shall adopt, strengthen and implement specific national standards, including emission, quality, product, and process standards, designed to prevent or abate harm to the environment or to restore or enhance environmental quality.

Article 39—Monitoring of Environmental Quality

1. Parties shall conduct scientific research and establish, strengthen, and implement scientific monitoring programs for the collection of environmental data and information to determine, *inter alia*,
   (a) the condition of all components of the environment, including changes in the status of natural resources; and
   (b) the effects, especially the cumulative or synergistic effects, of particular substances, activities, or combinations thereof on the environment.
2. To this end and as appropriate, Parties shall cooperate with each other and with competent international organizations.

Article 40—Scientific and Technical Cooperation

1. Parties shall promote scientific and technical cooperation in the field of environmental conservation and sustainable use of natural resources, in particular with developing countries. In promoting such cooperation, special attention should be given to the development and strengthening of national capacities, through the development of human resources, legislation and institutions.
2. Parties shall:
   (a) cooperate to establish comparable or standardized research techniques, harmonize international methods to measure environmental parameters, and promote widespread and effective participation of all States in establishing such international methodologies;
   (b) exchange, on a regular basis, appropriate scientific, technical and legal data, information and experience, in particular concerning the status of biological resources; and
   (c) inform each other on their environmental conservation measures and endeavor to coordinate such measures.

Article 41—Development and Transfer of Technology

Parties shall encourage and strengthen cooperation for the development and use, as well as access to and transfer of, environmentally sound technologies on mutually agreed terms, with a view to accelerating the transition to sustainable development, in particular by establishing joint research programs and joint ventures.

Parties shall designate appropriate national authorities to ensure that environmental impact assessments are effective and conducted under procedures accessible to concerned States, international organizations, persons and nongovernmental organization.

Article 42—Sharing Benefits of Biotechnology

Parties shall provide for the fair and equitable sharing of benefits arising out of biotechnologies based upon genetic resources with States providing access to such genetic resources on mutually agreed terms.

Article 43—Information and Knowledge

1. Parties shall facilitate the exchange of publicly available information relevant to the conservation and sustainable use of natural resources, taking into account the special needs of developing countries.
2. Parties shall require that access to indigenous knowledge be subject to the prior informed consent of the concerned communities and to specific regulations recognizing their rights to, and the appropriate economic value of, such knowledge.

Article 44—Education, Training and Public Awareness

1. Parties shall disseminate environmental knowledge by providing to their public and, in particular, to indigenous peoples and local communities, information, educational materials, and opportunities for environmental training and education.
2. Parties shall cooperate with each other, and where appropriate with competent international and national organizations, to promote environmental education, training, capacity building, and public awareness.

Article 45—National Financial Resources

1. Parties undertake to provide, in accordance with their capabilities, financial support and incentives for those national activities aimed at achieving the objectives of this Covenant.
2. Parties shall pursue innovative ways of generating new public and private financial resources for sustainable development, including the use of economic instruments, regulatory fees and taxes, and reallocation of resources at present committed to military purposes.

Article 46—International Financial Resources

1. Parties shall co-operate in establishing, maintaining, and strengthening ways and means of providing new and additional financial resources, particularly to developing countries for:
   (a) environmentally sound development programs and projects;
   (b) measures directed towards solving major environmental problems of global concern, and for the implementation measures of this Covenant where they would entail special or abnormal burdens, owing, in particular, to the lack of sufficient financial resources, expertise or technical capacity; and
   (c) making available, under favorable conditions, the transfer of environmentally sound technologies.
2. Parties, taking into account their respective capabilities and specific national and regional developmental priorities, objectives and circumstances, shall endeavor to augment their aid programs to reach the United Nations General Assembly target of 0.7 percent of Gross National Product for Official Development Assistance or such other agreed figure as may be established.
3. Parties shall consider ways and means of providing relief to debtor developing countries, including by way of cancellations, rescheduling or conversion of debts to investments, provided that such relief is limited to enable the debtor developing countries to further their sustainable development.
4. A Party that provides financial resources to a State for activities that may result in a significant adverse impact on the environment shall, in cooperation with the recipient State, ensure that an environmental impact is conducted. The resources provided shall include those necessary for the recipient State to carry out such assessment.

Part IX: Responsibility and Liability

Article 47—State Responsibility

Each State Party is responsible under international law for the breach of its obligations under this Covenant or of other rules of international law concerning the environment.

Article 48—State Liability

Each State Party is liable for significant harm to the environment of other States or of areas beyond the limits of national jurisdiction, as well as for injury to persons resulting therefrom, caused by acts or omissions of its organs or by activities under its jurisdiction or control.

Article 49—Cessation, Restitution and Compensation

1. Each State Party shall cease activities causing significant harm to the environment and shall, as far as practicable, reestablish the situation that would have existed if the harm had not occurred. Where that is not possible, the State Party of the origin of the harm shall provide compensation or other remedy for the harm. In particular, Parties shall co-operate to develop and improve means to remedy the harm, including measures for rehabilitation, restoration or reinstatement of habitats of particular conservation concern.
2. Where a State Party suffers such harm caused in part by its own negligence or that of persons under its jurisdiction or control, the extent of any redress or the level of any compensation due may be reduced to the extent that the harm is caused by negligence of that Party or persons under its jurisdiction or control.

Article 50—Consequences of Failure to Prevent Harm

Each State Party may be held responsible for significant harm to the environment resulting from its failure to carry out the obligations of prevention contained in this Covenant, in respect to its activities or those of its nationals.

Article 51—Exemptions

The State Party of origin of the harm shall not be responsible or liable if the harm,

(a) is directly due to an act of armed conflict or a hostile activity where the requirements under Article 32 of this Covenant are met, except an armed conflict initiated by the State Party of origin in violation of international law;

(b) is directly due to a natural phenomenon of an exceptional and inevitable character; or

(c) is caused wholly by an act or omission of a third party.

Article 52—Civil Remedies

1. Parties shall ensure the availability of effective civil remedies that provide for cessation of harmful activities as well as for compensation to victims of environmental harm irrespective of the nationality or the domicile of the victims.
2. Parties that do not provide such remedies shall ensure that compensation is paid for the damage caused by their acts or omissions or by activities of persons under their jurisdiction or control.
3. In cases of significant environmental harm, if an effective remedy is not provided in accordance with paragraph 1, the State Party of nationality of the victim shall espouse the victim's claim by presenting it to the State Party of origin of the harm. The State Party of origin shall not require the exhaustion of local remedies as a precondition for presentation of such claim.

Article 52 bis—Offenses

1. Parties shall establish, as appropriate, criminal or administrative offenses for violations of environmental law or for activities that cause or are likely to cause serious harm to the environment.
2. Parties shall establish sanctions for such offenses that take into account the seriousness of the offenses and may include fines, confiscation, suspension or cancellation of permits or other benefits, imprisonment, and the obligation to reinstate the environment.

Article 53—Recourse Under Domestic Law and Non-Discrimination

1. Each State Party of origin shall ensure that any person in another State Party who is adversely affected by transboundary environmental harm has the right of access to administrative and judicial procedures equal to that afforded nationals or residents of the State Party of origin in cases of domestic environmental harm.
2. Each State Party shall ensure that adversely affected persons have a right of recourse for violations of environmental regulations by that Party or any person or entity associated with that Party.

Article 54—Immunity from Jurisdiction

Parties may not claim sovereign immunity in respect of proceedings instituted under this Covenant.

Article 55—Environmental Harm in Areas Beyond National Jurisdiction

The provisions of Articles 47 to 54 may be invoked by any affected person for harm to the environment of areas beyond national jurisdiction.

PART X: APPLICATION AND COMPLIANCE

Article 56—Other Treaties

Parties shall endeavor to become and remain party to treaties relating to the subject matter of this Covenant and shall implement them.

Article 57—More Stringent Measures

1. The provisions of this Covenant shall not affect the right of Parties individually or jointly to adopt and implement more stringent measures than those required under this Covenant.
2. The provisions of this Covenant shall not prejudice any stricter obligation which Parties have entered into or may enter into under existing or future treaties.

Such procedures and mechanisms should improve and strengthen reporting requirements, and be simple, transparent, and non-confrontational.

Article 58—Areas Beyond the Limits of National Jurisdiction

In areas beyond the limits of national jurisdiction, Parties shall observe the provisions of the present Covenant to the full extent of their competence.

Article 59—Relations with Non-Parties

Parties shall encourage non-parties to act in a manner that is consistent with the objective of this Covenant.

Article 60—Reporting

1. Parties undertake to submit periodic reports on the measures they have adopted, progress made, and difficulties encountered in implementing their obligations under this Covenant.
2. All reports shall be submitted to the Secretary-General of the United Nations.

Article 61—Compliance and Dispute Avoidance

In the framework of environmental treaties to which they are party or by other means, Parties shall maintain or promote the establishment of procedures and institutional mechanisms, including enquiry and fact-finding, to assist and encourage States to comply fully with their obligations and to avoid environmental disputes. Such procedures and mechanisms should improve and strengthen reporting requirements, and be simple, transparent, and non-confrontational.

Article 62—Settlement of Disputes

1. Parties shall settle disputes concerning the interpretation or application of this Covenant by peaceful means, such as by negotiation, enquiry, mediation, conciliation, arbitration, judicial settlement, resort to regional agencies or arrangements, or by any other peaceful means of their own choice.
2. If parties to a dispute do not reach agreement on a solution or on a dispute settlement arrangement within one year following the notification by one party to another that a dispute exists, the dispute shall, at the request of one of the parties, be submitted to either an arbitral tribunal, including the Permanent Court of Arbitration, or to judicial settlement, including by the International Court of Justice and the International Tribunal for the Law of the Sea as appropriate.

4

Environmental Issues and Good Governance

A

Hassan P., "Elements of Good Environmental Governance," Keynote address presented at the Asia Pacific Forum on Environmental Governance and Sustainable Development: *Toward Partnership Building Among Parliamentarians, Civil Society Organizations, Private Sector and Government*, at United Nations University, Tokyo, Japan, UNDP, ESCAP and the Government of Japan, May 2001

Good environmental governance is an important pillar in the global partnership for sustainable development. Environmental governance may be described as the manner in which people exercise authority over nature. Natural resource management was internationalized by the *Stockholm Declaration* in 1972, echoing the earlier internationalization of human rights by the Universal Declaration of Human Rights in 1948. Today, good environmental governance is increasingly considered essential to development and natural resource management. The international financial institutions such as IBRD and IMF are requiring it as a condition to their assistance to any country. The *Asian Environmental Outlook 2000* prepared by the Asian Development Bank also spotlights good environmental governance as essential to sustainable development.

Good environmental governance is of particular importance to developing countries. It is only when policies in such societies are democratic, participative, transparent and founded on the rule of law and supported by a strong and independent judiciary that donor countries will have the confidence to deal with them. Dictatorial and corrupt regimes are not attractive for donors.

Good environmental governance thus emerges as an important condition for developing countries to receive the support of the developed states. Stockholm in 1972, the *World Charter of Nature* 1982 and the *Rio Declaration* 1992, each provided general principles for sustainable development. Good environmental governance is implementing these principles. Using recent opportunities, I identified and developed several elements of good environmental governance, particularly for developing countries. Let me repeat some of them, with particular reference to relevant experiences in Pakistan, to foster a debate on an important subject:

1. Good environmental governance would begin with a democratic dispensation that allows full participation to civil society in the running and administration of its affairs. Such a dispensation enables national and state parliaments to respond to the emerging needs of society for general and specific regimes and laws for environmental protection and sustainable development. Legislation is a major tool for achieving good environmental management and it is fortunate that we have this important constituency of parliamentarians from the Asia Pacific region present here today to share our vision for good environmental governance. The parliamentarians have a special role to play in this region, a role that has largely and unfortunately been ignored in most countries.
2. Rule of law, sanctity for human rights and a free and independent judiciary are essential for protecting and enforcing environmental protection regimes. In developing countries, particularly, the judiciary has played an activist role to innovate remedies against environmental degradation. In the internationally acclaimed *Shahla Zia* case, PLD 1994 SC 693, for example, I was able to persuade a full Bench of the Supreme Court of Pakistan that the right to a clean and healthy environment is inherent in the fundamental rights to life and dignity guaranteed in the Constitution of Pakistan. This was in spite of the fact that nowhere in the *travaux preparatoires* of the Constitution was there a discussion, in the drafting and discussion of Articles 9 and 14 dealing with the right to life and the right to dignity, on the quality of life. Yet the Supreme Court of Pakistan, following the equally important leadership provided by the superior courts of India and other States in the Asia and Pacific region, adopted an activist and liberal interpretation of the provisions of the Constitution well beyond the intent of its original drafters. It was, I believe, also because of the realization of the Judiciary that the Executive and the Legislature were not playing their due role to protect the environment and in the face of such insensitivity and growing environmental degradation, the Judiciary stepped in to light candles rather than be a part of the darkness.
3. However, notwithstanding the activist role played by the judiciary in some societies, in countries which have opportunities to redraft or amend their Constitutions or adopt new Constitutions, good environmental governance will be induced by a Constitutional provision on environmental protection and sustainable development. I want to emphasize to the parliamentarians here that a constitutional commitment to the environment—even in such general terms as it being a sacred trust for future generations—provides an effective framework for environment-friendly judicial pronouncements. In the Asia and Pacific region, the most activist judicial interventions to serve environmental protection and sustainable development have been by the Indian judiciary, particularly its Supreme Court. Using the constitutionally-protected fundamental right to life, the courts expanded this to include the right to live with human dignity, and the right to live in a healthy

environment. In 1976, the Constitution, through the 42nd amendment, guaranteed the right of Indian citizens to live in a clean environment. These constitutional provisions provided an opening for judicial activism which has generally served Indian civil society well. The *Shahla Zia case* in Pakistan the *Oposa case* in the Philippines and *Bulankulama case* in Sri Lanka (2000 SAELR 7(2)) are also important testaments to the potential role of the judiciary for environmental protection and sustainable development.

4. It is important to accept the principle of subsidiarity and decentralize decision making from the central government to participants and institutions at lower levels in the political administrative hierarchies. Governance by remote control from a distant capital ignores the role of locals and local communities that are affected by such decisions. There is improved efficiency and equity resulting from increased popular participation in public decision making.
5. Particularly for developing countries, good environmental governance promotes poverty alleviation specific policies through affirmative action programs. Poverty has been found to be an important degrader of the environment. Every possible effort must be made to eradicate it. As environmental degradation is a direct by-product of widespread poverty, sound environmental governance strategies can help a great deal towards mitigating the effects of poverty and ultimately benefit the environment.

The Asia and Pacific region is the most populous region in the world, home to about 55 percent of the world's population concentrated in about 23 percent of the total land surface. The region is also one of the most densely populated with a population density of about 93 persons per square kilometer. The region is home to about 900 million of the world's absolute poor: those who survive on less than one dollar per day. The largest concentration of severely impoverished people is in South Asia. This geographical incidence of poverty is governed by a wide range of factors, including the incidence of droughts, floods, environmental degradation and the insufficient provision of social services and infrastructure. This concentration of poverty can also sadly become self-perpetuating, as the weak and vulnerable in society are exposed to environmental and health risks arising from poor sanitation facilities, natural disasters and air and water pollution. While the world's looming environmental threat, destruction of biodiversity and water contamination is largely the byproducts of affluence, poverty can drive ecological deterioration through desperate overexploitation of a limited resource base.

In the Asia and the Pacific region, the poor suffer the most with environmental degradation as they live mostly in rural areas and depend directly or indirectly on the natural systems for their livelihoods. They are often landless and rely on various natural resources, such as soils and fisheries, many use wild foods and fuels to complement their diet, cooking and heat, and to supplement their income. The food, fuel wood and housing needs often force the poor in the rural and the mountainous areas to deforest woodlots and plough the mountain slopes. The results can be quite devastating over a longer period. The consequent decline in environment and destruction of the non-renewable resource base perpetuate poverty through diminishing yields. In the urban areas too, poverty usually results in the greater exposure of the poor to air pollution and concentration of huge number of people in a limited space (as in the slum areas of big cities) with poor water and sanitation facilities, leading to misery and disease.

Desperate overuse of natural resources can aggravate the problems of the poor especially where these resources are non-renewable or take a significant period of time for renewal. In such a situation, environmentally sound measures are necessary to arrest or reverse degradation of resources. These measures should have a cumulative impact on the productivity and welfare of the poor and may include soil and water conservation, afforestation, irrigation, drainage and water harvesting, management of livestock and pastures, and sand dune fixation. A recent example of this sound environmental management has been reclamation of sodic lands in the Uttar Pradesh State in India through a project of the World Bank in collaboration with the Indian government. This reclamation of land has also had numerous positive impacts both on the poor and the environment as it has enhanced the income level of beneficiaries by raising their farm income through increasing crop productivity.

Environmental education through a constructive dissemination of information should also be part of any poverty-focused environmental strategies. Educating the poor about the dangers of overexploitation of a limited resource base or the repercussions of the spread of disease through air pollution and poor water and sanitation facilities can enable them to take adequate preventive and/ or remedial measures.

All the environmental management strategies focused towards poverty alleviation should be conceived within a participatory and conservation oriented strategy which accords priority to the needs of the poor. It is also important to bring the poor onto the center stage of development and make them involved in a close partnership with federal and local governments, NGOs, grassroots institutions and other private and commercial entities. Only by forging such a partnership can the poor have a more facilitative participation in resource management and enhancement.

Pakistan, threatened with growing poverty, has made an important commitment to its alleviation. To meet its mounting external debt and to rejuvenate its private sector, it has been selling its "family silver" through a Privatization Commission. In past years, the sale proceeds realized by the Privatization Commission were generally not applied for the servicing of external debt and, in the face of this experience, we recently developed a comprehensive legislation on the privatization process which imposes a statutory obligation on the Government of Pakistan to utilize the sale proceeds from the Privatization Commission for the retirement of its external debt. In fact, the legislation provides that 90 percent of such proceeds shall be used to meet the repayment of Government debt; the important aspect of the law is also that 10 percent of the sale proceeds shall be used for poverty alleviation programs (Section 16).

This is an innovative way to emphasize a national policy for poverty reduction. The 10 percent from the Privatization Commission will be part of a greater national commitment but the statutory underpinnings of a well-publicized sale process highlights the rooting of an obligation in equity and good governance.

Good governance would similarly encompass a national commitment to reduce economic and opportunity disparities between its regions.

6. Civil society must be involved in the process of inducting environmental protection regimes. Such involvement will develop the ownership of civil society of environmental laws and policies and thus enhance their effectiveness. A public debate about an environmental law or policy before their adoption also helps in the dissemination of the proposed national priorities.

The experience in Pakistan with respect to the development of its national environmental protection legislation is instructive. The pioneering Pakistan *Environmental Protection Ordinance*, 1983 was promulgated by a military government, based on a draft that I had prepared. There was no national debate on its provisions; the country woke up one morning with the Ordinance. But when we got an opportunity over a decade later, we made sure that the Pakistan *Environmental Protection Act*, 1997, which repealed and replaced the Ordinance, had the benefit of an extended discussion in the public. We allowed for several months of a national debate and even took the proposed Act through a road show in the chambers of commerce and other fora of civil society. I chaired a national committee that over-sighted this process and I must attest that the public debate both improved the quality of the proposed Act, and developed an ownership of the Act by civil society. When Pakistan makes a commitment to the meaningful implementation of the Act, the national debate would have enhanced public participation in the effort.

7. The potential of nongovernmental organizations and similar stakeholders in civil society must be encouraged in the advocacy of environmental causes and dissemination of awareness. NGOs are increasingly involved in holding governments to good governance. Through their development and execution of environment-friendly projects, their public campaigns and public interest litigation, NGOs have become important leaders of sustainable development.

Many developing countries, some times, seek to regulate the NGOs. Such regulation is criticized in the developed countries. But this criticism can be uninformed. Recently, when a new law was being debated to regulate the working of NGOs in Pakistan, I opposed the main thrust of the Government policy but found that the proposed provisions on requiring the NGOs to disclose the sources of their financing, particularly foreign, and to have their accounts audited annually by Certified Public Accountants were unexceptionable.

8. A *Freedom of Information Act* is important for providing civil society access to information which can serve environmental causes, particularly public interest litigation The *Aarhus Convention*, 1998, has been a catalyst in this respect. Information is recognized as a prerequisite to effective national and

international environmental management, protection and cooperation. The availability of and access to information allows preventive and mitigation measures to be taken, ensures participation of citizens in national decision making processes and can influence consumer behavior. Information also allows the international community to determine whether States are complying with their legal obligations.

Access to information enhances transparency and accountability and reduces mala fide, corrupt and arbitrary decisions. Countries in the Asia and Pacific region are responding to this need; many former colonies inherited a long-standing culture of secrecy and non-involvement of peoples in governance and information-sharing. This is gradually being replaced by specific Freedom of Information Acts. But even when such statutes are introduced, Governments particularly with a legacy of colonial insecurities, are reluctant to make the quantum jump from historical secrecy to statute-based openness. Thus, while the Government of Pakistan promulgated the *Freedom of Information Ordinance*, 1997, the Ordinance was allowed to lapse after four months. Recent initiatives in this respect reflect the Government anxiety to restrict the scope of the new proposed legislation by continuing to restrict its application only to the Federal Government. During a recent visit to Thailand, I found that the 1997 *Freedom of Information Act* of Thailand has generated a similar debate about the adequacy of its provisions for transparency and disclosure.

9. Voluntary initiatives such as International Organization for Standardization (ISO), Codes of Conduct and Best Practices by Chambers of Commerce, Stock Exchanges, Farmers Associations, labor unions, research institutes and other groups facilitate good environmental management.
10. Community-based natural resource management, particularly in the fields of wildlife, forestry, irrigation and fisheries, has well-served sustainable development objectives. Involving the community in the management of natural resources on which the community depends for its sustenance has proved effective when laws with even penal provisions could not prevent significant resource or specie loss. Habitat loss because of exploding human populations, poverty levels, indiscriminate hunting and ineffective enforcement of laws, common characteristics of several developing countries, all contribute to dwindling wildlife. For decades, enforcement officials felt that this could be reversed by strict and harsh laws but this ignored the vital element of community participation. Contemporary experiences in resource management have shown that sustainable use of such resources is facilitated by involving the community. Such involvement essentially creates a stake of the community to protect the resource against loss and degradation.

The Northern Areas of Pakistan are host to some of the most exotic wildlife: marco polo sheep and ibex. Excessive poaching and hunting, in the recent past, threatened these species, the penalty provisions of our wildlife laws notwithstanding. The Worldwide Fund for Nature (Pakistan) has met this through an innovative scheme that involves the community. In the Bar Valley, trophy hunting/harvesting mature ibex was allowed through a predetermined quota by a license. The number of hunting licenses is based on an annual census of the area thus ensuring that the over-all wildlife population is not affected. The license fee for such culling is shared—at a level of 75 percent—with the local population, the Government retaining 25 percent as a management fee for the administration of the trophy scheme. When the local community found that 75 percent of the license fee is spent on health clinics and other welfare projects in the area such as a weaving center for women, the erstwhile poachers have become the guardians of the wildlife. Based upon the success of this initiative, this concept is being replicated in a number of other valleys in northern Pakistan.

Good environmental governance, thus, has to look to involving people and the community in natural resource management, whether the resource be wildlife, fishery or forests.

11. States must sign and ratify Multilateral Environmental Agreements and implement them at the national level. Good environmental governance cannot be achieved unless the State joins the mainstream of the global environmental agenda.
12. In many developing countries, the EPAs are under-staffed with little or no ability to monitor environmental laws and policies. States must allocate adequate funds to upgrade and strengthen the technical, administrative, professional and

financial capacities of the EPAs. Most countries, including the developing ones, generally have a comprehensive national environmental law which establishes a high-powered national environmental protection council supported by environmental protection agencies. But building an appropriate capacity to enforce environmental laws and regimes is at the core of good environmental governance. Experience has shown that it is not enough to have EPAs. They should, among others, have the appropriate laboratories and other scientific tools for testing water and air quality; they should have technical administrators to enforce the laws and environmental lawyers to prosecute offenders. This capacity is sadly lacking in most developing countries and the need to develop it can hardly be over-emphasized.

Let me give my favorite example of capacity building in my own field of interest, environmental law. Pakistan, as Chair of the Group of 77, incidentally led the debate on behalf of the developing countries at the Earth Summit in Rio de Janeiro in 1992; it has a population of over 140 million. Yet, in spite of such leadership and a significant population, Pakistan did not, until very recently, have a single law school teaching environmental law. This was typical of several other developing countries. How can the international community expect any degree of compliance with environmental treaties and regimes from such developing countries without any constituency of environmental lawyers? Who would draft national legislation to implement international treaty obligations? Who would seek to enforce the national laws, when drafted?

Recognizing the vital interdependence of capacity building and good environmental governance, I prioritized the development of a cadre of environmental lawyers in the developing countries in my capacity as the Chair of the Commission on Environmental law of IUCN–The World Conservation Union, 1990–1996. As a beginning, we established the Asia and Pacific Centre for Environmental Law (APCEL) in Singapore to jump-start the training of environmental lawyers in this region. APCEL trained the trainers from developing countries and, on return to their countries, these trainers initiated environmental law teaching in their Universities. Only early this year, four alumni of APCEL from Pakistan successfully launched the teaching of environmental law in the national premier law college, Punjab University Law College, at Lahore.

This effort toward capacity building needs to be replicated in other areas to facilitate a national commitment for good environmental governance.

13. Access to judicial and effective dispute resolution mechanisms is important to avoid continuing tension over environmental disputes. Dismantling technical hurdles such as standing to sue has facilitated public interest litigation in the service of sustainable development.
14. Strengthening linkages with journalists and promoting education and public awareness would give a steel-frame for environmental protection regimes. The journalists in developing countries, particularly, play an important role in identifying environmental causes and drawing national attention to the need to prioritize their redress. When I took to the road to environmental protection in the 1970s in Pakistan, it was a lonely journey. Both the military government and civil society then looked at the quest for environmental protection as a luxury which a developing country could ill-afford—and as a legacy of a Western education ill-suited to the developmental plans of Pakistan. It was hard to find allies and with the help of the United Nations Economic and Social Commission for Asia and the Pacific (ESCAP) and its dynamic environment chief, Dr. Kazi F. Jalal, we formed the Pakistan Forum of Environmental Journalists including the country's leading journalists who were widely read in Urdu and English newspapers. Things began to change and civil society, particularly NGOs, converted to friendship. The educational campuses followed and, over the years, environmental protection and sustainable development were legitimized as goals of civil society. The role of environmental journalism in this transformation has been significant and other developing societies may find some useful lessons in the Pakistan experience.

Pakistan did not, until very recently, have a single law school teaching environmental law. This was typical of several other developing countries.

Even as recently as last year, in 2000, journalists in Pakistan highlighted a national tragedy near my hometown, Lahore. The water supply to the villages of Kalalanwala and Manga Mandi, apparently affected by the untreated wastes of an adjoining factory, led to bone deformity and other physical ailments among over 100 children and women. As the tragedy was gradually but skillfully unveiled by the journalists, it became clear that environment administrators had failed to respond to the early complaints of the villagers.

Similar stories abound particularly in developing societies where enforcement of environmental regimes is lax but journalists have informed and educated civil society to good environmental governance. A free press and sensitivity in the journalist community to environmental issues can promote a qualitative environmental governance.

A free press and sensitivity in the journalist community to environmental issues can promote a qualitative environmental governance.

15. The empowerment of women, youth and marginalized groups and their utilization in resource management can be an important factor in the success of environmental governance. Women, in particular, have a crucial role to play in helping their respective societies and communities to achieve sustainable development through sound practices of environmental governance. As professionals, housewives, mothers or social mobilizers, women can both lead and influence in this respect. Women's awareness and concern for the environment can make them experienced managers of natural resources and their powers as consumers enables them to effect changes to production methods and material source choices. In spite of all this, the real and potential contribution of women to economic development, policy and decision making has yet to be adequately recognized. The countries in Asia and the Pacific should grasp this opportunity to positively utilize and further strengthen the role of women towards attaining sound environmental management.
16. The need for the developing countries to receive and for the developed countries to transfer resources, both financial and technological, is at the root of good environmental governance. Elsewhere, I have highlighted that the success of the global partnership that was structured at Stockholm and Rio depends on the transfer of such resources. Unfortunately, financial support from the developed to the developing countries, including through the Global Environment Facility (GEF) has decreased rather than increased in the post-Rio period. Consequently, there is the familiar spectacle of many developing countries with a plethora of national environmental legislation and policies but little or no enforcement or implementation of the same. Recent years have demonstrated that without financial resources and appropriate capacity building, it is difficult, if not impossible for developing countries to devote their meager resources for good environmental governance and sustainable development. Many developing countries are in a hopeless debt trap representing an unbearably onerous indebtedness to foreign donors. Donor countries should consider releasing these debts on a debt for sustainable development/nature/poverty reduction swap to enable developing countries to make an effective commitment to better natural resource management. Developing countries, in turn, should reduce their military spending to meet the same objectives of good environmental governance. Non-implementation and non-compliance of national and international environmental regimes stand out as the most compelling problems before the international community today. The conclusion is both unequivocal and compelling that if the global partnership structured at Stockholm in 1972 and Rio in 1992 is to move forward with any degree of success, it is essential that the developed countries must urgently respond to their global obligations to facilitate the transfer of financial resources and technology to the developing countries.

5

Armed Conflict and the Environment

A

Penna L.R., *Saving the Environment During Armed Conflicts*, unpublished paper, 2001

Wars endanger the environment. During the Vietnam War large-scale deforestation was carried out by the Americans. During the Gulf War Iraq had set on fire 7 million to 9 million barrels of oil in the Gulf. 590 oil well heads were damaged or destroyed. 508 oil wells were set on fire, and 82 were damaged so that oil was flowing freely from them.

The Government of Canada, working with the UN Secretary General hosted a conference of international experts in Ottawa to consider Iraq's wanton acts of destruction and their law of war implications. There was general agreement that the action constituted [a violation of] the laws of war, namely:

1. Art. 23g of the Annex to Hague IV prohibiting the destruction of enemy property not justified by military necessity.

2. United Nations Security Council Resolution 687 (3 April 1991) affirmed that Iraq was liable under international law to compensate any environmental damage and the depletion of national resources.

Protocol I Additional to the Geneva Conventions of 1949 prohibits the employment of methods or means of warfare which may cause long-term and severe damage to natural environment (Article 35.3), and enjoins that care shall be taken in warfare to avoid such damage (Article 55).

> "Art. 35. Basic rules
>
> In any armed conflict, the right of the Parties to the conflict to choose methods or means of warfare is not unlimited.
>
> It is prohibited to employ weapons, projectiles and material and methods of warfare of a nature to cause superfluous injury or unnecessary suffering.
>
> It is prohibited to employ methods or means of warfare which are intended, or may be expected, to cause widespread, long-term and severe damage to the natural environment...
>
> Article 55—Protection of the natural environment
>
> Care shall be taken in warfare to protect the natural environment against widespread, long term and severe damage. This protection includes a prohibition of the use of methods or means of warfare which are intended to or may be expected to cause such damage to the natural environment and thereby prejudice the health or survival of the population.
>
> Attacks against the natural environment by way of reprisals are prohibited."

The *Convention on the Prohibition of Military or Any Other Hostile Use of Environmental Modification Techniques* which entered into force on 5 October 1978 prohibits the deliberate manipulation of natural process in order to change "the dynamics, composition or structure of Earth, including its biota, lithosphere, hydrosphere, and atmosphere, or outer space."

> "Article I
>
> Each State Party to this Convention undertakes not to engage in military or any other hostile use of environmental modification techniques having widespread, long lasting or severe effects as the means of destruction, damage or injury to any other State Party.
>
> Each State Party to this Convention undertakes not to assist, encourage or induce any State, group of States or international organization to engage in activities contrary to the provisions of paragraph 1 of this article.
>
> Article II
>
> As used in article I, the term "environmental modification techniques" refers to any technique for changing—through the deliberate manipulation of natural processes—the dynamics, composition or structure of the Earth, including its biota, lithosphere, hydrosphere and atmosphere, or of outer space."

In spite of the international efforts in saving the environment during armed conflicts, in May 1999 NATO had used radioactive depleted-uranium weapons in Serbia and had bombed industrial plants containing dangerous chemicals. There is, thus a need for a provision in an international convention that would categorize environmental damage as a war crime and or crime against humanity. The wrongs and crimes are to be defined in the context of actual damages done or the potential damage that may be caused by the development of new weapons.

6

United Nations, World Summit on Sustainable Development, adopted at Johannesburg, South Africa, Plan of Implementation

http://www.johannesburgsummit.org/html/documents/summit_docs/2309_planfinal.htm

[*The World Summit on Sustainable Development (WSSD) concluded on September 4th 2002. This was ten years after the Earth Summit (Rio de Janeiro, 1992) and provided the opportunity to reflect and build on the Rio Declaration, Agenda 21 and the developments in international environmental law and policy. The WSSD was meant to accelerate the process towards sustainable development and many participants felt that this broad objective was not met. The event was not as high profile as the Earth Summit and there was a high priority given to trade liberalisation issues—possibly at the expense of energy efficiency targets. However, the Plan of Implementation demonstrates concrete commitments by governments such as halving the number of people without access to safe water and sanitation by 2015 (paragraph 7); maintaining and restoring fish stocks by 2015 (paragraph 30); significantly reducing the loss of biodiversity by 2010 (paragraph 42) and minimising the negative impacts of chemicals on human health and environment by 2020 (paragraph 22). There are also some significant statements supporting indigenous rights in the context of sustainable development. This demonstrates some progress but much remains to be done*].

Introduction

The United Nations Conference on Environment and Development (UNCED), held in Rio de Janeiro in 1992, provided the fundamental principles and the programme of action for achieving sustainable development. We strongly reaffirm our commitment to the Rio principles, the full implementation of Agenda 21 and the Programme for the Further Implementation of Agenda 21. We also commit ourselves to achieving the internationally agreed development goals, including those contained in the United Nations Millennium Declaration and in the outcomes of the major United Nations conferences and international agreements since 1992.

The present plan of implementation will further build on the achievements made since UNCED and expedite the realization of the remaining goals. To this end, we commit ourselves to undertaking concrete actions and measures at all levels and to enhancing international cooperation, taking into account the Rio Principles, including, inter alia, the principle of common but differentiated responsibilities as set out in principle 7 of the Rio Declaration on Environment and Development. These efforts will also promote the integration of the three components of sustainable development— economic development, social development and environmental protection—as interdependent and mutually reinforcing pillars. Poverty eradication, changing unsustainable patterns of production and consumption, and protecting and managing the natural resource base of economic and social development are overarching objectives of, and essential requirements for, sustainable development.

We recognize that the implementation of the outcomes of the Summit should benefit all, particularly women, youth, children and vulnerable groups. Furthermore, the implementation should involve all relevant actors through partnerships, especially between Governments of the North and South, on the one hand, and between Governments and major groups, on the other, to achieve the widely shared goals of sustainable development. As reflected in the Monterrey Consensus, such partnerships are key to pursuing sustainable development in a globalizing world.

Good governance within each country and at the international level is essential for sustainable development. At the domestic level, sound environmental, social and economic policies, democratic institutions responsive to the needs of the people, the rule of law, anti-corruption measures, gender equality and an enabling environment for investment are the basis for sustainable development. As a result of globalization, external factors have become critical in determining the success or failure of developing countries in their national efforts. The gap between developed and developing countries points to the continued need for a dynamic and enabling international economic environment supportive of international cooperation, particularly in the areas of finance, technology transfer, debt and trade, and full and effective participation of developing countries in global decision-making, if the momentum for global progress towards sustainable development is to be maintained and increased.

Peace, security, stability and respect for human rights and fundamental freedoms, including the right to development, as well as respect for cultural diversity, are essential for achieving sustainable development and ensuring that sustainable development benefits all.

We acknowledge the importance of ethics for sustainable development, and therefore we emphasize the need to consider ethics in the implementation of Agenda 21.

Poverty eradication

Eradicating poverty is the greatest global challenge facing the world today and an indispensable requirement for sustainable development, particularly for developing countries. Although each country has the primary responsibility for its own sustainable development and poverty eradication and the role of national policies and development strategies cannot be overemphasized, concerted and concrete measures are required at all levels to enable developing countries to achieve their sustainable development goals as related to the internationally agreed poverty-related targets and goals, including those contained in Agenda 21, the relevant outcomes of other United Nations conferences and the United Nations Millennium Declaration. This would include actions at all levels to:

(a) Halve, by the year 2015, the proportion of the world's people whose income is less than $1 a day and the proportion of people who suffer from hunger and, by the same date, to halve the proportion of people without access to safe drinking water;

(b) Establish a world solidarity fund to eradicate poverty and to promote social and human development in the developing countries pursuant to modalities to be determined by the General Assembly, while stressing the voluntary nature of the contributions, the need to avoid duplication of existing United Nations funds, and encouraging the role of the private sector and individual citizens relative to Governments in funding the endeavours;

(c) Develop national programmes for sustainable development and local and community development, where appropriate within country-owned poverty reduction strategies, to promote the empowerment of people living in poverty and their organizations. These programmes should reflect their priorities and enable them to increase access to productive resources, public services and institutions, in particular land, water, employment opportunities, credit, education and health;

(d) Promote women's equal access to and full participation, on the basis of equality with men, in decision-making at all levels, mainstreaming gender perspectives in all policies and strategies, eliminating all forms of violence and discrimination against women, and improving the status, health and economic welfare of women and girls through full and equal access to economic opportunity, land, credit, education and health-care services;

(e) Develop policies and ways and means to improve access by indigenous people and their communities to economic activities, and increase their employment through, where appropriate, such measures as training, technical assistance and credit facilities. Recognize that traditional and direct dependence on renewable resources and ecosystems, including sustainable harvesting, continues to be essential to the cultural, economic and physical well-being of indigenous people and their communities;

(f) Deliver basic health services for all and reduce environmental health threats, taking into account the special needs of children and the linkages between poverty, health and environment, with provision of financial resources, technical assistance and knowledge transfer to developing countries and countries with economies in transition;

(g) Ensure that children everywhere, boys and girls alike, will be able to complete a full course of primary schooling and will have equal access to all levels of education;

(h) Provide access to agricultural resources for people living in poverty, especially women and indigenous communities, and promote, as appropriate, land tenure arrangements that recognize and protect indigenous and common property resource management systems;

(i) Build basic rural infrastructure, diversify the economy and improve transportation and access to markets, market information and credit for the rural poor to support sustainable agriculture and rural development;

(j) Transfer basic sustainable agricultural techniques and knowledge, including natural resource management, to small and medium-scale farmers, fishers and the rural poor, especially in developing countries, including through multi-stakeholder approaches and public-private partnerships aimed at increasing agriculture production and food security;

(k) Increase food availability and affordability, including through harvest and food technology and management, as well as equitable and efficient distribution systems, by promoting, for example, community-based partnerships linking urban and rural people and enterprises;

(l) Combat desertification and mitigate the effects of drought and floods through such measures as improved use of climate and weather information and forecasts, early warning systems, land and natural resource management, agricultural practices and ecosystem conservation in order to reverse current trends and minimize degradation of land and water resources, including through the provision of adequate and predictable financial resources to implement the United Nations Convention to Combat Desertification in Those Countries Experiencing Serious Drought and/or Desertification, particularly in Africa, as one of the tools for poverty eradication;

(m) Increase access to sanitation to improve human health and reduce infant and child mortality, prioritizing water and sanitation in national sustainable development strategies and poverty reduction strategies where they exist.

The provision of clean drinking water and adequate sanitation is necessary to protect human health and the environment. In this respect, we agree to halve, by the year 2015, the proportion of people who are unable to reach or to afford safe drinking water (as outlined in the Millennium Declaration) and the proportion of people who do not have access to basic sanitation, which would include actions at all levels to:

(a) Develop and implement efficient household sanitation systems;
(b) Improve sanitation in public institutions, especially schools;
(c) Promote safe hygiene practices;
(d) Promote education and outreach focused on children, as agents of behavioural change;
(e) Promote affordable and socially and culturally acceptable technologies and practices;
(f) Develop innovative financing and partnership mechanisms;
(g) Integrate sanitation into water resources management strategies.

Take joint actions and improve efforts to work together at all levels to improve access to reliable and affordable energy services for sustainable development sufficient to facilitate the achievement of the millennium development goals, including the goal of halving the proportion of people in poverty by 2015, and as a means to generate other important services that mitigate poverty, bearing in mind that access to energy facilitates the eradication of poverty. This would include actions at all levels to:

(a) Improve access to reliable, affordable, economically viable, socially acceptable and environmentally sound energy services and resources, taking into account national specificities and circumstances, through various means, such as enhanced rural electrification and decentralized energy systems, increased use of renewables, cleaner liquid and gaseous fuels and enhanced energy efficiency, by intensifying regional and international cooperation in support of national efforts, including through capacity-building, financial and technological assistance and innovative financing mechanisms, including at the micro and meso levels, recognizing the specific factors for providing access to the poor;
(b) Improve access to modern biomass technologies and fuelwood sources and supplies, and commercialize biomass operations, including the use of agricultural residues, in rural areas and where such practices are sustainable;
(c) Promote a sustainable use of biomass and, as appropriate, other renewable energies through improvement of current patterns of use, such as management of resources, more efficient use of fuelwood and new or improved products and technologies;
(d) Support the transition to the cleaner use of liquid and gaseous fossil fuels, where considered more environmentally sound, socially acceptable and cost-effective;
(e) Develop national energy policies and regulatory frameworks that will help to create the necessary economic, social and institutional conditions in the energy sector to improve access to reliable, affordable, economically viable, socially acceptable and environmentally sound energy services for sustainable development and poverty eradication in rural, peri-urban and urban areas;
(f) Enhance international and regional cooperation to improve access to reliable, affordable, economically viable, socially acceptable and environmentally sound energy services, as an integral part of poverty reduction programmes, by facilitating the creation of enabling environments and addressing capacity-building needs, with special attention to rural and isolated areas, as appropriate;

(g) Assist and facilitate on an accelerated basis, with the financial and technical assistance of developed countries, including through public-private partnerships, the access of the poor to reliable, affordable, economically viable, socially acceptable and environmentally sound energy services, taking into account the instrumental role of developing national policies on energy for sustainable development, bearing in mind that in developing countries sharp increases in energy services are required to improve the standards of living of their populations and that energy services have positive impacts on poverty eradication and improve standards of living.

Strengthen the contribution of industrial development to poverty eradication and sustainable natural resource management. This would include actions at all levels to:

(a) Provide assistance and mobilize resources to enhance industrial productivity and competitiveness as well as industrial development in developing countries, including the transfer of environmentally sound technologies on preferential terms, as mutually agreed;

(b) Provide assistance to increase income-generating employment opportunities, taking into account the International Labour Organization (ILO) Declaration on Fundamental Principles and Rights at Work;

(c) Promote the development of micro, small and medium-sized enterprises, including by means of training, education and skill enhancement, with a special focus on agro-industry as a provider of livelihoods for rural communities;

(d) Provide financial and technological support, as appropriate, to rural communities of developing countries to enable them to benefit from safe and sustainable livelihood opportunities in small-scale mining ventures;

(e) Provide support to developing countries for the development of safe low-cost technologies that provide or conserve fuel for cooking and water heating;

(f) Provide support for natural resource management for creating sustainable livelihoods for the poor.

By 2020, achieve a significant improvement in the lives of at least 100 million slum dwellers, as proposed in the "Cities without slums" initiative. This would include actions at all levels to:

(a) Improve access to land and property, to adequate shelter and to basic services for the urban and rural poor, with special attention to female heads of household;

(b) Use low-cost and sustainable materials and appropriate technologies for the construction of adequate and secure housing for the poor, with financial and technological assistance to developing countries, taking into account their culture, climate, specific social conditions and vulnerability to natural disasters;

(c) Increase decent employment, credit and income for the urban poor, through appropriate national policies, promoting equal opportunities for women and men;

(d) Remove unnecessary regulatory and other obstacles for microenterprises and the informal sector;

(e) Support local authorities in elaborating slum upgrading programmes within the framework of urban development plans and facilitate access, particularly for the poor, to information on housing legislation.

Take immediate and effective measures to eliminate the worst forms of child labour as defined in ILO Convention No. 182, and elaborate and implement strategies for the elimination of child labour that is contrary to accepted international standards.

Promote international cooperation to assist developing countries, upon request, in addressing child labour and its root causes, inter alia, through social and economic policies aimed at poverty conditions, while stressing that labour standards should not be used for protectionist trade purposes.

Changing unsustainable patterns of consumption and production

Fundamental changes in the way societies produce and consume are indispensable for achieving global sustainable development. All countries should promote sustainable consumption and production patterns, with the developed countries taking the lead and with all countries benefiting from the process, taking into account the Rio principles, including, inter alia, the principle of common but differentiated responsibilities as set out in principle 7 of the Rio Declaration on Environment and Development. Governments, relevant international organizations, the private sector and all major groups should play an active role in changing unsustainable consumption and production patterns. This would include the actions at all levels set out below.

Encourage and promote the development of a 10-year framework of programmes in support of regional and national initiatives to accelerate the shift towards sustainable consumption and production to promote social and economic development within the carrying capacity of ecosystems by addressing and, where appropriate, delinking economic growth and environmental degradation through improving efficiency and sustainability in the use of resources and production processes, and reducing resource degradation, pollution and waste. All countries should take action, with developed countries taking the lead, taking into account the development needs and capabilities of developing countries through mobilization, from all sources, of financial and technical assistance and capacity-building for developing countries. This would require actions at all levels to:

(a) Identify specific activities, tools, policies, measures and monitoring and assessment mechanisms, including, where appropriate, life-cycle analysis and national indicators for measuring progress, bearing in mind that standards applied by some countries may be inappropriate and of unwarranted economic and social cost to other countries, in particular developing countries;

(b) Adopt and implement policies and measures aimed at promoting sustainable patterns of production and consumption, applying, inter alia, the polluter-pays principle described in principle 16 of the Rio Declaration on Environment and Development;

(c) Develop production and consumption policies to improve the products and services provided, while reducing environmental and health impacts, using, where appropriate, science-based approaches, such as life-cycle analysis;

(d) Develop awareness-raising programmes on the importance of sustainable production and consumption patterns, particularly among youth and the relevant segments in all countries, especially in developed countries, through, inter alia, education, public and consumer information, advertising and other media, taking into account local, national and regional cultural values;

(e) Develop and adopt, where appropriate, on a voluntary basis, effective, transparent, verifiable, non-misleading and non-discriminatory consumer information tools to provide information relating to sustainable consumption and production, including human health and safety aspects. These tools should not be used as disguised trade barriers;

(f) Increase eco-efficiency, with financial support from all sources, where mutually agreed, for capacity-building, technology transfer and exchange of technology with developing countries and countries with economies in transition, in cooperation with relevant international organizations.

Increase investment in cleaner production and eco-efficiency in all countries through, inter alia, incentives and support schemes and policies directed at establishing appropriate regulatory, financial and legal frameworks. This would include actions at all levels to:

(a) Establish and support cleaner production programmes and centres and more efficient production methods by providing, inter alia, incentives and capacity-building to assist enterprises, especially small and medium-sized enterprises and particularly in developing countries, in improving productivity and sustainable development;

(b) Provide incentives for investment in cleaner production and eco-efficiency in all countries, such as state-financed loans, venture capital, technical assistance and training programmes for small and medium-sized companies while avoiding trade-distorting measures inconsistent with WTO rules;

(c) Collect and disseminate information on cost-effective examples in cleaner production, eco-efficiency and environmental management, and promote the exchange of best practices and know-how on environmentally sound technologies between public and private institutions;

(d) Provide training programmes to small and medium-sized enterprises on the use of information and communication technologies.

Integrate the issue of production and consumption patterns into sustainable development policies, programmes and strategies, including, where applicable, into poverty reduction strategies.

Enhance corporate environmental and social responsibility and accountability. This would include actions at all levels to:

(a) Encourage industry to improve social and environmental performance through voluntary initiatives, including environmental management systems, codes of conduct, certification and public reporting on environmental and social issues, taking into account such initiatives as the International Organization for Standardization (ISO) standards and Global Reporting Initiative guidelines on sustainability reporting, bearing in mind principle 11 of the Rio Declaration on Environment and Development;

(b) Encourage dialogue between enterprises and the communities in which they operate and other stakeholders;

(c) Encourage financial institutions to incorporate sustainable development considerations into their decision-making processes;

(d) Develop workplace-based partnerships and programmes, including training and education programmes.

Encourage relevant authorities at all levels to take sustainable development considerations into account in decision-making, including on national and local development planning, investment in infrastructure, business development and public procurement. This would include actions at all levels to:

(a) Provide support for the development of sustainable development strategies and programmes, including in decision-making on investment in infrastructure and business development;

(b) Continue to promote the internalization of environmental costs and the use of economic instruments, taking into account the approach that the polluter should, in principle, bear the costs of pollution, with due regard to the public interest and without distorting international trade and investment;

(c) Promote public procurement policies that encourage development and diffusion of environmentally sound goods and services;

(d) Provide capacity-building and training to assist relevant authorities with regard to the implementation of the initiatives listed in the present paragraph;

(e) Use environmental impact assessment procedures.

***

Call upon Governments, as well as relevant regional and international organizations and other relevant stakeholders, to implement, taking into account national and regional specificities and circumstances, the recommendations and conclusions of the Commission on Sustainable Development concerning energy for sustainable development adopted at its ninth session, including the issues and options set out below, bearing in mind that in view of the different contributions to global environmental degradation, States have common but differentiated responsibilities. This would include actions at all levels to:

(a) Take further action to mobilize the provision of financial resources, technology transfer, capacity-building and the diffusion of environmentally sound technologies according to the recommendations and conclusions of the Commission on Sustainable Development as contained in section A, paragraph 3, and section D, paragraph 30, of its decision 9/1 on energy for sustainable development;

(b) Integrate energy considerations, including energy efficiency, affordability and accessibility, into socio-economic programmes, especially into policies of major energy-consuming sectors, and into the planning, operation and maintenance of long-lived energy consuming infrastructures, such as the public sector, transport, industry, agriculture, urban land use, tourism and construction sectors;

(c) Develop and disseminate alternative energy technologies with the aim of giving a greater share of the energy mix to renewable energies, improving energy efficiency and greater reliance on advanced energy technologies, including cleaner fossil fuel technologies;

(d) Combine, as appropriate, the increased use of renewable energy resources, more efficient use of energy, greater reliance on advanced energy technologies, including advanced and cleaner fossil fuel technologies, and the sustainable use of traditional energy resources, which could meet the growing need for energy services in the longer term to achieve sustainable development;

(e) Diversify energy supply by developing advanced, cleaner, more efficient, affordable and cost-effective energy technologies, including fossil fuel technologies and renewable energy technologies, hydro included, and their transfer to developing countries on concessional terms as mutually agreed. With a sense of urgency, substantially increase the global share of renewable energy sources with the objective of increasing its contribution to total energy supply, recognizing the role of national and voluntary regional targets as well as initiatives, where they exist, and ensuring that energy policies are supportive to developing countries' efforts to eradicate poverty, and regularly evaluate available data to review progress to this end;

(f) Support efforts, including through provision of financial and technical assistance to developing countries, with the involvement of the private sector, to reduce flaring and venting of gas associated with crude oil production;

(g) Develop and utilize indigenous energy sources and infrastructures for various local uses and promote rural community participation, including local Agenda 21 groups, with the support of the international community, in developing and utilizing renewable energy technologies to meet their daily energy needs to find simple and local solutions;

(h) Establish domestic programmes for energy efficiency, including, as appropriate, by accelerating the deployment of energy efficiency technologies, with the necessary support of the international community;

(i) Accelerate the development, dissemination and deployment of affordable and cleaner energy efficiency and energy conservation technologies, as well as the transfer of such technologies, in particular to developing countries, on favourable terms, including on concessional and preferential terms, as mutually agreed;

(j) Recommend that international financial institutions and other agencies' policies support developing countries, as well as countries with economies in transition, in their own efforts to establish policy and regulatory frameworks which create a level playing field between the following: renewable energy, energy efficiency, advanced energy technologies, including advanced and cleaner fossil fuel technologies, and centralized, distributed and decentralized energy systems;

(k) Promote increased research and development in the field of various energy technologies, including renewable energy, energy efficiency and advanced energy technologies, including advanced and cleaner fossil fuel technologies, both nationally and through international collaboration; strengthen national and regional research and development institutions/centres on reliable, affordable, economically viable, socially acceptable and environmentally sound energy for sustainable development;

(l) Promote networking between centres of excellence on energy for sustainable development, including regional networks, by linking competent centres on energy technologies for sustainable development that could support and promote efforts at capacity-building and technology transfer activities, particularly of developing countries, as well as serve as information clearing houses;

(m) Promote education to provide information for both men and women about available energy sources and technologies;

(n) Utilize financial instruments and mechanisms, in particular the Global Environment Facility (GEF), within its mandate, to provide financial resources to developing countries, in particular least developed countries and small island developing States, to meet their capacity needs for training, technical know-how and strengthening national institutions in reliable, affordable, economically viable, socially acceptable and environmentally sound energy, including promoting energy efficiency and conservation, renewable energy and advanced energy technologies, including advanced and cleaner fossil fuel technologies;

(o) Support efforts to improve the functioning, transparency and information about energy markets with respect to both supply and demand, with the aim of achieving greater stability and predictability and to ensure consumer access to reliable, affordable, economically viable, socially acceptable and environmentally sound energy services;

(p) Policies to reduce market distortions would promote energy systems compatible with sustainable development through the use of improved market signals and by removing market distortions, including restructuring taxation and phasing out harmful subsidies, where they exist, to reflect their environmental impacts, with such policies taking fully into account the specific needs and conditions of developing countries with the aim of minimizing the possible adverse impacts on their development;

(q) Take action, where appropriate, to phase out subsidies in this area that inhibit sustainable development, taking fully into account the specific conditions and different levels of development of individual countries and considering their adverse effect, particularly on developing countries;

(r) Governments are encouraged to improve the functioning of national energy markets in such a way that they support sustainable development, overcome market barriers and improve accessibility, taking fully into account that such policies should be decided by each country, and that its own characteristics and capabilities and level of development should be considered, especially as reflected in national sustainable development strategies, where they exist;

(s) Strengthen national and regional energy institutions or arrangements for enhancing regional and international cooperation on energy for sustainable development, in particular to assist developing countries in their domestic efforts to provide reliable, affordable, economically viable, socially acceptable and environmentally sound energy services to all sections of their populations;

(t) Countries are urged to develop and implement actions within the framework of the ninth session of the Commission on Sustainable Development, including through public-private partnerships, taking into account the different circumstances of countries, based on lessons learned by Governments, international institutions and stakeholders and including business and industry, in the field of access to energy, including renewable energy and energy-efficiency and advanced energy technologies, including advanced and cleaner fossil fuel technologies;

(u) Promote cooperation between international and regional institutions and bodies dealing with different aspects of energy for sustainable development within their existing mandate, bearing in mind paragraph 46 (h) of the Programme of Action for the Further Implementation of Agenda 21, strengthening, as appropriate, regional and national activities for the promotion of education and capacity-building regarding energy for sustainable development;

(v) Strengthen and facilitate, as appropriate, regional cooperation arrangements for promoting cross-border energy trade, including the interconnection of electricity grids and oil and natural gas pipelines;

(w) Strengthen and, where appropriate, facilitate dialogue forums among regional, national and international producers and consumers of energy.

* * *

Promote an integrated approach to policy-making at the national, regional and local levels for transport services and systems to promote sustainable development, including policies and planning for land use, infrastructure, public transport systems and goods delivery networks, with a view to providing safe, affordable and efficient transportation, increasing energy efficiency, reducing pollution, reducing congestion, reducing adverse health effects and limiting urban sprawl, taking into account national priorities and circumstances. This would include actions at all levels to:

(a) Implement transport strategies for sustainable development, reflecting specific regional, national and local conditions, so as to improve the affordability, efficiency and convenience of transportation, as well as improving urban air quality and health, and reduce greenhouse gas emissions, including through the development of better vehicle technologies that are more environmentally sound, affordable and socially acceptable;

(b) Promote investment and partnerships for the development of sustainable, energy efficient multi-modal transportation systems, including public mass transportation systems and better transportation systems in rural areas, with technical and financial assistance for developing countries and countries with economies in transition.

* * *

Prevent and minimize waste and maximize reuse, recycling and use of environmentally friendly alternative materials, with the participation of government authorities and all stakeholders, in order to minimize adverse effects on the environment and improve resource efficiency, with financial, technical and other assistance for developing countries. This would include actions at all levels to:

(a) Develop waste management systems, with highest priorities placed on waste prevention and minimization, reuse and recycling, and environmentally sound disposal facilities, including technology to recapture the energy contained in waste, and encourage small-scale waste-recycling initiatives that support urban and rural waste management and provide income-generating opportunities, with international support for developing countries;

(b) Promote waste prevention and minimization by encouraging production of reusable consumer goods and biodegradable products and developing the infrastructure required.

* * *

Renew the commitment, as advanced in Agenda 21, to sound management of chemicals throughout their life cycle and of hazardous wastes for sustainable development and for the protection of human health and the environment, inter alia, aiming to achieve by 2020 that chemicals are used and produced in ways that lead to the minimization of significant adverse effects on human health and the environment, using transparent science-based risk assessment procedures and science-based risk management procedures, taking into account the precautionary approach, as set out in principle 15 of the Rio Declaration on Environment and Development, and support developing countries in strengthening their capacity for the sound management of chemicals and hazardous wastes by providing technical and financial assistance. This would include actions at all levels to:

(a) Promote the ratification and implementation of relevant international instruments on chemicals and hazardous waste, including the Rotterdam Convention on Prior Informed Consent Procedures for Certain Hazardous Chemicals and Pesticides in International Trade so that it can enter into force by 2003 and the Stockholm Convention on Persistent Organic Pollutants so that it can enter into force by 2004, and encourage and improve coordination as well as supporting developing countries in their implementation;

(b) Further develop a strategic approach to international chemicals management based on the Bahia Declaration and Priorities for Action beyond 2000 of the Intergovernmental Forum on Chemical Safety (IFCS) by 2005, and urge that the United Nations Environment Programme (UNEP), IFCS, other international organizations dealing with chemical management, and other relevant international organizations and actors closely cooperate in this regard, as appropriate;

(c) Encourage countries to implement the new globally harmonized system for the classification and labelling of chemicals as soon as possible with a view to having the system fully operational by 2008;

(d) Encourage partnerships to promote activities aimed at enhancing environmentally sound management of chemicals and hazardous wastes, implementing multilateral environmental agreements, raising awareness of issues relating to chemicals and hazardous waste, and encouraging the collection and use of additional scientific data;

(e) Promote efforts to prevent international illegal trafficking of hazardous chemicals and hazardous wastes and to prevent damage resulting from the transboundary movement and disposal of hazardous wastes in a manner consistent with obligations under relevant international instruments, such as the Basel Convention on the Control of Transboundary Movements of Hazardous Wastes and Their Disposal;

(f) Encourage development of coherent and integrated information on chemicals, such as through national pollutant release and transfer registers;

(g) Promote reduction of the risks posed by heavy metals that are harmful to human health and the environment, including through a review of relevant studies, such as the UNEP global assessment of mercury and its compounds.

Protecting and managing the natural resource base of economic and social development

Human activities are having an increasing impact on the integrity of ecosystems that provide essential resources and services for human well-being and economic activities. Managing the natural resources base in a sustainable and integrated manner is essential for sustainable development. In this regard, to reverse the current trend in natural resource degradation as soon as possible, it is necessary to implement strategies which should include targets adopted at the national and, where appropriate, regional levels to protect ecosystems and to achieve integrated management of land, water and living resources, while strengthening regional, national and local capacities. This would include actions at all levels to:

Launch a programme of actions, with financial and technical assistance, to achieve the millennium development goal on safe drinking water. In this respect, we agree to halve, by the year 2015, the proportion of people who are unable to reach or to afford safe drinking water as outlined in the Millennium Declaration and the proportion of people without access to basic sanitation, which would include actions at all levels to:

(a) Mobilize international and domestic financial resources at all levels, transfer technology, promote best practice and support capacity-building for water and sanitation infrastructure and services development, ensuring that such infrastructure and services meet the needs of the poor and are gender-sensitive;

(b) Facilitate access to public information and participation, including by women, at all levels, in support of policy and decision-making related to water resources management and project implementation;

(c) Promote priority action by Governments, with the support of all stakeholders, in water management and capacity-building at the national level and, where appropriate, at the regional level, and promote and provide new and additional financial resources and innovative technologies to implement chapter 18 of Agenda 21;

(d) Intensify water pollution prevention to reduce health hazards and protect ecosystems by introducing technologies for affordable sanitation and industrial and domestic wastewater treatment, by mitigating the effects of groundwater contamination, and by establishing, at the national level, monitoring systems and effective legal frameworks;

(e) Adopt prevention and protection measures to promote sustainable water use and to address water shortages.

Develop integrated water resources management and water efficiency plans by 2005, with support to developing countries, through actions at all levels to:

(a) Develop and implement national/regional strategies, plans and programmes with regard to integrated river basin, watershed and groundwater management, and introduce measures to improve the efficiency of water infrastructure to reduce losses and increase recycling of water;

(b) Employ the full range of policy instruments, including regulation, monitoring, voluntary measures, market and information-based tools, land-use management and cost recovery of water services, without cost recovery objectives becoming a barrier to access to safe water by poor people, and adopt an integrated water basin approach;

(c) Improve the efficient use of water resources and promote their allocation among competing uses in a way that gives priority to the satisfaction of basic human needs and balances the requirement of preserving or restoring ecosystems and their functions, in particular in fragile environments, with human domestic, industrial and agriculture needs, including safeguarding drinking water quality;

(d) Develop programmes for mitigating the effects of extreme water-related events;

(e) Support the diffusion of technology and capacity-building for non-conventional water resources and conservation technologies, to developing countries and regions facing water scarcity conditions or subject to drought and desertification, through technical and financial support and capacity-building;

(f) Support, where appropriate, efforts and programmes for energy-efficient, sustainable and cost-effective desalination of seawater, water recycling and water harvesting from coastal fogs in developing countries, through such measures as technological, technical and financial assistance and other modalities;

(g) Facilitate the establishment of public-private partnerships and other forms of partnership that give priority to the needs of the poor, within stable and transparent national regulatory frameworks provided by Governments, while respecting local conditions, involving all concerned stakeholders, and monitoring the performance and improving accountability of public institutions and private companies.

Support developing countries and countries with economies in transition in their efforts to monitor and assess the quantity and quality of water resources, including through the establishment and/or further development of national monitoring networks and water resources databases and the development of relevant national indicators.

Improve water resource management and scientific understanding of the water cycle through cooperation in joint observation and research, and for this purpose encourage and promote knowledge-sharing and provide capacity-building and the transfer of technology, as mutually agreed, including remote-sensing and satellite technologies, particularly to developing countries and countries with economies in transition.

Promote effective coordination among the various international and intergovernmental bodies and processes working on water-related issues, both within the United Nations system and between the United Nations and international financial institutions, drawing on the contributions of other international institutions and civil society to inform intergovernmental decision-making; closer coordination should also be promoted to elaborate and support proposals and undertake activities related to the International Year of Freshwater 2003 and beyond.

* * *

Oceans, seas, islands and coastal areas form an integrated and essential component of the Earth's ecosystem and are critical for global food security and for sustaining economic prosperity and the well-being of many national economies, particularly in developing countries. Ensuring the sustainable development of the oceans requires effective coordination and cooperation, including at the global and regional levels, between relevant bodies, and actions at all levels to:

(a) Invite States to ratify or accede to and implement the United Nations Convention on the Law of the Sea, which provides the overall legal framework for ocean activities;

(b) Promote the implementation of chapter 17 of Agenda 21 which provides the programme of action for achieving the sustainable development of oceans, coastal areas and seas through its programme areas of integrated management and sustainable development of coastal areas, including exclusive economic zones; marine environmental protection; sustainable use and conservation of marine living resources; addressing critical uncertainties for the management of the marine environment and climate change; strengthening international, including regional, cooperation and coordination; and sustainable development of small islands;

(c) Establish an effective, transparent and regular inter-agency coordination mechanism on ocean and coastal issues within the United Nations system;

(d) Encourage the application by 2010 of the ecosystem approach, noting the Reykjavik Declaration on Responsible Fisheries in the Marine Ecosystem and decision 5/6 of the Conference of Parties to the Convention on Biological Diversity;

(e) Promote integrated, multidisciplinary and multisectoral coastal and ocean management at the national level, and encourage and assist coastal States in developing ocean policies and mechanisms on integrated coastal management;

(f) Strengthen regional cooperation and coordination between the relevant regional organizations and programmes, the UNEP regional seas programmes, regional fisheries management organizations and other regional science, health and development organizations;

(g) Assist developing countries in coordinating policies and programmes at the regional and subregional levels aimed at the conservation and sustainable management of fishery resources, and implement integrated coastal area management plans, including through the promotion of sustainable coastal and small-scale fishing activities and, where appropriate, the development of related infrastructure;

(h) Take note of the work of the open-ended informal consultative process established by the United

Nations General Assembly in its resolution 54/33 in order to facilitate the annual review by the Assembly of developments in ocean affairs and the upcoming review of its effectiveness and utility to be held at its fifty-seventh session under the terms of the above-mentioned resolution.

To achieve sustainable fisheries, the following actions are required at all levels:

(a) Maintain or restore stocks to levels that can produce the maximum sustainable yield with the aim of achieving these goals for depleted stocks on an urgent basis and where possible not later than 2015;

(b) Ratify or accede to and effectively implement the relevant United Nations and, where appropriate, associated regional fisheries agreements or arrangements, noting in particular the Agreement for the Implementation of the Provisions of the United Nations Convention on the Law of the Sea of 10 December 1982 relating to the Conservation and Management of Straddling Fish Stocks and Highly Migratory Fish Stocks and the 1993 Agreement to Promote Compliance with International Conservation and Management Measures by Fishing Vessels on the High Seas;

(c) Implement the 1995 Code of Conduct for Responsible Fisheries, taking note of the special requirements of developing countries as noted in its article 5, and the relevant Food and Agriculture Organization of the United Nations (FAO) international plans of action and technical guidelines;

(d) Urgently develop and implement national and, where appropriate, regional plans of action, to put into effect the FAO international plans of action, in particular the international plan of action for the management of fishing capacity by 2005 and the international plan of action to prevent, deter and eliminate illegal, unreported and unregulated fishing by 2004. Establish effective monitoring, reporting and enforcement, and control of fishing vessels, including by flag States, to further the international plan of action to prevent, deter and eliminate illegal, unreported and unregulated fishing;

(e) Encourage relevant regional fisheries management organizations and arrangements to give due consideration to the rights, duties and interests of coastal States and the special requirements of developing States when addressing the issue of the allocation of share of fishery resources for straddling stocks and highly migratory fish stocks, mindful of the provisions of the United Nations Convention on the Law of the Sea and the Agreement for the Implementation of the Provisions of the United Nations Convention on the Law of the Sea of 10 December 1982 Relating to the Conservation and Management of Straddling Fish Stocks and Highly Migratory Fish Stocks, on the high seas and within exclusive economic zones;

(f) Eliminate subsidies that contribute to illegal, unreported and unregulated fishing and to over-capacity, while completing the efforts undertaken at WTO to clarify and improve its disciplines on fisheries subsidies, taking into account the importance of this sector to developing countries;

(g) Strengthen donor coordination and partnerships between international financial institutions, bilateral agencies and other relevant stakeholders to enable developing countries, in particular the least developed countries and small island developing States and countries with economies in transition, to develop their national, regional and subregional capacities for infrastructure and integrated management and the sustainable use of fisheries;

(h) Support the sustainable development of aquaculture, including small-scale aquaculture, given its growing importance for food security and economic development.

In accordance with chapter 17 of Agenda 21, promote the conservation and management of the oceans through actions at all levels, giving due regard to the relevant international instruments to:

(a) Maintain the productivity and biodiversity of important and vulnerable marine and coastal areas, including in areas within and beyond national jurisdiction;

(b) Implement the work programme arising from the Jakarta Mandate on the Conservation and Sustainable Use of Marine and Coastal Biological Diversity of the Convention on Biological Diversity, including through the urgent mobilization of financial resources and technological assistance and the development of human and institutional capacity, particularly in developing countries;

(c) Develop and facilitate the use of diverse approaches and tools, including the ecosystem approach, the elimination of destructive fishing practices, the establishment of marine protected areas consistent with international law and based on scientific information, including representative networks by 2012 and time/area closures for the protection of nursery grounds and periods, proper coastal land use; and watershed planning and the integration of marine and coastal areas management into key sectors;

(d) Develop national, regional and international programmes for halting the loss of marine biodiversity, including in coral reefs and wetlands;

(e) Implement the RAMSAR Convention, including its joint work programme with the Convention on Biological Diversity, and the programme of action called for by the International Coral Reef Initiative to strengthen joint management plans and international networking for wetland ecosystems in coastal zones, including coral reefs, mangroves, seaweed beds and tidal mud flats.

Advance implementation of the Global Programme of Action for the Protection of the Marine Environment from Land-based Activities and the Montreal Declaration on the Protection of the Marine Environment from Land-based Activities, with particular emphasis in the period 2002–2006 on municipal wastewater, the physical alteration and destruction of habitats, and nutrients, by actions at all levels to:

(a) Facilitate partnerships, scientific research and diffusion of technical knowledge; mobilize domestic, regional and international resources; and promote human and institutional capacity-building, paying particular attention to the needs of developing countries;

(b) Strengthen the capacity of developing countries in the development of their national and regional programmes and mechanisms to mainstream the objectives of the Global Programme of Action and to manage the risks and impacts of ocean pollution;

(c) Elaborate regional programmes of action and improve the links with strategic plans for the sustainable development of coastal and marine resources, noting in particular areas which are subject to accelerated environmental changes and development pressures;

(d) Make every effort to achieve substantial progress by the next Global Programme of Action conference in 2006 to protect the marine environment from land-based activities.

Enhance maritime safety and protection of the marine environment from pollution by actions at all levels to:

(a) Invite States to ratify or accede to and implement the conventions and protocols and other relevant instruments of the International Maritime Organization (IMO) relating to the enhancement of maritime safety and protection of the marine environment from marine pollution and environmental damage caused by ships, including the use of toxic anti-fouling paints and urge IMO to consider stronger mechanisms to secure the implementation of IMO instruments by flag States;

(b) Accelerate the development of measures to address invasive alien species in ballast water. Urge IMO to finalize the IMO International Convention on the Control and Management of Ships' Ballast Water and Sediments.

Governments, taking into account their national circumstances, are encouraged, recalling paragraph 8 of resolution GC (44)/RES/17 of the General Conference of the International Atomic Energy Agency (IAEA) and taking into account the very serious potential for environment and human health impacts of radioactive wastes, to make efforts to examine and further improve measures and internationally agreed regulations regarding safety, while stressing the importance of having effective liability mechanisms in place, relevant to international maritime transportation and other transboundary movement of radioactive material, radioactive waste and spent fuel, including, inter alia, arrangements for prior notification and consultations done in accordance with relevant international instruments.

Improve the scientific understanding and assessment of marine and coastal ecosystems as a fundamental basis for sound decision-making, through actions at all levels to:

(a) Increase scientific and technical collaboration, including integrated assessment at the global and regional levels, including the appropriate transfer of marine science and marine technologies and techniques for the conservation and management of living and non-living marine resources and expanding ocean-observing capabilities for the timely prediction and assessment of the state of marine environment;

(b) Establish by 2004 a regular process under the United Nations for global reporting and assessment of the state of the marine environment, including socio-economic aspects, both current and foreseeable, building on existing regional assessments;

(c) Build capacity in marine science, information and management, through, inter alia, promoting the use of environmental impact assessments and environmental evaluation and reporting techniques, for projects or activities that are potentially harmful to the coastal and marine environments and their living and non-living resources;

(d) Strengthen the ability of the Intergovernmental Oceanographic Commission of the United Nations Educational, Scientific and Cultural Organization, FAO and other relevant international and regional and subregional organizations to build national and local capacity in marine science and the sustainable management of oceans and their resources.

***

An integrated, multi-hazard, inclusive approach to address vulnerability, risk assessment and disaster management, including prevention, mitigation, preparedness, response and recovery, is an essential element of a safer world in the twenty-first century. Actions are required at all levels to:

(a) Strengthen the role of the International Strategy for Disaster Reduction and encourage the international community to provide the necessary financial resources to its Trust Fund;

(b) Support the establishment of effective regional, subregional and national strategies and scientific and technical institutional support for disaster management;

(c) Strengthen the institutional capacities of countries and promote international joint observation and research, through improved surface-based monitoring and increased use of satellite data, dissemination of technical and scientific knowledge, and the provision of assistance to vulnerable countries;

(d) Reduce the risks of flooding and drought in vulnerable countries by, inter alia, promoting wetland and watershed protection and restoration, improved land-use planning, improving and applying more widely techniques and methodologies for assessing the potential adverse effects of climate change on wetlands and, as appropriate, assisting countries that are particularly vulnerable to those effects;

(e) Improve techniques and methodologies for assessing the effects of climate change, and encourage the continuing assessment of those adverse effects by the Intergovernmental Panel on Climate Change;

(f) Encourage the dissemination and use of traditional and indigenous knowledge to mitigate the impact of disasters, and promote community-based disaster management planning by local authorities, including through training activities and raising public awareness;

(g) Support the ongoing voluntary contribution of, as appropriate, non-governmental organizations, the scientific community and other partners in the management of natural disasters according to agreed, relevant guidelines;

(h) Develop and strengthen early warning systems and information networks in disaster management, consistent with the International Strategy for Disaster Reduction;

(i) Develop and strengthen capacity at all levels to collect and disseminate scientific and technical information, including the improvement of early warning systems for predicting extreme weather events, especially El Niño/La Niña, through the provision of assistance to institutions devoted to addressing such events, including the International Centre for the Study of the El Niño phenomenon;

(j) Promote cooperation for the prevention and mitigation of, preparedness for, response to and recovery from major technological and other disasters with an adverse impact on the environment in order to enhance the capabilities of affected countries to cope with such situations.

***

Change in the Earth's climate and its adverse effects are a common concern of humankind. We remain deeply concerned that all countries, particularly developing countries including the least developed countries and small island developing States, face increased risks of negative impacts of climate change and recognize that, in this context, the problems of poverty, land degradation, access to water and food and human health remain at the centre of global attention. The United Nations Framework Convention on Climate Change is the key instrument for addressing climate change, a global concern, and we reaffirm our commitment to achieving its ultimate objective of stabilization of greenhouse gas concentrations in the atmosphere at a level that would prevent dangerous anthropogenic interference with the climate system, within a time frame sufficient to allow ecosystems to adapt naturally to climate change, to ensure that food production is not threatened and to enable economic development to proceed in a sustainable manner, in accordance with our common but differentiated responsibilities and respective capabilities. Recalling the United Nations Millennium Declaration, in which heads of State and Government resolved to make every effort to ensure the entry into force of the Kyoto Protocol to the United Nations Framework Convention on Climate Change, preferably by the tenth anniversary of the United Nations Conference on Environment and Development in 2002, and to embark on the required reduction of emissions of greenhouse gases, States that have ratified the Kyoto Protocol strongly urge States that have not already done so to ratify the Kyoto Protocol in a timely manner. Actions at all levels are required to:

(a) Meet all the commitments and obligations under the UNFCCC;
(b) Work cooperatively towards achieving the objectives of the UNFCCC;
(c) Provide technical and financial assistance and capacity building to developing countries and countries with economies in transition in accordance with commitments under the UNFCCC, including the Marrakech accords;
(d) Build and enhance scientific and technological capabilities, inter alia through continuing support to the IPCC for the exchange of scientific data and information especially in developing countries;
(e) Develop and transfer technological solutions;
(f) Develop and disseminate innovative technologies in respect of key sectors of development, particularly energy, and of investment in this regard, including through private sector involvement, market-oriented approaches, as well as supportive public policies and international cooperation;
(g) Promote the systematic observation of the Earth's atmosphere, land and oceans by improving monitoring stations, increasing the use of satellites, and appropriate integration of these observations to produce high-quality data that could be disseminated for the use of all countries, in particular developing countries;
(h) Enhance the implementation of national, regional and international strategies to monitor the Earth's atmosphere, land and oceans including, as appropriate, strategies for integrated global observations, inter alia with the cooperation of relevant international organisations, especially the United Nations specialized agencies in cooperation with the UNFCCC;
(i) Support initiatives to assess the consequences of climate change, such as the Arctic Council initiative, including the environmental, economic and social impacts on local and indigenous communities.

Enhance cooperation at the international, regional and national levels to reduce air pollution, including transboundary air pollution, acid deposition and ozone depletion bearing in mind the Rio principles, including, inter alia, the principle that, in view of the different contributions to global environmental degradation, States have common but differentiated responsibilities, with actions at all levels to:

(a) Strengthen capacities of developing countries and countries with economies in transition to measure, reduce and assess the impacts of air pollution, including health impacts, and provide financial and technical support for these activities;
(b) Facilitate implementation of the Montreal Protocol on Substances that Deplete the Ozone Layer by ensuring adequate replenishment of its fund by 2003/2005;
(c) Further support the effective regime for the protection of the ozone layer established in the Vienna Convention for the Protection of the Ozone Layer and the Montreal Protocol, including its compliance mechanism;

(d) Improve access by developing countries to affordable, accessible, cost-effective, safe and environmentally sound alternatives to ozone-depleting substances by 2010, and assist them in complying with the phase-out schedule under the Montreal Protocol, bearing in mind that ozone depletion and climate change are scientifically and technically interrelated;

(e) Take measures to address illegal traffic in ozone-depleting substances.

* * *

Agriculture plays a crucial role in addressing the needs of a growing global population, and is inextricably linked to poverty eradication, especially in developing countries. Enhancing the role of women at all levels and in all aspects of rural development, agriculture, nutrition and food security is imperative. Sustainable agriculture and rural development are essential to the implementation of an integrated approach to increasing food production and enhancing food security and food safety in an environmentally sustainable way. This would include actions at all levels to:

(a) Achieve the Millennium Declaration target to halve by the year 2015 the proportion of the world's people who suffer from hunger and realize the right to a standard of living adequate for the health and well-being of themselves and their families, including food, including by promoting food security and fighting hunger in combination with measures which address poverty, consistent with the outcome of the World Food Summit and, for States Parties, with their obligations under article 11 of the International Covenant on Economic, Social and Cultural Rights;

(b) Develop and implement integrated land management and water-use plans that are based on sustainable use of renewable resources and on integrated assessments of socio-economic and environmental potentials, and strengthen the capacity of Governments, local authorities and communities to monitor and manage the quantity and quality of land and water resources;

(c) Increase understanding of the sustainable use, protection and management of water resources to advance long-term sustainability of freshwater, coastal and marine environments;

(d) Promote programmes to enhance in a sustainable manner the productivity of land and the efficient use of water resources in agriculture, forestry, wetlands, artisanal fisheries and aquaculture, especially through indigenous and local community-based approaches;

(e) Support the efforts of developing countries to protect oases from silt, land degradation and increasing salinity by providing appropriate technical and financial assistance;

(f) Enhance the participation of women in all aspects and at all levels relating to sustainable agriculture and food security;

(g) Integrate existing information systems on land-use practices by strengthening national research and extension services and farmer organizations to trigger farmer-to-farmer exchange on good practices, such as those related to environmentally sound, low-cost technologies, with the assistance of relevant international organizations;

(h) Enact, as appropriate, measures that protect indigenous resource management systems and support the contribution of all appropriate stakeholders, men and women alike, in rural planning and development;

(i) Adopt policies and implement laws that guarantee well defined and enforceable land and water use rights, and promote legal security of tenure, recognizing the existence of different national laws and/or systems of land access and tenure, and provide technical and financial assistance to developing countries as well as countries with economies in transition that are undertaking land tenure reform in order to enhance sustainable livelihoods;

(j) Reverse the declining trend in public sector finance for sustainable agriculture, provide appropriate technical and financial assistance, and promote private sector investment and support efforts in developing countries and countries with economies in transition to strengthen agricultural research and natural resource management capacity and dissemination of research results to the farming communities;

(k) Employ market-based incentives for agricultural enterprises and farmers to monitor and manage water use and quality, inter alia, by applying such methods as small-scale irrigation and wastewater recycling and reuse;

(l) Enhance access to existing markets and develop new markets for value-added agricultural products;

(m) Increase brown-field redevelopment in developed countries and countries with economies in transition, with appropriate technical assistance where contamination is a serious problem;

(n) Enhance international cooperation to combat the illicit cultivation of narcotic plants, taking into account their negative social, economic and environmental impacts;

(o) Promote programmes for the environmentally sound, effective and efficient use of soil fertility improvement practices and agricultural pest control;

(p) Strengthen and improve coordination of existing initiatives to enhance sustainable agricultural production and food security;

(q) Invite countries that have not done so to ratify the International Treaty on Plant Genetic Resources for Food and Agriculture;

(r) Promote the conservation, and sustainable use and management of traditional and indigenous agricultural systems and strengthen indigenous models of agricultural production.

* * *

Strengthen the implementation of the United Nations Convention to Combat Desertification in Those Countries Experiencing Serious Drought and/or Desertification, particularly in Africa, to address causes of desertification and land degradation in order to maintain and restore land, and to address poverty resulting from land degradation. This would include actions at all levels to:

(a) Mobilize adequate and predictable financial resources, transfer of technologies and capacity-building at all levels;

(b) Formulate national action programmes to ensure timely and effective implementation of the Convention and its related projects, with the support of the international community, including through decentralized projects at the local level;

(c) Encourage the United Nations Framework Convention on Climate Change, the Convention on Biological Diversity and the Convention to Combat Desertification to continue exploring and enhancing synergies, with due regard to their respective mandates, in the elaboration and implementation of plans and strategies under the respective Conventions;

(d) Integrate measures to prevent and combat desertification as well as to mitigate the effects of drought through relevant policies and programmes, such as land, water and forest management, agriculture, rural development, early warning systems, environment, energy, natural resources, health and education, and poverty eradication and sustainable development strategies;

(e) Provide affordable local access to information to improve monitoring and early warning related to desertification and drought;

(f) Call on the Second Assembly of the Global Environment Facility (GEF) to take action on the recommendations of the GEF Council concerning the designation of land degradation (desertification and deforestation) as a focal area of GEF as a means of GEF support for the successful implementation of the Convention to Combat Desertification; and consequently, consider making GEF a financial mechanism of the Convention, taking into account the prerogatives and decisions of the Conference of the Parties to the Convention, while recognizing the complementary roles of GEF and the Global Mechanism of the Convention in providing and mobilizing resources for the elaboration and implementation of action programmes;

(g) Improve the sustainability of grassland resources through strengthening management and law enforcement and providing financial and technical support by the international community to developing countries.

* * *

Mountain ecosystems support particular livelihoods, and include significant watershed resources, biological diversity and unique flora and fauna. Many are particularly fragile and vulnerable to the adverse effects of climate change and need specific protection. Actions at all levels are required to:

(a) Develop and promote programmes, policies and approaches that integrate environmental, economic and social components of sustainable mountain development and strengthen international cooperation for its positive impacts on poverty eradication programmes, especially in developing countries;

(b) Implement programmes to address, where appropriate, deforestation, erosion, land degradation, loss of biodiversity, disruption of water flows and retreat of glaciers;

(c) Develop and implement, where appropriate, gender-sensitive policies and programmes, including public and private investments that help eliminate inequities facing mountain communities;

(d) Implement programmes to promote diversification and traditional mountain economies, sustainable livelihoods and small-scale production systems, including specific training programmes and better access to national and international markets, communications and transport planning, taking into account the particular sensitivity of mountains;

(e) Promote full participation and involvement of mountain communities in decisions that affect them and integrate indigenous knowledge, heritage and values in all development initiatives;

(f) Mobilize national and international support for applied research and capacity-building, provide financial and technical assistance for the effective implementation of sustainable development of mountain ecosystems in developing countries and countries with economies in transition, and address the poverty among people living in mountains through concrete plans, projects and programmes, with sufficient support from all stakeholders, taking into account the spirit of the International Year of Mountains, 2002.

* * *

Promote sustainable tourism development, including non-consumptive and eco-tourism, taking into account the spirit of the International Year of Eco-tourism 2002, the United Nations Year for Cultural Heritage in 2002, the World Eco-tourism Summit 2002 and its Quebec Declaration, and the Global Code of Ethics for Tourism as adopted by the World Tourism Organization in order to increase the benefits from tourism resources for the population in host communities while maintaining the cultural and environmental integrity of the host communities and enhancing the protection of ecologically sensitive areas and natural heritages. Promote sustainable tourism development and capacity-building in order to contribute to the strengthening of rural and local communities. This would include actions at all levels to:

(a) Enhance international cooperation, foreign direct investment and partnerships with both private and public sectors, at all levels;

(b) Develop programmes, including education and training programmes, that encourage people to participate in eco-tourism, enable indigenous and local communities to develop and benefit from eco-tourism, and enhance stakeholder cooperation in tourism development and heritage preservation, in order to improve the protection of the environment, natural resources and cultural heritage;

(c) Provide technical assistance to developing countries and countries with economies in transition to support sustainable tourism business development and investment and tourism awareness programmes, to improve domestic tourism, and to stimulate entrepreneurial development;

(d) Assist host communities in managing visits to their tourism attractions for their maximum benefit, while ensuring the least negative impacts on and risks for their traditions, culture and environment, with the support of the World Tourism Organization and other relevant organizations;

(e) Promote the diversification of economic activities, including through the facilitation of access to markets and commercial information, and participation of emerging local enterprises, especially small and medium-sized enterprises.

* * *

Biodiversity, which plays a critical role in overall sustainable development and poverty eradication, is essential to our planet, human well-being and to the livelihood and cultural integrity of people. However, biodiversity is currently being lost at unprecedented rates due to human activities; this trend can only be reversed if the local people benefit from the conservation and sustainable use of biological diversity, in particular in countries of origin of genetic resources, in accordance with article 15 of the Convention on Biological Diversity. The Convention is the key instrument for the conservation and sustainable use of biological diversity and the fair and equitable sharing of benefits arising from use of genetic resources. A more efficient and coherent implementation of the three objectives of the Convention and the achievement by 2010 of a significant reduction in the current rate of loss of biological diversity will require the provision of new and additional financial and technical resources to developing countries, and includes actions at all levels to:

(a) Integrate the objectives of the Convention into global, regional and national sectoral and cross-sectoral programmes and policies, in particular in the programmes and policies of the economic sectors of countries and international financial institutions;

(b) Promote the ongoing work under the Convention on the sustainable use on biological diversity, including on sustainable tourism, as a cross-cutting issue relevant to different ecosystems, sectors and thematic areas;

(c) Encourage effective synergies between the Convention and other multilateral environmental agreements, inter alia, through the development of joint plans and programmes, with due regard to their respective mandates, regarding common responsibilities and concerns;

(d) Implement the Convention and its provisions, including active follow-up of its work programmes and decisions through national, regional and global action programmes, in particular the national biodiversity strategies and action plans, and strengthen their integration into relevant cross-sectoral strategies, programmes and policies, including those related to sustainable development and poverty eradication, including initiatives which promote community-based sustainable use of biological diversity;

(e) Promote the wide implementation and further development of the ecosystem approach, as being elaborated in the ongoing work of the Convention;

(f) Promote concrete international support and partnership for the conservation and sustainable use of biodiversity, including in ecosystems, at World Heritage sites and for the protection of endangered species, in particular through the appropriate channelling of financial resources and technology to developing countries and countries with economies in transition;

(g) To effectively conserve and sustainably use biodiversity, promote and support initiatives for hot spot areas and other areas essential for biodiversity and promote the development of national and regional ecological networks and corridors;

(h) Provide financial and technical support to developing countries, including capacity-building, in order to enhance indigenous and community-based biodiversity conservation efforts;

(i) Strengthen national, regional and international efforts to control invasive alien species, which are one of the main causes of biodiversity loss, and encourage the development of effective work programme on invasive alien species at all levels;

(j) Subject to national legislation, recognize the rights of local and indigenous communities who are holders of traditional knowledge, innovations and practices, and, with the approval and involvement of the holders of such knowledge, innovations and practices, develop and implement benefit-sharing mechanisms on mutually agreed terms for the use of such knowledge, innovations and practices;

(k) Encourage and enable all stakeholders to contribute to the implementation of the objectives of the Convention, and in particular recognize the specific role of youth, women and indigenous and local communities in conserving and using biodiversity in a sustainable way;

(l) Promote the effective participation of indigenous and local communities in decision and policy-making concerning the use of their traditional knowledge;

(m) Encourage technical and financial support to developing countries and countries with economies in transition in their efforts to develop and implement, as appropriate, inter alia, national sui generis systems and traditional systems according to national priorities and legislation, with a view to conserving and the sustainable use of biodiversity;

(n) Promote the wide implementation of and continued work on the Bonn Guidelines on Access to Genetic Resources and Fair and Equitable Sharing of Benefits arising out of their Utilization of the Convention, as an input to assist Parties to the Convention when developing and drafting legislative, administrative or policy measures on access and benefit-sharing, and contract and other arrangements under mutually agreed terms for access and benefit-sharing;

(o) Negotiate within the framework of the Convention on Biological Diversity, bearing in mind the Bonn Guidelines, an international regime to promote and safeguard the fair and equitable sharing of benefits arising out of the utilization of genetic resources;

(p) Encourage successful conclusion of existing processes under the World Intellectual Property Organization Intergovernmental Committee on Intellectual Property and Genetic Resources, Traditional Knowledge and Folklore, and in the ad hoc open-ended working group on article 8 (j) and related provisions of the Convention;

(q) Promote practicable measures for access to the results and benefits arising from biotechnologies based upon genetic resources, in accordance with articles 15 and 19 of the Convention, including through enhanced scientific and technical cooperation on biotechnology and biosafety, including the exchange of experts, training human resources and developing research-oriented institutional capacities;

(r) With a view to enhancing synergy and mutual supportiveness, taking into account the decisions under the relevant agreements, promote the discussions, without prejudging their outcome, with regard to the relationships between the Convention and agreements related to international trade and intellectual property rights, as outlined in the Doha Ministerial Declaration;

(s) Promote the implementation of the programme of work of the Global Taxonomy Initiative;

(t) Invite all States which have not already done so to ratify the Convention, the Cartagena Protocol on Biosafety and other biodiversity-related agreements, and invite those that have done so, to promote their effective implementation at the national, regional and international levels and to support developing countries and countries with economies in transition technically and financially in this regard.

* * *

Forests and trees cover nearly one third of the Earth's surface. Sustainable forest management of both natural and planted forests and for timber and non-timber products is essential to achieving sustainable development and is a critical means to eradicate poverty, significantly reduce deforestation and halt the loss of forest biodiversity and land and resource degradation, and improve food security and access to safe drinking water and affordable energy; highlights the multiple benefits of both natural and planted forests and trees; and contributes to the well-being of the planet and humanity. Achievement of sustainable forest management, nationally and globally, including through partnerships among interested Governments and stakeholders, including the private sector, indigenous and local communities and non-governmental organizations, is an essential goal of sustainable development. This would include actions at all levels to:

(a) Enhance political commitment to achieve sustainable forest management by endorsing it as a priority on the international political agenda, taking full account of the linkages between the forest sector and other sectors through integrated approaches;

(b) Support the United Nations Forum on Forests, with the assistance of the Collaborative Partnership on Forests, as key intergovernmental mechanisms to facilitate and coordinate the implementation of sustainable forest management at the national, regional and global levels, thus contributing, inter alia, to the conservation and sustainable use of forest biodiversity;

(c) Take immediate action on domestic forest law enforcement and illegal international trade in forest products, including in forest biological resources, with the support of the international community, and provide human and institutional capacity-building related to the enforcement of national legislation in those areas;

(d) Take immediate action at the national and international levels to promote and facilitate the means to achieve sustainable timber harvesting, and to facilitate the provision of financial resources and the transfer and development of environmentally sound technologies, and thereby address unsustainable timber-harvesting practices;

(e) Develop and implement initiatives to address the needs of those parts of the world that currently suffer from poverty and the highest rates of deforestation and where international cooperation would be welcomed by affected Governments;

(f) Create and strengthen partnerships and international cooperation to facilitate the provision of increased financial resources, the transfer of environmentally sound technologies, trade, capacity-building, forest law enforcement and governance at all levels, and integrated land and resource management to implement sustainable forest management, including the Intergovernmental Panel on Forests (IPF)/ Intergovernmental Forum on Forests (IFF) proposals for action;

(g) Accelerate implementation of the IPF/IFF proposals for action by countries and by the Collaborative Partnership on Forests, and intensify efforts on reporting to the United Nations Forum on Forests to contribute to an assessment of progress in 2005;

(h) Recognize and support indigenous and community-based forest management systems to ensure their full and effective participation in sustainable forest management;

(i) Implement the Convention on Biological Diversity's expanded action-oriented work programme on all types of forest biological diversity, in close cooperation with the Forum, Partnership members and other forest-related processes and conventions, with the involvement of all relevant stakeholders.

* * *

Mining, minerals and metals are important to the economic and social development of many countries. Minerals are essential for modern living. Enhancing the contribution of mining, minerals and metals to sustainable development includes actions at all levels to:

(a) Support efforts to address the environmental, economic, health and social impacts and benefits of mining, minerals and metals throughout their life cycle, including workers' health and safety, and use a range of partnerships, furthering existing activities at the national and international levels, among interested Governments, intergovernmental organizations, mining companies and workers, and other stakeholders, to promote transparency and accountability for sustainable mining and minerals development;

(b) Enhance the participation of stakeholders, including local and indigenous communities and women, to play an active role in minerals, metals and mining development throughout the life cycles of mining operations, including after closure for rehabilitation purposes, in accordance with national regulations and taking into account significant transboundary impacts;

(c) Foster sustainable mining practices through the provision of financial, technical and capacity-building support to developing countries and countries with economies in transition for the mining and processing of minerals, including small-scale mining, and, where possible and appropriate, improve value-added processing, upgrade scientific and technological information, and reclaim and rehabilitate degraded sites.

Sustainable development in a globalizing world

Globalization offers opportunities and challenges for sustainable development. We recognize that globalization and interdependence are offering new opportunities to trade, investment and capital flows and advances in technology, including information technology, for the growth of the world economy, development and the improvement of living standards around the world. At the same time, there remain serious challenges, including serious financial crises, insecurity, poverty, exclusion and inequality within and among societies. The developing countries and countries with economies in transition face special difficulties in responding to those challenges and opportunities. Globalization should be fully inclusive and equitable, and there is a strong need for policies and measures at the national and international levels, formulated and implemented with the full and effective participation of developing countries and countries with economies in transition, to help them to respond effectively to those challenges and opportunities. This will require urgent action at all levels to:

(a) Continue to promote open, equitable, rules-based, predictable and non-discriminatory multilateral trading and financial systems that benefit all countries in the pursuit of sustainable development. Support the successful completion of the work programme contained in the Doha

Ministerial Declaration and the implementation of the Monterrey Consensus. Welcome the decision contained in the Doha Ministerial Declaration to place the needs and interests of developing countries at the heart of the work programme of the Declaration, including through enhanced market access for products of interest to developing countries;

(b) Encourage ongoing efforts by international financial and trade institutions to ensure that decision-making processes and institutional structures are open and transparent;

(c) Enhance the capacities of developing countries, including the least developed countries, landlocked developing countries and small island developing States, to benefit from liberalized trade opportunities, through international cooperation and measures aimed at improving productivity, commodity diversification and competitiveness, community-based entrepreneurial capacity, and transportation and communication infrastructure development;

(d) Support the International Labour Organization and encourage its ongoing work on the social dimension of globalization, as stated in paragraph 64 of the Monterrey Consensus;

(e) Enhance the delivery of coordinated, effective and targeted trade-related technical assistance and capacity-building programmes, including to take advantage of existing and future market access opportunities, and to examine the relationship between trade, environment and development.

Implement the outcomes of the Doha Ministerial Conference by WTO members, further strengthen trade-related technical assistance and capacity-building, and ensure the meaningful, effective and full participation of developing countries in multilateral trade negotiations by placing their needs and interests at the heart of the WTO work programme.

Actively promote corporate responsibility and accountability, based on the Rio Principles, including through the full development and effective implementation of intergovernmental agreements and measures, international initiatives and public-private partnerships, and appropriate national regulations, and support continuous improvement in corporate practices in all countries.

Strengthen the capacities of developing countries to encourage public/private initiatives that enhance the ease of access, accuracy, timeliness and coverage of information on countries and financial markets. Multilateral and regional financial institutions could provide further assistance for these purposes.

Strengthen regional trade and cooperation agreements, consistent with the multilateral trading system, among developed and developing countries and countries with economies in transition, as well as among developing countries, with the support of international finance institutions and regional development banks, as appropriate, with a view to achieving the objectives of sustainable development.

Assist developing countries and countries with economies in transition in narrowing the digital divide, creating digital opportunities and harnessing the potential of information and communication technologies for development, through technology transfer on mutually agreed terms and the provision of financial and technical support, and in this context support the World Summit on the Information Society.

Health and sustainable development

The Rio Declaration on Environment and Development states that human beings are at the centre of concerns for sustainable development, and that they are entitled to a healthy and productive life, in harmony with nature. The goals of sustainable development can only be achieved in the absence of a high prevalence of debilitating diseases, while obtaining health gains for the whole population requires poverty eradication. There is an urgent need to address the causes of ill health, including environmental causes, and their impact on development, with particular emphasis on women and children, as well as vulnerable groups of society, such as people with disabilities, elderly persons and indigenous people.

Strengthen the capacity of health-care systems to deliver basic health services to all, in an efficient, accessible and affordable manner aimed at preventing, controlling and treating diseases, and to reduce environmental health threats, in conformity with human rights and fundamental freedoms and consistent with national laws and cultural and religious values, taking into account the reports of relevant United Nations conferences and summits and of special sessions of the General Assembly. This would include actions at all levels to:

(a) Integrate the health concerns, including those of the most vulnerable populations, into strategies, policies and programmes for poverty eradication and sustainable development;

(b) Promote equitable and improved access to affordable and efficient health-care services, including prevention, at all levels of the health system, essential and safe drugs at affordable prices, immunization services and safe vaccines, and medical technology;

(c) Provide technical and financial assistance to developing countries and countries with economies in transition to implement the Health for All Strategy, including health information systems and integrated databases on development hazards;

(d) Improve the development and management of human resources in health-care services;

(e) Promote and develop partnerships to enhance health education with the objective of achieving improved health literacy on a global basis by 2010, with the involvement of United Nations agencies, as appropriate;

(f) Develop programmes and initiatives to reduce, by the year 2015, mortality rates for infants and children under 5 by two thirds, and maternal mortality rates by three quarters, of the prevailing rate in 2000, and reduce disparities between and within developed and developing countries as quickly as possible, with particular attention to eliminating the pattern of disproportionate and preventable mortality among girl infants and children;

(g) Target research efforts and apply research results to priority public health issues, in particular those affecting susceptible and vulnerable populations, through the development of new vaccines, reducing exposures to health risks, building on equal access to health-care services, education, training and medical treatment and technology, and addressing the secondary effects of poor health;

(h) Promote the preservation, development and use of effective traditional medicine knowledge and practices, where appropriate, in combination with modern medicine, recognizing indigenous and local communities as custodians of traditional knowledge and practices, while promoting effective protection of traditional knowledge, as appropriate, consistent with international law;

(i) Ensure equal access of women to health-care services, giving particular attention to maternal and emergency obstetric care;

(j) Address effectively, for all individuals of appropriate age, the promotion of their healthy lives, including their reproductive and sexual health, consistent with the commitments and outcomes of recent United Nations conferences and summits, including the World Summit for Children, the United Nations Conference on Environment and Development, the International Conference of Population and Development, the World Summit for Social Development and the Fourth World Conference on Women, and their respective reviews and reports;

(k) Launch international capacity-building initiatives, as appropriate, that assess health and environment linkages and use the knowledge gained to create more effective national and regional policy responses to environmental threats to human health;

(l) Transfer and disseminate, on mutually agreed terms, including through public-private multisector partnerships, technologies for safe water, sanitation and waste management for rural and urban areas in developing countries and countries with economies in transition, with international financial support, taking into account country-specific conditions and gender equality including specific technology needs of women;

(m) Strengthen and promote ILO and World Health Organization (WHO) programmes to reduce occupational deaths, injuries and illnesses, and link occupational health with public health promotion as a means of promoting public health and education;

(n) Improve availability and access for all to sufficient, safe, culturally acceptable and nutritionally adequate food, increase consumer health protection, address issues of micronutrient deficiency, and implement existing internationally agreed commitments and relevant standards and guidelines;

(o) Develop or strengthen, where applicable, preventive, promotive and curative programmes to address non-communicable diseases and conditions, such as cardiovascular diseases, cancer, diabetes, chronic respiratory diseases, injuries, violence and mental health disorders and associated risk factors, including alcohol, tobacco, unhealthy diets and lack of physical activity.

Implement, within the agreed time frames, all commitments agreed in the Declaration of Commitment on HIV/AIDS adopted by the General Assembly at its twenty-sixth special session, emphasizing in particular the reduction of HIV prevalence among young men and women aged 15-24 by 25 per cent in the most affected countries by 2005 and globally by 2010, as well as combat malaria, tuberculosis and other diseases by, inter alia:

(a) Implementing national preventive and treatment strategies, regional and international cooperation measures, and the development of international initiatives to provide special assistance to children orphaned by HIV/AIDS;

(b) Fulfilling commitments for the provision of sufficient resources to support the Global Fund to Fight AIDS, Tuberculosis and Malaria, while promoting access to the Fund by countries most in need;

(c) Protecting the health of workers and promoting occupational safety, by, inter alia, taking into account, as appropriate the voluntary ILO code of practice on HIV/AIDS and the world of work, to improve conditions of the workplace;

(d) Mobilizing adequate public and encouraging private financial resources for research and development on diseases of the poor, such as HIV/AIDS, malaria, tuberculosis, directed at biomedical and health research, as well as new vaccine and drug development.

Reduce respiratory diseases and other health impacts resulting from air pollution, with particular attention to women and children, by:

(a) Strengthening regional and national programmes, including through public-private partnerships, with technical and financial assistance to developing countries;

(b) Supporting the phasing out of lead in gasoline;

(c) Strengthening and supporting efforts for the reduction of emissions, through the use of cleaner fuels and modern pollution control techniques;

(d) Assisting developing countries in providing affordable energy to rural communities, particularly to reduce dependence on traditional fuel sources for cooking and heating, which affect the health of women and children.

Phase out lead in lead-based paints and other sources of human exposure, work to prevent, in particular, children's exposure to lead, and strengthen monitoring and surveillance efforts and the treatment of lead poisoning.

Sustainable development of small island developing States

Small island developing States are a special case both for environment and development. Although they continue to take the lead in the path towards sustainable development in their countries, they are increasingly constrained by the interplay of adverse factors clearly underlined in Agenda 21, the Programme of Action for the Sustainable Development of Small Island Developing States and the decisions adopted at the twenty-second special session of the General Assembly. This would include actions at all levels to:

(a) Accelerate national and regional implementation of the Programme of Action, with adequate financial resources, including through GEF focal areas, transfer of environmentally sound technologies and assistance for capacity-building from the international community;

(b) Further implement sustainable fisheries management and improve financial returns from fisheries by supporting and strengthening relevant regional fisheries management organizations, as appropriate, such as the recently established Caribbean Regional Fisheries Mechanism and such agreements as the Convention on the Conservation and Management of Highly Migratory Fish Stocks in the Western and Central Pacific Ocean;

(c) Assist small island developing States, including through the elaboration of specific initiatives, in delimiting and managing in a sustainable manner their coastal areas and exclusive economic zones and the continental shelf (including, where appropriate, the continental shelf areas beyond 200 miles from coastal baselines), as well as relevant regional management initiatives within the context of the United Nations Convention on the Law of the Sea and the UNEP regional seas programmes;

(d) Provide support, including for capacity-building, for the development and further implementation of:
   (i) Small island developing States-specific components within programmes of work on marine and coastal biological diversity;
   (ii) Freshwater programmes for small island developing States, including through the GEF focal areas;

(e) Effectively reduce, prevent and control waste and pollution and their health-related impacts by undertaking by 2004 initiatives aimed at implementing the Global Programme of Action for the Protection of the Marine Environment from Land-based Activities in small island developing States;

(f) Work to ensure that, in the ongoing negotiations and elaboration of the WTO work programme on trade in small economies, due account is taken of small island developing States, which have severe structural handicaps in integrating into the global economy, within the context of the Doha development agenda;

(g) Develop community-based initiatives on sustainable tourism by 2004, and build the capacities necessary to diversify tourism products, while protecting culture and traditions, and effectively conserving and managing natural resources;

(h) Extend assistance to small island developing States in support of local communities and appropriate national and regional organizations of small island developing States for comprehensive hazard and risk management, disaster prevention, mitigation and preparedness, and help relieve the consequences of disasters, extreme weather events and other emergencies;

(i) Support the finalization and subsequent early operationalization, on agreed terms, of economic, social and environmental vulnerability indices and related indicators as tools for the achievement of the sustainable development of the small island developing States;

(j) Assist small island developing States in mobilizing adequate resources and partnerships for their adaptation needs relating to the adverse effects of climate change, sea level rise and climate variability, consistent with commitments under the United Nations Framework Convention on Climate Changes, where applicable;

(k) Support efforts by small island developing States to build capacities and institutional arrangements to implement intellectual property regimes;

Support the availability of adequate, affordable and environmentally sound energy services for the sustainable development of small island developing States by, inter alia:

(a) Strengthening ongoing and supporting new efforts on energy supply and services, by 2004, including through the United Nations system and partnership initiatives;

(b) Developing and promoting efficient use of sources of energy, including indigenous sources and renewable energy, and building the capacities of small island developing States for training, technical know-how and strengthening national institutions in the area of energy management;

Provide support to SIDS to develop capacity and strengthen:

(a) Health-care services for promoting equitable access to health care;

(b) Health systems for making available necessary drugs and technology in a sustainable and affordable manner to fight and control communicable and non-communicable diseases, in particular HIV/AIDS, tuberculosis, diabetes, malaria and dengue fever;

(c) Efforts to reduce and manage waste and pollution and building capacity for maintaining and managing systems to deliver water and sanitation services, in both rural and urban areas;

(d) Efforts to implement initiatives aimed at poverty eradication, which have been outlined in section II of the present document.

Undertake a full and comprehensive review of the implementation of the Barbados Programme of Action for the Sustainable Development of Small Island Developing States in 2004, in accordance with the provisions set forth in General Assembly resolution S-22/2, and in this context requests the General Assembly at its fifty-seventh session to consider convening an international meeting for the sustainable development of small island developing States.

Sustainable development for Africa

Since the United Nations Conference on Environment and Development, sustainable development has remained elusive for many African countries. Poverty remains a major challenge and most countries on the continent have not benefited fully from the opportunities of globalization, further exacerbating the continent's marginalization. Africa's efforts to achieve sustainable development have been hindered by conflicts, insufficient investment, limited market access opportunities and supply side constraints, unsustainable debt burdens, historically declining ODA levels and the impact of HIV/AIDS. The World Summit on Sustainable Development should reinvigorate the commitment of the international community to address these special challenges and give effect to a new vision based on concrete actions for the implementation of Agenda 21 in Africa. The New Partnership for Africa's Development (NEPAD) is a commitment by African leaders to the people of Africa. It recognizes that partnerships among African countries themselves and between them and with the international community are key elements of a shared and common vision to eradicate poverty, and furthermore it aims to place their countries, both individually and collectively, on a path of sustained economic growth and sustainable development, while participating actively in the world economy and body politic. It provides a framework for sustainable development on the continent to be shared by all Africa's people. The international community welcomes NEPAD and pledges its support to the implementation of this vision, including through utilization of the benefits of South-South cooperation supported, inter alia, by the Tokyo International Conference on African Development. It also pledges support for other existing development frameworks that are owned and driven nationally by African countries and that embody poverty reduction strategies, including poverty reduction strategy papers. Achieving sustainable development includes actions at all levels to:

(a) Create an enabling environment at the regional, subregional, national and local levels in order to achieve sustained economic growth and sustainable development and support African efforts for peace, stability and security, the resolution and prevention of conflicts, democracy, good governance, respect for human rights and fundamental freedoms, including the right to development and gender equality;

(b) Support the implementation of the vision of NEPAD and other established regional and subregional efforts, including through financing, technical cooperation and institutional cooperation, and human and institutional capacity-building at the regional, subregional and national levels, consistent with national policies, programmes and nationally owned and led strategies for poverty reduction and sustainable development, such as, where applicable, poverty reduction strategy papers;

(c) Promote technology development, transfer and diffusion to Africa and further develop technology and knowledge available in African centres of excellence;

(d) Support African countries to develop effective science and technology institutions and research activities capable of developing and adapting to world class technologies;

(e) Support the development of national programmes and strategies to promote education within the context of nationally owned and led strategies for poverty reduction, and strengthen research institutions in education in order to increase the capacity to fully support the achievement of internationally agreed development goals related to education, including those contained in the Millennium Declaration on ensuring that, by 2015, children everywhere, boys and girls alike, will be able to complete a full course of primary schooling, and that girls and boys will have equal access to all levels of education relevant to national needs;

(f) Enhance the industrial productivity, diversity and competitiveness of African countries through a combination of financial and technological support for the development of key infrastructure, access to technology, networking of research centres, adding value to export products, skills development and enhancing market access in support of sustainable development;

(g) Enhance the contribution of the industrial sector, in particular mining, minerals and metals, to the sustainable development of Africa by supporting the development of effective and transparent regulatory and management frameworks and value addition, broad-based participation, social and environmental responsibility and increased market access in order to create an attractive and conducive environment for investment;

(h) Provide financial and technical support to strengthen the capacity of African countries to undertake environmental legislative policy and institutional reform for sustainable development and to undertake environmental impact assessments and, as appropriate, to negotiate and implement multilateral environment agreements;

(i) Develop projects, programmes and partnerships with relevant stakeholders and mobilize resources for the effective implementation of the outcome of the African Process for the Protection and Development of the Marine and Coastal Environment;

(j) Deal effectively with energy problems in Africa, including through initiatives to:

  (i) Establish and promote programmes, partnerships and initiatives to support Africa's efforts to implement NEPAD objectives on energy, which seek to secure access for at least 35 per cent of the African population within 20 years, especially in rural areas;

  (ii) Provide support to implement other initiatives on energy, including the promotion of cleaner and more efficient use of natural gas and increased use of renewable energy, and to improve energy efficiency and access to advanced energy technologies, including cleaner fossil fuel technologies, particularly in rural and peri-urban areas;

(k) Assist African countries in mobilizing adequate resources for their adaptation needs relating to the adverse effects of climate change, extreme weather events, sea level rise and climate variability, and assist in developing national climate change strategies and mitigation programmes, and continue to take actions to mitigate the adverse effects on climate change in Africa, consistent with the United Nations Framework Convention on Climate Change;

(l) Support African efforts to develop affordable transport systems and infrastructure that promote sustainable development and connectivity in Africa;

(m) Further to paragraph 40 above, address the poverty affecting mountain communities in Africa;

(n) Provide financial and technical support for afforestation and reforestation in Africa and to build capacity for sustainable forest management, including combating deforestation and measures to improve the policy and legal framework of the forest sector.

Provide financial and technical support for Africa's efforts to implement the Convention to Combat Desertification at the national level and integrate indigenous knowledge systems into land and natural resources management practices, as appropriate, and improve extension services to rural communities and promote better land and watershed management practices, including through improved agricultural practices that address land degradation, in order to develop capacity for the implementation of national programmes.

Mobilize financial and other support to develop and strengthen health systems that aim at:

(a) Promoting equitable access to health-care services;

(b) Making available necessary drugs and technology in a sustainable and affordable manner to fight and control communicable diseases, including HIV/AIDS, malaria and tuberculosis, and trypanosomiasis, as well as non-communicable diseases, including those caused by poverty;

(c) Building capacity of medical and paramedical personnel;

(d) Promoting indigenous medical knowledge, as appropriate, including traditional medicine;

(e) Researching and controlling the Ebola disease.

Deal effectively with natural disasters and conflicts, including their humanitarian and environmental impacts, recognizing that conflicts in Africa have hindered and in many cases obliterated both the gains and efforts aimed at sustainable development, with the most vulnerable members of society, particularly women and children, being the most impacted victims, through efforts and initiatives, at all levels, to:

(a) Provide financial and technical assistance to strengthen the capacities of African countries, including institutional and human capacity, including at the local level, for effective disaster management, including observation and early warning systems, assessments, prevention, preparedness, response and recovery;

(b) Provide support to African countries to enable them to better deal with the displacement of people as a result of natural disasters and conflicts, and put in place rapid response mechanisms;

(c) Support Africa's efforts for the prevention and

resolution, management and mitigation of conflicts and its early response to emerging conflict situations to avert tragic humanitarian consequences;

(d) Provide support to refugee host countries in rehabilitating infrastructure and environment, including ecosystems and habitats, that were damaged in the process of receiving and settling refugees.

Promote integrated water resources development and optimize the upstream and downstream benefits therefrom, the development and effective management of water resources across all uses and the protection of water quality and aquatic ecosystems, including through initiatives at all levels, to:

(a) Provide access to potable domestic water, hygiene education and improved sanitation and waste management at the household level through initiatives to encourage public and private investment in water supply and sanitation that give priority to the needs of the poor, within stable and transparent national regulatory frameworks provided by Governments, while respecting local conditions involving all concerned stakeholders and monitoring the performance and improving the accountability of public institutions and private companies; and develop critical water supply, reticulation and treatment infrastructure, and build capacity to maintain and manage systems to deliver water and sanitation services, in both rural and urban areas;

(b) Develop and implement integrated river basin and watershed management strategies and plans for all major water bodies, consistent with paragraph 25 above;

(c) Strengthen regional, subregional and national capacities for data collection and processing, and for planning, research, monitoring, assessment and enforcement, as well as arrangements for water resource management;

(d) Protect water resources, including groundwater and wetland ecosystems, against pollution, as well as, in cases of most acute water scarcity, support efforts for developing non-conventional water resources, including the energy-efficient, cost-effective and sustainable desalination of seawater, rainwater harvesting and recycling of water.

Achieve significantly improved sustainable agricultural productivity and food security in furtherance of the agreed millennium development goals, including those contained in the Millennium Declaration, in particular to halve by 2015 the proportion of people who suffer from hunger, including through initiatives at all levels to:

(a) Support the development and implementation of national policies and programmes, including research programmes and development plans of African countries to regenerate their agricultural sector and sustainably develop their fisheries, and increase investment in infrastructure, technology and extension services, according to country needs. African countries should be in the process of developing and implementing food security strategies, within the context of national poverty eradication programmes, by 2005;

(b) Promote and support efforts and initiatives to secure equitable access to land tenure and clarify resource rights and responsibilities, through land and tenure reform processes which respect the rule of law and are enshrined in national law, and to provide access to credit to all, especially to women, and that enable economic and social empowerment and poverty eradication as well as efficient and ecologically sound utilization of land, and enable women producers to become decision makers and owners in the sector, including the right to inherit land;

(c) Improve market access for goods, including goods originating from African countries, in particular least developed countries, within the framework of the Doha Ministerial Declaration, without prejudging the outcome of the WTO negotiations and also within the framework of preferential agreements;

(d) Provide support for African countries to improve regional trade and economic integration between African countries. Attract and increase investment in regional market infrastructure;

(e) Support livestock development programmes aimed at progressive and effective control of animal diseases.

Achieve sound management of chemicals, with particular focus on hazardous chemicals and wastes, inter alia, through initiatives to assist African countries in elaborating national chemical profiles, and regional and national frameworks and strategies for chemical management and establishing chemical focal points.

Bridge the digital divide and create digital opportunity in terms of access infrastructure and technology transfer and application, through integrated initiatives for Africa. Create an enabling environment to attract investments, accelerate existing and new programmes and projects to connect essential institutions, and stimulate the adoption of information communication technologies in government and commerce programmes and other aspects of national economic and social life.

Support Africa's efforts to attain sustainable tourism that contributes to social, economic and infrastructure development through the following measures:

(a) Implementing projects at the local, national and subregional levels, with specific emphasis on marketing African tourism products, such as adventure tourism, eco-tourism and cultural tourism;

(b) Establishing and supporting national and cross-border conservation areas to promote ecosystem conservation according to the ecosystem approach, and to promote sustainable tourism;

(c) Respecting local traditions and cultures and promoting the use of indigenous knowledge in natural resource management and eco-tourism;

(d) Assisting host communities in managing their tourism projects for maximum benefit, while limiting negative impact on their traditions, culture and environment;

(e) Support the conservation of Africa's biological diversity, the sustainable use of its components and the fair and equitable sharing of the benefits arising out of the utilization of genetic resources, in accordance with commitments that countries have under biodiversity-related agreements to which they are parties, including such agreements as the Convention on Biological Diversity and the Convention on International Trade in Endangered Species of Wild Fauna and Flora, as well as regional biodiversity agreements.

Support African countries in their efforts to implement the Habitat Agenda and the Istanbul Declaration through initiatives to strengthen national and local institutional capacities in the areas of sustainable urbanization and human settlements, provide support for adequate shelter and basic services and the development of efficient and effective governance systems in cities and other human settlements, and strengthen, inter alia, the United Nations Human Settlements Programme/UNEP managing water for African cities programme.

Other regional initiatives

Important initiatives have been developed within other United Nations regions and regional, subregional and transregional forums to promote sustainable development. The international community welcomes these efforts and the results already achieved, and calls for actions at all levels for their further development, while encouraging interregional, intraregional and international cooperation in this respect, and expresses its support for their further development and implementation by the countries of the regions.

Sustainable development in Latin America and the Caribbean

The Initiative of Latin America and the Caribbean on Sustainable Development is an undertaking by the leaders of that region that, building on the Platform for Action on the Road to Johannesburg 2002, which was approved in Rio de Janeiro in October 2001, recognizes the importance of regional actions towards sustainable development and takes into account the region's singularities, shared visions and cultural diversity. It is targeted towards the adoption of concrete actions in different areas of sustainable development, such as biodiversity, water resources, vulnerabilities and sustainable cities, social aspects (including health and poverty), economic aspects (including energy) and institutional arrangements (including capacity-building, indicators and participation of civil society), taking into account ethics for sustainable development.

The Initiative envisages the development of actions among countries in the region that may foster South-South cooperation and may count with the support of groups of countries, as well as multilateral and regional organizations, including financial institutions. Being a framework for cooperation, the Initiative is open to partnerships with governments and all major groups.

Sustainable development in Asia and the Pacific

Bearing in mind the target of halving the number of people who live in poverty by the year 2015, as provided in the Millennium Declaration, the Phnom Penh Regional Platform on Sustainable Development for Asia and the Pacific recognized that the region contains over half of the world's population and the largest number of the world's people living in poverty. Hence, sustainable development in the region is critical to achieving sustainable development at the global level.

The Regional Platform identified seven initiatives for follow-up action: capacity-building for sustainable development; poverty reduction for sustainable development; cleaner production and sustainable energy; land management and biodiversity conservation; protection and management of and access to freshwater resources; oceans, coastal and marine resources and sustainable development of small island developing States; and action on atmosphere and climate change. Follow-up actions of these initiatives will be taken through national strategies and relevant regional and subregional initiatives, such as the Regional Action Programme for Environmentally Sound and Sustainable Development and the Kitakyushu Initiative for a Clean Environment, adopted at the Fourth Ministerial Conference on Environment and Development in Asia and the Pacific organized by the Economic and Social Commission for Asia and the Pacific.

Sustainable development in the West Asia region

The West Asia region is known for its scarce water and limited fertile land resources. The region has made progress to a more knowledge-based production of higher value-added commodities.

The regional preparatory meeting endorsed the following priorities: poverty alleviation, relief of debt burden; and sustainable management of natural resources, including, inter alia, integrated water resources management, implementation of programmes to combat desertification, integrated coastal zone management, and land and water pollution control.

Sustainable development in the Economic Commission for Europe region

The Economic Commission for Europe (ECE) regional ministerial meeting for the World Summit on Sustainable Development recognized that the region has a major role to play and responsibilities in global efforts to achieve sustainable development by concrete actions. The region recognized that different levels of economic development in countries of the region may require the application of different approaches and mechanisms to implement Agenda 21. In order to address the three pillars of sustainable development in a mutually reinforcing way, the region identified its priority actions for the ECE region for sustainable development in paragraphs 32-46 of a ministerial statement.

In furtherance of the region's commitment to sustainable development, there are ongoing efforts at the regional, subregional and transregional levels, including, inter alia, the Environment for Europe process; the fifth ECE ministerial conference, to be held in Kiev in May 2003; the development of an environmental strategy for the 12 countries of Eastern Europe; the Caucasus and Central Asia; the Central Asian Agenda 21; OECD work on sustainable development, the EU sustainable development strategy; and regional and subregional conventions and processes relevant to sustainable development, including, inter alia, the Aarhus Convention, the Alpine Convention, the North American Commission on Environmental Cooperation, the Boundary Waters Treaty, the Iqaluit Declaration of the Arctic Council, the Baltic Agenda 21 and the Mediterranean Agenda 21.

MEANS OF IMPLEMENTATION

The implementation of Agenda 21 and the achievement of the internationally agreed development goals, including those contained in the Millennium Declaration as well as in the present plan of action, require a substantially increased effort, both by countries themselves and by the rest of the international community, based on the recognition that each country has primary responsibility for its own development and that the role of national policies and development strategies cannot be overemphasized, taking fully into account the Rio principles, including, in particular, the principle of common but differentiated responsibilities, which states:

> "States shall cooperate in a spirit of global partnership to conserve, protect and restore the health and integrity of the Earth's ecosystem. In view of the different contributions to global environmental degradation, States have common but differentiated responsibilities. The developed countries acknowledge the responsibility that they bear in the international pursuit of sustainable development in view of the pressures their societies place on the global environment and of the technologies and financial resources they command."

The internationally agreed development goals, including those contained in the Millennium Declaration and Agenda 21, as well as in the present plan of action, will require significant increases in the flow of financial resources as elaborated in the Monterrey Consensus, including through new and additional financial resources, in particular to developing countries, to support the implementation of national policies and programmes developed by them, improved trade opportunities, access to and transfer of environmentally sound technologies on a concessional or preferential basis, as mutually agreed, education and awareness-raising, capacity-building, and information for decision-making and scientific capabilities within the agreed time frame required to meet these goals and initiatives. Progress to this end will require that the international community implement the outcomes of major United Nations conferences, such as the programmes of action adopted at the Third United Nations Conference on the Least Developed Countries, and the Global Conference on the Sustainable Development of Small Island Developing States, and relevant international agreements since 1992, particularly those of the International Conference on Financing for Development and the Fourth WTO Ministerial Conference, including building on them as part of a process of achieving sustainable development.

Mobilizing and increasing the effective use of financial resources and achieving the national and international economic conditions needed to fulfil internationally agreed development goals, including those contained in the Millennium Declaration, to eliminate poverty, improve social conditions and raise living standards and protect our environment, will be our first step to ensuring that the twenty-first century becomes the century of sustainable development for all.

In our common pursuit of growth, poverty eradication and sustainable development, a critical challenge is to ensure the necessary internal conditions for mobilizing domestic savings, both public and private, sustaining adequate levels of productive investment and increasing human capacity. A crucial task is to enhance the efficacy, coherence and consistency of macroeconomic policies. An enabling domestic environment is vital for mobilizing domestic resources, increasing productivity, reducing capital flight, encouraging the private sector, and attracting and making effective use of international investment and assistance. Efforts to create such an environment should be supported by the international community.

Facilitate greater flows of foreign direct investment so as to support the sustainable development activities, including the development of infrastructure, of developing countries, and enhance the benefits that developing countries can draw from foreign direct investment, with particular actions to:

(a) Create the necessary domestic and international conditions to facilitate significant increases in the flow of FDI to developing countries, in particular the least developed countries, which is critical to sustainable development, particularly FDI flows for infrastructure development and other priority areas in developing countries to supplement the domestic resources mobilized by them;

(b) Encourage foreign direct investment in developing countries and countries with economies in transition through export credits that could be instrumental to sustainable development;

Recognize that a substantial increase in ODA and other resources will be required if developing countries are to achieve the internationally agreed development goals and objectives, including those contained in the Millennium Declaration. To build support for ODA, we will cooperate to further improve policies and development strategies, both nationally and internationally, to enhance aid effectiveness, with actions to:

(a) Make available the increased ODA commitments announced by several developed countries at the International Conference on Financing for Development. Urge the developed countries that have not done so to make concrete efforts towards the target of 0.7 per cent of GNP as ODA to developing countries, and effectively implement their commitment on ODA to the least developed countries as contained in paragraph 83 of the Programme of Action for the Least Developed Countries for the Decade 2001–2010. We also encourage developing countries to build on progress achieved in ensuring that ODA is used effectively to help achieve development goals and targets in accordance with the outcome of the International Conference on Financing for Development. We acknowledge the efforts of all donors, commend those donors whose ODA contributions exceed, reach or are increasing towards the targets, and underline the importance of undertaking to examine the means and time frames for achieving the targets and goals;

(b) Encourage recipient and donor countries, as well as international institutions, to make ODA more efficient and effective for poverty eradication, sustained economic growth and sustainable development. In this regard, intensify efforts by the multilateral and bilateral financial and development institutions, in accordance with paragraph 43 of the Monterrey Consensus, in particular to harmonize their operational procedures at the highest standards, so as to reduce transaction costs and make ODA disbursement and delivery more flexible and more responsive to the needs of developing countries, taking into account national development needs and objectives under the ownership of recipient countries, and to use development frameworks that are owned and driven by developing countries and that embody poverty reduction strategies, including poverty reduction strategy papers, as vehicles for aid delivery, upon request.

Make full and effective use of existing financial mechanisms and institutions, including through actions at all levels to:

(a) Strengthen ongoing efforts to reform the existing international financial architecture, to foster a transparent, equitable and inclusive system that is able to provide for the effective participation of developing countries in the international economic decision-making processes and institutions, as well as for their effective and equitable participation in the formulation of financial standards and codes;

(b) Promote, inter alia, measures in source and destination countries to improve transparency and information about financial flows to contribute to stability in the international financial environment. Measures that mitigate the impact of excessive volatility of short-term capital flows are important and must be considered;

(c) Work to ensure that the funds are made available on a timely, more assured and predictable basis to international organizations and agencies, where appropriate, for their sustainable development activities, programmes and projects;

(d) Encourage the private sector, including transnational corporations, private foundations and civil society institutions, to provide financial and technical assistance to developing countries;

(e) Support new and existing public/private sector financing mechanisms for developing countries and countries with economies in transition, to benefit in particular small entrepreneurs and small, medium-sized and community-based enterprises and to improve their infrastructure, while ensuring the transparency and accountability of such mechanisms.

Welcome the successful and substantial third replenishment of the GEF, which will enable it to address the funding requirements of new focal areas and existing ones and continue to be responsive to the needs and concerns of its recipient countries, in particular developing countries, and further encourage GEF to leverage additional funds from key public and private organizations, improve the management of funds through more speedy and streamlined procedures and simplify its project cycle.

Explore ways of generating new public and private innovative sources of finance for development purposes, provided that those sources do not unduly burden developing countries, noting the proposal to use special drawing rights allocations for development purposes, as set forth in paragraph 44 of the Monterrey Consensus.

Reduce unsustainable debt burden through such actions as debt relief and, as appropriate, debt cancellation and other innovative mechanisms geared to comprehensively address the debt problems of developing countries, in particular the poorest and most heavily indebted ones. Therefore, debt relief measures should, where appropriate, be pursued vigorously and expeditiously, including within the Paris and London Clubs and other relevant forums, in order to contribute to debt sustainability and facilitate sustainable development, while recognizing that debtors and creditors must share responsibility for preventing and resolving unsustainable debt situations, and that external debt relief can play a key role in liberating resources that can then be directed towards activities consistent with attaining sustainable growth and development. Therefore, we support paragraphs 47 through 51 of the Monterrey Consensus dealing with external debt. Debt relief arrangements should seek to avoid imposing any unfair burdens on other developing countries. There should be an increase in the use of grants for the poorest, debt-vulnerable countries. Countries are encouraged to develop national comprehensive strategies to monitor and manage external liabilities as a key element in reducing national vulnerabilities. In this regard, actions are required to:

(a) Implement speedily, effectively and fully the enhanced heavily indebted poor countries (HIPC) initiative, which should be fully financed through additional resources, taking into consideration, as appropriate, measures to address any fundamental changes in the economic circumstances of those developing countries with unsustainable debt burden caused by natural catastrophes, severe terms-of-trade shocks or affected by conflict, taking into account initiatives which have been undertaken to reduce outstanding indebtedness;

(b) Encourage participation in the HIPC initiative of all creditors that have not yet done so;

(c) Bring international debtors and creditors together in relevant international forums to restructure unsustainable debt in a timely and efficient manner, taking into account the need to involve the private sector in the resolution of crises due to indebtedness, where appropriate;

(d) Acknowledge the problems of the debt sustainability of some non-HIPC low-income countries, in particular those facing exceptional circumstances;

(e) Encourage exploring innovative mechanisms to comprehensively address the debt problems of developing countries, including middle-income countries and countries with economies in transition. Such mechanisms may include debt-for-sustainable-development swaps;

(f) Encourage donor countries to take steps to ensure that resources provided for debt relief do not detract from ODA resources intended to be available for developing countries.

Recognizing the major role that trade can play in achieving sustainable development and in eradicating poverty, we encourage WTO members to pursue the work programme agreed at the Fourth WTO Ministerial Conference. In order for developing countries, especially the least developed among them, to secure their share in the growth of world trade commensurate with the needs of their economic development, we urge WTO members to take the following actions:

(a) Facilitate the accession of all developing countries, particularly the least developed countries, as well as countries with economies in transition, that apply for membership of WTO, in accordance with the Monterrey Consensus;

(b) Support the Doha work programme as an important commitment on the part of developed and developing countries to mainstream appropriate trade policies in their respective development policies and programmes;

(c) Implement substantial trade-related technical assistance and capacity-building measures and support the Doha Development Agenda Global Trust Fund established after the Fourth WTO Ministerial Conference as an important step forward in ensuring a sound and predictable basis for WTO-related technical assistance and capacity-building;

(d) Implement the New Strategy for WTO Technical Cooperation for Capacity-Building, Growth and Integration;

(e) Fully support the implementation of the Integrated Framework for Trade-Related Technical Assistance to Least Developed Countries, and urge development partners to significantly increase contributions to the Trust Fund of the Framework, in accordance with the Doha Ministerial Declaration.

In accordance with the Doha Declaration as well as with relevant decisions taken at Doha, we are determined to take concrete action to address issues and concerns raised by developing countries regarding the implementation of some WTO agreements and decisions, including the difficulties and resource constraints faced by them in fulfilling those agreements.

Call upon WTO members to fulfil the commitments made in the Doha Ministerial Declaration, notably in terms of market access, in particular for products of export interest to developing countries, especially least developed countries, by implementing the following actions, taking into account paragraph 45 of the Doha Ministerial Declaration:

(a) Review all special and differential treatment provisions with a view to strengthening them and making them more precise, effective and operational, in accordance with paragraph 44 of the Doha Ministerial Declaration;

(b) Aim to reduce or, as appropriate, eliminate tariffs on non-agricultural products, including the reduction or elimination of tariff peaks, high tariffs and tariff escalation, as well as non-tariff barriers, in particular on products of export interest to developing countries. Product coverage should be comprehensive and without a priori exclusions. The negotiations shall take fully into account the special needs and interests of developing and least developed countries, including through less than full reciprocity in reduction commitments, in accordance with the Doha Ministerial Declaration;

(c) Fulfil, without prejudging the outcome of the negotiations, the commitment for comprehensive negotiations initiated under article 20 of the Agreement on Agriculture as referred to in paragraphs 13 and 14 of the Doha Ministerial Declaration, aiming at substantial improvements in market access, reductions of with a view to phasing out all forms of export subsidies, and substantial reductions in trade-distorting domestic support, while agreeing that the provisions for special and differential treatment for developing countries shall be an integral part of all elements of the negotiations and shall be embodied in the schedules of concession and commitments and, as appropriate, in the rules and disciplines to be negotiated, so as to be operationally effective and to enable developing countries to effectively take account of their development needs, including food security and rural development. Take note of the non-trade concerns reflected in the negotiating proposals submitted by WTO members and confirm that non-trade concerns will be taken into account in the negotiations as provided for in the Agreement on Agriculture, in accordance with the Doha Ministerial Declaration.

Call on developed countries that have not already done so to work towards the objective of duty-free and quota-free access for all least developed countries' exports, as envisaged in the Programme of Action for the Least Developed Countries for the Decade 2001-2010, which was adopted in Brussels on 20 May 2001.

Commit to actively pursue the WTO work programme to address the trade-related issues and concerns affecting the fuller integration of small, vulnerable economies into the multilateral trading system in a manner commensurate with their special circumstances and in support of their efforts towards sustainable development, in accordance with paragraph 35 of the Doha Declaration.

Build the capacity of commodity-dependent countries to diversify exports through, inter alia, financial and technical assistance, international assistance for economic diversification and sustainable resource management, and address the instability of commodity prices and declining terms of trade, as well as strengthen the activities covered by the Second Account of the Common Fund for Commodities to support sustainable development.

Enhance the benefits for developing countries, as well as countries with economies in transition, from trade liberalization, including through public-private partnerships, through, inter alia, action at all levels, including through financial support for technical assistance, the development of technology and capacity-building to developing countries to:

(a) Enhance trade infrastructure and strengthen institutions;

(b) Increase developing country capacity to diversify and increase exports to cope with the instability of commodity prices and declining terms of trade;

(c) Increase the value added of developing country exports.

Continue to enhance the mutual supportiveness of trade, environment and development with a view to achieving sustainable development through actions at all levels to:

(a) Encourage the WTO Committee on Trade and Environment and the WTO Committee on Trade and Development, within their respective mandates, to each act as a forum to identify and debate developmental and environmental aspects of the negotiations, in order to help achieve an outcome which benefits sustainable development in accordance with the commitments made under the Doha Ministerial Declaration;

(b) Support the completion of the work programme of the Doha Ministerial Declaration on subsidies so as to promote sustainable development and enhance the environment, and encourage reform of subsidies that have considerable negative effects on the environment and are incompatible with sustainable development;

(c) Encourage efforts to promote cooperation on trade, environment and development, including in the field of providing technical assistance to developing countries, between the secretariats of WTO, UNCTAD, UNDP, UNEP and other relevant international environmental and development and regional organizations;

(d) Encourage the voluntary use of environmental impact assessments as an important national-level tool to better identify trade, environment and development interlinkages. Further encourage countries and international organizations with experience in this field to provide technical assistance to developing countries for these purposes.

Promote mutual supportiveness between the multilateral trading system and the multilateral environmental agreements, consistent with sustainable development goals, in support of the work programme agreed through WTO, while recognizing the importance of maintaining the integrity of both sets of instruments.

Complement and support the Doha Ministerial Declaration and the Monterrey Consensus by undertaking further action at the national, regional and international levels, including through public/private partnerships, to enhance the benefits, in particular for developing countries as well as for countries with economies in transition, of trade liberalization, through, inter alia, actions at all levels to:

(a) Establish and strengthen existing trade and cooperation agreements, consistent with the multilateral trading system, with a view to achieving sustainable development;

(b) Support voluntary WTO compatible market-based initiatives for the creation and expansion of domestic and international markets for environmentally friendly goods and services, including organic products, which maximize environmental and developmental benefits through, inter alia, capacity-building and technical assistance to developing countries;

(c) Support measures to simplify and make more transparent domestic regulations and procedures that affect trade so as to assist exporters, particularly those from developing countries.

Address the public health problems affecting many developing and least developed countries, especially those resulting from HIV/AIDS, tuberculosis, malaria and other epidemics, while noting the importance of the Doha Declaration on the TRIPS Agreement and Public Health, in which it has been agreed that the TRIPS Agreement does not and should not prevent WTO members from taking measures to protect public health. Accordingly, while reiterating our commitment to the TRIPS Agreement, we reaffirm that the Agreement can and should be interpreted and implemented in a manner supportive of WTO members' right to protect public health and in particular to promote access to medicines for all.

States should cooperate to promote a supportive and open international economic system that would lead to economic growth and sustainable development in all countries to better address the problems of environmental degradation. Trade policy measures for environmental purposes should not constitute a means of arbitrary or unjustifiable discrimination or a disguised restriction on international trade. Unilateral actions to deal with environmental challenges outside the jurisdiction of the importing country should be avoided. Environmental measures addressing transboundary or global environmental problems should, as far as possible, be based on an international consensus.

Take steps with a view to the avoidance of and refrain from any unilateral measure not in accordance with international law and the Charter of the United Nations that impedes the full achievement of economic and social development by the population of the affected countries, in particular women and children, that hinders their well-being and that creates obstacles to the full enjoyment of their human rights, including the right of everyone to a standard of living adequate for their health and well-being and their right to food, medical care and the necessary social services. Ensure that food and medicine are not used as tools for political pressure.

Take further effective measures to remove obstacles to the realization of the right of peoples to self-determination, in particular peoples living under colonial and foreign occupation, which continue to adversely affect their economic and social development and are incompatible with the dignity and worth of the human person and must be combated and eliminated. People under foreign occupation must be protected in accordance with the provisions of international humanitarian law.

In accordance with the Declaration on Principles of International Law concerning Friendly Relations and Cooperation among States in accordance with the Charter of the United Nations, this shall not be construed as authorizing or encouraging any action which would dismember or impair, totally or in part, the territorial integrity or political unity of sovereign and independent States conducting themselves in compliance with the principle of equal rights and self-determination of peoples and thus possessed of a Government representing the whole people belonging to the territory without distinction of any kind.

* * *

Promote, facilitate and finance, as appropriate, access to and the development, transfer and diffusion of environmentally sound technologies and corresponding know-how, in particular to developing countries and countries with economies in transition on favourable terms, including on concessional and preferential terms, as mutually agreed, as set out in chapter 34 of Agenda 21, including through urgent actions at all levels to:

(a) Provide information more effectively;

(b) Enhance existing national institutional capacity in developing countries to improve access to and the development, transfer and diffusion of environmentally sound technologies and corresponding know-how;

(c) Facilitate country-driven technology needs assessments;

(d) Establish legal and regulatory frameworks in both supplier and recipient countries that expedite the transfer of environmentally sound technologies in a cost-effective manner by both public and private sectors and support their implementation;

(e) Promote the access and transfer of technology related to early warning systems and to mitigation programmes to developing countries affected by natural disasters.

Improve the transfer of technologies to developing countries, in particular at the bilateral and regional levels, including through urgent actions at all levels to:

(a) Improve interaction and collaboration, stakeholder relationships and networks between and among universities, research institutions, government agencies and the private sector;

(b) Develop and strengthen networking of related institutional support structures, such as technology and productivity centres, research, training and development institutions, and national and regional cleaner production centres;

(c) Create partnerships conducive to investment and technology transfer, development and diffusion, to assist developing countries, as well as countries with economies in transition, in sharing best practices and promoting programmes of assistance, and encourage collaboration between corporations and research institutes to enhance industrial efficiency, agricultural productivity, environmental management and competitiveness;

(d) Provide assistance to developing countries, as well as countries with economies in transition, in accessing environmentally sound technologies that are publicly owned or in the public domain, as well as available knowledge in the public domain on science and technology, and in accessing the know-how and expertise required in order for them to make independent use of this knowledge in pursuing their development goals;

(e) Support existing mechanisms and, where appropriate, establish new mechanisms for the development, transfer and diffusion of environmentally sound technologies to developing countries and economies in transition.

* * *

Assist developing countries in building capacity to access a larger share of multilateral and global research and development programmes. In this regard, strengthen and, where appropriate, create centres for sustainable development in developing countries.

Build greater capacity in science and technology for sustainable development, with action to improve collaboration and partnerships on research and development and their widespread application among research institutions, universities, the private sector, governments, NGOs and networks, as well as between and among scientists and academics of developing and developed countries, and in this regard encourage networking with and between centres of scientific excellence in developing countries.

Improve policy and decision-making at all levels through, inter alia, improved collaboration between natural and social scientists, and between scientists and policy makers, including through urgent actions at all levels to:

(a) Increase the use of scientific knowledge and technology, and increase the beneficial use of local and indigenous knowledge in a manner respectful of the holders of that knowledge and consistent with national law;

(b) Make greater use of integrated scientific assessments, risk assessments and interdisciplinary and intersectoral approaches;

(c) Continue to support and collaborate with international scientific assessments supporting decision-making, including the ntergovernmental Panel on Climate Change, with the broad participation of developing country experts;

(d) Assist developing countries in developing and implementing science and technology policies;

(e) Establish partnerships between scientific, public

and private institutions, and by integrating scientists' advice into decision-making bodies in order to ensure a greater role for science, technology development and engineering sectors;

(f) Promote and improve science-based decision-making and reaffirm the precautionary approach as set out in principle 15 of the Rio Declaration on Environment and Development, which states:

> "In order to protect the environment, the precautionary approach shall be widely applied by States according to their capabilities. Where there are threats of serious or irreversible damage, lack of full scientific certainty shall not be used as a reason for postponing cost-effective measures to prevent environmental degradation."

Assist developing countries, through international cooperation, in enhancing their capacity in their efforts to address issues pertaining to environmental protection including in their formulation and implementation of policies for environmental management and protection, including through urgent actions at all levels to:

(a) Improve their use of science and technology for environmental monitoring, assessment models, accurate databases and integrated information systems;

(b) Promote and, where appropriate, improve their use of satellite technologies for quality data collection, verification and updating, and further improvement of aerial and ground-based observations, in support of their efforts to collect quality, accurate, long-term, consistent and reliable data;

(c) Set up and, where appropriate, further develop national statistical services capable of providing sound data on science education and research and development activities that are necessary for effective science and technology policy-making.

Establish regular channels between policy makers and the scientific community for requesting and receiving science and technology advice for the implementation of Agenda 21, and create and strengthen networks for science and education for sustainable development, at all levels, with the aim of sharing knowledge, experience and best practices and building scientific capacities, particularly in developing countries.

Use information and communication technologies, where appropriate, as tools to increase the frequency of communication and the sharing of experience and knowledge, and to improve the quality of and access to information and communications technology in all countries, building on the work facilitated by the United Nations Information and Communications Technology Task Force and the efforts of other relevant international and regional forums.

Support publicly funded research and development entities to engage in strategic alliances for the purpose of enhancing research and development to achieve cleaner production and product technologies, through, inter alia, the mobilization from all sources of adequate financial and technical resources, including new and additional resources, and encourage the transfer and diffusion of those technologies, in particular to developing countries.

Examine issues of global public interest through open, transparent and inclusive workshops to promote a better public understanding of such questions.

Further resolve to take concerted action against international terrorism, which causes serious obstacles to sustainable development.

* * *

Education is critical for promoting sustainable development. It is therefore essential to mobilize necessary resources, including financial resources at all levels, by bilateral and multilateral donors, including the World Bank and the regional development banks, by civil society and by foundations, to complement the efforts by national governments to pursue the following goals and actions:

(a) Meet the development goal contained in the Millennium Declaration of achieving universal primary education, ensuring that, by 2015, children everywhere, boys and girls alike, will be able to complete a full course of primary schooling;

(b) Provide all children, particularly those living in rural areas and those living in poverty, especially girls, with the access and opportunity to complete a full course of primary education;

Provide financial assistance and support to education, research, public awareness programmes and developmental institutions in developing countries and countries with economies in transition in order to:

(a) Sustain their educational infrastructures and programmes, including those related to environment and public health education;

(b) Consider means of avoiding the frequent, serious

financial constraints faced by many institutions of higher learning, including universities around the world, particularly in developing countries and countries in transition.

Address the impact of HIV/AIDS on the educational system in those countries seriously affected by the pandemic.

Allocate national and international resources for basic education as proposed by the Dakar Framework for Action on Education for All and for improved integration of sustainable development into education and in bilateral and multilateral development programmes, and improve integration between publicly funded research and development and development programmes.

Eliminate gender disparity in primary and secondary education by 2005, as provided in the Dakar Framework for Action on Education for All, and at all levels of education no later than 2015, to meet the development goals contained in the Millennium Declaration, with action to ensure, inter alia, equal access to all levels and forms of education, training and capacity-building by gender mainstreaming, and by creating a gender-sensitive educational system.

Integrate sustainable development into education systems at all levels of education in order to promote education as a key agent for change.

Develop, implement, monitor and review education action plans and programmes at the national, subnational and local levels, as appropriate, that reflect the Dakar Framework for Action on Education for All and that are relevant to local conditions and needs leading to the achievement of community development, and make education for sustainable development a part of those plans.

Provide all community members with a wide range of formal and non-formal continuing educational opportunities, including volunteer community service programmes, in order to end illiteracy and emphasize the importance of lifelong learning and promote sustainable development.

Support the use of education to promote sustainable development, including through urgent actions at all levels to:

(a) Integrate information and communications technology in school curriculum development to ensure its access by both rural and urban communities, and provide assistance particularly to developing countries, inter alia, for the establishment of an appropriate enabling environment required for such technology;

(b) Promote, as appropriate, affordable and increased access to programmes for students, researchers and engineers from developing countries in the universities and research institutions of developed countries in order to promote the exchange of experience and capacity that will benefit all partners;

(c) Continue to implement the work programme of the Commission on Sustainable Development on education for sustainable development;

(d) Recommend to the United Nations General Assembly that it consider adopting a decade of education for sustainable development, starting in 2005.

* * *

Enhance and accelerate human, institutional and infrastructure capacity-building initiatives, and promote partnerships in that regard that respond to the specific needs of developing countries in the context of sustainable development.

Support local, national, subregional and regional initiatives, with action to develop, use and adapt knowledge and techniques and to enhance local, national, subregional and regional centres of excellence for education, research and training in order to strengthen the knowledge capacity of developing countries and countries with economies in transition through, inter alia, the mobilization from all sources of adequate financial and other resources, including new and additional resources;

Provide technical and financial assistance to developing countries, including through the strengthening of capacity-building efforts, such as the United Nations Development Programme capacity 21 programme, to:

(a) Assess their own capacity development needs and opportunities at the individual, institutional and societal levels;

(b) Design programmes for capacity-building and support for local, national and community-level programmes that focus on meeting the challenges of globalization more effectively and attaining the internationally agreed development goals, including those contained in the Millennium Declaration;

(c) Develop the capacity of civil society, including youth, to participate, as appropriate, in designing, implementing and reviewing sustainable development policies and strategies at all levels;

(d) Build and, where appropriate, strengthen national

capacities for carrying out effective implementation of Agenda 21.

* * *

Ensure access, at the national level, to environmental information and judicial and administrative proceedings in environmental matters, as well as public participation in decision-making, so as to further principle 10 of the Rio Declaration on Environment and Development, taking into full account principles 5, 7 and 11 of the Declaration.

Strengthen national and regional information and statistical and analytical services relevant to sustainable development policies and programmes, including data disaggregated by sex, age and other factors, and encourage donors to provide financial and technical support to developing countries to enhance their capacity to formulate policies and implement programmes for sustainable development.

Encourage further work on indicators for sustainable development by countries at the national level, including integration of gender aspects, on a voluntary basis, in line with national conditions and priorities.

Promote further work on indicators, in conformity with paragraph 3 of decision 9/4 of the Commission on Sustainable Development.

Promote the development and wider use of earth observation technologies, including satellite remote sensing, global mapping and geographic information systems, to collect quality data on environmental impacts, land use and land-use changes, including through urgent actions at all levels to:

(a) Strengthen cooperation and coordination among global observing systems and research programmes for integrated global observations, taking into account the need for building capacity and sharing of data from ground-based observations, satellite remote sensing and other sources among all countries;

(b) Develop information systems that make the sharing of valuable data possible, including the active exchange of Earth observation data;

(c) Encourage initiatives and partnerships for global mapping.

Support countries, particularly developing countries, in their national efforts to:

(a) Collect data that are accurate, long-term, consistent and reliable;

(b) Use satellite and remote-sensing technologies for data collection and further improvement of ground-based observations;

(c) Access, explore and use geographic information by utilizing the technologies of satellite remote sensing, satellite global positioning, mapping and geographic information systems.

Support efforts to prevent and mitigate the impacts of natural disasters, including through urgent actions at all levels to:

(a) Provide affordable access to disaster-related information for early warning purposes;

(b) Translate available data, particularly from global meteorological observation systems, into timely and useful products.

Develop and promote the wider application of environmental impact assessments, inter alia, as a national instrument, as appropriate, to provide essential decision-support information on projects that could cause significant adverse effects to the environment.

Promote and further develop methodologies at policy, strategy and project levels for sustainable development decision-making at the local and national levels, and where relevant at the regional level. In this regard, emphasize that the choice of the appropriate methodology to be used in countries should be adequate to their country-specific conditions and circumstances, should be on a voluntary basis and should conform to their development priority needs.

INSTITUTIONAL FRAMEWORK FOR SUSTAINABLE DEVELOPMENT

An effective institutional framework for sustainable development at all levels is key to the full implementation of Agenda 21, the follow-up to the outcomes of the World Summit on Sustainable Development and meeting emerging sustainable development challenges. Measures aimed at strengthening such a framework should build on the provisions of Agenda 21 as well as the 1997 Programme for its further implementation and the principles of the Rio Declaration on Environment and Development and should promote the achievement of the internationally agreed development goals, including those contained in the Millennium Declaration, taking into account the Monterrey Consensus and relevant outcomes of other major United Nations conferences and international agreements since 1992. It should be responsive to the needs of all countries, taking into account the specific needs of developing countries including the means of implementation. It should lead to the strengthening of international bodies and organizations dealing with sustainable development, while respecting their existing mandates, as well as to the strengthening of relevant regional, national and local institutions.

Good governance is essential for sustainable development. Sound economic policies, solid democratic institutions responsive to the needs of the people and improved infrastructure are the basis for sustained economic growth, poverty eradication, and employment creation. Freedom, peace and security, domestic stability, respect for human rights, including the right to development, and the rule of law, gender equality, market-oriented policies, and an overall commitment to just and democratic societies are also essential and mutually reinforcing.

Objectives

Measures to strengthen sustainable development institutional arrangements at all levels should be taken within the framework of Agenda 21[1[1]] and should build on developments since UNCED, and should lead to the achievement of, inter alia, the following objectives:

(a) Strengthening commitments to sustainable development;

(b) Integration of the economic, social and environmental dimensions of sustainable development in a balanced manner;

(c) Strengthening of the implementation of Agenda 21, including through the mobilization of financial and technological resources, as well as capacity-building programmes, particularly for developing countries;

(d) Strengthening coherence, coordination and monitoring;

(e) Promoting the rule of law and strengthening of governmental institutions;

(f) Increasing effectiveness and efficiency through limiting overlap and duplication of activities of international organizations, within and outside the United Nations system, based on their mandates and comparative advantages;

(g) Enhancing participation and effective involvement of civil society and other relevant stakeholders in the implementation of Agenda 21, as well as promoting transparency and broad public participation;

(h) Strengthening capacities for sustainable development at all levels, including the local level, in particular those of developing countries;

(i) Strengthening international cooperation aimed at reinforcing the implementation of Agenda 21 and the outcomes of the Summit.

Strengthening the Institutional Framework for Sustainable Development at the International Level

The international community should:

(a) Enhance the integration of sustainable development goals as reflected in Agenda 21 and support for implementation of Agenda 21 and the outcomes of the Summit into the policies, work programmes and operational guidelines of relevant United Nations agencies, programmes and funds, GEF and international financial and trade institutions within their mandates, while stressing that their activities should take full account of national programmes and priorities, particularly those of developing countries, as well as, where appropriate, countries with economies in transition, to achieve sustainable development;

(b) Strengthen collaboration within and between the United Nations system, international financial institutions, the Global Environment Facility and WTO, utilizing the United Nations Chief Executives Board for Coordination (CEB), the United Nations Development Group, the Environment Management Group and other inter-agency coordinating bodies. Strengthened inter-agency collaboration should be pursued in all relevant contexts, with special emphasis on the operational level and involving partnership arrangements on specific issues to support, in particular, developing countries' efforts in implementing Agenda 21;

(c) Strengthen and better integrate the three dimensions of sustainable development policies and programmes, and promote the full integration of sustainable development objectives into programmes and policies of bodies that have a primary focus on social issues. In particular, the social dimension of sustainable development should be strengthened, inter alia, by emphasizing follow-up to the outcomes of the World Summit for Social Development and its five-year review, and taking into account their reports, and by support to social protection systems;

(d) Fully implement the outcomes of decision I on international environmental governance adopted by the UNEP Governing Council at its seventh special session, and invite the General Assembly at its fifty-seventh session to consider the important but complex issue of establishing universal membership for the Governing Council/ Global Ministerial Environment Forum;

(e) Engage actively and constructively in ensuring the timely completion of the negotiations on a comprehensive United Nations convention against corruption, including the question of repatriation of funds illicitly acquired to countries of origin;

(f) Promote corporate responsibility and accountability and the exchange of best practices in the context of sustainable development, including, as appropriate, through multi-stakeholder dialogue, such as through the Commission on Sustainable Development, and other initiatives;

(g) Take concrete action to implement the Monterrey Consensus at all levels.

Good governance at the international level is fundamental for achieving sustainable development. In order to ensure a dynamic and enabling international economic environment, it is important to promote global economic governance through addressing the international finance, trade, technology and investment patterns that have an impact on the development prospects of developing countries. To this effect, the international community should take all necessary and appropriate measures, including ensuring support for structural and macroeconomic reform, a comprehensive solution to the external debt problem and increasing market access for developing countries. Efforts to reform the international financial architecture need to be sustained with greater transparency and the effective participation of developing countries in decision-making processes. A universal, rule-based, open, non-discriminatory and equitable multilateral trading system, as well as meaningful trade liberalization, can substantially stimulate development worldwide, benefiting countries at all stages of development.

A vibrant and effective United Nations system is fundamental to the promotion of international cooperation for sustainable development and to a global economic system that works for all. To this effect, a firm commitment to the ideals of the United Nations and to the principles of international law and those enshrined in the Charter of the United Nations, and to strengthening the United Nations system and other multilateral institutions and promoting the improvement of their operations, is essential. States should also fulfil their commitment to negotiate and finalize as soon as possible a United Nations convention against corruption in all its aspects, including the question of repatriation of funds illicitly acquired to countries of origin and also to promoting stronger cooperation to eliminate money-laundering.

Role of the General Assembly

The General Assembly of the United Nations should adopt sustainable development as a key element of the overarching framework for United Nations activities, particularly for achieving the internationally agreed development goals, including those contained in the Millennium Declaration, and should give overall political direction to the implementation of Agenda 21 and its review.

Role of the Economic and Social Council

Pursuant to the relevant provisions of the Charter of the United Nations and Agenda 21 provisions regarding the Economic and Social Council and General Assembly resolutions 48/162 and 50/227, which reaffirmed the Council as the central mechanism for the coordination of the United Nations system and its specialized agencies and supervision of subsidiary bodies, in particular its functional commissions, and to promote the implementation of Agenda 21 by strengthening system-wide coordination, the Council should:

(a) Increase its role in overseeing system-wide coordination and the balanced integration of economic, social and environmental aspects of United Nations policies and programmes aimed at promoting sustainable development;

(b) Organize periodic consideration of sustainable development themes in regard to the implementation of Agenda 21, including the means of implementation. Recommendations in regard to such themes could be made by the Commission on Sustainable Development;

(c) Make full use of its high-level, coordination, operational activities and the general segments to effectively take into account all relevant aspects of the work of the United Nations on sustainable development. In this context, the Council should encourage the active participation of major groups in its high-level segment and the work of its relevant functional commissions, in accordance with the respective rules of procedure;

(d) Promote greater coordination, complementarity, effectiveness and efficiency of activities of its functional commissions and other subsidiary bodies that are relevant to the implementation of Agenda 21;

(e) Terminate the work of the Committee on Energy and Natural Resources for Development and transfer its work to the Commission on Sustainable Development;

(f) Ensure that there is a close link between the role of the Council in the follow-up to the Summit and its role in the follow-up to the Monterrey Consensus, in a sustained and coordinated manner. To that end, the Council should explore ways to develop arrangements relating to its meetings with the Bretton Woods institutions and WTO, as set out in the Monterrey Consensus;

(g) Intensify its efforts to ensure that gender mainstreaming is an integral part of its activities concerning the coordinated implementation of Agenda 21.

Role and function of the Commission on Sustainable Development

The Commission on Sustainable Development should continue to be the high-level commission on sustainable development within the United Nations system and serve as a forum for consideration of issues related to integration of the three dimensions of sustainable development. Although the role, functions and mandate of the Commission as set out in relevant parts of Agenda 21 and adopted in General Assembly resolution 47/191 continue to be relevant, the Commission needs to be strengthened, taking into account the role of relevant institutions and organizations. An enhanced role of the Commission should include reviewing and monitoring progress in the implementation of Agenda 21 and fostering coherence of implementation, initiatives and partnerships.

Within that context, the Commission should give more emphasis on actions that enable implementation at all levels, including promoting and facilitating partnerships involving Governments, international organizations and relevant stakeholders for the implementation of Agenda 21.

The Commission should:

(a) Review and evaluate progress and promote further implementation of Agenda 21;

(b) Focus on the cross-sectoral aspects of specific sectoral issues and provide a forum for better integration of policies, including through interaction among Ministers dealing with the various dimensions and sectors of sustainable development through the high-level segments;

(c) Address new challenges and opportunities related to the implementation of Agenda 21;

(d) Focus on actions related to implementation of Agenda 21, limiting negotiations in the sessions of the Commission to every two years;

(e) Limit the number of themes addressed in each session.

In relation to its role in facilitating implementation, the Commission should emphasize the following:

(a) Review progress and promote the further implementation of Agenda 21. In this context, the Commission should identify constraints on implementation and make recommendations to overcome those constraints;

(b) Serve as a focal point for the discussion of partnerships that promote sustainable development, including sharing lessons learned, progress made and best practices;

(c) Review issues related to financial assistance and transfer of technology for sustainable development, as well as capacity-building, while making full use of existing information. In this regard, the Commission on Sustainable Development could give consideration to more effective use of national reports and regional experience and to this end make appropriate recommendations;

(d) Provide a forum for analysis and exchange of experience on measures that assist sustainable development planning, decision-making and the implementation of sustainable development strategies. In this regard, the Commission could give consideration to more effective use of national and regional reports;

(e) Take into account significant legal developments in the field of sustainable development, with due regard to the role of relevant intergovernmental bodies in promoting the implementation of Agenda 21 relating to international legal instruments and mechanisms.

With regard to the practical modalities and programme of work of the Commission, specific decisions on those issues should be taken by the Commission at its next session, when the Commission's thematic work programme will be elaborated. In particular, the following issues should be considered:

(a) Giving a balanced consideration to implementation of all of the mandates of the Commission contained in General Assembly resolution 47/191;

(b) Continuing to provide for more direct and substantive involvement of international organizations and major groups in the work of the Commission;

(c) Give greater consideration to the scientific contributions to sustainable development through, for example, drawing on the scientific community and encouraging national, regional and international scientific networks to be involved in the Commission;

(d) Furthering the contribution of educators to sustainable development, including, where appropriate, in the activities of the Commission;

(e) The scheduling and duration of intersessional meetings.

Undertake further measures to promote best practices and lessons learned in sustainable development, and in addition promote the use of contemporary methods of data collection and dissemination, including broader use of information technologies.

Role of international institutions

Stress the need for international institutions both within and outside the United Nations system, including international financial institutions, WTO and GEF, to enhance, within their mandates, their cooperative efforts to:

(a) Promote effective and collective support to the implementation of Agenda 21 at all levels;

(b) Enhance the effectiveness and coordination of international institutions to implement Agenda 21, the outcomes of the World Summit on Sustainable Development, relevant sustainable development aspects of the Millennium Declaration, the Monterrey Consensus and the outcomes of the fourth WTO ministerial meeting, held in Doha in November 2001.

Request the Secretary-General of the United Nations, utilizing the United Nations System Chief Executives Board for Coordination, including through informal collaborative efforts, to further promote system-wide inter-agency cooperation and coordination on sustainable development, to take appropriate measures to facilitate exchange of information, and to continue to keep the Economic and Social Council and the Commission informed of actions being taken to implement Agenda 21.

Significantly strengthen support for UNDP capacity-building programmes for sustainable development, building on the experience gained from Capacity 21, as important mechanisms for supporting local and national development capacity-building efforts, in particular in developing countries.

Strengthen cooperation among UNEP and other United Nations bodies and specialized agencies, the Bretton Woods institutions and WTO, within their mandates.

UNEP, UN-Habitat, UNDP and UNCTAD, within their mandates, should strengthen their contribution to sustainable development programmes and the implementation of Agenda 21 at all levels, particularly in the area of promoting capacity-building.

To promote effective implementation of Agenda 21 at the international level, the following should also be undertaken:

(a) Streamline the international sustainable development meeting calendar and, as appropriate, reduce the number of meetings, the length of meetings and the amount of time spent on negotiated outcomes in favour of more time spent on practical matters related to implementation;

(b) Encourage partnership initiatives for implementation by all relevant actors to support the outcome of the World Summit on Sustainable Development. In this context, further development of partnerships and partnership follow-up should take note of the preparatory work for the Summit;

(c) Make full use of developments in the field of information and communication technologies.

Strengthening of the international institutional framework for sustainable development is an evolutionary process. It is necessary to keep under review relevant arrangements; identify gaps; eliminate duplication of functions; and continue to strive for greater integration, efficiency and coordination of the economic, social and environmental dimensions of sustainable development aiming at the implementation of Agenda 21.

Strengthening institutional arrangements for sustainable development at the regional level

Implementation of Agenda 21 and the outcomes of the Summit should be effectively pursued at the regional and subregional levels, through the regional commissions and other regional and subregional institutions and bodies.

Intraregional coordination and cooperation on sustainable development should be improved among the regional commissions, United Nations Funds, programmes and agencies, regional development banks, and other regional and subregional institutions and bodies. This should include, as appropriate, support for development, enhancement and implementation of agreed regional sustainable development strategies and action plans, reflecting national and regional priorities.

In particular and taking into account relevant provisions of Agenda 21, the regional commissions, in collaboration with other regional and subregional bodies, should:

(a) Promote the integration of the three dimensions of sustainable development into their work in a balanced way, including through implementation of Agenda 21. To this end, the regional commissions should enhance their capacity through internal action and be provided, as appropriate, with external support;

(b) Facilitate and promote a balanced integration of the economic, social and environmental dimensions of sustainable development into the work of regional, subregional and other bodies, for example by facilitating and strengthening the exchange of experiences, including national experience, best practices, case studies and partnership experience related to the implementation of Agenda 21;

(c) Assist in the mobilization of technical and financial assistance, and facilitate the provision of adequate financing for the implementation of regionally and subregionally agreed sustainable development programmes and projects, including addressing the objective of poverty eradication;

(d) Continue to promote multi-stakeholder participation and encourage partnerships to support the implementation of Agenda 21 at the regional and subregional levels.

Regionally and subregionally agreed sustainable development initiatives and programmes, such as the New Partnership for Africa's Development (NEPAD) and the interregional aspects of the globally agreed Programme of Action for the Sustainable Development of Small Island Developing States, should be supported.

Strengthening institutional frameworks for sustainable development at the national level

States should:

(a) Continue to promote coherent and coordinated approaches to institutional frameworks for sustainable development at all national levels, including through, as appropriate, the establishment or strengthening of existing authorities and mechanisms necessary for policy-making, coordination and implementation and enforcement of laws;

(b) Take immediate steps to make progress in the formulation and elaboration of national strategies for sustainable development and begin their implementation by 2005. To this end, as appropriate, strategies should be supported through international cooperation, taking into account the special needs of developing countries, in particular the least developed countries. Such strategies, which, where applicable, could be formulated as poverty reduction strategies that integrate economic, social and environmental aspects of sustainable development, should be pursued in accordance with each country's national priorities.

Each country has the primary responsibility for its own sustainable development, and the role of national policies and development strategies cannot be overemphasized. All countries should promote sustainable development at the national level by, inter alia, enacting and enforcing clear and effective laws that support sustainable development. All countries should strengthen governmental institutions, including by providing necessary infrastructure and by promoting transparency, accountability and fair administrative and judicial institutions.

All countries should also promote public participation, including through measures that provide access to information regarding legislation, regulations, activities, policies and programmes. They should also foster full public participation in sustainable development policy formulation and implementation. Women should be able to participate fully and equally in policy formulation and decision-making.

Further promote the establishment or enhancement of sustainable development councils and/or coordination structures at the national level, including at the local level, in order to provide a high-level focus on sustainable development policies. In that context, multi-stakeholder participation should be promoted.

Support efforts by all countries, particularly developing countries, as well as countries with economies in transition, to enhance national institutional arrangements for sustainable development, including at the local level. That could include promoting cross-sectoral approaches in the formulation of strategies and plans for sustainable development, such as, where applicable, poverty reduction strategies, aid coordination, encouraging participatory approaches and enhancing policy analysis, management capacity and implementation capacity, including mainstreaming a gender perspective in all those activities.

Enhance the role and capacity of local authorities as well as stakeholders in implementing Agenda 21 and the outcomes of the Summit and in strengthening the continuing support for local Agenda 21 programmes and associated initiatives and partnerships, and encourage, in particular, partnerships among and between local authorities and other levels of government and stakeholders to advance sustainable development as called for in, inter alia, the Habitat Agenda.

Participation of major groups

Enhance partnerships between governmental and non-governmental actors, including all major groups, as well as volunteer groups, on programmes and activities for the achievement of sustainable development at all levels.

Acknowledge the consideration being given to the possible relationship between environment and human rights, including the right to development, with full and transparent participation of Member States of the United Nations and observer States.

Promote and support youth participation in programmes and activities relating to sustainable development through, for example, supporting local youth councils or their equivalent, and by encouraging their establishment where they do not exist.

---

* Because the structure of chapter V was changed in the course of negotiations so that its paragraph numbering no longer corresponds to the earlier version contained in document A/CONF.199/L.1, Latin ordinal numbers (bis, ter etc.) are used after paragraph 45 until the end of the chapter in order not to disrupt the paragraph numbering of subsequent chapters which were not so changed.

* Because the structure of chapter IX was changed in the course of negotiations, so that its paragraph numbering no longer corresponds to the earlier version contained in document A/CONF.199/L.1, Latin ordinal numbers (bis, ter etc.) are used after paragraph 119 until the end of the chapter in order not to disrupt the paragraph numbering of the following chapter, which was not so changed.

[1] References in the present chapter to Agenda 21 are deemed to include Agenda 21, the Programme for the Further Implementation of Agenda 21 and the outcomes of the Summit.

7

References for Chapter 24

Arrow Kenneth, *et al.*, "Economic Growth, Carrying Capacity, and the Environment," 1995, *Science* 268:520–521.

Botero Marguerita Moreno de y Juan Tokatlian, *Ecodesarrollo, el pensamiento del decenio*, Inderena y Pnuna, Bogota, 1983.

Brenton T., *The Greening of Machiavelli: The Evolution of International Environmental Politics*, Earthscan/Royal Institute of International Affairs, London, 1994.

Cleveland H., "The Confidence Game," *Perspectives*, December 1995.

Condit R., Hubbel S.P., and Foster R.B, "Short-Term Dynamics of a Neotropical forest" *BioScience*, 42, 1992, pp 822–828.

Durning A.T., "Redesigning the Forest Economy," in Brown L.R. *et al., State of the World 1994*, W.W. Norton & Company, New York, 1994, pp 22-40.

Easterbrook G., *A Moment on the Earth: The Coming Age of Environmental Optimism*, Viking Press, New York, 1995.

Gadgil M., "Diversity: Cultural and Biological," *Trends in Ecology and Evolution* 2(12) 1987, pp 369-373.

Graeger N. and Smith D. (eds). *Environment, Poverty, Conflict*, International Peace Research Institute, PRIO Report No. 2/92, Oslo, 1994.

IUCN, "Regional Perspectives," *World Conservation*, IUCN magazine 1/99, p 7.

Kennedy P., *Preparing for the 21st Century*, HarperCollins, London, 1993, pp 428.

Korten D., *When Corporations Rule the World*, Earthscan, London, 1995.

Lutz W., Prinz C., and Langgassmer J., "World Population Projections and Possible Ecological Feedbacks," *POPNET* 23, 1993, pp 1-11.

MacNeill J., Winsemius P., and Yakushiji T., *Beyond Interdependence: The Meshing of the World's Economy and the Earth's Ecology*, Trilateral Commission, Oxford University Press, Oxford, 1991.

Martin P.H. and Lefebvre M.G., "Malaria and Climate: Sensitivity of Malaria Potential Transmission to Climate," *Ambio* 24(4), 1991, pp 200-209.

May J., "Influence of Environmental Transformation in Changing the Map of Disease," in Farvar, Taghi and Milton (eds), *The Careless Technology*, Natural History Press, Garden City, New York, 1972, pp 19-34.

May J., *The Ecology of Human Disease*, MD Publications, New York, 1958.

Maybury-Lewis D., *Millennium: Tribal Wisdom and the Modern World*, Viking Press, New York, 1958.

Meadows D.H., Meadows D.L., Randers J. and Behrens W.W. III, *The Limits to Growth: A Report for the Club of Rome's Project on the Predicament of Mankind*, Pan Books, Ltd., London, 1972.

Milsted D., "Even Geniuses Make Mistakes," *New Scientist* 19 August 1995, pp 49-50.

Myers N. and Simon J.L., *Scarcity or Abundance? A Debate on the Environment*, W.W. Norton and Company, New York, 1994.

Myers Norman and Kent J., *Perverse Subsidies: Tax Dollars Undercutting our Economies and Environments Alike*, International Institute for Sustainable Development, Winnipeg, Canada, 1998.

Pimentel D., Hunter M., LaGro J., *et al.*, "Benefits and Risks of Genetic Engineering in Agriculture" *BioScience* 39(9) 1989, pp 606-610.

Rennie J., "The Uncertainties of Technological Innovations," *Scientific American*, September 1995, pp 43-44.

Salim E, "Address to The South-East Asia and Pacific Ocean Law Conference (SEAPOL) May 1990," in Thammathirat S. (ed), *International Conference on the Implementation of the Law of the Sea Convention in the 1990's: Marine Protection and Other Issues*, 1990.

Sankaram A., *Global Agriculture: Perceptions, Prerequisites, Prescriptions*, M.S. Swaminathan Research Foundation, Madras, 1993.

Simon J.L. and Kahn H. (eds), *The Resourceful Earth: A Response to Global 2000*, Basil Blackwell, New York, 1984.

Slouka M., *War of the Words: Cyberspace and the High-Tech Assault on Reality*, Basic Books, New York, 1995.

Swain A., *Environment and Conflict: Analyzing the Developing World*, Report No. 37, Uppsala University, Uppsala, 1993.

UNDP, *Human Development Report 1992*, Oxford University Press, New York, 1992.

UNDP, *Conserving Indigenous Knowledge: Integrating Two Systems of Innovation*, United Nations Development Programme, New York, 1994.

Vitousek P.M., Ehrlich P.R., Ehrlich A.H., and Matson P.A., "Human Appropriation of the Products of Photosynthesis," *BioScience* 36 1986, pp 368-373.

Westing A.H. (ed.), *Global Resources and International Conflict: Environmental Factors in Strategic Policy and Action*, Oxford University Press, Oxford, 1986.

Westing A.H., "Human Instability and the Release of Dangerous Forces" in Polunin, N. and Burnett J. (eds.), *Surviving With the Biosphere*, Edinburgh University Press, Edinburgh, 1993, pp 307-319.

8

Additional References

Asian Development Bank, *Cambodia: Enhancing Governance for Sustainable Development*, 2000.

Ausubel J.H. 1993. 2020 vision. *The Sciences* 33(6): 14-19.

Barton N.H. and Hewitt G.M., "Adaptation, Speciation and Hybrid Zones" *Nature* 341, 1989, pp 497-503.

Bryson R.E., "Civilization and Rapid Climatic Change," *Environmental Conservation* 15(1), 1988, pp 7-15.

Burnet, MacFarlan, and White, *Natural History of Infectious Disease*, Cambridge University Press, Cambridge, 1972.

Comision, de desarrollo y medio ambiente de America Latina y el Caribe, *Nuestra Propia Agenda*, Banco InterAmericano de desarrollo y programa naciones unides para el desarrollo, Washington, DC, 1990.

Crowley T.J. and North G.R., "Abrupt Climate Change and Extinction Events in Earth History" *Science*, 240, 1988, pp 996-1,002.

Daly H.E., "Toward Some Operational Principles of Sustainable Development" *Ecological Economics* 2(1), 1990, pp 1-6.

Dasmann R., "National Parks, Nature Conservation, and 'Future Primitive,'" *Ecologist*, 65(5), 1975, pp 164-167.

Dogsé P. and von Droste B., *Debt-for-Nature Exchanges and Biosphere Reserves*, UNESCO, Paris, 1990.

Dubos R., *Mirage of Health: Utopias, Progress and Biological Change*, Harper Colophon Books, New York, 1979.

El-Sharkawy M.A., "Drought-Tolerant Cassava for Africa, Asia, and Latin America," *BioScience* 43(7), 1993, pp 441-451.

Garrett L., *The Coming Plague: Newly Emerging Diseases in a World Out of Balance*, Farrer, Straus and Girrux, New York, 1994.

Gates D.M., *Climate Change and its Biological Consequences*, Sinauer Associates, Inc., Sunderland, Massachusetts, 1993.

Goodland R., Daly H., and El Serafy S. (eds), *Environmentally Sustainable Economic Development: Building on Brundtland*, UNESCO, 1991.

Heywood V.H. and Watson R.T. (eds), *Global Biodiversity Assessment,* Cambridge University Press, Cambridge, 1995.

Hoffman C.A., "Ecological Risks of Genetic Engineering of Crop Plants," *BioScience* 40(6), 1990, pp 434-437.

Holling C.S., "Resilience of ecosystems: Local surprise and global change" in Clark, W.C., and R.E. Munn (eds). *Sustainable Development of the Biosphere*, Cambridge University Press, Cambridge, 1986, pp 292-317.

Homer-Dixon T.F., "Environmental Scarcities and Violent Conflict," *International Security,* Cambridge, Mass., 19(1) 1994-95, pp 5-40.

Houghton J.T., Jenkins G.J., and Ephraums J.J. (eds), *Climate Change: The IPCC Scientific Assessment*, Cambridge University Press, 1990.

IGES, Environmental Governance in Asia, 2001.

IGES, Urban Environmental Management, 2001.

IUCN, *Red Data Book*, IUCN, Gland, Switzerland, 1994.

IUCN, *1997 IUCN Red List of Threatened Plants*, IUCN, Gland, Switzerland, 1997.

KatesR.W., Turner B.L., and Clark W.C., "The Great Transformation," in Turner B.L., Clark W.C., Kates R.W., Richards J.F., Mathews J.T., and Meyer W.B. (eds), *The Earth as Transformed by Human Action*, Cambridge, University Press, New York, 1990, pp 1-17.

Lodge D.M., "Species Invasions and Deletions: Community Effects and Responses to Climate and Habitat Change," in Kareiva P.M., Kingsolver J.G., and Huey R.B. (eds), *Biotic Interactions and Global Change,* Sinauer Associates Inc., Sunderland, Massachusetts, 1993, pp. 367-387.

MacNeill J.P., Winsemius, and Yakushiji T., *Beyond Interdependence: The Meshing of the World's Economy and the Earth's Ecology*, Trilateral Commission, Oxford University Press, Oxford, 1991.

McNeely J.A., *Economics and Biological Diversity: Developing and Using Economic Incentives to Conserve Biological Resources*, IUCN, Gland, Switzerland, 1988.

McNeely J.A., "Climate Change and Biological Diversity: Policy Implications," in Boer, Mathius M., and DuGroot R.S. (eds), *Landscape-Ecological Impact of Climate Change* IOS Press, Amsterdam, 1990, pp 406-429.

McNeely J.A., "The Costs and Benefits of Alien Species" in *Proceedings*, Norway/UN Conference on Alien Species, Trondheim, Norway, 1996, pp 176-181.

Meyer A., "International Environmental Law and Human Rights: Towards the Explicit Recognition of Traditional Knowledge," *Review of European Community and International Environmental Law*, v.10 (1), 2001, pp 37-46.

Miller J.A., "Diseases for our Future" *BioScience* 39(8), 1989, pp 509-517.

Myers N., *Ultimate Security: The Environmental Basis of Political Stability*, W.W. Norton, New York, 1993.

Nikiforuk A., *The Fourth Horseman*, Penguin Books, Toronto, 1992, pp 200.

Norse E.A. (ed), *Global Marine Biological Diversity: A Strategy for Building Conservation into Decision-Making*, Island Press, California, 1993.

Ojima D.S., Galvin K.A., and Turner B.L., "The Global Impact of Land-Use Change" *BioScience* 44(5) 1994, pp 300-304.

Peters R.L. and Lovejoy T.E., *Global Warming and Biological Diversity*, Yale University Press, New Haven, 1992.

Popper F.J. and Popper D.E., "The Reinvention of the American Frontier" *The Almacus Journal*, Summer 1991, pp 4-7.

Postel S., "Carrying Capacity: Earth's Bottom Line" in Lester R. Brown *et al. State of the World 1994*, W.W. Norton and Company, New York, 1994, pp 3-21.

Rao I.M., Zeigler R.S., Vera R., and Sarkarung S., "Selection and Breeding for Acid-Soil Tolerance in Crops" *BioScience* 43(7), 1993, pp 454-465.

Rapalus, "Optimum Human Population about One-Third of Present Number," *Environmental Conservation* 21(2), 1994, pp 176-177.

Redford Kent H., "The Empty Forest," *BioScience* 42 (6), 1992, pp 412-422.

Shiva Vandana, *Staying Alive: Women, Ecology, and Development*, Colley for Women, New Delhi and Z Books, London, 1998.

Shiva Vandana, *Violence of the Green Revolution*, Third World Network, Panang and Z Books, London, 1991.

Shiva V., Bandyopadhyay J., Hegde P., Krishnamurthy B., Kurien J., Narendranath G., Ranprasad V., and Reddy S.T.S., *Ecology and the Politics of Survival: Conflicts Over Natural Resources in India*, UNU, Tokyo, 1991.

Simmons I.G., *Environmental History: A Concise Introduction*, Blackwell Publishers, Oxford, UK, 1993.

Smil Vaclav, *China's Environmental Crisis: An Enquiry into the Limits of National Development*, M.E. Sharpe, Inc., Armonk, New York, 1993.

Teale A., "Improving Control of Livestock Diseases," *BioScience*, 43(7) 1993, pp 475-483.

Tilman D., May R.M., Lehman C.L., and Nowak M.A., "Habitat Destruction and the Extinction Debt" *Nature* 371, 1994, pp 65-66.

Warrick R.A., Jones P.D., and Russell J.E., *The Greenhouse Effect, Climatic Change and Sea Level: An Overview*, paper prepared for Commonwealth Expert Group on Climatic Change and Sea Level Rise, London, May 1988.

WCMC, *Global Biodiversity: Status of the Earth's Living Resources*, Chapman and Hall, London, 1992.

World Resources Institute, *World Resources 1994-1995: A Guide to the Global Environment*, Oxford University Press, New York, 1994.

Appendix III

ASEAN Strategic Plan of Action on the Environment 1994 - 1998

OBJECTIVES

The Strategic Plan of Action on the Environment has the following five objectives :

a) to respond to specific recommendations of Agenda 21 requiring priority action in ASEAN;

b) to introduce policy measures and promote institutional development that encourage the integration of environmental factors in all developmental processes both at the national and regional levels;

c) to establish long term goals on environmental quality and work towards harmonised environmental quality standards for the ASEAN region;

d) to harmonise policy directions and enhance operational and technical cooperation on environmental matters, and undertake joint actions to address common environmental problems; and e) to study the implications of AFTA on the environment and take steps to integrate sound trade policies with sound environmental policies.

STRATEGIES

To attain these objectives, the following strategic thrusts and actions will be pursued :

Strategy 1: Support the development of a regional framework for integrating environment and development concerns in the decision-making process.

1.1 Continue support in the documentation of regional EIA experiences leading towards the harmonisation of procedures;

1.2 Initiate acctivities that will make use of natural resource and environmental accounting studies and approaches; and

1.3 Establish procedures that would initiate the integration of environmental concerns in the various ASEAN programmes activities.

Strategy 2: Promote government-private sector interactions that lead towards the development of policies that mutually support the thrust of each sector.

2.1 Initiate studies on development of environmental and trade policies which are supported to the principles of sustainable de velopment;

2.2 Establish mechanisms that encourage government and private sectors to adopt appropriate environmental standards backed up by sufficient economic incentives; and

2.3 Set up government-private sector information linkages/networks to include information on technology, expertise and facilities for environmental management.

Strategy 3: Strengthen the knowledge and information data base on environmental matters.

3.1 Pursue the establishment of basic environmental quality standards leading to the setting up of harmonised quality standards in the region;

3.2 Identify centers of excellence for environmental R&D and eventually build them as focal points of environmental networks; and

3.3 Establish a mechanism for the preparation of periodic reports on the state of the region's environment.

Strategy 4: Strengthen institutional and legal capacities to implement international agreements on environment.

4.1 Undertake a comparative study on the institutional structure and legislation structure and legislation on environmental management;

4.2 Establish capacities to support regional efforts to implement international agreements and participate effectively in the negotiation of new or revised agreements; and

4.3 Enhance collaboration with international bodies overseeing the implementation of international agreements and cooperation.

Strategy 5: Establish a regional framework on biological diversity conservation and sustainable utilization of its components.

5.1 Promote the development of a framework for the protection and conservation of heritage areas and endangered species; and

5.2 Strengthen capacities for R&D to enhance biodiversity conservation in the region.

Strategy 6: Promote the protection and management of coastal zones and marine resources.

6.1. Improve regional marine and coastal environmental coordination; and

6.2 Develop a framework for the integrated management of regional coastal zones.

Strategy 7: Promote environmentally sound management of toxic chemicals and hazardous wastes, and control of transboundary movement of hazardous wastes.

7.1 Establish a regional guidelines for assessing highly pollutive industries and safe handling of potentially harmful chemcials entering the ASEAN region; and

7.2 Strengthen the information network on the transboundary movement of toxic chemicals and hazardous waste.

Strategy 8: Develop a system for the promotion of environmentally sound technologies.

8.1 Establish linkages with existing clearing houses on environmentally sound technologies;

8.2 Establish mechanisms that identify end users of R&D results and encourage the participation of private sector;

8.3 Strengthen linkage and coordination with other ASEAN committees such as COST doing related R&D work on the environment; and

8.4 Support the promotion of indigenous technology or technologies that have been adapted to regional needs.

Strategy 9: Promote regional activities that strengthen the role of major groups in sustainable development.

9.1 Support the publication of regional environmental magazine and newsletters;

9.2 Strenthen regional information network and promote exchange of expertise on environmental education programmes; and

9.3 Develop strategic programmes of action that will strengthen the role and participation of major groups on environmental management and decision making.

Strategy 10: Strengthen the coordinative mechanism for the implementation and management of regional environment programmes.

10.1 Establish an operational system at the ASEAN Secretariat that could plan, monitor and facilitate the implementation of environmental projects; and

10.2 Source and match funding requirements for proposed projects.

Appendix IV

Kota Kinabalu Resolution on the Environment Kota Kinabalu, Sabah, Malaysia,

CONCERNED that the issues on environment are becoming more complex and challenging;

AWARE that to meet these challenges, there is a need to strengthen the institutional and organisational capacity within the ASEAN member countries;

REALISING that the Rio+10 Conference on Environment and Development, will provide new driving force for achieving environmentally sound and sustainable development;

EMPHASISING the need for enhancing ASEAN cooperation to address common environmental problems, promote technology transfer, information networking and to deal with the negative impacts of globalisation; and

RECOGNISING that the ASEAN Strategic Plan of Action on the Environment shall continue to be the guiding document for present and future initiatives toward achieving the balance between environmental protection and economic development.

WE, THE ASEAN MINISTERS FOR THE ENVIRONMENT HEREBY AGREED TO:

- synergise the ASEAN Strategic Plan of Action on the Environment with the Regional Action Plan for Environmentally Sound and Sustainable Development, 2001-2005 for Asia and the Pacific Region with a view to optimise the utilisation of limited resources in the implementation of the planned activities;
- adopt the approach of overcoming environmental pollution by working in collaboration with cities such as Kitakyushu which has successfully controlled pollution;
- adopt and implement the ASEAN Environmental Education Action Plan 2000-2005 and task ASOEN to implement the Plan;
- accelerate our efforts in the realisation of the Regional Action Plan for the Protection of the Marine Environment from Land and Sea-based activities by the year 2004;
- initiate the process of negotiation on the ASEAN Agreement on Transboundary Haze Pollution;
- continue and further enhance our collaboration to implement the Regional Haze Action Plan (RHAP) coherently and effectively;
- sustainably manage and wise use of our diverse biological resources and to exchange information on biodiversity conservation issues including biosafety and access to biological and genetic resources;
- stand firm on the common understanding that the developed countries must fulfill their commitment under the United Nations Framework Convention on Climate Change and subsequently the Kyoto Protocol;
- intensify our cooperation in enhancing national capacities in the negotiation and implementation of the multilateral environmental agreements;
- reiterate ASEAN's support on the proposal by Indonesia to host the "Rio + 10" Conference on Environment and Development, as stipulated at the 9th Environmental Congress for Asia and the Pacific (ECO ASIA 2000) on 3rd September 2000 and the Ministerial Conference on Environment and Development in Asia and the Pacific in Kitakyushu, Japan, 4-5 September 2000;
- support the proposal of Cambodia to host an Asia Pacific regional preparatory meeting in the run-up to the "Rio + 10" Conference on Environment and Development;
- enhance environmental co-operation between ASEAN and the 3 East Asian countries namely, China, Japan and the Republic of Korea;
- task ASEAN Secretariat to explore the possibility of establishing environmental co-operation between ASEAN and Central Asian countries;

support the proposal to organize an international forum on fire hazards arising from large-scale biomass burning; and

support to explore the possibility of seting up an Emergency Response and Rescue Institute.

Appendix V

ASEAN AGREEMENT ON TRANSBOUNDARY HAZE POLLUTION

The Parties to this Agreement,

REAFFIRMING the commitment to the aims and purposes of the Association of Southeast Asian Nations (ASEAN) as set forth in the Bangkok Declaration of 8 August 1967, in particular to promote regional co-operation in Southeast Asia in the spirit of equality and partnership and thereby contribute towards peace, progress and prosperity in theregion,

RECALLING the Kuala Lumpur Accord on Environment and Development which was adopted by the ASEAN Ministers of Environment on 19 June 1990 which calls for, inter alia, efforts leading towards the harmonisation of transboundary pollution prevention and abatement practices,

RECALLING ALSO the adoption of the 1995 ASEAN Co-operation Plan on Transboundary Pollution, which specifically addressed transboundary atmospheric pollution and called for, inter alia, establishing procedures and mechanisms for co-operation among ASEANMember States in the prevention and mitigation of land and/or forest fires and haze,

DETERMINED to give effect to the 1997 Regional Haze Action Plan and to the Hanoi Plan of Action which call for fully implementing the 1995 ASEAN Cooperation Plan on Transboundary Pollution, with particular emphasis on the Regional Haze Action Plan by the year 2001,

RECOGNISING the existence of possible adverse effects of transboundary haze pollution,

CONCERNED that a rise in the level of emissions of air pollutants within the region as forecast may increase such adverse effects,

RECOGNISING the need to study the root causes and the implications of the transboundary haze pollution and the need to seek solutions for the problems identified,

AFFIRMING their willingness to further strengthen international cooperation to develop national policies for preventing and monitoring transboundary haze pollution,

AFFIRMING ALSO their willingness to co-ordinate national action for preventing and monitoring transboundary haze pollution through exchange of information, consultation, research and monitoring,

DESIRING to undertake individual and joint action to assess the origin, causes, nature and extent of land and/or forest fires and the resulting haze, to prevent and control the sources of such land and/or forest fires and the resulting haze by applying environmentally sound policies, practices and technologies and to strengthen national and regional capabilities and cooperation in assessment, prevention, mitigation and management of land and/or forest fires and the resulting haze,

CONVINCED that an essential means to achieve such collective action is the conclusion and effective implementation of an Agreement,

Have agreed as follows:

PART I. GENERAL PROVISIONS

Article 1

Use of Terms

For the purposes of this Agreement:

1. "Assisting Party" means a State, international organisation, any other entity or person that offer and/or render assistance to a Requesting Party or a Receiving Party in the event of land and/or forest fires or haze pollution.
2. "Competent authorities" means one or more entities designated and authorised by each Party to act on its behalf in the implementation of this Agreement.
3. "Controlled burning" means any fire, combustion or smouldering that occurs in the open air, which is controlled by national laws, rules, regulations or guidelines and does not cause fire outbreaks and transboundary haze pollution.
4. "Fire prone areas" means areas defined by the national authorities as areas where fires are most likely to occur or have a higher tendency to occur.
5. "Focal point" means an entity designated and authorised by each Party to receive and transmit communications and data pursuant to the provisions of this Agreement.

6. "Haze pollution" means smoke resulting from land and/or forest fire which causes deleterious effects of such a nature as to endanger human health, harm living resources and ecosystems and material property and impair or interfere with amenities and other legitimate uses of the environment.
7. "Land and/or forest fires" means fires such as coal seam fires, peat fires, and plantation fires.
8. "Member State" means a Member State of the Association of Southeast Asian Nations.
9. "Open burning" means any fire, combustion or smouldering that occurs in the open air.
10. "Party" means a Member State of ASEAN that has consented to be bound by this Agreement and for which the Agreement is in force.
11. "Receiving Party" means a Party that accepts assistance offered by an Assisting Party or Parties in the event of land and/or forest fires or haze pollution.
12. "Requesting Party" means a Party that requests from another Party or Parties assistance in the event of land and/or forest fires or haze pollution.
13. "Transboundary haze pollution" means haze pollution whose physical origin is situated wholly or in part within the area under the national jurisdiction of one Member State and which is transported into the area under the jurisdiction of another Member State.
14. "Zero burning policy" means a policy that prohibits open burning but may allow some forms of controlled burning.

Article 2

Objective

The objective of this Agreement is to prevent and monitor transboundary haze pollution as a result of land and/or forest fires which should be mitigated, through concerted national efforts and intensified regional and international co-operation. This should be pursued in the overall context of sustainable development and in accordance with the provisions of this Agreement.

Article 3

Principles

The Parties shall be guided by the following principles in the implementation of this Agreement:

1. The Parties have, in accordance with the Charter of the United Nations and the principles of international law, the sovereign right to exploit their own resources pursuant to their own environmental and developmental policies, and the responsibility to ensure that activities within their jurisdiction or control do not cause damage to the environment and harm to human health of other States or of areas beyond the limits of national jurisdiction.
2. The Parties shall, in the spirit of solidarity and partnership and in accordance with their respective needs, capabilities and situations, strengthen co-operation and co-ordination to prevent and monitor transboundary haze pollution as a result of land and/or forest fires which should be mitigated.
3. The Parties should take precautionary measures to anticipate, prevent and monitor tranboundary haze pollution as a result of land and/or forest fires which should be mitigated, to minimise its adverse effects. Where there are threats of serious or irreversible damage from transboundary haze pollution, even without full scientific certainty, precautionary measures shall be taken by Parties concerned.
4. The Parties should manage and use their natural resources, including forest and land resources, in an ecologically sound and sustainable manner.
5. The Parties, in addressing transboundary haze pollution, should involve, as appropriate, all stakeholders, including local communities, non-governmental organisations, farmers and private enterprises.

Article 4

General Obligations

In pursuing the objective of this Agreement, the Parties shall:

1. Co-operate in developing and implementing measures to prevent and monitor transboundary haze pollution as a result of land and/or forest fires which should be mitigated, and to control sources of fires, including by the identification of fires, development of monitoring, assessment and early warning systems, exchange of information and technology, and the provision of mutual assistance.
2. When the transboundary haze pollution originates from within their territories, respond promptly to a request for relevant informationor consultations sought by a State or States that are or may be affected by such transboundary haze pollution, with a view to minimising the consequences of the transboundary haze pollution.
3. Take legislative, administrative and/or other measures to implement their obligations under this Agreement.

PART II. MONITORING, ASSESSMENT, PREVENTION AND RESPONSE

Article 5

ASEAN Co-ordinating Centre for Transboundary Haze Pollution Control

1. The ASEAN Co-ordinating Centre for Transboundary Haze Pollution Control, hereinafter referred to as "the ASEAN Centre", is hereby established for the purposes of facilitating co-operation and co-ordination among the Parties in managing the impact of land and/or forest fires in particular haze pollution arising from such fires.
2. The ASEAN Centre shall work on the basis that the national authority will act first to put out the fires. When the national authority declares an emergency situation, it may make a request to the ASEAN Centre to provide assistance.
3. A Committee composed of representatives of the national authorities of the Parties shall oversee the operation of the ASEAN Centre.
4. The ASEAN Centre shall carry out the functions as set out in Annex and any other functions as directed by the Conference of the Parties.

Article 6

Competent Authorities and Focal Points

1. Each Party shall designate one or more Competent Authorities and a Focal Point that shall be authorised to act on its behalf in the performance of the administrative functions required by this Agreement.
2. Each Party shall inform other Parties and the ASEAN Centre, of its Competent Authorities and Focal Point, and of any subsequent changes in their designations.
3. The ASEAN Centre shall regularly and expeditiously provide to Parties and relevant international organisations the information referred to in paragraph 2 above.

Article 7

Monitoring

1. Each Party shall take appropriate measures to monitor:
   a. all fire prone areas,
   b. all land and/or forest fires,
   c. the environmental conditions conducive to such land and/or forest fires, and
   d. haze pollution arising from such land and/or forest fires.
2. Each Party shall designate one or more bodies to function as National Monitoring Centres, to undertake monitoring referred to in paragraph 1 above in accordance with their respective national procedures.

3. The Parties, in the event that there are fires, shall initiate immediate action to control or to put out the fires.

Article 8

Assessment

1. Each Party shall ensure that its National Monitoring Centre, at agreed regular intervals, communicates to the ASEAN Centre, directly or through its Focal Point, data obtained relating to fire prone areas, land and/or forest fires, the environmental conditions conducive to such land and/or forest fires, and haze pollution arising from such land and/or forest fires.
2. The ASEAN Centre shall receive, consolidate and analyse the data communicated by the respective National Monitoring Centres or Focal Points.
3. On the basis of analysis of the data received, the ASEAN Centre shall, where possible, provide to each Party, through its Focal Point, an assessment of risks to human health or the environment arising from land and/or forest fires and the resulting transboundary haze pollution.

Article 9

Prevention

Each Party shall undertake measures to prevent and control activities related to land and/or forest fires that may lead to transboundary haze pollution, which include:

a. Developing and implementing legislative and other regulatory measures, as well as programmes and strategies to promote zero burning policy to deal with land and/or forest fires resulting in transboundary haze pollution;
b. Developing other appropriate policies to curb activities that may lead to land and/or forest fires;
c. Identifying and monitoring areas prone to occurrence of land and/or forest fires;
d. Strengthening local fire management and firefighting capability and co-ordination to prevent the occurrence of land and/or forest fires;
e. Promoting public education and awareness-building campaigns and strengthening community participation in fire management to prevent land and/or forest fires and haze pollution arising from such fires;
f. Promoting and utilising indigenous knowledge and practices in fire prevention and management; and
g. Ensuring that legislative, administrative and/or other relevant measures are taken to control open burning and to prevent land clearing using fire.

Article 10

Preparedness

1. The Parties shall, jointly or individually, develop strategies and response plans to identify, manage and control risks to human health and the environment arising from land and/or forest fires and related haze pollution arising from such fires.
2. The Parties shall, as appropriate, prepare standard operating procedures for regional co-operation and national action required under this Agreement.

Article 11

National Emergency Response

1. Each Party shall ensure that appropriate legislative, administrative and financial measures are taken to mobilise equipment, materials, human and financial resources required to respond to and mitigate the impact of land and/or forest fires and haze pollution arising from such fires.
2. Each Party shall forthwith inform other Parties and the ASEAN Centre of such measures.

Article 12

Joint Emergency Response through the Provision of Assistance

1. If a Party needs assistance in the event of land and/or forest fires or haze pollution arising from such fires within its territory, it may request such assistance from any other Party, directly or through the ASEAN Centre, or, where appropriate, from other States or international organisations.
2. Assistance can only be employed at the request of and with the consent of the requesting Party, or, when offered by another Party or Parties, with the consent of the receiving Party.
3. Each Party to which a request for assistance is directed shall promptly decide and notify the requesting Party, directly or through the ASEAN Centre, whether it is in a position to render the assistance requested, and of the scope and terms of such assistance.
4. Each Party to which an offer of assistance is directed shall promptly decide and notify the assisting Party, directly or through the ASEAN Centre, whether it is in a position to accept the assistance offered, and of the scope and terms of such assistance.
5. The requesting Party shall specify the scope and type of assistance required and, where practicable, provide the assisting Party with such information as may be necessary for that Party to determine the extent to which it is able to meet the request. In the event that it is not practicable for the requesting Party to specify the scope and type of assistance required, the requesting Party and assisting Party shall, in consultation, jointly assess and decide upon the scope and type of assistance required.
6. The Parties shall, within the limits of their capabilities, identify and notify the ASEAN Centre of experts, equipment and materials which could be made available for the provision of assistance to other Parties in the event of land and/or forest fires or haze pollution resulting from such fires as well as the terms, especially financial, under which such assistance could be provided.

Article 13

Direction and Control of Assistance

Unless otherwise agreed:

1. The requesting or receiving Party shall exercise the overall direction, control, co-ordination and supervision of the assistance within its territory. The assisting Party should, where the assistance involves personnel, designate in consultation with the requesting or receiving Party, the person or entity who should be in charge of and retain immediate operational supervision over the personnel and the equipment provided by it. The designated person or entity should exercise such supervision in co-operation with the appropriate authorities of the requesting or receiving Party.
2. The requesting or receiving Party shall provide, to the extent possible, local facilities and services for the proper and effective administration of the assistance. It shall also ensure the protection of personnel, equipment and materials brought into its territory by or on behalf of the assisting Party for such purposes.
3. A Party providing or receiving assistance in response to a request referred to in paragraph (1) above shall co-ordinate that assistance within its territory.

Article 14

Exemptions and Facilities in Respect of the Provision of Assistance

1. The requesting or receiving Party shall accord to personnel of the assisting Party and personnel acting on its behalf, the necessary exemptions and facilities for the performance of their functions.
2. The requesting or receiving Party shall accord the assisting Party exemptions from taxation, duties or other charges on the equipment and materials brought into the territory of the requesting or receiving Party for the purpose of the assistance.
3. The requesting or receiving Party shall facilitate the entry into, stay in and departure from its territory of personnel and of equipment and materials involved or used in the assistance.

Article 15

Transit of Personnel, Equipment and Materials in Respect of the Provision of Assistance

Each Party shall, at the request of the Party concerned, seek to facilitate the transit through its territory of duly notified personnel, equipment and materials involved or used in the assistance to the requesting or receiving Party.

PART III. TECHNICAL CO-OPERATION AND SCIENTIFIC RESEARCH

Article 16

Technical Co-operation

1. In order to increase the preparedness for and to mitigate the risks to human health and the environment arising from land and/or forest fires or haze pollution arising from such fires, the Parties shall undertake technical co-operation in this field, including the following:
   a. Facilitate mobilisation of appropriate resources within and outside the Parties;
   b. Promote the standardisation of the reporting format of data and information;
   c. Promote the exchange of relevant information, expertise, technology, techniques and know-how;
   d. Provide or make arrangements for relevant training, education and awareness-raising campaigns, in particular relating to the promotion of zero-burning practices and theimpact of haze pollution on human health and the environment;
   e. Develop or establish techniques on controlled burning particularly for shifting cultivators and small farmers, and to exchange and share experiences on controlled-burning practices;
   f. Facilitate exchange of experience and relevant information among enforcement authorities of the Parties;
   g. Promote the development of markets for the utilisation of biomass and appropriate methods for disposal of agricultural wastes;
   h. Develop training programmes for firefighters and trainers to be trained at local, national and regional levels; and
   i. Strengthen and enhance the technical capacity of the Parties to implement this Agreement.
2. The ASEAN Centre shall facilitate activities for technical cooperation as identified in paragraph 1 above.

Article 17

Scientific Research

The Parties shall individually or jointly, including in co-operation with appropriate international organisations, promote and, whenever possible, support scientific and technical research programmes related to the root causes and consequences of transboundary haze pollution and the means, methods, techniques and equipment for land and/or forest fire management, including fire fighting.

PART IV. INSTITUTIONAL ARRANGEMENTS

Article 18

Conference of the Parties

1. A Conference of the Parties is hereby established. The first meeting of the Conference of the Parties shall be convened by the Secretariat not later than one year after the entry into force of this Agreement. Thereafter, ordinary meetings of the Conference of the Parties shall be held at least once every year, in as far as possible in conjunction with appropriate meetings of ASEAN.
2. Extraordinary meetings shall be held at any other time upon the request of one Party provided that such request is supported by at least one other Party.
3. The Conference of the Parties shall keep under continuous review and evaluation the implementation of this Agreement and to this end shall:
   a. Take such action as is necessary to ensure the effective implementation of this Agreement;
   b. Consider reports and other information which may be submitted by a Party directly or through the Secretariat;
   c. Consider and adopt protocols in accordance with the Article 21 of this Agreement;

d. Consider and adopt any amendment to this Agreement;
e. Adopt, review and amend as required any Annexes to this Agreement;
f. Establish subsidiary bodies as may be required for the implementation of this Agreement; and
g. Consider and undertake any additional action that may be required for the achievement of the objective of this Agreement.

Article 19

Secretariat

1. A Secretariat is hereby established.

2. The functions of the Secretariat shall include:
   a. Arrange for and service meetings of the Conference of the Parties and of other bodies established by this Agreement;
   b. Transmit to the Parties notifications, reports and other information received in accordance with this Agreement;
   c. Consider inquiries by, and information from, the Parties, and to consult with them on questions relating to this Agreement;
   d. Ensure the necessary co-ordination with other relevant international bodies and in particular to enter into administrative arrangements as may be required for the effective discharge of the Secretariat functions; and
   e. Perform such other functions as may be assigned to it by the Parties.

3. The ASEAN Secretariat shall serve as the Secretariat to this Agreement.

Article 20

Financial Arrangements

1. A Fund is hereby established for the implementation of this Agreement.
2. It shall be known as the ASEAN Transboundary Haze Pollution Control Fund.
3. The Fund shall be administered by the ASEAN Secretariat under the guidance of the Conference of the Parties.
4. The Parties shall, in accordance with the decisions of the Conference of the Parties, make voluntary contributions to the Fund.
5. The Fund shall be open to contributions from other sources subject to the agreement of or approval by the Parties.
6. The Parties may, where necessary, mobilise additional resources required for the implementation of this Agreement from relevant international organisations, in particular regional financial institutions and the international donor community.

PART V. PROCEDURES

Article 21

Protocols

1. The Parties shall co-operate in the formulation and adoption of protocols to this Agreement, prescribing agreed measures, procedures and standards for the implementation of this Agreement.
2. The Conference of the Parties may, at ordinary meetings, adopt protocols to this Agreement by consensus of all Parties.
3. The text of any proposed protocol shall be communicated to the Parties by the Secretariat at least six months before such a session.
4. The requirements for the entry into force of any protocol shall be established by that instrument.

Article 22

Amendments to the Agreement

1. Any Party may propose amendments to the Agreement.
2. The text of any proposed amendment shall be communicated to the Parties by the Secretariat at least six

months before the Conference of the Parties at which it is proposed for adoption. The Secretariat shall also communicate proposed amendments to the signatories to the Agreement.

3. Amendments shall be adopted by consensus at an ordinary meeting of the Conference of the Parties.
4. Amendments to this Agreement shall be subject to acceptance. The Depositary shall circulate the adopted amendment to all Parties for their acceptance. The amendment shall enter into force on the thirtieth day after the deposit with the Depositary of the instruments of acceptance of all Parties.
5. After the entry into force of an amendment to this Agreement any new Party to this Agreement shall become a Party to this Agreement as amended.

Article 23

Adoption and Amendment of Annexes

1. Annexes to this Agreement shall form an integral part of the Agreement and, unless otherwise expressly provided, a reference to the Agreement constitutes at the same time a reference to the annexes thereto.
2. Annexes shall be adopted by consensus at an ordinary meeting of the Conference of the Parties.
3. Any Party may propose amendments to an Annex.
4. Amendments to an Annex shall be adopted by consensus at an ordinary meeting of the Conference of the Parties.
5. Annexes to this Agreement and amendments to Annexes shall be subject to acceptance. The Depositary shall circulate the adopted Annex or the adopted amendment to an Annex to all Parties for their acceptance. The Annex or the amendment to an Annex shall enter into force on the thirtieth day after the deposit with the Depositary of the instruments of acceptance of all Parties.

Article 24

Rules of Procedure and Financial Rules

The first Conference of the Parties shall by consensus adopt rules of procedure for itself and financial rules for the ASEAN Transboundary Haze Pollution Control Fund to determine in particular the financial participation of the Parties to this Agreement.

Article 25

Reports

The Parties shall transmit to the Secretariat reports on the measures taken for the implementation of this Agreement in such form and at such intervals as determined by the Conference of the Parties.

Article 26

Relationship with Other Agreements

The provisions of this Agreement shall in no way affect the rights and obligations of any Party with regard to any existing treaty, convention or agreement to which they are Parties.

Article 27

Settlement of Disputes

Any dispute between Parties as to the interpretation or application of, or compliance with, this Agreement or any protocol thereto, shall be settled amicably by consultation or negotiation.

PART VI. FINAL CLAUSES

Article 28

Ratification, Acceptance, Approval and Accession

This Agreement shall be subject to ratification, acceptance, approval or accession by the Member States. It shall be opened for accession from the day after the date on which the Agreement is closed for signature. Instruments of ratification, acceptance, approval or accession shall be deposited with the Depositary.

Article 29

Entry into Force

1. This Agreement shall enter into force on the sixtieth day after the deposit of the sixth instrument of ratification, acceptance, approval or accession.
2. For each Member State ratifying, accepting, approving or acceding to the Agreement after the deposit of the sixth instrument of ratification, acceptance, approval or accession, the Agreement shall enter into force on the sixtieth day after the deposit by such Member State of its instrument of ratification, acceptance, approval or accession.

Article 30

Reservations

Unless otherwise expressly provided by this Agreement no reservations may be made to the Agreement.

Article 31

Depositary

This Agreement shall be deposited with the Secretary General of ASEAN, who shall promptly furnish each Member State a certified copy thereof.

Article 32

Authentic Text

This Agreement shall be drawn up in the English language, and shall be the authentic text.

IN WITNESS WHEREOF the undersigned, being duly authorised by their respective Governments have signed this Agreement.

Done at **Kuala Lumpur, Malaysia** on the **tenth** day of **June** in the year **two thousand and two**.

For the Government of Brunei Darussalam

For the Government of the Kingdom of Cambodia
H.E. Mr. Keo Puth Reasmey
Ambassador
Royal Embassy of the Kingdom of Cambodia in Malaysia

For the Government of the Republic of Indonesia
Ms. Liana Bratasida
Deputy Minister for Environment Conservation
State Minister of Environment

For the Government of Lao People's Democratic Republic
H.E. Prof. Dr. Bountiem Phissamay
Minister to the Prime Minister's Office
Chairman of Science, Technology and Environment Agency

For the Government of Malaysia
H.E. Dato' Seri Law Hieng Ding
Minister of Science, Technology and the Environment

For the Government of the Union of Myanmar
U Thane Myint
Secretary, National Commission for Environmental Affairs
Director-General of the Ministry of Foreign Affairs

For the Government of the Republic of the Philippines

For the Government of the Republic of Singapore
H.E. Mr. Lim Swee Say
Minister for the Environment

For the Government of the Kingdom of Thailand
H.E. Mr. Chaisiri Anamarn
Ambassador Extraordinary and Plenipotentiary
Royal Thai Embassy in Malaysia

For the Government of the Socialist Republic of Viet Nam
H.E. Mr. Nguyen Van Dang
Vice Minister of Agriculture and Rural Development

ANNEX

Terms of Reference of the ASEAN Co-ordinating Centre for Transboundary Haze Pollution Control

The ASEAN Centre shall:

1. Establish and maintain regular contact with the respective National Monitoring Centres regarding the data, including those derived from satellite imagery and meteorological observation, relating to:

a. Land and /or forest fire;

b. Environmental conditions conducive to such fires; and

c. Air quality and levels of pollution, in particular haze arising from such fires.

2. Receive from the respective National Monitoring Centres or Focal Points the data above, consolidate, analyse and process the data into a

format that is easily understandable and accessible.

3. Facilitate co-operation and co-ordination among the Parties to increase their preparedness for and to respond to land and/or forest

fires or haze pollution arising from such fires.

4. Facilitate co-ordination among the Parties, other States and relevant organisations in taking effective measures to mitigate the impact of

land and/or forest fires or haze pollution arising from such fires.

5. Establish and maintain a list of experts from within and outside of the ASEAN region who may be utilised when taking measures to

mitigate the impact of land and/or forest fires or haze pollution arising from such fires, and make the list available to the Parties.

6. Establish and maintain a list of equipment and technical facilities from within and outside of the ASEAN which may be made available

when taking measures to mitigate the impact of land and/or forest fires or haze pollution arising from such fires, and make the list

available to the Parties.

7. Establish and maintain a list of experts from within and outside of the ASEAN region for the purpose of relevant training, education and

awareness-raising campaigns, and make the list available to the Parties.

8. Establish and maintain contact with prospective donor States and organisations for mobilising financial and other resources required for

the prevention and mitigation of land and/or forest fires or haze pollution arising from such fires and preparedness of the Parties,

including fire-fighting capabilities.

9. Establish and maintain a list of such donors, and make the list available to the Parties.

10. Respond to a request for or offer of assistance in the event of land and/or forest fires or haze pollution resulting from such fires by:

a. Transmitting promptly the request for assistance to other States and organisations; and

b. Co-ordinating such assistance, if so requested by the requesting Party or offered by the assisting Party.

11. Establish and maintain an information referral system for the exchange of relevant information, expertise, technology, techniques

and know-how, and make it available to the Parties in an easily accessible format.

12. Compile and disseminate to the Parties information concerning their experience and any other practical information related to the

implementation of the Agreement.

13. Assist the Parties in the preparation of standard operating procedures(SOP).